CHRONOLOGICAL TABLE

OF THE STATUTES

Chronological Table
of the Statutes

Part I
Covering the Acts of the Parliaments of
England, Great Britain and the United Kingdom
from 1235 to the end of 1968

Part II
Covering the Acts of the Parliaments
of the United Kingdom from 1969 to the end of 1992

Part III
**Covering the Acts of the Parliaments
of the United Kingdom from 1993 to the end of 2015**

**the Acts of the Parliaments of Scotland
from 1424 to 1707**

**the Acts of the Scottish Parliament
from 1999 to the end of 2015 and**

**the Acts of the National Assembly for Wales
from 2012 to the end of 2015**

**the Measures of the National Assembly for Wales
from 2008 to 2011 and**

**the Church Assembly Measures and General Synod Measures from
1920 to the end of 2015**

*Produced by The Stationery Office Limited for the
Controller of Her Majesty's Stationery Office and Queen's Printer of
Acts of Parliament and the Queen's Printer for Scotland*

Published by Authority

© Crown Copyright 2016
First published 2016

Published by TSO (The Stationery Office), part of Williams Lea Tag, and
available from:
Online
www.tsoshop.co.uk

Mail, Telephone, Fax & E-mail
TSO
PO Box 29, Norwich, NR3 1GN
Telephone orders/General enquiries: 0333 202 5070
Fax orders: 0333 202 5080
E-mail: customer.services@tso.co.uk
Textphone: 0333 202 5077

TSO@Blackwell and other Accredited Agents

ISBN 9780118405515

1993

c 1   **Gas (Exempt Supplies)**
        ss 1, 2 rep—Gas, 1995 c 45, s 17(5), sch 6
c 2   *British Coal and British Rail (Transfer Proposals)*—rep Coal Industry, 1994 c 21, s 67,
                sch 11 pt III
c 3   **Social Security**
        s 1 rep—Pension Schemes, 1993 c 48, s 188, sch 5 pt I
        s 2 rep in pt—Social Security Contributions (Trans of Functions, etc), 1999 c 2, ss 2, 26(3),
                sch 3 para 60(1)-(4), sch 10 pt I
            am—Pension Schemes, 1993 c 48, s 190, sch 8 para 45; Employment Rights, 1996 c 18,
                s 240, sch 1 para 58; Social Security Contributions (Trans of Functions, etc), 1999
                c 2, s 2, sch 3 para 60(1)-(3); Pensions, 2014 c 19, sch 12 para 29; (prosp) ibid, sch
                16 para 36
            appl—SIs 2003/963, art 4; 2004/889, art 5; 2005/878, art 5; 2006/624, art 5;
                2007/1052, art 5; 2014/475, art 5; 2015/588, art 4
        s 5 rep in pt—Pension Schemes, 1993 c 48, s 188, sch 5 pt I
c 4   *Consolidated Fund*—rep Appropriation, 1995 c 19, ss 2,3, sch (C)
c 5   *Damages (Scotland)*—rep Damages (S), 2011 asp 7, sch 2
c 6   **Bankruptcy (Scotland)**
        sch 1 rep in pt—Bankruptcy and Debt Advice (S), 2014 asp 11, sch 4
c 7   *Consolidated Fund (No 2)*—rep Appropriation, 1995 c 19, ss 2,3, sch (C)
c 8   **Judicial Pensions and Retirement**
        am—Employment Rights (Dispute Resolution), 1998 c 8, ss 1(2),16(3)(d)
        mod—Access to Justice, 1999 c 22, s 68(3)(b)
        power to am—SI 1986/1888 (NI 18) as am by 1993 c 8, s 31, sch 8 para 19(2); Human
                Rights, 1998 c 42, s 18(6), sch 4 paras 3, 4; Welfare Reform and Pensions,
                1999 c 30, s 43
        power to mod—Pension Schemes, 1993 c 48, ss 188-190, 191, 193(2), sch 6 pt II
                para 17(3)(j), sch 9 para 7
        power to mod—(NI) Pension Schemes (NI), 1993 c 49, ss 182-184, sch 5 pt II
                para 17(1)-(3)
        appl—Land Registration, 2002 c 9, s 107(3), sch 9, para 2(3)
        savings—SI 2007/2913, art 4
        Pt 1 (ss 1-18) appl (mods)—Parl Commnr, 1967 c 13, sch 1
            appl—SI 1995/639, reg 4.11(1)
            ext (mods)—SI 1996/1297, art 4(4), sch 1 para 6(1)-(4)
        s 1 am—Tribunals, Cts and Enforcement, 2007 c 15, s 48, sch 9 paras 14, 15; Public Service
                Pensions, 2013 c 25, sch 8 para 16
            rep in pt—Tribunals, Cts and Enforcement, 2007 c 15, s 146, sch 23
        s 2 am—Constitutional Reform, 2005 c 4, s 15(1), sch 4 pt 1 paras 226, 227; SI 2015/182,
                sch 3 para 12(2)(3)
        s 3 am—SI 2006/497, art 3; Income Tax, 2007 c 3, s 1027, sch 1 para 352; Statistics and
                Registration Service, 2007 c 18, s 60, sch 3 para 8
        s 4 appl—SI 1995/634, art 6(1)
        s 5 appl—SI 1995/634, art 6(1)
            am—SIs 2005/3325, arts 69, 70(2),(3)(a)(b),(4)-(6); 2015/182, sch 3 para 12(4)
            rep in pt—SI 2005/3325, arts 69, 70(3)(c)
        s 6 appl—SI 1995/634, art 6(1)
            am—SI 2005/3325, arts 69, 71
            appl (mods)—SI 2010/985, reg 5, sch 4
        s 7 appl—SI 1995/634, art 6(1)
        s 8 appl—SI 1995/634, art 6(1)
            am—SIs 2005/3325, arts 69, 72; 2015/182, sch 3 para 12(5)
        s 9 appl—SI 1995/634, art 6(1)
            am—SI 2005/3325, arts 69, 73; Tribunals, Cts and Enforcement, 2007 c 15, s 48, sch 9
                paras 14, 16
        s 9A added—Pensions, 2011 c 19, s 34
        s 10 am—Pension Schemes, 1993 c 48, s 190, sch 8 para 46(1)(a)-(d); (NI) Pension
                Schemes (NI), 1993 c 49, s 184, sch 7 para 43(1); SIs 1994/1696; 2001/3649,
                art 112(1)(2)(3)(a)(b)(4); 2006/497, art 4; 2007/126, reg 3, sch 6; Financial
                Services, 2012 c 21, sch 18 para 75(2); SI 2013/3115, sch 2 para 36
        s 11 am—Public Service Pensions, 2013 c 25, sch 8 para 17
        s 12 am—Tribunals, Cts and Enforcement, 2007 c 15, s 48, sch 9 paras 14, 17
            rep in pt—Tribunals, Cts and Enforcement, 2007 c 15, s 146, sch 23
        ss 12A, 12B added—Tribunals, Cts and Enforcement, 2007 c 15, s 48, sch 9 paras 14, 18

1993

c 8 *continued*

s 13 am—Pension Schemes, 1993 c 48, s 190, sch 8 para 46(2); (NI) Pension Schemes (NI), 1993 c 49, s 184, sch 7 para 43(2); SIs 1995/3213, art 165, sch 4 para 1; 2003/2916, regs 2, 4(1)(2)(3)(a)

    rep in pt—Pensions, 1995 c 26, ss 151, 177, sch 5 para 17, sch 7 pt III; SI 2003/2916, regs 2, 4(1)(3)(b)

s 16 am—Pension Schemes, 1993 c 48, s 190, sch 8 para 46(3); (NI) Pension Schemes (NI), 1993 c 49, s 184, sch 7 para 43(3)

s 17 subst—SI 2005/3325, arts 69, 74

s 18 rep—SI 2006/497, art 5

Pt 1A (s 18A) added—Pension Schemes, 2015 c 8, s 78(1)

s 19 appl (mods)—Parl Commnr, 1967 c 13, sch

    ext (mods)—SI 1996/1297, art 4(4), sch 1 para 6(2)-(4)

    rep in pt—SI 2006/497, art 6

s 20 am—SI 2005/3325, arts 69, 75

    appl (mods)—Parl Commnr, 1967 c 13, sch 1

    ext (mods)—SI 1996/1297, art 4(4), sch 1 para 6(2)-(4)

s 21 am—Loc Govt (W), 1994 c 19, s 66(6), sch 16 para 100

s 22 am—Pension Schemes, 2015 c 8, sch 5 para 5

s 23 appl (mods)—Parl Commnr, 1967 c 13, sch 1

    ext (mods)—SI 1996/1297, art 4(4), sch 1 para 6(2)-(4)

    am—Tribunals, Cts and Enforcement, 2007 c 15, s 48, sch 9 paras 14, 19

s 23A added—SI 2000/2986, reg 2

s 25 rep in pt—SIs 1996/1297, art 23(2), sch 5; 1996/1298, art 21(2), sch 6; 2004/1823, art 15

s 26 appl—Charities, 1993 c 10, sch 1B para 4; SI 1995/3192, art 4(a); Land Registration, 2002 c 9, ss 81, 100, 107(3), sch 9, para 1(3), sch 4, para 1(2), sch 5, para 2(2); Income Tax, 2007 c 3, s 704(3)

    mod—(transtl provn) Access to Justice, 1999 c 22, s 105, sch 14 pt V para 25

    saved—(NI) SIs 1998/1506, arts 6(3),8(7), sch 1, para 1; 1998/3162, art 82(3); Immigration and Asylum, 1999 c 33, ss 56(2), 57(3), sch 2 para 3(2), sch 3 para 3(2)

    restr—SI 1995/3192, arts 4(b)(i)(ii),5

    am—Merchant Shipping, 1995 c 21, s 314(2), sch 13 para 93(a); School Inspections, 1996 c 57, s 47(1), sch 6 para 6; Constitutional Reform, 2005 c 4, ss 15(1), 35(3), 38(3), 56(5), sch 4 pt 1 paras 226, 228(1)(2)(4)(5), sch 11 pt 2 para 4; Educ, 2005 c 18, s 61, sch 9 para 7; Tribunals, Cts and Enforcement, 2007 c 15, s 48, sch 8 para 31(1)-(4); ibid, s 54; ibid, s 56, sch 11 paras 11, 12; SI 2012/2595, art 6(3); Crime and Cts, 2013 c 22, sch 14 para 13(1); Tribunals (S), 2014 asp 10, sch 9 para 11(2)

    rep in pt—SIs (NI) 1998/1506, sch 7; 2001/3649, art 113; Communications, 2003 c 21, s 406(7), sch 19(1); Constitutional Reform, 2005 c 4, ss 15(1), 146, sch 4 pt 1 paras 226, 228(1)(3), sch 18 pt 2; SIs 2010/21, art 5, sch 1; 2012/2595, art 6(2); (prosp) Crime and Cts, 2013 c 22, sch 9 para 95; SI 2014/3248, sch 3 pt 2

s 27 am—Bail, Judicial Appointments etc (S), asp 9, s 12, sch para 5(1)

    rep in pt—Armed Forces, 2001 c 19, ss 34, 38, sch 6 pt 2, para 10, sch 7 pt 3; SSI 2014/155, art 2(2)

s 28 am—Pension Schemes, 2015 c 8, sch 5 para 6

s 28A added—SI 2010/976, art 15, sch 18

    am—Pension Schemes, 2015 c 8, sch 5 para 7

s 29 am—Pension Schemes, 2015 c 8, sch 5 para 8

s 30 am—Pension Schemes, 1993 c 48, s 190, sch 8 para 46(4); (NI) Pension Schemes (NI), 1993 c 49, s 184, sch 7 para 43(4); SI 2005/3325, arts 69, 76; Tribunals (S), 2014 asp 10, sch 9 para 11(3)

sch 1 am—Employment Tribunals, 1996 c 17, s 43, sch 1 para 10(2); SI 1996/1921, art 26, sch 1 para 9(a); (pt prosp) Social Security, 1998 c 14, s 86(1), sch 7, para 123(1); (NI) SI 1998/3162, art 105(1), sch 3; Access to Justice, 1999 c 22, s 78, sch 11 paras 39, 40; Immigration and Asylum, 1999 c 33, s 169(1), sch 14 para 98(1)(2); SIs 1999/1454, art 2; 1999/2283, art 2; Financial Services and Markets, 2000 c 8, s 432(1), sch 20 para 7(2); Nationality, Immigration and Asylum, 2002 c 41, s 114(3), sch 7, para 18; SIs 2002/1347, art 3; 2003/1311, art 2; 2003/2589, art 2; Asylum and Immigration (Treatment of Claimants, etc), 2004 c 19, s 26(7), sch 2 pt 1 para 8(1)(2); Pensions, 2004 c 35, s 102(4), sch 4

1993
c 8 *continued*

pt 4 para 17(1)(2); Constitutional Reform, 2005 c 4, ss 15(1), 37(2)(3), 59(5),
sch 4 pt 1 paras 226, 229, sch 11 pt 2 para 4; Gambling, 2005 c 19, s 140(2), sch
8 para 6; SIs 2005/53, art 2; 2006/391, art 2; (savings) 2007/675, art 2;
2007/2185, art 2; Tribunals, Cts and Enforcement, 2007 c 15, s 48, sch 8 para
31(1)(5); SIs 2008/171, art 2; 2008/2947, art 2; 2008/3139, art 2; Coroners and
Justice, 2009 c 25, s 177, sch 21 para 31; Crime and Cts, 2013 c 22, sch 14 para
13(2); SI 2015/109, art 2
rep in pt—(pt prosp) Social Security, 1998 c 14, s 86(1)(2), sch 7, para 123(2), sch 8;
SI 2002/3083, art 2; Courts, 2003 c 39, s 109(3), sch 10; SI 2003/2775, art 2;
Mental Capacity, 2005 c 9, s 67(1), sch 6 para 38(1)(2); Armed Forces, 2006 c
52, s 378, sch 17; SIs 2008/2833, art 6, sch 3; 2009/56, art 3, sch 1 para 190;
2009/1834, art 4, schs 1, 4; 2009/1307, art 5, sch 1; 2010/21, art 5, sch 1;
2010/22, art 5, sch 2; 2013/1036, sch 1 para 222(a)(b)
sch 1A added—SI 2005/3325, arts 69, 77
sch 2 appl (mods)—Parl Commnr, 1967 c 13, sch 1
am—Pension Schemes, 1993 c 48, s 190, sch 8 para 46(5); (NI) Pension Schemes (NI),
1993 c 49, s 184, sch 7 para 43(5); SIs 1994/1696; 2001/3649, art 114(1)-(6);
2011/1730, art 4; Financial Services, 2012 c 21, sch 18 para 75(3); Pension
Schemes, 2015 c 8, sch 4 paras 2, 48
ext (mods)—SI 1996/1297, art 4(4), sch 1 para 6(2)(3)(4)
sch 2A added—SI 2000/2986, reg 3
am—Pension Schemes, 2015 c 8, s 79
sch 4 rep in pt—Health Service Commrs, 1993 c 46, s 20, sch 3; SIs 1996/1297, art 23(2),
sch 5; 1996/1298 art 21(2), sch 6
sch 5 rep in pt—(pt prosp) Social Secrity, 1998 c 14, s 86, sch 7 para 24, sch 8; Financial
Services and Markets, 2000 c 8, s 432(1)(3), sch 20 para 7(3)(a), sch 22;
(prosp) Care Standards, 2000 c 14, s 117(2), sch 6; Bail, Judicial Appointments
etc (S), asp 9, s 12, sch para 5(2); Educ, 2002 c 32, s 215(2), sch 22 pt 3;
Communications, 2003 c 21, s 406(7), sch 19(1); Courts, 2003 c 39, s 109(3),
sch 10; Constitutional Reform, 2005 c 4, ss 15(1), 146, sch 4 pt 1 paras 226,
230, sch 18 pt 2; Mental Capacity, 2005 c 9, s 67(1), sch 6 para 38(1)(3); Nat
Health Service (Conseq Provns), 2006 c 43, s 2, sch 1 para 159; Armed Forces,
2006 c 52, s 378, sch 17; Tribunals, Cts and Enforcement, 2007 c 15, s 146,
sch 23; SIs 2008/2833, art 6, sch 3; 2009/56, art 3, sch 1 para 191; 2009/1307,
art 5, sch 1; 2010/21, art 5, sch 1; 2010/22, art 5, sch 2; 2013/294, art 2, sch;
2013/686, sch 1 para 6(2); 2013/1036, sch 1 para 223(a)(b); Courts Reform
(S), 2014 asp 18, sch 5 para 8(c)
am—Merchant Shipping, 1995 c 21, s 314(2), sch 13 para 93(b); SI 1995/3192, art 3;
Employment Tribunals, 1996 c 17, s 43, sch 1 para 10(3); Reserve Forces, 1996
c 14, s 131(1), sch 10 para 26; SI 1996/1921, art 26, sch 1 para 9(b); (pt prosp)
Social Security, 1998 c 14, s 86(1), sch 7 para 124(1); (NI) SI 1998/3162,
art 105(1), sch 3; Access to Justice, 1999 c 22, ss 78, 105, sch 11 para 41, sch 14
pt V para 25; Immigration and Asylum, 1999 c 33, s 169(1), sch 14
para 98(1)(3); SI 1999/1454, art 3; Financial Services and Markets, 2000 c 8,
s 432(1), sch 20 para 7(3)(b); Freedom of Information, 2000 c 36, ss 18(4),87(3),
sch 2 pt I para 11; Land Registration, 2002 c 9, s 133, sch 11, para 28;
Nationality, Immigration and Asylum, 2002 c 41, s 114(3), sch 7, para 19;
Courts, 2003 c 39, s 89(2); Asylum and Immigration (Treatment of Claimants,
etc), 2004 c 19, s 26(7), sch 2 pt 1 para 8(1)(3); Pensions, 2004 c 35, s 102(4),
sch 4 pt 4 para 17(1)(3); Constitutional Reform, 2005 c 4, ss 35(3), 59(5), sch
11 pt 2 para 4; Gambling, 2005 c 19, s 140(2), sch 8 para 3(4); SIs 2006/391,
art 3; 2006/2805, sch 2; 2007/675, art 4; 2007/2185, art 3; Tribunals, Cts and
Enforcement, 2007 c 15, s 48, sch 8 para 31(1)(6); ibid, s 56, sch 11 paras 11, 13;
Crime and Cts, 2013 c 22, sch 14 para 13(2); SI 2008/3139, art 3; SSI 2013/2,
art 2(1); Courts Reform (S), 2014 asp 18, sch 5 para 8(a)(b); Tribunals (S), 2014
asp 10, sch 9 para 11(4); SSI 2014/155, art 2(3)
saving—SI 2001/3650, art 17
sch 6 rep in pt—Value Added Tax, 1994 c 23, s 100(2), sch 15; Merchant Shipping, 1995
c 21, s 314(1), sch 12; Employment Tribunals, 1996 c 17, s 45, sch 3 pt I;
Education, 1996 c 56, s 582(2)(3), sch 38 pt I, sch 39; School Inspections,
1996 c 57, s 47(2), sch 7; Justices of the Peace, 1997, c 25, s 73(3), sch 6 pt I;
Plant Varieties, 1997 c 66, s 52, sch 4; Social Security, 1998 c 14, s 86(2),
sch 8; Data Protection, 1998 c 29, s 74(2), sch 16 pt I; (NI) SI 1998/3162,

1993
c 8 *continued*

art 105(4), sch 5; Immigration and Asylum, 1999 c 33, s 169(1)(3), sch 14
para 98(1)(4), sch 16; (prosp) Care Standards, 2000 c 14, s 117(2), sch 6;
SI 2001/3649, art 115(a)-(d); Courts, 2003 c 39, s 109(3), sch 10;
Communications, 2003 c 21, s 406(7), sch 19(1); Commons, 2006 c 26, s 53,
sch 6; SIs 2006/1031, reg 49, sch 9; 2006/2805, sch 2; 2008/2833, art 6, sch 3;
2013/686, sch 1 para 6(3)

sch 7 rep in pt—Social Security, 1998 c 14, s 86(1)(2), sch 7, para 125, sch 8; (prosp) Care
Standards, 2000 c 14, s 117(2), sch 6; Educ, 2002 c 32, s 215(2), sch 22 pt 3;
Communications, 2003 c 21, s 406(7), sch 19(1); Mental Capacity, 2005 c 9,
s 67(1), sch 6 para 38(1)(4); SIs 2006/2805, sch 2; 2009/1307, art 5, sch 1;
2010/22, art 5, sch 2; 2013/294, art 2, sch; 2013/686, sch 1 para 6(4)

am—Merchant Shipping, 1995 c 21, s 314(2), sch 13 para 93(c); Employment
Tribunals, 1996 c 17, s 43, sch 1 para 10(4); SI 1996/1921, art 26, sch 1
para 9(c); (NI) SI 1998/3162, art 105(1), sch 3; Freedom of Information, 2000
c 36, ss 18(4),87(3), sch 2 pt I para 12; Constitutional Reform, 2005 c 4, s 59(5),
sch 11 pt 2 para 4; Crime and Cts, 2013 c 22, sch 14 para 13(5)

restr—SI 1995/3192, art 4(b)(iii)

sch 8 rep in pt—Pension Schemes, 1993 c 48, s 188, sch 5 pt I; (NI) Pension Schemes (NI),
1993 c 49, s 182, sch 4 pt I; Social Security, 1998 c 14, s 86(2), sch 8

c 9   **Prisoners and Criminal Proceedings (Scotland)**
see—SI 1999/1748, art 4(2), sch 3, pts I, III paras 1-4, 10(2)
am—Crim Justice and Public Order, 1994 c 33, s 134(2); Crim Procedure (Conseq
Provns)(S), 1995 c 40, s 5, sch 4 para 86(2)
ext—Crime (Sentences), 1997 c 43, ss 41,56(1), sch 1 pt II, para 11, sch 5, para 12(1)(d)
power to mod—Police, Public Order and Crim Justice (S), 2006 asp 10, s 94(3)(4)
Pt 1 (ss 1-27) appl—Crim Procedure (S), 1995 c 46, s 209(7); Crime and Disorder, 1998
c 37, s 86(1)

ext—Crime (Sentences), 1997 c 43, ss 41,56(1), sch 1 pt II, para 10(5), sch 5,
para 11(1)(a)(d)(3)

mod—Crime and Punishment (S) Act 1997 c 48, ss 16(3), 33

rep (prosp)—Custodial Sentences and Weapons (S), 2007 asp 17, s 66, sch 5

s 1 mod—(pt retrosp) Repatriation of Prisoners, 1984 c 47, sch para 2
power to am—(1.2.2016) Prisoners (Control of Release) (S), 2015 asp 8, s 3(3)
am—Crime and Punishment (S) Act 1997 c 48, s 62(1), sch 1, para 14(2)(b); Crime and
Disorder, 1998 c 37, s 119, sch 8, para 98(1)(2)(3); Crim Justice (S), 2003 asp 7,
s 28(1)(2); Management of Offenders etc (S), 2005 asp 14, s 15(1)(2); (1.2.2016)
Prisoners (Control of Release) (S), 2015 asp 8, s 1(2); SSI 2015/409, art 3

rep in pt—Crime and Punishment (S) 1997 c 48, s 62(1)(2), sch 1, para 14(2)(a), sch 3;
Convention Rights (Compliance), 2001 asp 7, ss 1(1)(2), 4

appl (mods)—SI 1997/1776, art 2, sch 1, paras 5-7

ext—Crime (Sentences), 1997 c 43, ss 41,56(1), sch 1 pt II, paras 10(2)(a)(6)(7),
11(2)(a)(6), sch 5,paras11(1)(a)(d) (2)(3),12(1)(a)

excl—International Crim Court (S), 2001 asp 13, s 24(c)

s 1AA added—Management of Offenders etc (S), 2005 asp 14, s 15(1)(3)

s 1A added—Crime and Disorder, 1998 c 37, s 111(1)

excl—International Crim Court (S), 2001 asp 13, s 24(c)

am—Crim Justice (S), 2003 asp 7, ss 30, 85, sch 4 para 2(1)(2); Management of
Offenders etc (S), 2005 asp 14, s 15(1)(4)

s 2 ext—Crime (Sentences), 1997 c 43, ss 41,56(1), sch 1 pt II, paras 10(2)(6)(7),
11(2)(4)(6), sch 5, paras 11(1)(a)(d)(3), 12(1)(a)

appl (mods)—SI 1997/1776, art 2, sch 1, paras 5-7

restr—Crime and Punishment (S) Act 1997 c 48, ss 16(4)(a),33

am—Crime and Punishment (S) Act 1997 c 48, s 16(1)(b), 62(1), sch 1
para 14(3)(a)-(d); Convention Rights (Compliance) (S), 2001 asp 7,
ss 1(1)(3)(a)-(c)(e)(g)(i)(j), 4; Crim Justice (S), 2003 asp 7, s 29(1)(2); ibid, s 1(2),
sch 1 para 1(1)(2); Crim Cases (Punishment and Review (S), 2012 asp 7, s
1(2)(c)(d)

rep in pt—Crime and Punishment (S) Act 1997 c 48, ss 16(1)(b)(i),33, 62(2), sch 3;
Convention Rights (Compliance) (S), 2001 asp 7, ss 1(1)(3)(a)(b)(d)(f)(h)-(j), 4;
Crim Justice (S), 2003 asp 7, s 86, sch 5; Crim Cases (Punishment and Review
(S), 2012 asp 7, s 1(2)(a)(b)

mod—(pt retrosp) Repatriation of Prisoners, 1984 c 47, sch para 2; SI 1995/911, art 3

1993
c 9 s 2 *continued*

> excl—Crime and Punishment (S) Act 1997 c 48, ss 16(4)(b), 33; International Crim
> Court (S), 2001 asp 13, s 24(c)
ss 2A, 2B added—Crim Cases (Punishment and Review (S), 2012 asp 7, s 1(3)
s 3 ext—Crime (Sentences), 1997 c 43, ss 41,56(1), sch 1 pt II, paras 10(2)(6)(7), 11(2)(6),
> sch 5,paras 11(1)(a)(d)(3),12(1)(a)
> appl (mods)—SI 1997/1776, art 2, sch 1 paras 5-7
> am—Crim Procedure (Conseq Provns)(S), 1995 c 40, s 5, sch 4 para 86(3)
> excl—International Crim Court (S), 2001 asp 13, s 24(c)
s 3AA added—Management of Offenders etc (S), 2005 asp 14, s 15(1)(5)
> am—SSI 2008/126, art 2
s 3A added—Crime and Disorder, 1998 c 37, s 88
> am—Crim Justice (S), 2003 asp 7, s 31
s 4 am—(retrosp) Crime and Disorder, 1998 c 37, s 119, sch 8, para 99(1)(2); Mental
> Health (Care and Treatment) (S), 2003 asp 13, s 331(1), sch 4 para 6
> rep in pt—Mental Health (Care and Treatment) (S), 2003 asp 13, s 331(2), sch 5 pt 1
s 5 ext—Crime (Sentences), 1997 c 43, ss 41,56(1), sch 1 pt II, paras 10(2), sch 8
> paras 11(1)(a)(d)(3),12(1)(a)
> am—Crim Procedure (Conseq Provns) (S), 1995 c 40, s 5, sch 4 para 86; Crime and
> Disorder, 1998 c 37, s 119, sch 8, para 100(a)(b); Crim Justice (S), 2003 asp 7,
> ss 29(1)(3), 36(1)(2); Management of Offenders etc (S), 2005 asp 14, s 15(1)(6)
s 6 am—Crim Procedure (Conseq Provns)(S), 1995 c 40, s 5, sch 4 para 86(4); Crime and
> Punishment (S) Act 1997 c 48, s 62(1), sch 1, para 14(6)(b)(c)
> ext—Crime (Sentences), 1997 c 43, ss 41,56(1), sch 1 pt II, paras 10(2),11(2), sch 5,
> paras 11(1)(a)(d)(3), 12(1)(a)
> rep in pt—Convention Rights (Compliance) (S), 2001 asp 7, ss 1(1)(4), 4
s 7 am—Crim Justice, 1993 c 36, s 75(1); Crim Justice and Public Order, 1994 c 33,
> s 130(1); Crim Procedure (Conseq Provns)(S), 1995 c 40, s 5, sch 4 para 86(5);
> Crime and Disorder, 1998 c 37, s 119, sch 8, para 101(a)(b)(c)(d); Crim Justice (S),
> 2003 asp 7, s 38(1)(2)(a)(c)
> mod—(pt retrosp) Repatriation of Prisoners, 1984 c 47, sch para 2
> rep in pt—Crim Justice (S), 2003 asp 7, s 38(1)(2)(b)(d)
s 8 rep—Crim Procedure (Conseq Provns)(S), 1995 c 40, ss 4,6, sch 3 pt II paras 16, 17,
> sch 5
s 9 ext—Crime (Sentences), 1997 c 43, ss 41,56(1), sch 1 pt II, paras 10(2),11(2), sch 5,
> paras 11(1)(a)(d)(3) 12(1)(a)
> excl —International Crim Court (S), 2001 asp 13, s 24(c)
> am—Management of Offenders etc (S), 2005 asp 14, s 15(1)(7)
> rep in pt—Management of Offenders etc (S), 2005 asp 14, s 15(1)(7)(b)
s 10 rep in pt—Crim Justice, 1993 c 36, ss 76(2)(a), 79(14), sch 6 pt I; Convention Rights
> (Compliance) (S), 2001 asp 7, ss 3(1)(c)(ii)(e)(i), 4; Crim Justice, 2003 c 44,
> ss 304, 332, sch 32 pt 1 para 66(a)(i), sch 37 pt 7
> am—Crim Justice, 1993 c 36, s 76(2); Crim Justice and Public Order, 1994 c 33,
> s 133(a)(b)(i)(ii); Crime (Sentences), 1997 c 43, s 55(2), sch 4, para 16(1);Crime
> and Punishment (S) Act 1997 c 48, s 62(1), sch 1, para 14(8); Convention Rights
> (Compliance) (S), 2001 asp 7, ss 3(1)(a)(b)(c)(i)(iii)(d)(e)(ii) 4; Crim Justice,
> 2003 c 44, s 304, sch 32 pt 1 para 66(a)(ii)(iii)(b)(c); Crim Justice (S), 2003 asp
> 7, s 85, sch 4 para 2(1)(3); SSI 2005/465, art 2, sch 1 para 23(1)(2); Crim Justice
> and Immigration, 2008 c 4, s 148, sch 26 para 30
> excl —International Crim Court. (S), 2001 asp 13, s 24(c)
s 10A added —Convention Rights (Compliance) (S), 2001 asp 7, ss 3(2), 4
s 11 rep in pt—Crime and Disorder, 1998 c 37, ss 119,120(2), sch 8, para 102, sch 10
> am—Crim Justice (S), 1995 c 20, s 117(1), sch 6 pt I para 179(2); Crim Procedure
> (Conseq Provns)(S), 1995 c 40, s 5, sch 4 para 86(6); Management of Offenders
> etc (S), 2005 asp 14, s 15(1)(8)
> appl (mods)—SI 1997/1776 art 2, sch 1 para 5
> ext—Crime (Sentences), 1997 c 43, ss 41,56(1), sch 1 pt II, paras 10(2)(5), 11(2)(4)(6),
> sch 5, para 11(1)(3)
s 12 am—Crim Justice and Public Order, 1994 c 33, s 131;Crime and Punishment (S)
> Act 1997 c 48, s 62(1), sch 1, para 14(10)(b); Crim Justice and Court Services,
> 2000 c 43, s 74, sch 7 pt I para 4(1)(2); Crim Justice (S), 2003 asp 7, ss 28(1)(3),
> 35(1)(2); Management of Offenders etc (S), 2005 asp 14, s 15(1)(9); SIs
> 2005/886, art 2, sch para 50(1); 2008/912, art 3, sch 1
> appl (mods)—SI 1997/1776 art 2, sch 1 para 6

1993

c 9 s 12 *continued*

    ext—Crime (Sentences), 1997 c 43, ss 41,56(1), sch 1 pt II, paras 10(2)(5), 11(2)(4)(6), sch 5, para 11(1)(3)

ss 12AA, 12AB added—Management of Offenders etc (S), 2005 asp 14, s 15(1)(10)

s 12AA appl—SSI 2006/315, art 3

ss 12A, 12B added—Crim Justice (S), 2003 asp 7, s 35(1)(3)

    am—Management of Offenders etc (S), 2005 asp 14, s 15(1)(11)

s 13 appl (mods)—SI 1997/1776 art 2, sch 1 para 7

    ext—Crime (Sentences), 1997 c 43, ss 41,56(1), sch 1 pt II, paras 10(2)(5), 11(2)(4)(6), sch 5, para 11(1)(3)

s 14 am—Crim Procedure (Conseq Provns)(S), 1995 c 40, s 5, sch 4 para 86(7); Crime and Punishment (S) Act 1997 c 48, s 62(1), sch 1, para 14(11)(a); Access to Justice, 1999 c 22, s 90, sch 13 para 170; SI 2005/886, art 2, sch para 50(1)

    rep in pt—Crim Procedure (Conseq Provns)(S), 1995 c 40, ss 4,6, sch 3 pt II paras 16, 17, sch 5; Crime and Punishment (S) Act 1997 c 48, s 62(1)(2), sch 1, para 14(11)(a); Crime and Disorder, 1998 c 37, ss 119,120(2), sch 8, para 103, sch 10

    cert functions exercisable in S—SI 1999/1748, arts 4(1),8(1), sch 2 para 2

s 15 am—Crim Procedure (Conseq Provns)(S), 1995 c 40, s 5, sch 4 para 86(8); Crim Justice and Court Services, 2000 c 43, s 74, sch 7 pt I para 4(1)(2), pt II para 117; Crim Justice (S), 2003 asp 7, s 60(5); SI 2005/886, art 2, sch para 50(1); 2008/912, art 3, sch 1s

    ext—Crime (Sentences) 1997 c 43, ss 41,56(1), sch 1 pt II paras 10(2)(5)6)(7), 11(2)(4)(5)(6), sch 5, paras 11(1)(3),12(1)

    appl (mods)—SI 1997/1776, art 2, sch 1, paras 5-7

    cert functions exercisable in S—SI 1999/1748, arts 4(1), 8(1), sch 2 para 2

s 16 am—Crim Justice (S), 1995 c 20, s 117(1), sch 6 pt I para 179(3); Crim Procedure (Conseq Provns)(S), 1995 c 40, s 5, sch 4 para 86(9); Crime and Disorder, 1998 c 37, ss 111(2),119, sch 8, para 104(1)(2)

    ext—Crime(Sentences) 1997 c 43 ss 41,56(1), sch 1 pt II paras 10(2)(5), 11(2)(4), sch 5, paras 11(1)(3),12(1)

    rep in pt—Crime and Disorder, 1998 c 37, ss 119,120(2), sch 8, para 104(3), sch 10; Crim Justice (S), 2003 asp 7, s 36(1)(3)

s 17 mod—SI 1995/911, art 3; Crime and Disorder, 1998 c 37, s 111(7)

    ext—Crime(Sentences) 1997 c 43, ss 41,56(1), sch 1 pt II paras 10(2)(5)(6)(7), 11(2)(4), sch 5, paras 11(1)(3),12(1)

    appl (mods)—SI 1997/1776, art 2, sch 1, paras 5-7

    am—Crime and Disorder, 1998 c 37, s 119, sch 8, para 105; Convention Rights (Compliance) (S), 2001 asp 7, ss 1(1)(5)(b)(c), 4; Crim Justice (S), 2003 asp 7, s 36(1)(4); Management of Offenders etc (S), 2005 asp 14, s 15(1)(12)

    rep in pt—Convention Rights (Compliance) (S), 2001 asp 7, ss 1(1)(5)(a), 4

    restr—SSI 2001/315, rules 14(5), 18(3)

s 17A added—Management of Offenders etc (S), 2005 asp 14, s 15(1)(13)

s 18 am—(S) Loc Govt etc(S), 1994 c 39, s 180(1), sch 13 para 179(2); Crim Justice (S), 1995 c 20, s 117(1), sch 6 pt I para 179(4); Crim Justice (S), 2003 asp 7, s 60(6)

    ext—Crime(Sentences) 1997 c 43, ss 41,56(1), sch 1 pt II, paras 10(2)(5)(a)(6), 11(2)(4)(5), sch 5, paras 11(1)(3), 12(1)

    appl (mods)—SI 1997/1776, art 2, sch 1, paras 5-7

s 19 ext—Crime(Sentences) 1997 c 43 ss 41,56(1), sch 1 pt II paras 10(2)(5), 11(2)(4), sch 5, paras 11(1)-(3)(5),12(1)

    appl (mods)—SI 1997/1776, art 2, sch 1, paras 5-7

s 20 ext—Crime (Sentences), 1997 c 43, ss 41,56(1), sch 1 pt II, paras 10(2)(5), 11(2)(4)(5)(6)(7), sch 5, paras 11(1)(3),12

    am—Crime and Disorder, 1998 c 37, s 119, sch 8, para 106; Convention Rights (Compliance) (S), 2001 asp 7, s 5(1)(b)(c)(6)

    rep in pt—Convention Rights (Compliance) (S), 2001 asp 7, s 5(1)(a)(6); Crim Justice (S), 2003 asp 7, s 28(1)(4)

s 21 ext—Crime (Sentences), 1997 c 43, ss 41,56(1), sch 1 pt II, paras 10(2)(5), 11(2)(4), sch 5, paras 11(1)(3),12

s 26 rep—SSI 2005/465, art 3, sch 2

s 26A added—Crime and Disorder, 1998 c 37, s 87

    am—Crim Justice (S), 2003 asp 7, s 37

s 26B added—Crim Justice (S), 2003 asp 7, s 41

s 26C added (1.2.2016)—Prisoners (Control of Release) (S), 2015 asp 8, s 2(2)

1993

c 9 *continued*

s 27 am—(S) Loc Govt etc(S) 1994 c 39, s 180(1), sch 13 para 179(3); Crim Procedure (Conseq Provns)(S), 1995 c 40, ss 5,7(5), sch 4 para 86(10); Justices of the Peace, 1997 c 25, s 73(2), sch 5, para 33; Crime and Disorder, 1998 c 37, s 111(3), 119, sch 8, para 107; Crim Justice and Court Services, 2000 c 43, s 74, sch 7 pt II para 118; Crim Justice (S), 2003 asp 7, ss 1(2), 32(1)(2), sch 1 para 1(1)(3)(a)(b); Management of Offenders etc (S), 2005 asp 14, s 21(7); SI 2005/886, art 2, sch para 50(2); Crim Justice and Licensing (S), 2010 asp 13, s 71, sch 4 para 10

ext—Crime (Sentences), 1997 c 43, ss 41,56(1), sch 1 pt II, para 10(2)(4)(5), sch 5, paras 11(1)(3),12(1)

rep in pt—Crime and Punishment (S) Act 1997 c 48, s 62(1)(2), sch 1, para 14(16), sch 3; Convention Rights (Compliance) (S), 2001 asp 7, ss 1(1)(6), 4

excl—International Crim Court. (S), 2001 asp 13, s 24(c)

appl—Crime (Sentences), 1997 c 43, sch 1 para 8

ss 28-35,37-43 rep—Crim Procedure (Conseq Provns)(S), 1995 c 40, ss 4,6, sch 3 pt II paras 16,17, sch 5

s 45 am—Crim Justice and Public Order, 1994 c 33, s 130(2); Management of Offenders etc (S), 2005 asp 14, s 15(1)(14)

rep in pt—Crim Justice (S), 2003 asp 7, s 85, sch 4 para 2(1)(4)

sch 1 am—Crim Justice (S), 2003 asp 7, s 32(1)(3)(a)

sch 1 rep in pt—Crim Justice (S), 2003 asp 7, s 32(1)(3)(b)

sch 2 ext—Crime (Sentences), 1997 c 43, ss 41,56(1), sch 1 pt II, para 10(2), sch 5, paras 11(1)(3)(4),12(1)

rep in pt—SI 1999/1820, art 4, sch 2 pt I para 110 pt IV

am—Convention Rights (Compliance) (S), 2001 asp 7, s 5(2)-(6)

schs 3, 4 rep—Crim Procedure (Conseq Provns)(S), 1995 c 40, ss 4,6, sch 3 pt II paras 16, 17, sch 5

sch 5 rep in pt—Crim Procedure (Conseq Provns)(S), 1995 c 40, ss 4,6, sch 3 pt II paras 16, 17, sch 5; Mental Health (Care and Treatment) (S), 2003 asp 13, s 331(2), sch 5 pt 1; SSI 2015/39, sch para 2

sch 6 appl—Crime and Disorder, 1998 c 37, s 112; Crim Justice (S), 2003 asp 7, s 85, sch 4 para 1

am—Crim Justice, 1993 c 36, ss 75(2),76(3); Crim Justice and Public Order, 1994 c 33, ss 130(3)(a)(b), 134(1)(a)(b), 135; Children (S), 1995 c 36, s 105(4), sch 4 para 56(3);Crime (Sentences), 1997 c 43, s 55, sch 4 para 16(2);Crime and Punishment (S) Act 1997 c 48, s 62(1)(2), sch 1, para 14(18); Crime and Disorder, 1998 c 37, s 111(4)(a)(c)(d)(5)(6), 119, sch 8, paras 70(1), 108; Convention Rights (Compliance) (S), 2001 asp 7, ss 1(1)(7)(a)(i)(iii)(b)(ii), 4; Crim Justice (S), 2003 asp 7, s 33(3); SSI 2005/465, art 2, sch 1 para 23(1)(3)

rep in pt—Crime and Disorder, 1998 c 37, ss 111(4)(b),120(2), sch 10; Convention Rights (Compliance) (S), 2001 asp 7, ss 1(1)(7)(a)(ii)(b)(i), 3(3), 4

cert functions exercisable in S—SI 1999/1748, art 4(2), sch 3, pts II, III, paras 5-8, 10

ext—Crime (Sentences), 1997 c 43, ss 41,56(1), sch 1 pt II, paras 10(2)(5), 11(2), sch 5 paras 11(1)-(3), 12(1)(2)

mod—Repatriation of Prisoners, 1984 c 47, sch para 2

sch 8 rep in pt—Access to Justice, 1999 c 22, s 106, sch 15 pt I

c 10   *Charities*—rep Charities, 2011 c 25, sch 10

c 11   **Clean Air**

trans of powers —(W) SI 1999/672, art 2, sch 1

appl (mods)—SIs 1999/1736, art 15; 2011/939, art 9, sch 2

appl—(S) SSI 2001/50, reg 2(1), sch 5

mod—SIs 2010/1214, art 4, sch; 2010/1216, art 4, sch; 2010/1217, art 4, sch; 2010/1218, art 4, sch

s 1 power to excl—Clean Air, 1993 c 11, s 45(1)(a)

s 2 am—Environment, 1995 c 25, s 120(1), sch 22 para 195; SI 2015/664, sch 4 para 25

s 3 rep in pt—Environment, 1995 c 25, s 120(3), sch 24

s 5 power to excl—Clean Air, 1993 c 11, s 45(1)(a)

s 16 am—Building (S), 2003 asp 8, s 58, sch 6 para 20

s 17 rep—Environment, 1995 c 25, s 120(3), sch 24

s 18 ext—SI 2008/514, reg 2

s 19 see—(trans of functions) Environment, 1995 c 25, s 21(2)(c)

mod—Environment, 1995 c 25, s 33(5)(f)

am—(S) Environment, 1995 c 25, s 120(1), sch 22 para 196

ext—SI 2008/514, reg 2

1993

c 11 *continued*

s 20 power to excl—Clean Air, 1993 c 11, s 45(1)(a)

excl—SIs 1997/3009, art 2; (EW) 1999/1515, art 2; (S) SSI 1999/58, art 2; SIs (E)
2001/422, art 2, sch; (W) 1231(W 65), art 2, sch; (S) SSI 2001/16, art 2, sch;
SIs (E) 2003/2328, art 2; (W) 2727 (W 262), art 2, sch; (S) SSI 2003/436, art 2,
sch; (W) SIs 2005/426 (W 43), art 2, sch; (E) 2304, art 2, sch; (S) SSI 2005/615,
art 2, sch; SI 2008/515, art 2, sch; 2008/3101 (W 275), art 2, sch

appl (mod)—(E) SI 2007/2462, art 2

ext—SI 2008/514, reg 2

restr—SI 2013/561 (W 64), art 2

am—Regulatory Reform (S), 2014 asp 3, s 50(2); Deregulation, 2015 c 20, s 15(2)(3)

s 21 ext—SI 2008/514, reg 2

am—Regulatory Reform (S), 2014 asp 3, s 50(3); Deregulation, 2015 c 20, s 15(4)(5)

rep in pt—Regulatory Reform (S), 2014 asp 3, s 50(4); Deregulation, 2015 c 20, s
15(6)

ss 22-28 ext—SI 2008/514, reg 2

s 29 ext—SI 2008/514, reg 2

am—Regulatory Reform (S), 2014 asp 3, s 50(5); Deregulation, 2015 c 20, s 15(7)

s 30 rep in pt—SL(R), 1998 c 43, s 1(1), sch 1 pt X, Group 5; SL(R), 2004 c 14, s 1(1), sch
1 pt 13; Consumer Rights, 2015 c 15, sch 6 para 52(2)(4)

am—SL(R), 1998 c 43, s 1(2), sch 2, para 13; Consumer Rights, 2015 c 15, sch 6 para
52(3)(5)

s 31 am—SI 2000/1973, reg 39, sch 10 pt 1 paras 10,11; (S) SSI 2000/323, reg 36, sch 10
pt I para 4(2); SI 2013/755 (W 90), sch 2 para 343(2)(3); Regulatory Reform (S),
2014 asp 3, sch 3 para 4(2)(a)(ii)(b); Consumer Rights, 2015 c 15, sch 6 para 53

s 32 am—Consumer Rights, 2015 c 15, sch 6 para 54

s 33 am—Pollution Prevention and Control, 1999 c 24, s 6(1), sch 2 paras 9, 10; Regulatory
Reform (S), 2014 asp 3, sch 3 para 4(3)

rep in pt—(EW prosp) Pollution Prevention and Control, 1999 c 24, s 6(2), sch 3

s 35 am—Pollution Prevention and Control, 1999 c 24, s 6, sch 2, paras 9, 11; Regulatory
Reform (S), 2014 asp 3, sch 3 para 4(4)

rep in pt—(EW prosp) Pollution Prevention and Control, 1999 c 24, s 6, sch 3

s 36 rep in pt—(EW prosp) Pollution Prevention and Control, 1999 c 24, s 6, sch 3

am—SI 2000/1973, reg 39, sch 10 pt 1 paras 10,12; (S) SSI 2000/323, reg 36, sch 10
pt I para 4(3); SI 2013/755 (W 90), sch 2 para 344; Regulatory Reform (S), 2014
asp 3, sch 3 para 4(5)

excl—SI 2014/3318, reg 11, sch 3

s 40 am—SI 2013/755 (W 90), sch 2 para 345

s 41 rep—(EW prosp) Pollution Prevention and Control, 1999 c 24, s 6, sch 3

s 41A added—SI 2000/1973, reg 39, sch 10 pt 1 paras 10,13; (S) SSI 2000/323, reg 36,
sch 10 pt I para 4(4)

am—(EW) SIs 2007/3538, reg 73, sch 21; 2009/1799, reg 28, sch 2; 2010/675, reg
107, sch 26; Regulatory Reform (S), 2014 asp 3, sch 3 para 4(6)(7)

s 42 rep in pt—Environment, 1995 c 25, s 120(3), sch 24

am—Regulatory Reform (S), 2014 asp 3, sch 3 para 26

s 43 power to excl—Clean Air, 1993 c 11, s 45(1)(a)

s 46 am—Merchant Shipping, 1995 c 21, s 314(2), sch 13 para 94(a)

s 49 am—Consumer Rights, 2015 c 15, sch 6 para 55

s 51 rep in pt—Environment, 1995 c 25, s 120(3), sch 24

s 56 appl (mods)—SI 1994/2249

am—Consumer Rights, 2015 c 15, sch 6 para 56

s 57 appl (mods)—SI 1994/2249

s 58 appl (mods)—SI 1994/2249

rep in pt—Consumer Rights, 2015 c 15, sch 6 para 57(a)

am—Consumer Rights, 2015 c 15, sch 6 para 57(b)

s 59 am—Environment, 1995 c 25, s 120(1), sch 22 para 197

s 60 am—Environment, 1995 c 25, s 120(1), sch 22 para 198

s 61 rep in pt (S)—Public Health etc (S), 2008 asp 5, s 126, sch 3 pt 1

s 62 rep in pt—SL(R), 1993 c 50, s 1(1), sch 1 pt I; (S) Housing (Scotland), 2006 asp 1, s
192, sch 7

s 63 am—Environment, 1995 c 25, s 120(1), sch 22 para 199

s 64 am—Loc Govt (W), 1994 c 19, s 22(3), sch 9 para 18; (S) Loc Govt etc(S), 1994 c 39,
s 180(1), sch 13 para 180; Merchant Shipping, 1995 c 21, s 314(2), sch 13
para 94(b); Adults with Incapacity (S), 2000, asp 4, s 88(2), sch 5 para 25

1993

c 11 s 64 *continued*

rep in pt—Loc Govt (W), 1994 c 19, ss 22(3),66(8), sch 9 para 18, sch 18; (S) Public
Health etc (S), 2008 asp 5, s 126, sch 3 pt 1

s 66 rep (EW)—Clean Air, 1993 c 11, s 66(2); SI 1996/3056, art 2

s 68 rep in pt—SL(R), 2004 c 14, s 1(1), sch 1 pt 13

sch 3 rep (EW)—Clean Air, 1993 c 11, s 66(2); SI 1996/3056, art 2

c 12   **Radioactive Substances**

trans of functions—Environment, 1995 c 25, s 2(1)(e)

trans of powers —(W) SI 1999/672, art 2, sch 1

am—Environment, 1995 c 25, s 5(5)(h)

mod—Environment, 1995 c 25, ss 33(5)(g),120(1), sch 22 para 200; (prosp) Defence
Reform, 2014 c 20, sch 1 para 5

power to mod—Environmental Protection, 1990 c 43, ss 78YC(b)

appl—Nuclear Installations, 1965 c 57, ss 3(6A), 4(3A); (W) SI 1987/764, art 3(8); Energy,
2004 c 20, s 37(7); SI 2006/3169, art 2(2)

ss 1-7 rep (EW)—SI 2010/675, regs 107, 109, sch 26 para 11, sch 28

ss 1, 2 replaced (S) (by ss1A-1H, 1J)—SSI 2011/207, reg 3

s 8 am—Environment, 1995 c 25, s 120(1), sch 22 para 203; SI 2010/675, reg 107, sch 26
para 11(3)

rep in pt—(EW) SI 2010/675, regs 107, 109, sch 26 para 11, sch 28; (S) SSI 2011/207,
reg 8

ss 9, 10 rep (EW)—SI 2010/675, regs 107, 109, sch 26 para 11, sch 28

s 11 saved—SI 1999/3232, reg 30(2)

rep in pt—(EW) SI 2010/675, reg 107, schs 26, 28

am—(EW) SI 2010/675, reg 107, sch 26 para 11(4)

ss 12-14 rep (EW)—SI 2010/675, regs 107, 109, sch 26 para 11, sch 28

s 15 saved—SI 1999/3232, reg 30(2)

am—(S) SSI 2000/100, reg 2; (EW) SIs 2001/4005, reg 2; 2010/675, reg 107, sch 26
para 11(5); (S) SSI 2011/207, reg 4(2)

rep in pt—(EW) SI 2010/675, regs 107, 109, sch 26 para 11, sch 28; (S) SSI 2011/207,
reg 4(1)

excl—SI 2010/675 reg 2(4) (added by SI 2011/988, sch 3 para 2(b))

ss 16-39 rep (EW)—SI 2010/675, regs 107, 109, sch 26 para 11, sch 28

s 16 rep in pt (S)—Energy, 2013 c 32, sch 12 para 67(a)

am (S)—Energy, 2013 c 32, sch 12 para 67(b); Food (S), 2015 asp 1, sch para 5(2)

s 17 rep in pt (S)—Energy, 2013 c 32, sch 12 para 68(a)

am (S)—Energy, 2013 c 32, sch 12 para 68(b); Food (S), 2015 asp 1, sch para 5(3)

s 25 am (S)—Food (S), 2015 asp 1, sch para 5(4)

s 40 am—Environment, 1995 c 25, s 120(1), sch 22 para 224; Regulatory Reform (S), 2014
asp 3, sch 3 para 42(2)

ss 41, 42 rep (EW)—SI 2010/675, regs 107, 109, sch 26 para 11, sch 28

s 43 rep—Environment, 1995 c 25, s 120(1)(3), sch 22 para 221, sch 24

s 44 rep in pt—(EW) SI 2010/675, reg 109, sch 26 para 11, sch 28

ss 45, 46 rep (EW)—SI 2010/675, regs 107, 109, sch 26 para 11, sch 28

s 46 am (S)—Regulatory Reform (S), 2014 asp 3, sch 3 para 42(3)

s 47 subst (EW)—SI 2010/675, reg 107, sch 26 para 11(6)

am (S)—SSI 2011/207, reg 5(1)(2)

s 48 rep (EW)—SI 2010/675, regs 107, 109, sch 26 para 11, sch 28

am (S)—SSI 2011/207, reg 6

sch 1 rep (EW)—SI 2010/675, reg 107, sch 26 para 11, sch 28

sch 1A subst for sch 1 (S)—SSI 2011/207, reg 7, sch

sch 2 rep—Environment, 1995 c 25, s 120(1)(3), sch 22 para 229, sch 24

sch 3 am—Clean Air, 1993 c 11, s 66(1), sch 4 para 6; Environment, 1995 c 25, ss 107,
120(1), sch 17 para 8, sch 22 para 230.sch 3, para 14; Planning (Conseq Provns)
(S), 1997 c 11, s 4, sch 2, para 54; (NI) SI 1999/662, art 63(1), sch 7; (S) SSI
2006/181, art 2, sch; (EW) Marine and Coastal Access, 2009 c 23, s 184, sch 14
paras 16, 18; SI 2010/675, reg 107, sch 26 para 11(7); Regulatory Reform (S),
2014 asp 3, sch 3 para 27(b)(ii)

rep in pt—Environment, 1995 c 25, s 120(3), sch 24; Marine and Coastal Access,
2009 c 23, s 321, sch 22 pt 4; (EW) SI 2010/675, regs 107, 109, sch 26 para
11, sch 28; Regulatory Reform (S), 2014 asp 3, sch 3 para 27(a)(b)(i)

sch 4 rep in pt—(EW prosp) Pollution Prevention and Control, 1999 c 24, s 6, sch 3; Energy,
2013 c 32, sch 12 para 30

1993

c 12 *continued*

    sch 5 rep in pt—SL(R), 2004 c 14, s 1(1), sch 1 pt 16/1

    sch 6 rep (EW)—SI 2010/675, regs 107, 109, sch 26 para 11, sch 28

c 13   *Carrying of Knives etc (Scotland)*—rep Crim Procedure (Conseq Provns)(S), 1995 c 40, s 6, sch 5

c 14   **Disability (Grants)**

    power to am—Northern Ireland, 1998 c 47, s 87

    s 1 rep in pt—(prosp) Welfare Reform, 2007 c 5, s 67, sch 8

    am—(pt prosp) Welfare Reform, 2007 c 5, s 61(1)(2)

c 15   *Protection of Animals (Scotland)*—rep Animal Health and Welfare (S), 2006 asp 11, s 52, sch 2 para 9(o)

c 16   **Foreign Compensation (Amendment)**

c 17   **Non-Domestic Rating**

c 18   **Reinsurance (Acts of Terrorism)**

    trans of functions—(saving) SI 1997/2781, arts 2(1),7,8(1), sch pt II, paras 120-123

c 19   **Trade Union Reform and Employment Rights**

    ss 23-26 rep—Employment Rights, 1996 c 18, s 242, sch 3 pt I

    s 27 rep—SI 1995/31, reg 6, sch

    ss 28-31 rep—Employment Rights, 1996 c 18, s 242, sch 3 pt I

    s 33 rep—SI 2006/246, reg 20

    s 34 rep in pt—SI 1995/2587, reg 3(11); SL(R), 2004 c 14, s 1(1), sch 1 pt 8

    s 35 rep—SL(R), 2004 c 14, s 1(1), sch 1 pt 8

    ss 36-38 rep—Employment Tribunals, 1996 c 17, s 45, sch 3 pt I

    s 39 rep in pt—Employment Rights, 1996 c 18, s 242, sch 3 pt I; Equality, 2010 c 15, s 211, sch 26 para 25, sch 27, pt 1 (as subst by SI 2010/2279, schs 1, 2)

    ss 40-42 rep—Employment Tribunals, 1996 c 17, s 45, sch 3 pt I

    s 43 rep in pt—Employment Relations, 1999 c 26, s 44, sch 9(5)

    s 54 rep in pt—Employment Rights, 1996 c 18, s 242, sch 3 pt I

    schs 2-5 rep—Employment Rights, 1996 c 18, s 242, sch 3 pt I

    sch 6 rep in pt—Employment Rights, 1996 c 18, s 242, sch 3 pt I; Employment Rights (Dispute Resolution), 1998 c 8, s 15, sch 2; Equality, 2010 c 15, s 211, sch 26 para 26, sch 27, pt 1 (as subst by SI 2010/2279, schs 1, 2)

    sch 7 rep in pt—Employment Tribunals, 1996 c 17, s 45, sch 3 pt I; Employment Rights, 1996 c 18, s 242, sch 3 pt I; Employment Relations, 1999 c 26, s 44, sch 9(6); Equality, 2006 c 3, s 91, sch 4; Equality, 2010 c 15, s 211, sch 27 pt 1 (as subst by SI 2010/2279, sch 2)

    sch 8 rep in pt—Deregulation and Contracting Out, 1994 c 40, s 81, sch 17; Employment Tribunals, 1996 c 17, s 45, sch 3 pt I; Employment Rights, 1996 c 18, s 242, sch 3 pt I; Employment Relations, 1999 c 26, s 44, sch 9(6); SL(R), 2004 c 14, s 1(1), sch 1 pts 2/2, 8

    sch 9 rep in pt—Employment Rights, 1996 c 18, s 242, sch 3 pt I; SL(R), 2004 c 14, s 1(1), sch 1 pt 8; SI 2006/246, reg 20

c 20   *Licensing (Amendment) (Scotland)*—rep Licensing (S), 2005 asp 16, s 149, sch 7

c 21   **Osteopaths**

    saved—Scotland, 1998 c 46, s 30, sch 5 pt II, s G3(g)

    s 1 am—SI 2008/1774, art 2, sch 3; (prosp) Health and Social Care (Safety and Quality), 2015 c 28, sch para 3(2)

    rep in pt—SI 2008/1774, art 2, sch 3

    s 3 am—SI 2008/1774, art 2, sch 3

    s 5A added—SI 2007/3101, reg 207

    s 6 am—SI 2007/3101, reg 208

    s 8 am—SI 2007/3101, reg 209

    s 9 rep in pt—Chiropractors, 1994 c 17, s 42, sch 2 para 1(1)

    am—Chiropractors, 1994 c 17, s 42, sch 2 para 1(2)(3)

    s 10 am—Nat Health Service Reform and Health Care Professions, 2002 c 17, s 33(1)(2)(a)(b)(d); Crime and Cts, 2013 c 22, sch 9 para 116(a)(b)

    rep in pt—Nat Health Service Reform and Health Care Professions, 2002 c 17, ss 33(1)(2)(c), 37(2), sch 9 pt 2

    s 13 rep in pt—Chiropractors, 1994 c 17, s 42, sch 2 para 2(a)

    am—Chiropractors, 1994 c 17, s 42, sch 2 para 2(a)(b)

    s 17 am—SIs 2007/3101, reg 210; 2008/1774, art 2, sch 3

    s 18 am—Chiropractors, 1994 c 17, s 42, sch 2 para 3(1)(2)

    s 20 am—Chiropractors, 1994 c 17, s 42, sch 2 para 4; SI 2008/1774, art 2, sch 3; Policing and Crime, 2009 c 26, s 81(2)(3)(e)

1993

c 21 s 20 *continued*

rep in pt—SI 2008/1774, art 2, sch 3

s 22 am—Chiropractors, 1994 c 17, s 42, sch 2 para 5(1); Nat Health Service Reform and
Health Care Professions, 2002 c 17, s 33(1)(3)

rep in pt—Chiropractors, 1994 c 17, s 42, sch 2 para 5(2)

s 23 am—Nat Health Service Reform and Health Care Professions, 2002 c 17, s 33(1)(4)

ss 27, 28 rep in pt—Chiropractors, 1994 c 17, s 42, sch 2 para 6(2)(a)

am—Chiropractors, 1994 c 17, s 42, sch 2 para 6(2)(b)

s 29 am—Nat Health Service Reform and Health Care Professions, 2002 c 17, s 33(1)(5); SI
2007/3101, reg 211; Crime and Cts, 2013 c 22, sch 9 para 116(a)(b)

s 29A added—SI 2007/3101, reg 212

am—Crime and Cts, 2013 c 22, sch 9 para 116(a)(b)

s 30 am—Chiropractors, 1994 c 17, s 42, sch 2 para 7

s 31 am—Chiropractors, 1994 c 17, s 42, sch 2 para 8(a)(b); Nat Health Service Reform and
Health Care Professions, 2002 c 17, s 33(1)(6)(a)(b)(d)

rep in pt—Nat Health Service Reform and Health Care Professions, 2002 c 17, ss
33(1)(6)(c), 37(2), sch 9 pt 2

s 33 rep in pt—Competition 1998 c 41, s 74(1)(3), sch 12, para 16(a)(b), sch 14 pt I

am—Enterprise, 2002 c 40, s 278(1), sch 25, para 29

s 35 rep in pt—Nat Health Service Reform and Health Care Professions, 2002 c 17, ss
33(1)(7), 37(2), sch 9 pt 2; SI 2008/1774, art 2, sch 3

s 36 am—SI 2008/1774, art 2, sch 3

s 37 subst—SI 2014/1887, sch 1 para 9

s 38 rep—Data Protection, 1998 c 29, s 74(2), sch 16 pt I

s 39 rep—Police, 1997 c 50, ss 133(c),134(2), sch 10

s 40 am—SI 2008/948, art 3, sch 1

s 40A added—SI 2008/1774, art 2, sch 3

s 41 appl—Data Protection, 1998 c 29, s 69(1)(f)

am—Chiropractors, 1994 c 17, s 42, sch 2 para 9; SIs 2007/3101, reg 214; SI
2008/1774, art 2, sch 3

sch am—(pt retrosp) Chiropractors, 1994 c 17, s 42, sch 2 para 10(2)(3); Health and Social
Care (Community Health and Standards), 2003 c 43, s 187(8), sch 12 para 5; SI
2008/1774, art 2, sch 3; (prosp) Health and Social Care (Safety and Quality), 2015
c 28, sch para 3(3)(a)(b)

rep in pt—Health, 2006 c 28, s 80, sch 8 para 31, sch 9; SI 2008/1774, art 2, sch 3; SI
2009/1182, arts 4, 5-7, sch 5; Health and Social Care, 2012 c 7, sch 20 para
6(d)

c 22   *Merchant Shipping (Registration, etc)*—rep Merchant Shipping, 1995 c 21, s 314(1) sch 12;
(ext to Jersey) SI 2004/1284, art 3

c 23   **Asylum and Immigration Appeals**

am—Immigration and Asylum, 1999 c 33, s 65(1)

appl—Immigration, 1971 c 77, s 25(1A); Asylum and Immigration, 1996 c 49, ss 2(7),
11(6)

restr—Nationality, Immigration and Asylum, 2002 c 41, ss 77, 78

s 3 rep—Immigration and Asylum, 1999 c 33, s 169(1)(3), sch 14 paras 99, 100, sch 16

ss 4, 5 rep—Housing, 1996 c 52, s 227, sch 19 pt VIII; Immigration and Asylum, 1999 c 33,
ss 120(6), 121(3), 169(1)(3), sch 14 paras 99, 101, sch 16

s 6 excl—Asylum and Immigration, 1996 c 49, s 2(1)

rep—(retrosp to 26.7.1993) Immigration and Asylum, 1999 c 33, s 169(1)(3), sch 14
paras 99, 102(1)(2), sch 16

s 7 rep—Immigration and Asylum, 1999 c 33, s 169(1)(3), sch 14 paras 99, 103, sch 16

ext mods—(Iof M) SI 1997/275, art 2(2)

s 8 appl—SI 1994/1895

rep—Immigration and Asylum, 1999 c 33, s 169(1)(3), sch 14 paras 99, 104, sch 16

saving—(transtl provn) SI 2000/2444, art 3(2), sch 2 para 3(1)(2)(5)

s 9 rep—Immigration and Asylum, 1999 c 33, s 169(1)(3), sch 14 paras 99, 104, sch 16

s 9A inserted—Asylum and Immigration, 1996 c 49, s 12(2), sch 3 para 3

rep—Asylum and Immigration (Treatment of Claimants, etc), 2004 c 19, ss 26(7), 47,
sch 2 pt 1 para 9, sch 4

ss 10,11 rep—Immigration and Asylum, 1999 c 33, s 169(1)(3), sch 14 paras 99, 104,
sch 16

s 12 rep—Immigration and Asylum, 1999 c 33, s 169(1)(3), sch 14 paras 99, 107, sch 16

1993
c 23 *continued*

    sch 1 rep—Housing, 1996 c 52, s 227, sch 19 pt VIII; Immigration and Asylum, 1999 c 33, ss 120(6), 121(3), 169(1)(3), sch 14 paras 99, 101, sch 16

    sch 2 rep—Immigration and Asylum, 1999 c 33, s 169(1)(3), sch 14 paras 99, 104, sch 16

c 24   **Video Recordings**

    s 3 rep—Crim Justice and Public Order, 1994 c 33, s 168(3), sch 11

    s 5 rep—Crime and Punishment (S) Act 1997 c 48, ss 30(4),62(2), sch 3

    s 204 rep in pt—Finance, 2000 c 17, s 156, sch 40 pt III, Note 1

c 25   **Local Government (Overseas Assistance)**

    ext—Environment, 1995 c 25, s 70, sch 9 para 16

    s 1 am—Loc Govt (W), 1994 c 19, ss 20(4), 66(6), sch 6 pt II para 29, sch 16 para 103; (S) Loc Govt etc(S), 1994 c 39, s 180(1), sch 13 para 182; Environment, 1995 c 25, s 78, sch 10 para 36; GLA, 1999 c 29, ss 328(8),400, sch 29 pt I para 59; (E, W) SI 2001/3618, art 2; (EW) Fire and Rescue Services, 2004 c 21, s 53, sch 1 para 83; Civil Contingencies, 2004 c 36, s 32(1), sch 2 pt 1 para 10(3)(c); Loc Govt and Public Involvement in Health, 2007 c 28, s 209, sch 13 para 50; SI 2008/2840, art 4; Loc Democracy, Economic Development and Construction, 2009 c 20, s 119, sch 6 para 83

      rep in pt—Police and Magistrates' Cts, 1994 c 29, s 93, sch 9 pt I; Environment, 1995 c 25, s 120(3), sch 24; SI 2008/2840, art 4; Localism, 2011 c 20, sch 25 pt 32; Deregulation, 2015 c 20, sch 13 para 6(26)

c 26   **Bail (Amendment)**

    s 1 rep in pt—Extradition, 2003 c 41, ss 200(1)(4)(c)(7)(b), 220, sch 4

      am—Extradition, 2003 c 41, s 200(1)-(3)(4)(a)(b)(5)(6)(7)(a)(8)(9); Crim Justice, 2003 c 44, s 18; Constitutional Reform, 2005 c 4, s 15(1), sch 4 pt 1 para 231; Legal Aid, Sentencing and Punishment of Offenders, 2012 c 10, sch 11 para 32(2)-(5); ibid, sch 12 para 32

      appl—SI 2005/384, rules 19.16(11), 19.17(1)

c 27   **Local Government (Amendment)**

c 28   **Leasehold Reform, Housing and Urban Development**

    trans of powers—(W) SI 1999/672, art 2, sch 1

    s 1 rep in pt—Housing, 1996 c 52, ss 107(3),227, sch 19 pt V

      am—Housing, 1996 c 52, s 107, sch 10 para 2; (prosp) Commonhold and Leasehold Reform, 2002 c 15, s 124, sch 8, paras 2-4

    s 2 am—SI 1997/74, art 2, sch, para 9(a); (prosp) Commonhold and Leasehold Reform, 2002 c 15, s 124, sch 8, paras 2-4

      rep in pt—(prosp) Commonhold and Leasehold Reform, 2002 c 15, s 180, sch 14

    s 3 rep in pt—Housing, 1996 c 52, ss 107(1), 227, sch 19 pt V

    s 4 am—Housing, 1996 c 52, s 107(2); Commonhold and Leasehold Reform, 2002 c 15, ss 114-116

    ss 4A, 4B added (prosp)—Commonhold and Leasehold Reform, 2002 c 15, ss 114, 122

    s 4A appl—Finance, 2003 c 14, s 74(4)(a)

      am—SI 2009/1941, art 2, sch 1

    s 4C added—Commonhold and Leasehold Reform, 2002 c 15, ss 114, 122

      am—SI 2009/1941, art 2, sch 1

    s 5 am—Housing, 1996 c 52, s 106, sch 9 para 3(2); SIs 2009/1941, art 2, sch 1; 2011/1396, sch para 37(2)(g)

      rep in pt—Commonhold and Leasehold Reform, 2002 c 15, ss 114, 117(1), 180, sch 14

    s 6 rep—Commonhold and Leasehold Reform, 2002 c 15, s 180, sch 14

    s 7 am—SI 1997/627, art 2, sch, para 7; Civil Partnership, 2004 c 33, s 81, sch 8 para 47

      rep in pt—Commonhold and Leasehold Reform, 2002 c 15, s 180, sch 14

    ss 8, 8A rep—Commonhold and Leasehold Reform, 2002 c 15, s 180, sch 14

    s 8A added—Housing, 1996 c 52, s 106, sch 9 para 3(3)

    s 9 am—Housing, 1996 c 52, s 107, sch 10 para 3

    s 10 am—Housing, 1996 c 52, s 107, sch 10 para 4; Commonhold and Leasehold Reform, 2002 c 15, ss 114, 118; Civil Partnership, 2004 c 33, s 81, sch 8 para 48

      rep in pt—Housing, 1996 c 52, s 227, sch 19 pt V; Commonhold and Leasehold Reform, 2002 c 15, s 180, sch 14

      ext—Civil Partnership, 2004 c 33, ss 246, 247, sch 21 para 39

    s 11 am—Civil Evidence, 1995 c 38, s 15(1), sch 1 para 17; Housing, 1996 c 52, s 107, sch 10 para 5; (prosp) Commonhold and Leasehold Reform, 2002 c 15, s 124, sch 8, paras 2, 5

      rep in pt—Housing, 1996 c 52, s 227, sch 19 pt V; Commonhold and Leasehold Reform, 2002 c 15, s 180, sch 14

1993
c 28 *continued*

s 12 rep in pt—Commonhold and Leasehold Reform, 2002 c 15, s 180, sch 14

s 12A added—Commonhold and Leasehold Reform, 2002 c 15, s 114; (prosp) ibid, s 123(1)
  am—SI 2009/1941, art 2, sch 1

s 13 am—Housing, 1996 c 52, ss 106,107,111(2), sch 9 para 3(4), sch 10 para 6;
  Commonhold and Leasehold Reform, 2002 c 15, s 114; (prosp) ibid, ss 121,
  123(2), 124, sch 8, paras 2, 6
 rep in pt—Housing, 1996 c 52, ss 108, 227, sch 19 pt V; Commonhold and Leasehold
  Reform, 2002 c 15, ss 114, 119, 120, 180, sch 14

ss 14-16 rep (prosp)—Commonhold and Leasehold Reform, 2002 c 15, s 180, sch 14

s 17 am—Commonhold and Leasehold Reform, 2002 c 15, s 114; (pt prosp) ibid, ss 124,
  125, sch 8, paras 2, 7

s 18 am—Commonhold and Leasehold Reform, 2002 c 15, ss 114, 126(2); (prosp) ibid, s
  124, sch 8, paras 2, 8
 rep in pt—(prosp) Commonhold and Leasehold Reform, 2002 c 15, s 180, sch 14

s 19 am—Housing, 1996 c 52, s 107, sch 10 para 7

ss 20-36 am—(prosp) Commonhold and Leasehold Reform, 2002 c 15, s 124, sch 8, paras 2,
  9

s 21 am—Housing, 1996 c 52, s 107, sch 10 para 8; (prosp) Commonhold and Leasehold
  Reform, 2002 c 15, s 124, sch 8, paras 2,10

s 22 am—(prosp) Commonhold and Leasehold Reform, 2002 c 15, s 124, sch 8, paras 2, 11
 rep in pt—SI 2013/1036, sch 1 para 100

s 23 am—(prosp) Commonhold and Leasehold Reform, 2002 c 15, s 124, sch 8, paras 2, 12

s 24 am—(prosp) Commonhold and Leasehold Reform, 2002 c 15, s 124, sch 8, paras 2, 13;
  SI 2013/1036, sch 1 para 101

s 25 am—(prosp) Commonhold and Leasehold Reform, 2002 c 15, s 124, sch 8, paras 2, 14;
  SI 2013/1036, sch 1 para 102

s 26 am—Housing, 1996 c 52, s 107, sch 10 para 9; (prosp) Commonhold and Leasehold
  Reform, 2002 c 15, s 124, sch 8, paras 2, 15

s 27 am—(prosp) Commonhold and Leasehold Reform, 2002 c 15, s 124, sch 8, paras 2, 16;
  SI 2013/1036, sch 1 para 103

s 28 rep in pt—(prosp) Commonhold and Leasehold Reform, 2002 c 15, s 180, sch 14
 am—(prosp) Commonhold and Leasehold Reform, 2002 c 15, s 124, sch 8, paras 2, 17

s 29 rep in pt—(prosp) Commonhold and Leasehold Reform, 2002 c 15, s 180, sch 14; SI
  2003/2096, arts 4, 6, sch pt 1 para 20(a)
 am—SI 2003/2096, arts 4, 6, sch pt 1 para 20(b); (prosp) Commonhold and Leasehold
  Reform, 2002 c 15, s 124, sch 8, paras 2, 18; SI 2009/1941, art 2, sch 1

s 30 am—Housing, 1996 c 52, s 107, sch 10 para 10; (prosp) Commonhold and Leasehold
  Reform, 2002 c 15, s 124, sch 8, paras 2, 19

ss 31,32 am—(prosp) Commonhold and Leasehold Reform, 2002 c 15, s 124, sch 8, paras 2,
  20, 21

s 33 rep in pt—(prosp) Commonhold and Leasehold Reform, 2002 c 15, s 180, sch 14
 am—(prosp) Commonhold and Leasehold Reform, 2002 c 15, s 124, sch 8, paras 2, 22;
  SI 2013/1036, sch 1 para 104

s 34 am—Law of Property (Misc Provns), 1994 c 36, s 21(1), sch 1 para 12(1); Housing,
  1996 c 52, s 107, sch 10 para 11; Land Registration, 2002 c 9, s 133, sch 11, para
  30(1)(2); (prosp) Commonhold and Leasehold Reform, 2002 c 15, s 124, sch 8,
  paras 2, 23

s 35 am—(prosp) Commonhold and Leasehold Reform, 2002 c 15, s 124, sch 8, paras 2, 24

s 36 am—Housing, 1996 c 52, s 107, sch 10 para 12; (prosp) Commonhold and Leasehold
  Reform, 2002 c 15, s 124, sch 8, paras 2, 25

s 37A am—(prosp) Commonhold and Leasehold Reform, 2002 c 15, s 124, sch 8, paras 2,
  26
 rep in pt—(prosp) Commonhold and Leasehold Reform, 2002 c 15, s 180, sch 14

s 38 am—Housing, 1996 c 52, s 107, sch 10 para 13; SI 1997/74, art 2, sch para 9(b);
  (prosp) Commonhold and Leasehold Reform, 2002 c 15, s 124, sch 8, paras 2,
  27(1)-(4); SI 2013/1036, sch 1 para 105
 rep in pt—(prosp) Commonhold and Leasehold Reform, 2002 c 15, s 180, sch 14

s 39 am—Housing, 1996 c 52, ss 106, 112(2)-(4), sch 9 para 4(2); Commonhold and
  Leasehold Reform, 2002 c 15, ss 129, 130(1)(2), 132(1)
 rep in pt—Housing, 1996 c 52, s 227, sch 19 pt V; Commonhold and Leasehold
  Reform, 2002 c 15, ss 129, 130(1)(3), 131, 180, sch 14

s 41 am—(prosp) Commonhold and Leasehold Reform, 2002 c 15, s 124, sch 8, paras 2, 28

1993
c 28 *continued*

s 42 am—Housing, 1996 c 52, s 112(5); ibid, s 106, sch 9 para 4(3); Commonhold and
    Leasehold Reform, 2002 c 15, ss 129, 132(2)
    rep in pt—Commonhold and Leasehold Reform, 2002 c 15, s 180, sch 14
s 45 rep in pt—Commonhold and Leasehold Reform, 2002 c 15, s 180, sch 14
s 46 rep in pt—SI 2013/1036, sch 1 para 106
s 48 am—SI 2013/1036, sch 1 para 107
s 51 am—SI 2013/1036, sch 1 para 108
s 54 am—(prosp) Commonhold and Leasehold Reform, 2002 c 15, s 124, sch 8, paras 2, 29
s 57 am—Law of Property (Misc Provns), 1994 c 36, s 21(1), sch 1 para 12(2); Land
    Registration, 2002 c 9, s 133, sch 11, para 30(1)(2); Tribunals, Cts and
    Enforcement, 2007 c 15, s 86, sch 14 para 47
s 58A added—Housing, 1996 c 52, s 117
s 60 am—SI 2013/1036, sch 1 para 109
ss 61A,61B added—Housing, 1996 c 52, s 116, sch 11 para 3(1)
s 62 rep in pt—Commonhold and Leasehold Reform, 2002 c 15, s 180, sch 14
    am—SI 2013/1036, sch 1 para 110
s 65 rep (prosp)—Housing and Regeneration, 2008 c 17, s 321, sch 16
s 69 am—Housing, 1996 c 52, s 118(1)(2); Commonhold and Leasehold Reform, 2002 c 15,
    ss 114, 117(2); SI 2013/1036, sch 1 para 111(a)(b)
s 70 am—Housing, 1996 c 52, s 118(1)(3); Commonhold and Leasehold Reform, 2002 c 15,
    s 176, sch 13, paras 12, 13; SI 2013/1036, sch 1 para 112(b)
    rep in pt—SI 2013/1036, sch 1 para 112(a); (prosp) Infrastructure, 2015 c 7, sch 5 para
    38
s 71 am—Housing, 1996 c 52, s 118(1)(4)(b); SI 2013/1036, sch 1 para 113
    rep in pt—Housing, 1996 c 52, s 118(1)(4)(a)
    appl—SIs (E) 2003/2099, reg 3, sch 2 para 3(1)(b); (W) 2004/681 (W 69), reg 3, sch 2
    para 3(2)(b)
s 73 appl—SIs (E) 2003/2099, reg 3, sch 2 para 3(2)(c); (W) 2004/681 (W 69), reg 3, sch 2
    para 3(2)(c)
    am—SI 2013/1036, sch 1 para 114
s 74 am—(prosp) Commonhold and Leasehold Reform, 2002 c 15, s 124, sch 8, paras 2, 30
s 75 rep in pt—Commonhold and Leasehold Reform, 2002 c 15, s 180, sch 14
    am—SI 2013/1036, sch 1 para 115
Pt 1, Ch 5 (ss 76-84) appl (mods)—Commonhold and Leasehold Reform, 2002 c 15, s
    102(1), sch 7, para 14
    ext—(pt prosp) Commonhold and Leasehold Reform, 2002 c 15, s 172(1)(e)
s 78 appl—Housing, 1996 c 52, s 84(2)
    am —(prosp) Housing and Regeneration, 2008 c 17, s 303, sch 12 paras 14, 15
s 79 am—(prosp) Commonhold and Leasehold Reform, 2002 c 15, s 157, sch 10, paras
    16-19; (prosp) Housing and Regeneration, 2008 c 17, s 303, sch 12 paras 14, 16
ss 80-82 am—(prosp) Commonhold and Leasehold Reform, 2002 c 15, s 157, sch 10, paras
    16-19
s 84 power to am—Commonhold and Leasehold Reform, 2002 c 15, s 150, sch 9, para 13(a)
    am—Commonhold and Leasehold Reform, 2002 c 15, s 150, sch 9, para 10
s 87 am—Commonhold and Leasehold Reform, 2002 c 15, s 150, sch 9, para 11
    power to am—Commonhold and Leasehold Reform, 2002 c 15, s 150, sch 9, para 13(a)
s 88 am—Commonhold and Leasehold Reform, 2002 c 15, s 176, sch 13, paras 12, 14; SI
    2013/1036, sch 1 para 117(b)(c)
    rep in pt—Commonhold and Leasehold Reform, 2002 c 15, s 180, sch 14; SI
    2013/1036, sch 1 paras 116, 117(a)
s 90 am—Crime and Cts, 2013 c 22, sch 9 para 52; SI 2013/1036, sch 1 para 118
s 91 am—Housing, 1996 c 52, s 116, sch 11 para 3(2); Commonhold and Leasehold Reform,
    2002 c 15, ss 124, 176, sch 8, paras 2, 31, sch 13, paras 12, 15; SI 2013/1036,
    sch 1 para 119(b)-(d)
    rep in pt—Commonhold and Leasehold Reform, 2002 c 15, s 180, sch 14; SI
    2013/1036, sch 1 para 119(a)
s 92 am—Crime and Cts, 2013 c 22, sch 9 para 52
s 93 am—(prosp) Commonhold and Leasehold Reform, 2002 c 15, s 124, sch 8, paras 2, 32;
    Charities, 2011 c 25, sch 7 para 67; SI 2013/1036, sch 1 para 120
    rep in pt—(prosp) Commonhold and Leasehold Reform, 2002 c 15, s 180, sch 14
s 93A added—Housing, 1996 c 52, s 113
    rep in pt—Trusts of Land and Appointment of Trustees, 1996 c 47, s 25(2), sch 4

1993

c 28 s 93A *continued*

am—(prosp) Commonhold and Leasehold Reform, 2002 c 15, s 124, sch 8, paras 2, 33

s 94 am—Housing, 1996 c 52, ss 106,118(5), sch 9 para 5; Commonhold and Leasehold Reform, 2002 c 15, ss 129, 133; SI 2013/1036, sch 1 para 121

rep in pt—Commonhold and Leasehold Reform, 2002 c 15, s 180, sch 14

s 97 am—Land Registration, 2002 c 9, s 133, sch 11, para 30(1)(3)(4); (prosp) Commonhold and Leasehold Reform, 2002 c 15, s 124, sch 8, paras 2, 34, 35

rep in pt—Land Registration, 2002 c 9, s 135, sch 13

s 98 am—(prosp) Commonhold and Leasehold Reform, 2002 c 15, s 124, sch 8, paras 2, 34, 35

s 99 rep in pt—(prosp) Commonhold and Leasehold Reform, 2002 c 15, s 180, sch 14

am—Housing (W), 2014 anaw 7, s 140(1); Leasehold Reform (Amdt), 2014 c 10, s 1

s 101 rep in pt—Commonhold and Leasehold Reform, 2002 c 15, s 180, sch 14

am—Crime and Cts, 2013 c 22, sch 9 para 52; SI 2013/1036, sch 1 para 122

s 124 rep in pt—Housing, 1996 c 52, s 227, sch 19 pt IX

s 127 restr—SI s 1994/42; 1995/2720, art 2, sch

ss 130,131 rep—Housing, 1996 c 52, s 227, sch 19 pt X

s 134 rep—Housing, 1996 c 52, s 227, sch 19 pt I

s 135 rep —Housing and Regeneration, 2008 c 17, s 311, sch 16, sch 14 para 3(1), (2)

s 136 am—(retrosp) Finance, 1997 c 16, s 109; SI 2004/533, art 5(a); Housing and Regeneration, 2008 c 17, s 311, sch 14 para 3(1), (3), (5)

rep in pt—SI 2004/533, art 5(b)(c)

s 137 rep in pt—Housing and Regeneration, 2008 c 17, s 311, sch 16, sch 14 para 3(1), (4)

ss 141-143, 146-148, 152 rep—Housing (S), 2001 asp 10, s 112, sch 10, para 20

s 155 rep—Housing (S), 2001 asp 10, s 112, sch 10, para 20

s 156 rep in pt—(prosp) Housing (S), 2014 asp 14, sch 2 para 7

s 157 rep in pt—Housing (S), 2006 asp 1, s 192, sch 7

s 158 rep—Housing and Regeneration, 2008 c 17, ss 56, 321(1), sch 8 para 63 (1), (2)(a), sch 16

ss 159-161 rep—Housing and Regeneration, 2008 c 17, ss 56, 321(1), sch 8 para 63 (1), (2)(a), sch 16

ss 163-173 rep—Housing and Regeneration, 2008 c 17, ss 56, 321(1), sch 8 para 63 (1), (2)(a), sch 16

s 167 am—Loc Govt (W), 1994 c 19, s 66(6), sch 16 para 104

rep in pt—Coal Industry, 1994 c 21, s 67, sch 9 para 45, sch 11 pt IV; SI 1999/416, art 9

s 174 rep—Housing Grants, Construction and Regeneration, 1996 c 53, s 147, sch 3 pt III

ss 175, 177 rep—Housing and Regeneration, 2008 c 17, s 56, sch 16, sch 8 para 63 (1), (2)(a)

s 181 rep in pt—Govt of Wales, 1998 c 38, s 152, sch 18 pt V; Housing and Regeneration, 2008 c 17, s 321, sch 16

ss 183-185 rep—Housing and Regeneration, 2008 c 17, s 56, sch 16, sch 8 para 63 (1), (2)(a)

s 188 rep in pt—Housing Grants, Construction and Regeneration, 1996 c 53, s 147, sch 3 pt III; Housing and Regeneration, 2008 c 17, s 56, sch 16, sch 8 para 63 (1), (3)

sch 1 am—Housing, 1996 c 52, s 107, sch 10 paras 14, 15; (prosp) Commonhold and Leasehold Reform, 2002 c 15, s 124, sch 8, paras 2, 36(1)-(3); SI 2013/1036, sch 1 para 123

sch 2 am—Housing, 1996 c 52, s 107, sch 10 para 16; Trusts of Land and Appointment of Trustees, 1996 c 47, s 25(1), sch 3 para 27(2); (saving) GSM Cathedrals, 1999 (No 1), ss 36(2)(6), 38(2)(3); Mental Capacity, 2005 c 9, s 67(1), sch 6 para 39; GSM C of E (Misc Provns), 2006 No 1, s 14, sch 5 para 31(a)(b)(c); SI 2013/1036, sch 1 para 124

rep in pt—Trusts of Land and Appointment of Trustees, 1996 c 47, s 25(2), sch 4; GSM C of E (Misc Provns), 2006 No 1, s 14, sch 5 para 31(a)

sch 3 am—Housing, 1996 c 52, s 107, sch 10 para 17; (prosp) Commonhold and Leasehold Reform, 2002 c 15, s 124, sch 8, paras 2, 37(1)-(12)

rep in pt—(prosp) Commonhold and Leasehold Reform, 2002 c 15, s 180, sch 14

sch 4 am—(prosp) Commonhold and Leasehold Reform, 2002 c 15, s 124, sch 8, paras 2, 38

sch 5 am—(prosp) Commonhold and Leasehold Reform, 2002 c 15, s 124, sch 8, paras 2, 39; SI 2013/1036, sch 1 para 125

rep in pt—(prosp) Commonhold and Leasehold Reform, 2002 c 15, s 180, sch 14

1993

c 28 *continued*

sch 6 am—Housing, 1996 c 52, ss 107,109, sch 10 para 18; Commonhold and Leasehold Reform, 2002 c 15, ss 114,126(1),127,128; (prosp) ibid, s 124, sch 8, paras 2, 40(1)-(6)

rep in pt—Commonhold and Leasehold Reform, 2002 c 15, s 180, sch 14

sch 7 am—Law of Property (Misc Provns), 1994 c 36, s 21(1), sch 1 para 12(3); Housing, 1996 c 52, s 107, sch 10 para 19; (prosp) Commonhold and Leasehold Reform, 2002 c 15, s 124, sch 8, paras 2, 41

sch 8 am—(prosp) Commonhold and Leasehold Reform, 2002 c 15, s 124, sch 8, paras 2, 42(1)-(4); Crime and Cts, 2013 c 22, sch 9 para 52

sch 9 am—Housing, 1996 c 52, s 107, sch 10 para 20; SI 1997/74, art 2, sch para 9(d); (prosp) Commonhold and Leasehold Reform, 2002 c 15, s 124, sch 8, paras 2, 43; SI 2013/1036, sch 1 para 126(a)(b)

sch 9A added—Law of Property (Misc Provns), 1994 c 36, s 21(1), sch 1 para 12(4)

sch 10 rep in pt—Housing, 1996 c 52, s 227, sch 19 pt IX

am—(EW) SI 1996/2325, art 5(1), sch 2 para 21(3); SIs 1997/74, art 2, sch para 9(e); 2010/866, art 5, sch 2

sch 11 am—SI 2013/1036, sch 1 para 127

sch 13 am—Housing, 1996 c 52, s 110; Commonhold and Leasehold Reform, 2002 c 15, ss 129, 134-136; SI 2013/1036, sch 1 para 128

rep in pt—Commonhold and Leasehold Reform, 2002 c 15, s 180, sch 14

sch 14 am—Trusts of Land and Appointment of Trustees, 1996 c 47, s 25(1), sch 3 para 27(3); (saving) GSM Cathedrals, 1999 (No 1), ss 36(2)(6), 38(2)(3); Crime and Cts, 2013 c 22, sch 9 para 52; SI 2013/1036, sch 1 para 129

rep in pt—Crime and Cts, 2013 c 22, sch 9 para 100

sch 17 rep—Housing and Regeneration, 2008 c 17, ss 56, 321(1), sch 8 para 63(1), (2)(b), sch 16

sch 18 rep—Housing and Regeneration, 2008 c 17, ss 56, 321(1), sch 8 para 63(1), (2)(b), sch 16

sch 19 rep—Housing and Regeneration, 2008 c 17, ss 56, 321(1), sch 8 para 63(1), (2)(b), sch 16

sch 20 rep—Housing and Regeneration, 2008 c 17, ss 56, 321(1), sch 8 para 63(1), (2)(b), sch 16

sch 21 rep in pt—Land Registration, 2002 c 9, s 135, sch 13; Housing and Regeneration, 2008 c 17, s 321, sch 16; SI 2008/3002, arts 5, 6, schs 2, 3

am—SI 2008/3002, arts 4, 5, schs 1, 2

c 29 **Representation of the People**

power to am—SI 2006/3412, arts 3-5, sch 1

c 30 **Sexual Offences**

c 31 **Road Traffic (Driving Instruction by Disabled Persons)**

s 1 rep—Deregulation, 2015 c 20, sch 2 para 30(2)

s 2 rep (prosp)—Road Safety, 2006 c 49, s 59, sch 7(14)

rep in pt—Deregulation, 2015 c 20, sch 2 para 30(3)

sch rep in pt—(prosp) Road Safety, 2006 c 49, s 59, sch 7(14); Deregulation, 2015 c 20, sch 2 para 30(4)

c 32 **European Communities (Amendment)**

s 2 rep —European Union, 2011 c 12, s 14(3)(a)

s 3 am—SI 2012/1809, art 3(1), sch pt 1

s 4 am—SI 2012/1809, art 3(1), sch pt 1

s 5 am—SI 2012/1809, art 3(1), sch pt 1

s 6 am—Govt of Wales, 1998 c 38, s 125, sch 12, para 34; Scotland, 1998 c 46, s 125, sch 8, para 28; SIs 2001/3675, art 2; 2001/3719, art 2, sch, para 5; 2012/1809, art 3(1), sch pt 1

c 33 *Appropriation*—rep Appropriation, 1995 c 19, ss 2,3, sch(c)

c 34 **Finance**

mod—SI 1995/352, reg 13

s 4 rep in pt—(prosp) Finance, 1998 c 36, s 165, sch 27 pt I(1), Note

s 8 rep—Finance, 1995 c 4, ss 5(6)(7),162, sch 29 pt I

s 10 am—Finance, 2002 c 23, s 7(2); Finance, 2004 c 12, s 14

s 15 rep—Finance, 1994 c 9, ss 6, 258, schs 3,26 pt II, Note

s 16 rep in pt—Finance, 1994 c 9), ss 6, 258, schs 3,26 pt II, Note; Finance, 1995 c 4, s 162, sch 29 pt III

s 17 rep in pt—SI 1993/2452; Vehicle Excise and Registration, 1994 c 22, s 65, sch 5 pt I; (retrosp) Finance, 1994 c 9, s 258, sch 26 pt I

1993

c 34 *continued*

ss 18,19 rep—Vehicle Excise and Registration, 1994 c 22, s 65, sch 5 pt I

s 20 rep in pt—Vehicle Excise and Registration, 1994 c 22, s 65, sch 5 pt I; (retrosp)
Finance, 1994 c 9, s 258, sch 26 pt I

s 21 rep—Vehicle Excise and Registration, 1994 c 22, s 65, sch 5 pt I

s 22 rep—Finance, 2003 c 14, s 216, sch 43 pt 5(1)

s 23 rep—Vehicle Excise and Registration, 1994 c 22, s 65, sch 5 pt I

s 24 rep in pt—SL(R), 2004 c 14, s 1(1), sch 1 pt 17/3; Finance, 2007 c 11, s 114, sch 27 pt
6

am—Finance, 2007 c 11, s 105, sch 25 paras 13, 14; SI 2010/2959, art 2

s 27 am—Finance, 1994 c 9, s 9, sch 4 pt VI para 67

s 28 am—Finance, 1994 c 9, s 9, sch 4 pt VI para 68

s 29 am—Finance, 1994 c 9, s 9, sch 4 pt VI para 68; SI 2015/664, sch 2 para 6(2)

s 31 am—SI 2015/664, sch 2 para 6(3)

s 35 am—Finance, 1994 c 9, s 18(6)

s 36 rep in pt—Enterprise, 2002 c 40, s 278(2), sch 26

s 37 am—Finance, 2007 c 11, s 105, sch 25 paras 13, 15

s 39 rep in pt—Finance, 2002 c 23, s 141, sch 40 pt 1(4), Note 2

ss 42-50 rep—Value Added Tax, 1994 c 23, s 100(2), sch 15

ss 51, 52 rep—Income Tax, 2007 c 3, s 1031, sch 3

s 54 rep—Corporation Tax, 2010 c 4, s 1181, sch 3 pt 1

s 56 rep—Finance, 1999 c 16, s 139, sch 20 pt III(7), Note 4

s 57 rep in pt—Finance, 1994 c 9, ss 81,258, sch 9 para 12, sch 26 pt V(2), Note; Finance,
1999 c 16, s 139, sch 20 pt III(7), Note 4

s 59 rep—Income Tax, 2007 c 3, s 1031, sch 3

s 60 rep—Finance, 2002 c 23, s 141, sch 40 pt 3(10), Note 2

ss 61-63 rep—(saving) Finance, 1996 c 8, ss 105,205, sch 15 para 19(3), sch 41 pt V(3),
Note

ss 64,65 rep—(saving) Finance, 1996 c 8, ss 105,205, sch 15 para 19(3), sch 41 pt V(3),
Note

am—Finance, 1999 c 16, s 67(4)(8)

s 67 rep—SL(R), 2013 c 2, s 1, sch 1 pt 10(1)

s 66 rep—(saving) Finance, 1996 c 8, ss 105,205, sch 15 para 19(3), sch 41 pt V(3), Note

s 67 rep in pt—Corporation Tax, 2010 c 4, s 1181, sch 3 pt 1

s 68 rep—Income Tax (Earnings and Pensions), 2003 c 1, s 724(1), sch 8 pt 1

s 69 rep—Corporation Tax, 2009 c 4, s 1326, sch 3 pt 1

s 72 rep—Taxation (International and Other Provns), 2010 c 8, s 378, sch 10 pt 13

ss 73-76 rep—Income Tax (Earnings and Pensions), 2003 c 1, s 724(1), sch 8 pt 1

s 77 rep in pt—Finance, 1996 c 8, s 205, sch 41 pt V(1); Income Tax (Trading and Other
Income), 2005 c 5, s 884, sch 3; Corporation Tax, 2010 c 4, s 1181, sch 3 pt 1

s 78 rep—Finance, 1998 c 36, s 165, sch 27 pt III(2), Note

s 79 rep in pt—Finance, 1996 c 8, s 205, sch 41 pt V(1); Income Tax, 2007 c 3, s 1031, sch
3; SL(R), 2013 c 2, s 1, sch 1 pt 10(1)

s 80 rep—Income Tax, 2007 c 3, s 1027, sch 1 paras 354, 355, sch 3

s 81 rep—Finance, 1998 c 36, s 165, sch 27 pt III(2), Note

s 86 am—Finance, 2002 c 23, s 43(3)(4); Finance (No 2), 2005 c 22, s 41(5); Finance,
2012 c 14, s 37(2)

s 90 rep—Finance, 2000 c 17, s 156, sch 40 pt II(12), Note 10

s 91 rep in pt—Finance, 2007 c 11, s 114, sch 27 pt 2; Finance, 2012 c 14, sch 16 para 91

ss 92-92E rep—Corporation Tax, 2010 c 4, ss 1177, 1181, sch 1 paras 276, 277, sch 3 [for
insertions and replacements 2000-09 see Tables of Effect to Legislation in
Annual Volumes for those years — see Introduction]

s 96 rep—(retrosp) Finance, 1995 c 4, s 162, sch 29 pt VIII(5), Note 2

ss 97, 98 rep—SI 2006/3271, reg 43, sch

s 99 rep—(retrosp)Finance, 1995 c 4, s 162, sch 29 pt VIII(5), Note 2

s 100 rep in pt—(retrosp) Finance, 1995 c 4, s 162, sch 29 pt VIII(5), Note 2

s 101 rep—SI 2006/3271, reg 43, sch

s 102 rep—SI 2006/3271, reg 43, sch

s 103 rep in pt —(saving) Finance, 1996 c 8, s 205, sch 41 pt V(3), Note; Finance, 2012 c
14, sch 16 paras 247(e), 248

s 105 rep in pt—Income Tax (Earnings and Pensions), 2003 c 1, s 724(1), sch 8 pt 1

s 106 rep —Finance, 2004 c 12, s 326, sch 42 pt 3, Note

1993
c 34 *continued*

s 107 rep in pt—Finance, 2004 c 12, s 326, sch 42 pt 3, Note; Finance, 2009 c 10, s 5, sch 1
para 6(e); Taxation (International and Other Provns), 2010 c 8, s 378, sch 10 pt
13; SL(R), 2013 c 2, s 1, sch 1 pt 10(1)

s 108 rep—Corporation Tax, 2009 c 4, s 1326, sch 3 pt 1

s 109 rep in pt—Corporation Tax, 2009 c 4, s 1326, sch 3 pt 1; Corporation Tax, 2010 c 4, s
1181, sch 3 pt 1

s 110 rep—Corporation Tax, 2009 c 4, s 1326, sch 3 pt 1

s 111 rep—Income Tax, 2007 c 3, s 1031, sch 3

s 112 rep (saving)—Finance, 2004 c 12, s 326, sch 42 pt 3, Note
am—Income Tax (Trading and Other Income), 2005 c 5, s 882(1), sch 1 pt 2 paras
462, 463

ss 113-117 rep—Capital Allowances, 2001 c 2, s 580, sch 4

s 118 rep—Income Tax, 2007 c 3, s 1027, sch 1 paras 354, 356, sch 3

s 121 rep—Finance, 2001 c 9, ss 87(3)(a)(4), 110, sch 33 pt 2(12), Note

s 123 rep—Corporation Tax, 2009 c 4, s 1326, sch 3 pt 1

s 124 rep—Income Tax (Earnings and Pensions), 2003 c 1, s 724(1), sch 8 pt 1

Pt 2 (Ch 2, ss 125-170) power to am—Finance, 1994 c 9, s 177(6)(b)

ss 125-169 rep —Finance, 2002 c 23, ss 79(1)(b)(2)(3), 141, sch 23 pt 3, paras 25, 26, sch
40 pt 3(10), Note 2

Pt 2 Ch 3 (ss 171-184) appl—Finance, 1995 c 4, s 127(16)(a)
mod—SI 1997/2681, reg 3(1)(a)
appl—Finance, 1998 c 36, s 121, sch 20; Finance, 1999 c 16, s 83(1); SI 2001/1757,
reg 7(11)

s 171 am—Finance, 1994 c 9, s 228, sch 21 para 1(1); Finance (No 2), 1997 c 58,
s 22(1)(7); SI 2001/3629, arts 75, 82(a); Income Tax (Trading and Other
Income), 2005 c 5, s 882(1), sch 1 pt 2 paras 462, 464; Finance, 2008 c 9, s 34,
sch 12 para 16; Finance, 2009 c 10, s 40, sch 19 para 11
rep in pt—Finance, 1994 c 9, ss 228,258, sch 21 para 1(2)(3)(b), sch 26 pt V(25),
Note 2; Finance (No 2), 1997 c 58, ss 36,52, sch 6 para 20(2)(3), sch 8
pt II(11), Note
mod—SIs 1995/352, reg 13
appl—Income Tax (Trading and Other Income), 2005 c 5, s 397(6)

s 172 am—Finance, 1994 c 9, s 228, sch 21 para 2; SI 2001/3629, arts 75, 82(b)
mod—SI 1997/2681, reg 6(1)(b)

s 173 rep —Finance (No 2), 2005 c 22, ss 45(1)(9), 70, sch 11 pt 2(11), Note

s 174 am—Finance, 1994 c 9, s 228, sch 21 para 3; SI 2001/3629, arts 75, 82(c)
rep in pt—Finance, 1996 c 8, s 205, sch 41 pt V(18); Finance,1997 c 16, ss 76, 113,
sch 10 pt I paras 6(a), 7(1), sch 18 pt VI(10), Note 1

s 175 appl (mods)—SI 1995/351, reg 15(1)(c)
excl—SI 1997/2681, reg 7

s 176 rep in pt —(saving) Finance, 1996 c 8, s 205), sch 41 pt V(3), Note
mod—SI 1997/2681 reg 5(1)
am—Income Tax, 2007 c 3, s 1027, sch 1 paras 354, 357

s 177 rep—Finance, 2000 c 17, ss 107(11)(12),156, sch 40 pt II(16), Note 2

s 178 am—Finance, 1994 c 9, s 228, sch 21 para 5; Finance, 2002 c 23, s 86, sch 32, paras
1-4; Finance, 2008 c 9, s 118, sch 39 para 63
excl—SI 1995/351, reg 5(1)(c); 1997/2681 reg 4(1)

s 179 rep in pt—Finance, 1994 c 9, ss 228, 258, sch 21 para 6(1)(3), sch 26 pt V(25),
Note 3;
excl—SIs 1995/351, reg 14(2);1997/2681 reg 4(1

s 179A added—Finance, 1994 c 9, s 228, sch 21 para 6(2)(3)
excl—SIs 1995/351, reg 14(2);1997/2681 reg 4(1)

s 179B added—Finance, 2004 c 12, s 144, sch 25 paras 1, 2
am—SI 2014/3133, reg 3

s 180 excl—1997/2681 reg 8
am—Income Tax, 2007 c 3, s 1027, sch 1 paras 354, 358

s 182 rep in pt—Finance, 1994 c 9, ss 228,258, sch 21 para 7, sch 26 pt V(25), Note 4;
Finance, 1997 c 16, ss 76,113, sch 10 pt I,paras 6(a),7(1), sch 18 pt VI (10),
Note 1; Finance (No 2), 2005 c 22, ss 45(2)(8)(a)(9), 70, sch 11 pt 2(11), Note;
SL(R), 2013 c 2, s 1, sch 1 pt 10(1)
am—Finance, 1995 c 4, s 83(2); SI 2001/3629, arts 75, 79, 82(d)(e); Finance (No 2),
2005 c 22, s 45(3)(8)(a)(9); Income Tax, 2007 c 3, s 1027, sch 1 para 354, 359

1993
c 34 *continued*

s 183 rep in pt—Finance, 1993 c 34, s 213, sch 23 pt III(12), Notes 2,4; Finance, 1994 c 9,
    ss 228(2)(c),230,258, sch 26 pt V(25), Note 1; Income Tax (Trading and Other
    Income), 2005 c 5, s 884, sch 3; Income Tax, 2007 c 3, s 1031, sch 3

s 184 rep in pt—Finance, 1994 c 9, ss 228,258, sch 21 para 8(1)(a), sch 26 pt V(25), Note 6
    am—Finance, 1994 c 9, s 228, sch 21 para 8(1)(b)(2); Finance, 2002 c 23, s 86, sch
      32, paras 1, 5; SIs 2005/1538, art 2; 3338, regs 1(2), 16; 2006/3273, art 2;
      2013/636, sch para 3; 2014/3133, reg 4
    appl—Finance, 1995 c 4, s 127(16)(b)

s 185 am—Finance, 2007 c 11, s 102; Finance, 2008 c 9, s 107(1), (2), (3)(a), (4)-(6);
    Finance, 2009 c 10, s 91, sch 45 para 3(2)(c)
    rep in pt—Finance, 2008 c 9, s 107(1), (3)(b)

s 187 rep in pt—(savings) SI 2009/3054, arts 3, 5, sch
    am—SI 2009/56, art 3, sch 1 para 193

s 190 excl—Finance, 1994 c 9, s 238(2)
    rep in pt—Finance, 1994 c 9, s 258, sch 26 pt VI, Note 2

s 191 mod—Finance, 1994 c 9, ss 231,234, sch 22 pt II, para 13(2)

s 193 am—Corporation Tax, 2010 c 4, s 1177, sch 1 paras 276, 278

s 194 rep—Taxation (International and Other Provns), 2010 c 8, ss 374, 378, sch 8 paras 48,
    49, sch 10 pt 1

s 195 rep in pt—Taxation (International and Other Provns), 2010 c 8, ss 374, 378, sch 8
    paras 48, 50, sch 10 pt 1

s 201 rep—Finance, 1999 c 16, s 138, sch 20 pt V(2), Notes 1, 2

s 202 am—Finance, 1999 c 16, ss 112(4)(6), 122, sch 14 para 28

s 203 am—Finance, 1999 c 16, ss 112(4)(6), 122, sch 14 para 29

s 205 rep in pt—Finance, 2011 c 11, s 88(8)(a); SL(R), 2013 c 2, s 1, sch 1 pt 10(1)

s 206 rep in pt—Finance, 1996 c 8, s 205, sch 41 pt V(13); Finance (No 2), 1997 c 58, s 52,
    sch 8 pt III

s 208 rep in pt—Income Tax, 2007 c 3, s 1031, sch 3

s 209 rep—Finance, 1998 c 36, s 165, sch 27 pt V(3), Notes 1-2

s 211 rep—Finance, 1998 c 36, ss 160,165, sch 26, paras 2,3, sch 27 pt VI(2), Note

s 212 am—Income Tax, 2007 c 3, s 1027, sch 1 paras 354, 360

sch 2 rep—Value Added Tax, 1994 c 23, s 100(2), sch 15

schs 3-5 rep—Income Tax (Earnings and Pensions), 2003 c 1, s 724(1), sch 8 pt 1

sch 6 rep in pt—Finance, 1994 c 9, s 258, sch 26 pt V(2)(13), Notes; Finance, 1995 c 4,
    s 162, sch 29 pt VIII(8); Finance, 1996 c 8, s 205, sch 41 pt V(1)(2); (saving)
    ibid, pt V(3), Notes 206(3); Finance, 1997 c 16, ss 76,113, sch 10 pt I,
    para 7(1), sch 18 pt VI(10), Note 1; Finance (No 2), 1997 c 58, s 52, sch 8
    pt II(9), Note 3; Finance, 1998 c 36, s 165, sch 27 pt III(2)(29), Note;
    (2003-04) ibid, sch 27 pt III(31), Note; Finance, 1999 c 16, s 139, sch 20
    pt III(1), Note; Income Tax (Trading and Other Income), 2005 c 5, s 884, sch 3;
    Income Tax, 2007 c 3, s 1031, sch 3; Corporation Tax, 2009 c 4, s 1326, sch 3
    pt 1; Taxation (International and Other Provns), 2010 c 8, s 378, sch 10 pt 13;
    SL(R), 2013 c 2, s 1, sch 1 pt 10(1)

sch 7 rep in pt—(2003-04) Finance, 1998 c 36, s 165, sch 27 pt III(31), Note

sch 9 rep—SI 2006/3271, reg 43, sch

sch 10 rep—SI 2006/3271, reg 43, sch

sch 11 rep—SI 2006/3271, reg 43, sch

schs 12, 13 rep—Capital Allowances, 2001 c 2, s 580, sch 4

sch 14 rep in pt—Finance, 1998 c 36, s 165, sch 27 pt III(2)(28), Note; Finance, 2007 c 11,
    s 114, sch 27 pt 2; Corporation Tax, 2010 c 4, s 1181, sch 3 pt 1

schs 15-17 rep—Finance, 2002 c 23, s 141, sch 40 pt 3(10), Note 2

sch 18 rep in pt —(saving) Finance, 1996 c 8, s 205, sch 41 pt V(3), Note; Finance, 2002 c
    23, s 141, sch 40 pt 3(10), Note 2; SL(R), 2013 c 2, s 1, sch 1 pt 10(1)

sch 19 rep—Finance (No 2), 2005 c 22, ss 45(1)(9), 70, sch 11 pt 2(11), Note

sch 20 rep in pt—Finance, 1994 c 9, s 258, sch 26 pt V(25), Note 5; Finance (No 2), 1997
    c 58, ss34,52, sch 4 pt II para 30(1)(2), sch 8 pt II(10), Note
    mod—(temp) Finance, 1994 c 9, s 228, sch 21 para 14(3); SI 1995/353, reg 7
    am—Finance 1994 c 9 s 228, sch 21 paras 12(1)-(3),13(1),14(1)-(3), 15(1)-(3),
      16(2)(3); (retrosp) Finance, 1995 c 4, s 143; SI 1995/353, regs 3(3), 4(2),8;
      SIs 1999/3308, regs 3-6; 2001/3629, arts 75, 82(g)
    excl—SI 1997/2681, reg 7

sch 20A added—Finance, 2004 c 12, s 144, sch 25 paras 1, 3

1993

c 34 sch 20A *continued*

    am—Income Tax (Trading and Other Income), 2005 c 5, s 882(1), sch 1 pt 2 paras 462, 466; SI 2006/112, reg 2; Income Tax, 2007 c 3, s 1027, sch 1 paras 354, 361; SI 2009/56, art 3, sch 1 para 194(3); Finance, 2009 c 10, s 91, sch 45 para 3; Corporation Tax, 2010 c 4, s 1177, sch 1 paras 276, 279; SI 2014/3133, reg 5

    rep in pt—Income Tax, 2007 c 3, s 1031, sch 3; SI 2009/56, art 3, sch 1 para 194(2)(4)

  sch 20B added—Finance, 2008 c 9, s 107, sch 33 para 1

  sch 21 rep —SI 2009/3054, art 3, sch

  sch 23 rep in pt—SL(R), 2013 c 2, s 1, sch 1 pt 10(1)

c 35   *Education*—rep (savings) Education, 1996 c 56, s 582(2)(3), sch 38 pt I, sch 39 paras 9, 13, 21, 36

  sch 13 cont in force in pt—SI 1999/2267, reg 2

c 36   **Criminal Justice**

  s 1 am—Theft (Amdt), 1996 c 62, s 3; SI 2000/1878, art 2; Fraud, 2006 c 35, s 14, sch 1 para 24(1)(3); Identity Cards, 2006 c 15, s 30(1); Identity Documents, 2010 c 40, s 12, sch 1 para 8

    rep in pt—Fraud, 2006 c 35, s 14, sch 1 para 24(2), sch 3

    mod—Serious Crime, 2007 c 27, s 63, sch 6 para 21(a)

  s 2 am—Fraud, 2006 c 35, s 14, sch 1 para 25

  s 5 rep in pt—Crim Justice (Terrorism and Conspiracy), 1998 c 40, s 9(1)(2), sch 1 pt II, para 7(1), sch 2 pt II

    mod —Serious Crime, 2007 c 27, s 63, sch 6 para 21(b)

  s 6 rep in pt—Crim Justice (Terrorism and Conspiracy), 1998 c 40, s 9(1)(2), sch 1 pt II, para 7(2), sch 2 pt II

  ss 7-16,18 rep—Drug Trafficking, 1994 c 37, s 67, sch 3

  s 20 rep in pt—Drug Trafficking, 1994 c 37, s 67, sch 3

  s 21 rep in pt—Drug Trafficking, 1994 c 37, s 67, sch 3; Proceeds of Crime, 2002 c 29, s 457, sch 12; SL(R), 2004 c 14, s 1(1), sch 1 pt 2/1

    saved—Drug Trafficking, 1994 c 37, s 66, sch 2 para 8

  ss 22,24 rep in pt—Drug Trafficking, 1994 c 37, s 67, sch 3

  ss 25-35 rep—SL(R), 2004 c 14, s 1(1), sch 1 pt 2/1

  ss 37-45 rep—SL(R), 2004 c 14, s 1(1), sch 1 pt 2/1

  ss 38-48 rep—NI (Emergency Provns), 1996 c 22, s 63(7), sch 7 pt I

  s 47 rep—SL(R), 2004 c 14, s 1(1), sch 1 pt 2/1

  ss 49-51 rep—Terrorism, 2000 c 11, s 125(2), sch 16 pt I

  s 50 rep in pt—NI (Emergency Provns), 1996 c 22, s 63(7), sch 7 pt I

  Pt 5 (ss 52-64) appl—Financial Services and Markets, 2000 c 8, s 402(1)(a)

  s 59 rep—SL(R), 2004 c 14, s 1(1), sch 1 pt 2/1

  s 61A added—SI 2009/1941, art 2, sch 1

  s 62 rep in pt—SL(R), 2004 c 14, s 1(1), sch 1 pt 2/1

  s 64 rep in pt—SL(R), 2004 c 14, s 1(1), sch 1 pt 2/1

  s 65 rep in pt—Powers of Crim Cts (Sentencing), 2000 c 6, s 165(3)(4), sch 11 pt I para 2, sch 12 pt I

  s 66 rep—Powers of Crim Cts (Sentencing), 2000 c 6, s 165(3)(4), sch 11 pt I para 2, sch 12 pt I

  s 67 rep in pt—Crim Justice and Public Order, 1994 c 33, s 168(3), sch 11; Crim Justice, 2003 c 44, s 332, sch 37 pt 7

  ss 68,69 rep—Crim Procedure (Conseq Provns)(S), 1995 c 40, s 6, sch 5

  s 70 am—SIs 2000/2952, reg 6; 2006/3221, reg 29, sch 4; 2013/3115, sch 2 para 37

    rep in pt—SI 2000/2952, reg 6

  s 72 rep—Extradition, 2003 c 41, s 220, sch 4

  s 78 am—(retrosp) Crim Justice and Public Order 1994 c 33, s 168(1), sch 9 para 53; SI 2001/3649, art 340

    rep in pt—Drug Trafficking, 1994 c 37, s 67, sch 3; NI (Emergency Provns), 1996 c 22, s 63(7), sch 7 pt I; Terrorism, 2000 c 11, s 125(2), sch 16 pt I

  s 79 am—Drug Trafficking, 1994 c 37, s 65, sch 1 para 30(4)

    rep in pt—Drug Trafficking, 1994 c 37, ss 65, 67, sch 1 para 30(2)(3), sch 3; NI (Emergency Provns), 1996 c 22, s 63(7), sch 7 pt I; Northern Ireland, 1998 c 47, s 100(2), sch 15; Extradition, 2003 c 41, s 220, sch 4

  sch 1 am—SIs 2001/3649, art 341(1)-(3); 2005/381, reg 3; Financial Services, 2012 c 21, sch 18 para 76

  sch 2 appl (mods)—SI 2003/1633, reg 15, sch 2 para 8(1)(2)(f)

1993

c 36 *continued*

sch 3 rep—SL(R), 2004 c 14, s 1(1), sch 1 pt 2/1

sch 4 rep in pt—Drug Trafficking, 1994 c 37, s 67, sch 3; NI (Emergency Provns), 1996
c 22, s 63(7), sch 7 pt I; sch 4 para 5, Terrorism, 2000 c 11, s 125(2), sch 16
pt I; Proceeds of Crime, 2002 c 29, s 457, sch 12

saved—Drug Trafficking, 1994 c 37, s 66, sch 2 para 10

sch 5 rep in pt—Crim Procedure (Conseq Provns)(S), 1995 c 40, s 6, sch 5; NI (Emergency
Provns), 1996 c 22, s 63(7), sch 7 pt I; SI 2001/3649, art 342(a); Proceeds of
Crime, 2002 c 29, s 457, sch 12; Companies, 2006 c 46, s 1295, sch 16

sch 6 rep in pt—SI 2001/3649, art 342(b)

c 37 **Agriculture**

trans of powers in pt—(W) SI 1999/672, art 2, sch 1

Pt 1 (ss 1-24) mod—(retrosp) Finance, 1996 c 8, s 203

appl—Finance, 1996 c 8, s 203(11)

see—(trans of functions) SI 1999/3141, arts 2(1)(5), 3, sch

s 1 am—SIs 1994/282, 685

s 20 rep—Natural Environment and Rural Communities, 2006 c 16, s 105, sch 11 para 20,
sch 12

s 22 appl—SI 1994/2460

Pt 3 (ss 50-53) see—(trans of functions) SI 1999/3141, arts 2(1)(5), 3, sch

s 52 am—Crim Procedure (Conseq Provns)(S) 1995 c 40 s 5, sch 4 para 87

s 57 am—SI 2008/948, art 4, sch 3

s 58 see—(trans of functions) SI 2000/1812, arts 2,3, sch

sch 2 mod—(retrosp) Finance, 1996 c 8, s 203

am—Land Registration, 1997 c 2, s 4(1), sch 1 pt I, para 7(1)(2); Capital Allowances,
2001 c 2, s 578, sch 2, para 90; Income Tax, 2007 c 3, s 1027, sch 1 para 362

sch 4 am—Land Registration, 1997 c 2, s 4(1), sch 1 pt I, para 7(3)(4)

c 38 **Welsh Language**

mod—Welsh Language (W), 2011 nawm 1, sch 12 para 4

trans of powers—SI 1999/672, art 2, sch 1

s 1 rep —Welsh Language (W), 2011 nawm 1, s 143(5)(a)

s 2 rep —Welsh Language (W), 2011 nawm 1, s 143(5)(b)

s 3 rep —Welsh Language (W), 2011 nawm 1, s 144(3)(a)

s 4 rep —Welsh Language (W), 2011 nawm 1, s 143(5)(c); residue ibid, s 144(3)(b)

Pt 2 (ss 5-21) rep —Welsh Language (W), 2011 nawm 1, s 145(2)(a)

s 23 am—Constitutional Reform, 2005 c 4, s 15(1), sch 4 pt 1 para 232

s 25 am—Loc Govt (W), 1994 c 19, s 66(6), sch 16 para 106(2)

s 26 ext—European Parl Elections, 2002 c 24, s 7(5)

appl—Parl Voting System and Constituencies, 2011 c 1, sch 2 para 10(4); (4.3.2016)
Recall of MPs, 2015 c 25, s 21(5); European Union Referendum, 2015 c 36, s
9(6)

s 28 rep—Co-operative and Community Benefit Societies, 2014 c 14, sch 7

s 30 rep—Companies, 2006 c 46, s 1295, sch 16

ss 32, 33 rep —Charities, 2011 c 25, sch 10

s 34 rep —Welsh Language (W), 2011 nawm 1, ss 143(5)(d), 145(2)(b)

s 35 rep in pt—European Parl Elections, 2002 c 24, s 16, sch 4

sch 1 rep—Welsh Language (W), 2011 nawm 1, s 143(5)(e)

c 39 **National Lottery etc**

trans of functions—Nat Lottery, 1998 c 22, s 1(4)

trans of powers—(W) SI 1999/672, art 2, sch 1

appl—Nat Lottery, 1998 c 22, s 25(1)

mod—(W) SI 1999/672, art 5, sch 2

s 1 subst (prosp)—Nat Lottery, 2006 c 23, s 6, sch 1 para 2

am—Nat Lottery, 2006 c 23, s 3(a)

s 2 rep (E,W, S) —Gambling, 2005 c 19, s 356(4)(5), sch 17

s 3 rep—Nat Lottery, 1998 c 22, ss 1(2),26, sch 5 pt I

s 3A added—Nat Lottery, 1998 c 22, s 1(3)

am—SI 2013/2329, sch para 2(a)(c)

rep in pt—SI 2013/2329, sch para 2(b)

s 4 am—Horserace Betting and Olympic Lottery, 2004 c 25, s 34(1)(2)(a)(b); (prosp) Nat
Lottery, 2006 c 23, s 6, sch 1 para 4

see (functions made exercisable concurrently)—SI 2007/2129, art 3

s 4A added—Gambling, 2005 c 19, s 15(5), sch 3 para 2

rep—SI 2013/2329, sch para 3

1993
c 39 *continued*

    s 4B added—Nat Lottery, 2006 c 23, s 2
        am—Budget Responsibility and Nat Audit, 2011 c 4, sch 5 para 17; SI 2013/2329, sch
            para 4(a)-(d)
    s 4C added—Nat Lottery, 2006 c 23, s 2
        am—SI 2013/2329, sch para 5
    s 5 subst (prosp)—Nat Lottery, 2006 c 23, s 6, sch 1 para 4
        am—Horserace Betting and Olympic Lottery, 2004 c 25, s 34(1)(3)(4); Nat Lottery,
            2006 c 23, s 3(b)
        appl—SI 2015/85, art 5
    s 6 subst (prosp)—Nat Lottery, 2006 c 23, s 6, sch 1 para 4
    s 7 am—(prosp) Nat Lottery, 2006 c 23, s 6, sch 1 para 5; ibid, ss 3(d), 4
        rep in pt—Nat Lottery, 2006 c 23, s 21, sch 3; ibid, s 5(2)
    s 7A added—Nat Lottery, 2006 c 23, s 5(1)
        am—(prosp) Nat Lottery, 2006 c 23, s 6, sch 1 para 6
    s 8 am—(prosp) Nat Lottery, 2006 c 23, s 6, sch 1 para 7(a)
        rep in pt—(prosp) Nat Lottery, 2006 c 23, s 6, sch 1 para 7(b)
    s 9 am—Horserace Betting and Olympic Lottery, 2004 c 25, s 34(1)(5); (prosp) Nat Lottery,
            2006 c 23, s 6, sch 1 para 8
    s 10 am—(prosp) Nat Lottery, 2006 c 23, s 6, sch 1 para 9(a)(c)(d); ibid, ss 3(e), 5(3)
        rep in pt—(prosp) Nat Lottery, 2006 c 23, s 6, sch 1 para 9(b)
    s 10A added—Nat Lottery, 1998 c 22, s 2(1)(5)
        am—Horserace Betting and Olympic Lottery, 2004 c 25, s 34(1)(6); (prosp) Nat
            Lottery, 2006 c 23, s 6, sch 1 para 10
    s 10B added—Nat Lottery, 1998 c 22, s 3
    s 10C added —Gambling, 2005 c 19, s 15(5), sch 3 para 1
        am—(prosp) Nat Lottery, 2006 c 23, s 6, sch 1 para 11; SI 2013/2329, sch para
            6(a)(b)(i)
        rep in pt—SI 2013/2329, sch para 6(b)(ii)(c)
    s 11 am—Nat Lottery, 1998 c 22, s 2(2); Horserace Betting and Olympic Lottery, 2004 c 25,
            s 34(1)(7)
        see—(functions made exercisable concurrently) SI 2007/2129, art 3
    s 14 see—(trans of functions) Nat Lottery, 1998 c 22, s 1(5), sch 1 pt I, para 6(1)(b)
        rep in pt—Nat Lottery, 1998 c 22, ss 1(5),26, sch 1 pt I, para 6(5) pt III, para 13(a),
            sch 5 pt I; SI 2013/2329, sch para 7(c)
        am—Nat Lottery, 1998 c 22, s 1(5), sch 1 pt I, para 6(5) pt III, para 13(b); (S)
            SI 1999/1750, art 3, sch 2; SIs 1999/1750, art 6(1), sch 5 para 12; 1999/1756,
            art 2, sch para 15(1); 2013/2329, sch para 7(a)(b)
    s 17 rep—Horserace Betting and Olympic Lottery, 2004 c 25, ss 13, 38, sch 2 para 21, sch 6
    s 18 rep in pt —Gambling, 2005 c 19, s 356(4)(5), sch 17
    s 19 rep—Police, 1997 c 50, ss 133(d), 134(2), sch 10
    s 20 rep in pt—Nat Lottery, 1998 c 22, ss 1(5),26, sch 1 pt III, para 14(b), sch 5 pt I
        am—Nat Lottery, 1998 c 22, s 1(5), sch 1 pt III, para 14(a); Gambling, 2005 c 19,
            s 15(5), sch 3 para 3; SI 2013/2329, sch para 8
    s 21 am—Nat Lottery, 1998 c 22, s 2(3)
        rep in pt—Horserace Betting and Olympic Lottery, 2004 c 25, ss 34(1)(8)(9)(b), 38,
            sch 6
    s 22 am—Nat Lottery, 1998 c 22, s 6(2)-(6)(9), 17(9); SI 1999/344, arts 2, 3; SI 2000/3356,
            art 2; (retrosp) Nat Lottery (Funding of Endowments), 2003 c 23, s 1(1)(2);
            Horserace Betting and Olympic Lottery, 2004 c 25, s 34(1)(9)(a)(c); (prosp) Nat
            Lottery, 2006 c 23, ss 6, 7, sch 1 para 12; SIs 2010/2863, art 2; 2011/739, sch
            para 2; 2012/964, art 3(1), sch
        rep in pt—Nat Lottery, 1998 c 22, s 26, sch 5 pt II; Horserace Betting and Olympic
            Lottery, 2004 c 25, ss 34(1)(8)(9)(b), 38, sch 6
        appl—SI 2006/396, art 2
        trans of functions—SI 2011/739, art 2(1)(a)
    s 23 am—SI s 1994/1342; 1995/2088, art 2; 1996/3095, art 2; Nat Lottery, 1998 c 22,
            s 7(1); SI 1999/1563, art 2; SI 1999/2090, art 2; (S) SSI 2000/78, art 2; Nat
            Lottery, 2006 c 23, s 15(1); SI 2007/743, reg 2; SSI 2010/223, art 2; SI
            2011/685, art 2
        power to appl (mods)—Horserace Betting and Olympic Lottery, 2004 c 25,
            ss 26(2)(c)(4)(5), 28(3)(b)(4), 32(3)(b)(4)
        rep in pt—SSI 2010/223, art 2
    s 24 am—Nat Lottery, 2006 c 23, s 8(2)

1993
c 39 *continued*

s 25 am—Nat Heritage, 1997 c 14, s 3,sch 1 pt I, para 4; Nat Lottery, 1998 c 22, ss 9(1), 10; (retrosp) Nat Lottery (Funding of Endowments), 2003 c 23, s 1(1)(3); Nat Lottery, 2006 c 23, s 10; (pt prosp) ibid, s 13(1)

s 25A added—Nat Lottery, 1998 c 22, s 11(1)
    appl (mods)—Horserace Betting and Olympic Lottery, 2004 c 25, s 29, sch 5 pt 2 para 13(2)
    am—(pt prosp) Nat Lottery, 2006 c 23, s 13(2)

s 25B added—Nat Lottery, 1998 c 22, s 12(1)
    am—(retrosp) Nat Lottery (Funding of Endowments), 2003 c 23, s 1(1)(4)

s 25C added—Nat Lottery, 1998 c 22, s 13
    am—(S) SI 1999/1750, art 3, sch 2; Nat Lottery, 2006 c 23, s 19(2); SI 2011/739, sch para 3
    see—(cert functions trans (mods)) (S) SI 1999/1750, art 2, sch 1

s 25D added—SI 1999/1756, art 2, sch para 15(2)

s 25E added—Nat Lottery, 2006 c 23, s 11
    ext—Dormant Bank and Building Society Accounts, 2008 c 31, s 16, sch 3 para 14(2)

s 26 am—Nat Lottery, 1998 c 22, s 11(2)(3)(4); (S) SI 1999/1750, art 4, sch 3; Nat Lottery, 2006 c 23, s 19(3)
    see—(cert functions trans (mods)) (S) SI 1999/1750, art 2, sch 1

s 26A added—SI 1999/1756, art 2, sch para 15(3)
    am—(S) SI 1999/1750, art 4, sch 3

s 27 am—SIs 1999/1756, art 2, sch para 15(4); 2009/1941, art 2, sch 1
    see—(cert functions trans (mods)) (S) SI 1999/1750, art 2, sch 1

s 28 am—(S) SI 1999/1750, art 4, sch 3

s 29 am—(S) SI 1999/1750, art 4, sch 3; SI 1999/1756, art 2, sch para 15(5)
    see—(cert functions trans (mods)) (S) SI 1999/1750, art 2, sch 1

s 29A added—Nat Lottery, 2006 c 23, s 8(1)

s 30 am—Nat Lottery, 1998 c 22, s 6(7)(9); 2000/3355, art 2

s 30 rep—Horserace Betting and Olympic Lottery, 2004 c 25, ss 34(10), 38, sch 6

s 31 ext—Nat Lottery, 1998 c 22, ss 8(7),16(2), sch 4, para 11
    rep in pt—Nat Lottery, 1998 c 22, ss 1(5),26, sch 1 pt III, para 15(2)(a)(3), sch 5 pt I
    am—Nat Lottery, 1998 c 22, s 1(5), sch 1 pt III, para 15(2)(b)(4); SIs 2011/739, sch para 4; 2013/2329, sch para 9(a)(b)

s 32 appl—Nat Lottery, 1998 c 22, s 6(10)(c)
    am—(prosp) Nat Lottery, 2006 c 23, ss 6, 9(a), sch 1 para 13
    rep in pt—Nat Lottery, 2006 c 23, s 21, sch 3; ibid, s 9(b)

s 33 am—Nat Lottery, 1998 c 22, s 5(1)(2)(3)
    appl (mods)—Horserace Betting and Olympic Lottery, 2004 c 25, s 34(1)(11)
    see—(functions made exercisable concurrently) SI 2007/2129, art 3

s 34 am—(S) SI 1999/1750, art 3, sch 2; SI 1999/1750, art 6(1), sch 5 para 12; SI 1999/1756, art 2, sch para 15(6); Nat Lottery, 2006 c 23, s 12; SI 2011/739, sch para 5
    rep in pt—Nat Lottery, 2006 c 23, s 19(4)
    trans of functions—SI 2011/739, art 2(1)(b)

s 35 am—Nat Lottery, 1998 c 22, s 8(1); (S) SI 1999/1750, art 3, sch 2; SI 1999/1756, art 2, sch para 15(7); Nat Lottery, 2006 c 23, s 19(5)
    see—(cert functions trans (mods)) (S) SI 1999/1750, art 2, sch 1

s 36A added —Nat Lottery, 2006 c 23, s 14(1)

ss 36B-36E added—Nat Lottery, 2006 c 23, s 15(2)

s 36B trans of functions—SI 2011/739, art 2(1)(c)
    am—SI 2011/739, sch para 6

s 36E trans of functions—SI 2011/739, art 2(1)(d)(2)
    am—SI 2011/739, sch para 7(2)-(8)
    rep in pt—SI 2011/739, sch para 7(4)

ss 37-39 rep—Nat Lottery, 2006 c 23, s 19(6)(a)

ss 40-43 rep—Nat Lottery, 2006 c 23, s 19(6)(b)

ss 43A-43D added—Nat Lottery, 1998 c 22, s 7(2)
    rep—Nat Lottery, 2006 c 23, s 19(6)(c)

s 43CC added—SI 1999/1756, art 2, sch para 15(10)

s 44 am—Nat Heritage, 1997 c 14, s 3, sch 1 pt I, para 5, Nat Lottery, 1998 c 22, ss 6(8)(9), 8(2), 9(2), 12(2); (retrosp) Nat Lottery (Funding of Endowments), 2003 c 23, s 1(1)(8); Nat Lottery, 2006 c 23, s 20

1993
c 39 s 44 *continued*

       appl—(E) SIs 2004/691, art 2(2), sch para 2(1)(c); 2005/374, art 2(2), sch para 2(1)(c);
         608, sch para 1
       rep in pt—Nat Lottery, 2006 c 23, ss 19(7), 21, sch 3
    s 45 rep —Gambling, 2005 c 19, s 356(4)(5), sch 17
    s 46 rep in pt —Gambling, 2005 c 19, s 356(4)(5), sch 17
    ss 47-59 rep —Gambling, 2005 c 19, s 356(4)(5), sch 17
    s 60 excl—Nat Lottery, 1998 c 22, s 8(6)
       am—Nat Lottery, 1998 c 22, s 15(2)(3)(4)(5)(6); Nat Lottery, 2006 c 23, ss 8(3),
         19(8); SI 2011/739, sch para 8
    s 63 rep in pt—Northern Ireland, 1998 c 47, s 100(2), sch 15
    sch 1 am—Nat Lottery, 1998 c 22, s 2(4)
       rep in pt—Gambling, 2005 c 19, s 356(4)(5), sch 17
    sch 2 see—(trans of functions) SI 1995/269, art 3, sch para 22
       rep—Nat Lottery, 1998 c 22, ss 1(2),26, sch 5 pt I
    sch 2A added—Nat Lottery, 1998 c 22, s 1(5), sch 1 pt II, para 7
       am—Nat Lottery, 2006 c 23, s 1; SIs 2012/2404, sch 2 para 29(2); 2013/2329, sch
         para 10(a)
       rep in pt—SI 2013/2329, sch para 10(b)
    sch 3 rep in pt—Nat Lottery, 1998 c 22, ss 4(2)(5),26, sch 5 pt II; SI 2003/2096, arts 4, 6,
       sch pt 1 para 21(a)(b)
       am—Nat Lottery, 1998 c 22, s 4(2)(3)(4)(6); (prosp) Nat Lottery, 2006 c 23, s 6, sch
        1 para 14
    sch 3A added—Nat Lottery, 1998 c 22, s 12(3), sch 3
       am—(S) SI 1999/1750, art 4, sch 3; SI 1999/1756, art 2, sch para 15(12)
       see—(cert functions trans (mods)) (S) SI 1999/1750, art 2, sch 1
    sch 4 rep in pt—Nat Heritage, 1997 c 14, s 3, sch 1 pt I, para 6
    sch 4A added—Nat Lottery, 2006 c 23, s 14(2)
       appl —Dormant Bank and Building Society Accounts, 2008 c 31, s 22(8)
       am—Dormant Bank and Building Society Accounts, 2008 c 31, s 16, sch 3 para 11;
        SIs 2011/739, sch para 9(2)(3); 2011/2385, art 2; 2012/2404, sch 2 para 29(3)
       trans of functions—SI 2011/739, art 2(1)(e)
    sch 5 rep—Nat Lottery, 2006 c 23, s 19(9)(a)
    sch 6 rep—Nat Lottery, 2006 c 23, ss 19(9)(b), 21, sch 3
    sch 6A added—Nat Lottery, 1998 c 22, s 7(3), sch 2
       rep—Nat Lottery, 2006 c 23, ss 19(9)(b), 21, sch 3
    Schs 7-9 rep —Gambling, 2005 c 19, s 356(4)(5), sch 17

c 40   **Noise and Statutory Nuisance**
    trans of powers—(W) SI 1999/672, art 2, sch 1
    mod—SI 2010/1214, art 4, sch
    appl (mods)—SI 2011/939, art 9, sch 2
    s 6 rep—Environment, 1995 c 25, s 120(3), sch 24
    s 8 am—(S) Loc Govt etc (S), 1994 c 39, s 180(1), sch 13 para 183(2)
    s 9 am—(S) Loc Govt etc (S), 1994 c 39, s 180(1), sch 13 para 183(3)
       rep (EW)—Clean Neighbourhoods and Environment, 2005 c 16, s 107, sch 5 pt 7
    s 13 rep in pt—Environment, 1995 c 25, s 120(3), sch 24
    sch 1 rep—Environment, 1995 c 25, s 120(3), sch 24
    sch 2 am —(EW) Serious Organised Crime and Police, 2005 c 15, s 137(6)
    sch 3 am—(EW) Audit Commission, 1998 c 18, s 54(1), sch 3, para 26
       rep (EW) —Clean Neighbourhoods and Environment, 2005 c 16, s 107, sch 5 pt 7

c 41   **European Parliamentary Elections**
    ss 1, 2 rep—European Parl Elections, 1999 c 1, s 3(3), sch 4
    s 3 rep—European Parl Elections, 2002 c 24, s 16, sch 4
    sch rep—European Parl Elections, 1999 c 1, s 3(3), sch 4

c 42   **Cardiff Bay Barrage**
    am—SI 1996/593, reg 2, sch 1
    trans of powers—SI 1999/672, art 2, sch 1
    s 2 am—SI 2013/755 (W 90), sch 2 para 347
    s 3 am—SI 2013/755 (W 90), sch 2 para 348
    s 8 am—SI 2013/755 (W 90), sch 2 para 349(2)-(5)
    s 9 am—SI 2013/755 (W 90), sch 2 para 350
    s 12 am—SI 2013/755 (W 90), sch 2 para 351(2)(3)
    s 14 am—SI 2013/755 (W 90), sch 2 para 352
    s 15 am—SI 2013/755 (W 90), sch 2 para 353

1993

c 42 *continued*

s 16 rep in pt—SI 1996/525, art 3, sch pt I para 4(1); Loc Govt Byelaws (W), 2012 anaw 2, sch 2 para 15
    am—SI 2013/755 (W 90), sch 2 para 354
s 20 rep in pt—SI 1996/525, art 3, sch pt I para 4(2)
    am—SI 2013/755 (W 90), sch 2 para 355
s 26 am—SI 2013/755 (W 90), sch 2 para 356
s 33 am—SI 1996/525, art 3, sch pt I para 4(3)
sch 2 am—Communications, 2003 c 21, s 406(1), sch 17 para 124(a)(b); SIs 2009/1307, art 5, sch 1; 2013/755 (W 90), sch 2 para 357(2)(3)(a)(b)
sch 3 am—SI 2013/755 (W 90), sch 2 para 358(2)-(5)
sch 4 rep in pt—SI 1996/525, art 3, sch pt I para 4(4); Communications, 2003 c 21, s 406(7), sch 19(1)
    am—Communications, 2003 c 21, s 406(1), sch 17 para 125; SI 2013/755 (W 90), sch 2 para 359
sch 5 am—SI 2009/1307, art 5, sch 1
sch 7 saved—SI 1994/130L
    am—SI 1996/525, art 3, sch pt I para 4(5); Communications, 2003 c 21, s 406(1), sch 17 para 126; SI 2009/1307, art 5, sch 1
    rep in pt—SI 1996/525, art 3, sch pt I para 4(5)(e); Communications, 2003 c 21, s 406(7), sch 19(1)

c 43 **Railways**

am (spec provns and headings am)—SI 2015/1682, sch pt 1 para 1
appl—Fair Trading, 1973 c 41, s 50(2A); Finance, 1994 c 9, s 252, sch 24 para 1(1); Railway Heritage, 1996 c 42, s 7(2); Channel Tunnel Rail Link, 1996 c 61, s 22(5); (E) SIs 2005/927(L), art 58, sch 11 pt 3 para 2; 3523, art 51, sch 11 pt 3 para 18
mod—GLA, 1999 c 29, s 204(1)
trans of powers—(W) SI 1999/672, art 2, sch 1
saving—Edinburgh Airport Rail Link, 2007 asp 16, s 53
Pt 1 (ss 1-83) appl—Transport, 1962 c 46, s 3(1C); Transport 1968 c 73, ss 10(1)(viiia), 23A; Fair Trading 1973 c 41, sch 5 para 5; Capital Allowances, 1990 c 1, s 38A(5); (EW) Environmental Protection, 1990 c 43, s 79; Channel Tunnel Rail Link, 1996 c 61, ss 16(5), 17(5), 19(10), 37(5); ibid, s 9, sch 6 pt II, para 9(5), pt III para 17(5); GLA, 1999 c 29, s 177(4); SIs 2003/1075, art 40; 2003/1594, art 2(2)(c); 2004/389, art 38; Edinburgh Tram (Line Two), 2006 asp 6, s 78; Edinburgh Tram (Line One), 2006 asp 7, s 79
    mod—Channel Tunnel Rail Link, 1996 c 61, s 21
    savings—SIs (E) 2002/2398, art 5(5); 2003/3364, art 31(7); 2007/3234, art 6
    saved—SIs 2010/2136 (W 192), art 13; 2012/2635, art 35(2)
s 1 rep —Railways and Transport Safety, 2003 c 20, ss 16, 118, sch 2 pt 1 paras 1, 2, sch 8
ss 2, 3 rep—Railways, 2005 c 14, ss 21(1), 59, sch 13 pt 1
s 4 am—Competition, 1998 c 41, s 66(5), sch 10 pt II, para 6(3); Transport, 2000 c 38, ss 215, 224, sch 16 para 9; Pollution Prevention and Control, 1999 c 24, s 6, sch 2 para 12; Enterprise, 2002 c 40, s 278(1), sch 25, para 30(1)(2)(b); Railways and Transport Safety, 2003 c 20, s 16, sch 2 pt 1 paras 1, 3; Railways, 2005 c 14, s 3(1)-(3)(5)-(11); SI 2014/892, sch 1 para 100
    mod—(temp) London Olympic Games and Paralympic Games, 2006 c 12, ss 17 40(6); Crossrail, 2008 c 18, s 22(1)
    rep in pt—Transport, 2000 c 38, ss 224(3)(b), 274, sch 31 pt IV; Enterprise, 2002 c 40, s 278, sch 25, para 30(1)(2)(a)(c), sch 26; Railways and Transport Safety, 2003 c 20, ss 104, 118, sch 8; Railways, 2005 c 14, ss 3(1)(4), 59, sch 13 pt 1
    excl—SI 2010/1504, reg 13
s 5 rep—Transport, 2000 c 38, s 274, sch 31 pt IV
s 6 am—SI 1998/1340, reg 21(2)-(4); Railways and Transport Safety, 2003 c 20, s 16, sch 2 pt 1 paras 1, 3-6; SI 2005/3050, regs 3, 20, sch 1 pt 1 para 3(1)(3)(a)(4), sch 4 paras 1-4, 8-14
    excl—Channel Tunnel Rail Link, 1996 c 61, s 16(1); Crossrail, 2008 c 18, s 24(1)
    appl—Licensing, 2003 c 17, s 157(7); Licensing (S), 2005 asp 16, s 127(6)
    rep in pt—SI 2005/3050, regs 3, 20, sch 1 pt 1 para 3(1)(3)(b), sch 4 paras 1-4, 8-14
s 7 excl—GLA, 1999 c 29, s 199(1)(a)
power to ext—GLA, 1999 c 29, s 199(1)(a)(2)(3)
    am—Transport, 2000 c 38, s 216, sch 17 pt I para 2; Railways and Transport Safety, 2003 c 20, s 16, sch 2 pt 1 paras 1, 3-6; Railways, 2005 c 14, s 1, sch 1 pt 1 para 1(2)

1993

c 43 s 7 *continued*

    rep in pt—Transport, 2000 c 38, ss 252, 274, sch 27 para 18, sch 31 pt IV; Railways, 2005 c 14, ss 1, 59, sch 1 pt 1 para 1(1), sch 13 pt 1

  s 7A added—Transport, 2000 c 38, s 216, sch 17 pt I para 3

    rep—Railways, 2005 c 14, ss 1, 59, sch 1 pt 1 para 2, sch 13 pt 1

  s 8 restr—Channel Tunnel Rail Link, 1996 c 61, s 16(3)

    am—Transport, 2000 c 38, ss 215, 216, sch 16 para 10, sch 17 pt I para 4; Railways and Transport Safety, 2003 c 20, s 16, sch 2 pt 1 paras 1, 3-6; Railways, 2005 c 14, s 1, sch 1 pt 1 para 3(3)(4)(b)

    rep in pt—Transport, 2000 c 38, s 274, sch 31 pt IV; Railways, 2005 c 14, ss 1, 59, sch 1 pt 1 para 3(1)(2)(4)(a)(5), sch 13 pt 1

    appl—SIs 2005/2222, art 46, sch 10 pt 6 para 73(6); 3105, art 40, sch 10 para 2

  s 9 am—Transport, 2000 c 38, s 252, sch 27 para 19; Railways and Transport Safety, 2003 c 20, s 16, sch 2 pt 1 paras 1, 3-6; Railways, 2005 c 14, s 54, sch 11 paras 1, 2

  s 10 rep in pt—Railways, 2005 c 14, s 59, sch 13 pt 1

    appl—(W) SIs 2005/422 (W 40), reg 7(3); (E) 551, reg 6(4); (S) SSI 2005/127, art 7(4)

  s 11 rep in pt—Transport, 2000 c 38, ss 216, 274, sch 17 pt I para 5(3), sch 31 pt IV; Railways, 2005 c 14, ss 1, 59, sch 1 pt 1 para 4, sch 13 pt 1

    am—Transport, 2000 c 38, s 216, sch 17 pt I para 5(2)(4); Railways and Transport Safety, 2003 c 20, s 16, sch 2 pt 1 paras 1, 3

  s 12 am—Transport, 2000 c 38, s 216, sch 17 pt I para 6; Railways and Transport Safety, 2003 c 20, s 16, sch 2 pt 1 paras 1, 3; Railways, 2005 c 14, s 1, sch 1 pt 1 para 5(2)

    rep in pt—Railways, 2005 c 14, ss 1, 59, sch 1 pt 1 para 5(1), sch 13 pt 1

  s 13 am—Competition, 1998 c 41, s 66(5), sch 10 pt IV, para 15(2); SI 1999/506, art 33(a)(b); Transport, 2000 c 38, ss 216, 252, sch 17 pt I para 7, sch 27 para 20; Enterprise, 2002 c 40, s 278(1), sch 25, para 30(1)(3)(a); Railways and Transport Safety, 2003 c 20, s 16, sch 2 pt 1 paras 1, 3; Railways, 2005 c 14, s 1, sch 1 pt 1 paras 6(a), 10; Enterprise and Regulatory Reform, 2013 c 24, sch 6 para 70(2)(a)(b)(3)(a)(b)(4)(5)(a)(b)(6)(a)(b)(7)-(9)

    rep in pt—Transport, 2000 c 38, s 274, sch 31 pt IV; Enterprise, 2002 c 40, s 278, sch 25, para 30(1)(3)(b), sch 26; Railways, 2005 c 14, ss 1, 59, sch 1 pt 1 paras 6(b), 10, sch 13 pt 1

    appl (mods)—SIs 2005/3050, reg 14, sch 3 pt 1 para 1(b) pt 2 para 3

  s 13A added—Enterprise, 2002 c 40, s 278(1), sch 25, para 30(1)(4)

    am—Railways, 2005 c 14, s 1, sch 1 pt 1 paras 7, 10; Enterprise and Regulatory Reform, 2013 c 24, sch 6 para 71

  s 13B added—Enterprise, 2002 c 40, s 278(1), sch 25, para 30(1)(4)

    am—Communications, 2003 c 21, s 389(1), sch 16 para 4(1)(2); Enterprise and Regulatory Reform, 2013 c 24, sch 6 para 72(1)(a)(b); SI 2014/892, sch 1 para 101

  s 14 am—SI 1999/506, art 33(a)(b); Transport, 2000 c 38, s 216, sch 17 pt I para 8; Enterprise, 2002 c 40, s 278(1), sch 25, para 30(1)(5); Railways and Transport Safety, 2003 c 20, s 16, sch 2 pt 1 paras 1, 3; Railways, 2005 c 14, s 1, sch 1 pt 1 paras 8(a), 10; Enterprise and Regulatory Reform, 2013 c 24, sch 6 para 73(2)(3)(a)(b)(4)

    rep in pt—Competition, 1998 c 41, ss 66(5),74(3), sch 10 pt IV, para 15(3), sch 14 pt I; Railways, 2005 c 14, ss 1, 59, sch 1 pt 1 paras 8(b), 10, sch 13 pt 1

    appl (mods)—SI 2005/3050, reg 14, sch 3 pt 1 para 1(b)

  s 15 am—SI 1999/506, art 33(a)(b); Transport, 2000 c 38, ss 216, 242(1) sch 17 pt I para 9(2)(a)(3)-(8); Railways and Transport Safety, 2003 c 20, s 16, sch 2 pt 1 paras 1, 3; Enterprise and Regulatory Reform, 2013 c 24, sch 6 para 74

    rep in pt—Transport, 2000 c 38, ss 216, 274, sch 17 pt I para 9(2)(b), sch 31 pt IV; Railways and Transport Safety, 2003 c 20, ss 16, 118, sch 2 pt 1 paras 1, 7, sch 8; Railways, 2005 c 14, ss 1, 59, sch 1 pt 1 paras 9, 10, sch 13 pt 1

    appl (mods)—SI 2005/3050, reg 14, sch 3 pt 1 para 1(b) pt 2 para 4

  s 15A added—Transport, 2000 c 38, s 242(2)

    am—Railways and Transport Safety, 2003 c 20, s 16, sch 2 pt 1 paras 1, 3; Enterprise and Regulatory Reform, 2013 c 24, sch 6 para 75(2)(3)

    appl (mods)—SI 2005/3050, reg 14, sch 3 pt 1 para 1(b)

    rep in pt—Railways, 2005 c 14, ss 1, 59, sch 1 pt 1 para 10, sch 13 pt 1

  s 15B added—Transport, 2000 c 38, s 242(2)

1993

c 43 s 15B *continued*

am—Railways and Transport Safety, 2003 c 20, s 16, sch 2 pt 1 paras 1, 3; Enterprise and Regulatory Reform, 2013 c 24, sch 6 para 76(2)(3)

appl (mods)—SI 2005/3050, reg 14, sch 3 pt 1 para 1(b) pt 2 para 5

rep in pt—Railways, 2005 c 14, ss 1, 59, sch 1 pt 1 para 10, sch 13 pt 1

s 15C added—Transport, 2000 c 38, s 242(2)

am—Enterprise, 2002 c 40, s 278(1), sch 25, para 30(1)(6); Railways and Transport Safety, 2003 c 20, s 16, sch 2 pt 1 paras 1, 3, 8(a); Communications, 2003 c 21, s 389(1), sch 16 para 4(1)(3); Enterprise and Regulatory Reform, 2013 c 24, sch 6 para 77(2)(3)(4)(a)(b)(5); SI 2014/892, sch 1 para 102

rep in pt—Railways and Transport Safety, 2003 c 20, ss 16, 118, sch 2 pt 1 paras 1, 8(b), sch 8; Railways, 2005 c 14, ss 1, 59, sch 1 pt 1 para 10, sch 13 pt 1

appl (mods)—SI 2005/3050, reg 14, sch 3 pt 1 para 1(b)

s 16 rep in pt—Competition, 1998 c 41, ss 66(5),74(3), sch 10 pt IV, para 15(4)(a)(b)(ii)(c), sch 14 pt I; Railways, 2005 c 14, s 59, sch 13 pt 1

am—Competition, 1998 c 41, s 66(5), sch 10 pt IV, para 15(4)(b)(i); Transport, 2000 c 38, s 216, sch 17 pt I para 10; Enterprise, 2002 c 40, ss 86(5), 164(2), sch 9 pt 1, para 10; Railways and Transport Safety, 2003 c 20, s 16, sch 2 pt 1 paras 1, 3; SI 2003/1592, art 16, sch 4 para 12(1); Enterprise and Regulatory Reform, 2013 c 24, sch 6 para 78; SI 2014/892, sch 1 para 103

appl (mods)—SI 2005/3050, reg 14, sch 3 pt 1 para 1(b)

s 16A added—Transport, 2000 c 38, s 223

am—Railways, 2005 c 14, s 1, sch 1 pt 1 para 11(1)-(3)

s 16B added—Transport, 2000 c 38, s 223

am—Railways, 2005 c 14, s 1, sch 1 pt 1 para 11(4)(5)

s 16C added—Transport, 2000 c 38, s 223

am—Railways, 2005 c 14, s 1, sch 1 pt 1 para 11(1)

s 16D added—Transport, 2000 c 38, s 223

am—Railways, 2005 c 14, s 1, sch 1 pt 1 para 11(1)

s 16E added—Transport, 2000 c 38, s 223

am—Railways, 2005 c 14, s 1, sch 1 pt 1 para 11(1)

s 16F added—Transport, 2000 c 38, s 223

am—Railways, 2005 c 14, s 1, sch 1 pt 1 para 11(1)

s 16G added—Transport, 2000 c 38, s 223

am—Railways, 2005 c 14, s 1, sch 1 pt 1 para 11(1)

s 16H, 16I added—Transport, 2000 c 38, s 223

s 17 am—SI 1998/1340, reg 21(5)-(8); Transport, 2000 c 38, ss 215, 233(1), 252, sch 16 para 11, sch 27 para 21; Railways and Transport Safety, 2003 c 20, s 16, sch 2 pt 1 paras 1, 3; Railways, 2005 c 14, ss 1, 54, sch 1 pt 1 para 12(1)(2), sch 11 paras 1, 3(a); SI 2005/3049, reg 2(4), sch 1 pt 1 para 4(b)

rep in pt—Transport, 2000 c 38, s 274, sch 31 pt IV; SI 2005/3049, reg 2(4), sch 1 pt 1 para 4(a)

appl—SI 2003/3364, art 32, sch 7 para 1(2)

excl—SI 1994/606

restr—Channel Tunnel Rail Link, 1996 c 61, s 17(1)-(3)

s 18 am—Transport, 2000 c 38, ss 212(6), 215, 230(1)(2), 252, sch 16 para 12, sch 27 para 22; Railways and Transport Safety, 2003 c 20, s 16, sch 2 pt 1 paras 1, 3; Railways, 2005 c 14, s 1, sch 1 pt 1 para 12(1)(3)

excl—SI 1994/606

restr—Channel Tunnel Rail Link, 1996 c 61, s 17(1)-(3)

rep in pt—Transport, 2000 c 38, s 274, sch 31 pt IV; SI 2005/3049, reg 2(4), sch 1 pt 1 para 4(c)

s 19 restr—Channel Tunnel Rail Link, 1996 c 61, s 17(4)

am—Transport, 2000 c 38, ss 215, 230(3)(4), 233(2), sch 16 para 13; Railways and Transport Safety, 2003 c 20, s 16, sch 2 pt 1 paras 1, 3; Railways, 2005 c 14, ss 1, 54, sch 1 pt 1 para 12(1)(2), sch 11 paras 1, 3(b)

rep in pt—Transport, 2000 c 38, s 274, sch 31 pt IV

s 19A added—Transport, 2000 c 38, s 231(1)

s 20 am—Railways, 1993 c 43, s 36(3); Transport, 2000 c 38, s 252, sch 27 para 23(2)(4); Railways and Transport Safety, 2003 c 20, s 16, sch 2 pt 1 paras 1, 3, 9

excl—GLA, 1999 c 29, s 199(1)(b)

power to ext—GLA, 1999 c 29, s 199(1)(b)(2)(3)

rep in pt—Transport, 2000 c 38, ss 252, 274, sch 27 para 23(3), sch 31 pt IV

s 21 am—Railways and Transport Safety, 2003 c 20, s 16, sch 2 pt 1 paras 1, 3, 10(a)

1993

c 43 s 21 *continued*

        rep in pt—Railways and Transport Safety, 2003 c 20, ss 16, 118, sch 2 pt 1 paras 1,
           10(b), sch 8

  s 22 am—Competition, 1998 c 41, s 66(5), sch 10 pt IV, para 15(5); Transport, 2000 c 38,
        s 232(1); Enterprise, 2002 c 40, s 278(1), sch 25, para 30(1)(7); Railways and
        Transport Safety, 2003 c 20, s 16, sch 2 pt 1 paras 1, 3; SI 2014/892, sch 1 para
        104

        rep in pt—Transport, 2000 c 38, s 274, sch 31 pt IV

  s 22A added—Transport, 2000 c 38, s 232(2)

        am—Railways and Transport Safety, 2003 c 20, s 16, sch 2 pt 1 paras 1, 3; SI
           2005/3049, reg 2(4), sch 1 pt 1 para 4(d)(ii)

        rep in pt—SI 2005/3049, reg 2(4), sch 1 pt 1 para 4(d)(i)

  s 22B added—Transport, 2000 c 38, s 232(2)

  s 22C added—Transport, 2000 c 38, s 232(2)

        am—Railways and Transport Safety, 2003 c 20, s 16, sch 2 pt 1 paras 1, 3

        appl (mods)—SI 2005/3050, reg 14, sch 3 pt 2 para 9

  s 23 excl—SIs 1994/606; 1999/3112, art 3

        am—Transport, 2000 c 38, ss 212(1)(2), 215, 253, sch 16 para 14(1)-(3)(4), sch 28
           para 3; Railways, 2005 c 14, s 1, sch 1 pt 1 para 13(1)(2)(4)(5)

        appl—Enterprise, 2002 c 40, s 168(3)(i)(4)(k); SI 2003/1325, art 3(1)

        rep in pt—Railways, 2005 c 14, ss 1, 59, sch 1 pt 1 para 13(3), sch 13 pt 1

  s 24 am—Transport, 2000 c 38, s 215, sch 16 para 15; Railways and Transport Safety,
        2003 c 20, s 16, sch 2 pt 1 paras 1, 3; Railways, 2005 c 14, s 1, sch 1 pt 1 para 14

        rep in pt—Railways, 2005 c 14, s 59, sch 13 pt 1

  s 25 am—GLA, 1999 c 29, s 202; Loc Transport, 2008 c 26, s 77, sch 4 para 58(1), (2); SI
        2009/1941, art 2, sch 1; Loc Democracy, Economic Development and
        Construction, 2009 c 20, s 119, sch 6 paras 84, 85

        rep in pt—Transport, 2000 c 38, s 274, sch 31 pt IV

        excl—Crossrail, 2008 c 18, s 25(1)

  s 26 am—Transport, 2000 c 38, ss 212(3), 215, 253, sch 16 para 16, sch 28 para 3;
        Railways and Transport Safety, 2003 c 20, s 16, sch 2 pt 1 paras 1, 3; Railways,
        2005 c 14, s 1, sch 1 pt 1 para 15(1)-(3)(5)(6)

        rep in pt—Railways, 2005 c 14, ss 1, 59, sch 1 pt 1 para 15(1)(4), sch 13 pt 1

  ss 26A-26C added—Transport, 2000 c 38, ss 212(4), 253, sch 28 para 3

        replaced (by s 26ZA)—Railways, 2005 c 14, s 1, sch 1 pt 1 para 16

  s 27 am—Transport, 2000 c 38, ss 215, 252, sch 16 para 17, sch 27 para 24; Railways,
        2005 c 14, s 1, sch 1 pt 1 para 17; Tribunals, Cts and Enforcement, 2007 c 15, s
        62, sch 13 para 112

        rep in pt—Transport, 2000 c 38, s 274, sch 31 pt IV

  s 28 am—Transport, 2000 c 38, s 215, sch 16 para 18; Railways, 2005 c 14, s 1, sch 1 pt 1
        para 18

  s 29 am—Transport, 2000 c 38, s 215, sch 16 para 19; Railways, 2005 c 14, s 1, sch 1 pt 1
        para 19

        rep in pt—Transport, 2000 c 38, s 274, sch 31 pt IV

  s 30 subst—Transport, 2000 c 38, ss 212(5), 253, sch 28 para 3

        am—Railways, 2005 c 14, ss 1, 18, 54, sch 1 pt 1 para 20(1)(3)-(5), sch 11 paras 1, 4;
        Deregulation, 2015 c 20, sch 8 para 10(2)(3)

        rep in pt—Railways, 2005 c 14, ss 1, 59, sch 1 pt 1 para 20(2)(5), sch 13 pt 1

  ss 32, 33 rep—Transport, 2000 c 38, s 274, sch 31 pt IV

  s 34 am—Transport, 2000 c 38, ss 215, 246, 252, sch 16 para 20, sch 27 para 25

        rep in pt—Transport, 2000 c 38, s 274, sch 31 pt IV

        rep (saving) (S prosp)—Railways, 2005 c 14, ss 14, 59, sch 13 pt 1

        see—(exercise of functions) SSI 2005/598, arts 3-5, sch 1, sch 2 para 2

  s 35 am—Transport, 2000 c 38, ss 215, 252, sch 16 para 21; sch 27 para 26

        rep in pt—Transport, 2000 c 38, s 274, sch 31 pt IV

        rep (S) (prosp)—(saving) Railways, 2005 c 14, ss 14, 59, sch 13 pt 1

        see—(exercise of functions) SSI 2005/598, arts 3, 5, sch 1

  s 37-43 rep—Railways, 2005 c 14, s 59, sch 13 pt 1

  s 44 rep—Transport, 2000 c 38, ss 234(4), 253, 274, sch 28 paras 12, 17, sch 31 pt IV

  ss 45, 46 rep—Railways, 2005 c 14, s 59, sch 13 pt 1

  s 46A added—Transport, 2000 c 38, s 238

        rep—Railways, 2005 c 14, s 59, sch 13 pt 1

  s 46B added—Transport, 2000 c 38, s 216, sch 17 pt II para 25(3)

        rep—Railways, 2005 c 14, s 59, sch 13 pt 1

1993
c 43 *continued*

s 47 replaced (by ss 47,47A,47B)—Transport, 2000 c 38, s 215, sch 16 para 31
    rep—Railways, 2005 c 14, s 59, sch 13 pt 1
ss 48, 49 rep—Railways, 2005 c 14, s 59, sch 13 pt 1
s 50 excl—Greater Nottingham Light Rapid Transit, 1994 c xv, s 16(4)
    am—Transport, 2000 c 38, s 215, sch 16 para 33; Railways, 2005 c 14, s 54, sch 11
        paras 1, 5
    rep in pt—Transport, 2000 c 38, s 274, sch 31 pt IV; Railways, 2005 c 14, s 59, sch 13
        pt 1
ss 51-53 rep—Transport, 2000 c 38, s 274, sch 31 pt IV
s 54 appl—Transport 1968 c 73, s 56(2B)
    am—Transport, 2000 c 38, ss 215, 252, sch 16 para 34, sch 27 para 29; (pt prosp)
        Railways, 2005 c 14, s 54, sch 11 paras 1, 6
    rep in pt—Transport, 2000 c 38, s 274, sch 31 pt IV; (for specified purposes) Railways,
        2005 c 14, ss 54, 59, sch 11 paras 1, 6(3), sch 13 pt 1
s 55 am—Competition 1998 c 41, s 66(5), sch 10 para 15(6)(7)(a)(b); Transport, 2000 c 38,
        ss 215, 216, 225(2), 226(1), 236(3), 239(4), 252, 253, sch 16 para 35, sch 17 pt I
        para 11(2)(3)(4), pt II para 26, sch 27 para 30(2)(3)(4), sch 28 paras 6, 9, 13, 17;
        Railways and Transport Safety, 2003 c 20, s 16, sch 2 pt 1 paras 1, 3, 11;
        Railways, 2005 c 14, ss 1, 54, sch 1 pt 1 paras 21(1)(2)(4)-(7)(8)(b), 26, sch 11
        para 7(1)-(3)(5)(6); ibid, s 54, sch 11 paras 1, 7(4); Enterprise and Regulatory
        Reform, 2013 c 24, sch 14 para 12(2)(3)
    rep in pt—Transport, 2000 c 38, ss 226(1), 252, 253, 274, sch 27 para 30(5), sch 28
        paras 9, 17, sch 31 pt IV; Railways, 2005 c 14, ss 1, 59, sch 1 pt 1 paras
        21(8)(a), 26, sch 13 pt 1; ibid, ss 1, 59, sch 1 pt 1 paras 21(3), 26, sch 13 pt 1
    appl (mods)—SI 2005/3050, reg 14, sch 3 pt 1 para 1(c) pt 2 para 6
    appl—(saving) SI 2010/1504, reg 17
s 56 am—Transport, 2000 c 38, ss 215, 216, 226(2), 252, 253, sch 16 para 36, sch 17 pt I
        para 12, sch 27 para 31, sch 28 paras 9, 17; Railways and Transport Safety, 2003
        c 20, s 16, sch 2 pt 1 paras 1, 3; Railways, 2005 c 14, s 1, sch 1 pt 1 paras 22, 26
    appl (mods)—SI 2005/3050, reg 14, sch 3 pt 1 para 1(c)
    appl—(saving) SI 2010/1504, reg 17
s 57 am—Transport, 2000 c 38, ss 215, 252, sch 16 para 37, sch 27 para 32(3)-(5)
    rep in pt—Transport, 2000 c 38, ss 252, 274, sch 27 para 32(2), sch 31 pt IV
    appl (mods)—SI 2005/3050, reg 14, sch 3 pt 1 para 1(c)
    appl—Railways, 2005 c 14, s 44(1); (saving) SI 2010/1504, reg 17
ss 57A-57F added—Transport, 2000 c 38, s 225(1), 253, sch 28 paras 6-8, 17
s 57A am —Railways and Transport Safety, 2003 c 20, s 16, sch 2 pt 1 paras 1, 3, 12;
        Railways, 2005 c 14, s 1, sch 1 pt 1 paras 23, 26; Enterprise and Regulatory
        Reform, 2013 c 24, sch 14 para 13
    appl (mods)—SI 2005/3050, reg 14, sch 3 pt 1 para 1(c)
    appl—(saving) SI 2010/1504, reg 17
s 57B rep in pt —Railways and Transport Safety, 2003 c 20, ss 16, 118, sch 2 pt 1 paras 1,
        13, sch 8
    am—Railways and Transport Safety, 2003 c 20, s 16, sch 2 pt 1 paras 1, 3; Railways,
        2005 c 14, s 1, sch 1 pt 1 paras 24, 26
    appl (mods)—SI 2005/3050, reg 14, sch 3 pt 1 para 1(c)
    appl—(saving) SI 2010/1504, reg 17
s 57C appl (mods)—SI 2005/3050, reg 14, sch 3 pt 1 para 1(c)
    am—Railways, 2005 c 14, s 1, sch 1 pt 1 paras 25, 26
    appl—(saving) SI 2010/1504, reg 17
ss 57D, 57E appl (mods)—SI 2005/3050, reg 14, sch 3 pt 1 para 1(c)
    appl—SI 2010/1504, reg 17
s 57F appl (mods)—SI 2005/3050, reg 14, sch 3 pt 1 para 1(c)
    am—Railways, 2005 c 14, s 54, sch 11 paras 1, 8
    appl—(saving) SI 2010/1504, reg 17
s 58 am—Transport, 2000 c 38, ss 215, 252, sch 16 para 38, sch 27 para 33
    appl (mods)—SI 2005/3050, reg 14, sch 3 pt 1 para 1(c)
    appl—(saving) SI 2010/1504, reg 17
s 59 mod—Channel Tunnel Rail Link, 1996 c 61, s 19(1)
    appl—Insolvency, 1986 c 45, s 72GA(b); Enterprise, 2002 c 40, s 249(1)(b)
    am—Railways, 2005 c 14, s 49(1)(10)(11); SIs 2005/3050, regs 3, 20, sch 1 pt 1 para
        3(1)(5), sch 4 paras 1-4, 8-14; 2009/1941, art 2, sch 1
    rep in pt—Railways, 2005 c 14, s 59, sch 13 pt 1

1993
c 43 *continued*

s 60 restr—Channel Tunnel Rail Link, 1996 c 61, s 19(7)
    mod—Channel Tunnel Rail Link, 1996 c 61, s 19(2)(a)(3)
    am—Transport, 2000 c 38, ss 215, 252 sch 16 para 39, sch 27 para 34; Railways, 2005
      c 14, s 49(2)(3)(10)(11)
s 61 restr—Channel Tunnel Rail Link, 1996 c 61, s 19(7)
    mod—Channel Tunnel Rail Link, 1996 c 61, s 19(2)(a)
    am—Transport, 2000 c 38, s 215, sch 16 para 40; Railways, 2005 c 14,
      s 49(4)(a)(10)(11)
    rep in pt—Railways, 2005 c 14, ss 1, 59, sch 1 pt I para 27, sch 13 pt I
s 62 am—Transport, 2000 c 38, s 215, sch 16 para 41; Railways, 2005 c 14,
      s 49(4)(b)(10)(11)
    rep in pt—Railways, 2005 c 14, ss 1, 59, sch 1 pt I para 27, sch 13 pt I
s 63 saved—Scotland, 1998 c 46, s 30, sch 5 pt II, s E2(a)
    am—Railways, 2005 c 14, ss 50(1), 54, sch 11 paras 1, 9
    rep in pt—Railways, 2005 c 14, s 59, sch 13 pt I
ss 63-65 restr—Channel Tunnel Rail Link, 1996 c 61, s 19(7)
s 64A added—Railways, 2005 c 14, s 50(2)
s 65 am—SI 2009/1941, art 2, sch 1
s 66 am—Enterprise, 2002 c 40, s 278(1), sch 25, para 30(1)(8); SI 2003/1592, art 16, sch
      4 para 12(2)
    rep in pt—Enterprise, 2002 c 40, s 278(2), sch 26; SI 2003/1398, art 2, sch
      para 21(1)(2)
s 67 appl—Deregulation and Contracting Out, 1994 c 40, s 7, sch 2 para 11(2)
    am—Deregulation and Contracting Out, 1994 c 40, ss 7,12, sch 2 paras 12,13, sch 4
      paras 2(d),4; Competition, 1998 c 41, s 66(5), sch 10 para 6(5)(8)(9)(b);
      SI 1999/506, art 33(a)(b); Transport, 2000 c 38, ss 243, 252, sch 27 para 35;
      Enterprise, 2002 c 40, ss 168(9), 278(1), sch 9 pt 2, para
      21(1)-(4)(5)(a)(c)(6)(a)(c)(7), sch 25, para 30(1)(9)(b)(c); Railways and
      Transport Safety, 2003 c 20, s 16, sch 2 pt 1 paras 1, 3; SIs 2003/1398, art 2, sch
      para 21(1)(3); 2004/1261, reg 5, sch 2 para 6; 2012/1809, art 3(1), sch pt 1;
      Enterprise and Regulatory Reform, 2013 c 24, sch 14 para 14; ibid, sch 15 para 7;
      SI 2014/892, sch 1 para 105
    rep in pt—Deregulation and Contracting Out, 1994 c 40, ss 12,81 sch 4 para 4, sch 17;
      Competition, 1998 c 41, ss 66(5),74(3), sch 10 pt II, para 6(6)(7)(9)(a), sch 14
      pt I; Enterprise, 2002 c 40, ss 168(9), 278, sch 9 pt 2, para 21(1)(5)(b)(6)(b)(8),
      sch 25, para 30(1)(9)(a), sch 26; Railways, 2005 c 14, s 59, sch 13 pt I
    restr—Channel Tunnel Rail Link, 1996 c 61, s 22 (1) (4); Competition, 1998 c 41,
      s 66(5), sch 10 paras 6(1),16(3)
s 68 am—Transport, 2000 c 38, ss 216, 227, sch 17 pt I para 13, sch 22 pt I para 7;
      Railways and Transport Safety, 2003 c 20, s 16, sch 2 pt 1 paras 1, 3; Railways,
      2005 c 14, s 21(2); SI 2010/439, art 2, sch
    rep in pt—Transport, 2000 c 38, ss 234(6), 253, 274, sch 28 paras 12, 17, sch 31 pt IV;
      Railways, 2005 c 14, s 59, sch 13 pt I
    appl (mods)—SI 2005/3050, reg 14, sch 3 pt 1 para 1(d)
s 69 am—Transport, 2000 c 38, s 215, sch 16 para 42; Enterprise, 2002 c 40, s 278(1), sch
      25, para 30(1)(10); Railways and Transport Safety, 2003 c 20, s 16, sch 2 pt 1
      paras 1, 3; SI 2014/892, sch 1 para 106
    rep in pt—Railways, 2005 c 14, s 59, sch 13 pt I
s 70 rep—Transport, 2000 c 38, ss 216, 274, sch 17 pt II para 28(2), sch 31 pt IV
s 71 am—Enterprise, 2002 c 40, s 278(1), sch 25, para 30(1)(11); Railways and Transport
      Safety, 2003 c 20, s 16, sch 2 pt 1 paras 1, 3; SI 2014/892, sch 1 para 107
s 71A added—Transport, 2000 c 38, s 216, sch 17 pt I para 14
    rep—Railways, 2005 c 14, ss 1, 59, sch 1 pt I para 28, sch 13 pt I
s 71B added—Transport, 2000 c 38, ss 216, 253, sch 17 pt II para 28(1), sch 28 paras 15,
      17
    am—Railways, 2005 c 14, s 1, sch 1 pt I para 29
s 72 am—Transport, 2000 c 38, ss 215, 216, 230(5), 252, sch 16 para 43, sch 17 pt I
      para 15, sch 27 para 36; Railways and Transport Safety, 2003 c 20, s 16, sch 2 pt
      1 paras 1, 3; Railways, 2005 c 14, s 54, sch 11 paras 1, 10; SIs 2005/3050, regs 3,
      20, sch 1 pt 1 para 3(1)(6), sch 4 paras 1-4, 8-14; 2014/892, sch 1 para 108
    rep in pt—Transport, 2000 c 38, ss 216, 274, sch 17 pt II para 27(2), sch 31 pt IV;
      Railways, 2005 c 14, s 59, sch 13 pt I
    appl (mods)—SI 2005/3050, reg 14, sch 3 pt 1 para 1(e) pt 2 para 7

1993
c 43 *continued*

s 73 am—Transport, 2000 c 38, ss 215, 216, 252, sch 16 para 44, sch 17 pt I para 16, pt II
    para 27(1), sch 27 para 37; Railways and Transport Safety, 2003 c 20, s 16, sch 2
    pt I paras 1, 3; Railways, 2005 c 14, ss 1, 54, sch 1 pt I para 30(1)-(5)(7), sch 11
    para 11
  rep in pt—Transport, 2000 c 38, s 274, sch 31 pt IV; Railways, 2005 c 14, ss 1, 59, sch
    1 pt I para 30(6), sch 13 pt I
s 73A added—Railways, 2005 c 14, s 1, sch 1 pt I para 31
s 74 am—SI 1999/506, art 33(a)(b); (S) SI 1999/1750, art 3, sch 2; SI 1999/1750, art 6(1),
    sch 5 para 13; Enterprise, 2002 c 40, s 278(1), sch 25, para 30(1)(12); Railways
    and Transport Safety, 2003 c 20, s 16, sch 2 pt I paras 1, 3, 14(a); Enterprise and
    Regulatory Reform, 2013 c 24, sch 6 para 79(2)
  rep in pt—Transport, 2000 c 38, ss 216, 274, sch 17 pt II para 29(2), sch 31 pt IV;
    Railways and Transport Safety, 2003 c 20, ss 16, 118, sch 2 pt I paras 1, 14(b),
    sch 8; Enterprise and Regulatory Reform, 2013 c 24, sch 6 para 79(3)
s 75 rep—Railways, 2005 c 14, s 59, sch 13 pt I
s 76 am—(S) SI 1999/1750, art 3, sch 2; Transport, 2000 c 38, ss 215, 216, 227, 228,
    sch 16 para 46, sch 17 pt II para 20, sch 22 pt I para 8; Railways and Transport
    Safety, 2003 c 20, s 16, sch 2 pt I paras 1, 3, 15, 16; (pt prosp) Railways, 2005 c
    14, s 1, sch 1 pt I para 32(1)-(3); ibid, s 21, sch 6 para 5; SI 2010/439, art 2, sch
  appl—Transport, 1985 c 67, s 123
  excl—Transport, 2000 c 38, s 253, sch 28 para 10
  rep in pt—Transport, 2000 c 38, s 274, sch 31 pt IV; Railways, 2005 c 14, ss 1, 59, sch
    1 pt I para 32(4)(5), sch 13 pt I
  restr—SI 2003/1695, arts 3-5, sch
  appl (mods)—SIs 2003/1696, arts 3, 4; 2005/3050, reg 17(1); 2010/1504, reg 18
s 76A added—Railways, 2005 c 14, s 20
  am—SI 2010/439, art 2, sch
s 77 rep—Railways, 2005 c 14, s 59, sch 13 pt I
s 78 rep in pt—Transport, 2000 c 38, s 274, sch 31 pt IV
s 79 rep—Railways, 2005 c 14, s 59, sch 13 pt I
s 80 am—Transport, 2000 c 38, ss 215, 252, sch 16 para 48, sch 27 para 38(a); Railways,
    2005 c 14, ss 1, 54, sch 1 pt I para 33, sch 11 para 12; SI 2005/3050, regs 3, 20,
    sch 1 pt I para 3(1)(7), sch 4 paras 1-4, 8-14
  rep in pt—Transport, 2000 c 38, ss 252, 274, sch 27 para 38(b), sch 31 pt IV
s 81 appl—Capital Allowances, 1990 c 1, s 38A(5); (EW) Leasehold Reform, Housing and
    Urban Development, 1993 c 28, s 4(5)(c); Capital Allowances, 2001 c 2,
    s 95(5)(6)
s 82 appl—Scotland, 1998 c 46, s 30, sch 5 pt II, s E2, E2(b); SIs 2004/1573, art 10(1)(c);
    (W) 2005/422 (W 40), reg 7(3); (E) 551, reg 6(4); (S) SSI 2005/127, art 7(4)
s 83 am—SI 1998/1340, reg 21(9); Transport, 2000 c 38, ss 230(6), 233(3), 252, sch 27
    para 39; Enterprise, 2002 c 40, s 278(1), sch 25, para 30(1)(13)(b); Railways,
    2005 c 14, ss 1, 54, sch 1 pt 2 para 37, sch 11 para 13(a); ibid, s 54, sch 11 paras
    1, 13(b)(c); SI 2005/3050, regs 3, 20, sch 1 pt I para 3(1)(8)(a), sch 4 paras 1-4,
    8-14; Enterprise and Regulatory Reform, 2013 c 24, sch 6 para 80(a)
  appl—British Transport Commission, 1949 c xxix, s 53(3); Transport, 1968 c 73,
    s 23A; Finance, 1994 c 9, s 252, sch 24 para 19(7); Capital Allowances, 1990
    c 1, s 38A(5); Capital Allowances, 2001 c 2, s 95(5)(6); SIs 1999/2024,
    reg 3(2)(c); 2001/1451L, art 16(3); Enterprise, 2002 c 40,
    s 168(3)(i)(4)(j); (EW) SI 2002/2977, reg 6, sch pt 1, para 4(c); Licensing, 2003
    c 17, ss 157(7), 173(6); SIs 2004/568, reg 49(4); (W) 2004/3054 (W 263)(L),
    art 32, sch 6 para 18(2); (W) 2005/422 (W 40), reg 7(3); (E) 551, reg 6(4); (S)
    SSI 2005/127, art 7(4); Licensing (S), 2005 asp 16, s 127(6)
  rep in pt—Transport, 2000 c 38, s 274, sch 31 pt IV; Enterprise, 2002 c 40, s 278, sch
    25, para 30(1)(13)(a), sch 26; Railways, 2005 c 14, s 59, sch 13 pt I; ibid, s 59,
    sch 13 pt I; SI 2005/3050, regs 3, 20, sch 1 pt I para 3(1)(8)(b), sch 4 paras
    1-4, 8-14; Enterprise and Regulatory Reform, 2013 c 24, sch 6 para 80(b)
Pt 2 (ss 84-116) rep (prosp)—(prosp but rep of s 113 in force 15.1.2001) Transport, 2000
    c 38, s 274, sch 31 pt IV
  appl—Finance, 1994 c 9, s 252, sch 24 para 1(1)
  excl—Finance, 1994 c 9, s 252, sch 24 paras 4(1),8(4),17(2)
s 84 appl (mods)—Transport, 2000 c 38, s 241
s 85 appl—Finance, 1994 c 9, s 252, sch 24 para 1(1)
  appl (mods)—Transport, 2000 c 38, s 241

1993
c 43 *continued*

s 91 am—(temp) Constitutional Reform, 2005 c 4, s 15(1), sch 4 pt 2 paras 361(3), 382, 383

s 93 am—Employment Rights, 1996 c 18, s 240, sch 1 para 60(2)

s 94 am—SI 2008/948, art 3, sch 1

s 95 am—Railways and Transport Safety, 2003 c 20, s 16, sch 2 pt 1 paras 1, 3

s 106 am—SI 2008/948, art 3, sch 1

s 114 am—SI 2009/1941, art 2, sch 1

Pt 3 (ss 117-154) excl—Finance, 1994 c 9, s 252, sch 24 para 4(1)

s 118 rep in pt—Transport, 2000 c 38, ss 215, 274, sch 16 para 49(4)(b), sch 31 pt IV; Railways, 2005 c 14, s 59, sch 13 pt 1

am—Transport, 2000 c 38, s 215, sch 16 para 49(2)(3)(4)(a)(5); Railways and Transport Safety, 2003 c 20, s 16, sch 2 pt 1 paras 1, 3; Railways, 2005 c 14, s 54(1)

s 119 am—Railways, 2005 c 14, s 54(1)-(3)

s 121A added—Railways and Transport Safety, 2003 c 20, s 106

s 122 saved—SIs 2002/1066, art 43(3); 2004/757, art 50(3); 2005/3105, art 48(3); 2008/1261, art 27

s 125 rep and superseded—Railway Heritage, 1996 c 42, s 8(2)

ss 126-128 rep—Transport, 2000 c 38, s 274, sch 31 pt IV

s 129 rep—Transport, 2000 c 38, s 274, sch 31 pt IV

s 130 am—GLA, 1999 c 29, s 206; Transport, 2000 c 38, s 216, sch 17 pt II para 30; Railways, 2005 c 14, ss 1, 47, sch 1 pt 1 para 34(a)

rep in pt—Railways, 2005 c 14, ss 1, 59, sch 1 pt 1 para 34(b), sch 13 pt 1

s 131 rep—Competition, 1998 c 41, ss 66(5),74(3), sch 10 pt IV, para 15(8), sch 14 pt I

ss 132, 133 rep—Railways and Transport Safety, 2003 c 20, ss 73, 118, sch 5 para 2, sch 8

s 135 am—Transport, 2000 c 38, ss 215, 252, sch 16 para 50, sch 27 para 40; Railways, 2005 c 14, s 1, sch 1 pt 1 para 35

rep in pt—Transport, 2000 c 38, s 274, sch 31 pt IV

s 136 am—(S) Loc Govt etc(S), 1994 c 39, s 180(1), sch 13 para 184(2); Transport, 2000 c 38, s 215, sch 16 para 51; SI 2003/1615, art 2, sch 1 pt 1 para 19; Railways, 2005 c 14, s 54, sch 11 paras 1, 14; Loc Transport, 2008 c 26, s 77, sch 4 para 58(1), (3); SI 2010/402, reg 2

saved—Scotland, 1998 c 46, s 30, sch 5 pt II, s E2(c)

rep in pt—European Parliamentary Elections, 1993 c 41, s 136(2B); Railways, 2005 c 14, s 59, sch 13 pt 1

s 137, 139 rep—Transport, 2000 c 38, s 274, sch 31 pt IV

s 140 rep (S)—Transport (S), 2001 asp 2, s 71(6)

s 141 rep—Transport, 2000 c 38, s 274, sch 31 pt IV

s 143 am—Railways, 2005 c 14, s 54, sch 11 paras 1, 15

s 144 rep in pt—Transport, 2000 c 38, s 274, sch 31 pt IV; Railways, 2005 c 14, s 59, sch 13 pt 1

s 145 am—SI 1998/1340, reg 21(10); Competition, 1998 c 41, s 66(5), sch 10, para 15(9)(b)(10); GLA, 1999 c 29, s 252(2), sch 19 para 5(6); SI 1999/506, art 33(a)(b); Transport, 2000 c 38, ss 215, 227, 252, sch 16 para 52, sch 22 pt I para 11, sch 27 para 41; SIs 2001/3649, art 343; 2001/4050, art 2, sch pt IV, para 23; Enterprise, 2002 c 40, s 278(1), sch 25, para 30(1)(14); Railways and Transport Safety, 2003 c 20, s 16, sch 2 pt 1 paras 1, 3; Communications, 2003 c 21, s 406(1), sch 17 para 127; Railways, 2005 c 14, s 54, sch 11 paras 1, 16; SIs 2005/3049, reg 2(4), sch 1 pt 1 para 4(e)(ii); 3050, regs 3, 20, sch 1 pt 1 para 3(1)(9), sch 4 paras 1-4, 8-14; 2008/1277, reg 30, sch 2; 2009/1122, reg 3, sch; 2010/439, art 2, sch; Civil Aviation, 2012 c 19, sch 9 para 8; Financial Services, 2012 c 21, sch 18 para 77(2); Energy, 2013 c 32, sch 12 para 69; SI 2013/1881, sch para 5; SI 2014/892, sch 1 para 109(2)(a)(b)(ii)(3)-(5); SI 2015/786, reg 7(3)

rep in pt—Competition, 1998 c 41, s 66(5), 74(3), sch 10, para 15(9)(a), sch 14 pt I; Railways, 2005 c 14, s 59, sch 13 pt 1; SIs 2005/3049, reg 2(4), sch 1 pt 1 para 4(e)(i); 2008/960, art 22, sch 3; 2013/1575, sch para 1; 2014/892, sch 1 para 109(2)(b)(i); Deregulation, 2015 c 20, sch 6 para 22(9)

ext—Anti-terrorism, Crime and Security, 2001 c 24, s 17, sch 4 pt 1, para 34

excl—Railways and Transport Safety, 2003 c 20, s 115(1)(2)(j)

appl (mods)—SIs 2005/3050, reg 18; 2006/1391, art 2, sch; 2010/1504, reg 19

s 148 am—Crim Procedure (Conseq Provns)(S), 1995 c 40, s 5, sch 4 para 88

s 149 appl—SIs 1994/1432; 2001/3352, rule 9.9(1)

1993
c 43 s 149 *continued*

am—Loc Democracy, Economic Development and Construction, 2009 c 20, s 119, sch 6 paras 84, 86

s 149A added—SI 2006/2190, art 6

s 150 am—Transport, 2000 c 38, s 252, sch 27 para 42
rep in pt—Transport, 2000 c 38, s 274, sch 31 pt IV

s 151 rep in pt—(S) Loc Govt etc (S), 1994 c 39, s 180(1)(2), sch 13 para 184(3)(a), sch 14; SI 1999/506, art 33(c); Transport, 2000 c 38, s 274, sch 31 pt IV; Railways and Transport Safety, 2003 c 20, ss 16, 118, sch 2 pt 1 paras 1, 17, sch 8; Railways, 2005 c 14, s 59, sch 13 pt 1
am—Loc Govt (W), 1994 c 19, s 66(6), sch 16 para 107; (S) Loc Govt etc(S), 1994 c 39, s 180(1), sch 13 para 184(3)(b)(c); Transport, 2000 c 38, ss 215, 252, sch 16 para 53, sch 27 para 43; SIs 2001/3649, art 344; 2006/246, reg 20, sch 2; 2009/1941, art 2, sch 1; Financial Services, 2012 c 21, sch 18 para 77(3)
ext—Finance, 1994 c 9, s 252, sch 24 para 1(2)

s 152 rep in pt—Transport, 2000 c 38, s 274, sch 31 pt IV

s 154 am—Transport, 2000 c 38, s 252, sch 27 para 44

sch 1 rep—Railways and Transport Safety, 2003 c 20, ss 16, 118, sch 2 pt 1 paras 1, 2, sch 8

schs 2, 3 rep—Railways, 2005 c 14, s 59, sch 13 pt 1

sch 4 rep in pt—Transport, 2000 c 38, s 274, sch 31 pt IV
am—Enterprise, 2002 c 40, s 278(1), sch 25, para 30(1)(15)(a)-(c); Railways and Transport Safety, 2003 c 20, s 16, sch 2 pt 1 paras 1, 3; SI 2014/892, sch 1 paras 111, 112

sch 4A added—Transport, 2000 c 38, ss 231(2), 253, schs 24, 28 paras 11, 17
am—Railways and Transport Safety, 2003 c 20, s 16, sch 2 pt 1 paras 1, 3; Communications, 2003 c 21, s 389(1), sch 16 para 4(1)(4); Railways, 2005 c 14, s 4, sch 4 paras 1, 2, 4-11; Enterprise and Regulatory Reform, 2013 c 24, sch 6 para 81(2)-(4)(5)(a)(b)(6)(a)(b)(7)(a)(b)(i)(ii)(c); ibid, sch 6 para 81(8)-(12)(13)(a)(b)(c)(i)(ii)(d)
rep in pt—Railways, 2005 c 14, ss 4, 59, sch 4 paras 1, 3, 11, sch 13 pt 1

sch 5 rep—Railways, 2005 c 14, s 59, sch 13 pt 1

sch 6 mod—Channel Tunnel Rail Link, 1996 c 61, s 19(2)(b)(4)(5)
restr—Channel Tunnel Rail Link, 1996 c 61, s 19(7)
am—Transport, 2000 c 38, s 252, sch 27 para 48; Railways and Transport Safety, 2003 c 20, s 16, sch 2 pt 1 paras 1, 18; Railways, 2005 c 14, s 49(4)(c)(5)(6)(10)(11); SI 2009/1941, art 2, sch 1
appl—SI 2001/3352, rule 2.7(2)
rep in pt—Railways, 2005 c 14, s 59, sch 13 pt 1

sch 7 mod—Channel Tunnel Rail Link, 1996 c 61, s 19(6)
restr—Channel Tunnel Rail Link, 1996 c 61, s 19(7)
rep in pt—Transport, 2000 c 38, s 215, sch 16 para 54(5)(c); (pt prosp) ibid, s 274, sch 31 pt IV
am—Transport, 2000 c 38, s 215, sch 16 para 54(2)-(4)(5)(a)(b); SI 2005/3050, regs 3, 20, sch 1 pt 1 para 3(1)(10), sch 4 paras 1-4, 8-14; Railways, 2005 c 14, s 49(7)-(11)

sch 8 rep (prosp)—Transport, 2000 c 38, s 274, sch 31 pt IV
am—(temp) Constitutional Reform, 2005 c 4, s 15(1), sch 4 pt 2 paras 361(3), 382, 384

sch 9 rep (prosp)—Transport, 2000 c 38, s 274, sch 31 pt IV

sch 10 rep—Railways and Transport Safety, 2003 c 20, ss 73, 118, sch 5 para 2, sch 8
am—Transport, 2000 c 38, s 217, sch 18 pt I para 10

sch 11 rep in pt—SI 1995/31, reg 6, sch; Transport, 2000 c 38, s 274, sch 31 pt IV
am—Employment Rights, 1996 c 18, s 240, sch 1 para 60(3); Transport, 2000 c 38, ss 245(1), 252, sch 27 para 49(2)-(5); SI 2006/745, art 6
power to mod—Railways, 2005 c 14, s 1(8)(b)
rep in pt—Railways, 2005 c 14, s 59, sch 13 pt 1

sch 12 rep in pt—(pt prosp) Transport, 2000 c 38, s 274, sch 31 pt IV; Enterprise, 2002 c 40, s 278(2), sch 26

sch 13 rep—Transport, 2000 c 38, s 274, sch 31 pt IV

c 44 **Crofters (Scotland)**
appl—Transfer of Crofting Estates (S), 1997 c 26, s 7(2); Title Conditions (S), 2003 asp 9, s 90(3), sch 11 para 3(c); Civil Partnership, 2004 c 33, s 112(9)

1993
c 44 *continued*

     s 1 am—Crofting Reform etc, 2007 asp 7, s 1; ibid, s 39, sch 1 para 2(1)(2); Crofting
         Reform (S), 2010 asp 14, s 2(1)
       rep in pt—Crofting Reform (S), 2010 asp 14, s 55, sch 4 para 3(2)
     s 2 rep in pt—Crofting Reform (S), 2010 asp 14, s 55, sch 4 para 3(3)
     ss 2A-2D added —Crofting Reform (S), 2010 asp 14, s 2(2)
     s 3 appl—Town and Country Planning (S), 1997 c 8, s 122(1); SSI 2002/110, regs 9, 10, 32,
         sch 2 pt I, para 1(2)(a); Land Reform (S), 2003 asp 2, s 68(2)(a); SSIs 2003/1,
         art 15(2)(d); 2005/91, reg 10(2), sch 1 pt I para 1(2)(a)
       am—Crofting Reform etc, 2007 asp 7, s 21; Crofting Reform (S), 2010 asp 14, s
         22(1)(a)(b); Crofting (Amdt) (S), 2013 asp 10, sch para 1(2)
     s 3ZA added —Crofting Reform (S), 2010 asp 14, s 22(2)
     s 3A added—Crofting Reform etc, 2007 asp 7, s 6
       rep in pt—Crofting Reform (S), 2010 asp 14, s 23(1)-(3); ibid, s 55, sch 4 para 3(4);
     s 3AA added —Crofting Reform (S), 2010 asp 14, s 23(4)
     s 3B added—Crofting Reform etc, 2007 asp 7, s 6
       am—Crofting Reform (S), 2010 asp 14, s 23(5)
     s 3C added—Crofting Reform etc, 2007 asp 7, s 6
     s 4 am—Crofting Reform etc, 2007 asp 7, s 39, sch 1 para 2(1)(3)
       rep in pt—Crofting Reform etc, 2007 asp 7, s 42, sch 2
       subst —Crofting Reform (S), 2010 asp 14, s 46
     s 4A added—Crofting Reform etc, 2007 asp 7, s 9
       am—Crofting Reform (S), 2010 asp 14, s 55, sch 4 para 3(5)(a)
     s 5 am—Crofting Reform etc, 2007 asp 7, s 7(1)
       rep in pt—Crofting Reform (S), 2010 asp 14, s 55, sch 4 para 3(6)
     s 5A added—Crofting Reform etc, 2007 asp 7, s 8
       am—Crofting Reform (S), 2010 asp 14, s 55, sch 4 para 3(7)
     s 5AA added —Crofting Reform (S), 2010 asp 14, s 33(2)
     s 5B added—Crofting Reform etc, 2007 asp 7, s 8
       subst —Crofting Reform (S), 2010 asp 14, s 33(3)
     s 5C added —Crofting Reform (S), 2010 asp 14, s 33(3)
     s 6 am—Crofting Reform etc, 2007 asp 7, s 39, sch 1 para 2(1)(4)
     s 8 am—Crofting Reform etc, 2007 asp 7, s 12; Crofting Reform (S), 2010 asp 14, s 55, sch
         4 para 3(8)(a)(c)(d)
       rep in pt—Crofting Reform (S), 2010 asp 14, s 55, sch 4 para 3(8)(b)
     s 9 subst—Crofting Reform etc, 2007 asp 7, s 10
       am—Crofting Reform (S), 2010 asp 14, s 55, sch 4 para 3(9)(a)(c)
       rep in pt—Crofting Reform (S), 2010 asp 14, s 55, sch 4 para 3(9)(b)
     s 10 am—Crofting Reform etc, 2007 asp 7, s 13; Crofting Reform (S), 2010 asp 14, s
         49(1)-(7)
     s 11 am—SSI 2005/623, art 19; Crofting Reform etc, 2007 asp 7, s 17; Crofting Reform (S),
         2010 asp 14, ss 44(2), 55, sch 4 para 3(10)(a)-(c)(d)(i)(e)
       rep in pt—Crofting Reform (S), 2010 asp 14, s 55, sch 4 para 3(d)(ii)
     s 12 appl—Town and Country Planning (S), 1997 c 8, s 122(1); Civil Partnership, 2004 c
         33, s 112(9)
       restr (cond)—Land Reform (S), 2003 asp 2, ss 65(2), 84(2)
     s 13 am—Crofting Reform etc, 2007 asp 7, s 39, sch 1 para 2(1)(5); Crofting Reform (S),
         2010 asp 14, s 40
     s 14 am—Planning (Conseq Provns) (S), 1997 c 11, s 4, sch 2, para 55(1)(2); Crofting
         Reform (S), 2010 asp 14, s 41
     s 15 am—Planning (Conseq Provns) (S), 1997 c 11, s 4, sch 2, para 55(1)(2)
       rep in pt—Crofting Reform etc, 2007 asp 7, s 42, sch 2
     s 16 rep in pt—Abolition of Feudal Tenure etc (S), 2000 asp 5, s 76(1)(2), sch 12 pt I
         para 55(2), sch 13 pt I
       am—Abolition of Feudal Tenure etc (S), 2000 asp 5, s 76(1), sch 12 pt I para 55(2);
         Title Conditions (S), 2003 asp 9, s 128(1), sch 14 para 11
     s 17 rep in pt—Abolition of Feudal Tenure etc (S), 2000 asp 5, s 76(1)(2), sch 12 pt I
         para 55(3), sch 13 pt I
       am—Crofting (Amdt) (S), 2013 asp 10, sch para 1(3)
     s 19 rep in pt—Abolition of Feudal Tenure etc (S), 2000 asp 5, s 76(1)(2), sch 12 pt I
         para 55(4), sch 13 pt I; Housing (S), 2014 asp 14, s 92(3)
     s 19A added—Crofting Reform etc, 2007 asp 7, s 30(1)
     ss 19B-19D added—(s 19D(3) 30.11.2013) Crofting Reform (S), 2010 asp 14, s 34

1993
c 44 *continued*

s 20 am—Abolition of Feudal Tenure etc (S), 2000 asp 5, s 76(1), sch 12 pt I para 55(5);
Crofting Reform etc, 2007 asp 7, s 22(1)(2); Crofting Reform (S), 2010 asp 14, ss
42, 55, sch 4 para 3(11)(a)-(d)

s 21 am—Crofting Reform etc, 2007 asp 7, s 22(1)(2)

s 21A added—Crofting Reform etc, 2007 asp 7, s 22(3)
am—Crofting Reform (S), 2010 asp 14, s 55, sch 4 para 3(12)(a)
rep in pt—Crofting Reform (S), 2010 asp 14, s 55, sch 4 para 3(12)(b)

ss 21B-21D added —Crofting Reform (S), 2010 asp 14, s 35

s 22 rep in pt—Crofting Reform (S), 2010 asp 14, s 55, sch 4 para 3(13)

s 23 am—Crofting Reform etc, 2007 asp 7, s 24; Crofting Reform (S), 2010 asp 14, ss
44(3)(4)(a)(5)(6), 55, sch 4 para 3(14)(f)-(i); ibid, s 55, sch 4 para 3(14)(a)(c)(e);
Crofting (Amdt) (S), 2013 asp 10, sch para 1(4)(a)(b)(i)
rep in pt—Crofting Reform (S), 2010 asp 14, ss 44(4)(b), 55, sch 4 para 3(14)(b);
Crofting (Amdt) (S), 2013 asp 10, sch para 1(4)(b)(ii)

s 24 am—Crofting Reform etc, 2007 asp 7, ss 23(a), 39, sch 1 para 2(1)(3); Crofting
Reform (S), 2010 asp 14, s 45; ibid, s 55, sch 4 para 3(15)

ss 24A-24D added—Crofting (Amdt) (S), 2013 asp 10, s 1(2)

s 25 am—Crofting Reform etc, 2007 asp 7, ss 23(b), 39, sch 1 para 2(1)(4); Crofting
Reform (S), 2010 asp 14, s 43; ibid, s 55, sch 4 para 3(16)
rep in pt—Crofting Reform (S), 2010 asp 14, s 50(1)(a)
appl (mods)—Crofting (Amdt) (S), 2013 asp 10, s 4(3)(4)

s 26 am—Crofting Reform etc, 2007 asp 7, s 39, sch 1 para 2(1)(5); Crofting Reform (S),
2010 asp 14, s 55, sch 4 para 3(17)(a)(ii)-(c)
rep in pt—Crofting Reform (S), 2010 asp 14, s 55, sch 4 para 3(17)(a)(i)

ss 26A-26K added —Crofting Reform (S), 2010 asp 14, s 37

s 27 am—Crofting Reform etc, 2007 asp 7, s 11(1)
rep in pt—Crofting Reform (S), 2010 asp 14, s 55, sch 4 para 3(18)

s 28 rep—Crofting Reform etc, 2007 asp 7, s 11(2)

s 29 am—Agricultural Holdings (S), 2003 asp 11, s 94, sch para 49(a); Crofting Reform etc,
2007 asp 7, s 11(3)

s 29A added —Crofting Reform (S), 2010 asp 14, s 39

s 29B added—Crofting Reform (S), 2010 asp 14, s 39

s 30 am—Agricultural Holdings (S), 2003 asp 11, s 94, sch para 49(b); Crofting Reform etc,
2007 asp 7, s 25; Crofting Reform (S), 2010 asp 14, s 55, sch 4 para 3(19)(a)(b)
rep in pt—Crofting Reform etc, 2007 asp 7, s 42, sch 2

s 31 am—Crofting Reform (S), 2010 asp 14, s 55, sch 4 para 3(20)

s 38 am—Crofting Reform etc, 2007 asp 7, s 20(1)(2); Crofting Reform (S), 2010 asp 14, s
55, sch 4 para 3(21)

s 38A added—Crofting Reform etc, 2007 asp 7, s 20(1)(3)
am—Crofting Reform (S), 2010 asp 14, s 55, sch 4 para 3(22)
rep in pt—Crofting Reform (S), 2010 asp 14, s 50(1)(b)

s 39 rep in pt—Crofting Reform etc, 2007 asp 7, s 42, sch 2
am—Crofting Reform etc, 2007 asp 7, s 20(1)(4); Crofting Reform (S), 2010 asp 14, s
55, sch 4 para 3(23)(a)-(c)

s 40 am—Crofting Reform etc, 2007 asp 7, s 4; Crofting Reform (S), 2010 asp 14, s 55, sch
4 para 3(24)

s 40A added —Crofting Reform (S), 2010 asp 14, s 36

s 41 am—Crofting Reform etc, 2007 asp 7, ss 5, 39, sch 1 para 2(1)(9); Crofting Reform (S),
2010 asp 14, s 55, sch 4 para 3(25)(a)(b); Crofting (Amdt) (S), 2013 asp 10, sch
para 1(4)(c)
rep in pt—Crofting Reform etc, 2007 asp 7, s 42, sch 2

s 42 am—Crofting Reform etc, 2007 asp 7, s 39, sch 1 para 2(1)(10)

s 43 rep—Crofting Reform etc, 2007 asp 7, s 42, sch 2

s 44 am—Crofting Reform etc, 2007 asp 7, s 39, sch 1 para 2(1)(11)

s 45 am—Crofting Reform etc, 2007 asp 7, s 39, sch 1 para 2(1)(12); Crofting Reform (S),
2010 asp 14, s 55, sch 4 para 3(26)(a)
rep in pt—Crofting Reform (S), 2010 asp 14, s 55, sch 4 para 3(26)(b)

s 46 am—Crofting Reform etc, 2007 asp 7, s 39, sch 1 para 2(1)(13); Crofting Reform (S),
2010 asp 14, s 55, sch 4 para 3(27)(a)-(c)

s 46A added—Crofting Reform etc, 2007 asp 7, s 32
am—Crofting Reform (S), 2010 asp 14, s 55, sch 4 para 3(28)

s 47 am—Crofting Reform etc, 2007 asp 7, s 39, sch 1 para 2(1)(14)

1993
c 44 *continued*

s 48 am—Crofting Reform etc, 2007 asp 7, s 39, sch 1 para 2(1)(15); Crofting Reform (S),
　　　　　2010 asp 14, s 55, sch 4 para 3(29)(a)-(d)

s 49 am—Crofting Reform etc, 2007 asp 7, s 30(2); ibid, s 39, sch 1 para 2(1)(16)

s 49A added —Crofting Reform (S), 2010 asp 14, s 38

s 50 am—Crofting Reform etc, 2007 asp 7, s 26

s 50A added—Crofting Reform etc, 2007 asp 7, s 26

s 50B added—Crofting Reform etc, 2007 asp 7, s 26
　　　rep in pt—Crofting Reform (S), 2010 asp 14, s 55, sch 4 para 3(30)(a)(b)

s 51 subst —Crofting Reform (S), 2010 asp 14, s 47

s 51A added—Crofting Reform etc, 2007 asp 7, s 27
　　　rep in pt—Crofting Reform (S), 2010 asp 14, s 27(1)

s 51B added —Crofting Reform (S), 2010 asp 14, s 27(2)

s 52 am—Crofting Reform etc, 2007 asp 7, ss 28, 29, 39, sch 1 para 2(1)(17); Crofting
　　　　　Reform (S), 2010 asp 14, s 55, sch 4 para 3(31)(a)-(h)

s 52A added—Crofting Reform etc, 2007 asp 7, s 33(1)
　　　am—Crofting Reform (S), 2010 asp 14, ss 50(2), 55, sch 4 para 3(32)(a)
　　　rep in pt—Crofting Reform (S), 2010 asp 14, s 55, sch 4 para 3(32)(b)-(d); ibid, s
　　　　　50(1)(c)
　　　appl (mods)—Crofting Reform (S), 2010 asp 14, s 7(6); Crofting (Amdt) (S), 2013
　　　　　asp 10, s 4(1)(2)

s 53 am—Crofting Reform etc, 2007 asp 7, s 33(2); Crofting Reform (S), 2010 asp 14, s 55,
　　　　　sch 4 para 3(33)(a)(b)

s 53A added—Crofting Reform etc, 2007 asp 7, s 18

s 53B added—Crofting Reform etc, 2007 asp 7, s 19

s 54 rep—Crofting Reform etc, 2007 asp 7, s 42, sch 2

s 55 am—Crofting Reform etc, 2007 asp 7, s 39, sch 1 para 2(1)(18)

s 55A added—Crofting Reform etc, 2007 asp 7, s 35

s 56 am—Crofting Reform (S), 2010 asp 14, s 55, sch 4 para 3(34)
　　　appl—Crofting Reform (S), 2010 asp 14, s 13(4)

s 58A added—Crofting Reform etc, 2007 asp 7, s 3
　　　am—Crofting Reform (S), 2010 asp 14, s 48(2)(3)(b)(4)-(8)(10)
　　　rep in pt—Crofting Reform (S), 2010 asp 14, s 48(3)(9)(11)

s 58B added —Crofting Reform (S), 2010 asp 14, s 48(12)

s 59A added—Crofting Reform etc, 2007 asp 7, s 2

s 60 subst —Crofting Reform (S), 2010 asp 14, s 55, sch 4 para 3(35)

s 61 am—Planning (Conseq Provns) (S), 1997 c 11, s 4, sch 2, para 55(3); Civil Partnership,
　　　　　2004 c 33, s 261(2), sch 28 pt 4 para 58; Crofting Reform etc, 2007 asp 7, ss 36,
　　　　　37, 39, sch 1 para 2(1)(19); (pt prosp) Crofting Reform (S), 2010 asp 14, s 55,
　　　　　sch 4 para 3(36)(a)-(j)
　　　ext—Civil Partnership, 2004 c 33, ss 246, 247, sch 21 para 40

s 181 ext—SI 1996/207, reg 105(16)

sch 1 rep in pt—Requirements of Writing (S), 1995 c 7, s 14(2), sch 5; SI 1999/1820, art 4,
　　　　　sch 2 pt I para 111, pt IV
　　　subst —Crofting Reform (S), 2010 asp 14, s 1, sch 1

sch 2 am—Agricultural Holdings (S), 2003 asp 11, s 94, sch para 49(c)(i); (savings)
　　　　　Crofting Reform etc, 2007 asp 7, s 7(2)
　　　rep in pt—Agricultural Holdings (S), 2003 asp 11, s 94, sch para 49(c)(ii); Crofting
　　　　　Reform (S), 2010 asp 14, s 55, sch 4 para 3(37)(a)(b)

sch 3 am—Crofting Reform (S), 2010 asp 14, s 55, sch 4 para 3(4)

sch 4 rep—Crofting Reform etc, 2007 asp 7, s 20(1)(5)

sch 7 am—(retrosp) Crofting Reform etc, 2007 asp 7, s 39, sch 1 para 2(1)(21)(22)

c 45　　**Scottish Land Court**

appl—SSIs 2002/110, regs 9, 10, 32, sch 2 pt III, para 25; 2005/91, reg 10(2), sch 1 pt III
　　　　para 27

s 1 am—Scotland, 1998 c 46, s 125, sch 8, para 29(a)(b); Bail, Judicial Appointments etc
　　　　　(S), asp 9, s 12, sch para 6; Land Reform (S), 2003 asp 2, s 97(2); Agricultural
　　　　　Holdings (S), 2003 asp 11, s 82(a)(i)(ii)(iv)(b); Nature Conservation (S), 2004 asp
　　　　　6, s 57, sch 7 para 9; Crofting Reform etc, 2007 asp 7, s 39, sch 1 para 3; SSI
　　　　　2015/383, art 13
　　　rep in pt—Bail, Judicial Appointments etc (S), asp 9, s 12, sch para 6; Agricultural
　　　　　Holdings (S), 2003 asp 11, s 82(a)(iii)
　　　appl—Land Reform (S), 2003 asp 2, s 97(1)

sch 1 restr—Land Reform (S), 2003 asp 2, s 97(3)

1993

c 45 sch 1 *continued*

        saved—SSI 2009/376, regs 10, 11

        am—Agricultural Holdings (S), 2003 asp 11, s 82(c); Crofting Reform etc, 2007 asp 7, s 34; SSI 2013/2, art 2(2)(b); (1.4.2016) Courts Reform (S), 2014 asp 18, s 126(2)(3)

        rep in pt—SSI 2013/2, art 2(2)(a)

c 46   **Health Service Commissioners**

        rep (S)—S Public Services Ombudsman, 2002 asp 11, s 25(1), sch 6, para 14

        appl—SI 1999/686, art 5(1), sch pt II; (S) SSI 2001/137, art 5, sch pt II; (S) SSIs 2002/103, art 6(1), sch pt II; 2002/305, art 5, sch pt II; 2002/534, art 5, sch pt II

        appl (mods)—SI 1999/726, art 5(1)(2), sch pt II

        s 1 am—Govt of Wales, 1998 c 38, s 112, sch 10, para 2; SI 2004/1823, art 17(1)(2)(a)(i); Public Services Ombudsman (W), 2005 c 10, ss 38, 39(1), sch 6 paras 27-29, 30(1)(3)

           rep in pt—SI 2004/1823, art 17(1)(2)(a)(ii)(b); Public Services Ombudsman (W), 2005 c 10, ss 38, 39, sch 6 paras 27, 30(1)(2)(4), sch 7

        s 2 am—Health Authorities, 1995 c 17, s 2(1), sch 1 pt III para 126(2); Health Service Commrs (Amdt), 1996 c 5, s 4(1); Govt of Wales, 1998 c 38, s 112, sch 10, para 3(2)(4); Health, 1999 c 8, s 65, sch 4 para 85(2); Nat Health Service Reform and Health Care Professions, 2002 c 17, ss 1(3), 6(2), sch 1 pt 2, para 47, sch 5, para 38; Health and Social Care (Community Health and Standards), 2003 c 43, s 34, sch 4 paras 93, 94; ibid, s 184, sch 11 paras 60, 61; Public Services Ombudsman (W), 2005 c 10, ss 38, 39(1), sch 6 paras 27, 31(1)(2)(4); Health and Social Care, 2012 c 7, sch 5 para 68(c)

           rep in pt—Health Authorities 1995 c 17, ss 2(1),5(1), sch 1 pt III para 126(2), sch 3; Health Service Commrs (Amdt), 1996 c 5, ss 4(1), 13, sch 2; Govt of Wales 1998 c 38, ss 112,152, sch 10, para 3(3), sch 18 pt I; Nat Health Service Reform and Health Care Professions, 2002 c 17, ss 2(5), 37(2), sch 2 pt 2, para 61(1)(2), sch 9 pt 1; Health and Social Care (Community Health and Standards), 2003 c 43, ss 190(2), 196, sch 13 para 7, sch 14 pt 7; ibid, s 196, sch 14 pt 4; SI 2004/1823, art 17(1)(3); Public Services Ombudsman (W), 2005 c 10, ss 38, 39, sch 6 paras 27, 31(1)(3), sch 7; Health and Social Care, 2012 c 7, sch 5 para 68(a)(b); (prosp) ibid, sch 14 para 63

           appl—SI 2012/3072, art 2

        s 2A added—Health Service Commrs (Amdt), 1996 c 5, s 1

           am—Nat Health Service (Primary Care), 1997 c 46, s 41(10), sch 2 pt I, para 68(2)-(4); Health Service Commrs (Amdt), 2000 c 28, s 1(2); (E) SI 2002/2861, reg 26(b); Health and Social Care (Community Health and Standards), 2003 c 43, s 184, sch 11 paras 60, 62; SIs (temp) (E) 2004/288, art 7(1)(10)(a)(b); 2004/480 (W 49), art 6(1)(11)(a)(b); 2004/1823, art 17(1)(4)(b); Public Services Ombudsman (W), 2005 c 10, ss 38, 39(1), sch 6 paras 27, 32(1)(2)(4); Nat Health Service (Conseq Provns), 2006 c 43, s 2, sch 1 para 166; Health, 2006 c 28, s 80, sch 8 para 33; SI 2006/552, reg 3, sch 1; Health and Social Care, 2012 c 7, sch 5 para 69

           rep in pt—SIs (E) 2002/2861, reg 26(a); 2004/1823, art 17(1)(4)(a); Public Services Ombudsman (W), 2005 c 10, ss 38, 39, sch 6 paras 27, 32, sch 7; Nat Health Service (Conseq Provns), 2006 c 43, s 2, sch 1 para 166

        s 2B added—Health Service Commrs (Amdt), 1996 c 5, s 1

           am—Govt of Wales, 1998 c 38, s 112, sch 10, para 4; Health Service Commrs (Amdt), 2000 c 28, s 1(3); SI 2004/1823, art 17(1)(5)(b)(c); Public Services Ombudsman (W), 2005 c 10, ss 38, 39(1), sch 6 paras 27, 33(1)(2)(4); Health, 2009 c 21, s 12(1)-(3)

           rep in pt—SI 2004/1823, art 17(1)(5)(a); Public Services Ombudsman (W), 2005 c 10, ss 38, 39, sch 6 paras 27, 33(1)(3), sch 7

        s 3 am—Health Service Commrs (Amdt), 1996 c 5, ss 2,6(2);s 3(1ZA); Nat Health Service (Primary Care), 1997 c 46, s 41(10), sch 2 pt I, para 68(5); Govt of Wales, 1998 c 38, s 112, sch 10, para 5; Health and Social Care (Community Health and Standards), 2003 c 43, s 118; Public Services Ombudsman (W), 2005 c 10, ss 38, 39(1), sch 6 paras 27, 34, 35(1)(2); (prosp) NHS Redress, 2006 c 44, s 15(1)(2); Health, 2009 c 21, s 12(1)(4)

           rep in pt—Health, 1999 c 8, s 65, sch 4 para 85(3), sch 5; Public Services Ombudsman (W), 2005 c 10, ss 38, 39, sch 6 paras 27, 35(1)(3), sch 7

        saving—SI 1999/2541, art 11

1993
c 46 *continued*

s 4 am—Health Service Commrs (Amdt), 1996 c 5, ss 4(2),5; Health and Social Care
(Community Health and Standards), 2003 c 43, s 147, sch 9 para 11(1)(2); Public
Services Ombudsman (W), 2005 c 10, ss 38, 39(1), sch 6 paras 27, 36; (prosp)
NHS Redress, 2006 c 44, s 15(1)(3)

   rep in pt—(prosp) Health and Social Care (Community Health and Standards), 2003 c
43, s 196, sch 14 pt 2

s 5 rep—Health Service Commrs (Amdt), 1996 c 5, ss 6(1),13, sch 2

s 6 am—Health Authorities, 1995 c 17, s 2(1), sch 1 pt III para 126(3); Health Service
Commrs (Amdt), 1996 c 5, s 7(3); Nat Health Service Reform and Health Care
Professions, 2002 c 17, s 2(5), sch 2 pt 2, para 61(1)(3); Health and Social Care
(Community Health and Standards), 2003 c 43, s 184, sch 11 paras 60, 63(b); SIs
(temp) (E) 2004/288, art 7(1)(10)(c); (temp) (W) 2004/480 (W 49),
art 6(1)(11)(c); Public Services Ombudsman (W), 2005 c 10, ss 38, 39(1), sch 6
paras 27, 37(a); Nat Health Service (Conseq Provns), 2006 c 43, s 2, sch 1 para
167; Health, 2006 c 28, s 80, sch 8 para 34

   rep in pt—Health Service Commrs (Amdt), 1996 c 5, ss 7(2),13, sch 2; Health and
Social Care (Community Health and Standards), 2003 c 43, ss 184, 196, sch 11
paras 60, 63(a), sch 14 pt 4; Public Services Ombudsman (W), 2005 c 10, ss 38,
39, sch 6 paras 27, 37(b), sch 7

   transtl savings—SIs (E) 2004/865, art 113; (W) 2004/1016 (W 113), art 89

s 7 am—Health Service Commrs (Amdt), 1996 c 5, ss 3,8(2)(3), sch 1 para 2(3)-(5); Govt
of Wales, 1998 c 38, s 112, sch 10, para 6; Public Services Ombudsman (W), 2005
c 10, ss 38, 39(1), sch 6 paras 27, 38(1)(2)(a)(3)-(6); Nat Health Service (Conseq
Provns), 2006 c 43, s 2, sch 1 para 168; (prosp) NHS Redress, 2006 c 44, s
15(1)(4)(b); Health, 2009 c 21, s 12(1)(5)

   rep in pt—Health Service Commrs (Amdt) 1996 c 5 ss 3,13, sch 1 para 2(2), sch 2; SI
2004/1823, art 17(1)(6); Public Services Ombudsman (W), 2005 c 10, ss 38,
39, sch 6 paras 27, 38(1)(2)(b), sch 7; (prosp) NHS Redress, 2006 c 44, s
15(1)(4)(a)

s 7A added—Health Service Commrs (Amdt), 1996 c 5, s 4(3)

s 8 am—Govt of Wales, 1998 c 38, s 112, sch 10, para 7(a)(b); SI 1999/1820, art 4, sch 2
pt I para 112(2)

s 9 rep in pt—Health Service Commrs (Amdt), 1996 c 5, ss 9,13, sch 2

   am—Health Service Commrs (Amdt), 2000 c 28, s 2; Public Services Ombudsman (W),
2005 c 10, ss 38, 39, sch 6 paras 27, 39

s 10 am—Govt of Wales, 1998 c 38, s 112, sch 10, para 8; Public Services Ombudsman
(W), 2005 c 10, ss 38, 39(1), sch 6 paras 27, 40(1)(2)

   ext—Health and Social Care (Community Health and Standards), 2003 c 43,
s 113(4)(a)

   rep in pt—Public Services Ombudsman (W), 2005 c 10, ss 38, 39, sch 6 paras 27,
40(1)(3), sch 7

s 11 appl (mods)—SI 1996/709, art 9(3)

   am—Health Service Commrs (Amdt), 1996 c 5, s 3, sch 1 para 3; Govt of Wales, 1998
c 38, s 112, sch 10, para 9; Health and Social Care (Community Health and
Standards), 2003 c 43, s 147, sch 9 para 11(1)(3); Public Services Ombudsman
(W), 2005 c 10, ss 38, 39(1), sch 6 paras 27, 41(1)(2)(3)(a)(b); (prosp) NHS
Redress, 2006 c 44, s 15(1)(5)

   rep in pt—SI 2004/1823, art 17(1)(7); Public Services Ombudsman (W), 2005 c 10,
ss 38, 39, sch 6 paras 27, 41(1)(3)(c), sch 7

s 12 appl (mods)—SI 1996/709, art 9(3)

   am—Health Service Commrs (Amdt), 1996 c 5, s 3, sch 1 para 4; Health and Social
Care (Community Health and Standards), 2003 c 43, s 147, sch 9 para 11(1)(4);
Public Services Ombudsman (W), 2005 c 10, ss 38, 39(1), sch 6 paras 27, 42;
(prosp) NHS Redress, 2006 c 44, s 15(1)(6)

s 13 am—Public Services Ombudsman (W), 2005 c 10, ss 38, 39(1), sch 6 paras 27, 43

s 14 appl (mods)—SI 1996/709, art 9(3)

   am—Health Authorities, 1995 c 17, s 2(1), sch 1 pt III para 126(4); Health Service
Commrs (Amdt), 1996 c 5, ss 3,10, sch 1 para 5; Govt of Wales, 1998 c 38, s 112,
sch 10, para 10(2)-(4); SI 1999/1820, art 4, sch 2 pt I para 112(3); Health and
Social Care (Community Health and Standards), 2003 c 43, s 147, sch 9
para 11(1)(5); SI 2004/1823, art 17(1)(8)(d); Public Services Ombudsman (W),
2005 c 10, ss 38, 39(1), sch 6 paras 27, 44, 45; (prosp) NHS Redress, 2006 c 44,
s 15(1)(7); Health, 2009 c 21, s 12(1)(6); Health and Social Care, 2012 c 7, sch 5

1993
c 46 s 14   *continued*

para 70(2)(a),(3)(a),(4)(a),(6)(a); ibid, s 201; Health Service Commnr for E (Complaint Handling), 2015 c 29, s 1(2)(3)

rep in pt—Health Service Commrs (Amdt), 1996 c 5, ss 10(3)(b),13, sch 2; SI 2004/1823, art 17(1)(8); Health and Social Care, 2012 c 7, sch 5 para 70(2)(b), (3)(b),(4)(b),(5),(6)(b)

ss 14A,14B,14C added—Govt of Wales, 1998 c 38, s 112, sch 10, para 11

rep—Public Services Ombudsman (W), 2005 c 10, ss 38, 39, sch 6 paras 27, 46, sch 7

s 14A am—Health and Social Care (Community Health and Standards), 2003 c 43, s 147, sch 9 para 11(1)(6)

s 14B am—Health and Social Care (Community Health and Standards), 2003 c 43, s 147, sch 9 para 11(1)(7)

s 15 am—Health Service Commrs (Amdt), 1996 c 5, s 11; Govt of Wales, 1998 c 38, s 112, sch 10, para 12; (EW) Health, 1999 c 8, s 43(1)(2)(4)(a)(5) (see SI 1999/2540); Freedom of Information, 2000 c 36, s 76(2), sch 7 para 5; Public Services Ombudsman (W), 2005 c 10, ss 38, 39(1), sch 6 paras 27, 47(1)(2)(3)(4)(a); SI 2007/1889, art 11; Loc Govt and Public Involvement in Health, 2007 c 28, s 182, sch 12 para 15(1)(2)

rep in pt—Health Service Commrs (Amdt), 1996 c 5, ss 11(2),13, sch 1 para 2(2), sch 2; (EW) Health, 1999 c 8, ss 43(3)(4)(b), 65, sch 5 (see SI 1999/2540); Public Services Ombudsman (W), 2005 c 10, ss 38, 39, sch 6 paras 27, 47(1)(4)(b), sch 7

excl —Local Govt, 1974 c 7, s 34M

s 16 am—Public Services Ombudsman (W), 2005 c 10, ss 38, 39(1), sch 6 paras 27, 48

s 17 am—Govt of Wales, 1998 c 38, s 112, sch 10, para 13; SI 2004/2359, art 3; Public Services Ombudsman (W), 2005 c 10, ss 38, 39(1), sch 6 paras 27, 49(1)(2)(a)

ext—SI 1999/1351, art 17(5)(a)

rep in pt—Public Services Ombudsman (W), 2005 c 10, ss 38, 39, sch 6 paras 27, 49(1)(2)(b)(3), sch 7

s 18 am—Govt of Wales, 1998 c 38, s 112, sch 10, para 14(2)(3); Health and Social Care (Community Health and Standards), 2003 c 43, s 184, sch 11 paras 60, 64; Housing, 2004 c 34, s 265(1), sch 15 para 37(1)(2)(b); SI 2004/1823, art 17(1)(9)(a)(i)(ii)(b); Public Services Ombudsman (W), 2005 c 10, ss 38, 39(1), sch 6 paras 27, 50(1)(2)(a)(c)(3); (Health, 2009 c 21, s 35, sch 5 para 13

ext—SI 1999/1351, art 17(5)(a)

rep in pt—Govt of Wales, 1998 c 38, ss 112,152, sch 10, para 14(4), sch 18 pt I; Housing, 2004 c 34, ss 265(1), 266, sch 15 para 37(1)(2)(a)(3); SI 2004/1823, art 17(1)(9)(iii); Public Services Ombudsman (W), 2005 c 10, ss 38, 39, sch 6 paras 27, 50(1)(2)(b)(d), sch 7

s 18ZA added—SI 2007/1889, art 6

am—Loc Govt and Public Involvement in Health, 2007 c 28, s 182, sch 12 para 15(1)(3)

rep in pt—Loc Govt and Public Involvement in Health, 2007 c 28, s 241, sch 18

s 18A added—Freedom of Information, 2000 c 36, s 76(2), sch 7 para 6

am—Public Services Ombudsman (W), 2005 c 10, ss 38, 39(1), sch 6 paras 27, 51

s 19 am—Loc Govt (W), 1994 c 19, s 66(6), sch 16 para 108; Health Service Commrs (Amdt), 1996 c 5, s 3, sch 1 para 6; Govt of Wales, 1998 c 38, s 112, sch 10, para 15(2)-(4); Health, 2009 c 21, s 12(1)(7)

rep in pt—Loc Govt (W), 1994 c 19, s 66(6)(8), sch 16 para 108, sch 18; Health Service Commrs (Amdt), 1996 c 5, ss 3,13 sch 1 para 6(5), sch 2; Health, 1999 c 8, s 65, sch 4 para 85(4), sch 5; SI 2004/1823, art 17(1)(10); Public Services Ombudsman (W), 2005 c 10, ss 38, 39, sch 6 paras 27, 52, sch 7

s 24 am—Nat Health Service (Primary Care), 1997 c 46, s 41(10), sch 2 pt I, para 68(2)—(4)

sch 1 see—(trans of functions) SI 1995/269, art 3, sch para 24

am—Health Service Commrs (Amdt) 1996 c 5, s 3, sch 1 para 7; Govt of Wales 1998 c 38, s 112, sch 10, para 16(1)-(3)(4)(6)(a)(b)(8); SIs 1999/1820, art 4, sch 2 pt I para 112(4); 2004/1823, art 17(1)(11); Public Services Ombudsman (W), 2005 c 10, ss 38, 39(1), sch 6 paras 27, 53(1)(3)-(11); SI 2006/1031, reg 49, sch 8; Loc Govt and Public Involvement in Health, 2007 c 28, s 182, sch 12 para 15(1)(4); SI 2007/1889, arts 7, 14

ext—SI 1999/1351, art 17(5)(a)

1993
c 46 sch 1 *continued*

   rep in pt—Govt of Wales, 1998 c 38, ss 112,152, sch 10, para 16(5)(7), sch 18 pt I; SI
     2004/1823, art 17(1)(11); Public Services Ombudsman (W), 2005 c 10, ss 38,
     39, sch 6 paras 27, 53(1)(2), sch 7
  sch 1A added—Govt of Wales, 1998 c 38, s 112, sch 10, para 17
   rep—Public Services Ombudsman (W), 2005 c 10, ss 38, 39, sch 6 paras 27, 54, sch
     7
  sch 2 rep in pt—SI 2004/1823, art 17(1)(13); (prosp) Health, 2009 c 21, s 38, sch 6

c 47   *Probation Service*—rep Crim Justice and Court Services, 2000 c 43, s 75, sch 8
c 48   **Pension Schemes**
  am—Pensions, 1995 c 26, s 126, sch 4 pt I para 1
  appl—Matrimonial Causes, 1973 c 18, s 25D(3); Bankcruptcy (S), 1985 c 66, s 32(2A); SIs
    1987/1967, reg 42; 1971, reg 36(5); 1992/1814, reg 28(5); Scotland, 1998 c 46,
    s 126(1); Pensions 1995 c 26, s 124(5); SI 1996/207, reg 105; Welfare Reform and
    Pensions, 1999 c 30, s 26(1); SI 1999/3147, art 8(3), sch 1 para 2(4); Proceeds of
    Crime, 2002 c 29, s 275(4); SI 2002/1792, reg 18(5); Energy, 2004 c 20, s 80(7);
    Civil Partnership, 2004 c 33, s 72(1), sch 5 pt 4 para 16(5), pt 7 para 37(1); Pensions,
    2004 c 35, s 161(4)(a); ibid, s 165(1); (EW) SI 2005/550, art 7(6)(a)
  appl (mods)—SI 2011/245, sch 6 pt 1
  mod—SI 2009/317, art 3, sch
  power to am—Northern Ireland, 1998 c 47, s 87
  power to mod—Pensions, 1995 c 26, s 149(2); Social Security Contributions (Trans of
    Functions, etc), 1999 c 2, s 15(1)(2)(b); Welfare Reform and Pensions, 1999
    c 30, s 85; Pensions, 2004 c 35, ss 21(4), 321(1)(b)(2)(3)
  saved—SSI 2008/230, reg 43
  s 1 am—Welfare Reform and Pensions, 1999 c 30, s 18, sch 2 para 3(1); SI 1999/1820,
    art 4, sch 2 pt I para 113; Pensions, 2004 c 35, s 239(1)(3); Finance, 2007 c 11, s
    69, sch 20 paras 23(1), 24(1), sch 27; SI 2007/3014, reg 2, sch
   appl—Fire Services, 1947 c 41, s 27A(5); Police Pensions, 1976 c 35, s 8A(5);
    Transport, 1980 c 34, s 52B; Social Security Contributions and Benefits 1992 c 4,
    s 30DD(6); Railways, 1993 c 43, s 134(1),.sch 11 para 1(1); Jobseekers 1995
    c 18, s 35(1); Environment 1995 c 25, ss 3(8), 22(9), sch 2 pt I para 3(10);
    Pensions, 1995 c 26, ss 95, 176; SI 1995/300, reg B5; Employment Rights,1996
    c 18, ss 46(3), 58(3)(a),102(2); SIs 1996/2890,reg 2(1); (EW) (retrosp to
    1.1.2003) 1997/1612, reg 5B; GLA, 1999 c 29, s 411(10), sch 32 para 1;
    Welfare Reform and Pensions 1999 c 30, s 8(1); SIs 2002/427, regs 2(3)(b)(c), 11;
    2002/836, regs 2(3)(b)(c), 11; 2002/1792, reg 17B(2)(b)(i); (S) SSI 2002/494,
    reg 10, sch 2, para 8(d); Fire and Rescue Services, 2004 c 21, s 35(6); SI
    2004/1931, art 3(5)(c); (EW, NI) SI 2005/781, reg 22(d); (EW) SI 2005/1529,
    art 72(4), sch 1 pt II para 28
   am—Pensions, 2004 c 35, s 239(1)(2)(4)
  ss 2-5 rep—Pensions, 1995 c 26, ss 151, 177, sch 5 para 19, sch 7 pt III
  s 6 rep—Pensions, 2004 c 35, s 320, sch 13 pt 1
  Pt 3 (ss 7-68) appl (mods)—SI 1996/1977, reg 2(4)(a)-(f)
  mod—SIs 1995/1070, art 2(b); 2014/1711, reg 7(2)
  power to am & trans functions—Social Security Contributions (Trans of Functions, etc),
    1999 c 2, s 23
  power to mod—Pensions, 1995 c 26, s 149(1)
  am (heading am)—Pensions, 2014 c 19, sch 13 para 3
  Pt 3, Ch 1 (ss 7-39) heading am—Pensions, 2014 c 19, sch 13 para 4
  s 7 rep —(saving temp to 1.4.2019) Pensions, 2014 c 19, sch 13 para 5; SI 2015/1502, art
    2(1)(2)(a)
  ss 7A, 7B added—Pensions, 2014 c 19, sch 13 para 6
  s 8 appl—Pensions, 1995 c 26, ss 37(6)(b)(i),76(5)(b)(i), 77(3)(b)(i); SI 2001/117,
    reg 4(3)(d); (NI) SI 2005/1986, regs 17, 18(5), sch 2 para 1(2)
   am—Pensions, 1995 c 26, s 151, sch 5 paras 21,23(a); Social Security, 1998 c 14,
    s 86(1), sch 7, para 126; Social Security Contributions (Trans of Functions, etc),
    1999 c 2, s 1(1), sch 1 para 34; SI 2005/2050, art 2(1), sch 1 para 1; Pensions,
    2007 c 22, s 15, sch 4 paras 1, 3, 46, 47; Nat Insurance Contributions, 2008 c 16,
    sch 1 para 8(2)(3); Marriage (Same Sex Couples), 2013 c 30, sch 4 para 19;
    Pensions, 2014 c 19, sch 13 para 7; SI 2014/3229, sch 5 para 11(2)
   rep in pt—Pensions, 1995 c 26, ss 151, 177, sch 5 para 23(b), sch 7 pt III; Pensions,
    2007 c 22, s 27, sch 7 pt 7
   appl (mods)—SIs 1996/1461 reg 6(2); 1996/1462 regs 12,13, sch 2 paras 1, 6

1993
c 48 *continued*

s 9 rep—(saving temp to 1.4.2019) Pensions, 2014 c 19, sch 13 para 9; SI 2015/1502, art
   2(1)(2)(b)
s 10 rep —Pensions, 2008 c 30, s 148, sch 11, s 106(2)(a), (3)(a)
s 11 rep—(saving temp to 1.4.2019) Pensions, 2014 c 19, sch 13 para 9; SI 2015/1502, art
   2(1)(2)(c)
s 12 rep —Pensions, 2007 c 22, s 15, sch 4 para 6, sch 7
ss 12A-12D rep —(saving temp to 1.4.2019) Pensions, 2014 c 19, sch 13 para 11; SI
   2015/1502, art 2(1)(2)(d)
   saving—SI 2015/1502, art 2(3A) (added by 2015/2058, art 3(3)(c))
s 12E added —Pensions, 2014 c 19, sch 13 para 13(1)
s 13 rep in pt—Pensions, 1995 c 26, ss 151, 177, sch 5 para 26, sch 7 pt III
   saved—SI 1995/1019, reg D10(2)
   am—Pensions, 2007 c 22, s 14(1); Pensions, 2014 c 19, sch 13 paras 12, 14(a)
s 14 rep in pt—Pensions, 1995 c 26, ss 151, 177, sch 5 para 27(a), sch 7 pt III
   am—Pensions, 1995 c 26, s 151, sch 5 para 27(b); Social Security Contributions (Trans
   of Functions, etc), 1999 c 2, s 1(1), sch 1 para 38; Proceeds of Crime, 2002 c 29, s
   456, sch 11, para 22(1)(3); Pensions, 2014 c 19, sch 13 para 15
   appl (mods)—SIs 1996/1461, reg 6(4),1996/1462, regs 12,13, sch 2 paras 3,7
   mod—SI 1998/366, reg 36(1)
   appl—SI 1998/366, reg 36(3); (S) SSI 2005/393, reg E3(4); SI 2014/512, reg 224(8)
s 15 am—SIs 1994/542; 1995/559, arts 5,6(1)-(4); 1997/543, art 5(2); 1998/470, art 5(2);
   1999/264, art 5(2); 2000/440, arts 5,6; 2001/207, art 5(2); 2002/668, art 5;
   2003/526, art 5; 2004/552, arts 5, 6; 2005/522, arts 5, 6; 2011/821, arts 1, 5, 6;
   2013/574, art 5(2); 2014/516, art 5(2); 2015/457, art 5(2)
   appl (mods)—SI 2006/645, art 5
   mod—SI 2008/632, art 5
s 15A added—Welfare Reform and Pensions, 1999 c 30, s 32(3)
   mod—SIs 2015/182, sch 3 para 4; 319, reg 6; 370, reg 6; 372, reg 6; 390, reg 6; 432,
   reg 6; 436, reg 6; 848 (W 63), reg 6; SSIs 2015/117, reg 6; 118, reg 6; 145, reg
   6; 146, reg 6
s 16 am—Pensions, 1995 c 26, s 151, sch 5 para 28; Welfare Reform and Pensions, 1999
   c 30, s 18, sch 2 para 4; (saving) Pensions, 2014 c 19, sch 13 para 16 (and see SI
   2015/1502, art 2(3))
   cont in pt—SI 2015/1502, art 2(3)
   appl—SI 1998/366, reg 36(3); (S) SSI 2005/393, reg E3(4)
   mod—SIs 1996/1172, regs 65,66; 1996/1462, reg 13B(4)(5) (added by 2015/1452,
   reg 31(3))
   appl (mods)—SI s 1996/1461, reg 6(4); 1996/1462, reg 6(5)(6); ibid, reg 13B(3)(5)
   (added by 2015/1452, reg 31(3) and 2015/1677, reg 30(3))
s 17 am—Pensions, 1995 c 26, s 151, sch 5 para 29; Social Security Contributions (Trans of
   Functions, etc), 1999 c 2, s 1(1), sch 1 para 39; Child Support, Pensions and
   Social Security, 2000 c 19, s 56, sch 5 pt I para 1; SIs 2002/668, art 5; 2003/526,
   art 5; Pensions, 2004 c 35, s 284(2); SI 2005/2050, art 2(1), sch 1 para 4;
   Pensions, 2007 c 22, s 14(2); Marriage (Same Sex Couples), 2013 c 30, sch 4
   para 20(2)(a)(b)(3)(4)(5)(a)(b)(6); Pensions, 2014 c 19, sch 13 para 17; SIs
   2014/560, sch 1 para 25(a); 2014/3229, sch 5 para 11(3)
   rep in pt—Child Support, Pensions and Social Security, 2000 c 19, s 85, sch 9 pt III(4);
   SI 2014/560, sch 1 para 25(b)
   ext in pt—(S) Pension Schemes, 2015 c 8, s 81
s 18 appl—State Pension Credit, 2002 c 16, s 16(3)
s 19 appl—SI 1998/366, regs 36(3),58(5)(6); (S) SSI 2005/393, reg E3(1)(b)
   am—SIs 2001/3649, art 116(1)(2)(a); 2005/2050, art 2(1), sch 1 para 5; 2007/3014,
   reg 2, sch
   rep in pt—SI 2001/3649, art 116(1)(2)(b)(3)
s 20 appl (mods)—SI 1996/1462, regs 12,13, sch 2 paras 4,8
   am—Child Support, Pensions and Social Security, 2000 c 19, s 56, sch 5 pt I para 2(1);
   SI 2005/2050, art 2(1), sch 1 para 6; Pensions, 2007 c 22, s 15, sch 4 paras 7, 48;
   SI 2011/1730, arts 5(2), 9(2); Pensions, 2014 c 19, sch 13 para 18(a)(b)(ii)
   rep in pt—Pensions, 2007 c 22, s 27, sch 7 pt 7; Pensions, 2014 c 19, sch 13 para
   18(b)(i)
s 21 appl—SI 1998/366, reg 58(5)(6)
   am—Pensions, 2004 c 35, s 284(1); SI 2005/2050, art 2(1), sch 1 para 7
s 22 rep—Pensions, 1995 c 26, ss 151, 177, sch 5 para 30, sch 7 pt III

1993
c 48 *continued*

s 23 excl—Pensions, 1995 c 26, s 151, sch 5 para 31
    am—Pensions, 1995 c 26, s 151, sch 5 para 31(b); SI 2005/2050, art 2(1), sch 1 para 8
    rep in pt—Pensions, 1995 c 26, ss 151, 177, sch 5 para 32, sch 7 pt III; Pensions, 2014
        c 19, sch 13 para 19
s 24 rep—Pensions, 1995 c 26, ss 151, 177, sch 5 para 30, sch 7 pt III
ss 24A-24H added —Pensions, 2007 c 22, s 14(3)
s 24A am—Pensions, 2014 c 19, sch 13 para 20(a)
s 24D am—Marriage (Same Sex Couples), 2013 c 30, sch 4 para 21(2)(3)(a)(b)(4); SI
        2014/3229, sch 5 para 11(4)
    ext in pt—(S) Pension Schemes, 2015 c 8, s 81
s 24F rep in pt—Pension Schemes, 2015 c 8, sch 4 para 5
s 25 rep in pt—Pensions, 1995 c 26, ss 151, 177, sch 5 para 33(a), sch 7 pt III
    am—Pensions, 1995 c 26, s 151, sch 5 para 33(b); Social Security Contributions (Trans
        of Functions, etc), 1999 c 2, s 1(1), sch 1 para 40; Pensions, 2014 c 19, sch 13
        para 21
s 25A added (pt prosp)—Pensions, 2007 c 22, s 15, sch 4 para 9
    rep —Pensions, 2008 c 30, ss 106(2)(b), 148, sch 11
s 26 rep —Pensions, 2008 c 30, ss 106(2)(a), (3)(b), 148, sch 11
s 27 rep —Pensions, 2008 c 30, ss 106(2)(a), (3)(c), 148, sch 11
s 27A added —Pensions, 2007 c 22, s 15, sch 4 para 10
    rep —Pensions, 2008 c 30, ss 106(2)(b), 148, sch 11
s 28 rep in pt—Pensions, 1995 c 26, ss 151, 177, sch 5 para 34(b), sch 7 pt III; Welfare
        Reform and Pensions, 1999 c 30, ss 18, 28, sch 2 para 5, sch 13 pt I; Pensions,
        2004 c 35, ss 284(3)(b)(4)(6), 320, sch 13 pt 1
    rep —Pensions, 2007 c 22, s 15, sch 4 para 11, sch 7
s 28A added—Pensions, 1995 c 26, s 143
    am—SIs 2005/2050, art 2(1), sch 1 para 10; 2006/745, art 7
    mod—Finance, 2011 c 11, sch 16 para 58
s 28B added—Pensions, 1995 c 26, s 143
    am—Social Security Contributions (Trans of Functions, etc), 1999 c 2, s 1(1), sch 1
        para 41
s 29 am—Pensions, 1995 c 26, ss 144(2)-(4),151, sch 5 para 35; SI 2001/3649, art 117;
        Pensions, 2004 c 35, s 284(7)(a); SI 2005/2050, art 2(1), sch 1 para 11
    rep —Pensions, 2007 c 22, s 15, sch 4 para 11, sch 7
s 30 rep —Pensions, 2008 c 30, ss 106(2)(a), (3)(d), 148, sch 11
s 31 rep —Pensions, 2007 c 22, s 15, sch 4 para 49, sch 7
s 32 rep —Pensions, 2008 c 30, ss 106(2)(a), (3)(e), 148, sch 11
s 32A added—Pensions, 1995 c 26, s 146(1)
    rep —Pensions, 2008 c 30, ss 106(2)(b), 148, sch 11
s 33 rep—SI 2011/1730, art 9(3)
s 33A added—Pensions, 1995 c 26, s 147
    rep —Pensions, 2008 c 30, ss 106(2)(a), (3)(f), 148, sch 11
ss 34-36 rep—(saving temp to 1.4.2019) Pensions, 2014 c 19, sch 13 para 22; SI 2015/1502,
        art 2(1)(2)(e)
s 37 subst—Pensions, 1995 c 26, s 151, sch 5 para 39
    ext in pt—(S) Pension Schemes, 2015 c 8, s 81
    mod—SI 1998/1466, reg 2
    am—SIs 2005/2050, art 2(1), sch 1 para 12; 2011/1730, art 5(5); Marriage (Same Sex
        Couples), 2013 c 30, sch 4 para 22(2); Pensions, 2014 c 19, sch 13 paras 23, 24;
        SI 2014/3229, sch 5 para 11(5)
s 37A added —Pensions, 2014 c 19, sch 13 para 25
s 38 rep—SI 2011/1730, art 5(6)
s 38A added —Marriage (Same Sex Couples), 2013 c 30, sch 4 para 23
    ext—(S) Pension Schemes, 2015 c 8, s 81
s 39 am—SI 2011/1730, art 5(7)
Pt 3 Ch 2 (ss 40-49) heading subst—Pensions, 2014 c 19, sch 13 para 26
s 40 am—Pensions, 1995 c 26, s 137(1); Welfare Reform and Pensions, 1999 c 30, s 81,
        sch 11 para 21; Pensions, 2014 c 19, sch 13 para 27(b)
    rep in pt—(prosp) Pensions, 2007 c 22, s 15, sch 4 para 50; Pensions, 2014 c 19, sch 13
        para 27(a)
s 41 rep —(saving temp to 1.4.2019) Pensions, 2014 c 19, sch 13 para 29; SI 2015/1502,
        art 2(1)(2)(f)
s 42 rep —Pensions, 2014 c 19, sch 13 para 30(1)

1993

c 48 *continued*

s 42A added—Pensions, 1995 c 26, s 137(5)

    rep (prosp)—Pensions, 2007 c 22, s 15, sch 4 para 51, sch 7

    am—Social Security, 1998 c 14, s 86(1), sch 7, para 128; Social Security
        Contributions (Trans of Functions, etc), 1999 c 2, s 1(1), sch 1 para 46; Welfare
        Reform and Pensions, 1999 c 30, s 73, sch 9 pt II para 7; Nat Insurance
        Contributions, 2002 c 19, s 6, sch 1, paras 35, 37; Pensions, 2007 c 22, s 15, sch
        4 para 17; Nat Insurance Contributions, 2008 c 16, sch 1 para 11(1); SI
        2011/1730, arts 5(8), 9(4); Pensions, 2014 c 19, sch 13 para 2

    appl—SI 2006/1009, art 3

s 42B added—Pensions, 1995 c 26, s 137(5)

    rep—Pensions, 2007 c 22, s 15, sch 4 para 18, sch 7

s 43 am—Pensions, 1995 c 26, s 137(3)(4),151, sch 5 para 42; Social Security
      Contributions (Trans of Functions, etc), 1999 c 2, s 1(1), sch 1 para 47; Nat
      Insurance Contributions, 2002 c 19, s 6, sch 1, paras 35, 38; Pensions, 2007 c 22,
      s 15, sch 4 para 19; SI 2011/1730, arts 5(9), 9(5); Pensions, 2014 c 19, sch 13
      para 2

    rep (prosp)—Pensions, 2007 c 22, s 15, sch 4 para 52, sch 7

s 44 am—Pensions, 1995 c 26, s 164; Social Security Contributions (Trans of Functions,
      etc), 1999 c 2, s 1(1), sch 1 para 48

    rep —Pensions, 2007 c 22, s 15, sch 4 para 20, sch 7

s 45 rep in pt—Pensions, 1995 c 26, ss 138(3)(4),151, 177, sch 5 para 43, sch 7 pt III

    rep (prosp)—Pensions, 2007 c 22, s 15, sch 4 para 53, sch 7

    am—Pensions, 1995 c 26, s 138(2); Social Security Contributions (Trans of Functions,
        etc), 1999 c 2, s 1(1), sch 1 para 49; Pensions, 2007 c 22, s 15, sch 4 para 21; Nat
        Insurance Contributions, 2008 c 16, sch 1 para 12(1); Pensions, 2014 c 19, sch 13
        para 2

    appl (mods)—Finance, 2004 c 12, s 202(3)(a)

    appl—SI 2006/1009, art 4

ss 45A, 44B rep—Pensions, 2007 c 22, s 15, sch 4 para 22, sch 7

s 46 am—Social Security (Incapacity for Work), 1994 c 18, s 11, sch 1 pt II para 56(2)(4);
      Pensions, 1995 c 26, ss 126,151, sch 4 pt III para 22, sch 5 para 44; Welfare
      Reform and Pensions, 1999 c 30, s 70, sch 8 pt I para 18; (pt prosp) Pensions,
      2008 c 30, s 104, sch 4 paras 15, 16; (pt prosp) ibid, s 103(1)(2); (prosp) Pensions,
      2011 c 19, sch 3 para 10; SI 2014/3213, art 4

    rep in pt—Social Security (Incapacity for Work), 1994 c 18, s 11, sch 1 pt II
        para 56(3)(5)-(7), sch 2; (prosp) Welfare Reform, 2007 c 5, s 67, sch 8;
        Pensions, 2014 c 19, sch 12 para 71

    appl (mods)—SI 1996/1462, regs 12, 13, sch 2 para 2

    mod—SI 1996/1172, reg 49(1)

s 46A rep —Pensions, 2014 c 19, sch 12 para 95

s 47 am—Welfare Reform and Pensions, 1999 c 30, s 32(4); ibid, s 18, sch 2 para 6;
      SI 2001/3649, art 120; State Pension Credit, 2002 c 16, s 18; Proceeds of Crime,
      2002 c 29, s 456, sch 11, para 22(1)(4); Pensions, 2004 c 35, s 165(3); SI
      2005/2050, art 2(1), sch 1 para 14; Pensions, 2007 c 22, s 14(5); (prosp) Pensions,
      2008 c 30, s 104, sch 4 paras 15, 17; Marriage (Same Sex Couples), 2013 c 30,
      sch 4 para 24; SI 2014/3229, sch 5 para 11(6)

    rep in pt—Social Security (Incapacity for Work), 1994 c 18, s 11, sch 1 pt II para 57,
        sch 2

    appl (mods)—SI 1996/1461, reg 6(3)

    mod—SI 1996/1172, reg 49(1)

s 48 rep in pt—Pensions, 1995 c 26, ss 140(2), 177, sch 7 pt III; ibid, s 140(3)

    mod—SI 1996/1172, reg 49(1)

    am—SI 2005/2050, art 2(1), sch 1 para 15; (prosp) Pensions, 2008 c 30, s 104, sch 4
        paras 15, 18

s 48A added—Pensions, 1995 c 26, s 140(1)

    mod—SIs 1996/1172, reg 49(1); 2015/1452, reg 12(4); 1677, reg 12(4)

    saved—SI 1997/664, art 10

    am—Child Support, Pensions and Social Security, 2000 c 19, s 38; Nat Insurance
        Contributions, 2002 c 19, s 6, sch 1, paras 35, 39; Pensions, 2007 c 22, s 15, sch
        4 para 23; Pensions, 2014 c 19, sch 13 paras 2, 31

s 49 rep —Pensions, 2014 c 19, sch 13 para 32

s 50 rep —(saving) Pensions, 2014 c 19, sch 13 para 33; SI 2015/1502, art 2(3A) (added by
      2015/2058, art 3(3)(d))

1993
c 48 *continued*

s 51 am—Pensions, 1995 c 26, s 151, sch 5 para 46; Pensions, 2014 c 19, sch 13 para 34
　　　　mod—SI 1996/1172, reg 67
　　　　excl—SI 1996/1172, reg 69
s 52 subst —Pensions, 2014 c 19, sch 13 para 35
　　　　am—Pensions, 1995 c 26, s 151, sch 5 para 47(a)(b); Welfare Reform and Pensions,
　　　　　　1999 c 30, s 84, sch 12 para 30; (prosp) Pensions, 2007 c 22, s 15, sch 4 para 25;
　　　　　　SI 2011/1730, art 5(11)
　　　　rep in pt—Pensions, 1995 c 26, ss 151, 177, sch 5 para 47(c), sch 7 pt III; Pensions,
　　　　　　2008 c 30, s 148, sch 11 pt 2; SI 2011/1730, art 5(11)
　　　　ext—SI 1996/1172, reg 59
　　　　mod—SI 1996/1172, reg 76A(3) (subst by SI 2009/598, art 3)
s 53 am—Pensions, 1995 c 26, s 151, sch 5 para 48(a)(c); Social Security Contributions
　　　　　　(Trans of Functions, etc), 1999 c 2, s 1(1), sch 1 para 52; Pensions, 2004 c 35,
　　　　　　s 319(1), sch 12 paras 9,10; SI 2011/1730, art 5(12); Crime and Cts, 2013 c 22,
　　　　　　sch 9 para 52
　　　　rep in pt—Pensions, 1995 c 26, ss 151, 177, sch 5 para 48(b)(d), sch 7 pt III; (saving
　　　　　　temp to 1.4.2019) Pensions, 2014 c 19, sch 13 para 36 (with SI 2015/1502, art
　　　　　　2(1)(2)(h))
　　　　mod—SI 1996/1172, reg 76A(3) (subst by SI 2009/598, art 3)
s 54 rep—SI 2011/1730, art 5(13)
ss 55-68 rep —(saving) Pensions, 2014 c 19, sch 13 para 37 (with SI 2015/1502, art 2(4));
　　　　　　(saving temp to 1.4.2019) ibid, (with SI 2015/1502, art 2(1)(2)(i))
s 55 excl in pt (as saved)—SI 2015/1677, reg 10
ss 57, 60 mod (as saved)—SI 2015/1677, reg 11
s 68 am—Crim Justice and Cts, 2015 c 2, sch 11 para 12
Pt 3A (ss 68A-68D) added—Welfare Reform and Pensions, 1999 c 30, s 36
　　　　rep —Pensions, 2008 c 30, s 148, sch 11, s 100
Pt 4 Ch 1 (ss 69-82) mod—SIs 2015/182, sch 3 para 5; 319, reg 7; 370, reg 7; 372, reg 7;
　　　　　　390, reg 7; 432, reg 7; 436, reg 7; 848 (W 63), reg 7; SSIs 2015/117, reg 7;
　　　　　　118, reg 7; 145, reg 7; 146, reg 7
s 69 appl (mods)—SI 2005/3381, regs 14, 16, sch 2 paras 1, 3
s 70 am—SI 2005/2053, art 2, sch pt 3 para 11; (prosp) Pension Schemes, 2015 c 8, s
　　　　　　39(3)(a)
　　　　rep in pt—(prosp) Pension Schemes, 2015 c 8, s 39(3)(b)
　　　　appl (mods)—SI 2005/3381, regs 14, 16, sch 2 paras 1, 3
s 71 appl (mods)—SI 2005/3381, regs 14, 16, sch 2 paras 1, 3
　　　　mod—SI 2005/992, reg 2(1)-(3); SIs 2015/370, reg 16; 390, reg 16; 848 (W 63), reg
　　　　　　15(2); SSIs 2015/117, reg 15; 118, reg 16
　　　　am—(pt prosp) Public Service Pensions, 2013 c 25, sch 8 para 19(2)(3); Pensions,
　　　　　　2014 c 19, s 36; (prosp) Pension Schemes, 2015 c 8, s 39(2),(4)
s 72 appl (mods)—SI 2005/3381, regs 14, 16, sch 2 paras 1, 3
　　　　mod—SIs 2015/370, reg 16; 390, reg 16; 848 (W 63), reg 15; SSIs 2015/117, reg 15;
　　　　　　118, reg 16
s 73 rep in pt—Welfare Reform and Pensions, 1999 c 30, ss 18, 88, sch 2 para 3(2), sch 13
　　　　　　pt I
　　　　am—Pension Schemes, 2015 c 8, sch 4 para 7
　　　　appl (mods)—SI 2005/3381, regs 14, 16, sch 2 paras 1, 3
　　　　mod—SI 2005/992, reg 2(1)(4)-(7)
s 74 appl (mods)—SI 2005/3381, regs 14, 16, sch 2 paras 1, 3
　　　　am—(prosp) Pension Schemes, 2015 c 8, s 39(5)
　　　　mod—SIs 2015/370, reg 16; 390, reg 16; 848 (W 63), reg 15; SSIs 2015/117, reg 15;
　　　　　　118, reg 16
s 75 appl (mods)—SI 2005/3381, regs 14, 16, sch 2 paras 1, 3
　　　　mod—SIs 2005/992, reg 2(1)(4)-(7); 2015/370, reg 16; 390, reg 16; 848 (W 63), reg
　　　　　　15; SSIs 2015/117, reg 15; 118, reg 16
s 76 appl (mods)—SI 2005/3381, regs 14, 16, sch 2 paras 1, 3
ss 77-80 rep—Pensions, 1995 c 26, ss 122, 177, sch 3 para 24, sch 7 pt I
ss 81, 82 appl (mods)—SI 2005/3381, regs 14, 16, sch 2 paras 1, 3
Pt 4 Ch 2 (ss 83-86) mod—SIs 2015/182, sch 3 para 6; 319, reg 8; 370, reg 8; 372, reg 8;
　　　　　　390, reg 8; 432, reg 8; 436, reg 8; 848 (W 63), reg 8; SSIs 2015/117, reg 8;
　　　　　　118, reg 8; 145, reg 8; 146, reg 8
s 82A inserted (prosp) (into Pt 4 Ch 2)—Pension Schemes, 2015 c 8, sch 1 para 2

1993
c 48 *continued*

s 83 am—Welfare Reform and Pensions, 1999 c 30, s 84, sch 12 para 31; Pensions, 2004 c
    35, s 281; (pt prosp) Public Service Pensions, 2013 c 25, sch 8 para 20; (prosp)
    Pension Schemes, 2015 c 8, sch 1 para 3; (prosp) ibid, sch 2 para 2
    appl (mods)—SI 2005/3381, regs 14, 16, sch 2 paras 1, 3
s 84 replaced (prosp) (by ss 84, 84A-84F)—Pension Schemes, 2015 c 8, sch 1 para 4
    rep in pt—Pensions, 1995 c 26, ss 151, 177, sch 5 para 62, sch 7 pt III
    appl (mods)—SI 2005/3381, regs 14, 16, sch 2 paras 1, 3
    am—SI 2005/2053, art 2, sch pt 3 para 12; Statistics and Registration Service, 2007 c
        18, s 60, sch 3 para 9; Pensions, 2011 c 19, s 19(2); Marriage (Same Sex
        Couples), 2013 c 30, sch 4 para 25; SIs 2014/1954, reg 3; 2014/3229, sch 5 para
        11(7)
    mod—SI 2010/772, reg 37
    rep in pt—Pensions, 2011 c 19, s 19(3)
s 85 am—Welfare Reform and Pensions, 1999 c 30, s 84, sch 12 para 32
    appl (mods)—SI 2005/3381, regs 14, 16, sch 2 paras 1, 3
s 85A added (prosp)—Pension Schemes, 2015 c 8, sch 1 para 5
s 86 appl (mods)—SI 2005/3381, regs 14, 16, sch 2 paras 1, 3
ss 86A, 86B added (prosp)—Pension Schemes, 2015 c 8, sch 1 para 6
Pt 4 Ch 3 (ss 87-92) mod—SI 1997/1612, reg 90; SIs 2015/182, reg 1(3), sch 3 para 8; 319,
    regs 1(3),10; 370, regs 1(3),10; 372, regs 1(3),10; 390, regs 1(3),10; 432, regs
    1(3),10; 436, regs 1(3),10; 848 (W 63), regs 1(3),10; SSIs 2015/117, regs 1(3),
    10; 118, regs 1(3),10; 145, regs 1(3),10; 146, regs 1(3),10
    restr—(pt prosp) Child Support, Pensions and Social Security, 2000 c 19, s 56, sch 5
        pt II para 14
s 87 am—SI 2005/2050, art 2(1), sch 1 para 18; Pensions, 2007 c 22, s 15, sch 4 para 28;
    (saving) Pensions, 2014 c 19, sch 13 para 38 (with SI 2015/1502, art 2(6) (added
    by 2015/2058, art 3(3)(e))
ss 88-90 am—SI 2005/2050, art 2(1), sch 1 paras 19-21
Pt 4 Ch 4, 5 renumbered Ch 1, 2 in new Part 4ZA—Pension Schemes, 2015 c 8, sch 4 para
    4(1)
Pt 4ZA (ss 93-101AI) am (heading added)—Pension Schemes, 2015 c 8, sch 4 para 4(2)(a)
Pt 4ZA Ch. 1 (ss 93-101) am (heading subst)—Pension Schemes, 2015 c 8, sch 4 para
    4(2)(b)
    appl—SI 1994/1432
    power to mod—Pensions, 2004 c 35, s 24(7)
    mod—SIs 1998/366, regs 116-118; 2015/182, reg 11; 370, reg
        11; 372, reg 11; 390, reg 11; 432, reg 11; 436, reg 11; 848 (W 63), reg 11;
        SSIs 2015/117, reg 11; 118, reg 11; 145, reg 11; 146, reg 11
    saved—SI 2005/438, art 2(1), sch 1 pt F, rule F.1(2)
    excl—SI 2010/6, reg 2
s 93 subst—Pension Schemes, 2015 c 8, sch 4 para 8
    appl—Learning and Skills, 2000 c 21, s 135(4); SI 2008/239, reg 78; SSI 2008/228,
        reg 73
    appl (mods)—SI 2005/3381, regs 14, 16, sch 2 paras 1, 3
s 93A subst—Pension Schemes, 2015 c 8, sch 4 para 8
    appl (mods)—SI 2005/3381, regs 14, 16, sch 2 paras 1, 3
    appl—SIs 2005/590, reg 16(4); 2008/239, reg 78; SSI 2008/228, reg 73
    restr—SI 2014/1711, reg 31
    excl in pt—SI 2014/1711, reg 31
s 94 subst—Pension Schemes, 2015 c 8, sch 4 para 8
    ext—(pt prosp) Child Support, Pensions and Social Security, 2000 c 19, s 56, sch 5 pt II
        para 16(2)
    appl (mods)—SI 2005/3381, regs 14, 16, sch 2 paras 1, 3
    appl—SI 2005/590, reg 16(4); SSI 2008/228, reg 73; SI 2008/239, reg 78
s 95 am—Pensions, 1995 c 26, s 173, sch 6 para 3; Pension Schemes, 2015 c 8, s 68(2)-(5);
    ibid, sch 4 para 9(2)-(4)
    saved—SI 1995/639, reg 2.28(5)
    rep in pt—Child Support, Pensions and Social Security, 2000 c 19, sch 5 pt I para 7,
        sch 9 pt III(7); Pension Schemes, 2015 c 8, sch 4 para 9(5)
    appl (mods)—SI 2005/3381, regs 14, 16, sch 2 paras 1, 3
    appl—SSI 2008/228, reg 73; SI 2008/239, reg 78
s 96 appl —SI 1994/1662; SSI 2008/228, reg 73; SI 2008/239, reg 78
    appl (mods)—SI 2005/3381, regs 14, 16, sch 2 paras 1, 3

1993
c 48 s 96   *continued*

am—Pensions, 1995 c 26, s 151, sch 5 para 63; Welfare Reform and Pensions, 1999
c 30, s 84, sch 12 para 36; SIs 2001/3649, art 121; 2005/2053, art 2, sch pt 3
para 13; 2011/1730, art 5(14); Pension Schemes, 2015 c 8, s 68(6); ibid, sch 4
para 10(2)-(4)

rep in pt—Welfare Reform and Pensions, 1999 c 30, ss 18, 88, sch 2 para 3(2), sch 13
pt I; Pensions, 2007 c 22, s 15, sch 4 para 29, sch 7; SI 2011/1730, art 5(14);
Pensions, 2014 c 19, sch 13 para 39

s 97 am—Pensions, 1995 c 26, s 173, sch 6 para 4; Child Support, Pensions and Social
Security, 2000 c 19, s 56, sch 5 pt I para 8(1); Pension Schemes, 2015 c 8, s 69(2);
ibid, sch 4 para 11(2)(3)(5)

rep in pt—Pension Schemes, 2015 c 8, sch 4 para 11(4)

appl (mods)—SI 2005/3381, regs 14, 16, sch 2 paras 1, 3

appl—SSI 2008/228, reg 73; SI 2008/239, reg 78

ss 97A, 97B added—Pension Schemes, 2015 c 8, s 69(3)

s 97C added—Pension Schemes, 2015 c 8, s 69(4)

s 98 subst—Pension Schemes, 2015 c 8, sch 4 para 12

s 99 am—Pensions, 1995 c 26, s 173, sch 6 para 6; Pensions, 2004 c 35, s 319(1), sch 12
paras 9, 14; SI 2011/1730, art 5(15); Marriage (Same Sex Couples), 2013 c 30,
sch 7 para 32; SI 2014/3229, sch 5 para 11(8); Pension Schemes, 2015 c 8, s
50(2); ibid, sch 4 para 13(2)(5)

rep in pt—Pensions, 2004 c 35, s 320, sch 13 pt 1; Pension Schemes, 2015 c 8, sch 4
para 13(3)(4)

saved—SIs 1995/639, reg 2.28(5); 1997/664, art 5

appl—SSI 2008/228, reg 73; SI 2008/239, reg 78

appl (mods)—SIs 2005/686, reg 3; 3381, regs 14, 16, sch 2 paras 1, 3, 4

mod—SI 2005/992, regs 2(1), 3(1)

s 100 am—Welfare Reform and Pensions, 1999 c 30, s 84, sch 12 para 38; Pension Schemes,
2015 c 8, s 68(7)

appl (mods)—SI 2005/3381, regs 14, 16, sch 2 paras 1, 3

appl—SSI 2008/228, reg 73; SI 2008/239, reg 78

ss 100A-100D added—Pension Schemes, 2015 c 8, sch 4 para 14

s 101 appl (mods)—SI 2005/3381, regs 14, 16, sch 2 paras 1, 3

appl—SSI 2008/228, reg 73; SI 2008/239, reg 78

Pt 4ZA, Ch. 2 (ss 101AA-101AI) added —(as Pt 4 Ch 5) Pensions, 2004 c 35, s 264

am (heading subst)—Pension Schemes, 2015 c 8, sch 4 para 4(2)(c)

saved—SI 2005/438, art 2(1), sch 1 pt F, rule F.1(2)

appl (mods)—SI 2005/3381, regs 14, 16, sch 2 paras 1, 3

appl—SSI 2008/228, reg 73

excl—SI 2014/1711, reg 56(1)(c)

mod—SIs 2015/182, sch 3 para 11; 370, reg 13; 372, reg 13; 390, reg 13; 432, reg
13; 436, reg 13; SSIs 2015/118, reg 13; 145, reg 13; 146, reg 13

s 101AA am—Pensions, 2014 c 19, s 36(4)

s 101AG mod—SI 2005/992, regs 2(1), 3(3)

s 101AI am—(prosp) Pensions, 2014 c 19, sch 17 para 20(3); Pension Schemes, 2015 c 8, s
60(1)

Pt 4A (ss 101A-101Q) added—(EWS) Welfare Reform and Pensions, 1999 c 30, s 37

s 101A am—Pensions, 2014 c 19, sch 18 para 9(3); Pension Schemes, 2015 c 8, s 82(2)

s 101B am—Pensions, 2014 c 19, sch 18 para 9(3); Pension Schemes, 2015 c 8, s 82(3)

s 101C am—Pensions, 2014 c 19, sch 18 para 9(3); Pension Schemes, 2015 c 8, s 82(4)

s 101E am—Civil Partnership, 2004 c 33, s 261(1), sch 27 para 148

s 101F am—SI 2001/3649, art 122; Pensions, 2008 c 30, s 134(1),(3); Pension Schemes,
2015 c 8, sch 4 para 15(2)-(5)

appl—SI 2005/992, reg 3(2)

excl—SI 2010/6, reg 2

s 101G subst—Pension Schemes, 2015 c 8, sch 4 para 16

excl—SI 2010/6, reg 2

s 101H am—Pension Schemes, 2015 c 8, sch 4 para 17

excl—SI 2010/6, reg 2

s 101I excl—SI 2010/6, reg 2

s 101J am—Pensions, 2004 c 35, s 319(1), sch 12 paras 9, 15; Pension Schemes, 2015 c 8, s
50(3); ibid, sch 4 para 18

rep in pt—Pensions, 2004 c 35, s 320, sch 13 pt 1

appl—SSI 2008/228, reg 73

1993
c 48 s 101J *continued*
        excl—SI 2010/6, reg 2
    ss 101K, 101L excl—SI 2010/6, reg 2
    s 101M am—Pension Schemes, 2015 c 8, sch 4 para 19
        mod—SI 2005/992, regs 2(1), 3(2)
        excl—SI 2010/6, reg 2
    ss 101N excl—SI 2010/6, reg 2
    s 101NA added—Pension Schemes, 2015 c 8, sch 4 para 20
    s 101O excl—SI 2010/6, reg 2
    s 101P am—Pension Schemes, 2015 c 8, sch 4 para 21(2)(5)
        rep in pt—Pension Schemes, 2015 c 8, sch 4 para 21(3)(4)
        excl—SI 2010/6, reg 2
    s 101Q rep—Pension Schemes, 2015 c 8, sch 4 para 22
    ss 102-107 rep—Pensions 1995 c 26, ss 122, 177, sch 3 para 25, sch 7 pt I
    s 108 rep —(saving) Pensions 1995 c 26, ss 122, 177, sch 3 para 25, sch 7 pt I; SI 1997/664,
        art 6
    s 109 am—Pensions, 1995 c 26, ss 55,56; SI 2005/2050, art 2(1), sch 1 para 22
        rep in pt—Pensions, 2014 c 19, sch 13 para 40
    s 110 am—Pensions, 1995 c 26, s 53(4)(b); Pensions, 1995 c 26, ss 55,56; SI 2005/2050,
        art 2(1), sch 1 para 23
        rep in pt—Pensions, 1995 c 26, ss 53(4)(a), 177, sch 7 pt I
    s 111 rep—Pensions, 2004 c 35, ss 267(1), 320, sch 13 pt 1
    ss 111A, 111B added—Welfare Reform and Pensions, 1999 c 30, s 9
    s 111A appl—Pensions, 2004 c 35, s 17(3)(c)
        am—Pensions, 2004 c 35, s 268; Pensions, 2008 c 30, s 49
        rep in pt—Pensions, 2004 c 35, ss 319(1), 320, sch 12 paras 9, 16, sch 13 pt 1
    s 111B rep—Pensions, 2004 c 35, s 320, sch 13 pt 1
    s 112 rep—Pensions, 1995 c 26, ss 122, 177, sch 3 para 26, sch 7 pt I
    s 113 am—Child Support, Pensions and Social Security, 2000 c 19, s 52; Pensions, 2004 c
        35, s 319(1), sch 12 paras 9, 17; SI 2005/2053, art 2, sch pt 3 para 14; Pensions,
        2007 c 22, s 17, sch 5 para 6; (prosp) Pensions, 2014 c 19, s 44(1); (prosp)
        Pension Schemes, 2015 c 8, s 38(2)(a),(4)-(6); (prosp) ibid, sch 2 para 3
        rep in pt—(prosp) Pension Schemes, 2015 c 8, s 38(2)(b),(3)
    s 113A added—Pensions, 2004 c 35, s 319(1), sch 12 paras 9, 18
    s 114 rep—Pensions, 1995 c 26, ss 122, 177, sch 3 para 27, sch 7 pt I
        saved—SI 1997/664, art 7
    s 115 am—Crime and Cts, 2013 c 22, sch 9 para 52
    s 116 rep—Pensions, 1995 c 26, ss 122, 177, sch 3 para 28, sch 7 pt I
    s 118 rep—Pensions, 1995 c 26, ss 122, 177, sch 3 para 29, sch 7 pt I
    ss 119-122 rep—Pensions, 1995 c 26, ss 122, 177, sch 3 para 30, sch 7 pt I
    s 123 appl—Pensions, 1995 c 26, s 81(8)
        am—Employment Rights, 1996 c 18, s 240, sch 1 para 61(2); SI 2003/2096, arts 4, 6,
        sch pt 1 para 22(a)(ii)(b)(ii); Pensions, 2014 c 19, s 42(2)
        rep in pt—SI 2003/2096, arts 4, 6, sch pt 1 para 22(a)(i)(b)(i); Pensions, 2004 c 35,
        ss 319(1), 320, sch 12 paras 9, 19(a)(b), sch 13 pt I
    s 124 am—Pensions, 1995 c 26, s 90; Employment Rights, 1996 c 18, s 240, sch 1
        para 61(3); Child Support, Pensions and Social Security, 2000 c 19, s 56, sch 5
        pt I para 8(3); Pensions, 2004 c 35, s 319(1), sch 12 paras 9, 20; Pensions, 2014
        c 19, s 42(3); (prosp) Pension Schemes, 2015 c 8, sch 2 para 4
    s 127 am—SIs 2008/948, art 3, sch 1; 2009/1941, art 2, sch 1
    s 129 am—Pensions, 1995 c 26, s 122, sch 3 para 31(b); Pensions, 2004 c 35, s 319(1), sch
        12 paras 9, 21; SIs 2005/2053, art 2, sch pt 3 para 15; 3029, art 3, sch 1 para 2;
        Pension Schemes, 2015 c 8, sch 4 para 23
        rep in pt—Pensions, 1995 c 26, ss 122, 177, sch 3 para 31(a)(c), sch 7 pt I; Pensions,
        2004 c 35, s 320, sch 13 pt 1
        saved—(pt prosp) Child Support, Pensions and Social Security, 2000 c 19, s 56, sch 5
        pt II para 16(3)
    s 130 am—Pensions, 2004 c 35, s 319(1), sch 12 paras 9, 22; Pension Schemes, 2015 c 8,
        sch 4 para 24
    s 131 rep in pt—(prosp) Pensions, 2004 c 35, s 320, sch 13 pt 1
    s 132 rep in pt—Pensions, 1995 c 26, ss 122, 177, sch 3 para 32, sch 7 pt I; Pensions, 2004
        c 35, ss 267(2), 320, sch 13 pt 1
    s 133 rep—Pensions, 1995 c 26, ss 151, 177, sch 5 para 64, sch 7 pt III
    s 134 rep—Pensions, 1995 c 26, ss 151, 177, sch 5 para 64, sch 7 pt III

1993

c 48 s 134 *continued*

      saved—SI 1997/664, art 8

s 135 rep—Pensions, 1995 c 26, ss 151, 177, sch 5 para 64, sch 7 pt III

ss 136-140 rep—(savings) Pensions, 1995 c 26, ss 161, 177, sch 7 pt IV
      saved—SI 1997/664, art 9

ss 141-143 rep—(savings) Pensions, 1995 c 26, ss 161, 177, sch 7 pt IV

s 144 rep—Pensions, 1995 c 26, ss 122, 177, sch 3 para 38, sch 7 pt I
      saved—SI 1997/664, art 11(3)

s 145 am—Pensions, 1995 c 26, s 156; Pensions, 2004 c 35, s 274(1)(2); (prosp) ibid,
      s 319(1), sch 12 paras 9, 23; SI 2008/817, arts 9, 10

      rep in pt—Pensions, 1995 c 26, ss 173, 177, sch 6 para 7, sch 7 pt IV

s 145A added—Pensions, 2004 c 35, s 274(3)

s 146 am—Pensions, 1995 c 26, s 157(2)(3); Child Support, Pensions and Social Security,
      2000 c 19, s 53; Pensions, 2004 c 35, ss 275(1)(2), 319(1), sch 12 paras 9,
      24(a)(c); (prosp) ibid, para 24(b); SI 2005/2053, art 2, sch pt 3 para 16;
      Pensions, 2008 c 30, s 66

      rep in pt—Child Support, Pensions and Social Security, 2000 c 19, ss 53(9)(c),85,
      sch 9 pt III(3)

s 147 am—Pensions, 1995 c 26, s 157(4)(5)

s 148 am—Pensions, 1995 c 26, s 157(6); Child Support, Pensions and Social Security,
      2000 c 19, s 54(2)

      rep in pt—Pensions, 2004 c 35, ss 276(2)(a), 320, sch 13 pt 1

s 149 am—Pensions, 1995 c 26, ss 157(7),158(a),159(1); Bank of E, 1998 c 11, s 23, sch 5
      pt IV, Ch II, para 69(2); SI 2001/3649, art 123(b)(c); Pensions, 2004 c 35,
      s 319(1), sch 12 paras 9, 25; SI 2005/2743, art 2; Financial Services, 2012 c 21,
      sch 18 para 78(2); SI 2013/504, reg 21(2)

      rep in pt—Pensions, 1995 c 26, ss 158(b), 177, sch 7 pt IV; SI 2001/3649, art 123(a);
      Pensions, 2004 c 35, ss 276(2)(b)-(e), 320, sch 13 pt 1; SI 2009/1941, art 2,
      sch 1

s 150 am—Pensions, 1995 c 26, s 157(8); Crime and Cts, 2013 c 22, sch 9 para 52

s 151 am—Pensions, 1995 c 26, ss 157(9)—(11),159(2), 173, sch 6 para 8; Crime and Cts,
      2013 c 22, sch 9 para 52

s 151 rep in pt—Pensions, 2004 c 35, ss 276(2)(f)-(h), 320, sch 13 pt 1

s 151A added—Pensions, 1995 c 26, s 160

s 152 am—Crime and Cts, 2013 c 22, sch 9 para 119(a)(b)

s 153 rep in pt—Pensions, 1995 c 26, ss 122, 177, sch 3 para 39, sch 7 pt
      am—Pensions, 1995 c 26, ss 122, 177, sch 3 para 39(c), sch 7 pt I; Pension Schemes,
      2015 c 8, sch 4 para 25

s 154 am—Pensions, 1995 c 26, s 122, sch 3 para 40

s 155 rep in pt—Pensions, 1995 c 26, ss 151, 177, sch 5 para 65(a), sch 7 pt III
      am—Pensions, 1995 c 26, s 151, sch 5 para 65(b)(c); Social Security Contributions
      (Trans of Functions, etc), 1999 c 2, s 1(1), sch 1 para 59; SI 2011/1730, art
      5(15A) (added by SI 2012/709, art 2(3))

s 156 subst—Child Support, Pensions and Social Security, 2000 c 19, s 56, sch 5 pt I para 9
      am—(prosp) Pensions, 2007 c 22, s 15, sch 4 para 30; SI 2011/1730, art 5(16)

s 158 rep in pt—Pensions, 1995 c 26, ss 151, 177, sch 5 para 66, sch 7 pt III; Pensions,
      2004 c 35, s 320, sch 13 pt 1

      am—Pensions, 1995 c 26, s 151, sch 5 para 66(c)(i)(ii); (pt prosp) Social Security,
      1998 c 14, s 86(1), sch 7, para 129; Social Security Contributions (Trans of
      Functions, etc), 1999 c 2, s 6, sch 6 para 7; SI 2002/1397, art 12, sch pt I, para
      9(1)(2); Income Tax (Trading and Other Income), 2005 c 5, s 882(1), sch 1 pt 2
      paras 467, 468; Commrs for Revenue and Customs, 2005 c 11, s 50(6), sch 4
      para 51

s 158A added—Pensions, 1995 c 26, s 173, sch 6 para 9
      am—Bank of E 1998 c 11, s 23, sch 5 pt IV, Ch II, para 69(3); Social Security
      Contributions (Trans of Functions, etc), 1999 c 2, s 6, sch 6 para 8;
      SI 2001/3649, art 124(1)(3)(4); SI 2002/1397, art 12, sch pt I, para 9(1)(3);
      Pensions, 2004 c 35, s 319(1), sch 12 paras 9, 26; Financial Services, 2012 c
      21, sch 18 para 78(3)

      mod—(temp) SI 2001/2966, arts 3, 10

      rep in pt—SI 2001/3649, art 124(1)(2)

s 159 am—Pensions, 1995 c 26, s 122, sch 3 para 41; SI 2011/1730, art 5(17)(e) (subst by
      SI 2012/709, art 2(4))

1993

c 48 s 159 *continued*

   rep in pt—Welfare Reform and Pensions, 1999 c 30, s 88, sch 13 pt I; SI 2011/1730,
    art 5(17)(a)-(d) (subst by SI 2012/709, art 2(5))

   excl—Bankruptcy (S), 1985 c 66, ss 36C, 36F(2)(a); Insolvency, 1986 c 45, s 342C;
    Welfare Reform and Pensions, 1999 c 30, s 44(1); Proceeds of Crime, 2002 c
    29, s 273(5)(a); SI 2005/3181, art 184(5)(a)

   appl (mods)—SI 1996/1462, regs 12,13, sch 2 paras 5,9

   saved—SI 2000/1403, reg 13

s 159A added—Welfare Reform and Pensions, 1999 c 30, s 14(1)
   am—SI 2005/2053, art 2, sch pt 3 para 17

s 161 am—Pensions, 2014 c 19, s 42(4)

s 163 rep —Perpetuities and Accumulations, 2009 c 18, ss 4(c), 21, sch 1

s 164 rep in pt—Pensions 1995 c 26 ss 151, 173, 177, sch 5 para 67, sch 6 para 10, sch 7
   pt III; Employment Rights, 1996 c 18, s 242, sch 3 pt I; (prosp) Pensions, 2007
   c 22, s 15, sch 4 para 56, sch 7; SI 2011/1730, art 9(6)

   am—(prosp) Pensions, 2007 c 22, s 15, sch 4 para 32; (prosp) Pensions, 2008 c 30, s
   104, sch 4 paras 15, 20; SI 2011/1730, art 5(18) (subst by SI 2012/709, art
   2(5))

s 165 am—Pensions, 1995 c 26, s 151, sch 5 para 68; Employment Rights, 1996 c 18, s 240,
   sch 1;Petroleum, 1998 c 17, s 50, sch 4, para 37; (prosp) Pensions, 2008 c 30, s
   104, sch 4 paras 15, 21; Pensions, 2014 c 19, s 42(5)

   rep in pt—SI 2011/1730, art 5(18A) (added by SI 2012/709, art 2(6))

s 166 rep in pt—Pensions, 1995 c 26, ss 151, 173, 177, sch 5 para 69, sch 6 para 11, sch 7
   pt III

s 167 rep in pt—Northern Ireland, 1998 c 47, s 100(2), sch 15; (pt prosp) Social Security,
   1998 c 14, s 86(1)(2), sch 7, para 130(2), sch 8; Social Security Contributions
   (Trans of Functions, etc), 1999 c 2, ss 18, 26(3), sch 7 para 18(1)(3), sch 10
   pt I

   am—Social Security Contributions (Trans of Functions, etc), 1999 c 2, s 18, sch 7
   para 18(1)(2); SI 2005/3129, art 4(1), sch 1 para 5; (prosp) Pensions, 2008 c 30,
   s 104, sch 4 paras 15, 22

s 168 replaced (by, ss 168, 168A)—Pensions, 1995 c 26, s 155(1)

s 168 mod—Welfare Reform and Pensions, 1999 c 30, s 45(2)

   am—Pensions, 2004 c 35, s 319(1), sch 12 paras 9, 27

s 168A rep—Pensions, 2004 c 35, s 320, sch 13 pt 1

s 170 subst —(pt prosp) Social Security, 1998 c 14, s 86(1), sch 7, para 131

   am—Pensions, 1995 c 26, s 151, sch 5 para 70(a)(i)(iii)(c); Social Security
   Contributions (Trans of Functions, etc), 1999 c 2, s 16(2); Welfare Reform and
   Pensions, 1999 c 30, s 81, sch 11 para 22; SIs 2001/3649, art 125; 2005/2050,
   art 2(1), sch 1 para 24; 2008/2833, art 6, sch 3; 2011/1730, art 5(19)(20)

   certain functions trans—Social Security Contributions (Trans of Functions, etc), 1999
   c 2, s 16(1)

   mod—Social Security Contributions (Trans of Functions, etc), 1999 c 2, s 23(6);
   (temp) SI 1999/978, reg 2(1)(2)(b), sch

   power to am—Social Security Contributions (Trans of Functions, etc), 1999 c 2, s 23

   rep in pt—Pensions, 1995 c 26, ss 51,122, 177, sch 3 para 42, sch 5 para 70(a)(ii)(b),
   sch 7 pt I, sch 7 pts I, III

   saved—SI 1997/664, art 4(2)(3)

s 171 am—Pensions, 1995 c 26, s 151, sch 5 para 71; Social Security Contributions (Trans
   of Functions, etc), 1999 c 2, s 18, sch 7 para 19

   saved—SI 1997/664, art 4(2)(3)

   rep in pt—Pensions, 2014 c 19, sch 13 para 41

s 171A added—Social Security Contributions (Trans of Functions, etc), 1999 c 2, s 18,
   sch 7 para 20

   am—SI 2008/2833, art 6, sch 3

   rep in pt—Welfare Reform, 2012 c 5, sch 14 pt 14

ss 172, 173 rep—Pensions, 1995 c 26, ss 151, 177, sch 5 para 72, sch 7 pt III

s 174 am—Pensions, 1995 c 26, s 151, sch 5 para 73; Pensions, 2011 c 19, s 35(2)(3)

s 175 subst—Pensions, 1995 c 26, s 165

   appl (mods)—Welfare Reform and Pensions 1999 c 30, s 6, sch 1 para 1(2)(a)

   am—Pensions, 2004 c 35, ss 3, 319(1), sch 1 pt 5 para 26, sch 12 paras 9, 28; SI
   2010/22, art 5, sch 2

   rep in pt—Pensions, 2004 c 35, ss 3, 320, sch 1 pt 5 para 26, sch 13 pt 1

s 175A added—(prosp) Pensions, 2008 c 30, s 129, sch 10 para 1

1993
c 48 *continued*

s 176 am—Pensions, 1995 c 26, s 151, sch 5 para 74
s 177 am—Social Security Contributions (Trans of Functions, etc), 1999 c 2, s 1(1), sch 1
    para 61; (transtl savings) ibid, 1999 c 2, s 20(1)(a)(b)(5); Welfare Reform and
    Pensions, 1999 c 30, s 73, sch 9 pt II para 8; (prosp) Pensions, 2007 c 22, s 15,
    sch 4 para 33; SI 2011/1730, art 5(21) (subst by SI 2012/709, art 2(7))
  rep in pt—Pensions, 1995 c 26, ss 151, 177, sch 5 para 75, sch 7 pt III; Pensions,
    2004 c 35, s 320, sch 13 pt 1; (prosp) Pensions, 2007 c 22, s 15, sch 4 para 57,
    sch 7
s 178 am—Child Support, Pensions and Social Security, 2000 c 19, s 47(5); Child Support,
    Pensions and Social Security, 2000 c 19, s 56, sch 5 pt II para 17(9); Pensions,
    2004 c 35, s 319(1), sch 12 paras 9, 29; Pensions, 2014 c 19, sch 13 para 42(a)
  rep in pt—Welfare Reform and Pensions, 1999 c 30, s 88, sch 13 pt III; Child Support,
    Pensions and Social Security, 2000 c 19, s 85, sch 9 pt III(2); Pensions, 2014 c
    19, sch 13 para 42(b)
s 179 am—Pensions, 2004 c 35, s 319(1), sch 12 paras 9, 30; Pension Schemes, 2015 c 8,
    sch 4 para 26
  mod—SI 2005/992, reg 2(1)(8)(9)
s 180A added—SI 2001/3649, art 126
    am—Financial Services, 2012 c 21, sch 18 para 78(4)
s 181 rep in pt—Pensions, 1995 c 26, ss 122, 177, sch 3 para 44(a)(i), sch 7 pt I; ibid, ss 151,
    173, 177, sch 5 para 77(a)(i)(b)(c), sch 6 para 14 sch 7 pt III; Welfare Reform
    and Pensions, 1999 c 30, ss 18, 88, sch 2 para 3(2), sch 13 pts I, VI;
    SI 2001/3649, art 127(b); Pensions, 2004 c 35, ss 267(3), 320, sch 13 pt 1; SI
    2006/745, art 7; Pensions, 2007 c 22, s 27, sch 7; Pensions, 2008 c 30, s 148,
    sch 11 pt 2; Pensions, 2014 c 19, sch 13 para 43(3); (prosp) Pension Schemes,
    2015 c 8, sch 2 para 5(3)
  am—Pensions, 1995 c 26, ss 122,126, sch 3 para 44(a)(ii)(b), sch 4 pt III para 17;
    Employment Tribunals, 1996 c 17, s 43, sch 1 para 11; Welfare Reform and
    Pensions, 1999 c 30, ss 18, 32 sch 2 para 3(1); Child Support, Pensions and
    Social Security, 2000 c 19, s 56, sch 5 pt I para 2(3); SI 2001/3649, art 127(a);
    Proceeds of Crime, 2002 c 29, s 456, sch 11, para 22(1)(6); Income Tax
    (Earnings and Pensions), 2003 c 1, s 722, sch 6 pt 2 para 222; Pensions, 2004 c
    35, ss 7(1)(a)(2)(a), 282, 319(1), sch 12 paras 9, 31; SI 2005/2053, art 2, sch pt
    3 para 18; Pensions, 2007 c 22, s 12, sch 1 para 38; ibid, s 15, sch 4 paras 34, 58;
    Pensions, 2011 c 19, s 29(1); SI 2011/1730, arts 5(22), 9(7); Nat Insurance
    Contributions, 2014 c 7, sch 2 para 13; Pensions, 2014 c 19, sch 13 para
    43(2)(4)-(8); Pension Schemes, 2015 c 8, sch 4 para 27; (prosp) ibid, sch 2 para
    5(2)
  appl—Pension Schemes (NI), 1993 c 49, s 142(8); Pensions, 1995 c 26,
    ss 76(5)(b)(ii),77(3)(b)(ii); Welfare Reform and Pensions, 1999 c 30, s 1(4);
    Finance, 2004 c 12, ss 166, 168, sch 29 pt 1 para 5(3); SI 2005/704, reg 2(3)
  mod—SI 2005/992, reg 2(1)(4)-(7)
s 181A rep—Pensions, 2014 c 19, sch 13 para 44
s 181B added —Pensions, 2011 c 19, s 29(2)
s 182 rep in pt—Pensions, 1995 c 26, ss 151, 177, sch 5 para 78, sch 7 pt III
  am—Pension Schemes, 2015 c 8, s 70(1)
  saved—Welfare Reform and Pensions, 1999 c 30, s 7(3)
s 183 rep in pt—Pensions, 1995 c 26, ss 122,151, 173, 177, sch 3 para 45(b)(c), sch 5
    para 79, sch 6 para 15(a), sch 7 pts I,III,IV
  am—Pensions, 1995 c 26, ss 122, 173, sch 3 para 45(a), sch 6 para 15(b); Pensions,
    2004 c 35, s 319(1), sch 12 paras 9, 32; SI 2011/1730, art 5(23)
s 185 rep in pt—Pensions, 1995 c 26, ss 122,151, 177, sch 3 para 46, sch 5 para 80(c)(e),
    sch 7 pts I, III; SI 2013/2042, sch para 15; Pensions, 2014 c 19, sch 13 para 45
  am—Pensions, 1995 c 26, s 151, sch 5 para 80(a)(b)(d)(f); Welfare Reform and
    Pensions, 1999 c 30, s 81, sch 11 para 23; SI 2001/3649, art 128; Tribunals, Cts
    and Enforcement, 2007 c 15, s 48, sch 8 para 32; (prosp) Pensions, 2008 c 30, s
    103(1), (4); Financial Services, 2012 c 21, sch 18 para 78(5); Pension Schemes,
    2015 c 8, s 70(2)
s 186 rep in pt—Pensions, 1995 c 26, ss 151, 177, sch 5 para 81, sch 7 pt III
  am—Pensions, 1995 c 26, s 155(2); Pensions, 2007 c 22, s 14(12); (prosp) Pensions,
    2008 c 30, s 103(1),(5); Pension Schemes, 2015 c 8, s 70(3); (prosp) ibid, sch 1
    para 7
s 187 rep—Northern Ireland, 1998 c 47, s 100(2), sch 15

1993

c 48 *continued*

s 192 rep in pt—Pensions, 1995 c 26, ss 151, 177, sch 5 para 82, sch 7 pt III; Pensions, 2004 c 35, s 320, sch 13 pt 1

am—Pensions, 1995 c 26, s 151, sch 5 para 82; Pensions, 2004 c 35, s 319(1), sch 12 paras 9, 33

sch 1 rep—Pensions, 1995 c 26, ss 151, 177, sch 5 para 83, sch 7 pt III

sch 2 am—Pensions, 1995 c 26, ss 141(2)(a)(iii)(b), 151, sch 5 para 84(a)(b)(c)(ii)(e); Social Security Contributions (Trans of Functions, etc), 1999 c 2, s 1(1), sch 1 para 62(1)-(5); Pensions, 2007 c 22, s 15, sch 4 para 59; Pensions, 2014 c 19, sch 13 para 46(3)

rep in pt—Pensions, 1995 c 26, ss 141(2)(a)(i)(ii)(c),151, 177, sch 5 para 84(c)(i)(d), sch 7 pt III; SI 2011/1730, art 5(24); (saving temp to 1.4.2019) Pensions, 2014 c 19, sch 13 para 46(2)(4) (with SI 2015/1502, art 2(1)(2)(j))

sch 3 appl—Pension Schemes (NI), 1993 c 49, ss 80,98(3), sch 2 para 2(1)(2); Pensions, 1995 c 26, s 163(3)

power to am—Social Security Contributions (Trans of Functions, etc), 1999 c 2, s 23

am—SI 2005/2053, art 2, sch pt 3 para 19; Pensions, 2008 c 30, s 101, sch 2 paras 1-3; Pensions, 2011 c 19, s 19(5)(6); Marriage (Same Sex Couples), 2013 c 30, sch 4 para 26; SIs 2014/1954, reg 3(3); 2014/3229, sch 5 para 11(9); (prosp) Pension Schemes, 2015 c 8, sch 1 paras 8, 10

rep in pt—(prosp) Pension Schemes, 2015 c 8, sch 1 para 9

sch 4 am—Pensions, 1995 c 26, ss 137(6)(a)(b)(7), 151, sch 5 para 85; Welfare Reform and Pensions, 1999 c 30, s 18, sch 2 para 8; Pensions, 2007 c 22, s 12, sch 1 para 39; ibid, s 15, sch 4 para 60; SI 2008/948, art 3, sch 1; Pensions, 2014 c 19, sch 13 para 47(2)(3)

rep in pt—Pensions, 2007 c 22, s 27, sch 7 pt 7; Pensions, 2014 c 19, sch 13 para 47(4)

appl (mods)—Banking, 2009 c 1, ss 103, 145

sch 5 rep in pt—Crime and Cts, 2013 c 22, sch 13 para 89(2)(f)

sch 6 am—Social Security Contributions (Trans of Functions, etc), 1999 c 2, s 1(1), sch 1 para 63

rep in pt—Pensions, 1995 c 26, ss 151, 177, sch 5 para 86, sch 7 pt III

sch 7 rep in pt—Pensions, 1995 c 26, ss 122, 177, sch 3 para 47, sch 7 pt I; Crime and Cts, 2013 c 22, sch 13 para 89(2)(g)

sch 8 rep in pt—Police and Magistrates' Cts, 1994 c 29, s 93, sch 9 pt II; Pensions, 1995 c 26, s 177, sch 7 pts I,IV; Employment Rights, 1996 c 18, s 242, sch 3 pt I; Employment Tribunals, 1996 c 17, s 45, sch 3 pt I; (pt prosp) Social Security, 1998 c 14, s 86(2), sch 8; Welfare Reform and Pensions, 1999 c 30, s 88, sch 13 pt V; Child Support, Pensions and Social Security, 2000 c 19, s 85, sch 9 pt VI; SL(R), 2004 c 14, s 1(1), sch 1 pt 5/12; Finance, 2004 c 12, s 326, sch 42 pt 3, Note; Companies, 2006 c 46, s 1295, sch 16; (prosp) Welfare Reform, 2007 c 5, s 67, sch 8; SI 2008/948, art 3, sch 2

sch 9 rep in pt—Pensions, 1995 c 26, ss 173, 177, sch 6 para 16(2)(a)(c)(3), sch 7 pt IV; Pensions, 2004 c 35, s 320, sch 13 pt 1

am—Pensions, 1995 c 26, s 173, sch 6 para 16(2)(b)

c 49 *Pension Schemes (Northern Ireland)—N Irish*

c 50 **Statute Law (Repeals)**

s 1 excl—Flood Prevention and Land Drainage (S), 1997 c 36, s 6(1)

s 3 rep in pt—(prosp) SL(R), 1998 c 43, s 1(1), sch 1 pt X, Group 5

sch 1 excl—Flood Prevention and Land Drainage (S), 1997 c 36, s 6(1)

sch 2 rep in pt—Access to Justice, 1999 c 22, s 106, sch 15 pt III; SI 2001/1149, arts 3(2), 4(11), sch 2; Companies, 2006 c 46, s 1295, sch 16; Legal Services, 2007 c 29, s 210, sch 23; SL(R), 2008 c 12, s 1(1), sch 1 pt 3; Marine and Coastal Access, 2009 c 23, s 321, sch 22 pt 5

c 51 **European Economic Area**

s 2 restr—SI 1993/3183

excl—SI 1995/278, art 4

s 3 restr—SI 1995/484, reg 3

excl—SI 1995/732, reg 3

sch 1 rep in pt—SI 2006/5, reg 48, sch 7 para 6; (S) SSI 2006/1, reg 48, sch 7 para 1

2nd Session of 51st Parliament

c 52 *Consolidated Fund (No 3)*—rep Appropriation, 1995 c 19, ss 2, 3, sch(c)

1994

c 1   **Social Security (Contributions)**

c 2   **Statutory Sick Pay**

        s 1 rep in pt—SI 2006/1031, reg 49, sch 8

        s 5 am—Social Security Contributions (Trans of Functions, etc), 1999 c 2, s 1(1), sch 1
            para 64

c 3   **Non-Domestic Rating**

c 4   *Consolidated Fund*—rep Appropriation, 1996 c 45, s 3, sch(C)

c 5   *New Towns (Amendment)*—rep Housing and Regeneration, 2008 c 17, s 321, sch 16

c 6   *Mental Health (Amendment)*—rep SL(R), 2004 c 14, s 1(1), sch 1 pt 17/8

c 7   **Insolvency**

c 8   **Transport Police (Jurisdiction)**

c 9   **Finance**

        restr—Finance, 1995 c 4, s 86(11)(14)

        s 4 rep—Vehicle Excise and Registration, 1994 c 22, s 65, sch 5 pt I

        Pt 1 (Ch 2 ss 7-19) appl (mods)—SIs 2000/426, arts 4, 5; SI 2003/2758, art 4(a)

        s 7 subst—SI 2009/56, art 3, sch 1 para 197
            appl—SI 2010/594, art 4

        s 8 rep in pt—Finance, 2008 c 9, s 122, sch 40 para 21(d)(i)
            appl—SI 2010/594, art 4

        s 9 appl—Customs and Excise Management, 1979 c 2, ss 60B(2)(4), 92(6)(8), 100J, 101(4),
            107(2)(3), 108(4), 111(1), 114(2), 115(4), 116(3), 118G, 170A(1)(2); Alcoholic
            Liquor Duties, 1979 c 4, ss 8(2),10(2),13(3)(5), 15(4)(5)(7), 16(2)(3), 18(6),
            19(2), 20(1)(2), 21(3), 22(9), 24(4), 33(1)(5),34(2), 35(3), 41A(8), 44(2), 46(2),
            47(4)(5), 49(3), 54(5), 55(6), 55A(3), 56(2), 59(2), 61(2), 62(4)(6), 64(2), 67(2),
            69(3)(4), 71(1) (3), 75(5), 77(3)(4), 78(4), 82(2); Hydrocarbon Oil Duties, 1979
            c 5, ss 10(3)(4), 13(1)(2), 13AB(2)(5), 14(4)(5), 18(5), 20AA(4)(a), 20AAB(8),
            21(3), 22(1), 23(1)(1A), 24(4); Tobacco Products Duty, 1979 c 7, ss 7(2), 8E(3),
            8F(3), 8J(2); Betting and Gaming Duties, 1981 c 63, s 24(5), sch 1 paras 13(1)(2),
            14(3), sch 2 para 7(1)(2), sch 3 para 16(3), sch 4 para 16(1); Finance, 1993 c 34,
            ss 27(4), 28(3), 29(8); Finance, 1997 c 16, s 50(1), sch 5 pt I para 4(1); SI
            2010/594, art 4

            appl (mods)—Tobacco Products Duty, 1979 c 7, s 6B(2)(3)

            ext—Alcoholic Liquor Duties, 1979 c 4, sch 2A; Hydrocarbon Oil Duties, 1979 c 5,
            s 22(1AB); Finance, 1997 c 16, ss 12(5),13(1),15, sch 1 pt I paras 5(3),7 pt II
            para 10(3)

            am—Finance, 2000 c 17, s 28

        s 10 excl—Customs and Excise Management, 1979 c 2, ss 114(2),170A(2); Hydrocarbon
            Oil Duties, 1979 c 5, s 22(1A)
            appl—SI 2010/594, art 4

        s 10A added—Tribunals, Cts and Enforcement, 2007 c 15, s 62, sch 13 para 114
            rep—Finance, 2008 c 9, s 129, sch 43 para 3(1), (2)

        s 11 am—Finance, 1997 c 16, s 53(2)(9); Tribunals, Cts and Enforcement, 2007 c 15, s 62,
            sch 13 paras 113, 115
            appl—SI 2010/594, art 4

        s 11A added—Finance, 1995 c 4, s 16(1)(4)
            appl—SI 2010/594, art 4

        s 12 ext—Hydrocarbon Oil Duties, 1979 c 5, s 20AAB(5)
            am—Finance 1997 c 16, ss 13(2), 15, sch 2 pt II para 7, s 50(1)(2), sch 5 pt II
            para 6(2)(a), sch 6 paras 1(3), 7; Finance, 1998 c 36, s 20, sch 2, paras 7,12;
            SI 2001/3022, reg 9; Finance, 2004 c 12, s 4(3)(5); Finance, (No 3), 2010 c 33, s
            29, sch 13 para 3(1)-(5); Finance, 2012 c 14, sch 24 para 47; Finance, 2014 c 26,
            sch 28 para 16(b)
            mod—Serious Crime, 2007 c 27, s 63, sch 6 para 22
            appl—SI 2010/594, art 4; Finance, 2014 c 26, s 167(3)
            rep in pt—Finance (No 3), 2010 c 33, s 29, sch 13 para 3(6); Finance, 2014 c 26, sch
            28 para 16(a)

        s 12A added—Finance, 1997 c 16, s 50(2), sch 6 paras 1(1), 7
            rep in pt—Finance, 1998 c 36, s 165, sch 27 pt I(5), Note
            am—Finance, 1998 c 36, s 20, sch 2, paras 8(2)(3),12; Finance, 1998 c 36, s 20,
            sch 2, paras 8(3),12; Finance, 2002 c 23, s 4(1)(2), sch 1, para 4(1)(2); Finance,
            2008 c 9, s 16, sch 6 paras 17, 18, 33, 34; Finance (No 3), 2010 c 33, s 29, sch
            13 para 5
            saved —SI 2005/3472, reg 13(4)
            appl—SI 2010/594, art 4

1994
c 9 *continued*

s 12B added—Finance, 1997 c 16, s 50(2), sch 6 paras 1(1), 7
　　am—Finance, 1998 c 36, s 20, sch 2, paras 9(2)(3),12; Finance, 1998 c 36, s 20,
　　　　sch 2, paras 9(4),12; Finance, 2001 c 9, s 3(4); Finance, 2002 c 23, s 4(1)(2),
　　　　sch 1, para 4(1)(3); Finance, 2008 c 9, s 16, sch 6 paras 17, 19, 33, 35
　　mod—Finance, 1997 c 16, ss 12(6)(a), 15
　　rep in pt—Finance, 1997 c 16, s 113, sch 18 pt II Notes 1,2
　　appl—SI 2010/594, art 4
s 13 am—Finance, 1997 c 16, s 50(2), sch 6 paras 1(3), 7, s 53(3)(9)
　　appl—SI 2010/594, art 4
s 13A added—SI 2009/56, art 3, sch 1 para 198
　　mod—Finance, 2014 c 26, s 182(1)
　　appl—SI 2010/594, art 4
　　rep in pt—Finance, 2014 c 26, sch 28 para 17
　　am—Finance, 2012 c 14, sch 25 para 10; Finance, 2015 c 11, s 54(6)
s 14 appl—Betting and Gaming Duties, 1981 c 63,sch 4A para 6(1); SIs 1995/1046,
　　　　reg 7(3), 2351, reg 2; Finance, 1997 c 16, ss 11(7), 15; SI 2010/594, art 4
　　mod—Betting and Gaming Duties, 1981 c 63, sch 4 para 7A; Finance, 1995 c 4,
　　　　s 5(4)(6); Finance, 2014 c 26, s 182(3)
　　am—Finance, 1995 c 4, s 20(4)(5); Finance, 1997 c 16, s 50(2), sch 6 paras 1(2), 7;
　　　　Finance, 1998 c 36, s 20, sch 2, paras 10(a)(b)(c),12; Finance, 1999 c 16,
　　　　s 130(1)(4); Finance, 2002 c 23, s 4(1)(2), sch 1, para 4(1)(4); ibid, s 21(2)(3);
　　　　Finance, 2004 c 12, s 4(4)(5); Finance, 2008 c 9, s 16, sch 6 paras 17, 20, 33, 36;
　　　　SI 2009/56, art 3, sch 1 para 199
　　rep in pt—SI 2009/56, art 3, sch 1 para 199(5)
　　ext—Finance, 1997 c 16, ss 13(1), 15, sch 1 pt I para 8(11) pt II para 9(5), s 50(1),
　　　　sch 5 pt V; SI 1997/534, regs 3,5
s 14A added—SI 2009/56, art 3, sch 1 para 200
s 15 appl—SI 1995/1046, reg 7(3); Finance, 1997 c 16, ss 11(7), 15
　　mod—Betting and Gaming Duties, 1981 c 63, sch 4 para 7A; Finance, 1995 c 4,
　　　　s 5(4)(6); Finance, 2014 c 26, s 182(3)
　　ext—Finance, 1997 c 16, ss 13(1), 15, sch 1pt I para 8(11), pt II para 9(5), s 50(1),
　　　　sch 5 pt V para 19(1)
　　am—SI 2009/56, art 3, sch 1 para 201
ss 15A-15F added—SI 2009/56, art 3, sch 1 para 202
s 15A mod—Finance, 2014 c 26, ss 172(1), 182(3); ibid, sch 27 paras 2(3)(4), 4(3)(4),
　　　　6(4)(5),7(3)(4)
s 15B mod—Finance, 2014 c 26, s 182(3)
ss 15C-15F mod—Finance, 2014 c 26, ss 172(1), 182(3); ibid, sch 27 paras 2(3)(4), 4(3)(4),
　　　　6(40(5), 7(3)(4)
s 16 appl—SI 1995/1046, reg 7(3); Finance, 1997 c 16, ss 11(7), 15
　　am—Finance, 2001 c 9, s 15, sch 3 pt 4, paras 16, 21, 22; SIs 2009/56, art 3, sch 1
　　　　para 203; 2014/1264, art 2
　　mod—Betting and Gaming Duties, 1981 c 63, sch 4 para 7A; Finance, 1995 c 4,
　　　　s 5(4)(6); SIs 1995/2351, reg 3; 1997/534, regs 4,6; Finance, 2014 c 26, ss
　　　　172(1), 182(3); ibid, sch 27 paras 2(3)(4), 4(3)(4), 6(40(5), 7(3)(4)
　　am—Finance, 1995 c 4, s 16(3)(4); Finance, 1998 c 36, s 20, sch 2, paras 11,12
　　ext—Finance, 1997 c 16, ss 13(1), 15, sch 1 pt I para 8(11), pt II para 9(5), s 50(1),
　　　　sch 5 pt V para 19(1)
s 17 am—Vehicle Excise and Registration, 1994 c 22, s 63, sch 3 para 32; SI 2009/56, art 3,
　　　　sch 1 para 204
s 18 rep in pt—Value Added Tax, 1994 c 23, s 100(2), sch 15; Finance, 1997 c 16, s 113,
　　　　sch 18 pt V(2) Note
　　am—Finance, 1997 c 16, s 53(4)(9)
s 22 am—Crim Procedure (Conseq Provns)(S), 1995 c 40, s 5, sch 4 para 89(2)
　　rep in pt—Civil Evidence, 1995 c 38, s 15(2), sch 2; NI SI 1997/2983, art 13(2), sch 2;
　　　　Youth Justice and Crim Evidence, 1999 c 23, s 67, sch 6; (NI) SI 1999/2789,
　　　　art 40(3), sch 3; Crim Justice, 2003 c 44, s 332, sch 37 pt 6; SI 2004/1501,
　　　　art 46(2), sch 2
s 25 am—Crim Procedure (Conseq Provns)(S), 1995 c 40, s 5, sch 4 para 89(3)
s 28 am—Finance, 2012 c 14, sch 23 para 17
s 29 am—Finance, 2012 c 14, sch 23 para 18(2)(3)
　　rep in pt—Finance, 2012 c 14, sch 23 para 18(4)
s 29A added—Finance, 2012 c 14, sch 23 para 19

1994
c 9 *continued*

s 30 am—(retrosp) Finance, 1995 c 4, s 15(2)(3); Finance, 1997 c 16, s 9(1)-(3); Finance,
    2000 c 17, s 18(1)-(6)(8); Finance, 2002 c 23, s 121; SIs 2006/2693, art 2;
    2007/22, art 2; Finance, 2007 c 11, s 12(1)-(5); Finance, 2009 c 10, s 17(1), sch
    5 paras 1, 2(1)(2); SI 2009/193, art 2; Finance, 2010 c 13, s 14(1); Finance, 2012
    c 14, sch 23 paras 4(2)-(6), 8(2), 20; Finance, 2013 c 29, s
    185(2)(a)(b)(3)(a)(b)(4)(a)(b); Finance, 2014 c 26, ss 78, 79(4)(5)(a)(b)(e)
    rep in pt—Finance, 2002 c 23, ss 121(1)(2)(5), 141, sch 40 pt 4(1), Note; Finance,
    2008 c 9, s 153(1); Finance, 2009 c 10, s 17, sch 5 paras 1, 2(1)(3); Finance,
    2012 c 14, sch 23 para 8(3); Finance, 2014 c 26, s 79(3)(5)(c)(d)
s 30A added—Finance, 2012 c 14, sch 23 para 9
    am—Finance, 2012 c 14, sch 23 para 21; Finance, 2014 c 26, s 79(8) (9)(c)(ii)(iii)
    rep in pt—Finance, 2014 c 26, s 79(7)(9)(a)(b)(c)(i)
s 31 mod—SI 1994/1738
    am—Finance, 1996 c 8, s 13(1); Finance, 2000 c 17, s 19(1)(3)(6); Finance, 2015 c 11,
    s 57(1)
    rep in pt—Finance, 2000 c 17, ss 19(1)(2)(4)(6),156, sch 40 pt I(4), Note 1
s 32 am—Finance, 1996 c 8, s 13(2)(a)(b)
s 33 rep in pt—Finance, 2008 c 9, s 123, sch 41 para 25(e)(i)
    am—Finance, 2012 c 14, sch 23 para 10(2)-(5)
s 33A added—Finance, 2012 c 14, sch 23 para 11
s 34 am—Finance, 1998 c 36, s 15(2); Finance, 2012 c 14, sch 23 para 12(b)
    rep in pt—Finance, 2012 c 14, sch 23 para 12(a)
s 34A added—Finance, 1998 c 36, s 15(1)
s 38 am—Finance, 2013 c 29, s 186(1)
s 39 subst—Finance, 2009 c 10, s 17, sch 5 paras 1, 3
s 41 am—SI 2015/664, sch 2 para 7(2)
s 41A added—Finance, 2012 c 14, sch 23 para 13
s 42 am—Finance, 2009 c 10, s 17, sch 5 paras 1, 4
s 43 rep in pt—Finance, 2000 c 17, ss 19(5)(6),156, sch 40 pt I(4), Note 1
    am—Finance, 2012 c 14, sch 23 para 22(2)(3)
ss 45,47 rep—Value Added Tax, 1994 c 23, s 100(2), sch 15
s 50 am—Finance, 1997 c 16, ss 23(2), 24; SI 2012/266, art 2(2)
s 51 subst—Finance, 1997 c 16, ss 21(1), 24
    am—Finance, 1999 c 16, s 125; Finance (No 2), 2010 c 31, s 4(1); Finance (No. 2),
    2015 c 33, s 47(1)
ss 51A, 51B added—Finance, 1997 c 16, ss 22(1), 24, 25(1)(2)
s 52A added—Finance, 1997 c 16, s 25
    am—Finance, 1998 c 36, s 147(2)(3)(5); Corporation Tax, 2010 c 4, s 1177, sch 1
    paras 280, 281
    rep in pt—Finance, 1998 c 36, ss 147(4)(5),165, sch 27 pt V(1), Note
s 53 am—Finance, 1995 c 4, s 34, sch 5 paras 2(2)(a)(3)(4)
    rep in pt—Finance, 1995 c 4, ss 34,162, sch 5 para 2(2)(a)(b)(4), sch 29 pt VII
s 53A added—Finance, 1995 c 4, s 34, sch 5 para 4
    am—Finance, 1997 c 16, s 27(2)
s 53AA added—Finance, 1997 c 16, s 26
s 55 am—Finance, 1997 c 16, s 27(3)
ss 57, 58 rep—Finance, 2008 c 9, s 142(1)(a)
s 59 am—Finance, 1995 c 4, s 34, sch 5 para 5(2)-(4); Finance, 1997 c 16, s 27(6); SIs
    2009/56, art 3, sch 1 para 205; 2012/266, art 2(3)
    rep in pt—SI 2009/56, art 3, sch 1 para 205(4)
    ext—Finance, 1997 c 16, s 50(1), sch 5 pt V para 19(2)
ss 59A-59G added—SI 2009/56, art 3, sch 1 para 206
s 59G am—SI 2014/1264, art 3
s 60 ext—Finance, 1997 c 16, s 50(1), sch 5 pt V para 19(2)
    am—SI 2009/56, art 3, sch 1 para 207
    rep in pt—SI 2009/56, art 3, sch 1 para 207(3)(5)
s 62 am—Finance, 1997 c 16, s 27(7); SI 2003/2096, arts 4, 6, sch pt 1 para 23
s 63 am—Finance, 1997 c 16, s 27(8); SI 2009/1890, art 4
s 65 rep in pt—Finance, 2008 c 9, s 142(1)(b)
    am—Finance, 2008 c 9, s 143
s 67A added—Finance, 1997 c 16, s 29(1)(3)
    appl (mods)—Finance, 1998 c 36, s 146(5); Finance (No 2), 2010 c 31, s 4(3)
    mod—Finance (No. 2), 2015 c 33, s 47(5)

1994
c 9 *continued*

s 67B added—Finance, 1997 c 16, s 29(1)(3)
    appl (mods)—Finance, 1998 c 36, s 146(5)
    mod—Finance (No. 2), 2015 c 33, s 47(5)
s 67C added—Finance, 1997 c 16, s 29(1)(3)
    appl (mods)—Finance, 1998 c 36, s 146(5); Finance (No 2), 2010 c 31, s 4(3)
    mod—Finance (No. 2), 2015 c 33, s 47(5)
s 69 subst—Finance, 1997 c 16, ss 23(1), 24
    am—SI 2012/266, art 2(4)
ss 69A-69D added—SI 2012/266, art 2(5)
s 70 rep in pt—SI 1994/1698
    am—SI 1994/1698
s 72 am—Finance, 1997 c 16, ss 28(1)(2), 30(1)-(3); Finance, 2010 c 13, s 51(1)-(4)
s 73 am—Finance, 1995 c 4, s 34, sch 5 para 6; Finance, 1997 c 16, ss 21(2), 24, 27(9)(10);
    SIs 2009/56, art 3, sch 1 para 208; 2012/266, art 2(6)
    rep in pt—Finance, 2008 c 9, s 142(1)(c)
s 74 am—Finance, 1997 c 16, ss 22(2), 24; Finance, 2010 c 13, s 51(5)
ss 75, 76 rep—Income Tax, 2007 c 3, s 1031, sch 3
s 77 rep in pt—Finance, 1999 c 16, s 139, sch 20 pt III(3), Note 2; ibid, sch 20 pt III(4),
    Note; ibid, sch 20 pt III(5), Note 2; Income Tax, 2007 c 3, s 1031, sch 3;
    Finance, 2009 c 10, s 5, sch 1 para 6(f)
s 78 rep—Income Tax, 2007 c 3, s 1031, sch 3
s 79 rep in pt—Finance, 1999 c 16, s 139, sch 20 pt III(6), Note; Income Tax, 2007 c 3, s
    1031, sch 3
s 81 rep in pt—Finance, 1999 c 16, s 139, sch 20 pt III(7), Note 4
s 83 rep—Finance (No 2), 1997 c 58), s 52, sch 8 pt II(2), Note
s 84 rep—Finance, 1999 c 16, s 139, sch 20 pt III(15), Note
s 86 rep—Corporation Tax, 2010 c 4, s 1181, sch 3 pt 1
ss 88, 89 rep—Income Tax (Earnings and Pensions), 2003 c 1, s 724(1), sch 8 pt 1
s 92 rep—Finance, 1998 c 36, s 165, sch 27 pt III(31), Note
s 93 rep in pt—Finance, 2011 c 11, sch 11 para 10(a)
s 94 rep—Finance, 2011 c 11, sch 11 para 10(a)
ss 98, 99 rep—Finance, 1997 c 16, ss 61(2)(3), 113, sch 18 pt VI(3) Notes 1-3
ss 103-107 rep —Finance, 2004 c 12, s 326, sch 42 pt 3, Note
s 108 rep in pt—Income Tax (Earnings and Pensions), 2003 c 1, s 724(1), sch 8 pt 1
ss 109, 110 rep—Income Tax (Earnings and Pensions), 2003 c 1, s 724(1), sch 8 pt 1
s 111 rep—Finance, 1996 c 8, s 205, sch 41 pt V(1)
s 113 rep—Corporation Tax, 2010 c 4, s 1181, sch 3 pt 1
ss 114-116 rep—Finance, 2002 c 23, s 141, sch 40 pt 3(10), Note 2
s 117 rep—Capital Allowances, 2001 c 2, s 580, sch 4
s 118 rep in pt—Finance, 1994 c 9, s 258, sch 26 pt V Note 5; Finance, 2000 c 17,
      ss 73(1)(2),156, sch 40 pt II(8), Note 3; Capital Allowances, 2001 c 2, s 580,
      sch 4
    mod—Finance, 1996 c 8, s 135(5)
    am—Finance, 1996 c 8, s 135, sch 21 para 48; Finance, 1999 c 16, s 93(1)(2), sch 11
      para 8; Finance, 2000 c 17, s 73(1)(2)
s 119 rep in pt—Capital Allowances, 2001 c 2, s 580, sch 4
ss 120, 121 rep—Capital Allowances, 2001 c 2, s 580, sch 4
s 122 rep —Finance, 2007 c 11, s 114, sch 27 pt 2
s 123 rep in pt—Finance, 1997 c 16, ss 76, 113, sch 10 pt I para 7(1), sch 18 pt VI(10),
    Note 1; Income Tax, 2007 c 3, s 1031, sch 3
s 124 rep—Finance, 1996 c 8, s 205, sch 41 pt V(21)
ss 125-132 rep—Income Tax (Earnings and Pensions), 2003 c 1, s 724(1), sch 8 pt 1
s 134 rep—Finance, 2009 c 10, s 36, sch 16 para 5(b)
s 135 rep—Corporation Tax, 2010 c 4, s 1181, sch 3 pt 1
s 137 rep in pt—Income Tax, 2007 c 3, s 1031, sch 3 pt 2
s 139 rep—Income Tax (Earnings and Pensions), 2003 c 1, s 724(1), sch 8 pt 1
s 140 rep—Corporation Tax, 2010 c 4, s 1181, sch 3 pt 1
s 141 rep—Corporation Tax, 2009 c 4, s 1326, sch 3 pt 1
s 142 rep in pt—SI 2001/3629, art 109, sch
s 143 rep—Finance, 1995 c 4, s 162, sch 29, pt VIII, Note
ss 144, 145 rep —Corporation Tax, 2009 c 4, s 1326, sch 3 pt 1
Pt 4 Ch 2 (ss 147-177) excl—(saving) Finance, 1996 c 8, ss 101(1),105(1)
    restr—Finance, 1998 c 36, s 108, sch 16

1994
c 9 Pt 4 *continued*

    mod—(saving) Finance, 1996 c 8, s 105, sch 15 pt I para 25(2)(4)

    appl—(retrosp to 30.9.2002) Finance, 2003 c 14, s 177(9)(11)

ss 147-175 rep—Finance, 2002 c 23, ss 83(1)(c)(2)(3), 141, sch 28, sch 40 pt 3(13), Note 2

s 176 rep in pt—Finance, 1995 c 4, s 162, sch 29 pt VIII Note; SL(R), 2013 c 2, sch 1 pt
    10(1)

s 177 rep—Finance, 2002 c 23, ss 83(1)(c)(2)(3), 141, sch 28, sch 40 pt 3(13), Note 2

s 180 rep—Finance, 2001 c 9, s 110, sch 33 pt 2(13), Note

ss 181-183 rep—Finance, 1998 c 36, s 165, sch 27 pt III(28), Note

s 186 rep—Finance, 2001 c 9, s 110, sch 33 pt 2(13), Note

s 187 rep—Finance, 2008 c 9, s 113, sch 36 para 92(c)

ss 188, 189 rep—Finance, 2001 c 9, s 110, sch 33 pt 2(13), Note

ss 195,197 rep—Finance, 1998 c 36, s 165, sch 27 pt III(28), Note

s 198 rep and superseded—Finance, 1995 c 4, s 162, sch 29 pt VIII

ss 200-208 rep—Income Tax (Trading and Other Income), 2005 c 5, s 884, sch 3

ss 209, 210 rep—Income Tax, 2007 c 3, s 1031, sch 3

s 211 rep in pt—Capital Allowances, 2001 c 2, s 580, sch 4

ss 212-213 rep—Capital Allowances, 2001 c 2, s 580, sch 4

s 214 rep in pt—Capital Allowances, 2001 c 2, s 580, sch 4; Income Tax, 2007 c 3, s 1031,
    sch 3; Corporation Tax, 2010 c 4, s 1181, sch 3 pt 1

s 215 rep—Corporation Tax, 2009 c 4, s 1326, sch 3 pt 1

s 216 rep in pt—Income Tax (Trading and Other Income), 2005 c 5, s 884, sch 3

s 217 rep—Taxation (International and Other Provns), 2010 c 8, s 378, sch 10 pt 1

s 218 am—Finance, 1995 c 4, s 102(2)

Pt 4 Ch 5 (ss 219-230) appl—Finance, 1993 c 34, sch 20A; Finance, 1995 c 4,
    ss 127(16)(a), 129(4); Finance, 2003 c 14, s 152, sch 26 para 6(2)(a)

    mod—SI 1997/2681, reg 3(2)

s 219 am—Finance (No 2), 1997 c 58, s 22(2)(4)(7); SI 2001/3629, arts 83, 87(a);
    Corporation Tax, 2009 c 4, s 1322, sch 1 paras 391, 392; Corporation Tax,
    2010 c 4, s 1177, sch 1 paras 280, 282

    rep in pt—Finance, 1997 c 58, ss 22(3)(7), 52, sch 8 pt II(5), Note; Finance, 2003 c
    14, s 216, sch 43 pt 3(6), Note; Income Tax (Trading and Other Income), 2005
    c 5, s 884, sch 3; Finance, 2009 c 10, s 34, sch 14 para 18

s 220 am—SIs 2001/3629, arts 83, 87(b); 2007/1616, reg 2; Corporation Tax, 2009 c 4, s
    1322, sch 1 paras 391, 393

s 221 rep—Finance (No 2), 2005 c 22, ss 45(4)(9), 70, sch 11 pt 2(11), Note

s 222 am—SI 2001/3629, arts 83, 87(c)

    rep in pt—Finance, 1996 c 8, s 205, sch 41 pt V(18); Finance, 1997 c 16, ss 76,113,
    sch 10 pt I, paras 6(b),7(1), sch 18 pt VI(10), Note 1

s 223 mod—SI 1997/2681 reg 5(1)

s 224 rep—Finance, 2000 c 17, ss 107(11)(12),156, sch 40 pt II(16), Note 2

s 225 excl—SI 1995/351, reg 6(1)(c)

    am—Finance, 2002 c 23, s 86, sch 32, paras 6-9; Finance, 2008 c 9, s 118, sch 39
    para 64; Corporation Tax, 2009 c 4, s 1322, sch 1 paras 391, 394; Finance,
    2012 c 14, s 25(1)

s 226 am—SI 2001/3629, arts 83, 87(d); Finance, 2002 c 23, s 83(1)(b)(3), sch 27, para 16;
    Corporation Tax, 2009 c 4, s 1322, sch 1 paras 391, 395

    rep in pt—Finance, 2002 c 23, ss 80, 141, sch 24, para 7, sch 40 pt 3(10), Note 1,
    (11), Note

s 227 excl—SI 1997/2681 reg 4(2)

s 227A added—Finance, 2007 c 11, s 33

    am—Corporation Tax, 2010 c 4, s 1177, sch 1 paras 280, 283

s 227B added—Finance, 2007 c 11, s 43

    am—SI 2013/463, art 7(2)(a)-(c)

s 227C added—Finance, 2012 c 14, sch 20 para 8

s 229 am—Finance, 1995 c 4, s 83(2); SI 2001/3629, arts 83, 87(e); Finance, 2007 c 11, s
    47, sch 14 para 19; Corporation Tax, 2009 c 4, s 1322, sch 1 paras 391, 396

    rep in pt—Finance, 1997 c 16, ss 76,113, sch 10 pt I, paras 6(b),7(1), sch 18 pt VI(10),
    Note 1; Finance (No 2), 2005 c 22, s 70, sch 11 pt 2(11), Note

    am —(and renumbered) Finance (No 2), 2005 c 22, s 45(5)-(7)(8)(b)(9)

s 230 appl—Finance, 1995 c 4, s 127(16)(b); Finance, 1996 c 8, s 99, sch 11 pt II para 7(2);
    Finance, 2002 c 23, s 65(5); Finance, 2003 c 14, s 152, sch 26 para 6(2)(b)

    am—SI 2001/3629, arts 83, 85, 87(f); Finance, 2002 c 23, s 86, sch 32, paras 6, 10;
    SIs 2005/1538, art 3; 2006/3273, art 3; 2013/636, sch para 4

1994
c 9 *continued*

s 233 am—Finance, 1999 c 16, s 101(1)(2)
s 235 rep in pt—Finance, 2006 c 25, s 178, sch 26 pt 5(1)
Pt 6 (ss 239-245) heading am—SI 2005/82, reg 3(1)(2)
s 239 am —Finance (No 2), 2005 c 22, s 48(3)(5)
s 240 replaced (by, ss 240, 240A)—Finance, 1999 c 16, ss 109(3)(4), 122, sch 12 para 4
s 241 am—Finance, 1999 c 16, ss 112(4)(6), 122, sch 14 para 30
    rep in pt—Finance, 1999 c 16, s 138, sch 20 pt V(2), Notes 1, 2
s 242 am—Finance, 1999 c 16, ss 112(4)(6), 122, sch 14 para 31
s 243 am—Finance, 1999 c 16, ss 112(4)(6), 122, sch 14 para 32
s 245 rep in pt—SI 2003/2867, reg 2, sch pt 1 para 22(a)
    am—SI 2003/2867, reg 2, sch pt 1 para 22(b)(c); Finance (No 2), 2005 c 22,
      s 48(2)(5); SI 2005/82, reg 3(1)(3)
s 249 excl—(retrosp to 1.4.2002) Income and Corporation Taxes, 1988 c 1, s 747(1B)
    rep—Corporation Tax, 2009 c 4, ss 1322, 1326, sch 1 paras 391, 397, sch 3 pt 1
s 250 rep—Corporation Tax, 2009 c 4, ss 1322, 1326, sch 1 paras 391, 397, sch 3 pt 1
s 251 rep in pt —(saving) Finance, 1996 c 8, ss 105(1),205, sch 41 pt V(3), Note; Income
    Tax, 2007 c 3, s 1031, sch 3
s 255 rep—Finance, 2008 c 9, s 113, sch 36 para 92(c)
s 256 rep in pt—Finance (No 3), 2010 c 33, s 29, sch 13 para 2(a)
s 353 restr—Finance, 1995 c 4, s 123, sch 22 pt I para 2(3)-(5)
sch 2 rep in pt—Vehicle Excise and Registration, 1994 c 22, s 65, sch 5 pt I
sch 3 rep in pt—Finance, 1994 c 9, s 6, sch 3 para 3(10)(11); Finance, 1995 c 4, s 162,
    sch 29 pt III
sch 4 rep in pt—Finance, 1994 c 9, ss 5(6)(7), 162, sch 29 pt I; Finance, 1996 c 8, s 205,
    sch 41 pt I; Finance, 1997 c 16, s 113, sch 18 pt II Notes 1, 2; Finance, 2006 c
    25, s 178, sch 26 pt 1(1); Finance, 2008 c 9, s 123, sch 41 para 25(e)(ii);
    Finance, 2012 c 14, s 187(2)(c)
sch 5 appl—SI 1995/1046, reg 7(3)
    am—Finance, 1995 c 4, s 5, sch 2 para 8, s 16(2)(4); Finance, 1999 c 16, s 130(2)(4);
    Finance, 2000 c 17, s 10(5); Finance, 2001 c 9, s 15, sch 3 pt 4,
    paras 17(1)-(3)(4), 21, 22; Finance, 2002 c 23, s 12(1)(6)(7)(b), sch 4 pt 2, para
    12; Finance, 2008 c 9, ss 125, 126(1), sch 42 paras 1-7; Finance, 2014 c 26, sch
    21 para 9; ibid, sch 28 para 18(3)(b); Finance, 2015 c 11, s 54(7)
    rep in pt—Finance, 1995 c 4, ss 16(2)(4), 162, sch 29, pt IV; Finance, 2006 c 25, s
    178, sch 26 pt 1(1); Finance, 2012 c 14, s 187(2)(d); ibid, sch 39 para 52(2);
    Finance, 2014 c 26, sch 28 para 18(2)(3)(a)(4)
sch 5A added—Finance, 2009 c 10, s 17, sch 5 paras 1, 5
    am—Finance, 2013 c 29, s 186(2); Finance, 2014 c 26, s 80(1)(b)
    rep in pt—Finance, 2014 c 26, ss 79(10), 80(1)(a)
sch 6 power to am—Finance, 1996 c 8, s 197(2)(a)(7)
    am—Finance, 1996 c 8, s 197(6)(a)(7); (retrosp) Finance, 1997 c 16, s 50(1), sch 5
    pt III paras 7(2)-(4), 8(1)(2); SI 2009/56, art 3, sch 1 para 209
    rep in pt—Finance, 1996 c 8, s 205, sch 41 pt VIII(1); Finance, 1997 c 16, ss 50, 113,
    sch 5 pt III para 8(1)(2), sch 18 pt V(1) Note; Finance, 2001 c 9, ss 15, 110,
    sch 3 pt 4, paras 20-22, sch 33 pt 1(4), Note; Enterprise, 2002 c 40, s 278(2),
    sch 26
sch 6A added—Finance, 1997 c 16, ss 22(3), 24, sch 4
    am—Finance, 1998 c 36, s 146(1)(3); Finance, 2003 c 14, s 194; SI 2009/219, art 2;
    Corporation Tax, 2010 c 4, s 1177, sch 1 paras 280, 284; SI 2011/661, arts 3,
    4
sch 7 rep in pt—Civil Evidence, 1995 c 38, s 15(2), sch 2; Finance, 1996 c 8, s 205, sch 41
    pt VIII(1) Finance, 1997 c 16, s 113, sch 18 pt V(2), Note; (NI) SI 1997/2983,
    art 13(2), sch 2; Youth Justice and Crim Evidence, 1999 c 23, s 67, sch 6;
    SI 1999/2789, art 40(3), sch 3; Enterprise, 2002 c 40, s 278(2), sch 26; Crim
    Justice, 2003 c 44, s 332, sch 37 pt 6; SI 2004/1501, art 46(2), sch 2; Commrs
    for Revenue and Customs, 2005 c 11, ss 50(6), 52(2), sch 4 para 53, sch 5;
    Finance, 2007 c 11, ss 84, 114, sch 22 paras 3, 9, sch 27 pt 5; Finance, 2008 c
    9, s 122, sch 40 para 21(d)(ii); ibid, s 123, sch 41 para 25(e)(iii); ibid, s 129,
    sch 43 para 3(1), (3); ibid, s 138, sch 44 para 5(b); ibid, s 142(1)(d); SIs
    2009/3054, arts 3, 6, sch; 2010/530, art 2, sch
    power to am—Finance, 1996 c 8, s 197(2)(b)(7)
    power to mod—Finance, 1997 c 16, s 50(1), sch 5 pt I para 3

1994

c 9 sch 7 *continued*

am—Crim Procedure (Conseq Provns)(S), 1995 c 40, s 5, sch 4 para 89(4); Finance, 1995 c 4, s 34, sch 5 paras 7, 8(1)(2), 9; Finance, 1996 c 8, s 197(6)(b)(c)(7); Finance 1997 c 16, ss 27(1), 50(1), sch 5 pt I, pt II paras 5(2),6(2)(b), s 53(5)(9)(retrosp) ibid, s 50(1), sch 5 pt III paras 9(1)-(4),10(1)(2); SI 1997/2781 art 8(1), sch pt II para 124; Crim. Justice and Police, 2001 c 16, s 70, sch 2 pt 2, para 13(1)(2)(g); SIs 2002/1397, art 12, sch pt I, para 10; SI 2004/355, art 4; Tribunals, Cts and Enforcement, 2007 c 15, s 62, sch 13 paras 113, 116; Finance, 2008 c 9, s 138, sch 44 para 5(a); Finance, 2009 c 10, s 98, sch 50 para 1; ibid, s 99, sch 51 paras 1-4; SI 2009/571, art 8, sch 1; Financial Services, 2012 c 21, sch 18 para 79(2); SI 2015/664, sch 2 para 7(3)

ext—Finance, 1997 c 16, s 50(1), sch 5 pt I para 4(2); Crim. Justice and Police, 2001 c 16, s 50, sch 1 pt 1, para 57

see—(trans of functions) SI 1997/2781, arts 4(3), 7

excl—SI 2004/674, reg 22, sch 2 para 4(1)

appl (mods)—SI 2004/674, reg 22, sch 2 para 4(2)

sch 7A added—SIs 1994/1698

am—SIs 1997/1627,art 2(a)(b); 2001/3649, art 346(1)-(12); Finance, 2013 c 29, s 201(2)(a)(b)(3)(4); SI 2014/2856, arts 2, 3

rep in pt—SI 1996/2955, art 2; (prosp) Welfare Reform, 2012 c 5, sch 14 pt 9

sch 8 rep in pt—Finance, 1999 c 16, s 139, sch 20 pt III(3)-(5), Notes; Income Tax, 2007 c 3, s 1031, sch 3; Taxation (International and Other Provns), 2010 c 8, s 378, sch 10 pt 1

sch 9 rep in pt—Finance, 1995 c 4, s 42(3)-(5), 162, sch 29 pt VIII; Finance (No 2), 1997 c 58, s 52, sch 8 pt II(9) Note; Finance, 1999 c 16, s 139, sch 20 pt III)(7), 2 Note 4; Income Tax (Trading and Other Income), 2005 c 5, s 884, sch 3; Income Tax, 2007 c 3, s 1031, sch 3

sch 10 rep—Finance (No 2), 1997 c 58, s 52, sch 8 pt II(2) Note; Income Tax, 2007 c 3, s 1031, sch 3

sch 14 rep in pt—Corporation Tax, 2009 c 4, s 1326, sch 3 pt 1; Corporation Tax, 2010 c 4, s 1181, sch 3 pt 1; SL(R), 2013 c 2, s 1, sch 1 pt 10(1)

sch 15 rep in pt—Finance, 1996 c 8, s 205, sch 41 pt V(11); Finance, 1998 c 36, s 165, sch 27 pt III(13), Note 2; Finance, 2000 c 17, s 156, sch 40 pt II(5), Note 2; Finance, 2001 c 9, s 110, sch 33 pt 2(3), Notes 2, 5, 6; Income Tax, 2007 c 3, s 1031, sch 3

sch 16 rep in pt—Finance, 1995 c 4, s 162, sch 29 pt VIII, Note; Finance 1997 c 16, ss 76, 113, sch 10 pt I para 7(1), sch 18 pt VI (10) Note 1 Finance (No 2), 1997 c 58, s 52, sch 8 pt II(6)(11) Note; Finance, 1998 c 36, s 165, sch 27 pt III(2), Note; Finance, 2008 c 9, s 66(4)(e); SI 2009/2035, art 2, sch; SL(R), 2013 c 2, s 1, sch 1 pt 10(1)

sch 17 rep in pt—Finance, 1995 c 4, s 162, sch 29 pt VIII, Note; Finance, 1999 c 16, s 139, sch 20 pt III(7), Note 4; Finance, 2004 c 12, ss 77(2)-(6), 326, sch 42 pt 2(7), Note; Income Tax, 2007 c 3, s 1031, sch 3; Corporation Tax, 2010 c 4, s 1181, sch 3 pt 1; SL(R), 2013 c 2, s 1, sch 1 pt 10(1)

sch 18 rep—Finance, 2002 c 23, s 141, sch 40 pt 3(13), Note 2

sch 19 am—SI 1994/1813; Finance, 1995 c 4, s 74, sch 17 pt III para 22

rep in pt—SI 1994/1813; Finance, 1996 c 8, ss 131(3),205, sch 41 pt V(6)(12); Finance, 1998 c 36, s 165, sch 27 pt III(28), Note; Finance, 2001 c 9, s 110, sch 33 pt 2(13)(14), Note 2; Finance, 2007 c 11, s 114, sch 27 pt 5; Finance, 2008 c 9, s 113, sch 36 para 92(c); ibid, s 138, sch 44 para 11(a); Taxation (International and Other Provns), 2010 c 8, s 378, sch 10 pt 13; SL(R), 2013 c 2, s 1, sch 1 pt 10(1)

sch 20 mod—Finance, 1995 c 4, ss 122(4),123, sch 22 pt I paras 1(1)-(3),3(1)-(3), 5(3)(4), 6(1)-(3), 7(2)(3), 9(2)(3), 10(2)(3), 12-14

am—Finance, 1995 c 4, s 122(2)(4)(5); Income Tax (Trading and Other Income), 2005 c 5, s 882(1), sch 1 pt 2 paras 471, 472(1)(3)(b)(c); Income Tax, 2007 c 3, s 1027, sch 1 para 363

restr—Finance, 1998 c 36, s 56(5)(9)

appl—Finance, 1995 c 4, sch 22 paras 3(4), 7(4)

rep in pt—(saving) Income Tax (Trading and Other Income), 2005 c 5, ss 882(1), 883(4), 884, sch 1 pt 2 paras 471, 472(1)(2), sch 2 pt 3 paras 52(5), 54, sch 3; ibid, ss 882(1), 884, sch 1 pt 2 paras 471, 472(1)(3)(a)(4), sch 3; Income Tax, 2007 c 3, s 1031, sch 3

1994

c 9 *continued*

sch 21 rep in pt—Finance (No 2), 1997 c 58, s 52, sch 8 pt II(5)(11) Note; (pt prosp)
Finance (No 2), 2005 c 22, s 70, sch 11 pt 2(11), Note

sch 22 am—SI 2009/56, art 3, sch 1 paras 210-213

sch 24 rep in pt—SI 1995/31, reg 6, sch; (saving) Finance, 1996 c 8, ss 105(1),205, sch 41
pt V(3), Note; Finance, 2008 c 9, s 8, sch 2 para 70(b)(i); Corporation Tax,
2009 c 4, s 1322, sch 1 paras 391, 398; ibid, s 1326, sch 3 pt 1

am—Employment Rights, 1996 c 18, s 240, sch 1 para 62(a); Finance, 1998 c 36,
s 46(3), sch 7, para 9; Transport, 2000 c 38, s 252, sch 27 para 50(2)(3);
Capital Allowances, 2001 c 2, ss 578, 580, sch 2, para 91, sch 4; SI 2001/3629,
arts 83, 86; Income Tax (Earnings and Pensions), 2003 c 1, s 722, sch 6 pt 2
para 224(1)-(5); Income Tax (Trading and Other Income), 2005 c 5, s 882(1),
sch 1 pt 2 paras 471, 473; Financial Services, 2012 c 21, sch 18 para 79(3)

sch 25 am —Capital Allowances, 2001 c 2, ss 578, 580, sch 2, para 92, sch 4

rep in pt —Capital Allowances, 2001 c 2, ss 578, 580, sch 2, para 92(2)(a), sch 4;
Finance, 2008 c 9, s 8, sch 2 para 70(b)(ii)

c 10   *Race Relations (Remedies)*—rep Equality, 2010 c 15, s 211, sch 27 pt 1 (as subst by SI
2010/2279, sch 2)

c 11   **Road Traffic Regulation (Special Events)**

c 12   **Insolvency (No 2)**

c 13   **Intelligence Services**

appl—Water, 2003 c 37, s 1B

s 5 see—(trans of functions) (S) SI 1999/1750, art 2, sch 1; (cert functions exercisable in S)
SI 1999/1748, art 3, sch 1 para 16

ext (mods)—(Jersey, Guernsey) SI 1994/2955

am—Security Service, 1996 c 35, s 2; Regulation of Investigatory Powers, 2000 c 23,
ss 59(2)(a),74(1)(2); (prosp) Crim Justice and Court Services, 2000 c 43, s 74,
sch 7 pt II para 119

s 6 rep in pt—Regulation of Investigatory Powers, 2000 c 23, ss 74(3), 82(2), sch 5

am—SI 1999/1750, art 6(1), sch 5, para 14; Terrorism, 2006, c 11, s 31(1)-(4)

s 7 rep in pt—Regulation of Investigatory Powers, 2000 c 23, ss 74(3), 82(2), sch 5

am—Anti-terrorism, Crime and Security, 2001 c 24, s 116(1)(a)(b)(2); Terrorism, 2006,
c 11, s 31(5)(6)

s 7 am—Anti-terrorism, Crime and Security, 2001 c 24, s 116(1)(2)

s 8 rep—Regulation of Investigatory Powers, 2000 c 23, ss 59(8),82(2), sch 5

s 9 rep—(transtl savings) Regulation of Investigatory Powers, 2000 c 23, ss 70, 82(2), sch 5

s 10 rep—Justice and Security, 2013 c 18, sch 2 para 1(a)

s 11 ext (mods)—(Jersey, Guernsey) SI 1994/2955

am—Regulation of Investigatory Powers, 2000 c 23, s 74(4), s 82(1), sch 4 para 6;
Anti-terrorism, Crime and Security, 2001 c 24, s 116(3); Wireless Telegraphy,
2006 c 36, s 123, sch 7 para 14

rep in pt—Regulation of Investigatory Powers, 2000 c 23, s 82(2), sch 5; Justice and
Security, 2013 c 18, sch 2 para 1(b)

s 12 ext (mods)—(Jersey, Guernsey) SI 1994/2955

schs 1, 2 rep—(transtl savings) Regulation of Investigatory Powers, 2000 c 23, ss 70,82(2),
sch 5

sch 3 rep—Justice and Security, 2013 c 18, sch 2 para 1(c)

c 14   **Parliamentary Commissioner**

c 15   **Antarctic**

reprinted as am and ext (mods)—(specified Overseas Territories) SI 1995/1030 (am by
2015/823, arts 1,2, sch; (Guernsey) SI 1995/1033, arts 1(2)(3), 2; (Jersey) SI
1995/1034, arts 1(2)(3), 2; (Isle of Man); SI 1995/1035, arts 1(1)(3), 3, sch

s 3 am—Antarctic, 2013 c 15, s 14(6)

s 7 am—Antarctic, 2013 c 15, ss 14(2)(a), 16(2)(3)

s 8 am—Antarctic, 2013 c 15, ss 14(2)(b), 16(4)(5)

s 8A added—Antarctic, 2013 c 15, s 16(6)

s 8B added—Antarctic, 2013 c 15, s 16(8)

s 9 am—Antarctic, 2013 c 15, s 14(2)(c)

s 10 am—Antarctic, 2013 c 15, ss 14(2)(d), 15(2)(a)(b)

s 11 am—Antarctic, 2013 c 15, s 14(2)(e)(3)(a)(b)

s 12 am—Antarctic, 2013 c 15, ss 14(4)(a)-(c), 16(7)(a)(b)

s 15 am—Antarctic, 2013 c 15, s 15(3)

s 16 am—Antarctic, 2013 c 15, s 15(4)(a)(b)

s 17 appl—(prosp) Antarctic, 2013 c 15, s 11(1)(a)

1994

c 15 *continued*

        s 19 appl—(prosp) Antarctic, 2013 c 15, s 11(1)(b)

        s 27 am—Serious Crime, 2007 c 27, sch 6 para 23

        s 28 appl—(prosp) Antarctic, 2013 c 15, s 11(1)(c)

        s 29 appl—(prosp) Antarctic, 2013 c 15, s 11(1)(d)

        s 30 am—Antarctic, 2013 c 15, s 15(5)

        s 31 am—Antarctic, 2013 c 15, ss 14(5)(7), 16(9)(b)(c)(10)

            rep in pt—Antarctic, 2013 c 15, s 16(9)(a)

        s 34 appl—Antarctic, 2013 c 15, s 18(1)

c 16   **State Hospitals (Scotland)**

        s 2 rep in pt—Mental Health (Care and Treatment) (S), 2003 asp 13, s 331(2), sch 5 pt 1

c 17   **Chiropractors**

        saved—Scotland, 1998 c 46, s 30, sch 5 pt II, s G2(h)

        s 1 am—SI 2008/1774, art 2, sch 4; (prosp) Health and Social Care (Safety and Quality),

            2015 c 28, sch para 4(2)

          rep in pt—SI 2008/1774, art 2, sch 4;

        s 3 am—SI 2008/1774, art 2, sch 4

        s 5A added—SI 2007/3101, reg 219

        s 6 am—SI 2007/3101, reg 220

        s 8 am—SI 2007/3101, reg 221

        s 10 am—Nat Health Service Reform and Health Care Professions, 2002 c 17, s

            34(1)(2)(a)(b)(d); Crime and Cts, 2013 c 22, sch 9 para 65(a)(b)

          rep in pt—Nat Health Service Reform and Health Care Professions, 2002 c 17, ss

              34(1)(2)(c), 37(2), sch 9 pt 2

        s 17 am—SIs 2007/3101, reg 222; 2008/1774, art 2, sch 4

        s 20 am—SI 2008/1774, art 2, sch 4; Policing and Crime, 2009 c 26, s 81(2)(3)

          rep in pt—SI 2008/1774, art 2, sch 4

        s 22 am—Nat Health Service Reform and Health Care Professions, 2002 c 17, s 34(1)(3)

        s 23 am—Nat Health Service Reform and Health Care Professions, 2002 c 17, s 34(1)(4)

        s 27 ext—SI 2000/2865, sch, rule 2

        s 28 ext—SI 2000/2866, sch, rule 2

        s 29 am—Nat Health Service Reform and Health Care Professions, 2002 c 17, s 34(1)(5); SI

            2007/3101, reg 223; Crime and Cts, 2013 c 22, sch 9 para 65(a)(b)

        s 29A added—SI 2007/3101, reg 224

            am—Crime and Cts, 2013 c 22, sch 9 para 65(a)(b)

        s 31 am—Nat Health Service Reform and Health Care Professions, 2002 c 17, s

            34(1)(6)(a)(b)(d)

          rep in pt—Nat Health Service Reform and Health Care Professions, 2002 c 17, ss

              34(1)(6)(c), 37(2), sch 9 pt 2

        s 33 rep in pt—Competition 1998 c 41 s 74(1)(3), sch 12, para 17(a)(b), sch 14 pt I

          am—Enterprise, 2002 c 40, s 278(1), sch 25, para 31

        s 35 rep in pt—Nat Health Service Reform and Health Care Professions, 2002 c 17, ss

            34(1)(7), 37(2), sch 9 pt 2; SI 2008/1774, art 2, sch 4

        s 36 am—SI 2008/1774, art 2, sch 4

        s 37 subst—SI 2014/1887, sch 1 para 10

        s 38 rep—Data Protection, 1998 c 29, s 74(2), sch 16 pt I

        s 40 rep (prosp)—Police, 1997 c 50, ss 133(e), 134(2), sch 10

        s 41 am—SI 2008/948, art 3, sch 1

        s 41A added—SI 2008/1774, art 2, sch 4

        s 43 appl—Data Protection, 1998 c 29, s 69(1)(g)

          am—SIs 2007/3101, reg 226; 2008/1774, art 2, sch 4

        sch 1 am—(temp) SI 1998/2031, art 3(a)(b); Health and Social Care (Community Health

            and Standards), 2003 c 43, s 187(8), sch 12 para 6; SIs 2008/1774, art 2, sch 4;

            2009/1182, arts 4, 5-7, sch 5; (prosp) Health and Social Care (Safety and

            Quality), 2015 c 28, sch para 4(3)(a)(b)

          appl—SI 1999/1537, art 4(6)

          saved—SI 1999/1537, art 7(4)

          rep in pt—Health, 2006 c 28, s 80, sch 8 para 35, sch 9; SI 2008/1774, art 2, sch 4;

            Health and Social Care, 2012 c 7, sch 20 para 6(e)

c 18   **Social Security (Incapacity for Work)**

        excl—SI 1995/310, reg 16

        mod—Social Security, 1998 c 14, s 2(1)(2)(e)

        power to am—Northern Ireland, 1998 c 47, s 87

        s 1 rep (prosp)—Welfare Reform, 2007 c 5, s 67, sch 8

1994

c 18 *continued*

    s 2 rep in pt—Tax Credits, 2002 c 21, s 60, sch 6; (prosp) Welfare Reform, 2007 c 5, s 67,
        sch 8

    s 3 rep (prosp)—Welfare Reform, 2007 c 5, s 67, sch 8

    s 5 rep (prosp)—Welfare Reform, 2007 c 5, s 67, sch 8

    s 6 rep in pt—(pt prosp) Social Security, 1998 c 14, s 86(2), sch 8
        rep (prosp)—Welfare Reform, 2007 c 5, s 67, sch 8

    s 7 rep (prosp)—Welfare Reform, 2007 c 5, s 67, sch 8

    s 9 rep in pt—(saving) Welfare Reform and Pensions, 1999 c 30, s 88, sch 13 pt IV

    s 10 rep—Tax Credits, 2002 c 21, s 60, sch 6

    s 11 restr—SI 1995/310, reg 23

    s 13 excl—SI 1995/829, reg 25
        rep (prosp)—Welfare Reform, 2007 c 5, s 67, sch 8

    sch 1 am—SI 1994/2556
        rep in pt—Jobseekers, 1995 c 18, s 41(5), sch 3; Pensions, 1995 c 26, ss 126,177,
            sch 4 pt III paras 19,20, sch 7 pt II; Employment Rights, 1996 c 18, s 242,
            sch 3 pt I; (pt prosp) Social Security, 1998 c 14, s 86(2), sch 8; (saving)
            Welfare Reform and Pensions, 1999 c 30, s 88, sch 13 pt IV; Tax Credits, 2002
            c 21, s 60, sch 6; (prosp) Welfare Reform, 2007 c 5, s 67, sch 8; Pensions, 2007
            c 22, s 27, sch 7 pt 2; (prosp) Welfare Reform, 2009 c 24, s 58, sch 7 pt 2;
            Pensions, 2011 c 19, sch 2 para 4(a); (prosp) Welfare Reform, 2012 c 5, sch 14
            pt 7
        restr—SI 1995/310, reg 23

    sch 2 am—SI 1994/2556
        rep in pt—(saving) Welfare Reform and Pensions, 1999 c 30, s 88, sch 13 pt IV

c 19   **Local Government (Wales)**

    appl—Justices of the Peace, 1979 c 55, s 70; Loc Govt Finance, 1988 c 41, s 41A

    trans of powers—(W) SI 1999/672, art 2, sch 1

    s 6 rep—SL(R), 2004 c 14, s 1(1), sch 1 pt 10/1

    s 17 excl—Highways, 1980 c 66, s 329A; Public Passenger Vehicles, 1981 c 14, s 82(3);
        Road Traffic Regulation, 1984 c 27, s 142(1A); Town and Country Planning,
        1990 c 8, s 336(1A)

    s 19 rep in pt—Environment, 1995 c 25, s 120(3), sch 24

    s 21 rep—Education, 1996 c 56, s 582(2)(3), sch 38 pt I, sch 39

    s 24 rep—Police and Magistrates' Courts, 1994 c 29, s 93, sch 9 pt I

    s 26 rep—SL(R), 2004 c 14, s 1(1), sch 1 pt 10/3

    s 30 am—Education, 1996 c 56, s 582(1), sch 37 pt I para 123

    s 31 am—Education, 1996 c 56, s 582(1), sch 37 pt I para 124

    s 32 rep—SL(R), 2004 c 14, s 1(1), sch 1 pt 10/3

    s 38 am—Loc Govt, 2003 c 26, s 70(7)-(9)

    s 40 rep—SL(R), 2004 c 14, s 1(1), sch 1 pt 10/3

    s 41 am—Employment Rights, 1996 c 18, s 240, sch 1 para 63(2)

    s 43 am—Employment Rights, 1996 c 18, s 240, sch 1 para 63(3)

    s 44 am—Employment Rights, 1996 c 18, s 240, sch 1 para 63(4)(5); SI 1996/183, art 2(1)

    s 51 am—Loc Govt, 2003 c 26, s 127(1), sch 7 paras 56, 57
        rep in pt—Loc Govt, 2003 c 26, s 127(2), sch 8 pt I

    s 55 am—Justices of the Peace, 1997 c 25, s 73(2), sch 5 para 35(2); Access to Justice, 1999
        c 22, s 76, sch 10 para 46; Constitutional Reform, 2005 c 4, s 15(1), sch 4 pt 1
        para 233; SI 2005/886, art 2, sch para 51
        rep in pt—Access to Justice, 1999 c 22, s 106, sch 15 pt V(1)(3)

    s 61 rep in pt—Reserve Forces, 1996 c 14, s 131(2), sch 11; Lieutenancies, 1997 c 23,
        s 8(4), sch 3
        am—Lieutenancies, 1997 c 23, s 8(1)

    s 63 am—Loc Govt, 2003 c 26, s 127(1), sch 7 paras 56, 58

    s 64 appl—Loc Govt (W), 1994 c 19, s 1(3), sch 2 para 12(2); Reserve Forces, 1996 c 14,
        s 111, sch 4 para 10; Justices of the Peace, 1997 c 25, s 72(1)

    sch 2 rep in pt—Justices of the Peace, 1997 c 25, s 73(3), sch 6 pt I; Licensing, 2003 c 17,
        s 199, sch 7; Parly Voting System and Constituencies, 2011 c 1, sch 12 pt 2

    sch 5 appl—(temp) Town and Country Planning, 1990 c 8, s 28A

    sch 6 rep—Countryside and Rights of Way, 2000 c 37, s 102, sch 16 pt I

    sch 7 rep in pt—Traffic Management, 2004 c 18, s 98, sch 12 pt 1

    sch 8 rep in pt—Housing Grants, Construction and Regeneration, 1996 c 53, s 147, sch 3
        pt I; SI 2003/973 (W 132), art 13

1994

c 19 *continued*

　　　sch 9 rep in pt—SI 1996/3097, art 3(1)(e); SL(R), 1998 c 43, s 1(1), sch 1 pt X, Group 5;
　　　　　(prosp) Care Standards, 2000 c 14, s 117(2), sch 6; Scrap Metal Dealers, 2013
　　　　　c 10, s 19(1)(b)

　　　sch 10 rep in pt—Adoption and Children, 2002 c 38, s 139(3), sch 5; Nat Health Service
　　　　　Reform and Health Care Professions, 2002 c 17, s 37, sch 8, para 19, sch 9 pt 3;
　　　　　Nat Health Service (Conseq Provns), 2006 c 43, s 6, sch 4; SI 2010/1158, art 5,
　　　　　sch 3

　　　sch 12 rep in pt—Loc Govt, 1999 c 27, ss 30, 34, sch 2(2); Localism, 2011 c 20, sch 25 pt
　　　　　13

　　　sch 13 am—Audit Commission, 1998 c 18, s 54(1), sch 3, para 27; Govt of Wales, 1998
　　　　　c 38, s 150(2)(4); Justices of the Peach, 1997 c 25, s 73(2), sch 5 para 35(3)l
　　　　rep in pt—Govt of Wales, 1998 c 38, ss 150(3)(a)(b),152, sch 18 pt VII; Data
　　　　　Protection, 1998 c 29, s 74(2), sch 16 pt I; Race Relations (Amdt), 2000 c 34,
　　　　　s 9(2), sch 3

　　　sch 14 rep—SL(R), 2004 c 14, s 1(1), sch 1 pt 10/3

　　　sch 15 rep in pt—(prosp) Loc Govt, 2000 c 22, s 107, sch 6; Loc Govt, 2003 c 26, s 127(2),
　　　　　sch 8 pt 1; Licensing, 2003 c 17, s 199, sch 7; SI 2009/1375, art 2

　　　sch 16 rep in pt—Education, 1996 c 56, s 582(2)(3), sch 38 pt I, sch 39; SI 1996/655, reg 3;
　　　　　SL(R), 1998 c 43, s 1(1), sch 1 pt X, Group 5; Govt of Wales, 1998 c 38, s 152,
　　　　　sch 18, pts IV, V; European Parl Elections, 1999 c 1, s 3(3), sch 4; Loc Govt,
　　　　　1999 c 27, ss 30, 34, sch 2(2); Representation of the People, 2000 c 2, s 15(2),
　　　　　sch 7 pt I; Crim Justice and Court Services, 2000 c 43, s 75, sch 8;
　　　　　SI 2001/1149, arts 3(2), 4(11), sch 2; Licensing, 2003 c 17, s 199, sch 7;
　　　　　Communications, 2003 c 21, s 406(7), sch 19(1); SI 2003/1900, arts 2(1), 3(1),
　　　　　sch 1; SI 2003/3142, art 3(2); Loc Govt, 2003 c 26, s 127(2), sch 8 pt 1; Public
　　　　　Services Ombudsman (W), 2005 c 10, s 39(2), sch 7; Gambling, 2005 c 19,
　　　　　s 356(4)(5), sch 17; Commons, 2006 c 26, s 53, sch 6; Charities, 2006 c 50, s
　　　　　75, sch 9; SI 2008/1277, sch 4; Housing and Regeneration, 2008 c 17, s 321,
　　　　　sch 16; (pt prosp) Marine and Coastal Access, 2009 c 23, s 321, sch 22 pt 3;
　　　　　ibid, sch 22, pt 4; (S) Marine (S), 2010 asp 5, s 167, sch 4 para 7; Parly Voting
　　　　　System and Constituencies, 2011 c 1, sch 12 pt 2; Charities, 2011 c 25, sch 10;
　　　　　(savings) Mobile Homes (W), 2013 anaw 6, sch 4 para 7; SI 2014/3266 (W
　　　　　333), sch 2 para 2

　　　sch 17 saved—SI 1996/661, art 3(5)
　　　　am—Audit Commission, 1998 c 18, s 54(1), sch 3, para 28(2)(3)(a)(b)(c)(4)
　　　　rep in pt—(prosp) Coroners and Justice, 2009 c 25, s 178, sch 23 pt 1; (prosp)
　　　　　Infrastructure, 2015 c 7, sch 5 para 39

c 20　**Sunday Trading**

　　　s 2 appl—Christmas Day (Trading), 2004 c 26, s 2(4)
　　　s 5 rep—Deregulation and Contracting Out, 1994 c 40, s 81, sch 17
　　　s 8 appl—Christmas Day (Trading), 2004 c 26, s 3(5)
　　　s 36 rep in pt —(saving) SI 1996/1919, arts 256,257, schs 2,3
　　　sch 1 excl—SI 1994/3286L
　　　　am—Licensing, 2003 c 17, s 198, sch 6 para 110(1)(2)(a)(b)(3); Christmas Day
　　　　　(Trading), 2004 c 26, s 4(1)(2)(b); SIs 2004/470, art 2(1)(2)(a)(b)(d)(e);
　　　　　2006/2407, reg 44, sch 9; 2015/664, sch 4 para 26
　　　　appl (mods)—Christmas Day (Trading), 2004 c 26, s 1(4)(5)
　　　　rep in pt—Christmas Day (Trading), 2004 c 26, s 4(1)(2)(a); SI 2004/470,
　　　　　art 2(1)(2)(c)(f)
　　　　saved—Christmas Day (Trading), 2004 c 26, s 1(2)
　　　sch 2 appl (mods)—Christmas Day (Trading), 2004 c 26, s 3(3)
　　　　rep in pt—Consumer Rights, 2015 c 15, sch 6 para 58(2)
　　　　am—Consumer Rights, 2015 c 15, sch 6 para 58(3)
　　　　appl—Christmas Day (Trading), 2004 c 26, s 3(4)
　　　sch 3 am—SI 2004/470, art 2(1)(3); Christmas Day (Trading), 2004 c 26, s 4(3)
　　　　appl (mods)—Christmas Day (Trading), 2004 c 26, s 2(2)
　　　sch 4 rep in pt—Deregulation and Contracting Out, 1994 c 40, s 81, sch 17; Employment
　　　　　Tribunals, 1996 c 17, s 45, sch 3 pt I; Employment Rights, 1996 c 18, s 242,
　　　　　sch 3 pt I

c 21　**Coal Industry**

　　　　am—SIs 1996/593, reg 2, sch 1
　　　　appl—Statistics of Trade, 1947 c 39, s 9(5A); Opencast Coal, 1958 c 69, ss 4(1A), 15(1),
　　　　　16(2A),49(4B); Licensing, 1964 c 26, s 56(3); Gaming, 1968 c 65, s 52(2);

1994
c 21 *continued*

        Highways, 1980 c 66, s 290(5); Roads (S), 1984 c 54, s 140(3)(b); Finance, 2001 c 9,
            s 17(7); Licensing, 2003 c 17, s 66(4)(b)(i)

trans of powers—(W) SI 1999/672, art 2, sch 1

s 3 am—Petroleum, 1998 c 17, s 50, sch 4, para 38(2)

s 4 rep in pt—SI 2008/960, art 22, sch 3

ss 4A-4C added—(EW) Water, 2003 c 37, s 85(1)

s 4A am—Energy, 2011 c 16, s 115(2)

s 4CA added—Energy, 2011 c 16, s 115(1)

ss 4D-4F added—Water Services etc (S), 2005 asp 3, s 30(1)

s 4D am—Energy, 2011 c 16, s 116(2)

s 4G added—Energy, 2011 c 16, s 116(1)

s 8 am—Abolition of Feudal Tenure etc (S), 2000 asp 5, s 76(1), sch 12 pt I para 56(2)

s 9 am—Petroleum, 1998 c 17, s 50, sch 4, para 38(3)(a)(b)(c); Abolition of Feudal Tenure
        etc (S), 2000 asp 5, s 76(1), sch 12 pt I para 56(3)

s 10 appl—City of Edinburgh (Guided Busways) O Conf, 1998 c iii, s 1, s 40(2) of sch O
        rep in pt—Abolition of Feudal Tenure etc (S), 2000 asp 5, s 76(1)(2), sch 12 pt I
            para 56(4), sch 13 pt I

s 24 rep—SL(R), 2004 c 14, s 1(1), sch 1 pt 5/8

s 36 rep in pt—SI 2009/1941, art 2, sch 1

s 39 am—Enterprise, 2002 c 40, s 248(3), sch 17, para 48; SI 2009/1941, art 2, sch 1;
        (prosp) Planning (W), 2015 anaw 4, sch 2 para 18

s 41 am—(prosp) Planning (W), 2015 anaw 4, sch 2 para 19

s 43 appl—SI 1999/929, rule 3.3

s 47 am —SI 2009/1307, art 5, sch 1
        rep in pt—SI 2009/1307, art 5, sch 1

s 54 am—Planning (Conseq Provns) (S), 1997 c 11, s 4, sch 2 para 56(1); Financial Services,
        2012 c 21, sch 18 para 80

s 57 am—Petroleum, 1998 c 17, s 50, sch 4, para 38(4)

s 59 rep in pt—Competition, 1998 c 41, s 74(1)(3), sch 12, para 18(a), sch 14 pt I;
          SIs 2008/960, art 22, sch 3; 2008/1277, sch 4, reg 30, sch 2; 2014/892, sch 1
          para 113
        am—SI 1996,973,reg 16; Competition, 1998 c 41, s 74(1), sch 12, para 18(b);
          SI 1999/506, art 34; SI 2001/4050, art 2, sch pt IV, para 24; Enterprise, 2002 c
          40, s 278(1), sch 25, para 32; SI 2002/1555, art 23; Water, 2003 c 37, s 101(1),
          sch 7 pt 2 para 31; SIs 2008/1277, reg 30, sch 2; 2009/1307, art 5, sch 1; Energy,
          2013 c 32, sch 12 para 70; SIs 2013/755 (W 90), sch 2 para 360; 1882, art 10(2)
        ext—Anti-terrorism, Crime and Security, 2001 c 24, s 17, sch 4 pt 1, para 35

s 63 appl—Coal Mining Subsidence, 1991 c 45, s 51

s 65 am—SI 2009/1941, art 2, sch 1

s 65A added—SI 2007/2194, art 10, sch 4

s 66 am—Water Services etc (S), 2005 asp 3, s 30(2)

s 68 rep in pt—Planning (Conseq Provns) (S), 1997 c 11, s 3, sch 1 pt I; SL(R), 1998 c 43,
          s 1(1), sch 1 pt IV, Group 2; Gambling, 2005 c 19, s 356(4)(5), sch 17
        am—Water, 2003 c 37, s 85(3); Water Services etc (S), 2005 asp 3, s 30(3)

sch 1 am—SI 2012/2404, sch 2 para 30

sch 1A added—(EW) Water, 2003 c 37, s 85(2), sch 5

sch 1B added—(EW) Water, 2003 c 37, s 85(2), sch 6
        am—SI 2009/1307, art 5, sch 1

sch 1C added—Water Services etc (S), 2005 asp 3, s 30(4), sch 4

sch 3 am—SIs 2008/948, art 3, sch 1; 2009/1941, art 2, sch 1

sch 4 am—Capital Allowances, 2001 c 2, s 578, sch 2, para 93; Income Tax (Trading and
        Other Income), 2005 c 5, s 882(1), sch 1 pt 2 para 474
        rep in pt—Finance, 2008 c 9, s 8, sch 2 para 70(c)

sch 5 am—SI 2006/745, art 9

sch 7 am—2009/1307, art 5, sch 1

sch 9 rep in pt—Planning (Conseq Provns) (S), 1997 c 11, s 3, sch 1; SL(R), 1998 c 43,
          s 1(1), sch 1 pt IV, Group 2; Govt of Wales, 1998 c 38, s 152, sch 18, pts IV,V;
          Land Registration, 2002 c 9, s 135, sch 13; Enterprise, 2002 c 40, s 278(2), sch
          26; International Development, 2002 c 1, s 19(2), sch 4; Licensing, 2003 c 17,
          s 199, sch 7; Gambling, 2005 c 19, s 356(4)(5), sch 17; SI 2007/2194, art 10,
          sch 5; Land Registration etc (S), 2012 asp 5, sch 5 para 34
        am—SI 2007/2194, art 10, sch 4

1994

c 21 *continued*

      sch 10 rep in pt—Planning (Conseq Provns) (S), 1997 c 11, s 3, sch 1

        am—(S) Planning (Conseq Provns) (S), 1997 c 11, s 4, sch 2 para 56(2)

c 22   **Vehicle Excise and Registration**

      appl—Finance, 1995 c 4, s 19, sch 4 pt X paras 41(3), 42(5); Finance 1996 c 8,
        ss 17(10)(14), 23, sch 2 para 2; Income Tax (Earnings and Pensions), 2003 c 1,
        ss 140(2), 142(2)

      excl—SI 1999/1736, art 8(8)

      saved—Scotland, 1998 c 46, s 30, sch 5 pt II, s E1(e)

      constr with—Finance, 2000 c 17, s 23, sch 4

      s 1 am—Finance, 2002 c 23, s 19(1)(2), sch 5, paras 1, 2
        excl in pt—Road Traffic, 1988 c 52, s 12E(3)

      s 2 am—Finance, 1996 c 8, s 17(9)(14); SI 1999/1851, art 2(3)(c); Finance, 2002 c 23, s
        19(1)(2), sch 5, paras 1, 3

      s 3 am—Finance, 2009 c 10, s 14, sch 4 paras 1, 2; Finance, 2014 c 26, s 87(1)

      s 4 rep in pt—Finance, 2005 c 7, ss 7(1)(2)(13), 104, sch 11 pt 1, Note
        am—Finance, 2014 c 26, ss 88(2)(3), 89(2)

      s 5 am—Finance, 2007 c 11, s 106(1)

      s 7 am—Finance, 1996 c 8, ss 17(10)(14), 23, sch 2 para 2; Finance (No 2), 1997 c 58,
        s 14(1)(2); Vehicles (Crime), 2001 c 3, ss 32(1), 43, sch, para 3; Finance, 2002 c
        23, s 19(1)(2), sch 5, paras 1, 4; (prosp) Road Safety, 2006 c 49, s 47; HGV Road
        User Levy, 2013 c 7, s 15(1)(2)

        rep in pt—Finance, 2014 c 26, sch 19 para 2

        mod—Wireless Telegraphy, 2006 c 36, s 51(1)

      s 7A added—Finance, 2002 c 23, s 19(1)-(3), sch 5, paras 1, 5
        rep in pt—Finance (No 2), 2005 c 22, ss 66(1)(2)(7), 70, sch 11 pt 5(1), Note; Finance,
        2013 c 29, s 189(2); Finance, 2014 c 26, sch 19 para 3

        am—Finance (No 2), 2005 c 22, s 66(1)-(6)(8)

      s 7B added—Finance, 2002 c 23, s 19(1)-(3), sch 5, paras 1, 5
        am—Finance (No 2), 2005 c 22, s 66(1)(9)-(11); SI 2009/56, art 3, sch 1 para 215

      s 7C added—Finance, 2006 c 25, s 15

      s 9 am—SI 1996/2008, reg 2

      s 10 rep—Finance, 2014 c 26, sch 19 para 4

      s 11 am—Finance, 1996 c 8, s 23, sch 2 para 3
        saved—SI 2002/2742, reg 38, sch 6 pt II, para 9(b)

      s 13 am—Finance, 1996 c 8, s 18(4)(a)(b)(5); Finance, 1999 c 16, s 8(4)(5); Finance, 2002
        c 23, s 18(2)(3); Finance, 2005 c 7, s 7(1)(3)-(5)(14)(16); Finance, 2014 c 26, s
        89(3)(a)

        rep in pt—Finance, 2014 c 26, sch 18 para 10(a)

      s 14 am—Finance, 2014 c 26, sch 19 para 5(a)
        rep in pt—Finance, 2014 c 26, sch 19 para 5(b)

      s 15 restr—Finance, 1996 c 8, s 17(12)(13)
        am—Finance, 1998 c 36, s 16, sch 1, paras 13,17(1)
        mod—Finance, 1999 c 16, s 9, sch 1 para 9(3)-(5)
        rep in pt—Finance, 2014 c 26, sch 18 para 10(c)

      s 15A added—Finance, 2003 c 14, s 16(1)(3)

      s 16 rep—Finance, 2003 c 14, ss 16(2)(3), 216, sch 43 pt 1(4), Note

      s 19 am—Finance, 1996 c 8, s 23, sch 2 para 8; Finance, 2001 c 9, s 14(1)(2); Finance,
        2009 c 10, s 14, sch 4 paras 1, 3; Finance, 2013 c 29, sch 37 para 2(2)(3);
        Finance, 2014 c 26, sch 19 para 6
        mod—Finance, 2000 c 17, s 20(9); Finance, 2001 c 9, s 8(9)(12)
        restr—Finance, 2001 c 9, s 13(10)(14)
        rep in pt—Finance, 2001 c 9, ss 14(1)(3), 110, sch 33 pt 1(3), Note 1(a); Finance, 2009
        c 10, s 14, sch 4 paras 1, 3
        subst—Finance, 2008 c 9, s 144(1), (3)

      s 19A added—Finance, 1995 c 4, s 19, sch 4 para 32(1)(4)
        rep in pt—Finance, 2014 c 26, s 89(5)

      s 19B added—Finance, 1997 c 16, s 19(1)
        am—Finance, 2014 c 26, s 89(6)(a)(d)
        rep in pt—Finance, 2014 c 26, s 89(6)(b)(c)

      s 19C added—Finance, 2004 c 12, s 18(1)(2)(4)

      s 21 am—Finance, 1997 c 16, s 18, sch 3 paras 2,9

      s 22 am—Finance, 1996 c 8, s 23, sch 2 paras 4-7; Finance, 1997 c 16, s 18, sch 3 paras,
        s 18, sch 3 paras 3,9; Finance (No 2), 1997 c 58, s 14(3); Finance, 1998 c 36,

1994
c 22 *continued*

s 18; Vehicles (Crime), 2001 c 3, ss 32(2), 33(1), 43, sch, para 4; Finance, 2002 c 23, s 19(1)-(3), sch 5, paras 1, 6; (pt prosp) Road Safety, 2006 c 49, s 47; Finance, 2009 c 10, s 120

rep in pt—Finance, 1996 c 8, s 205, sch 41 pt II; Finance (No 2), 1997 c 58, s 52, sch 8 pt I Note; Finance, 1998 c 36, s 165, sch 27 pt I(4), Note; Finance, 2008 c 9, s 144(1), (4); Finance, 2014 c 26, sch 19 para 7

s 22ZA added—Finance, 2002 c 23, s 17

   am—Finance, 2003 c 14, s 15; Finance, 2013 c 29, sch 37 para 3(2)(3)(5)

   rep in pt—Finance, 2013 c 29, sch 37 para 3(4)

s 22A added—Vehicles (Crime), 2001 c 3, s 33(2)

   am—(prosp) Road Safety, 2006 c 49, s 48

s 26 am—Vehicle Registration Marks, 2007 c 14, s 1(1)(2)

s 27A added (prosp)—Vehicles (Crime), 2001 c 3, s 34

s 28A added—Serious Organised Crime and Police, 2005 c 15, s 151

s 29 am—Finance, 1996 c 8, s 23, sch 2 para 9; Finance, 2002 c 23, s 19(1)(2), sch 5, paras 1, 7; Finance, 2008 c 9, s 145, sch 45 paras 1, 2

   rep in pt—Finance, 2014 c 26, sch 19 para 8

   excl in pt—Road Traffic, 1988 c 52, s 12E(3)

s 30 am—Finance, 2008 c 9, s 145, sch 45 paras 1, 3

s 31 am—Finance, 2008 c 9, s 144(1), (5)(a)

   rep in pt—Finance, 2014 c 26, sch 19 para 9

ss 31A-31C added—Finance, 2002 c 23, s 19(1)-(3), sch 5, paras 1, 8

   rep in pt—Finance, 2014 c 26, sch 19 para 10

s 31B am—Finance, 2008 c 9, s 144(1), (5)(b)

   rep in pt—Finance, 2014 c 26, sch 19 para 11

s 31C am—Finance, 2008 c 9, s 144(1), (5)(c)

   rep in pt—Finance, 2014 c 26, sch 19 para 12

s 32 am—Powers of Crim Cts (Sentencing), 2000 c 6, s 165(1), sch 9 para 158; Finance, 2002 c 23, s 19(1)(2), sch 5, paras 1, 9(1)(2)

s 33 rep—Finance, 2014 c 26, sch 19 para 13

s 33A added—Finance, 2013 c 29, s 188(2)

   rep—Finance, 2014 c 26, sch 19 para 14

s 34 am—Finance, 2002 c 23, s 19(1)(2), sch 5, paras 1, 11

s 35 rep—Finance, 2014 c 26, sch 19 para 15

s 35A am—Finance, 1997 c 16, s 19(2); Finance, 1998 c 36, s 19(1)(2); Finance, 1999 c 16, s 8(4)(5); Finance, 2002 c 23, s 18(2)(4); Finance, 2005 c 7, s 7(1)(6)(15); Finance, 2014 c 26, s 89(7); ibid, sch 19 para 16(2)(4)(5)

   rep in pt—Finance, 2014 c 26, sch 19 para 16(3)

s 36 am—Finance, 1996 c 8, s 18(4)(c); Finance, 1998 c 36, s 19(3)(4); Finance, 1999 c 16, s 8(4)(5); Finance, 2002 c 23, s 18(2)(4); Finance, 2005 c 7, s 7(1)(6)(15); Finance, 2014 c 26, s 89(8); ibid, sch 19 para 17

s 41 am—Powers of Crim Cts (Sentencing), 2000 c 6, s 165(1), sch 9 para 159

s 42 am—Finance, 1996 c 8, s 22

s 43 am—SI 1999/1851, art 2(3)(b)

s 43A added—Finance, 1997 c 16, s 18, sch 3 paras 5,9

s 43B added—Vehicles (Crime), 2001 c 3, s 43, sch, para 5

s 43C added—Serious Organised Crime and Police, 2005 c 15, s 150(1)

s 44 am—Finance, 1997 c 16, s 18, sch 3 paras 6,9

   rep in pt—Finance, 2014 c 26, sch 19 para 18

s 45 am—Finance, 1996 c 8, s 23, sch 2 para 11; Finance, 1998 c 36, s 16, sch 1, paras 15, 17(2); (prosp) Road Safety, 2006 c 49, s 47

   rep in pt—Finance, 2014 c 26, sch 18 para 3(a)

   appl—Finance, 2000 c 17, s 20(10); Finance, 2001 c 9, s 8(10)(12)

   excl—Wireless Telegraphy, 2006 c 36, s 51(6)

s 46 am—Finance, 1997 c 16), s 18, sch 3 paras 7(1)(9)

s 46A added—Finance, 1996 c 8, s 23, sch 2 para 12

s 47 am—Finance, 1996 c 8, s 23, sch 2 para 14(1)(a)(3); Finance, 2002 c 23, s 19(1)(2), sch 5, paras 1, 12

s 48 am—Finance, 1996 c 8, s 23, sch 2 para 14(1)(b)(3); Finance, 2002 c 23, s 19(1)(2), sch 5, paras 1, 13

s 49 am—Crime and Cts, 2013 c 22, sch 9 para 36

s 51 am—Finance, 1997 c 16, s 18, sch 3 paras 7(2), 9; Courts, 2003 c 39, s 109(1), sch 8 para 362(a)

1994
c 22 *continued*

s 51A added—Finance, 1996 c 8, s 23, sch 2 para 13

s 52 rep in pt—(NI) SI 1997/2983, art 13(2), sch 2

s 53 am—Finance, 2002 c 23, s 19(1)(2), sch 5, paras 1, 14

s 54 am—Finance, 2002 c 23, s 19(1)(2), sch 5, paras 1, 15

s 55 am—Finance, 1996 c 8, s 23, sch 2 para 14(2)(3); Magistrates' Courts (Procedure),
    1998 c 15, s 4(1)(b)(2)(c); Courts, 2003 c 39, s 109(1), sch 8 para 362(b); Crim
    Justice and Cts, 2015 c 2, sch 11 para 13

s 57 rep in pt—Finance, 1996 c 8, ss 23,205, sch 2 para 16, sch 41 pt II; Finance, 2002 c 23,
        ss 20(2)(b), 141, sch 40 pt 1(5)
    am—Finance, 2002 c 23, s 19(1)-(3), sch 5, paras 1, 16

s 58 am—Finance, 2004 c 12, s 18(1)(3)(4)
    rep in pt—Finance, 2014 c 26, sch 19 para 19

s 59 am—Finance, 1996 c 8, s 23, sch 2 para 15

s 60 am—Finance, 2007 c 11, s 106(2)

s 60A added—Finance, 1995 c 4, s 19, sch 4 paras 16, 26, 29
    am—Finance, 2014 c 26, s 90(2)

s 61 am—Finance, 1996 c 8, s 22(4); Finance, 2014 c 26, s 90(3)
    am—Finance, 1996 c 8, s 15(3)(4)

s 61B added—Finance, 1998 c 36, s 16, sch 1, paras 2,17(2)
    rep—Finance, 2014 c 26, sch 18 para 2

s 62 am—Finance, 1997 c 16, s 18, sch 3 paras 7(3), 9; Finance, 2002 c 23, s 19(1)(2), sch
        5, paras 1, 17; Vehicle Registration Marks, 2007 c 14, s 1(3); Finance, 2009 c 10,
        s 14, sch 4 paras 1, 4; Finance, 2013 c 29, sch 37 para 4; Finance, 2014 c 26, sch
        19 para 20

s 66 excl—Finance, 1966 c 18, s 2(13)(a)

sch 1 am—Finance, 1996 c 8, ss 14,15(1)(2)(a)(4), 16,17,22(5)(6); (retrosp to 26.11.1996)
        Finance, 1997 c 16, s 16(1)(2); Finance (No 2), 1997 c 58, s 13(1)-(4); Finance,
        1998 c 36, s 16, sch 1, paras 3(1)(2)(3), 4, 5, 6(1)(2), 7(1)(2)(3), 8 (1)(2)(3), 9,
        10, 11(1)(2)(3), 12, 17(1); Finance, 1999 c 16, ss 8(1)-(3)(5), 9, sch 1
        paras 2(1)(2), 3-9; Finance, 2000 c 17, ss 20(1),21(1)(2),22,24 sch 3, sch 5
        paras 2,3,4,5,6(1)(a)(b)(2); Finance, 2001 c 9, ss 8(1)(12), 9, 10, 11,
        12(1)-(3)(5)(6), 13(2)(b)(4)(14), sch 2, paras 1-11; Finance, 2002 c 23, ss
        15(1)(2), 16, 18(1)(3), 20(1); Finance, 2003 c 14, s 14(1)-(4); Finance, 2005 c 7,
        s 7(1)(7)-(11)(12)(a)(b)(16); Finance, 2006 c 25, s 13(1)-(7); Finance, 2007 c
        11, s 11(1)-(9); Finance, 2008 c 9, ss 17(1)-(5), 146; Finance, 2009 c 10, s 13;
        ibid, s 14(1)-(4)(6)-(8); ibid, s 14, sch 4 paras 1, 5; Finance, 2010 c 13, s 11(1);
        Finance, 2011 c 11, ss 21(2)-(5), 22(2)-(5); Finance, 2012 c 14, s 195(2)-(5);
        Finance, 2013 c 29, s 187(2)-(5), sch 37 para 5; Finance, 2014 c 26, ss 81(2)-(5),
        82(1), 83(2)-(7)(8)(b); ibid, sch 18 para 6; Finance, 2015 c 11, s 58(2)(3);
        Finance (No. 2), 2015 c 33, s 46(2)
    rep in pt—Finance, 1996 c 8, ss 15(2)(b)(4), 17(7)(11)(15),18(2)(b)(5), 205, sch 41
        pt II; Finance, 1998 c 36, ss 16, 165, sch 1, paras 6(3),7(4), 8(4),11(4),17(1),
        17(1), sch 27 pt I(3), Note; Finance, 2001 c 9, ss 13(2)(a)(4)(14), 110, sch 33
        pt 1(3), Note 2; Finance, 2001 c 9, ss 13(3)(4)(14), 110, sch 33 pt 1(3), Note 2;
        Finance, 2002 c 23, ss 20(2)(a)(3)(4), 141, sch 40 pt 1(5), Note 1; Finance,
        2005 c 7, ss 7(1)(7)(12)(c)(16), 104, sch 11 pt 1, Note; Finance, 2014 c 26, s
        83(8)(a)(9); ibid, sch 18 paras 3(b), 4, 5, 7, 8, 9, 10(d)(e)
    appl—SI 2002/2742, reg 42(2); Income Tax (Earnings and Pensions), 2003 c 1,
        s 242(5)

sch 2 am—Value Added Tax, 1994 c 23, s 100(1), sch 14 para 14; Finance, 1996 c 8,
        s 15(5); (retrosp to 28.11.1995) ibid, s 20; (saving) ibid, s 21; Finance 1997 c 16,
        s 17; Finance, 1998 c 36, s 17; Finance, 1998 c 36, s 16, sch 1,
        paras 16(2)(3)(4)(5)(6)(7)(8),17(2); SIs 1999/2795, art 5; 2000/90, art 3(1),
        sch 1 para 28; Finance, 2001 c 9, s 12(4)(5); Finance, 2001 c 9, s 13(1)(4)(14);
        Vehicles (Crime), 2001 c 3, s 43, sch, para 6; Nat Health Service Reform and
        Health Care Professions, 2002 c 17, s 6(2), sch 5, para 39; Health and Social
        Care (Community Health and Standards), 2003 c 43, s 34, sch 4 paras 95, 96;
        (EW) Fire and Rescue Services, 2004 c 21, s 53, sch 1 para 85(1)-(3); SIs
        2004/2987, art 2(1)(g); (S) 2005/2060, art 3, sch pt 1 para 3; Nat Health Service
        (Conseq Provns), 2006 c 43, s 2, sch 1 paras 170-172; Finance, 2006 c 25, s
        13(8); SI 2006/1254, art 63, sch 3; Health and Social Care, 2008 c 14, s 95, sch
        5 para 62(b); Finance, 2009 c 10, s 14, sch 4 paras 1, 6; Police and Fire Reform
        (S), 2012 asp 8, sch 7 para 58; Finance, 2013 c 29, sch 37 para 6(2)-(5); Finance,

1994
c 22 *continued*

2014 c 26, ss 84(1), 85(1); ibid, sch 18 para 3(c)(i)(vi); Finance, 2015 c 11, s 59(1); Finance (No. 2), 2015 c 33, s 46(3)

rep in pt —(retrosp to 28.11.1995) Finance, 1996 c 8, ss 20(7)(c)(9)(a)(10), 205, sch 41 pt II; (saving) ibid, ss 21(5)-(7), 205, sch 41 pt II; Finance 1997 c 16, ss 18, 113, sch 3 paras 7(4), 9, sch 18 pt III Note; Health and Social Care, 2008 c 14, s 95, sch 15, sch 5 para 62(a); (prosp) Health and Social Care, 2012 c 7, sch 14 para 64; SI 2013/594, art 2; Finance, 2014 c 26, sch 18 para 3(c)(ii)(iii)(iv)(v)(vii)

sch 2A am—Finance, 1997 c 16, s 20(1)-(4); Finance, 2008 c 9, s 145, sch 45 paras 1, 4, 5(1)-(4)(a),(5)-8

rep in pt—Finance, 2008 c 9, s 145, sch 45 paras 1, 4, 5(4)(b); Finance, 2013 c 29, s 189(3)

sch 3 rep in pt—Value Added Tax, 1994 c 23, s 100(2), sch 15; Finance, 1996 c 8, ss 22(7)(a)(b),205, sch 41 pt II; Communications, 2003 c 21, s 406(7), sch 19(1); SI 2003/1900, arts 2(1), 3(1), sch 1; Income Tax (Earnings and Pensions), 2003 c 1, s 724(1), sch 8 pt 1; Nat Health Service (Conseq Provns), 2006 c 43, s 6, sch 4; Wireless Telegraphy, 2006 c 36, s 125, sch 9; SI 2006/1407, art 3, sch 2; SI 2009/818, reg 4; Scrap Metal Dealers, 2013 c 10, s 19(1)(c)

sch 4 am—Finance, 2002 c 23, s 18(2)(3); Finance, 2005 c 7, s 7(1)(4)(5)(14); Finance, 2014 c 26, s 89(4)(9)

rep in pt —Finance, 2009 c 10, s 14(1)(5); Finance, 2014 c 26, sch 18 para 10(b)

sch 5 am—Employment Rights, 1996 c 18, s 240, sch 1 para 64

c 23 **Value Added Tax**

ext—Finance, 1999 c 16, s 13(6)

mod—(retrosp to 4.12.1996) Finance, 1997 c 16, s 49(5)

see —(Crown status for the purposes of the Act ext) SI 1999/677, art 6

restr—(retrosp to 4.12.1996) Finance, 1997 c 16, s 49(3)

saved—SI 2008/568, art 4

appl (mod)—Finance (No 2), 2010 c 31, s 3, sch 2 para 20(2)

s 2 am—Finance (No 2), 1997 c 58), s 6; Finance, 2001 c 9, s 99(1)(2)(6)(7)(a)(9)(a), sch 31 pt 2, para 2; SI 2008/3020, art 3; Finance, 2009 c 10, s 9, sch 3 para 25(1)(2); Finance (No 2), 2010 c 31, s 3(1)

ext—Finance, 2000 c 17, s 30(1), sch 6 pt II para 9(4)

rep in pt—Finance, 2001 c 9, ss 99(1)(3)(7)(b)(8), 110, sch 33 pt 3(1), Notes 1(a), 2

mod—Finance, 2009 c 10, s 9(1)

see (power to am restr temp)—Finance (No. 2), 2015 c 33, s 2(1)(5)

s 3 am—Finance, 2000 c 17, s 136(1)(10)

s 3A added—Finance, 2003 c 14, s 23, sch 2 paras 1, 2

am—Finance, 2014 c 26, sch 22 paras 2, 12

s 5 am—SI 2007/2173

appl (mod)—Finance, 2008 c 9, s 113, sch 36 para 34(4)

s 6 am—Finance, 1996 c 8, ss 25,26, sch 3 para 1; (retrosp) Finance, 1998 c 36, s 22(2)(3); Finance, 2002 c 23, s 24(4)(a)(5)(6)

rep in pt—Finance, 2002 c 23, ss 24(1)(a)(5)(6), 141, sch 40 pt 2(2), Note; Finance, 2009 c 10, s 76, sch 36 paras 1, 2, 19

appl (mod)—Finance (No 2), 2010 c 31, s 3, sch 2 para 4(1)

s 7 am—Finance, 1996 c 8, ss 25,26, sch 3 para 2; Finance, 2009 c 10, s 76, sch 36 paras 1, 3(5); Finance, 2012 c 14, sch 28 para 3

rep in pt —Finance, 2009 c 10, s 76, sch 36 paras 1, 3(1)-(4)

s 7A added —Finance, 2009 c 10, s 76, sch 36 paras 1, 4

s 8 am—Finance, 1997 c 16, s 42; Finance, 2009 c 10, s 76, sch 36 paras 1, 5(1)-(4)(6)(7)

rep in pt —Finance, 2009 c 10, s 76, sch 36 paras 1, 5(1)(5)

s 9 subst —Finance, 2009 c 10, s 76, sch 36 paras 1, 6

s 9A added—Finance, 2004 c 12, s 21

am—Finance (No 3), 2010 c 33, s 20(1); Finance, 2014 c 26, s 104

s 11 appl (mod)—Finance, 2008 c 9, s 113, sch 36 para 34(4)

s 12 am—Finance, 1996 c 8, ss 25,26, sch 3 para 3

s 13 am—Finance, 1996 c 8, ss 25,26, sch 3 para 4

s 15 appl (mod)—Finance, 2008 c 9, s 113, sch 36 para 34(4)

s 16 am—Postal Services, 2000 c 26, s 127(4), sch 8 pt II para 22(2)

s 18 am—Finance (No 2), 2005 c 22, s 1

ss 18A-18F added—Finance, 1996 c 8, ss 25,26, sch 3 para 5

1994

c 23 s 18A-F *continued*

        appl—Income Tax (Earnings and Pensions), 2003 c 1, s 702(6)

s 18A am—SI 2007/2194, art 10, sch 4

s 18B rep in pt—Finance, 2012 c 14, sch 29 para 2(2)(3)
      am—Finance, 2012 c 14, sch 29 para 2(4)

s 18C rep in pt—Finance, 2012 c 14, sch 29 para 3(2)
      am—Finance, 2012 c 14, sch 29 para 3(3)

s 20 am—Finance, 1996 c 8, ss 25,26, sch 3 para 6

s 21 am—Finance, 1996 c 8, s 27(3)(4); Finance, 1999 c 16, s 12; Finance, 2006 c 25, s 18;
      SIs 2008/3020, art 4; 2009/730, art 17; Finance (No 2), A c 31, s 3(2)
      rep in pt—Finance, 1996 c 8, ss 27(2)(4),205, sch 41 pt I

s 22 rep—Finance, 1996 c 8, ss 28,205, sch 41 pt IV

s 23 subst by ss 23, 23A—Finance, 2012 c 14, sch 24 para 63

s 23A am—Finance, 2014 c 26, sch 28 para 19

s 24 am—Finance, 2003 c 14, s 17(1)(2)(8); Finance (No 3), 2010 c 33, s 19, sch 8 para
      1(3)-(6)
      rep in pt—Finance (No 3), 2010 c 33, s 19, sch 8 para 1(2)(7)

s 25 mod—Finance, 2008 c 9, s 121(2)

s 26 excl—Finance, 1999 c 16, s 13(1)
      am—Finance (No 3), 2010 c 33, s 19, sch 8 para 2

s 26A added—Finance, 2002 c 23, s 22(1)(3)

s 26AB added —Finance, 2006 c 25, s 19(2)

s 26B added—(retrosp to 24.4.2002) Finance, 2002 c 23, s 23(1)(4)

s 28 am—Finance, 1996 c 8, s 34; Finance, 1997 c 16, s 43

s 29 ext—SI 1999/3145, art 9(1)

s 29A added—Finance, 2001 c 9, s 99(1)(4)(7)(c)
      am—Finance, 2000 c 17, sch 6 pt II, para 9

s 29A see (power to am restr temp)—Finance (No. 2), 2015 c 33, s 2(2)(5)

s 30 am—Finance, 1996 c 8, ss 25,26,29(2)(5), sch 3 para 7

s 31 ext—SI 1999/3145, art 9(1); Finance, 1999 c 16, s 13(2)
      am—Finance, 2012 c 14, s 197(3)

s 33 rep in pt—(prosp) GLA, 1999 c 29, ss 325, 423, sch 27 para 68, sch 34 pt VII; (S)
          Public Health etc (S), 2008 asp 5, s 126, sch 3 pt 1
      am—Communications, 2003 c 21, s 406(1), sch 17 para 129(1)(2); Loc Transport,
          2008 c 26, s 77, sch 4 para 59; Police Reform and Social Responsibility, 2011 c
          13, sch 16 para 217

s 33A added—Finance, 2001 c 9, s 98(1)(2)(10)(11)
      am—Finance, 2008 c 9, s 118, sch 39 paras 32, 33

s 33B added—Finance, 2011 c 11, s 76(1)

ss 33C, 33D added—Finance, 2015 c 11, s 66(1)

s 35 am—Finance, 1996 c 8, s 30; SI 2001/2305, art 4; Finance, 2012 c 14, sch 29 para 4

s 36 rep in pt—Finance, 1997 c 16, ss 39, 113, sch 18 pt IV(3), Note; Finance, 1998 c 36,
          ss 23(1)(7),165, sch 27 pt II, Note; Finance, 2002 c 23, ss 22(2)(3), 141, sch
          40 pt 2(1), Note
      excl—Finance, 1997 c 16, s 39(1)
      am—(retrosp to 26.11.1996) Finance, 1997 c 16, s 39(2)-(4); Finance, 1998 c 36,
          s 23(2)(3)(4)(5)(6)(7); Finance, 1999 c 16, s 15(1)(2)(5)

s 36A added—Finance, 2002 c 23, s 25

s 37 ext—Finance, 1999 c 16, s 13(3)

s 38 ext—SI 1999/3145, art 9(1)

s 39 am—Finance, 2009 c 10, s 77(1)(2); Finance, 2012 c 14, sch 29 para 5(2)(3)

s 39A added—Finance, 2009 c 10, s 77(1)(3)

s 41 am—Govt of Wales, 1998 c 38, s 125, sch 12, para 35; Scotland, 1998 c 46, s 125,
          sch 8, para 30; Health, 1999 c 8, s 65, sch 4 para 86; SI 2000/90, art 3(1), sch 1
          para 29; Nat Health Service Reform and Health Care Professions, 2002 c 17, s
          6(2), sch 5, para 40; Health and Social Care (Community Health and Standards),
          2003 c 43, s 33(4); Govt of Wales, 2006 c 32, s 160, sch 10 para 39; Finance,
          2012 c 14, s 198(2)(b); (pt prosp) Health and Social Care, 2012 c 7, sch 14 para
          66; Finance, 2013 c 29, s 191(1); Finance, 2014 c 26, ss 106, 107; Finance, 2015
          c 11, s 67(1)
      rep in pt—SI 2000/90, art 3(1), sch 1 para 29; Finance, 2012 c 14, s 198(2)(a)
      ext—SI 1999/3145, art 8
      appl—Govt Resources and Accounts, 2000 c 20, s 21(3)
      appl (mod)—SI 2007/1118, art 4

1994
c 23 *continued*

s 41A added—Finance, 2012 c 14, s 198(3)
s 43 am—Finance, 1996 c 8, s 31(1); Finance, 1997 c 16, s 40(1)-(5);(retrosp) ibid,
    s 40(1)(3) (retrosp to 26.11.1996) ibid, s 41(1)(2); Finance, 1999 c 16, s 16, sch 2
    para 1(2); Finance, 2004 c 12, s 20(3); Finance, 2009 c 10, s 76, sch 36 paras 1,
    7(1)(2)(a)(b)(ii)(3)(a)(ii)(3)(b), 19; Corporation Tax, 2010 c 4, s 1177, sch 1 para
    285(a); Finance, 2012 c 14, s 200(2)
   rep in pt—Finance, 1996 c 8, s 205, sch 41 pt IV; Finance, 1999 c 16, ss 16, 139, sch 2
    para 1(3), sch 29 pt II(1)
s 43A added—Finance, 1999 c 16, s 16, sch 2 para 2
   am—SI 2009/1890, art 4
s 43AA added—Finance, 2004 c 12, s 20(1)
ss 43B, 43C added—Finance, 1999 c 16, s 16, sch 2 para 2
    am—Finance, 2004 c 12, s 20(4)
s 43D added—Finance, 2004 c 12, s 20(2)
s 46 am—SI 2003/2096, arts 4, 6, sch pt 1 paras 24, 25
s 48 am—Finance, 1997 c 16, s 53(6)(9); Finance, 2001 c 9, s 100; Finance, 2003 c 14,
    s 197(7); SI 2003/3092, art 2; Tribunals, Cts and Enforcement, 2007 c 15, s 62,
    sch 13 paras 117, 118; Finance, 2012 c 14, sch 29 para 6(2)(3)
s 49 rep in pt—Finance, 2007 c 11, s 114, sch 27 pt 6
   am—Finance, 2007 c 11, s 100(1)-(6)(10)
s 51B added—Finance, 2003 c 14, s 19, sch 1 paras 1, 4
s 54 am—Finance, 2012 c 14, sch 28 para 4; ibid, sch 29 para 7(b)
   rep in pt—Finance, 2012 c 14, sch 29 para 7(a)
s 55 am—Finance, 1996 c 8, ss 29(3)(5), 32; Finance, 2012 c 14, sch 28 para 5
   appl—SI 1999/3116, art 4
   excl—SI 1999/3117, art 8
   rep in pt—Finance, 1996 c 8, ss 29(3)(5),205, sch 41 pt IV
s 55A added—Finance, 2006 c 25, s 19(1)
   appl—SIs 2010/2239, art 4; 2014/1458, art 3(1) 4
   am—Finance, 2010 c 13, s 50(1); Finance, 2012 c 14, sch 28 para 6
s 56 rep —Finance, 2013 c 29, sch 38 para 4
   mod—Finance, 2013 c 29, sch 38 para 7(2)
s 57 rep —Finance, 2013 c 29, sch 38 para 4
   am—SIs 1996/2948, art 2; 1998/788, art 2; 2000/811, art 2; 2001/736, art 2;
    2002/1099, art 2; 2003/1057, art 2; 2004/776, art 2; Finance (No 2), 2005 c 22,
    s 2; SIs 2005/722, art 2; 2006/868, art 2; 2007/966, regs 2, 3, 4; 2008/722, arts 2,
    3; 2009/1030, art 2; 2010/919, art 2; 2011/898, art 2(2)(3); 2012/882, art 2(2);
    2013/659, art 2(2)
s 58A added—Finance, 2004 c 12, s 19, sch 2 pt 1 para 1
s 58B added—Finance, 2007 c 11, s 95(8)
s 59 am—Finance, 1996 c 8, s 35(3)(4)(8)
s 59A added—Finance, 1996 c 8, s 35(2)(8)
s 59B added—Finance, 1996 c 8, s 35(5)(8)
ss 60, 61 rep —Finance, 2007 c 11, s 97, sch 24 para 29(d), sch 27(5)
s 62 am—Finance, 1996 c 8, ss 25,26, sch 3 para 8; Finance, 1999 c 16, s 17(1)(2); Finance,
    2001 c 9, s 99(1)(6)(9)(b), sch 31 pt 2, para 3
   rep in pt—Finance, 1996 c 8, ss 25,26,205, sch 3 para 8(2), sch 41 pt IV
s 63, 64 rep—Finance, 2007 c 11, s 97, sch 24 para 29(d), sch 27(5)
s 65 am—Finance, 2006 c 25, s 19(3)
s 66 am—Finance, 2006 c 25, s 19(4); SI 2009/571, art 8, sch 1
s 67 rep—Finance, 2008 c 9, s 123, sch 41 para 25(f)
s 67A added—Tribunals, Cts and Enforcement, 2007 c 15, s 62, sch 13 para 119
   rep—Finance, 2008 c 9, s 129, sch 43 para 4
s 68 am—Finance, 1997 c 16, s 53(7)(9); Tribunals, Cts and Enforcement, 2007 c 15, s 62,
    sch 13 paras 117, 120
s 69 am—Finance, 1996 c 8, ss 25,26,35(6)(8), sch 3 para 9 (retrosp) Finance 1997 c 16,
    s 45(6); Finance, 2000 c 17, s 136(10); Finance, 2006 c 25, s 19(5); SI 2009/571,
    art 8, sch 1; Finance, 2012 c 14, sch 28 para 7
s 69A added—Finance, 2000 c 17, s 137(2)
   am—SI 2009/571, art 8, sch 1
s 69B added—Finance, 2006 c 25, s 21(2)
   am—SI 2009/571, art 8, sch 1
s 70 am—Finance, 2000 c 17, s 137(3); Finance, 2004 c 12, s 19, sch 2 pt 2 para 3

1994

c 23 *continued*

s 72 am—Finance, 2003 c 14, s 17(1)(5)(8); SI 2015/664, sch 2 para 8
　　　rep in pt—Finance, 2007 c 11, s 84, sch 22 paras 3, 8(a), sch 27
s 73 am—Finance, 1996 c 8, ss 25,26,197(6)(d)(7),sch 3 paras 10,11; SI 1996/165, art 2;
　　　Finance, 2000 c 17, s 136(4)(10); Finance, 2008 c 9, s 120(1); Finance, 2012 c
　　　14, sch 28 para 8
　　　rep in pt—Finance, 1996 c 8, s 205, sch 41 pt VIII
s 74 am—Finance, 2000 c 17, s 136(5)(10); SI 2010/530, art 2, sch; Finance, 2012 c 14,
　　　sch 28 para 9
s 76 am—Finance, 1996 c 8, ss 25,26,35(7)(8), sch 3 para 11 (retrosp) Finance 1997 c 16,
　　　s 45(6); Finance, 2000 c 17, s 137(4); Finance, 2006 c 25, s 21(3); Finance, 2007
　　　c 11, s 93(4)-(7); Finance, 2014 c 26, sch 22 para 13
　　　excl—SI 2004/674, reg 22, sch 2 para 3(1)
　　　appl—SI 2004/674, reg 22, sch 2 para 3(2)
　　　rep in pt —Finance, 2007 c 11, s 114, sch 27 pt 5
s 76A addded—Finance, 2014 c 26, sch 22 para 14
s 77 am—(retrosp) Finance, 1997 c 16, s 47(10); Finance, 1999 c 16, s 18(1)(2); Finance,
　　　2008 c 9, s 118, sch 39 paras 32, 34(1)-(4)(a); Finance, 2012 c 14, sch 28 para 10;
　　　Finance, 2014 c 26, sch 22 para 15
　　　rep in pt—Finance, 2008 c 9, s 118, sch 39 paras 32, 34(1), (4)(b)
s 77A added—Finance, 2003 c 14, s 18(1)(4)
　　　am—Finance, 2007 c 11, s 98(1); SI 2007/939, art 2
s 78 power to am—Finance, 1996 c 8, s 197(2)(c)(7)
　　　am—Finance 1996 c 8, s 197(6)(d)(7); Finance 1997 c 16, s 44(4)(5);(retrosp) ibid,
　　　　44(1)-(4)(6); Finance (No 2), 2005 c 22, s 4(1)(2)(6); Finance, 2008 c 9, s 118,
　　　　sch 39 paras 32, 35
s 78A added—(retrosp to 4.12.1996) Finance, 1997 c 16, s 45(1)(4)
　　　appl—(retrosp to 2.12.1996) Finance, 1997 c 16, s 49(4)
　　　ext—SI 2001/759, reg 4(3)
s 79 am—Finance, 1999 c 16, s 19(1)-(4)(5); Finance, 2001 c 9, s 98(1)(4)-(7)(10); Finance,
　　　2011 c 11, s 76(2); Finance, 2015 c 11, s 66(2)
　　　ext—Income Tax (Trading and Other Income), 2005 c 5, s 777
s 80 am—Finance, 1997 c 16, s 46(1)(4); (retrosp to 18.7.1996) ibid, s 47(1)(2)-(5);
　　　Finance (No 2), 2005 c 22, ss 3(1)-(11), 4(6); Finance, 2008 c 9, s 118, sch 39
　　　paras 32, 36; ibid, s 120(2)-(4); Finance, 2014 c 26, sch 22 para 16
　　　excl—Finance, 1997 c 16, s 47(4); (retrosp to 4.12.1996) ibid, s 47(6)(9)
　　　ext—Finance, 1997 c 16, s 47(12)
　　　mod—Finance, 2008 c 9, s 121(1)
s 80A added—Finance, c 16, s 46(2)
　　　am—Finance (No 2), 2005 c 22, s 4(1)(3)(6)
s 80B added—Finance, c 16, s 46(2)
　　　am—Finance (No 2), 2005 c 22, s 4(1)(4)(6)
s 81 am—(retrosp to 18.7.1996) Finance, 1997 c 16), s 48(1)(2); SI 2003/2096, arts 4, 6,
　　　sch pt 1 paras 24, 26(a)(b)(ii)(iii); Finance, 2008 c 9, s 132(1), (2), (3)(b), (c)
　　　rep in pt—SI 2003/2096, arts 4, 6, sch pt 1 paras 24, 26(b)(i); Finance, 2008 c 9,
　　　　s 132(1), (3)(a); Deregulation, 2015 c 20, sch 6 para 2(13)
Pt 5 (ss 82-87) appl (mod)—SIs 2007/2157, reg 44, sch 5 para 1 (subst by SI 2009/56, art
　　　3); 2007/3298 reg 12(2), sch 2 para 2 (subst by SI 2009/56, art 3)
　　　heading am—SI 2009/56, art 3, sch 1 para 217
s 82 subst—SI 2009/56, art 3, sch 1 para 218
　　　appl—SI 2007/3298, reg 13
s 83 am—Finance, 1996 c 8, ss 25,26,31(3), sch 3 para 12; (retrosp to 4.12.1996) Finance,
　　　1997 c 16, ss 45(2)(5), 46(3), 47(7)(9); SI 1997/2542, art 2; Finance, 1999 c 16,
　　　s 16, sch 2 para 3; Finance, 2000 c 17, s 137(5); SI 2001/3641, reg 17; Finance,
　　　2002 c 23, s 23(2)(4); ibid, s 24(4)(b)(5)(6); Finance, 2003 c 14, ss 17(1)(6)(8),
　　　18(2)(4); SI 2003/3075, reg 29, sch 2 pt I para 1; Finance, 2004 c 12, ss 19,
　　　22(1)(3), sch 2 pt 2 para 4; Finance (No 2), 2005 c 22, s 4(1)(5)(6); Finance,
　　　2006 c 25, s 21(4); Finance, 2007 c 11, s 93(8); SI 2009/56, art 3, sch 1 para 219;
　　　Finance, 2009 c 10, s 77(1)(4); Finance, 2012 c 14, s 200(3)
　　　appl—SI 2007/3298, reg 13
　　　rep in pt—SI 2007/2157, reg 51, sch 6
ss 83A-83G added—SI 2009/56, art 3, sch 1 para 220
s 83G am—SI 2014/1264, art 4

1994
c 23 *continued*

s 84 am—Finance, 1996 c 8, s 31(4); (retrosp to 4.12.1996) Finance, 1997 c 16),
    ss 31(3)(4), 43(3)(5); Finance, 1999 c 16, s 16, sch 2 para 4; Finance, 2002 c 23,
    s 23(3)(4); Finance, 2003 c 14, ss 17(1)(7)(8), 18(3)(4); Finance, 2004 c 12, s 19,
    sch 2 pt 2 para 5; Finance, 2006 c 25, s 21(5); Finance, 2007 c 11, s 93(9); SI
    2009/56, art 3, sch 1 para 221; Finance, 2014 c 26, sch 22 para 17
  rep in pt—SI 2009/56, art 3, sch 1 para 221(2)(8)
  appl (mods)—SI 2007/3298, reg 13, sch 2
s 85 mod—Finance, 2000 c 17, sch 6; Finance, 2001 c 9, s 42(7); Finance, 2003 c 14,
    s 37(1); SIs 2003/3102, reg 13; 2007/1509, reg 5; Saving Gateway Accounts,
    2009 c 8, s 56
  appl (mods)—SI 2003/3102, reg 13(1)
  appl—SI 2007/3298, reg 13
  am—Finance, 2000 c 17, s 30(1), sch 6 pt XI para 123(7); SI 2009/56, art 3, sch 1 para
    222(3)
  rep in pt—SI 2009/56, art 3, sch 1 para 222(2)
s 85A added—SI 2009/56, art 3, sch 1 para 223
s 85B added—SI 2009/56, art 3, sch 1 para 223
  mod—Finance, 1994 c 9, ss 16, 60 (amended by SI 2009/56, art 3, sch 1); Finance,
    2000 c 17, sch 6 (amended by SI 2009/56, art 3, sch 1);; Saving Gateway
    Accounts, 2009 c 8, s 56 (amended by SI 2009/56, art 3, sch 1);
  ss 86, 87 rep—SI 2009/56, art 3, sch 1 para 224
s 88 am—Finance, 2001 c 9, s 99(1)(6), sch 31 pt 2, para 4; Finance, 2002 c 23, s
    24(4)(c)(5)(6)
s 90 am—Finance, 2001 c 9, s 98(1)(8)(10); Finance, 2011 c 11, s 76(3); Finance, 2015 c
    11, s 66(3)
s 91 am—SI 1996/273, art 5(1), sch 2 para 27; SI 1999/1820, art 4, sch 2 pt I para 114(2);
    Statistics and Registration Service, 2007 c 18, s 46, sch 2 para 6
s 94 rep in pt—Finance, 1999 c 16, ss 20, 139, sch 20 pt II(2), Note
  am—Finance, 2007 c 11, s 100(7)(10)
s 95 am—SI 1994/3128
s 96 am—SI 1996/739 art 7(1), sch 1 pt I para 8; (retrosp) Finance c 16, s 35(1)(4); Finance,
    1998 c 36, s 24; Abolition of Feudal Tenure etc (S), 2000 asp 5, s 76(1), sch 12
    pt I para 57; Finance, 2001 c 9, s 99(1)(6), sch 31 pt 2, para 5; SI 2001/1149,
    art 3(1), sch 1, para 101; Finance, 2003 c 14, s 20; Finance, 2009 c 10, s 76, sch
    36 paras 1, 8(1)(2); SI 2009/56, art 3, sch 1 para 225
  rep in pt—Abolition of Feudal Tenure etc (S), 2000 asp 5, s 76(1)(2), sch 12 pt I
    para 57, sch 13 pt I; Finance, 2009 c 10, s 76, sch 36 paras 1, 8(1)(3); Finance
    (No 3), 2010 c 33, s 22(3)(a)
s 97 am—Finance, 1996 c 8, s 33(3); Finance, 2001 c 9, s 99(1)(6)(9)(a), sch 31 pt 2,
    para 6; Finance, 2004 c 12, ss 19, 20(5), 22(1)(4), sch 2 pt 2 para 6; Finance,
    2006 c 25, s 19(6); ibid, s 22(2); Finance, 2007 c 11, s 98(2); Finance, 2009 c 10,
    s 9, sch 3 para 25(1)(3); Finance, 2009 c 10, s 76, sch 36 paras 1, 9; Finance,
    2012 c 14, s 200(4); Finance, 2013 c 29, sch 38 para 5(a)(b)
  ext—Finance, 1999 c 16, s 13(6)
  rep in pt—Finance, 1996 c 8, s 205, sch 41 pt I; Finance, 2001 c 9, s 110, sch 33
    pt 3(1), Note 1(a); SI 2009/56, art 3, sch 1 para 226
s 97A added—(17.3.1998) (retrosp) Finance, 1998 c 36, s 22(1)(3)
  am—Finance, 2009 c 10, s 76, sch 36 paras 1, 10
  excl—Finance, 2014 c 26, s 105(1)
sch A1 am—SI 1998/1375, arts 3,4,5,6; Finance, 2000 c 17, s 135(1)(2), sch 35 paras 2-4,
    5-7,8(1)-(5),9,10; SI 2000/2954, arts 2,3,4; Finance, 2001 c 9, ss 96(1)(2)(3),
    97(1)(2)(3)
  rep & superseded—Finance, 2001 c 9, ss 99(1)(3)(7)(b), 110, sch 33 pt 3(1), Note 2
sch 1 rep in pt—Finance, 1997 c 16, ss 31(2) 113, sch 18 pt IV(1), Note
  am—SI 1994/2905; Finance, 1996 c 8, ss 25, 26, sch 3 para 13; SI 1996/2950, art 2;
    Finance, 1997 c 16, ss 31(1), 32; SIs 1997/1628, art 2(a)(b); 1998/761,
    art 2(a)(b); 1999/595, art 2; Finance, 2000 c 17, s 136(6)(10); SIs 2000/804,
    art 2; 2001/640, art 2; 2002/1098, art 2; 2003/1058, art 2; Finance, 2003 c 14,
    s 23, sch 2 paras 1, 3; SIs 2004/775, art 2; 2005/727, art 2; 2006/876, art 2;
    2007/941, reg 2; Finance, 2007 c 11, s 100(8)(10); SIs 2008/707, art 2;
    2009/1031, arts 2, 3; 2010/920, arts 2, 3; 2011/897, art 3(a)(b); Finance, 2012 c
    14, sch 28 paras 11(2)-(7), 12; ibid, sch 29 para 8; SIs 2012/883, art 3(a)(b);
    2013/660, art 3(a)-(c); 2014/703, art 3(a); 2015/750, art 3(a)-(c)

1994
c 23 *continued*

    sch 1A added—Finance, 2012 c 14, sch 28 para 1
        am—Finance, 2014 c 26, sch 22 para 18
    sch 2 am—Finance, 1996 c 8, ss 25,26, sch 3 para 14; Finance, 2012 c 14, sch 28 para 14;
        ibid, sch 29 para 9
        ext—SI 1999/3145, art 9(3)
    sch 3 am—SI 1994/2905; Finance 1996 c 8, ss 25,26, sch 3 para 15; SIs 1996/2950, art 3;
        1997/1628, art 3; 1998/761, art 3; 1999/595, art 3; Finance, 2000 c 17,
        s 136(7)(10); SIs 2000/804, art 3; 2001/640, art 3; 2002/1098, art 3; 2003/1058,
        art 3(a)(b); 2004/775, art 3; 2005/727, art 3; 2006/876, art 3; 2007/941, reg 3;
        2008/707, art 2; 2009/1031, arts 2, 4; 2010/920, arts 2, 4; 2011/897, art 4;
        Finance, 2012 c 14, sch 28 para 15; ibid, sch 29 para 10; SIs 2012/883, art 4;
        2013/660, art 4(a)(b); 2014/703, art 4; 2015/750, art 4(a)(b)
        ext—SI 1999/3145, art 9(3)
    sch 3A added—Finance, 2000 c 17, s 136(8)(10), sch 36
        am—Finance, 2012 c 14, sch 28 para 16; ibid, sch 29 para 11
    sch 3B added—Finance, 2003 c 14, s 23, sch 2 paras 1, 4
        am—Commrs for Revenue and Customs, 2005 c 11, s 50(6), sch 4 paras 54, 55; SI
        2009/56, art 3, sch 1 para 227; Finance, 2012 c 14, sch 28 para 17; Finance,
        2014 c 26, sch 22 paras 4, 5, 6(2)(3)(5)(b)(6)(a)(8), 7(2)(a)(b)(3)(a)(4)-(8), 8,
        9(2)-(6)(8), 10(2),(3)
        rep in pt—Finance, 2014 c 26, sch 22 para 6(4)(5)(a)(6)(b)(7), 7(2)(b)(c)(d)(3)(b),
        9(7), 10(4)
    sch 3BA added—Finance, 2014 c 26, sch 22 para 1
        excl—SI 1995/2518 pt 27, reg 223 (inserted by SI 2014/2430, reg 11)
    sch 4 am—Finance, 1996 c 8, s 33; (retrosp to 17.3.1998) Finance, 1998 c 36,
        s 21(1)(2)(3)(4)(5)(6); Finance, 2000 c 17, s 136(9)(10); SI 2000/266, art 2;
        SI 2001/735, art 2; Finance, 2003 c 14, ss 21, 22; Finance, 2007 c 11, s
        99(1)-(3)(6)-(7); ibid, s 100(9)(10); Finance (No 3), 2010 c 33, ss 19, 20(2), sch
        8 para 3(1); Finance, 2011 c 11, s 74(2)
        rep in pt—Finance, 1996 c 8, ss 29(4)(5),205, sch 41 pt IV; Finance, 2007 c 11, s 114,
        sch 27 pt 6; Finance, 2011 c 11, s 74(3)
        excl—SIs 2004/3150, art 2; 2010/2925, art 3
        appl (mod)—Finance, 2008 c 9, s 113, sch 36 para 34(4)
    sch 4A added —Finance, 2009 c 10, s 76, sch 36 paras 1, 11
        rep in pt —Finance, 2009 c 10, s 76, sch 36 paras 15(1)(2); SI 2014/2726, art 4(a)
        am—Finance, 2009 c 10, s 76, sch 36 paras 15(1)(3)(4); ibid, s 76, sch 36 para 17;
        SIs 2010/3017, art 2; 2012/2787, art 2; 2014/2726, arts 3, 4(b)
    sch 5 rep —Finance, 2009 c 10, s 76, sch 36 paras 1, 12
    sch 5A added—Finance, 1996 c 8, ss 25,26, sch 3 para 18
    sch 6 mod—SI 1997/1523, arts 7,8
        rep in pt—Finance, 2003 c 14, ss 19, 216, sch 1 paras 3, 4, sch 43 pt 2, Note
        am—Finance, 2004 c 12, s 22(1)(2)(5)(6); Finance (No 2), 2005 c 22, s 5; Finance,
        2007 c 11, s 99(4)(5); Corporation Tax, 2010 c 4, s 1177, sch 1 para 285(b);
        Finance, 2012 c 14, s 200(6)(7); Finance, 2013 c 29, sch 38 paras 2, 3, 6;
        Finance, 2014 c 26, s 108(1)
    sch 7 ext—SI 1999/3145, art 9(3)
        am—SI 2004/777, arts 2, 3; Corporation Tax, 2010 c 4, s 1177, sch 1 para 285(c)
    sch 7A added—Finance, 2001 c 9, s 99(1)(5)(7)(a), sch 31 pt 1
    sch 7A see (power to am restr temp)—Finance, (No. 2), 2015 c 33, s 2(3)(5)
        am—Tax Credits, 2002 c 21, s 47, sch 3, paras 47, 48; SIs 2002/1100, arts 2, 3-5;
        2005/726, arts 2, 3; 3329, art 3; 2006/1472, arts 3, 4; 2007/1601, arts 2-5;
        2007/3448, arts 2-4; 2008/2676, art 2; 2009/1359, arts 2-5; Finance, 2012 c
        14, sch 26 para 6(2)(3); Finance, 2013 c 29, s 193(2); SIs 2013/430, art
        2(2)(3); 601, art 2; 630, reg 9(2)
        rep in pt—(prosp) Welfare Reform, 2012 c 5, sch 14 pt 9; Finance, 2013 c 29, s
        193(3)
        mod—SI 2008/1410, arts 2, 3
    sch 8 am—SI s 1994/3014; 1996/1661, art 2(b); Planning (Conseq Provns) (S), 1997 c 11,
        s 4, sch 2 para 57(a)(b)(S) ibid, s 4, sch 2 para 57(a); (retrosp to 26.11.1996)
        Finance, 1997 c 16, ss 33(1)(2), 34(1)-(3); SIs 1997/50, art 2(a)(b); 2744, arts 3,
        4, 5, 7; (retrosp) Finance, 1999 c 16, s 14; SIs 1999/1642, art 2, 1820, art 4,
        sch 2 pt I para 114(3); Postal Services, 2000 c 26, s 127(4), sch 8 pt II
        para 22(3); SIs 2000/503, arts 3,4; 2000/805, arts 3,4,5-9; 2000/1517, arts 3,4,5;

2001/732, arts 2-6; 2001/753, arts 2, 3; 2001/754, arts 2-6; 2001/2305, art 3; 2002/1173, art 2; 2002/456, art 2(a)(b); 2002/1397, art 12, sch pt I, para 11; 2002/2813, arts 2-4; Tax Credits, 2002 c 21, s 47, sch 3, paras 47, 49; Health and Social Care (Community Health and Standards), 2003 c 43, s 34, sch 4 paras 97, 98; SI 2004/3343, art 2; Nat Health Service (Conseq Provns), 2006 c 43, s 2, sch 1 para 174; SIs 2006/1750, art 2; 2006/2407, reg 44, sch 9; 2007/289, art 67, sch 1; 2009/2972, arts 2, 3, 5, 6; 2009/2093, arts 2-4; Corporation Tax, 2010 c 4, s 1177, sch 1 para 285(d); Finance (No 3), 2010 c 33, ss 21(1)-(3), 22(1); SIs 2010/231, art 68, sch 4; 2010/486, art 2; Finance, 2011 c 11, s 75(2)(3); SI 2011/2085, sch 1 para 28(2); (pt prosp) Health and Social Care, 2012 c 7, sch 14 para 67(b); Finance, 2012 c 14, sch 26 paras 2(2)(4), 3(3)(4), 4(2)-(4), 5(2); ibid, sch 28 para 13; ibid, sch 34 para 42(a)(b)(i); SIs 2012/700, sch para 5(2); 2012/1916, sch 34 para 42(a)(b)(i); 2012/2907, art 3(1)(2); 2013/601, art 3(a)(b); 2013/630, reg 9(3)(b); 2014/1111, art 2

sch 8 see (power to am restr temp)—Finance (No. 2), 2015 c 33, s 2(4)(5)

    appl—SI 1995/2518, reg 84(8); Finance, 2012 c 14, sch 27 para 3(2)

    rep in pt—SIs 2006/1914, reg 75; 2007/3101, reg 65; 2009/2972, arts 2, 4, 7; 2010/2549, art 2; (prosp) Welfare Reform, 2012 c 5, sch 14 pt 9; (pt prosp) Health and Social Care, 2012 c 7, sch 14 para 67(a); Finance, 2012 c 14, sch 26 para 3(2)(5)(6); SI 2012/1916, sch 34 para 42(b)(ii)

    mod—SI 2012/1909, sch 7 para 15

    appl (mods)—SI 2013/349, sch 9 para 17

    am—SIs 2015/1862, sch 5 Table; 1949, art 2(2)

sch 9 am—SIs 1994/2969; 1995/2518, reg 84(5)(a)(6); Nursery Education and Grant-Maintained Schools, 1996 c 50, s 10, sch 3 para 15; Education, 1996 c 56, s 582(1), sch 37 pt I para 125; SIs 1996/1256, art 2(a), 2949, art 2; Finance, 1997 c 16, s 38(1)(2); Nurses, Midwives and Health Visitors, 1997 c 24, s 23(1), sch 4 para 6 SI 1997/510, art 2; School Standards and Framework, 1998 c 31, s 140(1), sch 30, para 51(a); (NI) SI 1998/1759, art 91(1), sch 5, pt II; SIs 1998/1294, art 2; 1999/594, arts 2,3,5-7, 1999/1575, art 2, 1999/1994, arts 2-5, 1999/2833, art 2(1)-(3), 2834, art 2, 1999/3116, art 2; Postal Services, 2000 c 26, s 127(4), sch 8 pt II para 22(4)(a)(b); Learning and Skills, 2000 c 21, s 149, sch 9 para 47; SIs 2000/802, art 3; 2001/3649, arts 347, 348; Finance, 2001 c 9, s 98(1)(9)(10); 2002/253, art 54(3), sch 5, para 12; SIs 254, art 48(3), sch 4, para 6; 762, arts 2-6; Finance, 2003 c 14, s 10(4)(b); SIs 2003/1569, art 2(a)(c); 2003/24, arts 2, 3; Communications, 2003 c 21, s 406(1), sch 17 para 129(1)(3); SIs 2003/1900, arts 2(1),3(1), sch 1; 2003/3142, art 3(2); 2004/3083, arts 2-4, 6; 3379, reg 4; 2005/3328, art 2; 3238 (W 243), arts 7, 9(1), sch 1 para 30; 2011, art 49, sch 6 pt 1 para 3 (for appt day(s) see Gazettes); 2006/2685, art 2; 2007/289, art 67, sch 1; 2007/206, arts 3-6; 2007/2163, arts 2-4; 2008/1892, art 2; 2008/2547, art 3; Corporation Tax, 2010 c 4, s 1177, sch 1 para 285(e); Finance (No 3), 2010 c 33, s 22(2); SIs 2010/231, art 68, sch 4; 2010/1080, art 2, sch 1; Finance, 2011 c 11, s 76(4); Educ, 2011 c 21, sch 16 para 9(2)-(5); SI 2011/2085, sch 1 para 28(3); Health and Social Care, 2012 c 7, ss 213(7)(g), 220(4); Finance, 2012 c 14, s 197(1)(2); ibid, sch 24 para 64(2)(3)(a)(4)(5)(a)(b); ibid, sch 26 para 5(2)-(6); Financial Services, 2012 c 21, sch 18 para 81; SIs 2012/58, art 2; 2013/1402, art 2(2)(3); Children and Families, 2014 c 6, sch 3 para 66; Finance, 2015 c 11, s 66(4); Deregulation, 2015 c 20, sch 14 para 41(3)(4)

    appl—SIs 1999/3115, art 2, 3121, art 3

    rep in pt—School Standards and Framework, 1998 c 31, s 140(1)(3), sch 30, para 51(b), sch 31; SI 1999/594, arts 2, 4; Standards in Scotland's Schools etc, 2000, asp 6, s 60(2), sch 3; SIs 2003/1568, art 2; 2003/1569, art 2(b)(d)-(i); 2004/3083, arts 2, 5; 2006/1914, reg 75; 2007/3101, reg 65; 2008/2547, art 3; 2008/1892, art 2; Health and Social Care, 2008 c 14, s 166, sch 15; Finance, 2009 c 10, s 113(1)-(3); SI 2010/1080, art 2, schs 1, 2; Educ, 2011 c 21, sch 16 para 9(2); SI 2011/2085, sch 1 para 28(3)(a), sch 2; Finance, 2012 c 14, sch 24 para 64(3)(b); SIs 2013/1773, sch 1 para 40(a)(b); 2013/1897, art 2; 2014/3185, art 2; Deregulation, 2015 c 20, sch 14 para 41(2)

sch 9A added—Finance, 1996 c 8, s 31(2), sch 4

    am—Finance, 1999 c 16, s 16, sch 2 para 5(2)-(4)

    renumbered—Finance, 1999 c 16, s 16, sch 2 para 5(2)

sch 10 subst—SI 2008/1146, art 2

1994

c 23 sch 10 *continued*

  am—SI 2009/1966, arts 2-8; Corporation Tax, 2010 c 4, s 1177, sch 1 para 285(f);
   SIs 2010/485, arts 3-6; 2011/86, arts 5, 6, 8; 2012/700, sch para 5(3)
  rep in pt—SIs 2010/485, arts 3, 4, 7; 2011/86, art 7
 sch 10A added—Finance, 2003 c 14, s 19, sch 1 paras 2, 4
  am—Finance, 2006 c 25, s 22(3); Finance, 2012 c 14, s 201(1)
 sch 11 am—Finance, 1996 c 8, s 38;Finance, 1997 c 16, s 113, sch 18 pt V(2) Note;
  Finance, 1999 c 16, s 15(3); Crim. Justice and Police, 2001 c 16, s 70, sch 2
  pt 2, para 13(1)(2)(f); Finance, 2003 c 14, s 17(1)(3)(4)(8); Commrs for
  Revenue and Customs, 2005 c 11, s 50(6), sch 4 paras 54, 56; Finance, 2006 c
  25, s 19(7); ibid, ss 20, 21(6); SI 2007/1421, art 2; Finance, 2008 c 9, s 115,
  sch 37 paras 4-6; Finance, 2009 c 10, s 78; Finance, 2010 c 13, s 50(2);
  Finance, 2012 c 14, s 202; ibid, sch 24 para 65(2)-(4); ibid, sch 29 para
  12(2)-(7)
  ext—Finance, 1999 c 16, s 13(6); Crim. Justice and Police, 2001 c 16, s 50, sch 1
  pt 1, para 58
  rep in pt—(NI) SI 1997/2983, (NI 21), art 13(2), sch 2; Youth Justice and Crim
  Evidence, 1999 c 23, s 67, sch 6; (NI) SI 1999/2789, art 40(3), sch 3; Finance,
  2002 c 23, ss 24(1)(b)(i)-(iii)(2)(3)(5)(6), 141, sch 40 pt 2(2), Note; Crim
  Justice, 2003 c 44, s 332, sch 37 pt 6; SI 2004/1501, art 46(2), sch 2; Finance,
  2007 c 11, s 84, sch 22 paras 3, 8(b), sch 27; Finance, 2008 c 9, s 113, sch 36
  para 87; ibid, s 138, sch 44 para 6
 sch 11A added—Finance, 2004 c 12, s 19, sch 2 pt 1 para 2
  am—Finance (No 2), 2005 c 22, s 6, sch 1 paras 1-4, 5(1)(2)(b)(3)(4), 6,
  7(1)(2)(b)(3)(4), 8; SIs 2008/954, art 20; 2009/571, art 8, sch 1
  rep in pt—Finance (No 2), 2005 c 22, ss 6, 70, sch 1 paras 1, 5(1)(2)(a), 7(1)(2)(a),
  sch 11 pt 1, Note
 sch 12 rep—SI 2009/56, art 3, sch 1 para 228
 sch 13 saved—Finance, 1997 c 16, s 47(12)
  rep in pt—Finance, 1997 c 16, ss 39(1), 113, sch 18 pt IV(3), Note
 sch 14 rep in pt—Capital Allowances, 2001 c 2, s 580, sch 4; (prosp) Enterprise, 2002 c 40,
  s 278(2), sch 26; SI 2009/56, art 3, sch 1 para 229

c 24 *Appropriation*—rep Appropriation, 1996 c 45, s 3, sch(C)

c 25 **Land Drainage**

c 26 **Trade Marks**
  appl—SI 1996/1908, reg 10(2)(3)
  appl (mods)—SIs (Isle of Man) 1996/729, art 2, sch; 2008/2206, art 3, schs 1-2
  mod—(Isle of Man) SI 2013/2601, art 2, sch
  s 1 appl—SI 2005/3468, reg 38(7)
  s 5 rep in pt—SI 2004/946, regs 3, 7(1)
   am—SI 2004/2332, regs 2, 3
  s 6 am—SIs 1999/1899, reg 13; 2004/2332, regs 2, 4
   mod—SI 2015/829, reg 13(3)(4)
  s 6A added—SI 2004/946, regs 3, 4, 8
   am—SI 2008/1067, regs 3, 4, 6
   mod—SI 2015/829, reg 13(5)(a)(6)
  s 10 am—SI 2004/946, regs 3, 7(2)(a)
   rep in pt—SI 2004/946, regs 3, 7(2)(b)
  ss 15-18 appl—SI 2006/1027, reg 5
  s 19 am—SI 2006/1028, reg 2, sch 2
   appl—SI 2006/1027, reg 5
  s 21 appl—SIs 1996/1908, reg 4; 2006/1027, reg 6
  ss 22-24 appl (mods)—SI 1996/714, art 5
  s 25 am—SI 2006/1028, reg 2, sch 2
   appl (mods)—SI 2008/2206, art 3, sch 2
  ss 33, 35 appl (mods)—SI 2008/2206, art 3, sch 2
  s 37 rep in pt—SI 2007/1976, arts 3, 6
   appl (mods)—SI 2008/2206, art 3, sch 2
  ss 38, 39 appl (mods)—SI 2008/2206, art 3, sch 2
  s 40 am—SI 2004/946, regs 3, 5, 8
  s 46 appl—SI 1996/1908, reg 3(3)
   appl (mods)—SI 1996/714, art 13
   mod—SI 2015/829, reg 13(7)(8)
  s 47 appl—SI 1996/1908, reg 3(3)

1994
c 26 s 47 *continued*
    appl (mods)—SI 1996/714, art 13
    am—SIs 2004/946, regs 3, 6, 9; 2008/1067, regs 3, 5, 7
    mod—SI 2015/829, reg 13(5)(b)(6)
s 48 appl—SI 1996/714, art 14
s 52 am—Legal Services, 2007 c 29, s 208, sch 21 paras 109, 110
s 53 am—SI 2004/2332, regs 2, 5
s 55 am—SIs 1999/1899, reg 13; 2006/1028, reg 2, sch 2
s 56 am—SI 1999/1899, reg 13
    saved—SI 1999/1899, reg 14(1)
ss 57, 58 am—SI 1999/1899, reg 13
s 61 rep—Finance, 2000 c 17, s 156, sch 40 pt III, Note 1
ss 63, 67 appl (mods)—SI 2008/2206, art 3, sch 2
s 69 am—Constitutional Reform, 2005 c 4, s 59(5), sch 11 pt 4 para 31
s 72 appl—SI 1996/1908, reg 3(3)
s 73 appl (mods)—SI 1996/714, art 15
s 74 appl—SI 1996/1908, reg 3(3)
    appl (mods)—SI 1996/714, art 15
s 75 am—SI 2005/587, art 4(1)(2); Crime and Cts, 2013 c 22, sch 9 para 134
s 76 appl—SI 1996/1908, reg 3(3)
    am—SI 2005/587, art 4(1)(3)
s 77 see—(trans of functions) (S) SIs 1999/678, art 2(1), sch; 1999/1750, art 2, sch 1; (cert
    functions exercisable in S) SI 1999/1748, art 3, sch 1 para 16
    am—Constitutional Reform, 2005 c 4, s 15(1), sch 4 pt 1 para 238; Tribunals, Cts and
    Enforcement, 2007 c 15, s 50, sch 10 para 25; SI 2012/2404, sch 2 para 31
s 82 am—Legal Services, 2007 c 29, s 184(1)(2)
s 83 subst—Legal Services, 2007 c 29, s 184(1)(3)
s 83A added—Legal Services, 2007 c 29, s 184(1)(3)
s 84 am—Legal Services, 2007 c 29, s 184(1)(4); ibid, s 208, sch 21 paras 109, 111
s 85 rep —Legal Services, 2007 c 29, s 184(1)(5), sch 23
s 86 am—Legal Services, 2007 c 29, s 208, sch 21 paras 109, 112
s 87 appl (mods)—SI 1996/1908, reg 5
    am —Legal Services, 2007 c 29, ss 184(1)(6), 208, sch 21 para 109
s 88 am—Legal Services, 2007 c 29, s 208, sch 21 para 113; SI 2009/3348, art 5
s 89 appl (mods)—SI s 1996/714, art 16; 1996/1908, reg 6
    appl—SI 2006/1027, reg 7
    am—SI 2004/1473, reg 13
s 90 rep in pt—Commrs for Revenue and Customs, 2005 c 11, ss 50(6), 52(2), sch 4 para 57,
    sch 5
    appl (mods)—SI s 1996/714, art 16; 1996/1908, reg 6
    appl—Olympic Symbol etc (Protection), 1995 c 32, s 12B(1); SI 2006/1027, reg 7
s 91 appl (mods)—SI s 1996/714, art 16; 1996/1908, reg 6
    am—Commrs for Revenue and Customs, 2005 c 11, s 50(6), sch 4 para 58;
    SI 2008/1277, reg 30, sch 2
    appl—SI 2006/1027, reg 7
s 92 appl (mods)—SI s 1996/714, art 17; 1908, reg 7
    appl—SI 2006/1027, reg 8
s 92A added —Copyright, etc and Trade Marks (Offences and Enforcement), 2002 c 25, s 6
    appl (mods)—(Isle of Man) SI 1996/729, sch, para 11A
    ext—Crim. Justice and Police, 2001 c 16, sch 1 pt 1 para 58A, pt 3 para 107A
    am—(EW) Serious Organised Crime and Police, 2005 c 15, s 174(1), sch 16 para 8
s 93 appl (mods)—SI s 1996/714, art 17; 1908, reg 7
    appl—SI 2006/1027, reg 8
    rep in pt—Consumer Rights, 2015 c 15, sch 6 para 59(2)(3)
    am—Consumer Rights, 2015 c 15, sch 6 para 59(4)
ss 97, 98 appl (mods)—SI s 1996/714, art 17; 1908, reg 7
    appl—SI 2006/1027, reg 8
    am—SI 2008/1277, reg 30, sch 2
s 104 am—SI 2004/2332, regs 2, 6; Legal Services, 2007 c 29, s 208, sch 21 paras 109,
    115
sch 4 rep in pt—Plant Varieties, 1997 c 66, s 52, sch 4; Northern Ireland, 1998 c 47,
    s 100(2), sch 15; SL(R), 2004 c 14, s 1(1), sch 1 pt 2/1; Companies, 2006 c 46,
    s 1295, sch 16; Legal Services, 2007 c 29, sch 23; SI 2009/1941, art 2, sch 2
c 27   **Inshore Fishing (Scotland)**

1994

c 28   **Merchant Shipping (Salvage and Pollution)**
       sch 2 rep in pt—Crime and Cts, 2013 c 22, sch 9 para 141

c 29   **Police and Magistrates' Courts**
       ss 1-26 rep—Police, 1996 c 16, s 103, sch 9 pt I
       s 27 rep in pt—Loc Govt, 1999 c 27, ss 30, 34, sch 2(2)
       ss 28, 29 rep—Police, 1996 c 16, s 103, sch 9 pt I
       s 30 rep (EW)—Loc Govt, 2003 c 26, s 127(2), sch 8 pt 1 (see SI 2003/2938)
       s 32 rep—Police, 1996 c 16, s 103, sch 9 pt I
       s 33 rep —SL(R), 2008 c 12, s 1(1), sch 1 pt 6
       ss 34-38 rep—Police, 1996 c 16, s 103, sch 9 pt I
       s 41 rep —SL(R), 2008 c 12, s 1(1), sch 1 pt 6
       s 45 rep—Police, 1996 c 16, s 103, sch 9 pt I
       Pt 3 (ss 66-68) rep—(saving) Police (NI), 1998 c 32, s 74(2)(3), schs 5,6
       ss 69-79 rep—Justices of the Peace, 1997 c 25, s 73(1)(3), sch 4 pt II para 11(3), sch 6 pt Is
       s 80 rep in pt—(saving) Justices of the Peace, 1997 c 25, s 73(1)(3), sch 4 pt II para 11(3),
          sch 6 pt I
       ss 81-90 rep—Justices of the Peace, 1997 c 25, s 73(1)(3), sch 4 pt II para 11(3), sch 6 pt I
       s 91 rep in pt—Justices of the Peace, 1997 c 25, s 73(1)(3), sch 4 pt II para 11(3), sch 6
       s 94 appl—Justices of the Peace, 1997 c 25, ss 73(1)(4),74(4), sch 4 pt II paras 7(8), 11(3),
          15(3)
       s 95 rep—Police, 1996 c 16, s 103, sch 9 pt I
       s 96 rep in pt —(saving) Police (NI), 1998 c 32, s 74(2)(3), schs 5,6
       schs 1-3 rep—Police, 1996 c 16, s 103, sch 9 pt I
       sch 4 rep in pt—Police, 1996 c 16, s 103, sch 9 pt; Justices of the Peace, 1997 c 25 s 73(3),
          sch 6 pt I; Audit Commission 1998 c 18 s 54(3), sch 5; (prosp) Loc Govt, 2000
          c 22, s 107, sch 6; Postal Services, 2000 c 26, s 127(6), sch 9; Race Relations
          (Amdt), 2000 c 34, s 9(2), sch 3
          am—Police, 1997 c 50, s 88, sch 6 para 22
       sch 5 rep in pt—Police, 1996 c 16, s 103, sch 9 pts I,II
       sch 8 rep in pt—Access to Justice, 1999 c 22, s 106, sch 15 pt V(1)(6); Crim Justice, 2003 c
          44, s 322, sch 37 pt 10
       sch 9 rep in pt—Police, 1996 c 16, s 103, sch 9 pt I

c 30   **Education**
       ext—Teaching and Higher Education, 1998 c 30, s 26(11)
       trans of powers—(W) SI 1999/672, art 2, sch 1
       power to mod—Educ, 2002 c 32, s 177(4)(5)
       excl—Higher Educ, 2004 c 8, s 29(3)
       ss 1-11 rep—Educ, 2005 c 18, ss 98, 99, 123, sch 14 para 11, sch 15, sch 19 pt 3
       s 11A added—Education, 1996 c 56, s 582(1), sch 37 pt I para 126
          rep—Educ, 2011 c 21, sch 5 para 7
       ss 12-17 rep—Educ, 2005 c 18, ss 98, 99, 123, sch 14 para 12, sch 15, sch 19 pt 3
       s 18 rep in pt—School Standards and Framework, 1998 c 31, s 140(3), sch 31
       s 18A added—Teaching and Higher Education, 1998 c 30, s 20
          replaced (by ss 18B, 18C)—Educ, 2005 c 18, ss 98, 99, sch 14 para 13, sch 15
       s 18B am—Educ and Inspections, 2006 c 40, s 157, sch 14 para 19(1)(2)(3)(6)(7); Educ
          and Skills, 2008 c 25, s 164; Educ, 2011 c 21, sch 5 para 8
          rep in pt—Educ and Inspections, 2006 c 40, s 157, sch 14 para 19(4)(5), sch 18; Educ,
          2011 c 21, sch 2 para 18, sch 5 para 9
       s 19 am—Education, 1996 c 56, s 582(1), sch 37 pt I para 128; Educ, 2002 c 32, s 215(1),
          sch 21, para 25; Educ, 2005 c 18, ss 98, 99, sch 14 para 14(b), sch 15
          rep in pt—Educ, 2005 c 18, ss 98, 99, 123, sch 14 para 14(a), sch 15, sch 19 pt 3
       s 20 mod—SI 2013/1793 (W 180), reg 3(c)
       s 21 am—SI 2010/1080, art 2, sch 1; Post-16 Educ (S), 2013 asp 12, sch para 3
       s 22 mod—SI 2013/1793 (W 180), reg 3(c)
       s 23 rep in pt—Educ, 2005 c 18, s 123, sch 19 pt 3
       s 27 rep in pt—Education, 1996 c 56, s 582(2)(3), sch 38 pt I, sch 39
       sch 1 rep—Educ, 2005 c 18, ss 98, 99, 123, sch 14 para 15, sch 15, sch 19 pt 3
       sch 2 rep in pt—Nursery Education and Grant-Maintained Schools, 1996 c 50, s 10, sch 4;
          Education, 1996 c 56, s 582(2)(3), sch 38 pt I sch 39; Audit Commission, 1998
          c 18, s 54(3), sch 5; Race Relations (Amdt), 2000 c 34, s 9(2), sch 3; Educ,
          2002 c 32, s 215(2), sch 22 pt 3; Educ, 2005 c 18, s 123, sch 19 pt 3

c 31   **Firearms (Amendment)**

c 32   **Sale of Goods (Amendment)**

1994

c 33   **Criminal Justice and Public Order**
    appl—(prosp) Prisoners' Earnings, 1996 c 33, s 4(3)
    trans of powers—(W) SI 1999/672, art 2, sch 1
    ss 1-4 rep & superseded—Crime and Disorder, 1998 c 37 ss 73(7)(b), 120(2), sch 10
        excl—SI 1999/3426, art 4(1)(b)
        saving—SI 1999/3426, art 4(5)
    s 1 power to restr—Crime and Disorder, 1998 c 37, s 116(1)(a)
    s 2 mod—(temp) SI 1998/1928, art 3
        power to mod—Crime and Disorder, 1998 c 37, s 116(2)
    s 4 mod—(temp) SI 1998/1928, art 3; Powers of Crim Cts (Sentencing), 2000 c 6,
        s 137(2)(f)
        power to mod—Crime and Disorder, 1998 c 37, s 116(2)
        am—Crime and Disorder, 1998 c 37, s 116(3)
        power to restr—Crime and Disorder, 1998 c 37, s 116(1)(b)
    s 9 am—Offender Management, 2007 c 21, s 16(2); ibid, s 39, sch 3 paras 19, 20
    s 9A added—Offender Management, 2007 c 21, s 17(3)
        mod—Serious Crime, 2007 c 27, s 63, sch 6 para 24
    s 11 am—Offender Management, 2007 c 21, s 17(4)
    s 12 am—Crime and Disorder, 1998 c 37, s 119, sch 8, para 111; Offender Management,
        2007 c 21, s 39, sch 3 paras 19, 21
    s 13 rep in pt—Offender Management, 2007 c 21, s 39, sch 3 paras 19, 22, sch 5
    s 14 am—Offender Management, 2007 c 21, s 39, sch 3 paras 19, 23
    s 15 am—Offender Management, 2007 c 21, s 39, sch 3 paras 19, 24
    s 16 rep—Powers of Crim Cts (Sentencing), 2000 c 6, s 165(3)(4), sch 11 pt I para 2, sch 12
        pt I
    s 18 rep in pt—Powers of Crim Cts (Sentencing), 2000 c 6, s 165(3)(4), sch 11 pt I para 2,
        sch 12 pt I
    s 19 rep in pt—Legal Aid, Sentencing and Punishment of Offenders, 2012 c 10, sch 12 para
        34
    s 20 rep & superseded—Crime and Disorder 1998 c 37, ss 97(5), 120(2), sch 10
    s 21 rep—Legal Aid, Sentencing and Punishment of Offenders, 2012 c 10, sch 12 para 34
    s 23 rep—Legal Aid, Sentencing and Punishment of Offenders, 2012 c 10, sch 12 para 34
    s 25 am—Crim Procedure (Conseq Provns) (S) 1995 c 40, s 5, sch 4 para 93(2); Crime and
        Disorder, 1998 c 37, s 56; Powers of Crim Cts (Sentencing), 2000 c 6, s 165(1),
        sch 9 para 160; Sexual Offences, 2003 c 42, s 139, sch 6 para 32(1)(2); Crim
        Justice, 2003 c 44, s 304, sch 32 pt 1 para 67(b); SI 2008/1779, art 16; Coroners
        and Justice, 2009 c 25, s 144, sch 17 para 3(1)(2)(4); Legal Aid, Sentencing and
        Punishment of Offenders, 2012 c 10, sch 11 para 33
        rep in pt—Crim Justice, 2003 c 44, ss 304, 332, sch 32 pt 1 para 67(a), sch 37 pt 7;
            Coroners and Justice, 2009 c 25, ss 144, 178, sch 17 para 3(1)(3), sch 23 pt 5
    s 26 rep (prosp)—Crim Justice, 2003 c 44, s 332, sch 37 pt 2
    s 29 rep in pt—Crim Justice, 2003 c 44, s 332, sch 37 pt 1
    s 31 rep—Crim Justice, 2003 c 44, s 332, sch 37 pt 5
    s 32 expld—Armed Forces, 1996 c 46, s 6(1)(2)
    s 34 am—Crim Procedure and Investigations, 1996 c 25, s 44(3)(7); Youth Justice and Crim
        Evidence, 1999 c 23, s 58(2), sch 7 para 8; Crim Justice, 2003 c 44, s 41, sch 3 pt
        2 para 64(1)(2)(b); Counter-Terrorism, 2008 c 28, s 22(9)
        appl (mods)—SIs 1997/16, art 2(1), sch; 2006/2326, art 3, sch 1; 2009/990, art 2, schs
        1, 2
        rep in pt—Crim Procedure and Investigations, 1996 c 25, ss 44(4)(7),80, sch 5 para 1;
        (pt prosp) Crim Justice, 2003 c 44, ss 41, 332, sch 3 pt 2 para 64(1)(2)(a), sch
        37 pt 4
        power to appl—Police, 1997 c 50, ss 37(2A)(d), 81(2A)(d)
    s 35 appl (mods)—SIs 1997/16, art 2(1), sch; 2009/990, art 2, schs 1, 2
        rep in pt—Crime and Disorder, 1998 c 37, ss 35(a)(b),120(1)(2), sch 9, para 2, sch 10
        am—Crim Justice, 2003 c 44, s 331, sch 36 pt 4 paras 62, 63
    s 36 am—Crim Procedure and Investigations, 1996 c 25, s 44(3)(7) Youth Justice and Crim
        Evidence, 1999 c 23, s 58(3), sch 7 para 8; Crim Justice, 2003 c 44, s 41, sch 3 pt
        2 para 64(1)(3)(b)
        appl (mods)—SIs 1997/16, art 2(1), sch; 2006/2326, art 3, sch 1; 2009/990, art 2, schs
        1, 2
        rep in pt—Crim Procedure and Investigations, 1996 c 25, ss 44(4)(7),80, sch 5 para 1;
        Crim Justice, 2003 c 44, ss 41, 332, sch 3 pt 2 para 64(1)(3)(a), sch 37 pt 4
        mod—Counter-Terrorism, 2008 c 28, s 22(10)

1994
c 33 *continued*

s 37 am—Youth Justice and Crim Evidence, 1999 c 23, s 58(4), sch 7 para 8; Crim Justice, 2003 c 44, s 41, sch 3 pt 2 para 64(1)(4)(b)

    appl (mods)—SIs 1997/16, art 2(1), sch; 2006/2326, art 3, sch 1; 2009/990, art 2, schs 1, 2

    rep in pt—Crim Procedure and Investigations, 1996 c 25, ss 44(4)(7),80, sch 5 para 1; Crim Justice, 2003 c 44, ss 41, 332, sch 3 pt 2 para 64(1)(4)(a), sch 37 pt 4

    mod—Counter-Terrorism, 2008 c 28, s 22(10)

s 38 am—Youth Justice and Crim Evidence, 1999 c 23, s 58(5), sch 7 para 8; Legal Services, 2007 c 29, s 208, sch 21 para 116

    appl (mods)—SIs 1997/16, art 2(1), sch; 2006/2326, art 3, sch 1; 2009/990, art 2, schs 1, 2

s 39 am—Armed Forces, 1996 c 46, s 5, sch 1 pt IV para 111; Armed Forces, 2006 c 52, s 378, sch 16 para 130

    rep in pt—Armed Forces, 2001 c 19, s 38, sch 7 pt 1

    mod—SI 2009/1059, art 205, sch 1

s 40 rep—Crim Justice, 2003 c 44, s 332, sch 37 pt 10

s 42 rep—Crim Justice, 2003 c 44, s 332, sch 37 pt 10

s 44 rep—(retrosp) Crim Procedure and Investigations, 1996 c 25, ss 44(2)(6),80, sch 5 para 1

s 47 rep in pt—(S) Crim Procedure (Conseq Provns) (S), 1995 c 40, ss 4,6, sch 3 pt II para 16, sch 5

s 48 rep—Powers of Crim Cts (Sentencing), 2000 c 6, s 165(3)(4), sch 11 pt I para 2, sch 12 pt I

s 50 rep—Youth Justice and Crim Evidence, 1999 c 23, s 67, sch 6

s 51 am—Crim Appeal, 1995 c 35, s 29(1), sch 2 para 19; Youth Justice and Crim Evidence, 1999 c 23, s 67, sch 4 paras 21, 22; (prosp) Crim Justice, 2003 c 44, s 331, sch 36 pt 2 para 11(1)-(3); ibid, pt 4 paras 62, 64; Crime and Cts, 2013 c 22, sch 17 para 36; Crim Justice and Cts, 2015 c 2, sch 11 para 14(2)(3)

s 52 rep in pt—Courts, 2003 c 39, s 109(3), sch 10

s 54 rep in pt—Police Reform, 2002 c 30, s 107(2), sch 8

s 55 rep in pt—(EW) Crim Evidence (Amdt), 1997 c 17, ss 1(1), 6(3)

s 57 rep—Protection of Freedoms, 2012 c 9, sch 10 pt 1

s 60 am—(S) Knives, 1997 c 21, s 8(2)(3)-(5)(6)-(10); Crime and Disorder, 1998 c 37, s 25(1); Anti-terrorism, Crime and Security, 2001 c 24, s 101, sch 7, paras 15, 16; Railways and Transport Safety, 2003 c 20, s 73, sch 5 para 4(1)(a)(2)(f); (EW) (prosp) Crim Justice, 2003 c 44, s 280(2)(3), sch 26 para 45(1)(2); SI 2004/1573, art 12(3)(a); Serious Crime, 2007 c 27, s 87

    ext—(S) Knives, 1997 c 21, s 8(11)

    rep in pt—Knives, 1997 c 21, s 8(3)(10); Anti-terrorism, Crime and Security, 2001 c 24, s 125, sch 8 pt 6; Railways and Transport Safety, 2003 c 20, s 73, sch 5 para 4(1)(b)(2)(f); SI 2004/1573, art 12(3)(b)

s 60A added—Crime and Disorder, 1998 c 37, s 26

    am—Anti-terrorism, Crime and Security, 2001 c 24, s 94(2)

s 60AA added—Anti-terrorism, Crime and Security, 2001 c 24, s 94(1)

    rep in pt—Railways and Transport Safety, 2003 c 20, s 73, sch 5 para 4(1)(b)(2)(f)

    am—Railways and Transport Safety, 2003 c 20, s 73, sch 5 para 4(1)(a)(2)(f); (EW) (prosp) Crim Justice, 2003 c 44, s 280(2)(3), sch 26 para 45(1)-(4)

s 60B added—Crime and Disorder, 1998 c 37, s 27(2)

s 61 am—Countryside and Rights of Way, 2000 c 37, s 51, sch 5 pt II para 17; (S) Land Reform (S), 2003 asp 2, s 99, sch 2 paras 10, 11; (W prosp) Commons, 2006 c 26, s 52, sch 5 para 5

    rep in pt—(EW) Serious Organised Crime and Police, 2005 c 15, ss 111, 174(2), sch 7 pt 1 para 31(1)(2), sch 17 pt 2

s 62A added—(EW) Anti-social Behaviour, 2003 c 38, s 60

    am—SI 2010/866, art 5, sch 2

s 62B added—(EW) Anti-social Behaviour, 2003 c 38, s 61

    am—(EW) (prosp) Crim Justice, 2003 c 44, s 280(2)(3), sch 26 para 45(1)(5)

    rep in pt—(EW) Serious Organised Crime and Police, 2005 c 15, ss 111, 174(2), sch 7 pt 1 para 31(1)(3), sch 17 pt 2

s 62C added—(EW) Anti-social Behaviour, 2003 c 38, s 62(1)

s 62D added—(EW) Anti-social Behaviour, 2003 c 38, s 63

s 62E added—(EW) Anti-social Behaviour, 2003 c 38, s 64

s 63 am—Licensing, 2003 c 17, s 198, sch 6 para 111

1994
c 33 s 63 *continued*

  rep in pt—Licensing, 2003 c 17, s 199, sch 7; (EW) Anti-social Behaviour, 2003 c 38,
   ss 58(1)-(6), 92, sch 3; (EW) (prosp) Crim Justice, 2003 c 44, s 280(2)(3), sch
   26 para 45(1)(6); (EW) Serious Organised Crime and Police, 2005 c 15, ss 111,
   174(2), sch 7 pt 1 para 31(1)(4), sch 17 pt 2
s 64 am—(S) Land Reform (S), 2003 asp 2, s 99, sch 2 paras 10, 12
s 65 rep in pt—(EW) Serious Organised Crime and Police, 2005 c 15, ss 111, 174(2), sch 7
   pt 1 para 31(1)(5), sch 17 pt 2
s 67 am—(EW) Anti-social Behaviour, 2003 c 38, s 62(2)
s 68 am—(EW) (prosp) Crim Justice, 2003 c 44, s 280(2)(3), sch 26 para 45(1)(7); (S)
   Land Reform (S), 2003 asp 2, s 99, sch 2 paras 10, 13
  rep in pt—(EW) Anti-social Behaviour, 2003 c 38, ss 59(1)(2), 92, sch 3; (EW) Serious
   Organised Crime and Police, 2005 c 15, ss 111, 174(2), sch 7 pt 1 para
   31(1)(6), sch 17 pt 2
s 69 rep in pt—Anti-social Behaviour, 2003 c 38, ss 59(1)(3), 92, sch 3; (EW) Serious
   Organised Crime and Police, 2005 c 15, ss 111, 174(2), sch 7 pt 1 para
   31(1)(7), sch 17 pt 2
  am—(EW) (prosp) Crim Justice, 2003 c 44, s 280(2)(3), sch 26 para 45(1)(8)
s 76 rep in pt—Serious Organised Crime and Police, 2005 c 15, ss 111, 174(2), sch 7 pt 1
   para 31(1)(8), sch 17 pt 2
s 80 rep in pt —Housing and Regeneration, 2008 c 17, s 321, sch 16
ss 81-83 rep—Terrorism, 2000 c 11, s 125(2), sch 16 pt 1
s 85 rep in pt —Serious Organised Crime and Police, 2005 c 15, s 174(2), sch 17 pt 2
s 92 rep (pt prosp)—Communications, 2003 c 21, s 406(7), sch 19(1); SI 2003/1900, arts
   2(1), 3(1), sch 1; SI 2003/3142, art 3(2)
s 97 rep in pt—Offender Management, 2007 c 21, s 39, sch 5 pt 2
s 100 am—SI 2007/2128, art 8, sch
s 102 am—Crim Procedure (Conseq Provns) (S), 1995 c 40, s 5, sch 4 para 93(3); Crim
   Justice (S), 2003 asp 7, s 76(1)(10); (S) SSI 2005/465, art 2, sch 1 para
   24(1)(2)(a)(b)(i)(ii)(aa)(bb)(iii); Police and Fire Reform (S), 2012 asp 8, sch 7
   para 9(2); SI 2013/602, sch 1 para 4(2)
  rep in pt—(S) SSI 2005/465, art 2, sch 1 para 24(1)(2)(b)(ii)(cc)
s 103 am—SI 1999/1820, art 4, sch 2 pt I para 115(2)
  rep in pt—SSI 2015/39, sch para 3(2)
s 104 am—Crim Procedure (Conseq Provns) (S), 1995 c 40, s 5, sch 4para 93(4)
s 106 am—SI 1999/1820, art 4, sch 2 pt I para 115(3); Agricultural Holdings (S), 2003 asp
   11, s 94, sch para 50
  appl—(S) Crim Procedure (S), 1995 c 46, s 307(1)
s 107 am—Crime and Punishment (S), 1997 c 48, s 43(4); SI 1999/1820, art 4, sch 2 pt I
   para 115(4); (S) Crim Justice and Licensing (S), 2010 asp 13, s 110(3)
  mod—SI 1994/1931 rule 2A(1)(2)(d) (as am by SI 1999/374, rule 2)
s 110 am—Crime and Punishment (S), 1997 c 48, ss 43(5), 62(1), sch 1 para 15;
   SI 1999/1820, art 4, sch 2 pt I para 115(5); (S) Crim Justice and Licensing (S),
   2010 asp 13, s 110(4)(a)(c); SSI 2015/39, sch para 3(3)
  rep in pt—(S) Crim Justice and Licensing (S), 2010 asp 13, s 110(4)(b)
s 111 am—SI 1999/1820, art 4, sch 2 pt I para 115(6); (S) Crim Justice and Licensing (S),
   2010 asp 13, s 110(5)
s 112 am—Crime and Punishment (S), 1997 c 48, s 43(6)
s 113 am—SI 1999/1820, art 4, sch 2 pt I para 115(7)
s 114 am—SI 1999/1820, art 4, sch 2 pt I para 115(8)
  appl—Law Reform (Misc Provns)(S), 1980 c 55, sch 1 pt I Crim Procedure (S), 1995
   c 46, s 307(1); Immigration and Asylum, 1999 c 33, s 147
s 115 am—SI 1999/1820, art 4, sch 2 pt I para 115(9)
s 116 rep in pt—SSI 2015/39, sch para 3(4)
s 117 am—Crim Procedure (Conseq Provns) (S), 1995 c 40, s 5, sch 4 para 93(5)
  rep in pt—(prosp) Crim Justice and Court Services, 2000 c 43, s 75, sch 8
s 117A added—SI 2010/976, art 6, sch 7
s 125 rep in pt—(prosp) Crim Justice and Court Services, 2000 c 43, s 75, sch 8
s 126 am—Employment Rights, 1996 c 18, s 240, sch 1 para 65; (saving) SI 1996/1919,
   arts 255,256, schs 1,2
s 127 am—SI 1999/1820, art 4, sch 2 pt I para 115(10); Crim Justice and Immigration,
   2008 c 4, s 138; SI 2010/976, art 6, sch 7; (prosp) Legal Aid, Sentencing and
   Punishment of Offenders, 2012 c 10, s 129(6)
  appl—Disability Discrimination, 1995 c 50, s 64(8)

1994
c 33 s 127 *continued*

   rep in pt—SI 2005/908, art 2

  s 127A added—Crim Justice and Immigration, 2008 c 4, s 139

   am—SI 2010/976, art 6, sch 7

  s 128 am—SIs 1999/1756, art 2, sch para 16; 2005/908, art 3; Offender Management, 2007
    c 21, s 25(2)

   see—(trans of functions) (S) SI 1999/1750, art 2, sch 1

   rep in pt—SI 2010/976, art 6, sch 7

  s 128A added—SI 2010/976, art 6, sch 7

  s 129 rep in pt—Crim Procedure (Conseq Provns) (S), 1995 c 40 ss 4,6 sch 3 pt II para 16
    sch 5

  s 130 rep in pt—Crime and Disorder, 1998 c 37, s 120(2), sch 10

  s 132 rep in pt—(S) Crim Procedure (Conseq Provns) (S), 1995 c 40 ss 4,6 sch 3 pt II
    para 16 sch 5

  s 134 rep in pt—Crim Justice (S), 2003 asp 7, s 86, sch 5

  s 136 am—Youth Justice and Crim Evidence, 1999 c 23, s 67, sch 4 paras 21, 23; Powers of
    Crim Cts (Sentencing), 2000 c 6, s 165(1)(3), sch 9 para 161, sch 11 pt III
    para 11(4); Anti-terrorism, Crime and Security, 2001 c 24, s 101, sch 7, paras 15,
    17; Crim Justice and Immigration, 2008 c 4, s 6, sch 4 para 42

   appl (mods)—Finance, 2007 c 11, s 87; Crime and Cts, 2013 c 22, s 55(7)(8)

  s 137 am—Anti-terrorism, Crime and Security, 2001 c 24, s 101, sch 7, paras 15, 18;
    Serious Organised Crime and Police, 2005 c 15, s 111, sch 7 pt 3 para
    47(1)(2)(5); SI 2011/1739, sch 2 para 1

   appl (mods)—Finance, 2007 c 11, s 87; Crime and Cts, 2013 c 22, s 55(7)(8)

  s 138 am—Crim Procedure (Conseq Provns) (S), 1995 c 40 s 5 sch 4 pt I para 93(6);
    Serious Organised Crime and Police, 2005 c 15, s 111, sch 7 pt 3 para
    47(1)(3)(5); SI 2011/1739, sch 2 para 2(2)(3)

   appl (mods)—Finance, 2007 c 11, s 87; Crime and Cts, 2013 c 22, s 55(7)(8)

  s 139 am—Terrorism, 2000 c 11, s 125(1), sch 15 para 9; Proceeds of Crime, 2002 c 29, s
    456, sch 11, para 24

   ext—Crim. Justice and Police, 2001 c 16, s 51, sch 1 pt 2, para 81

   appl (mods)—Finance, 2007 c 11, s 87; Crime and Cts, 2013 c 22, s 55(7)(8)

  s 140 am—Anti-terrorism, Crime and Security, 2001 c 24, s 101, sch 7, paras 15, 19;
    Serious Organised Crime and Police, 2005 c 15, s 111, sch 7 pt 3 para
    47(1)(4)(5)

  s 141 rep—Police, 1996 c 16, s 103, sch 9 pt I

  ss 142-144 rep—Sexual Offences, 2003 c 42, ss 139, 140, sch 6 para 32(1)(3), sch 7

  s 145 rep—Sexual Offences (Amdt), 2000 c 44, s 1(5)

  s 146 rep in pt—Armed Forces, 2006 c 52, s 378, sch 17

  s 147 rep in pt—Armed Forces, 2006 c 52, s 378, sch 17

  s 155 rep —Serious Organised Crime and Police, 2005 c 15, s 174(2), sch 17 pt 2

  s 157 rep in pt—(S) Crim Procedure (Conseq Provns) (S), 1995 c 40 ss 4.6 sch 3 pt II
    para 16 sch 5

  ss 158, 159 rep—Extradition, 2003 c 41, s 220, sch 4

  s 160 rep in pt—(retrosp) Police, 1996 c 16, s 103, sch 9 pt I

  s 161 rep—Data Protection, 1998 c 29, s 74(2), sch 16 pt I

  s 163 am—Communications, 2003 c 21, s 406(1), sch 17 para 130(1)-(5); SIs 2003/1900,
    arts 2(1), 3(1), sch 1; 2003/3142, art 3(2); Police and Fire Reform (S), 2012 asp
    8, sch 7 para 9(3); SI 2013/602, sch 1 para 4(3)(a)(b)(ii)

   rep in pt—Police and Fire Reform (S), 2012 asp 8, sch 8 pt 1; SI 2013/602, sch 1 para
    4(3)(b)(i)

  s 164 rep in pt—Crime (International Co-operation), 2003 c 32, s 91(2), sch 6; (S) Crim
    Justice and Licensing (S), 2010 asp 13, s 203, sch 7 para 20

   saving—SI 2004/787, arts 2, 3

  s 166 am—Football (Offences and Disorder), 1999 c 21, s 10; Football (Disorder), 2000
    c 25, s 1, sch 2 para 20; Violent Crime Reduction, 2006 c 38, s
    53(1)-(3)(a)(i)(3)(b)-(4)

   rep in pt—Football (Disorder), 2000 c 25, s 1, sch 2 para 20, sch 3; Serious Organised
    Crime and Police, 2005 c 15, s 174(2), sch 17 pt 2; Violent Crime Reduction,
    2006 c 38, ss 53(3)(a)(ii)(5), 65, sch 5

  s 166A added —Violent Crime Reduction, 2006 c 38, s 53(6)

  s 167 am—Transport, 2000 c 38, s 265(3)

   rep in pt—Serious Organised Crime and Police, 2005 c 15, s 174(2), sch 17 pt 2

1994
c 33 *continued*

s 170 am—Registration of Political Parties, 1998 c 48, s 15(1)(2(3); Political Parties, Elections and Referendums, 2000 c 41, s 158(1), sch 21 para 11

s 172 am—Knives, 1997 c 21, s 8(11); SI 2010/976, art 6, sch 7

sch 1 am—Crime and Disorder, 1998 c 37, s 119, sch 8, para 112; Powers of Crim Cts (Sentencing), 2000 c 6, s 165(1), sch 9 para 162; Offender Management, 2007 c 21, s 35; ibid, s 39, sch 3 paras 19, 25, 26

rep in pt—Offender Management, 2007 c 21, s 39, sch 5 pt 3

sch 2 am—Crime and Disorder, 1998 c 37, s 119, sch 8, para 113(1(2)

sch 4 rep—(retrosp) Crim Procedure and Investigations, 1996 c 25, ss 44(2)(6),80, sch 5 para 1

sch 8 rep in pt—Violent Crime Reduction, 2006 c 38, s 65, sch 5; (S) Aquaculture and Fisheries (S), 2007 asp 12, s 41, sch 1 para 5; Marine and Coastal Access, 2009 c 23, s 321, sch 22 pt 5; (S) Marine (S), 2010 asp 5, s 167, sch 4 para 13

sch 9 rep in pt—Drug Trafficking, 1994 c 37, s 67, sch 3; Crim Procedure and Investigations, 1996 c 25, s 80, sch 5 para 9; NI (Emergency Provns), 1996 c 22, s 63(7), sch 7 pt I; (pt prosp) Youth Justice and Crim Evidence, 1999 c 23, s 67, sch 6; Powers of Crim Cts (Sentencing), 2000 c 6, s 165(3)(4), sch 11 pt I para 2, sch 12 pt I; (prosp) Proceeds of Crime, 2002 c 29, s 457, sch 12; Crim Justice, 2003 c 44, s 332, sch 37 pts 4, 6; Legal Aid, Sentencing and Punishment of Offenders, 2012 c 10, sch 12 para 35; ibid, sch 25 pt 2; Deregulation, 2015 c 20, s 80(6)(c)

sch 10 rep in pt—Police, 1996 c 16, s 103, sch 9 pt I; NI (Emergency Provns), 1996 c 22, s 63(7), sch 7 pt I; SI 1996/1141, art 32(3), sch 5; Crime and Disorder, 1998 c 37, s 120(2), sch 10; Youth Justice and Crim Evidence, 1999 c 23, s 67, sch 6; Terrorism, 2000 c 11, s 125(2), sch 16 pt I; Powers of Crim Cts (Sentencing), 2000 c 6, s 165(3)(4), sch 11 pt I para 2, sch 12 pt I; Crim Justice and Court Services, 2000 c 43, s 75, sch 8; Crim Justice, 2003 c 44, s 332, sch 37 pt 10; (pt prosp) ibid, s 332, sch 37 pts 2, 4; Sexual Offences, 2003 c 42, ss 139, 140, sch 6 para 32(1)(4), sch 7; Serious Organised Crime and Police, 2005 c 15, s 174(2), sch 17 pt 2; Police and Justice, 2006 c 48, s 52, sch 15; Offender Management, 2007 c 21, s 39, sch 5 pt 2; Legal Aid, Sentencing and Punishment of Offenders, 2012 c 10, s 144(9); ibid, sch 25 pt 2; SSI 2015/39, sch para 3(5)

sch 11 rep in pt—(retrosp) Crim Procedure and Investigations 1996 c 25 ss 44(5)(6), 80, sch 5 para 1, Note 1; (retrosp) Youth Justice and Crim Evidence, 1999 c 23, s 67, sch 4, paras 21, 24

c 34 **Marriage**

c 35 **Sale and Supply of Goods**

sch 2 rep in pt—SI 2005/871, art 6, sch; Consumer Rights, 2015 c 15, sch 1 para 55(a)

c 36 **Law of Property (Miscellaneous Provisions)**

s 5 am—Commonhold and Leasehold Reform, 2002 c 15, s 68, sch 5, para 7

s 6 am—Land Registration, 2002 c 9, s 133, sch 11, para 31(1)(2)

s 9 rep in pt—SL(R), 2004 c 14, s 1(1), sch 1 pt 12

s 16 rep in pt—Trusts of Land and Appointment of Trustees, 1996 c 47, s 25(2), sch 4

s 17 am—Land Registration, 2002 c 9, s 133, sch 11, para 31(1)(3); Tribunals, Cts and Enforcement, 2007 c 15, s 48, sch 8 para 33; SI 2013/2042, sch para 16(a)(i)(ii)(b)

rep in pt—SI 2013/1036, sch 1 para 224

s 19 am—Public Trustee (Liability and Fees), 2002 c 35, s 2(4)

sch 1 rep in pt—SL(R), 1998 c 43, s 1(1), sch 1 pt IV, Group 2; Land Registration, 2002 c 9, s 135, sch 13

c 37 **Drug Trafficking**

mod—SI 1995/1967, art 2(1)

appl—Gas, 1995 c 45, s 205B(5); Crime (Sentences), 1997 c 43, s 3(5); (S) Proceeds of Crime, 2002 c 29, s 118(2)(i)

Pts I-III (ss 1-54) rep (pt prosp)—Proceeds of Crime, 2002 c 29, ss 456, 457, sch 11, para 25(1)(2)(a), sch 12 (prosp only for ss 39, 40 see SI 2003/333)

s 27 appl—(NI) SI 2005/3179, arts 5(5)(d), 12(7)(d), 17(5)(d), 40(3)(4)(d)

ss 39, 40 appl (mods)—(EW) SI 1996/2880, arts 3(2), 4-6, schs 1, 3

ext—(EW) SI 1996/2880, arts 3(1), 4-6, sch 1

ss 55-69 appl (mods)—(EW) SI 1996/2880, arts 3(2), 4-6, schs 1, 3

s 55 rep in pt—Proceeds of Crime, 2002 c 29, ss 456, 457, sch 11, para 25(1)(2)(b), sch 12

am—Courts, 2003 c 39, s 109(1), sch 8 para 364

1994
c 37 *continued*

s 56 ext—Crim. Justice and Police, 2001 c 16, ss 50, 55, sch 1 pt 1, para 59, pt 3, para 108
 rep in pt—Proceeds of Crime, 2002 c 29, ss 456, 457, sch 11, para 25(1)(2)(b), sch 12
s 59 rep in pt—Proceeds of Crime, 2002 c 29, ss 456, 457, sch 11, para 25(1)(2)(c), sch 12
 am—Proceeds of Crime, 2002 c 29, s 456, sch 11, para 25(1)(3)
s 59A added—Proceeds of Crime, 2002 c 29, s 456, sch 11, para 25(1)(4)
s 60 rep in pt—Proceeds of Crime, 2002 c 29, ss 456, 457, sch 11, para 25(1)(2)(d)-(f), sch
  12; Commrs for Revenue and Customs, 2005 c 11, ss 50(6), 52(2), sch 4 para
  59(c)(e), sch 5
 am—Proceeds of Crime, 2002 c 29, s 456, sch 11, para 25(1)(5); (prosp) Crim Justice,
  2003 c 44, s 331, sch 36 pt 2 para 12(1)-(3); Commrs for Revenue and Customs,
  2005 c 11, s 50(6), sch 4 para 59(a)(b)(d)(f); SI 2014/834, sch 2 para 9; Crim
  Justice and Cts, 2015 c 2, sch 11 para 15
 mod—Serious Crime, 2007 c 27, s 63, sch 6 para 25
s 61 rep in pt—Proceeds of Crime, 2002 c 29, ss 456, 457, sch 11, para 25(1)(2)(g), sch 12
 am—Proceeds of Crime, 2002 c 29, s 456, sch 11, para 25(1)(6)
s 62 rep—Proceeds of Crime, 2002 c 29, ss 456, 457, sch 11, para 25(1)(2)(h), sch 12
s 63 rep in pt—Proceeds of Crime, 2002 c 29, ss 456, 457, sch 11, para 25(1)(2)(h), sch 12
s 64 rep—Proceeds of Crime, 2002 c 29, ss 456, 457, sch 11, para 25(1)(2)(h), sch 12
s 68 am—Proceeds of Crime, 2002 c 29, s 456, sch 11, para 25(1)(7)
 rep in pt—Proceeds of Crime, 2002 c 29, ss 456, 457, sch 11, para 25(1)(2)(i)(j), sch
  12
sch 1 rep in pt—Land Registration, 2002 c 9, s 135, sch 13; Proceeds of Crime, 2002 c 29, s
  457, sch 12; Serious Organised Crime and Police, 2005 c 15, s 174(2), sch 17
  pt 2

c 38 **European Union (Accessions)**
c 39 **Local Government etc (Scotland)**
appl—Sewerage (S), 1968 c 47, s 10 Race Relations, 1976 c 71, s 71(2) Competition, 1980
  c 21, s 11(3)c c; Loc Govt etc(S), 1994 c 39, s 180(1), sch 13 para 2(3);
  Environmental Protection 1990 c 43, s 33A(13); Crime (Sentences), 1997 c 43, sch 1
  para 8); Crime and Disorder, 1998 c 37, s 19(8); SI 2002/2007, reg 8(2)(b)(ii)
excl—Town and Country Planning (S), 1997 c 8, s 24(5)(a)
appl—Crime and Disorder, 1998 c 37, s 95(1)
Pt 1 (ss 1-60) appl—Enterprise and New Towns (S), 1990 c 35, s 21(5)
s 2 appl—SI 1996/2890, reg 2(1); SSI 2002/167, reg 6(1)(b)(iii); Environmental Protection
  1990 c 43, s 44ZA(6); (E) SI 2005/3361, reg 24, sch 3 pt 6 para 51(2)
 excl—Loc Govt (S), 1973 c 65, s 23(1A)(1B)
s 3 excl—Loc Govt (S), 1973 c 65, s 23(1A)(1B)
s 4 am—S Loc Govt (Elections), 2002 asp 1, s 4(1)
 rep in pt—SSI 2007/265, reg 3
s 5 appl—Loc Govt (S), 1973 c 65, s 235(1); Representation of the People, 1983 c 2,
  s 18(3)(b); School Bds (S), 1988 c 47, s 22(2)
 am—S Loc Govt (Elections), 2002 asp 1, ss 1, 4(2); Scottish Loc Govt Elections, 2009
  asp 10, s 1(1)
 rep in pt—Scottish Loc Govt Elections, 2009 asp 10, s 1, sch para 2
s 8 rep in pt—Police and Fire Reform (S), 2012 asp 8, sch 8 pt 3
s 10 am—Employment Rights, 1996 c 18, s 240, sch 1 para 66(2)
s 13 am—Employment Rights, 1996 c 18, s 240, sch 1 para 66(3)
s 14 am—Employment Rights, 1996 c 18, s 240, sch 1 para 66(4)
s 27 am—Loc Govt in S, 2003 asp 1, s 32(2)
s 30 appl—Loc Govt (S), 1973 c 65, s 235(1); Social Security Admin, 1992 c 5, s 191
s 33 rep—Planning (Conseq Provns) (S), 1997 c 11, s 3, sch 1 pt I
s 36 rep—Fire (S), 2005 asp 5, s 89(2), sch 4
s 43 am—Fire (S), 2005 asp 5, s 89(1), sch 3 para 17; Police and Fire Reform (S), 2012 asp
  8, sch 7 para 75
s 46 rep—Licensing (S), 2005 asp 16, s 149, sch 7
s 51 rep in pt—Loc Electoral Admin and Registration Services (S), 2006 asp 14, s 59(3)
s 53 rep in pt—Public Records (S), 2011 asp 12, s 14(b)
s 55 rep in pt—Fire (S), 2005 asp 5, s 89(2), sch 4; Police and Fire Reform (S), 2012 asp 8,
  sch 8 pt 3
ss 62-64 rep—Water Industry (S), 2002 asp 3, s 71(2), sch 7, para 23(a)
s 63 am—Water Industry, 1999 c 9, s 15(1), sch 3 pt II, paras 7, 8
s 65 rep in pt—Water Industry (S), 2002 asp 3, s 71(2), sch 7, para 23(b)
s 66 rep—Water Industry (S), 2002 asp 3, s 71(2), sch 7, para 23(c)

1994

c 39 s 66 *continued*

transtl savings—SSI 2002/166, art 5

s 67 rep—Water Industry, 1999 c 9, s 15(2), sch 4 pt II

ss 67A, 68-83 rep—Water Industry (S), 2002 asp 3, s 71(2), sch 7, para 23(d)

s 76 transtl savings—SSI 2002/166, art 4

s 84 rep—Water Industry (S), 2002 asp 3, s 71(2), sch 7, para 23(d)

ss 85, 86 rep —Water Industry (S), 2002 asp 3, s 71(2), sch 7, para 23(d)

ss 87, 88 rep—Water Industry (S), 2002 asp 3, s 71(2), sch 7, para 23(d)

ss 89-100 rep —Water Industry (S), 2002 asp 3, s 71(2), sch 7, para 23(d)

ss 116-126 rep —Water Industry (S), 2002 asp 3, s 71(2), sch 7, para 23(e)

s 127 am—Crim Procedure (Conseq Provns) (S), 1995 c 40, s 5, sch 4 para 95(2)

s 128 appl—SI 1996/3261, rule 2

　　am—Children (S), 1995 c 36, s 105(4), sch 4 para 57; Crim Procedure (Conseq
　　　　Provns (S), 1995 c 40, s 5 sch 4 para 95(3)

s 130 am—Crim Procedure (Conseq Provns) (S), 1995 c 40, s 5, sch 4 para 95(4); Children
　　　　(S), 1995 c 36, s 105(4), sch 4 para 57

s 132 am—Children (S), 1995 c 36, s 105(4), sch 4 para 57

s 136 am—Public Finance and Accountability (S), 2000 asp 1, s 26, sch 4 para 12(1)(3)(a)
　　rep in pt—Public Finance and Accountability (S), 2000 asp 1, s 26, sch 4
　　　　para 12(1)(3)(a)(b)

s 139 rep—Children (S), 1995 c 36, s 105(5), sch 5

s 143 rep—Schools (Consultation) (S), 2010 asp 2, s 18, sch 3 para 2

s 150 see—(power to delegate functions) SI 1996/878, art 2, sch para 7

　　am—Police and Fire Reform (S), 2012 asp 8, sch 7 para 10

s 153 am—Climate Change (S), 2009 asp 12, s 67

s 157 rep—SI 2000/2040, art 2, sch pt I para 15 pt III

s 165 rep in pt—Environment, 1995 c 25, s 120(3), sch 24

s 172 rep in pt—Tourist Boards (S), 2006 asp 15, s 3(1)

ss 173-175 rep —Tourist Boards (S), 2006 asp 15, s 3(1)

s 177 rep in pt—Water Industry, 1999 c 9, s 15(1)(2), sch 3 pt II, paras 7, 16, sch 4 pt II

sch 2 rep in pt—Requirements of Writing (S), 1995 c 7, s 14(2), sch 5

sch 3 rep in pt—Requirements of Writing (S), 1995 c 7, s 14(2), sch 5

sch 4 rep—Planning (Conseq Provns) (S), 1997 c 11, s 3, sch 1 pt I

sch 5 rep in pt—Requirements of Writing (S), 1995 c 7, s 14(2), sch 5; Loc Governance (S),
　　　　2004 asp 9, s 5(2)

　　am—Loc Govt in S, 2003 asp 1, s 48

schs 7, 8 rep—Water Industry (S), 2002 asp 3, s 71(2), sch 7, para 23(f)

sch 9 rep in pt—Water Industry, 1999 c 9, s 15(1)(2), sch 3 pt II, paras 7, 17, sch 4 pt II;
　　　　SI 1999/1820, art 4, sch 2 pt I para 116 pt IV

schs 9A, 10, 11 rep—Water Industry (S), 2002 asp 3, s 71(2), sch 7, para 23(f)

sch 10 rep in pt—Abolition of Poindings and Warrant Sales, 2001 asp 1, s 3(1), sch pt 2

　　am—Debt Arrangement and Attachment (S), 2002 asp 17, s 61, sch 3 pt 1, para
　　　　23(1)-(3)

sch 12 rep in pt—Requirements of Writing (S), 1995 c 7, s 14(2), sch 5

sch 13 rep in pt—Housing, 1996 c 52, s 227, sch 19 pt VIII; ibid, s 227, sch 19 pt VI;
　　　　Reserve Forces, 1996 c 14, s 131(2), sch 11 SI 1996/3097, art 3(1)(f);
　　　　Planning (Conseq Provns) (S), 1997 c 11, s 3, sch 1 pt I; Lieutenancies, 1997
　　　　c 23, s 8(4), sch 3; S Legal Services Ombudsman and Commnr for Loc Admin
　　　　in S, 1997 c 35, s 10, sch; Data Protection, 1998 c 29, s 74(2), sch 16 pt I;
　　　　Water Industry, 1999 c 9, s 15(1)(2), sch 3 pt II, paras 7, 18, sch 4 pt II; Race
　　　　Relations (Amdt), 2000 c 34, s 9(2), sch 3; Powers of Crim Cts (Sentencing),
　　　　2000 c 6, s 165(3)(4), sch 11 pt I para 2, sch 12 pt I; Ethical Standards in
　　　　Public Life etc (S), 2000 asp 7, s 36, sch 4; SI 2001/1149, arts 3(2), 4(11),
　　　　sch 2; Housing (S), 2001 asp 10, s 112, sch 10, para 21; Water Industry (S),
　　　　2002 asp 3, s 71(2), sch 7, para 23(g); S Public Services Ombudsman, 2002
　　　　asp 11, s 25(1), sch 6, para 15; Building (S), 2003 asp 8, s 58, sch 6 para 21;
　　　　Civil Contingencies, 2004 c 36, s 32(2), sch 3; Licensing (S), 2005 asp 16,
　　　　s 149, sch 7; Fire (S), 2005 asp 5, s 89(2), sch 4; (prosp) Charities and Trustee
　　　　Investment (S), 2005 asp 10, s 104, sch 4 pt 1 para 11; Adoption and Children
　　　　(S), 2007 asp 4, s 120, sch 3; Welfare Reform, 2007 c 5, s 40, sch 5 para 11,
　　　　sch 8; Public Health etc (S), 2008 asp 5, s 126, sch 3 pt 1; SI 2008/1277, sch 4;
　　　　Flood Risk Management (S), 2009 asp 6, s 96, sch 3 para 6; Marine (S), 2010
　　　　asp 5, s 167, sch 4 para 8; Parly Voting System and Constituencies, 2011 c 1,
　　　　sch 12 pt 2; (1.4.2016) Reservoirs (S), 2011 asp 9, s 112(2); Regulatory

1994
c 39 *continued*

Reform (S), 2014 asp 3, sch 3 para 28; (prosp) Housing (S), 2014 asp 14, sch 2 para 8; (prosp) Community Empowerment (S), 2015 asp 6, sch 5; Deregulation, 2015 c 20, sch 23 para 34(6); SSI 2015/39, sch para 4

sch 14 rep in pt—Public Health etc (S), 2008 asp 5, s 126, sch 3 pt 1

c 40   **Deregulation and Contracting Out**

ss 1-5 rep—Regulatory Reform, 2001 c 6, s 12(1)(2)-(4); (saving) (S) Public Services Reform (S), 2010 asp 8, s 29, sch 7 para 1(2)(4)

s 6 see—(power to appl (mods)) Health, 1999 c 8, s 37(6)

am—(EW,NI) Regulatory Reform, 2001 c 6, s 13(1); (S) Public Services Reform (S), 2010 asp 8, s 29, sch 7 para 1(3)(a)(ii)(b)(c)

rep in pt—(S) Public Services Reform (S), 2010 asp 8, s 29, sch 7 para 1(3)(a)(i)

s 7 rep in pt—Enterprise, 2002 c 40, s 278(2), sch 26

am—Legislative and Regulatory Reform, 2006 c 51, s 31(1)

s 9 rep—Enterprise, 2002 c 40, s 278(2), sch 26

s 8 rep—Communications, 2003 c 21, s 406(7), sch 19(1)

ss 10, 11 rep—Competition, 1998 c 41, s 74(1)(3), sch 12, para 19(2), sch 14 pt I

s 12 rep in pt—Competition, 1998 c 41, s 74(1)(3), sch 12, para 19(3), sch 14 pt I

s 13 rep in pt—Companies, 2006 c 46, s 1295, sch 16

s 14 rep—SL(R), 2004 c 14, s 1(1), sch 1 pt 16/2

ss 16, 17 rep—Building Societies, 1997 c 32, s 46(2), sch 9

s 18 rep in pt—Licensing, 2003 c 17, s 199, sch 7

s 19 rep—Licensing, 2003 c 17, s 199, sch 7

s 20 rep —Gambling, 2005 c 19, s 356(4)(5), sch 17

s 21 rep—Licensing, 2003 c 17, ss 198, 199, sch 6 para 112, sch 7

s 22 rep (S) —SSI 2009/248, art 2, sch 2

ss 23, 24 rep—SL(R), 2004 c 14, s 1(1), sch 1 pt 16/2

s 28 rep—Charities, 2006 c 50, s 75, sch 9

s 29 rep in pt—Charities, 2006 c 50, s 75, sch 9; Charities, 2011 c 25, sch 10

s 30 rep—Charities, 2011 c 25, sch 10

s 36 rep in pt—Employment Rights, 1996 c 18, s 242, sch 13 pt I

s 37 am—Railways, 2005 c 14, s 59, sch 12 para 12; SI 2008/960, art 22, sch 3; Energy, 2013 c 32, sch 12 para 71(2)-(6); SI 2015/1682, sch pt 1 para 4(k)

Pt 1 (Ch 3 (ss 41-57)) rep—Goods Vehicles (Licensing of Operators), 1995 c 23, s 60(2), sch 8 pt I

s 62 rep in pt—SL(R), 2004 c 14, s 1(1), sch 1 pt 16/2

s 64 rep—SL(R), 2004 c 14, s 1(1), sch 1 pt 16/2

Pt 2 (ss 69-79) ext—(EW) Environment, 1995 c 25, s 65(7), sch 8 para 13; Nat Parks (S), 2000 asp 10, s 9, sch 2 para 14

saved—GLA, 1999 c 29, s 35(10)

mod—Care Standards, 2000 c 14, s 67

appl (mods)—Communications, 2003 c 21, s 1(7); SIs 2004/1777, art 34; 2004/1778, art 34

s 69 appl—SI 2000/2040, art 2, sch pt I para 16; Regulation of Care (S), 2001 asp 8, s 58(4)(b)(5)

ext—Learning and Skills, 2000 c 21, s 136(3)

s 70 am—GLA, 1999 c 29, s 40(1)-(3); SI 2001/2237, arts 2, 29; (W) SI 2002/808 (W 89), arts 2(n), 28; Loc Govt and Public Involvement in Health, 2007 c 28, s 239(1)

ext—Loc Govt, 1999 c 27, s 18

mod—Teaching and Higher Education, 1998 c 30, s 23(3)(b)

rep in pt—(prosp) GLA, 1999 c 29, s 423, sch 34 pt IX; Public Bodies, 2011 c 24, sch 6

s 71 am—(EW) Loc Govt, 2003 c 26, s 127(1), sch 7 para 59; (Planning, 2008 c 29, s 224(3)

rep in pt—Planning, 2008 c 29, s 224(3)

s 72 appl—Crime and Disorder, 1998 c 37, s 1F; Anti-social Behaviour, 2003 c 38, s 28A(7)

s 73 appl—Crime and Disorder, 1998 c 37, s 1F; Anti-social Behaviour, 2003 c 38, s 28A(7)

s 74 appl—Registration of Political Parties, 1998 c 48, s 23, sch 3, para 4

am—SIs 2009/1941, art 2, sch 1; 2013/1644, sch 1

s 75 appl—Crime and Disorder, 1998 c 37, s 1F; Anti-social Behaviour, 2003 c 38, s 28A(7)

1994

c 40 *continued*

s 79 am—Govt of Wales, 1998 c 38, s 125, sch 12, para 36; GLA, 1999 c 29, s 40(1)(4); SI 2001/3686, regs 6(11)(a)(i), 8; SI 2004/1823, art 18; Public Services Ombudsman (W), 2005 c 10, s 39(1), sch 6 para 55(a); Charities, 2006 c 50, s 75, sch 8 para 179; Loc Govt and Public Involvement in Health, 2007 c 28, s 239(2); SI 2009/1941, art 2, sch 1

ext—SI 1999/1351, art 17(2)(f)

rep in pt—SI 2001/3686, reg 6(11)(a)(ii)(b); Public Services Ombudsman (W), 2005 c 10, s 39, sch 6 para 55(b), sch 7; (prosp) Loc Govt and Public Involvement in Health, 2007 c 28, s 241, sch 18 pt 19

ss 79A-79C added—Loc Govt and Public Involvement in Health, 2007 c 28, s 239(3)

s 79A am—Loc Democracy, Economic Development and Construction, 2009 c 20, s 119, sch 6 para 87

rep in pt—Police Reform and Social Responsibility, 2011 c 13, sch 16 para 215; Deregulation, 2015 c 20, sch 13 para 6(27)

s 79B rep in pt—Police Reform and Social Responsibility, 2011 c 13, sch 16 para 216

s 80 am—SI 2001/3686, regs 6(11)(c), 8

s 82 rep in pt—SI 2003/1398, arts 2, 3(1), sch para 22; SL(R), 2004 c 14, s 1(1), sch 1 pt 16/2

sch 1 rep—Regulatory Reform, 2001 c 6, s 12(1)(2)-(4); (saving) (S) Public Services Reform (S), 2010 asp 8, s 29, sch 7 para 1(2)(4)

sch 2 rep—Enterprise, 2002 c 40, s 278(2), sch 26

am—Railways and Transport Safety, 2003 c 20, s 16, sch 2 pt 2 para 19(n)

sch 4 rep in pt—Competition, 1998 c 41, s 74(1)(3), sch 12, para 19(4), sch 14 pt I; Enterprise, 2002 c 40, s 278(2), sch 26; Communications, 2003 c 21, s 406(7), sch 19(1); SIs 2003/1900, arts 2(1), 3(1), sch 1; 2003/3142, art 3(2); SL(R), 2004 c 14, s 1(1), sch 1 pt 16/2; (S) Public Services Reform (S), 2010 asp 8, s 29, sch 7 para 2

am—Railways and Transport Safety, 2003 c 20, s 16, sch 2 pt 2 para 19(n)

sch 5 rep —Companies, 2006 c 46, s 1295, sch 16

sch 6 rep—Companies, 2006 c 46, s 1295, sch 16

sch 7 rep in pt—Licensing, 2003 c 17, s 199, sch 7

sch 8 rep—Employment Rights, 1996 c 18, s 242, sch 3 pt 1

sch 9 rep in pt—SI 1995/731, reg 28(1), sch 13; SSI 2012/321, sch 5 pt 1

see—(trans of functions) SI 1999/3141, arts 2(4)(5), 3

sch 10 rep in pt—SL(R), 2004 c 14, s 1(1), sch 1 pt 16/2

sch 11 rep in pt—Building Societies, 1997 c 32, s 46(2), sch 9; Competition, 1998 c 41, s 74(1)(3), sch 12, para 19(5), sch 14 pt I; Enterprise, 2002 c 40, s 278(2), sch 26; Licensing, 2003 c 17, s 199, sch 7; SI 2003/3180, arts 2, 3, sch para 5; SL(R), 2004 c 14, s 1(1), sch 1 pt 16/2; Charities, 2011 c 25, sch 10

schs 12,13 rep—Goods Vehicles (Licensing of Operators), 1995 c 23, s 60(2), sch 8

sch 15 mod—Rent (S), 1984 c 58, s 43C

am—Govt Resources and Accounts, 2000 c 20, s 29(1), sch 1 para 20(1)(2)

appl—Anti-social Behaviour, 2003 c 38, s 28A(7); Natural Environment and Rural Communities, 2006 c 16, s 85(4); Marine and Coastal Access, 2009 c 23, ss 21(4), 171(4); Care, 2014 c 23, s 79(8); Infrastructure, 2015 c 7, s 8(4)

sch 16 am—SI 2009/1941, art 2, sch 1

rep in pt—Social Security Admin (Fraud), 1997 c 47, s 22, sch 2; (pt prosp) Social Security, 1998 c 14, s 86(2), sch 8; Courts, 2003 c 39, s 109(3), sch 10; Companies, 2006 c 46, s 1295, sch 16

appl—Crime and Disorder, 1998 c 37, s 1F; Anti-social Behaviour, 2003 c 38, s 28A(7)

3rd Session of 51st Parliament

c 41 *Consolidated Fund (No 2)*—rep Appropriation, 1996 c 45, s 3, sch(C)

1995

c 1 *European Communities (Finance)*—rep & superseded European Communities (Finance), 2001 c 22, s 2(2)

c 2 *Consolidated Fund*—rep Appropriation, 1997 c 31, s 3, sch C

c 3 **South Africa**

s 1 rep in pt—Legal Aid, Sentencing and Punishment of Offenders, 2012 c 10, sch 10 para 7

sch rep in pt—Commonwealth, 2002 c 39, s 3, sch 3; Armed Forces, 2006 c 52, s 378, sch

1995
c 4   **Finance**
        mod—Income and Corporation Taxes, 1988 c 1, s 689A(2)
        s 1 rep in pt—SI 2010/1914, art 3
        s 4 rep in pt—SI 2015/2050, reg 2(2)(3)(b)(4)
            am—SI 2015/2050, reg 2(3)(a)
        s 5 appl—Licensing, 2003 c 17, s 191(2)
            am—SI 2009/56, art 3, sch 1
        s 15 rep—Finance, 2009 c 10, s 17, sch 5 para 6(a)
        s 17 rep in pt—Enterprise, 2002 c 40, s 278(2), sch 26
        s 21 rep—Finance, 2001 c 9, s 110, sch 33 pt 3(1), Note 2
        s 25 rep in pt—Finance, 1996 c 8, s 205, sch 41 pt IV(5)
        s 32 rep—Finance, 2008 c 9, s 123, sch 41 para 25(g)
        s 33 rep in pt—Finance, 1996 c 8, s 205, sch 41 pt IV(4)
        ss 35, 36 rep—Income Tax, 2007 c 3, s 1031, sch 3
        s 38 rep—Corporation Tax, 2010 c 4, s 1181, sch 3 pt 1
        s 39 rep—Finance, 1998 c 36, s 165, sch 27 pt III(4), Note
        s 40 rep in pt—Income Tax, 2007 c 3, s 1031, sch 3
        s 41 rep—Finance, 1998 c 36, s 165, sch 27 pt III(4), Note
        s 42 rep—Finance, 1999 c 16, s 139, sch 20 pt III(7), Note 4; SL(R), 2013 c 2, s 1, sch 1 pt
            10(1)
        ss 43-45 rep—Income Tax (Earnings and Pensions), 2003 c 1, s 724(1), sch 8 pt 1
        s 50 rep—Finance, 1996 c 8, s 205, sch 41 pt V(3)
        s 51 rep—Finance, 2012 c 14, sch 16 para 247(f)(i)
        s 52 rep in pt—SI 2001/3629, art 109, sch; Finance, 2002 c 23, s 141, sch 40 pt 3(10), Note
            2
        s 55 am—Finance, 1996 c 8, s 162(1); Finance, 2013 c 29, sch 9 para 6(1)
            rep in pt—Income Tax (Trading and Other Income), 2005 c 5, s 884, sch 3; Finance,
                2008 c 9, s 36, sch 14 para 17(d)
        s 56 rep—Income Tax (Trading and Other Income), 2005 c 5, ss 882(1), 884, sch 1 pt 2
            paras 475, 476, sch 3
        s 57 rep—SL(R), 2013 c 2, s 1, sch 1 pt 10(1)
        ss 58-61 rep —Finance, 2004 c 12, s 326, sch 42 pt 3, Note
        ss 62-65 rep—Income Tax (Trading and Other Income), 2005 c 5, s 884, sch 3
        s 66 rep—Income Tax, 2007 c 3, s 1031, sch 3
        ss 70, 71 rep—Income Tax, 2007 c 3, s 1031, sch 3
        s 72 rep in pt—Finance, 2004 c 12, s 326, sch 42 pt 2(13), Note 3, pt 2(14), Note 1
        s 73 rep—Income Tax, 2007 c 3, s 1027, sch 1 paras 364, 365, sch 3
        s 76 rep in pt—Finance (No 2), 1997 c 58, s 52, sch 8 pt II(11), Note; Income Tax (Trading
                and Other Income), 2005 c 5, s 884, sch 3; Corporation Tax, 2009 c 4, s 1326,
                sch 3 pt 1
        s 77 rep—Finance (No 2), 1997 c 58, s 52, sch 8 pt II(13), Note
        s 78 rep—Finance, 1998 c 36, s 165, sch 27 pt III(3), Note
        s 79 rep—Income Tax, 2007 c 3, s 1031, sch 3
        s 80 rep in pt—Finance, 1996 c 8, s 205, sch 41 pt V(21); Finance, 2007 c 11, s 114, sch 27
            pt 2
        s 81 rep—Finance, 2008 c 9, s 66(4)(f)
        s 82 rep—Finance, 1997 c 16, ss 76,113, sch 10 pt I para 7(1), sch 18 pt VI(10), Note 1
        s 83 rep in pt—Finance, 2008 c 9, s 43, sch 17 para 35(2)(a)
        ss 84, 85 rep—Finance, 1997 c 16, ss 76,113, sch 10 pt I para 7(1), sch 18 pt VI(10), Note 1
        s 86 rep—Income Tax, 2007 c 3, s 1031, sch 3
        s 87 rep—Corporation Tax, 2010 c 4, s 1181, sch 3 pt 1
        ss 88, 89 rep—Finance, 1996 c 8, s 205, sch 41 pt V(3)
        s 90 rep—Income Tax, 2007 c 3, s 1027, sch 1 paras 364, 366, sch 3
        ss 91-93 rep—Income Tax (Earnings and Pensions), 2003 c 1, s 724(1), sch 8 pt 1
        ss 94-101 rep—Capital Allowances, 2001 c 2, s 580, sch 4
        s 104 rep in pt—Finance, 1998 c 36, s 165, sch 27 pt III(28), Note
        s 105 rep in pt—Finance, 2008 c 9, s 115, sch 37 para 11(a)
        s 107 rep in pt—Finance, 1998 c 36, s 165, sch 27 pt III(28), Note
        s 108 rep—Income Tax (Earnings and Pensions), 2003 c 1, s 724(1), sch 8 pt 1
            revived—(retrosp to 6.4.2003) Finance, 2004 c 12, s 92, sch 17 para 6
        s 110 am—(retrosp) Finance, 1996 c 8, s 131(1)
        s 111 rep—Income Tax (Earnings and Pensions), 2003 c 1, s 724(1), sch 8 pt 1
        s 113 excl—Taxation of Chargeable Gains, 1992 c 12, s 71(2C)
        s 117 rep—Corporation Tax, 2009 c 4, s 1326, sch 3 pt 1

1995
c 4 *continued*

ss 118, 119 rep—Income Tax, 2007 c 3, s 1031, sch 3
ss 120, 121 rep—Corporation Tax, 2009 c 4, s 1326, sch 3 pt 1
s 122 rep—Income Tax (Trading and Other Income), 2005 c 5, s 884, sch 3
s 123 am—Income Tax (Trading and Other Income), 2005 c 5, s 882(1), sch 1 pt 2 paras
475, 478
s 124 rep—Income Tax (Trading and Other Income), 2005 c 5, s 884, sch 3
s 125 rep—Corporation Tax, 2009 c 4, s 1326, sch 3 pt 1
ss 126, 127 rep—Taxation (International and Other Provns), 2010 c 8, ss 374, 378, sch 8
paras 276, 277, sch 10 pt 11
s 128 appl—Finance, 1996 c 8, s 73, sch 6 para 15
rep in pt—Finance, 1996 c 8, ss 79,205, sch 7 paras 31,32-35, sch 41 pt V(2); Income
Tax, 2007 c 3, s 1031, sch 3
am—Income Tax (Earnings and Pensions), 2003 c 1, s 722, sch 6 pt 2 paras 225, 226;
Finance, 2003 c 14, s 155, sch 27 para 6; Income Tax (Trading and Other
Income), 2005 c 5, s 882(1), sch 1 pt 2 paras 475, 480; SI 2006/1963, reg 3;
Income Tax, 2007 c 3, s 1027, sch 1 paras 364, 368
s 129 rep—Finance, 2003 c 14, ss 155, 216, sch 27 para 7, sch 43 pt 3(6), Note
s 131 rep—Finance, 2002 c 23, ss 79(2)(3), 141, sch 23 pt 2, para 22(1)(2), pt 3, para 25,
sch 40 pt 3(10), Note 2
s 132 rep—Finance, 2002 c 23, s 141, sch 40 pt 3(13), Note 2
s 134 rep —SI 2009/3001, regs 13, schs 1, 2
s 135 rep—Corporation Tax, 2010 c 4, s 1181, sch 3 pt 1
s 136 rep—Finance, 1997 c 16, ss 61(2)(3),113, sch 18 pt VI(3) Notes 1-3
s 137 rep in pt—Finance, 1997 c 16, ss 61(2)(3),113, sch 18 pt VI(3) Notes 1-3
am—Income Tax (Earnings and Pensions), 2003 c 1, s 722, sch 6 pt 2 paras 225, 227
rep in pt—Income Tax (Earnings and Pensions), 2003 c 1, s 724(1), sch 8 pt 1
s 138 rep—Corporation Tax, 2010 c 4, s 1181, sch 3 pt 1
s 139 rep —Finance, 2004 c 12, ss 77, 326, sch 42 pt 2(7), Note
s 140 rep—Corporation Tax, 2009 c 4, s 1326, sch 3 pt 1
s 141 rep—Income Tax (Earnings and Pensions), 2003 c 1, s 724(1), sch 8 pt 1
s 142 rep—Finance, 1996 c 8, s 205, sch 41 pt V(15)
s 144 rep—Corporation Tax, 2010 c 4, s 1181, sch 3 pt 1
s 145 rep in pt—Income Tax (Trading and Other Income), 2005 c 5, s 884, sch 3
s 146 rep in pt—(retrosp) Finance, 2001 c 9, s 110, sch 33 pt 3(2), Note 2
s 151 am—Finance, 1999 c 16, ss 112(4)(6), 122, sch 14 para 33; Finance, 2000 c 17,
s 125; Corporation Tax, 2010 c 4, s 1177, sch 1 paras 286, 287
restr—(transtl savings) (retrosp to 24.4.2002) Finance, 2002 c 23, s 111, sch 34
s 152 am—Finance, 1999 c 16, s 122(4), sch 19 pt III para 13; SI 2001/3629, arts 88, 90;
Corporation Tax, 2010 c 4, s 1177, sch 1 paras 286, 288
saving—Income Tax (Trading and Other Income), 2005 c 5, s 883(4), sch 2 pt 5 para
78
s 153 rep—Finance, 1999 c 16, s 139, sch 20 pt VII, Notes 1, 2
s 154 appl—Capital Allowances, 2001 c 2, s 362(2)
am—Income Tax (Trading and Other Income), 2005 c 5, s 882(1), sch 1 pt 2 paras
475, 481; Income Tax, 2007 c 3, s 1027, sch 1 paras 364, 369
rep in pt—Income Tax, 2007 c 3, s 1031, sch 3; Corporation Tax, 2010 c 4, ss 1177,
1181, sch 1 paras 286, 289, sch 3
s 155 rep in pt—Finance, 1996 c 8, s 205, sch 41 pt VI
s 157 am—Income Tax (Trading and Other Income), 2005 c 5, s 882(1), sch 1 pt 2 paras
475, 482
s 158 rep—Commrs for Revenue and Customs, 2005 c 11, ss 50(6), 52(2), sch 4 para 60,
sch 5
s 160 rep—SL(R), 1998 c 43, s 1(1), sch 1 pt IV, Group 5
sch 2 rep in pt—Finance, 2006 c 25, s 178, sch 26 pt 1(1)
sch 3 rep in pt—Finance, 2002 c 23, s 141, sch 40 pt 1(3), Note; Finance, 2007 c 11, s 114,
sch 27 pt 5
sch 4 rep in pt—Civil Evidence, 1995 c 38, s 15(2) sch 2; Finance, 1996 c 8, s 205, sch 41
pt II(3); Finance, 1998 c 36, s 165, sch 27 pt I(3), Note; (retrosp) Finance,
2001 c 9, s 110, sch 33 pt 1(3), Note 2; Finance, 2002 c 23, s 141, sch 40 pts
1(5), 3(10), Note 2; Finance, 2005 c 7, s 104, sch 11 pt 1, Note
sch 5 rep in pt—Finance, 1997 c 16, s 113, sch 18 pt V(2), Note; SI 2009/3054, art 3, sch
sch 6 rep in pt—(saving) Finance, 1997 c 16, ss 85,113, sch 15 para 9(1), sch 18 pt VI(11),
Note; Finance, 1998 c 36, s 165, sch 27 pt III(4), Note; Finance, 1999 c 16,

1995
c 4 *continued*

s 139, sch 20 pt III(7), Note 4; Income Tax (Trading and Other Income), 2005 c 5, s 884, sch 3; Income Tax, 2007 c 3, s 1031, sch 3; Corporation Tax, 2009 c 4, s 1326, sch 3 pt 1; Corporation Tax, 2010 c 4, s 1181, sch 3 pt 1; SL(R), 2013 c 2, s 1, sch 1 pt 10(1)

sch 7 rep—Finance, 1996 c 8, s 205, sch 41 pt V(3)

sch 8 rep—Finance, 2012 c 14, sch 16 para 247(f)(ii)

    rep in pt—Finance, 1996 c 8, s 205, sch 41 pt V(3); Finance, 1997 c 16, s 113, sch 18 pt VI(6), Note; Finance (No 2), 1997 c 58, s 52, sch 8 pt II(4)(6), Note; ibid, pt VI(6) Note; Finance, 1998 c 36, s 165, sch 27 pt III(2), Note; Finance, 2001 c 9, s 110, sch 33 pt 2(12), Note; Capital Allowances, 2001 c 2, s 580, sch 4; Finance, 2004 c 12, s 326, sch 42 pt 2(3), Note; ibid, s 326, sch 42 pt 3, Note; SIs 2006/3271, reg 43, sch; 2007/2086, reg 6; Finance, 2007 c 11, s 114, sch 27 pt 2; Finance, 2008 c 9, s 43, sch 17 para 18(5)(c)

    mod—SI 2006/3271, reg 34

    am—Finance, 2007 c 11, s 40, sch 9 paras 15, 17(1)

sch 9 rep in pt—SI 2001/3629, art 109, sch, Note 1; Capital Allowances, 2001 c 2, s 580, sch 4; SI 2006/3271, reg 43, sch; Finance, 2007 c 11, s 114, sch 27 pt 2; Finance, 2012 c 14, sch 16 para 247(f)(iii)

sch 10 rep in pt—Finance, 2012 c 14, sch 18 para 23(c)

sch 11 rep —Finance, 2004 c 12, s 326, sch 42 pt 3, Note

sch 12 rep—Income Tax (Trading and Other Income), 2005 c 5, s 884, sch 3

sch 13 rep in pt—Finance, 2004 c 12, s 326, sch 42 pt 2(14), Note 1

schs 14, 15 rep—Income Tax, 2007 c 3, s 1031, sch 3

sch 16 rep—Finance, 2004 c 12, s 326, sch 42 pt 2(13), Note 3

sch 17 rep in pt—Finance, 1996 c 8, s 205, sch 41 pt V(12); Finance, 1999 c 16, s 139, sch 20 pt III(6), Note; Income Tax (Trading and Other Income), 2005 c 5, s 884, sch 3; Income Tax, 2007 c 3, s 1031, sch 3; Finance, 2008 c 9, s 8, sch 2 para 21(a); Corporation Tax, 2010 c 4, s 1181, sch 3 pt 1; SL(R), 2013 c 2, s 1, sch 1 pt 10(1)

sch 18 am—Income Tax (Trading and Other Income), 2005 c 5, s 882(1), sch 1 pt 2 paras 475, 483

    rep in pt—Corporation Tax, 2009 c 4, s 1326, sch 3 pt 1; Taxation (International and Other Provns), 2010 c 8, s 378, sch 10 pt 12

sch 19 rep—Finance, 1997 c 16, ss 76,113, sch 10 pt I para 7(1), sch 18 pt VI(10), Note 1

sch 22 am—Finance, 2001 c 9, s 88, sch 29 pt 5, para 37; Income Tax (Trading and Other Income), 2005 c 5, s 882(1), sch 1 pt 2 paras 475, 484(1)(3)(5)(7)(9)(10)(12); Income Tax, 2007 c 3, s 1027, sch 1 paras 364, 370; Corporation Tax, 2010 c 4, s 1177, sch 1 paras 286, 290

    appl—Income Tax (Trading and Other Income), 2005 c 5, s 883(4), sch 2 pt 3 paras 52(6), 53(4)

    rep in pt—Income Tax (Trading and Other Income), 2005 c 5, ss 882(1), 884, sch 1 pt 2 paras 475, 484(1)(2)(4)(6)(8)(11), sch 3

sch 23 rep—Taxation (International and Other Provns), 2010 c 8, ss 374, 378, sch 8 paras 276, 279, sch 10 pt 11

sch 24 rep in pt—Finance, 1996 c 8, s 205, sch 41 pt V(3); Finance, 1998 c 36, s 165, sch 27 pt III(2), Note; Corporation Tax, 2010 c 4, s 1181, sch 3 pt 1

    am—Finance, 2002 c 23, s 79(2)(3), sch 23 pt 2, para 22(1)(3), pt 3, para 25

sch 25 rep in pt—Finance, 2002 c 23, s 141, sch 40 pt 3(10), Note 2; Finance, 2005 c 7, s 104, sch 11 pt 2(6), Note

sch 26 rep—Corporation Tax, 2010 c 4, s 1181, sch 3 pt 1

sch 27 rep—Finance, 2004 c 12, ss 77, 326, sch 42 pt 2(7), Note

sch 28 rep—Finance, 1999 c 16, s 139, sch 20 pt VII, Notes 1, 2

c 5 **Building Societies (Joint Account Holders)**

c 6 **Civil Evidence (Family Mediation)(Scotland)**

s 1 am—Civil Partnership, 2004 c 33, s 261(2), sch 28 pt 4 para 59; Family Law (S), 2006 asp 2, s 45, sch 2 para 7

s 2 rep in pt—Adoption and Children (S), 2007 asp 4, s 120, sch 3

    am—Children (S), 1995 c 36, s 105(4) sch 4 para 59; Adoption and Children (S), 2007 asp 4, s 120, sch 2 para 8; SSIs 2010/21, art 2, sch; 2013/211, sch 1 para 8

    appl (mod)—SI 2010/985, reg 5, sch 4

    rep in pt—SSI 2013/211, sch 2

1995

c 7   **Requirements of Writing (Scotland)**

saved—SI 1996/2827, reg 54(3)

appl—SI 2011/2262, r 107(2)

am—SSI 2001/128, reg 5, sch 4 para 4

Pt 1 (s 1) heading added (pt prosp)—Land Registration etc (S), 2012 asp 5, s 96(4)

s 1 am—Abolition of Feudal Tenure etc (S), 2000 asp 5, s 76(1), sch 12 pt I para 58; SSI
     2006/491, art 3; (pt prosp) Land Registration etc (S), 2012 asp 5, s
     96(2)(a)(b)(i)(iii)(c)

excl in pt—SIs 2009/555, art 4; 2013/1388, reg 22(2)

rep in pt—(pt prosp) Land Registration etc (S), 2012 asp 5, s 96(2)(b)(ii); SSI 2014/190,
     art 3

restr—(temp) SSI 2014/41, art 3(3)

Pt 2 (ss 1A-9) heading added (pt prosp)—Land Registration etc (S), 2012 asp 5, sch 3 para 2

s 1A added (pt prosp)—Land Registration etc (S), 2012 asp 5, sch 3 para 2

s 2 appl—Title Conditions (S), 2003 asp 9, s 84(2)

am—(pt prosp) Land Registration etc (S), 2012 asp 5, sch 3 paras 3, 4

ss 2A-2C added—SSI 2006/491, art 3

rep (prosp)—Land Registration etc (S), 2012 asp 5, sch 3 para 5

restr—(temp) SSI 2014/41, art 3(3)

s 3 am—(pt prosp) Land Registration etc (S), 2012 asp 5, sch 3 para 6

s 3A added—SSI 2006/491, art 3

rep (prosp)—Land Registration etc (S), 2012 asp 5, sch 3 para 7

restr—(temp) SSI 2014/41, art 3(3)

s 4 am—(pt prosp) Land Registration etc (S), 2012 asp 5, sch 3 para 8

s 5 am—SSI 2006/491, art 3; (pt prosp) Land Registration etc (S), 2012 asp 5, sch 3 paras
     9(a)-(d), 10

rep in pt—(pt prosp) Land Registration etc (S), 2012 asp 5, sch 3 para 9(e)

s 6 am—(prosp) Bankruptcy and Diligence etc (S), 2007 asp 3, s 48(1); ibid, s 222(1)(2);
     (pt prosp) Land Registration etc (S), 2012 asp 5, sch 3 paras 11(b)-(g), 12

rep in pt—(prosp) Land Registration etc (S), 2012 asp 5, sch 3 para 11(a)

s 6A added—Bankruptcy and Diligence et. (S), 2007 asp 3, s 222(1)(3)

rep (prosp)—Land Registration etc (S), 2012 asp 5, sch 3 para 13

restr—(temp) SSI 2014/41, art 3(3)

s 7 am—(prosp) Land Registration etc (S), 2012 asp 5, sch 3 para 14

appl (mods)—(temp) SSI 2014/41, art 4

s 8 am—(prosp) Land Registration etc (S), 2012 asp 5, sch 3 paras, 15, 16

s 9 am—(prosp) Land Registration etc (S), 2012 asp 5, sch 3 para 17

Pt 3 (ss 9A-9F) added (pt prosp)—Land Registration etc (S), 2012 asp 5, s 97

Pt 4 (ss 10-15) renumbered as Pt 4 (pt prosp)—Land Registration etc (S), 2012 asp 5, sch 3
     para 21

title added (pt prosp)—Land Registration etc (S), 2012 asp 5, sch 3 para 22

s 11 rep (pt prosp)—Land Registration etc (S), 2012 asp 5, sch 3 para 18

s 12 am—Scotland, 1998 c 46, s 125, sch 8 para 31(a)(b); SIs 1999/1820, art 4, sch 2 pt I
     para 118; 2000/2040, art 2, sch pt I para 17; SSI 2006/491, art 3; SI 2009/1941,
     art 2, sch 1; (pt prosp) Land Registration etc (S), 2012 asp 5, sch 3 para
     19(a)(ii)(v)(vii)(ix)(b)

rep in pt—SI 2009/1941, art 2, sch 1; (prosp) Land Registration etc (S), 2012 asp 5, sch
     3 para 19(a)(i)(iii)(iv)(vi)(viii)

mod—(temp) SSI 2014/41, art 3(4)

s 13 rep in pt—Title Conditions (S), 2003 asp 9, s 128(2), sch 15

am—(pt prosp) Land Registration etc (S), 2012 asp 5, sch 3 para 20

sch 1 am—(prosp) Land Registration etc (S), 2012 asp 5, sch 3 paras 23, 24

sch 2 appl—SSIs (S) 2000/47, art 5, sch pt II; 2001/137, art 5, sch pt II; 2002/103, art 6(1),
     sch pt II; 2002/305, art 5, sch pt II; 2002/534, art 5, sch pt II

am—SSI 2001/128, reg 5, sch 4, para 5; SI 2008/948, art 3, sch 1; (prosp) Land
     Registration etc (S), 2012 asp 5, sch 3 para 25

appl (mods)—(temp) SSI 2014/41, art 4

sch 3 am—(prosp) Land Registration etc (S), 2012 asp 5, sch 3 para 26; SSI 2014/346, art
     2(2)

sch 4 rep in pt—Petroleum, 1998 c 17, s 51, sch 5 pt I; Housing (S), 2001 asp 10, s 112,
     sch 10 para 22; Companies, 2006 c 46, s 1295, sch 16; Co-operative and
     Community Benefit Societies, 2014 c 14, sch 7

am—(pt prosp) Land Registration etc (S), 2012 asp 5, sch 3 para 27; SSI 2014/346,
     art 2(1)

1995

c 8   **Agricultural Tenancies**

appl—Reserve and Auxiliary Forces (Protection of Civil Interests), 1951 c 65, s 27(5)(bb);
(EW) Opencast Coal, 1958 c 69, ss 14B(5)(625A(6)(7); ibid, sch 7 para 1A(3);
Leasehold Reform, 1967 c 88, s 1(3)(b); Agric (Misc Provns), 1968 c 34, s 12(1A);
Rent (Agric), 1976 c 80 sch 2 para 2; Rent, 1977 c 42, ss 10(2), 137(4)(c)(ii);
Landlord and Tenant, 1985 c 70, s 14(3); Housing, 1985 c 68 sch 1 para 8(2); Agric
Holdings, 1986 c 5 sch 6 para 6(1)(dd); Housing, 1988 c 50, s 24(2A), sch 1
para 7(3); Town and Country Planning, 1990 c 8, s 65(8); Coal Mining Subsidence,
1991 c 45, s 21(aa); Housing, 1996 c 52, s 81(4)(c)

mod—Opencast Coal, 1958 c 69, s 14B(3)

s 1 mod—Opencast Coal, 1958 c 69, s 14B(2)

s 4 am—SIs 2006/2805, art 12; 2013/1036, sch 1 para 216(b)

rep in pt—SIs 2006/2805, art 12, sch 2; 2013/1036, sch 1 para 216(a)

ss 5, 6 rep in pt—SI 2006/2805, art 13, sch 2

s 7 am—Civil Partnership, 2004 c 33, s 81, sch 8 para 49

rep in pt—SI 2006/2805, art 13, sch 2

s 9 rep in pt—SI 2006/2805, art 14, sch 2

am—SI 2006/2805, art 14

s 13 mod—Opencast Coal, 1958 c 69, s 14B(4), sch 7 para 3A

am—SI 2006/2805, art 15

Pt 3 (ss 15-27) mod—(EW) Opencast Coal, 1958 c 69, s 25A(3)(4)(7), sch 7 paras 1A,
22A(2), 3A

s 20 am—SI 2006/2805, art 16

s 22 restr—(EW) Opencast Coal, 1958 c 69, s 25A(2)

s 24 am—SI 2006/2805, art 17

s 28 rep in pt—Arbitration, 1996 c 23, s 107(2) sch 4; SI 2006/2805, art 14, sch 2

am—SI 2006/2805, art 14

s 33 rep in pt—Trusts of Land and Appointment of Trustees, 1996 c 47, s 25(2) sch 4

s 35 rep —Legal Services, 2007 c 29, s 210, sch 23

sch rep in pt—Housing, 1996 c 52, s 227, sch 19 pt IX

c 9   *Commonwealth Development Corporation*—rep Commonwealth Development Corpn, 1999
c 20, s 27, sch 4

c 10   **Home Energy Conservation**

rep (S)—Energy, 2011 c 16, s 118(1)(a)

trans of powers—(W) SI 1999/672, art 2, sch 1

restr —(EW) Sustainable Energy, 2003 c 30, s 4(5)(b); (W) Energy, 2011 c 16, s 118(1)(b)

s 1 am—Energy Conservation, 1996 c 38, s 1(2); (NI) SI 1999/659, art 8(1)(b); Housing,
2004 c 34, s 265(1), sch 15 para 38; (S) Housing (Scotland), 2006 asp 1, s 192,
sch 6 para 18; Energy, 2011 c 16, s 118(2)

rep in pt—(NI) SI 1999/659, art 8(1)(a)

appl—(EW) Sustainable Energy, 2003 c 30, ss 2(9), 4(15); (prosp) ibid, s 3(9); Housing,
2004 c 34, s 217(3)

s 2 power to am—Energy Conservation, 1996 c 38, s 2(3); Loc Govt, 2000 c 22, s 7(2)(b)

am—(EW) SI 1997/47, art 3(2)

excl—(E) SI 2005/157, art 4

ss 3, 4 power to am—Energy Conservation, 1996 c 38, s 2(3)

s 5 excl—(E) SI 2005/157, art 4

c 11   **Proceeds of Crime**

ss 1-13 rep—Proceeds of Crime, 2002 c 29, s 457, sch 12

s 15 rep in pt—Proceeds of Crime, 2002 c 29, ss 456, 457, sch 11, para 27, sch 12

s 16 rep in pt—Proceeds of Crime, 2002 c 29, s 457, sch 12

sch 1 rep—Proceeds of Crime, 2002 c 29, s 457, sch 12

c 12   **Carers (Recognition and Services)**

trans of powers—(W) SI 1999/672, art 2, sch 1

s 1 appl—SI 1996/693, art 2; Carers and Disabled Children, 2000 c 16, ss 1(2),6(2)

am—Carers and Disabled Children, 2000 c 16, s 4(1); Carers (Equal Opportunities),
2004 c 15, ss 1(1), 2(1); SI 2015/914, sch para 56(2)-(4)

c 13   **Road Traffic (New Drivers)**

saved—Scotland, 1998 c 46, s 30, sch 5 pt II, s E1(f)

s 1 am—SI 1996/1974, reg 5, sch 4 para 5(2)

s 2 am—Crime (International Co-operation), 2003 c 32, s 91(1), sch 5 paras 45, 46; Road
Safety, 2006 c 49, s 5, sch 1 para 25; ibid, s 10, sch 3 para 67

rep in pt—Road Safety, 2006 c 49, ss 5, 10, sch 1 para 25, sch 3 para 67, sch 7

1995

c 13 *continued*

s 3 am—Crime (International Co-operation), 2003 c 32, s 91(1), sch 5 paras 45, 47; Road Safety, 2006 c 49, s 5, sch 1 para 26; ibid, s 10, sch 3 para 68

s 4 am—Crime (International Co-operation), 2003 c 32, s 91(1), sch 5 paras 45, 48

s 5 am—Crime (International Co-operation), 2003 c 32, s 91(1), sch 5 paras 45, 49

s 7 am—Crime (International Co-operation), 2003 c 32, s 91(1), sch 5 paras 45, 50

s 9 am—SI 1996/1974, reg 5, sch 4 para 5(3); Crime (International Co-operation), 2003 c 32, s 91(1), sch 5 paras 45, 51

rep in pt—Road Safety, 2006 c 49, s 10, sch 3 para 69, sch 7

sch 1 am—Access to Justice, 1999 c 22, s 90, sch 13 para 173; Crime (International Co-operation), 2003 c 32, s 91(1), sch 5 paras 45, 52, 53-60; Courts, 2003 c 39, s 109(1), sch 8 para 365; Road Safety, 2006 c 49, s 5, sch 1 para 27; ibid, s 10, sch 3 para 70

rep in pt—Road Safety, 2006 c 49, s 10, sch 3 para 70, sch 7

sch 2 rep in pt—Road Safety, 2006 c 49, s 59, sch 7; SI 2015/583, sch 1 Table 1

c 14 **Land Registers (Scotland)**

s 1 am—Land Registration etc (S), 2012 asp 5, sch 5 para 35(a)

rep in pt—Land Registration etc (S), 2012 asp 5, sch 5 para 35(b)

c 15 **Activity Centres (Young Persons' Safety)**

trans of powers—(W) SI 1999/672, art 2, sch 1

s 1 am—SI 2008/960, art 22, sch 3

s 2 am—Health and Safety (Offences), 2008 c 20, s 2, sch 3 para 4

s 3 am—SI 2008/960, art 22, sch 3

c 16 **Prisoners (Return to Custody)**

s 1 am—(pt prosp) Crim Justice, 2003 c 44, s 186(5); Crim Justice and Cts, 2015 c 2, s 13; ibid, sch 9 para 11

saved—Crim Justice, 1991 c 53, s 46A; Crim Justice, 2003 c 44, ss 246(4)(b), 260(3)(b); ibid, sch 9 para 11

s 2 rep in pt—Crim Justice and Immigration, 2008 c 4, s 149, sch 28 pt 1

c 17 **Health Authorities**

trans of powers—(W) SI 1999/672, art 2, sch 1

s 1 rep —Nat Health Service Reform and Health Care Professions, 2002 c 17, s 37, sch 8, paras 20, 21, sch 9 pt 3

s 3 rep in pt—Nat Health Service (Amdt), 1995 c 31, s 3(10); Nat Health Service (Conseq Provns), 2006 c 43, s 6, sch 4

sch 1 rep in pt—Nat Health Service (Amdt), 1995 c 31, s 14(2) sch; Employment Rights, 1996 c 18, s 242, sch 3 pt I; Education, 1996 c 56 s 582(2)(3) sch 38 pt I, sch 39; Nurses, Midwives and Health Visitors, 1997c 24, s 23(3), sch 6; (saving) Nat Health Service (Primary Care), 1997 c 46, s 41(12), sch 3 pt I; Audit Commn, 1998 c 18, s 54(3), sch 5; Govt of Wales, 1998 c 38, s 152, sch 18 pt I; (pt prosp) Health, 1999 c 8, s 65, sch 5; Health and Social Care, 2001 c 15, s 67, sch 6 pts I, II; SI 2001/1149, arts 3(2), 4(11), sch 2; Nat Health Service Reform and Health Care Professions, 2002 c 17, s 37, sch 8, paras 20, 22, sch 9 pt 3; Adoption and Children, 2002 c 38, s 139(3), sch 5; International Development, 2002 c 1, s 19(2), sch 4; Nat Health Service Reform and Health Care Professions, 2002 c 17, s 37, sch 8, paras 20, 22, sch 9 pt 3; SI 2002/2469, reg 19(1), sch 13; (W, E) Health (W), 2003 c 4, s 7(2), sch 4; Health and Social Care (Community Health and Standards), 2003 c 43, s 196, sch 14 pts 2, 4; (W prosp) Water, 2003 c 37, s 101, sch 7 pt 3 para 41, sch 9 pt 3; Human Tissue, 2004 c 30, s 57, sch 7 pt 1; SL(R), 2004 c 14, s 1(1), sch 1 pt 10/1; (prosp) Nat Health Service Reform (S), 2004 asp 7, s 11(2), sch 2; Public Services Ombudsman (W), 2005 c 10, s 39(2), sch 7; Nat Health Service (Conseq Provns), 2006 c 43, s 6, sch 4; (pt prosp) Health, 2006 c 28, s 80, sch 9; SI 2006/1407, art 3, sch 2; Mental Health, 2007 c 12, s 55, sch 11 pt 6; Health and Social Care, 2012 c 7, s 39(4)(b)

sch 2 rep in pt—Health, 1999 c 8, s 65, sch 5; Health and Social Care, 2012 c 7, sch 5 para 71

am—Nat Health Service Reform and Health Care Professions, 2002 c 17, s 2(5), sch 2 pt 2, para 62; SIs 2002/2469, reg 4, sch 1 pt 1, para 20; 2003/2867, reg 2, sch pt 1 para 23; Nat Health Service (Conseq Provns), 2006 c 43, s 2, sch 1 para 176; (W) SI 2007/961 (W 85), art 3, sch

1995
c 18   **Jobseekers**
          see—SI 2009/1562, reg 2
          power to am—Northern Ireland, 1998 c 47, s 87; Social Security Contributions (Trans of
                  Functions, etc), 1999 c 2, s 9
          power to appl—Welfare Reform and Pensions, 1999 c 30, ss 60(3)(4), 72
          power to excl—Asylum and Immigration, 1996 c 49, s 11(1)(c)
          appl—Income and Corporation Taxes, 1988 c 1, ss 151A(9),347B(13); Social Security
                  Admin, 1992 c 5, s 191; Employment Tribunals, 1996 c 17 s 17(4); SIs 2002/1792,
                  reg 13B(1)(d); 2002/2007, reg 5(4)(c); (E) 2003/2098, reg 8(1)(b)
          appl (mod)—SI 2007/631, art 2
          excl—Immigration and Asylum, 1999 c 33, s 115(1)
          mod—SIs 1996/1927, art 2; 1996/1928, art 2, sch 1; Social Security, 1998 c 14,
                  s 2(1)(2)(f); (pt prosp) ibid, ss 8(1)(c)(4)(5), 11(1)(3); SIs 1999/779, art 2(1)(b)(2);
                  1999/2227, reg 2(2); 2003/2438, reg 5; 2007/2122, art 2; 2010/1907, reg 16
          restr—Children (Leaving Care), 2000 c 35, s 6
          s 1 am—Welfare Reform and Pensions, 1999 c 30, s 59, sch 7 para 2; Civil Partnership,
                  2004 c 33, s 254(1), sch 24 pt 7 para 118; Welfare Reform, 2007 c 5, s 28, sch 3
                  para 12(1)(2); (prosp) Welfare Reform, 2009 c 24, s 4(1)(2); (prosp) Welfare
                  Reform, 2012 c 5, s 44(2); (prosp) ibid, s 61(2)(3)
              appl—SIs 1996/2890, reg 2(1); 1996/3257, art 2(1); 2001/3210, reg 7(2)(a); (W)
                  2004/683 (W 71), reg 8(1)(b)
              appl (mods)—SI 1996/2567, reg 2(1)(2)-(4)
              mod—SIs 2000/721, regs 7, 9; 2004/934, reg 6(2); 959, reg 20; (temp) 2005/1125,
                  regs 6, 8
              rep in pt—Welfare Reform and Pensions, 1999 c 30, s 88, sch 13 pt V; (prosp) Welfare
                  Reform, 2012 c 5, s 49(2); (pt prosp) ibid, sch 14 pt 1
              excl in pt—SI 2013/276, reg 7(1)-(3)
          s 1A added (prosp)—Welfare Reform, 2009 c 24, s 4(1)(3)
              rep in pt —(prosp) Welfare Reform, 2009 c 24, s 58, sch 7 pt 1
          s 1B added (prosp)—Welfare Reform, 2009 c 24, s 4(1)(3)
          s 2 mod—SI 1996/207, reg 158
              appl (mods)—SIs 1996/207, reg 167; 2013/378, regs 69, 75
              am—Social Security, 1998 c 14, s 86(1), sch 7 para 133; Welfare Reform and Pensions,
                  1999 c 30, s 59, sch 7 para 3; Nat Insurance Contributions, 2002 c 19, s 6, sch 1,
                  para 45; Welfare Reform, 2009 c 24, s 12(1)-(4); ibid, s 12(5); (prosp) ibid, s 9, sch
                  2 paras 5, 6; Welfare Reform, 2012 c 5, sch 2 para 35
              rep in pt—(prosp) Welfare Reform, 2009 c 24, s 58, sch 7 pt 1; (pt prosp) Welfare
                  Reform, 2012 c 5, sch 14 pt 1
          s 3 rep (pt prosp)—Welfare Reform, 2012 c 5, sch 14 pt 1
              am—Welfare Reform and Pensions, 1999 c 30, s 59, sch 7 para 4(1); State Pension
                  Credit, 2002 c 16, s 14, sch 2 pt 3, paras 36, 37; Civil Partnership, 2004 c 33,
                  s 254(1), sch 24 pt 7 para 119; Welfare Reform, 2007 c 5, s 28, sch 3 para
                  12(1)(3)
              rep in pt —(prosp) Welfare Reform, 2009 c 24, s 58, sch 7 pt 1
          s 3A added—Welfare Reform and Pensions, 1999 c 30, sch 7 paras 1, 4(2)
              rep (pt prosp)—Welfare Reform, 2012 c 5, sch 14 pt 1
              am—State Pension Credit, 2002 c 16, s 14, sch 2 pt 3, paras 36, 38; Welfare Reform,
                  2007 c 5, s 28, sch 3 para 12(1)(4); (prosp) Welfare Reform, 2009 c 24, s 9, sch
                  2 paras 5, 7
              rep in pt—(prosp) Welfare Reform, 2009 c 24, s 58, sch 7 pt 1
          s 3B added—Welfare Reform and Pensions, 1999 c 30, sch 7 paras 1, 4(2)
              rep (pt prosp)—Welfare Reform, 2012 c 5, sch 14 pt 1
          s 4 am—Welfare Reform and Pensions, 1999 c 30, s 70, sch 8 pt V para 29(2); ibid, s 59,
                  sch 7 para 5; SI 2006/343, art 2, sch; (prosp) Welfare Reform, 2012 c 5, sch 5 para
                  5(a)
              rep in pt—(pt prosp) Welfare Reform, 2012 c 5, sch 14 pt 1; (prosp) ibid, sch 5 para 5(b)
              appl (mods)—SI 1996/2570, reg 3(1)(2)
          s 4A added—Welfare Reform and Pensions, 1999 c 30, s 59, sch 7 para 6
              rep (pt prosp)—Welfare Reform, 2012 c 5, sch 14 pt 1
          s 5 am—SI 1995/3276, reg 7(3)(a)
              rep in pt—(pt prosp) Welfare Reform, 2012 c 5, sch 14 pt 1
              mod—SI 2013/983, arts 12, 13
          ss 6-6L subst for ss 6-10 (pt prosp)—Welfare Reform, 2012 c 5, s 49(3)
          s 6 rep in pt—Social Security, 1998 c 14, s 86(1)(2), sch 7, para 134(1)(a), sch 8

1995
c 18 s 6 *continued*

>am—Social Security, 1998 c 14, s 86(1), sch 7 para 134(1)(b)(2)

s 7 rep in pt—Social Security, 1998 c 14, s 86(1)(2), sch 7 para 135, sch 8

s 8 am—Welfare Reform and Pensions, 1999 c 30, s 70, sch 8 pt V para 29(3); ibid, s 59, sch 7 para 7; (prosp) Welfare Reform, 2009 c 24, s 32(1)(3)(a); ibid, s 33(1)-(3); (prosp) ibid, s 32 (as subst by 2012 c 5, sch 7 para 16(3)); Welfare Reform, 2012 c 5, s 45; ibid, sch 7 para 2(2)(3)

>rep in pt —(prosp) Welfare Reform, 2009 c 24, s 58, sch 7 pt 3; Welfare Reform, 2012 c 5, sch 14 pt 3

s 9 subst—Welfare Reform, 2012 c 5, s 44(3)

s 9 am—(pt prosp) Social Security, 1998 c 14, s 86(1), sch 7 para 136(1)(2)(3); Welfare Reform and Pensions, 1999 c 30, s 70, sch 8 pt V para 29(2); Welfare Reform and Pensions, 1999 c 30, s 59, sch 7 paras 8,9; (prosp) Welfare Reform, 2009 c 24, s 31(1) (as amended by 2012 c 5, sch 7 para 15(2)(b)); (prosp) ibid, s 32(1)(3)(b) (as amended by 2012 c 5, sch 7 para 16(3)); SI 2011/1498, art 2(2)

>rep in pt—(pt prosp) Social Security, 1998 c 14, s 86(1)(2), sch 7 para 136(4), sch 8; (prosp) Welfare Reform, 2009 c 24, s 58, sch 7 pt 3

s 10 subst (prosp)—Welfare Reform, 2012 c 5, s 44(4)

>am—(pt prosp) Social Security, 1998 c 14, s 86(1), sch 7 para 137(1)(2)(3); (prosp) Welfare Reform, 2009 c 24, s 32(1)(3)(c); (prosp) ibid, s 32 (as substituted by 2012 c 5, sch 7 para 16(3)); SI 2011/1498, art 2(3)

>rep in pt—(pt prosp) Social Security, 1998 c 14, s 86(1)(2), sch 7 para 137(4), sch 8

s 11 rep —Social Security, 1998 c 14, s 86(1)(2), sch 7 para 138, sch 8

s 13 rep (pt prosp)—Welfare Reform, 2012 c 5, sch 14 pt 1

s 14 am—Employment Rights, 1996 c 18, s 240, sch 1 para 67(2)

>appl—SI 2003/2682, reg 64(11)

ss 15-17 rep (pt prosp)—Welfare Reform, 2012 c 5, sch 14 pt 1

s 15 excl—SI 1996/207, reg 171

>mod—SI 1996/207, reg 155

>am—Income Tax (Earnings and Pensions), 2003 c 1, s 722, sch 6 pt 2 paras 228, 229; Civil Partnership, 2004 c 33, s 254(1), sch 24 pt 7 para 120

s 15A added—Welfare Reform and Pensions, 1999 c 30, s 59, sch 7 para 10

>am—Civil Partnership, 2004 c 33, s 254(1), sch 24 pt 7 para 121

>rep in pt—(prosp) Welfare Reform, 2009 c 24, s 58, sch 7 pt 3

s 16 am—Social Security, 1998 c 14, s 86(1), sch 7 para 139(1)(2); (prosp) Welfare Reform, 2009 c 24, s 32(1)(3)(d); Welfare Reform, 2012 c 5, sch 7 para 3

>rep in pt—(prosp) Welfare Reform, 2009 c 24, s 58, sch 7 pt 1; (prosp) ibid, s 58, sch 7 pt 3

s 17 am—Welfare Reform and Pensions, 1999 c 30, s 70, sch 8 pt V para 29(4); ibid, s 59, sch 7 para 11; Welfare Reform, 2012 c 5, sch 7 para 3

s 17A added—Welfare Reform, 2009 c 24, s 1(1)(2)

>rep (pt prosp)—Welfare Reform, 2012 c 5, sch 14 pt 4

>am—(prosp) Welfare Reform, 2012 c 5, sch 7 para 4

>rep in pt—(prosp) Welfare Reform, 2009 c 24, s 58, sch 7 pt 3; (pt prosp) Welfare Reform, 2012 c 5, sch 14 pt 1; ibid, sch 14 pt 3

s 17B added—Welfare Reform, 2009 c 24, s 1(1)(2)

>rep (pt prosp)—Welfare Reform, 2012 c 5, sch 14 pt 4

s 17C added—Welfare Reform, 2009 c 24, s 11, sch 3 para 1

>rep —Welfare Reform, 2012 c 5, s 60(1)

s 18 rep (prosp)—Welfare Reform, 2012 c 5, sch 14 pt 1

ss 19-19C subst for s 19 —Welfare Reform, 2012 c 5, s 46(1)

>rep (pt prosp)—Welfare Reform, 2012 c 5, sch 14 pt 4

s 19 am—Employment Rights, 1996 c 18, s 240, sch 1 para 67(2); (pt prosp) Social Security, 1998 c 14, s 86(1), sch 7 para 141(1)(2); Welfare Reform and Pensions, 1999 c 30, s 59, sch 7 para 12; (prosp) Welfare Reform 2009 c 24, s 32 (substituted by 2012 c 5, sch 7 para 16(3))

>rep in pt—(prosp) Welfare Reform, 2009 c 24, s 58, sch 7 pt 3

>appl (mods)—SI 1996/2570, reg 3(1)(2)

>excl—SI 1996/2890, reg 2(3)

>expld—SI 1999/3156, reg 7

>ext—SI 1999/3156, reg 6(1)

>mod—SIs 1996/207, reg 159; 2004/959, reg 21

s 19A am—(prosp) Welfare Reform 2009 c 24, s 32 (substituted by 2012 c 5, sch 7 para 16(3))

1995

c 18 *continued*

s 20 am—Social Security, 1998 c 14, s 86(1), sch 7 para 142; Welfare Reform and Pensions, 1999 c 30, s 70, sch 8 pt V para 29(5); Welfare Reform, 2012 c 5, sch 7 para 5(a)-(d)

  mod—SI 1996/207, reg 159

  rep in pt—Social Security, 1998 c 14, s 86(2), sch 8; (pt prosp) Welfare Reform, 2012 c 5, sch 14 pt 3; (pt prosp) ibid, sch 14 pt 4

ss 20A, 20B added—Welfare Reform and Pensions, 1999 c 30, sch 7, paras 1, 13

  rep —Welfare Reform, 2012 c 5, sch 14 pt 3

ss 20C, 20D added (never in force)—Welfare Reform, 2009 c 24, s 25(1)(2)

  rep—Welfare Reform, 2012 c 5, sch 7 para 6

s 20E added (pt prosp)—Welfare Reform, 2009 c 24, s 32(1)(2)(5) (as am and rep in pt (pt prosp) by 2012 c 5, sch 7 para 16(2), sch 14 pts 2, 6)

  rep (pt prosp)—Welfare Reform, 2012 c 5, sch 14 pt 4

s 22 am—Welfare Reform, 2012 c 5, sch 7 para 7

  rep in pt—(pt prosp) Welfare Reform, 2012 c 5, sch 14 pt 4

s 23 rep (pt prosp)—Welfare Reform, 2012 c 5, sch 14 pt 1

  am—Civil Partnership, 2004 c 33, s 254(1), sch 24 pt 7 para 122; (temp) SI 2014/605, art 21(1)

s 25 rep (prosp)—Welfare Reform, 2012 c 5, sch 14 pt 1

s 26 rep (pt prosp)—Welfare Reform, 2012 c 5, sch 14 pt 1

  am—Income Tax (Earnings and Pensions), 2003 c 1, s 722, sch 6 pt 2 paras 228, 230

  rep in pt—(prosp) Welfare Reform, 2009 c 24, s 58, sch 7 pt 1

s 27 am—Social Security Contributions (Trans of Functions, etc), 1999 c 2, s 1(1), sch 1 para 65; Social Security Contributions (Trans of Functions, etc), 1999 c 2, ss 2, 8(1)(i),sch 3 para 61

  power to am—Social Security Contributions (Trans of Functions, etc), 1999 c 2, s 23(1)(d)(3)(a)(i)

  rep in pt—Social Security Contributions (Trans of Functions, etc), 1999 c 2, ss 2, 26(3), sch 3 para 61, sch 10 pt 1

s 28 rep (pt prosp)—Welfare Reform, 2012 c 5, sch 14 pt 1

  rep in pt—Social Security Admin (Fraud), 1997 c 47, s 22, sch 2; Social Security, 1998 c 14, s 86(2), sch 8; (prosp) Welfare Reform, 2009 c 24, s 58, sch 7 pt 1

s 29 am—Tax Credits, 1999 c 10, s 1(2), sch 1 paras 1, 6(h); Welfare Reform, 2009 c 24, s 28(1); (pt prosp) Welfare Reform, 2012 c 5, s 49(4)

  rep in pt—Tax Credits, 2002 c 21, s 60, sch 6

s 30 see—(trans of functions) (W) SI 2000/253, art 2, sch 1

s 31 rep (prosp)—Welfare Reform, 2009 c 24, s 58, sch 7 pt 1; Welfare Reform, 2012 c 5, sch 14 pt 1

  am—Social Security, 1998 c 14, s 86(1), sch 7 para 143; Welfare Reform and Pensions, 1999 c 30, s 59, sch 7 para 14; Civil Partnership, 2004 c 33, s 254(1), sch 24 pt 7 para 123

s 32 rep in pt—(prosp) Welfare Reform, 2012 c 5, sch 14 pt 8

s 33 rep—Child Support, Pensions and Social Security, 2000 c 19, s 85, sch 9 pt VI

s 34 appl—SI 1996/195, reg 12(2)

  rep in pt—Social Security Admin (Fraud), 1997 c 47, s 22, sch 2; Child Support, Pensions and Social Security, 2000 c 19, s 85, sch 9 pt VI

s 35 am—Social Security, 1998 c 14, s 86(1), sch 7 para 144(b); Social Security Contributions (Trans of Functions, etc), 1999 c 2, s 2, sch 3 para 62; Welfare Reform and Pensions, 1999 c 30, s 59, sch 7 para 15; Civil Partnership, 2004 c 33, s 254(1), sch 24 pt 7 para 124(1)-(3)(5); SIs 2006/343, art 2, sch; 2006/745, art 12; Welfare Reform, 2007 c 5, s 28, sch 3 para 12(1)(5); Welfare Reform, 2012 c 5, s 44(5); (pt prosp) ibid, s 49(5); ibid, sch 7 para 8; SIs 2014/560, sch 1 para 26(2); 2014/3229, sch 5 para 12(2)

  mod—SI 1996/207, reg 160

  rep in pt—Social Security, 1998 c 14, s 86(1)(2), sch 7 para 144(a), sch 8; Civil Partnership, 2004 c 33, ss 254(1), 261(4), sch 24 pt 7 para 124(1)(4), sch 30; (pt prosp) Welfare Reform, 2012 c 5, sch 14 pts 1, 3, 4; SIs 2014/560, sch 1 para 26(3); 2014/3229, sch 5 para 12(3)

  appl—SIs 1986/975, reg 13(3)(a)(b); 1987/818, reg 8(4)(a)(b)

  appl (mods)—SI 2013/378, reg 70

s 36 am—Social Security, 1998 c 14, s 86(1), sch 7 para 145; Social Security Contributions (Trans of Functions, etc), 1999 c 2, s 2, sch 3 para 63; Welfare Reform and

1995
c 18 *continued*

Pensions, 1999 c 30, s 70, sch 8 pt V para 29(6); Welfare Reform, 2009 c 24, s 1(1)(3); ibid, s 11, sch 3 para 3(1)(2); Welfare Reform, 2012 c 5, sch 7 para 9; rep in pt—(prosp) Welfare Reform, 2009 c 24, s 58, sch 7 pt 3; (pt prosp) Welfare Reform, 2012 c 5, sch 14 pt 4; ibid, sch 14 pt 6

s 37 am —Welfare Reform, 2009 c 24, s 11, sch 3 para 3(1)(3); ibid, s 29(1)(2); Welfare Reform, 2012 c 5, s 46(2); ibid, s 49(6)
    rep in pt—Welfare Reform, 2012 c 5, s 47; (pt prosp) ibid, sch 14 pt 4; ibid, sch 14 pt 6

s 38 am—Social Security Contributions (Trans of Functions, etc), 1999 c 2, s 1(1), sch 1 para 66; Social Security Contributions (Trans of Functions, etc), 1999 c 2, s 2, sch 3 para 64
    rep in pt—(pt prosp) Welfare Reform, 2012 c 5, sch 14 pt 1

s 40 rep (prosp)—Welfare Reform, 2012 c 5, sch 14 pt 1

sch A1 added—Welfare Reform, 2009 c 24, s 11, sch 3 para 2
    rep —Welfare Reform, 2012 c 5, s 60(1)

sch 1 am—Employment Rights, 1996 c 18, s 240, sch 1 para 67(3); (temp) Social Security, 1998 c 14, s 83, sch 6 para 5(2); Social Security, 1998 c 14, s 86(1), sch 7 para 146; Welfare Reform and Pensions, 1999 c 30, s 70, sch 8 pt V para 29(7); ibid, s 59, sch 7 para 16(2)-(5); Civil Partnership, 2004 c 33, s 254(1), sch 24 pt 7 para 125; Welfare Reform, 2007 c 5, s 28, sch 3 para 12(1)(6); Welfare Reform, 2009 c 24, s 11, sch 3 para 3(1)(4); ibid, s 29(1) (as amended by (prosp) 2012 c 5, sch 7 para 14); (prosp) ibid, s 30(1); ibid, s 34(3); Welfare Reform, 2012 c 5, s 46(3)(a)-(c); (prosp) ibid, s 61(4); ibid, s 105(5); (pt prosp) ibid, sch 7 para 10(2)(3); SI 2013/630, reg 10(a)(b)
    rep in pt—(pt prosp) Welfare Reform, 2012 c 5, sch 14 pt 1; (pt prosp) ibid, sch 14 pt 4; ibid, sch 14 pt 6
    excl—SIs 1996/207, reg 46(1); 1999/991, reg 14A(4); 2013/378, reg 36; 381, reg 48(5)

sch 2 rep in pt—Employment Tribunals, 1996 c 17, s 45, sch 3 pt I; Education, 1996 c 56, s 582(2)(3) sch 38 pt I, sch 39; Social Security (Recovery of Benefits), 1997 c 27, s 33(2), sch 4; Social Security Admin (Fraud), 1997 c 47, s 22, sch 2; (pt prosp) Social Security, 1998 c 14, s 86(2), sch 8; Child Support, Pensions and Social Security, 2000 c 19, s 85, sch 9 pt VI; SI 2002/1397, art 12, sch pt I, para 12; Courts, 2003 c 39, s 109(3), sch 10; Income Tax (Earnings and Pensions), 2003 c 1, s 724(1), sch 8 pt 1; Income Tax, 2007 c 3, s 1031, sch 3; Pensions, 2007 c 22, s 27, sch 7 pt 2; (pt prosp) Welfare Reform, 2007 c 5, s 67, sch 8; (prosp) Welfare Reform, 2009 c 24, s 58, sch 7 pt 1; (pt prosp) ibid, s 58, sch 7 pt 2; Taxation (International and Other Provns), 2010 c 8, s 378, sch 10 pt 12; (prosp) Welfare Reform, 2012 c 5, sch 14 pt 1; ibid, sch 14 pt 8
    am—Tax Credits, 2002 c 21, s 60, sch 6

sch 3 rep in pt—Welfare Reform, 2012 c 5, s 46(4)

c 19   *Appropriation*—rep Appropriation, 1997 c 31, s 3, sch C

c 20   **Criminal Justice (Scotland)**
    rep (S)—Crim Procedure (Conseq Provns) (S), 1995 c 40, ss 4,6, sch 3 pt II para 16(3) sch 5
    s 66 rep—Crime and Punishment (S), 1997 c 48, s 62(1)(2), sch 1 para 16, sch 3 [Note; ss 108,110 and sch 4 of, 1995 c 20 extended to EW]

c 21   **Merchant Shipping**
    appl—Aviation and Maritime Security, 1991 c 31, ss 18(3),46(1); Shipping and Trading Interests (Protection), 1995 c 22, s 9(2); Merchant Shipping and Maritime Security, 1997 c 28, s 9, sch 1 para 5(7)(8); Pollution Prevention and Control, 1999 c 24, s 3(2); SIs (EW) 2003/527, reg 10(3)(b); 2004/568, reg 5(5), sch 2 para 10(1)(a)(i); 2004/757, art 15(1)(c); (S) SSI 2004/257, reg 9(3)(b)
    ext (mods)—SIs 1997/1773, 2579-2590, 2598
    saved—Scotland, 1998 c 46, s 30, sch 5 pt II, s E3(i)
    am—Constitutional Reform, 2005 c 4, s 59(5), sch 11 pt 3 para 6
    s 3 am—SI 2015/664, sch 4 para 27(2)
    s 10 am—(S) SI 1999/1750, art 4, sch 3; SI 1999/1756, art 2, sch para 17
    s 15 am—SIs 2002/794, art 5(1), sch 1, para 36; 2015/664, sch 4 para 27(3)
      rep in pt—SI 2002/794, art 5(2), sch 2
    s 24 am—SI 2014/1614, reg 2(2)
    s 30 am—SI 2001/1149, art 3(1), sch 1, para 103; Postal Services, 2011 c 5, sch 12 para 147
      mod (temp)—SI 2011/2329, art 5
    s 32 am—SI 2014/1614, reg 2(3)

1995
c 21 *continued*

s 35 am—SI 2014/1614, reg 2(4)
s 47 am—Marine Navigation, 2013 c 23, s 10
s 53 am—SI 2002/3135, art 16(1), sch 1 pt I, para 12
s 55 saved—Education, 1996 c 56, s 560(3)(b)
　　　excl—School Standards and Framework, 1998 c 31, s 112(2)
　　　am—SI 2002/2125, reg 21, sch 2, para 1
s 56 am—Merchant Shipping and Maritime Security, 1997 c 28, s 17
s 57 rep in pt—(EW) (prosp) Crim Justice, 2003 c 44, ss 280(1)(3), 332, sch 25 para 96, sch
　　　　　37 pt 7
ss 62-67 appl—SI 2014/1613, reg 38(3)
s 68 am—Access to Justice, 1999 c 22, s 90, sch 13 para 174; Courts, 2003 c 39, s 109(1),
　　　　　sch 8 para 366
　　　appl—SI 2014/1613, reg 38(3)
s 69 appl—SI 2014/1613, reg 38(3)
s 70 am—SI 2014/1614, reg 2(5)
s 80 am—Merchant Shipping and Maritime Security, 1997 c 28, s 18(1)(2)
s 85 am—Merchant Shipping and Maritime Security, 1997 c 28, s 8(2)(3)(4)(b)(5); Health,
　　　　　2006 c 28, s 5(4)
　　　see—SI 1999/2029, arts 2, 5, sch 2
　　　rep in pt—Merchant Shipping and Maritime Security, 1997 c 28, ss 8(4)(a), 29(2),
　　　　　sch 7 pt I
s 86 see—SI 1999/2029, arts 2, 5, sch 2
　　　rep in pt—Merchant Shipping and Maritime Security, 1997 c 28, ss 8(6),29(2), sch 7
　　　　　pt I
s 89 rep—SI 1998/2241, reg 3(1)(a)
s 90 rep—SI 1998/2647, reg 1(2)(a)
s 91 rep in pt—SI 2002/1473, reg 3(1), sch 1, para 1(1)(2)
　　　am—SI 2002/1473, reg 3(2), sch 2, para 1; Communications, 2003 c 21, s 406(1), sch
　　　　　17 para 132; Wireless Telegraphy, 2006 c 36, s 123, sch 7 para 15
s 92 am—SI 2015/664, sch 4 para 27(4)
s 93 sidenote am—SI 1998/1691, reg 2(7)
　　　am—SI 1998/1691, reg 2(1)(2)(4)
　　　rep in pt—SI 1998/1691, reg 2(3)(5)(6)
s 94 am—Merchant Shipping and Maritime Security, 1997 c 28, s 9, sch 1 para 1
s 95 am—Merchant Shipping and Maritime Security, 1997 c 28, s 9, sch 1 para 2
s 96 appl—SIs 1995/3128, reg 10(2); 1997/2962, reg 30; 1998/2411, reg 16; 1998/2857,
　　　　　reg 13; 2002/2201, reg 12; 2006/2183, reg 41; 2006/2184, reg 24
　　　appl (mods)—SIs 1995/3128, reg 10(2); 1999/2205, reg 17; 2001/3209, reg 9(8);
　　　　　2001/3444, reg 13; 2002/2125, reg 18(1)(2)(a)(b); 2003/1809, reg 23;
　　　　　2004/1713, reg 17; 2006/3223, reg 26; 2011/2601, reg 14(2); 2015/410, reg
　　　　　49(3); 508, reg 27(3)
　　　rep in pt—Arbitration, 1996 c 23, s 107(2), sch 4
　　　mod—SI 2002/2055, reg 16; 2006/3224, reg 7
　　　am—Tribunals, Cts and Enforcement, 2007 c 15, s 50, sch 10 para 26
s 97 am—SI 1995/3128, reg 10(3)
　　　appl—SIs 1997/2962, reg 30; 1998/2411, reg 16; 1998/2857, reg 13; 2002/2201, reg
　　　　　12; 2006/2183, reg 41; 2006/2184, reg 24; 2006/3223, reg 26; 2006/3224, reg
　　　　　7
　　　appl (mods)—SIs 1999/2205, reg 17; 2001/3209, reg 9(8); 2001/3444, reg 13;
　　　　　2002/2125, reg 18(1)(2)(a)(c); 2003/1809, reg 23; 2004/1713, reg 17;
　　　　　2011/2601, reg 14(3); 2015/410, reg 49(3); 508, reg 27(3)
　　　mod—SI 2002/2055, reg 16
s 98 am—SI 2015/664, sch 4 para 27(5)
s 100 am—SI 2015/664, sch 4 para 27(6)
ss 100A, 100B added—Merchant Shipping and Maritime Security, 1997 c 28, s 1
s 100B am—SI 2015/664, sch 4 para 27(7)
ss 100C-100E rep—Marine Safety, 2003 c 16, s 3, sch 2 para 2(a), sch 3
ss 100F, 100G added—Merchant Shipping and Maritime Security, 1997 c 28, s 11
s 100G am—SI 2015/664, sch 4 para 27(8)
s 108 am—Coroners and Justice, 2009 c 25, s 177, sch 21 paras 32, 33
s 108A added—Marine Safety, 2003 c 16, s 1(1)
s 117 rep—Railways and Transport Safety, 2003 c 20, ss 87, 118, sch 8
s 123 mod—SI 1999/2998, reg 19

1995
c 21 *continued*

s 125 am—Merchant Shipping and Maritime Security, 1997 c 28, s 9, sch 1 para 3

s 128 am—Merchant Shipping and Maritime Security, 1997 c 28, s 29(1), sch 6 para 3(2);
Merchant Shipping (Pollution), 2006 c 8, s 2
appl—SI 2005/74, art 2

s 130 am—SI 2015/664, sch 4 para 88(a)(b)
Pt 6, Ch 1A (ss 130A-130E) added—Merchant Shipping and Maritime Security, 1997 c 28, s 5

s 131(3) amdt to earlier affecting provn SI 2006/2950 art 6—SI 2015/664, sch 4 para 71

s 131 appl—SIs 1996/282, art 3; 1996/2514, reg 36A(1)(2); 1996/3010, reg 14(1ZA);
(saving) Merchant Shipping and Maritime Security, 1997 c 28, s 7(1)(2)(5);
1998/1377, reg 14(2)
am—SIs 2009/1210, reg 3; 2015/664, sch 4 para 27(9)
mod—SI 2006/2950, art 6 (amended by 2015/664, sch 4 para 71)

s 135 am—(EW) Fire and Rescue Services, 2004 c 21, s 53, sch 1 para 87; (S) Fire (S),
2005 asp 5, s 89(1), sch 3 para 18; SI 2006/1254, art 63, sch 3; Police and Fire
Reform (S), 2012 asp 8, sch 7 para 59

s 136A added—(S NI prosp) Pollution Prevention and Control, 1999 c 24, s 6, sch 2 para 13
rep in pt—(EW prosp) Pollution Prevention and Control, 1999 c 24, s 6, sch 3
am—Regulatory Reform (S), 2014 asp 3, sch 3 para 6

ss 137-141 rep—Marine Safety, 2003 c 16, s 3, sch 2 para 2(b), sch 3

s 138A added—(saving) Merchant Shipping and Maritime Security, 1997 c 28, s 3(1)(2)

s 141 am—(saving) Merchant Shipping and Maritime Security, 1997 c 28, s 2(5)(6)

s 143 appl (mods)—SIs 1998/1377, reg 15(1); 2008/2924, reg 33; 2008/3257, reg 43;
2009/2796, reg 15
am—SI 2009/1941, art 2, sch 1

s 144 am—(saving) Merchant Shipping and Maritime Security, 1997 c 28, s (3)-(5)
appl—SIs 2008/2924, reg 29; 2008/3257, reg 39

s 145 am—(prosp) Crim Justice, 2003 c 44, s 331, sch 36 pt 2 para 13; SI 2007/3077, reg
16; Crim Justice and Cts, 2015 c 2, sch 11 para 16
appl—SIs 2007/3075, reg 17; 2007/3100, reg 20
appl (mods)—SIs 1997/2962 reg 27B(10) (added by 2014/1616, reg 2(18));
2002/2125 reg 17A(9) (added by 2014/308, reg 2(19)); 2008/2924, regs 28,
29; 2008/3257, regs 38, 39; 2009/2796, reg 12; 2010/323, reg 25; 2010/330,
reg 18; 2010/332, reg 20; 2010/2984, reg 24; 2010/2987, reg 14; 2013/1785,
reg 17(8); 2014/1512, reg 14(10); 2014/1613, reg 56(6)

s 146 appl (mods)—SIs 1998/1377, reg 15(2); 2008/2924, reg 32; 2008/3257, reg 44;
2009/2796, reg 10; 2010/323, reg 22; 2010/330, reg 15; 2010/332, reg 17;
2010/2984, reg 24; 2010/2987, reg 12
appl—SIs 2007/3075, reg 14; 2007/3077, reg 13; 2007/3100, reg 17

Pt 6, Ch 3 (ss 152-171) ext (mods)—(Guernsey) SI 1998/260, art 2, sch 1; (Cayman
Islands) SI 1998/1261, art 2, sch; (Montserrat) SI 1998/1262, art 2, sch; (St
Helena) SI 1998/1263, art 2, sch
am—SI 2006/1244

s 163 am—SI 2015/664, sch 4 para 27(10)

Pt 6, Ch 4 (ss 172-181) ext (mods)—(Guernsey) SI 1998/260, art 2, sch 1; (Cayman
Islands) SI 1998/1261, art 2, sch; (Montserrat) SI 1998/1262, art 2, sch; (St
Helena) SI 1998/1263, art 2, sch
am—SI 2006/1265

s 163A added —SI 2006/1244, regs 2, 17
am—SI 2009/1941, art 2, sch 1

s 165 am—(prosp) Third Parties (Rights against Insurers), 2010 c 10, s 20, sch 2 para 3

s 173 am—SI 2009/1941, art 2, sch 1

Pt 6, Ch 5 (ss 182A-182C) added—Merchant Shipping and Maritime Security, 1997 c 28,
s 14(1)

s 183 am—SI 2012/3152, reg 14

s 184 rep in pt—Consumer Rights, 2015 c 15, sch 4 para 29

s 185 am—Merchant Shipping and Maritime Security, 1997 c 28, s 15
saved—SI 1998/209, reg 4(3)

s 192A added—Merchant Shipping and Maritime Security, 1997 c 28, s 16
am—SI 2015/664, sch 4 para 89(a)(b)

Pt 8 (ss 193-233) appl—SI 1997/3016, art 2; Environmental Protection, 1990 c 43, s 79

s 193 am—Merchant Shipping and Maritime Security, 1997 c 28, s 29(1), sch 6 para 6;
Marine Navigation, 2013 c 23, s 8(1)

1995

c 21 s 193 *continued*

saved—SI 2008/1261, art 55

s 197 am—Merchant Shipping and Maritime Security, 1997 c 28, ss 19(1)(2),29(1), sch 6
para 7

rep in pt—Marine Navigation, 2013 c 23, s 9(2)

s 197A added—Marine Navigation, 2013 c 23, s 9(1)

s 201 am—Merchant Shipping and Maritime Security, 1997 c 28, s 29(1), sch 6 para 8

s 202 rep—Merchant Shipping and Maritime Security, 1997 c 28, s 29(1)(2), sch 6 para 9,
sch 7 pt I

s 203 am—Merchant Shipping and Maritime Security, 1997 c 28, s 29(1), sch 6 para 10

s 204 am—Merchant Shipping and Maritime Security, 1997 c 28, s 29(1), sch 6 para 11

s 205 am—Merchant Shipping and Maritime Security, 1997 c 28, s 29(1), sch 6 para 12

s 210 am—Merchant Shipping and Maritime Security, 1997 c 28, s 29(1), sch 6 para 13

appl—Colchester B.C., 2001 c. ii, s 5(2)(b)

s 214 am—Public Service Pensions, 2013 c 25, sch 8 para 21(2)(3)

s 221 am—SI 2003/2867, reg 2, sch pt 1 para 24

s 222A added—Merchant Shipping and Maritime Security, 1997 c 28, s 20

Pt 9 (ss 224-255) appl—Treasure, 1996 c 24, s 3(7); SIs 1997/2949L, art 13(1);
1999/403L, art 6; 1999/3444, art 12(9); 2002/2618(L), art 8(1);
2004/2469(L), art 6(3); (S) SSI 2005/353(L), arts 7(2), 10(6); (E) SI
2005/1137(L), art 9(1)(b)

s 232 am—Merchant Shipping and Maritime Security, 1997 c 28, s 29(1), sch 6 para 14

s 233 am—Merchant Shipping and Maritime Security, 1997 c 28, s 21

s 240 am—Merchant Shipping and Maritime Security, 1997 c 28, s 22

s 252 appl—SI 1997/2949L, art 14(1)

appl (mods)—SSIs 1999/202, art 24(1)-(5); 2000/233, arts 33, 34; 2002/410(L), arts
24, 25; SI 2007/3463, arts 25, 26

mod—SI 2012/1777, arts 19, 20

am—Marine Navigation, 2013 c 23, s 11(1)(2)

s 253 excl—SSI 1999/202, art 25(4)

appl (mods)—SSI 2000/233, arts 33,34

Pt 9A (ss 255A-255U) added —Wreck Removal Convention, 2011 c 8, s 1(2)

s 255B am—SI 2015/664, sch 4 para 27(11)

s 255C am—Marine Navigation, 2013 c 23, s 8(2)(a)

rep in pt—Marine Navigation, 2013 c 23, s 8(2)(b)

s 255D am—SI 2015/664, sch 4 para 27(12)

s 255E am—SI 2015/664, sch 4 para 27(13)

s 255F rep in pt—Marine Navigation, 2013 c 23, s 8(3)

s 255K am—SI 2015/664, sch 4 para 27(14)

s 256 ext—Shipping and Trading Interests (Protection), 1995 c 22, s 5(6)

am—Merchant Shipping and Maritime Security, 1997 c 28, s 29(1), sch 6 para 15

mod—SI 2015/398, reg 36(4)(a)

appl (mods)—SI 2015/398, reg 36(10)

s 256A added—SI 1999/1820, art 4, sch 2 pt I para 119

s 257 mod—Shipping and Trading Interests (Protection), 1995 c 22, s 5(6)

s 258 am—Merchant Shipping and Maritime Security, 1997 c 28, s 9, sch 1
para 4(2)(a)(b)(3)(4)

rep in pt—Merchant Shipping and Maritime Security, 1997 c 28, ss 9, 29(2), sch 1
para 4(2)(c), sch 7 pt I; Protection of Freedoms, 2012 c 9, sch 2 para 2(1), sch
10 pt 2

appl—SIs 2007/3077, reg 18; 2007/3075, reg 19; 2007/3100, reg 22; 2010/737, reg
19, 2987, reg 16

appl (mods)—SIs 1997/2962 reg 27A(2) (added by2014/1616, reg 2(18));
2002/2125 reg 14(3) (subst by 2014/308, reg 2(14)); 2008/2924, reg 26;
2008/3257, reg 36; 2009/2796, reg 10; 2010/323, reg 27, 330, reg 20, 332,
reg 22, 2984, reg 26; 2011/2601, reg 25(2); 2013/1785, reg 16(2); 2014/1613,
reg 54(2)

s 259 appl—SIs 2007/3075, reg 19, 3077, reg 18, 3100, reg 22; 2010/737, reg 19, 2987,
reg 16

appl (mods)—SIs 2002/2125 reg 14(4) (subst by 2014/308, reg 2(14)); 2008/2924,
reg 26, 3257, reg 38; 2009/2796, reg 10; 2010/323, reg 27, 330, reg 20, 332,
reg 22; 2010/2984, reg 26; 2013/1785, reg 16(3); 2014/1613, reg 54(3)

mod—SI 2015/398, reg 36(4)(b)

ext—SI 2015/508, reg 28(5)

1995
c 21 *continued*

s 260 appl—SIs 2007/3075, reg 19, 3077, reg 18, 3100, reg 22; 2010/737, reg 19, 2987, reg 16
    appl (mods)—SIs 1997/2962 reg 27A(3) (added by 2014/1616, reg 2(18));
    2002/2125 reg 14(4) (subst by 2014/308, reg 2(14)); 2009/2796, reg 10;
    2010/323, reg 27, 330, reg 20, 332, reg 22, 2984, reg 26; 2013/1785, reg
    16(3); 2014/1613, reg 54(3)
s 261 am—Merchant Shipping and Maritime Security, 1997 c 28, s 29(1), sch 6 para 16;
    SI 1998/2241, reg 3(1)(b); SI 1998/2647, reg 1(2)(b)
    appl—SIs 2007/3075, reg 19, 3077, reg 18, 3100, reg 22; 2010/737, reg 19, 2987, reg 16
    appl (mods)—SIs 1997/2962 reg 27A(5) (added by 2014/1616, reg 2(18));
    2002/2125 reg 14(6) (subst by 2014/308, reg 2(14)); 2009/2796, reg 10;
    2010/323, reg 27, 330, reg 20, 332, reg 22, 2984, reg 26; 2013/1785, reg
    16(5); 2014/1613, reg 54(5)
ss 262, 263 appl—SIs 2007/3075, reg 19, 3077, reg 18, 3100, reg 22; 2010/737, reg 19,
    2987, reg 16
    appl (mods)—SIs 1997/2962 reg 27A(5) (added by 2014/1616, reg 2(18));
    2002/2125 reg 14(6) (subst by 2014/308, reg 2(14)); 2009/2796, reg 10;
    2010/323, reg 27, 330, reg 20, 332, reg 22, 2984, reg 26; 2013/1785, reg
    16(5); 2014/1613, reg 54(5)
s 264 rep in pt—Arbitration, 1996 c 23, s 107(2) sch 4
    appl (mods)—SIs 1997/2962 reg 27A(5) (added by 2014/1616, reg 2(18)); 2001/152,
    reg 9(3); 2002/2125 reg 14(6) (subst by 2014/308, reg 2(14)); 2009/2796, reg
    10; 2010/323, reg 27, 330, reg 20; 2010/332, reg 22; 2010/2984, reg 26;
    2013/1785, reg 16(5); 2014/1613, reg 54(5);
    am—Tribunals, Cts and Enforcement, 2007 c 15, s 50, sch 10 para 26
    appl—SIs 2007/3075, reg 19, 3077, reg 18, 3100, reg 22; 2010/737, reg 19, 2987, reg 16
ss 265, 266 appl—SIs 2007/3075, reg 19, 3077, reg 18, 3100, reg 22; 2010/737, reg 19,
    2987, reg 16
    appl (mods)—SIs 1997/2962 reg 27A(5) (added by 2014/1616, reg 2(18));
    2002/2125 reg 14(6) (subst by 2014/308, reg 2(14)); 2009/2796, reg 10;
    2010/323, reg 27, 330, reg 20, 332, reg 22, 2984, reg 26; 2013/1785, reg
    16(5); 2014/1613, reg 54(5)
Pt 11 (ss 267-273) appl (mods)—SI 2002/1587, reg 17
s 269 rep in pt—Deregulation, 2015 c 20, s 55(a)(b)
s 271 am —Coroners and Justice, 2009 c 25, s 177, sch 21 paras 32, 34
s 273 am—Coroners and Justice, 2009 c 25, s 177, sch 21 paras 32, 35
Pt 12 (ss 274-291) appl—Shipping and Trading Interests (Protection), 1995 c 22 s 7(1)
s 277 appl—SI 1997/3022, reg 7
    ext (mods)—(Guernsey) SI 1998/260, art 2, sch 1
s 277A added—(Guernsey) SI 1998/260, art 3
s 278 appl—SI 1997/3022, reg 7
s 279 ext (mods)—(Guernsey) SI 1998/260, art 2, sch 1
s 280 appl—Magisrates Cts, 1980 c 43, s 3A; Supreme Court, 1981 c 54, s 46A
s 281 ext (mods)—(Guernsey) SI 1998/260, art 2, sch 1
    appl—Magisrates Cts, 1980 c 43, s 3A; Supreme Court, 1981 c 54, s 46A
s 282 appl—Magisrates Cts, 1980 c 43, s 3A; Supreme Court, 1981 c 54, s 46A
s 284 am—Merchant Shipping and Maritime Security, 1997 c 28, s 9, sch 1 para 5; SI
    2015/664, sch 4 para 27(15)
    appl—SIs 1997/2962, reg 29; 2002/2628, art 10(4); 2004/348, art 9(4); (EW)
    Animal Welfare, 2006 c 45, s 55(3)
    appl (mods)—SIs 1994/2464, reg 11; 1996/2154, regs 35, 35A(2); 3010,
    reg 15(3)(b); 1997/529, reg 8; 647, reg 12, 1320, reg 16(1), 2962 reg 27B(4)
    (added by 2014/1616, reg 2(18)); 1998/209, reg 9, 1012, reg 106, 1609,
    reg 10, 2514, reg 92, 2515, reg 74; 2647, reg 8, 2857, reg 12; 1999/1644,
    reg 17, 1957 reg 25, 2205, reg 16, 2723, reg 25, 2998, reg 18(2); 2001/9,
    reg 9, 3209, reg 9(7); 3444, reg 12; 2002/1473, reg 11, 2125, reg 17, 2201,
    reg 11, 2125 reg 17A(3) (added by 2014/308, reg 2(19)); Railways and Tpt
    Safety, 2003 c 20, s 84(3)(b)(4); SIs 2003/1809, reg 22, 2950, reg 9; 2004/302,
    reg 11, 1713, reg 16(3)(4), 2110, reg 21, 2884, reg 10; 2005/2286, reg 11;
    2007/3075, reg 20, 3077, reg 19, 3100, reg 23; 2008/2924, reg 28,3257, reg
    38; 2009/2796, reg 12; 2010/323, reg 28, 330, reg 20, 332, reg 23, 2984, reg

1995
c 21 s 284 *continued*

27, 2987, reg 17; 2011/2601, reg 3(5); 2012/2267, reg 9(2), 3152, reg 9(2); 2014/1512, reg 14(4)(5), 1613, reg 58(3); 2015/508, reg 27(1); 782, reg 54(1)(2)

ext (mods)—(Guernsey) SI 1998/260, art 2, ch 1; SI 1998/2771, reg 9

mod—SIs 1998/1419, reg 9; 1999/17, reg 9, 3210, reg 27(1); 2000/3216, reg 7; 2002/2055, reg 15; 2002/2125 reg 17B(4) (added by 2014/308, reg 2(19)); 2006/2183, reg 40, 2184, reg 23, 3224, reg 7; 2015/410, reg 49(4)

s 291 saved—Shipping and Trading Interests (Protection), 1995 c 22, s 7(3)

s 293 am—Merchant Shipping and Maritime Security, 1997 c 28, ss 6,29(1), sch 6 para 17; Petroleum, 1998 c 17, s 50, sch 4 para 39

s 297 am—Constitutional Reform, 2005 c 4, s 15(1), sch 4 pt 1 para 239

s 298 am—Merchant Shipping and Maritime Security, 1997 c 28, s 23

s 302 appl (mods)—2009/2796, reg 20

s 302A added—Merchant Shipping and Maritime Security, 1997 c 28, s 13, sch 2 para 1

s 303 rep—Commrs for Revenue and Customs, 2005 c 11, ss 50(6), 52(2), sch 4 para 61, sch 5

s 306 am—Merchant Shipping and Maritime Security, 1997 c 28, s 29(1), sch 6 para 18; Wreck Removal Convention, 2011 c 8, s 1(3)

rep in pt—SI 1998/2241, reg 3(1)(c)

s 306A added—Deregulation, 2015 c 20, s 106

s 308 ext (mods)—(Guernsey) SI 1998/260, art 2, sch 1

saved—SSI 1999/202, art 25(1)

s 311 rep—Railways and Transport Safety, 2003 c 20, ss 112(8), 118, sch 8

s 313 appl—SIs 1996/207, reg 156, 3153, art 2(1); 1999/1877, reg 17, sch para 9(2); 2000/3241, art 1

am—Merchant Shipping and Maritime Security, 1997 c 28, s 29(1), sch 6 para 19(2)(3)

ext (mods)—(Guernsey) SI 1998/260, art 2, sch 1

s 313A added—Merchant Shipping and Maritime Security, 1997 c 28, s 29(1), sch 6 para 20

s 314 ext—(Jersey) SI 2004/1284, art 3

s 315 mod—Wreck Removal Convention, 2011 c 8, s 1(5)

s 316 ext (mods)—(Guernsey) SI 1998/260, art 2, sch 1

sch 3 rep—SI 1998/2241, reg 3(1)(d)

sch 3A added—Marine Safety, 2003 c 16, s 1(2), sch 1

am—SIs 2004/2110, reg 22(1); 2009/1941, art 2, sch 1; 2015/664, sch 4 para 27(16)

sch 5 ext(mods)—(Guernsey) SI 1998/260, art 2, sch 1; (Cayman Islands) SI 1998/1261, art 2, sch; (Montserrat) SI 1998/1262, art 2, sch; (St Helena) SI 1998/1263, art 2, sch

sch 5 am—SI 2003/2559, art 2(1)(3)

sch 5ZA added—SI 2006/1265, art 12, sch

sch 5A added—Merchant Shipping and Maritime Security, 1997 c 28, s 14(2), sch 3

sch 6 am—Arbitration, 1996 c 23, s 107(1) sch 3 para 61; SI 2014/1361, art 2, sch

sch 7 am—SI 1998/1258, arts 3-7, 8, sch; SI 1999/1922, art 3; Damages (S), 2011 asp 7, sch 1 para 6

rep in pt—SI 2004/1273, art 2

sch 9 rep—Merchant Shipping and Maritime Security, 1997 c 28, s 29(1)(2), sch 6 para 9, sch 7 pt I

sch 11ZA added —Wreck Removal Convention, 2011 c 8, s 1(4), sch

sch 11A added—Merchant Shipping and Maritime Security, 1997 c 28, s 13, sch 2 para 2

sch 13 rep in pt—Education, 1996 c 56, s 582(2)(3) sch 38 pt I, sch 39; Petroleum, 1998 c 17, s 51, sch 5 pt I; SL(R), 1998 c 43, s 1(1), sch 1 pt VIII; Postal Services, 2000 c 26, s 127(6), sch 9; (saving) SIs 2001/3949, regs 9(2), 10-14, sch 2; 2005/1082, reg 28(1)(2), sch 5 pt 1 para 20, sch 6 pt 1; Wireless Telegraphy, 2006 c 36, s 125, sch 9; Marine and Coastal Access, 2009 c 23, s 321, sch 22 pt 5; Crime and Cts, 2013 c 22, sch 9 para 141; Deregulation, 2015 c 20, sch 23 para 32(3)

c 22 **Shipping and Trading Interests (Protection)**

saved—Scotland, 1998 c 46, s 30, sch 5 pt II, s E3(j)

s 3 ext—Anti-terrorism, Crime and Security, 2001 c 24, s 17, sch 4 pt I para 36

am—SI 2015/664, sch 4 para 28(2)

s 6 am—SI 2015/664, sch 4 para 28(3)

1995

c 23   **Goods Vehicles (Licensing of Operators)**
            mod—SI 1995/2181, art 3, sch para 12(1)
            saved—Scotland, 1998 c 46, s 30, sch 5 pt II, s E1(g)
            appl—(EW) Environmental Protection, 1990 c 43, s 79
            trans of functions—SI 2009/1885, art 2(3)
            s 1 am—Loc Transport, 2008 c 26, s 3(2)(b); SI 2013/1644, sch 1
            s 2 excl—SI 1996/2186, regs 4-17,20,22-30
                  appl (mods)—SI 1996/2186, regs 9,12,15,21,22,26,28-31, schs 4-6
                  am—Transport, 2000 c 38, s 261; SI 2011/2632, sch 2 para 2(2)(4)
                  rep in pt—SI 2011/2632, sch 2 para 2(3)
            s 2A added—Transport, 2000 c 38, s 262(1)
            s 2B added—SI 2011/996, reg 6(2)
            s 4 mod—SI 1995/2181, art 3, sch para 5(1)
                  rep in pt—SI 2011/2632, sch 2 para 3
            s 5 am—Transport, 2000 c 38, s 263; Loc Transport, 2008 c 26, s 125(1); SI 2013/1644,
                  sch 1
                  cont—SI 2013/1644, sch 1
            s 7 am—SI 2013/1644, sch 1
            s 8 am—SI 2013/1644, sch 1
            s 9 am—Road Safety, 2006 c 49, s 6; SI 2013/1644, sch 1
            s 10 am—SI 2013/1644, sch 1
            s 11 mod—SI 1995/2181, art 3, sch para 7
                  am—SI 2013/1644, sch 1
            s 12 am—(temp) Goods Vehicles (Licensing of Operators), 1995 c 23, s 59, sch 6 para 6;
                  (S) Planning (Conseq Provns) (S), 1997 c 11, s 4, sch 2 para 59(1); SIs
                  2011/2632, sch 2 para 4(2)(3); 2013/1644, sch 1
                  rep in pt—SI 2013/1644, sch 1
            ss 13-13D subst for s 13—SI 2011/2632, sch 2 para 5
            s 13A am—SI 2013/1644, sch 1
            s 13C am—SI 2013/1644, sch 1
            s 14 am—Planning (Conseq Provns) (S), 1997 c 11, s 4, sch 2 para 59; SI 2013/1644, sch 1
                  rep in pt—SI 2013/1644, sch 1
            s 15 am—SI 2011/2632, sch 2 para 6(2)(3)
            s 16 mod—SI 1995/2181, art 3, sch paras 2(4)3(4))
                  am—Mental Capacity, 2005 c 9, s 67(1), sch 6 para 40(1)(2); SI 2013/1644, sch 1
            s 17 mod—SI 1995/2181, art 3, sch para 6(1)
                  transtl provns—SI 2008/1474, regs 3, 4
                  excl (temp)—London Olympic Games and Paralympic Games, 2006 c 12, s 16E(3)
                  am—SIs 2011/2632, sch 2 para 7; 2013/1644, sch 1
            s 18 restr—SI 1995/2181, art 3, sch paras 8(19(1)
                  excl (temp)—London Olympic Games and Paralympic Games, 2006 c 12, s 16E(3)
                  mod—SI 1995/2181, art 3, sch paras 8(29(2)
                  am—SI 2013/1644, sch 1
            s 19 am—Planning (Conseq Provns) (S), 1997 c 11, s 4, sch 2 para 59; SI 2013/1644, sch 1
                  rep in pt—SI 2013/1644, sch 1
            s 20 am—SI 2013/1644, sch 1
                  rep in pt—SI 2013/1644, sch 1
            s 21 am—SI 2013/1644, sch 1
            s 22 am—SIs 2009/1941, art 2, sch 1; 2011/2632, sch 2 para 8(2); 2013/1644, sch 1
                  rep in pt—SI 2011/2632, sch 2 para 8(2)
            s 23 am—SI 2013/1644, sch 1
            s 24 transtl provns—SI 2008/1474, regs 3, 4
                  am—SIs 2009/1885, art 4, sch 1; 2011/2632, sch 2 para 9(a)(b); 2013/1644, sch 1
            s 25 transtl provns—SI 2008/1474, regs 3, 4
                  am—SI 2013/1644, sch 1
            s 26 mod—SI 1995/2181, art 3, sch para 11
                  am—Road Safety, 2006 c 49, s 6; SIs 2012/2404, sch 2 para 32; 2013/1644, sch 1
            s 27 am—SIs 2011/2632, sch 2 para 10(2)-(4); 2013/1644, sch 1
                  rep in pt—SI 2013/1644, sch 1
            s 28 am—SIs 2009/1941, art 2, sch 1; 2013/1644, sch 1
            s 29 am—SIs 2009/1885, art 4, sch 1; 2013/1644, sch 1
                  rep in pt—SI 2009/1885, art 4, sch 1
            s 30 excl—SI 1995/2181, art 3, sch para 12(1)(2)
                  am—SI 2013/1644, sch 1

1995
c 23 *continued*

   s 31 excl—SI 1995/2181, art 3, sch para 12(2)
    mod—SI 1995/2181, art 3, sch para 13(2)(3)
    saved—SI 1995/2869, reg 19
    am—SI 2013/1644, sch 1
   s 32 excl—SI 1995/2181, art 3, sch para 12(2)
    am—SI 2013/1644, sch 1
   s 34 am—SI 2013/1644, sch 1
   s 35 ext—Anti-terrorism, Crime and Security, 2001 c 24, s 17, sch 4 pt I para 38
    am—SIs 2009/1885, art 4, sch 1; 2011/2632, sch 2 para 11(2)-(5); 2013/1644, sch 1
   s 36 am—SI 2013/1644, sch 1
   s 37 am—SIs 2009/1885, art 4, sch 1; 2013/1644, sch 1
   s 38 am—Goods Vehicles (Licensing of Operators), 1995 c 23, s 50, sch 5 para 5(1); SI
    2011/2632, sch 2 para 12
   s 39 am—SI 2011/2632, sch 2 para 13
   s 41 am—Goods Vehicles (Licensing of Operators), 1995 c 23, s 50, sch 5 para 5(2)
   s 42 am—Goods Vehicles (Licensing of Operators), 1995 c 23, s 50, sch 5 para 5(3); SI
    2013/1644, sch 1
   s 43 am—SIs 2011/2632, sch 2 para 14; 2013/1644, sch 1
   s 44 am—SIs 2011/2632, sch 2 para 15; 2013/1644, sch 1
   s 45 excl—SI 1995/2181, art 3, sch para 14
    am—SI 2013/1644, sch 1
   s 46 rep in pt—SI 2011/2632, sch 2 para 16(a)
    am—SI 2011/2632, sch 2 para 16(b)
   s 48 am—Mental Capacity, 2005 c 9, s 67(1), sch 6 para 40(1)(3); SI 2013/1644, sch 1
    rep in pt—SI 2013/1644, sch 1
   s 49 see—(trans of functions) SI 1997/2971, art 3(3)(a)
    rep in pt—SI 1997/2971, art 6(1), sch para 24
    am—SIs 2011/2632, sch 2 para 17(a)(b); 2013/1644, sch 1
   s 56 rep—SL(R), 2004 c 14, s 1(1), sch 1 pt 14
   s 58 am—SIs 2009/1941, art 2, sch 1; 2011/2632, sch 2 para 18(3)-(5)
    rep in pt—SIs 2011/2632, sch 2 para 18(2); 2013/1644, sch 1
   sch 1 rep in pt—SI 2011/2632, sch 2 para 19(2)
    am—SI 2011/2632, sch 2 para 19(3)
   sch 1A added—Transport, 2000 c 38, s 262(2), sch 30
    am—Loc Transport, 2008 c 26, s 126; SIs 2009/1885, art 4, sch 1; 2013/1644, sch
     1
    rep in pt—SI 2009/1885, art 4, sch 1
   sch 2 am—Road Safety, 2006 c 49, s 6; (EW) SI 2007/3538, reg 73, sch 21; SIs 2010/675,
    reg 107, sch 26; 2013/1644, sch 1
   sch 3 am—SI 1999/2430, regs 2(1)(2), 4, 5(3)(4); (transtl savings) SI 1999/2430, regs 3,
    5(1)(2); Powers of Crim Cts (Sentencing), 2000 c 6, s 165(1), sch 9 para 174;
    Crim Justice, 2003 c 44, s 304, sch 32 pt 1 para 68; Armed Forces, 2006 c 52, s
    378, sch 16 para 131; SIs 2011/2298, sch para 12(2)(3); 2011/2632, sch 2 para
    20(4)-(8); Legal Aid, Sentencing and Punishment of Offenders, 2012 c 10, sch
    10 para 8; SI 2013/1644, sch 1
    mod—SIs 1999/2430, reg 5(4); 2009/1059, art 205, sch 1
    rep & superseded—SI 1999/2430, reg 5(5)
    rep in pt—SIs 2004/3222, reg 2; 2011/2298, sch para 12(3); 2011/2632, sch 2 para
     20(2)(3)
   sch 4 excl (temp)—London Olympic Games and Paralympic Games, 2006 c 12, s 16E(4)
    am—SIs 2011/2632, sch 2 para 21(a)(b); 2013/1644, sch 1
   sch 5 rep in pt—SI 2013/1644, sch 1
    am—SI 2013/1644, sch 1
   sch 6 rep in pt—SL(R), 2004 c 14, s 1(1), sch 1 pt 14
   sch 7 rep in pt—SL(R), 2004 c 14, s 1(1), sch 1 pt 14
c 24 **Crown Agents**
   s 5 am—SI 2008/948, art 3, sch 1
   s 6 am—SI 2009/1941, art 2, sch 1
   s 14 am—SI 2009/1941, art 2, sch 1
c 25 **Environment**
   trans of powers—(W) SI 1999/672, art 2, sch 1
   saved—Comhairle Nan Eilean Siar (Eriskay Causeway) O Conf, 2000 c i, s 1, sch, s 24(e)
   power to am—Flood and Water Management, 2010 c 29, s 28

1995
c 25 *continued*

Pt 1 (ss 1-56) appl—Water Resources, 1991 c 57, s 119(1)
s 1 trans of functions—SI 2013/1821, art 5
s 2 rep in pt —SL(R), 2004 c 14, s 1(1), sch 1 pt 13; (EW) SI 2009/463, reg 45, sch 2; (S)
SSI 2009/85, reg 48, sch 2
s 3 rep in pt—SL(R), 2004 c 14, s 1(1), sch 1 pt 13
s 4 am—Natural Environment and Rural Communities, 2006 c 16, s 105, sch 11 para 140;
SI 2013/755 (W 90), sch 2 para 362(2)-(5)
Pt 1 Ch 1A (ss 5-10) renumbered as Pt 1 Ch 1A and heading inserted—SI 2013/755 (W 90),
sch 2 para 363(1)(2)
s 5 am—SI 2013/755 (W 90), sch 2 para 364(2)-(6)
s 6 mod—SI 1999/1746, art 5(3)
am—(EW) Water, 2003 c 37, s 72; Water, 2003 c 37, ss 73, 101(1), sch 7 pt 1
para 15(1)(2); Marine and Coastal Access, 2009 c 23, s 230; Flood and Water
Management, 2010 c 29, s 31, sch 2 paras 51, 52; SI 2013/755 (W 90), sch 2 para
365(2)(4)-(7)(9)(10); Water, 2014 c 21, sch 10 para 16
rep in pt—(EW) SI 2009/463, reg 45, sch 2; (S) SSI 2009/85, reg 48, sch 2; SI
2013/755 (W 90), sch 2 para 365(3)(8)
s 8 rep in pt—Environment, 1995 c 25, s 120(3) sch 24; SI 2013/755 (W 90), sch 2 para
366(2)(a)
am—Countryside and Rights of Way, 2000 c 37, s 73(4), sch 8 para 1(t); Natural
Environment and Rural Communities, 2006 c 16, s 105, sch 11 para 141; SI
2013/755 (W 90), sch 2 para 366(2)(b)(c)(3)-(6)
s 9 am—SI 1999/416, art 3, sch 1 para 17(2); Countryside and Rights of Way, 2000 c 37,
s 73(4), sch 8 para 1(t); Natural Environment and Rural Communities, 2006 c 16, s
105, sch 11 para 142; SI 2013/755 (W 90), sch 2 para 367(2)(3)(4)(a)(5)(6)(b)(7)
rep in pt—SI 2013/755 (W 90), sch 2 para 367(4)(b)(c)(6)(a)
s 9A added—SI 2013/755 (W 90), sch 2 para 368
s 10 am—SI 2013/755 (W 90), sch 2 para 369(2)(b)-(d)(3)-(6)
s 11 rep—SI 2002/784 (W 85), art 2(2)
ss 12, 13 rep—SI 2013/755 (W 90), art 9(2)
ss 14-16 rep—Flood and Water Management, 2010 c 29, s 31, sch 2 paras 51, 53
s 16A added —(W) Water, 2003 c 37, s 67
rep—Flood and Water Management, 2010 c 29, s 31, sch 2 paras 51, 53
rep in pt—SI 2007/1388, art 3, sch 1
s 16B added—(W) Water, 2003 c 37, s 67
rep—Flood and Water Management, 2010 c 29, s 31, sch 2 paras 51, 53
s 17 rep—Flood and Water Management, 2010 c 29, s 31, sch 2 paras 51, 53
s 18 rep—Flood and Water Management, 2010 c 29, s 31, sch 2 paras 51, 53
s 18A added—Water, 2003 c 37, s 66(1)(2)
rep—Flood and Water Management, 2010 c 29, s 31, sch 2 paras 51, 53
s 19 rep—Flood and Water Management, 2010 c 29, s 31, sch 2 paras 51, 53
s 20A added—Regulatory Reform (S), 2014 asp 3, s 51
s 21 rep in pt—SL(R), 2004 c 14, s 1(1), sch 1 pt 13; Regulatory Reform (S), 2014 asp 3,
sch 3 para 29(2); SI 2015/374, art 6(2)
s 22 rep in pt—SL(R), 2004 c 14, s 1(1), sch 1 pt 13
s 23 rep—Regulatory Reform (S), 2014 asp 3, sch 3 para 29(3)
s 24 rep (S)—SSI 2006/181, art 2, sch
s 27 appl (mods) —(S) Flood Risk Management (S), 2009 asp 6, s 78
am—Regulatory Reform (S), 2014 asp 3, sch 3 para 43(2)
s 28 rep—Flood Risk Management (S), 2009 asp 6, s 96, sch 3 para 7
s 30 rep in pt—Public Records (S), 2011 asp 12, s 14(c)
am—Regulatory Reform (S), 2014 asp 3, sch 3 para 43(3)
s 31 am—SI 1999/1820, art 4, sch 2 pt I para 120(2)(a); Regulatory Reform (S), 2014 asp 3,
sch 3 para 14
rep in pt—SI 1999/1820, art 4, sch 2 pt I para 120(2)(b)(c) pt IV
see—(trans of functions) SI 2008/1776, art 2, sch
s 32 rep—Regulatory Reform (S), 2014 asp 3, sch 3 para 14(4)
s 33 am—Pollution Prevention and Control, 1999 c 24, s 6, sch 2, paras 14, 16; (S) SSI
2006/181, art 2, sch; Regulatory Reform (S), 2014 asp 3, sch 3 para
14(5)(a)(b)(i)(iv)(6)
rep in pt—(pt prosp) Pollution Prevention and Control, 1999 c 24, s 6, sch 3;
Regulatory Reform (S), 2014 asp 3, sch 3 para 14(5)(a)(b)(ii)(iii)
s 34 rep —Regulatory Reform (S), 2014 asp 3, sch 3 para 14(7)

1995

c 25 *continued*

s 35 rep—Nature Conservation (S), 2004 asp 6, s 57, sch 7 para 10(1)
s 36 rep—Regulatory Reform (S), 2014 asp 3, sch 3 para 14(8)
Pt I Ch 3 (ss 37-56) heading am—SI 2013/755 (W 90), sch 2 para 370
s 37 functions ceased to be exerciseable—SI 2013/1821, art 6
   am—Regulatory Reform (S), 2014 asp 3, sch 3 para 43(4)
s 38 mod—SI 1999/1746, art 5(1)
   am—Regulatory Reform (S), 2014 asp 3, sch 3 para 43(5)
   functions ceased to be exerciseable—SI 2013/1821, art 6
s 39 am—Regulatory Reform (S), 2014 asp 3, sch 3 para 14(9)(10)
s 40 mod—SI 1999/1746, art 5(2)
   saved—Railways, 1993 c 43, ss 44A, 44B
   appl (mods)—SI 2003/3242, reg 20(1)
   see—(trans of functions) SSI 2008/1776, art 2, sch
   am—(temp until 24.3.2012) SSI 2008/170, reg 21; SI 2013/755 (W 90), sch 2 para
     371; Regulatory Reform (S), 2014 asp 3, sch 3 para 43(6)
s 41 appl (mods)—SIs 1998/2746, reg 16(1); 2002/1559, sch 4 para 5(15)
   mod—(W) SI 1999/672, art 5, sch 2
   appl—(EW) Water Resources, 1991 c 57, s 61A(3); SSI 2014/258, sch para 8
   am—(S) SSI 2003/235, reg 21, sch 6 para 1; SIs 2003/1326, art 19; 2005/894,
     reg 59(1)(2); (W) 1806 (W 138), reg 59(1)(2); 2006/937, reg 3; 2007/1711, reg
     46; 2007/3106, art 9; 2008/3087, reg 18; (S) Climate Change (S), 2009 asp 12, s
     99, sch 2 para 2; SI 2009/890, reg 92, sch 8; Flood and Water Management, 2010
     c 29, s 33, sch 4 para 39; SIs 2011/988, sch 4 para 4(2); 2011/2911, sch para
     22(a)(b); 2012/1659, sch 3 para 13; 2013/755 (W 90), sch 2 para 372(2)-(4);
     2013/1821, art 16(2)(3); 2014/861, reg 22
   see—(trans of functions) SSI 2008/1776, art 2, sch
   rep in pt—SIs 2008/3087, reg 18; (savings) 2009/3381, regs 13, 16; 2012/2788, reg 4
   saved—SI 2009/890, regs 14, 55, 65
s 41A added—SIs 2005/925, reg 48, sch 6 para 1(1)(2)
   am—SIs 2011/2911, sch para 23(a)(c)-(f); 2012/2788, reg 5(2)-(7); 2013/1821, art
     17(2)-(7); 2013/3135, reg 13(2)(3)
   rep in pt—SI 2011/2911, sch para 23(b)
ss 41B, 41C added—SI 2013/1821, art 19
s 42 am—Foods Standards, 1999 c 28, s 40(1)(2), sch 5 para 44(1)(2)(a) (3)(5)(6);
     SIs 1999/1820, art 4, sch 2 pt I para 120(3); 2012/2788, reg 6(2)-(4)(5)(a)(6);
     2013/755 (W 90), sch 2 para 373(2)-(9); 2013/1821, arts 18(2)(3), 20(2)-(5);
     Food (S), 2015 asp 1, sch para 6
   appl (mods)—SIs 1998/2746, reg 16(1); 2002/1559, sch 4 para 5(15)
   mod—(W) SI 1999/672, art 5, sch 2; SI 2013/1821, art 21
   rep in pt—Foods Standards, 1999 c 28, s 40(1)(2)(4), sch 5 para 44(1)(2)(b)(4), sch 6;
     SI 2012/2788, reg 6(5)(b)
   see—(trans of functions) SI 2008/1776, art 2, sch
s 43 appl (mods)—SI 2002/1998, art 24(1)
   am—Regulatory Reform (S), 2014 asp 3, sch 3 para 43(7)
s 44 am—SI 1999/1820, art 4, sch 2 pt I para 120(4)(5)
   rep in pt—SI 1999/1820, art 4, sch 2 pt I para 120(5) pt IV
   functions ceased to be exerciseable—SI 2013/1821, art 6
s 45 am—SI 1999/1820, art 4, sch 2 pt I para 120(4)
   functions ceased to be exerciseable—SI 2013/1821, art 7
s 46 rep in pt—(S) Public Finance and Accountability (S), 2000 asp 1, s 26, sch 4
     para 13(1)(2)
   am—SIs 2007/2194, art 10, sch 4; 2008/948, art 3, sch 1
   functions ceased to be exerciseable—SI 2013/1821, art 10
s 46A added—(S) Public Finance and Accountability (S), 2000 asp 1, s 26, sch 4
     para 13(1)(3)
s 47 am—SI 1999/1820, art 4, sch 2 pt I para 120(4)
   functions ceased to be exerciseable—SI 2013/1821, art 8
s 48 am—(S) Public Finance and Accountability (S), 2000 asp 1, s 8, sch 1
     para 7(1)(2)(a)(c)
   rep in pt—(S) Public Finance and Accountability (S), 2000 asp 1, s 8, sch 1
     para 7(1)(2)(b)
   functions ceased to be exerciseable—SI 2013/1821, art 8
s 49 am—SI 1999/1820, art 4, sch 2 pt I para 120(4)

1995
c 25 s 49 *continued*

rep in pt—(S) Public Finance and Accountability (S), 2000 asp 1, s 8, sch 1
   para 7(1)(3)
functions ceased to be exerciseable—SI 2013/1821, arts 8, 10
s 50 am—SI 1999/1820, art 4, sch 2 pt I para 120(4)(6)
   functions ceased to be exerciseable—SI 2013/1821, art 8
s 51 functions ceased to be exerciseable—SI 2013/1821, art 8
   am—Revenue Scotland, 2014 asp 16, sch 4 para 2(2)
s 52 ext—SI 1999/1746, art 10(1)
   functions ceased to be exerciseable—SI 2013/1821, art 8
s 53 ext—(EW) Water Resources, 1991 c 57, sch 8 para 2
   trans of functions—SI 2013/1821, art 9(2)
   functions ceased to be exerciseable—SI 2013/1821, art 9(1)
   am—SI 2013/755 (W 90), sch 2 para 374(2)-(4); Regulatory Reform (S), 2014 asp 3,
      sch 3 para 43(8)
s 54 rep in pt—Legal Services, 2007 c 29, s 208, sch 21 para 117, sch 23
s 56 appl—Railways, 1993 c 43, s 54(2)
   am—Pollution Prevention and Control, 1999 c 24, s 6, sch 2 paras 14, 17;
      SI 2000/1973, reg 39, sch 10 pt 1 paras 14,15; (S) SSIs 2000/323, reg 36, sch 10
      pt I para 5(2); 2003/171, reg 2; (S) 2004/275, reg 2; (EW) 2005/883, reg 2; 925,
      reg 48, sch 6 para 1(1)(3); 1528, reg 3; (EW) 1728, reg 3; 2006/3289, reg 4; (S)
      SSI 2006/541, reg 10; (EW) SIs 2007/3538, reg 73, sch 21; (savings) 2009/3381,
      reg 13, 16; (S) SSIs 2009/247, reg 5; 2011/226, reg 3(2); SIs 2011/988, sch 4
      para 4(3); 2012/2788, reg 7(a)(i)(b); 2013/755 (W 90), sch 2 para 375(2)(3);
      2013/1821, art 30; 2013/3113, reg 94(a)-(d)(2); Regulatory Reform (S), 2014
      asp 3, sch 3 para 5(2)
   rep in pt—(EW prosp) Pollution Prevention and Control, 1999 c 24, s 6, sch 3; (S) SSI
      2006/181, art 2, sch; (saving) (EW) SI 2007/3538, reg 74, sch 23; SIs
      2010/675, regs 107, 109, sch 26, sch 28; 2012/2788, reg 7(a)(ii); Regulatory
      Reform (S), 2014 asp 3, sch 3 para 29(4)
s 60 rep in pt—SI 2010/675, reg 109, sch 28
s 66 am—SI 1999/416, art 3, sch 1 para 17(3); Countryside and Rights of Way, 2000 c 37,
      s 73(4), sch 8 para 1(t); Natural Environment and Rural Communities, 2006 c 16,
      s 105, sch 11 para 143; SI 2013/755 (W 90), sch 2 para 376; (prosp) Planning
      (W), 2015 anaw 4, sch 2 para 20(2)(3)
s 67 rep in pt—Planning and Compulsory Purchase, 2004 c 5, ss 118(2), 120, sch 7 para
      19(1)(2), sch 9
s 69 appl (mods)—SI 2011/1824, reg 50(1)(b)
s 71 am—Localism, 2011 c 20, sch 7 para 32
s 72 am—SI 1999/416, art 3, sch 1 para 17(4); Natural Environment and Rural
      Communities, 2006 c 16, s 105, sch 11 para 144; SI 2013/755 (W 90), sch 2 para
      376; Deregulation, 2015 c 20, sch 22 para 11(1)
s 73 rep—Loc Govt, 2003 c 26, s 127(2), sch 8 pt 1
s 75 am—Loc Govt and Public Involvement in Health, 2007 c 28, s 22, sch 1 para 18(1)(2)
s 79 am—Loc Govt and Public Involvement in Health, 2007 c 28, s 22, sch 1 para 18(1)(3)
   rep in pt—Loc Govt and Public Involvement in Health, 2007 c 28, s 241, sch 18
Pt 4 (ss 80-91) mod—GLA, 1999 c 29, s 364
   appl (mods)—(E) SI 2005/157, art 8(2)-(6)
s 80 am—SI 2013/755 (W 90), sch 2 paras 377, 378(2)(3)(b)
   rep in pt—SI 2013/755 (W 90), sch 2 para 378(3)(a)
s 81 rep in pt—Regulatory Reform (S), 2014 asp 3, sch 3 para 14(11)(a)
   am—Regulatory Reform (S), 2014 asp 3, sch 3 para 14(11)(b)(c)
s 82 functions made exercisable concurrently—SI 2011/908, art 10, sch 3 para 3
s 83 functions made exercisable concurrently—SI 2011/908, art 10, sch 3 para 4
s 84 functions made exercisable concurrently—SI 2011/908, art 10, sch 3 para 5
   see —(power to rep or am) Loc Govt, 2000 c 22, s 7(2)(c)
   excl—(E) SI 2005/157, art 8
   rep in pt—Regulatory Reform (S), 2014 asp 3, s 49(a); Deregulation, 2015 c 20, sch 13
      para 7(a)
   am—Regulatory Reform (S), 2014 asp 3, s 49(b); Deregulation, 2015 c 20, sch 13 para
      7(b)
s 85 am—GLA, 1999 c 29, s 367; SI 2001/3719, art 2, sch, para 6
   appl (mods)—SIs 2001/2315, reg 11(2); (E) 2003/2121, reg 14(2); 2010/1001, reg 31
s 86 rep in pt—Deregulation, 2015 c 20, sch 13 para 8(2)(a)

1995

c 25 *continued*

  s 86A added—GLA, 1999 c 29, s 368

  s 87 am—SI 2013/755 (W 90), sch 2 para 379; Regulatory Reform (S), 2014 asp 3, sch 3
    para 43(9)

  s 91 appl—GLA, 1999 c 29, s 366

    am—SI 2013/755 (W 90), sch 2 para 380; Regulatory Reform (S), 2014 asp 3, sch 3
      para 29(5); Deregulation, 2015 c 20, sch 13 para 8(2)(b)

  s 94 am—Competition, 1998 c 41, s 3(1)(b), sch 2 pt IV para 6(2)(3); SI 2013/755 (W 90),
    sch 2 para 381(2)(3)(a)(ii)(b)

    rep in pt—SIs 2000/311, art 28(2); 2004/1261, regs 5, 6(1)(2), sch 2 para
      7(1)(2)(a)-(c); 2013/755 (W 90), sch 2 para 381(3)(a)(i)

  s 94A rep—SI 2004/1261, regs 5, 6(1)(2), sch 2 para 7(1)(3)

  s 96 rep (S)—Planning (Conseq Provns) (S), 1997 c 11, s 3, sch 1 pt II
    rep in pt—(EW) Planning (Conseq Provns) (S), 1997 c 11, s 3, sch 1 pt III

  s 97 expld—SI 1997/1160, reg 4
    am—Deregulation, 2015 c 20, sch 22 para 12

  s 98 am—SI 1999/1820, art 4, sch 2 pt I para 120(7)
    appl—SI 1996/1030, art 3

  s 99 rep—Deregulation, 2015 c 20, sch 22 para 13

  s 101 rep in pt—Water, 2003 c 37, s 101, sch 7 pt 3 para 42, sch 9 pt 3

  s 102 rep —(EW) Marine and Coastal Access, 2009 c 23, s 321, sch 22 pt 4

  s 108 appl—SIs 1999/743, reg 22(7); (with savings) ibid, reg 20(3)(4); 2005/2773, reg 7;
    2006/1381, art 3; 2012/1715, reg 6(2); 2015/810, reg 31(2)

    appl (mods)—SIs 1997/648, reg 28; 2004/1769, reg 23, sch 1 para 2; 2005/3468,
      reg 35(1)-(4); 2007/871, reg 35; 2008/1097, reg 16; 2009/153, reg 31;
      2009/995 (W 81), reg 31

    excl—Water Resources, 1991 c 57, s 172(3A)

    see—(power to appoint persons to exercise powers) Pollution Prevention and Control,
      1999 c 24, s 2, sch 1 pt I para 14(2)

    rep in pt—(EW prosp) Pollution Prevention and Control, 1999 c 24, s 6, sch 3; SI
      2010/675, regs 107, 109, schs 26, 28; Regulatory Reform (S), 2014 asp 3, s
      46(2)(e),(h)(ii); SI 2015/374, art 6(3)

    am—SI 2000/1973, reg 39, sch 10 pt 1 paras 14,16; (S) SSI 2000/323, reg 36, sch 10
      pt I para 5(3); Anti-social Behaviour, 2003 c 38, s 55(6)-(9); (EW) Clean
      Neighbourhoods and Environment, 2005 c 16, s 53; (S) SSIs 2006/181, art 2,
      sch; (S) 2007/179, reg 16; Protection of Freedoms, 2012 c 9, sch 2 para 3(2)-(4);
      SI 2013/755 (W 90), sch 2 para 382(2)(3); Regulatory Reform (S), 2014 asp 3,
      s 46(2)(a)-(d),(f)(g), (h)(i); ibid, sch 3 paras 5(3), 43(10)

    ext (mods)—SI 2003/3310, reg 8

    ext—(S) SSI 2007/179, reg 19; SIs 2007/1711, reg 51, sch 5; 2011/1543, reg 8(3);
      2015/168, reg 13(3)

    mod—SIs 2006/1379, reg 18; 2006/2988 (W 277), reg 18

  s 108A added —Regulatory Reform (S), 2014 asp 3, s 46(3)

  s 109 appl—SI 2006/1381, art 3

  s 110 appl—SIs 2005/2773, reg 7; 2006/1381, art 3; 2012/1715, reg 6(2)
    am—Regulatory Reform (S), 2014 asp 3, sch 3 para 29(6)

  s 111 rep in pt—(EW prosp) Pollution Prevention and Control, 1999 c 24, s 6, sch 3; SL(R),
    2004 c 14, s 1(1), sch 1 pt 13

    am—SIs 2012/1715, reg 6(2); 2013/755 (W 90), sch 2 para 383

  s 113 am—Pollution Prevention and Control, 1999 c 24, s 6, sch 2 paras 14, 18(1)(2); (S)
    SI 1999/1750, art 3, sch 2; SIs 2000/1973, reg 39, sch 10 pt 1 paras 14,17;
    2013/755 (W 90), sch 2 para 384(2)(a)(b)(d)(e)(3)(4)(b); Regulatory Reform
    (S), 2014 asp 3, sch 3 para 43(11); Revenue Scotland, 2014 asp 16, sch 4 para
    2(3)

    rep in pt—(EW prosp) Pollution Prevention and Control, 1999 c 24, s 6, sch 3; SI
      2013/755 (W 90), sch 2 para 384(4)(a)

    saved—Waste and Emissions Trading, 2003 c 33, s 14(5)

  s 114 rep in pt—(EW prosp) Pollution Prevention and Control, 1999 c 24, s 6, sch 3;
    (saving) (EW) SI 2007/3538, reg 74, sch 23; SI 2010/675, regs 107, 109, sch
    26, sch 28; Regulatory Reform (S), 2014 asp 3, sch 3 para 29(7)

    am—SI 2000/1973, reg 39, sch 10 pt 1 paras 14,18; (S) SSI 2000/323, reg 36, sch 10,
      pt I, para 5(4); (EW) Water, 2003 c 37, ss 3(13), 8(7), 13(4), 21(4)(5); (S) SSIs
      2006/181, art 2, sch; 2011/226, sch para 1; Regulatory Reform (S), 2014 asp 3,
      sch 3 para 5(4)

1995

c 25 s 114 *continued*

        appl—(S) SSI 2000/95, reg 8(3); (EW) Water Resources, 1991 c 57, s 20B; (S) SSIs 2005/348, reg 49(3); 2011/209, reg 53(3)

s 115 am—(S) SI 1999/1750, art 3, sch 2; SI 2013/755 (W 90), sch 2 para 385

s 118 rep in pt—SL(R), 2004 c 14, s 1(1), sch 1 pt 13

s 122 appl—SI 2003/3242, reg 20(2)

        am—Regulatory Reform (S), 2014 asp 3, sch 3 para 43(12)

s 123 appl (mods)—Reservoirs 1975 c 23, s 22A; SI 1998/2746, reg 16(2)

        appl—(prosp) Resevoirs, 1975 c 23, s 22B (added by 2009 asp 6, s 86(2)); (S) SSI 2004/143, reg 24; Commons, 2006 c 26, s 46(10); SI 2010/699, art 16; Reservoirs (S), 2011 asp 9, s 106(1)

s 124 appl—SI 2006/1381, art 3

sch 1 am—SI 2012/2404, sch 2 para 33(2)

        trans of functions—SI 2013/1821, art 5

sch 2 am—Employment Rights, 1996 c 18, s 240, sch 1 para 68

        excl—SI 2011/1824, reg 50(2)

sch 3 rep—SI 2013/755 (W 90), art 9(2)

sch 4 rep—Flood and Water Management, 2010 c 29, s 31, sch 2 paras 51, 53

sch 5 rep—Flood and Water Management, 2010 c 29, s 31, sch 2 paras 51, 53

sch 6 rep in pt—Public Services Reform (S), 2010 asp 8, s 8(2)

        am—SI 2012/2404, sch 2 para 33(3); Regulatory Reform (S), 2014 asp 3, sch 3 para 43(13)

sch 7 am—SI 1999/416, art 3, sch 1 para 17(6); Natural Environment and Rural Communities, 2006 c 16, s 105, sch 11 para 146; ibid, s 61; (prosp) Loc Govt and Public Involvement in Health, 2007 c 28, ss 203(2), 216, sch 14 para 4; Local Government Byelaws (Wales), 2012 anaw 2, sch 2 para 16; SI 2013/755 (W 90), sch 2 para 386

        rep in pt—Employment Rights, 1996 c 18, s 242, sch 3 pt I; Audit Commn, 1998 c 18, s 54(3), sch 5; Loc Govt, 2000 c 22, s 107, sch 6; Loc Govt and Public Involvement in Health, 2007 c 28, s 241, sch 18; Loc Govt (W), 2011 nawm 4, sch 3 para 3, sch 4 pt F

        excl—SIs (W) 2001/2289, art 4; (temp) 2001/3577, art 3(1)(a)

        appl (mod)—SI 2007/1159, art 3

sch 8 rep in pt—Race Relations (Amdt), 2000 c 34, s 9(2), sch 3; (EW) Loc Govt, 2003 c 26, s 127(2), sch 8 pt 1; Loc Govt and Public Involvement in Health, 2007 c 28, s 239(4)

        am—Loc Democracy, Economic Development and Construction, 2009 c 20, s 67, sch 4 para 7; (W) Playing Fields (Community Involvement in Disposal Decisions) (W), 2010 nawm 6, s 3; Loc Govt (Religious etc. Observances), 2015 c 27, s 2(3)

sch 9 am—Countryside and Rights of Way, 2000 c 37, s 57, sch 6 pt II para 26; (pt prosp) Commons, 2006 c 26, s 52, sch 5 para 6; Charities, 2011 c 25, sch 7 para 68; (savings) Mobile Homes (W), 2013 anaw 6, sch 4 para 8(2)(3)

        rep in pt—Commons, 2006 c 26, s 53, sch 6

sch 10 rep in pt—Environment, 1995 c 25, ss 78,120(3) sch 10 para 32(18) sch 24; Justices of the Peace, 1997 c 25, s 73(3), sch 6 pt I; Govt of Wales, 1998 c 38, s 152, sch 18 pt IV, V; SL(R), 1998 c 43, s 1(1), sch 1 pt IV, Group 2; Countryside and Rights of Way, 2000 c 37, s 102, sch 16 pt V; Race Relations (Amdt), 2000 c 34, s 9, sch 3; (EW) Loc Govt, 2003 c 26, s 127(2), sch 8 pt 1; (prosp) Housing and Regeneration, 2008 c 17, s 321, sch 16

sch 11 am—GLA, 1999 c 29, s 369; Nat Parks (S), 2000 asp 10, s 36, sch 5 para 17; Regulatory Reform (S), 2014 asp 3, sch 3 para 43(14)

        rep in pt—Environment, 1995 c 25, s 120(3 sch 24; Regulatory Reform (S), 2014 asp 3, sch 3 para 29(8); Deregulation, 2015 c 20, sch 13 para 8(2)(c)

sch 13 rep (S)—Planning (Conseq Provns) (S), 1997 c 11, s 3, sch 1 pt II

        rep in pt—(EW) Planning (Conseq Provns) (S), 1997 c 11, s 3, sch 1 pt III

        am—Planning (Conseq Provns) (S), 1997 c 11, s 4, sch 2 para 60(1); Countryside and Rights of Way, 2000 c 37, ss 76(1),93, sch 10 pt II para 10, sch 15 pt I para 13; SIs (E) 2003/956, art 10(1)(2)(a)(b); (W) 2004/3156 (W 273), art 10(1)(2)(a)(b)

        excl—SIs 2009/3342 (W 293), reg 42; 2011/1824, reg 50(1)(a)

        appl (mods)—SI 2009/3342 (W 293), reg 45

        mod—SI 2011/1824, reg 50(5)

sch 14 rep (S)—Planning (Conseq Provns) (S), 1997 c 11, s 3, sch 1 pt II

1995
c 25 sch 14 *continued*

rep in pt—(EW) Planning (Conseq Provns) (S), 1997 c 11, s 3, sch 1 pt III; Growth
and Infrastructure, 2013 c 27, sch 3 para 8(3)(a)

am—Planning (Conseq Provns) (S), 1997 c 11, s 4, sch 2 para 60(2); (E) SI
2003/956, art 10(1)(3)(a)(b); Planning and Compulsory Purchase, 2004 c 5,
s 118(2), sch 7 para 19(1)(4); (W) SI 2004/3156 (W 273), art 10(1)(3)(a)(b);
Growth and Infrastructure, 2013 c 27, sch 3 paras 2, 3, 4, 5, 6(2)-(4), 7,
8(2)(3)(b), 9(2)(3)(4)(b)

excl—SIs 2009/3342 (W 293), reg 42; 2011/1824, reg 50(1)(a)

appl (mods)—SI 2009/3342 (W 293), reg 45

mod—SI 2011/1824, reg 50(5)

sch 15 rep in pt—Marine and Coastal Access, 2009 c 23, s 321, sch 22 pt 5; (EW) SI
2009/463, reg 45, sch 2; (S) SSI 2009/85, reg 48, sch 2

sch 17 rep in pt—(S) Public Health etc (S), 2008 asp 5, s 126, sch 3 pt 1

sch 18 appl (mods)—SIs 1997/648, reg 28(5)(6); 2004/1769, reg 23, sch 1 para 3;
2005/3468, reg 35(5)(6)

am—Regulatory Reform (S), 2014 asp 3, s 46(4)(a)(b)(i)

rep in pt—Regulatory Reform (S), 2014 asp 3, s 46(4)(b)(ii)

sch 20 rep in pt—Pollution Prevention and Control, 1999 c 24, s 6, sch 3; SI 2000/1973,
reg 39, sch 10 pt 1 paras 14,19; (S) SSI 2000/323, reg 36, sch 10 pt I para 5(5);
(saving) (EW) SI 2007/3538, reg 74, sch 23

am—SI 2000/1973, reg 39, sch 10 pt 1 paras 14,19; (S) SSIs 2000/323, reg 36,
sch 10 pt I para 5(5); (S) 2006/181, art 2, sch; (EW) SI 2007/3538, reg 73, sch
21; SSIs 2011/226, reg 3(3); 2012/360, sch 11 para 2(2); SI 2013/755 (W 90),
sch 2 para 387

appl—(S) SSI 2000/95, reg 8(3); (E) SI 2005/711, reg 6

power to appl (mods)—(EW) Anti-social Behaviour, 2003 c 38, s 72(6)

sch 21 rep in pt—Water Industry (S), 2002 asp 3, s 71(2), sch 7, para 24(1)(3)

sch 22 rep in pt—Planning (Conseq Provns) (S), 1997 c 11, s 3, sch 1 pt I; Crime and
Punishment (S) Act, 1997 c 48, ss 30(5),62(2), sch 3; Police, 1997 c 50,
s 134(2), sch 10; Pollution Prevention and Control, 1999 c 24, s 6, sch 3; Foods
Standards, 1999 c 28, s 40(4), sch 6; Utilities, 2000 c 27, s 108, sch 8; Water,
2003 c 37, s 101, sch 7 pt 1 para 15(1)(3), sch 9 pt 3; SL(R), 2004 c 14, s 1(1),
sch 1 pt 13; (saving) (EW) SI 2007/3538, reg 74, sch 23; SI 2010/675, reg 109,
sch 28; Energy, 2013 c 32, sch 12 para 30; Regulatory Reform (S), 2014 asp 3,
sch 3 para 29(10)(a)(b)(ii)(c)(d); SIs 2015/374, art 6(4); 664, sch 4 para 98

am—SI 2008/960, art 22, sch 3; Regulatory Reform (S), 2014 asp 3, sch 3 para
29(10)(b)(i)

sch 23 rep in pt—SL(R), 2004 c 14, s 1(1), sch 1 pt 13; SI 2013/755 (W 90), art 9(2);
Regulatory Reform (S), 2014 asp 3, sch 3 para 29(11)

sch 24 rep in pt—(S) Public Health etc (S), 2008 asp 5, s 126, sch 3 pt 1

c 26   **Pensions**

appl—SI 1995/3183, reg 2

appl (mods)—SI 2011/245, sch 6 pt 1

excl—Pension Schemes, 1993 c 48, s 6(8)

mod—Social Security Contributions and Benefits, 1992 c 4, s 55C(6); SIs 2009/317, art 3,
sch; 2010/1907, reg 16

power to am—Northern Ireland, 1998 c 47, s 87

power to mod—Insolvency, 2000 c 39, s 7(2); Pensions, 2004 c 35, s 321(1)(c)(2)(3)

Pt 1 (ss 1-125) appl (mods)—SI 1997/786, reg 2

appl—Welfare Reform and Pensions, 1999 c 30, s 38(4)(a); Armed Forces (Pensions
and Compensation), 2004 c 32, s 3(3); SI 2005/438, art 3(7)

transtl savings—SI 2005/3377, reg 20(2), sch 4 pt 2

s 1 rep—Pensions, 2004 c 35, s 320, sch 13 pt 1

s 2 rep—(saving) Pensions, 2004 c 35, s 320, sch 13 pt 1, SI 2005/695, art 6, sch 3

ss 3-11 appl (mods)—Welfare Reform and Pensions, 1999 c 30, s 6, sch 1 para 1(2)-(5)

s 3 subst—(saving) Pensions, 2004 c 35, s 33, SI 2005/695, art 6, sch 3

am—SI 2010/22, art 5, sch 2

rep in pt—SI 2010/22, art 5, sch 2

s 3A added—Pensions, 2014 c 19, s 46(2)

s 4 am—Insolvency, 2000 c 39, s 8, sch 4 pt II para 19(2); (saving) Pensions, 2004 c 35,
ss 34, 319(1), sch 12 paras 34, 35, SIs 2005/695, art 6, sch 3; 2009/1941, art 2,
sch 1; 2010/22, art 5, sch 2; 2012/2404, sch 2 para 34(2); Pensions, 2014 c 19, s
46(4)(5)

1995

c 26 s 4 *continued*

rep in pt—SI 2010/22, art 5, sch 2

s 5 rep—Pensions, 2004 c 35, s 320, sch 13 pt 1

s 6 am—Pensions, 2014 c 19, sch 19 para 2

s 7 rep in pt—Pensions, 2004 c 35, ss 35(1)(a), 319(1), 320, sch 12 paras 34, 36(a), sch 13
        pt 1; Pensions, 2008 c 30, ss 131(1)(b), 148, sch 11

am—Pensions, 2004 c 35, ss 35(1)(b), 319(1), sch 12 paras 34, 36(b); Pensions, 2008 c
        30, s 131(1)(a)(c); Pensions, 2014 c 19, sch 19 para 3

s 8 rep in pt—Welfare Reform and Pensions, 1999 c 30, ss 18, 88, sch 2 para 10, sch 13 pt I

am—(saving) Pensions, 2004 c 35, s 35(2), SI 2005/695, art 6, sch 3

s 9 am—Pensions, 2004 c 35, s 319(1), sch 12 paras 34, 37; Pensions, 2014 c 19, sch 19
        para 4

s 10 am—Welfare Reform and Pensions, 1999 c 30, s 18, sch 2 para 11; Tribunals, Cts and
        Enforcement, 2007 c 15, s 62, sch 13 para 121; Crime and Cts, 2013 c 22, sch 9
        para 52

power to appl—Pension Schemes, 2015 c 8, s 49(2)(c); (prosp) ibid, s 36(2)(b)

appl—(retrosp) SI 1987/257, reg M10(1)(b)(2); 1992/280, reg J10(1)(b)(2); Pension
        Schemes, 1993 c 48, ss 93A(4), 99(7)(8),101(4); ibid, s 93A(6) (subst by 2015 c
        8, sch 4 para 8); (retrosp) SI 1995/365, reg W10(1)(b)(2); (retrosp) SI 1998/366,
        reg 149(1)(b)(2); Welfare Reform and Pensions, 1999 c 30, ss 2(4), 33(1)-(3);
        (pt retrosp) ibid, s 3(7); Pensions, 2004 c 35, ss 70A, 231A(7); (S) SSI 2005/393,
        reg F9(1)(b)(2); SI 2005/3380, regs 3(4), 4(3), 6(4), 7(4), 8(2), 10(7), 12(4);
        SSIs 2008/228, reg 94; 2011/117, reg V10(1)(2); SI 2014/1711, regs 23(12),
        46(6); Pension Schemes, 2015 c 8, s 48(6); SIs 2015/118, reg 12(3); 742, reg
        12(7)

appl (mods)—Pension Schemes, 1993 c 48, s 111A(8)(9)(11); Pensions, 2004 c 35,
        s 314(a)

rep in pt—Pensions, 2004 c 35, ss 319(1), 320, sch 12 paras 34, 38, sch 13 pt 1

s 11 rep in pt—(saving) Pensions, 2004 c 35, ss 22(a), 320, sch 13 pt 1, SI 2005/695, art 6,
        sch 3

am—(saving) Pensions, 2004 c 35, s 22(b)-(d), SIs 2005/695, art 6, sch 3; 2009/1682,
        art 2, sch

s 12 appl (mods)—Welfare Reform and Pensions, 1999 c 30, s 6, sch 1 para 1(2)(3)

s 13 rep—Pensions, 2004 c 35, s 320, sch 13 pt 1

s 15 am—Pensions, 2004 c 35, s 319(1), sch 12 paras 34, 39

appl (mods)—Welfare Reform and Pensions, 1999 c 30, s 6, sch 1 para 1(2)(5)

ss 16-21 rep —Pensions, 2004 c 35, s 320, sch 13 pt 1

ss 22-26 mod—SIs 1997/252, regs 3,4; 2005/703, regs 10-12

excl—SI 1997/252, reg 5

s 22 am—Child Support, Pensions and Social Security, 2000 c 19, s 47(1); Pensions, 2004 c
        35, ss 36(1)(2), 319(1), sch 12 paras 34, 40; SI 2009/1941, art 2, sch 1

rep in pt—Pensions, 2004 c 35, ss 36(1)(2)(a), 320, sch 13 pt 1

ss 23, 24 replaced (by s 23)—Pensions, 2004 c 35, s 36(1)(3)

rep in pt—(prosp) Pension Schemes, 2015 c 8, s 44

s 25 am—Pensions, 2004 c 35, ss 36(1)(4), 319(1), sch 12 paras 34, 41(a)(b)(i)(c)(d)

rep in pt—Pensions, 2004 c 35, ss 319(1), 320, sch 12 paras 34, 41(b)(ii), sch 13 pt 1

s 26 am—Pensions, 2004 c 35, s 319(1), sch 12 paras 34, 42

ss 26A-26C rep—Pensions, 2004 c 35, ss 319(1), 320, sch 12 paras 34, 43, sch 13 pt 1

ss 27-36 appl (mods)—Welfare Reform and Pensions, 1999 c 30, s 6, sch 1 para 1(2)-(5)

s 28 rep in pt—Pensions, 2004 c 35, ss 319(1), 320, sch 12 paras 34, 44, sch 13 pt 1

s 29 am—Insolvency, 2000 c 39, s 8, sch 4 pt II para 19(3); Pensions, 2004 c 35, s 319(1),
        sch 12 paras 34, 45; SI 2004/1941, art 3, sch para 6; (S) SSI 2005/465, art 2, sch
        1 para 25; SI 2006/1722, art 2, sch 2; (prosp) Tribunals, Cts and Enforcement,
        2007 c 15, s 106, sch 16 para 8; SI 2009/1941, art 2, sch 1; 2012/2404, sch 2
        para 34(3)

rep in pt—Pensions, 2004 c 35, s 320, sch 13 pt 1

s 30 am—Child Support, Pensions and Social Security, 2000 c 19, s 56, sch 5 pt I
        para 10(1)(2); Pensions, 2004 c 35, ss 37, 319(1), sch 12 paras 34, 46(a)

rep in pt—Pensions, 2004 c 35, ss 319(1), 320, sch 12 paras 34, 46(b), sch 13 pt 1

s 30A rep—Pensions, 2004 c 35, ss 319(1), 320, sch 12 paras 34, 47, sch 13 pt 1

s 31 rep—Pensions, 2004 c 35, s 320, sch 13 pt 1

s 32 am—Pensions, 2004 c 35, s 319(1), sch 12 paras 34, 48

s 34 am—Trustee Delegation, 1999 c 15, s 5(3); SI 2001/3649, art 139; Pensions, 2004 c
        35, s 319(1), sch 12 paras 34, 49; (prosp) Pension Schemes, 2015 c 8, s 36(4)

1995
c 26 *continued*

s 35 subst—Pensions, 2004 c 35, s 244
    excl—SI 2005/3378, reg 6(1)
    appl—Constitutional Reform and Governance, 2010 c 25, s 40, sch 6 para 7(4)
s 36 am—SI 2001/3649, art 140; Pensions, 2004 c 35, s 245(1)(2)(4)-(6)
    rep in pt—Pensions, 2004 c 35, ss 245(1)(3), 320, sch 13 pt 1
s 36A added—Pensions, 2004 c 35, s 246
s 37 subst—Pensions, 2004 c 35, ss 250, 251
    excl—SIs 2006/802, reg 12; 2014/1711, reg 37(1)(a)
    mod—SI 2006/802, reg 14
    am—Pensions, 2008 c 30, s 130; (prosp) Pension Schemes, 2015 c 8, sch 2 para 7
s 38 am—Welfare Reform and Pensions, 1999 c 30, s 84, sch 12 pt I para 50(2)(4);
       Pensions, 2004 c 35, s 319(1), sch 12 paras 34, 50(1)(2)(a)(3); (prosp) Pension
       Schemes, 2015 c 8, sch 2 para 8
    power to mod—(prosp) Pension Schemes, 2015 c 8, s 26(3)(a)
    appl (mods)—SI 1996/3126, reg 12(3)
    excl—SI 1996/3126, reg 10
    rep in pt—Welfare Reform and Pensions, 1999 c 30, ss 84, 88, sch 12 pt I para 50(3),
         sch 13 pt III; Pensions, 2004 c 35, ss 319(1), 320, sch 12 paras 34, 50(1)(2)(b),
         sch 13 pt 1
s 39 appl (mods)—Welfare Reform and Pensions, 1999 c 30, s 6, sch 1 para 1(2)-(5)
s 40 rep in pt—SI 2001/3649, art 141(1)(2)
    am—SI 2001/3649, art 141(1)(3); Pensions, 2004 c 35, s 319(1), sch 12 paras 34, 51;
       SI 2004/355, art 5
s 41 am—Child Support, Pensions and Social Security, 2000 c 19, s 56, sch 5 pt I
       para 12(1); Pensions, 2004 c 35, s 319(1), sch 12 paras 34, 52; SI 2005/2053,
       art 2, sch pt 4 para 20
    appl (mods)—Welfare Reform and Pensions, 1999 c 30, s 6, sch 1 para 1(2)-(5)
    rep in pt—Pensions, 2004 c 35, s 320, sch 13 pt 1
ss 42-46 rep—Employment Rights, 1996 c 18, s 242, sch 3 pt I
s 47 appl (mods)—Welfare Reform and Pensions, 1999 c 30, s 6, sch 1 para 1(2)-(5)
    excl—SI 1996/1715, reg 3
    rep in pt—SI 2001/3649, art 142(1)(2)
    am—SI 2001/3649, art 142(1)(3); Pensions, 2004 c 35, s 319(1), sch 12 paras 34, 53
    appl—Pensions, 2004 c 35, s 182(10); ibid, s 151(8)
s 48 rep—Pensions, 2004 c 35, s 320, sch 13 pt 1
s 49 am—Welfare Reform and Pensions, 1999 c 30, ss 10(1),18, sch 2 para 12;
       SI 2001/3649, art 143(1)(2)(4)(5); Pensions, 2004 c 35, ss 269(1), s 319(1), sch
       12 paras 34, 54(a)(b)(ii); SI 2007/3014, reg 3; Financial Services, 2012 c 21, sch
       18 para 82(2)
    appl (mods)—Welfare Reform and Pensions, 1999 c 30, s 6, sch 1 para 1(2)-(5)
    rep in pt—SI 2001/3649, art 143(1)(3); Pensions, 2004 c 35, ss 319(1), 320, sch 12
         paras 34, 54(b)(i), sch 13 pt 1
s 49A added—Child Support, Pensions and Social Security, 2000 c 19, s 49(3)
    rep in pt—Pensions, 2004 c 35, ss 319(1), 320, sch 12 paras 34, 55, sch 13 pt 1
s 50 replaced (by ss 50, 50A, 50B)—Pensions, 2004 c 35, s 273
    appl (mods)—Welfare Reform and Pensions, 1999 c 30, s 6, sch 1 para 1(2)-(5); SI
       2005/3381, regs 14, 16, sch 2 paras 1, 2, 4
    transtl provns—SI 2008/649, reg 5
s 50A am—SI 2005/2053, art 2, sch pt 4 para 21
s 51 ext (mods)—SI 1997/784, regs 8,11(3)(e)(6)
    excl—SI 2014/1711, reg 26(1)
    am—Welfare Reform and Pensions, 1999 c 30, s 84, sch 12 pt I para 51; Child Support,
       Pensions and Social Security, 2000 c 19, s 51(1); Pensions, 2004 c 35,
       s 278(1)(2)(b)(c)(3)-(6); SI 2006/745, art 10; Pensions, 2011 c 19, ss 19(8),
       21(2)(3); Pensions, 2014 c 19, sch 13 para 59; Pension Schemes, 2015 c 8, s
       42(2); (prosp) ibid, s 41(1)(a)(b); (prosp) ibid, s 42(3); (prosp) ibid, s 43(1);
       (prosp) ibid, sch 2 para 9
    rep in pt—Pensions, 2004 c 35, ss 278(1)(2)(a), 320, sch 13 pt 1
    appl (mods)—SI 2005/3381, regs 14, 16, sch 2 paras 1, 3
s 51ZA added—Pensions, 2004 c 35, s 278(7)
    appl (mods)—SI 2005/3381, regs 14, 16, sch 2 paras 1, 3
    am—Pensions, 2008 c 30, s 101, sch 2 para 8
s 51ZB added—Pensions, 2011 c 19, s 21(4)

1995
c 26 *continued*

s 51A added—Child Support, Pensions and Social Security, 2000 c 19, s 51(2)
    appl (mods)—SI 2005/3381, regs 14, 16, sch 2 paras 1, 3
    am—SI 2011/1730, art 6(2); (prosp) Pension Schemes, 2015 c 8, sch 2 para 10
    rep in pt—SI 2011/1730, art 6(2)
s 52 ext (mods)—SI 1997/784, regs 8,11(3)(e)(6)
    appl (mods)—SI 2005/3381, regs 14, 16, sch 2 paras 1, 3
s 53 am—Welfare Reform and Pensions, 1999 c 30, s 84, sch 12 pt I para 52
    appl (mods)—SI 2005/3381, regs 14, 16, sch 2 paras 1, 3
s 54 am—Pensions, 2004 c 35, s 278(8)
    rep in pt—Pensions, 2004 c 35, s 320, sch 13 pt 1; Pensions, 2014 c 19, sch 13 para 60
    appl (mods)—SI 2005/3381, regs 14, 16, sch 2 paras 1, 3
ss 56-61 rep—Pensions, 2004 c 35, s 320, sch 13 pt 1
ss 62-65 rep—Equality, 2010 c 15, s 211, sch 27 pt 1 (as subst by SI 2010/2279, sch 2)
s 66A added—Child Support, Pensions and Social Security, 2000 c 19, s 55
    am—SI 2006/745, art 10
s 67 am—Welfare Reform and Pensions, 1999 c 30, s 84, sch 12 pt I para 53; (prosp)
    Pension Schemes, 2015 c 8, s 45(2)(b)
    appl—Railways and Transport Safety, 2003 c 20, s 18, sch 4 pt 3 para 24(5)
    replaced (by ss 67, 67A-67I)—Pensions, 2004 c 35, s 262
    rep in pt—(prosp) Pension Schemes, 2015 c 8, s 45(2)(a)
s 67A appl—Pensions, 2004 c 35, ss 229(3), 231(3); SI 2014/1711, reg 8(3)(b)
    appl (mods)—SI 2014/1711, reg 9(2)
    am—Pension Schemes, 2015 c 8, s 60(2); (prosp) ibid, s 45(3)-(6)
s 67D am—Pensions, 2007 c 22, s 17, sch 5 para 7
s 68 am—Pensions, 2004 c 35, s 319(1), sch 12 paras 34, 56
    appl (mods)—Welfare Reform and Pensions, 1999 c 30, s 6, sch 1 para 1(2)-(5)
s 69 subst —Pensions, 2014 c 19, sch 13 para 61
    rep in pt—Pensions, 2004 c 35, ss 319(1), 320, sch 12 paras 34, 57(b)-(d), sch 13 pt 1
    am—Pensions, 2004 c 35, s 319(1), sch 12 paras 34, 57(a); SI 2006/745, art 10
s 70 rep in pt—Pensions, 2014 c 19, sch 13 para 62
s 71 am—Pensions, 2004 c 35, s 263(1); Pensions, 2014 c 19, sch 13 para 63
s 71A added—Child Support, Pensions and Social Security, 2000 c 19, s 48
    appl—SI 2002/459, reg 8(2)(e)
    am—Pensions, 2004 c 35, s 319(1), sch 12 paras 34, 58
    rep in pt—Pensions, 2004 c 35, s 320, sch 13 pt 1
s 72 am—Pensions, 2004 c 35, s 263(2); Pensions, 2014 c 19, sch 13 para 64
s 72A added (pt prosp)—Child Support, Pensions and Social Security, 2000 c 19, s 49(1)
    appl—SI 2002/459, reg 9(1)
    rep in pt—Pensions, 2004 c 35, ss 319(1), 320, sch 12 paras 34, 59, sch 13 pt 1
s 72B added—Child Support, Pensions and Social Security, 2000 c 19, s 50
    rep in pt—(saving) Pensions, 2004 c 35, s 320, sch 13 pt 1, SI 2005/695, art 6, sch 3
s 72C added—Child Support, Pensions and Social Security, 2000 c 19, s 50
    rep in pt—Pensions, 2004 c 35, ss 319(1), 320, sch 12 paras 34, 60, sch 13 pt 1
s 73 appl (mods)—SIs 1996/3126, regs 3(1)(b)(c)(5)-(7)12(1); 2005/2159, reg 2
    appl—SI 2014/1711, regs 14(2), 15(5)(b), 16(4)
    am—SI 1996/3126, reg 3(1)(a)(4); Welfare Reform and Pensions, 1999 c 30, s 38(1);
    SI 2005/706, reg 4; Pension Schemes, 2015 c 8, sch 4 para 30; (prosp) ibid, sch 2
    para 11
    excl—(temp) SI 1997/664, art 11(1)
    replaced (by ss 73, 73A, 73B)—Pensions, 2004 c 35, s 270(1)
    rep in pt—Pensions, 2004 c 35, s 319(1), sch 12 para 34; (prosp) ibid, ss 319(1), 320,
    sch 12 para 61, sch 13 pt 1
    mod—SIs 1996/3126, reg 3; 2014/1711, regs 11(2), 13(2); (prosp) Pensions, 2014 c
    19, sch 20 para 15(2)
    power to mod—(prosp) Pension Schemes, 2015 c 8, s 26(3)(a)
s 73A saved—Pensions, 2004 c 35, s 150(4)
    mod—(prosp) Pensions, 2014 c 19, sch 20 para 15(2)(4)
    am—Pension Schemes, 2015 c 8, s 58(1)
s 73B power to mod—(prosp) Pension Schemes, 2015 c 8, s 26(3)(a)
    am—Pension Schemes, 2015 c 8, sch 4 para 31
s 74 am—Welfare Reform and Pensions, 1999 c 30, s 84, sch 12 pt I para 56; SI 2001/3649,
    art 144; Pensions, 2004 c 35, s 270(2)(a)(c)(d)(i)(f)
    power to mod—(prosp) Pension Schemes, 2015 c 8, s 26(3)(a)

1995
c 26 s 74　*continued*

　　　　　　appl (mods)—SIs 1996/3126, reg 12(2); 2005/2159, reg 2
　　　　　　excl—(temp) SI 1997/664, art 11(1)
　　　　　　rep in pt—Pensions, 2004 c 35, ss 270(2)(b)(d)(ii)(e), 320, sch 13 pt 1
　　　s 75 appl (mods)—SIs 1996/3128, regs 4(1)(2)-(5),5(1)(2),6(2)(3),7(1)-(9),8(1)(2),9;
　　　　　　　　1997/666, reg 11
　　　　　　appl—SI 2014/1711, regs 21(4), 22(3), 24(2)
　　　　　　excl—SIs 1996/3128, reg 10; 2008/2546, art 26, sch 3; 2014/1711, reg 20(1)
　　　　　　am—SI 1996/3128 reg 4(2); Pensions, 2004 c 35, s 271(1)-(5); (prosp) Pension
　　　　　　　　Schemes, 2015 c 8, sch 2 para 12
　　　　　　rep in pt—Pensions, 2004 c 35, ss 271(1)(6), 320, sch 13 pt 1
　　　s 75A added—Pensions, 2004 c 35, s 272
　　　s 76 excl—SIs 1996/2156, reg 14; 2006/802, reg 12; 2014/1711, reg 37(1)(b)
　　　　　　rep in pt—Pensions, 2004 c 35, ss 319(1), 320, sch 12 paras 34, 62(a)(b), sch 13 pt 1
　　　　　　power to mod—(prosp) Pension Schemes, 2015 c 8, s 26(3)(a)
　　　　　　am—Pensions, 2004 c 35, s 319(1), sch 12 paras 34, 62(c); SI 2006/745, art 10
　　　s 77 rep—SI 2006/745, art 10
　　　ss 78-82 rep—(saving) Pensions, 2004 c 35, s 320, sch 13 pt 1, SI 2005/1720, art 5
　　　s 83 rep—(saving) Pensions, 2004 c 35, s 320, sch 13 pt 1, SI 2005/1720, art 5
　　　　　　see—SI 2006/575, reg 44
　　　s 84 rep—(saving) Pensions, 2004 c 35, s 320, sch 13 pt 1, SI 2005/1720, art 5
　　　　　　see—SI 2006/575, reg 44
　　　　　　appl—SI 2014/1711, reg 25(4)
　　　ss 85, 86 rep—Pensions, 2004 c 35, s 320, sch 13 pt 1
　　　s 87 excl—(temp) SI 1997/664, art 12(1)
　　　　　　appl—Pensions, 2004 c 35, s 17(3)(b)
　　　　　　rep in pt—Pensions, 2004 c 35, ss 319(1), 320, sch 12 paras 34, 64, sch 13 pt 1
　　　　　　cont—(temp) SI 2014/1711, reg 68
　　　　　　am—(prosp) Pension Schemes, 2015 c 8, sch 2 paras 13, 14
　　　s 88 am—Child Support, Pensions and Social Security, 2000 c 19, s 56, sch 5 pt 1
　　　　　　　　para 12(4); Pensions, 2004 c 35, s 269(2); (prosp) Pension Schemes, 2015 c 8,
　　　　　　　　sch 2 para 15
　　　　　　rep in pt—Pensions, 2004 c 35, ss 319(1), 320, sch 12 paras 34, 65, sch 13 pt 1
　　　　　　cont—(temp) SI 2014/1711, reg 68
　　　s 89 am—Pensions, 2004 c 35, s 319(1), sch 12 paras 34, 66(a); (prosp) Pension Schemes,
　　　　　　　　2015 c 8, sch 2 para 16
　　　　　　rep in pt—Pensions, 2004 c 35, ss 319(1), 320, sch 12 paras 34, 66(b), sch 13 pt 1
　　　　　　cont—(temp) SI 2014/1711, reg 68
　　　s 91 saved—SIs 2000/1403, reg 13; 2010/990, reg 29
　　　　　　am—Welfare Reform and Pensions, 1999 c 30, s 84, sch 12 pt I para 57; Pensions,
　　　　　　　　2004 c 35, s 266; SI 2005/2053, art 2, sch pt 4 para 23
　　　　　　appl (mods)—Welfare Reform and Pensions, 1999 c 30, s 6, sch 1 para 1(2)-(5); SI
　　　　　　　　2005/3381, regs 14, 16, sch 2 paras 1, 3
　　　　　　appl—SI 2014/512, reg 180(2)
　　　　　　excl—Bankruptcy (S), 1985 c 66, ss 36C(1)(a), 36F(2)(a); (S) ibid, s 36C(2);
　　　　　　　　Insolvency, 1986 c 45, ss 342C(1)(a), 342F(5)(a); (EW) ibid, s 342C(2);
　　　　　　　　SI 1997/785, reg 8(1)-(4), (6); ibid, reg 8(7) (added by 2011/1801, reg 2);
　　　　　　　　Welfare Reform and Pensions, 1999 c 30, s 44(1); Proceeds of Crime, 2002 c 29,
　　　　　　　　s 273(5)(a); SI 2005/3181, art 184(5)(a); S Parliamentary Pensions, 2009 asp 1,
　　　　　　　　s 1(1), sch 1, rule 106
　　　　　　rep in pt—Welfare Reform and Pensions, 1999 c 30, s 88, sch 13 pt I; SI 2011/1730 art
　　　　　　　　6(2A) (added by 2012/709, art 2(8))
　　　s 92 am—Welfare Reform and Pensions, 1999 c 30, s 84, sch 12 pt I para 58; SI 2005/2053,
　　　　　　　　art 2, sch pt 4 para 24
　　　　　　appl (mods)—Welfare Reform and Pensions, 1999 c 30, s 6, sch 1 para 1(2)-(5); SI
　　　　　　　　2005/3381, regs 14, 16, sch 2 paras 1, 3
　　　　　　mod—SI 2015/1677, reg 19
　　　　　　excl—Bankruptcy (S), 1985 c 66, ss 36C(1)(a),36F(2)(a); (S) ibid, s 36C(2);
　　　　　　　　Insolvency, 1986 c 45, ss 342C(1)(a),342F(5)(a); (EW) ibid, s 342C(2);
　　　　　　　　SI 1997/785, reg 8(1)-(5); Welfare Reform and Pensions, 1999 c 30, s 44(1)
　　　　　　excl in pt—SI 2015/1452, reg 19
　　　　　　rep in pt—Welfare Reform and Pensions, 1999 c 30, ss 14(3), 88, sch 13 pt I
　　　　　　saved—SI 2000/1403, reg 13
　　　s 93 am—Welfare Reform and Pensions, 1999 c 30, s 84, sch 12 pt I paras 57,59

1995

c 26 s 93 *continued*

appl (mods)—Welfare Reform and Pensions, 1999 c 30, s 6, sch 1 para 1(2)-(5); SI 2005/3381, regs 14, 16, sch 2 paras 1, 3

excl—Bankruptcy (S), 1985 c 66, ss 36C(1)(a),36F(2)(a); (S) ibid, s 36C(2); Insolvency, 1986 c 45, ss 342C(1)(a),342F(5)(a); (EW) ibid, s 342C(2); SI 1997/785, reg 8(1)-(4); Welfare Reform and Pensions, 1999 c 30, s 44(1)

rep in pt—Welfare Reform and Pensions, 1999 c 30, s 88, sch 13 pt I

saved—SI 2000/1403, reg 13

s 94 am—Welfare Reform and Pensions, 1999 c 30, s 18, sch 2 para 17

appl (mods)—Welfare Reform and Pensions, 1999 c 30, s 6, sch 1 para 1(2)-(5); SI 2005/3381, regs 14, 16, sch 2 paras 1, 3

rep in pt—Welfare Reform and Pensions, 1999 c 30, s 88, sch 13 pt I

saved—SI 2000/1403, reg 13

excl—Bankruptcy (S), 1985 c 66, ss 36C(1)(a),36F(2)(a); (S) ibid, s 36C(2); Insolvency, 1986 c 45, ss 342C(1)(a),342F(5)(a); (EW) ibid, s 342C(2); SI 1997/785, reg 8(1)-(4); Welfare Reform and Pensions, 1999 c 30, s 44(1)

s 95 rep—Welfare Reform and Pensions, 1999 c 30, s 88, sch 13 pt I

ss 96-103 rep—(saving) Pensions, 2004 c 35, s 320, sch 13 pt 1, SI 2005/695, art 6, sch 3

ss 104-114 rep—Pensions, 2004 c 35, s 320, sch 13 pt 1

s 115 appl—Welfare Reform and Pensions, 1999 c 30, s 2(6)

s 116 appl (mods)—Pensions, 2004 c 35, s 314(b)

s 117 appl (mods)—Welfare Reform and Pensions, 1999 c 30, s 6, sch 1 para 1(2)-(5)

rep in pt—Pensions, 2004 c 35, s 320, sch 13 pt 1

s 118 am—Child Support, Pensions and Social Security, 2000 c 19, s 47(3)(4); Pensions, 2004 c 35, s 319(1), sch 12 paras 34, 67(a)

rep in pt—Pensions, 2004 c 35, ss 319(1), 320, sch 12 paras 34, 67(b), sch 13 pt 1

s 119 am—Pensions, 2004 c 35, s 319(1), sch 12 paras 34, 68; Pensions, 2007 c 22, s 17, sch 5 para 8

rep in pt—Pensions, 2004 c 35, s 320, sch 13 pt 1

s 123 appl—(S) SSI 2001/300, reg 14

s 124 am—Welfare Reform and Pensions, 1999 c 30, ss 18, 84, sch 2 para 18, sch 12 pt I para 61; Child Support, Pensions and Social Security, 2000 c 19, s 49(2); Pensions, 2004 c 35, ss 7(1)(b)(2)(b), 319(1), sch 12 paras 34, 69(1)-(4); SI 2005/2053, art 2, sch pt 4 para 25; Pension Schemes, 2015 c 8, sch 4 para 32; (prosp) ibid, s 45(7); (prosp) ibid, sch 2 paras 17, 18

appl—Disability Discrimination 1995 c 50, ss 4I, 4K; SI 2000/1403, regs 17, 23; Pensions, 2004 c 35, ss 151(8), 153(7), 170(4), 171(6)

appl (mods)—Welfare Reform and Pensions, 1999 c 30, s 6, sch 1 para 1(2)-(5)

restr—SI 2002/459, reg 12

rep in pt—(prosp) Pensions, 2004 c 35, s 320, sch 13 pt 1; SIs 2006/745, art 10; 2014/560, sch 1 para 27; 2014/3229, sch 5 para 13

s 125 appl (mods)—Welfare Reform and Pensions, 1999 c 30, s 6, sch 1 para 1(2)-(5)

am—(prosp) Pensions, 2004 c 35, s 240(1)

s 126 am—Pensions, 2007 c 22, s 13, sch 3 paras 1, 2; Pensions, 2011 c 19, sch 1 para 6

s 127 rep—Tax Credits, 2002 c 21, s 60, sch 6

s 128 am—Welfare Reform and Pensions, 1999 c 30, s 70, sch 8 pt I para 19; Child Support, Pensions and Social Security, 2000 c 19, s 33(4)

rep in pt—Pensions, 2014 c 19, sch 12 para 72

s 134 rep in pt—Pensions, 2004 c 35, s 320, sch 13 pt 1

s 136 rep in pt —Pensions, 2007 c 22, s 27, sch 7 pt 6; Pensions, 2014 c 19, sch 13 para 65

s 137 rep in pt—Social Security, 1998 c 14, s 86(2), sch 8; (pt prosp) Pensions, 2007 c 22, s 27, sch 7 pt 7; Pensions, 2014 c 19, sch 13 para 65

s 138 rep in pt—(pt prosp) Pensions, 2007 c 22, s 27, sch 7 pts 6, 7

s 139 rep —Pensions, 2007 c 22, s 27, sch 7 pt 7

s 142 rep—Pensions, 2007 c 22, s 27, sch 7 pt 6

ss 143-146 rep—Pensions, 2007 c 22, s 27, sch 7 pt 6

s 148 rep —Pensions, 2014 c 19, sch 13 para 65

s 149 rep—SI 2011/1730, art 6(3)

s 150 rep—SL(R), 2004 c 14, s 1(1), sch 1 pt 5/12

s 157 rep in pt—(prosp) Child Support, Pensions and Social Security, 2000 c 19, s 85, sch 9 pt III(3)

s 162 rep —SI 2011/1730, art 6(3)

s 163 rep—SI 2011/1730, art 6(3)

s 164 rep—Pensions, 2007 c 22, s 27, sch 7 pt 6

1995
c 26 *continued*

  s 166 am—Welfare Reform and Pensions, 1999 c 30, s 84, sch 12 pt I para 62; SI
    2005/3029, art 3, sch 1 para 4; Armed Forces, 2006 c 52, s 378, sch 16 para 132
  s 168 am—Pensions, 2008 c 30, s 138
  s 169 rep in pt—Child Support, Pensions and Social Security, 2000 c 19, s 85, sch 9 pt IV
  s 170 rep—Public Service Pensions, 2013 c 25, sch 11 para 7
  s 172 am—SI 2001/3649, art 148; Financial Services, 2012 c 21, sch 18 para 82(3)
  ss 174, 180 ext—Justices of the Peace, 1997 c 25, s 73(1), sch 4 pt II para 24(3)
  s 175 am—(prosp) Pensions, 2004 c 35, s 240(2); (prosp) Pension Schemes, 2015 c 8, s
    43(2)
    rep in pt—(prosp) Pensions, 2004 c 35, ss 240(2), 320, sch 13 pt 1; SI 2011/1730, art
      6(4)
  s 178 rep in pt—SL(R), 2004 c 14, s 1(1), sch 1 pt 5/12; Pensions, 2004 c 35, s 320, sch 13
    pt 1
  sch 1 rep—(saving) Pensions, 2004 c 35, s 320, sch 13 pt 1, SI 2005/695, art 6, sch 3
  sch 2 rep—(saving) Pensions, 2004 c 35, s 320, sch 13 pt 1, SI 2005/1720, art 5
  sch 3 rep in pt—Employment Rights, 1996 c 18, s 242, sch 3 pt I; Employment Tribunals,
    1996 c 17, s 45, sch 3 pt I; Child Support, Pensions and Social Security, 2000
    c 19, s 85, sch 9 pt III(2); SI 2001/3649, art 149(a); Companies (Audit,
    Investigations and Community Enterprise), 2004 c 27, s 64, sch 8; Pensions,
    2004 c 35, s 320, sch 13 pt 1
  sch 4 appl—(prosp) Transport (S), 2001 asp 2, s 68(7); Travel Concessions (Eligibility),
    2002 c 4, s 1(4); (S) Loc Govt in S, 2003 asp 1, s 44(3)
    am—State Pension Credit, 2002 c 16, s 14, sch 2 pt 3, para 39; Pensions, 2004 c 35,
      s 297(3); Welfare Reform, 2007 c 5, s 28, sch 3 para 13; Pensions, 2007 c 22, s
      13, sch 3 paras 3, 4; Pensions, 2011 c 19, s 1(2)(4)-(6); Pensions, 2014 c 19, s
      26, sch 12 para 30
    rep in pt—Pensions, 2004 c 35, s 320, sch 13 pt 1; (prosp) Welfare Reform, 2007 c 5,
      s 67, sch 8; Pensions, 2007 c 22, s 4(2), sch 7; Pensions, 2011 c 19, s 1(3);
      (prosp) ibid, sch 2 para 4(b); Pensions, 2014 c 19, sch 12 para 73
  sch 5 am—SI 1997/664, art 11(2)
    rep in pt—SI 1995/3213(NI 22), arts 147,168, sch 3 para 73, sch 5 pt III; Justices of
      the Peace, 1997 c 25, s 73(3), sch 6 pt I; (pt prosp) Social Security, 1998 c 14,
      s 86(2), sch 8; Social Security Contributions (Trans of Functions, etc), 1999 c 2,
      s 26(3), sch 10 pt I; Welfare Reform and Pensions, 1999 c 30, s 88, sch 13 pt I;
      Child Support, Pensions and Social Security, 2000 c 19, s 85, sch 9 pt VI; Child
      Support, Pensions and Social Security, 2000 c 19, s 85, sch 9 pt III(5)(6);
      SI 2001/3649, art 149(b); Finance, 2004 c 12, s 326, sch 42 pt 3, Note; (prosp)
      Pensions, 2004 c 35, s 320, sch 13 pt 1; (pt prosp) Pensions, 2007 c 22, s 27,
      sch 7
  sch 6 rep in pt—Pensions, 2004 c 35, s 320, sch 13 pt 1
  sch 7 rep in pt—SI 2001/3649, art 149(c)

c 27 **Geneva Conventions (Amendment)**
    ext (mods)—SIs 1999/1316, art 2; 2002/1076, art 2, schs 1, 2
    s 1 rep in pt—International Crim Court, 2001 c 17, s 83, sch 10
c 28 **Sale of Goods (Amendment)**
c 29 *Insurance Companies (Reserves)*—rep SI 2001/3649, art 3(1)(e)
c 30 **Landlord and Tenant (Covenants)**
    appl—Trustee, 1925 c, 19, s 26(1A)
    s 2 am—(EW) SI 1996/2325, art 5(1) sch 2 para 22
    s 3 am—Land Registration, 2002 c 9, s 133, sch 11, para 33(1)(2)
    s 15 am—Land Registration, 2002 c 9, s 133, sch 11, para 33(1)(2)
    s 20 am—Land Registration, 2002 c 9, s 133, sch 11, para 33(1)(3)(4)
c 31 **National Health Service (Amendment)**
    s 2 rep—Health and Social Care, 2001 c 15, s 67(2), sch 6 pt I, SI 2001/3738, art 2(5)(6)
    s 3 rep (prosp)—Health, 1999 c 8, s 65, sch 5
    ss 4-6 rep—Health and Social Care, 2001 c 15, s 67, sch 6 pt I, SI 2001/3738, art 2(5)(6)
    s 7 rep (prosp)—Health, 1999 c 8, s 65, sch 5
    s 8 am—Crime and Cts, 2013 c 22, sch 9 para 52
    s 9 rep (prosp)—Health, 1999 c 8, s 65, sch 5
    s 10 am—Crime and Cts, 2013 c 22, sch 9 para 52
    s 14 rep in pt —Health and Social Care, 2001 c 15, s 67(2), sch 6 pt I, SI 2001/3738,
      art 2(5)(6)

1995

c 32   **Olympic Symbol etc (Protection)**

        see—SIs 2003/2013; 2007/2129, art 3

        s 1 am—London Olympic Games and Paralympic Games, 2006 c 12, s 32, sch 3 para 2; SIs 2007/2129, art 5, sch; 2010/1551, art 11, sch

        s 3 am—London Olympic Games and Paralympic Games, 2006 c 12, s 32, sch 3 para 3(1)

        s 4 am—Northern Ireland, 1998 c 47, s 99, sch 13 para 15; SIs 1999/1042, art 3, sch 1 pt I para 12; 2003/2498, reg 2(1), sch 1 pt 2 para 20; London Olympic Games and Paralympic Games, 2006 c 12, s 32, sch 3 paras 3(2), 4; SIs 2007/1388, art 3, sch 1; 2007/2129, art 5, sch; 2010/1551, art 11, sch

        s 5 am—London Olympic Games and Paralympic Games, 2006 c 12, s 32, sch 3 para 5; SIs 2007/2129, art 5, sch; 2010/1551, art 11, sch

        s 5A added—London Olympic Games and Paralympic Games, 2006 c 12, s 32, sch 3 para 6

        s 7 am—London Olympic Games and Paralympic Games, 2006 c 12, s 32, sch 3 para 10; SIs 2007/2129, art 5, sch; 2010/1551, art 11, sch

        s 8 am—London Olympic Games and Paralympic Games, 2006 c 12, s 32, sch 3 para 11

        s 8A added —London Olympic Games and Paralympic Games, 2006 c 12, s 32, sch 3 para 12(1)

            rep in pt—Consumer Rights, 2015 c 15, sch 6 para 60(2)(3)

            am—Consumer Rights, 2015 c 15, sch 6 para 60(4)

        s 8B added —London Olympic Games and Paralympic Games, 2006 c 12, s 32, sch 3 para 13

        ss 12A, 12B added —London Olympic Games and Paralympic Games, 2006 c 12, s 32, sch 3 para 14

        s 13 rep in pt—(transtl provns) SI 2001/3949, regs 9(2), 10-14, sch 2

        s 15 am—SIs 2007/2129, art 5, sch; 2010/1551, art 11, sch

        s 18 am—London Olympic Games and Paralympic Games, 2006 c 12, s 32, sch 3 para 7; SIs 2007/2129, art 5, sch; 2010/1551, art 11, sch

c 33   *Licensing (Sunday Hours)*—rep Licensing, 2003 c 17, s 199, sch 7

c 34   **Child Support**

        mod—Social Security, 1998 c 14, s 2(1)(2)(g)

        saved—Scotland, 1998 c 46, s 30, sch 5 pt II, s F1, F2

        power to am—Northern Ireland, 1998 c 47, s 87

        ss 1-3, 6-9 rep (pt prosp)—Child Support, Pensions and Social Security, 2000 c 19, s 85, sch 9 pt I

        s 10 am—(GB) SI 1997/645, reg 2(1)-(3), sch paras 2,4 of memorandum; Income Tax (Earnings and Pensions), 2003 c 1, s 722, sch 6 pt 2 para 231; Civil Partnership, 2004 c 33, s 254(1), sch 24 pt 8 paras 126(1)-(3), 127

            ext—SI 1997/645, reg 2(2)(3)

            rep—Child Support, Pensions and Social Security, 2000 c 19, ss 23, 85, sch 9 pt I; Civil Partnership, 2004 c 33, ss 254(1), 261(4), sch 24 pt 8 para 126(1)(4), sch 30

            appl—Income Tax (Earnings and Pensions), 2003 c 1, ss 666, 670

        s 11 rep (pt prosp)—Child Support, Pensions and Social Security, 2000 c 19, s 85, sch 9 pt I

        ss 12, 13 rep—Social Security, 1998 c 14, s 86(2), sch 8

        s 14 rep in pt—Social Security, 1998 c 14, s 86(2), sch 8; (pt prosp) Child Support, Pensions and Social Security, 2000 c 19, s 85, sch 9 pt I

        ss 15, 16 rep—Social Security, 1998 c 14, s 86(2), sch 8

        s 17 rep—SI 2008/2833, art 6, sch 3

        s 18 rep in pt—(pt prosp) Child Support, Pensions and Social Security, 2000 c 19, ss 26, 85, sch 3 para 13(1)(2), sch 9 pt I

        s 19 rep (pt prosp)—Child Support, Pensions and Social Security, 2000 c 19, s 85, sch 9 pt I

        s 20 rep in pt—Child Support, Pensions and Social Security, 2000 c 19, s 85, sch 9 pt IX

        s 22 rep (pt prosp)—Child Support, Pensions and Social Security, 2000 c 19, s 85, sch 9 pt I

        s 24 rep—Child Support, Pensions and Social Security, 2000 c 19, ss 26,85, sch 3 para 13(1)(3), sch 9 pt I

        s 26 rep in pt—(pt prosp) Child Support, Pensions and Social Security, 2000 c 19, s 85, sch 9 pt I

        s 29 rep in pt and superseded—Northern Ireland, 1998 c 47, ss 87(8)(e),100(2), sch 15

        s 46 appl—SI 1999/991, reg 44(2)

        schs 1, 2 rep (pt prosp)—Child Support, Pensions and Social Security, 2000 c 19, s 85, sch 9 pt I

        sch 3 rep in pt—Social Security, 1998 c 14, s 86(2), sch 8; (pt prosp) Child Support, Pensions and Social Security, 2000 c 19, s 85, sch 9 pt I; Income Tax (Earnings and Pensions), 2003 c 1, s 724(1), sch 8 pt 1; (pt prosp) Child Maintenance and Other Payments, 2008 c 6, s 58, sch 8; SI 2008/2833, art 6, sch 3

1995

c 35 **Criminal Appeal**

ss 1, 2 am—Social Work (S), 1968 c 49, s 5B(4)(b)

ss 9, 10 am—Domestic Violence, Crime and Victims, 2004 c 28, s 58(1), sch 10 paras 31, 32

ss 12A, 12B added —Armed Forces, 2006 c 52, s 321, sch 11 para 2

    mod—SI 2009/1059, art 184

s 13 am—Armed Forces, 2006 c 52, s 321, sch 11 para 3

s 14 ext—(EW) Crim Appeal 1968 c 19, s 31(1)(aa); Crim Cases Review (Insanity), 1999 c 25, s 1(3); (NI) Crim Appeal (NI) 1980 c 47, s 45(3C)

    am—Crim Justice, 2003 c 44, s 315; Armed Forces, 2006 c 52, s 321, sch 11 para 4

s 15 am—Crim Justice, 2003 c 44, s 331, sch 36 pt 6 para 97; Armed Forces, 2006 c 52, s 321, sch 11 para 5

s 16 am—Armed Forces, 2006 c 52, s 321, sch 11 para 6; SI 2010/976, art 6, sch 6

s 17 appl—Disabled Persons (Services, Consultation and Representation, 1986 c 33, s 16(2A); Agric, 1986 c 49, s 28(3)

s 18 am—Armed Forces, 2006 c 52, s 321, sch 11 para 7

s 19 am—Armed Forces, 2006 c 52, s 321, sch 11 para 8

s 22 am—Police, 1996 c 16, s 103, sch 7 pt II para 47; SI 1996/1299, art 57(1) sch 3 para 19; Police, 1997 c 50, s 134(1), sch 9 para 71; Justice (NI), 2002 c 26, s 85(1), sch 12, para 49; Serious Organised Crime and Police, 2005 c 15, ss 59, 174(2), sch 4 para 63(1)(2)(b)(i)(iii)(c)(3); Commrs for Revenue and Customs, 2005 c 11, s 50(6), sch 4 para 62; Armed Forces, 2006 c 52, s 321, sch 11 para 9; Police Reform and Social Responsibility, 2011 c 13, sch 16 para 218; Crime and Cts, 2013 c 22, sch 8 para 186; Defence Reform, 2014 c 20, s 44(3)(4)

    rep in pt—NI (Emergency Provns), 1996 c 22, s 63(7) sch 7 pt I; Courts, 2003 c 39, s 109(1)(3), sch 8 para 367, sch 10; Serious Organised Crime and Police, 2005 c 15, ss 59, 174(2), sch 4 para 63(1)(2)(a)(b)(ii)(d), sch 17 pt 2; SI 014/834, sch 2 para 10

s 24 am—SI 2010/976, art 6, sch 6

s 30 am—Armed Forces, 2006 c 52, s 321, sch 11 para 10

    rep in pt—Armed Forces, 2006 c 52, s 378, sch 17

s 33 am—Armed Forces, 2006 c 52, s 321, sch 11 para 11

sch 1 am—SI 2010/976, art 6, sch 6

sch 2 rep in pt—Armed Forces, 1996 c 46, s 35(2) sch 7 pt III; Access to Justice, 1999 c 22, s 106, sch 15 pt I; Youth Justice and Crim Evidence, 1999 c 23, s 67, sch 6; (NI) SI 1999/2789, art 40(3), sch 3; Crim Justice, 2003 c 44, s 332, sch 37 pt 10

c 36 **Children (Scotland)**

appl—Factories, 1981 c 34, s 176(1); Foster Children (S), 1984 c 56, s 7(1)(dd); Child Trust Funds, 2004 c 6, s 3(9)(b); SI 2004/1031, reg 2(1), sch 1 pt 1 para 2

mod—SIs 1996/3255, reg 5; 2010/1907, reg 16

see—SIs 1997/291, rules 2.1-2.59, 3.1-3.64; 744, art 3

restr—Adoption and Children, 2002 c 38, s 46(2)(c)

ss 1-17 appl—SI 2004/1611, reg 25(5)

Pt 1 (ss 1-15) appl—Lands Clauses Consolidation (S) 1845 c, 19, ss 7,67,69,70; Age of Legal Capacity (S), 1991 c 50, ss 1(3)(f)(i5(1); Mental Health (Care and Treatment) (S), 2003 asp 13, ss 256(3) 278(3), 291(6)

    excl—Human Fertilisation and Embryology, 2008 c 22, s 53(4)(5)(l)

s 1 appl —Children and Young Persons (S), 1937 c 37, s 110(1); Mines and Quarries 1954 c 70 s 182(1); Education (S), 1962 c 47, s 145(33); Registration of Births, Deaths and Marriages (S), 1965 c 49, s 56(1); Social Work (S), 1968 c 59, ss 78(1)(a), 80(5); Sheriff Cts (S), 1971 c 58, s 37(2A);Employment of Children, 1973 c 24, s 2(2A); Domicile and Matrimonial Proceedings, 1973 c 45 sch 3 para 11(1); Sexual Offences (S), 1976 c 67, ss 11(1)14(1); Education (S), 1980 c 44, s 135(1); Family Law (S), 1985 c 37 s 2(2)(c); Law Reform (Parent and Child)(S) 1986 c 9, s 6(2); Disabled Persons (Services, Consultation and Representation), 1986 c 33, ss 1(3)(a)13(8)(b); Family Law, 1986 c 55, s 42(1); School Bds (S), 1988 c 47, s 22(2); Self-Governing Schools etc (S), 1989 c 39, s 80(1); Children, 1989 c 41, s 79(e); Access to Health Records, 1990 c 23, s 11; Horses (Protective Headgear for Young Riders) 1990 c 25 s 1(2)(a)(ii); Age of Legal Capacity (S), 1991 c 50, s 1(3)(g)(i)(ii); Crim Law (Consolidation) (S), 1995 c 39, s 12; Crim Procedure (S), 1995 c 46, ss 42(5)(a)45(5); Reserve Forces, 1996 c 14, s 9, sch 1 para 2(1)(b); SIs 1996/2447, reg 6(2); 1996/3256, reg 2(1); (pt prosp) Youth Justice and Crim Evidence, 1999 c 23, s 50(12);

1995
c 36 *continued*

SI 1999/3312, reg 2(1); Regulation of Care (S), 2001 asp 8, s 2(18)(b); Mental
Health (Care and Treatment) (S), 2003 asp 13, s 252(4); Vulnerable Witnesses
(S), 2004 asp 3, s 15(4)
   am—(S) Human Fertilisation and Embryology, 2008 c 22, s 56, sch 6 para 48
s 2 appl—Sheriff Cts (S), 1971 c 58, s 37(2A); Domicile and Matrimonial Proceedings,
1973 c 45 sch 3 para 11(1); Rehabilitation of Offenders, 1974 c 53 s 7(2)(c);
Civil Jurisdiction and Judgments, 1982 c 27 sch 9 para 2A; Family Law (S), 1985
c 37, s 2(2)(c); Family Law, 1986 c 55, s 42(1); Age of Legal Capacity (S), 1991
c 50 s 1(3)(g)(i)(ii); Crim Procedure (S) 1995 c 46 ss 42(5)(a), 45(5)
   am—Mental Health (Care and Treatment) (S), 2003 asp 13, s 252(4); (S) Human
Fertilisation and Embryology, 2008 c 22, s 56, sch 6 para 49
s 3 am—(temp) SI 1996/2203, art 4; (transtl provns) Family Law (S), 2006 asp 2, s 23; (S)
Human Fertilisation and Embryology, 2008 c 22, s 56, sch 6 para 50; (prosp)
Welfare Reform, 2009 c 24, s 56, sch 6 para 25; SSI 2013/211, sch 1 para 9(2)
s 4A added —(S) Human Fertilisation and Embryology, 2008 c 22, s 56, sch 6 para 51
s 7 am—(temp) SI 1996/2203, art 5
s 11 appl—Children 1975 c 72 s 51(5); Family Law (S) 1985 c 37, s 2(4)(c); SSI 2002/494,
reg 18(2)(p)
   am—(temp) SI 1996/2203, art 5; SSI 2001/36, reg 5; Family Law (S), 2006 asp 2, s 24;
Adoption and Children (S), 2007 asp 4, s 120, sch 2 para 9(1)(2); (S) Human
Fertilisation and Embryology, 2008 c 22, s 56, sch 6 para 52
   restr—Adoption (S), 1978 c 28, s 53C
   rep in pt—(S) SSI 2005/42, reg 9; Adoption and Children (S), 2007 asp 4, s 120, sch 3
s 11A added—Adoption and Children (S), 2007 asp 4, s 103
s 12 am—Civil Partnership, 2004 c 33, s 261(2), sch 28 pt 4 para 60; Family Law (S), 2006
asp 2, s 45, sch 2 para 8; Human Fertilisation and Embryology, 2008 c 22, s 56,
sch 6 para 53; Children's Hearings (S), 2011 asp 1, sch 5 para 2(2)
s 14 am—(S) SSI 2005/42, reg 5(1)(2)
s 15 appl—Disabled Persons (Services, Consultation and Representation, 1986 c 33,
s 1(3)(a); SIs 1996/3255, reg 2(1); 1996/3256, reg 2(1); 1996/3261,
rule 5(3)(b); 1996/3266, reg 19(2)(e)
   am—Adoption and Children (S), 2007 asp 4, s 120, sch 2 para 9(1)(3); (S) Human
Fertilisation and Embryology, 2008 c 22, s 56, sch 6 para 53; ibid, s 65, sch 7
para 17
Pt 2 (ss 16-93) appl—Adoption (S), 1978 c 28, ss 22A,65(1); Crim Procedure (S), 1995
c 46, ss 44(1), 51(1)(a)(i)(4)(a), 307(1); Crim Justice (S), 2003 asp 7, s 53(4);
SI 2004/1450, reg 33(1)
Pt 2, Ch 1 (ss 16-38) appl—Chronically Sick and Disabled Persons, 1970 c 4, s 29(2)(a);
Disabled Persons (Services, Consultation and Representation 1986 c 33, s 16
   mod—SI 1996/3255, reg 7(1)
s 16 rep in pt—Adoption and Children (S), 2007 asp 4, s 120, sch 3; Children's Hearings (S),
2011 asp 1, sch 5 para 2(3)
   am—Children's Hearings (S), 2011 asp 1, sch 5 para 2(3)
s 17 appl—Social Work (S), 1968 c 49, s 68(4); Childen, 1975 c 72, s 51(5); Foster
Children (S), 1984 c 56, s 2(6); Housing (S), 1987 c 26 ss 25(1A),61(4A);
SIs 1996/3262, reg 3(2)(b); 1996/3263, s 6(2); 1996/3256, reg 2(1); (pt prosp)
Youth Justice and Crim Evidence, 1999 c 23, s 50(12); SI 2001/155, reg 9(11);
(pt prosp) SI 2001/157, reg 21(2); Finance, 2003 c 14, s 176, sch 36 pt 1
para 4(3); SI 2004/747, reg 2(4)(e); Income Tax (Trading and Other Income),
2005 c 5, s 806(4)(b)
   am—Adoption and Children (S), 2007 asp 4, s 120, sch 2 para 9(1)(4); Children's
Hearings (S), 2011 asp 1, sch 5 para 2(4); SSI 2013/211, sch 1 para 9(3)
   rep in pt—Children's Hearings (S), 2011 asp 1, sch 5 para 2(4)
s 19 rep (prosp)—Children and Young People (S), 2014 asp 8, sch 5 para 4(2)
   appl—Crim Procedure (S), 1995 c 46, s 57A(16)
   am—Children's Hearings (S), 2011 asp 1, sch 5 para 2(5)
s 20 am—(prosp) Children and Young People (S), 2014 asp 8, sch 5 para 4(3)
s 21 saved—Mental Health (Care and Treatment) (S), 2003 asp 13, s 31(3)
s 22 am—Tax Credits, 1999 c 10, s 1(2), sch 1 paras 1, 6(j); Tax Credits, 2002 c 21, s 47,
sch 3, para 50; (S) Welfare Reform, 2007 c 5, s 28, sch 3 para 14; SSI 2013/137,
reg 5
   rep in pt—(prosp) Tax Credits, 2002 c 21, s 60, sch 6; (prosp) Welfare Reform, 2012 c
5, sch 14 pt 1

1995

c 36 s 22 *continued*

restr—Nationality, Immigration and Asylum, 2002 c 41, s 54, sch 3, paras 1(1)(i)(2)(3), 2-7

saved—Mental Health (Care and Treatment) (S), 2003 asp 13, s 29(1)(2)(b)

s 23 am—Community Care and Health (S), 2002 asp 5, s 10; Mental Health (Care and Treatment) (S), 2003 asp 13, ss 227(2), 331(1), sch 4 para 7

appl—Mental Health (Care and Treatment) (S), 2003 asp 13, s 62(8)

s 23A added (31.8.2016)—Children and Young People (S), 2014 asp 8, s 95

s 24 am—Community Care and Health (S), 2002 asp 5, s 11(1)

s 24A added—Community Care and Health (S), 2002 asp 5, s 11(2)

s 25 mod—Foster Children (S), 1984 c 56, s 12(5)

s 26 rep in pt—Adoption and Children (S), 2007 asp 4, s 120, sch 3

am—(E) (W prosp) Children and Young Persons, 2008 c 23, s 8, sch 1 para 9

s 26A added —Children and Young People (S), 2014 asp 8, s 67(1)

s 27 am—Children and Young People (S), 2014 asp 8, s 55(2)(3)

s 29 am—Regulation of Care (S), 2001 asp 8, s 73(1); Children and Young People (S), 2014 asp 8, ss 66(2)(a)(b)(c)(i)(d)-(h), 67(2)

restr—Nationality, Immigration and Asylum, 2002 c 41, s 54, sch 3, paras 1(1)(i)(2)(3), 2-7

rep in pt—Children and Young People (S), 2014 asp 8, s 66(2)(c)(ii)

s 30 restr—Nationality, Immigration and Asylum, 2002 c 41, s 54, sch 3, paras 1(1)(i)(2)(3), 2-7

am—Children and Young People (S), 2014 asp 8, s 66(3)(a)

rep in pt—Children and Young People (S), 2014 asp 8, s 66(3)(b)

s 33 am—Powers of Crim Cts (Sentencing), 2000 c 6, s 165(1), sch 9 para 175; Children's Hearings (S), 2011 asp 1, sch 5 para 2(6)

rep in pt—Children's Hearings (S), 2011 asp 1, sch 5 para 2(6); SI 2013/1465, sch 2 pt 2

ss 34, 37 rep—Regulation of Care (S), 2001 asp 8, s 80(1), sch 4

s 36 am—Regulation of Care (S), 2001 asp 8, s 79, sch 3 para 19(1)(2)(b); SSI 2005/465, art 2, sch 1 para 26; Joint Inspection of Children's Services and Inspection of Social Work Services (S), 2006 asp 3, s 8(1); SSI 2011/211, sch 1 para 6(a), sch 2 para 4

rep in pt—Regulation of Care (S), 2001 asp 8, s 79, sch 3 para 19(1)(2)(a)

s 38 expld—SI 1996/3259, reg 11

am—Regulation of Care (S), 2001 asp 8, s 79, sch 3 para 19(1)(3); Children's Hearings (S), 2011 asp 1, sch 5 para 2(7); SSI 2011/211, sch 1 para 6(b)

Pt 2, Chs 2,3 (ss 39-85) appl—Social Work (S), 1968 c 49, s 5(3); Crim Procedure (S), 1995 c 46, s 307(1)

s 39 appl—SIs 1996/3260, reg 2; 1996/3261, rule 2(1)

ext—SI 1996/3261, rule 4(1)

s 40 am—SI 1999/1042, art 4, sch 2 pt I para 10

rep in pt—SI 1999/1042, art 4, sch 2 pt III

s 44 am—Crim Justice (S), 2003 asp 7, s 52(a); Adoption and Children (S), 2007 asp 4, s 120, sch 2 para 9(1)(5); SI 2011/1740, sch 2 para 3(2); Children and Young People (S), 2014 asp 8, sch 5 para 4(4)(a); SI 2015/907, art 2(2)(a)

rep in pt—Children and Young People (S), 2014 asp 8, sch 5 para 4(4)(b); SI 2015/907, art 2(2)(b)

s 45 am—Crim Procedure (Conseq Provns) (S), 1995 c 40, s 5, sch 4 para 97(2); SI 1996/3261, rule 27, sch

s 48 excl—SSI 2013/150, art 2(3)

s 49 rep—Crim Procedure (Conseq Provns) (S), 1995 c 40, ss 4, 6, sch 3 pt II para 17, sch 5

s 50 am—Crim Procedure (Conseq Provns) (S), 1995 c 40, s 5, sch 4 para 97(3)

s 51 am—Antisocial Behaviour etc (S), 2004 asp 8, s 144(1), sch 4 para 4(1)(2)

s 52 am—Crim Procedure (Conseq Provns) (S), 1995 c 40, s 5, sch 4 para 97(4); Antisocial Behaviour etc (S), 2004 asp 8, s 12(2)(3); SSI 2010/21, art 2, sch

s 53 am—Crim Procedure (Conseq Provns) (S), 1995 c 40, s 5, sch 4 para 97(5); SSI 2013/119, sch 1 para 15

s 54 am—(temp) SI 1996/2203, art 6; Civil Partnership, 2004 c 33, s 261(2), sch 28 pt 4 para 61; Adoption and Children (S), 2007 asp 4, s 120, sch 2 para 9(1)(6)

s 55 restr—Adoption (S), 1978 c 28, s 53C

s 56 mod—SI 1996/3255, reg 8(3)

rep in pt—Antisocial Behaviour etc (S), 2004 asp 8, s 137(1)(2)(a)

am—Antisocial Behaviour etc (S), 2004 asp 8, s 137(1)(2)(b)

1995

c 36 *continued*

s 57 appl—SI 1996/3261, rule 2(1)

s 59 am—SI 1996/3261, rule 27, sch

s 60 am—SI 1996/3261, rule 28(1)-(5 sch

s 61 appl—SI 1996/3258, regs 12-16

s 63 am—Crim Procedure (Conseq Provns) (S), 1995 c 40, s 5, sch 4 para 97(6);
    SI 1996/3261, rule 27, sch

s 65 am—Antisocial Behaviour etc (S), 2004 asp 8, s 12(2)(4)

s 66 am—SI 1996/3261, rule 27, sch; Antisocial Behaviour etc (S), 2004 asp 8, s 144(1),
    sch 4 para 4(1)(3)

s 68 am—Antisocial Behaviour etc (S), 2004 asp 8, s 144(1), sch 4 para 4(1)(4)

ss 68A, 68B added—Vulnerable Witnesses (S), 2004 asp 3, s 23

s 69 am—SI 1996/3261, rules 27,28(1)-(5 sch; Antisocial Behaviour etc (S), 2004 asp 8,
    s 144(1), sch 4 para 4(1)(5)

s 70 appl—Social Work (S), s 94(1); Education (S), 1980 c 44, s 135(1); Foster Children
    (S), 1984 c 56, s 21(1); SI 1996/3260, reg 2; SSI 2006/15, regs 3, 6-8
    mod—SI 1996/3255, regs 6(111(112(1)
    saved—SI 1996/3261, rule 21(1)
    am—Antisocial Behaviour etc (S), 2004 asp 8, ss 135, 136(1)
    rep in pt—(EW) SI 2013/1465, art 20

s 71 am—Antisocial Behaviour etc (S), 2004 asp 8, s 136(2)

s 71A added—Antisocial Behaviour etc (S), 2004 asp 8, s 136(3)

s 73 am—SI 1996/3261, rule 28(1)-(5) sch; Antisocial Behaviour etc (S), 2004 asp 8,
    s 12(2)(5); Adoption and Children (S), 2007 asp 4, s 120, sch 2 para 9(1)(7)
    appl—Adoption (S), 1978 c 28, s 22A; (EW) SI 1996/3267, reg 4(2)(a); (NI) ibid,
    reg 5(2)(a)
    appl (mods)—SI 1996/3255, reg 6(3)
    saved—SI 1996/3261, rule 21(1)

s 74 rep—SI 2013/1465, sch 2 pt 2

s 75 am—Children's Hearings (S), 2011 asp 1, sch 5 para 2(8)

s 75A added—Antisocial Behaviour etc (S), 2004 asp 8, s 116

s 75B added—Antisocial Behaviour etc (S), 2004 asp 8, s 137(1)(3)

s 76 appl—Legal Aid (S), 1986 c 47, s 29
    am—SSI 2003/583, art 2, sch paras 1, 12; Children's Hearings (S), 2011 asp 1, sch 5
    para 2(9)(a)(b)

s 78 am—Crim Procedure (Conseq Provns) (S), 1995 c 40, s 5, sch 4 para 97(7); Police and
    Fire Reform (S), 2012 asp 8, sch 7 para 11(2)(a)(ii)(b)
    rep in pt—Police and Fire Reform (S), 2012 asp 8, sch 7 para 11(2)(a)(i)

s 79 appl—Legal Aid (S), 1986 c 47, s 29

s 82 rep—SI 2013/1465, sch 2 pt 2

s 83 rep—SI 2013/1465, sch 2 pt 2

Pt 2, Ch 4 (ss 86-92) mod—SI 1996/3255, reg 7(1)

s 86 rep —Adoption and Children (S), 2007 asp 4, s 120, sch 3

s 86A added —(S) SSI 2005/42, reg 5(1)(3)
    rep —Adoption and Children (S), 2007 asp 4, s 120, sch 3

ss 87-89 rep—Children and Children (S), 2007 asp 4, s 120, sch 3

s 93 appl—Children and Young Persons (S), 1937 c 37, s 110(1); Land Compensation (S),
    1973 c 56, s 80(1)(b); Education (S), 1980 c 44, s 135(1); Child Abduction and
    Custody, 1985 c 60, s 20(5); Legal Aid (S), 1986 c 47, s 29; SIs 1996/3255,
    3256, 3258, 3260, 3261, reg 2; 1997/291, rule 1.2
    am—(S prosp) Care Standards, 2000 c 14, s 116, sch 4 para 23; Regulation of Care (S),
    2001 asp 8, s 74; ibid, s 79, sch 3 para 19(1)(4)(a); Crim Justice (S), 2003 asp 7,
    s 52(b); Antisocial Behaviour etc (S), 2004 asp 8, s 137(1)(4); ibid, s 144(1), sch
    4 para 4(1)(6)(a)(b); Adoption and Children (S), 2007 asp 4, s 120, sch 2 para
    9(1)(8); Children's Hearings (S), 2011 asp 1, sch 5 para 2(10)(11); SI 2011/1740,
    sch 2 para 3(3); Police and Fire Reform (S), 2012 asp 8, sch 7 para 11(3); SSI
    2013/211, sch 1 para 9(4)(a)(b); SI 2013/1465, sch 1 para 5, sch 2 pt 1;
    2015/907, art 2(3)
    rep in pt—Regulation of Care (S), 2001 asp 8, s 79, sch 3 para 19(1)(4)(b); Adoption
    and Children (S), 2007 asp 4, s 120, sch 3; SI 2013/1465, sch 2 pt 2; SSI
    2013/211, sch 2

ss 94-98 rep—Adoption and Children (S), 2007 asp 4, s 120, sch 3

s 101 am—Adoption and Children (S), 2007 asp 4, s 120, sch 2 para 9(1)(9)

s 105 rep in pt—SI 2013/1465, sch 2 pt 2

1995

c 36 *continued*

> sch 1 am—Regulation of Care (S), 2001 asp 8, s 76
> sch 2 rep—Adoption and Children (S), 2007 asp 4, s 120, sch 3
> sch 3 am—Adoption and Children (S), 2007 asp 4, s 120, sch 2 para 9(1)(10)
> sch 4 rep in pt—Crim Procedure (Conseq Provns) (S), 1995 c 40, ss 4,6, sch 3 pt II para 17,
> > sch 5; Education, 1996 c 56, s 582(2)(3) sch 38 pt II, sch 39; Crime and
> > Punishment (S), 1997 c 48, s 62(1)(2), sch 1 para 17, sch 3; Regulation of Care
> > (S), 2001 asp 8, s 80(1), sch 4; Housing (S), 2001 asp 10, s 112, sch 10 para 23;
> > S Public Services Ombudsman, 2002 asp 11, s 25(1), sch 6, para 16; Mental
> > Health (Care and Treatment) (S), 2003 asp 13, s 331(2), sch 5 pt 1; Educ
> > (Additional Support for Learning) (S), 2004 asp 4, s 33, sch 3 para 9; Scottish
> > Schools (Parental Involvement), 2006 asp 8, s 23, sch; Joint Inspection of
> > Children's Services and Inspection of Social Work Services (S), 2006 asp 3, s
> > 8(4)(f); SL(R), 2008 c 12, s 1(1), sch 1 pt 11; SL(R), 2008 c 12, s 1, sch 1 pt
> > 11

c 37 **Atomic Energy Authority**

> ss 1-10 rep—Energy, 2004 c 20, s 197(9)(10), sch 23
> ss 12, 13 rep—Energy, 2004 c 20, s 197(9)(10), sch 23
> schs 1-4 rep—Energy, 2004 c 20, s 197(9)(10), sch 23

c 38 **Civil Evidence**

> appl—SI 2007/3588, rule 13
> s 2 ext—Proceeds of Crime, 2002 c 29, s 46(2); Civil Partnership, 2004 c 33, ss 246, 247,
> > sch 21 para 41
> > restr—SI 2003/421, rule 39
> > excl—SIs 2005/384, rule 61.8; 2010/60, rule 61.8; 2010/2955, rule 23.3; 2011/1434,
> > > rule 4; 2011/1709, rules 8, 61; 2012/1726, rule 61.8; 2013/1554, rule 61.8;
> > > 2014/1610, rule 61.8
> > excl in pt—SI 2015/1490, rule 33.39
> > appl—Proceeds of Crime, 2002 c 29, s 47Q (amended by 2009 c 26, s 55(1)(2)); SIs
> > > 2005/3180, art 10(2); 2005/3181, art 13(2)
> s 3 ext—Proceeds of Crime, 2002 c 29, s 46(2)
> > appl—Proceeds of Crime, 2002 c 29, s 47Q (amended by 2009 c 26, s 55(1)(2)); SIs
> > > 2005/3180, art 10(2); 2005/3181, art 13(2)
> s 4 ext—Proceeds of Crime, 2002 c 29, s 46(2)
> > appl—Proceeds of Crime, 2002 c 29, s 47Q (amended by 2009 c 26, s 55(1)(2)); SIs
> > > 2005/3180, art 10(2); 2005/3181, art 13(2)
> s 9 see—SI 1998/3132, rule 33.6(2)
> s 10 rep (prosp)—(NI) SI 1997/2983, art 13(2), sch 2
> s 16 am—SI 1999/1217, art 4(a)(b)
> > rep in pt—(NI) (prosp) SI 1997/2983, art 13(2), sch 2
> sch 1 rep in pt—Housing, 1996 c 52, s 227, sch 19 pt IX; Youth Justice and Crim Evidence,
> > 1999 c 23, s 67, sch 6; Crim Justice, 2003 c 44, s 332, sch 37 pt 6; Gambling,
> > 2005 c 19, s 356(4)(5), sch 17; Finance, 2008 c 9, ss 113, 114(8)(c), sch 36
> > para 92(d); SI 2009/3054, art 3, sch

c 39 **Criminal Law (Consolidation) (Scotland)**

> appl—Immigration and Asylum, 1999 c 33, s 139(1))
> ext—Crim Procedure (Conseq Provns) (S), 1995 c 40, ss 1,2(2)
> mod—Crim Procedure (S), 1995 c 46, s 46(3)
> s 1 am—(S) Human Fertilisation and Embryology, 2008 c 22, s 56, sch 6 para 55
> > excl—Human Fertilisation and Embryology, 2008 c 22, s 53(4)(5)(m)
> s 3 rep—Sexual Offences (S), 2009 asp 9, s 61, sch 6
> s 4 appl—Mental Health (Care and Treatment) (S), 2003 asp 13, s 319
> > am—Sexual Offences (S), 2009 asp 9, s 61, sch 5 para 1
> s 5 rep—Sexual Offences (S), 2009 asp 9, s 61, sch 6
> s 6 rep—Sexual Offences (S), 2009 asp 9, s 61, sch 6
> s 7 am—Crime and Punishment (S) Act, 1997 c 48, s 62(1), sch 1 para 18(3)
> > rep in pt —Sexual Offences (S), 2009 asp 9, s 61, sch 6
> s 8 rep in pt—Crim Justice (S), 2003 asp 7, s 19(2)(a)
> s 9 am —Sexual Offences (S), 2009 asp 9, s 61, sch 5 para 1(1)(4)(a)(i)(b)(c); Crim Justice
> > and Licensing (S), 2010 asp 13, s 71, sch 4 para 11(2)(b)(3)(b)
> > rep in pt—Sexual Offences (S), 2009 asp 9, s 61, sch 5 para 1(1)(4)(a)(ii); Crim Justice
> > > and Licensing (S), 2010 asp 13, s 71, sch 4 paras 11(2)(a)(3)(a)
> s 10 am —Sexual Offences (S), 2009 asp 9, s 61, sch 5 para 1(1)(5)
> s 11 am—Crim Justice and Licensing (S), 2010 asp 13, s 45(2)(a)-(d)

1995
c 39 *continued*

s 12 see—Crim Procedure (S), 1995 c 46, s 292(1) sch 10 para 6
s 12A added—Sexual Offences (S), 2009 asp 9, s 61, sch 5 para 1(1)(6)
s 13 am—Sexual Offences (Amdt), 2000 c 44, ss 1(3),2(4); Convention Rights
  (Compliance) (S), 2001 asp 7, s 10(b); Sexual Offences (S), 2009 asp 9, s 61, sch
  5 para 1(1)(7)(8); Crim Justice and Licensing (S), 2010 asp 13, s 45(3)
 rep in pt—Convention Rights (Compliance) (S), 2001 asp 7, s 10(a); Mental Health
  (Care and Treatment) (S), 2003 asp 13, s 331(2), sch 5 pt 1; Sexual Offences
  (S), 2009 asp 9, s 61, sch 5 para 1(1)(9), sch 6
s 14 rep—Sexual Offences (S), 2009 asp 9, s 61, sch 6
s 15 rep—Crim Justice (S), 2003 asp 7, s 19(2)(b)
s 16 rep—Crim Justice and Licensing (S), 2010 asp 13, s 203, sch 7 para 21
s 16A added—Sexual Offences (Conspiracy and Incitement), 1996 c 29, s 6
 rep—Sexual Offences (S), 2009 asp 9, s 61, sch 6
s 16B added—Sex Offenders, 1997 c 51, ss 8,10(3)
 rep—Sexual Offences (S), 2009 asp 9, s 61, sch 6
s 19 am—Crime and Punishment (S) Act, 1997 c 48, s 62(1), sch 1 para 18(4); SSI
  2009/248, art 2, sch 1
 rep in pt—Licensing (S), 2005 asp 16, s 149, sch 7; SSI 2009/248, art 2, sch 2
s 20 am—SI 2006/2407, reg 44, sch 9
s 21 am—Crime and Punishment (S) Act, 1997 c 48, s 62(1), sch 1 para 18(5)
s 22 am—Licensing (S), 2005 asp 16, s 144, sch 6 para 7(1)(2)
s 23 am—Crime and Punishment (S) Act, 1997 c 48, s 62(1), sch 1 para 18(6); Licensing
  (S), 2005 asp 16, s 144, sch 6 para 7(1)(3); SSI 2009/248, art 2, sch 1
 rep in pt—Crim Justice and Licensing (S), 2010 asp 13, s 203, sch 7 para 23
s 23A added—Finance, 2007 c 11, s 85, sch 23 paras 1, 3, 14
 am—Employment, 2008 c 24, s 12(2)
ss 23B-23P added—Finance, 2007 c 11, s 85, sch 23 paras 1, 3, 14
Pt 3 (ss 24-26) am—Finance, 2007 c 11, s 85, sch 23 paras 1, 2, 14
s 24 am—Crime and Disorder, 1998 c 37, s 110; Finance, 2007 c 11, s 85, sch 23 paras 1, 4,
  14; SI 2011/1739, sch 1 paras 2(a)(b), 5(2)(3); Crime and Cts, 2013 c 22, s
  55(10), sch 21 para 45(2)(3)
 rep in pt—Finance, 2007 c 11, s 114, sch 27 pt 5
ss 24A, 24B added—SI 2011/1739, sch 1 para 6
s 25 am—Finance, 2007 c 11, s 85, sch 23 paras 1, 5, 14; Crime and Cts, 2013 c 22, sch 21
  para 46
 rep in pt—SI 2011/1739, sch 1 para 3
s 25A added—SI 2011/1739, sch 1 para 4
 am—Crime and Cts, 2013 c 22, sch 21 para 47(2)(a)(i)(b)(c)(3)(4)
s 26 am—Crime and Punishment (S) Act, 1997 c 48, s 62(1), sch 1 para 18(7); Finance,
  2007 c 11, s 85, sch 23 paras 1, 6, 14
ss 26A, 26B added—Finance, 2007 c 11, s 85, sch 23 paras 1, 7, 14
s 26A am—Crime and Cts, 2013 c 22, s 55(11)
s 26B am—Crime and Cts, 2013 c 22, s 55(12), sch 21 para 48
s 26C added—Borders, Citizenship and Immigration, 2009 c 11, s 24(1)
s 27 am—Crime (International Co-operation), 2003 c 32, s 91(1), sch 5 paras 61, 62
s 28 am—Youth Justice and Crim Evidence, 1999 c 23, s 59, sch 3 para 25
 rep in pt—Crime (International Co-operation), 2003 c 32, s 91, sch 5 paras 61,
  63(a)-(c), sch 6
s 30 am—SI 2001/3649, art 234; Commrs for Revenue and Customs, 2005 c 11, s 50(6),
  sch 4 para 63; (prosp) Crim Justice and Licensing (S), 2010 asp 13, s 200(2)(a)
 rep in pt—SI 2009/1941, art 2, sch 1
Pt 5 (ss 31-43) rep—Proceeds of Crime, 2002 c 29, s 457, sch 12
s 44 excl—SI 2005/2055, reg 12(6)(c)
 am—(prosp) Crim Justice and Licensing (S), 2010 asp 13, s 200(2)(b)
s 45 am—Crime and Punishment (S) Act, 1997 c 48, s 62(1), sch 1 para 18(8); (prosp) Crim
  Justice and Licensing (S), 2010 asp 13, s 200(2)(c)
s 46 am—(prosp) Crim Justice and Licensing (S), 2010 asp 13, s 200(2)(d)(ii)
 rep in pt—(prosp) Crim Justice and Licensing (S), 2010 asp 13, s 200(2)(d)(i)
s 46A added—Crime (International Co-operation), 2003 c 32, s 89
s 47 am—Offensive Weapons, 1996 c 26, ss 2(2)(4); Police, Public Order and Crim Justice
  (S), 2006 asp 10, s 74(1)(2)(a); Crim Justice and Licensing (S), 2010 asp 13, s
  37(2)(a)-(c)
 rep in pt—Police, Public Order and Crim Justice (S), 2006 asp 10, s 74(1)(2)(b)

1995
c 39 *continued*

s 48 am—Police, Public Order and Crim Justice (S), 2006 asp 10, s 74(1)(3)

s 49 am—Police, Public Order and Crim Justice (S), 2006 asp 10, s 73(1)-(3); Crim Justice and Licensing (S), 2010 asp 13, s 37(3)(a)-(c)

s 49A added—Offensive Weapons, 1996 c 26, s 4(3)(4)

    am—Police, Public Order and Crim Justice (S), 2006 asp 10, s 73(1)(4)(5); Crim Justice and Licensing (S), 2010 asp 13, s 37(4)(a)(b)

s 49B added—Offensive Weapons, 1996 c 26, s 4(3)(4)

s 49C added—Custodial Sentences and Weapons (S), 2007 asp 17, s 63

    am—Crim Justice and Licensing (S), 2010 asp 13, s 37(5)

s 50 am—Offensive Weapons, 1996 c 26, s 1(2); Crim Justice and Licensing (S), 2010 asp 13, s 37(6)

    rep in pt—Police, Public Order and Crim Justice (S), 2006 asp 10, s 74(1)(4)

s 50A mod—Crime and Disorder, 1998 c 37, s 33

c 40   **Criminal Procedure (Consequential Provisions) (Scotland)**

ext—Crime and Punishment (S) Act, 1997 c 48, s 62(1), sch 1 para 6(2)

s 136 excl—Employment Agencies, 1973 c 35, s 11A(3)

sch 2 rep in pt—Housing Grants, Construction and Regeneration, 1996 c 53, s 147, sch 3 pt II; Crime and Punishment (S) Act, 1997 c 48, s 62(1)(2), sch 1 para 19(2), sch 3; SI 2001/1149, arts 3(2), 4(11), sch 2; Regulation of Care (S), 2001 asp 8, s 80(1), sch 4; Fire (S), 2005 asp 5, s 89(2), sch 4; Police, Public Order and Crim Justice (S), 2006 asp 10, s 101, sch 6 para 3; SSI 2006/536, reg 2, sch 3; (prosp) Public Health etc (S), 2008 asp 5, s 126, sch 3 pt 1; Police and Fire Reform (S), 2012 asp 8, sch 8 pt 1

sch 3 rep in pt—Proceeds of Crime, 2002 c 29, s 457, sch 12; Crim Justice and Licensing (S), 2010 asp 13, s 14, sch 2 para 39

sch 4 rep in pt—NI (Emergency Provns), 1996 c 22, s 63(7 sch 7 pt I; Crime and Punishment (S) Act, 1997 c 48, s 62(1)(2), sch 1 para 19(3), sch 3; Petroleum, 1998 c 17, s 51, sch 5 pt I; Terrorism, 2000 c 11, s 125(2), sch 16 pt I; Powers of Crim Cts (Sentencing), 2000 c 6, s 165(3)(4), sch 11 pt I para 2, sch 12 pt I; Proceeds of Crime, 2002 c 29, s 457, sch 12; (except in relation to the River Tweed or Upper Esk) Salmon and Freshwater Fisheries (Consolidation) (S), 2003 asp 15, s 70(2), sch 4 pt 2; Communications, 2003 c 21, s 406(7), sch 19(1); Mental Health (Care and Treatment) (S), 2003 asp 13, s 331(2), sch 5 pt 1; Antisocial Behaviour etc (S), 2004 asp 8, s 144(2), sch 5; SL(R), 2004 c 14, s 1(1), sch 1 pt 9/5 pt 16/2; Pensions, 2004 c 35, s 320, sch 13 pt 1; Licensing (S), 2005 asp 16, s 149, sch 7; Serious Organised Crime and Police, 2005 c 15, s 174(2), sch 17 pt 2; (prosp) Violent Crime Reduction, 2006 c 38, s 65, sch 5; Wireless Telegraphy, 2006 c 36, s 125, sch 9; Police and Justice, 2006 c 48, s 52, sch 15; (pt prosp) Companies, 2006 c 46, s 1295, sch 16; SI 2006/2319, art 76, sch 4; Finance, 2007 c 11, s 114, sch 27 pt 5; Finance, 2009 c 10, s 98, sch 50 para 2; Crim Justice and Licensing (S), 2010 asp 13, s 203, sch 7 para 24; Finance (No 3), 2010 c 33, s 29, sch 13 para 2(b); Public Services Reform (S), 2010 asp 8, s 29, sch 7 para 2; SSI 2013/211, sch 2; SI 2015/583, sch 1 Table 1

c 41   **Law Reform (Succession)**
c 42   **Private International Law (Miscellaneous Provisions)**

s 3 rep—Arbitration, 1996 c 23, s 107(2) sch 4

s 4 rep in pt—Proceeds of Crime, 2002 c 29, s 457, sch 12; SI 2006/2805, art 18, sch 2

s 15A added—SI 2008/2986, reg 2

s 15B added (S)—SSI 2008/404, reg 2

s 18 am—(S) SSI 2008/404, reg 2; SI 2008/2986, reg 3

sch rep in pt—Family Law, 1996 c 27, s 66(3) sch 10

c 43   **Proceeds of Crime (Scotland)**

appl—Gas, 1995 c 45, s 205B(5); Crim Law (Consolidation) (S), 1995 c 39, ss 41(3)43(1); Crime (Sentences), 1997 c 43, s 3(5)

appl (mods)—SI 2011/245, sch 6 pt 1

ext—Crim Procedure (Conseq Provns) (S), 1995 c 40, ss 1,2(2)

excl—Wireless Telegraphy, 2006 c 36, s 103, sch 5 para 7(b)

mod—SI 2009/317, art 3, sch

Pt 1 (ss 1-20) rep (except s 2(7))—Proceeds of Crime, 2002 c 29, ss 456, 457, sch 11, para 28(1)(2)(a), sch 12

s 2 restr—Crim Procedure (Conseq Provns) (S), 1995 c 40, s 4, sch 3 pt II para 15(3)

Pt 2 (ss 21-27) appl (mods)—SI 1999/675, art 4, sch 3 paras 2-7

1995
c 43 Pt 2 *continued*

restr—Road Traffic Offenders, 1988 c 53, s 33A; Crim Procedure (Conseq Provns) (S), 1995 c 40, s 4, sch 3 pt II para 15(2)

s 25 rep in pt—Crim Justice and Licensing (S), 2010 asp 13, s 14, sch 2 para 40(2)

s 26 rep in pt—Crim Justice and Licensing (S), 2010 asp 13, s 14, sch 2 para 40(3)

s 27 am—Crim Procedure and Investigations, 1996 c 25, s 73(2); SSI 2015/338, sch 2 para 4

Pt 3 (ss 28-34) appl (mods)—SI 1999/673, art 4, sch 3 paras 13-17; SI 1999/675, art 4, sch 3 paras 8-12

s 28 appl—Civic Govt (S), 1982 c 45, sch 2A para 8
am—Proceeds of Crime, 2002 c 29, s 456, sch 11, para 28(1)(5)
rep in pt—Proceeds of Crime, 2002 c 29, ss 456, 457, sch 11, para 28(1)(2)(b), sch 12

s 29 rep—Proceeds of Crime, 2002 c 29, ss 456, 457, sch 11, para 28(1)(2)(c), sch 12

s 31 rep in pt—Proceeds of Crime, 2002 c 29, ss 456, 457, sch 11, para 28(1)(2)(d), sch 12

s 32 am—Bankruptcy and Diligence etc (S), 2007 asp 3, s 226, sch 5 para 22
rep in pt—Bankruptcy and Diligence etc (S), 2007 asp 3, s 226, sch 6

s 33 ext—Proceeds of Crime (S), 1995 c 43, s 14(3)

ss 35-39 rep—Proceeds of Crime, 2002 c 29, ss 456, 457, sch 11, para 28(1)(2)(e), sch 12

s 40 rep in pt—Proceeds of Crime, 2002 c 29, ss 456, 457, sch 11, para 28(1)(2)(f), sch 12

s 42 am—Crime and Punishment (S) Act, 1997 c 48, s 62(1), sch 1 para 20; Terrorism, 2000 c 11, s 125(1), sch 15 para 11(3); Proceeds of Crime, 2002 c 29, s 456, sch 11, para 28(1)(6)
rep in pt—Proceeds of Crime, 2002 c 29, ss 456, 457, sch 11, para 28(1)(2)(g), sch 12

s 43 rep in pt—Proceeds of Crime, 2002 c 29, ss 456, 457, sch 11, para 28(1)(2)(h), sch 12

Pt 5 (ss 44-50) appl (mods)—SI 1999/675, art 4, sch 3 paras 13-17

s 45 rep in pt—Proceeds of Crime, 2002 c 29, ss 456, 457, sch 11, para 28(1)(2)(i), sch 12

s 47 rep—Proceeds of Crime, 2002 c 29, ss 456, 457, sch 11, para 28(1)(2)(j), sch 12

s 49 rep in pt—Terrorism, 2000 c 11, s 125(1)(2), sch 15 para 11(4), sch 16 pt I; Proceeds of Crime, 2002 c 29, ss 456, 457, sch 11, para 28(1)(2)(k), sch 12

s 65 am—Crim Procedure and Investigations, 1996 c 25, s 73(3)

sch 1 appl (mods)—SI 1999/673, art 4, sch 3 para 18; SI 1999/675, art 4, sch 3 para 18
mod—SI 1998/752, art 3(1)(g)
rep in pt—Proceeds of Crime, 2002 c 29, ss 456, 457, sch 11, para 28(1)(3)(a)-(g), sch 12; (pt prosp) Bankruptcy and Diligence etc (S), 2007 asp 3, s 226, sch 6
am—Debt Arrangement and Attachment (S), 2002 asp 17, s 61, sch 3 pt 1, para 24

sch 2 appl (mods)—SI 1999/675, art 4, sch 3 para 19
mod—Crim Procedure (Conseq Provns) (S), 1995 c 40, s 4, sch 3 pt II para 15(4)-(7)
rep in pt—Proceeds of Crime, 2002 c 29, ss 456, 457, sch 11, para 28(1)(4)(a)-(e), sch 12

sch 9 am—Crim Procedure and Investigations, 1996 c 25, s 73(4)

c 44 **Statute Law (Repeals)**
sch 2 rep in pt—SL(R), 2008 c 12, s 1(1), sch 1 pt 3; SL(R), 2008 c 12, s 1, sch 1 pt 3

c 45 **Gas**
trans of powers—(W) SI 1999/672, art 2, sch 1

ss 1,2 rep—Utilities, 2000 c 27, s 108, sch 8

s 3 rep in pt—(pt prosp) Utilities, 2000 c 27, s 108, sch 8

s 6 appl—SI 1996/752, art 3

s 8 rep in pt—Utilities, 2000 c 27, s 108, sch 8

s 10 am—SI 2000/245, art 2
rep in pt—Utilities, 2000 c 27, ss 89, 108, sch 8

s 12 appl—Energy, 1976 c 76, s 9(1)
am—SIs 2000/1937, reg 2(3), sch 3 paras 1, 2, 3, 4, 5(a)(b), 6; Energy, 2008 c 32, s 78(2)(a)(b); Energy, 2011 c 16, s 92(2)-(12)
rep in pt—SI 2000/1937, reg 2(3), sch 3 para 2; Energy, 2008 c 32, s 78(2)(a), sch 6

sch 1 rep (prosp)—Utilities, 2000 c 27, s 108, sch 8

sch 3 rep in pt—(prosp) Utilities, 2000 c 27, s 108, sch 8

sch 4 rep in pt—Planning (Conseq Provns) (S), 1997 c 11, s 3, sch 1 pt I; Loc Govt and Rating, 1997 c 29, s 33(2), sch 4; Govt of Wales, 1998 c 38, s 152, sch 18 pt IV; Postal Services, 2000 c 26, s 127(6), sch 9; Civil Contingencies, 2004 c 36, s 32(2), sch 3; SI 2005/1803, reg 47(1); (S) Flood Risk Management (S), 2009 asp 6, s 96, sch 3 para 8; Deregulation, 2015 c 20, sch 23 para 17(b)
am—Planning (Conseq Provns) (S), 1997 c 11, s 4, sch 2 para 61; Govt of Wales, 1998 c 38, s 135(2)(c); Housing, 2004 c 34, s 265(1), sch 15 para 39

sch 5 excl—SI 1996/449, art 21

1995
c 45 sch 5   *continued*
> rep in pt—Finance, 1998 c 36, s 165, sch 27 pt V(3), Note 1; Utilities, 2000 c 27,
>   s 108, sch 8; SI 2000/311, art 29

c 46   **Criminal Procedure (Scotland)**
> constr with—Crim Law (Consolidation) (S), 1995 c 39, s 43(2)
> excl—Crim Law (Consolidation) (S), 1995 c 39, s 46(3)
> ext—Crim Procedure (Conseq Provns) (S), 1995 c 40, ss 1,2(2)
> am—(temp) Crim Procedure (Conseq Provns) (S), 1995 c 40, s 4, sch 3 pt II para 5
> mod—SI 1996/3255, reg 5; Crim Proceedings etc (Reform) (S), 2007 asp 6, s 62(8)
> power to mod—Crim Proceedings etc (Reform) (S), 2007 asp 6, s 64(6)(7)
> appl—Legal Aid (S), 1986 c 47, s 25AA(1); Prisoners and Crim Proceedings (S), 1993 c 9,
>   s 2(3); Crime and Punishment (S), 1997 c 48, s 64; Sexual Offences, 2003 c 42, s 80,
>   sch 3 para 98; SSI 2008/356, reg 33; Offender Rehabilitation, 2014 c 11, sch 3 para
>   7 (inserting Crime (Sentences), 1997 c. 43 Sch 1 para 19B)
> appl (with or without mods)—(1.3.2016) Proceeds of Crime, 2002 c 29, s 118(2B)(c)
>   (added by 2015 c 9, s 19(1)(b))
> power to appl—Crim Proceedings etc (Reform) (S), 2007 asp 6, s 64(5)
> s 2 am—Crim Procedure (Amdt) (S), 2004 asp 5, s 25, sch paras 1, 2
> s 3 am—Crime and Punishment (S), 1997 c 48, s 13(1); Sexual Offences (S), 2009 asp 9, s
>   61, sch 5 para 2(1)(2)
> s 5 saved—Crim Procedure (Conseq Provns) (S), 1995 c 40, s 3(1) sch 1 para 2(3)
>   am—Crime and Punishment (S), 1997 c 48, s 13(2); Crim Proceedings etc (Reform) (S),
>   2007 asp 6, s 43
> s 5A added (pt prosp)—Crim Justice and Licensing (S), 2010 asp 13, s 203, sch 7 paras 25,
>   26
> s 6 am—Crim Proceedings etc (Reform) (S), 2007 asp 6, s 80, sch para 9(1)(4)(5);
>   (1.4.2016) Courts Reform (S), 2014 asp 18, sch 5 para 39(2)
>   power to am—(prosp) Crim Proceedings etc (Reform) (S), 2007 asp 6, s 63(2)
> s 7 am—Crim Proceedings etc (Reform) (S), 2007 asp 6, s 80, sch para 9(2)(4)(5); Sexual
>   Offences (S), 2009 asp 9, s 61, sch 5 para 2(1)(3)
>   rep in pt—Crim Proceedings etc (Reform) (S), 2007 asp 6, s 80, sch para 9(2)(4)(5);
>   (1.4.2016) Courts Reform (S), 2014 asp 18, sch 5 para 39(3)
> s 8 am—Crim Proceedings etc (Reform) (S), 2007 asp 6, s 80, sch para 9(3)(4)(5); Judiciary
>   and Cts (S), 2008 asp 6, s 59; SSI 2015/150, sch para 5
>   rep in pt—Crim Proceedings etc (Reform) (S), 2007 asp 6, s 80, sch para 9(3)(4)(5)
> s 9 am—Crim Proceedings etc (Reform) (S), 2007 asp 6, s 80, sch para 9(6)
> s 9A added—Crim Justice (S), 2003 asp 7, s 59
>   rep—Crim Proceedings etc (Reform) (S), 2007 asp 6, s 80, sch para 9(7)
> s 10 am—Crim Proceedings etc (Reform) (S), 2007 asp 6, s 80, sch para 10
> s 10A added—Crim Proceedings etc (Reform) (S), 2007 asp 6, s 80, sch para 11
>   am—Crim Justice and Licensing (S), 2010 asp 13, s 203, sch 7 paras 25,
>   27(a)(b)(ii)(iii)(c)
>   rep in pt—Crim Justice and Licensing (S), 2010 asp 13, s 203, sch 7 paras 25,
>   27(b)(i)
> s 11 am—Postal Services, 2000 c 26, s 127(4), sch 8 pt II para 24; Crim Justice and
>   Licensing (S), 2010 asp 13, s 203, sch 7 paras 25, 28(a)(b)
>   appl—Crim Justice (S), 2003 asp 7, s 69(2)(c)
> s 11A added—Criminal Justice (Terrorism and Conspiracy), 1998 c 40, s 7.
>   am—Crim Justice and Licensing (S), 2010 asp 13, s 50(2)(a)-(c)
> s 12 am—Police and Fire Reform (S), 2012 asp 8, sch 7 para 12(2)(a)
>   rep in pt—Police and Fire Reform (S), 2012 asp 8, sch 7 para 12(2)(b)
> s 13 am—Police, Public Order and Crim Justice (S), 2006 asp 10, s 81(1)-(5)
> s 14 am—Police, Public Order and Crim Justice (S), 2006 asp 10, s 81(6); Crim Procedure
>   (Legal Assistance, Detention and Appeals) (S), 2010 asp 15, ss 1(2), 3(1)
>   appl (mods)—Criminal Justice and Public Order, 1994 c 33, s 138(2)(2A)(6)-(9)
> s 14A added—Crim Procedure (Legal Assistance, Detention and Appeals) (S), 2010 asp 15,
>   s 3(2)
>   appl (mods)—Criminal Justice and Public Order, 1994 c 33, s 138(2)(2A)(6)-(9)
> s 14B added—Crim Procedure (Legal Assistance, Detention and Appeals) (S), 2010 asp 15,
>   s 3(2)
>   appl (mods)—Criminal Justice and Public Order, 1994 c 33, s 138(2)(2A)(6)-(9)
> s 15 appl—Terrorism, 2000 c 11, s 41(2), sch 8 pt I para 18(2)(b); Civil Partnership, 2004 c
>   33, s 116(4)

1995

c 46 s 15 *continued*

appl (mods)—Criminal Justice and Public Order, 1994 c 33, s 138(1A)(2)(2A)(6)-(9); Terrorism, 2000 c. 11 Sch 8 para 18(3) (inserted by Anti-social Behaviour, Crime and Policing, 2014 c 12, sch 9 para 5(12)(c))

am—Crime and Punishment (S), 1997 c 48, s 62(1), sch 1 para 21(2); Crim Procedure (Legal Assistance, Detention and Appeals) (S), 2010 asp 15, s 1(3)(a)(i)(b)(c)

rep in pt—Crim Procedure (Legal Assistance, Detention and Appeals) (S), 2010 asp 15, s 1(3)(a)(ii)

s 15A added—Crim Procedure (Legal Assistance, Detention and Appeals) (S), 2010 asp 15, s 1(4)

appl (mods)—Criminal Justice and Public Order, 1994 c 33, s 138(1B)(2)(2A)(6)-(9)

s 17 saved—Crim Law (Consolidation) (S), 1995 c 39, s 25(1)

s 17A added—Sexual Offences (Procedure and Evidence) (S), 2002 asp 9, s 3, sch, paras 1, 2

am—Crim Justice (S), 2003 asp 7, s 85, sch 4 para 3(1)(2); Crim Procedure (Amdt) (S), 2004 asp 5, s 25, sch paras 1, 3; Crim Justice and Licensing (S), 2010 asp 13, s 203, sch 7 paras 25, 29(a)(b)

s 18 appl (mods)—Criminal Justice and Public Order, 1994 c 33, s 138(2)(2A)(6)-(9); Terrorism, 2000 c 11, s 41(2), sch 8 pt I para 20

am—Crime and Punishment (S), 1997 c 48, s 47(1)(a)(b)(d); (retrosp) Crime and Disorder, 1998 c 37, s 119, sch 8 para 117(2); Crim Justice (S), 2003 asp 7, s 55(1)(2)(b); Police, Public Order and Crim Justice (S), 2006 asp 10, s 101, sch 6 para 4(1)(2); ibid, s 83(1); Crim Justice and Licensing (S), 2010 asp 13, ss 77(2), 203, sch 7 paras 25, 30; Protection of Freedoms, 2012 c 9, sch 1 para 6(2); Police and Fire Reform (S), 2012 asp 8, sch 7 para 12(3)

rep in pt—Crime and Punishment (S), 1997 c 48, ss 47(1)(c), 62(2), sch 3; Crim Justice (S), 2003 asp 7, s 55(1)(2)(a)

mod—Terrorism, 2000 11, sch 8 para 20(2)

appl—International Crim Court (S), 2001 asp 13, s 17, sch 4 para 1(3); Crim Justice (S), 2003 asp 7, s 56(8)

ext—International Crim Court (S), 2001 asp 13, s 17, sch 4 para 7

s 18A added —Police, Public Order and Crim Justice (S), 2006 asp 10, s 83(2)

am—Crim Justice and Licensing (S), 2010 asp 13, s 77(3); Police and Fire Reform (S), 2012 asp 8, sch 7 para 12(4)(a)

rep in pt—Police and Fire Reform (S), 2012 asp 8, sch 7 para 12(4)(b)

ss 18B, 18C added—Crim Justice and Licensing (S), 2010 asp 13, s 78

s 18C am—Police and Fire Reform (S), 2012 asp 8, sch 7 para 12(5)(a)

s rep in pt—Police and Fire Reform (S), 2012 asp 8, sch 7 para 12(5)(b)

s 18D added—Crim Justice and Licensing (S), 2010 asp 13, s 79

ss 18E, 18F added—Crim Justice and Licensing (S), 2010 asp 13, s 80

s 18E am—SSI 2013/211, sch 1 para 10(2)(a)(c)(d)(e)(i)-(iii)(f)

rep in pt—SSI 2013/211, sch 1 para 10(2)(b)

s 18F am—Police and Fire Reform (S), 2012 asp 8, sch 7 para 12(6)(a)

rep in pt—Police and Fire Reform (S), 2012 asp 8, sch 7 para 12(6)(b)

s 18G added—Protection of Freedoms, 2012 c 9, sch 1 para 6(3)

s 19 am—Crime and Punishment (S), 1997 c 48, ss 47(2)(a)(b)(c)(i), 48(1); Crim Justice (S), 2003 asp 7, s 55(1)(3)(b)(c); Police, Public Order and Crim Justice (S), 2006 asp 10, s 77(1)(3); Police and Fire Reform (S), 2012 asp 8, sch 7 para 12(7)

rep in pt—Crim Justice (S), 2003 asp 7, s 55(1)(3)(a); Crim Justice and Licensing (S), 2010 asp 13, s 203, sch 7 paras 25, 31

s 19A added—Crime and Punishment (S), 1997 c 48, s 48(2)

rep in pt—Crim Justice (S), 2003 asp 7, s 55(1)(3)(a); SSI 2005/465, art 2, sch 1 para 27(1)(2)(b); Sexual Offences (S), 2009 asp 9, s 61, sch 5 para 2(1)(4)(a)(ii)

am—Crim Justice (S), 2003 asp 7, s 55(1)(3)(b)(c); SSI 2005/465, art 2, sch 1 para 27(1)(2)(a); Police, Public Order and Crim Justice (S), 2006 asp 10, ss 77(1)(4), 101, sch 6 para 4(1)(3); Sexual Offences (S), 2009 asp 9, s 61, sch 5 para 2(1)(4)(a)(i)(iii)(b); Crim Justice and Licensing (S), 2010 asp 13, ss 81(a)(b), 203, sch 7 paras 25, 32; SSI 2010/421, art 2, sch

ss 19AA,19AB added—Police, Public Order and Crim Justice (S), 2006 asp 10, s 77(1)(2)

s 19AA am—Anti-social Behaviour, Crime and Policing, 2014 c 12, sch 11 para 51

s 19AB am—Anti-social Behaviour, Crime and Policing, 2014 c 12, sch 11 para 52

s 19B added—Crime and Punishment (S), 1997 c 48, s 48(2)

am—Crim Justice (S), 2003 asp 7, s 55(1)(4); Police, Public Order and Crim Justice (S), 2006 asp 10, s 77(1)(5)

1995
c 46 *continued*

s 19C added—Crim Justice and Licensing (S), 2010 asp 13, s 82
    am—SI 2011/2298, sch para 1(a)-(c); Police and Fire Reform (S), 2012 asp 8, sch 7 para 12(8)
s 20 rep—Crim Justice and Licensing (S), 2010 asp 13, s 203, sch 7 paras 25, 33
ss 20A, 20B added—Police, Public Order and Crim Justice (S), 2006 asp 10, s 84
s 21 rep in pt—Crim Proceedings etc (Reform) (S), 2007 asp 6, s 7(1)
s 22 excl—Terrorism, 2000 c 11, s 41(2), sch 8 pt II para 27(5)
    am—Crim Proceedings etc (Reform) (S), 2007 asp 6, ss 7(2), 80, sch para 26(a)
    rep in pt—Crim Justice and Licensing (S), 2010 asp 13, s 203, sch 7 paras 25, 34
ss 22ZA, 22ZB added—Crim Justice and Licensing (S), 2010 asp 13, s 55
s 22A added—Bail, Judicial Appointments etc (S), asp 9, s 1
    am—Crim Proceedings etc (Reform) (S), 2007 asp 6, s 6(1)
s 23 rep in pt—Bail, Judicial Appointments etc (S), asp 9, s 12, sch para 7(1)
    am—Bail, Judicial Appointments etc (S), asp 9, s 12, sch para 7(1); Crim Proceedings etc (Reform) (S), 2007 asp 6, s 6(2)
s 23A added—Bail, Judicial Appointments etc (S), asp 9, s 2
    am—Crim Procedure (Amdt) (S), 2004 asp 5, s 25, sch paras 1, 4 (see SSI 2004/405); Crim Justice and Licensing (S), 2010 asp 13, s 203, sch 7 paras 25, 35(a)(b)
s 23C added—Crim Proceedings etc (Reform) (S), 2007 asp 6, s 1
    am—Crim Justice and Licensing (S), 2010 asp 13, s 71, sch 4 para 2
s 23D added—Crim Proceedings etc (Reform) (S), 2007 asp 6, s 1
s 24 rep in pt—Bail, Judicial Appointments etc (S), asp 9, s 3(1); Sexual Offences (Procedure and Evidence) (S), 2002 asp 9, s 5(1)(a); Crim Justice and Licensing (S), 2010 asp 13, s 58(a)
    am—Sexual Offences (Procedure and Evidence) (S), 2002 asp 9, s 5(1)(b)(2); Crim Procedure (Amdt) (S), 2004 asp 5, s 25, sch paras 1, 5; Crim Proceedings etc (Reform) (S), 2007 asp 6, s 2; Crim Justice and Licensing (S), 2010 asp 13, s 58(b)
s 24A added—Extradition, 2003 c 41, s 199 (see SI 2003/3103, arts 2-5)
    renumbered (as s 24F)—SSI 2005/40, art 4(1)(2)
    rep—Crim Justice and Licensing (S), 2010 asp 13, s 59
ss 24A-24E added—Crim Procedure (Amdt) (S), 2004 asp 5, s 17
    rep—Crim Justice and Licensing (S), 2010 asp 13, s 59
s 24F added—SSI 2005/40, art 4(1)(2)
    rep—Crim Justice and Licensing (S), 2010 asp 13, s 59
s 25 am—Crim Procedure (Amdt) (S), 2004 asp 5, s 25, sch paras 1, 6 (see SSI 2004/405); ibid, s 18(1)(2); Crim Proceedings etc (Reform) (S), 2007 asp 6, s 2(2)
    appl—SSI 2007/480, art 4
s 25A added—Crim Procedure (Amdt) (S), 2004 asp 5, s 25, sch paras 1, 7 (see SSI 2004/405)
s 26 rep—Bail, Judicial Appointments etc (S), asp 9, s 3(2)
s 27 am—Crim Procedure (Amdt) (S), 2004 asp 5, s 25, sch paras 1, 8; Crim Proceedings etc (Reform) (S), 2007 asp 6, s 3(1)(2); ibid, s 80, sch para 26(c); Crim Justice and Licensing (S), 2010 asp 13, ss 62(1), 71, sch 4 para 3; (31.5.2016) Human Trafficking and Exploitation (S), 2015 asp 12, sch para 1
s 28 am—Crim Procedure (Amdt) (S), 2004 asp 5, s 25, sch paras 1, 9; Crim Proceedings etc (Reform) (S), 2007 asp 6, s 3(1)(2)
s 30 am—Crim Procedure (Amdt) (S), 2004 asp 5, s 18(1)(3)(4); Crim Proceedings etc (Reform) (S), 2007 asp 6, s 4(1); Crim Justice and Licensing (S), 2010 asp 13, s 57(2)(a)(b)
s 31 am—Crim Procedure (Amdt) (S), 2004 asp 5, ss 18(1)(3)(4), 25, sch paras 1, 10; Crim Justice and Licensing (S), 2010 asp 13, s 57(3)(a)
    rep in pt—Crim Justice and Licensing (S), 2010 asp 13, s 57(3)(b)
s 32 am—Bail, Judicial Appointments etc (S), asp 9, ss 4,12, sch para 7(2); Crim Procedure (Amdt) (S), 2004 asp 5, s 25, sch paras 1, 11; Crim Proceedings etc (Reform) (S), 2007 asp 6, s 4(2); Courts Reform (S), 2014 asp 18, s 122
    rep in pt—Bail, Judicial Appointments etc (S), asp 9, s 12, sch para 7(2)
s 32A added—Crim Proceedings etc (Reform) (S), 2007 asp 6, s 5
s 34A added—Crim Proceedings etc (Reform) (S), 2007 asp 6, s 31
s 33 am—Bail, Judicial Appointments etc (S), asp 9, s 12, sch para 7(3)
s 35 am—Sexual Offences (Procedure and Evidence) (S), 2002 asp 9, s 3, sch, paras 1, 3; Crim Justice (S), 2003 asp 7, s 85, sch 4 para 3(1)(2); Crim Procedure (Amdt) (S),

1995
c 46 *continued*

2004 asp 5, s 25, sch paras 1, 12; Crim Justice and Licensing (S), 2010 asp 13, s 203, sch 7 paras 25, 36(a)(b)

s 37 am—SI 1998/2635 para 2

s 41 am—Crim Justice and Licensing (S), 2010 asp 13, s 203, sch 7 paras 25, 41(c)

s 41A added—Crim Justice and Licensing (S), 2010 asp 13, s 52(2)

s 42 am—Crim Justice and Licensing (S), 2010 asp 13, s 52(3)(a)-(c)

s 43 mod—SI 1996/3255, reg 14(1)
    am—Crime and Punishment (S), 1997 c 48, s 55(2)(3)

s 44 mod—SI 1996/3255, reg 13(1)
    appl—SI 1996/3255, reg 2(1)
    am—Antisocial Behaviour etc (S), 2004 asp 8, s 10(1)(2); SI 2013/1465, sch 3 para 2(a)-(d); Children and Young People (S), 2014 asp 8, sch 5 para 5(2); SI 2015/907, art 3

s 44A added (1.2.2016)—Children and Young People (S), 2014 asp 8, s 91
    am—SSI 2015/402, sch para 3

s 46 am—Crime and Punishment (S), 1997 c 48, s 62(1), sch 1 para 21(4); SSI 2013/211, sch 1 para 10(3)(a)(b)

s 47 am—(1.9.2015) Victims and Witnesses (S), 2014 asp 1, s 15

s 48 am—SSI 2013/211, sch 1 para 10(4)

s 49 am—Crime and Punishment (S), 1997 c 48, s 23(a); (retrosp) Crime and Disorder, 1998 c 37, s 119, sch 8 para 118; Crim Justice, 2003 c 44, s 290(1)(2); Violent Crime Reduction, 2006 c 38, s 49, sch 1 para 4; Crim Proceedings etc (Reform) (S), 2007 asp 6, s 80, sch para 26(d); SSI 2013/211, sch 1 para 10(5)

s 50 am—Access to Justice, 1999 c 22, s 73(2)

s 51 mod—SI 1996/3255, reg 14(1)
    am—Crime and Punishment (S), 1997 c 48, s 56; Crim Justice (S), 2003 asp 7, s 23(3)(a)(ii)(b)(i)(iii)(c)(5)-(8); Crim Justice and Licensing (S), 2010 asp 13, s 64(3); SSI 2013/211, sch 1 para 10(6)(a)-(c)
    rep in pt—Crim Justice (S), 2003 asp 7, s 23(3)(a)(i)(b)(ii)(4); Crim Justice and Licensing (S), 2010 asp 13, s 64(2)
    appl—SSI 2014/337, sch 2 para 18(1)

ss 51A, 51B added—Crim Justice and Licensing (S), 2010 asp 13, s 168

s 52 rep in pt—Mental Health (Care and Treatment) (S), 2003 asp 13, s 331(2), sch 5 pt 1

ss 52A-52U added—Mental Health (Care and Treatment) (S), 2003 asp 13, s 130

s 52A am—Crim Proceedings etc (Reform) (S), 2007 asp 6, s 80, sch para 26(e)

s 52B am—Crim Proceedings etc (Reform) (S), 2007 asp 6, s 80, sch para 26(f); (prosp) Mental Health (S), 2015 asp 9, s 38(2)(a)

s 52C am—(prosp) Mental Health (S), 2015 asp 9, s 38(2)(b)

s 52D am—(prosp) Mental Health (S), 2015 asp 9, ss 38(2)(c), 40(2)

s 52F am—(prosp) Mental Health (S), 2015 asp 9, ss 38(2)(d), 40(3)

s 52G am—(prosp) Mental Health (S), 2015 asp 9, s 40(4)

s 52H rep in pt—Crim Justice and Licensing (S), 2010 asp 13, s 14, sch 2 para 2(a)(b)
    am—(prosp) Mental Health (S), 2015 asp 9, s 40(5)

s 52K am—(prosp) Mental Health (S), 2015 asp 9, s 38(2)(e)

s 52L am—(prosp) Mental Health (S), 2015 asp 9, s 38(2)(f)

s 52M am—(prosp) Mental Health (S), 2015 asp 9, ss 38(2)(g), 41(2)

s 52P am—(prosp) Mental Health (S), 2015 asp 9, ss 38(2)(h), 41(3)

s 52R rep in pt—Crim Justice and Licensing (S), 2010 asp 13, s 14, sch 2 para 3(a)(b)
    am—(prosp) Mental Health (S), 2015 asp 9, s 41(4)

s 53 am—Crime and Punishment (S) 1997 c 48, ss 11,62(1), sch 1 para 21(5)(a)-(f); Crim Justice and Licensing (S), 2010 asp 13, s 14, sch 2 para 4; (prosp) Mental Health (S), 2015 asp 9, s 42(2)
    rep in pt—Crime and Punishment (S), 1997 c 48, ss 10(1)(a),62(2), sch 3

s 53 replaced (by ss 53, 53A-53D)—Mental Health (Care and Treatment) (S), 2003 asp 13, s 131

s 53A am—(prosp) Mental Health (S), 2015 asp 9, s 42(3)

s 53B am—(prosp) Mental Health (S), 2015 asp 9, ss 42(4), 45(2)

s 53E added—Crim Justice and Licensing (S), 2010 asp 13, s 169

s 53F added—Crim Justice and Licensing (S), 2010 asp 13, s 170(1)

s 54 am—Mental Health (Care and Treatment) (S), 2003 asp 13, s 331(1), sch 4 para 8(1)(2)(a)-(d); Crim Procedure (Amdt) (S), 2004 asp 5, s 25, sch paras 1, 13; Crim Justice and Licensing (S), 2010 asp 13, s 170(2)(a)(ii)(b)(c); (prosp) Mental Health (S), 2015 asp 9, s 42(5)

1995
c 46 s 54 *continued*

    rep in pt—Crim Justice and Licensing (S), 2010 asp 13, s 170(2)(a)(ii)(3)
s 55 am—Crim Justice and Licensing (S), 2010 asp 13, s 203, sch 7 paras 25, 37(a)(b)
s 56 am—Crim Procedure (Amdt) (S), 2004 asp 5, s 25, sch paras 1, 14(a)
    rep in pt—Crim Procedure (Amdt) (S), 2004 asp 5, s 25, sch paras 1, 14(b)
s 57 ext—Crime and Punishment (S), 1997 c 48, s 9(1)(a)(2)(a)
    am—Adults with Incapacity (S), 2000, asp 4, s 88(2), sch 5 para 26(1); Crim Justice
        (S), 2003 asp 7, s 2; Mental Health (Care and Treatment) (S), 2003 asp 13,
        s 331(1), sch 4 para 8(1)(3); Crim Justice and Licensing (S), 2010 asp 13, s 203,
        sch 7 paras 25, 38; (prosp) Mental Health (S), 2015 asp 9, ss 39(2), 43(2)
s 57A added—Mental Health (Care and Treatment) (S), 2003 asp 13, s 133
    am—Crim Justice and Licensing (S), 2010 asp 13, s 14, sch 2 para 5; SSI 2011/211,
        sch 1 para 7; (prosp) Children and Young People (S), 2014 asp 8, sch 5 para
        5(3); SSI 2015/157, sch para 3
ss 57B-57D added—Mental Health (Care and Treatment) (S), 2003 asp 13, s 133
s 57B am—(prosp) Mental Health (S), 2015 asp 9, s 43(3)
s 57D am—(prosp) Mental Health (S), 2015 asp 9, s 43(4)
s 58 ext—Crime and Punishment (S), 1997 c 48, s 9(1)(a)(2)(b)
    am—Crime and Punishment (S), 1997 c 48, s 62(1), sch 1 para 21(6); Mental Health
        (Public Safety and Appeals) (S), 1999 asp 1, s 3(1)(b); Adults with Incapacity (S),
        2000, asp 4, s 88(2), sch 5 para 26(2); Mental Health (Care and Treatment) (S),
        2003 asp 13, s 331(1), sch 4 para 8(1)(4)(5); Adult Support and Protection (S),
        2007 asp 10, s 77, sch 1 para 4(a)(b); Crim Justice and Licensing (S), 2010 asp
        13, s 14, sch 2 para 6
    rep in pt—Mental Health (Care and Treatment) (S), 2003 asp 13, s 331(2), sch 5 pt 1
s 58A added—Adults with Incapacity (S), 2000, asp 4, s 84(2)
s 59 am—(temp) Crim Procedure (Conseq Provns) (S), 1995 c 40, s 4, sch 3 pt II para 10;
        Mental Health (Public Safety and Appeals) (S), 1999 asp 1, s 3(1)(b); Mental
        Health (Care and Treatment) (S), 2003 asp 13, s 331(1), sch 4 para 8(1)(4)(5)
    rep in pt—Adults with Incapacity (S), 2000, asp 4, s 88(3), sch 6; Mental Health (Care
        and Treatment) (S), 2003 asp 13, s 331(2), sch 5 pt 1
s 59A added—Crime and Punishment (S), 1997 c 48, s 6(1)
    ext—Crime and Punishment (S), 1997 c 48, s 9(1)(c)
    replaced (by ss 59A-59C)—Mental Health (Care and Treatment) (S), 2003 asp 13,
        s 331(1), sch 4 para 8(1)(6)
    am—(prosp) Mental Health (S), 2015 asp 9, s 44(2)
s 59C am—(prosp) Mental Health (S), 2015 asp 9, s 44(3)
s 60 am—Crime and Punishment (S), 1997 c 48, s 6(2); Mental Health (Care and
        Treatment) (S), 2003 asp 13, s 331(1), sch 4 para 8(1)(7)-(10)
s 60A added—Crime and Punishment (S), 1997 c 48, s 22; Adults with Incapacity (S), 2000,
        asp 4, s 88(2), sch 5 para 26(3)
    am—Mental Health (Care and Treatment) (S), 2003 asp 13, s 331(1), sch 4
        para 8(1)(7)-(10)
s 60B am—Mental Health (Care and Treatment) (S), 2003 asp 13, s 331(1), sch 4
        para 8(1)(7)-(10)
    rep in pt—Adult Support and Protection (S), 2007 asp 10, s 77, sch 1 para 4(c)
s 60C added—Mental Health (Care and Treatment) (S), 2003 asp 13, s 134
    am—Crim Justice and Licensing (S), 2010 asp 13, s 203, sch 7 paras 25, 40(a)
    rep in pt—Crim Justice and Licensing (S), 2010 asp 13, s 203, sch 7 paras 25, 40(b)
s 60D added—Mental Health (Care and Treatment) (S), 2003 asp 13, s 134
s 61 am—Crime and Punishment (S), 1997 c 48, s 10(2); Adults with Incapacity (S), 2000,
        asp 4, s 88(2), sch 5 para 26(4); Mental Health (Care and Treatment) (S), 2003
        asp 13, s 331(1), sch 4 para 8(1)(7)-(10); (prosp) Mental Health (S), 2015 asp 9, s
        46(2)
    rep in pt—Adults with Incapacity (S), 2000, asp 4, s 88(3), sch 6; Crim Justice and
        Licensing (S), 2010 asp 13, s 203, sch 7 paras 25, 41(a)(b)
s 61A added (prosp)—Mental Health (S), 2015 asp 9, s 46(3)
s 61B added (prosp)—Mental Health (S), 2015 asp 9, s 47(2)
s 62 am—Crime and Punishment (S), 1997 c 48, s 62(1), sch 1 para 21(7); Crim Justice and
        Licensing (S), 2010 asp 13, s 203, sch 7 paras 25, 42(a)(b); SSI 2015/338, sch 2
        para 5(2)
    power to mod—(pt prosp) Child Support, Pensions and Social Security, 2000 c 19,
        s 65(7)
s 63 rep in pt—Crime and Punishment (S), 1997 c 48, s 62(1)(2), sch 1 para 21(8)(a)(b)

1995
c 46 s 63 *continued*

am—Crime and Punishment (S), 1997 c 48, s 62(1), sch 1 para 21(8)(c); Crim Justice and Licensing (S), 2010 asp 13, s 203, sch 7 paras 25, 43(a)-(c); SSI 2015/338, sch 2 para 5(3)

s 64 am—Crim Justice and Licensing (S), 2010 asp 13, s 60(2)

s 65 am—Crime and Punishment (S), 1997 c 48, s 62(1), sch 1 para 21(9); Crim Procedure (Amdt) (S), 2004 asp 5, s 6(1)-(7)(9)-(11); Crim Proceedings etc (Reform) (S), 2007 asp 6, ss 26, 80, sch para 12(1)

  ext—Crime (Sentences), 1997 c 43, s 41, sch 1 pt II para 10(1)

  mod—Crime (Sentences), 1997 c 43, s 41, sch 1 pt II para 11(1)(a)

  appl (mods)—SI 1997/1776, art 2, sch 1 paras 5-7

  appl—Double Jeopardy (S), 2011 asp 16, s 6(7)(8)(a)

  rep in pt—Crim Procedure (Amdt) (S), 2004 asp 5, s 6(8)

s 66 am—Sexual Offences (Procedure and Evidence) (S), 2002 asp 9, s 3, sch, paras 1, 4; Crim Justice (S), 2003 asp 7, ss 61(1)(a)(b)(i)(c)-(e)(g), 85, sch 4 para 3(1)(2); Crim Procedure (Amdt) (S), 2004 asp 5, ss 1(1), 7(1)-(5), 10(5), 25, sch paras 1, 15(a)-(d); Crim Proceedings etc (Reform) (S), 2007 asp 6, s 35(1); Crim Justice and Licensing (S), 2010 asp 13, s 203, sch 7 paras 25, 44(a)(b)

  rep in pt—Crim Justice (S), 2003 asp 7, s 61(1)(b)(ii)(f); Crim Procedure (Amdt) (S), 2004 asp 5, ss 1(2), 7(6), 25, sch paras 1, 15(e)

s 67 am—Crim Procedure (Amdt) (S), 2004 asp 5, s 25, sch paras 1, 16(a)(i)(ii)(b)(c)

  rep in pt—Crim Procedure (Amdt) (S), 2004 asp 5, s 25, sch paras 1, 16(a)(iii)

s 67A added—Crime and Punishment (S), 1997 c 48, s 57(1)

  rep—Crim Procedure (Amdt) (S), 2004 asp 5, s 25, sch paras 1, 17

s 68 am—Crim Procedure (Amdt) (S), 2004 asp 5, s 25, sch paras 1, 18

s 69 am—Crim Justice (S), 2003 asp 7, s 1(2), sch 1 para 2(1)(2); Crim Procedure (Amdt) (S), 2004 asp 5, s 25, sch paras 1, 19; Crim Proceedings etc (Reform) (S), 2007 asp 6, s 53(1); Wildlife and Natural Environment (S), 2011 asp 6, s 40(3)(a)

s 70 ext—SI 1996/2827, reg 70(4)

  appl—Financial Services and Markets, 2000 c 8, s 403(4)(b); (prosp) Private Security Industry, 2001 c 12, s 23A (added by 2010 c 17, s 42, sch 1 para 10); Gangmasters (Licensing), 2004 c 11, ss 21(4)(b), 22(6)(b); Serious Crime, 2007 c 27, ss 31(6)(b)(ii), 32(5)(b)(ii); SIs 2007/1895, reg 6; 2007/2157, reg 47; 2007/3298, reg 16; Counter-Terrorism, 2008 c 28, s 62, sch 7 para 37(2)(b); Pensions, 2008 c 30, s 47(2)(b)(ii); SIs 2009/216, reg 10; 2009/209, reg 118; 2009/3263, reg 12; 2009/842, reg 28; 2009/261, reg 52; Bribery, 2010 c 23, s 15(2)(b)(iii); SIs 2010/265, reg 7; 2010/740, reg 24; 2014/3085, reg 23(4)(b); 2015/168, regs 11(5), 11(8)(b)(ii); 310, reg 30(6)(b)(ii); 979, reg 8(2)(b); 1945, reg 38(4)(b); 1946, reg 35(4)(b)

  appl (mods)—Political Parties, Elections and Referendums, 2000 c 41, s 153(4); Companies, 2006 c 46, s 1130; Terrorist Asset-Freezing etc, 2010 c 38, s 38(5)(b)(6); SIs 2011/2936, reg 16(2)(c); 2014/195, reg 15(2)(c); 2015/1896, reg 13(2)(c)

  am—SI 2001/1149, art 3(1), sch 1 para 104(1)(2); SSI 2001/128, reg 5, sch 4 para 1; Crim Procedure (Amdt) (S), 2004 asp 5, s 10(6) (see SSI 2004/405); Crim Proceedings etc (Reform) (S), 2007 asp 6, s 28; Crim Justice and Licensing (S), 2010 asp 13, s 66(1)-(12); Partnerships (Prosecution) (S), 2013 c 21, s 6(4)

s 70A added—Crim Justice and Licensing (S), 2010 asp 13, s 124(3)

s 71 am—Sexual Offences (Procedure and Evidence) (S), 2002 asp 9, ss 3, 8(2) sch, paras 1, 5; Vulnerable Witnesses (S), 2004 asp 3, s 2(1); (pt prosp) ibid, s 7(1)(a)(i)(iii)(b)(c); Crim Procedure (Amdt) (S), 2004 asp 5, ss 14(1), 19, 25, sch paras 1, 20(a); SSI 2005/40, art 4(1)(3); Crim Justice and Licensing (S), 2010 asp 13, s 203, sch 7 paras 25, 45; Victims and Witnesses (S), 2014 asp 1, s 11(1)

  rep in pt—(pt prosp) Vulnerable Witnesses (S), 2004 asp 3, s 7(1)(a)(ii); Crim Procedure (Amdt) (S), 2004 asp 5, s 25, sch paras 1, 20(b); Crim Proceedings etc (Reform) (S), 2007 asp 6, s 80, sch para 12(2)

s 71A rep—Crim Procedure (Amdt) (S), 2004 asp 5, s 25, sch paras 1, 21

ss 72, 72A, 73, 73A replaced (by ss 72, 72A-72D))—Crim Procedure (Amdt) (S), 2004 asp 5, s 1(3)

s 72 am—Victims and Witnesses (S), 2014 asp 1, s 11(2)

s 72A am—(pt prosp) Vulnerable Witnesses (S), 2004 asp 3, s 7(3)

s 72E added—Crim Procedure (Amdt) (S), 2004 asp 5, s 2

s 72F added—Crim Procedure (Amdt) (S), 2004 asp 5, s 8

  am—Crim Proceedings etc (Reform) (S), 2007 asp 6, s 80, sch para 13

1995
c 46 *continued*

s 72G added—Crim Procedure (Amdt) (S), 2004 asp 5, s 12
    am—Crim Proceedings etc (Reform) (S), 2007 asp 6, s 80, sch para 13
s 73 am—Sexual Offences (Procedure and Evidence) (S), 2002 asp 9, s 8(4); (prosp)
    Vulnerable Witnesses (S), 2004 asp 3, s 2(2)
s 73A added (prosp)—Vulnerable Witnesses (S), 2004 asp 3, s 2(3)
s 74 rep in pt—Crime and Punishment (S), 1997 c 48, s 62(1)(2), sch 1 para 21(10)(a),
    sch 3
    am—Crime and Punishment (S), 1997 c 48, s 62(1), sch 1 para 21(10)(b); Vulnerable
    Witnesses (S), 2004 asp 3, s 2(4); Crim Procedure (Amdt) (S), 2004 asp 5, ss 3,
    25, sch paras 1, 22; Crim Justice and Licensing (S), 2010 asp 13, s 72(2)
s 75 rep in pt—Crim Procedure (Amdt) (S), 2004 asp 5, s 25, sch paras 1, 23
s 75A added—Crim Procedure (Amdt) (S), 2004 asp 5, s 15
s 75B added—Crim Proceedings etc (Reform) (S), 2007 asp 6, s 39(1)
    am—SSI 2011/430, s 2(3)
s 75C added—SSI 2011/430, s 2(2)
s 76 am—Crim Procedure (Amdt) (S), 2004 asp 5, s 25, sch paras 1, 24
s 78 am—Sexual Offences (Procedure and Evidence) (S), 2002 asp 9, s 6(1); Crim
    Procedure (Amdt) (S), 2004 asp 5, s 25, sch paras 1, 25(b)-(d); Crim Justice and
    Licensing (S), 2010 asp 13, ss 124(4), 203, sch 7 paras 25, 46
    rep in pt—Crim Procedure (Amdt) (S), 2004 asp 5, s 25, sch paras 1, 25(a)
s 79 subst—Crim Procedure (Amdt) (S), 2004 asp 5, s 13(1)
    am —Antisocial Behaviour etc (S), 2004 asp 8, s 144(1), sch 4 para 5(1)(2); Crim
    Proceedings etc (Reform) (S), 2007 asp 6, s 80, sch para 14; Crim Justice and
    Licensing (S), 2010 asp 13, ss 90(2)(a), 203, sch 7 paras 25, 47
s 79A added—Crim Procedure (Amdt) (S), 2004 asp 5, s 14(2)
s 80 rep—Crim Procedure (Amdt) (S), 2004 asp 5, s 25, sch paras 1, 26
s 81 subst—Crim Procedure (Amdt) (S), 2004 asp 5, s 9
s 82 am—Crim Procedure (Amdt) (S), 2004 asp 5, s 25, sch paras 1, 27
s 83 am—Crime and Punishment (S), 1997 c 48, s 62(1), sch 1 para 21(12); Crim Justice
    (S), 2003 asp 7, s 58(1); Crim Procedure (Amdt) (S), 2004 asp 5, s 25, sch paras
    1, 28(a)(i)(b)(i)(c)
    rep in pt—Crim Procedure (Amdt) (S), 2004 asp 5, s 25, sch paras 1, 28(a)(ii)(b)(ii)(d)
s 83A added—Crim Procedure (Amdt) (S), 2004 asp 5, s 5
s 84 rep in pt—Crim Procedure (Amdt) (S), 2004 asp 5, s 25, sch paras 1, 29(a)(ii)(b)(ii)(c);
    Crim Justice and Licensing (S), 2010 asp 13, s 93(2)(d)
    am—Crim Procedure (Amdt) (S), 2004 asp 5, s 25, sch paras 1, 29(a)(i)(b)(i)(iii)(iv);
    Crim Justice and Licensing (S), 2010 asp 13, s 93(2)(a)-(c)
s 85 rep in pt—Crime and Punishment (S), 1997 c 48, ss 58(2),62(2), sch 3; Crim Justice
    and Licensing (S), 2010 asp 13, s 93(3)(b); Courts Reform (S), 2014 asp 18,
    sch 5 para 44
    am—Crime and Punishment (S), 1997 c 48, s 58(3); Crim Procedure (Amdt) (S), 2004
    asp 5, s 25, sch paras 1, 30; Crim Proceedings etc (Reform) (S), 2007 asp 6, s 29;
    Crim Justice and Licensing (S), 2010 asp 13, s 203, sch 7 paras 25, 48; ibid, s
    93(3)(a)(b)
s 87 am—Crim Procedure (Amdt) (S), 2004 asp 5, s 25, sch paras 1, 31
s 87A added—Crim Procedure (Amdt) (S), 2004 asp 5, s 13(2)
s 88 excl—SI 1996/513, sch 2 rule 141A(1)
ss 90A-90E added (pt prosp)—Crim Procedure (Amdt) (S), 2004 asp 5, s 11
s 90A rep in pt—Crim Proceedings etc (Reform) (S), 2007 asp 6, s 80, sch para 15(1)
s 90B am—Crim Proceedings etc (Reform) (S), 2007 asp 6, s 27(1)
s 90C am—Crim Proceedings etc (Reform) (S), 2007 asp 6, s 27(2)
s 90D am—Crim Proceedings etc (Reform) (S), 2007 asp 6, ss 27(3), 80, sch para 15(2);
    Crim Justice and Licensing (S), 2010 asp 13, s 203, sch 7 paras 25, 49
s 90E am—Crim Proceedings etc (Reform) (S), 2007 asp 6, s 80, sch para 15(3)
s 92 am—Crim Procedure (Amdt) (S), 2004 asp 5, s 10(1)(3)(4)
    rep in pt—Crim Procedure (Amdt) (S), 2004 asp 5, s 10(2)
s 93 appl—Crim Justice (S), 2003 asp 7, s 21(6)
s 94 am—Crim Justice (S), 2003 asp 7, s 65; Double Jeopardy (S), 2011 asp 16, sch para 7;
    (with trantl provns) SSI 2012/272, paras 2, 3
ss 97A-97D added—Crim Justice and Licensing (S), 2010 asp 13, s 73
s 99 am—Crim Justice (S), 2003 asp 7, s 79
s 101 rep in pt—Crime and Punishment (S), 1997 c 48, ss 31,62(2), sch 3

1995

c 46 s 101 *continued*

    am—Sexual Offences (Procedure and Evidence) (S), 2002 asp 9, s 10(1); Crim Justice (S), 2003 asp 7, s 1(2), sch 1 para 2(1)(3); ibid, s 57(1)(2); Crim Proceedings etc (Reform) (S), 2007 asp 6, s 53(2); Wildlife and Natural Environment (S), 2011 asp 6, s 40(3)(b)

s 101A added—Crim Justice and Licensing (S), 2010 asp 13, s 70(1)

s 102A added—Crim Proceedings etc (Reform) (S), 2007 asp 6, s 32

    am—SSI 2008/109, art 2; Crim Justice and Licensing (S), 2010 asp 13, s 203, sch 7 paras 25, 50

s 103 am—Crime and Punishment (S), 1997 c 48, s 62(1), sch 1 para 21(13); Crim Justice (S), 2003 asp 7, s 66(1)(2)

s 104 rep in pt—Crime and Punishment (S), 1997 c 48, s 62(1)(2), sch 1 para 21(14), sch 3

    am—Crim Justice and Licensing (S), 2010 asp 13, s 75

s 105 am—Crim Justice (S), 2003 asp 7, s 66(1)(3)

s 105A added—Crim Justice (S), 2003 asp 7, s 66(1)(4)

s 106 am—Proceeds of Crime (S), 1995 c 43, s 10(4);Crime and Punishment (S), 1997 c 48, s 17(1) 19(1),23(b); Crime and Disorder, 1998 c 37, s 94(2), sch 6 pt II para 5; (retrosp) ibid, s 119, sch 8 para 119; Protection of Children (S), 2003 asp 5, s 16(1)(2); Crim Justice (S), 2003 asp 7, s 1(2), sch 1 para 2(1)(4); Crim Justice and Licensing (S), 2010 asp 13, s 14, sch 2 para 7

    ext—Terrorism, 2000 c 11, ss 7(4)(b),8(1)(c)(ii); Terrorism Prevention and Investigation Measures, 2011 c 23, sch 3 para 4(3)(c)

    rep in pt—Protection of Vulnerable Groups (S), 2007 asp 14, s 88, sch 4 paras 13, 14

    appl—Counter-Terrorism and Security, 2015 c 6, sch 4 para 4(3)(c)

s 106A added (pt prosp)—Crime and Punishment (S), 1997 c 48, s 19(1)

s 107 am—Crime and Punishment (S), 1997 c 48, s 62(1), sch 1 para 21(15); Crim Justice (S), 2003 asp 7, s 62; Crim Proceedings etc (Reform) (S), 2007 asp 6, s 80, sch para 16(1); Double Jeopardy (S), 2011 asp 16, sch para 8

    appl (mods)—SSI 2002/387, para 3(1)(4)

ss 107A-107F added—Crim Justice and Licensing (S), 2010 asp 13, s 74

s 108 subst—Crime and Punishment (S), 1997 c 48, s 21(1)

    am—Crime and Disorder, 1998 c 37, s 94(2), sch 6 pt II para 6(2)(3); Proceeds of Crime, 2002 c 29, s 115(1)-(4); Crim Justice and Licensing (S), 2010 asp 13, s 14, sch 2 para 8(b); ibid, s 6(7); Regulatory Reform (S), 2014 asp 3, s 44(2); (1.3.2016) Serious Crime, 2015 c 9, s 17(2); (1.3.2016) ibid, sch 4 para 14

    rep in pt—Crim Justice and Licensing (S), 2010 asp 13, s 14, sch 2 para 8(a)

s 108A added—Crime and Punishment (S), 1997 c 48, s 18(2)

    am—(retrosp) Crime and Disorder, 1998 c 37, s 119, sch 8 para 120

s 109 restr—Proceeds of Crime (S), 1995 c 43, s 10(4)

    mod—Proceeds of Crime, 2002 c 29, s 100(6)

    am—Proceeds of Crime, 2002 c 29, s 456, sch 11, para 29(1)(2); Double Jeopardy (S), 2011 asp 16, sch para 9

s 110 am—Crime and Punishment (S), 1997 c 48, s 19(2); SSI 2002/387, para 2; Crim Procedure (Amdt) (S), 2004 asp 5, s 24(2); Crim Proceedings etc (Reform) (S), 2007 asp 6, s 80, sch para 16(2); Crim Justice and Licensing (S), 2010 asp 13, s 76(1); Double Jeopardy (S), 2011 asp 16, sch para 10

    rep in pt—Protection of Vulnerable Groups (S), 2007 asp 14, s 88, sch 4 paras 13, 15

s 111 am—Crim Procedure (Amdt) (S), 2004 asp 5, s 24(3); Crim Procedure (Legal Assistance, Detention and Appeals) (S), 2010 asp 15, s 5(2)

    rep in pt—Protection of Vulnerable Groups (S), 2007 asp 14, s 88, sch 4 paras 13, 16

s 112 am—Crime and Punishment (S), 1997 c 48, s 18(3); SI 1999/1042, art 3, sch 1 pt I para 13(2); Crim Justice (S), 2003 asp 7, s 66(1)(5); Scotland, 2012 c 11, s 36(10)

    rep in pt—Crim Proceedings etc (Reform) (S), 2007 asp 6, s 80, sch para 16(3)

s 113 am—Crime and Punishment (S), 1997 c 48, s 62(1), sch 1 para 21(16); Crim Justice and Licensing (S), 2010 asp 13, s 76(2); Double Jeopardy (S), 2011 asp 16, sch para 11(a)-(c)

    saving—(transtl provn) SI 1999/652, art 3(1)

    appl—SI 1996/513, rule 15.15(3)

s 113A added—Crim Justice and Licensing (S), 2010 asp 13, s 76(3)

s 114 am—SSI 2003/387 para 2(1)(2)(3)(a)

s 115 am—SSI 2003/387 para 2(1)(2)(3)(a)

    rep in pt—SSI 2003/387 para 2(1)(3)(b)

1995
c 46 *continued*

s 116 am—Crime and Punishment (S), 1997 c 48, s 18(4); Protection of Children (S), 2003
asp 5, s 16(1)(3); Crim Proceedings etc (Reform) (S), 2007 asp 6, s 80, sch para
16(4); Protection of Vulnerable Groups (S), 2007 asp 14, s 88, sch 4 paras 13,
17

s 118 am—Crime and Punishment (S), 1997 c 48, ss 18(5)(a)(b), s 62(1), sch 1
para 21(17)(b); Protection of Children (S), 2003 asp 5, s 16(1)(4); Mental
Health (Care and Treatment) (S), 2003 asp 13, s 331(1), sch 4 para 8(1)(11);
Crim Proceedings etc (Reform) (S), 2007 asp 6, s 80, sch para 16(5)(6);
Protection of Vulnerable Groups (S), 2007 asp 14, s 88, sch 4 paras 13, 18; Crim
Justice and Licensing (S), 2010 asp 13, ss 14, 203, sch 2 para 9, sch 7 paras 25,
51(a)(b); Double Jeopardy (S), 2011 asp 16, sch para 12

    rep in pt—Crime and Punishment (S), 1997 c 48, s 62(1)(2), sch 1 para 21(17)(a),
sch 3; (retrosp) Crime and Disorder, 1998 c 37, ss 119,120(2), sch 8 para 121,
sch 10

s 119 am—Crim Procedure (Amdt) (S), 2004 asp 5, s 25, sch paras 1, 32; Crim Justice and
Licensing (S), 2010 asp 13, s 76(4)(a)-(d)

s 121 am—Crime and Punishment (S), 1997 c 48, s 18(6); SI 1999/1042, art 3, sch 1 pt I
para 13(3); Scotland, 2012 c 11, s 36(10)

    excl—Double Jeopardy (S), 2011 asp 16, s 11(9)

s 121A added—Crime and Punishment (S), 1997 c 48, s 24(1)

    am—SI 1999/1042, art 3, sch 1 pt I para 13(4); Protection of Children (S), 2003 asp
5, s 16(1)(5); Crim Justice and Licensing (S), 2010 asp 13, s 14, sch 2 paras 1,
10; Scotland, 2012 c 11, s 36(10)

    rep in pt—Protection of Vulnerable Groups (S), 2007 asp 14, s 88, sch 4 paras 13,
19

s 122 am—SI 1999/1042, art 3, sch 1 pt I para 13(5); Scotland, 2012 c 11, s 36(10)

s 124 am—Crime and Punishment (S), 1997 c 48, s 62(1), sch 1 para 21(18)(a)(b);
SI 1999/1042, art 3, sch 1 pt I para 13(6); Scotland, 2012 c 11, s 36(11)

    rep in pt—Crime and Punishment (S), 1997 c 48, s 62(1)(2), sch 1 para 21(18)(c),
sch 3

s 125 am—Crime and Punishment (S), 1997 c 48, s 18(7)

s 126 am—Crime and Punishment (S), 1997 c 48, s 18(8)

s 130 rep—Crim Justice and Licensing (S), 2010 asp 13, s 86(2)

s 134 transtl provns—SSIs 2008/328, art 6; 2008/363, art 6

s 135 excl—Terrorism, 2000 c 11, s 41(2), sch 8 pt II para 27(4)(a)

    am—Crim Proceedings etc (Reform) (S), 2007 asp 6, ss 7(3), 80, sch para 17

s 136 appl—Water (Scotland) 1980 c 45, s 72(3C); Crim Justice, 1993 c 36, s 61A(3));
SIs 1996/1500, reg 16(5); 1996/2005, reg 11(4); 1996/2999, reg 11(4); (S)
SI 1998/955, reg 8(4); Nat Minimum Wage, 1998 c 39, s 33(5)(b);
SI 1999/3315, reg 8(5); SSI 1999/186, reg 8(6); SSIs 2000/418, reg 21(2);
2000/448, reg 14; 2001/300, reg 17(4); 2001/40, reg 11(4); 2001/140,
reg 16(5); 2001/208, 14(4); 2001/220, reg 11(4); 2001/225, reg 14(2);
2002/139, reg 20(2); 2002/278, reg 15(4); 2002/3026, reg 30(2C);
Communications, 2003 c 21, s 127(6); SI 2003/129, reg 22(2); Civil
Partnership, 2004 c 33, s 100(5); SSIs 2004/70, reg 21(2); 2004/520, reg
19A(5); Smoking, Health and Social Care (S), 2005 asp 13, s 5(2); SIs
2005/218, reg 12(10); 1259, art 10(3); 1803, reg 41(3); SSI 2006/319, art 10;
SI 2006/2657, art 14; Companies, 2006 c 46, s 1128; SIs 2007/281, art 13;
2007/1374, reg 13; Counter-Terrorism, 2008 c 28, s 62, sch 7 para 35(2);
Planning, 2008 c 29, s 58 (as mod (S) ibid, sch 12 para 9(b)); SI 2008/1277,
reg 14; SSIs 2008/64, reg 12; 2008/66, reg 23; 2008/159, reg 21; SIs
2009/847, reg 14, 886, art 12, 1495, reg 21, 1747, art 22, 3263, reg 10;
Terrorist Asset-Freezing etc, 2010 c 38, s 36(2)(b); SI 2010/1197, reg 1; SSI
2010/273, reg 21; SIs 2011/548, art 20 (added by SI 2011/605, art 15(3)(b)),
605, 1086, reg 15(3)(b), 1094, reg 15(3)(b), 1129, reg 15(3)(b), 1244, reg
15(3)(b), 1893, reg 15(3)(b), 2742, reg 15(3)(b); SSI 2011/416, sch 2 para
9(2); 2012/925, reg 22(3)(b); 1017, reg 71(3); 1102, reg 7(5); 1301, reg
14(3)(b); 1507, reg 14(3)(b); 1508, reg 14(3)(b); 1509, reg 14(3)(b); 1511, reg
14(3)(b); 1515, reg 14(3)(b); 1516, reg 14(3)(b); 1517, reg 14(3)(b); 1916, reg
339(2); 3032, reg 42(2)(b); Energy, 2013 c 32, sch 10 para 4(3)(c); SIs
2013/164, reg 14(3)(b), 1478, reg 22(2)(b), 1877, reg 17(3)(b); 2014/195, reg
13(4), 507, reg 13(3)(b), 587, reg 13(3)(b), 693, reg 13(3)(b), 1826, reg
13(3)(b), 1827, reg 13(3)(b), 2054, reg 7(3)(b), 3349, reg 13(5)(b); (prosp) Air

1995
c 46 *continued*

Weapons and Licensing (S), 2015 asp 10, s 32; SIs 2015/821, reg 16(8); 1361, reg 13(5)(b); 1553, reg 66(2)(b); 1740, reg 13(5)(b); 1896, reg 11(7); SSI 2015/359, reg 16(6)

excl—Nat Minimum Wage, 1998 c 39, s 33(4); SI 1999/1516, reg 9(5); Political Parties, Elections and Referendums, 2000 c 41, s 151(3); SIs 2001/947, art 16(8); 3365, art 10(6); 2002/111, art 20(9); 2628, art 16(8); 2003/1519, art 20(8); 2004/348, art 15(8); 2005/253, art 9(8); 281, reg 93; 1803, reg 41(2); 2008/1277, reg 14; 2009/886, art 12; 2009/1749, art 14(7); 2012/1017, reg 71(2); 2012/1102, reg 7(4); S Independence Referendum, 2013 asp 14, s 15(2); SI 2014/1615, reg 9(3)

ext—Crim Law (Consolidation) (S), 1995 c 39, s 4(3); SI 1999/1110, reg 7(6); SSI 2001/50, reg 18(2)

mod—Architects, 1997 c 22, s 21(4)(c); (saving) SI 2008/1276, reg 10

s 136A added—Crim Proceedings etc (Reform) (S), 2007 asp 6, s 23
    am—Crim Justice and Licensing (S), 2010 asp 13, s 203, sch 7 paras 25, 52(a)(b)
s 136B added—Crim Proceedings etc (Reform) (S), 2007 asp 6, s 54
s 137 transtl provns —SSIs 2008/328, art 6; 2008/363, art 6
s 137ZA added—Crim Proceedings etc (Reform) (S), 2007 asp 6, s 39(2)
    transtl provns—SSIs 2008/328, art 6; 2008/363, art 6
    am—SSI 2011/430, s 2(5)
s 137ZB added—SSI 2011/430, s 2(4)
ss 137A, 137B added—Crim Justice (S), 2003 asp 7, s 58(2)
s 137A am—Crim Proceedings etc (Reform) (S), 2007 asp 6, s 22(1)
s 137B am—Crim Proceedings etc (Reform) (S), 2007 asp 6, s 22(2); Crim Justice and Licensing (S), 2010 asp 13, s 203, sch 7 paras 25, 53
s 137C added—Crim Proceedings etc (Reform) (S), 2007 asp 6, s 22(3)
ss 137CA-137CC added—Crim Justice and Licensing (S), 2010 asp 13, s 61
s 137D added—Crim Proceedings etc (Reform) (S), 2007 asp 6, s 22(3)
s 137D appl—SSI 2007/480, art 4
s 140 am—Crime and Punishment (S), 1997 c 48, s 57(2)(a); Sexual Offences (Procedure and Evidence) (S), 2002 asp 9, s 3, sch, paras 1, 8; Crim Justice (S), 2003 asp 7, ss 61(2), 85, sch 4 para 3(1)(2); Crim Proceedings etc (Reform) (S), 2007 asp 6, s 35(2); Crim Justice and Licensing (S), 2010 asp 13, s 203, sch 7 paras 25, 54(a)(b)
    rep in pt—Crime and Punishment (S), 1997 c 48, ss 57(2)(b),62(2), sch 3; Crim Procedure (Amdt) (S), 2004 asp 5, s 25, sch paras 1, 33
s 141 rep in pt—Crime and Punishment (S), 1997 c 48, s 62(1)(2), sch 1 para 21(19)(a)(i), sch 3
    am—Crime and Punishment (S), 1997 c 48, s 62(1), sch 1 para 21(19)(a)(b); SSI 2001/128, reg 5, sch 4, para 2; Crim Justice (S), 2003 asp 7, s 61(3); Crim Proceedings etc (Reform) (S), 2007 asp 6, ss 8, 14(1); Crim Justice and Licensing (S), 2010 asp 13, s 68; Partnerships (Prosecution) (S), 2013 c 21, s 6(5)(a)(c)
s 141A added—Crim Justice and Licensing (S), 2010 asp 13, s 195(3)
s 143 am—SSI 2001/128, reg 5, sch 4, para 3; Crim Proceedings etc (Reform) (S), 2007 asp 6, s 17; Crim Justice and Licensing (S), 2010 asp 13, s 67(1)-(7)
    appl—(prosp) Private Security Industry, 2001 c 12, s 23A (added by 2010 c 17, s 42, sch 1 para 10); Gangmasters (Licensing), 2004 c 11,ss 21(4)(b), 22(6)(b); Companies, 2006 c 46, s 1130; Serious Crime, 2007 c 27, ss 31(6)(b)(ii), 32(5)(b)(ii); SIs 2009/3263, reg 12; 2010/740, reg 24; 2014/3085, reg 23(4)(b)
    appl (mods)—SIs 2011/2936, reg 16(2)(c); 2014/195, reg 15(2)(c); 2015/1896, reg 13(2)(c); 1945, reg 38(4)(b); 1946, reg 35(4)(b)
s 144 am—Sexual Offences (Procedure and Evidence) (S), 2002 asp 9, s 3, sch, paras 1, 9; Crim Justice (S), 2003 asp 7, ss 63(1)(2), 85, sch 4 para 3(1)(2); Crim Proceedings etc (Reform) (S), 2007 asp 6, s 9(1); Adult Support and Protection (S), 2007 asp 10, s 75(a); Crim Justice and Licensing (S), 2010 asp 13, s 203, sch 7 paras 25, 55
s 145 am—Crim Justice (S), 2003 asp 7, s 63(1)(3)
s 145ZA added—Adult Support and Protection (S), 2007 asp 10, s 75(b)
s 145A added—Crim Justice (S), 2003 asp 7, s 63(1)(4)
    am—Crim Proceedings etc (Reform) (S), 2007 asp 6, ss 9(2), 14(2)

1995
c 46 *continued*

s 146 am—Sexual Offences (Procedure and Evidence) (S), 2002 asp 9, s 3, sch, paras 1, 10;
    Crim Justice (S), 2003 asp 7, s 85, sch 4 para 3(1)(2); Crim Proceedings etc
    (Reform) (S), 2007 asp 6, s 10; Crim Justice and Licensing (S), 2010 asp 13, s
    203, sch 7 paras 25, 56
s 147 appl (mods)—SI 1997/1776, art 2, sch 1 paras 5-7
    mod—Crime (Sentences), 1997 c 43, s 41, sch 1 pt II para 11(1)(a)
    ext—Crime (Sentences), 1997 c 43, s 41, sch 1 pt II para 10(1)
    am—Crim Proceedings etc (Reform) (S), 2007 asp 6, s 11; SSI 2015/338, sch 2 para
        5(4)
    appl—Double Jeopardy (S), 2011 asp 16, s 6(7)(8)(b)
s 148 am—(retrosp) Crim Procedure (Intermediate Diets) (S), 1998 c 10, s 1(1)(2); Sexual
    Offences (Procedure and Evidence) (S), 2002 asp 9, s 8(5); Vulnerable
    Witnesses (S), 2004 asp 3, s 2(5); Crim Proceedings etc (Reform) (S), 2007 asp
    6, s 18; Crim Justice and Licensing (S), 2010 asp 13, s 90(2)(b); SSI 2014/242,
    para 2(2)
s 148A added—Sexual Offences (Procedure and Evidence) (S), 2002 asp 9, s 3, sch, paras 1,
    11
s 148B added—Vulnerable Witnesses (S), 2004 asp 3, s 9
ss 148C, 148D added—Crim Proceedings etc (Reform) (S), 2007 asp 6, s 21
s 149 subst—Crim Proceedings etc (Reform) (S), 2007 asp 6, s 19
s 149A added—Sexual Offences (Procedure and Evidence) (S), 2002 asp 9, s 6(2)
    subst—Crim Proceedings etc (Reform) (S), 2007 asp 6, s 19
s 149B added—Crim Proceedings etc (Reform) (S), 2007 asp 6, s 19
    am—Crim Justice and Licensing (S), 2010 asp 13, s 125(7)
s 150 am—SI 2001/1149, art 3(1), sch 1 para 104(1)(3); (retrosp) Crim Procedure (Amdt)
    (S), 2002 asp 4, s 1(1)(2)(4); Sexual Offences (Procedure and Evidence) (S),
    2002 asp 9, s 3, sch, paras 1, 12; Crim Proceedings etc (Reform) (S), 2007 asp 6,
    s 80, sch para 26(g); ibid, ss 14(3), 15; Crim Justice and Licensing (S), 2010 asp
    13, s 62(2)
s 150A added—Crim Proceedings etc (Reform) (S), 2007 asp 6, s 14(4)
s 152A added—Crim Proceedings etc (Reform) (S), 2007 asp 6, s 13
s 153 am—Crim Proceedings etc (Reform) (S), 2007 asp 6, s 14(5)
s 154 rep—Crime and Punishment (S), 1997 c 48, ss 28(1),62(2), sch 3
s 156 subst—Crim Proceedings etc (Reform) (S), 2007 asp 6, s 16
ss 156A-156D added—Crim Proceedings etc (Reform) (S), 2007 asp 6, s 16
s 156B appl—SSI 2007/480, art 4
s 156D am—SSI 2015/338, sch 2 para 5(5)(a)-(c)
s 157 am—Sexual Offences (Procedure and Evidence) (S), 2002 asp 9, s 8(6)
s 166 am—Sexual Offences (Procedure and Evidence) (S), 2002 asp 9, s 10(2); Crim
    Proceedings etc (Reform) (S), 2007 asp 6, s 53(3); Wildlife and Natural
    Environment (S), 2011 asp 6, s 40(3)(c)
    rep in pt—Crim Proceedings etc (Reform) (S), 2007 asp 6, s 12(1)
s 166A added—Crim Proceedings etc (Reform) (S), 2007 asp 6, s 12(2)
    subst—Crim Justice and Licensing (S), 2010 asp 13, s 70(2)
s 166B added—Crim Proceedings etc (Reform) (S), 2007 asp 6, s 12(2)
s 167 am—Crime and Disorder, 1998 c 37, s 119, sch 8 para 122; Crim Justice (S), 2003
    asp 7, s 26(2); (prosp) Custodial Sentences and Weapons (S), 2007 asp 17, s 66,
    sch 4 para 1; (prosp) Crim Justice and Licensing (S), 2010 asp 13, s 18, sch 3
    paras 15, 16(1)-(3)
    rep in pt—(prosp) Custodial Sentences and Weapons (S), 2007 asp 17, s 66, sch 5
s 169 rep—Crim Justice and Licensing (S), 2010 asp 13, s 16(2)
Pt 10 (ss 173-194) excl—Terrorism, 2000 c 11, ss 7(7)(b),8(1)(f)(ii)
    ext—Terrorism Prevention and Investigation Measures, 2011 c 23, sch 3 para 4(4)(e)
    appl—Counter-Terrorism and Security, 2015 c 6, sch 4 para 4(4)(e)
s 173 am—Protection of Children (S), 2003 asp 5, s 16(1)(6); Crim Justice and Licensing
    (S), 2010 asp 13, s 14, sch 2 para 11; Courts Reform (S), 2014 asp 18, sch 3
    para 2
    rep in pt—Protection of Vulnerable Groups (S), 2007 asp 14, s 88, sch 4 paras 13, 20
s 174 am—Crim Justice and Licensing (S), 2010 asp 13, s 72(3); Courts Reform (S), 2014
    asp 18, sch 3 para 3
s 175 am—Crime and Punishment (S), 1997 c 48, ss 17(2),21(2),23(c); Crime and Disorder,
    1998 c 37, s 94(2), sch 6 pt II para 7(2)(3)(4); Proceeds of Crime, 2002 c 29, s
    115(5)-(8); Protection of Children (S), 2003 asp 5, s 16(1)(7)(b)-(f); Protection

1995
c 46 *continued*

of Vulnerable Groups (S), 2007 asp 14, s 88, sch 4 paras 13, 21; Crim Justice
and Licensing (S), 2010 asp 13, s 14, sch 2 para 12(a)(i)(ii)(c); ibid, s 6(8);
Courts Reform (S), 2014 asp 18, sch 3 para 4; Regulatory Reform (S), 2014 asp
3, s 44(3); (1.3.2016) Serious Crime, 2015 c 9, sch 4 paras 15(2)(3), 17(3)

rep in pt—Crime and Disorder, 1998 c 37, ss 119,120(2), sch 8 para 123, sch 10;
Protection of Children (S), 2003 asp 5, s 16(1)(7)(a); Crim Justice and
Licensing (S), 2010 asp 13, s 14, sch 2 para 12(b)

s 175A added —Courts Reform (S), 2014 asp 18, s 120

s 176 mod—Proceeds of Crime, 2002 c 29, s 100(8)

am—Courts Reform (S), 2014 asp 18, sch 3 para 5

s 176A added—Double Jeopardy (S), 2011 asp 16, sch para 13

s 177 am—SI 1999/1042, art 3, sch 1 pt I para 13(7); Crim Proceedings etc (Reform) (S),
2007 asp 6, s 6(3); Scotland, 2012 c 11, s 36(10); Courts Reform (S), 2014 asp
18, sch 3 para 6(2)(3)

ext—International Crim Court, 2001 c 17, s 10(6)

rep in pt—Crim Proceedings etc (Reform) (S), 2007 asp 6, s 80, sch para 18(1)

s 178 am —Crim Proceedings etc (Reform) (S), 2007 asp 6, s 80, sch para 26(h); Double
Jeopardy (S), 2011 asp 16, sch para 14; Courts Reform (S), 2014 asp 18, sch 3
para 7

s 179 rep in pt—Crime and Punishment (S), 1997 c 48, s 62(1)(2), sch 1 para 21(20), sch 3
am—SSI 2009/108; Double Jeopardy (S), 2011 asp 16, sch para 15; Courts Reform
(S), 2014 asp 18, sch 3 para 8

excl in pt—Police, Public Order and Crim Justice, 2006 asp 10, s 96A(5)

s 180 am—Crim Proceedings etc (Reform) (S), 2007 asp 6, ss 25(1), 80, sch para 18(2);
Courts Reform (S), 2014 asp 18, sch 3 para 9

excl in pt—Police, Public Order and Crim Justice, 2006 asp 10, s 96A(5)

s 181 am—Crim Procedure (Amdt) (S), 2004 asp 5, s 24(4); Crim Procedure (Legal
Assistance, Detention and Appeals) (S), 2010 asp 15, s 5(3); (pt prosp) Courts
Reform (S), 2014 asp 18, sch 3 para 10

rep in pt—Protection of Vulnerable Groups (S), 2007 asp 14, s 88, sch 4 paras 13, 22

s 182 appl—Registered Designs, 1949 c 88 s 35ZD(10); Telecommunications, 1984 c 12,
s 81(8); SIs 1997/831, reg 19(1)-(4), sch 15 para 5(8); 2005/281, reg 98(8);
1803, reg 19(7); 2008/1597, reg 20, sch 5; 2013/1387, reg 9(9)

am—Courts Reform (S), 2014 asp 18, sch 3 para 11

rep in pt—Crime and Punishment (S), 1997 c 48, s 62(1)(2), sch 1 para 21(21), sch 3

ext—SI 2001/1701, reg 17, sch 13 para 14(8); Copyright, Designs and Patents, 1988
c 48, ss 114B(10), 297D(10)

s 183 am—Double Jeopardy (S), 2011 asp 16, sch para 16; Courts Reform (S), 2014 asp 18,
sch 3 para 12

s 184 am—Courts Reform (S), 2014 asp 18, sch 3 para 13

s 185 am—Courts Reform (S), 2014 asp 18, sch 3 para 14

s 186 am—Bail, Judicial Appointments etc (S), asp 9, s 12, sch para 7(4); Protection of
Children (S), 2003 asp 5, s 16(1)(8)(9); Crim Procedure (Amdt) (S), 2004 asp 5,
s 24(5)(b); Crim Proceedings etc (Reform) (S), 2007 asp 6, s 25(2); Protection of
Vulnerable Groups (S), 2007 asp 14, s 88, sch 4 paras 13, 23; Crim Justice and
Licensing (S), 2010 asp 13, s 14, sch 2 para 13; Courts Reform (S), 2014 asp 18,
sch 3 para 15

rep in pt—Crim Procedure (Amdt) (S), 2004 asp 5, s 24(5)(a)

excl in pt—Police, Public Order and Crim Justice, 2006 asp 10, s 96A(5)

s 187 am—Protection of Children (S), 2003 asp 5, s 16(1)(8)(9); Crim Proceedings etc
(Reform) (S), 2007 asp 6, s 25(3); ibid, s 80, sch para 18(3); Crim Justice and
Licensing (S), 2010 asp 13, s 14, sch 2 para 14; Courts Reform (S), 2014 asp 18,
sch 3 para 16

rep in pt—Protection of Vulnerable Groups (S), 2007 asp 14, s 88, sch 4 paras 13, 24

excl in pt—Police, Public Order and Crim Justice, 2006 asp 10, s 96A(5)

s 188 am—Courts Reform (S), 2014 asp 18, sch 3 para 17

s 189 rep in pt—Crime and Punishment (S), 1997 c 48, s 62(1)(2), sch 1 para 21(22), sch 3;
Protection of Vulnerable Groups (S), 2007 asp 14, s 88, sch 4 paras 13, 25

am—Protection of Children (S), 2003 asp 5, s 16(1)(10); Crim Justice and Licensing
(S), 2010 asp 13, s 14, sch 2 para 15; Courts Reform (S), 2014 asp 18, sch 3
para 18

1995
c 46 *continued*

s 190 am—Mental Health (Care and Treatment) (S), 2003 asp 13, s 331(1), sch 4
para 8(1)(12); Crim Justice and Licensing (S), 2010 asp 13, s 203, sch 7 paras
25, 57, 58(a)(b); Courts Reform (S), 2014 asp 18, sch 3 para 19
s 191 am—Courts Reform (S), 2014 asp 18, sch 3 para 20
s 191A added—Crim Procedure (Legal Assistance, Detention and Appeals) (S), 2010 asp 15,
s 6
am—Courts Reform (S), 2014 asp 18, sch 3 para 21
s 191B am—(prosp) Courts Reform (S), 2014 asp 18, sch 3 para 22
s 192 am—Courts Reform (S), 2014 asp 18, sch 3 para 23
s 193 excl—Double Jeopardy (S), 2011 asp 16, s 11(9)
s 193A added—Crime and Punishment (S), 1997 c 48, s 24(2)
am—Protection of Children (S), 2003 asp 5, s 16(1)(11); Antisocial Behaviour etc
(S), 2004 asp 8, s 144(1), sch 4 para 5(1)(3); Crim Justice and Licensing (S),
2010 asp 13, s 14, sch 2 para 16(a); Courts Reform (S), 2014 asp 18, sch 3
para 24
rep in pt—Protection of Vulnerable Groups (S), 2007 asp 14, s 88, sch 4 paras 13,
26; Crim Justice and Licensing (S), 2010 asp 13, s 14, sch 2 para 16(b)
s 194 am—Bail, Judicial Appointments etc (S), asp 9, s 12, sch para 7(5); Crim Proceedings
etc (Reform) (S), 2007 asp 6, s 25(4)
s 194ZA rep (prosp)—Courts Reform (S), 2014 asp 18, sch 3 para 25
Pt 10ZA (ss 194ZB-194ZL) added —Courts Reform (S), 2014 asp 18, s 119
Pt 10A (ss 194A-194L) added—Crime and Punishment (S), 1997 c 48, s 25(1)
ext—SI 1999/1181, art 2
s 194B am—SI 1999/1181, art 3; Crim Procedure (Legal Assistance, Detention and
Appeals) (S), 2010 asp 15, s 7(2); Courts Reform (S), 2014 asp 18, s 121(2)
s 194C am—Crim Procedure (Legal Assistance, Detention and Appeals) (S), 2010 asp 15, s
7(3)
s 194D am—Crim Justice and Licensing (S), 2010 asp 13, s 83
s 194DA added—Crim Procedure (Legal Assistance, Detention and Appeals) (S), 2010 asp
15, s 7(4)
s 194I am—SI 1999/1820, art 4, sch 2 pt I para 122(2); Police and Fire Reform (S), 2012
asp 8, sch 7 para 12(9)
rep in pt—Police and Fire Reform (S), 2012 asp 8, sch 8 pt 1
s 194IA added—Crim Justice and Licensing (S), 2010 asp 13, s 105
s 194J am—Crim Cases (Punishment and Review (S), 2012 asp 7, s 3(2)
ss 194M-194T added—Crim Cases (Punishment and Review (S), 2012 asp 7, s 3(3)
s 195 am—Crime and Punishment (S), 1997 c 48, s 13(3); Crim Justice (S), 2003 asp 7,
s 1(2), sch 1 para 2(1)(5)
s 196 am—Crime and Punishment (S), 1997 c 48, s 2(2); Crim Procedure (Amdt) (S), 2004
asp 5, s 20
s 199 am—Crime and Punishment (S), 1997 c 48, s 62(1), sch 1 para 21(23)
excl—Sexual Offences (S), 2009 asp 9, s 48(2)
s 200 am—Mental Health (Care and Treatment) (S), 2003 asp 13, ss 132(a)(b), 331(1), sch
4 para 8(1)(13); Crim Proceedings etc (Reform) (S), 2007 asp 6, s 6(4); SSI
2015/338, sch 2 para 5(6)
rep in pt—Mental Health (Care and Treatment) (S), 2003 asp 13, ss 132(c), 331(2),
sch 5 pt 1
s 201 saved—Proceeds of Crime (S), 1995 c 43, s 10(2); Proceeds of Crime, 2002 c 29, s
100(2)
appl—Crim Justice (S), 2003 asp 7, s 21(9)
am—Crim Justice (S), 2003 asp 7, ss 21(10), 67; Crim Proceedings etc (Reform) (S),
2007 asp 6, s 6(5); SSI 2015/338, sch 2 para 5(7)
rep in pt—Crim Proceedings etc (Reform) (S), 2007 asp 6, s 80, sch para 18(4)
s 202 saved—Proceeds of Crime (S), 1995 c 43, s 10(2); Proceeds of Crime, 2002 c 29, s
100(2)
am—Crime and Punishment (S), 1997 c 48, s 62(1), sch 1 para 21(24); Crim Justice
and Licensing (S), 2010 asp 13, s 71, sch 4 para 4
s 203 am—Crim Proceedings etc (Reform) (S), 2007 asp 6, s 80, sch para 26(i); ibid, s 24;
Crim Justice and Licensing (S), 2010 asp 13, s 20(2)
s 203A added—Crim Justice and Licensing (S), 2010 asp 13, s 22
s 204 rep in pt—Crime and Punishment (S), 1997 c 48, ss 6(3)(a),62(2), sch 3

1995
c 46 s 204 *continued*
am—Crime and Punishment (S), 1997 c 48, s 6(3)(b); Crim Justice (S), 2003 asp 7, s 1(2), sch 1 para 2(1)(6); Crim Justice and Licensing (S), 2010 asp 13, ss 17, 71, sch 4 para 5(a)(b)
s 204A added—Crime and Disorder, 1998 c 37, s 112
am—(prosp) Custodial Sentences and Weapons (S), 2007 asp 17, s 66, sch 4 para 2
s 204B added—Crim Justice (S), 2003 asp 7, s 26(1)
rep (pt prosp) —Custodial Sentences and Weapons (S), 2007 asp 17, s 66, sch 5
s 205 am—Convention Rights (Compliance) (S), 2001 asp 7, ss 2(1)(a), 4
rep in pt—Convention Rights (Compliance) (S), 2001 asp 7, ss 2(1)(b), 4
s 205B added—Crime and Punishment (S), 1997 c 48, s 2(1)
am—Proceeds of Crime, 2002 c 29, s 456, sch 11, para 29(1)(3); Crim Justice and Licensing (S), 2010 asp 13, s 71, sch 4 para 6(a)(b)
s 205C added—Crime and Punishment (S), 1997 c 48, s 3
s 205D added—Convention Rights (Compliance) (S), 2001 asp 7, ss 2(2), 4
s 206 subst—(temp) Crim Procedure (Conseq Provns) (S), 1995 c 40, s 4, sch 3 pt II para 4(1)
am—Crim Justice and Licensing (S), 2010 asp 13, s 16(3)(a)
rep in pt—Crim Justice and Licensing (S), 2010 asp 13, s 16(3)(b)
s 207 am—Crime and Punishment (S), 1997 c 48, ss 6(4), 62(1), sch 1 para 21(25); Violent Crime Reduction, 2006 c 38, s 49, sch 1 para 4(3)
s 208 renumbered and am—Crim Justice, 2003 c 44, s 290(1)(3); Antisocial Behaviour etc (S), 2004 asp 8, s 10(1)(3)(4)
am—Violent Crime Reduction, 2006 c 38, s 49, sch 1 para (4); Crim Justice and Licensing (S), 2010 asp 13, s 21(3)
s 209 am—Crime and Punishment (S), 1997 c 48, s 62(1), sch 1 para 21(26); Crime and Disorder, 1998 c 37, s 86(2)(a)(b); Crim Justice and Court Services, 2000 c 43, s 74, sch 7 pt I para 4(1)(2), pt II para 121; SI 2008/912, art 3, sch 1
rep in pt—Crime and Disorder, 1998 c 37, ss 86(2)(c),120(2), sch 10; SI 2008/912, art 3, sch 1
s 210 am—Crime and Punishment (S), 1997 c 48, s 12; Crime (International Co-operation), 2003 c 32, s 91(1), sch 5 paras 64, 65; Mental Health (Care and Treatment) (S), 2003 asp 13, s 331(1), sch 4 para 8(1)(14); Anti-social Behaviour, Crime and Policing, 2014 c 12, s 172(2)-(4)
rep in pt—Mental Health (Care and Treatment) (S), 2003 asp 13, s 331(2), sch 5 pt 1; Anti-social Behaviour, Crime and Policing, 2014 c 12, s 172(5)
s 210A added—Crime and Disorder, 1998 c 37, s 86(1)
appl—Prisons (S), 1989 c 45, s 39(7A)(7B); Prisoners and Crim Proceedings (S), 1993 c 9 s 26A; Crim Justice (S), 2003 asp 7, s 21(1)(a)
am—Sexual Offences (Amdt), 2000 c 44, s 6(2); Mental Health (Care and Treatment) (S), 2003 asp 13, s 312(b); SSI 2003/48, art 2; Crim Procedure (Amdt) (S), 2004 asp 5, s 21; Crim Proceedings etc (Reform) (S), 2007 asp 6, s 80, sch para 19; (prosp) Custodial Sentences and Weapons (S), 2007 asp 17, s 66, sch 4 para 3; Sexual Offences (S), 2009 asp 9, s 61, sch 5 para 2(1)(6); (prosp) Crim Justice and Licensing (S), 2010 asp 13, s 18, sch 3 paras 15, 17(1)-(3); ibid, s 23(a)(b); SSI 2010/421, art 2, sch
rep in pt—Mental Health (Care and Treatment) (S), 2003 asp 13, s 312(a); Sexual Offences (S), 2009 asp 9, s 61, sch 6
restr—SSI 2007/250, art 4
s 210AA added—Crim Justice (S), 2003 asp 7, s 20
ss 210B-210E added—Crim Justice (S), 2003 asp 7, s 1(1)
s 210EA added—Management of Offenders etc (S), 2005 asp 14, s 19
s 210F added—Crim Justice (S), 2003 asp 7, s 1(1)
am—Management of Offenders etc (S), 2005 asp 14, s 14
ss 210G, 210H added—Crim Justice (S), 2003 asp 7, s 1(1)
s 211 appl—Proceeds of Crime (S), 1995 c 43, ss 14(1) 34, sch 1 para 4(4); Proceeds of Crime, 2002 c 29, s 118(1)(2)(a)
saved—Crim Law (Consolidation) (S), 1995 c 39, s 41(1); SSI 2009/316, art 13
mod—Terrorism, 2000 c 11, s 23(9), sch 4 pt II para 16(3)
am—(pt prosp) Crim Proceedings etc (Reform) (S), 2007 asp 6, s 80, sch paras 20(1), 26(j); SSI 2009/342, arts 2, 7
s 214 appl (mods)—Proceeds of Crime (S), 1995 c 43, s 14(2)(a)-(i); Proceeds of Crime, 2002 c 29, s 118(1)(2)(b)

1995

c 46 s 214 *continued*

mod—Proceeds of Crime (S), 1995 c 43, s 15(2); Crime and Punishment (S), 1997 c 48, s 33(3), sch 2 para 1(3)

s 215 appl (mods)—Proceeds of Crime (S), 1995 c 43, s 14(2)(a)-(i)

s 216 appl (mods)—Proceeds of Crime (S), 1995 c 43, s 14(2)(a)-(i); Proceeds of Crime, 2002 c 29, s 118(1)(2)(c)

mod—SI 1996/3255, reg 14(1); Crime and Punishment (S), 1997 c 48, s 33(3), sch 2 para 1(3)

ss 217-220 appl (mods)—Proceeds of Crime (S), 1995 c 43, s 14(2)(a)-(i)

s 217 appl—Proceeds of Crime, 2002 c 29, s 118(1)(2)(d)

am—Crim Proceedings etc (Reform) (S), 2007 asp 6, s 80, sch para 20(2)

s 218 appl—Proceeds of Crime, 2002 c 29, s 118(1)(2)(e)

s 219 appl (mods)—Proceeds of Crime, 2002 c 29, s 118(1)(2)(f)

am—Proceeds of Crime, 2002 c 29, s 456, sch 11, para 29(1)(4); Antisocial Behaviour etc (S), 2004 asp 8, s 144(1), sch 4 para 5(1)(4); (1.3.2016) Serious Crime, 2015 c 9, s 19(3)

mod—(1.3.2016) Proceeds of Crime, 2002 c 29 s 118(2A) (added by 2015 c 9, s 19(1)(b))

power to am—(1.3.2016) Proceeds of Crime, 2002 c 29 s 118(2B)(a)(b) (added by 2015 c 9, s 19(1)(b))

s 220 appl (mods)—Proceeds of Crime, 2002 c 29, s 118(1)(2)(g)

am—Crim Justice (S), 2003 asp 7, s 85, sch 4 para 3(1)(3)

s 221 saved—SSIs 2000/7, art 5(1); 20, art 7; 26, art 5(1); 34, art 6(1); 53, art 5(1); 2001/117, art 6(1); 2002/51, art 6(1); 2003/56, art 13(1); 88, art 6(1); 2004/44, art 16(1); 209, art 7(1); 392, art 11(1); 2005/90, art 27(1); 330, art 6(1); 2010/100, art 5; 334, art 8

appl (mods)—Proceeds of Crime (S), 1995 c 43, s 14(2)(a)-(i)

appl—Proceeds of Crime, 2002 c 29, s 118(1)(2)(h); Fur Farming (Prohibition) (S), 2002 asp 10, s 3(2); SSI 2007/39, art 4; Glasgow Commonwealth Games, 2008 asp 4, s 36(3)

am—Debt Arrangement and Attachment (S), 2002 asp 17, s 61, sch 3 pt 1, para 25; Bankruptcy and Diligence etc (S), 2007 asp 3, s 226, sch 5 para 23

s 222 appl—SIs 2000/2230, art 5(3); 2015/191, art 3(4)

appl (mods)—Proceeds of Crime (S), 1995 c 43, s 14(2)(a)-(i); SSI 2001/117, art 6(4); Proceeds of Crime, 2002 c 29, s 118(1)(2)(i)

am—Crim Proceedings etc (Reform) (S), 2007 asp 6, s 80, sch para 20(3); (1.3.2016) Serious Crime, 2015 c 9, sch 4 para 16

mod—(1.3.2016) Proceeds of Crime, 2002 c 29 s 118(2C)(2D) (added by 2015 c 9, s 19(1)(b))

s 223 appl—Proceeds of Crime (S), 1995 c 43, s 14(2)(j)(k); Proceeds of Crime, 2002 c 29, s 118(1)(2)(j)

am—Crim Proceedings etc (Reform) (S), 2007 asp 6, s 80, sch para 20(4)

ss 223A-223T added—SSI 2009/342, arts 2, 3

s 223E am—SSI 2014/322, art 3

s 223FA added—SSI 2014/322, art 4

s 223G rep—SSI 2014/322, art 5

s 223H am—SSIs 2014/322, art 6(a); 2014/336, art 3

rep in pt—SSI 2014/322, art 6(b)

s 223I am—SSI 2014/322, art 7

s 223T am—SSI 2014/336, art 4

s 224 appl—Proceeds of Crime (S), 1995 c 43, s 14(2)(j)(k); Proceeds of Crime, 2002 c 29, s 118(1)(2)(k)

s 225 appl—Crim Law (Consolidation) (S), 1995 c 39, ss 13(7), 52(3)(b); Civil Aviation, 1982 c 16, s 105(1); Oil and Gas (Enterprise), 1982 c 23 s 28(1); Aviation Security, 1982 c 36, s 38(1); SI 1999/1379, arts 6(2), 7(1), sch 2

am—Crim Proceedings etc (Reform) (S), 2007 asp 6, s 48

ss 226A-226H added (pt prosp)—Crim Proceedings etc (Reform) (S), 2007 asp 6, s 55

s 226B am—SSI 2009/342, arts 2, 5

s 226HA added—SSI 2009/342, arts 2, 4

s 226I added (pt prosp)—Crim Proceedings etc (Reform) (S), 2007 asp 6, s 55

am—SSI 2009/342, arts 2, 6

ss 227A-227ZN added—Crim Justice and Licensing (S), 2010 asp 13, s 14(1)

s 227N am—SSI 2011/25, sch para 1(2)

s 227ZC am—SSI 2011/25, sch para 1(3)

1995
c 46 *continued*

s 227ZO added—SI 2011/2298, sch para 5

ss 228, 229 rep—Crim Justice and Licensing (S), 2010 asp 13, s 14, sch 2 para 17

s 229A added—Management of Offenders etc (S), 2005 asp 14, s 12(1)(2)

    rep—Crim Justice and Licensing (S), 2010 asp 13, s 14, sch 2 para 17

s 230 rep—Crim Justice and Licensing (S), 2010 asp 13, s 14, sch 2 para 17

s 230A added—Crim Justice (S), 2003 asp 7, s 46(1)(2)

    rep—Crim Justice and Licensing (S), 2010 asp 13, s 14, sch 2 para 17

ss 231-233 rep (S)—Crim Justice and Licensing (S), 2010 asp 13, s 14, sch 2 para 17

s 234 rep (S)—Crim Justice and Licensing (S), 2010 asp 13, s 14, sch 2 para 17

    rep in pt—(EW) SI 2011/2298, sch para 7(a)

s 234A added—Protection from Harassment, 1997 c 40, s 11

    rep in pt—Crime and Punishment (S), 1997 c 48, s 62(1)(2), sch 1 para 21(30), sch 3; Crim Justice (S), 2003 asp 7, s 49(1)(a)

    am—Crim Justice (S), 2003 asp 7, s 49(1)(b); Crim Justice and Licensing (S), 2010 asp 13, s 15(a)-(d)

s 234AA added —Antisocial Behaviour etc (S), 2004 asp 8, s 118

    rep in pt—Crim Justice and Licensing (S), 2010 asp 13, s 52(4)

s 234AB added —Antisocial Behaviour etc (S), 2004 asp 8, s 118

s 234B added—Crime and Disorder, 1998 c 37, s 89

    appl—Crim Justice (S), 2003 asp 7, s 42(10); SIs (E) 2003/762, reg 2(2)(n); (W) 2004/1748 (W 185), regs 3(1), 4, sch 1 para (n)

s 234C added—Crime and Disorder, 1998 c 37, s 90

s 234CA added—Crim Justice (S), 2003 asp 7, s 47(1)(2)

s 234D added—Crime and Disorder, 1998 c 37, s 91

    am—SI 2001/1149, art 3(1), sch 1 para 104(1)(5); Crim Justice (S), 2003 asp 7, s 42(11)(c)

s 234E added—Crime and Disorder, 1998 c 37, s 92

    am—Crim Justice (S), 2003 asp 7, ss 47(1)(3), 60(1)(c)

s 234F added—Crime and Disorder, 1998 c 37, s 92

    am—Crim Justice (S), 2003 asp 7, s 64

s 234G added—Crime and Disorder, 1998 c 37, s 93

    am—Crim Justice (S), 2003 asp 7, ss 47(1)(4), 60(1)(d)

s 234H added—Crime and Disorder, 1998 c 37, s 93

    am—Crim Justice (S), 2003 asp 7, s 42(11)(d); Crim Justice and Licensing (S), 2010 asp 13, s 14, sch 2 para 18(a)(b)

s 234J added—Crime and Disorder, 1998 c 37, s 94

    am—Crim Justice and Licensing (S), 2010 asp 13, s 14, sch 2 para 19(1)-(5)

s 234K added—Crime and Disorder, 1998 c 37, s 95(1)

    am—Crim Proceedings etc (Reform) (S), 2007 asp 6, s 80, sch para 26(k)

ss 235-245 rep (S)—Crim Justice and Licensing (S), 2010 asp 13, s 14, sch 2 para 20

s 244 rep (EW)—SI 2011/2298, sch para 7(b)

ss 245A-245I added—Crime and Punishment (S), 1997 c 48, s 5

s 245A am—Crim Justice (S), 2003 asp 7, ss 43(1)(2), 50(3)(a)(c); Crim Procedure (Amdt) (S), 2004 asp 5, s 25, sch paras 1, 35; Antisocial Behaviour etc (S), 2004 asp 8, s 121(1)(3); Crim Proceedings etc (Reform) (S), 2007 asp 6, s 80, sch para 26(m); Crim Justice and Licensing (S), 2010 asp 13, s 14, sch 2 paras 21(3)(4)

    rep in pt—Crim Justice (S), 2003 asp 7, s 50(3)(b); Antisocial Behaviour etc (S), 2004 asp 8, ss 121(1)(2), 144(2), sch 5; Crim Justice and Licensing (S), 2010 asp 13, s 14, sch 2 para 21(2); (1.4.2016) Courts Reform (S), 2014 asp 18, sch 5 para 39(4)

s 245C ext—Crim Justice, 2003 c 44, ss 188, 194, sch 11 pt 5 para 23, sch 13 pt 4 para 21

    appl—Crim Justice (S), 2003 asp 7, s 40(7); Prisoners and Crim Proceedings (S), 1993 c 9, s 12AB; SSI 2006/8, reg 5, sch 2; Offender Rehabilitation, 2014 c 11, sch 3 para 7 (inserting Crime (Sentences) 1997 c 43 Sch 1 para 19B)

    am—Crim Procedure (Amdt) (S), 2004 asp 5, s 25, sch paras 1, 36

s 245D subst—Crime and Disorder, 1998 c 37, s 94(2), sch 6 pt I para 3

    am—Antisocial Behaviour etc (S), 2004 asp 8, s 144(1), sch 4 para 5(1)(7)(a)(i)(ii)(b); Crim Justice and Licensing (S), 2010 asp 13, s 14, sch 2 para 22(1)-(3)(4)(b)(c)(5)(7)(a)(c)(8)(9)(a)

    rep in pt—Antisocial Behaviour etc (S), 2004 asp 8, s 144(1), sch 4 para 5(1)(7)(a)(iii); Crim Justice and Licensing (S), 2010 asp 13, s 14, sch 2 para 22(4)(a)(6)(7)(a)(ii)(b)(9)(b)

1995
c 46 *continued*

s 245E am—Crim Justice (S), 2003 asp 7, ss 43(1)(3), 60(1)(g)(h); Crim Procedure (Amdt)
(S), 2004 asp 5, s 25, sch paras 1, 37; Antisocial Behaviour etc (S), 2004 asp 8,
s 144(1), sch 4 para 5(1)(8)

s 245F am—Crim Justice (S), 2003 asp 7, ss 43(1)(4), 60(1)(g)(h); Crim Proceedings etc
(Reform) (S), 2007 asp 6, s 58

s 245G am—Crime and Disorder, 1998 c 37, s 94(2), sch 6 pt I para 4(2)(3); Antisocial
Behaviour etc (S), 2004 asp 8, s 144(1), sch 4 para 5(1)(9); Crim Justice and
Licensing (S), 2010 asp 13, s 14, sch 2 para 23(1)-(3)
rep in pt—Crim Justice and Licensing (S), 2010 asp 13, s 14, sch 2 para 23(4)

s 245H appl—Crim Justice, 2003 c 44, s 194, sch 13 pt 3 para 14(5)
am—Antisocial Behaviour etc (S), 2004 asp 8, s 144(1), sch 4 para 5(1)(10)

s 245J added—Crim Justice (S), 2003 asp 7, s 48
rep in pt—Crim Proceedings etc (Reform) (S), 2007 asp 6, s 80, sch para 21; Crim
Justice and Licensing (S), 2010 asp 13, s 14, sch 2 para 24(a)(iii)
am—Crim Proceedings etc (Reform) (S), 2007 asp 6, s 6(6); Crim Justice and
Licensing (S), 2010 asp 13, s 14, sch 2 para 24(a)(i)(ii)(c); SSI 2015/338, sch 2
para 5(8)

ss 245K-245Q added—Antisocial Behaviour etc (S), 2004 asp 8, s 120
rep—Crim Justice and Licensing (S), 2010 asp 13, s 14, sch 2 para 25

s 246 restr—Crim Procedure (Conseq Provns) (S), 1995 c 40, s 4, sch 3 pt II para 9
am—Crime and Punishment (S), 1997 c 48, s 62(1), sch 1 para 21(31)
rep in pt—Crim Justice and Licensing (S), 2010 asp 13, s 14, sch 2 para 26
excl—(1.3.2016) Serious Crime, 2007, c 27, s 36A(5)(6) (added by 2015 c 9, sch 1
para 25)

s 247 excl—Sexual Offences, 2003 c 42, s 134(1)(c)(2); (1.3.2016) Serious Crime, 2007, c
27, s 36A(5)(6) (added by 2015 c 9, sch 1 para 25); Coroners and Justice, 2009
c 25, s 158(3)(c); Double Jeopardy (S), 2011 asp 16, s 1(1)(4)(a)
am—Crim Justice and Licensing (S), 2010 asp 13, s 203, sch 7 paras 25, 59(a)
rep in pt—Crim Justice and Licensing (S), 2010 asp 13, s 203, sch 7 paras 25,
59(b)(c)

s 248 am—SI 1996/1974, reg 5, sch 4 para 6

ss 248A-248C added—Crime and Punishment (S), 1997 c 48, s 5

s 248C am—Crim Proceedings etc (Reform) (S), 2007 asp 6, s 80, sch paras 22, 26(o)
rep in pt—(prosp) Coroners and Justice, 2009 c 25, ss 177, 178, sch 21 para 91; (pt
prosp) ibid, sch 23 pt 4; (1.4.2016) Courts Reform (S), 2014 asp 18, sch 5 para
39(5)

ss 248D, 248E added (prosp) —Coroners and Justice, 2009 c 25, s 137, sch 16 para 3

s 248D excl—Crime (International Co-operation), 2003 c 32, s 54(3A)(b) (added by 2015 c
2, sch 7 para 2(4))

s 249 am—Crim Proceedings etc (Reform) (S), 2007 asp 6, ss 49(1), 80, sch paras 22, 26(p);
Crim Justice and Licensing (S), 2010 asp 13, ss 14, 115(1)(a)-(d)(f), sch 2 para
27; (prosp) Victims and Witnesses (S), 2014 asp 1, s 24; Regulatory Reform (S),
2014 asp 3, sch 3 para 12
rep in pt—Crim Justice and Licensing (S), 2010 asp 13, s 115(1)(e); (1.4.2016)
Courts Reform (S), 2014 asp 18, sch 5 para 39(6)
mod—Regulatory Reform (S), 2014 asp 3, s 34

s 251 am—Crim Proceedings etc (Reform) (S), 2007 asp 6, s 49(2); Crim Justice and
Licensing (S), 2010 asp 13, s 115(2)(b)
rep in pt—Crim Justice and Licensing (S), 2010 asp 13, s 115(2)(a)

s 252 am—Crime and Punishment (S), 1997 c 48, s 15(2)(b)
rep in pt—Crime and Punishment (S), 1997 c 48, ss 15(2)(a),62(2), sch 3

s 253 am—Crim Proceedings etc (Reform) (S), 2007 asp 6, s 49(3)

ss 253A-253E added (prosp)—Victims and Witnesses (S), 2014 asp 1, s 25

s 253A appl—(prosp) Proceeds of Crime, 2002, c 29, s 97A(9) (added by 2015 c 9, s 15(2))

ss 253F-253J added (pt prosp)—Victims and Witnesses (S), 2014 asp 1, s 26

s 254 am—Crim Justice and Licensing (S), 2010 asp 13, s 203, sch 7 paras 25, 60(a)(b)

s 254A-254E added—SSI 2015/107, reg 2(2)

s 254B am—SSI 2015/338, sch 2 para 5(9)

s 255 am—Crim Procedure (Amdt) (S), 2004 asp 5, s 25, sch paras 1, 38, 39

s 255A added—Crime and Punishment (S), 1997 c 48, s 27
am—Crim Procedure (Amdt) (S), 2004 asp 5, s 25, sch paras 1, 38, 39

s 256 saved—Proceeds of Crime (S), 1995 c 43, s 9(2)(5)

1995
c 46 *continued*

s 257 am—Crim Procedure (Amdt) (S), 2004 asp 5, ss 16, 25, sch paras 1, 40; Crim
 Proceedings etc (Reform) (S), 2007 asp 6, ss 20(1), 30
s 258 am—Crim Procedure (Amdt) (S), 2004 asp 5, s 25, sch paras 1, 41; Crim Proceedings
 etc (Reform) (S), 2007 asp 6, s 20(2); Crim Justice and Licensing (S), 2010 asp
 13, s 203, sch 7 paras 25, 61
ss 259-261 excl—Crim Procedure (Conseq Provns) (S), 1995 c 40, s 4, sch 3 pt II para 14
s 259 am—Crim Procedure (Amdt) (S), 2004 asp 5, s 25, sch paras 1, 42
s 260 am—Crim Procedure (Amdt) (S), 2004 asp 5, s 23
s 261A added—Crim Justice and Licensing (S), 2010 asp 13, s 85(2)
s 262 appl (mods)—Crim Justice and Licensing (S), 2010 asp 13, s 54(3)
 am—Crim Justice and Licensing (S), 2010 asp 13, s 85(3)(a)-(c); SSI 2013/211, sch 1
  para 10(7)
s 264 subst—Crim Justice and Licensing (S), 2010 asp 13, s 86(1)
s 266 am—Sexual Offences (Procedure and Evidence) (S), 2002 asp 9, s 10(3)
s 267A added—Crim Procedure (Amdt) (S), 2004 asp 5, s 22
s 267B added—Crim Proceedings etc (Reform) (S), 2007 asp 6, s 34
s 271 replaced (by ss 271, 271A-271M)—Vulnerable Witnesses (S), 2004 asp 3, s 1(1)
ss 271-271M appl (mods)—SSI 2015/447, art 3
 am—SSI 2005/465, art 2, sch 1 para 27(1)(3); Crim Justice and Licensing (S), 2010
  asp 13, ss 87(2)(a)(b)(ii), 88(a)(b); Victims and Witnesses (S), 2014 asp 1, ss
  10(a)(b)(d)(e), 11(3)
 appl—SSI 2005/574, rule 2(2)(b)(ii)
 rep in pt—Crim Justice and Licensing (S), 2010 asp 13, s 87(1)(b)(i); Victims and
  Witnesses (S), 2014 asp 1, s 10(c)
s 271A am—Crim Procedure (Amdt) (S), 2004 asp 5, s 25, sch paras 1, 43; Crim Justice
  and Licensing (S), 2010 asp 13, s 87(3)(a)-(h); Victims and Witnesses (S),
  2014 asp 1, s 11(4)(a)(i)(b)(i)(ii)(c)(d)(e)(i)(f)(g)(i)(ii)(iv)(h)(i)(i)(i)(m)(5);
  ibid, s 12(b); ibid, s 13; ibid, s 14(2)
 rep in pt—Victims and Witnesses (S), 2014 asp 1, s
  11(4)(a)(ii)(b)(iii)(c)(d)(e)(ii)(g)(iii)(v)(h)(ii)(i)(ii)(j)(k)(l); ibid, s 12(a)(i)
s 271BA added —Victims and Witnesses (S), 2014 asp 1, s 16(1)
s 271B am—Crim Justice and Licensing (S), 2010 asp 13, s 87(4)(a)-(c); Victims and
  Witnesses (S), 2014 asp 1, s 14(1)
s 271C am—Crim Procedure (Amdt) (S), 2004 asp 5, s 25, sch paras 1, 44; Crim Justice
  and Licensing (S), 2010 asp 13, s 87(5)(a)-(e); Victims and Witnesses (S),
  2014 asp 1, s 11(6); ibid, s 16(2); ibid, s 17
s 271D am—Crim Justice and Licensing (S), 2010 asp 13, s 87(6)(a)(b); Victims and
  Witnesses (S), 2014 asp 1, s 14(3); ibid, s 18
s 271E am—Victims and Witnesses (S), 2014 asp 1, s 11(7)
s 271F am—Crim Justice and Licensing (S), 2010 asp 13, s 87(7)(a)-(d); Victims and
  Witnesses (S), 2014 asp 1, ss 11(8)(a), 20(3)
 rep in pt—Victims and Witnesses (S), 2014 asp 1, s 11(8)(b)
s 271H am—Victims and Witnesses (S), 2014 asp 1, ss 20(1), 21(b)
 rep in pt—Victims and Witnesses (S), 2014 asp 1, s 21(a)(c)
s 271HA added —Victims and Witnesses (S), 2014 asp 1, s 19
s 271HB added —Victims and Witnesses (S), 2014 asp 1, s 20(2)
s 271I am—Crim Proceedings etc (Reform) (S), 2007 asp 6, s 35(3)
s 271J am—Crim Justice and Licensing (S), 2010 asp 13, s 87(8)(a)-(c)
s 271L am—Crim Justice and Licensing (S), 2010 asp 13, s 87(9)
ss 271N-271Z added—Crim Justice and Licensing (S), 2010 asp 13, s 90(1)
 appl—Crim Justice and Licensing (S), 2010 asp 13, s 90(3)
s 271V am—SSI 2015/338, sch 2 para 5(10)
s 271W am—SSI 2015/338, sch 2 para 5(11)
s 271X am—SSI 2015/338, sch 2 para 5(12)
s 271Y am—SSI 2015/338, sch 2 para 5(13)
s 271Z am—SSI 2015/338, sch 2 para 5(14)
s 272 am—Crim Proceedings etc (Reform) (S), 2007 asp 6, s 35(4)
s 273 power to appl—Crime (International Co-operation), 2003 c 32, s 29(2)
 am—Crim Justice and Licensing (S), 2010 asp 13, s 91(2)
s 273A added—Crim Justice and Licensing (S), 2010 asp 13, s 91(3)
s 274 subst—Sexual Offences (Procedure and Evidence) (S), 2002 asp 9, s 7
 am—SSI 2005/465, art 2, sch 1 para 27(1)(4)
s 275 subst—Sexual Offences (Procedure and Evidence) (S), 2002 asp 9, s 8(1)

1995
c 46 *continued*

ss 275A, 275B added—Sexual Offences (Procedure and Evidence) (S), 2002 asp 9, s 10(4)

s 275A am—Crim Proceedings etc (Reform) (S), 2007 asp 6, s 35(5); Crim Justice and
    Licensing (S), 2010 asp 13, s 71, sch 4 para 7(a)(ii)(b)
    rep in pt—Crim Justice and Licensing (S), 2010 asp 13, s 71, sch 4 para 7(a)(i)

s 275B am—Crim Procedure (Amdt) (S), 2004 asp 5, s 25, sch paras 1, 45

s 275C added—Vulnerable Witnesses (S), 2004 asp 3, s 5

s 277 am—Crim Procedure (Amdt) (S), 2004 asp 5, s 25, sch paras 1, 46, 47; Regulatory
    Reform (S), 2014 asp 3, sch 3 para 31(2)(a)(ii)(b)

s 278 am—Crim Procedure (Amdt) (S), 2004 asp 5, s 25, sch paras 1, 46, 47

s 279A added—Crime and Punishment (S), 1997 c 48, s 28(2)
    am—SI 1999/1820, art 4, sch 2 pt I para 122(4)

s 280 am—Crime and Punishment (S), 1997 c 48, s 62(1), sch 1 para 21(32); Crim
    Procedure (Amdt) (S), 2004 asp 5, s 25, sch paras 1, 48; Regulatory Reform (S),
    2014 asp 3, sch 3 para 31(3)
    rep in pt—Police and Fire Reform (S), 2012 asp 8, sch 8 pt 1

s 281 am—Crim Procedure (Amdt) (S), 2004 asp 5, s 25, sch paras 1, 49(a)(b)(ii)-(iv)
    rep in pt—Crim Procedure (Amdt) (S), 2004 asp 5, s 25, sch paras 1, 49(b)(i)

s 281A added—Vulnerable Witnesses (S), 2004 asp 3, s 4
    am—Crim Procedure (Amdt) (S), 2004 asp 5, s 25, sch paras 1, 50

s 282 am—Crim Procedure (Amdt) (S), 2004 asp 5, s 25, sch paras 1, 51

s 283 am—Crim Procedure (Amdt) (S), 2004 asp 5, s 25, sch paras 1, 52; Crim Proceedings
    etc (Reform) (S), 2007 asp 6, s 80, sch para 23

s 284 am—Crime and Punishment (S), 1997 c 48, s 47(4); Crim Justice (S), 2003 asp 7,
    s 54; Crim Procedure (Amdt) (S), 2004 asp 5, s 25, sch paras 1, 53

s 285 am—Crime and Punishment (S), 1997 c 48, ss 47(5), 59; SSI 2013/119, sch 1 para
    16(a)(i)-(iii)(b)(i)(ii)(iv)
    rep in pt—SSI 2013/119, sch 1 para 16(b)(iii)

s 286 am—Crim Justice (S), 2003 asp 7, s 57(1)(3); Crim Procedure (Amdt) (S), 2004 asp 5,
    s 25, sch paras 1, 54

s 286A added—Crim Justice (S), 2003 asp 7, s 57(1)(4)

s 287 am—SI 1999/1042, art 4, sch 2 pt I para 11; Crim Justice and Licensing (S), 2010 asp
    13, s 60(3)(a)(b)(i)(c)(d)
    rep in pt—SI 1999/1042, art 4, sch 2 pt III; Crim Justice and Licensing (S), 2010 asp
    13, s 60(3)(b)(ii)
    saved—Scotland, 1998 c 46, s 48(4)
    appl—SSI 2010/413, art 5

s 288ZA added—Scotland, 2012 c 11, s 34(3)
    mod—SI 2013/7, art 8

s 288ZB added—Scotland, 2012 c 11, s 35
    mod—SI 2013/7, art 6

ss 288A, 288B added—Scotland, 1998 c 46, s 125, sch 8 para 32(2)

s 288A am—Scotland, 2012 c 11, s 34(5)(7)(8)
    rep in pt—Scotland, 2012 c 11, s 34(6)

s 288AA added—Scotland, 2012 c 11, s 36(6)
    mod—SI 2013/7, arts 7, 9, 10
    appl—SI 2013/7, art 14

s 288B am—Constitutional Reform, 2005 c 4, s 40(4), sch 9 pt 2 para 86; Scotland, 2012 c
    11, s 36(8),(9)(a)
    rep in pt—Scotland, 2012 c 11, s 36(9)(b)

ss 288BA-288BC added—Crim Justice and Licensing (S), 2010 asp 13, s 63

s 288C added—Sexual Offences (Procedure and Evidence) (S), 2002 asp 9, s 1
    am—Crim Justice (S), 2003 asp 7, s 15(1)(2); Crim Procedure (Amdt) (S), 2004 asp
    5, s 4; ibid, s 25, sch paras 1, 55, 56; SSI 2005/465, art 2, sch 1 para 27(1)(5);
    Sexual Offences (S), 2009 asp 9, s 61, sch 5 para 2(1)(7); Crim Justice and
    Licensing (S), 2010 asp 13, s 69(2)(a); SSI 2010/421, art 2, sch
    rep in pt—Crim Justice and Licensing (S), 2010 asp 13, s 69(2)(b)

s 288D added—Sexual Offences (Procedure and Evidence) (S), 2002 asp 9, s 2(1)
    am—Crim Justice (S), 2003 asp 7, s 15(1)(3); Crim Procedure (Amdt) (S), 2004 asp
    5, s 4; ibid, s 25, sch paras 1, 55, 56; Crim Proceedings etc (Reform) (S), 2007
    asp 6, s 35(6); Crim Justice and Licensing (S), 2010 asp 13, s 69(3)(a)-(c)

ss 288E, 288F added—Vulnerable Witnesses (S), 2004 asp 3, s 6

1995

c 46 *continued*

s 288E am—Crim Procedure (Amdt) (S), 2004 asp 5, s 4; (Crim Proceedings etc (Reform)
(S), 2007 asp 6, s 80, sch para 26(q); Crim Justice and Licensing (S), 2010 asp
13, ss 69(4)(b)-(e), 87(10); Victims and Witnesses (S), 2014 asp 1, s 11(9)
rep in pt—Crim Justice and Licensing (S), 2010 asp 13, s 69(4)(a)(f)

s 288E, 288F appl (mods)—SSI 2015/447, arts 4, 5

s 288F am—Crim Procedure (Amdt) (S), 2004 asp 5, s 4; Crim Proceedings etc (Reform)
(S), 2007 asp 6, s 80, sch para 26(r); Crim Justice and Licensing (S), 2010 asp
13, s 69(5)(a)-(d)(f)
rep in pt—Crim Justice and Licensing (S), 2010 asp 13, s 69(5)(e)(g)

s 288G added —Vulnerable Witnesses (S), 2004 asp 3, s 10
am—Crim Proceedings etc (Reform) (S), 2007 asp 6, s 80, sch para 26(s)

s 291 am—Sexual Offences (Procedure and Evidence) (S), 2002 asp 9, s 4; Vulnerable
Witnesses (S), 2004 asp 3, s 8

s 292 rep in pt—Crim Proceedings etc (Reform) (S), 2007 asp 6, s 80, sch para 24

s 293 excl—Crim Procedure (Conseq Provns) (S), 1995 c 40, s 4, sch 3 pt II para 11

s 294 saved—(except in relation to the River Tweed or Upper Esk) Salmon and Freshwater
Fisheries (Consolidation) (S), 2003 asp 15, ss 1(3), 2(2), 5(2), 6(2), 8(2), 12(2),
71(3)-(5)

s 295 am—Crim Justice (S), 2003 asp 7, s 24(2)(a)(b)
rep in pt—Crim Justice (S), 2003 asp 7, s 24(2)(c)

s 297A added—Crim Proceedings etc (Reform) (S), 2007 asp 6, s 33

s 298 am—Crime and Punishment (S), 1997 c 48, s 62(1), sch 1 para 21(33); SSI 2015/338,
sch 2 para 5(15)
saved—Deer (S), 1996 c 58, s 24
saving—(transtl provn) SI 1999/652, art 3(1)
excl in pt—Police, Public Order and Crim Justice, 2006 asp 10, s 96A(5) (added by
SSI 2015/338, sch 2 para 9(6))

s 298A added—Crim Proceedings etc (Reform) (S), 2007 asp 6, s 38
am—SSI 2015/338, sch 2 para 5(16)

s 299 am—SSI 2015/338, sch 2 para 5(17)

s 300 am—SSI 2015/338, sch 2 para 5(18)

s 300A added—Crim Proceedings etc (Reform) (S), 2007 asp 6, s 40
am—SSI 2015/338, sch 2 para 5(19)

s 301A added—Crim Proceedings etc (Reform) (S), 2007 asp 6, s 37
appl—SSI 2007/480, art 4
am—SSI 2015/338, sch 2 para 5(20)

s 302 am—(pt prosp) Communications, 2003 c 21, s 406(1), sch 17 para 133(1)(2);
Wireless Telegraphy, 2006 c 36, s 123, sch 7 para 16; Crim Proceedings etc
(Reform) (S), 2007 asp 6, s 50(1); Crim Justice and Licensing (S), 2010 asp 13,
s 70(3)

ss 302A-302C added—Crim Proceedings etc (Reform) (S), 2007 asp 6, s 50(2)

s 302A am—Crim Justice and Licensing (S), 2010 asp 13, s 70(4)

s 303 am—Crim Proceedings etc (Reform) (S), 2007 asp 6, s 50(3); SI 2010/976, art 12,
sch 14
rep in pt—SI 2010/976, art 12, sch 14

s 303ZA added —Crim Proceedings etc (Reform) (S), 2007 asp 6, s 51
am—Crim Justice and Licensing (S), 2010 asp 13, s 70(5)(a)-(d)

s 303ZB added—Crim Proceedings etc (Reform) (S), 2007 asp 6, s 52

s 303A added—Crime and Punishment (S), 1997 c 48, s 20
am—SSI 2015/338, sch 2 para 5(21)

s 303B added—Crim Proceedings etc (Reform) (S), 2007 asp 6, s 41(1)

s 304 am—Crim Proceedings etc (Reform) (S), 2007 asp 6, s 80, sch para 26(t); Courts
Reform (S), 2014 asp 18, sch 5 para 15

s 305 saved—Terrorism, 2000 c 11, sch 6A para 5(2); Proceeds of Crime, 2002 c 29, ss
386(3)(a), 396(3)(a), 403(3)(a), 408(3)(a)
am—SSI 2015/338, art 2

s 307 appl—SI 1975/515, reg 5(1)(a); Crim Law (Consolidation) (S), 1995 c 39, s 16(6);
Chemical Weapons, 1996 c 6, ss 5(2)(b)7(7)(b)14(2)(b), 15(3)(b)29(1)(b);
Finance, 1996 c 8, s 60, sch 5 pt II paras 5(1)(b)7(1); (prosp) Nuclear
Explosions (Prohibition and Inspections), 1998 c 7, s 10(1)(b); Landmines,
1998 c 33, ss 8(2)(b), 10(7)(b),18(1)(b); Finance, 2001 c 9, s 29, sch 7
paras 7(1)(b), 8(1)

1995
c 46 s 307 *continued*

    am—Prisoners and Crim Proceedings (S), 1993 c 9, ss 15, 16B, 18; Crime and
        Punishment (S), 1997 c 48, ss 6(5),62(1), sch 1 para 21(34); Crime and Disorder,
        1998 c 37, ss 95(2), 119, sch 8 para 124(a)(b); Scotland, 1998 c 46, s 125, sch 8
        para 32(3); Crim Justice and Court Services, 2000 c 43, s 74, sch 7 pt II
        para 126; Regulation of Care (S), 2001 asp 8, s 79, sch 3 para 20; SI 2001/1149,
        art 3(1), sch 1 para 104(1)(7); Crim Justice (S), 2003 asp 7, s 1(2), sch 1
        para 2(1)(7); ibid, ss 57(1)(5)(a)(b), 60(2), 76(1)(11); Mental Health (Care and
        Treatment) (S), 2003 asp 13, s 331(1), sch 4 para 8(1)(16); Vulnerable
        Witnesses (S), 2004 asp 3, s 1(2); Crim Procedure (Amdt) (S), 2004 asp 5, s 25,
        sch paras 1, 57; Armed Forces, 2006 c 52, s 378, sch 16 para 133; Crim
        Proceedings etc (Reform) (S), 2007 asp 6, s 80, sch para 25; Finance, 2007 c 11,
        s 85, sch 23 paras 1, 8-10, 14; SI 2009/1182, arts 4, 5-7, sch 5; Crim Justice and
        Licensing (S), 2010 asp 13, s 14, sch 2 para 28(a)(i); ibid, ss 71, 200(3), sch 4
        para 8(a)(b); ibid, ss 65, 203, sch 7 paras 25, 62; Postal Services, 2011 c 5, sch
        12 para 146; Health and Social Care, 2012 c 7, s 213(8)(a); Police and Fire
        Reform (S), 2012 asp 8, sch 7 para 12(10); Crime and Cts, 2013 c 22, s 55(13);
        SSI 2013/211, sch 1 para 10(8)(a)-(e); Courts Reform (S), 2014 asp 18, sch 3
        para 26; (prosp) Mental Health (S), 2015 asp 9, s 53(2)
    rep in pt—Mental Health (Care and Treatment) (S), 2003 asp 13, s 331(2), sch 5 pt 1;
        Crim Justice and Licensing (S), 2010 asp 13, s 14, sch 2 para 28(a)(ii)(b); SSI
        2013/211, sch 2; Courts Reform (S), 2014 asp 18, sch 5 para 39(7)
    mod—SI 2009/1059, art 205, sch 1
  s 308A added —Crim Proceedings etc (Reform) (S), 2007 asp 6, s 41(2)
  s 309 am—SIs 2010/976, art 12, sch 14; 2011/2298, sch paras 8, 9
  s 337A am—(retrosp) Crim Procedure (Intermediate Diets) (S), 1998 c 10, s 1(3)
  sch 1 am—Prohibition of Female Genital Mutilation (S), 2005 asp 8, s 7(1); Protection of
        Children and Prevention of Sexual Offences (S), 2005 asp 9, s 18, sch para 2;
        Sexual Offences (S), 2009 asp 9, s 61, sch 5 para 2(1)(8); Crim Justice and
        Licensing (S), 2010 asp 13, s 41(2)
  sch 2 rep in pt—Crim Justice and Licensing (S), 2010 asp 13, s 60(5)
  sch 3 saved—Deer (S), 1996 c 58, s 24; (except in relation to the River Tweed or Upper
        Esk) Salmon and Freshwater Fisheries (Consolidation) (S), 2003 asp 15, ss 1(3),
        2(2), 5(2), 6(2), 8(2), 12(2), 71(3)-(5)
    am—Crime and Punishment (S), 1997 c 48, s 13(4); Crim Justice and Licensing (S),
        2010 asp 13, s 48
  sch 4 am—Crime and Punishment (S), 1997 c 48, s 62(1), sch 1 para 21(35); SSI 2005/465,
        art 2, sch 1 para 27(1)(6)
    rep in pt—Adults with Incapacity (S), 2000, asp 4, s 88(3), sch 6
  sch 5 rep in pt—SIs 2001/1149, arts 3(2), 4(11), sch 2; 2005/1082, reg 28(1)(2), sch 5 pt 1
        para 21, sch 6 pt 1; SSIs 2006/536, reg 2, sch 3; 2009/248, art 2, sch 2;
        2012/215, sch pt 3
  sch 6 rep—Crim Justice and Licensing (S), 2010 asp 13, s 14, sch 2 para 29
  sch 7 rep—Crim Justice and Licensing (S), 2010 asp 13, s 14, sch 2 para 29
  sch 8 am—SSI 2013/211, sch 1 para 10(9)
  sch 9 power to am or rep—Crim Procedure (S), 1995 c 46, s 280(2)
    am—Crime and Punishment (S), 1997 c 48, s 30(2)(3); SI 1999/1820, art 4, sch 2 pt I
        para 122(5); Communications, 2003 c 21, s 406(1)(7), sch 17 para 133(1)(3),
        sch 19(1); Building (S), 2003 asp 8, s 58, sch 6 para 22(b); Crim Procedure
        (Amdt) (S), 2004 asp 5, s 25, sch paras 1, 58; Antisocial Behaviour etc (S), 2004
        asp 8, s 144(1), sch 4 para 5(1)(12); SSIs 2006/181, art 2, sch; 2009/248, art 2,
        sch 1; Police and Fire Reform (S), 2012 asp 8, sch 7 para 12(11); SSI 2012/215,
        sch para 1; Regulatory Reform (S), 2014 asp 3, sch 3 para 31(4)(b); (prosp) Air
        Weapons and Licensing (S), 2015 asp 10, sch 2 para 2
    rep in pt—Building (S), 2003 asp 8, s 58, sch 6 para 22(a); SSI 2009/248, art 2, sch 2;
        Regulatory Reform (S), 2014 asp 3, sch 3 para 31(4)(a)
  sch 9A added—Crime and Punishment (S), 1997 c 48, s 25(2)
    rep in pt—SI 1999/1820, art 4, sch 2 pt I para 122(3) pt IV; Public Finance and
        Accountability (S), 2000 asp 1, s 26, sch 4 para 14(a)(b)(c)
  sch 10 rep in pt—SI 2001/1149, arts 3(2), 4(11), sch 2; SSI 2012/215, sch pt 3
  schs 11, 12 added—SSI 2009/342, arts 2, 8
  sch 12 am—SI 2012/1809, art 3(1), sch pt 1; SSIs 2014/322, art 8(b)(c); 2014/336, art 5
    rep in pt—SSI 2014/322, art 8(a)
  sch 13 added—SI 2011/2298, sch para 6

1995

c 47 **Northern Ireland (Remission of Sentences)**
s 1 am—NI (Emergency Provns, 1996 c 22, s 63(6) sch 6 para 18; Terrorism, 2000 c 11,
s 125(1), sch 15 para 12
cert functions restr from exercise in S—SI 1999/1748, art 8(2), sch 4 para 2
ext—Crime (Sentences), 1997 c 43, s 41, sch 1 pt II para 12(2)(a)(5)
s 3 restr—NI (Sentences), 1998 c 35, s 18

c 48 *Charities (Amendment)*—rep Charities, 2011 c 25, sch 10

c 49 *Town and Country Planning (Costs of Inquiries etc)*—rep SL(R), 2008 c 12, s 1(1), sch 1 pt 9

c 50 *Disability Discrimination)*—rep Equality, 2010 c 15, s 211, sch 27 pt 1

c 51 **Medical (Professional Performance)**
sch rep in pt—Health and Social Care (Community Health and Standards), 2003 c 43, s 196,
sch 14 pt 4

c 52 **Mental Health (Patients in the Community)**
Pt 1 (ss 1-64) appl—Housing Grants, Construction and Regeneration, 1996 c 53, s 101
s 1 rep in pt—Mental Health, 2007 c 12, s 55, sch 11 pt 5
ss 4-6 rep—Mental Health (Care and Treatment) (S), 2003 asp 13, s 331(2), sch 5 pt 1
sch 1 rep in pt—Mental Health, 2007 c 12, s 55, sch 11 pts 1, 5
sch 2 rep—Mental Health (Care and Treatment) (S), 2003 asp 13, s 331(2), sch 5 pt 1

c 53 **Criminal Injuries Compensation**
s 1 am—SI 1999/1747, art 3, sch 10 pt II para 2
rep in pt—SI 2008/2833, art 6, sch 3
s 5 am—SIs 1999/1747, art 3, sch 10 pt II para 2; 2008/2833, art 6, sch 3
see—(power to trans functions) Tribunals, Cts and Enforcement, 2007 c 15, s 30; SI
2008/2833, arts 3-5, sch 1
s 5A added (prosp)—Tribunals, Cts and Enforcement, 2007 c 15, s 48, sch 8 para 34
s 6 am—SI 1999/1820, art 4, sch 2 pt I para 123
ss 7A, 7B added—Domestic Violence, Crime and Victims, 2004 c 28, s 57(1)(2)
am—(S) Management of Offenders etc (S), 2005 asp 14, s 20(1)(2)(a)(b)
s 7C added—Domestic Violence, Crime and Victims, 2004 c 28, s 57(1)(2)
s 7D added—Domestic Violence, Crime and Victims, 2004 c 28, s 57(1)(2)
am—(S) Management of Offenders etc (S), 2005 asp 14, s 20(1)(2)(c)
s 8 rep—Finance, 1996 c 8, s 205, sch 41 pt V
s 9 am—SI 1999/1820, art 4, sch 2 pt I para 123; Domestic Violence, Crime and Victims,
2004 c 28, s 57(1)(3)
rep in pt—SI 2008/2833, art 6, sch 3
s 11 am—Sexual Offences, 2003 c 42, s 139, sch 6 para 34; Domestic Violence, Crime and
Victims, 2004 c 28, s 57(1)(4); (S) Management of Offenders etc (S), 2005 asp 14,
s 20(3); (S) Sexual Offences (S), 2009 asp 9, s 61, sch 5 para 3
rep in pt—SI 2008/2833, art 6, sch 3

4th Session of 51st Parliament

c 54 *Consolidated Fund (No 2)*—rep Appropriation, 1997 c 31, s 3, sch C

1996

c 1 **Humber Bridge (Debts)**

c 2 **Hong Kong (Overseas Public Servants)**
ss 2, 3 rep—SL(R), 2004 c 14, s 1(1), sch 1 pt 11
ss 5, 6 rep in pt—SL(R), 2004 c 14, s 1(1), sch 1 pt 11

c 3 **Wild Mammals (Protection)**
s 2 am—(S) Protection of Wild Mammals (S), 2002 asp 6, s 11, sch, para 6
restr—(EW) Hunting, 2004 c 37, s 13(1), sch 2 para 5
s 3 subst —(EW) Animal Welfare, 2006 c 45, s 64, sch 3 para 13; (S) SSI 2006/536, reg 2,
sch 1

c 4 *Consolidated Fund*—rep Appropriation, 1998 c 28, s 3, sch(C)
s 101 appl—SI 2000/54, reg 4(3)

c 5 **Health Service Commissioners (Amendment)**
sch 1 rep in pt—Health, 1999 c 8, s 65, sch 5

c 6 **Chemical Weapons**
ext (mods)—(I of M) SI 1998/2794, arts 2,3, sch; (Guernsey) SI 2000/743, art 3, sch
appl—Anti-terrorism, Crime and Security, 2001 c 24, s 75(2)(a)
appl (mods)—(Overseas Territories) SI 2005/854, art 2, schs 1-8
ss 1-32 ext (mods)—(Bailiwick of Jersey) SI 1998/2565, art 4, sch
s 1 appl—(E) SI 2000/227, reg 2(7)
appl (mods)—(W) SI 2001/2197, reg 2(7)

1996
c 6 *continued*

    s 2 ext (mods)—(Bailiwick of Jersey) SI 1998/2565, art 3
        ext—Terrorism, 2000 c 11, s 62(2)(c); Anti-terrorism, Crime and Security, 2001 c 24, s 50(1)(2)(b)
        appl—(Guernsey) SI 2000/743, art 2
    s 29 ext—Crim Justice and Police, 2001 c 16, s 50, sch 1 pt 1 para 60
    s 30A added—(EWNI) Anti-terrorism, Crime and Security, 2001 c 24, s 46
        am—Commrs for Revenue and Customs, 2005 c 11, s 50(6), sch 4 para 64(a)(b)(e); SI 2014/834, sch 2 para 11
        rep in pt—Commrs for Revenue and Customs, 2005 c 11, ss 50(6), 52(2), sch 4 para 64(c)(d), sch 5
        mod—Serious Crime, 2007 c 27, s 63, sch 6 para 28
    s 31 am—Justice (NI), 2002 c 26, s 28(1), sch 7, para 34
    s 32 ext—Anti-terrorism, Crime and Security, 2001 c 24, s 17, sch 4 pt 1 para 39
    ss 34-36,38,39 ext (mods)—(Bailiwick of Jersey) SI 1998/2565, art 4, sch
    sch ext (mods)—(Bailiwick of Jersey) SI 1998/2565, art 4, sch

c 7   *Prevention of Terrorism (Additional Powers)*—rep Terrorism, 2000 c 11, s 125(2), sch 16 pt 1

c 8   **Finance**
    mod—SI 2009/317, art 3, sch
    s 4 rep in pt—(retrosp) Finance, 2001 c 9, s 110, sch 33 pt 1(1), Note
    s 5 rep in pt—Finance, 2008 c 9, s 14, sch 5 para 25(b)
    s 9 rep in pt—Finance, 2007 c 11, s 40, sch 9 para 1(2)(e), 17(1)
    s 15 rep in pt—(retrosp) Finance, 2001 c 9, s 110, sch 33 pt 1(3), Note 2
    s 16 am—(retrosp) Finance, 2001 c 9, s 13(4)(13)(14)
        rep in pt—(retrosp) Finance, 2001 c 9, s 110, sch 33 pt 1(3), Note 2
    s 28 rep in pt—SI 2006/3271, reg 43, sch
    s 30 rep in pt—Finance, 2012 c 14, sch 29 para 13(a)
    s 36 rep—Finance, 2007 c 11, s 114, sch 27 pt 5
    s 37 rep—Finance, 2008 c 9, s 123, sch 41 para 25(h)(i)
    s 38 rep in pt—Finance, 2002 c 23, s 141, sch 40 pt 2(2), Note
    Pt 3 (ss 39-71) appl—Bankruptcy (S), 1985 c 66 sch 3 para 8B; Insolvency, 1986 c 45 sch 6 para 3B; Finance, 1998 c 36, s 148(4)
    s 40 am (transtl saving)—(with SI 2015/638) Scotland, 2012 c 11, s 31(2); SI 2015/599, art 6
        rep in pt—(17.2.2015 with qualifying provn) Wales, 2014 c 29, s 19(2)(3)
    s 42 am—Finance, 1999 c 16, s 124(1)(2); Finance, 2000 c 17, s 140; Finance, 2001 c 9, s 104; Finance, 2002 c 23, s 122; Finance, 2003 c 14, s 187(a)(b); Finance, 2005 c 7, s 99; Finance, 2006 c 25, s 170(1); Finance, 2007 c 11, s 15(1)-(5); Finance, 2008 c 9, s 18(1); Finance, 2009 c 10, s 18(1); Finance, 2010 c 13, s 15(1); Finance (No 3), 2010 c 33, s 24(1); Finance, 2011 c 11, s 25(1); Finance, 2012 c 14, s 205(1); Finance, 2013 c 29, s 198(2)(3); Finance, 2014 c 26, s 100(2)(3); Finance, 2015 c 11, s 64(2)(3); ibid, sch 15 para 2
    s 43 am—SI 2007/2909, art 2
    s 43A added—SI 1996/1529, art 3
        rep—SI 2008/2669, art 4
    s 43B added—SI 1996/1529, art 3
        am—SI 2008/2669, art 2
        rep in pt—SI 2008/2669, art 3; ibid, art 4
    s 43C added—SI 1999/2075, art 2
        rep—Finance, 2009 c 10, s 119, sch 60 paras 1, 10
    s 44A added—SI 1999/2075, art 2
        am—SI 2005/725, arts 2, 4
    s 45 am—SI 2005/725, arts 2, 5
    s 46 am—SI 2009/56, art 3, sch 1
    s 49 rep in pt—Finance, 2009 c 10, s 119, sch 60 paras 1, 12
    s 53 am—Finance, 2007 c 11, s 24; Finance, 2008 c 9, s 151(1)(2)
    s 54 am—SI 1996/1529, art 4; Finance, 2008 c 9, s 151(1)(3); SIs 2008/2669, art 3; 2009/56, art 3, sch 1
        ext—Finance, 1997 c 16, s 50(1), sch 5 pt V para 19(3)
        rep in pt—SIs 2008/2669, art 3; ibid, art 4; 2009/56, art 3, sch 1
    ss 54A-54G added—SI 2009/56, art 3, sch 1
    s 54G am—SI 2014/1264, art 5
    s 55 rep—Income Tax, 2007 c 3, s 1031, sch 3

1996
c 8 *continued*

s 56 ext—Finance, 1997 c 16, s 50(1), sch 5 pt V para 19(3)
rep in pt—SI 2009/56, art 3, sch 1
am—SI 2009/56, art 3, sch 1
s 57 rep—Income Tax, 2007 c 3, s 1031, sch 3
s 58 am—SI 2003/2096, arts 4, 6, sch pt 1 paras 27, 28
s 59 am—SI 2009/1890, art 4
s 60 am—Finance, 2000 c 17, s 142(1)(2)
s 62 rep—Finance, 2009 c 10, s 119, sch 60 paras 1, 4
s 63 am—Finance, 2015 c 11, sch 15 para 3
s 63A added—Finance, 2015 c 11, sch 15 para 4
s 65A added—Finance, 2009 c 10, s 119, sch 60 paras 1, 2
s 66 am —Pollution Prevention and Control, 1999 c 24, s 6, sch 2 para 19 (and see Finance,
2012 c 14, s 206 which provides for coming into force of para 19 (retrosp to
21.3.2000) in relation to S)
rep in pt (transtl saving)—(with SI 2015/638) Scotland, 2012 c 11, sch 4 para 3; SI
2015/599, art 6
s 67 am—SI 2000/1973, reg 39, sch 10 pt 1 paras 20,22; (S) SSI 2000/323, reg 36, sch 10
pt I para 6(3)
rep in pt (transtl saving)—(with SI 2015/638) Scotland, 2012 c 11, sch 4 para 2; SI
2015/599, art 6
s 70 am—SIs 1996/1529, arts 5,6; 2009/56, art 3, sch 1; 2013/755 (W 90), sch 2 para 389;
Finance, 2015 c 11, sch 15 para 5
rep in pt (transtl saving)—(with SI 2015/638) Scotland, 2012 c 11, sch 4 para 4; SI
2015/599, art 6
s 71 am—Finance, 2009 c 10, s 119, sch 60 paras 1, 3; Finance, 2015 c 11, sch 15 para 6
s 72 rep in pt—Finance, 2004 c 12, ss 77, 326, sch 42 pt 2(7), Note; Income Tax, 2007 c 3,
s 1031, sch 3
s 73 rep in pt—Income Tax, 2007 c 3, s 1031, sch 3
ss 74-76 rep—Income Tax, 2007 c 3, s 1031, sch 3
s 77 am—Finance, 2007 c 11, s 74(2)(4)
s 78 rep—Corporation Tax, 2010 c 4, s 1181, sch 3 pt 1
Pt 4, Ch 2 (ss 80-105) mod—(saving) Gas, 1986 c 44, s 60(3); (saving) Income and
Corporation Taxes, 1988 c 1, ss 56(4B), 477(3)(a), 494AA(5), 730A(6),
768B(10)(11), 768C(9)(10), 774B(5)(a); (saving) Legal Aid, 1988 c 35, s
11(7); Broadcasting, 1996 c 55, s 135, sch 7 para 11(2); Transport, 2000 c 38,
s 64, sch 7 para 17; Transport, 2000 c 38, s 250, sch 26 pt II para 7 pt III para
17 pt V para 29; Energy, 2004 c 20, s 47, sch 9 pt 1 para 11(2), pt 2 para 23(2)
appl—Income and Corporation Taxes, 1988 c 1, ss 43; (saving) Finance, 1993 c 34, ss
130,167(5A); Finance, 1994 c 9, s 160(2)(2A); Finance, 1996 c 8, ss 104,
105(1) sch 14 paras 23(2), 32(2); Finance, 2004 c 12, s 145, sch 26 para 1(6);
Energy, 2004 c 20, s 47, sch 9 pt 1 para 11(3), pt 2 para 23(3); Income Tax
(Trading and Other Income), 2005 c 5, s 149(4); Railways, 2005 c 14, s 53, sch
10 pt 3 para 28(2)
appl (mods)—Income and Corporation Taxes, 1988 c 1, s 730BB(6)(8)(9); Finance,
2005 c 7, ss 50(1)(2), 56
excl—(saving) Income and Corporation Taxes, 1988 c 1, ss 468L(5) 798(3A)
restr—(saving) Income and Corporation Taxes, 1988 c 1, ss 475(2)(b) 487(1)(3A),
494(2), 582(3A); Proceeds of Crime, 2002 c 29, s 448, sch 10 pt 2, paras 9, 10
ext—Income and Corporation Taxes, 1988 c 1, s 510A(6A)
ss 80-84 rep—Corporation Tax, 2009 c 4, ss 1322, 1326, sch 1 paras 402-407, sch 3 pt 1
s 84A added—Finance, 2002 c 23, s 79(2)(3), sch 23 pt 1, para 3, paras 25, 26(5)
rep—Corporation Tax, 2009 c 4, ss 1322, 1326, sch 1 paras 402, 408, sch 3 pt 1
ss 85, 86 replaced (by ss 85A, 85B)—Finance, 2004 c 12, s 52, sch 10 pt 1 para 3
s 85A rep—Corporation Tax, 2009 c 4, ss 1322, 1326, sch 1 paras 402, 409, sch 3 pt 1
s 85B ext—Finance, 2005 c 7, s 80, sch 4 pt 2 para 52
am—Finance, 2005 c 7, s 80, sch 4 pt 2 para 26
rep in pt—Finance (No 2), 2005 c 22, s 70, sch 11 pt 2(6), Note 3
appl (mods)—Crossrail, 2008 c 18, s 37, sch 13 para 14
s 85C rep—Corporation Tax, 2009 c 4, ss 1322, 1326, sch 1 paras 402, 411, sch 3 pt 1
s 87 rep—Corporation Tax, 2009 c 4, ss 1322, 1326, sch 1 paras 402, 412, sch 3 pt 1
s 87A rep—Corporation Tax, 2009 c 4, ss 1322, 1326, sch 1 paras 402, 413, sch 3 pt 1
s 88 rep—Corporation Tax, 2009 c 4, ss 1322, 1326, sch 1 paras 402, 414, sch 3 pt 1
s 88A rep—Corporation Tax, 2009 c 4, ss 1322, 1326, sch 1 paras 402, 415, sch 3 pt 1

1996
c 8 *continued*

s 89 rep—Finance, 2002 c 23, ss 82, 141, sch 25 pt 1, paras 1, 9, sch 40 pt 3(12), Note

s 90 rep (saving)—Finance, 2004 c 12, ss 52, 326, sch 10 pt 1 para 7, sch 42 pt 2(6), Note 1

s 90A rep—Corporation Tax, 2009 c 4, ss 1322, 1326, sch 1 paras 402, 416, sch 3 pt 1

s 91 rep—Finance, 2002 c 23, ss 82, 141, sch 25 pt 1, paras 1, 11, sch 40 pt 3(12), Note

ss 91A-91I rep—Corporation Tax, 2009 c 4, ss 1322, 1326, sch 1 paras 402, 417-425, sch 3 pt 1

s 92 rep (saving)—Finance, 2004 c 12, ss 52, 326, sch 10 pt 1 para 10, sch 42 pt 2(6), Notes 1, 2

am—Income Tax (Trading and Other Income), 2005 c 5, s 882(1), sch 1 pt 2 paras 485, 486

appl (mods)—Crossrail, 2008 c 18, s 37, sch 13 para 14

s 92A rep (saving)—Finance, 2004 c 12, ss 52, 326, sch 10 pt 1 para 10, sch 42 pt 2(6), Note 1

ss 93, 93A, 93B rep (saving)—Finance, 2004 c 12, ss 52, 326, sch 10 pt 1 para 11, sch 42 pt 2(6), Notes 1, 3

s 93C rep—Corporation Tax, 2009 c 4, ss 1322, 1326, sch 1 paras 402, 426, sch 3 pt 1

s 94 rep—Corporation Tax, 2009 c 4, ss 1322, 1326, sch 1 paras 402, 427, sch 3 pt 1

s 94A rep—Corporation Tax, 2009 c 4, ss 1322, 1326, sch 1 paras 402, 428, sch 3 pt 1

s 94B rep—Corporation Tax, 2009 c 4, ss 1322, 1326, sch 1 paras 402, 429, sch 3 pt 1

ss 95-101 rep—Corporation Tax, 2009 c 4, ss 1322, 1326, sch 1 paras 402, 430-436, sch 3 pt 1

s 102 rep—Income Tax (Trading and Other Income), 2005 c 5, ss 882(1), 884, sch 1 pt 2 paras 485, 487, sch 3

s 103 rep—Corporation Tax, 2009 c 4, ss 1322, 1326, sch 1 paras 402, 437, sch 3 pt 1

s 105 appl (mods)—Crossrail, 2008 c 18, s 37, sch 13 para 14

ss 106-110 rep—Income Tax (Earnings and Pensions), 2003 c 1, s 724(1), sch 8 pt 1

Pt 4, Ch 4 (ss 111-120) mod—(saving) Airports, 1986 c 31, s 77(3)

s 111 rep in pt—(retrosp to options granted on or after 2.12.2004) Finance (No 2), 2005 c 22, s 70, sch 11 pt 2(5), Note

ss 113-115 rep—Income Tax (Earnings and Pensions), 2003 c 1, s 724(1), sch 8 pt 1

s 120 rep in pt—Income Tax (Earnings and Pensions), 2003 c 1, s 724(1), sch 8 pt 1

s 121 rep in pt—Finance, 1998 c 36, s 165, sch 27 pt III(28), Note

s 122 rep in pt —Finance (No 2), 1997 c 58, s 52, sch 8 pt II(11), Note; Income Tax (Trading and Other Income), 2005 c 5, s 884, sch 3

s 123 rep in pt—Finance, 2001 c 9, s 110, sch 33 pt 2(13), Note; Finance, 2007 c 11, s 114, sch 27 pt 5

s 124 rep in pt—Finance, 2008 c 9, s 115, sch 37 para 11(b)

s 125 rep in pt—Finance, 2007 c 11, s 114, sch 27 pt 5

s 128 rep in pt—Finance, 2001 c 9, s 110, sch 33 pt 2(6), Note; Income Tax (Trading and Other Income), 2005 c 5, s 884, sch 3

s 129 rep in pt—(saving) Finance (No 2), 1997 c 58, s 52, sch 8 pt II(2), Note; Finance, 1999 c 16, s 139, sch 20 pt III(15), Note

s 135 rep in pt—Capital Allowances, 2001 c 2, s 580, sch 4

s 137 rep—Income Tax, 2007 c 3, s 1031, sch 3

s 139 rep—Finance, 1998 c 36, s 165, sch 27 pt III(2), Note

s 143 rep—Income Tax (Trading and Other Income), 2005 c 5, s 884, sch 3

s 144 rep—Finance, 1999 c 16, s 139, sch 20 pt III(15), Note

s 145 rep—Finance, 2008 c 9, s 70(3)

s 146 rep—Corporation Tax, 2010 c 4, s 1181, sch 3 pt 1

s 147 rep in pt—Corporation Tax, 2009 c 4, s 1326, sch 3 pt 1

s 148 am—SI 2001/3629, arts 92, 93(1)-(3); Finance, 2004 c 12, s 281(1), sch 35 paras 43, 44

s 149 rep—Finance, 1999 c 16, s 139, sch 20 pt III(6), Note

s 150 rep—Income Tax (Trading and Other Income), 2005 c 5, s 884, sch 3

s 151 am—Capital Allowances, 2001 c 2, s 578, sch 2 para 95

s 152 rep—Income Tax (Earnings and Pensions), 2003 c 1, s 724(1), sch 8 pt 1

s 153 rep—SL(R), 2013 c 2, s 1, sch 1 pt 10(1)

s 154 appl—Income and Corporation Taxes, 1988 c 1, s 118G(c)

am—Income Tax (Trading and Other Income), 2005 c 5, s 882(1), sch 1 pt 2 paras 485, 488(1)(2)

rep in pt—Income Tax (Trading and Other Income), 2005 c 5, ss 882(1), 884, sch 1 pt 2 paras 485, 488(1)(3)(4), sch 3; Corporation Tax, 2009 c 4, ss 1322, 1326, sch 1 paras 402, 438, sch 3 pt 1

1996
c 8 *continued*

s 155 rep—Income Tax, 2007 c 3, s 1031, sch 3
s 156 rep—SL(R), 2013 c 2, s 1, sch 1 pt 10(1)
s 158 rep—Income Tax, 2007 c 3, s 1031, sch 3
s 159 rep in pt—Finance, 1997 c 16, ss 76,113, sch 10 pt I para 7(1), sch 18 pt VI(10), Note
        1; Income Tax, 2007 c 3, s 1031, sch 3; Corporation Tax, 2010 c 4, s 1181, sch
        3 pt I
s 160 rep—Finance, 2006 c 25, s 143
s 161 rep—Income Tax, 2007 c 3, s 1031, sch 3
s 163 rep—Finance, 2012 c 14, sch 16 para 247(g)(i)
s 164 rep in pt—Finance (No 2), 1997 c 58, s 52, sch 8 pt II(6), Note; Finance, 2004 c 12, s
        326, sch 42 pt 2(3), Note; SI 2006/3271, reg 43, sch; Finance, 2008 c 9, s 43,
        sch 17 para 24(2)
s 165 rep in pt—Finance, 1997 c 16, s 113, sch 18 pt VI(6), Note; Corporation Tax, 2010 c
        4, s 1181, sch 3 pt I
s 166 rep (in relation to accounting periods ending on days to be specified by Treasury
        Order)—Finance, 2012 c 14, s 26(2)(b)(3)
s 167 rep in pt—Income Tax, 2007 c 3, s 1031, sch 3; Finance, 2007 c 11, s 114, sch 27 pt 2;
        Finance, 2012 c 14, sch 16 para 247(g)(ii); (prosp) ibid, sch 39 para 28(1)(3)
s 168 rep in pt—Finance, 2007 c 11, s 114, sch 27 pt 2; Finance, 2008 c 9, s 36, sch 14 para
        17(e); Finance, 2012 c 14, sch 16 para 247(g)(iii)
s 169 rep—Finance, 2001 c 9, s 110, sch 33 pt 2(12), Note
s 170 rep—Finance, 1998 c 36, s 165, sch 27 pt III(28), Note
s 171 rep —Finance, 2012 c 14, sch 18 para 23(d)
s 172 rep—Finance, 2004 c 12, s 326, sch 42 pt 3, Note
s 173 rep in pt—Corporation Tax, 2010 c 4, s 1181, sch 3 pt I
s 175 rep —Corporation Tax, 2010 c 4, s 1181, sch 3 pt I
s 176 rep—(2003-04) Finance, 1998 c 36, s 165, sch 27 pt III(31), Note
s 178 rep—Finance, 2004 c 12, ss 77, 326, sch 42 pt 2(7), Note
ss 179, 180 rep—Capital Allowances, 2001 c 2, s 580, sch 4
ss 186-196 rep—Finance, 1996 c 8, s 205, sch 41 pt VII, Note 4; Finance, 1997 c 16, s 113,
        sch 18 pt VII, Note 10
s 197 am—Finance, 1997 c 16, s 50(1), sch 5 pt V para 21; Finance, 1999 c 16, s 130(3)(4);
        Finance, 2000 c 17, s 30(2), sch 7 para 6; Finance, 2001 c 9, ss 15, 49(2), sch 3
        pt 4 paras 18, 21, 22; (retrosp) (to 1.4.2002) Finance, 2002 c 23, s 132(2)(3);
        Finance, 2009 c 10, s 105(6)(b); SI 2009/56, art 3, sch 1
    appl—Finance, 1997 c 16, s 50(1), sch 5 pt V para 17(1); Finance, 1999 c 16, ss
        126(2)(4)(8), 127(7)(11)
    ext—Finance, 1999 c 16, s 126(3)(4)(8)
    rep in pt—Finance, 1997 c 16, s 113, sch 18 pt V(1), Note; Finance, 1999 c 16, s 139,
        sch 20 pt VI
s 200 am—Representation of the People, 2000 c 2, s 15(1), sch 6 para 19; Taxation
        (International and Other Provns), 2010 c 8, s 371, sch 7 paras 73, 74(3)
    rep in pt—Taxation (International and Other Provns), 2010 c 8, ss 371, 378, sch 7
        paras 73, 74(2), sch 10 pt 12
s 202 saved—Income Tax (Trading and Other Income), 2005 c 5, ss 154(3), 452(2)
s 203 am—Corporation Tax, 2009 c 4, s 1322, sch 1 paras 402, 439
sch 1 am—SI 1998/1200, art 2; Finance, 2008 c 9, s 62, sch 22 para 3(1)
sch 1A am—Finance, 2007 c 11, s 41, sch 10 paras 6(1)(3), 17(2)
sch 2 rep in pt—Finance, 2001 c 9, s 110, sch 33 pt 1(3), Note 1(b); Finance, 2008 c 9, s
        118, sch 39 para 65(b)
sch 3 rep in pt—Finance, 2007 c 11, s 114, sch 27 pt 6; Finance, 2008 c 9, s 113, sch 36
        para 92(e)
sch 5 ext—Finance, 1997 c 16, s 50(1), sch 5 pt I para 4(3); Crim Justice and Police, 2001 c
        16, s 50, sch 1 pt 1 para 61
    power to mod—Finance, 1997 c 16, s 50(1), sch 5 pt I para 3
    rep in pt—Finance, 1997 c 16, s 113, sch 18 pt V(2), Note; (NI) SI 1997/2983, art
        13(2), sch 2; Youth Justice and Crim Evidence, 1999 c 23, s 67, sch 6; (NI) SI
        1999/2789, art 40(3), sch 3; Enterprise, 2002 c 40, s 278(2), sch 26; Crim
        Justice, 2003 c 44, s 332, sch 37 pt 6; SI 2004/1501, art 46(2), sch 2; Commrs
        for Revenue and Customs, 2005 c 11, ss 50(6), 52(2), sch 4 para 65, sch 5;
        Finance, 2007 c 11, ss 84, 114, sch 22 paras 3, 10, sch 27 pt 5; Finance, 2008 c
        9, ss 122, 123, 129, 138, sch 40 para 21(e), sch 41 para 25(h)(ii), sch 43 para 5,

1996
c 8 sch 5 *continued*

sch 44 para 7(b); (savings) SI 2009/3054, arts 3, 6, sch; Finance, 2009 c 10, s 99, sch 51 paras 37, 40(1)(6)(b)

am—Finance, 1997 c 16, ss 50(1),53(8)(9), sch 5 pt I pt II paras 5(3),6(2)(c) pt III para 12 pt IV para 13; (retrosp) ibid, s 50(1), sch 5 pt III para 11; Finance, 2000 c 17, s 142(3)(4), sch 37; Crim Justice and Police, 2001 c 16, s 70, sch 2 pt 2 para 13(1)(2)(h); Tribunals, Cts and Enforcement, 2007 c 15, s 62, sch 13 paras 122-124; Finance, 2008 c 9, s 138, sch 44 para 7(a); SI 2009/56, art 3, sch 1; Finance, 2009 c 10, s 98, sch 50 paras 21; ibid, s 99, sch 51 paras 37-39, 40(1)-(5)(6)(a); ibid, s 119, sch 60 paras 1, 5-9, 11; SIs 2009/571, art 8, sch 1; 2010/530, art 2, sch; 2013/755 (W 90), sch 2 para 390; Finance, 2015 c 11, sch 15 para 7; SI 2015/664, sch 2 para 9(a)-(e)

sch 6 rep in pt—Finance (No 2), 1997 c 58, s 52, sch 8 pt II(11), Note; Finance, 1997 c 16, ss 76,113, sch 10 pt I para 7(1), sch 18 pt VI(10), Note 1; Finance, 1998 c 36, s 165, sch 27, pt III(3), Note; Finance, 1999 c 16, s 139, sch 20 pt III(1), Note; Finance, 2003 c 14, s 216, sch 43 pt 3(12), Note 3; Income Tax (Trading and Other Income), 2005 c 5, s 884, sch 3; Income Tax, 2007 c 3, s 1031, sch 3; Finance, 2008 c 9, s 5, sch 1 para 49; Corporation Tax, 2009 c 4, s 1326, sch 3 pt 1; Corporation Tax, 2010 c 4, s 1181, sch 3 pt 1; SL(R), 2013 c 2, s 1, sch 1 pt 10(1)

sch 7 rep in pt—Finance, 2000 c 17, s 156, sch 40 pt II(17); Income Tax (Earnings and Pensions), 2003 c 1, s 724(1), sch 8 pt 1; Finance, 2003 c 14, s 216, sch 43 pt 5(3), Note; Income Tax (Trading and Other Income), 2005 c 5, s 884, sch 3; Income Tax, 2007 c 3, s 1031, sch 3; Finance, 2009 c 10, s 49, sch 25 para 9(3)(c); Corporation Tax, 2009 c 4, s 1326, sch 3 pt 1; Corporation Tax, 2010 c 4, s 1181, sch 3 pt 1; SL(R), 2013 c 2, s 1, sch 1 pt 10(1)

schs 8-11 rep—Corporation Tax, 2009 c 4, ss 1322, 1326, sch 1 paras 402, 440-443, sch 3 pt 1

sch 12 rep—Finance, 2002 c 23, ss 83(1)(b)(3), 141, sch 27, paras 17, 21, sch 40 pt 3(13), Note

sch 13 rep (saving)—(2005-06) Income Tax (Trading and Other Income), 2005 c 5, ss 882(1), 883(4), 884, sch 1 pt 2 paras 485, 490, sch 2 pt 5 paras 80, 81, sch 3

rep in pt—Corporation Tax, 2009 c 4, s 1326, sch 3 pt 1

sch 14 rep in pt—Finance (No 2), 1997 c 58, s 52, sch 8 pt II(4)(6), Note; Finance, 1997 c 16, ss 76,113, sch 10 pt I para 7(1), sch 18 pt VI(10), Note 1; Finance, 1998 c 36, s 165, sch 27 pt III(2)(4), Note; Finance, 2001 c 9, s 110, sch 33 pt 2(10), Note; Finance, 2002 c 23, s 141, sch 40 pt 3(10)(13), Note 2; Finance, 2004 c 12, s 326, sch 42 pt 2(3), Note; Income Tax (Trading and Other Income), 2005 c 5, s 884, sch 3; Income Tax, 2007 c 3, s 1031, sch 3; Finance, 2007 c 11, s 114, sch 27 pt 2; Finance, 2008 c 9, s 43, sch 17 para 18(5)(d); Corporation Tax, 2009 c 4, s 1326, sch 3 pt 1; Corporation Tax, 2010 c 4, s 1181, sch 3 pt 1; Taxation (International and Other Provns), 2010 c 8, s 378, sch 10 pts 1, 12; Finance, 2012 c 14, sch 16 para 247(g)(iv); SL(R), 2013 c 2, s 1, sch 1 pt 10(1)

sch 15 am—Finance, 1997 c 16, s 83, sch 13 paras 2-6, 7; Finance, 1999 c 16, s 67(1)-(3)(6)(7); Finance, 2000 c 17, s 102, sch 29 pt II para 45 pt III para 46(5); SI 2001/3629, arts 92, 96(1)(c); Finance, 2002 c 23, s 82, sch 25 pt 1, paras 1, 41, 42; Finance, 2003 c 14, s 155, sch 27 para 8; Income Tax (Trading and Other Income), 2005 c 5, s 882(1), sch 1 pt 2 paras 485, 491; SI 2005/3229, reg 130; Corporation Tax, 2009 c 4, s 1322, sch 1 paras 402, 444(1)(3)-(5)(7)-(9)(11)(12)(14)(b)(d)(15)(b)(c)(16)(b); Corporation Tax, 2010 c 4, s 1177, sch 1 paras 291, 293

ext—Finance, 1999 c 16, s 81(4)(5)(12)

mod—Finance (No 2), 1997 c 58, s 40(7)(9)

appl (mods)—Finance, 2002 c 23, s 82, sch 25 pt 3, para 64(6)

rep in pt—Finance, 2002 c 23, ss 79(2)(3), 141, sch 23 pt 1, paras 1, 16 pt 3, para 25, sch 40 pt 3(10)(13), Note 2; Finance, 2007 c 11, s 41, sch 10 paras 16(1)(5)(d), sch 27; Corporation Tax, 2009 c 4, ss 1322, 1326, sch 1 paras 402, 444(1)(2)(6)(10)(13)(14)(a)(c)(15)(a)(16)(a), sch 3 pt 1

sch 16 rep—Income Tax (Earnings and Pensions), 2003 c 1, s 724(1), sch 8 pt 1

sch 18 rep in pt—(saving) Finance (No 2), 1997 c 58, s 52, sch 8 pt II(2), Note; Finance, 1999 c 16, s 139, sch 20 pt III(15), Note; Income Tax (Trading and Other Income), 2005 c 5, s 884, sch 3; Finance, 2012 c 14, sch 39 para 28(1)(3)

1996
c 8 *continued*

sch 19 rep in pt—Finance, 1998 c 36, s 165, sch 27 pt III(28), Note; Finance, 2001 c 9, s 110, sch 33 pt 2(13), Note; Finance, 2008 c 9, s 113, sch 36 para 92(e)

sch 20 rep in pt—Finance, 1998 c 36, s 165, sch 27 pt III(4)(28), Note; (2003-04) ibid, pt III(31), Note; Finance, 1999 c 16, s 139, sch 20 pt III(7), Note 4; (2000-01) ibid, pt III(3), Note 2; ibid, pt III(4), Note; Finance, 2000 c 17, s 156, sch 40 pt II(3), Note; Capital Allowances, 2001 c 2, s 580, sch 4; Finance, 2002 c 23, s 141, sch 40 pt 3(13), Note 2; Income Tax (Earnings and Pensions), 2003 c 1, s 724(1), sch 8 pt 1; Income Tax (Trading and Other Income), 2005 c 5, s 884, sch 3; Income Tax, 2007 c 3, s 1031, sch 3; Finance, 2008 c 9, s 66(4)(g)(i); Finance, 2009 c 10, s 5, sch 1 para 6(g); Corporation Tax, 2009 c 4, s 1326, sch 3 pt 1; Corporation Tax, 2010 c 4, s 1181, sch 3 pt 1; Taxation (International and Other Provns), 2010 c 8, s 378, sch 10 pt 1; Finance, 2011 c 11, sch 9 para 5(a); Finance, 2012 c 14, sch 39 para 28(1)(3); SL(R), 2013 c 2, s 1, sch 1 pt 10(1)

sch 21 rep in pt—(savings) Finance, 1997 c 16, ss 85,113, sch 15 para 9(1), sch 18 pt VI(11), Note; Finance, 1998 c 36, s 165, sch 27, pt III(9)(23), Notes 1-2; (2003-04) ibid, pt III(31), Note; Finance, 1999 c 16, s 139, sch 20 pt III(3), Note 2, pt III(7), Note 4, pt III(6), Note; Finance, 2000 c 17, s 156, sch 40 pt II(4), Note 3; Capital Allowances, 2001 c 2, s 580, sch 4; Finance, 2004 c 12, s 326, sch 42 pt 3, Note; Income Tax (Trading and Other Income), 2005 c 5, s 884, sch 3; Income Tax, 2007 c 3, s 1031, sch 3; Finance, 2008 c 9, s 8, sch 2 para 75; Finance, 2009 c 10, s 5, sch 1 para 6(g); Corporation Tax, 2009 c 4, s 1326, sch 3 pt 1; Corporation Tax, 2010 c 4, s 1181, sch 3 pt 2; Taxation (International and Other Provns), 2010 c 8, s 378, sch 10 pts 1, 9; SL(R), 2013 c 2, s 1, sch 1 pt 10(1)

sch 22 rep in pt—Finance, 2001 c 9, s 110, sch 33 pt 2(13), Note; Finance, 2008 c 9, s 113, sch 36 para 92(e)

sch 23 rep—Income Tax, 2007 c 3, s 1031, sch 3

sch 24 rep in pt—Finance, 1998 c 36, s 165, sch 27 pt III(28), Note; Finance, 2001 c 9, s 110, sch 33 pt 2(13), Note; Corporation Tax, 2009 c 4, s 1326, sch 3 pt 1; Corporation Tax, 2010 c 4, s 1181, sch 3 pt 1

sch 25 rep—Finance, 1998 c 36, s 165, sch 27 pt III(2), Note

sch 26 rep—Income Tax (Trading and Other Income), 2005 c 5, s 884, sch 3

sch 27 rep in pt—Finance (No 2), 1997 c 58, s 52, sch 8 pt II(6)(11), Note

sch 28 rep in pt—SIs 2000/2188, art 6(2); 2009/3001, regs 13, schs 1, 2; Taxation (International and Other Provns), 2010 c 8, s 378, sch 10 pt 12

sch 29 rep—Finance, 2000 c 17, s 156, sch 40 pt II(17)

sch 30 rep—Finance, 2006 c 25, s 143, sch 26

sch 31 rep —Finance, 2012 c 14, sch 16 para 247(g)(v)

sch 32 rep (in relation to accounting periods ending on days to be specified by Treasury Order)—Finance, 2012 c 14, s 26(2)(b)(3)

sch 33 rep —Finance, 2012 c 14, sch 16 para 247(g)(vi)

sch 34 rep—Finance, 2001 c 9, s 110, sch 33 pt 2(12), Note

sch 35 rep—Capital Allowances, 2001 c 2, s 580, sch 4

sch 36 rep in pt—Finance, 1998 c 36, s 165, sch 27 pt III(27), Note; Finance, 2005 c 7, s 104, sch 11 pt 2(6), Note; Finance, 2009 c 10, s 36, sch 16 para 5 (c); SL(R), 2013 c 2, s 1, sch 1 pt 10(1)

sch 37 rep in pt—Income Tax, 2007 c 3, s 1031, sch 3; Corporation Tax, 2010 c 4, s 1181, sch 3 pt 1; SL(R), 2013 c 2, s 1, sch 1 pt 10(1)

sch 38 rep in pt—Finance (No 2), 1997 c 58, s 52, sch 8 pt II(11), Note; Finance, 2000 c 17, s 156, sch 40 pt II(10) Note 2,pt II(17); Income Tax (Trading and Other Income), 2005 c 5, s 884, sch 3; Income Tax, 2007 c 3, s 1031, sch 3; Finance, 2007 c 11, s 114, sch 27 pts 2, 6; Finance, 2008 c 9, s 66(4)(g)(ii); Corporation Tax, 2010 c 4, s 1181, sch 3 pt 1; Taxation (International and Other Provns), 2010 c 8, s 378, sch 10 pt 12

sch 39 rep in pt—Finance, 1998 c 36, s 165, sch 27 pt III(4), Note; (from year 2003-04) ibid, sch 27 pt III(31), Note; Capital Allowances, 2001 c 2, s 580, sch 4; Finance, 2004 c 12, s 326, sch 42 pt 3, Note

sch 40 rep in pt—Finance, 1999 c 16, s 138, sch 20 pt V(2), Notes 1, 2; Income Tax (Trading and Other Income), 2005 c 5, s 884, sch 3; Income Tax, 2007 c 3, s 1031, sch 3

c 9   *Education (Student Loans)*—rep Teaching and Higher Educ, 1998 c 30, s 44(2), sch 4

1996

c 10   **Audit (Miscellaneous Provisions)**
ss 1-3, 5, 6 rep—Audit Commission, 1998 c 18, s 54(3), sch 5

c 11   *Northern Ireland (Entry to Negotiations, etc)*—rep Northern Ireland, 1998 c 47, s 100(2), sch 15

c 12   **Rating (Caravans and Boats)**
sch am—Police and Fire Reform (S), 2012 asp 8, sch 7 para 60

c 13   **Non-Domestic Rating (Information)**
s 1 am—Business Rate Supplements, 2009 c 7, s 12(10)

c 14   **Reserve Forces**
ext (mods) —(to Isle of Man) SI 2010/2470, art 2, sch
am—Defence Reform, 2014 c 20, s 44(3)(4)
s 1 appl—SIs (E) 2001/475, reg 5, sch 1 para 36(i); (E) 2002/377, reg 5, sch 1, para 36(i);
2002/3199, reg 5, sch 2, para 20(i); (E) 2003/3170, reg 5, sch 3 para 20(i); (E)
2004/3131, reg 6, sch 3 para 21(i)
s 2 am—Armed Forces, 2006 c 52, s 358, sch 14 para 25
s 4 am—Armed Forces, 2006 c 52, s 358, sch 14 para 26
s 7 rep —Armed Forces, 2006 c 52, s 358, sch 14 para 27
s 9 am—Lieutenancies, 1997 c 23, s 8(2)
s 13 am—Armed Forces, 2006 c 52, s 358, sch 14 para 28
mod—SI 2009/1059, art 195
s 15 am—Armed Forces, 2006 c 52, s 358, sch 14 para 29
s 24 rep in pt—Armed Forces, 2006 c 52, s 358, sch 14 para 30
s 25 am—Armed Forces, 2006 c 52, s 358, sch 14 para 31
rep in pt—Armed Forces, 2006 c 52, s 358, sch 14 para 31
s 27 rep in pt—Armed Forces, 2006 c 52, s 358, sch 14 para 32
Pts 4-7 (ss 28-77) mod—Army, 1955 c 18, s 9(6A) sch 7 para 4(6A); Armed Forces, 1966 c
45, s 4(6A)
s 28 am—Defence Reform, 2014 c 20, s 45(1)
s 35 am—Armed Forces, 2001 c 19, s 34, sch 6 pt 3 para 11
s 41 rep in pt—Armed Forces, 2001 c 19, ss 34, 38, sch 6 pt 3 para 12, sch 7 pt 7
s 53 am—Armed Forces, 2006 c 52, s 358, sch 14 para 33
rep in pt—Armed Forces, 2006 c 52, s 358, sch 14 para 33
s 53A added—Armed Forces, 2006 c 52, s 358, sch 14 para 34
s 54 am—Defence Reform, 2014 c 20, s 45(3)
s 55 am—Armed Forces, 2006 c 52, s 358, sch 14 para 33
rep in pt—Armed Forces, 2006 c 52, s 358, sch 14 para 33
s 55A added—Armed Forces, 2006 c 52, s 358, sch 14 para 35
s 56 am—Armed Forces, 2011 c 18, s 28; Defence Reform, 2014 c 20, s 45(4)(5)
s 57 am—Armed Forces, 2006 c 52, s 358, sch 14 para 33; Defence Reform, 2014 c 20, s
45(6)
rep in pt—Armed Forces, 2006 c 52, s 358, sch 14 para 33
s 57A added—Armed Forces, 2006 c 52, s 358, sch 14 para 36
am—Defence Reform, 2014 c 20, s 45(7)
s 64 am—Defence Reform, 2014 c 20, s 45(8)
s 66 am—Armed Forces, 2006 c 52, s 358, sch 14 para 37
s 72 rep in pt—Armed Forces, 2006 c 52, s 358, sch 14 para 38
s 75 rep in pt—(EW) (prosp) Crim Justice, 2003 c 44, ss 280(1)(3), 332, sch 25 para 97, sch
37 pt 9
s 82 rep in pt—(EW) (prosp) Crim Justice, 2003 c 44, ss 280(1)(3), 332, sch 25 para 98, sch
37 pt 9
s 83 am—Defence Reform, 2014 c 20, sch 7 paras 2, 3
s 84 am—Defence Reform, 2014 c 20, sch 7 para 3
s 84A added—Defence Reform, 2014 c 20, s 46(1)
s 85 am—Defence Reform, 2014 c 20, sch 7 paras 4(2)(a)(c)(d)(3)-(6), 5
rep in pt—Defence Reform, 2014 c 20, sch 7 para 4(2)(b)
s 86 am—Defence Reform, 2014 c 20, sch 7 para 6(2)(5)
rep in pt—Defence Reform, 2014 c 20, sch 7 para 6(3)-(5)
s 87 rep in pt—(EW) (prosp) Crim Justice, 2003 c 44, ss 280(1)(3), 332, sch 25 para 99, sch
37 pt 9
am—Defence Reform, 2014 c 20, sch 7 para 7
s 89 am—Defence Reform, 2014 c 20, sch 7 para 8
ss 90, 91 am—(S) SI 1999/1750, art 4, sch 3; Constitutional Reform, 2005 c 4, s 15(1), sch
4 pt 1 paras 240-242
cert functs exercisable in S—SI 1999/1748, art 3, sch 1 para 18

1996

c 14 ss 90, 91 *continued*

see—(trans of functions) (S) SI 1999/678, art 2(1), sch

rep in pt—SI 1999/1750, art 6(1), sch 5 para 16

s 92 am—Constitutional Reform, 2005 c 4, s 15(1), sch 4 pt 1 paras 240, 243

s 92A added—Constitutional Reform, 2005 c 4, s 15(1), sch 4 pt 1 paras 240, 244

s 95 am—Armed Forces, 2006 c 52, s 358, sch 14 para 39

rep in pt—Armed Forces, 2006 c 52, s 358, sch 14 para 39; Armed Forces, 2011 c 18, s 15(2)(a), sch 5

s 96 am—Armed Forces, 2006 c 52, s 358, sch 14 para 40

s 97 am—Armed Forces, 2006 c 52, s 358, sch 14 para 41

s 98 am—Armed Forces, 2006 c 52, s 358, sch 14 para 42

rep in pt—Armed Forces, 2006 c 52, s 358, sch 14 para 42

mod—SI 2009/1059, art 201(3)

s 99 rep —Armed Forces, 2006 c 52, s 358, sch 14 para 43

s 100 rep—Armed Forces, 2006 c 52, s 358, sch 14 para 44

s 100A added—Armed Forces, 2006 c 52, s 358, sch 14 para 44

s 102 rep—Armed Forces, 2006 c 52, s 358, sch 14 para 45

s 103 rep—Armed Forces, 2006 c 52, s 378, sch 17

s 104 rep in pt—Armed Forces, 2006 c 52, s 358, sch 14 para 46

s 105 am—Armed Forces, 2006 c 52, s 358, sch 14 para 47

rep in pt—Armed Forces, 2006 c 52, s 358, sch 14 para 47

mod—SI 2009/1059, art 201(1)

s 106 rep—Armed Forces, 2006 c 52, s 358, sch 14 para 48

s 107 am—Armed Forces, 2006 c 52, s 358, sch 14 para 49

rep in pt—Armed Forces, 2006 c 52, s 358, sch 14 para 49

mod—2009/1059, art 201(5)(6)

s 108 am—Armed Forces, 2006 c 52, s 358, sch 14 para 50

s 113A added—Defence Reform, 2014 c 20, s 47

s 121 rep—Lieutenancies, 1997 c 23, s 8(4), sch 3

s 123 rep—Armed Forces, 2006 c 52, s 378, sch 17

s 124 rep—Armed Forces, 2006 c 52, s 358, sch 14 para 51

s 125 am—SI 1999/787, art 97, sch 8 para 1; Armed Forces, 2001 c 19, s 34, sch 6 pt 3 para 13

s 126 rep—Armed Forces, 2006 c 52, s 358, sch 14 para 52

s 127 rep in pt—SI 1998/3086, reg 10(5); Armed Forces, 2006 c 52, s 358, sch 14 para 53

am—Armed Forces, 2006 c 52, s 358, sch 14 para 53

s 129 am—Defence Reform, 2014 c 20, sch 6 paras 2, 3

sch 1 am—Armed Forces, 2006 c 52, s 358, sch 14 para 54

rep in pt—(EW) (prosp) Crim Justice, 2003 c 44, ss 280(1)(3), 332, sch 25 para 101, sch 37 pt 9; Armed Forces, 2006 c 52, s 358, sch 14 para 54

sch 2 rep —Armed Forces, 2006 c 52, s 358, sch 14 para 55

sch 3 rep—Armed Forces, 2006 c 52, s 358, sch 14 para 56

sch 5 rep in pt—SI 1999/678, art 5

see—(trans of functions) (S) SIs 1999/678, art 2, sch; 1999/1750, art 2, sch 1

am—Charities, 2006 c 50, s 75, sch 8 para 181; SI 2011/1396, sch para 36(b); Charities, 2011 c 25, sch 7 para 69(1)-(3)

sch 6 rep—Lieutenancies, 1997 c 23, s 8(4), sch 3

sch 7 rep—Armed Forces, 2006 c 52, s 358, sch 14 para 57

sch 9 rep in pt—Armed Forces, 2006 c 52, s 358, sch 14 para 58

am—Defence Reform, 2014 c 20, sch 6 paras 4, 5, sch 7 para 9

sch 10 rep in pt—Employment Rights, 1996 c 18, s 242, sch 3 pt I; Access to Justice, 1999 c 22, s 106, sch 15 pt V(8); Armed Forces, 2006 c 52, s 358, sch 14 para 59

sch 11 restr—SI 1997/306, reg 29

c 15 **National Health Service (Residual Liabilities)**

trans of powers—(W) SI 1999/672, art 2, sch 1

s 1 rep—Nat Health Service (Conseq Provns), 2006 c 43, s 6, sch 4

s 2 rep in pt—(prosp) Nat Health Service Reform (S), 2004 asp 7, s 11(2), sch 2

am—Public Bodies (Joint Working) (S), 2014 asp 9, s 64

c 16 **Police**

appl—Disability Discrimination, 1995 c 50, s 64A(7); (retrosp) SI 1997/1612, sch 2; Police (NI), 1998 c 32, s 51, sch 3 para 8(8); Prevention of Terrorism (Temp Provns) 1989 c 4, s 2A(11); Police (NI), 1998 c 32, s 73(1); Proceeds of Crime, 2002 c 29, s 313(2)(a); SIs 2002/1064, art 24(3)(a); 2003/1660, reg 11(7); 1661, reg 11(7); 2005/120, art 51(3)(a)(b); 1918, art 44(3); 2222, art 40(3); 3523, art 46(3)

1996
c 16 *continued*

power to mod—Insolvency, 2000 c 39, s 7(2)
power to appl (mods)—Railways and Transport Safety, 2003 c 20, ss 21(5)(a)(6),
22(6)(a)(7), 23(6)(a)(7)
appl (mods)—SI 2005/3181, art 210(2)(e)
s 1 appl—Crime and Disorder, 1998 c 37, s 18(1)
    rep in pt—GLA, 1999 c 29, ss 325, 423, sch 27 para 69, sch 34 pt VII
    am—Loc Govt and Public Involvement in Health, 2007 c 28, s 22, sch 1 para 19(1)(2);
        Police Reform and Social Responsibility, 2011 c 13, sch 16 para 2; Loc Govt
        (Democracy) (W), 2013 anaw 4, sch 1 para 2
s 2 am—Police Reform and Social Responsibility, 2011 c 13, sch 16 para 4(2)(3)
    rep in pt—Police Reform and Social Responsibility, 2011 c 13, sch 16 para 3
ss 3-5 rep —Police Reform and Social Responsibility, 2011 c 13, sch 16 para 5(a)
s 5A added—GLA, 1999 c 29, s 310(1)
    rep in pt—Police Reform and Social Responsibility, 2011 c 13, sch 16 para 5(b)
    am—Police Reform and Social Responsibility, 2011 c 13, sch 16 para 6(2)(3)
s 5B added—GLA, 1999 c 29, s 310(1)
    rep—Police Reform and Social Responsibility, 2011 c 13, sch 16 para 7
s 5C added—GLA, 1999 c 29, s 310(1)
    rep —Police Reform and Social Responsibility, 2011 c 13, sch 16 para 7
s 6 rep —Police Reform and Social Responsibility, 2011 c 13, sch 16 para 7
s 6AZA added—Police Reform and Social Responsibility, 2011 c 13, sch 16 para 9
s 6ZA added—Police and Justice, 2006 c 48, s 2, sch 2 para 8
    am—Police Reform and Social Responsibility, 2011 c 13, sch 16 para 10(2)-(5)
    rep in pt—Police Reform and Social Responsibility, 2011 c 13, sch 16 para 10(6)
s 6ZB added—Police and Justice, 2006 c 48, s 2, sch 2 para 9
    transtl provns—SI 2008/82, art 6
    am—Police Reform and Social Responsibility, 2011 c 13, sch 16 para 11(2)-(7)
    rep in pt—Police Reform and Social Responsibility, 2011 c 13, sch 16 para 11(8)(9)
s 6ZC added—Police and Justice, 2006 c 48, s 2, sch 2 para 9
    am—Police Reform and Social Responsibility, 2011 c 13, sch 16 para 12(2)-(4)
    rep in pt—Police Reform and Social Responsibility, 2011 c 13, sch 16 para 12(5)
s 6A added—Police Reform, 2002 c 30, s 92(1)
    rep—Police and Justice, 2006 c 48, s 2, sch 2 para 10, sch 15
ss 7, 8 rep—Police and Justice, 2006 c 48, s 2, sch 2 para 10, sch 15
s 8A added —Serious Organised Crime and Police, 2005 c 15, s 157
    rep —Police Reform and Social Responsibility, 2011 c 13, sch 16 para 13
s 9 rep—Police and Justice, 2006 c 48, s 2, sch 2 para 10, sch 15
s 9A added—GLA, 1999 c 29, s 314
    rep —Police Reform and Social Responsibility, 2011 c 13, sch 16 para 13
ss 9B-9D added—GLA, 1999 c 29, ss 315-317
        rep —Police Reform and Social Responsibility, 2011 c 13, sch 16 para 13
s 9E added—GLA, 1999 c 29, s 318
    rep —Police Reform and Social Responsibility, 2011 c 13, sch 16 para 13
s 9F added—GLA, 1999 c 29, s 319
    rep —Police Reform and Social Responsibility, 2011 c 13, sch 16 para 13
s 9FA added—Crim Justice and Police, 2001 c 16, s 122(1)
    rep—Police Reform and Social Responsibility, 2011 c 13, sch 16 para 13
s 9G added—GLA, 1999 c 29, s 320
    rep —Police Reform and Social Responsibility, 2011 c 13, sch 16 para 13
s 9H added—GLA, 1999 c 29, s 322
    am—Crim Justice and Police, 2001 c 16, ss 122(2), 125(1); Police Reform and Social
        Responsibility, 2011 c 13, sch 16 para 14
s 10 rep —Police Reform and Social Responsibility, 2011 c 13, sch 16 para 15
s 11 rep —Police Reform and Social Responsibility, 2011 c 13, sch 16 para 15
s 11A added —Crim Justice and Police, 2001 c 16, s 123(1)
    rep—Police Reform and Social Responsibility, 2011 c 13, sch 16 para 15
s 12 rep—Police Reform and Social Responsibility, 2011 c 13, sch 16 para 15
s 12A added—Crim Justice and Police, 2001 c 16, s 124(2)
    rep —Police Reform and Social Responsibility, 2011 c 13, sch 16 para 15
s 13 am—Crim Justice and Police, 2001 c 16, ss 123(2), 125(2)
    rep in pt—Crim Justice and Police, 2001 c 16, ss 123(2)(b), 137, sch 7 pt 4
ss 14-17 rep—Police Reform and Social Responsibility, 2011 c 13, sch 16 para 16
s 18 subst—Police Reform, 2002 c 30, s 101

1996
c 16 s 18 *continued*

am—Policing and Crime, 2009 c 26, s 112, sch 7 paras 1, 5; Police Reform and Social
   Responsibility, 2011 c 13, sch 16 paras 17, 18(3)(4)

rep in pt—Police Reform and Social Responsibility, 2011 c 13, sch 16 para 18(2)

ss 19-20 rep —Police Reform and Social Responsibility, 2011 c 13, sch 16 para 19

s 20A added—GLA, 1999 c 29, s 325, sch 27 para 78

rep—Police Reform and Social Responsibility, 2011 c 13, sch 16 para 19

s 21 rep—Police Reform and Social Responsibility, 2011 c 13, sch 16 para 19

s 22 am—GLA, 1999 c 29, s 325, sch 27 para 79(1)-(5); Police Reform and Social
   Responsibility, 2011 c 13, sch 16 para 21(2)-(7)

rep in pt—GLA, 1999 c 29, ss 325, 423, sch 27 para 79(6), sch 34 pt VII; Police
   Reform and Social Responsibility, 2011 c 13, sch 16 para 20

ss 22A-22C added—Police Reform and Social Responsibility, 2011 c 13, s 89(2)

s 23, with ss 23A-23I, subst for s 23—Policing and Crime, 2009 c 26, s 5

am—Police Reform and Social Responsibility, 2011 c 13, sch 12 para 2(2)(4)(6)(7);
   ibid, sch 16 para 22

rep in pt—Police Reform and Social Responsibility, 2011 c 13, sch 12 para 2(3)(5)(8)

s 23A am—Police Reform and Social Responsibility, 2011 c 13, sch 12 para
   3(2)(4)(5)(7)(8)

rep in pt—Police Reform and Social Responsibility, 2011 c 13, sch 12 para 3(3)(6)(9)

s 23AA added—Police Reform and Social Responsibility, 2011 c 13, sch 13 para 1

s 23B am—Police Reform and Social Responsibility, 2011 c 13, sch 12 para 4(2)-(4)

rep in pt—Police Reform and Social Responsibility, 2011 c 13, sch 12 para 4(5)

s 23C am—Police Reform and Social Responsibility, 2011 c 13, sch 12 para 5(3)

rep in pt—Police Reform and Social Responsibility, 2011 c 13, sch 12 para 5(2)

s 23D am—Police Reform and Social Responsibility, 2011 c 13, sch 12 para 6(2)-(5)

s 23E am—Police Reform and Social Responsibility, 2011 c 13, sch 12 para 7

s 23F am—Police Reform and Social Responsibility, 2011 c 13, sch 12 para 8

s 23FA added—Police Reform and Social Responsibility, 2011 c 13, s 89(3)

s 23G am—Police Reform and Social Responsibility, 2011 c 13, sch 12 para 9

s 23HA added—Police Reform and Social Responsibility, 2011 c 13, sch 12 para 10

s 23I am—Police Reform and Social Responsibility, 2011 c 13, sch 12 para 11(2)-(4)

s 24 am—Police, 1997 c 50, s 134(1), sch 9 para 74; Anti-terrorism, Crime and Security,
   2001 c 24, s 101, sch 7 paras 20, 22; Railways and Transport Safety, 2003 c 20, s
   73, sch 5 para 4(1)(a)(2)(h); SI 2004/1573, art 12(4)(b); Police and Justice, 2006
   c 48, s 2, sch 2 paras 17, 22; Police Reform and Social Responsibility, 2011 c 13,
   sch 16 para 23(2)-(5)

saved—Police Reform, 2002 c 30, s 16(7)

rep in pt—Serious Organised Crime and Police, 2005 c 15, ss 59, 174(2), sch 4 paras
   68, 70, sch 17 pt 2

s 25 am—Anti-terrorism, Crime and Security, 2001 c 24, s 101, sch 7 paras 20, 23;
   Railways and Transport Safety, 2003 c 20, s 73, sch 5 para 4(1)(a)(2)(h); SI
   2004/1573, art 12(1)(c); Police Reform and Social Responsibility, 2011 c 13, sch
   16 para 24(a)(b)

rep in pt—GLA, 1999 c 29, ss 325, 423, sch 27 para 80, sch 34 pt VII

s 26 rep in pt—GLA, 1999 c 29, ss 325, 423, sch 27 para 81, sch 34 pt VII; International
   Development, 2002 c 1, s 19(2), sch 4

am—Police Reform and Social Responsibility, 2011 c 13, sch 16 para 25(2)-(4)

s 27 am—Police and Justice, 2006 c 48, s 2, sch 2 para 23; Policing and Crime, 2009 c 26, s
   112, sch 7 paras 1, 6; Police Reform and Social Responsibility, 2011 c 13, sch 16
   para 26

s 28 rep in pt—GLA, 1999 c 29, ss 325, 423, sch 27 para 82, sch 34 pt VII

am—Police Reform and Social Responsibility, 2011 c 13, sch 16 para 27(a)(b)

s 29 rep in pt—GLA, 1999 c 29, ss 325, 423, sch 27 para 83, sch 34 pt VII

appl (mods)—Railways and Transport Safety, 2003 c 20, ss 24(3), 25(3)

s 30 am—Anti-terrorism, Crime and Security, 2001 c 24, s 101, sch 7 paras 20, 24;
   Railways and Transport Safety, 2003 c 20, s 73, sch 5 para 4(1)(a)(2)(h); Police
   and Justice, 2006 c 48, s 2, sch 2 para 21(1)(2); Policing and Crime, 2009 c 26, s
   112, sch 7 paras 1, 7; Police Reform and Social Responsibility, 2011 c 13, sch 16
   para 28(2)(3)

rep in pt—Police and Justice, 2006 c 48, s 2, sch 2 para 21(1)(3), sch 15

s 31 subst—Police Reform and Social Responsibility, 2011 c 13, sch 16 para 29

s 32 rep in pt—GLA, 1999 c 29, ss 325, 423, sch 27 para 84, sch 34 pt VII

am—Police Reform and Social Responsibility, 2011 c 13, sch 10 para 5(2)(3)

1996
c 16 *continued*

  s 33 am—GLA, 1999 c 29, s 325, sch 27 para 85(1)(3); Police Reform and Social
    Responsibility, 2011 c 13, sch 10 para 6
    rep in pt—GLA, 1999 c 29, ss 325,423, sch 27 para 85(1)(2), sch 34 pt VII
  s 34 am—Police Reform and Social Responsibility, 2011 c 13, sch 10 para 7(2)(3)(4)(b)(5)
    rep in pt—Police Reform and Social Responsibility, 2011 c 13, sch 10 para 7(4)(a)
  s 36 am—Crim Justice and Immigration, 2008 c 4, s 126, sch 22 paras 1, 2
    rep in pt—Anti-social Behaviour, Crime and Policing, 2014 c 12, sch 11 para 87
  s 36A added —Police Reform, 2002 c 30, s 1
    rep—Police and Justice, 2006 c 48, s 2, sch 2 para 24, sch 15
  s 37 rep—Police and Justice, 2006 c 48, s 2, sch 2 para 24, sch 15
  s 37A added—Police and Justice, 2006 c 48, s 2, sch 2 para 25
    subst —Police Reform and Social Responsibility, 2011 c 13, s 77
  s 38 rep—Police Reform and Social Responsibility, 2011 c 13, s 81(a)
  s 39 rep—Police Reform and Social Responsibility, 2011 c 13, s 81(b)
  s 39A added —Police Reform, 2002 c 30, s 2
    am—Police and Justice, 2006 c 48, ss 1, 6, sch 1 paras 61, 62, sch 4 para 3; Police
      Reform and Social Responsibility, 2011 c 13, sch 16 para 30(3); Anti-social
      Behaviour, Crime and Policing, 2014 c 12, s 124
    rep in pt—Police Reform and Social Responsibility, 2011 c 13, sch 16 para 30(2)
  s 40 subst —Police and Justice, 2006 c 48, s 2, sch 2 para 27
    am—Police Reform and Social Responsibility, 2011 c 13, s 91(2)
  s 40A added—Police and Justice, 2006 c 48, s 2, sch 2 para 27
    am—Police Reform and Social Responsibility, 2011 c 13, s 91(3)
  s 40B added—Police and Justice, 2006 c 48, s 2, sch 2 para 27
    am —Policing and Crime, 2009 c 26, s 112, sch 7 para 133; Police Reform and Social
      Responsibility, 2011 c 13, s 91(4)(5)
  s 40C added—Anti-social Behaviour, Crime and Policing, 2014 c 12, s 126
  s 41 am—Loc Govt, 1999 c 27, s 30, sch 1 pt II para 10; Police and Justice, 2006 c 48, s 2,
    sch 2 para 28; Police Reform and Social Responsibility, 2011 c 13, s 22(2)-(4);
    Localism, 2011 c 20, sch 6 para 33, sch 7 para 33
  ss 41A, 41B added —Police Reform, 2002 c 30, s 5
    rep—Police and Justice, 2006 c 48, s 2, sch 2 para 29, sch 15
  s 42 am—GLA, 1999 c 29, s 325, sch 27 para 90; Crim Justice and Police, 2001 c 16, s
    122(3); Crim Justice and Police, 2001 c 16, s 123(3); Police Reform, 2002 c 30, s
    33(1)-(6); Police Reform and Social Responsibility, 2011 c 13, s 82(3)-(10)
    rep in pt—Police Reform, 2002 c 30, ss 33(1)(7), 107(2), sch 8; Police Reform and
      Social Responsibility, 2011 c 13, s 82(11)
  s 42A added —Police Reform, 2002 c 30, s 34
    am—Police and Justice, 2006 c 48, s 6, sch 4 para 4; Police Reform and Social
      Responsibility, 2011 c 13, sch 16 para 31(2)(4)
    rep in pt—Police Reform and Social Responsibility, 2011 c 13, sch 16 para 31(3)
  s 43 rep—Police Reform and Social Responsibility, 2011 c 13, s 81(c)
  s 44 subst for ss 44, 45—Police Reform and Social Responsibility, 2011 c 13, s 92
  s 46 am—GLA, 1999 c 29, s 325, sch 27 para 92; Police Reform and Social Responsibility,
    2011 c 13, s 24(2)-(6)(8)(9); Anti-social Behaviour, Crime and Policing, 2014 c
    12, s 142(1)
  s 47 am—GLA, 1999 c 29, s 325, sch 27 para 93; Police Reform and Social Responsibility,
    2011 c 13, s 25(2)
    rep in pt—Anti-social Behaviour, Crime and Policing, 2014 c 12, s 142(2)(a)
  s 48 am—GLA, 1999 c 29, s 325, sch 27 para 94; Police Reform and Social Responsibility,
    2011 c 13, s 25(3)
  s 49 rep—Inquiries, 2005 c 12, ss 44(5), 48(1), 49(2), sch 2 pt 1 para 14, sch 3
  s 50 am—GLA, 1999 c 29, s 325, sch 27 para 95; Crim Justice and Police, 2001 c 16, s
    125(3)(4)(a); Crim Justice and Immigration, 2008 c 4, s 126, sch 22 paras 1,
    3(1)(2); Policing and Crime, 2009 c 26, s 3; Police Reform and Social
    Responsibility, 2011 c 13, s 82(12), sch 16 para 32; Public Service Pensions,
    2013 c 25, sch 8 para 23; Anti-social Behaviour, Crime and Policing, 2014 c 12, s
    123(1)
    ext—Police Reform, 2002 c 30, s 36(1)
    rep in pt—Crim Justice and Immigration, 2008 c 4, ss 126, 149, sch 22 paras 1, 3(1)(3),
      sch 28 pt 8
  s 51 am—Police, 1997 c 50, s 128(1); Police Reform, 2002 c 30, s 35; Crim Justice and
    Immigration, 2008 c 4, s 126, sch 22 paras 1, 4; Police Reform and Social

1996
c 16 *continued*

Responsibility, 2011 c 13, sch 16 para 33; Public Service Pensions, 2013 c 25, sch 8 para 24(2)(a)(3); Anti-social Behaviour, Crime and Policing, 2014 c 12, s 123(2)

ext —Police Reform, 2002 c 30, s 36(1)

rep in pt—Public Service Pensions, 2013 c 25, sch 8 para 24(2)(b)(4)

s 52 am—Police, 1997 c 50, s 128(2); Police Reform and Social Responsibility, 2011 c 13, sch 16 para 34; Public Service Pensions, 2013 c 25, sch 8 para 25; Anti-social Behaviour, Crime and Policing, 2014 c 12, s 133(4)

s 52A added —Anti-social Behaviour, Crime and Policing, 2014 c 12, s 133(1)

s 53 am—Police, 1997 c 50, s 134(1), sch 9 para 75; Police Reform, 2002 c 30, s 6; Police and Justice, 2006 c 48, s 6, sch 4 para 5; Policing and Crime, 2009 c 26, s 11; Police Reform and Social Responsibility, 2011 c 13, s 93(2)-(5)

s 53A added—Police Reform, 2002 c 30, s 7

appl (mods)—Railways and Transport Safety, 2003 c 20, s 45

am—Police and Justice, 2006 c 48, ss 1, 6, sch 1 paras 61, 63, sch 4 para 6; Policing and Crime, 2009 c 26, s 12; Police Reform and Social Responsibility, 2011 c 13, sch 16 para 35(3); Anti-social Behaviour, Crime and Policing, 2014 c 12, s 123(3)(a)(c)

rep in pt—Police Reform and Social Responsibility, 2011 c 13, sch 16 para 35(2)-(5); Anti-social Behaviour, Crime and Policing, 2014 c 12, s 123(3)(b)

ss 53B-53D added —Policing and Crime, 2009 c 26, s 2(1)

s 53E and cross-heading added—Anti-social Behaviour, Crime and Policing, 2014 c 12, s 125

s 54 am—Police, 1997 c 50, s 134(1), sch 9 para 76; Loc Govt, 1999 c 27, s 24(2); Crim Justice and Police, 2001 c 16, s 102, sch 4 para 7(1); Police Reform, 2002 c 30, ss 3(1), 84, 107(1), sch 7, para 15; Serious Organised Crime and Police, 2005 c 15, s 59, sch 4 paras 68, 71(1)(3); Police and Justice, 2006 c 48, s 29(1); Crim Justice and Immigration, 2008 c 4, s 129; Policing and Crime, 2009 c 26, s 1(2); Police Reform and Social Responsibility, 2011 c 13, s 83(4)(6)(7)

rep in pt—Crim Justice and Police, 2001 c 16, s 137, sch 7 pt 3; Serious Organised Crime and Police, 2005 c 15, ss 59, 174(2), sch 4 paras 68, 71(1)(2), 72, sch 17 pt 2; Crim Justice and Immigration, 2008 c 4, s 149, sch 28 pt 8; Policing and Crime, 2009 c 26, ss 2(2), 112, sch 8 pt 1; Police Reform and Social Responsibility, 2011 c 13, s 83(2)(3)(5)

power to appl (mods)—Commrs for Revenue and Customs, 2005 c 11, s 27(1)(2)(a)(i)

appl—SI 2012/2840, reg 11(1)

s 55 am—Police, 1997 c 50, s 134(1), sch 9 para 77; Loc Govt, 1999 c 27, s 24(3); Crim Justice and Police, 2001 c 16, s 102, sch 4 para 7(2); Police Reform, 2002 c 30, s 3(1); Police Reform and Social Responsibility, 2011 c 13, s 84(2)-(6)

rep in pt—GLA, 1999 c 29, ss 325, 423, sch 27 para 96, sch 34 pt VII; Serious Organised Crime and Police, 2005 c 15, ss 59, 174(2), sch 4 paras 68, 72, sch 17 pt 2; Police Reform and Social Responsibility, 2011 c 13, s 84(7)(8)

appl (mods)—Railways and Transport Safety, 2003 c 20, s 63(6)

power to appl (mods)—Commrs for Revenue and Customs, 2005 c 11, s 27(1)(2)(a)(i)

s 56 power to appl (mods)—Commrs for Revenue and Customs, 2005 c 11, s 27(1)(2)(a)(i)

appl (mods)—SI 2005/1133, reg 10(1)

s 57 am—Police, 1997 c 50, s 134(1), sch 9 para 78; Serious Organised Crime and Police, 2005 c 15, s 59, sch 4 paras 68, 73; Police and Justice, 2006 c 48, ss 1, 6, sch 1 paras 61, 64, sch 4 para 7; Crim Justice and Immigration, 2008 c 4, s 128; Policing and Crime, 2009 c 26, s 13; Police Reform and Social Responsibility, 2011 c 13, sch 16 para 36(2); Crime and Cts, 2013 c 22, sch 8 para 39

rep in pt—Police Reform and Social Responsibility, 2011 c 13, sch 16 para 36(3)

s 58 rep—Finance (No 2), 1997 c 58, s 52, sch 8 pt II(3)

s 59 am—Police, 1997 c 50, s 134(1), sch 9 para 79; Police and Justice, 2006 c 48, s 1, sch 1 paras 61, 65; Crim Justice and Immigration, 2008 c 4, s 126, sch 22 paras 1, 5; Police and Fire Reform (S), 2012 asp 8, sch 7 para 13(2); SI 2013/602, sch 1 para 5(2)

rep in pt—Finance (No 2), 1997 c 58, s 52, sch 8 pt II(3); Serious Organised Crime and Police, 2005 c 15, ss 59, 174(2), sch 4 paras 68, 74, sch 17 pt 2; Crime and Cts, 2013 c 22, sch 8 para 40

s 60 am—Police, 1997 c 50, s 134(1), sch 9 para 80; Police Reform and Social Responsibility, 2011 c 13, sch 16 para 37; Police and Fire Reform (S), 2012 asp 8, sch 7 para 13(3); SI 2013/602, sch 1 para 5(3)(a)-(c)

1996

c 16 s 60 *continued*

cert functions trans—(S) SI 1999/1750, art 2, sch 1

rep in pt—Serious Organised Crime and Police, 2005 c 15, ss 59, 174(2), sch 4 paras 68, 75, sch 17 pt 2

s 60A added—(S) Police, Public Order and Crim Justice (S), 2006 asp 10, s 101, sch 6 para 5(1)(2)

rep —Police and Fire Reform (S), 2012 asp 8, sch 8 pt 1

s 61 rep (S prosp)—Anti-social Behaviour, Crime and Policing, 2014 c 12, s 131(2)

am—Police, 1997 c 50, s 134(1), sch 9 para 81; SI 1999/1747, art 3, sch 21 pt II para 2; Police (NI), 2000 c 32, s 78, sch 6 para 12(2); Police and Justice, 2006 c 48, s 1, sch 1 paras 61, 66; (S) Police, Public Order and Crim Justice (S), 2006 asp 10, s 101, sch 6 para 5(1)(3); SI 2010/976, art 5, sch 3; Police Reform and Social Responsibility, 2011 c 13, sch 16 para 38

rep in pt—Serious Organised Crime and Police, 2005 c 15, ss 59, 174(2), sch 4 paras 68, 76, sch 17 pt 2; SI 2010/976, art 5, sch 3; Police and Fire Reform (S), 2012 asp 8, sch 8 pt 1; Crime and Cts, 2013 c 22, sch 8 para 41; SI 2013/602, sch 1 para 5(4)

s 62 rep (S prosp)—Anti-social Behaviour, Crime and Policing, 2014 c 12, s 131(2)

am—Police, 1997 c 50, s 134(1), sch 9 para 82; Police (NI), 1998 c 32, s 34(1)(2); SI 1999/1820, art 4, sch 2 pt I para 124(b)(c); Crim Justice and Police, 2001 c 16, s 128(1), sch 6 pt 2 para 77; Police Reform, 2002 c 30, ss 90(3), 91(3), 107(1), sch 7, para 16(1)(3); Serious Organised Crime and Police, 2005 c 15, s 59, sch 4 paras 68, 77(1)(5); Police and Justice, 2006 c 48, s 1, sch 1 paras 61, 67; (S) Police, Public Order and Crim Justice (S), 2006 asp 10, s 101, sch 6 para 5(1)(4); SI 2010/976, art 5, sch 3; Police and Fire Reform (S), 2012 asp 8, sch 7 para 13(4); SI 2013/602, sch 1 para 5(5); Crime and Cts, 2013 c 22, sch 8 para 42(4)

rep in pt—Police, 1997 c 50, s 134(2), sch 10; SI 1999/1820, art 4, sch 2 pt I para 124(a) pt IV; Police Reform, 2002 c 30, s 107, sch 7, para 16(1)(2), sch 8; Serious Organised Crime and Police, 2005 c 15, ss 59, 174(2), sch 4 paras 68, 77(1)-(4), sch 17 pt 2; SI 2010/976, art 5, sch 3; Police and Fire Reform (S), 2012 asp 8, sch 8 pt 1; Crime and Cts, 2013 c 22, sch 8 para 42(2)(3); SSI 2013/119, sch 1 para 17; SI 2013/602, sch 1 para 5(6)

excl—Police (NI), 2000 c 32, ss 49(4),78, sch 7 para 2

s 63 am—Police, 1997 c 50, s 134(1), sch 9 para 83; Police (NI), 1998 c 32, s 74(1), sch 4 para 20(2); Police Reform, 2002 c 30, ss 90(5), 91(5), 107(1), sch 7, para 17; Serious Organised Crime and Police, 2005 c 15, s 59, sch 4 paras 68, 78(1)(3); Police and Justice, 2006 c 48, s 1, sch 1 paras 61, 68; (S) Police, Public Order and Crim Justice (S), 2006 asp 10, s 101, sch 6 para 5(5); Crim Justice and Immigration, 2008 c 4, s 126, sch 22 paras 1, 6; Policing and Crime, 2009 c 26, s 10(3); Police Reform and Social Responsibility, 2011 c 13, sch 16 para 39; Police and Fire Reform (S), 2012 asp 8, s 97(2)(c); SI 2013/602 sch 1 para 5(7)(b); ibid, sch 2 para 25(2); Anti-social Behaviour, Crime and Policing, 2014 c 12, s 123(4); ibid, s 133(2)

rep in pt—Police Reform, 2002 c 30, s 107(2), sch 8; Serious Organised Crime and Police, 2005 c 15, ss 59, 174(2), sch 4 paras 68, 78(1)(2), sch 17 pt 2; Police and Fire Reform (S), 2012 asp 8, s 97(2)(a)(b); SI 2013/602, sch 1 para 5(7)(a)(i)(ii); Crime and Cts, 2013 c 22, sch 8 para 43

s 64 am—Police, 1997 c 50, s 134(1), sch 9 para 84; Police and Justice, 2006 c 48, s 1, sch 1 paras 61, 69

rep in pt—SI 2001/3649, art 349; Serious Organised Crime and Police, 2005 c 15, ss 59, 174(2), sch 4 paras 68, 79, sch 17 pt 2; Police and Fire Reform (S), 2012 asp 8, sch 8 pt 1; Crime and Cts, 2013 c 22, sch 8 para 44; SI 2013/602, sch 1 para 5(8)

mod—SI 2007/1098, art 6, sch 1

Pt 3A (ss 64A-64B) added—Anti-social Behaviour, Crime and Policing, 2014 c 12, s 132(1)

Pt 4, Ch 1 (ss 65-83) power to appl—Police, 1997 c 50, s 39(2)(c)

ss 65-77 rep—Police Reform, 2002 c 30, s 107(2), sch 8

s 78 rep—Police Reform, 2002 c 30, ss 26(9), 107(2), sch 8

ss 79-83 rep—Police Reform, 2002 c 30, s 107(2), sch 8

s 84 subst—Crim Justice and Immigration, 2008 c 4, s 126, sch 22 paras 1, 7

am—Police Reform and Social Responsibility, 2011 c 13, sch 16 para 40

s 85 appl—Police, 1997 c 50, s 82(2); SI 1999/731, reg 15(6)

am—Crim Justice and Immigration, 2008 c 4, s 126, sch 22 paras 1, 8

s 86 rep—Police Reform, 2002 c 30, s 107(2), sch 8

1996

c 16 *continued*

s 87 am—Police Reform, 2002 c 30, s 107(1), sch 7, para 18; Crim Justice and Immigration, 2008 c 4, s 126, sch 22 paras 1, 9; Police Reform and Social Responsibility, 2011 c 13, sch 16 para 41

s 88 am—Police, 1997 c 50, s 134(1), sch 9 para 85; Police Reform, 2002 c 30, ss 102(1)(2)(a)(4)(5)(a), 103(1); Serious Organised Crime and Police, 2005 c 15, s 59, sch 4 paras 68, 80(1)(3); Police Reform and Social Responsibility, 2011 c 13, sch 16 para 42(2)-(5); SI 2012/1809, art 3(1), sch pt 1; Crime and Cts, 2013 c 22, sch 8 para 45

appl (mods)—SI 1999/3272, art 3; Railways and Transport Safety, 2003 c 20, ss 25(5), 68(1)(3)

excl—Health and Safety at Work etc 1974 c 37, s 51A(2D)(2E)(b)

appl—Crime (International Co-operation), 2003 c 32, s 16(5)

rep in pt—Serious Organised Crime and Police, 2005 c 15, ss 59, 174(2), sch 4 paras 68, 80(1)(2), sch 17 pt 2

s 89 am—Police Reform, 2002 c 30, s 104(1); (prosp) Crim Justice, 2003 c 44, s 280(2)(3), sch 26 para 47; SIs 2012/1809, art 3(1), sch pt 1; 2013/602, sch 2 para 25(3)

ext—Crime (International Co-operation), 2003 c 32, s 84(1)

rep in pt—Serious Organised Crime and Police, 2005 c 15, ss 59, 174(2), sch 4 paras 68, 81, sch 17 pt 2

s 90 am—Anti-terrorism, Crime and Security, 2001 c 24, s 101, sch 7 paras 20, 25; Police and Justice, 2006 c 48, s 1, sch 1 paras 61, 70

appl (mods)—Railways and Transport Safety, 2003 c 20, s 68(1)-(3)

mod—Energy, 2004 c 20, s 68(2)

rep in pt—Crime and Cts, 2013 c 22, sch 8 para 46

s 91 am—Anti-terrorism, Crime and Security, 2001 c 24, s 101, sch 7 paras 20, 26; Railways and Transport Safety, 2003 c 20, s 73, sch 5 para 4(1)(a)(2)(h); Energy, 2004 c 20, s 68(3); Police and Justice, 2006 c 48, ss 1, 52, sch 1 paras 61, 71, sch 14 para 30

rep in pt—Crime and Cts, 2013 c 22, sch 8 para 47

s 92 am—GLA, 1999 c 29, s 325, sch 27 para 100; Police Reform and Social Responsibility, 2011 c 13, s 25(4)

rep in pt—Anti-social Behaviour, Crime and Policing, 2014 c 12, s 142(2)(b)

s 93 rep in pt—GLA, 1999 c 29, ss 325, 423, sch 27 para 101, sch 34 pt VII

am—Police Reform and Social Responsibility, 2011 c 13, s 25(5), sch 16 para 43

s 94 am—Police Reform and Social Responsibility, 2011 c 13, s 25(7)-(11)

s 95 am—GLA, 1999 c 29, s 325, sch 27 para 102(3)

rep in pt—GLA, 1999 c 29, ss 325, 423, sch 27 para 102(2), sch 34 pt VII

s 95A added—Anti-social Behaviour, Crime and Policing, 2014 c 12, s 127

s 96 am—GLA, 1999 c 29, s 325, sch 27 para 103(2); Police and Justice, 2006 c 48, s 2, sch 2 para 30; Police Reform and Social Responsibility, 2011 c 13, s 14(2)-(5)

rep in pt—GLA, 1999 c 29, ss 325, 423, sch 27 para 103(3), sch 34 pt VII; Police Reform and Social Responsibility, 2011 c 13, s 14(6)

s 96A added—GLA, 1999 c 29, s 325, sch 27 para 104

am—Police Reform and Social Responsibility, 2011 c 13, s 94(2)-(5)

rep in pt—Police Reform and Social Responsibility, 2011 c 13, s 94(6)

s 96B added—GLA, 1999 c 29, s 325, sch 27 para 104

rep—Police Reform and Social Responsibility, 2011 c 13, s 94(7)

s 97 am—Police, 1997 c 50, s 134(1), sch 9 para 86; Police (NI), 1998 c 32, s 74(1), sch 4 para 20(3)-(5); Police (NI), 2000 c 32, s 78, sch 6 para 12(3); Crim Justice and Police, 2001 c 16, s 102, sch 4 para 7(3); International Development, 2002 c 1, s 19(1), sch 3, para 11; Proceeds of Crime, 2002 c 29, s 456, sch 11, para 30; Police Reform, 2002 c 30, ss 102(1)(2)(b), 107(1), sch 7, para 19; Serious Organised Crime and Police, 2005 c 15, s 59, sch 4 paras 68, (1)(2)(b)(c)(3)(4); Police and Justice, 2006 c 48, s 1, sch 1 paras 61, 72; Safeguarding Vulnerable Groups, 2006 c 47, s 63, sch 9 para 13; Policing and Crime, 2009 c 26, s 81(2)(3)(g); Police Reform and Social Responsibility, 2011 c 13, sch 16 para 44; SIs 2012/2954, art 3(2)-(4); 3006, art 13(1)(2)(b); Crime and Cts, 2013 c 22, sch 8 para 48(2)(b)(3)(b)(5)

rep in pt—International Development, 2002 c 1, s 19(2), sch 4; Serious Organised Crime and Police, 2005 c 15, ss 59, 174(2), sch 4 paras 68, 82(1)(2)(a), sch 17 pt 2; Police and Justice, 2006 c 48, s 52, sch 15; Serious Crime, 2007 c 27, s 74, sch 8 para 155, sch 14; (pt prosp) Crim Justice and Immigration, 2008 c 4, s 126, sch 22 paras 1, 10; (prosp) ibid, s 149, sch 28 pt 8; Crime and Cts, 2013 c

1996
c 16 s 97 *continued*

        22, sch 8 para 48(2)(a)(i)(ii)(3)(a)(4); SI 2013/602, sch 2 para 25(4);
        Anti-social Behaviour, Crime and Policing, 2014 c 12, sch 11 para 88
    restr—Proceeds of Crime, 2002 c 29, s 313(2)(a)
    appl—Police, 1997 c 50, s 6(9)(b); Serious Organised Crime and Police, 2005 c 15, s
        58, sch 3 para 2(4)(b)
    appl (mods)—SI 2013/602, sch 3 para 5
    excl—Health and Safety at Work etc 1974 c 37, s 51A(2D)(2E)(c)
    mod—SI 2007/1098, art 6, sch 1
  s 97A added —Policing and Crime, 2009 c 26, s 10(1)
  s 98 am—Police, 1997 c 50, s 134(1), sch 9 para 87; Police (NI), 1998 c 32, s 74(1), sch 4
        para 20(6); Police (NI), 2000 c 32, s 78, sch 6 para 12(4)(5); Serious Organised
        Crime and Police, 2005 c 15, s 59, sch 4 paras 68, 83(1)(4)(b); Police Reform and
        Social Responsibility, 2011 c 13, sch 16 para 45(2)(3); SI 2013/602, sch 2 para
        25(5)(a)-(d)(e)(i)(ii)(f)(g)
    rep in pt—Police, 1997 c 50, s 134(2), sch 10; Serious Organised Crime and Police,
        2005 c 15, ss 59, 174(2), sch 4 paras 68, 83(1)-(4)(a)(c), sch 17 pt 2; SI
        2013/602, sch 2 para 25(5)(e)(iii)
  s 99 am—Police and Fire Reform (S), 2012 asp 8, sch 7 para 13(5); SI 2013/602, sch 1 para
        5(9)
  s 100 am—Loc Govt and Public Involvement in Health, 2007 c 28, s 22, sch 1 para 19(1)(3)
  s 100A, 100B added—Anti-social Behaviour, Crime and Policing, 2014 c 12, s 128
  s 101 am—GLA, 1999 c 29, s 312(1)(2)(3)(a); Anti-terrorism, Crime and Security, 2001 c
        24, s 101, sch 7 paras 20, 27; Police and Justice, 2006 c 48, s 6, sch 4 para 8;
        Police Reform and Social Responsibility, 2011 c 13, s 96(2)(a)(b)(d)(e)(3)
    rep in pt—GLA, 1999 c 29, ss 312(3)(b), 423, sch 34 pt VII; Railways and Transport
        Safety, 2003 c 20, s 73, sch 5 para 4(1)(b)(2)(h); Police Reform and Social
        Responsibility, 2011 c 13, s 96(2)(c)
    appl—Crime and Disorder, 1998 c 37, ss 18(1), 115(2)(c); SI 1999/2864, s 23(9);
        Finance, 2003 c 14, s 70, sch 9 para 1(3); Railways and Transport Safety, 2003
        c 20, s 18, sch 4 pt 1 para 7(2)(c); Civil Contingencies, 2004 c 36, ss 1-18, sch
        1 pt 1 para 3(1); Gambling, 2005 c 19, ss 39(6)(a), 219(7)(a)
  s 105 am—Anti-terrorism, Crime and Security, 2001 c 24, s 101, sch 7 paras 20, 28;
        Anti-social Behaviour, Crime and Policing, 2014 c 12, sch 11 para 89
    rep in pt—Police Reform, 2002 c 30, s 107(2), sch 8
  sch 1 am—Police, 1997 c 50, s 129; SIs 1997/1844-1847, 1849,1850,1855,1857;
        2009/119, art 3
    rep in pt—SI 1997/1844, art 3
    appl—Police Property, 1897 c 30, s 2(2B)(a)
  sch 2 rep—Police Reform and Social Responsibility, 2011 c 13, sch 16 para 46
  sch 2A added—GLA, 1999 c 29, s 310(2), sch 26
    rep —Police Reform and Social Responsibility, 2011 c 13, sch 16 para 46
  sch 3 rep—Police and Justice, 2006 c 48, s 2, sch 2 para 6
  sch 3A added—Courts, 2003 c 39, s 109(1), sch 8 para 376
    rep—Police and Justice, 2006 c 48, s 2, sch 2 para 6
  sch 4 subst—Police Reform, 2002 c 30, s 83
    am—SI 2002/2312, art 2
  sch 4A added—Police and Justice, 2006 c 48, s 29(2)
    rep in pt—Loc Govt and Public Involvement in Health, 2007 c 28, s 146, sch 9 para
        1(1)(2)(j), sch 18; Health and Social Care, 2008 c 14, s 95, sch 5 para
        63(1)(2)(a)(4)(a), sch 15; Police Reform and Social Responsibility, 2011 c 13,
        s 85(2)(3)(6); SI 2012/2401, sch 1 para 5(a)-(c); Loc Audit and Accountability,
        2014 c 2, sch 12 para 31(2)-(4)
    am—Health and Social Care, 2008 c 14, s 95, sch 5 para 63(1)(2)(b)(3)(4)(b); SI
        2008/912, art 3, sch 1; Police Reform and Social Responsibility, 2011 c 13, ss
        85(4)(5)(7), 86; SI 2012/2401, sch 1 para 5(d); Loc Audit and Accountability,
        2014 c 2, sch 12 para 31(5)
    transtl provns—SI 2008/2250, art 3
    appl—SI 2012/2840, regs 11(2), 12; Crime and Cts, 2013 c 22, s 11(5); SI
        2015/1792, sch paras 6-8
  sch 4B added —Anti-social Behaviour, Crime and Policing, 2014 c 12, s 132(2), sch 7
  sch 5 rep—Police Reform, 2002 c 30, s 107(2), sch 8
  sch 6 appl—Police, 1997 c 50, s 82(2)

1996
c 16 sch 6 *continued*
  am—Crim Justice and Police, 2001 c 16, s 125(5)(6); Police and Justice, 2006 c 48, s 2, sch 2 para 19; Tribunals, Cts and Enforcement, 2007 c 15, s 50, sch 10 para 27; Crim Justice and Immigration, 2008 c 4, s 126, sch 22 paras 1, 11(1)-(3)(5)(6); Police Reform and Social Responsibility, 2011 c 13, sch 16 para 47(2)(a)-(c)(3)(4)
  rep in pt—GLA, 1999 c 29, ss 325, 423, sch 27 para 107, sch 34 pt VII; Crim Justice and Immigration, 2008 c 4, ss 126, 149, sch 22 paras 1, 11(1)(4), sch 28 pt 8; Police Reform and Social Responsibility, 2011 c 13, sch 16 para 47(2)(d)
  sch 7 rep in pt—Justices of the Peace, 1997 c 25, s 73(3), sch 6 pt I; Audit Commission, 1998 c 18, s 54(3), sch 5; (saving) Police (NI), 1998 c 32, s 74(2)(3), schs 5, 6; Loc Govt, 1999 c 27, ss 30, 34, sch 2(2); (prosp) Loc Govt, 2000 c 22, s 107, sch 6; Football (Disorder), 2000 c 25, s 1, sch 3; Postal Services, 2000 c 26, s 127(6), sch 9; Race Relations (Amdt), 2000 c 34, s 9(2), sch 3; Loc Govt, 2003 c 26, s 127(2), sch 8 pt 1; Crim Justice, 2003 c 44, s 332, sch 37 pt 10; Protection of Freedoms, 2012 c 9, sch 10 pt 1; (S, NI prosp) Anti-social Behaviour, Crime and Policing, 2014 c 12, sch 11 para 102
c 17 **Employment Tribunals**
  see (citation am)—Employment Rights (Dispute Resolution) 1998 c 8 ss 1(2)(3), 16(2)(3)
  excl—SIs 1998/218, art 6; 1999/2256, art 6(1); (E) 2003/1964, art 6(1)
  saved—Scotland, 1998 c 46, s 30, sch 5 pt II, s H1(f)
  power to am, appl or make corres-ponding provn—Employment Relations, 2004 c 24, s 42(4)(d)
  mod—SI 2010/1907, reg 16
  s 1 rep in pt—Employment Rights (Dispute Resolution), 1998 c 8, s 15, sch 2
  s 3 see—(trans of functions) (S) SIs 1999/678, art 2(1), sch; 1999/1750, art 2, sch 1
  s 3A added—Tribunals, Cts and Enforcement, 2007 c 15, s 48, sch 8 paras 35, 36
   am—Crime and Cts, 2013 c 22, sch 14 para 13(1)
  s 4 am—Employment Rights (Dispute Resolution), 1998 c 8, ss 3(1)-(3)(4)(6), 5, 15, sch 1 para 12(1)-(4); (prosp) ibid, s 4; Nat Minimum Wage, 1998 c 39, s 27(1); SI 2006/246, reg 20, sch 2; Tribunals, Cts and Enforcement, 2007 c 15, s 48, sch 8 paras 35, 37, 38; Employment, 2008 c 24, s 9(3); SI 2012/988, art 2; (pt prosp) Enterprise and Regulatory Reform, 2013 c 24, s 11(1)
   mod—SIs 2001/1171, reg 7; (S) 2001/1170, reg 7; 2004/1861, reg 12
   rep in pt—Employment Rights (Dispute Resolution), 1998 c 8, ss 3(5),15, sch 2; Employment Relations, 1999 c 26, ss 41, 44, sch 8 para 2, sch 9(12)
  s 5 rep in pt—Employment Rights (Dispute Resolution), 1998 c 8, s 15, sch 2
   am—Employment Rights (Dispute Resolution), 1998 c 8, s 15, sch 1 para 13; Tribunals, Cts and Enforcement, 2007 c 15, s 48, sch 8 para 39; Equality, 2010 c 15, s 211, sch 26 para 28
  s 5A added—Tribunals, Cts and Enforcement, 2007 c 15, s 48, sch 8 paras 35, 40
   am—Crime and Cts, 2013 c 22, sch 14 para 13(1)
  s 5B added—Tribunals, Cts and Enforcement, 2007 c 15, s 48, sch 8 paras 35, 40
   am—Crime and Cts, 2013 c 22, sch 14 para 13(1)
  s 5C added—Tribunals, Cts and Enforcement, 2007 c 15, s 48, sch 8 paras 35, 40
  s 5D added—Tribunals, Cts and Enforcement, 2007 c 15, s 48, sch 8 paras 35, 40
   am—Crime and Cts, 2013 c 22, sch 14 para 12(2)-(7); ibid, sch 14 para 13(1)
  s 6 am—Arbitration, 1996 c 23, s 107(1) sch 3 para 62; (S) SSI 2010/220, art 2, sch
  s 7 rep in pt—Employment Rights (Dispute Resolution), 1998 c 8, s 15, sch 1 para 14(1)(2), sch 2
   am—Employment Rights (Dispute Resolution), 1998 c 8, ss 2, 15, sch 1, para 14(1)(3); Employment, 2002 c 22, ss 24(1), 25, 26; Employment, 2008 c 24, s 4; Equality, 2010 c 15, s 211, sch 26 para 29; Crime and Cts, 2013 c 22, sch 9 para 52; Enterprise and Regulatory Reform, 2013 c 24, sch 1 para 3; Small Business, Enterprise and Employment, 2015 c 26, s 151(2)
   ext—Trade Union and Labour Relations (Consolidation) 1992 c 52, s 239(4)(b)(c)
  s 7A added—Employment, 2002 c 22, s 27
   am—Tribunals, Cts and Enforcement, 2007 c 15, s 48, sch 8 paras 35, 41
  s 7B added—Tribunals, Cts and Enforcement, 2007 c 15, s 48, sch 8 paras 35, 42
   am—Enterprise and Regulatory Reform, 2013 c 24, sch 1 para 4; Crime and Cts, 2013 c 22, sch 14 para 13(1)
  s 9 am—Employment Rights (Dispute Resolution), 1998 c 8, s 15, sch 1 para 15; SI 2001/237, art 2; Employment, 2002 c 22, s 28; SI 2012/149, art 2; Enterprise and Regulatory Reform, 2013 c 24, s 21(2)(b)

1996
c 17 s 9 *continued*

    ext—Trade Union and Labour Relations (Consolidation) 1992 c 52, s 239(4)(b)(c)
    rep in pt—Enterprise and Regulatory Reform, 2013 c 24, s 21(2)(a)
  s 10 subst —Employment Relations, 1999 c 26, s 41, sch 8 para 3
    am—SI 1998/1833, reg 32(9); Employment Relations, 2004 c 24, ss 36, 57(1), sch 1
      para 24, SIs 2004/2566; 2010/493, reg 17; Crime and Cts, 2013 c 22, sch 14 para
      13(3)
  ss 10A,10B added—Employment Relations, 1999 c 26, s 41, sch 8 para 30
  s 12 am—SI 2003/1673, regs 3(2), 31(2); Equality, 2010 c 15, s 211, sch 26 para 29
  s 12A and cross-heading added—Enterprise and Regulatory Reform, 2013 c 24, s 16(1)
    appl (mods)—Trade Union and Labour Relations (Consolidation), 1992 c 52 s
        138(2A); Employment Rights, 1996 c 18 s 201(3A)
    am—(prosp) Small Business, Enterprise and Employment, 2015 c 26, s 150(3)
  s 13 rep in pt—Employment Relations, 1999 c 26, ss 9, 44, sch 4 pt III para 4, sch 9(2)
    am—Employment, 2002 c 22, s 22(1); Crime and Cts, 2013 c 22, sch 9 para 52;
      Enterprise and Regulatory Reform, 2013 c 24, sch 3 para 3; Small Business,
      Enterprise and Employment, 2015 c 26, s 151(3)
  s 13A added—Employment, 2002 c 22, s 22(2)
    am—Enterprise and Regulatory Reform, 2013 c 24, s 21(3)(a)(b); Small Business,
      Enterprise and Employment, 2015 c 26, s 151(4)
  s 15 am—Tribunals, Cts and Enforcement, 2007 c 15, s 48, sch 8 paras 35, 43; ibid, s 62,
      sch 13 para 125; Crime and Cts, 2013 c 22, sch 9 para 52
  s 16 rep in pt—Social Security, 1998 c 14, s 86(1)(2), sch 7 para 147(a), sch 8; SI
      2008/2833, art 6, sch 3; (prosp) Welfare Reform, 2009 c 24, s 58, sch 7 pt 1
    am—Social Security, 1998 c 14, s 86(1), sch 7 para 147(b); Welfare Reform, 2007 c 5,
      s 28, sch 3 para 15; SIs 2010/493, reg 17; 2013/630, reg 11(2)(a)(b)(3)
  s 17 am—Welfare Reform, 2007 c 5, s 28, sch 3 para 15; SI 2013/630, reg 11(4)
    rep in pt—(prosp) Welfare Reform, 2009 c 24, s 58, sch 7 pt 1
  s 18 am—Employment Rights (Dispute Resolution), 1998 c 8, ss 11(1), 15, sch 1 para 16;
      Nat Minimum Wage, 1998 c 39, s 30(1); SI 1998/1833, reg 33(b); Employment
      Relations, 1999 c 26, s 14(b); SIs 1999/3323, reg 33(1); 2000/1337, art 2;
      2000/1551, reg 10, sch para 1(a); 2001/1107, reg 2; Employment, 2002 c 22, ss
      24(2), 53, sch 7, para 23(1)(2); SI 2002/2034, reg 11, sch 2 pt 1, para 2(a)(ii);
      2003/1660, reg 39(2), sch 5 para 1(a)(ii); 2003/1661, reg 39, sch 5 para 1(a)(ii);
      2003/3049, reg 20, sch 2 para 2(1)(2); Employment Relations, 2004 c 24, s 57(1),
      sch 1 para 25, SIs 2004/2566; 2004/1713, reg 21, sch 2 para 1(1)(2); 2004/2326,
      regs 34(b)(c), 46; 2006/349, reg 17, sch; 2006/1031, reg 49, sch 8; 2006/2059,
      reg 35; 2007/2974, reg 52; 2008/1660, reg 19, sch 3; (pt prosp) Apprenticeships,
      Skills, Children and Learning, 2009 c 22, s 40, sch 1 para 16; SI 2009/2401, reg
      33; Equality, 2010 c 15, s 211, sch 26 para 31(a); SIs 2010/93, reg 25, sch 2;
      2010/493, reg 17; Enterprise and Regulatory Reform, 2013 c 24, sch 1 para
      5(2)(3)(4)(a)(b)(5)(7)(9); ibid, s 9(2)(3); SIs 2014/308, sch para 1(2); 2014/431,
      art 2; SI 2015/2054, art 2(2)
    rep in pt—SIs 1999/3323, reg 33(1); 2002/2034, reg 11, sch 2 pt 1, para 2(a)(i);
      2003/1660, reg 39(2), sch 5 para 1(a)(i); 2003/1661, reg 39, sch 5 para 1(a)(i);
      2003/3049, reg 20, sch 2 para 2(1)(2); 2004/3426, reg 34(a); Employment,
      2008 c 24, ss 6, 20, sch 1 pt 1; SIs 2008/1660, reg 19, sch 3; 2009/2401, reg
      33; Equality, 2010 c 15, s 211, sch 26 para 31(b); ibid, sch 27 pt 1; Enterprise
      and Regulatory Reform, 2013 c 24, sch 1 para 5(6)(8)
    appl—SI 2006/246, reg 12
  ss 18A, 18B added—Enterprise and Regulatory Reform, 2013 c 24, s 7(1)
  s 18C added—Enterprise and Regulatory Reform, 2013 c 24, sch 1 para 6
  s 19 rep in pt —Employment, 2002 c 22, ss 24(3), 54, sch 8(1); Employment, 2008 c 24, ss
      6, 20, sch 1 pt 1
    am—Employment, 2002 c 22, ss 24(4), 53, sch 7, para 23(1)(3)
  s 19A added —Tribunals, Cts and Enforcement, 2007 c 15, s 142
    am—Crime and Cts, 2013 c 22, sch 9 para 52; Enterprise and Regulatory Reform,
      2013 c 24, s 23(2)(a)(c)(2)(b)(i); ibid, sch 1 para 7; (prosp) Small Business,
      Enterprise and Employment, 2015 c 26, s 150(4)
    rep in pt—Enterprise and Regulatory Reform, 2013 c 24, s 23(2)(b)(ii)
  s 20 am—SIs 1999/3323, reg 35(2); 2004/2326, regs 36(2), 48(2), 49; 2006/2059, reg 37;
      2007/2974, reg 58; 2009/2401, reg 35
  s 21 rep in pt—Employment Rights (Dispute Resolution), 1998 c 8, s 15, sch 2; Nat
      Minimum Wage, 1998 c 39, s 53, sch 3; Tax Credits, 1999 c 10, ss 7, 19(4),

1996
c 17 *continued*

sch 3 para 5, sch 6; SI 1999/3323, reg 35(3); Tax Credits, 2002 c 21, s 60, sch 6; SIs 2002/2034, reg 11, sch 2 pt 1, para 2(b)(i); 2003/1660, reg 39(2), sch 5 para 1(b)(i); 1661, reg 39, sch 5 para 1(b)(i); 3049, reg 20, sch 2 para 2(1)(3); 2004/3426, reg 37(a); 2008/1660, reg 19, sch 3; 2009/2401, reg 36; Equality, 2010 c 15, s 211, sch 26 para 32(a); ibid, sch 27 pt 1

am—SI 1998/1833, reg 34(a)(b); (retrosp in pt) Employment Rights (Dispute Resolution), 1998 c 8, s 15, sch 1 para 17(1)(2)(3); Nat Minimum Wage, 1998 c 39,s 29; Tax Credits, 1999 c 10, s 7, sch 3 para 5; SIs 1999/3323, reg 35(3); 2000/1551, reg 10, sch para 1(b); 2002/2034, reg 11, sch 2 pt 1, para 2(b)(ii); 2003/1660, reg 39(2), sch 5 para 1(b)(ii); 2003/1661, reg 39, sch 5 para 1(b)(ii); 2003/3049, reg 20, sch 2 para 2(1)(3); 2004/2326, regs 48(2), 49; Employment Relations, 2004 c 24, s 38, SIs 2004/2566; 2004/1713, reg 21, sch 2 para 1(1)(3); 2004/3426, reg 37(b)(c); Equality, 2006 c 3, s 40, sch 3 para 57; SIs 2006/349, reg 17, sch; 1031, reg 49, sch 8; 2006/2059, reg 38; 2007/2974, reg 59; Pensions, 2008 c 30, s 59; SIs 2008/1660, reg 19, sch 3; 2009/2401, reg 36; 2010/93, reg 25, sch 2; 493, reg 17; Equality, 2010 c 15, s 211, sch 26 para 32(b); SI 2014/308, sch para 1(3)

s 22 am —Constitutional Reform, 2005 c 4, s 15(1), sch 4 pt 1 paras 245, 246(1)(2)(a)(3)-(5); Crime and Cts, 2013 c 22, sch 14 para 11(2)-(4)

rep in pt—Constitutional Reform, 2005 c 4, ss 15(1), 146, sch 4 pt 1 paras 245, 246(1)(2)(b), sch 18 pt 2

s 23 am —Constitutional Reform, 2005 c 4, s 15(1), sch 4 pt 1 paras 245, 247

s 24 am —Constitutional Reform, 2005 c 4, s 15(1), sch 4 pt 1 paras 245, 248

ss 24A, 24B added—Tribunals, Cts and Enforcement, 2007 c 15, s 48, sch 8 paras 35, 44

s 25 am —Constitutional Reform, 2005 c 4, s 15(1), sch 4 pt 1 paras 245, 249; SI 2012/2404, sch 2 para 35

s 27 am—Tribunals, Cts and Enforcement, 2007 c 15, s 48, sch 8 paras 35, 45

rep in pt—Tribunals, Cts and Enforcement, 2007 c 15, s 146, sch 23

s 28 rep in pt—Employment Relations, 1999 c 26, ss 41, 44, sch 8 para 4, sch 9(12)

am—Tribunals, Cts and Enforcement, 2007 c 15, s 48, sch 8 paras 35, 46; Enterprise and Regulatory Reform, 2013 c 24, s 12(2)

s 29A added—Tribunals, Cts and Enforcement, 2007 c 15, s 48, sch 8 paras 35, 47

s 30 am—Employment Relations, 1999 c 26, s 41, sch 8 para 5; SI 1999/3323, reg 35(4); Tribunals, Cts and Enforcement, 2007 c 15, s 48, sch 8 paras 35, 48; Crime and Cts, 2013 c 22, sch 14 para 13(3); Enterprise and Regulatory Reform, 2013 c 24, s 12(3)

rep in pt—Employment Relations, 2004 c 24, s 57, sch 1 para 26, sch 2, SI 2004/3342

s 33 see—(trans of functions) SI 1999/901, art 5, sch

am—Employment Relations, 2004 c 24, s 49(1)-(7)

s 34 subst—Employment, 2002 c 22, s 23

s 36 rep in pt—Employment Relations, 2004 c 24, s 57, sch 1 para 27, sch 2, SI 2004/3342

ss 37ZA-37ZC added (prosp)—Crim Justice and Cts, 2015 c 2, s

Pt 2A (ss 37A-37Q) added (prosp)—Small Business, Enterprise and Employment, 2015 c 26, s 150(2)

s 40 rep in pt—Enterprise and Regulatory Reform, 2013 c 24, sch 1 para 8

s 41 am—(pt prosp) Enterprise and Regulatory Reform, 2013 c 24, s 11(2); ibid, s 12(4); ibid, sch 3 para 4; (prosp) Small Business, Enterprise and Employment, 2015 c 26, s 150(5)

s 42 am—Employment Relations, 2004 c 24, s 49(8); Enterprise and Regulatory Reform, 2013 c 24, s 21(4); ibid, sch 1 para 9(a)(b); (prosp) Small Business, Enterprise and Employment, 2015 c 26, s 150(6)

s 50 am—Police, 1997 c 50, s 134(1), sch 9 para 88

s 105 am—SI 2000/1551, reg 10, sch para 2(1)

s 108 am—SI 2000/1551, reg 10, sch para 2(2)

s 109 am—SI 2000/1551, reg 10, sch para 2(3)

sch 1 rep in pt—(pt prosp) Social Security, 1998 c 14, s 86(2), sch 8; Equality, 2006 c 3, s 91, sch 4

sch 2 rep in pt—Equality, 2010 c 15, s 211, sch 27 pt 1

sch 3 rep in pt—(pt prosp) Social Security, 1998 c 14, s 86(2), sch 8

c 18   **Employment Rights**

restr—Employment Tribunals, 1996 c 17, s 21

appl—Trade Union and Labour Relations (Consolidation) 1992 c 52, s 212B; Housing Grants, Construction and Regeneration, 1996 c 53, s 104(3); Education, 1996 c 56, s

1996
c 18 *continued*

575(1); School Standards and Framework, 1998 c 31, ss 54, 55, 142(1), sch 16, para 27(3)(b), sch 17 paras 24(4)(b), 27; Postal Services, 2000 c 26, s 118(4); (S) Nat Parks (S), 2000 asp 10, s 29, sch 4 para 6(3); (retrosp) (to 16.2.2001) Political Parties, Elections and Referendums, 2000 c 41, sch 7 para 4; Income Tax (Earnings and Pensions), 2003 c 1, s 516, sch 3 pt 6 para 34(2)(a); Serious Organised Crime and Police, 2005 c 15, s 161(4)

mod—Highways, 1980 c 66, s 266B(7); (EW) Audit Commission, 1998 c 18, s 54(2), sch 4 para 9(2); Regional Development Agencies, 1998 c 45, s 6, sch 3 para 9(3); Access to Justice, 1999 c 22, s 105, sch 14 pt II paras 2(1)(b), 4(b), 7(2) pt V para 33(7)(b); GLA, 1999 c 29, s 410(5); SI 1999/2277, art 5(1); Utilities, 2000 c 27, s 3(8), sch 3 para 9(1)(2)(b); Transport, 2000 c 38, ss 211, 215(7), 217, 218, 220, 240, sch 15 para 11(2), sch 18 pt II para 16(b), sch 19 para 12(b), sch 21 para 13(b), sch 25 para 12(b); (EW) Crim Justice and Court Services, 2000 c 43, ss 21(4)-(6),22(5)-(8),23; (S) Public Finance and Accountability (S), 2000 asp 1, s 10, sch 2 para 8(3); SI 2009/317, art 3, sch

appl (mods)—SI 2011/245, sch 6 pt 1

am—Crim Justice and Court Services, 2000 c 43, s 4(3), sch 1 para 3(5)

power to am—Employment Relations, 1999 c 26, s 19(3)(f); Employment, 2002 c 22, s 45(3)(d)(i); Employment Relations, 2004 c 24, s 42(4)(d)

power to appl—Employment Relations, 1999 c 26, s 23(1)(b)

power to mod—Social Security Contributions (Trans of Functions, etc), 1999 c 2, s 15(1)(2)(b)

restr—Regional Development Agencies, 1998 c 45, s 6, sch 3 para 10

saved—Scotland, 1998 c 46, s 30, sch 5 pt II, s H1(g)

ext—(EW) Water, 2003 c 37, s 36(6), sch 3 para 9

excl—Crime and Cts, 2013 c 22, sch 5 para 15(1)(2)(b)

s 3 am—Employment, 2002 c 22, s 35
  rep in pt—Employment, 2002 c 22, ss 36, 54, sch 8(1); Pensions, 2014 c 19, sch 13 para 67

s 5 am—Employment Relations, 1999 c 26, s 32(3)

s 7 am—Employment, 2008 c 24, s 4

ss 7A, 7B added—Employment, 2002 c 22, s 37

s 11 power to appl—Nat Minimum Wage, 1998 c 39, s 12(4)(a)
  am—SI 2011/1133, reg 31; Enterprise and Regulatory Reform, 2013 c 24, sch 2 para 16; SI 2014/431, sch para 3
  rep in pt—Pensions, 2014 c 19, sch 13 para 68

s 12 power to appl—Nat Minimum Wage, 1998 c 39, s 12(4)(a)

Pt 2 (ss 13-27) mod—Nat Minimum Wage, 1998 c 39, s 18(1)(a)(2)

s 16 am—SI 2008/2833, sch 3 para 137

s 18 appl—SI 1999/3323, reg 33(1)
  am—Employment, 2008 c 24, s 5; Pensions, 2008 c 30, s 56(6)

s 23 appl—Govt of Wales, 1998 c 38, s 24(2)
  ext—Nat Minimum Wage, 1998 c 39, s 20(1)(a)
  am—Employment Rights (Dispute Resolution), 1998 c 8, s 15, sch 1 para 18; SI 2011/1133, reg 32; Enterprise and Regulatory Reform, 2013 c 24, sch 2 para 17; SI 2014/3322, reg 2
  restr—Employment, 2002 c 22, s 32, sch 4

s 24 am—Employment, 2008 c 24, s 7(1)

s 27 am—Employment, 2002 c 22, s 53, sch 7, paras 24, 25; Work and Families, 2006 c 18, s 11, sch 1 para 29; SI 2010/93, reg 25, sch 2; Children and Families, 2014 c 6, sch 7 para 30(a); ibid, sch 7 para 30(b)

Pt 2A (ss 27A, 27B) added—Small Business, Enterprise and Employment, 2015 c 26, s 153(2)

s 29 rep in pt—SI 2002/2034, reg 11, sch 2 pt 1, para 3(1)(2)

s 31 am—SI 1998/924, arts 3, 4, sch; Employment Relations, 1999 c 26, s 35; SIs 2001/21, arts 3, 4, sch; 2002/10, arts 3, 4, sch; 2927, arts 3, 4, sch; 2003/3038, arts 3, 4, sch; 2004/2989, arts 3, 4, sch; 2005/3352, arts 3, 4, sch; 2006/3045, art 3, sch; 2007/3570, arts 3, 4, sch; 2008/3055, arts 3, 4, sch; 2009/3274, arts 2, 3, sch; 2010/2926, art 3, sch; 2011/3006, art 3, sch; 2012/3007, art 3, sch; 2014/382, art 3, sch; 2015/226, art 3, sch
  power to am—Employment Relations, 1999 c 26, s 34(1)(a)-(e)

s 34 am—SI 2011/1133, reg 33; Enterprise and Regulatory Reform, 2013 c 24, sch 2 para 18

1996
c 18 *continued*

s 35 am—SI 2002/794, art 5(1), sch 1, para 37
 rep in pt—(W, S pt prosp) Enterprise and Regulatory Reform, 2013 c 24, sch 20 para 2
s 36 am—Sunday Working (S), 2003 c 18, s 1(1)(2)
s 37 rep in pt—Employment Relations, 1999 c 26, ss 9, 44, sch 4 pt III para 6, sch 9(2)
s 43 rep in pt—Employment Relations, 1999 c 26, ss 9, 44, sch 4 pt III para 7, sch 9(2)
Pt 4A (ss 43A-43L) added—Public Interest Disclosure, 1998 c 23, s 1
s 43A appl—SIs 1999/3323, regs 23(5), 28(4), 31(4); 2004/2326, reg 44(4); 2004/3426,
  regs 25(5), 30(4), 32(4)
s 43B am—Enterprise and Regulatory Reform, 2013 c 24, s 17
s 43C rep in pt—Enterprise and Regulatory Reform, 2013 c 24, s 18(1)(a)
s 43E am—SI 2000/2040, art 2, sch pt I para 19
 rep in pt—Enterprise and Regulatory Reform, 2013 c 24, s 18(1)(b)
s 43F expld—SI 1999/1549, art 2(1)
 rep in pt—Enterprise and Regulatory Reform, 2013 c 24, s 18(1)(c)
s 43FA added—(1.1.2016) Small Business, Enterprise and Employment, 2015 c 26, s
  148(2)
s 43G rep in pt—Enterprise and Regulatory Reform, 2013 c 24, s 18(2)(a)
 am—Enterprise and Regulatory Reform, 2013 c 24, s 18(2)(b)
s 43H rep in pt—Enterprise and Regulatory Reform, 2013 c 24, s 18(3)(a)
 am—Enterprise and Regulatory Reform, 2013 c 24, s 18(3)(b)
s 43K am—Nat Health Service Reform and Health Care Professions, 2002 c 17, s 2(5), sch
  2 pt 2, para 63; Health and Social Care (Community Health and Standards),
  2003 c 43, s 184, sch 11 para 65; SIs (E) 2004/288, art 7(1)(11); (W) 2004/480
  (W 49), art 6(1)(12); (S) 2004/957, art 2, sch para 8(a)(i)(b); Nat Health
  Service (Conseq Provns), 2006 c 43, s 2, sch 1 para 178; SI 2006/1056, art 2,
  sch; (pt prosp) Health, 2006 c 28, s 80, sch 8 para 37; (W) SI 2007/961 (W 85),
  art 3, sch; Health and Social Care, 2012 c 7, sch 5 para 73; Enterprise and
  Regulatory Reform, 2013 c 24, s 20(2)(a)(b)(3)(4)(7); SI 2015/491, art 2(2)(3)
 rep in pt—Health and Social Care (Community Health and Standards), 2003 c 43, s
  196, sch 14 pt 4; SI (S) 2004/957, art 2, sch para 8(a)(ii)(iii); Enterprise and
  Regulatory Reform, 2013 c 24, s 20(2)(c)(5)(6)
 mod—(temp) Enterprise and Regulatory Reform, 2013 c 24, s 20(10)
s 43KA added—Police Reform, 2002 c 30, s 37(1)
 am—Serious Organised Crime and Police, 2005 c 15, s 158(2)(a)(3)(5)(6); Crime
  and Cts, 2013 c 22, sch 8 para 50
s 43M added—Employment Relations, 2004 c 24, s 40(1)
 am—Coroners and Justice, 2009 c 25, s 177, sch 21 para 36
s 44 am—SI 1996/1513, reg 8; Employment Relations, 1999 c 26, s 18(2)
 rep in pt—Employment Relations, 1999 c 26, ss 18(2), 44, sch 9(3)
s 45A added—SI 1998/1833, reg 31(1)
 rep in pt—Employment Relations, 1999 c 26, ss 18(3), 44, sch 9(3)
 am—SIs 2003/3049, reg 20, sch 2 para 3(1)(2); 2004/1713, reg 21, sch 2 para
  2(1)(2); 2008/1660, reg 19, sch 3; 2014/308, sch para 2(2)
s 46 am—Employment Relations, 1999 c 26, s 18(2); Welfare Reform and Pensions, 1999 c
  30, s 18, sch 2 para 19
 appl—Welfare Reform and Pensions, 1999 c 30, s 6(1)(4)
 rep in pt—Employment Relations, 1999 c 26, ss 18(2), 44, sch 9(3)
s 47 am—Employment Relations, 1999 c 26, s 18(2); SIs 1999/1925, reg 12; 2006/246, reg
  20, sch 2
 rep in pt—Employment Relations, 1999 c 26, ss 18(2), 44, sch 9(3)
s 47A added—Teaching and Higher Educ, 1998 c 30, s 44(1), sch 3 para 10
 am—Employment Relations, 1999 c 26, s 18(2)
 rep in pt—Employment Relations, 1999 c 26, ss 18(2), 44, sch 9(3)
s 47AA added (prosp)—Educ and Skills, 2008 c 25, s 37
s 47B added—Public Interest Disclosure, 1998 c 23, s 2
 am—Employment Relations, 1999 c 26, s 18(2); Enterprise and Regulatory Reform,
  2013 c 24, s 19(1)
 rep in pt—Employment Relations, 1999 c 26, ss 18(2), 44, sch 9(3)
s 47C added—Employment Relations, 1999 c 26, s 9, sch 4 pt III para 8
 expld—SI 1999/3312, reg 19(1)(2)(4)
 am—Employment, 2002 c 22, s 53, sch 7, paras 24, 26; Work and Families, 2006 c
  18, s 11, sch 1 para 30; Children and Families, 2014 c 6, ss 127(2)(a), 128(2)(a),
  sch 7 para 31(a); ibid, s 129(1)

1996

c 18 s 47C *continued*

rep in pt—Children and Families, 2014 c 6, sch 7 para 31(b)

s 47D added —Tax Credits, 2002 c 21, s 27, sch 1, para 1(1)(2)

s 47E added—Employment, 2002 c 22, s 47(1)(3)

rep in pt—Children and Families, 2014 c 6, s 132(5)(a)

s 47F added (pt prosp)—Apprenticeships, Skills, Children and Learning, 2009 c 22, s 40(1)(3)

s 47G added—Growth and Infrastructure, 2013 c 27, s 31(2)

s 48 am—Public Interest Disclosure, 1998 c 23, s 3; Teaching and Higher Educ, 1998 c 30, s 44(1), sch 3 para 11(a)(b); SI 1998/1833, reg 31(2); Employment Relations, 1999 c 26, s 9, sch 4 pt III para 9; Tax Credits, 2002 c 21, s 27, sch 1, para 1(1)(3); Employment, 2002 c 22, s 53, sch 7, paras 24, 27; Employment Relations, 2004 c 24, ss 40(2), 41(3); (pt prosp) Apprenticeships, Skills, Children and Learning, 2009 c 22, s 40, sch 1 paras 1, 2; SI 2011/1133, reg 34; Enterprise and Regulatory Reform, 2013 c 24, s 19(2); ibid, sch 2 para 19; Growth and Infrastructure, 2013 c 27, s 31(3); Children and Families, 2014 c 6, s 129(2)

appl—Employment Relations, 1999 c 26, ss 12(2), 14, 15; SIs 2002/3207, reg 16(2); 2004/2326, reg 45(2)(3); 2006/349, reg 17, sch; 2010/155, reg 18

appl (mods)—Nat Minimum Wage, 1998 c 39, s 24(2)(a); SIs 1999/3323, reg 32(2)(a); 2004/3426, reg 33(2); Pensions, 2008 c 30, s 56(2); SI 2009/2401, reg 32

ext (mods)—Tax Credits, 1999 c 10, s 7, sch 3 para 2(2)(a)

restr—Employment, 2002 c 22, s 32, sch 4

s 49 am—SI 1998/1833, reg 31(3)(a)(b); Public Interest Disclosure, 1998 c 23, s 4(2)(3); Tax Credits, 2002 c 21, s 27, sch 1, para 1(1)(4); Enterprise and Regulatory Reform, 2013 c 24, s 18(4); Children and Families, 2014 c 6, s 129(3)

appl (mods)—Nat Minimum Wage, 1998 c 39, s 24(2)(a); SI 2004/3426, reg 33(2); Pensions, 2008 c 30, s 56(2)

ext (mods)—Tax Credits, 1999 c 10, s 7, sch 3 para 2(2)(a)

restr—Nat Minimum Wage, 1998 c 39, s 24(3)

appl—SIs 2004/2326, reg 45(2)(3); 2006/349, reg 17, sch; 2007/2974, reg 51; 2009/2401, reg 32

s 49A added—Police (Health and Safety), 1997 c 42, s 3

am—Serious Organised Crime and Police, 2005 c 15, s 158(2)(a)(3)(5)(6)

Pt 5A (s 49B) added—Small Business, Enterprise and Employment, 2015 c 26, s 149(2)

s 50 appl—SI 1998/633, art J12(2)

excl—SI 1998/633, art J12(1)

rep in pt—School Standards and Framework, 1998 c 31, s 140(3), sch 31; SI 2000/2463, art 2; (S) Standards in Scotland's Schools etc, 2000, asp 6, s 60(2), sch 3; Serious Organised Crime and Police, 2005 c 15, ss 59, 174(2), sch 4 paras 84, 86, sch 17 pt 2; Nat Health Service (Conseq Provns), 2006 c 43, s 2, sch 1 para 179; Police and Justice, 2006 c 48, s 52, sch 15; Police Reform and Social Responsibility, 2011 c 13, sch 16 para 219; SI 2011/2581, sch 3 para 2; Educ, 2011 c 21, sch 2 para 24; Health and Social Care, 2012 c 7, sch 5 para 74(a)(b); (prosp) ibid, sch 14 para 69; SSI 2015/39, sch para 5(a)(b)

am—SIs 2000/90, art 3(1), sch 1 para 30(2); 2000/1737, art 2; 2000/2463, art 2; (E) 2001/2237, arts 2, 30; (W) 2002/808 (W 89), arts 2(o), 29; 2002/2469, reg 4, sch 1 pt 1, para 22(1)(2); Health and Social Care (Community Health and Standards), 2003 c 43, s 34, sch 4 paras 99, 100; SI 2004/1822, art 2, sch pt 1 para 18; Nat Health Service (Conseq Provns), 2006 c 43, s 2, sch 1 para 179; Police and Justice, 2006 c 48, s 52, sch 14 para 31; Offender Management, 2007 c 21, s 39, sch 3 para 8; (W) SIs 2007/961 (W 85), art 3, sch; 2007/1837, art 2; 2010/1080, art 2, sch 1; 2010/1158, art 5, sch 2; Health and Social Care, 2012 c 7, sch 17 para 6(2), sch 19 para 6(2)

s 51 am—SI 2011/1133, reg 35; Enterprise and Regulatory Reform, 2013 c 24, sch 2 para 20

s 54 am—SI 2011/1133, reg 36; Enterprise and Regulatory Reform, 2013 c 24, sch 2 para 21

s 55 am—SIs 2002/253, art 54(3), sch 5, para 13; 2004/1771, art 3, sch pt 1 para 3

s 57 am—SI 2011/1133, reg 37; Enterprise and Regulatory Reform, 2013 c 24, sch 2 para 22; Children and Families, 2014 c 6, s 130(1)

ss 57ZA-57ZD added —SI 2010/93, reg 25, sch 2

s 57ZC am—Enterprise and Regulatory Reform, 2013 c 24, sch 2 para 23

am—Children and Families, 2014 c 6, s 130(2)

ss 57ZE-57ZI and cross-heading added—Children and Families, 2014 c 6, s 127(1)

1996

c 18 *continued*

  ss 57ZJ-57ZS and cross-heading added —Children and Families, 2014 c 6, s 128(1)

  s 57A added—Employment Relations, 1999 c 26, s 8, sch 4 pt II

   am—Civil Partnership, 2004 c 33, s 261(1), sch 27 para 151

  s 57B added—Employment Relations, 1999 c 26, s 8, sch 4 pt II

   am—SI 2011/1133, reg 38; Enterprise and Regulatory Reform, 2013 c 24, sch 2 para 24

  s 58 am—Teaching and Higher Educ, 1998 c 30, s 44(1), sch 3, para 12; Welfare Reform and Pensions, 1999 c 30, s 18, sch 2 para 19

   appl—Welfare Reform and Pensions, 1999 c 30, s 6(2)

   rep in pt—Pensions, 2004 c 35, s 320, sch 13 pt 1

  s 60 am—SI 2011/1133, reg 39; Enterprise and Regulatory Reform, 2013 c 24, sch 2 para 25

  s 61 am—SIs 1999/1925, reg 15; 2006/246, reg 20, sch 2

  s 63 am—SI 2011/1133, reg 40; Enterprise and Regulatory Reform, 2013 c 24, sch 2 para 26

  s 63A added—Teaching and Higher Educ, 1998 c 30, s 32

   see—(trans of functions) (S) SI 1999/1750, art 2, sch 1

   am—Learning and Skills, 2000 c 21, s 149, sch 9 para 50; Educ and Skills, 2008 c 25, s 39(1)(2)

  s 63B added—Teaching and Higher Educ, 1998 c 30, s 33

  s 63C added—Teaching and Higher Educ, 1998 c 30, s 33

   am—SI 2011/1133, reg 41; Enterprise and Regulatory Reform, 2013 c 24, sch 2 para 27

  ss 63D-63K added (pt prosp)—Apprenticeships, Skills, Children and Learning, 2009 c 22, s 40(1)(2)

  s 63I am—SI 2011/1133, reg 42; Enterprise and Regulatory Reform, 2013 c 24, sch 2 para 28

  s 64 am—SI 1999/3232, reg 41(1), sch 9 para 2

  s 65 rep in pt—SI 2002/2034, reg 11, sch 2 pt 1, para 3(1)(3)

  s 66 appl—SI 1999/3312, regs 19(2)(c), 20(3)(c)

   mod—SIs 1998/218, art 3, sch; 1999/2256, art 3, sch; 2006/1073, art 3

   appl (mods)—(E) SI 2003/1964, art 3, sch

  s 67 mod—SIs 1998/218, art 3, sch; 1999/2256, art 3, sch; 2006/1073, art 3

   saved—SI 1999/3242, reg 17

   appl (mods)—(E) SI 2003/1964, art 3, sch

  s 68 mod—SIs 1998/218, art 3, sch; 1999/2256, art 3, sch; 2006/1073, art 3

   appl (mods)—(E) SI 2003/1964, art 3, sch

  ss 68A-68D added —SI 2010/93, reg 25, sch 2

  s 69A added —SI 2010/93, reg 25, sch 2

  s 70 mod—SIs 1998/218, art 3, sch; 1999/2256, art 3, sch; 2006/1073, art 3

   appl (mods) —(E) SI 2003/1964, art 3, sch

   am—SI 2011/1133, reg 43; Enterprise and Regulatory Reform, 2013 c 24, sch 2 para 29

  s 70A added —SI 2010/93, reg 25, sch 2

   am—Enterprise and Regulatory Reform, 2013 c 24, sch 2 para 30

  Pt 8 (ss 71-80) subst—Employment Relations, 1999 c 26, s 7, sch 4 pt I

  s 71 mod—SIs 1998/218, art 3, sch; 1999/2256, art 3, sch; 2006/1073, art 3

   see—SI 1999/3312, regs 2(1), 4-12, 19-22

   restr—SI 1999/3312, reg 9

   am—Employment, 2002 c 22, s 17(1)-(3); Work and Families, 2006 c 18, s 11, sch 1 para 31; Children and Families, 2014 c 6, s 118(2)

   appl (mods) —(E) SI 2003/1964, art 3, sch

  s 72 expld—SI 1999/3312, reg 8

  s 73 see—SI 1999/3312, regs 2(1), 5-12, 17-22

   am—Employment, 2002 c 22, s 17(1)(4); Work and Families, 2006 c 18, s 11, sch 1 para 32; Children and Families, 2014 c 6, s 118(3)

  s 74 am—Employment, 2002 c 22, s 17(1)(5)

  Pt 8, Ch 1A (ss 75A-75D) added—Employment, 2002 c 22, s 3

  s 75A am—Work and Families, 2006 c 18, s 11, sch 1 para 33; Children and Families, 2014 c 6, ss 118(4), 121(1), 122(1)

   appl—SI 2014/3095, reg 2

  s 75B am—Work and Families, 2006 c 18, s 11, sch 1 para 34; Children and Families, 2014 c 6, ss 118(5), 122(2)

1996
c 18 s 75B *continued*

    appl—SI 2014/3095, reg 2
s 75D am—Children and Families, 2014 c 6, s 122(3)
Pt 8, Ch 1B (ss 75E-75K) added—Children and Families, 2014 c 6, s 117(1)
s 75G mod—SI 2014/3091, reg 2, sch
    appl (mods)—SI 2014/3095, reg 3, sch 1
s 75H mod—SI 2014/3091, reg 2, sch
    appl (mods)—SI 2014/3095, reg 3, sch 1
s 78 am —Employment, 2002 c 22, s 53, sch 7, paras 24, 28
s 80 am—SI 2011/1133, reg 44; Enterprise and Regulatory Reform, 2013 c 24, sch 2 para
    31
Pt 8, Ch 3 (ss 80A-80E) added —Employment, 2002 c 22, s 1
s 80A am—Work and Families, 2006 c 18, s 11, sch 1 para 35; Children and Families, 2014
    c 6, s 118(6)
    rep in pt—Children and Families, 2014 c 6, sch 7 para 32
    appl (mods)—SI 2014/3095, reg 4, sch 2
s 80AA added—Work and Families, 2006 c 18, s 3
    rep —Children and Families, 2014 c 6, s 125(1)
s 80B appl (mods)—SIs 2003/920, reg 2, sch; 2014/3095, reg 4, sch 2
    am—Work and Families, 2006 c 18, s 11, sch 1 para 36; Children and Families, 2014
    c 6, ss 118(7), 121(2)(a)(b), 122(4), 128(2)(b)
    rep in pt—Children and Families, 2014 c 6, sch 7 para 33
s 80BB added—Work and Families, 2006 c 18, s 4
    rep —Children and Families, 2014 c 6, s 125(1)
s 80C am—Work and Families, 2006 c 18, s 5; Children and Families, 2014 c 6, sch 7 para
    34(3)(d)(5)(c)(6)(7)
    rep in pt—Children and Families, 2014 c 6, sch 7 para
    34(2)(3)(a)(b)(4)(a)(b)(5)(a)(b)(d)
s 80D am—Work and Families, 2006 c 18, s 11, sch 1 para 37; Children and Families, 2014
    c 6, sch 7 para 35
s 80E am—Work and Families, 2006 c 18, s 11, sch 1 para 38; Children and Families, 2014
    c 6, sch 7 para 36(2)
    rep in pt—Children and Families, 2014 c 6, sch 7 para 36(3)
Pt 8A (ss 80F-80I) added—Employment, 2002 c 22, s 47(1)(2)
s 80F rep in pt—Work and Families, 2006 c 18, ss 12(4), 15, sch 2; Children and Families,
    2014 c 6, s 131(1)(2)(c)(d)
    am—Work and Families, 2006 c 18, s 12(1)(2)(3)(5); SI 2013/283, reg 2; Children
    and Families, 2014 c 6, s 131(2)(b)
s 80G am—Children and Families, 2014 c 6, s 132(2)-(4)
    rep in pt—Children and Families, 2014 c 6, s 132(5)(b)
s 80H am—SI 2011/1133, reg 45; Enterprise and Regulatory Reform, 2013 c 24, sch 2 para
    32; Children and Families, 2014 c 6, 133(2)(b)(3)-(6)
    rep in pt—Children and Families, 2014 c 6, s 132(5)(c)
s 80I rep in pt—Children and Families, 2014 c 6, s 132(5)(d)
s 86 rep in pt—SI 2002/2034, reg 11, sch 2 pt 1, para 3(1)(4)
s 88 am—Employment Relations, 1999 c 26, s 9, sch 4 pt III para 10; Employment, 2002 c
    22, s 53, sch 7, paras 24, 29; Work and Families, 2006 c 18, s 11, sch 1 para 39;
    Children and Families, 2014 c 6, sch 7 para 37(2)(a)(3)(b); ibid, sch 7 para
    37(2)(b)(3)(a)
s 89 am—Employment Relations, 1999 c 26, s 9, sch 4 pt III para 11; Employment, 2002 c
    22, s 53, sch 7, paras 24, 30; Work and Families, 2006 c 18, s 11, sch 1 para 40;
    Children and Families, 2014 c 6, sch 7 para 38(2)(a)(3)(b); ibid, sch 7 para
    38(2)(b)(3)(a)
s 90 am—SI 2008/1879, reg 2
s 92 am—Employment Relations, 1999 c 26, s 9, sch 4 pt III para 12; SI 1999/1436, arts
    2-4; Employment, 2002 c 22, s 53, sch 7, paras 24, 31; SI 2002/2034, reg 11, sch
    2 pt 1, para 3(1)(5)(6); Employment Relations, 2004 c 24, s 57(1), sch 1 para 28;
    SI 2012/989, art 2
    appl (mods)—SIs 1998/218, art 4(a); (E) 2003/1964, arts 3, 4(a), sch
    mod—SIs 1998/218, art 3, sch; 1999/2256, arts 3, 4(a), sch; 2006/1073, arts 3, 4
s 93 mod—SIs 1998/218, art 3, sch; 1999/2256, art 3, sch; 2006/1073, art 3
    appl (mods)—(E) SI 2003/1964, arts 3, 4(a), sch
Pt 10 (ss 94-134) am—Trade Union and Labour Relations (Consolidation) 1992 c 52, s
    238A(2)

1996
c 18 Pt 10 *continued*

appl—Nat Minimum Wage, 1998 c 39, s 23(4); Tax Credits, 1999 c 10, sch 3 para
1(3); Employment Relations, 1999 c 26, s 18(4)(5); SIs 2002/2034, reg 6(5);
2010/493, regs 13, 15

appl (mods)—SIs 1998/218, art 4(b); (E) 2003/1964, arts 3, 4(b), sch; 2009/2108, reg
33

expld—SI 1999/3312, reg 20

mod—SI 1998/218, art 3, sch; GSM Nat Institutions, 1998 (No 1), s 6(1), sch 3 para
3(1)(2); Trade Union and Labour Relations (Consolidation) 1992 c 52, s 70A,
sch A1 paras 161(1), 162; Employment Relations, 1999 c 26, ss 12(3)(6), 14,
15; SIs 1999/2256, arts 3, 4(b), sch; 2006/1073, arts 3, 4

ext—(subject to specified exclusions) SI 2000/1828, art 2(1)-(4)(6)

s 95 am—SI 2002/2034, reg 11, sch 2 pt 1, para 3(1)(7)

rep in pt—Employment Relations, 2004 c 24, s 57, sch 1 para 29, sch 2

s 96 rep—Employment Relations, 1999 c 26, ss 9, 44, sch 4 pt III para 13, sch 9(2)

s 97 rep in pt—Employment Relations, 1999 c 26, ss 9, 44, sch 4 pt III para 14, sch 9(2)

appl—SIs 2000/1338, art 4; 2002/2927, art 4(3)(f)

am—SI 2002/2034, reg 11, sch 2 pt 1, para 3(1)(8)

s 98 mod—GSM Nat Institutions, 1998 (No 1), s 6(1), sch 3 para 3(2)(b); SI 2006/246, reg
7(3)(b)

rep in pt—Employment Relations, 1999 c 26, ss 9, 44, sch 4 pt III para 15, sch 9(2); SI
2011/1069, reg 3(2)(a)

saved—GSM Nat Institutions, 1998 (No 1), s 6(1), sch 3 para 3(2)(b)

am—Employment, 2002 c 22, s 53, sch 7, paras 24, 32; Employment Relations, 2004 c
24, s 57(1), sch 1 para 30; SIs 2006/1031, reg 49, sch 8; 2011/1069, reg 3(2)(b)

ss 98ZA-98ZH added—SI 2006/1031, reg 49, sch 8

rep—SI 2011/1069, reg 3(3)

s 98A added—Employment, 2002 c 22, s 34(1)(2)

rep —Employment, 2008 c 24, ss 2, 20, sch 1 pt 1

s 98B added—Employment Relations, 2004 c 24, s 40(3)

am —Coroners and Justice, 2009 c 25, s 177, sch 21 para 36

s 99 subst—Employment Relations, 1999 c 26, s 9, sch 4 pt III para 16

am —Employment, 2002 c 22, s 53, sch 7, paras 24, 33; Work and Families, 2006 c 18,
s 11, sch 1 para 41; Children and Families, 2014 c 6, ss 127(2)(b), 128(2)(c), sch
7 para 39(a); ibid, sch 7 para 39(b)

s 101A added—SI 1998/1833, reg 32(1)

am—SIs 2003/3049, reg 20, sch 2 para 3(1)(3); 2004/1713, reg 21, sch 2 para
2(1)(3); 2008/1660, reg 19, sch 3; 2014/308, sch para 2(3)

s 101B added (prosp)—Educ and Skills, 2008 c 25, s 38

s 102 am—Welfare Reform and Pensions, 1999 c 30, s 18, sch 2 para 19

appl—Welfare Reform and Pensions, 1999 c 30, s 6(1)

s 103 renumbered—SI 1999/1925, reg 13

am—SIs 1999/1925, reg 13; 2006/246, reg 20, sch 2

s 103A added—Public Interest Disclosure, 1998 c 23, s 5

s 104 am—SI 1998/1833, reg 32(2)(b); Teaching and Higher Educ, 1998 c 30, s 44(1), sch
3 para 13; Employment, 2002 c 22, s 53, sch 7, paras 24, 34; SI 2003/3049, reg
20, sch 2 para 3(1)(4); Employment Relations, 2004 c 24, s 57(1), sch 1 para 31,
SIs 2004/2566; 2004/1713, reg 21, sch 2 para 2(1)(4); 2006/246, reg 19;
2008/1660, reg 19, sch 3; 2014/308, sch para 2(4)

s 104A added—Nat Minimum Wage, 1998 c 39, s 25(1)

mod—Agric Wages, 1948 c 47, s 3A(5); Agric Sector (W), 2014 anaw 6, s 5(8)

ext—(pt prosp) Agric Wages (S), 1949 c 30, s 3A(4) (added by Nat Minimum Wage,
1998 c 39, s 47, sch 2 para 13)

s 104B subst —Tax Credits, 2002 c 21, s 27, sch 1, para 3(1)(2)

s 104C added —Employment, 2002 c 22, s 47(1)(4)

mod—Pensions, 2008 c 30, s 56(5)

rep in pt—Children and Families, 2014 c 6, s 132(5)(e)

s 104D added —Pensions, 2008 c 30, s 57(1)(2)

s 104E added (pt prosp)—Apprenticeships, Skills, Children and Learning, 2009 c 22, s
40(1)(3)

s 104F added—SI 2010/493, reg 12

s 104G added—Growth and Infrastructure, 2013 c 27, s 31(4)

s 105 am—SI 1998/1833, reg 32(3); Public Interest Disclosure, 1998 c 23, s 6; Nat
Minimum Wage, 1998 c 39, s 25(2); Tax Credits, 1999 c 10, s 7, sch 3 para

1996
c 18 *continued*

3(2); Employment Relations, 1999 c 26, s 16, sch 5 para 5; SI 1999/3323, reg
29(1); Tax Credits, 2002 c 21, s 27, sch 1, para 3(1)(3); SI 2002/2034, reg 11,
sch 2 pt 1, para 3(1)(9)(10); Employment Relations, 2004 c 24, ss 40(4)(5),
41(4); SIs 2004/2326, reg 43(1); 3426, reg 31(1); 2006/349, reg 17, sch; 2059,
reg 32; 2007/825, reg 3; 2974, reg 48; (prosp) Educ and Skills, 2008 c 25, s
39(1)(3); Pensions, 2008 c 30, s 57(1)(4); (prosp) ibid, s 57(3); (pt prosp)
Apprenticeships, Skills, Children and Learning, 2009 c 22, s 40, sch 1 paras 1, 3;
SIs 2009/2401, reg 30; 2010/93, reg 25, sch 2; 493, reg 12

   rep in pt—Employment Relations, 1999 c 26, ss 9, 44, sch 4 pt III para 17, sch 9(2);
SI 2011/1069, reg 3(4)

s 106 am—Employment, 2002 c 22, s 53, sch 7, paras 24, 35; Work and Families, 2006 c
18, s 11, sch 1 para 42; Children and Families, 2014 c 6, sch 7 para 40

s 108 am—SI 1998/1833, reg 32(4); Public Interest Disclosure, 1998 c 23, s 7(1); Nat
Minimum Wage, 1998 c 39, s 25(3); Tax Credits, 1999 c 10, ss 7, 19(4), sch 3
para 3(3), sch 6; SIs 1999/1436, arts 2-4; 3323, reg 29(2); Tax Credits, 2002 c
21, s 27, sch 1, para 3(1)(4); SI 2002/2034, reg 11, sch 2 pt 1, para 3(1)(11);
Employment Relations, 2004 c 24, ss 40(6), 41(5), 57(1), sch 1 para 32; SIs
2004/2326, reg 43(2)(b)(3)(b); 3426, reg 31(2)(b); 2006/349, reg 17, sch; 1031,
reg 49, sch 8; 2059, reg 32; 2007/2974, reg 48; (prosp) Educ and Skills, 2008 c
25, s 39(1)(4); Pensions, 2008 c 30, s 57(1)(5); (pt prosp) Apprenticeships,
Skills, Children and Learning, 2009 c 22, s 40, sch 1 paras 1, 4; SIs 2009/2401,
reg 30; 2010/93, reg 25, sch 2; 493, reg 12; 2012/989, art 3; Enterprise and
Regulatory Reform, 2013 c 24, s 13; Growth and Infrastructure, 2013 c 27, s
31(5); Defence Reform, 2014 c 20, s 48(2)

   excl—Trade Union and Labour Relations (Consolidation) 1992 c 52, ss 70A, 154, sch
A1 para 164; Employment Relations, 1999 c 26, ss 12(4), 14, 15; SIs
2002/3207, reg 16(4); 2009/2108, reg 33(4); 2010/155, reg 18; 2015/2021,
reg 2(5)

   rep in pt—Nat Minimum Wage, 1998 c 39, ss 25(3),53, sch 3; Tax Credits, 1999 c 10,
ss 7, 19(4), sch 3 para 3(3), sch 6; Employment Relations, 1999 c 26, ss 9, 44,
sch 4 pt III para 18, sch 9(2); SIs 1999/3323, reg 29(2); 2002/2034, reg 11, sch
2 pt 1, para 3(1)(11); 2004/2326, reg 43(2)(a)(3)(a); 3426, reg 31(2)(a);
2009/2401, reg 30; 2011/1069, reg 3(5)

s 109 rep—SI 2006/1031, reg 49, sch 8

s 110 am—Employment Rights (Dispute Resolution), 1998 c 8, s 12(1)(2)(3)(5); (prosp)
Employment, 2002 c 22, s 44; Crime and Cts, 2013 c 22, sch 9 para 52

Pt 10, Ch 1 (ss 111-132) appl —SI 2010/155, reg 18

s 111 restr—Employment, 2002 c 22, s 32, sch 4

   am—SIs 2010/493, reg 12; 2011/1133, reg 46; Enterprise and Regulatory Reform,
2013 c 24, sch 2 para 33

s 111A added—Enterprise and Regulatory Reform, 2013 c 24, s 14

s 112 am—Employment Rights (Dispute Resolution), 1998 c 8, s 15, sch 1, para 19;
Employment, 2002 c 22, ss 34(1)(3), 53, sch 7, paras 24, 36; SI 2006/1031, reg
49, sch 8

   rep in pt—Employment Relations, 1999 c 26, s 44, sch 9(11); Employment, 2008 c 24,
s 20, sch 1 pt 1; SI 2011/1069, reg 3(6)

s 113 restr—Trade Union and Labour Relations (Consolidation), 1992 c 52, s 239(4)(a)

s 114 rep in pt—Employment Relations, 1999 c 26, ss 9, 44, sch 4 pt III para 20, sch 9(2)

s 115 rep in pt—Employment Relations, 1999 c 26, ss 9, 44, sch 4 pt III para 21, sch 9(2)

s 117 power to mod—Trade Union and Labour Relations (Consolidation), 1992 c 52, s
212A(8)(a)

   am—Employment Rights (Dispute Resolution), 1998 c 8, ss 14(1), 15, sch 1 para 20;
SI 1998/1833, reg 32(5); Employment Relations, 1999 c 26, s 33(2);
Employment, 2002 c 22, ss 34(1)(4), 53, sch 7, paras 24, 37

   rep in pt—Employment Rights (Dispute Resolution), 1998 c 8, s 15, sch 2;
Employment Relations, 1999 c 26, ss 33(1)(a)(2), 44, sch 9(10)(11)

   appl (mods)—SIs 1999/1548, reg 3; (EW) 2001/1185, arts 2, 5, sch para 160;
2004/753, art 6

s 118 am—Employment Rights (Dispute Resolution), 1998 c 8, s 15, sch 1, para 21(1)(2)(3);
SI 1998/1833, reg 32(5); Employment, 2002 c 22, s 53, sch 7, paras 24, 38

   rep in pt—Employment Relations, 1999 c 26, ss 9, 33(1)(a), 44, sch 4 pt III para 22,
sch 9(2)(10)(11); Employment, 2002 c 22, s 54, sch 8(1)

   appl (mods)—SI 1999/1548, reg 3

1996
c 18 *continued*

s 119 appl—Trade Union and Labour Relations (Consolidation), 1992 c 52, s 70A, sch A1
  para 160(2); Nat Minimum Wage, 1998 c 39, s 24(4)(a)
 rep in pt—Employment Relations, 1999 c 26, ss 9, 44, sch 4 pt III para 23, sch 9(2);
  SI 2006/1031, reg 49, sch 8
 appl (mods)—SI 1999/1548, reg 3
 mod—Pensions, 2008 c 30, s 56(4)(a)
s 120 am—SIs 1998/924, arts 3,4, sch; 1833, reg 32(5); 2001/21, arts 3, 4, sch;
  Employment, 2002 c 22, s 34(1)(6); SIs 2002/10, arts 3, 4, sch; 2927, arts 3, 4,
  sch; 2003/3038, arts 3, 4, sch; 2004/2989, arts 3, 4, sch; 2005/3352, arts 3, 4,
  sch; 2006/1031, reg 49, sch 8; 3045, art 3, sch; 2007/3570, arts 3, 4, sch;
  2008/3055, arts 3, 4, sch; 2010/493, reg 12; 2011/3006, art 3, sch; 2012/3007,
  art 3, sch; 2014/382, art 3, sch; 2015/226, art 3, sch
 power to am—Employment Relations, 1999 c 26, s 34(1)(a)-(e)
 rep in pt—Employment Relations, 1999 c 26, ss 36(1)(3), 44, sch 9(10); Employment,
  2008 c 24, s 20, sch 1 pt 1; SI 2011/1069, reg 3(7)
s 121 appl (mods)—SI 1999/1548, reg 3
s 122 am—SI 1998/1833, reg 32(5); Employment Rights (Dispute Resolution), 1998 c 8, s
  15, sch 1 para 22; SI 2010/493, reg 12
 appl (mods)—SI 1999/1548, reg 3
s 123 appl—Trade Union and Labour Relations (Consolidation), 1992 c 52, s 70A, sch A1
  para 160(2); Nat Minimum Wage, 1998 c 39, s 24(4)(b)
 appl (mods)—SI 1999/1548, reg 3
 am—Employment Rights (Dispute Resolution), 1998 c 8, s 15, sch 1 para 23;
  Employment, 2002 c 22, ss 34(1)(5), 53, sch 7, paras 24, 39; Enterprise and
  Regulatory Reform, 2013 c 24, s 18(5)
s 124 am—SI 1998/924, arts 3, 4, sch; Employment Relations, 1999 c 26, ss 34(4), 37(1);
  SIs 2001/21, arts 3, 4, sch; 2002/10, arts 3, 4, sch; 2927, arts 3, 4, sch;
  2003/3038, arts 3, 4, sch; 2004/2989, arts 3, 4, sch; 2005/3352, arts 3, 4, sch;
  2006/3045, art 3, sch; 2007/3570, arts 3, 4, sch; 2008/3055, arts 3, 4, sch;
  2009/3274, arts 2, 3, sch; 2011/3006, art 3, sch; 2012/3007, art 3, sch;
  2013/1949, art 2(2)(3); 2014/382, art 3, sch; 2015/226, art 3, sch
 appl—Trade Union and Labour Relations (Consolidation), 1992 c 52, s 70A, sch A1
  para 160(2); Nat Minimum Wage, 1998 c 39, s 24(4)(b)
 power to am—Employment Relations, 1999 c 26, s 34(1)(a)-(e); Enterprise and
  Regulatory Reform, 2013 c 24, s 15(1)-(9)
 rep in pt—Employment Relations, 1999 c 26, ss 36(1)(3), 44, sch 9(10)
 appl (mods)—SI 1999/1548, reg 3
s 124A added—Employment, 2002 c 22, s 39
 am—Employment, 2008 c 24, s 3(4)
s 125 rep—Employment Relations, 1999 c 26, ss 33(1)(a), 44, sch 9(10)
s 126 am—Employment Rights (Dispute Resolution), 1998 c 8, s 14(2)(3)(4)(b); SIs
  2003/1660, reg 39(2), sch 5 para 2(b); 1661, reg 39, sch 5 para 2(a)(ii)(b);
  2006/1031, reg 49, sch 8; Equality, 2010 c 15, s 211, sch 26 para 33
 appl (mods)—SI 1999/1548, reg 3
 rep in pt—Employment Rights (Dispute Resolution), 1998 c 8, ss 14(2)(4)(a), 15, sch
  2; SIs 2003/1660, reg 39(2), sch 5 para 2(a); 1661, reg 39, sch 5 para 2(a)(i)
s 127 rep—Employment Relations, 1999 c 26, ss 9, 44, sch 4 pt III para 24, sch 9(2)
s 127A rep—Employment, 2002 c 22, ss 53, 54, sch 7, paras 24, 40, sch 8(1)
s 127B rep—Employment Relations, 1999 c 26, ss 37(2), 44, sch 9(11)
s 128 am—SI 1998/1833, reg 32(5); Public Interest Disclosure, 1998 c 23, s 9;
  Employment Relations, 1999 c 26, s 6; SI 2010/493, reg 12
 appl—SIs 2002/3207, reg 16(5); 2010/155, reg 18
 ext—Employment Relations, 1999 c 26, ss 12(5), 14, 15
s 129 am—SI 1998/1833, reg 32(5); Public Interest Disclosure, 1998 c 23, s 9;
  Employment Relations, 1999 c 26, s 6; SI 2010/493, reg 12
 ext—Employment Relations, 1999 c 26, ss 12(5), 14, 15
 appl—SIs 2002/3207, reg 16(5); 2010/155, reg 18
ss 130-132 ext—Employment Relations, 1999 c 26, ss 12(5), 14, 15
 appl—SIs 2002/3207, reg 16(5); 2010/155, reg 18
s 134 am—Education, 1996 c 56, s 582(1) sch 37 pt I para 130; School Standards and
  Framework, 1998 c 31, s 140(1), sch 30 para 55; Educ, 2002 c 32, s 215(1), sch
  21, para 30; SI 2010/1158, art 5, sch 2
s 134A added—Police (Health and Safety), 1997 c 42, s 4

1996
c 18 s 134A   *continued*

        am—Serious Organised Crime and Police, 2005 c 15, ss 59, 158(2)(b)(3)(5)(6), sch 4 paras 84, 87; Crime and Cts, 2013 c 22, sch 8 para 51

       mod—SI 2006/1073, arts 3, 4

   Pt 11 (ss 135-181) mod—Highways, 1980 c 66, s 266B(6); Regional Development Agencies, 1998 c 45, ss 34,36, sch 8 para 9(3)(4), sch 9 para 9(3)(4); Access to Justice, 1999 c 22, s 105, sch 14 pt II paras 2(1)(b), 4(a), 7(2) pt V para 33(7)(a); GLA, 1999 c 29, ss 165(4), 217(7), s 410(4), sch 12 para 10(3); Learning and Skills, 2000 c 21, s 95(3); Transport, 2000 c 38, ss 217, 218, 220, 240, sch 18 pt II para 16(a), sch 19 para 12(a), sch 21 para 13(a), sch 25 para 12(a)

      excl—Utilities, 2000 c 27, s 3(8), sch 3 para 9(2)(a); (S) Public Finance and Accountability (S), 2000 asp 1, s 10 sch 2 para 8(4)(b); (S) Nat Parks (S), 2000 asp 10, s 29, sch 4 para 6(4)(b); Public Audit (W), 2004 c 23, s 68, sch 3 para 3(2)(a); Infrastructure, 2015 c 7, sch 3 para 9(1)(a)

   s 135 mod—SI 2006/246, reg 7(3)(b)

   s 136 am—SI 2002/2034, reg 11, sch 2 pt 1, para 3(1)(13)

   s 137 rep—Employment Relations, 1999 c 26, ss 9, 44, sch 4 pt III para 25, sch 9(2)

   s 139 appl—School Standards and Framework, 1998 c 31, s 57(6)(7); Educ, 2002 c 32, s 37(6)

      am—Educ, 2002 c 32, s 215(1), sch 21, para 31; SI 2010/1158, art 5, sch 2

   s 145 rep in pt—Employment Relations, 1999 c 26, ss 9, 44, sch 4 pt III para 26, sch 9(2)

      am—SI 2002/2034, reg 11, sch 2 pt 1, para 3(1)(14)

      appl—SI 2002/2927, art 4(3)(h)

   s 146 mod—SI 1999/2277, art 3, sch 2 pt I para 1

      rep in pt—Employment Relations, 1999 c 26, ss 9, 44, sch 4 pt III para 27, sch 9(2)

   s 153 appl —SI 2002/2927, art 4(3)(i)

   s 155 mod—SI 1999/2277, art 3, sch 2 pt I para 2

   s 156 rep—SI 2006/1031, reg 49, sch 8

   s 157 rep in pt—Employment Relations, 1999 c 26, ss 9, 44, sch 4 pt III para 29, sch 9(2)

   s 158 rep—SI 2006/1031, reg 49, sch 8

   s 161 ext—Civil Partnership, 2004 c 33, ss 246, 247, sch 21 para 42

   s 162 mod—SI 1999/2277, art 3, sch 2 pt I para 3

      rep in pt—Employment Relations, 1999 c 26, ss 9, 44, sch 4 pt III para 30, sch 9(2)

      am—SI 2006/1031, reg 49, sch 8

   s 163 restr—Employment, 2002 c 22, s 32, sch 4

      am—Employment, 2008 c 24, s 7(2)

   s 164 am—SI 2011/1133, reg 47; Enterprise and Regulatory Reform, 2013 c 24, sch 2 para 34

   s 166 rep in pt—Employment Rights (Dispute Resolution), 1998 c 8, s 15, sch 2; SI 2001/1090, reg 9(1), sch 5 para 18; Enterprise, 2002 c 40, ss 248(3), 278(2), sch 17, para 49(1)(2)(a), sch 26

      am—Employment Rights (Dispute Resolution), 1998 c 8, s 11(2); SI 2001/1090, reg 9(1), sch 5 para 18; Enterprise, 2002 c 40, s 248(3), sch 17, para 49(1)(2)(b); SI 2012/3014, art 3

   s 168 rep in pt—Employment Rights (Dispute Resolution), 1998 c 8, s 15, sch 2

      am—Employment Rights (Dispute Resolution), 1998 c 8, s 11(3); SI 1999/1925, reg 14

   s 171 am—Sovereign Grant, 2011 c 15, sch 1 para 31

   s 183 am—Enterprise, 2002 c 40, s 248(3), sch 17, para 49(1)(3)(b); Tribunals, Cts and Enforcement, 2007 c 15, s 108, sch 20; SI 2012/3014, art 4

      rep in pt—SI 2001/1090, reg 9(1), sch 5 para 19; Enterprise, 2002 c 40, ss 248(3), 278(2), sch 17, para 49(1)(3)(a), sch 26

   s 184 power to mod—Trade Union and Labour Relations (Consolidation), 1992 c 52, s 212A(9); Employment Rights (Dispute Resolution), 1998 c 8, s 7

      am—Employment Rights (Dispute Resolution), 1998 c 8, s 12(4)

   s 185 appl —SI 2002/2927, art 4(3)(j)

   s 186 am—SIs 1998/924, arts 3,4, sch; 2001/21, arts 3, 4, sch; 2002/10, arts 3, 4, sch; 2002/2927, arts 3, 4, sch; 2003/3038, arts 3, 4, sch; 2004/2989, arts 3, 4, sch; 2005/3352, arts 3, 4, sch; 2006/3045, art 3, sch; 2007/3570, arts 3, 4, sch; 2008/3055, arts 3, 4, sch; 2009/1903, art 2; 2010/2926, art 3, sch; 2012/3007, art 3, sch; 2014/382, art 3, sch; 2015/226, art 3, sch

      power to am—Employment Relations, 1999 c 26, s 34(1)(a)-(e)

      rep in pt—Employment Relations, 1999 c 26, ss 36(1)(3), 44, sch 9(10)

1996

c 18 *continued*

s 189 rep in pt—Enterprise, 2002 c 40, ss 248(3), 278(2), sch 17, para 49(1)(4), sch 26
am—SIs 2008/948, art 3, sch 1; 2011/3006, art 3, sch
s 191 am—Public Interest Disclosure, 1998 c 23, s 10; Employment, 2002 c 22, s 53, sch 7,
paras 24, 41; Employment Relations, 2004 c 24, s 57(1), sch 1 para 34
appl—Scotland, 1998 c 46, s 23(3)(b); Employment Relations, 1999 c 26, ss 13(1),
14, 15
rep in pt—Employment Relations, 2004 c 24, s 57, sch 1 para 34(1)(2), sch 2
s 192 am—Armed Forces, 1996 c 46, s 26; SI 1998/1833, reg 31(4); Employment Relations,
1999 c 26, s 9, sch 4 pt III para 31; Tax Credits, 2002 c 21, s 27, sch 1, para
1(1)(5); Employment, 2002 c 22, s 53, sch 7, paras 24, 42; Employment
Relations, 2004 c 24, s 57(1), sch 1 para 35; Armed Forces, 2006 c 52, s 378,
sch 16 para 136; Defence Reform, 2014 c 20, s 48(3)
rep in pt—(prosp) Tax Credits, 2002 c 21, s 60, sch 6
mod—SI 2009/1059, art 196
s 193 subst—Employment Relations, 1999 c 26, s 41, sch 8 para 1
s 194 am—SI 1998/1833, reg 31(5); Employment Relations, 1999 c 26, s 9, sch 4 pt III
para 32; Tax Credits, 2002 c 21, s 27, sch 1, para 1(1)(6)(a); Employment, 2002
c 22, s 53, sch 7, paras 24, 43; Employment Relations, 2004 c 24, ss 41(7),
57(1), sch 1 para 36; (prosp) Educ and Skills, 2008 c 25, s 39(1)(5); (pt prosp)
Apprenticeships, Skills, Children and Learning, 2009 c 22, s 40, sch 1 paras 1, 5;
Crime and Cts, 2013 c 22, sch 9 para 52
appl—Employment Relations, 1999 c 26, ss 13(1), 14, 15; SIs 2003/1660, regs 37(2),
38(2); 1661, regs 37(2), 38(2)
s 195 am—SI 1998/1833, reg 31(5); Employment Relations, 1999 c 26, s 9, sch 4 pt III
para 33; Tax Credits, 2002 c 21, s 27, sch 1, para 1(1)(6)(b); Employment, 2002
c 22, s 53, sch 7, paras 24, 43; Employment Relations, 2004 c 24, s 57(1), sch 1
para 37; (prosp) Educ and Skills, 2008 c 25, s 39(1)(6); (pt prosp)
Apprenticeships, Skills, Children and Learning, 2009 c 22, s 40, sch 1 paras 1, 6;
Crime and Cts, 2013 c 22, sch 9 para 52
appl—Employment Tribunals, 1996 c 17, s 39(5)
s 196 rep—Employment Relations, 1999 c 26, ss 32(3), 44, sch 9(9)
s 197 rep—SI 2002/2034, reg 11, sch 2 pt 1, para 3(1)(15), pt 2, para 5
s 199 am—Employment Relations, 1999 c 26, ss 9, 32(4), sch 4 pt III para 34(a)(b);
Employment, 2002 c 22, s 53, sch 7, paras 24, 44; Employment Relations, 2004
c 24, s 41(8); (pt prosp) Apprenticeships, Skills, Children and Learning, 2009 c
22, s 40, sch 1 paras 1, 7; SI 2014/1614, reg 3
rep in pt—Employment Relations, 1999 c 26, ss 9, 44, sch 4 pt III para 34(c), sch
9(2)(9); SI 2002/2034, reg 11, sch 2 pt 1, para 3(1)(16), pt 2, para 5
s 200 am—Police (Health and Safety), 1997 c 42, s 6(2)(b); SI 1998/1833, reg 31(6);
Public Interest Disclosure, 1998 c 23, s 13(a)(b); Employment Relations, 1999 c
26, s 9, sch 4 pt III para 35(a)-(c); Police Reform, 2002 c 30, s 37(2)(b)(c);
Employment Relations, 2004 c 24, s 57(1), sch 1 para 38
rep in pt—Police (Health and Safety), 1997 c 42, s 6(2)(a); Employment Relations,
1999 c 26, ss 9, 44, sch 4 pt III para 35(d), sch 9(2); Police Reform, 2002 c 30,
ss 37(2)(a), 107(2), sch 8
mod—SI 2010/782, reg 42(4)
s 201 am—Employment Rights, 1996 c 18, s 240, sch 1 para 18(1); (prosp) Petroleum,
1998 c 17, s 50, sch 4 para 40(2); Enterprise and Regulatory Reform, 2013 c 24,
sch 3 para 5
rep in pt—(prosp) Petroleum, 1998 c 17, ss 50, 51, sch 4 para 40(3), sch 5 pt I;
Employment Relations, 1999 c 26, s 44, sch 9(9)
s 202 am—SI 1998/1833, regs 31(5), 32(6)(a)(b); Employment Relations, 1999 c 26, s 9,
sch 4 pt III para 36; Employment Relations, 2004 c 24, s 57(1), sch 1 para 39
s 203 am—Employment Rights (Dispute Resolution), 1998 c 8, ss 8(5), 9(1)(2)(e),
10(1)(2)(e), 24(1)(2)(3); Employment Relations, 1999 c 26, s 14(a); SIs
2001/1107, reg 3; 2002/2034, reg 11, sch 2 pt 1, para 3(1)(17)(b); Legal
Services, 2007 c 29, s 208, sch 21 para 120; Enterprise and Regulatory Reform,
2013 c 24, s 23(1)(b); ibid, sch 1 para 10; SI 2014/431, sch para 4(a)-(c)
rep in pt—Employment Rights (Dispute Resolution), 1998 c 8, s 15, sch 2;
Employment Relations, 1999 c 26, s 44, sch 9(3); SIs 2002/2034, reg 11, sch 2
pt 1, para 3(1)(17)(a), pt 2, para 5; 2014/431, sch para 4(d)
appl—SIs 2000/1551, reg 9; 2002/2034, reg 10; 2006/246, reg 18; 2010/93, reg 15
s 204 rep in pt—Employment Relations, 1999 c 26, s 44, sch 9(9)

1996
c 18 *continued*

s 205 am—Public Interest Disclosure, 1998 c 23, s 14; SI 1998/1833, reg 31(7)
    appl—SI 2006/246, reg 16
s 205A and cross-heading added—Growth and Infrastructure, 2013 c 27, s 31(1)
s 206 am—SI 2005/3129, art 4(4), sch 4 para 11
s 207A added—SI 2011/1133, reg 48
s 207B added —Enterprise and Regulatory Reform, 2013 c 24, sch 2 para 35
s 208 rep—Employment Relations, 1999 c 26, ss 36(2)(3), 44, sch 9(10)
s 209 am—SI 1998/1833, reg 32(7)
    rep in pt—Employment Relations, 1999 c 26, ss 9, 23(6),44, sch 4 pt III para 37, sch
        9(2)(3)(4)(9); SI 2006/1031, reg 49, sch 8
Pt 14, Ch 1 (ss 210-219) appl—SI 1998/366, reg 13(7); GLA, 1999 c 29, s 411(10), sch 32
    para 3(8); SI 2002/2034, reg 8(4); (EW) Health and Social Care (Community
    Health and Standards), 2003 c 43, s 1(2), sch 1 para 3(3)
    ext—SI 2000/3386, art 1(5)
s 211 appl—Nat Health Service, 2006 c 41, s 30, sch 7 para 3(4)
    am—SI 2006/1031, reg 49, sch 8
s 212 am—Employment Relations, 1999 c 26, s 9, sch 4 pt III para 38(3)(a)
    rep in pt—Employment Relations, 1999 c 26, ss 9, 44, sch 4 pt III para
        38(2)(3)(b)(c)(4), sch 9(2)
s 214 excl—SI 1996/3147, reg 4
s 215 am—Social Security, 1998 c 14, s 86(1), sch 7 para 148; Social Security
    Contributions (Trans of Functions, etc), 1999 c 2, s 18, sch 7 para 21
s 218 am—SI 2000/90, art 3(1), sch 1 para 30(3); Educ, 2002 c 32, s 215(1), sch 21, para
    32; SI 2002/2469, reg 4, sch 1 pt 1, para 22(1)(3); Health and Social Care
    (Community Health and Standards), 2003 c 43, s 34, sch 4 paras 99, 101;
    Health Protection Agency, 2004 c 17, s 11(1), sch 3 para 13; Nat Health Service
    (Conseq Provns), 2006 c 43, s 2, sch 1 para 180; (W) SIs 2007/961 (W 85), art
    3, sch; 2010/1158, art 5, sch 2; Health and Social Care, 2012 c 7, sch 5 para
    75(a)(c)(e), sch 17 para 6(3), sch 19 para 6(3)
    rep in pt—Health and Social Care (Community Health and Standards), 2003 c 43, ss
        190(2), 196, sch 13 para 8, sch 14 pts 4, 7; Nat Health Service (Conseq Provns),
        2006 c 43, s 2, sch 1 para 180; Health and Social Care, 2012 c 7, sch 5 para
        75(b)(d), sch 7 para 9, sch 14 para 70
s 219 rep in pt—Employment Rights (Dispute Resolution), 1998 c 8, s 15, sch 1 para
        25(1)(2)(a)(3), sch 2
    am—Employment Rights (Dispute Resolution), 1998 c 8, s 15, sch 1, para
        25(1)(2)(b)(c)
Pt 14, Ch 2 (ss 220-229) appl—SI 1999/3312, reg 2(2); Employment, 2002 c 22, s 38(6);
    SIs 2002/3207, reg 15(4); 2004/2326, reg 40; 2004/3426, reg 28(2);
    2007/2974, reg 44; 2009/2401, reg 27; 2010/155, reg 17
    appl (mods)—Trade Union and Labour Relations (Consolidation) 1992 c 52, s 87(8);
        Employment Relations, 1999 c 26, ss 11(4), 14, 15; SI 2006/2914, reg 6
    ext—SI 1999/3323, reg 26(2)
    mod—SI 1999/3312, reg 22
s 220 appl (mods)—SI 1998/192, reg 37(1)
    appl—SI 2006/246, reg 16
ss 221-224 appl (mods)—SIs 1998/192, reg 37(1); 2003/3049, reg 11(4)(5); 2004/1713,
    reg 11(4)(5)
    appl—SI 2006/246, reg 16
s 225 subst—Employment Relations, 1999 c 26, s 9, sch 4 pt III para 39
    am—Employment, 2002 c 22, s 53, sch 7, paras 24, 45; (pt prosp) Apprenticeships,
        Skills, Children and Learning, 2009 c 22, s 40, sch 1 paras 1, 8; Children and
        Families, 2014 c 6, s 127(2)(c); ibid, s 128(2)(d)
    appl—SI 2006/246, reg 16
s 226 am—Employment Rights (Dispute Resolution), 1998 c 8, s 15, sch 1 para 26;
    Employment, 2002 c 22, s 53, sch 7, paras 24, 46; SI 2013/1949, art 3
    rep in pt—Employment Relations, 1999 c 26, ss 9, 44, sch 4 pt III para 40, sch 9(2)
    appl (mods)—SI 1998/192, reg 37(1)
    appl—SI 2006/246, reg 16
s 227 am—SIs 1998/924, arts 3,4, sch; 2001/21, arts 3, 4, sch; Employment, 2002 c 22, s
    53, sch 7, paras 24, 47; SIs 2002/10, arts 3, 4, sch; 2927, arts 3, 4, sch;
    2003/3038, arts 3, 4, sch; 2004/2989, arts 3, 4, sch; 2005/3352, arts 3, 4, sch;
    2006/3045, art 3, sch; 2007/3570, arts 3, 4, sch; 2008/3055, arts 3, 4, sch; (pt

1996
c 18 *continued*

prosp) Apprenticeships, Skills, Children and Learning, 2009 c 22, s 40, sch 1
paras 1, 9; SIs 2009/1903, art 2; 2010/2926, art 3, sch; 2011/3006, art 3, sch;
2012/3007, art 3, sch; 2014/382, art 3, sch; 2015/226, art 3, sch

appl—Employment Relations, 1999 c 26, ss 11(5), 14, 15; SIs 2002/3207, reg 15(5);
2006/246, reg 16; 2010/155, reg 17

power to am—Employment Relations, 1999 c 26, s 34(1)(a)-(e)

rep in pt—Employment Relations, 1999 c 26, s 44, sch 9(10)

appl (mods)—SI 1998/192, reg 37(1)

s 228 appl—SI 2006/246, reg 16

s 230 appl—(pt prosp) Data Protection, 1998 c 29, s 56(10)(a); Nat Minimum Wage, 1998
c 39, s 24(5); Employment Relations, 1999 c 26, ss 13(1)(2), 14, 15; Income
Tax (Earnings and Pensions), 2003 c 1, s 309(6); SI 2003/3319, reg 24(2)(4);
(EW) Educ, 2005 c 18, s 113(4)

am—Public Interest Disclosure, 1998 c 23, s 15(1); Children and Families, 2014 c 6,
sch 7 para 41; Small Business, Enterprise and Employment, 2015 c 26, s 149(3)

appl (mods)—SIs 1998/192, reg 37(1); 2006/2914, reg 6

ss 231, 232 appl (mods)—SIs 1998/192, reg 37(1); 2006/2914, reg 6

s 232 am—Licensing, 2003 c 17, s 198, sch 6 para 114; Sunday Working (S), 2003 c 18, s
1(1)(3)(b); (S) SSI 2009/248, art 2, sch 1

rep in pt—Sunday Working (S), 2003 c 18, s 1(1)(3)(a); (S) SSI 2009/248, art 2, sch
1

s 233 subst—Gambling, 2005 c 19, s 356(1)(2), sch 16 pt 2 para 11

appl (mods)—SI 2006/2914, reg 6

s 234 appl (mods)—SI 2006/2914, reg 6

appl—Educ and Skills, 2008 c 25, s 5(5)

s 235 am—Public Interest Disclosure, 1998 c 23, s 15(2); Employment, 2002 c 22, s 53, sch
7, paras 24, 48(1)-(3); SI 2002/2034, reg 11, sch 2 pt 1, para 3(1)(18); Work
and Families, 2006 c 18, s 11, sch 1 para 43; (pt prosp) Apprenticeships, Skills,
Children and Learning, 2009 c 22, s 40, sch 1 paras 1, 10; Children and Families,
2014 c 6, s 128(2)(e), sch 7 para 42(a), ibid, sch 7 para 42(b)(c)

rep in pt—Employment Relations, 1999 c 26, ss 9, 44, sch 4 pt III para 41, sch 9(2)

appl (mods)—SI 2006/2914, reg 6

s 236 am—Employment Relations, 1999 c 26, s 9, sch 4 pt III para 42; Employment, 2002 c
22, s 53, sch 7, paras 24, 49; Work and Families, 2006 c 18, s 11, sch 1 para 44;
(pt prosp) Apprenticeships, Skills, Children and Learning, 2009 c 22, s 40, sch 1
paras 1, 11; Enterprise and Regulatory Reform, 2013 c 24, s 20(8); Growth and
Infrastructure, 2013 c 27, s 31(6); Children and Families, 2014 c 6, s 117(2);
(1.1.2016) Small Business, Enterprise and Employment, 2015 c 26, s 148(3);
ibid, ss 149(3), 153(3)

rep in pt—Employment Relations, 1999 c 26, s 44, sch 9(10); Children and Families,
2014 c 6, sch 7 para 43(a)(b)

s 244 am—Sunday Working (S), 2003 c 18, s 1(1)(5)

sch 1 rep in pt—Education, 1996 c 56, s 582(2)(3) sch 38 pt I, sch 39; Employment Rights
(Dispute Resolution), 1998 c 8, s 15, sch 2; Petroleum, 1998 c 17, s 51, sch 5
pt I; (EW) Audit Commission, 1998 c 18, s 54(3), sch 5; Govt of Wales, 1998 c
38, s 152, sch 18, pts IV, VI; Access to Justice, 1999 c 22, s 106, sch 15 pt I;
Employment Relations, 1999 c 26, s 44, sch 9(10); Welfare Reform and
Pensions, 1999 c 30, s 88, sch 13 pt VI; (prosp) Transport, 2000 c 38, s 274,
sch 31 pt IV; SL(R), 2004 c 14, s 1(1), sch 1 pt 2/1; Gambling, 2005 c 19, s
356(4)(5), sch 17; Nat Health Service (Conseq Provns), 2006 c 43, s 6, sch 4;
SI 2008/1277, sch 4; (prosp) Welfare Reform, 2009 c 24, s 58, sch 7 pt 3;
Equality, 2010 c 15, s 211, sch 27 pt 1; Budget Responsibility and Nat Audit,
2011 c 4, sch 5 para 18

sch 2 rep in pt—Employment Rights (Dispute Resolution), 1998 c 8, s 15, sch 2; SL(R),
2004 c 14, s 1(1), sch 1 pt 8

c 19 **Law Reform (Year and a Day Rule)**

s 2 am—Domestic Violence, Crime and Victims, 2004 c 28, s 58(1), sch 10 para 33;
Coroners and Justice, 2009 c 25, s 177, sch 21 para 60; Domestic Violence, Crime
and Victims (Amdt), 2012 c 4, sch para 3

rep in pt—Domestic Violence, Crime and Victims, 2004 c 28, s 58(2), sch 11

c 20 *Dogs (Fouling of Land)* —rep Clean Neighbourhoods and Environment, 2005 c 16, ss 65, 107,
sch 5 pt 5

c 21 *London Regional Transport*—rep SL(R), 2008 c 12, s 1(1), sch 1 pt 5

1996

c 22   *Northern Ireland (Emergency Provisions)*—rep (subject to provns for cont in force with
amendments) Terrorism, 2000 c 11, ss 2(1)(b)(2),129(5), sch 1 paras 1-12, sch 16 pt
I; (cesser of continuance) SI 2001/421, arts 2, 3

c 23   **Arbitration**

excl—Arbitration (International Investment Disputes, 1966 c 41, s 3; Trade Union and
Labour Relations (Consolidation), 1992 c 52, s 212A(6); (NI) SIs 1998/3162, art
89(6); 2002/457, reg 9(b), sch 1, para 34; (W) 2002/897 (W 103), regs 9(b),
10(1)(b)(4)(b), 11(2), 33(5)(b)(iii), sch 1, para 34; 2005/465, regs 10(2), 11, 12(3),
39(4), sch 1 para 34

mod—Contracts (Rights of Third Parties), 1999 c 31, ss 8(1)(2), 10(2)(3)

power to appl—Housing Grants, Construction and Regeneration, 1996 c 53, s 108(6)

appl—Commonhold and Leasehold Reform, 2002 c 15, s 159(12); SIs (E) 2002/1711, reg
12(3)(b); (W) 2004/248 (W 25), reg 12(3)(b)

trans of functions—SI 2010/976, art 15, sch 17

Pt 1 (ss 1-84) excl—Multilateral Investment Guarantee Agency, 1988 c 8, s 6; Education,
1996 c 56, ss 336(4),476(4),582(4), sch 40 para 4; (EWS) (pt prosp) Social
Security, 1998 c 14, s 16(9); Protection of Children, 1999 c 14, s 9(4); SIs
2008/2685, r 3; 2686, r 3; 2698, r 3; 2699, r 3; 2009/273, rule 3; 1976, rule 3;
2013/1169, rule 4(2)

appl—Housing, 1996 c 52, s 81(1); Plant Varieties, 1997 c 66, s 52, sch 4;
Commonhold and Leasehold Reform, 2002 c 15, ss 158, 169(5), sch 11 pt 1,
para 6(5)

excl—Child Support, Pensions and Social Security, 2000 c 19, s 67, sch 7 para 10(8);
Equality, 2010 c 15, s 116, sch 17 para 6(6)

restr —Pensions Appeal Tribunals,1943 c 39, s 6D; Disability Discrimination, 1995 c
50, s 28J(7)

ss 8-10 appl—SI 2010/2600, art 30

s 12 appl—SI 2010/2600, art 30

s 14 appl—Merchant Shipping, 1894 c 60, s 496(5)

s 23 appl—SI 2010/2600, art 30

s 24 appl (mods)—SIs 2004/753, art 4, sch para 52EW; 2004/2333, sch para 52EW

ss 36, 38-44 power to appl—Arbitration (International Investment Disputes) 1966 s 3

s 42 appl (mods)—SI 1998/649, art 2, sch pt I para 24

s 45 appl (mods)—SIs 2004/753, art 4, sch para 110EW; 2004/2333, sch para 108EW

s 46 appl —(EW) SI 2004/2333, art 5

s 49 appl—SI 2010/2600, art 30

ss 57, 60 appl—SI 2010/2600, art 30

s 66 appl (mods)—SIs 2004/753, art 4, sch para 183EW; 2004/2333, sch para 135EW
appl—SI 2010/2600, art 30

s 67 appl (mods)—SIs 2004/753, art 4, sch para 187EW; 2004/2333, sch para 138EW

s 68 appl (mods)—SIs 2004/753, art 4, sch para 194EW; 2004/2333, sch para 145EW

s 69 appl (mods)—SIs 2004/753, art 4, sch para 200EW; 2004/2333, sch para 151EW

s 70 appl (mods)—SIs 2004/753, art 4, sch para 205EW; 2004/2333, sch para 156EW

s 71 appl (mods)—SIs 2004/753, art 4, sch para 212EW; 2004/2333, sch para 163EW

s 77 appl (mods)—SIs 2004/753, art 4, sch para 223EW; 2004/2333, sch para 174EW

s 78 appl (mods)—SIs 2004/753, art 4, sch para 224EW; 2004/2333, sch para 175EW

s 80 appl (mods)—SIs 2004/753, art 4, sch paras 209EW; 2004/2333, sch para 168EW

s 81 appl (mods)—SIs 2004/753, art 4, sch paras 217EW; 2004/2333, sch para 160EW

s 82 am—Crime and Cts, 2013 c 22, sch 9 para 60(1)

s 89 am—Consumer Rights, 2015 c 15, sch 4 para 31

s 90 subst—Consumer Rights, 2015 c 15, sch 4 para 32

s 91 rep in pt—SI 1999/678, art 6
see—(trans of functions) (S) SI 1999/678, art 2(1), sch
am—Consumer Rights, 2015 c 15, sch 4 para 33

s 105 am—Constitutional Reform, 2005 c 4, s 15(1), sch 4 pt 1 para 250; SI 2010/976, art
15, sch 18; Crime and Cts, 2013 c 22, sch 9 para 60(2)(a)-(e)
rep in pt—Crime and Cts, 2013 c 22, sch 9 para 60(2)(f)

sch 2 am —Constitutional Reform, 2005 c 4, s 40(4), sch 9 pt 1 para 60

sch 3 rep in pt—Housing, 1996 c 52, s 227, sch 19 pt III; Education, 1996 c 56 s 582(2)(3)
sch 38 pt I, sch 39; SI 1996/1921, art 28, sch 3; Plant Varieties, 1997 c 66, s 52,
sch 4; (NI) SIs 1998/3162, art 105(4), sch 5, 1506, art 78(2), sch 7; Care
Standards, 2000 c 14, s 117(2), sch 6; Communications, 2003 c 21, s 406(7),
sch 19(1); SIs 2003/1900, arts 2(1), 3(1), sch 1; 3142, art 3(2); SL(R), 2004 c
14, s 1(1), sch 1 pt 6/3; International Organisations, 2005 c 20, ss 1(2)(3), 9,

1996
c 23 *continued*

        sch; SIs 2006/2805, art 18, sch 2; 2009/1307, art 5, sch 4; 2013/686, sch 1
        para 7; Co-operative and Community Benefit Societies, 2014 c 14, sch 7

c 24   **Treasure**
    s 7 subst (prosp)—Coroners and Justice, 2009 c 25, s 177, sch 21 paras 37, 38
    s 8 am—(EW) (prosp) Crim Justice, 2003 c 44, s 280(2)(3), sch 26 para 48; (prosp)
        Coroners and Justice, 2009 c 25, s 177, sch 21 paras 37, 39
    s 8A added (prosp)—Coroners and Justice, 2009 c 25, s 30(1)(3)
    ss 8B, 8C added (prosp)—Coroners and Justice, 2009 c 25, s 177, sch 21 paras 37, 40
    s 9 subst (prosp)—Coroners and Justice, 2009 c 25, s 177, sch 21 paras 37, 41
    s 9A added (prosp)—Coroners and Justice, 2009 c 25, s 177, sch 21 paras 37, 41
    s 10 am —(prosp) Coroners and Justice, 2009 c 25, s 30(2)
    s 13 rep (prosp)—Coroners and Justice, 2009 c 25, ss 177, 178, sch 21 paras 37, 42, sch 23
        pt 1

c 25   **Criminal Procedure and Investigations**
    power to rep conferred—Crim Procedure and Investigations, 1996 c 25, s 78
    Pt 1 (ss 1-21) power to am—(NI) SI 1999/2789, art 26(7)
        power to mod—Youth Justice and Crim Evidence, 1999 c 23, s 38(7)(a)
    s 1 am—(prosp) Sexual Offences (Protected Material), 1997 c 39, s 9(4); Crime and
        Disorder, 1998 c 37, s 119, sch 8, para 125(a)(b); Crime and Cts, 2013 c 22, sch
        17 para 37(2)
        rep in pt—Justice (NI), 2002 c 26, s 86, sch 13; Crim Justice, 2003 c 44, ss 41, 332, sch
        3 pt 2 para 66(1)(2), sch 37 pt 4
    ss 3-5 excl—(prosp) Sexual Offences (Protected Material), 1997 c 39, s 9(2)
    s 3 am—Regulation of Investigatory Powers, 2000 c 23, s 82(1), sch 4 para 7(1); Crim
        Justice, 2003 c 44, ss 32, 331, sch 36 pt 3 paras 20, 21
        mod—Crim Procedure and Investigations, 1996 c 25, s 13(1) (now partially rep)
    s 4 am—Crim Justice, 2003 c 44, s 331, sch 36 pt 3 paras 20, 22
    s 5 am—Crime and Disorder, 1998 c 37, s 119, sch 8 para 126; Crim Justice, 2003 c 44, ss
        33(1), 41, sch 3 pt 2 para 66(1)(3)(a)(c)
        rep in pt—Crim Justice, 2003 c 44, s 331, sch 36 pt 3 paras 20, 23, sch 37 pt 3; ibid, ss
        41, 332, sch 3 pt 2 para 66(1)(3)(b), sch 37 pt 4
    s 6 rep in pt—Crim Justice, 2003 c 44, ss 331, 332, sch 36 pt 3 paras 20, 24, sch 37 pt 3
    s 6A added—(EW, NI) Crim Justice, 2003 c 44, s 33(2)
        am—Crim Justice and Immigration, 2008 c 4, s 60(1)
    s 6B added (EW, NI prosp)—Crim Justice, 2003 c 44, s 33(3)
    s 6C added (NI prosp)—(EW) Crim Justice, 2003 c 44, s 34
    s 6D added (EW, NI prosp)—Crim Justice, 2003 c 44, s 35
    s 6E added—(EW, NI) Crim Justice, 2003 c 44, s 36
    s 7 rep—Crim Justice, 2003 c 44, ss 331, 332, sch 36 pt 3 paras 20, 25, sch 37 pt 3
    s 7A added—(EW, NI) Crim Justice, 2003 c 44, s 37
        mod—Crim Procedure and Investigations, 1996 c 25, s 13(2)
    s 8 am—Regulation of Investigatory Powers, 2000 c 23, s 82(1), sch 4 para 7(1); Crim
        Justice, 2003 c 44, s 38
    s 9 rep—Crim Justice, 2003 c 44, ss 331, 332, sch 36 pt 3 paras 20, 26, sch 37 pt 3
    s 10 am—Crim Justice, 2003 c 44, s 331, sch 36 pt 3 paras 20, 27
    s 11 subst—(pt prosp) Crim Justice, 2003 c 44, s 39
        am—Crim Justice and Immigration, 2008 c 4, s 60(2)
    s 12 am—Crim Justice, 2003 c 44, s 331, sch 36 pt 3 paras 20, 28
    s 13 am—Crime and Disorder, 1998 c 37, s 119, sch 8, para 127(b); Access to Justice, 1999
        c 22, s 67(2); Crim Justice, 2003 c 44, s 331, sch 36 pt 3 paras 20, 29
        rep in pt—Access to Justice, 1999 c 22, s 106, sch 15 pt III; (pt prosp) Crim Justice,
        2003 c 44, ss 41, 332, sch 3 pt 2 para 66(1)(4), sch 37 pt 4
    s 14 am—Crim Justice, 2003 c 44, s 331, sch 36 pt 3 paras 20, 30
    s 15 am—Crim Justice, 2003 c 44, s 331, sch 36 pt 3 paras 20, 31
    s 16 am—Crim Justice, 2003 c 44, s 331, sch 36 pt 3 paras 20, 32
    ss 17, 18 excl—(prosp) Sexual Offences (Protected Material), 1997 c 39, s 9(3)
    s 17 am—Crim Justice, 2003 c 44, s 331, sch 36 pt 3 paras 20, 33
    s 19 am—Courts, 2003 c 39, s 109(1), sch 8 para 377; Crim Justice, 2003 c 44, s 331, sch
        36 pt 3 paras 20, 34; Constitutional Reform, 2005 c 4, s 15(1), sch 4 pt 1 para
        251
    s 20 excl—(prosp) Sexual Offences (Protected Material), 1997 c 39, s 9(2)
        am—Courts, 2003 c 39, s 109(1), sch 8 para 378; Crim Justice, 2003 c 44, s 331, sch
        36 pt 3 paras 20, 35(b)

1996

c 25 s 20 *continued*

        rep in pt—Crim Justice, 2003 c 44, ss 331, 332, sch 36 pt 3 paras 20, 35(a), sch 37 pt 3

s 21 am—Crim Justice, 2003 c 44, s 41, sch 3 pt 2 para 66(1)(5)

s 21A added—(EW, NI) Crim Justice, 2003 c 44, s 40

        rep in pt—Police and Justice, 2006 c 48, s 52, sch 15

Pt 2 (ss 22-27) appl—Police (NI), 1998 c 32, s 55

s 23 am—Regulation of Investigatory Powers, 2000 c 23, s 82(1), sch 4 para 7(2)

s 25 see —(code of practice in force 4.4.2005) (EW) SIs 2005/985, art 2; (code of practice

        in force 15.7.2005) (NI) 2005/2692, art 2

s 28 am—Crime and Disorder, 1998 c 37, s 119, sch 8 para 128; Crim Justice, 2003 c 44, s

        41, sch 3 pt 2 para 66(1)(6)(a); Crime and Cts, 2013 c 22, sch 17 para 37(3)

        rep in pt—(pt prosp) Crim Justice, 2003 c 44, ss 41, 332, sch 3 pt 2 para 66(1)(6)(b),

        sch 37 pt 4

Pt 3 (ss 28-38) appl—(pt prosp) Crim Justice, 2003 c 44, s 45(2)

s 29 am—(pt prosp) Crim Justice, 2003 c 44, ss 45(6)-(8), 309, 310(4), 331, sch 36 pt 4

        paras 65, 66; Terrorism, 2006, c 11, s 16

        appl (mods)—Domestic Violence, Crime and Victims, 2004 c 28, s 18(2)(3)

        see—SI 2005/384, rule 15.1

        mod—Serious Crime, 2007 c 27, s 63, sch 6 para 30

s 30 see —SI 2005/384, rule 15.1

s 31 mod—Crim Law, 1977 c 45, s 1A(10)

        am—Crim Justice, 2003 c 44, ss 310(5), 331, sch 36 pt 4 paras 65, 67

        rep in pt—Crim Justice, 2003 c 44, ss 331, 332, sch 36 pt 3 paras 20, 36, sch 37 pt 3

        see —SI 2005/384, rule 15.1

s 32 see —SI 2005/384, rule 15.1

s 33 am—Courts, 2003 c 39, s 109(1), sch 8 para 379(a)(b)

s 34 am—Crim Justice, 2003 c 44, s 331, sch 36 pt 4 paras 65, 68

s 35 am—(pt prosp) Crim Justice, 2003 c 44, ss 45(9), 331, sch 36 pt 4 paras 65, 69

        appl (mods)—Domestic Violence, Crime and Victims, 2004 c 28, s 18(5)

        rep in pt—Protection of Freedoms, 2012 c 9, sch 10 pt 10

s 36 am—Crim Justice, 2003 c 44, s 331, sch 36 pt 4 paras 65, 70; Constitutional Reform,

        2005 c 4, s 40(4), sch 9 pt 1 para 61(1)(2)

s 37 am—Access to Justice, 1999 c 22, s 24, sch 4 para 49; Crim Justice, 2003 c 44, s

        311(5)(6); Constitutional Reform, 2005 c 4, s 40(4), sch 9 pt 1 para 61(1)(3);

        Legal Aid, Sentencing and Punishment of Offenders, 2012 c 10, sch 5 para 42

s 38 am—Crim Justice, 2003 c 44, s 311(5)(7)

s 39 am—Crime and Disorder, 1998 c 37, s 119, sch 8 para 129; Crim Justice, 2003 c 44, ss

        41, 331, sch 3 pt 2 para 66(1)(7), sch 36 pt 4 paras 65, 71; Crime and Cts, 2013 c

        22, sch 17 para 37(4)

        rep in pt—Justice (NI), 2002 c 26, s 86, sch 13

ss 41, 42 appl (mods)—(NI) (pt prosp) Crim Justice, 2003 c 44, s 48A (added by 2003 c 44,

        s 50(1)(2)(14))

s 41 am—Crim Justice, 2003 c 44, s 311(5)(8)

s 44 rep in pt—Crim Justice, 2003 c 44, s 332, sch 37 pt 4

s 45 rep —Crim Justice, 2003 c 44, s 332, sch 37 pt 4

s 46 rep—SL(R), 2008 c 12, s 1(1), sch 1 pt 3

s 49 rep in pt—Crim Justice, 2003 c 44, s 332, sch 37 pt 4

s 56 rep in pt—Sexual Offences, 2003 c 42, s 140, sch 7

s 61 rep in pt—Coroners and Justice, 2009 c 25, s 178, sch 23 pt 2

s 62 rep—Youth Justice and Crim Evidence, 1999 c 23, s 67, sch 6; (NI) SI 1999/2789, art

        40(3), sch 3

s 65 rep—SL(R), 2008 c 12, s 1(1), sch 1 pt 3

s 67 appl—SI 1999/716, art 2

s 68 rep —Crim Justice, 2003 c 44, ss 41, 332, sch 3 pt 2 para 66(1)(8), sch 37 pt 4

s 69 rep—Deregulation, 2015 c 20, s 80(6)(d)

s 70 rep—(EW) Justices of the Peace, 1997 c 25, s 73(3), sch 6 pt 1

s 74 rep in pt—Armed Forces, 2006 c 52, s 378, sch 17

s 77 am—Crim Justice, 2003 c 44, s 331, sch 36 pt 3 paras 20, 37

s 78 subst—Armed Forces, 2006 c 52, s 378, sch 16 para 137

        mod—SI 2009/1059, art 205, sch 1

s 79 am—Crim Justice, 2003 c 44, s 311(5)(9)

        rep in pt—Armed Forces, 2006 c 52, s 378, sch 17

1996
c 25 *continued*
    sch 1 rep in pt—Youth Justice and Crim Evidence, 1999 c 23, s 67, sch 6; Powers of Crim
        Cts (Sentencing), 2000 c 6, s 165(3)(4), sch 11 pt I para 2, sch 12 pt I; Crim
        Justice, 2003 c 44, s 332, sch 37 pt 6, ibid, sch 37 pt 4
    sch 2 rep—Crim Justice, 2003 c 44, ss 41, 332, sch 3 pt 2 para 66(1)(8), sch 37 pt 4
    sch 3 rep in pt—Justice (NI), 2002 c 26, s 86, sch 13
        am—Crime and Cts, 2013 c 22, sch 17 para 37(5)
    sch 4 am—SI 1996/3160, art 58(1 sch 5 para 18; (ss 14A, 39 as set out in sch 4) Terrorism,
        2000 c 11, s 125(1), sch 15 para 13(2)(3); Crim Justice, 2003 c 44, s 331, sch
        36 pt 3 paras 20, 38; ibid, sch 36 pt 4 paras 65, 72(1)-(4); Courts, 2003 c 39, s
        109(1), sch 8 para 381; SI 2010/976, art 12, sch 14
        rep in pt—(NI) SI 1999/2789, art 40(3), sch 3; Crim Justice, 2003 c 44, ss 311(10),
        332, sch 37 pt 12
c 26   **Offensive Weapons**
    s 1 rep in pt —Serious Organised Crime and Police, 2005 c 15, s 174(2), sch 17 pt 2
    s 5 rep —(S) Crim Justice and Licensing (S), 2010 asp 13, s 203, sch 7 para 63
c 27   **Family Law**
    mod—Insolvency, 1986 c 45, s 337(3)
    s 1 am—Children and Families, 2014 c 6, s 18(4)
        rep in pt—Children and Families, 2014 c 6, s 18(2)(a)
    Pt 2 (ss 2-25) rep in pt—Children and Families, 2014 c 6, s 18(1)
    s 5 restr—Domicile and Matrimonial Proceedings, 1973 c 45 sch 1 para 10(1A) (as am by
        Family Law, 1996 c 27, s 19(5) sch 3 para 8)
    s 7 appl—(EW) Family Law, 1996 c 27, sch 2 para 6A
    s 8 am—Access to Justice, 1999 c 22, s 24, sch 4 paras 50, 51; Legal Aid, Sentencing and
        Punishment of Offenders, 2012 c 10, sch 5 para 44(2)-(4)
    s 9 restr—Domicile and Matrimonial Proceedings, 1973 c 45 sch 1 para 10(1A) (as am by
        Family Law, 1996 c 27, s 19(5) sch 3 para 8)
        rep in pt—Welfare Reform and Pensions, 1999 c 30, s 88, sch 13 pt II; Divorce
        (Religious Marriages), 2002 c 27, s 1(2)
    s 12 am—Constitutional Reform, 2005 c 4, s 12(2)(3), sch 1 pt 2 paras 22, 23, 25
    s 16 rep—Welfare Reform and Pensions, 1999 c 30, s 88, sch 13 pt II
    s 17 rep—Welfare Reform and Pensions, 1999 c 30, s 88, sch 13 pt II
    s 22 am—SI 2003/3191, arts 3(b), 6, sch para 2
    s 23 am—Access to Justice, 1999 c 22, s 24, sch 4 paras 50, 52; Legal Aid, Sentencing and
        Punishment of Offenders, 2012 c 10, sch 5 para 45(2)
        rep in pt—Access to Justice, 1999 c 22, s 106, sch 15 pt I; Legal Aid, Sentencing and
        Punishment of Offenders, 2012 c 10, sch 5 para 45(3)
    Pt 3 (ss 26-29) rep—Access to Justice, 1999 c 22, s 106, sch 15 pt I
    s 30 am—SI 1997/74, art 2, sch para 10(a); Civil Partnership, 2004 c 33, s 82, sch 9 pt 1
        para 1 pt 3 para 25; Prevention of Social Housing Fraud, 2013 c 3, sch para 6
        appl—Commonhold and Leasehold Reform, 2002 c 15, s 61
    s 31 am—Land Registration, 2002 c 9, s 133, sch 11, para 34(1)(2); Civil Partnership, 2004
        c 33, s 82, sch 9 pt 1 para 2 pt 3 para 25
        rep in pt—Land Registration, 2002 c 9, s 135, sch 13
    s 32 am—Civil Partnership, 2004 c 33, s 82, sch 9 pt 1 para 3 pt 3 para 25
    s 33 am—Civil Partnership, 2004 c 33, s 82, sch 9 pt 1 para 4 pt 3 para 25
    s 34 am—Civil Partnership, 2004 c 33, s 82, sch 9 pt 1 para 5 pt 3 para 25
    s 35 am—Civil Partnership, 2004 c 33, s 82, sch 9 pt 1 para 6 pt 3 para 25
    s 36 am—Domestic Violence, Crime and Victims, 2004 c 28, ss 2(2), 58(1), sch 10 para 34;
        Civil Partnership, 2004 c 33, s 82, sch 9 pt 1 para 7 pt 3 para 25
    s 37 am—Civil Partnership, 2004 c 33, s 82, sch 9 pt 1 para 8 pt 3 para 25
    s 38 am—Domestic Violence, Crime and Victims, 2004 c 28, s 58(1), sch 10 para 35
    s 41 rep—Domestic Violence, Crime and Victims, 2004 c 28, ss 2(1), 58(2), sch 11
    s 42 rep in pt—Domestic Violence, Crime and Victims, 2004 c 28, s 58, sch 10 para
        36(1)(3), sch 11
        am—Domestic Violence, Crime and Victims, 2004 c 28, s 58(1), sch 10 para 36(1)(2);
        Civil Partnership, 2004 c 33, s 82, sch 9 pt 1 para 9, pt 3 para 25
    s 42A added—Domestic Violence, Crime and Victims, 2004 c 28, ss 1, 59, sch 12 para 1
    s 44 am—Civil Partnership, 2004 c 33, s 82, sch 9 paras 10, 25
    s 45 am—Crime and Cts, 2013 c 22, sch 11 para 130
    s 46 am—Domestic Violence, Crime and Victims, 2004 c 28, s 58(1), sch 10 para 37; Crime
        and Cts, 2013 c 22, sch 11 para 131
    s 47 ext—Children, 1989 c 41, ss 38A, 38B, 44A, 44B

1996
c 27 s 47 *continued*

> rep in pt—Domestic Violence, Crime and Victims, 2004 c 28, s 58, sch 10 para
> 38(1)(2), sch 11; Crime and Cts, 2013 c 22, sch 11 para 132(a)
> am—Domestic Violence, Crime and Victims, 2004 c 28, s 58(1), sch 10 para
> 38(1)(3)-(5); Crime and Cts, 2013 c 22, sch 11 para 132(a)

s 48 ext—Children, 1989 c 41, ss 38A, 38B, 44A, 44B
> am—Mental Health, 2007 c 12, s 1, sch 1 paras 20

s 49 rep in pt—Domestic Violence, Crime and Victims, 2004 c 28, s 58, sch 10 para 39, sch
> 11
> am—Civil Partnership, 2004 c 33, s 82, sch 9 pt 1 para 11 pt 3 para 25

s 50 rep —Crime and Cts, 2013 c 22, sch 11 para 133
s 51 rep —Crime and Cts, 2013 c 22, sch 11 para 134
s 51 am—Mental Health, 2007 c 12, s 1, sch 1 para 20
s 54 am—Civil Partnership, 2004 c 33, s 82, sch 9 pt 1 para 12 pt 3 para 25
s 57 am —Constitutional Reform, 2005 c 4, s 15(1), sch 4 pt 1 paras 252, 253; Crime and
> Cts, 2013 c 22, sch 11 para 135(2)
> rep in pt—Crime and Cts, 2013 c 22, sch 11 para 135(3)

s 59 rep —Crime and Cts, 2013 c 22, sch 11 para 136
s 61 —Crime and Cts, 2013 c 22, sch 11 para 137
> am—Constitutional Reform, 2005 c 4, s 15(1), sch 4 pt 1 paras 252, 254; SI 2009/871,
> arts 8, 17

s 62 am—Adoption and Children, 2002 c 38, s 139(1), sch 3, paras 85-87; Domestic
> Violence, Crime and Victims, 2004 c 28, ss 3, 4, 58(1), sch 10 para 40; Civil
> Partnership, 2004 c 33, s 82, sch 9 pt 1 para 13 pt 3 para 25; SI 2011/1740, sch 1
> para 5
> rep in pt—SI 2011/1740, sch 1 pt 3

s 63 am—Adoption and Children, 2002 c 38, s 139(1), sch 3, paras 85, 88(a)(b); Domestic
> Violence, Crime and Victims, 2004 c 28, s 58(1), sch 10 para 41; Civil
> Partnership, 2004 c 33, s 82, sch 9 pt 1 para 14(1)(2)(4)(5), pt 3 para 25; Forced
> Marriage (Civil Protection), 2007 c 20, s 3, sch 2 para 3(1)(2); Human
> Fertilisation and Embryology, 2008 c 22, s 56, sch 6 para 37; Crime and Cts,
> 2013 c 22, sch 11 para 138
> appl—SI 2003/3319, reg 22(4)
> rep in pt—Civil Partnership, 2004 c 33, ss 82, 261(4), sch 9 pt 1 para 14(1)(3), pt 3
> para 25, sch 30; Children and Families, 2014 c 6, s 18(2)(b)
> ext—Civil Partnership, 2004 c 33, ss 246, 247, sch 21 para 43

ss 63A-63S added —Forced Marriage (Civil Protection), 2007 c 20, s 1
s 63CA added—Anti-social Behaviour, Crime and Policing, 2014 c 12, s 120(2)
s 63E am—Anti-social Behaviour, Crime and Policing, 2014 c 12, s 120(3)
s 63G rep in pt—Anti-social Behaviour, Crime and Policing, 2014 c 12, s 120(5)(a)
s 63H rep—Anti-social Behaviour, Crime and Policing, 2014 c 12, s 120(5)(b)
s 63I rep—Anti-social Behaviour, Crime and Policing, 2014 c 12, s 120(5)(c)
s 63J am—Anti-social Behaviour, Crime and Policing, 2014 c 12, s 120(4)
> rep in pt—Anti-social Behaviour, Crime and Policing, 2014 c 12, s 120(5)(d)

s 63K rep in pt—Anti-social Behaviour, Crime and Policing, 2014 c 12, s 120(5)(e)
s 63L rep in pt—Anti-social Behaviour, Crime and Policing, 2014 c 12, s 120(5)(f)
s 63M am—Crime and Cts, 2013 c 22, sch 11 para 139(2)
> rep in pt—(Crime and Cts, 2013 c 22, sch 11 para 139(3)

s 63N rep —Crime and Cts, 2013 c 22, sch 11 para 140
s 63P rep —Crime and Cts, 2013 c 22, sch 11 para 141
s 63S am—Crime and Cts, 2013 c 22, sch 11 para 142
s 64 am—Civil Partnership, 2004 c 33, s 261(1), sch 27 para 152(1)(3)
> rep in pt—Civil Partnership, 2004 c 33, s 261(1)(4), sch 27 para 152(1)(2), sch 30;
> Children and Families, 2014 c 6, s 18(2)(c)

s 65 am —Constitutional Reform, 2005 c 4, s 12(2)(3), sch 1 pt 2 paras 22, 24, 25; (pt
> prosp) Forced Marriage (Civil Protection), 2007 c 20, s 3, sch 2 para 3(1)(3)
> rep in pt—Crime and Cts, 2013 c 22, sch 11 para 143(a)(b); Children and Families,
> 2014 c 6, s 18(2)(d)

sch 2 am—Welfare Reform and Pensions, 1999 c 30, s 84, sch 12 pt I para 65(1)-(9)
sch 3 am—Children and Adoption, 2006 c 20, s 15, sch 2 para 12
sch 4 am—Land Registration, 2002 c 9, s 133, sch 11, para 34(1)(3); Civil Partnership,
> 2004 c 33, s 82, sch 9 pt 1 para 15, pt 3 para 25; Legal Services, 2007 c 29, s
> 208, sch 21 para 121

sch 5 ext—Children, 1989 c 41, ss 38A,38B,44A,44B

1996

c 27 sch 5 *continued*

am—Crime and Cts, 2013 c 22, sch 11 para 144(2)(3)

sch 7 appl—Matrimonial and Family Proceedings, 1984 c 42, s 22; Civil Partnership, 2004 c 33, s 72(4), sch 7 pt 1 para 13(1)(b)(3)

am—SI 1997/74, art 2, sch para 10(b); Civil Partnership, 2004 c 33, s 82, sch 9 pt 1 para 16, pt 3 para 25; Domestic Violence, Crime and Victims, 2004 c 28, s 58(1), sch 10 para 42; Crime and Cts, 2013 c 22, sch 11 para 145

rep in pt—Civil Partnership, 2004 c 33, ss 82, 261(4), sch 9 pt 1 para 16, pt 3 para 25, sch 30

sch 8 am—Welfare Reform and Pensions, 1999 c 30, s 84, sch 12 pt I paras 9(2), 19, 66(3)-(9)(12)-(14)

rep in pt—Access to Justice, 1999 c 22, s 106, sch 15 pts I, II; Land Registration, 2002 c 9, s 135, sch 13; Civil Partnership, 2004 c 33, s 261(4), sch 30; Housing and Regeneration, 2008 c 17, s 321, sch 16; Presumption of Death, 2013 c 13, sch 2 para 4; Crime and Cts, 2013 c 22, sch 10 para 99 Table; Children and Families, 2014 c 6, s 18(2)(e)

sch 9 rep in pt—Children and Families, 2014 c 6, s 18(2)(f)

sch 10 rep in pt—Children and Families, 2014 c 6, s 18(2)(j)

c 28   *Commonwealth Development Corporation*—rep Commonwealth Development Corpn, 1999 c 20, s 27, sch 4

c 29   **Sexual Offences (Conspiracy and Incitement)**

s 1 rep—Crim Justice (Terrorism and Conspiracy), 1998 c 40, s 9(1)(2), sch 1 pt II para 9(1), sch 2 pt II

s 2 am—Serious Crime, 2007 c 27, s 63, sch 6 para 60

mod—Serious Crime, 2007 c 27, s 63, sch 6 para 30

s 3 am—Crim Justice (Terrorism and Conspiracy), 1998 c 40, s 9(1), sch 1, pt II para 9(2)(a)(b)(ii)(f)

rep in pt—Crim Justice (Terrorism and Conspiracy), 1998 c 40, s 9(1)(2), sch 1 pt II para 9(2)(b)(i)(c)(d)(e), sch 2 pt II

mod—Serious Crime, 2007 c 27, s 63, sch 6 para 30

s 4 rep in pt—Crim Justice (Terrorism and Conspiracy), 1998 c 40, s 9(1)(2), sch 1 pt II para 9(3), sch 2 pt II

s 7 rep in pt—Crim Justice (Terrorism and Conspiracy), 1998 c 40, s 9(1)(2), sch 1 pt II para 9(4), sch 2 pt II

sch am—Sexual Offences, 2003 c 42, s 139, sch 6 para 35

rep in pt—Sexual Offences, 2003 c 42, s 140, sch 7

c 30   **Community Care (Direct Payments)**

trans of powers—(W) SI 1999/672, art 2, sch 1

ss 1-3 rep—Health and Social Care, 2001 c 15, s 67, sch 6 pt 3

s 4 rep—SSI 2014/90, sch pt 1

s 7 rep in pt —Health and Social Care, 2001 c 15, s 67, sch 6 pt 3

c 31   **Defamation**

appl—Govt of Wales, 1998 c 38, s 77(3); Scotland, 1998 c 46, s 41; Northern Ireland, 1998 c 47, s 50(3); NI (Elections), 1998 c 12, sch 1 para 8); (S) S Public Services Ombudsman, 2002 asp 11, ss 17(2), 18(2); (S) Mental Health (Care and Treatment) (S), 2003 asp 13, s 20(2); (S) Commr for Children and Young People (S), 2003 asp 17, s 15(2)

trans of functions—SI 2010/976, art 15, sch 17

s 9 am —Constitutional Reform, 2005 c 4, s 15(1), sch 4 pt 1 para 255; SI 2010/976, art 15, sch 18

s 13 rep—Serious Crime, 2015 c 9, sch 4 para 17

s 14 am—Defamation, 2013 c 26, s 7(1)

s 17 am—Scotland, 1998 c 46, s 125, sch 8 para 33(2)

s 20 rep in pt—(S) Crim Justice and Licensing (S), 2010 asp 13, s 203, sch 7 para 64

sch 1 ext—Govt of Wales, 1998 c 38, s 77(4)(a)

mod—Govt of Wales, 1998 c 38, s 77(4)(b)

am—Scotland, 1998 c 46, s 125, sch 8 para 33(3); SIs (E) 2001/2237, arts 2, 31; (W) 2002/808 (W 89), arts 2(p), 30; (E) 2002/1057, arts 2(h), 12; Govt of Wales, 2006 c 32, s 160, sch 10 para 40; SIs 2009/1941, art 2, sch 1; 2010/976, art 15, sch 18; Defamation, 2013 c 26, s 7(1), (4)-(11)

c 32   **Trading Schemes**

c 33   **Prisoners' Earnings**

s 1 am—(pt prosp) Child Support, Pensions and Social Security, 2000 c 19, s 26, sch 3 para 14

1996
c 33 *continued*
> s 4 rep in pt—(prosp) Crim Justice and Court Services, 2000 c 43, s 75, sch 8; (prosp) Legal
>> Aid, Sentencing and Punishment of Offenders, 2012 c 10, s 129(7)(a)
>> am—(prosp) Legal Aid, Sentencing and Punishment of Offenders, 2012 c 10, s 129(7)(b)
> s 5 am—(prosp) Legal Aid, Sentencing and Punishment of Offenders, 2012 c 10, s 129(8)

c 34 **Marriage Ceremony (Prescribed Words)**
c 35 **Security Service**
> s 1 rep in pt—Police, 1997 c 50, s 134(2), sch 10

c 36 *Licensing (Amendment) (Scotland)*—rep Licensing (S), 2005 asp 16, s 149, sch 7
c 37 **Noise**
> trans of powers—(W) SI 1999/672, art 2, sch 1
> s 1 am—(EW) Anti-social Behaviour, 2003 c 38, s 42(1)(2)
> s 2 am—(EW) Anti-social Behaviour, 2003 c 38, s 42(1)(3); Clean Neighbourhoods and
>> Environment, 2005 c 16, s 84, sch 1 paras 1, 3
>> rep in pt—(EW) Anti-social Behaviour, 2003 c 38, ss 42(1)(4), 92, sch 3; Clean
>>> Neighbourhoods and Environment, 2005 c 16, ss 84, 107, sch 1 para 2, sch 5 pt
>>> 7
> s 3 am —Clean Neighbourhoods and Environment, 2005 c 16, s 84, sch 1 para 4
> s 4 am —Clean Neighbourhoods and Environment, 2005 c 16, s 84, sch 1 para 5
> appl (mods)—London Local Authorities, 2007 c ii, s 31, sch 2
> s 4A added—Clean Neighbourhoods and Environment, 2005 c 16, s 84, sch 1 para 6
> s 5 am —Clean Neighbourhoods and Environment, 2005 c 16, s 84, sch 1 para 7
> s 6 am —Clean Neighbourhoods and Environment, 2005 c 16, s 84, sch 1 para 8
> s 7 am—Clean Neighbourhoods and Environment, 2005 c 16, s 84, sch 1 para 9
> s 8 rep in pt—Clean Neighbourhoods and Environment, 2005 c 16, ss 82, 107, sch 5 pt 7
>> am—Clean Neighbourhoods and Environment, 2005 c 16, s 84, sch 1 para 10
> s 8A added—Clean Neighbourhoods and Environment, 2005 c 16, s 82(2)
>> am—Clean Neighbourhoods and Environment, 2005 c 16, s 84, sch 1 para 11
> s 8B added—Clean Neighbourhoods and Environment, 2005 c 16, s 82(2)
> s 9 am—(EW) Anti-social Behaviour, 2003 c 38, s 42(1)(5); Clean Neighbourhoods and
>> Environment, 2005 c 16, ss 83, 84, sch 1 para 12
>> rep in pt—Clean Neighbourhoods and Environment, 2005 c 16, s 107, sch 5 pt 7
>> appl (mods)—London Local Authorities, 2007 c ii, s 31, sch 2
> s 10 am—Clean Neighbourhoods and Environment, 2005 c 16, s 84, sch 1 para 13
> s 11 am—(EW) Anti-social Behaviour, 2003 c 38, s 42(1)(6); Clean Neighbourhoods and
>> Environment, 2005 c 16, s 85
> s 12 am—(EW) Audit Commission, 1998 c 18, s 54(1), sch 3 para 31
>> rep in pt—Loc Audit and Accountability, 2014 c 2, sch 12 para 33
> s 14 am—Loc Audit and Accountability, 2014 c 2, sch 12 para 34
> sch am —Clean Neighbourhoods and Environment, 2005 c 16, s 84, sch 1 para 14

c 38 **Energy Conservation**
c 39 **Civil Aviation (Amendment)**
c 40 **Party Wall etc**
> trans of powers—(W) SI 1999/672, art 2, sch 1
> s 1 excl in pt—Crossrail, 2008 c 18, s 40, sch 14 para 17(1)(2)
> s 2 excl—Crossrail, 2008 c 18, s 40, sch 14 para 17(2)
> s 6 excl—Crossrail, 2008 c 18, s 40, sch 14 para 17(3)

c 41 **Hong Kong (War Wives and Widows)**
> s 1 rep in pt—Borders, Citizenship and Immigration, 2009 c 11, ss 47(2)(a), 56, sch 1 pt 2
>> am—Borders, Citizenship and Immigration, 2009 c 11, s 47(2)(b)
> s 2 rep in pt—SI 2003/1016, art 3, sch para 8(a)(d)
>> am—SI 2003/1016, art 3, sch para 8(b)(c)

c 42 **Railway Heritage**
> saved—Scotland, 1998 c 46, s 30, sch 5 pt II, s E2
> trans of functions—SI 2013/64, art 2(2)
> s 1 am—Transport, 2000 c 38, s 215, sch 16 para 55; Railways, 2005 c 14, s 59, sch 12
>> para 13(1)-(3)
>> rep in pt—Railways, 2005 c 14, s 59, sch 13 pt 1
> s 2 rep—SI 2013/64, art 2(3)(a)
> s 3 am—SI 2013/64, art 2(3)(b)
> s 4 am—Transport, 2000 c 38, s 252, sch 27 para 53; Railways, 2005 c 14, s 59, sch 12
>> para 13(1)(5); SI 2013/64, art 2(3)(c)
> s 5 am—SI 2013/64, art 2(3)(d)

1996

c 42 *continued*

        s 6 am—SI 2013/64, art 2(3)(e)

        s 7 am—SI 2013/64, art 2(3)(f)(i)(ii)

c 43   **Education (Scotland)**

        s 1 am—S Qualifications Authority, 2002 asp 14, s 1(3)(4)(a)(b)

          rep in pt—S Qualifications Authority, 2002 asp 14, s 1(3)(4)(c)

        s 4 am—Educ (Additional Support for Learning) (S), 2004 asp 4, s 33, sch 3 para 10(a)

        s 6 am—SI 2009/1941, art 2, sch 1

        s 7 rep in pt & am—S Qualifications Authority, 2002 asp 14, s 5

        s 16 rep in pt—Public Finance and Accountability (S), 2000 asp 1, s 26, sch 4 para 15(a)(c)

          am—Public Finance and Accountability (S), 2000 asp 1, s 26, sch 4 para 15(b)

        . Pt 2 (ss 23-27) rep—Standards in Scotland's Schools etc, 2000, asp 6, s 39

        ss 28-31 rep—Scottish Schools (Parental Involvement), 2006 asp 8, s 23, sch

        s 33 rep in pt—Educ (Additional Support for Learning) (S), 2004 asp 4, s 33, sch 3 para

          10(b)

        sch 1 rep in pt—S Qualifications Authority, 2002 asp 14, s 1(3)-(9), 2

        sch 4 rep—Scottish Schools (Parental Involvement), 2006 asp 8, s 23, sch

c 44   *Deer (Amendment)(Scotland)*—rep (saving) Deer (S), 1996 c 58, s 48(2)(5) schs 5,6, para 4

c 45   *Appropriation*—rep Appropriation, 1998 c 28, s 3, sch(C)

c 46   **Armed Forces**

        s 1 rep—Armed Forces, 2001 c 19, s 38, sch 7 pt 7

        ss 2-4 rep —Armed Forces, 2006 c 52, s 378, sch 17

        s 6 am—Armed Forces, 2006 c 52, s 378, sch 16 para 138

          rep in pt—Armed Forces, 2006 c 52, s 378, sch 17

        s 8 rep—Domestic Violence, Crime and Victims, 2004 c 28, s 58(2), sch 11

        ss 9-12 rep—Armed Forces, 2006 c 52, s 378, sch 17

        s 13 rep in pt—Legal Aid, Sentencing and Punishment of Offenders, 2012 c 10, sch 25 pt 2

        ss 15, 16 rep —Armed Forces, 2006 c 52, s 378, sch 17

        s 17 rep in pt—Armed Forces, 2006 c 52, s 378, sch 17

        s 20 rep —Armed Forces, 2006 c 52, s 378, sch 17

        ss 21, 23, 24 rep—Equality, 2010 c 15, s 211, sch 27 pt 1

        s 32 rep —Armed Forces, 2006 c 52, s 378, sch 17

        s 34 rep —Armed Forces, 2006 c 52, s 378, sch 17

        s 36 rep in pt—Armed Forces, 2006 c 52, s 378, sch 17

        sch 1 rep in pt—(prosp) Youth Justice and Crim Evidence, 1999 c 23, s 67, sch 6; Armed

          Forces, 2001 c 19, s 38, sch 7 pt 1; Armed Forces, 2006 c 52, s 378, sch 17

        sch 2 rep—Domestic Violence, Crime and Victims, 2004 c 28, s 58(2), sch 11

        sch 4 rep —Legal Aid, Sentencing and Punishment of Offenders, 2012 c 10, sch 25 pt 2

        sch 5 rep—Armed Forces, 2006 c 52, s 378, sch 17

        sch 6 rep in pt—Armed Forces, 2006 c 52, s 378, s 17

c 47   **Trusts of Land and Appointment of Trustees**

        appl—Interpretation, 1978 c 30 sch 1

        s 6 rep in pt—Trustee, 2000 c 29, s 40(1)(3), sch 2 pt II para 45(2), sch 4 pt II

          am—Trustee, 2000 c 29, s 40(1), sch 2 pt II para 45(1); Charities, 2006 c 50, s 75, sch 8

          para 182

        s 7 am—Commonhold and Leasehold Reform, 2002 c 15, s 68, sch 5, para 8

        s 9 rep in pt—Trustee, 2000 c 29, s 40(1)(3), sch 2 pt II para 46, sch 4 pt II

          am—Mental Capacity, 2005 c 9, s 67(1), sch 6 para 42(1)(2)

        s 9A added—Trustee, 2000 c 29, s 40(1), sch 2 pt II para 47

        s 11 saved—Trustee, 2000 c 29, s 13(3)(4)

          excl—Trustee, 2000 c 29, ss 13(3)(5),25-27,35,36(4)-(8),37,38

        s 17 rep in pt—Trustee, 2000 c 29, s 40(1)(3), sch 2 pt II para 48, sch 4 pt II

        s 20 am—Mental Capacity, 2005 c 9, s 67(1), sch 6 para 42(1)(3)

        s 23 am—Crime and Cts, 2013 c 22, sch 9 para 52

        sch 1 am—Civil Partnership, 2004 c 33, s 261(1), sch 27 para 153; Charities, 2011 c 25,

          sch 7 para 70

        sch 3 rep in pt—Trustee, 2000 c 29, s 40(1)(3), sch 2 pt II para 49, sch 4 pt II; Countryside

          and Rights of Way, 2000 c 37, s 102, sch 16 pt III; Land Registration, 2002 c 9,

          s 135, sch 13; Charities, 2011 c 25, sch 10

c 48   **Damages**

        trans of functions—SI 2010/976, art 15, sch 17

        s 1 am—SIs 1999/1820, art 4, sch 2 pt I para 126(2)(3); 2010/976, art 15, sch 18

        s 2 replaced (by ss 2, 2A, 2B)—(EW, NI) Courts, 2003 c 39, s 100(1)

          appl —(EW, NI) SI 2005/841, art 13(2)

1996
c 48 s 2 *continued*
>>> am—SI 2010/1504, reg 9
>>> s 2A appl —(EW, NI) SI 2005/841, art 3(b)
>>>>> am—SI 2010/976, art 15, sch 18
>>> s 2B am—SI 2010/976, art 15, sch 18
>>> ss 4, 5 replaced (by s 4)—Courts, 2003 c 39, s 101(1)
>>>>> saving—SI 2005/911, arts 13, 14
>>> s 6 am—Scotland, 1998 c 46, s 125, sch 8 para 34; SI 1999/1820, art 4, sch 2 pt I para
>>>>> 126(2)(3); Courts, 2003 c 39, s 101(2)
>>> s 7 am—Damages (S), 2011 asp 7, sch 1 para 7
>>> sch am—Courts, 2003 c 39, s 101(3)

c 49 **Asylum and Immigration**
>>> am—Immigration and Asylum, 1999 c 33, s 65(1)
>>> appl—Housing, 1996 c 52, ss 161(2)185(2)
>>> trans of powers—(W) SI 1999/672, art 2, sch 1
>>> restr—Nationality, Immigration and Asylum, 2002 c 41, ss 77, 78
>>> s 2 am—(retrosp) Immigration and Asylum, 1999 c 33, s 169(2), sch 15 para 2
>>>>> saving—(transtl provn) SI 2000/2444, art 3(2), sch 2 para 4(1)
>>> s 3 saving—(transtl provn) SI 2000/2444, art 3(2), sch 2 para 4(1)(2)
>>> ss 4,5 ext (mods)—(Jersey) SI 1998/1070, art 3, sch; (Guernsey) SI 1998/1264, art 3, sch
>>> s 5 rep (prosp)—Nationality, Immigration and Asylum, 2002 c 41, s 161, sch 9
>>> s 6 ext—SI 2008/680, art 12
>>> s 7 rep—Immigration and Asylum, 1999 c 33, s 169(1)(3), sch 14, paras 108, 109, sch 16
>>> s 8 rep—Immigration, Asylum and Nationality, 2006 c 13, s 26, sch 3
>>> s 8A added—Immigration and Asylum, 1999 c 33, s 22
>>>>> rep—Immigration, Asylum and Nationality, 2006 c 13, s 26, sch 3
>>> ss 9-11 rep—Immigration and Asylum, 1999 c 33, s 169(1)(3), sch 14, paras 108, 110-112,
>>>>> sch 16
>>> s 12 ext (mods)—(Jersey) SI 1998/1070, art 3, sch; (Guernsey) SI 1998/1264, art 3, sch
>>>>> ext—SI 2008/680, art 12
>>> s 13 ext (mods)—(Jersey) SI 1998/1070, art 3, sch; (Guernsey) SI 1998/1264, art 3, sch; SI
>>>>> 2008/680, art 12, sch 5
>>> sch 1 rep—Immigration and Asylum, 1999 c 33, s 169(1)(3), sch 14, paras 108, 113, sch 16
>>> sch 2 ext (mods)—(Jersey) SI 1998/1070, art 3, sch; (Guernsey) SI 1998/1264, art 3, sch
>>>>> rep in pt—Immigration and Asylum, 1999 c 33, s 169(1)(3), sch 14 paras 108, 114,
>>>>> sch 16
>>>>> ext—SI 2008/680, art 12
>>> sch 3 rep in pt—Immigration and Asylum, 1999 c 33, s 169(1)(3), sch 14 paras 108, 115,
>>>>> sch 16

c 50 *Nursery Education and Grant-Maintained Schools*—rep Educ, 2002 c 32, ss 18(1)(f),
>>> 215(2), sch 22 pt 3
c 51 **Social Security (Overpayments)**
c 52 **Housing**
>>> trans of powers—(W) SI 1999/672, art 2, sch 1
>>> power to mod—Insolvency, 2000 c 39, s 7(2)
>>> appl—SI 2003/1417, rules 181(2), 182(2), 183(4)
>>> see—(trans of cert functions) SI 2008/2839, art 2
>>> am—Co-operative and Community Benefit Societies, 2014 c 14, sch 4 para 56
>>> Pt 1 (ss 1-64) am—SI 1996/2325, art 3(1)(2); Govt of Wales, 1998 c 38, s 140, sch 16 para
>>>>> 82(1)(2); Housing and Regeneration, 2008 c 17, s 61(1); Housing (W), 2011
>>>>> nawm 5, sch para 2
>>>>> appl—Value Added Tax, 1994 c 23, sch 10,para 3(8)(a); Audit Commission, 1998 c 18,
>>>>> s 43; Immigration and Asylum, 1999 c 33, s 100(6); (EW) SI 1999/3056, reg
>>>>> 10(b); Crim Justice, 2003 c 44, s 325(9); Housing, 2004 c 34, s 80(6)
>>> s A1 added—Housing and Regeneration, 2008 c 17, s 61(1)(2)
>>> s 1 am—Govt of Wales, 1998 c 38, s 140, sch 16 para 83(3); Charities, 2006 c 50, s 75, sch
>>>>> 8 para 192; Housing and Regeneration, 2008 c 17, s 61(1)(3)(a)(7); Housing (W),
>>>>> 2014 anaw 7, sch 3 para 16
>>>>> rep in pt—Govt of Wales, 1998 c 38, ss 140,152, sch 16 para 83(2)(4), sch 18 pt VI;
>>>>> Housing and Regeneration, 2008 c 17, s 61(1)(3)(b), sch 16
>>>>> mod—SI 2008/2839, arts 3, 6, sch
>>> s 1A added —Housing and Regeneration, 2008 c 17, s 61(1)(4)
>>>>> am—Co-operative and Community Benefit Societies, 2014 c 14, sch 4 para 57
>>> s 2 ext—SIs 1999/985, art 2; 1206, art 2(1)

1996

c 52 s 2 *continued*

am—Housing and Regeneration, 2008 c 17, s 61(1)(5)(7); SI 2009/1941, art 2, sch 1; Co-operative and Community Benefit Societies, 2014 c 14, sch 4 para 58

s 3 am—SI 2001/3649, art 351; Charities, 2006 c 50, s 75, sch 8 para 184; Housing and Regeneration, 2008 c 17, s 61(1)(6)(7); SIs 2009/1941, art 2, sch 1; 2013/496, sch 11 para 5(1)(2)(a)

rep in pt—Deregulation, 2015 c 20, sch 13 para 6(28)

s 4 am—SI 2001/3649, art 352; Charities, 2006 c 50, s 75, sch 8 para 185; Housing and Regeneration, 2008 c 17, s 61(1)(7); SIs 2009/1941, art 2, sch 1; 2013/496, sch 11 para 5(1)(2)(b)

s 5 am—Housing and Regeneration, 2008 c 17, s 61(1)(7)

s 6 am—SI 2001/3649, art 353; Charities, 2006 c 50, s 75, sch 8 para 186; Housing and Regeneration, 2008 c 17, s 61(1)(7); SIs 2009/1941, art 2, sch 1; 2013/496, sch 11 para 5(1)(2)(c)

s 6A added—Housing (W), 2011 nawm 5, s 41

s 7 am—Housing and Regeneration, 2008 c 17, s 61(1)(7); Housing (W), 2011 nawm 5, sch para 3

s 8 am—Housing and Regeneration, 2008 c 17, s 61(1)(7)

s 9 rep in pt—Govt of Wales, 1998 c 38, ss 140,152, sch 16 para 84(2), sch 18 pt VI

am—Govt of Wales, 1998 c 38, s 140, sch 16 para 84(3); Housing and Regeneration, 2008 c 17, ss 61(1)(7), 62; SI 2010/866, art 5, sch 2

mod—SI 2008/2839, arts 3, 6, sch

s 10 am—Housing and Regeneration, 2008 c 17, s 61(1)(7); SI 2010/866, art 5, sch 2

s 11 rep in pt—Land Registration, 2002 c 9, s 135, sch 13

replaced (by ss 11, 11A, 11B) —Housing, 2004 c 34, s 199(1)-(5)

am—Housing and Regeneration, 2008 c 17, s 61(1)(7)

appl (mods)—Housing and Regeneration, 2008 c 17, s 179

s 11A am—Housing and Regeneration, 2008 c 17, s 61(1)(7)

appl (mods)—Housing and Regeneration, 2008 c 17, s 179

s 11B am—Housing and Regeneration, 2008 c 17, s 61(1)(7)

appl (mods)—Housing and Regeneration, 2008 c 17, s 179

s 12 am—Housing and Regeneration, 2008 c 17, s 307(7); ibid, s 61(1)(7)

appl (mods)—Housing and Regeneration, 2008 c 17, s 179

s 12A added —Housing, 2004 c 34, s 200(1)(3)

am—Housing and Regeneration, 2008 c 17, ss 61(1)(7), 62, 63

appl (mods)—Housing and Regeneration, 2008 c 17, s 179

s 12B added—Housing, 2004 c 34, s 200(1)(3)

am—Housing and Regeneration, 2008 c 17, s 61(1)(7)

appl (mods)—Housing and Regeneration, 2008 c 17, s 179

s 13 am—Countryside and Rights of Way, 2000 c 37, s 93, sch 15 pt I para 14; Land Registration, 2002 c 9, s 133, sch 11, para 35; Housing, 2004 c 34, s 200(2)(3); Housing and Regeneration, 2008 c 17, s 61(1)(7)

appl (mods)—Housing and Regeneration, 2008 c 17, s 179

s 14 am—Housing and Regeneration, 2008 c 17, s 61(1)(7)

appl (mods)—Housing and Regeneration, 2008 c 17, s 179

s 15 am—Civil Partnership, 2004 c 33, s 81, sch 8 para 50(1)-(3); Housing and Regeneration, 2008 c 17, s 61(1)(7)

rep in pt—Civil Partnership, 2004 c 33, s 261(4), sch 30

appl (mods)—Housing and Regeneration, 2008 c 17, s 179

s 15A added—Housing, 2004 c 34, s 201

am—Housing and Regeneration, 2008 c 17, ss 61(1)(7), 62, 63

s 16 appl—SI 1999/1135, art 2

am—(E) SI 2001/3257, art 2; Communications, 2003 c 21, s 406(1), sch 17 para 136; SIs 2003/1900, arts 2(1), 3(1), sch 1; 3142, art 3(2); Housing, 2004 c 34, s 202; Housing and Regeneration, 2008 c 17, ss 61(1)(7), 185(1); SI 2010/844, art 6, sch 2

mod—SI 2008/2839, arts 3, 6, sch

rep in pt —SI 2010/866, arts 5, 7, schs 2, 4

s 16A added (W prosp)—Housing, 2004 c 34, s 221

am—Housing and Regeneration, 2008 c 17, ss 61(1)(7), 185(2)

mod—SI 2008/2839, arts 3, 6, sch

s 17 ext—Housing, 2004 c 34, ss 192(3)(b), 194(4)(b)

am—Housing and Regeneration, 2008 c 17, ss 61(1)(7), 62, 63

appl (mods)—Housing and Regeneration, 2008 c 17, s 184

1996

c 52 *continued*

s 18 am—Govt of Wales, 1998 c 38, s 140, sch 16 para 85(2)(3); Housing and Regeneration, 2008 c 17, ss 61(1)(7), 62; SI 2010/866, art 5, sch 2

rep in pt —Housing, 2004 c 34, ss 218, 266, sch 11 paras 7, 8, sch 16; SI 2010/866, arts 5, 7, schs 2, 4

mod—SI 2008/2839, arts 3, 6, sch

s 19 am—Housing and Regeneration, 2008 c 17, s 61(1)(7)

s 20 rep in pt—Housing, 2004 c 34, ss 218, 266, sch 11 paras 7, 9, sch 16

am—Housing and Regeneration, 2008 c 17, ss 61(1)(7), 185(3); SI 2010/844, art 6, sch 2

mod—SI 2008/2839, arts 3, 6, sch

s 21 rep in pt—Housing, 2004 c 34, ss 218, 266, sch 11 paras 7, 10, sch 16

am—Housing and Regeneration, 2008 c 17, ss 61(1)(7), 185(4); SI 2010/844, art 6, sch 2

mod—SI 2008/2839, arts 3, 6, sch

s 22 am—Housing and Regeneration, 2008 c 17, s 61(1)(7)

s 23 am—Housing and Regeneration, 2008 c 17, ss 61(1)(7), 62

s 24 am—Housing and Regeneration, 2008 c 17, s 61(1)(7); SI 2010/866, arts 4, 5, sch 1, sch 2

ss 25, 26 am—Housing and Regeneration, 2008 c 17, s 61(1)(7)

s 27 am—Housing and Regeneration, 2008 c 17, s 61(1)(7)

mod—Housing and Regeneration, 2008 c 17, s 177(8); SI 2008/2839, arts 3, 6, sch

s 27A added (W pt prosp)—Housing, 2004 c 34, s 220

am—Housing and Regeneration, 2008 c 17, ss 61(1)(7), 62, 63

mod—SI 2008/2839, arts 3, 6, sch

rep in pt—SI 2010/866, arts 5, 7, schs 2, 4

s 27B added (W pt prosp)—Housing, 2004 c 34, s 220

am—Housing and Regeneration, 2008 c 17, s 61(1)(7)

mod—SI 2008/2839, arts 3, 6, sch

s 28 am—Housing, 2004 c 34, s 218, sch 11 paras 7, 11; Housing and Regeneration, 2008 c 17, ss 56, 61(1)(7), sch 8 para 65(1)(3)

rep in pt—Housing and Regeneration, 2008 c 17, ss 56, 321, sch 8 para 65(1)(2), sch 16

s 29 am—Housing and Regeneration, 2008 c 17, ss 61(1)(7), 62

mod—SI 2008/2839, arts 3, 6, sch

rep in pt—SI 2010/866, arts 5, 7, schs 2, 4

s 30 am—Govt of Wales, 1998 c 38, s 140, sch 16 para 86; Housing and Regeneration, 2008 c 17, ss 61(1)(7), 62

rep in pt—SI 2010/866, arts 5, 7, schs 2, 4

mod—SI 2008/2839, arts 3, 6, sch

appl (mods)—SI 2011/2866, sch 2

s 31 am—Housing, 2004 c 34, s 218, sch 11 paras 7, 12; Housing and Regeneration, 2008 c 17, s 61(1)(7)

ss 32, 33 am—Housing and Regeneration, 2008 c 17, s 61(1)(7)

s 33A added—Housing (W), 2011 nawm 5, s 35

am—Housing (W), 2014 anaw 7, sch 3 para 28(2)

s 33B added—Housing (W), 2011 nawm 5, s 36

am—Housing (W), 2014 anaw 7, sch 3 para 28(3)

s 33C added—Housing (W), 2011 nawm 5, s 37

am—Housing (W), 2014 anaw 7, sch 3 para 28(4)

s 34 am—Housing and Regeneration, 2008 c 17, s 61(1)(7); Housing (W), 2011 nawm 5, sch paras 4, 5

s 35—Housing and Regeneration, 2008 c 17, s 61(1)(7)

s 35A added—Housing (W), 2011 nawm 5, s 39

s 35B added—Housing (W), 2011 nawm 5, s 40

s 36 am—Govt of Wales, 1998 c 38, s 140, sch 16 para 87; Anti-social Behaviour, 2003 c 38, s 12(2); Housing, 2004 c 34, s 218, sch 11 paras 7, 13; Housing and Regeneration, 2008 c 17, s 61(1)(7); SI 2010/866, art 5, sch 2; Housing (W), 2011 nawm 5, sch paras 6, 7(a)

mod—SI 2008/2839, arts 3, 6, sch

rep in pt—SI 2010/866, arts 5, 7, schs 2, 4; Housing (W), 2011 nawm 5, sch para 7(b)

s 37 am—Housing and Regeneration, 2008 c 17, s 61(1)(7); Housing (W), 2011 nawm 5, s 42(2)(3), sch para 8

s 38 am—Housing and Regeneration, 2008 c 17, s 61(1)(7)

1996

c 52 *continued*

s 39 am—Housing and Regeneration, 2008 c 17, ss 61(1)(7), 62, 63; Housing (W), 2011 nawm 5, sch para 9

s 40 am—Enterprise, 2002 c 40, s 248(3), sch 17, paras 50, 51; Housing and Regeneration, 2008 c 17, s 61(1)(7); SI 2009/1941, art 2, sch 1

s 41 am—Enterprise, 2002 c 40, s 248(3), sch 17, paras 50, 52; Housing and Regeneration, 2008 c 17, s 61(1)(7); SI 2009/1941, art 2, sch 1

ss 42, 43 am—Housing and Regeneration, 2008 c 17, s 61(1)(7)

s 43A added—Housing (W), 2011 nawm 5, s 83

s 44 am—Charities, 2006 c 50, s 75, sch 8 para 187; Housing and Regeneration, 2008 c 17, s 61(1)(7); SI 2014/3486, art 29(2)

s 45 am—SI 2001/3649, art 354; Charities, 2006 c 50, s 75, sch 8 para 188; Housing and Regeneration, 2008 c 17, s 61(1)(7); SIs 2009/1941, art 2, sch 1; 2013/496, sch 11 para 5(1)(2)(d)

s 46 rep in pt—Govt of Wales, 1998 c 38, ss 140,152, sch 16 para 88(2), sch 18 pt VI

am—Govt of Wales, 1998 c 38, s 140, sch 16 para 88(3); Charities, 2006 c 50, s 75, sch 8 para 189; Housing and Regeneration, 2008 c 17, ss 61(1)(7), 62; SI 2010/866, art 5, sch 2; Housing (W), 2011 nawm 5, sch para 10

mod—SI 2008/2839, arts 3, 6, sch

s 47 am—Housing and Regeneration, 2008 c 17, s 61(1)(7)

appl (mods)—SI 2011/2866, sch 2

s 48 am—SI 2001/3649, art 355; Housing and Regeneration, 2008 c 17, s 61(1)(7); SI 2013/496, sch 11 para 5(1)(2)(e); Co-operative and Community Benefit Societies, 2014 c 14, sch 4 para 59

s 49 am—Govt of Wales, 1998 c 38, s 140, sch 16 para 89; Housing and Regeneration, 2008 c 17, s 61(1)(7)

mod—SI 2008/2839, arts 3, 6, sch

rep in pt—SI 2010/866, arts 5, 7, schs 2, 4

s 50 am—Housing and Regeneration, 2008 c 17, s 61(1)(7)

Pt 1 Ch 4A (ss 50A-50V) added—Housing (W), 2011 nawm 5, ss 50-71

s 50J am—SI 2015/664, sch 5 para 6

s 51 am—Govt of Wales, 1998 c 38, s 140, sch 16 para 90(a)(b); Housing, 2004 c 34, s 228(1); Public Services Ombudsman (W), 2005 c 10, ss 38, 39(1), sch 6 paras 56, 57; Housing and Regeneration, 2008 c 17, s 124(1)(2); ibid, s 311, sch 14 para 4(1)(2); SIs 2010/866, art 4, sch 1; 844, art 6, sch 2; (W prosp) Localism, 2011 c 20, s 181(3), sch 19 para 34(1)(2)(b)(3)

rep in pt—Localism, 2011 c 20, sch 19 para 34(1)(2)(a), sch 25 pt 31

mod—SI 2008/2839, arts 3, 6, sch

ss 51A-51C added—Housing, 2004 c 34, s 228(2)

rep—Public Services Ombudsman (W), 2005 c 10, ss 38, 39, sch 6 paras 56, 58, sch 7

s 52 am—Govt of Wales, 1998 c 38, s 140, sch 16 para 91; Housing, 2004 c 34, s 265(1), sch 15 paras 40, 41; Housing and Regeneration, 2008 c 17, ss 61(1)(7), 62; Housing (W), 2011 nawm 5, sch para 11

mod—Housing and Regeneration, 2008 c 17, s 177(8)

s 53 am—Govt of Wales, 1998 c 38, s 140, sch 16 para 92; Housing and Regeneration, 2008 c 17, ss 61(1)(7), 62

mod—SI 2008/2839, arts 3, 6, sch

rep in pt—SI 2010/866, arts 5, 7, schs 2, 4

s 54 rep—SI 2010/866, arts 5, 7, schs 2, 4

s 55 am—Housing and Regeneration, 2008 c 17, ss 61(1)(7), 62, 63

s 56 rep—Housing and Regeneration, 2008 c 17, s 61(1)(8), sch 16

s 57 rep in pt—SI 2001/3649, art 356(1)

am—Housing and Regeneration, 2008 c 17, s 61(1)(7); Co-operative and Community Benefit Societies, 2014 c 14, sch 4 para 60

s 58 am—Charities, 2006 c 50, s 75, sch 8 para 191(a); Housing and Regeneration, 2008 c 17, s 61(1)(7); SIs 2009/1941, art 2, sch 1; 2011/1396, sch para 45; Charities, 2011 c 25, sch 7 para 71; Housing (W), 2011 nawm 5, s 86

rep in pt—Charities, 2006 c 50, s 75, sch 8 para 191(b), sch 9

s 59 am—Housing and Regeneration, 2008 c 17, s 61(1)(7); SI 2009/1941, art 2, sch 1; Co-operative and Community Benefit Societies, 2014 c 14, sch 4 para 61

s 60 am—Housing and Regeneration, 2008 c 17, s 61(1)(7); SI 2009/1941, art 2, sch 1; Co-operative and Community Benefit Societies, 2014 c 14, sch 4 para 62

1996
c 52 *continued*

s 61 am—Housing and Regeneration, 2008 c 17, s 61(1)(7); SI 2009/1941, art 2, sch 1;
Co-operative and Community Benefit Societies, 2014 c 14, sch 4 para 63
s 62 am—Civil Partnership, 2004 c 33, s 81, sch 8 para 51; Housing and Regeneration,
2008 c 17, s 61(1)(7)
ext—Civil Partnership, 2004 c 33, ss 246, 247, sch 21 para 44
s 63 am—Housing and Regeneration, 2008 c 17, s 61(1)(7); SI 2009/1941, art 2, sch 1;
Housing (W), 2011 nawm 5, s 87
s 64 rep in pt—Govt of Wales, 1998 c 38, ss 140,152, sch 16 para 95(a), sch 18 pt VI; SIs
2001/3649, art 356(2); 2009/1941, art 2, sch 1; 2010/866, arts 5, 7, schs 2, 4;
Co-operative and Community Benefit Societies, 2014 c 14, sch 4 para 64(3)
am—Govt of Wales, 1998 c 38, s 140, sch 16 para 95(b); Housing and Regeneration,
2008 c 17, s 61(1)(7); SI 2009/1941, art 2, sch 1; Housing (W), 2011 nawm 5,
sch para 12; Co-operative and Community Benefit Societies, 2014 c 14, sch 4
para 64(2)(4)
ss 65-79 rep—Housing, 2004 c 34, s 266, sch 16
s 81 am—Commonhold and Leasehold Reform, 2002 c 15, ss 170, 176, sch 13, para 16; SI
2013/1036, sch 1 para 130(a)(b)
ext—Commonhold and Leasehold Reform, 2002 c 15, s 172(1)(f)
s 82 rep—Commonhold and Leasehold Reform, 2002 c 15, s 180, sch 14
s 83 rep in pt—Commonhold and Leasehold Reform, 2002 c 15, s 180, sch 14
s 84 appl (mods)—Commonhold and Leasehold Reform, 2002 c 15, s 102(1), sch 7, para 15
ext—Commonhold and Leasehold Reform, 2002 c 15, s 172(1)(g)
s 86 rep in pt—Commonhold and Leasehold Reform, 2002 c 15, s 180, sch 14
s 94 am—Housing and Regeneration, 2008 c 17, s 312(1)(2)
s 95 am—Crime and Cts, 2013 c 22, sch 9 para 52
s 105 rep in pt—Commonhold and Leasehold Reform, 2002 c 15, s 180, sch 14; Housing
and Regeneration, 2008 c 17, s 321, sch 16
ss 111, 112 rep—Commonhold and Leasehold Reform, 2002 c 15, s 180, sch 14
s 119 rep—Commonhold and Leasehold Reform, 2002 c 15, s 180, sch 14
Pt 4 (ss 120-123) heading am—SI 2013/630, reg 12(2)
s 122 am—(retrosp) (to 1.7.1997) Loc Govt, 2003 c 26, s 127(1), sch 7 para 60; Welfare
Reform, 2007 c 5, s 40, sch 5 para 12; Welfare Reform, 2012 c 5, sch 2 para 36;
(prosp) ibid, sch 4 para 13(2)(3)
rep in pt—Welfare Reform, 2007 c 5, s 67, sch 8; (prosp) Welfare Reform, 2012 c 5,
sch 14 pt 1
Pt 5, Ch 1 (ss 124-143) appl—Housing Grants, Construction and Regeneration, 1996 c 53, s
101; (W) SI 2003/3239 (W 319), reg 9(4)
s 124 saved—Housing, 2004 c 34, s 124(9)
am—SI 2010/866, art 5, sch 2
s 125 am—Housing, 2004 c 34, s 179(1)(2)(4); SI 2010/866, art 5, sch 2
ss 125A, 125B added—Housing, 2004 c 34, s 179(1)(3)(4)
s 125B appl—SI 2006/1077, reg 2
s 127 am—Housing and Regeneration, 2008 c 17, s 299, sch 11 paras 11(1)-(4), 14
rep in pt—Housing and Regeneration, 2008 c 17, s 299, sch 11 paras 11(1), (5), 14,
sch 16
s 130 am—Housing and Regeneration, 2008 c 17, s 299, sch 11 paras 12, 14
s 131 am—SI 2005/3336, art 20
s 132 am—Civil Partnership, 2004 c 33, s 81, sch 8 para 52
ext—Family Law, 1996 c 27, sch 7 para 7
s 133 am—Civil Partnership, 2004 c 33, s 81, sch 8 para 53
rep in pt—Civil Partnership, 2004 c 33, s 261(4), sch 30
s 134 am—Civil Partnership, 2004 c 33, s 81, sch 8 para 54
rep in pt—Civil Partnership, 2004 c 33, s 261(4), sch 30
s 137A added—Localism, 2011 c 20, s 155(6)
s 138 rep in pt —Constitutional Reform, 2005 c 4, ss 15(1), 146, sch 4 pt 1 paras 256, 257,
sch 18 pt 2
am—Crime and Cts, 2013 c 22, sch 9 para 52
s 140 am—Civil Partnership, 2004 c 33, s 81, sch 8 para 51
ext—Civil Partnership, 2004 c 33, ss 246, 247, sch 21 para 45
Pt 5, Ch 1A (ss 143A-143P) added—Anti-social Behaviour, 2003 c 38, s 14(5), sch 1 para 1
s 143C am—SI 2010/866, art 5, sch 2
s 143D am—Housing and Regeneration, 2008 c 17, s 299, sch 11 paras, 13(1)-(3), 14

1996
c 52 s 143D *continued*

rep in pt—Housing and Regeneration, 2008 c 17, s 299, sch 11 paras 13(1)(4), 14, sch 16

s 143H am—Civil Partnership, 2004 c 33, s 81, sch 8 para 55

s 143I am—Civil Partnership, 2004 c 33, s 81, sch 8 para 56

s 143J am—Civil Partnership, 2004 c 33, s 81, sch 8 para 57

s 143K am—Civil Partnership, 2004 c 33, s 81, sch 8 para 58

s 143MA added—Localism, 2011 c 20, s 155(7)

s 143N rep in pt —Constitutional Reform, 2005 c 4, ss 15(1), 146, sch 4 pt 1 paras 256, 258

am—Crime and Cts, 2013 c 22, sch 9 para 37(2)

s 143P am—Civil Partnership, 2004 c 33, s 81, sch 8 para 59

ext—Civil Partnership, 2004 c 33, ss 246, 247, sch 21 para 46

ss 152, 153 rep—Anti-social Behaviour, 2003 c 38, ss 13(1)(2), 92, sch 3

ss 153A-153E added—Anti-social Behaviour, 2003 c 38, s 13(1)(3)

rep —Anti-social Behaviour, Crime and Policing, 2014 c 12, sch 11 para 22

ss 154-158 rep —Anti-social Behaviour, Crime and Policing, 2014 c 12, sch 11 para 22

Pt 6 (ss 159-174) see—(cert functions exercisable by additional bodies) SI 1996/3205·art 2, sch 1

excl—SIs 1996/2753, reg 3(1); (E) SI 2000/702, reg 3; (W) SI 2000/1080, reg 2 (extending SI 2000/702, reg 3 to Wales)

restr—SIs (E) 2002/3264, reg 3; (W) 2003/239 (W 36), reg 3

mod—(pt prosp 1.4.2016) Immigration, 2014 c 22, sch 3 para 2(2)

s 159 am—Homelessness, 2002 c 7, s 13; SI 2010/866, art 5, sch 2; Localism, 2011 c 20, s 145(1)-(3)

excl in pt—(pt 1.4.2016) Immigration, 2014 c 22, sch 3 para 2(2)

s 160 am—Civil Partnership, 2004 c 33, s 81, sch 8 para 60; Localism, 2011 c 20, s 159(7)

rep in pt—Civil Partnership, 2004 c 33, s 261(4), sch 30

mod—(pt prosp 1.4.2016) Immigration, 2014 c 22, sch 3 para 2(3)

s 160ZA added—Localism, 2011 c 20, s 146(1)

am—SI 2013/630, reg 12(3)

s 160A added—(EW) Homelessness, 2002 c 7, s 14(2)(3)

am—Localism, 2011 c 20, s 146(2); SIs 2013/630, reg 12(4); 2015/1321 (W 119), art 2(2)

ss 161-165 rep—Homelessness, 2002 c 7, ss 14(1)(3), 18(2), sch 2

s 166 subst—Homelessness, 2002 c 7, s 15

am—Localism, 2011 c 20, s 147(2)

s 166A added—Localism, 2011 c 20, s 147(4)

am—SI 2012/2989, reg 2

s 167 appl—(W) SI 1997/45, reg 2

rep in pt—SI 1997/1902, reg 3

am—Homelessness, 2002 c 7, s 16; (W prosp) Housing, 2004 c 34, s 223; (pt prosp) Housing and Regeneration, 2008 c 17, s 314, sch 15 paras 1, 2; SI 2010/866, art 5, sch 2; Localism, 2011 c 20, s 147(3)(5); Housing (W), 2014 anaw 7, sch 3 para 3

s 168 am—Homelessness, 2002 c 7, s 18(1), sch 1, paras 2, 4

s 170 am—Homelessness, 2002 c 7, s 18(1), sch 1, paras 2, 5; SI 2010/866, art 5, sch 2

s 172 am—Localism, 2011 c 20, s 147(6)

s 174 am—Homelessness, 2002 c 7, s 18(1), sch 1, paras 2, 6; Localism, 2011 c 20, s 147(7)

rep in pt—Homelessness, 2002 c 7, s 18(2), sch 2

Pt 7 (ss 175-218) see—(certain functions exercisable by additional bodies) SI 1996/3205 art 3, sch 2

power to appl (mods)—Immigration and Asylum, 1999 c 33, s 169(2), sch 15 para 13

am (title am)—Housing (W), 2014 anaw 7, sch 3 para 4

s 177 am—Homelessness, 2002 c 7, s 10(1)

s 178 am—Adoption and Children, 2002 c 38, s 139(1), sch 3, paras 89-92; Civil Partnership, 2004 c 33, s 81, sch 8 para 61(1)-(7)

ext—Civil Partnership, 2004 c 33, ss 246, 247, sch 21 para 47

appl—Deregulation, 2015 c 20, s 34(4)

s 179 am—Housing (W), 2014 anaw 7, sch 3 para 5

s 180 appl—(E) SI 2003/3326, art 2

am—Housing (W), 2014 anaw 7, sch 3 para 6

s 182 am—Housing (W), 2014 anaw 7, sch 3 para 7

1996

c 52 *continued*

s 183 rep in pt—(prosp) Immigration and Asylum, 1999 c 33, s 169(1)(3), sch 14 para 116, sch 16

mod—SI 1997/797, art 2(1)-(3)

am—Housing (W), 2014 anaw 7, sch 3 para 8

s 184 mod—SI 1997/797, art 2(1)-(3)

am—(pt prosp) Housing and Regeneration, 2008 c 17, s 314, sch 15 paras 1, 3

s 185 am—Immigration and Asylum, 1999 c 33, s 117(4); Homelessness, 2002 c 7, s 18(1), sch 1, paras 2, 7; (pt prosp) Housing and Regeneration, 2008 c 17, s 314, sch 15 paras 1, 4; SI 2013/630, reg 12(5)

mod—SI 1997/797, art 2(1)-(3)

s 186 rep—Immigration and Asylum, 1999 c 33, ss 117(5), 169(3), sch 16

s 187 am—Immigration and Asylum, 1999 c 33, ss 117(6), 169(6); Housing (W), 2014 anaw 7, sch 3 para 9

mod—SI 1997/797, art 2(1)-(3)

ss 188-197 mod—SI 1997/797, art 2(1)-(3)

s 188 am—Homelessness, 2002 c 7, s 18(1), sch 1, paras 2, 8; (W prosp) Localism, 2011 c 20, s 149(2)

restr—Nationality, Immigration and Asylum, 2002 c 41, ss 54, 55(3)(4)(b), sch 3, paras 1(1)(j)(2)(3), 2-7

s 190 am—Homelessness, 2002 c 7, s 18(1), sch 1, paras 2, 9, 10

s 191 rep in pt—Homelessness, 2002 c 7, s 18(2), sch 2

s 192 am—Homelessness, 2002 c 7, ss 5(1), 18(1), sch 1, paras 2, 11, 12

s 193 am—Homelessness, 2002 c 7, ss 6(1)(2), 7(1)-(6), 8(1), 18(1), sch 1, paras 2, 13; (pt prosp) Housing and Regeneration, 2008 c 17, s 314, sch 15 paras 1, 5; (W prosp) Localism, 2011 c 20, s 148(1)(3)-(7)(9)(a)(b)(10)(11); Housing (W), 2014 anaw 7, sch 3 para 10(a)

rep in pt—Homelessness, 2002 c 7, ss 7(5)(6), 18(2), sch 2; (pt prosp) Localism, 2011 c 20, s 148(1)(2)(5)(a)(8)(9)(c), sch 25 pt 22; Housing (W), 2014 anaw 7, sch 3 para 10(b)

s 194 rep—Homelessness, 2002 c 7, ss 6(3)(4), 18(2), sch 2

s 195 am—Homelessness, 2002 c 7, ss 5(2), 18(1), sch 1, paras 2, 14; (pt prosp) Housing and Regeneration, 2008 c 17, s 314, sch 15 paras 1, 6; (W prosp) Localism, 2011 c 20, s 149(3)(b)

rep in pt—Homelessness, 2002 c 7, s 18(2), sch 2; (W pt prosp) Localism, 2011 c 20, s 149(3)(a), sch 25 pt 22

s 195A added (W prosp)—Localism, 2011 c 20, s 149(4)

s 196 rep in pt—Homelessness, 2002 c 7, s 18(2), sch 2

s 197 rep—Homelessness, 2002 c 7, ss 9(1)(2), 18(2), sch 2

s 198 mod—SIs 1997/797, art 2(1)-(3); (temp) 1999/3126, arts 3, 7

am—Homelessness, 2002 c 7, s 10(2); (W prosp) Localism, 2011 c 20, s 149(5)-(8); Housing (W), 2014 anaw 7, sch 3 para 11

rep in pt—Homelessness, 2002 c 7, s 18(2), sch 2

s 199 excl—SI 1997/797, art 2(1)(3)(b)

mod—SI 1997/797, art 2(1)-(3)

am—Armed Forces, 2001 c 19, s 34, sch 6 pt 5 para 30; Asylum and Immigration (Treatment of Claimants, etc.), 2004 c 19, s 11(1); Armed Forces, 2006 c 52, s 378, sch 16 para 139

rep in pt—Housing and Regeneration, 2008 c 17, s 315, sch 16

ss 200-205 mod—SI 1997/797, art 2(1)-(3)

s 200 am—Homelessness, 2002 c 7, s 18(1), sch 1, paras 2, 15; Housing (W), 2014 anaw 7, sch 3 para 12

rep in pt—Homelessness, 2002 c 7, s 18(2), sch 2

s 201A added —Housing (W), 2014 anaw 7, sch 3 para 13

s 202 am—Homelessness, 2002 c 7, ss 8(2), 18(1), sch 1, paras 2, 16; (pt prosp) Housing and Regeneration, 2008 c 17, s 314, sch 15 paras 1, 7; (W prosp) Localism, 2011 c 20, s 149(5)(9)

rep in pt—Housing and Regeneration, 2008 c 17, s 321, sch 16

s 203 am—Crime and Cts, 2013 c 22, sch 9 para 52

s 204 am—Homelessness, 2002 c 7, s 18(1), sch 1, paras 2, 17(a)(b)

restr—Nationality, Immigration and Asylum, 2002 c 41, ss 54, 55(3)(4)(b), sch 3, paras 1(1)(j)(2)(3), 2-7

s 204A added—Homelessness, 2002 c 7, s 11

s 205 am—Homelessness, 2002 c 7, s 18(1), sch 1, paras 2, 18

1996

c 52 s 205 *continued*

rep in pt—Homelessness, 2002 c 7, s 18(2), sch 2

s 206 mod—(temp) SI 1999/3126, arts 4-7

mod—SI 1997/797, art 2(1)-(3)

s 207 rep—Homelessness, 2002 c 7, s 18(2), sch 2

s 208 mod—(temp) SI 1999/3126, arts 4-7

mod—SI 1997/797, art 2(1)-(3)

s 209 subst—Homelessness, 2002 c 7, s 18(1), sch 1, paras 2, 19

s 210 mod—(temp) SI 1999/3126, arts 4-7

mod—SI 1997/797, art 2(1)-(3)

am—Housing, 2004 c 34, s 265(1), sch 15 paras 40, 43

ss 211-218 mod—SI 1997/797, art 2(1)-(3)

s 213 am—SI 2010/866, art 5, sch 2; Housing (W), 2014 anaw 7, sch 3 para 14

s 213A added—Homelessness, 2002 c 7, s 12

s 216 saving—Homelessness, 2002 c 7, s 20(4)

s 217 am—Homelessness, 2002 c 7, s 18(1), sch 1, paras 2, 20

s 218 am—Homelessness, 2002 c 7, s 18(1), sch 1, paras 2, 21; (pt prosp) Housing and
Regeneration, 2008 c 17, s 314, sch 15 paras 1, 8

rep in pt—Homelessness, 2002 c 7, s 18(2), sch 2

s 218A added—Anti-social Behaviour, 2003 c 38, s 12(1)

am—Police and Justice, 2006 c 48, s 52, sch 14 para 33; SI 2010/866, art 5, sch 2;
Anti-social Behaviour, Crime and Policing, 2014 c 12, sch 11 para 23

rep in pt—SI 2010/866, arts 5, 7, schs 2, 4

s 219 am—SIs 2008/3002, arts 4, 5, schs 1, 2; 2010/866, art 5, sch 2; Localism, 2011 c 20,
sch 19 para 35

rep in pt—SI 2010/866, arts 5, 7, schs 2, 4

s 220A added—Deregulation, 2015 c 20, s 48

s 231 am—SI 2013/630, reg 12(6)

sch 1 am—Govt of Wales, 1998 c 38, s 140, sch 16 para 96(2)(b)(5)(6)(b)(7)(8);
Insolvency, 2000 c 39, s 8, sch 4 pt II para 21; SIs 2001/3649, art 357(1)(2)(3);
2004/1941, art 3, sch para 8; Housing, 2004 c 34, s 218, sch 11 paras 7, 14,
17-21, 23-26; (prosp) ibid, sch 11 paras 15, 16; (prosp) Tribunals, Cts and
Enforcement, 2007 c 15, s 106, sch 16 para 10; SI 2007/2194, art 10, sch 4;
Housing and Regeneration, 2008 c 17, ss 61(1)(7), 62, 63, 311, sch 14 para
4(1)(3)(4); SIs 2008/948, art 3, sch 1; 2009/1941, art 2, sch 1; 2010/866, arts 4,
5, sch 1, sch 2; Housing (W), 2011 nawm 5, ss 43-49, 72-79, 80(2)(3), 81(1),
82(2)-(4), 84(2)(3)(a)(4), 85(2)-(7), sch paras 13(a), 14-19, 20(a); Charities,
2011 c 25, sch 7 para 72(2)-(4); SIs 2012/2404, sch 2 para 36; 2013/496, sch 11
para 5(1)(2)(f); Co-operative and Community Benefit Societies, 2014 c 14, sch 4
para 65

rep in pt—Govt of Wales, 1998 c 38, ss 140,152, sch 16 para 96(2)(6), sch 18 pt VI;
(prosp) Crim Justice, 2003 c 44, ss 280(1)(3), 332, sch 25 para 102, sch 37 pt 9;
Housing, 2004 c 34, ss 218, 266, sch 11 paras 7, 17, 20, 22, sch 16; Housing
(W), 2011 nawm 5, s 84(3)(b), sch paras 13(b), 20(b)

mod—SI 2008/2839, arts 3, 6, sch

sch 2 am—Govt of Wales, 1998 c 38, s 140, sch 16 para 97(2)(3); Housing and
Regeneration, 2008 c 17, s 124(1)(3)(5); (W pt prosp) Localism, 2011 c 20, ss
180(1), 181(4), 182(3)(8)

rep in pt—Housing and Regeneration, 2008 c 17, s 124(4), sch 16

mod—SI 2008/2839, arts 3, 6, sch

sch 2A added—Housing, 2004 c 34, s 228(3), sch 12

rep—Public Services Ombudsman (W), 2005 c 10, ss 38, 39, sch 6 paras 56, 58, sch
7

sch 3 rep in pt—Audit Commission, 1998 c 18, s 54(3), sch 5; Housing (S), 2001 asp 10, s
112, sch 10 para 24; SI 2009/484, art 6, sch 2; Corporation Tax, 2010 c 4, s
1181, sch 3 pt 1

am—Housing and Regeneration, 2008 c 17, s 61(1)(7)

sch 4 appl (mods)—Commonhold and Leasehold Reform, 2002 c 15, s 102(1), sch 7, para
15

ext—Commonhold and Leasehold Reform, 2002 c 15, s 172(1)(g)

power to am—Commonhold and Leasehold Reform, 2002 c 15, s 150, sch 9, para
13(a)

am—Commonhold and Leasehold Reform, 2002 c 15, s 150, sch 9, para 12

sch 5 am—SI 2009/1307, art 5, sch 1

1996
c 52 *continued*

sch 6 rep in pt—Commonhold and Leasehold Reform, 2002 c 15, s 180, sch 14
sch 9 rep in pt —Commonhold and Leasehold Reform, 2002 c 15, s 180, sch 14; Housing
    and Regeneration, 2008 c 17, s 321, sch 16
sch 10 rep in pt—Commonhold and Leasehold Reform, 2002 c 15, s 180, sch 14
sch 12 rep (prosp)—Welfare Reform, 2012 c 5, sch 14 pt 1
sch 13 rep in pt—Welfare Reform, 2007 c 5, s 67, sch 8; Housing and Regeneration, 2008 c
    17, s 321, sch 16; (prosp) Welfare Reform, 2012 c 5, sch 14 pt 1
sch 15 rep (prosp)—Anti-social Behaviour, Crime and Policing, 2014 c 12, sch 11 para 22
    am—Crime and Cts, 2013 c 22, sch 9 para 37(4)(a)
    rep in pt—Crime and Cts, 2013 c 22, sch 9 para 37(4)(b)
sch 18 rep in pt—Housing and Regeneration, 2008 c 17, s 321, sch 16
    am—SI 2010/866, art 5, sch 2

c 53   **Housing Grants, Construction and Regeneration**
restr—Architects, 1997 c 22, s 27, sch 2 para 17(3)
trans of powers—(W) SI 1999/672, art 2, sch 1
Pt 1, Ch 1 (ss 1-59) excl—SI 1996/2890, reg 3(1)
s 1 rep in pt—SI 2002/1860, arts 11,15, sch 3, paras 1, 2(a)(i)(b), sch 6
    am—SI 2002/1860, art 11, sch 3, paras 1, 2(a)(ii)(c); Housing, 2004 c 34, s
    224(1)(2)(9)
s 2 am—SIs 1996/2889, art 2; 1996/2891, reg 2, sch 1
    appl (mods)—SI 2010/2862, reg 23, sch 2
s 3 am—Police, 1997 c 50, s 134(1), sch 9 para 89; GLA, 1999 c 29, s 328(8), sch 29 pt I
    para 60; SIs 2000/90, art 3(1), sch 1 para 31(2); 2002/2469, reg 4, sch 1 pt 1, para
    23(1)(2); Health and Social Care (Community Health and Standards), 2003 c 43, s
    34, sch 4 paras 102, 103; (W) SI 2007/961 (W 85), art 3, sch; Loc Govt and Public
    Involvement in Health, 2007 c 28, s 209, sch 13 para 51; SI 2008/3002, arts 4, 5,
    schs 1, 2; Loc Democracy, Economic Development and Construction, 2009 c 20, s
    119, sch 6 para 88; Police Reform and Social Responsibility, 2011 c 13, sch 16
    para 220; Health and Social Care, 2012 c 7, sch 5 para 76(a); SI 2013/630, reg
    13(2)(3)
    rep in pt—Govt of Wales, 1998 c 38, s 152, sch 18 pt IV; GLA, 1999 c 29, s 423, sch 34
    pt VIII; Crim Justice and Police, 2001 c 16, ss 128(1), 137, sch 6 pt 2 paras 78,
    79, sch 7 pt 5(1); Health and Social Care, 2012 c 7, sch 5 para 76(b)(c); SI
    2013/1788 (W 178), reg 2(2)(3)
ss 4-18 rep—SI 2002/1860, arts 11,15, sch 3, paras 1, 3, sch 6
s 19 am—SI 2002/1860, art 11, sch 3, paras 1, 4(1)(2)(b)(3)(a); Housing, 2004 c 34, s
    224(1)(3)(9)
    rep in pt—SI 2002/1860, arts 11,15, sch 3, paras 1, 4(1)(2)(a)(3)(b)(4), sch 6
ss 20-22 rep in pt—SI 2002/1860, arts 11,15, sch 3, paras 1, 5, sch 6
s 22A added—SI 2002/1860, art 11, sch 3, paras 1, 6
    am—Housing, 2004 c 34, s 224(1)(4)(9)
s 23 am—SIs 1996/2888, arts 2, 3; 2002/1860, art 11, sch 3, paras 1, 7(a)(ii)(iii)(iv),
    8(a)(b); Housing, 2004 c 34, s 224(1)(5)(a)(b)(9)
    rep in pt—SI 2002/1860, arts 11,15, sch 3, paras 1, 7(a)(i)(b)(c), 8(c), sch 6
s 24 am—SI 2002/1860, art 11, sch 3, paras 1, 7(a)(ii)(iii)(iv), 8(a)(b); Housing, 2004 c 34,
    s 224(1)(5)(a)(b)(9)
    rep in pt—SI 2002/1860, arts 11,15, sch 3, paras 1, 7(a)(i)(b)(c), 8(c), sch 6; Housing,
    2004 c 34, ss 265(1), 266, sch 15 para 44, sch 16
ss 25-28 rep—SI 2002/1860, arts 11, sch 3, paras 1, 9, sch 6
s 29 am—SI 2002/1860, art 11, sch 3, paras 1, 10(a)(i); Housing, 2004 c 34, s
    224(1)(5)(c)(9)
    rep in pt—SI 2002/1860, arts 11,15, sch 3, paras 1, 10(a)(ii)(b)(c), 11, sch 6
s 30 appl—SI 1996/2890, reg 2(1)
    rep in pt—SI 2002/1860, arts 11,15, sch 3, paras 1, 10(a)(ii)(b)(c), 11, sch 6
    am—Civil Partnership, 2004 c 33, s 81, sch 8 para 62
s 31 am—SIs 1996/2890, reg 4; 2002/1860, art 11, sch 3, paras 1, 12(a)
    rep in pt—SI 2002/1860, arts 11,15, sch 3, paras 1, 12(b), sch 6
s 32 rep—SI 2002/1860, arts 11,15, sch 3, paras 1, 13, sch 6
s 33 rep in pt—SI 2002/1860, arts 11,15, sch 3, paras 1, 14, sch 6
s 36 am—SI 2002/1860, art 11, sch 3, paras 1, 15
s 40 am—SI 2002/1860, art 11, sch 3, paras 1, 16(b)
    rep in pt—SI 2002/1860, arts 11,15, sch 3, paras 1, 16(a)(c)-(e), 17(a), sch 6

1996
c 53 *continued*

s 41 am—SI 2002/1860, art 11, sch 3, paras 1, 17(b); Housing, 2004 c 34, s
224(1)(5)(d)(9)
rep in pt—SI 2002/1860, arts 11,15, sch 3, paras 1, 16(a)(c)-(e), 17(a), sch 6
s 43 rep in pt—SI 2002/1860, arts 11,15, sch 3, paras 1, 18(a)(c)(d)(i)(e), 19(b), sch 6
am—SI 2002/1860, art 11, sch 3, paras 1, 18(b)(d)(ii)
s 44 am—SI 2002/1860, art 11, sch 3, paras 1, 19(a)(c)
rep in pt—SI 2002/1860, arts 11,15, sch 3, paras 1, 18(a)(c)(d)(i)(e), 19(b), sch 6
ss 45-50 rep—SI 2002/1860, arts 11,15, sch 3, paras 1, 20, sch 6
s 52 am—SI 2002/1860, art 11, sch 3, paras 1, 21(c)
rep in pt—SI 2002/1860, arts 11,15, sch 3, paras 1, 21(a)(b), sch 6
ss 53, 54 rep—SI 2002/1860, arts 11,15, sch 3, paras 1, 22, sch 6
s 55 rep in pt—Trusts of Land and Appointment of Trustees, 1996 c 47, s 25(2), sch 4; SI
2002/1860, arts 11,15, sch 3, paras 1, 23, sch 6
s 57 am—SI 2002/1860, art 11, sch 3, paras 1, 24(a); Housing, 2004 c 34, s 224(1)(6)(9)
rep in pt—SI 2002/1860, arts 11,15, sch 3, paras 1, 24(b), sch 6
s 58 rep in pt—SI 2002/1860, arts 11,15, sch 3, paras 1, 25(a)(b), sch 6; Housing, 2004 c
34, ss 224(1)(7)(c)(9), 266, sch 16
am—SI 2002/1860, art 11, sch 3, paras 1, 25(c); Housing, 2004 c 34, s
224(1)(7)(a)(b)(9)
s 59 rep in pt—SI 2002/1860, arts 11,15, sch 3, paras 1, 26(a)-(l), sch 6; Housing, 2004 c
34, ss 224(1)(8)(b)(9), 266, sch 16; SI 2008/3002, arts 4-6, schs 1-3
am—SI 2002/1860, art 11, sch 3, paras 1, 26(m); Housing, 2004 c 34, s
224(1)(8)(a)(9); SI 2008/3002, arts 4, 5, schs 1, 2
Pt 1, Ch 2, 3 (ss 60-80) rep—SI 2002/1860, arts 11(1)(2)(b), 15(1)(2)(b), sch 3, para 27,
sch 6
Pt 1,Ch 4 (ss 81-91) rep—Housing, 2004 c 34, ss 51, 266, sch 16
ss 93-95 rep in pt—SI 2002/1860, arts 11, 15(1)(2)(b), sch 3, paras 28-30, 31(b), sch 6
s 95 am—SIs 2002/1860, art 11, sch 3, paras 28, 31(a); 2010/866, art 5, sch 2; Charities,
2011 c 25, sch 7 para 73
s 96 rep in pt—SI 2002/1860, arts 11, 15(1)(2)(b), sch 3, paras 28, 32, sch 6
s 97 rep—Housing, 2004 c 34, s 266, sch 16
s 98 rep in pt—Trusts of Land and Appointment of Trustees 1996 c 47s 25(2), sch 4; SI
2002/1860, arts 11, 15(1)(2)(b), sch 3 paras 28, 33, sch 6
s 100 am—SI 2015/914, sch para 57(2)(3)(a)
rep in pt—SI 2015/914, sch para 57(3)(b)
s 101 am—SIs 2002/1860, art 11, sch 3, paras 28, 34; 2008/3002, arts 4, 5, schs 1, 2
rep in pt—SIs 2002/1860, arts 11, 15(1)(2)(b), sch 3 paras 28, 34(a)(b), sch 6;
2008/3002, arts 4-6, schs 1-3
s 102 am—SI 2002/1860, art 11, sch 3, paras 28, 35
Pt 2 (ss 104-117) see—SI 1998/648, art 2
s 105 am—Communications, 2003 c 21, s 406(1), sch 17 para 137; SIs 2003/1900, arts
2(1), 3(1), sch 1; 3142, art 3(2)
s 106 rep in pt —Loc Democracy, Economic Development and Construction, 2009 c 20, ss
138(1)(2), 146, sch 7 pt 5
s 106A added —Loc Democracy, Economic Development and Construction, 2009 c 20, s
138(1)(3)
s 107 rep —Loc Democracy, Economic Development and Construction, 2009 c 20, ss
139(1), 146, sch 7 pt 5
s 108 excl—(S) Edinburgh Tram (Line One), 2006 asp 7, s 80(2); (S) Edinburgh Tram
(Line Two), 2006 asp 6, s 79(2); Glasgow Airport Rail Link, 2007 asp 1, s
35(4); Airdrie-Bathgate Railway and Linked Improvements, 2007 asp 19, s
55(3); Edinburgh Airport Rail Link, 2007 asp 16, s 56(3); SSI 2010/188, art
40
am—Loc Democracy, Economic Development and Construction, 2009 c 20, ss 139(2),
140
s 108A added—Loc Democracy, Economic Development and Construction, 2009 c 20, s
141
s 109 am—Loc Democracy, Economic Development and Construction, 2009 c 20, s 143(1)
s 110 am—Loc Democracy, Economic Development and Construction, 2009 c 20, s 142
rep in pt—Loc Democracy, Economic Development and Construction, 2009 c 20, s
143(1)(2); ibid, s 146, sch 7 pt 5
excl—SSI 2011/370, art 2
restr—SI 2011/2332, art 3

1996

c 53 *continued*

ss 110A, 110B added—Loc Democracy, Economic Development and Construction, 2009 c 20, s 143(1)(3)

s 111 subst—Loc Democracy, Economic Development and Construction, 2009 c 20, s 144(1)

s 112 am—Loc Democracy, Economic Development and Construction, 2009 c 20, ss 144(1)(2), 145

s 113 am—SI 2003/2096, arts 4, 6, sch pt 1 para 30

s 114 see—(trans of functions) (S) SI 1999/678, art 2(1), sch

Pt 3 (ss 118-125) rep—Architects, 1997 c 22, s 27, schs 2, 3

s 126 am—Equality, 2010 c 15, s 211, sch 26 para 34

s 129 rep—Housing and Regeneration, 2008 c 17, s 321, sch 16

ss 131-140 rep—SI 2002/1860, arts 11(1), 15(1), sch 3, paras 28, 36, sch 6

s 145 rep—Housing and Regeneration, 2008 c 17, s 321, sch 16

s 146 am—Loc Democracy, Economic Development and Construction, 2009 c 20, s 138(1)(4)

s 148 rep in pt—Architects, 1997 c 22, s 27, schs 2, 3

sch 1 rep in pt—(prosp) Commonhold and Leasehold Reform, 2002 c 15, s 180, sch 14; SI 2002/1860, art 15(1), sch 6; Housing, 2004 c 34, s 266, sch 16

sch 2 rep—(saving) Architects, 1997 c 22, s 27, sch 2 para 16, sch 3

c 54   **Statutory Instruments (Production and Sale)**

c 55   **Broadcasting**

saved—Scotland, 1998 c 46, s 30, sch 5 pt II, s K1; SI 2005/281, reg 73(1)(a)(iv); Wireless Telegraphy, 2006 c 36, s 111(3)(6)(i)

see—Tobacco Advertising and Promotion, 2002 c 36, s 12

ext—Communications, 2003 c 21, s 205(8)

ext (mods)—SIs (Guernsey) 2003/3192, art 2, sch 1; (Isle of Man) 2003/3193, art 2, sch 1; (Jersey) 2003/3203, art 2, sch 1

power to mod—Communications, 2003 c 21, ss 244(8), 262(4), 407(1)(b)

power exercised—Communications, 2003 c 21, ss 263(1)(a), 317

Pt 1 (ss 1-39) see—(cert functs trans) Communications, 2003 c 21, ss 2, 406(6), sch 1 para 3, sch 18 para 30

appl—Communications, 2003 c 21, ss 215(10)(c), 218(1), 406(6), sch 18 para 33(4)

am—Communications, 2003 c 21, s 241

power to appl—Communications, 2003 c 21, s 244(1)(b)

appl in pt (mods)—SI 2012/292, art 4, sch pt 1

s 1 am—SI 1998/3196, reg 2, sch para 8(2)(3); Communications, 2003 c 21, s 360(3), sch 15 pt 2 para 74; SI 2006/2131, art 4

rep in pt—SI 1998/3196, reg 2, sch para 8(4); Communications, 2003 c 21, s 406(7), sch 19(1)

s 2 am—Communications, 2003 c 21, s 360(3), sch 15 pt 2 para 75

rep in pt—Communications, 2003 c 21, s 406(7), sch 19(1)

s 3 am—Communications, 2003 c 21, s 360(3), sch 15 pt 2 para 76; Wireless Telegraphy, 2006 c 36, s 123, sch 7 para 17

excl in pt—SI 2008/1420, art 6

s 4 am—Communications, 2003 c 21, s 360(3), sch 15 pt 2 para 77(1)-(3)

rep in pt—Communications, 2003 c 21, ss 360(3), 406(7), sch 15 pt 2 para 77(1)(4), sch 19(1)

s 5 am—Communications, 2003 c 21, ss 350(2), 360(3), sch 15 pt 2 para 78(1)-(4)(5)(b)(6); SI 2011/1503, art 14

rep in pt—Communications, 2003 c 21, ss 360(3), 406(7), sch 15 pt 2 para 78(1)(5)(a), sch 19(1)

trans of powers—Communications, 2003 c 21, s 406(6), sch 18 para 54(5)(a)(c)

excl in pt—SI 2008/1420, art 6

s 6 rep—Communications, 2003 c 21, s 406(7), sch 19(1)

ss 7-16 power to replace—Communications, 2003 c 21, s 243(1)(2)

power to appl—Communications, 2003 c 21, s 243(1)(a)(2)

s 7 restr—(temp) SI 1996/2759, art 2

am—Communications, 2003 c 21, s 360(3), sch 15 pt 2 para 79

s 8 am—Communications, 2003 c 21, s 360(3), sch 15 pt 2 para 80

s 9 am—Communications, 2003 c 21, s 360(3), sch 15 pt 2 para 81

s 10 am—Communications, 2003 c 21, s 360(3), sch 15 pt 2 para 82

s 11 appl (mods)—SI 1996/2760, art 5(1)(2)(4)

1996

c 55 s 11 *continued*

rep in pt—Communications, 2003 c 21, ss 345, 406(7), sch 13 pt 2 paras 10, 11, sch
19(1)

am—Communications, 2003 c 21, ss 345, 360(3), sch 13 pt 2 paras 10, 11, sch 15 pt 2
para 83

s 12 am—SI 1998/3196, reg 2, sch para 9(2)-(4); Communications, 2003 c 21, ss 242,
360(3), 406(6), sch 15 pt 2 para 84, sch 18 para 33; SI 2013/2217, reg 4(2)

appl (mods)—SIs 1996/2760, art 5(1)(3)(4); 2008/1420, art 11

rep in pt—Communications, 2003 c 21, s 406(7), sch 19(1)

s 13 excl—SI 1996/2760, art 5(6)

appl (mods)—SI 1996/2760, art 5(1)(4)(5)

am—Communications, 2003 c 21, s 360(3), sch 15 pt 2 para 85

s 14 am—Communications, 2003 c 21, s 360(3), sch 15 pt 2 para 86(1)-(3)(4)(a)-(d)

s 15 am—Communications, 2003 c 21, ss 345, 360(3), sch 13 pt 2 paras 10, 12, sch 15 pt 2
para 87

s 16 appl (mods)—SI 1996/2760, art 5(1)(4)(7)

am—Communications, 2003 c 21, ss 360(3), 406(6), sch 15 pt 2 para 88, sch 18 para
50

rep in pt—Communications, 2003 c 21, s 406(7), sch 19(1)

s 17 am—Communications, 2003 c 21, s 345, 360(3), sch 13 pt 2 paras 10, 13, sch 15 pt 2
para 89

s 18 am—Communications, 2003 c 21, s 360(3), sch 15 pt 2 para 90(1)(2)

rep in pt—Communications, 2003 c 21, ss 360(3), 406(7), sch 15 pt 2 para 90(1)(3),
sch 19(1)

power to appl—Communications, 2003 c 21, s 243(1)(a)(2)

power to replace—Communications, 2003 c 21, s 243(1)(2)

appl (mods)—SI 2008/1420, art 6

s 19 rep in pt—Communications, 2003 c 21, ss 360(3), 406(7), sch 15 pt 2 para 91(1)(3),
sch 19(1)

am—Communications, 2003 c 21, s 360(3), sch 15 pt 2 para 91(1)(2)

power to appl—Communications, 2003 c 21, s 243(1)(a)(2)

power to replace—Communications, 2003 c 21, s 243(1)(2)

appl (mods)—SI 2008/1420, art 7

ss 20-22 rep—Communications, 2003 c 21, s 406(7), sch 19(1)

s 23 am—Communications, 2003 c 21, ss 345, 360(3), sch 13 pt 2 paras 10, 14, sch 15 pt 2
para 92

s 24 am—SI 1998/3196, reg 2, sch para 10; Communications, 2003 c 21, s 360(3), sch 15
pt 2 para 93

s 25 am—SI 1998/3196, reg 2, sch para 11; Communications, 2003 c 21, s 360(3), sch 15
pt 2 para 94(1)-(3)

rep in pt—Communications, 2003 c 21, ss 360(3), 406(7), sch 15 pt 2 para 94(1)(4),
sch 19(1)

s 26 am—Communications, 2003 c 21, s 360(3), sch 15 pt 2 para 95

s 27 am—Communications, 2003 c 21, ss 345, 360(3), sch 13 pt 2 paras 10, 15, sch 15 pt 2
para 96

s 28 rep—Communications, 2003 c 21, s 406(6)(7), sch 18 para 47, sch 19(1)

s 29 rep in pt—Communications, 2003 c 21, s 406(7), sch 19(1); SI 2009/1968, art 3

ss 30, 31 rep—Communications, 2003 c 21, s 406(7), sch 19(1)

s 32 am—Communications, 2003 c 21, s 360(3), sch 15 pt 2 para 97

s 33 see—(trans of functions) Communications, 2003 c 21, s 2, sch 1 para 11

am—Communications, 2003 c 21, s 360(3), sch 15 pt 2 para 98

rep in pt—Communications, 2003 c 21, s 406(7), sch 19(1)

s 34 rep—Communications, 2003 c 21, s 406(7), sch 19(1)

s 35 am—Communications, 2003 c 21, s 360(3), sch 15 pt 2 para 99

s 36 am—Communications, 2003 c 21, s 345, sch 13 pt 2 paras 10, 16

s 38 rep—Communications, 2003 c 21, s 406(7), sch 19(1)

s 39 am—Communications, 2003 c 21, s 360(3), sch 15 pt 2 para 100(a)(d); SIs 2006/2131,
art 5; 2013/2217, reg 4(3)(a)(b)

rep in pt—Communications, 2003 c 21, s 406(7), sch 19(1)

Pt 2 (ss 40-72) cert functs trans—Communications, 2003 c 21, ss 2, 406(6), sch 1 para 5,
sch 18 para 30

appl—Broadcasting, 1990 c 42, s 98; Communications, 2003 c 21, s 406(6), sch 18
para 33(4)

am—Communications, 2003 c 21, s 258

1996
c 55 Pt 2 *continued*

   power to appl—Communications, 2003 c 21, s 262(1)(b)(4)
 s 40 am—Communications, 2003 c 21, s 360(3), sch 15 pt 2 para 101(1)(2)(4)(5)
   rep in pt—Communications, 2003 c 21, ss 360(3), 406(7), sch 15 pt 2 para 101(1)(3),
    sch 19(1)
 s 41 am—Communications, 2003 c 21, s 256(1)
   appl—Broadcasting, 1990 c 42, s 126
 s 42 am—Communications, 2003 c 21, s 360(3), sch 15 pt 2 para 102; Wireless Telegraphy,
   2006 c 36, s 123, sch 7 para 18
 s 43 rep in pt—Communications, 2003 c 21, ss 360(3), 406(7), sch 15 pt 2 para
   103(1)(4)(5), sch 19(1)
   am—Communications, 2003 c 21, s 360(3), sch 15 pt 2 para 103(1)-(3)
 s 44 am—Communications, 2003 c 21, ss 350(2), 360(3), sch 15 pt 2 para
   104(1)-(4)(5)(b)(6); SI 2011/1503, art 15
   rep in pt—Communications, 2003 c 21, ss 360(3), 406(7), sch 15 pt 2 para
    104(1)(5)(a), sch 19(1)
   see—(trans of functions) Communications, 2003 c 21, s 406, sch 18 para 54(5)
 s 45 rep —Communications, 2003 c 21, s 406(7), sch 19(1)
 s 46 am—Communications, 2003 c 21, s 360(3), sch 15 pt 2 para 105; SI 2006/2131, art 5
   rep in pt—Communications, 2003 c 21, s 406(7), sch 19(1)
 s 47 am—Communications, 2003 c 21, s 360(3), sch 15 pt 2 para 106; SI 2006/2131, art 5
   rep in pt —Communications, 2003 c 21, s 406(7), sch 19(1)
 s 48 am—Communications, 2003 c 21, ss 360(3), 406(6), sch 15 pt 2 para 107, sch 18 para
   48
 s 49 see—(trans of functions) Communications, 2003 c 21, s 2, sch 1 para 12
   am —Communications, 2003 c 21, s 360(3), sch 15 pt 2 para 108; SI 2006/2131, art 5
 s 50 am —Communications, 2003 c 21, s 360(3), sch 15 pt 2 para 109; SI 2006/2131, art 5
 s 51 am —Communications, 2003 c 21, s 360(3), sch 15 pt 2 para 110; SI 2006/2131, art 5
 s 52 am —Communications, 2003 c 21, s 360(3), sch 15 pt 2 para 111
 s 53 am—Communications, 2003 c 21, ss 345, 360(3), sch 13 pt 2 paras 10, 17, sch 15 pt 2
   para 112
 s 54 am—SI 1998/1326, art 2; Communications, 2003 c 21, ss 259, 315, 360(3), sch 15 pt
   2 para 113; SIs 2006/2130, art 2; 2006/2131, art 5
   rep in pt —Communications, 2003 c 21, s 406(7), sch 19(1)
 s 54A added—Digital Economy, 2010 c 24, s 35
 s 55 am —Communications, 2003 c 21, s 360(3), sch 15 pt 2 para 114
 s 56 am —Communications, 2003 c 21, s 360(3), sch 15 pt 2 para
   115(1)(2)(a)(b)(d)(3)(4)(a)-(c); SI 2006/2131, art 5
   rep in pt —Communications, 2003 c 21, ss 360(3), 406(7), sch 15 pt 2 para
    115(1)(2)(c), sch 19(1)
 s 57 am—Communications, 2003 c 21, ss 345, 360(3), sch 13 pt 2 paras 10, 18, sch 15 pt 2
   para 116
 s 58 am—Communications, 2003 c 21, ss 261, 360(3), 406(6), sch 15 pt 2 para
   117(1)-(3)(5), sch 18 para 50; SI 2015/904, reg 2
   rep in pt —Communications, 2003 c 21, ss 360(3), 406(7), sch 15 pt 2 para 117(1)(4),
    sch 19(1)
 s 58ZA added—SI 2015/904, reg 3
 s 58A added—Digital Economy, 2010 c 24, s 36(1)
 s 59 am—Communications, 2003 c 21, ss 345, 360(3), sch 13 pt 2 paras 10, 19, sch 15 pt 2
   para 118
 s 60 am —Communications, 2003 c 21, ss 260(1), 360(3), sch 15 pt 2 para 119
   rep in pt —Communications, 2003 c 21, s 406(7), sch 19(1)
 s 61 am —Communications, 2003 c 21, s 360(3), sch 15 pt 2 para 120
   rep in pt —Communications, 2003 c 21, s 406(7), sch 19(1)
 s 62 am—Communications, 2003 c 21, ss 345, 360(3), sch 13 pt 2 paras 10, 20, sch 15 pt 2
   para 121
 s 63 am —Communications, 2003 c 21, s 260(2)(3); SI 2006/2131, art 5
 s 64 am —Communications, 2003 c 21, s 360(3), sch 15 pt 2 para 122
 s 65 am —Communications, 2003 c 21, s 360(3), sch 15 pt 2 para 123
 s 66 am—Communications, 2003 c 21, ss 345, 360(3), sch 13 pt 2 paras 10, 21, sch 15 pt 2
   para 124
 s 67 trans of functions—Communications, 2003 c 21, s 2, sch 1 para 11
   am —Communications, 2003 c 21, s 360(3), sch 15 pt 2 para 125
 s 68 rep —Communications, 2003 c 21, s 406(7), sch 19(1)

1996
c 55 *continued*

s 69 am —Communications, 2003 c 21, s 345, sch 13 pt 2 paras 10, 22

s 71 rep —Communications, 2003 c 21, s 406(7), sch 19(1)

s 72 am—Communications, 2003 c 21, ss 260(4), 360(3), sch 15 pt 2 para 126; SI 2006/2131, art 5; Digital Economy, 2010 c 24, s 36(2)

   rep in pt—Communications, 2003 c 21, s 406(7), sch 19(1)

ss 74-76 rep —Communications, 2003 c 21, s 406(7), sch 19(1)

s 77 rep in pt—Competition, 1998 c 41, s 74(1)(3), sch 12 para 21, sch 14 pt I

ss 78, 79 rep —Communications, 2003 c 21, s 406(7), sch 19(1)

s 80 rep in pt —Communications, 2003 c 21, s 406(7), sch 19(1)

ss 82-84 rep —Communications, 2003 c 21, s 406(7), sch 19(1)

s 86 rep in pt —Communications, 2003 c 21, s 406(7), sch 19(1)

ss 87-90 rep —Communications, 2003 c 21, s 406(7), sch 19(1)

ss 91, 93 rep —Communications, 2003 c 21, s 406(7), sch 19(1)

s 94 ext—(Guernsey) SI 1999/1314, art 2; (Jersey) SI 1999/1315, art 2

s 95 rep in pt —Communications, 2003 c 21, s 406(7), sch 19(1)

Pt 4 (ss 97-105) trans of functions—Communications, 2003 c 21, ss 2, 406(6), sch 1 para 13, sch 18 para 51

s 97 am —Communications, 2003 c 21, s 299(1)(3)(4)

   rep in pt —Communications, 2003 c 21, ss 299(2), 406(7), sch 19(1)

   excl—Communications, 2003 c 21, s 406(6), sch 18 para 51(5)

s 98 am —Communications, 2003 c 21, s 360(3), sch 15 pt 2 para 127; SI 2013/2217, reg 4(4)

   subst—SI 2000/54, reg 3, sch para 1

   saved—SI 2000/54, reg 4(2)

s 99 am—SI 2000/54, reg 3, sch para 2; (prosp) Communications, 2003 c 21, s 300(1); SI 2013/2217, reg 4(5)

s 100 saved—SI 2000/54, reg 4(1)

s 101 am—SI 2000/54, reg 3, sch para 3; (pt prosp) Communications, 2003 c 21, ss 300(2)-(4), 406(6), sch 18 para 51(3); ibid, s 360(3), sch 15 pt 2 para 128

   saved—SI 2000/54, reg 4(2)

s 101A added—SI 2000/54, reg 3, sch para 4

   am—SI 2013/2217, reg 4(6)(a)(b)

s 101B added—SI 2000/54, reg 3, sch para 4

   am —Communications, 2003 c 21, s 360(3), sch 15 pt 2 para 128; SI 2013/2217, reg 4(7)

   rep in pt—SI 2014/1184, reg 2

s 102 am—SI 2000/54, reg 3, sch para 5; (prosp) Communications, 2003 c 21, s 300(5); ibid, s 360(3), sch 15 pt 2 para 128

s 103 am—SI 2000/54, reg 3, sch para 6; Communications, 2003 c 21, ss 360(3), 406(6), sch 15 pt 2 para 128, sch 18 para 51(3); (prosp) ibid, s 300(6)

s 104 am—SI 2000/54, reg 3, sch para 7; Communications, 2003 c 21, ss 301, 360(3), 406(6), sch 15 pt 2 para 129(1)(2), sch 18 para 51(2)(3)

   rep in pt —Communications, 2003 c 21, ss 360(3), 406(7), sch 15 pt 2 para 129(1)(3), sch 19(1)

s 104ZA added—Communications, 2003 c 21, ss 302(1), 406(6), sch 18 para 51(3)

s 104A added—SI 2000/54, reg 3, sch para 8

   am —Communications, 2003 c 21, s 360(3), sch 15 pt 2 para 130

s 105 am—SI 2000/54, reg 3, sch para 9; Communications, 2003 c 21, s 302(2); SI 2013/2217, reg 4(8)(a)(b)

   rep in pt—Communications, 2003 c 21, ss 360(3), 406(7), sch 15 pt 2 para 131, sch 19(1)

Pt 5 (ss 106-130) cert functs trans—Communications, 2003 c 21, ss 2, 406, sch 1 para 14, sch 18 paras 52, 53

   restr—Communications, 2003 c 21, s 327(1)(2)

s 106 rep —Communications, 2003 c 21, s 406(7), sch 19(1)

s 107 am—Communications, 2003 c 21, s 360(3), sch 15 pt 2 paras 132, 133

   rep in pt —Communications, 2003 c 21, s 406(7), sch 19(1)

s 108 rep—Communications, 2003 c 21, s 406(6)(7), sch 18 para 43(1)(3), sch 19(1)

s 109 rep—Communications, 2003 c 21, s 406(7), sch 19(1)

s 110 am—Communications, 2003 c 21, s 360(3), sch 15 pt 2 para 132

   rep in pt—Communications, 2003 c 21, s 406(7), sch 19(1)

s 111 am—Communications, 2003 c 21, s 360(3), sch 15 pt 2 para 132

ss 112, 113 rep—Communications, 2003 c 21, s 406(7), sch 19(1)

1996
c 55 *continued*

    s 114 am—Communications, 2003 c 21, s 360(3), sch 15 pt 2 para 132
        rep in pt—Communications, 2003 c 21, s 406(7), sch 19(1)
    s 115 am—Communications, 2003 c 21, ss 327(1)(3), 360(3), sch 15 pt 2 paras 132, 134
        rep in pt—Communications, 2003 c 21, s 406(7), sch 19(1)
    s 116 rep—Communications, 2003 c 21, s 406(7), sch 19(1)
    s 117 am —Communications, 2003 c 21, s 360(3), sch 15 pt 2 para 135
    s 118 am —Communications, 2003 c 21, s 360(3), sch 15 pt 2 para 132
        rep in pt —Communications, 2003 c 21, s 406(7), sch 19(1)
    s 119 am —Communications, 2003 c 21, ss 327(1)(4), 360(3), sch 15 pt 2 paras 132,
          136(1)(2)(a)-(c)(e)(3)
        rep in pt —Communications, 2003 c 21, ss 360(3), 406(7), sch 15 pt 2 para
          136(1)(2)(d)(f), sch 19(1)
    s 120 am —Communications, 2003 c 21, ss 327(1)(5), 360(3), sch 15 pt 2 para 132
        rep in pt —Communications, 2003 c 21, s 406(7), sch 19(1)
    s 121 am —Communications, 2003 c 21, s 360(3), sch 15 pt 2 para 132
    ss 122-129 rep —Communications, 2003 c 21, s 406(7), sch 19(1)
    s 130 am —Communications, 2003 c 21, s 360(3), sch 15 pt 2 para 137
        rep in pt —Communications, 2003 c 21, s 406(7), sch 19(1)
    ss 131-133, 147,150 ext (mods)—SIs 1997/1755, 1756, 1757
    s 132 am—SI 2009/1941, art 2, sch 1
    s 137 am—SI 2003/2498, reg 2(1), sch 1 pt 2 para 21
        rep in pt—SI 2003/2498, reg 2(2), sch 2
    ss 140,141 rep—SI 2000/1175, reg 4
    s 142 rep —Communications, 2003 c 21, s 406(7), sch 19(1)
    s 143 rep in pt —Communications, 2003 c 21, ss 360(3), 406(7), sch 15 pt 2 para 138(1)(5),
          sch 19(1)
        am —Communications, 2003 c 21, s 360(3), sch 15 pt 2 para 138(1)-(4)(6)(7)
    s 144 am —Communications, 2003 c 21, s 360(3), sch 15 pt 2 para 139(1)-(3); (EW)
          (prosp) Crim Justice, 2003 c 44, ss 280(1)(3), 332, sch 25 para 103, sch 37 pt 9
        rep in pt —Communications, 2003 c 21, ss 360(3), 406(7), sch 15 pt 2 para 139(1)(4),
          sch 19(1)
    s 145 am —Communications, 2003 c 21, s 360(3), sch 15 pt 2 para 140(1)-(4)
        rep in pt—Communications, 2003 c 21, s 406(7), sch 19(1)
    s 146 rep in pt—SI 2003/3299, art 13(2)
    s 147 am—Communications, 2003 c 21, s 360(3), sch 15 pt 2 para 141
    sch 1 am—Communications, 2003 c 21, s 360(3), sch 15 pt 2 para 142
        mod—Communications, 2003 c 21, s 406(6), sch 18 para 37(2)
    sch 2 rep in pt —Communications, 2003 c 21, s 406(7), sch 19(1)
    schs 3, 4 rep—Communications, 2003 c 21, s 406(7), sch 19(1)
    sch 3 restr—(temp) SI 1999/1756, art 8(2)(e)
    sch 5 ext (mods)—SIs 1997/1755, 1756, 1757
        am—SI 2009/1941, art 2, sch 1
    sch 6 am—SIs 2008/948, art 3, sch 1; 2009/1941, art 2, sch 1
    sch 7 am—Capital Allowances, 2001 c 2, ss 578, 580, sch 2 para 97(1)(2), sch 4; SI
          2003/2867, reg 2, sch pt 1 para 25(1)-(4); Corporation Tax, 2009 c 4, s 1322,
          sch 1 paras 445, 446; SI 2009/1941, art 2, sch 1; Corporation Tax, 2010 c 4, s
          1177, sch 1 para 294; Taxation (International and Other Provns), 2010 c 8, s 374,
          sch 8 paras 245, 246, 293, 294
        rep in pt—Capital Allowances, 2001 c 2, ss 578, 580, sch 2 para 97(1), sch 4; Finance,
          2008 c 9, s 8, sch 2 para 70(d)
    sch 8 rep in pt—Communications, 2003 c 21, s 406(7), sch 19(1)
    sch 10 rep in pt—SI 1997/1682, reg 6(1); Political Parties, Elections and Referendums,
          2000 c 41, s 158(2), sch 22; Communications, 2003 c 21, s 406(7), sch 19(1)
        am—European Parl Elections, 2002 c 24, s 15, sch 3, para 5

c 56   **Education**
    constr with—School Inspections, 1996 c 57, s 46(4); Education, 1997 c 44, s 56(2);
        Education (Schools), 1997 c 59, s 4; Audit Commission, 1998 c 18, s 36(6);
        School Standards and Framework, 1998 c 31, s 142(8)(9); School Standards
        and Organisation (W), 2013 anaw 1, s 98(1); Qualifications Wales, 2015 anaw
        5, s 57(1)(2)
    power to delegate cert functions restricted —(W) SI 1999/2242, reg 42(1)(5)
    cert functions made exercisable concurrently—SIs 2014/863, sch 2 para 4; 2014/865, sch 2
        para 3; 2014/1012, art 12(1), sch 2 para 3

1996

c 56 *continued*

trans of powers—(W) SI 1999/672, art 2, sch 1

power to mod—Educ, 2002 c 32, s 177(4)(5)

am—SI 2010/1158, art 5, sch 2

appl—Income and Corporation Taxes, 1988 c 1, s 86(4)(b); Children, 1989 c 41, sch 9 para
3(3); Water Industry, 1991 c 56, sch 4A para 10; Further and Higher Educ, 1992 c
13, s 44(1); Employment Rights, 1996 c 18, ss 30(5), 63A(2)(a)(i)(b)); SIs 1997/599,
reg 2(2); 1612, sch 2; Data Protection, 1998 c 29, s 70(1); Teaching and Higher Educ,
1998 c 30, s 19(10)(c); School Standards and Framework, 1998 c 31, ss 36(2), 69,
73(8), 74, 76, 87(5)(b), 93, 100(2), 140(1), sch 10 para 1(7), sch 19 paras 2(4), 3(4),
sch 21 pt I para 1, sch 22 pt I para 3(2) pt III para 10(3)(4), sch 23 pt I para 1(1); (S)
ibid, ss 20, 48, 104(6), 105(10), 107(5)(b), 144(3)(a), sch 2 paras 1-3, sch 14 para
1(3)(a), sch 32 pt I para 5(7)(a) pt II paras 6(3), 9(3); (saving) ibid, ss 20(3), 21(2)(c);
SIs 1999/14, reg 2(2); 101, regs 1(4)(5)(9)-(11), 16(1)-(4); 129, reg 1; 362, regs 4(b),
55(7); 1469, reg 2; /2163, reg 58, sch 7 para 7(2)(a); 1999/2243, reg 48; 2000/478,
regs 17(1)(c),21(1); Learning and Skills, 2000 c 21, sch 7A; ibid, ss 5(4), 65(10),
83(11); SI 2001/1734, regs 18, 20(2), sch 2 pt III para 14(1)(b); Adoption and
Children, 2002 c 38, ss 4(9)(b), 8(2)(c); (prosp) Nationality, Immigration and
Asylum, 2002 c 41, ss 36(11), 37(8)(b); SIs 2002/195, reg 16(1)(b); (E) 377, regs 16,
24(1)(a)(2)(a)(b)(i), 26(2)(a)(b), sch 2, paras 15, 24; 1330, reg 18, sch 2 pt III, para
14(1)(b); 3200, reg 16(1)(b); Crim Justice, 2003 c 44, s 325(9); SIs 2003/1994, regs
18, 20(2), sch 2 pt 3 para 14(1)(b); (E) 3247, regs 14, 23(1)(a)(2), sch 1 paras 15, 24;
(S) SSI 2003/176, arts 6(1)(c)(ii), 9(b), sch 3 para 6; Carers (Equal Opportunities),
2004 c 15, s 3(7); Children, 2004 c 31, s 12(7)(e); (prosp) ibid, s 29(7)(e); SIs (W)
2004/1011 (W 108), reg 7(2)(c)(ii); (W) 2506 (W 224), reg 13, sch para 17; (E)
3130, regs 23(1)(a)(2)(a)(b)(i), 25(2)(a)(b); Income Tax (Trading and Other Income),
2005 c 5, s 71(1)(c);

appl (mods)—SI 2010/1907, reg 16

mod—SI 1998/1948, reg 3(1)(2), sch; School Standards and Framework, 1998 c 31, s 126;
Educ and Skills, 2008 c 25, s 168(2); Academies, 2010 c 32, ss 4(6), 17(4); SI
2013/1793 (W 180), reg 4; Children and Families, 2014 c 6, ss 83(7), 100(6)

s 1 rep in pt—School Standards and Framework, 1998 c 31, s 140(1)(3), sch 30 para 58, sch
31

mod—SI 1998/2670, reg 9

am—Learning and Skills, 2000 c 21, s 149, sch 9 para 51

s 2 am—Learning and Skills, 2000 c 21, s 110(1); Educ, 2002 c 32, ss 65(3), 156(2),
177(1)-(3), 215(1), sch 7 pt 2, para 6(1)(2), sch 21, para 33

appl—Learning and Skills, 2000 c 21, s 113A

rep in pt—Educ, 2002 c 32, s 215(2), sch 22 pt 3

appl—(W) SIs 2002/1187 (W 135), reg 18(2)(f); 2005/223, art 2, sch para 5

s 3 am—Education, 1997 c 44, s 57(1), sch 7 para 9; Educ, 2002 c 32, s 215(1), sch 21,
para 34

s 4 am—Education, 1997 c 44, ss 51,57(1), sch 7 para 10(a); Childcare, 2006 c 21, s 95; SI
2010/1080, art 2, sch 1; Educ, 2011 c 21, sch 13 para 9(2); (prosp) Higher Educ
(W), 2015 anaw 1, sch para 5

rep in pt—Education, 1997 c 44, s 57(1)(4), sch 7 para 10(b), sch 8; Educ, 2002 c 32, s
215(2), sch 22 pt 3

appl—School Standards and Framework, 1998 c 31, s 76, sch 22 pt I para 3(7); (E) SI
2004/118, art 2(2)(c); (E) SI 2005/1972, reg 2(1)(f)

restr—Learning and Skills, 2000 c 21, s 110(2)(3)

appl—Licensing, 2003 c 17, s 16(3)

s 5 am—School Standards and Framework, 1998 c 31, s 140(1), sch 30 para 59; Educ, 2005
c 18, s 72, sch 12 para 1; Educ and Inspections, 2006 c 40, s 30, sch 3 para 7;
Children, Schools and Families, 2010 c 26, s 1; School Standards and Organisation
(W), 2013 anaw 1, sch 5 para 17(2)(a)(b)

rep in pt—Educ, 2002 c 32, s 215(2), sch 22 pt 3

appl—SI 2005/2966, reg 2, sch 1 pts II, III

s 6 am—Education, 1997 c 44, s 57(1), sch 7 para 11; School Standards and Framework,
1998 c 31, s 140(1), sch 30 para 60; Educ, 2002 c 32, s 156(1); (prosp) Educ and
Skills, 2008 c 25, s 169, sch 1 paras 5, 6

rep in pt—Children and Families, 2014 c 6, sch 3 para 2(2)(3)

s 7 am —Apprenticeships, Skills, Children and Learning, 2009 c 22, s 126(2)(3)

s 8 am—Education, 1997 c 44, s 52(2)

1996

c 56 s 8 *continued*

  appl—SI 2003/118, reg 13(c); Civil Partnership, 2004 c 33, s 72(1)(3), sch 5 pt 9 para
   49(4), sch 6 pt 5 para 27(4)

s 9 am—School Standards and Framework, 1998 c 31, s 140(1), sch 30 para 61

s 10 am—Education, 1994 c 30, s 11A; Apprenticeships, Skills, Children and Learning,
  2009 c 22, s 126(2)(4)

s 11 am—Education, 1994 c 30, s 11A; Educ, 2011 c 21, sch 13 para 9(3)
  rep in pt—Apprenticeships, Skills, Children and Learning, 2009 c 22, s 126(2)(5)

s 12 rep—SI 2010/1158, arts 2, 5, sch 3

s 13 am—Learning and Skills, 2000 c 21, s 149, sch 9 para 52; SI 2005/3238 (W 243), arts
  7, 9(1), sch 1 paras 31, 32(b); Apprenticeships, Skills, Children and Learning,
  2009 c 22, s 59, sch 2 paras 1, 2; ibid, s 123, sch 6 para 12; Children and Families,
  2014 c 6, sch 3 para 3(2); Deregulation, 2015 c 20, sch 14 para 43
  rep in pt—SI 2005/3238 (W 243), arts 7, 9(1), sch 1 paras 31, 32(a); Children and
   Families, 2014 c 6, sch 3 para 3(3)

s 13A subst—Educ and Inspections, 2006 c 40, s 1; Apprenticeships, Skills, Children and
  Learning, 2009 c 22, s 59, sch 2 paras 1, 3
  am—Children and Families, 2014 c 6, sch 3 para 4

s 14 am—Education, 1997 c 44, s 57(1), sch 7 para 12; Educ, 2002 c 32, s 194(1); Educ
  and Inspections, 2006 c 40, s 2
  rep in pt—School Standards and Framework, 1998 c 31, s 140(1)(3), sch 30 para 62,
   sch 31

s 14A added—Educ and Inspections, 2006 c 40, s 3

s 15 rep—Learning and Skills, 2000 c 21, ss 149, 153, sch 9 para 53, sch 11

s 15ZA added —Apprenticeships, Skills, Children and Learning, 2009 c 22, s 41
  appl —Apprenticeships, Skills, Children and Learning, 2009 c 22, ss 83(4), 95(6)
  ext—SI 2011/908, art 10, sch 3 para 6
  am—Children and Families, 2014 c 6, sch 3 para 5; Deregulation, 2015 c 20, sch 14
   para 44; SI 2015/1852, art 2(2)

s 15ZB added —Apprenticeships, Skills, Children and Learning, 2009 c 22, s 41
  ext—SI 2011/908, art 10, sch 3 para 6
  functions made exercisable concurrently—SIs 2014/863, sch 2 para 4; 2014/865,
   sch 2 para 3; 2014/1012, art 12(1), sch 2 para 3

s 15ZC added—Apprenticeships, Skills, Children and Learning, 2009 c 22, s 42
  ext—SI 2011/908, art 10, sch 3 para 6
  functions made exercisable concurrently—SIs 2014/863, sch 2 para 4; 2014/865,
   sch 2 para 3; 2014/1012, art 12(1), sch 2 para 3
  am—SI 2015/1852, art 2(3)

s 15ZD added—Educ, 2011 c 21, sch 16 para 11

s 15A added—School Standards and Framework, 1998 c 31, s 140(1), sch 30 para 63
  restr—Learning and Skills, 2000 c 21, s 110(2)(4)
  am—Learning and Skills, 2000 c 21, s 149, sch 9 para 54; Apprenticeships, Skills,
   Children and Learning, 2009 c 22, s 59, sch 2 paras 1, 4(1)-(6); Children and
   Families, 2014 c 6, sch 3 para 6

s 15B added—Learning and Skills, 2000 c 21, s 149, sch 9 para 55
  am—Apprenticeships, Skills, Children and Learning, 2009 c 22, s 59, sch 2 paras 1, 5;
   Children and Families, 2014 c 6, sch 3 para 7

s 16 appl (mods) —Apprenticeships, Skills, Children and Learning, 2009 c 22, s 58(2)

s 17 am—Education, 1997 c 44, s 57(1), sch 7 para 13; (prosp) School Standards and
  Framework, 1998 c 31, s 140(1), sch 30 para 65; (W prosp) Childcare, 2006 c 21,
  s 103, sch 2 para 20

ss 17A-17D added —Apprenticeships, Skills, Children and Learning, 2009 c 22, s 45

s 17A ext—SI 2011/908, art 10, sch 3 para 6
  functions made exercisable concurrently—SIs 2014/863, sch 2 para 4; 2014/865, sch
   2 para 3; 2014/1012, art 12(1), sch 2 para 3

ss 17B-17D appl —Apprenticeships, Skills, Children and Learning, 2009 c 22, s 86(8)

s 18 rep —Apprenticeships, Skills, Children and Learning, 2009 c 22, s 269(2)(a)
  ext—SI 2011/908, art 10, sch 3 para 6

s 18A added —Apprenticeships, Skills, Children and Learning, 2009 c 22, s 48
  am—Children and Families, 2014 c 6, sch 3 para 8(b)
  rep in pt—Children and Families, 2014 c 6, sch 3 para 8(a)
  functions made exercisable concurrently—SIs 2014/863, sch 2 para 4; 2014/865, sch
   2 para 3; 2014/1012, art 12(1), sch 2 para 3

1996
c 56 *continued*

s 19 am—Education, 1997 c 44, s 47(4); Educ and Inspections, 2006 c 40, s 101; SI
    2007/1507, reg 2; Children, Schools and Families, 2010 c 26, s 3; (prosp) ibid, s
    25, sch 3 para 1
    rep in pt—Education, 1997 c 44, ss 47(2)(3),57(4), sch 8; (prosp) Children, Schools
        and Families, 2010 c 26, s 25, sch 4 pt 1
    appl—School Standards and Framework, 1998 c 31, s 10(6); (E) SI 2002/3199, reg 5,
        sch 2, para 9
    excl—(prosp) Nationality, Immigration and Asylum, 2002 c 41, s 36(5)(c)(10); (E) SI
        2007/1870, reg 5
    mod—SI 2012/1107, art 6(2)
ss 20-28 rep—School Standards and Framework, 1998 c 31, ss 133,140(1)(3), sch 30 para
    66, sch 31
s 29 am—Education, 1997 c 44, s 57(1), sch 7 para 14; Violence against Women, Domestic
    Abuse and Sexual Violence (W), 2015 anaw 3, s 9(2)
    rep in pt—School Standards and Framework, 1998 c 31, s 140(1)(3), sch 30 para
        67(a)(b), sch 31; Educ, 2002 c 32, s 215, sch 21, para 35, sch 22 pt 3
s 30 rep—School Standards and Framework, 1998 c 31, s 140(1)(3), sch 30, para 68, sch 31
Pt 2 (ss 31-182) rep—School Standards and Framework, 1998 c 31, s 140(1)(3), sch 30
    para 69, sch 31
ss 60, 61 am (as saved)—SI 2010/1158, art 5, sch 4
s 100 excl—(E) SI 2007/1870, reg 5
s 101 appl—SIs (E) 2002/377, reg 33, sch 4, para 1; (E) 2004/3130, reg 29, sch 3 para 1
Pt 3 (ss 183-311) rep (pt prosp in respect of Ch 6 (ss 244-258))—School Standards and
        Framework, 1998 c 31, s 140(1)(3), sch 30 para 70, sch 31
    appl—(E) SI 2002/377, reg 33, sch 4, para 2
ss 244-258 appl—(E) SI 2004/3130, reg 29, sch 3 para 2
s 244 savings—School Standards and Framework, 1998 c 31, s 144, sch 32 pt I para 2
s 245 mod—SI 999/274, reg 2
    savings—School Standards and Framework, 1998 c 31, s 144, sch 32 pt I para 2
s 246 mod—SI 1998/2670, reg 7(1)
    savings—School Standards and Framework, 1998 c 31, s 144, sch 32 pt I para 2
s 247 appl (mods)—SI 1999/274, reg 4
    mod—SIs 1998/2670, reg 7(2); 1999/274, reg 3; 532, reg 5(1)(2)
    see—(trans of functions) SI 1999/532, reg 4
    savings—School Standards and Framework, 1998 c 31, s 144, sch 32 pt I para 2
ss 248-254 savings—School Standards and Framework, 1998 c 31, s 144, sch 32 pt I para 2
s 311A added—Children and Families, 2014 c 6, sch 3 para 10
Pt 4, Ch 1 (ss 312-336A) excl—Children and Families, 2014 c 6, s 81
    title am—Children and Families, 2014 c 6, sch 3 para 9
s 312 am—Education, 1997 c 44, s 57(1), sch 7 para 23(a); School Standards and
    Framework, 1998 c 31, s 140(1), sch 30 para 71(b); Learning and Skills, 2000 c
    21, s 149, sch 9 para 56; Educ and Inspections, 2006 c 40, s 6, sch 1 paras 2, 3;
    Apprenticeships, Skills, Children and Learning, 2009 c 22, s 59, sch 2 paras 1, 6;
    Children and Families, 2014 c 6, sch 3 para 11
    appl—Education, 1997 c 44, s 26(6)(a); SIs 1999/606, reg 2(1); 2005/52, reg
        18(2)(b)
    rep in pt—Education, 1997 c 44, s 57(1)(4), sch 7 para 23(b), sch 8; School Standards
        and Framework, 1998 c 31, s 140(1)(3), sch 30 para 71(a), sch 31
s 312A added —Apprenticeships, Skills, Children and Learning, 2009 c 22, s 52(1)(2)
s 313 am—School Standards and Framework, 1998 c 31, s 140(1), sch 30 para 72; Special
    Educational Needs and Disability, 2001 c 10, s 42(1), sch 8 pt 1 paras 1, 2; Educ,
    2002 c 32, ss 195, 215(1), sch 18, paras 1, 2, 17, sch 21, para 36; (prosp) Educ
    and Skills, 2008 c 25, s 169, sch 1 paras 5, 7; SI 2008/2833, art 6, sch 3;
    Children and Families, 2014 c 6, sch 3 para 12(2)(3)(a)
    appl—(E) SI 2007/2979, reg 3, sch 1
    rep in pt—SI 2008/2833, art 6, sch 3; Children and Families, 2014 c 6, sch 3 para
        12(3)(b)
s 314 see—(appt day for code of practice) (W) SI 2002/156 (W 22), art 2
    am—Children and Families, 2014 c 6, sch 3 para 13
s 315 am—School Standards and Framework, 1998 c 31, s 140(1), sch 30 para 73; Educ,
    2002 c 32, s 215(1), sch 21, para 37
s 316 replaced (by ss 316, 316A)—Special Educational Needs and Disability, 2001 c 10, s 1
s 316 am—Educ, 2002 c 32, s 65(3), sch 7 pt 2, para 6(1)(3)

1996
c 56 s 316 *continued*
  excl—(prosp) Nationality, Immigration and Asylum, 2002 c 41, s 36(5)(d)(10)
  mod—SIs 2007/2599, art 3; 2013/1793 (W 180), reg 5
 s 316A rep in pt—Educ, 2002 c 32, s 215, sch 21, para 38(b), sch 22 pt 3; Children and
    Families, 2014 c 6, sch 3 para 14(3)(b)(4)(a)
  am—Educ, 2002 c 32, s 215(1), sch 21, para 38(a); Children and Families, 2014 c 6,
    sch 3 para 14(2)(3)(a)(4)(b)
  appl (mods)—SIs 2007/2599, art 4; 2007/3205, arts 3-6
 s 317 rep in pt—School Standards and Framework, 1998 c 31, s 140(1)(3), sch 30 para
    74(4)(a)(ii), sch 31; Educ, 2002 c 32, s 215, sch 21, para 39(1)(4)(b), sch 22 pt
    3; Children and Families, 2014 c 6, sch 3 para 15(b)
  am—School Standards and Framework, 1998 c 31, s 140(1), sch 30 para
    74(2)(3)(4)(a)(b)(i)(5)-(8); Special Educational Needs and Disability, 2001 c 10,
    s 14(2); ibid, s 42(1), sch 8 pt 1 paras 1, 5; Educ, 2002 c 32, s 215(1), sch 21,
    para 39(1)-(3)(4)(a)(5); Educ, 2005 c 18, s 117, sch 18 para 2; (W prosp) Educ
    and Inspections, 2006 c 40, s 173; Equality, 2010 c 15, s 211, sch 26 para 36;
    Children and Families, 2014 c 6, sch 3 para 15(a)
  appl (mods)—(E) SI 2007/2979, reg 3, sch 1
  mod—SI 2013/1793 (W 180), regs 6(1)(a), 7(a)
 s 317A added—Special Educational Needs and Disability, 2001 c 10, s 7(1)
  am—Educ, 2002 c 32, s 215(1), sch 21, para 40
 s 318 am—School Standards and Framework, 1998 c 31, s 140(1), sch 30 para 75; Educ,
    2002 c 32, ss 194(2), 215(1), sch 21, para 41; (W prosp) Childcare, 2006 c 21, s
    103, sch 2 para 21
  rep in pt—Educ, 2002 c 32, s 215(2), sch 22 pt 3; Children and Families, 2014 c 6,
    sch 3 para 16(2)(3)
 s 321 am—School Standards and Framework, 1998 c 31, s 140(1), sch 30 para 76(a)(b);
    Educ, 2002 c 32, s 215(1), sch 21, para 42
  appl—SI 2001/600, reg 43(1)
 s 322 am—SI 2000/90, art 3(1), sch 1 para 32(2); Nat Health Service (Conseq Provns),
    2006 c 43, s 2, sch 1 para 182; (W) SIs 2007/961 (W 85), art 3, sch; 2010/1158,
    art 5, sch 2; Health and Social Care, 2012 c 7, sch 5 para
    78(2)(a)(c)(3)(4)(a)(c)(5)(a)
  rep in pt—SI 2010/1158, art 5, sch 2, sch 3; Health and Social Care, 2012 c 7, sch 5
    para 78(2)(b)(4)(b)(5)(b)
 s 323 am—Special Educational Needs and Disability, 2001 c 10, s 42(1), sch 8 pt 1 paras 1,
    11(1)
 s 324 am—School Standards and Framework, 1998 c 31, s 140(1), sch 30 para 77; Special
    Educational Needs and Disability, 2001 c 10, s 9; Educ, 2002 c 32, s 215(1), sch
    21, para 43
  appl (mods)—SIs 1999/2666, reg 8, sch paras 1(a), 2-4; (W) 1999/2800, reg 7, sch
    paras 1, 2-8; (E) 2003/1041, reg 9, sch paras 1(a)(c), 2-5; (W) 2006/175, reg 9,
    sch
  appl—(E) SI 2001/3446, reg 12, sch 9 para 3
 s 325 am—Special Educational Needs and Disability, 2001 c 10, s 42(1)(6), sch 8 pt 1 paras
    1, 6(2)
  rep in pt—Special Educational Needs and Disability, 2001 c 10, s 42(1)(6), sch 8 pt 1
    paras 1, 6(1), sch 9
 s 326 am—Special Educational Needs and Disability, 2001 c 10, s 10, sch 1 pt 2 paras
    18-20; Educ (W), 2009 nawm 5, s 23, sch 1 paras 1, 2(b); Children and Families,
    2014 c 6, sch 3 para 17
  rep in pt—Educ (W), 2009 nawm 5, s 23, sch 1 paras 1, 2(a)
  restr—(prosp) Nationality, Immigration and Asylum, 2002 c 41, s 36(6)
 s 326A added—Special Educational Needs and Disability, 2001 c 10, s 5
  am—Educ, 2002 c 32, s 195, sch 18, paras 1, 3, 17; SI 2008/2833, art 6, sch 3;
    Children and Families, 2014 c 6, sch 3 para 18(2)(3)(a)
  rep in pt—Children and Families, 2014 c 6, sch 3 para 18(3)(b)
 s 327 am—School Standards and Framework, 1998 c 31, s 140(1), sch 30 para 78; Educ,
    2002 c 32, s 173; SI 2012/976, sch para 5
 s 328 am—Special Educational Needs and Disability, 2001 c 10, s 42(1), sch 8 pt 1 paras 1,
    7; Apprenticeships, Skills, Children and Learning, 2009 c 22, s 52
 s 328A added—Children, Schools and Families, 2010 c 26, s 2
  rep—Children and Families, 2014 c 6, sch 3 para 19(1)

1996
c 56 *continued*

s 329 am—Special Educational Needs and Disability, 2001 c 10, s 42(1), sch 8 pt 1 paras 1, 8

s 329A added—Special Educational Needs and Disability, 2001 c 10, s 8
  rep in pt—Educ, 2002 c 32, s 215, sch 21, para 44, sch 22 pt 3; Children and Families, 2014 c 6, sch 3 para 20(2)(b)(3)(a)
  appl (mods)—(prosp) Nationality, Immigration and Asylum, 2002 c 41, s 36(9)(b)
  am—(W prosp) Childcare, 2006 c 21, s 103, sch 2 para 22; Educ, 2011 c 21, sch 13 para 9(4); Children and Families, 2014 c 6, sch 3 para 20(2)(a)(3)(b)
  mod—(temp) Children and Families, 2014 c 6, sch 3 para 20(5)
s 330 rep—School Standards and Framework, 1998 c 31, s 140(1)(3), sch 30, para 79, sch 31
s 332 am—Education, 1997 c 44, s 57(1), sch 7 para 24; SI 2000/90, art 3(1), sch 1 para 32(3); Health and Social Care (Community Health and Standards), 2003 c 43, s 34, sch 4 paras 104, 105; Health and Social Care, 2012 c 7, sch 5 para 79(2)(a)(3)(4)
  rep in pt—Health and Social Care, 2012 c 7, sch 5 para 79(2)(b)
ss 332ZA-332ZC added —Educ (W), 2009 nawm 5, ss 1-3
s 332ZA rep in pt—Children and Families, 2014 c 6, sch 3 para 21(2)(3)
s 332ZB rep in pt—Children and Families, 2014 c 6, sch 3 para 22
s 332ZC rep in pt—Children and Families, 2014 c 6, sch 3 para 23
s 332A added—Special Educational Needs and Disability, 2001 c 10, s 2
  rep—Children and Families, 2014 c 6, sch 3 para 24(1)
s 332AA added —Educ (W), 2009 nawm 5, s 4(1)(3)
  rep in pt—Children and Families, 2014 c 6, sch 3 para 25(2)(3)
s 332B added—Special Educational Needs and Disability, 2001 c 10, s 2 3
  rep—Children and Families, 2014 c 6, sch 3 para 26(1)
s 332BA added—Educ (W), 2009 nawm 5, s 5(1)(3)
  rep in pt—Children and Families, 2014 c 6, sch 3 para 27(2)(3)
s 332BB added—Educ (W), 2009 nawm 5, s 6(1)(2)
  rep in pt—Children and Families, 2014 c 6, sch 3 para 28(2)(3)
ss 332C-332E added —Special Educational Needs (Information), 2008 c 11, s 1
  rep—Children and Families, 2014 c 6, sch 3 para 29(1)
ss 333-336 mod—(W) SI 1999/672, art 5, sch 2
s 333 appl—Special Educational Needs and Disability, 2001 c 10, s 17(3)
  am—Special Educational Needs and Disability, 2001 c 10, s 42(1), sch 8 pt 1 paras 1, 3; Educ, 2002 c 32, s 195, sch 18, paras 1, 4, 17; SI 2008/2833, art 6, sch 3; Educ (W), 2009 nawm 5, s 23, sch 1 paras 1, 4; Children and Families, 2014 c 6, sch 3 para 30
  see—(trans of functions) SI 2008/2833, arts 3-5, sch 1
  rep in pt—SI 2008/2833, art 6, sch 3; Children and Families, 2014 c 6, sch 3 para 31
s 334 am —Constitutional Reform, 2005 c 4, s 15(1), sch 4 pt 1 para 259; Tribunals, Cts and Enforcement, 2007 c 15, s 50, sch 10 para 28; SI 2008/2833, art 6, sch 3
s 335 am—SI 2008/2833, art 6, sch 3
  rep in pt—Children and Families, 2014 c 6, sch 3 para 32
s 336 am—Special Educational Needs and Disability, 2001 c 10, s 42(1), sch 8 pt 1 paras 1, 13; SI 2008/2833, art 6, sch 3; Educ (W), 2009 nawm 5, s 7(1)(3); Equality, 2010 c 15, s 211, sch 26 para 37; Crime and Cts, 2013 c 22, sch 9 para 52
  rep in pt—Special Educational Needs and Disability, 2001 c 10, s 42(1)(6), sch 8 pt 1 paras 1, 13, sch 9; Educ (W), 2009 nawm 5, s 7(1)(2); Children and Families, 2014 c 6, sch 3 para 33
s 336ZA added—Educ, 2002 c 32, s 195, sch 18, paras 1, 5, 17, 18
  rep—SI 2008/2833, art 6, sch 3
s 336ZB added—SI 2008/2833, art 6, sch 3
  rep in pt—Children and Families, 2014 c 6, sch 3 para 34(2)(3)
s 336A added—Special Educational Needs and Disability, 2001 c 10, s 4
  am—Educ, 2002 c 32, s 195, sch 18, paras 1, 6, 17, 18; SI 2008/2833, art 6, sch 3; Children and Families, 2014 c 6, sch 3 para 35(a)
  rep in pt—Children and Families, 2014 c 6, sch 3 para 35(b)
s 337 subst—Children and Families, 2014 c 6, sch 3 para 36
s 337A added —Educ and Skills, 2008 c 25, s 142(1)
ss 338-341 rep—School Standards and Framework, 1998 c 31, s 140(1)(3), sch 30 para 81, sch 31
s 342 subst—School Standards and Framework, 1998 c 31, s 140(1), sch 30, para 82

1996
c 56 s 342 *continued*

    am—Educ and Skills, 2008 c 25, ss 142(2)(3)(a)(4), 143; Children and Families, 2014 c 6, sch 3 para 37
    rep in pt—Educ and Skills, 2008 c 25, s 142(2)(3)(b), sch 2
s 342A added—Educ and Skills, 2008 c 25, s 144
ss 342B, 342C added —Educ and Skills, 2008 c 25, s 145
ss 343-346 rep—School Standards and Framework, 1998 c 31, s 140(1)(3), sch 30 para 83, sch 31
s 347 am—Special Educational Needs and Disability, 2001 c 10, s 42(1), sch 8 pt 1 paras 1, 12; Educ, 2002 c 32, s 174; Educ and Skills, 2008 c 25, s 146
s 348 am—School Standards and Framework, 1998 c 31, s 140(1), sch 30 para 84; Children and Families, 2014 c 6, sch 3 para 38(2)(3)
s 349 am—Educ and Skills, 2008 c 25, s 147(1)(2)(a)(b)(3); Academies, 2010 c 32, s 14, sch 2 para 3
    rep in pt—Educ and Skills, 2008 c 25, s 147(1)(2)(c), sch 2
Pt 5 (ss 350-374) mod—SI 1999/2262, reg 57
ss 350-369 rep—Educ, 2002 c 32, s 215(2), sch 22 pt 3
ss 370-374 rep—School Standards and Framework, 1998 c 31, s 140(1)(3), sch 30 para 91, sch 31
s 375 appl—School Standards and Framework, 1998 c 31, s 69, sch 19 para 1(2)
ss 376-389 rep—School Standards and Framework, 1998 c 31, s 140(1)(3), sch 30 para 92, sch 31
s 390 am—School Standards and Framework, 1998 c 31, s 140(1), sch 30 para 93
s 391 am—Education, 1997 c 44, s 57(1), sch 7 para 29; School Standards and Framework, 1998 c 31, s 140(1), sch 30 para 94(2); SI 2005/3239 (W 244), arts 7(1)-(3), 9(1), sch 1 para 5; Apprenticeships, Skills, Children and Learning, 2009 c 22, ss 174, 192, sch 12 paras 9, 10; Educ, 2011 c 21, sch 8 para 6
    rep in pt—School Standards and Framework, 1998 c 31, s 140(1)(3), sch 30 para 94(3), sch 31
s 392 rep in pt—School Standards and Framework, 1998 c 31, s 140(1)(3), sch 30 para 95, sch 31
s 393 rep—School Standards and Framework, 1998 c 31, s 140(1)(3), sch 30, para 96, sch 31
s 394 am—School Standards and Framework, 1998 c 31, s 140(1), sch 30 para 97(2)(a)-(c)(3)(4); Educ and Inspections, 2006 c 40, s 30, sch 3 para 9
    rep in pt—School Standards and Organisation (W), 2013 anaw 1, sch 5 para 17(3)
s 395 am—School Standards and Framework, 1998 c 31, s 140(1), sch 30 para 98
s 396 am—School Standards and Framework, 1998 c 31, s 140(1), sch 30 para 99
s 398 renumbered and am—Educ, 2005 c 18, ss 98, 99, sch 14 para 16, sch 15
    am—Educ, 2011 c 21, sch 5 para 11
s 399 am—School Standards and Framework, 1998 c 31, s 140(1), sch 30 para 100
ss 400, 401 rep—Education, 1997 c 44, ss 37(5),57(4), sch 8
s 402 am—School Standards and Framework, 1998 c 31, s 140(1), sch 30 para 101; Educ, 2002 c 32, s 215(1), sch 21, para 45
s 403 am—School Standards and Framework, 1998 c 31, s 140(1), sch 30 para 102; Learning and Skills, 2000 c 21, s 148(4)(5); Nat Health Service (Conseq Provns), 2006 c 43, s 2, sch 1 para 183; SI 2013/594, art 3
    rep in pt—Learning and Skills, 2000 c 21, ss 148(3),153, sch 11
s 404 am—School Standards and Framework, 1998 c 31, s 140(1), sch 30 para 103(a); Learning and Skills, 2000 c 21, s 148(6)
    rep in pt—School Standards and Framework, 1998 c 31, s 140(1)(3), sch 30 para 103(b), sch 31
    appl—(E) SIs 2005/2039, reg 3, sch 1 pt 1 para 1; (W) 2007/1069 (W 109), reg 3, sch 1; (E) 2007/2979, reg 3, sch 1
s 405 appl (mods) —(E) SIs 2005/2039, reg 3, sch 1 pt 1 para 2; (E) 2007/2979, reg 3, sch 1
    appl—(W) SI 2007/1069 (W 109), reg 3, sch 1
s 406 am—School Standards and Framework, 1998 c 31, s 140(1), sch 30 para 104
s 407 am—School Standards and Framework, 1998 c 31, s 140(1), sch 30 para 105
s 408 am—Education, 1997 c 44, s 57(1), sch 7 para 30(a); School Standards and Framework, 1998 c 31, s 140(1), sch 30 para 106(d)(ii); Learning and Skills, 2000 c 21, s 149, sch 9 para 57; Educ, 2002 c 32, s 215(1), sch 21, para 46(1)(2)(4)-(6); Apprenticeships, Skills, Children and Learning, 2009 c 22, ss 174, 192, sch 12 paras 9, 11; SI 2010/1158, art 5, sch 2; Educ, 2011 c 21, sch 8

1996
c 56 *continued*

    para 7; Qualifications Wales, 2015 anaw 5, sch 4 para 1(2)(a)(c); Violence
    against Women, Domestic Abuse and Sexual Violence (W), 2015 anaw 3, s 9(3)
  rep in pt—Education, 1997 c 44, s 57(1)(4), sch 7 para 30(b), sch 8; School Standards
    and Framework, 1998 c 31, s 140(1)(3), sch 30 para 106(a)-(c)(d)(i), sch 31;
    Educ, 2002 c 32, s 215, sch 21, para 46(1)(3), sch 22 pt 3; (pt prosp)
    Apprenticeships, Skills, Children and Learning, 2009 c 22, ss 223(1)(a), 266,
    sch 16 pt 7; SI 2010/1158, art 5, sch 2, sch 3; Qualifications Wales, 2015 anaw
    5, sch 4 para 1(2)(b)
s 409 rep (as to specified Local Authorities)—Apprenticeships, Skills, Children and
    Learning, 2009 c 22, ss 223(1)(b), 266, sch 16 pt 7; Note: repeal in force for
    specified Local Authorities see SIs 2010/303; 2011/1151. Affecting provns in
    2009 c 22 now rep by 2011 c 21, s 45(1)(2)(g)
  am—School Standards and Framework, 1998 c 31, s 140(1), sch 30 para 107(a)(b)(d);
    (W pt prosp) Educ, 2002 c 32, s 215(1), sch 21, para 47(1)(3)(4); Educ, 2011 c
    21, s 45(2)(a); School Standards and Organisation (W), 2013 anaw 1, sch 5 para
    2(2)
  rep in pt—School Standards and Framework, 1998 c 31, s 140(1)(3), sch 30 para
    107(c), sch 31; Educ, 2002 c 32, s 215, sch 21, para 47(1)(2), sch 22 pt 3;
    School Standards and Organisation (W), 2013 anaw 1, sch 5 para 17(4)
s 410 rep—Educ, 2002 c 32, ss 205, 215(2), sch 22 pt 3
ss 411-432 rep—School Standards and Framework, 1998 c 31, s 140(1)(3), sch 30 para 109,
    sch 31; SIs 1999/2800, reg 8(3)(5), 2484, art 2(4)
s 433 rep in pt—School Standards and Framework, 1998 c 31, s 140(1)(3), sch 30 para 110,
    sch 31
s 434 am—School Standards and Framework, 1998 c 31, s 140(1), sch 30, para 111(a); SI
    2013/1793 (W 180), reg 8(a)
  rep in pt—School Standards and Framework, 1998 c 31, s 140(1)(3), sch 30 para
    111(b), sch 31
  mod—SI 2011/1903, art 3
s 436 rep—School Standards and Framework, 1998 c 31, s 140(1)(3), sch 30, para 112, sch
    31
s 436A added—Educ and Inspections, 2006 c 40, s 4(1)
s 437 rep in pt—School Standards and Framework, 1998 c 31, s 140(1)(3), sch 30 para
    113(a), sch 31; Educ and Inspections, 2006 c 40, s 4(2), sch 18
  am—School Standards and Framework, 1998 c 31, s 140(1), sch 30, para 113(b)
s 438 am—(pt prosp) School Standards and Framework, 1998 c 31, s 140(1), sch 30 para
    114(a)(b); Children and Families, 2014 c 6, sch 3 para 39(2)(3)
  rep in pt—School Standards and Framework, 1998 c 31, s 140(1)(3), sch 30 para
    114(c), sch 31
s 439 am—School Standards and Framework, 1998 c 31, s 140(1), sch 30 para 115(2)(4);
    Educ, 2002 c 32, s 51, sch 4, para 14; (pt prosp) Educ and Skills, 2008 c 25, s
    169, sch 1 paras 48, 49
  appl (mods)—SIs 1999/2666, reg 8, sch paras 1(a), 2-4; (W) 1999/2800, reg 7, sch
    paras 1, 2-8; 2003/1041, reg 9, sch paras 1(a)(c), 2-5; (W) 2006/175, reg 9, sch
  mod—(temp) SI 1998/1948, reg 3(1)(2), sch para 8(1)(2)
  rep in pt—School Standards and Framework, 1998 c 31, s 140(1)(3), sch 30 para
    115(3), sch 31
s 440 am—School Standards and Framework, 1998 c 31, s 140(1), sch 30 para 116(a);
    Children and Families, 2014 c 6, sch 3 para 40(2)(3)
  rep in pt—School Standards and Framework, 1998 c 31, s 140(1)(3), sch 30 para
    116(a)(c), sch 31
s 441 am—Special Educational Needs and Disability, 2001 c 10, s 42(1)(6), sch 8 pt 1 paras
    1, 15(1)(3); Children and Families, 2014 c 6, sch 3 para 41
  rep in pt—Special Educational Needs and Disability, 2001 c 10, s 42(1)(6), sch 8 pt 1
    paras 1, 15(1)(2), sch 9
s 442 am—Children and Families, 2014 c 6, sch 3 para 42
s 444 rep in pt—School Standards and Framework, 1998 c 31, s 140(1)(3), sch 30 para 117,
    sch 31; Educ and Inspections, 2006 c 40, s 109(1)(5)(b), sch 18; (W) Learner
    Travel (W), 2008 nawm 2, s 26, sch 2
  am—Crim Justice and Court Services, 2000 c 43, s 72; (prosp) Crim Justice, 2003 c
    44, s 280(2)(3), sch 26 para 49(1)(2); Educ and Inspections, 2006 c 40, s 82;
    (savings) ibid, s 109(2),(3),(4),(5)(a),(6),(7),(8); (W) Learner Travel (W), 2008
    nawm 2, s 20; Educ, 2011 c 21, sch 13 para 9(7)

1996
c 56 *continued*

s 444ZA added—Educ, 2005 c 18, s 116
    am—Educ and Inspections, 2006 c 40, s 109(9); Educ, 2011 c 21, sch 1 para 6,
      sch 13 para 9(8)
    appl—Educ and Skills, 2008 c 25, s 155
s 444A added —Anti-social Behaviour, 2003 c 38, s 23(1)
    am—Educ, 2005 c 18, s 117, sch 18 para 3; Educ and Inspections, 2006 c 40, s 110;
      Educ and Skills, 2008 c 25, s 169, sch 1 paras 48, 50
    rep in pt—SI 2013/1657 (W 155), art 2(1)
s 444B added —Anti-social Behaviour, 2003 c 38, s 23(1)
    am—Educ, 2011 c 21, sch 13 para 9(9)
    rep in pt—SI 2013/1657 (W 155), art 2(1)
s 447 am—SI 2010/1158, art 5, sch 2
    rep in pt—SI 2010/1158, art 5, schs 2, 3
    mod—SI 2011/1329, rule 79(1)
s 448 rep—School Standards and Framework, 1998 c 31, s 140(1)(3), sch 30 para 118, sch
    31
s 449 am—School Standards and Framework, 1998 c 31, s 140(1), sch 30 para 119
Pt 6, Ch. 3 (ss 449-462) mod—SI 2013/1793 (W 180), reg 6(3)
s 450 am—Educ, 2005 c 18, ss 98, 99, sch 14 para 17, sch 15; Educ, 2011 c 21, sch 5 para
    12
    mod—SI 2013/1793 (W 180), reg 9
s 451 am—School Standards and Framework, 1998 c 31, s 140(1), sch 30 para 120(b)(c);
    Educ, 2002 c 32, s 215(1), sch 21, para 48; Childcare, 2006 c 21, s 17; (W
    prosp) Educ and Inspections, 2006 c 40, s 56(1)
    rep in pt—School Standards and Framework, 1998 c 31, s 140(1)(3), sch 30 para
      120(a)(d), sch 31
    excl—SI 2012/962, reg 2(1)
    mod—SI 2013/1793 (W 180), reg 6(1)(a)
ss 452-454 mod—SI 2013/1793 (W 180), reg 6(1)(a)
s 455 am—(pt prosp) Educ and Inspections, 2006 c 40, s 85, sch 10 para 3; (W) Learner
    Travel (W), 2008 nawm 2, s 22(1)(2)(a)(d)(e)
    rep in pt—(W) Learner Travel (W), 2008 nawm 2, s 22(1)(2)(b)(c), sch 2
    mod—SI 2013/1793 (W 180), reg 6(1)(a)
s 456 rep in pt—School Standards and Framework, 1998 c 31, s 140(1)(3), sch 30 para 121,
    sch 31
    am—(W prosp) Educ and Inspections, 2006 c 40, s 56(2); (W) Learner Travel (W),
      2008 nawm 2, s 22(1)(3); Educ, 2011 c 21, s 48(2)-(4)
s 457 am—Tax Credits, 1999 c 10, s 1(2), sch 1 paras 1, 6(p); Educ, 2002 c 32, s 200;
    Welfare Reform, 2007 c 5, s 28, sch 3 para 16(1)(2); Welfare Reform, 2012 c 5,
    sch 2 para 38
    rep in pt—School Standards and Framework, 1998 c 31, s 140(1)(3), sch 30 para
      122(a)(b), sch 31; (prosp) Welfare Reform, 2009 c 24, s 58, sch 7 pt 1; (prosp)
      Welfare Reform, 2012 c 5, sch 14 pt 1
    mod—SI 2013/1793 (W 180), reg 6(1)(a),(2)
s 458 am—School Standards and Framework, 1998 c 31, s 140(1), sch 30 para
    123(a)(i)(b)(ii)
    rep in pt—School Standards and Framework, 1998 c 31, s 140(1)(3), sch 30 para
      123(a)(ii)(b)(i)(c)(d), sch 31
s 460 mod—SI 2013/1793 (W 180), reg 6(1)(a)
s 462 mod—SI 2013/1793 (W 180), reg 6(1)(b)
s 463 subst—Educ, 2002 c 32, s 172
    appl—(E) SI 2004/118, art 2(2)(d)
    am—Children and Families, 2014 c 6, sch 3 para 43
ss 464-478 rep—Educ, 2002 c 32, s 215(2), sch 22 pt 3
s 479-481 rep—Education (Schools), 1997 c 59, ss 1(1)(a)(b)(3),6(3), sch pt I
s 482 rep—Educ, 2011 c 21, sch 14 para 16
s 483 rep—Academies, 2010 c 32, s 14, sch 2 para 5
s 483A added—Learning and Skills, 2000 c 21, s 133
    am—Educ, 2002 c 32, s 65(3), sch 7 pt 2, para 6(1)(4)(a); Educ and Skills, 2008 c
    25, s 147(4)-(7); Children and Families, 2014 c 6, sch 3 para 44
    rep in pt—Educ, 2002 c 32, ss 65(3), 215(2), sch 7 pt 2, para 6(1)(4)(b), sch 22 pt 3
s 484 power to ext—Teaching and Higher Educ, 1998 c 30, s 19(8)

1996
c 56 s 484 *continued*

> am—School Standards and Framework, 1998 c 31, s 7(10); School Standards and
> Framework, 1998 c 31, s 140(1), sch 30 para 125; Educ, 2002 c 32, s 215(1),
> sch 21, para 49(1)-(3); School Standards and Organisation (W), 2013 anaw 1,
> sch 5 para 2(3)
>
> restr—(E) Educ, 2002 c 32, s 18(2)
>
> rep in pt—Educ, 2002 c 32, s 215, sch 21, para 49(1)(4)(5), sch 22 pt 3

ss 486-488 rep—Educ, 2002 c 32, ss 18(1)(g), 215(2), sch 22 pt 3

s 489 am—School Standards and Framework, 1998 c 31, s 140(1), sch 30 para 126

s 490-492 rep—Educ, 2002 c 32, ss 18(1)(g)(h), 215(2), sch 22 pt 3

s 493 mod—(W) SI 1999/672, art 5, sch 2

> am—Educ, 2002 c 32, s 208(1)

s 494 mod—SIs 1998/2670, reg 8; (W) 1999/672, art 5, sch 2; 2012/1107, art 6(3)

> subst—School Standards and Framework, 1998 c 31, s 140(1), sch 30, para 128
>
> see—(trans of functions) Educ, 2002 c 32, s 208(2)(3)
>
> am—Educ, 2005 c 18, s 117, sch 18 para 5

s 495 ext—Education Reform, 1988 c 40, s 219

> mod—School Standards and Framework, 1998 c 31, s 44(7); (W) SI 1999/672, art 5,
> sch 2
>
> appl (mods)—(E) SI 2007/2979, reg 3, sch 1

s 496 mod—Education Reform, 1988 c 40, s 219; Education, 1997 c 44, s 43(4); School
> Standards and Framework, 1998 c 31, s 44(7); Learning and Skills, 2000 c 21,
> s 113(3); Education, 2002 c 32, s 135C(4); SI 2013/1721, art 3(3)(a)
>
> ext—Further and Higher Educ, 1992 c 13, s 57(6); School Standards and Framework,
> 1998 c 31, s 24, sch 4 para 10; Loc Govt, 2000 c 22, s 23, sch 1 para 10
>
> power to appl—School Standards and Framework, 1998 c 31, s 105(7); ibid, s 89C
>
> am—School Standards and Framework, 1998 c 31, s 140(1), sch 30 para 129(a)(b);
> Educ and Inspections, 2006 c 40, s 168(1); Apprenticeships, Skills, Children and
> Learning, 2009 c 22, s 59, sch 2 paras 1, 7; School Standards and Organisation
> (W), 2013 anaw 1, sch 5 para 2(4)(a)(b)
>
> appl—SIs (E) 2002/2903, reg 8; (E) 2002/2904, reg 8; 2007/194, reg 10; Loc Govt,
> 2000 c 22, sch A1 para 9(a); SI 2012/8, reg 32
>
> appl (mods)—(E) SIs 2007/2979, reg 3, sch 1; 2008/3090, reg 10; Equality, 2010 c
> 15, s 87
>
> rep in pt—Educ, 2011 c 21, s 45(2)(b)
>
> trans of functions—SI 2013/1721, art 2(b)(i)

s 497 mod—Education Reform, 1988 c 40, s 219; Education, 1997 c 44, s 43(4); School
> Standards and Framework, 1998 c 31, s 44(7); Learning and Skills, 2000 c 21,
> s 113(3); Education, 2002 c 32, s 135C(4); SI 2013/1721, art 3(3)(b)
>
> appl—SIs 1998/2876, reg 21; (E) 2002/2903, reg 8; (E) 2002/2904, reg 8; 2007/194,
> reg 10; Loc Govt, 2000 c 22, sch A1 para 9(b); SI 2012/8, reg 32
>
> ext—School Standards and Framework, 1998 c 31, s 24, sch 4, para 10; Loc Govt,
> 2000 c 22, s 23, sch 1 para 10
>
> power to appl—School Standards and Framework, 1998 c 31, s 105(7); ibid, s 89C
>
> am—School Standards and Framework, 1998 c 31, s 140(1), sch 30 para 130(a)(b);
> Educ and Inspections, 2006 c 40, s 168(2); Apprenticeships, Skills, Children and
> Learning, 2009 c 22, s 59, sch 2 paras 1, 8; SI 2010/1158, art 5, sch 2; School
> Standards and Organisation (W), 2013 anaw 1, sch 5 para 2(5)(a)(b)
>
> appl (mods)—(E) SIs 2007/1264, reg 10; 2008/3090, reg 10; Equality, 2010 c 15, s
> 87
>
> rep in pt—Educ, 2011 c 21, s 45(2)(c)
>
> trans of functions—SI 2013/1721, art 2(b)(ii)

s 497A added—School Standards and Framework, 1998 c 31, s 8

> mod—SIs 1998/3217, reg 2(b); 2013/1721, art 3(3)(c)
>
> rep in pt—Educ, 2002 c 32, ss 60(1)(5), 215(2), sch 22 pt 3
>
> am—Educ, 2002 c 32, s 60(1)-(4)(6)-(10); Apprenticeships, Skills, Children and
> Learning, 2009 c 22, s 59, sch 2 paras 1, 9; School Standards and Organisation
> (W), 2013 anaw 1, sch 5 para 2(6); Children and Families, 2014 c 6, s 101(2)
>
> appl—Children, 2004 c 31, s 50(1), (4)-(6)
>
> trans of functions—SI 2013/1721, art 2(b)(iii)

s 497AA added—Educ, 2002 c 32, s 61

> appl—Children, 2004 c 31, s 50(4)-(6)
>
> trans of functions—SI 2013/1721, art 2(b)(iv)
>
> mod—SI 2013/1721, art 3(3)(d)

1996

c 56 *continued*

s 497B added—School Standards and Framework, 1998 c 31, s 8
    mod—SIs 1998/3217, reg 2(b); 2013/1721, art 3(3)(e)
    am—Educ, 2002 c 32, s 62
    appl—Educ, 2002 c 32, s 64(4); Children, 2004 c 31, s 50(4)-(6)
s 498 ext—Education Reform, 1988 c 40, s 219
    mod—School Standards and Framework, 1998 c 31, s 44(7)
    am—School Standards and Framework, 1998 c 31, s 140(1), sch 30 para 131
s 499 am—School Standards and Framework, 1998 c 31, s 9; Educ, 2002 c 32, s 215(1),
    sch 21, para 50; SI 2010/1158, art 5, sch 2
ss 500-505 rep—School Standards and Framework, 1998 c 31, s 140(1)(3), sch 30 para 132,
    sch 31
s 507 rep—Inquiries, 2005 c 12, ss 44(5), 48(1), 49(2), sch 2 pt 1 para 15, sch 3
s 507A added—Educ and Inspections, 2006 c 40, s 6(1)
s 507B added—Educ and Inspections, 2006 c 40, s 6(1)
    am—SIs 2010/1080, art 2, sch 1; 2013/1721, art 3(2); Children and Families, 2014
    c 6, sch 3 para 45
    trans of functions—SI 2013/1721, art 2(a)
s 508 am—Learning and Skills, 2000 c 21, s 137; Educ and Inspections, 2006 c 40, s 6, sch
    1 para 4
s 508A added—Educ and Inspections, 2006 c 40, s 76
    am—Educ, 2011 c 21, sch 13 para 9(10)
ss 508B-508D added—Educ and Inspections, 2006 c 40, s 77(1)
s 508B appl (mods)—(E) SI 2007/1367, reg 2
s 508C am—Educ, 2011 c 21, sch 13 para 9(11)
s 508E added—Educ and Inspections, 2006 c 40, s 78(1)
ss 508F-508I added —Apprenticeships, Skills, Children and Learning, 2009 c 22, s 57(1)(2)
s 508F am—Children and Families, 2014 c 6, sch 3 para 46
s 508G am—Educ, 2011 c 21, sch 13 para 9(12)
s 508I am—Children and Families, 2014 c 6, sch 3 para 47
s 509 rep —Apprenticeships, Skills, Children and Learning, 2009 c 22, ss 57(1)(4), 266, sch
    16 pt 1
s 509A added—School Standards and Framework, 1998 c 31, s 124
    am—Educ, 2002 c 32, s 199, sch 19, paras 1, 6; (W prosp) Childcare, 2006 c 21, s
    103, sch 2 para 23; (W) Learner Travel (W), 2008 nawm 2, s 25, sch 1 para
    4(1)(5)(a)(b); Apprenticeships, Skills, Children and Learning, 2009 c 22, s 59,
    sch 2 paras 1, 10(3)
    rep in pt—Educ, 2002 c 32, s 215(2), sch 22 pt 3; (W) Learner Travel (W), 2008
    nawm 2, s 25, sch 1 para 4(1)(5)(c), sch 2
s 509AA added—Educ, 2002 c 32, s 199, sch 19, paras 1, 3
    am—SI 2005/3238 (W 243), arts 7, 9(1), sch 1 paras 31, 34; Educ and Inspections,
    2006 c 40, s 83(1); (W) Learner Travel (W), 2008 nawm 2, s 25, sch 1 para
    4(1)(2)(a)(c); Apprenticeships, Skills, Children and Learning, 2009 c 22, ss
    55(2), 56(1)(3), 59, sch 2 paras 1, 10(1); SI 2010/1080, art 2, sch 1; Educ,
    2011 c 21, sch 13 para 9(13)
    rep in pt—(W) Learner Travel (W), 2008 nawm 2, s 25, sch 1 para
    4(1)(2)(b)(d)(e), sch 2
s 509AB added—Educ, 2002 c 32, s 199, sch 19, paras 1, 4
    rep in pt—SI 2005/3238 (W 243), arts 7, 9(1), sch 1 paras 31, 35; (W) Learner
    Travel (W), 2008 nawm 2, s 25, sch 1 para 4(1)(3)(a)(c), sch 2; SI 2010/1080,
    art 2, schs 1, 2
    am—Educ and Inspections, 2006 c 40, ss 83(2), 85, sch 10 para 5; Loc Transport,
    2008 c 26, s 77, sch 4 para 60; Educ and Skills, 2008 c 25, s 83; (W) Learner
    Travel (W), 2008 nawm 2, s 25, sch 1 para 4(1)(3)(b); Apprenticeships, Skills,
    Children and Learning, 2009 c 22, ss 55(1), 53, 54 59, sch 2 paras 1, 10(2); SIs
    2010/1080, art 2, sch 1; 1158, art 5, sch 2; Children and Families, 2014 c 6,
    sch 3 para 48
s 509AC added—Educ, 2002 c 32, s 199, sch 19, paras 1, 5
    am—SI 2005/3238 (W 243), arts 7, 9(1), sch 1 paras 31, 36; Educ and Inspections,
    2006 c 40, s 83(3); SI 2010/1080, art 2, sch 1; Equality, 2010 c 15, s 211, sch
    26 para 38; Children and Families, 2014 c 6, sch 3 para 49
    rep in pt—(W) Learner Travel (W), 2008 nawm 2, s 25, sch 1 para 4(1)(4), sch 2;
    SI 2010/1080, art 2, schs 1, 2
s 509AD added—Educ and Inspections, 2006 c 40, s 84

1996

c 56 s 509AD *continued*

am—Educ and Skills, 2008 c 25, s 84; Apprenticeships, Skills, Children and Learning, 2009 c 22, s 57(1)(3)

s 509AE added—Apprenticeships, Skills, Children and Learning, 2009 c 22, s 56(1)(2)

s 510 rep in pt—School Standards and Framework, 1998 c 31, s 140(1)(3), sch 30 para 134(a)-(d), sch 31

am—Educ and Inspections, 2006 c 40, s 6, sch 1 para 5; Educ, 2011 c 21, sch 13 para 9(14)

s 512 replaced by ss 512, 512ZA, 512ZB—(pt prosp) Educ, 2002 c 32, s 201(1); SIs 2002/3185, 2003/124

am—School Standards and Framework, 1998 c 31, s 115(1)(4)(5); ibid, s 115(2)(3); Immigration and Asylum, 1999 c 33, s 169(1), sch 14 para 117; (W prosp) Childcare, 2006 c 21, s 103, sch 2 para 24; Educ and Inspections, 2006 c 40, s 86(2); Healthy Eating in Schools (W), 2009 nawm 3, s 8(2)

appl (mods)—(E) SI 1999/604, art 4; SI 1999/2164, art 4

mod—SIs 1999/610, art 5; 1999/1779, art 4

see—(trans of obligations) (specified schools) SI 1999/610, arts 2, 3

appl—Educ, 2005 c 18, s 110(8)

s 512ZA added—Educ, 2002 c 32, s 201(1)

appl (mods)—SI 1999/2164, reg 4

mod—SI 2004/592, art 2

am—Educ and Inspections, 2006 c 40, s 87(1); Educ, 2011 c 21, s 35(2)

rep in pt—School Standards and Organisation (W), 2013 anaw 1, s 91(2)(a)(b)

s 512ZB added (pt prosp)—Educ, 2002 c 32, s 201(1); SI 2003/124

am—Welfare Reform, 2007 c 5, s 28, sch 3 para 16(1)(3); Child Poverty, 2010 c 9, s 26(1)(a), (b)(i), (ii), (c), (d)(i),(ii),(e),(2),(3); Welfare Reform, 2012 c 5, sch 2 para 39(a)(b); Children and Families, 2014 c 6, s 106(2)

rep in pt—(prosp) Welfare Reform, 2009 c 24, s 58, sch 7 pt 1; Child Poverty, 2010 c 9, s 26(1)(b)(iii), (d)(iii), (2), (3); (prosp) Welfare Reform, 2012 c 5, sch 14 pt 1

s 512ZC added—Healthy Eating in Schools (W), 2009 nawm 3, s 7

s 512A added—School Standards and Framework, 1998 c 31, s 116

see—(W) SI 1999/2802, regs 3(1), 4(1)

am—Educ, 2002 c 32, ss 201(2), 215(1), sch 21, para 52; Educ, 2005 c 18, s 112

rep in pt—School Standards and Organisation (W), 2013 anaw 1, sch 5 para 31(1)

s 512B added—Children and Families, 2014 c 6, s 106(3)

s 514 am—School Standards and Framework, 1998 c 31, s 140(1), sch 30 para 135

s 514A added —Apprenticeships, Skills, Children and Learning, 2009 c 22, s 46

ext—SI 2011/908, art 10, sch 3 para 6

am—Children and Families, 2014 c 6, sch 3 para 50(2)(a)(3)

rep in pt—Children and Families, 2014 c 6, sch 3 para 50(2)(b)

functions made exercisable concurrently—SIs 2014/863, sch 2 para 4; 2014/865, sch 2 para 3

s 515 am—School Standards and Framework, 1998 c 31, s 140(1), sch 30 para 136; Childcare, 2006 c 21, s 103, sch 2 para 25

s 516 rep—School Standards and Framework, 1998 c 31, s 140(1)(3), sch 30, para 137, sch 31

s 517 rep (prosp)—School Standards and Framework, 1998 c 31, s 140(1)(3), sch 30 para 138, sch 31

mod—(temp) SI 1999/2260, reg 2(1)

am—Children and Families, 2014 c 6, sch 3 para 51

s 518 subst—(saving) School Standards and Framework, 1998 c 31, s 129; SI 1999/120, art 3(2)

s 519 am—School Standards and Framework, 1998 c 31, s 140(1), sch 30, para 139(2)(3)(4); SI 2012/976, sch para 6

s 520 rep in pt—School Standards and Framework, 1998 c 31, s 140(1)(3), sch 30 para 140, sch 31

am—(W pt prosp) Health and Social Care (Community Health and Standards), 2003 c 43, s 184, sch 11 para 66; Nat Health Service (Conseq Provns), 2006 c 43, s 2, sch 1 para 184

s 521 rep in pt—School Standards and Framework, 1998 c 31, s 140(1)(3), sch 30 para 141, sch 31

s 524 am—School Standards and Framework, 1998 c 31, s 140(1), sch 30 para 142(a)(c)

1996
c 56 s 524 *continued*

rep in pt—School Standards and Framework, 1998 c 31, s 140(1)(3), sch 30 para
142(b), sch 31

s 525 rep in pt—School Standards and Framework, 1998 c 31, s 140(1)(3), sch 30 para 143,
sch 31

s 527A added—Education, 1997 c 44, s 9
rep—Children, 2004 c 31, s 64, sch 5 pt 1

s 528 rep—Special Educational Needs and Disability, 2001 c 10, ss 34(3), 42(6), sch 9

s 529 am—School Standards and Framework, 1998 c 31, s 140(1), sch 30 para 145; Educ,
2005 c 18, s 72, sch 12 para 2; Educ and Inspections, 2006 c 40, s 30, sch 3 para
10; School Standards and Organisation (W), 2013 anaw 1, sch 5 para
17(5)(a)(b)

rep in pt—Educ and Inspections, 2006 c 40, s 184, sch 18

s 530 am—School Standards and Framework, 1998 c 31, s 140(1), sch 30 para 146; Educ,
2002 c 32, ss 70(9), 215(1), sch 8, para 9(2), sch 21, para 53; Educ, 2005 c 18,
s 72, sch 12 para 3; Educ and Inspections, 2006 c 40, s 30, sch 3 para 11; School
Standards and Organisation (W), 2013 anaw 1, sch 5 para 17(6)

rep in pt—SI 2010/1080, art 2, schs 1, 2

s 531 am—School Standards and Framework, 1998 c 31, s 140(1), sch 30 para 147

s 532 am—Children, 2004 c 31, s 18(9), sch 2 para 4(1)(2)

ss 532A-532C added—Educ, 2011 c 21, s 75(1)
rep —Educ, 2011 c 21, s 75(3)

s 533 am—School Standards and Framework, 1998 c 31, s 140(1), sch 30 para 148; Educ,
2002 c 32, s 215(1), sch 21, para 54; Educ and Inspections, 2006 c 40, s 87(2);
Educ, 2011 c 21, s 35(3)

rep in pt—School Standards and Organisation (W), 2013 anaw 1, s 91(3)(a)(b)

s 534 rep—School Standards and Framework, 1998 c 31, s 140(1)(3),sch 30, para 149, sch
31

s 535 am—School Standards and Framework, 1998 c 31, s 140(1), sch 30 para 150;
Childcare, 2006 c 21, s 103, sch 2 para 26

s 536 rep—School Standards and Framework, 1998 c 31, s 140(1)(3), sch 30 para 151, sch
31

s 537 am—Education, 1997 c 44, s 57(1), sch 7 para 37; School Standards and Framework,
1998 c 31, s 140(1), sch 30 para 152(a); Learning and Skills, 2000 c 21, s 149,
sch 9 para 60; Educ, 2002 c 32, s 65(3), sch 7 pt 2, para 6(1)(5); Educ, 2011 c
21, sch 13 para 9(15)

rep in pt—School Standards and Framework, 1998 c 31, s 140(1)(3), sch 30 para
152(b), sch 31; Educ, 2002 c 32, s 215(2), sch 22 pt 3

s 537A added—Education, 1997 c 44, s 20
subst—School Standards and Framework, 1998 c 31, s 140(1), sch 30, para 153
am—SI 2012/976, sch para 7

s 537AA added (prosp)—Educ and Skills, 2008 c 25, s 169, sch 1 paras 5, 8

s 537B added —Educ and Inspections, 2006 c 40, s 164
mod—SI 2012/1107, art 6(4)

s 537C added—SI 2010/501, reg 5, sch
subst—SI 2011/1726, reg 8
am—Charities, 2011 c 25, sch 7 para 74

s 538 am—School Standards and Framework, 1998 c 31, s 140(1), sch 30 para 154
appl (mods)—(E) SI 2007/2979, reg 3, sch 1

s 538A added—Educ, 2011 c 21, s 20

s 539 rep—School Standards and Framework, 1998 c 31, s 140(1)(3), sch 30 para 155, sch
31

s 540 am—School Standards and Framework, 1998 c 31, s 140(1), sch 30 para 156

s 541 subst—School Standards and Framework, 1998 c 31, s 140(1), sch 30 para 157
am—Learning and Skills, 2000 c 21, s 149, sch 9 para 61; Educ, 2002 c 32, s 65(3),
sch 7 pt 2, para 6(1)(6)

s 542 rep in pt—School Standards and Framework, 1998 c 31, s 140(1)(3), sch 30 paras
158(a)(b), 161, sch 31

am—School Standards and Framework, 1998 c 31, s 140(1), sch 30 para 158(c), sch
31

s 543 am—School Standards and Framework, 1998 c 31, s 140(1), sch 30 para 159(a)(b)

s 544 rep in pt—School Standards and Framework, 1998 c 31, s 140(1)(3), sch 30 para
160(a)(b)(ii),sch 31

am—School Standards and Framework, 1998 c 31, s 140(1), sch 30 para 160(b)(i)

1996
c 56 *continued*

s 545 rep in pt—Educ, 2002 c 32, s 215, sch 21, para 55, sch 22 pt 3

s 546 am—School Standards and Framework, 1998 c 31, s 140(1), sch 30 para 162(a)
    rep in pt—School Standards and Framework, 1998 c 31, s 140(1)(3), sch 30 para
        162(b), sch 31

s 547 rep in pt—School Standards and Framework, 1998 c 31, s 140(1)(3), sch 30 para
        163(a), sch 31
    am—School Standards and Framework, 1998 c 31, s 140(1), sch 30 para 163(b)(c);
        Educ, 2002 c 32, s 206, sch 20, para 1; Educ and Inspections, 2006 c 40, s 6, sch
        1 para 6; SI 2012/976, sch para 8

s 548 subst—School Standards and Framework, 1998 c 31, s 131(1)
    rep in pt—Educ, 2002 c 32, s 215(2), sch 22 pt 3
    am—(W prosp) Childcare, 2006 c 21, s 103, sch 2 para 27; (prosp) Educ and Skills,
        2008 c 25, s 169, sch 1 paras 5, 9

ss 549, 550 rep—School Standards and Framework, 1998 c 31, ss 131(2),140(1)(3), sch 30
        para 164, sch 31

s 550ZA added —Apprenticeships, Skills, Children and Learning, 2009 c 22, s 242(1)
    am—Educ, 2011 c 21, s 2(2)

s 550ZB added —Apprenticeships, Skills, Children and Learning, 2009 c 22, s 242(1)
    am—Educ, 2011 c 21, s 2(3)

s 550ZC added —Apprenticeships, Skills, Children and Learning, 2009 c 22, s 242(1)
    am—Educ, 2011 c 21, s 2(4)

s 550ZD added —Apprenticeships, Skills, Children and Learning, 2009 c 22, s 242(1)
    am—Educ, 2011 c 21, s 2(5)

s 550A added—Education, 1997 c 44, s 4
    rep —Educ and Inspections, 2006 c 40, s 96(a), sch 18

s 550AA added —Violent Crime Reduction, 2006 c 38, s 45
    am—Apprenticeships, Skills, Children and Learning, 2009 c 22, s 243(1)(2)(3)

s 550B added—Education, 1997 c 44, s 5
    rep —Educ and Inspections, 2006 c 40, s 96(a), sch 18
    rep in pt—School Standards and Framework, 1998 c 31, s 140(1)(3), sch 30 para
        165, sch 31
    am—Learning and Skills, 2000 c 21, s 149, sch 9 para 62; Educ, 2002 c 32, s 65(3),
        sch 7 pt 2, para 6(1)(7)

s 551 am—Education, 1997 c 44, s 57(1), sch 7 para 39; School Standards and Framework,
        1998 c 31, s 140(1), sch 30 para 166(a)
    rep in pt—School Standards and Framework, 1998 c 31, s 140(1)(3), sch 30 para
        166(b), sch 31

s 552 rep—School Standards and Framework, 1998 c 31, s 140(1)(3), sch 30 para 167, sch
        31

s 554 am—School Standards and Framework, 1998 c 31, s 140(1), sch 30 para 168

s 556 am—School Standards and Framework, 1998 c 31, s 140(1), sch 30 para 169

s 557 am—School Standards and Framework, 1998 c 31, s 140(1), sch 30 para 170; Educ,
        2002 c 32, s 69; SI 2009/1941, art 2, sch 1; Educ, 2011 c 21, sch 13 para 9(16)
    rep in pt—SI 2009/1941, art 2, sch 1

s 559 am—School Standards and Framework, 1998 c 31, s 140(1), sch 30 para 171; (prosp)
        Crim Justice, 2003 c 44, s 280(2)(3), sch 26 para 49(1)(3)
    rep in pt—SL(R), 2008 c 12, s 1(1), sch 1 pt 11; SL(R), 2008 c 12, s 1, sch 1 pt 11
    appl—SIs (E) 2005/2039, reg 3, sch 1 pt 1 para 3; (E) 2007/2979, reg 3, sch 1; (W)
        2007/1069 (W 109), reg 3, sch 1

s 560 am—School Standards and Framework, 1998 c 31, s 112(2); School Standards and
        Organisation (W), 2013 anaw 1, sch 5 para 2(7)
    rep in pt—School Standards and Framework, 1998 c 31, ss 112(3),140(3), sch 31

s 560A added —Apprenticeships, Skills, Children and Learning, 2009 c 22, s 47
    am—SI 2011/908, art 10, sch 3 para 6; Children and Families, 2014 c 6, sch 3 para
        54
    functions made exercisable concurrently—SIs 2014/863, sch 2 para 4; 2014/865,
        sch 2 para 3

s 561 excl—Educ and Skills, 2008 c 25, s 168(5)

s 562 am—Crim Justice, 2003 c 44, s 304, sch 32 pt 1 para 73; Crim Justice and
        Immigration, 2008 c 4, s 6, sch 4 para 47; (pt prosp) Apprenticeships, Skills,
        Children and Learning, 2009 c 22, s 49(1)-(6)
    excl—Educ and Skills, 2008 c 25, s 168(5); Apprenticeships, Skills, Children and
        Learning, 2009 c 22, s 264(4)

1996
c 56 *continued*

Pt 10, Ch 5A (ss 562A-562J) added (pt prosp)—Apprenticeships, Skills, Children and Learning, 2009 c 22, s 50

s 562C am—Children and Families, 2014 c 6, sch 3 para 55(2)(3)

s 562D am—Children and Families, 2014 c 6, sch 3 para 56

s 562G am—Children and Families, 2014 c 6, sch 3 para 57

s 562H am—Children and Families, 2014 c 6, sch 3 para 58(2)(3)

 rep in pt—Children and Families, 2014 c 6, sch 3 para 58(4)(5)

s 562J power to appl (mods)—Children and Families, 2014 c 6, s 70(7)

s 563 am—School Standards and Framework, 1998 c 31, s 140(1), sch 30 para 172(a)

 rep in pt—School Standards and Framework, 1998 c 31, s 140(1)(3), sch 30 para 172(b), sch 31

s 564 am—SIs 1996/3152, art 2, sch; 1997/2939, art 2, sch; 1998/3171, art 2, sch; 1999/3311, art 2, sch; 2002/3076, art 2, sch; 2010/441, art 2, sch; 2010/1158, art 5, sch 2

s 566 am—School Standards and Framework, 1998 c 31, s 140(1), sch 30 para 173; Children, 2004 c 31, s 18(9), sch 2 para 4(1)(3); Educ, 2005 c 18, s 117, sch 18 para 6; Educ and Skills, 2008 c 25, s 169, sch 1 paras 48, 51; SI 2010/1158, art 5, sch 2

s 567 rep—School Standards and Framework, 1998 c 31, s 140(1)(3), sch 30, para 174, sch 31

s 568 am—School Standards and Framework, 1998 c 31, s 140(1), sch 30 para 175(a); Educ, 2011 c 21, s 75(2)(3)

 rep in pt—School Standards and Framework, 1998 c 31, s 140(1)(3), sch 30 para 175(b)(c), sch 31; Educ, 2002 c 32, s 215(2), sch 22 pt 3

 saving—SI 1999/2323, art 16(3)

s 569 am—School Standards and Framework, 1998 c 31, s 140(1), sch 30 para 176; Apprenticeships, Skills, Children and Learning, 2009 c 22, s 242(2); Educ (W), 2009 nawm 5, s 8; Educ, 2011 c 21, s 2(6); SI 2013/1657 (W 155), art 2(2); Violence against Women, Domestic Abuse and Sexual Violence (W), 2015 anaw 3, s 9(4)

 rep in pt—Educ and Inspections, 2006 c 40, s 184, sch 18

s 569A added—Apprenticeships, Skills, Children and Learning, 2009 c 22, s 59, sch 2 paras 1, 11

s 570 am—School Standards and Framework, 1998 c 31, s 140(1), sch 30 para 177(a)(i)

 rep in pt—School Standards and Framework, 1998 c 31, s 140(1)(3), sch 30 para 177(a)(ii)(b), sch 31

 mod—SI 2013/1721, art 3(3)(f)

s 571 am—Education, 1997 c 44, s 57(1), sch 7 para 41(a)

 rep in pt—Education, 1997 c 44, s 57(1)(4), sch 7 para 41(b), sch 8

 trans of functions—SI 2013/1721, art 2(c)

 mod—SI 2013/1721, art 3(3)(g)

s 572 am—Anti-social Behaviour, 2003 c 38, s 23(2); SI 2004/2521, art 3

 appl—(W) SI 2005/2912 (W 209), reg 4

s 573 rep in pt—School Standards and Framework, 1998 c 31, s 140(1)(3), sch 30 para 178(a)(b), sch 31

s 575 rep—School Standards and Framework, 1998 c 31, s 140(1)(3), sch 30, para 179, sch 31

s 576 am—School Standards and Framework, 1998 c 31, s 140(1), sch 30 para 180(a)

 appl (mods)—School Standards and Framework, 1998 c 31, s 142(10)

 rep in pt—School Standards and Framework, 1998 c 31, s 140(1)(3), sch 30 para 180(b), sch 31

 appl—SIs 2001/600, reg 30(10); (E) 2003/507, reg 5(6); (W) 2004/1576 (W 162), reg 5(7); 2004/3109, reg 2, sch 2 para 2

 excl—SI 2013/2094, sch 1 para 18(3)

s 577 rep—School Standards and Framework, 1998 c 31, s 140(1)(3), sch 30, para 181, sch 31

s 578 am—Education, 1997 c 44, ss 57(1),58(2), sch 7 para 42; Education (Schools), 1997 c 59, ss 6(1)(2),7(2); Education (Student Loans), 1998 c 1, ss 6(1),7(2); Teaching and Higher Educ, 1998 c 30, ss 44(1), 46(2), sch 3, para 15; School Standards and Framework, 1998 c 31, ss 140(1),145(2), sch 30 para 182; (W) Learner Travel (W), 2008 nawm 2, s 29(2); Educ (W), 2011 nawm 7, s 34(2); Children and Families, 2014 c 6, s 140(2); Educ (W), 2014 anaw 5, s 45; Higher Educ (W), 2015 anaw 1, s 60(2); Qualifications Wales, 2015 anaw 5, s 61(2)

1996

c 56 s 578 *continued*

rep in pt—Teaching and Higher Educ, 1998 c 30, s 44(2), sch 4; Educ, 2002 c 32, s 215, sch 21, para 56, sch 22 pts 1,3; Educ, 2005 c 18, ss 61, 123, sch 9 para 9, sch 19 pt 1

appl—Disability Discrimination, 1995 c 50, s 28F(7); SIs (W) 2002/327 (W 40), reg 4(4); (E) 2003/514, reg 2, sch 2 para 2

s 579 am—Education, 1997 c 44, s 57(1), sch 7 para 43; School Standards and Framework, 1998 c 31, s 140(1), sch 30 para 183(a)(i)(iii)(iv); Educ, 2002 c 32, s 215(1), sch 21, para 57; (W) SI 2005/2913 (W 210), reg 4; Nat Health Service (Conseq Provns), 2006 c 43, s 2, sch 1 para 185; Welfare Reform, 2007 c 5, s 28, sch 3 para 16(1)(4); Apprenticeships, Skills, Children and Learning, 2009 c 22, s 59, sch 2 paras 1, 12; Academies, 2010 c 32, s 14, sch 2 para 6; SI 2010/1158, art 3; Educ, 2011 c 21, sch 13 para 9(17); Health and Social Care, 2012 c 7, sch 5 para 80; Children and Families, 2014 c 6, sch 3 para 59

appl—SI 1999/229, reg 2(1); Disability Discrimination, 1995 c 50, sch 4A, para 1(2); SIs 2002/195, reg 17(5)(a); (E) 2003/2045, reg 3; Licensing, 2003 c 17, s 16(3)

rep in pt—School Standards and Framework, 1998 c 31, s 140(1)(3), sch 30 para 183(a)(ii)(b), sch 31; (prosp) Welfare Reform, 2012 c 5, sch 14 pt 1

s 580 am—Education, 1997 c 44, s 57(1), sch 7 para 44; Learning and Skills, 2000 c 21, s 149, sch 9 para 63; (and set out as am) (W) SI 2000/1882, arts 2, 3, 4, sch 2; Educ, 2002 c 32, s 65(3), sch 7 pt 2, para 6(1)(8); Educ, 2005 c 18, s 72, sch 12 para 4; Educ and Inspections, 2006 c 40, s 4(3); (prosp) Educ and Skills, 2008 c 25, s 169, sch 1 paras 5, 10, 11; Apprenticeships, Skills, Children and Learning, 2009 c 22, s 59, sch 2 paras 1, 13; Academies, 2010 c 32, s 14, sch 2 para 7; Children, Schools and Families, 2010 c 26, s 25, sch 3 para 2; SI 2010/1158, art 5, sch 2; Educ, 2011 c 21, sch 13 para 9(18); Children and Families, 2014 c 6, sch 3 para 60

rep in pt—Education (Schools), 1997 c 59, s 6(3), sch pt I; SI 2000/1146, art 3; Educ, 2002 c 32, s 215(2), sch 22 pt 3; SI 2010/1158, art 5, schs 2, 3

s 583 rep in pt—Equality, 2010 c 15, s 211, sch 26 para 39, sch 27 pt 1

sch 1 am—Education, 1997 c 44, s 48; School Standards and Framework, 1998 c 31, s 140(1), sch 30 para 184(a)(i)(ii); Learning and Skills, 2000 c 21, s 149, sch 9 para 64; SIs (E) 2001/2237, arts 2, 32; (E) 2002/2953, reg 2(1); (W) 3184 (W 300), reg 5(6); (W) 808 (W 89), arts 2(q), 31; Apprenticeships, Skills, Children and Learning, 2009 c 22, s 249(3); Educ, 2011 c 21, ss 45(2)(d), 51(4), sch 13 para 9(19); School Standards and Organisation (W), 2013 anaw 1, sch 5 para 2(8)

rep in pt—School Standards and Framework, 1998 c 31, s 140(1)(3), sch 30 para 184(b)(c), sch 31; Educ, 2002 c 32, s 215(2), sch 22 pt 3; (E) SI 2002/2953, reg 2(2); Loc Govt, 2003 c 26, s 127(2), sch 8 pt 1; SI 2008/2840, art 5; Apprenticeships, Skills, Children and Learning, 2009 c 22, ss 223(1)(c), 266, sch 16 pt 7

excl—School Standards and Framework, 1998 c 31, s 45(3)(aa)

schs 2-10 rep—School Standards and Framework, 1998 c 31, s 140(1)(3), sch 30 para 185, sch 31

schs 11-13 rep—School Standards and Framework, 1998 c 31, s 140(1)(3), sch 30 para 185, sch 31

schs 14-16 rep—School Standards and Framework, 1998 c 31, s 140(1)(3), sch 30 para 185, sch 31

sch 17 rep—School Standards and Framework, 1998 c 31, s 140(1)(3), sch 30 para 185, sch 31

sch 18 rep—School Standards and Framework, 1998 c 31, s 140(1)(3), sch 30 para 185, sch 31

sch 19 rep—School Standards and Framework, 1998 c 31, s 140(1)(3), sch 30 para 185, sch 31

sch 20 rep—School Standards and Framework, 1998 c 31, s 140(1)(3), sch 30 para 185, sch 31

sch 21 rep—School Standards and Framework, 1998 c 31, s 140(1)(3), sch 30 para 185, sch 31

sch 22 rep (pt prosp)—School Standards and Framework, 1998 c 31, s 140(1)(3), sch 30 para 185, sch 31

sch 23 rep —(saving) School Standards and Framework, 1998 c 31, s 140(1)(3), sch 30 para 185, sch 31

1996
c 56 *continued*

schs 24,25 rep —School Standards and Framework, 1998 c 31, s 140(1)(3), sch 30 para 185, sch 31

sch 25A added—Education, 1997 c 44, s 8(2), sch 1 (s 8 and sch 1 now rep)
 rep—School Standards and Framework, 1998 c 31, s 140(1)(3), sch 30 paras 208(b), 222(a), sch 31

sch 26 am—Special Educational Needs and Disability, 2001 c 10, s 42(1), sch 8 pt 1 paras 1, 11(2), 14; (savings) Educ and Inspections, 2006 c 40, s 174(2)(4)

sch 27 am—School Standards and Framework, 1998 c 31, s 140(1), sch 30 para 186(2)(a)(b)(3); Special Educational Needs and Disability, 2001 c 10, ss 6, 10, 42(1)(6), sch 1 pt 1 paras 1-5, 7, 8-10, 11-13, 14, 15, 16, sch 8 pt 1 paras 1, 9, 10; Educ, 2002 c 32, s 215(1), sch 21, para 58(a)(b); (savings) Educ and Inspections, 2006 c 40, s 174(3)(4); Educ (W), 2009 nawm 5, s 23, sch 1 paras 1, 5
 appl (mods)—SI 1999/2666, reg 8, sch paras 1(b), 2-4; (W) SI 1999/2800, reg 7, sch paras 1, 2-8
 rep in pt—Special Educational Needs and Disability, 2001 c 10, ss 10, 42(6), sch 1 pt 1 paras 1, 6, 15, 16, 17, sch 9
 excl—(prosp) Nationality, Immigration and Asylum, 2002 c 41, s 36(5)(e)(10)

sch 28 rep—School Standards and Framework, 1998 c 31, s 140(1)(3), sch 30 para 187, sch 31

sch 29 rep—Education, 1997 c 44, s 57(4), sch 8

sch 30 rep and superseded—Education, 1997 c 44, ss 27(5),57(4), schs 5,8

sch 31 rep in pt—School Standards and Framework, 1998 c 31, s 140(1)(3), sch 30 para 188, sch 31

schs 32, 33 rep—School Standards and Framework, 1998 c 31, s 140(1)(3), sch 30 para 189(a)(b), sch 31

sch 33A added—Education, 1997 c 44, s 12(2), sch 2
 rep—School Standards and Framework, 1998 c 31, s 140(1)(3), sch 30 para 189(c), sch 31

sch 33B added—Education, 1997 c 44, s 14(2), sch 3
 rep—School Standards and Framework, 1998 c 31, s 140(1)(3), sch 30 para 189(d), sch 31

sch 34 rep—Educ, 2002 c 32, s 215(2), sch 22 pt 3

sch 35 rep—Educ (Schools), 1997 c 59, ss 1(1)c)(3),6(3), sch pt I

sch 35A added—Educ, 2002 c 32, s 65(3), sch 7 pt 1
 rep—Educ, 2011 c 21, sch 14 para 17

sch 35B added—Educ and Inspections, 2006 c 40, s 77, sch 8
 am—Educ and Skills, 2008 c 25, s 169, sch 1 paras 48, 52; Equality, 2010 c 15, s 211, sch 26 para 40; Educ, 2011 c 21, sch 1 para 7, sch 13 para 9(20); Children and Families, 2014 c 6, sch 3 para 61

sch 35C added—Educ and Inspections, 2006 c 40, s 78, sch 9
 am—Equality, 2010 c 15, s 211, sch 26 para 41
 appl (mods)—(E) SI 2007/1367, reg 2

sch 36 am—Educ, 2005 c 18, s 61, sch 9 para 10
 appl—SI 2007/2812, art 5, sch

sch 36A added—SI 2010/1158, arts 3, 5, schs 1, 4
 am—Equality, 2010 c 15, s 211, sch 26 para 42(3); Children and Families, 2014 c 6, sch 3 para 62(2); Qualifications Wales, 2015 anaw 5, sch 4 para 1(3)(b)
 rep in pt—Equality, 2010 c 15, s 211, sch 26 para 42(2), sch 27 pt 1; Children and Families, 2014 c 6, sch 3 para 62(3); Qualifications Wales, 2015 anaw 5, sch 4 para 1(3)(a)

sch 37 rep in pt—Education, 1997 c 44, s 57(4), sch 8; Audit Commission, 1998 c 18, s 54(3), sch 5; (prosp) Teaching and Higher Educ, 1998 c 30, s 44(2), sch 4; School Standards and Framework, 1998 c 31, s 140(1)(3), sch 30 para 189(e), sch 31; Powers of Crim Cts (Sentencing), 2000 c 6, s 165(3)(4), sch 11 pt I para 2, sch 12 pt I; Care Standards, 2000 c 14, s 117(2), sch 6; Learning and Skills, 2000 c 21, s 153, sch 11; Loc Govt, 2000 c 22, s 107, sch 6; Race Relations (Amdt), 2000 c 34, s 9(2), sch 3; Special Educational Needs and Disability, 2001 c 10, ss 38(14), 42(1)(6), sch 8 pt 1 paras 1, 4, sch 9; Educ, 2002 c 32, s 215(2), sch 22 pt 3; SI 2003/1398, art 2, sch para 25; SL(R), 2004 c 14, s 1(1), sch 1 pts 2/2, 10/2; (prosp) Sustainable and Secure Buildings, 2004 c 22, s 11(2), sch; Educ, 2005 c 18, s 123, sch 19 pt 3; Nat Health Service (Conseq Provns), 2006 c 43, s 6, sch 4; SI 2010/1158, art 5, sch 3;

1996
c 56 *continued*

Equality, 2010 c 15, s 211, sch 27 pt 1; Charities, 2011 c 25, sch 10; Children
and Young People (S), 2014 asp 8, sch 5 para 6
sch 39 appl—School Standards and Framework, 1998 c 31, s 142(8)(9)
rep in pt—School Standards and Framework, 1998 c 31, s 140(1)(3), sch 30 para
189(f), sch 31
am—SI 2010/1158, art 5, sch 2
sch 40 rep—School Standards and Framework, 1998 c 31, s 140(1)(3), sch 30, para 189(g),
sch 31
c 57   *School Inspections*—rep Educ, 2005 c 18, ss 60, 123, sch 19 pt 1; for trans provns and
savings, see SI 2005/2034, art 10, sch and SI 2006/1338, art 6, sch 4
c 58   **Deer (Scotland)**
am—Public Services Reform (S), 2010 asp 8, s 1, sch 1 paras 5, 6
trans of functions—Public Services Reform (S), 2010 asp 8, s 1(1)
Pt 1 (ss 1-4) am—Public Services Reform (S), 2010 asp 8, s 1, sch 1 paras 5, 7
s 1 am—Public Services Reform (S), 2010 asp 8, s 1, sch 1 paras 5, 8(1)-(4); Wildlife and
Natural Environment (S), 2011 asp 6, s 26(2)
rep in pt—Public Services Reform (S), 2010 asp 8, s 1, sch 1 paras 5, 8(5)
s 2 am—Public Services Reform (S), 2010 asp 8, s 1, sch 1 paras 5, 9(a)
rep in pt—Public Services Reform (S), 2010 asp 8, s 1, sch 1 paras 5, 9(b)
s 3 am—Public Services Reform (S), 2010 asp 8, s 1, sch 1 paras 5, 10; Wildlife and
Natural Environment (S), 2011 asp 6, s 26(3)
s 4 am—Public Services Reform (S), 2010 asp 8, s 1, sch 1 paras 5, 11; Wildlife and
Natural Environment (S), 2011 asp 6, s 26(4)
s 5 am—Public Services Reform (S), 2010 asp 8, s 1, sch 1 paras 5, 12; Wildlife and
Natural Environment (S), 2011 asp 6, s 29(2)(a)(i); ibid, s 29(2)(a)(ii)(b)
s 5A added—Wildlife and Natural Environment (S), 2011 asp 6, s 27(1)
s 7 am—Public Services Reform (S), 2010 asp 8, s 1, sch 1 paras 5, 13; Wildlife and
Natural Environment (S), 2011 asp 6, s 28(2)
s 8 am—Public Services Reform (S), 2010 asp 8, s 1, sch 1 paras 5, 14; Wildlife and
Natural Environment (S), 2011 asp 6, s 28(3)(a)(b)(d)
rep in pt—Wildlife and Natural Environment (S), 2011 asp 6, s 28(3)(c)
s 9 am—Public Services Reform (S), 2010 asp 8, s 1, sch 1 paras 5, 15
s 10 am—SSI 2006/367, art 3; Public Services Reform (S), 2010 asp 8, s 1, sch 1 paras 5,
16; Wildlife and Natural Environment (S), 2011 asp 6, s 28(4)
s 11 am—Public Services Reform (S), 2010 asp 8, s 1, sch 1 paras 5, 17; Wildlife and
Natural Environment (S), 2011 asp 6, s 28(5)
s 12 am—Public Services Reform (S), 2010 asp 8, s 1, sch 1 paras 5, 18
s 15 am—SSI 2006/367, art 3; Public Services Reform (S), 2010 asp 8, s 1, sch 1 paras 5,
19
s 16 am—SSI 2006/367, art 3; Public Services Reform (S), 2010 asp 8, s 1, sch 1 paras 5,
20
s 17 am—Wildlife and Natural Environment (S), 2011 asp 6, s 30(2)
rep in pt—Wildlife and Natural Environment (S), 2011 asp 6, s 30(3)
ss 17A, 17B added—Wildlife and Natural Environment (S), 2011 asp 6, s 30(4)
s 18 am—Public Services Reform (S), 2010 asp 8, s 1, sch 1 paras 5, 21; Wildlife and
Natural Environment (S), 2011 asp 6, ss 26(5), 30(5)
s 25 am—Wildlife and Natural Environment (S), 2011 asp 6, s 31(2)
s 26 am—SSI 2006/367, art 3; Crofting Reform etc., 2007 asp 7, s 39, sch 1 para 4;
Wildlife and Natural Environment (S), 2011 asp 6, s 29(3)
s 29 am—Wildlife and Natural Environment (S), 2011 asp 6, s 32(2)
s 29A added—Wildlife and Natural Environment (S), 2011 asp 6, s 32(3)
s 30 am—Wildlife and Natural Environment (S), 2011 asp 6, s 30(6)
s 31 am—Wildlife and Natural Environment (S), 2011 asp 6, s 30(7)
s 34 am—SSI 2006/367, art 3
s 37 am—SSI 2006/367, art 3; Public Services Reform (S), 2010 asp 8, s 1, sch 1 paras 5,
22; Wildlife and Natural Environment (S), 2011 asp 6, s 29(4)
s 38 rep —Wildlife and Natural Environment (S), 2011 asp 6, sch pt 2
s 39 am—Public Services Reform (S), 2010 asp 8, s 1, sch 1 paras 5, 23
s 40 am—SSI 2006/367, art 3; Public Services Reform (S), 2010 asp 8, s 1, sch 1 paras 5,
24
s 44 am—Wildlife and Natural Environment (S), 2011 asp 6, s 41(5)
s 45 am—Wildlife and Natural Environment (S), 2011 asp 6, ss 27(2), 30(8)
s 46 rep—Public Services Reform (S), 2010 asp 8, s 1, sch 1 paras 5, 25

1996

c 58 *continued*

    sch 1 rep—(with savings) Public Services Reform (S), 2010 asp 8, s 1, sch 1 paras 5, 26

    sch 2 am—Public Services Reform (S), 2010 asp 8, s 1, sch 1 paras 5, 27; Wildlife and
        Natural Environment (S), 2011 asp 6, s 28(6)(a)-(f)(h)(i)

    rep in pt—Wildlife and Natural Environment (S), 2011 asp 6, s 28(6)(g)

    sch 3 am—Nature Conservation (S), 2004 asp 6, s 57, sch 7 para 11; Wildlife and Natural
        Environment (S), 2011 asp 6, s 30(9)

c 59   *Public Order (Amendment)* —rep Serious Organised Crime and Police, 2005 c 15, s 174(2),
        sch 17 pt 2

c 60   *Consolidated Fund (No 2)*—rep Appropriation, 1998 c 28, s 3, sch(C)

c 61   **Channel Tunnel Rail Link**

    appl—SI 1999/107, reg 1(2)

    trans of functions—SI 1997/2971, art 3(3)(b)(4)(5)

    trans of obligations—SI 1999/391, art 2(2)(5)

    saved—SI 2002/1943, art 11

    s 1 rep in pt—SI 1999/537L, art 16

    ss 7, 8 appl (mods)—SIs 1999/537L, art 13(1), sch 3 paras 1-8; 2001/1451L, art 15(1), sch
        3 paras 1-7

    s 8 appl—SI 2002/1943, art 15(1)-(3)

    s 9 excl—SI 1999/107, reg 3

    s 11 am—SI 1997/2971, art 6(1), sch paras 25,26(a)(b)

    rep in pt—SI 1997/2971, art 6(1), sch paras 25,26(c)

    s 14 appl (mods)—SI 2001/1451L, art 15(1), sch 3 paras 1-7

    s 17 am —Railways and Transport Safety, 2003 c 20, s 16, sch 2 pt 2 para 19(o); SI
        2015/1682, sch pt 1 para 4(l)(i)

    rep in pt—Channel Tunnel Rail Link (Supplementary Provns), 2008 c 5, s 2

    s 19 am—Transport, 2000 c 38, s 215, sch 16 para 56

    rep in pt—Railways, 2005 c 14, s 59, sch 13 pt 1

    s 21 am—Competition, 1998 c 41, s 66(5), sch 10 pt IV para 16(2); Enterprise, 2002 c 40, s
        278(1), sch 25, para 35(1)(2); Railways and Transport Safety, 2003 c 20, s 16,
        sch 2 pt 2 paras 19(o), 20, 22; SIs 2014/892, sch 1 para 114; 2015/1682, sch pt 1
        para 4(l)(ii)(iii)

    rep in pt—Channel Tunnel Rail Link (Supplementary Provns), 2008 c 5, s 3

    s 21A added—Channel Tunnel Rail Link (Supplementary Provns), 2008 c 5, s 4

    am—SI 2015/1682, sch pt 1 para 4(l)(iv)

    s 22 rep—SI 2005/3049, reg 2(4), sch 1 pt 1 para 6

    s 23 rep—SI 2000/311, art 31(2)

    s 24 rep—SI 2003/1398, art 2, sch para 24(1)(3)

    s 25 rep—SI 2000/311, art 31(2)

    s 26 rep—SI 2003/1398, art 2, sch para 24(1)(3)

    ss 27-30 appl (mods)—SIs 1999/537L, art 13(1), sch 3 paras 1-8; 2001/1451L, art 15(1),
        sch 3 paras 1-7

    s 29 rep in pt—SI 1997/2971, art 6(1), sch paras 25, 27

    see—(trans of functions) SI 2001/2568, art 5

    am—SIs 2001/2568, art 16, sch para 15(1)(2); 2002/2626, art 20, sch 2, para 21(1)(2)

    s 34 appl—SIs 1999/537L, art 15(2); 2001/1451L, art 18(2); 2002/1943, art 16(2)

    ss 37, 39, 40 appl (mods)—SI 2001/1451L, art 15(1), sch 3 paras 1-7

    s 42A added—Transport, 2000 c 38, s 252, sch 27 para 55

    s 43 appl (mods)—SIs 1999/537L, art 13(1), sch 3 paras 1-8; 2001/1451L, art 15(1), sch 3
        paras 1-7

    rep in pt—SI 1997/2971, art 6(1), sch paras 25, 28

    s 50 am—SIs 1997/2971, art 6(1), sch paras 25, 29; 2001/2568, art 16, sch para 15(1)(3);
        2002/2626, art 20, sch 2, para 21(1)(3); 2007/3224, art 15, sch; 2009/229, art 9,
        sch 2

    appl (mods)—SI 2001/1451L, art 15(1), sch 3 paras 1-7

    trans of functions—SI 2009/229, art 4, sch 1(f)

    s 54 appl (mods)—SIs 1999/537L, art 13(1), sch 3 paras 1-8; 2001/1451L, art 15(1), sch 3
        paras 1-7

    appl—SI 2002/1943, art 15(4)

    s 56 am—Channel Tunnel Rail Link (Supplementary Provns), 2008 c 5, s 5

    sch 2 appl (mods)—SIs 1999/537L, art 13(1), sch 3 paras 1-8; 2001/1451L, art 15(1), sch 3
        paras 1-7

    appl—SI 2002/1943, art 15(1)-(3)

    am—Localism, 2011 c 20, sch 22 para 43

1996
c 61 *continued*

sch 3 am—GLA, 1999 c 29, s 328(8), sch 29 pt I para 61; SIs 2001/2568, art 16, sch para 15(1)(4); 2002/2626, art 20, sch 2, para 21(1)(4)

appl (mods)—SIs 1999/537L, art 13(1), sch 3 paras 1-8; 2001/1451L, art 15(1), sch 3 paras 1-7

am—SI 1997/2971, art 6(1), sch paras 25, 30

rep in pt—SIs 1997/2971, art 6(1), sch paras 25, 30; 1999/537L, art 16

see—(trans of functions) SI 2001/2568, art 5

sch 4 appl (mods)—SIs 1999/537L, art 13(1), sch 3 paras 1-8; 2001/1451L, art 15(1), sch 3 paras 1-7

am—Tribunals, Cts and Enforcement, 2007 c 15, s 139, sch 22 para 9; SI 2009/1307, art 5, sch 1

sch 5 appl (mods)—SIs 1999/537L, art 13(1), sch 3 paras 1-8; 2001/1451L, art 15(1), sch 3 paras 1-7

rep in pt and am—SI 1997/2971, art 6(1), sch paras 25, 31

sch 6 am—SIs 1997/2971, art 6(1), sch paras 25, 32; 1999/416, art 3, sch 1 para 18(2); Countryside and Rights of Way, 2000 c 37, s 73(4), sch 8 para 1(u); Communications, 2003 c 21, s 406(1), sch 17 para 138; SIs 2003/1900, arts 2(1), 3(1), sch 1; 3142, art 3(2); Natural Environment and Rural Communities, 2006 c 16, s 105, sch 11 para 147

rep in pt —SI 1997/2971, art 6(1), sch paras 25, 32

sch 7 am—SIs 1997/1744, art 2(2), sch para 6; 2971, art 6(1), sch paras 25, 33; 2001/2568, art 16, sch para 15(1)(5); 2002/2626, art 20, sch 2, para 21(1)(5); 2012/2590, sch para 2

sch 9 appl (mods)—SIs 1999/537L, art 13(1), sch 3 paras 1-8; 2001/1451L, art 15(1), sch 3 paras 1-7

am—Transport, 2000 c 38, s 252, sch 27 para 56

rep in pt—SL(R), 2013 c 2, s 1, sch 1 pt 9 Group 3(2)

sch 10 appl (mods)—SIs 1999/537L, art 13(1), sch 3 paras 1-8; 2001/1451L, art 15(1), sch 3 paras 1-7

am—Countryside and Rights of Way, 2000 c 37, s 76(1), sch 10 pt II para 11; SI 2001/1451L; art 15(1), sch 3 paras 1-7

appl—SI 2002/1943, art 15(1)-(3)

sch 14 am—SI 1999/416, art 3, sch 1 para 18(3); Countryside and Rights of Way, 2000 c 37, s 73(4), sch 8 para 1(u); SIs 2001/2568, art 16, sch para 15(1)(6); 2002/2626, art 20, sch 2, para 21(1)(6); Natural Environment and Rural Communities, 2006 c 16, s 105, sch 11 para 148; SIs 2007/3224, art 15, sch; 2009/229, art 9, sch 2

rep in pt and am—SI 1997/2971, art 6(1), sch paras 25, 34

trans of functions—SI 2009/229, art 4, sch 1(g)

appl (mods)—SI 2001/1451L, art 15(1), sch 3 paras 1-7

sch 15 appl (mods)—SIs 1999/537L, art 13(1), sch 3 paras 1-8; 2001/1451L, art 15(1), sch 3 paras 1-7

rep in pt—SI 1997/2971, art 6(1), sch paras 25, 35-37; Communications, 2003 c 21, s 406(7), sch 19(1); SIs 2003/1900, arts 2(1), 3(1), sch 1; 3142, art 3(2); 2012/1659, sch 3 para 14(3)(a)

am—SIs 1997/2971, art 6(1), sch paras 25, 35-37; 2001/2568, art 16, sch para 15(1)(7); 2002/2626, art 20, sch 2, para 21(1)(7); Communications, 2003 c 21, s 406(1), sch 17 para 139(1)-(4); SIs 2003/1900, arts 2(1), 3(1), sch 1; 3142, art 3(2); 2007/3224, art 15, sch; 2009/229, art 9, sch 2; 2012/1659, sch 3 para 14(2)(3)(b)

appl—SI 2002/1943, art 15(1)-(3)

trans of functions—SI 2009/229, art 4, sch 1(h)

c 62 **Theft (Amendment)**

s 1 rep—Fraud, 2006 c 35, s 14, sch 3

s 3 rep in pt—Fraud, 2006 c 35, s 14, sch 3

s 4 rep—Fraud, 2006 c 35, s 14, sch 3

5th Session of 51st Parliament
c 63 **Hong Kong Economic and Trade Office**

1997

c 1 *Horserace Totalisator Board*—rep Horserace Betting and Olympic Lottery, 2004 c 25, s 38, sch 6

1997

c 2   **Land Registration**
        ss 1-3 rep—Land Registration, 2002 c 9, s 135, sch 13
        s 5 rep in pt—Land Registration, 2002 c 9, s 135, sch 13
        sch 1 rep in pt—Land Registration, 2002 c 9, s 135, sch 13

c 3   **Sea Fisheries (Shellfish)(Amendment)**
        s 1 rep —Marine and Coastal Access, 2009 c 23, s 321, sch 22 pt 5(A)

c 4   *Telecommunications (Fraud)*—rep Communications, 2003 c 21, s 406(7), sch 19(1); SI
                2003/1900, arts 2(1), 3(1), sch 1; 3142, art 3(2)

c 5   **Firearms (Amendment)**
        s 1 excl—SI 1997/1535, art 5
            rep in pt—Firearms (Amdt)(No 2), 1997 c 64, s 2(7), sch
            am—Anti-social Behaviour, Crime and Policing, 2014 c 12, s 108(9)
        s 2 am—SI 1999/1750, art 6(1), sch 5 para 18; Anti-social Behaviour, Crime and Policing,
            2014 c 12, s 109(3)(a)
        s 3 am—SI 1999/1750, art 6(1), sch 5 para 18; Anti-social Behaviour, Crime and Policing,
            2014 c 12, s 109(3)(a)
        s 4 am—SI 1999/1750, art 6(1), sch 5 para 18; Anti-social Behaviour, Crime and Policing,
            2014 c 12, s 109(3)(a)
        s 5 am—SI 1999/1750, art 6(1), sch 5 para 18; Anti-social Behaviour, Crime and Policing,
            2014 c 12, s 109(3)(a)
        s 6 am—SI 1999/1750, art 6(1), sch 5 para 18; Anti-social Behaviour, Crime and Policing,
            2014 c 12, s 109(3)(a)
        s 7 see—(trans of functions) SI 1999/1750, art 2, sch 1
            am—SI 1999/1750, art 6(1), sch 5 para 18; Anti-social Behaviour, Crime and Policing,
            2014 c 12, s 109(3)(a)(b)
        s 8 am—SI 1999/1750, art 6(1), sch 5 para 18; Anti-social Behaviour, Crime and Policing,
            2014 c 12, s 109(3)(a)
        ss 11-14 rep—Firearms (Amdt)(No 2), 1997 c 64, s 2(7), sch
        s 15 am—Firearms (Amdt)(No 2), 1997 c 64, s 2(2)
        s 16 am—Firearms (Amdt)(No 2), 1997 c 64, s 2(3)
        s 17 am—Firearms (Amdt)(No 2), 1997 c 64, s 2(4)
        s 18 am—Firearms (Amdt)(No 2), 1997 c 64, s 2(5)
        ss 19-31 rep—Firearms (Amdt)(No 2), 1997 c 64, s 2(7), sch
        s 33 am—SI 2011/713, art 4(2)
        s 34 am—SI 2011/713, art 4(3)
        s 35 am—SI 2011/713, art 4(4)
        s 35A added—SI 2011/713, art 4(5)
            appl—SI 2013/602, sch 2 para 26
        s 39 am—SI 2015/860, reg 2(2)-(4)
        s 45 rep in pt—Firearms (Amdt)(No 2), 1997 c 64, s 2(7), sch
        s 46 rep—Firearms (Amdt)(No 2), 1997 c 64, s 2(7), sch
        ss 49,50 rep in pt—Firearms (Amdt)(No 2), 1997 c 64, s 2(7), sch
        s 51 ext—Firearms (Amdt)(No 2), 1997 c 64, s 2(6)
        sch 1 rep—Firearms (Amdt)(No 2), 1997 c 64, s 2(7), sch
        sch 2 rep in pt—Firearms (Amdt)(No 2), 1997 c 64, s 2(7), sch

c 6   **Local Government (Gaelic Names) (Scotland)**
c 7   **Northern Ireland Arms Decommissioning**
        s 2 am—NI Arms Decommissioning (Amdt), 2002 c 6, s 1; NI (Misc Provns), 2006 c 33, s
            21
        s 4 mod—Terrorism, 2000 c 11, s 125(1), sch 15 para 15(3)
        sch am—Terrorism, 2000 c 11, s 125(1), sch 15 para 15(1)(2)

c 8   **Town and Country Planning (Scotland)**
        see—SI 1999/677, art 2(1)(2)(4)(a)(5); (trans and exercise of cert funtions) SSI 2003/1,
            art 7(1)-(8)
        am—Planning (Listed Buildings and Conservation Areas) (S), 1997 c 9, s 81(4); Planning
            (Conseq Provns)(S), 1997 c 11, s 5, sch 3 para 8
        cont—SSI 2010/60, regs 5, 10
        appl—Finance, 1931 c 28, sch 2 para 2(b); Planning (Listed Buildings and Conservation
            Areas) (S), 1997 c 9, s 81(2)(3)(6); Planning (Hazardous Substances) (S), 1997 c 10,
            s 38(2); Planning (Conseq Provns)(S), 1997 c 11, s 1(2); City of Edinburgh (Guided
            Busways) O Conf, 1998 c iii, s 1, sch O, s 30(3); Railtrack (Waverley Station) O
            Conf, 2000 c vi, s 1, sch, s 6(1) of O; Finance, 2003 c 14, ss 61(3), 66(4);
            Stirling-Alloa-Kincardine Railway and Linked Improvements, 2004 asp 10, s 33(1);
            Licensing (S), 2005 asp 16, s 50(8); SSI 2005/489(L), art 15; Airdrie-Bathgate

1997
c 8 *continued*

Railway and Linked Improvements, 2007 asp 19, s 43(1); Glasgow Airport Rail Link, 2007 asp 1, s 38(1); Edinburgh Airport Rail Link, 2007 asp 16, s 43(1); SSIs 2008/188, art 53; 189, art 53; 190, art 53; Forth Crossing, 2011 asp 2, s 62(3)
appl (mods)—Stirling-Alloa-Kincardine Railway and Linked Improvements, 2004 asp 10, s 29, sch 9 paras 1-3, 6
excl—Planning (Listed Buildings and Conservation Areas) (S), 1997 c 9, s 45(4)
power to mod—Planning (Listed Buildings and Conservation Areas) (S), 1997 c 9, s 67(8)(9)
mod—Planning (Listed Buildings and Conservation Areas) (S), 1997 c 9, s 64(2)(a); SSI 2011/347, art 15(a)
saved—SSI 2002/410(L), art 57(3);
s 1 am—Planning etc. (S), 2006 asp 17, s 54(2)
Pt 1A (ss 3A-3D) added—Planning etc. (S), 2006 asp 17, s 1
s 3A mod—SSI 2011/228, sch 4 para 9
Pt 2 (ss 4-25) replaced by Pt 2 (ss 3E-25)—Planning etc. (S), 2006 asp 17, s 2
    power to appl—Nat Parks (S), 2000 asp 10, s 10(1)(b)
    transtl provns—SSI 2008/427, arts 2-5)
s 3F added —Climate Change (S), 2009 asp 12, s 72
s 6 excl—Edinburgh Tram (Line Two), 2006 asp 6, s 72(1)(a)(2)(a); Edinburgh Tram (Line One), 2006 asp 7, s 73(1)(a)(2)(a)
s 7 mod—SSI 2011/228, sch 4 para 9
s 15 mod—SSI 2011/228, sch 4 para 9
s 26 am—SSI 1999/1, reg 47; Water Environment and Water Services (S), 2003 asp 3, s 24(1)(2)(a)(i)(ii)(b)(iii)(v); SSI 2003/341, regs 2, 5; Planning and Compulsory Purchase, 2004 c 5, s 118(2), sch 7 para 20(1)(2); (pt prosp) Planning etc. (S), 2006 asp 17, s 3; SSI 2007/268, art 8; Marine (S), 2010 asp 5, s 63(2); SSI 2011/209, sch 11 paras 1, 5
    ext—SSI 1999/1, reg 44
    appl—Finance, 2003 c 14, s 60(5)(b); SSI 2007/268, art 14
    rep in pt—Water Environment and Water Services (S), 2003 asp 3, s 24(1)(2)(a)(iv)
    excl—SSI 2007/268, art 14
s 26AA added—Planning etc. (S), 2006 asp 17, s 4
    appl (mods)—SSI 2007/268, art 14
s 26AB added —Marine (S), 2010 asp 5, s 63(3)
s 26A added—Planning etc. (S), 2006 asp 17, s 5
s 27 am—SSI 2007/268, art 8
ss 27A-27CA added —Planning etc. (S), 2006 asp 17, s 6
s 28 am—Planning, 2008 c 29, s 36, sch 2 paras 54, 55
s 30 am—Planning etc. (S), 2006 asp 17, s 54(3)
s 31 ext—SSI 1999/1, reg 46
s 31A added—Planning etc. (S), 2006 asp 17, s 4
    appl (mods)—SSI 2007/268, art 14
    am—Aquaculture and Fisheries (S), 2013 asp 7, s 23(2)(3)(4)(b)
    rep in pt—Aquaculture and Fisheries (S), 2013 asp 7, s 23(4)(a)
s 32 subst —Planning etc. (S), 2006 asp 17, s 7
ss 32A, 32B added —Planning etc. (S), 2006 asp 17, s 8
s 33 am—Planning etc. (S), 2006 asp 17, s 54(4)
s 33A added—Planning etc. (S), 2006 asp 17, s 9
s 34 subst—Planning etc. (S), 2006 asp 17, s 10
    excl—Edinburgh Tram (Line One), 2006 asp 7, s 73(1)(b)(2)(b)
s 35 am—Agricultural Holdings (S), 2003 asp 11, s 94, sch para 51(a)(b)
ss 35A-35C added —Planning etc. (S), 2006 asp 17, s 11
    am—SSI 2013/25, art 2(2)
s 36 am—Planning etc. (S), 2006 asp 17, s 12; SSIs 2007/268, art 8; 2009/256, art 2
    appl (mods)—SSI 2011/139, reg 33(17)(b)(i)
s 36A added —Planning etc. (S), 2006 asp 17, s 13
s 37 am—Planning etc. (S), 2006 asp 17, s 54(5)
s 38 am—Planning etc. (S), 2006 asp 17, s 10
    mod—Edinburgh Tram (Line One), 2006 asp 7, s 73(1)(c)(2)(c); Edinburgh Tram (Line Two), 2006 asp 6, s 72(1)(c)(2)(c)
s 38A added—Planning etc. (S), 2006 asp 17, s 14
s 39 am—Planning etc. (S), 2006 asp 17, s 15; SSI 2013/26, art 2(2)
    rep in pt—Planning etc. (S), 2006 asp 17, s 15

1997
c 8 *continued*

s 40 am—Water Environment and Water Services (S), 2003 asp 3, s 24(1)(3)
ss 41, 42 rep in pt—Planning etc. (S), 2006 asp 17, s 56, sch
s 43 am—Planning etc. (S), 2006 asp 17, s 16
ss 43A, 43B added —Planning etc. (S), 2006 asp 17, s 17
　　　am—SSIs 2013/24, art 2(2); 2013/26, art 2(3)
s 45 rep—Planning etc. (S), 2006 asp 17, s 56, sch
s 46 rep in pt—Planning etc. (S), 2006 asp 17, s 56, sch
　　　am—Planning etc. (S), 2006 asp 17, s 18; SSI 2013/26, art 2(4)
s 47 mod—SSI 1999/1, reg 45
　　　see—SSI 1999/1, regs 9(1), 16(1)
　　　appl—SSI 2006/269, art 3
　　　am—Planning etc. (S), 2006 asp 17, s 19
　　　appl (mods)—SI 1984/467, reg 21(1)(1A) (subst by SSI 2013/154, reg 2(4)(a))
s 47A added —Planning etc. (S), 2006 asp 17, s 19
s 48 rep in pt—Planning etc. (S), 2006 asp 17, s 56, sch
　　　appl (mods)—SI 1984/467, reg 21(1)(1A) (subst by SSI 2013/154, reg 2(4)(a))
s 49 mod—Edinburgh Tram (Line One), 2006 asp 7, s 73(1)(d)(2)(d)
s 53 excl—Edinburgh Tram (Line One), 2006 asp 7, s 73(7); Edinburgh Tram (Line Two),
　　　2006 asp 6, s 72(7)
s 54 am—Nature Conservation (S), 2004 asp 6, s 57, sch 7 para 12(1)
s 55 am—SSI 2006/243, art 4
s 57 am—Transport and Works (S), 2007 asp 8, s 15(1); Flood Risk Management (S), 2009
　　　asp 6, s 65; Growth and Infrastructure, 2013 c 27, s 21(5)(6)
s 58 am—Planning etc. (S), 2006 asp 17, s 20
s 59 subst —Planning etc. (S), 2006 asp 17, s 21
　　　am—SSI 2013/26, art 2(5)
s 60 am—Planning etc. (S), 2006 asp 17, s 22; SSI 2009/256, art 2
　　　rep in pt—Planning etc. (S), 2006 asp 17, s 22; SSI 2009/256, art 2
s 61 am—Planning etc. (S), 2006 asp 17, s 22
s 65 am—SSI 2006/243, art 4
s 66 excl—Edinburgh Tram (Line Two), 2006 asp 6, s 72(5)
s 67 rep in pt—(prosp) Planning etc (S), 2006 asp 17, s 56, sch
　　　am—SSI 2006/243, art 4
s 71 am—SSI 2006/243, art 4; Planning etc (S), 2006 asp 17, s 22
s 75 subst—Planning etc (S), 2006 asp 17, s 23
　　　appl—SSI 2010/431, art 3(1) (am by SSI 2011/348, art 2(2))
　　　excl—SSI 2010/431, art 3(2) (am by SSI 2011/348, art 2(2))
s 75A added —Planning etc (S), 2006 asp 17, s 23
　　　appl—SSI 2010/431, art 3(1) (am by SSI 2011/348, art 2(2))
s 75B added —Planning etc (S), 2006 asp 17, s 23
　　　appl—SSI 2010/431, art 3(1) (am by SSI 2011/348, art 2(2))
s 75C added —Planning etc (S), 2006 asp 17, s 23
　　　saving—SSI 2010/431, art 3
　　　excl—SSI 2010/431, art 3(2) (am by SSI 2011/348, art 2(2))
ss 75D-75G added —Planning etc (S), 2006 asp 17, s 24
Pt 4 (ss 76-87) appl (mods)—SSI 2010/60, reg 31; SI 2010/490, regs 89, 93
s 77 am—SSI 2006/243, art 4
s 83 mod—SI 1998/2914, reg 6; (conditionally) ibid, reg 5
s 85 ext—Planning (Listed Buildings and Conservation Areas) (S), 1997 c 9, s 79(1)
　　　mod—Planning (Hazardous Substances) (S), 1997 c 10, ss 14(5),31
　　　appl—Planning (Hazardous Substances) (S), 1997 c 10, s 36
s 86 mod—Planning (Hazardous Substances) (S), 1997 c 10, ss 14(5),31
　　　appl—Planning (Hazardous Substances) (S), 1997 c 10, s 35(3)
s 87 mod—Planning (Hazardous Substances) (S), 1997 c 10, ss 14(5),31
s 88 am—Planning etc. (S), 2006 asp 17, s 22
s 88A added—Planning and Compulsory Purchase, 2004 c 5, s 90(4), sch 5 para 1
ss 90-92,94 power to mod—Loc Govt, Planning and Land 1980 c 65, sch 30 pt II paras 1-5
s 99 am—SI 2003/2155, art 3(1), sch 1 pt 2 para 13(3)
　　　power to mod—Loc Govt, Planning and Land 1980 c 65, sch 30 pt II paras 1-5
Pt 5, Ch 2 (ss 100-122) appl—Stirling-Alloa-Kincardine Railway and Linked Improvements,
　　　2004 asp 10, s 34(2)
　　　mod—Forth Crossing, 2011 asp 2, s 72
s 100 am—Planning, 2008 c 29, s 176(1)(3)

1997
c 8 *continued*

s 101 am—Planning, 2008 c 29, s 176(1)(4)
s 102 am—Planning, 2008 c 29, s 176(1)(5)
s 116A added —Planning, 2008 c 29, s 176(1)(6)
s 120 am—Planning, 2008 c 29, s 176(1)(7)
s 121 am—SI 1999/1820, art 4, sch 2 pt I para 127(2); Planning, 2008 c 29, s 176(1)(8)
s 122 am—Planning, 2008 c 29, s 176(1)(9)
Pt 6 (ss 123-158) appl (mods)—SSI 2010/60, reg 30
    mod—SI 2011/2305, reg 19(2)
s 123 am—Planning etc. (S), 2006 asp 17, ss 6, 9
s 125 am—SSI 2004/332, art 5(a)
s 130 power to appl—Planning (Hazardous Substances) (S), 1997 c 10, ss 23(1),31
    appl (mods)—SI 1984/467, reg 25(1)(2) (subst by SSI 2013/154, reg 2(6))
s 131 see—SSI 1999/1, regs 33, 34, 39(a)
    appl (mods)—SI 1984/467, reg 25(1)(2) (subst by SSI 2013/154, reg 2(6))
    appl—SSI 2015/181, reg 47
    rep in pt—SSI 2004/332, art 3(a); Planning etc. (S), 2006 asp 17, s 56, sch
    am—SSI 2004/332, art 3(a); Planning etc. (S), 2006 asp 17, s 54(6)
s 132 power to appl—Planning (Hazardous Substances) (S), 1997 c 10, ss 23(1),31
    appl (mods)—SI 1984/467, reg 25(1)(2) (subst by SSI 2013/154, reg 2(6))
s 133 restr—SSI 1999/1, reg 29
    power to appl—Planning (Hazardous Substances) (S), 1997 c 10, ss 23(1),31
    rep in pt—Planning etc. (S), 2006 asp 17, s 56, sch
s 134 power to appl—Planning (Hazardous Substances) (S), 1997 c 10, ss 23(1),31
    appl (mods)—SSI 2015/181, reg 48
s 135 am—Planning etc. (S), 2006 asp 17, s 54(7)
    power to mod—Planning (Hazardous Substances) (S), 1997 c 10, ss 23(1), 31
    appl (mods)—SIs 2010/105, reg 6; 2015/462, reg 9
    mod—SSI 2015/181, reg 49
s 136 power to mod—Planning (Hazardous Substances) (S), 1997 c 10, ss 23(1), 31
    mod—SSI 2015/181, reg 50
s 136A added —Planning etc. (S), 2006 asp 17, s 25
s 137 power to mod—Planning (Hazardous Substances) (S), 1997 c 10, ss 23(1), 31
    mod—SSI 2015/181, reg 51
s 138 power to mod—Planning (Hazardous Substances) (S), 1997 c 10, ss 23(1), 31
    mod—SSI 2015/181, reg 52
s 140 power to mod—Planning (Hazardous Substances) (S), 1997 c 10, ss 23(1), 31
s 141 power to mod—Planning (Hazardous Substances) (S), 1997 c 10, ss 23(1), 31
s 143 power to mod—Planning (Hazardous Substances) (S), 1997 c 10, ss 23(1), 31
    rep in pt—Planning etc. (S), 2006 asp 17, s 56, sch
s 144 power to mod—Planning (Hazardous Substances) (S), 1997 c 10, ss 23(1), 31
s 144A-144D added —Planning etc. (S), 2006 asp 17, s 26
s 145 power to mod—Planning (Hazardous Substances) (S), 1997 c 10, ss 23(1), 31
s 145A added —Planning etc. (S), 2006 asp 17, s 25
s 146 ext—Planning (Listed Buildings and Conservation Areas) (S), 1997 c 9, s 79(1)
s 147 power to mod—Planning (Hazardous Substances) (S), 1997 c 10, ss 23(1),31
    am—Planning etc. (S), 2006 asp 17, s 9
    mod—SSI 2015/181, reg 53
s 155 rep in pt—Planning etc. (S), 2006 asp 17, s 56, sch
s 156 am—Planning etc. (S), 2006 asp 17, s 54(8)
s 158A added—Planning etc. (S), 2006 asp 17, s 27
s 159 am—Planning etc. (S), 2006 asp 17, s 28
s 160 am—Planning etc. (S), 2006 asp 17, ss 28(2), 54(9); Planning, 2008 c 29, s 36, sch 2
    paras 54, 56
    appl—Edinburgh Tram (Line One), 2006 asp 7, s 59(3)(a)
    excl—Edinburgh Tram (Line Two), 2006 asp 6, s 59(3)(a)
s 161 am—Planning etc. (S), 2006 asp 17, s 28(3)
    cont—SSI 2010/431, art 2
s 161A added —Planning etc. (S), 2006 asp 17, s 28
s 162 subst—Planning and Compulsory Purchase, 2004 c 5, s 95
s 163 rep —Planning etc. (S), 2006 asp 17, s 56, sch
    cont—SSI 2010/431, art 2
s 164 am—Planning etc. (S), 2006 asp 17, s 28
s 168 am—Planning etc. (S), 2006 asp 17, s 28

1997
c 8 *continued*

s 169 rep in pt—Planning etc. (S), 2006 asp 17, s 56, sch
s 172 am—Planning and Compulsory Purchase, 2004 c 5, s 96; Planning, 2008 c 29, s 36,
　　　　sch 2 paras 54, 57
　　appl—Edinburgh Tram (Line One), 2006 asp 7, s 59(3)(b); Edinburgh Tram (Line
　　　　Two), 2006 asp 6, s 59(3)(b)
　　excl—SSI 2010/434, reg 8; Forth Crossing, 2011 asp 2, s 10(3)(b)
s 180 rep in pt—SSI 2009/256, art 2
s 182 rep in pt—(prosp) Planning etc. (S), 2006 asp 17, s 56, sch
　　am—(pt prosp) Planning etc. (S), 2006 asp 17, s 7
s 184 appl—Title Conditions (S), 2003 asp 9, s 21(7)
s 186 rep in pt—Planning (Conseq Provns)(S), 1997 c 11, s 3, sch 1 pt I
Pt 8 (ss 188-201) excl—SSI 2007/268, art 3
　　appl (mods)—Glasgow Commonwealth Games, 2008 asp 4, s 42
s 188 appl (mods)—Postal Services, 2000 c 26, s 95, sch 6 para 7
　　rep in pt—Loc Govt in S, 2003 asp 1, s 60(1)(i)(j)
s 189 rep in pt—Loc Govt in S, 2003 asp 1, s 60(1)(i)(j)
　　am—Planning and Compulsory Purchase, 2004 c 5, s 90(4), sch 5 para 3
s 190 am—Planning and Compulsory Purchase, 2004 c 5, s 90(4), sch 5 para 4
s 191 mod—Planning (Listed Buildings and Conservation Areas) (S), 1997 c 9, s 59(2)
　　rep in pt—Abolition of Feudal Tenure etc (S), 2000 asp 5, s 76(1)(2), sch 12 pt I
　　　　para 60(3), sch 13 pt I
s 193 mod—Planning (Listed Buildings and Conservation Areas) (S), 1997 c 9, s 59(2)
s 194 am—SI 2003/2155, art 3(1), sch 1 pt 2 para 13(1)(a)(2)
s 195 appl—SSIs 1999/201, art 26(1)(2); 1999/203, art 27(1); 2006/17, art 31; Edinburgh
　　　　Tram (Line One), 2006 asp 7, s 42(1); Edinburgh Tram (Line Two), 2006 asp
　　　　6, s 42(1); Waverley Railway (S), 2006 asp 13, s 42; Airdrie-Bathgate Railway
　　　　and Linked Improvements, 2007 asp 19, s 35
　　appl (mods)—Glasgow Airport Rail Link, 2007 asp 1, s 40; SSI 2010/188, art 24
　　ext—Planning (Listed Buildings and Conservation Areas) (S), 1997 c 9, s 79(1)
s 196 am—SI 2003/2155, art 3(1), sch 1 pt 2 para 13(1)(b)(2)
s 197 appl—Communications, 2003 c 21, s 118, sch 4 para 4(5)(6)(a); SIs 2003/1900, arts
　　　　2(1), 3(1), sch 1; 3142, art 3(2)
s 198 appl—Communications, 2003 c 21, s 118, sch 4 para 4(5)(6)(b); SIs 2003/1900, arts
　　　　2(1), 3(1), sch 1; 3142, art 3(2)
　　see—Stirling-Alloa-Kincardine Railway and Linked Improvements, 2004 asp 10,
　　　　s 27(4)(a)
s 202 am—SSI 2006/243, art 4
ss 203, 205, 206 power to mod—Loc Govt, Planning and Land 1980 c 65, sch 30 pt II
　　　　paras 6-8
s 205 am—SI 2003/2155, art 3(1), sch 1 pt 2 para 13(1)(c)(2)
s 207 am—SSI 2006/243, art 4
s 208 am—Land Reform (S), 2003 asp 2, s 99, sch 2 para 17; SSI 2006/243, art 4
s 211 excl—Stirling-Alloa-Kincardine Railway and Linked Improvements, 2004 asp 10,
　　　　s 27(4)(b)
s 212 am—SI 2003/2155, art 3(1), sch 1 pt 2 para 13(1)(d)(2)
Pt 10 (ss 214-236) appl (mods)—SSI 2010/60, reg 31
s 214 am—Transport, 2000 c 38, s 37, sch 5 para 10; SI 2001/1149, art 3(1), sch 1
　　　　para 112
　　appl—Land Reform (S), 2003 asp 2, s 40(7); Agricultural Holdings (S), 2003 asp 11,
　　　　s 27(4); Stirling-Alloa-Kincardine Railway and Linked Improvements, 2004
　　　　asp 10, s 29, sch 9 para 7; SSI 2005/127, arts 6(3), 7(4)
s 215 appl—City of Edinburgh (Guided Busways) O Conf, 1998 c iii, s 1, sch, O, s 3(2)
　　am—Transport, 2000 c 38, s 37, sch 5 para 11; SI 2001/1149, art 3(1), sch 1
　　　　para 113
s 216 subst—SI 2006/1157, art 2, sch
s 217 ext—Planning (Listed Buildings and Conservation Areas) (S), 1997 c 9, s 78(10);
　　　　Planning (Hazardous Substances) (S), 1997 c 10, s 35(8)
　　rep in pt—SIs 1997/2971, art 6(1), sch paras 38,39(a); 1999/1820, art 4, sch 2 pt 1
　　　　para 127(3), pt 4
　　am—SIs 1997/2971, art 6(1), sch paras 38,39(b); 2001/1149, art 3(1), sch 1 para 114
s 218 am—SI 1999/1820, art 4, sch 2 pt 1 para 127(4)(a); SSI 2013/26, art 2(6)(a)
　　rep in pt—SI 1999/1820, art 4, sch 2 pt 1 para 127(4)(b), pt 4; SSI 2013/26, art
　　　　2(6)(b)

1997
c 8 *continued*

s 220 am—SI 1999/1820, art 4, sch 2 pt 1 para 127(5)
ss 221-223 rep—SI 1999/1820, art 4, sch 2 pt 1 para 127(6), pt 4
s 224 am—SI 1999/1820, art 4, sch 2 pt 1 para 127(7)
    saved—Stirling-Alloa-Kincardine Railway and Linked Improvements, 2004 asp 10,
      s 22
    appl—Communications, 2003 c 21, s 118, sch 4 para 4(5)(6)(c); SIs 2003/1900, arts
      2(1), 3(1), sch 1; 3142, art 3(2); Edinburgh Tram (Line One), 2006 asp 7, ss 5,
      6, 72, sch 9 para 1; Edinburgh Tram (Line Two), 2006 asp 6, ss 5, 6, 57, 71,
      sch 8 para 1, sch 9 para 1; Glasgow Airport Rail Link, 2007 asp 1, s 34, sch 7
      para 1; SSI 2010/188, art 36, sch 7
    appl (mods)—Edinburgh Airport Rail Link, 2007 asp 16, s 40, sch 7 para 1; Forth
      Crossing, 2011 asp 2, s 57
s 225 am—SIs 1999/1820, art 4, sch 2 pt 1 para 127(8); 2003/2155, art 3(1), sch 1 pt 2
    para 13(1)(e)(2)
    saved—Stirling-Alloa-Kincardine Railway and Linked Improvements, 2004 asp 10,
      s 22
    appl—Communications, 2003 c 21, s 118, sch 4 para 4(5)(6)(c); SIs 2003/1900, arts
      2(1), 3(1), sch 1; 3142, art 3(2); Edinburgh Tram (Line One), 2006 asp 7, ss 5,
      6, 72, sch 9 para 1; Edinburgh Tram (Line Two), 2006 asp 6, ss 5, 6, 57, 71,
      sch 8 para 1, sch 9 para 1; Glasgow Airport Rail Link, 2007 asp 1, s 34, sch 7
      para 1
    appl (mods)—Edinburgh Airport Rail Link, 2007 asp 16, s 40, sch 7 para 1; SSI
      2010/188, art 36, sch 7; Forth Crossing, 2011 asp 2, s 57
s 226 rep in pt—SI 1999/1820, art 4, sch 2 pt 1 para 127(9), pt 4
    am—SIs 1999/1820, art 4, sch 2 pt 1 para 127(9), pt 4; 2003/2155, art 3(1), sch 1 pt
      2 para 13(1)(e)(2)
    appl—Communications, 2003 c 21, s 118, sch 4 para 4(5)(6)(c); SIs 2003/1900, arts
      2(1), 3(1), sch 1; 3142, art 3(2); Edinburgh Tram (Line Two), 2006 asp 6, ss 5,
      6, 57, 71, sch 8 para 1, sch 9 para 1; Glasgow Airport Rail Link, 2007 asp 1, s
      34, sch 7 para 1
    appl (mods)—Edinburgh Airport Rail Link, 2007 asp 16, s 40, sch 7 para 1; SSI
      2010/188, art 36, sch 7; Forth Crossing, 2011 asp 2, s 57
s 227 am—SIs 1999/1820, art 4, sch 2 pt 1 para 127(10)(a)(b); 2003/2155, art 3(1), sch 1
    pt 2 para 13(1)(e)(2)
    rep in pt—SI 1999/1820, art 4, sch 2 pt 1 para 127(10)(d), pt 4
    appl—Communications, 2003 c 21, s 118, sch 4 para 4(5)(6)(c); SIs 2003/1900, arts
      2(1), 3(1), sch 1; 3142, art 3(2); Capital Allowances, 2001 c 2, s 436;
      Edinburgh Tram (Line One), 2006 asp 7, sch 9 para 1; Edinburgh Tram (Line
      Two), 2006 asp 6, ss 5, 6, 57, 71, sch 8 para 1, sch 9 para 1; Glasgow Airport
      Rail Link, 2007 asp 1, s 34, sch 7 para 1
    appl (mods)—Edinburgh Airport Rail Link, 2007 asp 16, s 40, sch 7 para 1; SSI
      2010/188, art 36, sch 7; Forth Crossing, 2011 asp 2, s 57
s 228 rep in pt & am—SI 1999/1820, art 4, sch 2 pt 1 para 127(11), pt 4
s 229 rep in pt & am—SI 1999/1820, art 4, sch 2 pt 1 para 127(12), pt 4
s 230 am—SI 1999/1820, art 4, sch 2 pt 1 para 127(13)
s 231 am—SI 1999/1820, art 4, sch 2 pt 1 para 127(14)
    rep in pt—SI 1999/1820, art 4, sch 2 pt 1 para 127(14), pt 4
s 232 am—SIs 1999/1820, art 4, sch 2 pt 1 para 127(15); 2003/2155, art 3(1), sch 1 pt 2
    para 13(1)(f)(2); Planning etc. (S), 2006 asp 17, s 22
s 233 am—SIs 1999/1820, art 4, sch 2 pt 1 para 127(16); 2003/2155, art 3(1), sch 1 pt 2
    para 13(1)(f)(2)
s 235 am—SI 1999/1820, art 4, sch 2 pt 1 para 127(17)
Pt 11 (ss 237-241) mod—SSI 2011/139, regs 33(11), 42
s 237 power to appl—Planning (Hazardous Substances) (S), 1997 c 10, ss 23(1), 31
    am—Planning and Compulsory Purchase, 2004 c 5, s 92(2); Planning etc. (S), 2006
      asp 17, ss 19, 54(11)(a)(b)
    transtl provns—SSI 2008/427, arts 2-5
    appl (mods)—SSIs 2010/60, regs 5, 10; 2015/181, reg 54(1)(2)
s 238 am—Planning etc. (S), 2006 asp 17, ss 19, 54(12)(a)(d)
    rep in pt—Planning etc. (S), 2006 asp 17, s 54(12)(b)(c)
    transtl provns—SSI 2008/427, arts 2-5
s 239 power to appl—Planning (Hazardous Substances) (S), 1997 c 10, ss 23(1), 31
    ext—SSI 1999/1, reg 43

1997
c 8 s 239 *continued*

      am—Planning etc. (S), 2006 asp 17, s 19
      appl (mods)—SSIs 2010/60, regs 5, 10; 2015/181, reg 54(1)(3)
s 240 rep—SI 1999/1820, art 4, sch 2 pt 1 para 127(18), pt 4
s 241A added—Planning and Compulsory Purchase, 2004 c 5, s 90(1)
Pt 11A (ss 241A-241D) added (prosp)—Planning etc. (S), 2006 asp 17, s 29
Pt 12 (ss 242-251) appl—Planning and Compulsory Purchase, 2004 c 5, s 97(4)
s 242 appl—Scotland, 1998 c 46, s 122(2);:(S) SI 1999/1736, art 11(3); Transport (S),
      2005 asp 12, s 4, sch 1 para 6(2)(a)
      rep in pt—Planning and Compulsory Purchase, 2004 c 5, ss 90(4), 120, sch 5 para 23,
         sch 9
      am—Planning and Compulsory Purchase, 2004 c 5, s 90(4), sch 5 para 6(1)-(6)
s 242A added—Planning and Compulsory Purchase, 2004 c 5, s 92(1)
      am—Planning etc. (S), 2006 asp 17, s 54(13)
ss 243, 244 rep —Planning and Compulsory Purchase, 2004 c 5, ss 90(4), 120, sch 5 para 9,
      sch 9
s 245 rep—Planning and Compulsory Purchase, 2004 c 5, ss 94(1), 120, sch 9
s 245A added—Planning and Compulsory Purchase, 2004 c 5, s 94(2)
s 245B added—Planning and Compulsory Purchase, 2004 c 5, s 94(3)
s 246 rep —Planning and Compulsory Purchase, 2004 c 5, ss 90(4), 120, sch 5 para 23, sch
      9
s 247 subst—Planning and Compulsory Purchase, 2004 c 5, s 90(4), sch 5 para 24
s 247A added—Planning and Compulsory Purchase, 2004 c 5, s 90(4), sch 5 para 10(1)
s 248 rep—Planning and Compulsory Purchase, 2004 c 5, ss 90(4), 120, sch 5 para 10(2)(3),
      sch 9
s 249 ext—Planning (Conseq Provns)(S), 1997 c 11, s 5, sch 3 para 10(2)
s 249, 250 rep —Planning and Compulsory Purchase, 2004 c 5, ss 90(4), 120, sch 5 paras
      25, 26, sch 9
Pt 12A (s 251A-251D) added (prosp)—Planning etc. (S), 2006 asp 17, s 30
s 252 appl—Planning (Hazardous Substances) (S), 1997 c 10, s 29(3)
      rep in pt—Planning etc. (S), 2006 asp 17, s 56, sch; Regulatory Reform (S), 2014 asp
         3, s 55(c)
      am—Planning etc. (S), 2006 asp 17, s 31; Regulatory Reform (S), 2014 asp 3, s
         55(a)(b)
s 253 rep in pt—SI 1999/1820, art 4, sch 2 pt I para 127(19)
s 253A added—Planning etc. (S), 2006 asp 17, s 32
s 254 am—SSI 2006/243, art 4
s 255 am—Planning etc. (S), 2006 asp 17, s 54(14)
s 261 ext—Planning (Listed Buildings and Conservation Areas) (S), 1997 c 9, s 80(5);
      Planning (Hazardous Substances) (S), 1997 c 10, s 37(4)
s 262 rep in pt—SI 1999/1820, art 4, sch 2 pt 1 para 127(20), pt 4
s 263 rep—Planning etc. (S), 2006 asp 17, s 56, sch
s 263A added —Planning etc. (S), 2006 asp 17, s 50
s 264 rep—Nature Conservation (S), 2004 asp 6, s 57, sch 7 para 12(2)
s 264A added—Nat Parks (S), 2000 asp 10, s 36, sch 5 para 18
s 265 appl—Planning (Hazardous Substances) (S), 1997 c 10, ss 19,36, sch para 6(4)-(6);
      Land Reform (S), 2003 asp 2, ss 11(6), 18(6); Historic Environment Scotland,
      2014 asp 19, s 21(2) (adding (prosp) Ancient Monuments and Archaeological
      Areas, 1979 c 46, s 23A(3)); ibid, sch 2 para 34 (adding (prosp) Ancient
      Monuments and Archaeological Areas, 1979 c 46, sch 1A para 6(4))
s 265A added—Planning and Compulsory Purchase, 2004 c 5, s 91(1)
      appl—Planning (Listed Buildings and Conservation Areas) (S), 1997 c 9, s 79;
      Planning (Hazardous Substances) (S), 1997 c 10, s 36; Planning (Listed
      Buildings and Conservation Areas) (S), 1997 c 9, sch 3 para 6(7); Planning
      (Hazardous Substances) (S), 1997 c 10, sch para 6(7); Planning (Listed
      Buildings and Conservation Areas) (S), 1997 c 9, s 73B
s 266 ext—Planning (Listed Buildings and Conservation Areas) (S), 1997 c 9, s 79(1)
      appl—Planning (Hazardous Substances) (S), 1997 c 10, s 36
      am—SSI 2009/256, art 2
s 267 ext—Planning (Listed Buildings and Conservation Areas) (S), 1997 c 9, s 79(1)
      appl—Planning (Hazardous Substances) (S), 1997 c 10, s 36
      am—Planning etc. (S), 2006 asp 17, s 19
      rep in pt—Planning etc. (S), 2006 asp 17, s 19

1997
c 8 *continued*

s 269 appl (mods)—Communications, 2003 c 21, s 118, sch 4 para 7(3)(4); SIs 2003/1900,
　　　arts 2(1), 3(1), sch 1; 3142, art 3(2)
　　am—Planning etc. (S), 2006 asp 17, ss 26, 54(15)(a)
　　rep in pt—Planning etc. (S), 2006 asp 17, s 54(15)(b)
s 270 am—SI 1999/1820, art 4, sch 2 pt I para 127(21)
　　appl (mods)—Communications, 2003 c 21, s 118, sch 4 para 7(3)(4); SIs 2003/1900,
　　　arts 2(1), 3(1), sch 1; 3142, art 3(2)
s 270A added—Planning and Compulsory Purchase, 2004 c 5, s 90(4), sch 5 para 14
s 270B added—Planning etc. (S), 2006 asp 17, s 51
s 271 ext—Planning (Listed Buildings and Conservation Areas) (S), 1997 c 9, s 79(1)
　　appl—Planning (Hazardous Substances) (S), 1997 c 10, s 36; SSIs 2013/155, reg 48;
　　　2015/181, reg 59
　　am—SSI 2004/332, art 4
s 271A added—Planning and Compulsory Purchase, 2004 c 5, s 90(4), sch 5 para 17
　　appl—Planning (Listed Buildings and Conservation Areas) (S), 1997 c 9, s 79;
　　　Planning (Hazardous Substances) (S), 1997 c 10, s 36
s 272 ext—Planning (Listed Buildings and Conservation Areas) (S), 1997 c 9, s 79(1)
　　appl—Planning (Hazardous Substances) (S), 1997 c 10, s 36
　　power to mod—Loc Govt, Planning and Land 1980 c 65, sch 30 pt II para 9
　　rep in pt—Abolition of Feudal Tenure etc (S), 2000 asp 5, s 76(1)(2), sch 12 pt I
　　　para 60(4), sch 13 pt I
　　am—SSI 2004/332, art 5(b)
s 272A added—Planning and Compulsory Purchase, 2004 c 5, s 90(4), sch 5 para 18
　　appl—Planning (Hazardous Substances) (S), 1997 c 10, s 36; Planning (Listed
　　　Buildings and Conservation Areas) (S), 1997 c 9, s 79
s 273 ext—Planning (Listed Buildings and Conservation Areas) (S), 1997 c 9, s 79(1)
　　excl—Planning (Listed Buildings and Conservation Areas) (S), 1997 c 9, s 79(2)
　　appl—Planning (Hazardous Substances) (S), 1997 c 10, s 36
s 274 appl—Building (S), 2003 asp 8, s 33(4)
s 275 am—Water Environment and Water Services (S), 2003 asp 3, s 24(1)(4); Planning
　　　and Compulsory Purchase, 2004 c 5, s 118(2), sch 7 para 20(1)(3); Planning etc.
　　　(S), 2006 asp 17, s 54(16)(a)(b)(i), (c)-(f); (prosp) ibid, s 54(16)(b)(ii); Marine
　　　(S), 2010 asp 5, s 63(4); Regulatory Reform (S), 2014 asp 3, sch 3 para 32
　　rep in pt—SSI 2009/404, art 2, sch 4
s 275A added—Planning etc. (S), 2006 asp 17, s 52
s 276 ext—Planning (Listed Buildings and Conservation Areas) (S), 1997 c 9, s 79(1)
　　appl—Planning (Hazardous Substances) (S), 1997 c 10, s 36
s 277 am—SIs 1999/1820, art 4, sch 2 pt I para 127(22), pt 4; 2001/1149, art 3(1), sch 1
　　　para 115; SSIs 2004/332, art 6(1)-(3); 2006/243, art 4; Planning etc. (S), 2006
　　　asp 17, s 54(17)(a)(i)-(iv),(b); Planning, 2008 c 29, s 36, sch 2 paras 54, 58; SSI
　　　2009/256, art 2; Postal Services, 2011 c 5, sch 12 para 151; SSI 2011/226, reg 4
　　rep in pt—SI 1999/1820, art 4, sch 2 pt I para 127(22), pt 4; Abolition of Feudal
　　　Tenure etc (S), 2000 asp 5, s 76(1)(2), sch 12 pt I para 60(5), sch 13 pt I;
　　　Planning etc. (S), 2006 asp 17, s 56, sch
sch 1 am—Planning etc. (S), 2006 asp 17, s 53
　　rep in pt—Planning etc. (S), 2006 asp 17, s 53(5)
　　transtl provns—SSI 2008/427, art 6
sch 3 rep in pt—Planning etc. (S), 2006 asp 17, s 56, sch
sch 4 am—S Public Services Ombudsman, 2002 asp 11, s 25(1), sch 6, para 17; (pt prosp)
　　　Planning etc. (S), 2006 asp 17, s 54(18)
　　rep in pt—Planning etc. (S), 2006 asp 17, s 56, sch; SSI 2009/256, art 2
sch 5 am—Planning (Conseq Provns)(S), 1997 c 11, s 5, sch 3 para 14
sch 6 am—Tribunals, Cts and Enforcement, 2007 c 15, s 48, sch 8 paras 49, 50
　　rep in pt—SI 2013/2042, sch para 17(a)
sch 7 am—SI 1997/2971, art 6(1), sch paras 38, 40; SIs 2001/2568, art 16, sch
　　　para 16(a)(b); 2002/2626, art 20, sch 2, para 22; Tribunals, Cts and Enforcement,
　　　2007 c 15, s 48, sch 8 paras 49, 51
　　rep in pt—SI 2013/2042, sch para 17(b)
sch 8 appl (mods)—Planning and Compulsory Purchase, 2004 c 5, s 97(2)(b)(c); SSI
　　　2010/60, reg 29
　　appl—Planning and Compulsory Purchase, 2004 c 5, s 97(3)
　　restr—SSI 2011/139, reg 33(17)(a)
　　excl—SSI 2011/139, reg 33(18)

1997
c 8 sch 8 *continued*

mod—SSI 2011/139, reg 33(21)
sch 9 am—SSI 2004/332, art 7
restr—SSI 2011/139, reg 33(17)(a)
mod—SSI 2011/139, reg 33(21)
sch 10 am—Planning and Compulsory Purchase, 2004 c 5, s 118(2), sch 7 para
20(1)(4)(a)(b); SSI 2004/332, art 8
restr—SSI 2011/139, reg 33(17)(a)
mod—SSI 2011/139, reg 33(21)
sch 11 am—SSI 2006/243, art 4
sch 13 rep in pt—SI 1999/1820, art 4, sch 2 pt 1 para 127(23), pt 4
mod—SSI 2010/60, reg 31
sch 14 am—SI 2003/2155, art 3(1), sch 1 pt 2 para 13(4); Planning etc. (S), 2006 asp 17, s
54(19); Transport and Works (S), 2007 asp 8, s 15(2); Planning, 2008 c 29, s
176(1)(2)
appl—Edinburgh Airport Rail Link, 2007 asp 16, s 47
sch 15 appl (mods)—SSIs 1999/201, art 26(1)(2); 1999/203, art 27(1)(2); 2006/17, art 31;
Glasgow Airport Rail Link, 2007 asp 1, s 40; Forth Crossing, 2011 asp 2, s
35(2)
rep in pt—Abolition of Feudal Tenure etc (S), 2000 asp 5, s 76(1)(2), sch 12 pt I
para 60(6), sch 13 pt I
appl—Title Conditions (S), 2003 asp 9, ss 106(5)(c), 119(9); Edinburgh Tram (Line
One), 2006 asp 7, s 42; Edinburgh Tram (Line Two), 2006 asp 6, s 42;
Waverley Railway (S), 2006 asp 13, s 42; Airdrie-Bathgate Railway and
Linked Improvements, 2007 asp 19, s 35
excl—Glasgow Airport Rail Link, 2007 asp 1, s 13(3)
sch 16 am—SI 1999/1820, art 4, sch 2 pt I para 127(24); SSI 2006/243, art 4
sch 18 rep in pt—Planning etc. (S), 2006 asp 17, s 56, sch

c 9 **Planning (Listed Buildings and Conservation Areas) (Scotland)**
see—SI 1999/677, art 2(3)(4)(b)(5); SSI 2015/239, arts 13-18
am—Town and Country Planning (S), 1997 c 8, s 277(9); Planning (Conseq Provns)(S),
1997 c 11, s 5, sch 3 para 8
appl—Planning (Conseq Provns)(S), 1997 c 11, s 1(2); Railtrack (Waverley Station) O Conf,
2000 c vi, s 1, sch, s 6(1) of Order
appl (mods)—(specified sections appl (mods)) – SSI 2015/243, reg 15(1)(2); ibid, reg 15(3),
sch 3
mod—Town and Country Planning (S), 1997 c 8, s 24(4), sch 1 para 3
power to mod—Town and Country Planning (S), 1997 c 8, ss 2(2),20; Planning (Listed
Buildings and Conservation Areas) (S), 1997 c 9, s 67(8)(9)
restr—Town and Country Planning (S), 1997 c 8, ss 41(6),65(5), sch 3 pt I para 1(6)(a)
s 1 am—Historic Environment Scotland, 2014 asp 19, s 22(2); ibid, sch 3 para 2
s 1A added —Historic Environment Scotland, 2014 asp 19, sch 3 para 3
s 2 rep —Historic Environment Scotland, 2014 asp 19, sch 3 para 4
s 3 am—Historic Environment Scotland, 2014 asp 19, sch 3 para 5
s 5A added—Historic Environment (Amdt) (S), 2011 asp 3, s 18(1)
am—Historic Environment Scotland, 2014 asp 19, sch 3 para 6
s 6 excl—Stirling-Alloa-Kincardine Railway and Linked Improvements, 2004 asp 10, s 32,
sch 10 para 1(1)(a); Airdrie-Bathgate Railway and Linked Improvements, 2007
asp 19, s 42, sch 8 para 1(1)(a); Glasgow Airport Rail Link, 2007 asp 1, s 37, sch
8 para 1(1)(a); Edinburgh Airport Rail Link, 2007 asp 16, s 42, sch 8 para 1(1)(a);
Forth Crossing, 2011 asp 2, s 63(1)
s 7 am—Historic Environment Scotland, 2014 asp 19, sch 3 para 8(a)(c)
rep in pt—Historic Environment Scotland, 2014 asp 19, sch 3 para 8(b)
s 8 am—Historic Environment (Amdt) (S), 2011 asp 3, s 19
s 9 am—SSI 2006/243, art 5; (pt prosp) Planning etc. (S), 2006 asp 17, s 7; Historic
Environment Scotland, 2014 asp 19, sch 3 para 9(a)(ii)(b)
s 10A added—Historic Environment (Amdt) (S), 2011 asp 3, s 20(1)
mod—SSI 2011/377, art 5
s 11 see—(trans of cert functions) SSI 2003/1, art 7(3)-(8)
mod—SSI 2007/569, reg 5
rep in pt—Historic Environment (Amdt) (S), 2011 asp 3, s 21(a)
s 12 am—Historic Environment Scotland, 2014 asp 19, s 23(2)
s 13 am—Planning etc. (S), 2006 asp 17, s 55
rep in pt—Historic Environment Scotland, 2014 asp 19, s 23(3)(a)(b)

1997
c 9 *continued*

s 14 am—Historic Environment Scotland, 2014 asp 19, s 23(4)

s 15 am—SSI 2009/256, art 3

s 16 am—Planning etc. (S), 2006 asp 17, s 20

s 18 appl—SSI 2006/269, art 3
    am—Historic Environment (Amdt) (S), 2011 asp 3, s 20(2)

s 19 am—Historic Environment Scotland, 2014 asp 19, sch 3 para 19

s 20 rep in pt—Planning etc. (S), 2006 asp 17, s 56, sch
    am—Historic Environment Scotland, 2014 asp 19, sch 3 para 20

s 22 am—Historic Environment Scotland, 2014 asp 19, sch 3 para 10

s 23 am—Historic Environment Scotland, 2014 asp 19, sch 3 para 11

s 26 am—Historic Environment Scotland, 2014 asp 19, sch 3 para 25

s 28A added—Planning and Compulsory Purchase, 2004 c 5, s 90(4), sch 5 para 2

ss 29-32 power to mod—Loc Govt, Planning and Land 1980 c 65, sch 30 pt II paras 10-13

s 34 am—Historic Environment (Amdt) (S), 2011 asp 3, s 22(2)

s 35 rep in pt—SSI 2004/332, art 9(a)
    am—SSI 2004/332, art 9(b); Historic Environment (Amdt) (S), 2011 asp 3, s 22(3)

s 36 rep in pt—Planning etc. (S), 2006 asp 17, s 56, sch

s 37 am—Historic Environment Scotland, 2014 asp 19, sch 3 para 21

s 39 am—Historic Environment (Amdt) (S), 2011 asp 3, s 22(4)

s 39A added—Historic Environment (Amdt) (S), 2011 asp 3, s 24

s 40 am—Historic Environment (Amdt) (S), 2011 asp 3, s 22(5)

ss 41A-41I added—Historic Environment (Amdt) (S), 2011 asp 3, s 23(1)

s 42 am—Planning and Compulsory Purchase, 2004 c 5, s 90(4), sch 5 para 5

s 46 am—SI 2003/2155, art 3(1), sch 1 pt 2 para 14(1)(2)

s 49 am—Historic Environment (Amdt) (S), 2011 asp 3, s 25

s 50 am—Historic Environment (Amdt) (S), 2011 asp 3, s 26(2)

ss 50A-50G added—Historic Environment (Amdt) (S), 2011 asp 3, s 26(3)

s 51 am—Historic Environment (Amdt) (S), 2011 asp 3, s 27(2)

s 52 am—Historic Environment (Amdt) (S), 2011 asp 3, s 27(3)

s 53 excl—Forth Crossing, 2011 asp 2, s 63(4)

s 57 am—Planning and Compulsory Purchase, 2004 c 5, s 93(2); Historic Environment
    Scotland, 2014 asp 19, sch 3 para 22

s 58 appl—(prosp) Town and Country Planning (S), 1997 c 8, s 241C(4) (added by 2006
    asp 17, s 29)

s 61 am—Historic Environment Scotland, 2014 asp 19, sch 3 para 13

s 62 am—Historic Environment Scotland, 2014 asp 19, sch 3 para 14

s 65 power to appl—Town and Country Planning (S), 1997 c 8, s 182(2)(c)(3)(a)

s 66 excl—Stirling-Alloa-Kincardine Railway and Linked Improvements, 2004 asp 10, s 32,
    sch 10 para 1(4); Forth Crossing, 2011 asp 2, s 64
    am—SSI 2006/243, art 5; Historic Environment (Amdt) (S), 2011 asp 3, s 23(2);
    Historic Environment Scotland, 2014 asp 19, s 24(2)

s 69 rep in pt—SI 1999/1820, art 4, sch 2 pt 1 para 128(2), pt 4; Public Appointments and
    Public Bodies etc (S), 2003 asp 4, s 17, sch 4 para 13(a)
    am—SI 1999/1820, art 4, sch 2 pt 1 para 128(2), pt 4; Planning etc. (S), 2006 asp 17, s
    55

s 70 am—Historic Environment (Amdt) (S), 2011 asp 3, s 27(4)

s 71 rep in pt—Public Appointments and Public Bodies etc (S), 2003 asp 4, s 17, sch 4
    para 13(b)

s 72 rep in pt—Public Appointments and Public Bodies etc (S), 2003 asp 4, s 17, sch 4
    para 13(c); Planning etc. (S), 2006 asp 17, s 56, sch

s 73 am—Historic Environment Scotland, 2014 asp 19, sch 3 para 26(a)
    rep in pt—Historic Environment Scotland, 2014 asp 19, sch 3 para 26(b)

s 73A added—Planning and Compulsory Purchase, 2004 c 5, s 90(2)
    am—Historic Environment (Amdt) (S), 2011 asp 3, s 28

s 73B added—Planning and Compulsory Purchase, 2004 c 5, s 93(1)

s 73C added—Planning and Compulsory Purchase, 2004 c 5, s 90(4), sch 5 para 7

ss 73D, 73E added—Planning and Compulsory Purchase, 2004 c 5, s 94(4)

s 73F added—Planning and Compulsory Purchase, 2004 c 5, s 90(4), sch 5 para 11

ss 74, 75 rep —Planning and Compulsory Purchase, 2004 c 5, ss 90(4), 120, sch 5 para 19,
    sch 9

s 76 am—Historic Environment (Amdt) (S), 2011 asp 3, ss 18(2), 23(3); Historic
    Environment Scotland, 2014 asp 19, sch 3 para 27

s 78 rep in pt & am—SI 1999/1820, art 4, sch 2 pt 1 para 128(3) pt 4

1997
c 9 *continued*

s 78A added—Planning and Compulsory Purchase, 2004 c 5, s 90(4), sch 5 para 15
s 79 am—Planning and Compulsory Purchase, 2004 c 5, s 90(4), sch 5 para 20; SSI
    2004/332, art 10; Historic Environment (Amdt) (S), 2011 asp 3, s 29(1)
s 81 power to mod—Loc Govt, Planning and Land 1980 c 65, sch 30 pt II para 14
    am—Transport, 2000 c 38, s 37, sch 5 para 12; SIs 2001/1149, art 3(1), sch 1 para 116;
        2003/2155, art 3(1), sch 1 pt 2 para 14(1)(3); SSI 2004/332, art 11; (pt prosp)
        Planning etc. (S), 2006 asp 17, s 55; Historic Environment (Amdt) (S), 2011 asp
        3, s 23(4); Postal Services, 2011 c 5, sch 12 para 150
    rep in pt—Abolition of Feudal Tenure etc (S), 2000 asp 5, s 76(2), sch 13 pt I
s 82 am—(pt prosp) Planning etc. (S), 2006 asp 17, s 55; Historic Environment (Amdt) (S),
    2011 asp 3, s 30(2)-(6)
sch 1 am—Historic Environment Scotland, 2014 asp 19, sch 3 paras 15, 18
    rep in pt—Historic Environment Scotland, 2014 asp 19, sch 3 para 16
sch 2 am—Historic Environment Scotland, 2014 asp 19, sch 3 para 28
sch 3 am—SI 1999/1351, art 17(7)(b); S Public Services Ombudsman, 2002 asp 11, s 25(1),
    sch 6, para 18; Planning and Compulsory Purchase, 2004 c 5, s 91(2); Historic
    Environment Scotland, 2014 asp 19, sch 3 para 23(a)-(c)
    rep in pt—Historic Environment (Amdt) (S), 2011 asp 3, s 21(b); Historic
        Environment Scotland, 2014 asp 19, sch 3 para 23(d)
sch 4 ext—SI 1999/1351, art 17(7)(a)

c 10   **Planning (Hazardous Substances) (Scotland)**
am—Planning (Conseq Provns)(S), 1997 c 11, s 5, sch 3 para 8
appl—Planning (Conseq Provns)(S), 1997 c 11, s 1(2)
mod—Town and Country Planning (S), 1997 c 8, s 24(4), sch 1 para 3
power to mod—Town and Country Planning (S), 1997 c 8, ss 2(2), 20
s 2 am—SSI 2000/179, reg 2(2)
s 4 am—(temp) SSI 2000/179, reg 3(2); SSI 2006/269, art 5
s 5 am—SI 2014/469, sch 2 para 16
s 7 am—Planning, 2008 c 29, s 36, sch 2 paras 59, 60; SI 2014/469, sch 2 para 17
    appl—SSI 2015/181, reg 56(4)
s 8 am—Planning, 2008 c 29, s 36, sch 2 paras 59, 61; SI 2014/469, sch 2 para 18
s 10 mod—SSI 2007/569, reg 4
    am—Planning, 2008 c 29, s 36, sch 2 paras 59, 62; SI 2008/960, art 22, sch 3
ss 10A, 10B added—(temp) SSI 2000/179, reg 3(3)
s 12 am—Planning, 2008 c 29, s 36, sch 2 paras 59, 63
s 15 am—Planning and Compulsory Purchase, 2004 c 5, s 90(4), sch 5 para 21
    excl in pt—SSI 2015/181, reg 66
s 16 am—SI 2014/469, sch 2 para 19
s 18 cert functs made exercisable —SSI 2003/1, art 7(3)-(8)
    mod—SSI 2015/181, reg 56(3)
s 20 appl—(prosp) Town and Country Planning (S), 1997 c 8, s 241C(5) (added by 2006
        asp 17, s 29)
    mod—SSI 2015/181, reg 56(5)
s 27 am—SSI 2006/269, art 5
s 28 am—SI 2014/469, sch 2 para 20(2)(a)(3)-(6)
    rep in pt—SI 2014/469, sch 2 para 20(2)(b)
s 30A added—Planning and Compulsory Purchase, 2004 c 5, s 90(3)
ss 30B, 30C added—Planning and Compulsory Purchase, 2004 c 5, s 94(5)
s 30D added—SSI 2006/269, art 5
s 31 appl—SI 1999/1736, art 11(3)
    rep in pt—Planning and Compulsory Purchase, 2004 c 5, ss 90(4), 120, sch 5 para
        8(1)(2), sch 9
    am—Planning and Compulsory Purchase, 2004 c 5, s 90(4), sch 5 para 8(1)-(5)
s 32 rep —Planning and Compulsory Purchase, 2004 c 5, ss 90(4), 120, sch 5 para 12, sch 9
s 32A added—Planning and Compulsory Purchase, 2004 c 5, s 90(4), sch 5 para 13
s 35 rep in pt & am—SI 1999/1820, art 4, sch 2 pt I para 129 pt IV
s 35A added—Planning and Compulsory Purchase, 2004 c 5, s 90(4), sch 5 para 16
s 36 am—Planning and Compulsory Purchase, 2004 c 5, s 90(4), sch 5 para 22
s 38 am—Transport, 2000 c 38, s 37, sch 5 para 13; SI 2001/1149, art 3(1) sch 1, para 117;
    Planning, 2008 c 29, s 36, sch 2 paras 59, 64; SI 2009/1941, art 2, sch 1; Postal
    Services, 2011 c 5, sch 12 para 149; SI 2014/469, sch 2 para 20(7)
sch 1 am—SI 1999/1351, art 17(7)(c); S Public Services Ombudsman, 2002 asp 11, s 25(1),
    sch 6, para 19; Planning and Compulsory Purchase, 2004 c 5, s 91(3)

1997

c 11   **Planning (Consequential Provisions) (Scotland)**
          power to mod—Town and Country Planning (S), 1997 c 8, ss 2(2),20
          sch 2 rep in pt—SL(R), 1998 c 43, s 1(1), sch 1 pt IV, Group 2; SI 2001/1149, arts 3(2),
                  4(11), sch 2; Housing (S), 2001 asp 10, s 112, sch 10, para 25; Capital
                  Allowances, 2001 c 2, s 580, sch 4; Water Industry (S), 2002 asp 3, s 71(2),
                  sch 7, para 25; Building (S), 2003 asp 8, s 58, sch 6 para 23; Communications,
                  2003 c 21, s 406(7), sch 19(1); Flood Risk Management (S), 2009 asp 6, s 96,
                  sch 3 para 9; Regulatory Reform (S), 2014 asp 3, sch 3 para 33
          sch 3 mod—Town and Country Planning (S), 1997 c 8, s 247
c 12   **Civil Procedure**
          am—(except sch 1 para 1) Constitutional Reform, 2005 c 4, s 59(5), sch 11 pt 2 para 4
          s 1 am—Courts, 2003 c 39, s 82(1); Crime and Cts, 2013 c 22, sch 9 para 67(a); Anti-social
                  Behaviour, Crime and Policing, 2014 c 12, s 174(2)
              rep in pt—Constitutional Reform, 2005 c 4, ss 15(1), 146, sch 4 pt 1 paras 261, 262, sch
                  18 pt 2
          s 2 rep in pt —(prosp) Courts, 2003 c 39, ss 85(1), 109(3), sch 10
              am—Courts, 2003 c 39, s 83; Constitutional Reform, 2005 c 4, s 15(1), sch 4 pt 1 paras
                  261, 263; (temp) ibid, sch 4 pt 2 paras 361(3), 385; SI 2006/1847, art 2; Legal
                  Services, 2007 c 29, s 208, sch 21 para 122; Crime and Cts, 2013 c 22, sch 9 para
                  67(a)
          s 2A added—Courts, 2003 c 39, s 84
              am—Constitutional Reform, 2005 c 4, s 15(1), sch 4 pt 1 paras 261, 264
          s 3 subst (prosp)—Courts, 2003 c 39, s 85(2)
              am—Constitutional Reform, 2005 c 4, s 15(1), sch 4 pt 1 paras 261, 265(1)-(3)
              excl—Prevention of Terrorism, 2005 c 2, s 11(5), sch para 3(7)(a); (transtl provns)
                  Counter-Terrorism, 2008 c 28, s 72(6)(a); Terrorist Asset-Freezing etc, 2010 c 38,
                  s 29(9)(a), (11); Terrorism Prevention and Investigation Measures, 2011 c 23, sch
                  4 para 7(8)(a); Justice and Security, 2013 c 18, sch 3 para 3(9)(a);
                  Counter-Terrorism and Security, 2015 c 6, sch 3 para 8(a)
              rep in pt—Constitutional Reform, 2005 c 4, ss 15(1), 146, sch 4 pt 1 paras 261,
                  265(1)(4)(5), sch 18 pt 2
          s 3A added —Constitutional Reform, 2005 c 4, s 15(1), sch 4 pt 1 paras 261, 266
          s 4 am —Constitutional Reform, 2005 c 4, s 15(1), sch 4 pt 1 paras 261, 267
          s 5 subst—Constitutional Reform, 2005 c 4, s 13(2)(3), sch 2 pt 2 para 6
          s 6 am —Constitutional Reform, 2005 c 4, s 15(1), sch 4 pt 1 paras 261, 268
          s 7 am—Civil Partnership, 2004 c 33, s 261(1), sch 27 para 154
          sch 1 am—Crime and Cts, 2013 c 22, sch 9 para 67(b)(i)(ii)
          sch 2 rep in pt—Access to Justice, 1999 c 22, s 106, sch 15 pt III; Courts, 2003 c 39,
                  s 109(3), sch 10; Crime and Cts, 2013 c 22, sch 9 para 141
c 13   **United Nations Personnel**
          excl—Terrorism, 2000 c 11, s 63E
          ss 1-6 ext (mods) —(Guernsey) SI 1998/1075, art 2, sch
          ss 1-8 ext (mods)—(Jersey) SI 1998/1267, art 2; (I of M) SI 1998/1509, art 2
          s 4 am—Geneva Conventions and UN Personnel (Protocol), 2009 c 6, s 2
          s 5 am—Crime (International Co-operation), 2003 c 32, s 91(1), sch 5 paras 66, 67
          s 6 rep—Extradition, 2003 c 41, ss 219, 220, sch 3 paras 1, 10, sch 4 (see SI 2003/3103,
                  arts 2-5)
          s 8 ext (mods)—(Guernsey) SI 1998/1075, art 2, sch
          s 10 ext (mods)—(I of M) SI 1998/1509, art 2, sch
          sch ext (mods)—(Jersey) SI 1998/1267, art 2, sch; (I of M) SI 1998/1509, art 2, sch
c 14   **National Heritage**
c 15   *Consolidated Fund*—rep Appropriation, 1999 c 13, s 3, sch (C)
c 16   **Finance**
          s 7 rep in pt—Finance, 2000 c 17, s 156, sch 40 pt I(1), Note 1; Finance, 2008 c 9, ss 13(11),
                  14, sch 5 para 25(c)(i)
          s 8 rep in pt—Finance, 2008 c 9, s 13(11)
          s 9 rep—Finance, 2000 c 17, s 156, sch 40 pt I(4), Note 2
          s 10 am—Finance, 2002 c 23, s 11; Finance, 2007 c 11, s 105, sch 25 paras 16, 17; Finance,
                  2009 c 10, s 114(1)-(9); Finance, 2012 c 14, sch 24 para 48
              ext—SI 2007/2910, art 3
              rep in pt—Finance, 2007 c 11, s 114, sch 27 pt 6; Finance, 2012 c 14, sch 24 para 56
          s 11 am—(retrosp) Finance, 1998 c 36, s 11(1)-(3); Finance, 1999 c 16, s 7(1)(2); (Table
                  subst) Finance, 2001 c 9, s 7; Finance, 2002 c 23, s 10; Finance, 2003 c 14, s 13;
                  Finance, 2004 c 12, s 16; Finance, 2005 c 7, s 6; Finance, 2006 c 25, s 10;

1997
c 16 *continued*

Finance, 2007 c 11, ss 7(1)(2), 105, sch 25 paras 16, 18; Finance, 2008 c 9, s 22(1); Finance, 2009 c 10, s 19(1); SI 2009/56, art 3, sch 1 para 242; Finance, 2010 c 13, s 20(1); Finance, 2011 c 11, s 17(1); Finance, 2012 c 14, s 193(1); Finance, 2013 c 29, s 183(1); Finance, 2014 c 26, s 121(1); Finance, 2015 c 11, s 60(1)

rep in pt—Finance, 2009 c 10, s 113(5)(b)

s 14 am—Finance, 2009 c 10, s 114(1)(10)-(12)

s 15 am—Finance, 2007 c 11, s 105, sch 25 paras 16, 19; Finance, 2009 c 10, s 114(1)(13)-(15)

s 27 rep in pt—Finance, 2008 c 9, ss 123, 142(2), sch 41 para 25(i)

s 39 rep in pt—Finance, 2002 c 23, s 141, sch 40 pt 2(1), Note

s 47 rep in pt—Finance, 2008 c 9, s 118, sch 39 para 65(c)

s 51 am—Finance, 2000 c 17, s 30(2), sch 7 para 7(2); Finance, 2001 c 9, s 27, sch 5 para 14; Tribunals, Cts and Enforcement, 2007 c 15, s 62, sch 13 para 126

rep in pt—Tribunals, Cts and Enforcement, 2007 c 15, s 146, sch 23 pt 3; Finance, 2008 c 9, s 129, sch 43 para 6

s 52 rep—Finance, 2008 c 9, s 129, sch 43 para 15

s 54 rep in pt—Finance, 2004 c 12, ss 77, 326, sch 42 pt 2(7), Note; Income Tax, 2007 c 3, s 1031, sch 3

s 56 rep in pt—Finance, 2009 c 10, s 5, sch 1 para 6(h)

s 58 excl—Finance (No 2), 1997 c 58, s 18(1)

s 59 rep—Corporation Tax, 2010 c 4, s 1181, sch 3 pt 1

s 61 rep—SL(R), 2013 c 2, s 1, sch 1 pt 10(1)

ss 62, 63 rep—Income Tax (Earnings and Pensions), 2003 c 1, s 724(1), sch 8 pt 1

s 64 rep—Corporation Tax, 2010 c 4, s 1181, sch 3 pt 1

s 65 rep—Corporation Tax, 2009 c 4, s 1326, sch 3 pt 1

s 66 rep in pt—Capital Allowances, 2001 c 2, s 580, sch 4

s 67 rep—Finance, 2012 c 14, sch 16 para 247(h)

s 68 rep—Corporation Tax, 2010 c 4, s 1181, sch 3 pt 1

s 70 rep—Finance (No 2), 1997 c 58, s 52, sch 8 pt II(9), Note 3

s 71 rep—Finance (No 2), 1997 c 58, s 52, sch 8 pt II(4), Note

s 72 rep—Finance (No 2), 1997 c 58, s 52, sch 8 pt II(11), Note

s 73 rep—Finance, 2008 c 9, s 66(3)(a)

ss 74, 75 rep—Income Tax, 2007 c 3, s 1031, sch 3

s 77 rep—Finance, 2008 c 9, s 66(4)(h)

s 78 rep—Income Tax, 2007 c 3, s 1031, sch 3

s 79 rep—Finance, 2008 c 9, s 36, sch 14 para 17(f)

s 80 rep in pt—Income Tax (Trading and Other Income), 2005 c 5, s 884, sch 3; Income Tax, 2007 c 3, s 1031, sch 3

s 81 rep—Income Tax, 2007 c 3, s 1031, sch 3

s 82 rep—Taxation (International and Other Provns), 2010 c 8, ss 374, 378, sch 8 para 232(2), sch 10 pt 8

s 83 rep in pt—Finance, 2004 c 12, s 326, sch 42 pt 2(6), Note 1

ss 84, 86 rep—Capital Allowances, 2001 c 2, s 580, sch 4

s 89 am—Finance, 2008 c 9, s 8, sch 2 para 69(1)(2)

ss 90, 91 rep—Taxation (International and Other Provns), 2010 c 8, s 378, sch 10 pt 1

s 95 am—SI 2001/3629, arts 97, 99

s 96 am—SIs 2001/3629, arts 97, 100; 2004/3379, reg 5(1)(2)(3)(a); Financial Services, 2012 c 21, sch 18 para 83; 2015/575, sch 1 para 20(2)(3)(b)

rep in pt—SIs 2004/3379, reg 5(1)(3)(b); 2015/575, sch 1 para 20(3)(a)

ext—Finance, 1986 c 41, s 90; Finance, 1999 c 16, sch 19 para 6

ss 97-106 rep —Finance, 1997 c 16, s 113, sch 18 pt VII, Notes 1, 6

s 110 rep—Welfare Reform, 2012 c 5, sch 14 pt 13

s 111 rep—SL(R), 1998 c 43, s 1(1), sch 1 pt IV, Group 5

sch 1 am—Finance, 2007 c 11, s 105, sch 25 paras 16, 20(1)-(6); SIs 2009/56, art 3, sch 1 para 243; 1890, art 4; Finance, 2014 c 26, sch 28 para 20; SI 2015/664, sch 2 para 10

sch 2 rep in pt—Enterprise, 2002 c 40, s 278(2), sch 26; (prosp) Finance, 2007 c 11, s 114, sch 27 pt 5

sch 5 am—Finance, 2001 c 9, ss 15, 110, sch 3 pt 4, paras 19(1)-(5), 21, 22, sch 33 pt 1(4), Note; SI 2009/56, art 3, sch 1 para 244

rep in pt—Finance, 2001 c 9, ss 15, 110, sch 3 pt 4, paras 19(1)-(5), 21, 22, sch 33 pt 1(4), Note; Finance, 2009 c 10, s 99, sch 51 para 43(b)

1997

c 16 *continued*

sch 6 rep in pt—Finance, 2000 c 17, s 156, sch 40 pt I(1), Note 2; Finance, 2008 c 9, s 14, sch 5 para 25(c)(ii)

sch 7 excl—(retrosp to 26.11.1996) Income and Corporation Taxes, 1988 c 1, s 247(5B)-(5D); SI 1997/1154, reg 25(10)

restr—Finance (No 2), 1997 c 58, s 36(3)

am—Finance (No 2), 1997 c 58, s 24(14)(b)(15),25(6)-(8)

rep in pt—Finance (No 2), 1997 c 58, ss 36,52, sch 6 para 21(2)-(4), sch 8 pt II(11), Note; ibid, ss 24(14)(a)(15),52, sch 8 pt II(8) Note 1, pt II(9) Note 3, pt II(12) Notes 1,2; Income Tax (Trading and Other Income), 2005 c 5, s 884, sch 3; Income Tax, 2007 c 3, s 1031, sch 3

schs 8, 9 rep—Income Tax, 2007 c 3, s 1031, sch 3

sch 10 rep in pt—Finance (No 2), 1997 c 58, s 52, sch 8 pt II(11), Note; Income Tax, 2007 c 3, s 1031, sch 3; Corporation Tax, 2010 c 4, s 1181, sch 3 pt 1

sch 11 rep—Income Tax (Trading and Other Income), 2005 c 5, s 884, sch 3

sch 12 am—(retrosp) SI 1997/473, reg 53A; Finance, 1998 c 36, s 46(3), sch 7 para 12; Capital Allowances, 2001 c 2, ss 578, 580, sch 2 para 98(1)-(6), sch 4; SI 2001/3629, arts 97, 102(1)-(4); Finance, 2002 c 23, s 103(4)(e); Finance, 2005 c 7, ss 59, 80, sch 3 pt 3 paras 25, 31(2), sch 4 pt 1 para 18; Income Tax (Trading and Other Income), 2005 c 5, s 882(1), sch 1 pt 2 paras 492, 494; Finance (No 2), 2005 c 22, s 42, sch 9 para 19(3)(5); Finance, 2006 c 25, s 81, sch 9 para 7(1)-(3); Finance, 2008 c 9, s 8, sch 2 para 69(1)(3); SI 2008/954, art 22; Corporation Tax, 2009 c 4, s 1322, sch 1 paras 447, 448

excl—Finance, 1998 c 36, s 38, sch 5 pt IV para 74(1)(3)(4)

mod—SIs 1997/493, reg 53A; 1999/498, reg 16; 2005/2014, reg 42

rep in pt—Finance, 1998 c 36, s 165, sch 27 pt III(4), Note; Capital Allowances, 2001 c 2, ss 578, 580, sch 2 para 98(2)(7), sch 4; Finance, 2002 c 23, s 141, sch 40 pt 3(16); Finance, 2005 c 7, ss 80, 104, sch 4 pt 2 para 32, sch 11 pt 2(7), Note 2; Finance, 2007 c 11, s 41, sch 10 paras 4(4)(c), 16(1)(6), 17(2), sch 27; Finance, 2008 c 9, s 43, sch 17 para 17(10)(11)(d); Corporation Tax, 2010 c 4, ss 1177, 1181, sch 1 para 296(1)-(4), sch 3; Taxation (International and Other Provns), 2010 c 8, ss 374, 378, sch 8 para 232(3), sch 10 pt 8

sch 14 rep—Capital Allowances, 2001 c 2, s 580, sch 4

sch 15 rep in pt—Finance, 1998 c 36, s 165, sch 27 pt III(4), Note; Capital Allowances, 2001 c 2, s 580, sch 4

sch 16 rep—Capital Allowances, 2001 c 2, s 580, sch 4

sch 18 ext—Finance (No 2), 1997 c 58, s 4(1)(7)

rep in pt—Income Tax (Earnings and Pensions), 2003 c 1, s 724(1), sch 8 pt 1

sch 22 am—Finance, 2006 c 25, s 81, sch 9 paras 8-10

c 17 **Criminal Evidence (Amendment)**

s 1 am—Powers of Crim Cts (Sentencing), 2000 c 6, s 165(1), sch 9 para 180; Crime and Security, 2010 c 17, s 2(9)(a), (b)(i)

rep in pt—Crime and Security, 2010 c 17, s 2(9)(b)(ii)

s 2 am—Crime and Security, 2010 c 17, s 2(9), (10)

c 18 *Policyholders Protection*—rep SI 2001/3649, art 3(1)(f)

c 19 *Pharmacists (Fitness to Practise)*—rep SI 2007/289, art 67, sch 1 pt I, para 6

c 20 **British Nationality (Hong Kong)**

s 1 am —Borders, Citizenship and Immigration, 2009 c 11, s 47(3)

s 2 am—SI 2003/1016, art 3, sch para 9(b)(c)

rep in pt—SI 2003/1016, art 3, sch para 9(a)

c 21 **Knives**

appl (mods)—SI 2010/1907, reg 16

s 5 ext —Crim Justice and Police, 2001 c 16, s 50, sch 1 pt 1 para 63

s 11 am—SI 2010/976, art 12, sch 14

c 22 **Architects**

s 1A added—(savings) SI 2008/1331, regs 2, 3, 27

s 2 am—(savings) SI 2008/1331, regs 2, 4, 27

s 3 am—(savings) SI 2008/1331, regs 2, 5, 27

s 4 am—(savings) SIs 2008/1331, regs 2, 6, 27; 2011/2008, reg 2

s 4A added—(savings) SI 2008/1331, regs 2, 7, 27

s 5 rep (savings)—SI 2008/1331, regs 2, 7, 27

ss 5A-5E added—(savings) SI 2008/1331, regs 2, 8, 27

s 6 am—(savings) SI 2008/1331, regs 2, 9, 27

rep in pt—(savings) SI 2008/1331, regs 2, 9, 27

1997
c 22 *continued*

        s 6A added—(savings) SI 2008/1331, regs 2, 10, 27
        s 7 am—(savings) SI 2008/1331, regs 2, 11, 27
        s 8 am—(savings) SI 2008/1331, regs 2, 12, 27
            rep in pt—(savings) SI 2008/1331, regs 2, 12, 27
        s 9 am—(savings) SI 2008/1331, regs 2, 13, 27
            rep in pt—(savings) SI 2008/1331, regs 2, 13, 27
        s 10 am—(savings) SI 2008/1331, regs 2, 14, 27
        s 11 am—(savings) SI 2008/1331, regs 2, 15, 27
        s 12 rep (savings) —SI 2008/1331, regs 2, 16, 27
        s 15 rep in pt—(savings) SI 2008/1331, regs 2, 17, 29
        s 19 rep (savings)—SI 2008/1331, regs 2, 18, 27
        s 20 am—(savings) SI 2008/1331, regs 2, 19, 27
        s 22 subst—(savings) SI 2008/1331, regs 2, 20, 27
            am—Crime and Cts, 2013 c 22, sch 9 para 61
        ss 22B, 22C added—(savings) SI 2008/1331, regs 2, 21, 27
        s 25 am—(savings) SIs 2008/1331, regs 2, 22, 27; 2014/4, art 2(a)
            rep in pt—(savings) SI 2008/1331, regs 2, 22, 27
        sch 1 am—SIs 2004/655, arts 2-4; (savings) 2008/1331, regs 2, 23, 27; 2014/4, art 2(b)
        sch 1A added—(transtl provns and savings) SI 2008/1331, regs 2, 8, 26, 27

c 23   **Lieutenancies**
        saved—Scotland, 1998 c 46, s 30, sch 5 pt II, s B12
        s 2 trans of functions—(S) SIs 1999/1750, art 2, sch 1; 2001/3500, arts 3, 4(1)(c)(3)-(8),
               sch 1 para 1; 2010/1837, art 4
            am—SIs 2001/3500, art 8, sch 2 pt I para 5; 2010/1837, art 5, sch
        s 4 am—SI 2002/2842, arts 2, 3
        s 6 am—SI 2002/2842, arts 2, 4
        s 22A added—SI 2002/2842, arts 2, 5
        s 25 am—SI 2002/2842, arts 2, 6
        sch 1 am—SIs 1997/1992, reg 2; 2009/837, art 10

c 24   *Nurses, Midwives and Health Visitors*—rep Health, 1999 c 8, ss 60(3)(4), 65, sch 5
c 25   *Justices of the Peace*—rep (transtl savings) Courts, 2003 c 39, ss 6(4), 109(2)(3), sch 9
            paras 3-11, 14, sch 10
c 26   **Transfer of Crofting Estates (Scotland)**
c 27   **Social Security (Recovery of Benefits)**
        mod—Social Security, 1998 c 14, s 2(1)(2)(h); (EWS) (pt prosp) ibid, s 11(1)(3)
        power to am—Northern Ireland, 1998 c 47, s 87
        ext—Health and Social Care (Community Health and Standards), 2003 c 43, s 161(1)(5)
        appl (mods)—SI 2010/1907 reg 1
        s 1 appl—SI 1998/3132, rule 36.23
            appl (mods)—SI 2008/1596, regs 2, 5, sch 1
            am—Mesothelioma, 2014 c 1, sch 1 para 2
        s 1A added—Child Maintenance and Other Payments, 2008 c 6, s 54
            am—Mesothelioma, 2014 c 1, sch 1 para 17
        s 7 am—Tribunals, Cts and Enforcement, 2007 c 15, s 62, sch 13 para 127; Crime and Cts,
            2013 c 22, sch 9 para 52
        s 8A added—Mesothelioma, 2014 c 1, sch 1 para 3
        s 9 am—Mesothelioma, 2014 c 1, sch 1 para 8
        s 10 am—(pt prosp) Social Security, 1998 c 14, s 86(1), sch 7 para 149(1)(2);
            Mesothelioma, 2014 c 1, sch 1 para 4
            ext—SI 1999/991, reg 29(6)
            appl (mods)—SI 2008/1596, regs 2, 5, sch 1
        s 11 am—(pt prosp) Social Security, 1998 c 14, s 86(1), sch 7 para 150(1)(2); Welfare
            Reform, 2012 c 5, sch 11 para 10(2)(3); Mesothelioma, 2014 c 1, sch 1 paras 5, 8
            rep in pt—(pt prosp) Social Security, 1998 c 14, s 86(1)(2), sch 7 para 150(3), sch 8; SI
            2008/2833, art 6, sch 3
            appl (mods)—SI 2008/1596, regs 2, 5, sch 1
        s 12 am—(pt prosp) Social Security, 1998 c 14, s 86(1), sch 7, para 151(1)
            (2)(3)(a)(b)(4)(a)(b); SI 2008/2833, art 6, sch 3; Crime and Cts, 2013 c 22, sch
            11 para 148(2)
            rep in pt—(pt prosp) Social Security, 1998 c 14, s 86(1)(2), sch 7, para 151(5)(a)-(c),
            sch 8
            appl (mods)—SI 2008/1596, regs 2, 5, sch 1

1997
c 27 *continued*

s 13 am—(pt prosp) Social Security, 1998 c 14, s 86(1)(2), sch 7, para 152(1) (2)(a)(b)(3),
    sch 8; SI 2008/2833, art 6, sch 3; Mesothelioma, 2014 c 1, sch 1 paras 6, 8
  rep in pt—(pt prosp) Social Security, 1998 c 14, s 86(1)(2), sch 7 para 152(4), sch 8; SI
    2008/2833, art 6, sch 3
  appl (mods)—SI 2008/1596, regs 2, 5, sch 1
s 14 appl (mods)—SI 2008/1596, regs 2, 5, sch 1
  am—Mesothelioma, 2014 c 1, sch 1 para 8
s 15 appl (mods)—SI 2008/1596, reg 2, sch 1
ss 17, 18 appl (mods)—SI 2008/1596, regs 2, 5, sch 1
s 19 appl (mods)—SI 2008/1596, regs 2, 5, sch 1
  am—Mesothelioma, 2014 c 1, sch 1 para 8
s 20 appl (mods)—SI 2008/1596, regs 2, 5, sch 1
  am—Mesothelioma, 2014 c 1, sch 1 para 8
s 21 appl (mods)—SI 2008/1596, regs 2, 5, sch 1
  am—Mesothelioma, 2014 c 1, sch 1 para 8
s 22 appl (mods)—SI 2008/1596, regs 2, 5, sch 1
s 23 appl (mods)—SI 2008/1596, regs 2, 5, sch 1
  am—Mesothelioma, 2014 c 1, sch 1 para 19
s 26 appl (mods)—SI 2008/1596, regs 2, 5, sch 1
s 27 appl (mods)—SI 2008/1596, regs 2, 5, sch 1
s 28 appl (mods)—SI 2008/1596, regs 2, 5
s 29 am—Social Security, 1998 c 14, s 86(1), sch 7 para 153; SI 2008/1554, reg 50;
    Welfare Reform, 2012 c 5, sch 2 para 41, sch 9 para 35; Mesothelioma, 2014 c 1,
    sch 1 para 7
  rep in pt—SI 2008/2833, art 6, sch 3
  appl (mods)—SI 2008/1596, regs 2, 5, sch 1
s 30 appl (mods)—SI 2008/1596, reg 5
  am—Welfare Reform, 2012 c 5, sch 11 para 11(2)(3)
s 31 appl (mods)—SI 2008/1596, reg 5
s 32 appl (mods)—SI 2008/1596, reg 5
s 33 appl (mods)—SI 2008/1596, regs 2, 5
s 34 appl (mods)—SI 2008/1596, regs 2, 5
sch 1 am—Powers of Crim Cts (Sentencing), 2000 c 6, s 165(1), sch 9 para 181;
    SI 2001/3649, art 358(1)-(4); Armed Forces, 2006 c 52, s 378, sch 16 para 140;
    Financial Services, 2012 c 21, sch 18 para 84; Modern Slavery, 2015 c 30, sch 5
    para 13
  appl (mods)—SI 2008/1596, regs 2, 5, sch 1
  mod—SI 2009/1059, art 205, sch 1
sch 2 rep in pt—Tax Credits, 1999 c 10, ss 2, 19(4), sch 2 pt IV para 18(1)(a)(2), sch 6; (pt
    prosp) Welfare Reform, 2012 c 5, sch 14 pts 1, 9
  am—SI 2008/1554, reg 50; Welfare Reform, 2012 c 5, sch 2 para 42, sch 9 para 36
sch 3 rep in pt—Child Support, Pensions and Social Security, 2000 c 19, s 85, sch 9 pt VI
c 28 **Merchant Shipping and Maritime Security**
ss 2, 3 rep—Marine Safety, 2003 c 16, s 3(2), sch 3
s 4 rep—(EW) Fire and Rescue Services, 2004 c 21, s 54, sch 2; (S) Fire (S), 2005 asp 5,
    s 89(2), sch 4
s 7 rep in pt—SI 2015/664, sch 4 para 99
s 10 rep—Marine Safety, 2003 c 16, s 3(2), sch 3
s 24 saved—Scotland, 1998 c 46, s 30, sch 5 pt II, s E3(k)
  am—SI 2009/1941, art 2, sch 1
s 26 appl—Aviation Security, 1982 c 36, s 39(2)
  saved—Scotland, 1998 c 46, s 30, sch 5 pt II, s E3(k)
  appl (mods)—SI 2000/3059, art 4, sch 5
s 27, 28 saved—Scotland, 1998 c 46, s 30, sch 5 pt II, s E3(k)
sch 5 appl (mods)—SI 2000/3059, art 4, sch 5
c 29 **Local Government and Rating**
saving—SI 2007/3136, art 3
s 2 rep in pt—(prosp) Loc Govt, 2003 c 26, s 127(2), sch 8 pt 1
s 5 rep in pt—Loc Govt in S, 2003 asp 1, s 28(1)
s 8 am—Loc Govt in S, 2003 asp 1, s 28(2)
ss 9-25 rep—Loc Govt and Public Involvement in Health, 2007 c 28, s 101, sch 5 para 10,
    sch 18
sch 1 rep in pt—Localism, 2011 c 20, sch 25 pt 10

1997

c 29 *continued*

    sch 2 am—Postal Services, 2000 c 26, s 127(4), sch 8 pt II para 25; Loc Govt in S, 2003 asp
        1, ss 28(3)(4), 29; Postal Services, 2011 c 5, sch 12 para 148

    saved—SSIs 2000/92, reg 20(b); 2001/71, reg 17(b); 2002/91, reg 18(b); 2003/160,
        reg 19(b); 2008/85, reg 5

    sch 3 rep in pt—SI 2001/3649, art 359

c 30 **Police (Property)**

    rep (NI) —(saving) Police (NI), 1998 c 32, s 74(2)(3), schs 5, 6

    s 2 rep—Powers of Crim Cts (Sentencing), 2000 c 6, s 165(3)(4), sch 11 pt I para 2, sch 12
        pt I

    s 7 rep in pt—Powers of Crim Cts (Sentencing), 2000 c 6, s 165(3)(4), sch 11 pt I para 2,
        sch 12 pt I

c 31 *Appropriation*—rep Appropriation, 1999 c 13, s 3, sch (C)

c 32 **Building Societies**

    s 11 rep —Financial Services (Banking Reform), 2013 c 33, sch 9 para 4(3)(b)

    s 16 rep—SI 2001/2617, art 13(1), sch 3 pt II para 213(a)

    ss 19-24 rep—SI 2001/2617, art 13(1), sch 3 pt II para 213(b)

    ss 32-35 rep—SI 2001/2617, art 13(1), sch 3 pt II para 213(c)

    s 44 rep—SI 2001/2617, art 13(1), sch 3 pt II para 213(d)

    s 45 rep in pt—SI 2001/3629, art 109, sch

    sch 3 rep—SI 2001/2617, art 13(1)(2), sch 3 pt II para 213(e), sch 4

    sch 7 rep in pt—SI 2001/2617, art 13(1)(2), sch 3 pt II para 213(f), sch 4

    sch 8 rep in pt—SI 2001/2617, art 13(1)(2), sch 3 pt II para 213(g), sch 4

c 33 **Confiscation of Alcohol (Young Persons)**

    s 1 am—Crim Justice and Police, 2001 c 16, s 29; Licensing, 2003 c 17, ss 155(1)(b)(c),
        198, sch 6 para 115; Policing and Crime, 2009 c 26, s 29(1)(3)(5)(6)

    rep in pt—Licensing, 2003 c 17, ss 155(1)(a), 199, sch 7; Serious Organised Crime and
        Police, 2005 c 15, ss 111, 174(2), sch 7 pt 1 para 33, sch 17 pt 2; Policing and
        Crime, 2009 c 26, ss 29(1)(2)(4)(7), 112, sch 8 pt 3

c 34 **Contract (Scotland)**

c 35 **Scottish Legal Services Ombudsman and Commissioner for Local Administration in
    Scotland**

    ss 7, 8 rep—S Public Services Ombudsman, 2002 asp 11, s 25(1), sch 6, para 20

c 36 *Flood Prevention and Land Drainage (Scotland)* —Flood Risk Management (S), 2009 asp 6,
    s 96, sch 3 para 10

c 37 **Welsh Development Agency**

c 38 **Prisons (Alcohol Testing)**

c 39 **Sexual Offences (Protected Material)**

    ext—International Crim. Court., 2001 c 17, s 57

    Pt 1 (ss 1-21) power to mod—Youth Justice and Crim Evidence, 1999 c 23, s 38(7)(b)

    s 2 am—Crim Justice and Court Services, 2000 c 43, s 74, sch 7 pt II para 134; Legal
        Services, 2007 c 29, s 208, sch 21 para 123

    s 9 am —Crim Justice, 2003 c 44, s 311, sch 36 pt 3 paras 20, 39

    rep in pt—Crim Justice, 2003 c 44, ss 41, 332, sch 3 pt 2 para 67, sch 37 pt 4

    sch rep in pt—Sexual Offences, 2003 c 42, s 140, sch 7

    am—Sexual Offences, 2003 c 42, s 139, sch 6 para 36(a)(b)

    mod—Serious Crime, 2007 c 27, s 63, sch 6 para 34

c 40 **Protection from Harassment**

    s 1 am—Serious Organised Crime and Police, 2005 c 15, s 125(1)(2); Protection of
        Freedoms, 2012 c 9, sch 9 para 143(2)

    s 2 am—Serious Organised Crime and Police, 2005 c 15, s 125(1)(3)

    s 2A added—Protection of Freedoms, 2012 c 9, s 111(1)

    s 2B added—Protection of Freedoms, 2012 c 9, s 112

    s 3 am—Serious Organised Crime and Police, 2005 c 15, s 125(1)(4); Crime and Cts, 2013
        c 22, sch 9 para 39(a)(b)

    rep in pt—Crime and Cts, 2013 c 22, sch 9 para 39(c)

    s 2 rep in pt —Police Reform, 2002 c 30, s 107(2), sch 8

    s 3A added—Serious Organised Crime and Police, 2005 c 15, s 125(1)(5)

    am—Crime and Cts, 2013 c 22, sch 9 para 52

    s 4 am—Protection of Freedoms, 2012 c 9, sch 9 para 143(3)

    s 4A added—Protection of Freedoms, 2012 c 9, s 111(2)

    s 5 mod—Crime and Disorder, 1998 c 37, s 32(7); SI 2014/3300, regs 13, 17(7)

    rep in pt—Domestic Violence, Crime and Victims, 2004 c 28, ss 12(1), 58, 59, sch 10
        para 43(1)(3), sch 11, sch 12 para 5(1)

1997
c 40 s 5 *continued*
am—Domestic Violence, Crime and Victims, 2004 c 28, ss 12(2)-(4), 58(1), 59, sch 10
para 43(1)(2), sch 12 para 5(2)(3); Serious Organised Crime and Police, 2005 c 15,
s 125(1)(6)
s 5A added—Domestic Violence, Crime and Victims, 2004 c 28, s 12(5)
s 7 am—Crim Justice and Police, 2001 c 16, s 44; Domestic Violence, Crime and Victims,
2004 c 28, ss 58(1), 59, sch 10 para 44, sch 12 para 5(3); Serious Organised Crime
and Police, 2005 c 15, s 125(1)(7)
s 8 appl—(S) Housing (S) 1987 c 26, s 25(1B)
am—Domestic Abuse (S), 2011 asp 13, s 1(1)
rep in pt—Damages (S), 2011 asp 7, sch 2
s 8A added—(S) Domestic Abuse (S), 2011 asp 13, s 1(2)
s 9 rep in pt—Crim Justice (S), 2003 asp 7, s 49(2)(a)
am—Crim Justice (S), 2003 asp 7, s 49(2)(b); Domestic Abuse (S), 2011 asp 13, s 1(3)
c 41 **Building Societies (Distributions)**
c 42 **Police (Health and Safety)**
s 5 rep in pt—Serious Organised Crime and Police, 2005 c 15, ss 59, 174(2), sch 4 para 93,
sch 17 pt 2
am—Police Reform and Social Responsibility, 2011 c 13, sch 16 para 225; SI 2013/602,
sch 2 para 27(a)-(c)
c 43 **Crime (Sentences)**
cert functions restr from exercise in S—SI 1999/1748, art 8(2), sch 4 pt I para 1(1)
Pt 1 (ss 1-7) rep—Powers of Crim Cts (Sentencing), 2000 c 6, s 165(3)(4), sch 11 pt I para 2,
sch 12 pt I
Pt 2 (ss 8-34) appl (mods)—SI 1997/1776, art 2, sch 1 paras 2-4
s 8 rep—Crime and Disorder, 1998 c 37, ss 107(2),120(2), sch 10
ss 9, 9A rep—Powers of Crim Cts (Sentencing), 2000 c 6, s 165(3)(4), sch 11 pt I para 2,
sch 12 pt I
ss 10-27 rep—Crime and Disorder, 1998 c 37, ss 107(2),120(2), sch 10
Pt 2 Ch 2 (ss 28-34) appl—Crim Justice, 1991 c 53 sch 5 para 1(2); Crim Justice, 2003 c 44,
ss 225(4), 226(4)
excl—International Crim. Court., 2001 c 17, s 42, sch 7 para 3(1)
see (exercise of functions)—Crim Justice, 2003 c 44, s 239, sch 19 para 1
ss 28-30 cert functions restr from exercise in S—SI 1999/1748, art 8(2), sch 4 para 1(1)
s 28 am—Crime and Disorder, 1998 c 37, s 119, sch 8 para 130(1)(2); Powers of Crim Cts
(Sentencing), 2000 c 6, s 165(1), sch 9 para 182; Crim Justice and Court Services,
2000 c 43, s 74, sch 7 pt II paras 136(a),145; Crim Justice, 2003 c 44, s 275;
Crim Justice and Cts, 2015 c 2, s 11(1)
rep in pt—Crim Justice and Court Services, 2000 c 43, ss 74,75, sch 7 pt II
paras 136(b),145, sch 8
mod—Crim Justice and Court Services, 2000 c 43, s 74, sch 7 pt II paras 146-148;
Crim Justice, 2003 c 44, s 276, sch 22 para 16
ext—Crim Justice, 2003 c 44, ss 269(2), 276, sch 22 para 3
appl—(S) Prisoners and Criminal Proceedings (S) 1993 c 9, s 10(1)(a)(iii)
s 29 rep—Crim Justice, 2003 c 44, ss 303(b)(i), 332, sch 37 pt 8
s 31 am—Crime and Disorder, 1998 c 37, s 119, sch 8 para 131(2)(3); Crim Justice and
Court Services, 2000 c 43, s 74, sch 7 pt I para 4(1)(2); Crim Justice, 2003 c 44,
ss 230, 304, sch 18, para 1, sch 32 pt 1 paras 82, 83(1)(2)(4); SIs 2005/886, art 2,
sch para 53; 2008/912, art 3, sch 1; Crim Justice and Cts, 2015 c 2, sch 2 para 1
cert functions restr from exercise in S—SI 1999/1748, art 8(2), sch 4 para 1(1)(2)
mod—(temp) SI 1998/2327, art 5(1)(b)
rep in pt—Crime and Disorder, 1998 c 37, ss 119,120(2), sch 8 para 131(1), sch 10;
Crim Justice, 2003 c 44, ss 304, 332, sch 32 pt 1 paras 82, 83(1)(3), sch 37 pt
8; Children, 2004 c 31, s 64, sch 5 pt 4; Crim Justice and Immigration, 2008 c
4, s 149, sch 28 pt 2
s 31A added—(EW) Crim Justice, 2003 c 44, s 230, sch 18 para 2
am—Armed Forces, 2006 c 52, s 378, sch 16 para 141; Legal Aid, Sentencing and
Punishment of Offenders, 2012 c 10, s 117(10)(a)
s 32 cert functions restr from exercise in S—SI 1999/1748, art 8(2), sch 4 para 1(1)(2)
power to am—Legal Aid, Sentencing and Punishment of Offenders, 2012 c 10, s
128(3)(aa)
am—Crim Justice, 2003 c 44, s 304, sch 32 pt 1 paras 82, 84; Crim Justice and
Immigration, 2008 c 4, s 30; Crim Justice and Cts, 2015 c 2, s 11(2)
s 32ZA added—Crim Justice and Cts, 2015 c 2, s 12(1)

1997
c 43 *continued*

ss 32A, 32B added—Legal Aid, Sentencing and Punishment of Offenders, 2012 c 10, s 119
s 33 rep—Crim Justice, 2003 c 44, ss 303(b)(ii), 332, sch 37 pt 8
s 34 am—Crime and Disorder, 1998 c 37, ss 101(2),120(1), sch 9 para 11; Powers of Crim
 Cts (Sentencing), 2000 c 6, s 165(1), sch 9 para 183; Crim Justice, 2003 c 44,
 ss 230, 273(4), 276, sch 18 para 3, sch 22 para 17; Armed Forces, 2006 c 52, s
 378, sch 16 para 142; Legal Aid, Sentencing and Punishment of Offenders, 2012 c
 10, s 117(10)(b)
 appl—Crime and Disorder, 1998 c 37, ss 101(1),120(1), sch 9 para 11
 cert functions restr from exercise in S—SI 1999/1748, art 8(2), sch 4 para 1(1)(2)
 rep in pt—Crim Justice and Court Services, 2000 c 43, ss 74,75, sch 7 pt II paras 138,
 145, sch 8; Crim Justice, 2003 c 44, s 332, sch 37 pt 8; Armed Forces, 2006 c
 52, s 378, sch 16 para 142
 mod—SI 2009/1059, art 205, sch 1
s 35 rep (prosp)—Crim Justice, 2003 c 44, ss 303(b)(iii), 332, sch 37 pt 7
 rep in pt—Crime and Disorder, 1998 c 37, ss 106, 119, 120(2), sch 7, para 50(2)(3)(5),
 sch 8 para 132(3)(a),sch 10
 am—Crime and Disorder, 1998 c 37, ss 106, 119, sch 7 para 50(1)(3)-(6), sch 8
 para 132(1)(2)(3)(b); Access to Justice, 1999 c 22, s 66, sch 9 para 9; Powers of
 Crim Cts (Sentencing), 2000 c 6, s 165(1), sch 9 para 184; Proceeds of Crime,
 2002 c 29, s 456, sch 11, para 32(1)(2)
ss 36-39 rep—Powers of Crim Cts (Sentencing), 2000 c 6, s 165(3)(4), sch 11 pt I para 2,
 sch 12 pt I
s 40 rep (prosp)—Crim Justice, 2003 c 44, ss 303(b)(iii), 332, sch 37 pt 7
 rep in pt—SI 2015/583, sch 2 para 5
 am—Powers of Crim Cts (Sentencing), 2000 c 6, s 165(1), sch 9 para 185; Proceeds of
 Crime, 2002 c 29, s 456, sch 11, para 32(1)(3)
 appl—Prisons (S) 1989 c 45, s 13(b)
ss 43, 44, 50, 51 rep—Powers of Crim Cts (Sentencing), 2000 c 6, s 165(3)(4), sch 11 pt I
 para 2, sch 12 pt I
s 47 rep in pt—Domestic Violence, Crime and Victims, 2004 c 28, ss 58, 59, sch 10 para
 45(1)(2), sch 11 para 8(1)(2)(d)
 am—Domestic Violence, Crime and Victims, 2004 c 28, ss 58(1), 59, sch 10 para
 45(1)(3), sch 12 para 8(1)(2)(d); Armed Forces, 2006 c 52, s 378, sch 16 para
 143
s 52 rep—Sexual Offences, 2003 c 42, s 140, sch 7
s 54 rep in pt—Crime and Disorder, 1998 c 37, ss 119,120(2), sch 8 para 133, sch 10
 am—Crime and Disorder, 1998 c 37, s 106, sch 7 para 53; Crim Justice and Court
 Services, 2000 c 43, s 74, sch 7 pt II para 141
s 55 am—Crime and Disorder, 1998 c 37, s 106, sch 7 para 54
 rep in pt—Powers of Crim Cts (Sentencing), 2000 c 6, s 165(3)(4), sch 11 pt I para 2,
 sch 12 pt I; (prosp) Armed Forces, 2001 c 19, s 38, sch 7 pt 2
s 57 am—Crime and Disorder, 1998 c 37, s 119, sch 8 para 134; (retrosp) Crim Justice and
 Court Services, 2000 c 43, s 74, sch 7 pt II para 142; Armed Forces, 2006 c 52, s
 378, sch 16 para 144
sch 1 am—Crime and Disorder, 1998 c 37, s 119, sch 8 para 135(1)-(6)(9)(10);
 SI 1999/1820, art 4, sch 2 pt I para 130; Powers of Crim Cts (Sentencing), 2000
 c 6, s 165(1), sch 9 para 186(1)-(5); (retrosp) Crim Justice and Court Services,
 2000 c 43, s 74, sch 7 pt II para 143; (EW, NI) SI 2001/2565, art 3(1)(2); (S,
 NI) SI 2001/2565, art 3(1)(3); Crim Justice, 2003 c 44, s 304, sch 32 pt 1
 paras 82, 85(1)-(4); Justice (NI), 2004 c 4, s 13(1)(2)-7; Domestic Violence,
 Crime and Victims, 2004 c 28, s 58(1), sch 10 para 46; Management of
 Offenders etc. (S), 2005 asp 14, s 21(8); SI 2006/1055, art 2; Armed Forces,
 2006 c 52, s 378, sch 16 para 145; Offender Management, 2007 c 21, s 39, sch 3
 para 15; Crim Justice and Immigration, 2008 c 4, s 148, sch 26 paras 31,
 32(1)-(3)(5)-(9); SIs 2008/912, art 3, sch 1; 2010/976, art 6, sch 8; Legal Aid,
 Sentencing and Punishment of Offenders, 2012 c 10, sch 10 para 9(3)(a)(4)(a),
 sch 14 para 2, sch 16 paras 7, 8, sch 21 para 5; Offender Rehabilitation, 2014 c
 11, s 13(2)(3), sch 3 paras 2-4, 5(2)(3)(5), 6-8; Crim Justice and Cts, 2015 c 2,
 sch 1 para 12(2)(3)
 rep in pt—Crime and Disorder, 1998 c 37, ss 119,120(2), sch 8,
  para 135(4)(a)(d)(5)(c)(d)(6)(d)(7)(8), sch 10; Crm Justice, 2003 c 44, ss 304,
  332, sch 32 pt 1 paras 82, 85(1)(5), sch 37 pt 7; (EW) Children, 2004 c 31,
  s 64, sch 5 pt 4; Legal Aid, Sentencing and Punishment of Offenders, 2012 c 10,

1997
c 43 sch 1 *continued*

sch 10 para 9(2)(3)(b)(4)(b); Offender Rehabilitation, 2014 c 11, sch 3 para 5(4)

cert functions exercisable in S—SI 1999/1748, arts 4(1), 8(1), sch 2 para 3

excl—NI (Sentences), 1998 c 35, s 17, sch 3 para 9(1); SI 1998/2251, art 16(5); International Crim. Court., 2001 c 17, s 42(5)

ext (mods)—(I of M) SI 1997/1775, art 2, sch; Crime and Disorder, 1998 c 37, s 121(12); (Channel Is and I of M) SI 1998/2798, arts 2, 3, schs 1,2

mod—NI (Sentences), 1998 c 35, s 17, sch 3 para 9(5); (temp) SI 1998/2327, art 5(2)(c)(d); Crim Justice and Immigration, 2008 c 4, s 148, sch 26 paras 31, 32(1)(5); Crim Justice and Cts, 2015 c 2, s 97(1)

appl—International Crim Ct, 2001 c 17, s 46(1); SI 1994/1931, rule 14B(7)(a)(i); Justice (NI), 2002 c 26, s 70(3)

power mod—Offender Rehabilitation, 2014 c 11, s 23(6)

sch 2 rep in pt—Crime and Disorder, 1998 c 37, ss 119,120(2), sch 8 para 136, sch 10; (E, W, NI) SI 2001/2565, art 3(1)(4); Crim Justice, 2003 c 44, ss 304, 332, sch 32 pt 1 paras 82, 86, sch 37 pt 7

am—Crim Justice (S), 2003 asp 7, s 33(4); Crim Justice and Immigration, 2008 c 4, s 148, sch 26 paras 31, 33

sch 3 rep in pt—Mental Health (Care and Treatment) (S), 2003 asp 13, s 331(2), sch 5 pt 1

am—SI 2003 c 44, sch 32 para 125

sch 4 rep in pt—Crime and Disorder, 1998 c 37, ss 119,120(2), sch 8, para 137(a)(b)(c), sch 10; Powers of Crim Cts (Sentencing), 2000 c 6, s 165(3)(4), sch 11 pt I para 2, sch 12 pt I; (prosp) Armed Forces, 2001 c 19, s 38, sch 7 pt 2; Crim Justice, 2003 c 44, s 332, sch 37 pts 5, 7; Mental Health, 2007 c 12, s 55, sch 11 pt 5

am—Powers of Crim Cts (Sentencing), 2000 c 6, s 165(1), sch 9 para 187(1)(2)(3)(4)(5)

sch 5 am—Crime and Disorder, 1998 c 37, s 119, sch 8 para 138(2)(a)(3)(a)(b); SI 1999/1820, art 4, sch 2 pt I para 130; Powers of Crim Cts (Sentencing), 2000 c 6, s 165(1), sch 9 para 188

rep in pt—Crime and Disorder, 1998 c 37, ss 119,120(2), sch 8, para 138(1), sch 10; Crim Justice and Court Services, 2000 c 43, ss 74,75, sch 7 pt II paras 144,145, sch 8; Crim Justice and Immigration, 2008 c 4, s 149, sch 28 pt 2

sch 6 rep in pt—Crime and Disorder, 1998 c 37, ss 119,120(2), sch 8 para 139, sch 10

c 44 **Education**

trans of powers—(W) SI 1999/672, art 2, sch 1

power to mod—Educ, 2002 c 32, s 177(4)(5)

am—SI 2010/1158, art 5, sch 2

s 1 rep—Education (Schools), 1997 c 59, s 6(3), sch pt I

ss 2, 3 rep—School Standards and Framework, 1998 c 31, s 140(1)(3), sch 30, para 208(a), sch 31

ss 4, 5 rep —Educ and Inspections, 2006 c 40, s 184, sch 18

ss 6-8 rep—School Standards and Framework, 1998 c 31, s 140(1)(3), sch 30, para 208(b), sch 31

s 9 rep —Children, 2004 c 31, s 64, sch 5 pt 1

ss 10-14 rep—School Standards and Framework, 1998 c 31, s 140(1)(3), sch 30 para 208(c), sch 31

Pt 4, Ch 1 (ss 15-18) rep—Educ, 2002 c 32, ss 204, 215(2), sch 22 pt 3

s 19 am—School Standards and Framework, 1998 c 31, s 140(1), sch 30 para 213

ss 21-26 rep —Apprenticeships, Skills, Children and Learning, 2009 c 22, ss 174, 192, 266, sch 12 paras 12, 13, sch 16 pt 4

s 26A added—Educ, 2002 c 32, s 189, sch 17, para 4

rep —Apprenticeships, Skills, Children and Learning, 2009 c 22, ss 174, 192, 266, sch 12 paras 12, 13, sch 16 pt 4

Pt 5, Ch 2 (ss 27-32, 32A) am (heading subst)—SI 2005/3239 (W 244), arts 7(1)-(3), 9(1), sch 1 paras 6, 8

s 27 rep —SI 2005/3239 (W 244), arts 7(1)-(3), 9(1), sch 1 paras 6, 9

s 28 am —SI 2005/3239 (W 244), arts 7(1)-(3), 9(1), sch 1 paras 6, 10, 11

s 29 am—School Standards and Framework, 1998 c 31, s 140(1), sch 30 para 215; Educ, 2002 c 32, s 189, sch 17, para 5(1)(2)(3)(a)(4)(6); SI 2005/3239 (W 244), arts 7(1)-(3), 9(1), sch 1 paras 6, 12, 13(a); Apprenticeships, Skills, Children and Learning, 2009 c 22, ss 174, 192, sch 12 paras 12, 14; (W) Qualifications Wales, 2015 anaw 5, sch 4 para 2(2)

1997
c 44 s 29 *continued*

rep in pt—Educ, 2002 c 32, ss 189, 215(2), sch 17, para 5(1)(3)(b)(5), sch 22 pt 2; SI
2005/3239 (W 244), arts 7(1)-(3), 9(1), sch 1 paras 6, 13; School Standards
and Organisation (W), 2013 anaw 1, sch 5 para 18(2)(a)(b)
appl (mods)—(temp) (W) SI 2005/3239 (W 244), art 7(4)
s 30 rep—Qualifications Wales, 2015 anaw 5, sch 4 para 2(3)(a)
s 31 rep—SI 2005/3239 (W 244), arts 7(1)-(3), 9(1), sch 1 paras 6, 16
s 32 rep in pt —Educ, 2002 c 32, ss 189, 215(2), sch 17, para 7(1)(2), sch 22 pt 2; SI
2005/3239 (W 244), arts 7(1)-(3), 9(1), sch 1 paras 6, 18(a)(iii)(g);
Apprenticeships, Skills, Children and Learning, 2009 c 22, ss 174, 192, 266,
sch 12 paras 12, 16(4), sch 16 pt 4; Qualifications Wales, 2015 anaw 5, sch 4
para 2(3)(b)
am —Educ, 2002 c 32, ss 189, 215(1), sch 17, para 7(1)(3)(4), sch 21, para 70; SI
2005/3239 (W 244), arts 7(1)-(3), 9(1), sch 1 paras 6, 17, 18(a)(i)(ii)(b)-(f);
Educ and Skills, 2008 c 25, s 162(1)(6)-(9); Apprenticeships, Skills, Children
and Learning, 2009 c 22, ss 174, 192, sch 12 paras 12, 16(1)-(3)(5)
s 32ZA-32C rep—Qualifications Wales, 2015 anaw 5, sch 4 para 2(3)(c)
ss 33, 34 rep—SL(R), 2004 c 14, s 1(1), sch 1 pt 7
s 35 rep—Educ, 2011 c 21, sch 8 para 8
rep in pt —SI 2005/3239 (W 244), arts 7(1)-(3), 9(1), sch 1 paras 6, 21(a)
am —(W) SI 2005/3239 (W 244), arts 7(1)-(3), 9(1), sch 1 paras 6, 21(b);
Apprenticeships, Skills, Children and Learning, 2009 c 22, ss 174, 192, sch 12
paras 12, 20
s 36 rep—Apprenticeships, Skills, Children and Learning, 2009 c 22, ss 174, 192, 266, sch
12 paras 12, 21, sch 16 pt 4
s 37 rep—SL(R), 2004 c 14, s 1(1), sch 1 pt 7
s 38 ext—Disability Discrimination, 1995 c 50, s 28D(6)
am—Children, 2004 c 31, s 51; Educ, 2005 c 18, s 61, sch 9 para 11; Childcare, 2006
c 21, s 103, sch 2 para 28; Educ and Inspections, 2006 c 40, s 157, sch 14 para
22(4)(a); SI 2010/1158, art 5, sch 2; (1.4.2016) Well-being of Future Generations
(W), 2015 anaw 2, sch 4 para 1
appl—(E) SI 2005/1973, reg 2, sch para 2(1)(2)(a)
rep in pt—Educ and Inspections, 2006 c 40, s 157, sch 14 para 22(1), (2), (3), (4)(b),
sch 18
s 39 am—School Standards and Framework, 1998 c 31, s 134(3); Educ, 2005 c 18, s 61,
sch 9 para 12; Educ and Inspections, 2006 c 40, s 157, sch 14 para 23(b)
rep in pt—Educ and Inspections, 2006 c 40, s 157, sch 14 para 23(a), (c), sch 18
s 40 subst—Educ, 2002 c 32, s 180
am—Educ, 2005 c 18, s 61, sch 9 para 13
appl—(E) SI 2005/1973, reg 2, sch para 2(1)(2)(a)
s 41 rep—Educ and Inspections, 2006 c 40, s 157, sch 14 para 24, sch 18
s 41A added—Public Audit (W), 2004 c 23, s 66, sch 2 paras 17, 19
am—Public Audit (W), 2013 anaw 3, sch 4 para 4
s 42 rep—Educ, 2005 c 18, s 123, sch 19 pt 1
s 42A added—Educ, 2011 c 21, s 29(2)
appl (mods)—SI 2013/709, reg 2
excl in pt—SI 2013/709, reg 3
s 43 am—School Standards and Framework, 1998 c 31, s 140(1), sch 30, para 217(a)(c);
Learning and Skills, 2000 c 21, s 149, sch 9 para 71; Educ, 2002 c 32, s 65(3),
sch 7 pt 2, para 8; Educ and Skills, 2008 c 25, s 81(1)(2); Apprenticeships, Skills,
Children and Learning, 2009 c 22, s 250; Educ, 2011 c 21, s 29(3)(a)(g)(f)(i)
ext—(W) SI 2001/1987 (W 138), reg 2
ext (mods)—(E) SI 2003/2645, reg 2
rep in pt—Educ, 2011 c 21, s 29(3)(b)-(e)(f)(ii); School Standards and Organisation
(W), 2013 anaw 1, sch 5 para 18(3)
s 44 am—Learning and Skills, 2000 c 21, s 149, sch 9 para 72; Educ, 2011 c 21, s 29(4)
s 45 am—Educ and Skills, 2008 c 25, s 81(1)(3); Educ, 2011 c 21, s 29(5)(a)(d)(e)
rep in pt—Educ, 2011 c 21, s 29(5)(b)(c)
mod—SI 2013/1793 (W 180), regs 3(d), 7(b)
s 45A added—Educ and Skills, 2008 c 25, s 81(1)(4)
am—Educ, 2011 c 21, s 29(6)
s 45B added —Learning and Skills (W), 2009 nawm 1, s 45
am—Educ, 2011 c 21, s 29(7)
s 46 am—Educ, 2011 c 21, s 29(8)

1997
c 44 *continued*

s 49 rep—Educ, 2002 c 32, s 215, sch 21, para 71, sch 22 pt 3

s 50 rep—School Standards and Framework, 1998 c 31, s 140(1)(3), sch 30 para 218, sch 31

s 52 rep in pt—School Standards and Framework, 1998 c 31, s 140(1)(3), sch 30 para 219, sch 31

s 53A added—SI 2003/2867, reg 2, sch pt 1 para 26

s 54 rep in pt—Apprenticeships, Skills, Children and Learning, 2009 c 22, ss 174, 192, 266, sch 12 paras 12, 22, sch 16 pt 4; Qualifications Wales, 2015 anaw 5, sch 4 para 2(4)

am—Educ, 2011 c 21, s 24(7)

s 57 rep in pt—School Standards and Framework, 1998 c 31, s 140(1)(3), sch 30 para 220, sch 31

s 58 am —Educ, 2002 c 32, s 189, sch 17, para 9; Educ and Skills, 2008 c 25, s 163(2); Apprenticeships, Skills, Children and Learning, 2009 c 22, ss 174, 192, sch 12 paras 12, 23(b)

rep in pt—School Standards and Framework, 1998 c 31, s 140(1)(3), sch 30 para 221, sch 31; Apprenticeships, Skills, Children and Learning, 2009 c 22, ss 174, 192, 266, sch 12 paras 12, 23(a), sch 16 pt 4

schs 1-3 rep—School Standards and Framework, 1998 c 31, s 140(1)(3), sch 30 para 222(a), sch 31

sch 4 rep —Apprenticeships, Skills, Children and Learning, 2009 c 22, ss 174, 192, 266, sch 12 paras 12, 24, sch 16 pt 4

sch 5 rep —SI 2005/3239 (W 244), arts 7(1)-(3), 9(1), sch 1 paras 6, 25

sch 6 rep—Educ, 2005 c 18, s 123, sch 19 pt 1

sch 7 rep in pt—Audit Commn, 1998 c 18, s 54(3), sch 5; School Standards and Framework, 1998 c 31, s 140(1)(3), sch 30 para 223, sch 31; Finance, 1999 c 16, s 139, sch 20 pt III(15), Note; Educ, 2002 c 32, s 215(2), sch 22 pt 3; Apprenticeships, Skills, Children and Learning, 2009 c 22, ss 174, 192, 266, sch 12 paras 12, 25, sch 16 pt 4; Charities, 2011 c 25, sch 10

c 45   *Police (Insurance of Voluntary Assistants)*—rep SL(R), 2008 c 12, s 1(1), sch 1 pt 6

c 46   **National Health Service (Primary Care)**

am—(E) Health, 1999 c 8, s 39(3) (see SI 1999/2793)

ext (to the Isles of Scilly)—SI 2001/540, art 2

trans of powers—(W) SI 1999/672, art 2, sch 1

appl—(S) Freedom of Information (S), 2002 asp 13, ss 3(1)(a)(i), 75, sch 1 pt 4, para 35

Pt 1 (ss 1-20) rep (EW) —Health and Social Care (Community Health and Standards), 2003 c 43, ss 178, 196, sch 14 pt 4

restr (S)—Primary Medical Services (S), 2004 asp 1, s 3

power to mod—(prosp) Health, 1999 c 8, s 61(1)-(4)

transtl savings—(E) SI 2004/865, art 58

appl—(E) SI 2005/3477, reg 13(11)(d)

s 1 am—Health, 1999 c 8, s 65, sch 4 para 88(2); Health and Social Care, 2001 c 15, s 67, sch 5 pt 1 para 11(1)(2); Nat Health Service Reform and Health Care Professions, 2002 c 17, s 4(3), sch 3 pt 1, paras 1, 2(1)-(3); (S) Primary Medical Services (S), 2004 asp 1, s 8, sch para 2(1)(2); SIs (E) 2004/288, art 8(1)(3); (W) 2004/480 (W 49), art 7(1)(3); (S) (prosp) Smoking, Health and Social Care (S), 2005 asp 13, s 42(1), sch 2 para 4(1)(2)

appl—SI 2003/1250, arts 10(4)(a)(iii)(b)(iii), 31(4), sch 8 pt 2 para 22(2)(a)(iii)(b)(iii)

rep in pt—(S) Primary Medical Services (S), 2004 asp 1, s 8, sch para 2(1)(2); (prosp) Nat Health Service Reform (S), 2004 asp 7, s 11(2), sch 2; (S) (prosp) Smoking, Health and Social Care (S), 2005 asp 13, s 42(2), sch 3

s 2 am—Health, 1999 c 8, s 65, sch 4 para 88(3); SI 2003/1250, art 31(5), sch 9 para 6(a)

rep (S)—Primary Medical Services (S), 2004 asp 1, s 8, sch para 2(1)(3)

s 3 am—Health, 1999 c 8, s 65, sch 4 para 88(4); (S) (prosp) Smoking, Health and Social Care (S), 2005 asp 13, s 42(1), sch 2 para 4(1)(3)

rep in pt (S)—(prosp) Nat Health Service Reform (S), 2004 asp 7, s 11(2), sch 2

s 4 appl—(E) SI 2002/3048, reg 4(2)(b)

s 5 rep (S)—Primary Medical Services (S), 2004 asp 1, s 8, sch para 2(1)(4)

s 8ZA added—Health and Social Care, 2001 c 15, s 26(2)

am—Nat Health Service Reform and Health Care Professions, 2002 c 17, s 4(3), sch 3 pt 1, paras 1, 3

s 8A added—Health, 1999 c 8, s 6(1)

1997

c 46 s 8A *continued*

        am—Nat Health Service Reform and Health Care Professions, 2002 c 17, s 4(3), sch 3 pt 1, paras 1, 4

s 9 am—Health, 1999 c 8, s 65, sch 4 para 88(5); Nat Health Service Reform and Health Care Professions, 2002 c 17, s 4(1)

ss 11-13 rep (S)—Primary Medical Services (S), 2004 asp 1, s 8, sch para 2(1)(5)

s 12 am—Nat Health Service Reform and Health Care Professions, 2002 c 17, s 4(3), sch 3 pt 1, paras 1, 5

s 13 am—Nat Health Service Reform and Health Care Professions, 2002 c 17, s 4(3), sch 3 pt 1, paras 1, 6

s 14 rep—Health, 1999 c 8, s 65, sch 4 para 88(6), sch 5

s 15 rep (S)—Primary Medical Services (S), 2004 asp 1, s 8, sch para 2(1)(5)

s 17 am—(S) (prosp) Smoking, Health and Social Care (S), 2005 asp 13, s 42(1), sch 2 para 4(1)(4)

s 19 rep—Health, 1999 c 8, s 65, sch 4 para 88(6), sch 5

s 20 am —(S) Smoking, Health and Social Care (S), 2005 asp 13, s 12(1)(3)(a)

    rep in pt —(S) Smoking, Health and Social Care (S), 2005 asp 13, s 12(1)(3)(b)

s 21 am—Health and Social Care, 2001 c 15, s 67, sch 5 pt 1 para 11(1)(4); Nat Health Service Reform and Health Care Professions, 2002 c 17, s 4(3), sch 3 pt 1, paras 1, 7

    rep in pt—Nat Health Service (Conseq Provns), 2006 c 43, s 6, sch 4

s 22 am—Health and Social Care, 2001 c 15, s 27(5)(a); Nat Health Service Reform and Health Care Professions, 2002 c 17, s 4(3), sch 3 pt 1, paras 1, 8

    rep in pt—SI 2003/1250, art 31(5), sch 9 para 6(c); Nat Health Service (Conseq Provns), 2006 c 43, s 6, sch 4

s 23 rep in pt—(EW) Health and Social Care (Community Health and Standards), 2003 c 43, s 196, sch 14 pt 4, Note; (S) Primary Medical Services (S), 2004 asp 1, s 8, sch para 2(1)(6)

s 24 rep in pt—(EW) Health and Social Care (Community Health and Standards), 2003 c 43, s 196, sch 14 pt 4, Note

s 25 rep in pt —(EW) Health and Social Care (Community Health and Standards), 2003 c 43, s 196, sch 14 pt 4, Note

s 26 rep in pt—Nat Health Service (Conseq Provns), 2006 c 43, s 6, sch 4

ss 27-29 rep in pt —(prosp) Smoking, Health and Social Care (S), 2005 asp 13, s 42(2), sch 3; Nat Health Service (Conseq Provns), 2006 c 43, s 6, sch 4

s 31 rep in pt—Nat Health Service (Conseq Provns), 2006 c 43, s 6, sch 4

s 32 rep (EW)—Health and Social Care (Community Health and Standards), 2003 c 43, s 196, sch 14 pt 4, Note

s 33 rep (S)—Primary Medical Services (S), 2004 asp 1, s 8, sch para 2(1)(7)

s 34 rep in pt—Nat Health Service (Conseq Provns), 2006 c 43, s 6, sch 4

s 36 rep—Nat Health Service (Conseq Provns), 2006 c 43, s 6, sch 4

s 40 am—(W) Health and Social Care, 2001 c 15, s 26(3); Nat Health Service Reform and Health Care Professions, 2002 c 17, s 4(3), sch 3 pt 1, paras 1, 9

    rep in pt—(EW) Health and Social Care (Community Health and Standards), 2003 c 43, s 196, sch 14 pt 4, Note; (S) Primary Medical Services (S), 2004 asp 1, s 8, sch para 2(1)(8); Nat Health Service (Conseq Provns), 2006 c 43, s 6, sch 4; SI 2006/1407, art 2, sch 1

  saving—SI 2004/288, art 9

  see—SI 2004/288, art 6(2)(p)

ss 97, 97A saved—SI 1998/631, art 5

sch 1 rep—(EW) Health and Social Care (Community Health and Standards), 2003 c 43, s 196, sch 14 pt 4, Note; (S) Primary Medical Services (S), 2004 asp 1, s 8, sch para 2(1)(9)

sch 2 rep in pt—(pt prosp) Health, 1999 c 8, s 65, sch 5 (see SI 1999/2540); Health and Social Care, 2001 c 15, s 67, sch 6 pt 1; ibid, s 67, sch 6 pt 2; Community Care and Health (S), 2002 asp 5, s 25, sch 2, para 3; Nat Health Service Reform and Health Care Professions, 2002 c 17, s 37, sch 8, paras 23, 24, sch 9 pt 3; Public Appointments and Public Bodies etc (S), 2003 asp 4, s 17, sch 4 para 14(c); (EW) Health and Social Care (Community Health and Standards), 2003 c 43, s 196, sch 14 pt 4, Note; (S) Primary Medical Services (S), 2004 asp 1, s 8, sch para 2(1)(10)(a)(b); (S) (prosp) Smoking, Health and Social Care (S), 2005 asp 13, s 42(2), sch 3; Nat Health Service (Conseq Provns), 2006 c 43, s 6, sch 4; SI 2006/1407, art 3, sch 2

1997

c 46 *continued*

sch 3 rep in pt—(S) Public Appointments and Public Bodies etc (S), 2003 asp 4, s 17, sch 4 para 14(d); (S) (prosp) Smoking, Health and Social Care (S), 2005 asp 13, s 42(2), sch 3

c 47 **Social Security Administration (Fraud)**

s 3 rep (pt prosp)—Welfare Reform, 2012 c 5, sch 14 pt 1
    excl—Mental Health, 1983 c 20, s 37(1A)
s 4 excl—Mental Health, 1983 c 20, s 37(1A)
    rep in pt—(pt prosp) Welfare Reform, 2012 c 5, sch 14 pt 1
s 5 rep (pt prosp)—Welfare Reform, 2012 c 5, sch 14 pt 1
s 6 rep (EW)—Audit Commn, 1998 c 18, s 54(3), sch 5
ss 8-10 rep (pt prosp)—Welfare Reform, 2012 c 5, sch 14 pt 1
s 11 rep (prosp)—Welfare Reform, 2012 c 5, sch 14 pt 10
s 12 rep—Child Support, Pensions and Social Security, 2000 c 19, s 85, sch 9 pt VI
s 14 rep—Social Security Fraud, 2001 c 11, s 19, sch
s 16 rep (prosp)—Welfare Reform, 2012 c 5, sch 14 pt 1
ss 17, 18 rep (pt prosp)—Social Security, 1998 c 14, s 86(2), sch 8
sch 1 rep in pt—SI 1997/1182, art 19(2), sch 2; (EW) Audit Commn, 1998 c 18, s 54(3), sch 5; (pt prosp) Social Security, 1998 c 14, s 86(2), sch 8; Child Support, Pensions and Social Security, 2000 c 19, s 85, sch 9 pt VI; Employment, 2002 c 22, s 54, sch 8(1); Loc Govt, 2003 c 26, s 127(2), sch 8 pt 1; (pt prosp) Welfare Reform, 2012 c 5, sch 14 pt 1

c 48 **Crime and Punishment (Scotland)**

s 1 rep—Crim Justice (S), 2003 asp 7, s 19(3)
s 2 ext—Crime (Sentences) 1997 c 43 s 41, sch 1 pt II paras 10(5)(a)(6)(7), 11(5)
s 4 rep—Crime and Disorder, 1998 c 37, ss 119,120(2), sch 8 para 140, sch 10
ss 7, 8 rep—Mental Health (Care and Treatment) (S), 2003 asp 13, s 331(2), sch 5 pt 1
s 9 rep (prosp)—Mental Health (S), 2015 asp 9, s 49(a)
ss 11-13 ext—Crime (Sentences) 1997 c 43 s 41, sch 1 pt II paras 10(5)(a)(6)(7), 11(5)
s 13 rep in pt—Crim Justice and Licensing (S), 2010 asp 13, s 203, sch 7 paras 65, 67
s 15 rep in pt—Proceeds of Crime, 2002 c 29, ss 456, 457, sch 11, para 33(a), sch 12
s 16 am—(retrosp) Crime and Disorder, 1998 c 37, s 109(1)(2)(3); Convention Rights (Compliance) (S), 2001 asp 7, ss 1(8)(a)(i)(iii)(b)(ii), 4
    rep in pt—Convention Rights (Compliance) (S), 2001 asp 7, ss 1(8)(a)(ii)(b)(i), 4; Crim Justice (S), 2003 asp 7, s 86, sch 5
s 17 ext—Crime (Sentences) 1997 c 43 s 41, sch 1 pt II paras 10(5)(a)(6)(7), 11(5)
s 18 am—Crime and Disorder, 1998 c 37, s 119, sch 8 paras 119-121
s 26 rep—Crim Justice and Licensing (S), 2010 asp 13, s 14, sch 2 para 41(a)
s 30 am—Regulatory Reform (S), 2014 asp 3, sch 3 para 34(a)
    rep in pt—Regulatory Reform (S), 2014 asp 3, sch 3 para 34(b)
Pt 3 Ch 1 (ss 33-41) rep—Crime and Disorder, 1998 c 37, ss 108,120(2), sch 1
s 43 rep in pt—SSI 2015/39, sch para 6(a)
ss 45, 46 rep —Police and Fire Reform (S), 2012 asp 8, sch 8 pt 1
s 56 rep in pt—Crim Justice and Licensing (S), 2010 asp 13, s 203, sch 7 para 68
s 61 am —Licensing (S), 2005 asp 16, s 144, sch 6 para 8
s 63 rep in pt—Police and Fire Reform (S), 2012 asp 8, sch 8 pt 1
sch 1 am—Crime and Disorder, 1998 c 37, s 119, sch 8 para 141(2)
    rep in pt—Crime and Disorder, 1998 c 37, ss 119,120(2), sch 8, para 141(1)(a)(b), sch 10; Proceeds of Crime, 2002 c 29, ss 456, 457, sch 11, para 33(b), sch 12; Mental Health (Care and Treatment) (S), 2003 asp 13, s 331(2), sch 5 pt 1; Crim Justice, 2003 c 44, s 332, sch 37 pt 8; (prosp) Crim Justice (S), 2003 asp 7, s 85, sch 4 para 4; SSI 2006/536, reg 2, sch 3; Sexual Offences (S), 2009 asp 9, s 61, sch 6; Crim Justice and Licensing (S), 2010 asp 13, s 14, sch 2 para 41(b); SSI 2015/39, sch para 6(b)
sch 2 rep—Crime and Disorder, 1998 c 37, ss 119,120(2), sch 8 para 142, sch 10
sch 3 rep in pt—Crime and Disorder, 1998 c 37, ss 119,120(2), sch 8 para 143, sch 10; SSI 2006/536, reg 2, sch 3

c 49 *Public Entertainments Licences (Drug Misuse)*—rep Licensing, 2003 c 17, s 199, sch 7

c 50 **Police**

am—Police (NI), 2000 c 32, s 78, sch 6 para 20(2)(3)
power to mod—Insolvency, 2000 c 39, s 7(2)
ss 1-6 rep—Serious Organised Crime and Police, 2005 c 15, ss 59, 174(2), sch 4 paras 94, 95, sch 17 pt 2
s 7 rep—Crim Justice and Police, 2001 c 16, s 137, sch 7 pt 5(1)

1997
c 50 *continued*

ss 8-17A rep—Serious Organised Crime and Police, 2005 c 15, ss 59, 174(2), sch 4 paras
94, 95, sch 17 pt 2

s 18 rep—Crim Justice and Police, 2001 c 16, s 137, sch 7 pt 5(1)

ss 18A-43 rep—Serious Organised Crime and Police, 2005 c 15, ss 59, 174(2), sch 4 paras
94, 95, sch 17 pt 2

s 44 rep—Crim Justice and Police, 2001 c 16, s 137, sch 7 pt 5(1)

ss 45, 46 rep—Serious Organised Crime and Police, 2005 c 15, ss 59, 174(2), sch 4 paras
94, 95, sch 17 pt 2

ss 47-62A rep—Serious Organised Crime and Police, 2005 c 15, ss 59, 174(2), sch 4 paras
94-96, sch 17 pt 2

s 63 rep—Crim Justice and Police, 2001 c 16, s 137, sch 7 pt 5(1)

ss 64-66A rep—Serious Organised Crime and Police, 2005 c 15, ss 59, 174(2), sch 4 paras
94-96, sch 17 pt 2

ss 67, 68 rep—Crim Justice and Police, 2001 c 16, s 137, sch 7 pt 5(1)

ss 69-87 rep—Serious Organised Crime and Police, 2005 c 15, ss 59, 174(2), sch 4 paras
94-96, sch 17 pt 2

ss 89, 90 rep—Serious Organised Crime and Police, 2005 c 15, ss 59, 174(2), sch 4 paras
94-96, sch 17 pt 2

Pt 3 (ss 91-108) saved—Scotland, 1998 c 46, s 30, sch 5 pt II, s C10

power to mod—Police Reform, 2002 c 30, s 19(2)(b)

mod—(EW) SI 2004/815, art 2

s 91 am—SI 1999/1747, art 3, sch 6 pt II para 2(2)-(6); Regulation of Investigatory Powers,
2000 c 23, s 82(1), sch 4 para 8(1); Insolvency, 2000 c 39, s 8, sch 4 pt II
para 22(2); Railways and Transport Safety, 2003 c 20, s 73, sch 5
para 4(1)(b)(2)(i); SI 2004/1941, art 3, sch paras 9, 10; Constitutional Reform,
2005 c 4, s 145, sch 17 pt 2 para 27; (prosp) Tribunals, Cts and Enforcement,
2007 c 15, s 106, sch 16 para 11(1)(2); SI 2009/1941, art 2, sch 1; Anti-social
Behaviour, Crime and Policing, 2014 c 12, s 150

appl—Regulation of Investigatory Powers, 2000 c 23, s 63(5)

s 93 am—Regulation of Investigatory Powers, 2000 c 23, ss 75,82(1), sch 4 para 8(2);
(prosp) Crim Justice and Court Services, 2000 c 43, s 74, sch 7 pt II para 149;
Regulation of Investigatory Powers (Scotland) Act 2000 asp 11, s 23(1)-(4)(5)(b);
Enterprise, 2002 c 40, s 200(1)(2); Railways and Transport Safety, 2003 c 20,
s 73, sch 5 para 4(1)(a)(2)(i); Serious Organised Crime and Police, 2005 c 15,
s 59, sch 4 paras 94, 97(1)-(4); (S) Police, Public Order and Crim Justice (S),
2006 asp 10, s 101, sch 6 para 6(1)(2); Armed Forces, 2006 c 52, s 378, sch 16
para 146; Serious Crime, 2007 c 27, s 88, sch 12 para 1; Policing and Crime,
2009 c 26, s 6; (S) Crim Justice and Licensing (S), 2010 asp 13, s 107(2)(a)-(c);
Police and Fire Reform (S), 2012 asp 8, sch 7 para 14(2); Crime and Cts, 2013 c
22, s 55(1), sch 8 para 56(2)(3); ibid, sch 21 para 2(2)(3)(b)(4)(6); SIs 2013/602,
sch 1 para 6(2); 2014/892, sch 1 para 116

rep in pt —Serious Organised Crime and Police, 2005 c 15, ss 59, 174(2), sch 4 paras
94, 97(1)(5), sch 17 pt 2; Police and Fire Reform (S), 2012 asp 8, sch 8 pt 1

appl—SI 1986/1078, reg 37

s 94 rep in pt—Regulation of Investigatory Powers, 2000 c 23, s 82(1)(2), sch 4 para 8(4)(b),
sch 5; Serious Organised Crime and Police, 2005 c 15, ss 59, 174(2), sch 4
paras 94, 98(1)(2)(d)(4), sch 17 pt 2; (S) Police, Public Order and Crim Justice
(S), 2006 asp 10, s 101, sch 6 para 6(3)(b)(i); Police and Fire Reform (S), 2012
asp 8, sch 8 pt 1

appl—Regulation of Investigatory Powers, 2000 c 23, s 49(11), sch 2 para 2(7)

am—Regulation of Investigatory Powers, 2000 c 23, s 82(1), sch 4
para 8(3)(4)(a)(c)(5); Enterprise, 2002 c 40, s 200(1)(3); Railways and Transport
Safety, 2003 c 20, s 73, sch 5 para 4(1)(a)(2)(i); Serious Organised Crime and
Police, 2005 c 15, s 59, sch 4 paras 94, 98(1)(2)(a)-(c)(3); (S) Police, Public
Order and Crim Justice (S), 2006 asp 10, s 101, sch 6 para 6(1)(3)(a)(b)(ii)(c);
Police and Justice, 2006 c 48, s 52, sch 14 para 34; Armed Forces, 2006 c 52, s
378, sch 16 para 147; Serious Crime, 2007 c 27, s 88, sch 12 para 2; (S) Crim
Justice and Licensing (S), 2010 asp 13, s 107(3)(a)-(c); Police and Fire Reform
(S), 2012 asp 8, sch 7 para 14(3); SI 2013/602, sch 1 para 6(3)(a)(b); Crime and
Cts, 2013 c 22, sch 8 para 57, ibid, sch 21 para 3; SI 2014/892, sch 1 para 117

s 95 am—Regulation of Investigatory Powers, 2000 c 23, s 82(1), sch 4 para 8(6); Serious
Organised Crime and Police, 2005 c 15, s 59, sch 4 paras 94, 99; (S) Police,

1997
c 50 *continued*

Public Order and Crim Justice (S), 2006 asp 10, s 101, sch 6 para 6(4); Police and
Fire Reform (S), 2012 asp 8, sch 7 para 14(4); SI 2013/602, sch 1 para 6(4)

s 97 rep in pt—Regulation of Investigatory Powers, 2000 c 23, s 82(1)(2), sch 4 para 8(7),
sch 5

am—Regulation of Investigatory Powers, 2000 c 23, s 82(1), sch 4 para 8(7); Serious
Organised Crime and Police, 2005 c 15, s 59, sch 4 paras 94, 100; Crime and Cts,
2013 c 22, sch 8 para 58

s 101 am—SI 1999/1820, art 4, sch 2 pt I para 131(4); Railways and Transport Safety,
2003 c 20, s 73, sch 5 para 4(1)(b)(2)(i)

s 102 rep—Regulation of Investigatory Powers, 2000 c 23, ss 70,82(2), sch 5

s 103 am—Regulation of Investigatory Powers, 2000 c 23, s 82(1), sch 4 para 8(8)

s 104 rep in pt—Regulation of Investigatory Powers, 2000 c 23, s 82(1), sch 5

s 105 am—SI 1999/1747, art 3, sch 6 pt II para 2(2)-(6); Regulation of Investigatory
Powers, 2000 c 23, s 82(1)(2), sch 4 para 8(9), sch 5; Serious Organised Crime
and Police, 2005 c 15, s 59, sch 4 paras 94, 101; Police and Fire Reform (S),
2012 asp 8, sch 7 para 14(5); SI 2013/602, sch 1 para 6(5)

rep in pt—Regulation of Investigatory Powers, 2000 c 23, s 82(1)(2), sch 4 para 8(9),
sch 5

s 106 rep—Regulation of Investigatory Powers, 2000 c 23, s 82(1), sch 5

s 107 am—SI 1999/1747, art 3, sch 6 pt II para 2(2)-(6); Regulation of Investigatory
Powers, 2000 c 23, s 82(1), sch 4 para 8(10)(11); Serious Organised Crime and
Police, 2005 c 15, s 59, sch 4 paras 94, 102; (S) Police, Public Order and Crim
Justice (S), 2006 asp 10, s 101, sch 6 para 6(5); Serious Crime, 2007 c 27, s 88,
sch 12 para 3; Police Reform and Social Responsibility, 2011 c 13, sch 16 para
222; Police and Fire Reform (S), 2012 asp 8, sch 7 para 14(6); SI 2013/602, sch
1 para 6(6)(a)(b); Crime and Cts, 2013 c 22, sch 8 para 59; ibid, sch 21 para 4

appl—Regulation of Investigatory Powers, 2000 c 23, s 39(3)

rep in pt—Regulation of Investigatory Powers, 2000 c 23, s 82(1), sch 5; Police and
Fire Reform (S), 2012 asp 8, sch 8 pt 1

s 108 am—Regulation of Investigatory Powers, 2000 c 23, s 82(1), sch 4 para 8(12);
Wireless Telegraphy, 2006 c 36, s 123, sch 7 para 19; Armed Forces, 2006 c 52,
s 378, sch 16 para 148

rep in pt—Armed Forces, 2001 c 19, s 38, sch 7 pt 1; Serious Crime, 2007 c 27, s 88,
sch 12 para 4, sch 14

mod—SI 2009/1059, art 205, sch 1

ss 109-111 rep—Police and Justice, 2006 c 48, s 52, sch 15

Pt 5 (ss 112-127) appl—Police and Crim Evidence, 1984 c 60 s 27(4A); Crime and
Disorder, 1998 c 37, s 117(1)

expld—Data Protection, 1998 c 29, s 56(4)

power to mod (conditionally)—(EW) Serious Organised Crime and Police, 2005 c 15,
s 163(4)

power to ext—Serious Organised Crime and Police, 2005 c 15, s 168

ext in pt (mods)—(to Isle of Man) SI 2010/764, arts 3, 6, schs 1, 3; (to Guernsey) SI
2009/3215, art 3, schs 1, 3; (to Jersey) SI 2010/765, arts 3, 6, schs 1, 3

trans of functions—SI 2012/3006, arts 98, 99

s 112 am—(EW) Crim Justice, 2003 c 44, s 328, sch 35 paras 1, 2; (S) SSI 2006/50, art 2;
(prosp) (S) Protection of Vulnerable Groups (S), 2007 asp 14, s 78(1); Crim
Justice and Immigration, 2008 c 4, s 50(1)(2); Protection of Freedoms, 2012 c 9,
ss 80(1), 84; SI 2012/3006, art 37(a)

rep in pt—(S) Protection of Vulnerable Groups (S), 2007 asp 14, s 79; Policing and
Crime, 2009 c 26, ss 97(1)(2), 112, sch 8 pt 8

appl—(S) SSI 2006/96, regs 3, 5, 7

s 113 rep—Serious Organised Crime and Police, 2005 c 15, ss 163(1), 174(2), sch 17 pt 2

s 113A added —Serious Organised Crime and Police, 2005 c 15, s 163(2)

appl—(S) SSI 2006/96, regs 3, 6, 7

am—(EW) Safeguarding Vulnerable Groups, 2006 c 47, s 63, sch 9 para 14(1)(2);
Protection of Vulnerable Groups (S), 2007 asp 14, ss 78(2), 88, sch 4 paras 27,
28; Crim Justice and Immigration, 2008 c 4, s 50(1)(3); SIs 2009/203, arts 2, 3;
2010/1146, reg 4(2); Children's Hearings (S), 2011 asp 1, s 188; Protection of
Freedoms, 2012 c 9, s 80(1), sch 9 para 135; SIs 2012/3006, arts 37(b), 38;
2013/1200, arts 3, 4; SSI 2015/423, art 3(2)(a)(c)

rep in pt—(S) Protection of Vulnerable Groups (S), 2007 asp 14, s 79(1); Policing
and Crime, 2009 c 26, ss 97(1)(2), 112, sch 8 pt 8; Protection of Freedoms,

1997
c 50 s 113A *continued*

     2012 c 9, s 79(2)(a), sch 10 pt 6; ibid, sch 9 para 36, sch 10 pt 5; SSI 2015/423,
     art 3(2)(b)
    excl—SI 2010/1146, reg 4(1)
  s 113B added (EW pt prosp) —Serious Organised Crime and Police, 2005 c 15, s 163(2)
    am—(EW) Safeguarding Vulnerable Groups, 2006 c 47, s 63, sch 9 para 14(1)(3);
     Armed Forces, 2006 c 52, s 378, sch 16 para 149; (S) Protection of Vulnerable
     Groups (S), 2007 asp 14, s 80; SIs 2009/203, arts 2, 4; 2010/1146, reg 8; (S)
     Crim Justice and Licensing (S), 2010 asp 13, s 108(2); Protection of Freedoms,
     2012 c 9, ss 80(1), 82(1)(a)(c)(d)(2)(3)(a); SI 2012/3006, arts 37(c), 39;
     Crime and Cts, 2013 c 22, sch 8 para 60(b); SSI 2015/423, art 3(3)(a)(b)(ii)
    rep in pt—(S) Protection of Vulnerable Groups (S), 2007 asp 14, s 79(1); Policing
     and Crime, 2009 c 26, ss 97(1)(2), 112, sch 8 pt 8; Protection of Freedoms,
     2012 c 9, s 82(1)(b)(3)(b), sch 9 para 37, sch 10 pts 5, 6; (S 8.2.2016) ibid, s
     79(2)(b), sch 10 pt 6; Crime and Cts, 2013 c 22, sch 8 para 60(a); SSI
     2015/423, art 3(3)(b)(i),(c)-(e)
    appl—(S) SSI 2006/96, regs 3, 6, 7, 9
    appl (mods)—SI 2010/1146, regs 5-7
  s 113BA added (EW)—(EW) Safeguarding Vulnerable Groups, 2006 c 47, s 63, sch 9 para
    14(1)(4)
    (as added by 2006 c 47) am—Educ and Inspections, 2006 c 40, s 170(2); (W
     prosp) Educ and Skills, 2008 c 25, s 169, sch 1 para 12; Policing and Crime,
     2009 c 26, s 81(2)(3)(h)
    rep in pt—Protection of Freedoms, 2012 c 9, sch 9 para 38, sch 10 pt 5
  s 113BA added (S)—Crim Justice and Licensing (S), 2010 asp 13, s 108(3)
  s 113BB added (EW)—Safeguarding Vulnerable Groups, 2006 c 47, s 63, sch 9 para
    14(1)(4)
    am—Policing and Crime, 2009 c 26, s 81(2)(3)(h)
    rep in pt—Protection of Freedoms, 2012 c 9, sch 9 para 39, sch 10 pt 5
  s 113BC added (EW)—Safeguarding Vulnerable Groups, 2006 c 47, s 63, sch 9 para
    14(1)(4)
    am—Protection of Freedoms, 2012 c 9, sch 9 para 105
  s 113C rep—(EW) Safeguarding Vulnerable Groups, 2006 c 47, s 63, sch 10; (S) Proection
    of Vulnerable Groups (S), 2007 asp 14, s 88, sch 4 paras 27, 30
  ss 113CA-113CC added (S)—Protection of Vulnerable Groups (S), 2007 asp 14, s 88, sch 4
    paras 27, 29
  s 113CA am—Policing and Crime, 2009 c 26, s 81(2)(3)(h); SSI 2010/190, art 2;
    Anti-social Behaviour, Crime and Policing, 2014 c 12, sch 11 para 53
    rep in pt—SSI 2010/382, art 2
  s 113CB am—Policing and Crime, 2009 c 26, s 81(2)(3)(h); SSI 2010/190, art 3;
    Anti-social Behaviour, Crime and Policing, 2014 c 12, sch 11 para 54
    rep in pt—SSI 2010/382, art 3
  s 113CD added (EW) (prosp)—Policing and Crime, 2009 c 26, s 94
  ss 113D-113F rep —(EW) Safeguarding Vulnerable Groups, 2006 c 47, s 63, sch 10; (S)
    Protection of Vulnerable Groups (S), 2007 asp 14, s 88, sch 4 paras 27, 30
  s 114 am —Serious Organised Crime and Police, 2005 c 15, s 163(3), sch 14 paras 1, 2; (S)
    SSI 2006/50, art 2; (EW) Safeguarding Vulnerable Groups, 2006 c 47, s 63, sch
    9 para 14(1)(5); (S) Protection of Vulnerable Groups (S), 2007 asp 14, s 88, sch
    4 paras 27, 31; Protection of Freedoms, 2012 c 9, s 80(1), sch 9 para 106; SI
    2012/3006, art 37(e)
    appl—(S) SSI 2006/96, reg 3
    rep in pt—(S) Protection of Vulnerable Groups (S), 2007 asp 14, s 79(1); Policing and
     Crime, 2009 c 26, ss 97(1)(3), 112, sch 8 pt 8
  s 115 rep—Serious Organised Crime and Police, 2005 c 15, ss 163(1), 174(2), sch 17 pt 2
  s 116 am—Serious Organised Crime and Police, 2005 c 15, s 163(3), sch 14 paras 1, 3; (S)
    SSI 2006/50, art 2; (EW) Safeguarding Vulnerable Groups, 2006 c 47, s 63, sch
    9 para 14(6); Protection of Vulnerable Groups (S), 2007 asp 14, s 88, sch 4
    paras 27, 32; Protection of Freedoms, 2012 c 9, s 80(1), sch 9 para 107; SI
    2012/3006, art 37(f)
    appl—(S) SSI 2006/96, regs 3, 15
    rep in pt—(S) Protection of Vulnerable Groups (S), 2007 asp 14, s 79(1); Policing and
     Crime, 2009 c 26, ss 97(1)(3), 112, sch 8 pt 8
    mod—SI 2012/2157, art 9
  ss 116ZA, 116ZB added—SSI 2015/423, art 3(4)

1997
c 50 *continued*

s 116A added —Protection of Freedoms, 2012 c 9, s 83
  am—SI 2012/3006, art 37(g)
s 117 am—(S) Protection of Vulnerable Groups (S), 2007 asp 14, s 88, sch 4 paras 27, 33;
  Protection of Freedoms, 2012 c 9, s 82(4); ibid, sch 9 para 108(2)-(5); SI
  2012/3006, arts 37(h), 40; SSI 2015/423, art 3(5)(a)(b)
  rep in pt—(S) Protection of Vulnerable Groups (S), 2007 asp 14, s 79(2)
s 117A added—Protection of Freedoms, 2012 c 9, s 82(5)
  am—SI 2012/3006, art 37(i)
s 118 am —Serious Organised Crime and Police, 2005 c 15, s 164; (S) Protection of
  Vulnerable Groups (S), 2007 asp 14, s 88, sch 4 paras 27, 34; (prosp) Policing
  and Crime, 2009 c 26, s 95; Protection of Freedoms, 2012 c 9, sch 9 para
  109(2)-(4); SI 2012/3006, arts 37(j), 41
s 119 am—(EW, NI) Crim Justice and Police, 2001 c 16, s 134(2); (S) Crim Justice (S),
  2003 asp 7, s 70(1)(4); Serious Organised Crime and Police, 2005 c 15, s 165(1);
  ibid, s 163(3), sch 14 paras 1, 4; Safeguarding Vulnerable Groups, 2006 c 47, s
  63, sch 9 para 14(1)(7); (S) Protection of Vulnerable Groups (S), 2007 asp 14, s
  78(3)(4); Policing and Crime, 2009 c 26, s 112, sch 7 para 118; Police Reform
  and Social Responsibility, 2011 c 13, sch 16 para 223; Protection of Freedoms,
  2012 c 9, sch 9 para 110(2)-(6); ibid, sch 9 para 40(3)(b), sch 10 pt 5; SI
  2012/3006, arts 37(k), 42, 50, 51(1)-(3)
  rep in pt—GLA, 1999 c 29, ss 325, 423, sch 27 para 112, sch 34 pt VII; Protection of
  Freedoms, 2012 c 9, sch 9 para 40(2)(3)(a), sch 10 pt 5; SI 2012/3006, arts
  37(k), 42, 50, 51(1)(4)
  appl—(S) SSI 2006/96, reg 17
s 119A added (S)—Crim Justice (S), 2003 asp 7, s 70(1)(5)
  am—Serious Organised Crime and Police, 2005 c 15, s 163(3), sch 14 paras 1, 5;
  Protection of Vulnerable Groups (S), 2007 asp 14, s 78(3)(4)
s 119B added (EW, NI)—Safeguarding Vulnerable Groups, 2006 c 47, s 28
  am—SI 2010/976, art 12, sch 14; Protection of Freedoms, 2012 c 9, sch 9 para
  111(4)-(6); SI 2012/3006, art 37(l)
  rep in pt—Protection of Freedoms, 2012 c 9, sch 9 para 41, sch 10 pt 5; SI
  2012/3006, art 13(1)(2)(c)
s 120 rep in pt—(EW) Crim Justice, 2003 c 44, ss 328, 332, sch 35 paras 1, 6(1)(3), sch 37
  pt 11; (S) Protection of Vulnerable Groups (S), 2007 asp 14, s 79(2); Protection
  of Freedoms, 2012 c 9, sch 9 para 112(2)(c), sch 10 pt 6
  am—(EW, NI) Crim Justice and Police, 2001 c 16, s 134(3)(4); (S prosp) Crim
  Justice, 2003 c 44, s 328, sch 35 paras 1, 6(1)(2); (S) Crim Justice (S), 2003 asp
  7, s 70(1)(6); Serious Organised Crime and Police, 2005 c 15, s 163(3), sch 14
  paras 1, 6; (S) Protection of Vulnerable Groups (S), 2007 asp 14, ss 81(1), 88,
  sch 4 paras 27, 36; SI 2009/203, arts 2, 5; Protection of Freedoms, 2012 c 9, s
  80(2), sch 9 para 112(2)(3); SI 2012/3006, arts 37(m), 43
  appl—(S) SSI 2006/97, reg 10
s 120ZA added (EW)—Crim Justice, 2003 c 44, s 328, sch 35 paras 1, 7
  am—Serious Organised Crime and Police, 2005 c 15, s 163(3), sch 14 paras 1, 7;
  SIs 2009/203, arts 2, 6; 2012/3006, art 37(n)
s 120ZB added (S)—Protection of Vulnerable Groups (S), 2007 asp 14, s 81(2)
  am—Crim Justice and Licensing (S), 2010 asp 13, s 108(4)
s 120A added (EW)—Crim Justice and Police, 2001 c 16, s 134(1)
  (as added by 2001 c 16) am—Crim Justice, 2003 c 44, s 328, sch 35 paras 1, 8;
  Serious Organised Crime and Police, 2005 c 15, s 163(3), 165(2), sch 14 paras
  1, 8; SI 2009/203, arts 2, 7; Policing and Crime, 2009 c 26, s 96; Police and
  Fire Reform (S), 2012 asp 8, sch 7 para 14(7); Protection of Freedoms, 2012 c
  9, sch 9 para 42(4)(a)(b); SI 2012/3006, arts 37(o), 44
  (as added by 2001 c 16) rep in pt—Protection of Freedoms, 2012 c 9, sch 9 para
  42(2)(3)(4)(c), sch 10 pt 5
s 120A added (S)—Crim Justice (S), 2003 asp 7, s 70(1)(2)
  (as added by 2003 asp 7) am—Serious Organised Crime and Police, 2005 c 15,
  ss 163(3), 165(2), 166(1), sch 14 para 9; SSI 2006/50, art 2; Protection of
  Vulnerable Groups (S), 2007 asp 14, s 88, sch 4 paras 27, 37
  (as added by 2003 asp 7) appl—SSI 2006/97, reg 7
s 120AA added (EW)—Crim Justice, 2003 c 44, s 328, sch 35 paras 1, 9
  am—SI 2009/203, arts 2, 8; Protection of Freedoms, 2012 c 9, s 81; SI 2012/3006,
  art 37(p)

1997
c 50 *continued*

s 120AB added (EW)—Crim Justice, 2003 c 44, s 328, sch 35 paras 1, 9
    am—SIs 2009/203, arts 2, 9; 2012/3006, arts 37(q), 45
s 120AC added (EW)—Protection of Freedoms, 2012 c 9, s 79(3)
    am—SI 2012/3006, art 37(r)
s 120AD added—Protection of Freedoms, 2012 c 9, s 79(3)
    am—SI 2012/3006, art 37(s)
s 121 am—Serious Organised Crime and Police, 2005 c 15, s 163(3), sch 14 paras 1, 10
    rep (S)—Protection of Vulnerable Groups (S), 2007 asp 14, s 88, sch 4 paras 27, 38
s 122 am—(S) Crim Justice (S), 2003 asp 7, s 70(1)(7); Serious Organised Crime and
    Police, 2005 c 15, s 163(3), sch 14 paras 1, 11; Safeguarding Vulnerable Groups,
    2006 c 47, s 29; (S) Protection of Vulnerable Groups (S), 2007 asp 14, s 88, sch
    4 paras 27, 39; SI 2009/203, arts 2, 10; Protection of Freedoms, 2012 c 9, sch 9
    para 113; SI 2012/3006, arts 37(t), 46
    rep in pt—(prosp) Protection of Freedoms, 2012 c 9, sch 9 para 114, sch 10 pt 6
s 122A added (EW)—Crim Justice, 2003 c 44, s 328, sch 35 paras 1, 10
    rep—SI 2012/3006, art 51
s 122B added (S)—Protection of Vulnerable Groups (S), 2007 asp 14, s 88, sch 4 paras 27,
    40
s 124 am—Serious Organised Crime and Police, 2005 c 15, s 163(3), sch 14 paras 1, 12; SI
    2009/203, arts 2, 11; Protection of Freedoms, 2012 c 9, sch 9 para 115(2)(b)
    rep in pt—Protection of Freedoms, 2012 c 9, sch 9 para 115(2)(a)(3), sch 10 pt 6
s 124A added (EW)—Crim Justice, 2003 c 44, s 328, sch 35 paras 1, 11
    (as added by 2003 c 44) am—Serious Organised Crime and Police, 2005 c 15,
        s 165(3); Protection of Freedoms, 2012 c 9, sch 9 para 116(3); SI 2012/3006,
        art 37(u)
    (as added by 2003 c 44) rep in pt—Protection of Freedoms, 2012 c 9, sch 9 para
        116(2), sch 10 pt 6
s 124A added (S)—Crim Justice (S), 2003 asp 7, s 70(1)(8)
    (as added by 2003 asp 7) am—Protection of Vulnerable Groups (S), 2007 asp 14, s
        81(3)
s 124B added (EW)—Crim Justice, 2003 c 44, s 328, sch 35 paras 1, 11
    am—(prosp) Serious Organised Crime and Police, 2005 c 15, s 163(3), sch 14 paras
        1, 13
s 125 rep in pt —(EW) Crim Justice, 2003 c 44, ss 328, 332, sch 35 paras 1, 12, sch 37 pt
        11; (S) Serious Organised Crime and Police, 2005 c 15, s 174(2), sch 17 pt 2
    am—Serious Organised Crime and Police, 2005 c 15, s 163(3), sch 14 paras 1, 14;
        (EW, NI) SI 2005/3496, art 6(2); (S) SSI 2006/50, art 2; Anti-social Behaviour,
        Crime and Policing, 2014 c 12, s 151
s 125A added (S)—Protection of Vulnerable Groups (S), 2007 asp 14, s 79(3)
s 125B added (EW, NI)—Policing and Crime, 2009 c 26, s 97(1)
    am—Protection of Freedoms, 2012 c 9, sch 9 para 117; SI 2012/3006, art 37(v)
s 126 am—Serious Organised Crime and Police, 2005 c 15, s 166(2); (S) Protection of
    Vulnerable Groups (S), 2007 asp 14, s 88, sch 4 paras 27, 41; SI 2007/1351, art
    60, sch 7; Police Reform and Social Responsibility, 2011 c 13, sch 16 para 224;
    Police and Fire Reform (S), 2012 asp 8, sch 7 para 14(8); Protection of
    Freedoms, 2012 c 9, sch 9 para 118; SIs 2012/3006, art 47; 2013/602, sch 1
    para 6(7)(a)(b); SSI 2015/423, art 3(6)
s 126A added—SI 2010/976, art 12, sch 14
    rep in pt—SI 2012/3006, art 53
ss 130-132 rep—(saving) Police (NI), 1998 c 32, s 74(2)(3), schs 5, 6
s 133A added—Regulation of Investigatory Powers, 2000 c 23, s 82(1), sch 4 para 8(13)
ss 134-136 mod —(S) SSI 2009/4, arts 4, 5
ss 137 rep in pt—(saving) Police (NI), 1998 c 32, s 74(2)(3), schs 5, 6; Crim Justice and
    Police, 2001 c 16, s 137, sch 7 pt 5(1); Serious Organised Crime and Police,
    2005 c 15, ss 59, 174(2), sch 4 paras 94, 105, sch 17 pt 2
    mod (S)—SSI 2009/4, arts 4, 5
    am—(prosp) Anti-social Behaviour, Crime and Policing, 2014 c 12, sch 11 para 90
s 138 mod (S)—SSI 2009/4, arts 4, 5
schs 1-5 rep —Serious Organised Crime and Police, 2005 c 15, ss 59, 174(2), sch 4 paras 94,
    106, sch 17 pt 2
sch 6 rep in pt—(EW) Audit Commn, 1998 c 18, s 54(3), sch 5; (prosp) Loc Govt, 2000
    c 22, s 107, sch 6; Crim Justice and Police, 2001 c 16, s 137, sch 7 pt 5(1)
sch 7 rep—Regulation of Investigatory Powers, 2000 c 23, ss 70,82(2), sch 5

1997

c 50 *continued*

    sch 8 rep—Police and Justice, 2006 c 48, s 52, sch 15

    schs 8A, 8B added—SSI 2015/423, art 3(8)

    sch 9 rep in pt—(saving) Police (NI), 1998 c 32, s 74(2)(3), schs 5,6; Police (NI), 2000 c 32, s 78, sch 8; Race Relations (Amdt), 2000 c 34, s 9(2), sch 3; SI 2001/1149, arts 3(2), 4(11), sch 2; Crim Justice and Police, 2001 c 16, s 137, sch 7 pt 5(1); SI 2002/1860, arts 11(2)(b), 15(1)(2)(b), sch 6; Crim Justice, 2003 c 44, s 332, sch 37 pt 10; Courts, 2003 c 39, s 109(3), sch 10; Civil Contingencies, 2004 c 36, s 32(2), sch 3; Serious Organised Crime and Police, 2005 c 15, s 174(2), sch 17 pt 2; Police and Justice, 2006 c 48, s 52, sch 15

c 51   *Sex Offenders*—rep Sexual Offences, 2003 c 42, ss 93, 139, 140, 142(5), sch 4 para 7, sch 6 para 37, sch 7

c 52   **Police and Firemen's Pensions**

    s 1 rep in pt —Fire and Rescue Services, 2004 c 21, s 54, sch 2

      saving—SIs (E, S) 2004/2306, art 3, sch; (W) 2004/2918 (W 257), art 3, sch

    s 3 rep —Fire and Rescue Services, 2004 c 21, s 54, sch 2

c 53   **Dangerous Dogs (Amendment)**

c 54   **Road Traffic Reduction**

    trans of powers—(W) SI 1999/672, art 2, sch 1

    s 1 am—GLA, 1999 c 29, s 280(1)

    s 2 am—GLA, 1999 c 29, s 280(2)-(6)

      trans of functions—SI 2014/865, art 11(1)

c 55   **Birds (Registration Charges)**

    s 1 rep in pt—Countryside and Rights of Way, 2000 c 37, s 102, sch 16 pt IV

1st Session of 52nd Parliament

c 56   **National Health Service (Private Finance)**

    trans of powers—(W) SI 1999/672, art 2, sch 1

    s 1 rep—Nat Health Service (Conseq Provns), 2006 c 43, s 6, sch 4

c 57   **Appropriation (No 2)**

c 58   **Finance (No 2)**

    s 6 rep—Finance, 2001 c 9, s 110, sch 33 pt 3(1), Note 2

    s 15 rep—Finance, 1999 c 16, s 139, sch 20 pt III(7), Note 4; see also the Income Tax, 2007 c 3, s 1031, sch 3 pt 1

    s 16 rep in pt—Income Tax, 2007 c 3, s 1031, sch 3

    s 17 rep—SL(R), 2013 c 2, s 1, sch 1 pt 10(1)

    s 18 rep in pt—Corporation Tax, 2010 c 4, s 1181, sch 3 pt 1

    s 19 rep—Finance (No 2), 1997 c 58, s 52, sch 8 pt II(9), Note 3

    s 21 rep—Corporation Tax, 2009 c 4, s 1326, sch 3 pt 1

    s 22 rep in pt—Income Tax (Trading and Other Income), 2005 c 5, s 884, sch 3; Finance, 2009 c 10, s 34, sch 14 para 30(a)

    s 24 rep in pt—Finance, 2003 c 14, s 216, sch 43 pt 3(6), Note; Income Tax (Trading and Other Income), 2005 c 5, s 884, sch 3; Corporation Tax, 2009 c 4, s 1326, sch 3 pt 1

    s 25 rep in pt—Income Tax, 2007 c 3, s 1031, sch 3; SL(R), 2013 c 2, s 1, sch 1 pt 10(1)

    s 26 rep—Finance, 2008 c 9, s 66(4)(i)(i)

    s 27 rep—Corporation Tax, 2010 c 4, s 1181, sch 3 pt 1

    s 29 rep—Income Tax, 2007 c 3, s 1027, sch 1 paras 377, 378, sch 3

    s 30 mod—Finance, 1998 c 36, s 76(1)(2)

      excl—(temp) SI 1998/1871, reg 4(1)

      power to mod—Income and Corporation Taxes, 1988 c 1, s 333B

      restr—Finance, 1998 c 36, s 90(1)

      am—Income Tax (Trading and Other Income), 2005 c 5, s 882(1), sch 1 pt 2 paras 495, 496; Taxation (International and Other Provns), 2010 c 8, s 374, sch 8 paras 51, 52

      rep in pt—Income Tax (Trading and Other Income), 2005 c 5, s 884, sch 3; Corporation Tax, 2010 c 4, s 1181, sch 3 pt 1

    ss 31, 32 rep—Income Tax, 2007 c 3, s 1031, sch 3

    s 33 rep in pt—Income Tax, 2007 c 3, s 1031, sch 3; Corporation Tax, 2009 c 4, s 1326, sch 3 pt 1

    s 35 rep—Finance, 2011 c 11, sch 26 para 1(1)

    s 37 rep in pt—Finance, 1998 c 36, s 165, sch 27 pt III(3), Note; Income Tax, 2007 c 3, s 1031, sch 3

      am—Finance, 2000 c 17, s 111(5)(6)(a); Income Tax (Trading and Other Income), 2005 c 5, s 882(1), sch 1 pt 2 paras 495, 497

1997
c 58 *continued*

    s 38 rep—Finance, 2000 c 17, s 156, sch 40 pt II(17)

    s 39 rep—Corporation Tax, 2010 c 4, s 1181, sch 3 pt 1

    s 40 rep—Corporation Tax, 2009 c 4, ss 1322, 1326, sch 1 paras 449, 450, sch 3 pt 1

    s 41 rep —Corporation Tax, 2010 c 4, s 1181, sch 3 pt 1

    ss 42-47 rep—Capital Allowances, 2001 c 2, s 580, sch 4

    s 48 rep—Finance, 2006 c 25, s 178, sch 26 pt 3(4)

    s 49 rep—Finance, 1999 c 16, s 138, sch 20 pt V(2), Notes 1, 2

    s 50 rep in pt—Finance, 1998 c 36, s 165, sch 27 pt III(2), Note; Finance, 2011 c 11, s
        88(8)(b)

    sch 3 rep in pt—Finance, 1998 c 36, s 165, sch 27 pt III(2), Note; Finance, 2001 c 9, s 110,
        sch 33 pt 2(12), Note; Finance, 2004 c 12, s 326, sch 42 pt 2(3), Note; SI
        2006/3271, reg 43, sch; Finance, 2007 c 11, s 114, sch 27 pt 2; SL(R), 2013 c
        2, s 1, sch 1 pt 10(1)

        mod—Finance, 1998 c 36, s 90(3)

    sch 4 appl (mods)—(temp) SI 1998/1871, reg 4(2)

        mod—Finance, 1998 c 36, s 90(2)(a)(b)

        rep in pt—Finance, 1998 c 36, ss 31,165, sch 3 paras 45-48, sch 27, pt III(2)(28),
          Note; Finance, 1999 c 16, s 139, sch 20 pt III(1), Note; Income Tax (Trading
          and Other Income), 2005 c 5, s 884, sch 3; Income Tax, 2007 c 3, s 1031, sch 3;
          Finance, 2008 c 9, s 8, sch 2 para 21(b); Corporation Tax, 2010 c 4, s 1181,
          sch 3 pt 1; Taxation (International and Other Provns), 2010 c 8, s 378, sch 10
          pt 13; SL(R), 2013 c 2, s 1, sch 1 pt 10(1)

    sch 5 rep —Finance, 2011 c 11, sch 26 para 1(1)

    sch 6 rep in pt—Finance, 2004 c 12, s 326, sch 42 pt 2(3), Note; Finance, 2008 c 9, s
        66(4)(i)(ii)

    sch 7 rep—Corporation Tax, 2010 c 4, s 1181, sch 3 pt 1

    sch 8 restr—Finance, 1998 c 36, s 76(5), 90(4)

c 59   **Education (Schools)**

    trans of powers—(W) SI 1999/672, art 2, sch 1

    power to mod—Educ, 2002 c 32, s 177(4)(5)

    s 1 see—SI 1997/1968, reg 18(5)

    s 2 am—School Standards and Framework, 1998 c 31, s 140(1), sch 30 para 224

    s 3 am—School Standards and Framework, 1998 c 31, s 130(1)

    ss 6, 7 rep in pt—School Standards and Framework, 1998 c 31, s 140(3), sch 31

    s 19 rep (E)—Deregulation, 2015 c 20, s 66(1)

        am—Deregulation, 2015 c 20, s 66(2)(a)-(c)

c 60   **Law Officers**

    s 2 am—Justice (NI), 2002 c 26, s 27(2)

c 61   **Referendums (Scotland and Wales)**

c 62   **Ministerial and other Salaries**

c 63   *Local Government Finance (Supplementary Credit Approvals)*—rep Loc Govt, 2003 c 26,
        s 127(2), sch 8 pt 1

c 64   **Firearms (Amendment) (No 2)**

c 65   **Local Government (Contracts)**

    appl (mods)—SI 1999/1545, art 2

    power to appl—Govt of Wales, 1998 c 38, s 39

    trans of powers—(W) SI 1999/672, art 2, sch 1

    appl—Transport (S), 2005 asp 12, s 4, sch 1 para 16(1)(b)

    s 1 am—(prosp) GLA, 1999 c 29, ss 325, 423, sch 27 para 116, sch 34 pt VII; (EW) Loc
        Govt, 2003 c 26, s 127(1), sch 7 para 64

        rep in pt—(prosp) GLA, 1999 c 29, ss 325, 423, sch 27 para 116, sch 34 pt VII

        appl (mods)—SI 2007/1182, arts 2, 3, schs 1, 2

    ss 2-7 appl (mods)—SI 2007/1182, arts 2, 3, schs 1, 2

    s 8 am—(EW) Audit Commn, 1998 c 18, s 54(1)a, sch 3 para 34; Public Audit (W), 2004 c
        23, s 66, sch 2 para 20; (S prosp) Loc Audit and Accountability, 2014 c 2, sch 12
        para 35(2)(a)(c)

        appl (mods)—SI 2007/1182, arts 2, 3, schs 1, 2

        rep in pt—(S prosp) Loc Audit and Accountability, 2014 c 2, sch 12 para 35(2)(b)(3)

    s 9 appl (mods)—SI 2007/1182, arts 2, 3, schs 1, 2

    s 10 rep—Courts, 2003 c 39, s 109(3), sch 10

    s 11 appl (mods)—SI 2007/1182, art 2, sch 1

    s 12 rep in pt—Courts, 2003 c 39, s 109(3), sch 10

1997

c 66   **Plant Varieties**

    trans of functions—SI 1999/3141, arts 2(1)(5), 3, sch; (NI) 2002/2843, arts 8, 10

    trans of powers—(W) SI 1999/672, art 2, sch 1

    appl (mods)—SI 2002/247, reg 27

    appl—SI 2003/549, regs 2(1)(8), 3

    s 3 am—SI 2003/1016, art 3, sch para 10

    s 9 rep in pt —(E, NI) SI 2005/2726, art 2; (W) SI 2006/1261, art 2

    s 24 ext—SI 2002/247, reg 21

    s 26 ext in pt—SI 2002/247, reg 21

    s 28, 29 ext—SI 2002/247, reg 21

    s 33 rep—SI 2000/311, art 33

    s 38 appl—SI 1999/1801, reg 11(1)(b)

    s 44 ext—SI 2002/247, reg 21

    s 45 ext—SI 2002/247, reg 17(3)

    s 48 ext—SI 2002/247, reg 21

    sch 3 appl—SI 2001/3510, reg 17(2)

        appl (mods)—SI 2002/247, reg 19(2)(a)(b)

        am —Constitutional Reform, 2005 c 4, s 15(1), sch 4 pt 1 para 269; Northern Ireland,

            2009 c 3, s 2, sch 4 para 27; Crime and Cts, 2013 c 22, sch 9 para 120

c 67   *Consolidated Fund (No 2)*—rep Appropriation, 1999 c 13, s 3, sch (C)

c 68   **Special Immigration Appeals Commission**

    am—Immigration and Asylum, 1999 c 33, s 74

    restr—Immigration and Asylum, 1999 c 33, ss 73(9), 76(2)(3)

    power to appl—Nationality, Immigration and Asylum, 2002 c 41, s 109(2)(a)

    power to excl —Nationality, Immigration and Asylum, 2002 c 41, s 109(2)(c)

    s 1 am—Anti-terrorism, Crime and Security, 2001 c 24, s 35; (prosp) Crim Justice and Cts,

        2015 c 2, s 66(3)

        rep in pt—Prevention of Terrorism, 2005 c 2, s 16(2)(b)(4)

    s 2 subst—Nationality, Immigration and Asylum, 2002 c 41, s 114(3), sch 7, para 20

        am—Immigration, Asylum and Nationality, 2006 c 13, s 14, sch 1 para 14; Immigration,

            2014 c 22, sch 9 para 2

        excl in pt—Nationality, Immigration and Asylum, 2002 c 41, s 97A(2)(c)

        rep in pt—(prosp) Immigration, 2014 c 22, sch 9 para 26(2)

    s 2A rep—Nationality, Immigration and Asylum, 2002 c 41, ss 114(3), 161, sch 7, para 21,

        sch 9

    s 2B added—Nationality, Immigration and Asylum, 2002 c 41, s 4(2)

        am—Asylum and Immigration (Treatment of Claimants, etc.), 2004 c 19, s 26(7), sch

            2 pt 1 paras 10, 11

        rep in pt—(prosp) Immigration, 2014 c 22, sch 9 para 26(3)

    ss 2C, 2D added—Justice and Security, 2013 c 18, s 15

    s 2D am—Counter-Terrorism and Security, 2015 c 6, s 47

    s 2E added—Immigration, 2014 c 22, s 18

    s 4 rep—Nationality, Immigration and Asylum, 2002 c 41, ss 114(3), 161, sch 7, para 22,

        sch 9

    s 5 rep in pt—Regulation of Investigatory Powers, 2000 c 23, s 82(1), sch 5; Nationality,

        Immigration and Asylum, 2002 c 41, ss 114(3), 161, sch 7, para 23, sch 9

        am—Race Relations (Amdt), 2000 c 34, s 9(1), sch 2 para 28; Nationality, Immigration

            and Asylum, 2002 c 41, ss 4(3), 114(3), 161, sch 7, para 23, sch 9; SI 2010/21, art

            5, sch 1; Immigration, 2014 c 22, sch 9 para 10(2)

        appl—Nationality, Immigration and Asylum, 2002 c 41, s 97A(2K)

    s 6 see—(trans of functions) SI 1999/901, art 5, sch

        appl—Anti-terrorism, Crime and Security, 2001 c 24, s 30(3)(a); Nationality,

            Immigration and Asylum, 2002 c 41, s 97A(2K)

        ext—Anti-terrorism, Crime and Security, 2001 c 24, s 27(1)

        am—Counter-Terrorism, 2008 c 28, s 91(1)(2)

    s 6A added—Justice and Security, 2013 c 18, sch 2 para 9(2)

        am—Immigration, 2014 c 22, sch 9 para 26(4)

    s 7 rep in pt—Immigration and Asylum, 1999 c 33, s 169(1)(3), sch 14 paras 118, 123,

        sch 16

        appl—Anti-terrorism, Crime and Security, 2001 c 24, s 30(5)

        saved—Anti-terrorism, Crime and Security, 2001 c 24, s 33(9)

        ext—Anti-terrorism, Crime and Security, 2001 c 24, s 27(1)

        am—Justice and Security, 2013 c 18, sch 2 para 9(3); (prosp) Immigration, 2014 c 22,

            sch 9 para 26(5); (prosp) Crim Justice and Cts, 2015 c 2, s 66(4)

1997

c 68 *continued*

s 7A rep—Nationality, Immigration and Asylum, 2002 c 41, ss 114(3), 161, sch 7, para 24, sch 9

ss 7B-7D added (prosp)—Crim Justice and Cts, 2015 c 2, s 66(2)

s 8 am—(prosp) Crim Justice and Cts, 2015 c 2, s 66(5)(a)(6)

rep in pt—(prosp) Crim Justice and Cts, 2015 c 2, s 66(5)(a)(6)

s 9 mod—Crim Justice and Cts, 2015 c 2, s 97(2); Counter-Terrorism and Security, 2015 c 6, s 51(8)

sch 1 am—Immigration and Asylum, 1999 c 33, s 169(1), sch 14 paras 118, 125; Nationality, Immigration and Asylum, 2002 c 41, s 114(3), sch 7, para 25; Asylum and Immigration (Treatment of Claimants, etc.), 2004 c 19, s 26(7), sch 2 pt 1 paras 10, 12; Constitutional Reform, 2005 c 4, s 145, sch 17 pt 2 para 28; SI 2010/21, art 5, sch 1

sch 2 rep—Nationality, Immigration and Asylum, 2002 c 41, ss 114(3), 161, sch 7, para 26, sch 9

sch 3 am—Asylum and Immigration (Treatment of Claimants, etc.), 2004 c 19, s 26(7), sch 2 pt 1 paras 10, 13; SI 2010/21, art 5, sch 1; Immigration, 2014 c 22, sch 9 para 10(3)

c 69   *Supreme Court (Offices)*—rep SL(R), 2004 c 14, s 1(1), sch 1 pt 1/4

citation am—Constitutional Reform, 2005 c 4, s 59(5), sch 11 pt 1 para 2(1) pt 4 para 32

1998

c 1   *Education (Student Loans)*—rep Teaching and Higher Education, 1998 c 30, s 44(2), sch 4

c 2   *Public Processions (Northern Ireland)*—N Irish

c 3   **Greater London Authority (Referendum)**

s 1 excl in pt—Children and Families, 2014 c 6, s 43(3)

s 62 mod—(W) SI 2013/1793 (W 180), reg 6(1)(c)

c 4   *Consolidated Fund*—rep Appropriation, 2000 c 9, s 3, sch (C)

c 5   *Fossil Fuel Levy*—rep Utilities, 2000 c 27, s 108, sch 8

c 6   *Wireless Telegraphy*—rep Wireless Telegraphy, 2006 c 36, s 125, sch 9

c 7   **Nuclear Explosions (Prohibition and Inspections)**

s 10 ext—Crim Justice and Police, 2001 c 16, s 50, sch 1 pt 1 para 64

c 8   **Employment Rights (Dispute Resolution)**

ss 8-10 rep in pt—Equality, 2010 c 15, s 211, sch 27 pt 1 (subst by SI 2010/2279, sch 2)

s 13 rep—Employment, 2002 c 22, s 54, sch 8(1)

s 14 rep in pt & am—Employment Relations, 1999 c 26, ss 33(3), 44, sch 9(10)

s 17 rep in pt—SL(R), 2004 c 14, s 1(1), sch 1 pt 8

am—SI 2004/1862, reg 14(2)

sch 1 rep in pt—Employment, 2002 c 22, s 54, sch 8(1); Equality, 2010 c 15, s 211, sch 27 pt 1 (subst by SI 2010/2279, sch 2)

sch 5 rep in pt—Companies (Audit, Investigations and Community Enterprise), 2004 c 27, s 64, sch 8;

sch 11 mod—SI 1999/498, reg 15(2)-(5)

c 9   *Northern Ireland (Emergency Provisions)*—rep Terrorism, 2000 c 11, s 125(2), sch 16 pt I

c 10   **Criminal Procedure (Intermediate Diets)(Scotland)**

c 11   **Bank of England**

s 1 rep in pt—Banking, 2009 c 1, s 239(1)(2); Financial Services, 2012 c 21, sch 19

am—Banking, 2009 c 1, s 239(1)(3); Financial Services, 2012 c 21, s 1(1)

s 2 am—Banking, 2009 c 1, s 238(2)

ss 2A-2C added—Banking, 2009 c 1, s 238(1)

s 2A am—Financial Services, 2012 c 21, s 2(2)(3)

rep in pt—Financial Services, 2012 c 21, s 2(4)

s 2AA added—SI 2013/3115, sch 2 para 38(2)

am—SI 2014/894, reg 36(2)

ss 2B, 2C rep —Financial Services, 2012 c 21, s 4(4)

s 3 replaced by ss 3A-3F —Financial Services, 2012 c 21, s 3(2)

s 4 am—Financial Services, 2012 c 21, s 3(3); ibid, sch 1 pt 2 para 1; ibid, sch 2 para 4

s 7 am—SI 2008/948, art 3, sch 1; Financial Services (Banking Reform), 2013 c 33, s 137(2)

s 7A added —Financial Services (Banking Reform), 2013 c 33, s 137(3)

Pt 1A (ss 9A-9ZA) added) —Financial Services, 2012 c 21, s 4(1)

s 9H am—SI 2014/894, reg 36(3)

s 9I am—SI 2014/894, reg 36(4)

s 9Q am—SI 2014/894, reg 36(5)

1998

c 11 *continued*

    s 9U am—SI 2014/894, reg 36(6)

    s 13 am—Financial Services, 2012 c 21, s 1(2)

    s 15 am—Financial Services, 2012 c 21, sch 1 pt 2 para 2

    s 16 am—Financial Services, 2012 c 21, s 3(4)(a)(b)(d)

        rep in pt—Financial Services, 2012 c 21, s 3(4)(c)

    s 17 am—SIs 2000/2952, reg 7; 2001/3649, art 161; 2006/3221, reg 29, sch 4; Statistics
        and Registration Service, 2007 c 18, s 60, sch 3 para 10; SI 2008/948, art 3, sch 1;
        Financial Services, 2012 c 21, sch 18 para 85(2); SI 2013/3115, sch 2 para 38(3)

        appl (mods)—SI 2003/1633, reg 15, sch 2 para 8(1)(2)(g)

    s 21 rep —Financial Services, 2012 c 21, sch 18 para 85(3)(a)

    s 23 rep in pt—SI 2001/3649, art 162(b); Financial Services, 2012 c 21, sch 18 para
        85(3)(b)

    s 24 rep —Financial Services, 2012 c 21, sch 18 para 85(3)(c)

    ss 25-29 rep—SI 2001/3649, art 162(c)-(e)

    ss 31, 32 rep—SI 2001/3649, art 162(f)(g)

    s 35 rep—SI 2008/948, art 3, sch 2

    s 36 rep—SI 2001/3649, art 162(h)

    s 40 am—Financial Services, 2012 c 21, sch 1 pt 2 para 3

    s 41 subst—SI 2013/3115, sch 2 para 39

    sch 1 am—Banking, 2009 c 1, ss 240, 241(1), 242(1)(3)(b)(c), 243; Financial Services,
        2012 c 21, sch 2 para 1(2)(3), (5)-(14); SI 2012/2404, sch 2 para 38(2)

        rep in pt—Banking, 2009 c 1, s 242(1)(3)(a); Financial Services, 2012 c 21, sch 2
        para 1(4)

    sch 2 am—SI 2001/3649, art 163; Financial Services, 2012 c 21, sch 18 para 85(4); SI
        2013/721, art 2

    sch 2A added—Financial Services, 2012 c 21, sch 1 pt 1

    sch 2A mod—(temp) SIs 2013/161, art 12(2); 2013/1765, art 2

    sch 3 am—Financial Services, 2012 c 21, sch 2 para 2(2)(4), (5),(6)(b), (7)(8)(a),(10); SI
        2012/2404, sch 2 para 38(3)

        rep in pt—Financial Services, 2012 c 21, sch 2 para 2(3), (6)(a)(c), (8)(b),(9)

    sch 5 rep in pt—SI 2001/3649, art 162(b); Pensions, 2004 c 35, s 320, sch 13 pt 1; Legal
        Services, 2007 c 29, s 210, sch 23; SI 2009/1941, art 2, sch 2; Charities, 2011
        c 25, sch 10

        transtl provns—SI 2001/3648, regs 6(1), 7, 8

    sch 6 rep—SI 2001/3649, art 162(d)

    sch 7 am—SI 2001/3649, art 164; Statistics and Registration Service, 2007 c 18, s 46, sch 2
        para 7; Financial Services, 2012 c 21, sch 2 para 5; ibid, sch 18 para 85(5)(a)

        mod—(temp) SI 2001/2966, arts 3, 12

        ext—Anti-terrorism, Crime and Security, 2001 c 24, s 17, sch 4 pt 1 para 40(1)

        rep in pt—SI 2009/1941, art 2, sch 1; Financial Services, 2012 c 21, sch 18 para
        85(5)(b)

    sch 8 rep in pt—SI 2001/3649, art 162(i)

        ext—Anti-terrorism, Crime and Security, 2001 c 24, s 17, sch 4 pt 1 para 40(2)

    sch 9 rep in pt—SI 2001/3649, art 162(j)(i)(ii)

c 12   *Northern Ireland (Elections)—N Irish*

c 13   **Animal Health (Amendment)**

c 14   **Social Security**

    power to am—Northern Ireland, 1998 c 47, s 87

    power to mod—Social Security Contributions (Trans of Functions, etc), 1999 c 2,
        s 15(1)(2)(b)

    power to appl (mods)—Child Trust Funds, 2004 c 6, ss 23, 24(5)(a)

    appl (mods)—SI 2010/1907, reg 16, sch 2

    Pt 1 Ch 1 (ss 1-7) power to excl—Social Security Contributions (Trans of Functions, etc),
        1999 c 2, s 23(1)

        power to trans functions—Social Security Contributions (Trans of Functions, etc),
        1999 c 2, s 17

        see—(trans of functions) SI 2008/2833, arts 3-5, sch 1

    s 1 see—(cert functions trans) Tax Credits, 1999 c 10, s 2, sch 2 pt II para 5

    s 2 appl (mods)—(pt prosp) Pension Schemes, 1993 c 48 s 170(1) (as subst by Social
        Security, 1998 c 14, s 86(1), sch 7 para 131)

        am—State Pension Credit, 2002 c 16, s 11, sch 1 pt 2, paras 4, 5; Welfare Reform, 2007
        c 5, s 28, sch 3 para 17(1)(2); Welfare Reform, 2012 c 5, sch 2 para 44(b); ibid,

1998
c 14 s 2 *continued*

 sch 9 para 38; (6.4.2016) Pensions, 2014 c 19, sch 12 para 32; (prosp) ibid, sch 16 para 38

 rep in pt—State Pension Credit, 2002 c 16, s 21, sch 3; Welfare Reform, 2007 c 5, s 67, sch 8

s 3 am—Social Security Admin (NI), 1992 c 8, s 2B(9); Employment, 2002 c 22, s 50, sch 6, para 1; Pensions, 2004 c 35, s 236, sch 10 para 1; Child Maintenance and Other Payments, 2008 c 6, s 57, sch 7 para 3(1)(2)(b); Pensions, 2008 c 30, s 63(3); (prosp) Welfare Reform, 2009 c 24, s 25(4); Welfare Reform, 2012 c 5, s 127(10); Mesothelioma, 2014 c 1, sch 1 para 21

 ext—Social Security Admin, 1992 c 5, s 2(8)(9)

 rep in pt —Employment, 2002 c 22, ss 50, 54, sch 6, para 4, sch 8(1); Child Maintenance and Other Payments, 2008 c 6, s 57, sch 7 para 3(1)(2)(a); SI 2012/2007, sch para 64(a)

 appl (mods)—SI 1996/1434, sch 6

 excl—Educ and Skills, 2008 c 25, s 91(2)(a)

ss 4-7 rep—SI 2008/2833, art 6, sch 3

Pt 1 Ch 2 (ss 8-39) appl (mods)—Social Security Contributions (Trans of Functions, etc), 1999 c 2, s 18, sch 7 para 19(3); SI 2010/1907, regs 6(1)(2)(d)(3)

 cert functions trans—Tax Credits, 1999 c 10, s 2, sch 2 pt II para 5, pt III para 8(a); Tax Credits, 2002 c 21, ss 50(1)(2)(e), 54(2)(3)(5)(7)(9)

 mod—Tax Credits, 1999 c 10, s 2, sch 2 pt V para 21; Social Security Admin, 1992 c 5, s 2(B)(1)(3)(8); SIs 1999/2225, reg 2(2); 1999/2227, reg 2(2)

 power to appl—Welfare Reform and Pensions, 1999 c 30, s 52; Tax Credits, 2002 c 21, s 63(8)(a); (pt prosp) Childcare Payments, 2014 c 28, s 59(4)(a)

 am—Tax Credits, 2002 c 21, s 51, sch 4, paras 12, 15

 appl—Age-Related Payments, 2004 c 10, s 5(5); SI 2005/1983, reg 7(6)

s 8 am—Social Security Contributions (Trans of Functions, etc), 1999 c 2, s 18, sch 7 para 22; Tax Credits, 1999 c 10, s 1(2), sch 1 paras 1, 6(q); State Pension Credit, 2002 c 16, s 11, sch 1 pt 2, paras 4, 6; Welfare Reform, 2007 c 5, s 28, sch 3 para 17(1)(3); Welfare Reform, 2012 c 5, sch 2 para 45; ibid, sch 9 para 39; (6.4.2016) Pensions, 2014 c 19, sch 12 para 33; (prosp) ibid, sch 16 para 39

 mod—SIs 1995/310, reg 17(5); 1999/991, reg 15

 rep in pt—Social Security Contributions (Trans of Functions, etc), 1999 c 2, ss 18, 26(3), sch 7 para 22(2)(b), sch 10 pt I; Welfare Reform and Pensions, 1999 c 30, s 88, sch 13 pt VI; Tax Credits, 2002 c 21, s 60, sch 6; (prosp) Welfare Reform, 2009 c 24, s 58, sch 7 pt 1; Welfare Reform, 2012 c 5, sch 14 pt 8; (pt prosp) ibid, sch 14 pt 1

 appl (mods)—(pt prosp) Pension Schemes, 1993 c 48, s 170(2) (as subst by 1998 c 14, s 86(1), sch 7 para 131); Health and Social Care, 2008 c 14, s 132(8)

 appl—SI 2001/1002, regs 4, 7

s 9 am—(contingently) (transtl provn) Social Security Contributions (Trans of Functions, etc), 1999 c 2, s 26(1), sch 8 para 4

 rep in pt—Welfare Reform, 2012 c 5, sch 14 pt 8

 mod—Pension Schemes, 1993 c 48, s 170(4), s 9

 appl (mods)—(pt prosp) Pension Schemes, 1993 c 48, s 170(2) (as subst by 1998 c 14, s 86(1), sch 7 para 131); Health and Social Care, 2008 c 14, s 132(8); SI 2009/1377, arts 3, 4

 saved—SI 2000/729, reg 4(4); State Pension Credit, 2002 c 16, s 7(8)

s 10 ext—SI 1999/991, reg 14(2)

 mod—Pension Schemes, 1993 c 48, s 170(4); SI 1999/991, regs 14(4), 15

 am—Social Security Contributions (Trans of Functions, etc), 1999 c 2, s 18, sch 7 para 23; SI 2008/2833, art 6, sch 3; Welfare Reform, 2012 c 5, sch 12 para 4(2)(3)

 rep in pt—Social Security Contributions (Trans of Functions, etc), 1999 c 2, ss 18, 26(3), sch 7 para 23, sch 10 pt I; Welfare Reform, 2012 c 5, sch 14 pt 8

 restr—SI 1999/991, reg 7(1)

 appl (mods)—(pt prosp) Pension Schemes, 1993 c 48, s 170(2) (as subst by 1998 c 14, s 86(1), sch 7 para 131); Health and Social Care, 2008 c 14, s 132(8); SI 2009/1377, arts 3, 4

 saved—SI 2000/729, reg 4(4)

 appl—SI 2002/1792, reg 17(3)

s 10A added—Social Security Contributions (Trans of Functions, etc), 1999 c 2, s 18, sch 7 para 24

1998
c 14 s 10A *continued*
>>>am—SI 2009/56, art 3, sch 1 para 248
s 11 am—State Pension Credit, 2002 c 16, s 11, sch 1 pt 2, paras 4, 7; Welfare Reform,
>>>2007 c 5, s 28, sch 3 para 17(1)(4); Welfare Reform, 2012 c 5, sch 2 para 46; ibid,
>>>sch 9 para 40; (6.4.2016) Pensions, 2014 c 19, sch 12 para 34; (prosp) ibid, sch
>>>16 para 40
>>>rep in pt—State Pension Credit, 2002 c 16, s 21, sch 3
>>>appl (mods)—Health and Social Care, 2008 c 14, s 132(8); SI 2009/1377, arts 3, 4
s 12 am—Social Security Contributions (Trans of Functions, etc), 1999 c 2, s 18, sch 7
>>>para 25(1)(2)(a)(3); SI 2008/2833, art 6, sch 3; Welfare Reform, 2012 c 5, s
>>>102(2)-(4); ibid, s 105(6); SI 2014/886, art 4(1)
>>>appl (mods)—(pt prosp) Pension Schemes, 1993 c 48 s 170(4) (as subst by 1998 c 14,
>>>s 86(1), sch 7 para 131); SIs 2002/2926, regs 4-7; (temp) 2005/191, regs 6-12;
>>>Health and Social Care, 2008 c 14, s 132(8); SI 2009/1377, arts 3, 4
>>>appl—Tax Credits, 1999 c 10, s 10(4), sch 4 para 3(2)
>>>mod—Pension Schemes, 1993 c 48, s 170(6)
>>>rep in pt—Social Security Contributions (Trans of Functions, etc), 1999 c 2, ss 18,
>>>26(3), sch 7 para 25(1)(2)(b), sch 10 pt I
s 13 mod—Pension Schemes, 1993 c 48, s 170(7)
>>>am—Social Security Contributions (Trans of Functions, etc), 1999 c 2, s 18, sch 7
>>>para 26; SI 2008/2833, art 6, sch 3
>>>appl (mods)—(pt prosp) Pension Schemes, 1993 c 48 s 170(4) (as subst by 1998 c 14,
>>>s 86(1), sch 7 para 131); SIs 2002/2926, regs 4-7; (temp) 2005/191, regs 6-12;
>>>Health and Social Care, 2008 c 14, s 132(8); SI 2009/1377, arts 3, 4
>>>rep in pt—SI 2008/2833, art 6, sch 3
s 14 rep in pt—Social Security Contributions (Trans of Functions, etc), 1999 c 2, ss 18,
>>>26(3), sch 7 para 27, sch 10 pt I; SI 2008/2833, art 6, sch 3
>>>appl (mods)—(pt prosp) Pension Schemes, 1993 c 48 s 170(4) (as subst by 1998 c 14,
>>>s 86(1), sch 7 para 131); SIs 2002/2926, regs 4-7; (temp) 2005/191, regs 6-12;
>>>Child Maintenance and Other Payments, 2008 c 6, s 51(3); Health and Social
>>>Care, 2008 c 14, s 132(8); SI 2009/1377, arts 3, 4
>>>appl—Health and Social Care (Community Health and Standards), 2003 c 43,
>>>s 159(3)-(6)
>>>am—SI 2008/2833, art 6, sch 3
s 15 appl (mods)—(pt prosp) Pension Schemes, 1993 c 48 s 170(4) (as subst by 1998 c 14,
>>>s 86(1), sch 7 para 131); (temp) SI 2005/191, regs 6-12; Health and Social
>>>Care, 2008 c 14, s 132(8); SI 2009/1377, arts 3, 4
>>>appl—SI 2002/2926, reg 8
>>>am—SI 2008/2833, art 6, sch 3
>>>rep in pt—SI 2008/2833, art 6, sch 3
s 15A added—SI 2008/2833, art 6, sch 3
>>>rep in pt—SI 2012/2007, sch para 64(b); Deregulation, 2015 c 20, s 79
>>>appl (mods)—SI 2009/1377, arts 3, 4
s 16 rep in pt—(prosp) Social Security Contributions (Trans of Functions, etc), 1999 c 2,
>>>ss 18, 26(3), sch 7 para 28, sch 10 pt I; SI 2008/2833, art 6, sch 3
>>>appl (mods)—SIs 2002/2926, regs 9, 10; (temp) 2005/191, regs 6-12; Health and
>>>Social Care, 2008 c 14, s 132(8); SI 2009/1377, arts 3, 4
>>>appl—Pensions Appeal Tribunals 1943 c 39, s 6D
s 17 appl (mods)—SIs 2002/2926, regs 9, 10; (temp) 2005/191, regs 6-12; Health and
>>>Social Care, 2008 c 14, s 132(8); SI 2009/1377, arts 3, 4
>>>am—SI 2008/2833, art 6, sch 3
s 18 rep in pt & am—Social Security Contributions (Trans of Functions, etc), 1999 c 2,
>>>ss 18, 26(3), sch 7 para 29, sch 10 pt I
>>>am—Child Benefit, 2005 c 6, s 1(3), sch 1 pt 1 para 26; SI 2008/2833, art 6, sch 3
>>>saved—SI 1999/1958, art 3
>>>appl (mods)—Health and Social Care, 2008 c 14, s 132(8); SI 2009/1377, arts 3, 4
s 19 rep in pt—Social Security Contributions (Trans of Functions, etc), 1999 c 2, s 18, sch 7
>>>para 30
>>>saved—SI 1999/1958, art 3
>>>am—Welfare Reform, 2007 c 5, s 62(2)
>>>appl (mods)—Health and Social Care, 2008 c 14, s 132(8)
s 20 rep in pt—Social Security Contributions (Trans of Functions, etc), 1999 c 2, s 18, sch 7
>>>para 31; SI 2008/2833, art 6, sch 3
>>>am—Welfare Reform, 2007 c 5, s 62(3)(4); SI 2008/2833, art 6, sch 3

1998

c 14 s 20 *continued*

  appl (mods)—Health and Social Care, 2008 c 14, s 132(8)

s 20A added—SI 2008/2833, art 6, sch 3

s 21 rep in pt—Social Security Contributions (Trans of Functions, etc), 1999 c 2, ss 18,
   26(3), sch 7 para 32, sch 10 pt I

  am—SI 2008/2833, art 6, sch 3

  appl (mods)—Health and Social Care, 2008 c 14, s 132(8)

  appl—SI 2009/1377, art 3

s 22 am—State Pension Credit, 2002 c 16, s 11, sch 1 pt 2, paras 4, 8; Welfare Reform,
   2012 c 5, s 99(5)

  rep in pt—(prosp) Welfare Reform, 2012 c 5, sch 14 pt 10

  appl (mods)—Health and Social Care, 2008 c 14, s 132(8)

  appl —SI 2009/1377, art 3

s 23 appl (mods)—Health and Social Care, 2008 c 14, s 132(8)

  appl—SI 2009/1377, art 3

s 24 appl (mods)—Health and Social Care, 2008 c 14, s 132(8)

s 24A added—Social Security Contributions (Trans of Functions, etc), 1999 c 2, s 18, sch 7
   para 33

  am—SIs 2008/2833, art 6, sch 3; 2009/56, art 3, sch 1 para 249

  appl (mods)—Health and Social Care, 2008 c 14, s 132(8)

s 25 mod—Pension Schemes, 1993 c 48, s 170(7)

  appl (mods)—Health and Social Care, 2008 c 14, s 132(8); SI 2009/1377, arts 3, 4

  am—SI 2008/2833, art 6, sch 3

s 26 mod—Pension Schemes, 1993 c 48, s 170(7)

  am—Health and Social Care, 2008 c 14, s 132(8)

  appl (mods)—SI 2008/2833, art 6, sch 3; SI 2009/1377, arts 3, 4

s 27 restr—Tax Credits, 1999 c 10, s 2, sch 2 pt IV para 19(a)

  am—State Pension Credit, 2002 c 16, s 11, sch 1 pt 2, paras 4, 9; Constitutional
   Reform, 2005 c 4, s 40(4), sch 9 pt 1 para 64; Welfare Reform, 2007 c 5, s 28,
   sch 3 para 17(1)(5); Health and Social Care, 2008 c 14, s 132(8); Welfare
   Reform, 2012 c 5, sch 2 para 47; ibid, sch 9 para 41; (prosp) Pensions, 2014 c 19,
   sch 16 para 41; (6.4.2016) ibid, 2014 c 19, sch 12 para 35

  appl (mods)—SI 2008/2833, art 6, sch 3; SI 2009/1377, arts 3, 4

s 28 am—Social Security Contributions (Trans of Functions, etc), 1999 c 2, s 18, sch 7
   para 34; State Pension Credit, 2002 c 16, s 11, sch 1 pt 2, paras 4, 10; Welfare
   Reform, 2007 c 5, s 28, sch 3 para 17(1)(6); Health and Social Care, 2008 c 14, s
   132(8); Welfare Reform, 2012 c 5, sch 2 para 48(b); ibid, sch 9 para 42;
   (6.4.2016) Pensions, 2014 c 19, sch 12 para 36(b); (prosp) ibid, sch 16 para 42

  mod—Pension Schemes, 1993 c 48 s 170(7)

  rep in pt—State Pension Credit, 2002 c 16, s 21, sch 3; Welfare Reform, 2007 c 5, s 67,
   sch 8; SI 2008/2833, art 6, sch 3

  appl (mods)—SIs 2002/2926, reg 11; (temp) 2005/191, reg 13; 2008/2833, art 6, sch 3;
   2009/1377, arts 3, 4

s 29 am—Health and Social Care, 2008 c 14, s 132(8)

  rep in pt—Welfare Reform, 2012 c 5, s 68(1)

  appl (mods)—SI 2008/2833, art 6, sch 3

s 30 appl (mods)—Health and Social Care, 2008 c 14, s 132(8)

  rep in pt—Welfare Reform, 2012 c 5, s 68(2)

s 31 am—Welfare Reform, 2007 c 5, s 28, sch 3 para 17(1)(7)

  rep in pt—(prosp) Welfare Reform, 2007 c 5, s 67, sch 8

  appl (mods)—Health and Social Care, 2008 c 14, s 132(8)

ss 32, 33 appl (mods)—Health and Social Care, 2008 c 14, s 132(8)

s 34 rep (pt prosp)—Welfare Reform, 2012 c 5, sch 14 pt 1

  rep in pt—Child Support, Pensions and Social Security, 2000 c 19, ss 67, 85, sch 7
   para 22(1), sch 9 pt VII; (prosp) Welfare Reform, 2009 c 24, s 58, sch 7 pt 1

  transtl provns & savings—SI 2001/1264, reg 4(5)

  am—State Pension Credit, 2002 c 16, s 14, sch 2 pt 3, paras 40, 41

  appl (mods)—Health and Social Care, 2008 c 14, s 132(8)

s 35 rep —Child Support, Pensions and Social Security, 2000 c 19, ss 67, 85, sch 7
   para 22(1), sch 9 pt VII

s 36 rep —Welfare Reform, 2012 c 5, sch 14 pt 8

s 37 rep —Welfare Reform, 2012 c 5, sch 14 pt 8

s 38 rep —Welfare Reform, 2012 c 5, sch 14 pt 8

s 39ZA added—SI 2008/2833, art 6, sch 3

1998
c 14 s 39ZA *continued*
     appl (mods)—SI 2009/1377, arts 3, 4
s 39 am—Welfare Reform and Pensions, 1999 c 30, s 59, sch 7 para 17; Social Security
     Contributions (Trans of Functions, etc), 1999 c 2, s 18, sch 7 para 35(a)(b);
     Welfare Reform, 2007 c 5, s 62(5); Welfare Reform, 2012 c 5, sch 2 para 49
     appl (mods)—SIs 2002/2926, reg 12; (temp) 2005/191, reg 14; Health and Social Care,
     2008 c 14, s 132(8)
     rep in pt—SIs 2008/2833, art 6, sch 3; 2009/56, art 3, sch 1 para 250; (prosp) Welfare
     Reform, 2012 c 5, sch 14 pt 1
s 42 rep (pt prosp)—Child Support, Pensions and Social Security, 2000 c 19, s 85, sch 9 pt 1
s 50 rep in pt—Child Support, Pensions and Social Security, 2000 c 19, s 85, sch 9
     pt VIII(1), Note 1
s 51 rep—Welfare Reform and Pensions, 1999 c 30, s 88, sch 13 pt VI
s 52 rep—Child Support, Pensions and Social Security, 2000 c 19, s 85, sch 9 pt VIII(1),
     Note 1
s 58 rep—Social Security Contributions (Trans of Functions, etc), 1999 c 2, s 26(3), sch 10
     pt 1
s 59 rep in pt—Social Security Contributions (Trans of Functions, etc), 1999 c 2, s 26(3),
     sch 10 pt 1; Capital Allowances, 2001 c 2, s 580, sch 4
     saved—SI 1999/1958, art 3
s 60 saved—SI 1999/1958, art 3
s 61 rep in pt—Social Security Contributions (Trans of Functions, etc), 1999 c 2, s 26(3),
     sch 10 pt 1
     saved—SI 1999/1958, art 3
s 62 rep in pt—Social Security Contributions (Trans of Functions, etc), 1999 c 2, s 26(3),
     sch 10 pt 1; Finance, 2008 c 9, s 138, sch 44 para 11(b)
s 65 rep—Welfare Reform and Pensions, 1999 c 30, s 88, sch 13 pt VI
s 70 rep in pt—(prosp) Welfare Reform, 2012 c 5, sch 14 pt 8
s 71 rep (prosp)—Welfare Reform, 2012 c 5, sch 14 pt 8
s 72 trans of functions—Tax Credits, 2002 c 21, ss 49(1)(d), 54(1)(3)(4)(6)(8)
     am—Civil Partnership, 2004 c 33, s 254(1), sch 24 pt 11 para 138
s 74 rep (prosp)—Welfare Reform, 2012 c 5, sch 14 pt 10
s 75 rep (prosp)—Welfare Reform, 2012 c 5, sch 14 pt 8
s 77 rep (prosp)—Welfare Reform, 2007 c 5, s 67, sch 8
     rep in pt—Welfare Reform and Pensions, 1999 c 30, s 88, sch 13 pt IV
s 79 see—(cert functions made exercisable in S) SI 1999/1748, art 3, sch 1 para 19
     see—(trans of functions) (S) SIs 1999/678, art 2(1), sch; 1999/1750, art 2, sch 1
     mod—Tax Credits, 1999 c 10, s 2, sch 2 pt V para 20(g)
     am—Tax Credits, 2002 c 21, s 51, sch 4, paras 12, 13; SI 2008/2833, art 6, sch 3;
     Welfare Reform, 2012 c 5, s 104(2)
     appl—Pensions Appeal Tribunals 1943 c 39, s 11A
     appl (mods)—(temp) SI 2005/191, reg 15
     rep in pt—SI 2008/2833, art 6, sch 3; (pt prosp) Welfare Reform, 2012 c 5, sch 14 pt 1
s 80 mod—Tax Credits, 1999 c 10, s 2, sch 2 pt V para 20(h)
     am—Tax Credits, 2002 c 21, s 51, sch 4, paras 12, 14; Tribunals, Cts and Enforcement,
     2007 c 15, s 50, sch 10 para 29(1)(5); Welfare Reform, 2012 c 5, s 102(5)
     appl (mods) —(temp) SI 2005/191, reg 15
     rep in pt—SI 2008/2833, art 6, sch 3
s 81 rep—Welfare Reform, 2012 c 5, s 143
s 83 rep—Social Security, 1998 c 14, s 86(2), sch 8
s 84 appl (mods)—(temp) SI 2005/191, reg 15
s 164 saved—SI 1999/1958, art 3
sch 1 rep—SI 2008/2833, art 6, sch 3
sch 2 am—Welfare Reform and Pensions, 1999 c 30, s 84, sch 12 pt II para 87; (pt prosp)
     Child Support, Pensions and Social Security, 2000 c 19, s 26, sch 3 para 15; SI
     2002/1457, art 2(2), schedule, paras 1, 3(b); Employment, 2002 c 22, s 53, sch 7,
     para 51; State Pension Credit, 2002 c 16, s 11, sch 1 pt 2, paras 4, 11; Welfare
     Reform, 2007 c 5, s 28, sch 3 para 17(1)(8); Welfare Reform, 2012 c 5, s 97(6);
     (prosp) ibid, sch 2 para 50(2)(3)
     rep in pt—State Pension Credit, 2002 c 16, s 21, sch 3; Welfare Reform, 2007 c 5, s
     67, sch 8; (prosp) Welfare Reform, 2009 c 24, s 58, sch 7 pt 1; (prosp) Welfare
     Reform, 2012 c 5, sch 14 pt 1
sch 3 mod—Pension Schemes, 1993 c 48 s 170(7)

1998

c 14 sch 3 *continued*

      rep in pt—Social Security Contributions (Trans of Functions, etc), 1999 c 2, ss 18,
        26(3), sch 7 para 36, sch 10 pt I; (prosp) Child Support, Pensions and Social
        Security, 2000 c 19, s 85, sch 9 pt V; Social Security Fraud, 2001 c 11, s 19,
        sch; Welfare Reform, 2007 c 5, s 67, sch 8; Welfare Reform, 2009 c 24, s 58,
        sch 7 pt 3; (prosp) Welfare Reform, 2012 c 5, sch 14 pt 9; ibid, sch 14 pt 6;
        (prosp) ibid, sch 14 pt 1; (pt prosp) ibid, sch 14 pt 4
      saved—SI 1999/1958, art 3
      am—Child Support, Pensions and Social Security, 2000 c 19, s 66; Social Security
        Fraud, 2001 c 11, s 12(2); State Pension Credit, 2002 c 16, s 11, sch 1 pt 2,
        paras 4, 12; Welfare Reform, 2007 c 5, s 28, sch 3 para 17(1)(9); (pt prosp)
        Welfare Reform, 2012 c 5, s 105(7); ibid, sch 2 para 51; (prosp) ibid, sch 7 para
        11; ibid, sch 9 para 43(b); (6.4.2016) Pensions, 2014 c 19, sch 12 para 37
    sch 4 rep—SI 2008/2833, art 6, sch 3; Welfare Reform, 2009 c 24, ss 1(4), 11, sch 3 para 4;
      (prosp) ibid, s 4, sch 1 paras 1, 25; (prosp) ibid, s 33(4); (prosp) ibid, s 24, sch 4
      para 10
    sch 5 power to appl—Child Support, 1991 c 48 s 20(6)
      appl (mods)—SI 2002/2926, reg 9
      rep in pt—SI 2008/2833, art 6, sch 3
    sch 6 rep (pt prosp)—Social Security, 1998 c 14, s 86(2), sch 8
      am—SI 1999/1042, art 5, sch 3 pt I para 4
    sch 7 am—(pt prosp) Child Support, Pensions and Social Security, 2000 c 19, s 1(2)
      rep in pt—Social Security Contributions (Trans of Functions, etc), 1999 c 2, s 26(3),
        sch 10 pt I; Welfare Reform and Pensions, 1999 c 30, s 88, sch 13 pt VI; (pt
        prosp) Child Support, Pensions and Social Security, 2000 c 19, s 85, sch 9 pts I,
        VIII(1), Note 1, IX; Nat Insurance Contributions, 2002 c 19, s 7, sch 2;
        Pensions, 2007 c 22, s 27, sch 7 pt 6; (prosp) Tribunals, Cts and Enforcement,
        2007 c 15, s 146, sch 23; (pt prosp) Welfare Reform, 2007 c 5, s 67, sch 8; SI
        2008/2833, art 6, sch 3; (prosp) Welfare Reform, 2009 c 24, s 58, sch 7 pt 1;
        (prosp) Welfare Reform, 2012 c 5, sch 14 pt 8; (prosp) ibid, sch 14 pt 1; (prosp)
        ibid, sch 14 pt 4; ibid, sch 14 pt 3

c 15   **Magistrates' Courts (Procedure)**

c 16   *Tax Credits (Initial Expenditure)*—rep Tax Credits, 2002 c 21, s 60, sch 6

c 17   **Petroleum**

    power to mod —Energy, 2004 c 20, s 189
    Pt 1 (ss 1-9) appl—Energy, 2004 c 20, s 188(9)
      excl—Energy, 2008 c 32, s 33(2)
    s 1 appl—Pollution Prevention and Control, 1999 c 24, s 3(2)
    s 3 ext—SI 1999/360, reg 3(1)
    s 4 mod—Infrastructure, 2015 c 7, s 48
    s 4A added (6.4.2016)—Infrastructure, 2015 c 7, s 50
    s 4B added (pt 6.4.2016)—Infrastructure, 2015 c 7, s 50
    s 5 appl—SI 1999/160, art 2
      am—Energy, 2008 c 32, s 107, sch 5 paras 7, 8; Land Registration etc (S), 2012 asp 5,
        sch 5 para 36
    ss 5A-5C added —Energy, 2008 c 32, s 76
    s 5C am—SI 2014/834, sch 2 para 12
    Pt 1A (ss 9A-9I) added—Infrastructure, 2015 c 7, s 41
    s 10 am—Energy, 2004 c 20, s 103(3)
    s 11 ext—Communications, 2003 c 21, s 410(3); SI 2003/1900, arts 2(1), 3(1), sch 1; SI
        2003/3142, art 3(2)
      am—Energy, 2008 c 32, s 36, sch 1 paras 6, 7
    s 13 am—Energy, 2008 c 32, s 36, sch 1 paras 6, 8
    Pt 3 (ss 14-28) appl —Energy, 2004 c 20, ss 188(9), 189(6)
    s 14 restr—SI 2011/2305, reg 16(1)(a)
    s 15 am—SIs 2000/1937, reg 2(4), sch 4 para 1; 2011/2305, sch para 8; Energy, 2011 c 16,
        sch 2 para 9
    s 16 am—SIs 2000/1937, reg 2(4), sch 4 para 2; 2011/2305, sch para 9; Energy, 2011 c 16,
        sch 2 para 10
    s 17 am—SI 2000/1937, reg 2(4), sch 4 para 3; Energy, 2004 c 20, s 151(5)(a); SI
        2011/2305, sch para 10; Energy, 2011 c 16, sch 2 para 11
    ss 17A, 17B added—SI 2000/1937, reg 2(4), sch 4 para 4
      rep—Energy, 2004 c 20, ss 151(5)(b), 197(9), sch 23 pt 1
    s 17C added—SI 2000/1937, reg 2(4), sch 4 para 4

1998

c 17 s 17C *continued*

        rep—SI 2011/2704, reg 16(2)

    s 17D added—SI 2000/1937, reg 2(4), sch 4 para 4

        rep—SI 2011/2704, reg 16(3)

    s 17E added—SI 2000/1937, reg 2(4), sch 4 para 4

        rep—SI 2011/2704, reg 16(4)

    s 17F added—SI 2000/1937, reg 2(4), sch 4 para 4

        am—SI 2007/290, art 2, sch; Energy, 2011 c 16, sch 2 para 12

    s 17G added—SI 2000/1937, reg 2(4), sch 4 para 4

        am—Energy, 2011 c 16, sch 2 para 13

    ss 17GA, 17GB added—SI 2007/290, art 2, sch

    s 17H added—SI 2000/1937, reg 2(4), sch 4 para 4

        rep in pt—(prosp) Energy, 2004 c 20, s 197(9), sch 23 pt 1; SI 2011/2704, reg 16(5)(a)(i)(ii)(b)

        am—SIs 2004/2043, reg 2(3), sch 3 para 2; 2007/290, art 2, sch; 2011/2704, reg 16(5)(a)(iii)(iv)(c)

    s 18 am—SI 2000/1937, reg 2(4), sch 4 para 5; Energy, 2011 c 16, sch 2 para 14

    s 19 am—SI 2000/1937, reg 2(4), sch 4 para 6; Energy, 2011 c 16, sch 2 para 15

    s 21 am—SI 2000/1937, reg 2(4), sch 4 para 7

    s 24 am—Marine and Coastal Access, 2009 c 23, s 112(1), sch 8 para 7(1)-(4)

    s 26 am—Energy, 2008 c 32, s 78(3)(a)

        rep in pt—Energy, 2008 c 32, s 78(3)(b), sch 6

    s 27 am—SIs 2000/1937, reg 2(4), sch 4 para 8; 2007/290, art 2, sch

        rep in pt—Energy, 2004 c 20, s 197(9), sch 23 pt 1

    s 28 am—SIs 2000/1937, reg 2(4), sch 4 para 9; 2004/2043, reg 2(3), sch 3 para 3(a)(b); Energy, 2008 c 32, ss 36, 78(4), sch 1 paras 6, 9; SI 2011/2305, sch para 11

        rep in pt—Energy, 2004 c 20, s 197(9), sch 23 pt 1; Energy, 2008 c 32, s 78(4)(a), sch 6; SI 2011/2704, reg 16(6)

    Pt 4 (ss 29-45) see—(power to trans functions) Govt of Wales 1998 c 38 s 22(1)(c)(5), sch 3 pt I para 4(1)(b)

        appl—Capital Allowances, 2001 c 2, s 163(5); Energy, 2004 c 20, ss 188(9), 189(6); Energy, 2008 c 32, s 30(1)

    s 30 am—Energy, 2008 c 32, ss 36, 72(1)-(6), sch 1 paras 6, 10

        appl—Energy, 2008 c 32, s 30A(13); Finance, 2013 c 29, s 80(8)

    s 31 am—Energy, 2008 c 32, s 72(7)

        rep in pt—Energy, 2008 c 32, s 107, sch 5 paras 7, 9, sch 6

    ss 32, 33 mod—(W) SI 1999/672, art 5, sch 2

        am—(S) SI 1999/1750, art 4, sch 3

    s 34 mod—(W) SI 1999/672, art 5, sch 2

        am—(S) SI 1999/1750, art 4, sch 3; Energy, 2008 c 32, ss 72(8), 107, sch 5 paras 7, 10(a)

        rep in pt—Energy, 2008 c 32, s 107, sch 5 paras 7, 10(b), sch 6

    s 35 mod—(W) SI 1999/672, art 5, sch 2

        am—(S) SI 1999/1750, art 4, sch 3

    s 37 am—(S) SI 1999/1750, art 4, sch 3

        mod—(W) SI 1999/672, art 5, sch 2

    s 38 am—Energy, 2008 c 32, s 73

    ss 38A, 38B added—Energy, 2008 c 32, s 74(1)

    s 39 am—(S) SI 1999/1750, art 4, sch 3

        mod—(W) SI 1999/672, art 5, sch 2

    s 44 am—Energy, 2008 c 32, s 36, sch 1 paras 6, 11

    s 45 am—Energy, 2008 c 32, s 107, sch 5 paras 7, 11; Marine and Coastal Access, 2009 c 23, s 112(1), sch 8 para 8

    s 45A added—Energy, 2008 c 32, s 75(1)

    s 47A added —Energy, 2004 c 20, s 103(4)

        am—Energy, 2008 c 32, s 36, sch 1 paras 6, 12

    sch 1 expld—SI 1999/160, art 3

    sch 2 am—SI 2011/2305, sch para 12

    sch 4 rep in pt—(NI) SI 1998/3162, art 105(4), sch 5; SI 2000/311, art 34; Capital Allowances, 2001 c 2, s 580, sch 4; Communications, 2003 c 21, s 406(7), sch 19(1); SIs 2003/1900, arts 2(1), 3(1), sch 1; 2003/3142, art 3(2); Corporation Tax, 2010 c 4, s 1181, sch 3 pt 2; Taxation (International and Other Provns), 2010 c 8, s 378, sch 10 pts 6, 12; Deregulation, 2015 c 20, sch 23 para 17(c)

c 18   *Audit Commission*—rep Loc Audit and Accountability, 2014 c 2, s 1(2)

1998

c 19   **Community Care (Residential Accommodation)**
            s 1 rep (prosp)—Health and Social Care, 2001 c 15, s 67, sch 6 pt 3
            s 3 rep in pt—(prosp) Health and Social Care, 2001 c 15, s 67, sch 6 pt 3
            s 35 am—SI 1998/465, reg 2(11)
c 20   **Late Payment of Commercial Debts (Interest)**
            s 2 am—SI 1999/1820, art 4, sch 2 pt I para 132
                rep in pt—SI 2002/1674, regs 2(1)(2), 5; (S) SSI 2002/335, regs 2(1)(2), 4
            s 2A added—SSI 2002/335, regs 2(1)(3), 4
            s 3 rep in pt—SI 2002/1674, regs 2(1)(3), 5; (S) SSI 2002/335, regs 2(1)(4), 4
            s 4 am—SSI 2013/77, reg 2(2)(3)(b)(4)-(6); SIs 2013/395, reg 2(2)(3)(b)(4)-(6); 2015/102,
                sch 6 para 1; 1336, reg 2(2),(4)-(6); SSIs 2015/226, reg 2(2),(4)-(6); 446, sch 6
                para 1(2)
                rep in pt—SSI 2013/131, reg 2; SI 2013/908, reg 2; SI 2015/1336, reg 2(3); SSI
                    2015/226, reg 2(3)
            s 5A added—(S) SSI 2002/335, regs 2(1)(5), 4; SI 2002/1674, regs 2(1)(4), 5
                am—SSI 2013/77, reg 3(2)-(4); SI 2013/395, reg 3(2)-(4)
c 21   **European Communities (Amendment)**
c 22   **National Lottery**
            s 2 rep in pt—Nat Lottery, 1998 c 22, s 26, sch 5 pt I
            ss 6-8 rep in pt—Nat Lottery, 2006 c 23, s 21, sch 3
            s 11 rep in pt—Nat Lottery, 2006 c 23, s 21, sch 3
            s 14 rep—Nat Lottery, 2006 c 23, s 21, sch 3
            Pt 2 (ss16-25) rep —SI 2012/964, art 3(1), sch
            sch 1 rep in pt—SI 2013/2329, sch para 25
            sch 2 rep—Nat Lottery, 2006 c 23, s 21, sch 3
            sch 4 rep—SI 2012/964, art 3(1), sch
c 23   **Public Interest Disclosure**
            s 8 rep—Employment Relations, 1999 c 26, s 44, sch 9(11)
            s 11 rep—Employment Relations, 1999 c 26, s 44, sch 9(12)
            s 13 rep—Police Reform, 2002 c 30, ss 37(3), 107(2), sch 8
            s 18 rep in pt—Employment Relations, 1999 c 26, s 44, sch 9(11)
c 24   **Road Traffic Reduction (National Targets)**
            trans of powers—(W) SI 1999/672, art 2, sch 1
c 25   *Registered Establishments (Scotland)*—rep Regulation of Care (S), 2001 asp 8, s 80(1), sch 4
c 26   **Pesticides**
c 27   **Criminal Justice (International Co-operation)(Amendment)**
c 28   *Appropriation*—rep Appropriation, 2000 c 9, s 3, sch (C)
c 29   **Data Protection**
            appl—SIs 1993/1813, art 4(2); 1999/3145, art 9(4); 2010/89, reg 16
            see —(Crown status for the purposes of the Act ext) SI 1999/677, art 7(3)
            saved—Scotland, 1998 c 46, s 30, sch 5 pt II, s B2(a); Foods Standards, 1999 c 28, s 19(2);
                Anti-terrorism, Crime and Security, 2001 c 24, s 19(7); Enterprise, 2002 c 40, s
                237(4); Sexual Offences, 2003 c 42, s 94(6); SI 2003/2426, reg 4; Domestic
                Violence, Crime and Victims, 2004 c 28, s 54(7); Constitutional Reform, 2005 c 4,
                s 107(3)(a); Commrs for Revenue and Customs, 2005 c 11, ss 22(a), 41(6)(a);
                Serious Organised Crime and Police, 2005 c 15, ss 33(4)(a), 34(3)(a), 81(7);
                Gambling, 2005 c 19, s 352; Govt of Wales, 2006 c 32, s 94, sch 5 para 3; Statistics
                and Registration Service, 2007 c 18, s 54; Regulatory Enforcement and Sanctions,
                2008 c 13, s 70(4); Public Health etc (S), 2008 asp 5, s 117(6); Terrorist
                Asset-Freezing etc, 2010 c 38, s 25(2)(a)
            trans of powers—(W) SI 1999/672, art 2, sch 1
            excl—SIs 1993/1813, art 4(3); 2003/2818, art 8(2); 2014/3141, reg 50(1)
            cert functs trans—SIs 2001/3500, arts 3, 4(1)(3)-(8), sch 1 para 11; 2003/1887, art 4, sch 1
            ext—SI 2003/2818, art 11(4)
            power to am—Crim Justice and Immigration, 2008 c 4, s 77(5)
            s 1 appl—(W) SI 1999/450, art 4(2), sch 1 para 4; SIs 1999/450, art 4(2), sch 1 paras 4, 7;
                1999/787, art 3(2), sch 1 para 7; (S) Freedom of Information, 2002 asp 13, ss
                38(2)(a), 75; SIs 2002/318, reg 5(8); 2005/2042, reg 45(1)(d)(2)(a)
                am—Freedom of Information, 2000 c 36, ss 68(1)(2)(3), 87(3); SI 2004/3089,
                    art 2(1)(2)(a)-(c)
                rep in pt—Freedom of Information, 2000 c 36, s 86, sch 8 pt III
            s 2 appl—SI 1999/787, art 3(2), sch 1 para 4(2)
            s 5 am—SI 2014/3141, reg 52(a)

1998

c 29 *continued*

s 6 see—(cert functions trans and made exercisable in S) SIs 1999/678, art 2(1), sch; 1999/1748, art 3, sch 1 para 20; 1999/1750, art 2, sch 1

am—Freedom of Information, 2000 c 36, ss 18(4),87(3), sch 2 pt I para 13, pt II para 16; SIs 2001/3500, art 8, sch 2 pt I para 6(1)(a)-(f); 2003/1887, art 9, sch 2 para 9(1)(a); Tribunals, Cts and Enforcement, 2007 c 15, s 50, sch 10 para 30

appl—SI 2003/2426, reg 28(8)(a)

rep in pt—SI 2010/22, art 5, sch 2

s 7 mod—SIs 2000/413, ss 6,8; 2000/414, ss 6,7; 2000/415, ss 6,7

appl (mods)—SI 2014/3141, reg 44(1)

am—Freedom of Information, 2000 c 36, ss 69(1),73,87(3), sch 6 para 1; SIs 2001/3500, art 8, sch 2 pt I para 6(1)(a)-(f); 2003/1887, art 9, sch 2 para 9(1)(a)

appl—SI 2015/1945, reg 15(1)

s 8 am—SIs 2001/3500, art 8, sch 2 pt I para 6(1)(a)-(f); 2003/1887, art 9, sch 2 para 9(1)(a)

appl (mods)—SI 2014/3141, reg 44(1)

s 9 appl—SI 2015/1945, reg 15(1)

s 9A added—Freedom of Information, 2000 c 36, ss 69(2),87(3)

am—SIs 2001/3500, art 8, sch 2 pt I para 6(1)(a)-(f); 2003/1887, art 9, sch 2 para 9(1)(a)

s 10 am—SIs 2001/3500, art 8, sch 2 pt I para 6(1)(a)-(f); 2003/1887, art 9, sch 2 para 9(1)(a)

s 11 am—SI 1999/2093, reg 3(2)(3), sch 1 pt II para 3

s 12 am—SI 2001/3500, art 8, sch 2 pt I para 6(1)(g); SI 2003/1887, art 9, sch 2 para 9(1)(a)

s 15 am—Crime and Cts, 2013 c 22, sch 9 para 77

s 16 am—Freedom of Information, 2000 c 36, ss 71,87(3); SIs 2001/3500, art 8, sch 2 pt I para 6(1)(h); 2003/1887, art 9, sch 2 para 9(1)(a); Coroners and Justice, 2009 c 25, s 175, sch 20 para 1(b)

rep in pt—Coroners and Justice, 2009 c 25, ss 175, 178, sch 20 para 1(a), sch 23 pt 8

s 17 excl—SI 2000/188, reg 3, sch

am—SIs 2001/3500, art 8, sch 2 pt I para 6(1)(h); 2003/1887, art 9, sch 2 para 9(1)(a)

s 18 am—Coroners and Justice, 2009 c 25, s 175, sch 20 para 2

s 19 appl—(mods) SI 2000/188, reg 15

am—Coroners and Justice, 2009 c 25, s 175, sch 20 para 3

s 20 am—(prosp) Coroners and Justice, 2009 c 25, s 175, sch 20 para 4(b)(c)(d)

rep in pt—(prosp) Coroners and Justice, 2009 c 25, s 178, sch 20 para 4(a), sch 23 pt 8

ss 22, 23 am—SI 2001/3500, art 8, sch 2 pt I para 6(1)(j)(k); SI 2003/1887, art 9, sch 2 para 9(1)(a)

s 25 am—SI 2001/3500, art 8, sch 2 pt I para 6(1)(l)(2); SI 2003/1887, art 9, sch 2 para 9(1)(a)

s 26 am—Freedom of Information, 2000 c 36, s 18(4), sch 2 pt II para 17; SI 2001/3500, art 8, sch 2 pt I para 6(1)(m); SI 2003/1887, art 9, sch 2 para 9(1)(a); SI 2010/22, art 5, sch 2

s 28 see—(trans of functions) (S) SI 1999/679, art 2, sch

am—Crime (International Co-operation), 2003 c 32, s 91(1), sch 5 paras 68, 69

appl—SI 2003/2426, reg 28(8)(b)

s 30 ext—SI 1999/3145, art 9(3)

am—SI 2001/3500, art 8, sch 2 pt I para 6(1)(n); SI 2003/1887, art 9, sch 2 para 9(1)(a)

rep in pt—Standards in Scotland's Schools etc, 2000, asp 6, s 60(2), sch 3

s 31 ext—SI 1999/3145, art 9(3)

am—Financial Services and Markets, 2000 c 8, s 233; Enterprise, 2002 c 40, s 278(1), sch 25, para 37; Health and Social Care (Community Health and Standards), 2003 c 43, s 119; Companies (Audit, Investigations and Community Enterprise), 2004 c 27, s 59(3); SI 2004/1823, art 19(a)(i)(b)(i)(d)(e); Public Services Ombudsman (W), 2005 c 10, s 39(1), sch 6 para 60(c); (prosp) NHS Redress, 2006 c 44, s 14(10); SI 2006/3363, reg 29; Legal Services, 2007 c 29, ss 153, 170; (EW) Loc Govt and Public Involvement in Health, 2007 c 28, s 200; SI 2014/892, sch 1 para 118

saving—(transtl provn) SI 2001/2326, reg 11(4); SI 2004/454, art 11(4)

1998
c 29 s 31 *continued*

rep in pt—SI 2004/1823, art 19(a)(ii)(b)(ii)(c); Public Services Ombudsman (W), 2005
   c 10, s 39, sch 6 para 60(a)(b), sch 7; Educ and Inspections, 2006 c 40, s 157,
   sch 14 para 32, sch 18; Localism, 2011 c 20, sch 4 para 6(a), sch 25 pt 5

s 32 am—SIs 2001/3500, art 8, sch 2 pt I para 6(1)(o); 2003/1887, art 9, sch 2 para 9(1)(a)

s 33 appl—Mental Health (Care and Treatment) (S), 2003 asp 13, s 279(2)

s 33A added—Freedom of Information, 2000 c 36, ss 70(1),87(3)
   mod—SI 2007/1118, art 5

s 34 am—Freedom of Information, 2000 c 36, ss 72,87(3)

s 35A added—Freedom of Information, 2000 c 36, ss 73,87(3), sch 6 para 2

s 38 am—SI 2001/3500, art 8, sch 2 pt I para 6(1)(p); SI 2003/1887, art 9, sch 2
   para 9(1)(a)

Pt 5 (ss 40-50) ext (mods)—SI 1999/2093, reg 36(1), sch 4
   appl (mods)—SIs 2003/2426, reg 31, sch 1; 2014/3141, reg 51(1)(a); 2015/355, reg
     2(3)-(5)

s 40 appl—HFC Bank, 1999 c iv, s 6(15)(16)
   ext—SI 1999/2093, reg 34, sch 3 para 4
   ext (mods)—SI 1999/2093, reg 34, sch 3 para 5(2)

s 41 ext (mods)—SI 1999/2093, reg 34, sch 3 para 5(2)

ss 41A-41C added —Coroners and Justice, 2009 c 25, s 173

s 41C am—Protection of Freedoms, 2012 c 9, s 106(1)

s 42 ext (mods)—SI 1999/2093, reg 34, sch 3 para 5(2)

s 43 am—Coroners and Justice, 2009 c 25, s 175, sch 20 para 8; ibid, sch 20, para 10

s 44 am—Coroners and Justice, 2009 c 25, s 175, sch 20 para 9; ibid, sch 20, para 11

s 48 am—Coroners and Justice, 2009 c 25, s 175, sch 20 para 5

s 49 rep in pt—SI 2010/22, art 5, sch 2
   appl—SI 2010/910, art 7

Pt 6 (ss 51-75) appl (mods)—SI 2014/3141, reg 51(1)(b)

s 51 am—SIs 2001/3500, art 8, sch 2 pt I para 6(1)(q)(r); 2003/1887, art 9, sch 2
   para 9(1)(a); Coroners and Justice, 2009 c 25, s 174(2); Protection of Freedoms,
   2012 c 9, s 107(1)(a)(ii)(b)
   rep in pt—Protection of Freedoms, 2012 c 9, s 107(1)(a)(i), sch 10 pt 8

s 52 am—SI 2001/3500, art 8, sch 2 pt I para 6(1)(q)(r); SI 2003/1887, art 9, sch 2
   para 9(1)(a)

ss 52A-52E added —Coroners and Justice, 2009 c 25, s 174(1)

s 52B am—Protection of Freedoms, 2012 c 9, s 106(2)

s 54 am—SI 2001/3500, art 8, sch 2 pt I para 6(1)(s); SIs 2003/1887, art 9, sch 2
   para 9(1)(a); 2014/3141, reg 52(b)

s 54A added—Crime (International Co-operation), 2003 c 32, s 81

s 55 am—Freedom of Information, 2000 c 36, ss 70(2),87(3); (prosp) Crim Justice and
   Immigration, 2008 c 4, s 78

s 55A added—Crim Justice and Immigration, 2008 c 4, s 144(1)
   am—Coroners and Justice, 2009 c 25, s 175, sch 20 para 13

s 55B added—Crim Justice and Immigration, 2008 c 4, s 144(1)

s 55C added—Crim Justice and Immigration, 2008 c 4, s 144(1)
   am—Protection of Freedoms, 2012 c 9, s 106(3)

s 55D added—Crim Justice and Immigration, 2008 c 4, s 144(1)
   am—Crime and Cts, 2013 c 22, sch 9 para 52

s 55E added—Crim Justice and Immigration, 2008 c 4, s 144(1)
   am—SI 2010/22, art 5, sch 2
   rep in pt—SI 2010/22, art 5, sch 2

s 56 am—Powers of Crim Cts (Sentencing), 2000 c 6, s 165(1), sch 9 para 191; Freedom of
   Information, 2000 c 36, ss 68(4),87(3); SI 2001/3500, art 8, sch 2 pt I
   para 6(1)(t); SI 2003/1887, art 9, sch 2 para 9(1)(a); Serious Organised Crime
   and Police, 2005 c 15, s 59, sch 4 para 112; Safeguarding Vulnerable Groups,
   2006 c 47, s 63, sch 9 para 15(1)(2); SI 2007/1351, art 60, sch 7; Policing and
   Crime, 2009 c 26, s 81(2)(3)(i); SIs 2011/565, art 3(2); 2011/2425, reg 4(a);
   2012/3006, arts 16, 74; Crime and Cts, 2013 c 22, sch 8 para 187; SIs 2013/602,
   sch 2 para 28; 2013/630, reg 14(2)
   rep in pt—SI 2012/3006, art 73

s 58 appl (mods)—SI 1999/2093, reg 32(8)(b); SI 2003/2426, reg 28(8)(c)
   am—Freedom of Information, 2000 c 36, s 18(4), sch 2 pt II para 18

s 59 am—Freedom of Information, 2000 c 36, s 18(4), sch 2 pt II para 19
   ext—Anti-terrorism, Crime and Security, 2001 c 24, s 17, sch 4 pt 1 para 42

1998
c 29 *continued*

s 60 am—Crime (International Co-operation), 2003 c 32, s 91(1), sch 5 paras 68, 70
s 63 ext—SI 1999/3145, art 9(3)
    am—Crime (International Co-operation), 2003 c 32, s 91(1), sch 5 paras 68, 71
    mod—SI 2007/1118, art 5
s 63A added—Freedom of Information, 2000 c 36, ss 73,87(3), sch 6 para 3
    am—Justice and Security, 2013 c 18, sch 2 para 2(a)(b)
s 64 am—SI 2001/3500, art 8, sch 2 pt I para 6(1)(u); SI 2003/1887, art 9, sch 2
    para 9(1)(a)
s 67 am—Freedom of Information, 2000 c 36, ss 69(3),87(3); SI 2001/3500, art 8, sch 2 pt I
    para 6(1)(v); SI 2003/1887, art 9, sch 2 para 9(1)(a); Crim Justice and
    Immigration, 2008 c 4, s 144(2); Coroners and Justice, 2009 c 25, s 175, sch 20
    para 6; Protection of Freedoms, 2012 c 9, s 107(2)
    appl—SI 2003/2426, reg 28(8)(d)
    appl (mods)—SI 2014/3141, reg 44(1)
s 68 appl—(EW) Health, 1999 c 8, s 23(6)
s 69 appl—(EW) Health, 1999 c 8, s 24(10); (EW) SI 2002/1438, reg 7(3)
    am—SI 2000/90, art 3(1), sch 1 para 33; Nat Health Service Reform and Health Care
    Professions, 2002 c 17, s 6(2), sch 5, para 41; SIs 2002/253, art 54(3), sch 5, para
    14; 2002/254, art 48(3), sch 4, para 7; 2002/2469, reg 4, sch 1 pt 1, para 24;
    Health and Social Care (Community Health and Standards), 2003 c 43, s 34, sch
    4 paras 106, 107; SI 2003/1590, art 3, sch pt 1 para 1(a); SI 2005/848, arts 28,
    29, sch 1 pt 2 para 12, sch 2; Nat Health Service (Conseq Provns), 2006 c 43, s 2,
    sch 1 para 191; SIs 2007/289, art 67, sch 1; 2009/1182, arts 4, 5-7, sch 5;
    2010/231, art 68, sch 4; Health and Social Care, 2012 c 7, s 213(7)(h); ibid, s
    220(5); ibid, sch 5 para 82(a)(c); ibid, sch 17 para 7; (pt prsop) ibid, sch 19 para 7
    rep in pt—SI 2003/1590, art 3, sch pt 1 para 1(b); Health and Social Care, 2012 c 7,
    sch 5 para 82(b)(d); ibid, sch 14 para 74
s 70 am—SI 1999/1820, art 4, sch 2 pt I para 133; Freedom of Information, 2000 c 36,
    s 18(4), sch 2 pt I para 14(a); Freedom of Information, 2000 c 36, ss 18(4),87(3),
    sch 2 pt I para 14(b); Coroners and Justice, 2009 c 25, s 175, sch 20 para 7; SI
    2010/22, art 5, sch 2
s 71 am—Freedom of Information, 2000 c 36, ss 68(5),87(3)
s 75 am—SI 2001/3500, art 8, sch 2 pt I para 6(1)(w); SI 2003/1887, art 9, sch 2
    para 9(1)(a); Safeguarding Vulnerable Groups, 2006 c 47, s 63, sch 9 para
    15(1)(3); SI 2007/1351, art 60, sch 7; Policing and Crime, 2009 c 26, s
    81(2)(3)(i); SI 2011/565, art 3(3); 2011/2425, reg 4(b); Protection of Freedoms,
    2012 c 9, s 86; SI 2013/630, reg 14(3)
    rep in pt—SI 2012/3006, art 75
sch 1 am—SIs 2001/3500, art 8, sch 2 pt I para 6(1)(x); 2003/1887, art 9, sch 2
    para 9(1)(b)
    see—SI 2000/185
sch 2 am—Freedom of Information, 2000 c 36, ss 73,87(3), sch 6 para 4; SIs 2001/3500,
    art 8, sch 2 pt I para 6(1)(y); 2003/1887, art 9, sch 2 para 9(1)(b)
    mod—SI 2007/1118, art 5
sch 3 am—Freedom of Information, 2000 c 36, ss 73,87(3), sch 6 para 5; SIs 2001/3500,
    art 8, sch 2 pt I para 6(1)(z); 2003/1887, art 9, sch 2 para 9(1)(b); Serious Crime,
    2007 c 27, s 72
    mod—SI 2007/1118, art 5
sch 4 mod—Immigration and Asylum, 1999 c 33, s 13(4)
    am—SIs 2001/3500, art 8, sch 2 pt I para 6(1)(aa); 2003/1887, art 9, sch 2
    para 9(1)(b)
sch 5 am—Freedom of Information, 2000 c 36, s 18(4), sch 2 pt I para 15(1)(2); Freedom of
    Information, 2000 c 36, s 18(4), sch 2 pt II paras 20,21,22; SIs 2001/3500, art 8,
    sch 2 pt I para 6(1)(bb); SI 2003/1887, art 9, sch 2 para 9(1)(c)(2); Protection of
    Freedoms, 2012 c 9, s 105(1)(2)(4); ibid, s 108(2)
    restr—Freedom of Information, 2000 c 36, ss 18(7),87(3)
    rep in pt—Freedom of Information, 2000 c 36, s 18(4), sch 2 pt I para 15(1)(3);
    SI 2001/3500, art 8, sch 2 pt I para 6(3); SI 2010/22, art 5, sch 2; Protection of
    Freedoms, 2012 c 9, s 105(3); ibid, s 108(3); ibid, sch 10 pt 8
sch 6 appl (mods)—SI 1999/2093, reg 32(8); SI 2003/2426, reg 31, sch 1
    appl—Freedom of Information, 2000 c 36, ss 61,87(3); SI 2003/2426, reg 28(8)(b);
    SI 2010/910, art 7

1998

c 29 sch 6 *continued*

 am—Freedom of Information, 2000 c 36, ss 61(1),87(3), sch 4 paras 1-4;
  SI 2001/3500, art 8, sch 2 pt I para 6(1)c c; SI 2003/1887, art 9, sch 2
  para 9(1)(d); Constitutional Reform, 2005 c 4, s 15(1), sch 4 pt 1 para 275(1)(2);
  ibid, para 275(1)(3) pt 2 para 406; SI 2010/22, art 5, sch 2
 rep in pt—SI 2010/22, art 5, sch 2

sch 7 am—Northern Ireland, 1998 c 47, s 99, sch 13 para 21(1)(2); Freedom of Information,
  2000 c 36, ss 73,87(3), sch 6 paras 6, 7; SIs 2001/3500, art 8, sch 2 pt I
  para 6(1)(dd); 2002/1555, art 25(1)(3); 2003/1887, art 9, sch 2 para 9(1)(e);
  2007/126, reg 3, Sch 6; Coroners and Justice, 2009 c 25, s 175, sch 20 para 12;
  Financial Services, 2012 c 21, sch 18 para 86
 appl—SI 2000/184, art 2(3)
 rep in pt—SI 2002/1555, art 25(1)(2)
 mod—SI 2007/1118, art 5

sch 8 pt III excl—Freedom of Information, 2000 c 36, ss 40(6), 87(3); (S) Freedom of
  Information (S), 2002 asp 13, ss 38, 75; (S) SSI 2005/494, reg 39(4)
 am—Freedom of Information, 2000 c 36, ss 70(3), 87(3)

sch 9 appl (mods)—SI 1999/2093, reg 34, sch 3 para 5(3); SI 2003/2426, reg 31, sch 1
 ext—Crim Justice and Police, 2001 c 16, s 50, sch 1 pt 1 para 65
 am—Courts, 2003 c 39, s 65, sch 4 para 8; Coroners and Justice, 2009 c 25, s 175, sch
  20 para 14(1)-(7); ibid, s 178, sch 23 pt 8

sch 11 rep in pt—Standards in Scotland's Schools etc, 2000, asp 6, s 60(2), sch 3
 am—SI 2010/1158, art 5, sch 2

sch 12 rep in pt—(prosp) Housing (S), 2001 asp 10, s 112, sch 10 para 26

sch 13 am—Freedom of Information, 2000 c 36, ss 70(4),87(3)

sch 14 excl—SI 1999/2093, reg 34, sch 3 para 4
 rep in pt—Freedom of Information, 2000 c 36, ss 73,86, sch 6 para 8, sch 8 pt I

sch 15 rep in pt—Freedom of Information, 2000 c 36, s 86, sch 8 pt III; Violent Crime
  Reduction, 2006 c 38, s 65, sch 5

c 30   **Teaching and Higher Education**

 power to mod—(EW) Teaching and Higher Education, 1998 c 30, s 6, sch 2, para 7(3)
 trans of powers—(W) SI 1999/672, art 2, sch 1
 power to mod—Educ, 2002 c 32, s 177(4)(5)
 am—SI 2010/1158, art 5, sch 2
 ss 1-15 rep—Educ (W), 2014 anaw 5, sch 3 para 3
 s 15A am—Safeguarding Vulnerable Groups, 2006 c 47, s 63, sch 9 paras 2, 6; Educ, 2011
  c 21, sch 2 para 12(a)(c)(ii)
  rep in pt—Educ, 2011 c 21, sch 2 para 12(b)(c)(i)
 ss 16, 17 rep (S)—SSI 2011/215, sch 7
 s 18 rep—Educ, 2002 c 32, s 215, sch 21, para 84, sch 22 pt 3
 s 19 rep—Educ (W), 2014 anaw 5, sch 3 para 3
 s 20 rep—Educ, 2005 c 18, s 123, sch 19 pt 3
 s 22 see—SI 1998/2003, regs 3, 4
  am—Learning and Skills, 2000 c 21, s 146(2)(a); Income Tax (Earnings and Pensions),
   2003 c 1, s 722, sch 6 pt 2 para 236; Finance, 2003 c 14, s 147(3)(5); Higher
   Educ, 2004 c 8, s 42(1); ibid, s 43(1)(2); (savings) Apprenticeships, Skills,
   Children and Learning, 2009 c 22, s 257(1)(2)(4); Educ, 2011 c 21, s 76(1); SI
   2013/1881, sch para 6
  rep in pt—Learning and Skills, 2000 c 21, ss 146(2)(b),153, sch 11; Higher Educ, 2004
   c 8, ss 43(3), 50, sch 7; Educ, 2011 c 21, s 76(2)(a)
  transfer of cert functions—Higher Educ, 2004 c 8, s 44
 s 23 am—Learning and Skills, 2000 c 21, s 146(3); SIs (E) 2001/2237, arts 2, 34; (W)
   2002/808 (W 89), arts 2(s), 33
  rep in pt—SI 2010/1158, art 5, schs 2, 3
  transfer of cert functions—Higher Educ, 2004 c 8, s 44
 s 24 mod—Sale of Student Loans, 2008 c 10, s 7
  am—Further and Higher Educ (Governance and Information) (W), 2014 anaw 1, s 9
 s 26 rep —Higher Educ, 2004 c 8, ss 49, 50, sch 6 para 7, sch 7
 s 28 am—Learning and Skills, 2000 c 21, s 146(5); Learning and Skills, 2000 c 21, s 149,
   sch 9 para 75(c); Educ, 2005 c 18, ss 98, 99, sch 14 para 20, sch 15
  rep in pt—Learning and Skills, 2000 c 21, ss 149, 153, sch 9 para 75(a)(b), sch 11;
   Higher Educ, 2004 c 8, ss 49, 50, sch 6 para 8, sch 7
 s 34 rep—Learning and Skills, 2000 c 21, ss 149, 153, sch 9 para 76, sch 11
 s 35 rep—Educ, 2005 c 18, s 123, sch 19 pt 1

1998

c 30 *continued*

s 35A added—Learning and Skills, 2000 c 21, s 81

    rep—Educ, 2005 c 18, s 123, sch 19 pt 1

s 37 rep—Further and Higher Educ (S), 2005 asp 6, s 32, sch 3 para 7(a)

s 38 rep—Special Educational Needs and Disability, 2001 c 10, ss 38(15), 42(6), sch 9

s 41 rep —Charities, 2006 c 50, s 75, sch 9

s 42 am—Educ, 2002 c 32, s 148, sch 12 pt 1, paras 1, 9; (W prosp) Higher Educ, 2004 c 8, s 49, sch 6 para 9

    rep in pt—Educ, 2011 c 21, sch 2 para 15

s 43 am—(W prosp) Educ, 2002 c 32, s 148, sch 12 pt 1, paras 1, 10; SI 2010/1158, art 5, sch 2

s 46 am—Higher Educ, 2004 c 8, s 42(2); (savings) Apprenticeships, Skills, Children and Learning, 2009 c 22, s 257(1)(3)(4)

sch 1 rep —Educ (W), 2014 anaw 5, sch 3 para 3

sch 2 rep —Educ (W), 2014 anaw 5, sch 3 para 3

sch 3 rep in pt—Educ, 2002 c 32, s 215(2), sch 22 pt 3; Further and Higher Educ (S), 2005 asp 6, s 32, sch 3 para 7(b); Charities, 2006 c 50, s 75, sch 9

c 31   **School Standards and Framework**

am—(E) SI 1998/1973, reg 3(6); SI 2010/1158, art 5, sch 2

appl—SI 1999/101, regs 1(11), 16(1)-(4), 17(1)(d); 2000/478, regs 17(1)(d),21(1)(a); Educ, 2002 c 32, s 212(5); (E) SI 2002/377, regs 16, 24(1)(b)(2)(a), 26(2)(a), sch 2, paras 15, 24; (W) SI 2003/543 (W 77), reg 4(a); (E) SI 2003/3247, regs 14, 23(1)(b)(2), sch 1 paras 15, 24; (W) SI 2004/1576 (W 162), reg 10(2)(b); (W) SI 2004/2506 (W 224), reg 13, sch para 17; (E) SI 2004/3130, regs 14, 23(1)(b)(2)(a), 25(2)(a), sch 1 paras 15, 24

power to delegate certain functions restr —(W) SI 1999/2242, reg 42(1)(5)

trans of powers—(W) SI 1999/672, art 2, sch 1

power to mod—Educ, 2002 c 32, s 177(4)(5)

s 1 appl (mods)—SI 1999/2666, reg 8, sch paras 1(c), 2-8; (W) SI 1999/2800, reg 7, sch paras 1, 2-8; (E) SI 2003/1041, reg 9, sch paras 1(b)(c), 2-5; (W) 2006/175, reg 9, sch

    am—Educ, 2002 c 32, s 215(1), sch 21, para 87

    saved—(prosp) Nationality, Immigration and Asylum, 2002 c 41, s 37(5)

s 2 rep—Children, 2004 c 31, s 64, sch 5 pt 1

s 3 rep—Educ, 2002 c 32, ss 18(1)(i), 215(2), sch 22 pt 3

s 4 am—Educ, 2002 c 32, s 215(1), sch 21, para 88

s 5 rep—Educ and Inspections, 2006 c 40, s 184, sch 18

ss 6, 7 rep—Children, 2004 c 31, s 64, sch 5 pt 1

ss 8, 9 appl—Educ, 2002 c 32, s 63(4)

s 10 ext—SI 1999/362, reg 2(4)

    mod—SI 1998/1878, reg 2

    appl—Educ, 2002 c 32, s 4(2)(a)

    am—Educ, 2002 c 32, s 187, sch 15, paras 1, 2(1)(2)(4)(5), 8

    rep in pt—Educ, 2002 c 32, ss 187, 215(2), sch 15, paras 1, 2(3)(6), 8(2), sch 22 pt 3

s 11 ext—SI 1999/362, reg 2(4)

    rep in pt—Educ, 2002 c 32, ss 187, 215(2), sch 15, paras 1, 3, sch 22 pt 3

s 11A added—Educ, 2002 c 32, s 187, sch 15, paras 1, 4, 8(1)(4)

ss 11B, 11C added—Educ, 2002 c 32, s 187, sch 15, paras 1, 5

s 11D added—Educ, 2002 c 32, s 187, sch 15, paras 1, 6

s 12 am—Educ, 2002 c 32, ss 187, 215(1), sch 15, paras 1, 7, sch 21, para 90

s 13 rep—Educ, 2002 c 32, s 215, sch 21, para 91, sch 22 pt 1

Pt 1, Ch 4 (ss 14-19A) power to mod—Educ, 2002 c 32, s 25(1)(a)(2); Educ (W), 2011 nawm 7, s 18

    rep (W) —School Standards and Organisation (W), 2013 anaw 1, sch 5 para 4(2)

Pt 2 (ss 20-83) appl—(W prosp) Educ, 2002 c 32, s 12(1)(b); (E) SI 2005/2038, reg 4(2)

s 20 ext—SI 1999/362, reg 2(4)

    appl—SI 2001/3458, art 4(6); Disability Discrimination, 1995 c 50, sch 4A para 1(2); Education, 1996 c 56, s 512(6); Freedom of Information, 2000 c 36, sch 1, para 52; (prosp) Nationality, Immigration and Asylum, 2002 c 41, ss 36(4)(a), 37(8)(a); SIs (E) 2002/2316, reg 3(1); (E) 2002/2953, reg 5; 2003/3006, art 3(4); (W) 2004/1743 (W 182), reg 3; 2005/2966, reg 2, sch 1 pt III

    am—Educ, 2002 c 32, s 215(1), sch 21, para 95; Educ and Inspections, 2006 c 40, s 30, sch 3 para 20; (W) School Standards and Organisation (W), 2013 anaw 1, sch 5 para 19(2)

1998
c 31 *continued*

s 21 am—Educ and Inspections, 2006 c 40, s 30, sch 3 para 14; (W) School Standards and
         Organisation (W), 2013 anaw 1, sch 5 para 19(3)(a)(ii)(b)(i)(ii)
     rep in pt—Educ and Inspections, 2006 c 40, s 184, sch 18; (W) School Standards and
         Organisation (W), 2013 anaw 1, sch 5 para 19(3)(a)(i)(iii)(b)(i)
     appl (mods)—(E) SI 2007/1329
s 22 rep in pt—Educ, 2002 c 32, s 215, sch 21, para 96(1)(2), sch 22 pt 3
     appl—Freedom of Information, 2000 c 36, sch 1, para 52
     am—Educ, 2002 c 32, s 215(1), sch 21, para 96(1)(3)(4); (E) SI 2002/906, art 3; Educ
         and Inspections, 2006 c 40, s 30, sch 3 para 15
s 23 am—Charities, 2006 c 50, s 75, sch 8 para 194(3)(4)(5); SIs 2011/1725, sch para 3(a);
         2011/1396, sch para 46(1); Charities, 2011 c 25, sch 7 para 75(1)-(3)
     rep in pt—Charities, 2006 c 50, s 75, sch 8 para 194(1)(2), sch 9; SI 2011/1725, sch
         para 3(b)
s 23A added—Educ and Inspections, 2006 c 40, s 33(1)
     am—SIs 2010/1158, art 5, sch 2; 2011/1396, sch para 40(2)(d); Charities, 2011 c 25,
         sch 7 para 76
s 23B added—Educ and Inspections, 2006 c 40, s 33(1)
     am—Charities, 2011 c 25, sch 7 para 77
s 24 rep—Educ and Inspections, 2006 c 40, s 29, sch 18
s 25 am—Educ, 2005 c 18, s 72, sch 12 para 6; Educ and Inspections, 2006 c 40, s 30, sch 3
         para 16
s 26 rep—Children, 2004 c 31, s 64, sch 5 pt 1
ss 26A,26B added—Learning and Skills, 2000 c 21, s 149, sch 9 para 81
         rep—Children, 2004 c 31, s 64, sch 5 pt 1
s 27 rep—Educ and Inspections, 2006 c 40, s 30, sch 3 para 17, sch 18
Pt 2 Ch 2 (ss 28-35) mod—(transtl provn) SI 1999/704, reg 21, sch
s 28 rep—(W) School Standards and Organisation (W), 2013 anaw 1, sch 5 para 19(4)
s 28A added—Educ, 2005 c 18, s 65
         rep—Educ and Inspections, 2006 c 40, s 30, sch 3 para 19, sch 18
s 29 rep—(W) School Standards and Organisation (W), 2013 anaw 1, sch 5 para 19(4)
s 29A added—Educ and Skills, 2008 c 25, s 154
s 30 am—Learning and Skills, 2000 c 21, s 149, sch 9 para 83; SI 2005/3238 (W 243),
         arts 7, 9(1), sch 1 paras 37, 39; Educ and Inspections, 2006 c 40, s 30, sch 3 para
         21; SI 2010/1080, art 2, sch 1; Educ, 2011 c 21, sch 16 para 12; (W) School
         Standards and Organisation (W), 2013 anaw 1, sch 5 para 19(5)(a)(d)
     rep in pt—(W) School Standards and Organisation (W), 2013 anaw 1, sch 5 para
         19(5)(b)(c)
ss 31-35 rep (W)—School Standards and Organisation (W), 2013 anaw 1, sch 5 para 19(6)
ss 36-39 rep—Educ, 2002 c 32, s 215(2), sch 22 pt 3
s 40 rep (E prosp)—Educ, 2002 c 32, s 215(2), sch 22 pt 3
ss 41-44 rep—Educ, 2002 c 32, s 215(2), sch 22 pt 3
Pt 2, Ch 4 (ss 45-53) mod—SI 1998/2670, reg 3(1)(3)
     appl—(W) SIs 2002/1394 (W 137), reg 31(2)(d); (W) (for specified purposes)
         2005/2913 (W 210), reg 8; 2010/638 (W 64), reg 74; 2012/1035, reg 28;
         2014/1132 (W 111), regs 77, 78
     appl (mods)—(E) SI 2004/2042, regs 33, 34
ss 45-51A appl—(E) SI 2003/1965, reg 28
s 45 mod—SI 1998/2670, reg 3(4)
     am—Educ, 2002 c 32, s 215(1), sch 21, para 99; ibid, s 41(2); (E) SI 2002/2316, reg 2;
         Educ, 2005 c 18, s 101, sch 16 paras 2, 3(1)-(7); (pt prosp) Educ, 2011 c 21, s
         50(2)(3)
     appl—(EW) Educ, 1996 c 56, s 494(6)
s 45AA added —Educ, 2005 c 18, s 101, sch 16 para 4
ss 45AB, 45AC added —Educ, 2005 c 18, s 101, sch 16 para 4
         rep—SI 2010/823 (W 86), art 2
s 45A added—Educ, 2002 c 32, s 41(1)
     am —(EW) Loc Govt, 2003 c 26, s 127(1), sch 7 para 66(1)(3)(4); Educ, 2005 c 18,
         s 101, sch 16 paras 2, 3(1)-(7); Apprenticeships, Skills, Children and Learning,
         2009 c 22, s 202(1)(2); SI 2010/1158, art 5, sch 2
     rep in pt—Educ, 2005 c 18, ss 101, 123, sch 16 para 3(1)(8), sch 19 pt 4
     appl—SI 2006/468, regs 3, 5
s 45B added—Educ, 2002 c 32, s 42
     am—(EW) Loc Govt, 2003 c 26, s 127(1), sch 7 para 66(1)(5)(6)

1998
c 31 *continued*

s 45C added—Educ, 2002 c 32, s 42
ss 45B, 45C replaced (by ss 45B-45D) —Educ, 2005 c 18, s 101, sch 16 para 5
s 46 rep—Educ, 2002 c 32, ss 41(3), 215(2), sch 22 pt 3
s 47 appl—(E) SI 1999/604, art 3(1); SI 1999/1779, art 3(1)
   am—Educ, 2005 c 18, ss 101, 117, sch 16 paras 6, 7, sch 18 para 7
s 47ZA added —Apprenticeships, Skills, Children and Learning, 2009 c 22, s 202(1)(3)
s 47A added—Educ, 2002 c 32, s 43
   am—Educ, 2005 c 18, ss 101, 117, sch 16 paras 6, 7, sch 18 para 7; Educ and
      Inspections, 2006 c 40, s 57, sch 5 para 2(1)(2)(4); Educ and Skills, 2008 c 25,
      s 164(1)-(3); Apprenticeships, Skills, Children and Learning, 2009 c 22, s
      194(8)
   rep in pt—Educ and Inspections, 2006 c 40, s 57, sch 5 para 2(3), sch 18; Educ and
      Skills, 2008 c 25, s 165(1)(4), sch 2; SI 2010/1158, art 5, schs 2, 3, 4
   mod—SI 2008/2867, reg 25
s 48 excl—SI 1999/362, reg 6(5)
   am—Educ, 2002 c 32, s 40, sch 3, para 2; Educ, 2005 c 18, ss 101, 117, sch 16 paras 6,
      7, sch 18 para 7; Educ and Inspections, 2006 c 40, s 57, sch 5 para 3(1)(2)(3)(5)
   appl—(E) SI 2002/3199, reg 3(2)(i)
   rep in pt—Educ and Inspections, 2006 c 40, ss 57, 184, sch 5 para 3(4), sch 18
ss 49-51 power to mod—Educ, 2002 c 32, s 25(1)(b)(2); Educ (W), 2011 nawm 7, s 18
s 49 mod—SIs 1998/2670, reg 3(5); 2012/1035, reg 29, sch 8
   appl—School Standards and Organisation (W), 2013 anaw 1, sch 1 para 12(4)
   am—Educ, 2002 c 32, s 215(1), sch 21, para 100; (E) SI 2002/906, art 4; Educ and
      Inspections, 2006 c 40, s 57, sch 5 para 4; SI 2010/1158, art 5, sch 2; (W) School
      Standards and Organisation (W), 2013 anaw 1, sch 5 para 19(7)(b)
   rep in pt—(W) School Standards and Organisation (W), 2013 anaw 1, sch 5 para
      19(7)(a)
s 50 am—Educ, 2002 c 32, s 40, sch 3, para 3; ibid, s 215(1), sch 21, para 101; Educ, 2005
      c 18, s 117, sch 18 para 8; Children, Schools and Families, 2010 c 26, s 4(2), (3)
   appl (mods) —SIs (E) 2003/1965, reg 29; (E) 2007/960, reg 36; 2010/638 (W 64), reg
      75
   mod—SIs 2012/1035, reg 29, sch 8; 2014/1132 (W 111), reg 78
s 51 mod—SI 2012/1035, reg 29, sch 8
s 51A added—Educ, 2002 c 32, s 40, sch 3, para 4
   rep in pt—(W) School Standards and Organisation (W), 2013 anaw 1, sch 5 para
      4(3)(a)
   am—Educ, 2005 c 18, s 117, sch 18 paras 9, 10; Children, Schools and Families,
      2010 c 26, s 4(4); (W) School Standards and Organisation (W), 2013 anaw 1,
      sch 5 para 4(3)(b)
s 52 am & rep in pt—Educ, 2002 c 32, ss 45, 215(2), sch 22 pt 3
   am—(W prosp) Educ, 2005 c 18, s 117, sch 18 paras 9, 10; Apprenticeships, Skills,
      Children and Learning, 2009 c 22, s 253(1)(2); SI 2010/1158, art 5, sch 2
   appl—SI 2006/511, regs 3-5
s 53 rep —Apprenticeships, Skills, Children and Learning, 2009 c 22, ss 253(1)(3), 266, sch
      16 pt 9
s 53A added—(EW) Public Audit (W), 2004 c 23, s 66, sch 2 paras 39, 41
ss 54-57 rep—Educ, 2002 c 32, s 215(2), sch 22 pt 3
s 58 appl—Educ, 2002 c 32, s 35(6), sch 2 pt 1, para 4
   saved—SI 2003/1660, reg 39(1)(a)
   am—Educ, 2002 c 32, s 40, sch 3, para 6(1)-(6)
   rep in pt—Educ and Inspections, 2006 c 40, s 37(1), sch 18
s 59 appl—SI 1999/2243, regs 50(4), 51(2)(3)(4), 52(5)
   saved—SI 2003/1660, reg 39(1)(a)
   appl (mods)—SIs 1999/2243, reg 52(6); 1999/2262, regs 48, 49(2), 50(4)(5), 51(2),
      52(5)(6)
   mod—SI 1999/2243, reg 50(5)
   am—Educ, 2002 c 32, s 40, sch 3, para 7
s 60 appl—SI 1999/2243, regs 49(3), 50(5), 51(3), 52(6)
   saved—SI 2003/1660, reg 39(1)(a)
   appl (mods)—SI 1999/2262, regs 48, 49(3), 50(5), 51(3), 52(6)
   am—Educ, 2002 c 32, s 40, sch 3, para 8; Educ and Inspections, 2006 c 40, s 37(2)
s 61 rep—Educ and Inspections, 2006 c 40, s 96(b), sch 18

1998

c 31 *continued*

s 62 am—Educ, 2002 c 32, s 215(1), sch 21, para 103; Educ and Inspections, 2006 c 40, ss 71, 175, sch 7 para 14, sch 17 para 2; (W) School Standards and Organisation (W), 2013 anaw 1, sch 5 para 4(4)(a)(i)

rep in pt—(W) School Standards and Organisation (W), 2013 anaw 1, sch 5 para 4(4)(a)(ii)(b)

appl (mods)—SIs (E) 2005/2039, reg 3, sch 1 pt 1 para 6; (W) 2007/1069 (W 109), reg 3, sch 1; (E) 2007/2979, reg 3, sch 1

s 63 ext—SI 1999/129, reg 2

rep in pt—Educ, 2002 c 32, ss 53(1)(2)(4), 215(2), sch 22 pt 3

am—Educ, 2002 c 32, s 53(1)(3)

ss 64-68 rep—Educ, 2002 c 32, s 215(2), sch 22 pt 3

s 69 am—Educ, 2002 c 32, s 215(1), sch 21, para 104

s 71 am—Educ, 2002 c 32, s 215(1), sch 21, para 105; Educ and Inspections, 2006 c 40, s 55

s 72 appl—SIs 1999/2243, regs 9, 23, 30; 1999/2262, regs 9, 23, 30

am—Educ, 2002 c 32, s 215(1), sch 21, para 106

s 73 excl—SI 1999/362, reg 56

s 75 am—Educ and Inspections, 2006 c 40, s 36, sch 4 para 19

s 77 appl—SI 1999/2212, reg 3, sch 1 para 7; SI 1999/2213, reg 3, sch 1 para 9

mod—(temp) SI 1999/1, reg 2

restr—(E) Learning and Skills, 2000 c 21, s 131, sch 8 para 9(3)

excl—Education, 1996 c 56, sch 35A, at para 10(4); Academies, 2010 c 32, s 13, sch 1 para 10(2)(b)

rep in pt—Educ and Inspections, 2006 c 40, s 36, sch 4 para 18(6), sch 18; Educ, 2011 c 21, sch 14 para 18(4)

am—SI 2010/1158, art 5, sch 2; Educ, 2011 c 21, sch 13 para 10(2), sch 14 para 18(2)(b)(3)(5)

s 79 rep—Finance, 2007 c 11, s 79, sch 27

s 79A added—SI 2003/2867, reg 2, sch pt 1 para 28

rep—Finance, 2007 c 11, s 79, sch 27

s 80 excl—Educ, 2005 c 18, ss 95(5), 99, sch 15; (W) SI 2013/1793 (W 180), reg 10

s 81 am—Educ, 2002 c 32, s 215(1), sch 21, para 107

s 82 am—Educ, 2002 c 32, s 215(1), sch 21, para 108; Educ and Inspections, 2006 c 40, s 30, sch 3 para 28; Academies, 2010 c 32, s 14, sch 2 para 9; (W) School Standards and Organisation (W), 2013 anaw 1, sch 5 para 19(8)

s 83 mod—Educ and Inspections, 2006 c 40, s 70, sch 6 para 3(4)

Pt 3 (ss 84-109) excl (W) —SI 2013/1793 (W 180), reg 11(1)

s 84 appl (mods)—SI 1999/2666, reg 8, sch paras 1(c), 2-8; (W) SI 1999/2800, reg 7, sch paras 1, 2-8; (E) SI 2003/1041, reg 9, sch paras 1(b)(c), 2-5; (W) SI 2006/175, reg 9, sch

appl—SI 1999/1812, reg 7(1); (E) SI 2002/2897, reg 8(1)

mod—SI 1998/3130, reg 2; (temp) SI 1999/1064, reg 2; 2013/1553, arts 3, 4

am—Educ, 2002 c 32, s 51, sch 4, para 2; Educ and Inspections, 2006 c 40, s 40(1)(2)(3)(6)(7); Educ and Inspections, 2006 c 40, s 50(2); Apprenticeships, Skills, Children and Learning, 2009 c 22, s 43(1)(2)

rep in pt—Educ, 2002 c 32, s 215(2), sch 22 pt 3; Educ and Inspections, 2006 c 40, s 40(5), sch 18

s 85 see —(E) SI 2003/163, art 3

rep in pt—Educ and Inspections, 2006 c 40, s 40(8)(a), sch 18

am—(transtl provns) Educ and Inspections, 2006 c 40, s 40(8)(b)(9); SI 2007/1388, art 3, sch 1

s 85A added—Educ, 2002 c 32, s 46

appl (mods) —(E) SI 2003/1041, reg 9, sch paras 1(b)(c), 2-5; (W) SI 2006/175, reg 9, sch

rep in pt—Educ and Inspections, 2006 c 40, s 41(2)(a)(4)(a), sch 18; Educ, 2011 c 21, s 34(2)(a)(iii)(b)-(e)

am—Educ and Inspections, 2006 c 40, s 41(1)(2)(b)(3)(4)(b)(5)(6); Educ, 2011 c 21, s 34(2)(a)(i)(ii)

s 85B added—(W prosp) Educ, 2002 c 32, s 66

rep—Educ, 2011 c 21, sch 10 para 1(2)

s 86 appl (mods)—SI 1999/2666, reg 8, sch paras 1(c), 2-8; (W) SI 1999/2800, reg 7, sch paras 1, 2-8; (E) SI 2003/1041, reg 9, sch paras 1(b)(c), 2-5; (W) SI 2006/175, reg 9, sch

1998
c 31 s 86 *continued*
    appl—SI 1999/1812, reg 8, sch 2 para 5(b)
    mod—(temp) SI 1999/1064, regs 3-8
    am—Educ, 2002 c 32, ss 47(1), 51, sch 4, para 3(1)-(3)(4)(a)(5)(7)(8); (W) (transtl
        provns) SI 2006/173; Educ and Inspections, 2006 c 40, ss 42, 43(2); Educ and
        Skills, 2008 c 25, s 169, sch 1 paras 53, 54(1)-(3)(5)-(8)
    rep in pt—Educ, 2002 c 32, ss 51, 215(2), sch 4, para 3(1)(4)(b)(6), sch 22 pt 3; Educ
        and Skills, 2008 c 25, s 169, sch 1 paras 53, 54(1)(4)(9), sch 2
    excl—(prosp) Nationality, Immigration and Asylum, 2002 c 41, s 36(5)(a)(10); SIs (E)
        2005/2039, reg 4, sch 2 pt 1 para 1; (E) 2007/2979, reg 4, sch 2; (W)
        2007/1069 (W 109), reg 4, sch 2
  ss 86A, 86B added—Educ and Skills, 2008 c 25, s 150
  s 87 appl (mods)—SI 1999/2666, reg 8, sch paras 1(c), 2-8; (W) SI 1999/2800, reg 7, sch
        paras 1, 2-8; (E) SI 2003/1041, reg 9, sch paras 1(b)(c), 2-5; (W) SI 2006/175,
        reg 9, sch
    am—Educ, 2002 c 32, s 51, sch 4, para 4; Educ and Skills, 2008 c 25, s 169, sch 1
        paras 53, 55; Educ, 2011 c 21, sch 1 paras 9, 10(b)
    rep in pt—Educ, 2011 c 21, sch 1 para 10(a)
  s 88 mod—SIs 1998/3130, reg 3
    appl—SIs (E) 2001/475, reg 5, sch 1 para 19(c)(i); (E) 2002/377, reg 5, sch 1, para
        19(c)(i); 2002/3199, reg 5, sch 2, para 13(a); (E) SI 2004/3131, reg 6, sch 3
        para 14(a)
    am—Educ and Inspections, 2006 c 40, s 43(1); Educ and Skills, 2008 c 25, s 151(1)(2);
        Educ, 2011 c 21, s 64(2)(b), sch 13 para 10(3)
    rep in pt—Educ, 2011 c 21, s 64(2)(c)
  s 88A added—Educ and Inspections, 2006 c 40, s 44
    am—Educ and Skills, 2008 c 25, s 151(1)(3)
  ss 88B-88R added—Educ and Skills, 2008 c 25, s 151(1)(4)
  s 88C excl—SI 2008/3089, regs 23, 33
  s 88E mod—SI 2013/1553, arts 3, 5
  s 88F rep in pt—Educ, 2011 c 21, sch 10 para 1(3)
  s 88H am—Educ, 2011 c 21, ss 36(2)(5)(b), 64(3), sch 13 para 10(4)
    rep in pt—Educ, 2011 c 21, s 36(3)(4)(5)(a)(c)(d)(6)
  s 88I am—Educ, 2011 c 21, s 64(4), sch 13 para 10(5)
    rep in pt—Educ, 2011 c 21, s 34(3)
  s 88J rep—Educ, 2011 c 21, s 34(4)
  s 88K am—Educ, 2011 c 21, ss 36(7), 64(5), sch 10 para 4(2)(b)-(e), sch 13 para 10(6)
    rep in pt—Educ, 2011 c 21, sch 10 para 4(2)(a)(ii)
  s 88L rep—Educ, 2011 c 21, sch 10 para 4(3)
  s 88P am—Educ, 2011 c 21, s 34(5)(a), sch 13 para 10(7)
    rep in pt—Educ, 2011 c 21, s 34(5)(b)
  s 88Q am—Educ, 2011 c 21, sch 13 para 10(8)
    rep in pt—Educ, 2011 c 21, sch 10 para 1(4)
  s 89 appl—SIs 1999/1812, reg 8(3); (E) 2002/2898, reg 4(1)
    excl—SIs (temp) 1998/3198, arts 3, 4; (prosp) SI 2007/496, reg 4
    see—SI 1998/3165, regs 7-9
    am—Educ, 2002 c 32, s 51, sch 4, para 5; Educ, 2005 c 18, s 106; Educ and
        Inspections, 2006 c 40, ss 41(7), 46(1), 52(2); Educ and Skills, 2008 c 25, s 169,
        sch 1 paras 53, 57(1)(2)(4)(5)(7)
    rep in pt—Educ and Inspections, 2006 c 40, s 45(a), sch 18; ibid, s 50(3), sch 18; Educ
        and Skills, 2008 c 25, s 169, sch 1 paras 53, 57(1)(3)(6)(8), sch 2
  s 89A added—Educ, 2002 c 32, s 47(2)
    am—Educ and Skills, 2008 c 25, s 169, sch 1 paras 53, 58
  s 89B added—Educ, 2002 c 32, s 48
    appl (mods)—(E) SI 2003/1041, reg 9, sch paras 1(b)(c), 2-5; (W) SI 2006/175, reg 9,
        sch
    am—Educ and Skills, 2008 c 25, s 169, sch 1 paras 53, 59
  s 89C added—Educ, 2002 c 32, s 48
    appl (mods)—(E) SI 2003/1041, reg 9, sch paras 1(b)(c), 2-5; (W) SI 2006/175, reg 9,
        sch
    am—Educ and Inspections, 2006 c 40, s 43(3); Educ and Skills, 2008 c 25, s 169, sch
        1 paras 53, 60; (W) School Standards and Organisation (W), 2013 anaw 1, sch
        5 para 4(5)
  s 89D added—Educ and Inspections, 2006 c 40, s 46(2)

1998
c 31 s 89D *continued*

   rep—Educ and Skills, 2008 c 25, s 169, sch 1 paras 53, 61, sch 2

 s 90 am—Educ, 2002 c 32, s 51, sch 4, para 6; Educ and Inspections, 2006 c 40, s 41(8);
   ibid, s 47(1)(2)(4)(5); Educ and Skills, 2008 c 25, s 169, sch 1 paras 53,
   62(1)-(4)(6)-(7)(d)(f)(8)-(10)(b)(d)

  rep in pt—Educ and Inspections, 2006 c 40, s 47(3)(6); Educ and Skills, 2008 c 25, s
   169, sch 1 paras 53, 62(1)(5)(7)(e)(10)(c)(11), sch 2

 s 90ZA added—Educ and Skills, 2008 c 25, s 169, sch 1 paras 53, 63

 s 90A added—Educ and Inspections, 2006 c 40, s 46(3)

   rep—Educ and Skills, 2008 c 25, s 169, sch 1 paras 53, 64, sch 2

 s 91 rep—Educ, 2002 c 32, ss 49, 215(2), sch 22 pt 3

 s 92 appl (mods)—SI 1999/2666, reg 8, sch paras 1(c),2-8; (W) SI 1999/2800, reg 7, sch
   paras 1, 2-8; (E) SI 2003/1041, reg 9, sch paras 1(b)(c), 2-5; (W) SI 2006/175,
   reg 9, sch

  subst—Educ, 2002 c 32, s 51, sch 4, para 7

  am—Educ and Skills, 2008 c 25, s 169, sch 1 paras 53, 65

 s 93 rep —Educ, 2002 c 32, s 215(2), sch 22 pt 3

 s 94 appl (mods)—SI 1999/2666, reg 8, sch paras 1(c), 2-8; (W) SI 1999/2800, reg 7, sch
   paras 1, 2-8; (E) SI 2003/1041, reg 9, sch paras 1(b)(c), 2-5; (W) SI 2006/175,
   reg 9, sch

  mod—(temp) SI 1999/1064, regs 3-8

  am—Educ, 2002 c 32, ss 50, 51, sch 4, para 8; Educ and Inspections, 2006 c 40, s
   43(4); ibid, s 51(1); Educ and Skills, 2008 c 25, s 152; Loc Govt (W), 2011
   nawm 4, sch 3 para 4(2)

  excl—(prosp) Nationality, Immigration and Asylum, 2002 c 41, s 36(5)(b)(10); SIs (E)
   2005/2039, reg 4, sch 2 pt 1 para 1; (E) 2007/2979, reg 4, sch 2; (W)
   2007/1069 (W 109), reg 4, sch 2; (W) 2013/1793 (W 180), reg 11(4)

  rep in pt—Educ and Skills, 2008 c 25, s 169, sch 1 paras 53, 66, sch 2

 s 95 am—Educ, 2002 c 32, s 51, sch 4, para 9; Educ and Inspections, 2006 c 40, s 48(1);
   Educ and Skills, 2008 c 25, s 169, sch 1 paras 53, 67; SI 2010/1158, art 5, sch 2;
   Loc Govt (W), 2011 nawm 4, sch 3 para 4(3)

  appl (mods)—SI 1999/2666, reg 8, sch paras 1(c), 2-8; (W) SI 1999/2800, reg 7, sch
   paras 1, 2-8; (E) SI 2003/1041, reg 9, sch paras 1(b)(c), 2-5; (W) SI 2006/175,
   reg 9, sch

  excl—SI 2009/821 (W 72), reg 9

 s 95A added—Educ and Inspections, 2006 c 40, s 48(2)

  am—SI 2010/1158, art 5, sch 2

 s 96 am—Educ, 2002 c 32, s 51, sch 4, para 10; Educ and Inspections, 2006 c 40, s 51(2);
   Apprenticeships, Skills, Children and Learning, 2009 c 22, s 43(1)(3)

  appl (mods)—SI 1999/2666, reg 8, sch paras 1(c), 2-8;(W) SI 1999/2800, reg 7, sch
   paras 1, 2-8; (E) SI 2003/1041, reg 9, sch paras 1(b)(c), 2-5; (W) SI 2006/175,
   reg 9, sch

 s 97 am—Educ, 2002 c 32, s 51, sch 4, para 11; Educ and Inspections, 2006 c 40, s 49; SI
   2010/1080, art 2, sch 1

  appl (mods)—SI 1999/2666, reg 8, sch paras 1(c), 2-8;(W) SI 1999/2800, reg 7, sch
   paras 1, 2-8; (E) SI 2003/1041, reg 9, sch paras 1(b)(c), 2-5; (W) SI 2006/175,
   reg 9, sch

 ss 97A, 97B added—Educ and Inspections, 2006 c 40, s 50(1)

 s 97C added—Educ and Inspections, 2006 c 40, s 51(3)

 s 97D added—Educ and Inspections, 2006 c 40, s 52(1)

 s 98 mod—(temp) SI 1999/1064, regs 3-8

  appl (mods)—SI 1999/2666, reg 8, sch paras 1(c), 2-8;(W) SI 1999/2800, reg 7, sch
   paras 1, 2-8; (E) SI 2003/1041, reg 9, sch paras 1(b)(c), 2-5; (W) SI 2006/175,
   reg 9, sch

  am—Educ, 2002 c 32, s 51, sch 4, para 12; (E) SI 2002/2953, reg 4; (W) SI 2006/173,
   reg 10; Educ and Skills, 2008 c 25, s 169, sch 1 paras 53, 68; Children and
   Families, 2014 c 6, sch 3 para 68

 s 98A added —Educ and Skills, 2008 c 25, s 153

 s 99 appl (mods) —(E) SI 2003/1041, reg 9, sch paras 1(b)(c), 2-6; (W) SI 2006/175, reg 9,
   sch

  rep in pt—Educ and Inspections, 2006 c 40, s 39(4)(a), sch 18

  am—Educ and Inspections, 2006 c 40, s 39(4)(b)

  appl—Academies, 2010 c 32, s 6(4)

 s 100 am—Educ and Inspections, 2006 c 40, s 53

1998
c 31 *continued*

s 101 appl (mods)—SI 1999/2666, reg 8, sch paras 1(c), 2-8; (W) SI 1999/2800, reg 7, sch paras 1, 2-8; SI 2003/1041, reg 9, sch paras 1(b)(c), 2-5, 7; (W) SI 2006/175, reg 9, sch
mod—(temp) SI 1998/2230, reg 3
rep in pt—(W) School Standards and Organisation (W), 2013 anaw 1, sch 5 para 19(9)
am—Educ, 2002 c 32, s 215(1), sch 21, para 109; Educ and Inspections, 2006 c 40, s 54(1)
s 102 appl (mods)—(W) SI 1999/2800, reg 7, sch paras 1, 2-8; (E) SI 2003/1041, reg 9, sch paras 1(b)(c), 2-5; (W) SI 2006/175, reg 9, sch
am—Educ and Inspections, 2006 c 40, s 54(2)
s 103 appl (mods)—SIs 1999/2666, reg 8, sch paras 1(c), 2-4, 8; (W) 1999/2800, reg 7, sch paras 1, 2-8; (E) SI 2003/1041, reg 9, sch paras 1(b)(c), 2-5, 8; (W) SI 2006/175, reg 9, sch
mod—(temp) SI 1999/1064, regs 3-8
am—Educ and Inspections, 2006 c 40, s 54(3); Educ and Skills, 2008 c 25, s 169, sch 1 paras 53, 69; (W) School Standards and Organisation (W), 2013 anaw 1, sch 5 para 19(10)
s 105 expld—SI 1998/2876, reg 11(1)
s 107 mod—SI 1998/2670, reg 4
s 108 am—Educ and Skills, 2008 c 25, s 169, sch 1 paras 53, 70
s 109 am—Educ and Inspections, 2006 c 40, s 30, sch 3 para 29
ss 110, 111 rep—Deregulation, 2015 c 20, sch 16 para 2(1)
s 114 replaced by s 114A—Educ and Inspections, 2006 c 40, s 86(1)
s 114A am—Healthy Eating in Schools (W), 2009 nawm 3, s 8(1)
s 115 rep—Educ, 2002 c 32, s 215(2), sch 22 pt 3
Pt 5 (ss 117-124) power to appl—Educ, 2002 c 32, s 193(5)
s 117 appl—Nationality, Immigration and Asylum, 2002 c 41, s 36(4)(b)
s 118 am—Childcare, 2006 c 21, s 103, sch 2 para 30
s 118A added—Educ, 2002 c 32, s 149(1)
rep (W prosp)—Childcare, 2006 c 21, s 103, sch 3
am—(W prosp) Childcare, 2006 c 21, s 103, sch 2 para 31
s 119 am—Educ, 2002 c 32, s 150(1)(5); Childcare, 2006 c 21, s 103, sch 2 para 32
rep in pt—Educ, 2002 c 32, s 215(2), sch 22 pt 3; Children, 2004 c 31, s 64, sch 5 pt 1; Childcare, 2006 c 21, s 103, sch 2 para 32, sch 3
ss 120, 121 rep—Children, 2004 c 31, s 64, sch 5 pt 1
s 122 rep in pt—SL(R), 2004 c 14, s 1(1), sch 1 pt 7
appl (mods)—Education, 1996 c 56, s 329A(14)
am—Educ, 2005 c 18, s 53, sch 7 pt 2 para 7; Childcare, 2006 c 21, s 103, sch 2 para 33
s 123 am—Special Educational Needs and Disability, 2001 c 10, s 7(2); (W prosp) Childcare, 2006 c 21, s 103, sch 2 para 34; Children and Families, 2014 c 6, sch 3 para 69
Pt 5A (ss 124A, 124B) added—SI 2003/2037, regs 2, 3
am—Educ, 2011 c 21, s 62(4)(a)
s 124A am—Educ, 2011 c 21, s 62(2)
s 124AA added —Educ, 2011 c 21, s 62(3)
s 124B am—SI 2012/976, sch para 9
Pt 6 (ss 125, 126) rep—Learning and Skills, 2000 c 21, ss 149,153, sch 9 para 86, sch 11
s 127 rep (W) —School Standards and Organisation (W), 2013 anaw 1, s 96
see—SI 2001/435, art 2
appl—SI 1999/2022, art 2
rep in pt—Educ, 2002 c 32, s 215, sch 21, para 110(1)(3)(b), sch 22 pt 3; Educ, 2005 c 18, ss 61, 123, sch 9 para 21(a), sch 19 pt 1; Educ and Inspections, 2006 c 40, s 58(6), sch 18
am—Educ, 2002 c 32, s 215(1), sch 21, para 110(1)(2)(3)(a)(c); (E) SI 2003/2045, reg 4; (W) SI 2004/1743 (W 182), reg 4; Educ, 2005 c 18, s 61, sch 9 para 21(b); Educ and Inspections, 2006 c 40, s 58(1)(2)(3)(4)(5)(7)
s 128 rep —Apprenticeships, Skills, Children and Learning, 2009 c 22, ss 58(1)(a), 266, sch 16 pt 1
ss 131, 132 rep in pt—SL(R), 2004 c 14, s 1(1), sch 1 pt 7
s 133 rep—SL(R), 2004 c 14, s 1(1), sch 1 pt 7
s 134 rep in pt—SL(R), 2004 c 14, s 1(1), sch 1 pt 7; Educ, 2005 c 18, s 123, sch 19 pt 1

1998
c 31 *continued*

s 135 rep—Educ, 2005 c 18, s 123, sch 19 pt 1
s 137 am—Learning and Skills, 2000 c 21, s 149, sch 9 para 87
s 138 am—Educ, 2002 c 32, s 215(1), sch 21, para 111; Educ, 2005 c 18, ss 72, 101, sch
    12 para 9, sch 16 para 8; Educ and Inspections, 2006 c 40, s 175, sch 17 para 3;
    Educ, 2011 c 21, s 62(4)(b)
    rep in pt—Educ, 2002 c 32, s 215(2), sch 22 pt 3; Educ and Inspections, 2006 c 40, s
        184, sch 18; Deregulation, 2015 c 20, sch 16 para 2(2)(a)
s 138A added—Educ and Skills, 2008 c 25, s 169, sch 1 paras 53, 71
s 139 rep in pt—Educ and Inspections, 2006 c 40, s 157, sch 14 paras 33, 34, sch 18
s 141 appl (mods)—SI 1998/2763, reg 6(2); SI 1999/362, regs 8, 9, 27, 43; SI 1999/2243,
    reg 32(1)(2); SI 1999/2262, reg 32(1)(2)
    ext—SI 1999/362, reg 2(4)
s 142 rep in pt—Learning and Skills, 2000 c 21, ss 149, 153, sch 9 para 88, sch 11; (W)
    School Standards and Organisation (W), 2013 anaw 1, sch 5 para 4(6)
    am—Educ, 2002 c 32, s 215(1), sch 21, para 112; SI 2003/2037, regs 2, 4(1)-(3);
        Childcare, 2006 c 21, s 103, sch 2 para 35; Educ and Inspections, 2006 c 40, ss
        71, 175, sch 7 para 15, sch 17 para 4; Educ and Skills, 2008 c 25, s 169, sch 1
        paras 53, 72
    appl—(W) SI 1999/1671, sch 4 pt III para 18A; SI 2000/1979, reg 16(3); SI
        2002/2439, art 4, schedule pt 2, para 9(2)
s 143 am—Educ, 2002 c 32, s 215(1), sch 21, para 113; SI 2003/2037, regs 2, 5; Educ,
    2005 c 18, s 72, sch 12 para 10; Educ and Inspections, 2006 c 40, s 175, sch 17
    para 5; ibid, ss 30, 50(4), 71, sch 3 para 30(a)(i), sch 7 para 16; Educ and Skills,
    2008 c 25, s 169, sch 1 paras 53, 73; SI 2010/1158, art 5, sch 2
    rep in pt—Educ, 2002 c 32, s 215(2), sch 22 pt 3; Educ and Inspections, 2006 c 40, s
        30, sch 3 para 30(a)(ii)(b), sch 18; SI 2010/1158, art 5, schs 2, 3; (W) School
        Standards and Organisation (W), 2013 anaw 1, sch 5 para 4(7); ibid, sch 5 para
        19(11)(a)-(e)
s 144 see—(trans of functions) (W) SI 2000/253, art 2, sch 1
s 163 am—Educ and Inspections, 2006 c 40, s 163
sch 1 am—Charities, 2006 c 50, s 75, sch 8 para 195; Charities, 2011 c 25, sch 7 para 78;
    SI 2011/1396, sch para 46(2)
sch 1A added—Educ, 2002 c 32, s 59(2), sch 6
    rep (W) —School Standards and Organisation (W), 2013 anaw 1, sch 5 para 4(8)
sch 2 excl—SI 1998/1969, reg 17; (temp) SI 1998/1969, arts 18, 19(2)
sch 3 am—Educ, 2002 c 32, s 215(1), sch 21, para 114; SI (E) 2002/906, arts 5, 6,
    7(a)(c)(d), 8, 9, 10(a)-(c)(e)(f), 15; Educ and Inspections, 2006 c 40, ss 30, 35(3),
    36, sch 3 para 31, sch 4 para 22; (W) School Standards and Organisation (W),
    2013 anaw 1, sch 5 para 19(12)
    rep in pt—SI 2002/906, arts 7(b)(e), 10(d); Educ and Inspections, 2006 c 40, s
        35(1)(2), sch 18
    mod—(E) SI 2002/906, art 14(1)
    appl—Learning and Skills, 2000 c 21, sch 7A para 6(1); Educ and Inspections, 2006 c
        40, ss 7, 10-11, 15, sch 2 para 29(2)
sch 4 rep—Educ and Inspections, 2006 c 40, s 29, sch 18
sch 5 am—Race Relations (Amdt), 2000 c 34, s 9(1), sch 2 para 31; Special Educational
    Needs and Disability, 2001 c 10, s 42(1), sch 8 pt 2 para 23(1)(3); SI 2002/1397,
    art 12, schedule pt I, para 14; Educ, 2005 c 18, s 72, sch 12 para 12; Educ and
    Inspections, 2006 c 40, s 30, sch 3 para 32; SIs 2007/3224, art 15, sch;
    2010/1836, art 6, sch; Equality, 2010 c 15, s 211, sch 26 para 45 (as subst by SI
    2010/2279, sch 1); SI 2011/1060, art 5
    rep in pt—Special Educational Needs and Disability, 2001 c 10, s 42(1)(6), sch 8 pt 2
        para 23(1)(3), sch 9
schs 6-8 rep (W)—School Standards and Organisation (W), 2013 anaw 1, sch 5 para 19(13)
schs 9-12 rep—Educ, 2002 c 32, s 215(2), sch 22 pt 3
sch 13 rep (E prosp)—Educ, 2002 c 32, s 215(2), sch 22 pt 3
    saved—SI 1999/1502, reg 23
    appl (mods)—(E) SI 2007/2979, reg 3, sch 1
sch 14 am—Educ and Inspections, 2006 c 40, s 57, sch 5 para 5(1)(2)(3)(4)(b)(5); Educ,
    2011 c 21, s 46
    rep in pt—Educ and Inspections, 2006 c 40, s 57, sch 5 para 5(4), sch 18
    appl—SI 2006/468, reg 27
sch 15 mod—SIs 1998/2670, reg 6; 2012/1035, reg 29, sch 8

1998
c 31 sch 15 *continued*

power to mod—Educ (W), 2011 nawm 7, s 18
see—(power to mod) Educ, 2002 c 32, s 25(1)(b)(2)
am—Educ, 2002 c 32, s 40, sch 3, para 5; Educ, 2005 c 18, s 117, sch 18 para 11
rep in pt—Educ, 2002 c 32, s 40, sch 3, para 5; Educ and Inspections, 2006 c 40, s
57, sch 5 para 6
schs 16-18 rep—Educ, 2002 c 32, s 215(2), sch 22 pt 3
sch 19 am—Educ, 2002 c 32, s 215(1), sch 21, para 117(1)-(3)
sch 20 mod—(transtl provn) SI 1998/3172, reg 2(1)(3)
sch 22 am—Learning and Skills, 2000 c 21, s 149, sch 9 para 91; Educ, 2002 c 32, s 215(1),
sch 21, para 118(1)(6); Land Registration, 2002 c 9, s 133, sch 11, para 37; SI
2002/906, art 12; Educ, 2005 c 18, ss 72, 107, sch 12 para 15(1)(2), sch 17
paras 1-3, 5; ibid, s 107, sch 17 paras 4, 6; (W) SI 2005/3238 (W 243), arts 7,
9(1), sch 1 paras 37, 40; Educ and Inspections, 2006 c 40, s 36, sch 4 paras 1, 2,
3, 4(1)(2)(a)(b)(3)-(5), 5, 6, 7(1)(2)(a)-(c)(3)-(7), 8-17; SIs 2010/1080, art 2,
sch 1; 2010/1158, art 5, sch 2; Educ, 2011 c 21, sch 14 paras 3-8, 9(2)(3),
10-12, 13(2)-(4), 14(2)-(5), 15(2)-(4); SI 2011/1396, sch para 40(2)(d);
Charities, 2011 c 25, sch 7 para 79; (W) School Standards and Organisation
(W), 2013 anaw 1, sch 5 para 4(9); ibid, sch 5 para
19(14)(a)(b)(c)(ii)(iii)(v)(vi)(d); ibid, sch 5 para 19(14)
(e)(f)(i)(iii)(iv)(vi)(vii)(g)-(i); Children and Families, 2014 c 6, sch 3 para 70(a)
rep in pt—Learning and Skills, 2000 c 21, s 153, sch 11; (W) School Standards and
Organisation (W), 2013 anaw 1, sch 5 para 19(14)(c)(i)(iv)(vii)(f)(ii)(iv)(v);
ibid, sch 5 para 19(14)(c)(viii); Children and Families, 2014 c 6, sch 3 para
70(b)
excl—Academies, 2010 c 32, s 13, sch 1 para 10(2)(c)
schs 23-25 rep—Educ, 2002 c 32, s 215(2), sch 22 pt 3
sch 26 appl (mods)—(E pt prosp) Children, 1989 c 41, s 79P(3)(4) (added by 2000 c 14,
s 79(1))
am—Educ, 2002 c 32, s 155, sch 14, paras 1, 2(1)-(4), 3, 5, 7; (E pt prosp) Educ,
2005 c 18, s 53, sch 7 pt 2 paras 8, 9, 10(1)-(4)(6), 11, 20, 21, 24; ibid, s 53,
sch 7 pt 2 paras 8, 13, 14(1)(3)-(5)(7), 15(1)-(4), 16(1)(2)(4)(5), 17-19, 22, 23;
Childcare, 2006 c 21, s 103, sch 2 para 36; Educ and Inspections, 2006 c 40, s
157, sch 14 para 35(1)(2)
rep in pt—Educ, 2002 c 32, ss 155, 215(2), sch 14, para 2(1)(5), sch 22 pt 3; Educ,
2005 c 18, ss 53, 123, sch 7 pt 2 paras 8, 10(1)(5), 14(1)(2)(6), 15(1)(5),
16(1)(3), sch 19 pt 1; ibid, s 53, sch 7 pt 2 paras 8, 12; Childcare, 2006 c 21, s
103, sch 2 para 36, sch 3; Educ and Inspections, 2006 c 40, s 157, sch 14 para
35(3)(4), sch 18
saving—(E) SI 2002/2953, reg 6(1)(2)
appl—(E) SI 2005/1972, reg 2(1)(g)
sch 27 rep in pt—Learning and Skills, 2000 c 21, s 153, sch 11
sch 28 rep in pt—Educ, 2002 c 32, s 215(2), sch 22 pt 3; ibid, s 215(2), sch 22 pt 3; Educ,
2005 c 18, s 123, sch 19 pt 1
sch 30 rep in pt—SI 1999/638, reg 10; Learning and Skills, 2000 c 21, s 153, sch 11;
Special Educational Needs and Disability, 2001 c 10, s 42(1)(6), sch 8 pt 2
para 23(1)(4), sch 9; Educ, 2002 c 32, s 215(2), sch 22 pts 1, 3; (prosp) ibid,
sch 22 pt 2; Loc Govt, 2003 c 26, s 127(2), sch 8 pt 1; Children, 2004 c 31,
s 64, sch 5 pt 1; Educ, 2005 c 18, s 123, sch 19 pts 2, 3; ibid, sch 19 pt 2; ibid,
sch 19 pt 1; Nat Health Service (Conseq Provns), 2006 c 43, s 6, sch 4;
Charities, 2006 c 50, s 75, sch 9; Educ and Inspections, 2006 c 40, s 184, sch
18; (prosp) Educ and Skills, 2008 c 25, s 169, sch 2; (W) Learner Travel (W),
2008 nawm 2, s 26, sch 2; Apprenticeships, Skills, Children and Learning,
2009 c 22, s 266, sch 16; ibid, ss 58(1)(a), 266, sch 16 pt 4; Equality, 2010 c
15, s 211, sch 27 pt 1; Charities, 2011 c 25, sch 10; Children and Families,
2014 c 6, sch 3 para 16(4)(a); Loc Audit and Accountability, 2014 c 2, sch 1 pt
2
am—SI 2013/2042, sch para 18
sch 31 rep in pt—SI 2010/1080, art 2, schs 1, 2
sch 32 appl (mods)—(temp) SI 1998/2115, regs 3,4(1)(2)
mod—SI 1998/2670, reg 5(2)
rep in pt—Educ, 2002 c 32, s 215, sch 21, para 119, sch 22 pt 1
am—Educ and Inspections, 2006 c 40, s 36, sch 4 para 23

1998

c 32 **Police (Northern Ireland)**
trans of functions—Police (NI), 2000 c 32, s 2, sch 2 para 2
power to am—Police (NI), 2000 c 32, s 36A(4)
appl (mods)—SI 2005/3181, art 210(2)(f)
Pt 1 (ss 1-13) rep—Police (NI), 2000 c 32, s 78, sch 8
Pt 2 (ss 14-17) rep—Police (NI), 2000 c 32, s 78, sch 8
Pt 3 (ss 18-31) am—Police (NI), 2000 c 32, s 78, sch 6 para 23(2)(a)
ss 18-24 rep—Police (NI), 2000 c 32, s 78, sch 8
s 25 am—Police (NI), 2000 c 32, s 78, sch 6 para 23(2)(b); Police (NI), 2003 c 6, s 24(2);
    SI 2010/976, art 5, sch 3
s 26 am—Police (NI), 2000 c 32, ss 49(5), 78, sch 7 para 2; Police (NI), 2000 c 32, s 78,
    sch 6 para 23(2)(b); SI 2010/976, art 5, sch 3
s 27 am—Police (NI), 2000 c 32, ss 50, 78, sch 6 para 23(2)(b)(c); International
    Development, 2002 c 1, s 19(1), sch 3, para 12; Proceeds of Crime, 2002 c 29, s
    456, sch 11, para 34; Police Reform, 2002 c 30, ss 102(1)(2)(e), 107(1), sch 7,
    para 22; Police (NI), 2003 c 6, s 20(5), 25; Serious Organised Crime and Police,
    2005 c 15, s 59, sch 4 paras 113, 114(1)(2)(b)(3)(4); Police and Justice, 2006 c
    48, s 1, sch 1 para 73; SI 2010/976, art 5, sch 3
    rep in pt—Police (NI), 2000 c 32, s 78, sch 6 para 23(2)(c); International Development,
        2002 c 1, s 19(2), sch 4; Serious Organised Crime and Police, 2005 c 15, ss 59,
        174(2), sch 4 paras 113, 114(1)(2)(a), sch 17 pt 2; Police and Justice, 2006 c
        48, s 52, sch 15; Serious Crime, 2007 c 27, s 74, sch 8 para 156, sch 14
    appl—Serious Organised Crime and Police, 2005 c 15, s 58, sch 3 para 2(4)(c)
    excl—SI 1978/1039 (NI 9), art 2E(b)
s 28 am—Police (NI), 2000 c 32, s 78, sch 6 para 23(2)(d); SI 2010/976, art 5, sch 3
s 29 ext—Police (NI), 2000 c 32, s 41(1)(a)
    am—Police (NI), 2000 c 32, s 78, sch 6 para 23(2)(e)(f); Police Reform, 2002 c 30, ss
        102(1)(2)(f)(4)(5)(d), 103(5); Serious Organised Crime and Police, 2005 c 15,
        s 59, sch 4 paras 113, 115; SI 2010/976, art 5, sch 3
    excl—SI 1978/1039 (NI 9), art 2E(c)
    rep in pt—SI 2010/976, art 5, sch 3
s 31 am—Police (NI), 2000 c 32, s 78, sch 6 para 23(2)(g); SI 2010/976, art 5, sch 3
    excl—SI 1978/1047 (NI 17), sch para 2(2); Terrorism, 2006, c 11, s 28(7)(b)
s 32 ext—Police (NI), 2000 c 32, s 41(1)(a)
    am—SI 2010/976, art 5, sch 3
s 33 am—Police (NI), 2000 c 32, s 78, sch 6 para 23(3); SI 2010/976, art 5, sch 3
s 34 rep in pt—SI 2010/976, art 5, sch 3
s 35 ext—Police (NI), 2000 c 32, s 41(1)(a)
    am—SI 2010/976, art 5, sch 3
Pt 5 (ss 36-46) am—Police (NI), 2000 c 32, s 78, sch 6 para 23(4)(b); SI 2010/976, art 5,
    sch 3
s 36 rep—Police (NI), 2000 c 32, s 78, sch 8
s 37 rep—Police (NI), 2000 c 32, s 78, sch 6 para 23(4)(a), sch 8
s 38 rep—Police (NI), 2000 c 32, s 78, sch 8
s 39 rep—Police (NI), 2000 c 32, s 78, sch 6 para 23(4)(a), sch 8
s 40 rep in pt—Police and Justice, 2006 c 48, s 52, sch 15
    am—SI 2010/976, art 5, sch 3
s 41 am—(pt prosp) Police (NI), 2000 c 32, ss 30(9), 78, sch 6 para 23(4)(c); Police Reform,
    2002 c 30, s 3(2); Serious Organised Crime and Police, 2005 c 15, s 59, sch 4
    paras 113, 116; SI 2010/976, art 5, sch 3
    power to appl (mods)—Commrs for Revenue and Customs, 2005 c 11,
        s 27(1)(2)(a)(iii)
s 41A added—SI 2010/976, art 5, sch 3
s 42 am—(pt prosp) Police (NI), 2000 c 32, ss 30(10), 78, sch 6 para 23(4)(e); (prosp)
    Justice (NI), 2002 c 26, s 85(1), sch 12, para 61; Police Reform, 2002 c 30, s 3(2);
    SI 2010/976, art 5, sch 3
    power to appl (mods)—Commrs for Revenue and Customs, 2005 c 11,
        s 27(1)(2)(a)(iii)
    rep in pt —Serious Organised Crime and Police, 2005 c 15, ss 59, 174(2), sch 4 paras
        113, 117, sch 17 pt 2; SI 2010/976, art 5, sch 3
s 43 am—SI 2010/976, art 5, sch 3
s 44 rep—Inquiries, 2005 c 12, ss 44(5), 48(1), 49(2), sch 2 pt 1 para 17, sch 3; SI
    2010/976, art 5, sch 3
• ss 45, 46 am—Police (NI), 2000 c 32, s 78, sch 6 para 23(4)(c)

1998

c 32 *continued*

Pt 6 (ss 47-49) rep—Police (NI), 2000 c 32, s 78, sch 8

Pt 7 (ss 50-65) power to appl—Police (NI), 2003 c 6, s 34(3)

s 50 am—Police (NI), 2000 c 32, s 78, sch 6 para 23(5)(b); Justice (NI), 2002 c 26, s 34(1)(2)

    appl—Police (NI), 2000 c 32, s 74A(9)

s 52 am—Justice (NI), 2002 c 26, s 34(1)(3)

s 55 am—Police (NI), 2000 c 32, s 78, sch 6 para 23(5)(c); Justice (NI), 2002 c 26, s 34(1)(4); Justice (NI), 2004 c 4, s 6(1)(3)(4)

    rep in pt—Justice (NI), 2004 c 4, ss 6(1)(2)(5), 18, sch 4

s 56 am—Police (NI), 2000 c 32, s 78, sch 6 para 23(5)(d)

s 57 am—Police (NI), 2000 c 32, s 78, sch 6 para 23(5)(d)

s 58 rep in pt—Justice (NI), 2002 c 26, s 86, sch 13

s 58A added—Police (NI), 2000 c 32, s 62(1)

s 59 am—Police (NI), 2000 c 32, s 62(2)(3)

s 60 am—SI 2010/976, art 5, sch 3

s 60ZA added—Serious Organised Crime and Police, 2005 c 15, s 55(2)(a)

    am—Serious Crime, 2007 c 27, s 74, sch 8 para 157

s 60A added—Police (NI), 2003 c 6, s 13(1)

    am—SI 2010/976, art 5, sch 3

s 61 rep in pt—Police (NI), 2000 c 32, s 78, sch 8

    am —Serious Organised Crime and Police, 2005 c 15, s 55(2)(b); SI 2010/976, art 5, sch 3

s 61A rep—Police (NI), 2003 c 6, ss 13(2), 45, sch 4

s 61AA added—Police (NI), 2000 c 32, s 64

s 63 am—Police (NI), 2000 c 32, s 63(2); Police (NI), 2003 c 6, s 13(3); SI 2010/976, art 5, sch 3

    ext—Anti-terrorism, Crime and Security, 2001 c 24, s 17, sch 4 pt 1 para 43

s 64 am—Police (NI), 2000 c 32, ss 62(4), 65; Justice (NI), 2004 c 4, s 6(6); SI 2010/976, art 5, sch 3

    rep in pt—SI 2010/976, art 5, sch 3

s 64A added—SI 2010/976, art 5, sch 3

s 65 am—SI 2010/976, art 5, sch 3

s 66 am—Police Reform, 2002 c 30, s 104(3); Police (NI), 2003 c 6, ss 13(4), 38; SIs 2007/912, art 7; 2010/976, art 5, sch 3

    ext—Crime (International Co-operation), 2003 c 32, s 84(3)

    rep in pt—SI 2010/976, art 5, sch 3

s 67 ext—Police (NI), 2000 c 32, s 41(1)(a)

    am—Police (NI), 2003 c 6, s 39; SI 2007/912, art 7

s 68 ext—Police (NI), 2000 c 32, s 41(1)(a)

s 70 rep—Police (NI), 2000 c 32, s 78, sch 8

s 72 am—Police (NI), 2000 c 32, s 78, sch 6 para 23(6)(a); SI 2010/976, art 5, sch 3

    rep in pt—Police (NI), 2000 c 32, s 78, sch 8; SI 2010/976, art 5, sch 3

s 73 subst—Police (NI), 2000 c 32, s 78, sch 6 para 23(6)(b)

sch 1 rep—Police (NI), 2000 c 32, s 78, sch 8

sch 2 rep—Police (NI), 2000 c 32, s 78, sch 8

sch 3 am—Police (NI), 2000 c 32, s 78, sch 6 para 23(7)(a)(b)(c); Police Reform, 2002 c 30, s 102(1)(2)(g)(4)(5)(e); SI 2010/976, art 5, sch 3

    rep in pt—SI 2010/976, art 5, sch 3

sch 4 rep in pt—Police (NI), 2000 c 32, s 78, sch 8; (prosp) Police Reform, 2002 c 30, s 107(2), sch 8; Serious Organised Crime and Police, 2005 c 15, s 174(2), sch 17 pt 2

sch 5 am—Police (NI), 2000 c 32, s 78, sch 6 para 23(8)

c 33   **Landmines**

ext (mods)—(Guernsey) SI 2000/2769, art 3, sch; (I of Man) SI 2000/2770, art 3, sch; (Jersey) SI 2001/3930, arts 2, 3, sch

appl (mods)—(Overseas Territories) SI 2001/3499, art 2, schs 1-7

s 2 ext—(Guernsey corporations) SI 2000/2769, art 2; (I of Man corporations) SI 2000/2770, art 2

s 5 am—Armed Forces, 2006 c 52, s 378, sch 16 para 152

s 18 ext—Crim Justice and Police, 2001 c 16, s 50, sch 1 pt 1 para 66

s 19 ext—Anti-terrorism, Crime and Security, 2001 c 24, s 17, sch 4 pt 1 para 44

s 21 am—Commrs for Revenue and Customs, 2005 c 11, s 50(6), sch 4 para 66(a)(b)(g); SI 2014/834, sch 2 para 13

1998

c 33 s 21 *continued*

rep in pt—Commrs for Revenue and Customs, 2005 c 11, ss 50(6), 52(2), sch 4 para 66(c)(d)(f), sch 5

c 34 **Private Hire Vehicles (London)**

am (exc ss 37, 38, 40)—GLA, 1999 c 29, s 254(3), sch 21 para 2

trans of functions—GLA, 1999 c 29, s 254(1)(2)

excl—Public Passenger Vehicles, 1981 c 14, s 79A

s 1 rep in pt—Road Safety, 2006 c 49, s 54, sch 7

s 3 am—GLA, 1999 c 29, s 254(3), sch 21 para 3

s 4 am—Transport for London, 2008 c.i, s 25

ss 5, 6 appl (mods)—SI 2003/655, reg 8(a)-(c)

s 7 am—GLA, 1999 c 29, s 254(3), sch 21 para 4

s 8 am—GLA, 1999 c 29, s 254(3), sch 21 para 5

s 10 am—GLA, 1999 c 29, s 254(3), sch 21 para 6

s 12 appl (mods)—SI 2003/655, reg 8(d)

s 13 am—GLA, 1999 c 29, s 254(3), sch 21 para 7

mod—SI 2003/655, reg 7

s 14 am—GLA, 1999 c 29, s 254(3), sch 21 para 8; Transport for London, 2008 c.i, s 23

s 15 am—GLA, 1999 c 29, s 254(3), sch 21 para 9

s 17 am—GLA, 1999 c 29, s 254(3), sch 21 para 10

s 18 am—GLA, 1999 c 29, s 254(3), sch 21 para 11

s 19 am—GLA, 1999 c 29, s 254(3), sch 21 para 12

s 22 am—GLA, 1999 c 29, s 254(3), sch 21 para 13; Transport for London, 2008 c.i, s 24

s 23 am—Transport for London, 2008 c.i, s 26(1)(3)(4)

rep in pt—Transport for London, 2008 c.i, s 26(1)(2)

s 24 am—GLA, 1999 c 29, s 254(3), sch 21 para 14

s 25 am—SI 2005/886, art 2, sch para 54

s 30 am—GLA, 1999 c 29, s 254(3), sch 21 para 15

s 32 am—GLA, 1999 c 29, s 254(3), sch 21 para 16

s 36 am—GLA, 1999 c 29, s 254(3), sch 21 para 17; SI 2000/3145, art 3

appl (mods)—SI 2003/655, reg 8(e)

s 37 am—GLA, 1999 c 29, s 254(3), sch 21 para 18

s 38 rep—GLA, 1999 c 29, ss 254(3), 423, sch 21 para 19, sch 34 pt V

c 35 **Northern Ireland (Sentences)**

s 5 am—Terrorism, 2000 c 11, s 125(1), sch 15 para 16(2)

s 9 cert functions restr from exercise in S—SI 1999/1748, art 8(2), sch 4 para 2(1)(2)

s 10 am—SI 2000/2024, art 2

s 14 am—Terrorism, 2000 c 11, s 125(1), sch 15 paras 16(3), 17

mod—Serious Crime, 2007 c 27, s 63, sch 6 para 35

sch 2 am—Justice (NI), 2002 c 26, s 28(1), sch 7, para 20

c 36 **Finance**

appl (mods)—SI 2007/1050, regs 3-12

s 6 rep in pt—Finance, 2008 c 9, s 16, sch 6 para 8(c)

s 9 rep in pt—Finance, 2002 c 23, s 141, sch 40 pt 1(2), Note 2

s 17 rep in pt—Finance, 2009 c 10, s 36, sch 16 para 5 (d)

s 25 rep—Income Tax, 2007 c 3, s 1031, sch 3

s 26 rep—Finance, 1999 c 16, s 139, sch 20 pt III(4), Note

s 27 rep in pt—Finance, 2009 c 10, s 5, sch 1 para 6(i); Taxation (International and Other Provns), 2010 c 8, s 378, sch 10 pt 13

ss 28, 29 rep in pt—Corporation Tax, 2010 c 4, s 1181, sch 3 pt 1

s 30 rep in pt—SL(R), 2013 c 2, s 1, sch 1 pt 10(1)

s 32 am—(retrosp) Finance, 1999 c 16, s 91(4)(6); Finance, 2012 c 14, sch 20 para 16

appl—Energy, 2004 c 20, s 44(2)(k)

s 36 rep—Taxation (International and Other Provns), 2010 c 8, ss 371, 378, sch 7 paras 81, 82, sch 10 pt 12

s 37 rep in pt—Finance, 2001 c 9, s 110, sch 33 pt 2(12), Note

—Corporation Tax, 2009 c 4, ss 1322, 1326, sch 1 para 452, sch 3 pt 1

s 43 rep—Income Tax (Trading and Other Income), 2005 c 5, ss 882(1), 884, sch 1 pt 2 paras 499, 501, sch 3

s 44 rep—Finance, 2002 c 23, ss 64(6), 141, sch 40 pt 3(8), Note 2

s 45 rep—Finance, 2002 c 23, s 141, sch 40 pt 3(16)

s 46 am—Income Tax (Trading and Other Income), 2005 c 5, s 882(1), sch 1 pt 2 paras 499, 502

rep in pt—Corporation Tax, 2009 c 4, ss 1322, 1326, sch 1 para 453, sch 3 pt 1

1998
c 36 *continued*

s 47 rep—Finance, 1999 c 16, ss 55(2)(3), 139, sch 20 pt III(12), Note

s 48 rep—Finance, 2011 c 11, sch 26 para 2(1)

ss 49-53 rep—Income Tax (Earnings and Pensions), 2003 c 1, s 724(1), sch 8 pt 1

s 55 rep in pt—Income Tax (Earnings and Pensions), 2003 c 1, s 724(1), sch 8 pt 1; Finance, 2004 c 12, ss 77, 326, sch 42 pt 2(7), Note

s 56 am—Finance, 2004 c 12, ss 76, 77, sch 12 para 15; Income Tax, 2007 c 3, s 1027, sch 1 paras 380, 381

s 57 rep—Finance, 2004 c 12, ss 77, 326, sch 42 pt 2(7), Note

s 58 rep—Income Tax (Earnings and Pensions), 2003 c 1, s 724(1), sch 8 pt 1

ss 60, 61 rep—Income Tax (Earnings and Pensions), 2003 c 1, s 724(1), sch 8 pt 1

s 62 rep—SL(R), 2013 c 2, s 1, sch 1 pt 10(1)

ss 63-69 rep—Income Tax (Earnings and Pensions), 2003 c 1, s 724(1), sch 8 pt 1

s 70 rep in pt—Income Tax, 2007 c 3, s 1031, sch 3

ss 71-73 rep—Income Tax, 2007 c 3, s 1031, sch 3

s 74 rep in pt—Income Tax, 2007 c 3, s 1031, sch 3

s 75 rep—Income Tax (Trading and Other Income), 2005 c 5, s 884, sch 3

s 76 am—Income Tax (Trading and Other Income), 2005 c 5, s 882(1), sch 1 pt 2 paras 499, 503

rep in pt—Income Tax (Trading and Other Income), 2005 c 5, s 884, sch 3

s 77 rep—Finance, 2007 c 11, s 114, sch 27 pt 2

s 78 rep—Income Tax (Trading and Other Income), 2005 c 5, s 884, sch 3

s 79 rep in pt—Income Tax, 2007 c 3, s 1031, sch 3; Taxation (International and Other Provns), 2010 c 8, s 378, sch 10 pt 13

s 80 rep —Corporation Tax, 2010 c 4, s 1181, sch 3 pt 1

s 81 rep—Finance, 2000 c 17, s 156, sch 40 pt II(11), Note 2

s 82 rep in pt—Finance, 2002 c 23, s 141, sch 40 pt 3(12), Note; Corporation Tax, 2010 c 4, s 1181, sch 3 pt 1; Taxation (International and Other Provns), 2010 c 8, s 378, sch 10 pt 1

ss 83-85 rep—Capital Allowances, 2001 c 2, s 580, sch 4

s 88 rep—Finance, 2008 c 9, s 36, sch 14 para 17(g)

s 89 rep—Finance, 2008 c 9, s 36, sch 14 para 17(g)

s 90 rep in pt—Finance, 2001 c 9, s 110, sch 33 pt 2(12), Note

s 91 rep—Finance, 2001 c 9, s 110, sch 33 pt 2(12), Note

s 92 rep—Finance, 2004 c 12, s 326, sch 42 pt 3, Note

s 93 rep—Income Tax (Earnings and Pensions), 2003 c 1, s 724(1), sch 8 pt 1

ss 94-97 rep—Finance, 2004 c 12, s 326, sch 42 pt 3, Note

s 98 rep in pt—Finance, 2004 c 12, s 326, sch 42 pt 3, Note

s 99 rep in pt—Finance, 2002 c 23, s 141, sch 40 pt 3(13), Note 2; Income Tax (Trading and Other Income), 2005 c 5, s 884, sch 3

s 100 rep—Income Tax, 2007 c 3, s 1031, sch 3

s 102 rep in pt—Income Tax, 2007 c 3, s 1031, sch 3; Corporation Tax, 2010 c 4, s 1181, sch 3 pt 1

ss 103-105 rep—SL(R), 2013 c 2, s 1, sch 1 pt 10(1)

ss 106, 107 rep—Taxation (International and Other Provns), 2010 c 8, s 378, sch 10 pt 1

s 108 rep in pt—Finance, 2002 c 23, s 141, sch 40 pt 3(10), Note 2; Taxation (International and Other Provns), 2010 c 8, s 378, sch 10 pt 2

s 109 rep in pt—Finance, 2002 c 23, s 141, sch 40 pt 3(10), (13), Note 2

ss 110, 111 rep—Taxation (International and Other Provns), 2010 c 8, ss 374, 378, sch 8 paras 112, 113, sch 10 pt 2

ss 114-116 rep—Corporation Tax, 2010 c 4, s 1181, sch 3 pt 1

s 117 am—Capital Allowances, 2001 c 2, s 578, sch 2 para 100

s 118 rep—Taxation (International and Other Provns), 2010 c 8, ss 371, 378, sch 7 paras 87, 88, sch 10 pt 12

s 119 rep—Taxation (International and Other Provns), 2010 c 8, s 378, sch 10 pt 13

s 120 rep in pt—Finance, 2008 c 9, s 8, sch 2 para 21(c)(i)

s 121 rep in pt—Finance, 2008 c 9, s 8, sch 2 paras 55(a)(i), 82

s 123 am—Income Tax (Trading and Other Income), 2005 c 5, s 882(1), sch 1 pt 2 paras 499, 504

rep in pt—Finance, 2008 c 9, s 8, sch 2 para 96(a); Finance, 2012 c 14, sch 16 para 247(i)(i)

s 125 rep in pt—Finance, 2008 c 9, s 8, sch 2 para 96(b)

s 130 rep in pt—Finance, 2008 c 9, s 25, sch 7 para 114(a)

s 134 am—Income Tax, 2007 c 3, s 1027, sch 1 paras 380, 382

1998
c 36 *continued*

s 135 am—Income Tax, 2007 c 3, s 1027, sch 1 paras 380, 383

s 137 rep in pt—Finance, 2003 c 14, ss 170, 216, sch 33 para 16(6), sch 43 pt 3(12), Note 8; Finance, 2006 c 25, s 178, sch 26 pt 3(9)

s 138 rep—Finance, 2011 c 11, sch 11 para 10(b)

s 140 rep in pt—Finance, 2008 c 9, s 8, sch 2 para 55(a)(ii)

s 145 rep—Commrs for Revenue and Customs, 2005 c 11, ss 50(6), 52(2), sch 4 para 67, sch 5

s 148 rep in pt—Finance, 2001 c 9, s 110, sch 33 pt 3(3)

s 149 rep—Finance, 1999 c 16, s 138, sch 20 pt V(2), Notes 1, 2

s 152 rep in pt—Corporation Tax, 2010 c 4, s 1181, sch 3 pt 2; Taxation (International and Other Provns), 2010 c 8, s 378, sch 10 pt 6

s 153 rep—SL(R), 2013 c 2, s 1, sch 1 pt 10(1)

ss 155-157 rep—Budget Responsibility and Nat Audit, 2011 c 4, s 10(b)

s 161 am—Income Tax, 2007 c 3, s 1027, sch 1 paras 380, 384

s 162 rep in pt—Finance, 2003 c 14, s 216, sch 43 pt 5(4)

s 163 rep in pt—Finance, 2002 c 23, s 141, sch 40 pt 3(11), Note
    am—Commrs for Revenue and Customs, 2005 c 11, s 16, sch 2 pt 1 para 10

s 211 saved—SI 1999/2908, art 6(1)

s 490 rep in pt—Finance, 1998 c 36, ss 31,165, sch 3 para 28(2)(3), sch 27 pt III(2), Note

s 498 rep—Finance, 1998 c 36, ss 31,165, sch 3 para 30(1)(2), sch 27 pt III(2), Note

sch 2 savings—SI 2009/1022, art 3

sch 3 rep (except para 6)—Finance, 1998 c 36, s 165, sch 27 pt III(28), Note; Finance, 2001 c 9, s 110, sch 33 pt 2(10), Note; Finance, 2004 c 12, s 326, sch 42 pt 2(3), Note; Income Tax, 2007 c 3, s 1031, sch 3; Finance, 2009 c 10, s 5, sch 1 para 6(i); Corporation Tax, 2010 c 4, s 1181, sch 3 pt 1; SL(R), 2013 c 2, s 1, sch 1 pt 10(1)

sch 4 rep in pt—Finance, 2001 c 9, s 110, sch 33 pt 2(14), Note 2; Finance, 2002 c 23, s 141, sch 40 pt 3(10), Note 2; Corporation Tax, 2010 c 4, s 1181, sch 3 pt 1

sch 5 rep in pt—Finance, 1998 c 36, s 165, sch 27 pt III(5)(28), Note; Capital Allowances, 2001 c 2, s 580, sch 4; Income Tax (Trading and Other Income), 2005 c 5, s 884, sch 3; Income Tax, 2007 c 3, s 1031, sch 3; SI 2007/2086, reg 6; Corporation Tax, 2010 c 4, s 1181, sch 3 pt 1; Finance, 2012 c 14, sch 16 para 247(i)(ii), 248

sch 5A mod—SI 1999/2908, art 7(1)(2)

sch 6 rep—Finance, 2002 c 23, ss 64(6), 141, sch 40 pt 3(8), Note 2

sch 7 rep in pt—Capital Allowances, 2001 c 2, s 580, sch 4; Finance, 2002 c 23, s 141, sch 40 pt 3(1), (18), Note; Finance, 2004 c 12, s 326, sch 42 pt 2(3), Note; Income Tax (Trading and Other Income), 2005 c 5, s 884, sch 3; Income Tax, 2007 c 3, s 1031, sch 3; Corporation Tax, 2010 c 4, s 1181, sch 3 pts 1, 2; Taxation (International and Other Provns), 2010 c 8, s 378, sch 10 pts 8, 9, 11, 12, 13; SL(R), 2013 c 2, s 1, sch 1 pt 10(1)

sch 8 rep—Finance, 2004 c 12, ss 77, 326, sch 42 pt 2(7), Note

schs 9, 10 rep—Income Tax (Earnings and Pensions), 2003 c 1, s 724(1), sch 8 pt 1

sch 11 rep—SL(R), 2013 c 2, s 1, sch 1 pt 10(1)

sch 12 rep in pt—Income Tax, 2007 c 3, s 1031, sch 3

sch 13 rep in pt—Finance, 2001 c 9, s 110, sch 33 pt 2(3), Notes 2, 6; Finance, 2004 c 12, s 326, sch 42 pt 2(13), Note 6; Finance, 2006 c 25, s 178, sch 26 pt 3(13); Income Tax, 2007 c 3, s 1031, sch 3

sch 14 appl—Finance, 2003 c 14, s 171, sch 34 pt 2 para 12
    rep in pt—Income Tax (Trading and Other Income), 2005 c 5, s 884, sch 3; Finance, 2008 c 9, s 36, sch 14 para 17(g); Taxation (International and Other Provns), 2010 c 8, s 378, sch 10 pt 12

sch 15 rep—Finance, 2004 c 12, s 326, sch 42 pt 3, Note

sch 16 rep—Taxation (International and Other Provns), 2010 c 8, s 378, sch 10 pt 2

sch 17 rep in pt—Finance, 2004 c 12, s 326, sch 42 pt 2(1), Note; Finance, 2005 c 7, s 104, sch 11 pt 2(6), Note; Finance, 2009 c 10, s 36, sch 16 para 11(a); Finance, 2011 c 11, sch 12 para 13(a)

sch 18 see—Taxes Management, 1970 c 9, s 28ZC(1)(a)(5)(6); Finance, 2002 c 23, s 54(1), sch 13 pt 2, para 18(3), pt 5, para 28
    rep in pt—Finance, 2001 c 9, s 110, sch 33 pt 2(12), Note; Finance, 2002 c 23, s 141, sch 40 pt 3(16); Commrs for Revenue and Customs, 2005 c 11, ss 50(6), 52(2), sch 4 para 68(b), sch 5; Finance, 2006 c 25, ss 26(7), 178, sch 26 pt 3; Finance, 2007 c 11, ss 41, 97, sch 10 paras 14(1)(7), 16(1)(7), 17(2), sch 24 para 29(c),

1998
c 36 sch 18 *continued*

sch 27; Finance, 2008 c 9, ss 115, 122, 123, 138, sch 37 paras 7, 8(1)(7),
9(1)(3), sch 40 para 21(f), sch 41 para 25(j), sch 44 para 11(c); ibid, s
119(3)(10)(a); Corporation Tax, 2009 c 4, ss 1322, 1326, sch 1 para 454, sch 3
pt 1; SIs 2009/2035, art 2, sch; 2009/56, art 3, sch 1 para 253-267

am—Income and Corporation Taxes, 1988 c 1, s 349E; Finance, 1999 c 16,
ss 28(5)(6), 92(2)(3)(4)(7), 93(1)(2), sch 11 para 9; Finance, 2000 c 17,
ss 63(2)(4), 69(2), 97, 99, sch 16 para 5(2)(3)(4), sch 21 paras 2, 3, 4 sch 27
pt II paras 11,12(1); Finance, 2001 c 9, s 70(1)(3), sch 23 paras 4, 5, 6;
SI 2001/3629, art 103(1)(2); ibid, s 88, sch 29 pt 5 paras 13, 17(2)(3), 38(1)(4);
ibid, s 88, sch 29 pt 3 para 7; Capital Allowances, 2001 c 2, s 578, sch 2
para 103(1)(2); SI 2001/3629, art 103(1)(3)-(5); Finance, 2002 c 23, ss 54(2),
57(2)(3)(4)(c), 92(3)(4), sch 14, paras 2-5; Finance, 2004 c 12, ss 30(9), 37, 76,
77, sch 5 paras 9, 10, sch 12 para 16; Commrs for Revenue and Customs, 2005
c 11, s 50(6), sch 4 para 68(a); Finance, 2005 c 7, s 88(3)-(5); Finance (No 2),
2005 c 22, ss 29(1)(2), 31; Finance, 2006 c 25, ss 29, 42, 71(2)(3), sch 3 paras
1-9, sch 5 paras 27-29; Income Tax, 2007 c 3, s 1027, sch 1 paras 380, 385;
Finance, 2007 c 11, ss 39, 48, 58(2), sch 8 para 21, sch 15 paras 9, 10(1);
Finance, 2008 c 9, ss 115, 118, sch 37 paras 7, 8, 9(1)-(2)(4)(5), sch 39 paras
37-47; ibid, s 119(3)-(9)(10)(b)-(11); SI 2008/954, arts 23, 25; Corporation
Tax, 2009 c 4, s 1322, sch 1 para 454; SIs 2009/2035, art 2, sch; 2009/56, art
3, sch 1 paras 253-265; Finance, 2009 c 10, s 100, sch 52 paras 12-16; ibid, s
26, sch 7; para 25; Corporation Tax, 2010 c 4, s 1177, sch 1 para 297;
Taxation (International and Other Provns), 2010 c 8, s 371, sch 7 paras 107,
108; ibid, s 374, sch 8 paras 53, 54, 320, 321; Finance, 2010 c 13, s 32, sch 8
para 6; Finance, 2011 c 11, sch 19 paras 61, 62, 63(2)(3), 64(2)(3); SI
2011/1037, art 3(2)-(4); Finance, 2012 c 14, sch 15 paras 14(2)(3), 15(2)(3),
17(2)(3); Finance, 2013 c 29, ss 231(3), 232(3); ibid, sch 15 paras 5, 6(2)(3),
7(2)-(4); ibid, sch 18 paras 3(2)(3), 4(2)(3), 5(2)(3); ibid, sch 30 para 13(2)-(4);
SI 2013/636, sch para 5(2)-(4); Finance, 2014 c 26, s 277(4), sch 1 para 6, sch
4 paras 4-6; Finance, 2015 c 11, sch 2 para 2; Finance (No. 2), 2015 c 33, s
38(5); ibid, sch 3 para 3; ibid, sch 8 para 40

appl—Income and Corporation Taxes, 1988 c 1, ss 339(3B)(b), 804ZC(6)(b),
826(3AA)(3B), schs A2, 19B, 19C paras 14(2), 15(3), 28AA para 6C(6);
Taxation of Chargeable Gains, 1992 c 12, s 184I(6); SI 1995/3237 reg 2(1);
Finance, 2000 c 17, s 63(1)(4), sch 15 pt VI para 62(3); (except para 77)
Finance, 2000 c 17, s 82, sch 22 pt IX para 81(3); Finance (No 2), 2005 c 22,
ss 28(6), 31; Finance, 2007 c 11, s 42, sch 11 paras 2(7)(8), 5(1); Finance,
2008 c 9, ss 53, 113, sch 19 para 4(2), sch 36 para 88; Finance, 2010 c 13, s 22,
sch 1 para 23(5); Corporation Tax, 2010 c 4, ss 192(6)(b), 320(2), 321(3),
329I(7); Taxation (International and Other Provns), 2010 c 8, s 256(5);

excl—Income and Corporation Taxes, 1988 c 1, ss 444AD(3), 749A(4)(a),
sch 19AB para 1(6), sch 24 para 9(7); Capital Allowances, 1990 c 1 s 59C(7);
Capital Allowances, 1990 c 1, s 76B(5); Taxation of Chargeable Gains, 1992 c
12, s 213(8G); (retrosp) Finance, 1993 c 34, ss 94(10), 94AA, 94AB; Capital
Allowances, 2001 c 2, ss 201(5)(b), 227(5)(b); Taxation (International and
Other Provisions), 2010 c 8, s 371UB(5)(a); Finance, 2013 c 29, s 210(6)(b)

restr—Finance, 1994 c 9, s 118(7); Finance, 2004 c 12, ss 33(1)(3)(b)(4)(5)(b),
313(4)(e)

ext—Income and Corporation Taxes, 1988 c 1, ss 349E, 488(12); Capital
Allowances, 2001 c 2, s 135(5); Finance, 2004 c 12, ss 97(5), 101(6)

appl (mods)—Income and Corporation Taxes, 1988 c 1, s 349E; SI 1999/2975,
reg 10(3); 2001/1163, reg 8; Finance, 2004 c 12, ss 97(5), 101(7); Finance (No
2), 2005 c 22, s 61; SI 2005/3454, reg 13; SI 2005/3338, regs 1(2), 5(1)-(6),
6-8, 10(2)(a)(ii); Finance, 2010 c 13, s 22, sch 1 para 31; Taxation
(International and Other Provns), 2010 c 8, s 183(2); Localism, 2011 c 20, sch
24 para 8(2)

excl pt—Finance, 2014 c 26, s 208(10)(11)(c)

mod—Finance, 2014 c 26, s 225A(3)(4); ibid, sch 32 para 6A(3)(4)

sch 19 rep in pt—Finance, 1999 c 16, s 139, sch 20 pt VII, Notes 1, 2; Finance, 2001 c 9,
s 110, sch 33 pt 2(12)(13), Note; ibid, s 110, sch 33 pt 2(14), Note 2; Income
Tax (Trading and Other Income), 2005 c 5, s 884, sch 3; Finance, 2008 c 9, ss
113, 118, sch 36 para 92(f), sch 39 para 65(d); Corporation Tax, 2010 c 4, s
1181, sch 3 pt 1

1998

c 36 *continued*

　　　　sch 20 rep—Finance, 2008 c 9, s 8, sch 2 para 55(a)(iii)

　　　　sch 21 rep in pt —Finance, 2002 c 23, s 141, sch 40 pt 3(4), Note; Finance, 2008 c 9, ss 8, 25, sch 2 paras 21(c)(ii), 55(a)(iv), sch 7 para 114(a)

　　　　sch 24 rep—Finance, 2006 c 25, s 178, sch 26 pt 3(9)

c 37　**Crime and Disorder**

　　　　mod—Transport for London, 2008 c i, s 29

　　　　ss 1-1K rep—Anti-social Behaviour, Crime and Policing, 2014 c 12, sch 11 para 24(a)

　　　　ss 2, 2A, 2B, 3 rep—Sexual Offences, 2003 c 42, ss 139, 140, sch 6 para 38(1)(2), sch 7

　　　　s 4 rep —Anti-social Behaviour, Crime and Policing, 2014 c 12, sch 11 para 24(b)

　　　　s 5 am—SI 2000/90, art 3(1), sch 1 para 35(2); Crim Justice and Court Services, 2000 c 43, s 74, sch 7 pt II para 151; Police Reform, 2002 c 30, s 97(1)-(6), 15; Fire and Rescue Services, 2004 c 21, s 53, sch 1 para 89(1)(2)(a)(b); Police and Justice, 2006 c 48, ss 21, 22, sch 9 paras 1, 2; (W) SI 2007/961 (W 85), art 3, sch; SI 2008/912, art 3, sch 1; Policing and Crime, 2009 c 26, s 108(1)-(3); Police Reform and Social Responsibility, 2011 c 13, sch 11 paras 2(3)-(7), 3; Localism, 2011 c 20, sch 3 para 7; Health and Social Care, 2012 c 7, sch 5 para 84

　　　　　rep in pt —Police Reform, 2002 c 30, s 107(2), sch 8; Police Reform and Social Responsibility, 2011 c 13, sch 11 para 2(2); Police Reform and Social Responsibility, 2011 c 13, sch 11 para 2(8)

　　　　　appl (mods)—Police and Justice, 2006 c 48, s 15, sch 8 para 11(2)

　　　　s 6 subst—Police and Justice, 2006 c 48, s 22, sch 9 paras 1, 3

　　　　　am—Policing and Crime, 2009 c 26, s 108(1)(4)(5); Police Reform and Social Responsibility, 2011 c 13, sch 11 para 4(2)-(5)

　　　　　mod—SI 2010/970, art 2

　　　　s 6A added—Police Reform, 2002 c 30, s 98

　　　　　rep—Police and Justice, 2006 c 48, s 22, sch 9 paras 1, 3, sch 15

　　　　s 7 mod—SI 2010/970, art 2

　　　　　am—Police Reform and Social Responsibility, 2011 c 13, sch 11 para 4(2)-(5)

　　　　s 8 am—Youth Justice and Crim Evidence, 1999 c 23, s 67, sch 4, paras 25, 26; Powers of Crim Cts (Sentencing), 2000 c 6, s 165(1), sch 9 para 194; Crim Justice and Court Services, 2000 c 43, ss 73, 74, sch 7 pt I para 4(1)(2); Anti-social Behaviour, 2003 c 38, s 18; Children, 2004 c 31, ss 18(9), 60(1)(2), sch 2 para 5(1)(2); (pt prosp) Serious Organised Crime and Police, 2005 c 15, s 144, sch 10 pt 1 paras 1, 3; Violent Crime Reduction, 2006 c 38, s 60(2); SI 2008/912, art 3, sch 1; (prosp) Crime and Security, 2010 c 17, s 41(2); Anti-social Behaviour, Crime and Policing, 2014 c 12, sch 11 para 25(2)(4); ibid, sch 11 para 55(2)(3)

　　　　　rep in pt—Crim Justice, 2003 c 44, ss 324, 332, sch 34 para 1, sch 37 pt 12; Children, 2004 c 31, s 64, sch 5 pt 4; Anti-social Behaviour, Crime and Policing, 2014 c 12, sch 11 para 25(3)

　　　　　appl—Powers of Crim Cts (Sentencing), 2000 c 6, sch 1 pt 1A para 9D(7)

　　　　s 8A added —Crime and Security, 2010 c 17, s 41(3)

　　　　　rep —Anti-social Behaviour, Crime and Policing, 2014 c 12, sch 11 para 24(c)

　　　　s 9 am—Youth Justice and Crim Evidence, 1999 c 23, s 67, sch 4, paras 25, 27; Powers of Crim Cts (Sentencing), 2000 c 6, s 165(1), sch 9 para 195; Anti-social Behaviour, 2003 c 38, s 85(1)(8); Crim Justice, 2003 c 44, s 324, sch 34 para 2; SI 2008/912, art 3, sch 1; (prosp) Crime and Security, 2010 c 17, s 40(3); (pt prosp) ibid, s 41(4); Anti-social Behaviour, Crime and Policing, 2014 c 12, sch 11 para 26(3)

　　　　　appl—Powers of Crim Cts (Sentencing), 2000 c 6, sch 1 pt 1A para 9D(7); Anti-social Behaviour, 2003 c 38, ss 21(3), 27(3); (prosp) Educ and Skills, 2008 c 25, s 42(2)

　　　　　rep in pt—Children, 2004 c 31, s 64, sch 5 pt 4; (prosp) Crime and Security, 2010 c 17, s 41(4)(b); Anti-social Behaviour, Crime and Policing, 2014 c 12, sch 11 para 26(2)(4)(5)

　　　　s 10 appl—Powers of Crim Cts (Sentencing), 2000 c 6, sch 1 pt 1A para 9E(2); Anti-social Behaviour, 2003 c 38, ss 22(2), 28(2); (prosp) Educ and Skills, 2008 c 25, s 43(2)

　　　　　am—Constitutional Reform, 2005 c 4, s 15(1), sch 4 pt 1 paras 276, 277; SI 2009/871, arts 9, 18; (prosp) Crime and Security, 2010 c 17, s 41(5); Crime and Cts, 2013 c 22, sch 9 para 52

　　　　s 11 am—Children, 2004 c 31, s 60(1)(3); Crime and Cts, 2013 c 22, sch 11 para 147(2)

　　　　　rep in pt—Children, 2004 c 31, s 64, sch 5 pt 4; Policing and Crime, 2009 c 26, s 112, sch 8 pt 13; Crime and Cts, 2013 c 22, sch 11 para 147(3)

1998
c 37 *continued*

s 12 rep in pt—Children, 2004 c 31, ss 60(1)(4), 64, sch 5 pt 6; Crime and Cts, 2013 c 22, sch 11 para 148(4)

am—SI 2005/886, art 2, sch paras 56, 57; Crime and Cts, 2013 c 22, sch 11 para 148(3)

s 13 rep —Crime and Cts, 2013 c 22, sch 11 para 149

ss 13A-13E added (pt prosp)—Serious Organised Crime and Police, 2005 c 15, s 144, sch 10 pt 1 paras 1, 2, 6

s 13B am—Crime and Cts, 2013 c 22, sch 11 para 150; ibid, sch 16 para 27(a)

rep in pt—Crime and Cts, 2013 c 22, sch 16 para 27(b)

s 14 rep —Policing and Crime, 2009 c 26, s 112, sch 7 para 134(1)(2), sch 8 pt 13

s 15 rep —Policing and Crime, 2009 c 26, s 112, sch 7 para 134(1)(2), sch 8 pt 13

s 16 am —Police Reform, 2002 c 30, s 75(1)(2); Railways and Transport Safety, 2003 c 20, s 73, sch 5 para 4(1)(a)(2)(j); SI 2004/1573, art 12(5)(c); Educ and Inspections, 2006 c 40, s 108(1)-(6); ibid, s 109(10); Policing and Crime, 2009 c 26, s 112, sch 7 para 134(1)(3)

rep in pt—Railways and Transport Safety, 2003 c 20, s 73, sch 5 para 4(1)(b)(2)(j); SI 2004/1573, art 12(5)(d)

s 17 am—GLA, 1999 c 29, s 328(8), sch 29 pt I para 63; Police Reform, 2002 c 30, s 97(1)(12); Fire and Rescue Services, 2004 c 21, s 53, sch 1 para 89(1)(3); Police and Justice, 2006 c 48, s 22, sch 9 paras 1, 4; SI 2008/78, art 2; Policing and Crime, 2009 c 26, s 108(1)(6); Loc Democracy, Economic Development and Construction, 2009 c 20, s 119, sch 6 para 90; Police Reform and Social Responsibility, 2011 c 13, sch 16 para 233

rep in pt—Localism, 2011 c 20, sch 25 pt 32

s 17A am—Police and Justice, 2006 c 48, s 22, sch 9 paras 1, 5

s 18 am—Powers of Crim Cts (Sentencing), 2000 c 6, s 165(1), sch 9 para 196; Crim Justice and Court Services, 2000 c 43, s 74, sch 7 pt I para 4(1)(2); Crim Justice, 2003 c 44, ss 304, 323(1)(4), sch 32 pt I paras 87, 88(a); (pt prosp) Serious Organised Crime and Police, 2005 c 15, s 144, sch 10 pt 1 paras 1, 4; SIs 2005/886, art 2, sch para 58; 2008/912, art 3, sch 1; Police Reform and Social Responsibility, 2011 c 13, sch 16 para 234(2); Anti-social Behaviour, Crime and Policing, 2014 c 12, sch 11 para 27(3)(b)

rep in pt—Crim Justice, 2003 c 44, ss 304, 332, sch 32 pt I paras 87, 88(b), sch 37 pt 7; Children, 2004 c 31, s 64, sch 5 pt 4; Violent Crime Reduction, 2006 c 38, ss 60(3), 65, sch 5; Police Reform and Social Responsibility, 2011 c 13, sch 16 para 234(3); Anti-social Behaviour, Crime and Policing, 2014 c 12, sch 11 para 27(2)(3)(a)

appl—Powers of Crim Cts (Sentencing), 2000 c 6, sch 1 pt 1A para 9D(7)

s 19 rep—Antisocial Behaviour etc (S), 2004 asp 8, s 144(2), sch 5

s 20 rep—Sexual Offences, 2003 c 42, ss 139, 140, sch 6 para 38(1)(4), sch 7

ss 21, 22 rep—Antisocial Behaviour etc (S), 2004 asp 8, s 144(2), sch 5

s 22A rep—Antisocial Behaviour etc (S), 2004 asp 8, s 144(2), sch 5

s 23 rep in pt—Housing (S), 2001 asp 10, s 112, sch 10 para 27

s 25 rep in pt—Anti-terrorism, Crime and Security, 2001 c 24, s 125, sch 8 pt 6

s 27 rep in pt—Serious Organised Crime and Police, 2005 c 15, s 174(2), sch 17 pt 2

s 28 appl—Powers of Crim Cts (Sentencing), 2000 c 6, s 153(3); Anti-social Behaviour, 2003 c 38, s 47(2); Crim Justice, 2003 c 44, ss 145(3), 269(5), sch 21 para 2

am—Anti-terrorism, Crime and Security, 2001 c 24, s 39(1)-(4)

ss 29-32 am—Anti-terrorism, Crime and Security, 2001 c 24, s 39(1)(5)(6)

saved—Crim Justice, 2003 c 44, s 145(1)

s 31 rep in pt—Serious Organised Crime and Police, 2005 c 15, ss 111, 174(2), sch 7 pt 1 para 34, sch 17 pt 2

s 32 rep in pt—Police Reform, 2002 c 30, s 107(2), sch 8

am—Domestic Violence, Crime and Victims, 2004 c 28, ss 58, 59, sch 10 para 48, sch 11, sch 12 para 5(1); Protection of Freedoms, 2012 c 9, sch 9 para 144(2)(3)

s 35 rep—SL(R), 2008 c 12, s 1(1), sch 1 pt 3

s 36 rep in pt—SL(R), 2008 c 12, s 1(1), sch 1 pt 3

s 38 am—Youth Justice and Crim Evidence, 1999 c 23, s 67, sch 4, paras 25, 28; SI 2000/90, art 3(1), sch 1 para 35(3); Powers of Crim Cts (Sentencing), 2000 c 6, s 165(1)(3), sch 9 para 197, sch 11 pt III para 11(4); Crim Justice and Court Services, 2000 c 43, s 74, sch 7 pt II para 151; SI 2002/2469, reg 4, sch 1 pt 1, para 25(1)(2); Anti-social Behaviour, 2003 c 38, s 29(2); Crim Justice, 2003 c 44, ss 304, 323(1)(5), sch 32 pt 1 paras 87, 89; (prosp) Police and Justice, 2006 c 48,

CHRONOLOGICAL TABLE OF THE STATUTES

1998
c 37 *continued*

s 52, sch 14 para 36; Armed Forces, 2006 c 52, s 378, sch 16 para 153; Offender
Management, 2007 c 21, s 39, sch 3 para 3(1)(2); (W) SI 2007/961 (W 85), art 3,
sch; (pt prosp) Crim Justice and Immigration, 2008 c 4, ss 6, 148, sch 4 paras 48,
49(a)(b), sch 26 para 34; Police Reform and Social Responsibility, 2011 c 13, sch
16 para 235; Health and Social Care, 2012 c 7, sch 5 para 85(a); Legal Aid,
Sentencing and Punishment of Offenders, 2012 c 10, sch 24 para 15; ibid, sch 12
para 37; Offender Rehabilitation, 2014 c 11, sch 3 para 9(2)(3)

 rep in pt—Crim Justice, 2003 c 44, s 332, sch 37 pt 7; Crim Justice and Immigration,
2008 c 4, ss 6, 149, sch 4 paras 48, 49(c)(d), sch 28 pt 1; Health and Social
Care, 2012 c 7, sch 5 para 85(b)(c); Anti-social Behaviour, Crime and Policing,
2014 c 12, sch 11 para 28

s 39 am—SI 2000/90, art 3(1), sch 1 para 35(4); Crim Justice and Court Services, 2000
c 43, s 74, sch 7 pts I para 4(1)(2), II para 151; SI 2002/2469, reg 4, sch 1 pt 1,
para 25(1)(3); Children, 2004 c 31, s 18(9), sch 2 para 5(1)(3); (W) SI 2007/961
(W 85), art 3, sch; Offender Management, 2007 c 21, s 39, sch 3 para 3(1)(3);
Health and Social Care, 2012 c 7, sch 5 para 86(a); ibid, sch 5 para 87(a)

 rep in pt—Children, 2004 c 31, s 64, sch 5 pt 4; Health and Social Care, 2012 c 7, sch 5
para 86(b)(c); ibid, sch 5 para 87(b)

 appl (mods)—(E) SI 2005/157, art 5(2)-(5), sch 1

s 39A added —(E) Apprenticeships, Skills, Children and Learning, 2009 c 22, s 51

s 40 appl (mods)—(E) SI 2005/157, art 5(2)-(5), sch 1

 excl—(E) SI 2005/157, art 5

 rep in pt—Anti-social Behaviour, Crime and Policing, 2014 c 12, sch 11 para 50

s 41 am—SI 2000/90, art 3(1), sch 1 para 35(5); SI 2000/1160, art 3; Crim Justice and
Court Services, 2000 c 43, s 74, sch 7 pt II para 151; SI 2002/2469, reg 4, sch 1
pt 1, para 25(1)(4); Armed Forces, 2006 c 52, s 378, sch 16 para 154; Offender
Management, 2007 c 21, s 39, sch 3 para 3(1)(4); ibid, ss 32, 39, sch 3 para 16;
(W) SI 2007/961 (W 85), art 3, sch; Crime and Security, 2010 c 17, s 39(4);
Police Reform and Social Responsibility, 2011 c 13, sch 16 para 236; Health and
Social Care, 2012 c 7, sch 5 para 88(a)(b); Crim Justice and Cts, 2015 c 2, s
40(2); SI 2015/79, art 2(b)(c)

 rep in pt—SI 2000/1160, art 3; Legal Aid, Sentencing and Punishment of Offenders,
2012 c 10, sch 12 para 38; Health and Social Care, 2012 c 7, sch 5 para 88(c);
Crim Justice and Cts, 2015 c 2, s 40(3); SI 2015/79, art 2(a)

 appl (mods)—(E) SI 2005/157, art 5(2)-(5), sch 1

s 42 am—SI 2000/90, art 3(1), sch 1 para 35(6); Crim Justice and Court Services, 2000
c 43, s 74, sch 7 pt II para 151; SIs 2002/2469, reg 4, sch 1 pt 1, para 25(1)(5);
(W) 2007/961 (W 85), art 3, sch; (prosp) Crim Justice and Immigration, 2008 c 4,
s 9(4); SI 2010/1158, art 5, sch 2, 4; Health and Social Care, 2012 c 7, sch 5 para
89(a)(b)

 appl (mods)—(E) SI 2005/157, art 5(2)-(5), sch 1

 rep in pt—Police Reform and Social Responsibility, 2011 c 13, sch 16 para 237; Health
and Social Care, 2012 c 7, sch 5 para 89(c)

s 44 rep —Policing and Crime, 2009 c 26, s 112, sch 8 pt 13

s 47 rep in pt—Powers of Crim Cts (Sentencing), 2000 c 6, s 165(3)(4), sch 11 pt I para 2,
sch 12 pt I; Crim Justice, 2003 c 44, s 332, sch 37 pt 4; SI 2005/886, art 2, sch
para 59

s 48 rep (prosp)—Access to Justice, 1999 c 22, s 106, sch 15 pt V(2)

s 49 rep in pt—Access to Justice, 1999 c 22, s 106, sch 15 pt I

 am—SI 2004/2035, art 3, sch paras 35, 36

s 50 am—Access to Justice, 1999 c 22, s 24, sch 4 paras 53, 54; SI 2006/2493, reg 8; Legal
Aid, Sentencing and Punishment of Offenders, 2012 c 10, sch 5 para 47(2)

 ext—SI 1999/2784, rule 3(2)

 rep in pt—Access to Justice, 1999 c 22, s 106, sch 15 pt I; Crim Justice, 2003 c 44,
ss 41, 332, sch 3 pt 1 paras 15, 16, sch 37 pt 4; Legal Aid, Sentencing and
Punishment of Offenders, 2012 c 10, sch 5 para 47(3)

s 50A added—(EW) Crim Justice, 2003 c 44, s 41, sch 3 pt 1 paras 15, 17

s 51 see—SI 2005/384, rules 12.1, 13.1

 replaced (by ss 51, 51A-51E)—Crim Justice, 2003 c 44, s 41, sch 3 pt 1 paras 15, 18

 am—Crim Justice and Cts, 2015 c 2, s 52(2)

s 51A rep in pt—Violent Crime Reduction, 2006 c 38, ss 49, 65, sch 1 para 5, sch 5

 am—Violent Crime Reduction, 2006 c 38, s 49, sch 1 para 5; Legal Aid, Sentencing
and Punishment of Offenders, 2012 c 10, sch 21 para 5

1998

c 37 *continued*

s 51B am—Commrs for Revenue and Customs, 2005 c 11, s 50(6), sch 4 para 69; Legal Aid,
Sentencing and Punishment of Offenders, 2012 c 10, sch 5 para 48

rep in pt—SI 2014/834, sch 2 para 15

s 51C mod—Serious Crime, 2007 c 27, s 63, sch 6 para 36

s 52 see—SI 2005/384, rule 13.1

am —Crim Justice, 2003 c 44, s 41, sch 3 pt 2 paras 68, 69; Coroners and Justice, 2009
c 25, s 177, sch 21 para 78

ss 52A, 52B added—Crim Justice, 2003 c 44, s 41, sch 3 pt 1 paras 15, 19(1)

am—Legal Aid, Sentencing and Punishment of Offenders, 2012 c 10, sch 5 para 49

s 57 rep—Police and Justice, 2006 c 48, s 45

Pt 3A (ss 57A-57E) added—Police and Justice, 2006 c 48, s 45

Pt 3A title am—Coroners and Justice, 2009 c 25, s 109(3)

s 57A am—Coroners and Justice, 2009 c 25, s 109(2); Legal Aid, Sentencing and
Punishment of Offenders, 2012 c 10, sch 12 para 39

s 57B am—Coroners and Justice, 2009 c 25, s 106(1)(2)

s 57C am—Coroners and Justice, 2009 c 25, s 106(1)(3)(a)

rep in pt—Coroners and Justice, 2009 c 25, ss 106(1)(3)(b)(c)(d), 178, sch 23 pt 3

s 57D am—Coroners and Justice, 2009 c 25, s 106(1)(4)(a)(ii)

rep in pt —Coroners and Justice, 2009 c 25, ss 106(1)(4)(a)(i)(b), 178, sch 23 pt 3

s 57E appl—Serious Organised Crime and Police, 2005 c 15, s 75A

rep in pt—Coroners and Justice, 2009 c 25, ss 106(1)(5), 178, sch 23 pt 3

s 57F added—Coroners and Justice, 2009 c 25, s 109(1)

s 58 rep—Powers of Crim Cts (Sentencing), 2000 c 6, s 165(3)(4), sch 11 pt I para 2, sch 12
pt I

ss 59, 60 rep—Crim Justice, 2003 c 44, s 332, sch 37 pt 7

ss 61-64 rep—Powers of Crim Cts (Sentencing), 2000 c 6, s 165(3)(4), sch 11 pt I para 2,
sch 12 pt I

s 65 rep—Legal Aid, Sentencing and Punishment of Offenders, 2012 c 10, s 135(1)

s 66 rep —Legal Aid, Sentencing and Punishment of Offenders, 2012 c 10, s 135(1)

ss 66ZA, 66ZB added —Legal Aid, Sentencing and Punishment of Offenders, 2012 c 10, s
135(2)

rep in pt—Crim Justice and Cts, 2015 c 2, s 41(2)

ss 66A, 66B added—Crim Justice and Immigration, 2008 c 4, s 48, sch 9 paras 1, 3

s 66A rep in pt—Legal Aid, Sentencing and Punishment of Offenders, 2012 c 10, s 136

am—Legal Aid, Sentencing and Punishment of Offenders, 2012 c 10, ss 137, 138(2)

s 66B am—Legal Aid, Sentencing and Punishment of Offenders, 2012 c 10, s 138(3)

rep in pt—Crim Justice and Cts, 2015 c 2, s 41(3)

s 66BA added—Anti-social Behaviour, Crime and Policing, 2014 c 12, s 103(2)

s 66C added—Crim Justice and Immigration, 2008 c 4, s 48, sch 9 paras 1, 3

am—Legal Aid, Sentencing and Punishment of Offenders, 2012 c 10, s 138(4)

ss 66D, 66E, 66F added—Crim Justice and Immigration, 2008 c 4, s 48, sch 9 paras 1, 3

am—Legal Aid, Sentencing and Punishment of Offenders, 2012 c 10, s 138(5)

ss 66G,66H added—Crim Justice and Immigration, 2008 c 4, s 48, sch 9 paras 1, 3

s 66G am—Legal Aid, Sentencing and Punishment of Offenders, 2012 c 10, s 138(6)

s 66H am—Legal Aid, Sentencing and Punishment of Offenders, 2012 c 10, sch 24 para 16

rep in pt—SI 2014/834, sch 2 para 16

ss 67-79 rep—Powers of Crim Cts (Sentencing), 2000 c 6, s 165(3)(4), sch 11 pt I para 2,
sch 12 pt I

ss 80, 81 rep—Crim Justice, 2003 c 44, ss 303(c), 332, 333(6), sch 37 pt 7, sch 38 paras 2,
3

s 82 rep—Powers of Crim Cts (Sentencing), 2000 c 6, s 165(3)(4), sch 11 pt I para 2, sch 12
pt I

s 83 rep—Proceeds of Crime, 2002 c 29, s 457, sch 12

s 84 rep—Football (Disorder), 2000 c 25, s 1, sch 3; Police Reform, 2002 c 30, s 107(2),
sch 8

s 85 rep—Powers of Crim Cts (Sentencing), 2000 c 6, s 165(3)(4), sch 11 pt I para 2, sch 12
pt I

s 96 am—(S) Crim Justice and Licensing (S), 2010 asp 13, s 25(1)

s 97 rep —Legal Aid, Sentencing and Punishment of Offenders, 2012 c 10, sch 12 para 40

s 98 rep—Legal Aid, Sentencing and Punishment of Offenders, 2012 c 10, sch 12 para 40

ss 99, 100 rep—Crim Justice, 2003 c 44, s 332, sch 37 pt 7

s 101 rep in pt—Crim Justice, 2003 c 44, s 332, sch 37 pt 7

1998

c 37 *continued*

s 102 rep—Powers of Crim Cts (Sentencing), 2000 c 6, s 165(3)(4), sch 11 pt I para 2, sch 12 pt I

ss 103-105 rep—Crim Justice, 2003 c 44, s 332, sch 37 pt 7

ss 107, 108 rep—SL(R), 2008 c 12, s 1(1), sch 1 pt 3

s 113 rep—Serious Organised Crime and Police, 2005 c 15, ss 59, 174(2), sch 4 para 118, sch 17 pt 2

s 114 am—Powers of Crim Cts (Sentencing), 2000 c 6, s 165(1), sch 9 para 199; Police Reform, 2002 c 30, ss 62(2), 97(1)(13); (pt prosp) Serious Organised Crime and Police, 2005 c 15, ss 142(3), 144, sch 10 pt 1 paras 1, 5; Drugs, 2005 c 17, s 20(2); Police and Justice, 2006 c 48, s 22, sch 9 paras 1, 6(1)(2)(b)(3)(4); Crim Justice and Immigration, 2008 c 4, s 48, sch 9 paras 1, 4; (prosp) Crime and Security, 2010 c 17, s 40(4)

　　　rep in pt—Police and Justice, 2006 c 48, s 22, sch 9 paras 1, 6(1)(2)(a), sch 15; Anti-social Behaviour, Crime and Policing, 2014 c 12, sch 11 para 29

s 115 am—(EW) SI 2000/90, art 3(1), sch 1 para 35(7); Crim Justice and Court Services, 2000 c 43, s 74, sch 7 pt II para 151; Police Reform, 2002 c 30, s 97(1)(14); SI 2002/2469, reg 4, sch 1 pt 1, para 25(1)(6); (EW) Housing, 2004 c 34, s 219; Police and Justice, 2006 c 48, s 22, sch 9 paras 1, 7; (W) SIs 2007/961 (W 85), art 3, sch; 2008/912, art 3, sch 1; 2010/866, art 5, sch 2; Police Reform and Social Responsibility, 2011 c 13, sch 16 para 238; Health and Social Care, 2012 c 7, sch 5 para 90(b); SI 2013/602, sch 2 para 30

　　　appl (mods)—Transport for London, 2008 c.i, s 29(b)

　　　rep in pt—Health and Social Care, 2012 c 7, sch 5 para 90(a)(c)

s 116 rep—SL(R), 2008 c 12, s 1(1), sch 1 pt 3

s 117 am—Powers of Crim Cts (Sentencing), 2000 c 6, s 165(1), sch 9 para 200; Crim Justice and Court Services, 2000 c 43, s 74, sch 7 pt II para 152

　　　rep in pt—SI 2005/886, art 2, sch para 60

s 121 rep in pt—Powers of Crim Cts (Sentencing), 2000 c 6, s 165(3)(4), sch 11 pt I para 2, sch 12 pt I; Crim Justice, 2003 c 44, s 332, sch 37 pt 7; Legal Aid, Sentencing and Punishment of Offenders, 2012 c 10, sch 24 para 17

　　　am—Crim Justice, 2003 c 44, s 41, sch 3 pt 1 paras 15, 19(2), pt 2 para 70; ibid, s 68

sch 3 am—Access to Justice, 1999 c 22, s 67(1)(a)(b); ibid, s 90, sch 13 para 179(1)(2)(3); ibid, s 24, sch 4 paras 53, 55; Powers of Crim Cts (Sentencing), 2000 c 6, s 165(1), sch 9 para 201(1)(2)(3); (pt prosp) Crim Justice, 2003 c 44, ss 41, 331, sch 3 pt 1 paras 15, 20(1)(2)(3)(a)(4)-(11)(14), pt 2 paras 68, 71, 72, sch 36 pt 4 para 73; SI 2004/2035, art 3, sch paras 35, 37(1)-(3); Serious Organised Crime and Police, 2005 c 15, s 169(4); SI 2005/886, art 2, sch para 61(b)(c); Armed Forces, 2006 c 52, s 378, sch 16 para 155; Coroners and Justice, 2009 c 25, s 144, sch 17 para 5(1)(3); ibid, s 177, sch 21 para 81; Legal Aid, Sentencing and Punishment of Offenders, 2012 c 10, sch 5 para 50

　　　see—SIs 1998/3048, rules 2-4; 2005/384, rule 13.1

　　　rep in pt—Access to Justice, 1999 c 22, ss 67(1)(a), 106, sch 15 pt III; ibid, s 106, sch 15 pt V(7); Crim Justice, 2003 c 44, ss 130, 141, 332, sch 37 pt 6; (pt prosp) ibid, s 41, sch 3 pt 1 paras 15, 20(1)(3)(b)(c)(12), sch 37 pt 4; SI 2005/886, art 2, sch para 61(a); Coroners and Justice, 2009 c 25, ss 144, 178, sch 17 para 5(1)(2), sch 23 pt 5

　　　excl—Crim Appeal, 1968 c 19, sch 2 para 1(2); Crim Justice, 2003 c 44, s 84(7)

　　　mod—SI 2009/1059, art 205, sch 1

sch 4 rep in pt—Access to Justice, 1999 c 22, s 106, sch 15 pt IV; Powers of Crim Cts (Sentencing), 2000 c 6, s 165(3)(4), sch 11 pt I para 2, sch 12 pt I

sch 5 am—Access to Justice, 1999 c 22, s 66, sch 9 para 9; Youth Justice and Crim Evidence, 1999 c 23, s 67, sch 5 paras 5, 10(1)(2)(4), 11(1)(2)(4)(5)

　　　rep in pt—Powers of Crim Cts (Sentencing), 2000 c 6, s 165(3)(4), sch 11 pt I para 2, sch 12 pt I

sch 6 rep in pt—(S) Crim Justice and Licensing (S), 2010 asp 13, s 14, sch 2 para 42

sch 7 rep in pt—Powers of Crim Cts (Sentencing), 2000 c 6, s 165(3)(4), sch 11 pt I para 2, sch 12 pt I; (prosp) Crim Justice, 2003 c 44, s 332, sch 37 pt 7

sch 8 appl—SI 1999/3426, art 4(1)(a)(ii)

　　　rep in pt—Access to Justice, 1999 c 22, s 106, sch 15 pt III; ibid, sch 15 pts I, V(8); Powers of Crim Cts (Sentencing), 2000 c 6, s 165(3)(4), sch 11 pt I para 2, sch 12 pt I; Crim Justice and Court Services, 2000 c 43, ss 74,75, sch 7 pt II para 153, sch 8; Crim Justice and Police, 2001 c 16, s 137, sch 7 pt 2(1); Proceeds of Crime, 2002 c 29, ss 456, 457, sch 11, para 35, sch 12; Crim

1998

c 37 sch 8 *continued*

Justice, 2003 c 44, s 332, sch 37 pt 8; (prosp) ibid, sch 37 pts 4,7; Mental
Health (Care and Treatment) (S), 2003 asp 13, s 331(2), sch 5 pt 1; Sexual
Offences, 2003 c 42, ss 139, 140, sch 6 para 38(1)(8), sch 7; (prosp) (S)
Custodial Sentences and Weapons (S), 2007 asp 17, s 66, sch 5; Crim Justice
and Immigration, 2008 c 4, s 149, sch 28 pt 1; Legal Aid, Sentencing and
Punishment of Offenders, 2012 c 10, s 118(5); ibid, sch 25 pt 2; Crime and Cts,
2013 c 22, sch 10 para 99 Table

am—Powers of Crim Cts (Sentencing), 2000 c 6, s 165(1), sch 9 para 202; Crim
Justice and Immigration, 2008 c 4, s 6, sch 4 paras 48, 50

sch 9 rep in pt—Powers of Crim Cts (Sentencing), 2000 c 6, ss 165(3)(4), schs 11 pt I para 2,
sch 12 pt I; Proceeds of Crime, 2002 c 29, s 457, sch 12

am—Powers of Crim Cts (Sentencing), 2000 c 6, s 165(1), sch 9 para 203

c 38 **Government of Wales**

appl—SI 1999/1320, art 4(3)(b)

trans of powers—(W) SI 1999/672, art 2, sch 1

am—Constitutional Reform, 2005 c 4, s 59(5), sch 11 pt 2 para 4

ss 1-8 rep—Govt of Wales, 2006 c 32, s 163, sch 12

ss 9, 10 rep—SI 1999/450, arts 92-95, 100(3), 102, 103, 122(1)

ss 11-26 rep—Govt of Wales, 2006 c 32, s 163, sch 12

s 27 am —Nat Health Service Reform and Health Care Professions, 2002 c 17, s 37(1), sch
8, paras 25, 26; Health and Social Care (Community Health and Standards),
2003 c 43, s 192

rep in pt—(W) Health (W), 2003 c 4, s 7, sch 3 para 9, sch 4; Nat Health Service
(Conseq Provns), 2006 c 43, s 6, sch 4; Govt of Wales, 2006 c 32, s 163, sch
12

s 28 am—Govt of Wales, 2006 c 32, s 160, sch 10 para 42

s 29-34 rep—Govt of Wales, 2006 c 32, s 163, sch 12

s 34A added—Political Parties, Elections and Referendums, 2000 c 41, s 158(1), sch 21
para 12(4)

rep—Govt of Wales, 2006 c 32, s 163, sch 12

s 35-40 rep—Govt of Wales, 2006 c 32, s 163, sch 12

s 41A added—Public Audit (W), 2004 c 23, s 66, sch 2 paras 42, 43

rep—Govt of Wales, 2006 c 32, s 163, sch 12

ss 42-93 rep—Govt of Wales, 2006 c 32, s 163, sch 12

s 93A added—Public Audit (W), 2004 c 23, s 7

rep—Govt of Wales, 2006 c 32, s 163, sch 12

s 94 rep—Govt of Wales, 2006 c 32, s 163, sch 12

s 94A added—Public Audit (W), 2004 c 23, s 10

rep—Govt of Wales, 2006 c 32, s 163, sch 12

s 95 rep—Govt of Wales, 2006 c 32, s 163, sch 12

s 96 rep—Govt of Wales, 2006 c 32, s 163, sch 12

ss 96A-96C added—Public Audit (W), 2004 c 23, s 2

rep—Govt of Wales, 2006 c 32, s 163, sch 12

ss 97-101 rep—Govt of Wales, 2006 c 32, s 163, sch 12

s 101A added—Govt Resources and Accounts, 2000 c 20, s 29(1), sch 1 paras 21, 24

rep—Govt of Wales, 2006 c 32, s 163, sch 12

ss 102, 103 rep—Govt of Wales, 2006 c 32, s 163, sch 12

s 104 rep in pt—Learning and Skills, 2000 c 21, ss 149,153, sch 9 para 92(2), sch 11; Govt
of Wales, 2006 c 32, ss 160, 163, sch 10 para 43(8), sch 12

am—Learning and Skills, 2000 c 21, s 149, sch 9 para 92(3); Govt of Wales, 2006 c
32, s 160, sch 10 para 43

s 105 rep—SI 2013/1821, art 15(2)

s 106 rep—Govt of Wales, 2006 c 32, s 163, sch 12

s 107 rep—Govt of Wales, 2006 c 32, s 163, sch 12

ss 108-110 rep—Govt of Wales, 2006 c 32, s 163, sch 12

s 111 rep—Public Services Ombudsman (W), 2005 c 10, ss 38, 39, sch 6 paras 61, 65, sch 7

ss 112-124 rep—Govt of Wales, 2006 c 32, s 163, sch 12

s 132 rep—SI 2005/3226 (W 238), arts 3, 7(1)(b), sch 2 pt 1 para 11

s 138 rep—SI 2005/3226 (W 238), arts 3, 7(1)(b), sch 2 pt 1 para 11

s 144 am—Care Standards, 2000 c 14, s 72, sch 2 para 18; (W) Health (W), 2003 c 4,
s 7(1), sch 3 para 11; Public Audit (W), 2004 c 23, ss 65(1)-(3), 66, sch 2 paras
42, 46; Public Services Ombudsman (W), 2005 c 10, s 39(1), sch 6 paras 61,
66(a); Commnr for Older People (W), 2006 c 30, s 1, sch 1 para 20; Govt of

1998
c 38 *continued*

   Wales, 2006 c 32, s 160, sch 10 para 45; Health, 2006 c 28, s 80, sch 8 para 43;
    SI 2008/948, art 3, sch 1

  rep in pt—Public Audit (W), 2004 c 23, s 72, sch 4; Public Services Ombudsman (W),
    2005 c 10, s 39, sch 6 paras 61, 66(b), sch 7; Govt of Wales, 2006 c 32, ss 160,
    163, sch 10 para 45(6)(9), sch 12

  saved—Govt of Wales, 2006 c 32, s 94, sch 5 para 3

s 145 rep in pt—Public Audit (W), 2004 c 23, ss 66, 72, sch 2 paras 42, 47(1)(2), sch 4;
    Govt of Wales, 2006 c 32, ss 160, 163, sch 10 para 46(2), sch 12

  am—Public Audit (W), 2004 c 23, s 66, sch 2 paras 42, 47(1)(3); Govt of Wales,
    2006 c 32, s 160, sch 10 para 46(3)

  saved—Govt of Wales, 2006 c 32, s 94, sch 5 para 3

s 145A added—Public Audit (W), 2004 c 23, s 3

  saved—Govt of Wales, 2006 c 32, s 94, sch 5 para 3

  am—Govt of Wales, 2006 c 32, s 160, sch 10 para 47

s 145B added—Public Audit (W), 2004 c 23, s 4

  am—Educ, 2005 c 18, ss 98, 99, sch 14 para 21, sch 15; SI 2005/3238 (W 243),
    arts 7, 9(1), sch 1 paras 41, 43; Educ, 2011 c 21, sch 5 para 15(4); SI 2014/77
    (W 8), art 2

  rep in pt—Educ, 2011 c 21, sch 5 para 15(2)(3)(5)

s 145C added—Public Audit (W), 2004 c 23, s 5

  am—Govt of Wales, 2006 c 32, s 160, sch 10 para 48; SI 2010/866, art 5, sch 2;
    Public Audit (W), 2013 anaw 3, sch 4 para 6(3)(4)

  rep in pt—SI 2010/866, arts 5, 7, schs 2, 4; Public Audit (W), 2013 anaw 3, sch 4
    para 6(2)

s 145D added—Loc Govt and Public Involvement in Health, 2007 c 28, s 166

  am—SI 2010/866, art 5, sch 2; Public Audit (W), 2013 anaw 3, sch 4 para 7(2)-(4)

  rep in pt—SI 2010/866, arts 5, 7, schs 2, 4

s 146 rep in pt—Public Services Ombudsman (W), 2005 c 10, s 39, sch 6 paras 61, 67(b),
    sch 7

  am—Public Services Ombudsman (W), 2005 c 10, s 39(1), sch 6 paras 61, 67(a);
    Govt of Wales, 2006 c 32, s 160, sch 10 para 49; Public Audit (W), 2013 anaw
    3, sch 4 para 8

s 146A added—Public Audit (W), 2004 c 23, s 1

  saved—Govt of Wales, 2006 c 32, s 94, sch 5 para 3

  am—Govt of Wales, 2006 c 32, s 160, sch 10 para 50; SI 2010/866, art 5, sch 2;
    Public Audit (W), 2013 anaw 3, s 12

  rep in pt—SI 2010/866, arts 5, 7, schs 2, 4

s 147 rep—SI 2013/1821, art 11(2)

s 148 rep—Nat Health Service Reform and Health Care Professions, 2002 c 17, s 37, sch 8,
    paras 25, 27, sch 9 pt 3

s 151 am—Govt of Wales, 2006 c 32, s 160, sch 10 para 52

s 154 am—Govt of Wales, 2006 c 32, s 160, sch 10 para 53(2)

  rep in pt—Govt of Wales, 2006 c 32, ss 160, 163, sch 10 para 53(2)(4)(5)(6), sch 12;
    SI 2013/1821, arts 11(3), 15(3)(a)(b)

s 155 appl—SIs 2000/1503, art 7(2), 2001/650, art 5(2), 1631, art 13(1)(b), 2019, art 2;
    2003/2901, art 3, sch 2; 2004/1656 (W 170), reg 3(2), 1769, reg 6(4)(g)

  rep in pt—Govt of Wales, 2006 c 32, ss 160, 163, sch 10 para 53(2)(4)(5)(6), sch 12

  am—Govt of Wales, 2006 c 32, s 160, sch 10 para 54(2)(4)

s 156 rep—Govt of Wales, 2006 c 32, s 163, sch 12

schs 1-3 rep—Govt of Wales, 2006 c 32, s 163, sch 12

sch 4 am—Learning and Skills, 2000 c 21, s 149, sch 9 para 94; Care Standards, 2000 c 14,
    ss 6, 54, 66, sch 1 para 27(b)

  rep in pt—SIws 2002/253, art 54(3), sch 5, para 15; 2005/3238 (W 243), arts 7, 9(1),
    sch 1 paras 41, 44; 2005/3239 (W 244), arts 7(1)-(3), 9(1), sch 1 paras 26, 28;
    2006/63, art 3 (W 12); 2006/64, art 3 (W 13); Natural Environment and Rural
    Communities, 2006 c 16, s 105, sch 11 para 149, sch 12; SIs 2012/990 (W
    130), art 6; 2013/755 (W 90), art 2 para 392

sch 5 rep—Govt of Wales, 2006 c 32, s 163, sch 12

sch 6 am—Govt Resources and Accounts, 2000 c 20, s 29(1), sch 1 paras 21,23(b),27; Educ,
    2005 c 18, s 61, sch 9 para 22; Constitutional Reform and Governance, 2010 c
    25, s 19, sch 2 para 8

  rep in pt—Public Audit (W), 2004 c 23, ss 66, 72, sch 2 paras 42, 48, sch 4

1998

c 38 *continued*

sch 7 am—Govt Resources and Accounts, 2000 c 20, s 29(1), sch 1 paras 21, 23(c), 27;
Govt of Wales, 2006 c 32, s 160, sch 10 para 10

rep in pt—Public Audit (W), 2004 c 23, ss 66, 72, sch 2 paras 42, 49, sch 4; SIs
2013/755 (W 90), sch 2 para 393; 2013/1821, art 15(2)

sch 8 rep—Govt of Wales, 2006 c 32, s 163, sch 12

sch 9 cont—SI 1999/1791, art 4(5)

ext—SI 1999/1791, art 4(1)(2)

am—Care Standards, 2000 c 14, ss 6, 54, 66, sch 1 para 27(c); Govt Resources and
Accounts, 2000 c 20, s 29(1), sch 1 paras 21,23(d),27; Freedom of Information,
2000 c 36, s 76(2), sch 7 paras 7, 8; SI 2002/3146 (W 292), art 2(a)(b); (W)
Health (W), 2003 c 4, s 7(1), sch 3 para 13; SI 2004/2359, art 4; SI 2004/1823,
art 20(a)(ii)-(iv)(b)

rep in pt—Public Audit (W), 2004 c 23, ss 66, 72, sch 2 paras 42, 50, sch 4; SI
2004/1823, art 20(a)(i); Public Services Ombudsman (W), 2005 c 10, ss 38, 39,
sch 6 paras 61, 69, sch 7

sch 10 rep in pt—Public Services Ombudsman (W), 2005 c 10, s 39(2), sch 7

sch 11 rep—Govt of Wales, 2006 c 32, s 163, sch 12

sch 12 rep in pt—Crim Justice, 2003 c 44, s 332, sch 37 pt 10; Public Services Ombudsman
(W), 2005 c 10, s 39(2), sch 7; Govt of Wales, 2006 c 32, s 163, sch 12;
Budget Responsibility and Nat Audit, 2011 c 4, sch 5 para 19; Mental Health
(Discrimination), 2013 c 8, sch para 3

sch 13 am—SI 2009/1307, art 5, sch 1

sch 15 rep in pt—SI 2002/1860, arts 14(2), 15(1)(2)(d), sch 6; (prosp) Housing and
Regeneration, 2008 c 17, s 321, sch 16; (transtl provns and savings) SI
2008/3002, arts 5, 6, schs 2, 3

sch 16 rep in pt—Race Relations (Amdt), 2000 c 34, s 9(2), sch 3; Finance, 2004 c 12,
s 326, sch 42 pt 2(7), Note; Public Audit (W), 2004 c 23, s 72, sch 4; Loc Govt
and Public Involvement in Health, 2007 c 28, s 241, sch 18; Housing and
Regeneration, 2008 c 17, s 321, sch 16; SIs 2009/484, art 6, sch 2; 2010/866,
art 7, sch 4

sch 17 am—Care Standards, 2000 c 14, ss 6, 54, 66, sch 1 para 27(d); Nat Health Service
Reform and Health Care Professions, 2002 c 17, s 6(2), sch 5, para 42(1)(3);
Public Audit (W), 2004 c 23, s 66, sch 2 paras 42, 51; Nat Health Service
(Conseq Provns), 2006 c 43, s 2, sch 1 para 193

rep in pt—Nat Health Service Reform and Health Care Professions, 2002 c 17, ss
2(5), 37(2), sch 2 pt 2, para 66(1)(3), sch 9 pt 1; Public Audit (W), 2004 c 23,
ss 65(1)(4), 72, sch 4

c 39 **National Minimum Wage**

appl (mods)—Agricultural Wages, 1948 c 47, s 3A; Agricultural Wages (S), 1949 c 30,
s 3A; (NI) SI 1977/2151, art 8A

excl—Agricultural Wages, 1948 c 47, s 17A(1); Agricultural Wages (S), 1949 c 30,
s 17A(1); (NI) SI 1977/2151, art 2A(1)

restr (NI)—Northern Ireland, 1998 c 47, s 98(3)

saved—Scotland, 1998 c 46, s 30, sch 5 pt II, s H1(h)

trans of powers—(W) SI 1999/672, art 2, sch 1

s 1 ext—SI 1999/1128, art 2

s 3 am—SIs 1999/583, reg 2; 2007/2042, reg 2

s 8 rep in pt—SL(R), 2004 c 14, s 1(1), sch 1 pt 8

s 10 appl (mods)—Agric Sector (W), 2014 anaw 6, s 5(1)(2)(a)(3)-(7)

s 11 am—Enterprise and Regulatory Reform, 2013 c 24, sch 2 para 37

appl (mods)—Agric Sector (W), 2014 anaw 6, s 5(1)(2)(c)(3)-(7)

s 11A added —Enterprise and Regulatory Reform, 2013 c 24, sch 2 para 38

s 14 am—Civil Partnership, 2004 c 33, s 261(1), sch 27 para 155; (savings) Employment,
2008 c 24, s 10(1)(3)(4)

rep in pt—(savings) Employment, 2008 c 24, ss 10, 20, sch 1 pt 3

appl (mods)—Agric Sector (W), 2014 anaw 6, s 5(1)(2)(a)(3)-(7)

s 15 am—Finance, 2000 c 17, s 148; Employment Relations, 2004 c 24, s 57(1), sch 1 para
40; Employment, 2008 c 24, s 18(1)

s 16 appl—Employment Relations, 1999 c 26, s 39(2)

rep in pt—(W, S, NI prosp) Enterprise and Regulatory Reform, 2013 c 24, sch 20 para
2

am—Employment Relations, 2004 c 24, s 57(1), sch 1 para 41

s 16A added—Employment Relations, 2004 c 24, s 44

1998
c 39 s 16A *continued*

rep in pt—(W, S, NI prosp) Enterprise and Regulatory Reform, 2013 c 24, sch 20
  para 2
saved—Agricultural Wages, 1948 c 47, s 15A
s 17 am—SI 1999/750, regs 2(3) 3A(3A); (spec retrosp effect and saving) Employment,
  2008 c 24, s 8(1)-(5)(7)(8)
appl (mods)—Agricultural Wages, 1948 c 47, s 3A; Agric Sector (W), 2014 anaw 6, s
  5(1)(2)(c)(3)-(7)
s 19 am—Nat Minimum Wage (Enforcement Notices), 2003 c 8, s 1; Employment Relations,
  2004 c 24, ss 45, 46(2)(4)
subst—(savings) Employment, 2008 c 24, s 9(1)(7)
appl (mods)—Agric Sector (W), 2014 anaw 6, s 5(1)(2)(d)(3)-(7)
ss 19A-19D added—(savings) Employment, 2008 c 24, s 9(1)(2)(7)
s 19A am—SI 2014/547, reg 2(a)(b); Small Business, Enterprise and Employment, 2015 c
  26, s 152(2)(3)(5)
rep in pt—Small Business, Enterprise and Employment, 2015 c 26, s 152(4)
s 19C appl (mods)—Agric Sector (W), 2014 anaw 6, s 5(1)(2)(e)(3)-(7)
s 19D appl (mods)—Agric Sector (W), 2014 anaw 6, s 5(1)(2)(f)(3)-(7)
s 19E added—(savings) Employment, 2008 c 24, s 9(1)(2)(7)
  am—Crime and Cts, 2013 c 22, sch 9 para 52
ss 19F-19H added —(savings) Employment, 2008 c 24, s 9(1)(7)
s 19F appl (mods)—Agric Sector (W), 2014 anaw 6, s 5(1)(2)(g)(3)-(7)
s 19G appl (mods)—Agric Sector (W), 2014 anaw 6, s 5(1)(2)(h)(3)-(7)
s 19H appl (mods)—Agric Sector (W), 2014 anaw 6, s 5(1)(2)(i)(3)-(7)
ss 20-22 rep—(savings) Employment, 2008 c 24, s 9(1)(7)
ss 22A-22F added—Employment Relations, 2004 c 24, s 46(1)
  rep—(savings) Employment, 2008 c 24, s 9(1)(7)
s 23 rep in pt—Employment Relations, 1999 c 26, s 18(4); (saving) (NI) SI 1999/2790,
  arts 20(5), 40, sch 9(3)
appl (mods)—Agric Sector (W), 2014 anaw 6, s 5(1)(2)(j)(3)-(7)
s 24 restr—Employment, 2002 c 22, s 32, sch 4
  am—Enterprise and Regulatory Reform, 2013 c 24, sch 2 para 39
appl (mods)—Agric Sector (W), 2014 anaw 6, s 5(1)(2)(j)(3)-(7)
s 28 appl (mods)—Agric Sector (W), 2014 anaw 6, s 5(1)(2)(k)(3)-(7)
s 31 am—(savings) Employment, 2008 c 24, s 11(1)
appl (mods)—Agric Sector (W), 2014 anaw 6, s 5(1)(2)(l)(3)-(7)
s 33 am—Legal Services, 2007 c 29, s 208, sch 21 paras 124, 125
  rep in pt—Legal Services, 2007 c 29, s 210, sch 23; (savings) Employment, 2008 c 24,
    ss 11, 20, sch 1 pt 4
appl (mods)—Agric Sector (W), 2014 anaw 6, s 5(1)(2)(l)(3)-(7)
s 34 appl—Contracts (Rights of Third Parties), 1999 c 31, s 6(4)(c)
s 35 appl—Contracts (Rights of Third Parties), 1999 c 31, s 6(4)(b)
s 37A added —Employment, 2008 c 24, s 13
s 38 am—Crime and Cts, 2013 c 22, sch 9 para 52
s 39 am—Crime and Cts, 2013 c 22, sch 9 para 52
s 44 am—Employment, 2008 c 24, s 14; SI 2013/1465, sch 1 para 6
s 44A added—Employment Relations, 1999 c 26, s 22
  am—SI 2012/976, sch para 10
s 45 am—(prosp) Legal Aid, Sentencing and Punishment of Offenders, 2012 c 10, s 129(9)
s 45A added—Courts, 2003 c 39, s 109(1), sch 8 para 382
s 45B added—Immigration, Asylum and Nationality, 2006 c 13, s 59(2)
s 46 appl—Agricultural Wages, 1948 c 47, s 17A(2); Agricultural Wages (S), 1949 c 30,
  s 17A(2); (NI) SI 1977/2151, art 2A(2)
rep in pt—(W, S, NI prosp) Enterprise and Regulatory Reform, 2013 c 24, sch 20 para
  2
am—SI 2015/2001 (W 304), art 2(b)
s 47 appl—Agricultural Wages, 1948 c 47, s 17A(2); Agricultural Wages (S), 1949 c 30,
  s 17A(2); (NI) SI 1977/2151, art 2A(2)
rep in pt—(W, S, NI prosp) Enterprise and Regulatory Reform, 2013 c 24, sch 20 para
  2
s 48 appl (mods)—Agric Sector (W), 2014 anaw 6, s 5(1)(2)(m)(3)-(7)
s 49 am—Legal Services, 2007 c 29, s 208, sch 21 paras 124, 126; Enterprise and
  Regulatory Reform, 2013 c 24, s 23(3)(a)(b); ibid, sch 1 para 11; SI 2014/431,
  sch para 5

1998

c 39 s 49 *continued*

appl (mods)—Agric Sector (W), 2014 anaw 6, s 5(1)(2)(n)(3)-(7)

s 51 rep in pt—(savings) Employment, 2008 c 24, ss 9, 20, sch 1 pt 2

s 54 appl—Contracts (Rights of Third Parties), 1999 c 31, s 6(4)(a)

s 55 rep in pt—(W, S, NI prosp) Enterprise and Regulatory Reform, 2013 c 24, sch 20 para 2

sch 1 am—SI 2012/2404, sch 2 para 40

sch 2 rep in pt—SL(R), 2004 c 14, s 1(1), sch 1 pt 8; SI 2004/2178, reg 2(1), sch pt I; SSI 2004/384, reg 3, sch; (W, S, NI prosp) Enterprise and Regulatory Reform, 2013 c 24, sch 20 para 2

c 40 **Criminal Justice (Terrorism and Conspiracy)**

ss 1-3 rep—Terrorism, 2000 c 11, s 125(2), sch 16 pt I

s 4 rep—(subject to provns for cont in force) Terrorism, 2000 c 11, ss 2(2), 125(2), sch 1 paras 1(1)(c), 2-5, sch 16 pt I

s 8 rep—Crim Justice and Immigration, 2008 c 4, ss 62(1), 149, sch 28 pt 4; (S) Crim Justice and Licensing (S), 2010 asp 13, s 199

sch 1 rep in pt—Terrorism, 2000 c 11, s 125(2), sch 16 pt I; (prosp) (S) Sexual Offences (S), 2009 asp 9, s 61, sch 6

c 41 **Competition**

appl—Company Directors Disqualification 1986 c 46, s 9A(4)(a)(b)

power to mod—Enterprise, 2002 c 40, s 209(1)(2)(5)-(8)

saved—Communications, 2003 c 21, s 392(1)(6); Wireless Telegraphy, 2006 c 36, s 111(3)(6)(j)

Pt 1 (ss 1-60) cert functions made exercisable concurrently—Telecommunications, 1984 c 12, s 50(3); Financial Services and Markets, 2000 c 8, s 234J; Civil Aviation, 2012 c 19, s 62(1)-(3); Financial Services (Banking Reform), 2013 c 33, s 61(2)

mod—Health and Social Care, 2012 c 7, s 72(3)

am—(except in ss 38(pt),51) Transport, 2000 c 38, ss 86(1)(3)(7),89, 105(2)(d)(5); (except in ss 38(pt),51,52(pt),54) ibid, ss 86(4)(b)(5), 105(2)(d)(5)

appl—Enterprise, 2002 c 40, ss 16(6), 188(7), 209(3)

ext—(except ss 38(pt), 51) Communications, 2003 c 21, ss 371, 406(6), 408, sch 18 para 57; SI 2003/1900, arts 2(1), 3(1), sch 1; SI 2003/3142, art 3(2)

s 1 excl—SIs 2007/1896, art 4; 2008/1820, art 4

s 2 excl—Financial Services and Markets, 2000 c 8, ss 164(1)(2)(4), 311(9); SIs 2007/1896, art 4; 2008/1820, art 4; 2012/710, art 4

s 3 rep in pt—Enterprise, 2002 c 40, ss 207, 276(1), 278(2), sch 24, para 20(1)(b)(2)-(4), sch 26

am—Enterprise, 2002 c 40, s 278(1), sch 25, para 38(1)(2)

excl—SIs 2007/1896, art 4; 2008/1820, art 4

appl—Transport, 2000 c 38, sch 10

ss 4, 5 rep—SI 2004/1261, regs 4, 6(1)-(3), sch 1 para 3

s 6 am—Enterprise, 2002 c 40, s 278(1), sch 25, para 38(1)(5); SI 2004/1261, reg 4, sch 1 para 4; Enterprise and Regulatory Reform, 2013 c 24, sch 5 para 2

excl—SIs 2007/1896, art 4; 2008/1820, art 4

appl—Transport, 2000 c 38, sch 10

s 7 am—Enterprise, 2002 c 40, s 278(1), sch 25, para 38(1)(6)

rep in pt—SI 2004/1261, regs 4, 6(1)(2), sch 1 para 5

excl—SIs 2007/1896, art 4; 2008/1820, art 4

s 8 am—Enterprise, 2002 c 40, s 278(1), sch 25, para 38(1)(7); Enterprise and Regulatory Reform, 2013 c 24, sch 5 para 3

excl—SIs 2007/1896, art 4; 2008/1820, art 4

appl—Transport, 2000 c 38, sch 10

s 9 am—SI 2004/1261, reg 4, sch 1 para 6

excl—SIs 2007/1896, art 4; 2008/1820, art 4

s 10 am—Enterprise, 2002 c 40, s 278(1), sch 25, para 38(1)(8); SIs 2004/1261, regs 4, 7, sch 1 para 7(1)-(4); 2012/1809, art 3(1), sch pt 1; Enterprise and Regulatory Reform, 2013 c 24, sch 5 para 4

excl—SIs 2007/1896, art 4; 2008/1820, art 4

appl—Transport, 2000 c 38, sch 10

s 11 am—SIs 2004/1261, reg 4, sch 1 para 8; 2012/1809, art 3(1), sch pt 1

excl—SIs 2007/1896, art 4; 2008/1820, art 4

appl—Transport, 2000 c 38, sch 10

ss 12-16 rep—SI 2004/1261, regs 4, 6(1)(2), 9, sch 1 para 9

1998
c 41 *continued*

s 17 excl—SI 2007/1896, art 4
s 18 excl—Financial Services and Markets, 2000 c 8, ss 164(3)(5), 312; SI 2007/1896, art 4
s 19 excl—SI 2007/1896, art 4
ss 20-24 rep—SI 2004/1261, regs 4, 6(1)(2), sch 1 para 9
s 25 subst—SI 2004/1261, reg 4, sch 1 para 10
    appl—Transport, 2000 c 38, sch 10
    am—SI 2012/1809, art 3(1), sch pt 1; Enterprise and Regulatory Reform, 2013 c 24,
      sch 5 para 5(2)(3)
s 25A added —Enterprise and Regulatory Reform, 2013 c 24, s 42(2)
s 26 am—Enterprise, 2002 c 40, s 278(1), sch 25, para 38(1)(20); Enterprise and
      Regulatory Reform, 2013 c 24, s 39(3); ibid, sch 5 paras 6, 9
    rep in pt—SI 2004/1261, regs 4, 6(1)(2), sch 1 para 11
    appl—Company Directors Disqualification 1986 c 46, s 9C(2); Transport, 2000 c 38,
      sch 10
s 26A added —Enterprise and Regulatory Reform, 2013 c 24, s 39(2)
s 27 am —Crim Justice and Police, 2001 c 16, s 70, sch 2 pt 2 para 21; Enterprise, 2002 c
      40, s 278(1), sch 25, para 38(1)(21); SI 2004/1261, reg 4, sch 1 para
      12(1)(2)(a)(3)-(6); Enterprise and Regulatory Reform, 2013 c 24, sch 5 para 7
    rep in pt—SI 2004/1261, regs 4, 6(1)(2), sch 1 para 12(1)(2)(b)
    appl—Company Directors Disqualification 1986 c 46, s 9C(2); Transport, 2000 c 38,
      sch 10
s 28 ext—Crim Justice and Police, 2001 c 16, s 50, sch 1 pt 1 para 67
    am—Crim Justice and Police, 2001 c 16, s 70, sch 2 pt 2 para 21; Enterprise, 2002 c 40,
      ss 203(1)(2), 278(1), sch 25, para 38(1)(22); SI 2004/1261, reg 4, sch 1 para 13;
      Enterprise and Regulatory Reform, 2013 c 24, sch 5 para 8(2)(3)(a)(b); ibid, sch
      13 para 2(2)-(4)
    appl—Company Directors Disqualification 1986 c 46, s 9C(2); Transport, 2000 c 38,
      sch 10
s 28A added—SI 2004/1261, reg 4, sch 1 para 14
    appl—Transport, 2000 c 38, sch 10
    am—Enterprise and Regulatory Reform, 2013 c 24, sch 5 para 9; ibid, sch 13 para
      3(2)-(4)
s 29 am—SI 2004/1261, reg 4, sch 1 para 15
    appl—Company Directors Disqualification 1986 c 46, s 9C(2); Transport, 2000 c 38,
      sch 10
s 30 appl—Company Directors Disqualification 1986 c 46, s 9C(2); Transport, 2000 c 38,
      sch 10
s 30A added—Enterprise, 2002 c 40, s 198
    am—SI 2004/1261, reg 4, sch 1 para 16; Enterprise and Regulatory Reform, 2013 c
      24, s 39(5)-(7)
    appl—Transport, 2000 c 38, sch 10
s 31 subst—SI 2004/1261, reg 4, sch 1 para 17
    am—SI 2012/1809, art 3(1), sch pt 1; Enterprise and Regulatory Reform, 2013 c 24,
      sch 5 para 10
    appl—Transport, 2000 c 38, sch 10
ss 31A-31E added—SI 2004/1261, reg 4, sch 1 para 18
    appl—Transport, 2000 c 38, sch 10
s 31A am—Enterprise and Regulatory Reform, 2013 c 24, sch 5 para 11
s 31B am—Enterprise and Regulatory Reform, 2013 c 24, sch 5 para 12
s 31C am—Enterprise and Regulatory Reform, 2013 c 24, sch 5 para 13
s 31D am—Enterprise and Regulatory Reform, 2013 c 24, sch 5 para 14
s 31E am—Enterprise and Regulatory Reform, 2013 c 24, sch 5 para 15
s 31F added —Enterprise and Regulatory Reform, 2013 c 24, s 45
s 32 am—Enterprise, 2002 c 40, s 278(1), sch 25, para 38(1)(24); SIs 2004/1261, reg 4, sch
      1 para 19(1)(2); 2012/1809, art 3(1), sch pt 1; Enterprise and Regulatory Reform,
      2013 c 24, sch 5 para 16
    rep in pt—SI 2004/1261, regs 4, 6(1)(2), sch 1 para 19(1)(3)
    appl—Transport, 2000 c 38, sch 10
    mod—(prosp) Water Industry, 1991 c 56, s 40(5)(a)(7)(a) (subst by Water, 2014 c 21,
      s 8(1)); (prosp) ibid, ss 110A(7)(a), 110B(5)(a) (subst by Water, 2014 c 21, s
      9(1)); (prosp) ibid, ss 51B(9)(a), 51C(4)(a) (subst by Water, 2014 c 21, s 10(3));
      (prosp) ibid, ss 105ZA(9)(a), 105ZB(4)(a) (added by Water, 2014 c 21, s 11(3));

1998

c 41 s 32 *continued*

(prosp) ibid, s 66D(7)(a) (subst by Water, 2014 c 21, sch 2 para 3); (prosp) ibid, s 117E(7)(a) (added by Water, 2014 c 21, sch 4)

s 33 am—Enterprise, 2002 c 40, s 278(1), sch 25, para 38(1)(25); SIs 2004/1261, reg 4, sch 1 para 20(1)(2); 2012/1809, art 3(1), sch pt 1; Enterprise and Regulatory Reform, 2013 c 24, sch 5 para 17

rep in pt—SI 2004/1261, regs 4, 6(1)(2), sch 1 para 20(1)(3)

appl—Transport, 2000 c 38, sch 10

s 34 am—Enterprise, 2002 c 40, s 278(1), sch 25, para 38(1)(26); Enterprise and Regulatory Reform, 2013 c 24, sch 5 para 18

appl—Transport, 2000 c 38, sch 10

s 35 am—Enterprise, 2002 c 40, s 278(1), sch 25, para 38(1)(27); SIs 2004/1261, reg 4, sch 1 para 21; 2012/1809, art 3(1), sch pt 1; Enterprise and Regulatory Reform, 2013 c 24, s 43; ibid, sch 5 para 19

appl—Transport, 2000 c 38, sch 10

mod—(prosp) Water Industry, 1991 c 56, ss 40(7)(b), 40A(5)(b) (subst by Water, 2014 c 21, s 8(1)); (prosp) ibid, ss 110A(7)(b)(8), 110B(5)(b) (subst by Water, 2014 c 21, s 9(1)); (prosp) ibid, ss 51B(9)(b), 51C(4)(b) (subst by Water, 2014 c 21, s 10(3)); (prosp) ibid, ss 105ZA(9)(b), 105ZB(4)(b) (added by Water, 2014 c 21, s 11(3)); (prosp) ibid, s 117E(7)(b) (added by Water, 2014 c 21, sch 4)

s 36 am—Enterprise, 2002 c 40, s 278(1), sch 25, para 38(1)(28); SIs 2004/1261, reg 4, sch 1 para 22; 2012/1809, art 3(1), sch pt 1; Enterprise and Regulatory Reform, 2013 c 24, s 44(2); ibid, sch 5 para 20

s 37 am—Enterprise, 2002 c 40, s 278(1), sch 25, para 38(1)(29); Enterprise and Regulatory Reform, 2013 c 24, sch 5 para 21

s 38 am—Enterprise, 2002 c 40, s 278(1), sch 25, para 38(1)(30); SI 2004/1261, reg 4, sch 1 para 23; Constitutional Reform, 2005 c 4, s 40(4), sch 9 pt 1 para 65(1)(2); Enterprise and Regulatory Reform, 2013 c 24, ss 40(4)-(6), 44(3); ibid, sch 5 para 22; ibid, sch 15 para 10

s 39 am—Enterprise, 2002 c 40, s 278(1), sch 25, para 38(1)(31); SI 2004/1261, reg 4, sch 1 para 24; Enterprise and Regulatory Reform, 2013 c 24, sch 5 para 23

s 40 am—Enterprise, 2002 c 40, s 278(1), sch 25, para 38(1)(32); SI 2004/1261, reg 4, sch 1 para 25; Enterprise and Regulatory Reform, 2013 c 24, sch 5 para 24

appl—Transport, 2000 c 38, sch 10

ss 40A, 40B added —Enterprise and Regulatory Reform, 2013 c 24, s 40(2)

s 41 rep—SI 2004/1261, regs 4, 6(1)(2), sch 1 para 26

s 42 am—SI 2004/1261, reg 4, sch 1 para 27

appl—Transport, 2000 c 38, sch 10

rep in pt—Enterprise and Regulatory Reform, 2013 c 24, s 40(8)(9)

s 43 am—SI 2004/1261, reg 4, sch 1 para 28

appl—Transport, 2000 c 38, sch 10

s 44 appl—Financial Services and Markets, 2000 c 8, s 399; Transport, 2000 c 38, sch 10

am—Enterprise, 2002 c 40, s 278(1), sch 25, para 38(1)(34); Enterprise and Regulatory Reform, 2013 c 24, sch 5 para 25

Pt 1 Ch 4 (ss 45-49) rep in pt—Enterprise and Regulatory Reform, 2013 c 24, sch 5 para 219

am—Consumer Rights, 2015 c 15, sch 8 para 2

s 45 am—Enterprise, 2002 c 40, ss 187(1), 278(1), sch 25, para 38(1)(35)

rep—Enterprise and Regulatory Reform, 2013 c 24, sch 5 para 220

appl—Transport, 2000 c 38, sch 10

savings—SI 2014/892, art 3(7)

s 46 am—Enterprise, 2002 c 40, ss 21, 278(1), sch 5, paras 1, 2(a)(b), sch 25, para 38(1)(36); SIs 2004/1261, regs 4, 8(1)-(3)(a), sch 1 para 29; 2012/1809, art 3(1), sch pt 1; Enterprise and Regulatory Reform, 2013 c 24, sch 5 para 26; Consumer Rights, 2015 c 15, sch 8 para 3

rep in pt—Enterprise, 2002 c 40, ss 21, 278(2), sch 5, paras 1, 2(c), sch 26

appl—Transport, 2000 c 38, sch 10

s 47 subst—Enterprise, 2002 c 40, s 17

am—SIs 2003/767, art 4; 2004/1261, regs 4, 8(1)(3)(a), sch 1 para 30; 2007/1846, reg 3, sch; Enterprise and Regulatory Reform, 2013 c 24, sch 5 para 27

appl—Transport, 2000 c 38, sch 10

s 47A added—Enterprise, 2002 c 40, s 18

subst—Consumer Rights, 2015 c 15, sch 8 para 4(1)

savings—SI 2015/1648, rule 119(4)

1998

c 41 s 47A *continued*

    appl—Transport, 2000 c 38, sch 10

s 47B added—Enterprise, 2002 c 40, s 19
    subst—Consumer Rights, 2015 c 15, sch 8 para 5(1)
    appl—Transport, 2000 c 38, sch 10

s 47C added—Consumer Rights, 2015 c 15, sch 8 para 6

s 47D added—Consumer Rights, 2015 c 15, sch 8 para 7

s 47E added—Consumer Rights, 2015 c 15, sch 8 para 8(1)

s 48 rep—Enterprise, 2002 c 40, ss 21, 278(2), sch 5, paras 1, 3, sch 26

s 49 subst—Enterprise, 2002 c 40, s 21, sch 5, paras 1, 4
    appl—Transport, 2000 c 38, sch 10
    am—Consumer Rights, 2015 c 15, sch 8 para 9(2)(a),(3)-(5)
    rep in pt—Consumer Rights, 2015 c 15, sch 8 para 9(2)(b)

s 49A added—Consumer Rights, 2015 c 15, sch 8 para 10(1)

s 49B added—Consumer Rights, 2015 c 15, sch 8 para 11(1)

ss 49C-49E added—Consumer Rights, 2015 c 15, sch 8 para 12

s 50 am—Enterprise, 2002 c 40, s 278(1), sch 25, para 38(1)(37); Enterprise and
      Regulatory Reform, 2013 c 24, sch 5 para 29
    appl—Transport, 2000 c 38, sch 10

s 51 am—Enterprise, 2002 c 40, s 278(1), sch 25, para 38(1)(38); Enterprise and
      Regulatory Reform, 2013 c 24, sch 5 paras 30, 31(2)-(4)
    appl—Transport, 2000 c 38, sch 10

s 52 am—Enterprise, 2002 c 40, s 278(1), sch 25, para 38(1)(39); SIs 2004/1261, reg 4, sch
      1 para 31; 2012/1809, art 3(1), sch pt 1; Enterprise and Regulatory Reform, 2013
      c 24, sch 5 para 32(2)-(4)
    appl—Transport, 2000 c 38, sch 10

s 53 rep—SI 2004/1261, regs 4, 6(1)(2), sch 1 para 32

s 54 am—Transport, 2000 c 38, s 97, sch 8 pt IV para 14; Enterprise, 2002 c 40, s 278(1),
      sch 25, para 38(1)(41); Railways and Transport Safety, 2003 c 20, s 16, sch 2 pt
      2 para 19(p); Communications, 2003 c 21, s 371(5)(a)(b); SI 2003/1900, arts
      2(1), 3(1), sch 1; SI 2003/3142, art 3(2); Water, 2003 c 37, s 101(1), sch 7 pt 2
      para 32(1)(2); SI 2004/1261, reg 4, sch 1 para 33; Health and Social Care, 2012
      c 7, s 74(5)(b); Enterprise and Regulatory Reform, 2013 c 24, s 51(2)(a)(b)(3)(4);
      ibid, sch 5 para 33; ibid, sch 15 para 11(b); Financial Services (Banking Reform),
      2013 c 33, s 67(2); ibid, sch 8 para 9; SI 2015/1682, sch pt 1 para 4(m)
    rep in pt—Enterprise and Regulatory Reform, 2013 c 24, sch 15 para 11(a)
    appl—Enterprise, 2002 c 40, s 205(3)

ss 55, 56 rep—Enterprise, 2002 c 40, ss 247(j), 278(2), sch 26

s 57 am—Enterprise, 2002 c 40, s 278(1), sch 25, para 38(1)(42); Enterprise and
      Regulatory Reform, 2013 c 24, sch 5 para 34
    appl—Transport, 2000 c 38, sch 10

s 58 am—Enterprise, 2002 c 40, ss 21, 278(1), sch 5, paras 1, 5, sch 25, para 38(1)(43); SIs
      2004/1261, reg 4, sch 1 para 34(1)(3)(a)-(c); 2012/1809, art 3(1), sch pt 1;
      Enterprise and Regulatory Reform, 2013 c 24, sch 5 paras 35,
      36(2)(3)(a)(b)(4)(5); Consumer Rights, 2015 c 15, sch 8 para 13(2)-(5)
    rep in pt—SI 2004/1261, regs 4, 6(1)(2), sch 1 para 34(1)(2)
    appl—Transport, 2000 c 38, sch 10

s 58A added—Enterprise, 2002 c 40, s 20(1)(2)
    subst—Consumer Rights, 2015 c 15, sch 8 para 14(1)
    appl—Transport, 2000 c 38, sch 10

s 59 am—Enterprise, 2002 c 40, ss 20(1)(3), 21, 278(1), sch 5, paras 1, 6(b), sch 25, para
      38(1)(44)(a)(b); Communications, 2003 c 21, s 371(7); SI 2003/1900, arts 2(1),
      3(1), sch 1; SI 2003/3142, art 3(2); SIs 2004/1261, reg 4, sch 1 para
      35(1)(2)(a)-(d)(f)(h)(3); 2012/1809, art 3(1), sch pt 1; Enterprise and Regulatory
      Reform, 2013 c 24, sch 5 para 38(2)(a)(3); Consumer Rights, 2015 c 15, sch 8
      para 15(2)-(4)
    rep in pt—Enterprise, 2002 c 40, ss 21, 278(2), sch 5, paras 1, 6(a), sch 25, para
        38(1)(44), sch 26; SI 2004/1261, regs 4, 6(1)(2), sch 1 para 35(1)(2)(e);
        Enterprise and Regulatory Reform, 2013 c 24, sch 5 paras 38(2)(b), 221
    appl—Transport, 2000 c 38, sch 10

s 60 appl—Company Directors Disqualification 1986 c 46, s 9A(11); Transport, 2000 c 38,
      sch 10
    am—Enterprise, 2002 c 40, s 278(1), sch 25, para 38(1)(45); Enterprise and
      Regulatory Reform, 2013 c 24, sch 5 para 39

1998
c 41 *continued*

Pt 2 (ss 61-65) am—SI 2004/1261, reg 4, sch 1 para 36
s 61 subst—SI 2004/1261, reg 4, sch 1 para 36
    rep in pt—Enterprise and Regulatory Reform, 2013 c 24, sch 5 para 40(b)
    am—SI 2012/1809, art 3(1), sch pt 1; Enterprise and Regulatory Reform, 2013 c 24,
        sch 5 para 40(a); ibid, sch 13 para 4
    appl—Transport, 2000 c 38, sch 10
s 62 am—Enterprise, 2002 c 40, ss 203(1)(3), 278(1), sch 25, para 38(1)(47); SI
        2004/1261, reg 4, sch 1 para 37(1),(2)(a)(b)(c)(ii),(4)(a)(c)(d), (5)(a)(c)(i)(iii),
        (6)-(8); Enterprise and Regulatory Reform, 2013 c 24, sch 5 para 41; ibid, sch 13
        para 5(2)(3)
    rep in pt—SI 2004/1261, regs 4, 6(1)(2), sch 1 para 37(1),(3)(c)(i),(4)(b),(5)(b)(c)(ii)
    appl—Transport, 2000 c 38, sch 10
s 62A added—SI 2004/1261, reg 4, sch 1 para 38
    am—SI 2012/1809, art 3(1), sch pt 1; Enterprise and Regulatory Reform, 2013 c 24,
        sch 5 para 42; ibid, sch 13 para 6(2)(3)
    appl—Transport, 2000 c 38, sch 10
s 62B added—SI 2004/1261, reg 4, sch 1 para 39
    am—Enterprise and Regulatory Reform, 2013 c 24, sch 5 para 43
    appl—Transport, 2000 c 38, sch 10
s 63 am—Enterprise, 2002 c 40, ss 203(1)(4), 278(1), sch 25, para 38(1)(48); SI
        2004/1261, reg 4, sch 1 para 40(1)-(3)(b)(c)(ii),(4)(a)(b)(ii),(5)(a)(b)(ii), (6)-(9);
        Enterprise and Regulatory Reform, 2013 c 24, sch 5 para 44; ibid, sch 13 para
        7(2)(3)
    rep in pt—SI 2004/1261, regs 4, 6(1)(2), sch 1 para 40(1),(3)(c)(i),(4)(b)(i),(5)(b)(i)
    appl—Transport, 2000 c 38, sch 10
s 64 am—SI 2004/1261, reg 4, sch 1 para 41(1)-(4)
    appl—Transport, 2000 c 38, sch 10
s 65 am—SI 2004/1261, reg 4, sch 1 para 42
    appl—Transport, 2000 c 38, sch 10
ss 65A, 65B added—SI 2004/1261, reg 4, sch 1 para 43
    appl—Transport, 2000 c 38, sch 10
Pt 2A (ss 65C-65N) added—SI 2004/1261, reg 4, sch 1 para 44
    appl—Transport, 2000 c 38, sch 10
s 65C am—SI 2012/1809, art 3(1), sch pt 1; Enterprise and Regulatory Reform, 2013 c 24,
        sch 5 para 45(2)(3)(a)(4); ibid, sch 13 para 8
    rep in pt—Enterprise and Regulatory Reform, 2013 c 24, sch 5 para 45(3)(b)
s 65D am—SI 2012/1809, art 3(1), sch pt 1; Enterprise and Regulatory Reform, 2013 c 24,
        sch 5 para 46
s 65E am—Enterprise and Regulatory Reform, 2013 c 24, sch 5 para 47
s 65F am—Enterprise and Regulatory Reform, 2013 c 24, sch 5 para 48
s 65G am—Enterprise and Regulatory Reform, 2013 c 24, sch 5 para 49; ibid, sch 13 para
        9(2)-(4)
s 65H am—Enterprise and Regulatory Reform, 2013 c 24, sch 5 para 50; ibid, sch 13 para
        10(2)-(4)
s 65N am—Enterprise and Regulatory Reform, 2013 c 24, sch 5 para 51
ss 66, 67 rep—Enterprise, 2002 c 40, s 278(2), sch 26
ss 68-70 appl—Transport, 2000 c 38, sch 10
s 71 am—Enterprise, 2002 c 40, s 278(1), sch 25, para 38(1)(49); Consumer Rights, 2015 c
        15, sch 8 para 16
    appl—Transport, 2000 c 38, sch 10
s 72 am—SI 2004/1261, reg 4, sch 1 para 45
    appl—Transport, 2000 c 38, sch 10
s 73 am—SI 2004/1261, reg 4, sch 1 para 46(1)-(4)(6)
    rep in pt—SI 2004/1261, reg 4, sch 1 para 46(5)
    appl—Transport, 2000 c 38, sch 10
ss 74, 75 appl—Transport, 2000 c 38, sch 10
s 75A added—SI 2004/1261, reg 4, sch 1 para 47
    appl—Transport, 2000 c 38, sch 10
    am—Enterprise and Regulatory Reform, 2013 c 24, sch 5 para 52
s 76 appl—Transport, 2000 c 38, sch 10
ss 97, 98 mod—Loc Govt Finance, 1992 c 14, s 52V(3)
sch 1 ext—SI 2000/310, art 7

1998

c 41 sch 1 *continued*

am—Enterprise, 2002 c 40, s 278(1), sch 25, para 38(1)(50)(a)-(d); SI 2003/1592, art 16, sch 4 para 15(1); SI 2004/1261, reg 4, sch 1 para 48(1)(2)(a); SI 2004/1079, reg 2, sch para 1; Enterprise and Regulatory Reform, 2013 c 24, sch 5 para 53(2)(3); ibid, sch 15 para 12(2)(b)

rep in pt—Communications, 2003 c 21, s 406(7), sch 19(1); SI 2004/1261, regs 4, 6(1)(2), sch 1 para 48(1)(2)(b); Enterprise and Regulatory Reform, 2013 c 24, sch 15 para 12(2)(a)

sch 2 am—Communications, 2003 c 21, ss 291(3)(4), 371(6), 408; Enterprise and Regulatory Reform, 2013 c 24, sch 5 para 54

rep in pt—SI 2004/1261, regs 4, 6(1)(2), sch 1 para 49(1)(2); Companies (Audit, Investigations and Community Enterprise), 2004 c 27, s 64, sch 8; SI 2004/1261, regs 4, 6(1)(2), sch 1 para 49(1)(3); Financial Services, 2012 c 21, sch 19

sch 3 am—Enterprise, 2002 c 40, s 278(1), sch 25, para 38(1)(51)(a)(b); SIs 2004/1261, reg 4, sch 1 para 50(b)(i)-(iii); 2007/126, reg 3, sch 6; 2012/1809, art 3(1), sch pt 1; Enterprise and Regulatory Reform, 2013 c 24, sch 5 para 55(2)

rep in pt—SI 2004/1261, regs 4, 6(1)(2), sch 1 para 50(a)

sch 4 rep—Enterprise, 2002 c 40, ss 207, 276(1), 278(2), sch 24, para 20, sch 26

schs 5, 6 rep—SI 2004/1261, regs 4, 6(1)(2), sch 1 para 51

sch 6A added—SI 2004/1261, reg 4, sch 1 para 52

am—Enterprise and Regulatory Reform, 2013 c 24, sch 5 para 56(2)(3)(a)(b)(i)(ii)(4)-(14)

sch 7 rep —Enterprise and Regulatory Reform, 2013 c 24, sch 5 para 222

sch 7A added—Enterprise, 2002 c 40, s 187(4), sch 12

rep —Enterprise and Regulatory Reform, 2013 c 24, sch 5 para 223

sch 8 am—Enterprise, 2002 c 40, ss 21, 278(1), sch 5, paras 1, 8(1)(3)(4), sch 25, para 38(1)(54)(a)-(c); SI 2004/1261, regs 4, 8(1)-(3)(a), sch 1 para 53(1)(2)(4); Enterprise and Regulatory Reform, 2013 c 24, sch 5 para 57(2)-(4); Consumer Rights, 2015 c 15, sch 8 para 17

rep in pt—Enterprise, 2002 c 40, ss 21, 278(2), sch 5, paras 1, 8(1)(2), sch 26; SI 2004/1261, regs 4, 8(1)-(3), sch 1 para 53(3)

sch 9 am—Enterprise, 2002 c 40, s 278(1), sch 25, para 38(1)(55); SIs 2004/1261, reg 4, sch 1 para 54(1)-(5)(7)(9); 2012/1809, art 3(1), sch pt 1; Enterprise and Regulatory Reform, 2013 c 24, s 42(4)-(7); ibid, sch 5 para 58(2)-(7)(8)(a)(b)(9)(a)(b)(10)

rep in pt—SI 2004/1261, regs 4, 6(1)(2), 10, sch 1 para 54(1)(6)(8)

sch 10 rep in pt—Utilities, 2000 c 27, s 108, sch 8; Transport, 2000 c 38, s 274, sch 31 pt IV; Enterprise, 2002 c 40, s 278(2), sch 26; Communications, 2003 c 21, s 406(7), sch 19(1); SI 2003/1900, arts 2(1), 3(1), sch 1; SI 2003/3142, art 3(2); Water, 2003 c 37, s 101, sch 7 pt 2 para 32(1)(4)(b), sch 9 pt 3; ibid, s 101, sch 7 pt 2 para 32(1)(4)(a), sch 9 pt 3; SI 2003/1398, art 2, sch para 32(1)(2)

am—Railways and Transport Safety, 2003 c 20, s 16, sch 2 pt 2 para 19(p)

sch 11 rep—Enterprise, 2002 c 40, ss 247(j), 278(2), sch 26

am—Railways and Transport Safety, 2003 c 20, s 16, sch 2 pt 2 para 19(p)

sch 12 rep in pt—Enterprise, 2002 c 40, s 278(2), sch 26; SI 2003/1398, art 2, sch para 32(1)(3); SI 2003/3180, arts 2, 3, sch para 6; Communications, 2003 c 21, s 406(7), sch 19(1); Financial Services, 2012 c 21, sch 19

sch 13 am—Transport, 2000 c 38, s 97, sch 8 pt IV para 16(2)(3); SI 2000/311, art 2; 2000/2031, art 2; Water, 2003 c 37, s 101(1), sch 7 pt 2 para 32(1)(5); Constitutional Reform, 2005 c 4, s 40(4), sch 9 pt 1 para 65(1)(5)

ext—Communications, 2003 c 21, ss 371(8), 406(6), 408, sch 18 para 57; SI 2003/1900, arts 2(1), 3(1), sch 1; SI 2003/3142, art 3(2)

rep in pt—Communications, 2003 c 21, s 406(7), sch 19(1); SI 2003/1900, arts 2(1), 3(1), sch 1; SI 2003/3142, art 3(2); Financial Services, 2012 c 21, sch 19

c 42   **Human Rights**

appl—Govt of Wales, 1998 c 38, s 107(5); Scotland, 1998 c 46, s 126(1); Northern Ireland, 1998 c 47, ss 71(5), 98(1); Terrorism, 2000 c 11, sch 4 pt I para 11E, pt II para 25E, pt III para 41E; Proceeds of Crime, 2002 c 29, s 266(3)(b); Nationality, Immigration and Asylum, 2002 c 41, s 55(5)(a); Extradition, 2003 c 41, ss 21(1), 87(1); SIs 2005/930, reg 3(c); 2005/2795, rule 116(8); 2005/3181, arts 21(4), 68(4), 177(4)(b); (S) SSI 2005/581, art 15(4)

1998

c 42 *continued*

saved—Scotland, 1998 c 46, ss 29, 53(4), sch 4 pt I paras 1(2)(f), 9; Civil Contingencies, 2004 c 36, s 23(5)(b); Govt of Wales, 2006 c 32, s 94, sch 5 para 3; Statistics and Registration Service, 2007 c 18, s 54

cert functs trans—SI 2001/3500, arts 3, 4(1)(c)(3)-(8), sch 1 para 5; (except ss 5, 10, 18, 19, sch 4) SI 2003/1887, art 4, sch 1

ext —Civil Contingencies, 2004 c 36, s 30(2)

s 1 appl—Financial Services and Markets, 2000 c 8, s 300(5); Civil Contingencies, 2004 c 36, s 20(5)(b)(vi)

am—SI 2001/3500, art 8, sch 2 pt I para 7(a); SI 2003/1887, art 9, sch 2 para 10(1); SI 2004/1574, art 2(1)

s 2 rep in pt—SI 2003/1887, art 9, sch 2 para 10(2)

am—SI 2005/3429, arts 3(2), 5, 8, sch para 3

s 4 am—Constitutional Reform, 2005 c 4, s 40(4), sch 9 pt 1 para 66(1)-(3); Mental Capacity, 2005 c 9, s 67(1), sch 6 para 43; Crime and Cts, 2013 c 22, sch 14 para 5(5)

s 5 cert functs made exercisable concurrently—SI 2000/1830, art 2

am—Constitutional Reform, 2005 c 4, s 40(4), sch 9 pt 1 para 66(1)-(3); Armed Forces, 2006 c 52, s 378, sch 16 para 157

s 6 appl—Immigration and Asylum, 1999 c 33, s 65(2); Enterprise, 2002 c 40, s 238(3); Anti-social Behaviour, 2003 c 38, s 9(3)(b); Pensions, 2004 c 35, ss 83(2)(c)(ii), 87(2)(a)(ii), 201(2)(a)(ii); Care, 2014 c 23, s 73(2)(3)

excl—Infrastructure, 2015 c 7, s 8(3)(b)

rep in pt—Constitutional Reform, 2005 c 4, ss 40(4), 146, sch 9 pt 1 para 66(1)(4), sch 18 pt 5

s 7 mod—Terrorism, 2000 c 11, s 9

am—Regulation of Investigatory Powers, 2000 c 23, s 65(2)(a); SI 2005/3429, arts 3(2), 5, 8, sch para 3

power exercised—(S) SSI 2000/301, rule 3

excl—(S) SSI 2000/301, rule 4(2)

rep in pt—SI 2003/1887, art 9, sch 2 para 10(2)

appl—Prevention of Terrorism, 2005 c 2, s 11(2)

s 8 saving—(prosp) SI 2007/1351, art 57

s 9 power exercised—(S) SSI 2000/301, rule 4(1)

am—Justice (NI), 2002 c 26, s 10(6), sch 4, para 39

s 14 am—SI 2001/3500, art 8, sch 2 pt I para 7(b); SI 2003/1887, art 9, sch 2 para 10(1)

rep in pt—SI 2001/1216, art 2

appl—Prevention of Terrorism, 2005 c 2, s 1(10)

s 15 am—SI 2001/3500, art 8, sch 2 pt I para 7(c); SI 2003/1887, art 9, sch 2 para 10(1)

s 16 am—SI 2001/3500, art 8, sch 2 pt I para 7(d); SI 2003/1887, art 9, sch 2 para 10(1)

rep in pt—SI 2001/1216, art 3

s 18 am—Constitutional Reform, 2005 c 4, ss 15(1), 59(5), sch 4 pt 1 para 278, sch 11 pt 2 para 4

s 20 rep in pt—SI 2003/1887, art 9, sch 2 para 10(2)

am—SI 2005/3429, art 8, sch para 3

s 21 am—SI 2004/1574, art 2(2); Govt of Wales, 2006 c 32, s 160, sch 10 para 56

rep in pt—SI 2004/1574, art 2(2); Armed Forces, 2006 c 52, s 378, sch 17

s 22 rep in pt—Armed Forces, 2006 c 52, s 378, sch 17

sch 1 am—SI 2004/1574, art 2(3)

sch 2 am—SI 2000/2040, art 2, sch pt I para 21

sch 3 am—SI 2001/4032, art 2

rep in pt—SIs 2001/1216, art 4; 2005/1071, art 2

sch 4 am—Public Service Pensions, 2013 c 25, sch 8 para 26

c 43 **Statute Law (Repeals)**

sch 2 rep in pt—Courts, 2003 c 39, s 109(3), sch 10; Deregulation, 2015 c 20, sch 23 para 32(4)

c 44 **Waste Minimisation**

c 45 **Regional Development Agencies**

rep (pt prosp in respect of ss 14, 15,17)—Public Bodies, 2011 c 24, s 30, sch 6

ss 14, 15, 17 trans of functions—SI 2012/1471, art 2

c 46 **Scotland**

am—Road Traffic (NHS Charges), 1999 c 3, s 21(4); Crim Justice and Court Services, 2000 c 43, s 81(6); Scotland, 2012 c 11, s 12(2)(a)

1998

c 46 *continued*

appl—Disability Discrimination, 1995 c 50, s 49D; Foods Standards, 1999 c 28, s 24(10);
SI 1999/1320, art 4(3)(a); Anti-terrorism, Crime and Security, 2001 c 24, s 112(2);
Health Protection Agency, 2004 c 17, ss 1, 2(6)(a), 6(4), sch 1 para 6; Children, 2004
c 31, s 6(10); Inquiries, 2005 c 12, s 28(5)

ext—Adoption (Intercountry Aspects), 1999 c 18, s 16(2); Youth Justice and Crim Evidence,
1999 c 23, s 68(2); Foods Standards, 1999 c 28, ss 18(2), 35(1); Sexual Offences
(Amdt), 2000 c 44, s 7

mod—Health, 1999 c 8, s 66(1); Water Industry, 1999 c 9, s 14(3); Access to Justice, 1999
c 22, s 109(7); Pollution Prevention and Control, 1999 c 24, s 5(3); Welfare Reform
and Pensions, 1999 c 30, s 91(4); Political Parties, Elections and Referendums, 2000
c 41, s 133(2); SIs 2009/2231, art 3; 2012/700, art 3(1); 2014/3294, art 3(1);
2015/444, art 3(1)

s 2 excl—SI 1999/787, art 96

mod—Fixed-term Parliaments, 2011 c 14, s 4(2)

am—SI 2015/1764, art 4

s 4 mod—Powers of Crim Cts (Sentencing), 2000 c 6, s 167(5)

appl—International Organisations, 2005 c 20, s 10

s 5 am—Political Parties, Elections and Referendums, 2000 c 41, s 158(1), sch 21
para 13(2)

appl—International Organisations, 2005 c 20, s 10

s 7 appl—International Organisations, 2005 c 20, s 10

appl (mods)—SIs 2007/937, art 72; 2010/2999, art 4, sch 2

s 8 appl—International Organisations, 2005 c 20, s 10

mod—SI 2007/937, art 7, sch 2

am—SI 2010/2999, art 4, sch 2

s 9 appl—SI 1999/787, art 86

s 10 am—SIs 1999/787, art 88; 2002/2779, art 84; 2010/2999, art 87

s 12 am—Political Parties, Elections and Referendums, 2000 c 41, ss 7(2)(g), 8(2)(3)(b);
European Parl Elections, 2002 c 24, s 15, sch 3, para 7(1)(2); Scotland, 2012 c 11,
s 1(6)(7); ibid, s 1(2)(a)(b); ibid, s 1(3)(a)(b)(d)(e); ibid, s 1(8)

rep in pt—Political Parties, Elections and Referendums, 2000 c 41, s 158(1)(2), sch 21
para 13(3), sch 22; Scotland, 2012 c 11, s 1(2)(c); ibid, s 1(3)(c)(f); ibid, s
1(4)(5)

s 12A added —Scotland, 2012 c 11, s 1(9)

s 15 appl—SSI 2000/47, art 5, sch pt II

rep in pt—Constitutional Reform, 2005 c 4, ss 40(4), 146, sch 9 pt 2 paras 93, 94, sch
18 pt 5

s 16 am—House of Commons (Removal of Clergy Disqualification), 2001 c 13, s 1(3)(a),
sch 1 para 4

s 17 rep in pt—Mental Health (Discrimination), 2013 c 8, sch para 2(1)(a)

am—Mental Health (Discrimination), 2013 c 8, sch para 2(1)(b)

s 19 rep in pt—Scotland, 2012 c 11, s 4(2)

am—Scotland, 2012 c 11, s 4(3)-(5)

s 20 ext—SI 1999/1098, art 2(3)

s 21 restr—SI 1999/1082, arts B2, R1, sch 1 para 8, sch 6 para 14(2)

am—Scotland, 2012 c 11, s 5

s 23 ext—Foods Standards, 1999 c 28, s 35(1)(a)

mod—Energy, 2004 c 20, s 2(10), sch 1 pt 3 para 17(a)

ss 23, 27 appl—(S) S Parl Standards Commnr, 2002 asp 16, s 13(5)

s 29 am—Scotland, 2012 c 11, s 9(2)

excl in pt—Rehabilitation of Offenders, 1974 c 53, sch 3 para 9(1) (added by 2015 c 2,
s 19)

s 30 am—Scotland, 2012 c 11, s 9(1)

s 31 am—Scotland, 2012 c 11, s 6

s 32 am—Constitutional Reform, 2005 c 4, s 40(4), sch 9 pt 2 paras 93, 95(a)(b), 96(2),
97-99

rep in pt—Constitutional Reform, 2005 c 4, ss 40(4), 146, sch 9 pt 2 paras 93, 95(c),
sch 18 pt 5

s 33 am—Constitutional Reform, 2005 c 4, s 40(4), sch 9 pt 2 paras 93, 95(a)(b), 96(1),(2),
97-99

s 34 am—Constitutional Reform, 2005 c 4, s 40(4), sch 9 pt 2 paras 93, 95(a)(b), 96(2), 97;
SI 2012/1809, art 3(1), sch pt 1

s 35 am—Constitutional Reform, 2005 c 4, s 40(4), sch 9 pt 2 paras 93, 95(a)(b), 96(2), 98

1998
c 46 *continued*
s 36 am—Constitutional Reform, 2005 c 4, s 40(4), sch 9 pt 2 paras 93, 95(a)(b), 96(2), 99
s 39 appl (mods)—Interests of Members of the Scottish Parliament, 2006 asp 12, s 17(1)(2)
    am—Scotland, 2012 c 11, s 7(2)
s 43 rep —Bribery, 2010 c 23, s 17, sch 2
s 44 appl—(EWS) Disability Discrimination, 1995 c 50, s 4C(5)(f); SSI 2002/62, art 4, sch
    2 pt III; SI 2003/1660, reg 10(10)(b)(vi); SI 2003/1661, reg 10(10)(b)(vi); SI
    2004/1769, reg 6(4)(b)
s 49 appl—(EWS) Disability Discrimination, 1995 c 50 SI 2003/1660, reg 10(10)(b)(vi); SI
    2003/1661, reg 10(10)(b)(vi)
s 51 excl—SI 2006/242, art 2
    am—Constitutional Reform and Governance, 2010 c 25, s 19, sch 2 para 9(1)-(4)
    rep in pt—Constitutional Reform and Governance, 2010 c 25, s 19, sch 2 para 9(5)
s 53 excl—SI 1999/1746, art 3
    expld—(temp) SI 1999/1042, art 2
    see—SI 1999/1748, arts 3,5-7
    restr—SI 1999/1592, art 3(1), sch 1
s 54 appl—SI 2004/1769, reg 6(4)(a); Interpretation and Legislative Reform (S), 2009 asp
    10, s 27(4)
s 57 rep in pt—Scotland, 2012 c 11, s 36(2)
s 63 power exercised—SI 1999/1748, art 3, sch 1
    ext—Commrs for Revenue and Customs, 2005 c 11, s 8(2)(3)
s 64 excl—Dormant Bank and Building Society Accounts, 2008 c 31, s 26(9)
s 65 ext—(temp) Budget (Scotland) Act 2001 asp 4, s 4(1); Budget (S), 2002 asp 7, s 4;
    Budget (S), 2003 asp 6, s 4; Budget (S), 2004 asp 2, s 4; Budget (S), 2005 asp 4,
    s 4
s 66 am—Scotland, 2012 c 11, s 32(3)-(5); SI 2015/932, art 2
s 67 am—Scotland, 2012 c 11, s 32(7)(9)
    rep in pt—Scotland, 2012 c 11, s 32(8)
s 67A added —Scotland, 2012 c 11, s 32(10)
s 70 ext—Foods Standards, 1999 c 28, s 35(1)(b)
    mod—Energy, 2004 c 20, s 2(10), sch 1 pt 3 para 17(b)
Pt 4 (ss 73-80) rep—(end of tax year 2015-2016) Scotland, 2012 c 11, s 25(2) (with
    2015/2000, art 2)
s 75 am—(temp) Scotland, 2012 c 11, s 27
Pt 4A Ch 1 (ss 80A, 80B) added—Scotland, 2012 c 11, s 23(2)
    Ch 2 (ss 80C-80H) added—Scotland, 2012 c 11, s 25(3)
    Ch 2 see—(tax year 2016-17 appointed under s 25(3) of 2012 c 11) SI 2015/2000,
    art 3
    Ch 3 (ss 80I, 80J) added—Scotland, 2012 c 11, s 28
    Ch 4 (s 80K) added—Scotland, 2012 c 11, s 30(1)
s 80C am—Finance, 2014 c 26, sch 38 para 16(2)
s 80D am—Wales, 2014 c 29, ss 11(3)(4), 14(1)(7)(8)-(10) (prosp) (conditionally) ibid, ss
    11(5)
s 80DA added (prosp)—(conditionally) Wales, 2014 c 29, ss 11(6), 14(1)(7)(8)-(10)
s 80E am—(prosp) (conditionally) Wales, c 29, ss 11(7)(a), 14(1)(7)(8)-(10); ibid, s
    11(7)(b)
s 80F am—(prosp) (conditionally) Wales, c 29, ss 11(8)(a), 14(1)(7)(8)-(10); ibid, s
    11(8)(b)
s 80G am—Finance, 2014 c 26, sch 38 para 16(4)(5)(7)
    rep in pt—Finance, 2014 c 26, sch 38 para 16(6)
s 80HA added—Finance, 2014 c 26, s 297(1)
s 81 ext—SI 1999/1081, art 8
    am—Scotland, 2012 c 11, s 12(2)(b)
s 82 am—Constitutional Reform and Governance, 2010 c 25, s 38, sch 5 para 11
s 85 rep in pt—Crim Justice, 2003 c 44, s 332, sch 37 pt 10
s 86 rep—Parly Voting System and Constituencies, 2011 c 1, sch 12 pt 2
s 88 restr—SI 1999/1747, art 3, sch 2 pt II para 3(3), sch 4 pt II, sch 7 pt II para 3(3), sch 8
    para 3(3), sch 11 pt II para 4(3), sch 13 pt II para 3(3), sch 14 pt II para 3(3),
    sch 16 pt II para 3(3), sch 17 pt II para 3(3), sch 23 pt II para 2
    excl—SI 2000/1102, art 5
    appl—SI 2001/3458, art 5(6); SI 2003/3006, art 4(6); SI 2004/3125, art 3(6)
s 90A added—Scotland, 2012 c 11, s 16
s 91 mod —Energy, 2004 c 20, s 2(10), sch 1 pt 3 para 17(c)

1998
c 46 *continued*

 s 92 am—Interpretation and Legislative Reform (S), 2010 asp 10, s 45; Scotland, 2012 c 11,
  ss 9(3), 13(3)

 s 93 ext—Commrs for Revenue and Customs, 2005 c 11, s 15(1)
  am—Scotland, 2012 c 11, s 23(3)

 s 94 appl—(temp) SI 1999/1593, arts 2(1), 3
  ext—SI 1999/1750, art 6(2)(a)

 s 95 am—Constitutional Reform, 2005 c 4, s 40(4), sch 9 pt 2 paras 93, 100(a)(b)

 s 100 am—Justice (NI), 2002 c 26, s 28(1), sch 7, para 7; Convention Rights Proceedings
  (Amdt) (S), 2009 asp 11, s 1; Scotland, 2012 c 11, s 14(6)(7)
  rep in pt—Scotland, 2012 c 11, s 14(1)

 s 102 am—SI 1999/1347, rule 8(1)(a); Justice (NI), 2002 c 26, s 28(1), sch 7, para 10;
  Scotland, 2012 c 11, s 15; ibid, s 36(3)

 s 103 rep—Constitutional Reform, 2005 c 4, ss 40(4), 146, sch 9 pt 2 paras 93, 101, sch 18
  pt 5

 s 104 am—Scotland, 2012 c 11, s 13(4)

 s 108 ext—Commrs for Revenue and Customs, 2005 c 11, s 8(2)(3)

 s 110 am—(prosp) Scotland, 2012 c 11, sch 2 para 1(2); Finance, 2014 c 26, sch 38 para
  16(8)(a)
  rep in pt—Finance, 2014 c 26, sch 38 para 16(8)(b)

 s 111 am—SI 2006/2913, art 76, sch 4; Marine and Coastal Access, 2009 c 23, s 231

 s 112 am—Scotland, 2012 c 11, s 13(2)

 s 113 am—(prosp) Crim Justice, 2003 c 44, s 283(4)(7)(b), sch 27 para 7 (for savings see
  2012 c 11, s 39(5)); Scotland, 2012 c 11, s 3(1); ibid, s 39(2)(3)
  saving—Scotland, 2012 c 11, s 39(5)

 s 114 am—Scotland, 2012 c 11, s 32(11)

 ss 117-122 saving—SI 2001/1400, art 3

 s 117 ext—SI 1999/1750, art 6(2)(a);
  mod—SIs 1999/3321, art 3(2)(a); 2001/3504, arts 3, 4; 2007/2139, art 3
  ext (mods)—SI 2000/3253, art 5(1)(2); SI 2003/415, art 4; SI 2003/2617, art 5(1)(3)
  appl—SIs 2000/1563, art 7(1)(3)(4); 2006/1040, art 5; 2015/692, art 7(1)
  appl (mods)—SIs 2001/954, art 3; 2002/1630, art 3(1)(3); 2004/2030, arts 6, 7;
   2005/849, arts 5, 6; 2008/1776, art 3; 2014/2918, art 3

 s 118 excl—SI 1999/1096, art 3(6)
  ext—SI 1999/1750, art 6(2)(a)
  ext (mods)—SI 2000/3253, art 5(1)(2); SI 2003/415, art 4; SI 2003/2617, art 5(1)(3)
  mod—SIs 1999/3321, art 3(2)(a); 2001/3504, arts 3, 4; 2007/2139, art 3
  appl (mods)—SIs 1999/1747, art 4; 2004/2030, arts 6, 7; 2005/849, arts 5, 6;
   2008/1776, art 3
  appl—SIs 2000/1563, art 7(1)(3)(4); 2006/1040, art 5

 s 119 appl (mods)—SIs 1999/1747, art 4; 2001/954, art 3; 2002/1630, art 3(2)(3);
  2004/2030, arts 6, 7
  ext—SI 1999/1750, art 6(2)(b)
  mod—SI 1999/3321, art 3(2)(b); SI 2001/3504, arts 3, 4
  ext (mods)—SI 2003/415, art 4; SI 2003/2617, art 5(2)(3)

 ss 119-121 appl—SI 2000/1563, art 7(2)(3)(4)
  ext (mods)—SI 2000/3253, art 5(2)(3)

 s 120 appl (mods)—SI 1999/1747, art 4
  ext—SI 1999/1750, art 6(2)(b)
  mod—SI 1999/3321, art 3(2)(b)
  excl—(temp) SI 1999/441, art 23
  ext (mods)—SI 2003/415, art 4; SI 2003/2617, art 5(2)(3)

 s 121 appl (mods)—SIs 1999/1747, art 4; 2002/1630, art 3(2)(3)
  ext—SI 1999/1750, art 6(2)(b)
  excl—(temp) SI 1999/441, art 24
  ext (mods)—SI 2003/2617, art 5(2)(3)

 s 126 appl—Merchant Shipping, 1995 c 21, s 256A; SSI 2002/62, art 5, sch 3; Police, 1997
  c 50, s 119A(3)(b); SI 2004/1769, reg 6(4)(d)
  appl in pt—SSI 2015/446, reg 95(5)
  rep in pt—Welfare Reform and Pensions, 1999 c 30, s 88, sch 13 pt I

 s 127 ext—SI 1999/1379, art 6(3)
  am—Scotland, 2012 c 11, s 23(4)
  rep in pt—Constitutional Reform, 2005 c 4, ss 40(4), 146, sch 9 pt 2 paras 93, 102,
   sch 18 pt 5

1998
c 46 *continued*

sch 1 subst—Scottish Parliament (Constituencies), 2004 c 13, s 1(1)(3)(4), sch 1
subst (mods)—Scottish Parliament (Constituencies), 2004 c 13, s 1(1)-(4), sch 1, sch 2
am—SI 2010/2691, art 3; Scotland, 2012 c 11, sch 1 paras 2, 4(2), 5(2), 8, 9, 10(2)
rep in pt—SIs 2010/2691, art 3; Scotland, 2012 c 11, sch 1 paras 4(3), 5(3), 6(3), 7,
10(3); 2013/235, sch 2 para 39
sch 3 am—Scotland, 2012 c 11, s 4(6)
sch 4 am—SI 1999/1749, art 2(1); 2000/1831, arts 2,3; SI 2009/1380, art 2; Scotland,
2012 c 11, s 13(5); SIs 2015/692, art 3; 1764, art 2
excl—Rehabilitation of Offenders, 1974 c 53, sch 3 para 9(1) (added by 2015 c 2, s
19)
rep in pt—Scotland, 2012 c 11, s 14(3); (prosp) ibid, sch 2 para 1(3)
sch 5 am—Disability Rights Commn, 1999 c 17, s 14(1), sch 4 para 4; SIs 1999/1749,
arts 2(2),3,4,5,6(1); 2000/1113, art 2; 2000/3252, arts 2(1)(2), 3-5; 2001/1456,
art 2(1)(2); 2002/1629, art 2; European Parl Elections, 2002 c 24, s 15, sch 3,
para 7(1)(3); SIs 2004/3329, arts 2, 3, 4(a)(b); 2005/865, art 2(a); 2005/866,
art 2(1)-(4); 2006/609, art 2; Scotland, 2012 c 11, ss 10, 11, 23(5); SIs
2013/242, art 3; 2013/192, art 2(2)(3); Energy, 2013 c 32, sch 12 para 72;
Co-operative and Community Benefit Societies, 2014 c 14, sch 4 para 66; SI
2014/1559, arts 2(2), 3(2), 4(2), 5(2)-(4); SIs 2015/692, art 4(2)(3); 1379, art 2;
1764, art 3(2)(3)
appl—(temp) SI 1999/2210, art 3; Freedom of Information (S), 2002 asp 13, ss 4(2),
75; Loc Govt in S, 2003 asp 1, ss 1(7), 59(3); Mental Health (Care and
Treatment) (S), 2003 asp 13, s 3(4); Public Appointments and Public Bodies etc
(S), 2003 asp 4, s 2(10)(a); Antisocial Behaviour etc (S), 2004 asp 8, s 140(2);
Further and Higher Educ (S), 2005 asp 6, s 21(2); Transport (S), 2005 asp 12,
s 5(4); SI 2005/2966, reg 2, sch 1 pt I
rep in pt—SIs 2005/865, art 2(b)(c); 2008/960, art 22, sch 3; (prosp) Welfare Reform,
2012 c 5, sch 14 pt I
sch 6 appl—SIs 1999/1379, arts 6(2), 7(1), sch 2; SI 2004/1861, reg 16, sch 1 para 56(2);
Constitutional Reform, 2005 c 4, s 41(4)(b)
mod—SI 2013/7, arts 11, 12
am—Justice (NI), 2002 c 26, s 28(1), sch 7, para 4(a)-(c); Constitutional Reform,
2005 c 4, s 40(4), sch 9 pt 2 paras 93, 103(1)-(8), 104(1)-(8), 105(1)-(6), 106(1),
(3)-(5); Scotland, 2012 c 11, ss 36(4), 37
rep in pt—Constitutional Reform, 2005 c 4, ss 40(4), 146, sch 9 pt 2 paras 93,
106(1)(2), sch 18 pt 5
sch 7 rep in pt—Constitutional Reform, 2005 c 4, ss 40(4), 146, sch 9 pt 2 paras 93, 107,
sch 18 pt 5; Finance, 2014 c 26, sch 38 para 16(10)(a)(11)
am—Scotland, 2012 c 11, s 3(3)(4); ibid, s 23(6); ibid, s 32(12); ibid, s 39(4); (prosp)
ibid, sch 2 para 1(4)
sch 8 restr—SI 1999/1334, art 4
am—SI 2001/3649, art 360; Legislative and Regulatory Reform, 2006 c 51, s 27(4)
rep in pt—SI 2009/1307, art 5, sch 4; Mental Health (Discrimination), 2013 c 8, sch
para 2(2)
appl—Civil Partnership, 2004 c 33, s 260(5)(b)

c 47 **Northern Ireland**
see—(suspension and restoration of NI Assembly) Northern Ireland, 2000 c 1
mod (conditionally on 2001 c 1, s 1 being in force)—Northern Ireland, 2000 c 1, s 1(5)-(8),
sch
am—Tax Credits, 1999 c 10, s 16; Tax Credits, 2002 c 21, s 64(4)
appl—Finance, 2001 c 9, s 29, sch 7 para 14 (1)(c); Gangmasters (Licensing), 2004 c 11,
s 28, sch 2 para 15(3)(c); Children, 2004 c 31, s 7(10); Inquiries, 2005 c 12, ss 27(7),
30(8)
s 1 am—NI (St Andrews Agreement), 2006 c 53, s 8, sch 4
s 4 appl—Nat Health Service Reform and Health Care Professions, 2002 c 17, s 25(4), sch 7,
para 16(4)(b); Justice (NI), 2002 c 26, s 84(3); Gender Recognition, 2004 c 7,
s 23(4); Health Protection Agency, 2004 c 17, ss 1, 2(6)(b), 6(3), sch 1 para 26;
Civil Partnership, 2004 c 33, ss 247(9), 255(11), 259(11); SI 2004/1769,
reg 6(4)(c); Constitutional Reform, 2005 c 4, ss 5(4), 6(3)
am—NI (St Andrews Agreement), 2006 c 53, s 13; NI (Misc Provns), 2006 c 33, s 16
s 7 am—Justice (NI), 2002 c 26, s 84(1); NI (Misc Provns), 2006 c 33, s 30, sch 4 para 10
rep in pt—Justice (NI), 2002 c 26, s 86, sch 13

1998
c 47 *continued*

s 11 am—Justice (NI), 2002 c 26, s 28(1), sch 7, para 1(1)(2); Constitutional Reform, 2005 c 4, s 40(4), sch 9 pt 2 paras 108, 109(1), (2)(3), 110-112

s 12 am —Justice (NI), 2002 c 26, s 28(1), sch 7, para 1(1)(3); Constitutional Reform, 2005 c 4, s 40(4), sch 9 pt 2 paras 108, 109(2)(3), 110-112; SI 2012/1809, art 3(1), sch pt 1

s 13 am—Constitutional Reform, 2005 c 4, s 40(4), sch 9 pt 2 paras 108, 109(2)(3), 110-112

s 14 am —Justice (NI), 2002 c 26, s 28(1), sch 7, para 1(1)(4); Constitutional Reform, 2005 c 4, s 40(4), sch 9 pt 2 paras 108, 109(2)(3), 110-112

s 16 rep—NI (St Andrews Agreement), 2006 c 53, s 8(1)

ss 16A-16C added—NI (St Andrews Agreement), 2006 c 53, s 8(1)

s 16A excl—NI (St Andrews Agreement), 2006 c 53, s 2, sch 2 para 2(2)(5); Northern Ireland, 2009 c 3, s 1, sch 1 para 7(3)(a)

s 18 appl—(conditionally) Northern Ireland, 2000 c 1, s 3(1)(6)(7)(a)
    appl (mods)—NI (St Andrews Agreement), 2006 c 53, s 2, sch 2 para 2(6)
    am—NI (Monitoring Commn etc), 2003 c 25, ss 5(2)-(5), 10(2); NI (St Andrews Agreement), 2006 c 53, s 8, sch 5 paras 1, 2(1)(3)
    excl—Northern Ireland, 2006 c 17, s 2, sch 2 para 2(3); Northern Ireland, 2009 c 3, s 1, sch 1 para 6
    rep in pt—NI (St Andrews Agreement), 2006 c 53, s 8, sch 5 paras 1, 2(2)

s 19 appl—(conditionally) Northern Ireland, 2000 c 1, s 3(1)(6)(7)(b)

s 19A added—Disqualifications, 2000, c 42, s 2
    am—NI (St Andrews Agreement), 2006 c 53, s 8, sch 5 paras 1, 3

s 20 am—NI (St Andrews Agreement), 2006 c 53, s 5(1); SI 2010/976, art 23

s 21 appl—SI 2004/1769, reg 6(4)(f)

s 21A added —NI (Misc Provns), 2006 c 33, s 17
    am—Justice and Security (NI), 2007 c 6, s 44(1)-(5); Northern Ireland, 2009 c 3, s 1, sch 1 para 3

s 21B added—Justice and Security (NI), 2007 c 6, s 44(6)
    am—Northern Ireland, 2009 c 3, s 1, sch 1 para 9

s 21C added—Justice and Security (NI), 2007 c 6, s 44(7)
    am—Northern Ireland, 2009 c 3, s 1, sch 1 para 10

s 23 am—SI 2010/976, art 24

s 28 ext—Commrs for Revenue and Customs, 2005 c 11, s 15(2)

s 28A added—NI (St Andrews Agreement), 2006 c 53, s 5(2)

s 28B added—NI (St Andrews Agreement), 2006 c 53, s 6

s 28C added—NI (St Andrews Agreement), 2006 c 53, s 13

s 28D added—NI (St Andrews Agreement), 2006 c 53, s 16

s 29 appl—(conditionally) Northern Ireland, 2000 c 1, s 3(1)(6)(7)(c)
    appl (mods)—NI (St Andrews Agreement), 2006 c 53, s 2, sch 2 para 5(2)
    am—Disqualifications, 2000, c 42, s 3(1); NI (St Andrews Agreement), 2006 c 53, s 10

ss 29A, 29B added—NI (St Andrews Agreement), 2006 c 53, s 11(1)

s 29C added —Northern Ireland, 2009 c 3, s 2, sch 6 para 1

s 30 am—NI (Monitoring Commn etc), 2003 c 25, ss 4, 5(6)

s 30A added—NI (Monitoring Commn etc), 2003 c 25, s 5(1)

s 30A rep—NI (Monitoring Commn etc), 2003 c 25, s 12(3)

s 30B added—NI (Monitoring Commn etc), 2003 c 25, s 6

s 31 am—NI Assembly Elections, 2003 c 3, s 1(2)(a)(c); NI Assembly (Elections and Periods of Suspension), 2003 c 12, ss 1(1)(2), 7(1)(a)(i); NI (St Andrews Agreement), 2006 c 53, s 3(1)
    rep in pt—NI Assembly Elections, 2003 c 3, s 1(2)(b)
    power to cont—NI Assembly (Elections and Periods of Suspension), 2003 c 12, s 7(2)

s 32 am—NI (St Andrews Agreement), 2006 c 53, s 8, sch 5 paras 1, 4
    appl (mods)—Northern Ireland, 2009 c 3, s 1, sch 1 para 7(3)(b)

s 34 am—Political Parties, Elections and Referendums, 2000 c 42, s 7(2)(h)

s 36 rep in pt—Disqualifications, 2000, c 42, s 4; Constitutional Reform, 2005 c 4, s 146, sch 18 pt 5
    am—H of C (Removal of Clergy Disqualification), 2001 c 13, s 1(3)(a), sch 1 para 5

s 40 am—Disqualifications, 2000, c 42, s 3(2)

s 43 appl —Justice (NI), 2002 c 26, s 25(4)

s 44 am—Northern Ireland, 2000 c 1, s 9(3); NI (Misc Provns), 2006 c 33, s 18

s 47 excl—(conditionally) Northern Ireland, 2000 c 1, s 3(1)(8)
    rep in pt—Northern Ireland Assembly Members, 2010 c 16, s 1(4), (6), (14)

1998
c 47 s 47 *continued*
am—(NI) SI 2000/1110, arts 18(1)(2), 19; NI Assembly (Elections and Periods of
Suspension), 2003 c 12, s 4(1)-(3); Northern Ireland Assembly Members, 2010 c
16, s 1(1)-(3), (5), (7)-(12), (14)
mod—SI 2003/3039, art 2
appl (mods)—NI (St Andrews Agreement), 2006 c 53, s 4
ss 47A-47C added—NI (Monitoring Commn etc), 2003 c 25, s 7(1)
s 47B rep—NI (Monitoring Commn etc), 2003 c 25, s 12(3)
s 48 appl —Justice (NI), 2002 c 26, s 23(5)
am—NI (Monitoring Commn etc), 2003 c 25, s 7(2); Northern Ireland Assembly
Members, 2010 c 16, s 2
ss 51A-51C added—NI (Monitoring Commn etc), 2003 c 25, s 8
s 51B rep—NI (Monitoring Commn etc), 2003 c 25, s 12(3)
s 51D added—NI (Monitoring Commn etc), 2003 c 25, s 9
s 52 rep—NI (St Andrews Agreement), 2006 c 53, s 12
ss 52A-52C added—NI (St Andrews Agreement), 2006 c 53, s 12
s 53 am—NI (St Andrews Agreement), 2006 c 53, s 19, sch 7 paras 1, 2
s 63 excl—Finance, 1994 c 9, s 30A(11)(b)
s 69 am—Justice and Security (NI), 2007 c 6, s 18(1)
rep in pt—Justice and Security (NI), 2007 c 6, s 18(2)
appl (mods)—Justice and Security (NI), 2007 c 6, s 19
ss 69A, 69B added—Justice and Security (NI), 2007 c 6, s 15
s 69C added—Justice and Security (NI), 2007 c 6, s 16(1)
s 69D added—Justice and Security (NI), 2007 c 6, s 17(1)
s 71 am —Justice (NI), 2002 c 26, s 28(1), sch 7, para 5; Justice and Security (NI), 2007 c
6, s 14(1)(2)
s 72 rep—SL(R), 2004 c 14, s 1(1), sch 1 pt 5/11
s 75 am—Police (NI), 2000 c 32, s 78, sch 6 para 24(2); Justice (NI), 2002 c 26, ss
38(1)-(3), 85(1), sch 12, paras 62, 63; Serious Crime, 2007 c 27, s 74, sch 8 para
158
s 76 am—Police (NI), 2000 c 32, s 78, sch 6 para 24(3); SI 2001/1149, art 3(1), sch 1
para 121; Justice (NI), 2002 c 26, ss 38(1)(4)(5), 85(1), sch 12, paras 62, 64;
Serious Crime, 2007 c 27, s 74, sch 8 para 158
s 81 am—SI 1999/1347, rule 8(1)(b); Justice (NI), 2002 c 26, s 28(1), sch 7, para 8
s 82 rep—Constitutional Reform, 2005 c 4, ss 40(4), 146, sch 9 pt 2 paras 108, 113, sch 18
pt 5
s 84 am—Political Parties, Elections and Referendums, 2000 c 42, s 7(3); Elections, 2001
c 7, s 3(4)
ext—Elections, 2001 c 7, s 4, sch pt 4 para 33
s 85 excl—Youth Justice and Crim. Evidence, 1999 c 23, s.66(1)
restr—Crim Justice, 2003 c 44, s 334(1)-(3)
s 86 am—Northern Ireland, 2009 c 3, s 4
s 86A added—NI (Misc Provns), 2006 c 33, s 19
s 86B added—NI (Misc Provns), 2006 c 33, s 20
s 87 am—SIs 2000/741,art 2; 2000/3254, art 2; Tax Credits, 2002 c 21, s 64(1)(3); SIs
2002/265, art 2; 2003/1890, art 2; 2006/2659, art 2; 2008/1242, art 2; 2009/885,
art 2
s 88 am—Social Security Contributions (Trans of Functions, etc), 1999 c 2, s 2, sch 3
para 65
s 90 am—Constitutional Reform, 2005 c 4, s 15(2), sch 5 pt 1 paras 104-107
s 91 am—Justice (NI), 2002 c 26, s 28(1), sch 7, para 19; Constitutional Reform, 2005 c 4,
s 15(2), sch 5 pt 1 paras 104-107;
s 92 am—Constitutional Reform, 2005 c 4, s 15(2), sch 5 pt 1 paras 104-107
s 93 excl—SI 2006/612, art 3
s 95 saved—(NI) SI 1999/663, art 5(2)
am—Political Parties, Elections and Referendums, 2000 c 42, s 158(1), sch 21
para 14(3); Regulation of Investigatory Powers, 2000 c 23, s 82(1), sch 4 para 9
s 95A added—NI (Monitoring Commn etc), 2003 c 25, s 10(1)
s 96 am—NI Assembly (Elections and Periods of Suspension), 2003 c 12, ss 1(1)(3),
7(1)(a)(ii)(iii); NI (Misc Provns), 2006 c 33, s 30, sch 4 para 11; Justice and
Security (NI), 2007 c 6, s 16(2)
power to cont—NI Assembly (Elections and Periods of Suspension), 2003 c 12, s 7(2)
s 98 appl—SI 2003/2901, art 4, sch 3; Civil Partnership, 2004 c 33, ss 247(9), 255(11),
259(11); SI 2004/1769, reg 6(4)(e)

1998

c 47 s 98 *continued*

    rep in pt—Constitutional Reform, 2005 c 4, ss 40(4), 146, sch 9 pt 2 paras 108, 114, sch 18 pt 5

    am—NI (St Andrews Agreement), 2006 c 53, ss 8, 19, sch 5 paras 1, 5, sch 7 paras 1, 3

sch 1 am—Political Parties, Elections and Referendums, 2000 c 42, s 102

sch 2 ext—Food Standards 1999, c 28, s 35(4)

    am—Tax Credits, 2002 c 21, s 64(1)(2); Justice (NI), 2002 c 26, ss 9(13), 27(4), 82; Child Trust Funds, 2004 c 6, s 25; Constitutional Reform, 2005 c 4, ss 58(1)(2), 59(5), sch 11 pt 4 para 33(1)(2); NI (Misc Provns), 2006 c 33, s 30, sch 4 para 12(a)(c); NI (St Andrews Agreement), 2006 c 53, s 19, sch 7 paras 1, 4; Health and Social Care, 2008 c 14, s 137; (prosp) Saving Gateway Accounts, 2009 c 8, s 27; SI 2010/976, art 26; Small Charitable Donations, 2012 c 23, s 16

    rep in pt—Justice (NI), 2002 c 26, s 86, sch 13; NI (Misc Provns), 2006 c 33, s 30, sch 4 para 12(b), sch 5; Savings Accounts and Health in Pregnancy Grant, 2010 c 36, s 2(4)

    mod—Northern Ireland, 2009 c 3, s 1, sch 1 para 2

    excl—Finance, 1994 c 9, s 30A(11)(a)

sch 3 am—Postal Services, 2000 c 26, s 127(4), sch 8 pt II para 26; Police (NI), 2000 c 32, s 78, sch 6 para 24(4); Justice (NI), 2002 c 26, ss 83(a)-(c), 85(1), sch 12, paras 62, 65(1)-(3); SI 2003/3075, reg 29, sch 2 pt I para 2; Civil Contingencies, 2004 c 36, s 32(1), sch 2 pt 2 para 13; Higher Educ, 2004 c 8, s 7; Constitutional Reform, 2005 c 4, ss 58(1)(3), 59(5), sch 11 pt 4 para 33(1)(2); NI (Misc Provns), 2006 c 33, s 30, sch 4 para 13(1)(3); NI (St Andrews Agreement), 2006 c 53, s 19, sch 7 paras 1, 5; SIs 2007/3298, reg 19, sch 3; 2007/2157, reg 51, sch 6; 2010/977, arts 2-5, 7

    rep in pt—NI (Misc Provns), 2006 c 33, s 30, sch 4 para 13(1)(2), sch 5; SI 2010/977, arts 2, 6, 8

    excl—Finance, 1994 c 9, s 30A(11)(a)

sch 4 am—NI (St Andrews Agreement), 2006 c 53, s 7

sch 4A added —NI (Misc Provns), 2006 c 33, s 17, sch 2

    am—Northern Ireland, 2009 c 3, s 1, sch 1 para 4

sch 6 am—NI (St Andrews Agreement), 2006 c 53, s 17

sch 8 appl—SI 1999/1804, art 6(4)

sch 10 am—Justice (NI), 2002 c 26, s 28(1), sch 7, para 2(1)-(7); Constitutional Reform, 2005 c 4, s 40(4), sch 9 pt 2 paras 108, 115(1)-(6), 116(1)-(7), 117(1)-(8), 118(1),(3)-(5), 119

    rep in pt—Justice (NI), 2002 c 26, s 86, sch 13; Constitutional Reform, 2005 c 4, ss 40(4), 146, sch 9 pt 2 paras 108, 118(1)(2), sch 18 pt 5; SI 2010/976, art 15, sch 18

    appl—Constitutional Reform, 2005 c 4, s 41(4)(b)

sch 11 am—Justice (NI), 2002 c 26, s 5, sch 3, para 38(1)-(6); Constitutional Reform, 2005 c 4, s 15(2), sch 5 pt 1 paras 104, 108; Northern Ireland, 2009 c 3, s 2, sch 5 para 4

sch 12 am—Constitutional Reform, 2005 c 4, s 59(5), sch 11 pt 4 para 33(1)(3)

sch 12A added—NI (Monitoring Commn etc), 2003 c 25, s 10(3)

    am—NI (St Andrews Agreement), 2006 c 53, s 8, sch 5 paras 1, 6

sch 13 rep in pt—(NI) SI 2000/1110, art 16, sch 2; Govt of Wales, 2006 c 32, s 163, sch 12

c 48 **Registration of Political Parties**

    rep (exc ss 13, 15, 24, 26 & sch 2)—Political Parties, Elections and Referendums, 2000 c 41, s 158(2), sch 22

    restr—Political Parties, Elections and Referendums, 2000 c 41, s 163(7), sch 23 pt I paras 1, 7(1)

    s 15 ext—SI 1999/787, art 6, sch 2 para 9(4)

2nd Session of 52nd Parliament

c 49 *Consolidated Fund (No 2)*—rep Appropriation, 2000 c 9, s 3, sch (C)

1999

c 1 *European Parliamentary Elections*—rep European Parl Elections, 2002 c 24, s 16, sch 4

c 2 **Social Security Contributions (Transfer of Functions, etc)**

    s 3 rep in pt—Welfare Reform and Pensions, 1999 c 30, ss 81,88, sch 11 para 30, sch 13 pt VI

    am—Commrs for Revenue and Customs, 2005 c 11, s 50(6), sch 4 paras 73, 74

1999
c 2 *continued*
s 4 am—Welfare Reform and Pensions, 1999 c 30, s 81, sch 11 para 31; Nat Insurance
Contributions and Statutory Payments, 2004 c 3, s 11, sch 1 para 5(1)(2)(4); Nat
Insurance Contributions, 2015 c 5, sch 1 para 24
rep in pt—Nat Insurance Contributions and Statutory Payments, 2004 c 3, ss 11, 12, sch
1 para 5(1)(3)(4), sch 2 pt 1
s 7 rep—Commrs for Revenue and Customs, 2005 c 11, ss 50(6), 52(2), sch 4 paras 73, 75,
sch 5
Pt 2 (ss 8-19) appl—Social Security Admin, 1992 c 5, s 117A(3)
ext—Employment Rights, 1996 c 18, s 215(5)
mod—Nat Insurance Contributions, 2011 c 3, s 8(6)(a); SI 2015/828, art 2(a)
s 8 rep in pt—Welfare Reform and Pensions, 1999 c 30, s 88, sch 13 pt VI; Child Support,
Pensions and Social Security, 2000 c 19, ss 76(6)(a)(b)(7), 85, sch 9 pt VIII(1),
Note 2
am—Child Support, Pensions and Social Security, 2000 c 19, ss 76(6)(b)(7), 77(5);
Employment, 2002 c 22, s 9(1)-(3); Work and Families, 2006 c 18, s 11, sch 1 para
46; Children and Families, 2014 c 6, sch 7 para 45; Nat Insurance Contributions,
2015 c 5, sch 1 para 25
s 10 am—Child Support, Pensions and Social Security, 2000 c 19, s 77(6); SI 2009/56, art 3,
sch 1 para 269
s 11 am—Employment, 2002 c 22, s 9(1)(4); Work and Families, 2006 c 18, s 11, sch 1
para 47; SI 2009/56, art 3, sch 1 para 270; Children and Families, 2014 c 6, sch 7
para 46
s 12 am—Child Support, Pensions and Social Security, 2000 c 19, s 77(7); Finance, 2001
c 9, s 88, sch 29 pt 5 para 39; SI 2009/56, art 3, sch 1 para 271(2)
rep in pt—SI 2009/56, art 3, sch 1 para 271(3)
s 13 see—(cert functions made exercisable in S) SI 1999/1748, art 3, sch 1 para 22
see—(trans of functions) (S) SIs 1999/678, art 2(1), sch, 1750, art 2, sch 1
am—SI 2009/56, art 3, sch 1 para 272
rep in pt—SI 2009/56, art 3, sch 1 para 272(3)(a)(4)
s 14 am—Employment, 2002 c 22, s 9(1)(5); Work and Families, 2006 c 18, s 11, sch 1
para 48; SI 2009/56, art 3, sch 1 para 273; Children and Families, 2014 c 6, sch 7
para 47
s 16 excl—SI 1999/1662, art 4
s 19 subst—SI 2009/56, art 3, sch 1 para 274
s 20 rep in pt—Welfare Reform and Pensions, 1999 c 30, s 88, sch 13 pts VI, VII
s 22 am—SI 1999/979, art 2
s 24 am—Constitutional Reform and Governance, 2010 c 25, s 19, sch 2 para 10
sch 1 rep in pt—Welfare Reform and Pensions, 1999 c 30, ss 81, 88, sch 11 para 32, sch 13
pt VI; Child Support, Pensions and Social Security, 2000 c 19, s 85, sch 9
pt VIII(1), Note 1; Child Support, Pensions and Social Security, 2000 c 19,
s 85, sch 9 pt III(9); Employment, 2002 c 22, s 54, sch 8(1); Finance, 2004 c
12, s 326, sch 42 pt 3, Note; Pensions, 2004 c 35, s 320, sch 13 pt 1; Pensions,
2007 c 22, s 27, sch 7 pt 6
sch 2 am—(retrosp) Welfare Reform and Pensions, 1999 c 30, s 81, sch 11 para 33
sch 3 rep in pt—Welfare Reform and Pensions, 1999 c 30, s 88, sch 13 pt VI; Child Support,
Pensions and Social Security, 2000 c 19, s 85, sch 9 pt VIII(1), Note 1; Nat
Insurance Contributions, 2002 c 19, s 7, sch 2; Nat Insurance Contributions and
Statutory Payments, 2004 c 3, s 12, sch 2 pt 1; Nat Insurance Contributions,
2015 c 5, sch 1 para 26
sch 4 rep in pt—(saving) Finance, 2008 c 9, s 137(5)(7)
am—Crime and Cts, 2013 c 22, sch 9 para 129
sch 5 rep in pt—Child Support, Pensions and Social Security, 2000 c 19, s 85, sch 9 pt VI;
Nat Insurance Contributions and Statutory Payments, 2004 c 3, s 12, sch 2 pt 1;
Finance, 2008 c 9, s 129, sch 43 para 11(a)
sch 6 rep in pt—Welfare Reform, 2012 c 5, sch 14 pt 13
sch 7 rep in pt—Tribunals, Cts and Enforcement, 2007 c 15, s 146, sch 23; SI 2009/56, art 3,
sch 1 para 275
sch 8 rep in pt—Welfare Reform and Pensions, 1999 c 30, s 88, sch 13 pt VI
sch 9 rep in pt—Nat Insurance Contributions, 2015 c 5, sch 1 para 27
c 3   *Road Traffic (NHS Charges)*—rep (saving) Health and Social Care (Community Health and
Standards), 2003 c 43, ss 169(1), 196, sch 14 pt 3 (see SSI 2007/10, art 3)
c 4   *Consolidated Fund*—rep Appropriation, 2001 c 8, s 4, sch 3
c 5   *Scottish Enterprise*—rep Public Finance and Accountability (S), 2000 asp 1, s 8, sch 1 para 5

1999

c 6   **Rating (Valuation)**

c 7   **Northern Ireland (Location of Victims' Remains)**
         s 4 am—(prosp) Coroners and Justice, 2009 c 25, s 177, sch 21 para 43
         sch 1 rep in pt—Child Support, Pensions and Social Security, 2000 c 19, s 85, sch 9
                pt VIII(2), Note 1

c 8   **Health**
         Pt 1 (ss 1-44) appl—Health, 1999 c 8, s 64
                ext (mods)—(Isles of Scilly) SI 2001/448, art 2
         ss 2-12 rep—Nat Health Service (Conseq Provns), 2006 c 43, s 6, sch 4
         s 13 rep in pt—Nat Health Service (Conseq Provns), 2006 c 43, s 6, sch 4
         ss 14, 15 rep—Nat Health Service (Conseq Provns), 2006 c 43, s 6, sch 4
         s 16 am—Nat Health Service (Conseq Provns), 2006 c 43, s 2, sch 1 para 195; (prosp)
                Health and Social Care, 2012 c 7, sch 14 para 75
         s 17 rep—Nat Health Service (Conseq Provns), 2006 c 43, s 6, sch 4
         ss 18-24 rep—Health and Social Care (Community Health and Standards), 2003 c 43, s 196,
                sch 14 pt 2
         s 25 rep—SL(R), 2004 c 14, s 1(1), sch 1 pt 5/9
         ss 26-39 rep—Nat Health Service (Conseq Provns), 2006 c 43, s 6, sch 4
         s 40 rep—Health and Social Care, 2001 c 15, s 67, sch 6 pt 1
         ss 41, 42 rep—Nat Health Service (Conseq Provns), 2006 c 43, s 6, sch 4
         Pt 2 (ss 45-59) appl—Health, 1999 c 8, s 64
         ss 46-49 rep (prosp)—Nat Health Service Reform (S), 2004 asp 7, s 11(2), sch 2
         ss 53-55 rep (prosp)—Nat Health Service Reform (S), 2004 asp 7, s 11(2), sch 2
         s 56 rep in pt—(S) SSI 2004/167, art 2, sch para 5(a); Smoking, Health and Social Care (S),
                2005 asp 13, s 42(2), sch 3
         Pt 3 (ss 60-69) ext (mods)—(Isles of Scilly) SI 2001/448, art 2
         s 60 am—Nat Health Service Reform and Health Care Professions, 2002 c 17, s 26(9); SIs
                2002/253, art 54(3), sch 5, para 16(a); 2002/254, art 48(3), sch 4, para 8(a);
                Health and Social Care, 2008 c 14, ss 111, 127, sch 8 para 1(1)(2)(3)(b)(4), sch
                10 para 10; SI 2010/231, art 68, sch 4; Health and Social Care, 2012 c 7, ss
                209(2)-(10), 210,213(7)(i); ibid, sch 15 para 60; SI 2012/1916, sch 34 para 43
                rep in pt—Health, 2006 c 28, s 33; Health and Social Care, 2008 c 14, s 111, sch 15,
                       sch 8 para 1(1)(3)(a); Health and Social Care, 2012 c 7, sch 15 para 72(2)
         s 60A added—(savings) Health and Social Care, 2008 c 14, s 112
                am—Health and Social Care, 2012 c 7, s 209(11)-(13)
                rep in pt—Health and Social Care, 2012 c 7, sch 15 para 72(5)
         s 61 am—Nat Health Service Reform and Health Care Professions, 2002 c 17, s 1(3), sch 1
                pt 2, paras 48, 54; SI 2002/2469, reg 4, sch 1 pt 1, para 26; Nat Health Service
                (Conseq Provns), 2006 c 43, s 2, sch 1 para 196; Health and Social Care, 2012 c
                7, sch 5 para 92(a)(i)(ii)(b)(i)
                rep in pt—Health and Social Care (Community Health and Standards), 2003 c 43,
                       s 196, sch 14 pt 4; Health and Social Care, 2012 c 7, sch 5 para
                       92(a)(iii)(iv)(b)(ii)
         s 62 am—Health and Social Care, 2001 c 15, s 48(1)(3); Nat Health Service (Conseq
                Provns), 2006 c 43, s 2, sch 1 para 197; Health and Social Care, 2008 c 14, ss
                111, 127, sch 8 para 2, sch 10 para 11
                rep in pt—Health and Social Care (Community Health and Standards), 2003 c 43,
                       s 196, sch 14 pt 2; Nat Health Service (Conseq Provns), 2006 c 43, s 6, sch 4
         s 64 rep in pt—Health and Social Care (Community Health and Standards), 2003 c 43,
                s 196, sch 14 pt 2; Nat Health Service (Conseq Provns), 2006 c 43, s 6, sch 4
         s 66 rep in pt—Health and Social Care, 2001 c 15, s 67, sch 5 pt 1 para 12(1)(3), sch 6 pt 1;
                Health and Social Care (Community Health and Standards), 2003 c 43, s 196,
                sch 14 pt 2
         s 68 rep in pt—Nat Health Service (Conseq Provns), 2006 c 43, s 6, sch 4
         sch 1 rep—Nat Health Service (Conseq Provns), 2006 c 43, s 6, sch 4
         sch 2 rep—Health and Social Care (Community Health and Standards), 2003 c 43, s 196,
                sch 14 pt 2
         sch 2A added—Health and Social Care, 2001 c 15, s 48(1)(4), sch 4
                rep—Nat Health Service (Conseq Provns), 2006 c 43, s 6, sch 4
         sch 3 appl—Nat Health Service Reform and Health Care Professions, 2002 c 17, s 25(3)(i)
                am—Nat Health Service Reform and Health Care Professions, 2002 c 17, ss 26(10),
                       35; Health and Social Care (Community Health and Standards), 2003 c 43,
                       s 184, sch 11 para 67; Health and Social Care, 2008 c 14, s 111, sch 8 paras 4,

1999
c 8 sch 3 *continued*

5(2),6(1)(3),7, 8(a),9; ibid, s 127, sch 10 para 12; Health and Social Care, 2012 c 7, s 211(2)-(8); ibid, sch 15 para 61

rep in pt—SIs 2002/253, art 54(3), sch 5, para 16(b); 2002/254, art 48(3), sch 4, para 8(b); Health and Social Care (Community Health and Standards), 2003 c 43, s 196, sch 14 pt 4; Health and Social Care, 2008 c 14, s 111, sch 8 paras 5(3)(4), 6(2), 8(b),10, sch 15; Health and Social Care, 2012 c 7, sch 15 para 72(4)

sch 4 rep in pt—Health and Social Care, 2001 c 15, s 67, sch 6 pt 1; Nat Health Service Reform and Health Care Professions, 2002 c 17, s 37, sch 8, paras 28, 31, sch 9 pt 3; Community Care and Health (S), 2002 asp 5, s 25, sch 2, para 4; (W pt prosp) Health and Social Care (Community Health and Standards), 2003 c 43, s 196, sch 14 pts 2, 4; (EW) Health (W), 2003 c 4, s 7(2), sch 4; Mental Health (Care and Treatment) (S), 2003 asp 13, s 331(2), sch 5 pt 1; (S) SI 2004/957, art 2, sch para 9; (prosp) Nat Health Service Reform (S), 2004 asp 7, s 11(2), sch 2; (S) SSI 2004/167, art 2, sch para 5(b); Public Services Ombudsman (W), 2005 c 10, s 39(2), sch 7; Smoking, Health and Social Care (S), 2005 asp 13, s 42(2), sch 3; Nat Health Service (Conseq Provns), 2006 c 43, s 6, sch 4; (prosp) Health, 2006 c 28, s 80, sch 9; SI 2006/1407, art 3, sch 2; Corporation Tax, 2010 c 4, s 1181, sch 3 pt 1; Health and Social Care, 2012 c 7, sch 5 para 93

sch 5 rep in pt—Smoking, Health and Social Care (S), 2005 asp 13, s 42(2), sch 3

c 9 **Water Industry**
s 12 rep in pt—Water Industry (S), 2002 asp 3, s 71(2), sch 7, para 26(1)(2)(a)
s 13 rep—Water Industry (S), 2002 asp 3, s 71(2), sch 7, para 26(1)(2)(b)
sch 2 rep—Water Industry (S), 2002 asp 3, s 71(2), sch 7, para 26(1)(2)(c)
sch 3 rep in pt—Water Industry (S), 2002 asp 3, s 71(2), sch 7, para 26(1)(2)(d)

c 10 *Tax Credits*—rep (savings and transitional provns) Tax Credits, 2002 c 21, s 60, sch 6

c 11 **Breeding and Sale of Dogs (Welfare)**
rep (S) (prosp) —Animal Health and Welfare (S), 2006 asp 11, s 52, sch 2 para 9(p)
s 2 rep in pt—(prosp) Deregulation, 2015 c 20, sch 23 para 36(3)
s 8 am—(S) SI 1999/3321, art 3(1); (prosp) (EW) Crim Justice, 2003 c 44, s 280(1)(3), sch 25 para 104; (prosp) Deregulation, 2015 c 20, sch 23 para 41(4)
rep in pt—(prosp) Deregulation, 2015 c 20, sch 23 para 41(2)(3)
ext—(EW) SI 1999/3191, reg 2
see—SSI 1999/177, reg 2
see—(trans of functions) (S) SI 1999/3321, art 2(b)
s 9 am—Courts, 2003 c 39, s 109(1), sch 8 para 383
rep in pt—(prosp) (EW) Crim Justice, 2003 c 44, ss 280(1)(3), 332, sch 25 para 104, sch 37 pt 9

c 12 **Road Traffic (Vehicle Testing)**
s 6 rep—SL(R), 2004 c 14, s 1(1), sch 1 pt 14

c 13 *Appropriation*—rep Appropriation, 2001 c 8, s 4, sch 3

c 14 **Protection of Children**
appl—(EW pt prosp) Police 1997 c 50, s 113C (added by 2005 c 15, s 163(2)); Children, 2004 c 31, s 39(4)
appl (mods)—Children, 2004 c 31, s 39(1)
mod (S)—SSI 2009/4, art 4
s 1 added—Care Standards, 2000 c 14, s 95(2)
rep—Safeguarding Vulnerable Groups, 2006 c 47, s 63, sch 9 para 8(1)(2), sch 10
s 2 rep—Safeguarding Vulnerable Groups, 2006 c 47, s 63, sch 9 para 8(1)(2), sch 10
ss 2A-2D added—Care Standards, 2000 c 14, s 95(1)
rep—Safeguarding Vulnerable Groups, 2006 c 47, s 63, sch 9 para 8(1)(2), sch 10
s 3 rep —Safeguarding Vulnerable Groups, 2006 c 47, s 63, sch 9 para 8(1)(2), sch 10
ss 4A-4C added—Crim Justice and Court Services, 2000 c 43, s 74, sch 7 pt II para 155
rep—Safeguarding Vulnerable Groups, 2006 c 47, s 63, sch 9 para 8(1)(2), sch 10
s 5 rep—Educ, 2002 c 32, s 215, sch 21, para 120, sch 22 pt 3
s 6 rep—Crim Justice and Court Services, 2000 c 43, ss 74,75, sch 7 pt II para 156, sch 8
s 7 rep —Safeguarding Vulnerable Groups, 2006 c 47, s 63, sch 9 para 8(1)(2), sch 10
s 8 rep—Serious Organised Crime and Police, 2005 c 15, s 174, sch 17 pt 2
s 9 am—Care Standards, 2000 c 14, s 116, sch 4 para 26(3); Crim Justice and Court Services, 2000 c 43, s 74, sch 7 pt II para 157; Educ, 2002 c 32, ss 155, 215(1), sch 14, paras 6, 7, sch 21, para 122; Childcare, 2006 c 21, s 103, sch 2 para 38; Safeguarding Vulnerable Groups, 2006 c 47, s 63, sch 9 para 8(1)(3)(b)(ii); Educ

1999
c 14 *continued*

and Inspections, 2006 c 40, s 170(3); (transtl provns and savings) SI 2008/2833, art 6, schs 3, 4; (W) Children and Families (W), 2010 nawm 1, s 72, sch 1 paras 10, 12(c), (d); Crime and Cts, 2013 c 22, sch 9 para 123

rep in pt—Educ, 2002 c 32, s 215(2), sch 22 pt 3; Educ, 2005 c 18, ss 61, 123, sch 9 para 23, sch 19 pt 1; Childcare, 2006 c 21, s 103, sch 2 para 38, sch 3; Safeguarding Vulnerable Groups, 2006 c 47, s 63, sch 9 para 8, sch 10; (transtl provns and savings) SI 2008/2833, art 6, sch 3; (W) Children and Families (W), 2010 nawm 1, s 72, sch 1 paras 10, 12(a), (b)

see—(trans of functions) SI 2008/2833, arts 3-5, sch 1

s 10 rep—Care Standards, 2000 c 14, s 117(2), sch 6

s 12 am—Care Standards, 2000 c 14, s 116, sch 4 para 26(4)(a)(i)(b); Care Standards, 2000 c 14, s 116, sch 4 para 26(4)(a)(ii); Crim Justice and Court Services, 2000 c 43, s 74, sch 7 pt II para 158(a)(b); Educ, 2002 c 32, s 215(1), sch 21, para 123(1)(3); (transtl provns) SI 2008/2833, art 6, sch 3

rep in pt—(prosp) Care Standards, 2000 c 14, s 117(2), sch 6; Educ, 2002 c 32, s 215, sch 21, para 123(1)(2), sch 22 pt 3; Safeguarding Vulnerable Groups, 2006 c 47, s 63, sch 9 para 8(1)(4), sch 10

appl—SI 2002/233, reg 6(2)

s 13 rep—Safeguarding Vulnerable Groups, 2006 c 47, s 63, sch 10

s 14 am—Crim Justice and Court Services, 2000 c 43, s 74, sch 7 pt II para 159

s 72 am—Care Standards, 2000 c 14, s 116, sch 4 para 26(2)

sch rep—SI 2008/2833, art 6, sch 3

c 15   **Trustee Delegation**

ss 4, 6 rep—Mental Capacity, 2005 c 9, s 67(2), sch 7

s 7 rep in pt—Mental Capacity, 2005 c 9, s 67(2), sch 7

c 16   **Finance**

s 8 rep in pt—Finance, 2005 c 7, s 104, sch 11 pt 1, Note

s 13 rep in pt—Finance, 2008 c 9, s 113, sch 36 para 89

am—Finance, 2008 c 9, s 115, sch 37 para 10

s 15 rep in pt—SI 1999/3029, reg 5; Finance, 2008 c 9, s 113, sch 36 para 92(g)

s 21 rep—Govt Resources and Accounts, 2000 c 20, ss 21(4),29(2), sch 2

ss 22-24 rep—Income Tax, 2007 c 3, s 1031, sch 3

s 25 rep in pt—Income Tax, 2007 c 3, s 1031, sch 3; Finance, 2009 c 10, s 5, sch 1 para 6(j)

s 26 rep—Finance, 2008 c 9, s 8, sch 2 para 21(d)

s 28 rep—Finance, 2006 c 25, s 178, sch 26 pt 3(1)

s 30 rep—Tax Credits, 2002 c 21, s 60, sch 6

ss 31, 32 rep —Finance, 2009 c 10, s 5, sch 1 para 6(j)

s 35 rep—Income Tax, 2007 c 3, s 1031, sch 3

s 36 rep in pt—Income Tax, 2007 c 3, s 1031, sch 3

ss 42-45 rep—Income Tax (Earnings and Pensions), 2003 c 1, s 724(1), sch 8 pt 1

s 46 rep—SL(R), 2013 c 2, s 1, sch 1 pt 10(1)

s 47 rep—Finance, 2000 c 17, s 156, sch 40 pt II(3), Note

ss 48-51 rep—Income Tax (Earnings and Pensions), 2003 c 1, s 724(1), sch 8 pt 1

s 52 rep—Finance, 2004 c 12, s 326, sch 42 pt 3, Note

s 53 rep—Finance, 2004 c 12, ss 77, 326, sch 42 pt 2(7), Note

s 54 rep—Corporation Tax, 2009 c 4, ss 1322, 1326, sch 1 para 456, sch 3 pt 1

s 55 rep in pt—Corporation Tax, 2009 c 4, s 1326, sch 3 pt 1

ss 56, 57 rep—Finance, 2011 c 11, sch 26 para 2(2)(a)

s 58 rep—Corporation Tax, 2009 c 4, s 1326, sch 3 pt 1

s 60 rep—Income Tax (Trading and Other Income), 2005 c 5, s 884, sch 3

s 61 rep—Corporation Tax, 2009 c 4, s 1326, sch 3 pt 1

s 63 rep—Corporation Tax, 2009 c 4, ss 1322, 1326, sch 1 para 457, sch 3 pt 1

s 64 rep—Income Tax (Trading and Other Income), 2005 c 5, s 884, sch 3

s 65 rep in pt—Finance, 2004 c 12, s 326, sch 42 pt 2(6), Notes 1, 2; Income Tax (Trading and Other Income), 2005 c 5, ss 882(1), 884, sch 1 pt 2 paras 505, 507(1)(2), sch 3

am—Income Tax (Trading and Other Income), 2005 c 5, s 882(1), sch 1 pt 2 paras 505, 507(1)(3)-(5)

s 68 rep in pt—Corporation Tax, 2010 c 4, s 1181, sch 3 pt 1

s 69 rep—Income Tax, 2007 c 3, s 1031, sch 3

s 70 rep—Income Tax (Trading and Other Income), 2005 c 5, s 884, sch 3

s 71 rep—Income Tax, 2007 c 3, s 1031, sch 3

s 72 rep—Finance, 2008 c 9, s 8, sch 2 para 55(b)(i)

1999
c 16 *continued*

ss 77, 78 rep—Capital Allowances, 2001 c 2, s 580, sch 4
s 80 rep—Finance, 2008 c 9, s 36, sch 14 para 17(h)
s 81 am—Finance, 2002 c 23, s 67(3)(4)(b); Corporation Tax, 2009 c 4, s 1322, sch 1 para
    458; Finance, 2012 c 14, sch 16 para 93
    rep in pt—Corporation Tax, 2009 c 4, ss 1322, 1326, sch 1 para 458, sch 3 pt 1
s 85 rep—Taxation (International and Other Provns), 2010 c 8, ss 374, 378, sch 8 paras 115,
    116, sch 10 pt 2
s 86 rep—Taxation (International and Other Provns), 2010 c 8, s 378, sch 10 pt 2
s 87 rep—Taxation (International and Other Provns), 2010 c 8, ss 374, 378, sch 8 paras 115,
    118, sch 10 pt 2
s 88 rep—Finance, 2009 c 10, s 36, sch 16 para 5(e)
s 89 rep in pt—Corporation Tax, 2010 c 4, s 1181, sch 3 pt 1
s 91 rep in pt—Income Tax, 2007 c 3, s 1031, sch 3
s 97 am—Corporation Tax, 2010 c 4, s 1177, sch 1 paras 300, 301; Taxation (International
    and Other Provns), 2010 c 8, s 374, sch 8 paras 247, 248
s 98 am—Finance, 2004 c 12, s 285(5)(8), sch 37 pt 4 para 12; Corporation Tax, 2010 c 4,
    s 1177, sch 1 paras 300, 302; Taxation (International and Other Provns), 2010 c 8,
    s 374, sch 8 paras 187, 188
s 100 rep—Corporation Tax, 2010 c 4, s 1181, sch 3 pt 1
s 106 rep—SI 2009/3054, art 3, sch
s 108 rep in pt—Finance, 2008 c 9, s 122, sch 40 para 21(g)
s 110 appl—Finance, 2000 c 17, s 117, sch 33 para 5(2)
s 111 rep—Finance, 1999 c 16, s 138, sch 20 pt V(2), Notes 1, 2
ss 113, 116-121 rep (prosp)—Finance, 1999 c 16, ss 123(3)(4), 139, sch 20 pt V(6), Note
s 119 am—SI 2009/1890, art 11
s 122 mod—SI 1997/1156, reg 4(1)(2)-(7)
s 123 rep in pt—(prosp) Finance, 1999 c 16, ss 123(3)(4), 139, sch 20 pt V(6), Note;
        Finance, 2011 c 11, sch 26 para 7(2)(a)
    am—Finance, 2014 c 26, s 114(3)(a)
s 125 rep—Finance (No 2), 2010 c 31, s 4(4)
s 126 excl—SI 2004/674, reg 22, sch 2 para 2(1)
    appl (mods)—SI 2004/674, reg 22, sch 2 para 2(3)
s 127 am—(retrosp) Finance, 2000 c 17, s 29; SI 2000/633, art 2
s 132 am—Employment, 2002 c 22, s 53, sch 7, para 53; (pt prosp) Communications, 2003
        c 21, s 406(1), sch 17 para 156; SI 2003/1900, arts 2(1), 3(1),sch 1; SI
        2003/3142, art 3(2); Work and Families, 2006 c 18, s 11, sch 1 para 49
    appl—SIs 2002/2014, reg 3(4)(a); 2003/916, reg 4(2); 2003/2682, reg 189
    mod—Children and Families, 2014 c 6, sch 7 para 48
s 133 am—Employment, 2002 c 22, s 53, sch 7, para 53; Work and Families, 2006 c 18, s
        11, sch 1 para 49
    mod—Children and Families, 2014 c 6, sch 7 para 48
s 135 am—Commrs for Revenue and Customs, 2005 c 11, s 50(6), sch 4 para 76
sch 3 rep—Tax Credits, 2002 c 21, s 60, sch 6
sch 4 rep in pt—Income Tax, 2007 c 3, s 1031, sch 3; Finance, 2008 c 9, s 36, sch 14 para
        17(h); Corporation Tax, 2010 c 4, s 1181, sch 3 pt 1; Taxation (International
        and Other Provns), 2010 c 8, s 378, sch 10 pt 13; SL(R), 2013 c 2, s 1, sch 1 pt
        10(1)
sch 5 rep in pt—Capital Allowances, 2001 c 2, s 580, sch 4; Income Tax (Earnings and
        Pensions), 2003 c 1, s 724(1), sch 8 pt 1; Finance, 2004 c 12, s 326, sch 42 pt 3,
        Note
sch 6 rep—Corporation Tax, 2009 c 4, ss 1322, 1326, sch 1 paras 451, 459, sch 3 pt 1
sch 7 rep—Finance, 2008 c 9, s 8, sch 2 para 55(b)(ii)
sch 9 rep—Finance, 2011 c 11, sch 9 para 5(b)
sch 10 mod—SI 2000/1085, regs 3-8
    appl—(retrosp) (S) SI 1998/366, reg 152(2)
    rep in pt—Income Tax (Earnings and Pensions), 2003 c 1, s 724(1), sch 8 pt 1;
        Finance, 2004 c 12, s 326, sch 42 pt 3, Note
sch 11 rep in pt—Corporation Tax, 2009 c 4, s 1326, sch 3 pt 1; SI 2009/56, art 3, sch 1
        para 277; Corporation Tax, 2010 c 4, s 1181, sch 3 pt 1
sch 13 rep in pt—Finance, 1999 c 16, ss 123(3)(4), 139, sch 20 pt V(6), Note; Abolition of
        Feudal Tenure etc (S), 2000 asp 5, s 76(1)(2), sch 12 pt I para 61(2), sch 13
        pt I; (saving) Finance, 2008 c 9, s 99, sch 32 paras 9, 10(1)(3), 22; Finance,
        2011 c 11, sch 26 para 7(1)

1999
c 16 sch 13 *continued*

restr—Finance, 1991 c 31, 113(1); (saving) Finance, 1990 c 29, s 108(1) (see SI 2003/2899, art 2); Finance, 2003 c 14, ss 104, 125(1)(5)(8), 128(1)(3)(7), sch 15 para 33, sch 20 pt I para 1

mod—Finance, 2000 c 17, ss 118-122,129(3)(5)(6), sch 34 para 4; Finance, 2001 c 9, s 92(6)(8), sch 30 para 3; Finance, 2008 c 9, s 98(1)-(4)

excl—Finance, 2000 c 17, s 130; Finance, 2014 c 26, sch 24 para 5

am—Finance, 2000 c 17, ss 114, 115(1)(a)(b)(2)(3), 116; (conditionally) Finance, 2001 c 9, s 92(1)(6)(8), sch 30 para 1; (saving) Finance, 2003 c 14, ss 104, 125(4)(5)(8), sch 15 pt 3 para 13(2), sch 20 pt 2 para 6 (see SI 2003/2899, art 2); Finance, 2003 c 14, s 195(10)(12), sch 40 para 5; Finance, 2005 c 7, s 95(3)(5); Finance (No 2), 2005 c 22, s 58(3)(4); Finance, 2006 c 25, s 162(3); (saving) Finance, 2008 c 9, s 99, sch 32 paras 9, 10(1)(2), 22; SIs 2009/1890, art 11; 2013/1401, reg 5

appl—Finance, 2001 c 9, s 92A; SI 2001/3746, reg 3(4)

appl (mods)—Finance, 2002 c 23, s 116(2), sch 37, para 1

ext—Finance, 2002 c 23, s 116(2), sch 37, para 3

sch 14 rep in pt—(prosp) Finance, 1999 c 16, ss 123(3)(4), 139, sch 20 pt V(6), Note; Finance, 2008 c 9, s 100(2); (saving) ibid, s 99, sch 32 paras 20, 22; Finance, 2012 c 14, sch 39 paras 3(2)(c), 5(2)(b)

sch 15 mod—Finance, 1988 c 39, s 143(4)

restr—Finance, 1988 c 39, s 143(2)

rep in pt—(prosp) Finance, 1999 c 16, ss 123(3)(4), 139, sch 20 pt V(6), Note; Finance, 2008 c 9, s 99, sch 32 paras 9, 11(1)(2)(5)

am—Finance, 2008 c 9, s 99, sch 32 paras 9, 11(3)(4)

sch 16 rep in pt—(prosp) Finance, 1999 c 16, ss 123(3)(4), 139, sch 20 pt V(6), Note

sch 17 rep in pt—Finance, 1999 c 16, s 139, sch 20 pt V(5), Notes 1, 2; (pt prosp) Finance, 1999 c 16, ss 123(3)(4), 139, sch 20 pt V(6), Note

sch 17 am—SI 2009/56, art 3, sch 1 paras 278-283

rep in pt—SI 2009/56, art 3, sch 1 paras 281(3)(6), 283(1)

sch 18 am—Finance, 2003 c 14, s 206(3)-(5)

sch 19 appl—Finance, 1986 c 41 s 90(1B); Finance, 2001 c 9, s 94(3); Finance, 2014 c 26, s 114(6)

mod—SI 1997/1156, art 4, regs 4, 4A; Finance, 2001 c 9, s 94(1)(2)

rep in pt—(prosp) Finance, 1999 c 16, ss 123(3)(4), 139, sch 20 pt V(6), Note; Finance, 2014 c 26, s 114(1)

am—Finance, 2001 c 9, s 93(1)-(6); SI 2001/3629, art 104; Finance, 2004 c 12, s 281(1), sch 35 para 46(1)-(3); Finance, 2005 c 7, s 97(3)(4)(6); Finance, 2010 c 13, s 30, sch 6 para 15; Charities, 2011 c 25, sch 7 para 81

excl—SI 2006/964, reg 14A

sch 20 rep in pt—Finance, 2011 c 11, sch 26 para 7(2)(b)

c 17   *Disability Rights Commission*—rep (saving) Equality, 2006 c 3, ss 40, 91, sch 3 para 59, sch 4 (see SI 2007/2603, art 3)

s 1 appl —Children 1989 c 41, sch 1 para 6A(6)

c 18   **Adoption (Intercountry Aspects)**

transtl provns—SSI 2004/377, art 2

s 1 am—(S) Adoption and Children (S), 2007 asp 4, s 120, sch 2 para 10; SI 2011/1740, sch 2 para 4

s 2 am—Care Standards, 2000 c 14, s 116, sch 4 para 27; Regulation of Care (S), 2001 asp 8, s 79, sch 3 para 22(b); Adoption and Children, 2002 c 38, s 139(1)(3), sch 3, paras 96-99, sch 5

rep in pt—(prosp) Regulation of Care (S), 2001 asp 8, s 79, sch 3 para 22(a); Adoption and Children, 2002 c 38, s 139(1)(3), sch 3, paras 96-99, sch 5

s 3 rep —(EW) Adoption and Children, 2002 c 38, s 139(1), sch 3, para 95; (S) Adoption and Children (S), 2007 asp 4, s 120, sch 3

s 5 rep (S)—Adoption and Children (S), 2007 asp 4, s 120, sch 3

s 6 rep—(EW) Adoption and Children, 2002 c 38, s 139(1), sch 3, para 95; (S) Adoption and Children (S), 2007 asp 4, s 120, sch 3

s 7 rep in pt—Adoption and Children, 2002 c 38, s 139(3), sch 5

ss 8, 9 rep—(EW) Adoption and Children, 2002 c 38, s 139(1), sch 3, para 95; (S) Adoption and Children (S), 2007 asp 4, s 120, sch 3

s 10 rep (S, NI prosp)—Care Standards, 2000 c 14, s 117(2), sch 6

ss 11-13 rep—(EW) Adoption and Children, 2002 c 38, s 139(1), sch 3, para 95; (S) Adoption and Children (S), 2007 asp 4, s 120, sch 3

1999

c 18 *continued*

s 14 rep —Adoption and Children, 2002 c 38, s 139(1)(3), sch 3, para 100, sch 5

s 16 rep in pt—Adoption and Children, 2002 c 38, s 139(1)(3), sch 3, para 101, sch 5

s 18 rep in pt—Adoption and Children (S), 2007 asp 4, s 120, sch 3; SI 2011/1740, sch 2 pt 3

sch 2 rep in pt—Adoption and Children, 2002 c 38, s 139(3), sch 5; Adoption and Children (S), 2007 asp 4, s 120, sch 3; SI 2011/1740, sch 2 pt 3

c 19 **Company and Business Names (Chamber of Commerce, Etc)**

ss 1-3 am—SI 2009/1941, art 2, sch 1

c 20 **Commonwealth Development Corporation**

s 16 am—SI 2009/1941, art 2, sch 1

s 24 rep—Commonwealth Development Corporation, 1999 c 20, s 27, sch 4

s 26 am—SIs 2008/948, art 3, sch 1; 2009/1941, art 2, sch 1

sch 2 am—SIs 2007/2194, art 10, sch 4; 2008/948, arts 3, 4, schs 1, 3; 2009/1941, art 2, sch 1

rep in pt—SI 2009/1941, art 2, sch 1

sch 3 am—Income Tax (Trading and Other Income), 2005 c 5, s 882(1), sch 1 pt 2 para 510(1)-(3); Corporation Tax, 2009 c 4, s 1322, sch 1 paras 460, 461; Corporation Tax, 2010 c 4, s 1177, sch 1 para 303

rep in pt—Income Tax (Trading and Other Income), 2005 c 5, ss 882(1), 884, sch 1 pt 2 para 510(1)(4), sch 3

c 21 **Football (Offences and Disorder)**

s 1 rep—Football (Disorder), 2000 c 25, s 1, sch 3

s 2 rep in pt—Football (Disorder), 2000 c 25, s 1, sch 3; Violent Crime Reduction, 2006 c 38, s 65, sch 5

s 3 rep in pt—Football (Disorder), 2000 c 25, s 1, sch 3

s 4 rep—Football (Disorder), 2000 c 25, s 1, sch 3

s 5 rep in pt—Football (Disorder), 2000 c 25, s 1, sch 3

ss 6-8 rep—Football (Disorder), 2000 c 25, s 1, sch 3

c 22 **Access to Justice**

am—SI 2000/1119, reg 14, sch 3 pt 1

trans of functions —SI 2003/1887, art 4, sch 1

Pt 1 (ss 1-26) rep —Legal Aid, Sentencing and Punishment of Offenders, 2012 c 10, sch 5 para 51(a)

Pt 2 (ss 26-34) see —(trans of functions) SI 2005/3429, arts 3(1)(c), 4, 5

s 26 am—SIs 2003/1887, art 9, sch 2 para 11(1)(a); 2005/3429, art 8, sch para 4(a); Crim Defence Service, 2006 c 9, s 2(6); Crim Justice and Immigration, 2008 c 4, s 56(1)(5)

s 27 excl—(transtl provn) SI 2000/900, art 2(2)

s 28 am—SIs 2003/1887, art 9, sch 2 para 11(1)(b); 2005/3429, art 8, sch para 4(b)

s 29 rep —Legal Aid, Sentencing and Punishment of Offenders, 2012 c 10, s 46(2)

s 30 rep—Legal Aid, Sentencing and Punishment of Offenders, 2012 c 10, s 47(1)

appl—SI 2000/693, reg 3

excl—(transtl provn) SI 2000/900, art 4

am—SIs 2003/1887, art 9, sch 2 para 11(1)(c); 2005/3429, art 8, sch para 4(c)

s 33 rep—Tax Credits, 2002 c 21, s 60, sch 6

s 35 rep in pt—SL(R), 2004 c 14, s 1(1), sch 1; Legal Services, 2007 c 29, s 210, sch 23

ss 36, 37 rep —Legal Services, 2007 c 29, s 210, sch 23

ss 40-42 rep —Legal Services, 2007 c 29, s 210, sch 23

s 44 am—Legal Services, 2007 c 29, s 208, sch 21 paras 127, 129

rep in pt—Legal Services, 2007 c 29, s 210, sch 23

s 45 rep—SL(R), 2013 c 2, s 1, sch 1 pt 5

s 46 am—SIs 2001/135, art 2; 2003/1887, art 9, sch 2 para 11(1)(c)

rep in pt—Legal Services, 2007 c 29, s 208, sch 21 paras 127, 131, sch 23

s 47 rep—Legal Services, 2007 c 29, s 210, sch 23

ss 49-52 rep —Legal Services, 2007 c 29, s 210, sch 23

s 54 am —Crime and Cts, 2013 c 22, sch 9 para 52; ibid, sch 10 para 79

s 55 am—Crime and Cts, 2013 c 22, sch 9 para 52; ibid, sch 10 para 80

ss 56 am—Constitutional Reform, 2005 c 4, ss 15(1), 40(4), sch 4 pt 1 paras 279, 280, sch 9 pt 1 para 68(1)(2); Crime and Cts, 2013 c 22, sch 9 para 52; ibid, sch 10 para 81

s 57 am—Constitutional Reform, 2005 c 4, ss 15(1), 40(4), sch 4 pt 1 paras 279, 280, sch 9 pt 1 para 68(1)(2); Crime and Cts, 2013 c 22, sch 9 para 52; ibid, sch 10 para 82(a)(b)

1999
c 22 *continued*

s 58 rep in pt—Powers of Crim Cts (Sentencing), 2000 c 6, s 165(3)(4), sch 11 pt I para 2,
　　　　sch 12 pt I; Crim Justice, 2003 c 44, s 332, sch 37 pt 7
s 66 rep—Powers of Crim Cts (Sentencing), 2000 c 6, s 165(3)(4), sch 11 pt I para 2, sch 12
　　　　pt I
s 67 rep in pt—Crim Justice, 2003 c 44, s 332, sch 37 pt 4
s 68 excl—International Crim. Court., 2001 c 17, s 1(3), sch 1 para 7(3)(b)(5)(a)
　　　am—Constitutional Reform, 2005 c 4, s 15(1), sch 4 pt 1 paras 279, 281, 282; SSI
　　　　　2015/150, sch para 6
s 69 am—Constitutional Reform, 2005 c 4, s 15(1), sch 4 pt 1 paras 279, 281(1)(3)(4), 282
s 70 rep—SL(R), 2004 c 14, s 1(1), sch 1 pt 1/4
s 71 rep (prosp)—Coroners and Justice, 2009 c 25, s 178, sch 23 pt 1
s 72 rep (prosp)—Children, Schools and Families, 2010 c 26, s 25, sch 4 pt 2
ss 74, 75 rep—Courts, 2003 c 39, s 109(3), sch 10
s 77 rep—Courts, 2003 c 39, s 109(3), sch 10
s 78 rep in pt—Courts, 2003 c 39, s 109(3), sch 10
s 79 rep—SL(R), 2004 c 14, s 1(1), sch 1 pt 1/4
s 80-89 rep—Courts, 2003 c 39, s 109(3), sch 10
s 90 rep in pt—Courts, 2003 c 39, s 109(3), sch 10
s 91 rep—Courts, 2003 c 39, s 109(3), sch 10
s 93 rep in pt—Courts, 2003 c 39, s 109(3), sch 10
s 96 am—Powers of Crim Cts (Sentencing), 2000 c 6, s 165(1), sch 9 para 204
s 98 rep in pt—Justice (NI), 2002 c 26, s 86, sch 13; Courts, 2003 c 39, s 109(3), sch 10
ss 99, 100 rep—Courts, 2003 c 39, s 109(3), sch 10
ss 101-103 rep —Tribunals, Cts and Enforcement, 2007 c 15, s 146, sch 23
s 104 rep in pt—(prosp) Coroners and Justice, 2009 c 25, s 178, sch 23 pt 1
Pt 7 (ss 105-110) trans of functions—SI 2005/3429, arts 3(1)(c), 4, 5
s 108 trans of cert functions—(S) (saving) SI 2003/415, arts 2, 5, sch
　　　am—SI 2003/1887, art 9, sch 2 para 11(2)
sch 1 rep —Legal Aid, Sentencing and Punishment of Offenders, 2012 c 10, sch 5 para 51(a)
sch 2 rep—Legal Aid, Sentencing and Punishment of Offenders, 2012 c 10, sch 5 para 51(a)
　　　savings—SI 2013/534, art. 6
　　　am and rep in pt as saved—SI 2014/1773, art 3
sch 3 rep —Legal Aid, Sentencing and Punishment of Offenders, 2012 c 10, sch 5 para 51(a)
sch 3A added—Coroners and Justice, 2009 c 25, s 152(1)(4), sch 18
　　　rep—Legal Aid, Sentencing and Punishment of Offenders, 2012 c 10, sch 5 para
　　　　　51(a)
•　sch 4 mod—(temp) SI 2000/774, art 3
　　　rep in pt—Powers of Crim Cts (Sentencing), 2000 c 6, s 165(3)(4), sch 11 pt I para 2,
　　　　　sch 12 pt I; (prosp) Crim Justice, 2003 c 44, s 332, sch 37 pt 4; Courts, 2003 c
　　　　　39, s 109(3), sch 10; (pt prosp) Communications, 2003 c 21, s 406(7), sch
　　　　　19(1); SI 2003/1900, arts 2(1), 3(1),sch 1; SI 2003/3142, art 3(2); Equality,
　　　　　2006 c 3, s 91, sch 4; SI 2006/2493, reg 9; Legal Services, 2007 c 29, s 210,
　　　　　sch 23; (prosp) Welfare Reform, 2009 c 24, s 58, sch 7 pt 1; (prosp) Welfare
　　　　　Reform, 2012 c 5, sch 14 pt 1; Legal Aid, Sentencing and Punishment of
　　　　　Offenders, 2012 c 10, sch 5 pt 2; ibid, sch 12 para 41; Children and Families,
　　　　　2014 c 6, s 18(3)(a)
sch 5 rep in pt—(transtl savings) Powers of Crim Cts (Sentencing), 2000 c 6, s 165(3)(4),
　　　　　sch 11 paras 2,11, sch 12 pt I
sch 6 rep in pt—Legal Services, 2007 c 29, s 210, sch 23
sch 7 rep in pt—(transtl savings) Powers of Crim Cts (Sentencing), 2000 c 6, s 165(3)(4),
　　　　　sch 11 paras 2,11, sch 12 pt I; Legal Services, 2007 c 29, s 210, sch 23
sch 8 rep—Legal Services, 2007 c 29, s 159(2)(b)
sch 9 rep—Powers of Crim Cts (Sentencing), 2000 c 6, s 165(3)(4), sch 11 pt I para 2,
　　　　　sch 12 pt I
sch 10 rep in pt—Access to Justice, 1999 c 22, s 106, sch 15 pt V(6); ibid, sch 15 pt V(2);
　　　　　Crim Justice and Court Services, 2000 c 43, s 75, sch 8; Courts, 2003 c 39,
　　　　　s 109(3), sch 10; Licensing, 2003 c 17, s 199, sch 7; SL(R), 2004 c 14, s 1(1),
　　　　　sch 1 pt 6/5; Crime and Cts, 2013 c 22, sch 10 para 99 Table
sch 11 rep in pt—Access to Justice, 1999 c 22, s 106, sch 15 pt V(6); Crim Justice and
　　　　　Court Services, 2000 c 43, s 75, sch 8; Courts, 2003 c 39, s 109(3), sch 10;
　　　　　Licensing, 2003 c 17, s 199, sch 7; Extradition, 2003 c 41, s 220, sch 4 (see SI
　　　　　2003/3103, arts 2-5); Crim Justice, 2003 c 44, s 332, sch 37 pt 10; Inquiries,
　　　　　2005 c 12, ss 44(5), 49(2), sch 3; Loc Democracy, Economic Development and

1999
c 22 *continued*

Construction, 2009 c 20, s 146, sch 7 pt 3; Crime and Cts, 2013 c 22, sch 10 para 99 Table

sch 12 rep —Courts, 2003 c 39, s 109(3), sch 10

sch 13 rep in pt—Powers of Crim Cts (Sentencing), 2000 c 6, s 165(3)(4), sch 11 pt I para 2, sch 12 pt I; Adoption and Children, 2002 c 38, s 139(3), sch 5; Proceeds of Crime, 2002 c 29, s 457, sch 12; Courts, 2003 c 39, s 109(3), sch 10; Licensing, 2003 c 17, s 199, sch 7; (prosp) Crim Justice, 2003 c 44, s 332, sch 37 pt 4; (prosp) Domestic Violence, Crime and Victims, 2004 c 28, s 58(2), sch 11; Gambling, 2005 c 19, s 356(4)(5), sch 17; Licensing (S), 2005 asp 16, s 149, sch 7; Violent Crime Reduction, 2006 c 38, s 65, sch 5; Road Safety, 2006 c 49, s 59, sch 7(8); Finance, 2007 c 11, s 114, sch 27 pt 6; Crime and Cts, 2013 c 22, sch 11 para 210 Table

sch 14 rep in pt—Access to Justice, 1999 c 22, s 106, sch 15 pt V(6); Legal Services, 2007 c 29, s 210, sch 23; Legal Aid, Sentencing and Punishment of Offenders, 2012 c 10, sch 5 para 51(b)

appl—SI 2001/733, art 2(4)

am—SIs 2003/1887, art 9, sch 2 para 11(4); 2003/2867, reg 2, sch pt 1 para 29

see—(cert functs trans (S)) (saving) SI 2003/415, arts 2, 5, sch

c 23 **Youth Justice and Criminal Evidence**

am—Police and Justice, 2006 c 48, s 52, sch 14 para 37(1)(2)

ss 1-15 rep—(transtl savings) Powers of Crim Cts (Sentencing), 2000 c 6, s 165(3)(4), sch 11 paras 2,11, sch 12 pt I

ss 4, 15 rep in pt—Youth Justice and Crim Evidence, 1999 c 23, s 67, sch 6

Pt 2, Ch 1-3 (ss 16-43) ext—International Crim. Court., 2001 c 17, s 57

Pt 2, Ch 1 (ss 16-33) appl (mods) —Crime and Disorder, 1998 c 37, s 1I; Anti-social Behaviour, Crime and Policing, 2014 c 12, ss 16(1)-(3), 31(1)-(3)

s 16 appl (mods)—SIs 2006/2886, art 2, sch 1, 2887, art 2, sch 1, 2888, art 2, sch 1; 2009/2083, arts 3, 4

am—Coroners and Justice, 2009 c 25, s 98(1)(2)

s 17 appl (mods)—SIs 2006/2886, art 2, sch 1, 2887, art 2, sch 1, 2888, art 2, sch 1; 2009/2083, arts 3, 4

am—Coroners and Justice, 2009 c 25, s 99(1)(2); SI 2013/554, sch para 2; Modern Slavery, 2015 c 30, s 46(2)

s 18 appl (mods)—SIs 2006/2886, art 2, sch 1, 2888, art 2, sch 1; 2009/2083, arts 3, 4

appl—SI 2006/2887, art 2, sch 1

s 19 appl (mods)—SIs 2006/2886, art 2, sch 1, 2887, art 2, sch 1, 2888, art 2, sch 1; 2009/2083, arts 3, 4

s 20 am—Courts, 2003 c 39, s 109(1), sch 8 para 384(a)

appl (mods)—SIs 2006/2886, art 2, sch 1, 2887, art 2, sch 1, 2888, art 2, sch 1; 2009/2083, arts 3, 4

ss 21-23 appl (mods)—SIs 2006/2886, art 2, sch 1, 2887, art 2, sch 1, 2888, art 2, sch 1; 2009/2083, arts 3, 4

s 21 am—Coroners and Justice, 2009 c 25, s 100(1)(3)(4)(b)(5)(6)(8)(b)

rep in pt—Coroners and Justice, 2009 c 25, ss 100(1)(2)(4)(a)(7), 178, sch 23 pt 3

s 22 rep in pt—Coroners and Justice, 2009 c 25, ss 100(8)(a), 178, sch 23 pt 3

am—Coroners and Justice, 2009 c 25, ss 98(1)(4)(a), 100(8)(b)

s 22A added —Coroners and Justice, 2009 c 25, s 100

s 23 appl (mods)—SI 2009/2083, arts 3, 4

s 24 rep in pt—Courts, 2003 c 39, s 109(1)(3), sch 8 para 385, sch 10

appl (mods)—SIs 2006/2886, art 2, sch 1, 2887, art 2, sch 1, 2888, art 2, sch 1; 2009/2083, arts 3, 4

am—Coroners and Justice, 2009 c 25, s 102(1)

s 25 appl (mods)—SIs 2006/2886, art 2, sch 1; 2888, art 2, sch 1; 2009/2083, arts 3, 4

appl—SI 2006/2887, art 2, sch 1

am—SI 2013/554, sch para 3; Modern Slavery, 2015 c 30, s 46(3)

s 26 appl—SIs 2006/2887, art 2, sch 1, 2888, art 2, sch 1

appl (mod)—SI 2009/2083, arts 3, 4

s 27 am—Courts, 2003 c 39, s 109(1), sch 8 para 384(b); Coroners and Justice, 2009 c 25, ss 102(2),103(2)(3)(a)(5); ibid, s 177, sch 21 para 73

rep in pt—Crim Justice, 2003 c 44, ss 41, 332, sch 3 pt 2 para 73(1)(2), sch 37 pt 4; Coroners and Justice, 2009 c 25, ss 103(3)(b)(4), 178, sch 23 pt 3

appl (mods)—SIs 2006/2886, art 2, sch 1, 2887, art 2, sch 1, 2888, art 2, sch 1; 2009/2083, arts 3, 4

1999
c 23 *continued*

s 28 am—Courts, 2003 c 39, s 109(1), sch 8 para 384(c)
    appl (mods)—SI 2009/2083, arts 3, 4
s 29 am—Courts, 2003 c 39, s 109(1), sch 8 para 384(d)
    appl—SI 2005/384, rule 29.1(14)
    appl (mods)—SIs 2006/2886, art 2, sch 1, 2887, art 2, sch 1, 2888, art 2, sch 1;
      2009/2083, arts 3, 4
s 30 appl (mods)—SIs 2006/2886, art 2, sch 1, 2888, art 2, sch 1; 2009/2083, arts 3, 4
    appl—SI 2006/2887, art 2, sch 1
s 31 appl (mods)—SIs 2006/2886, art 2, sch 1, 2887, art 2, sch 1, 2888, art 2, sch 1;
      2009/2083, arts 3, 4
s 32 am—Crim Justice, 2003 c 44, s 331, sch 36 pt 4 paras 74, 75
    appl (mods)—SIs 2006/2886, art 2, sch 1, 2888, art 2, sch 1
s 33 appl (mods)—SIs 2006/2886, art 2, sch 1, 2888, art 2, sch 1; 2009/2083, arts 3, 4
    appl—SI 2006/2887, art 2, sch 1
    am—SIs 2013/554, sch para 4; 2013/2971, reg 2(a)(b); Modern Slavery, 2015 c 30, s
      46(4)
Pt 2, Ch IA heading am (prosp)—Coroners and Justice, 2009 c 25, s 104(2)
s 33A added—Police and Justice, 2006 c 48, s 47
    appl—SI 2009/2657, rule 14
    appl (mods)—SI 2009/2569, art 4
s 33B added—Police and Justice, 2006 c 48, s 47
    appl (mods)—SI 2009/2569, art 4
ss 33BA, 33BB added (prosp)—Coroners and Justice, 2009 c 25, s 104(1)
s 33C added—Police and Justice, 2006 c 48, s 47
    appl (mods)—SI 2009/2569, art 4
s 34 appl (mods)—SIs 2006/2886, art 2, sch 1, 2887, art 2, sch 1, 2888, art 2, sch 1;
      2009/2083, arts 5, 6
s 35 am—Sexual Offences, 2003 c 42, s 139, sch 6 para 41(1)(2); (spec retrosp effect) Crim
      Justice and Immigration, 2008 c 4, s 148, sch 26 paras 35, 36, 38; Coroners and
      Justice, 2009 c 25, s 105
    rep in pt—Sexual Offences, 2003 c 42, s 140, sch 7
    appl (mods)—SIs 2006/2886, art 2, sch 1, 2887, art 2, sch 1, 2888, art 2, sch 1;
      2009/2083, arts 5, 6
s 36 appl (mods)—SIs 2006/2886, art 2, sch 1, 2887, art 2, sch 1, 2888, art 2, sch 1;
      2009/2083, arts 5, 6
s 37 am—Courts, 2003 c 39, s 109(1), sch 8 para 384(e)
    appl (mods)—SIs 2006/2886, art 2, sch 1, 2887, art 2, sch 1, 2888, art 2, sch 1;
      2009/2083, arts 5, 6
s 38 am—Courts, 2003 c 39, s 109(1), sch 8 para 384(f)
    appl (mods)—SIs 2006/2886, art 2, sch 1, 2887, art 2, sch 1, 2888, art 2, sch 1;
      2009/2083, arts 5, 6
s 39 am—Crim Justice, 2003 c 44, s 331, sch 36 pt 4 paras 74, 76
    appl (mods)—SI 2006/2888, art 2, sch 1; 2009/2083, arts 5, 6
s 40 rep in pt—Access to Justice, 1999 c 22, s 106, sch 15 pt I
s 41 saved—Crim Justice, 2003 c 44, s 112(3)(b)
    appl (mods)—SIs 2006/2886, art 2, sch 1, 2887, art 2, sch 1, 2888, art 2, sch 1;
      2009/2083, arts 7, 8
    am—SI 2010/976, art 12, sch 14
s 42 am—Crim Justice, 2003 c 44, s 41, sch 3 pt 2 para 73(1)(3)(b)
    rep in pt—Crim Justice, 2003 c 44, ss 41, 332, sch 3 pt 2 para 73(1)(3)(a), sch 37 pt 4
    appl (mods)—SIs 2006/2886, art 2, sch 1, 2887, art 2, sch 1, 2888, art 2, sch 1;
      2009/2083, arts 7, 8
s 43 see—SI 2005/384, rule 36.1
    am—Courts, 2003 c 39, s 109(1), sch 8 para 384(g)
    appl (mods)—SIs 2006/2886, art 2, sch 1, 2887, art 2, sch 1, 2888, art 2, sch 1;
      2009/2083, arts 7, 8
s 44 am—Courts, 2003 c 39, s 109(1), sch 8 para 386; Armed Forces, 2006 c 52, s 378, sch
      16 para 158; SI 2010/976, art 12, sch 14
    appl (mods)—SI 2009/2083, art 13
    mod—SI 2009/1059, art 205, sch 1
s 45 appl—Crime and Disorder,1998 c 37, s 1; Violent Crime Reduction, 2006 c 38, s
      11(8)(b); Anti-social Behaviour, Crime and Policing, 2014 c 12, s 30(5)(b)

1999
c 23 s 45 *continued*
> appl (mods)—SIs 2006/2886, art 2, sch 1, 2887, art 2, sch 1, 2888, art 2, sch 1;
> 2009/2083, art 13
> s 45A added—Crim Justice and Cts, 2015 c 2, s 78(2)
> s 46 appl (mods)—SIs 2006/2886, art 2, sch 1, 2887, art 2, sch 1, 2888, art 2, sch 1;
> 2009/2083, art 13
> s 47 am—SI 1999/2789, art 40(1), sch 1 para 6; Police and Justice, 2006 c 48, s 52, sch 14
> para 37(1)(3)
> appl (mods) —Crime and Disorder, 1998 c 37, s 11; SIs 2006/2886, art 2, sch 2;
> 2006/2888, art 2, sch 2; 2009/2083, art 13; Anti-social Behaviour, Crime and
> Policing, 2014 c 12, ss 16(4), 31(4)
> s 49 appl (mods) —Crime and Disorder, 1998 c 37, s 11; 2009/2083, art 13
> appl—Anti-social Behaviour, Crime and Policing, 2014 c 12, ss 16(4), 31(4)
> am—Crim Justice and Cts, 2015 c 2, s 78(3)
> s 50 am—Crim Justice and Cts, 2015 c 2, s 78(4)
> s 51 appl (mods)—Crime and Disorder, 1998 c 37, s 11; 2009/2083, art 13
> appl—Anti-social Behaviour, Crime and Policing, 2014 c 12, ss 16(4), 31(4)
> s 52 appl (mods)—SIs 2006/2886, art 2, sch 2, 2888, art 2, sch 2; 2009/2083, art 13
> ss 53-57 appl (mods)—SIs 2006/2886, art 2, sch 1, 2887, art 2, sch 1, 2888, art 2, sch 1; SI
> 2009/2083, arts 9, 10
> s 62 am—Sexual Offences, 2003 c 42, s 139, sch 6 para 41(1)(3); (spec retrosp effect) Crim
> Justice and Immigration, 2008 c 4, s 148, sch 26 paras 35, 37, 38
> appl (mods)—SIs 2006/2887, art 2, sch 1; 2006/2888, art 2, sch 1; 2009/2083, arts 11,
> 12
> mod—Serious Crime, 2007 c 27, s 63, sch 6 para 37
> s 63 rep in pt—Armed Forces, 2001 c 19, s 38, sch 7 pt 1
> appl—(EW) Crime and Disorder, 1998 c 37, s 51C(7)
> appl (mods)—SIs 2006/2887, art 2, sch 1; 2006/2888, art 2, sch 1; 2009/2083, arts 11,
> 12, 13; 2009/2569, art 5
> am—Armed Forces, 2006 c 52, s 378, sch 16 para 159; Legal Services, 2007 c 29, s
> 208, sch 21 para 132
> s 64 rep in pt—Powers of Crim Cts (Sentencing), 2000 c 6, s 165(3)(4), sch 11 paras 2,11,
> sch 12 pt I
> am—Coroners and Justice, 2009 c 25, s 99(1)(3); SI 2010/976, art 12, sch 14
> s 65 am—Courts, 2003 c 39, s 109(1), sch 8 para 384(h); SI 2013/554, sch para 5
> rep in pt—Courts, 2003 c 39, s 109(1)(3), sch 8 para 387, sch 10
> appl (mods)—SIs 2006/2886, art 2, sch 1; 2006/2887, art 2, sch 1; 2006/2888, art 2,
> sch 1; 2009/2083, arts 11, 12, 13; 2009/2569, art 5
> s 67 rep in pt—Powers of Crim Cts (Sentencing), 2000 c 6, s 165(3)(4), sch 11 paras 2,11,
> sch 12 pt I
> s 68 rep in pt—(transtl savings) Powers of Crim Cts (Sentencing), 2000 c 6, s 165(3)(4),
> sch 11 paras 2,11, sch 12 pt I; Armed Forces, 2006 c 52, s 378, sch 17
> am—SI 2010/976, art 12, sch 14
> sch 1 rep—Powers of Crim Cts (Sentencing), 2000 c 6, s 165(3)(4), sch 11 paras 2,11,
> sch 12 pt I
> sch 1A added —Coroners and Justice, 2009 c 25, s 99, sch 14
> am—Legal Aid, Sentencing and Punishment of Offenders, 2012 c 10, sch 26 para
> 8(2)(3)
> sch 2 am—Powers of Crim Cts (Sentencing), 2000 c 6, s 165(1), sch 9 para 205
> rep in pt—Crim Justice and Cts, 2015 c 2, s 79(11)
> sch 2A added—Crim Justice and Cts, 2015 c 2, sch 15 para 2
> sch 3 rep in pt—Companies (Audit, Investigations and Community Enterprise), 2004 c 27,
> s 64, sch 8; SI 2009/1941, art 2, sch 2
> sch 4 rep in pt—Access to Justice, 1999 c 22, s 106, sch 15 pt V(8); Youth Justice and Crim
> Evidence, 1999 c 23, s 67, sch 6; Powers of Crim Cts (Sentencing), 2000 c 6,
> s 165(3)(4), sch 11 pt I para 2, sch 12 pt I; (EW) Crim Justice, 2003 c 44,
> s 332, sch 37 pts 5,6, 12; Companies, 2006 c 46, s 1295, sch 16; SI 2009/1941,
> art 2, sch 2; Legal Aid, Sentencing and Punishment of Offenders, 2012 c 10, sch
> 25 pt 2
> sch 5 rep—(transtl savings) Powers of Crim Cts (Sentencing), 2000 c 6, s 165(3)(4), sch 11
> paras 2,11, sch 12 pt I
> sch 7 rep in pt—(transtl savings) Powers of Crim Cts (Sentencing), 2000 c 6, s 165(3)(4),
> sch 11 paras 2,11, sch 12 pt I

1999

c 23 sch 7 *continued*

    am—Armed Forces, 2006 c 52, s 378, sch 16 para 161

    mod—SI 2009/1059, art 205, sch 1

c 24 **Pollution Prevention and Control**

   s 1 appl—(EW) Road Traffic Regulation, 1984 c 27, s 55

   spec provn(s) amdt to earlier commencing SSI 2015/74 art 2(2)—SSI 2015/139, art 2

    rep in pt—Regulatory Reform (S), 2014 asp 3, sch 3 para 7

   s 2 trans of certain functions—(W) SI 2005/1958, art 3; SI 2008/1776, art 2, sch

    rep in pt—(W) SI 2013/755 (W 90), sch 2 para 395(2)

    am—(W) SI 2013/755 (W 90), sch 2 para 395(3); Water, 2014 c 21, s 62(13)

   s 3 am—(W) SI 2013/755 (W 90), sch 2 para 396

   s 4 rep—(EW) (saving) SI 2007/3538, regs 73, 74, sch 21 para 26, sch 23

   sch 1 am—Waste and Emissions Trading, 2003 c 33, s 38; (S) Antisocial Behaviour etc (S),

    2004 asp 8, s 66, sch 2 pt 1 para 5; SI 2005/925, reg 48, sch 6 para 2; (EW)

    Clean Neighbourhoods and Environment, 2005 c 16, s 105; SIs 2012/2788, reg

    16; 2015/664, sch 4 para 90

    see—(trans of functions) SI 2008/1776, art 2, sch

   sch 2 rep in pt—Govt of Wales, 2006 c 32, s 163, sch 12; (EW) (saving) SI 2007/3538, reg

    74, sch 23

    see—(para 19 in force (S) retrosp to 21.3.2000) Finance, 2012 c 14, s 206(a)

   sch 3 rep in pt—Regulatory Reform (S), 2014 asp 3, sch 3 para 36

c 25 **Criminal Cases Review (Insanity)**

c 26 **Employment Relations**

   s 10 am—Employment Relations, 2004 c 24, s 37(1), SI 2004/2566

   s 11 power to appl—Employment Rights, 1996 c 18, s 80G(2)(n)

    rep in pt—Employment, 2002 c 22, s 54, sch 8(1)

    am—Employment Relations, 2004 c 24, s 37(2), SI 2004/2566; Enterprise and

    Regulatory Reform, 2013 c 24, sch 2 para 40

   s 12 power to appl—Employment Rights, 1996 c 18, s 80G(2)(n)

    am—Employment Relations, 2004 c 24, s 37(3), SI 2004/256

   s 13 power to appl—Employment Rights, 1996 c 18, s 80G(2)(n)

   s 14 am—SI 2014/431, sch para 6

   s 17 rep—Employment Relations, 2004 c 24, ss 31(8), 57(2), sch 2, SI 2004/2566

   s 18 rep in pt—Employment Relations, 1999 c 26, s 44, sch 9(3); Tax Credits, 2002 c 21, s

    60, sch 6

   s 23 rep in pt—Employment, 2002 c 22, s 41; Employment Relations, 2004 c 24,

    ss 39(1)(2), 57(2), sch 2

    am—Employment, 2002 c 22, s 53, sch 7, para 54; Employment Relations, 2004 c 24,

    s 39(1)(3)

   s 28 rep in pt—SL(R), 2004 c 14, s 1(1), sch 1 pt 8

   s 33 rep in pt—SL(R), 2004 c 14, s 1(1), sch 1 pt 8

   s 34 am—Employment Relations, 2004 c 24, s 57(1), sch 1 para 42, SI 2004/2566;

    Statistics and Registration Service, 2007 c 18, s 60, sch 3 para 11; Enterprise and

    Regulatory Reform, 2013 c 24, ss 15(10), 22(2)(b)(3)

    rep in pt—Enterprise and Regulatory Reform, 2013 c 24, s 22(2)(a)

    mod—SI 2009/1903, art 3

   s 37 rep in pt—SL(R), 2004 c 14, s 1(1), sch 1 pt 8

   s 40 rep—Educ, 2002 c 32, s 215(2), sch 22 pt 3

   sch 4 rep in pt—Tax Credits, 2002 c 21, s 60, sch 6; SL(R), 2004 c 14, s 1(1), sch 1 pt 8

   sch 6 rep in pt—SL(R), 2004 c 14, s 1(1), sch 1 pt 8

   sch 7 rep in pt—Employment, 2008 c 24, s 20, sch pt 5

   sch 8 rep in pt—Race Relations (Amdt), 2000 c 34, s 9(2), sch 3; SL(R), 2004 c 14, s 1(1),

    sch 1 pt 8

c 27 **Local Government**

   Pt 1 (ss 1-29) ext (mods)—(W pt prosp, S prosp) Loc Govt, 2003 c 26, s 101(1)(3)(4)

    appl—Public Audit (W), 2004 c 23, ss 54(1)(2)(b), 59(4)

   s 1 am—Fire and Rescue Services, 2004 c 21, s 53, sch 1 paras 90, 91; Public Audit (W),

    2004 c 23, s 50, sch 1 paras 1, 2; Police and Justice, 2006 c 48, s 4; Loc Govt and

    Public Involvement in Health, 2007 c 28, ss 136(1), 144, 209, sch 8 paras 1, 2, sch

    13 para 53; Loc Transport, 2008 c 26, s 77, sch 4 para 62; Loc Democracy,

    Economic Development and Construction, 2009 c 20, s 119, sch 6 para 91; Police

    Reform and Social Responsibility, 2011 c 13, sch 16 para 242(2)

    appl—(E) SI 2004/1705, art 1(2)(a)

1999
c 27 s 1 *continued*

rep in pt—Loc Govt and Public Involvement in Health, 2007 c 28, s 241, sch 18; Loc
Govt (W), 2009 nawm 2, s 51, sch 1 paras 9, 10; ibid, s 52, sch 4; Localism,
2011 c 20, sch 25 pt 32; Police Reform and Social Responsibility, 2011 c 13,
sch 16 para 242(3); Deregulation, 2015 c 20, sch 13 para 6(30)

s 2 am—Loc Govt and Public Involvement in Health, 2007 c 28, s 144, sch 8 paras 1, 3
rep in pt—Loc Govt and Public Involvement in Health, 2007 c 28, s 136(2), sch 18;
Learning and Skills (W), 2009 nawm 1, s 51, sch 1 paras 9, 11; Loc Govt (W),
2009 nawm 2, s 52, sch 1 paras 9, 11

s 2A added—Public Audit (W), 2004 c 23, s 50, sch 1 paras 1, 3
rep —Loc Govt (W), 2009 nawm 2, s 52, sch 4

s 3 am—Loc Govt and Public Involvement in Health, 2007 c 28, ss 137, 144, sch 8 paras 1,
5

s 3A added —Loc Govt and Public Involvement in Health, 2007 c 28, s 138(1)
rep —Deregulation, 2015 c 20, s 103(1)

s 4 rep —Loc Govt (W), 2009 nawm 2, s 52, sch 4

s 5 ext—(E) SI 2001/1299, reg 6(5); (W) SI 2001/2284, reg 6(6)
am—Loc Govt, 2003 c 26, s 100, sch 3 paras 4, 6 (see SI 2003/2938)
rep (W pt prosp)—Loc Govt and Public Involvement in Health, 2007 c 28, s 140, sch 18
pt 8

s 6 rep —Loc Govt (W), 2009 nawm 2, s 52, sch 4
am—Loc Govt, 2003 c 26, s 100, sch 3 paras 4, 7 (see SI 2003/2938); Loc Govt and
Public Involvement in Health, 2007 c 28, ss 139(3), 144, sch 8 paras 1, 7
rep in pt—Loc Govt and Public Involvement in Health, 2007 c 28, s 241, sch 18

s 7 rep —Loc Govt (W), 2009 nawm 2, s 52, sch 4

s 8 rep—Loc Govt and Public Involvement in Health, 2007 c 28, s 144, sch 8 paras 1, 10,
sch 18

ss 8A, 8B added—Public Audit (W), 2004 c 23, s 50, sch 1 paras 1, 7
rep —Loc Govt (W), 2009 nawm 2, s 52, sch 4

s 9 rep —Loc Govt (W), 2009 nawm 2, s 52, sch 4

s 10 subst—Loc Audit and Accountability, 2014 c 2, sch 10 para 2

s 10A added—Public Audit (W), 2004 c 23, s 50, sch 1 paras 1, 9
rep —Police Reform and Social Responsibility, 2011 c 13, sch 16 para 245

s 11 appl—Adoption (Intercountry Aspects), 1999 c 18, s 41A (see SI 2003/2938); Fire and
Rescue Services, 2004 c 21, s 24(1); (E) SI 2005/1973, reg 2, sch para 8
am—Public Audit (W), 2004 c 23, s 50, sch 1 paras 1, 10; Loc Govt and Public
Involvement in Health, 2007 c 28, ss 144, 151(2), sch 8 paras 1, 16; Loc Audit
and Accountability, 2014 c 2, sch 10 para 3
rep in pt—Loc Govt and Public Involvement in Health, 2007 c 28, s 241, sch 18; Public
Audit (W), 2013 anaw 3, sch 4 para 10

s 12 subst—Loc Audit and Accountability, 2014 c 2, sch 10 para 4

s 12A added—Public Audit (W), 2004 c 23, s 50, sch 1 paras 1, 12
rep —Public Audit (W), 2013 anaw 3, sch 4 para 11

s 13 appl (mods)—Fire and Rescue Services, 2004 c 21, s 24
am—Loc Govt and Public Involvement in Health, 2007 c 28, ss 144, 147(1), sch 8
paras 1, 18; Loc Audit and Accountability, 2014 c 2, sch 10 para
5(2)-(5)(6)(a)(7)
rep in pt—Loc Govt and Public Involvement in Health, 2007 c 28, s 241, sch 18; Loc
Audit and Accountability, 2014 c 2, sch 10 paras 5(6)(b), 11(a)

s 13A added—Public Audit (W), 2004 c 23, s 50, sch 1 paras 1, 13
rep —Public Audit (W), 2013 anaw 3, sch 4 para 12

s 14 rep (prosp)—Welfare Reform, 2012 c 5, sch 14 pt 1

s 15 am—Loc Govt and Public Involvement in Health, 2007 c 28, s 144, sch 8 paras 1, 20;
Children and Families, 2014 c 6, s 101(3)
rep in pt—Loc Govt (W), 2009 nawm 2, s 51, sch 1 paras 9, 16; ibid, s 52, sch 4; Loc
Audit and Accountability, 2014 c 2, sch 10 para 6

s 16 am—Loc Govt, 2003 c 26, s 100, sch 3 paras 4, 8 (see SI 2003/2938); Loc Govt and
Public Involvement in Health, 2007 c 28, ss 141(1), 142(1)
rep in pt—Loc Govt (W), 2009 nawm 2, s 51, sch 1 paras 9, 17; ibid, s 52, sch 4

s 17 am—Loc Govt, 2003 c 26, s 100, sch 3 paras 4, 9 (see SI 2003/2938)

ss 17A, 17B added—Loc Govt and Public Involvement in Health, 2007 c 28, s 142(2)(3)
rep —Loc Govt (W), 2009 nawm 2, s 52, sch 4

s 18 am—Loc Govt and Public Involvement in Health, 2007 c 28, s 239(5)

1999

c 27 *continued*

s 19 am—Loc Govt, 2003 c 26, s 100, sch 3 paras 4, 10 (see SI 2003/2938); Loc Govt and
Public Involvement in Health, 2007 c 28, s 136, sch 7 para 2(1)-(4); Loc Govt
(W), 2009 nawm 2, s 51, sch 1 paras 9, 18

s 21 rep—Loc Govt and Public Involvement in Health, 2007 c 28, s 241, sch 18

s 22 rep in pt—Loc Govt, 2003 c 26, s 127(2), sch 8 pt 1; Public Audit (W), 2004 c 23, s 72,
sch 4; Loc Govt and Public Involvement in Health, 2007 c 28, s 146, sch 9 para
1(1)(2)(m), sch 18; Loc Audit and Accountability, 2014 c 2, sch 1 pt 2; ibid,
sch 10 para 7

s 23 am—Public Audit (W), 2004 c 23, s 50, sch 1 paras 1, 14; Loc Govt and Public
Involvement in Health, 2007 c 28, s 144, sch 8 paras 1, 21; Loc Audit and
Accountability, 2014 c 2, sch 12 para 36(3)

rep in pt—Loc Govt and Public Involvement in Health, 2007 c 28, s 241, sch 18; Loc
Govt (W), 2009 nawm 2, s 51, sch 1 paras 9, 19; ibid, s 52, sch 4; Police
Reform and Social Responsibility, 2011 c 13, sch 16 para 246; Public Audit
(W), 2013 anaw 3, sch 4 para 13; Loc Audit and Accountability, 2014 c 2, sch
12 para 36(2); Deregulation, 2015 c 20, sch 22 para 14(1)

s 24 rep in pt—Police Reform, 2002 c 30, s 107(2), sch 8; (prosp) Police and Justice, 2006 c
48, s 52, sch 15

s 25 am—Health and Social Care (Community Health and Standards), 2003 c 43, s 147, sch
9 para 15; Public Audit (W), 2004 c 23, s 50, sch 1 paras 1, 15; Educ and
Inspections, 2006 c 40, s 157, sch 14 para 37; Health and Social Care, 2008 c 14,
s 95, sch 5 para 70; Loc Audit and Accountability, 2014 c 2, sch 10 para 8

rep in pt—Loc Govt (W), 2009 nawm 2, s 51, sch 1 paras 9, 20; ibid, s 52, sch 4;
Public Audit (W), 2013 anaw 3, sch 4 para 14

transtl provns—SI 2008/2250, art 3

s 26 am—Public Audit (W), 2004 c 23, s 50, sch 1 paras 1, 16; Loc Govt and Public
Involvement in Health, 2007 c 28, s 136, sch 7 para 2(1)(5)

rep in pt—Loc Govt and Public Involvement in Health, 2007 c 28, s 241, sch 18; Public
Audit (W), 2013 anaw 3, sch 4 para 15; Loc Audit and Accountability, 2014 c
2, sch 10 para 9

s 28 rep in pt—Loc Govt and Public Involvement in Health, 2007 c 28, s 241, sch 18; Loc
Govt (W), 2009 nawm 2, s 51, sch 1 paras 9, 21; ibid, s 52, sch 4; Deregulation,
2015 c 20, s 103(2)(a)

am—Loc Govt and Public Involvement in Health, 2007 c 28, s 138(2)

s 29 rep in pt—Fire and Rescue Services, 2004 c 21, ss 53, 54, sch 1 paras 90, 92, sch 2;
Loc Govt and Public Involvement in Health, 2007 c 28, s 241, sch 18; Loc
Govt (W), 2009 nawm 2, s 51, sch 1 paras 9, 22; ibid, s 52, sch 4; Police
Reform and Social Responsibility, 2011 c 13, sch 16 para 247; (E prosp)
Welfare Reform, 2012 c 5, sch 14 pt 1

am—Loc Govt and Public Involvement in Health, 2007 c 28, s 144, sch 8 paras 1, 22;
Welfare Reform, 2007 c 5, s 38(2)

s 31 rep—Loc Govt, 2003 c 26, ss 86, 127(2), sch 8 pt 1

s 33 am—Public Audit (W), 2004 c 23, s 50, sch 1 paras 1, 17; Loc Govt (W), 2009 nawm
2, s 36; Public Audit (W), 2013 anaw 3, sch 4 para 16

rep in pt—Loc Audit and Accountability, 2014 c 2, sch 10 para 10

sch 1 rep in pt—Localism, 2011 c 20, sch 25 pt 12

c 28   **Food Standards**

cert funct cease to be exercisble (S)—Food (S), 2015 asp 1, s 32

s 14 mod—Food Standards, 1999 c 28, ss 14(9), 38(3)

s 15 am—(EW) SI 2000/656, reg 11, sch 9; (S) SSI 2000/62, reg 11

s 17 rep (S)—Food (S), 2015 asp 1, sch para 7(2)

s 19 appl—(E) SIs 2005/2626, reg 7(6); (W) 3254 (W 247), reg 7(6); (S) SSIs 2005/616,
reg 8(6); 2007/522, art 8; SIs 2009/3255, reg 7(6); 2009/3376, reg 7(6)

appl (mods)—SIs (E) 2007/3185, reg 7; 2007/3294, reg 7; (S) SSI 2009/446, reg 7

s 22 am—SI 2007/1388, art 3, sch 1

s 24 see —(trans of functions) (S) SI 2005/849, arts 2, 6, sch

s 27 rep (S)—Food (S), 2015 asp 1, sch para 7(2)

s 29 see—(trans of functions) SI 2002/794, art 3(3)

am—SIs 2002/794, art 5(1), sch 1, para 38; 2006/2407, reg 44, sch 9

rep in pt—SI 2002/794, art 5(2), sch 2

s 30 rep in pt—SI 2002/794, art 5(2), sch 2

rep (S)—Food (S), 2015 asp 1, sch para 7(2)

am—SI 2004/3254, reg 13

1999

c 28 *continued*

s 32 am—SI 2007/1388, art 3, sch 1

s 43 am—Food (S), 2015 asp 1, sch para 7(3)

sch 1 am—SI 2012/2404, sch 2 para 43

sch 3 rep in pt—SIs 2010/675, regs 107, 109, schs 26, 28; 2015/978, sch pt 1

sch 4 am—Govt Resources and Accounts, 2000 c 20, s 29(1), sch 1 para 26(1)(2)(3); SI 2007/1388, art 3, sch 1

sch 5 rep in pt—SI 2004/1109, art 7, sch; SI 2010/675, reg 109, sch 28

c 29 **Greater London Authority**

appl—Representation of the People, 1983 c 2, s 203(1); SIs 2001/341, reg 103(1)(f); (E) 2002/2298, art 3(2); (EW) Loc Govt, 2003 c 26, ss 3(11), 23(1)(e), 29(7) (see SI 2003/2938)

am—Constitutional Reform, 2005 c 4, s 59(5), sch 11 pt 2 para 4

saving—SI 2007/3136, art 3

mod —Localism, 2011 c 20, s 35(6)(a)

excl—SI 2012/472, art 9(1)

Pt 1 (ss 1-29) appl—SI 2000/427, rule 2(2); (E) SI 2001/1298, reg 14(2)(g)

s 2 see—(power to transfer or mod functions) Political Parties, Elections and Referendums, 2000 c 41, s 18(3)(c); (E) SI 2001/3962, art 3(1)(2)(c)

am—(E) SI 2001/3962, art 9, sch 2 para 13; Loc Democracy, Economic Development and Construction, 2009 c 20, s 67, sch 4 paras 8, 9

s 3 excl—SI 2004/222, art 2(2)

s 4 appl—Representation of the People, 1983 c 2, s 203(1B)

am—Political Parties, Elections and Referendums, 2000 c 41, s 158(1), sch 21 para 15

s 6 am—Loc Govt, 2000 c 22, s 107, sch 5 para 31; Loc Govt and Public Involvement in Health, 2007 c 28, s 201(6)

appl—Localism, 2011 c 20, s 35(7)

rep in pt—Localism, 2011 c 20, sch 25 pt 5

s 7 am—Localism, 2011 c 20, s 34(13)

rep in pt—Loc Audit and Accountability, 2014 c 2, sch 12 para 38

s 7A excl—Regional Development Agencies, 1998 c 45, s 7B(6)

s 8 excl—Transport for London, 2008 c.i, s 5(3)

s 9 am—Localism, 2011 c 20, s 34(14)

rep in pt—Loc Audit and Accountability, 2014 c 2, sch 12 para 39

s 10 am—GLA, 2007 c 24, s 19

s 13 am—Loc Govt, 2000 c 22, s 107, sch 5 para 32; Loc Govt and Public Involvement in Health, 2007 c 28, s 201(6)

rep in pt—Localism, 2011 c 20, sch 25 pt 5

s 14 am—Localism, 2011 c 20, s 34(13)

rep in pt—Loc Audit and Accountability, 2014 c 2, sch 12 para 40

s 17A added—Representation of the People, 2000 c 2, s 14(2)

am—Political Parties, Elections and Referendums, 2000 c 41, s 7(2)(i); SI 2001/648, art 4(1), sch 1 para 14; Electoral Admin, 2006 c 22, s 10, sch 1 para 18; SI 2010/1837, art 5, sch; Postal Services, 2011 c 5, sch 12 para 155; SI 2015/1376, sch 2 para 6

see—(functions made exerciseable concurrently) SI 2010/1837, art 3

trans of funct—SI 2015/1376, art 3(1) sch 1

s 20 am—Electoral Admin, 2006 c 22, ss 17(5),18, sch 1 para 42; SI 2012/1809, art 3(1), sch

s 21 am—(E) SIs 2001/2237, arts 2, 35; 2006/1722, art 2, sch 2; 2012/2404, sch 2 para 42

rep in pt—Loc Audit and Accountability, 2014 c 2, sch 12 para 41

s 23 am—SI 2000/311, art 35

rep in pt—SI 2000/311, art 35

s 24 am—GLA, 2007 c 24, s 1(3)

s 25 am—SI 2011/3048, art 2(2)

s 26A added—GLA, 2007 c 24, s 1(1)

s 27 am—GLA, 2007 c 24, s 1(2)

s 28 see—(temp) (E) SI 2001/3575, art 4(g)

s 29 mod—SI 2000/308, art 3

rep in pt—SI 2000/1435, art 2, sch pt I paras 1,2

s 30 rep in pt—GLA, 2007 c 24, s 57, sch 2

am—GLA, 2007 c 24, ss 23, 40

appl—Localism, 2011 c 20, s 197(7)

1999

c 29 *continued*

s 31 am—Loc Govt, 2000 c 22, s 107, sch 5 para 33; Localism, 2011 c 20, s 186(4); ibid, sch 22 para 45(1)-(3); SI 2012/1530, art 2(2)(3); Infrastructure, 2015 c 7, s 33(1)

 rep in pt—Localism, 2011 c 20, s 186(2)(3), sch 25 pts 31, 32

s 33 appl—Police Reform and Social Responsibility, 2011 c 13, s 6(11)(a)

s 34 excl—Loc Govt, 2003 c 26, s 93(7)(b)

s 34A added —Localism, 2011 c 20, s 224(2)

 am—Co-operative and Community Benefit Societies Act 2014 c 14, sch 4 para 67

s 35 am—SI 2000/1435, art 2, sch pt I paras 1,3

s 38 excl—GLA, 1999 c 29, s 73(12); (EW) Loc Govt, 2003 c 26, s 3(9); SI 2008/1342, reg 7

 am—(E) SI 2001/2237, arts 2, 36; Planning, 2008 c 29, s 224(4); Localism, 2011 c 20, sch 19 para 37(1)-(5); ibid, sch 20 para 5; ibid, sch 22 para 46(1)-(4); Growth and Infrastructure, 2013 c 27, s 28(1)

 rep in pt—Localism, 2011 c 20, sch 25 pt 32

s 39 excl—SI 2008/1342, reg 7

s 39A added —Localism, 2011 c 20, s 223(2)

s 41 am—GLA, 2007 c 24, ss 24, 28(1)-(3), 41, 43(1), 44(1); Localism, 2011 c 20, ss 192(3), 227(1)-(3), sch 23 para 2(1)(2)(a)

 rep in pt—Localism, 2011 c 20, s 227(1)(4), sch 23 para 2(1)(2)(b)(3), sch 25 pt 33

 appl—Police Reform and Social Responsibility, 2011 c 13, s 6(11)(b)

s 42 excl—Regional Development Agencies, 1998 c 45, s 7B(6)

 am—GLA, 2007 c 24, s 2(1)

 appl—Police Reform and Social Responsibility, 2011 c 13, s 6(11)(c)

 rep in pt—Localism, 2011 c 20, sch 25 pt 33

s 42A added—GLA, 2007 c 24, s 2(2)

 rep —Localism, 2011 c 20, s 228(1), sch 25 pt 33

s 42B added —Localism, 2011 c 20, s 229

s 43 appl (mods)—Police Reform and Social Responsibility, 2011 c 13, s 6(11)(e)

s 44 appl—Police Reform and Social Responsibility, 2011 c 13, s 6(11)(f)

s 45 am—SI 2000/1435, art 2, sch pt I paras 1, 4; GLA, 2007 c 24, ss 3, 11(1)(2); Police Reform and Social Responsibility, 2011 c 13, sch 16 para 49

s 46 rep in pt—Localism, 2011 c 20, sch 25 pt 32

s 52 rep in pt—Loc Govt, 2003 c 26, s 127, sch 7 paras 68, 69(1)(4), sch 8 pt 1 (see SI 2003/2938)

 am—Loc Govt, 2003 c 26, s 127(1), sch 7 para 68, 69(1)-(3) (see SI 2003/2938)

s 54 excl—Loc Govt Finance, 1988 c 41, s 115A(10); Audit Commission, 1998 c 18, s 11A(12); GLA, 1999 c 29, s 73(12); Police Reform and Social Responsibility, 2011 c 13, s 32(6)(7); Loc Audit and Accountability, 2014 c 2, sch 7 para 7(5)

 rep in pt—GLA, 2007 c 24, s 57, sch 2; Police Reform and Social Responsibility, 2011 c 13, sch 16 para 50

 appl—Police Reform and Social Responsibility, 2011 c 13, s 32(9)

s 55 excl—Police Reform and Social Responsibility, 2011 c 13, s 32(6)(7)

s 58 rep in pt—Localism, 2011 c 20, sch 25 pt 32

s 60A added—GLA, 2007 c 24, s 4(1)

 am—SI 2008/2038, art 21; Police Reform and Social Responsibility, 2011 c 13, s 20(2)(a)(c); Localism, 2011 c 20, sch 22 para 47

 rep in pt—Police Reform and Social Responsibility, 2011 c 13, s 20(2)(b); Localism, 2011 c 20, sch 25 pt 32

s 61 am—GLA, 2007 c 24, ss 5, 11(1)(3); Loc Govt and Public Involvement in Health, 2007 c 28, s 203(3)(a)

 rep in pt—Police Reform and Social Responsibility, 2011 c 13, sch 16 para 51

 appl (mods)—Police Reform and Social Responsibility, 2011 c 13, s 33(9)(a)

s 62 appl (mods)—Police Reform and Social Responsibility, 2011 c 13, s 33(9)(b)

s 63 appl (mods)—Police Reform and Social Responsibility, 2011 c 13, s 33(9)(c)

s 64 am—(prosp) Crim Justice, 2003 c 44, s 280(2)(3), sch 26 para 52

 appl (mods)—Police Reform and Social Responsibility, 2011 c 13, s 33(9)(d)

s 65 appl (mods)—Police Reform and Social Responsibility, 2011 c 13, s 33(9)(e)

s 65A added—GLA, 2007 c 24, s 6

s 66 rep —Loc Govt, 2000 c 22, s 107, sch 5 para 34, sch 6

s 67 am—GLA, 2007 c 24, s 7

s 68 am—Loc Govt and Public Involvement in Health, 2007 c 28, s 203(3)(b); Localism, 2011 c 20, sch 22 para 48(1)-(5)

 rep in pt—Localism, 2011 c 20, sch 25 pt 32

1999

c 29 *continued*

s 70 restr—Loc Govt Finance, 1992 c 14, s 52U(2)-(11)
    appl (mods)—Further and Higher Education 1992 c 14, s 52J
    am—Loc Govt and Public Involvement in Health, 2007 c 28, s 203(3)(c)
s 71 restr—Loc Govt Finance, 1992 c 14, s 52U(2)-(11)
    appl (mods)—Further and Higher Education 1992 c 14, s 52J
s 72 restr—Loc Govt Finance, 1992 c 14, s 52U(2)-(11)
    rep in pt—GLA, 2007 c 24, s 57, sch 2
    am—GLA, 2007 c 24, s 8
s 73 restr—Loc Govt Finance, 1992 c 14, s 52U(2)-(11)
    appl (mods)—Further and Higher Education 1992 c 14, s 52J
    appl—Further and Higher Education 1992 c 14, ss 52J(9), 52U(12); Localism, 2011 c
      20, s 35(7)
    am—SI 2000/1435, art 2, sch pt I paras 1,5; GLA, 2007 c 24, s 9; Loc Govt and Public
      Involvement in Health, 2007 c 28, s 182, sch 12 para 16; Localism, 2011 c 20,
      sch 19 para 38; ibid, sch 22 para 49(1)-(4)
    rep in pt—GLA, 2007 c 24, s 57, sch 2; Localism, 2011 c 20, sch 25 pt 32
s 74 restr—Loc Govt Finance, 1992 c 14, s 52U(2)-(11)
    appl (mods)—Further and Higher Education 1992 c 14, s 52J
    appl—Further and Higher Education 1992 c 14, ss 52J(9), 52U(12)
s 75 restr—Loc Govt Finance, 1992 c 14, s 52U(2)-(11)
    appl (mods)—Further and Higher Education 1992 c 14, s 52J
s 85 mod—(E) SIs 2000/213, reg 6; (E) 2001/216, reg 6; 2010/219, reg 7; 2011/313, reg 7
    rep in pt—(E) SIs 2002/155, reg 6; 2003/195, reg 6; 2004/243, reg 6; (E) 2005/190,
      reg 6; (E) 2007/227, reg 7; Localism, 2011 c 20, s 76(1)(9)(10)(15), sch 25 pt
      13
    am—Loc Govt, 2003 c 26, s 127(1), sch 7 paras 68, 70 (see SI 2003/2938); SIs
      2006/247, reg 6; (E) 2007/227, reg 7; GLA, 2007 c 24, s 12(1)-(10); Localism,
      2011 c 20, s 76(1)(2); Localism, 2011 c 20, s 76(1)(3)-(8)(10)-(14)
    appl (mods)—SIs 2008/227, reg 7; 2009/206, reg 7
s 86 rep in pt—Crim. Justice and Police, 2001 c 16, s 137, sch 7 pt 5(1); SI 2014/389, art
      5(3)(4); Loc Govt Finance, 2012 c 17, s 3(10)(a)(ii),(b)(ii), (13)(14)
    am—GLA, 2007 c 24, s 12(11)-(14); Police Reform and Social Responsibility, 2011 c
      13, sch 16 para 52; Loc Govt Finance, 2012 c 17, s 3(10)(a)(i), (b)(i), (13)(14);
      SIs 2013/733, art 3(2)(a)(b); 2014/389, art 5(2)
s 87 am—Localism, 2011 c 20, sch 7 para 35
s 88 rep in pt—(E) SIs 2002/155, reg 7; 2003/195, reg 7; 2004/243, regs 7, 8; (E) 2005/190,
      regs 7, 8; (E) 2007/227, reg 8; Localism, 2011 c 20, s 77(1)(4), sch 25 pt 13
    am—SIs 2006/247, reg 7; (E) 2007/227, reg 8; Localism, 2011 c 20, s 77(1)-(3)(5)
    appl (mods)—SIs 2008/227, reg 8; 2009/206, reg 8
    mod—SIs 2010/219, reg 8; 2011/313, reg 8
s 89 am—SIs 2000/1435, art 2, sch pt I paras 1, 6; 2006/247, reg 8; (E) 2007/227, reg 9;
      Localism, 2011 c 20, s 77(6)(7)(9)
    mod—(E) SIs 2001/216, reg 7; 2010/219, reg 9; 2011/313, reg 9
    rep in pt—(E) SIs 2002/155, reg 8; 2003/195, reg 8; 2004/243, regs 7, 8; (E) 2005/190,
      regs 7, 8; (E) 2007/227, reg 9; Localism, 2011 c 20, s 77(6)(8), sch 25 pt 13
    appl (mods)—SIs 2008/227, reg 9; 2009/206, reg 9
s 90 am—Police Reform and Social Responsibility, 2011 c 13, sch 16 para 53(2)(3)
s 94 rep in pt—Localism, 2011 c 20, sch 25 pt 13
s 95 am—Police Reform and Social Responsibility, 2011 c 13, s 23(3)-(7); Localism, 2011
      c 20, sch 6 para 35, sch 7 para 36(1)(2)
    rep in pt—Localism, 2011 c 20, sch 7 para 36(1)(3)(4), sch 25 pt 13
    mod—Police, 1996 c 16, s 96B(6)
s 96 am—Police Reform and Social Responsibility, 2011 c 13, s 23(8); Localism, 2011 c 20,
      sch 6 para 36
s 97 am—Localism, 2011 c 20, sch 7 para 37
s 99 rep in pt—(E) SIs 2002/155, reg 9; 2003/195, reg 9; 2004/243, reg 9; (E) 2005/190,
      reg 9; (E) 2007/227, reg 10; Localism, 2011 c 20, sch 7 para 38(c), sch 25 pt
      13
    am—SI 2006/247, reg 9; GLA, 2007 c 24, s 12(15); Localism, 2011 c 20, sch 7 para
      38; SI 2013/733, art 3(3)
    appl (mods)—SIs 2008/227, reg 10; 2009/206, reg 10;
    mod—SIs 2010/219, reg 10; 2011/313, reg 10
Pt 3 Ch 2 (ss 100-103) am—SI 2013/733, art 3(4)

1999
c 29 *continued*

s 100 am—Loc Govt Finance, 2012 c 17, s 4
s 102 rep in pt—(E) SIs 2002/155, reg 10; 2003/195, reg 10; 2004/243, reg 10; (E)
            2005/190, reg 10; (E) 2007/227, reg 11; Localism, 2011 c 20, sch 7 para 39(a),
            sch 25 pt 13; Loc Govt Finance, 2012 c 17, s 3(11)(13)(14); SI 2014/389, art 6
        am—SIs 2006/247, reg 10; (E) 2007/227, reg 11; Localism, 2011 c 20, sch 7 para
            39(b); SI 2013/733, art 3(5)(a)(b)
        appl (mods)—SIs 2008/227, reg 11; 2009/206, reg 11
        mod—SIs 2010/219, reg 11; 2011/313, reg 11
s 104 rep in pt—Crim Justice and Police, 2001 c 16, s 137, sch 7 pt 5(1)
s 106 am—GLA, 2007 c 24, s 33
s 108 rep in pt—(E) Loc Govt, 2003 c 26, s 127(2), sch 8 pt 1 (see SI 2003/2938)
s 111 rep—Loc Govt, 2003 c 26, s 127(2), sch 8 pt 1 (see SI 2003/2938)
ss 112-118 rep—Loc Govt, 2003 c 26, s 127, sch 7 paras 68, 71, sch 8 pt 1 (see SI
            2003/2938)
s 119 am—Loc Govt, 2003 c 26, s 127(1), sch 7 paras 68, 72 (see SI 2003/2938)
        rep in pt—Loc Govt, 2003 c 26, s 127(2), sch 8 pt 1 (see SI 2003/2938)
s 120 am—Loc Govt, 2003 c 26, s 127(1), sch 7 paras 68, 73 (see SI 2003/2938)
s 121 am—Loc Govt, 2003 c 26, s 127(1), sch 7 paras 68, 74 (see SI 2003/2938)
s 122 am—Loc Govt, 2003 c 26, s 127(1), sch 7 paras 68, 75 (see SI 2003/2938)
        rep in pt—Loc Govt, 2003 c 26, s 127(2), sch 8 pt 1 (see SI 2003/2938)
s 123 am—Loc Govt, 2003 c 26, s 127(1), sch 7 paras 68, 76 (see SI 2003/2938)
s 124 am—Loc Govt, 2003 c 26, s 127(1), sch 7 paras 68, 77 (see SI 2003/2938)
        rep in pt—Loc Govt, 2003 c 26, s 127(2), sch 8 pt 1 (see SI 2003/2938)
s 125 rep in pt—Loc Govt and Public Involvement in Health, 2007 c 28, s 146, sch 9 para
            1(1)(2)(n), sch 18; Loc Audit and Accountability, 2014 c 2, sch 12 para 42
s 126 am—Loc Govt, 2003 c 26, s 127(1), sch 7 paras 68, 78 (see SI 2003/2938)
s 127 am—GLA, 2007 c 24, s 10(1); Localism, 2011 c 20, sch 20 para 6
s 127A added—GLA, 2007 c 24, s 10(2)
s 133 rep—Loc Audit and Accountability, 2014 c 2, sch 1 pt 2
s 134 am—Loc Audit and Accountability, 2014 c 2, sch 12 para 43(2)(3)(4)(a)
        rep in pt—Loc Audit and Accountability, 2014 c 2, sch 12 para 43(4)(b)
s 136 rep—Loc Govt, 2003 c 26, s 127(2), sch 8 pt 1; Localism, 2011 c 20, sch 25 pt 12
Pt 4 (ss 141-303) excl—(EW) Traffic Management, 2004 c 18, s 29(3)
        power to am—Concessionary Bus Travel, 2007 c 13, s 8(1)
s 154 excl—Crossrail, 2008 c 18, s 38(2)
s 155 excl—Crossrail, 2008 c 18, s 38(2)
s 157 am—Income Tax, 2007 c 3, s 1027, sch 1 paras 386, 387; SI 2009/1941, art 2, sch 1;
            Corporation Tax, 2010 c 4, s 1177, sch 1 paras 304, 305
        rep in pt—Income Tax, 2007 c 3, s 1031, sch 3
s 163 excl—SIs 2002/1066, art 41(5); 2004/757, art 48(5); 2005/3105, art 46(5);
            2014/3102, art 41(5); 2015/2044, art 38(5)
        am—GLA, 2007 c 24, s 17
s 164 excl—Transport for London, 2008 c.i, s 49(8)
s 169 see—SI 2000/1506, art 3
s 174 appl—(temp) SI 2000/1504, arts 2,4(1)(2)
s 175 rep in pt—Transport, 2000 c 38, ss 215, 274, sch 16 para 59(4), sch 31 pt IV;
            Railways, 2005 c 14, ss 15(1)(2)(b), 59, sch 13 pt 1
        am—Transport, 2000 c 38, s 215, sch 16 para 59(2)(3); Railways, 2005 c 14,
            ss 15(1)(2)(a)(3)-(7), 59, sch 12 para 14(1)(2)
s 177 am—Transport, 2000 c 38, s 215, sch 16 para 60
s 179 am—Transport, 2000 c 38, s 252, sch 27 para 58; Railways, 2005 c 14, s 59, sch 12
            para 14(1)(4)
s 180 mod—(temp) SI 2000/1462, arts 2,4(2)
s 185 mod—(temp) SI 2000/1462, arts 2,4(3)
s 189 am—Transport, 2000 c 38, s 267; SI 2009/1885, art 4, sch 1
        rep in pt—SI 2009/1885, art 4, sch 1
s 190 mod—SI 2000/1462, art 5
s 191 appl—SI 2000/1462, art 7(1)-(5)
        am—SI 2013/1644, sch 3
s 192 excl—SI 2000/1462, art 7(1)-(5)(8)-(10)
s 193 am—SI 2010/1158, art 5, sch 2
s 194 am—SI 2013/1644, sch 3
s 195 rep in pt—SI 2013/1644, sch 3

1999
c 29 *continued*

s 196 rep—Railways, 2005 c 14, s 59, sch 13 pt 1
s 197 rep—Railways, 2005 c 14, s 59, sch 13 pt 1
s 199 am—Transport, 2000 c 38, s 215, sch 16 para 63; Railways and Transport Safety,
    2003 c 20, s 16, sch 2 pt 2 para 19(q); SI 2015/1682, sch pt 1 para 4(n)(i)
    rep in pt—Transport, 2000 c 38, s 274, sch 31 pt IV; Railways, 2005 c 14, s 59, sch
      13 pt 1
s 200 am—Railways and Transport Safety, 2003 c 20, s 16, sch 2 pt 2 para 19(q); SI
    2015/1682, sch pt 1 para 4(n)(ii)
s 201 rep—Railways, 2005 c 14, ss 16(1), 59, sch 13 pt 1
s 203 rep—Railways, 2005 c 14, s 59, sch 13 pt 1
s 204 rep—Railways, 2005 c 14, s 59, sch 13 pt 1
s 207 excl—SIs 2000/1143, art 3; 2004/757, art 48(5); 2005/3105, art 46(5)
    excl in pt—SIs 2014/3102, art 41(5); 2015/2044, art 38(5)
    rep in pt—SI 2003/1613, art 4
    restr—SI 2005/763, art 3
s 209 am—Transport, 2000 c 38, s 252, sch 27 para 59
s 210 appl—Enterprise, 2002 c 40, s 249(1)(d)
s 211 am—Loc Transport, 2008 c 26, s 77, sch 4 para 63; SI 2009/1941, art 2, sch 1; Loc
    Democracy, Economic Development and Construction, 2009 c 20, s 119, sch 6
    para 92
s 216 am—Tribunals, Cts and Enforcement, 2007 c 15, s 62, sch 13 para 130
    excl —Crossrail, 2008 c 18, s 28(1)
s 218 appl—Land Registration, 2002 c 9, s 90(6)
s 219 rep—Land Registration, 2002 c 9, s 135, sch 13
s 220 am—SI 2009/1941, art 2, sch 1
s 224 am—SI 2009/1941, art 2, sch 1
s 228 am—Railways and Transport Safety, 2003 c 20, s 16, sch 2 pt 2 paras 19(q), 20, 23;
    SI 2015/1682, sch pt 1 para 4(n)(iii)
s 233 am—SI 2008/948, art 3, sch 1
s 235 rep in pt—Transport, 2000 c 38, ss 215, 274, sch 16 para 66(3), sch 31 pt IV;
    SI 2000/2031, art 20(2); Railways, 2005 c 14, s 59, sch 12 para 14(1)(5)(a),
    sch 13 pt 1; SIs 2005/3049, reg 2(4), sch 1 pt 1 para 5(b); 2008/960, art 22,
    sch 3; 2013/1575, sch para 2; 2014/892, sch 1 para 119(3); Deregulation,
    2015 c 20, sch 6 para 22(10)
    am—Transport, 2000 c 38, s 215, sch 16 para 66(2); SI 2000/2031, art 20(2);
    Enterprise, 2002 c 40, s 278(1), sch 25, para 39; Railways and Transport Safety,
    2003 c 20, s 16, sch 2 pt 2 para 19(q); (pt prosp) Communications, 2003 c 21,
    s 406(1), sch 17 para 157; SI 2003/1900, arts 2(1), 3(1),sch 1; SI 2003/3142,
    art 3(2); Railways, 2005 c 14, s 59, sch 12 para 14(1)(5)(b); SIs 2005/3049,
    reg 2(4), sch 1 pt 1 para 5(a); 2008/1277, reg 30, sch 2; 2009/1122, reg 3, sch;
    Civil Aviation, 2012 c 19, sch 9 para 10; Energy, 2013 c 32, sch 12 para 73; SIs
    2014/892, sch 1 para 119(2)-(4); 2015/1682, sch pt 1 para 4(n)(iv)
    appl (mods)—SI 2006/1391, art 2, sch
s 240 mod—(temp) SI 2000/1504, arts 2,5
    am—Transport, 2000 c 38, s 151(1)-(5); Transport, 2000 c 38, s 215, sch 16
    para 67(2); (EW) Travel Concessions (Eligibility), 2002 c 4, s 1(2); Railways,
    2005 c 14, s 59, sch 12 para 14(1)(6); Concessionary Bus Travel, 2007 c 13, s 4
    rep in pt—Transport, 2000 c 38, ss 215, 274, sch 16 para 67(3), sch 31 pt IV
    power to am—(EW) Travel Concessions (Eligibility), 2002 c 4, s 1(4)
    appl (mods)—SI 2010/459, art 2
s 241 mod—(temp) SI 2000/1504, arts 2,6
    am—Transport, 2000 c 38, s 151(1)(6); Concessionary Bus Travel, 2007 c 13, s 5
    rep in pt—Concessionary Bus Travel, 2007 c 13, s 13, sch 3
s 242 mod—(temp) SI 2000/1504, arts 2,7
    am—Transport, 2000 c 38, s 151(1)(7)-(12); SI 2005/3224, art 2(1)(2)(a);
    Concessionary Bus Travel, 2007 c 13, s 6
    rep in pt—SI 2005/3224, art 2(1)(2)(b); Concessionary Bus Travel, 2007 c 13, s 13,
    sch 3
s 243 am—Transport, 2000 c 38, s 151(1)(13); Concessionary Bus Travel, 2007 c 13, s 7
    rep in pt—Concessionary Bus Travel, 2007 c 13, s 13, sch 3
s 244 am—Concessionary Bus Travel, 2007 c 13, s 13, sch 2 paras 7, 8
s 247 am—Transport, 2000 c 38, ss 227, 252 sch 22 pt II para 22, sch 27 para 60; Railways,
    2005 c 14, ss 21, 59, sch 6 para 1, sch 12 para 14(1)(7)

1999
c 29 *continued*

    s 250 am—Transport, 2000 c 38, s 252, sch 27 para 61; Railways, 2005 c 14, s 59, sch 12
        para 14(1)(8)
    s 252 am—Transport, 2000 c 38, s 227, sch 22 pt II para 23
        rep in pt—Railways, 2005 c 14, s 59, sch 13 pt 1
    s 252A added—Railways, 2005 c 14, s 21, sch 6 para 2
    s 252B added—Railways, 2005 c 14, s 21, sch 6 para 3
        am—SIs 2010/439, art 2, sch; 2015/1682, sch pt 1 para 4(n)(v)
    s 252C added—Railways, 2005 c 14, s 21, sch 6 para 3
        appl (mods)—SIs 2005/3050, reg 19(1); 2010/1504, reg 18
        am—SI 2015/1682, sch pt 1 para 4(n)(vi)
    s 252D added—Railways, 2005 c 14, s 21, sch 6 para 3
        am—SI 2010/439, art 2, sch
    s 252E added—Railways, 2005 c 14, s 21, sch 6 para 4(1)
        am—SI 2010/439, art 2, sch
    s 269 am—SI 2000/1435, art 2, sch pt I paras 1,7
    s 283 rep in pt—(EW) Traffic Management, 2004 c 18, s 98, sch 12 pt 1
    s 284 rep (EW)—Traffic Management, 2004 c 18, s 98, sch 12 pt 1
    s 286 rep (EW)—Traffic Management, 2004 c 18, s 98, sch 12 pt 1
    ss 304-309 rep —Localism, 2011 c 20, sch 25 pt 32
    s 306 rep in pt—Loc Democracy, Economic Development and Construction, 2009 c 20, s
        146, sch 7 pt 4
    ss 309A-309D added—GLA, 2007 c 24, s 21(1)
    ss 309E-309H added—GLA, 2007 c 24, s 22(1)
    s 309E rep in pt—Health and Social Care, 2012 c 7, sch 5 para 94(a)(b); ibid, sch 14 para
        76
        am—Health and Social Care, 2012 c 7, sch 5 para 94(c)
    s 310 rep in pt—Police and Justice, 2006 c 48, s 52, sch 15
    s 326 rep—Crim Justice and Court Services, 2000 c 43, s 75, sch 8
    ss 328A, 328B added—GLA, 2007 c 24, s 27
    s 330 rep—Civil Contingencies, 2004 c 36, s 32(2), sch 3
    Pt 7A (ss 333ZA-333E) am (heading am)—Localism, 2011 c 20, s 187(1)(2)
    ss 333ZA-333ZJ added —Localism, 2011 c 20, s 187(3)
    s 333ZB am—Infrastructure, 2015 c 7, s 32(6)-(9)
    s 333A added—GLA, 2007 c 24, s 28(3)
        am—Housing and Regeneration, 2008 c 17, s 56, sch 8 paras 72,
        73(1)-(2)(b)(ii)(3)-(5)(b); SI 2010/866, art 5, sch 2; Localism, 2011 c 20, s
        188(1)(3)-(6)
        mod—(transtl provns and savings) SI 2008/2839, arts 3, 6, sch
        rep in pt—Housing and Regeneration, 2008 c 17, s 56, sch 8 para
        73(1)(2)(b)(iii)(5)(c), sch 16; SI 2010/866, arts 5, 7, schs 2, 4
    ss 333B, 333C added—GLA, 2007 c 24, s 28(3)
    s 333D added—GLA, 2007 c 24, s 28(3)
        am—Housing and Regeneration, 2008 c 17, s 56, sch 8 paras 72, 74; Localism,
        2011 c 20, s 188(7)-(9)
        mod—(transtl provns and savings) SI 2008/2839, arts 3, 6, sch
        rep in pt—Deregulation, 2015 c 20, s 29(6)(b)
    ss 333DA-333DC added—Infrastructure, 2015 c 7, s 31(6)
    s 333E added —Localism, 2011 c 20, s 187(4)
    Pt 7B (s 333F) added—Localism, 2011 c 20, s 192(2)
    Pt 8 (ss 334-350) appl—Town and Country Planning, 1990 c 8, s 336
    s 334 ext —Planning and Compulsory Purchase, 2004 c 5, s 113(9)(e)
    s 335 ext—Planning and Compulsory Purchase, 2004 c 5, s 113(9)(e)
        am—GLA, 2007 c 24, s 29; Localism, 2011 c 20, s 228(2)(b)(c)
        rep in pt—Localism, 2011 c 20, s 228(2)(a), sch 25 pt 33
    s 336 ext—Planning and Compulsory Purchase, 2004 c 5, s 113(9)(e)
    s 337 am—SI 2000/1435, art 2, sch pt I paras 1,8; Planning and Compulsory Purchase,
        2004 c 5, s 118(2), sch 7 para 22(1)(2)(a)
        ext —Planning and Compulsory Purchase, 2004 c 5, s 113(9)(e)
        rep in pt—Planning and Compulsory Purchase, 2004 c 5, s 118(2), sch 7 para
        22(1)(2)(b); (prosp) Localism, 2011 c 20, sch 8 para 4, sch 25 pt 16
    s 338 ext—Planning and Compulsory Purchase, 2004 c 5, s 113(9)(e)
        am—Tribunals, Cts and Enforcement, 2007 c 15, s 48, sch 8 para 52
        rep in pt—SI 2013/2042, sch para 19

1999
c 29 *continued*

s 339-341 ext—Planning and Compulsory Purchase, 2004 c 5, s 113(9)(e)
s 342 am—(W prosp) Planning and Compulsory Purchase, 2004 c 5, s 118(2), sch 7 para
22(1)(3); Loc Democracy, Economic Development and Construction, 2009 c 20,
s 85, sch 5 paras 9, 10
rep in pt—(prosp) Localism, 2011 c 20, sch 8 para 5, sch 25 pt 16
ext—Planning and Compulsory Purchase, 2004 c 5, s 113(9)(e)
s 343 ext—Planning and Compulsory Purchase, 2004 c 5, s 113(9)(e)
s 346 am—Planning and Compulsory Purchase, 2004 c 5, s 118(2), sch 7 para 22(1)(4)
s 347 am—Localism, 2011 c 20, sch 22 para 50
s 351 rep —Localism, 2011 c 20, s 226, sch 25 pt 33
ss 351A-351C added —Localism, 2011 c 20, s 225(1)
s 352 am—Countryside and Rights of Way, 2000 c 37, s 73(4), sch 8 para 1(v); Natural
Environment and Rural Communities, 2006 c 16, s 105, sch 11 para 151;
Localism, 2011 c 20, sch 23 para 3(1)-(4)
rep in pt—Localism, 2011 c 20, sch 23 para 3(1)(5), sch 25 pt 33
s 353 am—Waste and Emissions Trading, 2003 c 33, ss 17(8), 32(12); Localism, 2011 c 20,
sch 23 para 4(1)-(3); SI 2011/988, sch 4 para 5(2)
rep in pt—Waste and Emissions Trading, 2003 c 33, s 35(b); Localism, 2011 c 20, sch
23 para 4(1)(4), sch 25 pt 33
s 354 am—Waste and Emissions Trading, 2003 c 33, s 17(9); Localism, 2011 c 20, sch 23
para 5(1)(2)(3)(b); SI 2011/988, sch 4 para 5(3)
rep in pt—Localism, 2011 c 20, sch 23 para 5(1)(3)(a), sch 25 pt 33
s 355 am—GLA, 2007 c 24, s 37; Localism, 2011 c 20, sch 23 para 6(a); SI 2015/102, sch
6 para 3
rep in pt—Localism, 2011 c 20, sch 23 para 7, sch 25 pt 33
s 356 am—GLA, 2007 c 24, s 39(5); Localism, 2011 c 20, sch 23 para 6(b); SI 2015/102,
sch 6 para 4
ss 356A, 356B added—GLA, 2007 c 24, s 38(1)
s 356A am—Localism, 2011 c 20, sch 23 para 6(c)
s 357 am—Localism, 2011 c 20, sch 23 para 6(d)
s 358 am—GLA, 2007 c 24, s 39(1)-(4); Localism, 2011 c 20, sch 23 para 6(e); SI
2015/102, sch 6 para 5
s 359 am—GLA, 2007 c 24, s 11(1)(4); SI 2015/102, sch 6 para 6
s 360 am—(trans provns) SI 2006/5, reg 48, sch 7; GLA, 2007 c 24, s 39(6)-(8); SIs
2011/988, sch 4 para 5(4); 2015/102, sch 6 para 7(2)(a)(c),(3)(a),(4)(a)
rep in pt—Localism, 2011 c 20, sch 25 pt 33; SI 2015/102, sch 6 para 7(2)(b),
(3)(b)(c),(4)(b)(c)
s 361 rep—Waste and Emissions Trading, 2003 c 33, s 35(b)
s 361A added—GLA, 2007 c 24, s 42
s 361B added—GLA, 2007 c 24, s 43(2)
am—Localism, 2011 c 20, sch 23 para 8(1)-(6)
rep in pt—Localism, 2011 c 20, sch 23 para 8(1)(7), sch 25 pts 32, 33
s 361C added—GLA, 2007 c 24, s 43(2)
rep —Localism, 2011 c 20, sch 23 para 9, sch 25 pt 33
s 361D added—GLA, 2007 c 24, s 44(2)
am—Localism, 2011 c 20, sch 23 para 10(1)-(3)
rep in pt—Localism, 2011 c 20, sch 23 para 10(1)(4), sch 25 pt 33
s 361E added—GLA, 2007 c 24, s 44(2)
rep —Localism, 2011 c 20, sch 23 para 11, sch 25 pt 33
s 362 am—Localism, 2011 c 20, sch 20 para 7, sch 23 para 12(1)-(3)
rep in pt—Localism, 2011 c 20, sch 23 para 12(1)(4), sch 25 pt 33
s 363 am—Localism, 2011 c 20, sch 23 para 13(1)(2)(3)(b)
rep in pt—Localism, 2011 c 20, sch 23 para 13(1)(3)(a), sch 25 pt 33
s 364 am—Localism, 2011 c 20, sch 23 para 14
s 365 am—Localism, 2011 c 20, sch 23 para 15
s 367 am—SI 2000/1435, art 2, sch pt I paras 1,9
s 370 am—Localism, 2011 c 20, sch 23 para 16(1)-(4)
rep in pt—Localism, 2011 c 20, sch 23 para 16(1)(5), sch 25 pt 33
s 376 am—GLA, 2007 c 24, ss 2(3), 50(1)-(5)
rep in pt—SI 2012/147, sch
s 377A added—GLA, 2007 c 24, s 51(1)
s 378 am—SI 2005/3225 (W 237), arts 3, 6(2), sch 2 pt 1 para 3(1)(2)(a); (S) Tourist
Boards (S), 2006 asp 15, s 4, sch 2 para 5

1999
c 29 s 378 *continued*

        rep in pt—SI 2005/3225 (W 237), arts 3, 6(2), sch 2 pt 1 para 3(2)(b)
        mod—SI 2007/1103, art 2, sch
   s 380 am—(E) SI 2001/2237, arts 2, 37(a)-(d); GLA, 2007 c 24, s 51(2); Localism, 2011 c
        20, sch 20 para 8
        rep in pt—Localism, 2011 c 20, sch 25 pt 32
   s 385 am—SI 2001/3719, art 2, sch para 7; Police Reform and Social Responsibility, 2011 c
        13, ss 149(1), 150(3)
   s 389 am—Police Reform and Social Responsibility, 2011 c 13, sch 16 para 54
        rep in pt—Localism, 2011 c 20, sch 25 pt 32
   s 391 rep—Race Relations (Amdt), 2000 c 34, s 9(2), sch 3
   s 394 rep in pt—Localism, 2011 c 20, sch 25 pt 32
   s 400 rep in pt—Localism, 2011 c 20, sch 25 pt 32
   s 401 am—GLA, 2007 c 24, s 52(2)
   s 401A added—GLA, 2007 c 24, s 52(1)
        am—Localism, 2011 c 20, s 230(1)(2)(a)(b)(3)(4)-(8)
   s 404 rep—Equality, 2010 c 15, s 211, sch 27 pt 1
   s 408 am—Natural Environment and Rural Communities, 2006 c 16, s 105, sch 11 para
        152; Police Reform and Social Responsibility, 2011 c 13, sch 16 para 56;
        Localism, 2011 c 20, sch 22 para 51; Infrastructure, 2015 c 7, s 31(7)
        rep in pt—Housing and Regeneration, 2008 c 17, s 56, sch 8 paras 72, 75, sch 16;
        Localism, 2011 c 20, sch 25 pt 32; SI 2014/3184, sch para 13
   s 409 rep in pt—Housing and Regeneration, 2008 c 17, s 56, sch 8 paras 72, 76, sch 16;
        Localism, 2011 c 20, sch 25 pt 32
        am—Localism, 2011 c 20, s 223(3); Infrastructure, 2015 c 7, s 31(8)
   s 411 rep in pt—Police Reform and Social Responsibility, 2011 c 13, sch 16 para 57
   s 412 power to restr—Railways and Transport Safety, 2003 c 20, s 114(1)(3)
   s 414 appl—Police Reform and Social Responsibility, 2011 c 13, sch 15 para 22(1)
   s 415 excl—SI 2000/412, art 5
   s 419 am—Income Tax, 2007 c 3, s 1027, sch 1 paras 386, 388; Corporation Tax, 2010 c 4,
        s 1177, sch 1 paras 304, 306; Police Reform and Social Responsibility, 2011 c
        13, sch 16 para 58
        rep in pt—Income Tax, 2007 c 3, s 1031, sch 3
   s 420 am—Representation of the People, 2000 c 2, s 14(3); Transport, 2000 c 38, s 161,
        sch 11 para 23; ibid, s 267(8); Railways, 2005 c 14, s 21, sch 6 para 4(2);
        Concessionary Bus Travel, 2007 c 13, s 13, sch 2 paras 7, 9; GLA, 2007 c 24, ss
        4(3); 38(2), 43(3), 50(6), 51(3), 52(3); Localism, 2011 c 20, ss 224(3),
        230(1)(9); Infrastructure, 2015 c 7, s 31(9)
        rep in pt—Concessionary Bus Travel, 2007 c 13, s 13, sch 3
   s 424 am—GLA, 2007 c 24, ss 11(1)(6), 12(16), 21(2), 22(2); SI 2009/1941, art 2, sch 1;
        Police Reform and Social Responsibility, 2011 c 13, s 3(9); Localism, 2011 c 20,
        sch 22 para 52
        rep in pt—Localism, 2011 c 20, sch 25 pt 32
   s 425 rep in pt—Railways and Transport Safety, 2003 c 20, ss 114(6), 118, sch 8
   sch 1 see—(trans of functions) (E) SI 2001/3962, art 3(1)(2)(d)
        am—(E) SI 2001/3962, art 9, sch 2 para 14(1)(2)(a)-(e)(3)-(6)(8)(9); Concessionary
        Bus Travel, 2007 c 13, s 5, sch 1; Loc Democracy, Economic Development and
        Construction, 2009 c 20, s 67, sch 4 paras 8, 10(1)-(5)
        rep in pt—(E) SI 2001/3962, art 9, sch 2 para 14(1)(2)(f)(7); Loc Democracy,
        Economic Development and Construction, 2009 c 20, ss 67, 146, sch 4 paras 8,
        10(1)(6), sch 7 pt 3
   sch 2 appl—Representation of the People 1983 c 2, s 203(1B)
   sch 3 rep in pt—Political Parties, Elections and Referendums, 2000 c 41, s 158(2), sch 22
   sch 3A added—Representation of the People, 2000 c 2, s 14(4), sch 5
   sch 4 am—SI 2000/1435, art 2, sch pt I paras 1, 10; GLA, 2007 c 24, s 16
        rep in pt—GLA, 2007 c 24, s 57, sch 2; Police Reform and Social Responsibility,
        2011 c 13, sch 16 para 59
   sch 4A added—GLA, 2007 c 24, s 4(2), sch 1
        am—Police Reform and Social Responsibility, 2011 c 13, s 20(3)
   sch 6 appl (mods)—Local Govt Finance, 1992 c 14, s 52J
        am—GLA, 2007 c 24, s 13; SI 2010/2997, reg 2; Localism, 2011 c 20, sch 6 para
        37(1)-(8), sch 7 para 40; SIs 2012/15, reg 2; 2012/3125, reg 2; 2013/3178, reg
        2; 2014/389, art 7; 3308, reg 2; 2015/2032, reg 2
   sch 7 am—GLA, 2007 c 24, s 14; Localism, 2011 c 20, sch 6 para 38(1)-(3), sch 7 para 41

1999
c 29 sch 7 *continued*

appl—Loc Govt Finance, 1992 c 14, s 52ZU(11)
sch 8 rep—Loc Audit and Accountability, 2014 c 2, sch 1 pt 2
sch 9 rep—Localism, 2011 c 20, sch 25 pt 12
sch 10 excl—Loc Govt Finance, 1988 c 41, s 115(4A)
  am—Railways, 2005 c 14, s 17; GLA, 2007 c 24, s 18; SI 2009/1941, art 2, sch 1;
    Loc Democracy, Economic Development and Construction, 2009 c 20, s 85, sch
    5 paras 9, 11
  rep in pt—GLA, 2007 c 24, s 57, sch 2; (prosp) Localism, 2011 c 20, sch 8 para 6,
    sch 25 pt 16
sch 11 am—Transport for London, 2008 c.i, s 50
  appl (mods)—SI 2012/472, art 6(2)
  mod—SI 2012/472, art 6(1)
sch 12 appl—Railways and Transport Safety, 2003 c 20, s 114(2)
  restr—Railways and Transport Safety, 2003 c 20, s 114(4)
  power to restr—Railways and Transport Safety, 2003 c 20, s 114(2)(3)
sch 14 am—SI 2009/1941, art 2, sch 1
sch 16 mod—(temp) SI 2000/1504, arts 2,8
  rep in pt—Transport, 2000 c 38, s 274, sch 31 pt II
sch 17 appl (mods)—SI 2003/1614, art 2, sch 1
  appl —SI 2012/472, art 7
  am—(transtl provns) Transport for London, 2008 c.i, ss 27, 28
sch 18 am—Transport, 2000 c 38, ss 227, 252, sch 22 pt II para 24, sch 27 para 62(2)-(6);
    Railways and Transport Safety, 2003 c 20, s 16, sch 2 pt 2 para 19(q);
    Railways, 2005 c 14, s 59, sch 12 para 14(1)(9); SIs 2007/2194, art 10, sch 4;
    2008/948, art 3, sch 1; 2010/439, art 2, sch; 2015/1682, sch pt 1 para 4(n)(vii)
  rep in pt—Transport, 2000 c 38, ss 252, 274, sch 27 para 62(7), sch 31 pt IV; Loc
    Govt and Public Involvement in Health, 2007 c 28, s 241, sch 18
sch 19 rep in pt—Transport, 2000 c 38, s 274, sch 31 pt IV; Railways, 2005 c 14, s 59, sch
    13 pt 1
sch 20 rep in pt—SL(R), 2004 c 14, s 1(1), sch 1 pt 14
sch 23 am—Transport, 2000 c 38, s 199, sch 13 paras 2, 3(2)(3)(5), 4-9,10(2)(a)(3)(4)(5),
    11-17,18(b); Loc Transport, 2008 c 26, ss 112(2), 113(5)-(7), 115(3),
    116(4)-(8), 117(2), 118(6)-(9), 120, 121, sch 6 paras 9, 10(1)(3)(5), 11,
    12(1)(3)(4)(a)
  rep in pt—Transport, 2000 c 38, ss 199, 274, sch 13 paras 3(4), 10(2)(b),18(a),
    sch 31 pt III; Loc Transport, 2008 c 26, ss
    120(2)(3)(a)(4)(5)(6)(b)(7)(b)(d)(f)(ii), 121, sch 6 paras 9, 10(1)(2)(4)(6), 11,
    12(1)(2)(4)(b), sch 7
  power to appl (mods)—(W prosp) Transport, 2000 c 38, s 191, sch 12 para 12(2)(a)
  excl—Transport for London, 2008 c.i, ss 5(3), 6(1)
sch 24 rep in pt—Transport, 2000 c 38, ss 199, 274, sch 13 para 20(2)(4), 22(4),34(a)
    sch 31 pt III
  am—Transport, 2000 c 38, s 199, sch 13 paras 20(3)(5)(6),21, 22(2)(3)(5),23-33,
    34(b)
  power to appl (mods)—(W prosp) Transport, 2000 c 38, s 191, sch 12 para 12(2)(b)
sch 25 rep in pt—Localism, 2011 c 20, sch 25 pt 32; Public Bodies, 2011 c 24, sch 6
sch 26 rep—Police and Justice, 2006 c 48, s 52, sch 15
sch 27 rep in pt—Crim. Justice and Police, 2001 c 16, s 137, sch 7 pts 4, 5(1); Police
    Reform, 2002 c 30, s 107(2), sch 8; Courts, 2003 c 39, s 109(3), sch 10; SL(R),
    2004 c 14, s 1(1), sch 1 pt 10/2; Police and Justice, 2006 c 48, s 52, sch 15;
    (prosp) Crim Justice and Immigration, 2008 c 4, s 149, sch 28 pt 8; Anti-social
    Behaviour, Crime and Policing, 2014 c 12, sch 11 para 102
sch 28 am—GLA, 2007 c 24, s 25
  mod—SI 2013/2277, art 6
sch 29 rep in pt—SI 2001/1149, arts 3(2), 4(11), sch 2; Licensing, 2003 c 17, s 199, sch 7;
    Courts, 2003 c 39, s 109(3), sch 10; SL(R), 2004 c 14, s 1(1), sch 1 pt 10/2
sch 32 am—SIs 2000/1435, art 2, sch pt I paras 1,11; 2006/745, art 14; 2009/1941, art 2,
    sch 1
  see—SI 2000/3386, arts 2(2),3(2),4(5),5(8)
sch 33 am—Capital Allowances, 2001 c 2, ss 578, 580, sch 2 para 105, sch 4; Corporation
    Tax, 2010 c 4, s 1177, sch 1 paras 304, 307; Taxation (International and Other
    Provns), 2010 c 8, s 374, sch 8 paras 249, 250, 295, 296
  rep in pt—Capital Allowances, 2001 c 2, ss 578, 580, sch 2 para 105(9)(a), sch 4

1999
c 30   **Welfare Reform and Pensions**
             appl (mods)—SI 2010/1907, reg 16
             Pts I, II (ss 1-18) power to mod—Pensions, 2004 c 35, s 321(1)(c)(2)(3)
             Pt 1 mod—SI 2008/576, sch 4 para 5
             s 1 appl—SIs 2001/1335, art 4, sch 1 pt II para 20(2); 2005/1529, art 72(4); 2005/3378,
                     reg 8(2)
                 am—Pensions, 2004 c 35, ss 285(1)-(4), 319(1), sch 12 para 71; (prosp) ibid, para 72;
                     SI 2006/745, art 15; Pensions, 2007 c 22, s 15, sch 4 para 37
                 rep in pt—Pensions, 2007 c 22, s 27, sch 7 pt 6
             s 2 am—Pensions, 2004 c 35, ss 285(5), 319(1), sch 12 paras 71, 73; Pensions, 2007 c 22, s
                     15, sch 4 para 38
                 rep in pt—Pensions, 2004 c 35, s 320, sch 13 pt 1
             s 3 appl—Pensions, 2004 c 35, s 74(3)
                 am—Pensions, 2008 c 30, s 87(1)-(4)
                 rep in pt—Pensions, 2008 c 30, ss 87(1)(5)-(6)(b)(8)(10)(b)(12), 148, sch 11
             ss 4, 5 rep—Pensions, 2004 c 35, s 320, sch 13 pt 1
             s 6 rep in pt—Pensions, 2008 c 30, ss 87(1)(13), 148, sch 11
             s 7 rep—Pensions, 2007 c 22, s 15, sch 4 para 39, sch 7
             s 8 am—Pensions, 2004 c 35, ss 7(1)(c)(2)(c), 319(1), sch 12 paras 71, 74
                 rep in pt—Pensions, 2008 c 30, ss 87(1)(14), 148, sch 11
             s 11 appl—(EW) Insolvency, 1986 c 45, s 342A(8); (S) Bankcrupcy (S), 1985 c 66 s 36(8)
                 excl—Bankruptcy (S), 1985 c 66, s 32A(5)
                 am—SIs 2006/745, art 15; 2009/56, art 3, sch 1 para 284
             s 12 appl—(EW) Insolvency, 1986 c 45, s 342A(8); (S) Bankcrupcy (S), 1985 c 66 s 36(8)
                 excl—Bankruptcy (S), 1985 c 66, s 32A(5)
             s 12A restr—Family Law (S), 1985 c 37, s 8(4)(5)
             s 17 rep—Pensions, 2004 c 35, s 320, sch 13 pt 1
             Pt 3 (ss 19-26) appl—Proceeds of Crime, 2002 c 29, s 275(6)(a); SI 2005/3181,
                     art 186(4)(a)
                 power to mod—Pensions, 2004 c 35, s 321(1)(c)(2)(3)
             s 23 am—Civil Partnership, 2004 c 33, s 261(1), sch 27 para 157(1)(2)(3)(a)(4)(5)
                 rep in pt—Civil Partnership, 2004 c 33, s 261(1)(4), sch 27 para 157(1)(3)(b), sch 30
             s 24 am—Civil Partnership, 2004 c 33, s 261(1), sch 27 para 158
                 rep in pt—Civil Partnership, 2004 c 33, s 261(1)(4), sch 27 para 158(1)(3), sch 30
             s 26 appl—(EW) Civil Partnership, 2004 c 33, s 72(1), sch 5 pt 6 para 29(3)
                 am—SI 2006/745, art 15
             Pt 4 (ss 27-51) ext—SIs 1994/2924 reg 13A; 1997/3001, reg 11
                 appl—(retrosp) (S) SI 1991/1304, reg 12A
                 power to mod—Pensions, 2004 c 35, s 321(1)(c)(2)(3)
             Pt 4, Ch 1 (ss 27-46) power to mod—Pensions, 2004 c 35, s 220(2)
                 appl—(EW) Civil Partnership, 2004 c 33, s 72(1), sch 5 pt 4 para 16(2)(a); (NI) Civil
                     Partnership, 2004 c 33, s 196(1), sch 15 pt 3 para 11(2)(b); Pensions, 2004 c 35,
                     ss 133(9), 135(8), 220(3)
             s 27 mod—SI 2006/1690, reg 2
             s 28 appl—Family Law (S), 1985 c 37, s 8(7)(b); Income Tax (Earnings and Pensions),
                     2003 c 1, s 392(7)(a); Pensions, 2004 c 35, s 220(3)
                 am—Civil Partnership, 2004 c 33, s 261(1), sch 27 para 159(1)-(7)(9)(10)(b); Pensions,
                     2008 c 30, s 128(1)(2); Children and Families, 2014 c 6, s 18(5)
                 rep in pt—Civil Partnership, 2004 c 33, s 261(1)(4), sch 27 para 159(1)(8)(10)(a), sch
                     30; Children and Families, 2014 c 6, s 18(3)(b)(i)
             s 29 ext—(NI) SI 1999/3147, arts 32, 39(6), 40(5), sch 5 para 4(5)
             s 30 ext—(EW) Civil Partnership, 2004 c 33, s 72(1), sch 5 pt 6 para 28(2)(b)
                 mod—SI 2006/1690, reg 2
             s 32 appl—Welfare Reform and Pensions, 1999 c 30, s 32
             s 33 am—Pensions, 2004 c 35, s 7(1)(c)(2)(d)
                 mod—SI 2008/576, sch 4 para 5
             s 34 am—Civil Partnership, 2004 c 33, s 261(1), sch 27 para 160(1)(3)(b)
                 rep in pt—Civil Partnership, 2004 c 33, s 261(1)(4), sch 27 para 160(1)(2)(3)(a), sch
                     30
             s 36 rep—Pensions, 2008 c 30, s 148, sch 11 pt 2
             s 38 am—Pensions, 2004 c 35, s 319(1), sch 12 paras 71, 75; (prosp) Pension Schemes,
                     2015 c 8, sch 2 para 19
                 rep in pt—Pensions, 2004 c 35, s 320, sch 13 pt 1
             s 40 am—Pensions, 2004 c 35, s 280(1)-(5); Pensions, 2011 c 19, s 19(10)(11)

1999
c 30 s 40 *continued*

rep in pt—Pensions, 2008 c 30, s 148, sch 11 pt 2

s 41 ext—(EW) Civil Partnership, 2004 c 33, s 72(1), sch 5 pt 4 para 17(a); (NI) ibid, s 196(1), sch 15 pt 3 para 12(b)

s 44 am—Armed Forces, 2006 c 52, s 378, sch 16 para 162

s 46 rep in pt—(prosp) Pensions, 2004 c 35, s 320, sch 13 pt 1
    mod—SI 2006/1690, reg 2
    am—SI 2006/745, art 15

Pt 4, Ch 2 (ss 47-51) appl—Civil Partnership, 2004 c 33, s 72(1), sch 5 pt 4 para 16(3)(a); (NI) ibid, s 196(1), sch 15 pt 3 para 11(3)(b)

s 47 am—(6.4.2016) Pensions, 2014 c 19, sch 11 para 10(2)-(4)
    rep in pt—Pensions, 2014 c 19, sch 15 para 14

s 48 am—Civil Partnership, 2004 c 33, s 261(1), sch 27 para 161(1)-(7)(9)(10)(b); Pensions, 2008 c 30, s 128(1)(3); (6.4.2016) Pensions, 2014 c 19, sch 11 para 11
    rep in pt—Civil Partnership, 2004 c 33, s 261(1)(4), sch 27 para 161(1)(8)(10)(a), sch 30; Children and Families, 2014 c 6, s 18(3)(b)(ii)

s 49 am—Child Support, Pensions and Social Security, 2000 c 19, s 41(1); (6.4.2016) Pensions, 2014 c 19, sch 11 para 12(2)-(6)
    ext—(EW) Civil Partnership, 2004 c 33, s 72(1), sch 5 pt 6 para 28(2)(b)

s 49A added (6.4.2016)—Pensions, 2014 c 19, sch 11 para 13

s 50 rep in pt—Pensions, 2004 c 35, ss 297(4), 320, sch 11 pt 2 paras 23, 24, sch 13 pt 1

s 51 am—(6.4.2016) Pensions, 2014 c 19, sch 11 para 14

s 52 am—Child Support, Pensions and Social Security, 2000 c 19, s 39(3)-(5); Pensions, 2004 c 35, s 297(4), sch 11 pt 2 paras 23, 25; SI 2005/2053, art 2, sch pt 5 para 26

s 53 rep in pt—Employment, 2002 c 22, s 54, sch 8(1)

ss 57, 58 rep (pt prosp)—Welfare Reform, 2012 c 5, sch 14 pt 1

s 60 rep (prosp)—Welfare Reform, 2009 c 24, s 58, sch 7 pt 3
    expld—SI 2000/721, reg 4
    appl—Finance, 2000 c 17, s 85

ss 61-64 rep (prosp)—Welfare Reform, 2007 c 5, s 67, sch 8

s 67 rep (prosp)—Welfare Reform, 2012 c 5, sch 14 pt 9

s 72 ext—Pension Schemes, 1993 c 48, s 181(1)
    am—Employment, 2002 c 22, s 53, sch 7, para 55; Welfare Reform, 2007 c 5, s 28, sch 3 para 18; Educ and Skills, 2008 c 25, s 169, sch 1 para 74; Welfare Reform, 2009 c 24, ss 2(1)(5), 34(4); Welfare Reform, 2012 c 5, s 134(2); SI 2013/630, reg 15(b)
    rep in pt—Welfare Reform, 2007 c 5, s 67, sch 8; Educ and Skills, 2008 c 25, s 169, sch 2; (prosp) Welfare Reform, 2009 c 24, s 58, sch 7 pt 3; (prosp) Welfare Reform, 2012 c 5, s 134(3); ibid, sch 14 pt 1

s 79 am—SI 2010/866, art 5, sch 2

s 80 rep—Child Maintenance and Other Payments, 2008 c 6, s 58, sch 8

s 83 rep in pt—(prosp) Welfare Reform, 2009 c 24, s 58, sch 7 pt 3

sch 1 am—Pensions, 2004 c 35, s 319(1), sch 12 paras 71, 76
    rep in pt—Pensions, 2004 c 35, ss 319(1), 320, sch 12 paras 71, 76(2)(c), sch 13 pt 1; Children and Families, 2014 c 6, s 18(3)(c)

sch 2 rep in pt—Pensions, 2004 c 35, s 320, sch 13 pt 1; Pensions, 2007 c 22, s 27, sch 7 pt 6

sch 5 am—SI 2001/3649, art 159(1)(2)(a)(3); Pensions, 2004 c 35, s 319(1), sch 12 paras 71, 77(1)-(3); SIs 2006/745, art 15; 2007/3014, reg 2, sch; Pensions, 2007 c 22, s 15, sch 4 para 40
    rep in pt—SI 2001/3649, art 159(1)(2)(b); Pensions, 2007 c 22, s 27, sch 7 pt 6; Pensions, 2008 c 30, s 148, sch 11 pt 2
    appl—Pensions, 2004 c 35, s 133(9)
    mod—SI 2006/1690, reg 2

sch 7 rep in pt—(prosp) Welfare Reform, 2009 c 24, s 58, sch 7 pt 1; (prosp) ibid, s 58, sch 7 pt 3; Welfare Reform, 2012 c 5, sch 14 pt 3; (prosp) ibid, sch 14 pt 1

sch 8 rep in pt—Child Support, Pensions and Social Security, 2000 c 19, ss 32(3), 85, sch 9 pt II; (pt prosp) ibid, s 85, sch 9 pts III(1), VI; Tax Credits, 2002 c 21, s 60, sch 6; Income Tax (Earnings and Pensions), 2003 c 1, s 724(1), sch 8 pt 1; (prosp) Welfare Reform, 2007 c 5, s 67, sch 8; Welfare Reform, 2009 c 24, s 58, sch 7 pt 2; (prosp) ibid, s 58, sch 7 pt 1; (prosp) ibid, s 58, sch 7 pt 3; Welfare Reform, 2012 c 5, sch 14 pt 3; (pt prosp) ibid, sch 14 pt 1; (prosp) ibid, sch 14 pt 10

1999

c 30 *continued*

    sch 9 rep in pt—Nat Insurance Contributions, 2002 c 19, s 7, sch 2; (prosp) Pensions, 2007 c
        22, s 27, sch 7 pt 7

    sch 10 rep in pt—Nat Insurance Contributions, 2002 c 19, s 7, sch 2

    sch 11 rep in pt—Nat Insurance Contributions and Statutory Payments, 2004 c 3, s 12, sch 2
        pt 1; (prosp) Pensions, 2007 c 22, s 27, sch 7 pt 7; Finance, 2008 c 9, s 129, sch
        43 para 11(b); SI 2013/2042, sch para 20

    sch 12 rep in pt—Income Tax (Earnings and Pensions), 2003 c 1, s 724(1), sch 8 pt 1;
        Finance, 2004 c 12, s 326, sch 42 pt 3, Note; Pensions, 2004 c 35, s 320, sch
        13 pt 1; Pensions, 2008 c 30, s 148, sch 11 pt 2; (prosp) Welfare Reform, 2009
        c 24, s 58, sch 7 pt 3; (prosp) Welfare Reform, 2012 c 5, sch 14 pt 1; Children
        and Families, 2014 c 6, s 18(3)(b)(iii); (prosp) Pension Schemes, 2015 c 8, sch
        1 para 11(a)

c 31   **Contracts (Rights of Third Parties)**

    s 2 am—Crime and Cts, 2013 c 22, sch 9 para 71

    s 6 am—SI 2001/1090, reg 9(1), sch 5 para 20; SI 2005/2092, reg 9(2), sch 3 para 3; SI
        2009/1941, art 2, sch 1

    s 9 rep in pt—SI 2009/1941, art 2, sch 1

c 32   *Mental Health (Amendment) (Scotland)*—rep Mental Health (Care and Treatment) (S), 2003
        asp 13, s 331(2), sch 5 pt 1

c 33   **Immigration and Asylum**

    restr—Nationality, Immigration and Asylum, 2002 c 41, ss 54, 77, 78, sch 3, para
        1(1)(l)(2)(3)

    mod—SI 1994/1405, art 7 (as am by SIs 2007/3579, art 3; 2015/856, arts 5,6)

    ext (mods)—(Jersey) SI 2003/1252, art 2, sch; (Guernsey) SI 2003/2900, art 2, sch

    s 1 ext—SI 2008/680, art 14

    s 2 ext—SI 2008/680, art 14

    s 3 ext—SI 2008/680, art 14

    s 4 am—Nationality, Immigration and Asylum, 2002 c 41, s 49; Asylum and Immigration
        (Treatment of Claimants, etc.), 2004 c 19, s 10(1)(7); Immigration, Asylum and
        Nationality, 2006 c 13, s 43(7)

      power to restr—(prosp) Nationality, Immigration and Asylum, 2002 c 41, s 51(1)(2)(b)

      restr—(cond) Nationality, Immigration and Asylum, 2002 c 41, s 55(1)(2)(a)

      excl—(prosp) Crim Justice and Immigration, 2008 c 4, s 134(5)

    s 5 rep—Immigration, Asylum and Nationality, 2006 c 13, s 52, sch 2 para 3, sch 3

    ss 6-8 ext—SI 2008/680, art 14

    s 10 subst—Immigration, 2014 c 22, s 1

      am—Immigration, 2014 c 22, sch 1 para 2(3)

    ss 11, 12 rep—Asylum and Immigration (Treatment of Claimants, etc.), 2004 c 19, ss 33(2),
        47, sch 4, 2004/2523

    ss 13, 14 ext (mods)—SI 2008/680, art 14, sch 6

    s 15 rep—Nationality, Immigration and Asylum, 2002 c 41, ss 77(5), 161, sch 9

    ss 16, 17 ext (mods)—SI 2008/680, art 14, sch 6

    s 18 ext (mods)—SIs 2008/680, art 14, sch 6; 2011/2444, art 5, sch 3

      mod—SI 2012/1763, art 3, sch 2

    s 19 rep—Counter-Terrorism and Security, 2015 c 6, sch 5 para 3

    s 20 am—Nationality, Immigration and Asylum, 2002 c 41, s 132; Serious Organised Crime
        and Police, 2005 c 15, s 59, sch 4 paras 122, 123; Crime and Cts, 2013 c 22, sch
        8 para 65; SI 2013/602, sch 2 para 31

      rep in pt—UK Borders, 2007 c 30, s 58, sch

    s 21 am—Serious Organised Crime and Police, 2005 c 15, s 59, sch 4 paras 122, 124;
        Crime and Cts, 2013 c 22, sch 8 para 66(2)

      rep in pt—Crime and Cts, 2013 c 22, sch 8 para 66(3)

    s 22 ext—SI 2008/680, art 14

    s 23 rep—Immigration, 2014 c 22, sch 9 para 28

    s 24 am—SI 2008/678, art 5, sch 2; Immigration, 2014 c 22, ss 55(2), 56(2)

      ext (mods)—SI 2008/680, art 14, sch 6; ibid, sch 6 para 6A (added by SI 2011/1408,
        sch para 5)

      see—(trans of functions) SI 2008/678, art 3, sch 1

    s 24A added—Civil Partnership, 2004 c 33, s 261(1), sch 27 para 162

      am—SI 2008/678, art 5, sch 2; Immigration, 2014 c 22, ss 55(3), 56(3)

      see—(trans of functions) SI 2008/678, art 3, sch 1

    s 25 ext (mods)—SI 2008/680, art 14, sch 6

      am—Crime and Cts, 2013 c 22, sch 9 para 90(a)

1999

c 33 *continued*

s 26 ext (mods)—SI 2008/680, art 14, sch 6

s 27 rep—Immigration, Asylum and Nationality, 2006 c 13, s 52, sch 2 para 3, sch 3

s 28 ext—SI 2008/680, art 14

s 29 rep (prosp)—Nationality, Immigration and Asylum, 2002 c 41, s 161, sch 9

s 30 ext—SI 2008/680, art 14

s 31 am—Identity Cards, 2006 c 15, s 30(2); Identity Documents, 2010 c 40, s 12, sch 1
    para 10

s 32 appl (mods)—SI 2001/280, regs 3, 4(1)-(4), 5

    am—(pt prosp) Nationality, Immigration and Asylum, 2002 c 41, s 125, sch 8, paras 1,
    2 (see SI 2002/2811, art 4)

    see—SI 2004/251, art 2

    (ext mods)—SI 2008/680, art 14, sch 6

s 32A added (pt prosp)—Nationality, Immigration and Asylum, 2002 c 41, s 125, sch 8,
    paras 1, 3 (see SI 2002/2811, art 4)

    see—(code of practice in force 8 December 2002) SI 2002/2816, art 2

    (ext mods)—SI 2008/680, art 14, sch 6

s 33 see—SIs 2001/3233, art 2; 2004/250, art 2

    appl (mods)—SI 2001/280, regs 3, 4(1)(5), 5

    rep in pt—(pt prosp) Nationality, Immigration and Asylum, 2002 c 41, ss 125, 161, sch
    8, paras 1, 5, sch 9 (see SI 2002/2811, art 4)

    am—(pt prosp) Nationality, Immigration and Asylum, 2002 c 41, s 125, sch 8, paras 1,
    4 (see SI 2002/2811, art 4)

    (ext mods)—SI 2008/680, art 14, sch 6

s 34 appl (mods)—SI 2001/280, regs 3, 4(1)(6), 5

    am—(pt prosp) Nationality, Immigration and Asylum, 2002 c 41, s 125, sch 8, paras 1,
    6(1)(2)(4)(6) (see SI 2002/2811, art 4)

    rep in pt—(pt prosp) Nationality, Immigration and Asylum, 2002 c 41, s 125, 161, sch
    8, paras 1, 6(1)(3)(5), sch 9 (see SI 2002/2811, art 4)

    (ext mods)—SI 2008/680, art 14, sch 6

s 35 appl (mods)—SI 2001/280, regs 3, 4(1)(7), 5

    am—(pt prosp) Nationality, Immigration and Asylum, 2002 c 41, s 125, sch 8, paras 1,
    7 (see SI 2002/2811, art 4)

    (ext mods)—SI 2008/680, art 14, sch 6

s 35A added (pt prosp)—Nationality, Immigration and Asylum, 2002 c 41, s 125, sch 8,
    paras 1, 8 (see SI 2002/2811, art 4)

    (ext mods)—SI 2008/680, art 14, sch 6

s 36 appl (mods)—SI 2001/280, regs 3, 4(1)(8), 5

    am —(pt prosp) Nationality, Immigration and Asylum, 2002 c 41, ss 125, 161, sch 8,
    paras 1, 9, sch 9 (see SI 2002/2811, art 4)

    rep in pt—(pt prosp) Nationality, Immigration and Asylum, 2002 c 41, ss 125, 161,
    8, paras 1, 9, sch 9 (see SI 2002/2811, art 4)

    (ext mods)—SI 2008/680, art 14, sch 6

s 36A added (pt prosp)—Nationality, Immigration and Asylum, 2002 c 41, s 125, sch 8,
    paras 1, 10 (see SI 2002/2811, art 4)

    (ext mods)—SI 2008/680, art 14, sch 6

s 37 appl—SI 2001/280, regs 3, 4(1), 5

    rep in pt—(pt prosp) Nationality, Immigration and Asylum, 2002 c 41, ss 125, 161, sch
    8, paras 1, 11(4), sch 9 (see SI 2002/2811, art 4)

    am—(pt prosp) Nationality, Immigration and Asylum, 2002 c 41, s 125, sch 8, paras 1,
    11(1)-(3)(5)-(7) (see SI 2002/2811, art 4)

    (ext mods)—SI 2008/680, art 14, sch 6

s 38 rep in pt—(prosp) Nationality, Immigration and Asylum, 2002 c 41, s 161, sch 9

    ext—SI 2008/680, art 14

s 39 rep —Nationality, Immigration and Asylum, 2002 c 41, ss 125, 161, sch 8, paras 1, 12,
    sch 9 (see SI 2002/2811, art 4)

s 40 replaced (by ss 40, 40A, 40B)—Nationality, Immigration and Asylum, 2002 c 41, s
    125, sch 8, paras 1, 13

    (ext mods)—SI 2008/680, art 14, sch 6

ss 40A, 40B ext (mods)—SI 2008/680, art 14, sch 6

s 42 rep—Nationality, Immigration and Asylum, 2002 c 41, ss 125, 161, sch 8, paras 1, 14,
    sch 9

s 43 added & am (mods)—SI 2001/280, regs 3, 4(1)(9), 5

1999

c 33 s 43 *continued*

    am—Nationality, Immigration and Asylum, 2002 c 41, s 125, sch 8, paras 1, 15(a)(c)(e)-(h) (see SI 2002/2811, art 4); Crime and Cts, 2013 c 22, sch 9 paras 52, 90(b)

    rep in pt—Nationality, Immigration and Asylum, 2002 c 41, ss 125, 161, sch 8, paras 1, 15(b)(d), sch 9 (see SI 2002/2811, art 4)

    (ext mods)—SI 2008/680, art 14, sch 6

ss 44-52 rep—Nationality, Immigration and Asylum, 2002 c 41, ss 68(6)(a), 161, sch 9

s 53 am—Nationality, Immigration and Asylum, 2002 c 41, s 62(13); Constitutional Reform, 2005 c 4, s 15(1), sch 4 pt 1 paras 283, 284

    rep in pt—Nationality, Immigration and Asylum, 2002 c 41, ss 68(6)(b), 114(3), 161, sch 7, para 28, sch 9

s 54 ext—SI 2008/680, art 14

s 55 rep—Nationality, Immigration and Asylum, 2002 c 41, ss 68(6)(c), 161, sch 9

Pt 4 (ss 56-81) rep—Nationality, Immigration and Asylum, 2002 c 41, ss 114(1)(2), 161, sch 6, sch 9

s 82 am—Nationality, Immigration and Asylum, 2002 c 41, s 123(1)(2)(3); Legal Services, 2007 c 29, s 186, sch 18 paras 9, 10

    rep in pt—SI 2010/22, art 5, sch 2

s 83 am—Legal Services, 2007 c 29, s 186, sch 18 paras 9, 11

s 84 excl—(temp) SIs 2001/1393, arts 3, 4; 1403, arts 3, 4, sch 2, sch 3; (temp) 2002/9, art 3; (temp) 3025, art 3

    am—Asylum and Immigration (Treatment of Claimants, etc.), 2004 c 19, s 37(1); Legal Services, 2007 c 29, s 186, sch 18 paras 9, 12; Immigration, 2014 c 22, sch 7 para 5(1)

    rep in pt—Immigration, 2014 c 22, sch 7 para 2(1)(2)(a)(b)

s 85 rep in pt—Asylum and Immigration (Treatment of Claimants, etc.), 2004 c 19, ss 37(2), 47, sch 4

s 86 am—Asylum and Immigration (Treatment of Claimants, etc.), 2004 c 19, s 41(1)-(4); Legal Services, 2007 c 29, ss 186, 196(2), sch 18 paras 9, 13

    rep in pt—Legal Services, 2007 c 29, s 210, sch 23

s 86A added—Legal Services, 2007 c 29, s 186, sch 18 paras 9, 14

s 87 am—Nationality, Immigration and Asylum, 2002 c 41, s 140(3); SI 2010/22, art 5, sch 2; Immigration, 2014 c 22, sch 7 paras 4(1), 5(2)

    rep in pt—Asylum and Immigration (Treatment of Claimants, etc.), 2004 c 19, ss 40, 47, sch 4; SI 2010/22, art 5, sch 2; Immigration, 2014 c 22, sch 7 para 2(2)(c)

s 88 am—SI 2010/22, art 5, sch 2

    rep in pt—Immigration, 2014 c 22, sch 7 para 2(2)(d)

s 89 am—Asylum and Immigration (Treatment of Claimants, etc.), 2004 c 19, s 37(3); SI 2010/22, art 5, sch 2; Crime and Cts, 2013 c 22, sch 9 para 90(c); Immigration, 2014 c 22, sch 7 para 7(1)

    mod—Immigration, 2014 c 22, sch 9 paras 68, 69

    rep in pt—Immigration, 2014 c 22, sch 7 para 2(2)(e)

s 90 am—Asylum and Immigration (Treatment of Claimants, etc.), 2004 c 19, s 37(4); Legal Services, 2007 c 29, s 186, sch 18 paras 9, 15

s 91 am—SI 2010/22, art 5, sch 2

s 92 am—Crime and Cts, 2013 c 22, sch 9 para 90(c)

s 92A added—Asylum and Immigration (Treatment of Claimants, etc.), 2004 c 19, s 38(1)

s 92B added—Asylum and Immigration (Treatment of Claimants, etc.), 2004 c 19, s 39

Pt 6 (ss 94-127) appl (mods)—(prosp) Crim Justice and Immigration, 2008 c 4, ss 134(1)(2)(3)(5)(6), 135(1)-(5)

s 93 am—SI 2010/22, art 5, sch 2

s 94 appl—Nationality, Immigration and Asylum, 2002 c 41, ss 38(3)(a), 70(8)(a)

    am—Nationality, Immigration and Asylum, 2002 c 41, s 60(2); (prosp) ibid, s 44(1)(3)(4)

    rep in pt—(prosp) Nationality, Immigration and Asylum, 2002 c 41, ss 44(1)(5), 161, sch 9; SI 2008/2833, art 6, sch 3

    mod—Nationality, Immigration and Asylum, 2002 c 41, s 48

s 95 appl (mods)—Nat Assistance, 1948 c 29, s 21(1B)), ss 117(1), 169(2); Health Services and Public Health, 1968 c 46, ss 45(4B), 117(2), 169(2); Nat Health Service, 1977 c 49, sch 8 para 2(2B); Social Work (S), 1968 c 49, s 12(2B),13A(5), 13B(4); (prosp) Social Services and Well-being (W), 2014 anaw 4, s 46(2)(3); Care, 2014 c 23, s 21(2)(3)

    ext—(prosp) Nationality, Immigration and Asylum, 2002 c 41, s 22

1999

c 33 s 95 *continued*

am—(prosp) Nationality, Immigration and Asylum, 2002 c 41, s 44(1)(6); ibid, s 50(1)

power to restr—(prosp) Nationality, Immigration and Asylum, 2002 c 41, s 51(1)(2)(c)

restr—(cond) Nationality, Immigration and Asylum, 2002 c 41, s 55(1)(2)(a)

saved—Nationality, Immigration and Asylum, 2002 c 41, s 55(5)(b)

appl—Nat Health Service (W), 2006 c 42, s 192, sch 15 para 2(7); Nat Health Service, 2006 c 41, s 254, sch 20 para 2(7)

s 96 power to restr—Nationality, Immigration and Asylum, 2002 c 41, s 43

am—(prosp) Nationality, Immigration and Asylum, 2002 c 41, s 45(1)

rep in pt—Nationality, Immigration and Asylum, 2002 c 41, ss 61, 161, sch 9; SI 2002/782, art 2

s 97 am—(prosp) Nationality, Immigration and Asylum, 2002 c 41, s 45(2); (prosp) Welfare Reform, 2009 c 24, s 9, sch 2 para 8; Welfare Reform, 2012 c 5, sch 2 para 53

rep in pt—(prosp) Welfare Reform, 2012 c 5, sch 14 pt 1

s 98 power to restr—(prosp) Nationality, Immigration and Asylum, 2002 c 41, s 51(1)(2)(c)

restr—(cond) Nationality, Immigration and Asylum, 2002 c 41, s 55(1)(2)(a)

saved—Nationality, Immigration and Asylum, 2002 c 41, s 55(5)(c)

s 99 appl—(prosp) Nationality, Immigration and Asylum, 2002 c 41, s 24(2)

am—Nationality, Immigration and Asylum, 2002 c 41, s 56; Immigration, Asylum and Nationality, 2006 c 13, s 43(1)(2)

s 100 am—SI 2010/866, art 5, sch 2

s 102 rep—SI 2008/2833, art 6, sch 3

s 103 saved—(prosp) Nationality, Immigration and Asylum, 2002 c 41, s 26(4)

replaced (by ss 103, 103A, 103B) (prosp)—Nationality, Immigration and Asylum, 2002 c 41, s 53

(as enacted) am—Asylum and Immigration (Treatment of Claimants, etc.), 2004 c 19, s 10(3); (transtl provns) SI 2008/2833, art 6, sch 3

(as replaced by 2002 c 41) am—Asylum and Immigration (Treatment of Claimants, etc.), 2004 c 19, s 10(4); (transtl provns) SI 2008/2833, art 6, sch 3

(as enacted) rep in pt—(transtl provns) SI 2008/2833, art 6, sch 3

(as replaced by 2002 c 41) rep in pt—(transtl provns) SI 2008/2833, art 6, sch 3

s 103A am—Asylum and Immigration (Treatment of Claimants, etc.), 2004 c 19, s 10(5); SI 2008/2833, art 6, sch 3

s 104 rep—SI 2008/2833, art 6, sch 3

s 105 am—(prosp) (EW) Crim Justice, 2003 c 44, s 280(2)(3), sch 26 para 53(1)(2)

appl—(prosp) Nationality, Immigration and Asylum, 2002 c 41, s 35(1)(a)-(e)

ss 106, 107 appl—(prosp) Nationality, Immigration and Asylum, 2002 c 41, s 35(1)(a)-(e)

s 108 am—(prosp) (EW) Crim Justice, 2003 c 44, s 280(2)(3), sch 26 para 53(1)(3)

appl—(prosp) Nationality, Immigration and Asylum, 2002 c 41, s 35(1)(a)-(e)

s 109 appl—(prosp) Nationality, Immigration and Asylum, 2002 c 41, s 35(1)(a)-(e)

ss 109A, 109B added—UK Borders, 2007 c 30, s 18

s 110 appl—Nationality, Immigration and Asylum, 2002 c 41, ss 38(3)(b), 70(8)(b)

ext—Nationality, Immigration and Asylum, 2002 c 41, s 48

am—Nationality, Immigration and Asylum, 2002 c 41, s 60(1)

s 111 ext—Nationality, Immigration and Asylum, 2002 c 41, s 48

excl—(prosp) Crim Justice and Immigration, 2008 c 4, s 134(2)(f)

s 112 appl (mods)—(prosp) Nationality, Immigration and Asylum, 2002 c 41, s 35(1)(f)(2)

am—Crime and Cts, 2013 c 22, sch 9 para 90(c)

s 113 appl (mods)—(prosp) Nationality, Immigration and Asylum, 2002 c 41, s 35(1)(g)(3)

excl—(prosp) Crim Justice and Immigration, 2008 c 4, s 134(2)(g)

s 115 am—State Pension Credit, 2002 c 16, s 4(2); Tax Credits, 2002 c 21, s 51, sch 4, paras 20, 21; SI 2002/1457, art 2(2), schedule, paras 1, 3(c); Welfare Reform, 2007 c 5, s 28, sch 3 para 19; Health and Social Care, 2008 c 14, s 138(2)(3); Welfare Reform, 2012 c 5, sch 2 para 54; (prosp) ibid, sch 3 para 9; ibid, sch 9 para 44

appl—Tax Credits, 2002 c 21, s 42(2); SIs 2002/1792, reg 2(d); 1792, reg 5(1)(h)

rep in pt—Tax Credits, 2002 c 21, s 60, sch 6; (prosp) Welfare Reform, 2009 c 24, s 58, sch 7 pt 1; (prosp) Welfare Reform, 2012 c 5, sch 14 pt 1; (prosp) ibid, sch 14 pt 9

s 117 rep in pt—(EW) Homelessness, 2002 c 7, s 18(2), sch 2; Nat Health Service (Conseq Provns), 2006 c 43, s 6, sch 4

s 118 am—Immigration, Asylum and Nationality, 2006 c 13, s 43(3)

s 119 am—(pt prosp) Housing and Regeneration, 2008 c 17, s 314, sch 15 paras 17, 22

s 120 rep in pt—Mental Health (Care and Treatment) (S), 2003 asp 13, s 331(2), sch 5 pt 1

1999
c 33 *continued*

s 122 subst—(prosp) Nationality, Immigration and Asylum, 2002 c 41, s 47
    excl—SI 2000/705, reg 5

s 123 rep—Asylum and Immigration (Treatment of Claimants, etc), 2004 c 19, ss 12(1), 47,
    sch 4

s 124 appl—Nationality, Immigration and Asylum, 2002 c 41, s 35(1)(h)

s 127 am—SI 2001/1149, art 3(1), sch 1 para 124
    appl—(prosp) Nationality, Immigration and Asylum, 2002 c 41, s 35(1)(i)

ss 128-140 ext—SI 2008/680, art 14

s 141 appl—SI 2001/238, rule 5(4)
    am—Nationality, Immigration and Asylum, 2002 c 41, s 66(2)(3)(n); Asylum and
        Immigration (Treatment of Claimants, etc.), 2004 c 19, s 15; Immigration,
        Asylum and Nationality, 2006 c 13, s 28; Borders, Citizenship and Immigration,
        2009 c 11, s 51; Immigration, 2014 c 22, sch 9 para 29(2)-(4)
    rep in pt—Immigration, 2014 c 22, sch 9 para 29(5)
    appl (mods)—SI 2006/987, art 7
    mod—SI 1993/1813, art 7(1), sch 4 para 2A
    ext—SI 2002/2818, art 11(1)(f), sch 2 para 1A
    ext (mods)—SI 2008/680, art 14, sch 6

s 142 am—Immigration, Asylum and Nationality, 2006 c 13, s 29
    ext (mods)—SI 2008/680, art 14, sch 6

s 143 rep (prosp)—Immigration, 2014 c 22, sch 9 para 17(2)
    am—Anti-terrorism, Crime and Security, 2001 c 24, s 36(1)(b)(2)
    rep in pt—Anti-terrorism, Crime and Security, 2001 c 24, ss 36(1)(a)(c)(2), 125, sch 8
        pt 3
    appl (mods)—SI 2006/987, art 7
    ext—SI 2002/2818, art 11(1)(f), sch 2 para 1A
    ext (mods)—SI 2008/680, art 14, sch 6

s 144 am—Nationality, Immigration and Asylum, 2002 c 41, s 128; Immigration, 2014 c 22,
        sch 2 para 2(2)(3); (prosp) ibid, sch 9 para 17(3)
    ext (mods)—SI 2008/680, art 14, sch 6

s 144A added—Immigration, 2014 c 22, s 14(2)

s 145 am—Nationality, Immigration and Asylum, 2002 c 41, s 128
    ext (mods)—SI 2008/680, art 14, sch 6

s 146 am—Nationality, Immigration and Asylum, 2002 c 41, s 153(2); Immigration, 2014 c
        22, sch 1 para 5
    ext—SI 2008/680, art 14

s 147 am—Nationality, Immigration and Asylum, 2002 c 41, ss 62(14), 66(1)(b)(2)(3)(a);
        Borders, Citizenship and Immigration, 2009 c 11, s 25; Immigration, 2014 c 22,
        s 6(2)
    rep in pt—Nationality, Immigration and Asylum, 2002 c 41, ss 66(1)(a), 161, sch 9
    ext—SI 2003/2818, art 11(2)
    appl—(E) SI 2005/1972, reg 2(2)(b)

ss 148-153 am—Nationality, Immigration and Asylum, 2002 c 41, s 66(2)(3)(b)-(f)

s 149 ext—SI 2002/2538, reg 2
    am—Agricultural Holdings (S), 2003 asp 11, s 94, sch para 52

s 153A added—Immigration, Asylum and Nationality, 2006 c 13, s 59(1)

s 154 am—Nationality, Immigration and Asylum, 2002 c 41, s 65(1)

s 155 am—Nationality, Immigration and Asylum, 2002 c 41, s 66(2)(3)(g); Immigration,
        2014 c 22, s 6(3)

s 156 am—Asylum and Immigration (Treatment of Claimants, etc), 2004 c 19, s 26(7), sch
        2 pt 1 para 15; SI 2005/2078, art 15, sch 1 para 5(a)(b)(d); SI 2010/21, art 5,
        sch 1
    rep in pt—SI 2005/2078, art 15, sch 1 para 5(c)

ss 157-159 am—Nationality, Immigration and Asylum, 2002 c 41, s 66(2)(3)(h)-(j)

s 157A added—Immigration, 2014 c 22, s 6(4)

s 165 ext—SI 2008/680, art 14

s 166 rep in pt—Nationality, Immigration and Asylum, 2002 c 41, ss 61(b), 161, sch 9;
        (prosp) Immigration, 2014 c 22, sch 9 para 17(4)
    am—Asylum and Immigration (Treatment of Claimants, etc), 2004 c 19, ss 10(2),
        41(5); Civil Partnership, 2004 c 33, s 261(1), sch 27 para 163; Legal Services,
        2007 c 29, s 186, sch 18 paras 9, 16
    ext (mods)—SIs 2008/680, art 14, sch 6; 2011/2444, art 5, sch 2

1999

c 33 *continued*

s 167 appl—Anti-terrorism, Crime and Security, 2001 c 24, s 33(2)(8)(b); Access to Justice, 1999 c 22, sch 2 para 1; Extradition, 2003 c 41, s 40(4) (see SI 2003/3103, arts 2-5)

am—Nationality, Immigration and Asylum, 2002 c 41, s 158(4); Asylum and Immigration (Treatment of Claimants, etc.), 2004 c 19, s 44(4)(b)

appl (mods)—SI 2006/987, art 7

rep in pt—Immigration, Asylum and Nationality, 2006 c 13, s 64(3)(b), sch 3

ext (mods)—SI 2008/680, art 14, sch 6

s 168 ext (mods)—SI 2008/680, art 14, sch 6

s 169 ext—SI 2008/680, art 14

s 170 ext—SI 2008/680, art 14

sch 1 rep in pt—(subject to transtl provn(s)) (pt prosp) Nationality, Immigration and Asylum, 2002 c 41, ss 125, 161, sch 8, paras 1, 16(1)(2)(4)(5), sch 9 (see SI 2000/2811, art 4)

am—(subject to transtl provn(s)) (pt prosp) Nationality, Immigration and Asylum, 2002 c 41, s 125, sch 8, paras 1, 16(1)(3) (see SI 2000/2811, art 4)

schs 2-4 rep—Nationality, Immigration and Asylum, 2002 c 41, s 161, sch 9

sch 5 am—(subject to transtl provn(s)) Nationality, Immigration and Asylum, 2002 c 41, s 140(1) (see SI 2000/2811, art 5); Asylum and Immigration (Treatment of Claimants, etc.), 2004 c 19, ss 37(5)(a)-(k), 38(2), 41(6); Legal Services, 2007 c 29, ss 186, 196(2), sch 18 paras 9, 17; SI 2010/22, art 5, sch 2; Immigration, 2014 c 22, sch 7 paras 4(2)(b), 6, 7, 8(2)

rep in pt—Legal Services, 2007 c 29, s 210, sch 23; Immigration, 2014 c 22, sch 7 paras 2(2)(f), 4(2)(a), 8(1)

mod—Immigration, 2014 c 22, sch 9 paras 68, 69

sch 6 am—Nationality, Immigration and Asylum, 2002 c 41, s 140(2); Asylum and Immigration (Treatment of Claimants, etc.), 2004 c 19, s 37(6)(b); SI 2010/22, art 5, sch 2; Immigration, 2014 c 22, sch 7 paras 3(2)(a)(b)(3), 4(3)(b)(4), 5(3)

rep in pt—Asylum and Immigration (Treatment of Claimants, etc.), 2004 c 19, ss 37(6)(a), 47, sch 4; Immigration, 2014 c 22, sch 7 paras 2(2)(g), 4(3)(a)(c)

sch 7 rep—SI 2010/22, art 5, sch 2

sch 8 rep in pt—(prosp) Nationality, Immigration and Asylum, 2002 c 41, ss 45(3), 161, sch 9

am—Nationality, Immigration and Asylum, 2002 c 41, s 57

appl (mods)—Nat Assistance, 1948 c 29, s 21(1B)), ss 117(1), 169(2); Health Services and Public Health, 1968 c 46, s 45(4B)), ss 117(2), 169(2); Nat Health Service, 1977 c 49, sch 8 para 2(2B); Social Work (S), 1968 c 49, ss 12(2B),13A(5),13B(4)

sch 10 see—(trans of functions) SI 2007/275, art 3

am—SI 2007/275, art 6

rep in pt—SI 2008/2833, art 6, sch 3

sch 11 am—Nationality, Immigration and Asylum, 2002 c 41, ss 65(2), 66(2)(3)(k); Immigration, 2014 c 22, sch 9 para 12(2)

ext—SI 2003/2818, arts 11(2), 12(3)

sch 12 am—Nationality, Immigration and Asylum, 2002 c 41, ss 65(3), 66(2)(3)(l); Immigration, 2014 c 22, sch 9 para 12(3)

sch 13 am—Nationality, Immigration and Asylum, 2002 c 41, s 66(2)(3)(m)

ext—SI 2003/2818, art 11(2)

sch 14 rep in pt—Terrorism, 2000 c 11, s 125(2), sch 16 pt I; SI 2000/2326, regs 32(4),36; Nationality, Immigration and Asylum, 2002 c 41, s 161, sch 9; Nationality, Immigration and Asylum, 2002 c 41, s 161, sch 9; Nationality, Immigration and Asylum, 2002 c 41, s 161, sch 9; Educ, 2002 c 32, s 215(2), sch 22 pt 3; SIs 2008/2833, art 6, sch 3; 2010/22, art 5, sch 4

ext—SI 2008/680, art 14

sch 15 rep in pt—Mental Health (Care and Treatment) (S), 2003 asp 13, s 331(2), sch 5 pt 1

sch 16 ext—SI 2008/680, art 14

c 34 **House of Lords**

s 1 mod—Constitutional Reform and Governance, 2010 c 25, s 42(3), (8)

s 2 mod—Constitutional Reform and Governance, 2010 c 25, s 42(3), (8)

s 3 appl—SI 2001/84, art 2; House of Lords Reform, 2014 c 24, s 4(4)

excl—Constitutional Reform and Governance, 2010 c 25, s 42(3), (8)

3rd session of 52nd Parliament

c 35 *Consolidated Fund (No 2)*—rep Appropriation, 2001 c 8, s 4, sch 3

2000

c 1   *Northern Ireland*—rep NI (St Andrews Agreement), 2006 c 53, s 2, sch 4 (see SI 2007/1397,
         art 2)

c 2   **Representation of the People**
         mod—(E) SI 2001/1298, reg 10(1)(c); (NI) NI (Misc Provns) 2006 c 33, ss 11, 14, sch 1
         appl (mods)—(E) SI 2001/1298, regs 15-17, sch 5; (EW) SI 2002/185, reg 3(2), sch 2,
                  Table 3; SI 2004/1962, arts 6(1), 7, sch 2 pt 1, sch 3
         appl—SI 2004/1962, art 5(3)
         see—SI 2010/1837, art 3; (power to appl or incorp (mods)) Police Reform and Social
                  Responsibility, 2011 c 13, ss 54(5),58(1)-(3)(7)
         am (NI)—NI (Misc Provns) 2006 c 33, ss 11(8)(9), 12,13
         trans of functions—SI 2015/1376, art 3(1) sch 1
         s 10 am—Political Parties, Elections and Referendums, 2000 c 41, ss 9(1)(a)(b)(i), 158(1),
                  sch 21 para 16
              appl (mods)—SIs (E) 2001/1298, sch 3, Table 1; (W) 2004/870 (W 85), regs 8-12, 15,
                  sch 3, Table 1; (E) 2007/2089, regs 8, 11-13, sch 4; (W) 2008/1848 (W 177),
                  reg 8, sch 4; 2012/323, sch 4 para 1 Table 3; 2012/444, sch 4 para 1 Table 3;
                  2012/2031, regs 8, 12, 13, sch 4 pt 1 Table 3; 2012/2031, reg 17 sch 8 Table 2
                  (added by 2013/798, reg 7 sch 3)
              excl—European Parl and Loc Elections (Pilots), 2004 c 2, s 3
         s 11 am—Political Parties, Elections and Referendums, 2000 c 41, ss 9(1)(a)(b)(ii), 158(1),
                  sch 21 para 17
              appl (mods)—European Parl and Loc Elections (Pilots), 2004 c 2, s 5
         s 12 appl (mods)—SIs (E) 2001/1298, regs 8, 10(4), sch 3 Table 1; (W) 2004/870 (W 85),
                  regs 8-12, 15, sch 3, Table 1; (E) 2007/2089, regs 8, 11-13, sch 4; (W)
                  2008/1848 (W 177), reg 8, sch 4; 2012/323, sch 4 para 1 Table 3; 2012/444,
                  sch 4 para 1 Table 3; 2012/2031, regs 8, 12, 13, sch 4 pt 1 Table 3
              mod—(E) SI 2001/1298, reg 16(6), sch 5 pt I
         s 16A added—SI 2010/1837, art 5, sch
                  subst—SI 2015/1376, sch 2 para 7
         Pt 4 (ss 50-69) excl—(NI) (temp to 31.10.2007) NI (Misc Provns) 2006 c 33, s 11
         s 55 am—Electoral Admin, 2006 c 22, s 74, sch 1 para 147
         sch 1 rep in pt—Electoral Registration and Admin, 2013 c 6, sch 4 para 22
         sch 4 appl—City of London (Various Powers) 1957 c x, s 8(2); (E) SI 2007/2089, regs 11,
                  12
              appl (mods)—SIs (E) 2001/1298, regs 8, 10(4), sch 3 Table 1; (W) 2004/870 (W 85),
                  regs 8-12, 15, sch 3, Table 1; (E) 2007/2089, regs 8, 11-3, sch 4; (W)
                  2008/1848 (W 177), reg 8, sch 4; 2012/323, sch 4 para 1 Table 3; 2012/444,
                  sch 4 para 1 Table 3; 2012/2031, regs 8, 12, 13, sch 4 pt 1 Table 3
              mod—SIs (E) 2001/1298, reg 16(6), sch 5 pt I; 2007/1024, reg 3, sch 2
              trans of functions—SIs 2002/2626, art 11(1), sch 1; 2003/1887, art 4, sch 1
              am—Civil Partnership, 2004 c 33, s 261(1), sch 27 para 164(1)-(3); Electoral Admin,
                  2006 c 22, ss 10, 14(1)-(4), 35, 38(6), 74, sch 1 paras 19, 137; (S) Loc Electoral
                  Admin and Registration Services (S), 2006 asp 14, ss 27, 32; Electoral
                  Registration and Admin, 2013 c 6, ss 21(3), 22(1); Scottish Elections (Reduction
                  of Voting Age), 2015 asp 7, s 16(2)(3)
              rep in pt—Electoral Admin, 2006 c 22, s 74, sch 2; (S) Loc Electoral Admin and
                  Registration Services (S), 2006 asp 14, ss 20, 34
         sch 6 rep in pt—(prosp) Political Parties, Elections and Referendums, 2000 c 41, s 158(2),
                  sch 22; European Parl Elections, 2002 c 24, s 16, sch 4

c 3   *Consolidated Fund*—rep Appropriation, 2002 c 18, s 4, sch 3
c 4   *Armed Forces Discipline*—rep Armed Forces, 2006 c 52, s 378, sch 17
c 5   **Nuclear Safeguards**
         ext (mods)—(Jersey) SI 2004/1288, art 2(2), sch 2; (Isle of Man) SI 2004/1289, art 2(2),
                  sch 2; (Guernsey) SI 2004/1290, art 2(2), sch 2
         power to mod conferred—Energy, 2013 c 32, s 74(3)(d)(ii)
         s 1 am—Energy, 2013 c 32, sch 12 para 43(2)(3)
         s 2 am—Energy, 2013 c 32, sch 12 para 44(2)-(4)
         s 3 am—Energy, 2013 c 32, sch 12 para 45(2)-(6)
         s 4 rep—Energy, 2013 c 32, sch 12 para 46(1)
         s 5 am—Energy, 2013 c 32, sch 12 para 47(2)(3)
         s 6 ext—Anti-terrorism, Crime and Security, 2001 c 24, s 17, sch 4 pt 1 para 48
              am—Energy, 2013 c 32, sch 12 para 48
         s 7 am—Energy, 2013 c 32, sch 12 para 49

2000
c 5 *continued*

    s 8 ext—Crim Justice and Police, 2001 c 16, s 50, sch 1 pt 1 para 68
    am—Crim Justice and Police, 2001 c 16, s 70, sch 2 pt 2 para 22

c 6   **Powers of Criminal Courts (Sentencing)**
    saved—(EW) Crim Justice, 2003 c 44, s 189(6)
    appl—Sexual Offences, 2003 c 42, s 80, sch 3 para 96(a)
    appl (mods)—Criminal Procedure (Insanity), 1964 c 84, s 5A
    power to am—Offender Rehabilitation, 2014 c 11, s 7
    s 1 am—SI 2008/912, art 3, sch 1; Crime and Cts, 2013 c 22, sch 16 para 6
    ss 1, 2 replaced, by ss 1, 1A-1D—Crim Justice, 2003 c 44, s 278, sch 23 para 1
    s 1ZA added—Crime and Cts, 2013 c 22, sch 16 para 5
    s 1A am—SI 2008/912, art 3, sch 1
    s 3 excl—Magistrates' Cts, 1980 c 43, s 17D(2)(b)
        ext—Mental Health, 1983 c 20, s 43(4)
        rep in pt—(prosp) Crim Justice and Immigration, 2008 c 4, s 149, sch 28 pt 4
    s 3A added—Crim Justice, 2003 c 44, s 41, sch 3 pt 1 paras 21, 23
    s 3B added—Crim Justice, 2003 c 44, s 41, sch 3 pt 1 paras 21, 23
        ext—Mental Health, 1983 c 20, s 43(4)
        am—Crim Justice and Cts, 2015 c 2, s 53(1)(2)
    s 3C added—Crim Justice, 2003 c 44, s 41, sch 3 pt 1 paras 21, 23
    s 4 am—Crim Justice, 2003 c 44, s 41, sch 3 pt 1 paras 21, 24
        excl—Magistrates' Cts, 1980 c 43, s 17D(2)(b)
    s 4A added—Crim Justice, 2003 c 44, s 41, sch 3 pt 1 paras 21, 25
    s 5 subst—Crim Justice, 2003 c 44, s 41, sch 3 pt 1 paras 21, 26
    s 5A added—Crim Justice, 2003 c 44, s 41, sch 3 pt 1 paras 21, 27
    s 6 am—Crim Justice, 2003 c 44, s 304, sch 32 pt 1 paras 90, 91; ibid, s 41, sch 3 pt 1
        paras 21, 28
        rep in pt—Crim Justice, 2003 c 44, s 332, sch 37 pts 7, 9
    s 7 am—Crim Justice, 2003 c 44, s 304, sch 32 pt 1 paras 90, 92
    s 8 am—Crim Justice, 2003 c 44, s 41, sch 3 pt 2 para 74(1)(2); SI 2005/886, art 2, sch
        para 62
    s 9 rep in pt—SI 2005/886, art 2, sch para 63
    s 10 appl—SI 2005/384, rule 42.1(3)
    s 12 excl—Football Spectators 1989 c 37, s 14A(5); Violent Crime Reduction, 2006 c 38, s
        11(3); Serious Crime, 2007 c 27, s 36(5)(6)
        rep in pt—Crim Justice, 2003 c 44, ss 304, 332, sch 32 pt 1 paras 90, 93(b), sch 37 pt 7;
            Crim Justice and Cts, 2015 c 2, sch 12 para 9(2)(a)
        am—Crim Justice, 2003 c 44, s 304, sch 32 pt 1 paras 90, 93(a); Violent Crime
            Reduction, 2006 c 38, s 49, sch 1 para 6; Crim Justice and Immigration, 2008 c 4,
            s 148, sch 26 paras 40, 41; Legal Aid, Sentencing and Punishment of Offenders,
            2012 c 10, sch 19 para 4; ibid, sch 24 para 19; ibid, sch 26 para 10; Prevention of
            Social Housing Fraud, 2013 c 3, sch para 8; Crim Justice and Cts, 2015 c 2, sch 5
            para 4; ibid, sch 12 para 9(2)(b)(3)
        mod—Crime and Disorder, 1998 c 37, s 66F
    s 13 am—SI 2005/886, art 2, sch para 64
    s 14 excl—Football Spectators 1989 c 37, s 14A(5); Sexual Offences, 2003 c 42,
        s 134(1)(a)(2); Serious Crime, 2007 c 27, s 36(5)(6); Coroners and Justice, 2009
        c 25, s 158(3)(a); Modern Slavery, 2015 c 30, s 34(3)(a)
    s 16 restr—Crime and Disorder, 1998 c 37,s 1AB(4)
        am—Legal Aid, Sentencing and Punishment of Offenders, 2012 c 10, s 79(1)
    s 17 am—SI 2003/1605, reg 2; Crim Justice and Immigration, 2008 c 4, s 35(1)(2)(a)(b)(3);
        Coroners and Justice, 2009 c 25, s 144, sch 17 para 12; Legal Aid, Sentencing
        and Punishment of Offenders, 2012 c 10, s 79(2)(a)
        rep in pt—Crim Justice and Immigration, 2008 c 4, ss 35(1)(2)(c)(4), 149, sch 28 pt 2;
            Legal Aid, Sentencing and Punishment of Offenders, 2012 c 10, s 79(2)(b)
    s 18 am—Crim Justice and Cts, 2015 c 2, s 45(3)
    s 19 rep in pt—Crim Justice, 2003 c 44, ss 324, 332, sch 34 para 3(b), sch 37 pt 12
        am—Crim Justice, 2003 c 44, s 324, sch 34 para 3(a); Crim Justice and Immigration,
            2008 c 4, s 6, sch 4 paras 51, 52; Policing and Crime, 2009 c 26, s 112, sch 7
            para 22
    s 22 am—Crim Justice, 2003 c 44, s 324, sch 34 para 4; SI 2005/886, art 2, sch para 65
    s 24 am—Crim Justice and Immigration, 2008 c 4, s 148, sch 26 paras 40, 42
    s 27A added—Crim Justice and Immigration, 2008 c 4, s 36(1)(2)
    s 27B added—Crim Justice and Immigration, 2008 c 4, s 37(1)(2)

2000
c 6 *continued*

s 28 am—Crim Justice, 2003 c 44, s 324, sch 34 para 5(1)-(3); Crim Justice and
    Immigration, 2008 c 4, s 148, sch 26 paras 40, 43
s 31 am—SI 2004/2035, art 3, sch paras 39, 40(1)(2)
s 31 rep in pt—SI 2004/2035, art 3, sch paras 39, 40(1)(3)
Pt 4, Ch 1 (ss 33-36B) rep (prosp as to ss 33(1)(c), 36B)—Crim Justice and Immigration,
    2008 c 4, ss 6,149, sch 28 pt 1
s 33 am—Crim Justice, 2003 c 44, s 304, sch 32 pt 1 paras 90, 94; Crime and Cts, 2013 c
    22, sch 16 para 9
    appl—SIs 2002/2387(L), art 4, schedule pt III, para 7(1)(a); 2002/2662(L), art 4,
        schedule pt III, para 8(1)(a)
    subst—Crim Justice, 2003 c 44, s 304, sch 32 pt 1 paras 90, 95
ss 34-36A rep—Crim Justice, 2003 c 44, s 332, sch 37 pt 7
s 36B added (pt prosp)—Crim Justice and Ct Services, 2000 c 43, s 52
    am—Crim Justice, 2003 c 44, s 304, sch 32 pt 1 paras 90, 96; SI 2005/886, art 2, sch
        para 66
    rep in pt—Crim Justice, 2003 c 44, s 332, sch 37 pt 7
Pt 4, Ch 2 (ss 37-40C) rep —(with transtl provn(s)) Crim Justice and Immigration, 2008 c 4,
    ss 6,149, sch 28 pt 1
Pt 4, Ch 3 (ss 41-59) rep—(with transtl provn(s)) Crim Justice, 2003 c 44, ss 303(d)(i), 332,
    333(6), sch 37 pt 7, sch 38 para 4
Pt 4, Ch 4 (ss 60-62) rep—Crim Justice, 2003 c 44, s 332, sch 37 pt 7; (with transtl
    provn(s)) Crim Justice and Immigration, 2008 c 4, ss 6,149, sch 28 pt 1
Pt 4, Ch 5 (ss 63-72) rep—(with transtl provn(s)) Crim Justice and Immigration, 2008 c 4, ss
    6,149, sch 28 pt 1
s 73 am—Crim Justice and Ct Services, 2000 c 43, s 74, sch 7 pt I para 4; Crim Justice,
    2003 c 44, s 304, sch 32 pt 1 paras 90, 106(1)(2); Crim Justice and Immigration,
    2008 c 4, s 6, sch 4 paras 51, 53; SI 2008/912, art 3, sch 1
    rep in pt—Crim Justice, 2003 c 44, ss 304, 332, sch 32 pt 1 paras 90, 106(1)(3), sch 37
        pt 7; Children, 2004 c 31, s 64, sch 5 pt 4
s 74 am—Crim Justice and Ct Services, 2000 c 43, s 74, sch 7 pt I para 4; Crim Justice,
    2003 c 44, s 304, sch 32 pt 1 paras 90, 107; SIs 2005/886, art 2, sch para 76;
    2008/912, art 3, sch 1
    rep in pt—Children, 2004 c 31, s 64, sch 5 pt 4; (pt prosp) Crim Justice and
        Immigration, 2008 c 4, ss 6, 149, sch 4 paras 51, 54, sch 28 pt 1
s 75 rep in pt—Crim Justice and Immigration, 2008 c 4, ss 6, 149, sch 4 paras 51, 55, sch 28
    pt 1
s 76 rep in pt—(prosp) Crim Justice and Ct Services, 2000 c 43, ss 74, 75, sch 7 pt II
    para 176, sch 8
    appl—SIs 1975/515, reg 5(1)(a); 2002/2051, art 5(3)(a); Magistrates' Cts, 1980 c 43,
        s 20A(6); Serious Organised Crime and Police, 2005 c 15, s 73(8)(b)
    am—Crim Justice, 2003 c 44, s 304, sch 32 pt 1 paras 90, 108
s 78 rep (prosp)—Crim Justice, 2003 c 44, s 332, sch 37 pt 7
    am—Tribunals, Cts and Enforcement, 2007 c 15, s 62, sch 13 paras 131, 132
ss 79-82 rep—Crim Justice, 2003 c 44, s 332, sch 37 pt 7
s 82A added—Crim Justice and Ct Services, 2000 c 43, s 60(1)(3)
    mod—Crim Justice and Ct Services, 2000 c 43, s 60(4)
    am—Crim Justice, 2003 c 44, ss 230, 304, sch 18 para 4, sch 32 pt 1 paras 90,
        109(1)-(3)(4)(a); Armed Forces, 2006 c 52, s 378, sch 16 para 163; Crim
        Justice and Immigration, 2008 c 4, s 22(5); (prosp) ibid, s 19; Legal Aid,
        Sentencing and Punishment of Offenders, 2012 c 10, sch 13 para 10; Crim
        Justice and Cts, 2015 c 2, s 15(1)
    appl (mods)—Crim Justice, 2003 c 44, s 274(2)
    rep in pt—Crim Justice, 2003 c 44, ss 304, 332, sch 32 pt 1 paras 90, 109(1)(4)(b)(5),
        sch 37 pt 8
s 83 am—(prosp) Crim Justice and Ct Services, 2000 c 43, s 74, sch 7 pt II para 178; Crim
    Defence Service, 2006 c 9, s 4(2)(3)(c); Legal Aid, Sentencing and Punishment of
    Offenders, 2012 c 10, sch 5 para 53(2), (3)
s 84 rep—Crim Justice, 2003 c 44, s 332, sch 37 pt 7
    saved—Crim Justice and Immigration, 2008 c 4, s 20(5)
s 85 rep—Crim Justice, 2003 c 44, ss 303(d)(ii), 332, sch 37 pt 7
s 86 rep—Crim Justice, 2003 c 44, ss 303(d)(iii), 332, sch 37 pt 7; Legal Aid, Sentencing
    and Punishment of Offenders, 2012 c 10, s 121(4)
s 87 rep—Crim Justice, 2003 c 44, ss 303(d)(iii), 332, sch 37 pt 7

2000
c 6 *continued*

s 89 am—(prosp) Crim Justice and Ct Services, 2000 c 43, s 74, sch 7 pt II para 180; Crim Justice, 2003 c 44, s 41, sch 3 pt 2 para 74(1)(3)(b)

rep in pt—Crim Justice, 2003 c 44, ss 41, 332, sch 3 pt 2 para 74(1)(3)(a), sch 37 pt 4

s 90 am—Crim Justice and Ct Services, 2000 c 43, s 60(2)(3)

s 91 am—Sexual Offences, 2003 c 42, s 139, sch 6 para 43(1)(2); Crim Justice, 2003 c 44, ss 289, 304, sch 32 pt 1 paras 90, 110; Violent Crime Reduction, 2006 c 38, s 49, sch 1 para 7; Crim Justice and Immigration, 2008 c 4, s 6, sch 4 paras 51, 56

ext—Crim Justice, 2003 c 44, ss 226(2), 240(10), 250(4), 263(4), 264(7), 265(2)

saved—Crim Justice, 2003 c 44, s 238(4)

power to am—Firearms (Amdt), 1988 c 45, s 1(4A)(bb)

rep in pt—Crim Justice, 2003 c 44, s 332, sch 37 pt 7

s 92 rep in pt—Crim Justice and Immigration, 2008 c 4, ss 148, 149, sch 26 paras 40, 44, sch 28 pt 2

ss 93-96 rep (prosp)—Crim Justice and Ct Services, 2000 c 43, ss 74, 75, sch 7 pt II para 182, sch 8

s 97 rep (prosp)—Crim Justice and Ct Services, 2000 c 43, ss 74, 75, sch 7 pt II para 182, sch 8

rep in pt—Crim Justice and Cts, 2015 c 2, s 15(2)

appl—SI 2009/1059, art 205, sch 2 para 9

s 98 rep (prosp)—Crim Justice and Ct Services, 2000 c 43, ss 74, 75, sch 7 pt II para 182, sch 8

s 99 subst—Crim Justice, 2003 c 44, s 236

am—Armed Forces, 2006 c 52, s 378, sch 16 para 164; Offender Management, 2007 c 21, s 39, sch 3 para 9; Legal Aid, Sentencing and Punishment of Offenders, 2012 c 10, sch 22 para 15

mod—SI 2009/1059, art 205, sch 1

s 100 am—Crim Justice, 2003 c 44, s 304, sch 32 pt 1 paras 90, 111(1)(2); Legal Aid, Sentencing and Punishment of Offenders, 2012 c 10, sch 26 para 11; Crim Justice and Cts, 2015 c 2, sch 5 para 5

rep in pt—Crim Justice, 2003 c 44, ss 304, 332, sch 32 pt 1 paras 90, 111(1)(3), sch 37 pt 7

s 101 am—Terrorism, 2000 c 11, s 125(1), sch 15 para 20(3); (prosp) Crim Justice and Ct Services, 2000 c 43, s 74, sch 7 pt II para 185; Crim. Justice and Police, 2001 c 16, s 133(3); (prosp) Crim Justice, 2003 c 44, s 298; Police and Justice, 2006 c 48, s 42, sch 13 para 32; Crim Justice and Immigration, 2008 c 4, s 22(6); Legal Aid, Sentencing and Punishment of Offenders, 2012 c 10, sch 12 para 43(a); ibid, sch 13 para 11; Offender Rehabilitation, 2014 c 11, s 6(2)

rep in pt—Legal Aid, Sentencing and Punishment of Offenders, 2012 c 10, sch 12 para 43(b)

s 102 appl (mods)—Crime Sentences, 1997 c 43, sch 1 para 8

rep in pt—Offender Management, 2007 c 21, s 39, sch 5 part 3

am—Offender Management, 2007 c 21, ss 33, 34(1)(2)

s 103 am—Crim Justice and Ct Services, 2000 c 43, s 74, sch 7 pt I para 4; SIs 2005/886, art 2, sch paras 76, 77; 2008/912, art 3, sch 1; Offender Rehabilitation, 2014 c 11, s 6(3)

appl (mods)—Crime Sentences, 1997 c 43, sch 1 para 8

rep in pt—Children, 2004 c 31, s 64, sch 5 pt 4; Offender Rehabilitation, 2014 c 11, sch 3 para 11(2)(3)

s 104 appl (mods)—Crime Sentences, 1997 c 43, sch 1 para 8

am—Domestic Violence, Crime and Victims, 2004 c 28, s 29, sch 5 para 2(1)(3); SI 2005/886, art 2, sch paras 76, 77; Offender Management, 2007 c 21, s 34(1)(3); Legal Aid, Sentencing and Punishment of Offenders, 2012 c 10, s 80(2)-(6)

rep in pt—Domestic Violence, Crime and Victims, 2004 c 28, ss 29, 58(2), sch 5 para 2(1)(2), sch 11

mod (temp)—Legal Aid, Sentencing and Punishment of Offenders, 2012 c 10, s 80(8)

ss 104A, 104B added—Legal Aid, Sentencing and Punishment of Offenders, 2012 c 10, s 80(7)

s 105 am—(prosp) Crim Justice and Ct Services, 2000 c 43, s 74, sch 7 pt II para 186; Offender Management, 2007 c 21, s 34(1)(4)

s 106 rep in pt and am—(prosp) Crim Justice and Ct Services, 2000 c 43, ss 61(7), 74, 75, sch 7 pt II para 187, sch 8

am—Crim Justice, 2003 c 44, s 304, sch 32 pt 1 paras 90, 112; Crim Justice and Cts, 2015 c 2, s 15(3)

2000

c 6 s 106 *continued*

rep in pt—Crim Justice, 2003 c 44, s 332, sch 37 pt 7

appl—SI 2009/1059, art 205, sch 2 para 10

s 106A added—Crim Justice, 2003 c 44, s 304, sch 32 pt 1 paras 90, 113

    am—Armed Forces, 2006 c 52, s 378, sch 16 para 165; Legal Aid, Sentencing and Punishment of Offenders, 2012 c 10, sch 22 para 16

    mod—SI 2009/1059, art 205, sch 1

s 106B added —Offender Rehabilitation, 2014 c 11, s 6(4)

    appl (mods)—Crime (Sentences), 1997 c 43, sch 1 para 8 (as amended by Offender Rehabilitation, 2014 c 11, sch 3 para 3; ibid, sch 1 para 9 (as amended by Offender Rehabilitation, 2014 c 11, sch 3 para 5(2)(3)(5)

    mod—Armed Forces, 2006 c 52 s 213(1) (as amended by Offender Rehabilitation, 2014 c 11, sch 6 para 2)

s 107 am—Offender Management, 2007 c 21, s 34(1)(5)(6); Offender Rehabilitation, 2014 c 11, sch 3 para 12; Crim Justice and Cts, 2015 c 2, sch 9 para 12

s 108 rep (prosp)—Crim Justice and Ct Services, 2000 c 43, ss 74, 75, sch 7 pt II para 188, sch 8

    restr—(prosp) Crim Justice and Ct Services, 2000 c 43, s 61(2)

s 109 rep—Crim Justice, 2003 c 44, ss 303(3)(iv), 332, sch 37 pt 7

s 110 am—(prosp) Crim Justice and Ct Services, 2000 c 43, ss 74, 75, sch 7 pt II para 190, sch 8; Proceeds of Crime, 2002 c 29, s 456, sch 11, para 37(1)(2); Coroners and Justice, 2009 c 25, s 144, sch 17 para 10(1)(2)

    rep in pt—(prosp) Crim Justice and Ct Services, 2000 c 43, ss 74, 75, sch 7 pt II para 190, sch 8; Crim Justice, 2003 c 44, ss 304,332, sch 32 pt 1 paras 90, 114, sch 37 pt 7

    restr—Crim Justice, 2003 c 44, s 144(2)

    appl—Crim Justice, 2003 c 44, s 153(2)

s 111 am—(prosp) Crim Justice and Ct Services, 2000 c 43, s 74, sch 7 pt II para 191; Coroners and Justice, 2009 c 25, s 144, sch 17 para 10(1)(3)

    rep in pt—(prosp) Crim Justice and Ct Services, 2000 c 43, ss 74, 75, sch 7 pt II para 191, sch 8; Crim Justice, 2003 c 44, ss 304, 332, sch 32 pt 1 paras 90, 115, sch 37 pt 7;

    restr—Crim Justice, 2003 c 44, s 144(2)

    appl—Crim Justice, 2003 c 44, s 153(2)

s 112 rep in pt—Crim Justice, 2003 c 44, s 332, sch 37 pt 7

    appl (mods)—London Local Authorities, 2007 c ii, s 8(8)

s 113 rep in pt—Crim Justice, 2003 c 44, s 332, sch 37 pt 7; Coroners and Justice, 2009 c 25, s 178, sch 23 pt 5

    am—Coroners and Justice, 2009 c 25, s 144, sch 17 para 10(1)(4)

s 114 subst—Armed Forces, 2006 c 52, s 378, sch 16 para 166

    am—Serious Crime, 2007 c 27, s 60, sch 5 para 3; Coroners and Justice, 2009 c 25, s 144, sch 17 para 10(5)

    mod—SI 2009/1059, art 205, sch 1

s 115 rep in pt—Crim Justice, 2003 c 44, s 332, sch 37 pt 7

ss 116-129 rep—Crim Justice, 2003 c 44, ss 304, 332, sch 32 pt 1 paras 90, 116, sch 37 pt 7

s 130 am—Crim Justice, 2003 c 44, s 304, sch 32 pt 1 paras 90, 117; Violent Crime Reduction, 2006 c 38, s 49, sch 1 para 6; Fraud, 2006 c 35, s 14, sch 1 para 29; Crim Justice and Immigration, 2008 c 4, s 148, sch 26 paras 40, 46; Legal Aid, Sentencing and Punishment of Offenders, 2012 c 10, s 63(1); ibid, sch 19 para 5; ibid, sch 26 para 12; Crim Justice and Cts, 2015 c 2, sch 5 para 6

s 131 appl (mods)—Prevention of Social Housing Fraud, 2013 c 3, s 4(12)

    am—Crime and Cts, 2013 c 22, sch 16 para 8(2)-(5)

s 132 am—Domestic Violence, Crime and Victims, 2004 c 28, s 58(1), sch 10 para 49; SI 2004/2035, art 3, sch paras 39, 42; Constitutional Reform, 2005 c 4, s 40(4), sch 9 pt 1 para 69

    appl (mods)—Prevention of Social Housing Fraud, 2013 c 3, s 4(12); Modern Slavery, 2015 c 30, s 10(3)

s 133 am—Proceeds of Crime, 2002 c 29, s 456, sch 11, para 37(1)(3); Prevention of Social Housing Fraud, 2013 c 3, sch para 9; Modern Slavery, 2015 c 30, sch 5 para 14

    appl (mods)—Prevention of Social Housing Fraud, 2013 c 3, s 4(12); Modern Slavery, 2015 c 30, s 10(3)

s 134 am—Armed Forces, 2006 c 52, s 378, sch 16 para 167

    rep in pt—Armed Forces, 2006 c 52, s 378, sch 16 para 167

    mod—SI 2009/1059, art 205, sch 1

2000
c 6 s 134 *continued*

appl (mods)—Modern Slavery, 2015 c 30, s 10(3)

s 136 am—Crim Justice, 2003 c 44, s 304, sch 32 pt 1 paras 90, 118; Domestic Violence, Crime and Victims, 2004 c 28, s 58(1), sch 10 para 50

s 137 am—(E) SI 2001/2237, arts 2, 38; (W) SI 2002/808 (W 89), arts 2(t), 34; Domestic Violence, Crime and Victims, 2004 c 28, s 58(1), sch 10 paras 51(1)-(4), 52(1)-(3); Crim Justice and Immigration, 2008 c 4, s 6, sch 4 paras 51, 57(a)

rep in pt—(pt prosp) Crim Justice and Immigration, 2008 c 4, ss 6, 149, sch 4 paras 51, 57(b)(c), sch 28 pt 1

s 138 am—Crim Justice, 2003 c 44, s 304, sch 32 pt 1 paras 90, 119; Domestic Violence, Crime and Victims, 2004 c 28, s 58(1), sch 10 paras 51(1)-(4), 52(1)-(3)

s 139 rep in pt—(prosp) Crim Justice and Ct Services, 2000 c 43, ss 74, 75, sch 7 pt II para 193, sch 8

appl—Proceeds of Crime, 2002 c 29, ss 35(2), 36(2); Armed Forces c 52, ss 269A(2), 269B(4)

appl (mods)—Proceeds of Crime, 2002 c 29, s 35(2) (am by 2015 c 9, sch 4 para 30)

am—Constitutional Reform, 2005 c 4, s 40(4), sch 9 pt 1 para 69

s 140 rep in pt—(prosp) Crim Justice and Ct Services, 2000 c 43, ss 74, 75, sch 7 pt II para 194, sch 8; Crim Justice, 2003 c 44, ss 41, 332, sch 3 pt 2 para 74(1)(4)(a), sch 37 pt 4

appl—Proceeds of Crime, 2002 c 29, s 35(2)

am—Crim Justice, 2003 c 44, s 41, sch 3 pt 2 para 74(1)(4)(b); Constitutional Reform, 2005 c 4, s 40(4), sch 9 pt 1 para 69

s 142 am—Domestic Violence, Crime and Victims, 2004 c 28, s 58(1), sch 10 para 53; Prevention of Social Housing Fraud, 2013 c 3, sch para 10; Crim Justice and Cts, 2015 c 2, sch 12 para 10

s 143 am—Police Reform, 2002 c 30, s 56(6)

excl—Environmental Protection, 1990 c 43, s 33C; Wireless Telegraphy, 2006 c 36, s 103, sch 5 para 7(a)

s 146 rep in pt—Crime (International Co-operation), 2003 c 32, s 91, sch 5 paras 72, 73(a)(b), sch 6; Road Safety, 2006 c 49, s 10, sch 3 para 72, sch 7

am—Crime (International Co-operation), 2003 c 32, s 91(1), sch 5 paras 72, 73(a)(b); Crim Justice, 2003 c 44, s 304, sch 32 pt 1 paras 90, 120; Violent Crime Reduction, 2006 c 38, s 49, sch 1 para 6; Crim Justice and Immigration, 2008 c 4, s 148, sch 26 paras 40, 47; Legal Aid, Sentencing and Punishment of Offenders, 2012 c 10, sch 19 para 6; ibid, sch 26 para 13; Crim Justice and Cts, 2015 c 2, sch 5 para 7

s 147 rep in pt—Crime (International Co-operation), 2003 c 32, s 91, sch 5 paras 72, 74, sch 6; Road Safety, 2006 c 49, s 10, sch 3 para 73, sch 7

am—Crime (International Co-operation), 2003 c 32, s 91(1), sch 5 paras 72, 74; Road Safety, 2006 c 49, s 10, sch 3 para 73

mod—Serious Crime, 2007 c 27, s 63, sch 6 para 39

s 147A added —Coroners and Justice, 2009 c 25, s 137, sch 16 para 5(1)

rep in pt—Legal Aid, Sentencing and Punishment of Offenders, 2012 c 10, sch 10 para 10; ibid, sch 13 para 12(a); Crim Justice and Cts, 2015 c 2, s 30(2)(a)-(c)

am—Legal Aid, Sentencing and Punishment of Offenders, 2012 c 10, sch 13 para 12(b),(c); ibid, sch 14 para 3; Crim Justice and Cts, 2015 c 2, sch 1 para 13

excl—Crime (International Co-operation), 2003 c 32, s 54(3A)(c)

s 147B added —Coroners and Justice, 2009 c 25, s 137, sch 16 para 5(1)

s 148 am—Crim Justice, 2003 c 44, s 41, sch 3 pt 2 para 74(1)(5)

s 150 am—Crim Justice and Immigration, 2008 c 4, s 6, sch 4 paras 51, 58

ss 151-153 rep—Crim Justice, 2003 c 44, s 332, sch 37 pt 7

s 154 am—Crim Justice, 2003 c 44, s 304, sch 32 pt 1 paras 90, 121

s 155 am—SI 2004/2035, art 3, sch paras 39, 43; Crim Justice and Immigration, 2008 c 4, s 47, sch 8 para 28(1)(2)(a)(3); Legal Aid, Sentencing and Punishment of Offenders, 2012 c 10, sch 5 para 54

rep in pt—Crim Justice and Immigration, 2008 c 4, ss 47, 149, sch 8 para 28(1)(2)(b)(4), sch 28 pt 3

ss 156-158 rep—Crim Justice, 2003 c 44, s 332, sch 37 pt 7

s 159 am—Crim Justice, 2003 c 44, ss 278, 304, sch 23 para 2, sch 32 pt 1 paras 90, 122; (prosp) ibid, s 331, sch 36 pt 6 para 98; Crim Justice and Immigration, 2008 c 4, s 6, sch 4 paras 51, 59(a)

2000

c 6 s 159 *continued*

rep in pt—Crim Justice, 2003 c 44, s 332, sch 37 pt 7; Crim Justice and Immigration, 2008 c 4, ss 6, 149, sch 4 paras 51, 59(b)(d), sch 28 pt 1; (prosp) ibid, sch 4 paras 51, 59(c), sch 28 pt 1

s 160 am—Crim Justice and Ct Services, 2000 c 43, s 74, sch 7 pt II para 196; Offender Management, 2007 c 21, s 34(1)(7); Crim Justice and Immigration, 2008 c 4, s 6, sch 4 paras 51, 60(1)(3)(b); (prosp) Coroners and Justice, 2009 c 25, s 137, sch 16 para 5(2); ibid, s 177, sch 21 para 94; Crim Justice and Cts, 2015 c 2, s 43(4)

rep in pt—Crim Justice, 2003 c 44, s 332, sch 37 pt 7; Crim Justice and Immigration, 2008 c 4, ss 6, 149, sch 4 paras 51, 60(1)-(3)(a)(4), sch 28 pt 1

s 161 appl—Licensing, 2003 c 17, s 113, sch 4 paras 18, 19; Gambling, 2005 c 19, s 126, sch 7 pt 1 paras 8, 9

am—Sexual Offences, 2003 c 42, s 139, sch 6 para 43(1)(4)

rep in pt—Sexual Offences, 2003 c 42, s 140, sch 7; Crim Justice, 2003 c 44, s 332, sch 37 pt 7

s 162 rep—Crim Justice, 2003 c 44, s 332, sch 37 pt 7

s 163 am—Crim Justice and Ct Services, 2000 c 43, ss 43(2)(5),45(3), 70(4), 74, sch 7 pt I paras 1-3; (pt prosp) ibid, s 74, sch 7, pt II para 197; SI 2001/618, art 5(1)(5); Crim Justice, 2003 c 44, s 304, sch 32 pt 1 paras 90, 123(1)-(8); SI 2004/2035, art 3, sch paras 39, 44; SI 2005/886, art 2, sch para 80; Armed Forces, 2006 c 52, s 378, sch 16 para 168; Tribunals, Cts and Enforcement, 2007 c 15, s 62, sch 13 paras 131, 133; Crim Justice and Immigration, 2008 c 4, s 6, sch 4 paras 51, 61(c)

rep in pt—Crim Justice and Ct Services, 2000 c 43, ss, 74, 75, sch 7 pt II para 197(b), sch 8; Crim Justice, 2003 c 44, s 332, sch 37 pt 7; (pt prosp) Crim Justice and Immigration, 2008 c 4, ss 6, 149, sch 4 paras 51, 61(a)(b), sch 28 pt 1; Legal Aid, Sentencing and Punishment of Offenders, 2012 c 10, sch 9 para 1

appl—Crim Justice, 2003 c 44, ss 147(2)(a)(c), 174(6)

s 164 am—Crim Justice, 2003 c 44, s 304, sch 32 pt 1 paras 90, 124; Violent Crime Reduction, 2006 c 38, s 49, sch 1 para 8; Crim Justice and Immigration, 2008 c 4, s 148, sch 26 paras 40, 48; Legal Aid, Sentencing and Punishment of Offenders, 2012 c 10, sch 19 para 7; ibid, sch 26 para 14; Crim Justice and Cts, 2015 c 2, sch 5 para 8

rep in pt—Violent Crime Reduction, 2006 c 38, ss 49, 65, sch 1 para 8, sch 5

s 168 rep in pt—Crim Justice, 2003 c 44, s 332, sch 37 pt 7

s 246 am—Crim Justice and Cts, 2015 c 2, s 15(4)

s 250 am—Crim Justice and Cts, 2015 c 2, s 15(5)

s 260 am—Crim Justice and Cts, 2015 c 2, s 15(6)

sch 1 am—Crim Justice, 2003 c 44, s 324, sch 34 para 6; SI 2005/886, art 2, sch para 81(a), (b); Crim Justice and Immigration, 2008 c 4, ss 6, 36(1)(3), 37(1)(3), 148, sch 4 paras 106, 107, sch 26 paras 40, 49(1)(2)(3); Crim Justice and Cts, 2015 c 2, ss 43(3), 44

rep in pt—Crim Justice and Cts, 2015 c 2, s 44(2)(a)

sch 2 rep—Crim Justice, 2003 c 44, s 332, sch 37 pt 7

sch 3 rep —Crim Justice and Immigration, 2008 c 4, ss 6, 149, sch 28 pt 1

sch 4 rep—Crim Justice, 2003 c 44, s 332, sch 37 pt 7

sch 5 rep (prosp)—Crim Justice and Immigration, 2008 c 4, ss 6, 149, sch 28 pt 1

am—Crim Justice, 2003 c 44, s 304, sch 32 pt 1 paras 90, 126; Domestic Violence, Crime and Victims, 2004 c 28, s 29, sch 5 para 6(1)(3)(4); SI 2005/886, art 2, sch para 83(a)-(f)

rep in pt—Domestic Violence, Crime and Victims, 2004 c 28, s 29, sch 5 para 6(1)(2)

sch 6 rep —Crim Justice and Immigration, 2008 c 4, ss 6, 149, sch 28 pt 1

sch 7 rep —Crim Justice and Immigration, 2008 c 4, ss 6, 149, sch 28 pt 1

sch 8 am—Crim Justice and Ct Services, 2000 c 43, s 74, sch 7 pt II para 202(2); Crim Justice, 2003 c 44, s 304, sch 32 pt 1 paras 90, 129(a)(i)(ii)(iv)(b); SI 2005/886, art 2, sch para 85; Crim Justice and Immigration, 2008 c 4, s 6, sch 4 paras 51, 62(1)(4)(a)(7)(9), 106, 108(1)(3)-(6)

rep in pt—(prosp) Crim Justice and Ct Services, 2000 c 43, ss 74, 75, sch 7 pt II para 202(3), sch 8; Crim Justice, 2003 c 44, ss 304, 332, sch 32 pt 1 paras 90, 129(a)(iii), sch 37 pt 7; Crim Justice and Immigration, 2008 c 4, ss 6, 149, sch 4 paras 51, 62(1)-(3)(4)(b)-(6)(8), 106, 108(1)(2), sch 28 pt 1; Legal Aid, Sentencing and Punishment of Offenders, 2012 c 10, sch 24 paras 22, 23

2000

c 6 *continued*

sch 9 rep in pt—Crim Justice and Ct Services, 2000 c 43, ss 74,75, sch 7 pt II para 203(3), sch 8; (pt prosp) ibid, ss 74, 75, sch 7 pt II para 203(2)(5), sch 8; Football (Disorder), 2000 c 25, s 1, sch 3; (prosp) Armed Forces, 2001 c 19, s 38, sch 7 pt 2; Proceeds of Crime, 2002 c 29, s 457, sch 12; (pt prosp) Crim Justice, 2003 c 44, s 332, sch 37 pt 4; (prosp) ibid, sch 37 pt 7; ibid, s 332, sch 37 pts 2, 5, 12; Extradition, 2003 c 41, s 220, sch 4 (see SI 2003/3103, arts 2-5); Sexual Offences, 2003 c 42, ss 139, 140, sch 6 para 43(1)(5), sch 7; Domestic Violence, Crime and Victims, 2004 c 28, s 58(2), sch 11; Licensing (S), 2005 asp 16, s 149, sch 7; Inquiries, 2005 c 12, ss 44(5), 49(2), sch 3; (prosp) Police and Justice, 2006 c 48, s 52, sch 15 pt 3; Wireless Telegraphy, 2006 c 36, s 125, sch 9; Crim Justice and Immigration, 2008 c 4, s 149, sch 28 pt 1; (S) Crim Justice and Licensing (S), 2010 asp 13, s 14, sch 2 para 43; Legal Aid, Sentencing and Punishment of Offenders, 2012 c 10, sch 12 para 44; ibid, sch 24 para 20; ibid, sch 25 pt 2; Anti-social Behaviour, Crime and Policing, 2014 c 12, sch 11 para 50

sch 10 rep in pt—Crim Justice and Immigration, 2008 c 4, ss 6, 149, sch 4 paras 51, 63, sch 28 pt 1

sch 11 excl—Crim Justice and Ct Services, 2000 c 43, s 43(3)(b), 44(3)(b), 45(3)(b)

rep in pt—Crim Justice, 2003 c 44, ss 41, 322, sch 3 pt 2 para 74(1)(6), sch 37 pt 4; Crim Justice and Immigration, 2008 c 4, ss 6, 149, sch 4 paras 51, 64, sch 28 pt 1; Legal Aid, Sentencing and Punishment of Offenders, 2012 c 10, sch 25 pt 2

c 7 **Electronic Communications**

appl—Unsolicited Goods and Services, 1971 c 30, s 3(3C); (E) SI 2002/1278, reg 4(2); (S) SSI 2002/143, reg 9(10)(b); (EW) Anti-social Behaviour, 2003 c 38, s 80(7); SI 2003/1102, reg 15(8)(b); (E) SI 2003/2004, reg 5(4); SIs 2004/353, reg 15(7)(b), 1045, reg 17(8)(b), (E) 2885, reg 6(2); SSIs 2004/317, reg 25(2), 453, reg 5(2); (E) SI 2005/359, reg 7; SSIs 2005/328, reg 26(2), 329, reg 26(2)

Pt 1 (ss 1-6) rep—Electronic Communications, 2000 c 7, s 16(4)

s 7 appl—SIs 1997/1830, art 15(5); 2004/3315, art 4(2)

see—Land Registration, 2002 c 9, s 91(10)

s 8 saved —(S) Crim Justice (S), 2003 asp 7, s 82(1)

appl—(S) Crim Justice (S), 2003 asp 7, s 82(5)

mod—Social Security, 1998 c 14, s 79(6B); Social Security Admin, 1992 c 5, s 189(5B)

s 9 appl—(S) Crim Justice (S), 2003 asp 7, s 82(5)

mod—Social Security, 1998 c 14, s 79(6B); Social Security Admin, 1992 c 5, s 189(5B)

ss 11, 12 rep —Communications, 2003 c 21, s 406(7), sch 19(1); SI 2003/1900, arts 2(1), 3(1), sch 1; SI 2003/3142, art 3(2)

s 15 appl—SIs 1997/1830, art 15(5); 2002/761, reg 6(8); (E) 2002/1710, reg 61(4)(a); 2004/1604, reg 19(2); 2004/3315, art 5(3); (E) SIs 2005/659, reg 40(5)(a); (W) 2005/758 (W 63), reg 40(5)(a)

am—Communications, 2003 c 21, s 406(1), sch 17 para 158; SI 2003/1900, arts 2(1), 3(1),sch 1; SI 2003/3142, art 3(2)

c 8 **Financial Services and Markets**

see—SI 2004/2947, reg 12(1)(2)(b)

ext—Insolvency, 2000 c 39, s 15(2)

appl—Bankers' Books Evidence, 1879 c 11, s 10(c); Consumer Credit, 1974 c 39, s 146(5A)(a); Companies, 1985 c 6, sch 9 pt IV para 3; (temp) Financial Services, 1986 c 60, s 189, sch 14; Insolvency, 1986 c 45, s 124A(b)(ii); Law Reform (Misc Provns)(S), 1990 c 40, s 23; Pensions, 1995 c 26, ss 34(5)(b), 36(6)(a); Damages, 1996 c 48, s 4(3C); SIs 1969/1858, sch para 8; 1986/1032, sch 9 pt IV para 3(1)(b); 1994/1983, sch 4 para 18(1)(b); 1995/3213, arts 34(5)(b), 36(6)(a); 1996/1883, art 9(a), 2282, reg 3(2)(a)(b), 2424, reg 5(a)(b)(d)-(f); 1997/1612, sch 5A para 1(a), 1829, reg 3; 1998/504, reg 4(7), 1831, regs 3, 4, sch 1 para 4, 2888, reg 3(5), sch 1 para 4; 1999/1073, sch para 28; 2002/2706, reg 2(2)(a), 2848, art 2, sch, para 23(7)(a); Income Tax (Earnings and Pensions), 2003 c 1, s 702(1)(a)(i); Finance, 2003 c 14, s 101(4) (see SI 2003/2899, art 2); SSI 2003/231, arts 3-5, sch 2 pt 2, sch 3; SI 2005/1529, arts 16(2), 55(2), 70(2), 71(2)(a)

appl (mods)—SIs 2009/1342, art 34, sch; 2010/89, reg 13(2)

mod—Cts and Legal Services, 1990 c 41 s 107(17); SI 2000/1119, sch 3 pt I; Banking, 2009 c 1, s 249(1)

excl —Sale of Student Loans, 2008 c 10 s 8(1A); (pt prosp) Health and Social Care, 2012 c 7, s 134(5)

2000
c 8 *continued*

power to appl (temp until 15.5.2039)—(prosp) Water, 2014 c 21, s 79(4); (prosp) ibid, s
     81(10)
Pt 1 (ss 1-18) replaced (by Pt 1A (ss 1A-3S) —Financial Services, 2012 c. 21, s 6(1)
s 1A am—SI 2013/1773, sch 1 para 2
s 1B restr—SI 2013/1881, art 61(2)
     am—Pension Schemes, 2015 c 8, sch 3 para 3
s 1G am—SI 2013/655, art 3(2)
     mod—SIs 2001/544 arts 60LA(1)(3), 60S(1)(3) (added by SI 2014/366, art
          2(33)(37)); 2013/1881, art 65(3)(a)
s 1H am—SIs 2013/655, art 3(3); 2013/3115, sch 2 para 2
     rep in pt—SI 2013/1881, art 10(2)
s 1IA added (prosp)—Financial Services (Banking Reform), 2013 c 33, s 2
s 1L am—SI 2013/1773, sch 1 para 3
     mod—SI 2002/1775, reg 12(2) (am by 2013/472, sch 2 para 77(7)(a)(i))
     appl (mod)—SI 2013/1882, art 3(2)(a)(b)
s 1M am—Pension Schemes, 2015 c 8, sch 3 para 4
s 1Q am—Financial Services (Banking Reform), 2013 c 33, s 132
     mod—SI 2013/1881, art 65(3)(b)
s 1S am—Pension Schemes, 2015 c 8, sch 3 para 5
s 2B am—(prosp) Financial Services (Banking Reform), 2013 c 33, s 1(2)-(4)
s 2H subst—Financial Services (Banking Reform), 2013 c 33, s 130(1)
s 2J am—(prosp) Financial Services (Banking Reform), 2013 c 33, s 1(5)
s 3A am—Financial Services (Banking Reform), 2013 c 33, s 135(2)(b)
s 3B am—Financial Services (Banking Reform), 2013 c 33, s 130(2)
s 3I am—Financial Services (Banking Reform), 2013 c 33, sch 8 para 4; (prosp) ibid, s
     3(a)(b)
s 3M am—SIs 2013/3115, sch 2 para 3(a); 2014/3329, art 113
     rep in pt—SI 2013/3115, sch 2 para 3(b)
s 19 appl—Insolvency, 1986 c 45, s 8, sch B1, para 9(4); Data Protection, 1998 c 29, sch 7,
          para 6(3); Insolvency, 2000 c 39, sch 1; Consumer Credit, 1974 c 39, s 146(5D)
     excl (temp)—SI 2013/1773 reg 72(6B)(a) (added by SI 2014/1292, art 4(5)(b))
s 20 appl (mods)—SI 2006/2383, art 40, sch 1
     am—Financial Services, 2012 c. 21, sch 9 para 2
     mod—SIs 2013/655, art 10(3); 2015/369, art 7(3)
     excl—SI 2013/1773, regs 76(2), 78(4); ibid, reg 72(6B)(a) (added by SI 2014/1292,
          art 4(5)(b)
s 21 appl—SIs 2001/1335, arts 48, 50; 2001/3374, art 13, sch para 6; 2004/1484,
          reg 10(3)(4)
     appl (mods)—SI 2006/2383, art 40, sch 1
     excl—Enterprise and New Towns (S), 1990 c 35, s 31(2); Welsh Development Agency,
          1975 c 70, sch 1, para 21
     mod—SI 2013/1881, art 59(3)
s 22 appl—(EW) SIs 1975/1023, art 3(g); 2001/341, reg 114(6) (added by 2013/1881, sch
          para 22(b)); 2001/497, reg 113(6) (added by 2013/1881, sch para 23(b); SI
          2001/853, sch 1, para 14.1; Income Tax (Earnings and Pensions) 2003 c 1 s
          554O(6) (added by 2013/1881, sch para 9(c); SI 2004/400, reg 5(7) (added by
          2013/1881, sch para 25(b)); SI 2004/1045, reg 36(2)(a); Gambling, 2005 c 19,
          s 10(1); Income Tax, 2007 c 3 s 564B(1A) (added by 2013/1881, sch para
          12(b)); Legal Services, 2007 c 29, s 64(6)(b); SIs 2007/2157, reg 23(6) (added
          by 2013/1881, sch para 31(5)(b)); 2008/570 sch para 11(2) (subst by
          2013/1881, sch para 35); 2008/700 sch para 12(2) (subst by 2013/1881, sch
          para 36); 2008/1741, reg 112(5) (added by 2013/1881, sch para 37(b));
          Corporation Tax, 2009 c 4 s 502(1A) (added by 2013/1881, sch para 16(b));
          SSI 2011/141 sch 4 para (2) (subst by 2013/1881, sch para 43(a)); SIs
          2012/2079, reg 2(1A) (added by 2013/1881, sch para 44(a)(ii)); 2013/380 sch 6
          para 11(9) (added by 2013/1881, sch para 45(b)); SIs 2013/1046, rule 10(7)(a);
          2013/1877, reg 2(2)(a);
     see—Proceeds of Crime, 2002 c 29, s 330(12), sch 9 pt 1, para 1(3)
     am—Financial Services, 2012 c 21, s 7(1)
ss 22A, 22B added —Financial Services, 2012 c 21, s 9
s 23 am—Financial Services, 2012 c 21, sch 9 para 3
s 23A added —Financial Services, 2012 c 21, sch 9 para 4
s 24 rep in pt—SI 2015/664, sch 5 para 7

2000
c 8 *continued*

s 25 appl—SIs 2001/3374, art 13, sch para 6; 2013/1773, reg 52(2)(3)
s 26A added —Financial Services, 2012 c 21, sch 9 para 5
s 27 am—Financial Services, 2012 c 21, sch 9 para 6
s 28 am—Financial Services, 2012 c 21, sch 9 para 7
ss 28A, 28B added —Financial Services, 2012 c 21, sch 9 para 8
s 28A appl (mods)—SI 2014/208, art 2(2)
s 30 appl—SI 2013/1773, reg 52(5)
Pt 3 (ss 31-39A) am—SI 2013/504, reg 3(16)(e)
s 31 appl—(S) Sheriff Courts (S), 1907 c 51, sch 1, rules 27.5, 27.6; Building Societies,
    1986 c 53, s 101(4)(a); SIs 1987/1110, sch 1 para 9; (EW) 1975/1023, art 3(g);
    2002/376, reg 2(1)(a); 2004/1450, reg 14(2)(d)(i); SI 2005/382, reg 3(3)
    appl (mods)—SIs 2006/2383, art 40, sch 1; 2013/496, sch 1 para 4
    am—Financial Services, 2012 c. 21, s 11(1)
s 32 am—SI 2007/1973, regs 2, 3
s 33 am—Financial Services, 2012 c 21, sch 18 para 2(2)-(4)
    rep in pt—Financial Services, 2012 c 21, sch 18 para 2(5)
s 34 am—Financial Services, 2012 c 21, sch 4 para 27
s 35 am—Financial Services, 2012 c 21, sch 4 para 28
s 36 am—Financial Services, 2012 c 21, sch 18 para 3
s 38 am—Financial Services, 2012 c 21, sch 18 para 4
    mod—SIs 2013/655, art 10(5)(a); 2013/1881, art 59(2)(a); 2015/369, art 7(6)(a)
s 39 appl—Companies, 1985 c 6, s 249B(1)(d); SIs 1986/1032, art 257B(1)(d); 1997/1612,
    sch 5A, para 1(b); 2003/3075, reg 6(7); 2004/2615, art 5, sch paras 4, 7;
    2004/3351, art 5, sch paras 4, 7
    appl (mods)—SI 2015/910, art 17
    am—SI 2007/126, reg 3, sch 5; Financial Services, 2012 c 21, sch 18 para 5; ibid, s 10;
    SIs 2012/1906, art 3(2); 2013/3115, sch 2 para 4; 2015/910, sch 1 para 1(2)
    mod—SI 2013/1881, art 59(4)
s 39A added—SI 2007/126, reg 3, sch 5
    am—Financial Services, 2012 c. 21, sch 18 para 6
Pt 4 (ss 40-55) replaced (by Pt 4A (ss 55A-55Z4)) —Financial Services, 2012 c. 21, s 11(2)
Pt 4A (ss 55A-55Z4) excl—SI 1998/1870, reg 14(2)(c) (subst by SI 2013/472, sch 2 para
    22(5)(b))
    mod—SI 2013/1881, art 31(6)
s 55A excl—SI 2011/2832, art 5(3) (am by 2013/472, sch 2 para 220(a)(iii))
    mod—SIs 2013/655, art 10(5)(b); 2013/1881, art 59(2)(b); 2015/369, art 7(6)(b)
s 55B mod—SI 2013/1881, art 59(6)
s 55E mod—SIs 2013/655, art 10(5)(c); 2013/1881, art 59(2)(c); 2015/369, art 7(6)(c)
s 55F mod—SIs 2013/655, art 10(5)(d); 2013/1881, art 59(2)(c); 2015/369, art 7(6)(d)
s 55G am—SI 2013/504, reg 3(2)
s 55H am—SI 2013/1773, sch 1 para 4
s 55J mod—SIs 1995/1442, reg 49(2)) (subst by 2013/472, sch 2 para 12(c)(i)); 2013/440,
    art 8(1)
    am—SIs 2013/1773, sch 1 para 5(a)(ii)(b); 2013/3115, sch 2 para 5; 2015/910, sch 1
    paras 1(3), 2(2); 1882, reg 3(2)
s 55K mod—SI 2013/440, art 8(2)
s 55KA added—SI 2015/575, sch 1 para 3
s 55L mod—SIs 1995/1442, reg 49(2)) (subst by 2013/472, sch 2 para 12(c)(i)); 2013/655,
    art 10(4); 2015/369, art 7(4)(5)
s 55M mod—SIs 1995/1442, reg 49(2)) (subst by 2013/472, sch 2 para 12(c)(i))
s 55PA added—SI 2015/575, sch 1 para 4
s 55R am—SI 2013/3115, sch 2 para 6
s 55U excl—SI 2013/1881, arts 31(7), 33(5)
    appl (mods)—SI 2014/208, art 2(1)
    appl—SI 2014/366, art 4
s 55V mod—SI 2013/1881, arts 31(8), 32(3)(b), 33(6)
s 55V am—SIs 2013/1773, sch 1 para 6; (prosp) 2013/1797, sch 1 para 1(2)
    appl—SI 2013/1773, reg 22(4) (as subst by SI 2014/1292, art 4(3); ibid, reg 75(8)
    (added by SI 2014/1292,art 4(7)(e)); 2015/910, art 19(6)
    excl—SI 2013/1881, arts 35(2), 36(2), 37(3)(b), 38(3)(b), 39(2)(a)(i)(2)(b),
    40(2)(a)(i)(b), 41(2), 42(2); 2015/369, art 8(2)
s 55Z excl—SI 2013/1881, art 32(3)(a); 2015/369, art 5(7)
s 55Z1 appl (mods)—SI 2013/440, art 11(2)

2000
c 8 *continued*

s 55Z2 appl (mods)—SI 2013/440, art 12(2)
    am—SI 2013/3115, sch 2 para 7(b)(c); 2015/486, reg 13(2)
s 55Z2A added—SI 2013/3115, sch 2 para 8
s 55Z3 excl—SI 2013/1881, arts 34(3), 36(3), 38(4), 40(3), 42(3)
    appl—SIs 2013/1773 reg 22(4) (subst by SI 2014/1292, art 4(3)); ibid, reg 75(8)
        (added by SI 2014/1292, art 4(7)(e)); 2015/910, art 19(6)
Pt 5 (ss 56-71) mod—(EW) SI 1975/1023, art 3(g)
s 56 am—Financial Services, 2012 c. 21, s 13(2)-(8)
    rep in pt—Financial Services, 2012 c. 21, s 13(9)
s 57 am—Financial Services, 2012 c. 21, s 13(11)
s 58 am—Financial Services, 2012 c. 21, sch 5 para 2
s 59 appl—SIs 2003/1475, art 28(1); 2003/1476, arts 24(1), 26(1)
    mod—SI 2008/2546, art 15(1)
    am—Financial Services, 2012 c. 21, s 14(1); SI 2012/1906, art 3(4); (pt prosp)
        Financial Services (Banking Reform), 2013 c 33, s 18(3)(4); (prosp) ibid, sch 3
        para 1(2)(3)
    rep in pt—Financial Services, 2012 c. 21, sch 5 para 3; (pt prosp) Financial Services
        (Banking Reform), 2013 c 33, s 18(2)(5)
s 59ZA added—Financial Services (Banking Reform), 2013 c 33, s 19
ss 59A, 59B added —Financial Services, 2012 c. 21, s 14(2)
s 59A am—(pt prosp 7.3.2016) Financial Services (Banking Reform), 2013 c 33, sch 3 para
    2(2)(3)
s 60 ext—SI 2001/2511, reg 10
    am—Financial Services, 2012 c. 21, sch 5 para 4; (pt prosp 7.3.2016) Financial
        Services (Banking Reform), 2013 c 33, s 20(2)(3)
s 60A added (7.3.2016)—Financial Services (Banking Reform), 2013 c 33, s 21
s 61 excl—SIs 2003/1475, art 28(2); 2003/1476, arts 24(2), 26(2)
    am—Financial Services, 2012 c 21, sch 5 para 5; (7.3.2016) Financial Services
        (Banking Reform), 2013 c 33, ss 22(b), 23(2)-(6)
s 62 am—Financial Services, 2012 c 21, sch 5 para 6; (7.3.2016) Financial Services
    (Banking Reform), 2013 c 33, s 23(7)
s 62A added (7.3.2016)—Financial Services (Banking Reform), 2013 c 33, s 24
s 63 am—Financial Services, 2012 c 21, s 14(3); ibid, sch 5 para 7; (7.3.2016) Financial
    Services (Banking Reform), 2013 c 33, s 25; (7.3.2016) ibid, sch 3 para 3(2)(3)
ss 63ZA-63ZC added (7.3.2016)—Financial Services (Banking Reform), 2013 c 33, s 26
ss 63ZD, 63ZE added—Financial Services (Banking Reform), 2013 c 33, s 27
ss 63A-63D added—Financial Services, 2010 c 28, s 11
ss 63A-63C appl (mods)—SI 2013/441, art 2
s 63A am—Financial Services, 2012 c 21, sch 5 para 8; Financial Services (Banking
    Reform), 2013 c 33, s 28(2)(3); (7.3.2016) ibid, sch 3 para 4
s 63B am—Financial Services, 2012 c 21, sch 5 para 9
s 63C am—Financial Services, 2012 c 21, sch 5 para 10
s 63D am—Financial Services, 2012 c 21, sch 5 para 11
    excl—SIs 2013/655, art 9(2); 2015/369, art 6(2)(a)
ss 63E, 63F added (pt prosp 7.3.2016) —Financial Services (Banking Reform), 2013 c 33, s
    29
s 64 rep (pt prosp 7.3.2016)—Financial Services (Banking Reform), 2013 c 33, s 30(2)
    am—Financial Services, 2010 c 28, s 24, sch 2 para 7; Financial Services, 2012 c. 21, s
        14; ibid, sch 5 para 12
ss 64A, 64B added (pt prosp 7.3.2016)—Financial Services (Banking Reform), 2013 c 33, s
    30(3)
s 64C added (pt prosp 7.3.2016)—Financial Services (Banking Reform), 2013 c 33, s 31
s 65 rep (pt prosp 7.3.2016)—Financial Services (Banking Reform), 2013 c 33, s 30(2)
    am—Financial Services, 2012 c 21, sch 5 para 13
    excl—SI 2013/655, art 9(2)
s 66 power exercised—SIs 2001/2657, art 9; 2001/3083, art 9
    am—SI 2007/126, reg 3, sch 5; Financial Services, 2010 c 28, s 12(1)-(4); ibid, s 24,
        sch 2 para 8(2)(4); SI 2011/1613, reg 2(2); Financial Services, 2012 c. 21, sch 5
        para 14; SI 2012/1906, art 3(5); Financial Services (Banking Reform), 2013 c 33,
        s 28(5)(6); (7.3.2016) ibid, s 32(1)(a); (7.3.2016) ibid, sch 3 para 5; SI
        2013/1773, sch 1 para 8
    appl (mods)—SIs 2009/209, reg 95, sch 5 para 1; 2010/89, reg 19, sch; 2011/99, sch 3
        para 1; 2013/1882, art 3(3)

2000

c 8 s 66 *continued*

rep in pt—Financial Services, 2010 c 28, s 24, sch 2 para 8(3); (7.3.2016) Financial
Services (Banking Reform), 2013 c 33, s 32(1)(b)
ss 66A added (pt prosp)—Financial Services (Banking Reform), 2013 c 33, s 32(2)
am—SI 2015/1864, art 2(2)(3)
s 66B added (pt prosp)—Financial Services (Banking Reform), 2013 c 33, s 32(2)
s 67 appl—SIs 2009/209, reg 95, sch 5 para 1; 2010/89, reg 19, sch
appl (mods)—SIs 2011/99, sch 3 para 1; 2013/1882, art 3(3)
am—Financial Services, 2010 c 28, s 24, sch 2 para 9(1)-(7); Financial Services, 2012
c. 21, sch 5 para 15(2)(3), (4)(a); (7.3.2016) Financial Services (Banking
Reform), 2013 c 33, sch 3 para 6
rep in pt—Financial Services, 2012 c. 21, sch 5 para 15(4)(b)
s 68 appl—SIs 2009/209, reg 95, sch 5 para 1; 2010/89, reg 19, sch
appl (mods)—SIs 2011/99, sch 3 para 1; 2013/1882, art 3(3)
am—Financial Services, 2012 c 21, sch 5 para 16
s 69 appl—SIs 2009/209, reg 95, sch 5 para 1; 2013/1635, reg 29(1); 2014/3085, reg 28(1)
am—Financial Services, 2010 c 28, s 24, sch 2 para 10(1)-(3); Financial Services,
2012 c 21, sch 5 para 17; Financial Services (Banking Reform), 2013 c 33, sch 3
para 7
appl (mods)—SIs 2010/89, reg 19, sch; 2010/906, reg 22; 2011/99, sch 3 para 1
s 70 appl—SIs 2009/209, reg 95, sch 5 para 1; 2010/89, reg 19, sch; 2013/1635, reg 29(1);
2014/3085, reg 28(1)
appl (mods)—SI 2010/906, reg 22; 2011/99, sch 3 para 1
am—Financial Services, 2012 c. 21, sch 5 para 18
s 71A added—Financial Services (Banking Reform), 2013 c 33, s 33
Pt 6 (ss 72-103) appl (mods)—SI 1995/1537, sch 4 paras 3, 4
appl—Companies, 1985 c 6, s 262(1)
am —Financial Services, 2012 c. 21, s 16(2)(3)
ss 72, 73 rep —Financial Services, 2012 c. 21, s 16(14)
s 73A added—SI 2005/381, reg 4, sch 1 para 2
am—SI 2005/1433, reg 2(1), sch 1 para 1; Companies, 2006 c 46, s 1272, sch 15
paras 1, 3; Financial Services, 2012 c. 21, s 16(4)
s 74 appl—SI 2001/1335, art 71(2)
rep in pt—SIs 2005/381, reg 4, sch 1 para 3; 2005/1433, reg 2(1), sch 1 para 2
s 77 am—SI 2007/1973, regs 2, 5; Financial Services, 2012 c. 21, s 16(5); SI 2014/3329,
art 114
s 78 am—SIs 2007/1973, regs 2, 6; 2014/3329, art 115(2)(3)
s 78A added—SI 2007/1973, regs 2, 7
am—Financial Services, 2012 c. 21, s 17(2)
s 79 appl—SI 2001/1335, art 71(2)
rep in pt—SI 2005/1433, reg 2(1), sch 1 para 3(1)(2)
am—SI 2005/1433, reg 2(1), sch 1 para 3(1)(3)
s 83 rep—SI 2005/1433, reg 2(1), sch 1 para 4
ss 84-87 replaced (by ss 84-87, 87A-87R—SI 2005/1433, reg 2(1), sch 1 para 5
s 84 rep in pt—SI 2012/1538, reg 3(1)
s 86 am—SIs 2011/1668, reg 1(2); 2012/1538, regs 2(1), (2), 3; 2013/1125, reg 2;
2013/3115, sch 2 para 9; 2014/3293, reg 2(1)
s 87A am—SI 2012/1538, regs 2(3), 4; Financial Services, 2012 c. 21, s 16(6)
rep in pt—SI 2014/3293, reg 2(2)
s 87E am—Financial Services, 2012 c. 21, s 16(7); SI 2012/916, reg 2(3)
s 87F am—Financial Services, 2012 c. 21, s 16(8)
s 87FA added—SI 2014/3293, reg 3(1)
s 87FB added—SI 2014/3293, reg 3(2)
s 87G am—SI 2012/1538, reg 5(1)
s 87H am—Financial Services, 2012 c. 21, s 16(9); SI 2012/916, reg 2(4)
s 87I am—Financial Services, 2012 c. 21, s 16(10); SIs 2012/916, reg 2(5); 2012/1538, reg
6
rep in pt—Financial Services, 2012 c. 21, s 16(10)(a)(iii)
s 87K rep in pt—SI 2014/3293, reg 2(3)
s 87L rep in pt—SI 2014/3293, reg 2(4)
s 87P am—Financial Services, 2012 c. 21, s 16(11)
s 87Q am—SI 2012/1538, reg 5(2)
s 87R rep—SI 2012/1538, reg 3(3)
s 88 appl—(EW) SI 1975/1023, art 3(g)

2000
c 8 s 88 *continued*

    am—SI 2007/1973, regs 2, 9; Financial Services, 2012 c. 21, s 18(2)(3)
  s 89 replaced (by 88A-88F)—Financial Services, 2012 c. 21, s 18(4)
  s 88A restr—SI 2013/441, art 4
  s 89A added—Companies, 2006 c 46, s 1266(1)(2)
    rep in pt—SI 2015/1755, reg 2(1)
  s 89B added—Companies, 2006 c 46, s 1266(1)(2)
  s 89C added—Companies, 2006 c 46, s 1266(1)(2)
    am—SIs 2014/3293, reg 4(a); 2015/1755, reg 2(2)(a)(b)
    rep in pt—SIs 2014/3293, reg 4(b); 2015/1755, reg 2(2)(c)
  s 89E added—Companies, 2006 c 46, s 1266(1)(2)
    rep—SI 2015/1755, reg 2(3)
  s 89F added—Companies, 2006 c 46, s 1266(1)(2)
    am—SIs 2008/3053, art 2; 2015/1755, reg 2(4)(a)(i)-(iii)
    rep in pt—SI 2015/1755, reg 2(4)(a)(iv),(b)
  ss 89G, 89H added—Companies, 2006 c 46, s 1266(1)(2)
  s 89J added—Companies, 2006 c 46, s 1267
    rep in pt—SI 2015/1755, reg 2(5)
  ss 89K-89N added—Companies, 2006 c 46, s 1268
  s 89NA added—SI 2015/1755, reg 4(1)
  s 89O added—Companies, 2006 c 46, s 1269
  ss 89P-89V added —Financial Services, 2012 c. 21, s 19(1)
  s 89W added—SI 2015/1755, reg 3
  s 90 am—SI 2005/1433, reg 2(1), sch 1 para 6(1)(2)(3); Companies, 2006 c 46, s 1272, sch
    15 paras 1, 4, 5; SI 2012/1538, reg 7
  s 90ZA added—SI 2011/1613, reg 2(3)
    am—SI 2013/1388, reg 3(2)
  ss 90A, 90B added—Companies, 2006 c 46, s 1270
  s 90A subst—SI 2010/1192, regs 2, 3
  s 91 am—SIs 2005/381, reg 4, sch 1 para 4; 2005/1433, reg 2(1), sch 1 para 7(1)-(4);
    Companies, 2006 c 46, s 1272, sch 15 paras 1, 6; Financial Services, 2012 c. 21, s
    20; SI 2015/1755, reg 4(2)
  s 95 rep —Financial Services, 2012 c. 21, s 21
  s 96 appl—Banking, 2009 c 1, ss 39B(2) 48L(6A)
  s 96A added—SI 2005/381, reg 4, sch 1 para 6
    mod—SIs 2008/432, art 17, sch; 2008/2546, art 13, sch 1; 2009/814, art 7, sch
    am—SI 2012/1538, reg 8
  s 96B added—SI 2005/381, reg 4, sch 1 para 6
    am—Companies, 2006 c 46, s 1272, sch 15 paras 1, 7; SIs 2009/1941, art 2, sch 1
    para 181; 2009/2461, reg 2
    mod—SIs 2008/432, art 17, sch; 2009/814, art 7, sch
  s 96C added—SI 2005/381, reg 4, sch 1 para 6
  s 97 am—SIs 2005/381, reg 4, sch 1 para 7(a)(b); 2005/1433, reg 2(1), sch 1 para 8;
    Companies, 2006 c 46, s 1272, sch 15 paras 1, 8; Financial Services, 2012 c. 21,
    sch 18 para 7; SI 2015/1755, reg 4(3)
    rep in pt—SI 2005/381, reg 4, sch 1 para 7(c)
  s 98 rep—SI 2005/1433, reg 2(1), sch 1 para 9
  ss 99, 100 rep —Financial Services, 2012 c. 21, s 16(14)(c)(d)
  s 100A added—Companies, 2006 c 46, s 1271
    am—Financial Services, 2012 c. 21, s 16(12); SI 2012/916, reg 2(6)
  s 101 am—SI 2005/381, reg 4, sch 1 paras 9, 10
    rep in pt—Financial Services, 2012 c. 21, s 16(14)(e)
  s 102 rep —Financial Services, 2012 c. 21, s 16(14)(f)
  s 102A added —SI 2005/1433, reg 2(1), sch 1 para 11
    am—Companies, 2006 c 46, s 1272, sch 15 paras 1, 10; SIs 2008/3053, art 3;
    2015/1755, reg 5(1)
  s 102B added —SI 2005/1433, reg 2(1), sch 1 para 11
    am—SI 2007/126, reg 3, sch 5
  s 102C added —SI 2005/1433, reg 2(1), sch 1 para 11
    subst—SI 2015/1755, reg 5(2)
  s 103 subst —SI 2005/1433, reg 2(1), sch 1 para 11
  s 103 am—Companies, 2006 c 46, ss 1265, 1272, sch 15 paras 1, 11; SIs 2012/1538, reg 9;
    2014/3293, reg 5(2)(3)
    rep in pt— Financial Services, 2012 c. 21, s 16(14)(g); SI 2015/1755, reg 5(3)(b)

2000

c 8 s 103 *continued*

mod—SI 2014/1261, reg 2

s 103A added —Financial Services, 2012 c. 21, sch 6 para 2

    am—Financial Services (Banking Reform), 2013 c 33, sch 1 para 3

Pt 7 (ss 104-117) appl—Finance, 2003 c 14, s 63(7) (see SI 2003/2899, art 2)

    am—Financial Services (Banking Reform), 2013 c 33, sch 1 para 2

s 104 appl (mods)—(conditionally) SI 2001/3626, arts 3, 4, 5(1)

    rep in pt—Financial Services, 2012 c. 21, s 22(1)

s 105 appl—Finance, 2002 c 23, s 83, sch 26 pt 6, para 28(5)

    excl—Finance, 1989 c 26, s 82C(9)

    am—SIs 2007/3253, reg 2, sch 1; 2008/948, art 3, sch 1

    rep in pt—SI 2015/575, sch 1 para 5

s 106 am—SI 2008/948, art 3, sch 1; Financial Services (Banking Reform), 2013 c 33, sch
    1 para 4

s 106A added—Dormant Bank and Building Society Accounts, 2008 c 31, s 15, sch 2 para
    2

s 106B added—Financial Services (Banking Reform), 2013 c 33, sch 1 para 5

s 107 appl (mods)—(conditionally) SI 2001/3626, arts 3, 4, 5(1)

    am—Dormant Bank and Building Society Accounts, 2008 c 31, s 15, sch 2 para 3;
    Financial Services (Banking Reform), 2013 c 33, sch 1 para 6

s 108-110 appl (mods)—(conditionally) SI 2001/3626, arts 3, 4, 5(1)

s 109 am—Financial Services, 2012 c. 21, sch 6 para 3; Financial Services (Banking
    Reform), 2013 c 33, sch 1 para 7

s 109A added—Financial Services (Banking Reform), 2013 c 33, sch 1 para 8

s 110 am—Financial Services, 2012 c. 21, sch 6 para 4; Financial Services (Banking
    Reform), 2013 c 33, sch 1 para 9

s 111 appl (mods)—(conditionally) SI 2001/3626, arts 3, 4, 5(1)

    am—Dormant Bank and Building Society Accounts, 2008 c 31, s 15, sch 2 para 4;
    Financial Services (Banking Reform), 2013 c 33, sch 1 para 10

s 112 appl (mods)—(conditionally) SI 2001/3626, arts 3, 4, 5(1)

    am—SIs 2006/745, art 17; 2008/948, art 3, sch 1; 2008/1468, reg 2; Financial
    Services, 2012 c 21, sch 6 para 5; Financial Services (Banking Reform), 2013 c
    33, sch 1 para 11

    rep in pt—SI 2008/948, art 3, schs 1, 2

s 112ZA added —Financial Services, 2012 c. 21, sch 6 para 6

s 112A added—SI 2008/1468, reg 2

    am—Financial Services (Banking Reform), 2013 c 33, sch 1 para 12

s 113 appl (mods)—(conditionally) SI 2001/3626, arts 3, 4, 5(1)

    am—Financial Services, 2012 c. 21, sch 6 para 7

s 114 appl (mods)—(conditionally) SI 2001/3626, arts 3, 4, 5(1)

    am—SI 2007/3253, reg 2, sch 1

s 114A added—SI 2007/3253, reg 2, sch 1

s 115 am—Financial Services, 2012 c. 21, sch 6 para 8

s 116 am—SIs 2004/3379, reg 6(1)(2); 2015/575, sch 1 para 6(2)(a),(3)(4)

    rep in pt—SI 2015/575, sch 1 para 6(2)(b)

Pt 8 (ss 118-131A) appl (mods)—SI 2011/2699, reg 6, sch 1

    am (spec ss am)—Financial Services, 2012 c. 21, sch 9 para 9(1)(2)

s 118 subst—SI 2005/381, reg 5, sch 2 para 1

    am—SIs 2008/1439, reg 3; 2009/3128, reg 2; 2011/2928, reg 2(2); 2014/3081, reg
    2(2)(3)

s 118A subst—SI 2005/381, reg 5, sch 2 para 1

    am—SIs 2008/1439, reg 3; 2009/3128, reg 2; 2011/2928, reg 2(3); 2014/3081, reg
    2(4)

ss 118B, 118C added—SI 2005/381, reg 5, sch 2 para 1

s 119 am—SI 2005/381, reg 5, sch 2 para 2

s 121 am—Financial Services, 2012 c. 21, sch 9 para 9(3)

s 130 am—Financial Services, 2012 c. 21, sch 9 para 9(4)

s 130A added—SI 2005/381, reg 5, sch 2 para 3

s 131A added—SI 2005/381, reg 5, sch 2 para 4

    am—Financial Services, 2012 c. 21, sch 9 para 9(1)(2)

Pt 8A (ss 131B-131K) added—Financial Services, 2010 c 28, s 8

    am—Financial Services, 2012 c. 21, s 25

ss 131B-131D rep —SI 2012/2554, reg 2(2)

s 131E am—SI 2012/2554, reg 2(3)(a)-(c)

2000
c 8 s 131E *continued*

     rep in pt—SI 2012/2554, reg 2(3)(d)
  s 131F am—SI 2012/2554, reg 2(4)(b)
     rep in pt—SI 2012/2554, reg 2(4)(a)
  ss 131FA-131FC added—SI 2012/2554, reg 2(5)
  s 131G am—SI 2012/2554, reg 2(6), (7)
  s 131L added—SI 2012/2554, reg 2(8)
  Pt 9 (ss 132-137) appl (mods)—SIs 2007/2157, reg 44, sch 5; 2008/3249, art 2, sch;
     Banking, 2009 c 1, s 202(3); SIs 2009/209, reg 95, sch 5 para 2; 2009/1810,
     arts 13-18; 2010/89, reg 19, sch paras 7, 8; 2011/99, sch 3 para 2; 2012/3122,
     sch para 7; 2013/1635, reg 31(1); 2013/1882, art 3(4); 2014/3085, reg 30;
     2015/1945, reg 46; 1946, reg 43
    appl—SIs 2008/346, reg 40; 2013/504, reg 58; 2013/1773, reg 70(1); 2013/3115, reg
     42; 2014/894, reg 4; 2879, reg 5(12); 2015/575, s 56(2); 910, art 24(1)
    mod—SI 2014/3348, art 67(2)
  s 132 rep—SI 2010/22, art 5, sch 2
  s 133 subst—SI 2010/22, art 5, sch 2
    am—Financial Services, 2012 c. 21, s 23(2); (prosp) Financial Services (Banking
     Reform), 2013 c 33, s 4(2); SI 2013/1388, reg 3(3); Crime and Cts, 2013 c 22,
     sch 9 para 83; SI 2014/3329, art 116
    appl (mods)—SIs 2013/442, arts 12(2), 13(2); 2015/2038, sch 7 para 1
    appl—SI 2013/1881, art 55(3)
  s 133A added—SI 2010/22, art 5, sch 2
    am—Financial Services, 2012 c. 21, s 23(3)(a)(c)(d)
    rep in pt—Financial Services, 2012 c. 21, s 23(3)(b)
    mod—SI 2002/1775, reg 12(4) (am by 2013/472, sch 2 para 77(7)(b))
    appl (mods)—SIs 2013/442, arts 12(3), 13(3); 2015/2038, sch 7 para 1
  s 133B added—SI 2010/22, art 5, sch 2
    am—Financial Services, 2012 c. 21, s 23(4)
    appl (mods)—SI 2015/2038, sch 7 para 1
  ss 134-136 appl—SI 2007/3298, reg 13
  s 136 am—Financial Services, 2012 c. 21, s 23(5)
  s 137 rep—SI 2010/22, art 5, sch 2
  Pt 10 (ss 138-164) replaced (by Pt 9A, ss 137A-141A) —Financial Services, 2012 c. 21, s
    24(1)
  Pt 9A (ss 137A-141A) appl —Financial Services (Banking Reform), 2013 c 33, s 107(1)
  s 137A power to make rules mod—SI 2002/1775, reg 3(1)(4) (am by 2013/472, sch 2 para
    77(4)(a))
    mod—SIs 2002/1775, reg 3(2)(a) (subst by SI 2013/472, sch 2 para 77(4)(b));
     2008/432, art 15(1) (subst by SI 2013/472, sch 2 para 136(d)(i)); 2008/2546,
     art 37(1) (subst by 2013/472, sch 2 para 146(c)(i)); 2008/2644, art 27(1)
     (subst by 2013/472, sch 2 para 147(b)(i)); 2008/2666, art 18(1) (subst by
     2013/472, sch 2 para 148(b)(i)); 2008/2674, art 29(1) (subst by 2013/472, sch
     2 para 149(b)(i)); 2009/814, art 9(1) (subst by 2013/472, sch 2 para 167(b)(i));
     2009/3226, art 20(1) (subst by 2013/472, sch 2 para 182(a)(i))
    am—Financial Services (Banking Reform), 2013 c 33, s 131(1)
  s 137FA added—(prosp) Pensions, 2014 c 19, s 44(2)
    am—(prosp) Pension Schemes, 2015 c 8, sch 2 para 21(a)(c)
    rep in pt—(prosp) Pension Schemes, 2015 c 8, sch 2 para 21(b)
  s 137FB added—Pension Schemes, 2015 c 8, sch 3 para 6
  s 137G mod—SIs 2008/432, art 15(1A) (subst by 2013/472, sch 2 para 136(d)(i));
    2008/2546, art 37(1A) (subst by 2013/472, sch 2 para 146(c)(i)); 2008/2644,
    art 27(1A) (subst by 2013/472, sch 2 para 147(b)(i)); 2008/2666, art 18(1A)
    (subst by 2013/472, sch 2 para 148(b)(i)); 2008/2674, art 29(1A) (subst by
    2013/472, sch 2 para 149(b)(i)); 2009/814, art 9(1A) (subst by 2013/472, sch
    2 para 167(b)(i)); 2009/3226, art 20(1A) (subst by 2013/472, sch 2 para
    182(a)(i))
  s 137J am—SI 2014/3348, sch 3 para 2
  s 137K am—SI 2014/3348, sch 3 para 3
  s 137M rep—SI 2014/3348, sch 3 para 4
  s 137N am—SI 2014/3348, sch 3 para 5
  s 137R am—SI 2015/910, sch 1 para 1(4)
  s 137T mod—SI 2002/1775, reg 3(2)(a) (am by 2013/472, sch 2 para 77(4)(b))

2000
c 8 *continued*

s 138A mod—SIs 2001/1228, reg 7(3)(4) (am by 2013/472, sch 2 para 41(4)); 2002/1775, reg 3(2)(a) (am by 2013/472, sch 2 para 77(4)(b)); 2009/814, art 9 (am by 2013/472, sch 2 para 167(b))
appl (mods)—SI 2008/432, art 15(2) (am by 2013/472, sch 2 para 136(d)(ii)(aa))
appl—SIs 2008/2546, art 37(2) (am by 2013/472, sch 2 para 146(c)(ii)(aa)); 2008/2644, art 27(2) (subst by 2013/472, sch 2 para 147(b)(ii)(aa)); 2008/2666, art 18(2) (am by 2013/472, sch 2 para 148(b)(ii)(aa)); 2008/2674, art 29(2) (am by 2013/472, sch 2 para 149(b)(ii)(aa)); 2009/3226, art 20(2) (am by 2013/472, sch 2 para 182(a)(ii)(aa))
excl—SI 2006/3221, reg 8(2) (am by 2013/472, sch 2 para 118(h)(iii));
am—SI 2013/1388, reg 3(4); Financial Services (Banking Reform), 2013 c 33, sch 3 para 8
restr—SIs 2008/432, art 15(3) (am by 2013/472, sch 2 para 136(d)(iii)(aa)); 2008/2546, art 37(3) (am by 2013/472, sch 2 para 146(c)(iii)(aa)); 2008/2644, art 27(3) (am by 2013/472, sch 2 para 147(b)(ii)(aa)); 2008/2666, art 18(3) (am by 2013/472, sch 2 para 148(b)(iii)(aa)); 2008/2674, art 29(3) (am by 2013/472, sch 2 para 149(b)(iii)(aa)); 2009/3226, art 20(3) (am by 2013/472, sch 2 para 182(a)(iii)(aa))
s 138B mod—SI 2013/161, art 9(3)(4)
s 138D mod—SI 2002/1775, reg 3(2)(a) (am by 2013/472, sch 2 para 77(4)(b))
am—Financial Services (Banking Reform), 2013 c 33, sch 3 para 9
s 138F am—Pension Schemes, 2015 c 8, sch 3 para 7
s 138H mod—SI 2013/161, art 3(6); SI 2013/1881, art 64(4)
excl—SI 2002/1501, art 12(1) (am by 2013/472, sch 2 para 76(c)(i))
s 138I excl—SIs 2004/454, art 12(1) (am by 2013/472, sch 2 para 89(b)); 2006/3259, reg 4 (am by 2013/472, sch 2 para 120(b)(ii)); 2013/161, art 8(2); 2013/655, art 9(2); 015/369, art 6(2)(b); 909, art 4(2)(a)
appl (mods)—SIs 2013/1797, reg 6(3)-(7); 2013/1881, art 61(5)
appl —SI 2008/346, reg 42(4)(4A) (subst by 2013/472, sch 2 para 134(d))
excl—SIs 2013/1881, art 61(3); 2013/496, sch 1 para 6(2)(3)(a)
am—Pension Schemes, 2015 c 8, sch 3 para 8
s 138J appl (mods)—SIs 2013/1797, reg 6(3)-(7); 2013/1881, art 62(4)(5)
excl—SIs 2013/644, art 3(2); 2013/1881, art 62(2); 2015/905, art 5(2)(a); 909, art 4(2)(a)(b)
restr—SI 2013/442, art 70(3)
s 138K appl (mods)—SI 2013/1797, reg 6(3)-(7)
excl—SIs 2013/161, art 8(2); 2015/909, art 4(2)(a)(b)
am—Co-operative and Community Benefit Societies, 2014 c 14, sch 4 para 69
s 138L appl (mods)—SI 2013/1797, reg 6(3)-(7)
mod—SIs 2008/432, art 16(1) (am by 2013/472, sch 2 para 136(e)(i)(aa)); 2008/2546, art 38(1) (am by 2013/472, sch 2 para 146(d)(i)); 2008/2644, art 28(1) (am by 2013/472, sch 2 para 147(c)(i)); 2008/2666, art 19(1) (am by 2013/472, sch 2 para 148(c)(i)); 2008/2674, art 30(1) (am by 2013/472, sch 2 para 149(c)(i)); 2009/814, art 10(1) (am by 2013/472, sch 2 para 167(c)(i)); 2009/3226, art 21(1) (am by 2013/472, sch 2 para 182(b)(i))
s 139A mod—SIs 2008/432, art 16(2) (am by 2013/472, sch 2 para 136(e)(ii)(aa)); 2008/2546, art 38(2) (am by 2013/472, sch 2 para 146(d)(ii)); 2008/2644, art 28(2) (am by 2013/472, sch 2 para 147(c)(ii)(aa); 2008/2666, art 19(2) (am by 2013/472, sch 2 para 148(c)(ii)(aa)); 2008/2674, art 30(2) (am by 2013/472, sch 2 para 149(c)(ii)(aa); 2009/814, art 10(2) (am by 2013/472, sch 2 para 167(c)(ii); SI 2009/3226, art 21(2) (am by 2013/472, sch 2 para 182(b)(ii))
appl—SI 2013/496, sch 1 para 8
excl—SIs 2004/454, art 12(1) (am by 2013/472, sch 2 para 89(b)); 2006/3259, reg 4 (am by 2013/472, sch 2 para 120(b)(ii)); 2013/655, art 9(2); 2015/369, art 6(2)(c); 909, art 4(2)(a)
am—Pension Schemes, 2015 c 8, sch 3 para 9
s 139B appl—SI 2013/496, sch 1 para 8
s 140A rep in pt—(7.3.2016) Financial Services (Banking Reform), 2013 c 33, sch 3 para 10; 2014/892, sch 1 para 121(2)(i)(3)
am—SI 2014/892, sch 1 para 121(2)(ii); Pension Schemes, 2015 c 8, sch 3 para 10
s 140B am—SI 2014/892, sch 1 para 122(1)(3)
rep in pt—SI 2014/892, sch 1 para 122(2)
s 140C am—SI 2014/892, sch 1 para 123

2000

c 8 *continued*

s 140D am—SI 2014/892, sch 1 para 124

s 140E subst—SI 2014/892, sch 1 para 125

s 140F am—SI 2014/892, sch 1 para 126

s 140H am—SI 2014/892, sch 1 para 127

Pt 9B (ss 142A-142Z1) added (pt prosp)—Financial Services (Banking Reform), 2013 c 33, s 4(1)

 power to appl (mods) conferred—(prosp) Financial Services (Banking Reform), 2013 c 33, s 7(2)(b)

s 142X am—(prosp) Pension Schemes, 2015 c 8, sch 2 para 22

Pt 11 (ss 165-177) appl (mods)—SIs 2009/209, reg 95, sch 5 para 3; 2010/89, reg 19, sch para 2; 2011/99, sch 3 para 3; 2012/3122, sch para 2; 2013/1635, reg 13; 2013/1882, art 3(5); 2014/892, sch 1 para 127; 2015//910, art 23(2); 1945, reg 26; 1946, reg 23; 2038, sch 7 para 2

s 165 appl—SIs 2001/544, art 9G; 2013/1773, reg 71(1)(a)

 mod—SIs 2008/346, reg 46, sch; 2013/1881, art 50(1)

 appl (mods)—SIs 2009/209, reg 95, sch 5; 2013/1881, art 12(9); 2013/3115, reg 14

 am—Financial Services, 2010 c 28, s 24, sch 2 para 15; Financial Services, 2012 c. 21, sch 12 para 1; SI 2015/575, sch 1 para 7

 rep in pt—SI 2013/1773, sch 1 para 9

ss 165A-165C added—Financial Services, 2010 c 28, s 18(2)

s 165A am—Financial Services, 2012 c. 21, sch 12 para 2

s 165B am—Financial Services, 2012 c. 21, sch 12 para 3

s 165C am—Financial Services, 2012 c. 21, sch 12 para 4

s 166 subst —Financial Services, 2012 c. 21, sch 12 para 5

s 166 appl (mods)—SIs 2002/1775, reg 12(3); 2001/544, art 9G; 2013/3115, reg 14

 mod—SI 2008/346, reg 46, sch

 appl—SI 2013/1773, reg 71(1)(b)

s 166A added —Financial Services, 2012 c. 21, sch 12 para 6

 appl (mods)—SI 2008/346 sch para 4A (added by 2013/472, sch 2 para 134(g)(ii))

s 167 appl (mods)—SIs 2002/1775, reg 12(3); 2013/1881, art 12(9); 2013/3115, reg 14

 appl—SI 2013/1773, reg 71(1)(c)

 am—SI 2007/126, reg 3, sch 5; Financial Services, 2012 c. 21, sch 12 para 7; SI 2015/575, sch 1 para 8

s 168 appl (mods)—SIs 2002/1775, reg 12(3)(5); 2001/544, art 9G; 2013/1881, art 50(2); 2013/442, art 19(10)

 mod—SI 2015/910, art 23(3)

 am—SI 2007/126, reg 3, sch 5; Counter-Terrorism, 2008 c 28, s 62, sch 7 para 33(3); Financial Services, 2010 c 28, s 24, sch 2 para 16(1)-(3); SIs 2012/1906, art 3(7); 2012/2554, reg 2(11); Financial Services, 2012 c. 21, sch 12 para 8; SIs 2013/1773, sch 1 para 10; Pension Schemes, 2015 c 8, sch 3 para 11

 rep in pt—Financial Services, 2012 c. 21, sch 12 para 8(2)(a), (4)(f)

 appl—SI 2013/1773, regs 52(4), 53(3)

s 169 am—Financial Services, 2012 c. 21, sch 12 para 9

 appl—SI 2013/1773, reg 71(2)(a)

s 169A added—Financial Services, 2010 c 28, s 18(2)

 am—Financial Services, 2012 c. 21, sch 12 para 10

s 170 appl—(conditionally) SI 2001/1228, reg 30(4); SI 2013/1773, reg 71(2)(b)

 appl (mods)—SI 2013/3115, reg 14

 am—Financial Services, 2012 c. 21, sch 12 para 11

s 171 am—SI 2007/126, reg 3, sch 5

 appl—SI 2013/1773, reg 71(2)(c)

 appl (mods)—SI 2013/3115, reg 14

s 174 appl—SIs 2001/1228, reg 30(5); 2013/1773, reg 71(2)(d)

 appl (mods)—SI 2010/906, reg 16

 am—Financial Services, 2012 c. 21, sch 12 para 12

s 175 mod—SI 2001/1228, reg 30(6)

 appl—SI 2001/544, art 9G

 appl (mods)—SIs 2010/906, reg 17; 2013/3115, reg 14

 am—Financial Services, 2012 c. 21, sch 12 para 13

 appl—SI 2013/1773, reg 71(2)(e)

s 176 ext—Crim. Justice and Police, 2001 c 16, s 50, sch 1 pt 1 para 69

 appl (mods)—SIs 2001/1228, reg 30(7); 2001/544, art 9G; 2002/1775, reg 12(3); 2013/442, art 21; 2013/3115, reg 14

2000
c 8 s 176 *continued*
   appl—SIs 1995/1537, reg 23(1); 2013/1773, reg 71(1)(d)(2)(f)
   am—SI 2005/1433, reg 2(1), sch 1 para 12; Financial Services, 2010 c 28, s 24, sch 2
      para 17; Financial Services, 2012 c. 21, sch 12 para 14(2)-(5), (7)
   rep in pt—Financial Services, 2012 c. 21, sch 12 para 14(6)
s 176A added —Financial Services, 2012 c. 21, sch 12 para 15
   appl—SI 2013/1773, reg 71(2)(g)
   appl (mods)—SI 2013/3115, reg 14
s 177 am—SI 2001/1090, reg 9(1), sch 5 para 21; (prosp) (EW) Crim Justice, 2003 c 44,
      s 280(2)(3), sch 26 para 54(1)(2); Financial Services, 2012 c. 21, sch 18 para 8
   mod—SI 2001/1228, reg 30(6)
   appl—SIs 2001/544, art 9G; 2013/1773, reg 71(2)(h)
   appl (mods)—SIs 2010/906, reg 24; 2013/3115, reg 14
Pt 12 (ss 178-192) appl—SI 2001/2638, art 2(1)(b)(3)
   appl (mods)—SI 2011/99, sch 3 para 4
   am—Financial Services, 2012 c. 21, s 26(2)
   excl—SI 2013/1881, art 59(7)
s 178 subst—SI 2009/534, reg 3, sch 1
   am—Financial Services, 2012 c. 21, s 26(3)
ss 179-191 subst—SI 2009/534, regs 3, 8, sch 1
s 179 am—Financial Services, 2012 c. 21, s 26(4)
s 184 am—SIs 2011/1613, reg 2(6); 2013/3115, sch 2 para 10; 2015/1755, reg 6(1)(b)
   rep in pt—SI 2015/1755, reg 6(1)(a)
s 186 am—SI 2013/3115, sch 2 para 11
s 187 am—Financial Services, 2012 c. 21, s 26(5)
ss 187A-187C added —Financial Services, 2012 c. 21, s 26(6)
s 187A am—SI 2014/3329, art 117
s 188 am—SI 2013/3115, sch 2 para 12
s 189 am—SI 2014/3329, art 118
s 190 am—SIs 2013/3115, sch 2 para 13; 2014/3329, art 119; 2015/575, sch 1 para 9
ss 191A-191G added—SI 2009/534, regs 3, 8, sch 1
s 191A am—Financial Services, 2012 c 21, s 26(7)
s 191B am—Financial Services, 2012 c 21, s 26(8)
s 191C am—Financial Services, 2012 c 21, s 26(9)
s 191D am—Financial Services, 2012 c 21, s 26(10)
s 191E am—Financial Services, 2012 c 21, s 26(11)
s 191G am—Financial Services, 2012 c 21, s 26(12); SI 2013/3115, sch 2 para 14
s 192 am—SI 2009/534, reg 4
Pt 12A (ss 192A-192N) added —Financial Services, 2012 c. 21, s 27
s 192JA added (prosp)—Financial Services (Banking Reform), 2013 c 33, s 133(1)
s 192JB added —Financial Services (Banking Reform), 2013 c 33, s 133(1)
   am—SI 2014/3329, art 120
s 192K am—Financial Services (Banking Reform), 2013 c 33, s 133(2); SI 2014/3329, art
      121
s 192L am—SI 2014/3329, art 122
Pt 13 (ss 193-204) am—Financial Services, 2012 c 21, sch 4 para 30
   appl—SI 2013/1882, art 3(6)
s 193 am—SI 2011/1613, reg 2(7); Financial Services, 2012 c 21, sch 4 para 31; SI
      2013/1773, sch 1 para 11
s 194 am—Enterprise, 2002 c 40, s 278(1), sch 25, para 40(1)(6); Consumer Credit, 2006 c
      14, s 33(7); Financial Services, 2010 c 28, s 3(5)(a)(b); Financial Services, 2012
      c. 21, sch 4 para 32; SIs 2013/1773, sch 1 para 12; 2015/575, sch 1 para 10;
      2015/1882, reg 3(3)
   rep in pt—SI 2013/1881, art 10(3)
s 194A added—SI 2007/126, reg 3, sch 1
   am—Financial Services, 2012 c. 21, sch 4 para 33; SI 2012/916, reg 2(7)(a),(b)
   mod—SI 2001/3084, art 2(8)(a)
s 194B added (prosp)—SI 2013/3115, sch 2 para 15
s 194C added—SI 2015/910, sch 1 para 1(5)
s 195 rep in pt—SI 2005/1433, reg 2(1), sch 1 para 13; Financial Services, 2012 c 21, s
      16(14)(h); ibid, sch 4 para 34(5)(b)
   am—SI 2007/2194, art 10, sch 4; Financial Services, 2012 c 21, sch 4 para 34(2)-(4),
      (5)(a),(6)
s 195A added—SI /126, reg 3, sch 1

2000

c 8 s 195A *continued*

       subst—SI 2011/1613, reg 2(8)

       am—SI 2012/916, reg 2(8); Financial Services, 2012 c 21, sch 4 para 35; SIs
          2013/1773, sch 1 para 13; (prosp) 2013/1797, sch 1 para 1(3)

       mod—SI 2001/3084, art 2(8)(b) (subst by 2013/472, sch 2 para 58(b))

s 195B added—SI 2015/910, sch 1 para 1(6)

s 196 subst —Financial Services, 2012 c 21, sch 4 para 36

s 197 am—Financial Services, 2012 c. 21, sch 4 para 37

s 198 am—SIs 2004/3379, reg 6(1)(3); 2007/3253, reg 2, sch 1; Financial Services, 2012 c
       21, sch 4 para 38; SI 2015/575, sch 1 para 11

s 199 am—SIs 2007/126, reg 3, sch 1; 2007/3253, reg 2, sch 1; 2011/1613, reg 2(9)(a)-(d);
       Financial Services, 2012 c 21, sch 4 para 39; SI 2012/916, reg 2(9)(a),(b),(c); SI
       2013/1773, sch 1 para 14

       rep in pt—SI 2012/2015, reg 3

       excl—SI 2001/3084, art 2(8)(b) (subst by 2013/472, sch 2 para 58(b))

s 199A added—SI 2011/1613, reg 2(10)

       am—Financial Services, 2012 c. 21, sch 4 para 40

s 200 am—Financial Services, 2012 c. 21, sch 4 para 41

       appl (mods)—SI 2013/440, art 7(2A) (added by 2013/1765, art 11(3)(b))

s 201 subst —Financial Services, 2012 c. 21, sch 4 para 42

s 202 am—Financial Services, 2012 c. 21, sch 4 para 43

ss 203, 204 rep —SI 2013/1881, art 10(4)

Pt 14 (ss 204A-211) appl (mods)—SIs 2013/1881, art 12(10); 1882, art 3(7)

s 204A added —Financial Services, 2012 c. 21, sch 9 para 8

       mod—SIs 2013/441, art 11(5); 2015/910, art 23(1)(a)

       am—SIs 2013/1773, sch 1 para 15; 2015/1864, art 3(3)(4)

       rep in pt—SI 2015/1864, art 3(2)

s 205 mod—SI 2002/1775, reg 12(1)(1A)

       am—SIs 2007/126, reg 3, sch 5; 2011/1613, reg 2(11); Financial Services, 2012 c 21,
        sch 9 para 11; SI 2012/1906, art 3(8)

       appl—SIs 2013/1773, reg 71(1)(e); 2015/910, art 23(2)(n)

s 206 mod—SI 2002/1775, reg 12(1)(1A)

       am—SIs 2007/126, reg 3, sch 5; 2011/1613, reg 2(11); 2012/1906, art 3(9);
       Financial Services, 2012 c 21, sch 9 para 12

       rep in pt—Financial Services, 2010 c 28, s 10

       appl—SIs 2013/1773, reg 71(1)(f); 2015/910, art 23(2)(p)

s 206A added—Financial Services, 2010 c 28, s 9

       am—SIs 2011/99, sch 4 para 2(2); 2011/1613, reg 2(12); Financial Services, 2012
       c. 21, sch 9 para 13; SI 2012/1906, art 3(10)

       rep in pt—Financial Services, 2012 c 21, sch 9 para 13(4)(b)

s 207 mod—SI 2002/1775, reg 12(1)(1A)

       rep in pt—Financial Services, 2010 c 28, s 24, sch 2 para 18(2)

       am—Financial Services, 2010 c 28, s 24, sch 2 para 18(3); Financial Services, 2012 c.
       21, sch 9 para 14

       appl—SIs 2013/1773, reg 71(3); 2015/910, art 23(4)

s 208 mod—SI 2002/1775, reg 12(1)(1A)

       rep in pt—Financial Services, 2010 c 28, s 24, sch 2 para 19(2)(4)

       am—Financial Services, 2010 c 28, s 24, sch 2 para 19(3); Financial Services, 2012 c.
       21, sch 9 para 15

       appl—SIs 2013/1773, reg 71(3); 2015/910, art 23(4)

       excl—SI 2013/1881, art 45(3)

s 209 mod—SI 2002/1775, reg 12(1)(1A)

       am—Financial Services, 2012 c. 21, sch 9 para 16

       appl—SIs 2013/1773, reg 71(3); 2015/910, art 23(4)

s 210 appl—SIs 2008/346, reg 36; 2009/209, regs 86, 122-123; 2011/99, reg 53(6);
       2013/1773, reg 71(3); 2013/504, reg 10(8); 2013/1635, reg 29(2); 2014/2879,
       reg 5(8); 2014/3085, reg 28(2); 2015/910, art 23(4)

       appl (mods)—SIs 2010/89, reg 19, sch; 2010/906, reg 22; 2012/3122, sch para 3(1);
       2015/1945, reg 43; 1946, reg 40; 2038, reg 36(6)(7)

       am—Financial Services, 2010 c 28, s 24, sch 2 para 20(1)-(4); Financial Services,
       2012 c. 21, sch 9 para 17

       excl—SI 2013/1881, art 44(2)(8), 47(6)

       mod—SI 2013/1881, art 45(2)

2000

c 8 continued

s 211 appl—SIs 2008/346, reg 36; 2009/209, regs 86, 122-123; 2010/89, reg 19, sch;
2011/99, reg 53(6); 2013/1773, reg 71(3); 2013/504, reg 10(8); 2013/1635,
reg 29(2); 2014/2879, reg 5(8); 3085, reg 28(2); 2015/910, art 23(4); 1945,
reg 43(1); 2038, reg 36(6)
appl (mods)—SIs 2010/906, reg 22; 2012/3122, sch para 3(1); 2015/1946, reg 40(1)
am—Financial Services, 2012 c. 21, sch 9 para 18
Pt 15 (ss 212-224) restr—SI 2001/544, art 9J
mod—SI 2008/2546, art 29
s 212 appl—SIs 1997/1612, sch 5A para 1(f); 2003/1102, reg 32(3); 2004/353, reg 32(3)
am—Financial Services, 2010 c 28, s 24, sch 2 para 21; Financial Services, 2012 c 21,
sch 10 para 2(2)(3); Financial Services (Banking Reform), 2013 c 33, s 16(2)(3)
rep in pt—Financial Services, 2012 c. 21, sch 10 para 2(4)
s 213 appl (mods)—SI 2006/2383, art 40, sch 1
excl —SIs 2007/3510, art 8; 2013/1881, art 59(8)
am—(prosp) Banking, 2009 c 1, s 170(2); SI 2011/1613, reg 2(13); Financial
Services, 2012 c. 21, sch 10 para 3
s 214 am—Banking, 2009 c 1, s 174(1); Financial Services, 2012 c. 21, sch 10 para 4
s 214A added—Banking, 2009 c 1, s 160(1)
s 214B added—Banking, 2009 c 1, s 171(1)
subst—Financial Services, 2010 c 28, s 16(1)
appl (mods)—Banking, 2009 c 1, s 83(2)(h)(i); ibid, s 81CA(7); Financial Services,
2010 c 28, s 16(2)
am—Financial Services, 2012 c. 21, s 101(10)
ss 214C, 214D added—Financial Services, 2010 c 28, s 16(1)
appl (mods)—Financial Services, 2010 c 28, s 16(2)
s 215 appl (mods)—SIs 2001/1090, reg 6; 2011/245, sch 6 pt 2 para 3(2); 2014/229, art 5
am—Enterprise, 2002 c 40, s 248(3), sch 17, paras 53, 54; Banking, 2009 c 1, s 175;
Financial Services, 2012 c. 21, sch 10 para 5; SI 2015/486, reg 13(3)
mod—SI 2009/317, art 5
s 217 am—Financial Services, 2012 c. 21, sch 10 para 6
s 217A added —Financial Services, 2012 c. 21, sch 10 para 7
s 217B added —Financial Services, 2012 c. 21, sch 10 para 9
s 218 am—(prosp) Banking, 2009 c 1, s 170(3); Financial Services, 2012 c. 21, sch 10
paras 8, 10
s 218ZA added —Financial Services, 2012 c. 21, sch 10 para 11
s 218A added—Banking, 2009 c 1, s 176(1)
am—Financial Services, 2012 c. 21, sch 10 para 12; SI 2015/486, reg 13(4)
s 218B added—Financial Services (Banking Reform), 2013 c 33, s 15
s 219 appl (mods)—SIs 2008/2644, art 16; 2008/2666, art 13; 2008/2674, art 17
am—Banking, 2009 c 1, s 176(2)-(7)
rep in pt—Banking, 2009 c 1, s 176(8)-(9)
s 220 am—Banking, 2009 c 1, s 123(3); SI 2009/805, art 15
appl (mods)—SI 2011/245, sch 6 pt 2 para 3(3)
s 221 am—SI 2001/1090, reg 9(1), sch 5 para 21; Financial Services, 2012 c. 21, sch 10
para 13
s 221A added—Banking, 2009 c 1, s 179(1)
am—Financial Services, 2010 c 28, s 24, sch 2 para 22
s 222 mod—SI 2008/2546, art 32
ext—SIs 2008/2666, art 14; 2008/2674, art 18
am—Banking, 2009 c 1, s 179(2)
rep in pt—Financial Services, 2012 c. 21, sch 10 para 14
s 223 am—Banking, 2009 c 1, s 171(2); Financial Services, 2010 c 28, s 24, sch 2 para
24(1)-(3)
s 223A added (prosp)—Banking, 2009 c 1, s 172
s 223B added—Banking, 2009 c 1, s 173
s 223C added—Banking, 2009 c 1, s 177
s 224 am—Financial Services, 2012 c. 21, sch 10 para 15
s 224ZA added—Financial Services (Banking Reform), 2013 c 33, s 14
s 224A added—Banking, 2009 c 1, s 180;
am—Financial Services, 2010 c 28, s 24, sch 2 para 25(1)-(3)
Pt 15A (ss 224B-224F) added —Financial Services, 2010 c 28, s 17
s 224F am—Financial Services, 2012 c. 21, s 38(2)
Pt 16 (ss 225-234A) appl—SIs 2009/209, reg 125; 2011/99, reg 76(2)

2000
c 8 Pt 16   *continued*

         appl (mods)—SIs 2015/910, art 26; 1945, reg 17(1); 1946, reg 14

s 225 appl—(EW) SI 1975/1023, arts 3(g), 4(e); (S) SSI 2003/231, arts 3, 5, sch 2 pt 1
         para 2

s 226 am—SIs 2009/209, reg 126, sch 6; 2011/99, sch 4 para 2(3)(a); Financial Services,
         2012 c. 21, sch 11 para 1

s 226A added—Consumer Credit, 2006 c 14, s 59(1)
         rep —SI 2013/1881, art 10(5)

s 227 am—Consumer Credit, 2006 c 14, s 61(2); Financial Services, 2012 c. 21, sch 11
         para 3
         rep in pt—SI 2013/1881, art 10(6)

s 228 am—Consumer Credit, 2006 c 14, s 61(3); Financial Services, 2012 c. 21, sch 11
         para 4(3)(4)
         rep in pt—Financial Services, 2012 c. 21, sch 11 para 4(2); SI 2013/1881, art 10(7)

s 229 am—Consumer Credit, 2006 c 14, s 61(4)(5)(6)(7); Financial Services, 2012 c. 21,
         sch 11 para 5; SI 2013/1881, art 10(8)(d)
         rep in pt—SI 2013/1881, art 10(8)(a)(b)(c)(e)

s 230 am—Consumer Credit, 2006 c 14, s 61(8); Financial Services, 2012 c 21, sch 11 para
         6
         rep in pt—SI 2013/1881, art 10(9)(a)(b)

s 230A added —Financial Services, 2012 c 21, sch 11 para 7

s 232 am—Financial Services, 2012 c 21, sch 11 para 8

s 232A added —Financial Services, 2012 c 21, sch 11 para 9

s 234 am—SIs 2009/209, reg 126, sch 6; 2011/99, sch 4 para 2(3)(b); Financial Services,
         2012 c 21, sch 11 para 10

s 234A added—Consumer Credit, 2006 c 14, s 60
         rep —SI 2013/1881, art 10(10)

s 234B added —Financial Services, 2012 c 21, sch 11 para 12

Pt 16A (ss 234C-234H) added —Financial Services, 2012 c 21, s 43

s 234C am—Financial Services (Banking Reform), 2013 c 33, s 68(6)

s 234D rep in pt—SI 2013/1881, art 10(11)

s 234H rep —Financial Services (Banking Reform), 2013 c 33, sch 8 para 2

ss 234I-234O added —Financial Services (Banking Reform), 2013 c 33, sch 8 para 3

Pt 17 (ss 235-284) appl—Stock Transfer, 1963 c 18, s 1(4)
         am (spec ss am)—Financial Services, 2012 c 21, sch 18 para 9(1)(2)

s 235 appl—SI 1995/2724, sch 1 pt IV para 1(l)(ii)(C); Finance, 1996 c 8, ss 87(5A), 87A,
         sch 9, paras 2(1B), 18(1)(c), 20; SI 2002/376, reg 2(2); Finance, 2003 c 14,
         s 152, sch 26 para 5(4); Income Tax (Trading and Other Income), 2005 c 5,
         s 520(4)

s 235A added—SI 2013/1388, reg 3(5)

s 236 appl—Finance, 1996 c 8, sch 10 para 8(7A)(b); SI 1995/3103, reg 5(4)(a); Finance,
         2003 c 14, s 102(4) (see SI 2003/2899, art 2); Income Tax (Trading and Other
         Income), 2005 c 5, s 520(4)
         am—SI 2009/1941, art 2, sch 1 para 181

s 237 appl—Income and Corporation Taxes, 1988 c 1, sch 20 pt I para 6; (EW)
         SI 1975/1023, art 3(g); SIs 1990/2231, reg 4(l)(r); 2001/544, art 51(2);
         2001/1004, sch 2 para 3; (EW) 2004/266 para 6, sch 2 para 4(3); 2004/2095,
         reg 4(6); Finance (No 2), 2005 c 22, s 17(4)(a)
         am—SIs 2011/1613, reg 2(14); 2013/1388, reg 3(6)

s 238 appl—SIs 2001/3374, art 13, sch para 8; 2001/1060, arts 21(4)(a), 23(3)(a)
         am—SI 2013/1388, reg 3(7)

ss 239-241 appl—SI 2001/3374, art 13, sch para 8

s 241 am—SI 2013/636, sch para 6

s 243 am—SI 2011/1613, reg 2(15)

s 244 am—SI 2011/1613, reg 2(16)

s 247 am—SI 2011/1265, art 12(2)

s 249 appl—SI 2001/1228, reg 69, sch 5 para 20
         appl (mods)—SI 2013/441, art 12(2)
         am—Financial Services, 2012 c 21, sch 18 para 10; SI 2013/1388, reg 3(8)

s 250 am—SI 2007/1973, regs 2, 11; Financial Services, 2012 c 21, sch 18 para 11

s 251 am—SI 2011/1613, reg 2(17)

s 252 am—SI 2011/1613, reg 2(18)

s 252A added—SI 2011/1613, reg 2(19)

s 257 am—SI 2011/1613, reg 2(20); Financial Services, 2012 c 21, sch 18 para 12

2000
c 8 *continued*

s 258A added—SI 2011/1613, reg 2(21)
    am—SI 2013/1388, reg 3(9)(a)(b)
s 259 am—SIs 2011/1613, reg 2(22); 2013/1388, reg 3(10)
ss 261A, 261B added—SI 2011/1613, reg 2(23)
s 261B am—SI 2013/1388, reg 3(11)
Pt 17, Ch 3A (ss 261C-261Z5) added—SI 2013/1388, reg 3(12)
s 261D am—SI 2013/1773, sch 1 para 17
s 262 am—SI 2011/1265, art 12(3)
s 263 rep—Companies, 2006 c 46, s 129, sch 16
s 264 am—SIs 2011/1613, reg 2(24)(a)(b); 2012/2015, reg 4
    rep in pt—SI 2011/1613, reg 2(24)(c)
    appl (mods)—SI 2001/3084, art 3A (added by 2012/2017, art 2(3))
s 265 rep—SI 2011/1613, reg 2(25)
s 266 am—SI 2003/2066, reg 9
    appl—SI 2004/2095, reg 4(6)
s 267 am—Financial Services, 2012 c 21, sch 18 para 13
s 268 am—Financial Services, 2012 c 21, sch 18 para 14
s 269 am—Financial Services, 2012 c 21, sch 18 para 15
ss 270, 271 rep—SI 2013/1773, sch 1 para 18
s 272 am—SIs 2013/1773, sch 1 para 19(a); 2013/1388, reg 3(14)
    rep in pt—SI 2013/1773, sch 1 para 19(b)
    appl—SI 2001/3374, art 13, sch para 9
s 277 am—SI 2013/1773, sch 1 para 20
s 277A added—SI 2013/1773, sch 1 para 21
s 278 rep in pt—SI 2013/1773, sch 1 paras 22, 23
s 279 rep in pt—SI 2013/1773, sch 1 para 24
s 280 am—SI 2013/1773, sch 1 para 25(a)
    rep in pt—SI 2013/1773, sch 1 para 25(b)
s 281 am—SI 2013/1773, sch 1 para 26(b)
    rep in pt—SI 2013/1773, sch 1 para 26(a)
Pt 17 Ch 5A (ss 283A, 283B) added—SI 2011/1613, reg 2(26)
s 283A am—SI 2013/1388, reg 3(15)
s 284 am—Financial Services, 2012 c 21, sch 18 para 17
Pt 18 (ss 285-313) appl (mods)—SI 2011/2699, reg 7, sch 2
s 285 appl—Finance, 1986 c 41, ss 85(5), 106(4)(a), 107(4)(a), sch 18 para 10(2);
        Insolvency, 1986 c 45, sch A1 pt I, para 4E(3), sch 2A, para 2(3); Income and
        Corporation Taxes, 1988 c 1, s 203F(2)(a); Courts and Legal Services, 1990
        c 41, s 50(2)(e); Finance, 2002 c 23, s 83, sch 26 pt 6, para 31(9); SI 2005/824,
        art 7(2)(j)
    am—Financial Services, 2012 c 21, s 28; SI 2013/504, reg 3(3)
s 285A added —Financial Services, 2012 c 21, s 29
    am—SI 2013/504, reg 3(4)
s 286 am—SIs 2006/2975, reg 8; 2007/126, reg 3, sch 2; Financial Services, 2012 c 21, s
        30; ibid, sch 8 para 2
s 287 am—SI 2007/126, reg 3, sch 2; Financial Services, 2012 c 21, sch 8 para 3
s 288 am—Financial Services, 2012 c 21, sch 8 para 4; SI 2013/504, reg 3(5)
s 289 am—Financial Services, 2012 c 21, sch 8 para 5; SI 2013/504, reg 3(6)
s 290 am—SI 2007/126, reg 3, sch 2; Financial Services, 2012 c 21, sch 8 para 6(2)(3)(5);
        SI 2013/504, reg 3(7)
    rep in pt—Financial Services, 2012 c 21, sch 8 para 6(4)(6)
s 290ZA added—SI 2013/504, reg 3(8)
s 290A added—Investment, Exchange and Clearing Houses, 2006 c 55, s 4
    am—Financial Services, 2012 c 21, sch 8 para 7; SI 2013/504, reg 3(9)
s 291 appl (mods)—SI 2008/432, art 20
    mod—SI 2008/2546, art 39
s 292 am—SI 2006/2975, reg 9; Financial Services, 2012 c 21, sch 8 para 8; SI 2013/504,
        reg 3(10)
s 292A added—SI 2007/126, reg 3, sch 2
    am—Financial Services, 2012 c 21, sch 8 para 9
s 293 am—Financial Services, 2012 c 21, sch 8 para 10
s 293A added—SI 2007/126, reg 3, sch 2
    subst —Financial Services, 2012 c 21, sch 8 para 11
s 294 am—Financial Services, 2012 c 21, sch 8 para 12

2000
c 8 *continued*

s 295 am—Enterprise, 2002 c 40, s 278(1), sch 25, para 40(1)(9); Financial Services, 2012
     c 21, sch 8 para 13
s 296 appl—Companies, 1989 c 40, s 169(2)
     am—SI 2007/126, reg 3, sch 2; Financial Services, 2012 c 21, sch 8 para 14
s 296A added —Financial Services, 2012 c 21, s 31
     am—SI 2013/504, reg 3(11)(a)(b)(i)(c)
     rep in pt—SI 2013/504, reg 3(11)(b)(ii)
s 297 appl—Companies, 1989 c 40, s 169(2)
     am—SI 2007/126, reg 3, sch 2; Financial Services, 2012 c 21, sch 8 para 15; SIs
          2012/916, reg 2(10); 2013/504, reg 3(11)(b)(ii)
     rep in pt—Financial Services, 2012 c 21, sch 8 para 15(3)(a)(ii)
s 298 ext—SI 1999/2979, reg 7
     am—SI 2007/126, reg 3, sch 2; Financial Services, 2012 c 21, s 32(4)(6); ibid, sch 8
          para 16
     rep in pt—Financial Services, 2012 c 21, s 32(2)(3),(5)
     appl (mods)—Crim Justice (Terorrism and Conspiracy), 1998 c 40, s 170B(9)
s 299 am—Financial Services, 2012 c 21, sch 8 para 17
s 300A added—Investment, Exchange and Clearing Houses, 2006 c 55, s 1
     am—Financial Services, 2012 c 21, sch 8 para 18
ss 300B-300E added—Investment, Exchange and Clearing Houses, 2006 c 55, s 2
s 300B am—Financial Services, 2012 c 21, sch 8 para 19
s 300C am—Financial Services, 2012 c 21, sch 8 para 20
s 300D am—Financial Services, 2012 c 21, sch 8 para 21
s 300E am—SI 2013/504, reg 3(13)
s 301 am—Financial Services, 2012 c 21, sch 8 para 22
Pt 18, Ch 1A (ss 301A-301M) added—SIs 2007/126, reg 3, sch 2; 2009/534, regs 5,8, sch 2
s 301A am—Financial Services, 2012 c 21, sch 8 para 23; SI 2013/1908, reg 5(2)
s 301B am—Financial Services, 2012 c 21, sch 8 para 24
s 301C am—Financial Services, 2012 c 21, sch 8 para 25
s 301E rep in pt—SI 2015/1755, reg 6(2)(a)
s   am—SIs 2011/1613, reg 2(27); 2013/3115, sch 2 para 17; 2015/1755, reg 6(2)(b)
s 301F am—Financial Services, 2012 c 21, sch 8 para 26
s 301G am—Financial Services, 2012 c 21, sch 8 para 27
s 301H am—Financial Services, 2012 c 21, sch 8 para 28
s 301I am—Financial Services, 2012 c 21, sch 8 para 29
s 301J am—Financial Services, 2012 c 21, sch 8 para 30
s 301K am—Financial Services, 2012 c 21, sch 8 para 31
s 301L am—Financial Services, 2012 c 21, sch 8 para 32
s 301M am—SI 2013/3115, sch 2 para 18
Pt 18, Ch 2 (ss 302-310) rep—Financial Services, 2012 c 21, s 34(a)
Pt 18, Ch 3 (ss 311, 312) rep —Financial Services, 2012 c 21, s 34(b)
Pt 18, Ch 3A (ss 312A-312D) added—SI 2007/126, reg 3, sch 2
s 312A appl—SIs 2007/126, reg 5; 2011/2699, reg 8, sch 3
     am—Financial Services, 2012 c 21, sch 8 para 33
s 312B am—Financial Services, 2012 c 21, sch 8 para 34; SI 2012/916, reg 2(11)
s 312C excl—SI 2007/126, reg 5
     am—Financial Services, 2012 c 21, sch 8 para 35; SI 2012/916, reg 2(12)
Pt 18, Ch 3B added (ss 312E-312K) —Financial Services, 2012 c 21, s 33
ss 312E-312I restr—SI 2013/441, art 13
s 313 am—Enterprise, 2002 c 40, s 278(1), sch 25, para 40(1)(15); SI 2007/126, reg 3, sch
          2; Financial Services, 2012 c 21, sch 8 para 36; SI 2013/504, reg 3(14)(a)(b)
     rep in pt—SIs 2013/504, reg 3(14)(c); 2014/892, sch 1 para 129
Pt 18A (ss 313A-313D) added—SI 2007/126, reg 3, sch 3
     am—Financial Services, 2012 c 21, s 36
s 313A am—SI 2010/1193, reg 2
s 313B am—SI 2010/1193, reg 3
     rep in pt—SI 2010/1193, reg 3
ss 313BA-313BE added—SI 2010/1193, reg 4
s 313C am—SI 2010/1193, reg 5
s 313D am—SIs 2010/1193, reg 6; 2013/3115, sch 2 para 19
s 314 am—Financial Services, 2012 c 21, s 40(2)
s 314A added —Financial Services, 2012 c 21, s 40(3)
s 315 subst —Financial Services, 2012 c 21, s 40(4)

2000
c 8 *continued*

s 316 am—Financial Services, 2012 c 21, s 40(5); SI 2015/575, sch 1 para 12
s 317 am—Financial Services, 2012 c 21, s 40(6)
s 318 am—Financial Services, 2012 c 21, s 40(7)
s 319 am—Financial Services, 2012 c 21, s 40(8)
s 320 am—Financial Services, 2012 c 21, s 40(9)
s 321 am—Financial Services, 2012 c 21, s 40(10)
s 322 am—Financial Services, 2012 c 21, s 40(11)
s 323 am—SI 2008/1469, reg 2
s 324 appl—SI 2005/1998, reg 4(3)
Pt 20 (ss 325-332) appl (mods)—SI 2000/1119, sch 4 para 11
s 325 am—Financial Services, 2012 c 21, sch 16 para 1
s 326 appl—SIs 1993/1933, reg 15(2)(e); 1994/1757, reg 4(1)(e); 1997/1612, sch 5A
       para 1(d); 2001/192, reg 4(1)(e); 2001/192, reg 4(f)
s 327 restr—SI 2001/544, art 13(1)
       appl—SI 2001/1335, art 55(2); SI 2005/1529, art 55(3)(a)
s 328 am—SI 2003/1473, reg 9; Financial Services, 2012 c 21, sch 16 para 2; SI
       2013/1881, art 10(12)
       mod—SI 2001/544 arts 60LA(2)(3), 60S(2)(3) (added by SI 2014/366, art
       2(33)(37))
s 329 am—Financial Services, 2012 c 21, sch 16 para 3
s 330 am—Financial Services, 2012 c 21, sch 16 para 4
s 331 am—Financial Services, 2012 c 21, sch 16 para 5
s 332 restr—SI 2001/544, art 13(1)
       am—Financial Services, 2012 c 21, sch 16 para 6
Pt 20A (ss 333A-333R) added—Pension Schemes, 2015 c 8, sch 3 para 2
       trans of functions—SI 2015/2013, art 2
s 333B am—SI 2015/2013, sch para 1(2)
s 333C am—SI 2015/2013, sch para 1(3)
s 333D am—SI 2015/2013, sch para 1(4)
s 333E am—SI 2015/2013, sch para 1(5)
s 333F am—SI 2015/2013, sch para 1(6)
s 333G am—SI 2015/2013, sch para 1(7)
s 333J am—SI 2015/2013, sch para 1(8)
s 333K am—SI 2015/2013, sch para 1(9)
s 333L am—SI 2015/2013, sch para 1(10)
s 333M am—SI 2015/2013, sch para 1(11)(a)(b)
s 333M rep in pt—SI 2015/2013, sch para 1(11)(c)
s 333P am—SI 2015/2013, sch para 1(12)
s 333Q am—SI 2015/2013, sch para 1(13)
s 333R am—SI 2015/2013, sch para 1(14)
s 334 rep in pt—Financial Services, 2012 c 21, s 54(1)(a)
ss 335-339 rep—Financial Services, 2012 c 21, s 54(1)(b)-(f)
s 337 excl—SI 2003/1102, reg 4(6)
s 339A added —Financial Services, 2012 c 21, sch 13 para 2
       am—Financial Services (Banking Reform), 2013 c 33, s 134(3)
ss 339B, 339C added —Financial Services (Banking Reform), 2013 c 33, s 134(2)
Pt 22 (ss 340-346) appl (mods)—SI 2011/99, sch 3 para 5
s 340 am—Financial Services, 2012 c 21, sch 13 para 3
ss 341, 342 appl (mods)—SI 2009/209, reg 95, sch 5 para 4
s 342 am—Financial Services, 2012 c 21, sch 13 para 4; SI 2013/3115, sch 2 para 20
s 343 appl—SI 2003/1294, reg 2(3)(b)
       appl (mods)—SI 2009/209, reg 95, sch 5 para 4
       am—Financial Services, 2012 c 21, sch 13 para 5; SI 2013/3115, sch 2 para 21
ss 344-346 appl (mods)—SI 2009/209, reg 95, sch 5 para 4
s 344 am—Financial Services, 2012 c 21, sch 13 para 6
s 345 replaced (by ss 345, 345A-345E) —Financial Services, 2012 c 21, sch 13 para 7
s 345 appl (mods)—SI 2013/441, art 14(4)
s 347 am—SIs 2001/544, art 9K; 2007/126, reg 3, sch 5; Financial Services, 2012 c 21, sch
       12 para 16(2)(5); SI 2013/1388, reg 3(16); Financial Services (Banking
       Reform), 2013 c 33, sch 3 para 11; ibid, s 34; SI 2015/910, sch 1 para
       1(7)(a)(i)(ii)(b)-(d)
       rep in pt—Financial Services, 2012 c 21, sch 12 para 16(3)(4)
s 347A added —Financial Services, 2012 c 21, sch 12 para 17

2000
c 8 *continued*

s 348 ext—SI 2001/2188, reg 15
　　ext (mods)—SI 2001/3648, art 3(2)-(4)
　　appl—SIs 2003/1102, regs 16(2), 50(3)(4); 2004/353, regs 16(2), 50(3)(4);
　　　　2004/1045, regs 18(2)(3), 38(3)(4); 2008/346, reg 43; 2010/89, reg 16;
　　　　2015/910, art 18(3)
　　excl—SI 2006/1183, reg 18
　　appl (mods)—SI 2004/1045 regs 18(5), 38(8); Banking, 2009 c 1, s 89L; SIs
　　　　2009/209, reg 95, sch 5 para 5; 2010/89, reg 19, sch; 2011/99, sch 3 para 6;
　　　　2012/3122, sch para 4; 2013/1635, reg 11(1); 2014/3085, reg 12; 2015/1945,
　　　　regs 22(1), 25(1); 2038, sch 7 para 3; 1946, reg 22(1)
　　am—Financial Services, 2010 c 28, s 24, sch 2 para 26; Financial Services, 2012 c 21,
　　　　sch 12 para 18(2)(a), (3)(a),(c)(d), (4); Financial Services (Banking Reform),
　　　　2013 c 33, sch 8 para 5
　　rep in pt—Financial Services, 2012 c 21, sch 12 para 18(2)(b), (3)(b),(4)(c)
s 349 am—Companies, 2006 c 46, s 964(1)(4); SI 2006/1183, reg 18; Financial Services,
　　　　2012 c 21, sch 12 para 19
　　rep in pt—SI 2007/1093, art 7, sch 5
　　ext—SI 2001/2188, reg 15
　　ext (mods)—SI 2001/3648, art 3(2)
　　appl—SIs 2003/1102, regs 16(2), 50(3)(4); 2004/353, regs 16(2), 50(3)(4);
　　　　2004/1045, regs 18(2)(3), 38(3)(4); 2008/346, reg 43; 2010/89, reg 16;
　　　　2015/910, art 18(3)
　　appl (mods)—SI 2004/1045 regs 18(5), 38(8); Banking, 2009 c 1, s 89L; SIs
　　　　2009/209, reg 95, sch 5 para 5; 2010/89, reg 19, sch; 2011/99, sch 3 para 6;
　　　　2012/3122, sch para 4; 2013/1635, reg 11(1); 2014/3085, reg 12; 2015/1945,
　　　　regs 22(1), 25(1); 2038, sch 7 para 3; 1946, reg 22(1)
s 350 am—Financial Services, 2012 c 21, sch 12 para 20
s 351 rep —Financial Services, 2012 c 21, sch 12 para 21
　　appl—Enterprise, 2002 c 40, s 243(3)(c); SIs 2009/209, reg 95, sch 5 para 5; 2011/99,
　　　　sch 3 para 6
　　rep in pt—Enterprise, 2002 c 40, ss 247(k), 278(2), sch 26
s 351A added—SI 2011/1613, reg 2(28)
　　am—Financial Services, 2012 c 21, sch 12 para 22; SI 2013/1388, reg 3(17)
s 352 am—(prosp) (EW) Crim Justice, 2003 c 44, s 280(2)(3), sch 26 para 54(1)(3)
　　ext—SI 2001/2188, reg 15
　　ext (mods)—SI 2001/3648, art 3(2)
　　appl—SIs 2003/1102, regs 16(2), 50(3)(4); 2004/353, regs 16(2), 50(3)(4);
　　　　2004/1045, regs 18(2), 38(3)(4); 2008/346, reg 43; 2009/209, reg 95, sch 5
　　　　para 5; 2010/89, regs 16, 19, sch; 2011/99, sch 3 para 6; 2015/910, art 18(3)
　　appl (mods)—SI 2004/1045 regs 18(5), 38(8); Banking, 2009 c 1, s 89L; SIs
　　　　2012/3122, sch para 4; 2013/1635, reg 11(1); 2014/3085, reg 12; 2015/1945,
　　　　reg 25(1); 1946, reg 22(1); 2038, sch 7 para 3
s 353 am—Consumer Credit, 2006 c 14, s 61(9); Financial Services, 2012 c 21, sch 12 para
　　　　23
　　rep in pt—SI 2013/1881, art 10(13)
　　appl (mods)—Banking, 2009 c. 1, s 89L
s 353A added —Financial Services, 2012 c 21, sch 12 para 24
s 354 replaced (by ss 354A-354C) —Financial Services, 2012 c 21, sch 12 para 25
s 354A am—Financial Services (Banking Reform), 2013 c 33, sch 8 para 6
s 355 mod—SI 2009/317, art 5
　　am—Financial Services, 2012 c 21, sch 14 para 2; Co-operative and Community
　　　　Benefit Societies, 2014 c 14, sch 4 para 70
s 356 am—Insolvency, 2000 c 39, s 15(3); Financial Services, 2012 c 21, sch 14 para 3
　　appl (mods)—SIs 2001/1090, reg 6; 2014/229, art 6
s 357 am—Financial Services, 2012 c 21, sch 14 para 4
s 358 am—Financial Services, 2012 c 21, sch 14 para 5
s 359 subst—Enterprise, 2002 c 40, s 248(3), sch 17, paras 53, 55
　　am—Dormant Bank and Building Society Accounts, 2008 c 31, s 15, sch 2 para 6;
　　　　Financial Services, 2012 c 21, sch 14 para 6
　　rep in pt—Dormant Bank and Building Society Accounts, 2008 c 31, s 15, sch 2 para
　　　　6
　　appl (mods)—SIs 2009/209, reg 95, sch 5 para 6; 2011/99, sch 3 para 7; 2014/229,
　　　　art 7

2000
c 8 *continued*

s 361 subst—Enterprise, 2002 c 40, s 248(3), sch 17, paras 53, 56
    mod—SI 2009/317, art 5
    am—Financial Services, 2012 c 21, sch 14 para 7
    appl (mods)—SI 2014/229, art 8
s 362 appl (mods)—SIs 2001/1090, reg 6; 2011/245, sch 6 pt 2 para 3(4)
    am—Enterprise, 2002 c 40, s 248(3), sch 17, paras 53, 57; SI 2008/948, art 3, sch 1;
        Financial Services, 2012 c 21, sch 14 para 8(2)(b), (3)-(6)
    mod—SI 2009/317, art 5
    rep in pt—Financial Services, 2012 c 21, sch 14 para 8(2)(a)
    appl (mods)—SI 2014/229, art 9
s 362A added—Enterprise, 2002 c 40, s 248(3), sch 17, paras 53, 58
    am—Financial Services, 2012 c 21, sch 14 para 9
    appl (mods)—SI 2014/229, art 9
s 363 appl (mods)—SI 2001/1090, reg 6
    am—Financial Services, 2012 c 21, sch 14 para 10
s 364 appl (mods)—SI 2001/1090, reg 6
    am—Financial Services, 2012 c 21, sch 14 para 11
s 365 am—SI 2008/948, art 3, sch 1; Financial Services, 2012 c 21, sch 14 para 12
    appl (mods)—SI 2001/1090, reg 6
s 366 am—SI 2007/2194, art 10, sch 4; Financial Services, 2012 c 21, sch 14 para 13
s 367 mod—SI 2001/3650, arts 14, 15
    appl (mods)—SIs 2009/209, reg 95, sch 5 para 6; 2011/99, sch 3 para 7
    am—Financial Services, 2012 c 21, sch 14 para 14; SI 2015/575, sch 1 para 13
s 368 appl (mods)—SIs 2009/209, reg 95, sch 5 para 6; 2011/99, sch 3 para 7
    am—Financial Services, 2012 c 21, sch 14 para 15
s 369 am—Financial Services, 2012 c 21, sch 14 para 16
s 369A added—Dormant Bank and Building Society Accounts, 2008 c 31, s 15, sch 2 para
        7
    am—Financial Services, 2012 c 21, sch 14 para 17
s 370 subst —Financial Services, 2012 c 21, sch 14 para 18
    appl (mods)—SI 2001/1090, reg 6
    mod—SIs 2009/317, art 5; 2013/1388, reg 17(14)
s 371 appl (mods)—SI 2001/1090, reg 6
    am—SI 2008/948, art 3, sch 1; Financial Services, 2012 c 21, sch 14 para 19(2)(b),
        (3)-(5)
    rep in pt—Financial Services, 2012 c 21, sch 14 para 19(2)(a)
s 372 am—Financial Services, 2012 c 21, sch 14 para 20
s 373 am—Financial Services, 2012 c 21, sch 14 para 21(2)(b)(c),(3),(4)
    rep in pt—Financial Services, 2012 c 21, sch 14 para 21(2)(a)
s 374 am—Financial Services, 2012 c 21, sch 14 para 22(3)-(5)
    rep in pt—Financial Services, 2012 c 21, sch 14 para 22(2)
s 375 am—Financial Services, 2012 c 21, sch 14 para 23
    mod—SI 2009/317, art 5
    appl (mods)—SI 2011/245, sch 6 pt 2 para 3(5)
s 376 am—Financial Services, 2012 c 21, sch 14 para 24; Financial Services (Banking
        Reform), 2013 c 33, sch 10 para 2
s 377 excl—SI 2004/353, reg 4(7)
Pt 25 (ss 380-386) appl (mods)—SI 2013/1635, reg 24(1)
s 380 appl (mods)—SIs 2002/1775, reg 12(2); 2013/441, arts 15(2), 18(3); 2013/1882, art
        3(8)
    am—SIs 2007/126, reg 3, sch 5; 2011/1613, reg 2(29); Financial Services, 2012 c 21,
        sch 9 para 19(2)(3),(5); SIs 2012/1906, art 3(11); 2012/2554, reg 2(12); SI
        2013/1773, sch 1 para 27; Financial Services (Banking Reform), 2013 c 33, sch
        10 para 3(2); SI 2015/1755, reg 4(4)(a)-(c)
    rep in pt—Financial Services, 2012 c 21, sch 9 para 19(4)
    mod—SI 2015/910, art 23(1)(b)
s 381 am—Financial Services, 2012 c 21, sch 9 para 20
s 382 appl (mods)—SIs 2001/3755, reg 9(7); 2002/1775, reg 12(2); 2013/441, arts 16(2),
        18(3); 2013/1882, art 3(9)
    am—SIs 2007/126, reg 3, sch 5; 2011/1613, reg 2(29); Financial Services, 2012 c 21,
        sch 9 para 21; SIs 2012/1906, art 3(12); 2012/2554, reg 2(13); 2013/1773, sch
        1 para 28; Financial Services (Banking Reform), 2013 c 33, sch 10 para 3(3)
    mod—SI 2015/910, art 23(1)(c)

2000

c 8 s 382 *continued*

rep in pt—Financial Services, 2012 c 21, sch 9 para 21(6)

s 383 am—Financial Services, 2012 c 21, sch 9 para 22

s 384 appl (mods)—SIs 2002/1775, reg 12(1)(1A); 2013/441, arts 17(2), 18(3); 2013/1882, art 3(10)

    am—SIs 2007/126, reg 3, sch 5; 2011/1613, reg 2(29); Financial Services, 2012 c 21, sch 9 para 23(2)-(6),(8); SIs 2012/1906, art 3(13); 2013/1773, sch 1 para 29; Financial Services (Banking Reform), 2013 c 33, sch 10 para 3(4)

    rep in pt—Financial Services, 2012 c 21, sch 9 para 23(7)

    mod—SIs 2002/1775, reg 12(1)(1A) (subst by 2015/852, art 2(3)); 2015/910, art 23(1)(d)

s 385 am—Financial Services, 2012 c 21, sch 9 para 24

s 386 am—Financial Services, 2012 c 21, sch 9 para 25

Pt 26 (ss 387-396) appl—SIs 2002/1775, reg 11C(5) (added by 2015/852, art 2(2)); 2008/346, reg 44; 2013/1773, reg 70(2); 2015/910, art 24(2); 1945, reg 44; 1946, reg 41; 2038, sch 7 para 4

    appl (mods)—SIs 2009/209, reg 95, sch 5 para 7; 2010/89, reg 19, sch para 5; 2010/906, reg 30; 2011/99, sch 3 para 8; 2012/3122, sch para 5; 2013/1635, reg 30(1); 2013/1882, art 3(11); 2014/3085, reg 29

s 387 appl—SIs 2001/1228, reg 8(a)-(c); 2013/504, reg 56; 2014/2879, reg 5(10)

    appl (mods)—Banking, 2009 c 1, s 83ZT(2)-(4)

    am—Financial Services, 2012 c 21, sch 9 para 26; Financial Services (Banking Reform), 2013 c 33, sch 3 para 12

    excl—SI 2013/1881, arts 37(3)(a), 39(2)(a)(ii), 44(2)

s 388 appl—SIs 2001/1228, reg 8(a)-(c); 2013/504, reg 56; 2014/2879, reg 5(10)

    appl (mods)—Banking, 2009 c. 1, s 83ZU(6)(7); SIs 2013/1881, art 52

    am—Financial Services, 2012 c 21, sch 9 para 27; Financial Services (Banking Reform), 2013 c 33, sch 3 para 13

s 389 appl—SIs 2001/1228, reg 8(a)-(c); 2013/504, reg 56; 2014/2879, reg 5(10)

    appl (mods)—Banking, 2009 c. 1, s 83ZV

    am—Financial Services, 2012 c 21, sch 9 para 28

s 390 appl—SIs 2001/1228, reg 8(d); 2014/2879, reg 5(10)

    appl (mods)—Banking, 2009 c. 1, s 83ZV

    am—SI 2010/22, art 5, sch 2; Financial Services, 2012 c 21, sch 9 para 29

s 391 appl—SIs 2001/1228, reg 9; 2013/504, reg 56; 2014/2879, reg 5(11)

    appl (mods)—SIs 2009/209, Sch 4A paras 1(9)(10), 4(1)(c)(10)(11) (added by SI 2014/366, art 12(4)); 2011/99 Sch 2A para 1(9)(10)(12) (added by SI 2014/366, art 18(3))

    am—Financial Services, 2010 c 28, s 24, sch 2 para 28; Financial Services, 2012 c 21, s 24(2); ibid, sch 9 para 30; SI 2012/916, reg 2(13); (prosp) Financial Services (Banking Reform), 2013 c 33, s 4(3); SIs 2013/1388, reg 3(18); 2013/3115, sch 2 para 22; 2014/2879, reg 6(2); 2015/1755, reg 4(5)

    rep in pt—Financial Services, 2010 c 28, s 13(1)-(4)

    power to am—Financial Services, 2012 c 21, s 37(2)(a)

    restr in pt—SI 2013/441, art 33

    mod—SI 2013/1881, art 65(3)(c)

s 391A added —SI 2013/3115, sch 2 para 23

    am—SI 2015/1755, reg 4(6)

s 391B added—SI 2015/1755, reg 4(7)

s 392 am—SI 2007/126, reg 3, sch 5; Financial Services, 2010 c 28, s 24, sch 2 para 29(1)-(3); Financial Services, 2012 c 21, s 18(5); ibid, sch 8 para 37; ibid, sch 9 para 31; ibid, sch 13 para 8; (prosp) Financial Services (Banking Reform), 2013 c 33, s 4(4)(a)(b); SI 2013/1388, reg 3(19)

    appl (mods)—Banking, 2009 c 1, s 83ZV

s 393 am—Financial Services, 2012 c 21, sch 9 para 32

    appl—SIs 2001/1228, reg 24(3); 2001/544, art 95(10); 2013/504, reg 56; 2014/2879, reg 5(10)

    appl (mods)—Banking, 2009 c 1, s 83ZV

s 394 am—Regulation of Investigatory Powers, 2000 c 23, s 82(1), sch 4 para 11; Financial Services, 2012 c 21, sch 9 para 33

    appl—SIs 2001/1228, reg 24(3); 2001/544, art 95(10); 2013/504, reg 56; 2014/2879, reg 5(10)

    appl (mods)—Banking, 2009 c 1, s 83ZV

s 395 appl—SI 2001/1228, reg 10

2000

c 8 s 395 *continued*

am—SIs 2005/381, reg 7, 2005/1433, reg 2(1), sch 1 para 14; 2007/1973, regs 2, 8; 2009/534, reg 6; Financial Services, 2012 c 21, s 17(3); ibid, s 18(6); s 19(2); ibid, s 24(3); ibid, sch 9 para 34; Financial Services (Banking Reform), 2013 c 33, sch 3 para 14; SI 2013/1388, reg 3(20)

power to repeal—Financial Services, 2012 c 21, s 37(2)(b)

s 396 am—Financial Services, 2012 c 21, sch 9 para 35

Pt 27 (ss 397-403) appl—SI 2013/1881, art 50(3)

appl (mods)—SI 2013/1882, art 3(12)

s 397 rep —Financial Services, 2012 c 21, s 95

s 398 ext—SI 2001/3646, art 3(3)(b)(4)

am—Financial Services, 2012 c 21, sch 9 para 36; SIs 2012/2554, reg 2(14); 2013/1773, sch 1 para 30; 2015/1882, reg 3(4)

appl—SIs 1995/1537, reg 23(1); 2008/346, reg 38; 2012/2554, reg 5(5); 2013/3115, reg 45; 2015/2038, sch 7 para 5

appl (mods)—SI 2010/906, reg 25

mod—SI 2015/910, art 23(1)(e)

s 399 am—Enterprise, 2002 c 40, s 278(1), sch 25, para 40(1)(16); SI 2014/892, sch 1 para 130

s 400 appl—Companies (Audit, Investigations and Community Enterprise), 2004 c 27, s 15A; SIs 1995/1537, reg 23(1); 2008/346, reg 38; 2013/504, reg 57; 2013/504, reg 57

appl (mods)—SIs 2010/906, reg 26; 2013/441, art 34(2)

am—Financial Services, 2012 c 21, sch 9 para 37

s 401 appl—SI 1995/1537, reg 23(1); Companies (Audit, Investigations and Community Enterprise), 2004 c 27, s 15A; SI 2008/346, reg 38

am—Enterprise, 2002 c 40, s 278(1), sch 25, para 40(1)(17); Financial Services, 2012 c 21, sch 9 para 38

appl (mods)—SIs 2010/906, reg 27; 2015/2038, sch 7 para 6

rep in pt—SI 2013/1881, art 10(14)

s 402 am—Counter-Terrorism, 2008 c 28, s 62, sch 7 para 33(4); Financial Services, 2012 c 21, sch 9 para 39

appl—SI 2013/1881, art 49

s 403 appl—SIs 1995/1537, reg 23(1); 2008/948, art 3, sch 1; 2010/906, reg 28; 2013/504, reg 57

am—Financial Services, 2012 c 21, sch 9 para 40

s 404 subst —Financial Services, 2010 c 28, s 14(1)

am—SI 2011/99, sch 4 para 2(4)(a); Financial Services, 2012 c 21, sch 18 para 18

ss 404A-404G added—Financial Services, 2010 c 28, s 14(1)

s 404A am—Financial Services, 2012 c 21, sch 18 para 19

s 404B am—SI 2015/542, sch 7 para 1(2)

s 404E am—SI 2011/99, sch 4 para 2(4)(b)

mod—SI 2001/544, art 60LA(1)(3), 60S(1)(3) (added by SI 2014/366, art 2(33)(37))

rep in pt—SI 2013/1881, art 10(15)

s 404F am—SI 2011/99, sch 4 para 2(5); Financial Services, 2012 c 21, sch 18 para 20

s 405 am—SIs 2000/2952, reg 8(3); 2004/3379, reg 6(1)(4); 2006/3221, reg 29, sch 3; 2007/126, reg 3, sch 5; Financial Services, 2012 c 21, sch 18 para 21

rep in pt—SI 2015/575, sch 1 para 14

s 407 am—Financial Services, 2012 c 21, sch 18 para 22

s 409 rep in pt—SI 2011/1613, reg 2(30)

am—Financial Services, 2012 c 21, sch 18 para 23

s 410 appl—SI 1995/1537, reg 23(1)

am—Financial Services, 2012 c 21, s 47

rep in pt—Financial Services, 2012 c 21, s 16(14)(i)

ss 410A, 410B added—Financial Services (Banking Reform), 2013 c 33, s 135(1)

s 411 rep in pt—SI 2001/3629, art 109, sch

s 412 rep in pt—Gambling, 2005 c 19, ss 334(1)(e)(2), 356(4)(5), sch 17

s 412A added—SI 2007/126, reg 3, sch 5

am—Financial Services, 2012 c 21, sch 8 para 38

s 412B added—SI 2007/126, reg 3, sch 5

am—Financial Services, 2012 c 21, sch 8 para 39

s 413 appl—SIs 2009/209, reg 95, sch 5 para 8; 2010/89, reg 19, sch; 2011/99, sch 3 para 9; 2012/3122, sch para 6; 2015/1945, reg 27; 1946, reg 24; 2038, sch 7 para 7

2000
c 8 *continued*

s 414 appl (mods)—SIs 2015/1945, reg 42(1); 1946, reg 39(1)
s 415 appl—SI 1995/1537, reg 23(1)
    am—Financial Services, 2012 c 21, sch 18 para 24
    rep in pt—Financial Services, 2012 c 21, s 16(14)(j)
s 415A added—Financial Services, 2010 c 28, s 24, sch 2 para 30
    am—Financial Services, 2012 c 21, sch 18 para 25
s 415B added —Financial Services, 2012 c 21, sch 9 para 41
    rep in pt—(prosp) Financial Services (Banking Reform), 2013 c 33, sch 3 para
      15(2)(b)
    am—(prosp) Financial Services (Banking Reform), 2013 c 33, sch 3 para
      15(2)(a)(3)
s 417 am—Crim. Justice and Police, 2001 c 16, s 70, sch 2 pt 2 para 16(1)(2)(f); SI
      2002/1775, reg 13(1)(2)(a)-(c); SI 2005/1433, reg 2(1), sch 1 para 15;
      Companies, 2006 c 46, s 964(1)(6); SI 2007/126, reg 3, sch 5; Banking, 2009 c
      1, s 174(2); SI 2009/1941, art 2, sch 1 para 181; Financial Services, 2010 c 28,
      s 24, sch 2 para 31; SI 2010/22, art 5, sch 2; Financial Services, 2012 c 21, s
      48(1)(b)-(f),(i)-(n), (p)-(t); SIs 2012/916, reg 2(14); 2012/1809, art 3(1), sch pt
      1; 2012/1906, art 3(14); 2012/2554, reg 2(15); (prosp) Financial Services
      (Banking Reform), 2013 c 33, s 4(5); SIs 2013/504, reg 3(15); 2013/1773, sch
      1 para 31; 2013/3115, sch 2 para 24; 2014/2879, reg 6(3); Co-operative and
      Community Benefit Societies, 2014 c 14, sch 4 para 71(2); SIs 2015/575, sch 1
      para 15; 910, sch 1 para 1(8)
    rep in pt—Financial Services, 2012 c 21, s 48(1)(a),(g)(h),(o); SI 2014/892, sch 1
      para 131; Co-operative and Community Benefit Societies, 2014 c 14, sch 4
      para 71(1)
    appl—SIs 1995/3103, reg 13(2)(b); 2000/2316, reg 7
    mod—SI 2009/814, art 7
s 418 excl—SI 2002/682, art 9(9)(d)
    am—SIs 2002/1775, reg 13(1)(3); 2012/1906, art 3(15); (prosp) 2013/1797, sch 1
      para 1(4); 2014/1292, arts 2, 5
    rep in pt—(prosp) SI 2013/1797, sch 2 para 1
s 421 appl—SI 1995/1537, reg 7(12)
    am—SI 2008/948, art 3, sch 1
s 421ZA added —Financial Services, 2012 c 21, s 48(2)
s 421A added—SI 2008/948, art 3, sch 1
s 422 subst—SI 2009/534, regs 7, 8, sch 3
    am—SI 2013/3115, sch 2 para 25
s 422A added—SI 2009/534, regs 7, 8, sch 3
    am—SIs 2011/1613, reg 2(31); 2013/3115, sch 2 para 26; 2015/1755, reg 6(3)(b)
    rep in pt—SI 2015/1755, reg 6(3)(a)
s 423 appl—Companies, 1985 c 6, sch 9 pt IV, para 3(3); SIs 1995/3103, reg 13(2)(b);
      2000/2316, reg 7
s 424A added—SI 2006/2975, reg 10
    am—SI 2007/126, reg 3, sch 5
s 425 am—SIs 2000/2952, reg 8(4); 2003/1473, reg 2(1); 2003/2066, reg 2(1); 2004/3379,
      reg 6(1)(5)(a); 2006/2975, reg 11; 2007/126, reg 3, sch 5; 2007/3253, reg 2,
      sch 1; 2012/1906, art 3(16); 2013/1773, sch 1 para 32; 2013/3115, sch 2 para
      27; 2015/575, sch 1 para 16(b); 910, sch 1 para 1(9)
    rep in pt—SI 2004/3379, reg 6(1)(5)(b); 2015/575, sch 1 para 16(a)
s 425A added—Financial Services, 2010 c 28, s 24, sch 2 para 32
    am—SIs 2013/655, art 3(4); 2013/3115, sch 2 para 28
    mod—SI 2001/544, arts 60LA(1)(3), 60S(1)(3) (added by SI 2014/366, art
      2(33)(37)
s 425B added—Financial Services, 2010 c 28, s 24, sch 2 para 32
s 425C added —Financial Services, 2012 c 21, s 48(3)
s 426 am—Crim. Justice and Police, 2001 c 16, s 70, sch 2 pt 2 para 26
s 427 am—Enterprise, 2002 c 40, s 278(1), sch 25, para 40(1)(18); SI 2014/892, sch 1 para
      132
s 429 am—Companies, 2006 c 46, s 1272, sch 15 paras 1, 12; Banking, 2009 c 1, s 178;
      Financial Services, 2010 c 28, s 24, sch 2 para 33(2)(b); Financial Services,
      2012 c 21, s 49(2)(a),(3); Financial Services (Banking Reform), 2013 c 33, s
      136; Pension Schemes, 2015 c 8, sch 3 para 12

2000

c 8 s 429 *continued*

    rep in pt—Financial Services, 2010 c 28, s 24, sch 2 para 33(2)(a)(3)(4); Financial
      Services, 2012 c 21, s 49(2)(b)

sch 1 replaced (by schs 1ZA, 1ZB) —Financial Services, 2012 c 21, s 6(2), sch 3

sch 1ZA am—Financial Services (Banking Reform), 2013 c 33, ss 109(1), 131(2), sch 3
    para 16(b)(i), sch 8 para 7(2)(3), sch 10 para 4(2)-(5)(a)(b)(d); (prosp) ibid, s
    4(6); (prosp) ibid, sch 3 para 16(b)(ii); SIs 2013/1388, reg 3(21); 2013/1773,
    sch 1 para 33; Pension Schemes, 2015 c 8, sch 3 paras 13-16

    rep in pt—Financial Services (Banking Reform), 2013 c 33, sch 10 para 4(5)(c);
      (prosp) ibid, sch 3 para 16(a)

    mod—SIs 2007/3298, reg 4(4)) (am by 2013/472, sch 2 para 131(c)); 2008/346,
      reg 45 (am by 2013/472, sch 2 para 134(f); 2009/209, regs 92(1), 94 (am by
      2013/472, sch 2 para 155(3)(a)(4)); 2013/161, art 3(8)(a)(9); 2013/1635, reg
      8; 2013/1881, art 64(6); 2015/910, arts 23(5), 25; 1945, regs 21, 22; 2038, ss
      39, 41

    ext—SI 2011/99, reg 61 (am by 2013/472, sch 2 para 196(4))

    appl—Banking, 2009 c 1, ss 39B(2), 48L(6A); SIs 2012/3122, reg 16 (am by
      2013/472, sch 2 para 248(4)); 2013/161, art 7(3); 2013/1773, reg 71(3);
      2015/910, art 23(4); 1946, reg 18(1)(2)

    ext (mods)—SIs 2011/99, reg 59(1) (am by 2013/472, sch 2 para 196(3));
      2012/3122, reg 14 (am by 2013/472, sch 2 para 248(3))

    appl (mods)—SIs 2008/346, reg 37, sch para 5) (subst by 2013/472, sch 2 para
      134(b)(g)(iii)); 2013/1635, reg 7(2); 2014/3085, regs 6-8

sch 1ZB am—Financial Services (Banking Reform), 2013 c 33, s 130(3)(a)(i)(b), sch 3 para
    17(b)(i); (prosp) ibid, s 4(7); (prosp) ibid, s 5(2)(3); (prosp) ibid, s 109(2);
    (prosp) ibid, sch 3 para 17(b)(ii)

    rep in pt—Financial Services (Banking Reform), 2013 c 33, s 130(3)(a)(ii); (prosp)
      ibid, sch 3 para 17(a)

    mod—SIs 2013/161, art 3(8)(b); (temp) ibid, art 12(3)

    appl (mods)—SI 2013/442, art 4(2)

sch 1A added—Financial Services, 2010 c 28, s 2, sch 1

    am—SI 2011/99, sch 4 para 2(6); Financial Services, 2012 c 21, sch 15; SI
      2013/1881, art 10(16)(d)

    rep in pt—Financial Services, 2012 c 21, sch 15 para 4; SI 2013/1881, art
      10(16)(a)-(c)(e)

sch 2 see—Proceeds of Crime, 2002 c 29, s 330(12), sch 9 pt 1, para 1(3)

    am —Regulation of Financial Services (Land Transactions), 2005 c 24, s 1; Dormant
      Bank and Building Society Accounts, 2008 c 31, s 15, sch 2 para 1; Financial
      Services, 2012 c 21, ss 7(2)-(5), 8; SI 2013/1881, art 10(17)(a)

    appl (mods)—SI 2003/1633, reg 15, sch 2 paras 6(1)(2)(b), 8(1)(2)(h)

    appl—Income Tax (Earnings and Pensions, 2003 c 1 s 554O(6) (added by 2013/1881,
      sch para 9(c); SI 2004/1045, reg 36(2)(c); Income Tax, 2007 c 3 s 564B(1A)
      (added by SI 2013/1881, sch para 12(b); Legal Services, 2007 c 29, s 64(6)(b);
      Corporation Tax, 2009 c 4 s 502(1A) (added by SI 2013/1881, sch para 16(b);
      SIs 2001/341, reg 114(6) (added by 2013/1881, sch para 22(b); 2001/497, reg
      113(6) (added by 2013/1881, sch para 23(b); SI 2004/400, reg 5(7) (added by
      2013/1881, sch para 25(b)); 2007/2157, reg 23(6) (added by 2013/1881, sch
      para 31(5)(b); 2008/570 sch para 11(2) (subst by 2013/1881, sch para 35;
      2008/700 sch para 12(2) (subst by 2013/1881, sch para 36; 2008/1741, reg
      112(5) (added by 2013/1881, sch para 37(b); SSI 2011/141 sch 4 para 1(2)
      (subst by 2013/1881, sch para 43(a); 2012/2079, reg 2(1A) (added by
      2013/1881, sch para 44(a)(ii)); 2013/380 sch 6 para 11(9) (added by
      2013/1881, sch para 45(b); 2013/1877, reg 2(2)(c)

    rep in pt—SI 2013/1881, art 10(17)(b)

sch 3 am—SIs 2000/2952, reg 8(5); 2001/1376, reg 2(1)-(4)(6); Enterprise, 2002 c 40, s
    278(1), sch 25, para 40(1)(19)(a)(b); SIs 2003/1473, regs 2(2), 3(1)-(4),
    4(1)-(3), 5, 6(1)(2), 7; 2003/2066, regs 2(2), 3(1), 4(1); 2004/3379, reg 6(1)(6);
    2006/2975, reg 13; Consumer Credit, 2006 c 14, s 33(9)(10)(11)(12); SIs
    2006/3221, reg 29, sch 3; 2007/108, reg 2; 2007/126, reg 3, sch 4; 2007/3253,
    reg 2, sch 1; 2010/2628, regs 3, 13, sch 1; 2011/1613, reg 2(33); 2012/916, reg
    2(15); 2012/917, sch 1 para 2; 2012/1906, art 4; Financial Services, 2012 c 21,
    sch 4; SIs 2013/1162, reg 12; 2013/3115, sch 2 para 29(2)(4)-(10); 2013/1773,
    sch 1 para 34; 2015/575, sch 1 para 17(2)(a),(3),(5)-(8); 910, sch 1 para
    1(10)(a)-(l)

2000

c 8 sch 3 *continued*

    rep in pt—SIs 2001/1376, reg 2(1)(3); 2003/1473, regs 2(2)(a)(i)(c)(ii), 4(1)(2)(b); 2003/2066, reg 2(2)(a)(i)(c)(i); 2011/1613, reg 2(33)(f); Financial Services, 2012 c 21, sch 4 paras 2(4)(b), 3(5); (prosp) SIs 2013/1797, sch 1 para 1(5); 2013/1881, art 10(18)(a)(b); 2013/3115, sch 2 para 29(3); 2015/575, sch 1 para 17(2)(b),(4)

    appl—SIs 2001/3084, arts 2-4; 2002/376, reg 2(2); 2002/682, art 9(3)(4); (W) 2003/3239, reg 20

    mod—SI 2011/99, reg 78

  sch 4 appl—SI 2002/376, reg 2(2)

    rep in pt—Financial Services, 2010 c 28, s 24, sch 2 para 35(4)

  sch 5 am—SIs 2003/2066, reg 10(a)(b); 2013/1773, sch 1 para 35

    appl—SI 2004/1450, reg 14(2)(d)(i)

  sch 6 am—SIs 2001/2507, art 2; 2002/682, art 8; 2002/2707, art 2; 2003/1476, art 19; SI 2007/126, reg 3, sch 5; Financial Services, 2012 c 21, sch 18 para 26; SIs 2013/555, art 2; 2013/1773, sch 1 para 36; (prosp) 2013/1797, sch 1 para 1(6); 2013/1881, art 10(19); 2014/366, art 5; 2015/853, art 2(2)(3)(4)(a)

    rep in pt—Financial Services, 2012 c 21, s 11(3); SI 2015/853, art 2(4)(b)

  sch 7 rep —Financial Services, 2012 c 21, s 16(14)(k)

  sch 7 am—SI 2005/381, reg 4, sch 1 para 12

  sch 8 rep —Financial Services, 2012 c 21, s 16(14)(l)

  sch 9 rep—SI 2005/1433, reg 2(1), sch 1 para 16

  sch 10 am—Financial Services, 2012 c 21, s 16(13)

  sch 10A added—SI 2010/1192, regs 2, 3

  sch 11 rep—SI 2005/1433, reg 2(1), sch 1 para 16

  sch 11A added—SI 2005/1433, reg 2(2), sch 2

    am—SIs 2006/242, art 5; 2006/3221, reg 29, sch 3; Charities, 2011 c 25, sch 7 para 86; SIs 2011/99, sch 4 para 2(7); 2011/1668, reg 1(3); 2012/1538, reg 2(4),(5); 2013/3115, sch 2 para 30; Co-operative and Community Benefit Societies, 2014 c 14, sch 4 para 72

  sch 11B added—SI 2009/2461, reg 2, sch

    am—Charities, 2011 c 25, sch 7 para 87

  sch 12 am —SI 2004/3379, reg 6(1)(7); Constitutional Reform, 2005 c 4, s 15(1), sch 4 pt 1 para 286(3); SI 2007/2403, reg 2; 2007/3253, reg 2, sch 1; Dormant Bank and Building Society Accounts, 2008 c 31, s 15, sch 2 para 5; Financial Services, 2012 c 21, sch 6 paras 10-19; Financial Services (Banking Reform), 2013 c 33, sch 1 paras 2, 13; SI 2015/575, sch 1 para 18

    appl (mods)—SIs 2001/3626, arts 3, 4, 5(2); 2001/3626, art 5(2A) (added by 2013/1765, art 5(4)(c))

  sch 13 rep—SI 2010/22, art 5, sch 2

  sch 14 rep —Financial Services, 2012 c 21, s 24(4)

    am—Enterprise, 2002 c 40, s 278(1), sch 25, para 40(1)(20)(a)(b); Communications, 2003 c 21, s 389(1), sch 16 para 5; SI 2003/1900, arts 2(1), 3(1),sch 1; SI 2003/3142, art 3(2)

    rep in pt—Enterprise, 2002 c 40, s 278, sch 25, para 40(1)(20)(c), sch 26

  sch 15 mod—SI 2013/3128, art 4(4)

  sch 16 rep —SI 2013/1881, art 10(20)

  sch 17 am—Consumer Credit, 2006 c 14, ss 59(2), 61(10); Tribunals, Cts and Enforcement, 2007 c 15, s 62, sch 13 para 134; SIs 2009/209, reg 126, sch 6; 2011/99, sch 4 para 2(8); Financial Services, 2012 c 21, sch 11 paras 14-16, 18-30; Crime and Cts, 2013 c 22, sch 9 para 52; SI 2015/542, sch 7 para 1(3)(a)(b),(d)(e)

    rep in pt—SI 2013/1881, art 10(21); 2015/542, sch 7 para 1(3)(c)

    appl —(EW) SI 1975/1023, arts 3(g), 4(e); (S) SSI 2003/231, arts 3, 5, sch 2 pt 1 para 2; SI 2011/99, reg 76(2)

    excl—SI 2001/1821, art 4(1)

    appl (mods)—SI 2009/209, reg 127, sch 7 para 3

  sch 17A added —Financial Services, 2012 c 21, s 29(2) sch 7

    am—Financial Services (Banking Reform), 2013 c 33, sch 10 para 5; SIs 2013/504, reg 3(16)(a)-(g)(i), (h); 2014/2879, reg 6(4)

    rep in pt—SI 2013/504, reg 3(16)(g)(ii)

  sch 18 rep in pt—Co-operative and Community Benefit Societies, 2014 c 14, sch 7

  sch 19 rep—Enterprise, 2002 c 40, ss 247(k), 278(2), sch 26

2000

c 8 *continued*

sch 20 rep in pt—Income Tax, 2007 c 3, s 1031, sch 3; Finance, 2007 c 11, s 114, sch 27 pt 6; SI 2009/2035, art 2, sch; Corporation Tax, 2010 c 4, s 1181, sch 3 pt 1; SI 2010/22, art 5, sch 4

sch 22 appl—SI 2013/1046, rule 10(7)(c)

c 9   *Appropriation*—rep Appropriation, 2002 c 18, s 4, sch 3

c 10   **Crown Prosecution Service Inspectorate**

s 2 am—Police and Justice, 2006 c 48, s 30(1); Anti-social Behaviour, Crime and Policing, 2014 c 12, s 149(1)

rep in pt—SI 2014/834, sch 2 para 17

sch added—Police and Justice, 2006 c 48, s 30(2)

rep in pt—Loc Govt and Public Involvement in Health, 2007 c 28, s 146, sch 9 para 1(1)(2)(o), sch 18; Health and Social Care, 2008 c 14, s 95, sch 5 para 71(1)(2)(a)(3)(a), sch 15; SI 2012/2401, sch 1 para 9(a)-(c); (Loc Audit and Accountability, 2014 c 2, sch 12 para 44(2)(3)

am—Health and Social Care, 2008 c 14, s 95, sch 5 para 71(1)(2)(b)(3)(b); SIs 2008/912, art 3, sch 1; 2012/2401, sch 1 para 9(d); Loc Audit and Accountability, 2014 c 2, sch 12 para 44(4)

c 11   **Terrorism**

see—SIs 2001/425, art 2; 2001/427, art 2

mod—SIs 1994/1405, art 7 (as am by SIs 2007/3579, art 3; 2015/856, arts 5,6); 2009/317, art 3, sch; 2011/631, art 2-4, sch 1

appl (mods)—SI 2011/245, sch 6 pt 1

s 1 appl—Highways, 1980 c 66, s 329; Road Traffic Regulation, 1984 c 27, ss 22C(6), 67(1A); Roads (S), 1984 c 66, ss 39BA, 40; Railways, 1993 c 43, s 119; Anti-terrorism, Crime and Security, 2001 c 24, s 21(5)

am—Terrorism, 2006 c 11, s 34(a); Counter-Terrorism, 2008 c 28, s 75(1)(2)(a)

s 2 am—Commrs for Revenue and Customs, 2005 c 11, s 50(6), sch 4 para 77

s 3 am—Terrorism, 2006 c 11, ss 21, 22(2)

s 4 am—Terrorism, 2006 c 11, s 22(3)(4)

s 5 rep in pt—Terrorism, 2006 c 11, s 37, sch 3

am—Terrorism, 2006 c 11, s 22(5)(6)

s 6 am —Constitutional Reform, 2005 c 4, s 40(4), sch 9 pt 1 para 71

s 7 am—Terrorism, 2006 c 11, s 22(7)(8)

s 9 am—Regulation of Investigatory Powers, 2000 c 23, s 82(1), sch 4 para 12(1); Terrorism, 2006 c 11, s 22(9)

rep in pt—Terrorism, 2006 c 11, s 37, sch 3

ss 15-23 appl—SI 2001/192, reg 3

s 17A added—Counter-Terrorism and Security, 2015 c 6, s 42(1)

s 19 am—Anti-terrorism, Crime and Security, 2001 c 24, s 3, sch 2 pt 3 para 5(1)(3)(4); Serious Organised Crime and Police, 2005 c 15, s 59, sch 4 paras 125-127; Counter-Terrorism, 2008 c 28, s 77(1)(2); Crime and Cts, 2013 c 22, sch 8 para 68

excl—SI 2001/192, reg 4

s 20 am—Anti-terrorism, Crime and Security, 2001 c 24, s 3, sch 2 pt 3 para 5(1)(5); Serious Organised Crime and Police, 2005 c 15, s 59, sch 4 paras 125-127; Crime and Cts, 2013 c 22, sch 8 para 69

s 21 mod—Counter-Terrorism, 2008 c 28, s 77(4)

s 21ZA added—SI 2007/3398, reg 2, sch 1

am—Crime and Cts, 2013 c 22, sch 8 para 70

s 21ZB added—SI 2007/3398, reg 2, sch 1

am—Crime and Cts, 2013 c 22, sch 8 para 71

s 21ZC added—SI 2007/3398, reg 2, sch 1

s 21A added—Anti-terrorism, Crime and Security, 2001 c 24, s 3, sch 2 pt 3 para 5(1)(2)

am—Serious Organised Crime and Police, 2005 c 15, s 59, sch 4 paras 125, 128; SI 2007/3398, reg 2, sch 1; Crime and Cts, 2013 c 22, sch 8 para 72

mod—Counter-Terrorism, 2008 c 28, s 77(4)

s 21B added—Anti-terrorism, Crime and Security, 2001 c 24, s 3, sch 2 pt 3 para 5(1)(2)

am—Serious Organised Crime and Police, 2005 c 15, s 59, sch 4 paras 125, 129; SI 2007/3398, reg 2, sch 1; Crime and Cts, 2013 c 22, sch 8 para 73

s 21C added—SI 2007/3398, reg 2, sch 1

am—Crime and Cts, 2013 c 22, sch 8 para 74

s 21D added—SI 2007/3398, reg 2, sch 1

am—Crime and Cts, 2013 c 22, sch 8 para 75

2000

c 11 *continued*

ss 21E-21H added—SI 2007/3398, reg 2, sch 1

s 22A added—Counter-Terrorism, 2008 c 28, s 77(1)(3)(4)

s 23 subst—Counter-Terrorism, 2008 c 28, s 34

    am—Counter-Terrorism and Security, 2015 c 6, s 42(2)

s 23A added—Counter-Terrorism, 2008 c 28, s 35(1)

s 23B added—Counter-Terrorism, 2008 c 28, s 36

ss 24-31 rep—Anti-terrorism, Crime and Security, 2001 c 24, ss 1(4), 125, sch 8 pt 1

s 32 am—Terrorism, 2006 c 11, s 37(1)

s 34 am—Anti-terrorism, Crime and Security, 2001 c 24, s 101, sch 7 paras 29, 30;

    Railways and Transport Safety, 2003 c 20, s 73, sch 5 para 4(1)(a)(2)(k); SI

    2004/1573, art 12(6)(a)(b)

s 36 am—(prosp) (EW) Crim Justice, 2003 c 44, s 280(2)(3), sch 26 para 55(1)(2);

    Coroners and Justice, 2009 c 25, s 117(1)-(3)

s 38A added—Anti-terrorism, Crime and Security, 2001 c 24, s 3, sch 2 pt 1 para 1(1)(2)

s 38B added—Anti-terrorism, Crime and Security, 2001 c 24, s 117(1)(2)

s 39 am—Anti-terrorism, Crime and Security, 2001 c 24, s 117(1)(3); SI 2007/3398, reg 2,

    sch 1

    appl—SI 2001/192, reg 3

s 40 am—Protection of Freedoms, 2012 c 9, sch 9 para 24

s 43 ext—Crim. Justice and Police, 2001 c 16, s 51, sch 1 pt 2 para 82

    saved—Extradition, 2003 c 41, s 163(9) (see SI 2003/3103, arts 2-5)

    rep in pt—Protection of Freedoms, 2012 c 9, s 60(1), sch 10 pt 4

    am—Protection of Freedoms, 2012 c 9, s 60(2)

s 43A added—Protection of Freedoms, 2012 c 9, s 60(3)

ss 44-47 rep—Protection of Freedoms, 2012 c 9, s 59, sch 10 pt 4

s 47A added—Protection of Freedoms, 2012 c 9, s 61(1)

ss 47AA-47AE added—Protection of Freedoms, 2012 c 9, s 62

s 48 am—SI 2013/602, sch 2 para 32(2)

s 51 am—(prosp) (EW) Crim Justice, 2003 c 44, s 280(2)(3), sch 26 para 55(1)(3)

s 54 am—Anti-terrorism, Crime and Security, 2001 c 24, s 120(1); Crim Justice and Cts,

    2015 c 2, s 1(2)

    rep in pt—Counter-Terrorism, 2008 c 28, s 39, sch 3 paras 2, 3, sch 9

s 55 am—Anti-terrorism, Crime and Security, 2001 c 24, s 120(2)(a)(b)

    rep in pt—Anti-terrorism, Crime and Security, 2001 c 24, ss 120(2)(c), 125, sch 8 pt 7

s 57 am—Terrorism, 2006 c 11, s 13

s 58 rep in pt—Counter-Terrorism, 2008 c 28, s 39, sch 3 paras 2, 4, sch 9

s 58A added—Counter-Terrorism, 2008 c 28, s 76(1)(2)

ss 63A-63E added—Crime (International Co-operation), 2003 c 32, s 52

s 63A rep in pt—Terrorism, 2006 c 11, s 37, sch 3

s 63C am—SIs 2004/3224, reg 4; 2012/1809, art 3(1), sch pt 1

s 64 rep—Extradition, 2003 c 41, ss 219, 220, sch 3 paras 1, 11, sch 4 (see SI 2003/3103,

    arts 2-5)

Pt 7 (ss 65-113) see (provision for cesser)—Terrorism, 2000 c 11, s 112(1)(2)

    cont in force (except s 78)—(cont in force to 31.7.2007) Terrorism (NI), 2006 c 4, s 1

s 67 rep in pt—SI 2005/350, art 2(2)(a); Terrorism (NI), 2006 c 4, s 2(2), sch 1

ss 70, 71 rep—SI 2005/350, art 2(2)(b)(c); Terrorism (NI), 2006 c 4, s 2(2), sch 1

s 72 am—Justice (NI), 2002 c 26, s 28(1), sch 7, paras 21, 22; SI 2004/1500, art 29(2)

s 74 am —Constitutional Reform, 2005 c 4, s 15(1), sch 4 pt 1 paras 287, 288(1)(2)(a)(3)

s 74 rep in pt —Constitutional Reform, 2005 c 4, ss 15(1), 146, sch 4 pt 1 paras 287,

    288(1)(2)(b)(c)

s 75 saved—(pt prosp) Crim Justice, 2003 c 44, s 50(2); (NI) Domestic Violence, Crime and

    Victims, 2004 c 28, s 21(2)

s 76 rep—SI 2002/2141, art 2; Terrorism (NI), 2006 c 4, s 2(2), sch 1

s 78 rep—Terrorism (NI), 2006 c 4, s 2(2), sch 1

s 82 ext—Crim. Justice and Police, 2001 c 16, s 50, sch 1 pt 1 para 70

s 97 rep—Terrorism (NI), 2006 c 4, s 2(2), sch 1

s 100 rep—Terrorism (NI), 2006 c 4, s 2(2), sch 1

s 101 rep in pt—Armed Forces, 2001 c 19, s 38, sch 7 pt 1

    am—Police (NI), 2003 c 6, s 32(1), sch 3 para 8

s 103 am—Justice (NI), 2004 c 4, s 14

ss 104-111 cont in force—Terrorism (NI), 2006 c 4, s 1

s 112 am—Terrorism (NI), 2006 c 4, ss 1(4), 2(3)

s 117 am—Terrorism, 2006 c 11, s 37(2); Counter-Terrorism, 2008 c 28, s 29

2000

c 11 *continued*

s 118 am—Counter-Terrorism, 2008 c 28, s 76(3)

s 119 am—Counter-Terrorism, 2008 c 28, s 39, sch 3 paras 2, 5

s 120A added—Terrorism, 2006 c 11, s 37(3)

    subst—Counter-Terrorism, 2008 c 28, s 38(1)

s 121 am—Anti-terrorism, Crime and Security, 2001 c 24, s 101, sch 7 paras 29, 32; Crime (International Co-operation), 2003 c 32, s 91(1), sch 5 paras 75, 76

    rep in pt—Railways and Transport Safety, 2003 c 20, s 73, sch 5 para 4(1)(b)(2)(k); SI 2004/1573, art 12(6)(d)

    am—Railways and Transport Safety, 2003 c 20, s 73, sch 5 para 4(1)(a)(2)(k); Commrs for Revenue and Customs, 2005 c 11, s 50(6), sch 4 para 78

s 122 am—Anti-terrorism, Crime and Security, 2001 c 24, s 101, sch 7 paras 29, 33; Railways and Transport Safety, 2003 c 20, s 73, sch 5 para 4(1)(a)(2)(k)

    rep in pt—Anti-terrorism, Crime and Security, 2001 c 24, s 125, sch 8 pt 1

s 123 am—Crime (International Co-operation), 2003 c 32, ss 90, 91(1), sch 4 paras 1, 2, sch 5 paras 75, 77; Terrorism, 2006 c 11, s 22(1)(10); Counter-Terrorism, 2008 c 28, s 35(2); Protection of Freedoms, 2012 c 9, s 58(2), sch 9 para 25(2),(3)

    rep in pt—Terrorism (NI), 2006 c 4, s 51, sch 1

s 126 rep—Terrorism, 2006 c 11, s 37, sch 3

sch 2 am—SIs 2001/1261, art 2; 2002/2724, arts 2, 3; 2005/2892, art 2; 2006/2016, art 2; 2007/2184, art 2; 2008/1931, art 2; 2010/611, art 2; 2011/108, art 2; 2012/1771, art 2; 2013/1746, art 2; 2013/3172, art 2; 2014/927, art 2; 2014/1624, art 2; 2014/3189, art 2; 2015/55, art 2; 959, art 2

    rep in pt—SI 2008/1645, art 2

    mod—SIs 2011/2688, art 2(1); 2014/2210, art 2

    ext—SI 2013/2742, art 2

sch 3 am—Regulation of Investigatory Powers, 2000 c 23, s 82(1), sch 4 para 12(2); Pensions, 2004 c 35, s 319(1), sch 12 para 78; Constitutional Reform, 2005 c 4, ss 15(1), 145, sch 4 pt 1 paras 287, 289, sch 17 pt 2 para 29; Terrorism, 2006 c 11, s 22(1)(11); Counter-Terrorism, 2008 c 28, s 91(1)(2)

    rep in pt—Regulation of Investigatory Powers, 2000 c 23, s 82(1), sch 5

sch 3A added—Anti-terrorism, Crime and Security, 2001 c 24, s 3, sch 2 pt 3 para 5(1)(6)

    am—Enterprise, 2002 c 40, s 278(1), sch 25, para 41; SI 2003/3076, arts 2, 3, sch; Gambling, 2005 c 19, s 356(1)(2), sch 16 pt 2 para 13; SIs 2006/2384, art 2; 2006/3221, reg 29, sch 4; 2007/207, art 2; 2007/3288, art 2; 2008/948, art 3, sch 1; Localism, 2011 c 20, sch 18 para 1(a); SIs 2011/99, sch 4 para 3(a); 2011/2701, art 2; 2012/1534, art 2; 2012/2299, art 2(b); Financial Services, 2012 c 21, sch 18 para 87(2); SI 2013/3115, sch 2 para 40(2)(a)-(c)(d)(ii)(e); Co-operative and Community Benefit Societies, 2014 c 14, sch 4 para 73(2)(3); SI 2015/575, sch 1 para 21(2)(a),(b)(ii)

    rep in pt—Localism, 2011 c 20, sch 18 para 1(b), sch 25 pt 29; SIs 2012/2299, art 2(a); 2013/3115, sch 2 para 40(2)(d)(i); 2014/892, sch 1 para 148; 2015/575, sch 1 para 21(2)(b)(i)

sch 4 appl—(EW) SI 2001/3927, art 11(1); (S) SI 2001/3927, art 18; (NI) SI 2001/3927, art 25(1)

    appl (mods)—(EW) SI 2001/3927, art 11(1); (NI) SI 2001/3927, art 25(1)

    am—Anti-terrorism, Crime and Security, 2001 c 24, s 3, sch 2 pt 2 paras 2(1)-(7), 3(1)-(6), 4(1)-(5)(7); Land Registration, 2002 c 9, s 133, sch 11, para 38; Justice (NI), 2002 c 26, s 85(1), sch 12, para 80; Crime (International Co-operation), 2003 c 32, s 90, sch 4 paras 1, 3-9; Courts, 2003 c 39, s 109(1), sch 8 para 388(1)-(4); (prosp) Crim Justice, 2003 c 44, s 311, sch 36 pt 2 para 14; SI 2013/602, sch 2 para 32(3); Crim Justice and Cts, 2015 c 2, sch 11 para 17

    ext—(EW) SI 2001/3927, art 12; (S) SI 2001/3927, art 19; (NI) SI 2001/3927, art 26

    am—Anti-terrorism, Crime and Security, 2001 c 24, s 3, sch 2 pt 2 para 4(1)(6); Counter-Terrorism, 2008 c 28, ss 37, 39, sch 3 paras 2, 5(1)-(7)(9)-(29)

    rep in pt—Land Registration, 2002 c 9, s 135, sch 13; SI 2003/427, art 2(2)(b); Terrorism (NI), 2006 c 4, s 2(2), sch 1; (prosp) (S) Bankruptcy and Diligence etc (S), 2007 asp 3, s 226, sch 6; Counter-Terrorism, 2008 c 28, s 39, sch 3 paras 2, 5(1)(8)

sch 5 ext—Crim. Justice and Police, 2001 c 16, ss 50, 51, 55, sch 1 pt 1 para 71, pt 2 para 83, pt 3 para 109(1)(2)

    am—Anti-terrorism, Crime and Security, 2001 c 24, ss 121(1)(2)(b)(3); Crim. Justice and Police, 2001 c 16, s 70, sch 2 pt 2 para 27; (prosp) (EW) Crim Justice, 2003 c 44, s 280(2)(3), sch 26 para 55(1)(4)(a)(b); Courts, 2003 c 39, s 109(1), sch 8

2000

c 11 sch 5 *continued*

    para 389(1)-(3); ibid, s 65, sch 4 para 9; Terrorism, 2006 c 11, ss 26, 27; (S)
    Crim Justice and Licensing (S), 2010 asp 13, s 203, sch 7 para 69; Deregulation,
    2015 c 20, s 82(4)

   rep in pt—Anti-terrorism, Crime and Security, 2001 c 24, ss 121(1)(2)(a), 125, sch 8
    pt 7; SI 2003/427, art 2(2)(c); Terrorism (NI), 2006 c 4, s 2(2), sch 1;
    Terrorism, 2006 c 11, s 37, sch 3

  sch 6 am—SI 2000/2952, reg 9; Anti-terrorism, Crime and Security, 2001 c 24, s 3, sch 2
    pt 4 para 6; Anti-terrorism, Crime and Security, 2001 c 24, s 121(1)(4);
    SI 2001/3649, art 361(1)(2)(a)(c)(3); Courts, 2003 c 39, s 109, sch 8 para 390;
    ibid, s 65, sch 4 paras 10, 11; SIs 2004/3379, reg 7; 2006/3384, art 33;
    2006/3221, reg 29, sch 4; 2011/99, sch 4 para 3(b); Financial Services, 2012 c
    21, sch 18 para 87(3); SIs 2013/1773, sch 1 para 41; 2013/3115, sch 2 para
    40(3); 2015/575, sch 1 para 21(3)

   rep in pt—SI 2001/3649, art 361(1)(2)(b)

  sch 6A added—Anti-terrorism, Crime and Security, 2001 c 24, s 3, sch 2 pt 1 para 1(1)(3)

  sch 6B added—Protection of Freedoms, 2012 c 9, sch 5

   am—SI 2013/602, sch 2 para 32(4)

  sch 7 mod—SI 1993/1813, sch 4 para 3

   rep in pt—Anti-social Behaviour, Crime and Policing, 2014 c 12, sch 9 para 2(2)

   am—Anti-terrorism, Crime and Security, 2001 c 24, s 118(1)-(4); (prosp) (EW) Crim
    Justice, 2003 c 44, s 280(2)(3), sch 26 para 55(1)(5); Terrorism, 2006 c 11, s 29;
    SI 2011/1938, art 2(2); Anti-social Behaviour, Crime and Policing, 2014 c 12,
    sch 9 paras 1, 2(3), 3, 4; Counter-Terrorism and Security, 2015 c 6, sch 5 para 4,
    sch 8 para 1

   ext (mods)—SI 2003/2818, art 11(1)(b), sch 2 para 2(1)

   ext—SI 2003/2818, art 12(4)

  sch 8 see—SI 2001/159, art 2; (NI) SI 2001/402, art 2

   am—Anti-terrorism, Crime and Security, 2001 c 24, s 89(1)-(4); (EWNI) Crim.
    Justice and Police, 2001 c 16, ss 75, 84; Proceeds of Crime, 2002 c 29, s 456,
    sch 11, para 39(1)-(5); Crim Justice, 2003 c 44, s 306(1)-(4); Constitutional
    Reform, 2005 c 4, s 15(1), sch 4 pt 1 paras 287, 290; Serious Organised Crime
    and Police, 2005 c 15, s 111, sch 7 pt 3 para 48; Terrorism, 2006 c 11, ss 23, 24,
    25; Counter-Terrorism, 2008 c 28, ss 39, 82(1), sch 3 paras 2, 6; Protection of
    Freedoms, 2012 c 9, ss 57(1), 58(1); (pt prosp) ibid, sch 1 para 1(4); ibid, sch 1
    para 1(5)-(8)-(8); ibid, sch 9 para 26(2); Anti-social Behaviour, Crime and
    Policing, 2014 c 12, s 146(2); ibid, sch 9 para 5(2)(4)(6)(7)(8)(b)(9)(10)-(12),
    6(2)(3), 7(2)(a)(3); ibid, sch 9 para 7(2)(b); ibid, sch 11 para 125(2)(3)

   ext (mods)—SI 2003/2818, art 11(1)(b), sch 2 para 2(2)

   appl—SI 2003/1100, art 2

   appl (mods)—Prevention of Terrorism, 2005 c 2, s 5(8)

   rep in pt—Courts, 2003 c 39, s 109(1)(3), sch 8 para 391, sch 10; Terrorism, 2006 c
    11, ss 23(6), 25(4)(b)(c)(d), 37, sch 3; Counter-Terrorism, 2008 c 28, s 82(2);
    (prosp) ibid, s 16(1)(4), sch 9; Protection of Freedoms, 2012 c 9, sch 9 para
    26(3), (4), sch 10 pt 4; ibid, sch 1 para 1(2), (3), sch 10 pt 1; Anti-social
    Behaviour, Crime and Policing, 2014 c 12, sch 9 para 5(3)(5)(8)(a)

  sch 8A added—Counter-Terrorism, 2008 c 28, s 76, sch 8

   am—SI 2012/1809, art 3(1), sch pt 1

  sch 9 am—Justice (NI), 2002 c 26, s 28, sch 7, paras 21, 23; Justice (NI), 2004 c 4, s 11,
    sch 2 para 1(5); Fraud, 2006 c 35, s 14, sch 1 para 30(1)(2)(3); Terrorism (NI),
    2006 c 4, s 3(1)(c)(2)-(5); Terrorism, 2006 c 11, s 37(4)

   rep in pt—Fraud, 2006 c 35, s 14, sch 1 para 30(1), sch 3; Terrorism (NI), 2006 c 4, s
    3(1)(a)(b), sch 1

  sch 10 am—Wireless Telegraphy, 2006 c 36, s 123, sch 7 para 20

  sch 12 rep in pt—Fraud, 2006 c 35, s 14, sch 1 para 31(1), sch 3

   am—Fraud, 2006 c 35, s 14, sch 1 para 31(2)

  sch 14 am —Anti-terrorism, Crime and Security, 2001 c 24, s 2(4)-(7); Serious Organised
    Crime and Police, 2005 c 15, s 59, sch 4 paras 125, 130; Crime and Cts, 2013 c
    22, sch 8 para 76; Anti-social Behaviour, Crime and Policing, 2014 c 12, sch 9
    para 8

   ext (mods)—SI 2003/2818, art 11(1)(b), sch 2 para 2(3)

  sch 15 rep in pt—Proceeds of Crime, 2002 c 29, s 457, sch 12; Crim Justice, 2003 c 44,
    s 332, sch 37 pt 7; Serious Organised Crime and Police, 2005 c 15, s 174(2),

2000
c 11 *continued*

sch 17 pt 2; Legal Aid, Sentencing and Punishment of Offenders, 2012 c 10, sch 5 pt 2

c 12   **Limited Liability Partnerships**
ext (to EW, S and NI)—Limited Liability Partnership, 2000, s 19 (as am)
ext—Companies, 2006 c 46, s 1286(1)(a)
s 2 am—SIs 2002/915, reg 16, sch 2, para 1; 2009/1804, reg 85, sch 3 para 1
rep in pt—SI 2009/1804, reg 85, sch 3 para 1
s 3 am—SI 2009/1804, reg 85, sch 3 para 2
s 4 restr—Soc Security Contributions and Benefits, 1992 c 4, s 4AA(6)
s 4A added—SI 2009/1804, reg 85, sch 3 para 3
s 8 rep in pt—SI 2009/1804, reg 85, sch 3 para 4
s 9 am—SIs 2002/915, reg 16, sch 2, para 3; 2009/1804, reg 85, sch 3 para 5
rep in pt—SI 2009/1804, reg 85, sch 3 para 5
s 10 rep in pt—Income Tax, 2007 c 3, s 1031, sch 3; Corporation Tax, 2010 c 4, s 1181, sch 3 pt 1
s 14 am—SI 2009/1804, reg 85, sch 3 para 6
s 17 am—SI 2009/1804, reg 85, sch 3 para 7
s 18 appl—SI 2003/1375, art 6(c)
am and rep in pt—SI 2009/1804, reg 85, sch 3 para 8
s 19 am—SI 2009/1804, reg 85, sch 3 para 9
sch rep in pt—SI 2001/1228, reg 84, sch 7 pt I para 11; Companies, 2006 c 46, s 129, sch 16; SI 2009/1804, reg 85, sch 3 para 10
am—SI 2001/1228, reg 84, sch 7 pt I para 11; Companies (Audit, Investigations and Community Enterprise), 2004 c 27, s 33(6), sch 6 para 10; SI 2009/1804, reg 85, sch 3 para 10

c 13   **Royal Parks (Trading)**
ss 4-6 see—(power to apply) Parks Regulation (Amdt), 1926 c 36, s 2
s 4 appl—SI 1997/1639, reg 3C (added by 2012/957, reg 2(2))
am —Serious Organised Crime and Police, 2005 c 15, s 161(5), sch 13 pt 2 para 9
ss 5,6 appl—SI 1997/1639, reg 3C (added by 2012/957, reg 2(2))

c 14   **Care Standards**
appl—Educ, 2002 c 32, s 168(2)(a); Adoption and Children, 2002 c 38, s 8(1)(2); SI 2002/446, art 2(5); Sexual Offences, 2003 c 42, s 42(5); Crim Justice, 2003 c 44, s 207(2)(a); (E) SI 2005/1109, reg 4(2)(b)
s 1 appl—(E) SIs 1991/890, reg 2(2); 1991/895, reg 13; 1991/894, reg 11A; Sexual Offences, 2003 c 42, s 42(5); (E) SI 2005/1972, reg 2(1)(i)-(l)
am—Health and Social Care, 2008 c 14, s 95, sch 5 para 2
s 2 am—(E) SI 2001/3968, reg 3; (W) SI 2002/325 (W 38), reg 3(4); Health and Social Care (Community Health and Standards), 2003 c 43, s 106; Nat Health Service (Conseq Provns), 2006 c 43, s 2, sch 1 para 199; Health and Social Care, 2008 c 14, s 95, sch 5 para 3
appl—SIs 1988/1724, reg 1A; 1991/2890, reg 9 and 1991/2740, reg 7; Sexual Offences, 2003 c 42, s 42(5); Licensing, 2003 c 17, s 16(3); SIs 1992/1813, regs 40, 40ZA; 2001/157, regs 14, 15; (E) SI 2005/1972, reg 2(1)(i)-(l); Mental Capacity, 2005 c 9, s 38(7)(b)
s 3 appl—SIs 1988/1724, reg 1A; 1991/2890, reg 9; 1991/2740, reg 7; 1992/1813, regs 40, 40ZA; 2001/157, regs 14, 15; 2004/293, reg 10, sch 2 pt 2 para 16(d)(i); Mental Capacity, 2005 c 9, s 38(6)
am—Health and Social Care, 2008 c 14, s 95, sch 5 para 4
s 4 am—Adoption and Children, 2002 c 38, ss 8(3), 139(1), sch 3, paras 103-105; (E prosp) Health and Social Care (Community Health and Standards), 2003 c 43, s 107(1); SI 2004/1771, art 3, sch pt 1 para 2(a); (W prosp) Children and Young Persons, 2008 c 23, s 4(1); Health and Social Care, 2008 c 14, s 95, sch 5 para 5
appl—SI 2004/3136, reg 6, sch; (E) SI 2005/1972, reg 2(1)(m)-(p)
rep in pt—Deregulation, 2015 c 20, s 93(1)
s 5 am—Adoption and Children, 2002 c 38, s 139(1), sch 3, paras 103-105; Health and Social Care (Community Health and Standards), 2003 c 43, s 147, sch 9 paras 16, 17; Educ and Inspections, 2006 c 40, s 157, sch 14 para 38, 39; (W prosp) (conditional) Children and Young Persons, 2008 c 23, s 4(2); Health and Social Care, 2008 c 14, s 95, sch 5 para 6
rep in pt—(prosp) Children and Young Persons, 2008 c 23, s 42, sch 4; Deregulation, 2015 c 20, s 93(2)(a)(i)
s 5A added—Health and Social Care (Community Health and Standards), 2003 c 43, s 103

2000

c 14 s 5A *continued*

    rep—Health and Social Care, 2008 c 14, s 95, sch 5 para 7, sch 15

s 5B added—Health and Social Care (Community Health and Standards), 2003 c 43, s 104

    rep—Health and Social Care, 2008 c 14, s 95, sch 5 para 7, sch 15

ss 6, 7 rep—Health and Social Care (Community Health and Standards), 2003 c 43, s 196, sch 14 pt 2

s 8 am—Health and Social Care (Community Health and Standards), 2003 c 43, ss 109, 147, sch 9 paras 16, 18; Educ and Inspections, 2006 c 40, s 157, sch 14 para 40; Health and Social Care, 2008 c 14, s 95, sch 5 para 8(1)-(3)

    rep in pt—Health and Social Care, 2008 c 14, s 95, sch 5 para 8(1)(4), sch 15

s 9 rep—Health and Social Care (Community Health and Standards), 2003 c 43, s 196, sch 14 pt 2

s 10 rep in pt—Health and Social Care (Community Health and Standards), 2003 c 43, ss 147, 196, sch 9 paras 16, 19(a), sch 14 pt 2; Health and Social Care, 2008 c 14, s 95, sch 5 para 9, sch 15

    am—Health and Social Care (Community Health and Standards), 2003 c 43, s 147, sch 9 paras 16, 19(b); Educ and Inspections, 2006 c 40, s 157, sch 14 para 41

Pt 2 (ss 11-42) restr—Adoption and Children, 2002 c 38, s 2(4)

    trans of functions—Health and Social Care (Community Health and Standards), 2003 c 43, s 102(1)-(3)

    appl (mods)—(W) SI 2004/1756 (W 188), reg 3(3), sch 1; (E) SI 2004/2071, regs 40, 45, sch 5, sch 10

    appl—SI 2008/1976 (W 185), reg 3, sch 1

s 11 am—Adoption and Children, 2002 c 38, s 139(1), sch 3, paras 103, 106; Health and Social Care (Community Health and Standards), 2003 c 43, s 147, sch 9 paras 16, 20; Educ and Inspections, 2006 c 40, s 157, sch 14 para 42; Health and Social Care, 2008 c 14, s 95, sch 5 para 10(b)

    rep in pt—Health and Social Care, 2008 c 14, s 95, sch 5 para 10(a)(c), sch 15

    appl (mods)—SIs 2013/1394, sch 7 para 1; 2013/253, reg 2(1)(2)(a), sch

s 12 am—Health and Social Care (Community Health and Standards), 2003 c 43, s 105(1)(3); Educ and Inspections, 2006 c 40, s 157, sch 14 para 43; Health and Social Care, 2008 c 14, s 95, sch 5 para 11

    appl—SI 2006/878 (W 83), reg 3

    appl (mods)—SIs 2013/1394, sch 7 para 2; 2013/253, reg 2(1)(2)(b), sch

s 13 appl (mods)—SI 2013/1394, sch 7 para 3

s 14 am—Adoption and Children, 2002 c 38, s 139(1), sch 3, paras 103, 107; Health and Social Care, 2008 c 14, s 95, sch 5 para 12; (W prosp) Children and Young Persons, 2008 c 23, s 26(1)

    appl (mods)—(E) SIs 2004/1972, regs 2, 3; 2013/1394, sch 7 para 4; 2013/253, reg 2(1)(2)(c), sch

s 14A added —Health and Social Care, 2008 c 14, s 95, sch 5 para 13

    am—Children and Families, 2014 c 6, s 102(1)(a)(2)

    rep in pt—Children and Families, 2014 c 6, s 102(1)(b)

s 15 am—Health and Social Care (Community Health and Standards), 2003 c 43, s 105(1)(4)(5); Educ and Inspections, 2006 c 40, s 157, sch 14 para 44; Health and Social Care, 2008 c 14, s 95, sch 5 para 14; Children and Families, 2014 c 6, s 102(3)

    appl (mods)—(E) SIs 2004/1972, regs 2, 3; SI 2013/253, reg 2(1)(2)(d), sch

    appl—SI 2006/878 (W 83), reg 3

s 16 rep in pt—Adoption and Children, 2002 c 38, s 139(3), sch 3, paras 103, 108, sch 5

    am—Health and Social Care (Community Health and Standards), 2003 c 43, s 105(1)(6); Educ and Inspections, 2006 c 40, s 157, sch 14 para 45; Health and Social Care, 2008 c 14, s 95, sch 5 para 15

    appl (mods)—(E) SIs 2004/1972, regs 2, 3; 2013/253, reg 2(1)(2)(e) sch

    appl—SI 2006/878 (W 83), reg 3

s 17 appl (mods)—(E) SIs 2004/1972, regs 2, 3; 2013/1394, sch 7 para 5

    am—Health and Social Care, 2008 c 14, s 95, sch 5 para 16

s 18 appl (mods)—(E) SI 2004/1972, regs 2, 3

s 19 appl (mods)—(E) SIs 2004/1972, regs 2, 3; 2013/1394, sch 7 para 6

    am—Health and Social Care, 2008 c 14, s 95, sch 5 para 17(b)

    rep in pt—Health and Social Care, 2008 c 14, s 95, sch 5 para 17(a), sch 15

s 20 am—Nat Health Service Reform and Health Care Professions, 2002 c 17, s 2(5), sch 2 pt 2, para 70; (W) SI 2007/961 (W 85), art 3, sch; Health and Social Care, 2008 c 14, s 95, sch 5 para 18(1)-(6)

2000
c 14 s 20 *continued*
  appl (mods)—(E) SIs 2004/1972, regs 2, 3; 2013/1394, sch 7 para 7
 ss 20A, 20B added —Health and Social Care, 2008 c 14, s 95, sch 5 para 19
 s 20B am—Children and Families, 2014 c 6, s 102(4)(5)(a)
  rep in pt—Children and Families, 2014 c 6, s 102(5)(b)(6)(7)
 s 21 appl (mods)—(E) SIs 2004/1972, regs 2, 3; 2013/1394, sch 7 para 8
  rep in pt—(W 28.3.11) Children and Young Persons, 2008 c 23, ss 28(1)(5), 42, sch 4;
   Health and Social Care, 2008 c 14, s 95, sch 5 para 20(1)(5)(a), sch 15
  am—Health and Social Care, 2008 c 14, s 95, sch 5 para 20(1)-(4)(5)(b)(6); Children
   and Young Persons, 2008 c 23, s 28(1)-(4)
 s 22 am—Adoption and Children, 2002 c 38, s 139(1), sch 3, paras 103, 109; Health and
   Social Care (Community Health and Standards), 2003 c 43, s 105(1)(7); (E
   prosp) ibid, s 107(2)(b); Educ and Inspections, 2006 c 40, s 157, sch 14 para 46;
   (W prosp) Children and Young Persons, 2008 c 23, s 8, sch 1 para 11; Health and
   Social Care, 2008 c 14, s 95, sch 5 para 21; Children and Families, 2014 c 6, s
   103; (prosp) Social Services and Well-being (W), 2014 anaw 4, s 183
  rep in pt—(E prosp) Health and Social Care (Community Health and Standards), 2003
   c 43, ss 107(2)(a), 196, sch 14 pt 2
  appl (mods)—(E) SIs 2004/1972, regs 2, 3; 2013/253, reg 2(1)(2)(f), sch
  appl—SI 2006/878 (W 83), reg 3
 s 22A added (W prosp)—Children and Young Persons, 2008 c 23, s 26(2)
  appl (mods)—SI 2013/1394, sch 7 para 9
 s 22B added —Children and Young Persons, 2008 c 23, s 27
  appl (mods)—SI 2013/1394, sch 7 para 10
 s 23 am—Adoption and Children, 2002 c 38, s 139(1), sch 3, paras 103, 110; (W prosp)
   Health and Social Care (Community Health and Standards), 2003 c 43, s 147, sch
   9 paras 16, 21; Children and Young Persons, 2008 c 23, s 28(6); Children and
   Families, 2014 c 6, s 104
  appl (mods)—(E) SIs 2004/1972, regs 2, 3; 2013/253, reg 2(1)reg 2(2)(g) sch
 s 24 appl (mods)—(E) SIs 2004/1972, regs 2, 3; 2013/1394, sch 7 para 11
 s 24A added—Health and Social Care, 2008 c 14, s 95, sch 5 para 22
  appl (mods)—SI 2013/1394, sch 7 para 12
 s 25 appl (mods)—(E) SIs 2004/1972, regs 2, 3; 2013/253, reg 2(1)reg 2(2)(h) sch
 s 26 am—Health and Social Care, 2008 c 14, s 95, sch 5 para 23
  appl (mods)—(E) SIs 2004/1972, regs 2, 3; 2013/1394, sch 7 para 13
 s 27 appl (mods)—(E) SI 2004/1972, regs 2, 3
 s 28 appl (mods)—(E) SIs 2004/1972, regs 2, 3; 2008/1976 (W 185), reg 4; 2013/1394, sch
   7 para 14
 s 29 saved—(W) SI 2002/327 (W 40), reg 40(2)
  am—Health and Social Care (Community Health and Standards), 2003 c 43, s 147, sch
   9 paras 16, 22; Educ and Inspections, 2006 c 40, s 157, sch 14 para 47; Health
   and Social Care, 2008 c 14, s 95, sch 5 para 24
  appl (mods)—(E) SI 2004/1972, regs 2, 3
 s 30 appl (mods)—(E) SI 2004/1972, regs 2, 3
 ss 30ZA, 30ZB added—Health and Social Care, 2008 c 14, s 95, sch 5 para 25
 s 30ZB am—SI 2015/664, sch 5 para 8
 s 30A added —Children and Young Persons, 2008 c 23, s 29
  am—Health and Social Care, 2008 c 14, s 95, sch 5 para 26(1)(2)(4)
  rep in pt—Health and Social Care, 2008 c 14, s 95, sch 5 para 26(1)(3), sch 15;
   Deregulation, 2015 c 20, s 93(2)(a)(ii)
  appl (mods)—SIs 2013/253, reg 2(1)(2)(i), sch; 2013/1394, sch 7 para 15
 s 31 am—Adoption and Children, 2002 c 38, s 139(1), sch 3, paras 103, 111; Health and
   Social Care (Community Health and Standards), 2003 c 43, ss 108(1)-(3), 147,
   sch 9 paras 16, 23; Educ and Inspections, 2006 c 40, s 157, sch 14 para 48; (W
   prosp) Children and Young Persons, 2008 c 23, s 8, sch 1 para 12; Health and
   Social Care, 2008 c 14, s 95, sch 5 para 27
  rep in pt—Health and Social Care (Community Health and Standards), 2003 c 43,
   ss 108(1)(4), 196, sch 14 pt 2
  appl (mods)—(E) SIs 2004/1972, regs 2, 3; 2013/1394, sch 7 para 16; 2013/253, reg
   2(1)(2)(j), sch
  mod—SI 2008/1976, reg 4A (added by 2011/2686 (W 288), reg 2(4))
 s 32 rep in pt—Health and Social Care (Community Health and Standards), 2003 c 43,
   s 196, sch 14 pt 2
  appl (mods)—(E) SIs 2004/1972, regs 2, 3; 2013/1394, sch 7 para 17

2000
c 14 *continued*

ss 33-36 appl (mods)—(E) SIs 2004/1972, regs 2, 3; 2013/253, reg 2(1)(2)(k)-(n), sch

s 36A added—Adoption and Children, 2002 c 38, s 16

am—(temp) Adoption and Children, 2002 c 38, s 139(2), sch 4, para 4(2); Health and Social Care (Community Health and Standards), 2003 c 43, s 147, sch 9 paras 16, 24; Educ and Inspections, 2006 c 40, s 157, sch 14 para 49

s 37 appl (mods)—SI 2013/1394, sch 7 para 18

s 42 am—Health and Social Care (Community Health and Standards), 2003 c 43, ss 34, 147, sch 4 paras 110, 111, sch 9 paras 16, 25; Educ and Inspections, 2006 c 40, s 157, sch 14 para 50; (W) SI 2007/961 (W 85), art 3, sch; Health and Social Care, 2008 c 14, s 95, sch 5 para 28(1)-(4)(6)

rep in pt—Health and Social Care, 2008 c 14, s 95, sch 5 para 28(1)(5), sch 15; (pt prosp) Health and Social Care, 2012 c 7, sch 14 para 78

Pt 3 (ss 43-53) trans of functions—Health and Social Care (Community Health and Standards), 2003 c 43, s 102(4)

s 43 am—Adoption and Children, 2002 c 38, s 139(1), sch 3, paras 103, 112; (W prosp) Children and Young Persons, 2008 c 23, s 8, sch 1 para 13

s 44 rep—Health and Social Care (Community Health and Standards), 2003 c 43, s 196, sch 14 pt 2

s 45 am—Health and Social Care (Community Health and Standards), 2003 c 43, s 147, sch 9 paras 16, 26(b)(c)

rep in pt—Health and Social Care (Community Health and Standards), 2003 c 43, s 147, sch 9 paras 16, 26(a); ibid, s 196, sch 14 pt 2; Educ and Inspections, 2006 c 40, s 157, sch 14 para 51, sch 18

s 46 rep—Health and Social Care (Community Health and Standards), 2003 c 43, s 196, sch 14 pt 2

s 47 rep—Health and Social Care (Community Health and Standards), 2003 c 43, s 196, sch 14 pt 2

s 48 am—Adoption and Children, 2002 c 38, s 139(1), sch 3, paras 103, 114

s 49 rep in pt—Health and Social Care (Community Health and Standards), 2003 c 43, s 196, sch 14 pt 2

s 51 rep—Health and Social Care (Community Health and Standards), 2003 c 43, s 196, sch 14 pt 2

s 54 am—Health and Social Care, 2012 c 7, s 212(2), (b), (d), (e), (3)

rep in pt—Health and Social Care, 2012 c 7, s 212(2)(a), (c), (f)

s 55 am—Adoption and Children, 2002 c 38, s 139(1), sch 3, paras 103, 115; Health and Social Care (Community Health and Standards), 2003 c 43, s 147, sch 9 paras 16, 28; Educ and Inspections, 2006 c 40, s 157, sch 14 para 52; SI 2007/3101, reg 231; Health and Social Care, 2008 c 14, s 95, sch 5 para 29(1)(2)(3)(b); (W) Children and Families (W), 2010 nawm 1, s 72, sch 1 paras 13, 14; Health and Social Care, 2012 c 7, sch 15 para 2

rep in pt—Health and Social Care, 2008 c 14, s 95, sch 5 para 29(1)(3)(a), sch 15

s 56 am—SI 2007/3101, reg 232; Health and Social Care, 2012 c 7, sch 15 para 3

s 57 am—SI 2007/3101, reg 233; Health and Social Care, 2012 c 7, sch 15 para 4

s 58 am—Safeguarding Vulnerable Groups, 2006 c 47, s 63, sch 9 para 16; SI 2007/3101, reg 234; Health and Social Care, 2012 c 7, sch 15 para 5

s 58A added—SI 2007/3101, reg 235

am—Health and Social Care, 2012 c 7, sch 15 para 6

s 59 am—Health and Social Care, 2012 c 7, sch 15 para 7

s 60 am—SI 2007/3101, reg 236; Health and Social Care, 2012 c 7, sch 15 para 8

s 61 am—SI 2007/3101, reg 237; Health and Social Care, 2012 c 7, sch 15 para 9

s 62 am—Mental Health, 2007 c 12, s 20; Health and Social Care, 2012 c 7, sch 15 para 10

s 63 am—Health and Social Care, 2012 c 7, sch 15 para 11

s 64 am—SIs 2004/1947, reg 20(1)(2)(a)(c); 2007/3101, reg 238; Health and Social Care, 2012 c 7, sch 15 para 12(a),(c)

rep in pt—SI 2004/1947, reg 20(1)(2)(b); Health and Social Care, 2012 c 7, sch 15 para 12(b)

s 65 am—SI 2007/3101, reg 239; Health and Social Care, 2012 c 7, sch 15 para 13

s 66 am—SI 2007/3101, reg 240; Health and Social Care, 2012 c 7, sch 15 para 14

s 67 am—Health and Social Care, 2012 c 7, s 221, sch 15 para 15(a)

rep in pt—Health and Social Care, 2012 c 7, sch 15 para 15(b)

s 67A added—Health, 2006 c 28, s 72

s 68 am—SI 2007/3101, reg 241; Health and Social Care, 2012 c 7, sch 15 para 16 (for savings see SI 2012/1480, art 12(1))

2000
c 14 *continued*

s 69 am—Health and Social Care, 2012 c 7, sch 15 para 17

s 70 rep—Health and Social Care, 2012 c 7, sch 15 para 18

s 71 am—SI 2007/3101, reg 242; Health and Social Care, 2012 c 7, sch 15 para 19

s 72A added—Children's Commissioner for Wales, 2001 c 18, s 2

s 72B added—Children's Commissioner for Wales, 2001 c 18, s 3(1)
  am—SI 2007/1388, art 3, sch 1

s 73 am—Children's Commissioner for Wales, 2001 c 18, s 4(1)-(9); SI 2007/1388, art 3,
  sch 1

s 74 am—Children's Commissioner for Wales, 2001 c 18, s 5(2)

s 75ZA added—Commnr for Older People (W), 2006 c 30, s 22, sch 4 para 1
  am—Welsh Language (W), 2011 nawm 1, s 21 sch 3 paras 1,2

s 75A added—Children's Commissioner for Wales, 2001 c 18, s 5(1)
  am—SI 2007/1388, art 3, sch 1

s 76 am—Children's Commissioner for Wales, 2001 c 18, s 6; Children, 2004 c 31, s 61;
  Commnr for Older People (W), 2006 c 30, s 22, sch 4 para 1; Welsh Language
  (W), 2011 nawm 1, s 21, sch 3 paras, 1, 3

s 78 am—Children's Commissioner for Wales, 2001 c 18, s 1(1)-(3); SI 2007/1388, art 3,
  sch 1

Pt 7 (ss 80-104) appl —(EWS pt prosp) Police, 1997 c 50, s 113D (added by 2005 c 15,
  s 163(2))

ss 80-89 rep—Safeguarding Vulnerable Groups, 2006 c 47, s 63, sch 9 para 9, sch 10

s 90 rep —Serious Organised Crime and Police, 2005 c 15, s 174(2), sch 17 pt 2

ss 91-93 rep—Safeguarding Vulnerable Groups, 2006 c 47, s 63, sch 9 para 9

ss 94-99 rep—Safeguarding Vulnerable Groups, 2006 c 47, s 63, sch 10

s 100 rep—Educ, 2002 c 32, s 215(2), sch 22 pt 3

s 101 rep—Safeguarding Vulnerable Groups, 2006 c 47, s 63, sch 10

s 102 rep—Serious Organised Crime and Police, 2005 c 15, s 174(2), sch 17 pt 2

s 104 rep—Serious Organised Crime and Police, 2005 c 15, s 174(2), sch 17 pt 2

s 113 am—Health and Social Care (Community Health and Standards), 2003 c 43, s 147,
  sch 9 paras 16, 29
  rep in pt—Health and Social Care (Community Health and Standards), 2003 c 43,
   s 196, sch 14 pt 2; Health and Social Care, 2008 c 14, s 95, sch 5 para 30, sch
   15; Health and Social Care, 2012 c 7, sch 15 para 20

s 113A added—(pt prosp) Health and Social Care (Community Health and Standards), 2003
  c 43, s 105(1)(2)
  rep —Health and Social Care, 2008 c 14, s 95, sch 5 para 31, sch 15

s 114 rep in pt—Health and Social Care, 2012 c 7, sch 15 para 21

s 118 am—Children's Commissioner for Wales, 2001 c 18, s 7
  rep in pt—Health and Social Care, 2012 c 7, sch 15 para 22

s 118A added—Health and Social Care, 2008 c 14, s 95, sch 5 para 32

s 120 rep in pt—Health and Social Care, 2008 c 14, s 95, sch 5 para 33, sch 15

s 121 am—Nat Health Service Reform and Health Care Professions, 2002 c 17, s 6(2), sch 5,
  para 46; Adoption and Children, 2002 c 38, s 139(1), sch 3, paras 103,
  116(a)(b); SI 2002/2469, reg 4, sch 1 pt 1, para 27; Health and Social Care
  (Community Health and Standards), 2003 c 43, ss 34, 147, sch 4 paras 110, 112,
  sch 9 paras 16, 30; Nat Health Service (Conseq Provns), 2006 c 43, s 2, sch 1
  para 200; Educ and Inspections, 2006 c 40, s 157, sch 14 para 54; Mental
  Health, 2007 c 12, s 1, sch 1 para 22; (W prosp) Children and Young Persons,
  2008 c 23, s 4(3); SI 2008/2833, art 6, sch 3; Health and Social Care, 2012 c 7,
  sch 15 para 23(c)
  rep in pt—Health and Social Care (Community Health and Standards), 2003 c 43,
   s 196, sch 14 pt 2; Health and Social Care, 2008 c 14, s 95, sch 5 para 34, sch
   15; Health and Social Care, 2012 c 7, sch 5 para 95; ibid, sch 15 para 23(a),(b);
   Deregulation, 2015 c 20, s 93(2)(a)(iii)

s 122 rep in pt—Health and Social Care, 2012 c 7, sch 15 para 24

s 123 rep in pt—Health and Social Care, 2012 c 7, sch 15 para 25

sch 1 rep in pt—Health and Social Care (Community Health and Standards), 2003 c 43,
  s 196, sch 14 pt 2; Public Audit (W), 2004 c 23, s 72, sch 4; Public Services
  Ombudsman (W), 2005 c 10, s 39(2), sch 7; Govt of Wales, 2006 c 32, s 163,
  sch 12; Health and Social Care, 2012 c 7, sch 15 para 27

sch 1 am—Health and Social Care, 2012 c 7, sch 15 paras 28-43

sch 2 am—SI 2007/1388, art 3, sch 1
  rep in pt—SI 2011/1740, sch 2 pt 3

2000

c 14 *continued*

sch 2A added—Children's Commissioner for Wales, 2001 c 18, s 3(2), sch pt 1
    rep in pt—SI 2004/1771, art 3, sch pt 1 para 2(b); SIs 2005/3225 (W 237), arts 3,
      6(2), sch 2 pt 1 para 4, 2005/3226 (W 238), arts 3, 7(1)(b), sch 2 pt 1 para 12,
      2005/3238 (W 243), arts 7, 9(1), sch 1 paras 45, 46, 2005/3239 (W 244),
      arts 7(1)-(3), 9(1), sch 1 para 29; (pt prosp) Health and Social Care, 2012 c 7,
      sch 14 para 79
    am—(W) SIs 2007/961 (W 85), art 3, sch; 2012/990 (W 130), art 7; 2013/755 (W
      90), sch 2 para 397; Qualifications Wales, 2015 anaw 5, sch 1 para 36
sch 2B added—Children's Commissioner for Wales, 2001 c 18, s 4(10), sch pt 2
    rep in pt—SI 2005/3238 (W 243), arts 7, 9(1), sch 1 paras 45, 47; (pt prosp) Health
      and Social Care, 2012 c 7, sch 14 para 80
    am—SIs (W) 2007/961 (W 85), art 3, sch; 2007/1388, art 3, sch 1
sch 4 rep in pt—Children (Leaving Care), 2000 c 35, s 7(5)(a)(b); ibid, s 4(2); Adoption and
    Children, 2002 c 38, s 139(3), sch 5; Educ, 2002 c 32, s 215(2), sch 22 pt 3;
    Adoption and Children, 2002 c 38, s 139(1)(3), sch 3, paras 103, 117, sch 5;
    Sexual Offences, 2003 c 42, s 140, sch 7; Courts, 2003 c 39, s 109(3), sch 10;
    Income Tax (Earnings and Pensions), 2003 c 1, s 724(1), sch 8 pt 1; (prosp)
    Domestic Violence, Crime and Victims, 2004 c 28, s 58(2), sch 11; Mental
    Capacity, 2005 c 9, s 67(2), sch 7; Inquiries, 2005 c 12, ss 44(5), 49(2), sch 3;
    Serious Organised Crime and Police, 2005 c 15, s 174(2), sch 17 pt 2; (S)
    Adoption and Children (S), 2007 asp 4, s 120, sch 3; Crim Justice and
    Immigration, 2008 c 4, s 149, sch 28 pt 1; SIs 2008/2833, art 6, sch 3;
    2011/1740, sch 1 pt 3; Health and Social Care, 2012 c 7, s 39(4)(c); Legal Aid,
    Sentencing and Punishment of Offenders, 2012 c 10, sch 12 para 45

c 15   **Television Licences (Disclosure of Information)**
      s 5 am—Communications, 2003 c 21, s 406(1), sch 17 para 159(a)(b)

c 16   **Carers and Disabled Children**
      s 1 ext—Community Care (Delayed Discharges etc), 2003 c 5, s 4(10)
        am—Carers (Equal Opportunities), 2004 c 15, s 2(2); SI 2015/914, sch para 59
      s 2 ext—Community Care (Delayed Discharges etc), 2003 c 5, s 4(10)
      s 5 rep—Health and Social Care, 2001 c 15, s 67, sch 6 pt 3
      s 6 am—Carers (Equal Opportunities), 2004 c 15, s 2(3); SI 2015/914, sch para 60
      s 6A added—Carers (Equal Opportunities), 2004 c 15, s 1(2)
      s 7 am—(pt prosp) Health and Social Care, 2001 c 15, s 67, sch 5 pt 2 para 16
        rep in pt—Health and Social Care, 2001 c 15, s 67, sch 6 pt 3
      s 9 rep in pt—Health and Social Care, 2001 c 15, s 67, sch 6 pt 3
      s 11 am—SI 2015/914, sch para 61(2)(3)
      s 11 rep in pt—SI 2015/914, sch para 61(4)

c 17   **Finance**
      appl (mods)—SI 2011/245, sch 6 pt 1
      mod—SI 2009/317, art 3, sch
      s 5 rep in pt—(retrosp) Finance, 2001 c 9, s 110, sch 22 pt 1(1), Note; Finance, 2008 c 9, s
        13(11)
      s 18 rep in pt—Finance, 2009 c 10, s 17, sch 5 para 6(b)
      s 22 am—Income Tax, 2007 c 3, s 1027, sch 1 paras 389, 395
      ss 31, 32 rep—Income Tax, 2007 c 3, s 1031, sch 3
      s 33 rep—Income Tax (Trading and Other Income), 2005 c 5, s 884, sch 3
      s 34 rep—Tax Credits, 2002 c 21, s 60, sch 6
      s 36 rep—Corporation Tax, 2010 c 4, s 1181, sch 3 pt 1
      s 37 rep—Finance, 2008 c 9, s 8, sch 2 para 21(e)
      s 38 rep—Finance, 2011 c 11, sch 26 para 3(1)
      s 39 rep in pt—Income Tax, 2007 c 3, s 1031, sch 3; Finance, 2009 c 10, s 5, sch 1 para
        6(k)
      s 40 rep—Corporation Tax, 2010 c 4, s 1181, sch 3 pt 1
      s 41 rep in pt—Income Tax (Trading and Other Income), 2005 c 5, s 884, sch 3; Income
        Tax, 2007 c 3, s 1031, sch 3; Corporation Tax, 2010 c 4, s 1181, sch 3 pt 1
      s 42 rep—Finance, 2011 c 11, sch 26 para 2(2)(b)
      s 43 rep—Corporation Tax, 2010 c 4, s 1181, sch 3 pt 1
      s 44 rep in pt—Income Tax (Trading and Other Income), 2005 c 5, ss 882(1), 884, sch 1 pt
        2 paras 511, 512(1)(2), sch 3
        am—Income Tax (Trading and Other Income), 2005 c 5, s 882(1), sch 1 pt 2 paras 511,
        512(1)(3)(4); Income Tax, 2007 c 3, s 1027, sch 1 paras 389, 391

2000
c 17 *continued*

s 45 rep—Income Tax (Trading and Other Income), 2005 c 5, ss 882(1), 884, sch 1 pt 2 paras 511, 513, sch 3

s 46 rep—Corporation Tax, 2010 c 4, ss 1177, 1181, sch 1 paras 308, 309, sch 3 pt 1

s 47 rep—Income Tax (Earnings and Pensions), 2003 c 1, s 724(1), sch 8 pt 1

s 50 rep—Corporation Tax, 2009 c 4, ss 1322, 1326, sch 1 para 464, sch 3 pt 1

ss 56-60 rep—Income Tax (Earnings and Pensions), 2003 c 1, s 724(1), sch 8 pt 1

s 61 rep—Finance, 2004 c 12, s 326, sch 42 pt 3, Note

s 62 rep—Income Tax (Earnings and Pensions), 2003 c 1, s 724(1), sch 8 pt 1

s 63 rep in pt—Income Tax, 2007 c 3, s 1031, sch 3; Corporation Tax, 2010 c 4, s 1181, sch 3 pt 1

s 65 rep in pt—Income Tax, 2007 c 3, s 1031, sch 3

s 66 rep—Finance, 2008 c 9, s 8, sch 2 para 55(c)

s 67 rep—Finance, 2008 c 9, s 8, sch 2 para 55(c)

s 69 rep in pt—Corporation Tax, 2009 c 4, ss 1322, 1326, sch 1 para 465, sch 3 pt 1

ss 70-72 rep—Capital Allowances, 2001 c 2, s 580, sch 4

s 75 rep in pt—Capital Allowances, 2001 c 2, s 580, sch 4; SI 2006/3271, reg 43, sch

s 76 rep in pt—Capital Allowances, 2001 c 2, s 580, sch 4

s 77 rep—Capital Allowances, 2001 c 2, s 580, sch 4

s 78 rep—Taxation (International and Other Provns), 2010 c 8, s 378, sch 10 pt 13

ss 79-81 rep—Capital Allowances, 2001 c 2, s 580, sch 4

s 83 rep in pt—Income Tax, 2007 c 3, s 1031, sch 3

ss 84, 85 rep—Income Tax (Trading and Other Income), 2005 c 5, ss 882(1), 884, sch 1 pt 2 paras 511, 515, 516, sch 3

s 86 rep—Corporation Tax, 2010 c 4, s 1181, sch 3 pt 1

s 87 rep—Income Tax (Trading and Other Income), 2005 c 5, ss 882(1), 884, sch 1 pt 2 paras 511, 517, sch 3

ss 88, 89 rep—Corporation Tax, 2009 c 4, s 1326, sch 3 pt 1

s 98 rep—Corporation Tax, 2010 c 4, ss 1177, 1181, sch 1 paras 308, 310, sch 3 pt 1

s 100 rep—Corporation Tax, 2010 c 4, s 1181, sch 3 pt 1

s 105 am—Capital Allowances, 2001 c 2, s 578, sch 2 para 106

s 106 rep—Finance, 2002 c 23, s 141, sch 40 pt 3(10), Note 2

s 107 rep—Finance, 2007 c 11, s 114, sch 27 pt 2

ss 108, 109 rep —Finance, 2012 c 14, sch 16 para 247(j)

s 110 rep—Finance, 2006 c 25, s 178, sch 26

s 111 rep in pt—Income Tax, 2007 c 3, s 1031, sch 3

s 112 rep—Income Tax, 2007 c 3, s 1031, sch 3

s 113 rep—Capital Allowances, 2001 c 2, s 580, sch 4

s 119 am—Corporation Tax, 2010 c 4, s 1177, sch 1 paras 308, 311

s 120 am—Corporation Tax, 2010 c 4, s 1177, sch 1 paras 308, 312

s 121 am—Corporation Tax, 2010 c 4, s 1177, sch 1 paras 308, 313

s 126 rep in pt—Finance, 2008 c 9, s 149(2)(a)

s 127 rep in pt—Finance, 2012 c 14, sch 39 para 5(2)(c)

s 128 am—Land Registration, 2002 c 9, s 133, sch 11, para 39

s 130 rep—Finance, 2012 c 14, sch 39 para 6(1)

s 131 rep in pt—Finance, 2012 c 14, sch 39 para 6(2)

ss 133, 134 rep—Finance, 2000 c 17, s 156, sch 40 pt III, Note 3

s 135 rep—Finance, 2001 c 9, s 110, sch 33 pt 3(1), Note 2

s 136 rep in pt—Finance, 2008 c 9, s 123, sch 41 para 25(k)(i)

s 143 am—Income Tax (Trading and Other Income), 2005 c 5, s 882(1), sch 1 pt 2 paras 511, 518
    rep in pt—Corporation Tax, 2009 c 4, ss 1322, 1326, sch 1 para 466, sch 3 pt 1

s 144 rep—Taxation (International and Other Provns), 2010 c 8, ss 371, 378, sch 7 paras 96, 97, sch 10 pt 12

s 146 rep—Finance, 2006 c 25, s 178, sch 26 pt 8(2)

s 147 rep—Finance, 2006 c 25, s 178, sch 26 pt 8(2)

s 148 rep in pt—Commrs for Revenue and Customs, 2005 c 11, ss 50(6), 52(2), sch 4 paras 79, 80, sch 5

s 149 rep in pt—(prosp) Finance, 2007 c 11, s 114, sch 27 pt 5

s 150 rep (prosp)—Finance, 2007 c 11, s 114, sch 27 pt 5

s 155 am—Income Tax (Trading and Other Income), 2005 c 5, s 882(1), sch 1 pt 2 paras 511, 519; Income Tax, 2007 c 3, s 1027, sch 1 paras 389, 393

sch 1 rep in pt—(retrosp) Finance, 2001 c 9, s 110, sch 33 pt 1(1), Note

sch 2 rep in pt—Finance, 2009 c 10, s 22(11)(a)

2000

c 17 *continued*

sch 6 am—Finance, 2001 c 9, ss 99(1)(6), 105(1)(2)-(7), sch 31 pt 2, para 7; SI 2001/1139, reg 2; Crim. Justice and Police, 2001 c 16, s 70, sch 2 pt 2 para 13(1)(2)(i); Finance, 2002 c 23, ss 25(1)(a)(b)(2), 123, 124, 126, 127, 128; Finance, 2003 c 14, ss 188(1)(2)(a)-(d), 191(1)-(4), 192(1)(2)(a)(c)(3)-(7)(8)(b)(9)(10), 193(1)-(5); ibid, s 189(1)(2)(a)(3)(a)(5), 190(1)-(8); SI 2003/2096, arts 4, 6, sch pt 1 paras 31, 32(a)(b)(ii)(c)(d), 33; Finance, 2004 c 12, s 289(1)-(6); SI 2006/1848, reg 2; Finance, 2006 c 25, s 171(1); ibid, s 172(11)(a)(c)(d)(13)(a)(i)(14); Finance, 2007 c 11, ss 13, 23, sch 2; Tribunals, Cts and Enforcement, 2007 c 15, s 62, sch 13 paras 135-137; (EW) SI 2007/3538, reg 73, sch 21; Finance, 2008 c 9, ss 19(1), 138, 150, sch 44 para 8(a); Finance, 2009 c 10, ss 98, 99, 117, 118, sch 50 paras 18, 19(1)(2), sch 51 paras 32-36, sch 59; SIs 2009/56, art 3, sch 1 paras 286-292; 2009/571, art 8, sch 1; Corporation Tax, 2010 c 4, s 1177, sch 1 paras 308, 314; Finance, 2010 c 13, ss 17(1) 18(1), 67; SI 2010/675, reg 107, sch 26; Finance, 2011 c 11, s 23(1); ibid, sch 20 paras 2-7; Finance, 2012 c 14, sch 30 paras 1(1), 3-6, 8-11, 13, 14(c), 16(b), 20, 21; ibid, sch 31 paras 2-4, 6, 7(2)-(4)(a), (c), (d), 8(2)-(4)(b), 9, 10; ibid, sch 32 paras 2, 3, 4, 5(2)(a), (b), (3)-(6), 6-16, 20, 21; Finance, 2013 c 29, s 199(1); ibid, sch 42 paras 3-5, 6(2)-(4), 7, 8(2)(3), 9-18, 23(1), 24(1); Finance, 2014 c 26, ss 96(1), 97(2)(4), 98(1); ibid, sch 20 paras 7(a)(b), 12, 14(3); SI 2014/1264, art 6; Finance, 2015 c 11, s 63; (1.4.2016) ibid, s 62; Finance (No. 2), 2015 c 33, s 49; SI 2015/664, sch 2 para 11

ext—Crim Justice and Police, 2001 c 16, s 50, sch 1 pt 1 para 72

mod—Finance, 2011 c 11, s 79(2)(3); SI 2011/1023, art 2 3; Finance, 2013 c 29, sch 42 para 1(1)

excl—SI 2011/1025, art 2

rep in pt—Finance, 2001 c 9, s 110, sch 33 pt 3(1)(3), Note 1(b); ibid, 2001 c 9, s 110, sch 33 pt 3(3), Note; SI 2001/1139, reg 2(1)(4); Finance, 2002 c 23, ss 125(1)(c)(2), 141, sch 40 pt 4(2), Note; Finance, 2003 c 14, ss 189(1)(2)(b)(5), 192(1)(2)(b)(8)(a), 216, sch 43 pt 4(2), Note; ibid, ss 189(1)(3)(b)(4)(5), 216, sch 43 pt 4(2), Note; SI 2003/2096, arts 4, 6, sch pt 1 paras 31, 32(b)(i); Crim Justice, 2003 c 44, s 332, sch 37 pt 6; SI 2004/1501, art 46(2), sch 2; Commrs for Revenue and Customs, 2005 c 11, ss 50(6), 52(2), sch 4 paras 79, 81, sch 5; Finance, 2006 c 25, ss 172(7)(9)(10)(11)(b)(12)(13)(a)(ii)(13)(b)(14)(15), 178, sch 26; Finance, 2007 c 11, ss 84, 114, sch 22 paras 3, 11, sch 27; Finance, 2008 c 9, ss 122, 123, 129, 138, 149(1), sch 40 para 21(h), sch 41 para 25(k)(ii), sch 43 para 7, sch 44 para 8(b); Finance, 2009 c 10, ss 98, 99, sch 50 paras 18, 19(3), 20, sch 51 paras 32, 35(1)(4)(b), 36(1)(4)(b); SIs 2009/56, art 3, sch 1 paras 288(5), 290(3); (savings) 2009/3054, arts 3, 6, sch; Finance, 2011 c 11, s 79(1); Finance, 2012 c 14, sch 30 paras 7, 12, 14(a), (b), 15, 16(a); ibid, sch 31 paras 5, 7(4)(b), 8(4)(c); ibid, sch 32 paras 5(2)(c), 22; Finance, 2013 c 29, sch 42 para 6(5); ibid, sch 42 para 8(4); Finance, 2014 c 26, sch 20 paras 2-6, 7(c), 13, 14(2); Deregulation, 2015 c 20, sch 6 para 2(14)

sch 7 rep in pt—Enterprise, 2002 c 40, s 278(2), sch 26

sch 8 rep (subject to transtl provn(s))—Income Tax (Earnings and Pensions), 2003 c 1, ss 723(2), 724(1), sch 7 pt 7 paras 68, 69, 70 pt 11 para 92(1)(2)(b), sch 8 pt 1

am—Finance, 2001 c 9, ss 61, 95, sch 13 paras 1-4, 6, 8; (retrosp) ibid, 2001 c 9, s 61, sch 13, paras 1, 7; SI 2001/3629, arts 105, 107; Employee Share Schemes, 2002 c 34, ss 1(1)-(4), 2(1)-(4), 3(1)-(4); Finance, 2002 c 23, s 39(1)-(4)(6)(7); (saving) ibid, s 39(1)(5)(7)(8)

rep in pt—Finance, 2004 c 12, s 326, sch 42 pt 3, Note

schs 10, 11 rep—Income Tax (Earnings and Pensions), 2003 c 1, s 724(1), sch 8 pt 1

sch 12 am—Capital Allowances, 2001 c 2, s 578, sch 2 para 107; (2002-03 and subsequent years of assessment) Finance, 2001 c 9, s 57(3)(4), sch 12 pt 2 para 16; Finance, 2002 c 23, s 38(1)-(5); Income Tax (Earnings and Pensions), 2003 c 1, s 722, sch 6 pt 2 paras 242, 244

rep in pt—Income Tax (Earnings and Pensions), 2003 c 1, s 724(1), sch 8 pt 1; Income Tax (Trading and Other Income), 2005 c 5, s 882(1), sch 1 pt 2 paras 511, 520; Corporation Tax, 2009 c 4, ss 1322, 1326, sch 1 para 467, sch 3 pt 1

sch 13 rep—Finance, 2004 c 12, s 326, sch 42 pt 3, Note

sch 14 rep (savings)—Income Tax (Earnings and Pensions), 2003 c 1, ss 723(2), 724(1), sch 7 pt 7 paras 67(4)(b), 77, 78(2), 82, sch 8 pt 1

sch 15 am—Finance, 2001 c 9, s 64, sch 16 pt 2 paras 4, 5, 8; (retrosp in pt) ibid, s 64, sch 16 pt 2 paras 4, 6, 9; (retrosp) ibid, s 64, sch 16 pt 2 paras 4, 7; Finance,

2000
c 17 *continued*

2002 c 23, ss 44(2)(3), 45, 103(4)(f), sch 8 pt 2, para 5, sch 9 pt 2, para 6(1)-(5), pt 3, paras 7(1), 8(1); SI 2003/2096, arts 4, 6, sch pt 1 paras 31, 34(a)-(d); Finance, 2003 c 14, s 155, sch 27 para 9; Finance, 2004 c 12, s 95, sch 20 paras 1, 3, 4, 5(1)(2)(b)(c)(3)(4), 6, 7, 8(a)(ii)(b)(c), 9-15; ibid, s 146, sch 27 pt 2 para 6(1)-(3)(5)(6); Income Tax (Trading and Other Income), 2005 c 5, s 882(1), sch 1 pt 2 paras 511, 521; SI 2005/3229, regs 131, 132; Finance, 2006 c 25, ss 72(2)(e), 91, sch 14 para 3(1); (saving) Income Tax, 2007 c 3, s 51, sch 16 para 1; Finance, 2007 c 11, s 51, sch 16 paras 4(1)-(4), 8-10, 13-15, 18, sch 27; (transtl provns) Finance, 2008 c 9, s 32, sch 11 paras 1-3, 11; SI 2008/954, art 26; Finance, 2009 c 10, s 27, sch 8 para 8(1)(2)(4)-(6); SI 2009/56, art 3, sch 1 para 293; Corporation Tax, 2010 c 4, s 1177, sch 1 paras 308, 315(1)-(9)(11)(a)(c)-(15); Children and Families, 2014 c 6, sch 7 para 49

rep in pt—Finance, 2002 c 23, s 141, sch 40 pt 3(16); Finance, 2004 c 12, ss 95, 326, sch 20 paras 1, 5(1)(2)(a), 8(a)(i), 15, sch 42 pt 2(13), Note 6; ibid, ss 146, 326, sch 27 pt 2 para 6(1)(4)-(6), sch 42 pt 2(19), Note 3; Finance, 2007 c 11, s 114, sch 27 pt 2; SI 2008/954, arts 3, 26, sch; Corporation Tax, 2009 c 4, ss 1322, 1326, sch 1 para 468, sch 3 pt 1; Finance, 2009 c 10, s 27, sch 8 para 8(1)(3); Corporation Tax, 2010 c 4, ss 1177, 1181, sch 1 paras 308, 315(10)(11)(b), sch 3 pt 1

excl—Taxation of Chargeable Gains, 1992 c 12, sch 7AC, at para 4(4)

appl—Corporation Tax, 2010 c 4, s 71(5)

sch 16 rep in pt—Income Tax, 2007 c 3, s 1031, sch 3; Corporation Tax, 2010 c 4, s 1181, sch 3 pt 1

sch 17 rep in pt—Finance, 2001 c 9, s 110, sch 33 pt 2(3), Notes 2, 6; Income Tax, 2007 c 3, s 1031, sch 3

sch 18 rep in pt—Finance, 2006 c 25, s 178, sch 26; Income Tax, 2007 c 3, s 1031, sch 3

am—Income Tax, 2007 c 3, s 1027, sch 1 paras 389, 394

sch 19 rep in pt—Capital Allowances, 2001 c 2, s 580, sch 4; Corporation Tax, 2010 c 4, s 1181, sch 3 pt 1

sch 20 rep—Corporation Tax, 2009 c 4, ss 1322, 1326, sch 1 para 469, sch 3 pt 1

sch 22 mod—SI 2000/2303, regs 12,13(1); Taxation of Chargeable Gains, 1992 c 12, sch 7AB, at paras 1, 10

ext—Anti-terrorism, Crime and Security, 2001 c 24, s 17, sch 4 pt 1 para 49

am—Capital Allowances, 2001 c 2, ss 578, 580, sch 2 para 108, sch 4; (subject to transtl provn(s)) Finance, 2002 c 23, s 79(2)(3), sch 23 pt 2, para 23(1)-(3), pt 3, para 25; ibid, s 83(1)(b)(3), sch 27, paras 22, 23(1)-(3); (in relation to any lease entered into on or after 19.12.2002) Finance, 2003 c 14, s 169, sch 32 paras 1(1)(3)-(5), 2(1)(b), 3, 4(1)(2); ibid, s 169, sch 32 paras 2(2)(b), 3(1); Finance, 2004 c 12, ss 30(9), 37, sch 5 paras 11-13; (temp) SI 2005/1449, art 3; SI 2005/3229, regs 131, 133; Income Tax (Trading and Other Income), 2005 c 5, s 882(1), sch 1 pt 2 paras 511, 522; Finance, 2005 c 7, s 93, sch 7 pts 1, 2; Finance, 2008 c 9, ss 74, 80(5)-(7)(9)(b)(c), sch 24 para 19; Corporation Tax, 2009 c 4, s 1322, sch 1 para 470; SI 2009/56, art 3, sch 1 para 294; Corporation Tax, 2010 c 4, s 1177, sch 1 paras 308, 316; Taxation (International and Other Provns), 2010 c 8, s 374, sch 8 paras 55, 56, 119; Finance, 2011 c 11, ss 10(6)(7), 57; Finance, 2012 c 14, s 24(8); ibid, sch 20 paras 19, 20; SI 2013/2819, reg 35(b)(c); Finance, 2014 c 26, sch 1 para 7

rep in pt—Capital Allowances, 2001 c 2, ss 578, 580, sch 2 para 108(16), sch 4; Finance, 2002 c 23, s 141, sch 40 pt 3(10), Note 2; (in relation to any lease entered into on or after 19.12.2002) Finance, 2003 c 14, ss 169, 216, sch 32 paras 1(1)(2), 2(1)(a), 3(1), sch 43 pt 3(11), Note; ibid, ss 169, 216, sch 32 paras 2(2)(a), 3(1), sch 43 pt 3(11), Note; Finance, 2004 c 12, ss 146, 326, sch 27 pt 2 para 7, sch 42 pt 2(19), Note 4; Finance, 2005 c 7, ss 93, 104, sch 7 pt 1 paras 1, 16 pt 2 para 18(1), sch 11 pt 2(10), Note; Finance, 2008 c 9, s 84, sch 27 para 22; Finance, 2011 c 11, s 57(2)(d)(i)(iii)(6)(c); SI 2013/2819, reg 35(a)

appl—Income Tax (Earnings and Pensions), 2003 c 1, s 357(5)

excl—SIs 2006/333, art 3; 2007/850, art 3

sch 23 rep—(as to Corporation Tax) Finance, 2002 c 23, s 84(1), sch 29 pt 14, para 128; residue rep Income Tax (Trading and Other Income), 2005 c 5, ss 882(1), 884, sch 1 pt 2 paras 511, 523, sch 3

sch 26 rep in pt—Income Tax, 2007 c 3, s 1031, sch 3

2000

c 17 *continued*

sch 27 rep in pt—Finance, 2004 c 12, s 326, sch 42 pt 2(3), Note; Finance, 2006 c 25, s 178,
sch 26; Finance, 2007 c 11, s 114, sch 27 pt 2; Corporation Tax, 2010 c 4, s
1181, sch 3 pt 1

sch 28 rep—Corporation Tax, 2010 c 4, ss 1177, 1181, sch 1 paras 308, 317, sch 3 pt 1

sch 29 am—(retrosp) Finance, 2001 c 9, s 79

rep in pt—Finance, 2002 c 23, s 141, sch 40 pt 3(10), Note 2; Finance (No 2), 2005
c 22, s 70, sch 11 pt 2(8), Note; Finance, 2006 c 25, s 178, sch 26; SI
2006/3271, reg 43, sch; Finance, 2007 c 11, s 114, sch 27 pt 2; Corporation
Tax, 2009 c 4, s 1326, sch 3 pt 1; Finance, 2011 c 11, sch 9 para 5(c); ibid, sch
11 para 10(c)

sch 30 am—(retrosp) Finance, 2001 c 9, s 81, sch 27 para 7

rep in pt—Finance, 2002 c 23, s 141, sch 40 pt 3(13), Note 2; Finance, 2003 c 14,
s 216, sch 43 pt 3(12), Note 1; Finance, 2007 c 11, s 114, sch 27 pt 2; Finance,
2009 c 10, ss 34, 36, sch 14 para 30(b), sch 16 para 5(f); Taxation
(International and Other Provns), 2010 c 8, s 378, sch 10 pt 1; SL(R), 2013 c 2,
s 1, sch 1 pt 10(1)

sch 31 rep in pt—Finance, 2009 c 10, s 36, sch 16 para 11(b)

sch 33 rep in pt—Finance, 2000 c 17, s 156, sch 40 pt III, Note 4

sch 34 am—Corporation Tax, 2010 c 4, s 1177, sch 1 paras 308, 318

sch 35 rep—Finance, 2001 c 9, s 110, sch 33 pt 3(1), Note 2

sch 38 am—Communications, 2003 c 21, s 406(1), sch 17 para 160; SIs 2003/1900, arts
2(1), 3(1),sch 1; 2003/3142, art 3(2); 2009/56, art 3, sch 1 para 295

c 18 **Sea Fishing Grants (Charges)**

c 19 **Child Support, Pensions and Social Security**

appl (mods)—SI 2010/1907, reg 16

s 3 rep—Child Maintenance and Other Payments, 2008 c 6, s 58, sch 8

s 16 rep in pt—(prosp) Child Maintenance and Other Payments, 2008 c 6, s 58, sch 8;
(prosp) Welfare Reform, 2009 c 24, s 58, sch 7 pt 4

s 19 rep—Child Maintenance and Other Payments, 2008 c 6, s 58, sch 8

s 27 mod—SI 2002/1854, reg 2

s 28 rep—Child Maintenance and Other Payments, 2008 c 6, s 58, sch 8

s 32 rep in pt—Pensions, 2007 c 22, s 27, sch 7 pt 5

s 42 am—Pensions, 2004 c 35, s 298(1)(5)(a)(c); ibid, s 298(1)-(3)(4)(b)(5)(b); Pensions,
2014 c 19, sch 12 para 38

rep in pt—Pensions, 2004 c 35, ss 298(1)(4)(a), 320, sch 13 pt 1; Pensions, 2014 c 19,
sch 13 para 70

ss 43-46 rep—Pensions, 2004 c 35, s 320, sch 13 pt 1

s 47 rep in pt—Pensions, 2004 c 35, s 320, sch 13 pt 1

power to mod—Pensions, 2004 c 35, s 321(1)(e)(2)(3)

ss 48-53 power to mod—Pensions, 2004 c 35, s 321(1)(e)(2)(3)

s 54 rep—Pensions, 2004 c 35, ss 276(1), 320, sch 13 pt 1

ss 55, 56 power to mod—Pensions, 2004 c 35, s 321(1)(e)(2)(3)

s 57 rep in pt—SL(R), 2004 c 14, s 1(1), sch 1 pt 11; Armed Forces (Pensions and
Compensation), 2004 c 32, s 7(4), sch 3

s 62 rep —Welfare Reform, 2009 c 24, ss 26, 58, sch 7 pt 3
am—Social Security Fraud, 2001 c 11, s 12(1)

s 64 rep —Welfare Reform, 2009 c 24, ss 26, 58, sch 7 pt 3

s 65 rep —Welfare Reform, 2009 c 24, ss 26, 58, sch 7 pt 3

s 66 rep —Welfare Reform, 2009 c 24, ss 26, 58, sch 7 pt 3

s 68 rep (pt prosp)—Welfare Reform, 2012 c 5, sch 14 pt 1

s 69 am—Welfare Reform, 2012 c 5, sch 2 para 55; (prosp) ibid, sch 3 para 11(2)(a),(3)-(5);
(prosp) ibid, sch 4 para 14

rep in pt—(prosp) Welfare Reform, 2012 c 5, sch 3 para 11(2)(b)

s 70 am—(prosp) Welfare Reform, 2012 c 5, sch 3 para 12(2), (3), (4)(a)

rep in pt—Loc Govt, 2003 c 26, s 127(2), sch 8 pt 1 (see SI 2003/2938); (prosp)
Welfare Reform, 2012 c 5, sch 3 para 12(4)(b)

trans of functions—SI 2014/2918, art 2(1)

excl—SI 2014/2918, art 4(1)

s 70A added (prosp)—Welfare Reform, 2012 c 5, sch 3 para 13

s 71 rep (pt prosp)—Welfare Reform, 2012 c 5, sch 14 pt 1

s 75 rep in pt—Nat Insurance Contributions and Statutory Payments, 2004 c 3, s 12, sch 2 pt
1

2000

c 19 *continued*

s 79 rep in pt—Nat Insurance Contributions and Statutory Payments, 2004 c 3, s 12, sch 2 pt 1

s 83 rep in pt—Crime and Cts, 2013 c 22, sch 11 para 210 Table

sch 3 rep in pt—Income Tax, 2007 c 3, s 1031, sch 3; Child Maintenance and Other Payments, 2008 c 6, sch 8

sch 5 rep in pt—Pensions, 2004 c 35, s 320, sch 13 pt 1; Pensions, 2007 c 22, s 27, sch 7 pt 6; Pensions, 2014 c 19, sch 13 para 71

sch 6 rep in pt—Nat Insurance Contributions and Statutory Payments, 2004 c 3, s 12, sch 2 pt 1; (pt prosp) Welfare Reform, 2012 c 5, sch 14 pt 1

sch 7 rep (pt prosp)—Welfare Reform, 2012 c 5, sch 14 pt 1

    am—Constitutional Reform, 2005 c 4, s 40(4), sch 9 pt 1 para 72; (prosp) Welfare Reform, 2007 c 5, s 40, sch 5 para 13; ibid, s 30(3); SI 2008/2833, art 6, sch 3; (prosp) Welfare Reform, 2012 c 5, sch 11 para 13(3),(4), 14; ibid, sch 12 para 5

    rep in pt—SIs 2008/2833, art 6, sch 3; 2010/976, art 15, sch 18

sch 8 rep in pt—Legal Aid, Sentencing and Punishment of Offenders, 2012 c 10, sch 5 pt 2; Crime and Cts, 2013 c 22, sch 10 para 99 Table; ibid, sch 11 para 210 Table

sch 9 rep in pt—Pensions, 2004 c 35, s 320, sch 13 pt 1

c 20 **Government Resources and Accounts**

ss 1-3 rep in pt—SL(R), 2004 c 14, s 1(1), sch 1 pt 9/6

s 4A added—Constitutional Reform and Governance, 2010 c 25, s 43(2)

s 5 appl (mods)—SI 2002/794, art 6(12)

    rep in pt—SL(R), 2004 c 14, s 1(1), sch 1 pt 9/6

    am—SIs 2004/2947, reg 15, sch 7 pt 2 paras 1, 14(a); 2008/948, art 3, sch 1; Constitutional Reform and Governance, 2010 c 25, s 43(3)

s 6 rep in pt—SL(R), 2004 c 14, s 1(1), sch 1 pt 9/6

    appl (mods)—Budget Responsibility and Nat Audit, 2011 c 4, sch 5 para 25(6)

    am—Constitutional Reform and Governance, 2010 c 25, s 43(4)

    mod—SI 2013/148, art 2

s 7 rep in pt—SL(R), 2004 c 14, s 1(1), sch 1 pt 9/6

s 8 appl—SI 2003/1325, arts 2(1), 3(1), 4(1), 5(1)(2), 6(1)

    rep in pt—SL(R), 2004 c 14, s 1(1), sch 1 pt 9/6

s 9 am—SIs 2004/2947, reg 15, sch 7 pt 2 paras 1, 14(b); 2008/948, art 3, sch 1

s 10 am—Govt of Wales, 2006 c 32, s 160, sch 10 para 57

ss 12, 13 rep—Nat Health Service (Conseq Provns), 2006 c 43, s 6, sch 4

s 14 am—Health, 2006 c 28, s 80, sch 8 para 44; Health and Social Care, 2012 c 7, sch 5 para 96(4)

    rep in pt—Health and Social Care, 2012 c 7, sch 5 para 96(2),(3)

s 21 rep in pt—SL(R), 2004 c 14, s 1(1), sch 1 pt 9/6

s 25 appl (mods)—Budget Responsibility and Nat Audit, 2011 c 4, sch 5 para 25(6)

    am—Budget Responsibility and Nat Audit, 2011 c 4, s 19

s 26 rep in pt—SL(R), 2004 c 14, s 1(1), sch 1 pt 9/6

sch 1 rep in pt—Tax Credits, 2002 c 21, s 60, sch 6; SL(R), 2004 c 14, s 1(1), sch 1 pt 9/6; Public Services Ombudsman (W), 2005 c 10, s 39(2), sch 7; Govt of Wales, 2006 c 32, s 163, sch 12; Budget Responsibility and Nat Audit, 2011 c 4, sch 5 para 20

c 21 **Learning and Skills**

am—SI 2010/1158, art 5, sch 2

Pt 1 (ss 1-29) rep—Apprenticeships, Skills, Children and Learning, 2009 c 22, ss 123, 266, sch 6 paras 14-42, sch 16 pt 2

Pt 2 (ss 30-51) am—(heading am) SI 2005/3238 (W 243), arts 7, 9(1), sch 1 paras 48, 49

s 30 rep—SI 2005/3238 (W 243), arts 7, 9(1), sch 1 paras 48, 50

s 31 am—SI 2005/3238 (W 243), arts 7, 9(1), sch 1 paras 48, 51(a)(b); Learning and Skills (W), 2009 nawm 1, ss 21(1)(2)(a)(b), 47, sch paras 1, 4

    rep in pt—SI 2005/3238 (W 243), arts 7, 9(1), sch 1 paras 48, 51(c)(d); Learning and Skills (W), 2009 nawm 1, s 21(1)(2)(a)

s 32 am—SI 2005/3238 (W 243), arts 7, 9(1), sch 1 paras 48, 52(a)(c); Learning and Skills (W), 2009 nawm 1, s 47, sch paras 1, 2, 3, 5

    rep in pt—SI 2005/3238 (W 243), arts 7, 9(1), sch 1 paras 48, 52(b)(d)(e)

s 33 am—SI 2005/3238 (W 243), arts 7, 9(1), sch 1 paras 48, 53; Learning and Skills (W), 2009 nawm 1, s 47, sch paras 1, 2, 3

s 33A added—Learning and Skills (W), 2009 nawm 1, s 22

s 33B added—Learning and Skills (W), 2009 nawm 1, s 23

s 33C added—Learning and Skills (W), 2009 nawm 1, s 24

2000

c 21 *continued*

s 33D added—Learning and Skills (W), 2009 nawm 1, s 25
s 33E added—Learning and Skills (W), 2009 nawm 1, s 26
s 33F added—Learning and Skills (W), 2009 nawm 1, s 27
    am—Educ (W), 2009 nawm 5, s 22(1)(2)
s 33G added—Learning and Skills (W), 2009 nawm 1, s 28
s 33H added—Learning and Skills (W), 2009 nawm 1, s 29
s 33I added—Learning and Skills (W), 2009 nawm 1, s 30
s 33J added—Learning and Skills (W), 2009 nawm 1, s 31
    am—Further and Higher Educ (Governance and Information) (W), 2014 anaw 1, s
      6(1)
s 33K added—Learning and Skills (W), 2009 nawm 1, s 32
    am—Educ (W), 2011 nawm 7, s 9(2)(a)
    rep in pt—Educ (W), 2011 nawm 7, s 9(2)(b)
s 33L added—Learning and Skills (W), 2009 nawm 1, s 33
    am—Further and Higher Educ (Governance and Information) (W), 2014 anaw 1, s
      6(2)
s 33M added—Learning and Skills (W), 2009 nawm 1, s 34
s 33N added —Learning and Skills (W), 2009 nawm 1, s 35
    am—Educ (W), 2009 nawm 5, s 22(1)(3)
s 33O added—Learning and Skills (W), 2009 nawm 1, s 36
s 33P added—Learning and Skills (W), 2009 nawm 1, s 37
    rep in pt—School Standards and Organisation (W), 2013 anaw 1, sch 5 para 20(2)
s 33Q added —Learning and Skills (W), 2009 nawm 1, s 38
s 34 am—SI 2005/3238 (W 243), arts 7, 9(1), sch 1 paras 48, 54; Learning and Skills (W),
    2009 nawm 1, s 47, sch paras 1, 2, 3, 6
s 35 rep in pt—Special Educational Needs and Disability, 2001 c 10, ss 34(8), 42(6), sch 9;
    Children and Families, 2014 c 6, sch 3 para 72
    am—SI 2005/3238 (W 243), arts 7, 9(1), sch 1 paras 48, 55; Educ and Skills, 2008 c
      25, s 169, sch 1 paras 75, 76(c); Learning and Skills (W), 2009 nawm 1, s 47, sch
      paras 1, 2, 3, 7
s 36 am—Educ, 2002 c 32, s 215(1), sch 21, para 125; Educ, 2005 c 18, s 117, sch 18 para
      13; SI 2005/3238 (W 243), arts 7, 9(1), sch 1 paras 48, 56; Learning and Skills
      (W), 2009 nawm 1, s 47, sch paras 1, 2, 3; SI 2010/1158, art 5, sch 2
    transtl provns—(W) SI 2003/2959 (W 277), reg 5
s 37 am—SI 2005/3238 (W 243), arts 7, 9(1), sch 1 paras 48, 57; Learning and Skills (W),
    2009 nawm 1, s 47, sch paras 1, 2, 3, 8
s 38 am—SI 2005/3238 (W 243), arts 7, 9(1), sch 1 paras 48, 58(a); Learning and Skills
    (W), 2009 nawm 1, s 47, sch paras 1, 2, 3
    rep in pt—SI 2005/3238 (W 243), arts 7, 9(1), sch 1 paras 48, 58(b)
s 39 rep—Further and Higher Educ (Governance and Information) (W), 2014 anaw 1, sch 2
    para 2(a)
s 40 am—SI 2005/3238 (W 243), arts 7, 9(1), sch 1 paras 48, 60(b); Learning and Skills
    (W), 2009 nawm 1, s 47, sch paras 1, 2, 3, 9
    rep in pt—SI 2005/3238 (W 243), arts 7, 9(1), sch 1 paras 48, 60(a)
s 41 am—SI 2005/3238 (W 243), arts 7, 9(1), sch 1 paras 48, 61; Educ and Skills, 2008 c
      25, s 169, sch 1 paras 75, 76(d); Learning and Skills (W), 2009 nawm 1, s 47, sch
      paras 1, 2, 3, 10
    rep in pt—Children and Families, 2014 c 6, sch 3 para 73
ss 42-51 rep—SI 2005/3238 (W 243), arts 7, 9(1), sch 1 paras 48, 62
ss 52-72 rep —Educ and Inspections, 2006 c 40, s 157, sch 14 para 56, sch 18
s 74 am—SIs 2005/3238 (W 243), arts 7, 9(1), sch 1 paras 48, 63; 2010/1158, art 5, sch 2
s 75 am —Educ, 2005 c 18, s 61, sch 9 para 24; SI 2005/3238 (W 243), arts 7, 9(1), sch 1
    paras 48, 64
s 77 rep in pt—SI 2005/3238 (W 243), arts 7, 9(1), sch 1 paras 48, 65
    am—SI 2010/1158, art 5, sch 2
s 81 rep—Educ, 2005 c 18, s 123, sch 19 pt 1
s 82 am—Educ and Inspections, 2006 c 40, s 157, sch 14 para 57
s 83 am—Educ, 2002 c 32, s 178(1)(4); SIs 2005/3238 (W 243), arts 7, 9(1), sch 1 paras
      48, 66; 2010/1158, art 5, sch 2; School Standards and Organisation (W), 2013
      anaw 1, sch 5 para 20(3)
s 84 rep in pt—SI 2005/3238 (W 243), arts 7, 9(1), sch 1 paras 48, 67
    am—SI 2010/1158, art 5, sch 2
s 86 am —Educ, 2005 c 18, s 61, sch 9 para 25

2000

c 21 *continued*

s 90 rep—Educ and Inspections, 2006 c 40, s 157, sch 14 para 58(a), sch 18

s 91 rep—SI 2005/3238 (W 243), arts 7, 9(1), sch 1 paras 48, 68

s 92 rep in pt—Educ and Inspections, 2006 c 40, s 157, sch 14 para 58(b), sch 18

s 93 rep—SI 2005/3238 (W 243), arts 7, 9(1), sch 1 paras 48, 69

s 94 rep in pt —SI 2005/3238 (W 243), arts 7, 9(1), sch 1 paras 48, 70(a)

   am —SI 2005/3238 (W 243), arts 7, 9(1), sch 1 paras 48, 70(b); Educ and Inspections, 2006 c 40, s 157, sch 14 para 59

s 94A added—SI 2003/2867, reg 2, sch pt 1 para 31

s 95 rep in pt —SI 2005/3238 (W 243), arts 7, 9(1), sch 1 paras 48, 71(a)

   am —SI 2005/3238 (W 243), arts 7, 9(1), sch 1 paras 48, 71(b); Educ and Inspections, 2006 c 40, s 157, sch 14 para 60

s 96 appl—SI 2005/1739, art 2

   rep in pt—Qualifications Wales, 2015 anaw 5, sch 4 para 3(2)(a)(i)

   am—Apprenticeships, Skills, Children and Learning, 2009 c 22, ss 174, 192, sch 12 paras 26, 27; SI 2010/1158, art 5, schs 2, 4; Qualifications Wales, 2015 anaw 5, sch 4 para 3(2)(a)(ii)(b)(c),(3)

s 97 rep—Apprenticeships, Skills, Children and Learning, 2009 c 22, ss 123, 266, sch 6 paras 14, 43, sch 16 pt 2

s 98 am—Educ and Skills, 2008 c 25, s 98(1)(2); Apprenticeships, Skills, Children and Learning, 2009 c 22, ss 123, 174, 192, sch 6 paras 14, 44(1)(2), sch 12 paras 26, 28; Qualifications Wales, 2015 anaw 5, sch 4 para 3(4)

   rep in pt—Educ and Skills, 2008 c 25, s 159(1)(3), sch 2; Apprenticeships, Skills, Children and Learning, 2009 c 22, ss 123, 266, sch 6 paras 14, 44(3), sch 16 pt 2; Educ, 2011 c 21, sch 8 para 9; ibid, sch 16 para 14; Qualifications Wales, 2015 anaw 5, sch 4 para 3(4)

s 99 rep —Qualifications Wales, 2015 anaw 5, sch 4 para 3(5)

s 100 see—Education and Training (S), asp 2000 c 8, s 1(1)(b)(2)(d)(ii)(6)

   am —SI 2005/3238 (W 243), arts 7, 9(1), sch 1 paras 48, 72; Apprenticeships, Skills, Children and Learning, 2009 c 22, s 123, sch 6 paras 14, 46

   rep in pt—Qualifications Wales, 2015 anaw 5, sch 4 para 3(6)

s 101 am—Apprenticeships, Skills, Children and Learning, 2009 c 22, s 123, sch 6 paras 14, 47(a)(b); Qualifications Wales, 2015 anaw 5, sch 4 para 3(7)

   rep in pt—Apprenticeships, Skills, Children and Learning, 2009 c 22, ss 123, 266, sch 6 paras 14, 47(c), sch 16 pt 2; Qualifi Qualifications Wales, 2015 anaw 5, sch 4 para 3(7)

s 102 rep—Qualifications Wales, 2015 anaw 5, sch 4 para 3(8)

s 103 rep in pt—Apprenticeships, Skills, Children and Learning, 2009 c 22, s 266, sch 16 pt 2; Qualifications Wales, 2015 anaw 5, sch 4 para 3(9)

s 110 am—SI 2010/1158, art 5, sch 2; Educ, 2011 c 21, sch 12 para 44(2)

s 113 rep (W)—School Standards and Organisation (W), 2013 anaw 1, sch 5 para 20(4)

   am —Educ, 2005 c 18, s 46, sch 5 paras 1, 2; SIs 2010/1080, art 2, sch 1; 2010/1158, art 5, sch 2

   rep in pt—Educ and Inspections, 2006 c 40, s 30, sch 3 para 35, sch 18

s 113A added—Educ, 2002 c 32, s 72(1)

   rep (W)—School Standards and Organisation (W), 2013 anaw 1, sch 5 para 20(4)

   power to mod—Educ, 2002 c 32, s 74(1)(2)(b)

   rep in pt —SI 2005/3238 (W 243), arts 7, 9(1), sch 1 paras 48, 73(e); Apprenticeships, Skills, Children and Learning, 2009 c 22, ss 123, 266, sch 6 paras 14, 49, sch 16

   am—SI 2005/3238 (W 243), arts 7, 9(1), sch 1 paras 48, 73(i); ibid, arts 7, 9(1), sch 1 paras 48, 73(a)-(d)(f)-(h); Educ and Inspections, 2006 c 40, ss 30, 157, sch 3 para 36, sch 14 para 61; SI 2010/1158, art 5, schs 2, 4; Educ (W) 2011 nawm 7, s 26(4)

s 114 rep —Educ and Skills, 2008 c 25, s 79, sch 2

ss 115, 116 rep—Educ and Skills, 2008 c 25, s 79, sch 2

s 117 rep —Educ and Skills, 2008 c 25, s 79, sch 2

   am—Educ, 2002 c 32, s 65(3), sch 7 pt 2, para 10

s 118 rep—Educ and Skills, 2008 c 25, s 79, sch 2

s 119 rep —Educ and Skills, 2008 c 25, s 79, sch 2

s 120 rep —Educ and Skills, 2008 c 25, s 79, sch 2

   am—Crim Justice and Ct Services, 2000 c 43, s 74, sch 7 pt II para 209; SIs 2002/2469, reg 4, sch 1 pt 1, para 28(1)(3); 2008/912, art 3, sch 1

s 121 rep—Educ and Skills, 2008 c 25, s 79, sch 2

2000

c 21 *continued*

s 123 appl—Children, 2004 c 31, ss 25(10)(b)(ii), 30(2)(a)

s 125 rep in pt—SI 2005/3238 (W 243), arts 7, 9(1), sch 1 paras 48, 74

    mod—(W) SI 2007/961 (W 85), art 3, sch

    am—SI 2008/912, art 3, sch 1; Police Reform and Social Responsibility, 2011 c 13, sch 16 para 251

s 126 am—SI 2005/3238 (W 243), arts 7, 9(1), sch 1 paras 48, 75; Learning and Skills (W), 2009 nawm 1, s 42(1)(2)

    rep in pt—School Standards and Organisation (W), 2013 anaw 1, sch 5 para 20(5)

s 127 am—Learning and Skills (W), 2009 nawm 1, s 42(1)(3)

s 128 am—Educ, 2005 c 18, s 61, sch 9 para 27

s 129 rep in pt—Nat Health Service (Conseq Provns), 2006 c 43, s 2, sch 1 para 203; Police Reform and Social Responsibility, 2011 c 13, sch 16 para 252

    mod—(W) SI 2007/961 (W 85), art 3, sch

ss 130-132 rep (EW)—Educ, 2002 c 32, s 215(2), sch 22 pt 3

s 135 am—Pension Schemes, 2015 c 8, sch 4 para 33

s 138 am—Nat Health Service Reform and Health Care Professions, 2002 c 17, s 6(2), sch 5, para 47; SIs 2005/3238 (W 243), arts 7, 9(1), sch 1 paras 48, 76; 2008/912, art 3, sch 1

    mod—(W) SI 2007/961 (W 85), art 3, sch

ss 139A-139C added—Educ and Skills, 2008 c 25, s 80

    rep—Children and Families, 2014 c 6, sch 3 para 74

s 140 appl (mods)—(prosp) Nationality, Immigration and Asylum, 2002 c 41, s 36(9)(c)

    am—Educ and Skills, 2008 c 25, s 169, sch 1 paras 75, 77; SI 2010/1158, art 5, sch 2

    rep in pt—Educ and Skills, 2008 c 25, s 169, sch 1 paras 75, 77(g), sch 2

s 141 am—SI 2009/1941, art 2, sch 1 para 182

s 143 am—Educ, 2011 c 21, sch 12 para 44(3); Charities, 2011 c 25, sch 7 para 88

s 144 am—(W) SI 2005/3238 (W 243), arts 7, 9(1), sch 1 paras 48, 77; SI 2010/1080, art 2, sch 1; Educ, 2011 c 21, sch 16 para 15

    rep in pt—Deregulation, 2015 c 20, sch 14 para 45(a)(b)

s 145 am—SI 2010/1080, art 2, sch 1; Crime and Cts, 2013 c 22, sch 9 para 52

s 146 rep in pt—(prosp) Higher Educ, 2004 c 8, s 50, sch 7

s 148 rep in pt—(EW) Educ, 2002 c 32, s 215(2), sch 22 pt 3

s 150 am—(W) SI 2005/3238 (W 243), arts 7, 9(1), sch 1 paras 48, 78

    rep in pt—Educ and Inspections, 2006 c 40, s 157, sch 14 para 63, sch 18; Equality, 2010 c 15, s 211, sch 27 pt 1 (subst by SI 2010/2279, sch 2)

s 151 am—(W) SI 2005/3238 (W 243), arts 7, 9(1), sch 1 paras 48, 79(a)

    rep in pt—SI 2005/3238 (W 243), arts 7, 9(1), sch 1 paras 48, 79(b); Educ and Inspections, 2006 c 40, s 157, sch 14 para 64, sch 18

s 152 am—Further Education and Training, 2007 c 25, s 29, sch 1 paras 12, 15; Educ and Skills, 2008 c 25, s 86(1)(5)-(7); Learning and Skills (W), 2009 nawm 1, s 39

    rep in pt—SI 2010/1080, art 2, schs 1, 2

sch 1 rep —Apprenticeships, Skills, Children and Learning, 2009 c 22, ss 123, 266, sch 6 paras 14, 50, sch 16

sch 1A added—Educ and Skills, 2008 c 25, s 86(1)(7)

    rep (with transtl provn(s))—Apprenticeships, Skills, Children and Learning, 2009 c 22, ss 123, 266, sch 6 paras 14, 51, sch 16 pt 2

sch 2 rep—Further Education and Training, 2007 c 25, s 3(2)(b), sch 2

sch 3 rep—Apprenticeships, Skills, Children and Learning, 2009 c 22, ss 123, 266, sch 6 paras 14, 52, sch 16 pt 2

schs 4, 5 rep—SI 2005/3238 (W 243), arts 7, 9(1), sch 1 paras 48, 80, 81

sch 6 rep—Educ and Inspections, 2006 c 40, s 157, sch 14 para 65, sch 18

sch 7 rep (W)—School Standards and Organisation (W), 2013 anaw 1, sch 5 para 20(6)(a)

    appl (mods)—(E) SI 2001/798, reg 16, sch 4 paras 1-3

    am—Educ, 2002 c 32, ss, 75, 215(1), sch 10, paras 11, 15, sch 21, para 126(1)-(3); ibid, s 75, sch 10, paras 11-14; Educ, 2005 c 18, s 46, sch 5 paras 1, 3(1)(2)(3)(4)(10), sch 19 pt 1; ibid, s 46, sch 5 paras 1, 3(1)(5)-(8)(9)(11)-(14); SI 2005/3238 (W 243), arts 7, 9(1), sch 1 paras 48, 82; Educ and Inspections, 2006 c 40, ss 30, 71, 157, sch 3 paras 37, 38, 39, 40(1)(2)(a), 41, 42, 43(1)(2)(3)(5)(6), 44, 45, sch 7 para 18(1)(2), sch 14 para 66; SI 2010/1080, art 2, sch 1

    rep in pt—Educ, 2002 c 32, s 215(2), sch 22 pt 3; Children, 2004 c 31, s 64, sch 5 pt 1; Educ, 2005 c 18, ss 46, 123, sch 5 paras 1, 3(1)(15), sch 19 pt 1; Educ and

2000
c 21 sch 7 *continued*

Inspections, 2006 c 40, ss 30, 71, sch 3 paras 40(2)(b)(3), 43(4), sch 7 para 18(3), sch 18; SI 2010/1080, art 2, schs 1, 2
appl (mods)—(E) SI 2003/507, reg 27, sch 5
sch 7A added—Educ, 2002 c 32, s 72(2), sch 9
rep (W)—School Standards and Organisation (W), 2013 anaw 1, sch 5 para 20(6)(a)
power to mod—Educ, 2002 c 32, s 74(1)(2)(b)
am—(W) SI 2005/3238 (W 243), arts 7, 9(1), sch 1 paras 48, 83; Educ and Inspections, 2006 c 40, s 30, sch 3 para 46
rep in pt—Apprenticeships, Skills, Children and Learning, 2009 c 22, ss 123, 266, sch 6 paras 14, 53, sch 16 pt 2
sch 8 rep—Educ, 2002 c 32, s 215(2), sch 22 pt 3
sch 9 rep in pt—Race Relations (Amdt), 2000 c 34, s 9(2), sch 3; Special Educational Needs and Disability, 2001 c 10, ss 38(16), 42(6), sch 9; Educ, 2002 c 32, s 215(2), sch 22 pt 3; (EW) ibid, s 215(2), sch 22 pt 3; (prosp) Higher Educ, 2004 c 8, s 50, sch 7; Children, 2004 c 31, s 64, sch 5 pt 1; SI 2005/2467, reg 23(2)(a); Educ, 2005 c 18, s 123, sch 19 pt 3; ibid, s 123, sch 19 pt 1; Govt of Wales, 2006 c 32, s 163, sch 12; Educ and Inspections, 2006 c 40, s 184, sch 18; (W) Learner Travel (W), 2008 nawm 2, s 26, sch 2; Apprenticeships, Skills, Children and Learning, 2009 c 22, s 266, sch 16 pt 4; Equality, 2010 c 15, s 211, sch 27 pt 1 (subst by SI 2010/2279, sch 2); SI 2010/1080, art 2, schs 1, 2; Educ, 2011 c 21, s 29(9)(a), sch 16 para 16; School Standards and Organisation (W), 2013 anaw 1, sch 5 para 20(6)(b); Further and Higher Educ (Governance and Information) (W), 2014 anaw 1, sch 2 para 2(b); Deregulation, 2015 c 20, sch 16 para 2(2)(b)
sch 10 rep in pt—SI 2005/3238 (W 243), arts 7, 9(1), sch 1 paras 48, 84; Educ and Inspections, 2006 c 40, s 157, sch 14 para 67, sch 18

c 22 **Local Government**
appl—(W) Education, 1996 c 56, sch 1, para 15(3)
appl (mods)—SI 2010/1907, reg 16
see—(power to appl or incorp (mods)) Police Reform and Social Responsibility, 2011 c 13, s 58(1)-(3)(7); ibid, s 54(5)
trans of functions—SI 2015/1376, art 3(1) sch 1
s 1 am—Loc Govt and Public Involvement in Health, 2007 c 28, s 77; Loc Govt (W), 2011 nawm 4, s 126(1)
s 2 restr—(savings) Nationality, Immigration and Asylum, 2002 c 41, s 54, sch 3, paras 1(1)(k)(2)(3), 2-7; (cond) ibid, s 55(3)(4)(c)
am—Loc Govt and Public Involvement in Health, 2007 c 28, s 78(1)(2); Loc Govt (W), 2009 nawm 2, s 51, sch 2 paras 1, 2, sch 3; Localism, 2011 c 20, sch 1 para 3; Loc Govt (W), 2011 nawm 4, s 126(2); (1.4.2016) Well-being of Future Generations (W), 2015 anaw 2, sch 4 paras 3, 4
rep in pt—Localism, 2011 c 20, sch 25 pt 1
s 3 excl—Loc Govt, 2003 c 26, s 93(7)(c)
am—Loc Govt, 2003 c 26, s 100, sch 3 paras 11, 12 (see SI 2003/2938); Loc Govt and Public Involvement in Health, 2007 c 28, s 115(1)(2); Localism, 2011 c 20, sch 1 para 4
rep in pt—Localism, 2011 c 20, sch 25 pt 1
s 4 rep—Deregulation, 2015 c 20, s 100(1)
s 4A added—Loc Govt and Public Involvement in Health, 2007 c 28, s 78(1)(3)
rep—Deregulation, 2015 c 20, s 100(2)(a)
s 5 am—Loc Govt and Public Involvement in Health, 2007 c 28, s 115(1)(3)(4); Loc Govt (W), 2011 nawm 4, s 126(3)
s 6 am—Loc Govt and Public Involvement in Health, 2007 c 28, s 115(1)(5)
rep in pt—Loc Govt and Public Involvement in Health, 2007 c 28, s 241, sch 18
s 7 rep in pt—Waste and Emissions Trading, 2003 c 33, s 35(c); Loc Govt and Public Involvement in Health, 2007 c 28, s 241, sch 18
am—Loc Govt and Public Involvement in Health, 2007 c 28, s 115(1)(6); SI 2011/1011 (W 150), art 6
s 9 am—Loc Govt, 2003 c 26, s 100, sch 3 paras 11, 13 (see SI 2003/2938); Loc Govt and Public Involvement in Health, 2007 c 28, s 115(1)(7)
s 9A added—Loc Govt and Public Involvement in Health, 2007 c 28, s 115(1)(9)
Pt 1A (ss 9B-9R) added —Localism, 2011 c 20, sch 2 para 1
mod—SI 2013/643, art 2
s 9E see—(power to appl (mods)) Loc Govt, 2000 c 22 s 9EA(4)(c)(6)

2000

c 22 *continued*

    s 9F am—Health and Social Care, 2012 c 7, s 190(10)(c)

        appl (mods)—National Health Service, 2006 c 41, s 247A

        rep in pt—Health and Social Care, 2012 c 7, s 190(10)(a), (b)

    s 9FA appl (mods)—National Health Service, 2006 c 41, ss 247, 247A; SI 2013/218, reg
        30(2)

    s 9FF am—SI 2013/594, art 5(a)(b)

        rep in pt—SI 2013/594, art 5(c)

    s 9HE functions made exerciseable concurrently—SI 2013/2597, art 2(c)

        am—SIs 2013/2597, sch para 7(2)(a); 2015/1376, sch 2 para 8(2)(a)

    s 9KC appl (mods)—SI 2012/323, reg 17(8)

    s 9MG functions made exerciseable concurrently—SI 2013/2597, art 2(c)

        am—SIs 2013/2597, sch para 7(2)(b); 2015/1376, sch 2 para 8(2)(b)

    Pt 2 (ss 10-48) appl—(E) Patriotic Fund Reorganisation, 1903 c 20, sch 1, para 16; (E)
        Naval and Military War Pensions, &c, 1915 c 83, s 6(6); (E) Administration of
        Justice, 1973 c 15, sch 1 pt II, para 7B; (E) Finance, 1974 c 30, s 34(1); (E)
        Representation of the People, 1983 c 2, s 24(1A); (E) Local Government, 1985
        c 51, s 35(4); (W) Pilotage, 1987 c 21, s 3(10); (W) Local Government, 1988 c
        9, sch 2; (W) Local Government Finance, 1988 c 41, s 115B(2); (W) Water
        Industry, 1991 c 56, s 97(5); (W) Deregulation and Contracting Out, 1994 c 40,
        s 70(1A)(7); (W) Employment Rights, 1996 c 18, s 50(9A); (E) Defamation,
        1996 c 31, sch 1 pt II, para 11(2A); (W) Defamation, 1996 c 31, sch 1, para
        11(2); (W) Justices of the Peace, 1997 c 25, s 66(8); (W) Teaching and Higher
        Education, 1998 c 30, s 23(11); (W) SIs 1983/1964, reg 5(8)(a); 1992/613, reg
        4(3)(a); (E) SI 1995/2061, art 4B(2); (retrosp to 16.2.2001) Political Parties,
        Elections and Referendums, 2000 c 41, sch 7 para 4; (W) SI 2000/2993, reg 10;
        (E) SI 2003/2123, reg 4(1)(g); European Parl and Loc Elections (Pilots), 2004
        c 2, s 8, sch para 3(5); SI 2004/1412, art 2

        am—Localism, 2011 c 20, sch 3 para 9

    s 10 appl—(E) SI 2003/1115, art 4(2)

        appl (mods)—SI 2012/2734, reg 3-6, sch pt 3

        am—Localism, 2011 c 20, sch 3 para 10

    s 11 appl—(W) SI 1991/892, reg 2(a)(i); (W) Local Government Finance, 1992 c 14, s
        106(1)

        am—Loc Govt and Public Involvement in Health, 2007 c 28, s 62; Localism, 2011 c 20,
        sch 3 para 11

        rep in pt—Localism, 2011 c 20, sch 3 para 11(1)(3)(7)(b)(8)(9), sch 25 pt 4; Loc Govt
        (W), 2011 nawm 4, ss 34(2), 176(2), sch 4 pt B

    s 12 am—Localism, 2011 c 20, s 22, sch 3 para 12

    s 13 am—Loc Govt and Public Involvement in Health, 2007 c 28, s 236(9); Localism, 2011
        c 20, s 22, sch 3 para 13; Loc Govt (W), 2011 nawm 4, s 57(2)

        appl (mods)—SIs 2010/997, art 6; 2010/998, art 6

        rep in pt—Localism, 2011 c 20, ss 22, 237, sch 3 para 13(1)(4), sch 25 pt 4

    s 14 power to appl—Loc Govt, 2000 c 22, s 19(6)

        saved—(W) Weights and Measures, 1985 c 72, s 5(11)(d)

        am—Loc Govt and Public Involvement in Health, 2007 c 28, s 63; Localism, 2011 c 20,
        sch 3 para 14

        appl—Marine and Coastal Access, 2009 c 23, s 20(7)(a)

        appl (mods)—SIs 2010/997, arts 4, 6; 2010/998, arts 4, 6

        rep in pt—Localism, 2011 c 20, sch 3 para 14(1)(6), sch 25 pt 4

    s 15 power to appl—Loc Govt, 2000 c 22, s 19(6)

        appl—(E) SI 2000/2851, reg 4(2); Marine and Coastal Access, 2009 c 23, s 20(7)(a)

        saved—(W) Weights and Measures, 1985 c 72, s 5(11)(d)

        am—Loc Govt and Public Involvement in Health, 2007 c 28, s 63

    s 16 rep—Loc Govt (W), 2011 nawm 4, ss 34(1)(3), 176(2), sch 4 pt B

    s 17 appl (mods)—SI 2008/634, art 7

        mod—SI 2008/907, art 16

        am—Localism, 2011 c 20, sch 3 para 15

    s 18 appl—(W) Local Government and Housing, 1989 c 42, s 9(11)

        am—Localism, 2011 c 20, sch 3 para 16; Loc Govt (W), 2011 nawm 4, s 55

        rep in pt—Localism, 2011 c 20, sch 3 para 16(1)(4)(5), sch 25 pt 4

    s 19 am—Localism, 2011 c 20, sch 3 para 17

        rep in pt—Localism, 2011 c 20, sch 3 para 17(1)(2)(b), sch 25 pt 4

    s 20 am—Localism, 2011 c 20, sch 3 para 18

2000
c 22 *continued*

  s 21 am—Health and Social Care, 2001 c 15, s 7(1); Loc Govt, 2003 c 26, s 127(1), sch 7
    para 80 (see SI 2003/2938); Nat Health Service (Conseq Provns), 2006 c 43, s 2,
    sch 1 para 205; (prosp) Police and Justice, 2006 c 48, s 52, sch 14 para 38; Loc
    Govt and Public Involvement in Health, 2007 c 28, ss 120, 125, 127(1); Loc
    Democracy, Economic Development and Construction, 2009 c 20, s 32(2); Loc
    Govt (W), 2011 nawm 4, ss 57(2)(b), 58(5)(a), 75(4); (prosp) ibid, s 59;
    Localism, 2011 c 20, sch 3 para 19; (1.4.2016) Well-being of Future Generations
    (W), 2015 anaw 2, sch 4 para 5
    appl (mods)—Health and Social Care, 2001 c 15, s 10(3); (E) SI 2002/3048, reg 7(3);
    Nat Health Service, 2006 c 41, s 247(3)
    excl—Nat Health Service (W), 2006 c 42, s 185(7)(8); Nat Health Service, 2006 c 41,
    s 245(7)(8); SIs 2010/997, art 6; 2010/998, art 6
    rep in pt—Loc Govt and Public Involvement in Health, 2007 c 28, s 241, sch 18;
    Localism, 2011 c 20, sch 3 para 19, sch 25 pt 4; (temp) Health and Social Care,
    2012 c 7, s 190(9)(a)(i), (b)
  s 21ZA added—Loc Democracy, Economic Development and Construction, 2009 c 20, s 31
    rep —Localism, 2011 c 20, sch 3 para 20, sch 25 pt 4
  s 21A added—Loc Govt and Public Involvement in Health, 2007 c 28, s 119
    rep in pt—Loc Govt (W), 2011 nawm 4, ss 63(1)(2), 176(2), sch 4 pt D; Localism,
    2011 c 20, sch 3 para 21, sch 25 pt 4
    am—Loc Govt (W), 2011 nawm 4, s 63; ((temp) Health and Social Care, 2012 c 7, s
    190(9)(a)(ii)-(iv), (c)
  s 21B added—Loc Govt and Public Involvement in Health, 2007 c 28, s 122(1)
    am—Loc Govt (W), 2011 nawm 4, ss 64, 176(2), sch 4 pt D; (1.4.2016) Well-being
    of Future Generations (W), 2015 anaw 2, sch 4 para 6
  s 21C rep—Localism, 2011 c 20, sch 3 para 22, sch 25 pt 4
  s 21D added—Loc Govt and Public Involvement in Health, 2007 c 28, s 122(1)
    appl (mods)—SI 2008/634, art 7
    rep in pt—Localism, 2011 c 20, sch 3 para 23, sch 25 pt 4
    am—Loc Govt (W), 2011 nawm 4, s 65(1)(2); Localism, 2011 c 20, sch 3 para
    23(1)(4)(a)(ii)
  ss 21E, 21F rep—Localism, 2011 c 20, sch 3 para 24, sch 25 pt 4
  s 21G added —Loc Govt (W), 2011 nawm 4, s 61
    am—Localism, 2011 c 20, sch 3 para 27
  s 22 am—Loc Govt and Public Involvement in Health, 2007 c 28, s 122(2); Localism, 2011
    c 20, sch 3 para 28; Loc Govt (W), 2011 nawm 4, s 65(1)(3)(a)
    rep in pt—Loc Govt (W), 2011 nawm 4, ss 65(1)(3)(b), 176(2), sch 4, pt D; Localism,
    2011 c 20, sch 3 para 28(1)(3)(b), sch 25 pt 4
  s 22A added—Loc Govt and Public Involvement in Health, 2007 c 28, s 121(1)
    rep—Localism, 2011 c 20, sch 3 para 29, sch 25 pt 4
  s 25 am—Localism, 2011 c 20, sch 3 para 30
  s 26 rep in pt—Loc Govt (W), 2011 nawm 4, ss 34(1)(4), 176(2), sch 4 pt B
  s 27 appl (mods)—SIs (E) 2007/2089, regs 14, 17; 2008/1848 (W 177), regs 10, 13
    am—Localism, 2011 c 20, sch 3 para 31
  s 28 am—Localism, 2011 c 20, sch 3 para 32
  s 29 appl—(E) SI 2001/1003, reg 10(1); (W) SI 2002/2880 (W 276), reg 7(1); Loc Govt
    and Public Involvement in Health, 2007 c 28, s 71(7)
    am—Loc Govt and Public Involvement in Health, 2007 c 28, s 74, sch 3 paras 22, 23
    appl (mods)—SIs (E) 2007/2089, reg 17; 2008/1848 (W 177), reg 13
    rep in pt—Loc Govt (W), 2011 nawm 4, ss 36(1)(a), 176(2), sch 4 pt B
  s 30 rep—Loc Govt (W), 2011 nawm 4, ss 54(1)(2), 176(2), sch 4 pt C
  s 31 rep —Localism, 2011 c 20, sch 3 para 33, sch 25 pt 4
  s 32 rep —Localism, 2011 c 20, sch 3 para 34, sch 25 pt 4
  s 33 rep—Loc Govt (W), 2011 nawm 4, s 36(1)(d), sch 4 pt B
  s 33ZA added—Loc Govt (W), 2011 nawm 4, s 54(3)
    rep in pt—Localism, 2011 c 20, sch 3 para 35(1)(3), sch 25 pt 4
    am—Localism, 2011 c 20, sch 3 para 35(1)(2)
  ss 33A-33O added—Loc Govt and Public Involvement in Health, 2007 c 28, s 64
    rep—Localism, 2011 c 20, sch 3 paras 36-50, sch 25 pt 4
  s 34 am—Loc Govt and Public Involvement in Health, 2007 c 28, s 65; Localism, 2011 c 20,
    sch 3 para 51(1)(2); Loc Govt (W), 2011 nawm 4, s 36(1)(e)
    rep in pt—Localism, 2011 c 20, sch 3 para 51(1)(4), sch 25 pt 4

2000

c 22 *continued*

s 35 am—Loc Govt and Public Involvement in Health, 2007 c 28, s 65; Localism, 2011 c 20, sch 3 para 52; Loc Govt (W), 2011 nawm 4, s 36(1)(f)
rep in pt—Localism, 2011 c 20, sch 3 para 52(1)(4), sch 25 pt 1
s 36 am—Loc Govt and Public Involvement in Health, 2007 c 28, s 65; Localism, 2011 c 20, sch 3 para 53(1)(2); Loc Govt (W), 2011 nawm 4, s 36(1)(g)
rep in pt—Localism, 2011 c 20, sch 3 para 53(1)(3), sch 25 pt 4
s 37 am—Loc Govt and Public Involvement in Health, 2007 c 28, s 184(1); Localism, 2011 c 20, sch 3 para 54
s 38 am—Localism, 2011 c 20, sch 3 para 55
s 39 appl—SIs 2001/341, reg 103(1)(g); (E) 2004/555, reg 2(4)(c); 2004/557, reg 2(4)(j); (W) SI 2005/424 (W 42), reg 2(4)(h); (W) SI 2005/1510 (W 114), reg 2(3)(c)
am—Loc Govt and Public Involvement in Health, 2007 c 28, s 66; Localism, 2011 c 20, sch 3 para 56(1)(4)-(6)
rep in pt—Localism, 2011 c 20, sch 3 para 56(1)-(3)(7), sch 25 pt 4
s 41 am—Localism, 2011 c 20, sch 3 para 57
s 44 am—Political Parties, Elections and Referendums, 2000 c 41, s 158(1), sch 21 para 18(2); SI 2015/1376, sch 2 para 8(3)
see (functions made exercisable concurrently)—SI 2010/1837, art 3
ss 44A-44H added—Loc Govt and Public Involvement in Health, 2007 c 28, s 67
rep —Localism, 2011 c 20, sch 3 paras 58-65, sch 25 pt 4 (for savings in relation to ss 44A, 44B, 44D, 44E see SI 2012/1023, art 2(2))
s 45 am—Political Parties, Elections and Referendums, 2000 c 41, s 158(1), sch 21 para 18(3)(4); Loc Govt and Public Involvement in Health, 2007 c 28, s 69(7); Localism, 2011 c 20, sch 3 para 66; Loc Govt (W), 2011 nawm 4, s 54(4)
excl—Loc Govt and Public Involvement in Health, 2007 c 28, s 245, sch 4 para 10(4)
see —(functions made exercisable concurrently) SI 2010/1837, art 3
appl (mods)—Loc Govt (W), 2011 nawm 4, sch 1 para 4(3)
rep in pt—Localism, 2011 c 20, sch 3 para 66(1)(6), sch 25 pt 4
s 47 am—Loc Govt and Public Involvement in Health, 2007 c 28, s 68; Localism, 2011 c 20, sch 3 para 67(1)(2)
rep in pt—Localism, 2011 c 20, sch 3 para 67(1)(3)(4), sch 25 pt 4
s 48 appl—(E) SI 2001/1299, regs 12(5), 13(7)
am—Loc Govt and Public Involvement in Health, 2007 c 28, s 70; Localism, 2011 c 20, sch 3 para 68(1)(2)(6)
rep in pt—Loc Govt (W), 2011 nawm 4, ss 34(1)(5), 176(2), sch 4 pt B; Localism, 2011 c 20, sch 3 para 68, sch 25 pt 4
s 48A added—SI 2010/1837, art 5, sch
rep—SI 2015/1376, sch 2 para 8(4)
Pt 3 (ss 49-83) appl—Public Audit (W), 2004 c 23, s 54(2)(d); SIs 2010/497, art 17, sch 4; 2012/62, reg 29(2)
appl (mods)—SIs 2004/1777, art 14(1); 2004/1778, art 14(1); 2008/634, art 7(5)(6); 2011/3019, art 5(2)(3); 2012/2734, reg 3-6, sch pt 3
saving—Loc Govt and Public Involvement in Health, 2007 c 28, s 201(1)-(3)
mod—(transtl provns until 1.4.2009) SIs 2008/634, art 7(5)(6); 2008/907, art 16(8)
s 49 am—Fire and Rescue Services, 2004 c 21, s 53, sch 1 para 94; Public Audit (W), 2004 c 23, s 66, sch 2 paras 52, 53; Public Services Ombudsman (W), 2005 c 10, s 35, sch 4 paras 1, 2; (pt prosp) Loc Govt and Public Involvement in Health, 2007 c 28, s 183(1); ibid, s 183(7)(8); Loc Democracy, Economic Development and Construction, 2009 c 20, s 119, sch 6 para 93; Localism, 2011 c 20, sch 4 para 8(1)(6)
appl—Marine and Coastal Access, 2009 c 23, s 151(7)(c)
rep in pt—Police Reform and Social Responsibility, 2011 c 13, sch 16 para 257; Localism, 2011 c 20, sch 4 para 8, sch 25 pt 5
s 50 am—(pt prosp) Loc Govt and Public Involvement in Health, 2007 c 28, s 183(2); ibid, s 183(7)(8);
appl—Marine and Coastal Access, 2009 c 23, s 151(7)(c)
rep in pt—Police Reform and Social Responsibility, 2011 c 13, sch 16 para 258; Localism, 2011 c 20, sch 4 para 9, sch 25 pt 5
s 51 am—Public Services Ombudsman (W), 2005 c 10, s 35, sch 4 paras 1, 3; (pt prosp) Loc Govt and Public Involvement in Health, 2007 c 28, s 183(3)
appl—Marine and Coastal Access, 2009 c 23, s 151(7)(c)
appl (mods)—SI 2010/497, art 17, sch 4

2000

c 22 s 51 *continued*

rep in pt—Police Reform and Social Responsibility, 2011 c 13, sch 16 para 259; Localism, 2011 c 20, sch 4 para 10, sch 25 pt 5

s 52 rep in pt—(E prosp) Loc Govt and Public Involvement in Health, 2007 c 28, s 241, sch 18

am—Loc Govt and Public Involvement in Health, 2007 c 28, ss 183(4)-(6), 184(2); Localism, 2011 c 20, sch 4 para 11

appl—Marine and Coastal Access, 2009 c 23, s 151(7)(c)

s 53 am—Public Services Ombudsman (W), 2005 c 10, s 35, sch 4 paras 1, 4; Loc Govt and Public Involvement in Health, 2007 c 28, s 187; Loc Govt (Democracy) (W), 2013 anaw 4, s 68(2)

appl—Marine and Coastal Access, 2009 c 23, s 151(7)(c)

rep in pt—Localism, 2011 c 20, sch 4 para 12, sch 25 pt 5; Police Reform and Social Responsibility, 2011 c 13, sch 16 para 260

s 54 am—Loc Govt and Public Involvement in Health, 2007 c 28, s 184(3); Loc Govt (Democracy) (W), 2013 anaw 4, s 68(3)

appl—Marine and Coastal Access, 2009 c 23, s 151(7)(c)

rep in pt—Police Reform and Social Responsibility, 2011 c 13, sch 16 para 261; Localism, 2011 c 20, sch 4 para 13, sch 25 pt 5

s 54A added—Loc Govt, 2003 c 26, s 113(1)

rep in pt—Loc Govt and Public Involvement in Health, 2007 c 28, s 241, sch 18; Localism, 2011 c 20, sch 4 para 14, sch 25 pt 5; Police Reform and Social Responsibility, 2011 c 13, sch 16 para 262

am—Loc Govt and Public Involvement in Health, 2007 c 28, s 188(1)

appl—Marine and Coastal Access, 2009 c 23, s 151(7)(c)

s 55 rep —Localism, 2011 c 20, sch 4 para 15, sch 25 pt 5

s 56 appl—Marine and Coastal Access, 2009 c 23, s 151(7)(c)

s 56A added—Loc Govt and Public Involvement in Health, 2007 c 28, s 189

rep—Localism, 2011 c 20, sch 4 para 16, sch 25 pt 5

ss 57, 57A-57D, 58-65, 65A, 66, 66B, 66C, 67 rep—Localism, 2011 c 20, sch 4 para 30, sch 25 pt 5

s 68 am—Public Services Ombudsman (W), 2005 c 10, s 35, sch 4 paras 1, 9, 10; ibid, s 35, sch 4 paras 1, 11(a)-(c); Localism, 2011 c 20, sch 4 para 36(a)(ii)

rep in pt—Public Services Ombudsman (W), 2005 c 10, ss 35, 39(2), sch 4 paras 1, 11(d)(e), sch 7; Police Reform and Social Responsibility, 2011 c 13, sch 16 para 264; Localism, 2011 c 20, sch 4 para 36(a)(i)(b), sch 25 pt 5

s 69 am—Public Services Ombudsman (W), 2005 c 10, s 35, sch 4 paras 1, 12, 13

rep in pt—Localism, 2011 c 20, sch 4 para 37(1)(2), sch 25 pt 5

s 70 am—Public Services Ombudsman (W), 2005 c 10, s 35, sch 4 paras 1, 14-16; Localism, 2011 c 20, sch 4 para 38(1)(2); Social Services and Well-being (W), 2014 anaw 4, sch 3 para 12

rep in pt—Localism, 2011 c 20, sch 4 para 38(1)(3), sch 25 pt 5

s 71 am—Public Services Ombudsman (W), 2005 c 10, s 35, sch 4 paras 1, 14-16

rep in pt—Localism, 2011 c 20, sch 4 para 39, sch 25 pt 5

s 72 am—Public Services Ombudsman (W), 2005 c 10, s 35, sch 4 paras 1, 14-16

rep in pt—Localism, 2011 c 20, sch 4 para 39, sch 25 pt 5

s 73 am—Public Services Ombudsman (W), 2005 c 10, s 35, sch 4 paras 1, 17; Loc Govt and Public Involvement in Health, 2007 c 28, s 194(8); (Loc Govt (Democracy) (W), 2013 anaw 4, s 69(2)(a)-(c)(d)(ii)

rep in pt—Police Reform and Social Responsibility, 2011 c 13, sch 16 para 265; Localism, 2011 c 20, sch 4 para 41, sch 25 pt 5; Loc Govt (Democracy) (W), 2013 anaw 4, s 69(2)(d)(i)

s 74 am—Public Services Ombudsman (W), 2005 c 10, s 35, sch 4 paras 1, 18

s 75 am—SI 2010/22, art 5, sch 2

rep in pt—SI 2010/22, art 5, sch 2

s 76 am —Constitutional Reform, 2005 c 4, s 15(1), sch 4 pt 1 para 291; SI 2010/22, art 5, sch 2

rep in pt—SI 2010/22, art 5, sch 2

s 77 am —SI 2010/22, art 5, sch 2; Crime and Cts, 2013 c 22, sch 9 para 52

rep in pt—SI 2010/22, art 5, sch 2; Localism, 2011 c 20, sch 4 para 42, sch 25 pt 5

s 78 am—Public Services Ombudsman (W), 2005 c 10, s 35, sch 4 paras 1, 19; Loc Govt and Public Involvement in Health, 2007 c 28, s 197; SI 2010/22, art 5, sch 2; Localism, 2011 c 20, sch 4 para 43

appl (mods)—SI 2010/22, art 5, sch 5

2000

c 22 s 78 *continued*

rep in pt—Localism, 2011 c 20, sch 4 para 43, sch 25 pt 5

ss 78A, 78B rep—Localism, 2011 c 20, sch 4 paras 44, 45, sch 25 pt 5

s 79 am—Public Services Ombudsman (W), 2005 c 10, s 35, sch 4 paras 1, 20; Loc Govt
and Public Involvement in Health, 2007 c 28, s 199

rep in pt—Localism, 2011 c 20, sch 4 para 46, sch 25 pt 5

s 80 am—Public Services Ombudsman (W), 2005 c 10, s 35, sch 4 paras 1, 21, 22; SI
2010/22, art 5, sch 2; Localism, 2011 c 20, sch 4 para 47(1)(4)-(6)

rep in pt—Localism, 2011 c 20, sch 4 para 47(1)-(3)(7), sch 25 pt 5

s 81 am—Public Services Ombudsman (W), 2005 c 10, s 35, sch 4 paras 1, 21, 22;
Localism, 2011 c 20, sch 4 para 48(1)(2); Loc Govt (Democracy) (W), 2013
anaw 4, ss 58, 69(3)

rep in pt—Police Reform and Social Responsibility, 2011 c 13, sch 16 para 266;
Localism, 2011 c 20, sch 4 para 48(1)(3)(4), sch 25 pt 5

s 82 am—Public Audit (W), 2004 c 23, s 66, sch 2 paras 52, 55; Public Services
Ombudsman (W), 2005 c 10, s 35, sch 4 paras 1, 23; Localism, 2011 c 20, sch 4
para 49(1)(6)(b)

rep in pt—Police Reform and Social Responsibility, 2011 c 13, sch 16 para 267;
Localism, 2011 c 20, sch 4 para 49, sch 25 pt 5

s 82A added—Loc Govt, 2003 c 26, s 113(2)

am—Loc Govt and Public Involvement in Health, 2007 c 28, s 194(9)

rep in pt—Localism, 2011 c 20, sch 4 para 50, sch 25 pt 5

s 83 am—Public Services Ombudsman (W), 2005 c 10, s 35, 39(2), sch 4 paras 1, 24, sch 7;
Loc Govt and Public Involvement in Health, 2007 c 28, s 74, sch 3 paras 22, 26;
(prosp) Planning (W), 2015 anaw 4, sch 1 pt 2 pt 2 para 4

rep in pt—Loc Govt and Public Involvement in Health, 2007 c 28, s 146, sch 9 para
1(1)(2)(p), sch 18; SI 2010/22, art 5, sch 2; Police Reform and Social
Responsibility, 2011 c 13, sch 16 para 268; Localism, 2011 c 20, sch 4 para 51,
sch 25 pt 5

s 86 am—Loc Govt and Public Involvement in Health, 2007 c 28, s 54(3)(6)

s 89 rep in pt—Loc Democracy, Economic Development and Construction, 2009 c 20, s 146,
sch 7 pt 3

s 91 rep in pt—Loc Audit and Accountability, 2014 c 2, sch 1 pt 2

s 93 am—Adoption and Children, 2002 c 38, s 136

appl—SI 1987/1967, sch 9 para 76(1)(a), sch 10 para 66(1)(a); SI 1996/207, sch 7
para 72(1)(a), sch 8 para 59(1)(a); SI 1987/1971, sch 4 para 75(1)(a), sch 5
para 68(1)(a); SI 1992/1918, sch 4 para 74(1)(a), sch 5 para 68(1)(a)

s 94 rep—Welfare Reform, 2007 c 5, s 42(11), sch 8

s 95 rep—Welfare Reform, 2007 c 5, s 42(11), sch 8

s 96 rep (prosp)—Welfare Reform, 2012 c 5, sch 14 pt 1

s 99 am—Loc Govt (W), 2011 nawm 4, sch 3 para 5(2)

s 100 appl —(W) SI 2005/2915 (W 212), reg 7

rep (W)—Loc Govt (W), 2011 nawm 4, sch 3 para 5(3), sch. 4 pt F

s 101 rep in pt—Police Reform and Social Responsibility, 2011 c 13, sch 16 para 269

appl (mods)—SI 2012/2734, reg 3-6, sch pt 1

s 102 rep in pt—Children, 2004 c 31, ss 55(5)(a), 64, sch 5 pt 4

am—Children, 2004 c 31, s 55(5)(b)

s 104 rep—Loc Govt, 2003 c 26, s 127(2), sch 8 pt 1

s 105 am—Loc Govt, 2003 c 26, s 100, sch 3 paras 11, 14 (see SI 2003/2938); Loc Govt
and Public Involvement in Health, 2007 c 28, s 74, sch 3 paras 22, 27; (savings)
(EW) ibid, s 191(5); Localism, 2011 c 20, sch 3 para 70; SIs 2013/2597, sch
para 7(3); 2015/1376, sch 2 para 8(5)

rep in pt—Localism, 2011 c 20, sch 4 para 52, sch 25 pt 5

s 106 rep in pt—Localism, 2011 c 20, sch 3 para 71, sch 25 pt 4

am—Loc Govt (W), 2011 nawm 4, s 176(1); Loc Govt (Democracy) (W), 2013 anaw
4, s 68(4)

sch A1 added —Localism, 2011 c 20, sch 2 para 2

appl (mods)—Nat Health Service, 2006 c 41, s 247A(3)(d)

appl—SI 2012/1020, reg 11(5)

sch 1 am—(E) SI 2001/1517, arts 2, 6(2); (W) SI 2002/803 (W 88), arts 2, 6(2); Loc Govt,
2003 c 26, s 115 (see SI 2003/2938); Loc Govt and Public Involvement in
Health, 2007 c 28, s 74, sch 3 paras 22, 28, 29; SI 2010/1158, art 5, sch 2;
Localism, 2011 c 20, sch 3 para 72(1)-(3)(5)(8)(11); School Standards and
Organisation (W), 2013 anaw 1, sch 5 para 5(2)(3)

2000

c 22 sch 1 *continued*

rep in pt—Loc Govt (W), 2011 nawm 4, ss 34(1)(6), 176(2), sch 4 pt B; Localism, 2011 c 20, sch 3 para 72(1)(4)(6)(7)(9)(12), sch 25 pt 4

sch 4 rep —Localism, 2011 c 20, sch 4 para 53, sch 25 pt 5

sch 5 rep in pt—Adoption and Children, 2002 c 38, s 139(3), sch 5; Health and Social Care (Community Health and Standards), 2003 c 43, s 196, sch 14 pt 2; Fire and Rescue Services, 2004 c 21, s 54, sch 2; Inquiries, 2005 c 12, ss 44(5), 49(2), sch 3; Nat Health Service (Conseq Provns), 2006 c 43, s 6, sch 4; Loc Audit and Accountability, 2014 c 2, sch 1 pt 2

c 23　　**Regulation of Investigatory Powers**

cert functs made exercisable in S and trans to S Ministers—(saving) SI 2000/3253, arts 2,3,6, schs 1, 2

appl—Intelligence Services, 1994 c 13, s 7(9); Anti-terrorism, Crime and Security, 2001 c 24, s 19(9); Serious Organised Crime and Police, 2005 c 15, s 33(2)(d)

Pt 1 (ss 1-25) saved—Constitutional Reform, 2005 c 4, s 107(3)(b); Commrs for Revenue and Customs, 2005 c 11, ss 22(b), 41(6)(b); Serious Organised Crime and Police, 2005 c 15, ss 33(4)(b), 34(3)(b); Terrorist Asset-Freezing etc, 2010 c 38, s 25(2)(b)

Pt 1, Ch 1 (ss 1-20) see—(code of practice in force 1 July 2002) SI 2002/1693, art 2

s 1 am—SI 2011/1340, reg 2(1)

s 2 am—(temp until 31.12.2016) Data Retention and Investigatory Powers, 2014 c 27, s 5

s 3 am—Wireless Telegraphy, 2006 c 36, s 123, sch 7 paras 21, 22; Policing and Crime, 2009 c 26, s 100(1); SI 2011/1340, reg 3; Counter-Terrorism and Security, 2015 c 6, sch 8 para 2

s 4 am—Nat Health Service (Conseq Provns), 2006 c 43, s 2, sch 1 para 208; SI 2007/1388, art 3, sch 1; Health and Social Care, 2012 c 7, sch 5 para 98

s 5 trans of functions—SI 2007/2915, art 3, sch 2

am—(temp until 31.12.2016) Data Retention and Investigatory Powers, 2014 c 27, s 3(1)(2)

saved—SI 2008/648, art 1

s 6 am—Serious Organised Crime and Police, 2005 c 15, s 59, sch 4 paras 131, 132; Serious Crime, 2007 c 27, s 88, sch 12 paras 5, 6; Crime and Cts, 2013 c 22, sch 8 para 78; SI 2013/602, sch 2 para 33(2)(b)

rep in pt—SI 2013/602, sch 2 para 33(2)(a)

mod—SI 2007/1098, art 6, sch 1

s 7 am—SI 2000/3253, art 4(1), sch 3 pt II paras 3,4

s 9 am—SI 2000/3253, art 4(1), sch 3 pt II paras 3,5; Terrorism, 2006 c 11, s 32(1)(2)

trans of functions—SI 2007/2915, art 3, sch 2

s 10 am—SI 2000/3253, art 4(1), sch 3 pt II paras 3, 6; Terrorism, 2006 c 11, s 32(1)(3)(4)

trans of functions—SI 2007/2915, art 3, sch 2

s 11 am—(temp until 31.12.2016) Data Retention and Investigatory Powers, 2014 c 27, s 4(2)-(5)

s 12 am—(temp until 31.12.2016) Data Retention and Investigatory Powers, 2014 c 27, s 4(6)(7)

s 15 trans of functions—SI 2007/2915, art 3, sch 2

saved—SI 2008/648, art 1

s 16 am—Terrorism, 2006 c 11, s 32(1)(5)(6)(7)

s 17 saved—(EW, NI) Criminal Procedure and Investigations, 1996 c 25, s 7A(9)

am—Inquiries, 2005 c 12, s 48(1), sch 2 pt 1 para 20; Serious Organised Crime and Police, 2005 c 15, s 59, sch 4 paras 131, 133; Policing and Crime, 2009 c 26, s 100(2)

mod—SI 2007/1098, art 6, sch 1

rep in pt—Crime and Cts, 2013 c 22, sch 8 para 79; SI 2013/602, sch 2 para 33(3)

s 18 am—(transtl savings) SI 2001/1149, arts 3(1), 4(8), sch 1 para 135(1)(2); Prevention of Terrorism, 2005 c 2, s 11(5), sch para 9; Inquiries, 2005 c 12, s 48(1), sch 2 pt 1 para 21(1)(3)(4); Wireless Telegraphy, 2006 c 36, s 123, sch 7 paras 21, 23; Armed Forces, 2006 c 52, s 378, sch 16 para 169; Counter-Terrorism, 2008 c 28, ss 69, s 74(1); Terrorist Asset-Freezing etc, 2010 c 38, s 28(2)(3); Terrorism Prevention and Investigation Measures, 2011 c 23, sch 7 para 4(2)(b)(3)(a)(c); Justice and Security, 2013 c 18, s 16(2)(3)(a); ibid, sch 2 para 11; Counter-Terrorism and Security, 2015 c 6, s 15(3)

rep in pt—(transtl savings) SI 2001/1149, arts 3(2), 4(8)(11), sch 2; Communications, 2003 c 21, s 406(7), sch 19(1); SI 2003/1900, arts 2(1), 3(1), sch 1; SI 2003/3142, art 3(2); Inquiries, 2005 c 12, ss 44(5), 48(1), 49(2), sch 2 pt 1

2000

c 23 s 18 *continued*

para 21(1)(2), sch 3; Terrorism Prevention and Investigation Measures, 2011 c 23, sch 7 para 4(2)(a)(3)(b)

s 19 am—Serious Organised Crime and Police, 2005 c 15, s 59, sch 4 paras 131, 134
rep in pt—Crime and Cts, 2013 c 22, sch 8 para 80; SI 2013/602, sch 2 para 33(4)
mod—SI 2007/1098, art 6, sch 1

s 21 am—Serious Crime, 2007 c 27, s 88, sch 12 paras 5, 7

s 22 am—Policing and Crime, 2009 c 26, ss 7(1)(2), 112, sch 7 paras 12, 13; Protection of Freedoms, 2012 c 9, sch 9 para 7; SI 2013/602, sch 2 para 33(5)(b)(c)(6)(a)-(c); (temp until 31.12.2016) Data Retention and Investigatory Powers, 2014 c 27, ss 3(3)(4), 4(8)-(10)
rep in pt—SI 2013/602, sch 2 para 33(5)(a)

s 23 am—Policing and Crime, 2009 c 26, ss 7(1)(3)(4), 112, sch 7 paras 12, 14; Protection of Freedoms, 2012 c 9, sch 9 para 8; SI 2013/602, sch 2 para 33(6)(e)
rep in pt—SI 2013/602, sch 2 para 33(6)(d)

s 23A added—Protection of Freedoms, 2012 c 9, s 37
am—SI 2013/602, sch 2 para 33(7)

s 23B added—Protection of Freedoms, 2012 c 9, s 37

s 25 am—Serious Organised Crime and Police, 2005 c 15, s 59, sch 4 paras 131, 135(1)(2)(3)(4); Serious Crime, 2007 c 27, s 88, sch 12 paras 5, 8; Crime and Cts, 2013 c 22, sch 8 para 81
rep in pt—SI 2013/602, sch 2 para 33(8)
mod—SI 2007/1098, art 6, sch 1

Pt 2 (ss 26-48) appl (mods)—SI 2001/1057, arts 2-5
power to mod—Police Reform, 2002 c 30, s 19(2)(a)
see—(code of practice in force 1 August 2002) SIs 2002/1932, art 2; 2002/1933, art 2
mod—(EW) SI 2004/815, art 3

s 26 am—Communications, 2003 c 21, s 406(1), sch 17 para 161(1)(2)
appl—(EW, NI) Serious Organised Crime and Police, 2005 c 15, s 82, sch 5 para 27

s 27 am—Serious Crime, 2007 c 27, s 88, sch 12 paras 5, 9

s 28 see—SI 2010/521, arts 6-9

s 29 see—SI 2010/521, arts 6-9
mod—SI 2000/2793, art 4
am—Policing and Crime, 2009 c 26, s 8
rep in pt—SI 2013/602, sch 2 para 33(9)

s 31 rep in pt—SI 2001/3686, regs 6(17)(a), 8

s 32 am—Enterprise, 2002 c 40, s 199(1)(2); Serious Organised Crime and Police, 2005 c 15, s 59, sch 4 paras 131, 136; Armed Forces, 2006 c 52, s 378, sch 16 para 170; Serious Crime, 2007 c 27, s 88, sch 12 paras 5, 10; SI 2013/602, sch 2 para 33(10); Crime and Cts, 2013 c 22, s 55(2); ibid, sch 8 para 82; SI 2014/892, sch 1 para 134
rep in pt—Enterprise, 2002 c 40, s 278(2), sch 26

ss 32A, 32B added—Protection of Freedoms, 2012 c 9, s 38(1)

s 33 am—Enterprise, 2002 c 40, s 199(1)(3)(4); Serious Organised Crime and Police, 2005 c 15, s 59, sch 4 paras 131, 137(1)(3)(5)(6); Serious Crime, 2007 c 27, s 88, sch 12 paras 5, 11; Policing and Crime, 2009 c 26, s 9; SI 2013/602, sch 2 para 33(11)(a)(c)(g)(i)(aa)(ii); Crime and Cts, 2013 c 22, sch 8 para 83(2)(3)(a)(b)(4); ibid, sch 21 para 7(2)(3); SI 2014/892, sch 1 para 135
rep in pt —Serious Organised Crime and Police, 2005 c 15, ss 59, 174(2), sch 4 paras 131, 137(1)(2)(4)(7), sch 17 pt 2; SI 2013/602, sch 2 para 33(11)(b)(d)(e)(f)(g)(i)(bb)
mod—SI 2007/1098, art 6, sch 1

s 34 am—Enterprise, 2002 c 40, s 199(1)(5); Serious Organised Crime and Police, 2005 c 15, s 59, sch 4 paras 131, 138(1)-(4); Police and Justice, 2006 c 48, s 52, sch 14 para 39; Armed Forces, 2006 c 52, s 378, sch 16 para 172; Serious Crime, 2007 c 27, s 88, sch 12 paras 5, 12; Crime and Cts, 2013 c 22, sch 8 para 84(2)(3); ibid, sch 21 para 8(2)-(4); SIs 2013/602, sch 2 para 33(12)(a)(b); 2014/892, sch 1 para 136
rep in pt —Serious Organised Crime and Police, 2005 c 15, ss 59, 174(2), sch 4 paras 131, 138(1)(5)(6), sch 17 pt 2

s 35 see—SI 2000/2563, arts 3,4
am—Enterprise, 2002 c 40, s 199(1)(6); Serious Organised Crime and Police, 2005 c 15, s 59, sch 4 paras 131, 139; Serious Crime, 2007 c 27, s 88, sch 12 paras 5, 13;

2000
c 23 s 35 *continued*

Crime and Cts, 2013 c 22, sch 8 para 85(2)(3)(a); ibid, sch 21 para 9(2)(3)(a)(b); SI 2014/892, sch 1 para 137

rep in pt—Enterprise, 2002 c 40, s 278(2), sch 26

s 36 am—Enterprise, 2002 c 40, s 199(1)(7); Serious Organised Crime and Police, 2005 c 15, s 59, sch 4 paras 131, 140; Serious Crime, 2007 c 27, s 88, sch 12 paras 5, 14; Crime and Cts, 2013 c 22, sch 8 para 86(2)(3); ibid, sch 21 para 10(2)(3); SIs 2013/602, sch 2 para 33(13); 2014/892, sch 1 para 138

rep in pt—Enterprise, 2002 c 40, s 278(2), sch 26

s 37 am—Enterprise, 2002 c 40, s 199(1)(8); Serious Organised Crime and Police, 2005 c 15, s 59, sch 4 paras 131, 141; Serious Crime, 2007 c 27, s 88, sch 12 paras 5, 15; Crime and Cts, 2013 c 22, sch 8 para 87; ibid, sch 21 para 11; SI 2014/892, sch 1 para 139

rep in pt—Enterprise, 2002 c 40, s 278(2), sch 26

s 40 am—Enterprise, 2002 c 40, s 199(1)(9); Serious Organised Crime and Police, 2005 c 15, s 59, sch 4 paras 131, 142; Serious Crime, 2007 c 27, s 88, sch 12 paras 5, 16; Crime and Cts, 2013 c 22, sch 8 para 88; ibid, sch 21 para 12; SI 2014/892, sch 1 para 140

s 41 am—Armed Forces, 2006 c 52, s 378, sch 16 para 173

s 42 am—SI 2000/3253, art 4(1), sch 3 pt II paras 3,7

s 43 am—Protection of Freedoms, 2012 c 9, sch 9 para 9; ibid, s 38(2)

mod—SIs 2000/2793, art 6; 2013/2788, art 3

appl—SI 2009/3404, art 8

appl (mods)—SI 2010/123, art 8

s 44 am—SI 2000/3253, art 4(1), sch 3 pt II paras 3,8

s 45 am —Serious Organised Crime and Police, 2005 c 15, s 59, sch 4 paras 131, 143(a); SI 2013/602, sch 2 para 33(14)(a)(b)

rep in pt —Serious Organised Crime and Police, 2005 c 15, ss 59, 174(2), sch 4 paras 131, 143(b), sch 17 pt 2; SI 2013/602, sch 2 para 33(14)(c)

mod—SI 2007/1098, art 6, sch 1

s 46 am—Enterprise, 2002 c 40, s 199(1)(10); Energy, 2004 c 20, s 69(1), sch 14 para 8(1); Serious Organised Crime and Police, 2005 c 15, s 59, sch 4 paras 131, 144; Crime and Cts, 2013 c 22, sch 8 para 89; ibid, sch 21 para 13; SI 2014/892, sch 1 para 141

s 48 am—Enterprise, 2002 c 40, s 199(1)(11); Serious Crime, 2007 c 27, s 88, sch 12 paras 5, 18; SI 2014/892, sch 1 para 142(b)

rep in pt—SI 2014/892, sch 1 para 142(a)

s 49 am —Serious Organised Crime and Police, 2005 c 15, s 59, sch 4 paras 131, 145; Serious Crime, 2007 c 27, s 88, sch 12 paras 5, 19; Policing and Crime, 2009 c 26, s 112, sch 7 paras 12, 15; SI 2013/602, sch 2 para 33(15)(a); Crime and Cts, 2013 c 22, sch 8 para 90

rep in pt—SI 2013/602, sch 2 para 33(15)(b)

mod—SI 2007/1098, art 6, sch 1

s 51 am —Serious Organised Crime and Police, 2005 c 15, s 59, sch 4 paras 131, 146; Serious Crime, 2007 c 27, s 88, sch 12 paras 5, 20; Crime and Cts, 2013 c 22, sch 8 para 91(2)(a)(b)(3)

mod—SI 2007/1098, art 6, sch 1

rep in pt—SI 2013/602, sch 2 para 33(16)(b)(c)

s 53 am—Terrorism, 2006 c 11, s 15; Policing and Crime, 2009 c 26, s 26

s 54 am—Serious Organised Crime and Police, 2005 c 15, s 59, sch 4 paras 131, 147; Serious Crime, 2007 c 27, s 88, sch 12 paras 5, 21; Crime and Cts, 2013 c 22, sch 8 para 92

rep in pt—SI 2013/602, sch 2 para 33(17)

mod—SI 2007/1098, art 6, sch 1

s 55 am—Serious Organised Crime and Police, 2005 c 15, s 59, sch 4 paras 131, 148; Serious Crime, 2007 c 27, s 88, sch 12 paras 5, 22; Crime and Cts, 2013 c 22, sch 8 para 93(2)(3)

rep in pt—SI 2013/602, sch 2 para 33(18)(a)(b)

mod—SI 2007/1098, art 6, sch 1

s 56 am—Serious Organised Crime and Police, 2005 c 15, s 59, sch 4 paras 131, 149(b)(c); Armed Forces, 2006 c 52, s 378, sch 16 para 174; Crime and Cts, 2013 c 22, sch 8 para 94(a); SI 2013/602, sch 2 para 33(19)(a)(ii)

rep in pt—Serious Organised Crime and Police, 2005 c 15, ss 59, 174(2), sch 4 paras 131, 149(a), sch 17 pt 2; Serious Crime, 2007 c 27, s 88, sch 12 paras 5, 23,

2000

c 23 s 56 *continued*

    sch 14; Crime and Cts, 2013 c 22, sch 8 para 94(b); SI 2013/602, sch 2 para 33(19)(a)(i)(b)(c)

  mod—SI 2007/1098, art 6, sch 1

Pt 4 (ss 57-72) power to mod—Police Reform, 2002 c 30, s 19(2)(a)

  mod—(EW) SI 2004/815, art 3

s 57 am—SI 2000/3253, art 4(1), sch 3 pt II paras 3,9; Constitutional Reform, 2005 c 4, s 145, sch 17 pt 2 para 30(1)(2)(a); Protection of Freedoms, 2012 c 9, sch 9 para 10

s 58 am—SI 2000/3253, art 4(1), sch 3 pt II paras 3,10; Serious Organised Crime and Police, 2005 c 15, s 59, sch 4 paras 131, 150; Policing and Crime, 2009 c 26, s 112, sch 7 paras 12, 16; SI 2013/602, sch 2 para 33(20)(b); (temp until 31.12.2016) Data Retention and Investigatory Powers, 2014 c 27, s 6

  rep in pt—Crime and Cts, 2013 c 22, sch 8 para 95; SI 2013/602, sch 2 para 33(20)(a)

  mod—SI 2007/1098, art 6, sch 1

s 59 am—SI 2000/3253, art 4(1), sch 3 pt II paras 3,11; Constitutional Reform, 2005 c 4, s 145, sch 17 pt 2 para 30(1)(2)(b); Identity Cards, 2006 c 15, s 24(1)(2)

  rep in pt—Identity Documents, 2010 c 40, s 12, sch 1 paras 12, 13

s 59A added—Justice and Security, 2013 c 18, s 5

s 60 am—SI 2000/3253, art 4(1), sch 3 pt II paras 3,12; Serious Organised Crime and Police, 2005 c 15, s 59, sch 4 paras 131, 152; Policing and Crime, 2009 c 26, s 112, sch 7 paras 12, 17; Justice and Security, 2013 c 18, sch 2 para 4

s 61 am—Constitutional Reform, 2005 c 4, s 145, sch 17 pt 2 para 30(1)(3)

s 62 am—Protection of Freedoms, 2012 c 9, sch 9 para 11

s 65 am—Crime (International Co-operation), 2003 c 32, s 91(1), sch 5 paras 78, 79; Serious Organised Crime and Police, 2005 c 15, s 59, sch 4 paras 131, 151; Identity Cards, 2006 c 15, s 24(1)(3)(4)(5); Serious Crime, 2007 c 27, s 88, sch 12 paras 5, 24; Identity Documents, 2010 c 40, s 12, sch 1 paras 12, 14(3)(a); Protection of Freedoms, 2012 c 9, sch 9 para 12; SI 2013/602, sch 2 para 33(21)(a); Crime and Cts, 2013 c 22, sch 8 para 96

  mod—SI 2007/1098, art 6, sch 1

  rep in pt—Identity Documents, 2010 c 40, s 12, sch 1 paras 12, 14(2)(3)(b)(4); SI 2013/602, sch 2 para 33(21)(b)

s 67 am—Protection of Freedoms, 2012 c 9, sch 9 para 13

s 68 mod—SI 2007/1098, art 6, sch 1

  am—SI 2013/602, sch 2 para 33(22)(b)(c)

  rep in pt—Crime and Cts, 2013 c 22, sch 8 para 97; SI 2013/602, sch 2 para 33(22)(a)

s 71 am—Serious Crime, 2007 c 27, s 88, sch 12 paras 5, 25; SI 2011/1340, reg 2(2)(3); Protection of Freedoms, 2012 c 9, sch 9 para 14; Serious Crime, 2015 c 9, s 83; ibid, sch 4 para 18

  mod—SI 2014/2042, reg 10(3) 15(7)

s 72 mod—SI 2014/2042, reg 10(3) 15(7)

s 73 rep in pt—Wireless Telegraphy, 2006 c 36, s 125, sch 9

s 75 rep in pt—Serious Organised Crime and Police, 2005 c 15, ss 59, 174(2), sch 4 paras 131, 153, sch 17 pt 2

s 76A added—Crime (International Co-operation), 2003 c 32, s 83

  am—Serious Organised Crime and Police, 2005 c 15, s 59, sch 4 paras 131, 154(1)(2)(3)(a); (S) Police, Public Order and Crim Justice (S), 2006 asp 10, s 101, sch 6 para 8; Crime and Cts, 2013 c 22, sch 8 para 98(2)(3)

  rep in pt—Serious Organised Crime and Police, 2005 c 15, ss 59, 174(2), sch 4 paras 131, 154(1)(3)(b), sch 17 pt 2; SI 2013/602, sch 2 para 33(23)

  mod—SI 2007/1098, art 6, sch 1

s 77A added (pt prosp)—Protection of Freedoms, 2012 c 9, sch 9 para 15

s 77B added—Protection of Freedoms, 2012 c 9, sch 9 para 15

s 78 am—Crime (International Co-operation), 2003 c 32, s 91(1), sch 5 paras 78, 80; Protection of Freedoms, 2012 c 9, sch 9 para 16

s 81 am—(prosp) Crim Justice and Ct Services, 2000 c 43, ss 74, 75, sch 7 pt II para 211; Justice (NI), 2002 c 26, s 10(6), sch 4, para 40; Wireless Telegraphy, 2006 c 36, s 123, sch 7 paras 21, 24; Armed Forces, 2006 c 52, s 378, sch 16 para 175; Constitutional Reform and Governance, 2010 c 25, s 19, sch 2 para 11; Protection of Freedoms, 2012 c 9, sch 9 para 17; SI 2013/602, sch 2 para 33(24)

  appl—Intelligence Services, 1994 c 13, s 11(1A); Serious Organised Crime and Police, 2005 c 15, s 42(3); Identity Cards, 2006 c 15, s 42(9); Counter-Terrorism, 2008 c 28, s 21(4)

2000

c 23 s 81 *continued*

rep in pt—Armed Forces, 2001 c 19, s 38, sch 7 pt 1; Serious Crime, 2007 c 27, s 88, sch 12 paras 5, 27, sch 14

s 82 am —(transtl savings) SI 2001/1149, arts 3(1), 4(8), sch 1 para 135(1)(3); Postal Services, 2011 c 5, sch 12 para 160

rep in pt—(transtl savings) SI 2001/1149, arts 3(2), 4(8)(11), sch 2

sch A1 added—SI 2011/1340, reg 2(4), sch

am—Crime and Cts, 2013 c 22, sch 9 para 125

sch 1 am—SI 2001/2568, art 16, sch para 18(b); (transtl savings) SI 2001/1149, arts 3(1), 4(8), sch 1 para 135(1)(4); SIs 2002/794, art 5(1), sch 1, para 39; 2002/1397, art 12, schedule pt I, para 16(b); 2002/2626, art 20, sch 2, para 24(b); 2003/3171, arts 2(1)-(7), 3; Communications, 2003 c 21, s 406(1), sch 17 para 161(1)(3); Energy, 2004 c 20, s 69(1), sch 14 para 8(2); Serious Organised Crime and Police, 2005 c 15, s 59, sch 4 paras 131, 155; Gambling, 2005 c 19, s 356(1)(2), sch 16 pt 2 para 14; SI 2005/1084, art 2(1); Nat Health Service (Conseq Provns), 2006 c 43, s 2, sch 1 para 209; Educ and Inspections, 2006 c 40, s 157, sch 14 para 68; SIs 2006/1874, arts 2, 3; 2006/1926, art 9, sch 1; 2007/1388, art 3, sch 1; 2007/2128, art 8, sch; 2007/3224, art 15, sch; Serious Crime, 2007 c 27, s 88, sch 12 paras 5, 28; Health and Social Care, 2008 c 14, s 95, sch 5 para 72; SIs 2009/229, art 9, sch 2 para 3; 2009/2748, art 8, sch para 6(a); 2010/231, art 68, sch 4; 2010/521, art 2; 2010/976, art 6, sch 4; Postal Services, 2011 c 5, sch 12 para 161(b); Financial Services, 2012 c 21, sch 18 para 88; Crime and Cts, 2013 c 22, sch 8 para 99; (prosp) Energy, 2013 c 32, sch 12 para 74; SIs 2013/755 (W 90), sch 2 para 398; 2014/892, sch 1 para 143

rep in pt—SIs 2001/3686, regs 6(17)(b), 8; 2001/2568, art 16, sch para 18(a); 2002/794, art 5(2), sch 2; 2002/1397, art 12, schedule pt I, para 16(a); 2002/2626, art 20, sch 2, para 24(a); 2002/1555, art 26; Serious Organised Crime and Police, 2005 c 15, ss 161(5), 174(2), sch 13 pt 2 para 10, sch 17 pt 2; SIs 2005/1084, art 2(2); 2009/2748, art 8, sch para 6(b); 2010/521, art 2; 2010/976, art 6, sch 4; Postal Services, 2011 c 5, sch 12 para 161(a); SI 2013/602, sch 2 para 33(25)

mod—SI 2007/1098, art 6, sch 1; SI 2012/2007, sch para 65

sch 2 am—Courts, 2003 c 39, s 65, sch 4 para 12; Serious Organised Crime and Police, 2005 c 15, s 59, sch 4 paras 131, 156(1)(2)(3)-(5); Serious Crime, 2007 c 27, s 88, sch 12 paras 5, 29; Protection of Freedoms, 2012 c 9, sch 9 para 27; Crime and Cts, 2013 c 22, sch 8 para 100

rep in pt—SI 2013/602, sch 2 para 33(26)

mod—SIs 2007/1098, art 6, sch 1; 2011/631, sch 2 para 4

sch 3 am—Constitutional Reform, 2005 c 4, s 145, sch 17 pt 2 para 30(1)(2)(c); Tribunals, Cts and Enforcement, 2007 c 15, s 50, sch 10 para 33

sch 4 rep in pt—(transtl savings) SI 2001/1149, arts 3(2), 4(8)(11), sch 2; Communications, 2003 c 21, s 406(7), sch 19(1); SI 2003/1900, arts 2(1), 3(1),sch 1; SI 2003/3142, art 3(2); Serious Organised Crime and Police, 2005 c 15, s 174(2), sch 17 pt 2

c 24 **Census (Amendment)**

c 25 **Football Disorder**

s 2 rep—Serious Organised Crime and Police, 2005 c 15, ss 59, 174(2), sch 4 para 157, sch 17 pt 2

s 3 rep in pt—Football (Disorder) (Amdt), 2002 c 12, s 1(4)

s 5 am—Football (Disorder) (Amdt), 2002 c 12, s 1(1)(2)

rep in pt—Football (Disorder) (Amdt), 2002 c 12, s 1(1)(3); Violent Crime Reduction, 2006 c 38, ss 52(1), 65, sch 5

sch 2 rep in pt—Serious Organised Crime and Police, 2005 c 15, s 174(2), sch 17 pt 2; Violent Crime Reduction, 2006 c 38, s 65, sch 5

c 26 **Postal Services**

appl—(S) SI 1999/787, sch 4 para 10(5); SI 2001/3998, reg 6; (S) SI 2002/2779, arts 13(3), 58(6), 59(4), sch 4, para 11(5); SIs 2002/3113 pt I, s 4, reg 29, sch 19 pt I, para 4(2); 2003/284, art 135(2); Post Office, 1969 c 48, s 139; 1990 c xiv, s 14(16); London Loc Authorities, 2004 c i, s 13(3); SIs 2004/293, regs 63(6), 122(2), 124(5); (NI) 2004/1267, regs 58(5), 113(4); (E) 2004/2443, reg 7, sch 2 para 10(4)(a); (EW) SI 2005/384, rule 8.2

trans of functions—Consumers, Estate Agents and Redress, 2007 c 17, s 30(3)(b); SI 2009/1885, art 2

s 1 rep—Postal Services, 2011 c 5, sch 12 para 2

2000
c 26 *continued*

        s 2 rep—Consumers, Estate Agents and Redress, 2007 c 17, s 64, sch 8
        ss 3-5 rep—Postal Services, 2011 c 5, sch 12 para 2
        ss 6-41 rep—Postal Services, 2011 c 5, sch 12 para 3
        ss 44-50 rep—Postal Services, 2011 c 5, sch 12 para 4
        ss 51-59 rep—Consumers, Estate Agents and Redress, 2007 c 17, s 64, sch 8
        ss 60-61A rep—Postal Services, 2011 c 5, sch 12 para 5
        Pt 4 (ss 62-82) appl—SIs 2003/1542, art 2(5); 2003/2908, art 2(5)
        s 62 appl—SI 2001/1149, art 5; Insolvency, 1986 c 45, sch 2A, para 10(1)(h)
           rep in pt—Postal Services, 2011 c 5, sch 12 para 6
        s 63 appl—Insolvency, 1986 c 45, sch 2A, para 10(1)(i)
           subst—Postal Services, 2011 c 5, sch 12 para 7
        s 64 am—Postal Services, 2011 c 5, sch 12 para 8
           rep in pt—Postal Services, 2011 c 5, sch 12 para 8(5)
        ss 65-67 rep—Postal Services, 2011 c 5, s 1(1)
        s 68 am—Postal Services, 2011 c 5, sch 12 para 9
        s 69 am—Postal Services, 2011 c 5, sch 12 para 10
        s 70 am—Postal Services, 2011 c 5, sch 12 para 11
        s 71 am—Postal Services, 2011 c 5, sch 12 para 12
        s 72 am—SI 2008/948, art 3, sch 1; Postal Services, 2011 c 5, sch 12 para 13
        s 73 am—SI 2008/948, art 3, sch 1; Postal Services, 2011 c 5, sch 12 para 14
        s 74 appl (mods)—SI 2003/1633, reg 15, sch 2 para 8(1)(2)(i)
           am—Postal Services, 2011 c 5, sch 12 para 15
        s 75 rep—Postal Services, 2011 c 5, sch 12 para 16
        s 77 am—SI 2008/948, art 3, sch 1; Postal Services, 2011 c 5, sch 12 para 17; SI
           2013/1970, sch para 27
        s 78 am—Postal Services, 2011 c 5, sch 12 para 18
        s 79 rep—Postal Services, 2011 c 5, sch 12 para 19
        s 80 am—SIs 2007/2194, art 10, sch 4; 2008/948, art 4, sch 3; 2009/1941, art 2, sch 1 para
           183; Postal Services, 2011 c 5, sch 12 para 20
           rep in pt—SI 2007/2194, art 10, sch 5
        s 82 am—Postal Services, 2011 c 5, sch 12 para 21
        Pt 6 (ss 89-100) am —Postal Services, 2011 c 5, sch 12 para 22
        s 89 am—Postal Services, 2011 c 5, sch 12 para 23
           rep in pt—Postal Services, 2011 c 5, sch 12 para 23(4)(b)
        s 89A added—Postal Services, 2011 c 5, sch 12 para 24
        s 90 am—Postal Services, 2011 c 5, sch 12 para 25
        s 91 am—Postal Services, 2011 c 5, sch 12 para 26(1)-(5)
           rep in pt—Postal Services, 2011 c 5, sch 12 para 26(6)
        s 93 am—Postal Services, 2011 c 5, sch 12 para 27; SI 2014/631, sch 1 para 7(2)
        s 94 am—SI 2009/1885, art 4, sch 1
        s 97 am—Postal Services, 2011 c 5, sch 12 para 28
        s 98 am—Postal Services, 2011 c 5, sch 12 para 29
        s 99 am—Postal Services, 2011 c 5, sch 12 para 30
        s 100 rep in pt—Postal Services, 2011 c 5, sch 12 para 31(2)
           am—Postal Services, 2011 c 5, sch 12 para 31(3)(4)
        s 101 am—Postal Services, 2011 c 5, sch 12 para 32
        s 102 am—Postal Services, 2011 c 5, sch 12 para 33; SI 2014/631, sch 1 para 7(3)
        s 104 am—Tribunals, Cts and Enforcement, 2007 c 15, s 62, sch 13 para 138; Postal
           Services, 2011 c 5, sch 12 para 34(b); Counter-Terrorism and Security, 2015 c 6,
           sch 8 para 3
           rep in pt—Postal Services, 2011 c 5, sch 12 para 34(a)
        s 104A added—Postal Services, 2011 c 5, sch 12 para 35
        s 105 appl—SIs 2007/2195; 2011/3036, reg 5
           am—Policing and Crime, 2009 c 26, s 99(4); Postal Services, 2011 c 5, sch 12 para
           36
        s 105A added—Postal Services, 2011 c 5, sch 12 para 37
        s 106 am—Finance, 2010 c 13, s 57(2)
           rep in pt—Finance, 2010 c 13, s 57(3)(4)
        s 111 am—Postal Services, 2011 c 5, sch 12 para 38
           mod (temp)—SI 2011/2329, art 4
        s 112 am—Postal Services, 2011 c 5, sch 12 para 39
           mod (temp)—SI 2011/2329, art 4
        s 113 am—Postal Services, 2011 c 5, sch 12 para 40

2000

c 26 s 113 *continued*

mod (temp)—SI 2011/2329, art 4

s 114 am—Postal Services, 2011 c 5, sch 12 para 41

mod (temp)—SI 2011/2329, art 4

s 116 appl—SI 2005/3382, reg 17(4)

am—Postal Services, 2011 c 5, sch 12 para 42

s 117 rep—Postal Services, 2011 c 5, sch 12 para 43

s 118 rep—Postal Services, 2011 c 5, sch 12 para 44

s 119 rep—Postal Services, 2011 c 5, sch 12 para 45

s 122 am—Postal Services, 2011 c 5, sch 12 para 46

s 123 am—Postal Services, 2011 c 5, sch 12 para 47

s 124 rep in pt—Postal Services, 2011 c 5, sch 12 para 48

s 125 appl—SIs 2001/493, reg 6, sch para 2(4); 2001/494, reg 7, sch para 2(4); (S) Mental Health (Care and Treatment) (S), 2003 asp 13, s 281(9); (S) Antisocial Behaviour etc (S), 2004 asp 8, ss 8(8), 104(3)

am—SI 2002/3050, reg 7; Communications, 2003 c 21, s 406(1), sch 17 para 162(1)(2); SI 2003/1900, arts 2(1), 3(1),sch 1; SI 2003/3142, art 3(2); Consumers, Estate Agents and Redress, 2007 c 17, s 30(4)(c); SI 2009/1941, art 2, sch 1 para 183; Postal Services, 2011 c 5, sch 12 para 49; SI 2014/631, sch 1 para 7(4)(b)

rep in pt—SI 2014/631, sch 1 para 7(4)(a)

s 126 rep—Postal Services, 2011 c 5, sch 12 para 50

sch 1 rep—Postal Services, 2011 c 5, sch 12 para 51

sch 2 rep—Consumers, Estate Agents and Redress, 2007 c 17, s 64, sch 8

sch 3 am—Constitutional Reform, 2005 c 4, s 15(1), sch 4 pt 1 para 292

sch 3 rep in pt—Postal Services, 2011 c 5, sch 12 para 52(2)

sch 4 rep in pt—Postal Services, 2011 c 5, sch 12 para 53

sch 5 am—Tribunals, Cts and Enforcement, 2007 c 15, s 139, sch 22 para 11; SI 2009/1307, art 5, sch 1; Postal Services, 2011 c 5, sch 12 para 54

sch 6 am—SI 2009/1307, art 5, sch 1

sch 7 rep—Postal Services, 2011 c 5, sch 12 para 55

sch 8 rep in pt—SI 2007/2007, art 6, sch; Consumers, Estate Agents and Redress, 2007 c 17, s 64, sch 8; Finance (No 3), 2010 c 33, s 22(3)(b)

am—Consumers, Estate Agents and Redress, 2007 c 17, s 63, sch 7 paras 12, 17

c 27 **Utilities**

trans of functions—Consumers, Estate Agents and Redress, 2007 c 17, s 30(3)(a)

s 2 rep—Consumers, Estate Agents and Redress, 2007 c 17, s 64, sch 8

s 3 rep in pt—Consumers, Estate Agents and Redress, 2007 c 17, s 64, sch 8; SI 2014/631, sch 1 para 8(2)

s 3A added—SI 2011/2704, reg 22

s 4 rep in pt—Consumers, Estate Agents and Redress, 2007 c 17, s 63, sch 7 paras 18, 19, sch 8

am—SI 2014/631, sch 1 para 8(3)

s 4A added—Energy, 2013 c 32, s 137(2)

s 5 rep in pt—Enterprise and Regulatory Reform, 2013 c 24, sch 6 para 83(3)

am—SIs 2014/631, sch 1 para 8(4); 2015/862, reg 4

s 5ZA added—SI 2011/2704, reg 23

s 5A added—Sustainable Energy, 2003 c 30, s 6

am—SI 2012/2400, art 30(2)

s 7 rep—SI 2014/631, sch 1 para 8(5)

s 8 am—Consumers, Estate Agents and Redress, 2007 c 17, s 1, sch 1 para 29; SIs 2013/783, art 5(3)-(5)(6)(a); 2014/631, sch 1 para 8(6)(a)(ii)(iv)(v)(b)(c)(ii); 2014/892, sch 1 para 144

rep in pt—Consumers, Estate Agents and Redress, 2007 c 17, s 64, sch 8; SIs 2013/783, art 5(2)(6)(b); 2014/631, sch 1 para 8(6)(a)(i)(iii)(c)(i)(d)(i)(ii)

s 17 rep—Consumers, Estate Agents and Redress, 2007 c 17, s 64, sch 8

s 18 rep in pt—Consumers, Estate Agents and Redress, 2007 c 17, s 64, sch 8

s 19 rep—Consumers, Estate Agents and Redress, 2007 c 17, s 64, sch 8

s 20 rep in pt—Consumers, Estate Agents and Redress, 2007 c 17, s 64, sch 8

ss 21-27 rep—Consumers, Estate Agents and Redress, 2007 c 17, s 64, sch 8

s 28 rep in pt—Energy, 2004 c 20, s 197(9), sch 23 pt 1

s 33 am—Energy, 2004 c 20, s 143(1), sch 19 para 20(a)(c); Climate Change and Sustainable Energy, 2006 c 19, s 7(7)(b); Energy, 2008 c 32, s 107, sch 5 paras

2000
c 27 *continued*

     12, 13(b); Energy, 2010 c 27, s 35, sch 1 paras 11, 12(b); Energy, 2011 c 16, ss
     22(7), 77(5), 98(9); SI 2011/2704, reg 50(2); Energy, 2013 c 32, s 65(2)
    rep in pt—Energy, 2004 c 20, ss 143(1), 197(9), sch 19 para 20(b), sch 23 pt 1;
     Climate Change and Sustainable Energy, 2006 c 19, s 7(7)(a); Energy, 2008 c
     32, s 107, sch 5 paras 12, 13(a), sch 6; Energy, 2010 c 27, s 35, sch 1 paras 11,
     12(a); Energy, 2013 c 32, s 142(2)
  s 40 rep in pt—Enterprise, 2002 c 40, s 278(2), sch 26
  s 53 rep in pt—Energy, 2004 c 20, s 197(9), sch 23 pt 1
  s 67 trans of functions—(transtl & saving provn) (S) SI 2001/3504, art 2, 4, sch
    am—Energy, 2008 c 32, s 39
  s 69 rep—Energy, 2010 c 27, s 35, sch 1 paras 11, 13
  s 81 am—Energy, 2004 c 20, s 168(10); Energy, 2008 c 32, s 107, sch 5 paras 12, 14;
    Energy, 2010 c 27, s 35, sch 1 paras 11, 14; Energy, 2011 c 16, s 22(8), 77(6),
    98(10); SI 2011/2704, reg 49(2); Energy, 2013 c 32, s 142(3)
  s 98 rep—Energy, 2010 c 27, s 35, sch 1 paras 11, 15
  s 103 am—Climate Change and Sustainable Energy, 2006 c 19, s 17, sch para 7; Climate
    Change, 2008 c 27, s 79, sch 8 para 6; Energy, 2011 c 16, sch 1 para
    8(2)(a)(3)(a)(4); SI 2014/631, sch 1 para 8(7)
    rep in pt—Energy, 2011 c 16, sch 1 para 8(3)(b)(5)
  s 103A added—Energy, 2011 c 16, s 70
    am—SI 2014/631, sch 1 para 8(8)
  s 103B added—Energy, 2011 c 16, s 71
  s 104 rep —Enterprise and Regulatory Reform, 2013 c 24, sch 6 para 84
  s 105 ext—Anti-terrorism, Crime and Security, 2001 c 24, s 17, sch 4 pt 1 para 52
    am—SIs 2001/3649, art 363; 2001/4050, art 2, sch pt IV para 25; Enterprise, 2002 c
    40, s 278(1), sch 25, para 43(1)(3); SI 2002/1555, art 27(b); Railways and
    Transport Safety, 2003 c 20, s 16, sch 2 pt 2 para 19(s); Communications, 2003
    c 21, s 406(1), sch 17 para 163; SI 2003/1900, arts 2(1), 3(1),sch 1; SI
    2003/3142, art 3(2); Water, 2003 c 37,s 101(1), sch 7 pt 2 para 34; Energy,
    2004 c 20, s 186; Railways, 2005 c 14, s 59, sch 12 para 16; SI 2006/3336, art
    308, sch 12; Consumers, Estate Agents and Redress, 2007 c 17, s 63, sch 7 paras
    18, 20; Energy, 2008 c 32, s 107, sch 5 paras 12, 15; SI 2008/1277, reg 30, sch
    2; Energy, 2010 c 27, s 35, sch 1 paras 11, 16; Energy, 2011 c 16, sch 1 para 9;
    SI 2011/2704, reg 36(2); Civil Aviation, 2012 c 19, sch 9 para 11; Financial
    Services, 2012 c 21, sch 18 para 89; Energy, 2013 c 32, s 52; SIs 2013/1882, art
    10(3); 2014/469, sch 2 para 21; 2014/631, sch 1 para 8(9); 2014/892, sch 1
    para 146(2)(3)(a)(4)-(6); Infrastructure, 2015 c 7, s 51(9)(b); SIs 2015/862, reg
    5(a)-(f); 1682, sch pt 1 para 4(o)
    rep in pt—SI 2002/1555, art 27(a); Consumers, Estate Agents and Redress, 2007 c 17,
    s 64, sch 8; SIs 2008/960, art 22, sch 3; 2008/1277, reg 30, schs 2, 4;
    2014/892, sch 1 para 146(3)(b); Infrastructure, 2015 c 7, s 51(9)(a);
    Deregulation, 2015 c 20, sch 6 para 22(11)
    excl—Railways and Transport Safety, 2003 c 20, s 115(1)(2)(l); Energy, 2004 c 20,
    s 140(4); Energy, 2013 c 32, s 33(3)
    appl (mods)—SI 2006/1391, art 2, sch
    restr in pt—Energy, 2013 c 32, sch 2 para 10(4)(a)
  s 105A added—SI 2011/2704, reg 36(3)
  s 106 am—Consumers, Estate Agents and Redress, 2007 c 17, s 30(4)(d); SIs 2011/2704,
    reg 25; 2012/2400, art 30(3); 2014/631, sch 1 para 8(10)(a)
    rep in pt—SI 2014/631, sch 1 para 8(10)(b)
  sch 1 am—SI 2011/2704, reg 24; Enterprise and Regulatory Reform, 2013 c 24, sch 15 para
    13
  sch 2 rep—Consumers, Estate Agents and Redress, 2007 c 17, s 64, sch 8
  sch 6 rep in pt—Enterprise, 2002 c 40, s 278(2), sch 26; Energy, 2004 c 20, s 197(9), sch 23
    pt 1; Consumers, Estate Agents and Redress, 2007 c 17, s 64, sch 8
  sch 7 rep in pt—Consumers, Estate Agents and Redress, 2007 c 17, s 64, sch 8
c 28 **Health Service Commissioners (Amendment)**
c 29 **Trustee**
  saved—University of Manchester, 2004 c iv, s 12
  appl (mods)—SI 2010/917, art 16
  s 1 rep in pt—Public Services Ombudsman (W), 2005 c 10, s 39(2), sch 7
    appl—Charities, 1993 c 10, ss 73B(2), 73F(5)

2000

c 29 *continued*

    ss 4, 5 appl—People's Dispensary for Sick Animals, 1956 c lxvii, s 5(1A) (added by SI
        2015/198, sch Scheme para 4)

    s 5 excl—Settled Land, 1925 c 18, s 75A

    Pt 4 (ss 11-27) appl (mods)—People's Dispensary for Sick Animals, 1956 c lxvii, s
        5(1B)-(1D) (added by SI 2015/198, sch Scheme para 4); SI 2012/3012, reg 33;

    s 11 restr—Settled Land, 1925 c 18, s
        ext—Settled Land, 1925 c 18, s 107

    ss 13-15 ext—Settled Land, 1925 c 18, s 107

    s 19 am—Charities, 2006 c 50, s 75, sch 8 para 197; Corporation Tax, 2010 c 4, s 1177, sch
        1 para 319

    ss 21-23 ext—Settled Land, 1925 c 18, s 107

    s 29 am—Financial Services, 2012 c 21, sch 18 para 90

    s 32 ext—Settled Land, 1925 c 18, s 107
        appl (mods)—People's Dispensary for Sick Animals, 1956 c lxvii, s 5(1B)-(1D) (added
        by SI 2015/198, sch Scheme para 4); SI 2012/3012, reg 33

    s 38 am—Charities, 2011 c 25, sch 7 para 89

    s 39 am—Charities, 2011 c 25, sch 7 para 90

    sch 1 ext—Settled Land, 1925 c 18, s 107

    sch 2 rep in pt—Land Registration, 2002 c 9, s 135, sch 13; (prosp) Horserace Betting and
        Olympic Lottery, 2004 c 25, s 38, sch 6; Legal Services, 2007 c 29, s 210, sch
        23; SI 2008/576, art 18, sch; Health and Social Care, 2012 c 7, sch 20 para
        3(a)

c 30   *Licensing (Young Persons)*—rep Licensing, 2003 c 17, s 199, sch 7

c 31   **Warm Homes and Energy Conservation**

    ss 1A, 1B added —Energy, 2013 c 32, s 145(2)

    s 2 am—Consumers, Estate Agents and Redress, 2007 c 17, s 63, sch 7 para 21; Energy,
        2013 c 32, s 145(3)(a)(b); SI 2014/631, sch 1 para 9(2)
        rep in pt—Consumers, Estate Agents and Redress, 2007 c 17, s 64, sch 8; Energy, 2013 c
        32, s 145(3)(c)(d)

    s 4 am—SI 2014/631, sch 1 para 9(3)

c 32   **Police (Northern Ireland)**

    appl—Anti-terrorism, Crime and Security, 2001 c 24, s 1, sch 1 pt 4 para 10(7)(c); Proceeds
        of Crime, 2002 c 29, ss 220(9)(a), 302(7)(c)

    s 2 am—SI 2010/976, art 5, sch 3

    s 3 am—Police (NI), 2003 c 6, s 20(2); SI 2010/976, art 5, sch 3

    s 4 am—SIs 2010/976, art 5, sch 3; 2014/631, sch 1 para 9(3)

    s 5 am—SI 2010/976, art 5, sch 3

    s 5A added—Police (NI), 2003 c 6, s 5

    s 7 am—SI 2010/976, art 5, sch 3

    s 8 rep in pt—International Development, 2002 c 1, s 19(2), sch 4
        am—SI 2010/976, art 5, sch 3

    s 9 am—Police (NI), 2003 c 6, s 6(1)-(3)(12); SI 2010/976, art 5, sch 3

    s 10 am—Police (NI), 2003 c 6, s 6(1)(4)-(9)(12); SI 2010/976, art 5, sch 3

    s 12 am—Police (NI), 2003 c 6, s 7; SI 2010/976, art 5, sch 3

    s 15 appl—NI (St Andrews Agreement), 2006 c 53, s 20, sch 8 para 5(a)
        am—SI 2010/976, art 5, sch 3

    s 15A added—Police (NI), 2003 c 6, s 19, sch 1 paras 1, 2
        am—SI 2010/976, art 5, sch 3

    s 17 am—Police (NI), 2003 c 6, s 19, sch 1 paras 1, 3

    s 18 am—Police (NI), 2003 c 6, s 19, sch 1 paras 1, 4

    s 19 am—SI 2010/976, art 5, sch 3

    s 21 subst—Police (NI), 2003 c 6, s 19, sch 1 paras 1, 5

    ss 21A-21D added—Police (NI), 2003 c 6, s 19, sch 1 paras 1, 6-9

    s 22 am—Police (NI), 2003 c 6, s 19, sch 1 paras 1, 10

    s 24 am—Police (NI), 2003 c 6, s 1; SI 2010/976, art 5, sch 3

    s 25 rep in pt—Police (NI), 2003 c 6, ss 3(1)(2), 45, sch 4
        am—Police (NI), 2003 c 6, s 3(1)(3)

    s 26 am—SI 2010/976, art 5, sch 3

    s 27 am—Police (NI), 2003 c 6, ss 2, 6(1)(10)(12); SI 2010/976, art 5, sch 3

    s 28 rep in pt—Police (NI), 2003 c 6, ss 8(1)(2)(6), 45, sch 4
        am—Police (NI), 2003 c 6, s 8(1)(3)-(6); SI 2010/976, art 5, sch 3

    s 29 am—Police (NI), 2003 c 6, s 9(1)-(6)(9); SI 2010/976, art 5, sch 3

    s 30 am—SI 2010/976, art 5, sch 3

2000

c 32 *continued*

s 31 am—Police (NI), 2003 c 6, s 9(1)(7)-(9); SI 2010/976, art 5, sch 3

s 31A added—Police (NI), 2003 c 6, s 20(1)

s 32 rep in pt—Police (NI), 2003 c 6, ss 20(4), 45, sch 4

s 33 am—Police (NI), 2003 c 6, s 21

s 33A added—Police (NI), 2003 c 6, s 22

am—SI 2010/976, art 5, sch 3

ss 34, 35 am—SI 2010/976, art 5, sch 3

s 36 am—(temp) Police (NI), 2003 c 6, s 23(1)(2)(6)

s 36A added—Police (NI), 2003 c 6, s 24(1)

am—SI 2010/976, art 5, sch 3

s 41 mod—(temp) SI 2001/2513, art 2

am—SI 2010/976, art 5, sch 3

ss 42, 43 am—SI 2010/976, art 5, sch 3

s 44 see (provisions for expiry)—Police (NI), 2000 c 32, s 47

am—SI 2010/976, art 5, sch 3

ss 45, 46 see (provisions for expiry)—Police (NI), 2000 c 32, s 47

s 47A added—(temp) Police (NI), 2003 c 6, s 23(1)(3)(6)

s 48 am—SI 2010/976, art 5, sch 3

s 51 appl (mods)—Police (NI), 2003 c 6, s 36

am—SI 2010/976, art 5, sch 3

s 52 am—Justice (NI), 2004 c 4, s 8(6); SI 2010/976, art 5, sch 3

ss 53, 54 am—SI 2010/976, art 5, sch 3

s 57 am—Police (NI), 2003 c 6, s 20(3); SI 2010/976, art 5, sch 3

s 58 am—SI 2010/976, art 5, sch 3

s 59 am—Police (NI), 2003 c 6, ss 10, 27(2); SI 2010/976, art 5, sch 3

s 60 am—Police (NI), 2003 c 6, s 11; Inquiries, 2005 c 12, s 48(1), sch 2 pt 1 para 22; SI

2010/976, art 5, sch 3

s 61 am—SI 2010/976, art 5, sch 3

s 63 rep in pt—Police (NI), 2003 c 6, s 45, sch 4

s 66 am—SI 2010/976, art 5, sch 3

s 69 am—SI 2010/976, art 5, sch 3

ss 70, 71 am—SI 2010/976, art 5, sch 3

.s 73 am—SI 2010/976, arts 40, 81

s 74A added—Police (NI), 2003 c 6, s 27(1)

am—SI 2010/976, art 5, sch 3

s 76 am—SIs 2001/2513, art 3; 2010/976, art 5, sch 3

rep in pt—SI 2010/976, art 5, sch 3

s 76A added—Police (NI), 2003 c 6, s 29

am—SI 2010/976, art 5, sch 3

s 77 am—Police (NI), 2003 c 6, ss 6(1)(11)(12), 28(4); SI 2010/976, art 5, sch 3

sch 1 rep in pt—Police (NI), 2003 c 6, ss 4(2), 45, sch 4

am—Police (NI), 2003 c 6, s 19, sch 1 paras 1, 11(1)-(3); ibid, ss 4(1)(3), 12, 23(10),

28(1)-(3); (temp) ibid, s 23(1)(4)-(6); SI 2010/976, art 5, sch 3

appl (mods)—NI (St Andrews Agreement), 2006 c 53, s 2, sch 2 para 6(2)

sch 3 am—Police (NI), 2003 c 6, ss 15(1)-(6), 16; ibid, ss 14, 17; (retrosp to 23.11.2000)

ibid, s 18; ibid, s 19, sch 1 paras 1, 12, 16(1)-(4); SI 2005/861,

arts 3(1)(2)(3)-(7), 4, 5

appl (mods)—NI (St Andrews Agreement), 2006 c 53, s 20, sch 8 paras 1-4, 5(b)

sch 3A added—Police (NI), 2003 c 6, s 19, sch 1 paras 1, 13, 16(1)-(3)(5)

sch 6 rep in pt—Crim. Justice and Police, 2001 c 16, s 137, sch 7 pt 5(1); Serious Organised

Crime and Police, 2005 c 15, s 174(2), sch 17 pt 2; SI 2010/976, art 27

c 33 **Fur Farming (Prohibition)**

s 1 am—SI 2015/664, sch 4 para 29

s 5 am—SIs 2002/794, art 5(1), sch 1, para 40; 2009/1307, art 5, sch 1

s 6 am—SI 2002/794, art 5(1), sch 1, para 41

s 7 am—SI 2002/794, art 5(1), sch 1, para 42

c 34 **Race Relations (Amendment)**

s 1 rep—Equality, 2010 c 15, s 211, sch 27 pt 1 (subst by SI 2010/2279, sch 2)

s 2 rep—Equality, 2010 c 15 sch 27 pt 1A (am by 2011/1060, sch 30)

ss 3-10 rep—Equality, 2010 c 15, s 211, sch 27 pt 1 (subst by SI 2010/2279, sch 2)

sch 1 rep—Equality, 2010 c 15 sch 27 pt 1A (am by 2011/1060, sch 3)

sch 2 rep in pt—Nationality, Immigration and Asylum, 2002 c 41, s 161, sch 9; Equality,

2006 c 3, s 91, sch 4; Educ and Inspections, 2006 c 40, s 184, sch 18; Equality,

2000
c 34 *continued*

> 2010 c 15, s 211, sch 27 pt 1 (subst by SI 2010/2279, sch 2); ibid, sch 27 pt 1A (am by 2011/1060, sch 3)
>
> sch 3 rep—Equality, 2010 c 15, s 211, sch 27 pt 1 (subst by SI 2010/2279, sch 2)

c 35   **Children (Leaving Care)**
> s 6 excl—SI 2001/3074, reg 2(1)-(3)
> rep in pt—(prosp) Welfare Reform, 2009 c 24, s 58, sch 7 pt 1

c 36   **Freedom of Information**
> cert functs trans—SIs 2001/3500, arts 3, 4(1)(c)(3)-(8), sch 1 para 12; 2003/1887, art 4, sch 1
>
> appl—(S) Freedom of Information (S), 2002 asp 13, ss 3(4), 35(1)(g), 75
> appl (mods)—SIs 2009/3157, reg 11; 2012/2734, reg 3-6, sch Pts 1, 2, 3
> s 1 rep in pt—(W) Marine and Coastal Access, 2009 c 23, s 321, sch 22 pt 4
> s 2 am—Constitutional Reform and Governance, 2010 c 25, s 46, sch 7 para 2
> s 3 mod—SI 2008/2546, art 41; Budget Responsibility and Nat Audit, 2011 c 4, sch 3 para 13(2)
>> excl—SI 2009/814, art 8
> s 4 am—SIs 2001/3500, art 8, sch 2 pt I para 8(1)(a); 2003/1887, art 9, sch 2 para 12(1)(a); 2007/1388, art 3, sch 1; 2015/1897, sch para 2(2)(a
>> see—(functions exercisable concurrently) SI 2015/1897, art 3(1),(2)(a)
> s 5 am—SIs 2001/3500, art 8, sch 2 pt I para 8(1)(b); 2003/1887, art 9, sch 2 para 12(1)(a); 2015/1897, sch para 2(2)(b)
>> see—(functions exercisable concurrently) SI 2015/1897, art 3(1),(2)(b)
> s 6 am—Protection of Freedoms, 2012 c 9, s 103
> s 7 am—SIs 2001/3500, art 8, sch 2 pt I para 8(1)(c); 2003/1887, art 9, sch 2 para 12(1)(a); 2007/1388, art 3, sch 1; 2015/1897, sch para 2(2)(c)
>> see—(functions exercisable concurrently) SI 2015/1897, art 3(1),(2)(c)
> s 9 am—SIs 2001/3500, art 8, sch 2 pt I para 8(1)(d); 2003/1887, art 9, sch 2 para 12(1)(a); 2015/1897, sch para 2(3)(a)
>> trans of functions—SI 2015/1897, art 4(1),(2)(a)
> s 10 am—SIs 2001/3500, art 8, sch 2 pt I para 8(1)(e); 2003/1887, art 9, sch 2 para 12(1)(a); 2015/1897, sch para 2(3)(b)
>> mod—SI 2009/1369, reg 2
>> appl (mods)—SI 2010/2768, reg 2
>> trans of functions—SI 2015/1897, art 4(1),(2)(b)
> s 11 am—Protection of Freedoms, 2012 c 9, s 102(2)
> s 11A added—Protection of Freedoms, 2012 c 9, s 102(3)
>> am—SIs 2015/1415, reg 21(2); 1897, sch para 2(3)(c)
>> trans of functions—SI 2015/1897, art 4(1),(2)(c)
> s 11B added—Protection of Freedoms, 2012 c 9, s 102(3)
>> am—SI 2015/1897, sch para 2(3)(d)
> s 11B trans of functions—SI 2015/1897, art 4(1),(2)(d)
> s 12 am—SIs 2001/3500, art 8, sch 2 pt I para 8(1)(f); 2003/1887, art 9, sch 2 para 12(1)(a); 2015/1897, sch para 2(3)(e)
>> trans of functions—SI 2015/1897, art 4(1),(2)(e)
> s 13 am—SIs 2001/3500, art 8, sch 2 pt I para 8(1)(g); 2003/1887, art 9, sch 2 para 12(1)(a); 2015/1897, sch para 2(3)(f)
>> trans of functions—SI 2015/1897, art 4(1),(2)(f)
> s 15 am—SI 2015/1897, sch para 2(5)(a)
> s 18 rep in pt—SI 2010/22, art 5, sch 2; Protection of Freedoms, 2012 c 9, s 105(5), sch 10 pt 8
> s 19 am—Protection of Freedoms, 2012 c 9, s 102(4); SI 2015/1415, reg 21(3)
> s 22A added—Intellectual Property, 2014 c 18, s 20
> s 23 rep in pt —Serious Organised Crime and Police, 2005 c 15, ss 59, 174(2), sch 4 paras 158, 159, sch 17 pt 2
>> am—Serious Organised Crime and Police, 2005 c 15, ss 59, 174(2), sch 4 paras 158, 159, sch 17 pt 2; Crime and Cts, 2013 c 22, sch 8 para 102
> s 25 appl—SI 2004/3391, reg 15(6); Justice and Security, 2013 c 18, sch 2 para 5(2)
> s 26 excl—Statistics and Registration Service, 2007 c 18, s 40(3)
> s 28 am—SI 2007/1388, art 3, sch 1
> s 29 rep in pt—Armed Forces, 2001 c 19, s 38, sch 7 pt 1
> s 30 am—Armed Forces, 2006 c 52, s 378, sch 16 para 176
>> mod—SI 2009/1059, art 205, sch 1
> s 32 excl—Inquiries, 2005 c 12, s 18(3)

2000

c 36 s 32 *continued*

   am—Coroners and Justice, 2009 c 25, s 177, sch 21 para 44

s 35 am—SI 2007/1388, art 3, sch 1

s 36 am—SI 2007/1388, art 3, sch 1; Budget Responsibility and Nat Audit, 2011 c 4, sch 5
   para 22; Public Audit (W), 2013 anaw 3, sch 4 para 18

s 37 am—Constitutional Reform and Governance, 2010 c 25, s 46, sch 7 para 3

s 39 am—SI 2004/3391, reg 20

s 41 ext in pt—(savings) Mobile Homes (W), 2013 anaw 6, s 61(8)

s 44 excl—Statistics and Registration Service, 2007 c 18, s 40(1)

Pt 3 (ss 45-49) rep in pt —(heading rep in pt) SI 2001/3500, art 8, sch 2 pt I para 8(1)(h)

   am—SI 2015/1897, sch para 2(6)

   trans of cert functions—SI 2015/1897, arts 4(1),(2)(g)-(i), 6(1)(b),(3)(a)

s 45 am—SIs 2001/3500, art 8, sch 2 pt I para 8(1)(h); 2003/1887, art 9, sch 2
   para 12(1)(a); Protection of Freedoms, 2012 c 9, s 102(5); SI 2015/1897, sch
   para 2(3)(g), (7)

s 46 rep in pt—SI 2001/3500, art 8, sch 2 pt I para 8(2)

   am—SIs 2003/1887, art 9, sch 2 para 12(2); 2015/1897, sch para 2(3)(h),(5)(b)(c)

s 47 am—SIs 2001/3500, art 8, sch 2 pt I para 8(1)(i); 2003/1887, art 9, sch 2 para 12(1)(a);
   Protection of Freedoms, 2012 c 9, s 107(3)(a)(ii), (b); SI 2015/1897, sch para
   2(3)(i)

   rep in pt—Protection of Freedoms, 2012 c 9, s 107(3)(a)(i), sch 10 pt 8

   appl (mods)—SI 2004/3391, reg 16(5)(6)

s 48 appl (mods)—SI 2004/3391, reg 16(5)(6)

Pts 4, 5 (ss 50-61) appl (mods)—SIs 2004/3391, reg 18; 2015/1415, regs 18, 19

s 52 excl—SI 2015/1415, reg 22(7)

s 53 am—SIs 2001/3500, art 8, sch 2 pt I para 8(1)(j); 2003/1887, art 9, sch 2 para 12(1)(a);
   2007/1388, art 3, sch 1; 2015/1897, sch para 2(3)(j)

   trans of functions—SI 2015/1897, art 4(1),(2)(j)

s 54 excl—SI 2015/1415, reg 22(7)

ss 56-58 excl—SI 2015/1415, reg 22(7)

s 59 rep—SI 2010/22, art 5, sch 2

s 61 am—SI 2010/22, art 5, sch 2

s 62 am—Constitutional Reform and Governance, 2010 c 25, s 46, sch 7 para 4

s 63 am—Constitutional Reform and Governance, 2010 c 25, s 46, sch 7 para
   5(2)(b)(3)(b)(4)

   rep in pt—Constitutional Reform and Governance, 2010 c 25, s 46, sch 7 para
   5(2)(a)(3)(a)

s 65 trans of functions—SI 2015/1897, art 6(1)(b),(3)(b)(c)

   am—SI 2015/1897, sch para 2(5)(d)

s 66 am—SI 2015/1897, sch para 2(5)(e)

s 69 am—SI 2003/1887, art 9, sch 2 para 12(1)(b)

s 75 am—SIs 2001/3500, art 8, sch 2 pt I para 8(1)(k); 2003/1887, art 9, sch 2
   para 12(1)(c); 2015/1897, sch para 2(2)(d)

   see —(functions exercisable concurrently) SI 2015/1897, art 3(1),(2)(d)

s 76 am—(S) Public Services Ombudsman, 2002 asp 11, s 25(1), sch 6, para 23(1)(2)(b);
   Housing, 2004 c 34, s 265(1), sch 15 para 46; Public Services Ombudsman (W),
   2005 c 10, s 39(1), sch 6 paras 70, 71(b); Commnr for Older People (W), 2006 c
   30, s 1, sch 1 para 21; Health, 2009 c 21, s 35, sch 5 para 14

   rep in pt—(S) Public Services Ombudsman, 2002 asp 11, s 25(1), sch 6, para
   23(1)(2)(a); Public Services Ombudsman (W), 2005 c 10, s 39, sch 6 paras 70,
   71(a), sch 7

   appl—SI 2004/3391, reg 18(10)

s 76A added—SI 2004/3089, art 3(1)(2)

s 80 am—SI 2004/3089, art 3(1)(3)

s 80A added—Constitutional Reform and Governance, 2010 c 25, s 46, sch 7 para 6

   rep—Protection of Freedoms, 2012 c 9, s 104(1)(a), sch 10 pt 7

s 81 am—SI 2007/1388, art 3, sch 1

s 82 am—SIs 2001/3500, art 8, sch 2 pt I para 8(3); 2015/1897, sch para 2(2)(e)

   rep in pt—SI 2003/1887, art 9, sch 2 para 12(3)

s 83 am—SIs 2001/3500, art 8, sch 2 pt I para 8(1)(l); 2003/1887, art 9, sch 2 para 12(1)(c);
   2007/1388, art 3, sch 1; 2015/1897, sch para 2(2)(f)

   see —(functions exercisable concurrently) SI 2015/1897, art 3(1),(2)(d)

s 84 am—SIs 2001/3500, art 8, sch 2 pt I para 8(1)(m); 2003/1887, art 9, sch 2
   para 12(1)(c); 2007/1388, art 3, sch 1; 2010/22, sch 2; Protection of Freedoms,

2000
c 36 *continued*

> 2012 c 9, s 102(6); Crime and Cts, 2013 c 22, sch 8 para 103; SI 2015/1897, sch para 2(3)(k),(4)
>
> rep in pt—Crime and Cts, 2013 c 22, sch 8 para 103
>
> s 85 am—SIs 2001/3500, art 8, sch 2 pt I para 8(1)(n); 2003/1887, art 9, sch 2 para 12(1)(c); 2015/1897, sch para 2(2)(g)
>
> s 87 am—SIs 2001/3500, art 8, sch 2 pt I para 8(1)(o); 2003/1887, art 9, sch 2 para 12(1)(c)
>
> sch 1 am—Transport, 2000 c 38, s 204, sch 14 pt V para 30; Police (NI), 2000 c 32, s 78, sch 6 para 25(2)(3); (S, NI prosp) Health and Social Care, 2001 c 15, s 67, sch 5 pt 1 para 14; ibid, s 67, sch 5 pt 3, para 18; Private Security Industry, 2001 c 12, s 1(6), sch 1 para 23; Crim. Justice and Police, 2001 c 16, s 102, sch 4 para 8; SIs 2001/2565, art 4; 2002/2469, reg 4, sch 1 pt 1, para 29; Nat Health Service Reform and Health Care Professions, 2002 c 17, ss 6(2), 19(7), 20(11), 25(4), sch 5, para 48, sch 6, para 19, sch 7, para 24; SIs 2002/254, art 48(3), sch 4, para 9; 2002/2623, arts 2, 3, schs 1, 2; Educ, 2002 c 32, s 215(1), sch 21, para 127; Office of Communications, 2002 c 11, s 1(10), schedule, para 22; Police Reform, 2002 c 30, s 107(1), sch 7, para 23(a); SI 2002/253, art 54(3), sch 5, para 17; Justice (NI), 2002 c 26, ss 3, 23(9), 50(7), sch 2, para 20, sch 9, para 15; ibid, s 45(3), sch 8, para 16; (EW) Health (W), 2003 c 4, s 7(1), sch 3 paras 14, 15; Health and Social Care (Community Health and Standards), 2003 c 43, ss 34, 147, sch 4 paras 113, 114, sch 9 para 31; ibid, s 184, sch 11 para 68; Communications, 2003 c 21, s 406(1), sch 17 para 164; Loc Govt, 2003 c 26, s 105, sch 4 para 24 (see SI 2003/2938); SI 2003/1882, arts 2, 3, sch 1, sch 2; Police (NI), 2003 c 6, s 19, sch 1 paras 1, 15; Fire and Rescue Services, 2004 c 21, s 53, sch 1 para 95; SI 2004/938, art 2, sch 1; Civil Contingencies, 2004 c 36, s 32(1), sch 2 pt 1 para 10(3)(d); Energy, 2004 c 20, s 51(2), sch 10 pt 5 para 18; ibid, s 2(10), sch 1 pt 3 para 18; Higher Educ, 2004 c 8, s 49, sch 6 para 10; Gangmasters (Licensing), 2004 c 11, s 1, sch 1 para 6; Health Protection Agency, 2004 c 17, s 11(1), sch 3 para 15; Human Tissue, 2004 c 30, s 13, sch 2 para 27; Pensions, 2004 c 35, s 319(1), sch 12 para 79; SIs 2004/938, arts 3, 4, schs 2, 3; 2004/3327, art 3(5), sch 1 para 21; Justice (Northern Ireland), 2002 c 26, sch 3A; Constitutional Reform, 2005 c 4, ss 59(5), 61(2), 62(2), sch 11 pt 4 para 34(b), sch 12 pt 2 para 36(3), sch 13 para 17(3); Public Services Ombudsman (W), 2005 c 10, s 39(1), sch 6 paras 70, 72(b); Educ, 2005 c 18, ss 98, 99, sch 14 para 22, sch 15; Gambling, 2005 c 19, s 356(1)(2), sch 16 pt 2 para 16; SI 2005/3593, arts 2, 3, 4, 5, schs 1, 2, 3, 4; London Olympic Games and Paralympic Games, 2006 c 12, s 3, sch 1 para 23; Equality, 2006 c 3, s 2, sch 1 para 48; Commnr for Older People (W), 2006 c 30, s 1, sch 1 para 21; Police and Justice, 2006 c 48, s 1, sch 1 para 74; Nat Health Service (Conseq Provns), 2006 c 43, s 2, sch 1 para 211; Health, 2006 c 28, s 80, sch 8 para 45; Natural Environment and Rural Communities, 2006 c 16, s 105, sch 11 para 153(1)(2); ibid, s 105, sch 11 para 175; Educ and Inspections, 2006 c 40, s 157, sch 14 para 69(1)(2); Identity Cards, 2006 c 15, s 22(8); SIs 2006/1254, art 3, sch 1; 2006/2953, art 4, sch; 2006/3336, art 308, sch 12; Loc Govt and Public Involvement in Health, 2007 c 28, ss 22, 209, sch 1 para 20, sch 13 para 54; Consumers, Estate Agents and Redress, 2007 c 17, s 1, sch 1 para 35; Legal Services, 2007 c 29, ss 2, 114, sch 1 para 31, sch 15 para 32; Offender Management, 2007 c 21, s 39, sch 3 para 10; Pensions, 2007 c 22, s 20, sch 6 para 23; Tribunals, Cts and Enforcement, 2007 c 15, s 48, sch 8 para 53; SI 2007/1388, art 3, sch 1; (transtl provns) Regulatory Enforcement and Sanctions, 2008 c 13, s 1, sch 1 paras 19, 20; Health and Social Care, 2008 c 14, s 127, sch 10 para 13; ibid, ss 95, 160, sch 5 para 73(b), sch 14 para 4; Housing and Regeneration, 2008 c 17, ss 56, 277, sch 8 para 77(1)(2), sch 9 para 28(1)(2); Loc Transport, 2008 c 26, s 77, sch 4 para 64; Climate Change, 2008 c 27, s 32, sch 1 para 33; Planning, 2008 c 29, s 1, sch 1 para 27; Pensions, 2008 c 30, s 75, sch 1 para 24; Child Maintenance and Other Payments, 2008 c 6, s 1, sch 1 para 29; SIs 2008/576, art 18, sch; 2008/912, art 3, sch 1; 2008/1967, art 2; 2008/2833, art 6, sch 3; Parliamentary Standards, 2009 c 13, s 3(2), sch 1 para 27(1); ibid, s 3(4), sch 2 para 11; Loc Democracy, Economic Development and Construction, 2009 c 20, s 119, sch 6 para 94; ibid, s 55, sch 1 para 21; Apprenticeships, Skills, Children and Learning, 2009 c 22, ss 174, 192, sch 12 para 30; Marine and Coastal Access, 2009 c 23, s 1, sch 2 para 6; ibid, s 184, sch 14 para 19; Policing and Crime, 2009 c 26, s 2(4); Coroners and Justice, 2009 c

25, s 177, sch 21 para 82; Child Poverty, 2010 c 9, s 8, sch 1 para 21;
Constitutional Reform and Governance, 2010 c 25, s 19, sch 2 para 12;
Academies, 2010 c 32, s 14, sch 2 para 10; (W) NAW (Remuneration), 2010
nawm 4, s 17; SIs 2010/231, art 68, sch 4; 2010/937, arts 2, 3; 2010/1080, art 2,
sch 1; Budget Responsibility and Nat Audit, 2011 c 4, sch 1 para 27; ibid, sch 5
para 23(1); Postal Services, 2011 c 5, sch 12 para 157; Sports Grounds Safety
Authy, 2011 c 6, sch 2 para 8; Police Reform and Social Responsibility, 2011 c
13, s 87; ibid, sch 16 para 249; Localism, 2011 c 20, sch 22 para 53; SI
2011/1041, art 2(1), sch pt 1; ibid, art 2(2), sch pt 2; Financial Services, 2012 c
21, sch 18 para 91(b); Welfare Reform, 2012 c 5, sch 13 para 17(b); Health and
Social Care, 2012 c 7, s 189(4); ibid, sch 13 para 7(a); ibid, sch 5 para 99(b);
ibid, sch 15 paras 56(a), 69(2); ibid, sch 17 para 8; ibid, sch 19 para 8;
Protection of Freedoms, 2012 c 9, sch 9 para 133; SIs 2012/3006, art 17;
2012/990 (W 130), art 8; 2012/1659, sch 3 para 15(2)(b); Public Audit (W),
2013 anaw 3, sch 4 para 19; Justice and Security, 2013 c 18, sch 2 para 5(3);
Groceries Code Adjudicator, 2013 c 19, s 21(3); Energy, 2013 c 32, sch 12 para
75; Enterprise and Regulatory Reform, 2013 c 24, sch 4 para 25(a)(b); Financial
Services (Banking Reform), 2013 c 33, sch 4 para 15; SIs 2013/755 (W 90), sch
2 para 399(3); 783, art 7; 1644, sch 1; Transparency of Lobbying, Non-Party
Campaigning and Trade Union Admin, 2014 c 4, sch 2 para 13; Anti-social
Behaviour, Crime and Policing, 2014 c 12, sch 11 para 92; Defence Reform,
2014 c 20, sch 4 para 21(a); Water, 2014 c 21, sch 10 para 17; Care, 2014 c 23,
sch 5 para 34; ibid, sch 7 para 26; SI 2014/631, sch 1 para 10(2); Infrastructure,
2015 c 7, s 9(8); (prosp) Small Business, Enterprise and Employment, 2015 c 26,
sch 1 para 25; Modern Slavery, 2015 c 30, s 40(9); (prosp) Planning (W), 2015
anaw 4, sch 1 pt 2 para 5; Qualifications Wales, 2015 anaw 5, sch 1 para 37

rep in pt—(prosp) Transport, 2000 c 38, s 274, sch 31 pt IV; SI 2001/1283, art 3(7);
Police Reform, 2002 c 30, s 107, sch 7, para 23(b), sch 8; SIs 2002/253, art
54(3), sch 5, para 17; 2002/797, art 2(c); (pt prosp) Justice (NI), 2002 c 26, s
86, sch 13; Licensing, 2003 c 17, s 199, sch 7; Courts, 2003 c 39, s 109(1)(3),
sch 8 para 392, sch 10; Health and Social Care (Community Health and
Standards), 2003 c 43, s 196, sch 14 pt 2; (pt prosp) ibid, sch 14 pt 4; ibid,
ss 190(2), 196, sch 13 para 10, sch 14 pt 7; (pt prosp) Communications, 2003 c
21, s 406(7), sch 19(1); SI 2003/1883, art 2, sch 1; Health Protection Agency,
2004 c 17, s 11(2), sch 4; Horserace Betting and Olympic Lottery, 2004 c 25,
ss 13, 38, sch 2 para 22, sch 6; (prosp) ibid, s 17(2), sch 4 para 9; Pensions,
2004 c 35, s 320, sch 13 pt 1; SIs 2004/803 (W 83), art 3(3); 2004/1641,
arts 2, 3, schs 1, 2; 2004/3327, art 13, sch 4; Constitutional Reform, 2005 c 4,
ss 59(5), 146, sch 11 pt 4 para 34(a), sch 18 pt 5; Public Services Ombudsman
(W), 2005 c 10, s 39, sch 6 paras 70, 72(a), sch 7; Railways, 2005 c 14, s 59,
sch 13 pt 1; Serious Organised Crime and Police, 2005 c 15, ss 59, 174(2), sch
4 paras 158, 160, sch 17 pt 2; Educ, 2005 c 18, s 123, sch 19 pt 3; SIs
2005/3225 (W 237), arts 3, 6(2), sch 2 pt 1 para 5, 3226 (W 238), arts 3,
7(1)(b), sch 2 pt 1 para 13, 3238 (W 243), arts 7, 9(1), sch 1 para 85, 3239 (W
244), arts 7(1)-(3), 9(1), sch 1 para 31; SI 2005/3594, art 2, sch 1; Nat Health
Service (Conseq Provns), 2006 c 43, s 2, sch 1 para 211; Equality, 2006 c 3, s
40, sch 3 para 60, sch 4; Nat Lottery, 2006 c 23, s 21, sch 3; Natural
Environment and Rural Communities, 2006 c 16, s 105, sch 11 para 153(3),
sch 12; Educ and Inspections, 2006 c 40, s 157, sch 14 para 69(3), sch 18;
Police and Justice, 2006 c 48, s 52, sch 15; SIs 2006/63 (W 12), art 3; 2006/64
(W 13), art 3; 2006/1254, art 63, sch 4; 2006/3336, art 308, sch 13; Statistics
and Registration Service, 2007 c 18, s 73, sch 4; Offender Management, 2007 c
21, s 39, sch 5 pt 2; Consumers, Estate Agents and Redress, 2007 c 17, s 64,
sch 8; Loc Govt and Public Involvement in Health, 2007 c 28, s 146, sch 9 para
1(1)(2)(q), sch 18; Legal Services, 2007 c 29, s 210, sch 23; Tribunals, Cts and
Enforcement, 2007 c 15, s 146, sch 23; Health and Social Care, 2008 c 14, s
166, sch 15; ibid, s 95, sch 5 para 73(a), sch 15; Housing and Regeneration,
2008 c 17, ss 56, 277, 321, sch 8 para 77(1)(3), sch 9 para 28(1)(3), sch 16;
SIs 2008/576, art 18, sch; 2008/960, art 22, sch 3; Loc Democracy, Economic
Development and Construction, 2009 c 20, s 146, sch 7 pt 3; SI 2009/56, art 3,
sch 1 para 296; Identity Documents, 2010 c 40, s 12, sch 1 para 11; SIs
2010/231, art 68, sch 4, 234, art 7, sch 3, 939, arts 2,3, 1080, art 2, schs 1, 2;
Sports Grounds Safety Authy, 2011 c 6, sch 2 para 8, sch 3; Localism, 2011 c

2000
c 36 sch 1 *continued*

20, sch 5 para 16; ibid, sch 8 para 10; ibid, sch 16 para 17; ibid, sch 25 pts 5,
20, 26, 32; Educ, 2011 c 21, sch 2 para 25; Public Bodies, 2011 c 24, sch 6;
Financial Services, 2012 c 21, sch 18 para 91(a); Welfare Reform, 2012 c 5,
sch 13 para 17(a); ibid, sch 14 pt 8; Health and Social Care, 2012 c 7, sch 5
para 99(a),(c); ibid, sch 7 para 10; ibid, sch 13 para 7(b); (pt prosp) ibid, sch 14
para 81; ibid, sch 15 paras 50(e), 69(1)(d), 71(1)(c); ibid, sch 20 paras 1(b),
5(1)(c), 9(1)(c); Legal Aid, Sentencing and Punishment of Offenders, 2012 c 10,
sch 5 para 55; SIs 2012/246, art 4(2), sch 1 para 20, 964, art 3(1), sch, 990 (W
130), art 8, 1206, sch para 2, 1659, sch 3 para 15(2)(a), 1923, sch, 2398, sch 1
para 8, ibid, sch 2 para 3; 2654, sch; SL(R), 2013 c 2, s 1, sch 1 pt 10(3);
Crime and Cts, 2013 c 22, sch 8 para 104; Enterprise and Regulatory Reform,
2013 c 24, sch 20 para 2; SIs 2013/64, art 4; 252, sch pt 1; 687, sch 1 para 14;
755 (W 90), sch 2 para 399(2); 2042, sch para 22; 2329, sch para 26; 2352,
sch 1 para 13; (1.4.2017) Loc Audit and Accountability, 2014 c 2, sch 12 para
45; (pt prosp) Anti-social Behaviour, Crime and Policing, 2014 c 12, sch 11
para 102; Defence Reform, 2014 c 20, sch 4 para 21(b); 2014/631, sch 1 para
10(3); 892, sch 1 para 147; 1068, art 3(2); 1924, sch; 3184, sch para 14;
Deregulation, 2015 c 20, sch 13 para 6(31); ibid, sch 21 para 1(2)(b); SIs
2015/850, art 3(3); 978, sch pt 1
    ext—SI 2008/1271, art 2
  sch 2 rep in pt—SI 2010/22, art 5, sch 4
  sch 3 ext—Crim. Justice and Police, 2001 c 16, s 50, sch 1 pt 1 para 73
    am—Courts, 2003 c 39, s 65, sch 4 para 13
    appl (mods)—SI 2004/3391, reg 18
  sch 4 rep—SI 2010/22, art 5, sch 2
  sch 7 rep in pt—(S) Public Services Ombudsman, 2002 asp 11, s 25(1), sch 6, para 23(1)(3);
    Public Services Ombudsman (W), 2005 c 10, s 39(2), sch 7

c 37   **Countryside and Rights of Way**
  s 1 am—(W prosp) Commons, 2006 c 26, s 52, sch 5 para 7(1)(2)(a); Natural Environment
    and Rural Communities, 2006 c 16, s 105, sch 11 para 154; Marine and Coastal
    Access, 2009 c 23, s 303(2); SIs 2010/558, art 8, sch para 24; 2013/755 (W 90),
    sch 2 para 401
    rep in pt—(W prosp) Commons, 2006 c 26, s 52, sch 5 para 7(1)(2)(b)(3); Marine and
    Coastal Access, 2009 c 23, ss 303(2)(a), 321, sch 22 pt 7
  s 2 excl—Serious Organised Crime and Police, 2005 c 15, s 131(1)(a)
    am—Marine and Coastal Access, 2009 c 23, s 303(3)
  s 3 am—Marine and Coastal Access, 2009 c 23, s 303(4)
  s 3A added —Marine and Coastal Access, 2009 c 23, s 303(5)
  s 4 am—Natural Environment and Rural Communities, 2006 c 16, s 105, sch 11 para 155;
    SI 2013/755 (W 90), sch 2 para 402
  s 7 appl—Marine and Coastal Access, 2009 c 23, s 304, sch 20 para 4(4)
  s 8 appl—Marine and Coastal Access, 2009 c 23, s 304, sch 20 para 4(4)
  s 10 am—SI 2013/514, reg 2(2)(3)
  s 16 appl—(E) SI 2003/2004, reg 7(2)
    am—Marine and Coastal Access, 2009 c 23, s 303(6)
    rep in pt—Marine and Coastal Access, 2009 c 23, ss 303(6)(b), 321, sch 22 pt 7
  s 17 am—Communications, 2003 c 21, s 406(1), sch 17 para 165(1)(2); SI 2003/1900, arts
    2(1), 3(1),sch 1; SI 2003/3142, art 3(2)
  s 20 am—Natural Environment and Rural Communities, 2006 c 16, s 105, sch 11 para 156;
    (Marine and Coastal Access, 2009 c 23, s 303(7); SI 2013/755 (W 90), sch 2 para
    402
    rep in pt—Marine and Coastal Access, 2009 c 23, ss 303(7)(a) 321, sch 22 pt 7
  s 21 am—SIs 2010/558, art 8, sch para 15; 2013/755 (W 90), sch 2 para 403
  s 22 am—SI 2010/558, art 8, sch para 16
  s 23 am—SI 2010/558, art 8, sch para 17
  s 24 am—SI 2010/558, art 8, sch para 18
  s 25 am—SI 2010/558, art 8, sch para 19
  s 25A added—SI 2010/558, art 8, sch para 20
  s 26 am—Natural Environment and Rural Communities, 2006 c 16, s 105, sch 11 para 157;
    SIs 2010/558, art 8, sch para 21; 2013/755 (W 90), sch 2 para 404
  s 27 am—SI 2010/558, art 8, sch para 22
  s 29 am—SI 2002/794, art 5(1), sch 1, para 43
    rep in pt—SI 2002/794, art 5(2), sch 2

2000
c 37 *continued*

s 30 am—SI 2002/794, art 5(1), sch 1, para 44
    rep in pt—SI 2002/794, art 5(2), sch 2
s 31 am—SI 2010/558, art 8, sch para 23
s 33 am—Natural Environment and Rural Communities, 2006 c 16, s 105, sch 11 para 158;
    SI 2013/755 (W 90), sch 2 para 405(2)
    rep in pt—SI 2013/755 (W 90), sch 2 para 405(3)
ss 34-39 appl—Marine and Coastal Access, 2009 c 23, s 304, sch 20 para 1(1)
s 40 appl—Marine and Coastal Access, 2009 c 23, s 304, sch 20 para 9(3)
s 41 appl (mods)—Marine and Coastal Access, 2009 c 23, s 304, sch 20 para 9(4)
s 44 am—Marine and Coastal Access, 2009 c 23, s 303(8)
s 45 rep in pt—Communications, 2003 c 21, s 406(7), sch 19(1); SI 2003/1900, arts 2(1),
    3(1),sch 1; SI 2003/3142, art 3(2)
    am —(W prosp) Commons, 2006 c 26, s 52, sch 5 para 7(1)(4); Marine and Coastal
       Access, 2009 c 23, s 303(9)
s 46 am—Commons, 2006 c 26, s 52, sch 5 para 7(1)(5)
    rep in pt—Commons, 2006 c 26, s 53, sch 6
s 55A added—Deregulation, 2015 c 20, s 20
s 56 am—Deregulation, 2015 c 20, s 22(2)
s 56A added—Deregulation, 2015 c 20, s 21
s 56B added—Deregulation, 2015 c 20, s 22(1)
s 58 am—Natural Environment and Rural Communities, 2006 c 16, s 105, sch 11 para 159
s 60 excl—(E) SI 2005/157, art 6
s 61 am—Natural Environment and Rural Communities, 2006 c 16, s 105, sch 11 para 160
s 68 rep—Commons, 2006 c 26, s 51, sch 6
s 73 rep—Natural Environment and Rural Communities, 2006 c 16, s 105, sch 11 para 161,
    sch 12
s 74 rep—Natural Environment and Rural Communities, 2006 c 16, s 105, sch 11 para 162,
    sch 12
s 78 rep—SI 2015/664, sch 4 para 100
s 80 rep in pt—Natural Environment and Rural Communities, 2006 c 16, s 105, sch 12
s 81 rep in pt—Crim Justice, 2003 c 44, s 332, sch 37 pt 9
s 82 am—Natural Environment and Rural Communities, 2006 c 16, s 105, sch 11 para 163;
    SI 2013/755 (W 90), sch 2 para 407
s 83 am—Natural Environment and Rural Communities, 2006 c 16, s 105, sch 11 para
    164(a); SI 2013/755 (W 90), sch 2 para 408
s 84 am—Natural Environment and Rural Communities, 2006 c 16, s 105, sch 11 para
    164(b); SI 2013/755 (W 90), sch 2 para 408
s 85 am—Natural Environment and Rural Communities, 2006 c 16, s 105, sch 11 para 165;
    (prosp) Planning (W), 2015 anaw 4, sch 2 para 21
s 86 am—Planning and Compulsory Purchase, 2004 c 5, s 118(2), sch 7 para 23(b); Natural
    Environment and Rural Communities, 2006 c 16, s 105, sch 11 para 164(c); SI
    2013/755 (W 90), sch 2 para 408
    rep in pt—Planning and Compulsory Purchase, 2004 c 5, ss 118(2), 120, sch 7 para
       23(a), sch 9
s 87 rep in pt—Natural Environment and Rural Communities, 2006 c 16, s 105, sch 11 para
    166, sch 12
s 90 am—Natural Environment and Rural Communities, 2006 c 16, s 105, sch 11 para
    164(d); SI 2013/755 (W 90), sch 2 para 408
    rep in pt—Natural Environment and Rural Communities, 2006 c 16, s 105, sch 11 para
       167, sch 12
s 91 am—Natural Environment and Rural Communities, 2006 c 16, s 105, sch 11 para
    164(e); SI 2013/755 (W 90), sch 2 para 408
    rep in pt—Deregulation, 2015 c 20, sch 22 para 15(1)
s 92 rep in pt—Natural Environment and Rural Communities, 2006 c 16, s 105, sch 11 para
    168, sch 12; SI 2013/755 (W 90), sch 2 para 409(2)
    am—SI 2013/755 (W 90), sch 2 para 409(3)
s 98 rep—Commons, 2006 c 26, s 53, sch 6
s 101 rep in pt—Natural Environment and Rural Communities, 2006 c 16, s 105, sch 11
    para 169, sch 12
sch 1 am—Communications, 2003 c 21, s 406(1), sch 17 para 165(1)(3); SIs 2003/1900,
    arts 2(1), 3(1),sch 1; 2003/3142, art 3(2); 2010/558, art 8, sch paras 1-10; Postal
    Services, 2011 c 5, sch 12 para 156; 2013/755 (W 90), sch 2 para 410

2000

c 37 *continued*

sch 2 appl (mods)—(subject to transtl provn(s)) Greenham and Crookham Commons, 2002 c
i, ss 11(4)(7), 42(1)(b)

appl—(subject to transtl provn(s)) Greenham and Crookham Commons, 2002 c i, ss
11(4)(7), 42(1)(b)

am—SI 2010/558, art 8, sch paras 11-14

sch 3 appl—Marine and Coastal Access, 2009 c 23, s 304, sch 20 para 4(4)

sch 4 rep in pt—Natural Environment and Rural Communities, 2006 c 16, s 105, sch 12

sch 6 rep in pt—Growth and Infrastructure, 2013 c 27, s 13(7)

am—SI 2013/755 (W 90), sch 2 para 411(2)

sch 7 rep in pt—Natural Environment and Rural Communities, 2006 c 16, ss 70(8), 105, sch
12

sch 8 rep in pt—Natural Environment and Rural Communities, 2006 c 16, s 105, sch 12

sch 10 rep in pt—(EW) (saving) SI 2007/3538, reg 74, sch 23

sch 11 am—Natural Environment and Rural Communities, 2006 c 16, s 105, sch 11 para
170

sch 12 rep in pt—Police Reform, 2002 c 30, s 107(2), sch 8; Natural Environment and Rural
Communities, 2006 c 16, s 105, sch 12; SI 2007/1843, reg 8

sch 13 am—Natural Environment and Rural Communities, 2006 c 16, s 105, sch 11 para
164(f); SI 2013/755 (W 90), sch 2 para 412

rep in pt—Loc Audit and Accountability, 2014 c 2, sch 1 pt 2

sch 15 rep in pt—Natural Environment and Rural Communities, 2006 c 16, s 105, sch 12

c 38 **Transport**

appl—(conditionally) (E) SI 2005/157, art 7(4)-(6)

appl (mods)—(specified ss appl (mods)) (E) SI 2005/157, art 7(2)(a)(5)(6), sch 2 pt 1

s 5 am—SIs 2009/1941, art 2, sch 1 para 184; 2011/205, reg 2

rep in pt—SI 2011/205, reg 2

s 12 rep in pt—Enterprise, 2002 c 40, s 278, sch 25, para 44(1)(2), sch 26

am—Enterprise and Regulatory Reform, 2013 c 24, sch 6 para 86

ss 12A, 12B added—Enterprise, 2002 c 40, s 278(1), sch 25, para 44(1)(3)

s 12A am—Enterprise and Regulatory Reform, 2013 c 24, sch 6 para 87

s 12B am—Communications, 2003 c 21, s 389(1), sch 16 para 7(1)(2); Enterprise and
Regulatory Reform, 2013 c 24, sch 6 para 88; SI 2014/892, sch 1 para 150

s 13 am—Enterprise, 2002 c 40, s 278(1), sch 25, para 44(1)(4); Enterprise and Regulatory
Reform, 2013 c 24, sch 6 para 89

s 14 am—Enterprise and Regulatory Reform, 2013 c 24, sch 6 para 90

s 15 am—Enterprise and Regulatory Reform, 2013 c 24, sch 6 para 91

s 16 am—Enterprise and Regulatory Reform, 2013 c 24, sch 6 para 92

s 17 am—Enterprise and Regulatory Reform, 2013 c 24, sch 6 para 93

s 18 subst—Enterprise, 2002 c 40, s 278(1), sch 25, para 44(1)(5)

am—Communications, 2003 c 21, s 389(1), sch 16 para 7(1)(3); Enterprise and
Regulatory Reform, 2013 c 24, sch 6 para 94; SI 2014/892, sch 1 para 151

s 19 am—Enterprise, 2002 c 40, s 278(1), sch 25, para 44(1)(5); SI 2003/1592, art 16, sch
4 para 17; Enterprise and Regulatory Reform, 2013 c 24, sch 6 para 95; SI
2014/892, sch 1 para 152

s 21 rep in pt—Enterprise and Regulatory Reform, 2013 c 24, sch 14 para 15(2)

am—Enterprise and Regulatory Reform, 2013 c 24, sch 14 para 15(3)

s 26 appl—Enterprise, 2002 c 40, s 249(1)(c); Insolvency, 1986 c 45, s 72GA(c)

s 48 am—SI 2008/948, art 3, sch 1

s 49 am—SI 2009/1941, art 2, sch 1 para 184

s 56 am—SIs 2007/2194, art 10, sch 4; 2008/948, art 4, sch 3; 2009/1941, art 2, sch 1 para
184; 2015/17, sch 6 para 3

s 58 am—SI 2009/1941, art 2, sch 1 para 184

s 59 am—SI 2008/948, art 3, sch 1

s 61 am—Constitutional Reform, 2005 c 4, s 15(1), sch 4 pt 1 paras 293, 294

s 65 am—SI 2009/1941, art 2, sch 1 para 184

s 66 am—Civil Aviation, 2012 c 19, s 98(1)

s 67 am—Civil Aviation, 2012 c 19, s 98(2)

s 77 am—SI 2001/492, art 2

s 82 am—(prosp) (EW) Crim Justice, 2003 c 44, ss 280(1)(3), 304, sch 25 para 105, sch 32
pt 2 para 161

rep in pt—(prosp) (EW) Crim Justice, 2003 c 44, ss 280(1)(3), 332, sch 25 para 105,
sch 37 pt 9

s 85 rep in pt—Enterprise, 2002 c 40, ss 168(9), 278(2), sch 9 pt 2, para 23(1)(3)(a), sch 26

2000

c 38 s 85 *continued*

    am—Enterprise, 2002 c 40, ss 168(9), 278(1), sch 9 pt 2, para 23(1)(2)(3)(b), sch 25, para 44(1)(6); SI 2014/892, sch 1 para 153

s 86 am—Enterprise, 2002 c 40, ss 168(9), 278(1), sch 9 pt 2, para 24, sch 25, para 44(1)(7); SI 2004/1261, reg 5, sch 2 para 10; SI 2012/1809, art 3(1), sch pt 1; Enterprise and Regulatory Reform, 2013 c 24, sch 15 para 14; SI 2014/892, sch 1 para 154(2)-(6)(7)(b)(c)(8)-(10)

    rep in pt—SI 2014/892, sch 1 para 154(7)(a)

s 87 am—Enterprise, 2002 c 40, s 168(9), sch 9 pt 2, para 25

s 88 am—SI 2003/1398, art 2, sch para 37

s 89 am—Enterprise, 2002 c 40, ss 168(9), 278(1), sch 9 pt 2, para 26, sch 25, para 44(1)(8); SI 2014/892, sch 1 para 155

s 90 rep in pt—Enterprise, 2002 c 40, s 278, sch 25, para 44(1)(9)(b), sch 26

    am—Enterprise, 2002 c 40, s 278(1), sch 25, para 44(1)(9)(a); SI 2014/892, sch 1 para 156

s 91 rep in pt—Enterprise, 2002 c 40, s 278, sch 25, para 44(1)(10)(b), sch 26

    am—Enterprise, 2002 c 40, s 278(1), sch 25, para 44(1)(10)(a); SI 2014/892, sch 1 para 157

ss 93, 94 am —Constitutional Reform, 2005 c 4, s 15(1), sch 4 pt 1 paras 293, 295, 296

s 95 appl—(EW) Environmental Protection, 1990 c 43, s 79

Pt 2 (ss 108-162) power to am—Concessionary Bus Travel, 2007 c 13, ss 8(1), 9(1)(2), 10(1)(2)

    trans of functions—SIs 2014/865, art 8(1)(b); 2014/1012, art 8 9

s 108 appl—Transport (S), 2001 asp 2, ss 5(4)(d)(i), 15(e)(i); (E) SI 2004/2204, reg 15(3); (W) SI 2005/2839 (W 203), reg 13(3)

    excl—(E) SI 2005/157, art 7

    am—Transport (W), 2006 c 5, s 3, sch 1 paras 1, 2; Loc Transport, 2008 c 26, ss 7(1)(2), 8(1)(3)(4), 9(1), 77, sch 4 paras 41, 42; Loc Democracy, Economic Development and Construction, 2009 c 20, s 119, sch 6 para 96

    mod—SIs 2006/2993 (W 280), art 3; 2014/2178 (W 212), art 3

    rep in pt—Loc Transport, 2008 c 26, s 8(1)(2), sch 7

s 109 am—Transport (W), 2006 c 5, s 3, sch 1 paras 1, 3(1)-(4)(5)(a)(6); Loc Transport, 2008 c 26, s 9(2)-(4); Loc Democracy, Economic Development and Construction, 2009 c 20, s 119, sch 6 para 97

    rep in pt—Transport (W), 2006 c 5, s 3, sch 1 paras 1, 3(5)(b); Loc Transport, 2008 c 26, s 9(2)(5), sch 7

ss 109A, 109B added—Transport (W), 2006 c 5, s 3, sch 1 paras 1, 4

s 109A rep in pt—SI 2007/1388, art 3, sch 1

ss 110, 111 rep—Loc Transport, 2008 c 26, s 10(1)(2), sch 7

s 112 am—Loc Transport, 2008 c 26, ss 10(1)(3)(4)(a), 11; Equality, 2010 c 15, s 211, sch 26 para 48 (subst by SI 2010/2279, sch 1)

    rep in pt—Loc Transport, 2008 c 26, s 10(1)(3)(4)(b)(5), sch 7

s 113 am—Loc Transport, 2008 c 26, s 12(1)(3); Loc Democracy, Economic Development and Construction, 2009 c 20, s 119, sch 6 para 98

    rep in pt—Loc Transport, 2008 c 26, s 12(1)(2)(4), sch 7

s 113A added—Transport (W), 2006 c 5, s 3, sch 1 paras 1, 6

    am—Loc Transport, 2008 c 26, s 10(1)(6)

s 113B added—Transport (W), 2006 c 5, s 3, sch 1 paras 1, 6

    am—Loc Transport, 2008 c 26, s 10(1)(6)

s 114 excl—SIs 2005/3523, art 38; 2009/3293 (W 290), reg 4

    am—Loc Transport, 2008 c 26, s 13; SI 2013/1644, sch 3

s 115 am—Loc Transport, 2008 c 26, s 14; SI 2013/1644, sch 3

s 116 am—Loc Transport, 2008 c 26, s 15(1)-(5); SI 2013/1644, sch 3

    rep in pt—Loc Transport, 2008 c 26, s 131, sch 7

s 117 am—Loc Transport, 2008 c 26, s 16(1)(2); SI 2013/1644, sch 3

s 118 am—Loc Transport, 2008 c 26, s 17; SI 2013/1644, sch 3

s 122 am—Loc Transport, 2008 c 26, s 18; SI 2013/1644, sch 3

s 124 am—(EW) Railways, 2005 c 14, s 39(1)(2); Loc Transport, 2008 c 26, s 7, sch 1 paras 1, 2(1)(2); ibid, ss 19, 77, sch 4 paras 41, 43; Loc Democracy, Economic Development and Construction, 2009 c 20, s 119, sch 6 para 99

    rep in pt—Loc Transport, 2008 c 26, s 7, sch 1 paras 1, 2(1)(3), sch 7

s 125 am—(W prosp) Loc Transport, 2008 c 26, s 20(1)-(4)(b)(5); SI 2013/1644, sch 3

    rep in pt—(W prosp) Loc Transport, 2008 c 26, s 20(1)(4)(c), sch 7

2000
c 38 *continued*

s 126 am—(EW) Railways, 2005 c 14, s 39(3); (W prosp) Loc Transport, 2008 c 26, s
    21(1)-(5)(a)(6)
    rep in pt—(W prosp) Loc Transport, 2008 c 26, s 21(1)(5)(b), sch 7
s 126A added (W prosp)—Loc Transport, 2008 c 26, s 22(1)
s 126B added (W pt prosp)—Loc Transport, 2008 c 26, s 23
ss 126C, 126D added (W prosp) —Loc Transport, 2008 c 26, s 24
s 126E added (W pt prosp)—Loc Transport, 2008 c 26, s 25
s 127 am—(E) SI 2005/75, art 2; (W pt prosp) Loc Transport, 2008 c 26, s 26(1)-(8); SI
    2013/1644, sch 3
ss 127A, 127B added (W prosp)—Loc Transport, 2008 c 26, s 27(1)
s 127A trans of functions—SI 2015/65, art 2(2)(a)
    am—SI 2015/65, sch 1 para 5
s 127B trans of functions—SI 2015/65, art 2(2)(b)
    am—SI 2015/65, sch 1 para 5
s 128 am—(W prosp) Loc Transport, 2008 c 26, s 28; SI 2013/1644, sch 3
s 129 am—(W prosp) Loc Transport, 2008 c 26, s 29(1)-(3)
    rep in pt—(W prosp) Loc Transport, 2008 c 26, s 29(1)(4), sch 7
s 130 am—(W prosp) Loc Transport, 2008 c 26, s 30; SI 2013/1644, sch 3
s 131A added (W prosp)—Loc Transport, 2008 c 26, s 31
    am—SI 2013/1644, sch 3
s 131B added (W prosp)—Loc Transport, 2008 c 26, s 32
s 131C added (W prosp)—Loc Transport, 2008 c 26, s 33
s 131D added (W prosp)—Loc Transport, 2008 c 26, s 34
s 131E added (W pt prosp)—Loc Transport, 2008 c 26, s 35
    trans of functions—SI 2015/65, art 2(2)(c)
    am—SI 2015/65, sch 1 para 5
s 131F added (W prosp)—Loc Transport, 2008 c 26, s 36
    trans of funct—SI 2015/65, art 2(2)(d)
    am—SI 2015/65, sch 1 para 5
s 132 am—(EW) Railways, 2005 c 14, s 39(4)(5); (W prosp) Loc Transport, 2008 c 26, s
    37; SIs 2013/1644, sch 3; 2015/65, sch 1 para 5
    rep in pt—SI 2013/1644, sch 3
    trans of functions—SI 2015/65, art 2(2)(e)
s 132A added (W pt prosp)—Loc Transport, 2008 c 26, s 38
    trans of functions—SI 2015/65, art 2(2)(f)
    am—SI 2015/65, sch 1 para 5
s 132B added (W prosp)—Loc Transport, 2008 c 26, s 39
    trans of functions—SI 2015/65, art 2(2)(g)
    am—SI 2015/65, sch 1 para 5
s 132C added (W prosp)—Loc Transport, 2008 c 26, s 40(1)
s 132D added (W prosp)—Loc Transport, 2008 c 26, s 40(1)
    am—SI 2013/1644, sch 3
s 133 am—(W pt prosp) Loc Transport, 2008 c 26, s 41
s 134 am—(W prosp) Loc Transport, 2008 c 26, s 42
s 134A added (W prosp)—Loc Transport, 2008 c 26, s 43
s 134B added (W pt prosp)—Loc Transport, 2008 c 26, s 44(1)
s 135 am—Loc Transport, 2008 c 26, s 7, sch 1 paras 1, 3
s 136 am—SI 2013/1644, sch 3
s 137 am—Railways, 2005 c 14, s 59, sch 12 para 17(1)(2); SI 2013/1644, sch 3
s 139 am—Loc Transport, 2008 c 26, s 7, sch 1 paras 1, 4; SI 2013/1644, sch 3
s 140 am—SI 2013/1644, sch 3
s 143 ext—Anti-terrorism, Crime and Security, 2001 c 24, s 17, sch 4 pt 1 para 53(1)
s 144 rep (E prosp)—Traffic Management, 2004 c 18, s 98, sch 12 pt 1
    appl—SI 2006/1516, art 2
s 144 mod —(temp) Deregulation, 2015 c 20, sch 11 para 17
s 145 replaced (by s 145A)—Concessionary Bus Travel, 2007 c 13, s 1
s 145B added—Concessionary Bus Travel, 2007 c 13, s 13, sch 2 paras 10, 11
s 146 rep in pt—Transport, 2000 c 38, s 274, sch 31 pt II; (E) SI 2005/3224, art 3(1)(3)(5);
    Concessionary Bus Travel, 2007 c 13, s 13, sch 3
    power to am—(EW) Travel Concessions (Eligibility), 2002 c 4, s 1(4)
    am—(EW) Travel Concessions (Eligibility), 2002 c 4, s 1(3); Concessionary Bus
    Travel, 2007 c 13, ss 2, 13, sch 2 paras 10, 12; Loc Transport, 2008 c 26, s 77,
    sch 4 paras 41, 44; (E) SIs 2010/459, art 2; 2010/1179, arts 2, 3

2000
c 38 *continued*

s 147 am—Concessionary Bus Travel, 2007 c 13, s 13, sch 2 paras 10, 13
s 148 am—Concessionary Bus Travel, 2007 c 13, s 13, sch 2 paras 10, 14
s 149 am—Concessionary Bus Travel, 2007 c 13, s 3(1)(2)(3)
s 150 am—Concessionary Bus Travel, 2007 c 13, s 3(4)(5)(6)
s 151 rep in pt—Concessionary Bus Travel, 2007 c 13, s 13, sch 3
s 153 subst—Loc Transport, 2008 c 26, s 46(1)
s 155 am—Loc Transport, 2008 c 26, ss 63(2), 64(1)-(3)(5)(7)-(11), 65(1); (W pt prosp)
      ibid, s 44(3); SI 2009/1885, art 4, sch 1; SI 2013/1644, sch 3
    rep in pt—Loc Transport, 2008 c 26, s 64(1)(4)(6), sch 7
    trans of functions—SI 2009/1885, art 2
s 156 rep—Loc Transport, 2008 c 26, s 131, sch 7
s 157 am—Loc Transport, 2008 c 26, s 77, sch 4 paras 41, 45(1)(2); Loc Democracy,
      Economic Development and Construction, 2009 c 20, s 119, sch 6 para 100
s 158 rep—Transport, 2000 c 38, s 274, sch 31 pt II
s 160 am—Loc Transport, 2008 c 26, s 64(12)-(14)
s 162 rep in pt—(E) SI 2005/3224, art 3(1)(4)(5); Loc Transport, 2008 c 26, ss 12(5), 131,
      sch 7 pt 1; (W prosp) ibid, s 131, sch 7 pt 2
    am—Concessionary Bus Travel, 2007 c 13, s 13, sch 2 paras 10, 15; Loc Transport,
      2008 c 26, ss 7(1)(3), 10(1)(7), 15(6), 46(2), 77, sch 4 paras 41, 46; (W prosp)
      ibid, ss 22(2), 26(9), 27(2), 32(2), 40(2); Loc Democracy, Economic
      Development and Construction, 2009 c 20, s 119, sch 6 para 101
s 163 am—Loc Transport, 2008 c 26, ss 103, 109, sch 5 paras 1, 2; Loc Democracy,
      Economic Development and Construction, 2009 c 20, s 119, sch 6 para 102
s 164 am—Loc Transport, 2008 c 26, s 104; Loc Democracy, Economic Development and
      Construction, 2009 c 20, s 119, sch 6 para 103
s 165 am—Loc Transport, 2008 c 26, s 105; Loc Democracy, Economic Development and
      Construction, 2009 c 20, s 119, sch 6 para 104
s 165A added—Loc Transport, 2008 c 26, s 106
    am—Loc Democracy, Economic Development and Construction, 2009 c 20, s 119,
      sch 6 para 105
s 166 am—Loc Transport, 2008 c 26, s 107(1)-(2)(b)(3); Loc Democracy, Economic
      Development and Construction, 2009 c 20, s 119, sch 6 para 106
    rep in pt—Loc Transport, 2008 c 26, s 107(1)(2)(c), sch 7
s 166A added —Loc Transport, 2008 c 26, s 108
    am—Loc Democracy, Economic Development and Construction, 2009 c 20, s 119,
      sch 6 para 107
s 167 am—Loc Transport, 2008 c 26, s 109, sch 5 paras 1, 3; Loc Democracy, Economic
      Development and Construction, 2009 c 20, s 119, sch 6 para 108; Infrastructure,
      2015 c 7, sch 1 para 126
s 168 am—Loc Transport, 2008 c 26, s 109, sch 5 paras 1, 4; Loc Democracy, Economic
      Development and Construction, 2009 c 20, s 119, sch 6 para 109
s 169 am—Loc Transport, 2008 c 26, ss 109, 110(1)-(3), sch 5 paras 1, 5
    rep in pt—Loc Transport, 2008 c 26, s 110(1)(4), sch 7
s 170 am—Loc Transport, 2008 c 26, ss 109, 111(1)-(4), sch 5 paras 1, 6; Loc Democracy,
      Economic Development and Construction, 2009 c 20, s 119, sch 6 para 110
    rep in pt—Loc Transport, 2008 c 26, s 111(1)(5), sch 7
s 171 rep in pt—Loc Transport, 2008 c 26, s 131, sch 7
    am—Loc Transport, 2008 c 26, s 112(1)
s 172 am—Loc Transport, 2008 c 26, s 113(1)-(4)
s 172A added—Loc Transport, 2008 c 26, s 114
s 173 am—Loc Transport, 2008 c 26, s 115(1)
s 174 am—Loc Transport, 2008 c 26, s 115(2)
    appl—SI 2011/41, art 46(3)
s 175 appl—SI 2011/41, art 46(3)
s 176 am—Loc Transport, 2008 c 26, s 116(1)-(3); Infrastructure, 2015 c 7, sch 1 para 127
    appl—SI 2011/41, art 46(3)
s 177 am—Loc Transport, 2008 c 26, s 109, sch 5 paras 1, 7; Infrastructure, 2015 c 7, sch 1
      para 128
s 177A added—Loc Transport, 2008 c 26, s 117(1)
    am—Loc Democracy, Economic Development and Construction, 2009 c 20, s 119,
      sch 6 para 111
s 179 am—Loc Transport, 2008 c 26, s 7, sch 1 paras 1, 5
s 180 am—Loc Transport, 2008 c 26, s 7, sch 1 paras 1, 6

2000
c 38 *continued*

s 181 am—Loc Transport, 2008 c 26, s 7, sch 1 paras 1, 7(1)(2)(a)
 rep in pt—Loc Transport, 2008 c 26, s 7, sch 1 paras 1, 7(1)(2)(b), sch 7
s 184 excl—SI 2009/2085, reg 3
s 193 am—Loc Transport, 2008 c 26, s 109, sch 5 paras 1, 8; Loc Democracy, Economic
 Development and Construction, 2009 c 20, s 119, sch 6 para 112
s 194 am—Loc Transport, 2008 c 26, s 118(1)-(5); Loc Democracy, Economic
 Development and Construction, 2009 c 20, s 119, sch 6 para 113
s 197 am—Loc Transport, 2008 c 26, s 121, sch 6 para 8(1)(2)(b)
 rep in pt—Loc Transport, 2008 c 26, s 121, sch 6 para 8(1)(2)(a), sch 7
s 198 am—Loc Transport, 2008 c 26, ss 7(1)(4), 12(6)(a)(b), 77, 109, sch 4 paras 41, 47,
 sch 5 paras 1, 9; Loc Democracy, Economic Development and Construction,
 2009 c 20, s 119, sch 6 para 114
 rep in pt—Loc Transport, 2008 c 26, s 12(6)(c), sch 7
ss 201-211 rep—Railways, 2005 c 14, s 59, sch 13 pt 1
s 212 rep in pt—Railways, 2005 c 14, s 59, sch 13 pt 1
ss 213, 214 rep—Railways, 2005 c 14, ss 1, 59, sch 1 pt 1 para 36(a)(b), sch 13 pt 1
s 215 am—SI 2015/1682, sch pt 1 para 4(p)(i)
s 216 am—Railways and Transport Safety, 2003 c 20, s 16, sch 2 pt 2 para 19(t)(ii); SI
 2015/1682, sch pt 1 para 4(p)(ii)
s 217 rep in pt—Railways, 2005 c 14, s 59, sch 13 pt 1
ss 218-222 rep—(saving) Railways, 2005 c 14, ss 1, 46(4), 59, sch 1 pt 1 para 36(c), sch 13
s 224 rep in pt—Railways, 2005 c 14, s 59, sch 13 pt 1
s 226 rep in pt—Railways, 2005 c 14, s 59, sch 13 pt 1
s 227 rep in pt—Railways, 2005 c 14, s 59, sch 13 pt 1; SI 2010/439, art 2, sch
s 228 rep in pt—Railways, 2005 c 14, s 59, sch 13 pt 1
 am—Railways, 2005 c 14, s 59, sch 12 para 17(1)(3)
ss 234-239 rep—Railways, 2005 c 14, s 59, sch 13 pt 1
s 244 power to mod—Railways, 2005 c 14, s 1(8)(c)
s 246 rep (prosp)—Railways, 2005 c 14, s 59, sch 13 pt 1
s 248 am—Railways, 2005 c 14, s 59, sch 12 para 17(1)(4)(5)(6)(a)
s 248 rep in pt—Railways, 2005 c 14, s 59, sch 12 para 17(1)(6)(b), sch 13 pt 1
s 249 rep—Railways, 2005 c 14, s 59, sch 13 pt 1
s 251 rep—Railways, 2005 c 14, s 59, sch 13 pt 1
s 258 rep in pt—SI 2009/1885, art 4, schs 3, 4
s 259 rep in pt—(prosp) Road Safety, 2006 c 49, s 59, sch 7
 subst—SI 2013/1644, sch 1
s 263 am—Loc Transport, 2008 c 26, s 125(2)-(4); SI 2013/1644, sch 1
s 267 rep in pt—SI 2009/1885, art 4, schs 3, 4
s 269 rep—SL(R), 2004 c 14, s 1(1), sch 1 pt 14
s 272 see—(cert functs made exercisable in S and transferred to S Ministers) SI 2003/415,
 arts 3, 5
s 275 rep in pt—SL(R), 2004 c 14, s 1(1), sch 1 pt 14
s 278 rep in pt—Railways, 2005 c 14, s 59, sch 13 pt 1
sch 1 am—SI 2009/1941, art 2, sch 1 para 184
sch 3 am—SI 2009/1941, art 2, sch 1 para 184
sch 5 rep in pt—Housing, 2004 c 34, s 266, sch 16; Civil Contingencies, 2004 c 36, s 32(2),
 sch 3; Housing and Regeneration, 2008 c 17, s 321, sch 16; (S) Flood Risk
 Management (S), 2009 asp 6, s 96, sch 3 para 12
sch 6 am—Constitutional Reform, 2005 c 4, s 15(1), sch 4 pt 1 paras 293, 297
sch 7 mod—Transport, 2000 c 38, s 64, sch 7 para 20
 rep in pt—Finance, 2008 c 9, s 8, sch 2 para 70(e)(i)
 am—Corporation Tax, 2009 c 4, s 1322, sch 1 paras 471, 472; Corporation Tax, 2010
 c 4, s 1177, sch 1 paras 320, 321; Taxation (International and Other Provns),
 2010 c 8, s 374, sch 8 paras 251, 252
sch 8 rep in pt—Enterprise, 2002 c 40, s 278(2), sch 26; Communications, 2003 c 21,
 s 406(7), sch 19(1); SI 2003/1900, arts 2(1), 3(1),sch 1; SI 2003/3142, art 3(2);
 SI 2003/1400, art 7, sch 5; Civil Aviation, 2012 c 19, sch 9 para 17
sch 9 am—Enterprise, 2002 c 40, s 278(1), sch 25, para 44(1)(11)(a)(b); Railways and
 Transport Safety, 2003 c 20, s 16, sch 2 pt 2 para 19(t)(iii); Communications,
 2003 c 21, s 406(1), sch 17 para 166; SI 2003/1900, arts 2(1), 3(1),sch 1; SI
 2003/3142, art 3(2); Water, 2003 c 37,s 101(1), sch 7 pt 2 para 35; SI
 2003/1400, art 8, sch 6; Railways, 2005 c 14, s 59, sch 12 para 17(1)(7); SIs
 2008/1277, reg 30, sch 2; 2011/2491, sch 3 para 5; Civil Aviation, 2012 c 19,

2000
c 38 *continued*

        sch 9 para 12; SI 2012/1809, art 3(1), sch pt 1; Energy, 2013 c 32, sch 12 para 76; SIs 2014/892, sch 1 para 158(a)(b)(ii)(c)-(e); 2015/1682, sch pt 1 para 4(p)(iii)

        rep in pt—Communications, 2003 c 21, s 406(7), sch 19(1); SIs 2008/960, art 22, sch 3; 2013/1575, sch para 3; 2014/892, sch 1 para 158(b)(i); Deregulation, 2015 c 20, sch 6 para 22(12)

        appl (mods)—SI 2006/1391, art 2, sch

    sch 10 ext—Anti-terrorism, Crime and Security, 2001 c 24, s 17, sch 4 pt 1 para 53(2)

        am—Enterprise, 2002 c 40, s 278(1), sch 25, para 44(1)(12)(a)(b)(c)(i)-(iii)(d)-(l); Railways and Transport Safety, 2003 c 20, s 16, sch 2 pt 2 para 19(t)(iv); Loc Transport, 2008 c 26, s 46, sch 2 paras 1-4(2), 6, 9-14(2), 15, 16; Enterprise and Regulatory Reform, 2013 c 24, sch 6 para 96; SI 2015/1682, sch pt 1 para 4(p)(iv)

        rep in pt—Enterprise, 2002 c 40, s 278, sch 25, para 44(1)(12)(c)(iv), sch 26; Loc Transport, 2008 c 26, s 46, sch 2 paras 1, 4(3), 5, 7, 8, 14(3), sch 7

    sch 11 rep in pt—Transport, 2000 c 38, s 274, sch 31 pt II; Concessionary Bus Travel, 2007 c 13, s 13, sch 3; Loc Transport, 2008 c 26, s 131, sch 7

    sch 12 am—Loc Transport, 2008 c 26, ss 7, 109, 121, sch 1 paras 1, 8, sch 5 paras 1, 10-15, sch 6 paras 1, 2(1)(2), 4-6(3)(4)(b), 7(1)(4)(5); Loc Democracy, Economic Development and Construction, 2009 c 20, s 119, sch 6 para 115

        rep in pt—Loc Transport, 2008 c 26, s 121, sch 6 paras 1, 2(1)(3), 3, 6(4)(a), 7(1)-(3), sch 7

    schs 14, 15 rep—Railways, 2005 c 14, s 59, sch 13 pt 1

    sch 16 rep in pt—SI 2003/1400, art 7, sch 5; (pt prosp) Railways, 2005 c 14, s 59, sch 13 pt 1

    sch 17 am—Railways and Transport Safety, 2003 c 20, s 16, sch 2 pt 2 para 19(t)(v); 2015/1682, sch pt 1 para 4(p)(v)

        rep in pt—Railways, 2005 c 14, s 59, sch 13 pt 1; (saving) ibid, 2005 c 14, s 59, sch 13

    sch 18 rep in pt—Railways and Transport Safety, 2003 c 20, s 118, sch 8; Railways, 2005 c 14, s 59, sch 13 pt 1

    schs 19-21 rep—(saving) Railways, 2005 c 14, s 59, sch 13

    sch 22 rep in pt—Railways, 2005 c 14, s 59, sch 13 pt 1; SI 2010/439, art 2, sch

    sch 23 rep in pt—Railways, 2005 c 14, s 59, sch 13 pt 1

    sch 25 am—Railways, 2005 c 14, s 59, sch 12 para 17(1)(8)

    sch 25 rep in pt—Railways, 2005 c 14, s 59, sch 13 pt 1

    sch 26 rep in pt—Capital Allowances, 2001 c 2, ss 578, 580, sch 2 para 109(1)(a), sch 4; Finance, 2008 c 9, s 8, sch 2 para 70(e)(ii)

        am—Capital Allowances, 2001 c 2, ss 578, 580, sch 2 para 109(1)(b)(c), sch 4; ibid, sch 2 para 109(2), sch 4; Railways and Transport Safety, 2003 c 20, s 16, sch 2 pt 2 para 19(t)(vi); SI 2003/2867, reg 2, sch pt 1 para 32; Finance, 2004 c 12, s 52, sch 10 pt 1 para 46; Corporation Tax, 2009 c 4, s 1322, sch 1 paras 471, 473; Corporation Tax, 2010 c 4, s 1177, sch 1 paras 320, 322; SI 2015/1682, sch pt 1 para 4(p)(vi)

    sch 27 rep in pt—Railways and Transport Safety, 2003 c 20, s 118, sch 8; Railways, 2005 c 14, s 59, sch 13 pt 1

    sch 28 rep in pt—Railways, 2005 c 14, s 59, sch 13 pt 1

        am—Railways, 2005 c 14, s 59, sch 12 para 17(1)(9); SI 2010/439, art 2, sch

    sch 29 am—Capital Allowances, 2001 c 2, s 578, sch 2 para 109

        rep in pt—(prosp) Road Safety, 2006 c 49, s 59, sch 7

    sch 31 rep in pt—Railways, 2005 c 14, s 59, sch 13 pt 1

c 39   **Insolvency**

    s 4 rep in pt—Deregulation, 2015 c 20, sch 6 para 20(3)

    s 9 rep (prosp)—Enterprise, 2002 c 40, s 278(2), sch 26

    s 15 rep in pt—Financial Services, 2012 c 21, sch 19

    sch 1 am—SI 2002/1555, arts 29, 30

        rep in pt—SI 2002/1555, art 28

    sch 2 am—SI 2002/1555, art 31

    sch 4 rep in pt—Enterprise, 2002 c 40, s 278(3), sch 26; SI 2009/1941, art 2, sch 2; Charities, 2011 c 25, sch 10

c 40   *Protection of Animals (Amendment)*—rep Animal Welfare, 2006 c 45, s 65, sch 4

2000

c 41   **Political Parties, Elections and Referendums**

see—(functions exercisable concurrently (except s 70)) SI 2002/2626, art 11(1), sch 1;
(power to appl or incorp (mods)) Police Reform and Social Responsibility, 2011 c 13, s
58(1)-(3)(7); ibid, s 54(5)

power to am (NI)—SI 2008/1319, art 6

mod—(E) SI 2001/1298, reg 10(1)(c); (NI) (temp to 31.10.2010 with power to extend) SI
2008/1319, art 5(1),(2)-(7), sch 1; Parl Voting System and Constituencies, 2011 c 1,
s 6(1), sch 9;

appl—(E) SI 2001/1298, reg 10(4); SI 2004/1962, art 5(3); NI Assembly (Elections and
Periods of Suspension), 2003 c 12, s 3(9); NI (Misc Provns), 2006 c 33, s 14

appl (mods)—(EW) SI 2002/185, reg 3(2), sch 2

excl—NI (Misc Provns), 2006 c 33, s 11(1)(2)

trans of functions—SI 2015/1376, art 3(1) sch 1

s 1 am—Political Parties and Elections, 2009 c 12, s 6; ibid, s 39, sch 6 para 9

s 2 trans of functions—SIs 2001/3500, arts 5(2), 6(1)(c)(3)-(9); 2002/2626, art 11(2);
2010/1837, art 4; 2015/1376, art 5(1)(a)

am—SIs 2001/3500, art 8, sch 2 pt I para 9(1); 2002/2626, art 20, sch 2, para 25(1)(2);
2010/1837, art 5, sch; 2015/1376, sch 2 para 9(2)(a)

s 3 am—Electoral Admin, 2006 c 22, s 74, sch 1 para 139; Political Parties and Elections,
2009 c 12, ss 4, 5(1), 7(1), 39, sch 6 para 10

s 3A added—Political Parties and Elections, 2009 c 12, s 5(2)

am—Parl Voting System and Constituencies, 2011 c 1, sch 10 para 24

s 5 am—Electoral Admin, 2006 c 22, s 28; SI 2007/1388, art 3, sch 1; Police Reform and
Social Responsibility, 2011 c 13, sch 10 para 9; Loc Electoral Admin (S), 2011 asp
10, s 10; (4.3.2016) Recall of MPs, 2015 c 25, sch 6 para 3(2)

rep in pt—Police Reform and Social Responsibility, 2011 c 13, sch 10 para 9(b)

s 6 am—(4.3.2016) Recall of MPs, 2015 c 25, sch 6 para 3(3)

s 6A added—Electoral Admin, 2006 c 22, s 29

am—SI 2007/1388, art 3, sch 1; Police Reform and Social Responsibility, 2011 c 13,
sch 10 para 10; Loc Electoral Admin (S), 2011 asp 10, s 11(1); (4.3.2016) Recall
of MPs, 2015 c 25, sch 6 para 3(4)

appl (mods)—SIs (E) 2007/2089, regs 8, 11-13, sch 4; 2008/1848 (W 177), reg 8, sch
4; Parl Voting System and Constituencies, 2011 c 1, sch 4 para 4; SIs 2012/323,
sch 4 para 1 Table 4; 2012/444, sch 4 para 1 Table 4; 2012/2031, regs 8, 12,
13, sch 4 pt 1 Table 4; ibid, reg 17, sch 8 Table 3 (added by 2013/798, reg 7,
sch 3)

excl—SI 2008/1741, reg 72

saved—SIs 2010/2837, art 8, sch 2 paras 2, 3; 2010/2999, art 12, sch 4 paras 4, 5

ss 6B-6D added—Electoral Admin, 2006 c 22, s 29

appl (mods)—SIs (E) 2007/2089, regs 8, 11-13, sch 4; 2008/1848 (W 177), reg 8,
sch 4; SIs 2012/323, sch 4 para 1 Table 4; 2012/444, sch 4 para 1 Table 4;
2012/2031, regs 8, 12,13, sch 4 pt 1 Table 4; ibid, reg 17, sch 8 Table 3 (added
by 2013/798, reg 7, sch 3)

excl—SI 2008/1741, reg 72

saved—SIs 2010/2837, art 8, sch 2 paras 2, 3; 2010/2999, art 12, sch 4 paras 4, 5

s 6B rep in pt—Loc Electoral Admin (S), 2011 asp 10, s 11(2)

s 6C am—Loc Electoral Admin (S), 2011 asp 10, s 11(3)

s 6D am—Loc Electoral Admin (S), 2011 asp 10, s 11(4)

s 6E added—Electoral Admin, 2006 c 22, s 29

saved—SI 2010/2837, art 8, sch 2 paras 2, 3

mod—SI 2010/2999, art 12, sch 4 paras 4, 5; Parl Voting System and Constituencies,
2011 c 1, sch 5 para 4

appl (mods)—SIs 2012/444, sch 4 para 1 Table 4; 2012/2031, reg 8 12 13, sch 4 pt 1
Table 4; ibid, reg 17, sch 8 Table 3 (added by 2013/798, reg 7, sch 3)

s 6F added—Electoral Admin, 2006 c 22, s 29

am—Loc Electoral Admin (S), 2011 asp 10, s 11(5); (4.3.2016) Recall of MPs, 2015 c
25, sch 6 para 3(5)

s 6G added—Loc Electoral Admin (S), 2011 asp 10, s 11(6)

s 7 am—European Parl Elections, 2002 c 24, s 15, sch 3, para 8(1)(2); SI 2007/1388, art 3,
sch 1; Police Reform and Social Responsibility, 2011 c 13, sch 10 para 11; Loc
Electoral Admin (S), 2011 asp 10, s 12; Scotland, 2012 c 11, s 3(5); Electoral
Registration and Admin, 2013 c 6, s 22(2); Recall of MPs, 2015 c 25, sch 6 para
3(6)

2000

c 41 *continued*

s 8 am—European Parl Elections, 2002 c 24, s 15, sch 3, para 8(1)(3); Govt of Wales, 2006
c 32, s 160, sch 10 para 59; (prosp) Police Reform and Social Responsibility, 2011
c 13, sch 10 para 12; Scotland, 2012 c 11, s 3(6)

s 9A added—Electoral Admin, 2006 c 22, s 67

    am—Police Reform and Social Responsibility, 2011 c 13, sch 10 para 13; Loc
Electoral Admin (S), 2011 asp 10, s 13(1)

s 9B added—Electoral Admin, 2006 c 22, s 67

s 9C added—ectoral Admin, 2006 c 22, s 67

    appl (mods)—Parl Voting System and Constituencies, 2011 c 1, sch 4 para 5

s 10 am—Govt of Wales, 2006 c 32, s 160, sch 10 para 10; Loc Electoral Admin (S), 2011
asp 10, s 14(2); (4.3.2016) Recall of MPs, 2015 c 25, sch 6 para 3(7)

    appl (mods)—SI 2010/2837, art 28, sch 5

    rep in pt—Loc Electoral Admin (S), 2011 asp 10, s 14(3)

s 11 am—Communications, 2003 c 21, s 406(1), sch 17 para 167(1)(2)

    rep in pt—Communications, 2003 c 21, s 406(7), sch 19(1)

s 13 am—SI 2004/366, art 4(2), sch paras 1, 2; Govt of Wales, 2006 c 32, s 160, sch 10
para 61; Loc Electoral Admin (S), 2011 asp 10, ss 15(3), 16(2)(a)

    rep in pt—Political Parties and Elections, 2009 c 12, s 39, sch 7; ibid, s 8; Loc Electoral
Admin (S), 2011 asp 10, ss 15(2), 16(2)(b)

s 13A added—Loc Electoral Admin (S), 2011 asp 10, s 16(3)

s 14 rep —Loc Democracy, Economic Development and Construction, 2009 c 20, ss
61(3)(a), 146, sch 7 pt 3; (E) ibid, ss 61(2)(a), 146, sch 7 pt 3

s 15 rep —Loc Democracy, Economic Development and Construction, 2009 c 20, ss
61(2)(b), 146, sch 7 pt 3

s 16 rep —Loc Democracy, Economic Development and Construction, 2009 c 20, ss
61(3)(b), 146, sch 7 pt 3

s 17 rep —Loc Democracy, Economic Development and Construction, 2009 c 20, ss
61(3)(b), 146, sch 7 pt 3

s 18 rep —Loc Democracy, Economic Development and Construction, 2009 c 20, ss 66(b),
146, sch 7 pt 3

s 19 rep —Loc Democracy, Economic Development and Construction, 2009 c 20, ss
61(3)(c), 146, sch 7 pt 3

s 20 rep—Loc Democracy, Economic Development and Construction, 2009 c 20, ss 61(3)(c),
146, sch 7 pt 3

s 20A added—Electoral Administration Act 2006, s 4(1)

    rep—Electoral Registration and Admin, 2013 c 6, s 23(2)

s 21 am—(4.3.2016) Recall of MPs, 2015 c 25, sch 6 para 3(8)

s 22 am—(pt prosp) Electoral Admin, 2006 c 22, s 52(4)(5)(6); Fixed-term Parls, 2011 c 14,
sch para 19; SI 2012/1917, art 24(2)

s 24 appl—(EW) SI 2001/341, reg 105(1); (S) SI 2001/497, reg 104(1); (NI) SI 2001/400,
reg 99(1)

    am—SI 2004/366, art 4(2), sch paras 1, 3; Electoral Admin, 2006 c 22, s 74, sch 1 para
140; (4.3.2016) Recall of MPs, 2015 c 25, sch 6 para 4(2); SI 2015/1982, sch
para 1

s 25 am—Recall of MPs, 2015 c 25, sch 6 para 4(3)

s 26 am—Co-operative and Community Benefit Societies, 2014 c 14, sch 4 para 75

s 28 am—SI 2004/366, art 4(2), sch paras 1, 4(a)(b); Electoral Admin, 2006 c 22, s 48

    rep in pt—SI 2004/366, art 4(2), sch paras 1, 4(b)

ss 28A, 28B added—Electoral Admin, 2006 c 22, s 49(1)

s 29 am—Electoral Admin, 2006 c 22, s 74, sch 1 para 142

s 30 am—SI 2004/366, art 4(2), sch paras 1, 5; Electoral Admin, 2006 c 22, s 49(2)

s 31 am—SI 2004/366, art 4(2), sch paras 1, 6

s 32 am—Electoral Admin, 2006 c 22, s 50

s 33 am—Electoral Admin, 2006 c 22, s 51

s 34 am—(pt prosp) Electoral Admin, 2006 c 22, s 74, sch 1 para 143

s 37 appl—Communications, 2003 c 21, ss 333(3), 338, sch 12 pt 2 para 18(4)

    am—SI 2004/366, art 4(2), sch paras 1, 7

s 40 am—SI 2004/366, art 4(2), sch paras 1, 8

s 42 rep in pt—NI (Misc Provns), 2006 c 33, s 11(8)(a)(I), sch 5

    am—Electoral Admin, 2006 c 22, s 53

s 44 am—SI 2004/366, art 4(2), sch paras 1, 9

s 45 am—Electoral Admin, 2006 c 22, s 54

s 47 am—Political Parties and Elections, 2009 c 12, s 13(1)(2)(a)(b)

2000
c 41 s 47 *continued*
  rep in pt—Loc Democracy, Economic Development and Construction, 2009 c 20, ss
    13(1)(2)(c), 61(3)(b), 146, sch 7 pt 3
s 48 am—SI 2004/366, art 4(2), sch paras 1, 10; Crime and Cts, 2013 c 22, sch 9 para
    121(a)
Pt 4 (ss 50-71) appl—European Parl (Representation), 2003 c 7, s 12(4)
ss 50-69 excl—(until 16.2.2007) (NI) SI 2005/299, art 2
s 50 rep in pt—Electoral Admin, 2006 c 22, s 74, sch 1 para 144, sch 2
  appl—Companies, 2006 c 46, s 364(4)
s 52 am—SI 2004/366, art 4(2), sch paras 1, 11; Electoral Admin, 2006 c 22, s 74, sch 1
    para 145; Political Parties and Elections, 2009 c 12, s 20(1)
  rep in pt—Electoral Admin, 2006 c 22, ss 55, 74, sch 2
s 53 am—Electoral Admin, 2006 c 22, s 74, sch 1 para 146
  rep in pt—Electoral Admin, 2006 c 22, s 74, sch 2
  appl—Companies, 2006 c 46, s 364(2)(b)(3)(b)(4)
s 54 am—SIs 2001/1184, reg 11(b); 2004/366, art 4(2), sch paras 1, 12; 2007/2501, art 6,
    sch 2; (prosp) Political Parties and Elections, 2009 c 12, ss 9(1), 10(1)-(3), 39, sch
    6 para 12; ibid, s 20(1); SIs 2009/185, art 2, sch; 2009/1941, art 2, sch 1 para
    185; Co-operative and Community Benefit Societies, 2014 c 14, sch 4 para 76; SI
    2015/1982, sch para 2(a)(b)(d)
  appl (mods)—NI (Misc Provns), 2006 c 33, s 11(4)
  rep in pt—Political Parties and Elections, 2009 c 12, s 39, sch 7; SI 2009/1941, art 2,
    sch 1 para 185; SI 2015/1982, sch para 2(c)
s 54A added (prosp)—Political Parties and Elections, 2009 c 12, s 9(2)
s 54B added (prosp)—Political Parties and Elections, 2009 c 12, s 10(4)
s 55 am—SI 2004/366, art 4(2), sch paras 1, 13; Electoral Admin, 2006 c 22, s 74, sch 1
    para 147; (prosp) Political Parties and Elections, 2009 c 12, s 39, sch 6 para 13
s 56 appl (mods)—Representation of the People, 1983 c 2 sch 2A para 7; SIs 2004/293,
    reg 42, sch 6 pt 2 para 7 pt 3 para 12(4); (NI) 2004/1267, reg 38, sch 4 pt II
    para 7; 2007/236, art 41, sch 6; 2012/1917, sch 5 para 7
  appl—SI 2003/284, art 39, sch 6 para 7
  am—SI 2007/2501, art 6, sch 2; (prosp) Political Parties and Elections, 2009 c 12, ss
    9(3)(4), 10(5), 39, sch 6 para 14; ibid, s 12
s 57 appl (mods)—Representation of the People, 1983 c 2 sch 2A para 7; SIs (NI)
    2004/1267, reg 38, sch 4 pt II para 7; 2007/236, art 41, sch 6; 2012/1917, sch
    5 para 7
  appl—SI 2003/284, art 39, sch 6 para 7
s 57A added—SI 2004/366, art 4(2), sch paras 1, 14
  rep—SI 2009/185, art 2, sch
s 58 am—SI 2004/366, art 4(2), sch paras 1, 15; (prosp) Political Parties and Elections,
    2009 c 12, s 39, sch 6 para 15
  appl (mods)—Representation of the People, 1983 c 2 sch 2A para 7; SIs (NI)
    2004/1267, reg 38, sch 4 pt II para 7; 2007/236, art 41, sch 6; 2012/1917, sch
    5 para 7
  appl—SI 2003/284, art 39, sch 6 para 7
s 59 am—SI 2004/366, art 4(2), sch paras 1, 16
  appl (mods)—Representation of the People, 1983 c 2 sch 2A para 7; SIs (NI)
    2004/1267, reg 38, sch 4 pt II para 7; 2007/236, art 41, sch 6; 2012/1917, sch
    5 para 7
  appl—SI 2003/284, art 39, sch 6 para 7
s 60 am—SI 2004/366, art 4(2), sch paras 1, 17
  appl (mods)—Representation of the People, 1983 c 2 sch 2A para 7; SIs (NI)
    2004/1267, reg 38, sch 4 pt II para 7; 2007/236, art 41, sch 6; 2012/1917, sch
    5 para 7
  appl—SI 2003/284, art 39, sch 6 para 7
s 61 appl (mods)—Representation of the People, 1983 c 2 sch 2A para 9; SIs 2004/293,
    reg 42, sch 6 pt 2 para 9; (NI) 2004/1267, reg 38, sch 4 pt II para 9; 2007/236,
    art 41, sch 6; 2012/1917, sch 5 para 9
  appl—SI 2003/284, art 39, sch 6 para 9
s 62 am—Electoral Admin, 2006 c 22, s 74, sch 1 para 148; Political Parties and Elections,
    2009 c 12, s 20(2)(3); (prosp) ibid, s 39, sch 6 para 16
s 62A added—Electoral Admin, 2006 c 22, s 56
s 63 am—Political Parties and Elections, 2009 c 12, s 20(3); Fixed-term Parls, 2011 c 14,
    sch para 20

2000

c 41 *continued*

s 65 am—Electoral Admin, 2006 c 22, s 10, sch 1 para 24; Political Parties and Elections, 2009 c 12, s 13(1)(3)(a); (prosp) ibid, s 39, sch 6 para 17

rep in pt—Political Parties and Elections, 2009 c 12, ss 13(1)(3)(b), 39, sch 7

s 67 am—(prosp) Political Parties and Elections, 2009 c 12, s 39, sch 6 para 18; SI 2012/1917, art 24(3)

s 68 rep—Electoral Admin, 2006 c 22, ss 57, 74, sch 2

s 69 rep in pt—Electoral Admin, 2006 c 22, s 74, sch 1 para 149, sch 2

am—Electoral Admin, 2006 c 22, s 58; SI 2007/2501, art 6, sch 2

s 70 rep—NI (Misc Provns), 2006 c 33, s 11(8)(a)(ii), sch 5

ss 71A-71C added—NI (Misc Provns), 2006 c 33, s 12

ss 71D, 71E added—NI (Misc Provns), 2006 c 33, s 14, sch 1 para 1

Pt 4A (ss 71F-71Y) added —(EWS pt prosp) Electoral Admin, 2006 c 22, ss 61(1), 74, sch 1 para 98

renumbered as Pt 4A, Ch 1—SI 2008/1319, art 3(1)

mod—European Union Referendum, 2015 c 36, sch 1 paras 26, 28; ibid, sch 2 para 10(2)

s 71F am—Political Parties and Elections, 2009 c 12, s 20(1)

s 71GA added—SI 2009/185, art 2, sch

s 71H mod—SI 2009/185, art 2, sch

am—(prosp) Political Parties and Elections, 2009 c 12, s 39, sch 6 para 19; SI 2009/185, art 2, sch

s 71HZA added (prosp)—Political Parties and Elections, 2009 c 12, s 11(1)

s 71HA added—SI 2009/185, art 2, sch

s 71I mod—SI 2009/185, art 2, sch; European Union Referendum, 2015 c 36, sch 2 para 12

s 71J mod—SI 2009/185, art 2, sch

s 71L am—(prosp) Political Parties and Elections, 2009 c 12, s 11(2)

mod—SI 2009/185, art 2, sch; European Union Referendum, 2015 c 36, sch 2 para 13

s 71M am—Political Parties and Elections, 2009 c 12, s 20(2)(3)

s 71O am—SI 2009/185, art 2, sch

s 71Q am—Political Parties and Elections, 2009 c 12, s 20(3)

s 71R am—SI 2009/185, art 2, sch

s 71S am—Political Parties and Elections, 2009 c 12, s 13(1)(4)(a); SI 2009/185, art 2, sch

rep in pt—Political Parties and Elections, 2009 c 12, ss 13(1)(4)(b), 39, sch 7

s 71U am—(prosp) Political Parties and Elections, 2009 c 12, s 39, sch 6 para 20; SI 2009/185, art 2, sch

s 71W am—SI 2009/185, art 2, sch

s 71X am—SI 2009/185, art 2, sch

Pt 4A Ch 2 (ss 71Z, 71Z1, 71Z2) added—SI 2008/1319, art 3(2)

Ch 2 mod (temp)—(ss 71Z3, 71Z4 added (temp to 31.10.2010) SI 2008/1319, art 5, sch 1

s 72 am—Recall of MPs, 2015 c 25, sch 6 para 5(2)

s 73 am—SI 2004/366, art 4(2), sch paras 1, 18

s 74 am—SI 2004/366, art 4(2), sch paras 1, 19; Recall of MPs, 2015 c 25, sch 6 para 5(3); SI 2015/1982, sch para 3

s 77 am—SI 2004/366, art 4(2), sch paras 1, 20; Electoral Admin, 2006 c 22, s 65(1); Crime and Cts, 2013 c 22, sch 9 para 121(b)(c)

rep in pt—Electoral Admin, 2006 c 22, ss 20, 74, sch 1 para 54, sch 2

appl (mods)—S Independence Referendum, 2013 asp 14, sch 4 para 15(8)

s 79 am—Transparency of Lobbying, Non-Party Campaigning and Trade Union Admin, 2014 c 4, s 30(2)

s 80 am—Transparency of Lobbying, Non-Party Campaigning and Trade Union Admin, 2014 c 4, s 30(3)

s 85 appl—(EW) SI 2001/341, reg 106(1)(b); (S) SI 2001/497, reg 105(1)(b); (NI) SI 2001/400, reg 100(1)(b)

am—SI 2004/366, art 4(2), sch paras 1, 21; Transparency of Lobbying, Non-Party Campaigning and Trade Union Admin, 2014 c 4, ss 26(2)(4)(a)(b)(i)(iii)(c)(5)(6), 32(7)

rep in pt—Transparency of Lobbying, Non-Party Campaigning and Trade Union Admin, 2014 c 4, s 26(3)(4)(b)(ii)

s 87 am—SI 2004/366, art 4(2), sch paras 1, 22; Transparency of Lobbying, Non-Party Campaigning and Trade Union Admin, 2014 c 4, s 30(5); Recall of MPs, 2015 c 25, sch 6 para 6(2)

2000
c 41 s 87 *continued*

rep in pt—Transparency of Lobbying, Non-Party Campaigning and Trade Union Admin, 2014 c 4, s 26(7)(a)(b)

s 88 am—SI 2004/366, art 4(2), sch paras 1, 23; Political Parties and Elections, 2009 c 12, s 18; Transparency of Lobbying, Non-Party Campaigning and Trade Union Admin, 2014 c 4, s 32(2)-(6)

rep in pt—SI 2015/1982, sch para 4

s 90 am—SI 2004/366, art 4(2), sch paras 1, 24; Transparency of Lobbying, Non-Party Campaigning and Trade Union Admin, 2014 c 4, s 35(2)

s 91 am—SI 2004/366, art 4(2), sch paras 1, 25

s 92 am—SI 2004/366, art 4(2), sch paras 1, 26; Electoral Admin, 2006 c 22, s 65(2); Crime and Cts, 2013 c 22, sch 9 para 121(b)(c)

s 94 am—SI 2004/366, art 4(2), sch paras 1, 27; Transparency of Lobbying, Non-Party Campaigning and Trade Union Admin, 2014 c 4, ss 26(9)(10), 27(2), 28(2)-(6), 29(2), 30(6)(7)(a)(b), 35(2)

ss 94A, 94B added—Transparency of Lobbying, Non-Party Campaigning and Trade Union Admin, 2014 c 4, s 27(3)

ss 94C-94H added—Transparency of Lobbying, Non-Party Campaigning and Trade Union Admin, 2014 c 4, s 30(8)

ss 95A-95F added—Transparency of Lobbying, Non-Party Campaigning and Trade Union Admin, 2014 c 4, s 33(2)

s 96 am—Transparency of Lobbying, Non-Party Campaigning and Trade Union Admin, 2014 c 4, ss 29(3)(a)(b), 34(2)(3)(a)

rep in pt—Transparency of Lobbying, Non-Party Campaigning and Trade Union Admin, 2014 c 4, s 34(3)(b)

s 96A added—Transparency of Lobbying, Non-Party Campaigning and Trade Union Admin, 2014 c 4, s 35(3)

s 97 am—Transparency of Lobbying, Non-Party Campaigning and Trade Union Admin, 2014 c 4, s 35(4)

s 98 am—Transparency of Lobbying, Non-Party Campaigning and Trade Union Admin, 2014 c 4, s 35(5)(6)

s 99 am—Transparency of Lobbying, Non-Party Campaigning and Trade Union Admin, 2014 c 4, s 27(4)

s 99A added—Transparency of Lobbying, Non-Party Campaigning and Trade Union Admin, 2014 c 4, s 35(7)

s 100 am—Transparency of Lobbying, Non-Party Campaigning and Trade Union Admin, 2014 c 4, s 35(8)

Pt 7 (ss 101-129) appl—Regional Assemblies (Preparations), 2003 c 10, s 12(5); European Union Referendum, 2015 c 36, s 3

restr—Parl Voting System and Constituencies, 2011 c 1, s 5(c); European Union Referendum, 2015 c 36, sch 1 para 21

ext—(Gibraltar) European Union Referendum, 2015 c 36, s 12(2)

excl—European Union Referendum, 2015 c 36, sch 1 para 19

s 101 am—SI 2007/1388, art 3, sch 1

Pt 7, Ch 2 (ss 111-124) see —(power to mod) Regional Assemblies (Preparations), 2003 c 10, s 2(10)(c)

s 101 appl—(EW) Mental Capacity, 2005 c 9, s 29(2)

s 105 appl—(EW) SI 2001/341, s 106(1)(c)(4)(b); (S) SI 2001/497, reg 105(1)(c)(4)(b); (NI) SI 2001/400, reg 100(1)(c)

restr—European Union Referendum, 2015 c 36, sch 1 para 7(2)

mod—European Union Referendum, 2015 c 36, sch 1 paras 2, 5; European Union Referendum, 2015 c 36, sch 1 paras 35, 37(1)

s 106 mod—European Union Referendum, 2015 c 36, sch 1 paras 3(1), 6, 7(1)

s 107 mod—European Union Referendum, 2015 c 36, sch 1 para 4

restr—European Union Referendum, 2015 c 36, sch 1 para 7(2)

s 108 power to appl (mods)—Wales, 2014 c 29, s 12(7), sch 1 para 8

mod—European Union Referendum, 2015 c 36, sch 1 para 9

s 109 appl (mods)—SIs 2004/1963, art 6(1); 2010/2985, art 3

power to appl (mods)—Wales, 2014 c 29, s 12(7), sch 1 para 8

mod—European Union Referendum, 2015 c 36, sch 1 paras 10, 12

s 110 power to appl (mods)—Wales, 2014 c 29, s 12(7), sch 1 para 8

mod—European Union Referendum, 2015 c 36, sch 1 paras 11(1)-(3), 13(3)(4)

s 112 excl—SI 2013/242, art 4(3)(a)

appl—European Union Referendum, 2015 c 36, sch 1 para 22(7)(a)

2000
c 41 *continued*

s 113 appl—European Union Referendum, 2015 c 36, sch 1 para 22(7)(b)
s 115 am—Electoral Admin, 2006 c 22, s 65(3); Crime and Cts, 2013 c 22, sch 9 para
    121(b)
    mod—European Union Referendum, 2015 c 36, sch 1 para 24
s 117 mod—European Union Referendum, 2015 c 36, sch 1 paras 20, 22(3)(a)(5)
s 117 appl—European Union Referendum, 2015 c 36, sch 1 para 22(7)(c)
s 118 mod—European Union Referendum, 2015 c 36, sch 1 para 22
s 120 mod—Parl Voting System and Constituencies, 2011 c 1, s 6(2); European Union
    Referendum, 2015 c 36, sch 1 para 23, sch 2 para 2(1)
s 123 mod—Parl Voting System and Constituencies, 2011 c 1, s 6(3); European Union
    Referendum, 2015 c 36, sch 1 para 36, sch 2 para 2(2)
s 124 mod—Parl Voting System and Constituencies, 2011 c 1, s 6(4); European Union
    Referendum, 2015 c 36, sch 2 para 2(3)
s 125 power to mod—European Union Referendum, 2015 c 36, s 8
    mod—European Union Referendum, 2015 c 36, sch 1 para 38
s 126 excl—Regional Assemblies (Preparations), 2003 c 10, s 12(3); Wales, 2014 c 29, s
    12(7), sch 1 para 10
    am—Electoral Admin, 2006 c 22, s 66(1)
s 127 appl—Communications, 2003 c 21, ss 333(3), 338, sch 12 pt 2 para 18(4)(7)
    appl (mods)—SI 2013/242, art 4(1)(a)(2)
    mod—European Union Referendum, 2015 c 36, sch 1 paras 11(4), 43
s 128 appl (mods)—Parl Voting System and Constituencies, 2011 c 1, sch 4 para 6
    mod—European Union Referendum, 2015 c 36, sch 3 paras 2, 4, 6(4)
s 129 saved—Regional Assemblies (Preparations), 2003 c 10, s 12(1)
    see—Regional Assemblies (Preparations), 2003 c 10, s 29(5)(c)
s 132 rep in pt—(S) Loc Electoral Admin and Registration Services (S), 2006 asp 14, s 18
s 134 rep in pt—Loc Governance (S), 2004 asp 9, s 14(1)(2)
s 135 rep in pt—Loc Governance (S), 2004 asp 9, s 14(1)(2)
s 138 am—Loc Governance (S), 2004 asp 9, s 14(1)(3); (S) Loc Electoral Admin and
    Registration Services (S), 2006 asp 14, s 28
Pt 9 (ss 139, 140) am—Political Parties and Elections, 2009 c 12, s 39, sch 6 para 21
s 139 rep—Companies, 2006 c 46, s 129, sch 16
s 140 rep—Companies, 2006 c 46, s 129, sch 16
s 140A added—Political Parties and Elections, 2009 c 12, s 19(1)
s 142 rep—European Parl Elections, 2002 c 24, s 16, sch 4
s 143 see—Election Publications, 2001 c 5, ss 1(a), 3(3)(4)(6)
    am—Electoral Admin, 2006 c 22, s 66(2); Transparency of Lobbying, Non-Party
    Campaigning and Trade Union Admin, 2014 c 4, s 26(11)(a)(i)(b)
    rep in pt—Transparency of Lobbying, Non-Party Campaigning and Trade Union
    Admin, 2014 c 4, s 26(11)(a)(ii)
s 143A added—Transparency of Lobbying, Non-Party Campaigning and Trade Union
    Admin, 2014 c 4, s 26(12)
s 145 am—Political Parties and Elections, 2009 c 12, s 1; ibid, s 39, sch 6 para 22;
    Transparency of Lobbying, Non-Party Campaigning and Trade Union Admin,
    2014 c 4, s 38(2)-(4)
    rep in pt—Political Parties and Elections, 2009 c 12, s 39, sch 7
    appl in pt—European Union Referendum, 2015 c 36, sch 1 para 44(1), sch 2 para 9(1)
s 146 subst —Political Parties and Elections, 2009 c 12, s 2(1)
    am—Electoral Admin, 2006 c 22, s 74, sch 1 para 150
s 147 subst —Political Parties and Elections, 2009 c 12, s 3(1)
    am—Electoral Admin, 2006 c 22, s 61(2)
s 148 am—Electoral Admin, 2006 c 22, s 74, sch 1 para 151; Political Parties and Elections,
    2009 c 12, s 39, sch 6 para 23
    mod—European Union Referendum, 2015 c 36, sch 1 para 44(2),, sch 2 para 9(2)
s 149 am—Electoral Admin, 2006 c 22, s 61(3); Political Parties and Elections, 2009 c 12, s
    39, sch 6 para 24; Transparency of Lobbying, Non-Party Campaigning and
    Trade Union Admin, 2014 c 4, s 33(3)
    mod—SI 2008/1319, art 5, sch 1
    rep in pt—Political Parties and Elections, 2009 c 12, s 39, sch 7
    appl in pt—European Union Referendum, 2015 c 36, sch 1 para 42, sch 2 para 8
s 150 am—SIs 2004/366, art 4(2), sch paras 1, 28; 2008/1319, art 7, sch 2; 2015/1982, sch
    para 5
s 151 am—SIs 2004/366, art 4(2), sch paras 1, 29; 2015/1982, sch para 6

2000

c 41 s 151 *continued*

    appl—European Union Referendum, 2015 c 36, sch 1 para 44(3), sch 2 para 9(3);
        (4.3.2016) Recall of MPs, 2015 c 25, sch 4 para 21(1)(a)

s 152 appl—(4.3.2016) Recall of MPs, 2015 c 25, sch 4 para 21(1)(b)

s 153 am—SIs 2004/366, art 4(2), sch paras 1, 30; 2015/1982, sch para 7
    appl—(4.3.2016) Recall of MPs, 2015 c 25, sch 4 para 21(1)(c)

s 154 appl—(4.3.2016) Recall of MPs, 2015 c 25, sch 4 para 21(1)(d); European Union
        Referendum, 2015 c 36, sch 1 para 44(3), sch 2 para 9(3)

s 155 am—Political Parties and Elections, 2009 c 12, s 20(4); Transparency of Lobbying,
        Non-Party Campaigning and Trade Union Admin, 2014 c 4, ss 31(2)(3), 33(4)

s 156 am—NI (Misc Provns), 2006 c 33, s 13(1); Electoral Admin, 2006 c 22, s 61, sch 1
        para 100; SI 2008/1319, art 4; Political Parties and Elections, 2009 c 12, ss 3(4),
        39, sch 6 para 25; Transparency of Lobbying, Non-Party Campaigning and
        Trade Union Admin, 2014 c 4, s 26(13)
    rep in pt—NI (Misc Provns), 2006 c 33, s 11(8)(a)(iii), sch 5; Loc Democracy,
        Economic Development and Construction, 2009 c 20, s 146, sch 7 pt 3

s 158 am—Loc Governance (S), 2004 asp 9, s 14(1)(4); (S) Loc Electoral Admin and
        Registration Services (S), 2006 asp 14, s 28

s 159A added—SI 2002/2626, art 20, sch 2, para 25(1)(3)
    am—NI (Misc Provns), 2006 c 33, s 11(9); ibid, s 13(2); SIs 2008/1319, art 4;
        2010/1837, art 5, sch; 2015/1376, sch 2 para 9(2)(b)

s 160 appl—(EW) SI 2001/341, reg 106(1)(a); (S) SI 2001/497, reg 105(1)(a); (NI) SI
        2001/400, reg 100(1)(a)
    am—SIs 2004/366, art 4(2), sch paras 1, 31(a)(b); 2007/1388, art 3, sch 1; 2008/948,
        art 3, sch 1; 2009/185, art 2, sch; Political Parties and Elections, 2009 c 12, s 39,
        sch 6 para 26; SI 2015/1982, sch para 8(b)-(d)
    mod—European Union Referendum, 2015 c 36, sch 1 para 45
    rep in pt—SI 2015/1982, sch para 8(a)

s 161 appl—(NI) SI 2004/1267, reg 38, sch 4 pt II para 6(2); European Union Referendum,
        2015 c 36, sch 1 para 39(14)

s 162 appl—Representation of the People, 1983 c 2 sch 2A para 6(2); SIs 2004/293, reg 42,
        sch 6 pt 2 para 6(2); 2007/236, art 41, sch 6; SI 2012/1917, sch 5 para 6(2)
    am—SI 2004/366, art 4(2), sch paras 1, 32

s 163 am—SIs 2004/366, art 4(1); 2009/185, art 2

sch 1 am—Electoral Admin, 2006 c 22, s 74, sch 1 para 152; SI 2007/1388, art 3, sch 1;
        Political Parties and Elections, 2009 c 12, ss 7(2)(3), 39, sch 6 para
        27(1)-(3)(4)(b); Loc Electoral Admin (S), 2011 asp 10, ss 16(4), 17; SI
        2012/2404, sch 2 para 44; Transparency of Lobbying, Non-Party Campaigning
        and Trade Union Admin, 2014 c 4, s 33(5); Deregulation, 2015 c 20, s 94(3)-(6);
        (4.3.2016) Recall of MPs, 2015 c 25, sch 6 para 3(9)
    mod—S Independence Referendum, 2013 asp 14, s 28(2)
    excl—S Independence Referendum, 2013 asp 14, s 29(5)
    restr—S Independence Referendum, 2013 asp 14, s 27(5)
    rep in pt—Political Parties and Elections, 2009 c 12, s 39, sch 6 para 27(1)(4)(a), sch
        7; Loc Democracy, Economic Development and Construction, 2009 c 20, s 146,
        sch 7 pt 3

sch 2 am—SIs 2001/3500, art 8, sch 2 pt I para 9(2); 2002/2626, art 20, sch 2, para
        25(1)(4); 2010/1837, art 5, sch; 2015/1376, sch 2 para 9(2)(c)

sch 3 rep in pt—Scottish Parl (Constituencies), c 13, s 1(5); Govt of Wales, 2006 c 32, s 163,
        sch 12; Loc Democracy, Economic Development and Construction, 2009 c 20,
        ss 61(3)(d), 146, sch 7 pt 3

sch 6 excl—(until 16.2.2007) (NI) SI 2005/299, art 2
    mod—European Union Referendum, 2015 c 36, sch 1 para 27
    am—SI 2004/366, art 4(2), sch paras 1, 33(a)-(k); Electoral Admin, 2006 c 22, ss 10,
        74, sch 1 paras 26, 153; SI 2007/2501, art 5, sch 1; (prosp) Political Parties and
        Elections, 2009 c 12, ss 9(5)(6), 10(6); SI 2009/185, art 2, sch; Co-operative and
        Community Benefit Societies, 2014 c 14, sch 4 para 77
    rep in pt—SI 2015/1982, sch para 9

sch 6A added (pt prosp)—Electoral Admin, 2006 c 22, s 61(5)
    am—SI 2008/1737, art 5, sch 1; (prosp) Political Parties and Elections, 2009 c 12, s
        11(3); SI 2009/185, art 2, sch; Co-operative and Community Benefit Societies,
        2014 c 14, sch 4 para 78
    mod—European Union Referendum, 2015 c 36, sch 2 para 11
    rep in pt—SI 2015/1982, sch para 10(a)(b)

2000
c 41 *continued*

sch 7 excl—(until 16.2.2007) (NI) SI 2005/299, art 3; NI (Misc Provns), 2006 c 33, s 11(3)
   appl—(EW) SI 2001/341, reg 104(1)(a); (S) SI 2001/497, reg 103(1)(a); (NI) SI
      2001/400, reg 98(1)(a); (until 16.2.2007) SI 2005/299, art 5
   am—(retrosp to 16.2.2001) Loc Govt, 2003 c 26, s 114(1)-(3); (retrosp to 16.2.2001)
      (S) Loc Govt in S, 2003 asp 1, s 42(1)(2); SI 2004/366, art 4(2), sch paras 1,
      34(a)(b); Electoral Admin, 2006 c 22, ss 10, 61, sch 1 paras 28, 99; (pt prosp)
      ibid, s 59; SI 2007/2501, art 6, sch 2; Political Parties and Elections, 2009 c 12,
      ss 13(1)(5)(a)(b), 14(1)-(4), 15(1), 20; (prosp) ibid, ss 9, 10, 39, sch 3 paras 1-3,
      sch 4 paras 1-3, sch 6 para 28; SI 2012/1917, art 24(4)
   rep in pt—Electoral Admin, 2006 c 22, s 74, sch 2; NI (Misc Provns), 2006 c 33, s
      11(8)(iv), sch 5; Political Parties and Elections, 2009 c 12, ss 13(1)(5)(c), 39,
      sch 7; (pt prosp) ibid, s 39, sch 7
sch 7A added (pt prosp)—Electoral Admin, 2006 c 22, s 61, sch 1 pt 6, paras 97, 99, 102
   am—SI 2008/1737, art 6, sch 2; (prosp) Political Parties and Elections, 2009 c 12, s
      11(4)-(6); ibid, ss 13(1)(6)(a)(b), 16(1)(2)(b)(3), 17, 20; SI 2009/185, art 2,
      sch
   rep in pt—Political Parties and Elections, 2009 c 12, ss 13(1)(6)(c), 16(1)(2)(a), 39,
      sch 7
sch 8 am—SI 2004/366, art 7
sch 8A added —Transparency of Lobbying, Non-Party Campaigning and Trade Union
      Admin, 2014 c 4, sch 3
sch 9 appl (mods)—NI Assembly Elections, 2003 c 3, s 1(4); NI Assembly (Elections and
      Periods of Suspension), 2003 c 12, s 1(4)(b); Electoral Admin, 2006 c 22, s 64
   disappl (cond) (retrosp)—Transparency of Lobbying, Non-Party Campaigning and
      Trade Union Admin, 2014 c 4, s 46(3)(a)
   mod—Transparency of Lobbying, Non-Party Campaigning and Trade Union Admin,
      2014 c 4, s 46(3)(b)(4)
   am—SIs 2004/366, art 4(2), sch paras 1, 35(a)(b); 2007/1388, art 3, sch 1; Fixed-term
      Parls, 2011 c 14, sch para 21
sch 10 appl (mods)—NI Assembly Elections, 2003 c 3, s 1(4); NI Assembly (Elections and
      Periods of Suspension), 2003 c 12, s 1(4)(b)
   mod—Transparency of Lobbying, Non-Party Campaigning and Trade Union Admin,
      2014 c 4, s 46(5)(6)
   am—SIs 2004/366, art 4(2), sch paras 1, 36(a)-(c); 2007/1388, art 3, sch 1;
      Fixed-term Parls, 2011 c 14, sch para 22; Transparency of Lobbying, Non-Party
      Campaigning and Trade Union Admin, 2014 c 4, ss 28(7), 29(5)-(9)
   disappl (cond) (retrosp)—Transparency of Lobbying, Non-Party Campaigning and
      Trade Union Admin, 2014 c 4, s 46(5)(a)
sch 11 am—SI 2004/366, art 4(2), sch paras 1, 37; Electoral Admin, 2006 c 22, s 10, sch 1
      para 29; Political Parties and Elections, 2009 c 12, s 20; (prosp) ibid, ss 9, 10,
      39, sch 3 paras 4-6, sch 4 paras 4-6, sch 6 para 29; Transparency of Lobbying,
      Non-Party Campaigning and Trade Union Admin, 2014 c 4, s 33(6)
   rep in pt —(prosp) Political Parties and Elections, 2009 c 12, s 39, sch 7
sch 11A added —Transparency of Lobbying, Non-Party Campaigning and Trade Union
      Admin, 2014 c 4, sch 4
sch 12 am—Communications, 2003 c 21, s 406(1), sch 17 para 167(1)(3); SI 2010/1158,
      art 5, sch 2; Postal Services, 2011 c 5, sch 12 para 158
   rep in pt—Communications, 2003 c 21, s 406(7), sch 19(1)
   appl (mods)—SI 2010/2837, art 28, sch 5; 2013/242, art 4(1)(b)(2)
   mod—European Union Referendum, 2015 c 36, sch 1 para 14
   power to appl (mods)—Wales, 2014 c 29, s 12(7), sch 1 para 8
sch 13 appl (mods)—SI 2010/2985, art 5
   excl—SI 2013/242, art 4(3)(b)
   mod—European Union Referendum, 2015 c 36, sch 1 para 18
sch 14 mod—European Union Referendum, 2015 c 36, sch 1 paras 22, 25
sch 15 am—Electoral Admin, 2006 c 22, s 10, sch 1 para 30; Political Parties and Elections,
      2009 c 12, s 20; (prosp) ibid, ss 9, 10, 39, sch 3 paras 7-9, sch 4 paras 7-9, sch
      6 para 30(1)(2)(b)-(4)
   rep in pt—Political Parties and Elections, 2009 c 12, s 39, sch 6 para 30(1)(2)(a);
      (prosp) ibid, s 39, sch 7
   mod—Parl Voting System and Constituencies, 2011 c 1, s 6(5); European Union
      Referendum, 2015 c 36, sch 1 paras 29-34, sch 2 para 2(4)(5)
sch 18 see—Election Publications, 2001 c 5, ss 1(b), 3(3)(4)(6)

2000
c 41 sch 18 *continued*

rep in pt—Electoral Admin, 2006 c 22, s 74, sch 2
sch 19 rep—Companies, 2006 c 46, s 129, sch 16
sch 19A added—Political Parties and Elections, 2009 c 12, s 19(2), sch 5
    am—(4.3.2016) Recall of MPs, 2015 c 25, sch 6 para 7(2)(a)-(c)
    mod—European Union Referendum, 2015 c 36, sch 2 para 2(6)
sch 19B added —Political Parties and Elections, 2009 c 12, s 2(2), sch 1
    mod—European Union Referendum, 2015 c 36, sch 1 para 44(4), sch 2 para 9(4)
sch 19C added —Political Parties and Elections, 2009 c 12, s 3(2), sch 2
    mod—Parl Voting System and Constituencies, 2011 c 1, s 6(6)(7), sch 9; European
        Union Referendum, 2015 c 36, sch 1 paras 37(1), 44(4), sch 2 paras 2(7), 9(5)
    am—Crime and Cts, 2013 c 22, sch 9 para 121(d); SIs 2013/602, sch 2 para 34;
        2015/664, sch 5 para 9
sch 20 am—Electoral Admin, 2006 c 22, s 61, sch 1 para 101; NI (Misc Provns), 2006 c 33,
    s 14, sch 1 para 2; (prosp) Political Parties and Elections, 2009 c 12, ss 9, 10,
    11(7), 39, sch 3 para 10, sch 4 para 10, sch 6 para 31; ibid, ss 2(3), 3(3), 14(5),
    15(2), 19(3); Transparency of Lobbying, Non-Party Campaigning and Trade
    Union Admin, 2014 c 4, ss 30(9), 33(8), 35(9); SI 2015/664, sch 4 para
    30(a)(b)
    rep in pt—Electoral Admin, 2006 c 22, s 74, sch 1 para 155, sch 2; Political Parties
        and Elections, 2009 c 12, s 39, sch 7
    mod—SI 2008/1319, art 5, sch 1
sch 21 rep in pt—European Parl Elections, 2002 c 24, s 16, sch 4; Communications, 2003 c
    21, s 406(7), sch 19(1); Govt of Wales, 2006 c 32, s 163, sch 12; Loc
    Democracy, Economic Development and Construction, 2009 c 20, s 146, sch 7
    pt 3
sch 22 rep in pt—Loc Democracy, Economic Development and Construction, 2009 c 20, ss
    61(3)(e), 146, sch 7 pt 3
sch 23 rep in pt—Companies, 2006 c 46, s 129, sch 16

c 42   **Disqualifications**
c 43   **Criminal Justice and Court Services**
    s 1 rep—Offender Management, 2007 c 21, s 39, sch 5 pt 1
    ss 2, 3 rep —Offender Management, 2007 c 21, s 39, sch 5 pt 1
    s 4 rep—Offender Management, 2007 c 21, s 39, sch 5 pt 1
    s 5 rep —Offender Management, 2007 c 21, s 39, sch 5 pt 1
    s 5A added—Armed Forces, 2006 c 52, s 378, sch 16 para 178
        subst—Armed Forces, 2006 c 52, s 327
        mod—SI 2009/1059, art 205, sch 1
    s 6 rep in pt—Offender Management, 2007 c 21, s 39, sch 5 pt 1
    s 7 am—Police and Justice, 2006 c 48, s 31(1)
    s 8 rep —Offender Management, 2007 c 21, s 39, sch 5 pt 1
    s 9 rep—Offender Management, 2007 c 21, s 39, sch 5 pt 1
    s 10 rep —Offender Management, 2007 c 21, s 39, sch 5 pt 1
    s 11 appl—Children, 2004 c 31, s 41(2)
    s 12 rep in pt—Adoption and Children, 2002 c 38, s 139(1)(3), sch 3, para 118, sch 5
        trans of functions—SI 2003/3191, art 3(d)
        appl—Children, 2004 c 31, s 35(3); SI 2004/2187, reg 3
        am—Children, 2004 c 31, s 40, sch 3 paras 12, 13
    s 15 am—Legal Services, 2007 c 29, s 208, sch 21 para 133
    s 17 rep—Courts, 2003 c 39, s 109(3), sch 10
    s 18 rep in pt—Offender Management, 2007 c 21, s 39, sch 5 pt 1
    s 19 am—SIs 2003/2867, reg 2, sch pt 1 para 30; 2003/3191, arts 3(d), 6, sch para 4(1)(2)
    s 20 am—SI 2003/3191, arts 3(d), 6, sch para 4(1)(2)
        rep in pt—Offender Management, 2007 c 21, s 39, sch 5 pt 1
    s 21 rep in pt—Offender Management, 2007 c 21, s 39, sch 5 pt 1
    s 22 rep —Offender Management, 2007 c 21, s 39, sch 5 pt 1
    s 23 rep—Offender Management, 2007 c 21, s 39, sch 5 pt 1
        am—SI 2003/3191, arts 3(d), 6, sch para 4(1)(2)
    s 24 rep —Safeguarding Vulnerable Groups, 2006 c 47, s 63, sch 10
    s 25 rep in pt—SI 2003/3191, art 6, sch para 4(1)(3)(a); Offender Management, 2007 c 21,
        s 39, sch 5 pt 1
        am—SI 2003/3191, art 6, sch para 4(1)(3)(b)
    ss 26-29 rep —Safeguarding Vulnerable Groups, 2006 c 47, s 63, sch 10
    ss 29A, 29B added—Crim Justice, 2003 c 44, s 299, sch 30 paras 1, 2

2000

c 43 ss 29A, 29B *continued*

　　　　rep —Safeguarding Vulnerable Groups, 2006 c 47, s 63, sch 10

ss 30-34 rep —Safeguarding Vulnerable Groups, 2006 c 47, s 63, sch 10

s 35 rep —Safeguarding Vulnerable Groups, 2006 c 47, s 63, sch 10; SI 2007/1351, art 60, sch 8

s 36 rep —(EW) Safeguarding Vulnerable Groups, 2006 c 47, s 63, sch 10; SI 2007/1351, art 60, sch 8

　　　　rep in pt—Children and Families, 2014 c 6, sch 5 para 9(2)

s 37 rep —Safeguarding Vulnerable Groups, 2006 c 47, s 63, sch 10

s 38 rep (pt prosp)—Safeguarding Vulnerable Groups, 2006 c 47, s 63, sch 10

s 39 rep—Sexual Offences, 2003 c 42, ss 139, 140, sch 6 para 44(1)(2), sch 7

s 42 am—Crim Justice, 2003 c 44, s 304, sch 32 pt 1 paras 133, 135; Nat Health Service (Conseq Provns), 2006 c 43, s 2, sch 1 para 213; Childcare, 2006 c 21, s 103, sch 2 para 40; Armed Forces, 2006 c 52, s 378, sch 16 para 183; SI 2011/1396, sch para 48(a); Charities, 2011 c 25, sch 7 para 91

　　　　rep in pt—Safeguarding Vulnerable Groups, 2006 c 47, s 63, sch 10; Armed Forces, 2006 c 52, s 378, sch 16 para 183; SI 2008/2833, art 6, sch 3

Pt 3 (ss 43-70) appl—Bail, 1976 c 63, s 3(6E), sch 1 pt I para 6B; (prosp) Crim Justice, 2003 c 44, s 161(8)

s 46 rep—Crim Justice and Immigration, 2008 c 4, s 149, sch 28 pt 1

s 52 rep (prosp)—Crim Justice and Immigration, 2008 c 4, s 149, sch 28 pt 1

ss 47-51 rep—Crim Justice, 2003 c 44, s 332, sch 37 pt 7

ss 53-55 rep—Crim Justice, 2003 c 44, s 332, sch 37 pt 7

s 56 rep in pt—Legal Aid, Sentencing and Punishment of Offenders, 2012 c 10, sch 24 para 24

s 57 rep in pt—Drugs, 2005 c 17, s 23, sch 1 para 5, sch 2

s 62 appl—Crim Justice, 2003 c 44, ss 250(2)(b)(i)(4)(b)(i), 251(2)(b)(i); Crime (Sentences), 1997 c 43, sch 1 para 8; Serious Organised Crime and Police, 2005 c 15, s 112(8)(a)

　　　　am—Crim Justice, 2003 c 44, s 304, sch 32 pt 1 paras 133, 136; Armed Forces, 2006 c 52, s 378, sch 16 para 184; Legal Aid, Sentencing and Punishment of Offenders, 2012 c 10, sch 21 para 17; ibid, sch 22 para 18; Crim Justice and Cts, 2015 c 2, sch 2 para 2(3)

　　　　rep in pt—Armed Forces, 2006 c 52, s 378, sch 17; Crim Justice and Cts, 2015 c 2, sch 2 para 2(2)

s 63 rep—Crim Justice, 2003 c 44, s 332, sch 37 pt 7

s 64 appl—Crim Justice, 2003 c 44, ss 250(2)(b)(i)(4)(b)(i), 251(2)(b)(i)

　　　　am—Armed Forces, 2006 c 52, s 378, sch 16 para 185; SI 2008/912, art 3, sch 1; Legal Aid, Sentencing and Punishment of Offenders, 2012 c 10, sch 21 para 18; ibid, sch 22 para 19; Offender Rehabilitation, 2014 c 11, s 11(2)(b)-(e); ibid, sch 3 para 13

　　　　appl—Crime (Sentences), 1997 c 43, sch 1 para 8

　　　　rep in pt—(prosp) Crim Justice, 2003 c 44, s 332, sch 37 pt 7; Children, 2004 c 31, s 64, sch 5 pt 4; Armed Forces, 2006 c 52, s 378, sch 17; Offender Rehabilitation, 2014 c 11, s 11(2)(a)

s 64A added —Offender Rehabilitation, 2014 c 11, s 12(1)

　　　　appl (mods)—Crime (Sentences), 1997 c. 43, sch 1 paras 8, 9 (amended by 2014 c 11, s 13(2)(a),(3)(a))

s 66 rep—Sexual Offences, 2003 c 42, ss 139, 140, sch 6 para 44(1)(2), sch 7

ss 67, 68 rep—Crim Justice, 2003 c 44, s 332, sch 37 pt 12

s 69 rep—Domestic Violence, Crime and Victims, 2004 c 28, s 58, sch 10 paras 54, 55, sch 11

s 70 am—Crim Justice, 2003 c 44, s 304, sch 32 pt 1 paras 133, 138; Offender Rehabilitation, 2014 c 11, s 11(3)

　　　　rep in pt—Crim Justice and Immigration, 2008 c 4, ss 6, 149, sch 4 paras 68, 70, sch 28 pt 1

s 71 am—Serious Organised Crime and Police, 2005 c 15, ss 59, 123(1), sch 4 para 161; Police and Justice, 2006 c 48, s 1, sch 1 para 75; Police Reform and Social Responsibility, 2011 c 13, sch 16 para 248; Crime and Cts, 2013 c 22, sch 8 para 105(2)(b)(3)(b)(i)(ii)(c); SI 2013/602, sch 2 para 35

　　　　rep in pt—Policing and Crime, 2009 c 26, s 112, sch 8 pt 13; Crime and Cts, 2013 c 22, sch 8 para 105(2)(a)(3)(a)(b)(iii)

ss 76, 77 rep in pt—Constitutional Reform, 2005 c 4, s 146, sch 18 pt 2

2000

c 43 *continued*

s 78 rep in pt—Crim Justice, 2003 c 44, s 332, sch 37 pt 7; Offender Management, 2007 c 21, s 39, sch 5 pt 1

s 81 am—Armed Forces, 2006 c 52, s 378, sch 16 para 186

rep in pt—Armed Forces, 2006 c 52, s 378, sch 16 para 186

s 85 appl (mods)—SI 2014/3141, sch 3 para 5(7)

sch 1 rep—Offender Management, 2007 c 21, s 39, sch 5 pt 1

sch 1A added—Police and Justice, 2006 c 48, s 31(2)

rep in pt—Loc Govt and Public Involvement in Health, 2007 c 28, s 146, sch 9 para 1(1)(2), sch 18; Health and Social Care, 2008 c 14, s 95, sch 5 para 74(1)(2)(a)(3)(a)(4)(a), sch 15; SI 2012/2401, sch 1 para 11(a)-(c); Loc Audit and Accountability, 2014 c 2, sch 12 para 46(2)-(4)

am—Health and Social Care, 2008 c 14, s 95, sch 5 para 74(1)(2)(b)(3)(b)(4)(b); SI 2012/2401, sch 1 para 11(d); Loc Audit and Accountability, 2014 c 2, sch 12 para 46(5)(a)(b)

sch 2 am—SI 2003/3191, arts 3(d), 6, sch para 4(1)(4); Children, 2004 c 31, s 40, sch 3 paras 12, 14

sch 3 am—SI 2003/3191, arts 3(d), 6, sch para 4(1)(2)

sch 4 rep—Safeguarding Vulnerable Groups, 2006 c 47, s 63, sch 10

sch 5 rep—Sexual Offences, 2003 c 42, ss 139, 140, sch 6 para 44(1)(6), sch 7

sch 6 am—SI 2004/1892, art 2(1)-(3); Fraud, 2006 c 35, s 14, sch 1 para 32(2); SI 2007/2171, art 2

rep in pt—Fraud, 2006 c 35, s 14, sch 1 para 32(1), sch 3

sch 7 rep in pt—Adoption and Children, 2002 c 38, s 139(3), sch 5; Educ, 2002 c 32, s 215(2), sch 22 pt 3; Police Reform, 2002 c 30, s 107(2), sch 8; Crim Justice, 2003 c 44, s 332, sch 37 pt 7; ibid, s 332, sch 37 pt 10; Courts, 2003 c 39, s 109(3), sch 10; Domestic Violence, Crime and Victims, 2004 c 28, s 58(2), sch 11; Serious Organised Crime and Police, 2005 c 15, s 174(2), sch 17 pt 2; Safeguarding Vulnerable Groups, 2006 c 47, s 63, sch 10; Educ and Skills, 2008 c 25, s 169, sch 2; (pt prosp) Crim Justice and Immigration, 2008 c 4, s 149, sch 28 pt 1; Welfare Reform, 2009 c 24, s 58, sch 7 pt 3; (S) Crim Justice and Licensing (S), 2010 asp 13, s 14, sch 2 para 44(3); Legal Aid, Sentencing and Punishment of Offenders, 2012 c 10, sch 12 para 46(2),(3); ibid, sch 25 pt 2

am—SI 2005/886, art 2, sch para 87; (S) Crim Justice and Licensing (S), 2010 asp 13, s 14, sch 2 para 44(2)

c 44 **Sexual Offences (Amendment)**

rep (S)—Sexual Offences (S), 2009 asp 9, s 61, sch 6

s 1 rep in pt—Sexual Offences, 2003 c 42, ss 139, 140, sch 6 para 45(1)(2), sch 7

s 2 rep in pt—Sexual Offences, 2003 c 42, ss 139, 140, sch 6 para 45(1)(3), sch 7

s 3 rep (EW,NI)—Sexual Offences, 2003 c 42, ss 139, 140, sch 6 para 45(1)(4), sch 7

am—Civil Partnership, 2004 c 33, s 261(2), sch 28 pt 4 para 62

s 4 rep (EW,NI)—Sexual Offences, 2003 c 42, ss 139, 140, sch 6 para 45(1)(4), sch 7

am—Regulation of Care (S), 2001 asp 8, s 79, sch 3 para 25(1)(2)(b),(3)(a); (S) SSI 2005/465, art 2, sch 1 para 29(1)(2)(b)(c)

rep in pt—Regulation of Care (S), 2001 asp 8, s 79, sch 3 para 25(1)(2)(a), (3)(b)(c); (S) SSI 2005/465, art 2, sch 1 para 29(1)(2)(a)

s 5 rep—Sexual Offences, 2003 c 42, ss 139, 140, sch 6 para 45(1)(5), sch 7

s 6 rep in pt—Sexual Offences, 2003 c 42, ss 139, 140, sch 6 para 45(1)(6), sch 7

4th session of the 52nd Parliament

c 45 *Consolidated Fund (No 2)*—rep Appropriation, 2002 c 18, s 4, sch 3

2001

c 1 *Consolidated Fund*—rep Appropriation, 2003 c 13, s 4, sch 3

c 2 **Capital Allowances**

appl—Finance, 2002 c 23, s 84(1), sch 29 pt 15, para 133(2); Income Tax (Trading and Other Income), 2005 c 5, s 824(3); Railways, 2005 c 14, s 53, sch 10 pt 2 para 14(1)(d)(2); Income Tax, 2007 c 3, ss 513(4), 959, 963; Corporation Tax, 2009 c 4, ss 47(1)(2), 212(a)(b); Corporation Tax, 2010 c 4, ss 332(2), 817(b), 992(2); Taxation (International and Other Provns), 2010 c 8, s 220(2)

appl (mods)—Finance, 2003 c 14, s 176, sch 36 pt 3 paras 16, 17(1)(2); Income Tax (Trading and Other Income), 2005 c 5, ss 825(3), 825A(2); Income Tax, 2007 c 3, ss 414, 467, 474, 573, 576, 578, 597, 711, 970; SI 2009/470, reg 57;

2001
c 2 *continued*

Corporation Tax, 2010 c 4, ss 675(2), 687(4), 948(1)-(4), 954(2)-(5), 955(2)-(6), 992(2), 996(2)

am—Commrs for Revenue and Customs, 2005 c 11, s 50(6), sch 4 paras 82, 83

saved—Taxation of Chargeable Gains, 1992 c 12, s 151X(4); Income Tax, 2007 c 3, s 962; ibid, s 564V(4)

mod—Income Tax, 2007 c 3, s 988; Corporation Tax, 2009 c 4, s 294(2); SI 2015/1540, regs 7, 8

excl—Corporation Tax, 2009 c 4, s 3; Corporation Tax, 2010 c 4, s 48(4); Taxation (International and Other Provns), 2010 c 8, ss 79(2)(a), 174(2)(b)

ext—Corporation Tax, 2009 c 4, s 969(4)(b)

s 1 am—Finance, 2001 c 9, s 67, sch 19 pt 2 para 1; Finance, 2005 c 7, s 92, sch 6 pt 2 para 2; Finance, 2013 c 29, sch 4 para 46

   rep in pt—Finance, 2008 c 9, s 84, sch 27 paras 1, 2; Finance, 2012 c 14, sch 39 para 38(2)

s 2 am—Finance, 2001 c 9, s 67, sch 19 pt 2 para 2; Finance, 2005 c 7, s 92, sch 6 pt 2 para 3; Finance, 2008 c 9, s 74, sch 25 paras 1, 2; Corporation Tax, 2009 c 4, s 1322, sch 1 paras 474, 475

   rep in pt—Finance, 2008 c 9, s 84, sch 27 paras 1, 3; Finance, 2012 c 14, sch 39 para 38(3)

s 3 am—Finance, 2005 c 7, s 92, sch 6 pt 2 para 4; Finance, 2008 c 9, s 74, sch 25 paras 1, 3

   excl—Finance, 2006 c 25, s 120(7); Corporation Tax, 2010 c 4, s 599(8)

   rep in pt—Finance, 2008 c 9, s 84, sch 27 paras 1, 4

s 4 am—Income Tax (Earnings and Pensions), 2003 c 1, s 722, sch 6 pt 2 paras 246, 247; Finance, 2004 c 12, s 281(1), sch 35 paras 47, 48; Income Tax (Trading and Other Income), 2005 c 5, s 882(1), sch 1 pt 2 paras 524, 525; Income Tax, 2007 c 3, s 1027, sch 1 paras 396, 397

   appl—Income and Corporation Taxes, 1988 c 1, s 349ZA; Income Tax (Trading and Other Income), 2005 c 5, s 608; Income Tax, 2007 c 3, s 910(5); Corporation Tax, 2009 c 4, s 931

   rep in pt—Income Tax, 2007 c 3, s 1031, sch 3

s 5 appl (mods)—(retrosp to 2.12.2004) Finance (No 2), 1992 c 48, s 42(8B)

   appl—Pensions Regulator Tribunal (Trans of Functions) (NI), 2010 c 4, s 356JA; Corporation Tax, 2010 c 4, ss 332K(1), 356JN

Pt 1 Ch 1A (ss 6A-6E) added (prosp)—Corporation Tax (NI) 2015, sch 1 para 2

s 9 am—Finance, 2012 c 14, sch 10 para 7

Pt 2 (ss 11-270) appl—Energy, 2004 c 20, s 47, sch 9 pt 2 para 21(6); Railways, 2005 c 14, s 53, sch 10 pt 2 para 14(7); Crossrail, 2008 c 18, s 37, sch 13 para 37(2)

   mod—Finance, 2013 c 29, s 73(7)-(11)

s 12 excl—Finance, 2009 c 10, s 24(6)

   am—(prosp) Corporation Tax (NI), 2015, sch 1 para 3

s 13 appl (mods)—Finance, 2003 c 14, s 176, sch 36 pt 3 paras 16, 17(1)(3), 19; Income Tax (Trading and Other Income), 2005 c 5, ss 825(4), 825C(2), 827

   mod—Corporation Tax, 2009 c 4, s 18C(2)

   appl—Corporation Tax, 2010 c 4, s 126(2)

   rep in pt—(spec retrosp effect) Finance, 2008 c 9, s 55, sch 20 para 6(1)(2)(19)

s 13A added—Finance, 2006 c 25, s 81, sch 8 para 2

s 13B added—Finance, 2011 c 11, sch 14 para 12(2)

s 15 am—SI 2004/2310, arts 1(2), 2, sch para 52; Income Tax (Trading and Other Income), 2005 c 5, s 882(1), sch 1 pt 2 paras 524, 526; Corporation Tax, 2009 c 4, s 1322, sch 1 paras 474, 476; Finance, 2011 c 11, sch 13 para 15; ibid, sch 14 para 12(3); Finance, 2012 c 14, sch 20 para 9; (prosp) Corporation Tax (NI), 2015, sch 1 para 4

s 16 am—Income Tax (Trading and Other Income), 2005 c 5, s 882(1), sch 1 pt 2 paras 524, 527; Finance, 2011 c 11, sch 14 para 12(4)

   rep in pt—Corporation Tax, 2009 c 4, ss 1322, 1326, sch 1 paras 474, 477, sch 3 pt 1

s 17 am—Income Tax (Trading and Other Income), 2005 c 5, s 882(1), sch 1 pt 2 paras 524, 528; Corporation Tax, 2009 c 4, s 1322, sch 1 paras 474, 478(1)(3); Finance, 2011 c 11, sch 14 para 12(5)

   rep in pt—Corporation Tax, 2009 c 4, ss 1322, 1326, sch 1 paras 474, 478(1)(2), sch 3 pt 1

ss 17A, 17B added—Finance, 2011 c 11, sch 14 para 12(6)

s 18 subst—SI 2004/2310, arts 1(2), 2, sch para 53

2001

c 2 s 18 *continued*

am—Corporation Tax, 2009 c 4, s 1322, sch 1 paras 474, 479; Finance, 2013 c 29, sch 18 para 21(4)

s 19 am—Finance, 2012 c 14, sch 16 para 95

s 20 am—Income Tax (Earnings and Pensions), 2003 c 1, s 722, sch 6 pt 2 paras 246, 248; Income Tax (Trading and Other Income), 2005 c 5, s 882(1), sch 1 pt 2 paras 524, 529

s 23 am—Income Tax (Trading and Other Income), 2005 c 5, s 882(1), sch 1 pt 2 paras 524, 530; Finance, 2008 c 9, s 73(1)(a)(b)(iii); Finance, 2012 c 14, s 41(1)

rep in pt—Finance, 2008 c 9, ss 71(7), 72(2), 73(1)(b)(i)(ii); Finance, 2012 c 14, sch 39 para 34(2)

s 26 am—Finance, 2008 c 9, s 109, sch 34 paras 2, 3; Finance, 2013 c 29, sch 32 para 3

s 27 am—Finance, 2012 c 14, sch 39 para 34(3)

s 28 am—Finance, 2001 c 9, s 69, sch 21 para 1; Income Tax (Trading and Other Income), 2005 c 5, s 882(1), sch 1 pt 2 paras 524, 531; Finance, 2008 c 9, s 71(1)-(3); Corporation Tax, 2009 c 4, s 1322, sch 1 paras 474, 480; Finance, 2011 c 11, sch 14 para 12(7)

rep in pt—Finance, 2008 c 9, s 71(1)(4)-(6)

s 29 rep—Finance, 2008 c 9, s 72(1)

ss 30-32 rep—Finance, 2012 c 14, sch 39 para 33

s 33 am—Income Tax (Trading and Other Income), 2005 c 5, s 882(1), sch 1 pt 2 paras 524, 532; Finance, 2011 c 11, sch 14 para 12(8)

rep in pt—Finance, 2009 c 10, s 30, sch 11 paras 12, 13, 30, 31

s 33A added—Finance, 2008 c 9, s 73(1)(2)

appl—Corporation Tax, 2009 c 4, s 60

excl —Income Tax (Trading and Other Income), 2005 c 5, s 55A(2)

s 33B added—Finance, 2008 c 9, s 73(1)(2)

s 34A added—Finance, 2006 c 25, s 81, sch 8 para 3

s 35 am—Income Tax (Trading and Other Income), 2005 c 5, s 882(1), sch 1 pt 2 paras 524, 533; Finance, 2011 c 11, sch 14 para 12(9)

s 36 subst—Finance, 2001 c 9, s 59(1), (3), (4)

s 38 am—Income Tax (Trading and Other Income), 2005 c 5, s 882(1), sch 1 pt 2 paras 524, 534; Corporation Tax, 2009 c 4, s 1322, sch 1 paras 474, 481

s 38ZA added—Finance, 2013 c 29, sch 5 para 5(2)

s 38A added—Finance, 2008 c 9, s 74, sch 24 paras 1, 2

s 38B added—Finance, 2008 c 9, s 74, sch 24 paras 1, 2

am—Finance, 2009 c 10, s 30, sch 11 paras 1, 2, 30, 31; Corporation Tax, 2010 c 4, s 1177, sch 1 paras 323, 324

s 39 am—Finance, 2001 c 9, s 65, sch 17 para 1; Finance, 2002 c 23, ss 59, 61, 63, sch 19, paras 1, 2, sch 20, paras 1, 2, sch 21 pt 1, paras 1, 2; Finance, 2003 c 14, s 167, sch 30 paras 1, 2(a)(c); Finance (No 3), 2010 c 33, s 18, sch 7 para 2; Finance, 2012 c 14, sch 11 para 2

rep in pt—Finance, 2001 c 9, s 110, sch 33 pt 2(4), Note; Finance, 2002 c 23, s 141, sch 40 pt 3(7), Note; Finance, 2003 c 14, ss 167, 216, sch 30 paras 1, 2(b), sch 43 pt 3(9), Note; (saving) Finance, 2008 c 9, s 75(1)(3)(a)(6)(7); ibid, s 76(1)(5)(a)

appl (mods)—Finance, 2009 c 10, s 24(1)(a)

ss 40-45 rep (saving)—Finance, 2008 c 9, s 76(1)(2)(7)(8)

ss 45A-45C added—Finance, 2001 c 9, s 65, sch 17 paras 2, 6

s 45A am—Finance, 2012 c 14, s 45(2)

s 45AA added—Finance, 2012 c 14, s 45(3)

am—Finance, 2013 c 29, s 67

s 45B appl—SI 2001/2541, art 4(2)

s 45D added—Finance, 2002 c 23, s 59, sch 19, paras 1, 3

am—(transtl provns) Finance, 2008 c 9, s 77(1)-(3)(6); Finance, 2009 c 10, s 30, sch 11 paras 12, 14(1)-(5)(7)(9), 30, 31; Finance, 2013 c 29, s 68(1); Finance, 2014 c 26, s 64(2); SI 2015/60, art 4

rep in pt—Finance, 2009 c 10, s 30, sch 11 paras 12, 14(6), 30, 31

ss 45DA, 45DB added—Finance (No 3), 2010 c 33, s 18, sch 7 para 3

s 45DA am—Finance, 2014 c 26, s 64(3); Finance, 2015 c 11, s 45(2)

s 45DB am—Finance, 2014 c 26, sch 13 para 2; Finance, 2015 c 11, s 45(7)

rep in pt—Finance, 2015 c 11, s 45(4)-(6)

s 45E added—Finance, 2002 c 23, s 61, sch 20, paras 1, 3

2001

c 2 s 45E *continued*

        am—Finance, 2008 c 9, s 78(1)-(4); Finance, 2013 c 29, s 69; Finance, 2014 c 26, s
            64(4); SI 2015/60, art 5

s 45F added—Finance, 2002 c 23, s 63, sch 21 pt 1, paras 1, 3

        am—Corporation Tax, 2010 c 4, s 1177, sch 1 paras 323, 325

s 45G added—Finance, 2002 c 23, s 63, sch 21 pt 1, paras 1, 4

ss 45H-45J added—Finance, 2003 c 14, s 167, sch 30 paras 1, 3, 7

ss 45K-45N added—Finance, 2012 c 14, sch 11 para 3

s 45K am—Finance, 2014 c 26, s 64(5); ibid, sch 13 para 3

s 45M am—Finance, 2014 c 26, sch 13 para 4(2)-(5)(7)-(9)

        rep in pt—Finance, 2014 c 26, sch 13 para 4(6)

s 45N am—Finance, 2014 c 26, sch 13 para 5(2)(3)

s 46 am—Finance, 2001 c 9, s 65, sch 17 para 3; Finance, 2002 c 23, ss 59, 61, 62, 63, sch
            19, paras 1, 4, sch 20, paras 1, 4, sch 21 pt 1, paras 1, 5; Finance, 2003 c 14,
            s 167, sch 30 paras 1, 4(1)(a)(c)(2); Finance, 2006 c 25, s 81, sch 8 para 4, sch 9
            para 11; Finance, 2009 c 10, s 30, sch 11 paras 1, 3, 30, 31; Finance (No 3), 2010
            c 33, s 18, sch 7 para 4; Finance, 2012 c 14, sch 11 para 4

        rep in pt—Finance, 2001 c 9, s 110, sch 33 pt 2(4), Note; Finance, 2002 c 23, s 141,
            sch 40 pt 3(7), Note; Finance, 2003 c 14, ss 167, 216, sch 30 paras 1, 4(1)(b),
            sch 43 pt 3(9), Note; (saving) Finance, 2008 c 9, s 75(1)(3)(b)(6)(7); ibid, s
            76(1)(5)(b); Finance, 2013 c 29, ss 68(2), 70(1)

ss 47-49 rep (saving)—Finance, 2008 c 9, s 75(1)(3)(b)(c)(6)(7)

s 51 rep—Finance, 2008 c 9, s 76(1)(5)(c)

s 51A added—Finance, 2008 c 9, s 74, sch 24 paras 1, 3

        am—(retrosp effect) Finance, 2009 c 10, s 64, sch 32 paras 12, 17, 18, 22; Finance,
            2010 c 13, s 5(1); Finance, 2011 c 11, s 11; Finance (No. 2), 2015 c 33, s 8(1)

        mod—Finance, 2013 c 29, s 7 sch 1; Finance, 2014 c 26, s 10

ss 51B-51N added—Finance, 2008 c 9, s 74, sch 24 paras 1, 3

s 51JA added (prosp)—Corporation Tax (NI), 2015, sch 1 para 5

s 52 am—Finance, 2001 c 9, s 65, sch 17 para 4; Finance, 2002 c 23, ss 59, 61, 63, sch 19,
            paras 1, 5, sch 20, paras 1, 5, sch 21 pt 1, paras 1, 6; Finance, 2003 c 14, s 167,
            sch 30 paras 1, 5; Finance, 2004 c 12, s 142(3); Finance, 2006 c 25, s 30(3);
            Finance, 2008 c 9, s 108(1); Finance, 2009 c 10, s 24(1)(b); (retrosp effect) ibid, s
            64, sch 32 paras 13, 17, 19, 22; Finance (No 3), 2010 c 33, s 18, sch 7 para
            5(2)(3)(a)(b); Finance, 2012 c 14, sch 11 para 5

        appl (mods)—Finance, 2006 c 25, s 30(1)

        rep in pt—Finance, 2008 c 9, s 76(1)(5)(d); (spec retrosp effect) ibid, s 55, sch 20 para
            6(1)(3)(19); (saving) ibid, s 75(1)(3)(c)(6)(7)

s 52A added—Finance, 2008 c 9, s 74, sch 24 paras 1, 4

        am—Finance, 2012 c 14, sch 11 para 6

s 54 am—Finance, 2008 c 9, s 82, sch 26 paras 1, 3

        rep in pt—Finance, 2009 c 10, s 30, sch 11 paras 12, 15, 30, 31

s 55 am—Finance, 2009 c 10, s 30, sch 11 paras 12, 30, 31

s 56 am—Finance, 2008 c 9, ss 80(1)-(4)(9)(a), 81(1)(2), 82, sch 26 paras 1, 4; Corporation
            Tax, 2010 c 4, s 1177, sch 1 paras 323, 326; Finance, 2011 c 11, s 10(2)(4)(b)

s 56A added—Finance, 2008 c 9, s 81(1), (3)

s 57 am—(retrosp for specified purposes) Finance, 2001 c 9, s 68, sch 20 pt 2 paras 5(2),
            9(1)-(4), (8); Finance, 2008 c 9, s 109, sch 34 paras 2, 4; (retrosp effect) Finance,
            2009 c 10, s 64, sch 32 paras 14, 17, 20, 22; Finance, 2012 c 14, sch 9 para 2;
            ibid, sch 10 para 8; Finance, 2013 c 29, sch 32 para 4

        rep in pt—(spec retrosp effect) Finance, 2008 c 9, s 55, sch 20 para 6(1)(4)(19)

s 58 am—Finance, 2008 c 9, s 74, sch 24 paras 1, 5

s 59 am—Finance, 2008 c 9, s 81(1)(4); Finance, 2013 c 29, sch 4 para 47; ibid, sch 5 para
            5(3)

        appl—Income Tax (Trading and Other Income), 2005 c 5 s 240C(6)

s 60 appl—Income and Corporation Taxes, 1988 c 1, s 785A(6)

        am—Corporation Tax, 2010 c 4, s 1177, sch 1 paras 323, 327; Taxation (International
            and Other Provns), 2010 c 8, s 374, sch 8 paras 233, 234

s 61 am—Proceeds of Crime, 2002 c 29, s 448, sch 10 pt 2, paras 12-17; Income Tax
            (Earnings and Pensions), 2003 c 1, s 722, sch 6 pt 2 paras 246, 249; Finance,
            2006 c 25, s 81, sch 8 para 5; (spec retrosp effect) Finance, 2008 c 9, s 55, sch 20
            para 4(1)-(4); (retrosp effect) Finance, 2009 c 10, s 64, sch 32 paras 1(1)-(3), 5(1);
            Finance, 2011 c 11, sch 13 para 16; (prosp) Corporation Tax (NI), 2015, sch 1
            para 6

2001

c 2 s 61 *continued*

> appl (mods)—Crossrail, 2008 c 18, s 37, sch 13 paras 19(2), 35(2)
> rep in pt—(retrosp effect) Finance, 2009 c 10, s 64, sch 32 paras 1(1)(4), 5(1)

s 62A added—Finance, 2011 c 11, sch 13 para 17

s 63 appl (mods)—Finance, 2002 c 23, s 58(1)(4), sch 18 pt 3, para 9(3)(c)

> appl—Railways, 2005 c 14, s 53, sch 10 pt 1 paras 2(5), 3(4) pt 3 paras 22(5), 23(4)
> am—Income Tax (Earnings and Pensions), 2003 c 1, s 722, sch 6 pt 2 paras 246, 250;
> Income Tax (Trading and Other Income), 2005 c 5, s 882(1), sch 1 pt 2 paras 524,
> 535; Corporation Tax, 2009 c 4, s 1322, sch 1 paras 474, 482; Corporation Tax,
> 2010 c 4, s 1177, sch 1 paras 323, 328; Finance, 2011 c 11, sch 3 para 4; ibid, sch
> 14 para 12(10)
> rep in pt—Finance, 2010 c 13, s 30, sch 6 para 16

s 64A added—Finance, 2010 c 13, s 27, sch 5 para 3(1)

s 65 am—Finance, 2008 c 9, s 82, sch 26 paras 1, 5; Finance, 2009 c 10, s 30, sch 11 paras
12, 17, 30, 31; Finance, 2011 c 11, s 12(3)

s 66 am—Finance, 2006 c 25, s 84(2); Finance, 2008 c 9, s 82, sch 26 paras 1, 6; Finance,
2009 c 10, s 30, sch 11 paras 12, 18(b), 30, 31; (retrosp effect) ibid, s 64, sch 32
paras 6, 8

> rep in pt—(spec retrosp effect) Finance, 2008 c 9, s 55, sch 20 para 6(1)(5)(19);
> Finance, 2009 c 10, s 30, sch 11 paras 12, 18(a), 30, 31

s 66A added—Finance, 2013 c 29, sch 4 para 48

ss 66B-66E added (prosp)—Corporation Tax (NI), 2015, sch 1 para 7

s 67 am—Finance, 2006 c 25, s 81, sch 9 para 12

s 68 appl—Railways, 2005 c 14, s 53, sch 10 pt 1 para 2(5) pt 3 para 22(5)

ss 70A, 70B added—Finance, 2006 c 25, s 81, sch 8 para 6

s 70C added—Finance, 2006 c 25, s 81, sch 8 para 6

> am—Finance, 2011 c 11, s 33(2)

s 70D added—Finance, 2006 c 25, s 81, sch 8 para 6

s 70DA added—(retrosp effect) Finance, 2009 c 10, s 64, sch 32 paras 15, 17

> am—Finance, 2015 c 11, sch 10 para 2

s 70E added—Finance, 2006 c 25, s 81, sch 8 para 6

> am—Finance, 2009 c 10, s 64, sch 32 paras 7, 8; Corporation Tax, 2010 c 4, s 1177,
> sch 1 paras 323, 329(b); Finance, 2011 c 11, s 33(4)(5); Finance, 2012 c 14, s
> 46
> rep in pt—Corporation Tax, 2010 c 4, ss 1177, 1181, sch 1 paras 323, 329(a), sch 3

Pt 2 Ch 6A (ss 70F-70Y,70YA-70YJ) added—Finance, 2006 c 25, s 81, sch 8 para 7

> appl—Finance, 2008 c 9, s 55, sch 20 para 11(12); Corporation Tax, 2010 c 4, s
> 381(1)

s 70G am—Finance, 2009 c 10, s 126(5)(a)

s 70H am—(spec retrosp effect) Finance, 2008 c 9, s 55, sch 20 para 7; Finance, 2009 c 10,
s 126(5)(a); (retrosp effect) ibid, s 64, sch 32 paras 16, 17; ibid, s 100, sch 52
para 9; Corporation Tax, 2010 c 4, s 1177, sch 1 paras 323, 330(b)

> rep in pt—Corporation Tax, 2010 c 4, ss 1177, 1181, sch 1 paras 323, 330(a), sch 3

s 70I am—(transtl provns) Finance, 2008 c 9, s 55, sch 20 para 6(1)(6)(20)

s 70J am—Finance, 2010 c 13, s 28(5)

s 70K appl—Corporation Tax, 2009 c 4, s 18C

s 70O am—Finance, 2009 c 10, s 126(5)(a)

s 70V am—Income Tax, 2007 c 3, s 1027, sch 1 paras 396, 397; Corporation Tax, 2010 c 4,
s 1177, sch 1 paras 323, 331

s 70YI rep in pt—Income Tax, 2007 c 3, s 1027, sch 1 paras 396, 399, sch 3

s 72 am—Income Tax (Earnings and Pensions), 2003 c 1, s 722, sch 6 pt 2 paras 246, 251

ss 74-79 rep—Finance, 2009 c 10, s 30, sch 11 paras 1, 4, 30, 31

s 80 rep—(2002-03) Finance, 2001 c 9, ss 59(2)-(4), 110, sch 33 pt 2(1), Note

s 81 rep—Finance, 2009 c 10, s 30, sch 11 paras 1, 5, 30, 31

s 82 rep—Finance, 2009 c 10, s 30, sch 11 paras 1, 5, 30, 31, 68

s 84 am—Finance, 2006 c 25, s 81, sch 8 para 8; Finance, 2008 c 9, s 82, sch 26 paras 1, 7;
Finance, 2009 c 10, s 30, sch 11 paras 1, 6, 12, 19, 30, 31

s 86 am—Finance, 2009 c 10, s 30, sch 11 paras 12, 20, 30, 31; Finance, 2011 c 11, s 12(2)

s 87 am—Finance, 2011 c 11, s 12(4)

s 88 am—Income Tax (Earnings and Pensions), 2003 c 1, s 722, sch 6 pt 2 paras 246, 252

> excl—Railways, 2005 c 14, s 53, sch 10 pt 1 para 2(4) pt 3 para 22(4); Crossrail, 2008
> c 18, s 37, sch 13 paras 19(4), 35(4); SI 2015/1540, reg 7(8)

s 89 am—(spec retrosp effect) Finance, 2008 c 9, s 55, sch 20 para 6(1)(7)(19); Finance,
2011 c 11, s 12(5)

2001
c 2 *continued*

s 92 rep—Finance, 2008 c 9, s 82, sch 26 paras 1, 8

s 94 rep in pt—Finance, 2004 c 12, ss 146, 326, sch 27 pt 2 paras 8, 11, sch 42 pt 2(19),
Note 5

s 96 am—Finance, 2009 c 10, s 30, sch 11, pars 12, 20. 30, 31

s 99 appl (mods)—Finance, 1993 c 34, s 93A
am—Corporation Tax, 2010 c 4, s 1177, sch 1 paras 323, 332; Finance, 2014 c 26, sch
1 para 8(a)
rep in pt—Finance, 2014 c 26, sch 1 para 8(b)

s 101 subst—Finance, 2008 c 9, s 82, sch 26 paras 1, 9

s 102 subst—Finance, 2008 c 9, s 82, sch 26 paras 1, 10
appl (mods)—Finance, 2008 c 9, s 83(2)

s 104A added—Finance, 2008 c 9, s 82, sch 26 paras 1, 2
am—Finance, 2009 c 10, s 30, sch 11 paras 1, 7(1)(2)(a)(c)(3)(4), 30, 31; Finance,
2010 c 13, s 28(6)(b); Finance, 2012 c 14, s 45(4)
rep in pt—Finance, 2009 c 10, s 30, sch 11 paras 1, 7(1)(2)(b), 30, 31; Finance,
2010 c 13, s 28(6)(a)

s 104AA added—Finance, 2009 c 10, s 30, sch 11 paras 1, 8, 30, 31
am—Finance, 2013 c 29, s 68(3)

ss 104B-104D added—Finance, 2008 c 9, s 82, sch 26 paras 1, 2

s 104D am—Finance, 2011 c 11, s 10(3)(4)(a)

s 104E added—Finance, 2008 c 9, s 82, sch 26 paras 1, 2
mod—Finance, 2008 c 9, s 83(7)(a)
am—Finance, 2011 c 11, s 10(4)(b)

s 104F added—Finance, 2009 c 10, s 30, sch 11 paras 9, 30, 31
am—Corporation Tax, 2010 c 4, s 1177, sch 1 paras 323, 333

s 104G added—Finance, 2010 c 13, s 28(7)

s 105 am—Finance, 2006 c 25, s 81, sch 9 para 13; Corporation Tax, 2009 c 4, s 1322, sch
1 paras 474, 483; Finance, 2009 c 10, s 126(5)(a); Taxation (International and
Other Provns), 2010 c 8, s 374, sch 8 paras 57, 58

s 106 am—Income Tax (Trading and Other Income), 2005 c 5, s 882(1), sch 1 pt 2 paras
524, 536(1)(2); Corporation Tax, 2009 c 4, s 1322, sch 1 paras 474, 484
rep in pt—Income Tax (Trading and Other Income), 2005 c 5, ss 882(1), 884, sch 1 pt
2 paras 524, 536(1)(3), sch 3

s 108 am—Income Tax (Trading and Other Income), 2005 c 5, s 882(1), sch 1 pt 2 paras
524, 537(1)(2); Corporation Tax, 2009 c 4, s 1322, sch 1 paras 474, 485;
Corporation Tax, 2010 c 4, s 1177, sch 1 paras 323, 334
rep in pt—Income Tax (Trading and Other Income), 2005 c 5, ss 882(1), 884, sch 1 pt
2 paras 524, 537(1)(3), sch 3

s 112 am—Income Tax (Trading and Other Income), 2005 c 5, s 882(1), sch 1 pt 2 paras
524, 538(1)(2); Corporation Tax, 2009 c 4, s 1322, sch 1 paras 474, 486;
Corporation Tax, 2010 c 4, s 1177, sch 1 paras 323, 335
rep in pt—Income Tax (Trading and Other Income), 2005 c 5, ss 882(1), 884, sch 1 pt
2 paras 524, 538(1)(3), sch 3

s 115 am—Income Tax (Trading and Other Income), 2005 c 5, s 882(1), sch 1 pt 2 paras
524, 539(1)(2); Corporation Tax, 2009 c 4, s 1322, sch 1 paras 474, 487;
Corporation Tax, 2010 c 4, s 1177, sch 1 paras 323, 336
rep in pt—Income Tax (Trading and Other Income), 2005 c 5, ss 882(1), 884, sch 1 pt
2 paras 524, 539(1)(3), sch 3

s 122 am—Income Tax (Trading and Other Income), 2005 c 5, s 882(1), sch 1 pt 2 paras
524, 540(1)(2); Corporation Tax, 2009 c 4, s 1322, sch 1 paras 474, 488
rep in pt—Income Tax (Trading and Other Income), 2005 c 5, ss 882(1), 884, sch 1 pt
2 paras 524, 540(1)(3), sch 3

s 125 am—Income Tax (Trading and Other Income), 2005 c 5, s 882(1), sch 1 pt 2 paras
524, 540(1)(2); Corporation Tax, 2009 c 4, s 1322, sch 1 paras 474, 489
rep in pt—Income Tax (Trading and Other Income), 2005 c 5, ss 882(1), 884, sch 1 pt
2 paras 524, 540(1)(3), sch 3

ss 130, 135 restr—Finance, 2000 c 17, sch 22 para 22F(2)(4)

s 131 am—Corporation Tax, 2010 c 4, s 1177, sch 1 paras 323, 337

s 138 am—Income Tax, 2007 c 3, s 1027, sch 1 paras 396, 400; Corporation Tax, 2010 c 4,
s 1177, sch 1 paras 323, 338

s 153 am—Finance, 2004 c 12, s 146, sch 27 pt 2 paras 9(1)(2), 11
rep in pt—Finance, 2004 c 12, ss 146, 326, sch 27 pt 2 paras 9(1)(3), 11, sch 42 pt
2(19), Note 5

2001

c 2 *continued*

s 154 am—Income Tax (Trading and Other Income), 2005 c 5, s 882(1), sch 1 pt 2 paras 524, 542; Corporation Tax, 2010 c 4, s 1177, sch 1 paras 323, 339

s 155 am—Income Tax (Trading and Other Income), 2005 c 5, s 882(1), sch 1 pt 2 paras 524, 543; Corporation Tax, 2010 c 4, s 1177, sch 1 paras 323, 340

s 156 am—Income Tax (Trading and Other Income), 2005 c 5, s 882(1), sch 1 pt 2 paras 524, 544; Income Tax, 2007 c 3, s 1027, sch 1 paras 396, 401; Corporation Tax, 2010 c 4, s 1177, sch 1 paras 323, 341

s 158 am—Corporation Tax, 2010 c 4, s 1177, sch 1 paras 323, 342

s 160 am—Finance, 2014 c 26, s 67(4)

s 161 am—Finance, 2014 c 26, s 67(5)(6)

ss 161A-161D added—(retrosp for specified purposes) Finance, 2001 c 9, s 68, sch 20 pt 2 paras 5(1), 9(1)-(4), (8)

s 161C am—Finance, 2013 c 29, sch 32 para 5

s 162 am—Income Tax (Trading and Other Income), 2005 c 5, s 882(1), sch 1 pt 2 paras 524, 545; Corporation Tax, 2010 c 4, s 1177, sch 1 paras 323, 343

s 163 am—(retrosp for specified purposes) Finance, 2001 c 9, s 68, sch 20 pt 2 paras 6, 9(1), (5), (8); Finance, 2008 c 9, s 109(1)-(4); Finance, 2009 c 10, ss 84, 87, sch 38 paras 1, 2, sch 41 para 5; Finance, 2013 c 29, s 90

rep in pt—Finance, 2008 c 9, s 109(1)(5)

s 164 am—(retrosp) (in pt and for specified purposes) Finance, 2001 c 9, s 68, sch 20 pt 2 paras 7(1)-(3), (5), (6), 9(1), (5), (8), (9); Finance, 2008 c 9, s 109, sch 34 paras 2, 5; Finance, 2009 c 10, s 84, sch 38 paras 1, 3(1)-(3)(4)(b)(5)-(7); Finance, 2013 c 29, s 91(1); ibid, sch 32 para 6

rep in pt—(retrosp for specified purposes) Finance, 2001 c 9, ss 68, 110, sch 20 pt 2 paras 7(1), (4), 9(1), (5), (8), sch 33 pt 2(5), Note 1; Finance, 2009 c 10, s 84, sch 38 paras 1, 3(1)(4)(a)

s 165 am—(retrosp for specified purposes) Finance, 2001 c 9, s 68, sch 20 pt 2 paras 8(1), (3), (4), 9(1), (5), (8); Finance, 2008 c 9, ss 109, 110(1)-(5), sch 34 paras 2, 6; Finance, 2009 c 10, s 84, sch 38 paras 1, 4; (retrosp effect) ibid, s 87, sch 41 para 6; Finance, 2013 c 29, sch 32 para 7

rep in pt—(retrosp) Finance, 2001 c 9, ss 68, 110, sch 20 pt 2, paras 8(1), (2), 9(9), sch 33 pt 2(5), Note 2

ss 165A-165E added—Finance, 2013 c 29, sch 32 para 2

s 172 am—Finance, 2001 c 9, s 66, sch 18 para 1; Finance, 2006 c 25, s 81, sch 8 para 9(1)

s 172A added—Finance, 2006 c 25, s 81, sch 8 para 9(2)

s 175A added—Finance, 2001 c 9, s 66, sch 18 para 2

s 176 am—Finance, 2001 c 9, s 66, sch 18 para 3

s 179 am—Finance, 2002 c 23, s 103(4)(g)

rep in pt—Finance, 2002 c 23, s 141, sch 40 pt 3(16)

s 180A added—Finance, 2001 c 9, s 66, sch 18 para 4

s 181 am—Finance, 2001 c 9, ss 66, 69, sch 18 para 5, sch 21 para 2(1)(2)

mod—SI 2015/1540, reg 8(4)(b)

s 182 am—Finance, 2001 c 9, s 69, sch 21 para 2(3)

mod—SI 2015/1540, reg 8(4)(b)

s 182A added—Finance, 2001 c 9, s 66, sch 18 para 6

s 184 am—Finance, 2001 c 9, s 69, sch 21 para 2(4)

s 186 am—Finance, 2008 c 9, s 84, sch 27 paras 1, 5; Finance, 2009 c 10, s 126(5)(a)

s 186A added—Finance, 2012 c 14, sch 10 para 6

ss 187A, 187B added—Finance, 2012 c 14, sch 10 para 1

s 188 am—Finance, 2001 c 9, s 66, sch 18 para 7

s 192A added—Finance, 2001 c 9, s 66, sch 18 para 8

ss 195A, 195B added—Finance, 2001 c 9, s 66, sch 18 para 9

s 196 am—Finance, 2001 c 9, s 66, sch 18 para 10

appl (mods)—Crossrail, 2008 c 18, s 37, sch 13 paras 20(2), 36(2)

mod—SI 2015/1540, reg 8(2)

s 198 am—Finance, 2012 c 14, sch 10 paras 3, 9

s 199 am—Finance, 2012 c 14, sch 10 para 10

s 201 am—Finance, 2012 c 14, sch 10 para 4

s 203 am—Finance, 2001 c 9, s 66, sch 18 para 11

s 204 am—SI 2009/56, art 3, sch 1 para 298

s 205 am—Finance, 2008 c 9, s 74, sch 24 paras 1, 6

s 208 appl (mods)—Finance, 1993 c 34, s 93A

s 208A added—Finance, 2009 c 10, s 30, sch 11 paras 10, 30, 31

2001

c 2 *continued*

s 210 am—Finance, 2008 c 9, s 74, sch 24 paras 1, 7
s 211 excl—Corporation Tax, 2010 c 4, s 599(3)
Pt 2 Ch 16ZA (ss 212ZA-212ZF) added (prosp)—Corporation Tax (NI) 2015, sch 1 para 8
Pt II Ch 16A (ss 212A-212S) added—Finance, 2010 c 13, s 26, sch 4 para 2
       am—Finance, 2013 c 29, sch 26 para 4
s 212B am—Finance, 2013 c 29, sch 26 paras 2,5
s 212C am—Finance, 2013 c 29, sch 26 para 6
s 212I am—Finance, 2013 c 29, sch 26 para 7
s 212J am—Finance, 2013 c 29, sch 26 para 8
s 212K am—Finance, 2013 c 29, sch 26 para 9
s 212LA added—Finance, 2013 c 29, sch 26 para 3
s 212N am—Finance, 2013 c 29, sch 26 para 10
s 212P am—Finance, 2013 c 29, sch 26 para 11
s 212Q am—Finance, 2013 c 29, sch 26 para 12
Pt 2 Ch 16B (ss 212T, 212U) added—Finance (No 3), 2010 c 33, s 18, sch 7 para 6
       am—Finance, 2012 c 14, sch 11 para 7(2)
s 212T am—Finance, 2014 c 26, sch 13 para 6
s 212U am—Finance, 2014 c 26, sch 13 para 7
Pt 2 Ch 17 (ss 213-233) am—Finance, 2010 c 13, s 26, sch 4 para 3
s 214 am—Finance, 2012 c 14, sch 9 para 3
s 215 subst—Finance, 2012 c 14, sch 9 para 1
s 216 am—Finance, 2009 c 10, s 64, sch 32 para 23; Finance, 2012 c 14, sch 9 para 4
s 217 am—(spec retrosp effect) Finance, 2008 c 9, ss 55, 74, sch 20 para 6(1)(8)(19), sch 24
      paras 1, 8
s 218 am—(spec retrosp effect) Finance, 2008 c 9, s 55, sch 20 para 6(1)(9)(19); Finance,
      2012 c 14, sch 9 para 5; Finance, 2015 c 11, sch 10 para 3
s 218ZA added—Finance, 2012 c 14, sch 9 para 6
s 218A added—Finance, 2008 c 9, s 74, sch 24 paras 1, 9
s 219 am—Finance, 2002 c 23, s 103(4)(g); Finance, 2005 c 7, s 80, sch 4 pt 2 para 33;
      Finance, 2006 c 25, s 81, sch 9 para 14
   rep in pt—Finance, 2002 c 23, s 141, sch 40 pt 3(16); (spec retrosp effect) Finance,
      2008 c 9, s 55, sch 20 para 6(1)(10)(19)
s 220 am—Finance, 2006 c 25, s 81, sch 9 para 15; Corporation Tax, 2010 c 4, s 1177, sch
      1 paras 323, 344
   rep in pt—Income Tax, 2007 c 3, s 1027, sch 1 paras 396, 402
s 221 am—Finance, 2001 c 9, s 69, sch 21 para 3; (spec retrosp effect) Finance, 2008 c 9, s
      55, sch 20 para 6(1)(11)(19); Finance, 2009 c 10, s 64, sch 32 para 24
   appl—Corporation Tax, 2010 c 4, s 771(8)
ss 222-224 rep —(spec retrosp effect) Finance, 2008 c 9, s 55, sch 20 para
      6(1)(12)(a)(b)(c)(19)
s 226 rep—(spec retrosp effect)Finance, 2008 c 9, s 55, sch 20 para 6(1)(12)(d)(19)
s 227 rep in pt—(spec retrosp effect) Finance, 2008 c 9, s 55, sch 20 para 6(1)(13)(a)(19)
      am—(spec retrosp effect) Finance, 2008 c 9, s 55, sch 20 para 6(1)(13)(b)(19)
s 228 rep in pt—(spec retrosp effect) Finance, 2008 c 9, s 55, sch 20 para 6(1)(14)(19)
s 228A-228J added—Finance, 2004 c 12, s 134, sch 23
s 228A subst—(spec retrosp effect) Finance, 2008 c 9, s 55, sch 20 para 12(1)(2)(12)
s 228B am—(spec retrosp effect) Finance, 2008 c 9, s 55, sch 20 para 12(1)(3)(12); ibid, s
      55, sch 20 para 13(1)-(3)
s 228C am—(spec retrosp effect) Finance, 2008 c 9, s 55, sch 20 para 12(1)(4)(12)
ss 228D-228F rep—(spec retrosp effect) Finance, 2008 c 9, s 55, sch 20 para 12(1)(5)(12)
s 228G am—(spec retrosp effect) Finance, 2008 c 9, s 55, sch 20 para 12(1)(6)(12)
s 228H am—(spec retrosp effect) Finance, 2008 c 9, s 55, sch 20 para 12(1)(7),
      (8)(a)(c)(e)(f), (9); Corporation Tax, 2010 c 4, s 1177, sch 1 paras 323, 345
   rep in pt—(spec retrosp effect) Finance, 2008 c 9, s 55, sch 20 para 12(1)(7),
      (8)(b)(d)(f)
s 228J am—(spec retrosp effect) Finance, 2008 c 9, s 55, sch 20 para 12(1)(10)(12)
ss 228K-228M added—Finance, 2006 c 25, s 84(3)
s 228M am—Corporation Tax, 2010 c 4, s 1177, sch 1 paras 323, 346
ss 228MA-228MC added—Finance, 2010 c 13, s 27, sch 5 para 1(1)
s 229A added—(retrosp effect) Finance, 2009 c 10, s 64, sch 32 paras 21, 22
      am—Finance, 2015 c 11, sch 10 para 4
s 230 am—(spec retrosp effect) Finance, 2008 c 9, s 55, sch 20 para 6(1)(15)(19); Finance,
      2012 c 14, sch 9 para 7(2)

2001
c 2 s 230 *continued*
    rep in pt—Finance, 2012 c 14, sch 9 para 7(3)
s 232 am—Income Tax, 2007 c 3, s 1027, sch 1 paras 396, 403
s 236 am—Finance, 2008 c 9, s 74, sch 24 paras 1, 10
s 237 am—Finance, 2008 c 9, s 74, sch 24 paras 1, 11
    rep in pt—Finance, 2008 c 9, s 76(1)(5)(e)
s 241 rep in pt—(spec retrosp effect) Finance, 2008 c 9, s 55, sch 20 para 6(1)(16)(19)
    am—(spec retrosp effect) Finance, 2008 c 9, s 74, sch 24 paras 1, 12
s 242 am—Finance, 2015 c 11, sch 10 para 5(2)(3)(4)(b)(5)
    rep in pt—Finance, 2015 c 11, sch 10 para 5(4)(a)
s 243 rep —Finance, 2008 c 9, s 55, sch 20 para 6(1)(17)(19)
s 247 am—Finance, 2010 c 13, s 26, sch 4 para 4; (prosp) (prosp) Corporation Tax (NI),
    2015, sch 1 para 9
s 248 am—Income Tax (Trading and Other Income), 2005 c 5, s 882(1), sch 1 pt 2 paras
    524, 546; Finance, 2011 c 11, sch 14 para 12(11)
s 249 am—Corporation Tax, 2010 c 4, s 1177, sch 1 paras 323, 347; Finance, 2011 c 11,
    sch 14 para 12(12)
s 250 am—Finance, 2011 c 11, sch 14 para 12(13)
s 250A added—Finance, 2011 c 11, sch 14 para 12(14)
s 252 am—Income Tax (Trading and Other Income), 2005 c 5, s 882(1), sch 1 pt 2 paras
    524, 547; Corporation Tax, 2009 c 4, s 1322, sch 1 paras 474, 490
s 253 am—SI 2004/2310, arts 1(2), 2, sch para 54(1)-(3); Corporation Tax, 2009 c 4, s
    1322, sch 1 paras 474, 491; Corporation Tax, 2010 c 4, s 1177, sch 1 paras 323,
    348; Finance, 2015 c 11, sch 5 para 8
s 254 am—Finance, 2012 c 14, sch 16 paras 96, 97
s 255 subst—Finance, 2012 c 14, sch 16 para 98
s 256 mod—SI 1997/473, reg 53C; SI 2004/2680, regs 20, 21; SI 2005/2014, reg 44
    am—SI 2004/2310, arts 1(2), 2, sch paras 55, 56; Finance, 2007 c 11, ss 38, 39, sch 7
    paras 68, 70, sch 8 paras 22, 23; Corporation Tax, 2009 c 4, s 1322, sch 1 paras
    474, 492; Finance, 2012 c 14, sch 16 para 99(2),(3),(5)
    appl—Corporation Tax, 2010 c 4, ss 4(4), 37(9), 45(6), 62(6), 66(4)
    rep in pt—Finance, 2012 c 14, sch 16 para 99(4)
s 257 am—SI 2004/2310, arts 1(2), 2, sch paras 55, 56; Finance, 2007 c 11, s 39, sch 8
    paras 22, 24; Corporation Tax, 2009 c 4, s 1322, sch 1 paras 474, 493; Finance,
    2009 c 10, s 126(5)(a); Finance, 2012 c 14, sch 16 para 100
    rep in pt—Finance, 2007 c 11, s 41, sch 10 paras 14(1)(8)(a), 17(2), sch 27
    appl (mods)—SI 2008/1942, regs 2, 3, 8
s 258 am—Income Tax (Trading and Other Income), 2005 c 5, s 882(1), sch 1 pt 2 paras
    524, 548; Income Tax, 2007 c 3, s 1027, sch 1 paras 396, 404
s 260 am—Corporation Tax, 2009 c 4, s 1322, sch 1 paras 474, 494; Corporation Tax,
    2010 c 4, s 1177, sch 1 paras 323, 349
    appl (mods)—Corporation Tax, 2010 c 4, s 101(2)
s 261 am—Corporation Tax, 2010 c 4, s 1177, sch 1 paras 323, 350; Finance, 2012 c 14,
    sch 16 para 101
s 261A added—Finance, 2006 c 25, s 83(3)
    am—Corporation Tax, 2010 c 4, s 1177, sch 1 paras 323, 351
s 262 am—Income Tax (Earnings and Pensions), 2003 c 1, s 722, sch 6 pt 2 paras 246, 253
s 262A added—Finance, 2008 c 9, s 74, sch 25 paras 1, 4
s 263 am—Finance, 2001 c 9, s 69, sch 21 para 4(1); Income Tax (Trading and Other
    Income), 2005 c 5, s 882(1), sch 1 pt 2 paras 524, 549; Finance, 2008 c 9, s 74,
    sch 24 paras 1, 13; Corporation Tax, 2009 c 4, s 1322, sch 1 paras 474, 495
s 265 am—Income Tax (Trading and Other Income), 2005 c 5, s 882(1), sch 1 pt 2 paras
    524, 550; Finance, 2008 c 9, s 74, sch 24 paras 1, 14; Corporation Tax, 2009 c
    4, s 1322, sch 1 paras 494, 496
    excl—Crossrail, 2008 c 18, s 37, sch 13 para 37(2)
s 266 am—Finance, 2006 c 25, s 85(2); Income Tax, 2007 c 3, s 1027, sch 1 paras 396, 405;
    Finance, 2008 c 9, s 82, sch 26 paras 1, 11
s 267 am—Finance, 2006 c 25, s 85(3)
s 267A added—Finance, 2006 c 25, s 85(4)
    am—Corporation Tax, 2010 c 4, s 1177, sch 1 paras 323, 352; Finance, 2011 c 11,
    sch 6 para 23
s 268 am—Income Tax (Trading and Other Income), 2005 c 5, s 882(1), sch 1 pt 2 paras
    524, 551
ss 268A-268C added—Finance, 2009 c 10, s 30, sch 11 paras 11, 30, 31

2001
c 2 *continued*

s 268D added—Finance, 2009 c 10, s 30, sch 11 paras 12, 21, 30, 31
    rep in pt—(prosp) Welfare Reform, 2012 c 5, sch 14 pt 9
    am—Finance, 2013 c 29, s 72(1)
s 286E added—Finance, 2012 c 14, sch 9 para 8
Pt 3 (ss 287-360) rep —Finance, 2008 c 9, s 84(2)
Pt 3A (ss 360A-360Z4) added—Finance, 2005 c 7, s 92, sch 6 pt 1 para 1
s 360B am—Finance, 2009 c 10, s 126(5)(a); Finance, 2014 c 26, s 66(2)-(6)
s 360BA added—Finance, 2014 c 26, s 66(7)
s 360C am—Finance, 2009 c 10, s 126(5)(a)
    rep in pt—Finance, 2012 c 14, sch 39 para 8(2)(a)
s 360L subst—Finance, 2014 c 26, s 66(8)
s 360M am—Finance, 2014 c 26, s 66(9)
s 360Z am—(prosp) Corporation Tax (NI), 2015, sch 1 para 11
Pt 4 (ss 361-393) rep —Finance, 2008 c 9, s 84(2)
Pt 4A (ss 393A-393W) added—Finance, 2001 c 9, s 67, sch 19 pt 1
    rep—Finance, 2012 c 14, sch 39 para 37
s 394 am—Finance, 2014 c 26, s 67(2); (prosp) Corporation Tax (NI), 2015, sch 1 para 12
s 395 am—Finance, 2013 c 29, sch 32 para 10
s 396 appl—Income Tax (Trading and Other Income), 2005 c 5, s 161(3)
    am—Finance, 2014 c 26, s 67(2)
s 398 am—Finance, 2014 c 26, s 68(2)
s 399 am—Finance, 2014 c 26, s 68(3)
s 403 am—Finance, 2013 c 29, s 92(3)
s 406 am—Income Tax (Trading and Other Income), 2005 c 5, s 882(1), sch 1 pt 2 paras
    524, 561; Corporation Tax, 2009 c 4, s 1322, sch 1 paras 474, 508
s 416 am—Finance, 2013 c 29, s 92(4)
ss 416ZA, 416ZB added—Finance, 2013 c 29, s 92(5)
ss 416ZC-416ZE added—Finance, 2013 c 29, sch 32 para 9
Pt 5, Ch 5A (ss 416A-416C) added—Finance, 2002 c 23, s 63, sch 21 pt 2, paras 8, 9
s 416B am—Corporation Tax, 2010 c 4, s 1177, sch 1 paras 323, 355; Finance, 2013 c 29,
    s 92(6)
ss 416D, 416E added—Finance, 2002 c 23, s 63, sch 21 pt 2, paras 8, 10, 11
s 418 am—Finance, 2002 c 23, s 63, sch 21 pt 2, paras 8, 12
s 419 am—Finance, 2002 c 23, s 63, sch 21 pt 2, paras 8, 13
s 420 am—Corporation Tax, 2010 c 4, s 1177, sch 1 paras 323, 356; Taxation
    (International and Other Provns), 2010 c 8, s 374, sch 8 paras 233, 235
s 423 am—Income Tax (Earnings and Pensions), 2003 c 1, s 722, sch 6 pt 2 paras 246, 254
ss 431A-431C added—Finance, 2014 c 26, s 67(7)
s 432 am—(prosp) Corporation Tax (NI), 2015, sch 1 para 13
Pt 6 (ss 437-451) am—Proceeds of Crime, 2002 c 29, s 448, sch 10 pt 2, paras 26-29
s 437 am—Finance, 2002 c 23, s 103(4)(g); Income Tax, 2007 c 3, s 1027, sch 1 paras 396,
    407
s 439A added (prosp)—Corporation Tax (NI), 2015, sch 1 para 14
s 441 appl—Income and Corporation Taxes, 1988 c 1, sch 19B, at para 14
s 443 rep in pt—Finance, 2008 c 9, s 84, sch 27 paras 1, 6
s 448 rep in pt—Finance, 2008 c 9, s 84, sch 27 paras 1, 7
s 450 am—(prosp) Corporation Tax (NI), 2015, sch 1 para 15
s 454 am—Income Tax (Trading and Other Income), 2005 c 5, s 882(1), sch 1 pt 2 paras
    524, 562; Corporation Tax, 2009 c 4, s 1322, sch 1 paras 474, 509
s 455 am—Income Tax (Trading and Other Income), 2005 c 5, s 882(1), sch 1 pt 2 paras
    524, 563; Corporation Tax, 2009 c 4, s 1322, sch 1 paras 474, 510
s 462 am—Income Tax (Trading and Other Income), 2005 c 5, s 882(1), sch 1 pt 2 paras
    524, 564; Corporation Tax, 2009 c 4, s 1322, sch 1 paras 474, 511
s 476 am—Corporation Tax, 2010 c 4, s 1177, sch 1 paras 323, 357; Taxation
    (International and Other Provns), 2010 c 8, s 374, sch 8 paras 233, 236
s 479 am—Income Tax (Trading and Other Income), 2005 c 5, s 882(1), sch 1 pt 2 paras
    524, 565; Income Tax, 2007 c 3, s 1027, sch 1 paras 396, 408
s 481 am—Income Tax (Trading and Other Income), 2005 c 5, s 882(1), sch 1 pt 2 paras
    524, 566; Corporation Tax, 2009 c 4, s 1322, sch 1 paras 474, 512
s 483 am—Income Tax (Trading and Other Income), 2005 c 5, s 882(1), sch 1 pt 2 paras
    524, 567; Corporation Tax, 2009 c 4, s 1322, sch 1 paras 474, 513
s 484 am—(prosp) Corporation Tax (NI), 2015, sch 1 para 16

2001

c 2 *continued*

s 488 am—Income Tax (Trading and Other Income), 2005 c 5, s 882(1), sch 1 pt 2 paras
524, 568; Corporation Tax, 2009 c 4, s 1322, sch 1 paras 474, 514

s 489 am—(prosp) Corporation Tax (NI), 2015, sch 1 para 17

s 505 am—Corporation Tax, 2010 c 4, s 1177, sch 1 paras 323, 358

s 529 am—Income Tax (Trading and Other Income), 2005 c 5, s 882(1), sch 1 pt 2 paras
524, 569; Corporation Tax, 2009 c 4, s 1322, sch 1 paras 474, 515(1)(3)(b)

rep in pt—Corporation Tax, 2009 c 4, ss 1322, 1326, sch 1 paras 474,
515(1)(2)(3)(a)(4), sch 3 pt 1

s 534 excl—Income Tax (Trading and Other Income), 2005 c 5, s 225L; Corporation Tax,
2010 c 4, s 290(3)

s 536 am—Income Tax (Trading and Other Income), 2005 c 5, s 882(1), sch 1 pt 2 paras
524, 570; Corporation Tax, 2009 c 4, s 1322, sch 1 paras 474, 516; Finance,
2011 c 11, sch 14 para 12(15)

s 537 am—Finance, 2001 c 9, s 67, sch 19 pt 2 para 3; Finance, 2005 c 7, s 92, sch 6 pt 2
para 5

rep in pt—Finance, 2008 c 9, s 84, sch 27 paras 1, 7

s 538 am—Finance, 2013 c 29, s 73

ss 539, 540 rep —Finance, 2008 c 9, s 84, sch 27 paras 1, 9, 10

s 542 am—Finance, 2001 c 9, s 67, sch 19 pt 2 para 4; Finance, 2008 c 9, s 84, sch 27 paras
1, 11

rep in pt—SL(R), 2013 c 2, s 1, sch 1 pt 10(1)

Pt 12 Ch 1 (ss 544, 545) am—Finance, 2012 c 14, sch 16 para 102

s 544 am—SI 2004/2310, arts 1(2), 2, sch para 57; Finance, 2012 c 14, sch 16 para 103(2)

rep in pt—Finance, 2007 c 11, s 41, sch 10 paras 14(1)(8)(b), 17(2), sch 27; Finance,
2012 c 14, sch 16 para 103(3)

s 545 am—(retrosp) Finance, 2001 c 9, s 76, sch 25 para 7; Finance, 2007 c 11, s 38, sch 7
paras 68, 71; Corporation Tax, 2009 c 4, s 1322, sch 1 paras 474, 517; Finance,
2012 c 14, sch 16 para 104

s 546 am—Finance, 2005 c 7, s 92, sch 6 pt 2 para 6

rep in pt—Finance, 2008 c 9, s 84, sch 27 paras 1, 12

s 555 appl—Income and Corporation Taxes, 1988 c 1, sch 19B, at para 11(3)

s 558 am—Finance, 2001 c 9, s 69, sch 21 para 4(2); Income Tax (Trading and Other
Income), 2005 c 5, s 882(1), sch 1 pt 2 paras 524, 571; Corporation Tax, 2009 c
4, s 1322, sch 1 paras 474, 518

s 559 am—Income Tax (Trading and Other Income), 2005 c 5, s 882(1), sch 1 pt 2 paras
524, 572; Corporation Tax, 2009 c 4, s 1322, sch 1 paras 474, 519

excl—Crossrail, 2008 c 18, s 37, sch 13 para 10

s 560 am—SI 2001/3629, art 108; Finance, 2003 c 14, s 153(1)(d)(4); Finance, 2012 c 14,
sch 16 para 105(3); SI 2015/575, sch 1 para 22

rep in pt—SI 2001/3629, art 108; Finance, 2007 c 11, ss 40, 41, sch 9 paras 1(2)(f),
17(1), sch 10 paras 14(1)(8)(c), 17(2), sch 27; Finance, 2012 c 14, sch 16 para
105(2)

mod—SI 1997/473, reg 53D

s 560A added—Corporation Tax, 2010 c 4, s 1177, sch 1 paras 323, 359

s 561 am—Finance, 2003 c 14, s 153(1)(d)(4); (spec retrosp effect) SI 2007/3186, reg 3,
sch 1; Corporation Tax, 2010 c 4, s 1177, sch 1 paras 323, 360

s 561A added—Finance (No 2), 2005 c 22, s 56

subst—(spec retrosp effect) SI 2007/3186, reg 3, sch 2

am—Corporation Tax, 2010 c 4, s 1177, sch 1 paras 323, 361

s 563 appl—Income Tax (Trading and Other Income), 2005 c 5, ss 193(5), 607(1);
Corporation Tax, 2009 c 4, ss 177(5), 930(1)

rep in pt—SI 2009/56, art 3, sch 1 para 299(2)

am—SI 2009/56, art 3, sch 1 para 299(3); Finance, 2012 c 14, sch 10 para 5

s 564 am—Finance, 2008 c 9, s 84, sch 27 paras 1, 13(a)

rep in pt—Finance, 2008 c 9, s 84, sch 27 paras 1, 13(b)

s 567 am—Finance, 2001 c 9, s 67, sch 19 pt 2 para 5; Finance, 2005 c 7, s 92, sch 6 pt 2
para 7

excl—Railways, 2005 c 14, s 53, sch 10 pt 1 para 4(4) pt 3 para 24(4); Crossrail,
2008 c 18, s 37, sch 13 paras 21(6), 38(6)

rep in pt—Finance, 2008 c 9, s 84, sch 27 paras 1, 14; Finance, 2012 c 14, sch 39
para 38(4)

s 568 excl—Railways, 2005 c 14, s 53, sch 10 pt 1 para 4(4) pt 3 para 24(4); Crossrail,
2008 c 18, s 37, sch 13 paras 21(6), 38(6)

2001

c 2 *continued*

s 569 excl—Railways, 2005 c 14, s 53, sch 10 pt 1 para 4(4) pt 3 para 24(4); Crossrail,
2008 c 18, s 37, sch 13 paras 21(6), 38(6)

rep in pt—Finance, 2008 c 9, s 84, sch 27 paras 1, 15

s 570 am—Finance, 2001 c 9, s 67, sch 19 pt 2 para 6; Finance, 2005 c 7, s 92, sch 6 pt 2
para 8

excl—Railways, 2005 c 14, s 53, sch 10 pt 1 para 4(4) pt 3 para 24(4); Crossrail,
2008 c 18, s 37, sch 13 paras 21(6), 38(6)

rep in pt—Finance, 2008 c 9, s 84, sch 27 paras 1, 16; Finance, 2012 c 14, sch 39
para 38(5)

s 570A added—(transtl savings) Finance, 2003 c 14, s 164

am—Finance, 2005 c 7, s 92, sch 6 pt 2 para 9

rep in pt—Finance, 2008 c 9, s 84, sch 27 paras 1, 17; Finance, 2012 c 14, sch 39
para 38(6)

s 570B added—Income Tax, 2007 c 3, s 1027, sch 1 paras 396, 409

s 573 am—Finance, 2001 c 9, s 67, sch 19 pt 2 para 7; Finance, 2005 c 7, s 92, sch 6 pt 2
para 10

excl—Railways, 2005 c 14, s 53, sch 10 pt 2 para 15(2); Crossrail, 2008 c 18, s 37,
sch 13 para 10

rep in pt—Finance, 2008 c 9, s 84, sch 27 paras 1, 18; Finance, 2012 c 14, sch 39
para 38(7)

s 574 am—Income Tax, 2007 c 3, s 1027, sch 1 paras 396, 410

s 575 subst—Income Tax, 2007 c 3, s 1027, sch 1 paras 396, 411

s 575A added—Income Tax, 2007 c 3, s 1027, sch 1 paras 396, 411

am—Corporation Tax, 2010 c 4, s 1177, sch 1 paras 323, 362

s 576 rep—Commrs for Revenue and Customs, 2005 c 11, ss 50(6), 52(2), sch 4 paras 82,
85, sch 5

s 577 am—Income Tax (Trading and Other Income), 2005 c 5, s 882(1), sch 1 pt 2 paras
524, 573; Corporation Tax, 2009 c 4, s 1322, sch 1 paras 474, 520; Corporation
Tax, 2010 c 4, s 1177, sch 1 paras 323, 363

rep in pt—Income Tax, 2007 c 3, s 1027, sch 1 paras 396, 412, sch 3; Corporation
Tax, 2009 c 4, ss 1322, 1326, sch 1 paras 474, 520(1)(2), sch 3 pt 1

excl—Corporation Tax, 2010 c 4, s 675(2)

sch A1 added—Finance, 2008 c 9, s 74, sch 25 paras 1, 5

am—Corporation Tax, 2009 c 4, s 1322, sch 1 paras 474, 521; Corporation Tax,
2010 c 4, s 1177, sch 1 paras 323, 364; Finance, 2011 c 11, sch 14 para 12(16);
(prosp) Welfare Reform, 2012 c 5, sch 3 para 14; Finance, 2012 c 14, sch 16
para 106; Finance, 2014 c 26, sch 4 para 7; (prosp) Corporation Tax (NI),
2015, sch 1 para 10

rep in pt—(pt prosp) Welfare Reform, 2012 c 5, sch 14 pt 1; Finance, 2013 c 29, sch
18 para 6

sch 1 am—Finance, 2001 c 9, s 67, sch 19 pt 2 para 8; Income Tax (Earnings and Pensions),
2003 c 1, s 722, sch 6 pt 2 paras 246, 255, 256; Finance, 2004 c 12, s 281(1),
sch 35 paras 47, 49; ibid, s 146, sch 27 pt 2 paras 10, 11; Income Tax (Trading
and Other Income), 2005 c 5, s 882(1), sch 1 pt 2 paras 524, 574(1)(2)(3);
Finance, 2005 c 7, s 92, sch 6 pt 2 para 11; Finance, 2006 c 25, s 84(4); Income
Tax, 2007 c 3, s 1027, sch 1 paras 396, 413; Finance, 2008 c 9, ss 74, 82, sch 24
paras 1, 6, 15, sch 26 paras 1, 12; Corporation Tax, 2009 c 4, s 1322, sch 1
paras 474, 522(2)(3)(a)-(c)(e); Finance, 2009 c 10, ss 30, 126(3), sch 11 paras
12, 23; Corporation Tax, 2010 c 4, s 1177, sch 1 paras 323, 365; Finance, 2011
c 11, s 12(6)(a), sch 14 para 12(17)(b); Finance, 2012 c 14, sch 16 para 107(3);
Finance, 2013 c 29, sch 18 para 6; SI 2013/464, art 2; Finance, 2014 c 26, sch 1
para 9; (prosp) Corporation Tax (NI), 2015, sch 1 para 18

rep in pt—Finance, 2003 c 14, s 216, sch 43 pt 3(9), Note; Commrs for Revenue and
Customs, 2005 c 11, ss 50(6), 52(2), sch 4 paras 82, 86, sch 5; Income Tax,
2007 c 3, s 1031, sch 3; Finance, 2008 c 9, s 84, sch 27 paras 1, 19;
Corporation Tax, 2009 c 4, ss 1322, 1326, sch 1 paras 474, 522(3)(d), sch 3 pt
1; Finance, 2009 c 10, s 126(3)(4); Finance, 2011 c 11, s 12(6)(b), sch 14 para
12(17)(a); Finance, 2012 c 14, sch 16 para 107(2); ibid, sch 39 para 38(8),(9)

sch 2 rep in pt—Finance, 2002 c 23, s 141, sch 40 pt 3(8), Note 2; Income Tax (Earnings
and Pensions), 2003 c 1, s 724(1), sch 8 pt 1; Finance, 2004 c 12, s 326, sch 42
pt 2(3)(6), Note; ibid, s 326, sch 42 pt 3, Note; Income Tax (Trading and Other
Income), 2005 c 5, s 884, sch 3; Finance, 2005 c 7, s 104, sch 11 pt 2(6), Note;
Finance, 2006 c 25, s 178, sch 26; SI 2006/3271, reg 43, sch; Income Tax,

2001
c 2 *continued*

2007 c 3, s 1031, sch 3; Corporation Tax, 2009 c 4, s 1326, sch 3 pt 1; SI
2009/56, art 3, sch 1 para 300; Corporation Tax, 2010 c 4, s 1181, sch 3 pts 1,
2; Taxation (International and Other Provns), 2010 c 8, s 378, sch 10 pts 2, 6, 8,
9, 12; Finance, 2012 c 14, sch 39 para 19(2)(a)

    sch 3 am—(retrosp to 2.12.2004) Finance, 2005 c 7, s 59, sch 3 pt 3 paras 27, 31(3);
Finance, 2009 c 10, s 126(5)(a); SI 2009/56, art 3, sch 1 para 301

    rep in pt—Income Tax (Trading and Other Income), 2005 c 5, s 884, sch 3; (saving)
Finance, 2008 c 9, s 76(1)(4); ibid, s 76(1)(5)(f); ibid, s 84, sch 27 paras 1, 20;
Finance, 2009 c 10, s 30, sch 11 paras 12, 24

c 3   **Vehicles (Crime)**

    Pt 1 (ss 1-16) rep—Scrap Metal Dealers, 2013 c 10, s 19(1)(d)(i)

    s 17 rep in pt—Road Safety, 2006 c 49, s 46, sch 7

    s 18 am—Serious Organised Crime and Police, 2005 c 15, s 123(2); Police and Justice,
2006 c 48, s 1, sch 1 paras 76, 77; Road Safety, 2006 c 49, s 46; Police Reform
and Social Responsibility, 2011 c 13, sch 16 para 275; SI 2013/602, sch 2 para
36

    rep in pt—Crime and Cts, 2013 c 22, sch 8 para 106

    s 20 am—Road Safety, 2006 c 49, s 46

    s 23 subst—Road Safety, 2006 c 49, s 46

    s 24 appl—SIs 2002/2977, reg 7(3); 2008/1715

    s 25 appl—SIs 2002/2977, reg 6(7); 2008/1715, reg 6

    s 26 am—Road Safety, 2006 c 49, ss 44, 46

    s 28 am—Road Safety, 2006 c 49, s 45

    s 30 am—Road Safety, 2006 c 49, ss 44, 46

    s 31 am—Communications, 2003 c 21, s 406(1), sch 17 para 168; SI 2003/1900, arts 2(1),
3(1),sch 1; SI 2003/3142, art 3(2); Road Safety, 2006 c 49, ss 44, 45, 46

    s 35 rep—Scrap Metal Dealers, 2013 c 10, s 19(1)(d)(ii)

    s 36 rep —Policing and Crime, 2009 c 26, s 112, sch 7 para 131, sch 8 pt 13

    s 38 am—Courts, 2003 c 39, s 109(1), sch 8 para 394(a); Serious Organised Crime and
Police, 2005 c 15, s 123(3); Police and Justice, 2006 c 48, s 1, sch 1 paras 76, 78;
(prosp) Road Safety, 2006 c 49, s 2; Police Reform and Social Responsibility,
2011 c 13, sch 16 para 276

    rep in pt—Courts, 2003 c 39, s 109(1)(3), sch 8 para 394(b), sch 10

    s 39 am—Road Safety, 2006 c 49, s 46

    s 40 am—Communications, 2003 c 21, s 406(1), sch 17 para 168; SI 2003/1900, arts 2(1),
3(1),sch 1; SI 2003/3142, art 3(2)

    s 45 am—Road Safety, 2006 c 49, s 46

    rep in pt—Policing and Crime, 2009 c 26, s 112, sch 8 pt 13

    sch rep in pt—Courts, 2003 c 39, s 109(3), sch 10; Scrap Metal Dealers, 2013 c 10, s
19(1)(d)(iii)

c 4   *Criminal Defence Service (Advice and Assistance)*— rep Legal Aid, Sentencing and
Punishment of Offenders, 2012 c 10, sch 5 pt 2

c 5   **Election Publications**

    trans of functions—SIs 2002/2626, art 11(1), sch 1; 2003/1887, art 4, sch 1

    s 1 rep in pt—(savings) SI 2006/3416, art 4

    s 2 am—SI 2002/2626, art 20, sch 2, para 26

    rep in pt—SI 2003/1887, art 9, sch 2 para 13

c 6   **Regulatory Reform**

    ss 1-12 rep —Legislative and Regulatory Reform, 2006 c 51, s 30, sch

    s 13 rep in pt—Legislative and Regulatory Reform, 2006 c 51, s 30, sch

    s 14 rep in pt—Legislative and Regulatory Reform, 2006 c 51, s 30, sch

    s 15 rep in pt—Legislative and Regulatory Reform, 2006 c 51, s 30, sch

    s 21 appl (mods)—SI 2007/3544, arts 2, 3, sch

    s 22 appl (mods)—SI 2007/3544, arts 2, 4, sch

c 7   **Elections**

    sch am—SI 2010/2977, art 6

    rep in pt—SI 2010/2977, art 6

c 8   *Appropriation*—rep Appropriation, 2003 c 13, s 4, sch 3

c 9   **Finance**

    s 2 rep in pt—Finance, 2008 c 9, s 13(11)

    am —Finance, 2002 c 23, ss 129(2), 130(1)(3), 132(1)(3), sch 38, paras 1,
3(1)-(3)(4)(a); Finance, 2007 c 11, s 22; Finance, 2015 c 11, s 61(3); (retrosp to
1.4.2014) Finance (No. 2), 2015 c 33, s 48(4)(a)

2001
c 9 s 17 *continued*

   rep in pt—Finance, 2002 c 23, ss 130(2)(3), 131(1)(4), 132(1)(3), 141, sch 38, paras 1,
    3(1)(4)(b), sch 40 pt 4(3), Note 2; Finance, 2007 c 11, s 114, sch 27 pt 1;
    (retrosp to 1.4.2014) Finance (No. 2), 2015 c 33, s 48(4)(b)
  s 18 am—Finance, 2002 c 23, ss 131(2)(4), 132(1)(3), sch 38, paras 1, 4(1)(2); (retrosp to
    1.4.2014) Finance (No. 2), 2015 c 33, s 48(5)
   rep in pt—Finance, 2002 c 23, ss 132(1)(3), 141, sch 38, paras 1, 4(1)(3), sch 40 pt
    4(3), Note 2
  s 19 appl—SI 2001/4027, art 3(4)
   am—Finance, 2002 c 23, s 132(1)(3), sch 38, paras 1, 5
  s 20 rep in pt—Finance, 2002 c 23, ss 131(3)(a), 141, sch 40 pt 4(3), Note 2
  s 21 rep in pt—Finance, 2002 c 23, ss 131(3)(b), 141, sch 40 pt 4(3), Note 2
  s 22 am—Finance, 2002 c 23, s 132(1)(3), sch 38, paras 1, 6
  s 24 rep in pt—Finance, 2002 c 23, ss 131(3)(c), 141, sch 40 pt 4(3), Note 2
   am—Finance, 2002 c 23, s 132(1)(3), sch 38, paras 1, 7
  s 25 am—SI 2009/571, art 8, sch 1
  s 26 am—SI 2015/664, sch 2 para 12(2)
  s 30A added—Finance, 2002 c 23, s 129(1)
   am—Finance, 2004 c 12, s 290; Finance, 2011 c 11, s 81(2)(4)
   subst—Finance, 2004 c 12, s 291(1)(2)(4)
   rep in pt—Finance, 2011 c 11, s 81(3)
  s 30B-30D added—Finance, 2015 c 11, s 61(2)
  s 32 am—Finance, 2009 c 10, s 99, sch 51 paras 27, 28
  s 37 rep in pt—Finance, 2002 c 23, ss 132(1)(3), 141, sch 38, paras 1, 8, sch 40 pt 4(3),
    Note 2; Deregulation, 2015 c 20, sch 6 para 2(15)(a)
   am—SI 2003/2096, arts 4, 6, sch pt 1 paras 35, 36
  s 40 am—SI 2009/56, art 3, sch 1 para 303
   rep in pt—SI 2009/56, art 3, sch 1 para 303(4)
  ss 40A-40G added—SI 2009/56, art 3, sch 1 para 304
  s 40G am—SI 2014/1264, art 7
  s 41 am—SI 2009/56, art 3, sch 1 para 305
   rep in pt—SI 2009/56, art 3, sch 1 para 305(3)
  s 42 am—SI 2009/56, art 3, sch 1 para 306
   rep in pt—SI 2009/56, art 3, sch 1 para 306(2)(a)
  s 43 am—SI 2009/571, art 8, sch 1
  s 45 am—SI 2009/571, art 8, sch 1
  s 48 appl—SI 2001/4027, art 11
   am—Finance, 2004 c 12, s 291(1)(3)(4); SI 2009/56, art 3, sch 1 para 307; Finance,
    2015 c 11, s 61(4)
  ss 50, 51 rep—Income Tax, 2007 c 3, s 1031, sch 3
  ss 52, 53 rep—Tax Credits, 2002 c 21, s 60, sch 6
  s 55 rep—Corporation Tax, 2010 c 4, s 1181, sch 3 pt 1
  s 57 rep in pt—Income Tax (Earnings and Pensions), 2003 c 1, s 724(1), sch 8 pt 1
  s 58 rep—Income Tax (Earnings and Pensions), 2003 c 1, s 724(1), sch 8 pt 1
  ss 60-62 rep—Income Tax (Earnings and Pensions), 2003 c 1, s 724(1), sch 8 pt 1
  s 64 rep in pt—Income Tax, 2007 c 3, s 1031, sch 3
  s 67 rep—Finance, 2012 c 14, sch 39 para 39(a)
  s 70 rep in pt—Corporation Tax, 2009 c 4, ss 1322, 1326, sch 1 paras 523, 524, sch 3 pt 1
  s 71 rep in pt—Income Tax (Trading and Other Income), 2005 c 5, s 884, sch 3
  s 73 rep—Corporation Tax, 2009 c 4, s 1326, sch 3 pt 1
  s 74 rep—Finance, 2004 c 12, s 326, sch 42 pt 3, Note
  s 75 rep in pt—Corporation Tax, 2009 c 4, s 1326, sch 3 pt 1
  s 78 rep—Finance, 2008 c 9, s 8, sch 2 para 55(d)(i)
  s 81 rep—SL(R), 2013 c 2, s 1, sch 1 pt 10(1)
  s 82 rep—Finance, 2009 c 10, s 36, sch 16 para 5(g)
  s 83 rep in pt—Finance, 2008 c 9, s 36, sch 14 para 17(j)
  s 84 rep—Corporation Tax, 2010 c 4, s 1181, sch 3 pt 1
  s 85 rep in pt—Income Tax, 2007 c 3, s 1031, sch 3
  s 86 rep—Corporation Tax, 2010 c 4, s 1181, sch 3 pt 1
  s 87 rep in pt—Finance, 2007 c 11, s 41, sch 10 paras 16(1)(9), sch 27
  s 89 rep in pt—Finance, 2008 c 9, s 138, sch 44 para 11(e)
  s 92 rep—Finance, 2012 c 14, sch 39 para 7(1)
  ss 92A, 92B added—Finance, 2002 c 23, s 110(3)(6)
  ss 92A, 92B rep—Finance, 2012 c 14, sch 39 para 7(1)

2001
c 9 *continued*

ss 93, 94 rep—Finance, 2014 c 26, s 114(3)(b)

s 95 subst—Income Tax (Earnings and Pensions), 2003 c 1, s 722, sch 6 pt 2 para 257

s 98 rep in pt—Finance, 2007 c 11, s 114, sch 27 pt 5

s 105 rep in pt—Finance, 2011 c 11, s 79(4)

s 107 rep (spec retrosp effect) (saving)—Finance, 2008 c 9, s 135(13)

sch 1 rep in pt—Finance, 2002 c 23, s 141, sch 40 pt 1(4), Note 2

sch 2 rep in pt—Finance, 2005 c 7, s 104, sch 11 pt 1, Note

sch 3 am—SI 2009/56, art 3, sch 1 para 308; Finance (No 3), 2010 c 33, s 29, sch 13 para 8

sch 4 am—Finance, 2002 c 23, s 132(1)(3), sch 38, paras 1, 9; SI 2009/571, art 8, sch 1

    rep in pt—Finance, 2008 c 9, s 123, sch 41 para 25(l)

sch 5 rep in pt—Enterprise, 2002 c 40, s 278(2), sch 26; Finance, 2008 c 9, s 129, sch 43
    para 8; Finance, 2009 c 10, s 99, sch 51 paras 27, 29(4)(b)

    am—Tribunals, Courts and Enforcement, 2007 c 15, s 62, sch 13 paras 139-141;
    Finance, 2009 c 10, s 99, sch 51 paras 27, 29

sch 6 am—(retrosp to 1.5.2002) Finance, 2002 c 23, s 133(1)(2)(a)(3)-(6); SI 2009/56, art
    3, sch 1 para 309; Finance, 2015 c 11, s 61(5); SI 2015/664, sch 2 para 12(3)

    rep in pt—(retrosp to 1.5.2002) Finance, 2002 c 23, ss 133(1)(2)(b)(c)(6), 141, sch 40
    pt 4(3), Note 1; Finance, 2007 c 11, s 84, sch 22 paras 3, 12, sch 27; Finance,
    2008 c 9, s 122, sch 40 para 21(i)

sch 7 rep in pt—Crim Justice, 2003 c 44, s 332, sch 37 pt 6; SI 2004/1501, art 46(2), sch 2;
    Finance, 2007 c 11, s 84, sch 22 paras 3, 12, sch 27; Finance, 2008 c 9, s 138,
    sch 44 para 9(b); Finance, 2009 c 10, s 98, sch 50 paras 15, 16(3), 17;
    (savings) SI 2009/3054, arts 3, 6, sch

    am—Finance, 2008 c 9, s 138, sch 44 para 9(a); Finance, 2009 c 10, s 98, sch 50
    paras 15, 16(1)(2); SI 2009/571, art 8, sch 1

sch 8 rep in pt—Finance, 2002 c 23, ss 132(1)(3), 141, sch 38, paras 1, 10, sch 40 pt 4(3),
    Note 2; SI 2003/2096, arts 4, 6, sch pt 1 paras 35, 37(b)(i); Deregulation, 2015
    c 20, sch 6 para 2(15)(b)

    am—SI 2003/2096, arts 4, 6, sch pt 1 paras 35, 37(a)(b)(ii)(c)(d); Finance, 2009 c 10,
    s 99, sch 51 paras 27, 30; Finance, 2015 c 11, s 61(6)

sch 9 am—SI 2009/1890, art 4

sch 10 am—Finance, 2009 c 10, s 99, sch 51 paras 27, 31(1)-(3)(4)(a)

    rep in pt—Finance, 2009 c 10, s 99, sch 51 paras 31(1)(4)(b)

sch 11 rep—Tax Credits, 2002 c 21, s 60, sch 6

sch 12 rep in pt—Income Tax (Earnings and Pensions), 2003 c 1, s 724(1), sch 8 pt 1

schs 13, 14 rep—Income Tax (Earnings and Pensions), 2003 c 1, s 724(1), sch 8 pt 1

sch 15 rep in pt—Income Tax, 2007 c 3, s 1031, sch 3; Finance, 2009 c 10, s 27, sch 8 para
    10(a)

sch 16 rep in pt—Income Tax, 2007 c 3, s 1031, sch 3

sch 19 rep—Finance, 2012 c 14, sch 39 para 39(a)

sch 21 rep in pt—Income Tax (Trading and Other Income), 2005 c 5, s 884, sch 3; Finance,
    2008 c 9, s 84, sch 27 para 23(1)(3)

sch 22 rep—Corporation Tax, 2009 c 4, ss 1322, 1326, sch 1 paras 523, 525, sch 3 pt 1

sch 23 rep in pt—Corporation Tax, 2009 c 4, s 1326, sch 3 pt 1

sch 24 rep in pt—Income Tax (Trading and Other Income), 2005 c 5, s 884, sch 3; Income
    Tax, 2007 c 3, s 1031, sch 3; SI 2009/56, art 3, sch 1 para 310

sch 25 rep in pt—Income Tax, 2007 c 3, s 1031, sch 3; Finance, 2007 c 11, s 114, sch 27 pt
    2; Corporation Tax, 2010 c 4, s 1181, sch 3 pt 1

sch 26 rep—Finance, 2008 c 9, s 8, sch 2 para 55(d)(ii)

sch 27 rep in pt—Finance, 2005 c 7, s 104, sch 11 pt 2(9), Note; Finance, 2009 c 10, s 34,
    sch 14 para 30(c); Taxation (International and Other Provns), 2010 c 8, s 378,
    sch 10 pt 1; SL(R), 2013 c 2, s 1, sch 1 pt 10(1)

sch 28 rep in pt—Finance, 2004 c 12, s 326, sch 42 pt 2(17), Note; Income Tax (Trading
    and Other Income), 2005 c 5, s 884, sch 3; Finance, 2008 c 9, s 36, sch 14 para
    17(j)

sch 29 rep in pt—(pt prosp) Finance (No 2), 2005 c 22, s 70, sch 11 pt 2(11), Note; Income
    Tax, 2007 c 3, s 1031, sch 3; Finance, 2007 c 11, s 114, sch 27 pt 5; Finance,
    2008 c 9, s 113, sch 36 para 92(h); SI 2009/56, art 3, sch 1 para 311; Taxation
    (International and Other Provns), 2010 c 8, s 378, sch 10 pt 2

sch 30 excl—SI 2001/3746, regs 4(1)(b), (2), 5, 6

    am—Finance, 2002 c 23, s 110(4)(5); Corporation Tax, 2010 c 4, s 1177, sch 1 para
    366

2001

c 10 **Special Educational Needs and Disability**
    s 2 rep—Children and Families, 2014 c 6, sch 3 para 24(2)
    s 3 rep—Children and Families, 2014 c 6, sch 3 para 26(2)
    ss 11-33 rep—Equality, 2010 c 15, s 211, sch 27 pt 1 (subst by SI 2010/2279, sch 2)
    s 34 rep in pt—Equality, 2010 c 15, s 211, sch 27 pt 1 (subst by SI 2010/2279, sch 2)
    ss 35-37 rep—Equality, 2006 c 3, s 91, sch 4
    ss 38-40 rep—Equality, 2010 c 15, s 211, sch 27 pt 1 (subst by SI 2010/2279, sch 2)
    s 42 rep in pt—(saving) Educ, 2002 c 32, s 195, sch 18, paras 16, 17
    schs 2-6 rep—Equality, 2010 c 15, s 211, sch 27 pt 1 (subst by SI 2010/2279, sch 2)
    sch 7 rep—Equality, 2006 c 3, s 91, sch 4
    sch 8 rep in pt—Educ, 2002 c 32, s 215(2), sch 22 pt 2; (saving) (EW) Educ, 2005 c 18,
        s 123, sch 19 pt 4; Educ and Inspections, 2006 c 40, s 184, sch 18; SI
        2008/2833, art 6, sch 3

c 11 **Social Security Fraud**
    appl (mods)—SI 2010/1907, reg 16
    s 1 rep in pt—(pt prosp) Welfare Reform, 2012 c 5, sch 14 pt 1
    s 2 rep in pt—(pt prosp) Welfare Reform, 2012 c 5, sch 14 pt 1
    s 4 am—SI 2004/1822, art 2, sch pt 1 para 19
    s 6 rep—(pt prosp) Welfare Reform, 2012 c 5, sch 14 pt 1
    s 6A added —Welfare Reform, 2009 c 24, s 24(1); Pensions, 2014 c 19, sch 12 para 40;
        (prosp) ibid, sch 16 para 44
       am—Welfare Reform, 2012 c 5, s 117; ibid, sch 2 para 57; ibid, sch 9 para 46
       rep in pt—(prosp) Welfare Reform, 2012 c 5, sch 14 pt 1; (prosp) ibid, sch 14 pt 9
    s 6B added—Welfare Reform, 2009 c 24, s 24(1)
       am—(prosp) Welfare Reform, 2009 c 24, s 9, sch 2 paras 9, 10; Welfare Reform, 2012
        c 5, ss 118(3)-(6), 119(2); (prosp) ibid, s 121(1)(a), (b), (d); ibid, sch 2 para
        58(1)-(3); (prosp) ibid, sch 2 para 58(4); (pt prosp) ibid, sch 3 para 16
       rep in pt—(prosp) Welfare Reform, 2009 c 24, s 58, sch 7 pt 1; Welfare Reform, 2012
        c 5, s 113(8)(a); (prosp) ibid, s 121(1)(c); (pt prosp) ibid, sch 14 pt 1; (prosp)
        ibid, sch 14 pt 12
       excl—SI 2013/386, reg 35(3)(b)
    s 6C added—Welfare Reform, 2009 c 24, s 24(1)
       rep in pt—(S) Crim Justice and Licensing (S), 2010 asp 13, s 14, sch 2 para 45(2); SI
        2011/2298, sch para 13(2); (prosp) Welfare Reform, 2012 c 5, sch 14 pt 12
       am—Welfare Reform, 2012 c 5, s 113(8)(b)
    s 7 am—State Pension Credit, 2002 c 16, s 14, sch 2 pt 3, paras 44, 45; Welfare Reform,
        2007 c 5, s 28, sch 3 para 23(1)-(3); (savings) ibid, s 49; Welfare Reform, 2009 c
        24, s 24, sch 4 paras 1, 2(1)(2)(a)(3)(5); (prosp) ibid, s 9, sch 2 paras 9, 11;
        Welfare Reform, 2012 c 5, ss 118(7), 119(4)-(11); ibid, sch 2 para 59(2), (3);
        (prosp) ibid, sch 2 para 59(4); (pt prosp) ibid, sch 3 para 17
       rep in pt—Tax Credits, 2002 c 21, s 60, sch 6; Welfare Reform, 2009 c 24, ss 24, 58, sch
        4 paras 1, 2(1)(2)(b)(4), sch 7 pt 1; (S) Crim Justice and Licensing (S), 2010
        asp 13, s 14, sch 2 para 45(3); SI 2011/2298, sch para 13(3); (pt prosp)
        Welfare Reform, 2012 c 5, sch 14 pt 1
       appl—SI 2001/1002, reg 7(2)(g)
       excl—SI 2013/386, reg 35(3)(b)
    s 8 rep (pt prosp)—Welfare Reform, 2012 c 5, sch 14 pt 1
       am—Welfare Reform, 2009 c 24, s 1(5); ibid, s 24, sch 4 paras 1, 3; Welfare Reform,
        2012 c 5, s 113(8)(b); ibid, sch 7 para 12(2); (prosp) ibid, sch 2 para 60(2), (3)
       rep in pt—Welfare Reform, 2009 c 24, s 58, sch 7 pt 3; Welfare Reform, 2012 c 5, sch 7
        para 12(5); (prosp) ibid, sch 2 para 60(4); (prosp) ibid, sch 14 pt 12
    s 9 am—State Pension Credit, 2002 c 16, s 14, sch 2 pt 3, paras 44, 46; Welfare Reform,
        2007 c 5, s 28, sch 3 para 23(1)(4)(5); Welfare Reform, 2009 c 24, s 24, sch 4
        paras 1, 4; Welfare Reform, 2012 c 5, sch 2 para 61(1)-(4); (prosp) ibid, sch 2 para
        61(5); ibid, s 113(8)(b)
       rep in pt—(prosp) Welfare Reform, 2009 c 24, s 58, sch 7 pt 1; (pt prosp) Welfare
        Reform, 2012 c 5, sch 14 pt 1; (prosp) ibid, sch 14 pt 12
    s 10 am—State Pension Credit, 2002 c 16, s 14, sch 2 pt 3, paras 44, 47; Welfare Reform,
        2007 c 5, s 28, sch 3 para 23(1)(6); Welfare Reform, 2009 c 24, s 24, sch 4 paras
        1, 5; Welfare Reform, 2012 c 5, sch 9 para 47; ibid, sch 2 para 62; Pensions, 2014
        c 19, sch 12 para 41; (prosp) ibid, 2014 c 19, sch 16 para 45
       rep in pt—State Pension Credit, 2002 c 16, s 21, sch 3; (pt prosp) Welfare Reform,
        2012 c 5, sch 14 pt 1

2001

c 11 *continued*

s 11 am—State Pension Credit, 2002 c 16, s 14, sch 2 pt 3, paras 44, 48; Welfare Reform; 2007 c 5, s 28, sch 3 para 23(1)(7); Welfare Reform, 2009 c 24, s 24, sch 4 paras 1, 6; Welfare Reform, 2012 c 5, ss 118(8), 119(12), sch 2 para 63(2), (3); (pt prosp) ibid, sch 3 para 18

rep in pt—(prosp) Welfare Reform, 2009 c 24, s 58, sch 7 pt 1; (pt prosp) Welfare Reform, 2012 c 5, sch 14 pt 1

s 12 rep in pt—Welfare Reform, 2009 c 24, s 58, sch 7 pt 3

s 13 am—State Pension Credit, 2002 c 16, s 14, sch 2 pt 3, paras 44, 49; Welfare Reform, 2007 c 5, s 28, sch 3 para 23(1)(8); Welfare Reform, 2009 c 24, s 24, sch 4 paras 1, 7(1)-(3)(5)

rep in pt—Welfare Reform, 2009 c 24, ss 24, 58, sch 4 paras 1, 7(1)(4), sch 7 pt 3; (pt prosp) Welfare Reform, 2012 c 5, sch 14 pt 1; (prosp) ibid, sch 14 pt 12

s 14 rep (pt prosp)—Welfare Reform, 2012 c 5, sch 14 pt 1

s 21 am—Welfare Reform, 2009 c 24, s 24, sch 4 paras 1, 8

c 12 **Private Security Industry**

s 2 am—Serious Organised Crime and Police, 2005 c 15, s 171(1), sch 15 paras 1, 2; SI 2010/976, art 14, sch 16; Police Reform and Social Responsibility, 2011 c 13, sch 16 para 273

s 2A added—Serious Organised Crime and Police, 2005 c 15, s 171(1), sch 15 paras 1, 3

s 3 am—Serious Organised Crime and Police, 2005 c 15, s 171(1), sch 15 paras 1, 4; SI 2010/976, art 14, sch 16; (prosp) Crime and Security, 2010 c 17, s 42, sch 1 para 2, 3(1)-(4); Protection of Freedoms, 2012 c 9, sch 9 para 20(2)(a)

rep in pt—Protection of Freedoms, 2012 c 9, sch 9 para 20(2)(b), sch 10 pt 3

s 4 am—Violent Crime Reduction, 2006 c 38, s 63; SIs 2009/1941, art 2, sch 1 para 188(2); 2009/3017, art 2; (prosp) Crime and Security, 2010 c 17, s 42, sch 1 para 4 (amended by SI 2012/2595, art 22(3)(a))

ss 4A, 4B added (prosp)—Crime and Security, 2010 c 17, s 42(2)

s 4A rep in pt—Protection of Freedoms, 2012 c 9, sch 9 para 20(3), sch 10 pt 3

s 5 am—(prosp) Crime and Security, 2010 c 17, s 42, sch 1 paras 5, 6

s 6 rep—Protection of Freedoms, 2012 c 9, sch 9 para 20(4), sch 10 pt 3

s 7 am—Serious Organised Crime and Police, 2005 c 15, s 171(1), sch 15 paras 1, 5; SI 2010/976, art 14, sch 16

s 8 am—(prosp) Crime and Security, 2010 c 17, s 42, sch 1 para 8

s 9 am—(prosp) Crime and Security, 2010 c 17, s 42(4) (amended by SI 2012/2595, art 22(3)(b))

s 11 am—Courts, 2003 c 39, s 109(1), sch 8 para 395(1)(2)(4)(b); Serious Organised Crime and Police, 2005 c 15, s 171(1), sch 15 paras 1, 6

rep in pt—Courts, 2003 c 39, s 109(1)(3), sch 8 para 395(1)(3)(4)(a), sch 10

s 13 am—Serious Organised Crime and Police, 2005 c 15, s 171(1), sch 15 paras 1, 7

s 14 am—(prosp) Crime and Security, 2010 c 17, s 43(1)-(3)

s 15 am—Serious Organised Crime and Police, 2005 c 15, s 171(1), sch 15 paras 1, 8; (prosp) Crime and Security, 2010 c 17, s 43(4)-(6)

appl—SI 2006/425, regs 3-5

s 16 rep in pt—(prosp) Crime and Security, 2010 c 17, s 43(7)

s 17 am—(prosp) Crime and Security, 2010 c 17, s 43(8)-(10)

s 18 am—Courts, 2003 c 39, s 109(1), sch 8 para 396(1)(2)(4)(b); Serious Organised Crime and Police, 2005 c 15, s 171(1), sch 15 paras 1, 9

rep in pt—Courts, 2003 c 39, s 109(1)(3), sch 8 para 396(1)(3)(4)(a), sch 10

s 19 am—(prosp) Crime and Security, 2010 c 17, s 42(5); (prosp) ibid, s 42, sch 1 para 9

s 21 rep (EW)—Crim Justice, 2003 c 44, s 332, sch 37 pt 11

s 22A added (prosp)—Crime and Security, 2010 c 17, s 44(2) (never in force—repealed)

rep—Protection of Freedoms, 2012 c 9, sch 9 para 20(5), sch 10 pt 3

s 22B added (prosp)—Crime and Security, 2010 c 17, s 44(2) (as amended by SI 2012/3595, art 22(4)) (never in force—repealed)

s 23 am—Serious Organised Crime and Police, 2005 c 15, s 171(1), sch 15 paras 1, 10; (prosp) Crime and Security, 2010 c 17, s 42(6)

s 23A added (prosp)—Crime and Security, 2010 c 17, s 42, sch 1 para 10

s 24 am—Serious Organised Crime and Police, 2005 c 15, s 171(1), sch 15 paras 1, 11; SI 2010/976, art 14, sch 16

rep in pt—Protection of Freedoms, 2012 c 9, sch 9 para 20(6), sch 10 pt 3

s 25 am—SIs 2007/2194, art 10, sch 4; 2009/1941, art 2, sch 1 para 188(3); 2010/976, art 14, sch 16; (prosp) Crime and Security, 2010 c 17, s 42(7); (prosp) ibid, s 42, sch 1 para 11

2001

c 12 s 25 *continued*

    rep in pt—Protection of Freedoms, 2012 c 9, sch 9 para 20(7), sch 10 pt 3

s 26 rep in pt—(EW) Crim Justice, 2003 c 44, s 332, sch 37 pt 11

    am—Serious Organised Crime and Police, 2005 c 15, s 171(1), sch 15 paras 1, 12

sch 1 am—Serious Organised Crime and Police, 2005 c 15, s 171(1), sch 15 paras 1, 13; SI 2010/976, art 14, sch 16; SI 2012/2404, sch 2 para 45

sch 2 am—Licensing, 2003 c 17, s 198, sch 6 para 118; SI 2005/224, arts 2, 3, 4; Serious Organised Crime and Police, 2005 c 15, s 171(1), sch 15 paras 1, 14; Gambling, 2005 c 19, s 356(1)(2), sch 16 pt 2 para 17; SI 2006/1831, arts 2-5; Offender Management, 2007 c 21, s 13(7); SI 2007/2201, regs 2-5; (S) SSI 2009/248, art 2, sch 1; SIs 2009/3017, art 3; 2009/3043, arts 2-7; SI 2013/1465, sch 1 para 7; Crim Justice and Cts, 2015 c 2, sch 10 para 32

    rep in pt—(S) SSI 2009/248, art 2, schs 1, 2; SI 2009/3043, art 7; Protection of Freedoms, 2012 c 9, sch 9 para 20(8), sch 10 pt 3

c 13 **House of Commons (Removal of Clergy Disqualification)**

sch 1 rep in pt—European Parl Elections, 2002 c 24, s 16, sch 4; Govt of Wales, 2006 c 32, s 163, sch 12

c 14 **Rating (Former Agricultural Premises and Rural Shops)**

s 1 rep in pt—Loc Govt, 2003 c 26, s 127(2), sch 8 pt 1

s 2 rep—Localism, 2011 c 20, sch 25 pt 10

c 15 **Health and Social Care**

ss 1-4 rep—Nat Health Service (Conseq Provns), 2006 c 43, s 6, sch 4

s 5 ext—(Is of Scilly) SI 2003/49, art 2(1)(2)(a)

s 6 rep—Nat Health Service (Conseq Provns), 2006 c 43, s 6, sch 4

s 7 ext (mods)—(Is of Scilly) SI 2004/1425, art 2

    rep in pt—Nat Health Service (Conseq Provns), 2006 c 43, s 6, sch 4

ss 8-13 rep—Nat Health Service (Conseq Provns), 2006 c 43, s 6, sch 4

s 14 ext—(Is of Scilly) SI 2003/49, art 2(1)(2)(a)

    am—Nat Health Service (Conseq Provns), 2006 c 43, s 2, sch 1 para 215

    rep in pt—Nat Health Service (Conseq Provns), 2006 c 43, s 6, sch 4

s 15 rep—Health and Social Care (Community Health and Standards), 2003 c 43, s 196, sch 14 pt 4

s 16 rep—Nat Health Service (Conseq Provns), 2006 c 43, s 6, sch 4

s 17 rep—Health and Social Care (Community Health and Standards), 2003 c 43, s 196, sch 14 pt 4

s 18 rep—Health and Social Care (Community Health and Standards), 2003 c 43, ss 184, 196, sch 11 paras 69, 70, sch 14 pt 4

s 19 rep—Crim Justice, 2003 c 44, s 332, sch 37 pt 11; Serious Organised Crime and Police, 2005 c 15, s 174(2), sch 17 pt 2

ss 20, 21 rep—Nat Health Service (Conseq Provns), 2006 c 43, s 6, sch 4

s 22 rep—Health and Social Care (Community Health and Standards), 2003 c 43, s 196, sch 14 pt 4

s 23 rep—Nat Health Service (Conseq Provns), 2006 c 43, s 6, sch 4

s 24 ext—(Is of Scilly) SI 2003/49, art 2(1)(2)(a)

s 25 rep—Nat Health Service (Conseq Provns), 2006 c 43, s 6, sch 4

s 26 rep—Health and Social Care (Community Health and Standards), 2003 c 43, s 196, sch 14 pt 4

s 27 rep—Nat Health Service (Conseq Provns), 2006 c 43, s 6, sch 4

Pt 2 (ss 28-43) ext—(Is of Scilly) SI 2003/49, art 2(1)(2)(b)

ss 28-38 rep—Nat Health Service (Conseq Provns), 2006 c 43, s 6, sch 4

s 39 am—Nat Health Service (Conseq Provns), 2006 c 43, s 2, sch 1 para 216

ss 40-43 rep—Nat Health Service (Conseq Provns), 2006 c 43, s 6, sch 4

Pt 3 (ss 45-48) rep—Nat Health Service (Conseq Provns), 2006 c 43, s 6, sch 4

s 49 ext (mods)—(Is of Scilly) SI 2003/761, art 2(1)(2)(a)

s 50 rep in pt—SI 2015/914, sch para 63

s 54 ext (mods)—(Is of Scilly) SI 2003/761, art 2(1)(2)(a)

    rep in pt—Health and Social Care, 2008 c 14, s 166, sch 15

s 55 ext (mods)—(Is of Scilly) SI 2003/761, art 2(1)(2)(a)

    am—SI 2015/914, sch para 64

s 56 ext (mods)—(Is of Scilly) SI 2003/761, art 2(1)(2)(a)

s 57 ext (mods)—(Is of Scilly) SI 2003/761, art 2(1)(2)(a)

    am—Health and Social Care, 2008 c 14, s 146(1)-(7); (W) Social Care Charges (W), 2010 nawm 2, s 16; SI 2015/914, sch para 65(2)-(6)

    rep in pt—SI 2015/914, sch para 65(3)

2001
c 15 *continued*
>>s 58 ext (mods)—(Is of Scilly) SI 2003/761, art 2(1)(2)(a)
>>s 59 ext (mods)—(Is of Scilly) SI 2003/761, art 2(1)(2)(a)
>>>am—SI 2015/914, sch para 66(3)(a)(b)
>>>rep in pt—SI 2015/914, sch para 66(2)
>>ss 60, 61 rep—Nat Health Service (Conseq Provns), 2006 c 43, s 6, sch 4
>>s 64 rep in pt—Nat Health Service (Conseq Provns), 2006 c 43, s 6, sch 4
>>>am—Health and Social Care, 2008 c 14, s 146(8)
>>s 66 rep in pt—Nat Health Service (Conseq Provns), 2006 c 43, s 2, sch 1 para 217
>>s 67 ext—(Is of Scilly) SI 2003/49, art 2(1)(2)(d)
>>>ext (mods)—(Is of Scilly) SI 2003/761, art 2(1)(2)(b)(c)
>>s 68 am—Nat Health Service (Conseq Provns), 2006 c 43, s 2, sch 1 para 218
>>>rep in pt—Nat Health Service (Conseq Provns), 2006 c 43, s 6, sch 4
>>schs 1-4 rep—Nat Health Service (Conseq Provns), 2006 c 43, s 6, sch 4
>>sch 5 am—(temp) (E) SI 2001/3294, art 4(2), sch pt II; (temp) (W) SI 2002/1919, art 3(2), schedule pt III; Nat Health Service Reform and Health Care Professions, 2002 c 17, s 2(5), sch 2 pt 2, paras 71, 82
>>>rep in pt—Nat Health Service Reform and Health Care Professions, 2002 c 17, s 37, sch 8, paras 32, 37, sch 9 pt 3; Health and Social Care (Community Health and Standards), 2003 c 43, s 196, sch 14 pt 4; SI 2006/1407, art 3, sch 2; Health and Social Care, 2008 c 14, s 166, sch 15; SI 2010/22, art 5, sch 4
>>>ext —(Is of Scilly) (in pt with mods) SI 2003/49, art 2(1)(2)(b)(d)
>>sch 6 ext—(Is of Scilly) SI 2003/49, art 2(1)(2)(d)
>>>ext (mods)—(Is of Scilly) SI 2003/761, art 2(1)(2)(c)

c 16 **Criminal Justice and Police**
>appl—SI 1982/1109, rule 38(1)
>s 1 am—SI 2002/1934, art 2; Licensing, 2003 c 17, s 198, sch 6 paras 119, 120; Communications, 2003 c 21, s 406(1), sch 17 para 169; SI 2003/1900, arts 2(1), 3(1),sch 1; SI 2003/3142, art 3(2); Fire and Rescue Services, 2004 c 21, s 53, sch 1 para 97(1)(3); SI 2004/2540, art 2(1)(2)(3)(a)(4)-(7); SIs 2005/1090, art 2; 2005/3048, art 2; 2009/110, art 2; 2012/1430, art 2; 2014/1365, art 2
>>rep in pt—Licensing, 2003 c 17, s 199, sch 7; Communications, 2003 c 21, s 406(7), sch 19(1); SI 2003/1900, arts 2(1), 3(1),sch 1; SI 2003/3142, art 3(2); (prosp) Fireworks, 2003 c 22, s 15, sch; Fire and Rescue Services, 2004 c 21, ss 53, 54, sch 1 para 97(1)(2), sch 2; SI 2004/2540, art 2(1)(3)(b); SI 2005/3048, art 2; Legal Aid, Sentencing and Punishment of Offenders, 2012 c 10, sch 23 para 2
>s 2 am—Anti-social Behaviour, 2003 c 38, s 87(1)-(3); SI 2004/3166, art 2; Legal Aid, Sentencing and Punishment of Offenders, 2012 c 10, sch 23 para 3(2), (3), (6), (7)
>>rep in pt—Legal Aid, Sentencing and Punishment of Offenders, 2012 c 10, sch 23 para 3(4), (5), (8), (9)
>s 2A added—Legal Aid, Sentencing and Punishment of Offenders, 2012 c 10, sch 23 para 4
>s 3 am—Anti-social Behaviour, 2003 c 38, s 87(1)(4); Courts, 2003 c 39, s 109(1), sch 8 para 397; Domestic Violence, Crime and Victims, 2004 c 28, s 15; SI 2004/2540, art 3; Legal Aid, Sentencing and Punishment of Offenders, 2012 c 10, sch 23 para 5(3)
>>rep in pt—SI 2010/64, art 2; Legal Aid, Sentencing and Punishment of Offenders, 2012 c 10, sch 23 para 5(2),(4)
>s 4 mod—SI 2004/3166, art 6(1)-(3)
>>am—Legal Aid, Sentencing and Punishment of Offenders, 2012 c 10, sch 23 para 6
>s 5 mod—SI 2004/3166, art 6(1)-(3)
>>am—Legal Aid, Sentencing and Punishment of Offenders, 2012 c 10, sch 23 para 7
>s 6 am—Legal Aid, Sentencing and Punishment of Offenders, 2012 c 10, sch 23 para 8
>s 7 am—Courts, 2003 c 39, s 109(1), sch 8 para 398
>>mod—SI 2004/3166, art 6(1)(4)
>s 8 am—Courts, 2003 c 39, s 109(1), sch 8 para 399; Legal Aid, Sentencing and Punishment of Offenders, 2012 c 10, sch 23 para 9
>s 9 am—Courts, 2003 c 39, s 109(1), sch 8 para 400
>s 10 mod—SI 2004/3166, art 6(1)(5)(6)
>>am—Legal Aid, Sentencing and Punishment of Offenders, 2012 c 10, sch 23 para 10
>s 10A added —Legal Aid, Sentencing and Punishment of Offenders, 2012 c 10, sch 23 para 11
>s 11 am—Legal Aid, Sentencing and Punishment of Offenders, 2012 c 10, sch 23 para 12
>ss 12-16 rep—Anti-social Behaviour, Crime and Policing, 2014 c 12, sch 11 para 30
>ss 17, 18 rep —Licensing, 2003 c 17, s 199, sch 7

2001
c 16 *continued*

s 19 am—Licensing, 2003 c 17, s 198, sch 6 paras 119, 126(a)

s 20 am—Licensing, 2003 c 17, s 198, sch 6 paras 119, 126(b)
rep in pt—SI 2005/886, art 2, sch para 88

s 21 am—Licensing, 2003 c 17, s 198, sch 6 paras 119, 126(c); Courts, 2003 c 39, s 109(1), sch 8 para 401

s 22 am—Courts, 2003 c 39, s 109(1), sch 8 para 402

s 23 rep in pt—SI 2005/886, art 2, sch para 88

s 25 am—(prosp) Crim Justice, 2003 c 44, s 280(2)(3), sch 26 para 56(1)(2); SI 2015/664, sch 4 para 31

s 27 am—Licensing, 2003 c 17, s 198, sch 6 paras 119, 126(d)

s 28 rep in pt—Licensing, 2003 c 17, ss 198, 199, sch 6 paras 119, 127(b), sch 7
am—Licensing, 2003 c 17, s 198, sch 6 paras 119, 127(a)(c)

ss 30-32 rep —Licensing, 2003 c 17, s 199, sch 7

s 33 am—Identity Cards, 2006 c 15, s 39(3)(4); Identity Documents, 2010 c 40, s 12, sch 1 paras 15, 16

s 34 mod—Serious Crime, 2007 c 27, s 63, sch 6 para 41

ss 35, 36 am—Identity Cards, 2006 c 15, s 39(3); Identity Documents, 2010 c 40, s 12, sch 1 paras 15, 17

s 38 rep—Drugs, 2005 c 17, s 23, sch 1 para 6, sch 2

s 42 am—(prosp) Crim Justice, 2003 c 44, s 280(2)(3), sch 26 para 56(1)(3); Serious Organised Crime and Police, 2005 c 15, s 127
rep in pt—Serious Organised Crime and Police, 2005 c 15, ss 111, 174(2), sch 7 pt 1 para 35(a), sch 17 pt 2

s 42A added—Serious Organised Crime and Police, 2005 c 15, s 126(1)

s 45 rep—Companies, 2006 c 46, s 129, sch 16

s 46 rep in pt—Police Reform, 2002 c 30, s 107(2), sch 8

s 47 rep in pt—Serious Organised Crime and Police, 2005 c 15, ss 111, 174(2), sch 7 pt 1 para 35(b), sch 17 pt 2

ss 48, 49 rep —Policing and Crime, 2009 c 26, s 112, sch 8 pt 13

s 52 am—SI 2010/976, art 12, sch 14

s 55 rep in pt & am—Proceeds of Crime, 2002 c 29, ss 456, 457, sch 11, para 40(1)(2), sch 12

s 56 rep in pt—SIs 2001/3649, art 364(a); 2009/1941, art 2, sch 1 para 189
appl (mods)—(NI) Police (NI), 2003 c 6, sch 2 pt 1 para 10(b)
am—Crim Justice, 2003 c 44, s 12, sch 1 para 14

s 57 rep in pt—SI 2001/3649, art 364(b); Finance, 2007 c 11, s 84, sch 22 paras 3, 13(1)(a), sch 27; SI 2009/1941, art 2, sch 1 para 189; Consumer Rights, 2015 c 15, sch 6 para 62(a)
am—Human Tissue, 2004 c 30, s 56, sch 6 para 5(1)(2); (S NI prosp) Animal Welfare, 2006 c 45, s 64, sch 3 para 14(1); (transtl provns) SI 2006/659, reg 1, sch 1; SI 2006/3363, reg 25; Human Fertilisation and Embryology, 2008 c 22, s 65, sch 7 para 19; Financial Services, 2012 c 21, sch 18 para 92; Consumer Rights, 2015 c 15, sch 6 para 62(b)

s 59 am—Deregulation, 2015 c 20, s 82(5)

s 60 rep in pt & am—Proceeds of Crime, 2002 c 29, ss 456, 457, sch 11, para 40(1)(3), sch 12

s 63 rep in pt—Gambling, 2005 c 19, s 356(4)(5), sch 17; Finance, 2007 c 11, s 84, sch 22 paras 3, 13(1)(b), sch 27
am—Finance, 2007 c 11, s 85, sch 23 paras 11, 12, 14

s 64 am—Proceeds of Crime, 2002 c 29, s 456, sch 11 para 40(1)(4); Serious Crime, 2007 c 27, s 77, sch 10 para 27
rep in pt—Proceeds of Crime, 2002 c 29, s 457, sch 12; Policing and Crime, 2009 c 26, s 112, sch 7 para 115, sch 8 pt 5; SI 2009/1941, art 2, sch 1 para 189

s 65 am—Proceeds of Crime, 2002 c 29, s 456, sch 11, para 40(1)(5); SIs 2006/3363, reg 26; 2010/2960, reg 36, sch 6; 2011/1065, reg 2(2); Consumer Rights, 2015 c 15, sch 6 para 63(3)(4)(b)
rep in pt—Finance, 2007 c 11, s 84, sch 22 paras 3, 13(1)(c), sch 27; SI 2009/1941, art 2, sch 1 para 189; Consumer Rights, 2015 c 15, sch 6 para 63(2), (4)(a)(c)

s 66 rep in pt—SIs 2001/3649, art 364(c); 2008/1277, sch 4; Human Fertilisation and Embryology, 2008 c 22, s 65, sch 7 para 20(b), sch 8; SIs 2009/1941, art 2, sch 1 para 189; 2010/2960, reg 36, schs 6, 8; 2013/1575, sch para 5; Consumer Rights, 2015 c 15, sch 6 para 64(a)

2001

c 16 s 66 *continued*

am—Human Tissue, 2004 c 30, s 56, sch 6 para 5(1)(3); SI 2005/1803, reg 47(2)(3); (S NI prosp) Animal Welfare, 2006 c 45, s 64, sch 3 para 14(2); (transtl provns) SI 2006/659, reg 1, sch 1; SI 2006/3363, reg 27; Consumers, Estate Agents and Redress, 2007 c 17, s 63, sch 7 para 22(a); Human Fertilisation and Embryology, 2008 c 22, s 65, sch 7 para 20(a); SI 2008/1277, reg 30, sch 2; Marine and Coastal Access, 2009 c 23, s 253(6); SIs 2010/2960, reg 36, sch 6; 2011/1065, reg 2(3); Consumer Rights, 2015 c 15, sch 6 para 64(b)-(d)

s 67 am—Finance, 2007 c 11, s 84, sch 22 para 2

s 68 rep in pt—SI 2001/3649, art 364(d)
  am—SI 2007/3298, reg 19, sch 3

s 69 am—SI 2010/976, art 12, sch 14

s 71 rep—Police Reform, 2002 c 30, s 107(2), sch 8

s 78 rep in pt—Policing and Crime, 2009 c 26, s 112, sch 8 pt 13

s 80 rep in pt—Police Reform, 2002 c 30, s 107(2), sch 8; Policing and Crime, 2009 c 26, s 112, sch 8 pt 13

ss 82, 84 rep—Protection of Freedoms, 2012 c 9, sch 10 pt 1

ss 87-96 rep—Police and Justice, 2006 c 48, s 52, sch 15

s 97 am—Police and Justice, 2006 c 48, ss 1, 6, sch 1 para 97, sch 4 para 10; Police Reform and Social Responsibility, 2011 c 13, sch 16 para 271; Anti-social Behaviour, Crime and Policing, 2014 c 12, s 123(5)(a)
  rep in pt—Police and Justice, 2006 c 48, s 52, sch 15; Crime and Cts, 2013 c 22, sch 8 para 107; Anti-social Behaviour, Crime and Policing, 2014 c 12, s 123(5)(b)

s 98 am—Police Reform and Social Responsibility, 2011 c 13, sch 16 para 272

s 101 rep in pt—Police and Justice, 2006 c 48, s 52, sch 15

s 104 am—Serious Organised Crime and Police, 2005 c 15, s 59, sch 4 paras 162, 164(1)(3)(a)

s 104 rep in pt—Serious Organised Crime and Police, 2005 c 15, ss 59, 174(2), sch 4 paras 162, 164(1)(2)(3)(b)(4), sch 17 pt 2; (prosp) Police and Justice, 2006 c 48, s 52, sch 15

ss 105, 106 rep (prosp)—Police and Justice, 2006 c 48, s 52, sch 15

s 107 rep in pt—Serious Organised Crime and Police, 2005 c 15, ss 59, 174(2), sch 4 paras 162, 165, sch 17 pt 2
  rep (prosp)—Police and Justice, 2006 c 48, s 52, sch 15

ss 108-121 rep—Serious Organised Crime and Police, 2005 c 15, ss 59, 174(2), sch 4 paras 162, 166, sch 17 pt 2

s 122 rep in pt—Police Reform, 2002 c 30, s 107(2), sch 8

s 123 rep in pt—Police Reform, 2002 c 30, s 107(2), sch 8

s 125 rep in pt—Police Reform, 2002 c 30, s 107(2), sch 8; (prosp) Crim Justice and Immigration, 2008 c 4, s 149, sch 28 pt 8

ss 130, 132 rep—Legal Aid, Sentencing and Punishment of Offenders, 2012 c 10, sch 12 para 47

s 133 rep in pt—Legal Aid, Sentencing and Punishment of Offenders 2012 c 10, sch 12 para 47

s 134 rep in pt—(EW) Crim Justice, 2003 c 44, s 332, sch 37 pt 11; (prosp) Policing and Crime, 2009 c 26, s 112, sch 8 pt 8

s 138 rep in pt—Serious Organised Crime and Police, 2005 c 15, ss 59, 174(2), sch 4 paras 162, 167, sch 17 pt 2; SI 2009/1941, art 2, sch 2

sch 1 rep in pt—SI 2001/3649, art 364(e); Proceeds of Crime, 2002 c 29, s 457, sch 12; Licensing, 2003 c 17, s 199, sch 7; Crime (International Co-operation), 2003 c 32, ss 26(3)(a), 91(2), sch 6; Gambling, 2005 c 19, s 356(1)(2)(4)(5), sch 16 pt 2 para 18(1), sch 17; Finance, 2007 c 11, s 84, sch 22 paras 3, 13(2), sch 27; SIs 2008/1277, sch 4; 2009/1941, art 2, sch 1 para 189; 2010/2960, reg 36, schs 6, 8; 2013/1575, sch para 6; 2013/1881, sch para 7; Finance, 2014 c 26, sch 28 para 21; Consumer Rights, 2015 c 15, sch 6 para 65(2)
  am—Proceeds of Crime, 2002 c 29, s 456, sch 11, para 40(1)(6)(7); Enterprise, 2002 c 40, s 194(5); Licensing, 2003 c 17, s 198, sch 6 paras 119, 128(a)(b); Crime (International Co-operation), 2003 c 32, s 26(3)(b); Extradition, 2003 c 41, s 165(1)-(3) (see SI 2003/3103, arts 2-5); SI 2003/934, arts 2(1)-(4), 3(1)-(3); Human Tissue, 2004 c 30, s 56, sch 6 para 5(1)(4); SI 2005/1803, reg 47(2)(4)(5); Serious Organised Crime and Police, 2005 c 15, s 68; Gambling, 2005 c 19, s 356(1)(2), sch 16 pt 2 para 18(1); (transtl provns) SI 2006/659, reg 1, sch 1; Charities, 2006 c 50, s 26(2); Terrorism, 2006 c 11, s 28(6); SI 2006/3363, reg 28; Consumer Credit, 2006 c 14, s 51(7); SI 2007/3298, reg 19,

2001
c 16 sch 1 *continued*

              sch 3; Consumers, Estate Agents and Redress, 2007 c 17, s 63, sch 7 para 22(b); Finance, 2007 c 11, s 85, sch 23 paras 11, 13, 14; SI 2007/2157, reg 51, sch 6; Human Fertilisation and Embryology, 2008 c 22, s 65, sch 7 para 21; SI 2008/1277, reg 30, sch 2; Cluster Munitions (Prohibitions), 2010 c 11, s 31, sch 3 para 1; (S) Marine (S), 2010 asp 5, s 141(6); SI 2010/2960, reg 36, sch 6; Charities, 2011 c 25, sch 7 para 92; SI 2011/1065, reg 2(4); Protection of Freedoms, 2012 c 9, sch 9 paras 28, 29, 145; Consumer Rights, 2015 c 15, sch 6 para 65(3)-(5)

          saving—SI 2004/787, arts 2, 3

       sch 2 rep in pt—SI 2001/3649, art 364(f); Companies, 2006 c 46, s 129, sch 16; (EWS prosp) Police and Justice, 2006 c 48, s 52, sch 15; (prosp) Finance, 2007 c 11, s 114, sch 27 pt 5; SI 2008/1277, sch 4; Human Fertilisation and Embryology, 2008 c 22, s 66, sch 8; SI 2013/1575, sch para 7; Consumer Rights, 2015 c 15, sch 6 para 66(2)

          am—Companies (Audit, Investigations and Community Enterprise), 2004 c 27, s 25(1), sch 2 pt 3 para 30; SI 2008/1277, reg 30, sch 2; Consumer Rights, 2015 c 15, sch 6 para 66(3)-(8)

       sch 3 rep—Police and Justice, 2006 c 48, s 52, sch 15

       sch 4 rep in pt—Serious Organised Crime and Police, 2005 c 15, s 174(2), sch 17 pt 2; Police and Justice, 2006 c 48, s 52, sch 15

       sch 5 rep—Serious Organised Crime and Police, 2005 c 15, s 174(2), sch 17 pt 2

       sch 6 rep in pt—Police Reform, 2002 c 30, s 107(2), sch 8; (subject to transtl provn(s)) SI 2002/1860, arts 11(2)(b), 15(1)(2)(b), sch 6; (EW) Loc Govt, 2003 c 26, s 127(2), sch 8 pt 1 (see SI 2003/2938); Serious Organised Crime and Police, 2005 c 15, s 174(2), sch 17 pt 2

c 17   **International Criminal Court**

       ext (mods)—SI 2009/1738, annex 1

       mod—SI 2009/317, art 3, sch

       appl (mods)—SI 2011/245, sch 6 pt 1

       s 7 am—Courts, 2003 c 39, s 109(1), sch 8 para 403(a)

       s 6 am—Legal Aid, Sentencing and Punishment of Offenders, 2012 c 10, sch 5 para 56

       s 9 am—Constitutional Reform, 2005 c 4, s 40(4), sch 9 pt 1 para 75

       s 13 am—Courts, 2003 c 39, s 109(1), sch 8 para 403(b)

       s 23 ext—(I of Man) SIs 2004/714, art 2(a); (Jersey) 2014/2706, art 2(a) sch

       s 26 rep in pt—Courts, 2003 c 39, s 109(1)(3), sch 8 para 404, sch 10

          am—Constitutional Reform, 2005 c 4, s 15(1), sch 4 pt 1 para 299

       s 32 am—SI 2003/1016, art 3, sch paras 12, 13; Armed Forces, 2006 c 52, s 378, sch 16 para 188

          mod—SI 2009/1059, art 205, sch 1

       s 33 am—Serious Organised Crime and Police, 2005 c 15, s 111, sch 7 pt 3 para 49(1)(2)(4)

       s 35 am—Coroners and Justice, 2009 c 25, s 177, sch 21 para 45

       s 42 ext—(I of Man) SI 2004/714, art 2(b)

          appl (mods)—SI 2007/2140, art 2

       s 43 appl (mods)—SI 2007/2140, art 2

       s 44 ext (mods)—(I of Man) SI 2004/714, art 2(c), sch paras 1, 2; (Jersey) 2014/2706, art 2(b) sch

          appl (mods)—SI 2007/2140, art 2

       s 45 ext (mods)—(Jersey) 2014/2706, art 2(b) sch

          appl (mods)—SI 2007/2140, art 2

       ss 46-48 appl (mods)—SI 2007/2140, art 2

       s 53 am—Coroners and Justice, 2009 c 25, s 70(1)(2)

       s 54 mod—SI 2009/1059, art 205, sch 1

          am—Bribery, 2010 c 23, s 17, sch 1 paras 3, 4

       s 55 appl—Extradition, 2003 c 41, ss 64(7)(c), 65(7)(c), 137(6)(c), 138(6)(c) (see SI 2003/3103, arts 2-5)

          am—Serious Organised Crime and Police, 2005 c 15, s 111, sch 7 pt 3 para 49(1)(3)(4)

          mod—Serious Crime, 2007 c 27, s 63, sch 6 para 42

          rep in pt—Serious Crime, 2007 c 27, s 63, sch 6 para 61(1)(2), sch 14

       s 60 am—Coroners and Justice, 2009 c 25, s 70(1)(2)

       s 61 am—Bribery, 2010 c 23, s 17, sch 1 paras 3, 5

       s 62 appl—Extradition, 2003 c 41, ss 64(7)(c), 65(7)(c), 137(6)(c), 138(6)(c) (see SI 2003/3103, arts 2-5)

          mod—Serious Crime, 2007 c 27, s 63, sch 6 para 42

2001

c 17 s 62 *continued*
> rep in pt—Serious Crime, 2007 c 27, s 63, sch 6 para 61(1)(3), sch 14

s 65A added—Coroners and Justice, 2009 c 25, s 70(1)(3)

s 65B added—Coroners and Justice, 2009 c 25, s 70(1)(3)

s 67 am—Armed Forces, 2006 c 52, s 378, sch 16 para 189

s 67A added —Coroners and Justice, 2009 c 25, s 70(1)(4)

s 68 mod—SI 2009/1059, art 205, sch 1

s 70 ext (mods)—(I of Man) SIs 2004/714, art 2(d), sch para 3; 2010/2965, art 3; (Jersey) 2014/2706, art 2(c) sch

s 71 rep—Extradition, 2003 c 41, ss 219, 220, sch 3 paras 1, 12, sch 4 (see SI 2003/3103, arts 2-5)

ss 72, 73 rep—Extradition, 2003 c 41, s 220, sch 4 (see SI 2003/3103, arts 2-5)

s 74 rep—Armed Forces, 2006 c 52, s 378, sch 17

s 75 am—Armed Forces, 2006 c 52, s 378, sch 16 para 190

s 77A added—(EW) International Tribunals (Sierra Leone), 2007 c 7, s 1

s 79 rep in pt—Armed Forces, 2006 c 52, s 378, sch 17

s 83 ext—(I of Man) SI 2004/714, art 2(e)
> ext (mods)—SIs 2010/2965, art 3; (Jersey) 2014/2706, art 2(d) sch

sch 1 ext—International Crim. Ct. (S), 2001 asp 13, s 27
> am—International Organisations, 2005 c 20, s 6(1)(2)(a)(c)(3)
> rep in pt—International Organisations, 2005 c 20, ss 6(1)(2)(b), 9, sch

sch 2 am—Extradition, 2003 c 41, s 219, sch 3 paras 1, 13(1)-(5) (see SI 2003/3103, arts 2-5); Armed Forces, 2006 c 52, s 378, sch 16 para 191
> rep in pt—Extradition, 2003 c 41, ss 219, 220, sch 3 paras 1, 13(1)(6), sch 4 (see SI 2003/3103, arts 2-5)

sch 4 am—Crime and Security, 2010 c 17, s 5(2); (prosp) ibid, s 11(2); Protection of Freedoms, 2012 c 9, sch 1 para 2

sch 5 am—Courts, 2003 c 39, s 65, sch 4 para 14; ibid, s 109(1), sch 8 para 405
> ext—Crim Justice and Police, 2001 c 16, sch 1 pt 1 para 73A

sch 6 am—Land Registration, 2002 c 9, s 133, sch 11, para 40
> rep in pt—Land Registration, 2002 c 9, s 135, sch 13

sch 7 am—SI 2001/2565, art 5; Crim Justice, 2003 c 44, s 304, sch 32 pt 1 para 139; Crim Justice and Immigration, 2008 c 4, s 22(7); Legal Aid, Sentencing and Punishment of Offenders, 2012 c 10, sch 13 para 13; ibid, sch 14 para 4

sch 10 ext—(I of Man) SI 2004/714, art 2(e)
> ext (mods)—SI 2010/2965, art 3; (Jersey) SI 2014/2706, art 2(d) sch
> rep in pt—Armed Forces, 2006 c 52, s 378, sch 17

c 18 **Children's Commissioner for Wales**

c 19 **Armed Forces**
ss 1-12 rep—Armed Forces, 2006 c 52, s 378, sch 17

s 13 rep in pt—Armed Forces, 2006 c 52, s 378, sch 17

ss 14-22 rep—Armed Forces, 2006 c 52, s 378, sch 17

ss 24, 25 rep—Armed Forces, 2006 c 52, s 378, sch 17

s 26 am—Armed Forces, 2006 c 52, s 378, sch 16 para 192
> rep in pt—Armed Forces, 2006 c 52, s 378, sch 16 para 192

s 27 appl—SI 1997/169, rule 43
> am—Armed Forces, 2006 c 52, s 378, sch 16 para 193

s 28 am—Armed Forces, 2006 c 52, s 378, sch 16 para 194
> rep in pt—Armed Forces, 2006 c 52, s 378, sch 16 para 194
> mod—SI 2009/1059, art 205, sch 1

s 29 rep—Armed Forces, 2006 c 52, s 378, sch 17

s 30 am—Constitutional Reform, 2005 c 4, s 40(4), sch 9 pt 1 para 76; Armed Forces, 2006 c 52, s 378, sch 16 para 195

ss 31-33 rep—Armed Forces, 2006 c 52, s 378, sch 17

ss 35, 36 rep in pt—Armed Forces, 2006 c 52, s 378, sch 17

s 37 rep—Armed Forces, 2006 c 52, s 378, sch 17

schs 1-5 rep—Armed Forces, 2006 c 52, s 378, sch 17

sch 6 rep in pt—Sexual Offences, 2003 c 42, s 140, sch 7; Armed Forces, 2006 c 52, s 378, sch 17; Housing and Regeneration, 2008 c 17, s 321, sch 16

c 20 **Social Security Contributions (Share Option)**
s 2 appl—Income Tax (Earnings and Pensions), 2003 c 1, s 481(4)
> am—Income Tax (Earnings and Pensions), 2003 c 1, s 722, sch 6 pt 2 paras 259, 260; Finance, 2003 c 14, s 140, sch 22 paras 55, 56

2001

c 20 *continued*

> s 3 am—Income Tax (Earnings and Pensions), 2003 c 1, s 722, sch 6 pt 2 paras 259, 261; Finance, 2003 c 14, s 140, sch 22 paras 55, 57
>
> s 4 rep—Income Tax (Earnings and Pensions), 2003 c 1, s 724(1), sch 8 pt 1
>
> s 5 am—Income Tax (Earnings and Pensions), 2003 c 1, s 722, sch 6 pt 2 paras 259, 262; Finance, 2003 c 14, s 140, sch 22 paras 55, 58

1st session of the 53rd Parliament

c 21   *Appropriation (No2)*—rep Appropriation, 2003 c 13, s 4, sch 3

c 22   *European Communities (Finance)*—rep European Communities (Finance), 2008 c 1, s 2(2)

c 23   *Human Reproductive Cloning*—rep Human Fertilisation and Embryology, 2008 c 22, s 3(6), sch 8

c 24   **Anti-terrorism, Crime and Security**

> Act mod (temp)—SI 2014/469, art 7(2)(3)
>
> s 2 rep in pt—Legal Aid, Sentencing and Punishment of Offenders, 2012 c 10, sch 5 pt 2
>
> s 17 saved—Communications, 2003 c 21, s 393(2)(d); SIs 2003/1900, arts 2(1), 3(1),sch 1; 2003/3142, art 3(2); Wireless Telegraphy, 2006 c 36, s 111(3)
>
> s 18 appl (mods)—Proceeds of Crime, 2002 c 29, s 442
>
> > appl—Communications, 2003 c 21, s 393(9); SI 2003/1900, arts 2(1), 3(1),sch 1; SI 2003/3142, art 3(2); Identity Cards, 2006 c 15, s 18(3); Wireless Telegraphy, 2006 c 36, s 111(8); Cluster Munitions (Prohibitions), 2010 c 11, s 23(3); Energy, 2013 c 32, sch 9 para 19(2)
> >
> > ext—Pensions, 2004 c 35, ss 83(3), 87(11), 201(11)
>
> s 19 rep in pt—Counter-Terrorism, 2008 c 28, s 20, sch 1 para 1, sch 9
>
> ss 21-32 rep—Prevention of Terrorism, 2005 c 2, s 16(2)(a)(4)
>
> s 33 rep—Immigration, Asylum and Nationality, 2006 c 13, s 55(6), sch 3
>
> s 34 appl—Nationality, Immigration and Asylum, 2002 c 41, s 72(8)
>
> s 36 rep (prosp)—Immigration, 2014 c 22, sch 9 para 18
>
> ss 37, 38 rep—SL(R), 2008 c 12, s 1(1), sch 1 pt 3
>
> s 39 rep in pt—Crim Justice, 2003 c 44, s 332, sch 37 pt 7; Serious Organised Crime and Police, 2005 c 15, s 174(2), sch 17 pt 2
>
> s 47 rep in pt—Anti-terrorism, Crime and Security, 2001 c 24, s 47(9)
>
> ss 50-56 appl (mods)—(Overseas Territories) SI 2005/854, art 3, schs 2, 3, 4A, 5A, 8A
>
> s 53 am—Commrs for Revenue and Customs, 2005 c 11, s 50(6), sch 4 para 87(a)(b)(e); SI 2014/834, sch 2 para 18
>
> > rep in pt—Commrs for Revenue and Customs, 2005 c 11, ss 50(6), 52(2), sch 4 para 87(c)(d), sch 5
> >
> > mod—Serious Crime, 2007 c 27, s 63, sch 6 para 43
>
> s 55 am—Justice (NI), 2002 c 26, s 28(1), sch 7, para 36(a)
>
> s 58 appl (mods)—SI 2007/926, art 2, sch
>
> > mod—SI 2007/926, art 2, sch
> >
> > excl—SI 2007/932, regs 2, 3
>
> ss 59-72 appl (mods)—SI 2007/926, art 2, sch
>
> s 73 appl (mods)—SI 2007/926, art 2, sch
>
> > mod—SI 2007/926, art 2, sch
>
> s 74 appl (mods)—SI 2007/926, art 2, sch
>
> > am—SI 2013/602, sch 2 para 37(2)
>
> s 76 rep (saving)—Energy, 2004 c 20, s 197(9)(10), sch 23
>
> s 77 am—Energy, 2004 c 20, s 69(1), sch 14 para 10(1); ibid, s 77(1)-(4)(5)(a)(b); SI 2008/960, art 22, sch 3; Energy, 2011 c 16, s 105; Energy, 2013 c 32, sch 12 para 32
>
> s 78 rep in pt—Energy, 2004 c 20, s 197(9), sch 23 pt 1
>
> s 79 am—Energy, 2004 c 20, s 69(1), sch 14 para 10(2)
>
> s 80 am—Energy, 2013 c 32, sch 12 para 33
>
> s 80A added—Energy, 2008 c 32, s 101
>
> s 81 am—Justice (NI), 2002 c 26, s 28(1), sch 7, para 36(b)
>
> s 82 rep in pt—Police Reform, 2002 c 30, s 107(2), sch 8
>
> > am—Aviation (Offences), 2003 c 19, s 1(3)
>
> s 91 rep in pt—(prosp) SI 2004/1500, art 35, sch 3
>
> s 94 rep in pt—Police Reform, 2002 c 30, s 107(2), sch 8
>
> s 98 rep in pt—Energy, 2004 c 20, s 197(9), sch 23 pt 1
>
> s 100 am—Railways and Transport Safety, 2003 c 20, s 73, sch 5 para 4(1)(a)(2)(l); Energy, 2004 c 20, s 69(1), sch 14 para 10(3); SI 2013/602, sch 2 para 37(3); Infrastructure, 2015 c 7, s 22(1)(a)

2001

c 24 s 100 *continued*

rep in pt—Railways and Transport Safety, 2003 c 20, s 73, sch 5 para 4(1)(b)(2)(l); Energy, 2004 c 20, s 197(9), sch 23 pt 1; Infrastructure, 2015 c 7, s 22(1)(b)

ss 102, 103 see—SI 2003/3175, art 2

s 104 rep—Anti-terrorism, Crime and Security, 2001 c 24, s 105(1)-(5)

ss 108-110 rep—Bribery, 2010 c 23, s 17, sch 2

s 113 am—Terrorism, 2006 c 11, s 34(b)

s 113A added—Crime (International Co-operation), 2003 c 32, s 53

am—Counter-Terrorism, 2008 c 28, s 75(1)(2)(b)

s 113B added—Crime (International Co-operation), 2003 c 32, s 53

ss 122, 123 rep—SL(R), 2008 c 12, s 1(1), sch 1 pt 3

sch 1 am—Crim Justice, 2003 c 44, s 331, sch 36 pt 4 para 77; Armed Forces, 2006 c 52, s 378, sch 16 para 196; Terrorism, 2006 c 11, s 35; Counter-Terrorism, 2008 c 28, ss 83, 84; Financial Services, 2012 c 21, sch 18 para 93(a); SI 2013/602, sch 2 para 37(4)

rep in pt—Financial Services, 2012 c 21, sch 18 para 93(b)

mod—SI 2009/1059, art 205, sch 1

sch 3 am—Counter-Terrorism, 2008 c 28, s 70

sch 4 rep in pt—Enterprise, 2002 c 40, s 278(2), sch 26; Communications, 2003 c 21, s 406(7), sch 19(1); Pensions, 2004 c 35, s 320, sch 13 pt 1; Nat Health Service (Conseq Provns), 2006 c 43, s 2, sch 1 para 220; Equality, 2006 c 3, s 40, sch 3 para 61(a), sch 4; SI 2009/1941, art 2, sch 1 para 190, sch 2; Postal Services, 2011 c 5, sch 12 para 162(a); Legal Aid, Sentencing and Punishment of Offenders, 2012 c 10, sch 5 para 57(a); Loc Audit and Accountability, 2014 c 2, sch 12 para 48(a)

am—Health and Social Care (Community Health and Standards), 2003 c 43, s 34, sch 4 paras 119, 120; Companies (Audit, Investigations and Community Enterprise), 2004 c 27, s 25(1), sch 2 pt 3 para 31; Nat Health Service (Conseq Provns), 2006 c 43, s 2, sch 1 paras 221, 222; Equality, 2006 c 3, s 40, sch 3 para 61(b); Postal Services, 2011 c 5, sch 12 para 162; Legal Aid, Sentencing and Punishment of Offenders, 2012 c 10, sch 5 para 57(b); Loc Audit and Accountability, 2014 c 2, sch 12 para 48(b)

appl in pt (mods)—SIs 2015/184, sch para 34; 192, sch para 17

sch 5 mod—SIs 2007/926, art 2, sch; 2007/929, regs 2-7

am—SI 2012/1466, art 2(a)

rep in pt—SI 2012/1466, art 2(b),(c)

sch 6 am—Constitutional Reform, 2005 c 4, ss 15(1), 145, sch 4 pt 1 para 300, sch 17 pt 2 para 31; Counter-Terrorism, 2008 c 28, s 91(1)(2)

sch 7 rep in pt—Railways and Transport Safety, 2003 c 20, ss 73, 118, sch 5 para 3, sch 8; Energy, 2004 c 20, s 197(9), sch 23 pt 1; Protection of Freedoms, 2012 c 9, sch 10 pt 4; Anti-social Behaviour, Crime and Policing, 2014 c 12, s 112(2)(b)

c 25　*Consolidated Fund (No 2)*—rep Appropriation, 2003 c 13, s 4, sch 3

2002

c 1　**International Development**

s 1 am—International Development (Gender Equality), 2014 c 9, s 1(2)

s 3 am—International Development (Gender Equality), 2014 c 9, s 1(3)

s 9 am—SI 2005/3225 (W 237), arts 3, 6(2), sch 2 pt 1 para 6(1)

s 14 am—Educ, 2011 c 21, sch 13 para 12

sch 1 am—SI 2002/2469, reg 4, sch 1 pt 1, para 31; Health and Social Care (Community Health and Standards), 2003 c 43, s 34, sch 4 paras 121, 122; Health Protection Agency, 2004 c 17, s 11(1), sch 3 para 16; SI 2005/3225 (W 237), arts 3, 6(2), sch 2 pt 1 para 6(2); Nat Health Service (Conseq Provns), 2006 c 43, s 2, sch 1 para 224; Health and Social Care, 2012 c 7, sch 5 para 100(a); ibid, sch 17 para 9

rep in pt—Health and Social Care (Community Health and Standards), 2003 c 43, ss 190(2), 196, sch 13 para 11, sch 14 pt 7; Health and Social Care, 2012 c 7, sch 5 para 100(b),(c); ibid, sch 7 para 11; (pt prosp) ibid, sch 14 para 82

mod—(W) SI 2007/961 (W 85), art 3, sch

sch 3 rep in pt—Income Tax (Earnings and Pensions), 2003 c 1, s 724(1), sch 8 pt 1; Serious Organised Crime and Police, 2005 c 15, s 174(2), sch 17 pt 2

c 2　**Sex Discrimination (Election Candidates)**

trans of functions—SIs 2007/2914, art 3; 2010/1839, art 3

s 1 rep—Equality, 2010 c 15, s 211, sch 27 pt 1 (subst by SI 2010/2279, sch 2)

2002
c 2 *continued*
        s 3 am—SI 2010/1839, art 7, sch; Equality, 2010 c 15, s 105(3)
        sch 3 am—SI 2007/2914, art 8, sch
c 3   **European Communities (Amendment)**
        s 1 rep in pt—European Union, 2011 c 12, s 14(3)(b)
        s 90 rep—Finance, 2012 c 14, sch 20 para 21
c 4   **Travel Concessions (Eligibility)**
c 5   *Civil Defence (Grant)*—rep Civil Contingencies, 2004 c 36, s 32(2), sch 3
c 6   **Northern Ireland Arms Decommissioning (Amendment)**
c 7   **Homelessness**
        mod—SI 2008/2867, reg 27
        s 1 excl—(E) SI 2005/157, art 3
          am—Housing (W), 2014 anaw 7, sch 3 para 17
        s 3 am—Loc Govt, 2003 c 26, s 127(1), sch 7 para 81; Localism, 2011 c 20, s 153
          rep in pt—Housing (W), 2014 anaw 7, sch 3 para 18
        s 7 rep in pt—(prosp) Localism, 2011 c 20, sch 25 pt 22
        s 8 rep in pt—(prosp) Localism, 2011 c 20, sch 25 pt 22
c 8   **British Overseas Territories**
c 9   **Land Registration**
        appl—Commonhold and Leasehold Reform, 2002 c 15, s 65(2)(a); SIs 2004/1830, rule 3(1);
           2005/3180, art 11; 3181, arts 14(1)(2)(b), 153(1)(2)(b); 2005/3181 art 141L (added
           by 2013/2604, art 3)
        saving—Proceeds of Crime, 2002 c 29, s 47(1)(2)(c)(3)
        ext (saving)—Proceeds of Crime, 2002 c 29, s 248(1)(2)(c)(3)
        trans functions—SI 2011/2436, sch 1 para 3
        s 3 am—Localism, 2011 c 20, s 157(2)
        s 4 rep in pt—SI 2008/2872, art 2
          am—SI 2008/2872, art 2; Charities, 2011 c 25, sch 7 para 94; Localism, 2011 c 20, s
           157(3)
        s 5 am—SI 2011/2436, sch 2 para 4(2)
        s 7 am—SI 2008/2872, art 3
        s 9 appl (mods)—SI 2003/1417, rule 196A
        s 10 appl (mods)—SI 2003/1417, rule 196A
        s 11 appl (mods)—SI 2003/1417, rule 196B
        s 12 appl (mods)—SI 2003/1417, rule 196B
        s 22 appl—SI 2003/1417, rule 39
        s 27 am—(E pt prosp) (W prosp) Commons, 2006 c 26, s 52, sch 5 para 8(1)(2); Localism,
           2011 c 20, s 157(4)
        s 29 appl (mods)—SI 2003/1417 rule 196B
        s 33 am—(E pt prosp) (W prosp) Commons, 2006 c 26, s 52, sch 5 para 8(1)(3); Localism,
           2011 c 20, s 157(5)
        s 62 transtl provns—SI 2003/1953, art 15
          am—SI 2011/2436, sch 2 para 4(2)
        s 73 am—SI 2013/1036, sch 1 para 226
        s 75 am—Crime and Cts, 2013 c 22, sch 9 para 52
        s 76 am—Crime and Cts, 2013 c 22, sch 9 para 52
        s 80 am—SI 2011/2436, sch 2 para 4(2)
        s 87 am—Deregulation, 2015 c 20, sch 6 para 2(16)(a)
          rep in pt—Deregulation, 2015 c 20, sch 6 para 2(16)(b)-(d)
        s 91 am—Co-operatives and Community Benefit Societies, 2003 c 15, s 5(8); SIs
           2005/1906, art 10(1), sch 1 para 17; 2008/948, art 3, sch 1; Co-operative and
           Community Benefit Societies, 2014 c 14, sch 4 para 80
        s 93 am—SI 2011/2436, sch 2 para 4(2)
        s 99 am—SI 2011/2436, sch 2 para 4(2)
        s 100 am—SI 2011/2436, sch 2 para 4(2); (prosp) Infrastructure, 2015 c 7, sch 5 para 18
        s 101 am—SI 2011/2436, sch 2 para 4(2)
        s 102 am—SI 2011/2436, sch 2 para 4(2)
        s 105 am—Infrastructure, 2015 c 7, s 35
        s 106 am—SI 2009/1941, art 2, sch 1; (prosp) Infrastructure, 2015 c 7, sch 5 para 19
        s 107 rep—SI 2013/1036, sch 1 para 227
        s 108 am—SI 2013/1036, sch 1 para 228
        s 109 rep—SI 2013/1036, sch 1 para 229
        s 110 am—SI 2013/1036, sch 1 para 230
        s 111 am—SI 2013/1036, sch 1 para 231

2002
c 9 *continued*

s 112 am—SI 2013/1036, sch 1 para 232
ss 113, 114 rep—SI 2013/1036, sch 1 paras 233, 234
s 118 am—SI 2011/2436, sch 2 para 4(2)
s 121 subst—SI 2009/1941, art 2, sch 1
am—SI 2011/2436, sch 2 para 4(2)
s 125 am—Civil Partnership, 2004 c 33, s 261(1), sch 27 para 167
s 127 am—Constitutional Reform, 2005 c 4, s 15(1), sch 4 pt 1 paras 301, 302; SI
2011/2436, sch 2 para 4(2); Infrastructure, 2015 c 7, s 36(1)
s 128 am—SIs 2011/2436, sch 2 para 4(3); 2013/1036, sch 1 para 235(a)
rep in pt—SI 2013/1036, sch 1 para 235(b)
s 130 am—SI 2011/2436, sch 2 para 4(2)
s 132 am—Localism, 2011 c 20, s 157(6); Crime and Cts, 2013 c 22, sch 9 para 52
rep in pt—SI 2013/1036, sch 1 para 236
s 134 am—SI 2011/2436, sch 2 para 4(2)
sch 1 am—Localism, 2011 c 20, s 157(7)
sch 3 am—(W prosp) Commons, 2006 c 26, s 52, sch 5 para 8(1)(4); Localism, 2011 c 20, s
157(8)
sch 4 excl—Commonhold and Leasehold Reform, 2002 c 15, s 6(2)
sch 5 am—SIs 2011/2436, sch 2 para 4(2); 2013/1036, sch 1 para 237(a)(b)
rep in pt—SI 2013/1036, sch 1 para 237(c)
sch 6 appl —SI 2003/1417, rule 31(4)
am—SI 2011/1133, regs 50-53
sch 7 am—SI 2011/2436, sch 2 para 4(2); (prosp) Infrastructure, 2015 c 7, sch 5 para 20
sch 9 rep—SI 2013/1036, sch 1 para 238
sch 11 rep in pt—(prosp) Proceeds of Crime, 2002 c 29, s 457, sch 12; (prosp) Commons,
2006 c 26, s 53, sch 6; Charities, 2011 c 25, sch 10
sch 12 am—SI 2003/1953, art 17
excl—SI 2003/1953, arts 7(2), 24(1)
c 10   *Consolidated Fund*—rep Appropriation, 2004 c 9, s 4, sch 3
c 11   **Office of Communications**
saved—Communications, 2003 c 21, ss 393(6)(b), 408; SI 2003/1900, arts 2(1), 3(1),sch 1;
SI 2003/3142, art 3(2)
s 1 ext (mods)—(Guernsey) SI 2003/3195, art 5, sch 1 para 1; (Jersey) SI 2003/3197, art 5,
sch 1 para 1; (I of Man) SI 2003/3198, art 5, sch 1 para 1
s 2 rep—Communications, 2003 c 21, s 406(1)(7), sch 17 para 171, sch 19(1)
ss 4-6 rep—Communications, 2003 c 21, s 406(1)(7), sch 17 para 171, sch 19(1)
s 7 ext (mods)—(Guernsey) SI 2003/3195, art 5, sch 1 para 3; (Jersey) SI 2003/3197, art 5,
sch 1 para 2; (I of Man) SI 2003/3198, art 5, sch 1 para 2
sch appl—Communications, 2003 c 21, s 400(8)
ext —Communications, 2003 c 21, s 12(13)(14)
ext (mods)—(Guernsey) SI 2003/3195, art 5, sch 1 para 4; (Jersey) SI 2003/3197, art 5,
sch 1 para 3; (I of Man) SI 2003/3198, art 5, sch 1 para 3
rep in pt—Communications, 2003 c 21, s 406(1)(7), sch 17 para 172(1)(2)(a)-(d), sch
19(1)
am—Communications, 2003 c 21, s 406(1), sch 17 para 172(1)(3)(4); Postal Services,
2011 c 5, sch 12 para 168; SIs 2011/1210, sch 1 para 3; 2012/2404, sch 2 para 46;
Enterprise and Regulatory Reform, 2013 c 24, sch 15 para 40
c 12   **Football (Disorder) (Amendment)**
ss 1-3 rep—Violent Crime Reduction, 2006 c 38, s 65, sch 5
c 13   **Electoral Fraud (Northern Ireland)**
ss 2, 3 rep in pt—Electoral Admin, 2006 c 22, s 74, sch 2
s 6 rep in pt—(prosp) Political Parties and Elections, 2009 c 12, s 39, sch 7
s 8 am—Electoral Admin, 2006 c 22, s 15(9)
c 14   **National Heritage**
s 16 am—Sovereign Grant, 2011 c 15, sch 1 para 33
c 15   **Commonhold and Leasehold Reform**
Pt 1 (ss 1-70) appl—Disability Discrimination, 1995 c 50, ss 22A, 24L
s 1 am—SI 2009/1941, art 2, sch 1 para 194(2)
s 5 am—SI 2009/1941, art 2, sch 1 para 194(3)
s 8 am—SI 2009/1941, art 2, sch 1 para 194(4)
s 13 am—SI 2009/1941, art 2, sch 1 para 194(5)
s 31 am—SI 2009/1941, art 2, sch 1 para 194(6)
s 34 am—SI 2009/1941, art 2, sch 1 para 194(7)

2002
c 15 *continued*

    s 36 am—SI 2009/1941, art 2, sch 1 para 194(8)
    s 37 am—SI 2009/1941, art 2, sch 1 para 194(9)
    s 40 am—SI 2009/1941, art 2, sch 1 para 194(10)
    s 51 am—SI 2009/1941, art 2, sch 1 para 194(11)
    s 57 am—SI 2009/1941, art 2, sch 1 para 194(12)
    s 58 am—SI 2009/1941, art 2, sch 1 para 194(13)
    s 61 am—Civil Partnership, 2004 c 33, s 82, sch 9 pt 2 para 24
    s 62 am—Housing and Regeneration, 2008 c 17, s 319(1)(2)
    s 65 trans of functions—SI 2011/2436, sch 1 para 4
        am—SI 2011/2436, sch 2 para 5
    s 66 am—Crime and Cts, 2013 c 22, sch 9 para 52
    s 69 am—SI 2009/1941, art 2, sch 1 para 194(14)
    Pt 2, Ch 1 (ss 71-113) appl—(E) SI 2003/2099, reg 3, sch 2 para 4(1); (W) SI 2004/681 (W
        69), reg 3, sch 2 para 4(1)
    s 73 am—SI 2009/1941, art 2, sch 1 para 194(15)
    s 74 am—SI 2009/1941, art 2, sch 1 para 194(16)
    s 75 appl—(E) SI 2003/1988, regs 3(2)(j), 8(1), sch 1, Note 1
    s 76 am—Civil Partnership, 2004 c 33, s 81, sch 8 para 64
    s 77 am—Civil Partnership, 2004 c 33, s 81, sch 8 para 65
    s 78 am—SI 2009/1941, art 2, sch 1 para 194(17)
    s 79 rep in pt—SI 2013/1036, sch 1 para 132
    s 84 am—SI 2013/1036, sch 1 para 133
    s 85 am—SI 2013/1036, sch 1 para 134(a)
        rep in pt—SI 2013/1036, sch 1 para 134(b)
    s 87 rep in pt—SI 2003/2096, arts 4, 6, sch pt 1 paras 38, 39(a)
        am—SIs 2003/2096, arts 4, 6, sch pt 1 paras 38, 39(b); 2009/1941, art 2, sch 1 para
        194(18)
    s 88 am—SI 2013/1036, sch 1 para 135
    s 91 appl—(E) SI 2003/1988, regs 4(e), 8(2), sch 2, Note 3
    s 94 am—SI 2013/1036, sch 1 para 136
    s 99 am—SI 2013/1036, sch 1 para 137
    s 104 rep—Commonhold and Leasehold Reform, 2002 c 15, s 180, sch 14
    s 105 rep in pt—SI 2003/2096, arts 4, 6, sch pt 1 paras 38, 40(a)
        am—SIs 2003/2096, arts 4, 6, sch pt 1 paras 38, 40(b); 2009/1941, art 2, sch 1 para
        194(19)
    s 107 am—Crime and Cts, 2013 c 22, sch 9 para 52
    s 112 am—SI 2013/1036, sch 1 para 138
    s 141 rep (prosp)—Housing and Regeneration, 2008 c 17, s 321, sch 16
    s 144 rep in pt—SI 2010/866, art 5, sch 2
    s 156 rep in pt—(prosp) Housing and Regeneration, 2008 c 17, s 321, sch 16
    s 159 am—SI 2013/1036, sch 1 para 139(a)
    s 160 rep in pt—SI 2013/1036, sch 1 para 140
    s 164 appl—(W) SI 2005/1354 (W 102), reg 3, sch
    s 168 am—SI 2013/1036, sch 1 para 141
    s 172 am—SI 2013/1036, sch 1 para 142
    s 175 am—SI 2009/1307, art 5, sch 1 para 269
        rep in pt—SIs 2009/1307, art 5, sch 1 para 269; 2010/22, art 5, sch 2; 2013/1036, sch
        1 para 143
    Pt 2, Ch 6A (ss 176A-176C) added—SI 2013/1036, sch 1 para 144
    sch 1 am—SI 2009/1941, art 2, sch 1 para 194(20)
    sch 3 am—Companies, 2006 c 46, s 1283; SI 2009/1941, art 2, sch 1 para 195
        rep in pt—SI 2009/1941, art 2, sch 1 para 195
    sch 6 am—Civil Partnership, 2004 c 33, s 81, sch 8 para 66; SI 2013/1036, sch 1 para 145
        ext—Civil Partnership, 2004 c 33, ss 246, 247, sch 21 para 52
    sch 7 am—SI 2013/1036, sch 1 para 146(b)
        rep in pt—SI 2013/1036, sch 1 para 146(a)
    sch 10 rep in pt—(prosp) Housing and Regeneration, 2008 c 17, s 321, sch 16
    sch 11 am—Crime and Cts, 2013 c 22, sch 9 para 69; SI 2013/1036, sch 1 para 147
    sch 12 am—SI 2013/1036, sch 1 para 148
c 16   **State Pension Credit**
    appl—SIs 1987/1971, reg 25(1)(c); 2002/2008, reg 4
    appl (mods)—SI 2010/1925, reg 3, sch
    s 1 appl—(E) SI 1992/2977, sch 3 pt 1 para 28H

2002
c 16 s 1 *continued*
am—(prosp) Welfare Reform, 2012 c 5, sch 4 paras 2, 3; (prosp) ibid, s 75
s 2 am—Civil Partnership, 2004 c 33, s 254(1), sch 24 pt 13 paras 140, 141; (prosp)
Welfare Reform, 2012 c 5, s 74(2)
s 3 mod—SI 2002/1792, reg 8, sch III, para 1(1)(2)
am—Civil Partnership, 2004 c 33, s 254(1), sch 24 pt 13 para 140; (6.4.2024) Pensions,
2007 c 22, s 13, sch 1 para 44; Pensions, 2014 c 19, sch 12 para 89
s 3ZA added —Pensions, 2014 c 19, sch 12 para 90
s 3A added (prosp)—Welfare Reform, 2012 c 5, sch 4 para 4
s 4 mod—SI 2002/1792, reg 8, sch III, para 1(1)(3)
am—Civil Partnership, 2004 c 33, s 254(1), sch 24 pt 13 para 140; (prosp) Welfare
Reform, 2012 c 5, sch 2 para 64
s 5 mod—SI 2002/1792, reg 8, sch III, para 1(1)(4)
am—Civil Partnership, 2004 c 33, s 254(1), sch 24 pt 13 para 140
s 6 am—Civil Partnership, 2004 c 33, s 254(1), sch 24 pt 13 para 140; Pensions, 2014 c 19,
s 28(1)(2)
s 7 am—SI 2006/343, art 2, sch; (prosp) Welfare Reform, 2012 c 5, sch 4 para 5; Pensions,
2014 c 19, sch 12 para 43
s 9 am—Civil Partnership, 2004 c 33, s 254(1), sch 24 pt 13 para 140; Pensions, 2008 c 30,
s 29(2)(b); ibid, s 105(1)-(4); (cond) Pensions, 2014 c 19, s 29(2)(b)
restr—Pensions, 2014 c 19, s 29(2)(a)
mod—Pensions, 2014 c 19, s 28(3)
s 12 am—(prosp) Welfare Reform, 2012 c 5, sch 4 para 6
s 15 rep in pt—(pt prosp) Welfare Reform, 2012 c 5, sch 14 pt 1
s 16 am—SI 2002/1792, reg 16; Sovereign Grant, 2011 c 15, sch 1 para 32; Pensions, 2014
c 19, sch 11 para 15, sch 12 para 44
s 17 am—Income Tax (Earnings and Pensions), 2003 c 1, s 722, sch 6 pt 2 para 263; Civil
Partnership, 2004 c 33, s 254(1), sch 24 pt 13 paras 142(1)-(3)(5), 143; SI
2006/343, art 2, sch; (prosp) Welfare Reform, 2012 c 5, s 74(3); (prosp) ibid, sch
4 para 7; SIs 2014/560, sch 1 para 28(2); 2014/3229, sch 5 para 14(2)
rep in pt—Civil Partnership, 2004 c 33, ss 254(1), 261(4), sch 24 pt 13 para 142(1)(4),
sch 30; (prosp) Welfare Reform, 2012 c 5, sch 14 pt 1; SIs 2014/560, sch 1
para 28(3); 2014/3229, sch 5 para 14(3)
s 18A added—Welfare Reform, 2009 c 24, s 27(1)(2)
rep in pt—(prosp) Welfare Reform, 2012 c 5, sch 14 pt 1
s 19 am—Welfare Reform, 2009 c 24, s 27(1)(3); (prosp) Welfare Reform, 2012 c 5, s
75(2)
sch 2 rep in pt—Courts, 2003 c 39, s 109(3), sch 10; Income Tax (Earnings and Pensions),
2003 c 1, s 724(1), sch 8 pt 1; Asylum and Immigration (Treatment of
Claimants, etc), 2004 c 19, s 47, sch 4; (prosp) Welfare Reform, 2007 c 5, s 67,
sch 8; Welfare Reform, 2009 c 24, s 58, sch 7 pt 3; (prosp) ibid, sch 7 pt 1;
(prosp) Welfare Reform, 2012 c 5, sch 4 para 8; (pt prosp) ibid, sch 14 pt 1;
(prosp) ibid, sch 14 pt 12
c 17 **National Health Service Reform and Health Care Professions**
ext (except ss 6, 9, 24, schs 4, 5)—(Is of Scilly) SI 2003/50, art 2
ss 1, 2 rep in pt—Nat Health Service (Conseq Provns), 2006 c 43, s 6, sch 4
s 3 rep—Nat Health Service (Conseq Provns), 2006 c 43, s 6, sch 4
s 4 rep in pt—Health and Social Care (Community Health and Standards), 2003 c 43, s 196,
sch 14 pt 4; Nat Health Service (Conseq Provns), 2006 c 43, s 6, sch 4
s 5 rep—Nat Health Service (Conseq Provns), 2006 c 43, s 6, sch 4
s 6 rep—Nat Health Service (Conseq Provns), 2006 c 43, s 6, sch 4
s 7 rep—Nat Health Service (Conseq Provns), 2006 c 43, s 6, sch 4
ss 8-10 rep—Nat Health Service (Conseq Provns), 2006 c 43, s 6, sch 4
ss 11-14 rep—Health and Social Care (Community Health and Standards), 2003 c 43, s 196,
sch 14 pt 2
s 15 rep—Nat Health Service (Conseq Provns), 2006 c 43, s 6, sch 4
s 16 rep—Nat Health Service (Conseq Provns), 2006 c 43, s 6, sch 4
s 17 rep—Nat Health Service (Conseq Provns), 2006 c 43, s 6, sch 4
s 18 rep—Nat Health Service (Conseq Provns), 2006 c 43, s 6, sch 4
s 19 am—Health and Social Care (Community Health and Standards), 2003 c 43, s 31(1)(5)
rep in pt—Nat Health Service (Conseq Provns), 2006 c 43, s 6, sch 4; Loc Govt and
Public Involvement in Health, 2007 c 28, s 241, sch 18
s 20 rep—Nat Health Service (Conseq Provns), 2006 c 43, s 6, sch 4
s 21 rep—Nat Health Service (Conseq Provns), 2006 c 43, s 6, sch 4

2002

c 17 *continued*

s 22 rep in pt—(prosp) Health (W), 2003 c 4, s 7, sch 3 para 16, sch 4; Nat Health Service (Conseq Provns), 2006 c 43, s 6, sch 4

　　　am—Nat Health Service (Conseq Provns), 2006 c 43, s 2, sch 1 para 226

s 23 rep—Nat Health Service (Conseq Provns), 2006 c 43, s 6, sch 4

s 24 rep—Nat Health Service (Conseq Provns), 2006 c 43, s 6, sch 4

Pt 2 (ss 25-35) am—Health and Social Care, 2012 c 7, s 222(5)

s 25 power to mod—Health, 1999 c 8, s 60(1)

　　　am—Health and Social Care, 2008 c 14, ss 113(2)(3), 127, sch 10 paras 16, 17(1)-(3); SI 2010/231, art 68, sch 4; Health and Social Care, 2012 c 7, ss 220(6), 222, 223(1), (2); ibid, s 224(2); ibid, sch 15 paras 56(b), 62(a); (prosp) Health and Social Care (Safety and Quality), 2015 c 28, s 5(1)

　　　rep in pt—Health and Social Care, 2008 c 14, s 127, sch 10 para 17(1)(4), sch 15

　　　excl—Female Genital Mutilation, 2003 c 31, s 5B(12)(a)(b)

s 25A added—Health and Social Care, 2012 c 7, s 224(1)

s 25B added —Health and Social Care, 2012 c 7, s 225(1)

s 25C added—Health and Social Care, 2012 c 7, s 227

ss 25D-25F added—Health and Social Care, 2012 c 7, s 228

ss 25G-25I added—Health and Social Care, 2012 c 7, s 229(1)

s 26 am—SI 2007/289, art 67, sch 1; Health and Social Care, 2008 c 14, s 115; Health and Social Care, 2012 c 7, sch 15 paras 62(b)(i), 63; ibid, s 229

　　　rep in pt—Health and Social Care, 2008 c 14, s 116(2), sch 15; SI 2010/231, art 68, sch 4; Health and Social Care, 2012 c 7, sch 15 para 64

s 26A added—Health and Social Care, 2008 c 14, s 116(1)

　　　am—Health and Social Care, 2012 c 7, sch 15 paras 62(c), 65; ibid, s 223(3),(5); ibid, s 229(6); (1.2.2016) ibid, s 223(4)

s 26B added—Health and Social Care, 2008 c 14, s 117

　　　am—Health and Social Care, 2012 c 7, sch 15 para 62(d); ibid, s 223(6); ibid, s 229(7)-(9)

s 27 am—Health and Social Care, 2012 c 7, sch 15 paras 62(e)(i), 63; (prosp) ibid, s 223(7), (8)(a)

　　　rep in pt—(prosp) Health and Social Care, 2012 c 7, s 223(8)(b)

s 28 am—Health and Social Care, 2012 c 7, s 225(2); ibid, sch 15 para 62(f)

s 29 am—SIs 2002/3135, art 16(1), sch 1 pt I, para 13; 2004/1771, art 3, sch pt 1 para 1; 2005/848, arts 28, 29, sch 1 pt 2 para 13, sch 2; 2011, art 49, sch 6 pt 1 para 4; 2007/289, art 67, sch 1; Health and Social Care, 2008 c 14, s 118(1)(2)(a)(e)-(g)(3)(4); SI 2010/231, art 68, sch 4; Health and Social Care, 2012 c 7, s 213(7)(j); ibid, sch 15 paras 62(g)(i), 63; ibid, s 223(9),(10); SI 2015/794, art 18(1)-(8)

　　　rep in pt—(transtl provns) Health and Social Care, 2008 c 14, s 118(1)(2)(c)(5)(6), sch 15; Health and Social Care, 2012 c 7, sch 15 para 73(1)

s 29A added—SI 2015/794, art 18(9)

s 35 rep (prosp)—Health, 2006 c 28, s 80, sch 9

s 36 rep—Nat Health Service (Conseq Provns), 2006 c 43, s 6, sch 4; SI 2006/1407, art 3, sch 2

s 38 rep in pt—Nat Health Service (Conseq Provns), 2006 c 43, s 6, sch 4; SI 2006/1407, arts 2, 3, schs 1, 2; (pt prosp) Health and Social Care, 2012 c 7, s 223(11); ibid, s 225(3)

　　　am—(pt prosp) Health and Social Care, 2012 c 7, s 223(12),(13); ibid, s 224(3); (pt prosp) ibid, s 226(9); ibid, s 230(5)

s 42 rep in pt—Crim Justice, 2003 c 44, s 332, sch 37 pt 11; Nat Health Service (Conseq Provns), 2006 c 43, s 6, sch 4

sch 1 rep —Health and Social Care, 2012 c 7, sch 5 para 102

sch 2 rep—Health and Social Care, 2012 c 7, sch 5 para 103

sch 3 rep in pt—Health and Social Care (Community Health and Standards), 2003 c 43, s 196, sch 14 pt 4; Nat Health Service (Conseq Provns), 2006 c 43, s 6, sch 4; SI 2006/1407, art 2, sch 1; Health and Social Care, 2012 c 7, sch 21 para 3(4)

sch 4 rep—Nat Health Service (Conseq Provns), 2006 c 43, s 6, sch 4

sch 5 rep in pt—(EW) Health (W), 2003 c 4, s 7(2), sch 4; Health and Social Care (Community Health and Standards), 2003 c 43, s 196, sch 14 pt 2; Public Services Ombudsman (W), 2005 c 10, s 39(2), sch 7; Nat Health Service (Conseq Provns), 2006 c 43, s 6, sch 4; Health, 2006 c 28, s 80, sch 9; SI 2006/1407, art 3, sch 2; Corporation Tax, 2010 c 4, s 1181, sch 3 pt 1

2002

c 17 *continued*

sch 6 rep in pt—Nat Health Service (Conseq Provns), 2006 c 43, s 6, sch 4; Health, 2006 c 28, s 80, sch 8 para 51, sch 9; SI 2006/1407, art 2, sch 1; Loc Govt and Public Involvement in Health, 2007 c 28, s 241, sch 18

sch 7 am—Health, 2006 c 28, s 80, sch 8 para 52; Health and Social Care, 2008 c 14, sS 114, 127, sch 10 para 19; Health and Social Care, 2012 c 7, s 223(14); ibid, s 224(4); ibid, sch 15 paras 63, 65, 62(h), (j), 63, 66; ibid, s 226(2)-(5),(6)(a), (b)(ii), (7), (8)

rep in pt—Health and Social Care, 2008 c 14, s 166, sch 15; Health and Social Care, 2012 c 7, s 224(5); (pt prosp) ibid, s 226(6)(b)(i)

sch 8 rep in pt—Health and Social Care (Community Health and Standards), 2003 c 43, s 196, sch 14 pts 2, 4; (EW) Health (W), 2003 c 4, s 7(2), sch 4; Nat Health Service (Conseq Provns), 2006 c 43, s 6, sch 4; SI 2006/1407, art 3, sch 2

c 18   *Appropriation*—rep Appropriation, 2004 c 9, s 4, sch 3

-c 19   **National Insurance Contributions**

sch 1 rep in pt—(prosp) Pensions, 2007 c 22, s 27, sch 7 pt 7; (prosp) Welfare Reform, 2007 c 5, s 67, sch 8

am—Welfare Reform, 2009 c 24, s 12(6)

c 20   *Industrial and Provident Societies*—rep Co-operative and Community Benefit Societies, 2014 c 14, sch 7

c 21   **Tax Credits**

appl—(S) Crim Justice, 2003 c 44, s 53(3)

appl (mods)—SI 2014/1230, reg 12(2)-(6); ibid, reg 12A(2) Sch 1626, reg 4(1) (added by SI 2014/1626, reg 4(1))

see—SI 2011/2910, art 2

Pt 1 (ss 1-48) rep (prosp)—Welfare Reform, 2012 c 5, sch 14 pt 1

appl (mods)—SIs 2003/653, regs 4, 5; 2003/742, regs 3-21

appl—(E) SI 2000/1280, reg 4(1)(e)

s 2 subst—Commrs for Revenue and Customs, 2005 c 11, s 50(6), sch 4 paras 88, 92

funct exercisable concurrently—SI 2014/3280, art 3

s 3 am—Civil Partnership, 2004 c 33, s 254(1), sch 24 pt 14 para 144

rep in pt—Corporation Tax, 2009 c 4, s 1326, sch 3 pt 1

s 4 am—Civil Partnership, 2004 c 33, s 254(1), sch 24 pt 14 paras 145, 146

s 5 excl—SI 2005/773, art 6

s 6 am—SI 2005/828, art 2

s 7 am—SI 2013/386, sch para 2

s 7 appl—Child Trust Funds, 2004 c 6, s 9(6)

s 11 am—Civil Partnership, 2004 c 33, s 254(1), sch 24 pt 14 para 145

s 17 am—Civil Partnership, 2004 c 33, s 254(1), sch 24 pt 14 paras 145, 146; SI 2013/386, sch para 3(a)-(d)

rep in pt—SI 2013/386, sch para 3(e)

s 18 appl—Child Trust Funds, 2004 c 6, s 9(5)

am—SIs 2013/386, sch para 4(a)(c)(d)(iv); 2014/886, art 2(2)

rep in pt—SI 2013/386, sch para 4(b)(d)(i)-(iii)

s 19 appl—Child Trust Funds, 2004 c 6, s 9(5)

am—SIs 2009/56, art 3, sch 1 para 313; 2013/386, sch para 5; 2014/886, art 2(3)

s 20 appl—Child Trust Funds, 2004 c 6, s 9(5)

am—SIs 2013/386, sch para 6; 2014/886, art 2(4)(5)

s 21 appl—Child Trust Funds, 2004 c 6, s 9(5)

am—SI 2013/386, sch para 7

ss 21A, 21B added—SI 2014/886, art 2(6)

s 23 am—SIs 2013/386, sch para 8(a)(b)(ii); 2014/886, art 2(7)

rep in pt—SI 2013/386, sch para 8(b)(i)

s 24 am—Civil Partnership, 2004 c 33, s 254(1), sch 24 pt 14 para 145

s 25 appl—SI 2002/2014, reg 30(3)

am—Income Tax (Earnings and Pensions), 2003 c 1, s 722, sch 6 pt 2 paras 264, 265(1)-(3)

rep in pt—Income Tax (Earnings and Pensions), 2003 c 1, ss 722, 724(1), sch 6 pt 2 paras 264, 265(1)(4), sch 8 pt 1; Finance, 2008 c 9, s 113, sch 36 para 90

s 28 am—SIs 2013/386, sch para 9(a)(b); 2014/886, art 2(8)

rep in pt—SI 2013/386, sch para 9(c)(d)

s 29 am—Income Tax (Earnings and Pensions), 2003 c 1, s 722, sch 6 pt 2 paras 264, 266; Finance, 2009 c 10, s 110, sch 58 para 8; SI 2013/386, sch para 10

s 30 am—SIs 2013/386, sch para 11; 2014/886, art 2(8)

2002

c 21 *continued*

 s 31 am—SI 2014/886, art 2(9)

 s 32 am—Civil Partnership, 2004 c 33, s 254(1), sch 24 pt 14 para 145

 s 35 am—(prosp) Welfare Reform, 2012 c 5, s 124

 s 36 rep in pt—Finance, 2007 c 11, s 84, sch 22 paras 3, 14, sch 27; (prosp) Welfare Reform, 2012 c 5, sch 14 pt 12

 ss 36A-36D added —Welfare Reform, 2012 c 5, s 120(2)

 s 36A rep in pt—(prosp) Welfare Reform, 2012 c 5, s 121(2); (prosp) ibid, sch 14 pt 12

 s 36B rep in pt—(prosp) Welfare Reform, 2012 c 5, sch 14 pt 12

 s 38 am—Welfare Reform, 2012 c 5, s 120(3); SIs 2013/386, sch para 12; 2014/886, art 2(10)(11)

 s 39 am—SIs 2002/3196, regs 4, 5; 2009/56, art 3, sch 1 para 314(3); 2014/886, art 2(13)(b)

  rep in pt—SIs 2009/56, art 3, sch 1 para 314(2)(4); 2014/886, art 2(12)(13)(a)

 s 39A added—SI 2014/885, art 2(2)

 s 40 rep in pt—Commrs for Revenue and Customs, 2005 c 11, ss 50(6), 52(2), sch 4 paras 89, 92, sch 5

 s 48 am—Civil Partnership, 2004 c 33, s 254(1), sch 24 pt 14 para 147(1)-(3); SI 2013/386, sch para 13

  rep in pt—Civil Partnership, 2004 c 33, ss 254(1), 261(4), sch 24 pt 14 para 147(2), sch 30; SI 2009/56, art 3, sch 1 para 315

 s 49 rep in pt—(EW, S) Child Benefit, 2005 c 6, s 3(a), sch 2 pt 1; (NI) ibid, sch 2 pt 2

 s 52 am—Constitutional Reform and Governance, 2010 c 25, s 19, sch 2 para 13

 s 53 subst—Commrs for Revenue and Customs, 2005 c 11, s 50(6), sch 4 paras 90, 92

 s 63 appl—SI 2002/2173, reg 11(5)(6)

  am—SIs 2008/2833, art 6, sch 3; 2009/56, art 3, sch 1 para 316; 2012/533, art 2(2)

  rep in pt—SI 2009/56, art 3, sch 1 para 316(5)(b)(8)

 s 65 am—SI 2010/976, art 15, sch 18

 s 66 am—Welfare Reform, 2012 c 5, s 120(4)

 s 67 rep (prosp)—Welfare Reform, 2012 c 5, sch 14 pt 12

  am—Welfare Reform, 2012 c 5, s 120(5)

 sch 2 am—SIs 2009/56, art 3, sch 1 paras 317-320; 2013/386, sch para 14

 sch 3 rep in pt—Courts, 2003 c 39, s 109(3), sch 10; Income Tax (Earnings and Pensions), 2003 c 1, s 724(1), sch 8 pt 1; (pt prosp) Welfare Reform, 2007 c 5, s 67, sch 8; (prosp) Welfare Reform, 2009 c 24, s 58, sch 7 pt 1; ibid, s 58, sch 7 pt 2

 sch 4 rep in pt—Asylum and Immigration (Treatment of Claimants, etc), 2004 c 19, s 47, sch 4; Welfare Reform, 2012 c 5, s 107(3)

 sch 5 am—Children, 2004 c 31, s 63; Child Maintenance and Other Payments, 2008 c 6, s 57, sch 7 para 4; SI 2013/1465, sch 1 para 8

  rep in pt—Commrs for Revenue and Customs, 2005 c 11, ss 50(6), 52(2), sch 4 paras 91, 92, sch 5; Educ and Skills, 2008 c 25, s 169, sch 1 para 78; ibid, sch 2; Welfare Reform, 2012 c 5, sch 14 pt 13

c 22 **Employment**

 s 5 rep—Commrs for Revenue and Customs, 2005 c 11, ss 50(6), 52(2), sch 4 para 93, sch 5

 s 6 rep in pt—Work and Families, 2006 c 18, s 15, sch 2

 s 7 am—Work and Families, 2006 c 18, s 11, sch 1 para 50; Children and Families, 2014 c 6, sch 7 para 51(2)(a)(3)(a)(i)(3)(b)(i); ibid, sch 7 para 51(2)(b)(3)(a)(ii)(b)(ii)(4)

 s 8 am—Work and Families, 2006 c 18, s 11, sch 1 para 51; Children and Families, 2014 c 6, sch 7 para 52(2)(a)(3)(a)(i)(b)(i)(c)(i); ibid, sch 7 para 52(2)(b)(3)(a)(ii)(b)(ii)(c)(ii)

 s 10 am—Work and Families, 2006 c 18, s 11, sch 1 para 52; Children and Families, 2014 c 6, sch 7 para 53(2)(a)(3)(a); ibid, sch 7 para 53(2)(b)(3)(b)

 s 11 am—Work and Families, 2006 c 18, s 11, sch 1 para 53; Children and Families, 2014 c 6, sch 7 para 54(a); ibid, sch 7 para 54(b)

 s 12 am—Work and Families, 2006 c 18, s 11, sch 1 para 54; Children and Families, 2014 c 6, sch 7 para 55(3)(5)

  rep in pt—Children and Families, 2014 c 6, sch 7 para 55(2)(4)(6)

 s 13 am—Work and Families, 2006 c 18, s 11, sch 1 para 55; SI 2008/2656, reg 2; Children and Families, 2014 c 6, sch 7 para 56(a); ibid, sch 7 para 56(b)

  rep in pt—SI 2012/2007, sch para 66

 s 14 am—Work and Families, 2006 c 18, s 11, sch 1 para 56; Children and Families, 2014 c 6, sch 7 para 57(2)(a)(3)(a); ibid, sch 7 para 57(2)(b)(3)(b)

 s 15 am—Work and Families, 2006 c 18, s 11, sch 1 para 57; Children and Families, 2014 c 6, sch 7 para 58(d); Pensions, 2014 c 19, sch 13 para 72

2002

c 22 s 15 *continued*

    rep in pt—Children and Families, 2014 c 6, sch 7 para 58(a)(b)

s 18 rep—Work and Families, 2006 c 18, s 15, sch 2

s 24 rep in pt—Employment, 2008 c 24, s 20, sch pt 1

ss 29-33 rep—Employment, 2008 c 24, s 20, s 1, sch pt 1

s 41 rep —Employment Relations, 2004 c 24, s 57(2), sch 2

s 42 rep—Equality, 2010 c 15, s 211, sch 27 pt 1 (subst by SI 2010/2279, sch 2)

s 49 rep (prosp)—Welfare Reform, 2012 c 5, sch 14 pt 1

s 51 rep in pt—Employment, 2008 c 24, s 20, sch pt 1

s 55 am—Work and Families, 2006 c 18, s 11, sch 1 para 58; Children and Families, 2014 c
    6, sch 7 para 59(a); ibid, sch 7 para 59(b)(c)

sch 1 am—SI 2009/56, art 3, sch 1 paras 321-324
    rep in pt—SI 2009/56, art 3, sch 1 para 325

schs 2, 3 rep—Employment, 2008 c 24, s 20, s 1, sch pt 1

sch 4 rep in pt—Tax Credits, 2002 c 21, s 60, sch 6; Employment, 2008 c 24, s 20, s 1, sch
    pt 1

    am—SIs 2003/1660, reg 39(2), sch 5 para 4; 2003/1661, reg 39, sch 5 para 4;
        2003/1673, regs 3(2), 31(3); Employment Relations, 2004 c 24, s 57(1), sch 1
        para 43, 2004/2566; SI 2006/1031, reg 49, sch 8; 2007/30, art 2; 2007/2974,
        reg 63; 2008/1660, reg 19, sch 3

    mod—SI 2006/1073, art 3

sch 5 rep in pt—Tax Credits, 2002 c 21, s 60, sch 6; Equality, 2010 c 15, s 211, sch 26 para
        49(2) (subst by SI 2010/2279, sch 1); ibid, s 211, sch 27 pt 1 (subst by SI
        2010/2279, sch 2)

    am—SIs 2003/1660, reg 39(2), sch 5 para 4; 2003/1661, reg 39, sch 5 para 4;
        2003/1673, regs 3(2), 31(3); Employment Relations, 2004 c 24, s 57(1), sch 1
        para 43, 2004/2566; SIs 2006/2059, reg 34; 2006/1031, reg 49, sch 8; 2007/30,
        art 2; 2007/2974, reg 63; 2008/1660, reg 19, sch 3; Equality, 2010 c 15, s 211,
        sch 26 para 49(3) (subst by SI 2010/2279, sch 1)

sch 6 rep in pt—Tax Credits, 2002 c 21, s 60, sch 6; Pensions, 2004 c 35, s 320, sch 13 pt 1;
        (prosp) Child Maintenance and Other Payments, 2008 c 6, s 58, sch 8; (prosp)
        Welfare Reform, 2012 c 5, sch 14 pt 1; ibid, sch 14 pt 13

sch 7 rep in pt—Tax Credits, 2002 c 21, s 60, sch 6; Work and Families, 2006 c 18, s 15,
        sch 2; (prosp) Welfare Reform, 2009 c 24, s 58, sch 7 pt 3; (prosp) Welfare
        Reform, 2012 c 5, sch 14 pt 1; ibid, sch 14 pt 13

c 23   **Finance**

appl (mods)—SI 2007/1050, regs 3-12

mod—SI 2009/317, art 3, sch

s 5 rep in pt—Finance, 2008 c 9, s 14, sch 5 para 25(d)(i)

s 11 rep—Finance, 2009 c 10, s 114(16)(a)

s 13 rep—Finance, 2007 c 11, s 114, sch 27 pt 6

ss 26-28 rep—Income Tax, 2007 c 3, s 1031, sch 3

s 29 rep—Income Tax, 2007 c 3, s 1031, sch 3
    am—(spec retrosp effect) SI 2007/3186, reg 3, sch 3

s 31 rep—Corporation Tax, 2010 c 4, s 1181, sch 3 pt 1

ss 33-37 rep—Income Tax (Earnings and Pensions), 2003 c 1, s 724(1), sch 8 pt 1

s 38 rep in pt—Income Tax (Earnings and Pensions), 2003 c 1, s 724(1), sch 8 pt 1

s 39 rep—Income Tax (Earnings and Pensions), 2003 c 1, s 724(1), sch 8 pt 1

s 40 rep in pt—Finance, 2004 c 12, ss 77, 326, sch 42 pt 2(7), Note

s 41 rep—Income Tax (Earnings and Pensions), 2003 c 1, s 724(1), sch 8 pt 1

s 42 rep in pt—Finance, 2011 c 11, sch 10 para 8(b)

s 43 rep in pt—Finance, 2012 c 14, s 37(3)

s 46 rep—Finance, 2008 c 9, s 8, sch 2 para 55(e)(i)

s 47 rep—Finance, 2008 c 9, s 8, sch 2 para 55(e)(i)

s 48 rep—Income Tax, 2007 c 3, s 1031, sch 3

s 53 rep—Corporation Tax, 2009 c 4, ss 1322, 1326, sch 1 para 527, sch 3 pt 1

s 54 rep—Corporation Tax, 2009 c 4, ss 1322, 1326, sch 1 para 528, sch 3 pt 1

s 55 rep—Corporation Tax, 2009 c 4, ss 1322, 1326, sch 1 para 529, sch 3 pt 1

s 56 rep—Corporation Tax, 2009 c 4, s 1326, sch 3 pt 1

s 57 rep in pt—Corporation Tax, 2010 c 4, ss 1177, 1181, sch 1 paras 368, 369, sch 3 pt 1

s 58 rep—Corporation Tax, 2010 c 4, ss 1177, 1181, sch 1 paras 368, 370, sch 3 pt 1

s 60 rep—Corporation Tax, 2009 c 4, s 1326, sch 3 pt 1

s 62 rep—Finance, 2006 c 25, s 178, sch 26 pt 3(13)

s 63 am—Corporation Tax, 2010 c 4, s 1177, sch 1 paras 368, 371

2002
c 23 *continued*

s 64 rep—Corporation Tax, 2009 c 4, ss 1322, 1326, sch 1 para 530, sch 3 pt 1
s 65 am—Corporation Tax, 2009 c 4, s 1322, sch 1 para 531
 rep in pt—Corporation Tax, 2009 c 4, s 1326, sch 3 pt 1
s 66 mod—SIs 1997/473, reg 53E; 2006/3271, reg 38
 am—(retrosp to1.1.2003) SI 2004/2200, reg 11(1)(2)(a)(b); Finance, 2007 c 11, s 40,
  sch 9 para 1(4), 17(1)
 rep in pt—Finance, 2007 c 11, ss 41, 114, sch 10 paras 14(1)(10)(a), 17(2), sch 27
s 67 rep in pt—Corporation Tax, 2009 c 4, s 1326, sch 3 pt 1
s 68 rep—Corporation Tax, 2009 c 4, s 1326, sch 3 pt 1
ss 69, 70 rep—Finance, 2002 c 23, s 141, sch 40 pt 3(13), Note 2
s 71 rep—Corporation Tax, 2009 c 4, ss 1322, 1326, sch 1 para 532, sch 3 pt 1
ss 72-77 rep—Finance, 2004 c 12, ss 52(3), 326, sch 42 pt 2(6), Notes 1-3
s 78 rep—Finance, 2002 c 23, ss 83(1)(b)(3), 141, sch 27, paras 24, 25, sch 40 pt 3(13),
  Note 2
s 79 appl—(retrosp to 30.9.2002) Finance, 2003 c 14, s 177(1)(4)(a)(5)(8)(11)
s 80 appl—(retrosp to 30.9.2002) Finance, 2003 c 14, s 177(1)(4)(b)(5)(8)(11)
s 81 appl—(retrosp to 30.9.2002) Finance, 2003 c 14, s 177(1)(6)(a)(8)(11)
 am—Corporation Tax, 2009 c 4, s 1322, sch 1 para 533
s 82 rep—Finance, 2008 c 9, s 36, sch 14 para 17(k)
s 83 appl—(retrosp to 30.9.2002) Finance, 2003 c 14, s 177(1)(4)(c)(5)(8)(11)
 rep in pt—Corporation Tax, 2009 c 4, ss 1322, 1326, sch 1 para 534, sch 3 pt 1
s 84 rep in pt—Corporation Tax, 2009 c 4, ss 1322, 1326, sch 1 para 535, sch 3 pt 1
s 88 rep in pt—Finance, 2006 c 25, s 178, sch 26 pt 8(2); Taxation (International and Other
  Provns), 2010 c 8, s 378, sch 10 pt 1; SL(R), 2013 c 2, s 1, sch 1 pt 10(1)
s 90 am—Finance, 2006 c 25, s 78(1)-(8)
s 91 rep—Corporation Tax, 2010 c 4, s 1181, sch 3 pt 1
s 92 rep in pt—Corporation Tax, 2010 c 4, s 1181, sch 3 pt 1
s 94 rep in pt—Income Tax, 2007 c 3, s 1031, sch 3
s 95 rep—Income Tax, 2007 c 3, s 1031, sch 3
s 96 rep in pt—Finance, 2003 c 14, s 216, sch 43 pt 5(3), Note; Income Tax, 2007 c 3, s
  1031, sch 3
s 97 rep—Corporation Tax, 2010 c 4, s 1181, sch 3 pt 1
s 98 rep—Income Tax, 2007 c 3, s 1027, sch 1 paras 414, 415, sch 3
ss 99, 100 rep—Finance, 2006 c 25, s 178, sch 26 pt 3(4)
s 101 rep—(retrosp to 2.12.2004) Finance, 2005 c 7, ss 59, 104, sch 3 pt 1 para 2, sch 11 pt
  2(3), Note 4; Finance, 2006 c 25, s 178, sch 26 pt 3(4)
s 102 rep—Corporation Tax, 2010 c 4, s 1181, sch 3 pt 1
s 103 rep in pt—Income Tax (Earnings and Pensions), 2003 c 1, s 724(1), sch 8 pt 1;
  Finance, 2004 c 12, ss 52(3), 326, sch 42 pt 2(6), Note 1; Income Tax (Trading
  and Other Income), 2005 c 5, s 884, sch 3; Finance, 2005 c 7, s 104, sch 11 pt
  2(7), Note 2; Finance, 2006 c 25, s 178, sch 26 pt 3(12); Income Tax, 2007 c 3,
  s 1031, sch 3; Corporation Tax, 2009 c 4, s 1326, sch 3 pt 1; Corporation Tax,
  2010 c 4, s 1181, sch 3 pts 1, 2; Taxation (International and Other Provns),
  2010 c 8, s 378, sch 10 pt 8
s 104 rep—Income Tax (Trading and Other Income), 2005 c 5, ss 883(4), 884, sch 2 pt 5
  para 79, sch 3
s 105 rep in pt—Corporation Tax, 2009 c 4, s 1326, sch 3 pt 1
s 106 rep—Corporation Tax, 2009 c 4, s 1326, sch 3 pt 1
s 107 rep—Corporation Tax, 2010 c 4, s 1181, sch 3 pt 2; Taxation (International and Other
  Provns), 2010 c 8, s 378, sch 10 pt 12
ss 108, 109 rep—Income Tax, 2007 c 3, s 1031, sch 3
s 110 rep—Finance, 2012 c 14, sch 39 para 7(2)(a)
s 111 am—Finance, 2003 c 14, ss 124, 126(1)-(5)(9)-(11), sch 19 para 6(2) (see SI
  2003/2899, art 2)
s 112 rep—Finance, 2012 c 14, sch 39 para 5(2)(d)
s 113 rep—Finance, 2012 c 14, sch 39 para 5(1)(b)
s 117 rep—SI 2005/2007, art 2
s 121 rep—Finance, 2009 c 10, s 17, sch 5 para 6(c)
ss 123, 124 rep—Finance, 2012 c 14, sch 32 para 22(3)
s 133 rep in pt—Finance, 2008 c 9, s 122, sch 40 para 21(j)
s 134 rep—Finance, 2011 c 11, sch 25 para 17(1)
s 135 appl—SI 2001/1004, regs 90A(2)

2002

c 23 s 135 *continued*

am—Commrs for Revenue and Customs, 2005 c 11, ss 16, 50(6), sch 2 pt 1 para 12,
sch 4 paras 94, 95(1)(a)(b) (c), (2); Finance, 2007 c 11, s 93(1)-(3)

s 137 am—Finance, 2004 c 12, s 292; Finance, 2005 c 7, s 100

s 142 am—Income Tax, 2007 c 3, s 1027, sch 1 paras 414, 416

sch 2 rep in pt—Finance, 2008 c 9, s 14, sch 5 para 25(d)(ii)

sch 4 rep in pt—Finance, 2007 c 11, s 114, sch 27 pt 6

sch 6 rep—Income Tax (Earnings and Pensions), 2003 c 1, s 724(1), sch 8 pt 1

sch 9 rep in pt—Income Tax, 2007 c 3, s 1031, sch 3; Finance, 2007 c 11, s 114, sch 27 pt 2;
Finance, 2008 c 9, s 8, sch 2 para 55(e)(ii); Corporation Tax, 2009 c 4, s 1326,
sch 3 pt 1; SI 2009/3001, reg 13, sch 2; Corporation Tax, 2010 c 4, s 1181, sch
3 pt 1; Finance, 2011 c 11, sch 9 para 5(d)

sch 10 rep—Finance, 2008 c 9, s 8, sch 2 para 55(e)(iii)

sch 11 rep in pt—Finance, 2008 c 9, ss 8, 25, sch 2 para 55(e)(iv), sch 7 para 114(b)

sch 12 rep—Corporation Tax, 2009 c 4, ss 1322, 1326, sch 1 para 536, sch 3 pt 1

sch 13 rep—Corporation Tax, 2009 c 4, ss 1322, 1326, sch 1 para 537, sch 3 pt 1

sch 14 rep—Corporation Tax, 2009 c 4, s 1326, sch 3 pt 1

sch 15 rep—Corporation Tax, 2009 c 4, s 1326, sch 3 pt 1

sch 16 rep —Corporation Tax, 2010 c 4, ss 1177, 1180, 1181, sch 1 paras 368, 373, schs 2,
3

sch 17 rep in pt—Income Tax, 2007 c 3, s 1031, sch 3; Corporation Tax, 2010 c 4, s 1181,
sch 3 pt 1

sch 18 rep—Corporation Tax, 2010 c 4, ss 1177, 1181, sch 1 paras 368, 374, sch 3 pt 1

sch 19 rep in pt—Finance, 2009 c 10, s 30, sch 11 para 25

sch 22 rep—Corporation Tax, 2009 c 4, ss 1322, 1326, sch 1 para 540, sch 3 pt 1

sch 23 rep in pt—Finance, 2004 c 12, ss 52(3), 326, sch 42 pt 2(6), Notes 1, 2; (prosp)
Finance (No 2), 2005 c 22, s 70, sch 11 pt 2(6), Note 3; Finance, 2005 c 7,
s 104, sch 11 pt 2(6), Note; Corporation Tax, 2009 c 4, ss 1322, 1326, sch 1
para 541(1)(2), sch 3 pt 1; Corporation Tax, 2010 c 4, s 1181, sch 3 pt 1;
Taxation (International and Other Provns), 2010 c 8, s 378, sch 10 pt 2

am—Corporation Tax, 2009 c 4, s 1322, sch 1 para 541(1)(3)

sch 24 appl—(retrosp to 30.9.2002) Finance, 2003 c 14, s 177(1)(4)(b)(5)(8)(11)

rep in pt—Finance, 2004 c 12, ss 52(3), 326, sch 42 pt 2(6), Note 1

sch 25 rep in pt—Finance, 2003 c 14, s 216, sch 43 pt 3(12), Note 1; Finance, 2004 c 12,
ss 52(3), 326, sch 42 pt 2(6), Note 1; SI 2004/2310, arts 1(2), 2, sch para 66;
Finance, 2005 c 7, s 104, sch 11 pt 2(5)(7), Note, Note 2; Finance (No 2), 2005
c 22, s 70, sch 11 pt 2(7)-(9), Note; SI 2005/646, arts 2, 8; Income Tax, 2007 c
3, s 1031, sch 3; Finance, 2007 c 11, s 114, sch 27 pt 2; Finance, 2008 c 9, s 36,
sch 14 para 17(k); Corporation Tax, 2009 c 4, ss 1322, 1326, sch 1 para 542,
sch 3 pt 1; Corporation Tax, 2010 c 4, s 1181, sch 3 pt 1;Taxation
(International and Other Provns), 2010 c 8, s 378, sch 10 pt 1

am—(retrosp) Finance, 2003 c 14, s 178, sch 37 pt 2 para 6; Income Tax (Trading
and Other Income), 2005 c 5, s 882(1), sch 1 pt 2 paras 575, 579; Income Tax,
2007 c 3, s 1027, sch 1 paras 414, 421

sch 26 rep—Corporation Tax, 2009 c 4, ss 1322, 1326, sch 1 para 543, sch 3 pt 1

sch 27 appl—(retrosp to 30.9.2002) Finance, 2003 c 14, s 177(1)(4)(c)(5)(8)(11)

rep in pt—Finance, 2004 c 12, ss 52(3), 326, sch 42 pt 2(6), Notes 1, 3; Income Tax
(Trading and Other Income), 2005 c 5, s 884, sch 3; Finance, 2007 c 11, s 114,
sch 27 pt 2; Corporation Tax, 2010 c 4, s 1181, sch 3 pt 1; Taxation
(International and Other Provns), 2010 c 8, s 378, sch 10 pt 1; ibid, s 378, sch
10 pt 2

sch 28 appl (mods)—(retrosp to 30.9.2002) Finance, 2003 c 14, s 177(1)(6)(b)(7)(8)(11)

rep in pt—Corporation Tax, 2009 c 4, ss 1322, 1326, sch 1 para 544(1)(2)(4), sch 3
pt 1

am—Corporation Tax, 2009 c 4, s 1322, sch 1 para 544(1)(3)(5)-(7)

sch 29 rep—Corporation Tax, 2009 c 4, ss 1322, 1326, sch 1 para 545, sch 3 pt 1

sch 30 rep in pt—Income Tax, 2007 c 3, s 1031, sch 3; Corporation Tax, 2010 c 4, s 1181,
sch 3 pt 1; Taxation (International and Other Provns), 2010 c 8, s 378, sch 10
pt 1; Finance, 2011 c 11, sch 9 para 5(e)

sch 33 rep—Income Tax, 2007 c 3, s 1027, sch 1 paras 414, 422, sch 3

sch 34 am—Finance, 2003 c 14, ss 124, 126(6)-(11), sch 19 para 6(2) (see SI 2003/2899,
art 2); Legal Services, 2007 c 29, s 208, sch 21 paras 134, 135; Corporation
Tax, 2010 c 4, s 1177, sch 1 paras 368, 375

sch 35 rep—Finance, 2012 c 14, sch 39 para 5(1)(b)

2002

c 23 *continued*

sch 37 am—Corporation Tax, 2010 c 4, s 1177, sch 1 paras 368, 377
sch 39 rep—Finance, 2011 c 11, sch 25 para 17(1)

c 24 **European Parliamentary Elections**

see—(functions made exerciseable concurrently) SI 2010/1837, art 3; (power to appl or incorp (mods)) Police Reform and Social Responsibility, 2011 c 13, s 58(1)-(3)(7); ibid, s 54(5)

ext—(Gibraltar) European Parl (Representation), 2003 c 7, s 19

trans of functions—SIs 2003/1887, art 4, sch 1; 2015/1376, art 3(1), sch 1

s 1 subst—European Parl (Representation), 2003 c 7, s 1

power to am—European Parl (Representation), 2003 c 7, s 5(1)

am—SIs 2004/366, art 3(1)(2); 2004/1245, art 2; (saving) 2008/1954, arts 1, 2; European Union, 2011 c 12, s 16

s 1A added—European Parl (Representation), 2003 c 7, s 7(1)

s 2 am—SI 2004/366, art 3(1)(3)(a)(b)

appl—SI 2004/293, reg 9, sch 1 pt 3 paras 54(2)(4), 55(1)(3), 56(1)(b)(ii)

s 5 am—Political Parties and Elections, 2009 c 12, s 26(1)

s 6 am—European Parl (Representation), 2003 c 7, s 20(1)-(4); Political Parties and Elections, 2009 c 12, s 27

restr—(EW) SI 2004/294, reg 7(1)(2)(5)

excl—SI 2008/2857, art 7

s 7 am—European Parl (Representation), 2003 c 7, s 22

s 8 am—European Parl (Representation), 2003 c 7, s 15(3)

s 9 am—SIs 2004/366, art 3(1)(4); 2004/1374, reg 2(1)(2)

s 10 am—European Parl (Representation), 2003 c 7, s 21(1)(2); SI 2004/1374, reg 2(1)(3); Electoral Admin, 2006 c 22, s 18, sch 1 para 41; SI 2013/2876, reg 3

rep in pt—Constitutional Reform, 2005 c 4, ss 145, 146, sch 17 pt 2 para 32, sch 18 pt 5

s 11 am—European Parl (Representation), 2003 c 7, s 21(1)(2); SI 2004/366, art 3(1)(5)

s 12 rep—European Union, 2011 c 12, s 14(3)(c)

s 13 rep in pt—European Parl (Representation), 2003 c 7, s 8(1)(2)

am—European Parl (Representation), 2003 c 7, s 21(3)

s 16A added—SI 2002/2626, art 20, sch 2, para 27

rep—SI 2003/1887, art 9, sch 2 para 14

s 16B added—SI 2010/1837, art 5, sch

subst—SI 2015/1376, sch 2 para 10

s 17 am—European Parl (Representation), 2003 c 7, s 20(5)

sch 1 rep in pt—European Parl (Representation), 2003 c 7, s 8(1)(3)(c)

am—European Parl (Representation), 2003 c 7, s 8(1)(3)(a)(b); SIs 2004/366, art 3(1)(6)(a)-(d); 2009/837, art 26

excl in pt—European Union Referendum, 2015 c 36, sch 3 para 5(4)

sch 1A added—European Parl (Representation), 2003 c 7, s 7(2), sch

appl—European Parl (Representation), 2003 c 7, s 4(2)

am—SI 2004/1374, reg 2(1)(4)

sch 3 rep in pt—Crim Justice, 2003 c 44, s 332, sch 37 pt 10; Govt of Wales, 2006 c 32, s 163, sch 12

c 25 **Copyright etc and Trade Marks (Offences and Enforcement)**

c 26 **Justice (Northern Ireland)**

am —Constitutional Reform, 2005 c 4, s 59(5), sch 11 pt 3 para 6

trans of functions—SI 2010/976 art 15, sch 17

s 1 subst—Constitutional Reform, 2005 c 4, s 4(1)

s 2 am—Justice (NI), 2004 c 4, s 1, sch 1 para 1; Northern Ireland, 2009 c 3, s 2, sch 3 para 1(1)(3)

rep in pt—Northern Ireland, 2009 c 3, s 2, sch 3 para 1(1)-(2); SI 2010/976, art 15, sch 18

s 3 am—Justice (NI), 2004 c 4, ss 1, 2(1), sch 1 para 2

rep in pt—SI 2010/976, art 15, sch 18

s 4 rep —Northern Ireland, 2009 c 3, s 2, sch 3 para 2

s 5 subst—(savings) Northern Ireland, 2009 c 3, s 2, sch 3 para 3, sch 6

s 5A added —Constitutional Reform, 2005 c 4, s 123

am—Northern Ireland, 2009 c 3, s 2, sch 3 para 4

s 6 rep —Northern Ireland, 2009 c 3, s 2, sch 3 para 5

s 7 am—Northern Ireland, 2009 c 3, s 2, sch 3 para 6(1)-(4)(6)-(7)(b)

rep in pt—Northern Ireland, 2009 c 3, s 2, sch 3 para 6(1)(5)(7)(c)

2002

c 26 *continued*

s 8 subst—Northern Ireland, 2009 c 3, s 2, sch 3 para 7

--s 9 am—Justice (NI), 2002 c 26, s 5, sch 3, paras 40, 41; Constitutional Reform, 2005 c 4, ss 15(2), 145, sch 5 pt 1 paras 115-117, sch 17 pt 2 para 33(1)(2)(a); Northern Ireland, 2009 c 3, s 2, sch 4 para 33, sch 6

rep in pt—Justice (NI), 2002 c 26, s 86, sch 13; Constitutional Reform, 2005 c 4, s 124(1)

s 9A added—Constitutional Reform, 2005 c 4, s 124(2)

s 9B added (pt prosp)—Constitutional Reform, 2005 c 4, s 125

rep in pt—(savings) Northern Ireland, 2009 c 3, s 2, sch 3 para 8(1)(2), sch 6; SI 2009/56, art 3, sch 1 para 330

am—Northern Ireland, 2009 c 3, s 2, sch 3 para 8(1)(3)

ss 9C-9F added—Constitutional Reform, 2005 c 4, ss 126-129

s 9F am—SI 2010/976, art 15, sch 18

s 9G added—Constitutional Reform, 2005 c 4, s 130

rep—(savings) Northern Ireland, 2009 c 3, s 2, sch 3 para 9

s 9H added—Constitutional Reform, 2005 c 4, s 131

rep in pt—(savings) Northern Ireland, 2009 c 3, s 2, sch 3 para 10

s 9I added—Constitutional Reform, 2005 c 4, s 132

am—Northern Ireland, 2009 c 3, s 2, sch 3 para 11(1)-(2)(4)

rep in pt—Northern Ireland, 2009 c 3, s 2, sch 3 para 11(1)(3)

s 10 am—Constitutional Reform, 2005 c 4, s 15(2), sch 5 pt 1 paras 115, 118

s 12 am—Constitutional Reform, 2005 c 4, s 11

rep in pt—Constitutional Reform, 2005 c 4, ss 15(2), 146, sch 5 pt 1 paras 115, 119, sch 18 pt 3

s 18 rep in pt—Courts, 2003 c 39, s 109(3), sch 10; Constitutional Reform, 2005 c 4, ss 145, 146, sch 17 pt 2 para 33(1)(3), sch 18 pt 5

s 19 rep in pt—SI 2010/976, art 15, sch 18

s 24 am—(pt prosp) Constitutional Reform, 2005 c 4, s 15(2), sch 5 pt 1 para 115; ibid, sch 5 pt 1 para 120; ibid, s 154, sch 17 pt 2 para 33(1)(2)(b)

s 27 am—(temp) Terrorism, 2000 c 11, s 63E

s 29 am—SI 2010/976, art 11, sch 13

s 30 am—SI 2010/976, art 11, sch 13

excl—Crim Justice, 2003 c 44, s 92(1) (as modified by 2003 c 44, s 96(1)(17))

s 30A added—Northern Ireland, 2009 c 3, s 3(2)

s 31A added—Extradition, 2003 c 41, s 192(5)(6) (see SI 2003/3103, arts 2-5)

s 32A added—Justice (NI), 2004 c 4, s 7

s 34 rep in pt—Justice (NI), 2004 c 4, s 18, sch 4

s 36 am—Extradition, 2003 c 41, s 192(5)(7) (see SI 2003/3103, arts 2-5)

excl—Crim Justice, 2003 c 44, s 92(1) (as modified by 2003 c 44, s 96(1)(17)); Bribery, 2010 c 23, s 10(10)

s 37 am—Justice (NI), 2004 c 4, s 8(7)(8)

s 41 ext—Crim Justice, 2003 c 44, s 334(4)

s 43 am—(pt prosp) Constitutional Reform, 2005 c 4, s 15(2), sch 5 pt 1 para 115; ibid, sch 5 pt 1 para 121; ibid, s 145, sch 17 pt 2 para 33(1)(2)(c)

s 44 am—Extradition, 2003 c 41, s 192(5)(8) (see SI 2003/3103, arts 2-5)

s 45 am—SI 2010/976, art 11, sch 13

s 46 am—Justice (NI), 2004 c 4, s 9(1)(2)(4); SI 2010/976, art 11, sch 13

rep in pt—Justice (NI), 2004 c 4, ss 9(1)(3), 18, sch 4

s 47 am—Justice (NI), 2002 c 26, s 28(1), sch 7, paras 15, 16; SI 2010/976, art 11, sch 13

rep in pt—SI 2010/976, art 15, sch 18

s 49 am—Justice (NI), 2002 c 26, s 28(1), sch 7, paras 15, 17; SI 2010/976, art 11, sch 13

rep in pt—SI 2010/976, art 15, sch 18

s 50 am—SI 2010/976, art 11, sch 13

rep in pt—SI 2010/976, art 15, sch 18

s 51 am—SI 2010/976, art 11, sch 13

rep in pt—SI 2010/976, art 15, sch 18

s 52 subst—SI 2010/976, art 11, sch 13

s 56 am—SI 2010/976, art 11, sch 13

s 63 am—SI 2010/976, art 11, sch 13

ss 68, 69 am—SI 2010/976, art 11, sch 13

ss 69A, 69B added—Domestic Violence, Crime and Victims, 2004 c 28, s 46(1)(2)

am—SI 2010/976, art 11, sch 13

s 70 am—Domestic Violence, Crime and Victims, 2004 c 28, s 46(1)(3)

2002

c 26 s 70 *continued*

    rep in pt—SI 2010/976, art 11, sch 13

    ss 71-73 am—SI 2010/976, art 11, sch 13

    ss 79-81 rep—Justice (NI), 2004 c 4, s 18, sch 4

    s 83 rep—SI 2010/976, art 27

    s 85 am—SI 2010/976, art 11, sch 13

    s 87 am—SI 2010/976, art 11, sch 13

    s 88 appl—Constitutional Reform, 2005 c 4, s 120(7)(b)

        am—Northern Ireland, 2009 c 3, s 2, sch 3 para 12

    s 89 am—SI 2010/976, art 11, sch 13

    s 90 rep in pt—Justice (NI), 2004 c 4, ss 1, 18, sch 1 para 4(1)(2), sch 4; Northern Ireland,
        2009 c 3, s 2, sch 4 para 34(1)(4), sch 6; SI 2010/976, art 11, sch 13

        am—Justice (NI), 2004 c 4, s 1, sch 1 para 4(1)(3)(4); Domestic Violence, Crime and
        Victims, 2004 c 28, s 46(1)(4); Northern Ireland, 2009 c 3, s 2, sch 4 para
        34(1)-(3); SI 2010/976, art 11, sch 13

    s 91 am—Constitutional Reform, 2005 c 4, s 4(2)

    sch 1 am—(pt prosp) Constitutional Reform, 2005 c 4, s 15(2), sch 5 pt 1 paras 115, 122;
        Northern Ireland, 2009 c 3, s 2, sch 4 para 35(1)-(4)

        rep in pt—SI 2009/56, art 3, sch 1 para 331

    sch 2 am—Justice (NI), 2004 c 4, ss 1, 2(2), sch 1 para 5(1)-(14); SI 2010/976, art 15, sch
        18

        rep in pt—SI 2010/976, art 15, sch 18

    sch 3 subst —Northern Ireland, 2009 c 3, s 2, sch 3 para 13

    sch 3A added —Constitutional Reform, 2005 c 4, s 124(3), sch 15

        am—Northern Ireland, 2009 c 3, s 2, sch 3 para 14; SI 2010/976, art 15, sch 18

    sch 4 am—Constitutional Reform, 2005 c 4, s 15(2), sch 5 pt 1 paras 115, 124(1)-(4)

        rep in pt—Police and Justice, 2006 c 48, s 52, sch 15; Armed Forces, 2006 c 52, s 378,
        sch 17; Northern Ireland, 2009 c 3, s 2, sch 4 para 36; (S) Crim Justice and
        Licensing (S), 2010 asp 13, s 14, sch 2 para 46

    sch 5 rep—Constitutional Reform, 2005 c 4, ss 15(2), 146, sch 5 pt 1 paras 115, 125, sch 18
        pt 3

    sch 6 rep in pt—(pt prosp) Justice (NI), 2002 c 26, s 86, sch 13; SI 2009/56, art 3, sch 1
        para 332

        am—(pt prosp) Constitutional Reform, 2005 c 4, s 15(2), sch 5 pt 1 paras 115, 126;
        Northern Ireland, 2009 c 3, s 2, sch 4 para 35(1)-(3)

    sch 7 am—Justice (NI), 2004 c 4, s 8(9)

        rep in pt—Terrorism, 2006 c 11, s 37, sch 3; Wireless Telegraphy, 2006 c 36, s 125,
        sch 9; Govt of Wales, 2006 c 32, s 163, sch 12

    sch 8 am—SI 2010/976, art 11, sch 13

        rep in pt—SI 2010/976, art 11, sch 13

    sch 9 am—SI 2010/976, art 11, sch 13

        rep in pt—SI 2010/976, art 11, sch 13

    sch 11 rep in pt—Terrorism (NI), 2006 c 4, s 51, sch 1

    sch 12 rep in pt—Justice (NI), 2004 c 4, s 18, sch 4; Legislative and Regulatory Reform,
        2006 c 51, s 30, sch 1; SI 2008/2833, art 6, sch 3; Northern Ireland, 2009 c 3, s
        2, sch 4 para 37; SI 2010/976, art 27

        am—(pt prosp) Constitutional Reform, 2005 c 4, s 15(2), sch 5 pt 1 para 115; ibid,
        sch 5 pt 1 para 127

    sch 13 rep in pt—(pt prosp) Constitutional Reform, 2005 c 4, s 15(2), sch 5 pt 1 para 115;
        ibid, ss 15(2), 146, sch 5 pt 1 para 128(1)(2), sch 18 pt 3; Northern Ireland,
        2009 c 3, s 2, sch 4 para 38

        am—(pt prosp) Constitutional Reform, 2005 c 4, s 15(2), sch 5 pt 1 para 115; ibid, ss
        15(2), 145, sch 5 pt 1 para 128(1)(3), sch 17 pt 3 para 37

c 27   **Divorce (Religious Marriages)**

c 28   **Export Control**

    s 5 am—SI 2012/1809, art 3(1), sch pt 1

    s 9 ext (mods)—SIs 2004/3101, art 4, sch 3; 2004/3102, art 4, sch 3; 2004/3103, art 4, sch
        3

    s 11 am—SI 2012/1809, art 3(1), sch pt 1

c 29   **Proceeds of Crime**

    mod—SI 2009/317, art 3, sch

    appl (mods)—SI 2011/245, sch 6 pt 1

    ss 1, 2 rep—Serious Crime, 2007 c 27, s 74, sch 8 paras 121, 123, sch 14

    ss 2A-2C added—Serious Crime, 2007 c 27, s 74, sch 8 paras 121, 124

2002

c 29 *continued*

s 2A am—Crime and Cts, 2013 c 22, sch 8 para 109
    rep in pt—SI 2014/834, sch 2 para 20
s 2B am—Crime and Cts, 2013 c 22, sch 8 para 110(2)(4)
    rep in pt—Crime and Cts, 2013 c 22, sch 8 para 110(3)(5)
s 2C am—Serious Crime, 2007 c 27, s 84(2)
    rep in pt—SI 2014/834, sch 2 para 21
s 3 am—Serious Crime, 2007 c 27, s 74, sch 8 paras 120, 121; Crime and Cts, 2013 c 22,
    sch 8 para 111
    rep in pt—Serious Crime, 2007 c 27, s 92, sch 14
ss 4, 5 rep—Serious Crime, 2007 c 27, s 74, sch 8 paras 121, 125
Pt 2 (ss 6-91) power to mod—Serious Organised Crime and Police, 2005 c 15, s 97; Crime
    and Cts, 2013 c 22, s 47
    appl (mods)—SIs 2014/3141, regs 10(5), 15(5); 2015/868, reg 5
s 6 am—Crim Justice, 2003 c 44, s 41, sch 3 pt 2 para 75(1)(2); Prevention of Social
    Housing Fraud, 2013 c 3, sch para 12; Serious Crime, 2015 c 9, sch 4 para 19
    appl—SI 2005/3181, art 189(10)(a)
    rep in pt—Serious Crime, 2007 c 27, s 74, sch 8 paras 1, 2, sch 14
s 7 am—Policing and Crime, 2009 c 26, s 112, sch 7 paras 99, 100; Prevention of Social
    Housing Fraud, 2013 c 3, sch para 13
s 9 am—SI 2007/3287, arts 2, 3
s 10A added—Serious Crime, 2015 c 9, s 1
s 11 rep in pt—Serious Crime, 2007 c 27, s 74, sch 8 paras 1, 3, sch 14
    subst—Serious Crime, 2015 c 9, s 5(1)
s 12 disappl—SI 2014/3141, reg 15(6)
    am—Serious Crime, 2015 c 9, s 5(2); ibid, sch 4 para 20
s 13 am—Counter-Terrorism, 2008 c 28, s 39, sch 3 para 7(1)(2); Prevention of Social
    Housing Fraud, 2013 c 3, sch para 14; Crim Justice and Cts, 2015 c 2, sch 12
    para 11; Serious Crime, 2015 c 9, s 6; (17.3.2016) Modern Slavery, 2015 c 30,
    sch 5 para 15(2)(3)(a)(d)(4)
    rep in pt—(17.3.2016) Modern Slavery, 2015 c 30, sch 5 para 15(3)(b)(c)(e)(f)
ss 13A, 13B added—Serious Crime, 2015 c 9, s 7
s 14 rep in pt—Serious Crime, 2007 c 27, s 74, sch 8 paras 1, 4, sch 14
    am—Prevention of Social Housing Fraud, 2013 c 3, sch para 15; Serious Crime, 2015 c
    9, sch 4 para 21
s 15 am—Prevention of Social Housing Fraud, 2013 c 3, sch para 16; Serious Crime, 2015 c
    9, sch 4 para 22
s 16 rep in pt—Serious Crime, 2007 c 27, s 74, sch 8 paras 1, 5-12, sch 14
    am—Serious Crime, 2015 c 9, s 2(1)
s 17 rep in pt—Serious Crime, 2007 c 27, s 74, sch 8 paras 1, 5-12, sch 14
s 18 rep in pt—Serious Crime, 2007 c 27, s 74, sch 8 paras 1, 5-12, sch 14
    am—Serious Crime, 2015 c 9, s 2(2)
s 18A added—Serious Crime, 2015 c 9, s 2(3)
s 19 rep in pt—Serious Crime, 2007 c 27, s 74, sch 8 paras 1, 5-12, sch 14
    am—Prevention of Social Housing Fraud, 2013 c 3, sch para 17; Serious Crime, 2015 c
    9, sch 4 para 23; Modern Slavery, 2015 c 30, sch 5 para 16
s 20 rep in pt—Serious Crime, 2007 c 27, s 74, sch 8 paras 1, 5-12, sch 14
    am—Prevention of Social Housing Fraud, 2013 c 3, sch para 18; Serious Crime, 2015 c
    9, sch 4 para 24; Modern Slavery, 2015 c 30, sch 5 para 17
s 21 rep in pt—Serious Crime, 2007 c 27, s 74, sch 8 paras 1, 5-12, sch 14
    am—Prevention of Social Housing Fraud, 2013 c 3, sch para 19; Serious Crime, 2015 c
    9, sch 4 para 25
s 22 rep in pt—Serious Crime, 2007 c 27, s 74, sch 8 paras 1, 5-12, sch 14
    am—Serious Crime, 2015 c 9, sch 4 para 26
s 23 rep in pt—Serious Crime, 2007 c 27, s 74, sch 8 paras 1, 5-12, sch 14
    am—Serious Crime, 2015 c 9, s 8(1)
s 24 am—Courts, 2003 c 39, s 109(1), sch 8 para 406(a)
s 25 am—Courts, 2003 c 39, s 109(1), sch 8 para 406(b)
s 25A added—Serious Crime, 2015 c 9, s 8(2)
s 26 rep in pt—Serious Crime, 2007 c 27, s 74, sch 8 paras 1, 13, sch 14
s 27 am—Crim Justice, 2003 c 44, s 41, sch 3 pt 2 para 75(1)(3); Serious Crime, 2015 c 9, s
    9(1)(2)
    rep in pt—Serious Crime, 2007 c 27, s 74, sch 8 paras 1, 14, sch 14
s 28 rep in pt—Serious Crime, 2007 c 27, s 74, sch 8 paras 1, 15, sch 14

2002

c 29 s 28 *continued*

am—Serious Crime, 2015 c 9, s 9(3)(4)

s 31 rep in pt—Serious Crime, 2007 c 27, s 74, sch 8 paras 1, 16, sch 14
am—Serious Crime, 2015 c 9, s 3(1); ibid, sch 4 para 27

s 32 am—Prevention of Social Housing Fraud, 2013 c 3, sch para 20; Serious Crime, 2015 c
9, s 3(2); ibid, sch 4 para 28; Modern Slavery, 2015 c 30, sch 5 para 18

s 33 am —Constitutional Reform, 2005 c 4, s 40(4), sch 9 pt 1 para 77(1)(2); Prevention of
Social Housing Fraud, 2013 c 3, sch para 21; Serious Crime, 2015 c 9, s 3(3);
ibid, sch 4 para 29; Modern Slavery, 2015 c 30, sch 5 para 19
rep in pt—Serious Crime, 2007 c 27, s 74, sch 8 paras 1, 17, sch 14

s 34 rep—Serious Crime, 2007 c 27, s 74, sch 8 paras 1, 18, sch 14

s 35 am—Serious Crime, 2007 c 27, s 74, sch 8 paras 1, 19; Serious Crime, 2015 c 9, s
10(1); ibid, sch 4 para 30
rep in pt—Serious Crime, 2007 c 27, s 92, sch 14
disappl—SI 2014/3141, reg 15(6)

ss 36, 37 rep—Serious Crime, 2007 c 27, s 74, sch 8 paras 1, 20, sch 14

s 38 am—Crim Justice, 2003 c 44, s 304, sch 32 pt 1 para 141
disappl—SI 2014/3141, reg 15(6)

s 39 am—Serious Crime, 2007 c 27, s 74, sch 8 paras 1, 21
rep in pt—Serious Crime, 2007 c 27, s 92, sch 14
disappl—SI 2014/3141, reg 15(6)

s 40 rep in pt—Serious Crime, 2007 c 27, s 74, sch 8 paras 1, 22, sch 14
am—Serious Crime, 2015 c 9, s 11(1)

s 41 am—Crime and Cts, 2013 c 22, s 46(2)(3)(a)(4)-(6); Serious Crime, 2015 c 9, s 11(2);
ibid, sch 4 para 31
rep in pt—Crime and Cts, 2013 c 22, s 46(3)(b)

s 41A added —Policing and Crime, 2009 c 26, s 52(2)
am—Crime and Cts, 2013 c 22, sch 8 para 112; ibid, sch 21 para 15

s 42 rep in pt—Serious Crime, 2007 c 27, s 74, sch 8 paras 1, 23, sch 14
am—Serious Crime, 2015 c 9, s 12; ibid, sch 4 para 32

s 44 am—Constitutional Reform, 2005 c 4, s 40(4), sch 9 pt 1 para 77(1)(3)

s 44A added —Policing and Crime, 2009 c 26, s 52(3)

s 45 rep —Policing and Crime, 2009 c 26, ss 55(3), 112, sch 8 pt 4

ss 47A-47S added —Policing and Crime, 2009 c 26, s 55(2)

s 47A am—Crime and Cts, 2013 c 22, s 55(4)(a)

s 47B am—Serious Crime, 2015 c 9, s 13(1)

s 47C am—Crime and Cts, 2013 c 22, sch 21 para 16

s 47G am—Crime and Cts, 2013 c 22, sch 21 para 17; Serious Crime, 2015 c 9, s 13(2)

s 47M am—Crime and Cts, 2013 c 22, sch 21 para 18

s 49 am—Serious Crime, 2007 c 27, s 82(1)

s 51 am—Serious Crime, 2007 c 27, s 82(2); Serious Crime, 2015 c 9, s 4

ss 52, 53 rep—Serious Crime, 2007 c 27, s 74, sch 8 paras 1, 24, sch 14

s 54 am—Courts, 2003 c 39, s 109(1), sch 8 para 407

s 55 am—Courts, 2003 c 39, s 109(1), sch 8 para 408; Policing and Crime, 2009 c 26, s
51(2); ibid, s 58(4)(5); Police Reform and Social Responsibility, 2011 c 13, sch
16 para 305(a); Prevention of Social Housing Fraud, 2013 c 3, sch para 22;
Crime and Cts, 2013 c 22, sch 8 para 113; Serious Crime, 2015 c 9, sch 4 para 33;
(17.3.2016) Modern Slavery, 2015 c 30, sch 5 para 20
rep in pt—Police Reform and Social Responsibility, 2011 c 13, sch 16 para 305(b); SI
2014/834, sch 2 para 22

ss 56, 57 rep—Serious Crime, 2007 c 27, s 74, sch 8 paras 1, 25, sch 14

s 58 am—Serious Crime, 2007 c 27, s 74, sch 8 paras 1, 26; Tribunals, Courts and
Enforcement, 2007 c 15, s 62, sch 13 paras 142, 143

s 59 am—Tribunals, Courts and Enforcement, 2007 c 15, s 62, sch 13 paras 142, 144

s 60 rep—Serious Crime, 2007 c 27, s 74, sch 8 paras 1, 27, sch 14

ss 61, 62 am—Serious Crime, 2007 c 27, s 74, sch 8 paras 1, 28, 29

s 63 am—Serious Crime, 2007 c 27, s 74, sch 8 paras 1, 30
rep in pt—Serious Crime, 2007 c 27, s 92, sch 14

s 64 rep in pt—Serious Crime, 2007 c 27, s 74, sch 8 paras 1, 31, sch 14

s 65 rep in pt—Serious Crime, 2007 c 27, s 74, sch 8 paras 1, 32, sch 14

s 66 am—Constitutional Reform, 2005 c 4, s 40(4), sch 9 pt 1 para 77(1)(3)

s 67 am—Courts, 2003 c 39, s 109(1), sch 8 para 409; Policing and Crime, 2009 c 26, s
58(3); Serious Crime, 2015 c 9, s 14(1)-(3)
rep in pt—Serious Crime, 2007 c 27, s 74, sch 8 paras 1, 33, sch 14

2002

c 29 *continued*

ss 67A-67D added —Policing and Crime, 2009 c 26, s 58(2)

s 67A am—Serious Crime, 2015 c 9, s 14(4)

s 69 am—Serious Crime, 2007 c 27, s 74, sch 8 paras 1, 34; Policing and Crime, 2009 c 26, ss 55(4), 112, sch 7 paras 66, 67

s 70 am—(pt prosp) Crim Justice, 2003 c 44, s 41, sch 3 pt 2 para 75(1)(4)

s 72 am—Commrs for Revenue and Customs, 2005 c 11, s 50(6), sch 4 para 97; Policing and Crime, 2009 c 26, s 61(2); Crime and Cts, 2013 c 22, sch 8 para 114; ibid, sch 21 para 19

rep in pt—SI 2014/834, sch 2 para 23

s 74 rep in pt—Serious Crime, 2007 c 27, s 74, sch 8 paras 1, 35, sch 14

s 82 am—Serious Organised Crime and Police, 2005 c 15, s 109, sch 6 paras 4, 5; Counter-Terrorism, 2008 c 28, s 39, sch 3 para 7(1)(3); Policing and Crime, 2009 c 26, s 112, sch 7 paras 99, 101

appl—SI 2005/3181, art 49(2)

s 84 appl—SI 2005/3181, art 49(3)

s 85 am—Crim Justice, 2003 c 44, s 331, sch 36 pt 2 para 15; Constitutional Reform, 2005 c 4, s 40(4), sch 9 pt 1 para 77(1)(4); Policing and Crime, 2009 c 26, s 112, sch 7 paras 66, 68; Crime and Cts, 2013 c 22, sch 17 para 38; Crim Justice and Cts, 2015 c 2, sch 11 para 18

ext—SI 2003/428, rule 5(4)

s 87 rep in pt—Policing and Crime, 2009 c 26, s 112, sch 7 paras 66, 69, sch 8 pt 4

am—Serious Crime, 2015 c 9, s 5(3)

s 87A added —Policing and Crime, 2009 c 26, s 112, sch 7 paras 66, 70

s 88 appl—SI 2005/384, rule 58.12(4)

s 89 am—Courts, 2003 c 39, s 94(1)-(3); Serious Crime, 2015 c 9, sch 4 para 34

s 90 am—Constitutional Reform, 2005 c 4, s 40(4), sch 9 pt 1 para 77(1)(5)

s 91 am—Courts, 2003 c 39, ss 94(4), 109(1), sch 8 para 410

Pt 3 (ss 92-155) appl—SI 2014/3141, sch 1 paras 6(5), 11(5)

s 92 appl—SI 2005/3181, art 189(10)(a)

am—(1.3.2016) Serious Crime, 2015 c 9, sch 4 para 35

s 93 am—Policing and Crime, 2009 c 26, s 112, sch 7 paras 99, 102

s 97 am—Counter-Terrorism, 2008 c 28, s 39, sch 3 para 7(1)(4); (prosp) Serious Crime, 2015 c 9, s 15(1)

s 97A added (prosp)—Serious Crime, 2015 c 9, s 15(2)

ss 97B-97D added (1.3.2016)—Serious Crime, 2015 c 9, s 16

s 99 am—(prosp) Serious Crime, 2015 c 9, sch 4 para 36

s 100 am—(prosp) Serious Crime, 2015 c 9, sch 4 para 37

s 104 am—(prosp) Serious Crime, 2015 c 9, sch 4 para 38

s 105 am—(prosp) Serious Crime, 2015 c 9, sch 4 para 39

s 106 am—(prosp) Serious Crime, 2015 c 9, sch 4 para 40

s 107 am—(prosp) Serious Crime, 2015 c 9, sch 4 para 41

s 111 am—(1.3.2016) Serious Crime, 2015 c 9, s 18(1)(2)

s 112 am—(1.3.2016) Serious Crime, 2015 c 9, s 18(3)(4)

s 117 disappl—SI 2014/3141, sch 1 para 11(6)

s 118 disappl—SI 2014/3141, sch 1 para 11(6)

am—(1.3.2016) Serious Crime, 2015 c 9, s 19(1)(a)(b)

rep in pt—(1.3.2016) Serious Crime, 2015 c 9, sch 4 para 42

s 119 am—(1.3.2016) Serious Crime, 2015 c 9, s 20(1)

s 120 am—(1.3.2016) Serious Crime, 2015 c 9, s 20(2)

s 120A added —Policing and Crime, 2009 c 26, s 53(2)

am—Crime and Cts, 2013 c 22, sch 8 para 115; ibid, sch 21 para 20

s 121 am—(1.3.2016) Serious Crime, 2015 c 9, s 21; (1.3.2016) ibid, sch 4 para 43

s 122A added —Policing and Crime, 2009 c 26, s 53(3)

s 123 am—(S) Bankruptcy and Diligence etc (S), 2007 asp 3, s 226, sch 5 para 29

rep in pt—(S) (pt prosp) Bankruptcy and Diligence etc (S), 2007 asp 3, s 226, sch 6

s 126 rep —Policing and Crime, 2009 c 26, ss 56(3), 112, sch 8 pt 4

ss 127A-127R added —Policing and Crime, 2009 c 26, s 56(2)

s 127A am—Crime and Cts, 2013 c 22, s 55(4)(b)

s 127B am—(1.3.2016) Serious Crime, 2015 c 9, s 22(1)

s 127C am—Crime and Cts, 2013 c 22, sch 21 para 21

s 127G am—Crime and Cts, 2013 c 22, sch 21 para 22; (1.3.2016) Serious Crime, 2015 c 9, s 22(2)

s 127M am—Crime and Cts, 2013 c 22, sch 21 para 23

2002

c 29 *continued*

s 131 am—Policing and Crime, 2009 c 26, s 59(3); (prosp) Serious Crime, 2015 c 9, sch 4 para 44

ss 131A-131D added —Policing and Crime, 2009 c 26, s 59(2)

s 132 am—Policing and Crime, 2009 c 26, ss 56(4), 112, sch 7 paras 66, 71

s 139 am—Policing and Crime, 2009 c 26, s 61(3); SSI 2013/119, sch 1 para 19(2); Crime and Cts, 2013 c 22, sch 8 para 116

s 142 am—SSI 2011/231, art 3

s 148 am—Serious Organised Crime and Police, 2005 c 15, s 109, sch 6 paras 4, 6; Counter-Terrorism, 2008 c 28, s 39, sch 3 para 7(1)(5); Policing and Crime, 2009 c 26, s 112, sch 7 paras 99, 103

s 150 appl—SI 2005/3181, art 87(2)

s 153 rep in pt—Policing and Crime, 2009 c 26, s 112, sch 7 paras 66, 72, sch 8 pt 4; (1.3.2016) Serious Crime, 2015 c 9, sch 4 para 45

s 153A added —Policing and Crime, 2009 c 26, s 112, sch 7 paras 66, 73

Pt 4 (ss 156-239) power to mod—Serious Organised Crime and Police, 2005 c 15, s 97 appl—SI 2014/3141, sch 2 paras 6(5), 11(5)

s 156 appl—SI 2005/3181, art 189(10)(a)
    rep in pt—Serious Crime, 2007 c 27, s 74, sch 8 paras 1, 36, sch 14
    am—Serious Crime, 2015 c 9, sch 4 para 46

s 157 am—Policing and Crime, 2009 c 26, s 112, sch 7 paras 99, 104

s 160A added—Serious Crime, 2015 c 9, s 24

s 161 subst—Serious Crime, 2015 c 9, s 28(1)

s 162 disappl—SI 2014/3141, sch 2 para 11(6)
    am—Serious Crime, 2015 c 9, s 28(2); ibid, sch 4 para 47

s 163 am—Counter-Terrorism, 2008 c 28, s 39, sch 3 para 7(1)(6)

ss 163A, 163B added—Serious Crime, 2015 c 9, s 29

s 164 rep in pt—Serious Crime, 2007 c 27, s 74, sch 8 paras 1, 38, sch 14

ss 166-173 rep in pt—Serious Crime, 2007 c 27, s 74, sch 8 paras 1, 39-46, sch 14

s 166 am—Serious Crime, 2015 c 9, s 25(1)

s 167 rep in pt—Serious Crime, 2007 c 27, s 74, sch 8 paras 1, 40, sch 14

s 168 rep in pt—Serious Crime, 2007 c 27, s 74, sch 8 paras 1, 41, sch 14
    am—Serious Crime, 2015 c 9, s 25(2)

s 168A added—Serious Crime, 2015 c 9, s 25(3)

ss 169-172 rep in pt—Serious Crime, 2007 c 27, s 74, sch 8 paras 1, 42-45, sch 14

s 173 rep in pt—Serious Crime, 2007 c 27, s 74, sch 8 paras 1, 46, sch 14
    am—Serious Crime, 2015 c 9, s 30(1)

ss 174, 175 am—SI 2010/976, art 12, sch 14

s 175A added—Serious Crime, 2015 c 9, s 30(2)

s 176 rep in pt—Serious Crime, 2007 c 27, s 74, sch 8 paras 1, 47-49, sch 14

s 177 rep in pt—Serious Crime, 2007 c 27, s 74, sch 8 paras 1, 48, sch 14
    am—Serious Crime, 2015 c 9, s 31(1)(2)

s 178 rep in pt—Serious Crime, 2007 c 27, s 74, sch 8 paras 1, 49, sch 14

s 181 rep in pt—Serious Crime, 2007 c 27, s 74, sch 8 paras 1, 50
    am—Serious Crime, 2015 c 9, s 26(1)(2); ibid, sch 4 para 48

s 183 am—Constitutional Reform, 2005 c 4, s 40(4), sch 9 pt 1 para 77(1)(6); Serious Crime, 2015 c 9, s 26(3)
    rep in pt—Serious Crime, 2007 c 27, s 74, sch 8 paras 1, 51, sch 14

s 184 rep—Serious Crime, 2007 c 27, s 74, sch 8 paras 1, 52, sch 14

s 185 disappl—SI 2014/3141, sch 2 para 11(6)
    am—Serious Crime, 2015 c 9, s 32(1); ibid, sch 4 para 49

s 186 rep—Serious Crime, 2007 c 27, s 74, sch 8 paras 1, 53, sch 14

s 187 disappl—SI 2014/3141, sch 2 para 11(6)

s 188 am—Serious Crime, 2007 c 27, s 74, sch 8 paras 1, 54
    disappl—SI 2014/3141, sch 2 para 11(6)

s 189 rep in pt—Serious Crime, 2007 c 27, s 74, sch 8 paras 1, 55, sch 14
    am—Serious Crime, 2015 c 9, s 33(1)

s 190 am—Serious Crime, 2015 c 9, s 33(2); ibid, sch 4 para 50

s 190A added (1.3.2016)—Policing and Crime, 2009 c 26, s 54(2)
    am—Crime and Cts, 2013 c 22, sch 8 para 117; ibid, sch 21 para 24

s 191 rep in pt—Serious Crime, 2007 c 27, s 74, sch 8 paras 1, 56, sch 14
    am—Serious Crime, 2015 c 9, s 34; ibid, sch 4 para 51

s 193 am—Constitutional Reform, 2005 c 4, s 40(4), sch 9 pt 1 para 77(1)(7)

s 193A added (1.3.2016)—Policing and Crime, 2009 c 26, s 54(3)

2002

c 29 *continued*

s 194 rep (1.3.2016)—Policing and Crime, 2009 c 26, ss 57(2), 112, sch 8 pt 4
    am—Serious Crime, 2007 c 27, s 78(3)(4)
ss 195A-195S added (1.3.2016)—Policing and Crime, 2009 c 26, s 57(2)
s 195A am—Crime and Cts, 2013 c 22, s 55(4)(c)
s 195B am—Serious Crime, 2015 c 9, s 35(1)
s 195C am—Crime and Cts, 2013 c 22, sch 21 para 25
s 195G am—Crime and Cts, 2013 c 22, sch 21 para 26; Serious Crime, 2015 c 9, s 35(2)
ss 195H, 195I am—(1.3.2016) Policing and Crime, 2009 c 26, s 57(2) (amended by SI
    2012/2595, art 18(2)(a)-(h))
s 195M am—Crime and Cts, 2013 c 22, sch 21 para 27
s 195S am—(pt prosp 1.3.2016) Policing and Crime, 2009 c 26, s 57(2) (amended by SI
    2012/2595, art 18(2)(i)-(l)); Crime and Cts, 2013 c 22, sch 8 para 118; SI
    2015/230, art 2
s 195T added (pt 1.3.2016)—Policing and Crime, 2009 c 26, s 57(2) (amended by SI
    2012/2595, art 18(2)(m))
s 197 am—Serious Crime, 2007 c 27, s 82(3)
s 199 am—Serious Crime, 2007 c 27, s 82(4); Serious Crime, 2015 c 9, s 27
ss 200, 201 rep—Serious Crime, 2007 c 27, s 74, sch 8 paras 1, 57, sch 14
s 203 am—Policing and Crime, 2009 c 26, s 51(3); (1.3.2016) ibid, s 60(4)(5); Crime and
    Cts, 2013 c 22, sch 8 para 119
ss 204, 205 rep—Serious Crime, 2007 c 27, s 74, sch 8 paras 1, 58, sch 14
s 206 am—Serious Crime, 2007 c 27, s 74, sch 8 paras 1, 59
s 208 rep—Serious Crime, 2007 c 27, s 74, sch 8 paras 1, 60, sch 14
s 209 am—Serious Crime, 2007 c 27, s 74, sch 8 paras 1, 61
s 210 am—Serious Crime, 2007 c 27, s 74, sch 8 paras 1, 62
    rep in pt—Serious Crime, 2007 c 27, s 92, sch 14
s 211 am—Serious Crime, 2007 c 27, s 74, sch 8 paras 1, 63
    rep in pt—Serious Crime, 2007 c 27, s 92, sch 14
ss 212, 213 rep in pt—Serious Crime, 2007 c 27, s 74, sch 8 paras 1, 64, 65, sch 14
s 214 am—Constitutional Reform, 2005 c 4, s 40(4), sch 9 pt 1 para 77(1)(7)
s 215 rep in pt—Serious Crime, 2007 c 27, s 74, sch 8 paras 1, 66, sch 14
    am—(1.3.2016) Policing and Crime, 2009 c 26, s 60(3); SI 2010/976, art 12, sch 14;
    Serious Crime, 2015 c 9, s 36(1)-(3)
ss 215A-215D added (1.3.2016)—Policing and Crime, 2009 c 26, s 60(2)
s 215A am—Serious Crime, 2015 c 9, s 36(4)
s 217 am—Serious Crime, 2007 c 27, s 74, sch 8 paras 1, 67; (1.3.2016) Policing and
    Crime, 2009 c 26, ss 57(2), 112, sch 7 paras 66, 74
s 220 am—Policing and Crime, 2009 c 26, s 61(4)-(7); Crime and Cts, 2013 c 22, sch 8
    para 120
s 222 rep in pt—Serious Crime, 2007 c 27, s 74, sch 8 paras 1, 68, sch 14
s 223 am—SI 2010/976, art 12, sch 14
s 230 am—Serious Organised Crime and Police, 2005 c 15, s 109, sch 6 paras 4, 7;
    Counter-Terrorism, 2008 c 28, s 39, sch 3 para 7(1)(7); Policing and Crime,
    2009 c 26, s 112, sch 7 paras 99, 105
    appl—SI 2005/3181, art 135(2)
s 232 appl—SI 2005/3181, art 135(2)
s 233 am—Constitutional Reform, 2005 c 4, s 40(4), sch 9 pt 1 para 77(1)(8); Policing and
    Crime, 2009 c 26, s 112, sch 7 paras 66, 75
s 235 rep in pt—(1.3.2016) Policing and Crime, 2009 c 26, s 112, sch 7 paras 66, 76, sch 8
    pt 4
    am—Serious Crime, 2015 c 9, s 28(3)
s 235A added —Policing and Crime, 2009 c 26, s 112, sch 7 paras 66, 77
s 237 am—SI 2010/976, art 12, sch 14
s 238 am—Constitutional Reform, 2005 c 4, s 40(4), sch 9 pt 1 para 77(1)(9); SI 2010/976,
    art 12, sch 14
s 241 am—Serious Organised Crime and Police, 2005 c 15, s 109, sch 6 paras 4, 8
    appl—SI 2005/3181, art 192(3)(a)
s 242 appl—SI 2005/3181, art 189(8)(b)
Pt 5, Ch 2 (ss 243-288) power to mod —Crime and Cts, 2013 c 22, sch 25 para 7
s 243 am—Serious Organised Crime and Police, 2005 c 15, s 109, sch 6 paras 4, 9
ss 245A-245D added—Serious Organised Crime and Police, 2005 c 15, s 98(1)
s 245C am—Legal Aid, Sentencing and Punishment of Offenders, 2012 c 10, sch 5 para 59
ss 245E-245G added—Serious Crime, 2007 c 27, s 83(1)

2002

c 29 *continued*

s 246 am—Serious Crime, 2007 c 27, s 74, sch 8 paras 85, 86, sch 14

s 248 rep in pt—(prosp) Proceeds of Crime, 2002 c 29, s 457, sch 12

 am—Serious Organised Crime and Police, 2005 c 15, s 109, sch 6 paras 4, 11, 12

s 249 am—Serious Organised Crime and Police, 2005 c 15, s 109, sch 6 paras 4, 11, 12

ss 250, 251 am—Serious Organised Crime and Police, 2005 c 15, s 109, sch 6 paras 4, 13

s 252 am—Serious Organised Crime and Police, 2005 c 15, s 109, sch 6 paras 4, 13, 14;

 Legal Aid, Sentencing and Punishment of Offenders, 2012 c 10, sch 5 para 60

s 253 am—Serious Organised Crime and Police, 2005 c 15, s 109, sch 6 paras 4, 13;

 Tribunals, Courts and Enforcement, 2007 c 15, s 62, sch 13 paras 142, 146

ss 254, 255 am—Serious Organised Crime and Police, 2005 c 15, s 109, sch 6 paras 4, 13

ss 255A-255F added—Serious Organised Crime and Police, 2005 c 15, s 98(2)

ss 255G-255I added (1.3.2016)—Serious Crime, 2015 c 9, s 23(2)

s 266 am—Serious Organised Crime and Police, 2005 c 15, s 109, sch 6 paras 4, 15

s 271 am—Serious Organised Crime and Police, 2005 c 15, s 109, sch 6 paras 4, 16

s 272 am—Serious Organised Crime and Police, 2005 c 15, s 109, sch 6 paras 4, 17;

 Serious Crime, 2007 c 27, s 74, sch 8 paras 85, 87

s 273 am—Serious Crime, 2007 c 27, s 83(2); Serious Crime, 2015 c 9, sch 4 para 52

s 275 am—SI 2010/976, art 12, sch 14

s 277 am—Serious Crime, 2007 c 27, s 83(2); Serious Crime, 2015 c 9, sch 4 para 53

s 278 am—Policing and Crime, 2009 c 26, s 112, sch 7 paras 99, 106

s 280 am—Serious Organised Crime and Police, 2005 c 15, ss 99(1)(2), 109, sch 6 paras 4,

 18; Serious Crime, 2007 c 27, s 74, sch 8 paras 85, 88; SI 2008/949, art 2;

 Crime and Cts, 2013 c 22, sch 18 para 5

s 282 am—SI 2010/976, art 12, sch 14; Financial Services, 2012 c. 21, sch 18 para 94(2)

s 282A added—Crime and Cts, 2013 c 22, s 48(2)

 power to mod—Crime and Cts, 2013 c 22, sch 25 para 4(2)(a)

ss 282B-282F added —Crime and Cts, 2013 c 22, sch 18 para 6

s 282CA added (1.3.2016)—Serious Crime, 2015 c 9, s 23(3)

s 283 am—Serious Organised Crime and Police, 2005 c 15, s 109, sch 6 paras 4, 19;

 Serious Crime, 2007 c 27, s 74, sch 8 paras 85, 89

s 284 am—Serious Organised Crime and Police, 2005 c 15, s 99(1)(3)(a)(b)

s 285 am—(saving) Debt Arrangement and Attachment (S), 2002 asp 17, ss 59, 61, sch 3 pt

 1, para 29(1)

 rep in pt—(S) (pt prosp) Bankruptcy and Diligence etc (S), 2007 asp 3, s 226, sch 6

s 286 rep—Crime and Cts, 2013 c 22, s 48(4)

ss 286A, 286B added—Serious Organised Crime and Police, 2005 c 15, s 109, sch 6 paras 4,

 20

s 287 am—Serious Organised Crime and Police, 2005 c 15, s 109, sch 6 paras 4, 21; SI

 2010/976, art 12, sch 14

s 289 am—Serious Crime, 2007 c 27, s 79, sch 11 paras 1, 2; Policing and Crime, 2009 c

 26, s 63; SI 2010/976, art 12, sch 14; Finance, 2013 c 29, sch 48 para 2

 appl—UK Borders, 2007 c 30, s 24

s 290 am—Serious Organised Crime and Police, 2005 c 15, s 100(1)(3); Serious Crime,

 2007 c 27, s 79, sch 11 paras 1, 3; SI 2010/976, art 12, sch 14; Finance, 2013 c

 29, sch 48 para 3

 appl—UK Borders, 2007 c 30, s 24

s 291 am—Serious Crime, 2007 c 27, s 79, sch 11 paras 1, 4; SI 2010/976, art 12, sch 14;

 Finance, 2013 c 29, sch 48 para 4

 appl—UK Borders, 2007 c 30, s 24

s 292 see—SI 2002/3115, art 2

 appl—UK Borders, 2007 c 30, s 24

 am—SI 2010/976, art 12, sch 14; Finance, 2013 c 29, sch 48 para 5

 rep in pt—SI 2010/976, art 12, sch 14

s 293 see—SSI 2002/569, art 2

 appl—UK Borders, 2007 c 30, s 24

s 293A added—SI 2010/976, art 12, sch 14

s 294 appl—UK Borders, 2007 c 30, s 24

 am—Serious Crime, 2007 c 27, s 79, sch 11 paras 1, 6; Finance, 2013 c 29, sch 48

 para 6

s 295 am—Serious Organised Crime and Police, 2005 c 15, s 100(1)(2); Serious Crime,

 2007 c 27, s 79, sch 11 paras 1, 7; Policing and Crime, 2009 c 26, s 64; Finance,

 2013 c 29, sch 48 para 7

 appl—UK Borders, 2007 c 30, s 24

2002
c 29 *continued*

s 296 am—Serious Organised Crime and Police, 2005 c 15, s 100(1)(3); Serious Crime, 2007 c 27, s 79, sch 11 paras 1, 8; Finance, 2013 c 29, sch 48 para 8
 appl—UK Borders, 2007 c 30, s 24
s 297 appl—UK Borders, 2007 c 30, s 24
 am—Serious Crime, 2007 c 27, s 79, sch 11 paras 1, 9; Finance, 2013 c 29, sch 48 para 9
ss 297A-297G added (pt prosp 1.3.2016)—Policing and Crime, 2009 c 26, s 65(1)(4)
s 297A am—Crime and Cts, 2013 c 22, sch 21 para 28
s 297F am—Crime and Cts, 2013 c 22, sch 21 para 29
s 298 appl—UK Borders, 2007 c 30, s 24
 am—Serious Crime, 2007 c 27, s 79, sch 11 paras 1, 10; Policing and Crime, 2009 c 26, s 65(2)
s 299 subst—Serious Organised Crime and Police, 2005 c 15, s 101 (see SI 2005/1521)
 appl—UK Borders, 2007 c 30, s 24
 am—Policing and Crime, 2009 c 26, s 65(3)
s 300 appl—UK Borders, 2007 c 30, s 24
 am—Policing and Crime, 2009 c 26, s 112, sch 7 paras 99, 107
s 301 appl—UK Borders, 2007 c 30, s 24
 am—Policing and Crime, 2009 c 26, s 112, sch 7 paras 99, 108
s 302 am—Serious Organised Crime and Police, 2005 c 15, s 100(1)(3); Serious Crime, 2007 c 27, s 79, sch 11 paras 1, 11; (pt prosp 1.3.2016) Policing and Crime, 2009 c 26, s 112, sch 7 paras 99, 109; SI 2010/976, art 12, sch 14; Police Reform and Social Responsibility, 2011 c 13, sch 16 para 306; Finance, 2013 c 29, sch 48 para 10; SSI 2013/119, sch 1 para 19(3)
 appl—UK Borders, 2007 c 30, s 24
s 302A added—Serious Crime, 2007 c 27, s 84
 am—Serious Crime, 2007 c 27, s 79, sch 11 paras 1, 12; SI 2014/834, sch 2 para 24
s 303 appl—UK Borders, 2007 c 30, s 24
 am—SI 2010/976, art 12, sch 14
s 303A added—Serious Crime, 2007 c 27, s 79, sch 11 paras 1, 13
Pt 5 Ch 4 (ss 304-316) power to mod —Crime and Cts, 2013 c 22, sch 25 para 7
s 308 am—Armed Forces, 2006 c 52, s 378, sch 16 para 197; (pt prosp 1.3.2016) Policing and Crime, 2009 c 26, s 112, sch 7 paras 66, 78; Financial Services, 2012 c. 21, sch 18 para 94(3)(a); Prevention of Social Housing Fraud, 2013 c 3, sch para 23; (EW) Modern Slavery, 2015 c 30, sch 5 para 21
 rep in pt—Financial Services, 2012 c. 21, sch 18 para 94(3)(b)
 mod—SI 2009/1059, art 205, sch 1
s 309 am—SI 2010/976, art 12, sch 14
s 313 rep—Serious Crime, 2007 c 27, s 74, sch 8 paras 85, 90, sch 14
s 316 am—Crim Justice, 2003 c 44, s 331, sch 36 pt 4 para 78; Serious Organised Crime and Police, 2005 c 15, s 109, sch 6 paras 4, 22(1)-(3); Serious Crime, 2007 c 27, s 74, sch 8 paras 85, 91; SI 2010/976, art 12, sch 14; Crime and Cts, 2013 c 22, s 48(5); ibid, sch 8 para 12; Serious Crime, 2015 c 9, sch 4 para 541
 rep in pt—SI 2014/834, sch 2 para 25
 power to mod—Crime and Cts, 2013 c 22, sch 25 para 4(2)(f)
Pt 6 (ss 317-326) power to rep—Serious Crime, 2007 c 27, s 74, sch 8 para 102
s 317 am—Serious Crime, 2007 c 27, s 74, sch 8 paras 92-94; Crime and Cts, 2013 c 22, sch 8 para 122
s 318 am—Serious Crime, 2007 c 27, s 74, sch 8 paras 92-94; Crime and Cts, 2013 c 22, sch 8 para 123
s 319 am—Income Tax (Trading and Other Income), 2005 c 5, s 882(1), sch 1 pt 2 paras 581, 582; Serious Crime, 2007 c 27, s 74, sch 8 paras 92, 95; Crime and Cts, 2013 c 22, sch 8 para 124
s 320 rep—SI 2009/56, art 3, sch 1 para 333
s 321 am—Serious Crime, 2007 c 27, s 74, sch 8 paras 92, 97; Crime and Cts, 2013 c 22, sch 8 para 125
s 322 am—Serious Crime, 2007 c 27, s 74, sch 8 paras 92, 98; Crime and Cts, 2013 c 22, sch 8 para 126
s 323 am—Children and Families, 2014 c 6, sch 7 para 60(2)(c)(3)(b)(c); ibid, sch 7 para 60(3)(a); ibid, sch 7 para 60(4)
 rep in pt—Finance, 2007 c 11, s 84, sch 22 paras 3, 15, sch 27; Children and Families, 2014 c 6, sch 7 para 60(2)(a)(b)

2002

c 29 *continued*

s 324 am—Serious Crime, 2007 c 27, s 74, sch 8 paras 92, 99; Crime and Cts, 2013 c 22, sch 8 para 127

s 325 am—Serious Crime, 2007 c 27, s 74, sch 8 paras 92, 100; Crime and Cts, 2013 c 22, sch 8 para 128(1)

rep in pt—Serious Crime, 2007 c 27, s 92, sch 14

Pt 7 (ss 327-340) appl—SI 2003/173, reg 3

ss 327-329 transtl savings (am)—SI 130, art 3

s 327 am—Serious Organised Crime and Police, 2005 c 15, ss 102(1)(2), 103(1)(2)

appl—SI 2006/1070, reg 2

s 328 am—Serious Organised Crime and Police, 2005 c 15, ss 102(1)(3), 103(1)(3)

appl—SI 2006/1070, reg 2

s 329 am—Serious Organised Crime and Police, 2005 c 15, ss 102(1)(4), 103(1)(4)

appl—SI 2006/1070, reg 2

s 330 am—Serious Organised Crime and Police, 2005 c 15, ss 59, 102(1)(5), 104(1)-(3), 106(1)(2), sch 4 paras 168, 170; SI 2006/308, art 2; Serious Crime, 2007 c 27, s 74, sch 8 paras 121, 126; Crime and Cts, 2013 c 22, sch 8 para 129

rep in pt—Serious Organised Crime and Police, 2005 c 15, ss 105(1)(2), 174(2), sch 17 pt 2; SI 2007/3398, reg 3, sch 2

s 331 am—Serious Organised Crime and Police, 2005 c 15, ss 59, 102(1)(6), 104(1)(4), sch 4 paras 168, 171; Serious Crime, 2007 c 27, s 74, sch 8 paras 121, 127; Crime and Cts, 2013 c 22, sch 8 para 130

s 332 am—Serious Organised Crime and Police, 2005 c 15, ss 59, 102(1)(7), 104(1)(5)(6), sch 4 paras 168, 172; Serious Crime, 2007 c 27, s 74, sch 8 paras 121, 128; Crime and Cts, 2013 c 22, sch 8 para 131

s 333 rep—SI 2007/3398, reg 3, sch 2

ss 333A-333E added—SI 2007/3398, reg 3, sch 2

s 333A am—Crime and Cts, 2013 c 22, sch 8 para 132

s 334 am—Serious Organised Crime and Police, 2005 c 15, s 105(1)(3); SI 2007/3398, reg 3, sch 2

s 336 am—Serious Organised Crime and Police, 2005 c 15, s 59, sch 4 paras 168, 173; Serious Crime, 2007 c 27, s 74, sch 8 paras 121, 129; Crime and Cts, 2013 c 22, sch 8 para 133

s 337 am—Serious Organised Crime and Police, 2005 c 15, ss 104(1)(7), 106(1)(3)

s 337 rep in pt—Serious Organised Crime and Police, 2005 c 15, ss 105(1)(2), 174(2), sch 17 pt 2

s 338 rep in pt—Serious Organised Crime and Police, 2005 c 15, ss 105(1)(2)(4), 174(2), sch 17 pt 2

am—Serious Organised Crime and Police, 2005 c 15, s 106(1)(4)-(6); SI 2007/3398, reg 3, sch 2; Serious Crime, 2015 c 9, s 37

s 339 am—Serious Organised Crime and Police, 2005 c 15, s 105(1)(5)

rep in pt—Serious Organised Crime and Police, 2005 c 15, s 174(2), sch 17 pt 2

s 339ZA added—SI 2007/3398, reg 3, sch 2

am—Crime and Cts, 2013 c 22, sch 8 para 134

s 339A added—Serious Organised Crime and Police, 2005 c 15, s 103(1)(5)

s 340 am—Serious Organised Crime and Police, 2005 c 15, ss 59, 103(1)(6), sch 4 paras 168, 174; Serious Crime, 2007 c 27, s 74, sch 8 paras 121, 130; Crime and Cts, 2013 c 22, sch 8 para 135

mod—Serious Crime, 2007 c 27, s 63, sch 6 para 44(a)

Pt 8, Ch 1 (ss 341, 342) power to mod—Crime and Cts, 2013 c 22, s 47

s 341 appl—SI 2005/384, rule 62.3(3)

am—Serious Crime, 2007 c 27, s 75(1); Coroners and Justice, 2009 c 25, s 169, sch 19 paras 1, 2; Policing and Crime, 2009 c 26, s 112, sch 7 paras 99, 110; Crime and Cts, 2013 c 22, sch 19 para 2; ibid, sch 19 para 25(a); (1.3.2016) Serious Crime, 2015 c 9, s 38(1)

rep in pt—Crime and Cts, 2013 c 22, sch 19 para 25(b)

s 341A added —Crime and Cts, 2013 c 22, sch 19 para 3

s 342 appl—SI 2003/173, reg 3

transtl savings (am)—SI 130, art 5(1)

am—Serious Crime, 2007 c 27, s 77, sch 10 paras 1, 2; SI 2007/3398, reg 3, sch 2; Coroners and Justice, 2009 c 25, s 169, sch 19 paras 1, 3

Pt 8, Ch 2 (ss 343-379) power to mod—Crime and Cts, 2013 c 22, s 47

s 343 am—Serious Crime, 2007 c 27, s 77, sch 10 paras 1, 3; Coroners and Justice, 2009 c 25, s 169, sch 19 paras 1, 4; Policing and Crime, 2009 c 26, s 66(2)(a)

2002
c 29 s 343 *continued*
rep in pt—Policing and Crime, 2009 c 26, ss 66(2)(b), 112, sch 8 pt 5
s 344 am—Serious Crime, 2007 c 27, s 77, sch 10 paras 1, 4; Coroners and Justice, 2009 c 25, s 169, sch 19 paras 1, 5; Policing and Crime, 2009 c 26, ss 66(3)(a), 112, sch 8 pt 5
rep in pt—Policing and Crime, 2009 c 26, s 66(3)(b)
s 345 ext (mods)—SI 2003/425, arts 3, 13, 23, 24
am—Serious Crime, 2007 c 27, s 75(2); Coroners and Justice, 2009 c 25, s 169, sch 19 paras 1, 6; Crime and Cts, 2013 c 22, sch 19 para 4
s 346 am—Serious Crime, 2007 c 27, s 75(3); Coroners and Justice, 2009 c 25, s 169, sch 19 paras 1, 7; Crime and Cts, 2013 c 22, sch 19 para 5
s 347 ext (mods)—SI 2003/425, arts 3, 13, 23, 24
s 348 ext (mods)—SI 2003/425, arts 3, 13, 23, 24
s 349 ext (mods)—SI 2003/425, arts 3, 13, 23, 24
s 350 ext (mods)—SI 2003/425, arts 3, 13, 23, 24
am—Serious Crime, 2007 c 27, s 77, sch 10 paras 1, 5; Coroners and Justice, 2009 c 25, s 169, sch 19 paras 1, 8; Policing and Crime, 2009 c 26, s 66(4)(a)
rep in pt—Policing and Crime, 2009 c 26, ss 66(4)(b), 112, sch 8 pt 5
s 351 am—Serious Crime, 2007 c 27, ss 74, 77, sch 8 paras 103, 104, sch 10 paras 1, 6; Coroners and Justice, 2009 c 25, s 169, sch 19 paras 1, 9; Crime and Cts, 2013 c 22, sch 8 para 136; ibid, sch 21 para 30; Finance, 2013 c 29, sch 48 para 11
rep in pt—Policing and Crime, 2009 c 26, ss 66(5), 112, sch 8 pt 5
s 352 ext (mods)—SI 2003/425, arts 5, 15, 25
am—Serious Crime, 2007 c 27, ss 74, 76(1), 77, 80(1)(2), sch 8 paras 103, 105, sch 10 paras 1, 7; Coroners and Justice, 2009 c 25, s 169, sch 19 paras 1, 10; Crime and Cts, 2013 c 22, sch 21 para 31; ibid, sch 8 para 137; ibid, sch 19 para 6; Deregulation, 2015 c 20, s 82(6)
rep in pt—Finance, 2013 c 29, sch 48 para 12; SI 2014/834, sch 2 para 26
s 353 am—Serious Crime, 2007 c 27, ss 74, 76(2)(3), 77, 80(3)(4), sch 8 paras 103, 106, sch 10 paras 1, 8; Coroners and Justice, 2009 c 25, s 169, sch 19 paras 1, 11; Crime and Cts, 2013 c 22, sch 21 para 32(a)(b); ibid, sch 8 para 138; ibid, sch 19 para 7; Finance, 2013 c 29, sch 48 para 13(2)(b); (1.3.2016) Serious Crime, 2015 c 9, s 38(2)
rep in pt—Finance, 2013 c 29, sch 48 para 13(2)(a)(3)
s 354 ext (mods)—SI 2003/425, arts 5, 15, 25
s 355 am—Policing and Crime, 2009 c 26, s 66(6); SI 2010/976, art 12, sch 14
s 356 am—Serious Crime, 2007 c 27, ss 74, 77, 80(5)(6), sch 8 paras 103, 107, sch 10 paras 1, 9; Coroners and Justice, 2009 c 25, s 169, sch 19 paras 1, 12; Policing and Crime, 2009 c 26, s 66(7)(c); Crime and Cts, 2013 c 22, sch 21 para 33; Crime and Cts, 2013 c 22, sch 21 para 33
rep in pt—Serious Crime, 2007 c 27, s 92, sch 14; Policing and Crime, 2009 c 26, s 66(7)(a)(b)(d), sch 8 pt 5
s 357 am—Serious Crime, 2007 c 27, ss 74, 77, sch 8 paras 103, 108, sch 10 paras 1, 10; Coroners and Justice, 2009 c 25, s 169, sch 19 paras 1, 13; Crime and Cts, 2013 c 22, sch 8 para 139; ibid, sch 21 para 34; ibid, sch 19 para 8; SI 2014/834, sch 2 para 27
s 358 am—Coroners and Justice, 2009 c 25, s 169, sch 19 paras 1, 14; Crime and Cts, 2013 c 22, sch 19 para 9
ss 359, 360 ext (mods)—SI 2003/425, arts 7, 17, 27, 28
s 361 ext (mods)—SI 2003/425, arts 7, 17, 27, 28
am—Serious Crime, 2007 c 27, s 74, sch 8 paras 103, 109
s 362 am—Serious Crime, 2007 c 27, s 74, sch 8 paras 103, 110; Coroners and Justice, 2009 c 25, s 169, sch 19 paras 1, 15; Crime and Cts, 2013 c 22, sch 8 para 140
s 363 am—Serious Crime, 2007 c 27, s 77, sch 10 paras 1, 11; Crime and Cts, 2013 c 22, sch 19 para 10(a)
rep in pt—Crime and Cts, 2013 c 22, sch 19 para 10(b)
s 364 appl (mods)—(EW,NI) Crime (International Co-operation), 2003 c 32, s 32(6)
am—Serious Organised Crime and Police, 2005 c 15, s 107(1)(2); SI 2009/1941, art 2, sch 1
s 365 am—Crime and Cts, 2013 c 22, sch 19 para 11
s 366 ext (mods)—SI 2003/425, arts 9, 10, 19, 20
s 367 ext (mods)—SI 2003/425, arts 9, 19, 29, 30
s 368 ext (mods)—SI 2003/425, arts 9, 10, 19, 20

2002
c 29 *continued*

        s 369 am—Serious Crime, 2007 c 27, s 74, sch 8 paras 103, 111; Crime and Cts, 2013 c 22,
            sch 8 para 141; ibid, sch 21 para 35; Finance, 2013 c 29, sch 48 para 14
        s 370 ext (mods)—SI 2003/425, arts 11, 21, 31, 32
            am—Serious Crime, 2007 c 27, s 77, sch 10 paras 1, 12; Coroners and Justice, 2009 c
            25, s 169, sch 19 paras 1, 17; Crime and Cts, 2013 c 22, sch 19 para 12(a)
            rep in pt—Crime and Cts, 2013 c 22, sch 19 para 12(b)
        s 371 am—Crime and Cts, 2013 c 22, sch 19 para 13
        s 372 ext (mods)—SI 2003/425, arts 11, 21, 31, 32
        s 374 ext (mods)—SI 2003/425, arts 11, 12, 21, 22
        s 375 am—Serious Crime, 2007 c 27, s 74, sch 8 paras 103, 112; Crime and Cts, 2013 c 22,
            sch 8 para 142; ibid, sch 21 para 36; Finance, 2013 c 29, sch 48 para 15
        ss 375A, 375B added —Crime and Cts, 2013 c 22, sch 19 para 26
        s 375C added —Finance, 2013 c 29, sch 48 para 16
        s 376 rep—Serious Crime, 2007 c 27, s 74, sch 8 paras 103, 113
        s 377 see—SI 2003/334, art 2
            am—Serious Crime, 2007 c 27, s 74, sch 8 paras 103, 114; SI 2010/976, art 12, sch
            14; Crime and Cts, 2013 c 22, sch 8 para 143; ibid, sch 21 para 37; Finance,
            2013 c 29, sch 48 para 17
            rep in pt—SI 2010/976, art 12, sch 14
        ss 377ZA, 377ZB added—SI 2010/976, art 12, sch 14
        s 377A added—Serious Crime, 2007 c 27, s 74, sch 8 paras 103, 115
            rep in pt—SI 2014/834, sch 2 para 28
        s 378 am—Serious Organised Crime and Police, 2005 c 15, s 59, sch 4 paras 168, 175;
            Serious Crime, 2007 c 27, ss 74, 77, 80(7)(8), sch 8 paras 103, 116, sch 10
            paras 1, 13; Coroners and Justice, 2009 c 25, s 169, sch 19 paras 1, 18; Finance,
            2013 c 29, sch 48 para 18; Crime and Cts, 2013 c 22, s 55(5); ibid, sch 8 para
            144; ibid, sch 19 paras 27, 29, 30
            appl—SI 2005/384, rules 56.4(4), 62.1(3), 62.2(2), 62.3(3)
            rep in pt—Serious Crime, 2007 c 27, s 92, sch 14
        s 380 ext (mods)—SI 2003/425, arts 4, 14
            am—Serious Crime, 2007 c 27, s 77, sch 10 paras 1, 14; (S) ibid, s 75(4); Crime and
            Cts, 2013 c 22, sch 19 para 14(3)
            rep in pt—Crime and Cts, 2013 c 22, sch 19 para 14(2)
        s 381 am—(S) Serious Crime, 2007 c 27, s 75(5); Crime and Cts, 2013 c 22, sch 19 para 15
        ss 382-384 ext (mods)—SI 2003/425, arts 4, 14
        s 385 ext (mods)—SI 2003/425, arts 4, 14
            am—Serious Crime, 2007 c 27, s 77, sch 10 paras 1, 15
        s 386 am—Serious Crime, 2007 c 27, s 77, sch 10 paras 1, 16
        s 387 ext (mods)—SI 2003/425, arts 6, 16
            am—Serious Crime, 2007 c 27, s 77, sch 10 paras 1, 17; (S) ibid, ss 76(4), 86; Crime
            and Cts, 2013 c 22, sch 19 para 16(3)
            rep in pt—Crime and Cts, 2013 c 22, sch 19 para 16(2)
        s 388 am—Serious Crime, 2007 c 27, s 77, sch 10 paras 1, 18; (S) ibid, s 76(5)(6); Crime
            and Cts, 2013 c 22, sch 19 para 17; (prosp) Serious Crime, 2015 c 9, s 38(3)
        s 389 ext (mods)—SI 2003/425, arts 6, 16
        s 390 ext (mods)—SI 2003/425, arts 6, 16, 25
            am—Serious Crime, 2007 c 27, s 77, sch 10 paras 1, 19
        s 391 am—Serious Crime, 2007 c 27, s 77, sch 10 paras 1, 20; Crime and Cts, 2013 c 22,
            sch 19 para 18
        s 392 am—Crime and Cts, 2013 c 22, sch 19 para 19
        s 393 ext (mods)—SI 2003/425, arts 8, 18, 27, 28
        ss 394, 395 ext (mods)—SI 2003/425, arts 8, 18
        s 397 am—Serious Crime, 2007 c 27, s 77, sch 10 paras 1, 21; Crime and Cts, 2013 c 22,
            sch 19 para 20(3)(a)
            rep in pt—Crime and Cts, 2013 c 22, sch 19 para 20(2)(3)(b)
        s 398 appl (mods)—(S) Crime (International Co-operation), 2003 c 32, s 37(6)
            am—Serious Organised Crime and Police, 2005 c 15, s 107(1)(3); SI 2009/1941, art
            2, sch 1
        s 399 am—Crime and Cts, 2013 c 22, sch 19 para 21
        s 400 ext (mods)—SI 2003/425, arts 29, 30
        s 401 ext (mods)—SI 2003/425, arts 10, 20
        s 402 ext (mods)—SI 2003/425, arts 29, 30
        s 404 ext (mods)—SI 2003/425, arts 12, 22

2002

c 29 s 404 *continued*

am—Serious Crime, 2007 c 27, s 77, sch 10 paras 1, 22; Crime and Cts, 2013 c 22, sch 19 para 22(3)(a)

rep in pt—Crime and Cts, 2013 c 22, sch 19 para 22(2)(3)(b)

s 405 am—Crime and Cts, 2013 c 22, sch 19 para 23

s 406 ext (mods)—SI 2003/425, arts 12, 22

s 407 ext (mods)—SI 2003/425, arts 31, 32

ss 408A, 408B added —Crime and Cts, 2013 c 22, sch 19 para 28

s 408C added—Finance, 2013 c 29, sch 48 para 19

s 409 appl (mods)—Crime (International Co-operation), 2003 c 32, ss 22(6), 38(5), 41(5)

s 410 see—SSI 2003/94, art 2

s 412 appl—Serious Organised Crime and Police, 2005 c 15, s 64(7)

am—Serious Crime, 2007 c 27, s 77, sch 10 paras 1, 23; Crime and Cts, 2013 c 22, sch 21 para 38; Finance, 2013 c 29, sch 48 para 20

Pt 8, Ch 4 (ss 413-416) power to mod—Crime and Cts, 2013 c 22, s 47

s 415 am—Serious Organised Crime and Police, 2005 c 15, s 107(1)(4)

mod—Serious Crime, 2007 c 27, s 63, sch 6 para 44(b)

s 416 am—Serious Crime, 2007 c 27, ss 74, 77, sch 8 paras 103, 117, sch 10 paras 1, 24; Crime and Cts, 2013 c 22, sch 8 para 145; Serious Crime, 2015 c 9, sch 4 para 56

s 417 rep in pt—Serious Crime, 2007 c 27, s 74, sch 8 paras 1, 69, sch 14

am—(pt prosp 1.3.2016) Policing and Crime, 2009 c 26, s 112, sch 7 paras 66, 79

s 418 am—Serious Crime, 2007 c 27, s 74, sch 8 paras 1, 70; Policing and Crime, 2009 c 26, s 112, sch 7 paras 66, 80

s 419 am—Serious Crime, 2007 c 27, s 74, sch 8 paras 1, 71; Policing and Crime, 2009 c 26, s 112, sch 7 paras 66, 81

rep in pt—Serious Crime, 2007 c 27, s 92, sch 14; Policing and Crime, 2009 c 26, s 112, sch 8 pt 4

s 420 rep in pt—Serious Crime, 2007 c 27, s 74, sch 8 paras 1, 72, sch 14

am—Policing and Crime, 2009 c 26, s 112, sch 7 paras 66, 82

s 421 am—Serious Crime, 2007 c 27, s 74, sch 8 paras 1, 73; Policing and Crime, 2009 c 26, s 112, sch 7 paras 66, 83

s 422 am—Serious Crime, 2007 c 27, s 74, sch 8 paras 1, 74; (pt prosp 1.3.2016) Policing and Crime, 2009 c 26, s 112, sch 7 paras 66, 84

rep in pt—Serious Crime, 2007 c 27, s 92, sch 14; Policing and Crime, 2009 c 26, s 112, sch 8 pt 4

s 423 rep in pt—Serious Crime, 2007 c 27, s 74, sch 8 paras 1, 75, sch 14

am—(pt prosp 1.3.2016) Policing and Crime, 2009 c 26, s 112, sch 7 paras 66, 85

s 424 am—Serious Crime, 2007 c 27, s 74, sch 8 paras 1, 76; Policing and Crime, 2009 c 26, s 112, sch 7 paras 66, 86

s 425 am—Serious Crime, 2007 c 27, s 74, sch 8 paras 1, 77; (pt prosp 1.3.2016) Policing and Crime, 2009 c 26, s 112, sch 7 paras 66, 87

rep in pt—Serious Crime, 2007 c 27, s 92, sch 14

s 426 am—Serious Crime, 2007 c 27, s 74, sch 8 paras 1, 78; (pt prosp 1.3.2016) Policing and Crime, 2009 c 26, s 112, sch 7 paras 66, 88

rep in pt—Serious Crime, 2007 c 27, s 92, sch 14

s 427 am—Serious Crime, 2007 c 27, s 74, sch 8 paras 1, 79; (pt prosp 1.3.2016) Policing and Crime, 2009 c 26, s 112, sch 7 paras 66, 89

rep in pt—Serious Crime, 2007 c 27, s 92, sch 14; Policing and Crime, 2009 c 26, s 112, sch 8 pt 4

s 428 am—Serious Crime, 2007 c 27, s 74, sch 8 paras 1, 80; (pt prosp 1.3.2016) Policing and Crime, 2009 c 26, s 112, sch 7 paras 66, 90

rep in pt—Serious Crime, 2007 c 27, s 92, sch 14

s 429 am—Serious Crime, 2007 c 27, s 74, sch 8 paras 1, 81; (pt prosp 1.3.2016) Policing and Crime, 2009 c 26, s 112, sch 7 paras 66, 91

rep in pt—Serious Crime, 2007 c 27, s 92, sch 14; Policing and Crime, 2009 c 26, s 112, sch 8 pt 4

s 430 am—Serious Crime, 2007 c 27, s 74, sch 8 paras 1, 82; (pt prosp 1.3.2016) Policing and Crime, 2009 c 26, s 112, sch 7 paras 66, 92

rep in pt—Serious Crime, 2007 c 27, s 92, sch 14

s 432 am—Serious Organised Crime and Police, 2005 c 15, s 109, sch 6 paras 4, 23; Serious Crime, 2007 c 27, s 74, sch 8 paras 1, 83; (pt prosp 1.3.2016) Policing and Crime, 2009 c 26, s 112, sch 7 paras 66, 93

s 435 subst—Serious Crime, 2007 c 27, s 74, sch 8 paras 121, 131

2002
c 29 *continued*

s 436 am—Commrs for Revenue and Customs, 2005 c 11, s 50(6), sch 4 para 98; Serious
Organised Crime and Police, 2005 c 15, s 59, sch 4 paras 168, 176; Serious
Crime, 2007 c 27, s 74, sch 8 paras 121, 132; SI 2010/976, art 12, sch 14
rep in pt—Serious Crime, 2007 c 27, s 92, sch 14
ext—SI 2008/1909, art 2, sch
s 437 am—Serious Crime, 2007 c 27, s 74, sch 8 paras 121, 133
s 438 am—Serious Crime, 2007 c 27, ss 74, 79, sch 8 paras 121, 134, sch 11 para 14;
Crime and Cts, 2013 c 22, sch 8 para 146; SI 2014/834, sch 2 para 29
rep in pt—Serious Crime, 2007 c 27, s 92, sch 14
ext—SI 2008/1909, art 3
s 439 am—Serious Organised Crime and Police, 2005 c 15, s 59, sch 4 paras 168, 177;
Serious Crime, 2007 c 27, s 74, sch 8 paras 121, 135; Crime and Cts, 2013 c 22,
sch 8 para 147
rep in pt—SI 2014/834, sch 2 para 30
s 441 am—Serious Crime, 2007 c 27, s 74, sch 8 paras 121, 136
rep in pt—SI 2014/834, sch 2 para 31
s 443 am—Serious Crime, 2007 c 27, s 74, sch 8 paras 121, 137; Crime and Cts, 2013 c 22,
sch 8 para 148
s 444 am—Serious Organised Crime and Police, 2005 c 15, s 108(1)-(3); Serious Crime,
2007 c 27, s 74, sch 8 paras 121, 138; SI 2010/976, art 12, sch 14; Crime and
Cts, 2013 c 22, sch 8 para 149; SI 2014/834, sch 2 para 32(a)
rep in pt—SI 2014/834, sch 2 para 32(b)
s 445 am—Serious Organised Crime and Police, 2005 c 15, s 59, sch 4 paras 168, 178;
Serious Crime, 2007 c 27, s 74, sch 8 paras 121, 139; SI 2010/976, art 12, sch
14; Crime and Cts, 2013 c 22, sch 8 para 150
rep in pt—SI 2014/834, sch 2 para 33
s 447 am—Serious Organised Crime and Police, 2005 c 15, s 108(1)(4); Serious Crime,
2015 c 9, s 39
rep in pt—Serious Organised Crime and Police, 2005 c 15, s 174(2), sch 17 pt 2
appl—SI 2005/3181, arts 7(4), 55, 57(4), 68(7), 82(3)(a), 92, 94(4), 107(7), 141,
177(1)(2)(a), 202(1)(2)
mod—Serious Crime, 2007 c 27, s 63, sch 6 para 44(c)
s 449 rep in pt—Serious Crime, 2007 c 27, s 74, sch 8 paras 121, 140
am—Crime and Cts, 2013 c 22, sch 8 para 151
s 449A added—Serious Crime, 2007 c 27, s 74, sch 8 paras 103, 118
s 450 am—Serious Crime, 2007 c 27, s 77, sch 10 paras 1, 25
s 451 am—Commrs for Revenue and Customs, 2005 c 11, s 50(6), sch 4 para 99(e); SI
2014/834, sch 2 para 34
rep in pt—Commrs for Revenue and Customs, 2005 c 11, ss 50(6), 52(2), sch 4 para
99(c), sch 5
mod—Serious Crime, 2007 c 27, s 63, sch 6 para 44(d)
s 452 am—SI 2010/976, art 12, sch 14
s 453 am—Serious Crime, 2007 c 27, s 81(1)
s 453A added—Serious Crime, 2007 c 27, s 81(2)
am—(pt prosp 1.3.2016) Policing and Crime, 2009 c 26, s 112, sch 7 paras 66, 94
s 458 am—SI 2010/976, art 12, sch 14
s 459 am—Serious Organised Crime and Police, 2005 c 15, s 103(1)(7); Serious Crime,
2007 c 27, ss 74, 79, sch 8 paras 103, 119, sch 11 para 15; Policing and Crime,
2009 c 26, s 112, sch 7 paras 66, 95; ibid, s 57(5) (added by SI 2012/2595, art
18(2)(n)); SI 2010/976, art 12, sch 14; Crime and Cts, 2013 c 22, s 46(7);
Serious Crime, 2015 c 9, ss 10(2),14(5),19(2),32(2), 36(5); ibid, sch 4 para 57
rep in pt—SI 2010/976, art 12, sch 14
s 460 am—Serious Crime, 2007 c 27, s 74, sch 8 paras 121, 141; SI 2010/976, art 12, sch
14
rep in pt—SI 2014/834, sch 2 para 35
sch 1 rep—Serious Crime, 2007 c 27, s 74, sch 8 paras 121, 142
sch 2 am—Nationality, Immigration and Asylum, 2002 c 41, s 114(3), sch 7, para 31;
Sexual Offences, 2003 c 42, s 139, sch 6 para 46(1)-(3); Gangmasters
(Licensing), 2004 c 11, s 14(4); Asylum and Immigration (Treatment of
Claimants, etc), 2004 c 19, s 5(7); Serious Crime, 2007 c 27, s 63, sch 6 para 62;
Protection of Freedoms, 2012 c 9, sch 9 para 138; Serious Crime, 2015 c 9, sch 4
para 58; Modern Slavery, 2015 c 30, s 7(2)(3)(b)
rep in pt—Modern Slavery, 2015 c 30, s 7(3)(a)

2002
c 29 *continued*

sch 3 am—(saving) Debt Arrangement and Attachment (S), 2002 asp 17, ss 59, 61, sch 3 pt 1, para 29(2)

rep in pt—(S) Bankruptcy and Diligence etc (S), 2007 asp 3, s 226, sch 6

sch 4 am—Nationality, Immigration and Asylum, 2002 c 41, s 114(3), sch 7, para 32; SSI 2003/594, art 3; Gangmasters (Licensing), 2004 c 11, s 14(4); Asylum and Immigration (Treatment of Claimants, etc), 2004 c 19, s 5(8); SSIs 2011/231, art 4; 2014/187, art 3; (31.5.2016) Human Trafficking and Exploitation (S), 2015 asp 12, s 15(a)(b)

rep in pt—SI 2013/1881, sch para 8

sch 5 am—Nationality, Immigration and Asylum, 2002 c 41, s 114(3), sch 7, para 33; Sexual Offences, 2003 c 42, s 139, sch 6 para 46(1)(4)(5)(a); Asylum and Immigration (Treatment of Claimants, etc), 2004 c 19, s 5(9); Gangmasters (Licensing), 2004 c 11, s 14(4); Serious Crime, 2007 c 27, s 63, sch 6 para 62

rep in pt—Sexual Offences, 2003 c 42, ss 139, 140, sch 6 para 46(1)(5)(b), sch 7

sch 7A added—Crime and Cts, 2013 c 22, s 48(3)

sch 8 am—Commrs for Revenue and Customs, 2005 c 11, s 50(6), sch 4 para 100; Serious Crime, 2007 c 27, s 74, sch 8 paras 92, 101; Crime and Cts, 2013 c 22, sch 8 para 152

rep in pt—Serious Crime, 2007 c 27, s 92, sch 14

sch 9 am—SI 2003/3074, arts 1-4, sch; Pensions, 2004 c 35, s 319(1), sch 12 para 80; Gambling, 2005 c 19, s 356(1)(2), sch 16 pt 2 para 19; SIs 2006/2385, art 2; 2006/3221, reg 29, sch 4; 2007/209, art 2; Localism, 2011 c 20, sch 18 para 2(a); SIs 2011/99, sch 4 para 4; 2011/2701, art 3; Financial Services, 2012 c 21, sch 18 para 94(4); SIs 2012/1534, art 3; 2013/3115, sch 2 para 41(2)-(4)(5)(b); Co-operative and Community Benefit Societies, 2014 c 14, sch 4 para 81; SI 2015/575, sch 1 para 23(2)(3)(b)

rep in pt—Localism, 2011 c 20, sch 18 para 2(b), sch 25 pt 29; SIs 2012/2299, art 3; 2013/3115, sch 2 para 41(5)(a); 2014/892, sch 1 para 159

sch 10 am—Income Tax (Trading and Other Income), 2005 c 5, s 882(1), sch 1 pt 2 paras 581, 583(1)-(6); Income Tax, 2007 c 3, s 1027, sch 1 paras 414, 424; Serious Crime, 2007 c 27, ss 74, 83(3), sch 8 paras 1, 84; Corporation Tax, 2009 c 4, s 1322, sch 1 paras 546, 547; Policing and Crime, 2009 c 26, s 112, sch 7 paras 99, 111; Serious Crime, 2015 c 9, sch 4 para 59

rep in pt—Finance, 2008 c 9, s 84, sch 27 para 24; SI 2015/575, sch 1 para 23(3)(a)

sch 11 rep in pt—Extradition, 2003 c 41, s 220, sch 4 (see SI 2003/3103, arts 2-5); (prosp) Crim Justice, 2003 c 44, s 332, sch 37 pt 7; Serious Organised Crime and Police, 2005 c 15, s 174(2), sch 17 pt 2; Serious Crime, 2007 c 27, s 92, sch 14; Pensions, 2008 c 30, s 148, sch 11 pt 2; Financial Services, 2012 c. 21, sch 19; Legal Aid, Sentencing and Punishment of Offenders, 2012 c 10, s 148(5); Modern Slavery, 2015 c 30, sch 5 para 22

c 30 **Police Reform**

s 1 rep (prosp)—Police and Justice, 2006 c 48, s 52, sch 15

s 5 rep—Police and Justice, 2006 c 48, s 52, sch 15

s 8 rep—Serious Organised Crime and Police, 2005 c 15, ss 59, 174(2), sch 4 paras 179, 180, sch 17 pt 2

Pt 2 (ss 9-29) transtl provns—SI 2004/671, arts 2(1)(2), 3

see —(power to appl, am or mod) Police Reform and Social Responsibility, 2011 c 13, sch 7 para 7(1)

power to appl (mods)—Commrs for Revenue and Customs, 2005 c 11, s 28(1)(2)(a)

appl (mods)—SIs 2005/3311, reg 3(1)(2)(6)(a), sch 1; 2012/1204, regs 27, 35(1); 2013/1778, reg 2

mod—SI 2015/431, reg 4 sch

s 9 am—Serious Organised Crime and Police, 2005 c 15, s 55(1), sch 2 paras 1, 2(a); Police and Justice, 2006 c 48, ss 1, 52, sch 1 paras 80, 81, sch 14 para 40; Police Reform and Social Responsibility, 2011 c 13, sch 14 para 2; Crime and Cts, 2013 c 22, sch 8 para 153(1)(c)

rep in pt—Serious Organised Crime and Police, 2005 c 15, ss 55(1), 174(2), sch 2 paras 1, 2(b), sch 17 pt 2; Crime and Cts, 2013 c 22, sch 8 para 153(1)(a)(b)

appl—SI 2008/212, reg 5

appl (mods)—SIs 2009/2133, reg 4; 2010/782, reg 4; 2010/1813, reg 5; 2013/2325, reg 5

2002

c 30 *continued*

s 10 rep in pt—Serious Organised Crime and Police, 2005 c 15, ss 55(1), 174(2), sch 2
paras 1, 3(1)(2)(a)(b)(3)(a)(c)(4); Police and Justice, 2006 c 48, s 52, sch 15;
Police Reform and Social Responsibility, 2011 c 13, sch 14 para 6(a)

am—Serious Organised Crime and Police, 2005 c 15, ss 55(1), 160, sch 2 paras 1,
3(1)(2)(c)(3)(b)(4), sch 12 paras 1, 2; Police and Justice, 2006 c 48, s 1, sch 1
paras 80, 82; Serious Crime, 2007 c 27, s 74, sch 8 para 160; Police Reform and
Social Responsibility, 2011 c 13, sch 16 para 278(2); Crime and Cts, 2013 c 22,
sch 6 para 9(2)(a)(3)

appl (mods)—SIs 2008/212, reg 5, sch 1; 2012/62, reg 3(5)

rep in pt—Crime and Cts, 2013 c 22, sch 6 para 9(2)(b)(4)

s 11 am—Serious Organised Crime and Police, 2005 c 15, s 55(1), sch 2 paras 1, 4; Police
and Justice, 2006 c 48, s 1, sch 1 paras 80, 83; Police Reform and Social
Responsibility, 2011 c 13, sch 16 para 279; Crime and Cts, 2013 c 22, sch 6 para
10(2)(b)(3)(5)(c)

rep in pt—Police and Justice, 2006 c 48, s 52, sch 15; Crime and Cts, 2013 c 22, sch 6
para 10(2)(a)(4)(5)(a)

appl (mods)—SI 2008/212, reg 5, sch 1

s 12 am—Serious Organised Crime and Police, 2005 c 15, s 160, sch 12 paras 1, 3; Police
Reform and Social Responsibility, 2011 c 13, sch 16 para 280; Police
(Complaints and Conduct), 2012 c 22, s 2(3); Anti-social Behaviour, Crime and
Policing, 2014 c 12, s 135

appl (mods)—SI 2008/212, reg 5, sch 1

rep in pt—Police Reform and Social Responsibility, 2011 c 13, sch 14 para 8(6)(a)

s 13 am—Serious Organised Crime and Police, 2005 c 15, s 160, sch 12 paras 1, 4(a)-(c)

appl—SI 2008/212, reg 5

rep in pt—Police Reform and Social Responsibility, 2011 c 13, sch 14 para 6(b)

s 14 rep—Police Reform and Social Responsibility, 2011 c 13, sch 14 para 4

s 15 am—Serious Organised Crime and Police, 2005 c 15, s 55(1), sch 2 paras 1,
5(1)-(5)(6)(a)(b)(7)(8); Police and Justice, 2006 c 48, s 1, sch 1 paras 80, 84;
Police Reform and Social Responsibility, 2011 c 13, sch 14 para 7, sch 16 para
281; Crime and Cts, 2013 c 22, sch 6 para 11(2)(4)-(8)(10)

rep in pt—Serious Organised Crime and Police, 2005 c 15, ss 55(1), 174(2), sch 2
paras 1, 5(1)(6)(c), sch 17 pt 2; Crime and Cts, 2013 c 22, sch 6 para
11(3)(9)(11)

appl (mods)—SI 2008/212, reg 5, sch 1

s 16 am—Serious Organised Crime and Police, 2005 c 15, s 55(1), sch 2 paras 1, 6; ibid, sch
12 paras 1, 5; Police Reform and Social Responsibility, 2011 c 13, sch 16 para
282; Crime and Cts, 2013 c 22, sch 6 para 12

appl (mods)—SI 2008/212, reg 5, sch 1

s 16A added—Police and Justice, 2006 c 48, s 1, sch 1 paras 80, 85

rep—Crime and Cts, 2013 c 22, sch 6 para 13

s 17 am—Police and Justice, 2006 c 48, s 1, sch 1 paras 80, 86; Police Reform and Social
Responsibility, 2011 c 13, sch 16 para 284

appl (mods)—SI 2008/212, reg 5, sch 1

rep in pt—Crime and Cts, 2013 c 22, sch 6 para 14

s 18 am—Serious Organised Crime and Police, 2005 c 15, s 160, sch 12 paras 1, 6; Police
Reform and Social Responsibility, 2011 c 13, sch 16 para 285

appl (mods)—SI 2008/212, reg 5, sch 1

s 19 appl—SI 2008/212, reg 5

appl (mods)—SIs 2009/2133, reg 4; 2010/782, reg 4; 2010/1813, reg 5; 2013/2325,
reg 5

s 20 appl (mods)—SI 2008/212, reg 5, sch 1

am—Police Reform and Social Responsibility, 2011 c 13, sch 16 para 286

s 21 appl—SI 2004/645, reg 29(7)

am—Serious Organised Crime and Police, 2005 c 15, s 160, sch 12 paras 1, 7

appl (mods)—SI 2008/212, reg 5, sch 1

s 22 am—Serious Organised Crime and Police, 2005 c 15, s 160, sch 12 paras 1, 8, 9; Police
and Justice, 2006 c 48, s 6, sch 4 para 11; Police Reform and Social
Responsibility, 2011 c 13, sch 16 para 287

appl (mods)—SIs 2008/212, reg 5, sch 1; 2009/2133, reg 4; 2010/782, reg 4;
2010/1813, reg 5; 2012/62, reg 4; 2013/2325, reg 5

rep in pt—Police Reform and Social Responsibility, 2011 c 13, sch 14 para 9(3)

2002
c 30 *continued*

s 23 am—Serious Organised Crime and Police, 2005 c 15, s 160, sch 12 paras 1, 8, 9; Crim Justice and Immigration, 2008 c 4, s 127, sch 23 paras 1, 2; Police Reform and Social Responsibility, 2011 c 13, sch 16 para 288
appl (mods)—SIs 2008/212, reg 5, sch 1; 2009/2133, reg 4; 2010/782, reg 4; 2010/1813, reg 5
s 24 am—Police and Justice, 2006 c 48, s 6, sch 4 para 12; Police Reform and Social Responsibility, 2011 c 13, sch 16 para 289
appl (mods)—SIs 2008/212, reg 5, sch 1; 2009/2133, reg 4; 2010/782, reg 4; 2010/1813, reg 5; 2013/2325, reg 5
s 25 rep—Serious Organised Crime and Police, 2005 c 15, ss 55(1), 174(2), sch 2 paras 1, 7, sch 17 pt 2
s 26 am—Railways and Transport Safety, 2003 c 20, s 73, sch 5 para 4(1)(a)(2)(m); Police Reform and Social Responsibility, 2011 c 13, sch 16 para 290
appl (mods)—SI 2008/212, reg 5, sch 1
s 26A added—Serious Organised Crime and Police, 2005 c 15, s 55(1), sch 2 paras 1, 8
rep—Crime and Cts, 2013 c 22, sch 6 para 15
s 26B added—Police and Justice, 2006 c 48, s 1, sch 1 paras 80, 87
rep—Crime and Cts, 2013 c 22, sch 6 para 15
s 26BA added—Anti-social Behaviour, Crime and Policing, 2014 c 12, s 130
s 26C added—Crime and Cts, 2013 c 22, s 11(6)
s 27 appl—SI 2008/212, reg 5
appl (mods)—SIs 2009/2133, reg 4; 2010/782, reg 4; 2013/2325, reg 5
s 28 appl—SI 2008/212, reg 5
s 28A added—Police (Complaints and Conduct), 2012 c 22, s 2(2)
s 29 am—Serious Organised Crime and Police, 2005 c 15, ss 55(1), 160, sch 2 paras 1, 9, sch 12 paras 1, 10(1)(3); ibid, s 160, sch 12 paras 1, 10(1)(2)(a)(b); Police and Justice, 2006 c 48, s 1, sch 1 paras 80, 88; Police Reform and Social Responsibility, 2011 c 13, sch 16 para 291(a); ibid, sch 14 para 5(1); Police (Complaints and Conduct), 2012 c 22, s 2(4); Crime and Cts, 2013 c 22, sch 6 para 16; Anti-social Behaviour, Crime and Policing, 2014 c 12, sch 11 para 93
rep in pt—Police and Justice, 2006 c 48, s 52, sch 15; Police Reform and Social Responsibility, 2011 c 13, sch 16 para 291(b); ibid, sch 14 para 8(6)(b)
appl (mods)—SI 2008/212, reg 5, sch 1
s 38 appl (mods)—(EW) Railways and Transport Safety, 2003 c 20, s 28(1)(a)(b)(2)
rep in pt—Serious Organised Crime and Police, 2005 c 15, ss 59, 174(2), sch 4 paras 179, 181, sch 17 pt 2; Policing and Crime, 2009 c 26, s 112, sch 7 para 125(2), sch 8 pt 13
am—Police and Justice, 2006 c 48, ss 7(1), 9, sch 5 paras 1, 2; Police Reform and Social Responsibility, 2011 c 13, sch 16 para 292
s 38A added—Police and Justice, 2006 c 48, s 7(2)
am—Police Reform and Social Responsibility, 2011 c 13, sch 16 para 293
ss 38B, 38C added —Police Reform and Social Responsibility, 2011 c 13, sch 13 para 3
s 39 appl (mods)—(EW) Railways and Transport Safety, 2003 c 20, s 28(1)(a)(b)(2)
am—Police and Justice, 2006 c 48, s 6, sch 4 para 13; Police Reform and Social Responsibility, 2011 c 13, sch 16 para 294
rep in pt—Anti-social Behaviour, Crime and Policing, 2014 c 12, sch 11 para 94
s 40 rep in pt—Police Reform and Social Responsibility, 2011 c 13, sch 16 para 295(4)(b)
am—Police Reform and Social Responsibility, 2011 c 13, sch 16 para 295(2)(3)(4)(a)(c)
s 41 am—Police and Justice, 2006 c 48, s 52, sch 14 para 42
s 41A added—Police and Justice, 2006 c 48, s 15(1)
s 41B added—Police and Justice, 2006 c 48, s 16
s 42 appl (mods)—(EW) Railways and Transport Safety, 2003 c 20, s 28(1)(c)(2)
rep in pt—Serious Organised Crime and Police, 2005 c 15, ss 59, 174(2), sch 4 paras 179, 182, sch 17 pt 2
am—Serious Organised Crime and Police, 2005 c 15, s 122(1)(2); Police and Justice, 2006 c 48, ss 9, 52, sch 5 paras 1, 3, sch 14 para 43; Police Reform and Social Responsibility, 2011 c 13, sch 13 para 4, sch 16 para 296
s 43 am—Railways and Transport Safety, 2003 c 20, s 73, sch 5 para 4(1)(a)(2)(m); SI 2004/1573, art 12(7)(a)(b); Police and Justice, 2006 c 48, s 6, sch 4 para 14; Police Reform and Social Responsibility, 2011 c 13, sch 16 para 297
rep in pt—SI 2004/1573, art 12(7)(c); Legal Aid, Sentencing and Punishment of Offenders, 2012 c 10, sch 23 para 14(2)

2002
c 30 *continued*

s 45 appl (mods)—(EW) Railways and Transport Safety, 2003 c 20, s 28(1)(d)-(f)(2)
    rep in pt—Serious Organised Crime and Police, 2005 c 15, ss 59, 174(2), sch 4 paras
        179, 183, sch 17 pt 2
    am—Police and Justice, 2006 c 48, s 6, sch 4 para 15; Police Reform and Social
        Responsibility, 2011 c 13, sch 16 para 298
s 46 am—(prosp) Crim Justice, 2003 c 44, s 280(2)(3), sch 26 para 57; Police and Justice,
        2006 c 48, s 52, sch 14 para 44; Police Reform and Social Responsibility, 2011 c
        13, sch 13 para 5
    appl (mods)—(EW) Railways and Transport Safety, 2003 c 20, s 28(1)(d)-(f)(2)
s 47 appl (mods)—(EW) Railways and Transport Safety, 2003 c 20, s 28(1)(d)-(f)(2)
    rep in pt—Serious Organised Crime and Police, 2005 c 15, ss 59, 174(2), sch 4 paras
        179, 184, sch 17 pt 2
    am—Police and Justice, 2006 c 48, s 52, sch 14 para 45
s 48 rep—Serious Organised Crime and Police, 2005 c 15, s 174(2), sch 17 pt 2
s 49 rep in pt—Serious Organised Crime and Police, 2005 c 15, s 174(2), sch 17 pt 2
s 50 rep in pt—Anti-social Behaviour, Crime and Policing, 2014 c 12, sch 11 para 31(2)
    am—Anti-social Behaviour, Crime and Policing, 2014 c 12, sch 11 para 31(3)
s 51 am—Police and Justice, 2006 c 48, s 6, sch 4 para 16; Coroners and Justice, 2009 c 25,
        s 117(4)-(8); Police Reform and Social Responsibility, 2011 c 13, sch 16 para
        299
ss 61-66 rep —Anti-social Behaviour, Crime and Policing, 2014 c 12, sch 11 para 50
ss 67-74 rep—Sexual Offences, 2003 c 42, s 140, sch 7
s 76 rep in pt—Road Safety, 2006 c 49, s 59, sch 7
s 82 am—Railways and Transport Safety, 2003 c 20, s 73, sch 5 para 4(1)(a)(2)(m); Energy,
        2004 c 20, s 69(1), sch 14 para 11; Serious Organised Crime and Police, 2005 c
        15, ss 59, 161(5), sch 4 paras 179, 185(1)(3)(a)(4)(a)(5), sch 13 pt 2 paras 1,
        12(1)(2)(a)(3); SI 2013/602, sch 2 para 39(2)(a)(ii)(b)(c)
    rep in pt—Energy, 2004 c 20, s 197(9), sch 23 pt 1; Serious Organised Crime and
        Police, 2005 c 15, ss 59, 161(5), 174(2), sch 4 paras 179,
        185(1)(2)(3)(b)(4)(b), sch 13 pt 2 paras 11, 12(1)(2)(b)(4), sch 17 pt 2; SI
        2013/602, sch 2 para 39(2)(a)(i)
s 84 rep—Policing and Crime, 2009 c 26, s 112, sch 8 pt 1
ss 85-91 rep—Serious Organised Crime and Police, 2005 c 15, ss 59, 174(2), sch 4 paras
        179, 186, sch 17 pt 2
    rep (prosp)—Police and Justice, 2006 c 48, s 52, sch 15
s 93 rep—Serious Organised Crime and Police, 2005 c 15, ss 59, 174(2), sch 4 paras 179,
        187, sch 17 pt 2
s 94 rep—Police and Justice, 2006 c 48, s 52, sch 15
s 95 rep—Serious Organised Crime and Police, 2005 c 15, ss 158(4)(a)(6), 174(2), sch 17
        pt 1
s 96 rep in pt—Police and Justice, 2006 c 48, s 6, sch 4 para 17, sch 15
s 97 rep in pt—Police and Justice, 2006 c 48, s 52, sch 15
ss 98, 99 rep—Police and Justice, 2006 c 48, s 52, sch 15
s 102 rep in pt—Serious Organised Crime and Police, 2005 c 15, ss 59, 174(2), sch 4 paras
        179, 188, 189, sch 17 pt 2; Police and Justice, 2006 c 48, s 52, sch 15
s 103 rep in pt—Serious Organised Crime and Police, 2005 c 15, ss 59, 174(2), sch 4 paras
        179, 188, 189, sch 17 pt 2; SI 2013/602, sch 2 para 39(3)
s 105 am—Anti-social Behaviour, 2003 c 38, s 89(1)(2); Police and Justice, 2006 c 48, ss 9,
        52, sch 5 paras 1, 4, sch 14 para 46
    rep in pt—Police and Justice, 2006 c 48, s 52, sch 15
s 106 rep in pt—Railways and Transport Safety, 2003 c 20, s 73, sch 5 para 4(1)(b)(2)(m)
    am—Police and Justice, 2006 c 48, s 6, sch 4 para 18
s 108 rep in pt—Serious Organised Crime and Police, 2005 c 15, ss 55(1), 174(2), sch 2
        paras 1, 10, sch 17 pt 2; Police and Justice, 2006 c 48, s 52, sch 15
    am—Police (Complaints and Conduct), c 22, s 1(4)
sch 1 rep—Serious Organised Crime and Police, 2005 c 15, s 174(2), sch 17 pt 2
sch 2 appl (mods)—SIs 2005/3311, reg 3(1)(3)(6)(a), sch 2; 2013/2325, reg 5
    am—(prosp) Tribunals, Courts and Enforcement, 2007 c 15, s 106, sch 16 para 13;
        SIs 2009/1941, art 2, sch 1; 2013/602, sch 2 para 39(4)
    appl—SIs 2009/2133, reg 5; 2010/782, reg 5
    rep in pt—Police Reform and Social Responsibility, 2011 c 13, sch 14 para 3
sch 3 transtl provns—SI 2004/671, art 4(2)

2002
c 30 sch 3 *continued*

appl (mods) —SIs 2005/3311, reg 3(1)(4)(6)(a), sch 3; ibid, reg 3(1)(5)(6)(b), sch 3; 2008/212, reg 5, sch 2; SI 2012/62, regs 20(3), 23

am—Serious Organised Crime and Police, 2005 c 15, ss 159, 160, sch 11, paras 1, 3, 4, sch 12 paras 1, 11-13, 16, 17, 19, 20, 21, 22(1)(3), 23, 24; ibid, ss 55(1), 160, sch 2 paras 1, 11, sch 12 paras 1, 11, 14, 15; ibid, ss 159, 160, sch 11 paras 1, 2, sch 12 paras 1, 11, 18; Police and Justice, 2006 c 48, s 1, sch 1 paras 80, 89; Crim Justice and Immigration, 2008 c 4, s 127, sch 23 paras 1, 3-6(4), 7(1)(2), 8, 9(1)(2)(4), 11, 12(1)(2)(a)(3)(4), 13-19; Police Reform and Social Responsibility, 2011 c 13, sch 14 paras 5(2), 8(2)(5), 9(1)(2), 10(2)(5)(6)(7)(8)(a), 11(2)-(5), 12(2)(a)(3)(4)(5), 13(4)-(7), 14, 16, 17(2), 18, 19(2), 20-22; ibid, sch 16, paras 300-303; Police (Complaints and Conduct), 2012 c 22, s 1(2),(3); Crime and Cts, 2013 c 22, sch 6 para 17; ibid, sch 8 para 153(2); Anti-social Behaviour, Crime and Policing, 2014 c 12, ss 136, 138(1)(3)(4), 139; ibid, s 137; ibid, sch 11 para 95(2) (3)(4)(b)(5)(b)(6)(b) (7)(8)(a)(b)(9)

rep in pt—Crim Justice and Immigration, 2008 c 4, ss 127, 149, sch 23 paras 1, 6(1)(5), 7(1)(3), 9(1)(3), 10, 12(2)(b), sch 28 pt 8; Police Reform and Social Responsibility, 2011 c 13, sch 14 paras 8(3)(4), 10(4)(8)(b), 12(2)(b), 13(2), 20(1)(11)(c)(d); Anti-social Behaviour, Crime and Policing, 2014 c 12, sch 11 para 95(4)(a)(5)(a)(6)(a)(6)(a)(8)(c)

sch 4 appl (mods)—(EW) Railways and Transport Safety, 2003 c 20, s 28(1)(g)(2)

appl—Police and Criminal Evidence, 1984 c 60, s 64A; SI 2007/3202, art 2

am—Anti-social Behaviour, 2003 c 38, ss 23(3)-(5), 33(1)-(3), 46(1)(b), 89(1)(3)(4); Crim Justice, 2003 c 44, s 12, sch 1 paras 16-20; Serious Organised Crime and Police, 2005 c 15, ss 122(1)(3)(a)(b)(7), 161(5), sch 8 pt 1 paras 1, 4-7, 10, 11, 13-15, sch 9 paras 1, 3-9, sch 13 pt 2 paras 11, 13(1)(3)(4); ibid, ss 122(7), 161(1), sch 8 pt 1 paras 1, 3(1)-(5)(6)(b)(7)(8)(10), sch 9 paras 1, 2, sch 13 pt 2 paras 11, 13(1)(2); ibid, s 122(7), sch 8 pt 1 paras 1, 4, 8, 9, 12, 16; ibid, s 122(7), sch 8 pt 1 paras 1, 2; Drugs, 2005 c 17, s 5(2)(a)(b); Clean Neighbourhoods and Environment, 2005 c 16, s 62(1)(2); Police and Justice, 2006 c 48, ss 8, 9, sch 5 para 1(1)-(6)(7)(a)(b)(8)-(10); Violent Crime Reduction, 2006 c 38, s 24(6); Educ and Inspections, 2006 c 40, ss 107(2)(3), 108(7); (prosp) Loc Govt and Public Involvement in Health, 2007 c 28, ss 129, 133, sch 6 para 4; UK Borders, 2007 c 30, s 47; Loc Transport, 2008 c 26, s 77, sch 4 para 65; Coroners and Justice, 2009 c 25, s 108(3); Loc Democracy, Economic Development and Construction, 2009 c 20, s 119, sch 6 para 116; Policing and Crime, 2009 c 26, s 112, sch 7 para 125(3)(b); ibid, s 112, sch 7 para 27; Crime and Security, 2010 c 17, ss 4(6), 6(4); Protection of Freedoms, 2012 c 9, sch 9 para 30; Anti-social Behaviour, Crime and Policing, 2014 c 12, ss 40(2)(3), 53(5)(6), 69(1)(2); ibid, sch 10 paras 2-6

rep in pt—Anti-social Behaviour, 2003 c 38, ss 46(1)(a), 92, sch 3; Clean Neighbourhoods and Environment, 2005 c 16, s 107, sch 5 pt 5; Serious Organised Crime and Police, 2005 c 15, ss 59, 174(2), sch 4 paras 179, 190, sch 17 pt 2; Police and Justice, 2006 c 48, s 52, sch 15; Policing and Crime, 2009 c 26, s 112, sch 8 para 125(3)(a), sch 8 pt 13; Legal Aid, Sentencing and Punishment of Offenders, 2012 c 10, sch 23 para 14(3); Anti-social Behaviour, Crime and Policing, 2014 c 12, sch 11 para 32

restr—SI 2004/2540, art 4

mod—SI 2011/631, sch 2 para 5; Canterbury City Council, 2013 c i, s 13(2)

sch 5 appl—Police and Criminal Evidence, 1984 c 60, s 64A

am—Anti-social Behaviour, 2003 c 38, ss 23(6)-(8), 46(2)(b), 89(1)(5)-(7); Serious Organised Crime and Police, 2005 c 15, s 122(1)(4)(5)(b)(6)(7), sch 8 pt 2 paras 17-20; ibid, s 122(7), sch 8 pt 2 paras 17, 21; Clean Neighbourhoods and Environment, 2005 c 16, s 62(1)(3); Police and Justice, 2006 c 48, s 9, sch 5 paras 1, 6; Educ and Inspections, 2006 c 40, s 107(4)(5)(6); (prosp) Loc Govt and Public Involvement in Health, 2007 c 28, ss 129, 133, sch 6 para 4; Policing and Crime, 2009 c 26, s 112, sch 7 para 27

rep in pt—Anti-social Behaviour, 2003 c 38, ss 46(2)(a), 92, sch 3; Serious Organised Crime and Police, 2005 c 15, ss 122(1)(4)(5)(a), 174(2), sch 17 pt 2; Clean Neighbourhoods and Environment, 2005 c 16, s 107, sch 5 pt 5; Legal Aid, Sentencing and Punishment of Offenders, 2012 c 10, sch 23 para 14(4); Anti-social Behaviour, Crime and Policing, 2014 c 12, sch 11 para 33

restr—SI 2004/2540, art 5

2002

c 30 *continued*

   sch 5A added—Police and Justice, 2006 c 48, s 15(2)

    rep in pt—Legal Aid, Sentencing and Punishment of Offenders, 2012 c 10, sch 23
     para 14(5)

   sch 6 rep—Serious Organised Crime and Police, 2005 c 15, s 174(2), sch 17 pt 2

   sch 7 rep in pt—Crim Justice, 2003 c 44, s 332, sch 37 pt 1; Courts, 2003 c 39, s 109(3),
     sch 10; Serious Organised Crime and Police, 2005 c 15, s 174(2), sch 17 pt 2;
     (pt prosp) Police and Justice, 2006 c 48, s 52, sch 15

   sch 8 rep in pt—Serious Organised Crime and Police, 2005 c 15, ss 158(4)(b)(6), 174(2),
     sch 17 pt 1

c 31 **Mobile Telephones (Re-programming)**

   s 1 rep in pt—Violent Crime Reduction, 2006 c 38, ss 62, 65, sch 5

    am—Violent Crime Reduction, 2006 c 38, s 62

c 32 **Education**

   transtl provns (am)—SIs 2002/2439, sch pt 2 para 4; (W) 2003/2959 (W 277), regs 3-9

   appl—(W) SI 2004/1576 (W 162), reg 10(2)(b)

   am—SI 2010/1158, art 5, sch 2

   s 1 am—Educ and Inspections, 2006 c 40, s 157, sch 14 paras 70, 71; ibid, s 161, sch 16
     para 1(1)-(4)(c); (prosp) Educ and Skills, 2008 c 25, s 169, sch 1 paras 13, 14

    rep in pt—Educ and Inspections, 2006 c 40, s 161, sch 16 para 1(4)(d), sch 18

   s 2 rep in pt—Legislative and Regulatory Reform, 2006 c 51, s 30, sch 1; Educ and
     Inspections, 2006 c 40, s 161, sch 16 para 2(3), sch 18

    am—Educ and Inspections, 2006 c 40, s 161, sch 16 para 2(1)(2)

   s 4 am—Educ and Inspections, 2006 c 40, s 161, sch 16 para 3

   s 11 am—SIs 2009/1941, art 2, sch 1; 2010/1158, art 5, sch 2

   s 13 am—SI 2009/1941, art 2, sch 1

   s 14 am—Children, 2004 c 31, s 59(1)-(5); Educ, 2005 c 18, ss 98, 99, sch 14 para
     23(1)-(3), sch 15; SI 2010/1158, art 5, sch 2; Educ, 2011 c 21, s 15(2)

   s 15 am—SI 2010/1158, art 5, sch 2

   s 16 am—Educ, 2011 c 21, s 15(3)

   s 19 excl—(until 30.3.2007) SI 2004/657, arts 2(a), 5

    appl—(W) SI 2005/2913 (W 210), reg 7(2)-(4); (E) SI 2007/2979, reg 3, sch 1

    am—Educ, 2011 c 21, s 38; Educ (W), 2011 nawm 7, s 19(2)

    rep in pt—School Standards and Organisation (W), 2013 anaw 1, sch 5 para 21(2)

   s 20 excl—(until 30.3.2007) SI 2004/657, arts 2(b), 5

    appl—(W) SI 2005/2913 (W 210), reg 7(2)-(4)

    am—Educ (W), 2011 nawm 7, s 19(3)

   s 21 appl (mods)—(until 30.3.2007) SI 2004/657, arts 3(e)(f), 5; (E) SI 2007/2979, reg 3,
     sch 1

    am—(transtl provn) (W) SI 2004/1743 (W 182), reg 3; Educ and Inspections, 2006 c
     40, s 38(1); Apprenticeships, Skills, Children and Learning, 2009 c 22, s 194(9);
     (1.4.2016) Well-being of Future Generations (W), 2015 anaw 2, sch 4 para 7

    rep in pt—SI 2010/1158, art 5, schs 2-4

   s 22 am—Educ (W), 2011 nawm 7, s 22(8)

   s 23 appl —(W) SI 2005/2913 (W 210), reg 7(2)-(4)

   s 24 appl—(EW) Educ, 2005 c 18, s 68(2)

    am—Educ (W), 2011 nawm 7, s 19(4)

   s 25 am—Educ and Inspections, 2006 c 40, s 71, sch 7 para 19; Educ (W), 2011 nawm 7, s
     19(5)(b)

    rep in pt—Educ (W), 2011 nawm 7, s 19(5)(a)

   s 26 am—Educ (W), 2011 nawm 7, s 9(3)(a)

   s 27 mod—(temp) (E) SIs 2002/2113, reg 3(1); 2002/2316, reg 3(1); (temp) (W) SI
     2003/1717 (W 184), reg 3(1)(2)

    appl (mods)—(E) SIs 2003/1558, reg 31; 2007/958, reg 30; (E) 2007/2979, reg 3, sch
     1

    am—(prosp) Children, Schools and Families, 2010 c 26, s 4(1)

   s 28 mod—(temp) (E) SIs 2002/2113, reg 3(2); (temp) (W) 2003/1717 (W 184),
     reg 3(1)(2)

    appl (mods)—(E) SIs 2003/1558, reg 31; 2007/958, reg 30; (E) 2007/2979, reg 3, sch
     1

    am—Educ and Inspections, 2006 c 40, s 38(2); Children and Families, 2014 c 6, s
     88(2)(4)(a)

    rep in pt—Children and Families, 2014 c 6, s 88(3)(4)(b)

   s 28A added—Educ, 2005 c 18, s 68(2)

2002
c 32 *continued*

s 29 see—(E) SI 2002/2018, art 2

　appl—(E) SIs 2005/2039, reg 3, sch 1 pt 1 para 7; (W) 2007/1069 (W 109), reg 3, sch 1

　mod—(temp) (W) SIs 2003/1717 (W 184), reg 3(1)(2); (W) 2013/1793 (W 180), reg 6(1)(d)

　am—Educ, 2005 c 18, ss 103(1)(a)(b), 115; (prosp) Apprenticeships, Skills, Children and Learning, 2009 c 22, s 260

　appl (mods)—(E) SI 2007/2979, reg 3, sch 1

s 29A added—Educ and Skills, 2008 c 25, s 154

s 29B added (prosp)—Educ and Skills, 2008 c 25, s 157

s 30 mod—(temp) (E) SI 2002/2316, reg 3(1)

　am—(transtl provn) (W) SI 2004/1743 (W 182), reg 3; Educ, 2005 c 18, s 103(1)(c); ibid, ss 103(1)(a)(b), 115; Healthy Eating in Schools (W), 2009 nawm 3, s 2; SI 2010/1158, art 5, sch 2

　power to rep—Educ, 2005 c 18, s 103(3)(a)

　appl (mods)—(E) SIs 2005/2039, reg 3, sch 1 pt 1 para 8; (E) 2007/2979, reg 3, sch 1; (W) 2007/1069 (W 109), reg 3, sch 1

s 30A added—Educ, 2005 c 18, s 104

　rep—Educ, 2011 c 21, s 32(1)

s 32 appl (mods)—(E) 2007/2979, reg 3, sch 1; (W) 2007/1069 (W 109), reg 3, sch 1

　am—(W) Learner Travel (W), 2008 nawm 2, s 21(1)(2); Educ (W), 2014 anaw 5, sch 3 para 1(2)(a)(i)(b)(i)(d); Deregulation, 2015 c 20, sch 16 para 3(3)(4)

　rep in pt—Educ (W), 2014 anaw 5, sch 3 para 1(2)(a)(ii)(b)(ii)(c); Deregulation, 2015 c 20, sch 16 para 3(2)

ss 32A-32C added—Educ (W), 2014 anaw 5, s 42

s 33 rep (W)—School Standards and Organisation (W), 2013 anaw 1, s 95

　am—Educ, 2005 c 18, s 103(2)(a)(b)

　power to rep—Educ, 2005 c 18, s 103(3)(b)

　appl—(W) SI 2005/2913 (W 210), reg 7(2)-(4)

s 34 appl—(W) SI 2005/2913 (W 210), reg 7(2)-(4)

　am—(W) School Standards and Organisation (W), 2013 anaw 1, sch 5 para 6(2)

s 35 rep in pt—(W) School Standards and Organisation (W), 2013 anaw 1, sch 5 para 6(3)(a); Deregulation, 2015 c 20, sch 16 para 4(1)

　am—Educ, 2011 c 21, s 19(1); (W) School Standards and Organisation (W), 2013 anaw 1, sch 5 para 6(3)(b); Deregulation, 2015 c 20, sch 16 para 4(2)

　appl (mods)—SI 2007/2979, sch 1 para 17A (added by 2012/3158, reg 3(2))

s 36 rep in pt—(W) School Standards and Organisation (W), 2013 anaw 1, sch 5 para 6(4)(a); (E) Deregulation, 2015 c 20, sch 16 para 5(1)

s 36 am—Educ, 2011 c 21, s 19(2); (W) School Standards and Organisation (W), 2013 anaw 1, sch 5 para 6(4)(b); Deregulation, 2015 c 20, sch 16 para 5(2)

s 37 mod—(temp) (E) SI 2002/2316, reg 3(1)

　am—Educ, 2005 c 18, s 117, sch 18 para 14; Educ, 2011 c 21, s 47(2)(3); (W) School Standards and Organisation (W), 2013 anaw 1, sch 5 para 6(5)(b)

　rep in pt—(W) School Standards and Organisation (W), 2013 anaw 1, sch 5 para 6(5)(a)

s 39 appl—(W) SI 2005/2913 (W 210), reg 7(2)-(4)

　appl (mods)—SI 2007/2979, sch 1 para 17B (added by 2012/3158, reg 3(2))

　am—Educ (W), 2011 nawm 7, s 19(6)

s 41 am—(W) SI 2002/3184 (W 300), reg 4; Loc Govt, 2003 c 26, s 127(1), sch 7 para 66(2)-(4) (see SI 2003/2938)

　rep in pt—Educ, 2005 c 18, s 123, sch 19 pt 4

s 42 am—Loc Govt, 2003 c 26, s 127(1), sch 7 para 66(2)(5)(6) (see SI 2003/2938)

　rep —Educ, 2005 c 18, s 123, sch 19 pt 4

s 51A added—Educ, 2011 c 21, s 4(2)

　appl (mods)—SI 2012/1033, reg 21

s 52 mod—SIs (temp) (E) 2002/2953, reg 5; 2008/532, reg 4; (W) 2013/1793 (W 180), reg 8(b)

　appl (mods)—(until 30.3.2007) SI 2004/657, arts 3(h), 5

　appl—(W) SI 2005/2913 (W 210), reg 7(2)-(4)

　am—Educ, 2011 c 21, s 4(3)(a)(b); Local Government (W), 2011 nawm 4, sch 3 para 6

　rep in pt—Educ, 2011 c 21, s 4(3)(c)

s 53 appl—(W) SI 2005/2913 (W 210), reg 7(2)-(4)

2002

c 32 *continued*

s 54 rep—Educ, 2005 c 18, s 123, sch 19 pt 1

ss 55-59 rep (W)—School Standards and Organisation (W), 2013 anaw 1, sch 5 para 6(6)

s 56 rep in pt—Educ, 2005 c 18, s 123, sch 19 pt 1

s 62A added—Educ and Inspections, 2006 c 40, s 71, sch 7 para 20
    appl (mods)—(E) SI 2007/2979, reg 3, sch 1
    am—Apprenticeships, Skills, Children and Learning, 2009 c 22, s 204

s 63 rep (W)—School Standards and Organisation (W), 2013 anaw 1, sch 5 para 6(6)
    am—Educ, 2005 c 18, s 61, sch 9 para 28; Educ and Inspections, 2006 c 40, ss 71, 175, sch 7 para 21(1)(2)(3)(5), sch 17 para 6
    rep in pt—Educ and Inspections, 2006 c 40, s 71, sch 7 para 21(4), sch 18

s 64 am—Educ and Inspections, 2006 c 40, s 71, sch 7 para 22
    rep in pt—(W) School Standards and Organisation (W), 2013 anaw 1, sch 5 para 6(7)

s 65 rep in pt—Academies, 2010 c 32, s 14, sch 2 paras 11, 12; Educ, 2011 c 21, sch 14 para 19

s 66 rep—Educ, 2011 c 21, sch 10 para 2

s 67 rep—Academies, 2010 c 32, s 14, sch 2 paras 11, 13

s 68 rep—Academies, 2010 c 32, s 14, sch 2 paras 11, 14

ss 70, 71 rep—Educ, 2005 c 18, ss 66(14), 123, sch 19 pt 2

s 72 rep (W)—School Standards and Organisation (W), 2013 anaw 1, sch 5 para 21(3)

s 73 rep—Educ and Inspections, 2006 c 40, s 184, sch 18

s 74 rep—Educ, 2005 c 18, s 123, sch 19 pt 2

s 76 am—Childcare, 2006 c 21, s 48, sch 1 para 3; Apprenticeships, Skills, Children and Learning, 2009 c 22, ss 174, 192, sch 12 para 32
    rep in pt—Childcare, 2006 c 21, ss 48, 103, sch 1 para 3, sch 3; Apprenticeships, Skills, Children and Learning, 2009 c 22, s 266, sch 16 pt 4

s 77 rep—Childcare, 2006 c 21, ss 48, 103, sch 1 para 4, sch 3

s 78 rep in pt—Childcare, 2006 c 21, ss 48, 103, sch 1 para 5, sch 3

s 79 mod—(temp) (E) SI 2002/2316, reg 4(a)
    am—Childcare, 2006 c 21, s 48, sch 1 para 6
    rep in pt—Childcare, 2006 c 21, ss 48, 103, sch 1 para 6, sch 3

s 80 appl—(E) SIs 2005/2039, reg 3, sch 1 pt 1 para 10; (E) 2007/2979, reg 3, sch 1
    am—Childcare, 2006 c 21, s 48, sch 1 para 7

s 81 rep—Childcare, 2006 c 21, s 48, sch 1 para 8

s 83 rep—Childcare, 2006 c 21, ss 48, 103, sch 1 para 9, sch 3

s 84 am—SIs 2013/2092, art 2; 2013/2093, art 2

s 85 subst—(subject to transtl provn(s)) SI 2003/2946, arts 2, 3; (prosp) Educ and Inspections, 2006 c 40, s 74(1)
    mod—Educ and Inspections, 2006 c 40, s 74(4)
    am—Apprenticeships, Skills, Children and Learning, 2009 c 22, ss 174, 192, sch 12 para 33; Educ, 2011 c 21, sch 8 para 12; SI 2013/2092, art 3
    rep in pt—SI 2012/2056, art 2

s 85A added —(prosp) Educ and Inspections, 2006 c 40, s 74(1)
    am—Apprenticeships, Skills, Children and Learning, 2009 c 22, ss 174, 192, sch 12 para 34

s 86 am—(prosp) Educ and Inspections, 2006 c 40, s 74(2)

s 87 am—Childcare, 2006 c 21, s 48, sch 1 para 10; Apprenticeships, Skills, Children and Learning, 2009 c 22, ss 159, 174, 192, sch 12 para 35(1)(2)(3)(b)(5)(6)
    rep in pt—Childcare, 2006 c 21, ss 48, 103, sch 1 para 10, sch 3; Apprenticeships, Skills, Children and Learning, 2009 c 22, ss 174, 192, 266, sch 12 para 35, sch 16 pt 4; Educ, 2011 c 21, sch 8 para 13

s 88 am—Educ and Skills, 2008 c 25, s 156
    rep in pt—SI 2010/1080, art 2, sch 1

s 89 rep—Childcare, 2006 c 21, ss 48, 103, sch 1 para 11, sch 3

s 90 mod —(temp) (E) SI 2002/2316, reg 4(c)(d)
    appl (mods)—(until 30.3.2007) SIs 2004/657, arts 3(i), 5; 2007/958, reg 30
    rep in pt—Childcare, 2006 c 21, ss 48, 103, sch 1 para 12, sch 3; Educ, 2011 c 21, sch 8 para 14(2)(b)(3)(6)
    am—Apprenticeships, Skills, Children and Learning, 2009 c 22, ss 174, 192, sch 12 para 36; Educ, 2011 c 21, sch 8 para 14(2)(a)(4)(5)(7)

s 92 am—Children and Families, 2014 c 6, sch 3 para 77

s 93 rep in pt—Childcare, 2006 c 21, ss 48, 103, sch 1 para 13, sch 3

s 94 mod—(temp) (E) SI 2002/2316, reg 4(e)
    rep in pt—Childcare, 2006 c 21, ss 48, 103, sch 1 para 14, sch 3

2002

c 32 s 94 *continued*

am—Children and Families, 2014 c 6, sch 3 para 78
s 95 mod—(temp) (E) SI 2002/2316, reg 4(f)(g)
  appl (mods)—(until 30.3.2007) SI 2004/657, arts 3(j), 5
s 96 subst—Educ, 2011 c 21, sch 8 para 15
s 97 am—Learning and Skills (W), 2009 nawm 1, s 1; Educ (W), 2009 nawm 5, s 21(2)
  rep in pt—(W) School Standards and Organisation (W), 2013 anaw 1, sch 5 para 21(4)
s 99 mod—(temp) (W) SI 2002/3184 (W 300), reg 5(1)(2)
s 100 mod—(temp) (W) SI 2002/3184 (W 300), reg 5(1)-(3)
  rep in pt—Learning and Skills (W), 2009 nawm 1, s 2(2)
  am—Learning and Skills (W), 2009 nawm 1, s 47, sch 1 paras 11, 12, 13, 14; ibid, s
    2(3)
s 101 mod—(temp) (W) SI 2002/3184 (W 300), reg 5(1)(4)
  am—SIs 2003/932 (W 122), art 2(1)-(3); (W) 2008/1899 (W 181), art 2; Learning
    and Skills (W), 2009 nawm 1, s 47, sch 1 paras 11, 12, 13; ibid, s 3(3)
  appl—(W) SI 2007/1069 (W 109), reg 3, sch 1
  rep in pt—Learning and Skills (W), 2009 nawm 1, s 3(2)
s 102 am—Learning and Skills (W), 2009 nawm 1, s 47, sch 1 paras 11, 12, 13; Educ (W),
    2009 nawm 5, s 21(3)
  appl—SI 2014/1999 (W 200), art 2(2)
s 103 am—Learning and Skills (W), 2009 nawm 1, s 47, sch 1 paras 11, 12, 13
  rep in pt—Educ (W), 2009 nawm 5, s 21(4)
  appl—SI 2014/1999 (W 200), art 2(3)
s 104 am—Educ (W), 2009 nawm 5, s 21(5)
s 105 excl—SI 2008/1736 (W 170), reg 3
  am—(W) SI 2008/1899 (W 181), art 3; Learning and Skills (W), 2009 nawm 1, s 47,
    sch 1 paras 11, 12, 13
  rep in pt—Educ (W), 2009 nawm 5, s 21(6)
s 107 am—Learning and Skills (W), 2009 nawm 1, s 19
s 108 mod—(temp) (W) SI 2002/3184 (W 300), reg 5(1)(5)
  am—Learning and Skills (W), 2009 nawm 1, s 47, sch 1 paras 11, 12, 13, 15; () Educ
    (W), 2009 nawm 5, s 21(7)(a)
  rep in pt—Educ (W), 2009 nawm 5, s 21(7)(b)
s 110 am—Educ (W), 2009 nawm 5, s 21(8)
s 111 mod—(temp) (W) SI 2002/3184 (W 300), reg 5(1)(2)
  rep in pt—SI 2005/3239 (W 244), arts 7(1)-(3), 9(1), sch 1 para 32(a)(i)(b)
  am—SI 2005/3239 (W 244), arts 7(1)-(3), 9(1), sch 1 para 32(a)(ii)(iii); Learning
    and Skills (W), 2009 nawm 1, s 47, sch 1 paras 11, 12, 13, 16, 17; (W) School
    Standards and Organisation (W), 2013 anaw 1, sch 5 para 21(5)
s 114 mod—(temp) (W) SI 2002/3184 (W 300), reg 5(1)(2)
  am—Learning and Skills (W), 2009 nawm 1, s 47, sch 1 paras 11, 12, 13, 18
s 115 mod—(temp) (W) SI 2002/3184 (W 300), reg 5(1)(2)
s 116A added—Learning and Skills (W), 2009 nawm 1, s 4
s 116B added —Learning and Skills (W), 2009 nawm 1, s 5
s 116C added —Learning and Skills (W), 2009 nawm 1, s 6
s 116D added—Learning and Skills (W), 2009 nawm 1, s 7
s 116E added —Learning and Skills (W), 2009 nawm 1, s 8
s 116F added—Learning and Skills (W), 2009 nawm 1, s 9
s 116G added —Learning and Skills (W), 2009 nawm 1, s 10
s 116H added—Learning and Skills (W), 2009 nawm 1, s 11
s 116I added—Learning and Skills (W), 2009 nawm 1, s 12
  am—Further and Higher Educ (Governance and Information) (W), 2014 anaw 1, s
    6(3)
s 116J added—Learning and Skills (W), 2009 nawm 1, s 13
  am—Educ (W), 2011 nawm 7, s 9(3)(b)(i)
  rep in pt—Educ (W), 2011 nawm 7, s 9(3)(b)(ii)
s 116K added—Learning and Skills (W), 2009 nawm 1, s 14
  am—Further and Higher Educ (Governance and Information) (W), 2014 anaw 1, s
    6(4)
s 116L added—Learning and Skills (W), 2009 nawm 1, s 15
s 116M added —Learning and Skills (W), 2009 nawm 1, s 16
s 116N added—Learning and Skills (W), 2009 nawm 1, s 17
  rep in pt—School Standards and Organisation (W), 2013 anaw 1, sch 5 para 21(6)
s 116O added—Learning and Skills (W), 2009 nawm 1, s 18

2002

c 32 *continued*

s 117 am—Learning and Skills (W), 2009 nawm 1, s 47, sch 1 paras 11, 19

s 118 am—Learning and Skills (W), 2009 nawm 1, s 47, sch 1 paras 11, 12, 13, 20

s 122 mod—(temp) (W) SI 2002/3184 (W 300), reg 6(2)

    appl—SIs 2001/2897, sch 2 para 5; 2003/2169, art 2; 2003/2640, art 1(2); (W) 2003/543, sch 1 para 5; 2005/539, art 1(2)

s 129 am—Educ, 2005 c 18, s 72, sch 12 para 16; Educ and Inspections, 2006 c 40, s 30, sch 3 para 47; SI 2006/246, reg 20, sch 2; (W) School Standards and Organisation (W), 2013 anaw 1, sch 5 para 21(7)

s 131 am—SI 2005/3238 (W 243), arts 7, 9(1), sch 1 paras 86, 87(a); (prosp) Educ (W), 2014 anaw 5, sch 3 para 1(3)

    rep in pt—SIs 2005/3238 (W 243), arts 7, 9(1), sch 1 paras 86, 87(b); 2010/1080, art 2, schs 1, 2; (prosp) Educ (W), 2014 anaw 5, sch 3 para 3

s 132 mod—(temp) (W) SI 2002/3184 (W 300), reg 6(1)

    appl—SI 2003/1994, reg 12(6)

    rep in pt—Educ, 2011 c 21, sch 2 para 19(2)

    am—Educ (W), 2014 anaw 5, sch 3 para 1(4)

s 133 am—Educ (W), 2014 anaw 5, sch 3 para 1(5)

s 134 rep —Educ (W), 2014 anaw 5, sch 3 para 3

ss 135A-135C added—Educ, 2011 c 21, s 9

s 135A am—Educ, 2011 c 21, sch 13 para 13(2); SI 2012/976, sch para 12

s 136 rep in pt—(E) Deregulation, 2015 c 20, sch 15 para 8(1)(a)(b)

    am—Deregulation, 2015 c 20, sch 15 para 8(2)(a)(b)

s 137 rep (E)—Deregulation, 2015 c 20, sch 15 para 8(1)(c)

    am—(W prosp) Further Education and Training, 2007 c 25, s 23; Deregulation, 2015 c 20, sch 15 para 8(2)(c)

s 138 rep (E)—Deregulation, 2015 c 20, sch 15 para 8(1)(d)

    rep in pt—Deregulation, 2015 c 20, sch 15 para 8(2)(d)

s 139 rep—Further and Higher Educ (Governance and Information) (W), 2014 anaw 1, s 7

s 140 am—(prosp) Higher Educ (W), 2015 anaw 1, sch para 6

s 141 am—SI 2010/1158, art 5, sch 2

ss 141A-141E added—Educ, 2011 c 21, s 8(1)

s 141A am—Educ, 2011 c 21, sch 13 para 13(3)(4)

ss 141F-141H added—Educ, 2011 c 21, s 13(1)

s 141F am—Crim Justice and Cts, 2015 c 2, sch 11 para 19(2)(3)

s 142 am—SI 2010/1158, art 5, sch 2

    rep (pt prosp)—Safeguarding Vulnerable Groups, 2006 c 47, s 63, sch 10

s 143 rep (pt prosp)—Safeguarding Vulnerable Groups, 2006 c 47, s 63, sch 10

s 144 rep (pt prosp)—Safeguarding Vulnerable Groups, 2006 c 47, s 63, sch 10

    am—SI 2008/2833, art 6, sch 3

    saved—SI 2009/12, art 6

s 145 am—Educ, 2005 c 18, ss 98, 99, sch 14 para 24, sch 15

    rep in pt—Educ, 2011 c 21, sch 2 para 19(4), sch 5, para 17

s 149 rep in pt—(W prosp) Childcare, 2006 c 21, s 103, sch 3

s 150 rep in pt—Children, 2004 c 31, s 64, sch 5 pt 1; (W prosp) Childcare, 2006 c 21, s 103, sch 3

s 151 am—Educ and Inspections, 2006 c 40, s 157, sch 14 para 72

s 153 am—Childcare, 2006 c 21, s 103, sch 2 para 41

    rep in pt—Childcare, 2006 c 21, s 103, sch 2 para 41, sch 3; (W) School Standards and Organisation (W), 2013 anaw 1, sch 5 para 21(8)

s 154 rep (W)—School Standards and Organisation (W), 2013 anaw 1, sch 5 para 21(9)

s 156A added—Educ and Skills, 2008 c 25, s 169, sch 1 paras 13, 15

s 156AA added—SI 2012/976, sch para 13

s 157 am—Childcare, 2006 c 21, s 47

    rep in pt—Educ and Skills, 2008 c 25, s 169, sch 1 paras 13, 16, sch 2

s 158 rep in pt—Educ and Skills, 2008 c 25, s 169, sch 1 paras 13, 17(a), sch 2

    am—Educ and Skills, 2008 c 25, s 169, sch 1 paras 13, 17(b)

s 159 am—Educ, 2005 c 18, s 61, sch 9 para 29

    rep in pt—Educ and Inspections, 2006 c 40, s 172(3), sch 18

ss 162A, 162B added—Educ, 2005 c 18, s 54, sch 8 paras 1, 2

    rep —Educ and Skills, 2008 c 25, s 169, sch 1 paras 13, 18, sch 2

s 163 subst—Educ, 2005 c 18, s 54, sch 8 paras 1, 3

    rep in pt—Educ and Skills, 2008 c 25, s 169, sch 1 paras 13, 19(a)(b)(c), sch 2

s 164 subst—Educ, 2005 c 18, s 54, sch 8 paras 1, 3

2002

c 32 s 164 *continued*

rep in pt—Educ and Skills, 2008 c 25, s 169, sch 1 paras 13, 20, sch 2

s 165 am—Educ, 2005 c 18, s 54, sch 8 paras 1, 4

rep in pt—Educ and Skills, 2008 c 25, s 169, sch 1 paras 13, 21, sch 2

ss 166, 167 am—SI 2008/2833, art 6, sch 3

s 167A added (E prosp)—Educ and Inspections, 2006 c 40, s 169

rep in pt—Educ and Skills, 2008 c 25, s 169, sch 1 paras 13, 22, sch 2

s 167B added (E prosp)—Educ and Inspections, 2006 c 40, s 169

am—SI 2008/2833, art 6, sch 3 para 196

s 167C added (E prosp)—Educ and Inspections, 2006 c 40, s 169

subst—Educ and Skills, 2008 c 25, s 169, sch 1 paras 13, 23

am—Educ and Skills, 2008 c 25, sch 1 para 23; Policing and Crime, 2009 c 26, s 81(2)(3)(k)(4)(a); SI 2012/3006, art 13(1), (2)(e)

s 167D added (E prosp)—Educ and Inspections, 2006 c 40, s 169

subst —Educ and Skills, 2008 c 25, s 169, sch 1 paras 13, 23

s 168A added —Educ and Inspections, 2006 c 40, s 172(2)

s 168B added—Educ and Inspections, 2006 c 40, s 172(2)

s 168C added—Educ and Inspections, 2006 c 40, s 172(2)

s 169 am—(E prosp) Educ and Inspections, 2006 c 40, s 170(1)

s 171 rep in pt—Educ, 2005 c 18, ss 54, 123, sch 8 paras 1, 5, sch 19 pt 1; Educ and Skills, 2008 c 25, s 169, sch 1 paras 13, 24(1)-(4), sch 2

am—Educ and Inspections, 2006 c 40, s 157, sch 14 para 75; Childcare, 2006 c 21, s 47; Educ and Skills, 2008 c 25, s 169, sch 1 paras 13, 24(1)(5)

s 175 appl—Children, 2004 c 31, s 12(7)(c); (prosp) ibid, 29(7)(c)

am—SI 2010/1158, art 5, sch 2

appl (mods)—SI 2007/2979, sch 1 para 19A (added by 2012/3158, reg 3(3))

s 176 am—Educ and Inspections, 2006 c 40, s 167; (prosp) Educ and Skills, 2008 c 25, s 158(a)(c)

rep (W)—Children and Families (W), 2010 nawm 1, ss 12(3), 73, sch 2

rep in pt—Educ and Inspections, 2006 c 40, s 184, sch 18; (prosp) Educ and Skills, 2008 c 25, ss 158(b), 169; ibid, sch 2

s 178 rep in pt—Educ and Inspections, 2006 c 40, s 184, sch 18; SI 2010/1080, art 2, schs 1, 2

s 179 rep—Educ, 2005 c 18, s 123, sch 19 pt 1

s 183 rep in pt—Educ, 2005 c 18, s 123, sch 19 pt 1; SI 2010/1080, art 2, sch 1; Educ, 2011 c 21, sch 16 para 19; Deregulation, 2015 c 20, sch 14 para 46(a)(b)

s 188 rep—Educ, 2005 c 18, s 123, sch 19 pt 1

ss 191-193 rep (W)—School Standards and Organisation (W), 2013 anaw 1, sch 5 para 21(10)

s 194 rep in pt—Children and Families, 2014 c 6, sch 3 para 16(4)(b)

s 203 am—Educ, 2011 c 21, sch 13 para 13(5)

s 207 am—Apprenticeships, Skills, Children and Learning, 2009 c 22, s 59, sch 2 paras 1, 14

s 208A added —Apprenticeships, Skills, Children and Learning, 2009 c 22, s 123, sch 6 paras 54, 55

rep—Educ, 2011 c 21, sch 16 para 20

s 209 rep—Further Education and Training, 2007 c 25, s 30, sch 2

s 210 rep in pt—Childcare, 2006 c 21, ss 48, 103, sch 1 para 16, sch 3; Educ, 2011 c 21, sch 16 para 21

am—Childcare, 2006 c 21, s 48, sch 1 para 16; (W) Learner Travel (W), 2008 nawm 2, s 21(1)(3); Learning and Skills (W), 2009 nawm 1, s 20; Apprenticeships, Skills, Children and Learning, 2009 c 22, s 123, sch 6 paras 54, 56; Educ (W), 2014 anaw 5, sch 3 para 1(6)

s 210A added (prosp)—Educ and Skills, 2008 c 25, s 169, sch 1 para 79

s 212 am—SI 2010/1158, art 5, sch 2

s 215 appl—(W) SI 2005/2913 (W 210), reg 7(2)-(4)

s 216 rep in pt—Apprenticeships, Skills, Children and Learning, 2009 c 22, s 266, sch 16 pt 4

sch 1 mod—(temp) (E) SIs 2002/2316, reg 3; 2002/2113, reg 3(1)(3); (temp) (W) SI 2003/1717 (W 184), reg 3(2)(3)

appl (mods)—Social Security Administration, 1992 c 5, ss 113A, 113B; (E) SIs 2003/1558, regs 31, 32; 2007/958, regs 30, 31; 2007/2979, sch 1 para 20 (added by 2012/3158, reg 3(4))

appl—(W) SIs 2005/2913 (W 210), reg 7(2)-(4); (E) 2007/2979, reg 3, sch 1

2002

c 32 sch 1 *continued*

        am—Educ and Inspections, 2006 c 40, s 30, sch 3 para 48; Children, Schools and Families, 2010 c 26, s 6; Academies, 2010 c 32, s 14, sch 2 paras 11, 15; Educ (W), 2011 nawm 7, s 19(7); Educ, 2011 c 21, s 39; (W) School Standards and Organisation (W), 2013 anaw 1, sch 5 para 21(11)

        rep in pt—SI 2010/1080, art 2, schs 1, 2

    sch 2 appl—(E) SI 2003/1963, regs 36, 37

        appl (mods)—SIs 2006/873 (W 81), regs 35, 38, 39; 2007/2979, sch 1 para 20A (added by 2012/3158, reg 3(5))

        am—Apprenticeships, Skills, Children and Learning, 2009 c 22, s 237(7)

    sch 4 rep in pt—Educ and Skills, 2008 c 25, s 169, sch 2

    sch 5 rep (W)—School Standards and Organisation (W), 2013 anaw 1, sch 5 para 6(8)

    sch 6 rep (W)—School Standards and Organisation (W), 2013 anaw 1, sch 5 para 6(8)

    sch 7 rep in pt—Educ, 2005 c 18, s 123, sch 19 pt 1; Educ and Skills, 2008 c 25, s 169, sch 2; Equality, 2010 c 15, s 211, sch 27 pt 1 (subst by SI 2010/2279, sch 2); Educ, 2011 c 21, s 29(9)(b); Deregulation, 2015 c 20, sch 16 para 2(2)(c)

    sch 8 rep—Educ, 2005 c 18, ss 66(14), 123, sch 19 pt 2

    schs 9, 10 rep (W)—School Standards and Organisation (W), 2013 anaw 1, sch 5 para 21(12)

    sch 11 am—SI 2012/2404, sch 2 para 47

    sch 11A added —Educ, 2011 c 21, s 8(2)

        am—SI 2012/3006, art 13(1), (2)(e)

    sch 11B added—Educ, 2011 c 21, sch 4

        am—SI 2012/1809, art 3(1), sch pt 1

    sch 12 rep in pt—Serious Organised Crime and Police, 2005 c 15, s 174(2), sch 17 pt 2; Educ, 2011 c 21, sch 2 para 19(5)

    sch 13 rep in pt—Serious Organised Crime and Police, 2005 c 15, s 174(2), sch 17 pt 2

    sch 14 rep in pt—Educ, 2005 c 18, s 123, sch 19 pt 1

    sch 16 rep—Educ, 2005 c 18, s 123, sch 19 pt 1

    sch 17 rep in pt—Childcare, 2006 c 21, s 103, sch 3; Educ and Skills, 2008 c 25, s 169, sch 2; Apprenticeships, Skills, Children and Learning, 2009 c 22, s 266, sch 16 pt 4; Qualifications Wales, 2015 anaw 5, sch 4 para 4

    sch 18 rep in pt—SIs 2008/2833, art 6, sch 3; Equality, 2010 c 15, s 211, sch 27 pt 1 (subst by SI 2010/2279, sch 2)

    sch 19 rep in pt—(W) Learner Travel (W), 2008 nawm 2, s 26, sch 2

    sch 21 rep in pt—(prosp) Sustainable and Secure Buildings, 2004 c 22, s 11(2), sch; Educ, 2005 c 18, s 123, sch 19 pts 1-3; (E pt prosp) ibid, s 123, sch 19 pt 4; Serious Organised Crime and Police, 2005 c 15, s 174(2), sch 17 pt 2; (pt prosp) Safeguarding Vulnerable Groups, 2006 c 47, s 63, sch 10; Educ and Inspections, 2006 c 40, s 184, sch 18; ibid, s 184, sch 18; ibid, s 184, sch 18; (W) Learner Travel (W), 2008 nawm 2, s 26, sch 2; Apprenticeships, Skills, Children and Learning, 2009 c 22, s 266, sch 16 pt 4; Equality, 2010 c 15, s 211, sch 27 pt 1 (subst by SI 2010/2279, sch 2); SIs 2010/1080, art 2, schs 1, 2; 2010/1158, art 5, sch 3; (W) School Standards and Organisation (W), 2013 anaw 1, sch 5 paras 6(9), 21(13), 32

        am—SI 2013/2042, sch para 23

        appl—(W) SI 2005/2913 (W 210), reg 7(2)-(4)

    sch 22 appl—(W) SI 2005/2913 (W 210), reg 7(2)-(4)

c 33   *Copyright (Visually Impaired Persons)*—rep SI 2014/1384, sch para 8 Table

c 34   *Employee Share Schemes*—rep Income Tax (Earnings and Pensions), 2003 c 1, s 724(1), sch 8 pt 1

c 35   **Public Trustee (Liability and Fees)**

c 36   **Tobacco Advertising and Promotion**

    mod—SSI 2013/85, reg 17

    see—SI 2002/2013

    s 2 transtl provns—(EW, NI) SI 2002/2865, art 3; (S) SSI 2002/512, art 3

        am—SI 2006/2369, reg 2

    s 3 transtl provns—(EW, NI) SI 2002/2865, art 3; (S) SSI 2002/512, art 3

    s 3A added—SI 2006/2369, reg 3

    s 4 am—SI 2006/2369, reg 4

    s 5 am—SI 2006/2369, reg 5

    s 6 am—Health, 2009 c 21, s 20; ibid, s 24, sch 4 paras 2, 3

        rep in pt—(S) Tobacco and Primary Medical Services (S), 2010 asp 3, s 41, sch 2 para 3 (with SSI 2010/77, art 2)

2002

c 36 *continued*

ss 7A-7C added—Health, 2009 c 21, s 21

s 7D added (pt prosp)—Health, 2009 c 21, s 21

s 8 am—SI 2006/2369, reg 6; Health, 2009 c 21, s 24, sch 4 paras 2, 4

    rep in pt—(S) Tobacco and Primary Medical Services (S), 2010 asp 3, s 41, sch 2 para 4
        (with SSI 2010/77, art 2)

s 9 transtl provns—(EW, NI) SI 2002/2865, art 3; (S) SSI 2002/512, art 3

    am—Health, 2009 c 21, s 24, sch 4 paras 2, 5

s 10 transtl provns—(EW, NI) SI 2002/2865, art 3; (S) SSI 2002/512, art 3

s 11 am—Health, 2009 c 21, s 24, sch 4 paras 2, 6

s 12 am—Communications, 2003 c 21, s 406(1), sch 17 para 173

    rep in pt—Communications, 2003 c 21, s 406(7), sch 19(1)

s 13 am—Health, 2009 c 21, s 24, sch 4 paras 2, 7(2); (EW prosp) ibid, sch 4 paras 2, 7(1),
        (3); (W prosp) ibid, sch 4 paras 2, 7(5); ibid, sch 4 para 7(6)

    rep in pt—(EW prosp) Health, 2009 c 21, ss 24, 38, sch 4 paras 2, 7(4), sch 6

    appl—Children and Young Persons (Protection from Tobacco), 1991 c 23, s 3A

s 14 rep in pt—Health, 2009 c 21, ss 24, 38, sch 4 paras 2, 8(2)(3)(a), sch 6

    am—Health, 2009 c 21, s 24, sch 4 paras 2, 8(3)(b)(c)

    appl—Children and Young Persons (Protection from Tobacco), 1991 c 23, s 3A

s 15 appl—Children and Young Persons (Protection from Tobacco), 1991 c 23, s 3A

s 16 am—SI 2006/2369, reg 7; Health, 2009 c 21, s 24, sch 4 paras 2, 9(3)

    rep in pt—Health, 2009 c 21, ss 24, 38, sch 4 paras 2, 9(2)(4), sch 6

s 17 am—Health, 2009 c 21, s 24, sch 4 paras 2, 10

s 19 am—Health, 2009 c 21, s 24, sch 4 paras 2, 11

s 21 am—SI 2006/2369, reg 8; Health, 2009 c 21, s 24, sch 4 paras 2, 12

    sch 1 added—SI 2006/2369, reg 9

        am—(pt prosp) Health, 2009 c 21, s 24, sch 4 paras 2, 13

c 37 **Private Hire Vehicles (Carriage of Guide Dogs etc)**

s 1 rep—Equality, 2010 c 15, s 211, sch 27 pt 1 (subst by SI 2010/2279, sch 2)

ss 3-5 rep—Equality, 2010 c 15, s 211, sch 27 pt 1 (subst by SI 2010/2279, sch 2)

c 38 **Adoption and Children**

appl—Civil Partnership, 2004 c 33, s 3(2), sch 2 pt 1 para 2; Mental Capacity, 2005 c 9,
    s 27(2)(a)

appl (mods)—SI 2005/392, regs 11, 52-58

s 1 appl (mods)—SI 2010/985, reg 2, sch 1

    am—Children and Families, 2014 c 6, ss 3(2)(3), 9(2)

s 2 appl (mods)—SI 2010/985, reg 2, sch 1

    appl—Income and Corporation Taxes, 1988 c 1, s 327A(1)(k)

s 3A added—Children and Families, 2014 c 6, s 4(1); Social Services and Well-being (W),
    2014 anaw 4, s 170

s 4 appl—Income and Corporation Taxes, 1988 c 1, s 327A(1)(k)

    am—SI 2010/1158, art 5, sch 2; Health and Social Care, 2012 c 7, sch 5 para 105(a),
    (c)(i)

    rep in pt—Health and Social Care, 2012 c 7, sch 5 para 105(b), (c)(ii)

s 4A added (prosp)—Children and Families, 2014 c 6, s 5

s 4B added—Children and Families, 2014 c 6, s 6

s 5 rep—Children, 2004 c 31, s 64, sch 5 pt 1

s 8 am—Health and Social Care (Community Health and Standards), 2003 c 43, s 34, sch 4
    paras 125, 126; SI 2010/1158, art 5, sch 2; Health and Social Care, 2012 c 7, sch 5
    para 106(a), (b)(ii)

    rep in pt—SI 2010/1158, art 5, sch 2; Health and Social Care, 2012 c 7, sch 5 para
    106(b)(i)

s 12 am—Children, 2004 c 31, s 57; Children and Young Persons, 2008 c 23, s
    34(1)(2)(b)(4)-(7)

    rep in pt—Children and Young Persons, 2008 c 23, s 34(1)(2)(a)(3), sch 4

s 13 am—Courts, 2003 c 39, s 109(1), sch 8 para 411; Crime and Cts, 2013 c 22, sch 11
    para 152

s 17 rep—Inquiries, 2005 c 12, ss 44(5), 48(1), 49(2), sch 2 pt 1 para 23, sch 3

Pt 1 Ch 3 (ss 18-65) appl (mods)—SI 2005/392, regs 6-9

s 21 am—Civil Partnership, 2004 c 33, s 79(1)(2)

s 22 am—Children and Families, 2014 c 6, s 2(3)

s 22C am—Children and Families, 2014 c 6, s 2(2)

s 25 mod—(S) Adoption and Children (S), 2007 asp 4, s 78(1)(2)(a)

2002
c 38 *continued*

s 26 am—Children and Adoption, 2006 c 20, s 15, sch 2 paras 13, 14; Children and
　　　　Families, 2014 c 6, sch 2 para 60(2)(3)(4)(b)(5)-(7)
　　rep in pt—Children and Families, 2014 c 6, s 9(3); ibid, sch 2 para 60(4)(a)
s 28 mod—(S) Adoption and Children (S), 2007 asp 4, s 78(1)(2)(b)
　　　am—Children and Families, 2014 c 6, sch 2 para 61
s 29 rep in pt—Children and Families, 2014 c 6, sch 2 para 62(2)
　　　am—Children and Families, 2014 c 6, sch 2 para 62(3)(4)
s 32 am—Children and Families, 2014 c 6, sch 2 para 63
s 35 am—Children and Families, 2014 c 6, sch 2 para 64
ss 36, 37 appl (mods)—SI 2010/985, reg 2, sch 1
s 41 appl (mods)—SI 2010/985, reg 2, sch 1
s 46 appl (mods)—SI 2010/985, reg 2, sch 1
　　　am—SI 2013/1465, sch 1 para 9
s 47 am—Civil Partnership, 2004 c 33, s 79(1)(3); SI 2011/1740, sch 1 para 6(2)
　　　appl (mods)—SI 2010/2469, art 3
s 48 appl (mods)—SI 2010/985, reg 2, sch 1
s 51 am—Human Fertilisation and Embryology (Deceased Fathers), 2003 c 24, ss 2(1), 3(1),
　　　　sch para 18; Civil Partnership, 2004 c 33, s 79(1)(4)(5); Human Fertilisation and
　　　　Embryology, 2008 c 22, s 56, sch 6 para 39
ss 51A, 51B added—Children and Families, 2014 c 6, s 9(1)
s 52 am—Mental Capacity, 2005 c 9, s 67(1), sch 6 para 45
s 55 am—Courts, 2003 c 39, s 109(1), sch 8 para 412
　　rep in pt—Crime and Cts, 2013 c 22, sch 11 para 153
s 60 appl (mods)—SI 2010/985, reg 2, sch 1
　　　am—Crime and Cts, 2013 c 22, sch 11 para 154
s 64 am—Civil Partnership, 2004 c 33, s 79(1)(6)
　　　appl (mods)—SI 2010/985, reg 2, sch 1
s 65 appl—(W) SI 2005/2689 (W 189), reg 18(3)
　　　appl (mods)—SI 2010/985, reg 2, sch 1
s 67 excl—Sexual Offences, 2003 c 42, ss 27(1)(b), 29(1)(b)
　　　appl (mods)—SI 2010/985, reg 2, sch 1
ss 68, 69 appl (mods)—SI 2010/985, reg 2, sch 1
s 69 am—Inheritance and Trustees' Powers, 2014 c 16, s 4(1)
ss 71-73 appl (mods)—SI 2010/985, reg 2, sch
s 74 am—Sexual Offences, 2003 c 42, s 139, sch 6 para 47; Civil Partnership, 2004 c 33,
　　　　s 79(1)(7)
　　　mod—Sexual Offences, 2003 c 42, ss 64, 65
　　　appl (mods)—SI 2010/985, reg 2, sch
　　　appl (mods)—SI 2010/985, reg 2, sch
s 76 appl (mods)—SI 2010/985, reg 2, sch
s 77 appl (mods)—SI 2010/985, reg 2, sch
s 78 trans of functions—SI 2008/678, art 3, sch 1
　　　am—SI 2008/678, art 5, sch 2
　　　appl (mods)—SIs 2010/985, reg 2, sch; 2010/1205, reg 2
s 79 am—Civil Partnership, 2004 c 33, s 79(1)(8); SIs 2005/3542, art 4; 2008/678, art 5,
　　　　sch 2
　　　trans of functions—SI 2008/678, art 3, sch 1
　　　appl (mods)—SI 2010/985, reg 2, sch
s 81 am—Civil Partnership, 2004 c 33, s 79(1)(9); SI 2008/678, art 5, sch 2
　　　trans of functions—SI 2008/678, art 3, sch 1
s 82 appl (mods)—SI 2010/985, reg 2, sch 1
s 83 am—Children and Adoption, 2006 c 20, s 14(1)(2)
　　　appl (mods)—SI 2010/985, reg 2, sch 1
s 85 am—SI 2011/1740, sch 1 para 6(3)
　　　excl—(6.4.2016) Social Services and Well-being (W), 2014 anaw 4, s 124(6)
s 91A added—Children and Adoption, 2006 c 20, s 13
s 92 restr—SI 2005/3222, regs 3-5
　　　am—Crime and Cts, 2013 c 22, sch 11 para 155
s 93 restr—SI 2005/3222, regs 3-5
　　　am—SI 2015/664, sch 4 para 32(2)
s 95 am—Crime and Cts, 2013 c 22, sch 11 para 156; SI 2015/664, sch 4 para 32(3)
s 96 am—SI 2011/1740, sch 1 para 6(4); Children and Families, 2014 c 6, s 9(4)

2002

c 38 *continued*

s 98 am—Civil Partnership, 2004 c 33, s 79(1)(10); SI 2008/678, art 5, sch 2; Children and Families, 2014 c 6, s 1

trans of functions—SI 2008/678, art 3, sch 1

s 99 am—Health and Social Care (Community Health and Standards), 2003 c 43, s 147, sch 9 para 32; Educ and Inspections, 2006 c 40, s 157, sch 14 para 76

s 100 rep—Crime and Cts, 2013 c 22, sch 11 para 210 Table

s 101 appl (mods)—SI 2010/985, reg 2, sch 1

am—Crime and Cts, 2013 c 22, sch 11 para 157

s 102 am—Children, 2004 c 31, s 40, sch 3 paras 15, 16

appl (mods)—SI 2010/985, reg 2, sch 1

s 103 am—Children, 2004 c 31, s 40, sch 3 paras 15, 17

s 104 appl (mods)—SI 2010/985, reg 2, sch 1

s 105 appl (mods)—SIs 2010/985, reg 2, sch 1; 2010/2469, art 4

am—SI 2011/1740, sch 1 para 6(5)

s 106 appl (mods)—SI 2010/985, reg 2, sch 1

s 107 appl (mods)—SI 2010/985, reg 2, sch 1

am—SI 2011/1740, sch 1 para 6(6)

s 109 am—Children and Families, 2014 c 6, s 14(8)

s 118 rep in pt—(W prosp) Children and Young Persons, 2008 c 23, s 42, sch 4

s 121 rep in pt—Children and Families, 2014 c 6, s 15(3)

s 123 restr—SI 2005/3222, regs 3-5

am—(S) Adoption and Children (S), 2007 asp 4, s 120, sch 2 para 12; SI 2011/1740, sch 2 para 5

rep in pt—(S) Adoption and Children (S), 2007 asp 4, s 120, sch 3; SI 2011/1740, sch 2 pt 3

s 124 restr—SI 2005/3222, regs 3-5

excl—SI 2005/3222, reg 11

s 125 am—Children and Families, 2014 c 6, s 7(2); ibid, sch 1 para 2

rep in pt—Children and Families, 2014 c 6, sch 1 para 11(1)

s 126 rep in pt—Children and Families, 2014 c 6, sch 1 paras 3, 11(1)

s 127 am—Children and Families, 2014 c 6, sch 1 para 4(2)

rep in pt—Children and Families, 2014 c 6, sch 1 paras 4(3)(4), 11(1)

s 128 am—Children and Families, 2014 c 6, s 7(3); ibid, sch 1 para 5

rep in pt—Children and Families, 2014 c 6, sch 1 para 11(1)

s 128A added—Children and Families, 2014 c 6, s 7(4)

rep in pt—Children and Families, 2014 c 6, sch 1 para 11(1)

s 129 am—Children and Families, 2014 c 6, s 7(5); ibid, sch 1 para 6(2)-(4)(6)(7)

rep in pt—Children and Families, 2014 c 6, sch 1 paras 6(5), 11(1)

s 130 rep—Children and Families, 2014 c 6, sch 1 para 7

s 131 am—SI 2011/2581, sch 2 para 4(a); Children and Families, 2014 c 6, sch 1 para 8(2)(a)-(c)(3)(4)

rep in pt—Children and Families, 2014 c 6, sch 1 paras 8(2)(d)(5), 11(1)

ss 132-134 rep—(S) Adoption and Children (S), 2007 asp 4, s 120, sch 3; SI 2011/1740, sch 2 pt 3

s 135 rep—Serious Organised Crime and Police, 2005 c 15, s 174(2), sch 17 pt 2

s 140 appl (mods)—SI 2010/985, reg 2, sch 1

am—Children and Families, 2014 c 6, ss 4(2), 7(6)

s 141 am—Courts, 2003 c 39, s 109(1), sch 8 para 413(1)(2); Children, 2004 c 31, s 62(6); Constitutional Reform, 2005 c 4, s 12(2)(3), sch 1 pt 2 paras 26-28

rep in pt—Courts, 2003 c 39, s 109(1)(3), sch 8 para 413(1)(3), sch 10; Crime and Cts, 2013 c 22, sch 11 para 158

appl (mods)—SI 2010/985, regs 2, 7, sch 1

s 142 am—Constitutional Reform, 2005 c 4, s 12(2)(3), sch 1 pt 2 paras 26-28; SI 2008/678, art 5, sch 2

rep in pt—Children and Families, 2014 c 6, sch 1 para 9

trans of functions—SI 2008/678, art 3, sch 1

s 144 am—Courts, 2003 c 39, s 109(1), sch 8 para 414; Civil Partnership, 2004 c 33, s 79(1)(11)(12); SIs 2011/1740, sch 1 para 6(7); 2011/2581, sch 2 para 4(b); Crime and Cts, 2013 c 22, sch 11 para 159

rep in pt—Children and Families, 2014 c 6, sch 1 para 10

appl (mods)—SI 2010/985, reg 2, sch 1

s 149 rep in pt—Children and Families, 2014 c 6, sch 1 para 11(2)

sch 1 trans of functions—SI 2008/678, art 3, sch 1

2002

c 38 sch 1 *continued*

        am—SI 2008/678, art 5, sch 2

        appl (mods)—SI 2010/985, reg 2, sch 1

    sch 2 trans of functions—SI 2008/678, art 3, sch 1

        am—SIs 2008/678, art 5, sch 2; 2011/1740, sch 1 para 6(8)

    sch 3 rep in pt—Courts, 2003 c 39, s 109(3), sch 10; Serious Organised Crime and Police, 2005 c 15, s 174(2), sch 17 pt 2; Nat Health Service (Conseq Provns), 2006 c 43, s 6, sch 4; (prosp) Safeguarding Vulnerable Groups, 2006 c 47, s 63, sch 10; (S) Adoption and Children (S), 2007 asp 4, s 120, sch 3; SI 2011/1740, sch 2 pt 3; Legal Aid, Sentencing and Punishment of Offenders, 2012 c 10, sch 5 pt 2; Crime and Cts, 2013 c 22, sch 10 para 99 Table, sch 11 para 210 Table

    sch 4 rep in pt—Adoption and Children, 2002 c 38, s 139(3), sch 5

    sch 6 am—(W prosp) Children and Young Persons, 2008 c 23, s 8, sch 1 para 14; Children and Families, 2014 c 6, sch 2 para 65(2)

        rep in pt—Children and Families, 2014 c 6, sch 2 para 65(3)

c 39   **Commonwealth**

    sch 2 rep in pt—Armed Forces, 2006 c 52, s 378, sch 17

c 40   **Enterprise**

    appl—(E) SI 2005/397, reg 2, sch 1 para 8(5)

    saved—Wireless Telegraphy, 2006 c 36, s 111(3)(6)(k)

    mod—Consumers, Estate Agents and Redress, 2007 c 17, s 29(4); Civil Aviation, 2012 c 19, s 60(3)

    Pt 1 (ss 1-11) am —Enterprise and Regulatory Reform, 2013 c 24, sch 5 para 65

    functions trans—SI 2013/783, art 2

    ss 1-4 rep —Enterprise and Regulatory Reform, 2013 c 24, sch 5 para 229

    s 2 savings—SI 2014/892, art 3(7)

    s 5 am—Enterprise and Regulatory Reform, 2013 c 24, sch 5 para 60

    s 6 am—Enterprise and Regulatory Reform, 2013 c 24, sch 5 para 61

    s 7 am—Enterprise and Regulatory Reform, 2013 c 24, sch 5 para 62; Small Business, Enterprise and Employment, 2015 c 26, s 37

    s 8 rep —Enterprise and Regulatory Reform, 2013 c 24, sch 5 para 63

    s 8A added—SI 2013/783, art 3

        am—SI 2014/892, sch 1 para 2

    s 10 rep in pt—SI 2008/1277, reg 30, schs 2, 4

    s 11 appl—SI 2003/1368, art 2

        am—Enterprise and Regulatory Reform, 2013 c 24, sch 5 para 64

    s 12 am—Consumer Rights, 2015 c 15, s 82(1)

    s 14 am—Educ and Inspections, 2006 c 40, s 161, sch 16 para 4; Enterprise and Regulatory Reform, 2013 c 24, s 48(6); Consumer Rights, 2015 c 15, s 82(2); ibid, sch 8 para 19

        appl—SI 2009/209, regs 106, 122-123

    s 15 appl—SI 2009/209, regs 106, 122-123

        am—Consumer Rights, 2015 c 15, sch 8 para 20

    s 16 am—SI 2012/1809, art 3(1), sch pt 1; Crime and Cts, 2013 c 22, sch 9 para 81(a); Consumer Rights, 2015 c 15, sch 8 para 21

    Pt 3 (ss 22-130) mod—(EW) SI 2004/3202 (as am by 2015/1936, regs 3-20), regs 2-9, 10(1), 11-35; Health and Social Care, 2012 c 7, s 79; Enterprise and Regulatory Reform, 2013 c 24, sch 4 para 56

    appl (mods)—SI 2003/1592, art 15, sch 3

    excl—SI 2008/2546, art 40

    s 22 rep in pt—Communications, 2003 c 21, s 406(7), sch 19(1); SI 2004/1079, reg 2, sch para 2(1)(2)(a); Enterprise and Regulatory Reform, 2013 c 24, sch 5 para 67(3)(b), sch 8 para 2(b)

        am—SI 2004/1079, reg 2, sch para 2(1)(2)(b)(3)(4); Enterprise and Regulatory Reform, 2013 c 24, sch 5 para 67(2)(3)(a)(4)(5), sch 8 para 2(a)

    s 23 appl (mods)—SI 2003/1592, art 2, sch 1

        mod—SI 2003/1592 art 5A(c) (added by SI 2014/891, art 7)

        am—Enterprise and Regulatory Reform, 2013 c 24, sch 5 para 68

    s 24 appl (mods)—SI 2003/1592, art 2, sch 1

        am—Enterprise and Regulatory Reform, 2013 c 24, sch 5 para 69

    s 25 appl (mods)—SI 2003/1592, art 2, sch 1

        am—SI 2004/1079, reg 2, sch para 2(1)(5); Enterprise and Regulatory Reform, 2013 c 24, sch 5 para 70, sch 15 para 16

    s 26 appl (mods)—SI 2003/1592, art 2, sch 1

2002
c 40 *continued*

s 27 appl (mods)—SIs 2003/1592, art 2, sch 1; 2003/1595, art 3(a)
s 28 appl (mods)—SI 2003/1592, art 2, sch 1
 am—Enterprise and Regulatory Reform, 2013 c 24, sch 5 para 71
s 29 appl (mods)—SIs 2003/1592, art 2, sch 1; 2003/1595, art 3(b)
s 30 appl (mods)—SI 2003/1592, art 2, sch 1
s 31 rep—Enterprise and Regulatory Reform, 2013 c 24, sch 15 para 17
s 32 appl (mods)—SI 2003/1592, art 2, sch 1
 am—Enterprise and Regulatory Reform, 2013 c 24, sch 15 para 18(4)
 rep in pt—Enterprise and Regulatory Reform, 2013 c 24, sch 15 para 18(2)(3)
s 33 rep in pt—Communications, 2003 c 21, s 406(7), sch 19(1); SI 2004/1079, reg 2, sch
  para 2(1)(6)(a); Enterprise and Regulatory Reform, 2013 c 24, sch 5 para
  72(3)(b)(c), sch 8 para 3(b)
 am—SI 2004/1079, reg 2, sch para 2(1)(6)(b)(7)(8); Enterprise and Regulatory Reform,
  2013 c 24, sch 5 para 72(2)(3)(a)(4), sch 8 para 3(a)
ss 34ZA, 34ZB added —Enterprise and Regulatory Reform, 2013 c 24, sch 8 para 4
s 34A added—SI 2004/1079, reg 2, sch para 2(1)(9)
 am—Enterprise and Regulatory Reform, 2013 c 24, sch 5 para 73(2)(3)(a)(4)(5), sch
  15 para 19(2)(3)
 rep in pt—Enterprise and Regulatory Reform, 2013 c 24, sch 5 para 73(3)(b), sch 15
  para 19(4)
s 34B added—SI 2004/1079, reg 2, sch para 2(1)(9)
 rep —Enterprise and Regulatory Reform, 2013 c 24, sch 15 para 20
s 34C added —Enterprise and Regulatory Reform, 2013 c 24, sch 5 para 74
 mod—Enterprise and Regulatory Reform, 2013 c 24, sch 4 para 47(2)
s 35 am—Enterprise and Regulatory Reform, 2013 c 24, sch 5 para 75
s 36 am—Enterprise and Regulatory Reform, 2013 c 24, sch 5 para 76
s 37 am—Enterprise and Regulatory Reform, 2013 c 24, sch 5 para 77(2)(3)(5)
 rep in pt—Enterprise and Regulatory Reform, 2013 c 24, sch 5 para 77(4)
s 38 am—Enterprise and Regulatory Reform, 2013 c 24, sch 5 para 78(2)
 rep in pt —Enterprise and Regulatory Reform, 2013 c 24, sch 5 para 78(3)
s 39 rep in pt—SI 2004/1079, reg 2, sch para 2(1)(10)
 am—Enterprise and Regulatory Reform, 2013 c 24, sch 5 para 79, sch 8 para 5
s 40 rep in pt—SI 2004/1079, reg 2, sch para 2(1)(11)
 am—Enterprise and Regulatory Reform, 2013 c 24, sch 5 para 80
s 41 am—Enterprise and Regulatory Reform, 2013 c 24, sch 5 para 81
ss 41A, 41B added —Enterprise and Regulatory Reform, 2013 c 24, sch 8 para 6
s 42 am—Enterprise and Regulatory Reform, 2013 c 24, sch 5 para 82(2)(3), sch 15 para
  21(2)-(5)(6)(b)(7)(9)
 rep in pt—Enterprise and Regulatory Reform, 2013 c 24, sch 15 para 21(6)(a)(8)(10)
s 43 am—Communications, 2003 c 21, s 389(1), sch 16 para 8; Enterprise and Regulatory
  Reform, 2013 c 24, sch 5 para 83(2)
s 44 am—Communications, 2003 c 21, s 376; Enterprise and Regulatory Reform, 2013 c 24,
  sch 5 para 84(2)(3)(a)(4)(5)
 rep in pt—Enterprise and Regulatory Reform, 2013 c 24, sch 5 para 84(3)(b)
s 44A added—Communications, 2003 c 21, s 377
s 45 am—Communications, 2003 c 21, s 389(1), sch 16 para 9; Enterprise and Regulatory
  Reform, 2013 c 24, sch 5 para 85
s 46 rep in pt—Communications, 2003 c 21, s 406(7), sch 19(1); SI 2004/1079, reg 2, sch
  para 2(1)(12)(a); Enterprise and Regulatory Reform, 2013 c 24, sch 15 para 22
 am—SI 2004/1079, reg 2, sch para 2(1)(12)(b)(13)(14); Enterprise and Regulatory
  Reform, 2013 c 24, sch 5 para 86
s 46A added—SI 2004/1079, reg 2, sch para 2(1)(15)
 am—Enterprise and Regulatory Reform, 2013 c 24, sch 5 para 87(2)
 rep in pt—Enterprise and Regulatory Reform, 2013 c 24, sch 5 para 87(3)
s 46B added—SI 2004/1079, reg 2, sch para 2(1)(15)
 am—Enterprise and Regulatory Reform, 2013 c 24, sch 15 para 23(2)(4)
 rep in pt—Enterprise and Regulatory Reform, 2013 c 24, sch 15 para 23(3)(5)
s 46C added—SI 2004/1079, reg 2, sch para 2(1)(15)
 rep—Enterprise and Regulatory Reform, 2013 c 24, sch 15 para 24
s 46D added —Enterprise and Regulatory Reform, 2013 c 24, sch 15 para 24
 mod—Enterprise and Regulatory Reform, 2013 c 24, sch 4 para 47(2)
s 47 am—Enterprise and Regulatory Reform, 2013 c 24, sch 5 para 89
s 48 am—Enterprise and Regulatory Reform, 2013 c 24, sch 5 para 90

2002

c 40 *continued*

s 49 am—Enterprise and Regulatory Reform, 2013 c 24, sch 5 para 91, sch 15 para 25(4)(b)
    rep in pt—Enterprise and Regulatory Reform, 2013 c 24, sch 15 para 25(2)(3)(4)(a)(5)

s 50 am—Communications, 2003 c 21, s 389(1), sch 16 para 10; Enterprise and Regulatory
    Reform, 2013 c 24, sch 5 para 92

s 51 rep in pt—SI 2004/1079, reg 2, sch para 2(1)(16)
    am—Enterprise and Regulatory Reform, 2013 c 24, sch 5 para 93

s 52 rep in pt—SI 2004/1079, reg 2, sch para 2(1)(17)
    am—Enterprise and Regulatory Reform, 2013 c 24, sch 5 para 94

s 53 am—SI 2004/1079, reg 2, sch para 2(1)(18)(a); Enterprise and Regulatory Reform,
    2013 c 24, sch 5 para 95(2)(3)(b)(4)
    rep in pt—SI 2004/1079, reg 2, sch para 2(1)(18)(b)(c); Enterprise and Regulatory
    Reform, 2013 c 24, sch 5 para 95(3)(a)

s 54 am—Enterprise and Regulatory Reform, 2013 c 24, sch 5 para 96(2)(4)(5)(b)(c)
    rep in pt—Enterprise and Regulatory Reform, 2013 c 24, sch 5 para 96(3)(5)(a)

s 55 am—Enterprise and Regulatory Reform, 2013 c 24, sch 5 para 97

s 56 am—Enterprise and Regulatory Reform, 2013 c 24, sch 5 para
    98(2)(3)(a)(b)(4)(5)(a)(6)(7)(a)(b)(d)
    rep in pt—Enterprise and Regulatory Reform, 2013 c 24, sch 5 para
    98(3)(c)(5)(b)(7)(c)

s 57 am—Communications, 2003 c 21, s 389(1), sch 16 para 11; Enterprise and Regulatory
    Reform, 2013 c 24, sch 5 para 99

s 58 am—Communications, 2003 c 21, ss 375(1), 389(1), sch 16 para 12; SIs 2004/1079,
    reg 2, sch para 2(1)(19); 2008/2645, art 2; Enterprise and Regulatory Reform,
    2013 c 24, sch 5 para 100

s 58A added—Communications, 2003 c 21, s 375(2)

s 59 am—Communications, 2003 c 21, s 378(1)(2); Enterprise and Regulatory Reform,
    2013 c 24, sch 5 para 101(2)(3), sch 15 para 26(3)(4)(7)
    rep in pt—Enterprise and Regulatory Reform, 2013 c 24, sch 15 para 26(2)(5)(6)(8)

s 59A added—Communications, 2003 c 21, s 378(1)(3)

s 60 am—Communications, 2003 c 21, s 389(1), sch 16 para 13; Enterprise and Regulatory
    Reform, 2013 c 24, sch 5 para 102(2)

s 61 am—Communications, 2003 c 21, s 379; Enterprise and Regulatory Reform, 2013 c 24,
    sch 5 para 103

s 61A added—Communications, 2003 c 21, s 380

s 62 am—Communications, 2003 c 21, s 389(1), sch 16 para 14; Enterprise and Regulatory
    Reform, 2013 c 24, sch 5 para 104
    rep in pt—Communications, 2003 c 21, s 406(7), sch 19(1)

s 62A added —Enterprise and Regulatory Reform, 2013 c 24, sch 5 para 105
    mod—Enterprise and Regulatory Reform, 2013 c 24, sch 4 para 47(2)

s 63 am—Enterprise and Regulatory Reform, 2013 c 24, sch 5 para 106

s 64 am—Enterprise and Regulatory Reform, 2013 c 24, sch 5 para 107, sch 15 para
    27(3)(b)
    rep in pt—Enterprise and Regulatory Reform, 2013 c 24, sch 15 para 27(3)(a)(4)

s 65 am—Communications, 2003 c 21, s 389(1), sch 16 para 15; Enterprise and Regulatory
    Reform, 2013 c 24, sch 5 para 108

s 66 am—Enterprise and Regulatory Reform, 2013 c 24, sch 5 para 109

s 67 rep in pt—Communications, 2003 c 21, ss 389(1), 406(7), sch 16 para 16(a), sch 19(1)
    am—Communications, 2003 c 21, s 389(1), sch 16 para 16(b)(c); SI 2004/1079, reg 2,
    sch para 2(1)(20); Enterprise and Regulatory Reform, 2013 c 24, sch 5 para 110,
    sch 15 para 28

s 68 am—Communications, 2003 c 21, s 389(1), sch 16 para 17(b); SI 2004/1079, reg 2,
    sch para 2(1)(21); Enterprise and Regulatory Reform, 2013 c 24, sch 5 para 111,
    sch 15 para 29
    rep in pt—Communications, 2003 c 21, ss 389(1), 406(7), sch 16 para 17(a), sch 19(1)

s 69 rep (transtl provns and savings)—Communications, 2003 c 21, ss 374, 406(6)(7), sch
    18 paras 59, 60, sch 19(1)

s 71 rep —Enterprise and Regulatory Reform, 2013 c 24, s 30(1)

s 72 am—Enterprise and Regulatory Reform, 2013 c 24, s 30(3)(5)-(9), sch 5 para 112, sch
    7 para 5(3)(b)
    rep in pt—Enterprise and Regulatory Reform, 2013 c 24, s 30(4), sch 7 para 5(2)(3)(a)

s 73 am—Enterprise and Regulatory Reform, 2013 c 24, sch 5 para 113

ss 73A, 73B added —Enterprise and Regulatory Reform, 2013 c 24, sch 8 para 7

s 74 am—Enterprise and Regulatory Reform, 2013 c 24, sch 5 para 114

2002
c 40 *continued*

s 75 am—Enterprise and Regulatory Reform, 2013 c 24, sch 5 para 115
s 76 am—Enterprise and Regulatory Reform, 2013 c 24, sch 5 para 116
s 77 am—Enterprise and Regulatory Reform, 2013 c 24, sch 5 para 117
    rep in pt—Enterprise and Regulatory Reform, 2013 c 24, sch 15 para 30
s 78 am—Enterprise and Regulatory Reform, 2013 c 24, sch 5 para 118, sch 15 para 31
s 79 appl (mods)—SI 2003/1592, art 13, sch 2 para 8(9)(10); 2014/891, art 17(9)(10)
    am—SI 2009/1941, art 2, sch 1; Enterprise and Regulatory Reform, 2013 c 24, sch 5
      para 119
s 80 am—Enterprise and Regulatory Reform, 2013 c 24, sch 5 para 120(2)(3), sch 7 para
      2(2)-(4)(6)
    rep in pt—Enterprise and Regulatory Reform, 2013 c 24, sch 7 para 2(5)(7)
s 81 am—Enterprise and Regulatory Reform, 2013 c 24, sch 5 para 121(2)(3), sch 7 para
      3(2)-(4)(6)
    rep in pt—Enterprise and Regulatory Reform, 2013 c 24, sch 7 para 3(5)(7)
s 82 am—Enterprise and Regulatory Reform, 2013 c 24, sch 5 para 122
s 83 am—Enterprise and Regulatory Reform, 2013 c 24, sch 5 para 123(2)-(4)
    rep in pt—Enterprise and Regulatory Reform, 2013 c 24, sch 5 para 123(5)
s 84 am—Enterprise and Regulatory Reform, 2013 c 24, sch 5 para 124(2)
    rep in pt—Enterprise and Regulatory Reform, 2013 c 24, sch 5 para 124(3)
s 85 am—Enterprise and Regulatory Reform, 2013 c 24, sch 5 para 125
s 89 rep in pt—Enterprise and Regulatory Reform, 2013 c 24, sch 15 para 32
s 90 appl—Communications, 2003 c 21, s 406(6), sch 18 para 62(7)(9)
s 91 appl—Communications, 2003 c 21, s 406(6), sch 18 para 62(7)(9)
    am—Enterprise and Regulatory Reform, 2013 c 24, sch 5 para 126
s 92 appl—Communications, 2003 c 21, s 406(6), sch 18 para 62(7)(9)
    am—Enterprise and Regulatory Reform, 2013 c 24, sch 5 paras 127,
      128(2)(3)(a)(i)(4)(5)(a)(c)(6)
    rep in pt—Enterprise and Regulatory Reform, 2013 c 24, sch 5 para 128(3)(a)(ii)
      (b)(i)(ii)(c)(5)(b)
s 93 appl—Communications, 2003 c 21, s 406(6), sch 18 para 62(7)(9)
    am—Enterprise and Regulatory Reform, 2013 c 24, sch 5 para
      129(3)(a)-(c)(4)(5)(a)(b)(6)(7)
    rep in pt—Enterprise and Regulatory Reform, 2013 c 24, sch 5 para 129(2)(3)(d)(5)(c),
      sch 15 para 33(4)
s 94 appl—Communications, 2003 c 21, s 406(6), sch 18 para 62(7)(9)
    am—Enterprise and Regulatory Reform, 2013 c 24, sch 5 para 130(2)
    rep in pt—Enterprise and Regulatory Reform, 2013 c 24, sch 5 para 130(3), sch 15
      para 34
ss 94A, 94B added —Enterprise and Regulatory Reform, 2013 c 24, s 31(1)
s 95 am—Enterprise and Regulatory Reform, 2013 c 24, sch 5 para 131
s 96 am—Enterprise and Regulatory Reform, 2013 c 24, sch 5 para 132(2), sch 8 para
      8(2)-(4)
    rep in pt—Enterprise and Regulatory Reform, 2013 c 24, sch 8 para 8(5)
s 97 rep —Enterprise and Regulatory Reform, 2013 c 24, sch 8 para 9
    am—SI 2004/1079, reg 2, sch para 2(1)(22)
s 98 rep —Enterprise and Regulatory Reform, 2013 c 24, sch 8 para 9
s 99 am—SI 2004/1079, reg 2, sch para 2(1)(23); Enterprise and Regulatory Reform, 2013
      c 24, sch 5 para 133(2)-(4), sch 8 para 10(2)(3), sch 15 para 35(3)
    rep in pt—Enterprise and Regulatory Reform, 2013 c 24, sch 15 para 35(2)
s 100 am—Enterprise and Regulatory Reform, 2013 c 24, sch 5 para 134, sch 8 para
      11(2)(a)-(c)(f)(3)(a)(b)(4)
    rep in pt—Enterprise and Regulatory Reform, 2013 c 24, sch 8 para 11(2)(d)(e)
s 101 rep in pt—Enterprise and Regulatory Reform, 2013 c 24, sch 8 para 12
s 103 am—Enterprise and Regulatory Reform, 2013 c 24, s 32(1)
s 104 am—Enterprise and Regulatory Reform, 2013 c 24, sch 5 para 135(2)(3)(a)(b)
    rep in pt—Enterprise and Regulatory Reform, 2013 c 24, sch 5 para 135(3)(c)
    mod—SI 2003/1592 art 5A(d) (added by SI 2014/891, art 7)
s 104A added—Communications, 2003 c 21, s 381
    am—Enterprise and Regulatory Reform, 2013 c 24, sch 5 para 136
    mod—SI 2003/1592 art 5A(d) (added by SI 2014/891, art 7)
s 105 am—Communications, 2003 c 21, s 382; Enterprise and Regulatory Reform, 2013 c
      24, sch 5 para 137(2)(3)(a)(i)(c)(ii)(4)(5)(a)(b)(6)-(9)(11)

2002
c 40 s 105 *continued*

  rep in pt—Enterprise and Regulatory Reform, 2013 c 24, sch 5 para
    137(3)(a)(ii)(b)(c)(i)(5)(c)(10)
s 106 am—Enterprise and Regulatory Reform, 2013 c 24, sch 5 para 138(2)(b)(c)(3)(5)-(8)
  rep in pt—Enterprise and Regulatory Reform, 2013 c 24, sch 5 para 138(2)(a)(4)(9)
s 106A added—Communications, 2003 c 21, s 383
  am—Enterprise and Regulatory Reform, 2013 c 24, sch 5 para 139
s 106B added—Communications, 2003 c 21, s 384
  am—Enterprise and Regulatory Reform, 2013 c 24, sch 5 para 140
s 107 am—Communications, 2003 c 21, s 389(1), sch 16 para 18; Enterprise and
    Regulatory Reform, 2013 c 24, sch 5 para 141(2)(a)(3)-(7), sch 15 para
    36(2)(3)(5)-(8)
  rep in pt—Enterprise and Regulatory Reform, 2013 c 24, sch 5 para 141(2)(b)(c), sch
    15 para 36(4)(9)
s 108 am—Communications, 2003 c 21, s 389(1), sch 16 para 19; Enterprise and
    Regulatory Reform, 2013 c 24, sch 5 para 142
s 109 appl (mods)—Competition, 1980 c 21, s 11B(1A); Gas, 1986 c 44, s 41EB(1A);
    Electricity, 1989 c 29, s 56CB(1A); (EW) Water Industry, 1991 c 56,
    ss 14B(1A), 16B, 17M, 17Q; SI 1992/231 (NI 1), arts 15B(1A), 17A(14A);
    Railways, 1993 c 43, ss 13B(1A), 15C(2DA), Sch 4A paras 10A(1A),
    15(2DA); SIs 1996/275 (NI 2), arts 15B(1A), 17A(17A); 1999/3088, reg 8;
    Transport, 2000 c 38, ss 12B(1A), 18(6A); (S) SIs 2003/419 (NI 6), Sch 2
    para 5(1A), 10(3A)(7); 2005/3172, arts 5(1)(a)(5); SI 2006/3336 (NI 21), arts
    23(1A), 27(6A); Legal Services, 2007 c 29, s 60(9); SI 2011/2749, arts 3(a), 4;
    Health and Social Care, 2012 c 7, Sch 10 para 10(1)(a)(2A)(12)
  appl—SIs 2006/3336, arts 23, 27; 2014/549, sch 2 para 3
  mod—SI 2003/1592 art 5A(e) (added by SI 2014/891, art 7)
  am—Enterprise and Regulatory Reform, 2013 c 29, sch 5 para 143; SI 2014/892,
    sch 1 para 3
  savings—SIs 2014/549, sch 1 para 6; 2014/892, sch 2 para 1
s 110 appl (mods)—(EW) Water Industry, 1991 c 56, ss 16B, 17M, 17Q; SIs 1999/3088,
    reg 8; (S) 2005/3172, arts 5(1)(b)(2)(5), 10(3)(b)(4)(7); Legal Services, 2007 c
    29, s 60(9); SI 2011/2749, arts 3(b), 4; Health and Social Care, 2012 c 7, sch
    10 para 10(1)(b), (2)-(4), (12)
  appl—SI 2006/3336, arts 23, 27
  mod—SI 2003/1592, art 5A(f) (added by SI 2014/891, art 7)
  am—Enterprise and Regulatory Reform, 2013 c 24, sch 5 para 144
  rep in pt—Enterprise and Regulatory Reform, 2013 c 24, s 29(10)
  savings—SIs 2014/549, sch 1 para 6; 2014/892, sch 2 para 1
ss 110A, 110B added —Enterprise and Regulatory Reform, 2013 c 24, s 29(11)(12)(b)
  appl (mods)—Competition, 1980 c 21, s 11B(1)(ba)(2A); Legal Services, 2007 c 29,
    s 60(9)
  savings—SI 2014/892, sch 2 para 1
  mod—SI 2003/1592, art 5A(f) (added by SI 2014/891, art 7)
s 110B savings—SIs 2014/549, sch 1 para 6; 2014/892, sch 2 para 1
  mod—SI 2003/1592, art 5A(f) (added by SI 2014/891, art 7)
s 111 appl (mods)—(EW) Water Industry, 1991 c 56, ss 16B, 17M, 17Q; SIs 1999/3088,
    reg 8; (S) 2005/3172, arts 5(1)(c)(3)(5), 10(3)(c)(5)(7); Legal Services, 2007 c
    29, s 60(9); SI 2011/2749, arts 3(c), 4; Health and Social Care, 2012 c 7, sch
    10 para 10(1)(c), (2), (5)-(7), (12)
  appl—SI 2006/3336, arts 23, 27
  am—Enterprise and Regulatory Reform, 2013 c 24, sch 5 para 145
  rep in pt—Enterprise and Regulatory Reform, 2013 c 24, s 29(12)(a)
  savings—SIs 2014/549, sch 1 para 6; 2014/892, sch 2 para 1
  mod—SI 2003/1592, art 5A(f) (added by SI 2014/891, art 7)
ss 112-115 appl (mods)—(EW) Water Industry, 1991 c 56, ss 16B, 17M, 17Q; SIs
    1999/3088, reg 8; (S) 2005/3172, arts 5(1)(d)-(g)(5), 10(3)(d)-(g)(7); Legal
    Services, 2007 c 29, s 60(9); Health and Social Care, 2012 c 7, sch 10 para
    10(1)(d)-(g), (2), (8)-(10), (12)
  appl—Competition, 1998 c 41 s 40A(9); SI 2006/3336, arts 23, 27; Legal
    Services, 2007 c 29, s 60(9)
s 112 appl—SIs 2011/2749, art 3(d)
  am—Enterprise and Regulatory Reform, 2013 c 24, sch 5 para 146
  mod—SI 2003/1592, art 5A(f) (added by SI 2014/891, art 7)

2002
c 40 *continued*

s 113 appl—SIs 2011/2749, art 3(e)
    am—Enterprise and Regulatory Reform, 2013 c 24, sch 5 para 147
    mod—SI 2003/1592, art 5A(f) (added by SI 2014/891, art 7)
s 114 appl—SIs 2011/2749, art 3(f)
    am—Enterprise and Regulatory Reform, 2013 c 24, sch 5 para 148
    mod—SI 2003/1592, art 5A(f) (added by SI 2014/891, art 7)
s 115 appl—SIs 2011/2749, art 3(g)
    am—Enterprise and Regulatory Reform, 2013 c 24, sch 5 para 149
    mod—SI 2003/1592, art 5A(f) (added by SI 2014/891, art 7)
s 116 appl (mods)—(EW) Water Industry, 1991 c 56, ss 16B, 17M, 17Q; SIs 1999/3088,
        reg 8; (S) 2005/3172, arts 5(1)(h)(5), 10(3)(h)(7); Health and Social Care,
        2012 c 7, sch 10 para 10(1)(h), (2),(11), (12)
    appl—SIs 2006/3336, arts 23, 27; 2011/2749, art 3(h)
    am—Enterprise and Regulatory Reform, 2013 c 24, sch 5 para 150
s 117 appl—SI 1990/1715, reg 5; Communications, 2003 c 21, s 193(8); SI 2003/1900,
        arts 2(1), 3(1),sch 1; SI 2003/3142, art 3(2)
    appl (mods)—(subject to transtl mods) Communications, 2003 c 21, ss 370(10), 408;
        SIs 2003/1900, arts 2(1), 3(1),sch 1; 2003/3142, art 3(2); (S) 2005/3172,
        arts 5(1)(a)-(i)(2)-(5), 10(3)(a)-(i)(4)-(7); 2011/2749, arts 3(i), 4; Health and
        Social Care, 2012 c 7, sch 10 para 10(1)(i), (2), (12)
    am—Communications, 2003 c 21, s 389(1), sch 16 para 20; Enterprise and
        Regulatory Reform, 2013 c 24, sch 5 para 151
    mod—SI 2006/3336, art 29; Health and Social Care, 2012 c 7, s 73(6)
s 118 am—Communications, 2003 c 21, s 389(1), sch 16 para 21; Enterprise and
        Regulatory Reform, 2013 c 24, sch 5 para 152
    mod—SI 2003/1592, art 5A(g) (added by SI 2014/891, art 7)
s 119 am—Enterprise and Regulatory Reform, 2013 c 24, sch 5 para 153(20(b)(3)
    rep in pt—Enterprise and Regulatory Reform, 2013 c 24, sch 5 para 153(2)(a)
s 119A added—Communications, 2003 c 21, s 385
s 119B added—Communications, 2003 c 21, s 386
    am—Enterprise and Regulatory Reform, 2013 c 24, sch 5 para 154(2)(3)
s 120 am—Communications, 2003 c 21, s 389(1), sch 16 para 22; Enterprise and
        Regulatory Reform, 2013 c 24, s 31(2), sch 5 para 155
    mod—SI 2003/1592, art 5A(h) (added by SI 2014/891, art 7)
    appl—Energy, 2004 c 20, s 141, sch 18 para 15
s 121 am—Communications, 2003 c 21, s 389(1), sch 16 para 23(1)(2)(a)(3)(a)(5)(a);
        Enterprise and Regulatory Reform, 2013 c 24, sch 5 para 156
    rep in pt—Communications, 2003 c 21, ss 389(1), 406(7), sch 16
        para 23(1)(2)(b)(3)(b)(4)(5)(b)(6), sch 19(1)
s 122 am—SI 2004/1079, reg 2, sch para 2(1)(24); Enterprise and Regulatory Reform,
        2013 c 24, sch 5 para 157(2)(b)(3)
    rep in pt—Enterprise and Regulatory Reform, 2013 c 24, sch 5 para 157(2)(a)
s 123 am—Enterprise and Regulatory Reform, 2013 c 24, sch 5 para 158
s 124 am—Communications, 2003 c 21, s 389(1), sch 16 para 24; Enterprise and
        Regulatory Reform, 2013 c 24, s 31(3), sch 8 para 13(2)
s 125 appl (mods)—(S) SI 2005/3172, arts 5(1)(j)(2)-(5), 10(3)(j)(4)-(7); Health and Social
        Care, 2012 c 7, sch 10 para 10(1)(j), (2), (12)
s 126 am—Communications, 2003 c 21, s 406(1), sch 17 para 174(1)(2); SI 2003/1900,
        arts 2(1), 3(1),sch 1; SI 2003/3142, art 3(2)
s 127 am—Communications, 2003 c 21, s 375(3); Civil Partnership, 2004 c 33, s 261(1),
        sch 27 para 168
    appl—SIs 2003/1370, art 2, sch para 7; (EW) 2004/3206, reg 2(b), sch para 7
    ext—Civil Partnership, 2004 c 33, ss 246, 247, sch 21 para 53
s 128 am—Communications, 2003 c 21, s 406(1), sch 17 para 174(1)(3)
s 129 rep in pt—SI 2004/1079, reg 2, sch para 2(1)(25)(a)
    am—SIs 2004/1079, reg 2, sch para 2(1)(25)(b); 2008/2645, art 3; 2009/1941, art 2,
        sch 1
s 130 am—Communications, 2003 c 21, s 389(1), sch 16 para 25; SIs 2004/1079, reg 2, sch
        para 2(1)(26)(b); 2008/2645, art 3; Enterprise and Regulatory Reform, 2013 c
        24, sch 5 para 159(2)(4)
    rep in pt—SI 2004/1079, reg 2, sch para 2(1)(26)(a); Enterprise and Regulatory
        Reform, 2013 c 24, sch 5 para 159(3), sch 15 para 37
s 130A added —Enterprise and Regulatory Reform, 2013 c 24, sch 12 para 1

2002
c 40 s 130A *continued*

mod—Financial Services (Banking Reform), 2013 c 33, s 59(6); Financial Services (Banking Reform), 2013 c 33, sch 8 para 3 (adding 2000 c 8 s 234I(6))

appl (mods)—Gas, 1986 c 44, s 36A(2C); Electricity, 1989 c 29, s 43(2C)); Water Industry, 1991 c 56, s 31(4ZA); SI 1992/231 (NI 1), art 46(2C); Railways, 1993 c 43, s 67(2C)); SI 1996/275 (NI 2), art 23(2C); Transport, 2000 c 38, s 86(5A); Communications, 2003 c 21, s 370(3A); SI 2006/3336 (NI 21), art 29(4A); Health and Social Care, 2012 c 7, s 73(3A); Civil Aviation, 2012 c 19, s 60(4A)

Pt 4 (ss 131-184 (except ss 166, 171)) ext—Communications, 2003 c 21, ss 370, 406(6), 408, sch 18 para 56; SI 2003/1900, arts 2(1), 3(1),sch 1; SI 2003/3142, art 3(2)

appl (mods)—Gas, 1986 c 44, s 36A; Electricity, 1989 c 29, s 43(2B); Water Industry, 1991 c 56, s 31(4); Railways, 1993 c 43, s 67(4)(d); Transport, 2000 c 38, s 86(4A); Health and Social Care, 2012 c 7, s 73(3)(b); Civil Aviation, 2012 c 19, s 60(3A)

mod —Health and Social Care, 2012 c 7, s 73; Civil Aviation, 2012 c 19, s 60; Enterprise and Regulatory Reform, 2013 c 24, sch 4 para 57

functions made exercisable concurrently —Civil Aviation, 2012 c 19, s 60; Financial Services (Banking Reform), 2013 c 33, s 59(1)-(5)

am—Enterprise and Regulatory Reform, 2013 c 24, sch 12 para 8

Pt 4, Ch 1 (ss 131-138) am—Enterprise and Regulatory Reform, 2013 c 24, sch 12 para 9

s 131 am—Enterprise and Regulatory Reform, 2013 c 24, s 33, sch 5 para 163(2)(3), sch 10 para 2

ss 131A-131C added —Enterprise and Regulatory Reform, 2013 c 24, sch 12 para 2

s 132 am—Enterprise and Regulatory Reform, 2013 c 24, s 34(2)(3), sch 5 para 164(2)(3), sch 10 para 3(a)(b), sch 12 para 10(2)(3)

s 133 am—Enterprise and Regulatory Reform, 2013 c 24, sch 5 para 165, sch 9 para 2

s 133A added —Enterprise and Regulatory Reform, 2013 c 24, sch 5 para 166

s 134 am—Enterprise and Regulatory Reform, 2013 c 24, sch 5 para 167, sch 9 para 3

s 135 am—Enterprise and Regulatory Reform, 2013 c 24, sch 5 para 168(2)(3)(b)(c)(4), sch 10 para 4

rep in pt—Enterprise and Regulatory Reform, 2013 c 24, sch 5 para 168(3)(a), sch 12 para 11

s 136 am—Railways and Transport Safety, 2003 c 20, s 16, sch 2 pt 2 para 19(u); Communications, 2003 c 21, s 406(1), sch 17 para 174(1)(4); SI 2003/1900, arts 2(1), 3(1),sch 1; SI 2003/3142, art 3(2); Water, 2003 c 37,s 101(1), sch 7 pt 2 para 36(1)(2); SI 2006/3336, art 308, sch 12; Civil Aviation, 2012 c 19, s 61(11); Health and Social Care, 2012 c 7, s 74(6); Enterprise and Regulatory Reform, 2013 c 24, sch 5 para 169(2)(3)(4); Financial Services (Banking Reform), 2013 c 33, s 67(3); (ibid, sch 8 para 10(2)(3); SI 2015/1682, sch pt 1 para 4(q)(i)

rep in pt—Communications, 2003 c 21, s 406(7), sch 19(1); SIs 2003/1900, arts 2(1), 3(1), sch 1; 2003/3142, art 3(2); 2006/3336, art 308, sch 13; Enterprise and Regulatory Reform, 2013 c 24, sch 5 para 169(5)

s 137 am—Enterprise and Regulatory Reform, 2013 c 24, sch 5 para 170, sch 12 para 3

s 138 am—Enterprise and Regulatory Reform, 2013 c 24, sch 5 para 171, sch 9 para 4, sch 12 para 4

ss 138A, 138B added —Enterprise and Regulatory Reform, 2013 c 24, sch 12 para 5

s 139 am—Enterprise and Regulatory Reform, 2013 c 24, s 35, sch 5 para 172

s 140 am—Enterprise and Regulatory Reform, 2013 c 24, sch 5 para 173, sch 10 para 5

s 140A added —Enterprise and Regulatory Reform, 2013 c 24, s 35(8)

s 140B added —Enterprise and Regulatory Reform, 2013 c 24, sch 10 para 6

s 141 am—Enterprise and Regulatory Reform, 2013 c 24, sch 5 para 174, sch 9 para 5, sch 10 para 7(2)(3)

ss 141A, 141B added —Enterprise and Regulatory Reform, 2013 c 24, s 35(9)

s 142 am—Enterprise and Regulatory Reform, 2013 c 24, sch 5 para 175, sch 10 para 8

s 143 am—Enterprise and Regulatory Reform, 2013 c 24, sch 5 para 176, sch 10 para 9(2)(3)(5)(7)

rep in pt—Enterprise and Regulatory Reform, 2013 c 24, sch 10 para 9(4)(6)

s 143A added —Enterprise and Regulatory Reform, 2013 c 24, sch 10 para 10

s 144 am—Enterprise and Regulatory Reform, 2013 c 24, sch 5 para 177, sch 10 para 11, sch 12 para 6

s 145 am—Enterprise and Regulatory Reform, 2013 c 24, sch 5 para 178, sch 10 para 12

2002

c 40 *continued*

s 146 am—Enterprise and Regulatory Reform, 2013 c 24, sch 5 para 179, sch 10 para 13

s 146A added —Enterprise and Regulatory Reform, 2013 c 24, sch 10 para 14

s 147 am—Enterprise and Regulatory Reform, 2013 c 24, sch 5 para 180, sch 9 para 6, sch 10 para 15

s 147A added —Enterprise and Regulatory Reform, 2013 c 24, sch 10 para 16

s 148 am—Enterprise and Regulatory Reform, 2013 c 24, sch 5 para 181, sch 10 para 17(3)

    rep in pt—Enterprise and Regulatory Reform, 2013 c 24, sch 10 para 17(2)

s 148A added —Enterprise and Regulatory Reform, 2013 c 24, sch 10 para 18

s 149 am—Enterprise and Regulatory Reform, 2013 c 24, sch 5 para 182, sch 10 para 19

s 150 am—Enterprise and Regulatory Reform, 2013 c 24, sch 5 para 183, sch 10 para 20

s 151 am—Enterprise and Regulatory Reform, 2013 c 24, sch 5 para 184, sch 10 para 21

s 152 am—Enterprise and Regulatory Reform, 2013 c 24, sch 5 para 185

    rep in pt—Enterprise and Regulatory Reform, 2013 c 24, sch 10 para 22

s 153 am—SI 2004/1079, reg 2, sch para 2(1)(27); Enterprise and Regulatory Reform, 2013 c 24, sch 5 para 186(a)(b)

    rep in pt—Enterprise and Regulatory Reform, 2013 c 24, sch 5 para 186(c)

s 154 am—Enterprise and Regulatory Reform, 2013 c 24, sch 5 paras 187, 188, sch 9 para 7

s 155 am—Enterprise and Regulatory Reform, 2013 c 24, sch 10 para 23

s 156 am—Enterprise and Regulatory Reform, 2013 c 24, sch 5 para 189, sch 9 para 8, sch 12 para 12

s 157 am—Enterprise and Regulatory Reform, 2013 c 24, s 37(2)(3), sch 10 para 24

s 158 am—Enterprise and Regulatory Reform, 2013 c 24, s 37(4)(5), sch 10 para 25

s 159 am—Enterprise and Regulatory Reform, 2013 c 24, sch 5 para 190, sch 10 para 26

s 160 am—Enterprise and Regulatory Reform, 2013 c 24, sch 5 para 191, sch 10 para 27

s 161 am—Enterprise and Regulatory Reform, 2013 c 24, sch 5 para 192(2)(3), sch 10 para 28

    excl—Groceries Code Adjudicator, 2013 c 19, s 21(5)

s 162 am—Enterprise and Regulatory Reform, 2013 c 24, sch 5 para 193, sch 5 para 194(2)(3)(a)(i)(d) (4)(5)(6)(a)(c)(7)

    rep in pt—Enterprise and Regulatory Reform, 2013 c 24, sch 5 para 194(3)(a)(ii)(b)(i)(ii)(c)(6)(b)

s 163 am—Enterprise and Regulatory Reform, 2013 c 24, sch 5 para 195(3)-(8)

    rep in pt—Enterprise and Regulatory Reform, 2013 c 24, sch 5 para 195(2)

s 166 am—Enterprise and Regulatory Reform, 2013 c 24, sch 5 para 196(2)(3)(a)(4)

    rep in pt—Enterprise and Regulatory Reform, 2013 c 24, sch 5 para 196(3)(b)(c)(5)(6)

s 167 am—Enterprise and Regulatory Reform, 2013 c 24, sch 5 para 197(2)(3)(5)

    rep in pt—Enterprise and Regulatory Reform, 2013 c 24, sch 5 para 197(4)

s 168 am—Railways and Transport Safety, 2003 c 20, s 16, sch 2 pt 2 para 19(u); Communications, 2003 c 21, s 406(1), sch 17 para 174(1)(5); Water, 2003 c 37, s 101(1), sch 7 pt 2 para 36(1)(3), sch 8 para 55(1)(2); Railways, 2005 c 14, s 59, sch 12 para 18(1)(2)(c)(3); SI 2006/3336, art 308, sch 12; Postal Services, 2011 c 5, sch 12 para 164(2)(3); SI 2012/2400, art 31; Health and Social Care, 2012 c 7, s 74(7); Civil Aviation, 2012 c 19, sch 9 para 14(2)(b),(3)(b); Enterprise and Regulatory Reform, 2013 c 24, sch 5 para 198; (prosp) Water, 2014 c 21, sch 7 para 129; SI 2015/1682, sch pt 1 para 4(q)(ii)

    rep in pt—Communications, 2003 c 21, s 406(7), sch 19(1); SIs 2003/1900, arts 2(1), 3(1), sch 1; 2003/3142, art 3(2); Railways, 2005 c 14, s 59, sch 12 para 18(1)(2)(a)(b), sch 13 pt 1; Postal Services, 2011 c 5, sch 12 para 164(4); Civil Aviation, 2012 c 19, sch 9 para 14(2)(a),(3)(a)

    appl (mods)—SI 2005/3050, reg 14, sch 3 pt 1 paras 1(f), 8

s 169 am—Enterprise and Regulatory Reform, 2013 c 24, sch 5 para 199(a)-(c), sch 10 para 29, sch 12 para 13(a)

    rep in pt—Enterprise and Regulatory Reform, 2013 c 24, sch 5 para 199(d), sch 12 para 13(b)

s 170 am—Enterprise and Regulatory Reform, 2013 c 24, sch 5 para 200(3)(4)

    rep in pt—Enterprise and Regulatory Reform, 2013 c 24, sch 5 para 200(2)(5)

s 171 am—Enterprise and Regulatory Reform, 2013 c 24, sch 5 para 201(2)(b)(c)(3)(5)(6)(b)(7)(b)(8)(9)

    rep in pt—Enterprise and Regulatory Reform, 2013 c 24, sch 5 para 201(2)(a)(4)(6)(a)(7)(a)(10)

s 172 am—Enterprise and Regulatory Reform, 2013 c 24, sch 5 para 202, sch 10 para 30(2)(4)(a)(b)(6)(7)(8), sch 12 para 14(2)(3)(a)(b)(4)

2002

c 40 s 172 *continued*

rep in pt—Enterprise and Regulatory Reform, 2013 c 24, sch 10 para 30(3)(5)

s 173 am—Enterprise and Regulatory Reform, 2013 c 24, sch 5 para 203(a)(b)
  rep in pt—Enterprise and Regulatory Reform, 2013 c 24, sch 5 para 203(c)

s 174 am—Enterprise and Regulatory Reform, 2013 c 24, s 36, sch 5 para 204
  mod—Legal Services, 2007 c 29, s 57(5)
  savings—SI 2014/892, sch 2 para 3

ss 174A-174E added —Enterprise and Regulatory Reform, 2013 c 24, sch 11 para 1

s 174B mod—Financial Services and Markets, 2000 c 8, s 140D(2); Legal Services, 2007 c 29, s 57(5A)

s 175 rep —Enterprise and Regulatory Reform, 2013 c 24, sch 11 para 3
  savings—SI 2014/892, sch 2 para 3

s 176 rep —Enterprise and Regulatory Reform, 2013 c 24, sch 11 para 4

s 177 am—Enterprise and Regulatory Reform, 2013 c 24, sch 5 para 205
  rep in pt—Enterprise and Regulatory Reform, 2013 c 24, sch 10 para 31

s 178 am—Enterprise and Regulatory Reform, 2013 c 24, sch 5 para 206(2)(b)(3)
  rep in pt—Enterprise and Regulatory Reform, 2013 c 24, sch 5 para 206(2)(a)

s 179 am—Enterprise and Regulatory Reform, 2013 c 24, sch 5 para 207, sch 11 para 5, sch 12 para 15

s 180 am—Communications, 2003 c 21, s 389(1), sch 16 para 26

s 181 am—Enterprise and Regulatory Reform, 2013 c 24, sch 11 para 6(2)(3)(b), sch 12 para 16(2)(3)
  rep in pt—Enterprise and Regulatory Reform, 2013 c 24, sch 11 para 6(3)(a)

s 183 am—Enterprise and Regulatory Reform, 2013 c 24, sch 5 para 208, sch 10 para 32(2)(3)(a)(b)(d)(f)(h)-(k)(4)(5)(6)
  rep in pt—Enterprise and Regulatory Reform, 2013 c 24, sch 10 para 32(3)(c)(e)(g)

s 184 am—Enterprise and Regulatory Reform, 2013 c 24, sch 5 para 209(2)(4), sch 9 para 9, sch 10 para 33, sch 12 para 17
  rep in pt—Enterprise and Regulatory Reform, 2013 c 24, sch 5 para 209(3)

ss 185-187 rep —Enterprise and Regulatory Reform, 2013 c 24, sch 5 para 225

s 188 am—Enterprise and Regulatory Reform, 2013 c 24, s 47(4)
  rep in pt—Enterprise and Regulatory Reform, 2013 c 24, s 47(2)(3)

s 188A added —Enterprise and Regulatory Reform, 2013 c 24, s 47(5)

s 188B added —Enterprise and Regulatory Reform, 2013 c 24, s 47(6)

s 190 am—Enterprise and Regulatory Reform, 2013 c 24, sch 5 para 210

s 190A added —Enterprise and Regulatory Reform, 2013 c 24, s 47(7)

s 191 rep—Extradition, 2003 c 41, ss 219, 220, sch 3 paras 1, 14, sch 4 (see SI 2003/3103, arts 2-5)

s 192 am—Enterprise and Regulatory Reform, 2013 c 24, sch 5 para 211

s 193 am—Enterprise and Regulatory Reform, 2013 c 24, sch 5 para 212

s 194 am—Enterprise and Regulatory Reform, 2013 c 24, s 48(2)-(4), sch 5 para 213

s 195 am—Enterprise and Regulatory Reform, 2013 c 24, sch 5 para 214

s 196 am—Enterprise and Regulatory Reform, 2013 c 24, sch 5 para 215

s 201 am—Enterprise and Regulatory Reform, 2013 c 24, sch 5 para 216

s 205 am—SI 2014/892, sch 1 para 4

s 206 am—SI 2014/892, sch 1 para 5

s 209 am—SI 2012/1809, art 3(1), sch pt 1

s 210 am—SI 2006/3363, regs 4, 5
  rep in pt—Consumer Rights, 2015 c 15, sch 7 para 2

s 211 rep in pt—Consumer Rights, 2015 c 15, sch 7 para 3(2)
  am—Consumer Rights, 2015 c 15, sch 7 para 3(3)

s 212 rep in pt—SI 2006/3363, reg 6
  am—SIs 2006/3363, regs 7, 8, 9, 11; 2007/528, reg 2

s 213 am—SIs 2006/3363, reg 10; 2011/1208, reg 16(a); Financial Services, 2012 c. 21, sch 18 para 95(2); SI 2014/892, sch 1 para 6; Consumer Rights, 2015 c 15, sch 7 para 4

s 214 am—SIs 2013/783, art 9; 2014/892, sch 1 para 7; Consumer Rights, 2015 c 15, sch 7 para 5

s 215 am—SI 2006/3363, reg 12; Crime and Cts, 2013 c 22, sch 9 para 81(c); SI 2014/892, sch 1 para 8
  rep in pt—Crime and Cts, 2013 c 22, sch 9 para 81(b)

s 216 am—SI 2014/892, sch 1 para 9

s 217 am—Consumer Rights, 2015 c 15, sch 7 para 6

s 218A added—SI 2008/1277, reg 27

2002

c 40 *continued*

s 219 am—SIs 2006/3363, reg 13; 2014/892, sch 1 para 10; Consumer Rights, 2015 c 15, sch 7 para 7

ss 219A-219C added—Consumer Rights, 2015 c 15, sch 7 para 8

s 220 am—SI 2014/892, sch 1 para 11; Consumer Rights, 2015 c 15, sch 7 para 9

s 221 am—SI 2006/3363, reg 14

s 222 am—Civil Partnership, 2004 c 33, s 261(1), sch 27 para 169

s 223 am—SI 2009/1941, art 2, sch 1

s 223A added—Consumer Rights, 2015 c 15, sch 6 para 78

ss 224-227 rep—Consumer Rights, 2015 c 15, sch 6 paras 68-71

ss 227A-227F added—SI 2006/3363, reg 17

    rep—Consumer Rights, 2015 c 15, sch 6 paras 72-77

s 228 am—SI 2006/3363, reg 18

    rep in pt—Consumer Rights, 2015 c 15, sch 6 para 79

s 229 am—SIs 2006/3363, reg 19; 2014/892, sch 1 para 14; Consumer Rights, 2015 c 15, sch 7 para 10

s 230 saved—SI 2008/1277, reg 30, sch 3

    am—SI 2014/892, sch 1 para 15(2)(a)(3)(a)(4)

    rep in pt—SI 2014/892, sch 1 para 15(2)(b)(3)(b)

    cont—SI 2010/2960, reg 36, sch 7

s 231 am—SI 2014/892, sch 1 para 16

    rep in pt—SI 2014/631, sch 2 para 4

s 234 am—Communications, 2003 c 21, s 406(1), sch 17 para 174(1)(6); SI 2003/1900, arts 2(1), 3(1),sch 1; SI 2003/3142, art 3(2)

ss 235A, 235B added—SI 2006/3363, reg 20

s 236 subst—SI 2006/3363, reg 21

    rep in pt—Consumer Rights, 2015 c 15, sch 6 para 80

Pt 9 (ss 237-247) appl—SI 1990/1715, reg 5; (subject to transtl mods) Communications, 2003 c 21, ss 393(8), 408; SIs 2003/1900, arts 2(1), 3(1), sch 1; 2003/3142, art 3(2); 2009/209, regs 107, 122-123

s 237 excl—Railways and Transport Safety, 2003 c 20, s 115(1)(2)(m)

s 241 am—Enterprise and Regulatory Reform, 2013 c 24, s 55

s 241A added—Companies, 2006 c 46, s 1281

    rep in pt—Financial Services, 2012 c. 21, sch 19

s 243 rep in pt—Financial Services, 2012 c. 21, sch 19

s 247 rep in pt—SI 2013/1575, sch para 9

s 248 mod—Energy, 2004 c 20, s 170(1)(2)(a); Postal Services, 2011 c 5, s 84(a)

    see —(power to mod ext) Energy, 2011 c 16, s 100(2)(a)

s 249 am—Water, 2003 c 37,s 101(1), sch 8 para 55(1)(3); (prosp) Water, 2014 c 21, sch 7 para 130

    rep in pt—(prosp) Flood and Water Management, 2010 c 29, s 34, sch 5 para 6(3)

    appl (mods)—SI 2013/1582, sch 1 para 7(1)

s 253 see (power restr)—SI 2004/353, reg 4(8)

s 254 mod—Energy, 2004 c 20, s 170(1)(2)(b); Postal Services, 2011 c 5, s 84(b)

    restr—SI 2004/1045, reg 3(7)

    see —(power to mod ext) Energy, 2011 c 16, s 100(2)(b)

s 255 am—SIs 2008/948, art 3, sch 1; 2010/866, art 5, sch 2; 2012/700, sch para 6

    rep in pt—Co-operative and Community Benefit Societies, 2014 c 14, sch 7

s 264 rep in pt—Small Business, Enterprise and Employment, 2015 c 26, s 135(3)(a)

s 265 rep —Courts, 2003 c 39, s 109(3), sch 10

s 268 mod—Loc Govt, 2003 c 26, s 105, sch 4 para 25 (see SI 2003/2938)

    ext—Human Tissue, 2004 c 30, s 56, sch 6 para 6(1)

    mod—Human Tissue, 2004 c 30, s 56, sch 6 para 6(2)

    am—Constitutional Reform, 2005 c 4, s 15(1), sch 4 pt 1 paras 304, 305(1)(2)(b)(3)

    rep in pt—Constitutional Reform, 2005 c 4, ss 15(1), 146, sch 4 pt 1 paras 304, 305(1)(2)(a), sch 18 pt 2

s 270 rep in pt—Deregulation, 2015 c 20, sch 6 para 22(13)

s 273 rep in pt—Enterprise and Regulatory Reform, 2013 c 24, sch 5 para 217(3)

    am—Enterprise and Regulatory Reform, 2013 c 24, sch 5 para 217(2)

s 276 appl—Communications, 2003 c 21, s 389(2)

s 277 appl—Communications, 2003 c 21, s 389(2)(3)

    mod—Energy, 2004 c 20, s 170(1)(2)(a); Postal Services, 2011 c 5, s 84(a); Co-operative and Community Benefit Societies, 2014 c 14, s 118(6)

    see —(power to mod ext) Energy, 2011 c 16, s 100(2)(a)

2002
c 40 *continued*

sch 1 rep —Enterprise and Regulatory Reform, 2013 c 24, sch 5 para 229

sch 2 am —Constitutional Reform, 2005 c 4, s 15(1), sch 4 pt 1 paras 304, 306; Tribunals, Courts and Enforcement, 2007 c 15, s 50, sch 10 para 36

sch 3 rep in pt—Enterprise and Regulatory Reform, 2013 c 24, sch 5 para 226

sch 4 appl (mods)—Communications, 2003 c 21, ss 195(8), 294, sch 11 para 10(7); SI 2003/1900, arts 2(1), 3(1), sch 1; SI 2003/3142, art 3(2)

    am—Crime and Cts, 2013 c 22, sch 9 para 81(d); Enterprise and Regulatory Reform, 2013 c 24, s 48(5), sch 5 para 66; Consumer Rights, 2015 c 15, s 82(3); ibid, sch 8 paras 23-30

sch 7 appl (mods)—Communications, 2003 c 21, s 406(6), sch 18 para 62(6)(8)

    am—Enterprise and Regulatory Reform, 2013 c 24, sch 5 para 160, sch 7 para 4(3)(4)(5)(b)(7)(8), sch 15 para 38

    rep in pt—Enterprise and Regulatory Reform, 2013 c 24, sch 7 para 4(2)(5)(a)(c)(6)

sch 8 am—Communications, 2003 c 21, s 387; SIs 2008/2645, art 4; 2009/1941, art 2, sch 1; Enterprise and Regulatory Reform, 2013 c 24, s 49; s 50(4)(a)(b)(5), sch 5 para 161(2)(3)(4)(b)

    rep in pt—Enterprise and Regulatory Reform, 2013 c 24, s 50(2)(6), sch 5 para 161(4)(a)

sch 9 rep in pt—Communications, 2003 c 21, s 406(7), sch 19(1); SI 2003/1900, arts 2(1), 3(1),sch 1; SI 2003/3142, art 3(2); Postal Services, 2011 c 5, sch 12 para 165; Civil Aviation, 2012 c 19, sch 9 para 17

sch 10 appl—Communications, 2003 c 21, s 406(6), sch 18 para 62(7)(a)

    am—Enterprise and Regulatory Reform, 2013 c 24, sch 5 para 162

    mod—SI 2004/3202, reg 36 (added by 2015/1936, reg 21)

sch 11 rep —Enterprise and Regulatory Reform, 2013 c 24, sch 5 para 227

sch 12 rep —Enterprise and Regulatory Reform, 2013 c 24, sch 5 para 228

sch 13 am—SIs 2003/1374, art 2; 2004/2095, reg 26; 2005/2759, reg 4, sch para 19; 2006/3363, reg 22; 2008/1277, regs 26, 30, sch 2; 2009/2999, reg 48; 2010/1010, regs 46,101; 2010/2960, reg 36, sch 6; 2011/1208, reg 16(b); 2014/2908, art 3; SIs 2015/542, reg 20(1); 1392, reg 6(a)(b); 1911, reg 18(2)

    rep in pt—SI 2008/1277, reg 30, schs 2, 4; 2010/1010, regs 46,101; 2010/2960, reg 36, schs 6, 8

sch 14 am—(pt prosp) Fireworks, 2003 c 22, s 12(3); SIs 2003/1400, art 3, sch 1; 2003/2580, art 3, sch; 2007/2977, art 2; Financial Services, 2012 c. 21, sch 18 para 95(3); Groceries Code Adjudicator, 2013 c 19, s 21(4); SI 2014/892, sch 1 para 17; Consumer Rights, 2015 c 15, sch 6 para 81; (prosp) Small Business, Enterprise and Employment, 2015 c 26, sch 1 para 26; SI 2015/1726, sch para 3

    rep in pt—SIs 2008/1277, sch 4; 2010/2960, reg 36, schs 6, 8; 2013/1575, sch para 10

sch 15 am—(pt prosp) Fireworks, 2003 c 22, s 12(3); Communications, 2003 c 21, s 406(1), sch 17 para 174(1)(7); SI 2003/1900, arts 2(1), 3(1),sch 1; SI 2003/3142, art 3(2); Water, 2003 c 37,s 101(1), sch 7 pt 2 para 36(1)(4); SI 2003/1400, art 4, sch 2; Railways, 2005 c 14, s 59, sch 12 para 18(1)(4); SIs 2006/2909, art 2; 2006/3336, art 308, sch 12; 2007/2194, art 10, sch 4; 2007/2977, art 2; Postal Services, 2011 c 5, sch 12 para 166; SI 2011/2491, sch 3 para 6; Civil Aviation, 2012 c 19, sch 9 para 15; Groceries Code Adjudicator, 2013 c 19, s 21(4); Enterprise and Regulatory Reform, 2013 c 24, sch 15 para 39; SIs 2014/469, sch 2 para 22; 2014/892, sch 1 para 17; 2014/2807, art 2; Consumer Rights, 2015 c 15, sch 4 para 35; (prosp) Small Business, Enterprise and Employment, 2015 c 26, sch 1 para 26; SIs 2015/1726, sch para 4; 1911, reg 18(3)

    appl (mods)—SI 2006/1391, art 2, sch

    rep in pt—SIs 2007/2194, art 10, sch 5; 2009/1941, art 2, sch 1; 2010/2960, reg 36, schs 6, 8; 2013/1575, sch para 11; Deregulation, 2015 c 20, sch 23 para 28(6)

sch 16 am—SI 2003/2096, art 2(1)-(5)

sch 17 rep in pt—Companies, 2006 c 46, s 129, sch 16; Small Business, Enterprise and Employment, 2015 c 26, s 107(5)

sch 19 am—SI 2003/2096, art 3

sch 22 rep in pt—Small Business, Enterprise and Employment, 2015 c 26, s 135(3)(b)

    rep in pt—Small Business, Enterprise and Employment, 2015 c 26, s 135(3)(c)

sch 24 appl—SI 2006/354, art 3

    rep in pt—SIs 2013/294, art 2 sch; 2014/892, sch 1 para 18(2)

    am—SI 2014/892, sch 1 para 18(3)-(6)

2002
c 40 *continued*

    sch 25 rep in pt—SI 2003/3180, arts 2, 3, sch para 7; Communications, 2003 c 21, s 406(7),
        sch 19(1); SI 2003/1900, arts 2(1), 3(1),sch 1; SI 2003/3142, art 3(2);
        Companies (Audit, Investigations and Community Enterprise), 2004 c 27, s 64,
        sch 8; Consumer Credit, 2006 c 14, s 70, sch 4; Consumers, Estate Agents and
        Redress, 2007 c 17, s 64, sch 8; Legal Services, 2007 c 29, s 210, sch 23; SI
        2008/1277, sch 4; Loc Transport, 2008 c 26, s 131, sch 7; Postal Services,
        2011 c 5, sch 12 para 167; Civil Aviation, 2012 c 19, sch 9 para 17; Financial
        Services, 2012 c. 21, sch 19; SI 2013/294, art 2 sch; Consumer Rights, 2015 c
        15, sch 6 para 85(c)

c 41   **Nationality, Immigration and Asylum**
    cert provns ext (mods) to I of Man with transtl provns)—SI 2008/680, art 16, sch 7, with art
        4, sch 2
    see—SI 2011/1158, art 4 6
    s 6 rep in pt—Equality, 2010 c 15, sch 27 pt 1A (amended by SI 2011/1060, art 4(b)); SI
        2011/1060, art 4(a)
    s 10 rep in pt—Immigration, Asylum and Nationality, 2006 c 13, s 52, sch 2 para 4(a), sch 3
        am—Immigration, Asylum and Nationality, 2006 c 13, ss 50(5), 52, sch 2 para 4(b)
    s 11 rep—(savings) Borders, Citizenship and Immigration, 2009 c 11, ss 48(2)(3), 56, sch 1
        pt 2
    s 16 rep in pt—Constitutional Reform, 2005 c 4, s 146, sch 18 pt 2
    s 34 rep—UK Borders, 2007 c 30, s 54(b), sch
    s 36 am—Educ, 2005 c 18, s 61, sch 9 para 30; SIs 2008/2833, art 6, sch 3; 2010/1158, art
        5, sch 2; Children and Families, 2014 c 6, sch 3 para 79(2)-(4)(6)(7)
        rep in pt—Children and Families, 2014 c 6, sch 3 para 79(5)
    s 37 am—SI 2010/1158, art 5, sch 2
    s 45 rep in pt—Nat Health Service (Conseq Provns), 2006 c 43, s 6, sch 4
    s 46 am—SI 2005/2078, art 15, sch 1 para 6
    s 52 rep—Asylum and Immigration (Treatment of Claimants, etc), 2004 c 19, s 47, sch 4
    s 55 am—SI 2012/961, sch 1 para 3
    s 62 rep in pt—Prevention of Terrorism, 2005 c 2, s 16(2)(c)(4); Immigration, 2014 c 22,
        sch 9 para 3(2)(c)
        am—Immigration, 2014 c 22, sch 9 paras 3(2)(a)(b), 13
    s 69 appl—(prosp) Crim Justice and Immigration, 2008 c 4, s 133(4)
    s 72 rep in pt—Asylum and Immigration (Treatment of Claimants, etc), 2004 c 19, s 26(7),
        sch 2 pt 1 paras 16, 17; Immigration, 2014 c 22, sch 9 para 31(a)
        am—Immigration, Asylum and Nationality, 2006 c 13, s 14, sch 1 para 2; UK Borders,
            2007 c 30, s 39; SI 2010/21, art 5, sch 1; Immigration, 2014 c 22, sch 9 para
            31(b)
        appl—Immigration, Asylum and Nationality, 2006 c 13, s 55(5)
        excl—(prosp) Crim Justice and Immigration, 2008 c 4, s 131(5)(6)
    s 73 rep in pt—Immigration, 2014 c 22, sch 9 para 7 table
    s 74 rep—Immigration, 2014 c 22, sch 9 para 7 table
    s 75 rep in pt—Immigration, 2014 c 22, sch 9 para 7 table
    s 76 rep in pt—Immigration, 2014 c 22, sch 9 paras 3(3), 7 table
    s 78A added—Immigration, 2014 c 22, s 2
    s 79 am—(pt prosp) UK Borders, 2007 c 30, s 35(1)(2); Immigration, 2014 c 22, sch 9 para
        32
    s 80 rep—Asylum and Immigration (Treatment of Claimants, etc), 2004 c 19, ss 33(3)(a),
        47, sch 4, SI 2004/2523
    Pt 5 (ss 81-117) heading subst—Immigration, 2014 c 22, sch 9 para 33
    s 81 subst—SI 2010/21, art 5, sch 1
    s 82 appl—(S) SI 1994/1443, rule 41.47(5)
        subst—Immigration, 2014 c 22, s 15(2)
    s 83 rep—Immigration, 2014 c 22, s 15(3)
    s 83A added—Immigration, Asylum and Nationality, 2006 c 13, s 1
        rep—Immigration, 2014 c 22, s 15(3)
    s 84 appl—SI 2000/2326, sch 2
        subst—Immigration, 2014 c 22, s 15(4)
    s 85 appl—SI 2000/2326, sch 2
        appl in pt—SI 2006/1003, sch 2 para 4(10) (subst by 2015/694, sch 2 para 16(b))
        am—Asylum and Immigration (Treatment of Claimants, etc), 2004 c 19, s 26(7), sch 2
            pt 1 paras 16, 18; Immigration, Asylum and Nationality, 2006 c 13, s 14, sch 1

2002

c 41 s 85 *continued*

paras 3; UK Borders, 2007 c 30, s 19(1); Immigration, 2014 c 22, s 15(5); ibid, sch 9 para 34(a)

rep in pt—Immigration, 2014 c 22, sch 9 para 34(b)

s 85A added—UK Borders, 2007 c 30, s 19(2)

rep—Immigration, 2014 c 22, sch 9 para 35

s 86 appl—SI 2000/2326, sch 2

am—Asylum and Immigration (Treatment of Claimants, etc), 2004 c 19, s 26(7), sch 2 pt 1 paras 16, 18; Immigration, Asylum and Nationality, 2006 c 13, s 14, sch 1 paras 4

rep in pt—Immigration, 2014 c 22, sch 9 para 36

ss 87-91 rep—Immigration, 2014 c 22, sch 9 para 37

s 92 subst—Immigration, 2014 c 22, s 17(2)

mod (temp)—SI 2014/1820, art 4

s 93 rep—Asylum and Immigration (Treatment of Claimants, etc), 2004 c 19, ss 33(3)(b), 47, sch 4, SI 2004/2523

s 94 am—SIs 2003/970, art 3; 2003/1919, art 2; Asylum and Immigration (Treatment of Claimants, etc), 2004 c 19, s 27(1)-(3)(5)-(8); (for specific purposes) SIs 2005/330, art 2; 2005/3306, art 2; 2006/3215, art 2; 2006/3275, art 2; (prosp) Immigration, Asylum and Nationality, 2006 c 13, s 13; ibid, s 47(8); SIs 2007/2221, arts 1-3; 2007/3187, reg 3; 2010/561, art 3; Immigration, 2014 c 22, sch 9 para 38(2)-(7)

rep in pt—Asylum and Immigration (Treatment of Claimants, etc), 2004 c 19, ss 27(1)(4), 47, sch 4; SI 2005/1016, art 2; Immigration, 2014 c 22, sch 9 para 38(8)

s 94A added—SI 2007/3187, reg 4

am—Immigration, 2014 c 22, sch 9 para 39

s 94B am—Immigration, 2014 c 22, s 17(3)

s 95 rep—Immigration, 2014 c 22, sch 9 para 40

s 96 am—Asylum and Immigration (Treatment of Claimants, etc), 2004 c 19, s 30; Immigration, 2014 c 22, sch 9 para 41(2)(a),(c)(d),(3)

rep in pt—Immigration, 2014 c 22, sch 9 para 41(2)(b)

s 97 am—Immigration, Asylum and Nationality, 2006 c 13, s 14, sch 1 para 6

rep in pt—Immigration, 2014 c 22, sch 9 para 42

s 97A added—Immigration, Asylum and Nationality, 2006 c 13, s 7

appl (mods)—SI 2006/1003, reg 28A (added by 2013/3032, sch 1 para 24)

am—Crime and Cts, 2013 c 22, s 54; Immigration, 2014 c 22, sch 9 para 43(a)

rep in pt—Immigration, 2014 c 22, sch 9 para 43(b)

s 97B added—Crime and Cts, 2013 c 22, s 53(3)

rep—Immigration, 2014 c 22, sch 9 para 44

s 98B rep—Immigration, 2014 c 22, sch 9 para 45

s 99 am—Crime and Cts, 2013 c 22, s 51(2)(b); Immigration, 2014 c 22, sch 9 para 46(a)

rep in pt—Crime and Cts, 2013 c 22, s 51(2)(a); Immigration, 2014 c 22, sch 9 para 46(b)

s 100 rep—Asylum and Immigration (Treatment of Claimants, etc), 2004 c 19, ss 26(5)(a), 47, sch 4

ss 101-103 rep—Asylum and Immigration (Treatment of Claimants, etc), 2004 c 19, ss 26(5)(a), 47, sch 4

ss 103A-103E added—Asylum and Immigration (Treatment of Claimants, etc), 2004 c 19, s 26(6)(7), sch 2 pt 2

rep—SI 2010/21, art 5, sch 1

s 104 am—Asylum and Immigration (Treatment of Claimants, etc), 2004 c 19, s 26(7), sch 2 pt 1 paras 16, 20(a); Immigration, Asylum and Nationality, 2006 c 13, s 9; SI 2010/21, art 5, sch 1; Immigration, 2014 c 22, sch 9 para 47(3)(4)(a)

rep in pt—Asylum and Immigration (Treatment of Claimants, etc), 2004 c 19, ss 26(7), 47, sch 2 pt 1 paras 16, 20(b) sch 4; Immigration, 2014 c 22, sch 9 para 47(2)(4)(b)(5)

s 105 see —(power to appl or modify regs under s 105) Asylum and Immigration (Treatment of Claimants, etc), 2004 c 19, s 8(10)

am—Immigration, 2014 c 22, sch 9 para 48

s 106 am—Asylum and Immigration (Treatment of Claimants, etc), 2004 c 19, s 26(7), sch 2 pt 1 paras 16, 21(a)-(d)(f)(g)(o)(s); Immigration, Asylum and Nationality, 2006 c 13, s 14, sch 1 para 9; UK Borders, 2007 c 30, s 19(3); SI 2010/21, art 5, sch 1

2002

c 41 s 106 *continued*

rep in pt—Asylum and Immigration (Treatment of Claimants, etc), 2004 c 19,
ss 26(7), 47, sch 2 pt 1 paras 16, 21(e)(h)-(n)(p)-(r)(t), sch 4; SI 2010/21, art 5,
sch 1; Immigration, 2014 c 22, sch 9 para 49

s 107 am—Asylum and Immigration (Treatment of Claimants, etc), 2004 c 19, s 26(7), sch
2 pt 1 paras 16, 22(1)(a)(c); Tribunals, Courts and Enforcement, 2007 c 15, s 48,
sch 8 para 54(1)-(3); SI 2010/21, art 5, sch 1

rep in pt—Asylum and Immigration (Treatment of Claimants, etc), 2004 c 19,
ss 26(7), 47, sch 2 pt 1 paras 16, 22(1)(b), sch 4; SI 2010/21, art 5, sch 1;
Immigration, 2014 c 22, sch 9 para 50

s 108 am—Asylum and Immigration (Treatment of Claimants, etc), 2004 c 19, s 26(7), sch
2 pt 1 paras 16, 23; Immigration, Asylum and Nationality, 2006 c 13, s 14, sch 1
para 10

rep in pt—Immigration, 2014 c 22, sch 9 para 51

s 110 rep—Immigration, Asylum and Nationality, 2006 c 13, s 10, sch 3

s 111 rep—UK Borders, 2007 c 30, s 54(c), sch

s 112 am—Asylum and Immigration (Treatment of Claimants, etc), 2004 c 19, ss 26, 27,
29(2), sch 2 pt 1 paras 16, 24; (prosp) Immigration, Asylum and Nationality,
2006 c 13, s 14, sch 1 para 11; ibid, s 7; SI 2010/21, art 5, sch 1

rep in pt—SI 2010/21, art 5, sch 1; Immigration, 2014 c 22, sch 9 para 52

s 113 appl—Anti-terrorism, Crime and Security, 2001 c 24, s 33; Asylum and Immigration
(Treatment of Claimants, etc), 2004 c 19, s 8(7)

am—(prosp) Immigration, Asylum and Nationality, 2006 c 13, s 12; Immigration,
2014 c 22, sch 9 para 53(2)(a)(i)(b)(d)

rep in pt—Immigration, 2014 c 22, sch 9 para 53(2)(a)(ii)(c)(3)

s 115 rep—Immigration, 2014 c 22, sch 9 para 54

s 116 rep—Legal Aid, Sentencing and Punishment of Offenders, 2012 c 10, sch 5 pt 2

Pt 5A (ss 117A-117D) added—Immigration, 2014 c 22, s 19

s 120 subst—Immigration, 2014 c 22, sch 9 para 55

appl (mods)—SI 2006/1003, sch 2 para 4(8)(9) (subst by 2015/694, sch 2 para 16(b))

s 122 rep—Immigration, Asylum and Nationality, 2006 c 13, s 52, sch 2 para 5, sch 3

s 124 rep—Counter-Terrorism and Security, 2015 c 6, s 22(10)

s 126 appl—British Nationality, 1981 c 61 s 41(IZB)

am—Immigration, 2014 c 22, s 8; ibid, sch 2 para 3(2)-(4)

rep in pt—Immigration, 2014 c 22, sch 9 para 19; ibid, sch 2 para 3(5)

s 127 am—Immigration, 2014 c 22, sch 2 para 4(2)(3)(4)(a)

rep in pt—Immigration, 2014 c 22, sch 2 para 4(4)(b)(c)

s 130 rep—UK Borders, 2007 c 30, s 58, sch

s 131 am—UK Borders, 2007 c 30, s 43; Borders, Citizenship and Immigration, 2009 c 11,
s 47(4)

s 133 am—Health and Social Care (Community Health and Standards), 2003 c 43, ss 34,
190(2), sch 4 paras 127, 128, sch 13 para 12; Health Protection Agency, 2004 c
17, s 11(1)(2), sch 3 para 17(1)-(3)(4)(b)(5)(b); Nat Health Service (Conseq
Provns), 2006 c 43, s 2, sch 1 para 228; SI 2011/2581, sch 2 para 5; Health and
Social Care, 2012 c 7, sch 5 para 107(b); ibid, sch 7 para 12(2)(a), (3)(a), (4)(a),
(b), (5)(a)

rep in pt—Health and Social Care (Community Health and Standards), 2003 c 43,
ss 190(2), 196, sch 13 para 12, sch 14 pt 7; Health Protection Agency, 2004 c
17, s 11(1)(2), sch 3 para 17(1)(4)(a)(5)(a), sch 4; Health and Social Care,
2012 c 7, sch 5 para 107(a), (c); ibid, sch 7 para 12(2)(b), (3)(b), (4)(c),(5)(b);
(pt prosp) ibid, sch 14 para 83

see—SI 2011/1408, sch para 6

s 135 am—Financial Services, 2012 c. 21, sch 18 para 96

s 137 am—(prosp) Crim Justice, 2003 c 44, s 280(2)(3), sch 26 para 58

s 142 rep—UK Borders, 2007 c 30, s 54(d), sch

ss 145, 146 rep—Sexual Offences, 2003 c 42, ss 139, 140, sch 6 para 48, sch 7

s 158 rep—Immigration, Asylum and Nationality, 2006 c 13, s 64(3)(c), sch 3

sch 3 am—Asylum and Immigration (Treatment of Claimants, etc), 2004 c 19, s 9(1)(2), SI
2004/2999; (transtl provn) SI 2004/2999, arts 3, 4; Nat Health Service (Conseq
Provns), 2006 c 43, s 2, sch 1 para 229; Children and Young Persons, 2008 c 23,
s 22(6); Borders, Citizenship and Immigration, 2009 c 11, s 48(6); SI 2012/961,
sch 1 para 4; SI 2015/914, sch para 67(3)(4)

rep in pt—SI 2015/914, sch para 67(2)

sch 4 rep—SI 2010/21, art 5, sch 1

2002

c 41 *continued*

        sch 5 rep —Asylum and Immigration (Treatment of Claimants, etc), 2004 c 19, ss 26(5)(b), 47, sch 4

        sch 7 rep in pt—Prevention of Terrorism, 2005 c 2, s 16(2)(c)(4); Equality, 2006 c 3, s 91, sch 4; Equality, 2010 c 15, s 211, sch 27 pt 1 (subst by SI 2010/2279, sch 2); Immigration, 2014 c 22, sch 9 para 60 table

c 42   **Animal Health**

        s 6 rep—Deregulation, 2015 c 20, sch 23 para 38

        sch rep—Deregulation, 2015 c 20, sch 23 para 38

2nd session of the 53rd Parliament

c 43   *Consolidated Fund (No 2)*—rep Appropriation, 2004 c 9, s 4, sch 3

c 44   *Appropriation (No 2)*—rep Appropriation, 2004 c 9, s 4, sch 3

2003

c 1   **Income Tax (Earnings and Pensions)**

        appl—SI 2002/2006, regs 5(3), 7(5); Income Tax, 2007 c 3, ss 513(4), 959, 963; Taxation (International and Other Provns), 2010 c 8, s 220(2); Corporation Tax, 2010 c 4, ss 332(2), 817(b)

        appl (mods)—Income Tax, 2007 c 3, ss 414, 467, 474, 573, 576, 578, 597, 711, 970; Corporation Tax, 2009 c 4, s 969(4)(b); SI 2009/470, reg 57; Corporation Tax, 2010 c 4, s 996(2); SI 2010/1907, reg 16

        am—Commrs for Revenue and Customs, 2005 c 11, s 50(6), sch 4 paras 101, 102(1)(2)(3)(a)(d)-(k), 103(1)-(3), 104-118, 121(a)-(d), 122(a)-(e), 123(a)-(e), 124(a)-(e)

        saved—Taxation of Chargeable Gains, 1992 c 12, s 151X(4); Income Tax, 2007 c 3, ss 564V(4), 962

        mod—Income Tax, 2007 c 3, s 988; Corporation Tax, 2009 c 4, s 294(2)

        excl—Corporation Tax, 2009 c 4, s 3; Taxation (International and Other Provns), 2010 c 8, ss 79(2)(a), 174(2)(b)

        s 1 rep in pt—Income Tax, 2007 c 3, s 1027, sch 1 paras 425, 426, sch 3

          am—Finance, 2011 c 11, sch 2 para 3; SI 2011/1583, art 2(2); Finance, 2012 c 14, sch 1 para 5(2)

        Pt 2 (ss 3-61) appl—Corporation Tax, 2009 c 4, s 969(4)(a)

        s 3 am—Finance, 2003 c 14, s 140, sch 22 paras 1, 16; Finance, 2011 c 11, sch 2 para 4

        s 4 appl—SI 2004/1865, reg 3(2)

        s 6 am—Income Tax (Trading and Other Income), 2005 c 5, s 882(1), sch 1 pt 2 paras 584, 585; Finance, 2008 c 9, s 25, sch 7 paras 2, 3; Finance, 2014 c 26, sch 9 para 3

        s 7 am—Finance, 2003 c 14, s 140, sch 22 paras 1, 17; Finance, 2007 c 11, s 25, sch 3 paras 1, 2; Finance, 2011 c 11, sch 2 para 5; Finance, 2015 c 11, sch 1 para 2

        s 10 appl—Finance, 2004 c 12, s 244, sch 34 paras 10(2), 11(2)

          am—Finance, 2008 c 9, s 25, sch 7 paras 2, 4; Finance, 2011 c 11, sch 2 para 6; Finance, 2014 c 26, sch 9 para 4

        s 11 am—Income Tax, 2007 c 3, s 1027, sch 1 paras 425, 427

        s 13 am—Finance, 2008 c 9, s 25, sch 7 paras 2, 5; Finance, 2011 c 11, sch 2 para 7

        Pt 2 Ch 4 (ss 14-19) subst—Finance, 2008 c 9, s 25, sch 7 paras 2, 6

        s 14 am—Finance, 2008 c 9, s 25, sch 7 paras 2, 7

        Pt 2 Ch 5 (ss 15-41) am—Finance, 2008 c 9, s 25, sch 7 paras 2, 10

        s 15 am—Finance, 2008 c 9, s 25, sch 7 paras 2, 8, 9; Finance, 2013 c 29, sch 6 para 2; ibid, sch 45 para 58

        s 17 am—Finance, 2015 c 11, sch 1 para 3

        s 19 am—Finance, 2013 c 29, sch 23 para 2

        s 20 appl—Income Tax (Trading and Other Income), 2005 c 5, s 392(4)(b)

          am—Finance, 2008 c 9, s 25, sch 7 paras 2, 11(1)(2)(4)

        s 21 rep—Finance, 2008 c 9, s 25, sch 7 paras 2, 13

          heading subst—Finance, 2008 c 9, s 25, sch 7 paras 2, 12

        s 22 am—(transtl provns) Finance, 2008 c 9, s 25, sch 7 paras 2, 14(1)(2)-(3)(5)-(7); Finance, 2013 c 29, sch 45 para 59; ibid, sch 46 para 7(1)(2)

          rep in pt—(transtl provns) Finance, 2008 c 9, s 25, sch 7 paras 2, 14(1)(4), 82

        s 23 am—Finance, 2004 c 12, s 281(1), sch 35 paras 54, 55; Finance, 2008 c 9, s 25, sch 7 paras 2, 15; Finance, 2013 c 29, sch 45 para 60; ibid, sch 46 para 8; Finance, 2014 c 26, sch 3 para 2

        s 24 am—Income Tax, 2007 c 3, s 1027, sch 1 paras 425, 428; Finance, 2008 c 9, s 25, sch 7 paras 2, 16; Corporation Tax, 2010 c 4, s 1177, sch 1 paras 378, 379; Finance, 2013 c 29, sch 45 para 61

2003
c 1 continued

ss 24A, 24B added—Finance, 2014 c 26, sch 3 para 3

s 25 rep—Finance, 2008 c 9, s 25, sch 7 paras 2, 18
    heading subst—Finance, 2008 c 9, s 25, sch 7 paras 2, 17

s 26 am—(transtl provns) Finance, 2008 c 9, s 25, sch 7 paras 2, 19, 82; Finance, 2013 c 29,
    sch 45 para 62; ibid, sch 46 para 9

s 26A added—Finance, 2013 c 29, sch 46 para 10

s 27 am—Finance, 2008 c 9, s 25, sch 7 paras 2, 20; Finance, 2013 c 29, sch 45 para 149

s 28 appl—(2003-04) Finance, 1990 c 29, s 25; Finance, 2004 c 12, s 189(4)

s 30 am—Finance, 2015 c 11, sch 1 para 4

ss 31-37 rep—Finance, 2008 c 9, s 25, sch 7 paras 2, 21

s 40 am—Finance, 2004 c 12, s 146, sch 27 pt 2 paras 12, 16

s 41ZA added—Finance, 2013 c 29, sch 6 para 3

ss 41A, 41B added—Finance, 2008 c 9, s 25, sch 7 paras 2, 22

s 41C added—Finance, 2008 c 9, s 25, sch 7 paras 2, 22
    am—Finance, 2013 c 29, sch 46 para 11; Finance, 2014 c 26, sch 3 para 4

ss 41D, 41E added—Finance, 2008 c 9, s 25, sch 7 paras 2, 22

Pt 2 Ch 5B (ss 41F-41L) subst for Pt 2 Ch 5A—Finance, 2014 c 26, sch 9 para 5

ss 42, 43 rep—Finance, 2008 c 9, s 25, sch 7 paras 2, 23

s 43 am (as saved)—SI 2009/56, art 3, sch 1 para 335

s 44 subst—Finance, 2014 c 26, s 16(2)

s 45 rep in pt—Finance, 2014 c 26, s 16(3)(4)(a)

s 46 am—Finance, 2014 c 26, s 16(4)(b)

s 46A added—Finance, 2014 c 26, s 16(5)

s 47 rep in pt—Finance, 2014 c 26, s 16(6)

Pt 2 Ch 8 (ss 48-61) appl—Income Tax (Trading and Other Income), 2005 c 5, ss 163(5),
    164(4)

s 48 am—Income Tax, 2007 c 3, s 1027, sch 1 paras 425, 429; Finance, 2007 c 11, s 25,
    sch 3 paras 1, 3

s 49 am—Finance, 2003 c 14, s 136(1)(2)(4); Finance, 2013 c 29, s 22(1)
    rep in pt—Finance, 2003 c 14, ss 136(1)(3)(a)(4), 216, sch 43 pt 3(1), Note

s 51 am—Corporation Tax, 2010 c 4, s 1177, sch 1 paras 378, 380

s 52 am—SI 2005/3229, regs 137, 138

s 54 am—Finance, 2004 c 12, ss 76, 77, sch 12 para 17; ibid, s 281(1), sch 35 paras 54, 56
    appl—SIs 2005/1907, regs 4, 13; 2006/575, reg 39

s 56 am—Finance, 2003 c 14, s 136(1)(3)(b)(i)(4); Finance, 2004 c 12, s 281(1), sch 35
    paras 54, 57; Finance, 2013 c 29, sch 46 para 30(a)
    rep in pt—Finance, 2003 c 14, ss 136(1)(3)(b)(ii)(4), 216, sch 43 pt 3(1), Note;
        Finance, 2004 c 12, s 326, sch 42 pt 3, Note; Finance, 2013 c 29, sch 46 para
        30(b)

s 60 am—Corporation Tax, 2010 c 4, s 1177, sch 1 paras 378, 381

s 61 am—Income Tax (Trading and Other Income), 2005 c 5, s 882(1), sch 1 pt 2 paras 584,
    586; SI 2005/3229, regs 137, 139; Corporation Tax, 2009 c 4, s 1322, sch 1
    paras 548, 549; Corporation Tax, 2010 c 4, s 1177, sch 1 paras 378, 382

ss 61A-61J added—Finance, 2007 c 11, s 25, sch 3 paras 1, 4

s 61G am—Finance, 2013 c 29, sch 46 para 31(a)
    rep in pt—Finance, 2013 c 29, sch 46 para 31(b)

Pt 3 (ss 62-226) see—(2005-06) Finance, 2004 c 12, s 84, sch 15 para 19
    ext—Finance, 2002 c 23, sch 29 para 92(4A)

s 63 rep in pt—Finance, 2003 c 14, ss 140, 216, sch 22 paras 1, 20, sch 43 pt 3(4), Note;
    Finance, 2015 c 11, sch 1 para 5(2)(b),(3)
    appl—Finance, 2004 c 12, s 173(10)
    am—Finance, 2011 c 11, sch 2 para 8; Finance, 2015 c 11, sch 1 para 5(2)(a)

s 64 rep in pt—Finance, 2003 c 14, ss 140, 216, sch 22 paras 1, 21, sch 43 pt 3(4), Note

s 65 rep—Finance, 2015 c 11, s 12(2)

s 66 appl—SI 2003/2682, reg 85(3)
    am—Finance, 2015 c 11, sch 1 para 6

s 67 appl—(W) SI 1998/105, sch para 3; Finance, 2003 c 14, s 62, sch 7 pt 1 para 5(4), pt 2
    para 12(5)(a) (see SI 2003/2899, art 2); Finance, 2004 c 12, ss 64, 77, sch 11 pt
    3 para 11(3); ibid, s 173(10)

s 68 appl—Finance, 2004 c 12, s 173(10)
    am—SI 2005/3229, regs 137, 140; Corporation Tax, 2010 c 4, s 1177, sch 1 paras 378,
    383

s 69 appl—(W) SI 1998/105, sch para 3

2003

c 1 s 69 *continued*

      am—Income Tax, 2007 c 3, s 1027, sch 1 paras 425, 430

s 72 am—SI 2014/211, art 3

s 84 am—(2005-06) Finance, 2004 c 12, s 78, sch 13 para 2(1)(2)

s 86 am—SI 2009/1890, art 4

s 87 am—(2005-06) Finance, 2004 c 12, s 78, sch 13 para 2(1)(3)

      rep in pt—Finance, 2012 c 14, sch 39 para 50(2)

s 89 rep—Finance, 2012 c 14, sch 39 para 50(1)

s 95 am—(2005-06) Finance, 2004 c 12, s 78, sch 13 para 2(1)(4)

      rep in pt—Finance, 2015 c 11, s 12(4)(a)

s 96 rep—Finance, 2015 c 11, s 12(3)

s 96A added—Finance, 2006 c 25, s 63

s 99 am—Finance, 2010 c 13, s 30, sch 6 para 17(2)

ss 100A, 100B added—(spec retrosp effect) Finance, 2008 c 9, s 45(1)

s 105 am—Finance, 2009 c 10, s 71(1)(2)

ss 105A, 105B added—Finance, 2009 c 10, s 71(1)(3)

s 111 am—SI 2009/56, art 3, sch 1 para 336(3)

      rep in pt—SI 2009/56, art 3, sch 1 para 336(2)

s 114 am—(2005-06) Finance, 2004 c 12, s 80, sch 14 paras 1, 2

      rep in pt—(2005-06) Finance, 2004 c 12, s 326, sch 42 pt 2(9), Note; Finance, 2014 c 26, s 23(1)

s 116 am—(2005-06) Finance, 2004 c 12, s 80, sch 14 paras 1, 3; Finance, 2009 c 10, s 54(1)(2)

s 119 am—(2005-06) Finance, 2004 c 12, s 80, sch 14 paras 1, 4

s 121 am—Finance, 2009 c 10, s 53, sch 28 paras 1, 2(1)(2); ibid, s 54(1)(3); SI 2012/266, art 3(2)

      rep in pt—Finance, 2009 c 10, s 53, sch 28 paras 1, 2(1)(3)

s 122 am—Finance, 2009 c 10, s 54(1)(4)

s 123-125 appl (mods)—Vehicle Excise and Registration, 1994 c 22, s 1GF(3)(4)

s 124A added—Finance, 2009 c 10, s 54(1)(5)

s 125 appl—SI 2003/2682, reg 90(4)

      am—Finance, 2012 c 14, s 14(2)

s 125A added—Finance, 2012 c 14, s 14(3)

ss 127-130 appl (mods)—Vehicle Excise and Registration, 1994 c 22, s 1GF(3)(4)

s 133 am—Finance, 2014 c 26, s 24(2)(a)(c)

      rep in pt—Finance, 2014 c 26, s 24(2)(b)

s 139 rep in pt—Finance, 2003 c 14, ss 138(1)(2), 216, sch 43 pt 3(2); Finance, 2010 c 13, s 58(6)

      am—Finance, 2003 c 14, s 138(1)(3); Finance, 2006 c 25, s 59(1)-(6)(7); Finance, 2008 c 9, s 47(1); Finance, 2009 c 10, s 53, sch 28 paras 1, 6; Finance, 2010 c 13, s 58(3)-(5); Finance, 2011 c 11, s 51(1); Finance, 2012 c 14, s 17(1); Finance, 2013 c 29, s 23(3)(4)(5)(b)(6)(b); Finance, 2014 c 26, s 24(3)-(5); (tax year 2017-18) Finance, 2015 c 11, s 7(3)(4); (tax year 2018-19 and subsequent) ibid, s 8(3)(4)

      subst (prosp)—Finance, 2010 c 13, s 59(2)

      rep in pt—Finance, 2013 c 29, s 23(2)(5)(a)(6)(a); Finance, 2014 c 26, s 24(3)(6)

s 140 am—Finance, 2009 c 10, s 53, sch 28 paras 1, 7; Finance, 2010 c 13, s 58(7)-(9); Finance, 2013 c 29, s 23(8)(9)(a)(10); Finance, 2014 c 26, s 24(7)s 24(8)(9); (tax year 2017-18) Finance, 2015 c 11, s 7(5); (tax year 2018-19 and subsequent) ibid, s 8(5)

      rep in pt—Finance, 2010 c 13, s 58(10); Finance, 2013 c 29, s 23(10); Finance, 2014 c 26, s 24(7)(10)

s 141 rep (2016-17 and subsequent tax years)—Finance, 2014 c 26, s 24(11)

      am (temp)—(2015-16 tax year) Finance, 2015 c 11, s 9(1)

s 142 am—Finance, 2014 c 26, s 24(12)-(14); (tax year 2017-18) Finance, 2015 c 11, s 7(6); (tax year 2018-19 and subsequent) ibid, s 8(6)

      rep in pt—Finance, 2009 c 10, s 53, sch 28 paras 1, 8(b)

s 144 am—Finance, 2014 c 26, s 25(1)

s 145 am—Finance, 2009 c 10, s 53, sch 28 paras 1, 3

s 147 am—Finance, 2009 c 10, s 53, sch 28 paras 1, 4

s 148 rep in pt—SI 2012/266, art 3(3)(a); Finance, 2015 c 11, sch 1 para 7

      am—SI 2012/266, art 3(3)(b)(c)

s 149 am—Finance, 2010 c 13, s 58(11)

2003
c 1 *continued*

s 150 am—SIs 2008/511, art 2; 2010/406, art 2; 2011/895, art 2; 2012/915, art 2; 3037, art
2; 2013/3033, art 2; 2014/2896, arts 2, 3; 2015/1979, art 2

ss 155-166 replaced, by ss 155-164—(2005-06) Finance, 2004 c 12, s 80, sch 14 paras 1, 5

s 155 am—Finance, 2010 c 13, s 58(12); SI 2013/3033, art 3; Finance, 2015 c 11, s 10(2);
SI 2015/1979, art 3

s 156 am—Finance, 2010 c 13, s 58(13)(a); Finance, 2015 c 11, s 10(3)

s 157 rep in pt—Finance, 2015 c 11, sch 1 para 8

s 158 am—Finance, 2010 c 13, s 58(13)(b); Finance, 2014 c 26, s 25(2); Finance, 2015 c
11, s 10(4)

s 160 am—Finance, 2010 c 13, s 58(14)(a); Finance, 2015 c 11, s 10(5)
rep in pt—Finance, 2010 c 13, s 58(14)(b)

s 161 am—SIs 2010/406, art 3; 2012/3037, art 3; 2013/3033, art 4; 2014/2896, art 4;
2015/1979, art 4

s 169 am—Finance, 2015 c 11, sch 1 para 9(2)

s 169 rep in pt—Finance, 2015 c 11, sch 1 para 9(3)

s 169A added—(2005-06) Finance, 2004 c 12, s 80, sch 14 paras 1, 6
am—Finance, 2015 c 11, sch 1 para 10(2)
rep in pt—Finance, 2015 c 11, sch 1 para 10(3)

s 170 am—Finance, 2003 c 14, s 138(4); (2005-06) Finance, 2004 c 12, s 80, sch 14 paras
1, 7; Finance, 2006 c 25, s 59(8); Finance, 2009 c 10, s 53, sch 28 paras 1, 5;
Finance, 2010 c 13, ss 58(15), 59(3)(b); Finance, 2014 c 26, s 24(15); Finance,
2015 c 11, s 10(6)
rep in pt—Finance, 2010 c 13, s 59(3)(a)

s 171 rep in pt—(2007-08) Finance, 2004 c 12, s 326, sch 42 pt 2(9), Note

s 173A added—Taxation (International and Other Provns), 2010 c 8, s 365, sch 2 paras 48,
49

s 174 am—SI 2005/3229, regs 137, 141

s 178 am—Income Tax (Trading and Other Income), 2005 c 5, s 882(1), sch 1 pt 2 paras
584, 587; Income Tax, 2007 c 3, s 1027, sch 1 paras 425, 431, sch 3;
Corporation Tax, 2009 c 4, s 1322, sch 1 paras 548, 550; Corporation Tax,
2009 c 4, s 1322, sch 1 paras 548, 550

s 180 am—Income Tax (Trading and Other Income), 2005 c 5, s 882(1), sch 1 pt 2 paras
584, 588; Income Tax, 2007 c 3, s 1027, sch 1 paras 425, 432; Corporation Tax,
2009 c 4, s 1322, sch 1 paras 548, 551; Finance, 2014 c 26, s 22(1)

s 181 appl—SI 2005/724, reg 3(2)

s 184 am—Finance, 2015 c 11, sch 1 para 11

s 188 am—Finance, 2015 c 11, sch 1 para 12(2)(3)

s 189 am—Income Tax (Trading and Other Income), 2005 c 5, s 882(1), sch 1 pt 2 paras
584, 589

Pt 3, Ch 8 (ss 192-197) rep—Finance, 2003 c 14, ss 140, 216, sch 22 paras 1, 22, sch 43 pt
3(4), Note

Pt 3, Ch 9 (ss 198-200) rep—Finance, 2003 c 14, ss 140, 216, sch 22 paras 1, 23, sch 43 pt
3(4), Note

s 201 appl—SI 2002/2006, reg 4(3)

s 206 am—Finance, 2005 c 7, s 17

s 211 am—Taxation (International and Other Provns), 2010 c 8, s 374, sch 8 paras 297, 298

s 215 appl—Income Tax (Trading and Other Income), 2005 c 5, s 776(2)
am—Income Tax (Trading and Other Income), 2005 c 5, s 882(1), sch 1 pt 2 paras
584, 590; Taxation (International and Other Provns), 2010 c 8, s 374, sch 8
paras 297, 299

Pt 3, Ch 11 (ss 216-220) rep—Finance, 2015 c 11, s 13(1)

Pt 3, Ch 12 (ss 221-226) am—Finance, 2013 c 29, sch 23 para 4(a)

s 221 am—Finance, 2013 c 29, sch 23 para 4(b)

s 222 am—Finance, 2003 c 14, s 144; Finance, 2006 c 25, s 94(2); Finance, 2011 c 11, sch
2 para 10; Finance, 2014 c 26, ss 19(1), 21(2)

s 223 am—Finance, 2010 c 13, s 30, sch 6 para 17(4)

s 224 rep—Finance, 2004 c 12, s 326, sch 42 pt 3, Note

s 225 am—Finance, 2008 c 9, s 25, sch 7 paras 2, 24

ss 226A-226D added—Finance, 2013 c 29, sch 23 para 3

s 227 rep in pt—Finance, 2003 c 14, ss 140, 216, sch 22 paras 1, 25(1)(3)(4)(b), sch 43 pt
3(4), Note; Finance, 2014 c 26, sch 8 paras 45, 130, 191
am—Finance, 2003 c 14, s 140, sch 22 paras 1, 25(1)(2)(4); Finance, 2011 c 11, sch
2 para 11

2003
c 1 *continued*

s 228 am—Finance, 2015 c 11, s 14(3); ibid, sch 1 para 13; Pension Schemes, 2015 c 8, s
54(2)
s 229 appl—SI 2001/1004, reg 22A
am—(2016-17 and subsequent tax years) Finance (No. 2), 2015 c 33, s 29(2)
s 230 appl—SI 2001/1004, reg 22A
am—Income Tax, 2007 c 3, s 1027, sch 1 paras 425, 433; Corporation Tax, 2010 c 4,
s 1177, sch 1 paras 378, 384; SI 2011/896, reg 2
s 232 am—Finance, 2013 c 29, sch 45 para 63
s 235 appl—SI 2001/1004, reg 22A
s 235A added—(2016-17 and subsequent tax years) Finance (No. 2), 2015 c 33, s 29(3)
s 236 am—Finance, 2004 c 12, s 81(2)(3); (2016-17 and subsequent tax years) Finance
(No. 2), 2015 c 33, s 29(4)
s 237 am—(2005-06) Finance, 2004 c 12, s 80, sch 14 paras 1, 8; Finance, 2005 c 7,
s 16(1)(2)(7)
s 239 am—Finance, 2008 c 9, s 48(1); Finance, 2015 c 11, sch 1 para 14(2)
rep in pt—Finance, 2015 c 11, sch 1 para 14(3)
s 240 am—SI 2005/3229, regs 137, 143
ss 241A, 241B added—SI 2014/211, art 2(1)
s 244 am—Finance, 2005 c 7, s 16(1)(3)(7)
s 246 appl—SI 2002/2006, reg 4
s 248A added—Finance, 2004 c 12, s 81(1)(3)
s 251 appl—SI 2002/2006, reg 4
s 256 appl—SI 2002/2006, reg 4
s 264 am—SI 2003/1361, art 2
s 266 rep in pt—Finance, 2006 c 25, s 178, sch 26; Finance, 2009 c 10, s 55(1)(2)
am—Finance, 2006 c 25, ss 60(1), 62(3); Finance, 2014 c 26, s 12; Finance, 2015 c
11, sch 1 para 15
s 267 rep in pt—Finance, 2006 c 25, s 178, sch 26
am—Finance, 2006 c 25, ss 60(2), 62(4); Finance, 2015 c 11, sch 1 para 16
s 269 am—Finance, 2008 c 9, s 48(2); Finance, 2015 c 11, sch 1 para 17
s 270A added—(2005-06) Finance, 2004 c 12, s 78, sch 13 para 3
am—Finance, 2005 c 7, ss 15, 16(1)(4)(7); SI 2006/882, art 2; Finance, 2011 c 11,
s 36(1), sch 8 para 2; SI 2013/513, art 2(2); (prosp) Childcare Payments, 2014
c 28, s 63(2)(3)
s 270AA added (prosp)—Childcare Payments, 2014 c 28, s 63(4)
s 270B added—Finance, 2011 c 11, sch 8 para 3
s 271 am—Finance, 2008 c 9, s 25, sch 7 paras 2, 25; Finance, 2011 c 11, sch 2 para 12;
Finance, 2013 c 29, sch 46 para 12
s 272 appl—SI 2003/2682, reg 4(2)
s 277 am—Finance, 2003 c 14, s 123(1), sch 18 para 6 (see SI 2003/2899, art 2)
s 279A added—Finance, 2007 c 11, s 64
s 286 am—Finance, 2004 c 12, s 92, sch 17 para 9(1)(2)
s 287 am—Finance, 2011 c 11, sch 2 para 13
Pt 4, Ch 7A (ss 289A-289E) added—Finance, 2015 c 11, s 11(1)
s 290 rep in pt—Finance, 2010 c 13, s 30, sch 6 para 17(5)
am—Finance, 2015 c 11, sch 1 para 18
s 290A added—SI 2010/157, art 2
am—Finance, 2015 c 11, sch 1 para 19(a)(c)
rep in pt—Finance, 2015 c 11, sch 1 para 19(b)
s 290B added—SI 2010/157, art 2
am—Finance, 2015 c 11, sch 1 para 20(a)-(c)
ss 290C-290F added—Finance, 2015 c 11, s 13(2)
s 291 am—SI 2007/1388, art 3, sch 1; Finance, 2008 c 9, s 52(1)(3); Finance, 2009 c 10, s
56(2); Finance, 2012 c 14, s 15(1)
rep in pt—Finance, 2008 c 9, s 52(1)(2)
s 292 subst—Finance (No 2), 2010 c 31, s 7, sch 4 paras 1(2)(4)(5)
am—Finance, 2011 c 11, s 37(1)
s 293 am—SI 2007/1388, art 3, sch 1
s 293A added—Finance (No 2), 2010 c 31, s 7, sch 4 para 2
s 293B added—Finance, 2013 c 29, s 10(1)
s 294 am—Finance, 2004 c 12, s 82; SI 2007/1388, art 3, sch 1; Finance (No 2), 2010 c 31,
s 7, sch 4 para 3
s 295 am—SI 2007/1388, art 3, sch 1

2003

c 1 *continued*

s 295A added—(2016-17 and subsequent tax years) Finance (No. 2), 2015 c 33, s 29(5)

s 297A added—Finance, 2007 c 11, s 64(1)

    am—Finance, 2012 c 14, s 16(2)

s 297B added—Finance, 2008 c 9, s 51(1)

    am—Finance, 2012 c 14, s 16(3)

s 297C added—Finance, 2012 c 14, s 16(4)

s 299 am—SI 2003/2922, art 3

s 302 am—Income Tax (Trading and Other Income), 2005 c 5, s 882(1), sch 1 pt 2 paras 584, 591

s 303 am—Finance, 2012 c 14, sch 37 para 4(2)-(5)

s 304A added—Finance, 2011 c 11, s 38(1)

s 305 appl—SI 2002/2006, reg 4

    rep in pt—Finance, 2004 c 12, ss 146, 326, sch 27 pt 2 paras 13, 16, sch 42 pt 2(19), Note 6

s 306A added—Finance, 2015 c 11, s 14(2)

s 307 am—Finance, 2004 c 12, s 201(1); (2004-05) ibid, s 248

    appl—SIs 2005/1907, regs 4, 14; 2006/575, reg 40

s 308 subst—Finance, 2004 c 12, s 201(2)

    am—Finance, 2013 c 29, s 11(1)

s 308A added—Finance, 2004 c 12, s 243, sch 33 para 3

s 308B added—Pension Schemes, 2015 c 8, s 54(1)

s 310 rep in pt—Finance, 2005 c 7, ss 18(1)(2)(5), 104, sch 11 pt 2(1), Note

s 311 appl—SI 2002/2006, reg 4; Income Tax (Trading and Other Income), 2005 c 5, s 74(2)

    am—Finance, 2005 c 7, s 18(1)(3)(a)(b)(5)

    rep in pt—Finance, 2005 c 7, ss 18(1)(3)(c)(4)(5), 104, sch 11 pt 2(1), Note

Pt 4 Ch 10A (ss 312A-312I) added—Finance, 2014 c 26, sch 37 para 5

s 315 am—Finance, 2004 c 12, s 281(1), sch 35 paras 54, 59

s 316A added—Finance, 2003 c 14, s 137

    appl—SI 2002/2006, reg 4

s 317 appl—SI 2002/2006, reg 4

    am—Finance, 2004 c 12, s 92, sch 17 para 1; Finance, 2010 c 13, s 60(4)

s 318 replaced, by ss 318, 318A-318D—Finance, 2004 c 12, s 78, sch 13 para 1

s 318 am—Finance, 2005 c 7, s 16(1)(5)(7); SIs 2008/2170, reg 2; 2011/775, reg 2; 2011/2581, sch 2 para 6(a)

    rep in pt—SIs 2008/2170, reg 2; 2009/2888, reg 2

s 318A am—Finance, 2005 c 7, s 16(1)(6)(7); SI 2006/882, art 2; Finance, 2011 c 11, s 36(2), sch 8 para 4; SI 2013/513, art 2(3); (prosp) Childcare Payments, 2014 c 28, s 64(2)(3)

s 318ZA added (prosp)—Childcare Payments, 2014 c 28, s 64(4)

s 318AA added—Finance, 2011 c 11, sch 8 para 5

s 318B am—Finance, 2013 c 29, s 12(1); (prosp) Childcare Payments, 2014 c 28, s 64(5); SI 2015/346, reg 2(2)

s 318C rep in pt—SIs 2005/770, regs 2, 3(a); 2008/2170, reg 3; 2009/1544, reg 3; 2009/2888, reg 2; 2011/775, reg 3(3)(b)(4)(a)(6)

    am—SIs 2005/770, regs 2, 3(b), 4-6; 2005/3229, regs 137, 144; 2007/849, reg 2; 2007/2478, reg 2; 2008/2170, reg 3; 2009/1544, reg 3; 2009/2888, reg 2; 2011/775, reg 3; 2011/2581, sch 2 para 6

s 318D am—Finance, 2011 c 11, sch 8 para 6; SI 2013/630, reg 16(2)

s 319 subst—Finance, 2006 c 25, s 60(3)

s 320 rep—Finance, 2006 c 25, ss 61(1), 178, sch 26

s 320A added—Finance, 2006 c 25, s 62(2)

s 320B added—Finance, 2009 c 10, s 55(1)(4)

s 320C added—Finance, 2014 c 26, s 12(2)

s 323 am—SI 2003/1361, art 3

s 324 am—SI 2003/1361, art 4

s 325A added—Income Tax (Trading and Other Income), 2005 c 5, s 882(1), sch 1 pt 2 paras 584, 592

    am—SI 2005/3229, regs 137, 145

s 326 appl—SI 2002/2006, reg 4

s 326A added—Finance, 2011 c 11, s 39(1)

    am—SI 2013/1133, art 2

s 326B added—Finance, 2013 c 29, sch 23 para 37

2003

c 1 *continued*

s 327 rep in pt—Finance, 2004 c 12, ss 281(1), 326, sch 35 paras 54, 60(1)(2), sch 42 pt 3, Note

am—Finance, 2004 c 12, s 281(1), sch 35 paras 54, 60(1)(3)

s 328 rep in pt—Finance, 2013 c 29, sch 46 para 32

s 329 am—Income Tax, 2007 c 3, s 1027, sch 1 paras 425, 434; Finance, 2013 c 29, sch 45 para 64

s 331 am—Taxation (International and Other Provns), 2010 c 8, s 374, sch 8 paras 297, 300

Pt 5, Ch 2 (ss 333-360) restr—Finance, 2004 c 12, ss 243, 283, sch 33 para 1(5), sch 36 pt 4 para 51

s 335 rep in pt—Finance, 2008 c 9, s 25, sch 7 paras 2, 26

s 340A added—SI 2014/211, art 2(2)

s 341 am—Finance, 2013 c 29, sch 46 para 33

s 342 am—Finance, 2013 c 29, sch 46 para 34

s 343 am—SIs 2003/1652, art 2; 2004/1360, art 2; 2005/1091, art 2; 2005/2011, art 49, sch 6 pt 1 para 5; Legal Services, 2007 c 29, s 208, sch 21 para 137; SIs 2007/289, art 67, sch 1; 2008/836, art 2; 2010/231, art 68, sch 4; Health and Social Care, 2012 c 7, sch 15 para 56(d); SI 2012/3004, art 2; SIs 2014/859, art 2; 2015/886, art 2

rep in pt—Health and Social Care, 2008 c 14, s 166, sch 15; SI 2009/1182, arts 4, 5-7, sch 5; Educ, 2011 c 21, sch 2 para 26; Health and Social Care, 2012 c 7, sch 15 para 51

saved—SI 2010/231, art 69, sch 6

s 345 rep in pt—SI 2009/56, art 3, sch 1 para 337

s 346 am—Finance, 2009 c 10, s 67(1)(2)

s 347 am—Income Tax, 2007 c 3, s 1027, sch 1 paras 425, 435

s 351 rep in pt—Finance, 2010 c 13, s 30, sch 6 para 17(6)

s 355 restr—Finance, 1988 c 39, s 38(9)

s 357 am—SI 2004/2310, arts 1(2), 2, sch para 68; Income Tax (Trading and Other Income), 2005 c 5, s 882(1), sch 1 pt 2 paras 584, 593; Income Tax, 2007 c 3, s 1027, sch 1 paras 425, 436; Corporation Tax, 2009 c 4, s 1322, sch 1 paras 548, 552; Corporation Tax, 2010 c 4, s 1177, sch 1 paras 378, 385(b); Finance, 2012 c 14, sch 16 para 111

rep in pt—Corporation Tax, 2010 c 4, ss 1177, 1181, sch 1 paras 378, 385(a), sch 3

s 360 am—Finance (No 2), 2010 c 31, s 7, sch 4 para 1(3)

s 360A added—Income Tax (Trading and Other Income), 2005 c 5, s 882(1), sch 1 pt 2 paras 584, 594

s 370 am—Finance, 2008 c 9, s 25, sch 7 paras 2, 27

rep in pt—Finance, 2013 c 29, sch 46 para 35

s 371 am—SI 2005/3229, regs 137, 146(1)-(3); Finance, 2008 c 9, s 25, sch 7 paras 2, 28

s 372 am—SI 2005/3229, regs 137, 147

s 374 am—SI 2005/3229, regs 137, 148(1)-(3)

s 376 am—Finance, 2013 c 29, sch 46 para 36

s 378 am—Finance, 2008 c 9, s 25, sch 7 paras 2, 29; Finance (No 3), 2010 c 33, s 4(1)-(3); Finance, 2013 c 29, sch 46 para 37(2)(3)

rep in pt—Finance, 2013 c 29, sch 46 para 37(4)

s 381 am—Finance, 2004 c 12, s 281(1), sch 35 paras 54, 61

s 385 subst—Finance, 2004 c 12, s 146, sch 27 pt 2 paras 14, 16

Pt 6, Ch 1 (ss 386-392) rep —Finance, 2004 c 12, ss 247, 283, 326, sch 36 pt 4 para 52, sch 42 pt 3, Note

s 393 replaced, by ss 393, 393A, 393B—Finance, 2004 c 12, s 249(1)(3)

s 393 am—Finance, 2004 c 12, s 249(1)(2); Finance, 2005 c 7, s 19(1)(2)(7)

s 393A appl—Income and Corporation Taxes, 1988 c 1, s 266A; Finance, 2004 c 12, ss 246(4), 251(3), 252(4); ibid,ss 196A(5), 246A(5)

s 393B appl—Income and Corporation Taxes, 1988 c 1, s 266A; Finance, 2004 c 12, ss 196A(5), 246A(5), 251(3), 252(4); SIs 2005/3377, reg 17(2), 3380, reg 15(3); 2006/132, reg 2

am—Finance, 2004 c 12, s 249; Finance, 2007 c 11, s 69, sch 20 para 21; Finance, 2015 c 11, sch 4 para 18

s 394 am—Finance, 2004 c 12, s 249(1)(4)-(7); Income Tax (Trading and Other Income), 2005 c 5, s 882(1), sch 1 pt 2 paras 584, 595; SI 2010/536, art 2; Finance, 2011 c 11, sch 2 para 14; Finance, 2012 c 14, s 1(4); Finance, 2013 c 29, sch 45 para 65

transtl provns—Finance, 2004 c 12, s 283, sch 36 pt 4 paras 53-55

2003
c 1 *continued*

s 394A added—Finance, 2013 c 29, sch 45 para 125
ss 395-397 replaced, by s 395—Finance, 2004 c 12, s 249(1)(8)
s 395 transtl provns—Finance, 2004 c 12, s 283, sch 36 pt 4 para 55
    am—Finance, 2004 c 12, s 249
s 395A added—SI 2009/730, art 2
s 395B added—SI 2014/211, art 5(2)
s 396 am—SI 2005/3229, regs 137, 150
s 397 am—Income Tax (Trading and Other Income), 2005 c 5, s 882(1), sch 1 pt 2 paras
    584, 596
s 399 am—Finance, 2004 c 12, s 249(1)(9)(10)
    rep in pt—Income Tax (Trading and Other Income), 2005 c 5, ss 882(1), 884, sch 1 pt
      2 paras 584, 597, sch 3
s 399A added—Finance, 2004 c 12, s 249(1)(11)
    appl—Finance, 2004 c 12, s 252(8); SI 2005/3455, reg 2(5)(b)
s 400 subst—Finance, 2004 c 12, s 249(1)(11)
    am—SI 2005/3229, regs 137, 151
s 401 am—SIs 2005/3229, regs 137, 152; 2011/1037, art 10(2); 2014/211, art 5(3)(a)
s 404A added—Income Tax, 2007 c 3, s 1027, sch 1 paras 425, 437
s 407 am—Finance, 2004 c 12, s 281(1), sch 35 paras 54, 62(1)(2)
    rep in pt—Finance, 2004 c 12, ss 281(1), 326, sch 35 paras 54, 62(1)(3), sch 42 pt 3,
      Note
s 408 rep in pt—Finance, 2004 c 12, ss 281(1), 326, sch 35 paras 54, 63(1)(3), sch 42 pt 3,
      Note
    am—Finance, 2004 c 12, s 281(1), sch 35 paras 54, 63(1)(2)(4); SI 2006/1963, reg 2
s 411 am—Finance, 2007 c 11, s 63
s 413 am—Finance, 2008 c 9, s 25, sch 7 paras 2, 30; Finance, 2013 c 29, sch 46 para 38
s 413A added—SI 2011/1037, art 10(3)
    am—SI 2013/234, art 3(1)(a)
    rep in pt—SI 2013/234, art 3(1)(b)
s 414A added—SI 2014/211, art 5(3)(b)
Pt 7 (ss 417-554) appl—SI 2001/1004, sch 4 pt II para 7(5A)(c)
    mod—Finance, 2005 c 7, s 21(8)(c)
Pt 7, Chs 1-4 (ss 417-450) appl—Taxation of Chargeable Gains, 1992 c 12, ss 119A(7),
    149AA(4)-(6)
Pt 7, Ch 1 (ss 417-421) replaced, by ss 417-421, 421A-421L—(pt prosp) Finance, 2003 c
    14, s 140, sch 22 paras 1, 2
s 417 rep in pt—Finance, 2014 c 26, sch 8 paras 46, 131, 192
s 418 am—Finance, 2014 c 26, sch 9 para 7
    rep in pt—Finance, 2008 c 9, s 50(2)(a)
s 420 appl—SI 2004/1863, reg 2, sch pt 1 para 3(1)
    am—Finance (No 2), 2005 c 22, s 12, sch 2 paras 1, 2(1)-(5)(6)(a)(8); Finance, 2006
      c 25, s 92(1)-(4); Corporation Tax, 2009 c 4, s 1322, sch 1 paras 548, 553;
      Finance, 2009 c 10, s 126(5)(b); Taxation (International and Other Provns),
      2010 c 8, s 374, sch 8 paras 203, 204
    rep in pt—Finance (No 2), 2005 c 22, ss 12, 70, sch 2 paras 1, 2(1)(6)(b)(8), sch 11 pt
      2(1), Note
s 421B appl—SI 2001/1004, reg 22(7)(a)
    am—Finance, 2005 c 7, s 20(2)(3)(5)
s 421C am—Finance, 2004 c 12, s 90(1)(2)(5)
    appl—Finance, 2005 c 7, s 21(11)
s 421D am—Finance, 2005 c 7, s 20(2)(3)(c)(5); Finance, 2014 c 26, sch 9 para 35
s 421E rep—Finance, 2014 c 26, sch 9 para 8
s 421F am—Finance, 2004 c 12, s 89
s 421G rep—Finance, 2004 c 12, ss 88(1)(2)(11), 326, sch 42 pt 2(11), Note 2
s 421H am—Corporation Tax, 2010 c 4, s 1177, sch 1 paras 378, 386
s 421J rep in pt—Finance, 2014 c 26, sch 8 para 227
ss 421JA-421JF added—Finance, 2014 c 26, sch 8 para 228
s 421K am—Finance, 2005 c 7, s 20(2)(4)(5); Finance, 2014 c 26, sch 8 para 229
s 421L am—Finance, 2007 c 11, s 109, sch 26 para 10(1)(2); Finance, 2014 c 26, s 21(3),
    sch 8 para 230
Pt 7, Ch 2 (ss 422-434) replaced, by Pt 7, Ch 2 (ss 422-432)—Finance, 2003 c 14, s 140,
    sch 22 paras 1, 3
s 422 appl (mods) —Finance (No 2), 2005 c 22, s 12, sch 2 para 4(4)

2003
c 1 *continued*

s 424 am—Finance (No 2), 2005 c 22, s 12, sch 2 paras 1, 3, 4(1)(2)(a)(3)(4)
    rep in pt—Finance (No 2), 2005 c 22, ss 12, 70, sch 2 paras 1, 3, 4(1)(2)(b)(4), sch 11
        pt 2(1), Note
s 425 am—Finance, 2014 c 26, sch 9 para 9
s 426 am—Finance, 2004 c 12, s 85, sch 16 para 1(1)(2)
s 428 excl—Finance, 2003 c 14, sch 23 pt 4 para 21(7) (as subst by 2003 c 14, s 140, sch
        22 paras 59, 68); Corporation Tax, 2009 c 4, s 1027(4)(b)
    am—Finance (No 2), 2005 c 22, s 12, sch 2 paras 1, 3, 5; Finance, 2008 c 9, s
        49(2)(3)(4); Finance, 2011 c 11, sch 2 para 15; Finance, 2013 c 29, sch 23 para
        5; Finance, 2014 c 26, sch 9 para 10
s 428A added—Finance, 2004 c 12, s 85, sch 16 para 1(1)(3)
s 429 am—Finance, 2004 c 12, s 86(1)(2)(a)(3)-(5)(8); Finance (No 2), 2005 c 22, s 12, sch
        2 paras 1, 3, 6
    rep in pt—Finance, 2004 c 12, ss 86(1)(2)(5)-(8), 326, sch 42 pt 2(11), Note 1
s 430 am—Finance, 2014 c 26, sch 9 para 11
s 430A added—Finance, 2014 c 26, sch 9 para 36
s 431 am—Finance, 2011 c 11, sch 2 para 16; Finance, 2013 c 29, sch 23 para 6; Finance,
        2014 c 26, sch 9 para 12
s 431A added—Finance, 2004 c 12, s 88(1)(3)(11)(12)
    am—Finance, 2014 c 26, sch 8 paras 47, 132, 193
s 431B added—Finance (No 2), 2005 c 22, s 12, sch 2 paras 1, 3, 7
    am—SI 2015/360, reg 2(a)(b)
Pt 7, Ch 3 (ss 435-446) replaced, by ss 435-444—Finance, 2003 c 14, s 140, sch 22 paras 1,
    4
s 436 appl—Finance, 2005 c 7, s 21(11)
    am—Finance (No 2), 2005 c 22, s 12, sch 2 paras 1, 8, 9(1)(4)
s 437 am—Finance (No 2), 2005 c 22, s 12, sch 2 paras 1, 8, 9(2)-(4); Finance, 2011 c 11,
        sch 2 para 17; Finance, 2013 c 29, sch 23 para 7
    excl—Finance, 2003 c 14, sch 23 para 22C(4A))
s 438 am—Finance, 2004 c 12, s 85, sch 16 para 2(1)(2)
s 439 am—Equality, 2010 c 15, s 211, sch 26 para 51 (subst by SI 2010/2279, sch 1)
s 440 am—Finance (No 2), 2005 c 22, s 12, sch 2 paras 1, 8, 10
s 441 am—Finance, 2011 c 11, sch 2 para 18
s 442A added—Finance, 2004 c 12, s 85, sch 16 para 2(1)(3)
s 443 am—Finance, 2004 c 12, s 86(1)(2)(b)(3)-(5)(8); Finance (No 2), 2005 c 22, s 12, sch
        2 paras 1, 8, 11
    rep in pt—Finance, 2004 c 12, ss 86(1)(2)(5)(8), 326, sch 42 pt 2(11), Note 1
Pt 7, Ch 3A (ss 446A-446J) added—Finance, 2003 c 14, s 140, sch 22 paras 1, 5
s 446A am—Corporation Tax, 2010 c 4, s 1177, sch 1 paras 378, 387
s 446B am—Finance, 2011 c 11, sch 2 para 19; Finance, 2013 c 29, sch 23 para 8
s 446C am—Finance, 2011 c 11, sch 2 para 20
s 446E excl —Finance, 2003 c 14, sch 23 pt 4 para 21(8); Corporation Tax, 2009 c 4, s
        1026(4)(b); ibid, s 1027(4)(b)
    am—Finance, 2004 c 12, s 87
s 446G excl—Finance, 2003 c 14, sch 23 pt 4A para 22C(8); Corporation Tax, 2009 c 4, s
        1033(4)(b); ibid, s 1034(4)
s 446H excl—Finance, 2003 c 14, sch 23 pt 4A para 22C(8); Corporation Tax, 2009 c 4, s
        1033(4)(b); ibid, s 1034(4)
s 446IA added—Finance, 2004 c 12, s 86(6)(8)
Pt 7, Ch 3B (ss 446K-446P) added—Finance, 2003 c 14, s 140, sch 22 paras 1, 6
s 446K am—Corporation Tax, 2010 c 4, s 1177, sch 1 paras 378, 388
s 446N am—Finance, 2008 c 9, s 25, sch 7 paras 2, 32
s 446NA added—Finance, 2004 c 12, s 86(7)(8)
s 446O transtl provns—Finance, 2004 c 12, ss 88(13), 89(5)
    appl (mods)—Finance (No 2), 2005 c 22, s 12, sch 2 para 2(8)
Pt 7, Ch 3C (ss 446Q-446W) added—Finance, 2003 c 14, s 140, sch 22 paras 1, 7
s 446R am—Finance, 2004 c 12, s 86(1)(2)(c)(3)-(5)(8); Finance (No 2), 2005 c 22, s 12,
        sch 2 paras 1, 12, 13
    rep in pt—Finance, 2004 c 12, ss 86(1)(2)(5)(8), 326, sch 42 pt 2(11), Note 1
s 446S am—Finance, 2011 c 11, sch 2 para 21
s 446T am—Finance, 2008 c 9, s 49(2)(5); Finance, 2011 c 11, sch 2 para 22; Finance,
        2013 c 29, sch 23 para 9; Finance, 2014 c 26, sch 9 para 13

2003

c 1 *continued*

s 446U am—Finance (No 2), 2005 c 22, s 12, sch 2 paras 1, 12, 14; Finance, 2014 c 26, sch
 9 para 37

s 446UA added—Finance (No 2), 2005 c 22, s 12, sch 2 paras 1, 12, 15

s 446V am—Finance, 2011 c 11, sch 2 para 23; Finance, 2013 c 29, sch 23 para 10

Pt 7, Ch 3D (ss 446X-446Z) added—Finance, 2003 c 14, s 140, sch 22 paras 1, 8

Pt 7, Ch 4 (ss 447-470) replaced, by ss 447-450—Finance, 2003 c 14, s 140, sch 22 paras 1,
 9

s 447 am—Finance (No 2), 2005 c 22, s 12, sch 2 paras 1, 17, 18

s 449 am—Finance, 2004 c 12, s 86(1)(2)(d)(3)-(5)(8); Finance (No 2), 2005 c 22, s 12, sch
 2 paras 1, 17, 19

 rep in pt—Finance, 2004 c 12, ss 86(1)(2)(5)(8), 326, sch 42 pt 2(11), Note 1

Pt 7, Ch 4A added (ss 451-469) —Finance, 2005 c 7, ss 20(1)(5)-(7), 21(1)-(7)(11)

s 452 am—Finance, 2011 c 11, sch 2 para 24; Finance, 2013 c 29, sch 23 para 11

s 459 am—Corporation Tax, 2010 c 4, s 1177, sch 1 paras 378, 389

Pt 7, Ch 5 (ss 471-487) replaced, by Pt 7, Ch 5 (ss 471-484)—Finance, 2003 c 14, s 140,
 sch 22 paras 1, 10

 appl—Taxation of Chargeable Gains, 1992 c 12, ss 144ZB, 149A, 288; ibid,
 s 288(1A)

s 471 appl—SI 2001/1004, sch 3 pt IX para 7A

s 472 am—Finance, 2004 c 12, s 90(1)(3)(5)

s 473 am—Finance, 2014 c 26, sch 8 paras 133, 194

s 474 rep—Finance, 2014 c 26, sch 9 para 14

s 476 am—Finance, 2004 c 12, s 85, sch 16 para 3(1)(2); Income Tax (Trading and Other
 Income), 2005 c 5, s 882(1), sch 1 pt 2 paras 584, 598; Income Tax, 2007 c 3, s
 1027, sch 1 paras 425, 438

 rep in pt—Finance, 2014 c 26, sch 8 paras 134, 195, 196

s 477 am—Finance, 2004 c 12, s 90(1)(4)(5); Income Tax (Trading and Other Income),
 2005 c 5, s 882(1), sch 1 pt 2 paras 584, 599; Equality, 2010 c 15, s 211, sch 26
 para 52 (subst by SI 2010/2279, sch 1)

s 479 am—Corporation Tax, 2010 c 4, s 1177, sch 1 paras 378, 390; Finance, 2013 c 29,
 sch 23 para 12

s 480 rep in pt—Finance, 2004 c 12, ss 85, 326, sch 16 para 3(1)(3), sch 42 pt 2(10), Note 1;
 Finance, 2014 c 26, sch 8 para 197

 am—Finance, 2008 c 9, s 49(2)(6); Finance, 2011 c 11, sch 2 para 25; Finance, 2014
 c 26, sch 9 para 15

s 481 am—Finance, 2004 c 12, s 85, sch 16 para 3(1)(4)

s 482 am—Finance, 2004 c 12, s 85, sch 16 para 3(1)(5)

s 484 rep in pt—Finance, 2004 c 12, ss 85, 326, sch 16 para 7(1), sch 42 pt 2(10), Note 1

Pt 7 Ch 6 (ss 488-515) title rep in pt—Finance, 2014 c 26, sch 8 para 2

s 488 appl—Finance, 2004 c 12, s 195(5)

 ext—Income Tax (Trading and Other Income), 2005 c 5, s 770(5)

 rep in pt—Finance, 2014 c 26, sch 8 para 3(2)(3)(a),(4)(5)(a)

 am—Finance, 2014 c 26, sch 8 para 3(3)(b),(5)(b)

s 489 am—Finance, 2004 c 12, s 88(1)(4)(11); Finance, 2014 c 26, sch 8 para 4

s 491 rep—Finance, 2003 c 14, ss 140, 216, sch 22 paras 1, 26, sch 43 pt 3(4), Note

s 492 rep in pt—Finance, 2004 c 12, s 326, sch 42 pt 3, Note

s 493 rep in pt—Income Tax (Trading and Other Income), 2005 c 5, ss 882(1), 884, sch 1 pt
 2 paras 584, 600(1)(2), sch 3

 am—Income Tax (Trading and Other Income), 2005 c 5, s 882(1), sch 1 pt 2 paras
 584, 600(1)(3); Corporation Tax, 2010 c 4, s 1177, sch 1 paras 378, 391

s 494 rep—Finance, 2003 c 14, ss 140, 216, sch 22 paras 1, 27, sch 43 pt 3(4), Note

s 495 rep—Finance, 2003 c 14, ss 140, 216, sch 22 paras 1, 28, sch 43 pt 3(4), Note

s 496 subst—Income Tax (Trading and Other Income), 2005 c 5, s 882(1), sch 1 pt 2 paras
 584, 601

s 497 am—Income Tax (Trading and Other Income), 2005 c 5, s 882(1), sch 1 pt 2 paras
 584, 602

s 498 appl—Income Tax (Trading and Other Income), 2005 c 5, s 402(3)

 am—SI 2006/246, reg 20, sch 2; Finance, 2013 c 29, sch 2 para 19

 rep in pt—Finance, 2013 c 29, sch 2 para 2

s 500 am—Finance, 2014 c 26, sch 8 para 6

s 502 am—Income Tax (Trading and Other Income), 2005 c 5, s 882(1), sch 1 pt 2 paras
 584, 603

s 503 am—Finance, 2014 c 26, sch 8 para 7

2003
c 1 *continued*

s 505 am—Finance, 2004 c 12, s 88(1)(5)

s 506 am—Finance, 2004 c 12, s 88(1)(11); Finance, 2014 c 26, sch 8 para 8(2)

s 509 am—Finance, 2003 c 14, s 140, sch 22 paras 1, 11; Finance, 2014 c 26, sch 8 para 9

s 510 am—Finance, 2014 c 26, sch 8 para 10

s 511 am—Finance, 2014 c 26, sch 8 para 11

s 515 rep in pt—Income Tax (Trading and Other Income), 2005 c 5, ss 882(1), 884, sch 1 pt 2 paras 584, 604(1)-(3), sch 3; Income Tax, 2007 c 3, s 1031, sch 3; Corporation Tax, 2009 c 4, ss 1322, 1326, sch 1 paras 548, 554(1)(2)(3)(a), sch 3 pt 1

    am—Income Tax (Trading and Other Income), 2005 c 5, s 882(1), sch 1 pt 2 paras 584, 604(1)(4); Income Tax, 2007 c 3, s 1027, sch 1 paras 425, 439; Corporation Tax, 2009 c 4, s 1322, sch 1 paras 548, 554(1)(3)(b); Finance, 2014 c 26, sch 8 para 12

Pt 7 Ch 7 (ss 516-520) title rep in pt—Finance, 2014 c 26, sch 8 para 98

s 516 appl—Finance, 2004 c 12, s 195(5); Income Tax (Trading and Other Income), 2005 c 5, s 703(3)

    am—Income Tax (Trading and Other Income), 2005 c 5, s 882(1), sch 1 pt 2 paras 584, 605; Finance, 2014 c 26, sch 8 para 99(3)(b),(5)(6)(b)

    rep in pt—Finance, 2014 c 26, sch 8 para 99(2)(3)(a),(4),(6)(a)

s 517 am—Finance, 2014 c 26, sch 8 para 100

s 518 rep—Finance, 2003 c 14, ss 140, 216, sch 22 paras 1, 29, sch 43 pt 3(4), Note

s 519 rep in pt—Finance, 2003 c 14, ss 140, 216, sch 22 paras 1, 30, sch 43 pt 3(4), Note; Finance, 2004 c 12, s 326, sch 42 pt 2(11), Note 2

    am—Finance, 2004 c 12, s 88(1)(6)(11); Finance, 2013 c 29, sch 2 para 21; Finance, 2014 c 26, sch 8 para 101

s 520 rep—Finance, 2003 c 14, ss 140, 216, sch 22 paras 1, 31, sch 43 pt 3(4), Note

Pt 7 Ch 8 (ss 521-526) title rep in pt—Finance, 2014 c 26, sch 8 para 159

s 521 am—Finance, 2014 c 26, sch 8 para 160(3)(b)(5)(6)(b)

    rep in pt—Finance, 2014 c 26, sch 8 para 160(2)(3)(a)(4)(6)(a)

s 522 am—Finance, 2014 c 26, sch 8 para 161

s 523 rep—Finance, 2003 c 14, ss 140, 216, sch 22 paras 1, 32, sch 43 pt 3(4), Note

s 524 am—Finance, 2003 c 14, s 139, sch 21 pt 3 paras 13, 14(1)-(3)(5); Finance, 2004 c 12, s 88(1)(7)(11); Finance, 2013 c 29, sch 2 para 26; Finance, 2014 c 26, sch 8 para 162

    rep in pt—Finance, 2003 c 14, ss 140, 216, sch 22 paras 1, 33, sch 43 pt 3(4), Note; Finance, 2004 c 12, s 326, sch 42 pt 2(11), Note 2; Finance, 2013 c 29, sch 2 para 14

s 525 rep—Finance, 2003 c 14, ss 140, 216, sch 22 paras 1, 34, sch 43 pt 3(4), Note

s 526 am—Finance, 2003 c 14, s 140, sch 22 paras 1, 35

s 527 appl—Taxation of Chargeable Gains, 1992 c 12, s 105A

s 528 rep—Finance, 2003 c 14, ss 140, 216, sch 22 paras 1, 36, sch 43 pt 3(4), Note

s 531 am—Finance, 2003 c 14, s 140, sch 22 paras 1, 37; Finance, 2013 c 29, sch 23 para 13

s 532 am—Finance, 2003 c 14, s 140, sch 22 paras 1, 38; Finance, 2013 c 29, sch 2 para 94(1); ibid, sch 23 para 14

s 536 am—SIs 2008/706, reg 2; 2012/1360, art 2(2)(c)

s 538 am—Finance, 2003 c 14, s 140, sch 22 paras 1, 39; Corporation Tax, 2010 c 4, s 1177, sch 1 paras 378, 392

s 539 am—Finance, 2014 c 26, sch 8 para 198

s 540 am—Finance, 2003 c 14, s 140, sch 22 paras 1, 40; Finance, 2008 c 9, s 25, sch 7 paras 2, 34

    rep in pt—Finance, 2014 c 26, sch 9 para 16

s 541 am—Finance, 2003 c 14, s 140, sch 22 paras 1, 41

s 549 am—Corporation Tax, 2010 c 4, s 1177, sch 1 paras 378, 393

    rep in pt—Finance, 2014 c 26, sch 8 paras 48, 135, 199

s 551 am—SI 2005/3229, regs 137, 153

ss 552, 553 appl—Income Tax, 2007 c 3, s 395(5)

s 554 am—Finance, 2004 c 12, s 92, sch 17 para 9(1)(3)

    appl—Income Tax, 2007 c 3, s 395(5)

Pt 7A (ss 554A-554Z21) added—Finance, 2011 c 11, sch 2 para 1

s 554E am—Finance, 2014 c 26, sch 8 paras 49, 136, 200

s 554L am—Finance, 2014 c 26, sch 9 para 18

s 554M am—Finance, 2014 c 26, sch 9 para 19

2003

c 1 *continued*

s 554N am—Finance, 2013 c 29, sch 23 para 15; Finance, 2014 c 26, sch 9 paras 20(6), 38
    rep in pt—Finance, 2014 c 26, sch 9 para 20(2)-(5)
s 554O am—SI 2013/1881, sch para 9
s 554S mod—SI 2011/2696, reg 5
s 554Z1 appl (mods)—Income Tax (Trading and Other Income), 2005 c 5, s 39(3)
Pt 7A, Ch 2 (ss 554Z2-554Z16) excl—SI 2011/2696, regs 3, 4
s 554Z4 am—Finance, 2013 c 29, sch 45 para 68(2)(3)
s 554Z4A added—Finance, 2013 c 29, sch 45 para 126
s 554Z6 am—Finance, 2013 c 29, sch 45 para 69
s 554Z9 am—Finance, 2013 c 29, sch 45 para 70; ibid, sch 46 para 13; Finance, 2014 c 26,
    sch 3 para 5
s 554Z10 am—Finance, 2013 c 29, sch 45 para 71; ibid, sch 46 para 14(1)(c)(2)
s 554Z11A added—Finance, 2013 c 29, sch 45 para 127
s 554Z12 am—Finance, 2013 c 29, sch 45 para 128
s 555 am—Income Tax, 2007 c 3, s 1027, sch 1 paras 425, 440
s 556A added—Finance, 2009 c 10, s 67(1)(3)
s 563 am—Finance, 2004 c 12, s 281(1), sch 35 paras 54, 64
Pt 9 (ss 565-654) power to am conferred—Taxation of Pensions, 2014 c 30, s 4(3)
    excl—Finance, 2004 c 12, sch 36 para 45A(1)
s 565 am—Finance, 2004 c 12, s 204(1), sch 31 paras 1, 2
s 566 am—Finance, 2004 c 12, s 204(1), sch 31 paras 1, 3(1)(2)(4)
    rep in pt—Finance, 2004 c 12, ss 204(1), 326, sch 31 paras 1, 3(1)(3), sch 42 pt 3,
        Note
    appl—Income and Corporation Tax, 1988 c 1, s 775A
s 567 am—Finance, 2004 c 12, s 204(1), sch 31 paras 1, 4; Finance, 2011 c 11, sch 2 para
    26
s 567A added—Finance, 2011 c 11, sch 2 para 27
s 568 am—Finance, 2004 c 12, s 204(1), sch 31 paras 1, 5
s 572A added—Finance, 2013 c 29, sch 45 para 129
s 573 am—Taxation of Pensions, 2014 c 30, sch 2 para 25(2)(7); Finance, 2015 c 11, sch 4
    para 20
s 574 am—SI 2005/3229, regs 137, 154; Finance, 2011 c 11, sch 16 para 21(2); Taxation
    of Pensions, 2014 c 30, sch 2 para 25(3)(a)(ii)(b),(7)
    rep in pt—Taxation of Pensions, 2014 c 30, sch 2 para 25(3)(a)(i),(7)
s 575 saved—Income Tax (Trading and Other Income), 2005 c 5, s 840(3)
    am—Income Tax (Trading and Other Income), 2005 c 5, s 882(1), sch 1 pt 2 paras
        584, 606; Finance, 2011 c 11, sch 16 para 21(3); Finance, 2013 c 29, sch 45
        para 72
    rep in pt—Finance, 2008 c 9, s 25, sch 7 para 45
s 576A added—Finance, 2011 c 11, sch 16 para 21(4)
    subst—Finance, 2013 c 29, sch 45 para 116
    mod—Taxation of Pensions, 2014 c 30, sch 1 para 84
    am—Taxation of Pensions, 2014 c 30, sch 1 para 83
s 577 am—Finance, 2004 c 12, s 92, sch 17 para 9(1)(4)(a); Finance (No 2), 2005 c 22,
    s 10(1)(2); Pensions, 2014 c 19, sch 12 paras 45, 74
    rep in pt—Finance, 2004 c 12, ss 92, 326, sch 17 para 9(1)(4)(b), sch 42 pt 2(12)
Pt 9, Ch 5A (ss 579A-579D) added—Finance, 2004 c 12, ss 204(1), 283, sch 31 paras 1, 6,
    sch 36 pt 4 paras 43(2), 44, 45
    mod—SI 2012/764, regs 23, 24
s 579A appl—SI 2006/575, reg 41
    am—Taxation of Pensions, 2014 c 30, sch 2 para 25(4)(7); Finance, 2015 c 11, sch
        4 para 22
s 579B am—Finance, 2011 c 11, sch 16 para 22(2)
s 579CZA added—Taxation of Pensions, 2014 c 30, sch 2 para 25(5)(7)
    am—Finance, 2015 c 11, sch 4 para 23(1)
s 579CA added—Finance, 2011 c 11, sch 16 para 22(3)
    subst—Finance, 2013 c 29, sch 45 para 117
    mod—Taxation of Pensions, 2014 c 30, sch 1 para 82
    am—Taxation of Pensions, 2014 c 30, sch 1 para 81; Finance (No. 2), 2015 c 33, s
        22(6)(7)
s 579D subst—Finance, 2011 c 11, sch 16 para 22(4)
    am—Taxation of Pensions, 2014 c 30, sch 2 para 25(6)

2003

c 1 *continued*

Pt 9, Chs 6-8 (ss 580-604) rep—Finance, 2004 c 12, ss 204(1), 326, sch 31 paras 1, 7, sch 42 pt 3, Note

Pt 9, Ch 9 (ss 605-608) rep—Finance, 2004 c 12, ss 204(1), 283, 326, sch 31 paras 1, 7, sch 36 pt 4 para 43(1), sch 42 pt 3, Note

s 609 am—Income Tax, 2007 c 3, s 1027, sch 1 paras 425, 441; Finance, 2012 c 14, sch 39 para 32(4)(5)

s 610 am—Finance, 2004 c 12, s 204(1), sch 31 paras 1, 8

s 611 am—Finance, 2004 c 12, s 204(1), sch 31 paras 1, 9

s 611A added—Finance, 2015 c 11, sch 4 para 21

s 613 saved—Income Tax (Trading and Other Income), 2005 c 5, s 840(3)
    am—Income Tax (Trading and Other Income), 2005 c 5, s 882(1), sch 1 pt 2 paras 584, 607

s 615 am—SI 2005/3229, regs 137, 158

Pt 9, Ch 13 (ss 623-628) rep —Finance, 2004 c 12, ss 204(1), 326, sch 31 paras 1, 10, sch 42 pt 3, Note

s 631 am—Income Tax (Trading and Other Income), 2005 c 5, s 882(1), sch 1 pt 2 paras 584, 608

s 633 am—SI 2005/3229, regs 137, 159

s 635 saved—Income Tax (Trading and Other Income), 2005 c 5, s 840(3)
    am—Income Tax (Trading and Other Income), 2005 c 5, s 882(1), sch 1 pt 2 paras 584, 609

Pt 9, Ch 15A (ss 636A-636C) added—Finance, 2004 c 12, ss 204(1), 283, sch 31 paras 1, 11, sch 36 pt 3 para 35(4)

s 636A am—Finance, 2007 c 11, s 69, sch 19 paras 28, 29(3); Finance, 2011 c 11, sch 16 para 42; Finance, 2014 c 26, sch 5 para 5(3); Taxation of Pensions, 2014 c 30, sch 1 paras 31, 62; Finance (No. 2), 2015 c 33, s 22(2),(3)(a),(4)
    rep in pt—Finance, 2007 c 11, s 114, sch 27 pt 3; SI 2009/1171, reg 3A(2)(6); Finance, 2011 c 11, sch 16 para 42(5)(c); Taxation of Pensions, 2014 c 30, sch 2 para 19(3); Finance (No. 2), 2015 c 33, s 22(3)(b)
    appl—SI 2010/1187, reg 4 (added by Finance, 2014 c 26, sch 5 para 6)
    mod—SI 2006/207, reg 18 (added by 2014 c 30, sch 1 para 96(15))

s 636AA added—Finance (No. 2), 2015 c 33, s 22(5)

s 636B am—Finance, 2005 c 7, s 101, sch 10 paras 59, 64(1); SI 2006/572, art 37
    appl (mods)—SI 2009/1171, reg 3A(4)(5); Finance, 2004 c 12, sch 29 para 11A(5)(6)

Pt 9, Ch 16 (s 637) rep —Finance, 2004 c 12, ss 204, 326, sch 31 paras 1, 12, sch 42 pt 3, Note

s 639 am—(retrosp) Finance, 2005 c 7, s 19(1)(3)(4)(8)

s 640A added—Finance, 2005 c 7, s 19(1)(5)(9)
    am—Finance, 2015 c 11, s 15(1)

s 641 am—Finance, 2005 c 7, s 19(1)(6)(9)
    rep in pt—SL(R), 2008 c 12, s 1(1), sch 1 pt 1, group 4

s 643 am—SI 2005/3229, regs 137, 160; Taxation (International and Other Provns), 2010 c 8, s 374, sch 8 paras 59, 60

s 644 am—Finance, 2004 c 12, s 204(1), sch 31 paras 1, 13

s 644A added—Income Tax (Trading and Other Income), 2005 c 5, s 882(1), sch 1 pt 2 paras 584, 610
    am—SI 2005/3229, regs 137, 161

s 646 am—SI 2005/3229, regs 137, 162

s 646A added—Income Tax (Trading and Other Income), 2005 c 5, s 882(1), sch 1 pt 2 paras 584, 611
    am—Finance, 2015 c 11, s 15(1)

ss 646B-646F added—Finance, 2015 c 11, sch 4 para 17(1)

s 655 am—Income Tax (Trading and Other Income), 2005 c 5, s 882(1), sch 1 pt 2 paras 584, 612; Finance, 2012 c 14, sch 1 para 5(3)

s 658 am—Welfare Reform, 2007 c 5, s 28, sch 3 para 24(1)(2)
    rep in pt—(prosp) Welfare Reform, 2007 c 5, s 67, sch 8

s 660 am—Work and Families, 2006 c 18, s 11, sch 1 para 60; Welfare Reform, 2007 c 5, s 28, sch 3 para 24(1)(3); SI 2013/630, reg 16(3); Children and Families, 2014 c 6, sch 7 para 62(3); ibid, sch 7 para 62(4)(5)(c)
    rep in pt—Work and Families, 2006 c 18, s 15, sch 2; (prosp) Welfare Reform, 2007 c 5, s 67, sch 8; Children and Families, 2014 c 6, sch 7 para 62(2)(5)(a)(b); (prosp) Pensions, 2014 c 19, sch 16 para 47

2003

c 1 *continued*

s 661 am—Welfare Reform, 2007 c 5, s 28, sch 3 para 24(1)(4)
> rep in pt—(prosp) Welfare Reform, 2007 c 5, s 67, sch 8

ss 663, 664 rep (prosp)—Welfare Reform, 2007 c 5, s 67, sch 8

s 665 am—SI 2005/3229, regs 137, 163(b)
> rep in pt—SI 2005/3229, regs 137, 163(a)

s 669 rep in pt—SI 2005/3229, regs 137, 164(c)
> am—SI 2005/3229, regs 137, 164(a)(b)

ss 673, 674 rep in pt—SI 2005/3229, regs 137, 165, 166

s 675 am—SIs 2005/3229, regs 137, 167; 2013/630, reg 16(4)

s 677 rep in pt—Finance, 2004 c 12, ss 92, 326, sch 17 para 9(1)(5), sch 42 pt 2(12);
> (prosp) Welfare Reform, 2012 c 5, sch 14 pt 9; (prosp) Pensions, 2014 c 19, sch
> 16 para 48
> am—Welfare Reform, 2007 c 5, s 28, sch 3 para 24(1)(5); Finance, 2008 c 9, s 46(1);
> Health and Social Care, 2008 c 14, s 138(4); Welfare Reform, 2012 c 5, sch 9
> para 49; Finance, 2013 c 29, s 13(1); SI 2014/606, reg 3; Finance, 2015 c 11, s
> 16(2)

s 679 am—Income Tax (Trading and Other Income), 2005 c 5, s 882(1), sch 1 pt 2 paras
> 584, 613

s 681A added—Income Tax (Trading and Other Income), 2005 c 5, s 882(1), sch 1 pt 2
> paras 584, 614
> am—Finance, 2013 c 29, sch 46 para 39(1)

Pt 10, Ch 8 (ss 681B-681H) added—Finance, 2012 c 14, sch 1 para 1

Pt 11 (ss 682-712) power to amend or repeal—Finance, 2009 c 10, s 110, sch 58 para 10

s 682 am—Finance, 2009 c 10, s 110, sch 58 para 9(1)(2)

s 683 appl—SI 2003/2682, reg 4(2)
> am—Finance, 2004 c 12, s 204(1), sch 31 paras 1, 14(1)-(3); Finance (No 2), 2005 c
> 22, s 10(1)(3)(4); Finance, 2005 c 7, s 101, sch 10 paras 60, 64(2); Finance,
> 2011 c 11, sch 16 para 60; Finance, 2013 c 29, sch 45 para 130; Finance (No. 2),
> 2015 c 33, s 22(8)
> rep in pt—Finance, 2004 c 12, ss 204(1), 326, sch 31 paras 1, 14(1)(4), sch 42 pt 3,
> Note

s 684 am—Finance, 2003 c 14, s 145(1)(2); Finance, 2006 c 25, s 94(3); Finance, 2009 c
> 10, s 110, sch 58 paras 1, 3(1)(2)(4)-(6), 4-7; SI 2009/56, art 3, sch 1 para 338;
> Finance, 2011 c 11, s 85; SI 2011/1585, art 2(2)(3); Finance, 2012 c 14, s
> 225(2)-(4), sch 1 para 5(4); SIs 2014/992, art 7(a)(b); 2438, art 2(2); Finance,
> 2015 c 11, s 17(2)(3)
> rep in pt—Finance, 2009 c 10, s 110, sch 58 paras 1, 2, 3(3)
> appl—SI 2001/1004, sch 4 pt 3B para 29X

s 685 am—Finance, 2003 c 14, s 145(3)(4); SI 2011/1583, art 2(4)(5); Finance, 2012 c 14,
> sch 1 para 5(5)
> rep in pt—Finance, 2009 c 10, s 110, sch 58 para 9(1)(3)(a)

s 686 am—Finance (No 2), 2005 c 22, s 10(1)(5)(6)

s 687 am—Finance, 2011 c 11, sch 2 para 28; SI 2011/1583, art 2(6)

s 687A added—Finance, 2011 c 11, sch 2 para 29

s 688 am—Finance, 2014 c 26, ss 16(8)-(10), 17(3)(4)

s 688A added—Finance, 2007 c 11, s 25, sch 3 paras 1, 6

s 689 am—Finance, 2011 c 11, sch 2 para 30; SI 2011/1583, art 2(7); Finance, 2014 c 26,
> ss 20(2)(3), 21(4)

s 689A added—Finance, 2014 c 26, s 21(5)
> am—Finance, 2014 c 26, s 21(8)

s 690 am—Finance, 2008 c 9, s 25, sch 7 paras 2, 35; SI 2011/1583, art 2(8); Finance,
> 2013 c 29, sch 45 para 73; ibid, sch 46 para 15; Finance, 2014 c 26, s 21(6)

s 691 am—SI 2011/1583, art 2(9)

s 695A added—Finance, 2011 c 11, sch 2 para 31

s 696 am—Finance, 2011 c 11, sch 2 para 32

s 697 am—Finance, 2014 c 26, sch 8 paras 137(b)(c), 201
> rep in pt—Finance, 2014 c 26, sch 8 para 137(a)

ss 698, 699 replaced, by s 698 —(with savings) Finance, 2003 c 14, s 140, sch 22 paras 1,
> 12

s 698 am—Finance, 2004 c 12, s 85, sch 16 para 4(1)(2); Finance (No 2), 2005 c 22, s 12,
> sch 2 paras 1, 12, 16; Finance, 2008 c 9, s 25, sch 7 paras 2, 36

s 700 subst—Finance, 2003 c 14, s 140, sch 22 paras 1, 13

2003

c 1 s 700 *continued*

am—Finance, 2004 c 12, s 85, sch 16 para 4(1)(3); Finance, 2008 c 9, s 25, sch 7 paras 2, 37

s 700A added—Finance, 2008 c 9, s 25, sch 7 paras 2, 38

am—Finance, 2014 c 26, sch 9 para 21

s 701 rep in pt—Finance, 2003 c 14, ss 139, 140, 216, sch 21 pt 3 paras 13, 18(1)(2)(5), sch 22 paras 1, 14, sch 43 pt 3(3)(4), Note; Finance, 2004 c 12, ss 88(1)(8), (9)(b)(11), 326, sch 42 pt 2(11), Note 2; Finance, 2014 c 26, sch 8 para 138(a)

am—Finance, 2003 c 14, s 139, sch 21 pt 3 paras 13, 18(1)(3)-(5); Finance, 2004 c 12, s 88(1)(8), (9)(a)(c), (10)(11); Finance, 2014 c 26, sch 8 paras 138(b), 202

s 702 am—(subject to transtl provn(s)) Finance, 2003 c 14, s 140, sch 22 paras 1, 15(1)(2)(4); ibid,s 140, sch 22 paras 1, 15(1)(3); Corporation Tax, 2009 c 4, s 1322, sch 1 paras 548, 555 Finance, 2009 c 10, s 126(5)(b)

appl—SIs 2001/1004, sch 3 pt 3 para 1; 2005/724, reg 5(2)

s 707 am—Finance, 2003 c 14, s 145(5)

s 710 am—Finance, 2003 c 14, s 145(6); Finance, 2006 c 25, s 94(4); Finance, 2011 c 11, sch 2 para 33; Finance, 2014 c 26, s 21(7)(a)(b)

s 711 am—Finance, 2008 c 9, s 118, sch 39 para 49

s 712 am—SI 2011/1583, art 2(10)

s 713 am—Finance, 2011 c 11, sch 3 para 5

s 714 appl—Income Tax (Trading and Other Income), 2005 c 5, s 72(3)

am—Corporation Tax, 2010 c 4, s 1177, sch 1 paras 378, 394

rep in pt—Finance, 2010 c 13, s 30, sch 6 para 17(7)

s 715 rep in pt—SIs 2009/56, art 3, sch 1 para 339; 2009/3054, art 3, sch

s 716A added—Income Tax (Trading and Other Income), 2005 c 5, s 882(1), sch 1 pt 2 paras 584, 615

am—Finance, 2011 c 11, sch 2 para 34

s 716B added—Finance, 2014 c 26, s 18(1)

s 717 am—Commrs for Revenue and Customs, 2005 c 11, s 50(6), sch 4 paras 101, 102(3)(l); Finance, 2007 c 11, ss 25, 109, sch 3 paras 1, 7, sch 26 para 10(1)(3); Finance, 2012 c 14, sch 1 para 5(6); Finance, 2014 c 26, sch 3 para 6; ibid, sch 37 para 6; (prosp) Childcare Payments, 2014 c 28, s 63(5); (prosp) ibid, s 64(6)

s 718 am—Income Tax, 2007 c 3, s 1027, sch 1 paras 425, 442

s 719 am—Income Tax, 2007 c 3, s 1027, sch 1 paras 425, 443

s 720 rep—Commrs for Revenue and Customs, 2005 c 11, ss 50(6), 52(2), sch 4 paras 101, 119, sch 5

s 721 am—Finance, 2004 c 12, s 85, sch 16 para 7(2); SI 2005/3229, regs 137, 168; Income Tax, 2007 c 3, s 1027, sch 1 paras 425, 444; (transtl provns) Finance, 2008 c 9, s 25, sch 7 paras 2, 39, 82

appl—Finance, 2004 c 12, s 173(11)

rep in pt—Income Tax, 2007 c 3, s 1031, sch 3

sch 1 rep in pt—Finance, 2003 c 14, ss 140, 216, sch 22 paras 1, 42(1)(2)(4), sch 43 pt 3(4), Note; (2007-08) Finance, 2004 c 12, s 326, sch 42 pt 2(9), Note; ibid,s 326, sch 42 pt 3, Note; Commrs for Revenue and Customs, 2005 c 11, ss 50(6), 52(2), sch 4 paras 101, 120, sch 5; Income Tax, 2007 c 3, s 1031, sch 3; Finance, 2008 c 9, s 25, sch 7 paras 2, 40; Corporation Tax, 2009 c 4, ss 1322, 1326, sch 1 paras 548, 556(b), sch 3 pt 1; Finance, 2009 c 10, s 126(3)(4); SI 2009/56, art 3, sch 1 para 340; Finance, 2015 c 11, sch 1 para 21(2)

am—Finance, 2003 c 14, s 140, sch 22 paras 1, 42(1)(3)(4); Finance, 2004 c 12, ss 85, 146, sch 16 para 7(3), sch 27 pt 2 paras 15, 16; ibid,ss 204(1), 249(1)(12), 281(1), sch 31 paras 1, 15, sch 35 paras 54, 65(1)-(3); Income Tax (Trading and Other Income), 2005 c 5, s 882(1), sch 1 pt 2 paras 584, 616(1)-(3); Finance (No 2), 2005 c 22, ss 10(1)(7), 12, sch 2 paras 1, 2(7)(8); SI 2005/3229, regs 137, 169; Income Tax, 2007 c 3, s 1027, sch 1 paras 425, 445, 446; Welfare Reform, 2007 c 5, s 28, sch 3 para 24(1)(6); Finance, 2007 c 11, s 25, sch 3 paras 1, 8; Finance, 2008 c 9, s 46(2); Corporation Tax, 2009 c 4, s 1322, sch 1 paras 548, 556(a); Finance, 2009 c 10, s 126(3); ibid, s 40, sch 19 para 12; SI 2009/56, art 3, sch 1 para 340; Corporation Tax, 2010 c 4, s 1177, sch 1 paras 378, 395; Taxation (International and Other Provns), 2010 c 8, s 374, sch 8 paras 322, 323; Finance, 2011 c 11, sch 16 para 61; SI 2011/1583, art 2(11); Finance, 2012 c 14, s 14(4), sch 1 para 5(7); Welfare Reform, 2012 c 5, sch 9 para 50; Finance, 2013 c 29, sch 45 para 105; Finance, 2014 c 26, sch 37 para 7; Finance, 2015 c 11, s 16(3); ibid, sch 1 para 21(3); (2016-17 and subsequent tax years) Finance (No. 2), 2015 c 33, s 29(6)

2003
c 1 *continued*

sch 2 appl—SI 2001/1004, sch 3 pt IX para 7; Income Tax (Trading and Other Income),
2005 c. 5, ss 394(3C), 396, 405, 407(3C), 770(6)(7)

am—Finance, 2003 c 14, ss 139, 140, 142(3), sch 21 pt 1 paras 1-4, 6, 7(1)-(5), 8(a),
sch 22 paras 1, 43; SI 2005/3229, regs 137, 170; Income Tax (Trading and
Other Income), 2005 c 5, s 882(1), sch 1 pt 2 paras 584, 617(1)-(6); SI
2006/246, reg 20, sch 2; Income Tax, 2007 c 3, s 1027, sch 1 paras 425, 447;
Finance, 2008 c 9, s 25, sch 7 paras 2, 41; Corporation Tax, 2009 c 4, s 1322,
sch 1 paras 548, 557; Finance, 2009 c 10, s 126(5)(b); SI 2009/56, art 3, sch 1
paras 341-343; Corporation Tax, 2010 c 4, s 1177, sch 1 paras 378, 396;
Finance, 2010 c 13, s 42(1)-(3); Financial Services, 2012 c 21, sch 18 para
97(2)(3); Finance, 2013 c 29, sch 2 paras 20(1), 34(a)(b), 47(a), 50, 52,
53(2)(a)(3), 55, 56, 57, 79, 80, 83, 84, 85, 92(a); Co-operative and Community
Benefit Societies, 2014 c 14, sch 4 para 82(2)(3); Finance, 2014 c 26, ss
49(2)(3), 50(2)-(4); ibid, sch 8 paras 15, 16, 18, 19(2)(3), 20-28, 30, 31, 32(b);
ibid, sch 37 para 19

rep in pt—Finance, 2003 c 14, ss 139, 216, sch 21 pt 1 paras 1, 5, 8(b), sch 43 pt 3(3);
Commrs for Revenue and Customs, 2005 c 11, ss 50(6), 52(2), sch 4 paras 101,
103(4)(a), 121(e), sch 5; SI 2009/56, art 3, sch 1 paras 341-343; Finance, 2013
c 29, sch 2 paras 3,5,6, 34(b), 35(b), 36, 37, 47(b), 48, 49, 51, 53(2)(b), 87, 88,
90, 92(b), 93(1); ibid, sch 46 para 40(1); Finance, 2014 c 26, sch 8 paras 14,
17, 19(4), 29, 32(a)

sch 3 am—Finance, 2003 c 14, s 139, 140, sch 21 pt 2 paras 9, 10, 11(1)(2)(3)(a)(4),
12(1)-(5), sch 22 paras 1, 44; Income Tax (Trading and Other Income), 2005 c 5,
s 882(1), sch 1 pt 2 paras 584, 618(1)-(6)(8)-(12); SI 2005/3229, regs 137, 171;
Income Tax, 2007 c 3, s 1027, sch 1 paras 425, 448; SI 2007/1093, art 6, sch 3;
Finance, 2008 c 9, s 25, sch 7 paras 2, 42; SIs 2008/954, arts 31, 32; 2009/56,
art 3, sch 1 paras 344-347; Corporation Tax, 2010 c 4, s 1177, sch 1 paras 378,
397; Finance, 2013 c 29, sch 2 paras 8(b), 9(a), 23-25, 60(a), 62, 63, 65, 66;
ibid, sch 46 para 41(1)(a); Finance, 2014 c 26, sch 8 paras 104, 105, 108-110,
111(2), 112, 113(b), 114-119, 120(b); ibid, sch 37 para 20; SI 2014/402, art
2(2)

rep in pt—Finance, 2003 c 14, ss 139, 216, sch 21 pt 2 paras 9, 11(1)(3)(b), sch 43 pt
3(3); Income Tax (Trading and Other Income), 2005 c 5, ss 882(1), 884, sch 1
pt 2 paras 584, 618(1)(7), sch 3; Commrs for Revenue and Customs, 2005 c 11,
ss 50(6), 52(2), sch 4 paras 101, 103(4)(b), 122(f), sch 5; Income Tax, 2007 c
3, s 1031, sch 3; SI 2009/56, art 3, sch 1 paras 344-347; Finance, 2013 c 29,
sch 2 paras 8(a)(c), 9(b), 10-12, 13, 40-42, 60(b), 61; ibid, sch 46 para
41(1)(b); Finance, 2014 c 26, sch 8 paras 103, 106, 107, 111(3), 113(a),
120(a)

appl—Income Tax (Trading and Other Income), 2005 c 5, s 703(3)

sch 4 am—Finance, 2003 c 14, s 139, sch 21 pt 3 paras 13, 15(1), 16, 17(1)-(5); Income
Tax (Trading and Other Income), 2005 c 5, s 882(1), sch 1 pt 2 paras 584, 619;
SI 2005/3229, regs 137, 172; Income Tax, 2007 c 3, s 1027, sch 1 paras 425,
449; SIs 2007/2194, art 10, sch 4; 2008/954, arts 31, 33; 2009/56, art 3, sch 1
paras 348-351; Corporation Tax, 2010 c 4, s 1177, sch 1 paras 378, 398;
Finance, 2010 c 13, s 39(2)(a)(i); Financial Services, 2012 c 21, sch 18 para
97(4); Finance, 2013 c 29, sch 2 paras 28-30, 44(1), 68, 70(a), 72, 73, 75, 76;
Finance, 2014 c 26, sch 8 paras 50, 165, 166, 169-173, 174(2)(b)(3), 175(3)(4),
176-181, 182(b); ibid, sch 37 para 21(1)

rep in pt—Commrs for Revenue and Customs, 2005 c 11, ss 50(6), 52(2), sch 4 paras
101, 103(4)(c), 123(f), sch 5; Income Tax, 2007 c 3, s 1031, sch 3; Finance,
2010 c 13, s 39(2)(a)(ii)(iii)(b); Finance, 2013 c 29, sch 2 para 15, 70(b), 71;
Finance, 2014 c 26, sch 8 paras 164, 167, 168, 174(2)(a)(4)(5), 182(a)

sch 5 am—Finance, 2003 c 14, s 140, sch 22 paras 1, 45; Finance, 2004 c 12,
ss 96(1)-(3)(4)(b)-(d)(f)(5)(6), 146, sch 27 pt 2 para 17(1)-(3)(5)-(7); Income
Tax (Trading and Other Income), 2005 c 5, s 882(1), sch 1 pt 2 paras 584,
620(1)-(3); SI 2005/3229, regs 137, 173; Finance, 2005 c 7, s 80, sch 4 pt 2
para 48; SI 2007/2194, art 10, sch 4; Income Tax, 2007 c 3, s 1027, sch 1 paras
425, 450; Finance, 2007 c 11, s 61; Finance, 2008 c 9, ss 25, 33(1)-(5), sch 7
paras 2, 43; SIs 2008/706, reg 2; 954, arts 31, 34; 2009/56, art 3, sch 1 paras
352-357; Corporation Tax, 2010 c 4, s 1177, sch 1 paras 378, 399; Finance (No
3), 2010 c 33, s 6(1)-(3); SI 2012/1360, art 2(2); Finance, 2013 c 29, sch 2 para

2003
c 1 *continued*

        31(1); Children and Families, 2014 c 6, sch 7 para 63; Finance, 2014 c 26, sch 8
        paras 51, 203, 217(3)(4)(b)(5)(6), 218-220; ibid, sch 37 para 22(1)
      rep in pt—Finance, 2004 c 12, ss 96(1)(4)(a)(e)(6), 146, 326, sch 27 pt 2 para
        17(1)(4)(6)(7), sch 42 pt 2(13)(19), Notes 5, 7; Commrs for Revenue and
        Customs, 2005 c 11, ss 50(6), 52(2), sch 4 paras 101, 124(f), sch 5; SI 2009/56,
        art 3, sch 1 paras 352-357; Finance (No 3), 2010 c 33, s 6(2)(4); Finance, 2013
        c 29, sch 46 para 42; Finance, 2014 c 26, sch 8 para 217(2)
    sch 6 rep in pt—Finance, 2004 c 12, s 326, sch 42 pt 2(12), Note 1; ibid, s 326, sch 42 pt 3,
        Note; (2003-04) ibid,ss 92, 326, sch 17 para 5(2), sch 42 pt 2(12), Note 2; ibid,
        ss 77, 326, sch 42 pt 2(7), Note; Income Tax (Trading and Other Income),
        2005 c 5, s 884, sch 3; Income Tax, 2007 c 3, s 1031, sch 3; (prosp) Welfare
        Reform, 2007 c 5, s 67, sch 8; Finance, 2008 c 9, ss 25, 138, sch 7 para 79(a),
        sch 44 para 11(f); Corporation Tax, 2009 c 4, s 1326, sch 3 pt 1; Finance, 2009
        c 10, s 5, sch 1 para 6(l); (prosp) Welfare Reform, 2009 c 24, s 58, sch 7 pt 1;
        SI 2009/56, art 3, sch 1 para 358; Corporation Tax, 2010 c 4, s 1181, sch 3 pts
        1, 2; Taxation (International and Other Provns), 2010 c 8, s 378, sch 10 pts 1, 9,
        12; Finance, 2011 c 11, sch 26 para 3(2)(a); (prosp) Finance, 2012 c 14, sch 39
        para 28(1); (prosp) Scotland, 2012 c 11, sch 2 para 2; (pt prosp) Welfare
        Reform, 2012 c 5, sch 14 pt 1
    sch 7 am—Finance, 2003 c 14, s 140, sch 22 paras 1, 46; Finance, 2009 c 10, s 126(5)(b);
        SI 2009/2035, art 2, sch; Finance, 2015 c 11, sch 1 para 22(2)(a)(3)
      rep in pt—Finance, 2003 c 14, ss 140, 216, sch 22 paras 1, 46(1)(2)(9)(11)(12),
        (14)(b), (17)(18)(20)(24)(25), (26)(a)-(c), sch 43 pt 3(4), Note; (2005-06)
        Finance, 2004 c 12, s 326, sch 42 pt 2(9), Note; ibid,s 326, sch 42 pt 3, Note;
        Finance, 2008 c 9, ss 8, 25, 50(2)(b), sch 2 para 52, sch 7 paras 2, 44; SI
        2009/2035, art 2, sch; Finance, 2012 c 14, sch 39 para 50(3); Finance, 2015 c
        11, s 12(4)(b); ibid, sch 1 para 22(2)(b)
    sch 8 rep in pt—(retrosp) Finance, 2004 c 12, s 92, sch 17 para 6
c 2   *Consolidated Fund*—rep Appropriation (No 3), 2005 c 21, s 4, sch 3
c 3   **Northern Ireland Assembly Elections**
    s 1 rep in pt—NI Assembly (Elections and Periods of Suspension), 2003 c 12, s 1(5)
c 4   **Health (Wales)**
    s 1 rep in pt—Nat Health Service (Conseq Provns), 2006 c 43, s 6, sch 4; SI 2006/1407, art
        3, sch 2
    s 3 trans of functions—SI 2009/2623, art 3
    s 4 am—Health and Social Care, 2012 c 7, sch 15 para 56(c)
    sch 1 rep—Nat Health Service (Conseq Provns), 2006 c 43, s 6, sch 4
    sch 2 rep in pt—Public Audit (W), 2004 c 23, ss 66, 72, sch 2 para 56, sch 4
    sch 3 rep in pt—Nat Health Service (Conseq Provns), 2006 c 43, s 6, sch 4; Govt of Wales,
        2006 c 32, s 163, sch 12
c 5   **Community Care (Delayed Discharges etc)**
    s 1 am—Health and Social Care (Community Health and Standards), 2003 c 43, s 34, sch 4
        paras 129, 130; (pt prosp) Health and Social Care, 2012 c 7, sch 14 para 84; SI
        2013/2341, art 3
    rep in pt—Health and Social Care, 2012 c 7, sch 5 para 109; SI 2015/914, sch para 69
    s 4 am—SI 2015/914, sch para 70(2)-(4)
    s 9 rep in pt—Health and Social Care, 2012 c 7, sch 5 para 110(a)(c)(i)(ii)(d)(ii)(iii)(e)
      am—Health and Social Care, 2012 c 7, sch 5 para 110(b)(d)(i)
    s 12 am—Nat Health Service (Conseq Provns), 2006 c 43, s 2, sch 1 para 231; SI 2010/813,
        art 11; SI 2015/914, sch para 71(2)(3)
      rep in pt—SI 2015/914, sch para 71(4)
    s 14 am—SI 2015/914, sch para 72(2)(3)
    s 15 rep—SI 2015/914, sch para 73
    s 16 subst—SI 2015/914, sch para 74
c 6   **Police (Northern Ireland)**—*N Irish*
c 7   **European Parliament (Representation)**
    see (functions made exerciseable concurrently)—SI 2010/1837, art 3
    trans of functions—SIs 2003/1887, art 4, sch 1; 2015/1376, art 3(1) sch 1
    appl (mods)—SI 2004/293, reg 13, sch 5 paras 1-3
    ss 3,5,6,10,11 am—SI 2003/1887, art 9, sch 2 para 15(1)(a)
    s 12 rep in pt—Communications, 2003 c 21, s 406(7), sch 19(1)
        am—SI 2003/1887, art 9, sch 2 para 15(1)(a); Electoral Admin, 2006 c 22, s 74, sch 1
        para 156

2003

c 7 *continued*

ss 13,17,18 am—SI 2003/1887, art 9, sch 2 para 15(1)(a)
s 21 am—SI 2003/1887, art 9, sch 2 para 15(1)(b)
s 26 rep—SI 2003/1887, art 9, sch 2 para 15(2)
s 26A added—SI 2010/1837, art 5, sch
 subst—SI 2015/1376, sch 2 para 11
s 28 am—SI 2003/1887, art 9, sch 2 para 15(1)(c)

c 8   *National Minimum Wage (Enforcement Notices)*—rep Employment, 2008 c 24, s 20, sch pt 2

c 9   **Electricity (Miscellaneous Provisions)**
s 1 appl—Energy, 2004 c 20, s 79(2)
 am—SI 2009/1941, art 2, sch 1

c 10   *Regional Assemblies (Preparations)*—rep Loc Democracy, Economic Development and
  Construction, 2009 c 20, s 146, sch 7 pt 4

c 11   *Industrial Development (Financial Assistance)*—rep Industry and Export (Financial Support),
  2009 c 5, s 1(2)

c 12   **Northern Ireland Assembly (Elections and Periods of Suspension)**
s 308A mod—SI 2006/572, art 17
s 636A mod—SI 2006/572, art 7

c 13   *Appropriation*—rep Appropriation (No 3), 2005 c 21, s 4, sch 3

c 14   **Finance**
mod—SI 2009/317, art 3, sch
appl (mods)—SI 2011/245, sch 6 pt 1
s 9 rep in pt—Finance, 2007 c 11, s 114, sch 27 pt 6
s 14 rep in pt—Finance, 2005 c 7, s 104, sch 11 pt 1, Note
s 17A am—Finance, 2006 c 25, s 164, sch 25 paras 2, 4-6
s 22 rep in pt—Finance, 2007 c 11, s 114, sch 27 pt 6
s 24 am—SI 2009/56, art 3, sch 1 para 360
ss 26, 27 appl—Finance, 2014 c 26, s 102(2)
s 29 appl—Finance, 2014 c 26, s 102(2)
s 30 am—SI 2009/56, art 3, sch 1 para 361
 appl—Finance, 2014 c 26, s 102(2)
ss 31, 32 appl—Finance, 2014 c 26, s 102(2)
s 33 am—SI 2009/56, art 3, sch 1 paras 362,363
 appl—Finance, 2014 c 26, s 102(2)
ss 33A-33F added—SI 2009/56, art 3, sch 1 para 364
 appl—Finance, 2014 c 26, s 102(2)
s 33 F am—SI 2014/1264, art 8
ss 34-36 rep—SI 2009/56, art 3, sch 1 para 365
s 37 subst—SI 2009/56, art 3, sch 1 para 366
 appl—Finance, 2014 c 26, s 102(2)
s 38 rep—Corporation Tax, 2009 c 4, s 1326, sch 3 pt 1
ss 39-41 appl—Finance, 2014 c 26, s 102(2)
Pt 4 (ss 42-124) appl—Finance, 2005 c 7, s 96, sch 9 para 4(4); Finance (No 2), 2005 c 22,
 s 49, sch 10 pt 1 para 16(9) pt 2 para 22(5); Finance, 2014 c 26, s 223(8),
 (9)(d)
appl (mod)—Finance, 2009 c 10, s 10(1)
mod (S)—(Stamp Duty Land Tax disappl (S)) Scotland, 2012 c 11, s 29(2) (with SI
 2015/637)
mod—Finance, 2013 c 29, s 194(8)-(12)
s 43 am—Finance, 2004 c 12, ss 296, 297(1)(2)(9), sch 39 pt 1 paras 1, 2, 13(3)
 rep in pt—Finance, 2004 c 12, s 326, sch 42 pt 4(2), Note 2
s 44 am—SIs 2003/2760, reg 2, sch para 1; 2003/2816, reg 2, sch para 1; Finance, 2004 c
 12, s 296, sch 39 pt 1 paras 1, 3, 13(3), 14(1), 15, 26; Corporation Tax, 2010 c 4,
 s 1177, sch 1 paras 400, 401
 rep in pt—(with SI 2015/637) Scotland, 2012 c 11, sch 3 para 3
s 44A added—Finance, 2004 c 12, s 296, sch 39 pt 1 paras 1, 4(1), 13(1)
s 45 subst—Finance, 2013 c 29, sch 39 para 2
 am—Finance, 2013 c 29, s 194
s 45A added—Finance, 2004 c 12, s 296, sch 39 pt 1 paras 1, 5(5), 13(2)
 am—Corporation Tax, 2010 c 4, s 1177, sch 1 paras 400, 403
s 47 rep in pt—SIs 2003/2760, reg 2, sch para 3(5); 2003/2816, reg 2, sch para 3(5);
 Finance, 2004 c 12, s 326, sch 42 pt 4(2), Note 3; SI 2004/1069, regs 2, 3(a)
 am—SI 2004/1069, regs 2, 3(b); Finance, 2007 c 11, s 76(1)(3)

2003
c 14 *continued*

s 48 am—Finance, 2004 c 12, ss 296, 297(1)(3)(9), sch 39 pt 1 paras 1, 4(2), 13(1);
　　　　Finance, 2007 c 11, s 75(2)(4); (with SI 2015/637) Scotland, 2012 c 11, s
　　　　29(2)(3)(a), sch 3 para 4(c); (17.2.2015 with qualifying provns) Wales, 2014 c 29,
　　　　s 16(3)(4)-(7), sch 2 para 3(2)
　　rep in pt—(with SI 2015/637) Scotland, 2012 c 11, sch 3 para 4(a)(b); (17.2.2015 with
　　　　qualifying provns) Wales, 2014 c 29, s 16(2)-(7), sch 2 para 3(3)
s 48A added—(17.2.2015 with qualifying provns) Wales, 2014 c 29, s 16(3)(4)-(7), sch 2
　　　　para 4
s 51 am—SIs 2003/2760, reg 2, sch para 8(3); 2003/2816, reg 2, sch para 8(3); Finance,
　　　　2004 c 12, s 296, sch 39 pt 2 paras 14(1), 22(3), 26
• 　s 53 am—Finance, 2004 c 12, s 297(1)(4)(9); Corporation Tax, 2010 c 4, s 1177, sch 1
　　　　paras 400, 404
s 54 am—Corporation Tax, 2010 c 4, s 1177, sch 1 paras 400, 405
s 55 am—Finance, 2005 c 7, s 95(1)(4); Finance, 2006 c 25, s 162(1); Finance, 2009 c 10, s
　　　　80(6); Finance, 2010 c 13, s 7(1); Finance, 2012 c 14, s 213(1), sch 35 para 2;
　　　　(with SI 2015/637) Scotland, 2012 c 11, sch 3 para 5(b); Stamp Duty Land Tax,
　　　　2015 c 1, s 1(2)-(6)
　　excl—SI 2007/3437, reg 9
　　appl (mod)—Finance, 2009 c 10, s 10(1)(a)
　　rep in pt—(with SI 2015/637) Scotland, 2012 c 11, sch 3 para 5(a); Stamp Duty Land
　　　　Tax, 2015 c 1, s 1(7)
s 55A added—Finance, 2012 c 14, sch 35 para 3
s 57 rep—Finance, 2012 c 14, sch 39 para 8(1)
s 57AA added—Finance, 2010 c 13, s 6(2)
　　　　am—(with SI 2015/637) Scotland, 2012 c 11, sch 3 para 6(a)
　　　　rep in pt—(with SI 2015/637) Scotland, 2012 c 11, sch 3 para 6(b)
s 57A added—SIs 2003/2760, reg 2, sch para 2; 2003/2816, reg 2, sch para 2; Finance,
　　　　2004 c 12, s 296, sch 39 pt 2 paras 14(1), 19(1), 26
　　rep in pt—(temp) Finance, 2004 c 12, s 296, sch 39 pt 1 paras 1, 6(1)(4), 13(3)(5);
　　　　Finance, 2013 c 29, sch 39 para 4(a)
　　am—(temp) Finance, 2004 c 12, s 296, sch 39 pt 1 paras 1, 6(1)-(3), 13(3)(5);
　　　　Finance, 2013 c 29, sch 39 para 4(b)
ss 58, 59 replaced, by s 58A—SIs 2003/2760, reg 2, sch para 3(1); 2003/2816, reg 2, sch
　　　　para 3(1); Finance, 2004 c 12, s 296, sch 39 pt 2 paras 14(1), 17(1), 26
s 58B added—Finance, 2007 c 11, s 19(1)
　　　　am—(spec retrosp effect) Finance, 2008 c 9, s 93(1)(2)
s 58C added—Finance, 2007 c 11, s 19(1)
　　　　am—(spec retrosp effect) Finance, 2008 c 9, s 93(1)(3)-(6)
s 58D added—Finance, 2011 c 11, sch 22 para 2
s 60 rep in pt—(with SI 2015/637) Scotland, 2012 c 11, sch 3 para 7; (17.2.2015 with
　　　　qualifying provns) Wales, 2014 c 29, s 16(3)(4)-(7), sch 2 paras 5, 35
s 61 am—Nat Health Service (Conseq Provns), 2006 c 43, s 2, sch para 233; Govt of
　　　　Wales, 2006 c 32, s 160, sch 10 para 63; SI 2011/2581, sch 2 para 7
　　rep in pt—(prosp) Health and Social Care, 2012 c 7, sch 14 para 86; (with SI
　　　　2015/637) Scotland, 2012 c 11, sch 3 para 8(2)(3)
s 63 am—Financial Services, 2012 c 21, sch 18 para 98; SI 2015/575, sch 1 para 24(2)(4)
　　rep in pt—SI 2015/575, sch 1 para 24(3)
s 64A rep—Finance, 2006 c 25, ss 166(2), 178, sch 26
s 66 am—Finance (No 2), 2005 c 22, s 49, sch 10 pt 2 paras 17, 18, 22; Nat Health Service
　　　　(Conseq Provns), 2006 c 43, s 2, sch 1 para 234; Govt of Wales, 2006 c 32, s 160,
　　　　sch 10 para 64; SI 2009/1890, art 3; (prosp) Planning (W), 2015 anaw 4, sch 2
　　　　para 22
　　rep in pt—SI 2009/1890, art 3; (prosp) Health and Social Care, 2012 c 7, sch 14 para
　　　　87
　　mod—Finance, 2013 c 29, s 153(3)
s 67A added—Finance, 2012 c 14, s 216(1)
s 69 rep in pt—SI 2012/964, art 3(1), sch
s 71 am—SI 2006/3337, art 3, sch; Housing and Regeneration, 2008 c 17, s 56, sch 8 paras
　　　　78, 79; ibid,s 277, sch 9 paras 29, 30; Finance, 2009 c 10, s 81(1)-(4); Localism,
　　　　2011 c 20, sch 19 para 40
s 71A added—(EW, NI) Finance, 2005 c 7, s 94, sch 8 paras 1, 2, 7(1)
　　rep in pt—Finance, 2006 c 25, ss 168(2), 178, sch 26; Finance, 2011 c 11, sch 21
　　　　para 3(1); (with SI 2015/637) Scotland, 2012 c 11, sch 3 para 9

2003

c 14 s 71A *continued*

    am—Finance, 2006 c 25, s 168(1); Finance, 2007 c 11, s 75(3)(4); Taxation (International and Other Provns), 2010 c 8, s 374, sch 8 paras 205, 206

ss 72, 72A rep —(with SI 2015/637) Scotland, 2012 c 11, sch 3 para 10

s 73 am—Finance, 2005 c 7, s 94, sch 8 paras 1, 5, 7; Finance, 2006 c 25, s 168(1)(3); Finance, 2007 c 11, s 75(3)(4); Taxation (International and Other Provns), 2010 c 8, s 374, sch 8 paras 205, 209

    rep in pt—Finance, 2006 c 25, s 168(2); Finance, 2011 c 11, sch 21 para 3(1); (with SI 2015/637) Scotland, 2012 c 11, sch 3 para 11; (17.2.2015 with qualifying provns) Wales, 2014 c 29, s 16(3)(4)-(7), sch 2 para 6

s 73A added—Finance, 2006 c 25, s 168(4)

    am—Finance, 2008 c 9, s 155(1)(2)

s 73AB added—Finance, 2008 c 9, s 155(1)(3)

    am—Corporation Tax, 2010 c 4, s 1177, sch 1 paras 400, 406; (with SI 2015/637) Scotland, 2012 c 11, sch 3 para 12(2)

    rep in pt—(with SI 2015/637) Scotland, 2012 c 11, sch 3 paras 12(1), 13(4)

s 73B added—Finance, 2007 c 11, s 75(1)(4)

    rep in pt—(with SI 2015/637) Scotland, 2012 c 11, sch 3 paras 13(2)(3), 14

s 73BA added—Finance, 2011 c 11, sch 21 para 3(2)

    am—Finance, 2015 c 11, s 68(2)

s 73C added—Finance, 2009 c 10, s 123, sch 61 paras 24, 25

    am—Taxation (International and Other Provns), 2010 c 8, s 374, sch 8 paras 205, 210

s 73CA added—Finance, 2010 c 13, s 6(3)

    rep in pt—(with SI 2015/637) Scotland, 2012 c 11, sch 3 para 14

s 74 am—Finance, 2009 c 10, s 80(1)(2)(3)(b)(4)(5); Finance, 2012 c 14, sch 35 para 5; Finance, 2014 c 26, s 112(1); Stamp Duty Land Tax, 2015 c 1, sch para 2(2)(3)

    rep in pt—Finance, 2009 c 10, s 80(1)(3)(a)

s 75 rep—(with SI 2015/637) Scotland, 2012 c 11, sch 3 para 15

s 75A added—SI 2006/3237, reg 2, sch

    subst—Finance, 2007 c 11, s 71

    am—Corporation Tax, 2010 c 4, s 1177, sch 1 paras 400, 407

s 75B added—Finance, 2007 c 11, s 71

s 75C added—Finance, 2007 c 11, s 71

    rep in pt —Finance, 2010 c 13, s 55(1)(a)

    am—Finance, 2010 c 13, s 55(1)(b); (with SI 2015/637) Scotland, 2012 c 11, sch 3 para 16

s 76 appl—Railways, 2005 c 14, s 53, sch 10 pt 4 para 30(3)

    rep in pt—Finance, 2007 c 11, s 80(1)(2)(9)(a), sch 27

s 76 mod—Finance, 2013 c 29, s 194(8)-(12)

s 77 subst—Finance, 2008 c 9, s 94(1)(2)

    rep in pt—(with SI 2015/637) Scotland, 2012 c 11, sch 3 para 17

    am—Finance, 2013 c 29, sch 39 para 5; Stamp Duty Land Tax, 2015 c 1, sch para 9

s 77A added—Finance, 2008 c 9, s 94(1)(2)

    am—SI 2008/2338, reg 2; Stamp Duty Land Tax, 2015 c 1, sch para 10

s 78A added—Finance (No 2), 2005 c 22, s 48(1)(5)

    am—Loc Govt and Public Involvement in Health, 2007 c 28, s 220, sch 16 para 9

    rep in pt—Loc Govt and Public Involvement in Health, 2007 c 28, s 241, sch 18

s 79 am—Finance, 2004 c 12, ss 296, 297(1)(5)-(7)(10), 298(1)(3), sch 39 pt 1 paras 1, 7, 13(1)-(3); Finance (No 2), 2005 c 22, s 47(2); Finance, 2008 c 9, s 94, sch 30 paras 1, 2(1)(3); Finance, 2013 c 29, sch 39 para 6(b)

    rep in pt—(with SI 2015/637) Scotland, 2012 c 11, sch 3 para 18; Finance, 2013 c 29, sch 39 para 6(a)

s 80 rep in pt—SIs 2003/2760, reg 2, sch para 5(2); 2003/2816, reg 2, sch para 5(2); Finance, 2004 c 12, s 326, sch 42 pt 4(2), Note 3; Stamp Duty Land Tax, 2015 c 1, sch para 4(1)(b)

    am—SIs 2003/2760, reg 2, sch paras 5(3), 8(5); 2003/2816, reg 2, sch paras 5(3), 8(5); Finance, 2004 c 12, ss 296, 299(1)(4), sch 39 pt 2 paras 14(1), 22(4), 26; Finance (No 2), 2005 c 22, s 49, sch 10 pt 1 paras 1, 15, 16(5)-(9); Finance, 2007 c 11, s 80(1)(3)(9)(b); Stamp Duty Land Tax, 2015 c 1, sch para 4(1)(a)(2)

    excl—SI 2003/2837, reg 26

s 81 am—SIs 2003/2760, reg 2, sch para 3(3); 2003/2816, reg 2, sch para 3(3); Finance, 2004 c 12, ss 296, 302(5)(7), sch 39 pt 2 paras 14(1), 17(3), 19(2), 26; Finance, 2007 c 11, s 80(1)(4)(9)(c); Finance, 2013 c 29, sch 40 para 3

2003

c 14 s 81 *continued*

  rep in pt—Finance, 2007 c 11, s 114, sch 27 pt 4

s 81ZA added—Finance, 2013 c 29, sch 40 para 4

  mod—Finance, 2013 c 29, sch 40 para 9(2)

  am—Stamp Duty Land Tax, 2015 c 1, sch para 5

s 81A added—SIs 2003/2760, reg 2, sch para 5(1); 2003/2816, reg 2, sch para 5(1); Finance, 2004 c 12, s 296, sch 39 pt 2 paras 14(1), 19(1), 26

  am—Finance, 2007 c 11, s 80(1)(5)(9)(d); Stamp Duty Land Tax, 2015 c 1, sch para 6(a)

  rep in pt—Stamp Duty Land Tax, 2015 c 1, sch para 6(b)

s 81B added—SIs 2003/2760, reg 2, sch para 6; 2003/2816, reg 2, sch para 6; Finance, 2004 c 12, s 296, sch 39 pt 2 paras 14(1), 20, 26

  rep in pt—Finance, 2008 c 9, s 94, sch 30 paras 1, 3; Finance, 2012 c 14, s 222(4)(e)

s 82 am—SI 2009/56, art 3, sch 1 para 367

s 82A added—Finance, 2004 c 12, s 299(1)(2)

s 85 am—Finance, 2013 c 29, sch 40 para 5

s 86 am—Finance, 2007 c 11, s 80(1)(6)(9)(e); Finance, 2009 c 10, s 123, sch 61 paras 24, 26; Finance, 2013 c 29, sch 40 para 6

s 87 am—SIs 2003/2760, reg 2, sch paras 3(4), 5(4), 8(6); 2003/2816, reg 2, sch paras 3(4), 5(4), 8(6); Finance, 2004 c 12, ss 296, 302(6)(7), sch 39 pt 2 paras 14(1), 17(4), 19(3), 22(5), 26; Finance, 2011 c 11, sch 22 para 5; Finance, 2013 c 29, sch 41 para 4(a)

  rep in pt—Finance, 2013 c 29, sch 41 para 4(b)

s 90 am—SIs 2003/2760, reg 2, sch para 8(7); 2003/2816, reg 2, sch para 8(7); Finance, 2004 c 12, s 296, sch 39 pt 2 paras 14(1), 22(6), 26; SI 2009/56, art 3, sch 1 para 368

s 93 am—SI 2009/3054, art 3, sch

  rep in pt—(with savings) SI 2009/3054, arts 3, 7, sch; Finance, 2012 c 14, sch 38 para 58(2)

s 94 rep in pt—(with savings) SI 2009/3054, arts 3, 7, sch

s 96 rep—Finance, 2012 c 14, sch 38 para 58(3)

s 99 am—Finance, 2004 c 12, s 298(1)(4)

s 101 rep in pt—Finance, 2006 c 25, s 178, sch 26

  am—Finance, 2006 c 25, s 166(3); Corporation Tax, 2010 c 4, s 1177, sch 1 paras 400, 408

s 103 am—SI 2009/56, art 3, sch 1 para 369

s 104 am—Finance, 2004 c 12, s 304, sch 41 paras 2(a), 3

s 106 rep in pt—Finance, 2012 c 14, s 222(2)

s 107 am—SIs 2003/2760, reg 2, sch para 7; 2003/2816, reg 2, sch para 7; Finance, 2004 c 12, s 296, sch 39 pt 2 paras 14(1), 21, 26; Govt of Wales, 2006 c 32, s 160, sch 10 para 65

s 108 am—Finance, 2007 c 11, s 76(2)(3); Corporation Tax, 2010 c 4, s 1177, sch 1 paras 400, 409; (with SI 2015/637) Scotland, 2012 c 11, sch 3 para 19; (17.2.2015 with qualifying provns) Wales, 2014 c 29, s 16(3)(4)-(7), sch 2 para 7

s 109 am—Finance, 2012 c 14, sch 35 para 6(2)(3); Stamp Duty Land Tax, 2015 c 1, sch para 11

s 110 am—Finance, 2010 c 13, s 6(4)

s 111 am—Finance, 2004 c 12, s 299(1)(5)

s 112 rep in pt—Finance, 2012 c 14, sch 39 para 8(2)(b)(i)

s 113 am—Finance, 2004 c 12, s 299(1)(6)

  rep in pt—Finance, 2008 c 9, s 25, sch 7 para 114(c); Finance (No 3), 2010 c 33, s 28, sch 12 para 3

s 114 excl—Finance (No 2), 2005 c 22, s 48(6)

  am—Finance, 2007 c 11, s 19(2)

s 115 rep—SI 2009/56, art 3, sch 1 para 370

s 116 mod—Finance, 2013 c 29, s 114(2)

s 116M added—(17.2.2015 with qualifying provns) Wales, 2014 c 29, s 17(1)(2)

s 117 rep in pt—(with SI 2015/637) Scotland, 2012 c 11, sch 3 para 20; (17.2.2015 with qualifying provns) Wales, 2014 c 29, s 16(3)(4)-(7), sch 2 para 8

s 119 appl—SI 2003/2837, reg 5(6)

  am—Finance, 2004 c 12, s 296, sch 39 pt 1 paras 1, 8, 13(1)-(3); Finance (No 2), 2005 c 22, s 47(3); Finance, 2013 c 29, sch 39 para 7; ibid, sch 41 para 5

  rep in pt—Finance, 2004 c 12, s 326, sch 42 pt 4(2), Note 2; (with SI 2015/637) Scotland, 2012 c 11, sch 3 para 21

2003
c 14 *continued*

s 120 subst—Finance, 2004 c 12, s 296, sch 39 pt 2 paras 14(1), 22(1), 26

s 121 am—SIs 2009/56, art 3, sch 1 para 371; 2012/700, sch para 7(2); Finance, 2013 c 29, sch 39 para 8

    rep in pt—(with SI 2015/637) Scotland, 2012 c 11, sch 3 para 22; (17.2.2015 with qualifying provns) Wales, 2014 c 29, s 16(3)(4)-(7), sch 2 para 9

s 122 am—SIs 2003/2760, reg 2, sch paras 8(8), 11(4); 2003/2816, reg 2, sch paras 8(8), 11(4); Finance, 2004 c 12, s 296, sch 39 pt 1 paras 1, 5(6), 13(2), pt 2 paras 14(1), 22(7), 25(4), 26; Finance, 2005 c 7, s 94, sch 8 paras 1, 6, 7; SI 2009/56, art 3, sch 1 para 372; Finance, 2013 c 29, sch 40 para 7

    rep in pt—(with SI 2015/637) Scotland, 2012 c 11, sch 3 para 23; Stamp Duty Land Tax, 2015 c 1, sch para 12

s 125 am—SI 2003/2760, reg 2, sch para 9; 2003/2816, reg 2, sch para 9; Finance, 2004 c 12, ss 296, 304, sch 39 pt 2 paras 14(1), 23, 26, sch 41 paras 2(b), 3

s 127 rep—Finance, 2012 c 14, sch 39 para 5(2)(e)(i)

s 128 rep—Finance, 2012 c 14, sch 39 para 9(1)(a)

s 129 rep—Finance, 2012 c 14, sch 39 para 9(1)(b)

s 130 am—Commrs for Revenue and Customs, 2005 c 11, s 50(6), sch 4 paras 125, 127

    rep in pt—Finance, 2012 c 14, sch 39 para 9(1)(c)

ss 131, 132 rep—Income Tax, 2007 c 3, s 1031, sch 3

s 134 rep—Corporation Tax, 2010 c 4, s 1181, sch 3 pt 1

s 138 rep in pt—Finance, 2008 c 9, s 47(2)(a)

s 141 rep—Corporation Tax, 2009 c 4, ss 1322, 1326, sch 1 paras 558, 559, sch 3 pt 1

s 143 rep—Corporation Tax, 2009 c 4, ss 1322, 1326, sch 1 paras 558, 560, sch 3 pt 1

s 146 rep—Finance, 2011 c 11, sch 26 para 3(2)(b)

s 147 rep in pt—(prosp) Finance, 2004 c 12, s 326, sch 42 pt 2(7), Note

s 148 rep—Corporation Tax, 2010 c 4, ss 1177, 1181, sch 1 paras 400, 410, sch 3 pt 1

s 149 rep in pt—Corporation Tax, 2009 c 4, s 1326, sch 3 pt 1; Corporation Tax, 2010 c 4, s 1181, sch 3 pt 1

s 150 rep—Corporation Tax, 2010 c 4, ss 1177, 1181, sch 1 paras 400, 411, sch 3 pt 1

s 151 rep—Income Tax, 2007 c 3, s 1027, sch 1 paras 451, 452, sch 3

s 152 rep—Corporation Tax, 2010 c 4, ss 1177, 1181, sch 1 paras 400, 412, sch 3 pt 1

s 153 rep in pt—Finance, 2004 c 12, s 326, sch 42 pt 3, Note; Income Tax (Trading and Other Income), 2005 c 5, s 884, sch 3; Income Tax, 2007 c 3, ss 114, 1031, sch 3, sch 27 pt 2; Finance, 2007 c 11, s 114, sch 27 pt 2; Corporation Tax, 2009 c 4, s 1326, sch 3 pt 1; Corporation Tax, 2010 c 4, s 1181, sch 3 pt 1; Taxation (International and Other Provns), 2010 c 8, s 378, sch 10 pt 1; Finance, 2012 c 14, s 26(2)(c); SL(R), 2013 c 2, s 1, sch 1 pt 10(1)

    am—Income Tax, 2007 c 3, s 1027, sch 1 paras 451, 454

s 154 rep—Taxation (International and Other Provns), 2010 c 8, s 378, sch 10 pt 1

s 156 rep—Finance, 2012 c 14, sch 16 para 109

s 160 rep—Finance, 2008 c 9, s 8, sch 2 para 55(f)(i)

s 168 rep—Corporation Tax, 2009 c 4, s 1326, sch 3 pt 1

s 171 rep—Finance, 2008 c 9, s 36, sch 14 para 17(l)

s 174 rep—Finance, 2004 c 12, s 326, sch 42 pt 3, Note

s 175 rep—Income Tax (Trading and Other Income), 2005 c 5, s 884, sch 3

s 176 rep—Income Tax (Trading and Other Income), 2005 c 5, ss 882(1), 884, sch 1 pt 2 paras 621, 623, sch 3

s 177 am—Corporation Tax, 2009 c 4, s 1322, sch 1 paras 558, 564

ss 178, 179 rep—Corporation Tax, 2009 c 4, s 1326, sch 3 pt 1

s 180 rep in pt—Corporation Tax, 2009 c 4, s 1326, sch 3 pt 1

s 183 rep—Corporation Tax, 2010 c 4, s 1181, sch 3 pt 1

s 184 rep—Corporation Tax, 2009 c 4, s 1326, sch 3 pt 1

s 188 rep—Finance, 2012 c 14, sch 30 para 17

s 192 rep in pt—Finance, 2008 c 9, s 122, sch 40 para 21(k)(i)

s 193 rep in pt—Finance, 2012 c 14, sch 32 para 22(4)

s 195 am—Corporation Tax, 2009 c 4, s 1322, sch 1 paras 558, 565; Corporation Tax, 2010 c 4, s 1177, sch 1 paras 400, 413

s 197 rep—SI 2012/3062, sch

s 198 rep—Finance, 2006 c 25, s 178, sch 26 pt 8(2)

s 199 rep—Taxation (International and Other Provns), 2010 c 8, ss 371, 378, sch 7 paras 105, 106, sch 10 pt 12

s 202 rep—Income Tax, 2007 c 3, s 1031, sch 3

s 204 am—Finance, 2007 c 11, s 94(1)-(7)

2003

c 14 *continued*

s 205 am—Finance, 2007 c 11, s 94(8)

s 207 rep in pt—SL(R), 2013 c 2, s 1, sch 1 pt 10(1)

sch 2A added—Finance, 2013 c 29, sch 39 para 3

sch 3 am—(retrosp) Finance, 2004 c 12, ss 300, 301(1)(7); SI 2005/3229, reg 174; Housing and Regeneration, 2008 c 17, s 277, sch 9 paras 29, 31

sch 4 rep in pt—SIs 2003/2760, reg 2, sch paras 3(5), 8(11); 2003/2816, reg 2, sch paras 3(5), 8(11); 2003/3293, reg 2(1)(2)(a); Finance, 2004 c 12, s 326, sch 42 pt 4(2), Note 3; SI 2004/1069, regs 2, 4(1)(2)(a); (with SI 2015/637) Scotland, 2012 c 11, sch 3 para 24

    am—SIs 2003/3293, reg 2(1)(2)(b)(3)-(5); 2004/1069, regs 2, 4(1)(2)(b)(3); Finance, 2004 c 12, ss 296, 297(1)(8)(9), 301(2)-(4)(6), sch 39 pt 1 paras 1, 9(1)-(3), 13(3); (retrosp) ibid,s 301(2)(5)(7); SIs 2004/1206, regs 2, 3; 2006/875, reg 3; Corporation Tax, 2010 c 4, s 1177, sch 1 paras 400, 414; SI 2010/1080, art 2, sch 1; Educ, 2011 c 21, sch 15 para 1; Finance, 2011 c 11, sch 21 para 4(2)(3); Finance, 2014 c 26, s 111(2)(3)

    excl—SI 2006/575, reg 43

sch 4A added—Finance, 2012 c 14, sch 35 para 4

    am—Finance, 2013 c 29, sch 40 para 2; Stamp Duty Land Tax, 2015 c 1, sch para 13; Finance, 2015 c 11, s 68(3)

    mod—Finance, 2013 c 29, sch 40 para 9(3)

sch 5 am—SI 2003/2914, reg 2, sch paras 1, 2; Finance, 2004 c 12, s 296, sch 39 pt 1 paras 1, 10, 13(3); Finance, 2005 c 7, s 95(2)(4); Finance, 2006 c 25, ss 162(2), 164(2); Finance, 2008 c 9, s 95(1)(2)(a)(3); Finance, 2011 c 11, sch 22 para 6; Finance, 2012 c 14, sch 35 para 7(2)(3)

    rep in pt—SIs 2003/2760, reg 2, sch para 8(9)(11); 2003/2816, reg 2, sch para 8(9)(11); Finance, 2004 c 12, s 326, sch 42 pt 4(2), Note 3; Finance, 2008 c 9, s 95(1)(2)(b)

    appl (mod)—Finance, 2009 c 10, s 10(1)(b)

sch 6 rep—Finance, 2012 c 14, sch 39 para 8(1)

sch 6A added—SIs 2003/2760, reg 2, sch para 3(2); 2003/2816, reg 2, sch para 3(2); Finance, 2004 c 12, s 296, sch 39 pt 2 paras 14(1), 17(2), 26

    am—Corporation Tax, 2010 c 4, s 1177, sch 1 paras 400, 415

sch 6B added—Finance, 2011 c 11, sch 22 para 3

    rep in pt—Stamp Duty Land Tax, 2015 c 1, sch para 7(3)(8)

    am—Finance, 2012 c 14, sch 35 para 8; Finance, 2013 c 29, sch 39 para 9; Stamp Duty Land Tax, 2015 c 1, sch para 7(2)(4)-(7); Finance, 2015 c 11, s 69(1)

sch 7 am—Finance (No 2), 2005 c 22, s 49, sch 10 pt 1 paras 1, 3, 4, 5, 6, 8, 9, 16(1)-(9), pt 2 paras 17, 19, 20, 22; Finance, 2006 c 25, s 167; Finance, 2007 c 11, s 74(3)(5); Finance, 2008 c 9, s 96(1)(2)(3)(b)-(5); Corporation Tax, 2010 c 4, s 1177, sch 1 paras 400, 416; SI 2013/234, arts 7, 8; Stamp Duty Land Tax, 2015 c 1, sch para 8

    rep in pt—Finance, 2008 c 9, s 96(1)(3)(a); (17.2.2015 with qualifying provns) Wales, 2014 c 29, s 16(3)(4)-(7), sch 2 para 10

    excl—SI 2009/2971, reg 33

sch 8 am—Finance, 2004 c 12, s 302(1)-(4)(7); Finance, 2008 c 9, s 95(7); Finance, 2014 c 26, sch 23 paras 2(b)(c), 3, 4

    rep in pt—Finance, 2010 c 13, s 30, sch 6 paras 18-20; Finance, 2014 c 26, sch 23 para 2(a)

sch 9 am—Finance, 2004 c 12, s 303(1)(2)(4); Finance, 2007 c 11, ss 77, 78; Finance, 2008 c 9, s 95(8)(10); Housing and Regeneration, 2008 c 17, s 56, sch 8 paras 78, 80; ibid,s 277, sch 9 paras 29, 32; Finance, 2009 c 10, s 81(5)(6)(7)(b); ibid, s 82(1); Corporation Tax, 2010 c 4, s 1177, sch 1 paras 400, 417; Finance, 2010 c 13, s 6(5); SI 2010/844, art 6, sch 2; Localism, 2011 c 20, sch 19 para 41; Police Reform and Social Responsibility, 2011 c 13, sch 16 para 314; SI 2013/602, sch 2 para 40; Stamp Duty Land Tax, 2015 c 1, sch paras 14, 15

    rep in pt—SI 2005/3226 (W 238), arts 3, 7(1)(b), sch 2 pt 1 para 14; Finance, 2008 c 9, s 95(9); Finance, 2009 c 10, s 81(5)(7)(a); (17.2.2015 with qualifying provn) Wales, 2014 c 29, s 16(3)(4)-(7), sch 2 para 11

    mod—(transtl provns and savings) SI 2008/2839, arts 3, 6, sch

    appl—Finance, 2009 c 10, s 82(1)(3)

sch 10 am—SI 2004/3208, regs 2, 3(a)(b), 4, 5(1)(2)(b)(3); Finance, 2004 c 12, s 299(1)(7)(a)(8)(a); Finance (No 2), 2005 c 22, s 47(4); Finance, 2009 c 10, s 99, sch 51 paras 14-16; SIs 2009/56, art 3, sch 1 paras 373-394; 2009/1307,

2003

c 14 *continued*

art 5, sch 1; Finance (No 3), 2010 c 33, s 28, sch 12 paras 2, 4; Finance, 2011 c
11, sch 22 para 7; Finance, 2013 c 29, s 231(4); Finance, 2014 c 26, ss
224(3)(4), 225(2); Finance (No. 2), 2015 c 33, sch 8 para 41

restr—Finance, 2004 c 12, s 313(4)(f)

rep in pt—Finance, 2004 c 12, ss 299(1)(7)(b)(8)(b)(c), 326, sch 42 pt 4(2), Note 1;
SI 2004/3208, regs 2, 5(1)(2)(a); Finance, 2007 c 11, s 80(1)(7)(9)(f); Finance,
2008 c 9, s 122, sch 40 para 21(k)(ii); SIs 2009/56, art 3, sch 1 paras 373-394;
(with savings) 2009/3054, arts 3, 7, sch; (with SI 2015/637) Scotland, 2012 c
11, sch 3 para 25; (17.2.2015 with qualifying provn) Wales, 2014 c 29, s
16(3)(4)-(7), sch 2 para 12

appl (mod)—Finance, 2009 c 10, s 123, sch 61 para 7(9)

appl—SI 2003/2837, reg 20

excl—Finance, 2014 c 26, s 208(10)s 208(11)(d)

mod—Finance, 2014 c 26, ss 227(9)(c), 277(5)

sch 11 am—Finance, 2009 c 10, s 98, sch 50 paras 3, 8-11; SI 2009/56, art 3, sch 1 para
394

sch 11A added—Finance, 2004 c 12, s 299(1)(3), sch 40

am—Finance, 2009 c 10, s 98, sch 50 paras 3, 12, 13(1)(3), 14; SI 2009/56, art 3,
sch 1 paras 395-400; Finance (No 3), 2010 c 33, s 28, sch 12 para 5(a)

rep in pt—Finance, 2009 c 10, s 98, sch 50 paras 3, 12, 13(2); SI 2009/56, art 3,
sch 1 paras 395-400; (with savings) 2009/3054, arts 3, 7, sch; Finance (No 3),
2010 c 33, s 28, sch 12 para 5(b)

appl—Finance, 2013 c 29, s 210(6)(e); ibid, sch 33 paras 28(2), 31(3)

sch 12 am—(S) Bankruptcy and Diligence etc (S), 2007 asp 3, s 226, sch 5 para 32;
Tribunals, Cts and Enforcement, 2007 c 15, s 62, sch 13 para 147; Crime and
Cts, 2013 c 22, sch 9 para 52

rep in pt—(saving) Finance, 2008 c 9, s 137(6)(7); ibid,ss 129, 138, sch 43 paras 9,
16, sch 44 para 10

appl—Finance, 2013 c 29, s 165

sch 13 am—Legal Services, 2007 c 29, s 208, sch 21 para 138; SIs 2009/56, art 3, sch 1
paras 401-409; 3054, art 3, sch; Finance, 2012 c 14, sch 38 para 58(4)(b)

rep in pt—Finance, 2007 c 11, s 84, sch 22 paras 3, 16, sch 27; SIs 2009/56, art 3,
sch 1 paras 401-409; 3054, art 3, sch; Finance, 2012 c 14, sch 38 para 58(4)(a)

sch 14 am—SI 2009/56, art 3, sch 1 paras 410-412

rep in pt—SI 2009/56, art 3, sch 1 paras 410-412

sch 15 am—Finance, 2004 c 12, ss 304, 305, sch 41 paras 1, 2(c), 3; Finance (No 2), 2005 c
22, s 49, sch 10 pt 1 paras 1, 10, 16(3)(6)-(9), pt 2 paras 17, 21(1)-(4)(6),
22(4); SI 2006/3237, reg 2, sch; Finance, 2006 c 25, s 163, sch 24 paras 1-10;
Finance, 2007 c 11, s 72; Finance, 2008 c 9, s 95(11); transtl provns) ibid,s 97,
sch 31 paras 1-9, 11; Corporation Tax, 2010 c 4, s 1177, sch 1 paras 400, 418;
Finance, 2011 c 11, sch 22 para 8; Finance, 2012 c 14, sch 35 para 9, sch 39
para 8(3); Finance, 2014 c 26, sch 24 para 11(2)(3)(a)(b)(d)-(f); Stamp Duty
Land Tax, 2015 c 1, sch para 16

rep in pt—Finance (No 2), 2005 c 22, ss 49, 70, sch 10 pt 2 paras 17, 21(1)(5), 22(4),
sch 11 pt 3(1), Note; Finance, 2006 c 25, ss 163, 178, sch 24 paras 2(2), 5(2),
sch 26; Finance, 2007 c 11, s 114, sch 27 pt 4; Finance, 2012 c 14, sch 39 para
8(2)(b)(ii); (with SI 2015/637) Scotland, 2012 c 11, sch 3 para 26; Finance,
2014 c 26, sch 24 para 11(3)(c)

sch 16 am—Finance (No 2), 2005 c 22, s 49, sch 10 pt 1 paras 1, 11, 16(4)(6)-(9); Finance,
2006 c 25, s 165(1); Finance, 2007 c 11, s 72

sch 17 rep—SI 2009/56, art 3, sch 1 para 413

sch 17A added—Finance, 2004 c 12, s 296, sch 39 pt 2 paras 14(1), 22(2), 26 (replacing SI
2003/2816, reg 2, sch para 8(2))

am—(temp) Finance, 2004 c 12, s 296, sch 39 pt 1 paras 1, 11(1)-(5), 13(3)-(5);
Finance (No 2), 2005 c 22, s 49, sch 10 pt 1 paras 1, 7, 12-14, 16(1)(4)-(9); SI
2006/875, reg 4; Finance, 2006 c 25, s 164, sch 25 paras 3, 7, 8; Finance, 2007
c 11, s 80(1)(8)(9)(g); Finance, 2008 c 9, ss 94, 95(12), sch 30 paras 1, 14;
Corporation Tax, 2010 c 4, s 1177, sch 1 paras 400, 419; (with SI 2015/637)
Scotland, 2012 c 11, sch 3 para 27(2)(8); SI 2012/1667, reg 3; Finance, 2013 c
29, sch 39 para 10; ibid, sch 41 paras 2, 3, 6(2)(3); Stamp Duty Land Tax,
2015 c 1, sch paras 17(a), 18(a)

appl—SI 2006/1958, regs 7, 8

mod—SI 2010/814, reg 2

2003

c 14 sch 17A *continued*

        rep in pt—Finance, 2012 c 14, sch 39 para 8(2)(b)(iii); (with SI 2015/637)
             Scotland, 2012 c 11, sch 3 para 27(3)-(7)(9); Finance, 2013 c 29, sch 41 para
             7(1); Stamp Duty Land Tax, 2015 c 1, sch paras 17(b), 18(b)

    sch 18 rep in pt—Corporation Tax, 2010 c 4, s 1181, sch 3 pt 1

    sch 19 am—SIs 2003/2760, reg 2, sch paras 8(10), 10, 11(1); 2003/2816, reg 2, sch
        paras 8(10), 10, 11(1)-(3); (saving) Finance, 2004 c 12, s 296, sch 39 pt 1
        paras 1, 12, 13(3)(4); ibid,s 296, sch 39 pt 2 paras 14(1), 22(8), 24, 25(1)-(3),
        26; (retrosp to 1.12.2003) ibid,s 303(3)(5); Stamp Duty Land Tax, 2015 c 1,
        sch paras 19, 20

        rep in pt—SIs 2003/2760, reg 2, sch para 11(1); 2003/2816, reg 2, sch para 11(1);
             Finance, 2004 c 12, s 326, sch 42 pt 4(2), Note 3; Finance, 2012 c 14, sch 39
             para 5(2)(e)(ii)

    sch 20 am—Corporation Tax, 2010 c 4, s 1177, sch 1 paras 400, 420

    sch 21 rep in pt—Finance, 2004 c 12, s 326, sch 42 pt 2(11), Note 2

    sch 22 rep in pt—Corporation Tax, 2009 c 4, s 1326, sch 3 pt 1

    schs 23-25 rep—Corporation Tax, 2009 c 4, ss 1322, 1326, sch 1 paras 558, 566, sch 3 pt 1

    sch 26 rep—Corporation Tax, 2010 c 4, ss 1177, 1181, sch 1 paras 400, 421, sch 3 pt 1

    sch 27 rep in pt—Finance, 2004 c 12, s 326, sch 42 pt 3, Note; ibid,s 52(3), 326, sch 42 pt
        2(6), Note 1; Finance, 2006 c 25, s 178, sch 26; Income Tax, 2007 c 3, s 1031,
        sch 3; Taxation (International and Other Provns), 2010 c 8, s 378, sch 10 pts 1,
        11

    sch 28 rep in pt—SI 2009/2035, art 2, sch

    sch 29 rep in pt—Finance, 2008 c 9, ss 8, 25, sch 2 para 55(f)(ii), sch 7 para 146

    sch 30 rep in pt—Finance, 2006 c 25, s 178, sch 26

    sch 31 rep —Corporation Tax, 2009 c 4, s 1326, sch 3 pt 1

    sch 33 rep in pt—Finance, 2004 c 12, s 326, sch 42 pt 2(1)(3), Note; SI 2005/3465,
        art 10(a); Finance, 2007 c 11, s 114, sch 27 pt 2; Finance, 2008 c 9, s 43, sch
        17 paras 3(b), 18(5)(e); SI 2008/381, art 31, sch; Taxation (International and
        Other Provns), 2010 c 8, s 378, sch 10 pt 1; Finance, 2012 c 14, sch 16 para
        247(k)

    sch 34 rep—Finance, 2008 c 9, s 36, sch 14 para 17(l)

    sch 35 rep in pt—Income Tax (Trading and Other Income), 2005 c 5, s 884, sch 3; Income
        Tax, 2007 c 3, s 1031, sch 3; Corporation Tax, 2009 c 4, s 1326, sch 3 pt 1

    sch 36 rep—Income Tax (Trading and Other Income), 2005 c 5, ss 882(1), 883(4), 884, sch
        1 pt 2 paras 621, 626, sch 2 pt 10 para 149, sch 3

    sch 37 rep—Corporation Tax, 2009 c 4, s 1326, sch 3 pt 1

    sch 38 rep in pt—Income Tax, 2007 c 3, s 1031, sch 3; Finance, 2007 c 11, s 114, sch 27 pt
        2; Finance, 2008 c 9, s 66(4)(j)

    sch 39 rep in pt—Income Tax (Trading and Other Income), 2005 c 5, s 884, sch 3; Income
        Tax, 2007 c 3, s 1031, sch 3

    sch 40 rep in pt—Income Tax, 2007 c 3, s 1031, sch 3; Finance, 2008 c 9, s 99, sch 32 para
        21

    sch 41 rep in pt—SI 2008/381, art 31, sch; Corporation Tax, 2009 c 4, s 1326, sch 3 pt 1;
        Corporation Tax, 2010 c 4, s 1181, sch 3 pt 1

    sch 42 rep in pt—Finance, 2009 c 10, s 36, sch 16 para 11(c)

c 15   *Co-operatives and Community Benefit Societies*—rep Co-operative and Community Benefit
        Societies, 2014 c 14, sch 7

c 16   **Marine Safety**
    s 2 rep—Fire and Rescue Services, 2004 c 21, s 54, sch 2

c 17   **Licensing**
    appl—Noise, 1996 c 37, s 2; Anti-social Behaviour, 2003 c 38, s 41(3)
    mod—SI 2009/1724, arts 2, 3
    s 2 am—Deregulation, 2015 c 20, s 67(1)
    s 5 mod—(temp) Licensing, 2003 c 17, s 200, sch 8 pt 4 para 29; SI 2008/2867, reg 12
        am—Fire and Rescue Services, 2004 c 21, s 53, sch 1 para 98(1)(2)(3)(a); Police
            Reform and Social Responsibility, 2011 c 13, ss 104(2), 122(2)(a)(4)-(7); Health
            and Social Care, 2012 c 7, sch 5 para 112(b)
        rep in pt—Police Reform and Social Responsibility, 2011 c 13, s 122(2)(b)(3); Health
            and Social Care, 2012 c 7, sch 5 para 112(a)
    s 7 appl—Gambling, 2005 c 19, s 232(2)(a)
        am—Police Reform and Social Responsibility, 2011 c 13, s 119(2)
    s 9 appl—Gambling, 2005 c 19, s 232(4)
    s 10 appl (mods)—Gambling, 2005 c 19, s 232(2)(b)(3)

2003

c 17 s 10 *continued*

am—Violent Crime Reduction, 2006 c 38, s 22(1); (prosp) Police Reform and Social
Responsibility, 2011 c 13, s 121(3)(b)

rep in pt—(prosp) Police Reform and Social Responsibility, 2011 c 13, s 121(3)(a);
Deregulation, 2015 c 20, sch 18 para 2

s 11 appl—SI 2005/3468, reg 38(5)(ii)

s 13 am—Fire and Rescue Services, 2004 c 21, s 53, sch 1 para 98(1)(2)(3)(b); SI
2005/1541, art 53(1), sch 2 para 50(1)(2); Policing and Crime, 2009 c 26, s 33(1);
Police Reform and Social Responsibility, 2011 c 13, ss 103(2)(a), 104(3); Health
and Social Care, 2012 c 7, sch 5 para 113(b); SI 2012/1659, sch 3 para 16(2)

rep in pt—Police Reform and Social Responsibility, 2011 c 13, ss 103(2)(b), 105(2);
Health and Social Care, 2012 c 7, sch 5 para 113(a)

s 14 appl—SI 2005/3468, reg 38(5)(iii)

s 16 am—Nat Health Service (Conseq Provns), 2006 c 43, s 2, sch 1 para 236; SI 2010/813,
art 12

rep in pt—Charities, 2011 c 25, sch 7 para 95, sch 10; (prosp) Health and Social Care,
2012 c 7, sch 5 para 114, sch 14 para 88

s 17 am—SI 2009/2999, reg 49; Police Reform and Social Responsibility, 2011 c 13, s
105(3)

rep in pt—SI 2009/2999, reg 49

s 18 am—Police Reform and Social Responsibility, 2011 c 13, ss 105(4), 109(2)

s 19 am—Policing and Crime, 2009 c 26, s 32, sch 4 para 1

s 19A added —Policing and Crime, 2009 c 26, s 32, sch 4 para 2

s 21 am—Violent Crime Reduction, 2006 c 38, s 25

s 22 am—Police Reform and Social Responsibility, 2011 c 13, s 109(3)

s 24 am—Policing and Crime, 2009 c 26, s 112, sch 7 paras 29, 30

s 25 rep in pt—Deregulation, 2015 c 20, s 72(a)

s 25A added—SI 2009/1724, arts 2, 3

am—Policing and Crime, 2009 c 26, s 112, sch 7 paras 29, 31; Police Reform and
Social Responsibility, 2011 c 13, s 109(4)

s 26 am—Police Reform and Social Responsibility, 2011 c 13, s 120(2)

s 27 am—Mental Capacity, 2005 c 9, s 67(1), sch 6 para 46(1)(2)

rep in pt—Deregulation, 2015 c 20, sch 6 para 2(17)

s 31 am—Police Reform and Social Responsibility, 2011 c 13, ss 105(5); 109(5)

s 34 am—SI 2009/2999, reg 49

s 35 am—Policing and Crime, 2009 c 26, s 112, sch 7 paras 29, 32; Police Reform and
Social Responsibility, 2011 c 13, ss 105(6), 109(6)

s 37 am—SI 2009/2999, reg 49

s 39 am—Police Reform and Social Responsibility, 2011 c 13, s 109(7)

ss 41A-41C added—SI 2009/1772, art 2

s 41B am—Police Reform and Social Responsibility, 2011 c 13, s 105(7)

s 41D added—SI 2009/1724, arts 2, 4

am—Policing and Crime, 2009 c 26, s 112, sch 7 paras 29, 33; Police Reform and
Social Responsibility, 2011 c 13, ss 105(8), 109(8)

s 42 am—SI 2009/2999, reg 49

s 43 appl—Gambling, 2005 c 19, s 283, sch 13 para 20(3)

s 44 am—Police Reform and Social Responsibility, 2011 c 13, s 109(9)

s 47 am—Mental Capacity, 2005 c 9, s 67(1), sch 6 para 46(1)(3)(a); SIs 2009/2999, reg
49; 2010/2452, arts 2, 4

rep in pt—Mental Capacity, 2005 c 9, s 67(1)(2), sch 6 para 46(1)(3)(b), sch 7

s 48 am—SI 2010/2452, arts 2, 4; Police Reform and Social Responsibility, 2011 c 13, s
109(10)

s 51 am—Police Reform and Social Responsibility, 2011 c 13, s 106(2)

s 52 am—Policing and Crime, 2009 c 26, s 112, sch 7 paras 29, 34; Police Reform and
Social Responsibility, 2011 c 13, ss 106(3), 109(11)

s 52A added—SI 2009/1724, arts 2, 5

am—Policing and Crime, 2009 c 26, s 112, sch 7 paras 29, 35

ss 53A-53C added—Violent Crime Reduction, 2006 c 38, s 21

s 53A excl—SI 2007/2502, reg 2

am—Police Reform and Social Responsibility, 2011 c 13, s 106(4)

s 53B am—Police Reform and Social Responsibility, 2011 c 13, s 109(12)

s 53C am—Policing and Crime, 2009 c 26, s 112, sch 7 paras 29, 36; Police Reform and
Social Responsibility, 2011 c 13, ss 106(5), 109(13)

s 55 am—Police Reform and Social Responsibility, 2011 c 13, s 139(2)

2003

c 17 *continued*

s 55A added—Police Reform and Social Responsibility, 2011 c 13, s 120(3)
 appl (mods)—Police Reform and Social Responsibility, 2011 c 13, s 129(6)(a)
s 57 am—Policing and Crime, 2009 c 26, s 112, sch 7 paras 29, 37
s 58 am—Legal Services, 2007 c 29, s 208, sch 21 paras 139, 140
s 64 am—Co-operative and Community Benefit Societies, 2014 c 14, sch 4 para 84
s 65 am—Co-operative and Community Benefit Societies, 2014 c 14, sch 4 para 85
s 69 am—Fire and Rescue Services, 2004 c 21, s 53, sch 1 para 98(1)(2)(3)(c); SI
 2005/1541, art 53(1), sch 2 para 50(1)(2); Policing and Crime, 2009 c 26, s 33(2);
 Police Reform and Social Responsibility, 2011 c 13, ss 103(3)(a), 104(4); Health
 and Social Care, 2012 c 7, sch 5 para 115(b); SI 2012/1659, sch 3 para 16(3)
 rep in pt—Police Reform and Social Responsibility, 2011 c 13, ss 103(3)(b), 107(2);
  Health and Social Care, 2012 c 7, sch 5 para 115(a)
s 71 am—SI 2009/2999, reg 49; Police Reform and Social Responsibility, 2011 c 13, s
 107(3)
 rep in pt—SI 2009/2999, reg 49
s 72 am—Policing and Crime, 2009 c 26, s 112, sch 7 paras 29, 38; Police Reform and
 Social Responsibility, 2011 c 13, ss 107(4), 110(2)
s 73A added —Policing and Crime, 2009 c 26, s 32, sch 4 para 3
s 73B added —Policing and Crime, 2009 c 26, s 32, sch 4 para 4
s 76 am—Police Reform and Social Responsibility, 2011 c 13, s 110(3)
s 78 am—Policing and Crime, 2009 c 26, s 112, sch 7 paras 29, 39
s 79 rep in pt—Deregulation, 2015 c 20, s 72(b)
s 80 am—Police Reform and Social Responsibility, 2011 c 13, s 120(4)
s 84 am—SI 2009/2999, reg 49
s 85 am—Policing and Crime, 2009 c 26, s 112, sch 7 paras 29, 40; Police Reform and
 Social Responsibility, 2011 c 13, ss 107(5), 110(4)
ss 86A-86C added—SI 2009/1772, art 3
s 86B am—Police Reform and Social Responsibility, 2011 c 13, s 107(6)
s 87 am—Police Reform and Social Responsibility, 2011 c 13, s 108(2)(3)
s 88 am—Policing and Crime, 2009 c 26, s 112, sch 7 paras 29, 41; Police Reform and
 Social Responsibility, 2011 c 13, ss 108(4), 110(5)
s 92 am—Police Reform and Social Responsibility, 2011 c 13, s 139(3)
s 92A added—Police Reform and Social Responsibility, 2011 c 13, s 120(5)
 appl (mods)—Police Reform and Social Responsibility, 2011 c 13, s 129(6)(b)
s 94 am—Policing and Crime, 2009 c 26, s 112, sch 7 paras 29, 42
s 95 am—Legal Services, 2007 c 29, s 208, sch 21 paras 139, 141
s 98 am—Police Reform and Social Responsibility, 2011 c 13, ss 113(2), 114(2)
s 99A added—Police Reform and Social Responsibility, 2011 c 13, s 112(2)
s 100 rep in pt—SI 2009/2999, reg 49
 am—Police Reform and Social Responsibility, 2011 c 13, ss 114(3), 115(2)
s 100A added—Police Reform and Social Responsibility, 2011 c 13, s 114(4)
s 101 am—Civil Partnership, 2004 c 33, s 261(1), sch 27 para 170
s 102 am—Police Reform and Social Responsibility, 2011 c 13, ss 114(5), 116(1)(a)
 rep in pt—Police Reform and Social Responsibility, 2011 c 13, s 116(1)(b)
s 104 am—SIs 2009/2999, reg 49; 2010/2452, arts 3, 4; Police Reform and Social
 Responsibility, 2011 c 13, ss 112(3)-(7), 114(6)(b), 117(1)
 rep in pt—Police Reform and Social Responsibility, 2011 c 13, ss 112(8), 114(6)(a)
s 104A added—Police Reform and Social Responsibility, 2011 c 13, s 114(7)
s 105 rep in pt—Police Reform and Social Responsibility, 2011 c 13, ss 112(9)(a),
 114(8)(c)
 am—Police Reform and Social Responsibility, 2011 c 13, ss 111(2), 112(9)(b)-(e),
 114(8)
s 106 rep in pt—Police Reform and Social Responsibility, 2011 c 13, s 112(10)(a)
 am—Police Reform and Social Responsibility, 2011 c 13, ss 112(10)(b)-(e), 114(9)
s 106A added—Police Reform and Social Responsibility, 2011 c 13, s 113(3)
s 107 am—Police Reform and Social Responsibility, 2011 c 13, ss 112(11), 114(10),
 115(3); Deregulation, 2015 c 20, s 68(1)
s 109 am—Police Reform and Social Responsibility, 2011 c 13, s 113(4)
s 110 am—Police Reform and Social Responsibility, 2011 c 13, s 113(5); Deregulation,
 2015 c 20, s 72(c)
Pt 5A (ss 110A-110N) added—Deregulation, 2015 c 20, sch 17
s 115 am—Deregulation, 2015 c 20, s 69(1)
 rep in pt—Deregulation, 2015 c 20, sch 18 para 3

2003

c 17 *continued*

s 117 rep in pt—Deregulation, 2015 c 20, sch 18 para 4(1)-(3)(5)
    am—Deregulation, 2015 c 20, sch 18 para 4(4)
s 119 rep—Deregulation, 2015 c 20, sch 18 para 5
s 120 am—Police Reform and Social Responsibility, 2011 c 13, s 111(3)
s 121 rep—Deregulation, 2015 c 20, sch 18 para 6
s 122 rep in pt—Deregulation, 2015 c 20, sch 18 para 8
s 123 rep in pt—Deregulation, 2015 c 20, sch 18 para 9
s 124 am—Police Reform and Social Responsibility, 2011 c 13, s 111(5)
s 126 rep in pt—Deregulation, 2015 c 20, s 72(d)
s 128 rep in pt—Deregulation, 2015 c 20, sch 18 para 10
s 130 am—Constitutional Reform, 2005 c 4, s 40(4), sch 9 pt 1 para 78
s 134 rep in pt—Deregulation, 2015 c 20, sch 18 para 11
s 136 am—Deregulation, 2015 c 20, s 67(3); SI 2015/664, sch 4 para 33(2)
s 137 am—SI 2015/664, sch 4 para 33(3)
s 140 am—Deregulation, 2015 c 20, s 67(4)
s 141 am—Deregulation, 2015 c 20, s 67(5)
s 143 am—Deregulation, 2015 c 20, s 67(6)
s 144 am—Deregulation, 2015 c 20, s 67(7)
s 147A added—Violent Crime Reduction, 2006 c 38, s 23(1)
    am—Policing and Crime, 2009 c 26, s 28; Police Reform and Social Responsibility,
        2011 c 13, s 118(2); Deregulation, 2015 c 20, s 67(8); SI 2015/664, sch 4 para
        33(4)
s 147B added—Violent Crime Reduction, 2006 c 38, s 23(1)
s 148 rep—Deregulation, 2015 c 20, s 70
s 153 am—Deregulation, 2015 c 20, s 67(9)
s 155 rep in pt—Policing and Crime, 2009 c 26, s 112, sch 8 pt 3; Anti-social Behaviour,
        Crime and Policing, 2014 c 12, sch 11 para 50
s 156 am—SI 2015/664, sch 4 para 33(5)
s 157 am—SIs 2005/886, art 2, sch para 89; 2015/664, sch 4 para 33(6)
s 158 rep in pt—Deregulation, 2015 c 20, sch 18 para 12
s 159 am—Deregulation, 2015 c 20, s 67(10)
s 160 am—SI 2005/886, art 2, sch para 90
ss 161-166 rep—Anti-social Behaviour, Crime and Policing, 2014 c 12, sch 11 para 34
s 167 am—Policing and Crime, 2009 c 26, s 112, sch 7 paras 29, 43; Police Reform and
        Social Responsibility, 2011 c 13, ss 106(6), 111(6); Anti-social Behaviour,
        Crime and Policing, 2014 c 12, sch 11 para 35
s 168 am—Anti-social Behaviour, Crime and Policing, 2014 c 12, sch 11 para 36; SI
        2015/664, sch 4 para 33(9)
s 169 rep—Anti-social Behaviour, Crime and Policing, 2014 c 12, sch 11 para 37
s 169A added—Violent Crime Reduction, 2006 c 38, s 24(1)
    am—Police Reform and Social Responsibility, 2011 c 13, s 118(3)
s 169B added—Violent Crime Reduction, 2006 c 38, s 24(1)
s 170 am—Violent Crime Reduction, 2006 c 38, s 24(2)-(4); Police Reform and Social
        Responsibility, 2011 c 13, sch 16 para 315
    rep in pt—Anti-social Behaviour, Crime and Policing, 2014 c 12, sch 11 para 38
s 171 am—SI 2005/886, art 2, sch para 92; Violent Crime Reduction, 2006 c 38, s 24(5);
        Anti-social Behaviour, Crime and Policing, 2014 c 12, sch 11 para 39(2)
    rep in pt—Anti-social Behaviour, Crime and Policing, 2014 c 12, sch 11 para 39(3)(4)
ss 172A-172E added —Crime and Security, 2010 c 17, s 55(2) (amending provn never in
        force)
    subst—Police Reform and Social Responsibility, 2011 c 13, s 119(3)
s 172B am—Health and Social Care, 2012 c 7, sch 5 para 116(b)
    rep in pt—Health and Social Care, 2012 c 7, sch 5 para 116(a)
s 175 subst—Gambling, 2005 c 19, s 356(1)(2), sch 16 pt 2 para 20(1)(2)
s 177 am—Fire and Rescue Services, 2004 c 21, s 53, sch 1 para 98(1)(2)(3)(d); Police
        Reform and Social Responsibility, 2011 c 13, s 109(14); Live Music, 2012 c 2, s
        1(1)(a)(d)(i)
    rep in pt—SI 2005/1541, art 53(1), sch 2 para 50(1)(3); Live Music, 2012 c 2, s
        1(1)(b)(c)(d)(ii)(iii)(e)
s 177A added—Live Music, 2012 c 2, s 1(2)
    am—SI 2014/3253, art 2
s 186 am—Violent Crime Reduction, 2006 c 38, s 23(2)
s 191 appl—SI 2005/3468, reg 38(5)(i)(iv)

2003

c 17 s 191 *continued*

am—SI 2006/2407, reg 44, sch 9

s 192 appl—SI 2005/3468, reg 38(5)(i)(iv)

s 193 am—SIs 2009/1724, arts 2, 6; 2009/2999, reg 49

s 194 am—SIs 2009/1724, arts 2, 6; 2009/2999, reg 49; Police Reform and Social
Responsibility, 2011 c 13, ss 112(12), 114(11); Deregulation, 2015 c 20, s
67(11)

rep in pt—Police Reform and Social Responsibility, 2011 c 13, ss 105(9), 107(7)

s 195 mod—SI 2007/1118, art 6

s 197 am—Violent Crime Reduction, 2006 c 38, s 23(30); Policing and Crime, 2009 c 26, s
112, sch 7 paras 29, 44; Deregulation, 2015 c 20, s 67(12)

ss 197A, 197B added (prosp)—Police Reform and Social Responsibility, 2011 c 13, s
121(2)

sch 1 am—Gambling, 2005 c 19, s 356(1)(2), sch 16 pt 2 para 20(1)(3); Policing and Crime,
2009 c 26, s 112, sch 7 para 23; Live Music, 2012 c 2, ss 2(2)(4)(5) (8)(9), 3;
SIs 2013/1578, arts 2-4; 2014/3253, arts 3, 4; Deregulation, 2015 c 20, s 76

appl—SI 2005/1541, art 37(11)(a)

rep in pt—Live Music, 2012 c 2, s 2(3)(6)(7)(10)-(15)

sch 2 am—Charities, 2006 c 50, s 75, sch 8 para 199; Charities, 2011 c 25, sch 7 para 96;
Deregulation, 2015 c 20, s 71

sch 3 am—Anti-social Behaviour, Crime and Policing, 2014 c 12, sch 11 para 40

rep in pt—Deregulation, 2015 c 20, sch 18 para 13

sch 4 am—SI 2005/2366, art 2; Gambling, 2005 c 19, s 356(1)(2), sch 16 pt 2 para
20(1)(4); Fraud, 2006 c 35, s 14, sch 1 para 34; SIs 2007/2075, art 2;
2008/1277, reg 30, sch 2; Police Reform and Social Responsibility, 2011 c 13, s
123

sch 5 am—SI 2005/886, art 2, sch para 93(a)(b)(c)(ii); Violent Crime Reduction, 2006 c 38,
s 22(2); Police Reform and Social Responsibility, 2011 c 13, ss 112(13)(a)(b)(d),
114(12)

rep in pt—SI 2005/886, art 2, sch para 93(c)(i)(d); Police Reform and Social
Responsibility, 2011 c 13, s 112(13)(c); Deregulation, 2015 c 20, sch 18 para
14

sch 6 rep in pt—(EW) (pt prosp) Crim Justice, 2003 c 44, s 332, sch 37 pt 11; Gambling,
2005 c 19, s 356(4)(5), sch 17; (S) Licensing (S), 2005 asp 16, s 149, sch 7;
Serious Organised Crime and Police, 2005 c 15, s 174(2), sch 17 pt 2; (prosp)
Violent Crime Reduction, 2006 c 38, s 65, sch 5; Finance, 2006 c 25, s 178,
sch 26; SL(R), 2008 c 12, s 1(1), sch 1 pt 3; Anti-social Behaviour, Crime and
Policing, 2014 c 12, sch 11 para 50

sch 8 am—SI 2005/886, art 2, sch para 94

c 18 **Sunday Working (Scotland)**

c 19 **Aviation (Offences)**

s 1 rep in pt—Serious Organised Crime and Police, 2005 c 15, s 174(2), sch 17 pt 2

c 20 **Railways and Transport Safety**

appl—SIs 2005/1918, art 44(3)(b); 2005/3523, art 46(3)(b)

s 1 rep in pt—Deregulation, 2015 c 20, s 54(3)

s 14 rep in pt—Deregulation, 2015 c 20, s 54(2)

Pt 2 (ss 15-17) am—SI 2015/1682, sch pt 1 para 2(a)

s 15 am—SI 2015/1682, sch pt 1 para 2(b)

s 15A added—Infrastructure, 2015 c 7, s 10(9)

s 19 am—Police and Justice, 2006 c 48, s 52, sch 14 para 47(a)

rep in pt—Police and Justice, 2006 c 48, s 52, sch 14 para 47(b), sch 15

s 24 am—Policing and Crime, 2009 c 26, s 112, sch 7 paras 8, 9; SI 2013/602, sch 2 para
41(2)

s 25 am—Police Reform and Social Responsibility, 2011 c 13, sch 16 para 323; SI
2013/602, sch 2 para 41(3)

s 27 am—Policing and Crime, 2009 c 26, s 112, sch 7 paras 8, 10

s 28 am—Police and Justice, 2006 c 48, s 52, sch 14 para 28; Police Reform and Social
Responsibility, 2011 c 13, sch 13 para 6, sch 16 para 324

s 36 am—Crim Justice and Immigration, 2008 c 4, s 126, sch 22 para 17, 18

s 37 am—Crim Justice and Immigration, 2008 c 4, s 126, sch 22 paras 17, 19

s 42 am—Crim Justice and Immigration, 2008 c 4, s 126, sch 22 paras 17, 20

s 43 rep—Crim Justice and Immigration, 2008 c 4, ss 126, 149, sch 22 paras 17, 20, sch 28
pt 8

s 45 rep in pt—Police Reform and Social Responsibility, 2011 c 13, sch 16 para 325

2003
c 20 *continued*
s 50 am—Police and Justice, 2006 c 48, s 52, sch 14 para 49
   rep in pt—Police Reform and Social Responsibility, 2011 c 13, sch 16 para 326(b)
s 52 am—Police and Justice, 2006 c 48, s 52, sch 14 para 50
s 54 am—Loc Govt and Public Involvement in Health, 2007 c 28, s 144, sch 8
s 55 am—Police and Justice, 2006 c 48, s 52, sch 14 para 51
   rep in pt—Police Reform and Social Responsibility, 2011 c 13, sch 16 para 327(b)
s 62 rep in pt —Railways, 2005 c 14, s 59, sch 13 pt 1
   am—SI 2015/1682, sch pt 1 para 2(c)
s 63 am—SI 2013/602, sch 2 para 41(4)
s 64 am—SI 2013/602, sch 2 para 41(5)
s 67 am—SI 2013/602, sch 2 para 41(6)
s 69 rep in pt—Road Safety, 2006 c 49, s 59, sch 7
s 73 rep in pt—Railways, 2005 c 14, s 59, sch 13 pt 1
ss 75, 76 rep in pt—Police and Justice, 2006 c 48, s 52, sch 15
s 81 am—SI 2015/1730, reg 2
s 83 am—Deregulation, 2015 c 20, sch 11 para 14(2)-(8)
s 90 am—Armed Forces, 2006 c 52, s 378, sch 16 para 198
s 96 am—Deregulation, 2015 c 20, sch 11 para 16(2)-(5),(6)(a),(7)(8)
s 96 rep in pt—Deregulation, 2015 c 20, sch 11 para 16(6)(b)
s 101 am—Armed Forces, 2006 c 52, s 378, sch 16 para 199
s 104 rep—Railways, 2005 c 14, s 59, sch 13 pt 1
s 109 rep —Road Safety, 2006 c 49, s 59, sch 7
sch 1 am—SI 2012/2404, sch 2 para 48(2); Enterprise and Regulatory Reform, 2013 c 24,
      sch 15 para 41
sch 2 rep in pt—Railways, 2005 c 14, s 59, sch 13 pt 1; Postal Services, 2011 c 5, sch 12
      para 169; SI 2015/1682, sch pt 1 para 2(d)
sch 3 rep in pt—SIs 2005/3049, reg 2(4), sch 1 pt 1 para 7; 2015/1682, sch pt 1 para 2(e)
sch 4 rep in pt—Railways, 2005 c 14, s 59, sch 13 pt 1
   am—SI 2005/913, art 3(2)-(4); Police and Justice, 2006 c 48, s 52, sch 14 para 52;
      (prosp) Tribunals, Cts and Enforcement, 2007 c 15, s 106, sch 16 para 14; SI
      2009/1941, art 2, sch 1; Police Reform and Social Responsibility, 2011 c 13, sch
      16 para 328; SI 2012/2404, sch 2 para 48(3); SI 2013/602, sch 2 para 41(7)
sch 5 rep in pt—Protection of Freedoms, 2012 c 9, sch 10 pt 4
c 21 **Communications**
appl—Water Industry, 1991 c 56, s 2(2E); (EW) Anti-social Behaviour, 2003 c 38, s 80(7);
      Pensions, 2004 c 35, s 304(11); (S) Stirling-Alloa-Kincardine Railway and Linked
      Improvements, 2004 asp 10, s 29, sch 9 para 7; (E) SI 2005/927(L), art 49, sch 10
      para 1(6)
mod—SI 2004/1944, art 4, sch pt 2 (as am by 2010/118, art 5; 2015/1000, art 8)
ext in pt (mods)—(Guernsey) SI 2003/3195, arts 1(4), 6, sch 2; (I of Man) SI 2003/3198,
      arts 1(4), 6, sch 2
ext (mods)—(Jersey) SI 2003/3197, arts 1(3)-(5), 6, sch 2; (Guernsey) SI 2013/243, art 5
      sch Pt 2
saved—Wireless Telegraphy, 2006 c 36, s 111(1)(3)(6)(7)
s 3 am—Postal Services, 2011 c 5, sch 12 para 57
s 4 am—SIs 2011/1210, sch 1 para 5; 2012/1809, art 3(1), sch pt 1
s 4A added—SI 2011/1210, sch 1 para 6
s 5 saved—Wireless Telegraphy, 2006 c 36, s 5(5)
   am—SI 2011/1210, sch 1 para 7
s 14 am—Wireless Telegraphy, 2006 c 36, s 123, sch 7 paras 25, 26; Postal Services, 2011
      c 5, sch 12 para 58
s 16 am—Postal Services, 2011 c 5, sch 12 para 59
s 17 am—Consumers, Estate Agents and Redress, 2007 c 17, s 40; SI 2014/631, sch 1 para
      11(2)
s 22 am—Postal Services, 2011 c 5, sch 12 para 60
s 26 am—Postal Services, 2011 c 5, sch 12 para 61(2)(3); SI 2011/1210, sch 1 para 8
s 27 am—Equality, 2010 c 15, s 211, sch 26 para 54 (subst by SI 2010/2279, sch 1)
Pt 2, Ch 1 (ss 32-151) appl—SI 2004/945, art 3(2)
s 32 appl—SI 2003/1901, reg 4(1); Fire and Rescue Services, 2004 c 21, s 48(1)(a);
      Housing, 2004 c 34, s 248(4); Civil Contingencies, 2004 c 36, ss 1-18, sch 1 pt
      3 para 22(2)(a)(b), pt 4 para 33(2)(a)(b); (EW) SI 2005/1541, art 48(7)(a); SI
      2005/2024, reg 4(4)-(6)
   am—SI 2011/1210, sch 1 para 9

2003
c 21 *continued*

s 35 am—SI 2011/1210, sch 1 para 10(a)
  rep in pt—SI 2011/1210, sch 1 para 10(b)
s 35A added—SI 2011/1210, sch 1 para 11
s 36 am—SI 2011/1210, sch 1 para 12
s 37 rep—SI 2011/1210, sch 1 para 13
s 38 rep in pt—SI 2011/1210, sch 1 para 14
s 40 am—SI 2011/1210, sch 1 para 15(a)
  rep in pt—SI 2011/1210, sch 1 para 15(b)
s 41 rep in pt—SI 2011/1210, sch 1 para 16(a)
  am—SI 2011/1210, sch 1 para 16(b)
s 42 am—SI 2011/1210, sch 1 para 17
s 43 am—SI 2011/1210, sch 1 para 18
s 45 am—SI 2011/1210, sch 1 para 19
s 46 am—SI 2011/1210, sch 1 para 20
s 47 am—SI 2011/1210, sch 1 para 21
s 48 am—SI 2011/1210, sch 1 para 22
  rep in pt—SI 2011/1210, sch 1 para 22(c)
ss 48A-48C added—SI 2011/1210, sch 1 para 23
s 49 am—SI 2011/1210, sch 1 para 24
ss 49A-49C added—SI 2011/1210, sch 1 para 25
s 50 rep—SI 2011/1210, sch 1 para 26
s 51 am—SI 2011/1210, sch 1 para 27
s 52 am—SI 2011/1210, sch 1 para 28
s 54 am—SI 2011/1210, sch 1 para 29
s 56 appl—SI 2003/2426, reg 18(8)
  am—SI 2011/1210, sch 1 para 30
s 56A added—SI 2011/1210, sch 1 para 31
s 58 am—SI 2011/1210, sch 1 para 32
s 61 am—SI 2011/1210, sch 1 para 33
s 64 am—SI 2011/1210, sch 1 para 34
s 65 am—SI 2011/1210, sch 1 para 35
s 67 am—SIs 2008/948, art 3, sch 1; 2011/1210, sch 1 para 36
s 68 am—SI 2011/1210, sch 1 para 37
s 73 am—SI 2011/1210, sch 1 para 38
  rep in pt—SI 2011/1210, sch 1 para 38(d)
s 74 am—SI 2011/1210, sch 1 para 39
s 75 rep in pt—SI 2011/1210, sch 1 para 40
s 76A added—SI 2011/1210, sch 1 para 41
s 77 am—SIs 2008/948, art 3, sch 1; 2012/1809, art 3(1), sch pt 1
s 80 am—SI 2011/1210, sch 1 para 42
ss 80A, 80B added—SI 2011/1210, sch 1 para 43
s 81 subst—SI 2011/1210, sch 1 para 44
s 82 rep—SI 2011/1210, sch 1 para 45
s 84 am—SI 2011/1210, sch 1 para 46(a)
  rep in pt—SI 2011/1210, sch 1 para 46(b)
s 84A added—SI 2011/1210, sch 1 para 47
s 85 am—SI 2011/1210, sch 1 para 48
s 87 am—SI 2011/1210, sch 1 para 49
ss 89A-89C added—SI 2011/1210, sch 1 para 50
s 90 rep—SI 2011/1210, sch 1 para 51
s 91 am—SIs 2008/948, art 3, sch 1; 2011/1210, sch 1 para 52(a)
  rep in pt—SI 2011/1210, sch 1 para 52(b)
s 92 rep—SI 2011/1210, sch 1 para 53
s 94 appl (mods)—SI 2000/730, reg 18(5)
  am—SI 2011/1210, sch 1 para 54; Enterprise and Regulatory Reform, 2013 c 24, sch
   14 para 17
s 95 appl (mods)—SI 2000/730, reg 18(5)
s 96 appl (mods)—SI 2000/730, reg 18(5)
ss 96A-96C added—SI 2011/1210, sch 1 para 55
s 96A am—Enterprise and Regulatory Reform, 2013 c 24, sch 14 para 18
s 97 appl (mods)—SI 2000/730, reg 18(5)
  am—SI 2011/1210, sch 1 para 56
  rep in pt—SI 2011/1210, sch 1 para 56(f)

2003
c 21 *continued*

s 98 am—SI 2011/1210, sch 1 para 57(a)
  rep in pt—SI 2011/1210, sch 1 para 57(b)(c)
s 99 am—SI 2011/1210, sch 1 para 58
s 100 am—SI 2011/1210, sch 1 para 59
s 100A added—SI 2011/1210, sch 1 para 60
s 102 am—SI 2011/1210, sch 1 para 61
s 103 am—SI 2011/1210, sch 1 para 62
s 104 am—SI 2011/1210, sch 1 para 63
s 105 rep—SI 2011/1210, sch 1 para 64
ss 105A-105D added—SI 2011/1210, sch 1 para 65
s 107 am—SI 2011/1210, sch 1 para 66
s 109 am—SI 2011/1210, sch 1 para 67; Growth and Infrastructure, 2013 c 27, s 9(1)(2)
  mod—Growth and Infrastructure, 2013 c 27, s 9(4)
s 110 am—SI 2011/1210, sch 1 para 68(a)(b)
  rep in pt—SI 2011/1210, sch 1 para 68(c)
s 110A added—SI 2011/1210, sch 1 para 69
s 111 am—SI 2011/1210, sch 1 para 70
ss 111A, 111B added—SI 2011/1210, sch 1 para 71
s 112 rep—SI 2011/1210, sch 1 para 72
s 113 am—SI 2011/1210, sch 1 para 73
s 114 am—SI 2011/1210, sch 1 para 74
s 115 am—SI 2011/1210, sch 1 para 75
s 119 am—Legal Aid, Sentencing and Punishment of Offenders, 2012 c 10, sch 5 para 61
s 120 am—SI 2011/1210, sch 1 para 76(a); Consumer Rights, 2015 c 15, s 80(1)
  rep in pt—SI 2011/1210, sch 1 para 76(b)
s 120A added—SI 2011/1210, sch 1 para 77
s 121 am—Consumer Rights, 2015 c 15, s 80(2)
s 123 am—SI 2005/3469, art 2; Consumer Rights, 2015 c 15, s 80(3)-(5)
s 124A added—Digital Economy, 2010 c 24, s 3
s 124B added—Digital Economy, 2010 c 24, s 4
s 124C added—Digital Economy, 2010 c 24, s 5
s 124D added—Digital Economy, 2010 c 24, s 6
s 124E added—Digital Economy, 2010 c 24, s 7
s 124F added—Digital Economy, 2010 c 24, s 8
s 124G added—Digital Economy, 2010 c 24, s 9
s 124H added—Digital Economy, 2010 c 24, s 10
s 124I added—Digital Economy, 2010 c 24, s 11
s 124J added—Digital Economy, 2010 c 24, s 12
s 124K added—Digital Economy, 2010 c 24, s 13
s 124L added—Digital Economy, 2010 c 24, s 14
s 124M added—Digital Economy, 2010 c 24, s 15
s 124N added—Digital Economy, 2010 c 24, s 16(1)
s 124O added (prosp)—Digital Economy, 2010 c 24, s 19
s 124P added (prosp)—Digital Economy, 2010 c 24, s 20(1)
s 124Q added (prosp)—Digital Economy, 2010 c 24, s 20(1)
  am—Crime and Cts, 2013 c 22, sch 9 para 52
s 124R added (prosp)—Digital Economy, 2010 c 24, s 21
s 125 rep in pt—SI 2003/2498, reg 2(2), sch 2
s 127 am—Crim Justice and Cts, 2015 c 2, s 51(1)
s 130 am—SIs 2006/1032, art 2; 2010/2291, art 2
ss 134A-134C added—Digital Economy, 2010 c 24, s 1(1)
s 135 am—Digital Economy, 2010 c 24, ss 1(2), 16(2); SI 2011/1210, sch 1 para
  79(a)(ii)(b)
  rep in pt—SI 2011/1210, sch 1 para 79(a)(i)
s 137 am—SI 2011/1210, sch 1 para 80
s 138 am—SI 2011/1210, sch 1 para 81(a)(c)
  rep in pt—SI 2011/1210, sch 1 para 81(b)
s 139 am—SIs 2011/1210, sch 1 para 82, 1773, art 2(1)
  rep in pt—SI 2011/1210, sch 1 para 82(c)(g)
ss 139A-139C added—SI 2011/1210, sch 1 para 83
s 140 am—SI 2011/1210, sch 1 para 84
s 142 am—SI 2011/1210, sch 1 para 85

2003
c 21 *continued*

s 143 am—SI 2011/1210, sch 1 para 86
s 144 am—SI 2011/1210, sch 1 para 87
s 146A added—SI 2011/1210, sch 1 para 88
s 150A added—SI 2011/1210, sch 1 para 89
s 151 appl—Civil Contingencies, 2004 c 36, ss 1-18, sch 1 pt 3 para 22(2)(b), pt 4 para
    33(2)(b); SIs 2004/757, art 41, sch 12 para 1(6); (W) 3054 (W 263)(L), art 30,
    sch 4 para 1(6); 2005/8(L), art 13, sch 2 para 6; 120, arts 11(7), 40(5), 64, sch
    11 para 1(6); 2222, arts 46, 47, sch 10 pt 4 para 45(2), sch 11 para 1(6)
    am—SI 2011/1210, sch 1 para 90
ss 152-180 rep—Wireless Telegraphy, 2006 c 36, s 125, sch 9
s 181 rep—Wireless Telegraphy, 2006 c 36, s 125, sch 9
ss 182-184 rep—Wireless Telegraphy, 2006 c 36, s 125, sch 9
s 185 rep in pt—SI 2011/1210, sch 1 para 91(a)
    am—SI 2011/1210, sch 1 para 91(b)-(d)
s 185A added—SI 2011/1210, sch 1 para 92
s 186 am—SI 2011/1210, sch 1 para 93
s 189 am—SI 2011/1210, sch 1 para 94
s 190 am—Wireless Telegraphy, 2006 c 36, s 123, sch 7 paras 25, 27; SI 2011/1210, sch 1
    para 95(a)-(c)
    rep in pt—SI 2011/1210, sch 1 para 95(d)
s 191 rep in pt—SI 2011/1210, sch 1 para 96
s 192 am—Wireless Telegraphy, 2006 c 36, s 123, sch 7 paras 25, 28; (prosp) Digital
    Economy, 2010 c 24, s 20(2); Enterprise and Regulatory Reform, 2013 c 24, sch
    15 para 43
Pt III (ss 198-362) am—Digital Economy, 2010 c 24, s 22(4)
    appl in pt—SI 2012/292, art 4, sch pt 2
s 193 am—Enterprise and Regulatory Reform, 2013 c 24, sch 6 para 98; ibid, sch 15 para
    44
s 193A added—Enterprise and Regulatory Reform, 2013 c 24, s 54
s 194 rep—Enterprise and Regulatory Reform, 2013 c 24, sch 6 para 99
s 195 am—Enterprise and Regulatory Reform, 2013 c 24, sch 15 para 45
s 197 am—Enterprise and Regulatory Reform, 2013 c 24, sch 6 para 100
s 198 am—SI 2009/2979, reg 3
s 198A added—Digital Economy, 2010 c 24, s 22(1)
ss 198B-D added—Digital Economy, 2010 c 24, s 23(1)
s 199 am—Digital Economy, 2010 c 24, s 22(2)
s 204 am—SI 2009/1968, art 2
s 211 am—SI 2009/2979, reg 8
s 214 am—Digital Economy, 2010 c 24, s 26(2)
s 216 am—Digital Economy, 2010 c 24, ss 24(2)-(6), 26(2)
s 216A added—Digital Economy, 2010 c 24, s 24(7)
s 217 am—Digital Economy, 2010 c 24, s 24(8)
s 218 am—(prosp) Digital Economy, 2010 c 24, s 28(2)(3)(a)(4)
    rep in pt—(prosp) Digital Economy, 2010 c 24, ss 28(3)(b), 45, sch 2
s 218A added—Digital Economy, 2010 c 24, s 27
s 219 am—Digital Economy, 2010 c 24, s 26(3)
s 221 rep (prosp)—Digital Economy, 2010 c 24, ss 28(5), 45, sch 2
s 222 am—Digital Economy, 2010 c 24, s 26(3)
s 224 am—Digital Economy, 2010 c 24, s 25(1)-(3)
    rep in pt—Digital Economy, 2010 c 24, s 45, sch 2, s 25(4)
s 225 am—Digital Economy, 2010 c 24, s 26(4)
s 228 am—Digital Economy, 2010 c 24, s 26(5)
s 229 am—Digital Economy, 2010 c 24, s 26(6)-(12)
s 230 am—Digital Economy, 2010 c 24, s 26(13)-(18)
s 232 am—SIs 2006/2131, art 2; 2009/2979, reg 6
s 233 am—SI 2006/2131, art 2
    rep in pt—SI 2009/2979, reg 6
s 235 am—SI 2006/2131, art 3
Pt 3, Ch 3 (ss 245-262) mod —SI 2004/1944, sch para 10A (added by 2010/118, art 5, with
    2015/1000, para 8)
s 245 mod—SI 2004/1944, sch para 10
s 263 am—Digital Economy, 2010 c 24, s 37
s 264A added—Digital Economy, 2010 c 24, s 2

2003

c 21 *continued*

s 271A added—Digital Economy, 2010 c 24, s 23(2)

s 276 am—(prosp) Digital Economy, 2010 c 24, s 28(6)

s 281 am—SI 2003/3299, art 13(1)

s 310 am—SI 2011/3003, art 2

s 314 am—Digital Economy, 2010 c 24, s 34(2)(4)-(6)

   rep in pt—Digital Economy, 2010 c 24, s 45, sch 2, s 34(2)(3)

s 319 am—SI 2010/831, reg 2

s 321 am—SI 2010/831, reg 3

   rep in pt—SI 2010/831, reg 3

s 324 am—SI 2010/831, reg 4

s 325 am—SI 2010/831, reg 5

   rep in pt—SI 2010/831, reg 5

s 329 am—SI 2009/2979, reg 8

s 335A added—SI 2009/2979, reg 7

   am—SI 2010/1883, reg 4

s 337 am—Equality, 2010 c 15, s 211, sch 26 para 55 (subst by SI 2010/2279, sch 1)

s 341 am—SI 2009/2979, reg 5

s 343 am—SI 2013/1126, art 2(2)(3)

s 361 am—SI 2009/2979, reg 9

   rep in pt—SI 2009/2979, reg 9

s 362 am—(prosp) Digital Economy, 2010 c 24, s 28(7); SIs 2010/831, reg 6; 2013/2217,
   reg 7

s 363 ext (mods)—(Guernsey) SI 2004/307, arts 4, 5, sch para 1; (Jersey) SI 2004/308,
   arts 4, 5, sch 1 para 1

   mod—SI 2007/1118, art 7

s 364 ext (mods)—(Guernsey) SI 2004/307, arts 4, 5, sch para 2; (Jersey) SI 2004/308,
   arts 4, 5, sch 1 para 2

   am—Wireless Telegraphy, 2006 c 36, s 123, sch 7 paras 25, 29

s 365 ext (mods)—(Guernsey) SI 2004/307, arts 4, 5, sch para 3; (Jersey) SI 2004/308,
   arts 4, 5, sch 1 para 3

s 366 ext (mods)—(Guernsey) SI 2004/307, arts 4, 5, sch para 4; (Jersey) SI 2004/308,
   arts 4, 5, sch 1 para 4

   am—Wireless Telegraphy, 2006 c 36, s 123, sch 7 paras 25, 30

s 367 rep—Enterprise and Regulatory Reform, 2013 c 24, sch 21 para 2

s 368 ext (mods)—(Guernsey) SI 2004/307, arts 4, 5; (Jersey) SI 2004/308, arts 4, 5

Pt 4A (ss 368A-368R) added—SI 2009/2979, reg 2

s 368B am—SIs 2010/419, regs 2, 3; 2014/2916, regs 2, 3

s 368BA added—SI 2010/419, regs 2, 4, 13

s 368BB added—SI 2010/419, regs 2, 4

s 368D am—SI 2010/419, regs 2, 5

s 368G am—SI 2010/419, regs 2, 6

s 368H am—SI 2010/831, reg 7

s 368J am—SI 2010/419, regs 2, 7

s 368K am—SI 2010/419, regs 2, 8

s 368NA added—SI 2010/419, regs 2, 9, 13

s 368O am—SI 2010/419, regs 2, 10

s 368P am—SI 2010/419, regs 2, 11

   rep in pt—SI 2010/419, regs 2, 11

s 368Q am—SI 2010/419, regs 2, 12

s 368R am—SIs 2010/831, reg 8; 2012/1916, sch 34 para 44

s 369 am—Postal Services, 2011 c 5, sch 12 para 62

s 370 am—Postal Services, 2011 c 5, sch 12 para 63; SI 2014/892, sch 1 para 161

s 371 am—SI 2004/1261, reg 5, sch 2 para 11; Postal Services, 2011 c 5, sch 12 para 64; SI
   2012/1809, art 3(1), sch pt 1; Enterprise and Regulatory Reform, 2013 c 24, sch
   15 para 46; SI 2014/892, sch 1 para 162

s 388 rep—SI 2014/892, sch 1 para 163

s 393 am—Wireless Telegraphy, 2006 c 36, s 123, sch 7 paras 25, 31; SIs 2008/1277, reg
   30, sch 2; 2011/1210, sch 1 para 97; 2014/892, sch 1 para 164(1)(a)(i)(b)(c)

   rep in pt—Wireless Telegraphy, 2006 c 36, s 125, sch 9; Enterprise and Regulatory
   Reform, 2013 c 24, sch 21 para 2; SI 2014/892, sch 1 para 164(1)(a)(ii)

s 394 rep in pt—Wireless Telegraphy, 2006 c 36, s 125, sch 9

   am—Postal Services, 2011 c 5, sch 12 para 65

s 395 am—SI 2011/1210, sch 1 para 98

2003
c 21 *continued*

s 400 am—Wireless Telegraphy, 2006 c 36, s 123, sch 7 paras 25, 32; Digital Economy,
2010 c 24, s 39(3); Postal Services, 2011 c 5, sch 12 para 66
s 401 am—Wireless Telegraphy, 2006 c 36, s 123, sch 7 paras 25, 33
s 402 rep in pt—Childcare, 2006 c 21, s 125, sch 9
am—(prosp) Digital Economy, 2010 c 24, s 20(3)
s 403 appl—Postal Services, 2011 c 5, s 63
s 404 rep in pt—Wireless Telegraphy, 2006 c 36, s 125, sch 9; Enterprise and Regulatory
Reform, 2013 c 24, sch 21 para 2
am—Postal Services, 2011 c 5, sch 12 para 67
s 405 am—Wireless Telegraphy, 2006 c 36, s 123, sch 7 paras 25, 34; SIs 2009/2979, reg
11; 2010/1883, reg 5; Postal Services, 2011 c 5, sch 12 para 68; SI 2011/1210,
sch 1 para 99
s 407 rep—Wireless Telegraphy, 2006 c 36, s 125, sch 9
s 408 appl—SI 2003/2155, art 3(1), sch 1 pt 5 para 45(2)
s 410 am—Energy, 2004 c 20, s 87(5); Wireless Telegraphy, 2006 c 36, s 123, sch 7 paras
25, 35
sch 1 rep in pt—Wireless Telegraphy, 2006 c 36, s 125, sch 9
sch 2 am—SI 2003/2867, reg 2, sch pt 1 para 33
sch 4 appl—SI 2003/3299, art 4(4)
sch 5 rep—Wireless Telegraphy, 2006 c 36, s 125, sch 9
sch 6 rep—Wireless Telegraphy, 2006 c 36, s 125, sch 9
sch 7 rep—Wireless Telegraphy, 2006 c 36, s 125, sch 9
sch 8 am—Wireless Telegraphy, 2006 c 36, s 123, sch 7 paras 25, 36; Digital Economy,
2010 c 24, s 16(3)
rep in pt—Wireless Telegraphy, 2006 c 36, ss 123, 125, sch 7 paras 25, 36, sch 9
sch 9 am—Digital Economy, 2010 c 24, s 22(3)
sch 11 am—SIs 2012/1809, art 3(1), sch pt 1; 2014/892, sch 1 para 165
sch 11A added—SI 2010/831, reg 9
sch 12 am—SIs 2009/2979, regs 3, 4; 2010/419, reg 14; 2010/831, reg 10; Equality, 2010
c 15, s 211, sch 26 para 56 (subst by SI 2010/2279, sch 1)
rep in pt—SI 2010/831, reg 10
excl in pt—SI 2013/242, art 4(3)(c)
sch 14 am—SIs 2003/3299, art 14(1)(2)(4); 2011/1503, arts 6(3)(4), 7, 9
rep in pt—SIs 2003/3299, art 14(1)(3); 2011/1503, arts 3, 6(2), 8
sch 15 rep in pt—(prosp) Digital Economy, 2010 c 24, s 45, sch 2
sch 16 rep in pt—Postal Services, 2011 c 5, sch 12 para 69; Financial Services, 2012 c 21,
sch 19
sch 17 am—SI 2003/2498, reg 2(1), sch 1 pt 2 para 23
rep in pt—Commons, 2006 c 26, s 53, sch 6; Wireless Telegraphy, 2006 c 36, s 125,
sch 9; Armed Forces, 2006 c 52, s 378, sch 17; Finance, 2006 c 25, s 178, sch
26; SI 2006/3336, art 308, sch 13; Housing and Regeneration, 2008 c 17, s
321, sch 16; Taxation (International and Other Provns), 2010 c 8, s 378, sch 10
pt 12; SI 2010/866, art 7, sch 4; Postal Services, 2011 c 5, sch 12 para 70;
Public Bodies, 2011 c 24, sch 6; Scrap Metal Dealers, 2013 c 10, s 19(1)(e);
Enterprise and Regulatory Reform, 2013 c 24, sch 21 para 2
sch 18 saved—SI 2005/281, reg 73(1)(e)
rep in pt—Wireless Telegraphy, 2006 c 36, s 125, sch 9
am—SI 2011/1210, sch 1 para 100
sch 19 rep in pt—Wireless Telegraphy, 2006 c 36, s 125, sch 9

c 22   **Fireworks**
cert functs made exercisable concurrently—(S) SI 2004/2030, arts 4, 7, sch
appl—Police and Criminal Evidence, 1984 c 60, s 1
s 2 am—SI 2008/960, art 22, sch 3
ss 11A, 11B added—(S) Police, Public Order and Crim Justice (S), 2006 asp 10, s 76
s 12 rep in pt—Consumer Rights, 2015 c 15, sch 6 para 82(2)(a)
am—Consumer Rights, 2015 c 15, sch 6 para 82(2)(b)(3)
s 14 am—SI 2014/1638, sch 13 para 7

c 23   **National Lottery (Funding of Endowments)**
s 1 rep in pt—Nat Lottery, 2006 c 23, s 21, sch 3

c 24   **Human Fertilisation and Embryology (Deceased Fathers)**
s 2 rep in pt—Legislative and Regulatory Reform, 2006 c 51, s 30, sch 1
sch rep in pt—(S) Adoption and Children (S), 2007 asp 4, s 120, sch 3; Human Fertilisation
and Embryology, 2008 c 22, s 66, sch 8

2003

c 25   **Northern Ireland (Monitoring Commission etc)**
ss 1-3 rep—NI (Monitoring Commn etc.), 2003 c 25, s 12(3)
s 11 rep—NI (Monitoring Commn etc.), 2003 c 25, s 12(3)

c 26   **Local Government**
Pt 1 (ss 1-24) appl—Humber Bridge, 2013 c vi, s 8(4); (specified ss appl) Police Reform and
Social Responsibility, 2011 c. 13, sch 2 para 7A(4)(7)(8)
appl (mods)—(specified ss appl (mods)) Police Reform and Social Responsibility, 2011
c. 13, sch 4 para 4A(4)(5)
s 11 am—Localism, 2011 c 20, s 174
s 13 excl—SI 2004/533, art 7(8)(9)
s 18 am—(prosp) Loc Govt and Public Involvement in Health, 2007 c 28, s 216, sch 14 para
5(1)(2)
s 21 am—Loc Govt and Public Involvement in Health, 2007 c 28, s 238(2); Localism, 2011
c 20, s 73; Loc Audit and Accountability, 2014 c 2, sch 12 para 50(3)
rep in pt—Loc Audit and Accountability, 2014 c 2, sch 12 para 50(2)
s 22 am—Loc Audit and Accountability, 2014 c 2, sch 12 para 51
s 23 am—Fire and Rescue Services, 2004 c 21, s 53, sch 1 paras 99, 100; Civil
Contingencies, 2004 c 36, s 32(1), sch 2 pt 1 para 10(3)(e); Loc Govt and Public
Involvement in Health, 2007 c 28, s 209, sch 13 para 55(1)(2); Loc Democracy,
Economic Development and Construction, 2009 c 20, s 119, sch 6 para 117(1)(2);
Police Reform and Social Responsibility, 2011 c 13, sch 16 para 317
rep in pt—SI 2005/886, art 2, sch para 96; Deregulation, 2015 c 20, sch 13 para
6(32)(a)
s 24 am—(pt prosp) Loc Govt and Public Involvement in Health, 2007 c 28, ss 216, 238(3),
sch 14 para 5(1)(3); Loc Audit and Accountability, 2014 c 2, sch 12 para 52
s 25 am—Localism, 2011 c 20, sch 7 para 43; Police Reform and Social Responsibility,
2011 c 13, sch 16 para 318
s 26 am—Localism, 2011 c 20, sch 7 para 44
s 27 am—Localism, 2011 c 20, sch 7 para 45
s 28 am—Localism, 2011 c 20, sch 7 para 46
s 33 am—Fire and Rescue Services, 2004 c 21, s 53, sch 1 paras 99, 101; Civil
Contingencies, 2004 c 36, s 32(1), sch 2 pt 1 para 10(3)(e); Loc Govt and Public
Involvement in Health, 2007 c 28, s 209, sch 13 para 55(1)(2); Loc Democracy,
Economic Development and Construction, 2009 c 20, s 119, sch 6 para 117(1)(3);
Police Reform and Social Responsibility, 2011 c 13, s 27(4), sch 16 para 319;
Deregulation, 2015 c 20, sch 13 para 6(32)(b)
rep in pt—SI 2005/886, art 2, sch para 96
ss 34, 35 rep—Loc Govt and Public Involvement in Health, 2007 c 28, s 136, sch 7 para
3(1)(2), sch 18
s 36 am—Loc Govt and Public Involvement in Health, 2007 c 28, s 144, sch 8 para 25(1)(2);
Loc Govt (W), 2009 nawm 2, s 51, sch 1 paras 23, 24
s 36A added—Loc Govt and Public Involvement in Health, 2007 c 28, s 143
am—Loc Govt (W), 2009 nawm 2, s 51, sch 1 paras 23, 25
s 36B added—Loc Govt and Public Involvement in Health, 2007 c 28, s 143
am—Loc Govt (W), 2009 nawm 2, s 51, sch 1 paras 23, 26
Pt 4 (ss 41-59) mod—SI 2004/2443 reg 1A(2) (added by 2013/2265, reg 3(2))
appl (mods)—SI 2014/3204, sch 5 para 1
s 43 appl (mod)—Business Rate Supplements, 2009 c 7, s 16, sch 2 para 9(1)(a)(2)
s 44 appl (mod)—Business Rate Supplements, 2009 c 7, s 16, sch 2 para 9(1)(b)(2)
mod—SI 2014/3204, regs 18(5)(b), 19(3)(b)
s 46 appl (mod)—Business Rate Supplements, 2009 c 7, s 16, sch 2 para 9(1)(c)(2)
mod—SI 2014/3204, regs 18(5)(b), 19(3)(b)
s 47 appl (mod)—Business Rate Supplements, 2009 c 7, s 16, sch 2 para 9(1)(3)
mod—SI 2014/3204, regs 18(5)(b), 19(3)(b)
s 51 appl (mod)—Business Rate Supplements, 2009 c 7, s 16, sch 2 para 9(1)(d)(2)
s 52 appl (mod)—Business Rate Supplements, 2009 c 7, s 16, sch 2 para 9(1)(e)(2)
s 53 appl (mod)—Business Rate Supplements, 2009 c 7, s 16, sch 2 para 9(1)(f)(2)
rep in pt—Deregulation, 2015 c 20, sch 22 para 18
s 54 appl (mod)—Business Rate Supplements, 2009 c 7, s 16, sch 2 para 9(1)(g)(2)
s 61 rep in pt—Localism, 2011 c 20, sch 25 pt 10
s 63 rep in pt—Localism, 2011 c 20, sch 25 pt 10
s 64 rep in pt—Rating (Empty Properties), 2007 c 9, s 2, sch 2; Localism, 2011 c 20, sch 25
pt 10
s 70 rep in pt—(2013-2014) Loc Govt Finance, 2012 c 17, s 5, sch 3 para 33

2003
c 26 *continued*

s 76 rep—Loc Gov Finance, 2012 c 17, sch 4 para 9

s 83 am—(W) SI 2005/2929 (W 214), art 2

s 87 rep (E)—Deregulation, 2015 c 20, s 29(1)

am—Housing, 2004 c 34, s 265(1), sch 15 para 47; Housing (W), 2014 anaw 7, sch 3 para 23(1)(b); Deregulation, 2015 c 20, s 29(2)-(5)

rep in pt—Housing (W), 2014 anaw 7, sch 3 para 23(1)(a)

s 88 am—Deregulation, 2015 c 20, s 29(6)(a)

s 89 rep in pt—(prosp) Localism, 2011 c 20, sch 25 pt 24

s 93 am—Loc Govt and Public Involvement in Health, 2007 c 28, s 136, sch 7 para 3(1)(3); Loc Govt (W), 2009 nawm 2, s 51, sch 1 paras 23, 27; Localism, 2011 c 20, ss 12(4), 14(2)

excl—SIs 2008/2909, art 3; 2009/55 (W 19), art 3; 2015/619, art 4

s 94 am—Loc Govt and Public Involvement in Health, 2007 c 28, s 136, sch 7 para 3(1)(4)

s 95 am—Loc Govt and Public Involvement in Health, 2007 c 28, s 136, sch 7 para 3(1)(5); (prosp) ibid, s 216, sch 14 para 5(1)(4); Loc Govt (W), 2009 nawm 2, s 51, sch 1 paras 23, 28; Localism, 2011 c 20, s 12(5); Police Reform and Social Responsibility, 2011 c 13, sch 16 para 320(b)

rep in pt—(prosp) Loc Govt and Public Involvement in Health, 2007 c 28, s 241, sch 18 pt 16; ibid, sch 18 pt 8; Localism, 2011 c 20, sch 25 pt 32; Police Reform and Social Responsibility, 2011 c 13, sch 16 para 320(a)

s 96 am—Loc Govt and Public Involvement in Health, 2007 c 28, s 136, sch 7 para 3(1)(6); (prosp) ibid, s 216, sch 14 para 5(1)(5)

s 97 am—Loc Govt and Public Involvement in Health, 2007 c 28, s 136, sch 7 para 3(1)(7); Loc Govt and Public Involvement in Health, 2007 c 28, s 141(2); Loc Govt (W), 2009 nawm 2, s 51, sch 1 paras 23, 29

s 98 am—Loc Govt and Public Involvement in Health, 2007 c 28, ss 136, 141(3), 144, sch 7 para 3(1)(8), sch 8 para 25(1)(3)

s 99 rep —Loc Audit and Accountability, 2014 c 2, sch 12 para 53

s 100 ext—Planning (Listed Buildings and Conservation Areas) 1990 c 9, s 93(6B)

am—Traffic Management, 2004 c 18, s 95(4); Children, 2004 c 31, s 17(4); Legislative and Regulatory Reform, 2006 c 51, s 31(2); (prosp) Loc Govt and Public Involvement in Health, 2007 c 28, s 216, sch 14 para 5(1)(6); Loc Audit and Accountability, 2014 c 2, sch 12 para 54(3)

rep in pt—Clean Neighbourhoods and Environment, 2005 c 16, s 107, sch 5 pt 9; Loc Govt and Public Involvement in Health, 2007 c 28, s 241, sch 18; Loc Audit and Accountability, 2014 c 2, sch 12 para 54(2)(4)

s 101 am—Fire and Rescue Services, 2004 c 21, s 53, sch 1 paras 99, 103; Loc Govt and Public Involvement in Health, 2007 c 28, ss 136, 144, sch 7 para 3(1)(9), sch 8 para 25(1)(4); Loc Govt (W), 2009 nawm 2, s 51, sch 1 paras 23, 30

rep in pt—Fire and Rescue Services, 2004 c 21, s 54, sch 2; Loc Govt and Public Involvement in Health, 2007 c 28, s 241, sch 18; Police Reform and Social Responsibility, 2011 c 13, sch 16 para 321

s 102 am—SI 2006/246, reg 20, sch 2; Loc Govt and Public Involvement in Health, 2007 c 28, s 136, sch 7 para 3(1)(10)(11)

rep in pt—Loc Govt and Public Involvement in Health, 2007 c 28, s 241, sch 18

s 105 am—Loc Govt and Public Involvement in Health, 2007 c 28, s 220, sch 16 para 11; Loc Govt Finance, 2012 c 17, sch 4 para 10

ss 107, 108 rep —Loc Audit and Accountability, 2014 c 2, sch 1 pt 2

s 109 rep —Housing and Regeneration, 2008 c 17, s 321, sch 16

s 110 rep —Loc Audit and Accountability, 2014 c 2, sch 1 pt 2

s 111 rep —Loc Audit and Accountability, 2014 c 2, sch 1 pt 2

s 112 rep—Localism, 2011 c 20, sch 25 pt 5

s 115 rep—Localism, 2011 c 20, sch 25 pt 4

s 119 rep—Clean Neighbourhoods and Environment, 2005 c 16, s 107, sch 5 pt 9

s 121 rep—Fire and Rescue Services, 2004 c 21, s 54, sch 2

s 124 rep in pt—Loc Govt and Public Involvement in Health, 2007 c 28, s 220, sch 14 para 12

am—Loc Govt (W), 2009 nawm 2, s 51, sch 1 paras 23, 31

s 129 am—(S) Housing (S), 2010 asp 17, s 157(2)

sch 4 am—Civil Partnership, 2004 c 33, s 261(1), sch 27 para 171; Loc Govt and Public Involvement in Health, 2007 c 28, s 220, sch 16 para 13; SI 2012/2404, sch 2 para 49

2003
c 26 *continued*
    sch 7 rep in pt—Fire and Rescue Services, 2004 c 21, s 54, sch 2; Public Services
        Ombudsman (W), 2005 c 10, s 39(2), sch 7; Educ, 2005 c 18, s 123, sch 19 pt
        4; Council Tax (New Valuations List for E), 2006 c 7, s 1(7); Govt of Wales,
        2006 c 32, s 163, sch 12; Loc Govt and Public Involvement in Health, 2007 c
        28, s 241, sch 18 pt 14; (prosp) ibid, sch 18 pt 17; Localism, 2011 c 20, sch 25
        pts 4, 13, 14; (2013-2014) Loc Govt Finance, 2012 c 17, ss 1(5)(6)(7),
        3(12)(b)(13)(14), 5, sch 3 para 34; (prosp) Welfare Reform, 2012 c 5, sch 14 pt
        1; Loc Audit and Accountability, 2014 c 2, sch 1 pt 2
c 27   **Dealing in Cultural Objects (Offences)**
    s 4 am—Commrs for Revenue and Customs, 2005 c 11, s 50(6), sch 4 para 128(a)(b)(e); SI
        2014/834, sch 2 para 36
    rep in pt—Commrs for Revenue and Customs, 2005 c 11, ss 50(6), 52(2), sch 4 para
        128(c)(d), sch 5
    mod—Serious Crime, 2007 c 27, s 63, sch 6 para 45
c 28   **Legal Deposit Libraries**
    appl—SI 2013/777, reg 13(1)
    s 10 rep in pt—(EW,NI) Coroners and Justice, 2009 c 25, s 178, sch 23 pt 2; (S) Crim
        Justice and Licensing (S), 2010 asp 13, s 203, sch 7 para 72(a)-(f)
    s 12 rep in pt—Nat Library of S, 2012 asp 3, sch 2 para 7(a)(i)(iii)(iv)
      am—Nat Library of S, 2012 asp 3, sch 2 para 7(a)(ii)
    s 14 am—Nat Library of S, 2012 asp 3, sch 2 para 7(b)(i)
      rep in pt—Nat Library of S, 2012 asp 3, sch 2 para 7(b)(ii)
    s 15 rep in pt—Nat Library of S, 2012 asp 3, sch 3
c 29   **Household Waste Recycling**
    sch 5 am—Prevention of Social Housing Fraud, 2013 c 3, sch para 27(a)
c 30   **Sustainable Energy**
    s 1 am—Energy, 2004 c 20, s 81; Climate Change and Sustainable Energy, 2006 c 19, ss
        6(b), 12(2)(b)(3), 22; Energy, 2008 c 32, s 87(1)(a)(d)(e); Energy, 2011 c 16, s
        118(2)
    appl—Energy, 2004 c 20, s 82(9); Climate Change and Sustainable Energy, 2006 c 19, s
        5(2)
    rep in pt—Climate Change and Sustainable Energy, 2006 c 19, ss 6(a), 12(2)(a); Energy,
        2008 c 32, s 87(1)(b)(c), sch 6; Energy, 2011 c 16, s 118(3); Deregulation,
        2015 c 20, s 57(4)(a)
    s 2 saved—Housing, 2004 c 34, s 217(2)
      rep in pt—Energy, 2011 c 16, s 110(3)
    s 4 rep in pt—Energy, 2011 c 16, s 118(4)
    s 7 rep—Deregulation, 2015 c 20, sch 23 para 19
    s 9 rep in pt—Energy, 2011 c 16, s 110(4)
c 31   **Female Genital Mutilation**
    s 3 rep in pt—Serious Crime, 2015 c 9, s 70(1)(a)
    s 3A added—Serious Crime, 2015 c 9, s 72(2)
    s 4 rep in pt—Serious Crime, 2015 c 9, s 70(1)(b)
      am—Serious Crime, 2015 c 9, s 72(3)
    s 4A added—Serious Crime, 2015 c 9, s 71(1)
    s 5 am—Serious Crime, 2015 c 9, s 72(4)
    s 5A added—Serious Crime, 2015 c 9, s 73(1)
    s 5B added—Serious Crime, 2015 c 9, s 74
    s 5C added—Serious Crime, 2015 c 9, s 75(1)
    s 6 am—Serious Crime, 2015 c 9, s 70(1)(c)
    s 8 am—(prosp) Serious Crime, 2015 c 9, sch 4 para 60
    sch 1 added—Serious Crime, 2015 c 9, s 71(2)
    sch 2 added—Serious Crime, 2015 c 9, s 73(2)
c 32   **Crime (International Co-operation)**
    ss 4A, 4B added (prosp)—Crim Justice, 2003 c 44, s 331, sch 36 pt 2 para 16
    s 4A am—Crim Justice and Cts, 2015 c 2, sch 11 para 21
    s 4B am—Crim Justice and Cts, 2015 c 2, sch 11 para 22
    s 8 appl—Criminal Procedure (S), 1995 c 46, s 194IA(4)
    s 9 rep in pt—Crim Justice, 2003 c 44, s 332, sch 37 pt 6; SI 2004/1501, art 46(2)
      appl—Criminal Procedure (S), 1995 c 46, s 194IA(5)
    s 16, am—Serious Organised Crime and Police, 2005 c 15, s 111, sch 7 pt 3 para
        51(1)-(3)(a)(4)

2003
c 32 *continued*

    s 17 am—Serious Organised Crime and Police, 2005 c 15, s 111, sch 7 pt 3 para
        51(1)-(3)(a)(4)
        rep in pt—Serious Organised Crime and Police, 2005 c 15, ss 111, 174(2), sch 7 pt 3
            para 51(1)(3)(b)(4), sch 17 pt 2
    s 18 am—SI 2013/602, sch 2 para 42(2)
    s 27 am—Crim Justice and Immigration, 2008 c 4, s 97(1)
    s 29 rep in pt—SI 2010/976, art 12, sch 14
        am—SI 2010/976, art 12, sch 14
    s 47 am—Armed Forces, 2006 c 52, s 378(1), sch 16 para 237
    s 48 am—Crim Justice and Immigration, 2008 c 4, s 148, sch 26 para 52
    s 50 am—SI 2010/976, art 12, sch 14
    s 51 appl—SIs 1982/1109, rule 30(6); 2005/384, rules 32.1(6), 32.2(2)
        am—SI 2013/602, sch 2 para 42(3)
    Pt 3, Ch 1 (ss 54-75) am—(prosp) Crim Justice and Cts, 2015 c 2, s 31(2)
    s 54 am—(prosp) Coroners and Justice, 2009 c 25, s 177, sch 21 para 93; (prosp) Crim
        Justice and Cts, 2015 c 2, s 31(3); ibid, sch 7 para 2
    s 55 am—(prosp) Crim Justice and Cts, 2015 c 2, sch 7 para 3(2); SI 2015/583, sch 2 para
        6(a)
        excl—(temp)(retrosp to 1.12.2014) Crim Justice and Cts, 2015 c 2, sch 7 para 24(a)
    s 56 am—(prosp) Crim Justice and Cts, 2015 c 2, s 31(4); ibid, sch 7 para 5(2)-(4)(9)(10)
        rep in pt—(prosp) Crim Justice and Cts, 2015 c 2, sch 7 para 5(5)-(8)
    s 57 am—(prosp) Crim Justice and Cts, 2015 c 2, sch 7 para 6
        excl—(temp)(retrosp to 1.12.2014) Crim Justice and Cts, 2015 c 2, sch 7 para 24(b)
    s 58 am—(prosp) Crim Justice and Cts, 2015 c 2, sch 7 para 7
    s 59 rep in pt—SI 2005/886, art 2, sch para 97
    ss 60, 62 am—Constitutional Reform, 2005 c 4, s 40(4), sch 9 pt 1 para 79
    s 63 am—Road Safety, 2006 c 49, s 10, sch 3 para 75; (prosp) Crim Justice and Cts, 2015 c
        2, sch 7 para 8(2)
        rep in pt—Road Safety, 2006 c 49, s 10, sch 3 para 75, sch 7; (prosp) Crim Justice and
            Cts, 2015 c 2, sch 7 para 8(3)
    s 64 am—(prosp) Road Safety, 2006 c 49, s 10, sch 3 para 76; (prosp) Crim Justice and Cts,
        2015 c 2, sch 7 para 9(2)
        rep in pt—(prosp) Road Safety, 2006 c 49, s 10, sch 3 para 76, sch 7; (prosp) Crim
            Justice and Cts, 2015 c 2, sch 7 para 9(3)
    s 65 am—(prosp) Crim Justice and Cts, 2015 c 2, sch 7 para 10
    s 68 am—Road Safety, 2006 c 49, s 10, sch 3 para 77; (prosp) Crim Justice and Cts, 2015 c
        2, sch 7 para 11; SI 2015/583, sch 2 para 6(b)
    s 69 am—(prosp) Road Safety, 2006 c 49, s 10, sch 3 para 78; (prosp) Crim Justice and Cts,
        2015 c 2, sch 7 para 12
    s 70 excl—(temp)(retrosp to 1.12.2014) Crim Justice and Cts, 2015 c 2, sch 7 para 24(c)
    s 71 am—(prosp) Crim Justice and Cts, 2015 c 2, sch 7 para 13
    s 71A added—(prosp) Crim Justice and Cts, 2015 c 2, s 31(5)
    s 72 am—(prosp) Crim Justice and Cts, 2015 c 2, sch 7 para 14
    s 73 am—(prosp) Crim Justice and Cts, 2015 c 2, sch 7 para 15
    s 74 rep in pt—(prosp) Road Safety, 2006 c 49, s 10, sch 3 para 79, sch 7; (prosp) Crim
            Justice and Cts, 2015 c 2, sch 7 para 16(4)(6); SI 2015/583, sch 2 para 6(c)
        am—(prosp) Crim Justice and Cts, 2015 c 2, sch 7 paras 16(2)(3)(5)(7), 17, 18
    s 84 am—SI 2013/602, sch 2 para 42(4)
    s 85 rep—Serious Organised Crime and Police, 2005 c 15, ss 59, 174(2), sch 4 para 191,
        sch 17 pt 2
    ss 86, 87 rep—SI 2004/1897, art 2
    sch 3 am—Road Safety, 2006 c 49, ss 20, 21; Legal Aid, Sentencing and Punishment of
        Offenders, 2012 c 10, sch 27 para 10; Crime and Cts, 2013 c 22, sch 22 para 16;
        Crim Justice and Cts, 2015 c 2, sch 6 para 10(3); (prosp) ibid, sch 7 para
        19(2)(3)
        rep in pt—Crim Justice and Cts, 2015 c 2, sch 6 para 10(2); (prosp) ibid, sch 7 para
            19(4)-(8)
    sch 3A added (prosp)—Crim Justice and Cts, 2015 c 2, sch 7 para 20
    sch 3B added (prosp)—Crim Justice and Cts, 2015 c 2, sch 7 para 21
    sch 5 rep in pt—Road Safety, 2006 c 49, s 59, sch 7(2); Serious Crime, 2007 c 27, s 92, sch
        14; SI 2015/583, sch 1 Table 1

2003

c 33   **Waste and Emissions Trading**
s 4 am—SIs 2011/2499, regs 3(a), 4; 2013/141, reg 3
s 5 am—SI 2011/2499, reg 5
s 9 am—SI 2011/2499, reg 3(b)
    excl—SI 2011/2499, reg 8
s 10 am—SI 2011/2499, reg 3(c)
s 11 am—SI 2011/2499, reg 3(d)
s 12 am—SI 2011/2499, reg 3(e)
s 19 am—(W) SI 2013/755 (W 90), sch 2 para 413
s 21 am—SI 2011/2499, reg 6
s 23 am—SI 2004/1936, reg 2
s 24 am—Loc Govt and Public Involvement in Health, 2007 c 28, s 209(1); Deregulation,
    2015 c 20, sch 13 para 6(33)(a)
    rep in pt—SI 2013/141, reg 3(4); Deregulation, 2015 c 20, sch 13 para 6(33)(b)
s 25 am—(E) SIs 2005/894, reg 77, sch 11 pt 1; (W) 2005/1806 (W 138), reg 73, sch 11 pt
    1 paras 3, 4; 2011/2499, reg 7
s 26 excl—SI 2011/2499, reg 8
s 32 mod—SI 2007/63, art 4
s 37 subst—SSI 2011/226, sch para 2
    am—SI 2011/988, sch 4 para 6

c 34   **Arms Control and Disarmament (Inspections)**
c 35   **European Union (Accessions)**
s 2 am—SI 2012/1809, art 3(1), sch pt 1
c 36   **Fire Services**
s 1 am—Fire and Rescue Services, 2004 c 21, s 53, sch 1 paras 104, 105(1)(2)(4)
    rep in pt—Fire and Rescue Services, 2004 c 21, ss 53, 54, sch 1 paras 104, 105(1)(3),
    sch 2
s 3 rep in pt—Fire and Rescue Services, 2004 c 21, ss 53, 54, sch 1 paras 104,
    106(1)(2)(b)(3)(4)(c), sch 2
    am—Fire and Rescue Services, 2004 c 21, s 53, sch 1 paras 104,
    106(1)(2)(a)(c)(4)(a)(b)
c 37   **Water**
s 3 am—(W) SI 2013/755 (W 90), sch 2 para 415
s 4 am—(W) SIs 2013/755 (W 90), sch 2 para 416; 2015/664, sch 4 para 34
s 7 am—(W) SI 2013/755 (W 90), sch 2 para 417(2)
s 10 am—(W) SI 2013/755 (W 90), sch 2 para 418
s 27 am—(W) SI 2013/755 (W 90), sch 2 para 419
s 33 am—(W) SI 2013/755 (W 90), sch 2 para 420
s 40 rep (prosp)—Water, 2014 c 21, sch 7 para 132
s 52 am—(W) SI 2013/755 (W 90), sch 2 para 421; (1.4.2016) Water, 2014 c 21, sch 7
    para 133
s 57 rep in pt—SI 2015/664, sch 4 para 101(2)
s 58 am—(1.4.2016) Water, 2014 c 21, sch 7 para 134
ss 60, 61 rep—SI 2015/664, sch 4 para 101(3)(4)
s 75 ext to S—(prosp) Flood Risk Management (S), 2009 asp 6, s 87
s 102 am—(W) SI 2013/755 (W 90), sch 2 para 422
s 103 am—(W) SI 2013/755 (W 90), sch 2 para 423
s 105 am—(W) SI 2013/755 (W 90), sch 2 para 424
sch 1 rep in pt—Natural Environment and Rural Communities, 2006 c 16, s 105, sch 11
    para 172, sch 12
sch 7 rep in pt—Equality, 2010 c 15, sch 27 pt 1A (added by SI 2011/1060, sch 3); Postal
    Services, 2011 c 5, sch 12 para 170
c 38   **Anti-social Behaviour**
am—Police and Justice, 2006 c 48, s 52, sch 14 para 53
Pt 1 (ss 1-11) rep—Anti-social Behaviour, Crime and Policing, 2014 c 12, sch 11 para 41(a)
Pt 1A (ss 11A-11L) added—Crim Justice and Immigration, 2008 c 4, s 118, sch 20
    rep—Anti-social Behaviour, Crime and Policing, 2014 c 12, sch 11 para 41(b)
s 13 rep —Anti-social Behaviour, Crime and Policing, 2014 c 12, sch 11 para 50
    rep in pt—Police and Justice, 2006 c 48, s 52, sch 15
    am—Crime and Cts, 2013 c 22, sch 9 para 52
s 14 rep in pt—Housing and Regeneration, 2008 c 17, s 321, sch 16; Anti-social Behaviour,
    Crime and Policing, 2014 c 12, sch 11 para 50
s 19 am—Educ, 2005 c 18, s 117, sch 18 para 15; Educ and Inspections, 2006 c 40, s 97;
    Educ and Skills, 2008 c 25, s 169, sch 1 para 80; SI 2010/1158, art 5, sch 2

2003
c 38 *continued*

　　s 20 am—Educ and Inspections, 2006 c 40, s 98; SI 2010/1158, art 5, sch 2
　　s 21 am—Educ and Inspections, 2006 c 40, s 99(2)(a)(b)(d); SI 2010/1158, art 5, sch 2
　　　　rep in pt—Educ and Inspections, 2006 c 40, s 99(2)(c), sch 18
　　s 22A added—Educ and Inspections, 2006 c 40, s 99(3)
　　　　am—SI 2010/1158, art 5, sch 2
　　s 23 rep in pt—Serious Organised Crime and Police, 2005 c 15, s 174(2), sch 17 pt 2
　　　　am—Educ, 2005 c 18, s 117, sch 18 para 4
　　s 24 am—Educ and Inspections, 2006 c 40, s 99(4); SI 2010/1158, art 5, sch 2; Educ, 2011
　　　　c 21, sch 13 para 11
　　ss 25A, 25B added—Police and Justice, 2006 c 48, s 23(1)
　　s 25B am—SI 2010/866, art 5, sch 2
　　s 26 am—Police and Justice, 2006 c 48, s 52, sch 14 para 54
　　s 26A added—Police and Justice, 2006 c 48, s 24
　　　　am—Crime and Cts, 2013 c 22, sch 9 para 52
　　s 26B added—Police and Justice, 2006 c 48, s 24
　　　　am—Crim Justice and Immigration, 2008 c 4, s 125(1)(3); SI 2010/866, art 5, sch 2;
　　　　Crime and Cts, 2013 c 22, sch 9 para 52
　　s 26C added—Police and Justice, 2006 c 48, s 24
　　　　am—SI 2010/866, art 5, sch 2; Crime and Cts, 2013 c 22, sch 9 para 52
　　s 27 am—Police and Justice, 2006 c 48, s 52, sch 14 para 55; Crim Justice and Immigration,
　　　　2008 c 4, s 125(1)(4); SI 2010/866, art 5, sch 2; Crime and Cts, 2013 c 22, sch 9
　　　　para 52
　　s 28 am—Police and Justice, 2006 c 48, s 52, sch 14 para 56; Crime and Cts, 2013 c 22, sch
　　　　9 para 52
　　s 28A added—Police and Justice, 2006 c 48, s 25
　　s 29 am—Police and Justice, 2006 c 48, ss 23(2), 52, sch 14 para 57; Crim Justice and
　　　　Immigration, 2008 c 4, s 125(1)(2); SI 2010/866, art 5, sch 2
　　Pt 4 (ss 30-36 rep)—Anti-social Behaviour, Crime and Policing, 2014 c 12, sch 11 para
　　　　41(c)
　　s 37 rep in pt—Serious Organised Crime and Police, 2005 c 15, s 174(2), sch 17 pt 2;
　　　　Violent Crime Reduction, 2006 c 38, s 65, sch 5
　　s 38 rep in pt—Violent Crime Reduction, 2006 c 38, s 65, sch 5
　　ss 40, 41 rep—Anti-social Behaviour, Crime and Policing, 2014 c 12, sch 11 para 41(d)
　　s 41 am—Clean Neighbourhoods and Environment, 2005 c 16, s 106, sch 4 para 13
　　s 43 rep in pt—Clean Neighbourhoods and Environment, 2005 c 16, ss 28, 107, sch 5 pt 3
　　s 43A added—Clean Neighbourhoods and Environment, 2005 c 16, s 28(2)
　　s 43B added—Clean Neighbourhoods and Environment, 2005 c 16, s 29
　　s 45 am—Clean Neighbourhoods and Environment, 2005 c 16, s 106, sch 4 para 14
　　　　rep in pt—Clean Neighbourhoods and Environment, 2005 c 16, s 107, sch 5 pt 9
　　s 47 am—Clean Neighbourhoods and Environment, 2005 c 16, ss 30, 106, sch 4 para 15
　　ss 48-52 rep—Anti-social Behaviour, Crime and Policing, 2014 c 12, sch 11 para 41(e)
　　s 54A added—Clean Neighbourhoods and Environment, 2005 c 16, s 32
　　s 56 rep in pt—Anti-social Behaviour, Crime and Policing, 2014 c 12, sch 11 para 50
　　s 85 rep in pt—Anti-social Behaviour, Crime and Policing, 2014 c 12, sch 11 para 50
　　s 86 rep in pt—Anti-social Behaviour, Crime and Policing, 2014 c 12, sch 11 para 50
　　s 87 rep—Legal Aid, Sentencing and Punishment of Offenders, 2012 c 10, sch 23 para 15
　　s 88 rep—Crim Justice and Immigration, 2008 c 4, s 149, sch 28 pt 1
　　s 91 rep—Police and Justice, 2006 c 48, s 52, sch 15
　　sch 2 rep—Crim Justice and Immigration, 2008 c 4, s 149, sch 28 pt 1

c 39　　**Courts**
　　am (except ss 102(1)(a), 103(8))—Constitutional Reform, 2005 c 4, s 59(5), sch 11 pt 2
　　　　para 4
　　appl—SI 1998/644, reg 3; Criminal Justice, 2003 c 44, s 56
　　s 1 am—Mental Capacity, 2005 c 9, s 67(1), sch 6 para 47(1)(2); Crime and Cts, 2013 c 22,
　　　　sch 9 para 40(a); ibid, sch 10 para 84
　　s 2 am—Constitutional Reform, 2005 c 4, s 15(1), sch 4 pt 1 paras 308, 309
　　s 4 rep—SI 2012/1206, sch para 4
　　s 5 rep—SI 2012/1206, sch para 5
　　s 8 am—Constitutional Reform, 2005 c 4, s 15(1), sch 4 pt 1 paras 308, 312; Police Reform
　　　　and Social Responsibility, 2011 c 13, sch 16 para 311
　　　　rep in pt—SI 2012/1206, sch para 6
　　s 10 am—Constitutional Reform, 2005 c 4, ss 15(1), 106, sch 4 pt 1 paras 308, 313, 314;
　　　　Crime and Cts, 2013 c 22, sch 13 para 39

2003
c 39 *continued*

s 11 am—Constitutional Reform, 2005 c 4, ss 15(1), 106, sch 4 pt 1 paras 308, 313, 314
ss 13-17 am—Constitutional Reform, 2005 c 4, s 15(1), sch 4 pt 1 paras 308, 315-319
s 18 rep in pt—Crime and Cts, 2013 c 22, sch 10 para 85
s 19 am—Constitutional Reform, 2005 c 4, s 15(1), sch 4 pt 1 paras 308, 320; Crime and
   Cts, 2013 c 22, sch 10 para 86
s 20 am—Constitutional Reform, 2005 c 4, s 15(1), sch 4 pt 1 paras 308, 321; SI
   2012/2398, sch 2 para 5(a)
   rep in pt—SI 2012/2398, sch 2 para 5(b)
s 21 am—Constitutional Reform, 2005 c 4, s 15(1), sch 4 pt 1 paras 308, 322(1)-(4)
s 22 am—Constitutional Reform, 2005 c 4, s 15(1), sch 4 pt 1 paras 308, 323; Tribunals,
   Cts and Enforcement, 2007 c 15, s 50, sch 10 para 38(1)(2)
s 23 am—Constitutional Reform, 2005 c 4, s 14, sch 3 para 5
s 24 am—Constitutional Reform, 2005 c 4, s 15(1), sch 4 pt 1 paras 308, 324; Tribunals,
   Cts and Enforcement, 2007 c 15, s 50, sch 10 para 38(1)(3); Crime and Cts, 2013
   c 22, sch 13 para 38
s 25 am—Constitutional Reform, 2005 c 4, s 15(1), sch 4 pt 1 paras 308, 325
s 26 rep in pt—Crime and Cts, 2013 c 22, sch 10 para 99 Table
s 27 am—Constitutional Reform, 2005 c 4, s 15(1), sch 4 pt 1 paras 308, 326
s 28 am—Constitutional Reform, 2005 c 4, s 15(1), sch 4 pt 1 paras 308, 327; SI
   2012/2398, sch 2 para 6(a); Crime and Cts, 2013 c 22, sch 10 para 87(2)(3)
   rep in pt—SI 2012/2398, sch 2 para 6(b); Crime and Cts, 2013 c 22, sch 10 para 87(4)
s 30 am—Constitutional Reform, 2005 c 4, s 15(1), sch 4 pt 1 paras 308, 328
   rep in pt—Crime and Cts, 2013 c 22, sch 10 para 88
s 34 am—Constitutional Reform, 2005 c 4, s 15(1), sch 4 pt 1 paras 308, 329; Crime and
   Cts, 2013 c 22, sch 10 para 89
s 36A added—Crime and Cts, 2013 c 22, s 26(2)
s 41 am—Serious Organised Crime and Police, 2005 c 15, s 59, sch 4 para 192; Loc
   Democracy, Economic Development and Construction, 2009 c 20, s 119, sch 6
   para 118; Police Reform and Social Responsibility, 2011 c 13, sch 16 para 312
   rep in pt—Crime and Cts, 2013 c 22, sch 8 para 189
s 49 rep in pt—Crime and Cts, 2013 c 22, sch 10 para 99 Table
Pt 4 (ss 51-57) appl (mods)—SI 2014/786, art 3 4(a)
s 54A added—Crim Justice and Cts, 2015 c 2, s 70(2)
s 55 am—Coroners and Justice, 2009 c 25, s 146(1)(2); Crim Justice and Cts, 2015 c 2, s
   70(3)
s 55A added—Coroners and Justice, 2009 c 25, s 146(1)(3)
s 56 am—Coroners and Justice, 2009 c 25, s 146(1)(4); Crim Justice and Cts, 2015 c 2, s
   70(4)
Pt 5 (ss 58-61A) rep—SI 2012/2401, sch 1 para 13
s 61A added—Police and Justice, 2006 c 48, s 32(1)
s 62 subst—Constitutional Reform, 2005 c 4, s 15(1), sch 4 pt 1 paras 308, 330
s 64 am—Constitutional Reform, 2005 c 4, s 15(1), sch 4 pt 1 paras 308,
   331(1)(2)(b)(3)(4)(b)(5); Mental Capacity, 2005 c 9, s 67(1), sch 6 para
   47(1)(3)(b); Tribunals, Cts and Enforcement, 2007 c 15, s 56, sch 11 para 14;
   Crime and Cts, 2013 c 22, sch 9 para 40(b)
   rep in pt—Constitutional Reform, 2005 c 4, ss 15(1), 146, sch 4 pt 1 paras 308,
     331(1)(2)(a)(4)(a), sch 18 pt 2; Mental Capacity, 2005 c 9, s 67(1)(2), sch 6
     para 47(1)(3)(a), sch 7; Crime and Cts, 2013 c 22, sch 13 para 89(2)(i)
s 65 rep in pt—Armed Forces, 2011 c 18, sch 5
s 66 am—Armed Forces, 2011 c 18, sch 2 para 6; Crime and Cts, 2013 c 22, sch 14 para 4
   rep in pt—Crime and Cts, 2013 c 22, sch 10 para 90
s 68 am—Anti-social Behaviour, Crime and Policing, 2014 c 12, s 174(1)
s 69 rep in pt—Constitutional Reform, 2005 c 4, ss 15(1), 146, sch 4 pt 1 paras 308, 332,
   sch 18 pt 2
s 70 am—Constitutional Reform, 2005 c 4, s 15(1), sch 4 pt 1 paras 308, 333; SIs
   2005/2625, art 2(b); 2007/2128, art 8, sch; Legal Services, 2007 c 29, s 208, sch
   21 paras 142, 143
   rep in pt—SI 2005/2625, art 2(a)
   see—(trans of functions) SI 2007/2128, art 4
s 71 am—Constitutional Reform, 2005 c 4, s 15(1), sch 4 pt 1 paras 308, 334
s 72 am—Constitutional Reform, 2005 c 4, s 15(1), sch 4 pt 1 paras 308, 335
   rep in pt—Constitutional Reform, 2005 c 4, sch 18 pt 2; SI 2007/2128, art 8, sch
   see—(trans of functions) SI 2007/2128, art 4

2003
c 39 *continued*

s 72A added—Constitutional Reform, 2005 c 4, s 15(1), sch 4 pt 1 paras 308, 336
    see—(trans of functions) SI 2007/2128, art 4
    rep in pt—SI 2007/2128, art 8, sch
s 73 am—Constitutional Reform, 2005 c 4, s 15(1), sch 4 pt 1 paras 308, 337
    see—(trans of functions) SI 2007/2128, art 4
    rep in pt—SI 2007/2128, art 8, sch
s 74 am—Constitutional Reform, 2005 c 4, s 13(2)(3), sch 2 pt 2 paras 7, 8
s 75 rep in pt—Constitutional Reform, 2005 c 4, s 15(1), 146, sch 4 pt 1 paras 308, 338, sch
    18 pt 2; Crime and Cts, 2013 c 22, sch 10 para 91(2)
    am—Crime and Cts, 2013 c 22, sch 10 para 91(3)(4)
s 76 rep in pt—Constitutional Reform, 2005 c 4, ss 12(2)(3), 146, sch 1 pt 2 para 29, sch 18
    pt 2; Crime and Cts, 2013 c 22, sch 10 para 92(2)(b)(3)
    am—Children, 2004 c 31, s 62(7); Civil Partnership, 2004 c 33, s 261(1), sch 27 para
    172; Children, Schools and Families, 2010 c 26, s 25, sch 3 para 14; Crime and
    Cts, 2013 c 22, sch 10 para 92(2)(a)
s 77 rep in pt—Constitutional Reform, 2005 c 4, ss 15(1), 146, sch 4 pt 1 paras 308, 338,
    339(1)(6), sch 18 pt 2; Crime and Cts, 2013 c 22, sch 10 para 93(2)
    am—Constitutional Reform, 2005 c 4, s 15(1), sch 4 pt 1 paras 308, 339(1)-(5)(7)(8);
    Legal Services, 2007 c 29, s 208, sch 21 paras 142, 143; Crime and Cts, 2013 c
    22, sch 10 para 93(3)
s 78 am—Constitutional Reform, 2005 c 4, s 15(1), sch 4 pt 1 paras 308, 340
s 79 am—Constitutional Reform, 2005 c 4, s 15(1), sch 4 pt 1 paras 308, 341
    rep in pt—Constitutional Reform, 2005 c 4, s 146, sch 18 pt 2
s 79A added—Constitutional Reform, 2005 c 4, s 15(1), sch 4 pt 1 paras 308, 342
s 80 am—Constitutional Reform, 2005 c 4, s 15(1), sch 4 pt 1 paras 308, 343
s 81 am—Constitutional Reform, 2005 c 4, ss 13(2)(3), 15(1), sch 2 pt 2 paras 7, 9, sch 4 pt
    1 paras 308, 344; Crime and Cts, 2013 c 22, sch 9 para 40(a); (props) ibid, sch 10
    para 94(2)-(5)
    rep in pt—Crime and Cts, 2013 c 22, sch 10 para 94(6)
s 88 am—Constitutional Reform, 2005 c 4, s 40(4), sch 9 pt 1 para 80(1)(2)
s 91 am—Constitutional Reform, 2005 c 4, ss 15(1), 40(4), sch 4 pt 1 paras 308, 345, sch 9
    pt 1 para 80(1)(3)
s 92 am—Constitutional Reform, 2005 c 4, ss 15(1), 40(4), sch 4 pt 1 paras 308, 345, sch 9
    pt 1 para 80(1)(3); Crime and Cts, 2013 c 22, sch 9 para 40(a); ibid, sch 10 para
    95
s 98 am—Tribunals, Cts and Enforcement, 2007 c 15, s 48, sch 8 para 55; (prosp) ibid, ss
    106, 107(3), sch 16 para 15; Crime and Cts, 2013 c 22, sch 9 para 40(a)(c)
    appl—(temp until 15.4.2022) SI 2015/930, reg 8(5)(a)
    mod—Immigration, 2014 c 22, s 45 (subst Immigration, Asylum and Nationality, 2006
    c 13, s 18(1D)); (pt prosp) ibid, s 31(5)(a); (temp until 31.3.2022) SIs 2015/957,
    reg 7(5)(a); 961, reg 8(5)(a)
s 100 rep in pt—Income Tax (Trading and Other Income), 2005 c 5, s 884, sch 3
s 101 am—Income Tax (Trading and Other Income), 2005 c 5, s 882(1), sch 1 pt 2 para 627
s 102 am—Constitutional Reform, 2005 c 4, ss 15(1), 59(5), sch 4 pt 1 paras 308, 346(1)(3),
    sch 11 pt 3 para 6; Justice and Security (NI), 2007 c 6, s 47; SI 2010/976, art 15,
    sch 18
    rep in pt—Constitutional Reform, 2005 c 4, s 15(1), sch 4 pt 1 paras 308, 346(1)(2)
s 103 am—Constitutional Reform, 2005 c 4, s 59(5), sch 11 pt 3 para 6
s 107 rep in pt—Constitutional Reform, 2005 c 4, ss 15(1), 146, sch 4 pt 1 paras 308, 347;
    SI 2012/2398, sch 2 para 7
s 108 am—Constitutional Reform, 2005 c 4, s 15(1), sch 4 pt 1 paras 308, 348; SI
    2010/976, art 15, sch 18
s 109 power to rep or am (ext)—Domestic Violence, Crime and Victims, 2004 c 28, s 29,
    sch 5 para 10
    am—Constitutional Reform, 2005 c 4, s 15(1), sch 4 pt 1 paras 308, 349; SI
    2010/976, art 15, sch 18
s 111 am—Crime and Cts, 2013 c 22, s 27(14)
sch 1 rep—SI 2012/1206, sch para 7
sch 3A rep—SI 2012/2401, sch 1 para 14
    added—Police and Justice, 2006 c 48, s 32(2)
sch 4 rep in pt—Police and Justice, 2006 c 48, s 52, sch 15
sch 5 power to am or excl—Domestic Violence, Crime and Victims, 2004 c 28, ss 14(5), 59,
    sch 12 para 7

2003
c 39 sch 5 *continued*

am—Domestic Violence, Crime and Victims, 2004 c 28, ss 14(4), 59, sch 12 para 7; Disability Discrimination, 2005 c 13, s 19(1), sch 1 pt 2 para 47(1)(2)(3); SI 2006/1737, arts 4-33; Tribunals, Cts and Enforcement, 2007 c 15, s 62, sch 13 paras 148, 149; Crim Justice and Immigration, 2008 c 4, ss 41, 80(1); (prosp) Welfare Reform, 2009 c 24, s 9, sch 2 paras 12, 13; Legal Aid, Sentencing and Punishment of Offenders, 2012 c 10, s 88; Prevention of Social Housing Fraud, 2013 c 3, sch paras 25, 26, 27(b); Crime and Cts, 2013 c 22, s 27(3)-(10)(12); ibid, sch 16 para 28(2); (prosp) ibid, s 26(3); SI 2013/630, reg 17(2); Crim Justice and Cts, 2015 c 2, s 56(2),(3)(b)(d)(e),(4),(5)(a)(c),(6); Modern Slavery, 2015 c 30, sch 5 para 23(2)(b)(3)(4)

rep in pt—SI 2006/1737, arts 4-33; Crime and Cts, 2013 c 22, s 27(11); Crim Justice and Cts, 2015 c 2, s 56(3)(a)(c),(5)(b); Modern Slavery, 2015 c 30, sch 5 para 23(2)(a)

ext—Crime and Cts, 2013 c 22, s 27(13)

sch 6 see —(power to am or excl) Domestic Violence, Crime and Victims, 2004 c 28, ss 14(5), 59, sch 12 para 7

appl—(specified areas) SI 2004/2198, art 2, sch

am—Tribunals, Cts and Enforcement, 2007 c 15, s 62, sch 13 paras 148, 150; (prosp) Welfare Reform, 2009 c 24, s 9, sch 2 paras 12, 14; Crime and Cts, 2013 c 22, sch 16 para 28(3); SI 2013/630, reg 17(3)

sch 7 am—Constitutional Reform, 2005 c 4, s 15(1), sch 4 pt 1 paras 308, 351; Tribunals, Cts and Enforcement, 2007 c 15, s 62, sch 13 paras 148, 151; ibid, s 140; Crime and Cts, 2013 c 22, sch 9 para 40(d)(ii)

rep in pt—Tribunals, Cts and Enforcement, 2007 c 15, s 146, sch 23; Crime and Cts, 2013 c 22, sch 9 para 40(d)(i)

sch 8 rep in pt—(S) Constitutional Reform, 2005 c 4, s 15(1), sch 4 pt 1 paras 308, 351; Serious Organised Crime and Police, 2005 c 15, s 174(2), sch 17 pt 2; Gambling, 2005 c 19, s 356(4)(5), sch 17; (pt prosp) Violent Crime Reduction, 2006 c 38, s 65, sch 5; (pt prosp) Road Safety, 2006 c 49, s 59, sch 7; Police and Justice, 2006 c 48, s 52, sch 15; (S) Adult Support and Protection (S), 2007 asp 10, s 77, sch 2; SI 2007/2007, art 6, sch; Finance, 2007 c 11, s 114, sch 27 pt 6; Health and Social Care, 2008 c 14, s 166, sch 15; Marine and Coastal Access, 2009 c 23, s 321, sch 22 pt 5(C); (prosp) Coroners and Justice, 2009 c 25, s 178, sch 23 pt 1; Equality, 2010 c 15, sch 27 Pt 1A (added by SI 2011/1060, sch 3); Armed Forces, 2011 c 18, sch 5; Legal Aid, Sentencing and Punishment of Offenders, 2012 c 10, sch 12 para 48; SI 2012/2398, sch 2 para 8; Crime and Cts, 2013 c 22, sch 10 para 99 Table; ibid, sch 11 para 210 Table; Serious Crime, 2015 c 9, sch 4 para 61

sch 9 rep in pt—SI 2012/2401, sch 1 para 15

c 40 **Ragwort Control**
c 41 **Extradition**

mod—(specified sections mod) SI 2003/3150, art 2(2), sch

s 2 am—Police and Justice, 2006 c 48, s 42, sch 13 para 1(1); Anti-social Behaviour, Crime and Policing, 2014 c 12, s 157(3)

s 3 am—Armed Forces, 2006 c 52, s 378, sch 16 para 200
rep in pt—Armed Forces, 2006 c 52, s 378, sch 16 para 200

s 5 am—Armed Forces, 2006 c 52, s 378, sch 16 para 201

s 6 am—Policing and Crime, 2009 c 26, s 77(1)-(5)

s 7 am—Police and Justice, 2006 c 48, s 42, sch 13 para 16(1)(2); Policing and Crime, 2009 c 26, s 77(1)(6)

s 8 am—Police and Justice, 2006 c 48, s 42, sch 13 para 16(1)(2); Anti-social Behaviour, Crime and Policing, 2014 c 12, s 155

ss 8A, 8B added—Policing and Crime, 2009 c 26, s 69

s 9 am—Police and Justice, 2006 c 48, s 42, sch 13 para 16(1)(2)

s 11 am—Police and Justice, 2006 c 48, s 42, sch 13 para 3(1); (S prosp) Crime and Cts, 2013 c 22, sch 20 para 2; Anti-social Behaviour, Crime and Policing, 2014 c 12, ss 156(1), 157(1), sch 11 para 104
rep in pt—Anti-social Behaviour, Crime and Policing, 2014 c 12, s 158(2)

s 12A added—Anti-social Behaviour, Crime and Policing, 2014 c 12, s 156(2)

s 14 am—Police and Justice, 2006 c 48, s 42, sch 13 para 2(1)

s 16 rep—Anti-social Behaviour, Crime and Policing, 2014 c 12, s 158(1)

s 19A added—Police and Justice, 2006 c 48, s 42, sch 13 para 3(2)

ss 19B-19F added (S prosp)—Crime and Cts, 2013 c 22, sch 20 para 3

2003
c 41 *continued*

s 21 am—Police and Justice, 2006 c 48, s 42, sch 13 para 16(1)(2); Anti-social Behaviour, Crime and Policing, 2014 c 12, sch 11 para 105(2)

rep in pt—Anti-social Behaviour, Crime and Policing, 2014 c 12, sch 11 para 105(3)

s 21A added—Anti-social Behaviour, Crime and Policing, 2014 c 12, s 157(2)(4)

s 21B added—Anti-social Behaviour, Crime and Policing, 2014 c 12, s 159

s 22 am—Policing and Crime, 2009 c 26, s 71(1)(2)

s 23 am—Police and Justice, 2006 c 48, s 42, sch 13 para 7; Policing and Crime, 2009 c 26, s 71(1)(3)

s 24 am—Police and Justice, 2006 c 48, s 42, sch 13 para 16(1)(2)

s 26 am—Anti-social Behaviour, Crime and Policing, 2014 c 12, s 160(1); ibid, sch 11 para 106

s 28 am—Anti-social Behaviour, Crime and Policing, 2014 c 12, s 160(2); ibid, sch 11 para 107

s 29 am—Police and Justice, 2006 c 48, s 42, sch 13 para 8(1)

s 30 am—Constitutional Reform, 2005 c 4, s 40(4), sch 9 pt 1 para 81(1)(4)(a); Police and Justice, 2006 c 48, s 42, sch 13 paras 8(2), 16(1)(2); Crime and Cts, 2013 c 22, sch 20 para 17(1)

s 30A added—Crime and Cts, 2013 c 22, sch 20 para 17(2)

   am—SI 2015/992, art 3(2)

s 32 am—Constitutional Reform, 2005 c 4, s 40(4), sch 9 pt 1 para 81(1)(2)(4)(b); Police and Justice, 2006 c 48, s 42, sch 13 para 8(3)

s 33 am—Constitutional Reform, 2005 c 4, s 40(4), sch 9 pt 1 para 81(1)(2)(4)(b); Police and Justice, 2006 c 48, s 42, sch 13 para 8(4)

s 33ZA added—Crime and Cts, 2013 c 22, sch 20 para 18

s 33A added—Police and Justice, 2006 c 48, s 42, sch 13 para 8(5)

s 33B added—Crime and Cts, 2013 c 22, sch 20 para 19

s 34 am—Crime and Cts, 2013 c 22, sch 20 para 20

s 35 am—Police and Justice, 2006 c 48, s 42, sch 13 para 9(1); Anti-social Behaviour, Crime and Policing, 2014 c 12, sch 11 para 108; SI 2015/992, art 3(3)

s 36 am—Constitutional Reform, 2005 c 4, s 40(4), sch 9 pt 1 para 81(1)(4)(c); Crime and Cts, 2013 c 22, sch 20 para 21(1); Anti-social Behaviour, Crime and Policing, 2014 c 12, sch 11 para 109

s 36A added—Crime and Cts, 2013 c 22, sch 20 para 21(2); Anti-social Behaviour, Crime and Policing, 2014 c 12, s 161(1)

s 36B added—Anti-social Behaviour, Crime and Policing, 2014 c 12, s 161(1)

s 37 am—Police and Justice, 2006 c 48, s 42, sch 13 paras 9(2), 10; SI 2015/992, art 3(4)

s 38 am—Police and Justice, 2006 c 48, s 42, sch 13 para 9(3); SI 2015/992, art 3(5)

s 39 am—Anti-social Behaviour, Crime and Policing, 2014 c 12, s 162(1)(b)

   rep in pt—Anti-social Behaviour, Crime and Policing, 2014 c 12, s 162(1)(a)

s 40 rep in pt—Anti-social Behaviour, Crime and Policing, 2014 c 12, sch 11 para 121(4)(a)

s 42 am—SI 2015/992, art 3(6)

s 43 am—Constitutional Reform, 2005 c 4, s 40(4), sch 9 pt 1 para 81(1)(4)(d)

s 44 am—Police and Justice, 2006 c 48, s 42, sch 13 para 16(1)(2)

s 45 am—Legal Aid, Sentencing and Punishment of Offenders, 2012 c 10, sch 5 para 63

   rep in pt—Anti-social Behaviour, Crime and Policing, 2014 c 12, s 163(a)

s 46 am—Police and Justice, 2006 c 48, s 42, sch 13 para 16(1)(2)

s 47 mod—Extradition, 2003 c 41, ss 23(3)(b), 89(3)(b)

ss 50, 51 am—Police and Justice, 2006 c 48, s 42, sch 13 para 16(1)(2)

s 52 am—Police and Justice, 2006 c 48, s 42, sch 13 para 11

s 59 subst—Policing and Crime, 2009 c 26, s 72

   rep in pt—Legal Aid, Sentencing and Punishment of Offenders, 2012 c 10, sch 10 para 11(2)(a), sch 16 para 10(a)

   am—Legal Aid, Sentencing and Punishment of Offenders, 2012 c 10, sch 16 para 10(b)

s 60 am—Constitutional Reform, 2005 c 4, s 40(4), sch 9 pt 1 para 81(1)(4)(e)(f); SI 2015/992, art 3(7)

s 61 am—Constitutional Reform, 2005 c 4, s 40(4), sch 9 pt 1 para 81(1)(4)(e)(f); SI 2010/976, art 15, sch 18; Legal Aid, Sentencing and Punishment of Offenders, 2012 c 10, sch 7 para 13(2); SI 2015/992, art 3(8)

s 62 rep in pt—Legal Aid, Sentencing and Punishment of Offenders, 2012 c 10, sch 7 para 14

ss 62A, 62B added—Legal Aid, Sentencing and Punishment of Offenders, 2012 c 10, sch 7 para 15

ss 64, 65 subst—Anti-social Behaviour, Crime and Policing, 2014 c 12, s 164(1)

2003

c 41 *continued*

s 66 am—Anti-social Behaviour, Crime and Policing, 2014 c 12, s 164(2), sch 11 para 110

s 67 am—Constitutional Reform, 2005 c 4, s 15(1), sch 4 pt 1 paras 352, 353; Police and Justice, 2006 c 48, s 42, sch 13 para 15(1); SI 2010/976, art 15, sch 18

s 68A added—Police and Justice, 2006 c 48, s 42, sch 13 para 2(2)

s 70 am—Police and Justice, 2006 c 48, s 42, sch 13 paras 1(2), 17; (S prosp) Crime and Cts, 2013 c 22, sch 20 paras 5, 11

rep in pt—Anti-social Behaviour, Crime and Policing, 2014 c 12, sch 11 para 121(4)(b)

s 71 am—Armed Forces, 2006 c 52, s 378, sch 16 para 202

rep in pt—Armed Forces, 2006 c 52, s 378, sch 16 para 202

s 72 am—Police and Justice, 2006 c 48, s 42, sch 13 para 16(1)(2)

s 73 am—Armed Forces, 2006 c 52, s 378, sch 16 para 203

rep in pt—Armed Forces, 2006 c 52, s 378, sch 16 para 203

s 74 am—Police and Justice, 2006 c 48, s 42, sch 13 para 16(1)(2)

ss 76A, 76B added —Policing and Crime, 2009 c 26, s 70

s 77 am—Police and Justice, 2006 c 48, s 42, sch 13 para 16(1)(2)

s 82 am—Police and Justice, 2006 c 48, s 42, sch 13 para 2(3)

s 83 am—Police and Justice, 2006 c 48, s 42, sch 13 para 18

ss 83A-83E added (S prosp)—Crime and Cts, 2013 c 22, sch 20 para 6

s 88 am—Policing and Crime, 2009 c 26, s 71(1)(4)

s 89 am—Police and Justice, 2006 c 48, s 42, sch 13 para 7; Policing and Crime, 2009 c 26, s 71(1)(5)

ss 90, 92 am—Police and Justice, 2006 c 48, s 42, sch 13 para 16(1)(2)

s 93 am—Police and Justice, 2006 c 48, s 42, sch 13 para 3(4); Anti-social Behaviour, Crime and Policing, 2014 c 12, s 162(3)

s 96A added—Police and Justice, 2006 c 48, s 42, sch 13 para 3(4)

s 97 am—Policing and Crime, 2009 c 26, s 71(1)(6)

s 98 am—Policing and Crime, 2009 c 26, s 71(1)(7)

s 99 am—Police and Justice, 2006 c 48, s 42, sch 13 para 19

s 101 am—Constitutional Reform and Governance, 2010 c 25, s 19, sch 2 para 14

s 102 am—Policing and Crime, 2009 c 26, s 71(1)(8)

s 103 am—Anti-social Behaviour, Crime and Policing, 2014 c 12, s 160(3); ibid, sch 11 para 111

s 104 am—Police and Justice, 2006 c 48, s 42, sch 13 para 8(6)

s 105 am—Anti-social Behaviour, Crime and Policing, 2014 c 12, s 160(4); ibid, sch 11 para 112

s 106 am—Police and Justice, 2006 c 48, s 42, sch 13 para 8(7)

s 107 am—Constitutional Reform, 2005 c 4, s 40(4), sch 9 pt 1 para 81(1)(4)(g); Police and Justice, 2006 c 48, s 42, sch 13 paras 8(8), 16(1)(2); Crime and Cts, 2013 c 22, sch 20 para 23(1)

s 107A added—Crime and Cts, 2013 c 22, sch 20 para 23(2)

am—SI 2015/992, art 3(9)

s 108 am—(S prosp) Crime and Cts, 2013 c 22, sch 20 para 12; Anti-social Behaviour, Crime and Policing, 2014 c 12, s 160(5); ibid, sch 11 para 113

s 110 am—Anti-social Behaviour, Crime and Policing, 2014 c 12, s 160(6); ibid, sch 11 para 114

s 111 am—Police and Justice, 2006 c 48, s 42, sch 13 para 8(9)

s 112 subst—Police and Justice, 2006 c 48, s 42, sch 13 para 8(10)

am—Crime and Cts, 2013 c 22, sch 20 para 24(1)

s 112A added—Crime and Cts, 2013 c 22, sch 20 para 24(2)

s 114 am—Constitutional Reform, 2005 c 4, s 40(4), sch 9 pt 1 para 81(1)(3)(4)(i); Police and Justice, 2006 c 48, s 42, sch 13 para 8(11)

s 115 am—Constitutional Reform, 2005 c 4, s 40(4), sch 9 pt 1 para 81(1)(3)(4)(i); Police and Justice, 2006 c 48, s 42, sch 13 para 8(12)

s 115A added—Police and Justice, 2006 c 48, s 42, sch 13 para 8(13)

s 115B added—Crime and Cts, 2013 c 22, sch 20 para 25

s 116 am—Crime and Cts, 2013 c 22, sch 20 para 26

s 117 am—(S prosp) Crime and Cts, 2013 c 22, sch 20 para 13; Anti-social Behaviour, Crime and Policing, 2014 c 12, sch 11 para 115; SI 2015/992, art 3(10)

s 118 am—Constitutional Reform, 2005 c 4, s 40(4), sch 9 pt 1 para 81(1)(4)(j); Crime and Cts, 2013 c 22, sch 20 para 27(1); Anti-social Behaviour, Crime and Policing, 2014 c 12, sch 11 para 116

s 118A added—Crime and Cts, 2013 c 22, sch 20 para 27(2); Anti-social Behaviour, Crime and Policing, 2014 c 12, s 161(2)

2003

c 41 *continued*

s 118B added—Crime and Cts, 2013 c 22, sch 20 para 2; Anti-social Behaviour, Crime and
    Policing, 2014 c 12, s 161(2)8

s 119 am—Police and Justice, 2006 c 48, s 42, sch 13 para 13

s 121 am—Anti-social Behaviour, Crime and Policing, 2014 c 12, s 162(2)(b)
    rep in pt—Anti-social Behaviour, Crime and Policing, 2014 c 12, s 162(2)(a)

s 124 am—SI 2015/992, art 3(11)

s 125 am—Constitutional Reform, 2005 c 4, s 40(4), sch 9 pt 1 para 81(1)(4)(k)

s 127 am—Legal Aid, Sentencing and Punishment of Offenders, 2012 c 10, sch 5 para 64

s 128 rep in pt—Anti-social Behaviour, Crime and Policing, 2014 c 12, s 163(b)

s 132 subst—Policing and Crime, 2009 c 26, s 73
    rep in pt—Legal Aid, Sentencing and Punishment of Offenders, 2012 c 10, sch 10 para
        11(2)(b), sch 16 para 11(a)
    am—Legal Aid, Sentencing and Punishment of Offenders, 2012 c 10, sch 16 para
        11(b)

s 133 am—Constitutional Reform, 2005 c 4, s 40(4), sch 9 pt 1 para 81(1)(4)(l)(m); SI
    2015/992, art 3(12)

s 134 am—Constitutional Reform, 2005 c 4, s 40(4), sch 9 pt 1 para 81(1)(4)(l)(m); SI
    2010/976, art 15, sch 18; Legal Aid, Sentencing and Punishment of Offenders,
    2012 c 10, sch 7 para 16(2); SI 2015/992, art 3(13)

s 135 rep in pt—Legal Aid, Sentencing and Punishment of Offenders, 2012 c 10, sch 7 para
    17

ss 135A, 135B added—Legal Aid, Sentencing and Punishment of Offenders, 2012 c 10, sch
    7 para 18

s 137 am—Anti-social Behaviour, Crime and Policing, 2014 c 12, s 164(3)(4)
    rep in pt—Anti-social Behaviour, Crime and Policing, 2014 c 12, sch 11 para 117

s 138 am—Anti-social Behaviour, Crime and Policing, 2014 c 12, s 164(5)(6)
    rep in pt—Anti-social Behaviour, Crime and Policing, 2014 c 12, sch 11 para 118

s 139 am—Constitutional Reform, 2005 c 4, s 15(1), sch 4 pt 1 paras 352, 354; Police and
    Justice, 2006 c 48, s 42, sch 13 para 15(1); SI 2010/976, art 15, sch 18

s 140A added—Police and Justice, 2006 c 48, s 42, sch 13 para 2(4)

s 141 am—Police and Justice, 2006 c 48, s 42, sch 13 para 20

s 142 am—Police and Justice, 2006 c 48, s 42, sch 13 paras 1(3), 21, 22; Anti-social
    Behaviour, Crime and Policing, 2014 c 12, s 165
    mod—Serious Crime, 2007 c 27, s 63, sch 6 para 46
    appl (mods)—SI 2014/3141, reg 98(8)

ss 143, 144 rep —Policing and Crime, 2009 c 26, ss 74(1)(2), 112, sch 8 pt 6

s 145 am—Policing and Crime, 2009 c 26, s 75(1)(2)

s 146 am—Police and Justice, 2006 c 48, s 42, sch 13 para 23

s 148 am—Police and Justice, 2006 c 48, s 42, sch 13 para 2(6)

s 150 am—Anti-social Behaviour, Crime and Policing, 2014 c 12, s 166(1)

s 151 rep —Policing and Crime, 2009 c 26, ss 76(1)(2), 112, sch 8 pt 6

s 151A added—Policing and Crime, 2009 c 26, s 76(1)(3)
    am—Anti-social Behaviour, Crime and Policing, 2014 c 12, s 166(1)

s 151B added—Anti-social Behaviour, Crime and Policing, 2014 c 12, s 166(2)

s 152 am—Policing and Crime, 2009 c 26, s 75(1)(3)

s 153 am—Policing and Crime, 2009 c 26, s 74(1)(4)

ss 153A-153D added —Policing and Crime, 2009 c 26, s 74(1)(3)

s 153B rep in pt—Legal Aid, Sentencing and Punishment of Offenders, 2012 c 10, sch 10
    para 11(2)(c), sch 16 para 12(a)
    am—Legal Aid, Sentencing and Punishment of Offenders, 2012 c 10, sch 16 para
    12(b)

s 153D rep in pt—Anti-social Behaviour, Crime and Policing, 2014 c 12, sch 11 para
    121(4)(c)

s 155 am—Armed Forces, 2006 c 52, s 378, sch 16 para 204

s 155A added—Police and Justice, 2006 c 48, s 42, sch 13 para 24

s 157 am—Anti-social Behaviour, Crime and Policing, 2014 c 12, s 174(3)

s 160 am—Anti-social Behaviour, Crime and Policing, 2014 c 12, s 174(4)

s 173 see—SI 2003/3336, art 2

ss 177, 178 ext—Legal Aid, Sentencing and Punishment of Offenders, 2012 c 10, s 153(2)

s 179 am—Police and Justice, 2006 c 48, s 42, sch 13 para 2(7)

s 180 am—Anti-social Behaviour, Crime and Policing, 2014 c 12, s 167(1)

s 181 am—Anti-social Behaviour, Crime and Policing, 2014 c 12, s 167(2)

s 182 rep—Legal Aid, Sentencing and Punishment of Offenders, 2012 c 10, sch 5 pt 2

2003
c 41 *continued*

s 184 am—Constitutional Reform, 2005 c 4, ss 15(1), 40(4), sch 4 pt 1 paras 352, 355, sch 9 pt 1 para 81(1)(4)(n)(5)

s 185 am—Constitutional Reform, 2005 c 4, ss 15(1), 40(4), sch 4 pt 1 paras 352, 355, sch 9 pt 1 para 81(1)(4)(n)(5); Policing and Crime, 2009 c 26, s 112, sch 7 para 117; SI 2010/976, art 15, sch 18

s 187 am—Police and Justice, 2006 c 48, s 42, sch 13 para 15(2)

s 188 am—Police and Justice, 2006 c 48, s 42, sch 13 para 2(8)

s 189 am—Police and Justice, 2006 c 48, s 42, sch 13 para 2(9)

ss 189A-189E added (prosp)—Anti-social Behaviour, Crime and Policing, 2014 c 12, s 168

s 193 subst—Anti-social Behaviour, Crime and Policing, 2014 c 12, s 169

s 197 am—Policing and Crime, 2009 c 26, s 74(1)(5); Anti-social Behaviour, Crime and Policing, 2014 c 12, sch 11 para 119

s 197A added—Police and Justice, 2006 c 48, s 42, sch 13 para 25

    am—Policing and Crime, 2009 c 26, s 71(1)(9)

s 200 rep in pt—Legal Aid, Sentencing and Punishment of Offenders, 2012 c 10, sch 11 para 35

s 201 rep—Legal Aid, Sentencing and Punishment of Offenders, 2012 c 10, sch 12 para 49

s 202 am—Police and Justice, 2006 c 48, s 42, sch 13 para 26

s 204 subst—Policing and Crime, 2009 c 26, s 67

    am—Anti-social Behaviour, Crime and Policing, 2014 c 12, s 170, sch 11 para 120(2)(3)(a)

    rep in pt—Anti-social Behaviour, Crime and Policing, 2014 c 12, sch 11 para 120(3)(b)

ss 206A-206C added—Policing and Crime, 2009 c 26, s 78

s 208 am—Constitutional Reform, 2005 c 4, s 40(4), sch 9 pt 1 para 81(1)(4)(o); SI 2015/992, art 3(14)

s 212 am—Policing and Crime, 2009 c 26, s 68

s 213 am—Constitutional Reform, 2005 c 4, s 40(4), sch 9 pt 1 para 81(1)(4)(p)(q); SI 2015/992, art 3(15)

s 214 am—Constitutional Reform, 2005 c 4, s 40(4), sch 9 pt 1 para 81(1)(4)(p)(q)

s 216 am—Armed Forces, 2006 c 52, s 378, sch 16 para 205; Policing and Crime, 2009 c 26, s 71(1)(10); Armed Forces, 2011 c 18, sch 4 para 2; Anti-social Behaviour, Crime and Policing, 2014 c 12, sch 11 para 121

    rep in pt—Legal Aid, Sentencing and Punishment of Offenders, 2012 c 10, sch 10 para 11(3)

s 222 ext—Legal Aid, Sentencing and Punishment of Offenders, 2012 c 10, s 153(2)

s 223 am—SI 2010/976, art 15, sch 18; Legal Aid, Sentencing and Punishment of Offenders, 2012 c 10, sch 7 para 19; (prosp) Anti-social Behaviour, Crime and Policing, 2014 c 12, sch 11 para 122

s 226 am—Anti-social Behaviour, Crime and Policing, 2014 c 12, sch 11 para 123

sch 1 am—Police and Justice, 2006 c 48, s 42, sch 13 para 16(1)(2); Anti-social Behaviour, Crime and Policing, 2014 c 12, sch 11 para 124

c 42   **Sexual Offences**

see—SI 2002/2013

s 15 am—Crim Justice and Immigration, 2008 c 4, s 73, sch 15 para 1; Crim Justice and Cts, 2015 c 2, s 36(1)

s 15A added—Serious Crime, 2015 c 9, s 67

s 21 am—Children, 2004 c 31, s 40, sch 3 para 18; (W prosp) Children and Young Persons, 2008 c 23, s 8, sch 1 para 15; Educ and Skills, 2008 c 25, s 169, sch 1 para 81; SIs 2010/813, art 13; 2011/1045, art 15

s 22 am—Nat Health Service (Conseq Provns), 2006 c 43, s 2, sch 1 para 238; SI 2010/813, art 13

    rep in pt—SI 2010/813, art 13

s 23 am—Civil Partnership, 2004 c 33, s 261(1), sch 27 para 173

s 27 am—Crim Justice and Immigration, 2008 c 4, s 73, sch 15 paras 2, 3; (W prosp) Children and Young Persons, 2008 c 23, s 8, sch 1 para 16

s 28 am—Civil Partnership, 2004 c 33, s 261(1), sch 27 para 174

s 29 am—Crim Justice and Immigration, 2008 c 4, s 73, sch 15 paras 2, 4

s 42 mod—(W) SI 2007/961 (W 85), art 3, sch

    am—SI 2010/813, art 13; Health and Social Care, 2012 c 7, sch 5 para 117(a)

    rep in pt—Health and Social Care, 2012 c 7, sch 5 para 117(b)

s 43 am—Civil Partnership, 2004 c 33, s 261(1), sch 27 para 175

s 48 am—Serious Crime, 2015 c 9, s 68(2)(3)

2003

c 42 *continued*

s 49 am—Serious Crime, 2015 c 9, s 68(4)

s 50 am—Serious Crime, 2015 c 9, s 68(5)

s 51 rep in pt—Serious Crime, 2015 c 9, s 68(6)(a)

am—Serious Crime, 2015 c 9, s 68(6)(b)

s 51A added—Policing and Crime, 2009 c 26, s 19

s 53A added—Policing and Crime, 2009 c 26, s 14

s 54 am—Policing and Crime, 2009 c 26, s 112, sch 7 para 24; Serious Crime, 2015 c 9, sch 4 para 62

ss 57-59 replaced (by s 59A)—Protection of Freedoms, 2012 c 9, s 109(2)

s 59A rep (EW)—Modern Slavery, 2015 c 30, sch 5 para 5(2)

s 60 am—UK Borders, 2007 c 30, s 31(4); Protection of Freedoms, 2012 c 9, s 109(3)(5)

rep in pt—Protection of Freedoms, 2012 c 9, s 109(4), sch 10 pt 9

ss 60A-60C added—Violent Crime Reduction, 2006 c 38, s 54, sch 4 para 2

rep (EW)—Modern Slavery, 2015 c 30, sch 5 para 5(2)

s 60A am—Protection of Freedoms, 2012 c 9, sch 9 para 140(2)

s 60B am—Protection of Freedoms, 2012 c 9, sch 9 para 140(3)

s 64 am—Crim Justice and Immigration, 2008 c 4, s 73, sch 15 paras 2, 5

appl (mods)—SI 2010/985, reg 5, sch 4

s 65 am—Crim Justice and Immigration, 2008 c 4, s 73, sch 15 paras 2, 6

appl (mods)—SI 2010/985, reg 5, sch 4

s 72 subst—Crim Justice and Immigration, 2008 c 4, s 72(1)

s 78 am—(prosp) Serious Crime, 2015 c 9, sch 4 para 63

s 80 appl—(S) Protection of Children and Prevention of Sexual Offences (S), 2005 asp 9, s 8(5)

s 81 rep in pt—Armed Forces, 2006 c 52, s 378, sch 16 para 206

s 82 am—(S) Management of Offenders etc (S), 2005 asp 14, s 17; Violent Crime Reduction, 2006 c 38, s 57(1); SSI 2011/25, sch para 2(2)

s 83 am—(S) Police, Public Order and Crim Justice (S), 2006 asp 10, s 78(1)-(3); Crim Justice and Immigration, 2008 c 4, ss 142(1), 148, sch 26 paras 53, 54

s 84 am—(S) Police, Public Order and Crim Justice (S), 2006 asp 10, s 78(4)(b)(c)(6); Crim Justice and Immigration, 2008 c 4, s 142(2)-(5)

rep in pt—(S) Police, Public Order and Crim Justice (S), 2006 asp 10, s 78(4)(5)(a)

s 85 am—Crim Justice and Immigration, 2008 c 4, ss 142(6)-(9), 148, sch 26 paras 53, 55; (S) Crim Justice and Licensing (S), 2010 asp 13, s 102(2)(a)-(c)

s 86 rep in pt—Crim Justice and Immigration, 2008 c 4, s 149, sch 28 pt 4; (S) Crim Justice and Licensing (S), 2010 asp 13, s 102(3)

s 87 am—(S) Police, Public Order and Crim Justice (S), 2006 asp 10, ss 77(6)(7), 78(7)

rep in pt—Crim Justice and Immigration, 2008 c 4, s 149, sch 28 pt 4; (S) Crim Justice and Licensing (S), 2010 asp 13, s 102(4); (S) SSI 2013/119, sch 1 para 20(2)

s 88 appl—(S) SSI 2004/205, reg 10(1)(a)

am—(S) Police, Public Order and Crim Justice (S), 2006 asp 10, s 77(6)(8); Anti-social Behaviour, Crime and Policing, 2014 c 12, sch 11 para 56

rep in pt—(S) SSI 2013/119, sch 1 para 20(3)

ss 88A-88I added—(S) SSIs 2010/370, arts 2, 3; 2011/45, art 3

s 88C am—(S) SSI 2013/119, sch 1 para 20(4)

s 89 am—(S) SSI 2013/119, sch 1 para 20(5)(a); Anti-social Behaviour, Crime and Policing, 2014 c 12, sch 11 para 57

rep in pt—(S) SSI 2013/119, sch 1 para 20(5)(b)

s 90 am—(S) SSI 2013/119, sch 1 para 20(6)

s 91 am—(S) Management of Offenders etc (S), 2005 asp 14, s 18; (S) Police, Public Order and Crim Justice (S), 2006 asp 10, ss 77(6)(9), 78(8)

ss 91A-91F added—SI 2012/1883, art 3

s 91A am—Anti-social Behaviour, Crime and Policing, 2014 c 12, sch 11 para 58

s 94 am—Serious Organised Crime and Police, 2005 c 15, s 59, sch 4 paras 193-195; Police and Justice, 2006 c 48, s 1, sch 1 para 90; SI 2008/2656, reg 3; SI 2013/602, sch 2 para 43; Crime and Cts, 2013 c 22, sch 8 para 154

rep in pt—SI 2012/2007, sch para 68

s 95 am—Serious Organised Crime and Police, 2005 c 15, s 59, sch 4 paras 193-195; SIs 2008/2656, reg 3; 2013/602, sch 2 para 43

rep in pt—SI 2012/2007, sch para 69

s 96 am—(S) Police, Public Order and Crim Justice (S), 2006 asp 10, s 79

rep in pt—(S) Crim Justice and Licensing (S), 2010 asp 13, s 102(5)

s 96A added (S)—Police, Public Order and Crim Justice (S), 2006 asp 10, s 80

2003

c 42 s 96A *continued*

    am—(S) SSI 2013/119, sch 1 para 20(7)(a)(ii)(bi)(c)(ii)

    mod—(S) SSI 2013/121, art 14

    rep in pt—(S) SSI 2013/119, sch 1 para 20(7)(a)(i)(c)(i)

s 96B added—Violent Crime Reduction, 2006 c 38, s 58(1)

ss 103-114 see—SI 2005/384, rule 50.1

s 103 am—(S) SSI 2013/119, sch 1 para 20(8)(a)

    rep in pt—(S) SSI 2013/119, sch 1 para 20(8)(b)

ss 103A-130K added—Anti-social Behaviour, Crime and Policing, 2014 c 12, sch 5 para 2

ss 104-122 rep (S NI prosp)—Anti-social Behaviour, Crime and Policing, 2014 c 12, sch 5
    para 3

s 104 am—Anti-social Behaviour, Crime and Policing, 2014 c 12, sch 11 para 59

s 105 am—(S) Protection of Children and Prevention of Sexual Offences (S), 2005 asp 9,
    s 17(1); (S) SSI 2013/119, sch 1 para 20(9)

s 106 am—Crim Justice and Immigration, 2008 c 4, s 141(1)

    rep in pt—(S) Crim Justice and Licensing (S), 2010 asp 13, s 100(2)(a)

s 107 am—SSI 2011/45, art 4(1)

s 108 am—(prosp) Armed Forces, 2011 c 18, s 17(2)

    rep in pt—Anti-social Behaviour, Crime and Policing, 2014 c 12, sch 11 para 60

s 109 am—(S) Crim Justice and Licensing (S), 2010 asp 13, s 100(2)(b)

    rep in pt—Anti-social Behaviour, Crime and Policing, 2014 c 12, sch 11 para 61

s 110 am—Anti-social Behaviour, Crime and Policing, 2014 c 12, sch 11 para 62

s 111 rep in pt—(S) Protection of Children and Prevention of Sexual Offences (S), 2005 asp
    9, s 17(2)(a)(i)(b)

    am—(S) Protection of Children and Prevention of Sexual Offences (S), 2005 asp 9,
    s 17(2)(a)(ii)(iii)(c); SSIs 2011/25, sch para 2(3); 2015/338, sch 2 para 8

s 111A added —(S) Crim Justice and Licensing (S), 2010 asp 13, s 100(2)(c)

s 112 rep in pt—(S) Protection of Children and Prevention of Sexual Offences (S), 2005 asp
    9, s 17(4)(a)(c)(i)(e)(ii)

    am—(S) Protection of Children and Prevention of Sexual Offences (S), 2005 asp 9,
    s 17(4)(b)(c)(ii)(iii)-(v)(d)(e)(i)(iii)(iv)(f)(5); (S) Crim Justice and Licensing (S),
    2010 asp 13, s 100(2)(d); (S) SSI 2013/119, sch 1 para 20(10)

s 113 am—SSI 2011/25, sch para 2(4); Anti-social Behaviour, Crime and Policing, 2014 c
    12, sch 11 para 63(2)(4)

    rep in pt—Anti-social Behaviour, Crime and Policing, 2014 c 12, sch 11 para 63(3)

s 114 am—Anti-social Behaviour, Crime and Policing, 2014 c 12, sch 11 para 64

s 115 am—Policing and Crime, 2009 c 26, s 23(1)(a)(2); (S) Crim Justice and Licensing (S),
    2010 asp 13, s 101(2)

    rep in pt—(EW, NI) Policing and Crime, 2009 c 26, s 112, sch 8 pt 2

s 116 am—Armed Forces, 2006 c 52, s 378, sch 16 para 207; Policing and Crime, 2009 c
    26, s 23(1)(b)(2); (S) Crim Justice and Licensing (S), 2010 asp 13, s 101(3)

s 117 am—Policing and Crime, 2009 c 26, s 24; (S) Crim Justice and Licensing (S), 2010
    asp 13, s 101(4)

s 117A added—Policing and Crime, 2009 c 26, s 25(1)(2)(4)

    am—Anti-social Behaviour, Crime and Policing, 2014 c 12, sch 11 para 65

s 117B added—(S) Crim Justice and Licensing (S), 2010 asp 13, s 101(5)

    am—Anti-social Behaviour, Crime and Policing, 2014 c 12, sch 11 para 66

s 119 am—Anti-social Behaviour, Crime and Policing, 2014 c 12, sch 11 para 67

s 121 am—(S) SSI 2013/119, sch 1 para 20(11)

s 122 am—Policing and Crime, 2009 c 26, s 25(1)(3); (S) Crim Justice and Licensing (S),
    2010 asp 13, s 101(6); SI 2011/2298, sch para 3(1); SSI 2011/25, sch para 2(5);
    Anti-social Behaviour, Crime and Policing, 2014 c 12, sch 11 para 68(2)(3)

    rep in pt—Anti-social Behaviour, Crime and Policing, 2014 c 12, sch 11 para 68(4)

ss 122A-122K added —Anti-social Behaviour, Crime and Policing, 2014 c 12, sch 5 para 4

ss 123-129 rep (S NI prosp)—Anti-social Behaviour, Crime and Policing, 2014 c 12, sch 5
    para 5(1)

s 123 am—(Anti-social Behaviour, Crime and Policing, 2014 c 12, sch 11 para 69; ibid, sch
    11 para 70(2)

    rep in pt—Anti-social Behaviour, Crime and Policing, 2014 c 12, sch 11 para 70(3)

s 125 am—Anti-social Behaviour, Crime and Policing, 2014 c 12, sch 11 para 71

s 126 am—Anti-social Behaviour, Crime and Policing, 2014 c 12, sch 11 para 72

s 127 am—Anti-social Behaviour, Crime and Policing, 2014 c 12, sch 11 para 73

s 128 am—Violent Crime Reduction, 2006 c 38, s 56(2); Anti-social Behaviour, Crime and
    Policing, 2014 c 12, sch 11 para 74

2003
c 42 *continued*

s 129 am—Violent Crime Reduction, 2006 c 38, s 56(3); Anti-social Behaviour, Crime and Policing, 2014 c 12, sch 11 para 75

s 131 am—Crim Justice, 2003 c 44, s 304, sch 32 pt 1 paras 142, 143; Armed Forces, 2006 c 52, s 378, sch 16 para 208; Legal Aid, Sentencing and Punishment of Offenders, 2012 c 10, sch 21 para 19, sch 22 para 20

s 132A added —Policing and Crime, 2009 c 26, s 22(1)(2)(4)

s 133 am—Crim Justice, 2003 c 44, s 304, sch 32 pt 1 paras 142, 144; Domestic Violence, Crime and Victims, 2004 c 28, s 58(1)(3), sch 10 para 57(1)(2); (EW) SI 2005/2078, art 15, sch 1 para 7; (S) SSI 2005/465, art 2, sch 1 para 33; Armed Forces, 2006 c 52, s 378, sch 16 para 209; Crim Justice and Immigration, 2008 c 4, s 148, sch 26 paras 53, 56; (S) SSIs 2010/370, art 4(1); 2011/25, sch para 2(6); 2011/45, art 4(2); Anti-social Behaviour, Crime and Policing, 2014 c 12, sch 11 para 76(2)

rep in pt—(S) SSI 2005/465, art 3, sch 2; Armed Forces, 2006 c 52, s 378, sch 16 para 209; Legal Aid, Sentencing and Punishment of Offenders, 2012 c 10, sch 24 para 25

mod—SI 2009/1059, art 205, sch 1

s 134 am—Armed Forces, 2006 c 52, s 378, sch 16 para 210; SSI 2011/25, sch para 2(7)

s 135 rep in pt—Domestic Violence, Crime and Victims, 2004 c 28, s 58, sch 10 para 58, sch 11

appl—Crim Justice, 2003 c 44, s 327B

am—(S) Crim Justice and Licensing (S), 2010 asp 13, s 203, sch 7 para 73

s 136 am—Violent Crime Reduction, 2006 c 38, s 58(2); Policing and Crime, 2009 c 26, s 22(1)(3)(4); SI 2010/976, art 12, sch 14; Anti-social Behaviour, Crime and Policing, 2014 c 12, sch 11 para 77

power to am conferred—(prosp) Anti-social Behaviour, Crime and Policing, 2014 c 12, s 181(3)

ss 136ZA-136ZD added —Anti-social Behaviour, Crime and Policing, 2014 c 12, sch 5 para 6

Pt 2A (ss 136A-136R) added (NI prosp)—Policing and Crime, 2009 c 26, s 21, sch 2 para 1

s 136A am—Anti-social Behaviour, Crime and Policing, 2014 c 12, sch 6 para 2(4)(6); Serious Crime, 2015 c 9, sch 4 paras 64, 65

rep in pt—Anti-social Behaviour, Crime and Policing, 2014 c 12, sch 6 para 2(2)(3)(5)

s 136B am—Anti-social Behaviour, Crime and Policing, 2014 c 12, sch 6 para 3

s 136BA added—Anti-social Behaviour, Crime and Policing, 2014 c 12, sch 6 para 4

s 136C am—Anti-social Behaviour, Crime and Policing, 2014 c 12, sch 6 para 5

s 136D am—Anti-social Behaviour, Crime and Policing, 2014 c 12, sch 6 para 6

s 136H am—Anti-social Behaviour, Crime and Policing, 2014 c 12, sch 6 para 7

s 136I am—Anti-social Behaviour, Crime and Policing, 2014 c 12, sch 6 para 8

s 136J am—Anti-social Behaviour, Crime and Policing, 2014 c 12, sch 6 para 9

s 136M am—Police Reform and Social Responsibility, 2011 c 13, sch 16 para 329

s 136O am—Anti-social Behaviour, Crime and Policing, 2014 c 12, sch 6 para 10

s 136R am—Anti-social Behaviour, Crime and Policing, 2014 c 12, sch 6 para 11

s 137 am—Armed Forces, 2006 c 52, s 378, sch 16 para 211; Anti-social Behaviour, Crime and Policing, 2014 c 12, sch 5 para 7

mod—SI 2009/1059, art 205, sch 1

s 138 am—(S) Police, Public Order and Crim Justice (S), 2006 asp 10, s 78(9); Crim Justice and Immigration, 2008 c 4, ss 142(10), 148, sch 26 paras 53, 57; (NI prosp) Policing and Crime, 2009 c 26, s 21, sch 2 para 2; (S) Crim Justice and Licensing (S), 2010 asp 13, s 102(6); (S) SSI 2010/370, arts 4(2); SI 2010/976, art 12, sch 14; SSI 2011/45, art 4(3)

appl (mods)—(S)(temp) SSI 2010/370, art 4(3)

mod—SSI 2011/45, art 4(4)

s 142 am—(S) Protection of Children and Prevention of Sexual Offences (S), 2005 asp 9, s 17(6); Violent Crime Reduction, 2006 c 38, s 54, sch 4 para 3; (NI prosp) Policing and Crime, 2009 c 26, s 21, sch 2 para 3; Anti-social Behaviour, Crime and Policing, 2014 c 12, s 113(2)

rep in pt—(S) Sexual Offences (S), 2009 asp 9, s 61, sch 6

power to am conferred—Anti-social Behaviour, Crime and Policing, 2014 c 12, s 181(3)

sch 1 rep in pt—Policing and Crime, 2009 c 26, s 112, sch 8 pt 2

sch 2 mod—Serious Crime, 2007 c 27, s 63, sch 6 para 47

2003

c 42 sch 2 *continued*

am—Crim Justice and Immigration, 2008 c 4, s 72(2)(3)(a)(b)(4)

rep in pt—Crim Justice and Immigration, 2008 c 4, ss 72(2)(3)(c), 149, sch 28 pt 5

sch 3 am—(S) Protection of Children and Prevention of Sexual Offences (S), 2005 asp 9, s 18, sch para 3(a)-(d); Armed Forces, 2006 c 52, s 378, sch 16 para 212; SI 2007/296, art 2; Serious Crime, 2007 c 27, ss 60, 63, sch 5 para 4(1)(2), sch 6 para 63(1)(2); Crim Justice and Immigration, 2008 c 4, s 148, sch 26 paras 53, 58; Coroners and Justice, 2009 c 25, s 177, sch 21 para 62(1)(2)(4)(5); ibid, s 177, sch 21 para 62(3); (S) Sexual Offences (S), 2009 asp 9, s 61, sch 5 para 5; (S) Crim Justice and Licensing (S), 2010 asp 13, ss 41(3)(a)(b), 42(3); SSI 2010/421, art 2, sch; Serious Crime, 2015 c 9, sch 4 para 66(3)(4); (prosp) ibid, sch 4 para 66(2)

rep in pt—Armed Forces, 2006 c 52, s 378, sch 16 para 212; (S) Sexual Offences (S), 2009 asp 9, s 61, sch 6

mod—SI 2009/1059, art 205, sch 1

ext—SI 2011/2298, sch para 3(2)

sch 5 am—Domestic Violence, Crime and Victims, 2004 c 28, s 58(1), sch 10 para 59(1)-(4); Armed Forces, 2006 c 52, s 378, sch 16 para 213; SI 2007/296, art 3; Serious Crime, 2007 c 27, ss 60, 63, sch 5 para 4(1)(3), sch 6 para 63(1)(3); Policing and Crime, 2009 c 26, s 112, sch 7 paras 24, 25; Domestic Violence, Crime and Victims (Amendment), 2012 c 4, sch para 5; Protection of Freedoms, 2012 c 9, sch 9 paras 140(4), 146; (EW) Modern Slavery, 2015 c 30, sch 5 para 5(3)

sch 6 rep in pt—Serious Organised Crime and Police, 2005 c 15, s 174(2), sch 17 pt 2; Armed Forces, 2006 c 52, s 378, sch 17; (S) Sexual Offences (S), 2009 asp 9, s 61, sch 6; Anti-social Behaviour, Crime and Policing, 2014 c 12, sch 11 para 50; (EW) Modern Slavery, 2015 c 30, sch 5 para 5(4)

c 43   **Health and Social Care (Community Health and Standards)**

appl—(Is of Scilly) SI 2004/567, art 2

mod—SI 2009/462,art 9, sch 3

ss 1-32 rep—Nat Health Service (Conseq Provns), 2006 c 43, s 6, sch 4

s 33 am—Nat Health Service (Conseq Provns), 2006 c 43, s 2, sch 1 para 240

rep in pt—Nat Health Service (Conseq Provns), 2006 c 43, s 6, sch 4; Corporation Tax, 2010 c 4, s 1181, sch 3 pt 1

ss 35-40 rep—Nat Health Service (Conseq Provns), 2006 c 43, s 6, sch 4

ss 41-44 rep—Health and Social Care, 2008 c 14, s 95, sch 5 para 36, sch 15

s 45 appl—(E) SIs 2005/1972, reg 2(1)(u); (E) 2005/1973, reg 2, sch para 7(1)

am—Nat Health Service (Conseq Provns), 2006 c 43, s 2, sch 1 para 241; Health and Social Care, 2008 c 14, s 95, sch 5 para 37; Health, 2009 c 21, s 13, sch 1 para 5

s 46 rep—Health and Social Care, 2008 c 14, s 95, sch 5 para 38, sch 15

s 47 am—Health, 2006 c 28, s 14

ss 47A-47C added—Health, 2006 c 28, s 14

rep—Health and Social Care, 2008 c 14, s 95, sch 5 para 39, sch 15

ss 48-69 rep—Health and Social Care, 2008 c 14, s 95, sch 5 para 40, sch 15

s 69A added—Public Audit (W), 2004 c 23, s 66, sch 2 paras 57, 59

rep —Health and Social Care, 2008 c 14, s 95, sch 5 para 40, sch 15

s 70 am—Public Audit (W), 2004 c 23, s 66, sch 2 paras 57, 60

s 71 am—Health and Social Care, 2012 c 7, sch 5 para 119(a)

rep in pt—Health and Social Care, 2012 c 7, sch 5 para 119(b)

s 75 am—Health, 2006 c 28, s 80, sch 8 para 54

ss 76-87 rep—Health and Social Care, 2008 c 14, s 95, sch 5 para 41, sch 15

ss 88-91 rep —Health and Social Care, 2008 c 14, s 95, sch 5 para 41, sch 15

Pt 2, Ch 6 (ss 92-101) appl (mods)—Children, 2004 c 31, s 30(1)

s 94 ext—Public Audit (W), 2004 c 23, s 41(6)

appl—SI 2006/878 (W 83), reg 5

s 95 ext—Public Audit (W), 2004 c 23, ss 41(6), 42(4)

rep in pt—Loc Audit and Accountability, 2014 c 2, sch 12 para 56

s 96 subst—Educ and Inspections, 2006 c 40, s 157, sch 14 para 88

am—Health and Social Care, 2008 c 14, s 95, sch 5 para 42

s 100 am—Health and Social Care, 2008 c 14, s 95, sch 5 para 43

ss 102-104 rep—Health and Social Care, 2008 c 14, s 95, sch 5 para 44, sch 15

s 110 rep—Educ and Inspections, 2006 c 40, s 157, sch 14 para 89, sch 18

s 112 rep—Educ and Inspections, 2006 c 40, s 157, sch 14 para 90, sch 18

2003
c 43 *continued*

s 113 am—Public Services Ombudsman (W), 2005 c 10, s 39(1), sch 6 paras 74, 75; Nat Health Service (Conseq Provns), 2006 c 43, s 2, sch 1 para 242; GSM C of E Marriage, 2008 No 1, s 10; (W) NHS Redress (W), 2008 nawm 1, s 10; Health and Social Care, 2012 c 7, sch 5 para 120

  rep in pt—Health and Social Care, 2008 c 14, s 95, sch 5 para 45, sch 15

s 114 rep in pt—Public Services Ombudsman (W), 2005 c 10, s 39, sch 6 paras 74, 76(a), sch 7; Health and Social Care, 2008 c 14, s 95, sch 5 para 46, sch 15

  am—Public Services Ombudsman (W), 2005 c 10, s 39(1), sch 6 paras 74, 76(b); Nat Health Service (Conseq Provns), 2006 c 43, s 2, sch 1 para 243; Loc Govt and Public Involvement in Health, 2007 c 28, s 182, sch 12 para 18

s 115 appl—Nat Health Service, 2006 c 41, s 73C(5)

s 116 rep in pt—Educ and Inspections, 2006 c 40, s 184, sch 18

ss 120-141 rep—Health and Social Care, 2008 c 14, s 95, sch 5 para 47, sch 15

s 143 subst—Health and Social Care, 2008 c 14, s 95, sch 5 para 48

s 144 rep—Health and Social Care, 2008 c 14, s 95, sch 5 para 49, sch 15

s 145 rep—Health and Social Care, 2008 c 14, s 95, sch 5 para 50, sch 15

s 145A added—Public Audit (W), 2004 c 23, s 66, sch 2 paras 57, 61

  rep—Health and Social Care, 2008 c 14, s 95, sch 5 para 50, sch 15

s 148 appl—Public Audit (W), 2004 c 23, s 64(3); Mental Capacity, 2005 c 9, s 49(10); (E) SI 2005/1972, reg 2(1)(v)

  am—Nat Health Service (Conseq Provns), 2006 c 43, s 2, sch 1 para 246; Educ and Inspections, 2006 c 40, s 157, sch 14 para 93; Health and Social Care, 2012 c 7, sch 5 para 121(c); SI 2012/961, sch 1 para 6

  rep in pt—Loc Govt and Public Involvement in Health, 2007 c 28, s 146, sch 9 para 1(1)(2)(v), sch 18; Health and Social Care, 2008 c 14, s 95, sch 5 para 51, sch 15; Health and Social Care, 2012 c 7, sch 5 para 121(a)(b); (prosp) ibid, sch 14 para 90; Loc Audit and Accountability, 2014 c 2, sch 12 para 57

s 150 am—Nat Health Service (Conseq Provns), 2006 c 43, s 2, sch 1 para 247; Health, 2006 c 28, s 80, sch 8 para 55

s 153 subst—Health, 2006 c 28, s 73

s 155 am—Tribunals, Cts and Enforcement, 2007 c 15, s 62, sch 13 para 152; Crime and Cts, 2013 c 22, sch 9 para 52

s 157 am—SI 2008/2833, art 6, sch 3

  rep in pt—SI 2008/2833, art 6, sch 3

s 158 am—SI 2008/2833, art 6, sch 3

  rep in pt—SI 2008/2833, art 6, sch 3

s 159 rep—SI 2008/2833, art 6, sch 3

s 160 am—Nat Health Service (Conseq Provns), 2006 c 43, s 2, sch 1 para 248; Health and Social Care, 2012 c 7, sch 5 para 122(a)

  rep in pt—Health and Social Care, 2012 c 7, sch 5 para 122(b); (prosp) ibid, sch 14 para 91

s 162 am—Nat Health Service (Conseq Provns), 2006 c 43, s 2, sch 1 para 249; (prosp) Health and Social Care, 2012 c 7, sch 14 para 92(a)

  rep in pt—(prosp) Health and Social Care, 2012 c 7, sch 14 para 92(b)-(d)

s 165 am—Nat Health Service (Conseq Provns), 2006 c 43, s 2, sch 1 para 250; Health and Social Care, 2012 c 7, sch 5 para 123(b)

  rep in pt—Health and Social Care, 2012 c 7, sch 5 para 123(a); (prosp) ibid, sch 14 para 93

s 168 am—Nat Health Service (Conseq Provns), 2006 c 43, s 2, sch 1 para 251

ss 170-172 rep—Nat Health Service (Conseq Provns), 2006 c 43, s 6, sch 4

ss 174, 175 rep—Nat Health Service (Conseq Provns), 2006 c 43, s 6, sch 4

ss 177-183 rep—Nat Health Service (Conseq Provns), 2006 c 43, s 6, sch 4

s 187 rep in pt—Health, 2006 c 28, s 80, sch 8 para 56, sch 9

s 188 rep—Health, 2006 c 28, s 80, sch 8 para 57, sch 9

s 189 rep in pt—Legislative and Regulatory Reform, 2006 c 51, s 30, sch 1; Safeguarding Vulnerable Groups, 2006 c 47, s 63, sch 10

ss 191, 192 rep—Nat Health Service (Conseq Provns), 2006 c 43, s 6, sch 4

s 194 am—Nat Health Service (Conseq Provns), 2006 c 43, s 2, sch 1 para 252

s 195 rep in pt—Nat Health Service (Conseq Provns), 2006 c 43, s 6, sch 4

s 338 power mod—Offender Rehabilitation, 2014 c 11, s 23(7)

sch 1 rep—Nat Health Service (Conseq Provns), 2006 c 43, s 6, sch 4

sch 2 rep in pt—Nat Health Service (Conseq Provns), 2006 c 43, s 6, sch 4; Health and Social Care, 2012 c 7, sch 13 paras 3(2), 5(2), 6(2)

2003
c 43 *continued*

sch 4 rep in pt—Inquiries, 2005 c 12, ss 44(5), 49(2), sch 3; Mental Health, 2007 c 12, s 55, sch 11 pt 3; Equality, 2010 c 15, sch 27 pt 1A (added by SI 2011/1060, sch 3); Health and Social Care, 2012 c 7, s 39(4)(d)

schs 6-8 rep—Health and Social Care, 2008 c 14, s 95, sch 5 para 52, sch 15

sch 9 rep in pt—(prosp) Health and Social Care (Community Health and Standards), 2003 c 43, s 196, sch 14 pt 2; Safeguarding Vulnerable Groups, 2006 c 47, s 63, sch 10; Educ and Inspections, 2006 c 40, s 184, sch 18; Loc Govt and Public Involvement in Health, 2007 c 28, s 241, sch 18; Loc Audit and Accountability, 2014 c 2, sch 1 pt 2

sch 10 am—Damages (S), 2011 asp 7, sch 1 para 8; Financial Services, 2012 c 21, sch 18 para 99; Modern Slavery, 2015 c 30, sch 5 para 26

sch 11 rep in pt—Public Services Ombudsman (W), 2005 c 10, s 39(2), sch 7; Nat Health Service (Conseq Provns), 2006 c 43, s 6, sch 4; (prosp) Health, 2006 c 28, s 80, sch 9

sch 12 rep in pt—Health, 2006 c 28, s 80, sch 9

sch 13 rep in pt—Nat Health Service (Conseq Provns), 2006 c 43, s 6, sch 4; Corporation Tax, 2010 c 4, s 1181, sch 3 pt 1

c 44 **Criminal Justice**

power to am conferred—Offender Rehabilitation, 2014 c 11, s 7

s 3 rep—Serious Organised Crime and Police, 2005 c 15, s 174(2), sch 17 pt 2

s 5 rep in pt—Drugs, 2005 c 17, s 23, sch 1 para 8, sch 2

s 20 am—(temp) SI 2004/829, art 2(3)(a)(i)(b)
rep in pt—(temp) SI 2004/829, art 2(3)(a)(ii)

Pt 3 (ss 22-27) excl—Crim Justice and Cts, 2015 c 2, s 17(8)(a)

s 22 am—(pt prosp) Police and Justice, 2006 c 48, s 17(1)-(3); Legal Aid, Sentencing and Punishment of Offenders, 2012 c 10, ss 133(1), 134(a)(b)

s 23 am—Legal Aid, Sentencing and Punishment of Offenders, 2012 c 10, s 133(3)

s 23ZA added—Anti-social Behaviour, Crime and Policing, 2014 c 12, s 103(1)

s 23A added—Police and Justice, 2006 c 48, s 17(1)(4)
am—Crim Justice and Immigration, 2008 c 4, s 148, sch 26 paras 59, 60(1)-(4); Legal Aid, Sentencing and Punishment of Offenders, 2012 c 10, s 133(4); SI 2015/664, sch 5 para 10
rep in pt—Crim Justice and Immigration, 2008 c 4, s 148, sch 26 paras 59, 60(1)(5); ibid, s 149, sch 28 pt 4

s 23B added —Crim Justice and Immigration, 2008 c 4, s 148, sch 26 paras 59, 61
am—Legal Aid, Sentencing and Punishment of Offenders, 2012 c 10, s 133(5)

s 24A added—Police and Justice, 2006 c 48, s 18(1)(2)
appl—Crime and Disorder, 1998 c 37, s 66E

s 24B added—Police and Justice, 2006 c 48, s 18(1)
appl—Crime and Disorder, 1998 c 37, s 66E

s 25 see—SI 2004/1683, art 2
am—Police and Justice, 2006 c 48, s 52, sch 14 para 58; Legal Aid, Sentencing and Punishment of Offenders, 2012 c 10, s 133(6)
rep in pt—Police and Justice, 2006 c 48, s 52, sch 15

s 27 am—Commrs for Revenue and Customs, 2005 c 11, s 50(6), sch 4 para 129
rep in pt—Commrs for Revenue and Customs, 2005 c 11, ss 50(6), 52(2), sch 4 para 129(b), sch 5; SI 2014/834, sch 2 para 38

s 29 am—Serious Organised Crime and Police, 2005 c 15, s 59, sch 4 para 196; Commrs for Revenue and Customs, 2005 c 11, s 50(6), sch 4 para 130; Crime and Cts, 2013 c 22, sch 8 para 187; Crim Justice and Cts, 2015 c 2, s 46
rep in pt—SI 2014/834, sch 2 para 39

s 30 am—SI 2004/2035, art 3, sch paras 45, 46(1)(2); Crim Justice and Cts, 2015 c 2, s 47
rep in pt—SI 2004/2035, art 3, sch paras 45, 46(1)(3)

s 32 rep in pt—(S) Crim Justice and Licensing (S), 2010 asp 13, s 14, sch 2 para 49

s 43 rep—Protection of Freedoms, 2012 c 9, s 113, sch 10 pt 10

s 45 rep in pt—Terrorism, 2006 c 11, s 37, sch 3; Protection of Freedoms, 2012 c 9, sch 9 para 148(2)(b)(c), sch 10 pt 10
am—Protection of Freedoms, 2012 c 9, sch 9 para 148(2)(a)

s 46 rep in pt—Protection of Freedoms, 2012 c 9, sch 9 para 148(3), sch 10 pt 10

s 48 am—Domestic Violence, Crime and Victims, 2004 c 28, ss 58(1), 59, sch 10 para 60, sch 12 para 8(1)(2)(d)
rep in pt—Protection of Freedoms, 2012 c 9, sch 9 para 148(4), sch 10 pt 10

2003

c 44 *continued*

s 50 am—Domestic Violence, Crime and Victims, 2004 c 28, ss 58(1), 59, sch 10 para 61, sch 12 para 8(1)(2)(d); Constitutional Reform, 2005 c 4, s 40(4), sch 9 pt 1 para 82(1)(2); SI 2010/976, art 12, sch 14

s 53 am—SI 2005/886, art 2, sch para 99

s 55 am—SI 2004/2035, art 3, sch paras 45, 47

s 56 rep in pt—SIs 2004/2035, art 3, sch paras 45, 48; 2005/886, art 2, sch para 100
   am—SI 2005/886, art 2, sch para 100; Legal Services, 2007 c 29, s 208, sch 21 paras 145, 146

s 58 am—Domestic Violence, Crime and Victims, 2004 c 28, s 30

s 61 am—Crim Justice and Immigration, 2008 c 4, s 44

s 62 am—Crim Justice and Cts, 2015 c 2, s 7(2)

ss 62A, 62B added—Crim Justice and Cts, 2015 c 2, s 7(3)

s 71 am—Constitutional Reform, 2005 c 4, s 40(4), sch 9 pt 1 para 82(1)(3); Legal Aid, Sentencing and Punishment of Offenders, 2012 c 10, sch 5 para 65

s 74 am—Domestic Violence, Crime and Victims, 2004 c 28, s 58(1), sch 10 para 62

s 76 am—SI 2012/1809, art 3(1), sch pt 1

s 81 am—Constitutional Reform, 2005 c 4, s 40(4), sch 9 pt 1 para 82(1)(4)

s 88 am—Crim Justice and Immigration, 2008 c 4, sch 26 paras 59, 63

s 89 am—Crim Justice and Immigration, 2008 c 4, sch 26 paras 59, 63

s 91 am—Crim Justice and Immigration, 2008 c 4, sch 26 paras 59, 63

s 94 am—Armed Forces, 2006 c 52, s 378, sch 16 para 214

s 97 rep in pt—SI 2010/976, art 12, sch 14
   am—SI 2010/976, art 12, sch 14

s 98 appl—SI 2005/384, rule 35.1

s 103 am—Coroners and Justice, 2009 c 25, s 144, sch 17 para 1(1)(2)

s 108 am—Coroners and Justice, 2009 c 25, s 144, sch 17 para 1(1)(3)

s 111 am—SI 2004/2035, art 3, sch paras 45, 49

s 112 am—Armed Forces, 2006 c 52, s 378, sch 16 para 215
   mod—SI 2009/1059, art 205, sch 1

s 117 mod—SI 2009/1059, art 205, sch 1

s 120 appl (mods)—SI 2007/236, art 120
   rep in pt—Coroners and Justice, 2009 c 25, ss 112, 178 sch 23 pt 3

s 127 am—SI 2004/2035, art 3, sch paras 45, 50(a)
   rep in pt—SI 2004/2035, art 3, sch paras 45, 50(b)(c)

s 132 am—SI 2004/2035, art 3, sch paras 45, 51

s 134 mod—SI 2009/1059, art 205, sch 1

s 138 rep in pt—Coroners and Justice, 2009 c 25, ss 111, 178, sch 23 pt 3

Pt 12 (ss 142-305) mod—(temp) SI 2005/643, arts 2, 3
   am (heading)—Offender Rehabilitation, 2014 c 11, sch 3 para 20

Pt 12, Ch 1 (ss 142-176) power to am—Crim Justice and Immigration, 2008 c 4, s 4(3)

s 142 am—Violent Crime Reduction, 2006 c 38, s 49, sch 1 para 9(2); Crim Justice and Immigration, 2008 c 4, ss 9(2)(a), 148, sch 26 paras 59, 64; Legal Aid, Sentencing and Punishment of Offenders, 2012 c 10, sch 19 para 9, sch 26 para 16(2)(3); Crim Justice and Cts, 2015 c 2, sch 5 para 10
   rep in pt—(prosp) Crim Justice and Immigration, 2008 c 4, ss 9(2), 149, sch 28 pt 2

s 142A added (prosp)—Crim Justice and Immigration, 2008 c 4, s 9(1)
   am—Legal Aid, Sentencing and Punishment of Offenders, 2012 c 10, sch 26 para 17(2)(3); Crim Justice and Cts, 2015 c 2, sch 5 para 11

s 143 am—Armed Forces, 2006 c 52, s 378, sch 16 para 216; Coroners and Justice, 2009 c 25, s 144, sch 17 para 6(1)(2)(b)(3)
   rep in pt—Coroners and Justice, 2009 c 25, ss 144, 178, sch 17 para 6(1)(2)(a), sch 23 pt 5
   mod—SI 2009/1059, art 205, sch 1
   appl (mod)—SI 2009/2042, regs 3, 4, 10

s 144 am—Legal Aid, Sentencing and Punishment of Offenders, 2012 c 10, sch 26 para 18; Crim Justice and Cts, 2015 c 2, sch 5 para 12

s 146 am—Legal Aid, Sentencing and Punishment of Offenders, 2012 c 10, s 65(3)-(6)

s 147 am—Crim Justice and Immigration, 2008 c 4, s 6, sch 4 paras 71, 72(1)(2)(b)
   rep in pt—Crim Justice and Immigration, 2008 c 4, ss 6, 149, sch 4 paras 71, 72(1)(2)(a)(3), sch 28 pt 1

s 148 appl—(transtl provns) Crim Justice and Immigration, 2008 c 4, s 1(6)(a)
   excl —Crim Justice and Immigration, 2008 c 4, s 1, sch 1 para 5(2)(b)

2003
c 44 s 148 *continued*

        rep in pt—Crim Justice and Immigration, 2008 c 4, ss 6, 149, sch 4 paras 71, 73(1)(2)(a)(4), sch 28 pt 1

        am—Crim Justice and Immigration, 2008 c 4, s 6, sch 4 paras 71, 73(1)(2)(b)(3); ibid, s 10; Crime and Cts, 2013 c 22, sch 16 para 3

s 149 am—Crim Justice and Immigration, 2008 c 4, s 6, sch 4 paras 71, 74

s 150 am—Violent Crime Reduction, 2006 c 38, s 49, sch 1 para 9(3); Crim Justice and Immigration, 2008 c 4, s 6, sch 4 paras 71, 75; ibid,s 148, sch 26 paras 59, 65; Legal Aid, Sentencing and Punishment of Offenders, 2012 c 10, sch 19 para 10; Crime and Cts, 2013 c 22, sch 16 para 23(1); Crim Justice and Cts, 2015 c 2, sch 5 para 13

        rep in pt—Violent Crime Reduction, 2006 c 38, ss 49, 65, sch 1 para 9(3), sch 5

        appl—(transtl provns) Crim Justice and Immigration, 2008 c 4, s 1(6)(a)

s 150A added—Crim Justice and Immigration, 2008 c 4, s 11(1)

s 151 am—Domestic Violence, Crime and Victims, 2004 c 28, s 58(1), sch 10 para 63; Armed Forces, 2006 c 52, s 378, sch 16 para 217; Crim Justice and Immigration, 2008 c 4, ss 6, 11(2)-(6), sch 4 paras 71, 76; (prosp) Coroners and Justice, 2009 c 25, s 144, sch 17 para 8; Prevention of Social Housing Fraud, 2013 c 3, sch para 29; Crim Justice and Cts, 2015 c 2, sch 12 para 13; Modern Slavery, 2015 c 30, sch 5 para 24

s 152 am—Violent Crime Reduction, 2006 c 38, s 49, sch 1 para 9(4); Crim Justice and Immigration, 2008 c 4, s 148, sch 26 paras 59, 66; Legal Aid, Sentencing and Punishment of Offenders, 2012 c 10, sch 19 para 11, sch 26 para 20; Crim Justice and Cts, 2015 c 2, sch 5 para 14

        appl—Crim Justice and Immigration, 2008 c 4, s 2, sch 2 para 6(14)

s 153 am—Violent Crime Reduction, 2006 c 38, s 49, sch 1 para 9(5); Legal Aid, Sentencing and Punishment of Offenders, 2012 c 10, sch 19 para 12, sch 21 para 21, sch 26 para 21; Crim Justice and Cts, 2015 c 2, sch 5 para 15

        rep in pt—Crim Justice and Immigration, 2008 c 4, ss 148, 149, sch 26 paras 59, 67, sch 28 pt 2

s 154 am—Tribunals, Cts and Enforcement, 2007 c 15, s 62, sch 13 paras 153, 154

        transtl provns—SI 2008/1098, art 10

        appl (mods)—SI 2010/2837, art 27, sch 4

s 156 am—Crim Justice and Immigration, 2008 c 4, s 6, sch 4 paras 71, 77(1)(2)(4); Legal Aid, Sentencing and Punishment of Offenders, 2012 c 10, sch 19 para 13, sch 21 para 22(2)(3)

        rep in pt—Crim Justice and Immigration, 2008 c 4, ss 6, 149, sch 4 paras 71, 77(1)(3), sch 28 pt 1

s 157 am—Health and Social Care, 2012 c 7, s 38(5)(d)

s 158 rep in pt—Children, 2004 c 31, s 64, sch 5 pt 4

        am—Crim Justice and Immigration, 2008 c 4, s 12; SI 2008/912, art 3, sch 1

s 159 am—Legal Services, 2007 c 29, s 208, sch 21 paras 145, 147

s 160 am—Legal Services, 2007 c 29, s 208, sch 21 paras 145, 148; SI 2008/912, art 3, sch 1

s 161 rep in pt—Children, 2004 c 31, s 64, sch 5 pt 4; Crim Justice and Immigration, 2008 c 4, ss 6, 149, sch 4 paras 71, 78, sch 28 pt 1

s 161A added—Domestic Violence, Crime and Victims, 2004 c 28, ss 14(1), 59, sch 12 para 7

        excl—SIs 2007/707, art 2; 1079, art 3; 2012/1696, art 2

        am—Prevention of Social Housing Fraud, 2013 c 3, sch para 30; Modern Slavery, 2015 c 30, sch 5 para 25

s 161B added—Domestic Violence, Crime and Victims, 2004 c 28, ss 14(1), 59, sch 12 para 7

s 162 am—Crime and Cts, 2013 c 22, sch 16 para 24

s 163 am—Crim Justice and Immigration, 2008 c 4, s 148, sch 26 paras 59, 68; Legal Aid, Sentencing and Punishment of Offenders, 2012 c 10, sch 19 para 14

s 164 am—Domestic Violence, Crime and Victims, 2004 c 28, ss 14(2), 59, sch 12 para 7; Crim Justice and Cts, 2015 c 2, sch 11 para 23

s 166 am—Crim Justice and Immigration, 2008 c 4, s 11(6)

ss 167, 168 rep—Coroners and Justice, 2009 c 25, s 178, sch 23 pt 4

ss 170-173 rep —Coroners and Justice, 2009 c 25, s 178, sch 23 pt 4

s 174 subst—Legal Aid, Sentencing and Punishment of Offenders, 2012 c 10, s 64(2)

s 176 rep in pt—Crim Justice and Immigration, 2008 c 4, ss 6, 149, sch 4 paras 71, 81(a), sch 28 pt 1; Coroners and Justice, 2009 c 25, s 178, sch 23 pt 4

2003

c 44 s 176 *continued*

    am—Crim Justice and Immigration, 2008 c 4, s 6, sch 4 paras 71, 81(b)

s 177 am—Crim Justice and Immigration, 2008 c 4, s 6, sch 4 paras 71, 82; Legal Aid,
    Sentencing and Punishment of Offenders, 2012 c 10, s 66(1)(a)(2), 72(1)(2); (pt
    prosp) ibid, s 76(2)(3); Crime and Cts, 2013 c 22, sch 16 para 2; (prosp) ibid,
    sch 16 para 12(2)-(4); Offender Rehabilitation, 2014 c 11, s 15(2); ibid, sch 5
    para 2(4)(a)

    rep in pt—Legal Aid, Sentencing and Punishment of Offenders, 2012 c 10, ss 66(1)(b),
    70(1); (prosp) Crime and Cts, 2013 c 22, sch 16 para 12(5); Offender
    Rehabilitation, 2014 c 11, sch 5 para 2(2)(3)(4)(b)

    mod—Armed Forces, 2006 c 52 s 182(3A)

Pt 12 Ch 3 (ss 181-195) am—(heading subst) Legal Aid, Sentencing and Punishment of
    Offenders, 2012 c 10, sch 9 para 3

ss 181-188 rep—Legal Aid, Sentencing and Punishment of Offenders, 2012 c 10, s 89(1)(a)

s 189 mod—(temp) Legal Aid, Sentencing and Punishment of Offenders, 2012 c 10, sch 9
    para 20

    am—Legal Aid, Sentencing and Punishment of Offenders, 2012 c 10, s 68

s 190 am—Legal Aid, Sentencing and Punishment of Offenders, 2012 c 10, s 72(3)(4), sch 9
    para 4; (prosp) ibid, s 76(4)(5); (prosp) Crime and Cts, 2013 c 22, sch 16 para
    13(2)-(4); Offender Rehabilitation, 2014 c 11, s 15(2); ibid, sch 5 para 3(4)(a)

    rep in pt—Legal Aid, Sentencing and Punishment of Offenders, 2012 c 10, s 70(2);
    (prosp) Crime and Cts, 2013 c 22, sch 16 para 13(5); Offender Rehabilitation,
    2014 c 11, sch 5 para 3(2)(3)(4)(b)

s 191 am—Legal Aid, Sentencing and Punishment of Offenders, 2012 c 10, sch 9 para 5;
    Offender Rehabilitation, 2014 c 11, sch 4 para 2

s 192 rep in pt—SI 2005/886, art 2, sch para 101; Offender Rehabilitation, 2014 c 11, sch 4
    para 3(2)(a)

    am—(prosp) Crime and Cts, 2013 c 22, sch 16 para 14; Offender Rehabilitation, 2014
    c 11, sch 4 para 3(2)(b)(3)

s 195 am—Legal Aid, Sentencing and Punishment of Offenders, 2012 c 10, sch 9 para 6

    rep in pt—Legal Aid, Sentencing and Punishment of Offenders, 2012 c 10, sch 10 para
    13

Pt 12 Ch 4 (ss 196-223) appl (mods)—Children, 1989 c 41, sch A1 paras 1-3

s 196 am—Legal Aid, Sentencing and Punishment of Offenders, 2012 c 10, sch 9 para
    7(2)(3), sch 10 para 14(2)(a)

    rep in pt—Legal Aid, Sentencing and Punishment of Offenders, 2012 c 10, sch 10 para
    14(2)(b)(c)(3)

s 197 subst—Offender Rehabilitation, 2014 c 11, s 14(1)

s 198 mod—Armed Forces, 2006 c 52 s 183(1A)

    am—Offender Rehabilitation, 2014 c 11, sch 4 para 11(2)(a)

    rep in pt—Offender Rehabilitation, 2014 c 11, sch 4 para 11(2)(b)(3)

s 199 rep in pt—Children, 2004 c 31, s 64, sch 5 pt 4; Crim Justice and Immigration, 2008 c
    4, ss 6, 149, sch 4 paras 71, 84(b), sch 28 pt 1

    am—Crim Justice and Immigration, 2008 c 4, s 6, sch 4 paras 71, 84(a); SI 2008/912,
    art 3, sch 1

s 200 am—Legal Aid, Sentencing and Punishment of Offenders, 2012 c 10, sch 9 para 8

s 200A added —Offender Rehabilitation, 2014 c 11, s 15(3)

s 201 rep —Offender Rehabilitation, 2014 c 11, s 15(4)

s 202 rep in pt—Offender Management, 2007 c 21, s 39, sch 5 pt 3; SI 2008/912, art 3, sch
    1; Legal Aid, Sentencing and Punishment of Offenders, 2012 c 10, s 70(5), sch
    10 para 16; Offender Rehabilitation, 2014 c 11, s 16(2)

    am—Offender Management, 2007 c 21, s 31; Crim Justice and Immigration, 2008 c 4,
    s 6, sch 4 paras 71, 86; SI 2008/912, art 3, sch 1; Legal Aid, Sentencing and
    Punishment of Offenders, 2012 c 10, s 70(4)(6)(a)(b)(7)

s 203 am—Crim Justice and Immigration, 2008 c 4, s 6, sch 4 paras 71, 87; SI 2008/912,
    art 3, sch 1

    rep in pt—SI 2008/912, art 3, sch 1

s 204 am—Legal Aid, Sentencing and Punishment of Offenders, 2012 c 10, s 71(2)(3)

    rep in pt—Legal Aid, Sentencing and Punishment of Offenders, 2012 c 10, sch 10 para
    17

s 206 mod—Armed Forces, 2006 c 52, s 182, sch 6 para 3

    am—SI 2008/912, art 3, sch 1

s 206A added—Legal Aid, Sentencing and Punishment of Offenders, 2012 c 10, s 72(5)

s 207 mod—Armed Forces, 2006 c 52, s 182, sch 6 para 4

2003
c 44 s 207 *continued*

am—SIs 2009/1182, arts 4, 5-7, sch 5; 2010/813, art 14; Health and Social Care,
2012 c 7, s 213(8)(b); Legal Aid, Sentencing and Punishment of Offenders, 2012
c 10, s 73(2)(b)

rep in pt—Legal Aid, Sentencing and Punishment of Offenders, 2012 c 10, s
73(2)(a)(3)

s 208 mod—Armed Forces, 2006 c 52, s 182, sch 6 para 4

s 209 mod—Armed Forces, 2006 c 52, s 182, sch 6 para 5

am—Crim Justice and Immigration, 2008 c 4, s 6, sch 4 paras 71, 88; SI 2008/912,
art 3, sch 1

rep in pt—SI 2008/912, art 3, sch 1; Legal Aid, Sentencing and Punishment of
Offenders, 2012 c 10, s 74(1)

s 210 am—Offender Rehabilitation, 2014 c 11, sch 4 para 4

s 211 rep in pt—SI 2005/886, art 2, sch para 101; Crim Justice and Immigration, 2008 c 4,
ss 6, 149, sch 4 paras 71, 89, sch 28 pt 1; Legal Aid, Sentencing and
Punishment of Offenders, 2012 c 10, s 74(2)(b); Offender Rehabilitation, 2014
c 11, sch 4 para 5(2)(a)

am—Legal Aid, Sentencing and Punishment of Offenders, 2012 c 10, s 74(2)(a);
Offender Rehabilitation, 2014 c 11, sch 4 para 5(2)(b)(3)

s 212 rep in pt—Legal Aid, Sentencing and Punishment of Offenders, 2012 c 10, s 75(1)

s 212A added (pt prosp)—Legal Aid, Sentencing and Punishment of Offenders, 2012 c 10, s
76(1)

s 213 rep —Offender Rehabilitation, 2014 c 11, s 15(4)

s 214 rep in pt—Crim Justice and Immigration, 2008 c 4, s 6, sch 4 paras 71, 90

am—Offender Rehabilitation, 2014 c 11, s 17(3)(a)(b)(4)(5)

s 215 am—(pt prosp) Legal Aid, Sentencing and Punishment of Offenders, 2012 c 10, s
76(6); (prosp) Crime and Cts, 2013 c 22, sch 16 para 16

s 215A added (prosp)—Crime and Cts, 2013 c 22, sch 16 para 17

excl—(prosp) Armed Forces, 2006 c 52, s 183(1) (amended by 2013 c 22, sch 16
para 37(3))

s 216 am—SI 2005/886, art 2, sch para 103

rep in pt—Legal Aid, Sentencing and Punishment of Offenders, 2012 c 10, sch 10 para
19

s 217 am—Crim Justice and Immigration, 2008 c 4, s 6, sch 4 paras 71, 91

s 218 am—SI 2005/886, art 2, sch para 104; (prosp) Crime and Cts, 2013 c 22, sch 16 para
18; Offender Rehabilitation, 2014 c 11, s 17(7)(8)

rep in pt—Offender Rehabilitation, 2014 c 11, sch 5 para 4

s 219 am—SIs 2005/886, art 2, sch para 105; 2008/912, art 3, sch 1; Offender
Rehabilitation, 2014 c 11, sch 4 para 12

s 220 rep in pt—Offender Rehabilitation, 2014 c 11, s 18(3)

s 220A added —Offender Rehabilitation, 2014 c 11, s 18(2)

mod—Armed Forces, 2006 c 52, s 183(3A)

excl—Armed Forces, 2006 c 52, s 183(1)

s 221 rep in pt—(pt prosp) Crim Justice and Immigration, 2008 c 4, ss 6, 149, sch 4 paras
71, 92(a)(c), sch 28 pt 1

am—Crim Justice and Immigration, 2008 c 4, s 6, sch 4 paras 71, 92(b)(3); ibid, s
148, sch 26 para 2(1)(2); Police Reform and Social Responsibility, 2011 c 13,
sch 16 para 313

s 222 am—SI 2008/912, art 3, sch 1; Offender Rehabilitation, 2014 c 11, sch 5 para 5(b)

rep in pt—Offender Rehabilitation, 2014 c 11, sch 5 para 5(a)

s 223 am—(pt prosp) Legal Aid, Sentencing and Punishment of Offenders, 2012 c 10, s
76(7)

rep in pt—Legal Aid, Sentencing and Punishment of Offenders, 2012 c 10, ss 74(3),
75(2)

s 224 rep in pt—Crim Justice and Immigration, 2008 c 4, ss 148, 149, sch 26 paras 59, 69,
sch 28 pt 2

am—Legal Aid, Sentencing and Punishment of Offenders, 2012 c 10, sch 19 paras 15,
16

s 224A added—Legal Aid, Sentencing and Punishment of Offenders, 2012 c 10, s 122

am—Legal Aid, Sentencing and Punishment of Offenders, 2012 c 10, sch 19 para 17;
Crim Justice and Cts, 2015 c 2, s 5(1)

mod—(temp) Legal Aid, Sentencing and Punishment of Offenders, 2012 c 10, sch
19 para 24(2)(a)(b)

s 225 am—Crim Justice and Immigration, 2008 c 4, s 13(1)

2003

c 44 s 225 *continued*

transtl provns—SI 2008/1587, art 2

rep in pt—Legal Aid, Sentencing and Punishment of Offenders, 2012 c 10, s 123(a), sch 21 para 23

s 226 am—Crim Justice and Immigration, 2008 c 4, s 14

appl—Armed Forces, 2006 c 52, s 226

rep in pt—Legal Aid, Sentencing and Punishment of Offenders, 2012 c 10, s 123(b), sch 21 para 24

s 226A added—Legal Aid, Sentencing and Punishment of Offenders, 2012 c 10, s 124

mod—(temp) Legal Aid, Sentencing and Punishment of Offenders, 2012 c 10, sch 21 para 36(2)

appl (mods)—Armed Forces, 2006 c 52, s 219A(4)(5)

am—Offender Rehabilitation, 2014 c 11, s 8(2)(3)

s 226B added—Legal Aid, Sentencing and Punishment of Offenders, 2012 c 10, s 124

mod—(temp) Legal Aid, Sentencing and Punishment of Offenders, 2012 c 10, sch 21 para 36(3)

appl (mods)—Armed Forces, 2006 c 52, s 221A(2)-(7)

s 227 rep—Legal Aid, Sentencing and Punishment of Offenders, 2012 c 10, s 123(c)

s 228 rep—Legal Aid, Sentencing and Punishment of Offenders, 2012 c 10, s 123(d)

s 229 rep in pt—Crim Justice and Immigration, 2008 c 4, ss 17(1)(2)(a)(4), 149, sch 28 pt 2

am—Crim Justice and Immigration, 2008 c 4, s 17(1)(2)(b)(c)(3)

mod—SI 2009/1059, art 205, sch 1

s 231 am—Crim Justice and Immigration, 2008 c 4, s 18(1); Legal Aid, Sentencing and Punishment of Offenders, 2012 c 10, sch 19 paras 19, 20(2)-(4), sch 21 paras 25(a)(b)(i)(ii)(c)

s 232 rep—Legal Aid, Sentencing and Punishment of Offenders, 2012 c 10, sch 21 para 26

s 232A added—Legal Aid, Sentencing and Punishment of Offenders, 2012 c 10, sch 19 para 21

am—Crim Justice and Cts, 2015 c 2, s 5(2)

s 233 rep—Crim Justice and Immigration, 2008 c 4, ss 148, 149, sch 26 paras 59, 70, sch 28

s 234 rep—Crim Justice and Immigration, 2008 c 4, ss 18(3), 49, sch 28 pt 2

s 235 am—Legal Aid, Sentencing and Punishment of Offenders, 2012 c 10, sch 21 paras 27, 28

appl—Armed Forces, 2006 c 52, s 224

Pt 12 Ch 5A (s 236A) added—Crim Justice and Cts, 2015 c 2, sch 1 para 2

s 236A appl in pt—Armed Forces, 2006 c 52, s 224A(2)

Pt 12 Ch 6 (ss 237-268) ext—Legal Aid, Sentencing and Punishment of Offenders, 2012 c 10, s 121

am—Legal Aid, Sentencing and Punishment of Offenders, 2012 c 10, sch 14 para 16; Offender Rehabilitation, 2014 c 11, sch 3 para 15

appl—Offender Rehabilitation, 2014 c 11, sch 7 para 2(a)

s 237 am—Armed Forces, 2006 c 52, s 378, sch 16 para 219; Crim Justice and Immigration, 2008 c 4, s 21(1)(2); Legal Aid, Sentencing and Punishment of Offenders, 2012 c 10, ss 110(2), 117(2)(3), sch 20 para 2(2), sch 22 para 21; Offender Rehabilitation, 2014 c 11, s 2(3); Crim Justice and Cts, 2015 c 2, sch 1 para 15

mod—SI 2009/1059, art 205, sch 1

s 238 am—Legal Aid, Sentencing and Punishment of Offenders, 2012 c 10, sch 20 para 3

s 239 am—(prosp) Crim Justice and Cts, 2015 c 2, sch 3 para 6

s 239A added (prosp)—Crim Justice and Cts, 2015 c 2, s 8(1)

s 240 rep—Legal Aid, Sentencing and Punishment of Offenders, 2012 c 10, s 108(1)

s 240ZA added—Legal Aid, Sentencing and Punishment of Offenders, 2012 c 10, s 108(2)

am—Legal Aid, Sentencing and Punishment of Offenders, 2012 c 10, sch 20 para 4; Offender Rehabilitation, 2014 c 11, s 9(6); Crim Justice and Cts, 2015 c 2, sch 1 para 16

s 240A added—Crim Justice and Immigration, 2008 c 4, s 21(1)(4)

excl—International Criminal Court, 2001 c 17, sch 7; SI 2008/2793, arts 2-4

rep in pt—Legal Aid, Sentencing and Punishment of Offenders, 2012 c 10, s 109(4)(a)(5)(7)(b), sch 16 para 14

am—Legal Aid, Sentencing and Punishment of Offenders, 2012 c 10, s 109(2)(3)(4)(b)(6)(7)(a)(8); Offender Rehabilitation, 2014 c 11, s 9(7)

s 241 mod—(transtl provn) SI 2003/3283, art 3

2003

c 44 s 241 *continued*

am—Armed Forces, 2006 c 52, s 378, sch 16 para 220; Crim Justice and Immigration, 2008 c 4, s 21(1)(5); Legal Aid, Sentencing and Punishment of Offenders, 2012 c 10, s 110(4)-(7)

rep in pt—Legal Aid, Sentencing and Punishment of Offenders, 2012 c 10, sch 10 para 20

s 242 am—Crim Justice and Immigration, 2008 c 4, s 21(1)(6); Legal Aid, Sentencing and Punishment of Offenders, 2012 c 10, s 110(7)

rep in pt—Legal Aid, Sentencing and Punishment of Offenders, 2012 c 10, sch 12 para 51

s 243 rep in pt—SI 2004/1897, art 3

am—Police and Justice, 2006 c 48, s 42, sch 13 para 31; Legal Aid, Sentencing and Punishment of Offenders, 2012 c 10, s 110(8)

appl—Powers of Criminal Courts (Sentencing), 2000 c 6, s 101(12A)

s 243A added—Legal Aid, Sentencing and Punishment of Offenders, 2012 c 10, s 111(1)

am—Offender Rehabilitation, 2014 c 11, s 1; ibid, sch 3 paras 16, 17

s 244 am—Domestic Violence, Crime and Victims, 2004 c 28, s 31, sch 6 paras 1, 2; Legal Aid, Sentencing and Punishment of Offenders, 2012 c 10, ss 114(2), 117(4), 125(2), sch 14 para 6(2)(3)(a)(b), sch 17 para 2; Offender Rehabilitation, 2014 c 11, s 9(2); ibid, sch 3 para 18; Crim Justice and Cts, 2015 c 2, sch 1 para 5

rep in pt—Legal Aid, Sentencing and Punishment of Offenders, 2012 c 10, sch 10 para 21(2)(3)

s 244A added—Crim Justice and Cts, 2015 c 2, sch 1 para 6

s 245 rep—Legal Aid, Sentencing and Punishment of Offenders, 2012 c 10, sch 10 para 22

s 246 am—Domestic Violence, Crime and Victims, 2004 c 28, s 31, sch 6 paras 1, 3; Armed Forces, 2006 c 52, s 378, sch 16 para 221; Crim Justice and Immigration, 2008 c 4, ss 22(1)(2), 24; Legal Aid, Sentencing and Punishment of Offenders, 2012 c 10, ss 110(9), 112(2)-(6), sch 14 para 7, sch 20 para 5(2)(3); Crim Justice and Cts, 2015 c 2, sch 1 para 7

rep in pt—(prosp) Domestic Violence, Crime and Victims, 2004 c 28, s 58(2), sch 11; Legal Aid, Sentencing and Punishment of Offenders, 2012 c 10, sch 10 para 23(2)-(6)

s 246A added—Legal Aid, Sentencing and Punishment of Offenders, 2012 c 10, s 125(3)

am—Crim Justice and Cts, 2015 c 2, s 4

s 247 rep in pt—Crim Justice and Immigration, 2008 c 4, ss 25, 149, sch 28 pt 2

am—Legal Aid, Sentencing and Punishment of Offenders, 2012 c 10, sch 17 para 3; Crim Justice and Cts, 2015 c 2, s 14(3)

s 248 rep in pt—Legal Aid, Sentencing and Punishment of Offenders, 2012 c 10, s 116(2)

s 249 am—Domestic Violence, Crime and Victims, 2004 c 28, s 31, sch 6 paras 1, 4, 5; Legal Aid, Sentencing and Punishment of Offenders, 2012 c 10, sch 10 para 24(a), sch 14 para 8(2)(3)(4)(a), sch 17 para 4; Offender Rehabilitation, 2014 c 11, s 5(4)

appl (mods)—Crim Justice, 1991 c 53, s 50A

rep in pt—Legal Aid, Sentencing and Punishment of Offenders, 2012 c 10, sch 10 para 24(b)-(d), sch 14 para 8(4)(b)

s 250 am—Domestic Violence, Crime and Victims, 2004 c 28, s 31, sch 6 paras 1, 4, 5; Armed Forces, 2006 c 52, s 378, sch 16 para 222; Offender Management, 2007 c 21, s 28(5); Legal Aid, Sentencing and Punishment of Offenders, 2012 c 10, s 117(5), sch 10 para 25(b), sch 20 para 6(2)(3); Offender Rehabilitation, 2014 c 11, s 12(2); Crim Justice and Cts, 2015 c 2, sch 1 para 17; ibid, sch 2 para 4; (prosp) ibid, sch 3 para 7

appl—Crim Justice, 1991 c 53, s 37ZA

appl (mods)—Crim Justice, 1991 c 53, s 50A

rep in pt—Legal Aid, Sentencing and Punishment of Offenders, 2012 c 10, sch 10 para 25(a), sch 14 para 9; Offender Rehabilitation, 2014 c 11, s 5(5)

s 251 rep—Legal Aid, Sentencing and Punishment of Offenders, 2012 c 10, sch 10 para 26

s 252 am—Armed Forces, 2006 c 52, s 378, sch 16 para 224; Legal Aid, Sentencing and Punishment of Offenders, 2012 c 10, sch 10 para 27(a)

appl—Crim Justice, 1991 c 53, s 50A

rep in pt—Legal Aid, Sentencing and Punishment of Offenders, 2012 c 10, sch 10 para 27(b)

s 253 am—SI 2008/912, art 3, sch 1; Legal Aid, Sentencing and Punishment of Offenders, 2012 c 10, s 114(3), sch 14 para 10; Crim Justice and Cts, 2015 c 2, sch 2 para 5(2)

2003
c 44 s 253 *continued*

rep in pt—Legal Aid, Sentencing and Punishment of Offenders, 2012 c 10, sch 10 para 28; Crim Justice and Cts, 2015 c 2, sch 2 para 5(3)

s 254 am—Crim Justice and Immigration, 2008 c 4, s 29(1)(b); Legal Aid, Sentencing and Punishment of Offenders, 2012 c 10, s 113(1)

appl—Crim Justice, 1991 c 53, s 50A

rep in pt—Crim Justice and Immigration, 2008 c 4, ss 29(1)(a), 149, sch 28 pt 2

s 255 am—Legal Aid, Sentencing and Punishment of Offenders, 2012 c 10, s 113(2); Offender Rehabilitation, 2014 c 11, s 9(3)

s 255ZA added—Crim Justice and Cts, 2015 c 2, s 12(2)

ss 255A-255D added —Crim Justice and Immigration, 2008 c 4, s 29(2)

replaced by s 255A-255C—Legal Aid, Sentencing and Punishment of Offenders, 2012 c 10, s 114(1)

s 255A am—Legal Aid, Sentencing and Punishment of Offenders, 2012 c 10, sch 20 para 7; Offender Rehabilitation, 2014 c 11, s 9(4)(b)-(d); (prosp) Crim Justice and Cts, 2015 c 2, s 9(2)

rep in pt—Offender Rehabilitation, 2014 c 11, s 9(4)(a)

s 255B am—Offender Rehabilitation, 2014 c 11, s 9(5); (prosp) Crim Justice and Cts, 2015 c 2, s 9(3)

s 255C am—(prosp) Crim Justice and Cts, 2015 c 2, s 9(4)

s 256 rep (prosp)—Crim Justice and Cts, 2015 c 2, s 9(5)

am—Crim Justice and Immigration, 2008 c 4, ss 29(3), 30(1)(2)(5); Legal Aid, Sentencing and Punishment of Offenders, 2012 c 10, ss 114(4), 116(3)

appl—Crim Justice, 1991 c 53, s 50A

rep in pt—Crim Justice and Immigration, 2008 c 4, ss 30(1)(3)(4), 149, sch 28 pt 2

s 256A added—Crim Justice and Immigration, 2008 c 4, s 30(6)

appl—Crim Justice, 1991 c 53, s 50A

am—Legal Aid, Sentencing and Punishment of Offenders, 2012 c 10, s 116(4); (prosp) Crim Justice and Cts, 2015 c 2, s 9(6)

s 256AZA added—(prosp) Crim Justice and Cts, 2015 c 2, s 10(1)

s 256AA added —Offender Rehabilitation, 2014 c 11, s 2(2)

appl (mods)—(pt prosp) Crime (Sentences), 1997 c 43, sch 1 para 8(2)(4)(8)-(12) (as amended by 2014 c 11, sch 3 para 3(2)(3)(5)); Powers of Crim Cts (Sentencing), 2000 c 6, s 106B(2)-(7)

am—Crim Justice and Cts, 2015 c 2, sch 1 para 18

s 256AB added —Offender Rehabilitation, 2014 c 11, sch 1 para 1

appl (mods)—(pt prosp) Crime (Sentences), 1997 c 43, sch 1 para 8(2)(4)(8)-(12) (as amended by 2014 c 11, sch 3 para 3(2)(3)(5))

s 256AC added —Offender Rehabilitation, 2014 c 11, s 3(1)

appl (mods)—(pt prosp) Crime (Sentences), 1997 c 43, sch 1 para 8(2)(4)(8)-(12) (as amended by 2014 c 11, sch 3 para 3(2)(3)(5)); Powers of Crim Cts (Sentencing), 2000 c 6, s 106B(2)-(7)

am—Crim Justice and Cts, 2015 c 2, sch 12 para 14

ss 256B, 256C added—Legal Aid, Sentencing and Punishment of Offenders, 2012 c 10, s 115

s 256B am—Offender Rehabilitation, 2014 c 11, s 4(2)(4)(a)(5)(7); Crim Justice and Cts, 2015 c 2, sch 2 para 6

rep in pt—Offender Rehabilitation, 2014 c 11, s 4(3)(6)(8); ibid, sch 3 para 19

appl (mods) —(pt prosp) Crime (Sentences), 1997 c 43, sch 1 para 8(2)(4)(8)-(12) (as amended by 2014 c 11, sch 3 para 3(2)(3)(5))

s 256C am—Offender Rehabilitation, 2014 c 11, sch 3 paras 21, 22

appl (mods) —(pt prosp) Crime (Sentences), 1997 c 43, sch 1 para 8(2)(4)(8)-(12) (as amended by 2014 c 11, sch 3 para 3(2)(3)(5))

s 256D added —Offender Rehabilitation, 2014 c 11, sch 1 para 2

appl (mods)—(pt prosp) Crime (Sentences), 1997 c 43, sch 1 para 8(2)(4)(8)-(12) (as amended by 2014 c 11, sch 3 para 3(2)(3)(5)); Powers of Crim Cts (Sentencing), 2000 c 6, s 106B(2)-(7)

s 256E added —Offender Rehabilitation, 2014 c 11, sch 1 para 2

appl (mods) —(pt prosp) Crime (Sentences), 1997 c 43, sch 1 para 8(2)(4)(8)-(12) (as amended by 2014 c 11, sch 3 para 3(2)(3)(5)); Powers of Crim Cts (Sentencing), 2000 c 6, s 106B(2)-(7)

s 257 am—Police and Justice, 2006 c 48, s 32(1)(4)

2003
c 44 *continued*

s 258 am—Legal Aid, Sentencing and Punishment of Offenders, 2012 c 10, s 117(6), sch 17
para 5(2)(3), sch 20 para 8; Crim Justice and Cts, 2015 c 2, sch 1 para 19;
Serious Crime, 2015 c 9, s 10(3)

ext—Legal Aid, Sentencing and Punishment of Offenders, 2012 c 10, s 121(2)

s 259A added—Crim Justice and Immigration, 2008 c 4, s 34(1)(2)

s 260 am—Armed Forces, 2006 c 52, s 378, sch 16 para 225; Crim Justice and Immigration,
2008 c 4, s 34(1)(3)-(5)(8)(c)(9); SI 2008/978, art 2; Legal Aid, Sentencing and
Punishment of Offenders, 2012 c 10, s 116(5), sch 14 para 11, sch 17 para 6, sch
20 para 9(2)-(4); Crim Justice and Cts, 2015 c 2, sch 1 para 20; (prosp) ibid, sch
3 para 8

rep in pt—(pt prosp) Crim Justice and Immigration, 2008 c 4, ss 34(1)(6)(8)(a)(b),
149, sch 28 pt 2; Legal Aid, Sentencing and Punishment of Offenders, 2012 c
10, sch 10 para 29; Crim Justice and Cts, 2015 c 2, s 14(4)

s 261 am—Legal Aid, Sentencing and Punishment of Offenders, 2012 c 10, s 116(6)(7), sch
14 para 12(2)(3)(a)(b), sch 20 para 10(2)(3); Crim Justice and Cts, 2015 c 2, s
14(5)(b)(ii); ibid, sch 1 para 21

rep in pt—Legal Aid, Sentencing and Punishment of Offenders, 2012 c 10, sch 10 para
30; Crim Justice and Cts, 2015 c 2, s 14(5)(a),(b)(i),(c)

s 262 rep—Legal Aid, Sentencing and Punishment of Offenders, 2012 c 10, sch 16 para 16

s 263 rep in pt—Armed Forces, 2006 c 52, s 378, sch 16 para 226; Legal Aid, Sentencing
and Punishment of Offenders, 2012 c 10, sch 10 para 31

am—Legal Aid, Sentencing and Punishment of Offenders, 2012 c 10, ss 116(8)(9),
117(7), sch 14 para 13, sch 17 para 7, sch 20 para 11; Crim Justice and Cts,
2015 c 2, sch 1 para 22

s 264 am—Domestic Violence, Crime and Victims, 2004 c 28, s 31, sch 6 paras 1, 6; Crim
Justice and Immigration, 2008 c 4, s 148, sch 26 paras 59, 71; Legal Aid,
Sentencing and Punishment of Offenders, 2012 c 10, s 117(8), sch 14 para
14(b)(c)(e), sch 17 para 8, sch 20 para 12(2)(3); Offender Rehabilitation, 2014 c
11, s 5(2); Crim Justice and Cts, 2015 c 2, sch 1 para 23

rep in pt—(prosp) Domestic Violence, Crime and Victims, 2004 c 28, s 58(2), sch 11;
Legal Aid, Sentencing and Punishment of Offenders, 2012 c 10, sch 10 para
32(2)(3)(a)(b), sch 14 para 14(a)(d)(f)

s 264A added—Domestic Violence, Crime and Victims, 2004 c 28, s 31, sch 6 paras 1, 7

rep—Legal Aid, Sentencing and Punishment of Offenders, 2012 c 10, sch 10 para 33

s 264B added —Offender Rehabilitation, 2014 c 11, s 5(3)

appl—(pt prosp) Crime (Sentences), 1997 c 43, sch 1 paras 8(2)(a), 9(2)(a)(4)(a) (as
amended by 2014 c 11, sch 3 paras 3(2)(a), 5(2)(3)

s 265 am—Crim Justice and Immigration, 2008 c 4, s 18(1)(4); Legal Aid, Sentencing and
Punishment of Offenders, 2012 c 10, s 117(9), sch 20 para 13; Crim Justice and
Cts, 2015 c 2, sch 1 para 24

rep in pt—Legal Aid, Sentencing and Punishment of Offenders, 2012 c 10, sch 10 para
34, sch 16 para 17

s 266 rep—Legal Aid, Sentencing and Punishment of Offenders, 2012 c 10, s 118(2)

s 267 am—Legal Aid, Sentencing and Punishment of Offenders, 2012 c 10, sch 14 para 15

s 267A added—Legal Aid, Sentencing and Punishment of Offenders, 2012 c 10, sch 16 para
2

s 267B added—Legal Aid, Sentencing and Punishment of Offenders, 2012 c 10, sch 17 para
9

s 268 am—Armed Forces, 2006 c 52, s 378, sch 16 para 227; Offender Rehabilitation, 2014
c 11, sch 3 para 23; Crim Justice and Cts, 2015 c 2, s 14(2); (prosp) ibid, sch 3
para 9

rep in pt—Legal Aid, Sentencing and Punishment of Offenders, 2012 c 10, sch 10 para
35

s 269 am—Armed Forces, 2006 c 52, s 378, sch 16 para 228; Crim Justice and Immigration,
2008 c 4, s 22(1)(3); Coroners and Justice, 2009 c 25, s 177, sch 21 paras 83, 85;
Legal Aid, Sentencing and Punishment of Offenders, 2012 c 10, s 110(10)

s 270 restr (cond)—Serious Organised Crime and Police, 2005 c 15, s 73(7)

am—Legal Aid, Sentencing and Punishment of Offenders, 2012 c 10, s 64(3)

s 272 rep in pt—Armed Forces, 2006 c 52, s 378, sch 16 para 229; (prosp) Crim Justice and
Immigration, 2008 c 4, s 149, sch 28 pt 3

s 273 am—Crim Justice and Immigration, 2008 c 4, s 148, sch 26 paras 59, 73

s 274 am—Constitutional Reform, 2005 c 4, s 40(4), sch 9 pt 1 para 82(1)(5)

2003

c 44 *continued*

s 277 am—Armed Forces, 2006 c 52, s 378, sch 16 para 230; Coroners and Justice, 2009 c 25, s 177, sch 21 paras 83, 85

s 279 rep—Crim Justice and Immigration, 2008 c 4, ss 6, 149, sch 4 paras 71, 94, sch 28 pt 1

s 281 appl—(prosp) Horserace Betting and Olympic Lottery, 2004 c 25, s 10(3)

   appl (mods)—SIs 2007/236, arts 35, 36; 2010/2837, art 27, sch 4

   transtl provns—Crossrail, 2008 c 18, s 35, sch 11 para 7(3)

   mod—Defence Reform, 2014 c 20, sch 7 para 10 11

s 282 appl—(prosp) Horserace Betting and Olympic Lottery, 2004 c 25, s 10(3); Violent Crime Reduction, 2006 c 38, s 56(4)

s 291 am—Violent Crime Reduction, 2006 c 38, s 49, sch 1 para 9(7)

s 299 rep (prosp)—Safeguarding Vulnerable Groups, 2006 c 47, s 63, sch 10

s 300 am—Crim Justice and Immigration, 2008 c 4, s 40; (prosp) ibid, s 148, sch 26 para 2(3)(a)(i)

   rep in pt—(prosp) Crim Justice and Immigration, 2008 c 4, ss 148, 149, sch 26 para 2(3)(a)(ii)(b), sch 28 pt 2

s 301 rep in pt—Road Safety, 2006 c 49, s 10, sch 3 para 80, sch 7

s 302 rep in pt—Legal Aid, Sentencing and Punishment of Offenders, 2012 c 10, sch 10 para 36

   am—Offender Rehabilitation, 2014 c 11, sch 3 para 24(2)(4)

s 305 am—(prosp) Domestic Violence, Crime and Victims, 2004 c 28, s 58(1), sch 10 para 64; Violent Crime Reduction, 2006 c 38, s 49, sch 1 para 9(8); Armed Forces, 2006 c 52, s 378, sch 16 para 231; Tribunals, Cts and Enforcement, 2007 c 15, s 62, sch 13 paras 153, 155; Crim Justice and Immigration, 2008 c 4, s 148, sch 26 paras 59, 72(a); Legal Aid, Sentencing and Punishment of Offenders, 2012 c 10, s 72(6), sch 19 para 22, sch 26 para 22(2)(3); (pt prosp) ibid, s 76(8); Offender Rehabilitation, 2014 c 11, sch 5 para 6(2); Crim Justice and Cts, 2015 c 2, sch 5 para 16

   rep in pt—Crim Justice and Immigration, 2008 c 4, ss 148, 149, sch 26 paras 59, 72(b), sch 28 pt 2; Legal Aid, Sentencing and Punishment of Offenders, 2012 c 10, sch 10 para 37; Offender Rehabilitation, 2014 c 11, sch 5 para 6(3)

   transtl provns—SI 2008/1587, art 2

   mod—(temp) Legal Aid, Sentencing and Punishment of Offenders, 2012 c 10, sch 19 para 24(3)

s 306 rep in pt—Terrorism, 2006 c 11, s 37, sch 3

s 322 rep (prosp)—Anti-social Behaviour, Crime and Policing, 2014 c 12, sch 11 para 50

   am—Children, 2004 c 31, s 18(9), sch 2 para 8

s 323 rep (prosp)—Anti-social Behaviour, Crime and Policing, 2014 c 12, sch 11 para 50

s 325 am—Nat Health Service (Conseq Provns), 2006 c 43, s 2, sch 1 para 254; Crim Justice and Immigration, 2008 c 4, s 148, sch 26 paras 59, 74; SIs 2008/912, art 3, sch 1; 2010/866, art 5, sch 2; 1158, art 5, sch 2; 2011/1733, art 2; Health and Social Care, 2012 c 7, sch 5 para 124(a)(b)(d)(i)

   rep in pt—SI 2010/1158, art 5, schs 2, 3; Health and Social Care, 2012 c 7, sch 5 para 124(c)(d)(ii)

s 326 am—Crim Justice and Immigration, 2008 c 4, s 148, sch 26 paras 59, 75

   transtl savings—SI 2004/829, art 2(5)

s 327 am—(temp) SI 2004/829, art 2(6); Legal Aid, Sentencing and Punishment of Offenders, 2012 c 10, sch 21 para 29; Deregulation, 2015 c 20, s 83(2)-(5),(7)

   rep in pt—Deregulation, 2015 c 20, s 83(6)

s 327A added—Crim Justice and Immigration, 2008 c 4, s 140(1)

s 327B added—Crim Justice and Immigration, 2008 c 4, s 140(1)

   rep in pt—Legal Aid, Sentencing and Punishment of Offenders, 2012 c 10, sch 24 para 26

s 329 am—Armed Forces, 2006 c 52, s 378, sch 16 para 232; Crime and Cts, 2013 c 22, sch 9 para 52

   mod—SI 2009/1059, art 205, sch 1

s 330 am—Constitutional Reform, 2005 c 4, s 15(1), sch 4 pt 1 paras 356, 359; (pt prosp) Police and Justice, 2006 c 48, s 17(1)(5); Crim Justice and Immigration, 2008 c 4, ss 21(7), 148, sch 26 paras 59, 76; Coroners and Justice, 2009 c 25, s 177, sch 21 paras 83, 87; Legal Aid, Sentencing and Punishment of Offenders, 2012 c 10, s 110(12)(a); Offender Rehabilitation, 2014 c 11, sch 3 para 25; Crim Justice and Cts, 2015 c 2, sch 1 para 3; (prosp) ibid, s 10(2); Serious Crime, 2015 c 9, s 10(4)

2003
c 44 s 330 *continued*

rep in pt—Constitutional Reform, 2005 c 4, s 146, sch 18 pt 2; Crim Justice and
    Immigration, 2008 c 4, ss 6, 149, sch 4 paras 71, 95, sch 28 pt 1; Legal Aid,
    Sentencing and Punishment of Offenders, 2012 c 10, s 110(12)(b), sch 21 para
    30; Protection of Freedoms, 2012 c 9, sch 9 para 148(5), sch 10 pt 10; Offender
    Rehabilitation, 2014 c 11, sch 4 para 13

s 330A added—SI 2010/976, art 12, sch 14

s 333 am—SI 2010/976, art 12, sch 14

s 336 am—SI 2010/976, art 12, sch 14

s 337 am—Serious Organised Crime and Police, 2005 c 15, s 167; Armed Forces, 2006 c 52,
    s 378, sch 16 para 233

    rep in pt—Armed Forces, 2006 c 52, s 378, sch 16 para 233

    mod—SI 2009/1059, art 205, sch 1

s 338 ext—Legal Aid, Sentencing and Punishment of Offenders, 2012 c 10, s 153(3)

    mod—Crim Justice and Cts, 2015 c 2, s 97(3)

sch 1 rep in pt—Armed Forces, 2006 c 52, s 378, sch 17

sch 3 rep in pt—Armed Forces, 2006 c 52, s 378, sch 17; Crim Justice and Immigration,
    2008 c 4, ss 53, 149, sch 13 paras 1, 6, 7, sch 28 pt 4; (prosp) Coroners and
    Justice, 2009 c 25, s 178, sch 23 pt 1; Serious Crime, 2015 c 9, sch 4 para 67

    am—Crim Justice and Immigration, 2008 c 4, s 53, sch 13 paras 1-5, 8-10

sch 4 am—Corporate Manslaughter and Corporate Homicide, 2007 c 19, s 26, sch 1 para 2

sch 5 am—Corporate Manslaughter and Corporate Homicide, 2007 c 19, s 26, sch 1 para 3

sch 6 am—SI 2004/2035, art 3, sch paras 45, 52; Armed Forces, 2006 c 52, s 378, sch 16
    para 234

sch 7 am—SI 2004/2035, art 3, sch paras 45, 53; Armed Forces, 2006 c 52, s 378, sch 16
    para 235

    rep in pt—Armed Forces, 2006 c 52, s 378, sch 16 para 235

sch 8 rep in pt—Domestic Violence, Crime and Victims, 2004 c 28, s 29, sch 5 para 7(1)(2);
    Crim Justice and Immigration, 2008 c 4, ss 6, 149, sch 4 paras 71, 96, sch 28 pt
    1; Offender Rehabilitation, 2014 c 11, s 18(4)(6)

    am—Domestic Violence, Crime and Victims, 2004 c 28, s 29, sch 5 para 7(1)(3)-(5);
    SI 2005/886, art 2, sch para 106(a)-(f); Crim Justice and Immigration, 2008 c 4,
    s 6, sch 4 para 109; ibid,s 38; SI 2008/912, art 3, sch 1; Legal Aid, Sentencing
    and Punishment of Offenders, 2012 c 10, ss 66(3)-(5), 67(2)-(7); Crime and Cts,
    2013 c 22, sch 16 para 22(2); (prosp) ibid, sch 16 para 19; Offender
    Rehabilitation, 2014 c 11, sch 4 paras 6, 14; ibid, s 18(5); Crim Justice and Cts,
    2015 c 2, sch 12 para 15

    mod—Armed Forces, 2006 c 52, s 181, sch 5 paras 1-22

sch 9 am—SIs 2005/886, art 2, sch para 107; 2011/2298, sch para 14; (pt prosp) Legal Aid,
    Sentencing and Punishment of Offenders, 2012 c 10, s 76(9); (prosp) Crime and
    Cts, 2013 c 22, sch 16 para 20; Offender Rehabilitation, 2014 c 11, sch 5 para
    7(2)(4)(5)

sch 9 rep in pt—Offender Rehabilitation, 2014 c 11, s 16(3); ibid, sch 5 para 7(3)

sch 10 rep—Legal Aid, Sentencing and Punishment of Offenders, 2012 c 10, s 89(1)(b)

sch 11 rep—Legal Aid, Sentencing and Punishment of Offenders, 2012 c 10, s 89(1)(b)

sch 12 rep in pt—Domestic Violence, Crime and Victims, 2004 c 28, s 29, sch 5 para
    8(1)(2); Legal Aid, Sentencing and Punishment of Offenders, 2012 c 10, sch 10
    para 38(2)(a)(3)(a)(b); Offender Rehabilitation, 2014 c 11, s 18(7)(9)

    am—Domestic Violence, Crime and Victims, 2004 c 28, s 29, sch 5 para 8(1)(3)-(5);
    SIs 2005/886, art 2, sch para 110; 2008/912, art 3, sch 1; Legal Aid,
    Sentencing and Punishment of Offenders, 2012 c 10, s 69(2)(3), sch 9 paras 10,
    11, sch 10 para 38(2)(b); (prosp) Crime and Cts, 2013 c 22, sch 16 para 21;
    Offender Rehabilitation, 2014 c 11, sch 4 paras 7, 15; (pt prosp) ibid, s 18(8);
    Crim Justice and Cts, 2015 c 2, sch 12 para 16

    mod—Armed Forces, 2006 c 52, s 206, sch 7 paras 1-9

sch 13 am—Domestic Violence, Crime and Victims, 2004 c 28, s 29, sch 5 para 9; SIs
    2005/886, art 2, sch para 111; 2008/912, art 3, sch 1; Legal Aid, Sentencing
    and Punishment of Offenders, 2012 c 10, sch 9 para 12(2)(3); (pt prosp) ibid, s
    76(10); (prosp) Crime and Cts, 2013 c 22, sch 16 para 20; Offender
    Rehabilitation, 2014 c 11, sch 5 para 8(2)(4)

    rep in pt—Offender Rehabilitation, 2014 c 11, s 16(4); ibid, sch 5 para 8(3)(5)

sch 14 rep in pt—Offender Rehabilitation, 2014 c 11, s 17(9); ibid, sch 5 para 9

sch 15 am—Domestic Violence, Crime and Victims, 2004 c 28, s 58(1), sch 10 para 65;
    Coroners and Justice, 2009 c 25, s 138; Domestic Violence, Crime and Victims

2003
c 44 *continued*

(Amendment), 2012 c 4, sch para 6; Protection of Freedoms, 2012 c 9, sch 9 paras 139, 147; Crim Justice and Cts, 2015 c 2, s 2(2)-(4),(6)(7); ibid, sch 6 para 11; Serious Crime, 2015 c 9, sch 4 para 68(3)-(5); (prosp) ibid, sch 4 para 68(2); Modern Slavery, 2015 c 30, s 6(2)(3)

rep in pt—Crim Justice and Cts, 2015 c 2, s 2(5)

mod—Serious Crime, 2007 c 27, s 63, sch 6 para 48(a)

sch 15A added—Crim Justice and Immigration, 2008 c 4, s 13(2), sch 5

rep—Legal Aid, Sentencing and Punishment of Offenders, 2012 c 10, sch 21 para 31

sch 15B added—Legal Aid, Sentencing and Punishment of Offenders, 2012 c 10, sch 18

am—Crim Justice and Cts, 2015 c 2, s 3(2)-(5)(7)(8); Serious Crime, 2015 c 9, sch 4 para 69; Modern Slavery, 2015 c 30, s 6(4)

schs 16, 17 rep—Crim Justice and Immigration, 2008 c 4, ss 17(5), 149, sch 28 pt 2

sch 18 rep in pt—Legal Aid, Sentencing and Punishment of Offenders, 2012 c 10, sch 21 para 35(a)

sch 18A added—Crim Justice and Cts, 2015 c 2, sch 1 para 4

mod—Armed Forces, 2006 c 52, s 224A(4)

sch 19A added —Offender Rehabilitation, 2014 c 11, sch 2

appl (mods)—Crime (Sentences), 1997 c. 43 sch 1 para 8(2)(4)(8)-(12); Powers of Crim Cts (Sentencing), 2000, c 6, s 106B(2)(c)(3)-(7)

sch 20 rep—Legal Aid, Sentencing and Punishment of Offenders, 2012 c 10, sch 16 para 16

sch 20A added—Legal Aid, Sentencing and Punishment of Offenders, 2012 c 10, sch 16 para 3

appl—Crime (Sentences), 1997 c. 43, sch 1 paras 8(2)(a), 9(2)(a)(4)(a) (as amended by 2014 c 11, sch 3 para 3(2)(b),(3)(b))

rep in pt—(prosp) Crim Justice and Cts, 2015 c 2, s 9(7)

am—Crim Justice and Cts, 2015 c 2, ss 14(6)(b), 15(7)(a)(b),(d)

sch 20B added—Legal Aid, Sentencing and Punishment of Offenders, 2012 c 10, sch 17 para 10

appl—Crime (Sentences), 1997 c. 43, sch 1 paras 8(2)(a), 9(2)(a)(4)(a) (as amended by 2014 c 11, sch 3 para 3(2)(b),(3)(b))

am—Offender Rehabilitation, 2014 c 11, s 5(7)(8); Crim Justice and Cts, 2015 c 2, s 15(9); (prosp) ibid, sch 3 paras 10, 11(a)(b)

rep in pt—Crim Justice and Cts, 2015 c 2, s 15(8)

sch 21 am—Armed Forces, 2006 c 52, s 378, sch 16 para 236; Counter-Terrorism, 2008 c 28, s 75(1)(2)(c); Coroners and Justice, 2009 c 25, s 177, sch 21 para 52(b); SI 2010/197, arts 2, 3; Legal Aid, Sentencing and Punishment of Offenders, 2012 c 10, s 65(8)(9); Crim Justice and Cts, 2015 c 2, s 27(2)

rep in pt—Coroners and Justice, 2009 c 25, ss 177, 178, sch 21 para 52(a), sch 23 pt 2; Crim Justice and Cts, 2015 c 2, s 27(3)

sch 22 am—Constitutional Reform, 2005 c 4, s 40(4), sch 9 pt 1 para 82(1)(6)

mod—SI 2009/1059, art 205, sch 1

sch 24 rep—Crim Justice and Immigration, 2008 c 4, ss 6, 149, sch 4 paras 71, 97, sch 28

sch 25 rep in pt—Gambling, 2005 c 19, s 356(4)(5), sch 17; Nat Health Service (Conseq Provns), 2006 c 43, s 6, sch 4; Wireless Telegraphy, 2006 c 36, s 125, sch 9; Armed Forces, 2006 c 52, s 378, sch 17; SL(R), 2008 c 12, s 1(1), sch 1 pt 1, group 4; Marine and Coastal Access, 2009 c 23, s 321, sch 22 pt 5(B)(C); (W S prosp) Enterprise and Regulatory Reform, 2013 c 24, sch 20 para 2; Co-operative and Community Benefit Societies, 2014 c 14, sch 7

sch 26 rep in pt—(pt prosp) Violent Crime Reduction, 2006 c 38, s 65, sch 5; Govt of Wales, 2006 c 32, s 163, sch 12; Health and Social Care, 2008 c 14, s 166, sch 15; SI 2008/576, art 18, sch; Legal Aid, Sentencing and Punishment of Offenders, 2012 c 10, sch 5 pt 2; Anti-social Behaviour, Crime and Policing, 2014 c 12, sch 11 para 50

sch 27 rep in pt—Legislative and Regulatory Reform, 2006 c 51, s 30, sch 1; SI 2008/576, art 18, sch

sch 30 rep (prosp)—Safeguarding Vulnerable Groups, 2006 c 47, s 63, sch 10

sch 31 am—Crim Justice and Immigration, 2008 c 4, s 148, sch 26 para 2(1)(4)(6); Offender Rehabilitation, 2014 c 11, s 18(10)(11)

rep in pt—Crim Justice and Immigration, 2008 c 4, ss 148, 149, sch 26 para 2(1)(5), sch 28 pt 2

sch 32 am—SI 2005/886, art 2, sch para 112

2003
c 44 sch 32 *continued*
    rep in pt—Armed Forces, 2006 c 52, s 378, sch 17; SL(R), 2008 c 12, s 1(1), sch 1 pt
      1, group 4; (pt prosp) Crim Justice and Immigration, 2008 c 4, s 149, sch 28 pt
      1; Welfare Reform, 2009 c 24, s 58, sch 7 pt 3; Legal Aid, Sentencing and
      Punishment of Offenders, 2012 c 10, sch 10 para 39, sch 12 para 52; ibid, sch
      25 pt 2
   sch 34A added—Crim Justice and Immigration, 2008 c 4, s 140, sch 24
    am—Coroners and Justice, 2009 c 25, s 177, sch 21 para 63; Serious Crime, 2015
      c 9, sch 4 para 70(3)(4); (prosp) ibid, sch 4 para 70(2)
   sch 35 rep in pt—(S prosp) Serious Organised Crime and Police, 2005 c 15, s 174(2), sch 17
      pt 2; Policing and Crime, 2009 c 26, s 112, sch 8 pt 8
   sch 36 rep in pt—Armed Forces, 2006 c 52, s 378, sch 17; (prosp) Crim Justice and
      Immigration, 2008 c 4, s 149, sch 28 pt 4
   sch 37 rep in pt—Crim Justice and Immigration, 2008 c 4, ss 148, 149, sch 26 paras 59, 77,
      sch 28 pt 4; Marine and Coastal Access, 2009 c 23, s 321, sch 22 pt 5(B)
   sch 38 rep in pt—Children, 2004 c 31, s 64, sch 5 pt 4; Coroners and Justice, 2009 c 25, ss
      177, 178, sch 21 paras 83, 88, sch 23 pt 4
3rd session of 53rd Parliament
c 45 *Consolidated Fund (No 2)*—rep Appropriation (No 3), 2005 c 21, s 4, sch 3

2004

c 1 *Consolidated Fund*—rep Appropriation (No 2), 2006 c 24, s 4, sch 3
c 2 **European Parliamentary and Local Elections (Pilots)**
c 3 **National Insurance Contributions and Statutory Payments**
   s 5 rep in pt—Finance, 2008 c 9, s 129, sch 43 para 11(c)
c 4 **Justice (Northern Ireland)**
   ss 3-5 rep —Northern Ireland, 2009 c 3, s 2, sch 5 para 5
   s 8 am—Justice (NI), 2002 c 26, sch 7 para 7A; SI 2010/976, art 12, sch 14
    rep in pt—SI 2010/976, art 12, sch 14
   s 10 am—Police and Justice, 2006 c 48, s 42, sch 13 para 29
    rep in pt—Police and Justice, 2006 c 48, s 52, sch 15
   s 10A added—Police and Justice, 2006 c 48, s 42, sch 13 para 30
   s 11 am—Terrorism (NI), 2006 c 4, s 1(5)
   s 21 am—Coroners and Justice, 2009 c 25, s 147(1)(5); SI 2010/976, art 12, sch 14
   sch 1 rep in pt—Northern Ireland, 2009 c 3, s 2, sch 5 para 5
   sch 3 am—Coroners and Justice, 2009 c 25, s 147(1)-(4); SI 2010/976, art 15, sch 18
c 5 **Planning and Compulsory Purchase**
   Pt 1 (ss 1-12) rep —Loc Democracy, Economic Development and Construction, 2009 c 20,
      ss 85, 146, sch 5 para 13, sch 7 pt 4
   Pt 2 (ss 13-37) mod—SI 2008/2867, regs 21-24
   s 15 am—Greater London Authority, 2007 c 24, s 30; Planning, 2008 c 29, s
      180(1)(2)(b)(c)(e); Localism, 2011 c 20, s 111
    rep in pt—Planning, 2008 c 29, s 180(1)(2)(a)(d), sch 13; Localism, 2011 c 20, s
      111(1)(2) ibid, sch 25 pt 17; (prosp) ibid, sch 8 para 8, sch 25 pt 16
    appl (mods)—SIs 2008/1572, art 4; 2010/497, art 16, sch 3; 2011/1455, art 4(2)
   s 16 am—Localism, 2011 c 20, s 110(2)
   s 17 am—Planning, 2008 c 29, s 180(1)(3)(b)-(d)
    rep in pt—Planning, 2008 c 29, s 180(1)(3)(a), sch 13
    mod—SI 2010/490, reg 39
   s 18 am—Planning, 2008 c 29, s 180(1)(4)(a)(b); Localism, 2011 c 20, sch 12 para 28
    rep in pt—Planning, 2008 c 29, s 180(1)(4)(c), sch 13
   s 19 am—Loc Democracy, Economic Development and Construction, 2009 c 20, s 85, sch 5
      para 14; (prosp) Planning (W), 2015 anaw 4, sch 2 para 24
    rep in pt—(prosp) Localism, 2011 c 20, sch 8 para 9, sch 25 pt 16; Deregulation, 2015
      c 20, s 100(2)(b)
   s 20 am—Localism, 2011 c 20, ss 110(3), 112(2)
   s 21 am—Localism, 2011 c 20, s 112(5)
   s 22 rep in pt—Localism, 2011 c 20, s 112(4), sch 25 pt 17
   s 23 am—Localism, 2011 c 20, s 112(3)
   s 24 am—Loc Democracy, Economic Development and Construction, 2009 c 20, s 85, sch 5
      para 15(1)(2)(4); Localism, 2011 c 20, sch 22 para 55; (prosp) ibid, sch 8 para
      10(1)(2)

2004
c 5 s 24 *continued*

    rep in pt—Loc Democracy, Economic Development and Construction, 2009 c 20, ss 85,
        146, sch 5 para 15(1)(3)(5), sch 7 pt 4; (prosp) Localism, 2011 c 20, sch 8 para
        10(1)(3), sch 25 pt 16

s 28 am—Loc Democracy, Economic Development and Construction, 2009 c 20, s 85, sch 5
    para 16

    rep in pt—(prosp) Localism, 2011 c 20, sch 8 para 11, sch 25 pt 16

s 33 appl (mods)—London Olympic Games and Paralympic Games, 2006 c 12, s
    5(1)(b)(2)(3)(c)

s 33A added—Localism, 2011 c 20, s 110(1)

s 35 am—Localism, 2011 c 20, s 113

    rep in pt—Localism, 2011 c 20, s 113(1)(2), sch 25 pt 17

s 37 am—Housing and Regeneration, 2008 c 17, s 56, sch 8 para 81; Planning, 2008 c 29, s
    180(1)(6); Loc Democracy, Economic Development and Construction, 2009 c 20,
    s 85, sch 5 para 17; Localism, 2011 c 20, sch 22 para 56

    mod—SI 2008/2897, reg 19(2) (added by SI 2009/276, reg 14)

    transtl saving—SI 2010/497, art 17, sch 4

    rep in pt—(prosp) Localism, 2011 c 20, sch 8 para 12, sch 25 pt 16

s 38 am—Planning, 2008 c 29, s 180(1)(7); Loc Democracy, Economic Development and
    Construction, 2009 c 20, s 82(1); Localism, 2011 c 20, sch 8 para 13(1); ibid, sch
    9 para 6; (prosp) Planning (W), 2015 anaw 4, s 9

    rep in pt—(prosp) Localism, 2011 c 20, sch 8 para 13(2), sch 25 pt 16

ss 38A-38C added—Localism, 2011 c 20, sch 9 para 7

s 39 am—(W prosp) Planning, 2008 c 29, s 183; Loc Democracy, Economic Development
    and Construction, 2009 c 20, s 85, sch 5 para 18(2)(b)(c)(3)

    rep in pt—Loc Democracy, Economic Development and Construction, 2009 c 20, ss 85,
        146, sch 5 para 18(2)(a), sch 7 pt 4; (1.4.2016) Planning (W), 2015 anaw 4, s
        2(6)

s 40 rep in pt—Localism, 2011 c 20, sch 12 para 29, sch 25 pt 18

s 42 rep in pt—(W prosp) Planning, 2008 c 29, s 238, sch 13

s 45 am—(prosp) Localism, 2011 c 20, sch 8 para 14(2)(3)

    rep in pt—(prosp) Localism, 2011 c 20, sch 8 para 14, sch 25 pt 16

ss 46-48 rep—Planning, 2008 c 29, ss 225(1)(a), 238, sch 13

s 51 rep in pt—(16.3.2016) Planning (W), 2015 anaw 4, ss 35(8), 36(7)

s 53 rep (W prosp)—Planning, 2008 c 29, s 238, sch 13

s 56 am—Planning, 2008 c 29, s 184; SI 2014/1770 (W 182), art 3(2)(a)

    rep in pt—SI 2014/1770 (W 182), art 3(2)(b)(3)

s 59 am—Growth and Infrastructure, 2013 c 27, sch 1 para 12; (pt 1.3.2016) (pt prosp)
    Planning (W), 2015 anaw 4, sch 3 para 2

s 60 subst (4.1.2016)—Planning (W), 2015 anaw 4, s 3

ss 60A, 60B added (4.1.2016)—Planning (W), 2015 anaw 4, s 3

s 60C added (prosp)—Planning (W), 2015 anaw 4, s 3

s 60D-60G added—Planning (W), 2015 anaw 4, s 4(1)

s 60H added (prosp)—Planning (W), 2015 anaw 4, s 5

s 60I, 60J added (prosp)—Planning (W), 2015 anaw 4, s 6

s 61 am—(4.1.2016) Planning (W), 2015 anaw 4, s 11(2)

s 62 appl—Planning and Energy, 2008 c 21, s 1(4)(b)

    am—Loc Govt (W), 2009 nawm 2, s 51, sch 2 paras 4, 5, 6, sch 3; (prosp) Planning
        (W), 2015 anaw 4, sch 2 para 25; (1.4.2016) Well-being of Future Generations
        (W), 2015 anaw 2, sch 4 paras 9, 10

    mod—SI 2010/490, reg 39

    rep in pt—(prosp) Localism, 2011 c 20, sch 8 para 15, sch 25 pt 16

s 66 replaced (by s 66A)—(4.1.2016) Planning (W), 2015 anaw 4, s 13

s 68A added (prosp)—Planning (W), 2015 anaw 4, s 8(1)

s 69 am—(prosp) Planning (W), 2015 anaw 4, s 8(2)

s 72 am—Planning (W), 2015 anaw 4, s 14(3); (4.1.2016) ibid, s 14(2),(4)-(10)

s 74 am—(prosp) Planning (W), 2015 anaw 4, sch 2 para 26

s 78 rep in pt—(prosp) Localism, 2011 c 20, sch 8 para 16, sch 25 pt 16

    am—(16.3.2016) Planning (W), 2015 anaw 4, s 15(2)

s 113 am—Planning, 2008 c 29, s 185; Loc Democracy, Economic Development and
    Construction, 2009 c 20, s 85, sch 5 para 19; (prosp) Localism, 2011 c 20, sch 8
    para 17(1)(2)(b); Crim Justice and Cts, 2015 c 2, sch 16 para 8(2),(4); (prosp)
    Planning (W), 2015 anaw 4, sch 2 para 27

2004

c 5 s 113 *continued*

rep in pt—(prosp) Localism, 2011 c 20, sch 8 para 17, sch 25 pt 16; Crim Justice and
Cts, 2015 c 2, sch 16 para 8(3),(5)

s 116 am—Localism, 2011 c 20, sch 12 para 30

s 121 am—Planning, 2008 c 29, s 187, sch 7 para 7

s 122 rep in pt—Planning, 2008 c 29, s 238, sch 13

am—(prosp) Planning (W), 2015 anaw 4, sch 7 para 1

sch 2A added—Planning (W), 2015 anaw 4, sch 1 para 1

sch 6 rep in pt—Planning, 2008 c 29, ss 225(1)(b), 238, sch 13

sch 7 rep in pt—SI 2008/3002, arts 5, 6, schs 2, 3; (prosp) Localism, 2011 c 20, sch 25 pt
16

sch 8 am—SI 2012/961, sch 3 para 1(2)

c 6   **Child Trust Funds**

s 1 appl—(EW) SI 2005/1529, art 73(3)

s 2 appl—SI 2005/990, reg 12(1)(a)(2)

am—SI 2009/1117, reg 3, sch 2; Savings Accounts and Health in Pregnancy Grant,
2010 c 36, s 1

s 3 appl—SI 2005/990, reg 12(1)(a)(2)

am—(prosp) Welfare Reform, 2009 c 24, s 9, sch 2 para 15; Deregulation, 2015 c 20, ss
60(2)(3), 61(2), 62(4)

rep in pt—Deregulation, 2015 c 20, s 61(3)(4)

s 7A added—Deregulation, 2015 c 20, s 62(2)

s 7B added—Deregulation, 2015 c 20, s 62(3)

s 7C added—Deregulation, 2015 c 20, s 63

s 14 rep—Finance, 2007 c 11, s 114, sch 27 pt 2

s 15 am—SI 2009/3054, art 3, sch

rep in pt—SI 2009/3054, art 3, sch

s 16 am—Deregulation, 2015 c 20, s 60(4)

s 20 am—Deregulation, 2015 c 20, s 62(5)

s 21 am—SI 2009/56, art 3, sch 1 para 415

s 22 appl—SI 2005/990, reg 12(1)(a)(2)

s 23 am—SI 2009/56, art 3, sch 1 para 416(2)(4)

rep in pt—SI 2009/56, art 3, sch 1 para 416(3)(5)

s 24 rep—SI 2009/56, art 3, sch 1 para 417

s 29 am—SI 2009/56, art 3, sch 1 para 418

rep in pt—SI 2009/56, art 3, sch 1 para 418(3)

c 7   **Gender Recognition**

see—Offences (Aggravation by Prejudice) (S), 2009 asp 8, s 2(8)(a)

s 2 am—Marriage (Same Sex Couples), 2013 c 30, sch 5 para 16; Marriage and Civil
Partnership (S), 2014 asp 5, sch 2 para 14; SI 2014/3229, sch 5 para 15(2)

s 3 am—Civil Partnership, 2004 c 33, s 250(2)(a); SI 2009/1182, arts 4, 5-7, sch 5 para 8;
Marriage (Same Sex Couples), 2013 c 30, sch 5 paras 2, 18; Marriage and Civil
Partnership (S), 2014 asp 5, sch 2 paras 3, 16; SI 2014/3229, sch 5 para 15(3)

s 3A added—Marriage (Same Sex Couples), 2013 c 30, sch 5 para 17

s 3B added—Marriage (Same Sex Couples), 2013 c 30, sch 5 para 19

s 3C added—Marriage and Civil Partnership (S), 2014 asp 5, sch 2 para 15

s 3D added—Marriage and Civil Partnership (S), 2014 asp 5, sch 2 para 17

ss 3E, 3F added—SI 2014/3229, sch 5 para 15(4)

s 4 am—Civil Partnership, 2004 c 33, s 250(2)(b); Marriage (Same Sex Couples), 2013 c
30, sch 5 para 3; Marriage and Civil Partnership (S), 2014 asp 5, sch 2 para
4(a)(b)(i)(c)(d)

rep in pt—Marriage and Civil Partnership (S), 2014 asp 5, sch 2 para 4(b)(ii)

ss 4A, 4B added—Marriage (Same Sex Couples), 2013 c 30, sch 5 para 4

ss 4C-4F added—Marriage and Civil Partnership (S), 2014 asp 5, sch 2 para 5

s 4C mod—SSI 2014/361, reg 8(2); SI 2014/3229, art 15(2)

s 4F mod—SSI 2014/361, reg 8(3); SI 2014/3229, art 15(3)

s 5 am—Civil Partnership, 2004 c 33, s 250(3); Marriage and Civil Partnership (S), 2014
asp 5, sch 2 para 6

s 5A added—Civil Partnership, 2004 c 33, s 250(4)

s 5B added—Marriage (Same Sex Couples), 2013 c 30, sch 5 para 5

ss 5C, 5D added—Marriage and Civil Partnership (S), 2014 asp 5, sch 2 para 7

s 6 am—Marriage (Same Sex Couples), 2013 c 30, sch 5 para 6

s 7 am—Civil Partnership, 2004 c 33, s 250(5)(a); Marriage (Same Sex Couples), 2013 c
30, sch 5 para 7; Marriage and Civil Partnership (S), 2014 asp 5, sch 2 para 19(1)

2004

c 7 s 7 *continued*

    appl—SI 2006/758, art 2

s 8 am—Civil Partnership, 2004 c 33, s 250(5)(b); Crime and Cts, 2013 c 22, sch 11 para 160; Marriage (Same Sex Couples), 2013 c 30, sch 5 para 8; Marriage and Civil Partnership (S), 2014 asp 5, sch 2 para 8; SI 2014/3229, sch 5 para 15(5)

s 10 am—Marriage (Same Sex Couples), 2013 c 30, sch 5 para 9(1); Marriage and Civil Partnership (S), 2014 asp 5, sch 2 para 9(1)

s 11A added—Marriage (Same Sex Couples), 2013 c 30, sch 5 para 10

s 11B added—Marriage (Same Sex Couples), 2013 c 30, sch 5 para 11

s 11C added—Marriage and Civil Partnership (S), 2014 asp 5, sch 2 para 10; SI 2014/3229, sch 5 para 15(6)

s 11D added—Marriage and Civil Partnership (S), 2014 asp 5, sch 2 para 11; SI 2014/3229, sch 5 para 15(6)

s 19 rep—Equality, 2010 c 15, s 211, sch 27 pt 1 (subst by SI 2010/2279, sch 2)

s 21 am—Civil Partnership, 2004 c 33, s 250(6); Marriage (Same Sex Couples), 2013 c 30, sch 5 para 12

s 21 rep in pt—Marriage and Civil Partnership (S), 2014 asp 5, sch 2 para 12; SI 2014/3229, sch 5 para 15(7)

s 22 am—Civil Partnership, 2004 c 33, s 250(5)(c); SI 2010/976, art 12, sch 14; Marriage (Same Sex Couples), 2013 c 30, sch 5 para 13; Marriage and Civil Partnership (S), 2014 asp 5, sch 2 para 19(2)

s 23 mod—Pensions, 2014 c 19, sch 12 para 47

s 24 rep in pt—Legislative and Regulatory Reform, 2006 c 51, s 30, sch 1
    am—Marriage and Civil Partnership (S), 2014 asp 5, sch 2 para 19(3)

s 25 am—Civil Partnership, 2004 c 33, s 250(7); Health and Social Care, 2012 c 7, s 213(8)(d); Marriage (Same Sex Couples), 2013 c 30, sch 5 para 14; Marriage and Civil Partnership (S), 2014 asp 5, sch 2 para 2
    rep in pt—SI 2009/1182, arts 4, 5-7, sch 5 para 8

s 27 am—SI 2009/1182, arts 4, 5-7, sch 5 para 8

sch 1 am—Civil Partnership, 2004 c 33, s 250(8); SI 2006/1016, art 2, sch 1; Tribunals, Cts and Enforcement, 2007 c 15, s 48, sch 8 para 60; SI 2009/1182, arts 4, 5-7, sch 5 para 8; Marriage (Same Sex Couples), 2013 c 30, sch 5 para 20; SI 2013/2042, sch para 28(b)(c); Marriage and Civil Partnership (S), 2014 asp 5, sch 2 para 18
    rep in pt—SI 2013/2042, sch para 28(a)

sch 3 am—Civil Partnership, 2004 c 33, s 250(9); (S) SSI 2006/596, art 2; SI 2008/678, art 5, sch 2; Marriage (Same Sex Couples), 2013 c 30, sch 5 para 9(2); Marriage and Civil Partnership (S), 2014 asp 5, sch 2 para 9(2)
    rep in pt—Legislative and Regulatory Reform, 2006 c 51, s 30, sch 1
    see—(trans of functions) SI 2008/678, sch 1

sch 4 rep in pt—Civil Partnership, 2004 c 33, s 261(4), sch 30; SI 2006/1945, art 5

sch 5 am—Pensions, 2014 c 19, sch 11 para 16, sch 12 paras 48, 76
    rep in pt—Pensions, 2014 c 19, sch 12 para 83

sch 6 rep in pt—Equality, 2010 c 15, s 211, sch 27 pt 1 (subst by SI 2010/2279, sch 2)

c 8   **Higher Education**

s 11 am—Consumer Rights, 2015 c 15, s 89(2)

s 12 am—Consumer Rights, 2015 c 15, s 89(3)

s 19 rep—Equality, 2010 c 15, s 211, sch 27 pt 1 (subst by SI 2010/2279, sch2)

s 22 am—Higher Educ (W), 2015 anaw 1, sch para 8

s 23 subst—Educ, 2011 c 21, sch 5 para 19

s 24 am—Educ, 2005 c 18, ss 98, 99, sch 14 para 26, sch 15; Educ, 2011 c 21, sch 5 para 20

s 26 appl—SI 2006/507, reg 2

ss 27, 28 rep—Higher Educ (W), 2015 anaw 1, sch para 9

s 29 am—Educ, 2005 c 18, ss 98, 99, sch 14 para 29, sch 15; Educ, 2011 c 21, sch 5 para 23; Higher Educ (W), 2015 anaw 1, sch para 10(4)(a)(c),(5)
    rep in pt—Higher Educ (W), 2015 anaw 1, sch para 10(2)(3),(4)(b)

s 30 rep in pt—Higher Educ (W), 2015 anaw 1, sch para 11

s 31 am—Educ, 2005 c 18, ss 98, 99, sch 14 para 30, sch 15; Educ, 2011 c 21, sch 5 para 24

s 32 rep in pt—Higher Educ (W), 2015 anaw 1, sch para 12

s 33 am—Higher Educ (W), 2015 anaw 1, sch para 13(2),(7)
    rep in pt—Higher Educ (W), 2015 anaw 1, sch para 13(3)-(6)

s 34 am—Educ, 2005 c 18, ss 98, 99, sch 14 para 31, sch 15; Educ, 2011 c 21, sch 5 para 25; Higher Educ (W), 2015 anaw 1, sch para 14(2)(a),(3)

2004

c 8 s 34 *continued*

rep in pt—Higher Educ (W), 2015 anaw 1, sch para 14(2)(b)

s 35 rep in pt—Higher Educ (W), 2015 anaw 1, sch para 15

s 36 rep in pt—Higher Educ (W), 2015 anaw 1, sch para 16

s 37 am—Educ, 2005 c 18, ss 98, 99, sch 14 para 32, sch 15; Educ, 2011 c 21, sch 5 para 26

rep in pt—Higher Educ (W), 2015 anaw 1, sch para 17

s 38 rep—Higher Educ (W), 2015 anaw 1, sch para 18

s 39 am—Higher Educ (W), 2015 anaw 1, sch para 19(a)

rep in pt—Higher Educ (W), 2015 anaw 1, sch para 19(b)(c)

s 40 am—Educ, 2005 c 18, ss 98, 99, sch 14 para 34, sch 15; SI 2010/501, reg 5, sch; Charities, 2011 c 25, sch 7 para 97; Educ, 2011 c 21, sch 5 para 28

rep in pt—Educ, 2011 c 21, sch 5 para 28(2)

s 40A added—SI 2011/658 (W 96), reg 3(2)

rep—Higher Educ (W), 2015 anaw 1, sch para 20

s 41 am—Educ, 2005 c 18, ss 98, 99, sch 14 para 35(1)(3)-(5), sch 15; SIs 2010/1080, art 2, sch 1; 1158, art 5, sch 2; Educ, 2011 c 21, sch 5 para 29(b)

appl—Income Tax (Earnings and Pensions), 2003 c 1, s 457

rep in pt—Educ, 2011 c 21, s 77(1), sch 5 para 29(a), sch 16 para 22; Higher Educ (W), 2015 anaw 1, sch para 21

s 48 am—Educ, 2005 c 18, ss 98, 99, sch 14 para 36(b), sch 15

rep in pt—Educ, 2005 c 18, ss 98, 99, 123, sch 14 para 36(a), sch 15, sch 19 pt 3

c 9   *Appropriation*—rep Appropriation (No 2), 2006 c 24, s 4, sch 3

c 10   **Age-Related Payments**

s 2 am—(prosp) Welfare Reform, 2009 c 24, s 9, sch 2 para 16

rep in pt—(prosp) Welfare Reform, 2009 c 24, s 58, sch 7 pt 1

s 6 appl—SI 2013/2980, reg 5

s 7 am—SI 2013/1442, art 3

functions made exerciseable concurrently—SI 2013/1442, art 2

s 8 rep in pt—(prosp) Welfare Reform, 2009 c 24, s 58, sch 7 pt 1

am—SI 2011/2581, sch 2 para 8

c 11   **Gangmasters (Licensing)**

s 3 am—(EW) SI 2009/463, reg 45, sch 2; (S) SSI 2009/85, reg 48, sch 2

s 14 am—Serious Organised Crime and Police, 2005 c 15, s 111, sch 7 pt 4 para 62

mod—Serious Crime, 2007 c 27, s 63, sch 6 para 50

s 15 am—Deregulation, 2015 c 20, s 92

sch 2 am—Serious Organised Crime and Police, 2005 c 15, s 111, sch 7 pt 4 para 62

c 12   **Finance**

appl (mods)—Income Tax, 2007 c 3, ss 414, 467, 474, 573, 576, 578, 597, 711, 970

appl—Income Tax, 2007 c 3, ss 513(4), 959, 963

saved—Income Tax, 2007 c 3, s 962

mod—Income Tax, 2007 c 3, s 988

s 7 rep in pt—Finance, 2008 c 9, ss 13(11), 14, sch 5 para 25(e)(i)

s 8 rep in pt—Finance, 2008 c 9, s 13(11)

s 10 rep in pt—Finance, 2008 c 9, s 14, sch 5 para 25(e)(ii)

ss 23, 24 rep—Income Tax, 2007 c 3, s 1031, sch 3

s 26 rep—Corporation Tax, 2010 c 4, s 1181, sch 3 pt 1

s 29 rep—Income Tax, 2007 c 3, s 1031, sch 3

ss 30-32 rep—Taxation (International and Other Provns), 2010 c 8, s 378, sch 10 pt 2

s 34 rep in pt—Corporation Tax, 2009 c 4, s 1326, sch 3 pt 1; Taxation (International and Other Provns), 2010 c 8, s 378, sch 10 pt 2

ss 35, 36 rep—Taxation (International and Other Provns), 2010 c 8, s 378, sch 10 pt 2

s 39 rep—Corporation Tax, 2009 c 4, s 1326, sch 3 pt 1

ss 40, 41 rep—Finance, 2012 c 14, sch 16 paras 247(1)(i)

s 44 rep—Finance, 2012 c 14, sch 16 paras 247(1)(ii), 148

s 45 rep in pt—Corporation Tax, 2009 c 4, s 1326, sch 3 pt 1; Corporation Tax, 2010 c 4, s 1181, sch 3 pt 1

s 48 rep—Corporation Tax, 2009 c 4, s 1326, sch 3 pt 1

ss 50, 51 rep—Corporation Tax, 2010 c 4, ss 1177, 1181, sch 1 paras 423, 424, sch 3 pt 1

s 52 rep in pt—(retrosp) Finance, 2005 c 7, ss 80, 104, sch 4 pt 2 para 50, sch 11 pt 2(7), Note 1

s 54 rep—Corporation Tax, 2009 c 4, s 1326, sch 3 pt 1

s 56 rep—Corporation Tax, 2010 c 4, s 1181, sch 3 pt 1

2004
c 12 *continued*

s 59 am—Nat Health Service (Conseq Provns), 2006 c 43, s 2, sch 1 para 256; Income Tax, 2007 c 3, s 1027, sch 1 paras 456, 459; SI 2007/1388, art 3, sch 1; Housing and Regeneration, 2008 c 17, s 56, sch 8 para 82; ibid, s 277, sch 9 para 33; SI 2009/56, art 3, sch 1 para 420; Corporation Tax, 2010 c 4, s 1177, sch 1 paras 423, 426; Localism, 2011 c 20, sch 19 para 42

   mod—(transtl provns and savings) SI 2008/2839, arts 3, 6, sch

   rep in pt—(pt prosp) Health and Social Care, 2012 c 7, sch 14 para 94

s 65 am—Income Tax, 2007 c 3, s 1027, sch 1 paras 456, 460

s 67 rep in pt—SI 2009/56, art 3, sch 1 para 421(5)

   am—SI 2009/56, art 3, sch 1 para 421

s 71 am—Income Tax (Trading and Other Income), 2005 c 5, s 882(1), sch 1 pt 2 paras 629, 630

   rep in pt—Corporation Tax, 2009 c 4, ss 1322, 1326, sch 1 paras 569, 570, sch 3 pt 1

s 72 am—Finance, 2007 c 11, s 101

s 73A added—Income Tax, 2007 c 3, s 1027, sch 1 paras 456, 461

s 79 rep—Finance, 2006 c 25, s 178, sch 26

s 83 rep—Corporation Tax, 2010 c 4, ss 1177, 1181, sch 1 paras 423, 427, sch 3 pt 1

s 86 rep in pt—Finance (No 2), 2005 c 22, s 70, sch 11 pt 2(1), Note

s 91 rep—Income Tax, 2007 c 3, s 1031, sch 3

s 94 rep in pt—Income Tax, 2007 c 3, s 1031, sch 3

s 97 rep—Income Tax (Trading and Other Income), 2005 c 5, ss 882(1), 884, sch 1 pt 2 paras 629, 631, sch 3

   see—SI 2005/2899, art 2 and explanatory note

ss 98-100 rep—Income Tax (Trading and Other Income), 2005 c 5, ss 882(1), 884, sch 1 pt 2 paras 629, 632-634, sch 3

ss 101, 102 rep—Income Tax, 2007 c 3, s 1027, sch 1 paras 456, 463, sch 3

ss 103, 104 rep—Income Tax (Trading and Other Income), 2005 c 5, ss 882(1), 884, sch 1 pt 2 paras 629, 637, 638, sch 3

s 105 rep in pt—Income Tax (Trading and Other Income), 2005 c 5, s 884, sch 3

s 106 rep—Income Tax (Trading and Other Income), 2005 c 5, ss 882(1), 884, sch 1 pt 2 paras 629, 639, sch 3

ss 107-114 rep—Taxation (International and Other Provns), 2010 c 8, ss 374, 378, sch 8 paras 61, 62(a)(b), sch 10 pt 1

s 115 rep—Taxation (International and Other Provns), 2010 c 8, s 374, sch 8 paras 61, 62(c); residue ibid, s 378, sch 10 pt 1

ss 119-122 rep—Income Tax, 2007 c 3, s 1027, sch 1 paras 456, 464, sch 3

s 122A added—(retrosp to 2.12.2004) Finance, 2005 c 7, s 79(1)(4)

   rep—Income Tax, 2007 c 3, s 1027, sch 1 paras 456, 464, sch 3

s 123 rep—Income Tax, 2007 c 3, s 1027, sch 1 paras 456, 464, sch 3

ss 126-130 rep—Income Tax, 2007 c 3, s 1027, sch 1 paras 456, 465, sch 3

s 131 rep—Finance, 2009 c 10, s 48, sch 24 para 8(b)

s 132 rep—Finance, 2009 c 10, s 48, sch 24 para 8(b)

s 135 rep—Finance, 2009 c 10, s 49, sch 25 para 9(3)(d)

s 137 rep in pt—Corporation Tax, 2009 c 4, s 1326, sch 3 pt 1; Corporation Tax, 2010 c 4, s 1181, sch 3 pt 1

s 138 rep—Income Tax (Trading and Other Income), 2005 c 5, s 884, sch 3

s 139 rep—Corporation Tax, 2010 c 4, s 1181, sch 3 pt 1

s 140 rep—Income Tax (Trading and Other Income), 2005 c 5, s 884, sch 3

s 141 rep—Corporation Tax, 2009 c 4, s 1326, sch 3 pt 1

s 142 rep—Finance, 2008 c 9, s 75(4)(a)

s 143 rep—Income Tax (Trading and Other Income), 2005 c 5, s 884, sch 3

s 147 rep in pt—Income Tax (Trading and Other Income), 2005 c 5, s 884, sch 3; Finance, 2007 c 11, s 114, sch 27 pt 2

s 148 rep—Corporation Tax, 2010 c 4, s 1181, sch 3 pt 1

Pt 4 (ss 149-284) appl (mods)—Finance, 2009 c 10, s 72, sch 35 para 18; SI 2009/470, reg 57; Finance, 2013 c 29, sch 22 para 1(2)

   saved—Taxation of Chargeable Gains, 1992 c 12, s 151X(4); Income Tax, 2007 c 3, s 564V(4)

   mod—Finance, 2011 c 11, sch 18 para 14(3); Finance, 2014 c 26, sch 6 para 1(2)(3)

   power to am conferred—Taxation of Pensions, 2014 c 30, s 4(3)

s 150 appl—Finance (No 2), 2005 c 22, s 18(3)(b)(ii); SI 2005/3458, reg 2(2)(a)

   am—Finance, 2013 c 29, s 53(1)

s 151 appl (mods)—SI 2006/575, reg 5

2004

c 12 s 151 *continued*

  am—Finance, 2006 c 25, s 161, sch 23 para 2

s 152 appl (mods)—SI 2006/575, reg 6

s 153 am—Finance, 2005 c 7, s 101, sch 10 paras 1-3, 64(1); Finance, 2014 c 26, sch 7 para 2

ss 153A-153F added—Finance, 2014 c 26, sch 7 para 3

s 154 power to am ext—Pensions, 2004 c 35, s 239(6)

  am—Finance, 2007 c 11, s 69, sch 20 paras 1, 2, 24(1)

  rep in pt—Finance, 2007 c 11, s 114, sch 27 pt 3

s 155 rep—Finance, 2007 c 11, s 69, sch 20 paras 1, 3, 24(1), sch 27

s 156 am—SI 2009/56, art 3, sch 1 para 423

  rep in pt—SI 2009/56, art 3, sch 1 para 423(2)(5)(c)

s 156A added—Finance, 2014 c 26, sch 7 para 4

s 158 am—SI 2013/1114, art 2; Finance, 2014 c 26, sch 7 para 6

s 159 am—SI 2009/56, art 3, sch 1 para 424

  rep in pt—SI 2009/56, art 3, sch 1 para 424(2)(5)(b)

ss 159A-159D added—Finance, 2014 c 26, sch 7 para 7

s 160 am—Finance, 2006 c 25, ss 158, 161, sch 21 para 3, sch 23 para 3; Finance, 2007 c 11, s 69, sch 20 paras 1, 5, 24(2)

s 161 am—Finance, 2005 c 7, s 101, sch 10 paras 1, 5, 64(1); Finance, 2006 c 25, s 161, sch 23 para 4; Income Tax, 2007 c 3, s 1027, sch 1 paras 456, 467

s 162 am—Finance, 2005 c 7, s 101, sch 10 paras 1, 6, 64(1); Finance, 2006 c 25, s 161, sch 23 para 5; Income Tax, 2007 c 3, s 1027, sch 1 paras 456, 468

s 163 appl—Finance, 2011 c 11, s 68(5)

s 164 appl—SI 2006/134, reg 2

  appl (mods)—SI 2006/575, reg 8

  am—Finance, 2006 c 25, s 161, sch 23 para 6; Finance, 2008 c 9, s 92, sch 29 para 1(1)(2); Finance, 2011 c 11, sch 16 para 63; Taxation of Pensions, 2014 c 30, sch 1 para 85

  rep in pt—Finance, 2009 c 10, s 75(2)(a)

s 165 am—Finance, 2005 c 7, s 101, sch 10 paras 1, 7, 64(1); Finance, 2007 c 11, s 69, sch 19 paras 1, 2(1)-(3), 29(1)(2); Finance, 2011 c 11, sch 16 paras 1(2)(3), 64; Finance, 2013 c 29, s 50(1); Finance, 2014 c 26, s 41(1); Taxation of Pensions, 2014 c 30, sch 1 paras 1, 41

  mod—SIs 2006/207, reg 6 (substituted by SI 2012/1795, reg 3); 572, art 4; Finance, 2011 c 11, sch 16 paras 90(2)(a), 91(2)(a)

  appl (mods)—SI 2006/207, reg 6; Finance (No 2), 2010 c 31, s 6, sch 3 paras 2(2)(a)

  rep in pt—Finance, 2011 c 11, sch 16 para 1(2)(c); Taxation of Pensions, 2014 c 30, sch 1 para 32(1)

s 166 appl (mods)—SI 2006/575, reg 11

  am—Finance, 2007 c 11, s 69, sch 20 paras 1, 9, 24(3); Taxation of Pensions, 2014 c 30, sch 1 paras 54, 55; Finance, 2014 c 26, sch 5 paras 2(2), 5(1), 13

  mod—SI 2006/572, arts 23B, 23ZC(2), 23ZE(2) (added by SI 2011/732, art 3)

s 167 mod—SIs 2006/207, reg 7; 572, art 4 (substituted by SI 2012/1795, reg 4); Finance, 2011 c 11, sch 16 paras 98(2)(a), 99(2)(a)

  appl (mods)—SI 2006/207, reg 7; Finance (No 2), 2010 c 31, s 6, sch 3 paras 2(2)(c)

  am—Finance, 2007 c 11, s 69, sch 19 paras 4, 29(2), sch 20 paras 22(1), 24(3); Finance, 2011 c 11, sch 16 para 11(2)(3); Finance, 2013 c 29, s 50(2); Finance, 2014 c 26, s 41(2); Taxation of Pensions, 2014 c 30, sch 1 para 6; ibid, sch 2 para 2; Finance, 2015 c 11, sch 4 para 2

  rep in pt—Finance, 2011 c 11, sch 16 para 11(2)(c); Taxation of Pensions, 2014 c 30, sch 1 para 32(1)(c)(d)

s 168 mod—SI 2006/572, art 8

  appl—SI 2006/575, reg 14

  rep in pt—Finance, 2007 c 11, s 69, sch 19 paras 1, 5, 29(3), sch 27

  am—Finance, 2011 c 11, sch 16 para 65; Taxation of Pensions, 2014 c 30, sch 1 para 7; Finance (No. 2), 2015 c 33, s 22(9)

s 169 am—Finance, 2005 c 7, s 101, sch 10 paras 1, 36, 64(1); Finance, 2011 c 11, sch 16 para 66(a); Finance, 2013 c 29, s 53; Taxation of Pensions, 2014 c 30, sch 1 paras 8, 92; ibid, sch 2 para 4; Finance, 2014 c 26, sch 7 para 23(a)

  rep in pt—Finance, 2011 c 11, sch 16 para 66(b)

s 170 am—SI 2009/56, art 3, sch 1 para 425

  rep in pt—SI 2009/56, art 3, sch 1 para 425(2)(5)(b)

s 171 am—Finance, 2006 c 25, s 161, sch 23 para 7

2004
c 12 *continued*

s 172 am—Finance, 2005 c 7, s 101, sch 10 paras 1, 37, 64(1); (spec retrosp effect) Finance, 2008 c 9, s 91, sch 28 paras 1, 2, 15(1); Taxation of Pensions, 2014 c 30, sch 2 para 5; Finance, 2015 c 11, sch 4 para 8

s 172A added—Finance, 2005 c 7, s 101, sch 10 paras 1, 38, 64(1)

    am—Income Tax, 2007 c 3, s 1027, sch 1 paras 456, 469, sch 3; Finance, 2007 c 11, s 69, sch 20 paras 1, 6, 24(3); (spec retrosp effect) Finance, 2008 c 9, s 91, sch 28 paras 1, 3, 15(2); Equality, 2010 c 15, s 211, sch 26 para 58 (subst by SI 2010/2279, sch 1); Taxation of Pensions, 2014 c 30, sch 2 para 6-10; Finance, 2014 c 26, sch 7 para 10(3); Finance, 2015 c 11, sch 4 para 9

    rep in pt—Finance, 2014 c 26, sch 7 para 10(2)

s 172B added—Finance, 2005 c 7, s 101, sch 10 paras 1, 38, 64(1)

    am—Income Tax, 2007 c 3, s 1027, sch 1 paras 456, 470, sch 3; Finance, 2007 c 11, s 69, sch 19 paras 1, 12(1)-(4), 29(5); (retrosp to 6.4.2006) ibid, s 69, sch 19 paras 1, 12(1)(5), 29(4); Finance, 2008 c 9, s 91, sch 28 paras 1, 4(1)-(3)(4)(b)(5); Finance, 2011 c 11, sch 16 para 67(2)(3); Taxation of Pensions, 2014 c 30, sch 1 paras 9, 10; ibid, sch 2 paras 11, 12; Finance, 2015 c 11, sch 4 para 10

    rep in pt—Finance, 2007 c 11, s 69, sch 19 paras 1, 6, 29(3), sch 27; Finance, 2008 c 9, s 91, sch 28 paras 1, 4(1)(4)(a); Finance, 2011 c 11, sch 16 para 67(4)

s 172BA added—Finance, 2007 c 11, s 69, sch 19 paras 1, 13, 29(5)

    rep—Finance, 2011 c 11, sch 16 para 68

s 172C added—Finance, 2005 c 7, s 101, sch 10 paras 1, 38, 64(1)

    am—Income Tax, 2007 c 3, s 1027, sch 1 paras 456, 471

s 172D added—Finance, 2005 c 7, s 101, sch 10 paras 1, 38, 64(1)

    am—Income Tax, 2007 c 3, s 1027, sch 1 paras 456, 472; Finance, 2011 c 11, sch 17 para 2

s 173 am—Finance, 2006 c 25, ss 158, 161, sch 21 para 4, sch 23 para 8; Finance, 2015 c 11, sch 1 para 25

s 174 am—Finance, 2006 c 25, s 161, sch 23 para 174

s 174A added—Finance, 2006 c 25, s 158, sch 21 para 5

s 175 excl—SI 2006/575, reg 15

    am—Finance, 2006 c 25, s 161, sch 23 para 10

ss 176-178 excl—SI 2006/575, reg 15

s 179 excl—SI 2006/575, reg 15

    am—Finance, 2006 c 25, s 161, sch 23 para 11

s 180 excl—SI 2006/575, reg 15

    am—Finance, 2006 c 25, s 161, sch 23 para 12

    mod—SI 2012/1258, reg 2

s 181 excl—SI 2006/575, reg 15

    am—Finance, 2006 c 25, s 161, sch 23 para 13

s 181A added—Finance, 2007 c 11, s 69, sch 19 paras 1, 14, 29(2)

    rep—Finance, 2011 c 11, sch 16 para 69

s 182 excl—SI 2006/575, reg 16

    restr—Finance, 2011 c 11, s 68(1)

    mod—Finance, 2011 c 11, s 68(2)

    am—Finance, 2011 c 11, sch 16 para 70; Taxation of Pensions, 2014 c 30, sch 1 paras 11, 12; ibid, sch 2 para 13

s 183 excl—SI 2006/575, reg 16

    mod—Finance, 2011 c 11, s 68(2)

ss 184, 185 excl—SI 2006/575, reg 16

ss 185A-185F added—Finance, 2006 c 25, s 158, sch 21 para 6

    restr—SI 2006/207, reg 4B

s 185G added—Finance, 2006 c 25, s 158, sch 21 para 6

    restr—SI 2006/207, reg 4B

    rep in pt—Finance, 2008 c 9, s 8, sch 2 para 53; Finance, 2013 c 29, sch 46 para 120

ss 185H, 185I added—Finance, 2006 c 25, s 158, sch 21 para 6

    restr—SI 2006/207, reg 4B

s 185J added—Finance, 2014 c 26, sch 5 para 3

s 186 am—Income Tax (Trading and Other Income), 2005 c 5, ss 882(1), 883(4), sch 1 pt 2 paras 629, 644, sch 2 pt 12 para 161; Finance, 2006 c 25, s 158, sch 21 para 7

    appl (mods)—SI 2006/575, reg 17

s 188 am—Finance, 2007 c 11, s 68, sch 18 paras 1, 2; Finance, 2014 c 26, sch 7 para 13

2004
c 12 s 188 *continued*

rep in pt—Finance, 2007 c 11, s 69, sch 19 paras 1, 7, 29(3), sch 27; Finance, 2013 c 29, s 52(2)(3)

s 189 am—Income Tax (Trading and Other Income), 2005 c 5, ss 882(1), 883(4), sch 1 pt 2 paras 629, 645, sch 2 pt 12 para 161; SI 2005/3229, regs 1(7), 175, 176; Income Tax, 2007 c 3, s 1027, sch 1 paras 456, 473; Taxation (International and Other Provns), 2010 c 8, s 374, sch 8 paras 61, 63; Finance, 2011 c 11, sch 14 para 1; Finance, 2014 c 26, sch 17 para 18

rep in pt—Income Tax, 2007 c 3, s 1031, sch 3

s 190 rep in pt—Finance, 2013 c 29, s 52(4)

s 192 am—SI 2005/3229, regs 1(7), 175, 177; Finance, 2009 c 10, s 6, sch 2 paras 10, 11; SI 2015/1810, art 3

rep in pt—Income Tax, 2007 c 3, s 1027, sch 1 paras 456, 474, sch 3

ss 192A, 192B added—SI 2015/1810, art 4

s 193 am—Income Tax, 2007 c 3, s 1027, sch 1 paras 456, 475

s 194 am—Income Tax, 2007 c 3, s 1027, sch 1 paras 456, 476

s 195 rep in pt—Finance, 2014 c 26, sch 8 paras 52, 139

s 195A added—Finance, 2007 c 11, s 68, sch 18 paras 1, 3

s 196 am—Income Tax (Trading and Other Income), 2005 c 5, ss 882(1), 883(4), sch 1 pt 2 paras 629, 646, sch 2 pt 12 para 161; Corporation Tax, 2009 c 4, s 1322, sch 1 paras 569, 573; Finance, 2012 c 14, sch 16 para 113

rep in pt—Finance, 2013 c 29, s 52(5)

s 196A added—Finance, 2005 c 7, s 101, sch 10 paras 1, 39, 64(1)

am—Corporation Tax, 2009 c 4, s 1322, sch 1 paras 569, 574; Finance, 2012 c 14, sch 16 para 114

ss 196B-196J added (in relation to contributions paid during period 29.11.2011 to 21.2.2012)—Finance, 2012 c 14, sch 13 paras 1, 3

ss 196B-196L added (in relation to contributions paid on or after 22.2.2012)—(with transtl provns) Finance, 2012 c 14, sch 13 paras 15, 16-31

s 196L am—Finance, 2012 c 14, sch 16 para 115

s 197 am—Income Tax (Trading and Other Income), 2005 c 5, ss 882(1), 883(4), sch 1 pt 2 paras 629, 647, sch 2 pt 12 para 161; Finance, 2008 c 9, s 92, sch 29 para 14(1)-(3); Corporation Tax, 2009 c 4, s 1322, sch 1 paras 569, 575; Finance, 2012 c 14, sch 16 para 116

excl—SI 2006/575, reg 20

s 198 excl—SI 2006/575, reg 20

s 199 am—Income Tax (Trading and Other Income), 2005 c 5, ss 882(1), 883(4), sch 1 pt 2 paras 629, 648, sch 2 pt 12 para 161; Finance, 2012 c 14, sch 16 para 117

appl (mods)—SI 2006/575, reg 20

appl—SI 2010/1187, reg 3

s 199A added—Finance, 2008 c 9, s 90(1)

am—Corporation Tax, 2009 c 4, s 1322, sch 1 paras 569, 576; Finance, 2012 c 14, sch 16 para 118

s 200 am—Income Tax (Trading and Other Income), 2005 c 5, ss 882(1), 883(4), sch 1 pt 2 paras 629, 649, sch 2 pt 12 para 161; Corporation Tax, 2009 c 4, s 1322, sch 1 paras 569, 577; Finance, 2012 c 14, sch 16 para 119

appl—SI 2010/1187, reg 3

s 202 rep in pt—Finance, 2013 c 29, s 52(6)

s 203 am—SI 2005/3229, regs 1(7), 175, 178

s 205 am—SI 2010/536, art 3

rep in pt—Finance, 2013 c 29, sch 46 para 121

s 205A added—Finance, 2011 c 11, sch 16 para 40

rep in pt—Finance, 2013 c 29, sch 46 para 122

am—Taxation of Pensions, 2014 c 30, s 2(4)

s 206 appl—SI 2006/136

am—Finance, 2011 c 11, sch 16 para 41; Taxation of Pensions, 2014 c 30, s 2, sch 1 para 13, sch 2 para 17; Finance (No. 2), 2015 c 33, s 21

rep in pt—Finance, 2013 c 29, sch 46 para 123

s 207 rep in pt—Finance, 2013 c 29, sch 46 para 124

am—Finance, 2014 c 26, sch 7 para 11

s 208 am—Finance, 2006 c 25, s 161, sch 23 para 14; Finance, 2009 c 10, s 6, sch 2 paras 10, 12

mod—SI 2012/764, reg 24

rep in pt—Finance, 2013 c 29, sch 46 para 125

2004
c 12 *continued*

s 209 am—SI 2006/569, reg 3; Finance, 2006 c 25, s 161, sch 23 para 15; Finance, 2009 c
10, s 6, sch 2 paras 10, 13
mod—SI 2012/764, reg 24
rep in pt—Finance, 2013 c 29, sch 46 para 126
s 210 am—Finance, 2006 c 25, s 161, sch 23 para 16
s 211 am—Finance, 2006 c 25, s 161, sch 23 para 17; Finance, 2011 c 11, sch 16 para 71;
Taxation of Pensions, 2014 c 30, sch 1 para 14
s 212 appl—Income Tax (Earnings and Pensions), 2003 c 1, s 636B(3)
mod—SI 2006/572, art 10
am—Finance, 2006 c 25, s 161, sch 23 para 18; Finance, 2011 c 11, sch 16 para 72;
Taxation of Pensions, 2014 c 30, sch 1 para 15
s 213 excl—SI 2006/575, reg 20
am—Finance, 2006 c 25, s 161, sch 23 para 19
ss 213A-213P added—Finance, 2010 c 13, s 23, sch 2 para 2
s 214 appl (mods)—SI 2010/1187, regs 5, 6-9
mod—SI 2012/764, reg 24
s 215 rep in pt—Finance, 2005 c 7, ss 101, 104, sch 10 paras 1, 41, 64(1), sch 11 pt 4, Note
2
am—Finance, 2008 c 9, s 92, sch 29 para 15; Finance, 2009 c 10, s 6, sch 2 paras 10,
14
appl (mods)—SI 2010/1187, regs 5, 6-9
s 216 am—Finance, 2005 c 7, s 101, sch 10 paras 1, 31, 42, 64(1); Finance, 2006 c 25, s
161, sch 23 para 30; Finance, 2008 c 9, s 92, sch 29 para 1(1)(3); (spec retrosp
effect) ibid, s 92, sch 29 paras 4, 5; Finance, 2011 c 11, sch 16 paras 43, 73;
Taxation of Pensions, 2014 c 30, sch 1 para 16, sch 2 para 21; Finance, 2015 c
11, sch 4 para 4
appl—SI 2006/575, reg 23
mod—SI 2006/572, art 29A; reg 13 or 14 of SIs 2015/319, 370, 372, 390, 432, 436,
848 (W 63); SSIs 2015/117, 118, 145, 146
appl (mods)—Finance (No 2), 2010 c 31, s 6, sch 3 para 6(1); SI 2010/1187, regs 5,
6-9
s 217 appl (mods)—SI 2010/1187, regs 5
rep in pt—Finance, 2013 c 29, sch 46 para 127
am—Taxation of Pensions, 2014 c 30, sch 2 para 22; Finance, 2015 c 11, sch 4 para 5
s 218 appl (mods)—SI 2010/1187, regs 5, 6-9
am—Finance, 2011 c 11, sch 18 para 2; Finance, 2013 c 29, s 48(2)(3); ibid, sch 22
para 6
s 219 am—Finance, 2006 c 25, s 161, sch 23 para 31; Finance, 2007 c 11, s 69, sch 20
paras 1, 10, 24(3); Finance, 2013 c 29, sch 22 para 7(1); Finance, 2014 c 26,
sch 6 para 10(1); Taxation of Pensions, 2014 c 30, sch 2 para 23(2)(a)(c)(3);
Finance, 2015 c 11, sch 4 para 6
rep in pt—Taxation of Pensions, 2014 c 30, sch 2 para 23(2)(b)
appl (mods)—SI 2010/1187, regs 5, 6-9
s 220 am—Finance, 2005 c 7, s 101, sch 10 paras 1, 45, 64(1)
appl (mods)—SI 2010/1187, regs 5, 6-9
s 221 appl (mods)—SI 2010/1187, regs 5, 6-9
ss 222, 223 mod—SI 2006/572, arts 13, 14
appl (mods)—SI 2010/1187, regs 5, 6-9
ss 224-226 appl (mods)—SI 2010/1187, regs 5, 6-9
s 227 appl (mods)—SI 2006/207, reg 8
am—Finance, 2009 c 10, s 6, sch 2 paras 10, 15; Finance, 2011 c 11, sch 16 para
45(1), sch 17 para 3(3)(4)(6); Taxation of Pensions, 2014 c 30, sch 1 para 63;
Finance (No. 2), 2015 c 33, sch 4 para 11(2)(a); SI 2015/1810, art 7(2)
rep in pt—Finance, 2011 c 11, sch 17 para 3(2)(5); Taxation of Pensions, 2014 c 30,
sch 1 para 66(2)(a); Finance (No. 2), 2015 c 33, sch 4 para 11(2)(b)
mod—SI 2012/764, reg 24
s 227A added—Finance, 2011 c 11, sch 16 para 45(2)
rep—Taxation of Pensions, 2014 c 30, sch 1 para 66(1)
s 227ZA added—Taxation of Pensions, 2014 c 30, sch 1 para 64
am—Finance (No. 2), 2015 c 33, sch 4 para 11(3)
ss 227B-227G added—Taxation of Pensions, 2014 c 30, sch 1 para 65(1)
s 227B rep in pt—Finance (No. 2), 2015 c 33, sch 4 para 4(2)(a)(i)(iii)
am—Finance (No. 2), 2015 c 33, sch 4 para 4(2)(a)(ii)

2004
c 12 *continued*

s 227C rep in pt—Finance (No. 2), 2015 c 33, sch 4 para 4(2)(b)
    am—Finance (No. 2), 2015 c 33, sch 4 para 4(2)(c)
s 227D rep in pt—Finance (No. 2), 2015 c 33, sch 4 para 4(2)(d)
s 227E rep—Finance (No. 2), 2015 c 33, sch 4 para 4(1)
s 228 subst —Finance, 2011 c 11, sch 17 para 4
    am—Finance, 2013 c 29, s 49(2)(3)
ss 228ZA, 228ZB added—(2016-17 and subsequent tax years) Finance (No. 2), 2015 c 33,
    sch 4 para 10(1)
s 228A added—Finance, 2011 c 11, sch 17 para 5
    appl (mods)—Finance, 2011 c 11, sch 17 paras 29, 30
    am—Taxation of Pensions, 2014 c 30, sch 1 para 67(1)
s 228B added—SI 2015/80, art 11
s 228C added—Finance (No. 2), 2015 c 33, sch 4 para 6
s 229 appl—Finance, 2009 c 10, s 72, sch 35 para 4(1)
    am—Finance, 2011 c 11, sch 17 para 6; Finance (No. 2), 2015 c 33, sch 4 para 8
s 230 appl (mods) —SI 2005/3458, reg 5(1)-(4); Finance, 2009 c 10, s 72, sch 35 para
    5(1)(2); SI 2009/2031, arts 2, 5, 6, 7, 10
    am—Finance, 2011 c 11, sch 17 para 7; SI 2015/80, art 12
s 231 appl (mods)—SI 2006/207, reg 9; Finance, 2009 c 10, s 72, sch 35 para 5(2)
    am—Finance, 2011 c 11, sch 17 para 8
s 232 appl (mods) —SI 2005/3458, regs 5(1)(2), 6, 7(1)-(4); Finance, 2009 c 10, s 72, sch
    35 para 5(2)
    am—Finance, 2011 c 11, sch 17 para 9; SI 2015/80, art 13(a)(i),(b),(c)(i),(d)(e),(g)
    rep in pt—Finance, 2011 c 11, sch 17 para 9(5)(7)(9); SI 2015/80, art 13(a)(ii),(c)(ii),
    (f)
s 233 appl (mods)—SI 2005/3458, regs 5(1)(2), 6, 7(1)-(4); Finance, 2009 c 10, s 72, sch
    35 para 5(1)(2); SI 2009/2031, arts 2, 5
    rep in pt—Finance, 2013 c 29, s 52(7)
    am—SI 2015/80, art 14
s 234 appl (mods)—SI 2005/3458, regs 5(1)(2), 6, 7(1)-(4); Finance, 2009 c 10, s 72, sch
    35 para 5(1)(2); SI 2009/2031, arts 2, 5; Finance, 2011 c 11, sch 17 para 28(6)
    am—Finance, 2011 c 11, sch 17 para 10; SI 2015/80, art 15
    mod—reg 14 or 15 of SIs 2015/319, 370, 372, 390, 432, 436, 848 (W 63); SSIs
    2015/117, 118, 145, 146
s 235 appl—SI 2006/130, reg 2
    appl (mods)—SI 2006/207, reg 10; Finance, 2009 c 10, s 72, sch 35 para 5(2)
    rep in pt—Finance, 2011 c 11, sch 17 para 11(2)
    am—Finance, 2011 c 11, sch 17 para 11(3)
s 236 appl (mods) —SI 2005/3458, regs 7(1)(2), 8; Finance, 2009 c 10, s 72, sch 35 paras
    5(2), 6(6)
    am—Finance, 2011 c 11, sch 17 para 12; SI 2015/80, art 16(a)(i),(b),(c)(i),(d)-(f)
    rep in pt—Finance, 2011 c 11, sch 17 para 12(7); SI 2015/80, art 16(a)(ii),(c)(ii)
s 236A added—Finance, 2011 c 11, sch 17 para 13
s 237 appl (mod)—Finance, 2009 c 10, s 72, sch 35 para 5(2), 6(6); SI 2009/2031, arts 2, 5
    am—Finance, 2011 c 11, sch 17 para 14
s 237ZA added—Finance (No. 2), 2015 c 33, sch 4 para 9
ss 237A-237F added—Finance, 2011 c 11, sch 17 para 15
s 237A rep in pt—Finance, 2013 c 29, sch 46 para 128
s 237B appl (mods)—Finance, 2011 c 11, sch 17 para 32
    rep in pt—Finance, 2013 c 29, sch 46 para 129; SI 2015/80, art 17(a)(ii)(iii)
    am—Taxation of Pensions, 2014 c 30, sch 1 para 68; SIs 2015/80, art 17(a)(i),(b);
    1810, art 7(3)
s 238 am—Finance, 2011 c 11, sch 17 para 16; Finance (No. 2), 2015 c 33, sch 4 para 2
    rep in pt—Finance, 2011 c 11, sch 17 para 16(4)(a)
ss 238ZA, 238ZB added—Finance (No. 2), 2015 c 33, sch 4 para 3
s 238A added—Finance, 2011 c 11, sch 17 para 17
s 239 am—Finance, 2006 c 25, s 158, sch 21 para 8; Finance, 2014 c 26, sch 5 para 12
    rep in pt—Finance, 2013 c 29, sch 46 para 130
    mod—SI 2006/572, art 18 (amended by Finance, 2014 c 26, sch 5 para 12(4))
s 240 am—Finance, 2009 c 10, s 6, sch 2 paras 10, 16
s 241 am—Finance, 2006 c 25, s 158, sch 21 para 9; Finance, 2007 c 11, s 69, sch 19 paras
    1, 15, 29(2)
    rep in pt—Finance, 2011 c 11, sch 16 para 74

2004
c 12 *continued*

s 242 excl—SI 2006/575, reg 25
    am—Finance, 2009 c 10, s 6, sch 2 paras 10, 17
    rep in pt—Finance, 2013 c 29, sch 46 para 131
s 245 mod—SI 2006/572, art 16
    rep in pt—Finance, 2007 c 11, s 114, sch 27 pt 2
s 246 am—Income Tax (Trading and Other Income), 2005 c 5, ss 882(1), 883(4), sch 1 pt 2
    paras 629, 650, sch 2 pt 12 para 161; Corporation Tax, 2009 c 4, s 1322, sch 1
    paras 569, 578; Finance, 2012 c 14, sch 16 paras 120(2)(3), 121
s 246A added—Finance, 2005 c 7, s 101, sch 10 paras 1, 40, 64(1)
    am—Corporation Tax, 2009 c 4, s 1322, sch 1 paras 569, 579
s 249 am—Income Tax (Trading and Other Income), 2005 c 5, ss 882(1), 883(3), sch 1 pt 2
    paras 629, 651, sch 2 pt 12 para 161
s 251 am—Finance, 2005 c 7, s 101, sch 10 paras 1, 47, 64(1); Finance, 2010 c 13, s 49;
    Taxation of Pensions, 2014 c 30, sch 1 para 93; Finance (No. 2), 2015 c 33, s
    21(6)
s 252 rep —SI 2009/3054, art 3, sch
s 253 rep —(with savings) SI 2009/3054, arts 3, 8, sch
s 254 appl—SI 2006/136, reg 2
    appl (mods)—Finance, 2011 c 11, sch 17 para 33
    am—Finance, 2011 c 11, sch 17 para 18
s 255 am—Finance, 2011 c 11, sch 17 para 19; Finance, 2014 c 26, sch 7 para 17
ss 255A, 225B added—Finance, 2005 c 7, s 101, sch 10 paras 1, 48, 64(1)
s 256 am—Finance, 2006 c 25, s 161, sch 23 para 42
s 257 am—Finance, 2014 c 26, sch 7 para 23(b)
s 259 rep —(with savings) SI 2009/3054, arts 3, 8, sch
s 260 appl—SI 2006/136, reg 2
    rep in pt—SIs 2011/702, art 14; 2013/1114, art 5
s 261 appl (mods)—SI 2010/1187, reg 11
    am—Finance, 2014 c 26, sch 7 para 23(c)
s 262 appl (mods)—SI 2010/1187, reg 11
s 264 am—Finance, 2014 c 26, sch 7 para 23(d)
s 266A added—Finance, 2005 c 7, s 101, sch 10 paras 1, 4, 64(1)
    am—Income Tax, 2007 c 3, s 1027, sch 1 paras 456, 477; Finance, 2014 c 26, sch 7
    para 14
s 266B added—Finance, 2005 c 7, s 101, sch 10 paras 1, 4, 64(1)
    am—Finance, 2014 c 26, sch 7 para 15
s 268 am—Finance, 2007 c 11, s 69, sch 19 paras 1, 17, 29(7); Finance, 2014 c 26, sch 5
    para 12(3)
    rep in pt—Finance, 2011 c 11, sch 16 para 75
s 269 am—SI 2009/56, art 3, sch 1 para 427; Finance, 2011 c 11, sch 17 para 20
    rep in pt—SI 2009/56, art 3, sch 1 para 427(2)(6)(b)
s 270 appl—SI 2006/569, reg 3
    am—Finance, 2014 c 26, sch 7 para 9(1)
s 271 am—SI 2009/56, art 3, sch 1 para 428
    rep in pt—SI 2009/56, art 3, sch 1 para 428(2)(5)(b)
s 272 appl (mods)—SI 2006/569, reg 3
    am—Finance, 2014 c 26, sch 7 para 18
ss 272A-272C added—Finance, 2014 c 26, sch 7 para 19
s 273 appl (mods)—SI 2006/569, reg 3
    excl—SI 2006/575, reg 28
    am—Income Tax, 2007 c 3, s 1027, sch 1 paras 456, 478; Corporation Tax, 2010 c 4,
    s 1177, sch 1 paras 423, 428; Finance, 2014 c 26, sch 7 para 20
    rep in pt—Finance, 2007 c 11, s 69, sch 20 paras 1, 4, 24(1), sch 27
s 273ZA added—Finance, 2006 c 25, s 158, sch 21 para 10
s 273A added—Finance, 2005 c 7, s 101, sch 10 paras 1, 49(1), 64(1)
    appl (mods)—SI 2006/569, reg 3
    am—Finance, 2011 c 11, sch 16 para 76; Taxation of Pensions, 2014 c 30, sch 1
    para 17
s 273B added—Taxation of Pensions, 2014 c 30, sch 1 para 79
    am—Finance, 2015 c 11, sch 4 para 11
s 274 am—Finance, 2005 c 7, s 101, sch 10 paras 1, 49(2), 64(1); Finance, 2014 c 26, sch 7
    para 21
    appl (mods)—SI 2006/569, reg 3

2004

c 12 *continued*

s 274A added—Finance, 2005 c 7, s 101, sch 10 paras 1, 50, 64(1)

s 275 appl (mods)—SI 2006/207, reg 11

s 276 appl (mods)—SI 2006/207, reg 12

s 278 am—Finance, 2006 c 25, s 158, sch 21 para 11; Income Tax, 2007 c 3, s 1027, sch 1 paras 456, 479

s 279 am—Finance, 2005 c 7, s 101, sch 10 paras 1, 9, 64(1); Finance, 2006 c 25, s 161, sch 23 para 33; Income Tax, 2007 c 3, s 1027, sch 1 paras 456, 480; Finance, 2011 c 11, sch 17 para 21

    appl (mods)—SI 2006/207, reg 13

    rep in pt—Income Tax, 2007 c 3, s 1031, sch 3

s 280 rep in pt—Income Tax (Trading and Other Income), 2005 c 5, ss 882(1), 884, sch 1 pt 2 paras 629, 652, sch 3; Income Tax, 2007 c 3, s 1031, sch 3; Finance, 2007 c 11, s 69, sch 19 paras 1, 8, 29(3), sch 27; Corporation Tax, 2009 c 4, ss 1322, 1326, sch 1 paras 569, 580(a), sch 3 pt 1; Finance, 2011 c 11, sch 16 para 77(2)(3)(5); Finance, 2012 c 14, sch 13 para 2(a)

    am—Income Tax (Trading and Other Income), 2005 c 5, s 882(1), sch 1 pt 2 paras 629, 652; Finance, 2005 c 7, s 101, sch 10 paras 1, 10, 17, 33, 64(1); Finance, 2006 c 25, ss 158, 161, sch 21 para 12, sch 23 para 26; Income Tax, 2007 c 3, s 1027, sch 1 paras 456, 481; Finance, 2007 c 11, s 69, sch 20 paras 22(2), 24(3); Corporation Tax, 2009 c 4, s 1322, sch 1 paras 569, 580(b); Finance, 2010 c 13, s 68(1)-(4); Finance, 2011 c 11, sch 16 para 77(4), sch 17 para 22; Finance, 2012 c 14, sch 13 paras 2(b), 16; ibid, sch 16 para 122; Finance, 2013 c 29, s 53(8); Finance, 2014 c 26, sch 5 para 5(4); Taxation of Pensions, 2014 c 30, sch 1 paras 18, 56, sch 2 paras 14, 18; Finance, 2015 c 11, sch 4 para 12; Finance (No. 2), 2015 c 33, sch 4 para 5; SI 2015/1810, art 7(4)

s 281 am—Finance, 2006 c 25, s 161, sch 23 para 34

    rep in pt—Finance, 2009 c 10, s 75(2)(b)

s 282 am—Finance, 2009 c 10, s 6, sch 2 paras 10, 18; ibid, s 75(1); Finance, 2010 c 13, s 23, sch 2 para 3; Finance, 2011 c 11, sch 17 para 23; Finance, 2014 c 26, sch 5 para 14

    mod—Finance, 2011 c 11, sch 16 para 108(2)

s 283 am—Finance, 2006 c 25, sch 23 para 35

    rep in pt—Finance, 2009 c 10, s 75(2)(c)

s 285 rep in pt—Corporation Tax, 2010 c 4, s 1181, sch 3 pt 2; Taxation (International and Other Provns), 2010 c 8, s 378, sch 10 pt 6

s 295 rep in pt—Finance, 2008 c 9, s 122, sch 41 para 21(l)

s 298 rep in pt—Finance, 2012 c 14, sch 39 para 8(2)(c); Scotland, 2012 c 11, sch 3 para 28

Pt 7 (ss 306-319) excl—Finance, 2014 c 26, sch 35 para 13(b)

s 306A added—Finance, 2007 c 11, s 108(1)(2)(10)

    am—SI 2009/56, art 3, sch 1 para 429

s 307 am—Finance, 2007 c 11, s 108(3)(10); Corporation Tax, 2010 c 4, s 1177, sch 1 paras 423, 429; Finance, 2010 c 13, s 56, sch 17 para 2

s 308 appl—SI 2004/1865, reg 2(2)(a)

    am—Finance, 2008 c 9, s 116, sch 38 paras 1, 2; SI 2009/56, art 3, sch 1 para 430; Finance, 2010 c 13, s 56, sch 17 para 3; Finance, 2012 c 14, s 215

s 308A added—Finance, 2007 c 11, s 108(4)(10)

s 310A added—Finance, 2014 c 26, s 284(2)

    appl—Finance, 2014 c 26, s 284(11)

s 310B added—Finance, 2014 c 26, s 284(2)

s 310C added—Finance, 2015 c 11, sch 17 para 1

s 311 am—Finance, 2008 c 9, s 116, sch 38 paras 1, 3(a)(c)(d); Finance, 2015 c 11, sch 17 para 4

    rep in pt—Finance, 2008 c 9, s 116, sch 38 paras 1, 3(b)

s 312 subst —Finance, 2008 c 9, s 116, sch 38 paras 1, 4

s 312A added —Finance, 2008 c 9, s 116, sch 38 paras 1, 4

    am—Finance, 2013 c 29, s 223(2)

s 313 rep in pt—Finance, 2008 c 9, s 116, sch 38 paras 1, 5(1)(2)

    am—Finance, 2008 c 9, s 116, sch 38 paras 1, 5(1)(3)(4); SI 2009/571, art 8, sch 1; Finance, 2015 c 11, sch 17 para 6

s 313ZA added—Finance, 2010 c 13, s 56, sch 17 para 6

s 313ZB added—Finance, 2013 c 29, s 223(3)

s 313ZC added—Finance, 2015 c 11, sch 17 para 9

s 313A added—Finance, 2007 c 11, s 108(5)(10)

2004

c 12 s 313A *continued*

   am—Finance, 2010 c 13, s 56, sch 17 para 4

  s 313B added—Finance, 2007 c 11, s 108(5)(10)

   am—SI 2009/56, art 3, sch 1 para 431

  s 313C added—Finance, 2010 c 13, s 56, sch 17 para 9

   am—Finance, 2015 c 11, sch 17 para 12

  s 314A added—Finance, 2007 c 11, s 108(6)(10)

   am—SI 2009/56, art 3, sch 1 para 432

  s 316 subst—Finance, 2008 c 9, s 116, sch 38 paras 1, 6

   am—Finance, 2010 c 13, s 56, sch 17 para 7; Finance, 2014 c 26, s 284(3); Finance,
    2015 c 11, sch 17 paras 2, 7, 10

  s 316A added—Finance, 2015 c 11, sch 17 para 14

  s 316B added—Finance, 2015 c 11, sch 17 para 16

  s 316C, 316D added—Finance, 2015 c 11, sch 17 para 17

  s 317 am—Finance, 2010 c 13, s 56, sch 17 para 8

  s 317A added—Finance, 2007 c 11, s 108(7)(10)

   am—SI 2009/56, art 3, sch 1 para 433

  s 318 am—Finance, 2007 c 11, s 108(8)(10); SI 2009/56, art 3, sch 1 para 434(3); Taxation
    (International and Other Provns), 2010 c 8, s 374, sch 8 paras 301, 302(2);
    Finance, 2010 c 13, s 56, sch 17 para 5; Finance, 2013 c 29, sch 35 para 2(b);
    Finance, 2014 c 26, s 284(4)

   rep in pt—SI 2009/56, art 3, sch 1 para 434(2); Taxation (International and Other
    Provns), 2010 c 8, ss 374, 378, sch 8 paras 301, 302(3), sch 10; Finance, 2013
    c 29, sch 35 para 2(a)

  s 322 am—Finance, 2011 c 11, sch 25 para 18

  s 324 am—SI 2012/1809, art 3(1), sch pt 1

  sch 4 rep in pt—Income Tax (Trading and Other Income), 2005 c 5, s 884, sch 3; Income
    Tax, 2007 c 3, s 1031, sch 3

   am—SI 2010/1080, art 2, sch 1

  sch 5 rep in pt—Corporation Tax, 2009 c 4, s 1326, sch 3 pt 1; Corporation Tax, 2010 c 4, s
    1181, sch 3 pt 1; Taxation (International and Other Provns), 2010 c 8, s 378,
    sch 10 pt 2

  sch 6 rep—Finance, 2012 c 14, sch 16 paras 247(l)(iii), 248

  sch 7 rep in pt—Finance, 2007 c 11, s 114, sch 27 pt 2; Finance, 2008 c 9, s 43, sch 17 para
    18(5)(e); SI 2008/381, art 31, sch; Taxation (International and Other Provns),
    2010 c 8, s 378, sch 10 pt 1; Finance, 2012 c 14, sch 16 para 247(l)(iv)

  sch 8 rep —Corporation Tax, 2009 c 4, s 1326, sch 3 pt 1

   am—SI 2006/207, reg 14(3)(ba)(ea) (added by Taxation of Pensions, 2014 c 30, sch 1
    para 33(3)(a)(c))

  sch 9 rep—Corporation Tax, 2009 c 4, s 1326, sch 3 pt 1

   excl—SI 2014/512, reg 167

  sch 10 rep in pt—Finance, 2005 c 7, ss 80, 104, sch 4 pt 2 para 27(1), sch 11 pt 2(7), Note 2;
    ibid, s 104, sch 11 pt 2(5), Note; (prosp) Finance (No 2), 2005 c 22, s 70, sch
    11 pt 2(6), Note 3; Finance, 2007 c 11, s 114, sch 27 pt 2; Corporation Tax,
    2009 c 4, s 1326, sch 3 pt 1; Corporation Tax, 2010 c 4, s 1181, sch 3 pt 1

   am—Finance, 2005 c 7, s 80, sch 4 pt 2 para 51; Finance, 2008 c 9, s 94, sch 30
    paras 1, 7

  sch 11 rep in pt—Finance, 2008 c 9, s 94, sch 30 paras 1, 8, 9(1)(4), 10

   am—Finance, 2008 c 9, s 94, sch 30 paras 1, 9(1)-(4), 11; SI 2009/1890, art 6;
    Corporation Tax, 2010 c 4, s 1177, sch 1 paras 423, 430; SI 2015/789, arts 2,
    3

  sch 12 rep in pt—Income Tax, 2007 c 3, s 1031, sch 3; Taxation (International and Other
    Provns), 2010 c 8, s 378, sch 10 pt 12

  sch 15 am—Income Tax (Trading and Other Income), 2005 c 5, s 882(1), sch 1 pt 2 paras
    629, 653(1)-(5); SI 2005/3229, regs 175, 179(a)(b); Finance, 2006 c 25, s
    80(1)-(4); Income Tax, 2007 c 3, s 1027, sch 1 paras 456, 482; Finance, 2007
    c 11, s 66

   appl—SI 2005/724, reg 6(6)

   rep in pt—Finance, 2008 c 9, s 94, sch 30 paras 1, 12

  sch 16 rep in pt—Finance, 2008 c 9, s 94, sch 30 paras 1, 13; Corporation Tax, 2009 c 4, s
    1326, sch 3 pt 1

  sch 17 rep in pt—Finance, 2004 c 12, s 326, sch 42 pt 3, Note; Income Tax (Trading and
    Other Income), 2005 c 5, s 884, sch 3; Income Tax, 2007 c 3, s 1031, sch 3;
    Corporation Tax, 2009 c 4, s 1326, sch 3 pt 1

2004
c 12 *continued*

sch 18 rep in pt—Finance, 2006 c 25, s 178, sch 26; Income Tax, 2007 c 3, s 1031, sch 3; Finance, 2007 c 11, s 114, sch 27 pt 2; Finance, 2009 c 10, s 27, sch 8 para 10(b)

sch 19 rep in pt—Income Tax (Trading and Other Income), 2005 c 5, s 884, sch 3; Income Tax, 2007 c 3, s 1031, sch 3

sch 20 rep in pt—Finance, 2007 c 11, s 114, sch 27 pt 2

sch 21 rep in pt—Finance, 2008 c 9, s 8, sch 2 paras 21(g), 55(g); SI 2009/2035, art 2, sch

sch 22 rep in pt—Finance, 2007 c 11, s 114, sch 27 pt 3

sch 24 am—Income Tax (Trading and Other Income), 2005 c 5, s 882(1), sch 1 pt 2 paras 629, 654

    rep in pt—Income Tax (Trading and Other Income), 2005 c 5, s 884, sch 3; Income Tax, 2007 c 3, s 1031, sch 3; Finance, 2013 c 29, sch 29 para 11

sch 26 excl—SI 2004/2572, regs 6, 7

    rep in pt—Corporation Tax, 2009 c 4, s 1326, sch 3 pt 1; SI 2009/3001, reg 13, sch 2; Corporation Tax, 2010 c 4, s 1181, sch 3 pt 1

    am—Corporation Tax, 2009 c 4, s 1322, sch 1 paras 569, 581

sch 27 am—Income Tax, 2007 c 3, s 1027, sch 1 paras 456, 483

    rep in pt—Income Tax, 2007 c 3, s 1031, sch 3; Corporation Tax, 2010 c 4, s 1181, sch 3 pt 1

sch 28 rep in pt—Finance, 2005 c 7, ss 101, 104, sch 10 paras 11(1)(2)(6), 64(1), sch 11 pt 4, Note 2; Finance, 2005 c 7, ss 101, 104, sch 10 paras 13(4), 14(5), 16(5), 27(1)(2)(3)(b)(5), 64(1), sch 11 pt 4, Note 2; Finance, 2007 c 11, s 69, sch 19 paras 1, 3, 29(1), sch 27; Finance, 2008 c 9, s 91, sch 28 paras 1, 5; Finance, 2009 c 10, s 75(2)(d); Finance, 2011 c 11, sch 16 paras 4(b), 6(4), 14(b), 78(a)-(d); Taxation of Pensions, 2014 c 30, sch 1 para 32(1)(e); Finance, 2015 c 11, sch 4 paras 3, 13

    am—Finance, 2005 c 7, s 101, sch 10 paras 11(1)(3)-(9), 12, 13(1)-(3), 14(1)-(4), 15, 16(1)-(4), 18-23, 26, 27(1)(3)(a)(4), 28, 29, 64(1); SI 2005/3229, regs 1(7), 175, 180; Finance, 2006 c 25, s 161, sch 23 para 20; SI 2007/493, reg 2; Finance, 2007 c 11, s 69, sch 19 paras 11, 29(4); ibid, sch 20 paras 7(1)-(3), 8, 24(3)-(5); Finance, 2008 c 9, s 92, sch 29 para 2; Finance, 2011 c 11, sch 16 paras 3, 4(a), 5-10, 13, 14(a), 15-20; Financial Services, 2012 c 21, sch 18 para 100; Finance, 2013 c 29, s 51(2); Finance, 2014 c 26, s 41(3)(4); Taxation of Pensions, 2014 c 30, sch 1 paras 2, 3(1), 4(1), 19-21, 37-40, 43-51, sch 2 para 3(1)

    mod—SIs 2006/207, reg 14 (substituted by SI 2012/1795, reg 5); 572, arts 5, 24, 29; Finance, 2011 c 11, sch 16 paras 87, 88, 89(2), 90(2)(b)(8), 92, 93(2), 95, 96, 97(2), 98(2)(b), 100(2)

    appl—Income Tax (Earnings and Pensions), 2003 c 1, s 579CZA(9); ibid, ss 646B(5)(6), 646C(9), 646D(5)(6)

    appl (mods)—SIs 2006/207, reg 14; 2006/572, arts 5A, 34; Finance (No 2), 2010 c 31, s 6, sch 3 paras 2(2)(b)(2)(d), 34; Finance, 2011 c 11, sch 16 paras 90(7), 98(7)(8)

sch 29 am—Finance, 2005 c 7, s 101, sch 10 paras 1, 24, 30, 34, 35(1)-(3), 64(1); Finance, 2006 c 25, ss 159(1), 161, sch 23 paras 21-23, 27-29; Finance, 2007 c 11, s 69, sch 19 paras 1, 16(1)(2)(4), 29(4); ibid, s 69, sch 19 paras 16(1)(3)(5)(6), 29(4)(6), sch 20 paras 11-13, 24(3)(6)(7); SI 2010/1187, reg 19; Finance, 2011 c 11, sch 16 paras 24(2)(b)(3)(4), 25-27, 28(3), 31, 33, 34(3), 35(2)(b)(c)(3), 36(3), 37, 38, 79(3)(4), sch 18 paras 4-7; Finance, 2013 c 29, sch 22 para 8(2)(4); Finance, 2014 c 26, s 42(1), sch 5 paras 1, 2(1), 4, 5(2), 22-25, 57-60, 70, 71, 74; Taxation of Pensions, 2014 c 30, sch 2 para 15; Finance, 2015 c 11, sch 4 paras 14, 15

    rep in pt—Finance, 2007 c 11, ss 69, 114, sch 19 paras 1, 9, 29(3), sch 27; Finance, 2011 c 11, sch 16 paras 24(2)(a), 28(2), 29, 30, 33(3), 34(2), 35(2)(a), 36(2), 37(3)(b), 38, 79(2); Finance, 2013 c 29, ss 51(3), 52(8); Finance, 2014 c 26, s 42(2); Taxation of Pensions, 2014 c 30, sch 1 para 75(1), sch 2 para 19(1); Finance (No. 2), 2015 c 33, s 21(8)

    appl—SI 2006/135; Income Tax (Earnings and Pensions), 2003 c 1, s 646B(7)

    appl (mods)—SI 2006/207, reg 15; Finance (No 2), 2010 c 31, s 6, sch 3 paras 2(2)(e), 7, 88(2)

    mod—SIs 2006/207, reg 15 (substituted by SI 2012/1795, reg 6); 572, art 8; 2009/1172, arts 2, 3

    excl—SI 2006/575, reg 11

2004

c 12 *continued*

  sch 29A added—Finance, 2006 c 25, s 158, sch 21 para 13
      appl—SI 2006/1958, regs 3-6
      mod—SI 2006/207, regs 4C, 4D
      am—Income Tax, 2007 c 3, s 1027, sch 1 paras 456, 484; Finance, 2007 c 11, s 69,
          sch 20 paras 1, 14, 24(8); (spec retrosp effect) Finance, 2008 c 9, s 92, sch 29
          para 3(1); Corporation Tax, 2010 c 4, s 1177, sch 1 paras 423, 431; SI
          2013/636, sch para 7
      rep in pt—Finance, 2007 c 11, s 114, sch 27 pt 3; Finance, 2009 c 10, s 75(2)(e)
  sch 31 am—SI 2006/569, reg 3
  sch 32 am—Finance, 2005 c 7, s 101, sch 10 paras 1, 8(1)-(6), 25(1)-(3), 32,
          43(1)(2)(3)(a)(4)-(8), 44, 64(1); (spec retrosp effect) Finance, 2008 c 9, s 92,
          sch 29 paras 6-10; Finance, 2011 c 11, sch 16 paras 44, 80; Taxation of
          Pensions, 2014 c 30, sch 1 paras 26, 27, 61, 76(1), sch 2 paras 19(2), 24;
          Finance, 2015 c 11, sch 4 para 7; Finance (No. 2), 2015 c 33, s 21(7)
      rep in pt—Finance, 2005 c 7, ss 101, 104, sch 10 paras 1, 43(1)(3)(b), 64(1), sch 11
          pt 4, Note 2; Finance, 2011 c 11, sch 16 para 80(4)
      appl (mods)—SI 2006/207, reg 16
      appl—SI 2006/575, reg 23
      mod—Finance, 2011 c 11, sch 16 para 104(3)
  sch 33 am—Finance, 2005 c 7, s 101, sch 10 paras 1, 46, 64(1); Finance, 2006 c 25, s 161,
          sch 23 para 32; SI 2009/56, art 3, sch 1 para 435; Taxation of Pensions, 2014 c
          30, sch 1 para 94
      appl (mods)—SI 2005/3458, reg 2(2)(b)
      appl—Income Tax (Trading and Other Income), 2005 c 5, ss 38(4), 866(5)
      rep in pt—SI 2009/56, art 3, sch 1 para 435(2)(5)(a)
  sch 34 appl (mods)—SI 2006/207, reg 17
      am—Finance, 2006 c 25, s 158, sch 21 para 14; Finance, 2007 c 11, s 69, sch 19
          paras 1, 18(4); Finance, 2008 c 9, s 92, sch 29 para 16; (transtl provns) ibid, s
          92, sch 29 para 19(1)-(3)(5)(a)(6); Taxation (International and Other Provns),
          2010 c 8, s 374, sch 8 paras 61, 64; Finance, 2010 c 13, s 23, sch 2 para 4;
          Finance, 2011 c 11, sch 2 para 51, sch 16 para 81, sch 17 para 24; Finance,
          2014 c 26, s 45; Taxation of Pensions, 2014 c 30, sch 1 para 95; Finance (No.
          2), 2015 c 33, s 22(10)
      rep in pt—Finance, 2007 c 11, s 69, sch 19 paras 1, 18(1)-(3), 29(3), sch 27; Finance,
          2011 c 11, sch 16 para 81(5); Taxation of Pensions, 2014 c 30, sch 1 para
          32(1)(f)
  sch 35 rep in pt—Income Tax (Trading and Other Income), 2005 c 5, s 884, sch 3; Income
          Tax, 2007 c 3, s 1031, sch 3; Finance, 2007 c 11, s 114, sch 27 pt 2; Finance,
          2008 c 9, s 36, sch 14 para 17(n); Corporation Tax, 2009 c 4, s 1326, sch 3 pt
          1; Finance, 2009 c 10, s 5, sch 1 para 6(m); ibid, s 126(6)(a); Corporation Tax,
          2010 c 4, s 1181, sch 3 pt 1; Finance, 2012 c 14, sch 16 para 247(1)(v); ibid,
          sch 39 para 31(2)(b); ibid, sch 39 para 28(1)(3)
      am—SI 2005/3229, regs 1(7), 175, 181; Income Tax (Trading and Other Income),
          2005 c 5, ss 882(1), 883(4), sch 1 pt 2 paras 629, 655, sch 2 pt 12 para 161;
          Finance (No 2), 2005 c 22, s 42, sch 9 para 18(1)-(7); SI 2006/569, reg 3;
          Finance, 2014 c 26, s 114(3)(c)
  sch 36 am—Finance, 2005 c 7, s 101, sch 10 paras 1, 51, 52(1)(2)(3)(b)(4)-(6)(7)(b)(8)(9),
          53(1)-(16), 54(1)(3)-(7), 55(1)-(7), 56, 57, 58(1)-(3) 64(1); Income Tax
          (Trading and Other Income), 2005 c 5, s 882(1), sch 1 pt 2 paras 629,
          656(1)-(3); SI 2005/3229, regs 175, 182(a)(b); Finance, 2006 c 25, ss 158,
          161, sch 21 para 15, sch 23 paras 24, 25, 36-41, 43-46; Income Tax, 2007 c 3,
          s 1027, sch 1 paras 456, 485; Finance, 2007 c 11, s 69, sch 19 paras 1, 10,
          29(3), sch 20 paras 1, 15-19, 24(3); (spec retrosp effect) Finance, 2008 c 9, s 92,
          sch 29 para 18(7); Finance, 2009 c 10, s 72, sch 35 para 22; Corporation Tax,
          2010 c 4, s 1177, sch 1 paras 423, 432; Equality, 2010 c 15, s 211, sch 26 para
          59 (subst by SI 2010/2279, sch 1); Finance, 2011 c 11, sch 16 para 82, sch 18
          paras 9-11; SI 2013/1114, art 3; Finance, 2014 c 26, sch 5 para 7-10; Taxation
          of Pensions, 2014 c 30, sch 1 paras 28, 29, 77(1), 78(1); Finance, 2015 c 11,
          sch 4 para 19
      rep in pt—Finance, 2005 c 7, ss 101, 104, sch 10 paras 1, 52(1)(3)(a) (6)(7)(a),
          54(1)(2), 61(a)(b), 64(1)(2), sch 11 pt 4, Note 1, Note 2; SI 2006/572, art 523;
          Finance, 2007 c 11, s 114, sch 27 pt 3; Finance, 2011 c 11, sch 16 para 82(6),
          sch 17 para 25; Finance, 2013 c 29, s 52(9)

2004

c 12 sch 36 *continued*

    mod—SI 2006/572, arts 11, 18, 22, 23, 23D, 23ZA(2), 23ZC(3), 23ZD(2), 23ZE(3)(4), 42(3), 43(4)

    appl—Income Tax (Earnings and Pensions), 2003 c 1, s 554U(2); SI 2006/575, reg 30; Finance, 2011 c 11, sch 18 para 14(9)-(11); Finance, 2013 c 29, sch 22 para 1(8)-(10)

    appl (mods)—SI 2010/1187, regs 5, 10; Finance, 2011 c 11, sch 18 para 14(8); Finance, 2013 c 29, sch 22 para 1(7); Finance, 2014 c 26, sch 6 para 2(3)(4)(7)(8)

  sch 37 rep in pt—Corporation Tax, 2010 c 4, s 1181, sch 3 pt 2; Taxation (International and Other Provns), 2010 c 8, s 378, sch 10 pt 6

  sch 39 rep in pt—Finance, 2004 c 12, s 326, sch 42 pt 4(2), Note 3; Finance, 2006 c 25, s 178, sch 26

  sch 42 excl—Finance, 2005 c 7, s 80, sch 4 pt 2 para 27(1)

c 13   **Scottish Parliament (Constituencies)**

  s 1 rep in pt—Scotland, 2012 c 11, s 8(1)

  sch 2 rep—Scotland, 2012 c 11, s 8(1)

c 14   **Statute Law (Repeals)**

  s 1 rep in pt—Legislative and Regulatory Reform, 2006 c 51, s 30, sch 1

c 15   **Carers (Equal Opportunities)**

  s 3 appl (mods)—(Isles of Scilly) SI 2005/1096, art 2

    rep in pt—SI 2010/1158, art 5, schs 2, 3; Health and Social Care, 2012 c 7, sch 5 para 125(4)(b)(ii)

    am—Health and Social Care, 2012 c 7, sch 5 para 125(2)(b)(3)(4)(a)(b)(i); SI 2015/914, sch para 76

  s 6 rep in pt—SI 2015/914, sch para 77

c 16   **Patents**

  s 2 rep in pt—SI 2006/1028, reg 2, sch 4

c 17   **Health Protection Agency**

  rep (except sch 3 para 3 and s 11(1) as relating)—Health and Social Care, 2012 c 7, s 56(2)(3)

c 18   **Traffic Management**

  s 1 am—Infrastructure, 2015 c 7, sch 1 para 130

  s 7 saved—Road Traffic Regulation, 1984 c 27, s 67(1A)

  s 11 am—Infrastructure, 2015 c 7, sch 1 para 131

  s 12 am—Infrastructure, 2015 c 7, sch 1 para 132

  s 15 am—Infrastructure, 2015 c 7, sch 1 para 133

  Pt 2 (ss 16-31) am—Infrastructure, 2015 c 7, sch 1 paras 134, 135-147

  ss 32-39 appl—SI 2014/2384, arts 10(4A) 11(5A) 16(2A) (added by 2015/723, sch Table 2)

  s 33 rep in pt —Infrastructure, 2015 c 7, sch 1 para 148

    am—Deregulation, 2015 c 20, sch 10 para 5

  s 33A added—Deregulation, 2015 c 20, sch 10 para 6

  s 34 am—Deregulation, 2015 c 20, sch 10 para 7

  s 36 subst—Deregulation, 2015 c 20, sch 10 para 8

  s 37 am—Deregulation, 2015 c 20, sch 10 para 9(2)(a),(3)(4)

    rep in pt—Deregulation, 2015 c 20, sch 10 para 9(2)(b)

  s 39 am—Deregulation, 2015 c 20, sch 10 para 10

  s 60 appl—Highways, 1980 c 66, s 129A

    am—Infrastructure, 2015 c 7, sch 1 para 149

  s 61 appl—Highways, 1980 c 66, s 129A

    am—Infrastructure, 2015 c 7, sch 1 para 150

  s 65 am—Infrastructure, 2015 c 7, sch 1 para 151

  s 76 am—Loc Transport, 2008 c 26, s 127(1)(2)

  s 78A added—Deregulation, 2015 c 20, s 53(2)

  s 79 am—Disability Discrimination, 2005 c 13, s 19(1), sch 1 pt 2 para 48(1)-(3)

    rep in pt—Disability Discrimination, 2005 c 13, s 19(1), sch 1 pt 2 para 48(1)(2)

  s 81 am—SI 2006/1016, art 2, sch 1; Tribunals, Cts and Enforcement, 2007 c 15, s 50, sch 10 para 39

  s 82 rep in pt—Tribunals, Cts and Enforcement, 2007 c 15, s 62, sch 13 para 156(a), sch 23

    am—Crime and Cts, 2013 c 22, sch 9 para 135

  s 83 rep—Tribunals, Cts and Enforcement, 2007 c 15, s 62, sch 13 para 156(b), sch 23 (for savings see SI 2014/600, art 5)

  s 85 am—Loc Transport, 2008 c 26, s 127(1)(3); Deregulation, 2015 c 20, sch 9 para 2

2004

c 18 *continued*

    s 86 am—Loc Transport, 2008 c 26, s 127(1)(4); Deregulation, 2015 c 20, sch 9 para 3

    s 87 am—Loc Transport, 2008 c 26, s 127(1)(5)

    s 87A added—Deregulation, 2015 c 20, s 53(3)

    s 95 rep in pt—Loc Audit and Accountability, 2014 c 2, sch 12 para 123(a)

    sch 7 mod—SIs 2011/1072, art 37(4)(b); 2013/2587, art 41(6)

      am—SIs 2012/12, reg 2; 2013/362, reg 28

      appl—SI 2014/2269, art 37(6)(b)

    sch 8 am—Deregulation, 2015 c 20, sch 11 para 19

    sch 9 saved—SI 2008/613 (W 65), art 2, sch

      appl in pt—London Loc Authorities and Transport for London, 2003 c iii, s 4(12)

c 19 **Asylum and Immigration (Treatment of Claimants, etc)**

    s 1 ext—SI 2008/680, art 18

    s 2 am—(EW) Serious Organised Crime and Police, 2005 c 15, s 111, sch 7 pt 4 para 63(a)

      ext (mods)—SI 2008/680, art 18, sch 8

    s 3 rep—Identity Cards, 2006 c 15, s 44, sch 2

    s 4 rep (EW)—Modern Slavery, 2015 c 30, sch 5 para 6(2)

      rep (S) (prosp)—Human Trafficking and Exploitation (S), 2015 asp 12, sch para 4

      am—Human Tissue, 2004 c 30, s 56, sch 6 para 7; UK Borders, 2007 c 30, s 31(1); (S)

        SSI 2008/259, art 2; Borders, Citizenship and Immigration, 2009 c 11, s 54; (S)

        Crim Justice and Licensing (S), 2010 asp 13, s 46(2)(a)(c)(d); Protection of

        Freedoms, 2012 c 9, s 110(2)(3)(a)(ii)(b)(c)(4)

      rep in pt—(S) Crim Justice and Licensing (S), 2010 asp 13, s 46(2)(b); Protection of

        Freedoms, 2012 c 9, s 110(3)(a)(i), sch 10 pt 9

      ext (mods)—SI 2008/680, art 18, sch 8

    s 5 rep (S) (prosp)—Human Trafficking and Exploitation (S), 2015 asp 12, sch para 4

      am—UK Borders, 2007 c 30, s 31(2); (S) Crim Justice and Licensing (S), 2010 asp 13, s

        46(3)(a)(b)(ii)(c); Protection of Freedoms, 2012 c 9, s 110(6)

      rep in pt—(S) Crim Justice and Licensing (S), 2010 asp 13, s 46(3)(b)(i); Protection of

        Freedoms, 2012 c 9, s 110(5), sch 9 para 141(2)(a)(b), sch 10 pt 9; (EW)

        Modern Slavery, 2015 c 30, sch 5 para 6(3)

      ext (mods)—SI 2008/680, art 18, sch 8

    s 6 ext (mods)—SI 2008/680, art 18, sch 8

    s 8 am—SI 2010/21, art 5, sch 1

      rep in pt—SI 2010/21, art 5, sch 1; Immigration, 2014 c 22, sch 9 para 4

    s 9 am—(temp) (until coming into force of 2002 c 41, s 44) SI 2004/2999, art 3; SI

      2008/2833, art 6, sch 3

    s 13 am—Immigration, Asylum and Nationality, 2006 c 13, s 45

    s 14 rep in pt—Fraud, 2006 c 35, s 14, sch 1 para 35(1), sch 3; Identity Cards, 2006 c 15, s

        44, sch 2; SI 2014/3229, sch 5 para 16(a); (EW) Modern Slavery, 2015 c 30,

        sch 5 para 6(4)(a)

      am—Fraud, 2006 c 35, s 14, sch 1 para 35; Identity Cards, 2006 c 15, s 30(3); Identity

        Documents, 2010 c 40, s 12, sch 1 para 18; Protection of Freedoms, 2012 c 9, sch

        9 para 141(3); SI 2014/3229, sch 5 para 16(b); (EW) Modern Slavery, 2015 c 30,

        sch 5 para 6(4)(b)

      ext (mods)—SI 2008/680, art 18, sch 8

    s 15 ext—SI 2008/680, art 18

      rep in pt—Immigration, 2014 c 22, sch 9 para 60 table

    s 16 ext—SI 2008/680, art 18

    s 17 ext (mods)—SI 2008/680, art 18, sch 8

    s 18 ext—SI 2008/680, art 18

    s 19 ext (mods)—SI 2008/680, art 18, sch 8

      rep in pt—SI 2011/1158, art 2(1)

      am—Immigration, 2014 c 22, s 58(2)(3)

    s 20 rep in pt—Legislative and Regulatory Reform, 2006 c 51, s 30, sch 1

      ext (mods)—SI 2008/680, art 18, sch 8

      am—SI 2011/1158, art 2(1)(c)(2)

    s 21 am—(S) Loc Electoral Admin and Registration Services (S), 2006 asp 14, s 59(4); SIs

        2011/1158, art 2(1)(e)(f); 2015/396, sch 2 paras 2, 3

      rep in pt—SI 2011/1158, art 2(1)(d)

    s 22 am—SI 2011/1158, art 2(1)(g)(i)

    s 23 rep in pt—SI 2011/1158, art 2(1)(h)(j)-(l)

    s 25 rep—Immigration, Asylum and Nationality, 2006 c 13, s 50(3)(b), sch 3; SI 2011/1158,

      art 2(3)

2004

c 19 *continued*

s 26 ext (mods)—SI 2008/680, art 18, sch 8
    rep in pt—SI 2010/21, art 5, sch 3; Immigration, 2014 c 22, sch 9 para 60 table
s 27 ext—SI 2008/680, art 18
    rep in pt—Immigration, 2014 c 22, sch 9 para 60 table
ss 28, 29 rep—Immigration, 2014 c 22, sch 9 para 60 table
s 30 ext—SI 2008/680, art 18
s 31 rep—Immigration, 2014 c 22, sch 9 para 60 table
s 32 rep—Prevention of Terrorism, 2005 c 2, s 16(2)(d)(4)
s 34 ext—SI 2008/680, art 18
s 35 am—(EW) Serious Organised Crime and Police, 2005 c 15, s 111, sch 7 pt 4 para
        63(b); Immigration, 2014 c 22, sch 2 para 5
    ext (mods)—SI 2008/680, art 18, sch 8
s 36 appl—(prosp) Crim Justice and Immigration, 2008 c 4, s 133(3)
    ext (mods)—SI 2008/680, art 18, sch 8
    am—SI 2010/21, art 5, sch 1
    rep in pt—SI 2010/21, art 5, sch 1
s 42 am—Immigration, Asylum and Nationality, 2006 c 13, s 52, sch 2 para 6; UK Borders,
        2007 c 30, s 20; Immigration, 2014 c 22, sch 9 para 73(3)
    rep in pt—Immigration, Asylum and Nationality, 2006 c 13, s 52, sch 2 para 6(2)(b),
        sch 3; Immigration, 2014 c 22, sch 9 para 73(2)(4)(5)
    ext (mods)—SI 2008/680, art 18, sch 8
s 44 rep—Immigration, Asylum and Nationality, 2006 c 13, s 64(3)(d), sch 3
s 45 ext (mods)—SI 2008/680, art 18, sch 8
s 47 ext—SI 2008/680, art 18
s 50 ext—SI 2008/680, art 18
s 56 rep in pt—SI 2010/21, art 5, sch 3
sch 1 rep—SI 2010/21, art 5, sch 3
sch 2 ext—SI 2008/680, art 18
    rep in pt—SI 2010/21, art 5, sch 3; Immigration, 2014 c 22, sch 9 para 60 table
sch 3 am—SIs 2006/3393, art 2; 2010/2802, art 2; Immigration, 2014 c 22, sch 9 para
        56(2)(3)(b)(c)(4)(b)(c)(5)(c)(6)(b)(c)
    rep in pt—SI 2010/2802, art 2; Immigration, 2014 c 22, sch 9 para
        56(3)(a)(4)(a)(5)(a)(b)(6)(a)
sch 4 ext—SI 2008/680, art 18
sch 23 am—(S) Loc Electoral Admin and Registration Services (S), 2006 asp 14, s 59(5)

c 20 **Energy**

s 10 am—SI 2010/675, reg 107, sch 26
s 14 am—Energy, 2013 c 32, sch 12 para 78; (W) SI 2013/755 (W 90), sch 2 para 426
s 27 am—Corporation Tax, 2009 c 4, s 1322, sch 1 paras 582, 583; Corporation Tax, 2010
        c 4, s 1177, sch 1 paras 433, 434
s 28 am—Corporation Tax, 2009 c 4, s 1322, sch 1 paras 582, 584(1)-(3)(4); Corporation
        Tax, 2010 c 4, s 1177, sch 1 paras 433, 435
s 29 am—Finance, 2006 c 25, s 99(1)-(5); SI 2008/948, art 3, sch 1
s 30 rep in pt—Finance, 2006 c 25, ss 100(2)(b), 178, sch 26
    am—Finance, 2006 c 25, s 100(1)-(5); SI 2008/948, art 3, sch 1
s 37 am—SIs 2009/1941, art 2, sch 1; 2010/675, reg 107, sch 26
s 44 am—SI 2004/2310, arts 1(2), 2, sch para 72; Corporation Tax, 2009 c 4, s 1322, sch 1
        paras 582, 585; Corporation Tax, 2010 c 4, s 1177, sch 1 paras 433, 436
s 50 am—SI 2009/1941, art 2, sch 1
s 55 am—Policing and Crime, 2009 c 26, s 112, sch 7 para 11
s 57 rep—Protection of Freedoms, 2012 c 9, sch 10 pt 4
s 59 rep in pt—Serious Organised Crime and Police, 2005 c 15, ss 59, 174(2), sch 4 paras
        197, 198, sch 17 pt 2
    am—SI 2013/602, sch 2 para 44(2)
s 59A added—Serious Organised Crime and Police, 2005 c 15, s 59, sch 4 paras 197, 199
    am—Crime and Cts, 2013 c 22, sch 8 para 155
s 62 am—SI 2013/602, sch 2 para 44(3)
s 64 am—SI 2013/602, sch 2 para 44(4)
s 66 am—SI 2013/602, sch 2 para 44(5)
s 68 rep in pt—SI 2013/602, sch 2 para 44(6)
ss 72-75 rep—SI 2010/675, reg 109, sch 28
s 78 rep in pt—Energy, 2013 c 32, sch 12 para 30
s 81 rep in pt—Energy, 2008 c 32, s 108, sch 6

2004

c 20 *continued*

s 84 am—Marine and Coastal Access, 2009 c 23, ss 41, 43, sch 4 para 4

s 90 am—Energy, 2011 c 16, s 104(1)

s 91 am—Energy, 2011 c 16, s 104(2)

s 95 mod—Marine and Coastal Access, 2009 c 23, s 13(5)(a)
am—Marine and Coastal Access, 2009 c 23, s 13(7)

s 96 excl—SI 2007/1948, reg 9

s 99 rep in pt—(S) Marine (S), 2010 asp 5, s 167, sch 4 para 3

s 105 rep in pt—Energy, 2008 c 32, s 107, sch 5 paras 16, 17, sch 6
am—Energy, 2008 c 32, s 69(1)-(3)

s 105A added—Energy, 2008 c 32, s 69(1)(4)

s 106 appl (mods)—SI 2015/1386, art 42(4)(5)(a)

s 107 rep in pt—Energy, 2008 c 32, s 107, sch 5 paras 16, 18, sch 6

s 108 am—Energy, 2008 c 32, s 69(1)(5)
appl (mods)—SI 2015/1386, art 42(4)(5)(b)

s 109 appl (mods)—SI 2015/1386, art 42(4)(5)(c)

s 110 appl (mods)—SI 2015/1386, art 42(4)(5)(d)

s 110A added —Energy, 2008 c 32, s 70(1)
appl (mods)—SI 2015/1386, art 42(4)(5)(e)

s 110B added —Energy, 2008 c 32, s 70(1)
appl (mods)—SI 2015/1386, art 42(4)(5)(f)

s 112 appl (mods)—SI 2015/1386, art 42(4)(5)(g)

s 112A added—Energy, 2008 c 32, s 71
appl (mods)—SI 2015/1386, art 42(4)(5)(h)

s 114 am—Energy, 2008 c 32, s 70(2)

s 115 see—(trans of functions) (S) SI 2005/849, arts 2, 6, sch

s 116 rep—Energy, 2008 c 32, s 108, sch 6

ss 117-119 see—(trans of functions) (S) SI 2005/849, arts 2, 6, sch

s 121 am—Energy, 2008 c 32, s 40(1)

s 125 subst —Climate Change, 2008 c 27, s 78, sch 7 paras 1, 2

ss 125A-125C added —Climate Change, 2008 c 27, s 78, sch 7 paras 1, 2

s 126 am—Climate Change, 2008 c 27, s 78, sch 7 paras 1, 3

s 128 am—Climate Change, 2008 c 27, s 78, sch 7 paras 1, 4

s 129 am—Climate Change, 2008 c 27, s 78, sch 7 paras 1, 5

ss 131A-131C added—Climate Change, 2008 c 27, s 78, sch 7 paras 1, 6

s 132 am—Energy, 2008 c 32, s 107, sch 5 paras 16, 19; Climate Change, 2008 c 27, s 78,
sch 7 paras 1, 7(1)-(3); SI 2012/2723, regs 3, 4, 5

s 137 am—Energy, 2011 c 16, s 117; SI 2011/2704, reg 50(3); Energy, 2013 c 32, s 65(3)

s 146 am—Energy, 2011 c 16, s 98(11); SI 2011/2704, reg 50(4); Energy, 2013 c 32, s
65(4)

s 150 am—Energy, 2011 c 16, s 98(12); SI 2011/2704, reg 49(3)

ss 154-171 mod—SI 2013/1046, rule 205(2)-(4)

s 154 am—Energy, 2013 c 32, s 48(2)

s 155 am—Energy, 2013 c 32, s 48(3)

ss 156-158 appl (mods)—Energy, 2011 c 16, s 96(1)(2)

s 159 am—Energy, 2011 c 16, s 97
appl (mods)—Energy, 2011 c 16, s 96(1)(2)

ss 160-165 appl (mods)—Energy, 2011 c 16, s 96(1)(2)

s 166 am—Energy, 2011 c 16, s 93
appl (mods)—Energy, 2011 c 16, s 96(1)(2)

s 167 appl (mods)—Energy, 2011 c 16, s 96(1)(2)

s 169 appl—SI 2005/2483, rule 80

s 170 am—Energy, 2011 c 16, s 100(3)

s 171 am—SI 2009/1941, art 2, sch 1
appl (mods)—Energy, 2011 c 16, s 96(5)(6)

s 172 am—Energy, 2011 c 16, s 80(2)
power to am conferred—Energy, 2013 c 32, s 38(b)

s 173 am—Energy, 2011 c 16, s 81(4); Enterprise and Regulatory Reform, 2013 c 24, sch 6
para 102(2)(b)(3)(4)
rep in pt—Enterprise and Regulatory Reform, 2013 c 24, sch 6 para 102(2)(a)

s 174 am—Enterprise and Regulatory Reform, 2013 c 24, sch 6 para 103(4)
rep in pt—Enterprise and Regulatory Reform, 2013 c 24, sch 6 para 103(2)

s 175 am—Energy, 2011 c 16, s 81(5); Enterprise and Regulatory Reform, 2013 c 24, sch 6
para 104

2004

c 20 *continued*

s 176 rep—Enterprise and Regulatory Reform, 2013 c 24, sch 6 para 105
s 177 rep—Enterprise and Regulatory Reform, 2013 c 24, sch 6 para 106
s 179 rep in pt—Consumers, Estate Agents and Redress, 2007 c 17, s 64, sch 8
s 180 rep in pt—Energy, 2008 c 32, s 108, sch 6
s 185 am—Climate Change and Sustainable Energy, 2006 c 19, s 25; Energy, 2008 c 32, s 107, sch 5 paras 16, 20; Energy, 2011 c 16, s 111
s 188 am—Energy, 2008 c 32, s 36, sch 1 para 13
s 193 appl—SI 2007/3072, art 24
s 196 am—Climate Change, 2008 c 27, s 78, sch 7 paras 1, 7(1)(4); SI 2009/1941, art 2, sch 1
    rep in pt—(S prosp) SI 2010/675, regs 107, 109, schs 26, 28
    appl (mods)—Energy, 2011 c 16, s 96(5)(6)
sch 1 am—SI 2012/2404, sch 2 para 50(2)
sch 2 am—Energy, 2013 c 32, sch 12 para 79; (W) SI 2013/755 (W 90), sch 2 para 427
sch 3 am—Energy, 2013 c 32, sch 12 para 80; (W) SI 2013/755 (W 90), sch 2 para 428
sch 4 rep in pt—Finance, 2008 c 9, s 84, sch 27 para 25
    am—Corporation Tax, 2010 c 4, s 1177, sch 1 paras 433, 437
sch 5 am—SI 2006/246, reg 20, sch 2
sch 6 am—SIs 2008/948, art 3, sch 1; 2009/1941, art 2, sch 1
sch 7 am—SIs 2008/948, art 3, sch 1; 2009/1941, art 2, sch 1
sch 8 am—SI 2009/1941, art 2, sch 1
sch 9 rep in pt—Finance, 2008 c 9, s 8, sch 2 para 70(f)
    am—Corporation Tax, 2009 c 4, s 1322, sch 1 paras 582, 586; Corporation Tax, 2010 c 4, s 1177, sch 1 paras 433, 438
sch 10 am—SI 2012/2404, sch 2 para 50(3)
sch 12 am—Police and Justice, 2006 c 48, s 52, sch 14 para 59
sch 13 am—Energy, 2008 c 32, s 107, sch 5 paras 16, 21
sch 14 rep in pt—Serious Organised Crime and Police, 2005 c 15, s 174(2), sch 17 pt 2; Police and Justice, 2006 c 48, s 52, sch 15; Equality, 2010 c 15, sch 27 pt 1A (added by SI 2011/1060, sch 3)
sch 15 rep—SI 2010/675, reg 109, sch 28
sch 16 mod—Marine and Coastal Access, 2009 c 23, s 13(5)(b)(6)
sch 20 am—SIs 2008/948, art 3, sch 1; 2009/1941, art 2, sch 1; Energy, 2011 c 16, s 101(2); Financial Services, 2012 c 21, sch 18 para 101
    rep in pt—SI 2009/1941, art 2, sch 1
    appl (mods)—Energy, 2011 c 16, s 96(1)-(3)
    power to mod ext in pt—Energy, 2011 c 16, s 101(1)
    mod—SI 2013/1046, rule 205(2)-(4)
sch 21 appl (mods)—Energy, 2011 c 16, s 96(1)(2)(4)
    mod—SI 2013/1046, rule 205(2)-(4)
sch 22 am—SI 2006/1519, art 2; Energy, 2011 c 16, s 81(6); Enterprise and Regulatory Reform, 2013 c 24, sch 6 para 107(2)-(5)(6)(b)(d)(7)(8)(9)(a)(b)(i)(c)(10)-(14)(15)(a)(c)
    rep in pt—Enterprise and Regulatory Reform, 2013 c 24, sch 6 para 107(6)(a)(c)(9)(b)(ii)(15)(b)(d)

c 21 **Fire and Rescue Services**
    appl—Housing, 2004 c 34, s 254, sch 14 para 2(2); ibid, s 10(4)
s 1 appl—Civil Contingencies, 2004 c 36, ss 1-18, sch 1 pt 1 para 4
s 2 am—Loc Govt and Public Involvement in Health, 2007 c 28, s 22, sch 1 para 22(1)(2); Deregulation, 2015 c 20, sch 22 para 16(2)
    rep in pt—Loc Democracy, Economic Development and Construction, 2009 c 20, s 146, sch 7 pt 4
s 4 am—Loc Govt and Public Involvement in Health, 2007 c 28, s 22, sch 1 para 22; Loc Democracy, Economic Development and Construction, 2009 c 20, s 146, sch 7 pt 4; Deregulation, 2015 c 20, sch 22 para 16(3)
s 5 rep—Localism, 2011 c 20, s 9(2), sch 25 pt 2
ss 5A-5L added—Localism, 2011 c 20, s 9(1)
s 5B am—Co-operative and Community Benefit Societies, 2014 c 14, sch 4 para 86
ss 18A-18C added—Localism, 2011 c 20, s 10(2)
s 19 rep—Localism, 2011 c 20, s 10(3), sch 25 pt 2
s 24 am—Loc Govt and Public Involvement in Health, 2007 c 28, s 144, sch 8 para 26; Loc Govt (W), 2009 nawm 2, s 51, sch 1 paras 32, 33
s 27 rep—Inquiries, 2005 c 12, ss 44(5), 48(1), 49(2), sch 2 pt 1 para 24, sch 3

2004

c 21 *continued*

s 34 am—Fire (S), 2005 asp 5, s 89(1), sch 3 para 24; Police and Fire Reform (S), 2012 asp 8, sch 7 para 66(2); Public Service Pensions, 2013 c 25, sch 8 para 27; SI 2013/602, sch 1 para 7(2)

see—(trans of functions) (S) SI 2005/849, arts 2, 6, sch

s 35 see—(trans of functions) (S) SI 2005/849, arts 2, 6, sch

am—Financial Services, 2012 c 21, sch 18 para 102; Police and Fire Reform (S), 2012 asp 8, sch 7 para 66(3); SI 2013/602, sch 1 para 7(3)

s 36 see—(trans of functions) (S) SI 2005/849, arts 2, 6, sch

s 44 rep in pt—Emergency Workers (Obstruction), 2006 c 39, s 6

appl (mods)—SI 2013/602, art 17(2)

s 45 appl—SI 2013/602, art 17(3)

s 46 appl—SI 2013/602, art 17(3)

s 60 see—(trans of functions for specified purposes) (S) SI 2005/849, arts 2, 6, sch

am—Localism, 2011 c 20, s 9(3)-(6)

s 62 am—Localism, 2011 c 20, ss 9(7), 10(4)

rep in pt—Localism, 2011 c 20, s 9(7)(c), sch 25 pt 2

sch 1 rep in pt—(prosp) Road Safety, 2006 c 49, s 59, sch 7; Finance, 2008 c 9, s 72(3)(a); SI 2009/818, reg 4; Corporation Tax, 2010 c 4, s 1181, sch 3 pt 1; Equality, 2010 c 15, sch 27 pt 1A (added by SI 2011/1060, sch 3); Co-operative and Community Benefit Societies, 2014 c 14, sch 7; (S prosp) Loc Audit and Accountability, 2014 c 2, sch 1 pt 2; (S prosp) ibid, sch 12

c 22 **Sustainable and Secure Buildings**

trans of funct—SI 2009/3019, art 2

c 23 **Public Audit (Wales)**

appl (mods)—Public Audit (W), 2013 anaw 3, sch 3 para 2(3)

s 2 rep—Govt of Wales, 2006 c 32, s 163, sch 12

ss 6-11 rep—Govt of Wales, 2006 c 32, s 163, sch 12

s 12 am—Offender Management, 2007 c 21, s 5, sch 1 para 13(5)(a); (with transtl provns and savings) Police Reform and Social Responsibility, 2011 c 13, sch 16 para 337

s 13 subst—Public Audit (W), 2013 anaw 3, s 11(1)

ss 14, 15 rep—Public Audit (W), 2013 anaw 3, sch 4 para 21

s 16 rep—Public Audit (W), 2013 anaw 3, sch 4 para 22

s 17 am—Public Audit (W), 2013 anaw 3, sch 4 para 23(2)(4)

rep in pt—Public Audit (W), 2013 anaw 3, sch 4 para 23(3)

ss 18, 19 rep—Public Audit (W), 2013 anaw 3, sch 4 para 24

s 20 am—Public Audit (W), 2013 anaw 3, sch 4 para 25(2)-(5)(7)(8)(a)(9)

rep in pt—Public Audit (W), 2013 anaw 3, sch 4 para 25(6)(8)(b)(10)

s 21 rep—Public Audit (W), 2013 anaw 3, sch 4 para 26

s 22 am—Public Audit (W), 2013 anaw 3, sch 4 para 27(2)

rep in pt—Public Audit (W), 2013 anaw 3, sch 4 para 27(3)(4)

s 23 am—Public Audit (W), 2013 anaw 3, sch 4 para 28

s 24 am—Offender Management, 2007 c 21, s 5, sch 1 para 13(5)(b); Public Audit (W), 2013 anaw 3, sch 4 para 29

s 25 am—Offender Management, 2007 c 21, s 5, sch 1 para 13(5)(c); Public Audit (W), 2013 anaw 3, sch 4 para 30

s 26 am—Public Audit (W), 2013 anaw 3, sch 4 para 31

s 27 am—Public Audit (W), 2013 anaw 3, sch 4 para 32

s 28 am—Public Audit (W), 2013 anaw 3, sch 4 para 33(2)

rep in pt—Public Audit (W), 2013 anaw 3, sch 4 para 33(3)

s 29 am—Public Audit (W), 2013 anaw 3, sch 4 para 34

s 30 am—Public Audit (W), 2013 anaw 3, sch 4 para 35

s 31 am—Public Audit (W), 2013 anaw 3, sch 4 para 36

s 32 am—Public Audit (W), 2013 anaw 3, sch 4 para 37; Crime and Cts, 2013 c 22, sch 9 para 124

s 33 am—Public Audit (W), 2013 anaw 3, sch 4 para 38(2)-(7)

rep in pt—Public Audit (W), 2013 anaw 3, sch 4 para 38(8)

s 34 am—Public Audit (W), 2013 anaw 3, sch 4 para 39

s 35 am—Public Audit (W), 2013 anaw 3, sch 4 para 40

s 36 am—Public Audit (W), 2013 anaw 3, sch 4 para 41

s 37 am—Public Audit (W), 2013 anaw 3, sch 4 para 42(2)(6)

rep in pt—Public Audit (W), 2013 anaw 3, sch 4 para 42(3)-(5)

s 38 am—Public Audit (W), 2013 anaw 3, sch 4 para 43

s 39 am—Public Audit (W), 2013 anaw 3, sch 4 para 44

2004

c 23 *continued*

s 40 am—(with transtl provns and savings) Police Reform and Social Responsibility, 2011 c 13, sch 16 para 338; Public Audit (W), 2013 anaw 3, sch 4 para 45

s 41 am—Loc Govt and Public Involvement in Health, 2007 c 28, s 144, sch 8 para 27(1)(2); Loc Govt (W), 2009 nawm 2, s 51, sch 1 para 35; Public Audit (W), 2013 anaw 3, sch 4 para 46(4)

    rep in pt—Public Audit (W), 2013 anaw 3, sch 4 para 46(2)(3)

s 42 am—Public Audit (W), 2013 anaw 3, sch 4 para 47(2)(b)(3)

    rep in pt—Public Audit (W), 2013 anaw 3, sch 4 para 47(2)(a)(4)(5)

s 43 rep —Loc Audit and Accountability, 2014 c 2, sch 12 para 60

s 44 rep in pt—Public Audit (W), 2013 anaw 3, sch 4 para 48

s 45 am—Public Audit (W), 2013 anaw 3, sch 4 para 49

s 46 am—(with transtl provns and savings) Police Reform and Social Responsibility, 2011 c 13, sch 16 para 339; Public Audit (W), 2013 anaw 3, sch 4 para 50

s 47 am—Public Audit (W), 2013 anaw 3, sch 4 para 51

s 48 am—(prosp) Loc Govt and Public Involvement in Health, 2007 c 28, s 216, sch 14 para 6

s 51 am—Public Audit (W), 2013 anaw 3, sch 4 para 52(3)

    rep in pt—Public Audit (W), 2013 anaw 3, sch 4 para 52(2)

s 52 am—Public Audit (W), 2013 anaw 3, sch 4 para 53(2)(4)(5)

    rep in pt—Public Audit (W), 2013 anaw 3, sch 4 para 53(3)

s 53 am—Public Audit (W), 2013 anaw 3, sch 4 para 54

s 54 am—Public Services Ombudsman (W), 2005 c 10, s 39(1), sch 6 para 77; SI 2005/1018, art 2(1)(3); Loc Govt and Public Involvement in Health, 2007 c 28, s 167(1)-(5)(8); Loc Govt (W), 2009 nawm 2, s 51, sch 1 paras 34, 36; Public Audit (W), 2013 anaw 3, sch 4 para 55(2)(4)(b)

    rep in pt—SI 2005/1018, art 2(1)(2); Loc Govt and Public Involvement in Health, 2007 c 28, s 241, sch 18; Public Audit (W), 2013 anaw 3, sch 4 para 55(3)(4)(a)(5)(6)(7)

s 54ZA added—Loc Govt and Public Involvement in Health, 2007 c 28, s 167(1)(6)(8)

    rep in pt—Public Audit (W), 2013 anaw 3, sch 4 para 56(2)

    am—Public Audit (W), 2013 anaw 3, sch 4 para 56(3)

s 54A added—SI 2005/1018, art 2(4)

    rep—Loc Govt and Public Involvement in Health, 2007 c 28, s 167(1)(7)(8), sch 18

s 56 rep in pt—Public Audit (W), 2013 anaw 3, sch 4 para 57

s 57 rep —Loc Audit and Accountability, 2014 c 2, sch 12 para 61

s 58 am—Public Audit (W), 2013 anaw 3, sch 4 para 58

s 59 am—Loc Govt and Public Involvement in Health, 2007 c 28, s 144, sch 8 para 27(1)(3)

    rep in pt—Loc Govt and Public Involvement in Health, 2007 c 28, s 241, sch 18; Public Audit (W), 2013 anaw 3, sch 4 para 59

s 60 am—Nat Health Service (Conseq Provns), 2006 c 43, s 2, sch 1 para 261

s 61 am—Health, 2006 c 28, s 80, sch 8 para 62; Public Audit (W), 2013 anaw 3, sch 4 para 60

s 62 am—Health and Social Care, 2008 c 14, s 95, sch 5 para 76; Public Audit (W), 2013 anaw 3, sch 4 para 61(2)(3)

    transtl provns—SI 2008/2250, art 3

    rep in pt—Loc Audit and Accountability, 2014 c 2, sch 12 para 62(2)(3)

s 64 am—Health and Social Care, 2008 c 14, s 95, sch 5 para 77

ss 64A-64H added—Serious Crime, 2007 c 27, s 73, sch 7 para 4

s 64A rep in pt—Public Audit (W), 2013 anaw 3, sch 4 para 62

s 64B am—Public Audit (W), 2013 anaw 3, sch 4 para 63

s 64C am—Public Audit (W), 2013 anaw 3, sch 4 para 64

s 64D am—Public Audit (W), 2013 anaw 3, sch 4 para 65; Loc Audit and Accountability, 2014 c 2, sch 12 para 63

s 64E rep in pt—Public Audit (W), 2013 anaw 3, sch 4 para 66

s 64F am—Public Audit (W), 2013 anaw 3, sch 4 para 67

s 64G am—Public Audit (W), 2013 anaw 3, sch 4 para 68

s 65 rep in pt—Govt of Wales, 2006 c 32, s 163, sch 12

s 67A added—Police and Justice, 2006 c 48, s 52, sch 14 para 60

    am—SI 2008/912, art 3, sch 1; Public Audit (W), 2013 anaw 3, sch 4 para 69

    rep in pt—SI 2012/2401, sch 1 para 17

s 68 am—SI 2014/77 (W 8), art 3(2)(3)

s 69 rep —Loc Audit and Accountability, 2014 c 2, sch 12 para 64

s 70 rep —Loc Audit and Accountability, 2014 c 2, sch 12 para 64

2004

c 23 s 70 *continued*

    rep in pt—Loc Govt and Public Involvement in Health, 2007 c 28, s 241, sch 18

    s 71 rep in pt—Loc Govt and Public Involvement in Health, 2007 c 28, s 146, sch 9 para 1(1)(2)(w), sch 18

    sch 1 rep in pt—Loc Govt and Public Involvement in Health, 2007 c 28, s 241, sch 18; Loc Audit and Accountability, 2014 c 2, sch 12 para 123(c)

    sch 2 rep in pt—Nat Health Service (Conseq Provns), 2006 c 43, s 6, sch 4; Govt of Wales, 2006 c 32, s 163, sch 12; ibid, s 163, sch 12; Educ and Inspections, 2006 c 40, s 184, sch 18; Loc Govt and Public Involvement in Health, 2007 c 28, s 241, sch 18; Housing and Regeneration, 2008 c 17, s 321, sch 16; Apprenticeships, Skills, Children and Learning, 2009 c 22, s 266, sch 16; SI 2010/866, art 7, sch 4; Localism, 2011 c 20, sch 25 pt 5; (pt prosp) Welfare Reform, 2012 c 5, sch 14 pt 1; Loc Audit and Accountability, 2014 c 2, sch 1 pt 2; ibid, sch 12 para 123(c)

    sch 3 am—Loc Audit and Accountability, 2014 c 2, sch 12 para 65(3)(a); SI 2014/77 (W 8), art 3(4)

    rep in pt—Loc Audit and Accountability, 2014 c 2, sch 12 para 65(2)(3)(b)

c 24 **Employment Relations**

    s 41 rep in pt—(prosp) Pensions, 2008 c 30, s 148, sch 11 pt 1

    ss 45, 46 rep—Employment, 2008 c 24, s 20, sch pt 2

    s 47 rep (prosp W & S)—Enterprise and Regulatory Reform, 2013 c 24, sch 20 para 2

    sch 1 rep in pt—(prosp W, S) Enterprise and Regulatory Reform, 2013 c 24, sch 20 para 2

c 25 **Horserace Betting and Olympic Lottery**

    see—SI 2007/2129, art 3

    s 2 am—SI 2009/1941, art 2, sch 1

    s 3 am—SI 2006/246, reg 20, sch 2

    s 5 am—SI 2009/1941, art 2, sch 1

    s 6 am—SI 2008/948, art 3, sch 1

    s 9 am—Crime and Cts, 2013 c 22, sch 9 para 52

    s 7 am—SI 2007/2194, art 10, sch 4

    s 12 am—SI 2008/948, art 3, sch 1

    s 21 am—(prosp) Nat Lottery, 2006 c 23, s 6, sch 1 para 16(2)(a); SI 2013/2329, sch para 27(a)

    rep in pt—(prosp) Nat Lottery, 2006 c 23, s 6, sch 1 para 16(2)(b)

    s 22 am—(prosp) Nat Lottery, 2006 c 23, s 6, sch 1 para 16(3); SIs 2007/2129, art 5, sch; 2013/2329, sch para 27(b)

    rep in pt—SI 2010/1551, art 11, sch

    s 23 am—SI 2007/2129, art 5, sch

    rep in pt—SI 2010/1551, art 11, sch

    s 24 am—(prosp) Nat Lottery, 2006 c 23, s 6, sch 1 para 16(4)

    s 26 am—(prosp) Nat Lottery, 2006 c 23, s 6, sch 1 para 16(5)(6); SIs 2007/2129, art 5, sch; 2013/2329, sch para 27(c)

    rep in pt—SI 2010/1551, art 11, sch

    s 28 am—SI 2007/2129, art 5, sch

    rep in pt—SI 2010/1551, art 11, sch

    s 30 am—SI 2007/2129, art 5, sch

    rep in pt—SI 2010/1551, art 11, sch

    s 31 am—SIs 2007/2129, art 5, sch; 2013/2329, sch para 27(d)

    rep in pt—SI 2010/1551, art 11, sch

    s 32 am—(prosp) Nat Lottery, 2006 c 23, s 6, sch 1 para 16(7); SIs 2006/246, reg 20, sch 2; 2007/2129, art 5, sch; 2010/1551, art 11, sch

    rep in pt—SI 2010/1551, art 11, sch

    s 34 am—SIs 2007/2129, art 5, sch; 2010/1551, art 11, sch

    rep in pt—SIs 2007/2129, art 5, sch; 2010/1551, art 11, sch

    s 35 am—SI 2007/2129, art 5, sch

    rep in pt—SI 2010/1551, art 11, sch

    sch 3 am—SI 2006/246, reg 20, sch 2

    sch 5 am—SIs 2007/2129, art 5, sch; 2010/1551, art 11, sch

    rep in pt—SI 2010/1551, art 11, sch

c 26 **Christmas Day (Trading)**

    s 1 am—SI 2015/664, sch 4 para 36

    s 3 rep in pt—Consumer Rights, 2015 c 15, sch 6 para 83(2)

    am—Consumer Rights, 2015 c 15, sch 6 para 83(3)

2004
c 27   **Companies (Audit, Investigations and Community Enterprise)**

appl (mods)—Companies, 2006 c 46, ss 1(1), 288, 540, 546-548, 583, 628, 629, 738, 1118, 1125, 1129, 1156, 1158

ext—Companies, 2006 c 46, s 1284(1)

ss 1-10 rep —Companies, 2006 c 46, s 1295, sch 16

s 11 rep in pt—Companies, 2006 c 46, s 1295, sch 16

ss 12, 13 rep—Companies, 2006 c 46, s 1295, sch 16

s 14 am—SI 2005/1433, reg 2(3), sch 3 para 5; Companies, 2006 c 46, s 1272, sch 15 paras 13, 14; SI 2008/948, art 3, sch 1; Financial Services, 2012 c 21, sch 18 para 103

s 15 subst—(EWS) SI 2008/948, art 3, sch 1

    rep—(NI) SI 2008/948, art 3, sch 2

ss 15A-15E added—SI 2008/948, art 3, sch 1

s 15D am—SI 2012/1439, art 6(1); Co-operative and Community Benefit Societies, 2014 c 14, sch 4 para 88(3)(4)

    rep in pt—Co-operative and Community Benefit Societies, 2014 c 14, sch 4 para 88(2)

s 16 am—SI 2005/1433, reg 2(3), sch 3 para 6; Companies, 2006 c 46, ss 1238, 1247, 1264, 1274, 1276(1)-(4), sch 14 para 1; SIs 2008/948, art 3, sch 1; 2009/1941, art 2, sch 1; 2011/1856, reg 2; Pensions, 2014 c 19, s 47; Loc Audit and Accountability, 2014 c 2, sch 12 para 67

    rep in pt—SI 2009/1941, art 2, sch 1

s 17 am—Companies, 2006 c 46, s 1275(1)-(6)

s 18 rep (prosp)—Small Business, Enterprise and Employment, 2015 c 26, s 38(2)

s 18A added (prosp)—Small Business, Enterprise and Employment, 2015 c 26, s 38(1)

s 19 rep—Companies, 2006 c 46, s 1295, sch 16

s 20 rep—Companies, 2006 c 46, s 1295, sch 16

Pt 2 (ss 26-63) appl (mod)—Companies, 2006 c.46, ss 1170A, 1170B; SI 2009/1941, art 12, sch 3

    excl—SI 2009/2437, regs 18, 24

    ext—SI 2011/1265, sch 1 para 2

s 26 am—SIs 2006/242, art 5; 2007/1093, art 6, sch 4

s 32 am—SIs 2007/1093, art 6, sch 4; 2009/1941, art 2, sch 1

    rep in pt—SI 2009/1941, art 2, sch 1

s 33 am—SIs 2007/1093, art 6, sch 4; 2009/1941, art 2, sch 1

    rep in pt—SI 2009/1941, art 2, schs 1, 2

s 34 am—SIs 2007/1093, art 6, sch 4; 2007/2194, art 10, sch 4; 2008/948, art 3, sch 1

    rep in pt—SI 2008/948, art 3, schs 1, 2

s 35 am—SIs 2007/1093, art 6, sch 4; 2009/1941, art 2, sch 1

s 36 am—SIs 2007/1093, art 6, sch 4; 2009/1941, art 2, sch 1

ss 36A, 36B added—SI 2009/1941, art 2, sch 1

s 37 subst—SI 2009/1941, art 2, sch 1

ss 37A-37C added—SI 2009/1941, art 2, sch 1

s 38 subst—SI 2009/1941, art 2, sch 1

s 38A added—SI 2009/1941, art 2, sch 1

s 39 am—Charities, 2006 c 50, s 75, sch 8 para 201; SIs 2007/1093, art 6, sch 4; 2009/1941, art 2, sch 1

s 40 am—SI 2006/242, art 5; Charities, 2006 c 50, s 75, sch 8 para 202; SIs 2007/1093, art 6, sch 4; 2009/1941, art 2, sch 1

    rep in pt—SI 2009/1941, art 2

s 40A added—SI 2007/1093, art 6, sch 4

    am—SI 2009/1941, art 2, sch 1

s 43 am—SIs 2007/1093, art 6, sch 4; 2007/2194, art 10, sch 4; 2008/948, art 3, sch 1

    rep in pt—SI 2007/2194, art 10, sch 5

s 45 am—SIs 2007/1093, art 6, sch 4; 2009/1941, art 2, sch 1; 2015/664, sch 3 para 8

    rep in pt—SI 2008/948, art 3, schs 1, 2

s 46 am—SIs 2007/1093, art 6, sch 4; 2009/1941, art 2, sch 1

s 47 am—SI 2007/1093, art 6, sch 4

s 48 am—SI 2007/1093, art 6, sch 4

s 49 am—SI 2009/1941, art 2, sch 1

ss 51, 52 am—SIs 2007/1093, art 6, sch 4; 2009/1941, art 2, sch 1

s 53 see—(power to apply or disapply) Charities, 1993 c 10, s 69J; Charities, 2011 c 25, s 234(2)(a)

    rep in pt—SI 2008/948, art 3, schs 1, 2

2004

c 27 s 53 *continued*

        am—SI 2009/1941, art 2, sch 1; Co-operative and Community Benefit Societies, 2014
           c 14, sch 4 para 89

    s 54 subst—SI 2009/1941, art 2, sch 1

        see—(power to apply or disapply) Charities, 1993 c 10, s 69J; Charities, 2011 c 25, s
           234(2)(a)

    ss 54A-54C added—SI 2009/1941, art 2, sch 1

    s 54C am—Corporation Tax, 2010 c 4, s 1177, sch 1 para 439; Charities, 2011 c 25, sch 7
        para 98

    s 55 subst—SI 2009/1941, art 2, sch 1

        see—(power to apply or disapply) Charities, 1993 c 10, s 69J

    s 55A added—SI 2009/1941, art 2, sch 1

    s 56 am—SI 2007/1093, art 6, sch 4; Co-operative and Community Benefit Societies, 2014
        c 14, sch 4 para 90(2)(3)

    s 58 rep—SI 2009/1941, art 2, sch 1

    s 59 am—SI 2007/1093, art 6, sch 4

    s 60 am—SI 2009/1941, art 2, sch 1

    s 62 am—SI 2009/1941, art 2, sch 1

    s 63 am—SIs 2006/242, art 5; 2007/1093, art 6, sch 4; 2011/1396, sch para 47; Charities,
        2011 c 25, sch 7 para 99

        rep in pt—SI 2009/1941, art 2, sch 1

    s 66 am—Companies, 2006 c 46, s 1276(6); SI 2007/1093, art 6, sch 4; Small Business,
        Enterprise and Employment, 2015 c 26, s 38(3)

    sch 1 rep—Companies, 2006 c 46, s 1295, sch 16

    sch 2 rep in pt—Companies, 2006 c 46, s 1295, sch 16; Small Business, Enterprise and
        Employment, 2015 c 26, sch 7 para 24

    sch 3 am—Charities, 2006 c 50, s 75, sch 8 para 204; Charities, 2011 c 25, sch 7 para 100

    sch 6 rep in pt—Companies, 2006 c 46, s 1295, sch 16; SI 2009/1941, art 2, sch 2

    sch 7 am—SI 2007/1093, art 6, sch 4

    sch 9 am—(prosp) Crim Justice and Cts, 2015 c 2, sch 3 para 12

c 28   **Domestic Violence, Crime and Victims**

    s 5 am—Domestic Violence, Crime and Victims (Amdt), 2012 c 4, s 1

    s 6 am—Domestic Violence, Crime and Victims (Amdt), 2012 c 4, sch para 8

    s 6A added—Domestic Violence, Crime and Victims (Amdt), 2012 c 4, s 2

    s 8 am—Armed Forces, 2006 c 52, s 378, sch 16 para 238; Domestic Violence, Crime and
        Victims (Amdt), 2012 c 4, sch para 9

        mod—SI 2009/1059, art 205, sch 1

    s 9 am—Nat Health Service (Conseq Provns), 2006 c 43, s 2, sch 1 para 263; SIs 2008/912,
        art 3, sch 1; 2010/976, art 12, sch 14; Health and Social Care, 2012 c 7, sch 5 para
        126(a)

        rep in pt—Health and Social Care, 2012 c 7, sch 5 para 126(b)(c); (prosp) ibid, sch 14
        para 95

    s 10 rep in pt—Serious Organised Crime and Police, 2005 c 15, s 174(2), sch 17 pt 2

    s 14 rep in pt—SI 2006/1737, art 54

    s 16 rep in pt—Road Safety, 2006 c 49, s 59, sch 7

    s 18A rep in pt—SI 2010/976, art 12, sch 14

        am—SI 2010/976, art 12, sch 14

    s 31 rep—Legal Aid, Sentencing and Punishment of Offenders, 2012 c 10, sch 10 para 40(2)

    s 32 see—(trans of functions) SI 2007/2128, art 4

        am—SI 2007/2128, art 8, sch

    s 33 see—(trans of functions) SI 2007/2128, arts 4, 5

        am—SI 2007/2128, art 8, sch

    s 35 am—SI 2008/912, art 3, sch 1

    s 36 am—Mental Health, 2007 c 12, s 39, sch 5 paras 1, 2; SI 2008/912, art 3, sch 1

    s 36A added—Mental Health, 2007 c 12, s 39, sch 5 paras 1, 3

    s 37 am—Mental Health, 2007 c 12, s 39, sch 5 paras 1, 4; SIs 2008/912, art 3, sch 1; 2833,
        art 6, sch 3

    s 37A added—Mental Health, 2007 c 12, s 39, sch 5 paras 1, 5

        am—SI 2008/2833, art 6, sch 3

        rep in pt—Health and Social Care, 2012 c 7, s 39(4)(e)(i)(ii)

    s 38 am—Mental Health, 2007 c 12, s 39, sch 5 paras 1, 6; SIs 2008/912, art 3, sch 1; 2833,
        art 6, sch 3

    s 38A added—Mental Health, 2007 c 12, s 39, sch 5 paras 1, 7

        am—SI 2008/2833, art 6, sch 3

2004

c 28 s 38A *continued*

    rep in pt—Health and Social Care, 2012 c 7, s 39(4)(e)(i)

 s 38B added—Mental Health, 2007 c 12, s 39, sch 5 paras 1, 7

 s 39 am—Mental Health, 2007 c 12, s 39, sch 5 paras 1, 8; SI 2008/912, art 3, sch 1

 s 40 am—SIs 2008/912, art 3, sch 1; 2008/2833, art 6, sch 3

 s 41 am—SIs 2008/912, art 3, sch 1; 2008/2833, art 6, sch 3

 s 41A added—Mental Health, 2007 c 12, s 39, sch 5 paras 1, 9

 s 42 am—Mental Health, 2007 c 12, s 39, sch 5 paras 1, 10; SI 2008/912, art 3, sch 1

 s 42A added—Mental Health, 2007 c 12, s 39, sch 5 paras 1, 11

 s 43 am—Mental Health, 2007 c 12, s 39, sch 5 paras 1, 12; SIs 2008/912, art 3, sch 1;
    2833, art 6, sch 3

 s 43A added—Mental Health, 2007 c 12, s 39, sch 5 paras 1, 13

   am—SI 2008/2833, art 6, sch 3

   rep in pt—Health and Social Care, 2012 c 7, s 39(4)(e)(i)(iii)

 s 44 am—Mental Health, 2007 c 12, s 39, sch 5 paras 1, 14; SIs 2008/912, art 3, sch 1;
    2833, art 6, sch 3

 s 44A added—Mental Health, 2007 c 12, s 39, sch 5 paras 1, 15

   am—SI 2008/2833, art 6, sch 3

   rep in pt—Health and Social Care, 2012 c 7, s 39(4)(e)(i)

 s 44B added—Mental Health, 2007 c 12, s 39, sch 5 paras 1, 15

 s 45 am—Armed Forces, 2006 c 52, s 378, sch 16 para 239; Mental Health, 2007 c 12, s 39,
    sch 5 paras 1, 16

 s 48 see—(trans of functions) SI 2007/2128, arts 4, 5

   am—SI 2007/2128, art 8, sch; Coroners and Justice, 2009 c 25, s 142(1)(2)(b)

   rep in pt—Coroners and Justice, 2009 c 25, ss 142(1)(2)(a), 178, sch 23 pt 5

 s 49 see—(trans of functions) SI 2007/2128, arts 4, 5

   am—SI 2007/2128, art 8, sch; Coroners and Justice, 2009 c 25, s 142(1)(3)(c)

 s 50 rep in pt—Coroners and Justice, 2009 c 25, ss 142(1)(4), 178, sch 23 pt 5

 s 53 see—(trans of functions) SI 2007/2128, arts 4, 5

   am—SI 2007/2128, art 8, sch

 s 54 see—(trans of functions) SI 2007/2128, arts 4, 5

   am—SIs 2007/2128, art 8, sch; 2008/912, art 3, sch 1

 s 55 rep—SI 2013/2853, art 2(2)(b)

 s 56 am—SI 2010/976, art 12, sch 14

 s 57 ext (mods) —(S) Management of Offenders etc. (S), 2005 asp 14, s 20(1)(2)

 s 61 am—SI 2010/976, art 12, sch 14

 s 62 am—Armed Forces, 2006 c 52, s 378, sch 16 para 240; Domestic Violence, Crime and
    Victims (Amdt), 2012 c 4, sch para 10

 sch 3 rep in pt—Armed Forces, 2006 c 52, s 378, sch 17

 sch 5 am—SI 2005/886, art 2, sch para 113

 sch 6 rep—Legal Aid, Sentencing and Punishment of Offenders, 2012 c 10, sch 10 para
    40(2)

 sch 8 rep —Coroners and Justice, 2009 c 25, ss 142(6), 178, sch 23 pt 5

 sch 9 am—Serious Organised Crime and Police, 2005 c 15, s 59, sch 4 para 200; SIs
    2006/1926, art 9, sch 1; 2007/2128, art 8, sch; 3224, art 15, sch; 2008/912, art 3,
    sch 1; 2833, art 6, sch 3; 2009/2748, art 8, sch; 2010/1836, art 6, sch; Crime and
    Cts, 2013 c 22, sch 8 para 186; SI 2014/469, sch 2 para 23

   rep in pt—SI 2008/960, art 22, sch 3; Coroners and Justice, 2009 c 25, s 178, sch 23
    pt 5; SIs 2009/2748, art 8, sch; 2010/1836, art 6, sch; Legal Aid, Sentencing
    and Punishment of Offenders, 2012 c 10, sch 5 para 66

 sch 10 rep in pt—Serious Organised Crime and Police, 2005 c 15, s 174(2), sch 17 pt 2;
    (prosp) Coroners and Justice, 2009 c 25, s 178, sch 23 pt 1; Legal Aid,
    Sentencing and Punishment of Offenders, 2012 c 10, sch 16 para 18

 sch 11 rep in pt—Legal Aid, Sentencing and Punishment of Offenders, 2012 c 10, sch 10
    para 40(3)

c 29 **Highways (Obstruction by Body Corporate)**

c 30 **Human Tissue**

 s 1 appl—SI 2006/1260, reg 2

   rep in pt—SI 2015/865, art 2(2)(a)(c)

   am—Human Fertilisation and Embryology, 2008 c 22, sch 7 para 22; (prosp) Coroners
    and Justice, 2009 c 25, s 177, sch 21 paras 47, 48; Human Transplantation (W),
    2013 anaw 5, s 16(2); SI 2015/865, art 2(2)(b)

 s 4 am—SI 2015/865, art 2(3)

 s 6 appl—SI 2006/1659, regs 3, 4

2004

c 30 s 6 *continued*

> am—Human Transplantation (W), 2013 anaw 5, s 16(3)
> s 8 am—Human Transplantation (W), 2013 anaw 5, s 16(4)
> s 14 am—SI 2007/1523, reg 30; Human Fertilisation and Embryology, 2008 c 22, s 65, sch
> > 7 para 23; SI 2012/1501, reg 25(2)
> > ext (mods)—(S) SI 2012/1501, reg 7(1)(a)
> s 15 ext (mods)—SIs 2007/1523, reg 9; (S) 2012/1501, reg 7(1)(b)(2)
> > am—Human Transplantation (W), 2013 anaw 5, s 16(5)
> s 16 appl—SI 2006/1260, reg 3
> > am—SI 2007/1523, reg 31
> s 17 appl—SI 2007/1523, reg 8
> s 19 appl—SI 2007/1523, reg 8
> > appl (mods)—SI 2012/1501, reg 6
> s 20 appl—SI 2007/1523, reg 8
> > appl (mods)—SI 2012/1501, reg 6
> s 21 appl—SI 2007/1523, reg 8
> > appl (mods)—SI 2012/1501, reg 6
> s 22 appl (mods)—SIs 2007/1523, reg 8; 2012/1501, reg 6
> s 23 appl—SI 2007/1523, reg 8
> > appl (mods)—SI 2012/1501, reg 6
> s 24 appl—SI 2007/1523, reg 8
> > appl (mods)—SI 2012/1501, reg 6
> s 26 ext (mods)—SI 2007/1523, reg 9
> > am—Human Transplantation (W), 2013 anaw 5, s 15(2)
> s 27 am—SI 2005/3129, art 4(4), sch 4 para 12(1)(2); Human Transplantation (W), 2013
> > anaw 5, s 15(3)
> s 29 am—(pt prosp) Human Transplantation (W), 2013 anaw 5, s 15(4)
> s 32 am—SIs 2012/1501, reg 25(3); 2014/1459, reg 12
> s 33 appl—SI 2006/1659, regs 10, 11
> > excl—SI 2006/1997, art 8(2)
> s 34 appl—SI 2006/1659, reg 9
> s 36 am—Human Transplantation (W), 2013 anaw 5, s 16(6)
> s 37 appl (mods)—SIs 2007/1523, reg 8; 2012/1501, reg 6
> s 39 am—Armed Forces, 2006 c 52, s 378, sch 16 para 241
> > mod—SI 2009/1059, art 205, sch 1
> s 41 am—SIs 2007/1523, reg 32; 2012/1501, reg 25(4)
> s 43 am—(prosp) Coroners and Justice, 2009 c 25, s 177, sch 21 paras 47, 50; Human
> > Transplantation (W), 2013 anaw 5, s 16(7)
> s 52 am—Human Transplantation (W), 2013 anaw 5, s 15(5); ibid, s 16(8)
> s 54 am—SI 2005/3129, art 4(4), sch 4 para 12(1)(3); Human Fertilisation and Embryology,
> > 2008 c 22, s 65, sch 7 para 24
> s 58 am—Human Transplantation (W), 2013 anaw 5, s 16(9)
> s 59 am—SI 2012/1501, reg 25(5)
> s 60 am—Human Transplantation (W), 2013 anaw 5, s 16(10)
> sch 2 am—Health, 2009 c 21, s 19, sch 3 paras 7, 19; SIs 2012/1501, reg 25(6); 2404, sch 2
> > para 51; Human Transplantation (W), 2013 anaw 5, s 16(11)
> sch 3 appl (mods)—SIs 2007/1523, reg 8; 2012/1501, reg 6
> > am—SIs 2007/1523, reg 33; 2012/1501, reg 25(7)
> sch 4 appl—SIs 2006/1260, reg 2; 2006/1659, regs 5-7
> > am—Armed Forces, 2006 c 52, s 378, sch 16 para 242
> > mod—SI 2009/1059, art 205, sch 1
> sch 5 am—(prosp) Coroners and Justice, 2009 c 25, s 177, sch 21 paras 47, 49; Human
> > Transplantation (W), 2013 anaw 5, s 16(12)
> sch 6 rep in pt—(prosp) Coroners and Justice, 2009 c 25, s 178, sch 23 pt 1

c 31 **Children**

> appl—(EW) Educ, 2005 c 18, s 113(5)
> ss 2-2C subst for s 2—Children and Families, 2014 c 6, s 107
> s 2D added—Children and Families, 2014 c 6, s 108
> s 2E added—Children and Families, 2014 c 6, s 109
> s 2F added—Children and Families, 2014 c 6, s 110
> s 3 am—Children and Families, 2014 c 6, sch 5 para 1(3)
> > rep in pt—Children and Families, 2014 c 6, sch 5 para 1(2)
> s 4 rep—Children and Families, 2014 c 6, sch 5 para 2(1)
> s 5 am—Children and Families, 2014 c 6, sch 5 para 3

2004

c 31 s 5 *continued*

    rep in pt—Children and Families, 2014 c 6, sch 5 para 2(2)(a)

s 6 am—Children and Families, 2014 c 6, sch 5 para 4

    rep in pt—Children and Families, 2014 c 6, sch 5 para 2(2)(b)

s 7 am—Children and Families, 2014 c 6, sch 5 para 5

    rep in pt—Children and Families, 2014 c 6, sch 5 para 2(2)(c)

s 7A added—Children and Families, 2014 c 6, s 111

s 7B added—Children and Families, 2014 c 6, s 112

s 8 am—Children and Families, 2014 c 6, s 113(2)(b)(3)-(6)

    rep in pt—Children and Families, 2014 c 6, s 113(2)(a)(c)

s 8A added—Children and Families, 2014 c 6, s 114

s 9 subst—Children and Families, 2014 c 6, sch 5 para 6(1)

Pt 2 (ss 9A-24) am—SI 2010/1158, art 5, sch 2

s 9A added —Apprenticeships, Skills, Children and Learning, 2009 c 22, s 195(1)

s 10 am—Offender Management, 2007 c 21, s 39, sch 3 para 4(1)(2); Educ and Skills, 2008
      c 25, s 169, sch 1 paras 82, 83; SIs 2010/1080, art 2, sch 1; 1158, art 5, sch 2;
      Police Reform and Social Responsibility, 2011 c 13, sch 16 para 331; Health and
      Social Care, 2012 c 7, sch 5 para 128(a)(b); Children and Families, 2014 c 6, sch
      3 para 80

    rep in pt—Apprenticeships, Skills, Children and Learning, 2009 c 22, ss
         193(1)(2)(b)(4), 266, sch 16 pt 5; SI 2010/1158, art 5, sch 3; Educ, 2011 c 21,
         sch 16 para 23; Health and Social Care, 2012 c 7, sch 5 para 128(c)

    appl (mods)—SI 2007/2979, sch 1 para 20B (added by SI 2012/1201, reg 3)

s 11 am—Offender Management, 2007 c 21, s 39, sch 3 para 4(1)(3); Educ and Skills, 2008
      c 25, s 169, sch 1 paras 82, 84; Police Reform and Social Responsibility, 2011 c
      13, sch 16 para 332; Health and Social Care, 2012 c 7, sch 5 para 129(a)(b);
      Crime and Cts, 2013 c 22, s 8(1); Crim Justice and Cts, 2015 c 2, sch 9 para 14

    rep in pt—(pt prosp) Health and Social Care, 2012 c 7, sch 5 para 129(c)(d), sch 14
         para 97

s 12 am—Nat Health Service (Conseq Provns), 2006 c 43, s 2, sch 1 para 265; Childcare,
      2006 c 21, s 103, sch 2 para 43; Apprenticeships, Skills, Children and Learning,
      2009 c 22, s 193(1)(2)(a)(3)(5); SIs 2010/866, art 5, sch 2; 2012/976, sch para
      14

ss 12A-12D added —Apprenticeships, Skills, Children and Learning, 2009 c 22, s 194(1)(2)

s 12A am—Health and Social Care, 2012 c 7, sch 5 para 130

s 13 am—Offender Management, 2007 c 21, s 39, sch 3 para 4(1)(4); Educ and Skills, 2008
      c 25, s 169, sch 1 paras 82, 85; Apprenticeships, Skills, Children and Learning,
      2009 c 22, s 196(1)(2); Health and Social Care, 2012 c 7, sch 5 para 131(a)(b);
      Crim Justice and Cts, 2015 c 2, sch 9 para 15

    rep in pt—(pt prosp) Health and Social Care, 2012 c 7, sch 5 para 131(c), sch 14 para
         98

s 14 am—Apprenticeships, Skills, Children and Learning, 2009 c 22, s 196(3)

s 14A added —Apprenticeships, Skills, Children and Learning, 2009 c 22, s 197

s 14B added—Children, Schools and Families, 2010 c 26, s 8

s 15 am—Crim Justice and Cts, 2015 c 2, sch 9 para 16; ibid, sch 10 para 34(a)(b)

s 15A added—Children, Schools and Families, 2010 c 26, s 10

s 17 subst—Apprenticeships, Skills, Children and Learning, 2009 c 22, s 194(3)

s 17A added—Apprenticeships, Skills, Children and Learning, 2009 c 22, s 194(3)

s 18 am—Nat Health Service (Conseq Provns), 2006 c 43, s 2, sch 1 para 266; Childcare,
      2006 c 21, s 16(2); Apprenticeships, Skills, Children and Learning, 2009 c 22, s
      194(4); SI 2010/1158, art 5, sch 2

    rep in pt—Childcare, 2006 c 21, ss 16(2)(a)(b), 103, sch 3; Further Education and
         Training, 2007 c 25, s 30, sch 2; SI 2010/1158, art 5, schs 2, 3

s 20 rep in pt—Educ and Inspections, 2006 c 40, s 157, sch 14 para 96(2), sch 18; Loc Govt
         and Public Involvement in Health, 2007 c 28, s 146, sch 9 para 1(1)(2)(x), sch
         18; SI 2012/2401, sch 1 para 19; Loc Audit and Accountability, 2014 c 2, sch
         12 para 68

    am—Educ and Inspections, 2006 c 40, s 157, sch 14 paras 95, 96(1)(2); Health and
         Social Care, 2008 c 14, s 95, sch 5 para 78; SI 2008/912, art 3, sch 1

s 23 rep in pt—Childcare, 2006 c 21, ss 16(3), 103, sch 3

    am—Educ and Inspections, 2006 c 40, s 157, sch 14 para 97; Childcare, 2006 c 21, s
         16(3); Apprenticeships, Skills, Children and Learning, 2009 c 22, s 194(5)

s 24 rep—Educ and Inspections, 2006 c 40, s 184, sch 18

Pt 3 (ss 25-34) am—SI 2010/1158, art 5, sch 2

2004

c 31 *continued*

s 25 am—SI 2005/3238 (W 243), arts 7, 9(1), sch 1 paras 89, 90; Offender Management, 2007 c 21, s 39, sch 3 para 4(1)(5); Police Reform and Social Responsibility, 2011 c 13, sch 16 para 333; (prosp) Social Services and Well-being (W), 2014 anaw 4, s 163; Crim Justice and Cts, 2015 c 2, sch 9 para 17; (1.4.2016) Well-being of Future Generations (W), 2015 anaw 2, sch 4 para 12

s 26 rep (1.4.2016)—(1.4.2016) Well-being of Future Generations (W), 2015 anaw 2, sch 4 para 13

    am—(W) Children and Families (W), 2010 nawm 1, s 4(2)(3); (W) Mental Health (W), 2010 nawm 7, s 11; (prosp) Social Services and Well-being (W), 2014 anaw 4, s 14(4)

s 27 am—(1.4.2016) Well-being of Future Generations (W), 2015 anaw 2, sch 4 para 14

s 28 am—Offender Management, 2007 c 21, s 39, sch 3 para 4(1)(6); Police Reform and Social Responsibility, 2011 c 13, sch 16 para 334; Crime and Cts, 2013 c 22, s 8(2); Crim Justice and Cts, 2015 c 2, sch 9 para 18

    rep in pt—(prosp) Health and Social Care, 2012 c 7, sch 14 para 99

s 29 am—SI 2005/3238 (W 243), arts 7, 9(1), sch 1 paras 89, 91; Nat Health Service (Conseq Provns), 2006 c 43, s 2, sch 1 para 267; (W) Children and Families (W), 2010 nawm 1, s 72, sch 1 paras 15, 16; SI 2010/866, art 5, sch 2

s 30 rep in pt—(1.4.2016) Well-being of Future Generations (W), 2015 anaw 2, sch 4 para 15

s 31 am—Offender Management, 2007 c 21, s 39, sch 3 para 4(1)(7); Crim Justice and Cts, 2015 c 2, sch 9 para 19

s 32A added (prosp)—Children, Schools and Families, 2010 c 26, s 9

s 33 am—Crim Justice and Cts, 2015 c 2, sch 9 para 20; ibid, sch 10 para 35

s 37 am—Legal Services, 2007 c 29, s 208, sch 21 para 149

s 38 rep—Educ and Inspections, 2006 c 40, s 156, sch 18

s 39 rep—Safeguarding Vulnerable Groups, 2006 c 47, s 63, sch 10

s 45 am—SI 2010/1158, art 5, sch 2

s 46 am—SI 2010/1158, art 5, sch 2

s 47 rep in pt—Children and Young Persons, 2008 c 23, s 35

s 49 am—(W 6.4.2016) Children and Young Persons, 2008 c 23, s 8, sch 1 para 17; SI 2010/1158, art 5, sch 2

s 50 am—Apprenticeships, Skills, Children and Learning, 2009 c 22, s 194(6); SI 2010/1158, art 5, sch 2; School Standards and Organisation (W), 2013 anaw 1, sch 5 para 7(2)(a)(c)

    rep in pt—SI 2010/1158, art 5, sch 3; School Standards and Organisation (W), 2013 anaw 1, sch 5 para 7(2)(b)

s 50A added—School Standards and Organisation (W), 2013 anaw 1, sch 5 para 7(3)

    rep in pt—(1.4.2016) Well-being of Future Generations (W), 2015 anaw 2, sch 4 para 16

s 65 am—SI 2010/1158, art 4; Crim Justice and Cts, 2015 c 2, sch 10 para 36(2)(3)

    rep in pt—SI 2010/1158, art 4; ibid, art 5, sch 3

s 66 am—Apprenticeships, Skills, Children and Learning, 2009 c 22, s 194(7); ibid, s 195(2); (W) Children and Families (W), 2010 nawm 1, s 4(2)(4); (6.4.2016) Social Services and Well-being (W), 2014 anaw 4, s 163(8)

    rep in pt—(1.4.2016) Well-being of Future Generations (W), 2015 anaw 2, sch 4 para 17

sch 1 rep in pt —(prosp) Safeguarding Vulnerable Groups, 2006 c 47, s 63, sch 10; Children and Families, 2014 c 6, sch 5 para 9(1)

    am—Children and Families, 2014 c 6, sch 5 paras 7, 8

sch 2 rep in pt —(prosp) Safeguarding Vulnerable Groups, 2006 c 47, s 63, sch 10; Anti-social Behaviour, Crime and Policing, 2014 c 12, sch 11 para 50

c 32 **Armed Forces (Pensions and Compensation)**

s 1 am—Public Service Pensions, 2013 c 25, sch 8 para 28

s 3 mod—SI 2009/262, art 2

s 7 rep in pt—SI 2008/2833, art 6, sch 3

sch 1 rep in pt—Constitutional Reform, 2005 c 4, s 146, sch 18 pt 2

c 33 **Civil Partnership**

trans of functions—SI 2010/1839, art 3

power to appl (mods) conferred—Marriage and Civil Partnership (S), 2014 asp 5, s 30(5)(b)

s 1 am—Marriage (Same Sex Couples), 2013 c 30, sch 7 para 34; Marriage and Civil Partnership (S), 2014 asp 5, s 11(9)

s 4 am—Marriage (Same Sex Couples), 2013 c 30, sch 7 para 35

2004
c 33 *continued*

s 6 am—SI 2005/2000, art 3, sch paras 1, 2(1)(2)
    rep in pt—SI 2005/2000, art 3, sch paras 1, 2(1)(3); Equality, 2010 c 15, s 202(2); ibid,
        s 211, sch 27 pt 1 (subst by SI 2010/2279, sch 2)
s 6A added—SI 2005/2000, art 3, sch paras 1, 3
    see—(trans of functions) SI 2008/678, art 3, sch 1
    am—SI 2008/678, art 5, sch 2; Equality, 2010 c 15, s 202(3)
s 8 am—SI 2005/2000, art 3, sch paras 1, 4, 5(1)(2), 6; Immigration, 2014 c 22, sch 4 para
    19(2)(3)
s 8A added—Immigration, 2014 c 22, sch 4 para 20
ss 9-9F subst for s 9—Immigration, 2014 c 22, sch 4 para 21
s 10 am—SI 2005/2000, art 3, sch paras 1, 4, 5(1)(2), 6
s 11 am—Immigration, 2014 c 22, sch 4 para 22
s 12 am—Immigration, 2014 c 22, sch 4 para 23
s 12A added—Immigration, 2014 c 22, sch 4 para 24
s 14 am—Immigration, 2014 c 22, sch 4 para 26(1)
s 14A added —Immigration, 2014 c 22, sch 4 para 26(2)
s 15 am—Immigration, 2014 c 22, sch 4 para 26(3)
s 16 am—Immigration, 2014 c 22, sch 4 para 26(4)
s 17 am—SI 2005/2000, art 3, sch paras 1, 7; Protection of Freedoms, 2012 c 9, s 114(3)(a)
    rep in pt—Protection of Freedoms, 2012 c 9, s 114(3)(b), sch 10 pt 11
s 20 rep in pt—SI 2005/2000, art 3, sch paras 1, 8(1)(3)(6)(a)(7)
    am—SI 2005/2000, art 3, sch paras 1, 8(1)(2)(4)(5)(6)(b)
s 22 am—SI 2005/2000, art 3, sch paras 1, 9
s 29 rep in pt—SI 2005/2000, art 3, sch paras 1, 10
s 30A added—Immigration, 2014 c 22, sch 4 para 27
s 31 am—SI 2005/2000, art 3, sch paras 1, 11
    rep in pt—Protection of Freedoms, 2012 c 9, s 114(4), sch 10 pt 11
s 34 am—SIs 2005/2000, art 3, sch paras 1, 12; 2008/678, art 5, sch 2
    see—(trans of functions) SI 2008/678, art 3, sch 1
s 35 rep in pt—Legislative and Regulatory Reform, 2006 c 51, s 30, sch 1
    see—(trans of functions) SI 2008/678, art 3, sch 1
    am—SI 2008/678, art 5, sch 2
s 36 am—SIs 2005/2000, art 3, sch paras 1, 13; 2008/678, art 5, sch 2; Immigration, 2014 c
    22, sch 4 para 28; Deregulation, 2015 c 20, s 99(2)
    see—(trans of functions) SI 2008/678, art 3, sch 1
s 37 am—Crime and Cts, 2013 c 22, sch 11 para 162
s 40 rep in pt—Children and Families, 2014 c 6, s 17(6)
s 41 appl (mods)—SI 2005/3042, art 3(1)
s 42 am—Legal Services, 2007 c 29, s 208, sch 21 para 150
s 45 am—Crime and Cts, 2013 c 22, sch 11 para 163
s 49 rep in pt—SI 2005/2000, art 3, sch paras 1, 14(1)(2)
    am—SI 2005/2000, art 3, sch paras 1, 14(1)(3)
s 52 am—SI 2005/2000, art 3, sch paras 1, 15(1)(2); Immigration, 2014 c 22, sch 4 para 29
    rep in pt—SI 2005/2000, art 3, sch paras 1, 15(1)(3)
s 56 rep in pt—Children and Families, 2014 c 6, s 17(7)
s 58 am—Crime and Cts, 2013 c 22, sch 11 para 164
s 63 rep—Children and Families, 2014 c 6, s 17(1)(b)
s 65 appl (mods)—SI 2005/3042, art 3(2)
s 66 am—Crime and Cts, 2013 c 22, sch 11 para 165(2)
    rep in pt—Crime and Cts, 2013 c 22, sch 11 para 165(3)
s 70A added (prosp)—Equality, 2010 c 15, s 201(1)
s 85 am—Marriage and Civil Partnership (S), 2014 asp 5, s 24(2)
s 86 am—(S) Family Law (S), 2006 asp 2, s 33, sch 1 paras 1, 2; SI 2009/1892, arts 2, 4,
    schs 1, 4; Marriage and Civil Partnership (S), 2014 asp 5, s 24(3)(a)-(c)(d)(i)(e)(i)
    rep in pt—(S) Family Law (S), 2006 asp 2, s 45, sch 3; Marriage and Civil Partnership
      (S), 2014 asp 5, s 24(3)(d)(ii)(e)(ii)
s 87 am—Marriage and Civil Partnership (S), 2014 asp 5, s 24(4)
s 88 rep in pt—(S) Loc Electoral Admin and Registration Services (S), 2006 asp 14, s
      52(2)(a)
    am—(S) Loc Electoral Admin and Registration Services (S), 2006 asp 14, s
      52(2)(b)(c)(d); Marriage and Civil Partnership (S), 2014 asp 5, ss 24(5), 25
ss 88A-88F added—SI 2015/396, sch 3 para 2

2004
c 33 *continued*

s 89 am—Marriage and Civil Partnership (S), 2014 asp 5, s 24(6); SI 2015/396, sch 3 para 4

s 90 am—(S) Loc Electoral Admin and Registration Services (S), 2006 asp 14, s 52(3); Marriage and Civil Partnership (S), 2014 asp 5, s 24(7)(a)(c); ibid, s 24(7)(b)

s 91 am—Marriage and Civil Partnership (S), 2014 asp 5, s 24(8); SI 2015/396, sch 3 para 5

s 92 am—(S) Loc Electoral Admin and Registration Services (S), 2006 asp 14, s 52(4); Marriage and Civil Partnership (S), 2014 asp 5, s 24(9)(a)(c)
rep in pt—Marriage and Civil Partnership (S), 2014 asp 5, s 24(9)(b)(ii)

s 93 am—(S) Loc Electoral Admin and Registration Services (S), 2006 asp 14, s 51; Marriage and Civil Partnership (S), 2014 asp 5, s 24(10)(a)(b)(d)
rep in pt—Marriage and Civil Partnership (S), 2014 asp 5, s 24(10)(c)

s 93A added (S)—Marriage and Civil Partnership (S), 2014 asp 5, s 24(11)

s 94 am—Marriage and Civil Partnership (S), 2014 asp 5, s 24(12)

ss 94A-94E added (S)—Marriage and Civil Partnership (S), 2014 asp 5, s 24(13)

s 94A added—SI 2015/396, sch 3 para 6

s 95 am—Marriage and Civil Partnership (S), 2014 asp 5, s 24(14)

s 95ZA added (S)—Marriage and Civil Partnership (S), 2014 asp 5, s 24(15)

s 95A added (S)—Loc Electoral Admin and Registration Services (S), 2006 asp 14, s 52(5)
am—Marriage and Civil Partnership (S), 2014 asp 5, s 24(16)

s 96 am—Marriage and Civil Partnership (S), 2014 asp 5, s 24(17)

s 97 am—Marriage and Civil Partnership (S), 2014 asp 5, s 24(18)

s 98 subst (pt prosp)—(S) Loc Electoral Admin and Registration Services (S), 2006 asp 14, s 52(6)

s 100 am—Marriage and Civil Partnership (S), 2014 asp 5, ss 24(19), 28(2)

s 101 am—(S) Family Law (S), 2006 asp 2, s 33, sch 1 paras 1, 3

s 103 am—(S) Family Law (S), 2006 asp 2, s 33, sch 1 paras 1, 4

s 106 am—(S) Family Law (S), 2006 asp 2, s 33, sch 1 paras 1, 5

s 107 am—(S) Family Law (S), 2006 asp 2, s 33, sch 1 paras 1, 6

s 108 am—(S) SSI 2006/384, art 9

s 111A added (S)—Family Law (S), 2006 asp 2, s 33, sch 1 paras 1, 7

s 112 am—Land Registration etc. (S), 2012 asp 5, sch 5 para 44

s 113 am—(S) Family Law (S), 2006 asp 2, s 33, sch 1 paras 1, 8
rep in pt—(S) Family Law (S), 2006 asp 2, s 45, sch 3; (S) SSI 2006/384, art 10

ss 114, 115 rep (S)—Family Law (S), 2006 asp 2, s 45, sch 3

s 116 rep (S)—Family Law (S), 2006 asp 2, s 45, sch 3

s 117 am—(S) Family Law (S), 2006 asp 2, s 33, sch 1 paras 1, 9
rep in pt—(S) Family Law (S), 2006 asp 2, s 45, sch 3

s 119 rep in pt—(S) Family Law (S), 2006 asp 2, s 45, sch 3

s 122 am—(S) Loc Electoral Admin and Registration Services (S), 2006 asp 14, s 52(7)

s 123 rep in pt—(S) Family Law (S), 2006 asp 2, s 33, sch 1 paras 1, 10(c)(d)
am—(S) Family Law (S), 2006 asp 2, s 33, sch 1 paras 1, 10(a)(b)

s 124A added (S)—Family Law (S), 2006 asp 2, s 33, sch 1 paras 1, 11

s 126 am—Marriage and Civil Partnership (S), 2014 asp 5, s 24(20); SI 2015/396, sch 3 para 7

s 129 rep (S)—Family Law (S), 2006 asp 2, s 45, sch 3

s 135 am—(S) Family Law (S), 2006 asp 2, s 33, sch 1 paras 1, 12; Marriage and Civil Partnership (S), 2014 asp 5, s 24(21); SI 2015/396, sch 3 para 8
rep in pt—(S) Family Law (S), 2006 asp 2, s 45, sch 3

s 150 rep—SI 2005/2000, art 3, sch paras 1, 16

s 188 am—SI 2006/1016, art 2, sch 1

s 210 am—SI 2012/3100, art 2(2)-(4); Marriage (Same Sex Couples), 2013 c 30, sch 7 para 36

s 212 appl (mods)—(EW) SI 2005/3042, art 5
am—SI 2014/560, sch 1 para 29(2)

s 213 see—(trans of functions) SI 2007/2914, art 3
am—SI 2007/2914, art 8, sch; 2010/1839, art 7, sch; (prosp) Marriage (Same Sex Couples), 2013 c 30, sch 2 para 5(2)

s 214 am—Marriage and Civil Partnership (S), 2014 asp 5, s 26(2)

s 219 am—SI 2010/976, art 15, sch 18
rep in pt—SI 2010/976, art 15, sch 18

s 220 am—Crime and Cts, 2013 c 22, sch 11 para 166

s 222 am—Presumption of Death, 2013 c 13, sch 2 para 3(2)(4)

2004

c 33 s 222 *continued*

    rep in pt—Presumption of Death, 2013 c 13, sch 2 para 3(3)

s 227 am—SI 2011/1484, sch 7 para 16(2)

ss 235, 236 appl (mods)—(EW, NI) SI 2005/3104, regs 2(1)-(5), 3-6; (S) SSI 2005/567, regs 2(1)-(5), 3-6

s 237 appl (mods) —(EW, NI) SI 2005/3104, reg 2(1)(6); (S) SSI 2005/567, reg 2(1)(6)
    am—SI 2010/976, art 15, sch 18

s 239 am—SI 2005/2000, art 3, sch paras 1, 17(1)(2)
    rep in pt—SI 2005/2000, art 3, sch paras 1, 17(1)(3)(4)

s 245 am—Armed Forces, 2006 c 52, s 378, sch 16 para 243

s 246 appl—SI 2005/3137, art 3, sch

sch 1 appl (mods)—SI 2010/985, reg 5, sch 4
    rep in pt—Crime and Cts, 2013 c 22, sch 11 para 167(2)
    am—Crime and Cts, 2013 c 22, sch 11 para 167(3)

sch 2 am—Crime and Cts, 2013 c 22, sch 11 para 168(2)(3)(a); Children and Families, 2014 c 6, sch 2 para 66; SI 2014/560, sch 1 para 29(3)
    rep in pt—Crime and Cts, 2013 c 22, sch 11 para 168(3)(a)

sch 3 am—SI 2005/2000, art 3, sch paras 1, 18(1)(2)(4)(5)(6)(b)
    rep in pt—SI 2005/2000, art 3, sch paras 1, 18(1)(3)(6)(a)(7)

sch 3A added —Immigration, 2014 c 22, sch 4 para 25

sch 5 appl (mods)—SI 2005/3042, art 3(3)
    mod—SI 2006/1934, regs 2, 4
    am—Pensions, 2008 c 30, s 120, sch 6 paras 14, 15-19; SI 2011/1484, sch 7 para 16(3)(4); Legal Aid, Sentencing and Punishment of Offenders, 2012 c 10, ss 52, 53, 54; Crime and Cts, 2013 c 22, sch 11 paras 170, 171(2), 172(2)(4)(a)(5), 173(b), 176, 177; Inheritance and Trustees' Powers, 2014 c 16, sch 3 para 5
    rep in pt—Pensions, 2008 c 30, s 120, sch 6 paras 14, 15-17, sch 11; Crime and Cts, 2013 c 22, sch 11 paras 171(3), 172(3), 173(a), 174, 175

sch 6 appl (mods)—SI 2005/3042, art 3(4)
    am—SIs 2006/1016, art 2, sch 1; 2011/1484, sch 7 para 16(5); Crime and Cts, 2013 c 22, sch 11 paras 179, 181, 182, 183(2)(a), 185(2)(3)(a), 187-190, 192(a), 193(a), 193(b)(ii), 194, 195, 197(2), 197(3)(a), 199(3)(4), 200
    rep in pt—Crime and Cts, 2013 c 22, sch 11 paras 180, 183(2)(b)(3), 184, 185(3)(b), 186, 191, 192(b), 193(b)(i), 196, 197(3)(b)(c)(4), (5), 198(a), 198(b), 199(2)

sch 7 am—Pensions, 2008 c 30, s 120, sch 6 paras 14, 20(1)(2)(4); SI 2011/1484, sch 7 para 16(6); Crime and Cts, 2013 c 22, sch 11 para 201
    rep in pt—Pensions, 2008 c 30, s 120, sch 6 paras 14, 20(1)(3), sch 11

sch 9 rep in pt—(prosp) Housing and Regeneration, 2008 c 17, s 321, sch 16

sch 10 subst—Marriage and Civil Partnership (S), 2014 asp 5, s 24(22)

sch 10A added—SI 2015/396, sch 3 para 3

sch 11 am—SI 2007/1655, reg 5, sch 1; 2011/1484, sch 7 para 16(7)

sch 12 rep in pt—SI 2006/1945, art 4

sch 15 am—SIs 2010/976, art 15, sch 18; 2011/1484, sch 7 para 16(8)(9)

sch 16 rep in pt—SI 2006/1945, art 6
    am—SIs 2006/1016, art 2, sch 1; 2010/976, art 15, sch 18

sch 17 am—SIs 2010/976, art 15, sch 18; 2011/1484, sch 7 para 16(10)

sch 18 rep in pt—SI 2006/1459, art 75, sch 5

sch 20 am—SIs 2005/3129, art 3; 2005/3135, art 2; 2012/2976, sch paras 2-19
    rep in pt—Marriage and Civil Partnership (S), 2014 asp 5, s 26(3)

sch 21 am—SSI 2005/568, art 2; SI 2005/3137, art 2(a)-(g); Welfare Reform, 2007 c 5, s 59(4)
    rep in pt—(prosp) Safeguarding Vulnerable Groups, 2006 c 47, s 63, sch 10; Charities, 2011 c 25, sch 10

sch 22 rep in pt—SI 2009/1941, art 2, sch 1

sch 23 rep in pt—SI 2005/2000, art 3, sch paras 1, 19(1)(2)(a); (prosp) Immigration, Asylum and Nationality, 2006 c 13, s 50(6), sch 3; SI 2011/1158, art 5(1)(a)-(c)(e)-(g)(i)
    am—SIs 2005/2000, art 3, sch paras 1, 19(1)(2)(b)(3); 2011/1158, art 5(1)(d)(h)(2); Immigration, 2014 c 22, s 58(5)-(9)

sch 24 rep in pt—Welfare Reform, 2007 c 5, s 40, sch 5 para 14, sch 8; (pt prosp) ibid, s 67, sch 8; Pensions, 2007 c 22, s 27, sch 7; Child Maintenance and Other Payments, 2008 c 6, s 58, sch 8; (prosp) Welfare Reform, 2009 c 24, s 58, sch 7 pt 1; (prosp) ibid, s 58, sch 7 pt 3; ibid, s 58, sch 7 pt 2; (pt prosp) Welfare Reform, 2012 c 5, sch 14 pts 1, 7, 8; Pensions, 2014 c 19, sch 12 para 75

2004

c 33 *continued*

sch 25 rep in pt—Public Service Pensions, 2013 c 25, sch 11 para 7

sch 26 rep in pt—Armed Forces, 2011 c 18, sch 5

sch 27 rep in pt—Electoral Admin, 2006 c 22, s 74, sch 2; (pt prosp) Companies, 2006 c 46, s 1295, sch 16; SI 2007/438, art 3; Mental Health, 2007 c 12, s 55, sch 11 pts 3, 5; Legal Aid, Sentencing and Punishment of Offenders, 2012 c 10, sch 5 pt 2; Crime and Cts, 2013 c 22, sch 10 para 99 Table; Co-operative and Community Benefit Societies, 2014 c 14, sch 7; Consumer Rights, 2015 c 15, sch 6 para 85(d)

sch 28 rep in pt—(S) Family Law (S), 2006 asp 2, s 45, sch 3; (prosp) (S) SSI 2013/211, sch 2

sch 29 rep in pt—SI 2007/2194, art 10, sch 5; SI 2009/1941, art 2, sch 2

sch 30 rep—Damages (S), 2011 asp 7, sch 2

c 34   **Housing**

appl—SI 2005/1541, art 31(7)

s 22 am—SI 2013/1036, sch 1 para 150

s 34 am—SI 2013/1036, sch 1 para 151

s 42 am—SI 2009/1307, art 5, sch 1

s 45 am—SI 2013/1036, sch 1 para 152

s 50 am—SI 2009/1307, art 5, sch 1

Pt 2 (ss 55-78) mod—(W) SI 2007/3231 (W 283), regs 2-10

ss 55-60 appl—SI 2007/1904, reg 2

s 61 appl (mods)—SI 2007/1904, regs 2, 3

s 62 appl—SI 2007/1904, reg 2

am—SI 2013/1036, sch 1 para 153

s 63 appl—SI 2007/1904, reg 2

ss 64, 65 appl (mods)—SI 2007/1904, regs 2, 4, 5

s 66 appl—SI 2007/1904, reg 2

s 67 appl (mods)—SI 2007/1904, regs 2, 6

ss 68-72 appl—SI 2007/1904, reg 2

s 72 am—SIs 2013/1036, sch 1 para 154; 2015/664, sch 4 para 37(2)

s 73 appl (mods)—SI 2007/1904, regs 2, 7

am—SIs 2013/630, reg 18(2); (W) 2013/1788 (W 178), reg 3(2); 2013/1036, sch 1 para 155

s 74 appl—SI 2007/1904, reg 2

am—SIs 2013/630, reg 18(3); (W) 2013/1788 (W 178), reg 3(3)

s 75 appl (mods)—SI 2007/1904, regs 2, 8

ss 76, 77 appl—SI 2007/1904, reg 2

s 78 appl (mods)—SI 2007/1904, regs 2, 9

ss 79, 80 am—SI 2010/866, art 5, sch 2

s 86 am—SI 2013/1036, sch 1 para 156

s 95 am—SIs 2013/1036, sch 1 para 157; 2015/664, sch 4 para 37(3)

s 96 am—SIs 2013/630, reg 18(4); (W) 2013/1788 (W 178), reg 3(4); 2013/1036, sch 1 para 158

s 97 am—SIs 2013/630, reg 18(5); (W) 2013/1788 (W 178), reg 3(5)

s 102 am—SI 2013/1036, sch 1 para 159

s 103 am—SI 2013/1036, sch 1 para 160

s 105 am—SI 2013/1036, sch 1 para 161

s 110 am—SI 2013/1036, sch 1 para 162

s 114 am—SI 2013/1036, sch 1 para 163

s 120 am—SI 2013/1036, sch 1 para 164

s 126 am—SI 2013/1036, sch 1 para 165

s 130 am—SI 2013/1036, sch 1 para 166

s 133 am—SI 2013/1036, sch 1 para 167

s 134 am—SI 2013/1036, sch 1 para 168

s 138 am—SI 2013/1036, sch 1 para 169

s 139 mod—(W) SI 2007/3231 (W 283), reg 11

appl (mods)—SI 2007/1904, reg 11

s 143 am—SIs 2009/1307, art 5, sch 1; 2013/1036, sch 1 para 170

s 144 am—SI 2013/1036, sch 1 para 171

Pt 5 (ss 148-178) rep—Localism, 2011 c 20, s 183(1), sch 25 pt 29

s 181 am—SIs 2009/1307, art 5, sch 1; 2013/1036, sch 1 para 172

ss 209-211 rep (S)—Housing (Scotland), 2006 asp 1, s 192, sch 7

s 212 excl in pt—SI 2007/797, arts 2(5), 3 (added by 2015 c 20, s 30(2)(3))

2004
c 34 *continued*

s 213 am—Localism, 2011 c 20, s 184(2)
s 214 am—Localism, 2011 c 20, s 184(3)-(9); Crime and Cts, 2013 c 22, sch 9 para 52; Deregulation, 2015 c 20, s 31(2)(3)
s 215 am—Localism, 2011 c 20, s 184(10)-(13); Crime and Cts, 2013 c 22, sch 9 para 52
ss 215A-215C added—Deregulation, 2015 c 20, s 32
s 217 rep—Energy, 2011 c 16, s 118(5)
s 225 am—Housing (W), 2014 anaw 7, sch 3 para 24(2)
s 226 am—Housing (W), 2014 anaw 7, sch 3 para 24(3)
s 228 rep in pt—Public Services Ombudsman (W), 2005 c 10, s 39(2), sch 7
s 229 am—SI 2013/1036, sch 1 para 173
s 230 am—SIs 2011/1005, art 4(2); (W) 2012/899 (W 119), art 4(2); 2013/1036, sch 1 para 174; (savings) (W) Mobile Homes (W), 2013 anaw 6, sch 4 para 9(2); Mobile Homes, 2013 c 14, s 7(2)
s 231 am—SIs 2009/1307, art 5, sch 1; 2013/1036, sch 1 para 175
rep in pt—SI 2009/1307, art 5, sch 1
s 231A added—SI 2013/1036, sch 1 para 176
am—SI 2014/1900, sch 1 para 13
s 231B added—SI 2013/1036, sch 1 para 176
am—SI 2014/1900, sch 1 para 14
s 231C added—SI 2013/1036, sch 1 para 176
am—SI 2014/1900, sch 1 para 15
s 231D added—SI 2013/1036, sch 1 para 176
am—SI 2014/1900, sch 1 para 16
s 244 am—SI 2013/1036, sch 1 para 177
s 250 rep in pt—Localism, 2011 c 20, sch 25 pt 29
s 255 am—SIs 2009/1307, art 5, sch 1; 2013/1036, sch 1 para 178
s 256 am—SI 2013/1036, sch 1 para 179
s 261 am—SI 2013/1036, sch 1 para 180
s 262 rep in pt—Localism, 2011 c 20, sch 25 pt 29
s 263 mod—SIs (W) 2007/3231 (W 283), reg 12; 1904, reg 12
s 270 rep in pt—Localism, 2011 c 20, sch 25 pt 29
sch 1 am—SIs 2009/1307, art 5, sch 1; 2013/1036, sch 1 para 181(a)
rep in pt—SI 2013/1036, sch 1 para 181(b)
sch 2 am—SIs 2009/1307, art 5, sch 1; 2013/1036, sch 1 para 182(a)(b)
rep in pt—SI 2013/1036, sch 1 para 182(c)
sch 3 am—SIs 2009/1307, art 5, sch 1; 2013/1036, sch 1 para 183
sch 4 appl (mods)—SI 2007/1904, regs 2, 10
am—SI 2015/1693, reg 15(1)(a)-(c)
sch 5 am—SIs 2009/1307, art 5, sch 1; 2013/1036, sch 1 para 184(a)(b)
rep in pt—SI 2013/1036, sch 1 para 184(c)
sch 6 am—SIs 2009/1307, art 5, sch 1; 2013/1036, sch 1 para 185(a)(b)
rep in pt—SI 2013/1036, sch 1 para 185(c)
sch 7 am—SIs 2009/1307, art 5, sch 1; 2013/1036, sch 1 para 186(a)-(c)
rep in pt—SI 2013/1036, sch 1 para 186(d)
sch 8 rep—Localism, 2011 c 20, sch 25 pt 29
sch 10 am—SI 2007/796, regs 2-12; Localism, 2011 c 20, s 184(14)
sch 11 rep in pt—SI 2010/866, art 7, sch 4
sch 12 rep—Public Services Ombudsman (W), 2005 c 10, s 39(2), sch 7
sch 13 am—SIs 2011/1005, art 4(3); (W) 2012/899 (W 119), art 4(3); (W) (savings) Mobile Homes (W), 2013 anaw 6, sch 4 para 9(3); Mobile Homes, 2013 c 14, s 7(3); Crime and Cts, 2013 c 22, sch 9 paras 52, 89; SI 2013/1036, sch 1 para 187
sch 14 am—SI 2010/866, art 5, sch 2; Localism, 2011 c 20, s 185(1); (with transtl provns and savings) Police Reform and Social Responsibility, 2011 c 13, sch 16 para 335; Co-operative and Community Benefit Societies, 2014 c 14, sch 4 para 91
sch 15 rep in pt—Public Services Ombudsman (W), 2005 c 10, s 39(2), sch 7; SI 2010/866, art 7, sch 4

c 35 **Pensions**
power to mod conferred—Pensions, 2014 c 19, s 45(1)
mod—SI 2009/317, art 3, sch
appl (mods)—SI 2011/245, sch 6 pt 1
s 5 am—Pensions, 2008 c 30, s 65; Pensions, 2014 c 19, s 48
s 10 am—SI 2005/2113, reg 2(1)(3); Pensions, 2014 c 19, sch 19 para 6

2004
c 35 *continued*

s 11 am—Public Service Pensions, 2013 c 25, sch 4 para 2

s 13 am—Public Service Pensions, 2013 c 25, sch 4 para 3; Pension Schemes, 2015 c 8, sch 2 para 24; SI 2015/879, reg 25

s 14A added—Public Service Pensions, 2013 c 25, sch 4 para 4

s 17 am—Public Service Pensions, 2013 c 25, sch 4 para 5; (prosp) Pension Schemes, 2015 c 8, sch 2 para 25

s 18 am—Pensions, 2014 c 19, s 52; Pension Schemes, 2015 c 8, sch 4 para 35(2)-(4)
     rep in pt—Pension Schemes, 2015 c 8, sch 4 para 35(5)

s 23 am—(prosp) Pension Schemes, 2015 c 8, sch 2 para 26

s 24 am—SI 2005/2053, art 2, sch pt 6 para 27(a)(c); Pension Schemes, 2015 c 8, sch 4 para 37
     rep in pt—SI 2005/2053, art 2, sch pt 6 para 27(b)

s 34 rep in pt—SI 2010/22, art 5, sch 4

s 38 appl (mods)—SI 2005/2188, reg 16
     mod —SI 2009/814, art 5
     am—(spec retrosp effect) Pensions, 2008 c 30, s 126, sch 9 paras 1, 2(1), 7, 8, 15(1)(2); Pensions, 2011 c 19, s 26(2)(3); (prosp) Pension Schemes, 2015 c 8, sch 2 para 27
     excl—SI 2008/2546, art 26, sch 3
     rep in pt—(spec retrosp effect) Pensions, 2008 c 30, s 126, sch 9 paras 1, 7, 15(1), sch 11

s 38A added—(spec retrosp effect) Pensions, 2008 c 30, s 126, sch 9 paras 1, 2(2), 15(1)

s 38B added—(spec retrosp effect) Pensions, 2008 c 30, s 126, sch 9 paras 1, 2(2), 15(1)

s 39 appl (mods)—SI 2005/2188, reg 16

s 39A added—(spec retrosp effect) Pensions, 2008 c 30, s 126, sch 9 paras 1, 9, 15(3)

s 39B added—(spec retrosp effect) (transtl provns) Pensions, 2008 c 30, s 126, sch 9 paras 1, 9, 15(3), 16(1)

ss 40-42 appl (mods)—SI 2005/2188, reg 16

s 43 appl (mods)—SI 2005/2188, reg 16
     mod—SI 2009/814, art 5
     am—Pensions, 2011 c 19, s 26(5)(6); (prosp) Pension Schemes, 2015 c 8, sch 2 para 28

s 43A added—(spec retrosp effect) Pensions, 2008 c 30, s 126, sch 9 paras 1, 10, 15(3)

s 43B added—(spec retrosp effect) (transtl provns) Pensions, 2008 c 30, s 126, sch 9 paras 1, 10, 15(3), 16(2)

s 44 appl (mods)—SI 2005/2188, reg 16
     am—(spec retrosp effect) Pensions, 2008 c 30, s 126, sch 9 paras 1, 14, 15(4); SI 2009/1941, art 2, sch 1

ss 45-51 appl (mods)—SI 2005/2188, reg 16

s 45 am—SI 2009/1941, art 2, sch 1

s 51 am—SI 2009/1941, art 2, sch 1

s 52 appl (mods)—SI 2005/2188, reg 16
     excl—SI 2008/2546, art 26, sch 3
     am—(prosp) Pension Schemes, 2015 c 8, sch 2 para 29

ss 53-56 appl (mods)—SI 2005/2188, reg 16

s 57 appl—SIs 2005/590, reg 5(2)(b); (NI) 1986, reg 13(6)
     am—SI 2009/1941, art 2, sch 1

s 58 am—Pensions, 2011 c 19, sch 4 para 2

s 60 appl (mods) —SI 2005/597, reg 3(3)

s 63 am—Pensions, 2014 c 19, s 49(2)

s 66 am—Pensions, 2014 c 19, sch 19 para 7

s 68 appl (mods) —(NI) SI 2005/1986, reg 4(1)(2)(a)(3)(5), sch 1

s 70 am—Public Service Pensions, 2013 c 25, sch 4 para 6

s 70A added —Public Service Pensions, 2013 c 25, sch 4 para 7

s 71 am—Public Service Pensions, 2013 c 25, sch 4 para 8

s 72 am—Pensions, 2008 c 30, s 61(1)(2); Public Service Pensions, 2013 c 25, sch 4 para 9; Pensions, 2014 c 19, s 41(2)

s 73 am—Public Service Pensions, 2013 c 25, sch 4 para 10; Pension Schemes, 2015 c 8, sch 4 para 38

s 74 am—Pensions, 2008 c 30, s 61(1)(3)

s 75 am—Pensions, 2008 c 30, s 61(1)(4)

s 76 am—Pensions, 2008 c 30, s 61(1)(5)

s 80 am—Pensions, 2008 c 30, s 48(1)
     rep in pt—Pensions, 2008 c 30, ss 48(2), 148, sch 11

s 82 appl (mods)—SI 2005/597, reg 5(3)

2004

c 35 s 82 *continued*

am—Pensions, 2008 c 30, ss 62(1), 64(1)(2)

s 84 am—Pensions, 2008 c 30, s 83

s 85 appl (mods)—(NI) SI 2005/1986, reg 4(1)(2)(b)(3)(5), sch 1

s 87 am—SI 2009/1941, art 2, sch 1

s 88 subst—Pensions, 2008 c 30, s 62(1)

s 89 am—Public Service Pensions, 2013 c 25, sch 4 para 11

s 89A added —Public Service Pensions, 2013 c 25, sch 4 para 12

s 90 am—Pensions, 2008 c 30, s 126, sch 9 paras 1, 3; Public Service Pensions, 2013 c 25, sch 4 para 13; Pension Schemes, 2015 c 8, sch 2 para 30

s 90A added—Public Service Pensions, 2013 c 25, sch 4 para 14

s 91 see —(code of practice in force 6.4.2005) SI 2005/1108, art 2

am—Public Service Pensions, 2013 c 25, sch 4 para 15

s 92 am—Public Service Pensions, 2013 c 25, sch 4 para 16

s 93 am—Public Service Pensions, 2013 c 25, sch 4 para 17

s 96 am—Pensions, 2008 c 30, s 126, sch 9 paras 1, 4; SI 2010/22, art 5, sch 2; Pensions, 2011 c 19, s 26(7); Pensions, 2014 c 19, sch 19 para 8

rep in pt—SI 2010/22, art 5, sch 2

s 97 am—Pensions, 2007 c 22, s 14(6); Pensions, 2014 c 19, sch 19 para 9

s 99 am—SI 2010/22, art 5, sch 2

rep in pt—SI 2010/22, art 5, sch 2

s 102 rep—SI 2010/22, art 5, sch 2

s 102A added—SI 2010/22, art 5, sch 2

s 103 am—SI 2010/22, art 5, sch 2; Crime and Cts, 2013 c 22, sch 9 para 52

rep in pt—SI 2010/22, art 5, sch 2

ss 104, 105 rep—SI 2010/22, art 5, sch 2

s 106 am—SI 2010/22, art 5, sch 2

Pt 2 (ss 107-220) appl (mods)—SIs 2005/277, regs 2-9, 10(1)-(3); 441, regs 2-75

appl—(EW) Civil Partnership, 2004 c 33, s 72(1), sch 5 pt 7 para 37(1); (NI) ibid, s 196(1), sch 15 pt 6 para 32(1); SI 2014/1711, reg 42(1) 53 57

s 113 appl (mods)—SI 2005/1851, reg 4, sch 1 (as amended by 2009/1851, regs 3, 5, 36-38)

s 114 appl (mods)—SI 2005/1986, reg 4(2)(ba) (substituted SI 2009/1851, reg 5)

s 115 appl (mods)—SI 2005/1986, reg 4(2)(bb) (added by 2009/1851, reg 5)

am—Financial Services, 2012 c 21, sch 18 para 104(2)

s 117 appl (mods)—SI 2005/1986, reg 4(2)(bd) (added by 2009/1851, reg 5)

s 117A added (prosp)—Pensions, 2008 c 30, s 129, sch 10 paras 2, 3

s 119 appl (mods)—SI 2005/1986, reg 4(2)(be) (added by 2009/1851, reg 5)

s 121 appl—SI 2005/626, reg 8(3)

am—SIs 2005/2893, art 2; 2009/1941, art 2, sch 1

appl mods—SI 2011/245, sch 6 pt 2 para 4

rep in pt—Deregulation, 2015 c 20, sch 6 para 2(18)

Pt 2, Ch 3 (ss 126-181) appl—(EW) Civil Partnership, 2004 c 33, s 72(1), sch 5 pt 7 paras 30(3)(a), 37(1)(2)(a); (NI) ibid, s 196(1), sch 15 pt 6 paras 23(3)(a), 32(1)(2)(a)

s 126 appl—SI 2005/3377, reg 8(8)

mod—(prosp) Pensions, 2014 c 19, sch 20 para 17

am—(prosp) Pension Schemes, 2015 c 8, sch 2 para 31

s 134 appl (mods)—SIs 2005/449, reg 3(1); 2005/1986, reg 4(2)(bf) (added by 2009/1851, reg 5)

s 135 am—Pension Schemes, 2015 c 8, s 58(3); ibid, sch 4 para 39

s 138 mod—(prosp) Pensions, 2014 c 19, sch 20 para 14(3)

am—Pension Schemes, 2015 c 8, s 59(2)(3),(5)-(12); ibid, sch 4 para 40

rep in pt—Pension Schemes, 2015 c 8, s 59(4)

s 141 am—Pensions, 2011 c 19, sch 4 para 3

s 142 am—Pensions, 2011 c 19, sch 4 para 4

s 143 am—SI 2005/705, reg 2(1)-(3); Pensions, 2011 c 19, sch 4 para 5

s 143A added—Pensions, 2011 c 19, sch 4 para 6

mod—SI 2005/441, reg 68 (amended by SI 2012/1688, reg 2(20))

s 144 am—Pensions, 2011 c 19, sch 4 para 7

s 145 am—Pensions, 2011 c 19, sch 4 para 8

s 151 am—Pensions, 2011 c 19, sch 4 paras 9, 14

s 152 am—Pensions, 2011 c 19, sch 4 para 15(2)-(4)(6)(8)(9)

rep in pt—Pensions, 2011 c 19, sch 4 para 15(5)(7)

2004

c 35 *continued*

s 154 am—Pensions, 2011 c 19, sch 4 paras 10, 16(a); Public Service Pensions, 2013 c 25, sch 4 para 18

s 158 am—SI 2005/705, reg 2(4); Pensions, 2011 c 19, sch 4 para 11

s 160 am—Pensions, 2011 c 19, sch 4 paras 12, 17(2)(a)
     rep in pt—Pensions, 2011 c 19, sch 4 para 17(2)(b)

s 162 appl—Finance, 2005 c 7, s 102(4)
     mod—(prosp) Pensions, 2014 c 19, sch 20 para 13

s 168 appl (mods)—(NI) SI 2005/1986, reg 4(1)(2)(c)(3)(5), sch 1
     excl—SI 2006/1503, reg 32

s 168A added—Pensions, 2008 c 30, s 121

s 170 rep in pt—SI 2011/1730, art 7(a)
     am—SI 2011/1730, art 7(b)

s 172 rep in pt—Pensions, 2011 c 19, sch 4 para 17(3)
     am—Pensions, 2011 c 19, sch 4 para 16(b)

s 173 am—Pensions, 2008 c 30, ss 123(1)(2)(a), 129, sch 10 paras 2, 4
     rep in pt—Pensions, 2008 c 30, ss 123(1)(2)(b), 148, sch 11

s 174 appl (mods)—SI 2005/441, regs 14(2), 16(2), 63(2)

s 175 appl (mods)—SI 2005/441, regs 14(2), 16(2), 63(2)
     appl—SI 2006/672, reg 2
     mod—SI 2006/566, regs 3-5

s 176 appl (mods)—SI 2005/441, regs 14(2), 16(2), 63(2)

s 177 appl (mods)—SI 2005/441, regs 14(2), 16(2), 63(2)
     appl—SI 2006/742, art 2
     mod—SI 2006/2692, reg 2

s 178 appl (mods)—SI 2005/441, regs 14(2), 16(2), 63(2)
     appl—SI 2006/2692, regs 3, 4

s 179 appl (mods)—SI 2005/441, regs 14(2), 16(2), 63(2)

s 180 appl (mods)—SI 2005/441, regs 14(2), 16(2), 63(2)
     appl—SI 2006/566, reg 2

s 181 appl (mods)—SI 2005/441, regs 14(2), 16(2), 63(2)
     excl—SIs 2005/842, reg 12(2); 2006/580, reg 20 (amended by 2010/196, reg 8)

s 181A added —Pensions, 2008 c 30, s 129, sch 10 paras 2, 5

s 182 appl—Finance, 2005 c 7, s 102(5)(c)

ss 182-184 appl (mods)—SI 2005/2184, regs 10-20

s 185 appl (mods)—SI 2005/2184, regs 10-20
     appl—SI 2006/575, reg 44

s 186 appl (mods)—SI 2005/2184, regs 10-20
     appl—SI 2006/575, reg 44

s 188 am—(prosp) Pensions, 2008 c 30, s 129, sch 10 paras 2, 6

s 189A added (prosp)—Pensions, 2008 c 30, s 129, sch 10 paras 2, 7

ss 190-200 appl (mods)—SIs 2005/441, regs 14-27, 61-70; (NI) 1986, reg 4(1)(2)(d)(3)(5), sch 1

s 201 appl (mods)—SIs 2005/441, regs 14-27, 61-70; (NI) 1986, reg 4(1)(2)(d)(3)(5), sch 1
     rep in pt—SI 2009/1941, art 2, sch 1

s 202 appl (mods)—SI 2005/441, regs 14-27, 61-70

ss 203,204 appl (mods)—SIs 2005/441, regs 14-27, 61-70; (NI) 1986, reg 4(1)(2)(d)(3)(5), sch 1

ss 205-208 appl (mods)—SI 2005/441, regs 14-27, 61-70

s 209 appl—SI 2005/590, reg 2(8)
     appl (mods)—SIs 2005/441, regs 14-27, 61-70; 3256, regs 2, 3(1)
     am—(prosp) Pensions, 2008 c 30, s 129, sch 10 paras 2, 8

ss 210,211 appl (mods)—SI 2005/441, regs 14-27, 61-70

s 212 appl (mods)—SIs 2005/441, regs 14-27, 61-70; 3256, regs 2, 3(2)

s 212A added—SI 2008/817, arts 8, 10

s 213 appl (mods)—SIs 2005/441, regs 14-27, 61-70; 3256, regs 2, 3(3)

s 214 appl (mods)—SI 2005/441, regs 14-27, 61-70

s 215 appl (mods)—SIs 2005/441, regs 14-27, 61-70; 3256, regs 2, 3(4)

s 216 appl (mods)—SIs 2005/441, regs 14-27, 61-70; 3256, regs 2, 3(5)-(8)

s 217 appl (mods)—SIs 2005/441, regs 14-27, 61-70; 3256, regs 2, 3(5)-(8)
     am—Crime and Cts, 2013 c 22, sch 9 para 52

s 218 appl (mods)—SIs 2005/441, regs 14-27, 61-70; 3256, regs 2, 3(5)-(8)
     am—Crime and Cts, 2013 c 22, sch 9 para 52

ss 219, 220 appl (mods)—SI 2005/441, regs 14-27, 61-70

2004
c 35 *continued*

Pt 3 (ss 221-233) restr—SI 2005/3377, reg 17
appl (mods)—SI 2005/3377, reg 19, sch 2 paras 1, 3-5, 7, 10
excl—SIs 2008/2546, art 26, sch 3; 2014/1711, reg 63
appl—SI 2014/1711, reg 64
s 221 subst (prosp)—Pension Schemes, 2015 c 8, sch 2 para 32
appl (mods)—SI 2005/3380, reg 5(1)(a)
s 222 appl—SI 2005/3378, reg 4(11)
s 224 appl (mods)—SIs 2005/3377, reg 19, sch 2 para 6(1)(2)(a), 8, 11; 3380, reg 5(1)(b)
mod—SI 2014/1711, reg 65
s 226 appl (mods)—SIs 2005/3377, reg 19, sch 2 para 6(1)(2)(b)(3); 3380, reg 5(1)(c)(d)
s 227 appl (mods)—SIs 2005/3377, reg 19, sch 2 para 6(1)(2)(c), 9(5)(7)(8), 12(1)(2);
3380, reg 5(1)(c)(d)
s 229 appl (mods)—SI 2005/3377, reg 19, sch 2 paras 2, 8, 9(1)(2)(4)
s 230 am—Pensions, 2007 c 22, s 17, sch 5 para 9
rep in pt—Pensions, 2007 c 22, s 27, sch 7 pt 7
s 231 appl (mods)—SIs 2005/3377, reg 19, sch 2 para 6(1)(2)(d); 3380, reg 5(1)(e)
am—Pensions, 2008 c 30, s 132
s 231A added—SI 2006/1733, reg 2
ss 241, 242 appl (mods)—SI 2006/714, reg 5
s 243 am—SI 2009/1941, art 2, sch 1
s 248 am—SI 2009/1941, art 2, sch 1
appl (mods)—SI 2010/8, reg 2
s 248A added —Public Service Pensions, 2013 c 25, sch 4 para 19
s 249A added—SI 2005/3379, reg 2
am—SI 2009/1682, art 2, sch; Constitutional Reform and Governance, 2010 c 25, s
40, sch 6 para 46; Public Service Pensions, 2013 c 25, sch 4 para 20
s 249B added —Public Service Pensions, 2013 c 25, sch 4 para 21
s 251 am—Pensions, 2011 c 19, s 25
s 25, am—SI 2007/3014, reg 4
s 254 am—SI 2007/3014, reg 4; Pension Schemes, 2015 c 8, sch 2 para 33
s 256 am—Pensions, 2011 c 19, s 17; Pensions, 2014 c 19, sch 18 para 10; (prosp) ibid, sch
17 para 21
s 257 am—SI 2006/246, reg 20, sch 2
rep in pt—Pensions, 2007 c 22, ss 15, 27, sch 4 para 41, sch 7 pt 6
appl—(saving) SI 2008/2546, art 27
appl (mods)—SIs 2009/3226, art 12; 2009/814, art 4
s 258 appl (mods)—SIs 2008/2546, art 27; 2009/3226, art 12; 2009/814, art 4
am—Pensions, 2014 c 19, sch 13 para 73; (prosp) Pension Schemes, 2015 c 8, sch 2
para 34
s 259 appl (mods)—SI 2006/16, reg 2
s 261 appl (mods)—SI 2006/16, reg 2
s 273 am—Pensions, 2007 c 22, s 16
ss 284, 285 rep in pt—Pensions, 2007 c 22, s 27, sch 7 pt 6
s 286 appl (mods)—SI 2005/441, reg 76 (Pt 10)
appl—SI 2014/1711, reg 72(3)
am—Pensions, 2007 c 22, s 18(1)-(3); (pt prosp) Pensions, 2008 c 30, s
124(1)-(5)(7)-(10); Pensions, 2011 c 19, ss 23(1), 24; (prosp) Pension Schemes,
2015 c 8, sch 2 para 35
rep in pt—Pensions, 2008 c 30, ss 124(1)(6), 148, sch 11
s 286A added—(spec retrosp effect) Pensions, 2008 c 30, s 125(1)(2)
s 287 am—SI 2007/3014, reg 4
excl—SI 2014/1711, reg 77(1)(2)
ss 289, 290 am—SI 2007/3014, reg 4
s 291 am—SI 2007/3014, reg 4; Pension Schemes, 2015 c 8, sch 2 para 36
s 292A added (pt prosp)—Pensions, 2011 c 19, s 18
rep—Pensions, 2014 c 19, s 38(3)(a)
ss 293-295 am—SI 2007/3014, reg 4
s 299 see—(EW) SI 2014/560, sch 2 para 5(ggg); (S) SI 2014/3229, sch 2 para 6(qq))
ss 303-305 mod—Pensions, 2008 c 30, s 144A
s 306 am—Pensions, 2008 c 30, s 126, sch 9 paras 1, 11; SI 2009/1941, art 2, sch 1
s 307 appl—SI 2005/842, regs 16(3), 17
am—Pensions, 2011 c 19, s 31(2); (prosp) Pension Schemes, 2015 c 8, sch 2 para 37
s 310 am—SI 2010/22, art 5, sch 2

2004
c 35 *continued*

s 316 am—Pensions, 2008 c 30, ss 125(3), 126, sch 9 paras 1, 5, 12; Pensions, 2011 c 19, sch 4 para 18(3)(4); (prosp) Pensions, 2014 c 19, sch 20 para 5
    rep in pt—Pensions, 2011 c 19, sch 4 para 18(2)
s 318 appl (mods)—SI 2005/277, reg 11
    rep in pt—SI 2010/22, art 5, sch 2; (prosp) Pension Schemes, 2015 c 8, sch 2 para 38(2)(b)
    am—Public Service Pensions, 2013 c 25, sch 4 para 22; Pension Schemes, 2015 c 8, s 60(3); ibid, sch 4 para 41; (prosp) ibid, sch 2 para 38(2)(a)(3)
s 323 am—(pt prosp) Pensions, 2008 c 30, ss 63(2), 129, sch 10 paras 2, 9
sch 1 am—(transtl provns) Pensions, 2008 c 30, s 133(1)-(4)(6)
    rep in pt—Pensions, 2008 c 30, ss 133(1)(5), 148, sch 11
sch 2 am—SIs 2005/703, reg 5; 2005/2113, reg 2(2)(3); 2006/349, reg 20; Pensions, 2007 c 22, s 14(7); Pensions, 2008 c 30, ss 126, 131(2), sch 9 paras 1, 13; SI 2010/22, art 5, sch 2; Pensions, 2014 c 19, sch 19 para 10
sch 3 am—Income Tax (Trading and Other Income), 2005 c 5, s 882(1), sch 1 pt 2 paras 657, 658(b); SIs 2006/745, art 18; 2937, art 2; Charities, 2006 c 50, s 75, sch 8 para 206; Companies, 2006 c 46, s 1275(7); Income Tax, 2007 c 3, s 1027, sch 1 paras 486, 487; SIs 2009/1941, art 2, sch 1; 2010/22, art 5, sch 2; Charities, 2011 c 25, sch 7 para 101; Financial Services, 2012 c 21, sch 18 para 104(3); SIs 2012/691, art 2(1); 3006, art 84; 2013/504, reg 23(2)
    rep in pt—Income Tax (Trading and Other Income), 2005 c 5, ss 882(1), 884, sch 1 pt 2 paras 657, 658(a), sch 3; Income Tax, 2007 c 3, s 1031, sch 3; SI 2009/1941, art 2, sch 1
sch 4 rep—SI 2010/22, art 5, sch 2
sch 5 appl (mods)—SIs 2005/650, reg 18; 669, reg 26; 2005/1986, reg 4(2)(da)
    appl—SIs 2006/597, regs 3, 6; 2014/1711, reg 42(1) 53 57
    am—Pensions, 2008 c 30, s 123(1)(3)-(5)
sch 6 appl (mods)—SIs 2005/441, regs 26(3), 70(2)(3); 277, regs 2, 10(4)(5)
sch 7 appl (mods)—SIs 2005/441, regs 26(3), 70(2)(3); 277, regs 2, 10(4)(5); 449, reg 3(2)-(4)
    am—SI 2005/705, reg 3; Statistics and Registration Service, 2007 c 18, s 60, sch 3 para 15; (pt prosp) Pensions, 2008 c 30, s 122, sch 8 paras 1-18; Pensions, 2011 c 19, s 20, sch 4 paras 19, 37; ibid, sch 4 paras 22-25, 26(1)(b)(2), 27, 28; Pensions, 2014 c 19, s 51; (prosp) ibid, sch 20 paras 2, 3, 6; Pension Schemes, 2015 c 8, sch 4 para 42
    appl—SI 2006/347, art 2; Pensions, 2008 c 30, s 116, sch 5 para 17(5); SI 2014/1711, reg 42(1) 53 57
    mod—SI 2006/1690, reg 3; (prosp) Pensions, 2014 c 19, sch 20 para 8(1)-(4); (prosp) ibid, sch 20 para 12
    rep in pt—Pensions, 2011 c 19, sch 4 para 26(1)(a)
sch 8 rep in pt—Income Tax (Trading and Other Income), 2005 c 5, ss 882(1), 884, sch 1 pt 2 paras 657, 659(a), sch 3; Income Tax, 2007 c 3, s 1031, sch 3; SI 2009/1941, art 2, sch 1
    am—Income Tax (Trading and Other Income), 2005 c 5, s 882(1), sch 1 pt 2 paras 657, 659(b); SI 2006/2937, art 3; Charities, 2006 c 50, s 75, sch 8 para 207; Income Tax, 2007 c 3, s 1027, sch 1 paras 486, 488; SI 2010/22, art 5, sch 2; Charities, 2011 c 25, sch 7 para 102; Financial Services, 2012 c 21, sch 18 para 104(4); SIs 2012/3006, art 85; 2013/504, reg 23(3)
    appl (mods) —(NI) SI 2005/1986, reg 4(1)(2)(e)(3)(5), sch 1
sch 9 mod—SI 2005/600, reg 3
    am—SIs 2005/600, reg 4(a)(b); 2113, reg 3; 2006/685, reg 2; 2007/771, reg 8; 2010/560, reg 2; Pensions, 2011 c 19, sch 4 para 13; SIs 2011/731, reg 35; 2014/1954, reg 4
sch 10 am—Pensions, 2008 c 30, s 63(1)
    rep in pt—(pt prosp) Welfare Reform, 2012 c 5, sch 14 pt 1
sch 11 rep in pt—Pensions, 2007 c 22, s 27, sch 7 pt 1; (prosp) Pensions, 2011 c 19, sch 2 para 4(c)
sch 12 rep in pt—SI 2006/745, art 18; Pension Schemes, 2015 c 8, s 38(7)
sch 14 am—Nat Health Service (Conseq Provns), 2006 c 43, s 2, sch 1 para 269
c 36   **Civil Contingencies**
    saved—Govt of Wales, 2006 c 32, s 94, sch 5 para 3
    ss 1-3 am—SI 2010/976, art 5, sch 3
    ss 5-7 am—SI 2010/976, art 5, sch 3

2004
c 36 *continued*
   ss 9, 10 am—SI 2010/976, art 5, sch 3
   s 12A added—SI 2010/976, art 5, sch 3
   s 13 am—SI 2010/976, art 5, sch 3
   s 14A added—SI 2010/976, art 5, sch 3
   s 15 am—SI 2010/976, art 5, sch 3
   s 15A added—SI 2010/976, art 5, sch 3
   ss 17, 18 am—SI 2010/976, art 5, sch 3
   s 25 rep—SI 2013/2042, sch para 29
   s 28 rep—Finance, 2006 c 25, s 178, sch 26
   sch 1 am—SIs 2005/2043, art 2(a)(b); 3050, reg 3, sch 1 pt 1 para 4(a)(b); Nat Health
     Service (Conseq Provns), 2006 c 43, s 2, sch 1 para 271; SI 2011/1223, art 2;
     Civil Aviation, 2012 c 19, sch 9 para 16(2)(3); Health and Social Care, 2012 c 7,
     sch 5 para 132(2)(a)(3)(a), sch 7 para 16; Energy, 2013 c 32, sch 12 para 81; (S)
     SSI 2013/119, sch 3 para 1; (W) SI 2013/755 (W 90), sch 2 para 429;
     Infrastructure, 2015 c 7, sch 1 para 152
     rep in pt—Marine and Coastal Access, 2009 c 23, ss 312, 321, sch 22 pt 8; (pt prosp)
      Health and Social Care, 2012 c 7, sch 5 para 132(2)(b)(3)(b), sch 14 para 100
   sch 2 rep in pt—Equality, 2010 c 15, sch 27 pt 1A
   sch 3 rep—Finance, 2006 c 25, s 178, sch 26
 c 37 **Hunting**
   s 7 rep—Serious Organised Crime and Police, 2005 c 15, ss 111, 174(2), sch 7 pt 1 para 37,
     sch 17 pt 2
4th session of 53rd Parliament
 c 38 *Appropriation*—rep Appropriation (No 2), 2006 c 24, s 4, sch 3

2005

 c 1 **Electoral Registration (Northern Ireland)**
 c 2 *Prevention of Terrorism*—rep Terrorism Prevention and Investigation Measures, 2011 c 23, s
   1
 c 3 *Appropriation*—rep Appropriation (No 2), 2007 c 10, s 4, sch 3
 c 4 **Constitutional Reform**
   s 3 am—Tribunals, Cts and Enforcement, 2007 c 15, s 1; Crime and Cts, 2013 c 22, sch 14
     para 13(1)
     rep in pt—SI 2008/2833, art 6, sch 3
   s 5 am—Crim Justice and Cts, 2015 c 2, s 81
   s 7 am—Crime and Cts, 2013 c 22, sch 9 para 42, sch 10 para 97
   s 8 am—Police and Justice, 2006 c 48, s 52, sch 14 para 61
   s 16 excl—SI 2013/2192, reg 3
   s 23 am—Crime and Cts, 2013 c 22, sch 13 para 2(2)(3)(5)
     rep in pt—Crime and Cts, 2013 c 22, sch 13 para 2(4)
   s 25 am—Tribunals, Cts and Enforcement, 2007 c 15, s 50, sch 10 para 41
     rep in pt—Tribunals, Cts and Enforcement, 2007 c 15, s 146, sch 23
   s 26 am—Crime and Cts, 2013 c 22, sch 13 paras 3, 7
   s 27 am—SIs 2007/1388, art 3, sch 1; 2010/976, art 12, sch 14; Crime and Cts, 2013 c 22,
     sch 13 paras 4(1)(2), 7(6)(7) (9)
     rep in pt—Crime and Cts, 2013 c 22, sch 13 para 7(1)(a)
   s 27A added—Crime and Cts, 2013 c 22, sch 13 para 5
   s 27B added—Crime and Cts, 2013 c 22, sch 13 para 6
   ss 28-31 rep —Crime and Cts, 2013 c 22, sch 13 para 7(1)(b)
   s 39 am—Crim Justice and Cts, 2015 c 2, s 82
   s 40 rep in pt—(prosp) Courts Reform (S), 2014 asp 18, sch 5 para 33; SI 2015/700, sch
     para 13
   s 41 am—SIs 2007/1388, art 3, sch 1; 2009/2958, art 7; 2011/1011 (W 150), art 9
   ss 45, 46 mod—SI 2006/227, art 2
   s 48 am—Crime and Cts, 2013 c 22, ss 29(1), 30(2)
   s 49 am—Crime and Cts, 2013 c 22, s 29(3)-(5)
   ss 51A-51E added—Crime and Cts, 2013 c 22, s 30(1)
   s 54 am—SI 2007/1388, art 3, sch 1
   s 58 rep in pt—SI 2010/976, art 27
   s 60 rep in pt—Crime and Cts, 2013 c 22, sch 13 para 7(1)(b)
   s 63 am—Crime and Cts, 2013 c 22, sch 13 para 10
   s 66 am—Crime and Cts, 2013 c 22, sch 13 para 55
   s 67 am—Crime and Cts, 2013 c 22, sch 13 para 56

2005
c 4 *continued*

    s 69 am—Crime and Cts, 2013 c 22, sch 13 para 57
    s 70 am—Crime and Cts, 2013 c 22, sch 13 para 58(2)(3)(5), 82(2)
        rep in pt—Crime and Cts, 2013 c 22, sch 13 para 58(4)(6)
    s 71 subst by ss 71-71B—Crime and Cts, 2013 c 22, sch 13 para 82(3)
    ss 71-75 rep—Crime and Cts, 2013 c 22, sch 13 para 53(2)(a)
    ss 75A-75G added—Tribunals, Cts and Enforcement, 2007 c 15, s 2, sch 1 para 4
    s 75A am—Crime and Cts, 2013 c 22, sch 13 para 59
    s 75B am—Crime and Cts, 2013 c 22, sch 13 para 60
    ss 75C-75G rep—Crime and Cts, 2013 c 22, sch 13 para 53(2)(b)
    s 76 am—Crime and Cts, 2013 c 22, sch 13 para 61
    s 78 am—Crime and Cts, 2013 c 22, sch 13 para 62
    s 79 am—Crime and Cts, 2013 c 22, sch 13 para 63
    ss 80-84 rep—Crime and Cts, 2013 c 22, sch 13 para 53(2)(c)
    s 85 am—Tribunals, Cts and Enforcement, 2007 c 15, s 53(1)(3)(4); Crime and Cts, 2013 c
        22, sch 13 para 64; ibid, sch 14 para 3(4)
    s 86 am—Crime and Cts, 2013 c 22, sch 13 para 65
    s 87 am—Crime and Cts, 2013 c 22, sch 13 para 66
    s 88 am—Crime and Cts, 2013 c 22, sch 13 para 67(a)(b)
        rep in pt—Crime and Cts, 2013 c 22, sch 13 para 67(c)(d)
    ss 89-93 rep—Crime and Cts, 2013 c 22, sch 13 para 53(2)(d)
    s 94 subst—Crime and Cts, 2013 c 22, sch 13 para 68
    s 94A added—Tribunals, Cts and Enforcement, 2007 c 15, s 53(1)(2)
        am—Crime and Cts, 2013 c 22, sch 13 para 40
    s 94AA added—Crime and Cts, 2013 c 22, sch 14 para 3(3)
    s 94B added—Tribunals, Cts and Enforcement, 2007 c 15, s 53(1)(2)
        rep in pt—SI 2008/2833, art 6, sch 3
        am—Crime and Cts, 2013 c 22, sch 13 para 48
    s 94C added—Crime and Cts, 2013 c 22, sch 13 para 53(3)
    s 95 am—Tribunals, Cts and Enforcement, 2007 c 15, s 2, sch 1 para 5; Crime and Cts,
        2013 c 22, sch 13 para 69
    s 96 rep—Crime and Cts, 2013 c 22, sch 13 para 53(2)(e)
    s 97 am—Tribunals, Cts and Enforcement, 2007 c 15, s 53(1)(5)-(7); Crime and Cts, 2013 c
        22, sch 13 para 70(2)(b)(3)
        rep in pt—Crime and Cts, 2013 c 22, sch 13 para 70(2)(a)
    s 99 am—Crime and Cts, 2013 c 22, sch 13 para 71(1)
    s 100 am—Crime and Cts, 2013 c 22, sch 13 para 72
    s 101 am—Crime and Cts, 2013 c 22, sch 13 para 73
    s 102 am—Crime and Cts, 2013 c 22, sch 13 para 74
    s 103 am—Crime and Cts, 2013 c 22, sch 13 para 75
    s 104 am—Crime and Cts, 2013 c 22, sch 13 para 76
    s 105 am—Crime and Cts, 2013 c 22, sch 13 para 77
    s 107 am—SI 2013/602, sch 2 para 45
    ss 108-121 appl (mod)—Coroners and Justice, 2009 c 25, s 23, sch 3 para 14
    s 108 appl—SI 2006/676, reg 39
    s 109 am—Tribunals, Cts and Enforcement, 2007 c 15, s 48, sch 8 paras 62, 63
    ss 110-113 appl—SI 2006/676, reg 44
        appl (mods)—SI 2014/1919, reg 22
    s 122 am—Crime and Cts, 2013 c 22, sch 13 para 26
    s 132 am—Crim Justice and Cts, 2015 c 2, s 83(1)
    s 134 saved—Northern Ireland, 2009 c 3, s 2, sch 6 para 11(2)
    s 135 saved—Northern Ireland, 2009 c 3, s 2, sch 6 para 11(2)(3)
    s 137A added—Crime and Cts, 2013 c 22, sch 13 para 11
    s 139 am—Crime and Cts, 2013 c 22, sch 13 para 7(8)
    s 144 am—Crime and Cts, 2013 c 22, sch 13 paras 7(9)(10), 27, 78
    sch 1 rep in pt—(prosp) Coroners and Justice, 2009 c 25, s 178, sch 23 pt 1
        mod—Matrimonial and Family Proceedings, 1984 c 42 s 31D(7)
        excl—Matrimonial and Family Proceedings, 1984 c 42 s 31D(8)
    sch 2 am—Crime and Cts, 2013 c 22, sch 13 para 25
    sch 3 rep in pt—Tribunals, Cts and Enforcement, 2007 c 15, s 146, sch 23
    sch 4 rep in pt—Nat Health Service (Conseq Provns), 2006 c 43, s 6, sch 4; Legal Services,
        2007 c 29, s 210, sch 23; Tribunals, Cts and Enforcement, 2007 c 15, s 146,
        sch 23 pt 1; (prosp) ibid, sch 23 pt 6; SI 2008/2833, art 6, sch 3; (prosp)
        Coroners and Justice, 2009 c 25, s 178, sch 23 pt 1; ibid, s 178, sch 23 pt 4; SI

2005
c 4 *continued*

2009/1307, art 5, sch 4; SIs 2010/22, art 5, sch 4 pts 1, 2; 2012/1206, sch para 9; 2398, sch 1 para 9, sch 2 para 9; Crime and Cts, 2013 c 22, sch 13 paras 34(7), 89(2)(j); ibid, sch 9 para 141, sch 10 para 99 Table; SI 2013/686, sch 1 para 8(2); (prosp) Infrastructure, 2015 c 7, sch 5 paras 8(6), 12(2); Deregulation, 2015 c 20, sch 6 para 2(19)(a)

sch 5 rep in pt—Tribunals, Cts and Enforcement, 2007 c 15, s 146, sch 23 pt 1; Northern Ireland, 2009 c 3, s 2, sch 5 para 6

sch 6 rep in pt—Budget Responsibility and Nat Audit, 2011 c 4, sch 5 para 25

sch 7 am—Nat Health Service (Conseq Provns), 2006 c 43, s 2, sch 1 para 273; Income Tax, 2007 c 3, s 1027, sch 1 paras 489, 490; Tribunals, Cts and Enforcement, 2007 c 15, ss 48, 144, sch 8 paras 62, 64(b); (prosp) ibid, sch 8 para 64(a); Loc Govt and Public Involvement in Health, 2007 c 28, s 220, sch 16 paras 14, 15; Legal Services, 2007 c 29, s 199; SIs 2007/275, art 5; 2007/2128, art 8, sch; 2008/2833, art 6, sch 3; Northern Ireland, 2009 c 3, s 2, sch 5 para 7(1)(3)-(6); Coroners and Justice, 2009 c 25, s 134; SI 2010/976, art 15, sch 18; Pensions, 2011 c 19, sch 5 para 3; Crime and Cts, 2013 c 22, sch 13 para 32(4), 35(6), 36(6), 37(7), 38(4), 79; Public Service Pensions, 2013 c 25, sch 8 para 29; Marriage (Same Sex Couples), 2013 c 30, s 8(6); SI 2013/1036, sch 1 para 240; Intellectual Property, 2014 c 18, s 10(10)

rep in pt—Nat Health Service (Conseq Provns), 2006 c 43, s 6, sch 4; Commons, 2006 c 26, s 53, sch 6; SI 2006/2805, art 18, sch 2; Tribunals, Cts and Enforcement, 2007 c 15, s 86, sch 14 para 48, sch 23 pt 4; Health and Social Care, 2008 c 14, s 166, sch 15; SI 2008/2833, art 6, sch 3; Northern Ireland, 2009 c 3, s 2, sch 5 para 7(1)-(2); (prosp) Coroners and Justice, 2009 c 25, s 178, sch 23 pt 1; SIs 2009/1307, art 5, sch 1; 2010/22, art 5, sch 2; 2010/976, art 15, sch 18; Financial Services, 2012 c 21, sch 19; SI 2013/686, sch 1 para 8(3); Co-operative and Community Benefit Societies, 2014 c 14, sch 7

sch 8 rep in pt—Crime and Cts, 2013 c 22, sch 13 para 7(1)(a)(11)(12)

sch 9 rep in pt—Govt of Wales, 2006 c 32, s 163, sch 12; Loc Transport, 2008 c 26, s 131, sch 7; SI 2009/1836, art 5, schs 2, 3; Financial Services, 2012 c 21, sch 19; Legal Aid, Sentencing and Punishment of Offenders, 2012 c 10, sch 5 pt 2; SI 2013/686, sch 1 para 8(4)

am—Police and Justice, 2006 c 48, s 42, sch 13 para 35

sch 11 rep in pt—(prosp) Safeguarding Vulnerable Groups, 2006 c 47, s 63, sch 10; (prosp) Companies, 2006 c 46, s 129, sch 16; Armed Forces, 2006 c 52, s 378, sch 17; Legal Services, 2007 c 29, s 210, sch 23; Health and Social Care, 2008 c 14, s 166, sch 15; SIs 2009/1307, art 5, sch 4; 2009/1941, art 2, sch 2; Corporation Tax, 2010 c 4, s 1181, sch 3 pt 1; SI 2013/294, art 2 sch; Deregulation, 2015 c 20, sch 6 para 2(19)(b)

sch 12 am—Tribunals, Cts and Enforcement, 2007 c 15, s 48, sch 8 paras 62, 65; SI 2012/2404, sch 2 para 52(2); Crime and Cts, 2013 c 22, sch 13 paras 17, 19, 20-24, 80, 82(4)

rep in pt—Tribunals, Cts and Enforcement, 2007 c 15, s 146, sch 23; Crime and Cts, 2013 c 22, sch 13 para 18

sch 13 am—SI 2012/2404, sch 2 para 52(3)

sch 14 am—Nat Health Service (Conseq Provns), 2006 c 43, s 2, sch 1 para 274; SI 2006/1551, art 2; Charities, 2006 c 50, s 75, sch 8 para 208; Armed Forces, 2006 c 52, s 378, sch 16 para 244; Income Tax, 2007 c 3, s 1027, sch 1 paras 489, 491; Tribunals, Cts and Enforcement, 2007 c 15, s 48, sch 8 paras 62, 66; ibid, ss 57(7), 59; Loc Govt and Public Involvement in Health, 2007 c 28, s 220, sch 16 paras 14, 16; (pt prosp) Coroners and Justice, 2009 c 25, s 177, sch 21 para 51; SIs 2009/1307, art 5, sch 1; 2010/490, reg 132, sch 6; Crime and Cts, 2013 c 22, sch 13 paras 29(2)(3)(5), 41(2)(3), 49; ibid, sch 14 paras 3(1), 13(2); (pt prosp) ibid, sch 13 para 41(4); SI 2014/2040, art 2

rep in pt—Commons, 2006 c 26, s 53, sch 6; Armed Forces, 2006 c 52, s 378, sch 17; SI 2006/2805, art 18, sch 2; Tribunals, Cts and Enforcement, 2007 c 15, ss 56, 146, sch 11 para 15, sch 23 pt 2; (pt prosp) sch 23 pt 1; SI 2008/2833, art 6, sch 3; SIs 2009/56, art 3, sch 1 para 436; 2009/1834, art 4, schs 1, 4; 2010/21, art 5, schs 1, 2; Crime and Cts, 2013 c 22, sch 13 paras 29(4), 41(5)(6), 89(2)(k); SIs 2013/294, art 2 sch; 2013/686, sch 1 para 8(5); 2013/1036, sch 1 para 241; 2014/3248, sch 3 pt 2; Deregulation, 2015 c 20, sch 6 para 22(14)

2005

c 5   Income Tax (Trading and Other Income)
am—Commrs for Revenue and Customs, 2005 c 11, s 50(6), sch 4 paras 131,
    132(1)(2)(3)(b)-(g)(i), 133
appl—Income Tax, 2007 c 3, ss 513(4), 959, 963; Corporation Tax, 2010 c 4, ss 332(2),
    817(b); Taxation (International and Other Provns), 2010 c 8, ss 220(2), 681BD(3))
appl (mods)—Income Tax, 2007 c 3, ss 414, 467, 474, 573, 576, 578, 597, 711, 970; SI
    2009/470, reg 57; Corporation Tax, 2010 c 4, s 996(2)
saved—Taxation and Chargeable Gains 1992 c 12, s 151X(4); Income Tax, 2007 c 3, s 962;
    ibid, s 564V(4)
mod—Income Tax, 2007 c 3, s 988; Corporation Tax, 2009 c 4, s 294(2)
excl—Corporation Tax, 2009 c 4, s 3; Taxation (International and Other Provns), 2010 c 8,
    ss 79(2)(a), 174(2)(b)
s 1 rep in pt—Income Tax, 2007 c 3, ss 1027, 1031, sch 1 paras 492, 493, sch 3
    am—Finance (No 3), 2010 c 33, s 1, sch 1 paras 30, 31
s 4 rep in pt—Corporation Tax, 2009 c 4, ss 1322, 1326, sch 1 para 647(1)(3)(b), sch 3 pt 1
s 6 am—Finance, 2013 c 29, sch 45 para 75
s 12 am—Income Tax, 2007 c 3, s 1027, sch 1 paras 492, 494
s 13 am—Income Tax, 2007 c 3, s 1027, sch 1 paras 492, 495
    rep in pt—Income Tax, 2007 c 3, s 1031, sch 3
s 16 am—Taxation (International and Other Provns), 2010 c 8, s 374, sch 8 paras 189, 190
    appl—Taxation (International and Other Provns), 2010 c 8, s 206(3)(b)(4)(b)
s 17 am—Income Tax, 2007 c 3, s 1027, sch 1 paras 492, 496; Finance, 2013 c 29, sch 45
    para 76
s 22 am—Corporation Tax, 2009 c 4, s 1322, sch 1 para 588
s 23 am—Finance (No 3), 2010 c 33, s 1, sch 1 paras 30, 32
s 25 am—SI 2008/954, arts 35, 36; Finance, 2013 c 29, sch 4 para 3
s 25A added—Finance, 2013 c 29, sch 4 para 4
s 31 am—Finance, 2007 c 11, s 67(1)-(3)(7); Finance, 2013 c 29, s 78(1); ibid, sch 4 para
    49; ibid, sch 5 para 3
    rep in pt—Finance, 2009 c 10, s 30, sch 11 paras 34, 35
Pt 2 Ch 3A (ss 31A-31F) added—Finance, 2013 c 29, sch 4 para 5
s 32A added—Finance, 2013 c 29, sch 4 para 7
s 33A added—Finance, 2013 c 29, sch 4 para 8
s 38 am—Finance, 2007 c 11, s 34(7)(8)(13); Finance, 2013 c 29, sch 4 para 9
s 39 am—Finance, 2007 c 11, s 34(7)(9)(13); Finance, 2011 c 11, sch 2 para 36
s 40 am—Finance, 2011 c 11, sch 2 para 37
s 41 am—Finance, 2007 c 11, s 34(7)(10)(13); Finance, 2011 c 11, sch 2 para 38
s 42 am—Finance, 2007 c 11, s 34(7)(11)(13)
s 44 am—Finance, 2011 c 11, sch 2 para 39
s 48 am—Corporation Tax, 2009 c 4, s 1322, sch 1 para 589(1) (2)(4); Finance, 2009 c 10,
    s 30, sch 11 paras 34, 36(1)-(4); Finance, 2012 c 14, sch 16 para 126
    rep in pt—Corporation Tax, 2009 c 4, ss 1322, 1326, sch 1 para 589(1)(3), sch 3 pt 1;
    Finance, 2009 c 10, s 30, sch 11 paras 34, 36(1)(5)(6)
s 49 am—Corporation Tax, 2009 c 4, s 1322, sch 1 para 590; Finance, 2009 c 10, s 30, sch
    11 paras 34, 37; Taxation (International and Other Provns), 2010 c 8, s 374, sch 8
    paras 253, 254(3)
    rep in pt—Finance, 2009 c 10, s 30, sch 11 paras 34, 37(1)(2)(a)(b), (4)(a)(b)(5);
    Taxation (International and Other Provns), 2010 c 8, ss 374, 378, sch 8 paras
    253, 254(2), sch 10
s 50 rep—Finance, 2009 c 10, s 30, sch 11 paras 34, 38
ss 50A, 50B added—Finance, 2009 c 10, s 30, sch 11 paras 34, 39
s 51 rep—Income Tax, 2007 c 3, s 1027, sch 1 paras 492, 497, sch 3
s 51A added—Finance, 2013 c 29, sch 4 para 10
s 52 am—Income Tax, 2007 c 3, s 1027, sch 1 paras 492, 498
s 54 am—SIs 2009/56, art 3, sch 1 para 438; 2009/571, art 8, sch 1; 2010/530, art 2, sch;
    2014/1283, sch para 5
s 55A added—Finance, 2008 c 9, s 73(4)
    am—Finance, 2013 c 29, sch 4 para 11
s 55B added—Finance, 2010 c 13, s 27, sch 5 para 2(1)
s 56 am—Finance, 2013 c 29, sch 4 para 50
s 56A added—Finance, 2013 c 29, sch 4 para 13
s 57A added—SI 2009/730, art 3
s 57B added—Finance, 2013 c 29, sch 4 para 14
s 58 ext—Finance, 2005 c 7, ss 51(3)(5), 56

2005

c 5 s 58 *continued*

        mod—Income Tax 2007 c 3, s 564N(3)

        am—Finance, 2013 c 29, sch 4 para 15

s 60 am—Corporation Tax, 2009 c 4, s 1322, sch 1 para 591

s 61 am—Finance, 2013 c 29, sch 28 para 2

s 64 am—Corporation Tax, 2009 c 4, s 1322, sch 1 para 592

s 65 am—Corporation Tax, 2009 c 4, s 1322, sch 1 para 593

s 66 am—Corporation Tax, 2009 c 4, s 1322, sch 1 para 594

s 67 am—Corporation Tax, 2009 c 4, s 1322, sch 1 para 595(1)-(3)

s 71 am—Corporation Tax, 2009 c 4, s 1322, sch 1 para 596; SI 2010/1158, art 5, sch 2;
        Educ, 2011 c 21, sch 13 para 14; SI 2012/976, sch para 15

s 72 am—Finance, 2013 c 29, sch 4 para 16

s 75 rep in pt—SI 2009/2035, art 2, sch

s 79 rep in pt—Corporation Tax, 2009 c 4, ss 1322, 1326, sch 1 para 597, sch 3 pt 1

s 79A added—Corporation Tax, 2009 c 4, s 1322, sch 1 para 598

s 80 am—Corporation Tax, 2009 c 4, s 1322, sch 1 para 599

ss 86A, 86B added—Finance, 2015 c 11, sch 5 para 1

s 87 am—Income Tax, 2007 c 3, s 1027, sch 1 paras 492, 499

s 88 am—(prosp) Finance (No 2), 2005 c 22, s 14(1)(2)(4)(5); Corporation Tax, 2009 c 4, s
        1322, sch 1 para 600

        rep in pt—(prosp) Finance (No 2), 2005 c 22, ss 14(1)(3)(5), 70, sch 11 pt 2(2), Note 1

s 94 am—SI 2005/3229, regs 183, 184

s 94A added—Taxation (International and Other Provns), 2010 c 8, s 371, sch 7 paras 27,
        28

        am—Finance, 2013 c 29, sch 4 para 17; Finance, 2014 c 26, sch 8 para
        140(3)(a)(b)(4)(5)

        rep in pt—Finance, 2014 c 26, sch 8 para 140(2)(a)(b)(3)(c)

s 94AA added—Finance, 2014 c 26, sch 17 para 3(2)

Pt 2 Ch 5A (ss 94B-94I) added—Finance, 2013 c 29, sch 5 para 2

s 95A added—Finance, 2013 c 29, sch 4 para 19

s 96A added—Finance, 2013 c 29, sch 4 para 20

ss 97A, 97B added—Finance, 2013 c 29, sch 4 para 21

s 100 am—Corporation Tax, 2010 c 4, s 1177, sch 1 paras 444, 445; Taxation
        (International and Other Provns), 2010 c 8, s 374, sch 8 paras 253, 255

s 105 am—Finance, 2013 c 29, sch 4 para 22

Pt 2 Ch 6A (ss 106A-106E) added—Finance, 2013 c 29, sch 4 para 23

s 108 rep in pt—Income Tax, 2007 c 3, s 1027, sch 1 paras 492, 500, sch 3; SI 2012/964,
        art 3(1), sch

        excl—Income Tax, 2007 c 3, s 445(1)(a)

        am—Corporation Tax, 2010 c 4, s 1177, sch 1 paras 444, 446; Finance, 2011 c 11,
        sch 3 para 6

s 111A added—Finance, 2013 c 29, sch 4 para 24

s 128 rep—SI 2009/2035, art 2, sch

s 130 rep in pt—Finance, 2006 c 25, s 178, sch 26, pt 3(4), Note 1

s 130A added—Finance, 2013 c 29, sch 4 para 25

s 131 rep—Finance, 2006 c 25, s 178, sch 26, pt 3(4), Note 1

s 132 rep in pt—Finance, 2006 c 25, s 178, sch 26, pt 3(4), Note 1

        appl (mods)—SI 2007/1050, reg 12

s 134 rep in pt—Finance, 2006 c 25, s 178, sch 26, pt 3(4)

        excl—Finance, 2006 c 25, ss 47(1), 53

s 135 excl—Finance, 2006 c 25, ss 47(1), 53

        rep in pt—Finance, 2006 c 25, s 178, sch 26, pt 3(4), Note 1

        am—Finance, 2006 c 25, s 178, sch 26, pt 3(4), Note 2(a)(b)

ss 136-144 rep—Finance, 2006 c 25, s 178, sch 26, pt 3(4), Note 1

s 144A added—Finance, 2013 c 29, sch 4 para 26

s 146 am—Wireless Telegraphy, 2006 c 36, s 123, sch 7 para 37

s 148ZA added—Finance, 2013 c 29, sch 4 para 27

s 148A added—Finance, 2006 c 25, s 81, sch 8 para 13

        excl—Finance, 2008 c 9, s 55, sch 20 para 11(2); Finance, 2009 c 10, s 65, sch 33
        para 5

s 148B added—Finance, 2006 c 25, s 81, sch 8 para 13

        excl—Finance, 2008 c 9, s 55, sch 20 para 11(8); Finance, 2009 c 10, s 65, sch 33
        para 7

s 148C added—Finance, 2006 c 25, s 81, sch 8 para 13

2005
c 5 *continued*

ss 148D-148F added—Finance, 2006 c 25, s 81, sch 8 para 13
s 148D subst—Corporation Tax, 2010 c 4, s 1177, sch 1 paras 444, 447
ss 148DA, 148DB added—Corporation Tax, 2010 c 4, s 1177, sch 1 paras 444, 448
s 148E subst—Corporation Tax, 2010 c 4, s 1177, sch 1 paras 444, 449
ss 148EA, 148EB added—Corporation Tax, 2010 c 4, s 1177, sch 1 paras 444, 450
s 148F added (retrosp effect)—Finance, 2009 c 10, s 65, sch 33 paras 2, 3
    subst—Corporation Tax, 2010 c 4, s 1177, sch 1 paras 444, 451
s 148FA added—(spec retrosp effect) Finance, 2008 c 9, s 55, sch 20 para 10(1)(2)(5)
s 148FB added—(spec retrosp effect) Finance, 2008 c 9, s 55, sch 20 para 10(1)(3)(6)
s 148FC added—(spec retrosp effect) Finance, 2008 c 9, s 55, sch 20 para 10(1)(4)(7)
ss 148G-148J added—Finance, 2006 c 25, s 81, sch 8 para 13
s 148K added—Finance, 2013 c 29, sch 4 para 28
s 149 am—Finance, 2009 c 10, s 44, sch 22 para 11(3)(a)
s 150 am—Finance, 2009 c 10, s 44, sch 22 para 11(3)(b)
s 154A added—Taxation (International and Other Provns), 2010 c 8, s 371, sch 7 paras 42,
    43
    rep in pt—Finance, 2013 c 29, sch 46 para 44
s 155 rep in pt—Corporation Tax, 2009 c 4, ss 1322, 1326, sch 1 para 601(1)(2), sch 3 pt 1
    am—Corporation Tax, 2009 c 4, s 1322, sch 1 para 601(1)(3)-(6)
s 157 rep—Finance, 2012 c 14, sch 39 para 43(1)(a)
s 158 am—Corporation Tax, 2009 c 4, s 1322, sch 1 para 602
s 160 rep—Finance, 2013 c 29, sch 4 para 51
s 162 rep—Finance, 2012 c 14, sch 39 para 21(1)(a)
s 164A added—Finance, 2007 c 11, s 25, sch 3 para 9
s 167 rep in pt—SI 2010/675, reg 107, sch 26; ibid, reg 109, sch 28
    am—SI 2015/374, art 7(2)
s 168 am—Finance, 2012 c 14, s 53
s 169 am—SI 2012/266, art 4(2)
s 170 am—Corporation Tax, 2009 c 4, s 1322, sch 1 para 603; SI 2012/266, art 4(3)
s 171 am—Corporation Tax, 2009 c 4, s 1322, sch 1 para 604
ss 172ZA-172ZE added—SI 2012/266, art 4(4)
ss 172A-172F added—Finance, 2008 c 9, s 37, sch 15 paras 1, 2
s 172AA added—Finance, 2013 c 29, sch 4 para 29
s 172F am—Taxation (International and Other Provns), 2010 c 8, s 374, sch 8 paras 120,
    121; Finance (No. 2), 2015 c 33, s 40(2)
Pt 2, Ch 2 (ss 173-186) am—Finance, 2008 c 9, s 37, sch 15 paras 1, 3
s 173 am—Taxation (International and Other Provns), 2010 c 8, s 374, sch 8 paras 120, 122;
    Finance (No. 2), 2015 c 33, s 41(2)
s 175 am—Corporation Tax, 2009 c 4, s 1322, sch 1 para 605
s 176 am—Corporation Tax, 2009 c 4, s 1322, sch 1 para 606
s 177 am—Corporation Tax, 2009 c 4, s 1322, sch 1 para 607
s 178 am—Corporation Tax, 2009 c 4, s 1322, sch 1 para 608
s 179 am—Income Tax, 2007 c 3, s 1027, sch 1 paras 492, 501
s 180 am—Corporation Tax, 2009 c 4, s 1322, sch 1 para 609
s 184 am—Corporation Tax, 2009 c 4, s 1322, sch 1 para 610
s 186 rep in pt—SI 2009/56, art 3, sch 1 para 439
s 188AA added—Finance, 2013 c 29, sch 4 para 30
s 191A added—Finance, 2013 c 29, sch 4 para 31
s 194 am—Corporation Tax, 2009 c 4, s 1322, sch 1 para 611
Pt 2, Ch 15 (ss 196-220) appl (mods)—Income and Corporation Taxes, 1988 c 1, s 118ZO;
    Finance, 2005 c 7, ss 72(8), 76(2)
    excl—SI 1997/2681, reg 6(1)(a)
s 203 appl—Income Tax, 2007 c 3, s 90
s 218 am—SI 2009/56, art 3, sch 1 para 440
s 221 am—SI 2012/266, art 7
s 221A added—Finance, 2013 c 29, sch 4 para 32
Pt 2 Ch 16ZA (ss 225ZA-225ZG) added—SI 2012/266, art 6
s 225ZAA added—Finance, 2013 c 29, sch 4 para 33
s 225ZH added—Finance, 2013 c 29, sch 4 para 34
Pt 2 Ch 16A (ss 225A-225U) added—Taxation (International and Other Provns), 2010 c 8,
    s 364, sch 1
s 225N am—Finance, 2013 c 29, sch 31 paras 1(2), 14(3)(4)
    rep in pt—Finance, 2013 c 29, sch 31 paras 6(2), 14(2)

2005

c 5 *continued*

s 225O rep—Finance, 2013 c 29, sch 31 para 6(3)
ss 225P, 225Q rep—Finance, 2013 c 29, sch 31 para 15
s 225R am—Finance, 2013 c 29, sch 31 paras 1(3)(b)-(d), 16
 rep in pt—Finance, 2013 c 29, sch 31 paras 1(3)(a)
s 225T rep—Finance, 2013 c 29, sch 31 para 9
s 225V added—Finance, 2013 c 29, sch 31 para 22
s 227 am—Finance (No 2), 2005 c 22, s 37, sch 6 para 2; Finance, 2012 c 14, s 54(1)
s 227A added—Finance, 2013 c 29, sch 4 para 36
s 229 am—Finance, 2013 c 29, sch 4 para 52(2)
s 232 am—Income Tax, 2007 c 3, s 1027, sch 1 paras 492, 502
 appl—Income Tax, 2007 c 3, ss 524(5), 526(6)
ss 235, 236 appl—Income Tax, 2007 c 3, ss 524(6), 526(6)
ss 238, 239 rep—Finance, 2013 c 29, sch 4 para 52(3)
ss 239A, 239B added—Finance, 2013 c 29, sch 4 para 37
Pt 2, Ch 17A (ss 240A-240E) added—Finance, 2013 c 29, sch 4 para 38
s 243 am—Finance, 2013 c 29, sch 45 para 77
s 246 am—Corporation Tax, 2009 c 4, s 1322, sch 1 para 612; Finance, 2013 c 29, sch 4
 para 39(2)
s 247 rep in pt—Finance, 2009 c 10, s 30, sch 11 paras 34, 40
s 248 am—Income Tax, 2007 c 3, s 1027, sch 1 paras 492, 503
s 249 am—Corporation Tax, 2009 c 4, s 1322, sch 1 para 613
s 250 am—Income Tax, 2007 c 3, s 1027, sch 1 paras 492, 504
s 254 am—Income Tax, 2007 c 3, s 1027, sch 1 paras 492, 505; Finance, 2013 c 29, sch 4
 para 39(3); ibid, sch 5 para 4
s 256 rep in pt—Income Tax, 2007 c 3, s 1027, sch 1 paras 492, 506, sch 3
s 259 subst—Finance (No 2), 2005 c 22, s 37, sch 6 para 3
 am—SI 2008/954, arts 35, 37
s 260 am—Finance, 2008 c 9, s 25, sch 7 paras 46, 47(a)
 rep in pt—Finance, 2008 c 9, s 25, sch 7 paras 46, 47(b)
s 263 appl—Finance, 2005 c 7, s 57
s 267 rep in pt—Finance, 2009 c 10, s 55(1)(3)
s 268A added—Finance, 2006 c 25, s 64(4)
s 269 rep in pt—Finance, 2008 c 9, s 25, sch 7 paras 46, 48
s 270 am—Finance, 2013 c 29, sch 45 para 81
s 272 am—Finance, 2006 c 25, s 81, sch 8 para 14; Finance, 2008 c 9, s 73(5); Finance,
 2009 c 10, s 30, sch 11 paras 34, 41(a); Taxation (International and Other
 Provns), 2010 c 8, s 371, sch 7 paras 27, 29; Finance, 2014 c 26, sch 17 para
 3(3); Finance, 2015 c 11, sch 5 para 2
 rep in pt—Income Tax, 2007 c 3, s 1027, sch 1 paras 492, 507, sch 3; Finance, 2009 c
 10, s 30, sch 11 paras 34, 41(b)
s 272A added—Finance (No. 2), 2015 c 33, s 24(2)
 excl in pt—SI 2013/2819, reg 12(3A) (added by 2015/2053, reg 3)
s 272B added—Finance (No. 2), 2015 c 33, s 24(2)
s 274 am—Finance, 2007 c 11, s 67(4)-(7); Finance, 2013 c 29, s 78(2); Finance (No. 2),
 2015 c 33, s 24(3)(4)
 rep in pt—Finance, 2009 c 10, s 30, sch 11 paras 34, 42
ss 274A, 274B added—Finance (No. 2), 2015 c 33, s 24(5)
s 276 am—Corporation Tax, 2009 c 4, s 1322, sch 1 para 614
ss 277-281 excl—Income and Corporation Taxes, 1988 c 1, s 774G(7)
s 279 am—Corporation Tax, 2009 c 4, s 1322, sch 1 para 615
s 281 am—Corporation Tax, 2009 c 4, s 1322, sch 1 para 615
s 281A added—Taxation (International and Other Provns), 2010 c 8, s 374, sch 8 paras 269,
 270
s 287 am—Corporation Tax, 2009 c 4, s 1322, sch 1 para 617(1)(2)(3)(b)(c)(d)
 rep in pt—Corporation Tax, 2009 c 4, ss 1322, 1326, sch 1 para 617(1)(3)(a), sch 3 pt
 1
s 288 am—Corporation Tax, 2009 c 4, s 1322, sch 1 para 618(1)(2)(3)(b)
 rep in pt—Corporation Tax, 2009 c 4, ss 1322, 1326, sch 1 para 618(1)(3)(a), sch 3 pt
 1
s 290 am—Corporation Tax, 2009 c 4, s 1322, sch 1 para 619
s 292 am—Finance, 2013 c 29, sch 28 para 3
s 293 am—Corporation Tax, 2009 c 4, s 1322, sch 1 para 620
s 294 am—Corporation Tax, 2009 c 4, s 1322, sch 1 para 621

2005
c 5 *continued*

s 295 am—Corporation Tax, 2009 c 4, s 1322, sch 1 para 622
s 296 am—Corporation Tax, 2009 c 4, s 1322, sch 1 para 623
s 298 am—Corporation Tax, 2009 c 4, s 1322, sch 1 para 624
s 299 am—Corporation Tax, 2009 c 4, s 1322, sch 1 para 625
s 301 am—Finance, 2008 c 9, s 118, sch 39 paras 50, 51
s 302 am—Finance, 2008 c 9, s 118, sch 39 paras 50, 52
ss 302A-302C added—Taxation (International and Other Provns), 2010 c 8, s 371, sch 7
    paras 21, 22
s 302B rep in pt—Finance, 2011 c 11, sch 23 paras 57(2), 65
s 303 appl —Capital Allowances, 2001 c 2, s 360I
    am—Corporation Tax, 2009 c 4, s 1322, sch 1 para 626
s 304 am—Corporation Tax, 2009 c 4, s 1322, sch 1 para 627
s 305 rep—SI 2009/2035, art 2, sch
ss 308A-308C added—SI 2011/1037, art 11(2)
s 312 appl—SI 2006/912, reg 2
    am—Finance, 2007 c 11, s 18(1)-(3)(6)
s 313 am—Finance, 2007 c 11, s 18(4)(6)
s 314 am—Finance, 2007 c 11, s 18(5)(7)
s 318 am—Corporation Tax, 2009 c 4, s 1322, sch 1 para 628
s 319 rep—Finance, 2012 c 14, sch 39 para 43(1)(b)
s 322 am—Income Tax, 2007 c 3, s 1027, sch 1 paras 492, 508; Finance, 2011 c 11, sch 14
    para 2(2); Finance (No. 2), 2015 c 33, s 24(6)
    rep in pt—Income Tax, 2007 c 3, s 1031, sch 3
s 325 am—Finance, 2011 c 11, sch 14 para 2(3)
s 326 am—Finance, 2011 c 11, sch 14 para 2(4)
s 326A added—Finance, 2011 c 11, sch 14 para 2(5)
s 327 am—Income Tax, 2007 c 3, s 1027, sch 1 paras 492, 509; Finance, 2011 c 11, sch 14
    para 2(6); SI 2011/1037, art 11(3)
s 328 am—Income Tax, 2007 c 3, s 1027, sch 1 paras 492, 510; Finance, 2011 c 11, sch 14
    para 2(7)
    rep in pt—Income Tax, 2007 c 3, s 1031, sch 3
ss 328A, 328B added—Finance, 2011 c 11, sch 14 para 2(8)
s 333 am—Income Tax, 2007 c 3, s 1027, sch 1 paras 492, 511
s 337 rep in pt—Finance, 2012 c 14, sch 39 para 43(2)(a)(i)
s 339 rep in pt—Finance, 2012 c 14, sch 39 para 43(2)(a)(ii)
ss 340-343 rep—Finance, 2012 c 14, sch 39 para 43(1)(c)
s 354 am—Income Tax, 2007 c 3, s 1027, sch 1 paras 492, 512
    rep in pt—Finance, 2009 c 10, s 30, sch 11 paras 34, 43
s 356 am—Corporation Tax, 2009 c 4, s 1322, sch 1 para 629(1)-(5)
ss 357-360 rep—Finance, 2008 c 9, s 25, sch 7 paras 46, 49
s 365 am—Finance, 2013 c 29, sch 12 para 2(a)
    rep in pt—Finance, 2013 c 29, sch 12 para 2(b); SI 2013/2819, reg 36(2)
s 367 am—Finance, 2009 c 10, s 39(1)(4); Co-operative and Community Benefit Societies,
    2014 c 14, sch 4 para 93
s 368 am—Finance, 2013 c 29, sch 45 para 83
s 368A added—Finance, 2013 c 29, sch 45 para 132
s 369 am—Finance, 2006 c 25, s 64(1); Income Tax, 2007 c 3, s 1027, sch 1 paras 492, 513;
    (retrosp effect) Finance, 2009 c 10, s 33(1)(2); ibid, s 39(1)(2); Taxation
    (International and Other Provns), 2010 c 8, s 371, sch 7 paras 66, 67; Finance,
    2011 c 11, s 69(2); Co-operative and Community Benefit Societies, 2014 c 14,
    sch 4 para 93; SI 2014/992, art 8(2)
    rep in pt—Finance, 2012 c 14, sch 39 para 53(2)
s 370A added—Finance, 2013 c 29, sch 11 para 6
s 372 am—Income Tax, 2007 c 3, s 1027, sch 1 paras 492, 514
    excl—SI 2013/460, reg 3(1)(b)
s 373 rep in pt —Finance (No 2), 2005 c 22, ss 17(1)(d), 19, 70, sch 11 pt 2(3), Note 2
    am—SI 2006/964, reg 91
s 374 am—SI 2006/964, reg 96
s 375 am—SI 2006/964, reg 96; Corporation Tax, 2010 c 4, s 1177, sch 1 paras 444, 452
s 376 rep in pt—Finance (No 2), 2005 c 22, ss 17(1)(e), 19, 70, sch 11 pt 2(3), Note 2
    am—SI 2006/964, reg 96
s 378A added—Finance, 2009 c 10, s 39(1)(3)
    ext—SI 2009/3001 regs 95(3), 96(3)

2005

c 5 s 378A *continued*

> am—SI 2009/3001, reg 128; Taxation (International and Other Provns), 2010 c 8, s 374, sch 8 paras 167, 168

s 379 am—Co-operative and Community Benefit Societies, 2014 c 14, sch 4 para 94

s 380 ext—Finance, 2005 c 7, ss 55, 56, sch 2 para 10
> am—Finance, 2013 c 29, sch 11 para 7

s 380A added (retrosp effect)—Finance, 2009 c 10, s 33(1)(3)

s 381 appl—Income Tax 2007 c 3, s 564R(2)

Pt 4, Ch 2A (ss 381A-381E) added—Finance, 2013 c 29, sch 12 para 3

Pt 4, Ch 3 (ss 382-401) am—Finance, 2008 c 9, s 34, sch 12 paras 1, 2

s 382 am—Finance, 2014 c 26, sch 8 para 54; Finance, 2015 c 11, s 19(3)

s 385 am—Finance, 2015 c 11, s 19(4)

s 385A added—Finance, 2013 c 29, sch 23 para 16

s 387 am—SI 2006/964, reg 96

s 388 am—SI 2006/964, reg 96; Corporation Tax, 2010 c 4, s 1177, sch 1 paras 444, 453

s 389 am—Corporation Tax, 2010 c 4, s 1177, sch 1 paras 444, 454

s 390 am—SI 2006/964, reg 96

s 392 am—Finance, 2014 c 26, sch 8 paras 55, 56

s 394 am—Finance, 2014 c 26, sch 8 para 57

s 395 am—Finance, 2014 c 26, sch 8 para 58

s 396 rep in pt—Finance, 2014 c 26, sch 8 para 59

s 396A added—Finance, 2015 c 11, s 19(2)

s 397 excl—Finance, 2006 c 25, s 121(5); Income Tax, 2007 c 3, s 504(4)(b); Corporation Tax, 2010 c 4, s 549(2); SI 2013/2819, reg 12(3)(a)
> am—Income Tax, 2007 c 3, s 1027, sch 1 paras 492, 515; Finance, 2008 c 9, s 34, sch 12 paras 1, 3; Finance, 2013 c 29, sch 29 para 13; Finance, 2015 c 11, s 19(5)
> rep in pt—SI 2013/2819, reg 36(3)

ss 397A-397C added—Finance, 2008 c 9, s 34, sch 12 paras 1, 4

s 397A am—Finance, 2009 c 10, s 40, sch 19 paras 1, 2(1)-(3); Taxation (International and Other Provns), 2010 c 8, s 374, sch 8 paras 65, 66; Finance, 2013 c 29, sch 29 para 14(a)
> rep in pt—Finance, 2009 c 10, s 40, sch 19 paras 1, 2(1)(4); Finance, 2013 c 29, sch 29 para 14(b); SI 2013/2819, reg 36(4)
> excl—SI 2013/2819, reg 12(3)(a)
> appl—SI 2009/3001, reg 95(4)

s 397AA added—Finance, 2009 c 10, s 40, sch 19 paras 1, 3
> mod—SI 2009/3333, reg 2

s 397BA added—Finance, 2009 c 10, s 40, sch 19 paras 1, 5
> am—Taxation (International and Other Provns), 2010 c 8, s 374, sch 8 paras 65, 67

s 397B rep—Finance, 2013 c 29, sch 29 para 15

s 397C am—Finance, 2009 c 10, s 40, sch 19 paras 1, 6

s 398 am—Finance, 2008 c 9, s 34, sch 12 paras 1, 5; Finance, 2009 c 10, s 40, sch 19 paras 1, 7

s 399 am—Income Tax, 2007 c 3, s 1027, sch 1 paras 492, 516; Finance, 2008 c 9, s 34, sch 12 paras 1, 6; Finance, 2015 c 11, s 19(6)
> rep in pt—SI 2013/2819, reg 36(5)
> excl—Income Tax, 2007 c 3, ss 504(4)(c), 592(3), 593(3); SI 2013/2819, reg 12(3)(b)
> appl—Income Tax, 2007 c 3, s 594(3)

s 400 am—Income Tax, 2007 c 3, s 1027, sch 1 paras 492, 517
> rep in pt—SI 2013/2819, reg 36(6)
> excl—Income Tax, 2007 c 3, s 504(4)(d); SI 2013/2819, reg 12(3)(c)

s 401 am—Income Tax, 2007 c 3, s 1027, sch 1 paras 492, 518; Corporation Tax, 2010 c 4, s 1177, sch 1 paras 444, 455

s 401A added—Corporation Tax, 2010 c 4, s 1177, sch 1 paras 444, 456

s 401B added—Corporation Tax, 2010 c 4, s 1177, sch 1 paras 444, 457

s 401C added—Finance, 2013 c 29, sch 45 para 133

s 403 rep in pt—Finance, 2008 c 9, s 34, sch 12 paras 17, 18

s 405 am—Finance, 2014 c 26, sch 8 paras 61, 62(2)
> rep in pt—Finance, 2014 c 26, sch 8 para 62(3)

s 406 am—Finance, 2008 c 9, s 34, sch 12 paras 17, 19

s 407 am—Finance, 2008 c 9, s 34, sch 12 paras 17, 20; Finance, 2014 c 26, sch 8 para 63

2005
c 5 *continued*

s 408 am—Finance, 2008 c 9, s 34, sch 12 paras 17, 21; Finance, 2014 c 26, sch 8 para 64

s 408A added—Finance, 2013 c 29, sch 45 para 134

s 409 excl—Corporation Tax c 4, s 549(2A)

s 410 am—Income Tax, 2007 c 3, s 1027, sch 1 paras 492, 519; Corporation Tax, 2010 c 4, s 1177, sch 1 paras 444, 458; Finance, 2010 c 13, s 30, sch 6 para 21(2); SI 2013/2819, reg 36(7)

    excl—Corporation Tax 2010 c 4, s 549(2A)

s 410A added—Corporation Tax, 2010 c 4, s 1177, sch 1 paras 444, 459

    excl—Corporation Tax 2010 c 4, s 549(2A)

s 411 excl—Corporation Tax 2010 c 4, s 549(2A)

s 412 am—Corporation Tax, 2010 c 4, s 1177, sch 1 paras 444, 460

    appl—Corporation Tax 2010 c 4, s 599A(2)

    excl—Corporation Tax 2010 c 4, s 549(2A)

s 413 am—Corporation Tax, 2009 c 4, s 1322, sch 1 para 630;

    excl—Corporation Tax 2010 c 4, s 549(2A)

s 413A added—Finance, 2013 c 29, sch 45 para 135

s 414 am—Income Tax, 2007 c 3, s 1027, sch 1 paras 492, 520

    excl—Corporation Tax 2010 c 4, s 549(2A)

s 414A added—Corporation Tax, 2010 c 4, s 1177, sch 1 paras 444, 461

s 415 am—Corporation Tax, 2010 c 4, s 1177, sch 1 paras 444, 462; SI 2013/463, art 8

s 417 am—Finance, 2006 c 25, s 89, sch 13 para 31(1)(a); Finance, 2013 c 29, sch 30 para 14(1)

s 418 am—Income Tax, 2007 c 3, s 1027, sch 1 paras 492, 521

s 419 am—Corporation Tax, 2009 c 4, s 1322, sch 1 para 631; Corporation Tax, 2010 c 4, s 1177, sch 1 paras 444, 463

s 420 am—Finance, 2006 c 25, s 89, sch 13 para 31(1); Corporation Tax, 2010 c 4, s 1177, sch 1 paras 444, 464

s 420A added—Finance, 2013 c 29, sch 45 para 136

s 421 am—Income Tax, 2007 c 3, s 1027, sch 1 paras 492, 522

s 421A added—Corporation Tax, 2010 c 4, s 1177, sch 1 paras 444, 465

s 426 am—Income Tax, 2007 c 3, s 1027, sch 1 paras 492, 523

    rep in pt—Income Tax, 2007 c 3, s 1031, sch 3

Pt 4 Ch 8 (ss 427-460) appl—Corporation Tax, 2009 c 4, s 406

s 430 am —(retrosp) Finance (No 2), 2005 c 22, s 39, sch 7 para 25(1)(2)(10)

    rep in pt —(retrosp) Finance (No 2), 2005 c 22, ss 39, 70, sch 7 para 25(1)(2)(10), sch 11 pt 2(8), Note

s 437 am —(retrosp) Finance (No 2), 2005 c 22, s 39, sch 7 para 25(1)(3)(10)

s 438 am —(retrosp) Finance (No 2), 2005 c 22, s 39, sch 7 para 25(1)(4)(10)

s 440 am —(retrosp) Finance (No 2), 2005 c 22, s 39, sch 7 para 25(1)(5)(10)

s 441 am —(retrosp) Finance (No 2), 2005 c 22, s 39, sch 7 para 25(1)(6)(10)

s 443 am—Finance, 2007 c 11, s 109, sch 26 para 11(1)(2)

    rep in pt—Finance, 2007 c 11, s 114, sch 27 pt 6

s 444 am —(retrosp) Finance (No 2), 2005 c 22, s 39, sch 7 para 25(1)(7)(10)

s 446 am—Income Tax, 2007 c 3, s 1027, sch 1 paras 492, 524

s 450 subst —Finance, 2007 c 11, s 109, sch 26 para 5

s 451 rep —Finance, 2007 c 11, s 109, sch 26 para 5

ss 452A-452G added—(retrosp) Finance (No 2), 2005 c 22, s 39, sch 7 para 25(1)(8)(10)

s 452G saved—Taxation of Chargeable Gains, 1992 c 12, s 151D

s 454 am—Income Tax, 2007 c 3, s 1027, sch 1 paras 492, 525

s 455 am—Finance, 2012 c 14, sch 39 para 48(1)

s 456 am—Corporation Tax, 2010 c 4, s 1177, sch 1 paras 444, 466

s 457 rep in pt—Finance, 2006 c 25, ss 89, 178, sch 13 para 32(1)(a), sch 26; Income Tax, 2007 c 3, s 1031, sch 3

    am—Finance, 2006 c 25, s 89, sch 13 para 32(2); Income Tax, 2007 c 3, s 1027, sch 1 paras 492, 526

s 459 am—Income Tax, 2007 c 3, s 1027, sch 1 paras 492, 527; Finance, 2013 c 29, sch 46 para 45

s 460 am—Income Tax, 2007 c 3, s 1027, sch 1 paras 492, 528; Finance, 2008 c 9, s 25, sch 7 paras 74, 78; Corporation Tax, 2010 c 4, s 1177, sch 1 paras 444, 467

    rep in pt—Finance, 2007 c 11, s 109, sch 26 para 11(1)(3), sch 27

Pt 4, Ch 9 (ss 461-546) appl (mods)—SI 2004/1450, reg 38 (amended by 2010/582, reg 18)

    power to exclude conferred—Finance, 2012 c 14, s 61

ss 463A-463E added—Finance, 2013 c 29, sch 9 para 8

2005
c 5 *continued*

s 465 am—Finance, 2013 c 29, sch 45 paras 84, 150
    appl—Income and Corporation Taxes, 1988 c 1 sch 15 pt A1 para A5(4)(a); ibid, sch
        15 pt 1 para B2(4) (added by Finance, 2013 c 29, sch 9 para 3)
s 465A added—Income Tax, 2007 c 3, s 1027, sch 1 paras 492, 529
    am—Finance, 2008 c 9, s 5, sch 1 paras 50, 51
s 465B added—Finance, 2013 c 29, sch 45 para 140
s 466 am—Income Tax, 2007 c 3, s 1027, sch 1 paras 492, 530; Finance, 2008 c 9, s 5, sch
        1 paras 50, 52; Corporation Tax, 2009 c 4, s 1322, sch 1 para 632
s 467 am—Finance, 2006 c 25, s 89, sch 13 para 32(3); Income Tax, 2007 c 3, s 1027, sch
        1 paras 492, 531; Finance, 2008 c 9, ss 5, 36, sch 1 paras 50, 53, sch 14 paras
        10, 11; Finance, 2013 c 29, sch 45 para 85
s 468 am—Finance, 2006 c 25, s 79, sch 7 para 7(1)-(4); Income Tax, 2007 c 3, s 1027, sch
        1 paras 492, 532; Finance, 2013 c 29, sch 45 para 141; ibid, sch 46 para 46
s 469 am—Finance, 2008 c 9, s 36, sch 14 paras 10, 12
s 473 appl—Income and Corporation Taxes, 1988 c 1, s 775A
    am—Finance, 2007 c 11, s 38, sch 7 paras 76, 77; Finance, 2012 c 14, sch 16 paras
        125, 127, 128
    rep in pt—Finance, 2008 c 9, s 36, sch 14 para 17(n)
s 473A added—Finance, 2012 c 14, s 11(1)
s 476 am—Finance, 2007 c 11, s 38, sch 7 paras 76, 78; Finance, 2012 c 14, sch 16 para
        128; Finance, 2013 c 29, sch 8 para 2(a)(d)
    rep in pt—(spec retrosp effect) Finance, 2008 c 9, s 43, sch 17 para 27(1)(3); Finance,
        2013 c 29, sch 8 para 2(b)
s 482 am—Income Tax, 2007 c 3, s 1027, sch 1 paras 492, 533; Corporation Tax, 2010 c 4,
        s 1177, sch 1 paras 444, 468
    rep in pt—Income Tax, 2007 c 3, s 1031, sch 3
s 483 am—Co-operative and Community Benefit Societies, 2014 c 14, sch 4 para 95
s 485 am—Finance, 2013 c 29, sch 9 para 9
s 486 rep—Finance, 2008 c 9, s 36, sch 14 paras 10, 13
s 487 am—SI 2005/3229, regs 183, 185
s 491 am—Finance, 2012 c 14, s 11(2)
s 496 am—Corporation Tax, 2009 c 4, s 1322, sch 1 para 633
s 501 am—Finance, 2008 c 9, s 36, sch 14 paras 10, 14(a)
    rep in pt—Finance, 2008 c 9, s 36, sch 14 paras 10, 14(b)
s 504 am—Finance, 2012 c 14, sch 16 para 129
s 514 am—Finance, 2013 c 29, sch 45 para 142
s 520 am—Income Tax, 2007 c 3, s 1027, sch 1 paras 492, 534; Corporation Tax, 2010 c 4,
        s 1177, sch 1 paras 444, 469; SI 2013/636, sch para 8
s 528 subst—Finance, 2013 c 29, sch 8 para 3
    am—Finance, 2013 c 29, sch 45 para 86
    excl—Income and Corporation Taxes, 1988 c 1 s 552(14) (added by Finance, 2013 c
        29, sch 8 para 6)
s 528A added—Finance, 2013 c 29, sch 8 para 3
    am—Finance, 2013 c 29, sch 45 para 87
    excl—Income and Corporation Taxes, 1988 c 1 s 552(14)
s 529 rep—Finance, 2013 c 29, sch 8 para 4
s 530 am—Income Tax, 2007 c 3, s 1027, sch 1 paras 492, 535; Finance, 2008 c 9, s 5, sch
        1 paras 50, 54(1)(2)
    rep in pt—Finance, 2008 c 9, s 5, sch 1 paras 50, 54(1)(3)
s 531 am—Finance, 2012 c 14, sch 16 para 130(2)(3), sch 18 para 18
s 535 am—Income Tax, 2007 c 3, s 1027, sch 1 paras 492, 536; Finance, 2008 c 9, s 5, sch
        1 paras 50, 55
s 536 am—Income Tax, 2007 c 3, s 1027, sch 1 paras 492, 537; Finance, 2008 c 9, s 5, sch
        1 paras 50, 56; Finance, 2013 c 29, sch 8 para 5; ibid, sch 45 para 88(3)(5)
s 537 am—Income Tax, 2007 c 3, s 1027, sch 1 paras 492, 538; Finance, 2008 c 9, s 5, sch
        1 paras 50, 57
s 539 subst—Income Tax, 2007 c 3, s 1027, sch 1 paras 492, 539
    rep in pt—Finance, 2008 c 9, s 5, sch 1 paras 50, 58
    am—SI 2015/1810, art 9(2)(3)
s 541 am—Finance, 2013 c 29, sch 45 para 143
s 541A added—Finance, 2007 c 11, s 29(3)
s 541B added—Finance, 2007 c 11, s 29(3)
        rep in pt—Finance, 2008 c 9, s 36, sch 14 paras 10, 15

      s 545 rep in pt—Finance, 2010 c 13, s 30, sch 6 para 21(3)

          appl—Income and Corporation Taxes, 1988 c 1 sch 15 pt A1 para A5(4)(b) (added by
              Finance, 2013 c 29, sch 9 para 2)

      s 546 am—Income Tax, 2007 c 3, s 1027, sch 1 paras 492, 540

      Pt 4, Ch 10 (ss 547-550) rep —SI 2013/2819, reg 36(8)

      s 552 rep in pt—Finance, 2009 c 10, s 49, sch 25 para 9(2)(a)(ii)

      Pt 4, Ch 12 (ss 555-569) rep—Finance, 2013 c 29, sch 12 para 13(2)

      ss 570-573 rep—Finance, 2009 c 10, s 49, sch 25 para 9(2)(b)

      s 577 am—Finance, 2013 c 29, sch 45 para 89

      s 595 am—Income Tax, 2007 c 3, s 1027, sch 1 paras 492, 546

      ss 597-599 appl—Income Tax, 2007 c 3, s 910(4)

      s 601 am—Income Tax, 2007 c 3, s 1027, sch 1 paras 492, 547

      s 602 am—Income Tax, 2007 c 3, s 1027, sch 1 paras 492, 548

      s 618 am—Income Tax, 2007 c 3, s 1027, sch 1 paras 492, 549

          rep in pt—Income Tax, 2007 c 3, s 1031, sch 3

      Pt 5, Ch 5 (ss 619-648) appl—Corporation Tax, 2010 c 4, s 817(a)

      s 619 am—SI 2005/3229, regs 183, 186; Finance, 2006 c 25, s 89, sch 13 para 5(1);
              Income Tax, 2007 c 3, s 1027, sch 1 paras 492, 550

      s 619A added—Income Tax, 2007 c 3, s 1027, sch 1 paras 492, 551

      s 620 am—Income Tax, 2007 c 3, s 1027, sch 1 paras 492, 552; SI 2012/964, art 3(1), sch
          appl—Finance, 2011 c 11, sch 23 para 26(2)
          rep in pt—SI 2012/964, art 3(1), sch

      s 623 subst—Finance, 2006 c 25, s 89, sch 13 para 31(2)

      s 624 am—SI 2005/3229, regs 183, 187; Income Tax, 2007 c 3, s 1027, sch 1 paras 492,
              553

      s 625 am—SI 2005/3229, regs 183, 188

      s 626 am—SI 2005/3229, regs 183, 189

      s 627 am—SI 2005/3229, regs 183, 190; Income Tax, 2007 c 3, s 1027, sch 1 paras 492,
              554; Finance, 2012 c 14, s 12(2)

      s 628 am—SI 2005/3229, regs 183, 191; Finance, 2006 c 25, s 89, sch 13 para 33(1)(2);
              Income Tax, 2007 c 3, s 1027, sch 1 paras 492, 555; SI 2012/964, art 3(1), sch
          rep in pt—Income Tax, 2007 c 3, s 1031, sch 3; SIs 2012/964, art 3(1), sch;
              2014/3062, art 2

      s 629 am—SI 2005/3229, regs 183, 192(1)(2)(3)(b)(c)(4)(5); Finance, 2006 c 25, s 89, sch
              13 para 34
          rep in pt—SI 2005/3229, regs 183, 192(1)(3)(a)

      s 630 am —SI 2005/3229, regs 183, 192(1)(5); Finance, 2006 c 25, s 89, sch 13 para
              33(1)(3)

      s 631 am—SI 2005/3229, regs 183, 192(1)(5), 193; Finance, 2006 c 25, s 89, sch 13 para
              33(4); Income Tax, 2007 c 3, s 1027, sch 1 paras 492, 556

      s 632 am—SIs 2005/3229, regs 183, 192(1)(5); 2009/3001, reg 128

      s 634 am—SI 2005/3229, regs 183, 194

      s 635 am—Income Tax, 2007 c 3, s 1027, sch 1 paras 492, 557

      s 636 am—Income Tax, 2007 c 3, s 1027, sch 1 paras 492, 558; Finance, 2013 c 29, sch 46
              para 48(1)

      s 637 am—SI 2005/3229, regs 183, 195

      s 640 am—Income Tax, 2007 c 3, s 1027, sch 1 paras 492, 559; Finance, 2009 c 10, s 6,
              sch 2 paras 19, 20(b); Finance, 2012 c 14, s 1(5)
          rep in pt—Finance, 2009 c 10, s 6, sch 2 paras 19, 20(a)

      s 643 am—Corporation Tax, 2010 c 4, s 1177, sch 1 paras 444, 470

      s 645 am—Finance, 2012 c 14, s 12(3)

      s 646 am—SI 2009/56, art 3, sch 1 para 441; Finance (No 3), 2010 c 33, s 7(1)-(5)

      s 646A added—Income Tax, 2007 c 3, s 1027, sch 1 paras 492, 560

      s 647 rep —Finance, 2011 c 11, sch 23 paras 57(3), 65

      s 648 am—Finance, 2009 c 10, s 51, sch 27 para 13; Finance, 2013 c 29, sch 46 para 49

      s 650 appl—Corporation Tax, 2009 c 4, s 952(6)

      s 651 rep in pt—Finance, 2013 c 29, sch 46 para 50

      s 664 rep in pt—Finance, 2013 c 29, sch 46 para 51

      s 669 am—Income Tax, 2007 c 3, s 1027, sch 1 paras 492, 561; Finance, 2008 c 9, s 5, sch
              1 paras 50, 59; Finance, 2009 c 10, s 6, sch 2 paras 19, 21; SI 2015/1810, art 10

      s 671 am—Corporation Tax, 2009 c 4, s 1322, sch 1 para 634

      s 677 am—Income Tax, 2007 c 3, s 1027, sch 1 paras 492, 562

      s 678 am—Income Tax, 2007 c 3, s 1027, sch 1 paras 492, 563

2005
c 5 *continued*

s 679 am—Income Tax, 2007 c 3, s 1027, sch 1 paras 492, 564
 rep in pt—Finance, 2008 c 9, s 5, sch 1 paras 50, 60
s 680 am—Income Tax, 2007 c 3, s 1027, sch 1 paras 492, 565; Finance, 2008 c 9, s 5, sch 1 paras 50, 61
s 680A added—Income Tax, 2007 c 3, s 1027, sch 1 paras 492, 566
 am—Finance, 2008 c 9, s 5, sch 1 paras 50, 62(1)(2)(a)(4)(5)(a)(7)
s 682 am—Income Tax, 2007 c 3, s 1027, sch 1 paras 492, 567
s 682A added—Taxation (International and Other Provns), 2010 c 8, s 371, sch 7 paras 46, 47
s 683 rep in pt—Finance, 2012 c 14, sch 39 para 21(2)
s 684 am—Income Tax, 2007 c 3, s 1027, sch 1 paras 492, 568
s 685A added—Finance, 2006 c 25, s 89, sch 13 para 6(1)
 am—Income Tax, 2007 c 3, ss 1027, 1031, sch 1 paras 492, 569, sch 3; (spec retrosp effect) Finance, 2008 c 9, s 67(1); Finance, 2009 c 10, s 6, sch 2 paras 19, 22; SI 2015/1810, art 11
s 686 am—Income Tax, 2007 c 3, s 1027, sch 1 paras 492, 570
 rep in pt—Income Tax, 2007 c 3, s 1031, sch 3
Pt 5, Ch 8 (ss 687-689) appl (mods)—SI 2006/964, reg 85N (added by SI 2010/294, regs 2, 21)
s 687 am—Finance, 2013 c 29, sch 12 para 13(3)
s 688 rep in pt—Finance, 2008 c 9, s 34, sch 12 paras 17, 22
 excl—SI 2009/3001, reg18, 96(3)
 am—Finance (No 3), 2010 c 33, s 1, sch 1 paras 30, 33
s 689 excl—SI 2009/3001, regs 18 96(3)
s 689A added—Finance, 2013 c 29, sch 45 para 137
s 691 rep—Finance, 2011 c 11, sch 26 para 4
s 694 am—Finance, 2011 c 11, s 40(2)
s 695A added—Finance, 2011 c 11, s 40(3)
s 699 am—Finance, 2011 c 11, s 40(4)
s 700 rep—SI 2009/3054, art 3, sch
s 701 am—Finance, 2008 c 9, s 40; Finance, 2011 c 11, s 40(5)
s 703 am—Finance, 2014 c 26, sch 8 para 141
s 704 am—Income Tax, 2007 c 3, s 1027, sch 1 paras 492, 571
s 705 am—Finance, 2009 c 10, s 50, sch 26 para 2
s 706 am—Finance, 2009 c 10, s 50, sch 26 para 3
s 706 rep in pt—Finance, 2009 c 10, s 50, sch 26 para 6(a), 7, 8
s 707 am—Finance, 2009 c 10, s 50, sch 26 para 4
s 708 am—Finance, 2009 c 10, s 50, sch 26 paras 5, 6(b)
s 714 am—Income Tax, 2007 c 3, s 1027, sch 1 paras 492, 572
s 715 am—Finance, 2013 c 29, sch 46 para 52
s 717 rep in pt—Finance, 2007 c 11, s 46(5)(9), sch 27
s 718 mod—Income and Corporation Taxes, 1988 c 1, s 437
s 723 rep—Finance, 2007 c 11, s 46(6)(9), sch 27
s 724 rep in pt—Income Tax, 2007 c 3, s 1027, sch 1 paras 492, 573, sch 3; Finance, 2007 c 11, s 114, sch 27 pt 2
 am—Finance, 2007 c 11, s 46(7)(9)
s 726 am—SIs 2010/813, art 16; 2011/2581, sch 2 para 9
ss 729, 730 am—SI 2005/3229, regs 183, 196
s 730 am—SI 2005/3229, regs 183, 197
s 731 appl (mods)—SIs 2010/673, art 2; 2011/1157, art 2(1)
s 732 am—Crime and Security, 2010 c 17, s 48, sch 2 para 3
s 733 appl (mods)—SIs 2010/673, art 2; 2011/1157, art 2(1)
s 734 appl (mods)—SIs 2010/673, art 2; 2011/1157, art 2(1)
s 742 am—SI 2005/3229, regs 183, 198; Finance (No 3), 2010 c 33, s 2(3)(a)-(c)
s 744 am—Finance (No 3), 2010 c 33, s 2(2)(a), (d); Children and Families, 2014 c 6, sch 2 para 68
 rep in pt—Finance (No 3), 2010 c 33, s 2(2)(b)
s 745 am—(S) Adoption and Children (S), 2007 asp 4, s 120, sch 2 para 13; SI 2011/1740, sch 2 para 6
 rep in pt—(S) Adoption and Children (S), 2007 asp 4, s 120, sch 3; Finance (No 3), 2010 c 33, s 2(3)(b); SI 2011/1740, sch 2 pt 3
s 746 am—Finance (No 3), 2010 c 33, s 2(4)(a)-(d)
 rep in pt—Finance (No 3), 2010 c 33, s 2(4)(b)

2005
c 5 *continued*

s 748 rep—Finance, 2012 c 14, sch 39 para 21(1)(b)
s 749 am—SI 2014/992, art 8(1)(a)
s 749A added—Corporation Tax, 2009 c 4, s 1322, sch 1 para 635
s 750 rep—Finance, 2012 c 14, sch 39 para 53(1)(a)
s 752 am —SI 2009/1890, art 12
s 753A added—Finance, 2011 c 11, s 69(3)
s 755 am—Income Tax, 2007 c 3, s 1027, sch 1 paras 492, 574; SI 2009/1890, art 3
s 756A added—Finance, 2006 c 25, s 64(2)
      am—Income Tax, 2007 c 3, s 1027, sch 1 paras 492, 575
s 757 am—SIs 2005/2899, art 3; 2006/3288, art 2; Income Tax, 2007 c 3, s 1027, sch 1
      paras 492, 576
s 763 am—Taxation (International and Other Provns), 2010 c 8, s 374, sch 8 paras 61, 68
s 764 am—Taxation (International and Other Provns), 2010 c 8, s 374, sch 8 paras 65, 69
s 767 am—Income Tax, 2007 c 3, s 1027, sch 1 paras 492, 577
s 770 am—Finance, 2014 c 26, sch 8 paras 66, 67(2)
     rep in pt—Finance, 2014 c 26, sch 8 para 67(3)
s 771 am—Finance, 2013 c 29, sch 46 para 53(1)
s 776 am—Children and Young Persons, 2008 c 23, s 21(4)
s 780 am—Nat Health Service (Conseq Provns), 2006 c 43, s 2, sch 1 para 276
s 782 am—Deregulation, 2015 c 20, s 57(3)(b)
s 782A added—Finance, 2007 c 11, s 20
      am—Deregulation, 2015 c 20, s 57(3)(b)
s 782B added—Finance, 2007 c 11, s 21(1)(3)
s 783 am—Finance, 2006 c 25, s 64(3)
Pt 7 (ss 784-828) am—Finance (No 3), 2010 c 33, s 1, sch 1 paras 30, 34
s 786 am—Finance, 2013 c 29, sch 4 para 40
s 789 am—SI 2015/1539, art 2
Pt 7, Ch 2 (ss 803-828) am—Finance (No 3), 2010 c 33, s 1, sch 1 para 29
s 803 am—Finance (No 3), 2010 c 33, s 1, sch 1 para 2
s 804 am—Finance (No 3), 2010 c 33, s 1, sch 1 para 3
s 804A added—Finance (No 3), 2010 c 33, s 1, sch 1 para 4
s 805 am—Finance (No 3), 2010 c 33, s 1, sch 1 para 5; Finance, 2013 c 29, sch 4 para 42
s 805A added—Finance (No 3), 2010 c 33, s 1, sch 1 para 6
s 806 am—(W 6.4.2016) Children and Young Persons, 2008 c 23, s 8, sch 1 para
      18(1)(2)(3)(b); SI 2013/1465, sch 1 para 10(a)(c)(d); Children and Families,
      2014 c 6, sch 2 para 69
     rep in pt—(W 6.4.2016) Children and Young Persons, 2008 c 23, s 8, sch 1 para
      18(1)(3)(a), sch 4; SI 2013/1465, sch 1 para 10(b)
s 806A added—Finance (No 3), 2010 c 33, s 1, sch 1 para 6
s 806B added—Finance (No 3), 2010 c 33, s 1, sch 1 para 7
s 807 am—Finance (No 3), 2010 c 33, s 1, sch 1 para 8
s 808 am—Finance (No 3), 2010 c 33, s 1, sch 1 para 9
s 809 subst—Finance (No 3), 2010 c 33, s 1, sch 1 para 10
s 810 am—Finance (No 3), 2010 c 33, s 1, sch 1 para 11
s 811 am—Finance (No 3), 2010 c 33, s 1, sch 1 para 12
s 812 subst—Finance (No 3), 2010 c 33, s 1, sch 1 para 13
s 813 am—Finance (No 3), 2010 c 33, s 1, sch 1 para 14
s 814 am—Finance (No 3), 2010 c 33, s 1, sch 1 para 15
s 815 am—Finance (No 3), 2010 c 33, s 1, sch 1 para 16
s 816 am—Finance (No 3), 2010 c 33, s 1, sch 1 para 17
s 817 am—Finance (No 3), 2010 c 33, s 1, sch 1 para 18
s 818 am—Finance (No 3), 2010 c 33, s 1, sch 1 para 19
s 819 am—Finance (No 3), 2010 c 33, s 1, sch 1 para 20
s 820 am—Finance (No 3), 2010 c 33, s 1, sch 1 para 21; Finance, 2013 c 29, sch 4 para 43
s 821 am—Finance (No 3), 2010 c 33, s 1, sch 1 para 22
s 822 am—Finance (No 3), 2010 c 33, s 1, sch 1 para 23
s 823 am—Finance (No 3), 2010 c 33, s 1, sch 1 para 24
s 824 am—Finance (No 3), 2010 c 33, ss 1, 3(2), sch 1 para 25
s 825 subst—Finance (No 3), 2010 c 33, s 3(3)
ss 825A-825D added—Finance (No 3), 2010 c 33, s 3(3)
s 826 am—Finance (No 3), 2010 c 33, s 1, sch 1 para 27
s 827 am—Finance (No 3), 2010 c 33, s 1, sch 1 para 28
s 829 am—Finance, 2008 c 9, s 25, sch 7 paras 46, 50

2005

c 5 *continued*

s 830 am—Finance, 2008 c 9, s 25, sch 7 paras 46, 51(1)(2), 96, 156(b), 162; SI 2009/3001, reg 128

rep in pt—Finance, 2008 c 9, s 25, sch 7 paras 46, 51(1)(3), 156(a)

s 831 rep—Finance, 2008 c 9, s 25, sch 7 paras 46, 52

s 832 subst—(transtl provns) Finance, 2008 c 9, s 25, sch 7 paras 46, 53, 83

s 832 am—Finance, 2013 c 29, sch 45 para 90(2)

s 832A added—(transtl provns) Finance, 2008 c 9, s 25, sch 7 paras 46, 53, 83

subst—Finance, 2013 c 29, sch 45 para 118

s 832B added—Finance, 2008 c 9, s 25, sch 7 paras 46, 53

ss 833-837 rep—Finance, 2008 c 9, s 25, sch 7 paras 46, 54

s 839 rep in pt—Finance, 2008 c 9, s 25, sch 7 paras 66, 67; Corporation Tax, 2009 c 4, ss 1322, 1326, sch 1 para 637(1)(3)(b), sch 3 pt 1; SI 2013/2819, reg 36(9)(a)

am—Corporation Tax, 2009 c 4, s 1322, sch 1 para 637(1)(2)(3)(a)(4); SI 2013/2819, reg 36(9)(b)(c)

s 840 rep in pt—Finance, 2008 c 9, s 25, sch 7 paras 66, 68

s 840A added—Finance, 2008 c 9, s 25, sch 7 paras 66, 69

am—Finance, 2008 c 9, s 118, sch 39 paras 50, 53

s 841 am—Income Tax, 2007 c 3, s 1027, sch 1 paras 492, 578

Pt 9 (ss 846-863) mod—Income and Corporation Taxes, 1988 c 1, s 774D(4)

appl—Income Tax 2007 c 3, ss 809BZH(4), 809BZK(4)

s 847 am—Corporation Tax, 2009 c 4, s 1322, sch 1 para 638

s 849 appl—Income and Corporation Taxes, 1988 c 1, s 118ZO; Finance, 2005 c 7, ss 72(9)(a), 76(3)(a)

am—Corporation Tax, 2009 c 4, s 1322, sch 1 para 639; Finance, 2013 c 29, sch 45 para 78

s 850 subst—Corporation Tax, 2009 c 4, s 1322, sch 1 para 640

am—Finance, 2014 c 26, sch 17 para 7(2)

ss 850A, 850B added—Corporation Tax, 2009 c 4, s 1322, sch 1 para 640

ss 850C-850E added—Finance, 2014 c 26, sch 17 para 7(3)

s 850C appl—Corporation Tax, 2009 c 4, s 1264A(1)

s 850D appl—Corporation Tax, 2009 c. 4, s 1264A(1)

s 852 am—Income Tax, 2007 c 3, s 1027, sch 1 paras 492, 579; Finance, 2013 c 29, sch 45 para 79

s 854 am—Finance, 2013 c 29, sch 45 para 80

s 857 am—Finance, 2008 c 9, s 25, sch 7 paras 66, 70(1)(2)(4)

rep in pt—Finance, 2008 c 9, s 25, sch 7 paras 66, 70(1)(3)

s 858 am—(spec retrosp effect) Finance, 2008 c 9, s 58(3); Taxation (International and Other Provns), 2010 c 8, s 374, sch 8 paras 65, 70

s 860 am—Corporation Tax, 2009 c 4, s 1322, sch 1 para 641

s 861 am—Corporation Tax, 2009 c 4, s 1322, sch 1 para 642

s 862 am—Corporation Tax, 2009 c 4, s 1322, sch 1 para 643(1)(2)

rep in pt—Corporation Tax, 2009 c 4, ss 1322, 1326, sch 1 para 643(1)(3), sch 3 pt 1

s 863 am—Income Tax, 2007 c 3, s 1027, sch 1 paras 492, 580

ss 863A-863G added—Finance, 2014 c 26, sch 17 para 1

ss 863H-863L added—Finance, 2014 c 26, sch 17 para 15

s 869 am—SIs 2009/56, art 3, sch 1 para 442; 2009/571, art 8, sch 1; 2010/530, art 2, sch

s 871 am—Income Tax, 2007 c 3, s 1027, sch 1 paras 492, 581

s 872 am—Income Tax, 2007 c 3, s 1027, sch 1 paras 492, 582

s 873 am—Commrs for Revenue and Customs, 2005 c 11, s 50(6), sch 4 paras 131, 132(3)(h); Finance, 2009 c 10, s 40, sch 19 paras 1, 8

rep in pt—Finance, 2007 c 11, s 46(8), sch 27

ss 876, 877 rep—Income Tax, 2007 c 3, s 1027, sch 1 paras 492, 583, 584, sch 3

s 878 rep in pt—Commrs for Revenue and Customs, 2005 c 11, ss 50(6), 52(2), sch 4 paras 131, 134(1), sch 5; Income Tax, 2007 c 3, s 1031, sch 3; Finance, 2008 c 9, s 25, sch 7 paras 66, 71

am—Income Tax, 2007 c 3, s 1027, sch 1 paras 492, 585; Taxation (International and Other Provns), 2010 c 8, s 371, sch 7 paras 89, 90

s 879 rep in pt—Income Tax, 2007 c 3, s 1027, sch 1 paras 492, 586, sch 3

s 881rep—Corporation Tax, 2009 c 4, ss 1322, 1326, sch 1 para 644, sch 3 pt 1

s 885 am—Income Tax, 2007 c 3, s 1027, sch 1 paras 492, 587

sch 1 rep in pt—(pt prosp) Finance (No 2), 2005 c 22, s 70, sch 11 pt 2(2) Note 2, (3) Notes 1, 2, (8) Note, (12) Note; SI 2005/3338, regs 1(2), 17; Finance, 2006 c 25, s 178, sch 26; Income Tax, 2007 c 3, s 1031, sch 3; Finance, 2007 c 11, s 114,

2005

c 5 *continued*

        sch 27 pt 2; Finance, 2008 c 9, ss 8, 25, 36, 66(4)(k), 92, sch 2 para 21(h), sch 7 para 79(b), sch 14 paras 10, 16, 17(n), sch 29 para 14(4); ibid, s 84, sch 27 para 26; Health and Social Care, 2008 c 14, s 166, sch 15; Corporation Tax, 2009 c 4, s 1322, sch 1 para 645; ibid, s 1326, sch 3 pt 1; Finance, 2009 c 10, s 5, sch 1 para 6(n); ibid, s 49, sch 25 para 9(3)(e); SIs 2009/56, art 3, sch 1 para 443; 2009/2035, art 2, sch; 2009/3001, reg 13, sch 2; Corporation Tax, 2010 c 4, s 1181, sch 3 pts 1, 2; Taxation (International and Other Provns), 2010 c 8, s 378, sch 10 pts 1, 2, 6, 8-13; Finance, 2012 c 14, sch 16 para 247(n); ibid, sch 39 paras 19(2)(b), 31(2)(c), 39(b); SL(R), 2013 c 2, s 1, sch 1 pt 10(1); Finance, 2013 c 29, sch 12 para 13(4)

    sch 2 am—Finance, 2005 c 7, s 59, sch 3 pt 3 paras 30(1)(4), 31(2); SI 2005/3229, regs 183, 199; Income Tax, 2007 c 3, s 1027, sch 1 paras 492, 589, 590; Finance, 2007 c 11, s 38, sch 7 paras 76, 79; Corporation Tax, 2009 c 4, s 1322, sch 1 para 646; SI 2009/2035, art 2, sch; Corporation Tax, 2010 c 4, s 1177, sch 1 paras 444, 471; Finance, 2012 c 14, sch 16 para 131

      rep in pt—Finance, 2007 c 11, s 114, sch 27 pt 2; Income Tax, 2007 c 3, s 1027, sch 1 paras 492, 588, sch 3; Finance, 2008 c 9, ss 25, 36, sch 7 paras 66, 72, sch 14 para 17(n); Finance, 2009 c 10, s 30, sch 11 paras 34, 44; SI 2009/56, art 3, sch 1 para 444; Taxation (International and Other Provns), 2010 c 8, ss 371, 378, sch 7 paras 61, 62, sch 10 pt 12; Finance, 2013 c 29, sch 12 para 13(5)

    sch 4 rep in pt —Commrs for Revenue and Customs, 2005 c 11, ss 50(6), 52(2), sch 4 paras 131, 134(2), sch 5; Income Tax, 2007 c 3, s 1031, sch 3; Finance, 2008 c 9, s 25, sch 7 paras 66, 73; Finance, 2009 c 10, s 126(3)(4); Finance, 2010 c 13, s 30, sch 6 para 21(5)(a)(i); Finance (No 3), 2010 c 33, s 1, sch 1 paras 30, 35(a); Finance, 2013 c 29, sch 12 para 13(6)

      am —(retrosp) Finance (No 2), 2005 c 22, s 39, sch 7 para 25(1)(9)(10); SI 2005/3229, regs 183, 200; Income Tax, 2007 c 3, s 1027, sch 1 paras 492, 591, 592; Finance, 2008 c 9, s 37, sch 15 paras 1, 4; Corporation Tax, 2009 c 4, s 1322, sch 1 para 647(1)(2)(a); Finance, 2009 c 10, s 6, sch 2 paras 19, 23; ibid, s 126(3); Corporation Tax, 2010 c 4, s 1177, sch 1 paras 444, 472; Taxation (International and Other Provns), 2010 c 8, s 374, sch 8 paras 189, 191, 211, 212, 324, 325; Finance, 2010 c 13, s 30, sch 6 para 21(5)(a)(ii)(b); Finance (No 3), 2010 c 33, s 1, sch 1 paras 30, 35(b); SI 2012/266, art 8; Finance, 2013 c 29, sch 4 para 53; ibid, sch 45 para 106; SI 2015/1810, art 12

    sch 6 rep in pt—Finance, 2012 c 14, s 54(4)

c 6   **Child Benefit**

    sch 1 rep in pt—Pensions, 2007 c 22, s 27, sch 7pt 2; Welfare Reform, 2009 c 24, s 58, sch 7 pt 2

c 7   **Finance**

    ss 8, 9 rep—Income Tax, 2007 c 3, s 1031, sch 3

    s 11 rep—Corporation Tax, 2010 c 4, s 1181, sch 3 pt 1

    s 14 rep—Income Tax, 2007 c 3, s 1031, sch 3

    s 23 am—Finance, 2006 c 25, s 89, sch 13 para 35(2)(a); Finance, 2008 c 9, sch 2 para 12

    s 24 am—Finance, 2006 c 25, s 89, sch 13 para 35(2)(b)

    s 25 am—Finance, 2006 c 25, s 89, sch 13 para 35(2)(c)(3)

    s 26 am—Income Tax, 2007 c 3, s 1027, sch 1 paras 593, 594; Finance, 2008 c 9, sch 2 para 13

    s 27 am—Finance, 2006 c 25, s 89, sch 13 para 35(4); Income Tax, 2007 c 3, s 1027, sch 1 paras 593, 595

    s 28 am—Finance, 2008 c 9, sch 2 para 14(2)-(4); Finance, 2013 c 29, sch 45 para 151(2)

    s 28A added—Finance, 2006 c 25, s 89, sch 13 para 36(1)

    s 30 am—Finance, 2006 c 25, s 88, sch 12 para 48(1); Finance, 2008 c 9, sch 2 para 15; Finance, 2013 c 29, sch 45 para 151(3)(a); ibid, sch 46 para 133(1)

      rep in pt—Finance, 2013 c 29, sch 45 para 151(3)(b)

    s 31 am—Finance, 2008 c 9, sch 2 para 16(2),(3); Finance, 2013 c 29, sch 45 para 151(4)

    s 32 am—Finance, 2008 c 9, sch 2 para 17(2),(3); Finance, 2013 c 29, sch 45 para 151(5)

    s 33 rep—Finance, 2008 c 9, sch 2 para 18

    s 34 am—Finance, 2006 c 25, s 88, sch 12 para 48(2); Finance, 2013 c 29, sch 44 para 15

    s 35 am—Finance, 2006 c 25, s 88, sch 12 para 48(3); Crime and Security, 2010 c 17, s 48, sch 2 para 4; Finance, 2013 c 29, sch 44 para 16

    s 37 am—Finance, 2006 c 25, ss 80, 89, sch 12 para 48(4), sch 13 para 35(2)(d)

    s 38 subst—Finance, 2013 c 29, sch 44 para 17

    s 40 rep in pt—SI 2009/56, art 3, sch 1 para 445

2005

c 7 continued

s 41 rep in pt—Income Tax, 2007 c 3, s 1027, sch 1 paras 593, 596, sch 3; Finance, 2008 c
9, s 8, sch 2 para 102(a); Finance, 2013 c 29, sch 45 para 151(6)(b)

    am—Finance, 2013 c 29, sch 45 para 151(6)(a)

s 42 rep in pt—Finance, 2006 c 25, ss 89, 178, sch 13 para 35(5), sch 26 pt 3(15)

s 43 am—Finance, 2006 c 25, s 89, sch 13 para 35(6)

s 44 rep in pt—Income Tax, 2007 c 3, s 1031, sch 3; Finance, 2008 c 9, s 8, sch 2 para 21(i)

ss 46-48A rep—Taxation (International and Other Provns), 2010 c 8, ss 374, 378, sch 8
    paras 213, 214, sch 10 pt 7

s 48B added—Finance, 2007 c 11, s 53(1)(14)

    am—Corporation Tax, 2009 c 4, s 1322, sch 1 para 651; Finance, 2009 c 10, s 123,
        sch 61 para 27

    rep in pt—Corporation Tax, 2009 c 4, ss 1322, 1326, sch 1 para 651(c)(iii), sch 3 pt 1;
        Corporation Tax, 2010 c 4, ss 1177, 1181, sch 1 paras 473, 474sch 3; Taxation
        (International and Other Provns), 2010 c 8, ss 374, 378, sch 8 paras 213, 214,
        sch 10 pts 7, 13

    appl—Finance, 2009 c 10, s 123, sch 61 paras 2-4

ss 49, 49A rep—Taxation (International and Other Provns), 2010 c 8, ss 374, 378, sch 8
    paras 213, 214, sch 10 pt 7

s 50 rep—Corporation Tax, 2009 c 4, ss 1322, 1326, sch 1 para 654, sch 3 pt 1

ss 51-53 rep—Taxation (International and Other Provns), 2010 c 8, ss 374, 378, sch 8 paras
    213, 214, sch 10 pt 7

s 54 rep—Corporation Tax, 2009 c 4, ss 1322, 1326, sch 1 para 657, sch 3

ss 54A-57 rep—Taxation (International and Other Provns), 2010 c 8, ss 374, 378, sch 8
    paras 213, 214, sch 10 pt 7

ss 58-71 rep—Finance, 2006 c 25, s 178, sch 26 pt 3(4) Note 1

s 73 rep—Income Tax, 2007 c 3, s 1031, sch 3

s 74 rep—Income Tax, 2007 c 3, ss 1027, 1031, sch 1 paras 593, 600, sch 3

ss 75-78 rep—Income Tax, 2007 c 3, s 1027, sch 1 paras 593, 600, sch 3

s 79 rep—Income Tax, 2007 c 3, s 1031, sch 3

s 81 rep—Corporation Tax, 2009 c 4, s 1326, sch 3 pt 1

s 83 excl—SI 2006/3296, reg 21

    rep in pt—Finance, 2006 c 25, ss 101(3)(a), 178, sch 26

    am—Finance, 2006 c 25, s 101; Finance, 2007 c 11, s 59; Corporation Tax, 2009 c 4, s
        1322, sch 1 para 662

    appl—(savings) SI 2007/3338, reg 2

s 84 rep—Corporation Tax, 2010 c 4, ss 1177, 1181, sch 1 paras 473, 476, sch 3

s 85 rep—Taxation (International and Other Provns), 2010 c 8, s 378, sch 10 pt 1

s 86 rep in pt—Taxation (International and Other Provns), 2010 c 8, s 378, sch 10 pt 1

s 87 rep—Taxation (International and Other Provns), 2010 c 8, s 378, sch 10 pt 1

s 88 rep in pt—Taxation (International and Other Provns), 2010 c 8, s 378, sch 10 pt 1

ss 89, 90 rep—Finance, 2009 c 10, s 36, sch 16 para 5(h)

s 91 rep in pt—Corporation Tax, 2009 c 4, s 1326, sch 3 pt 1; Taxation (International and
    Other Provns), 2010 c 8, s 378, sch 10 pt 1

s 95 rep—Finance, 2006 c 25, s 178, sch 26

s 96 rep—Finance, 2012 c 14, sch 39 para 8(2)(d)(i)

s 97 rep in pt—Finance, 2014 c 26, s 114(3)(d)

s 102 am—Corporation Tax, 2010 c 4, s 1177, sch 1 paras 473, 477

s 105 am—Income Tax, 2007 c 3, s 1027, sch 1 paras 593, 601; Corporation Tax, 2009 c 4,
    s 1322, sch 1 para 663

sch 1A added—Finance, 2013 c 29, sch 44 para 19

    am—Finance, 2014 c 26, s 291(2)(a)(3)

    rep in pt—Finance, 2014 c 26, s 291(2)(b)(4)

sch 2 am—SI 2006/964, reg 92; Finance, 2006 c 25, s 95(8); Income Tax, 2007 c 3, s 1027,
    sch 1 paras 593, 602; Finance, 2007 c 11, s 53(9)(13)

    rep in pt—Income Tax, 2007 c 3, s 1031, sch 3; Corporation Tax, 2009 c 4, ss 1322,
        1326, sch 1 para 664, sch 3 pt 1; Taxation (International and Other Provns),
        2010 c 8, ss 374, 378, sch 8 paras 213, 215, sch 10 pts 7, 13; Finance, 2011 c
        11, sch 23 paras 58, 65

sch 3 rep—Finance, 2006 c 25, s 178, sch 26 pt 3(4) Note 1

sch 4 rep in pt—Finance (No 2), 2005 c 22, ss 37, 70, sch 6 para 4(1)(6), sch 11 pt 2(6),
    Notes 1, 2; Corporation Tax, 2009 c 4, ss 1322, 1326, sch 1 para 665, sch 3 pt
    1; ibid, s 1326, sch 3 pt 1; Corporation Tax, 2010 c 4, s 1181, sch 3 pt 1;
    Taxation (International and Other Provns), 2010 c 8, s 378, sch 10 pt 1

2005

c 7 *continued*

> sch 5 rep—Taxation (International and Other Provns), 2010 c 8, s 378, sch 10 pt 1
> sch 9 rep in pt—Finance, 2012 c 14, sch 39 paras 7(2)(b), 8(2)(d)(ii)
> sch 10 rep in pt—Finance, 2008 c 9, s 92, sch 29 para 11; Finance, 2011 c 11, sch 16 para
>> 84(a); Finance, 2015 c 11, sch 4 para 16

c 8   *Appropriation (No 2)*—rep Appropriation (No 2), 2007 c 10, s 4, sch 3

c 9   **Mental Capacity**

> appl (pt prosp)—Care, 2014 c 23, s 80(2)
> s 2 appl—SI 2014/2936, reg 8(3)
> s 3 appl—SI 2014/2936, reg 8(3)
> s 4 appl—SIs 2010/781, reg 18 (substituted by SI 2012/1513, reg 5); 1000, reg 1(3)
> ss 4A, 4B added—Mental Health, 2007 c 12, s 50(1)(2)
> s 6 rep in pt—Mental Health, 2007 c 12, s 50(1)(4)(a), sch 11
> s 9 appl—SI 2014/2936, reg 14(5)
> s 10 am—SI 2012/2404, sch 2 para 53(2)
> s 11 rep in pt—Mental Health, 2007 c 12, s 50(1)(4)(b), sch 11
> s 13 am—SI 2012/2404, sch 2 para 53(3)
> s 16A added—Mental Health, 2007 c 12, s 50(1)(3)
> s 20 rep in pt—Mental Health, 2007 c 12, s 50(1)(4)(c), sch 11
>> am—Mental Health, 2007 c 12, s 51
> s 21 am—SI 2006/1016, art 2, sch 1
> s 21A added—Mental Health, 2007 c 12, s 50, sch 9 paras 1, 2
> s 27 am—Human Fertilisation and Embryology, 2008 c 22, sch 6 para 40
>> restr—SI 2014/1530, reg 65
>> excl in pt—SI 2015/62, reg 33
> s 28 am—Mental Health, 2007 c 12, ss 28(1)(10), 35(4)(5)
> s 30 am—Human Fertilisation and Embryology, 2008 c 22, sch 7 para 25
> s 35 am—Mental Health, 2007 c 12, s 50, sch 9 paras 1, 3; SI 2010/813, art 17; Health and
>> Social Care, 2012 c 7, sch 5 para 134
> s 37 excl—SI 2006/2883, reg 3
>> am—Mental Health, 2007 c 12, s 35(4)(6)
> s 38 excl—SI 2006/2883, reg 3
>> am—Nat Health Service (Conseq Provns), 2006 c 43, s 2, sch 1 para 278; Mental
>> Health, 2007 c 12, s 50, sch 9 paras 1, 4; SI 2010/813, art 17
> s 39 excl—SI 2006/2883, reg 3
>> am—Mental Health, 2007 c 12, s 50, sch 9 paras 1, 5; SI 2015/914, sch para 79
> ss 39A-39E added—Mental Health, 2007 c 12, s 50, sch 9 paras 1, 6
> s 40 subst—Mental Health, 2007 c 12, s 49
>> am—Mental Health, 2007 c 12, s 50, sch 9 paras 1, 7
> s 42 am—Mental Health, 2007 c 12, s 50, sch 9 paras 1, 8
> s 45 am—SI 2006/1016, art 2, sch 1
> s 46 am—SI 2006/1016, art 2, sch 1; Crime and Cts, 2013 c 22, sch 14 para 5
> s 49 am—SI 2010/813, art 17
> s 50 am—Mental Health, 2007 c 12, s 50, sch 9 paras 1, 9
> s 51 am—SI 2006/1016, art 2, sch 1
> s 52 subst—SI 2006/1016, art 2, sch 1
> s 53 am—Crim Justice and Cts, 2015 c 2, s 62(2)(3)
>> rep in pt—Crim Justice and Cts, 2015 c 2, s 62(4)
> s 58 am—SI 2010/813, art 17
> s 59 rep—SI 2012/2401, sch 2 para 2
> s 61 am—SI 2010/813, art 17
> s 64 am—Mental Health, 2007 c 12, s 50, sch 9 paras 1, 10; Health and Social Care, 2012 c
>> 7, sch 5 para 135; SI 2012/2404, sch 2 para 53(4)
> s 65 am—SI 2006/1016, art 2, sch 1; Mental Health, 2007 c 12, s 50, sch 9 paras 1, 11
> sch A1 added —Mental Health, 2007 c 12, s 50, sch 7
>> am—SI 2010/813, art 17; Health and Social Care, 2012 c 7, sch 5 para 136(2)(c);
>> SI 2014/560, sch 1 para 30
>> rep in pt—Health and Social Care, 2012 c 7, sch 5 para 136(2)(a)(b)(d)(3)-(6)
> sch 1 am—SI 2012/2404, sch 2 para 53(5)
> sch 1A added—Mental Health, 2007 c 12, s 50, sch 8
>> am—SI 2015/914, sch para 80
> sch 3 am—SI 2010/1898, reg 17, sch
> sch 4 am—Mental Health, 2007 c 12, s 1, sch 1 para 23; SI 2012/2404, sch 2 para 53(6)
>> rep in pt—Mental Health, 2007 c 12, s 55, sch 11 pt 1

2005
c 9 *continued*

sch 6 rep in pt—Legal Services, 2007 c 29, s 210, sch 23; Legal Aid, Sentencing and
Punishment of Offenders, 2012 c 10, sch 5 pt 2; Co-operative and Community
Benefit Societies, 2014 c 14, sch 7; Deregulation, 2015 c 20, sch 6 para 20(4)

c 10 **Public Services Ombudsman (Wales)**

Pt 2 (ss 2-34) appl (mods)—SI 2012/2734, regs 3-6, sch pt 3
am—Social Services and Well-being (W), 2014 anaw 4, sch 3 para 14
s 2 am—Social Services and Well-being (W), 2014 anaw 4, sch 3 para 15
s 4 am—Social Services and Well-being (W), 2014 anaw 4, sch 3 para 16
s 7 am—Govt of Wales, 2006 c 32, s 160, sch 10 para 68; Social Services and Well-being
(W), 2014 anaw 4, sch 3 para 17
s 8 am—Govt of Wales, 2006 c 32, s 160, sch 10 para 69
s 9 am—Govt of Wales, 2006 c 32, s 160, sch 10 para 70; Social Services and Well-being
(W), 2014 anaw 4, sch 3 para 18
s 10 am—Govt of Wales, 2006 c 32, s 160, sch 10 para 71; Social Services and Well-being
(W), 2014 anaw 4, sch 3 para 19
s 12 rep in pt—Govt of Wales, 2006 c 32, ss 160, 163, sch 10 para 72, sch 12
s 13 am—Legal Services, 2007 c 29, s 208, sch 21 para 151
s 14 am—Social Services and Well-being (W), 2014 anaw 4, sch 3 para 20
s 16 am—Govt of Wales, 2006 c 32, s 160, sch 10 para 73
rep in pt—Govt of Wales, 2006 c 32, ss 160, 163, sch 10 para 73(3), sch 12
s 21 rep in pt—Govt of Wales, 2006 c 32, ss 160, 163, sch 10 para 74, sch 12
s 23 rep in pt—Govt of Wales, 2006 c 32, ss 160, 163, sch 10 para 75, sch 12
am—Social Services and Well-being (W), 2014 anaw 4, sch 3 para 21
s 24 rep in pt—Govt of Wales, 2006 c 32, ss 160, 163, sch 10 para 76(5), sch 12
am—Govt of Wales, 2006 c 32, s 160, sch 10 para 76
s 25 rep—Social Services and Well-being (W), 2014 anaw 4, sch 3 para 23
ss 25A, 25B added—Commrs for Older People (W), 2006 c 30, ss 22, 23, Sch 4, para 2(2)
rep—Social Services and Well-being (W), 2014 anaw 4, sch 3 para 23
s 26 rep—Social Services and Well-being (W), 2014 anaw 4, sch 3 paras 24, 25
s 27 rep—Social Services and Well-being (W), 2014 anaw 4, sch 3 para 25
s 28 am—Govt of Wales, 2006 c 32, s 160, sch 10 para 78
s 29 am—Govt of Wales, 2006 c 32, s 160, sch 10 para 79
s 30 am—Govt of Wales, 2006 c 32, s 160, sch 10 para 80
s 32 rep—Social Services and Well-being (W), 2014 anaw 4, sch 3 para 26
Pts 2A (ss 34A-34T), 2B (ss 34U-34Z) added—Social Services and Well-being (W), 2014
anaw 4, sch 3 para 2
s 40 am—Govt of Wales, 2006 c 32, s 160, sch 10 para 81
s 41 am—Nat Health Service (Conseq Provns), 2006 c 43, s 2, sch 1 para 280; SI 2006/363
(W 49), art 4; Commnr for Older People (W), 2006 c 30, s 22, sch 4 para 2; Govt
of Wales, 2006 c 32, s 160, sch 10 para 82; Social Services and Well-being (W),
2014 anaw 4, sch 3 para 27
rep in pt—Nat Health Service (Conseq Provns), 2006 c 43, s 2, sch 1 para 280; Govt of
Wales, 2006 c 32, ss 160, 163, sch 10 para 82(2)(a), sch 12
mod—SI 2006/363 (W 49), arts 5, 6, 7
s 42 am—Govt of Wales, 2006 c 32, s 160, sch 10 para 83; Social Services and Well-being
(W), 2014 anaw 4, sch 3 paras 28, 29
s 43 am—Govt of Wales, 2006 c 32, s 160, sch 10 para 84
s 44 am—Govt of Wales, 2006 c 32, s 160, sch 10 para 85(2)
rep in pt—Govt of Wales, 2006 c 32, ss 160, 163, sch 10 para 85(3), sch 12
sch 1 excl—SI 2006/1011 (W 104), art 3
am—Govt of Wales, 2006 c 32, s 160, sch 10 para 86; Constitutional Reform and
Governance, 2010 c 25, s 44(7); Social Services and Well-being (W), 2014 anaw
4, sch 3 para 30
rep in pt—Govt of Wales, 2006 c 32, ss 160, 163, sch 10 para 86(12)(b)(ii), sch 12
sch 2 rep in pt—SI 2005/3238 (W 243), arts 7, 9(1), sch 1 paras 92, 93
am—SI 2006/363 (W 49), art 2; Govt of Wales, 2006 c 32, s 160, sch 10 para 87;
Police Reform and Social Responsibility, 2011 c 13, sch 16 para 342; Social
Services and Well-being (W), 2014 anaw 4, sch 3 para 31
appl (mods)—SI 2012/2734, regs 3-6, sch pt 3
sch 3 rep in pt—SIs 2005/3225 (W 237), arts 3, 6(2), sch 2 pt 1 para 7; 3226 (W 238),
arts 3, 7(1)(b), sch 2 pt 1 para 15; 3238 (W 243), arts 7, 9(1), sch 1 paras 92,
94

2005

c 10 sch 3 *continued*

    am—SI 2006/363 (W 49), art 3; Govt of Wales, 2006 c 32, s 160, sch 10 para 88; Climate Change, 2008 c 27, s 32, sch 1 para 35; SI 2009/3019, art 12; Police Reform and Social Responsibility, 2011 c 13, sch 16 para 343; SI 2012/990 (W 130), art 9; Loc Govt (Democracy) (W), 2013 anaw 4, sch 1 para 3; SI 2013/755 (W 90), sch 2 para 430; Water, 2014 c 21, sch 10 para 18; Planning (W), 2015 anaw 4, sch 1 para 6; Qualifications Wales, 2015 anaw 5, sch 1 para 38

    sch 3A added—Social Services and Well-being (W), 2014 anaw 4, sch 3 para 4

    sch 4 rep in pt—Localism, 2011 c 20, sch 25 pt 5

    sch 6 rep in pt—Nat Health Service (Conseq Provns), 2006 c 43, s 6, sch 4; Govt of Wales, 2006 c 32, s 163, sch 12; Loc Govt and Public Involvement in Health, 2007 c 28, s 241, sch 18; (prosp) Health, 2009 c 21, s 38, sch 6; Loc Audit and Accountability, 2014 c 2, sch 1 pt 2

c 11   **Commissioners for Revenue and Customs**

    s 5 am—(prosp) Welfare Reform, 2012 c 5, sch 3 para 20

    rep in pt—(prosp) Welfare Reform, 2012 c 5, sch 14 pt 1

    ss 6, 7 mod—Serious Crime, 2007 c 27, s 88, sch 12 para 31; Finance, 2007 c 11, s 84(2)

    saving—Finance, 2007 c 11, s 84(2)

    restr—Finance, 2013 c 29, sch 48 para 22

    s 8A added—Infrastructure, 2015 c 7, s 40

    ss 13, 14 rep in pt—Finance, 2007 c 11, ss 84, 114, sch 22 paras 3, 17, sch 27 pt 5

    s 15 am—Wales, 2014 c 29, s 7

    s 16A added—Finance, 2009 c 10, s 92(1)

    mod—Finance, 2009 c 10, s 92(2)

    s 18 appl (mods)—Teaching and Higher Education, 1998 c 30, s 24

    excl —Income Tax, 2007 c. 3, s 257SI(1)(2)

    mod—Corporation Tax, 2009 c 4, s 1206(1)

    am—Scotland, 2012 c 11, s 24(3)(4); SI 2014/3294, art 4(1)(a); Wales, 2014 c 29, s 7(7)(b)(8)(9)

    rep in pt—Wales, 2014 c 29, s 7(7)(a)

    restr—Corporation Tax, 2009 c 4 ss 1216CM, 1217CM; Finance, 2013 c 29, s 80(6)

    s 19 appl—Olympic Symbol etc (Protection), 1995 c 32, s 12B(2); Gambling, 2005 c 19, s 352A; Income Tax, 2007 c 3, s 257SI(6); Criminal Justice (NI), 2013 c 7, s 14A(3); (prosp) (conditionally) Childcare Payments, 2014 c 28, s 28; Deregulation, 2015 c 20, s 5(4); Small Business, Enterprise and Employment, 2015 c 26, s 9(5)

    appl (mods)—Teaching and Higher Education, 1998 c 30, s 24

    mod—Finance, 1994 c 9, s 41A(3)

    am—Scotland, 2012 c 11, s 24(5); SI 2014/834, sch 1 para 6

    rep in pt—SI 2014/3294, art 4(1)(b)

    s 20 am—Police and Justice, 2006 c 48, s 1, sch 1 para 91; Crime and Cts, 2013 c 22, sch 8 para 156

    s 21 am—Serious Crime, 2007 c 27, s 74, sch 8 para 164; SI 2014/834, sch 1 para 7(3)-(6)

    rep in pt—Serious Crime, 2007 c 27, s 92, sch 14; SI 2014/834, sch 1 para 7(2)

    s 23 am—Borders, Citizenship and Immigration, 2009 c 11, s 19(4)

    s 25 am—Finance, 2008 c 9, s 137(1); Crime and Cts, 2013 c 22, sch 9 para 68

    s 25A added—Finance, 2008 c 9, s 138(1)

    s 27 am—SI 2013/602, sch 2 para 46

    s 29 am—SI 2014/834, sch 1 para 8

    s 35 am—Serious Crime, 2007 c 27, s 74, sch 8 para 165

    s 37 appl (mods) —Serious Organised Crime and Police, 2005 c 15, s 38(6)

    am—Serious Crime, 2007 c 27, s 74, sch 8 para 166

    s 38 appl (mods)—Serious Organised Crime and Police, 2005 c 15, s 38(6)

    am—Serious Crime, 2007 c 27, s 84(3)

    ss 34-39 rep—SI 2014/834, sch 1 para 9

    s 40 am—Serious Crime, 2007 c 27, ss 74, 79, sch 8 para 167, sch 11 para 16; Crime and Cts, 2013 c 22, sch 8 para 186; SI 2014/834, sch 1 para 10(2)(3); Wales, 2014 c 29, s 7(10)

    rep in pt—SI 2014/834, sch 1 para 10(3)(c)(d), (5)(d),(8)

    mod—SI 2014/834, art 9

    s 41 rep—SI 2014/834, sch 1 para 11

    s 42 rep—SI 2014/834, sch 1 para 12

2005

c 11 *continued*

s 44 am—Sale of Student Loans, 2008 c 10, s 6(5); Finance, 2012 c 14, sch 23 para 14;
(prosp) Welfare Reform, 2012 c 5, sch 3 para 21
excl—VAT, 1994 c 23, Sch 3BA paras 13, 15A
rep in pt—Employment, 2008 c 24, ss 9, 20, sch pt 2; (prosp) Scotland, 2012 c 11, sch
2 para 3(2); (prosp) Welfare Reform, 2012 c 5, sch 14 pt 1

s 49 rep—SI 2014/834, sch 1 para 13

s 51 am—Scotland, 2012 c 11, s 24(6); Wales, 2014 c 29, s 7(12)(13)

s 54 rep in pt—(prosp) Welfare Reform, 2012 c 5, sch 14 pt 1

s 55 appl—Olympic Symbol etc (Protection), 1995 c 32, s 12B(2)

sch 1 am—Work and Families, 2006 c 18, s 11, sch 1 para 61; Children and Families, 2014
c 6, sch 7 para 64(2); ibid, sch 7 para 64(4)
rep in pt—(prosp) Welfare Reform, 2012 c 5, sch 14 pt 1; Children and Families, 2014
c 6, sch 7 para 64(3)

sch 2 am—Wireless Telegraphy, 2006 c 36, s 123, sch 7 para 38; Serious Crime, 2007 c 27,
s 77, sch 10 para 28
rep in pt—UK Borders, 2007 c 30, s 58, sch; Serious Crime, 2007 c 27, s 88, sch 12
para 30, sch 14; Finance, 2007 c 11, ss 84(1), 114, sch 27; Criminal Justice and
Immigration, 2008 c 4,ss 97(2), 149, sch 28 pt 6; Finance, c 11, sch 23 paras
59, 65; Finance, 2013 c 29, sch 48 para 21

sch 3 rep—SI 2014/834, sch 1 para 14

sch 4 rep in pt—Finance, 2006 c 25, s 178, sch 26 pt 8(2); Serious Crime, 2007 c 27, s 92,
sch 14; Finance, 2007 c 11, s 114, sch 27 pt 2; ibid, s 114, sch 27 pt 5; Finance,
2008 c 9, s 25, sch 7 para 79(c); SIs 2009/2035, art 2, sch; 2009/3054, art 3,
sch; Taxation (International and Other Provns), 2010 c 8, s 378, sch 10 pt 1;
Finance, 2012 c 14, sch 39 paras 9(2), 43(2)(b); (prosp) Scotland, 2012 c 11,
sch 2 para 3(3); Welfare Reform, 2012 c 5, sch 14 pt 13; SI 2014/834, sch 1
para 15

c 12 **Inquiries**

s 1 am—Govt of Wales, 2006 c 32, s 160, sch 10 para 90
rep in pt—Govt of Wales, 2006 c 32, ss 160, 163, sch 10 para 90, sch 12

s 10 am—SSI 2015/150, sch para 8(2)
rep in pt—SSI 2015/150, sch para 8(3)

s 14 appl—Counter-Terrorism, 2008 c 28, s 74(3)

s 23 am—Financial Services, 2012 c 21, sch 18 para 105

s 27 am—Govt of Wales, 2006 c 32, s 160, sch 10 para 91

s 28 am—Govt of Wales, 2006 c 32, s 160, sch 10 para 92

s 29 am—Govt of Wales, 2006 c 32, s 160, sch 10 para 93

s 30 am—NI (Misc Provns), 2006 c 33, s 30, sch 4 para 14; Govt of Wales, 2006 c 32, s
160, sch 10 para 94

s 41 am—Govt of Wales, 2006 c 32, s 160, sch 10 para 95

s 43 am—Govt of Wales, 2006 c 32, s 160, sch 10 para 96

s 46 rep —Financial Services, 2012 c 21, sch 19

s 51 am—Govt of Wales, 2006 c 32, s 160, sch 10 para 97

sch 2 rep in pt—Safeguarding Vulnerable Groups, 2006 c 47, s 63, sch 10; (S) Protection of
Vulnerable Groups (S), 2007 asp 14, s 88, sch 4 para 45

c 13 **Disability Discrimination**

rep (except s 9, sch 1 (pt))—Equality, 2010 c 15, s 211, sch 27 pt 1 (subst by SI 2010/2279,
sch 2); ibid, sch 27 pt 1A (added by SI 2011/1060, sch 3)

sch 1 rep in pt—Equality, 2006 c 3, s 91, sch 4; SI 2008/2828, art 6

c 14 **Railways**

s 1 am—SI 2010/439, art 2, sch

s 6 explained—Channel Tunnel Rail Link (Supplementary Provns), 2008 c 5, s 1

Pt 3 (ss 9-21) am—SI 2010/439, art 2, sch

s 13 am—Loc Transport, 2008 c 26, s 77, sch 4 para 66(1)(2); Deregulation, 2015 c 20, sch
8 para 7

s 16 am—SI 2009/1941, art 2, sch 1

s 17 rep in pt—Greater London Authority, 2007 c 24, s 57, sch 2; (prosp) Localism, 2011 c
20, sch 25 pt 16

s 19 am—SI 2010/439, arts 2, 4, sch

s 19A added —Loc Transport, 2008 c 26, s 74
am—SI 2010/439, art 2, sch

s 22 am—SI 2015/1682, sch pt 1 para 3(a)
excl—SIs 1994/573, reg 6(4) (added by 2009/3336, art 2); 2013/339, art 7

2005

c 14 *continued*

s 23 am—SI 2015/1682, sch pt 1 para 3(b)
  excl—SIs 1994/573, reg 6(4) (added by 2009/3336, art 2); 2013/339, art 7
s 24 am—SI 2015/1682, sch pt 1 para 3(c)
  excl—SIs 1994/573, reg 6(4) (added by 2009/3336, art 2); 2013/339, art 7
s 25 excl—SI 2013/2587, art 3(3)
  am—SI 2015/1682, sch pt 1 para 3(d)
s 26 am—SI 2015/1682, sch pt 1 para 3(e)
  excl—SI 2013/339, art 8
s 27 am—SI 2015/1682, sch pt 1 para 3(f)
  excl—SI 2013/339, art 8
s 28 am—SI 2015/1682, sch pt 1 para 3(g)
  excl—SI 2013/339, art 8
s 29 am—SI 2015/1682, sch pt 1 para 3(h)
  excl—SIs 1994/573, reg 6(5) (added by 2009/3336, art 2); 2013/339, art 9
s 30 am—SI 2015/1682, sch pt 1 para 3(i)
  excl—SIs 1994/573, reg 6(5) (added by 2009/3336, art 2); 2013/339, art 9
s 31 am—SI 2015/1682, sch pt 1 para 3(j)
  excl—SIs 1994/573, reg 6(5) (added by 2009/3336, art 2); 2013/339, art 9
s 32 am—SI 2015/1682, sch pt 1 para 3(k)
s 33 am—Loc Transport, 2008 c 26, s 77, sch 4 para 66(1)(3); Loc Democracy, Economic
  Development and Construction, 2009 c 20, s 119, sch 6 para 119; SI 2015/1682,
  sch pt 1 para 3(l)
s 34 am—SI 2015/1682, sch pt 1 para 3(m)
s 36 am—SI 2015/1682, sch pt 1 para 3(n)
s 37 am—SI 2015/1682, sch pt 1 para 3(o)
s 45 am—SI 2015/1682, sch pt 1 para 3(p)
s 46 rep in pt—SI 2005/3050, reg 3, sch 1 pt 1 para 5(a)
  am—SI 2005/3050, reg 3, sch 1 pt 1 para 5(b)
s 51 am—SI 2015/1682, sch pt 1 para 3(q)
s 58 am—Loc Transport, 2008 c 26, s 77, sch 4 para 66(1)(4)
s 59 am—SI 2005/3050, reg 3, sch 1 pt 1 para 6
  appl (mods) —SI 2005/3050, reg 14, sch 3 pt 1 para 1(g)
sch 1 appl (mods)—SI 2005/3050, reg 14, sch 3 pt 1 para 1(h)
  am—SIs 2010/439, art 2, sch; 2015/1682, sch pt 1 para 3(r)
sch 2 am—SI 2009/1941, art 2, sch 1
sch 3 rep in pt—Legislative and Regulatory Reform, 2006 c 51, s 30, sch 1; SI 2008/960,
  art 22, sch 3
  am—SI 2006/556, reg 2; Road Safety, 2006 c 49, s 51; SI 2008/960, art 22, sch 3;
   Energy, 2013 c 32, sch 12 paras 83-85; SI 2015/1682, sch pt 1 para 3(s)
sch 4 am—SI 2015/1682, sch pt 1 para 3(t)
sch 5 am—SIs 2010/439, arts 2, 5, sch; 2015/1682, sch pt 1 para 3(u)
  rep in pt—SI 2010/439, art 5
sch 7 am—SI 2010/439, art 2, sch
sch 10 rep in pt—Finance, 2008 c 9, s 8, sch 2 para 70(g)
  am—Corporation Tax, 2009 c 4, s 1322, sch 1 para 667; Corporation Tax, 2010 c 4,
   s 1177, sch 1 para 478; SI 2015/1682, sch pt 1 para 3(v)
sch 12 rep in pt—Postal Services, 2011 c 5, sch 12 para 173

c 15 **Serious Organised Crime and Police**
Pt 1 (ss 1-59) rep—Crime and Cts, 2013 c 22, sch 8 para 158
s 60 am—NI (Misc Provns), 2006 c 33, s 26, sch 3 paras 1, 2; Terrorism, 2006 c 11, s
  33(1)(2)
  rep in pt—(prosp) NI (Misc Provns), 2006 c 33, s 30, sch 5; SI 2014/834, sch 2 para 41
  ext—NI (Misc Provns), 2006 c 33, s 26
s 61 am—SI 2006/1629, art 2; NI (Misc Provns), 2006 c 33, s 26, sch 3 paras 1, 3; Bribery,
  2010 c 23, s 17, sch 1 paras 7, 8
  ext—Identity Cards, 2006 c 15, s 26; NI (Misc Provns), 2006 c 33, s 26
s 62 am—NI (Misc Provns), 2006 c 33, s 26, sch 3 paras 1, 4; Terrorism, 2006 c 11, s 33(3);
  Crime and Cts, 2013 c 22, sch 8 para 159
  ext—NI (Misc Provns), 2006 c 33, s 26
s 63 ext—NI (Misc Provns), 2006 c 33, s 26
s 64 ext—NI (Misc Provns), 2006 c 33, s 26
  am—NI (Misc Provns), 2006 c 33, s 26, sch 3 paras 1, 5

2005

c 15 *continued*

s 65 am—NI (Misc Provns), 2006 c 33, s 26, sch 3 paras 1, 6; (S) Crim Justice and
Licensing (S), 2010 asp 13, s 203, sch 7 para 77

ext—NI (Misc Provns), 2006 c 33, s 26

s 66 ext—NI (Misc Provns), 2006 c 33, s 26

am—NI (Misc Provns), 2006 c 33, s 26, sch 3 paras 1, 7

s 67 am—NI (Misc Provns), 2006 c 33, s 26, sch 3 paras 1, 8

s 69 ext—NI (Misc Provns), 2006 c 33, s 26

s 70 ext—NI (Misc Provns), 2006 c 33, s 26

am—Terrorism, 2006 c 11, s 33(4)

s 71 am—Coroners and Justice, 2009 c 25, s 113(1)-(4); Financial Services, 2012 c 21, sch
18 para 106

rep in pt—SI 2014/834, sch 2 para 42

s 72 am—Coroners and Justice, 2009 c 25, s 113(1)(5)(6)

s 74 am—SI 2010/976, art 13, sch 15

s 75A added—Police and Justice, 2006 c 48, s 52, sch 14 para 62

s 75B added—Coroners and Justice, 2009 c 25, s 113(1)(7)

s 76 rep—Serious Crime, 2015 c 9, s 50(1)(a)

s 77 rep—Serious Crime, 2015 c 9, s 50(1)(b)

s 78 rep—Serious Crime, 2015 c 9, s 50(1)(c)

ss 79-81 rep (1.3.2016)—Serious Crime, 2015 c 9, sch 4 para 71

s 79 appl—(S) SSI 2006/170, art 2; Coroners and Justice, 2009 c 25, s 168(5)

ss 80, 81 appl—Coroners and Justice, 2009 c 25, s 168(5)

s 82 am—(S) Police, Public Order and Crim Justice (S), 2006 asp 10, s 101, sch 6 para
13(1)(9); SIs 2010/976, art 13, sch 15; 2013/602, sch 2 para 48(13)(a); Crime
and Cts, 2013 c 22, sch 8 para 160; Anti-social Behaviour, Crime and Policing,
2014 c 12, s 178(2)(a)-(c)

mod—SI 2007/1098, art 6, sch 1

rep in pt—SI 2013/602, sch 2 para 48(13)(b); Anti-social Behaviour, Crime and
Policing, 2014 c 12, s 178(2)(d)

s 87 am—SI 2010/976, art 13, sch 15

rep in pt—SI 2010/976, art 13, sch 15

s 89 am—SI 2010/976, art 13, sch 15

rep in pt—SI 2010/976, art 13, sch 15

ss 91, 92 rep—Anti-social Behaviour, Crime and Policing, 2014 c 12, s 178(3)

s 93 rep in pt—Anti-social Behaviour, Crime and Policing, 2014 c 12, s 178(4)

s 94 rep in pt—(S) Police, Public Order and Crim Justice (S), 2006 asp 10, s 101, sch 6 para
13(1)(10)

mod—SI 2007/1098, art 6, sch 1

s 97 am—SI 2010/976, art 13, sch 15; Serious Crime, 2015 c 9, s 40(2)(4)

rep in pt—SI 2010/976, art 13, sch 15; Serious Crime, 2015 c 9, s 40(3)

s 99 rep in pt—Serious Crime, 2007 c 27, s 92, sch 14

s 112 rep in pt—Serious Organised Crime and Police, 2005 c 15, s 174(2), sch 17 pt 2

s 117 rep in pt—Protection of Freedoms, 2012 c 9, sch 10 pt 1

s 118 rep in pt—Protection of Freedoms, 2012 c 9, sch 10 pt 1

s 120 rep—Policing and Crime, 2009 c 26, s 112, sch 8 pt 13

s 121 rep in pt—Policing and Crime, 2009 c 26, s 112, sch 8 pt 13

s 123 rep in pt—Policing and Crime, 2009 c 26, s 112, sch 8 pt 13

s 126 rep in pt—Serious Organised Crime and Police, 2005 c 15, s 174(2), sch 17 pt 2

s 128 am—Terrorism, 2006 c 11, s 12(1)-(3)

s 129 am—Terrorism, 2006 c 11, s 12(1)(2)(4)

s 130 rep in pt—Serious Organised Crime and Police, 2005 c 15, s 174(2), sch 17 pt 2

ss 132-138 rep —Police Reform and Social Responsibility, 2011 c 13, s 141(1)

s 139 rep in pt—Anti-social Behaviour, Crime and Policing, 2014 c 12, sch 11 para 50

s 140 rep in pt—Anti-social Behaviour, Crime and Policing, 2014 c 12, sch 11 para 50

ss 141-143 rep —Anti-social Behaviour, Crime and Policing, 2014 c 12, sch 11 para 50

s 146 am—Charities, 2011 c 25, sch 7 para 103

s 148 am—SI 2012/3039, reg 28(2)-(5)(b)

rep in pt—SI 2012/3039, reg 28(5)(c)

s 153 am—Police and Justice, 2006 c 48, s 1, sch 1 para 92; Crime and Cts, 2013 c 22, sch
8 para 161(2)(3)

rep in pt—Crime and Cts, 2013 c 22, sch 8 para 161(4)

s 154 rep in pt—Deregulation, 2015 c 20, sch 11 para 1(4)

s 155 am—Police Reform and Social Responsibility, 2011 c 13, sch 16 para 349

2005

c 15 *continued*

s 156 am—SI 2013/602, sch 2 para 48(14)(a)
    rep in pt—SI 2013/602, sch 2 para 48(14)(b)
s 170 rep—Armed Forces, 2006 c 52, s 378, sch 17
s 172 am—SI 2010/976, art 13, sch 15; Serious Crime, 2015 c 9, s 40(5)
    rep in pt—Crime and Cts, 2013 c 22, sch 8 para 162; Anti-social Behaviour, Crime
        and Policing, 2014 c 12, s 178(5)
s 173 am—SI 2010/976, art 13, sch 15
s 175 am—Serious Crime, 2007 c 27, s 63, sch 6 para 64(1)(3)
    rep in pt—Crime and Cts, 2013 c 22, sch 8 para 163; Serious Crime, 2015 c 9, sch 4
        para 72
s 177 rep in pt—Crime and Cts, 2013 c 22, sch 8 para 164
s 178 am—SI 2010/976, art 13, sch 15
s 179 am—SI 2005/3496, arts 3, 4; NI (Misc Provns), 2006 c 33, s 26, sch 3 paras 1, 9;
    (1.3.2016) Serious Crime, 2015 c 9, sch 4 para 73(2)(4)
    rep in pt—(1.3.2016) Serious Crime, 2015 c 9, sch 4 para 73(3)(5)
sch 1 am—Serious Crime, 2007 c 27, s 74, sch 8 para 174; Policing and Crime, 2009 c 26, s
    109; SIs 2010/976, art 13, sch 15; 2012/2404, sch 2 para 54(2)(3)
sch 4 rep in pt—(prosp) Road Safety, 2006 c 49, s 59, sch 7; Police and Justice, 2006 c 48, s
      52, sch 15; Serious Crime, 2007 c 27, s 92, sch 14; Policing and Crime, 2009 c
      26, s 112, sch 8 pt 13; Equality, 2010 c 15 sch 27 pt 1A (added by SI
      2011/1060, sch 3); (prosp) Loc Audit and Accountability, 2014 c 2, sch 1 pt 2
    am—SI 2013/2042, sch para 30
sch 5 rep—Anti-social Behaviour, Crime and Policing, 2014 c 12, s 178(6)
sch 7 rep in pt—Armed Forces, 2006 c 52, s 378, sch 17; Legal Services, 2007 c 29, s 210,
      sch 23; Anti-social Behaviour, Crime and Policing, 2014 c 12, sch 11 para 50
sch 9 rep in pt—Policing and Crime, 2009 c 26, s 112, sch 8 pt 13
sch 10 rep in pt—(prosp) Anti-social Behaviour, Crime and Policing, 2014 c 12, sch 11 para
    50
sch 14 rep in pt—(prosp) Safeguarding Vulnerable Groups, 2006 c 47, s 63, sch 10; (prosp)
      SI 2007/1351, art 60, sch 8; (prosp) Policing and Crime, 2009 c 26, s 112, sch
      8 pt 8
sch 15 rep in pt—Protection of Freedoms, 2012 c 9, sch 10 pt 3
sch 16 rep in pt—Wireless Telegraphy, 2006 c 36, s 125, sch 9; Police and Justice, 2006 c
      48, s 52, sch 15
sch 17 rep in pt—SI 2005/3496, art 5

c 16　　**Clean Neighbourhoods and Environment**

s 1 rep—Police and Justice, 2006 c 48, s 52, sch 15
s 2 rep—Anti-social Behaviour, Crime and Policing, 2014 c 12, sch 11 para 50
s 20 rep in pt—Anti-social Behaviour, Crime and Policing, 2014 c 12, sch 11 para 50
s 21 rep—Anti-social Behaviour, Crime and Policing, 2014 c 12, sch 11 para 50
s 22 rep—Anti-social Behaviour, Crime and Policing, 2014 c 12, sch 11 para 50
s 31 rep—Anti-social Behaviour, Crime and Policing, 2014 c 12, sch 11 para 50
s 46 am—SI 2005/2900, reg 3(1)-(3)
Pt 6, Ch 1 (ss 55-67) excl—(W) SIs 2007/701 (W 58), reg 3; 2009/2829, art 3, sch
s 54 am—Waste (W), 2010 nawm 8, s 18, sch 1 para 1(1)-(3)
    rep in pt—Waste (W), 2010 nawm 8, s 18, sch 1 para 1(4)
ss 55-64 rep—Anti-social Behaviour, Crime and Policing, 2014 c 12, sch 11 para 42
ss 66, 67 rep—Anti-social Behaviour, Crime and Policing, 2014 c 12, sch 11 para 42
ss 87-89 rep —SI 2012/147, sch
s 90 am—SI 2006/246, reg 20, sch 2
s 94 rep in pt—SI 2012/147, sch
s 95 rep in pt—SI 2012/147, sch
s 105 am—Climate Change, 2008 c 27, s 88(1)
sch 2 rep in pt—SI 2012/147, sch
sch 3 rep in pt—SI 2012/147, sch
sch 4 rep in pt—Anti-social Behaviour, Crime and Policing, 2014 c 12, sch 11 para 50

c 17　　**Drugs**

s 19 am—Police Reform and Social Responsibility, 2011 c 13, sch 16 para 340
s 2 rep—Policing and Crime, 2009 c 26, s 112, sch 8 pt 13

c 18　　**Education**

am—SI 2010/1158, art 5, sch 2
Pt 1 (ss 1-63) appl (mods)—(E) SI 2005/2039, reg 3, sch 1 pt 1 para 11
ss 1-4 rep—Educ and Inspections, 2006 c 40, s 157, sch 14 para 99, sch 18

2005
c 18 *continued*

s 5 am—Educ and Inspections, 2006 c 40, ss 71, 154(b), sch 7 para 23; (prosp) Educ and
Skills, 2008 c 25, s 169, sch 1 paras 25, 26; Academies, 2010 c 32, s 14, sch 2
paras 16, 17; Educ, 2011 c 21, ss 40(2), 41(1); ibid, sch 13 para 15(2)
rep in pt—Educ and Inspections, 2006 c 40, s 154(a), sch 18
appl (mods)—(W) SI 2007/1069 (W 109), reg 3, sch 1; (E) SI 2007/2979, reg 3, sch 1
s 6 appl (mods)—(W) SI 2007/1069 (W 109), reg 3, sch 1; (E) SI 2007/2979, reg 3, sch 1
am—Educ, 2011 c 21, s 40(3)(b)
rep in pt—Educ, 2011 c 21, s 40(3)(a)
s 7 appl (mods)—(W) SI 2007/1069 (W 109), reg 3, sch 1; (E) SI 2007/2979, reg 3, sch 1
s 8 subst—Educ and Inspections, 2006 c 40, s 157, sch 14 para 100
appl (mods)—(W) SI 2007/1069 (W 109), reg 3, sch 1
appl—(E) SI 2007/2979, reg 3, sch 1
am—Educ, 2011 c 21, s 40(4)
s 9 rep in pt—Educ and Inspections, 2006 c 40, s 157, sch 14 para 101, sch 18
appl (mods)—(W) SI 2007/1069 (W 109), reg 3, sch 1
appl—(E) SI 2007/2979, reg 3, sch 1
am—Educ, 2011 c 21, s 40(5)
s 10 appl—SIs (E) SI 2005/1973, reg 2, sch para 4(1)(2)(b); (E) 2007/2979, reg 3, sch 1;
2015/1792, sch para 3
appl (mods)—(W) SI 2007/1069 (W 109), reg 3, sch 1
s 10A added—Apprenticeships, Skills, Children and Learning, 2009 c 22, s 225(1)(2)
s 11 rep in pt—Educ and Inspections, 2006 c 40, s 157, sch 14 para 102, sch 18
appl (mods)—(W) SI 2007/1069 (W 109), reg 3, sch 1
appl—(E) SI 2007/2979, reg 3, sch 1; Educ and Skills, 2008 c 25, s 75(6)
ss 11A-11C added—Educ and Inspections, 2006 c 40, s 160
s 11C rep in pt—Deregulation, 2015 c 20, sch 16 para 6(2)(a)
s 12 am—Educ and Inspections, 2006 c 40, s 157, sch 14 para 103; Educ, 2011 c 21, s
40(6)
appl (mods)—(W) SI 2007/1069 (W 109), reg 3, sch 1
appl—(E) SI 2007/2979, reg 3, sch 1
s 13 appl (mods)—(E) SI 2007/2979, reg 3, sch 1
s 14 appl (mods)—(E) SI 2007/2979, reg 3, sch 1
am—Apprenticeships, Skills, Children and Learning, 2009 c 22, s 225(3); SI
2010/1080, art 2, sch 1; Deregulation, 2015 c 20, sch 16 para 6(3)
rep in pt—Educ, 2011 c 21, sch 16 para 25
s 14A added—Apprenticeships, Skills, Children and Learning, 2009 c 22, s 225(1)(4)
rep in pt—Educ, 2011 c 21, sch 16 para 26; Deregulation, 2015 c 20, sch 16 para
6(2)(b)
s 15 am—Educ and Inspections, 2006 c 40, s 71, sch 7 para 1; Educ, 2011 c 21, s 40(7)
appl—(E) SI 2007/2979, reg 3, sch 1
s 16 appl—(E) SI 2007/2979, reg 3, sch 1
am—Apprenticeships, Skills, Children and Learning, 2009 c 22, s 225(1)(5)
s 16A added—Apprenticeships, Skills, Children and Learning, 2009 c 22, s 225(1)(6)
s 17 am—Educ and Inspections, 2006 c 40, s 71, sch 7 para 2(1)(2)(a)(3)(4)(5); Educ, 2011
c 21, s 40(8)
rep in pt—Educ and Inspections, 2006 c 40, s 71, sch 7 para 2(2)(b), sch 18
appl—(E) SI 2007/2979, reg 3, sch 1
s 18 rep in pt—Educ and Inspections, 2006 c 40, s 71, sch 7 para 24, sch 18
am—Educ and Inspections, 2006 c 40, s 157, sch 14 para 104; Apprenticeships, Skills,
Children and Learning, 2009 c 22, s 225(1)(7)
appl (mods)—(E) SI 2007/2979, reg 3, sch 1
ss 19-27 appl—(E) SI 2007/2979, reg 3, sch 1
s 19 rep in pt—Educ (W), 2014 anaw 5, s 43
s 20 am—Healthy Eating in Schools (W), 2009 nawm 3, s 3(1)(2)
s 28 am—(W) SI 2005/3238 (W 243), arts 7, 9(1), sch 1 paras 95, 96; (prosp) Educ and
Skills, 2008 c 25, s 169, sch 1 paras 25, 27; (W) School Standards and
Organisation (W), 2013 anaw 1, sch 5 para 22(2)(b)(ii)(iii)
appl—(E) SI 2007/2979, reg 3, sch 1
rep in pt—(W) School Standards and Organisation (W), 2013 anaw 1, sch 5 para
22(2)(a)(b)(i)(iii)(iv)
ss 29-37 appl—(E) SI 2007/2979, reg 3, sch 1
s 31 am—Healthy Eating in Schools (W), 2009 nawm 3, s 3(1)(3)
rep in pt—(W) School Standards and Organisation (W), 2013 anaw 1, sch 5 para 22(3)

2005
c 18 *continued*

s 38 am—SI 2005/3238 (W 243), arts 7, 9(1), sch 1 paras 95, 97
    appl—(E) SI 2007/2979, reg 3, sch 1
ss 39-57 appl—(E) SI 2007/2979, reg 3, sch 1
s 41 rep in pt—(W) School Standards and Organisation (W), 2013 anaw 1, sch 5 para 22(4)
s 42 rep in pt—(W) School Standards and Organisation (W), 2013 anaw 1, sch 5 para 22(5)
s 43 rep in pt—(W) School Standards and Organisation (W), 2013 anaw 1, sch 5 para 22(6)
ss 44A-44F added—(W) School Standards and Organisation (W), 2013 anaw 1, s 77
s 45 rep (W)—School Standards and Organisation (W), 2013 anaw 1, sch 5 para 8(2)
s 46 rep (W)—School Standards and Organisation (W), 2013 anaw 1, sch 5 para 22(7)(a)
s 49 am—Deregulation, 2015 c 20, sch 16 para 6(4)
s 51 am—SI 2010/1158, art 5, sch 2
s 58 appl—SIs (E) 2005/1973, reg 2, sch paras 2(1)(2)(b), 4(1)(2)(b); Childcare, 2006 c 21,
    s 78A(7); (E) 2007/2979, reg 3, sch 1; Educ and Skills, 2008 c 25, s 97(2); SI
    2015/1792, sch para 3
s 59 am—Childcare, 2006 c 21, s 103, sch 2 para 44; Educ and Inspections, 2006 c 40, s
    157, sch 14 para 105; Educ and Skills, 2008 c 25, s 169, sch 1 paras 25, 28; (W)
    Children and Families (W), 2010 nawm 1, s 72, sch 1 paras 17, 18
    rep in pt—Childcare, 2006 c 21, s 103, sch 2 para 44, sch 3; Educ and Skills, 2008 c 25,
    s 169, sch 2
    appl—(E) SI 2007/2979, reg 3, sch 1
ss 60, 61 appl—(E) SI 2007/2979, reg 3, sch 1
s 62 appl—(E) SI 2007/2979, reg 3, sch 1
    am—Educ and Skills, 2008 c 25, s 169, sch 1 paras 25, 29
s 63 appl—(E) SI 2007/2979, reg 3, sch 1
ss 64-67 rep—Educ and Inspections, 2006 c 40, s 30, sch 3 para 49, sch 18
s 68 rep (W)—School Standards and Organisation (W), 2013 anaw 1, sch 5 para 22(7)(b)
    am—Educ and Inspections, 2006 c 40, s 30, sch 3 para 50(1)(2)(3)(b)
    rep in pt—Educ and Inspections, 2006 c 40, s 30, sch 3 para 50(3)(a)(3)(c), sch 18
s 69 rep (W)—School Standards and Organisation (W), 2013 anaw 1, sch 5 para 22(7)(b)
    rep in pt—Educ and Inspections, 2006 c 40, s 184, sch 18
ss 70,71 rep (W)—School Standards and Organisation (W), 2013 anaw 1, sch 5 para
    22(7)(b)
s 73 rep—Educ and Inspections, 2006 c 40, s 30, sch 3 para 51, sch 18
ss 74-84 rep —Educ, 2011 c 21, s 14
ss 84A, 84B added—Educ, 2011 c 21, s 15(5)
s 92 am—SIs 2005/3238 (W 243), arts 7, 9(1), sch 1 paras 95, 98; 2010/501, reg 5, sch;
    2010/1080, art 2, sch 1; Charities, 2011 c 25, sch 7 para 104; Educ, 2011 c 21, s
    15(6)(a)(c)
    rep in pt—Educ, 2011 c 21, s 15(6)(b)(d), sch 16 para 27; Deregulation, 2015 c 20, sch
    14 para 48
s 93 am—Educ, 2011 c 21, s 15(7)
s 94 subst—Educ, 2011 c 21, s 15(8)
s 99 rep—Educ, 2011 c 21, sch 5 para 31
s 100 am—Educ and Inspections, 2006 c 40, s 157, sch 14 para 106; Educ, 2011 c 21, s
    15(9)(b)-(d)
    rep in pt—Educ, 2011 c 21, s 15(9)(a)
s 102 rep—Deregulation, 2015 c 20, s 66(3)
s 103 rep in pt—(W) School Standards and Organisation (W), 2013 anaw 1, sch 5 para 33
s 104 rep—Educ, 2011 c 21, s 32(2)
s 106 rep—Educ and Skills, 2008 c 25, s 169, sch 2
s 108 am—Apprenticeships, Skills, Children and Learning, 2009 c 22, s 123, sch 6 para 57
    rep in pt—Educ, 2011 c 21, sch 16 para 28; (prosp) Welfare Reform, 2012 c 5, sch 14
    pt 1; Deregulation, 2015 c 20, sch 14 para 49
s 110 am—Academies, 2010 c 32, s 14, sch 2 paras 16, 18
    rep in pt—(prosp) Welfare Reform, 2012 c 5, sch 14 pt 1
s 113 am—SI 2010/1158, art 5, sch 2; Educ, 2011 c 21, sch 13 para 15(3)
    rep in pt—SI 2010/1158, art 5, schs 2, 3
s 114 am—SI 2010/1158, art 5, sch 2; (W) School Standards and Organisation (W), 2013
    anaw 1, sch 5 para 8(3)
    rep in pt—SI 2010/1158, art 5, schs 2, 3
s 121 am—Educ, 2011 c 21, s 40(9)
s 122 am—SI 2010/1158, art 5, sch 2
    rep in pt—Deregulation, 2015 c 20, s 66(4)

2005

c 18 *continued*

 sch 1 rep—Educ and Inspections, 2006 c 40, s 157, sch 14 para 107, sch 18

 sch 3 am—SI 2006/1016, art 2, sch 1; Tribunals, Cts and Enforcement, 2007 c 15, s 50, sch
  10 para 42

 sch 4 rep in pt—(W) School Standards and Organisation (W), 2013 anaw 1, sch 5 para
  22(8)

 sch 5 rep (W)—School Standards and Organisation (W), 2013 anaw 1, sch 5 para 22(9)(a)
  rep in pt—Educ and Inspections, 2006 c 40, s 184, sch 18; SI 2010/1080, art 2, sch 2

 sch 7 rep in pt—Childcare, 2006 c 21, s 103, sch 3; Educ and Inspections, 2006 c 40, s 184,
  sch 18

 sch 8 rep in pt—Educ and Skills, 2008 c 25, s 169, sch 2

 sch 9 rep in pt—Educ and Inspections, 2006 c 40, s 184, sch 18; (prosp) Educ and Skills,
  2008 c 25, s 169, sch 2; Equality, 2010 c 15, s 211, sch 27, pt 1 (subst by SI
  2010/2279, sch 2); (W) School Standards and Organisation (W), 2013 anaw 1,
  sch 5 para 8(4)

 sch 10 rep—Educ and Inspections, 2006 c 40, s 30, sch 3 para 53, sch 18

 sch 11 rep—Educ and Inspections, 2006 c 40, s 30, sch 3 para 53, sch 18

 sch 12 rep in pt—Educ and Inspections, 2006 c 40, s 184, sch 18; (W) School Standards and
  Organisation (W), 2013 anaw 1, sch 5 para 22(9)(b)

 sch 13 rep—Educ, 2011 c 21, s 14

 sch 14 rep in pt—Equality, 2010 c 15, s 211, sch 27 pt 1 (subst by SI 2010/2279, sch 2);
  ibid, sch 27 pt 1A (added by SI 2011/1060, sch 3); Educ, 2011 c 21, sch 5 para
  32; Loc Audit and Accountability, 2014 c 2, sch 1 pt 2; Higher Educ (W), 2015
  anaw 1, sch para 22

 sch 15 rep —Educ, 2011 c 21, sch 5 para 33

c 19 **Gambling**

 appl (mods)—SI 2014/1641, art 4(1)

 s 2 am—(S) SSI 2009/248, art 2, sch 1

 s 19 am—Charities, 2011 c 25, sch 7 para 105

 s 23 am—SI 2013/602, sch 2 para 49(2)

 s 24 am—SI 2013/602, sch 2 para 49(3)

 s 25 am—(S) SSI 2009/248, art 2, sch 1; SI 2013/602, sch 2 para 49(4)

 s 30 am—SI 2013/2329, sch para 12

 s 31 rep—SI 2013/2329, sch para 13

 s 33 mod—SI 2007/2102, art 3

 s 33 am—(pt prosp) Gambling (Licensing and Advertising), 2014 c 17, s 1(1)

 s 36 am—(pt prosp) Gambling (Licensing and Advertising), 2014 c 17, s 1(2)

 s 54 mod—SI 2007/2158, reg 6

 s 66 mod—SI 2006/3267, reg 2, sch, Table 2

 s 67 mod—SI 2006/3267, reg 2, sch, Table 2
  am—Finance, 2014 c 26, sch 28 para 23

 s 69 mod—SIs 2006/3267, reg 2, sch, Table 2; 2009/1059, art 205, sch 1

 s 70 mod—SI 2006/3267, reg 2, sch, Table 2

 s 71 mod—SIs 2006/3267, reg 2, sch, Table 2; 2009/1059, art 205, sch 1

 s 72 excl—SI 2006/3267, reg 2, sch, Table 1

 s 73 mod—SI 2006/3267, reg 2, sch, Table 2
  am—Protection of Freedoms, 2012 c 9, sch 9 para 119(a)

 s 75 mod—SI 2006/3267, reg 2, sch, Table 2

 s 79 mod—SI 2006/3267, reg 2, sch, Table 2

 ss 80, 81 excl—SI 2006/3267, reg 2, sch, Table 1

 ss 82-84 mod—SI 2006/3267, reg 2, sch, Table 2

 ss 85-87 excl—SI 2006/3267, reg 2, sch, Table 1

 s 88 mod—SI 2006/3267, reg 2, sch, Table 2

 s 89 excl—SI 2006/3267, reg 2, sch, Table 1
  rep in pt—SI 2007/2321, reg 2

 ss 90-99 excl—SI 2006/3267, reg 2, sch, Table 1

 s 99 am—SI 2009/207, art 2

 s 102 excl—SI 2006/3267, reg 2, sch, Table 1
  am—SI 2009/1941, art 2, sch 1

 ss 103,110-112 excl—SI 2006/3267, reg 2, sch, Table 1

 s 114 mod—SI 2006/3267, reg 2, sch, Table 2
  am—SI 2012/2404, sch 2 para 55(2)

 s 116 mod—SIs 2006/3267, reg 2, sch, Table 2; 2007/2159, art 3

 s 117 mod—SIs 2006/3267, reg 2, sch, Table 2; 2007/2159, art 3

2005

c 19 s 117 *continued*

    rep in pt—SI 2007/2321, reg 2

s 118 mod—SI 2007/2159, art 3

    am—Finance, 2014 c 26, sch 28 para 24

s 118A added—Finance, 2014 c 26, sch 28 para 25

s 119 mod—SIs 2006/3267, reg 2, sch, Table 2; 2007/2159, art 3

    am—Finance, 2014 c 26, sch 28 para 26

s 120 mod—SIs 2006/3267, reg 2, sch, Table 2; 2007/2159, art 3

s 123 excl—SI 2006/3267, reg 2, sch, Table 1

s 126 mod—SI 2006/3267, reg 2, sch, Table 2

s 140 subst—SI 2010/22, art 5, sch 2

ss 142, 143 rep—SI 2010/22, art 5, sch 2

ss 144, 145 am—SI 2010/22, art 5, sch 2

s 146 am—SI 2010/22, art 5, sch 2

    rep in pt—SI 2010/22, art 5, sch 2

s 147 rep—SI 2010/22, art 5, sch 2

s 148 rep in pt—SI 2010/22, art 5, sch 2

s 149 rep—SI 2010/22, art 5, sch 2

s 150 mod—SI 2007/2158, reg 6

s 155 appl—(S) SSI 2007/505, reg 5

    am—(S) SSI 2009/248, art 2, sch 1

s 157 am—(S) SSI 2006/475, art 2, sch 1; Police and Fire Reform (S), 2012 asp 8, sch 7
        para 69; SI 2013/602, sch 1 para 8

s 163 mod—SI 2007/2102, art 4

s 172 mod—SI 2007/2158, reg 6

    am—SIs 2009/324, art 2; 2011/1710, arts 2, 3

s 180 saved—SI 2007/1409, regs 16, 17, sch 6

s 182 am—SI 2007/1410, art 2

s 194 am—SI 2012/2404, sch 2 para 55(3)

s 211 am—SI 2012/1659, sch 3 para 17(2)

s 231 am—SI 2012/1659, sch 3 para 17(3)

s 233 am—(S) SSI 2009/248, art 2, sch 1

s 245 rep—SI 2007/2321, reg 2

s 271 am—SI 2007/2158, reg 6

s 273 mod—SI 2007/2158, reg 6

s 274 rep in pt—(S) SSI 2009/248, art 2, sch 2

s 277 am—(S) SSI 2009/248, art 2, sch 1

s 285 am—(S) SSI 2009/248, art 2, sch 1

    rep in pt—(S) SSI 2009/248, art 2, sch 1

s 291 excl—SI 2007/2257, reg 3

s 304 am—(S) SI 2006/3267, reg 2, sch

s 331 rep—Gambling (Licensing and Advertising), 2014 c 17, s 3(1)

s 332 rep in pt—Gambling (Licensing and Advertising), 2014 c 17, ss 3(2), 4(2)(3)

s 333 am—SI 2010/1883, reg 6

ss 336-338 mod—SI 2007/2102, art 5

s 337 mod—SI 2007/2102, art 5

    am—SI 2010/22, art 5, sch 2

    rep in pt—SI 2010/22, art 5, sch 2

s 338 mod—SI 2007/2102, art 5

s 349 mod—SI 2008/2867, reg 12

s 352A added—Finance, 2006 c 25, s 177(1)

s 353 am—SI 2007/2194, art 10, sch 4

s 354 am—Armed Forces, 2006 c 52, s 378, sch 16 para 245; (S) SSI 2006/475, art 2, sch 1

s 361 rep in pt—Gambling (Licensing and Advertising), 2014 c 17, s 3(2)(a)(iii)

sch 1 am—SI 2007/2689, reg 2, sch

sch 3 rep in pt—SI 2013/2329, sch para 14

sch 4 am—SI 2013/2329, sch para 15

sch 6 am—SI 2007/2101, art 2; Serious Crime, 2007 c 27, s 74, sch 8 para 176; SI 2010/22,
        art 5, sch 2; Financial Services, 2012 c 21, sch 18 para 107(b); SI 2012/1633,
        arts 2(b), 3(a)-(e)(g)(h)(j)-(l); Crime and Cts, 2013 c 22, sch 8 para 166(a); SI
        2014/892, sch 1 para 166

    rep in pt—Serious Crime, 2007 c 27, s 92, sch 14; Financial Services, 2012 c 21, sch
        18 para 107(a); SI 2012/1633, arts 2(a), 3(f)(i); Crime and Cts, 2013 c 22, sch
        8 para 166(b); SI 2013/2329, sch para 16

2005

c 19 *continued*

sch 7 am—Armed Forces, 2006 c 52, s 378, sch 16 para 246; SI 2006/3391, arts 2, 3; Fraud, 2006 c 35, s 14, sch 1 para 38; Serious Crime, 2007 c 27, s 60, sch 5 para 6

sch 8 rep—SI 2010/22, art 5, sch 2

sch 10 am—SI 2012/2404, sch 2 para 55(4)

sch 11 am—(S) SSI 2009/248, art 2, sch 1

sch 14 am—SI 2012/2404, sch 2 para 55(5)

sch 16 rep in pt—Policing and Crime, 2009 c 26, s 112, sch 8 pt 13; Equality, 2010 c 15, sch 27 pt 1A; Postal Services, 2011 c 5, sch 12 para 172

c 20 **International Organisations**

1st session of 54th Parliament

c 21 *Appropriation (No 3)*—rep Appropriation (No 2), 2007 c 10, s 4, sch 3

c 22 **Finance (No 2)**

s 7 am—Income Tax, 2007 c 3, s 1027, sch 1 paras 603, 604; Finance, 2008 c 9, s 5, sch 1 para 65(b); Finance, 2009 c 10, s 6, sch 2 para 24; SI 2015/1810, art 13

rep in pt—Finance, 2008 c 9, s 5, sch 1 para 64(a); Finance, 2013 c 29, sch 46 para 135(1)

s 8 rep in pt—Corporation Tax, 2009 c 4, s 1326, sch 3 pt 1

am—Pensions, 2014 c 19, sch 12 para 50(2)(3)

s 9 am—Pensions, 2014 c 19, sch 12 para 51

s 10 rep in pt—Finance, 2009 c 10, s 126(6)(b)

s 11 rep—Income Tax, 2007 c 3, s 1031, sch 3

s 13 rep—Corporation Tax, 2010 c 4, s 1181, sch 3 pt 1

s 16 rep—Corporation Tax, 2010 c 4, s 1181, sch 3 pt 1

s 17 rep in pt—Corporation Tax, 2009 c 4, s 1326, sch 3 pt 1

am—Corporation Tax, 2010 c 4, s 1177, sch 1 para 479

s 18 am—Income Tax, 2007 c 3, s 1027, sch 1 paras 603, 605; Corporation Tax, 2009 c 4, s 1322, sch 1 para 669; Financial Services, 2012 c 21, sch 18 para 108; ibid, sch 16 para 124

rep in pt—Finance, 2010 c 13, s 30, sch 6 para 22; Finance, 2013 c 29, sch 46 para 136

s 23 rep—SI 2009/3001, reg 13, sch 2

ss 24-31 rep—Taxation (International and Other Provns), 2010 c 8, ss 374, 378, sch 8 paras 151, 152, sch 10 pt 3

s 38 rep in pt—Income Tax, 2007 c 3, s 1031, sch 3; Corporation Tax, 2010 c 4, s 1181, sch 3 pt 1

s 41 rep—Corporation Tax, 2009 c 4, s 1326, sch 3 pt 1

s 43 rep—Taxation (International and Other Provns), 2010 c 8, s 378, sch 10 pt 1

s 47 rep in pt—Scotland, 2012 c 11, sch 3 para 29(a)(b)

s 48 rep in pt—Finance, 2012 c 14, sch 16 para 126(c)

s 50 rep—Finance, 2007 c 11, s 73, sch 21 para 8, sch 27

s 54 rep in pt—Corporation Tax, 2009 c 4, s 1326, sch 3 pt 1

s 55 rep—Corporation Tax, 2009 c 4, s 1326, sch 3 pt 1

s 59 rep in pt—Finance, 2008 c 9, s 8, sch 2 para 70(h); Taxation (International and Other Provns), 2010 c 8, s 378, sch 10 pt 1

s 60 rep—Corporation Tax, 2009 c 4, s 1326, sch 3 pt 1

s 61 rep—Taxation (International and Other Provns), 2010 c 8, ss 371, 378, sch 7 paras 109, 110, sch 10 pt 12

s 65 rep in pt—Finance, 2011 c 11, sch 11 para 10(d)

s 68 rep—SI 2012/3062, sch

s 71 am—Income Tax, 2007 c 3, s 1027, sch 1 paras 603, 606; Corporation Tax, 2009 c 4, s 1322, sch 1 para 672

sch 3 rep—Taxation (International and Other Provns), 2010 c 8, ss 374, 378 sch 8 paras 151, 155, sch 10 pt 3

sch 4 rep in pt—Income Tax, 2007 c 3, s 1031, sch 3; Finance, 2011 c 11, sch 10 para 8(c)

sch 6 am—Finance, 2008 c 9, s 62, sch 22 para 18(2)

sch 7 rep in pt—Finance, 2006 c 25, s 178, sch 26; Income Tax, 2007 c 3, s 1031, sch 3; Finance, 2007 c 11, s 114, sch 27 pt 2; Finance, 2008 c 9, s 62, sch 22 para 19(2)(b); Corporation Tax, 2009 c 4, s 1326, sch 3 pt 1; Finance, 2009 c 10, s 48, sch 24 para 9(c); ibid, sch 25 para 9(3)(f); Corporation Tax, 2010 c 4, s 1181, sch 3 pt 1

am—Corporation Tax, 2009 c 4, s 1322, sch 1 para 674

sch 8 rep in pt—Taxation (International and Other Provns), 2010 c 8, s 378, sch 10 pts 2, 13

2005

c 22 *continued*

    sch 9 rep in pt—SI 2005/3465, art 10(b); Finance, 2007 c 11, s 114, sch 27 pt 2; Finance, 2008 c 9, s 43, sch 17 para 17(10)(11)(f); SI 2008/381, art 31, sch; Finance, 2012 c 14, sch 16 para 247(m)

    sch 11 rep in pt—Corporation Tax, 2009 c 4, s 1326, sch 3 pt 1

c 23   *Consolidated Fund*—rep Appropriation (No 2), 2007 c 10, s 4, sch 3

c 24   **Regulation of Financial Services (Land Transactions)**

2006

c 1   **Racial and Religious Hatred**

c 2   **European Union (Accessions)**

    s 2 am—SI 2012/1809, art 3(1), sch pt 1

c 3   **Equality**

    s 1 am—SI 2010/1839, art 7, sch

    s 4 am—SIs 2007/2914, art 8, sch; 2010/1839, art 7, sch

    s 7 rep in pt—Enterprise and Regulatory Reform, 2013 c 24, s 64(4)

    s 8 am—Equality, 2010 c 15, s 211, sch 26 para 62 (subst by SI 2010/2279, sch 1)

    s 9 rep in pt—Enterprise and Regulatory Reform, 2013 c 24, s 64(5)

    s 10 am—SIs 2007/2914, art 8, sch; 2010/1839, art 7, sch; Equality, 2010 c 15, s 211, sch 26 para 63 (subst by SI 2010/2279, sch 1)

        rep in pt—Enterprise and Regulatory Reform, 2013 c 24, s 64(1)(a)

    s 11 am—SI 2007/1388, art 3, sch 1; Equality, 2010 c 15, s 211, sch 26 para 64 (subst by SI 2010/2279, sch 1)

    s 12 am—SIs 2007/2914, art 8, sch; 2010/1839, art 7, sch; Enterprise and Regulatory Reform, 2013 c 24, s 64(2)(6)

    s 13 am—Enterprise and Regulatory Reform, 2013 c 24, s 64(7)

    s 14 am—SIs 2006/1031, reg 49, sch 8; 2007/1388, art 3, sch 1, 2914, art 8, sch; 2010/1839, art 7, sch; Equality, 2010 c 15, s 211, sch 26 para 65(1)-(5) (subst by SI 2010/2279, sch 1); ibid, s 211, sch 26 para 65(6) (subst by SI 2010/2279, sch 1)

    s 15 am—SIs 2007/2914, art 8, sch; 2010/1839, art 7, sch

    s 16 am—Equality, 2010 c 15, s 211, sch 26 para 66 (subst by SI 2010/2279, sch 1); Enterprise and Regulatory Reform, 2013 c 24, s 64(8)

    s 17 am—Enterprise and Regulatory Reform, 2013 c 24, s 64(9)

    s 21 am—Equality, 2010 c 15, s 211, sch 26 para 67 (subst by SI 2010/2279, sch 1); Crime and Cts, 2013 c 22, sch 9 para 52

    s 22 am—Crime and Cts, 2013 c 22, sch 9 para 52

    s 24 am—Crime and Cts, 2013 c 22, sch 9 para 52

    s 24A added—Equality, 2010 c 15, s 211, sch 26 para 68 (subst by SI 2010/2279, sch 1)

    ss 25, 26 rep—Equality, 2010 c 15, s 211, sch 26 paras 69, 70, sch 27 pt 1 (subst by SI 2010/2279, schs 1, 2)

    s 27 rep—Enterprise and Regulatory Reform, 2013 c 24, s 64(1)(b)

    s 28 am—SIs 2007/2914, art 8, sch; 2010/1839, art 7, sch; Equality, 2010 c 15, s 211, sch 26 para 72 (subst by SI 2010/2279, sch 1); Enterprise and Regulatory Reform, 2013 c 24, s 23(4)

    s 29 am—SIs 2007/2914, art 8, sch; 2010/1839, art 7, sch; Legal Aid, Sentencing and Punishment of Offenders, 2012 c 10, sch 5 para 67

    s 31 am—Equality, 2010 c 15, s 211, sch 26 para 73 (subst by SI 2010/2279, sch 1)

    s 32 am—Equality, 2010 c 15, s 211, sch 26 para 74 (subst by SI 2010/2279, sch 1); Crime and Cts, 2013 c 22, sch 9 para 52

    s 33 rep—Equality, 2010 c 15, s 211, sch 26 para 75, sch 27 pt 1 (subst by SI 2010/2279, schs 1, 2)

    s 34 am—(pt prosp) Equality, 2010 c 15, s 211, sch 26 para 76 (subst by SI 2010/2279, sch 1)

    s 35 am—SI 2007/2914, art 8, sch; Equality, 2010 c 15, s 211, sch 26 para 77 (subst by SI 2010/2279, sch 1)

        rep in pt—SI 2010/1839, art 7, sch

    s 39 am—SIs 2006/246, reg 20, sch 2; Equality, 2010 c 15, s 211, sch 26 para 78 (subst by SI 2010/2279, sch 1); Enterprise and Regulatory Reform, 2013 c 24, s 64(10)

    s 43 rep—Equality, 2010 c 15, s 211, sch 26 para 79, sch 27 pt 1 (subst by SI 2010/2279, schs 1, 2)

    Pt 2 (ss 44-80) rep—Equality, 2010 c 15, s 211, sch 26 para 80, sch 27 pt 1 (subst by SI 2010/2279, schs 1, 2)

2006

c 3 *continued*

    s 81 rep—Equality, 2010 c 15, s 211, sch 26 para 81, sch 27 pt 1 (subst by SI 2010/2279, schs 1, 2)

    s 83 rep —Equality, 2010 c 15, s 211, sch 26 para 82, sch 27 pt 1 (subst by SI 2010/2279, schs 1, 2)

    ss 84, 85 rep—Equality, 2010 c 15, s 211, sch 26 para 82, sch 27 pt 1 (subst by SI 2010/2279, schs 1, 2)

    s 86 rep—Equality, 2006 c 3, s 91, sch 4

    s 87 rep —Equality, 2010 c 15, s 211, sch 26 para 82, sch 27 pt 1 (subst by SI 2010/2279, schs 1, 2)

    ss 88-90 rep —Equality, 2010 c 15, s 211, sch 26 para 82), sch 27 pt 1 (subst by SI 2010/2279, schs 1, 2)

    s 92 am—SI 2007/1388, art 3, sch 1

    s 94 rep in pt—Equality, 2010 c 15, s 211, sch 26 para 83, sch 27 pt 1 (subst by SI 2010/2279, schs 1, 2)

    sch 1 am—SIs 2007/1388, art 3, sch 1, 2914, art 8, sch, 3555, art 2; Equality, 2010 c 15, s 211, sch 26 para 84 (subst by SI 2010/2279, sch 1); Enterprise and Regulatory Reform, 2013 c 24, s 64(11)(c)

        rep in pt—Enterprise and Regulatory Reform, 2013 c 24, s 64(11)(a)(b)(d); SI 2014/406, art 3(1)(2)

    sch 2 am—Legal Services, 2007 c 29, s 208, sch 21 para 152; Justice and Security, 2013 c 18, sch 2 para 6; Crime and Cts, 2013 c 22, sch 9 para 52

    sch 3 rep in pt—Equality, 2010 c 15, s 211, sch 26 para 85, sch 27 pt 1 (subst by SI 2010/2279, schs 1, 2)

    sch 5 am—SI 2010/1838, arts 2, 3

c 4   **Terrorism (Northern Ireland)**

c 5   **Transport (Wales)**

    s 2 rep in pt—SI 2007/1388, art 3, sch 1

    s 5 mod—SI 2007/1388, art 3, sch 1

    s 7 am—Loc Transport, 2008 c 26, s 69

    s 25 excl —(temp) SI 2010/1909, art 2

    s 109C added—Transport (W), 2006 c 5, s 3, sch 1 paras 1, 4

    sch rep in pt—Loc Transport, 2008 c 26, s 131, sch 7

c 6   *Appropriation*—rep Appropriation (No 2), 2008 c 8, s 4, sch 3

c 7   **Council Tax (New Valuation Lists for England)**

c 8   **Merchant Shipping (Pollution)**

c 9   **Criminal Defence Service**

    ss 1-3 rep—Legal Aid, Sentencing and Punishment of Offenders, 2012 c 10, sch 5 pt 2

    s 4 rep in pt—Legal Aid, Sentencing and Punishment of Offenders, 2012 c 10, sch 12 para 53; ibid, sch 5 pt 2

c 10   **National Insurance Contributions**

c 11   **Terrorism**

    s 6 am—Crim Justice and Cts, 2015 c 2, s 1(3)

    s 7 am—Counter-Terrorism, 2008 c 28, s 38(2)

    s 11A added —Counter-Terrorism, 2008 c 28, s 38(3)

    s 14 rep (prosp)—Crim Justice and Immigration, 2008 c 4, s 149, sch 28 pt 5

    s 17 mod—Serious Crime, 2007 c 27, s 63, sch 6 para 52(a)

        rep in pt—Serious Crime, 2015 c 9, sch 4 para 74

        am—Serious Crime, 2015 c 9, s 81

    s 19 am—Counter-Terrorism, 2008 c 28, s 29

    s 23 rep in pt—Protection of Freedoms, 2012 c 9, sch 10 pt 4

    s 25 rep—Protection of Freedoms, 2012 c 9, s 57(2), sch 10 pt 4

    s 30 rep—Protection of Freedoms, 2012 c 9, sch 10 pt 4

    s 36 am—Protection of Freedoms, 2012 c 9, s 58(3), sch 9 para 32; Counter-Terrorism and Security, 2015 c 6, s 45(1)

    s 39 mod—Crim Justice and Cts, 2015 c 2, s 97(4); Counter-Terrorism and Security, 2015 c 6, s 51(4)

    sch 1 mod—Serious Crime, 2007 c 27, s 63, sch 6 para 52(b)

        am—Crim Justice and Immigration, 2008 c 4, s 148, sch 26 para 79(1)-(5)

c 12   **London Olympic Games and Paralympic Games**

    s 2 am—SI 2007/2129, art 5, sch

        rep in pt—SI 2010/1551, art 11, sch

    ss 3-8 rep—SI 2014/3184, sch para 2

    s 9 am—SI 2007/2129, art 5, sch

2006

c 12 s 9 *continued*

    rep in pt—SI 2010/1551, art 11, sch

    ss 10-18 rep (14.9.2012)—London Olympic Games and Paralympic Games, 2006 c 12, s
      40(6)

    s 19 am—SI 2007/2129, art 5, sch

     rep in pt—SI 2010/1551, art 11, sch

    s 20 am—SI 2007/2129, art 5, sch; London Olympic Games and Paralympic Games (Amdt),
      2011 c 22, s 2(1)

     rep in pt—SIs 2010/1551, art 11, sch; 2014/3184, sch paras 3, 4

    s 21 am—Police Reform and Social Responsibility, 2011 c 13, sch 16 para 355

     rep in pt—London Olympic Games and Paralympic Games (Amdt), 2011 c 22, s 1(1)

    s 22 am—London Olympic Games and Paralympic Games (Amdt), 2011 c 22, s 1(2)-(4);
      Police Reform and Social Responsibility, 2011 c 13, sch 16 para 356

    s 23 rep—SI 2014/3184, sch para 2(g)

    s 24 am—SI 2010/1551, art 11, sch

     rep in pt—SI 2010/1551, art 11, sch

    s 25 am—SI 2010/1551, art 11, sch

     rep in pt—SIs 2010/1551, art 11, sch; 2014/3184, sch para 2(h)

    s 26 am—SI 2007/2129, art 5, sch; London Olympic Games and Paralympic Games (Amdt),
      2011 c 22, s 2(3)

     rep in pt—SIs 2010/1551, art 11, sch; 2014/3184, sch para 5

    s 28 am—London Olympic Games and Paralympic Games (Amdt), 2011 c 22, s
      1(5)(a)(7)(8); Police Reform and Social Responsibility, 2011 c 13, sch 16 para
      357

     rep in pt—London Olympic Games and Paralympic Games (Amdt), 2011 c 22, s
      1(5)(b)(6); SI 2014/3184, sch para 6

    s 29 rep—SI 2014/3184, sch para 2(i)

    s 30 am—SI 2007/2129, art 5, sch;

     rep in pt—SI 2010/1551, art 11, sch

    s 31 am—London Olympic Games and Paralympic Games (Amdt), 2011 c 22, s 3(1)

    ss 31A-31E added—London Olympic Games and Paralympic Games (Amdt), 2011 c 22, s
      1(9)

     rep—SI 2014/3184, sch para 2(j)-(n)

    s 33 rep (14.9.2012)—London Olympic Games and Paralympic Games, 2006 c 12, s 40(8)

    s 34 am—SI 2007/2129, art 5, sch

     rep in pt—SI 2010/1551, art 11, sch; Localism, 2011 c 20, sch 25 pt 32

    s 35 am—SI 2007/2129, art 5, sch

     rep in pt—SI 2010/1551, art 11, sch

    s 36 rep (pt prosp)—Public Bodies, 2011 c 24, sch 6

     am—SI 2007/2129, art 5, sch

     rep in pt—SI 2010/1551, art 11, sch

    s 37 am—SI 2007/2129, art 5, sch; London Olympic Games and Paralympic Games (Amdt),
      2011 c 22, ss 1(11), 2(5)(6)

     rep in pt—SI 2010/1551, art 11, sch; London Olympic Games and Paralympic Games
      (Amdt), 2011 c 22, s 1(10)(11); SI 2014/3184, sch para 7(a)-(d)

    s 38 rep in pt—London Olympic Games and Paralympic Games (Amdt), 2011 c 22, s 1(12)

    s 40 am—SI 2007/2129, art 5, sch

     rep in pt—SI 2010/1551, art 11, sch

    s 41 am—SI 2007/2129, art 5, sch

     rep in pt—SIs 2010/1551, art 11, sch; 2014/3184, sch para 2(o)

    sch 1 rep—SI 2014/3184, sch para 2(p)

    sch 2 rep—SI 2014/3184, sch para 2(q)

    sch 4 rep (14.9.2012)—London Olympic Games and Paralympic Games, 2006 c 12, s 40(8)

c 13 **Immigration, Asylum and Nationality**

    mod—SI 1994/1405, art.7 (as am by SIs 2007/3579, art 3; 2015/856, arts 5,6)

    ext in pt (mods) —(to I of Man) SI 2008/680, art 20, sch 9

    ss 1-6 rep—Immigration, 2014 c 22, sch 9 para 60 table

    s 11 rep in pt—Immigration, 2014 c 22, sch 9 para 60 table

    s 12 am—Immigration, 2014 c 22, sch 9 para 57(2)(a)

     rep in pt—Immigration, 2014 c 22, sch 9 para 57(2)(c)

    s 13 rep—Immigration, 2014 c 22, sch 9 para 57(3)

    s 15 am—Immigration, 2014 c 22, sch 9 para 61

    s 17 am—Crime and Cts, 2013 c 22, sch 9 para 52; Immigration, 2014 c 22, s 44

    s 18 am—Immigration, 2014 c 22, s 45

2006

c 13 *continued*

s 23 am—Equality, 2010 c 15, s 211, sch 26 para 81 (subst by SI 2010/2279, sch 1)

s 27 ext (mods)—SIs (Jersey) 2015/1532, art 2(1) sch 1; (Guernsey) 1533, art 4 sch 1

s 31 ext (mods)—(Isle of Man) SI 2008/680, art 20, sch 9 (amended by SI 2011/1408, sch paras 8(1)(2), 9(b)); (Guernsey) SI 2011/2444, art 4, sch 1; (Jersey) SI 2012/1763, art 2, sch 1

s 32 am—(prosp) Police and Justice, 2006 c 48, s 14(1)-(3); Counter-Terrorism and Security, 2015 c 6, sch 5 para 6

ext (mods)—(Isle of Man) SI 2008/680, art 20, sch 9 (amended by SI 2011/1408, sch paras 8(1)(2), 9(b)); (Guernsey) SI 2011/2444, art 4, sch 1; (Jersey) SI 2012/1763, art 2, sch 1

rep in pt—(prosp) Police and Justice, 2006 c 48, s 52, sch 15 pt 2

ss 32A, 32B added—Counter-Terrorism and Security, 2015 c 6, sch 5 para 7

s 33 rep in pt—(prosp) Police and Justice, 2006 c 48, s 52, sch 15 pt 2

am—(prosp) Police and Justice, 2006 c 48, s 14(1)(3)

s 34 ext (mods)—(Isle of Man) SI 2008/680, art 20, sch 9 (amended by SI 2011/1408, sch paras 8(1)(2)(b)); (Guernsey) SI 2011/2444, art 4, sch 1; (Jersey) SI 2012/1763, art 2, sch 1

s 34 am—Counter-Terrorism and Security, 2015 c 6, sch 5 para 8

s 36 am—(prosp) Police and Justice, 2006 c 48, s 14(1)(4); Borders, Citizenship and Immigration, 2009 c 11, s 21; SI 2013/602, sch 2 para 50(2)

rep in pt—(prosp) Police and Justice, 2006 c 48, s 52, sch 15 pt 2

ext (mods)—(Isle of Man) SI 2008/680, art 20, sch 9 (amended by SI 2011/1408, sch paras 8(1)(2), 9(b))

s 37 ext (mods)—(Isle of Man) SI 2008/680, art 20, sch 9 (amended by SI 2011/1408, sch paras 8(1)(2), 9(b))

s 38 rep—Counter-Terrorism, 2008 c 28, s 20, sch 9, sch 1 para 4

s 39 ext (mods)—(Isle of Man) SI 2008/680, art 20, sch 9 (amended by SI 2011/1408, sch paras 8(1)(2), 9(b)); (Guernsey) SI 2011/2444, art 4, sch 1; (Jersey) SI 2012/1763, art 2, sch 1

am—Crime and Cts, 2013 c 22, sch 8 para 186; SI 2013/602, sch 2 para 50(3)

ss 40, 41 ext—SI 2003/2818, art 11(1)(g)

s 42 ext (mods)—SIs (Jersey) 2015/1532, art 2(1) sch 1; (Guernsey) 1533, art 4 sch 1

s 47 rep—Immigration, 2014 c 22, sch 9 para 5

s 48 rep—Immigration, 2014 c 22, sch 9 para 7 table

ss 50, 51 appl—UK Borders, 2007 c 30, s 15(2)

s 51 rep—Immigration, 2014 c 22, sch 9 para 74

s 52 rep—Immigration, 2014 c 22, sch 9 para 74

s 55 am—SI 2010/21, art 5, sch 1; Immigration, 2014 c 22, sch 9 para 57(4)(b)

rep in pt—Immigration, 2014 c 22, sch 9 para 57(4)(a)

s 57 rep in pt—Immigration, 2014 c 22, sch 9 para 60 table

s 58 rep —Borders, Citizenship and Immigration, 2009 c 11, s 56, sch pt 2

s 62 mod—Crime and Cts, 2013 c 22, s 52(7)

s 63 am—Police and Justice, 2006 c 48, s 54(7)

s 64 rep in pt—UK Borders, 2007 c 30, s 58, sch; ibid, s 61(3)

sch 1 rep in pt—SI 2010/21, art 5, sch 3; Immigration, 2014 c 22, sch 9 para 57(5); ibid, sch 9 para 60 table

sch 2 rep in pt—Immigration, 2014 c 22, sch 9 para 76(a)

c 14 **Consumer Credit**

s 2 rep in pt—SI 2013/1881, sch para 10(a)

ss 3, 4 rep —SI 2013/1881, sch para 10(a)

s 5 rep in pt—SI 2013/1881, sch para 10(a)

s 22 rep in pt—SI 2013/1881, sch para 10(a)

s 24 rep in pt—SI 2013/1881, sch para 10(a)

s 25 rep in pt—SI 2013/1881, sch para 10(a)

s 26 rep —SI 2013/1881, sch para 10(a)

s 27 rep in pt—SI 2013/1881, sch para 10(a)

ss 28-50 rep —SI 2013/1881, sch para 10(a)

s 51 rep in pt—SI 2013/1881, sch para 10(a); Consumer Rights, 2015 c 15, sch 6 para 85(g)

ss 52-54 rep —SI 2013/1881, sch para 10(a)

s 55 rep—SI 2009/1835, art 4, sch 3

s 56 rep in pt—SI 2009/1835, art 4, sch 3

ss 57, 58 rep—SI 2009/1835, art 4, sch 3

ss 59, 60 rep —SI 2013/1881, sch para 10(a)

2006

c 14 *continued*

    s 61 rep in pt—SI 2013/1881, sch para 10(a)

    ss 62, 65 rep —SI 2013/1881, sch para 10(a)

    sch 1 rep—SI 2009/1835, art 4, sch 3

    sch 2 rep —SI 2013/1881, sch para 10(b)

    sch 3 rep in pt—SI 2008/2826, art 6; SI 2013/1881, sch para 10(c)

c 15   *Identity Cards*—rep Identity Documents, 2010 c 40, s 1(1)

c 16   **Natural Environment and Rural Communities**

    s 1 am—Marine and Coastal Access, 2009 c 23, s 311

    s 12 rep in pt—Legal Services, 2007 c 29, s 208, sch 21 para 153, sch 23

    Pt 1 Ch 2 (ss 17-25) rep in pt_—SI 2012/2654, sch

    s 26 rep in pt—Public Bodies, 2011 c 24, sch 6

    s 32 am—(W) SI 2013/755 (W 90), sch 2 para 432

    s 40 am—(prosp) Planning (W), 2015 anaw 4, sch 2 para 28

    s 42 am—(W) SI 2013/755 (W 90), sch 2 para 433

    s 43 am—SI 2013/1506, sch 5 para 2

    ss 73-77 rep—SI 2012/1658, art 5, sch

    ss 78-80 am—SI 2009/229, art 9, sch 2

    s 81 am—SIs 2009/229, art 9, sch 2; 2010/501, reg 5, sch; Charities, 2011 c 25, sch 7 para 109

    ss 82, 86, 98 am—SI 2009/229, art 9, sch 2

    s 108 rep in pt—SI 2012/1658, art 5, sch

    sch 1 am—SI 2012/2404, sch 2 para 56(2)

    sch 2 rep—SI 2012/2654, sch

    sch 4 am—SI 2012/2404, sch 2 para 56(4)

    sch 5 am—Crim Justice and Immigration, 2008 c 4, s 148, sch 26 para 80

    sch 7 am—Marine and Coastal Access, 2009 c 23, s 184, sch 14, para 20; SI 2012/1659, sch 3 para 18

        rep in pt—SI 2014/1924, sch

    sch 10 am—SI 2009/1941, art 2, sch 1

    sch 11 rep in pt—(saving) SI 2007/3538, reg 74, sch 23; Marine and Coastal Access, 2009 c 23, s 321, sch 22, pts 4, 8; Equality, 2010 c 15, sch 27 pt 1A (added by SI 2011/1060, sch 3); SI 2012/1658, art 5, sch; Deregulation, 2015 c 20, sch 22 paras 7(2), 11(2), 15(2)

c 17   *Northern Ireland*—rep NI (St Andrews Agreement), 2006 c 53, s 22

c 18   **Work and Families**

    ss 3-10 rep —Children and Families, 2014 c 6, sch 7 para 66

    s 11 rep in pt—Children and Families, 2014 c 6, sch 7 para 67

    sch 1 rep in pt—Welfare Reform, 2012 c 5, sch 14 pt 13; Children and Families, 2014 c 6, sch 7 para 68

c 19   **Climate Change and Sustainable Energy**

    ss 3-5 rep—Deregulation, 2015 c 20, s 57(1)(a)(b)

    s 7 rep in pt—Deregulation, 2015 c 20, s 57(1)(c)

    s 8 rep—Deregulation, 2015 c 20, s 57(1)(c)

    s 10 rep—Deregulation, 2015 c 20, s 57(1)(d)

    s 12 rep—Deregulation, 2015 c 20, s 57(1)(e)

    s 14 trans of functions—SI 2009/3019, arts 2(b), 5

        excl—Deregulation, 2015 c 20, s 57(1)(c)

    s 18 rep—Deregulation, 2015 c 20, s 57(1)(c)

    s 21 rep—Deregulation, 2015 c 20, s 57(1)(f)

    s 22 rep in pt—Deregulation, 2015 c 20, s 57(1)(d)

    ss 23, 24 rep—Deregulation, 2015 c 20, s 57(1)(e)

    s 26 am—SI 2008/1767, art 2

c 20   **Children and Adoption**

    sch 2 rep in pt—Children and Families, 2014 c 6, s 18(3)(d)

c 21   **Childcare**

    savings—SI 2008/2261, arts 3, 4, schs 1, 2

    power to am rep (cond)—Children and Families, 2014 c 6, s 137(2) (5)

    power to mod (cond)—Children and Families, 2014 c 6, s 137(2) (5)

    s 3 am—Apprenticeships, Skills, Children and Learning, 2009 c 22, s 201

    s 4 am—Health and Social Care, 2012 c 7, sch 5 para 137(a)(b)(i)

        rep in pt—Health and Social Care, 2012 c 7, sch 5 para 137(b)(ii)(iii)

2006

c 21 *continued*

ss 5A-5G added—Apprenticeships, Skills, Children and Learning, 2009 c 22, s 198

s 6 am—Equality, 2010 c 15, s 211, sch 26 para 88 (added by SI 2010/2279, sch 1); SI 2013/630, reg 19(2)

s 7 subst —Educ, 2011 c 21, s 1(2)

s 7A added—Children and Families, 2014 c 6, s 87(2)

s 9A added—Children and Families, 2014 c 6, s 87(3)

s 11 rep—Children and Families, 2014 c 6, s 86

s 12 am—Equality, 2010 c 15, s 211, sch 26 para 89 (added by SI 2010/2279, sch 1)

s 13 am—Educ and Skills, 2008 c 25, s 169, sch 1 paras 30, 31; SI 2012/976, sch para 17

s 13A added—Educ, 2011 c 21, s 1(3)

    am—Small Business, Enterprise and Employment, 2015 c 26, s 74(1)

    rep in pt—(prosp) Welfare Reform, 2012 c 5, sch 14 pt 1

s 13B added—Educ, 2011 c 21, s 1(3)

    am—Small Business, Enterprise and Employment, 2015 c 26, s 74(2)

s 14 rep—Educ and Inspections, 2006 c 40, s 157, sch 14 para 109, sch 18

s 15 am—SI 2010/1158, art 5, sch 2

    rep in pt—SI 2010/1158, art 5, schs 2, 3

s 18 am—(W prosp) Children and Young Persons, 2008 c 23, s 8, sch 1 para 19(1), (2), (3)(b); SI 2010/813, art 18; Crim Justice and Cts, 2015 c 2, sch 9 para 21

    rep in pt—(W prosp) Children and Young Persons, 2008 c 23, s 8, sch 1 para 19(1), (3)(a), sch 4; SI 2010/813, art 18

s 21 rep in pt—SI 2010/1080, art 2, schs 1, 2

s 22 am—Equality, 2010 c 15, s 211, sch 26 para 90 (added by SI 2010/2279, sch 1); (W) SI 2013/1788 (W 178), reg 4

s 27 am—Equality, 2010 c 15, s 211, sch 26 para 91 (added by SI 2010/2279, sch 1)

s 28 am—SI 2010/1158, art 5, sch 2

s 29 subst (W)—School Standards and Organisation (W), 2013 anaw 1, sch 5 para 10

    am—SI 2010/1158, art 5, sch 2

    rep in pt—SI 2010/1158, art 5, schs 2, 3

s 30 am—(W) Children and Families (W), 2010 nawm 1, s 72, sch 1 paras 21, 22

s 31 rep—Educ and Inspections, 2006 c 40, s 157, sch 14 para 110, sch 18

s 32 am—Children and Families, 2014 c 6, sch 4 para 2(2)(a)(c)(3)(4)(a)(c)(5)(6)

    rep in pt—Children and Families, 2014 c 6, sch 4 para 2(2)(b)(4)(b)

s 33 mod—SI 2008/979, arts 2, 3, 6, 8

    am—Children and Families, 2014 c 6, sch 4 para 4

s 34 am—Educ and Skills, 2008 c 25, s 169, sch 1 paras 30, 32; Children and Families, 2014 c 6, sch 4 para 5

    mod—SI 2008/979, arts 2, 4-9

    rep in pt—Small Business, Enterprise and Employment, 2015 c 26, ss 75(1), 76(6); (1.1.2016) ibid, sch 2 para 2

s 35 am—Children and Families, 2014 c 6, sch 4 para 6

s 36 am—Children and Families, 2014 c 6, sch 4 para 7

    rep in pt—(1.1.2016) Small Business, Enterprise and Employment, 2015 c 26, sch 2 para 3

s 37 am—Children and Families, 2014 c 6, sch 4 para 8

    rep in pt—(1.1.2016) Small Business, Enterprise and Employment, 2015 c 26, sch 2 para 4

s 37A added—Children and Families, 2014 c 6, sch 4 para 9

    rep in pt—(1.1.2016) Small Business, Enterprise and Employment, 2015 c 26, sch 2 para 5

s 38 am—Children and Families, 2014 c 6, sch 4 para 10

s 40 am—Small Business, Enterprise and Employment, 2015 c 26, s 75(2)

s 41 am—Apprenticeships, Skills, Children and Learning, 2009 c 22, ss 160, 174, 192, sch 12 paras 38, 39

s 42 am—Apprenticeships, Skills, Children and Learning, 2009 c 22, ss, 174, 192, sch 12 paras 38, 40(1)(2)(b)(4)(5); (pt prosp) ibid, s 160

    rep in pt—Apprenticeships, Skills, Children and Learning, 2009 c 22, ss 174, 192, 266, sch 12 paras 38, 40(1)(2)(a)(3), sch 16; Educ, 2011 c 21, sch 8 para 17

s 44 am—Apprenticeships, Skills, Children and Learning, 2009 c 22, ss 174, 192, sch 12 paras 38, 41; Children and Families, 2014 c 6, sch 4 para 11(2)(a)(3)(4)

    rep in pt—Children and Families, 2014 c 6, sch 4 para 11(2)(b)

2006

c 21 *continued*

s 46 am—Apprenticeships, Skills, Children and Learning, 2009 c 22, ss 174, 192, sch 12
    paras 38, 42; Educ, 2011 c 21, sch 8 para 18(2)(4)
  rep in pt—Educ, 2011 c 21, sch 8 para 18(3)
s 47 rep in pt—Educ and Skills, 2008 c 25, s 169, sch 2
s 49 am—(prosp) Educ and Skills, 2008 c 25, s 169, sch 1 paras 30, 33; SI 2012/976, sch
    para 18; Children and Families, 2014 c 6, s 85; ibid, sch 4 para 12
s 50 rep in pt—Educ and Inspections, 2006 c 40, s 157, sch 14 para 111, sch 18
Pt 3 Ch 2A (ss 51A-51F) added—Children and Families, 2014 c 6, sch 4 para 13
s 52 mod—SI 2008/979, arts 2, 3, 6, 8
  am—Children and Families, 2014 c 6, sch 4 para 15
s 53 am—Educ and Skills, 2008 c 25, s 169, sch 1 paras 30, 34; SI 2012/976, sch para 19;
    Children and Families, 2014 c 6, sch 4 para 16; Small Business, Enterprise and
    Employment, 2015 c 26, s 76(7)(a)
  mod—SI 2008/979, arts 2, 4-8
  rep in pt—Small Business, Enterprise and Employment, 2015 c 26, s 76(7)(b);
    (1.1.2016) ibid, sch 2 para 6
s 54 am—Children and Families, 2014 c 6, sch 4 para 17
s 55 am—Children and Families, 2014 c 6, sch 4 para 18
  rep in pt—(1.1.2016) Small Business, Enterprise and Employment, 2015 c 26, sch 2
    para 7
s 56 am—Children and Families, 2014 c 6, sch 4 para 19
  rep in pt—(1.1.2016) Small Business, Enterprise and Employment, 2015 c 26, sch 2
    para 8
s 56A am—Children and Families, 2014 c 6, sch 4 para 20
  rep in pt—(1.1.2016) Small Business, Enterprise and Employment, 2015 c 26, sch 2
    para 9
s 57 am—Children and Families, 2014 c 6, sch 4 para 21
  rep in pt—(1.1.2016) Small Business, Enterprise and Employment, 2015 c 26, sch 2
    para 10
s 57A added—Children and Families, 2014 c 6, sch 4 para 22
  rep in pt—(1.1.2016) Small Business, Enterprise and Employment, 2015 c 26, sch 2
    para 11
s 58 am—Children and Families, 2014 c 6, sch 4 para 23
s 59 am—Children and Families, 2014 c 6, sch 4 para 24(2)(a)(3)(a)(4)
  rep in pt—Children and Families, 2014 c 6, sch 4 para 24(2)(b)(3)(b)
s 60 am—Children and Families, 2014 c 6, sch 4 para 25
s 61 rep in pt—Educ and Inspections, 2006 c 40, s 157, sch 14 para 112, sch 18
Pt 3 Ch 3A (ss 61A-61G) added—Children and Families, 2014 c 6, sch 4 para 26
s 63 am—Educ and Skills, 2008 c 25, s 169, sch 1 paras 30, 35; SI 2012/976, sch para 20;
    Small Business, Enterprise and Employment, 2015 c 26, s 75(3)
  rep in pt—(1.1.2016) Small Business, Enterprise and Employment, 2015 c 26, sch 2
    para 12
s 64 rep in pt—(1.1.2016) Small Business, Enterprise and Employment, 2015 c 26, sch 2
    para 13
s 65 am—Children and Families, 2014 c 6, sch 4 para 26
  rep in pt—(1.1.2016) Small Business, Enterprise and Employment, 2015 c 26, sch 2
    para 14
s 65A added—Children and Families, 2014 c 6, sch 4 para 29
  rep in pt—(1.1.2016) Small Business, Enterprise and Employment, 2015 c 26, sch 2
    para 15
s 66 am—Children and Families, 2014 c 6, sch 4 para 30
s 67 am—Children and Families, 2014 c 6, sch 4 para 31(2)(a)(3)(a)(4)
  rep in pt—Children and Families, 2014 c 6, sch 4 para 31(2)(b)(3)(b)
s 68 am—Children and Families, 2014 c 6, sch 4 para 33
s 69 am —SI 2008/2833, art 6, sch 3; Children and Families, 2014 c 6, sch 4 para 34; Small
    Business, Enterprise and Employment, 2015 c 26, sch 2 para 16
s 69A added—Children and Families, 2014 c 6, sch 4 para 35
s 69B, 69C added—Children and Families, 2014 c 6, sch 4 para 36
s 70 am—Children and Families, 2014 c 6, sch 4 para 37
s 70A added—Children and Families, 2014 c 6, sch 4 para 38
s 71 am—Children and Families, 2014 c 6, sch 4 para 39
s 72 am—Crime and Cts, 2013 c 22, sch 11 para 203; Children and Families, 2014 c 6, sch
    4 para 40

2006

c 21 *continued*

s 73 am—Children and Families, 2014 c 6, sch 4 para 41
s 74 am—Children and Families, 2014 c 6, sch 4 para 42
s 75 am—Safeguarding Vulnerable Groups, 2006 c 47, s 63, sch 9 para 10; (W) Children
    and Families (W), 2010 nawm 1, s 72, sch 1 paras 21, 23; Children and Families,
    2014 c 6, sch 4 paras 43, 44
    rep in pt—(prosp) Safeguarding Vulnerable Groups, 2006 c 47, s 63, sch 10; Legal Aid,
      Sentencing and Punishment of Offenders, 2012 c 10, sch 24 para 27
s 76 am—Children and Families, 2014 c 6, sch 4 para 45
ss 76A, 76B added—Children and Families, 2014 c 6, sch 4 para 46
s 77 rep in pt—Educ and Inspections, 2006 c 40, s 157, sch 14 para 113(2)(4), sch 18
    am—Educ and Inspections, 2006 c 40, s 157, sch 14 para 113(1)(3); Children and
      Families, 2014 c 6, sch 4 para 47
s 78 am—Children and Families, 2014 c 6, sch 4 para 48
ss 78A, 78B added—Children and Families, 2014 c 6, sch 4 para 49
s 79 am—Educ and Inspections, 2006 c 40, s 157, sch 14 para 114; Crime and Cts, 2013 c
    22, sch 11 para 204(b); Children and Families, 2014 c 6, sch 4 para 50
    rep in pt—Crime and Cts, 2013 c 22, sch 11 para 204(a)
ss 80, 81 rep—Educ and Inspections, 2006 c 40, s 157, sch 14 para 115, sch 18
s 82 am—Children and Families, 2014 c 6, sch 4 para 51
s 83 am—SI 2013/630, reg 19(3); Children and Families, 2014 c 6, sch 4 para 52
s 83A added—Children and Families, 2014 c 6, sch 4 para 53
    am—(pt prosp) Childcare Payments, 2014 c 28, s 29
s 84 am—Children and Families, 2014 c 6, sch 4 para 54
s 84A added—Children and Families, 2014 c 6, sch 4 para 55
s 85 am—Children and Families, 2014 c 6, sch 4 para 56
s 85A added—Small Business, Enterprise and Employment, 2015 c 26, sch 2 para 17
s 87 am—Children and Families, 2014 c 6, sch 4 para 57
s 89 am—Children and Families, 2014 c 6, sch 4 para 58
s 90 am—Children and Families, 2014 c 6, sch 4 para 59(2)
    rep in pt—Children and Families, 2014 c 6, sch 4 para 59(3)
s 93 am—Children and Families, 2014 c 6, sch 4 para 60(2)(a)(3)(4)(a)
    rep in pt—Children and Families, 2014 c 6, sch 4 para 60(4)(b)
s 94 rep (1.1.2016)—Small Business, Enterprise and Employment, 2015 c 26, sch 2 para 18
    am—Children and Families, 2014 c 6, sch 4 para 61
s 96 rep in pt—Small Business, Enterprise and Employment, 2015 c 26, s 76(2)(a),(3)(b),
    (4)(a),(5)(b)
    am—Small Business, Enterprise and Employment, 2015 c 26, s 76(2)(b),(3)(a),(4)(b),
    (5)(a)
s 98 am—Educ and Inspections, 2006 c 40, s 157, sch 14 para 117; Children and Families,
    2014 c 6, sch 4 para 62
    rep in pt—SI 2010/1080, art 2, schs 1, 2
Pt 3A (ss 98A-98G) added —Apprenticeships, Skills, Children and Learning, 2009 c 22,
    s 199
s 98F am—Crime and Cts, 2013 c 22, sch 11 para 205(b)
    rep in pt—Crime and Cts, 2013 c 22, sch 11 para 205(a)
s 99 mod—Childcare, 2006 c 21, s 100
    am—Children and Families, 2014 c 6, sch 4 para 63; Small Business, Enterprise and
      Employment, 2015 c 26, s 75(4)
    rep in pt—SI 2010/1080, art 2, schs 1, 2
s 100 rep—Educ, 2011 c 21, s 1(4)
s 101 am—(W) Children and Families (W), 2010 nawm 1, s 72, sch 1 paras 21, 24; SI
    2010/1158, art 5, sch 2
s 105 rep in pt—(1.1.2016) Small Business, Enterprise and Employment, 2015 c 26, sch 2
    para 19
s 106 am—Educ and Skills, 2008 c 25, s 169, sch 1 paras 30, 36; SI 2010/1080, art 2, sch 1
s 110 am—(W) Learner Travel (W), 2008 nawm 2, s 25, sch 1 para 5
sch 1 rep in pt—Apprenticeships, Skills, Children and Learning, 2009 c 22, s 266, sch 16
sch 2 rep in pt—Educ and Inspections, 2006 c 40, s 184, sch 18; (W) Children and Families
    (W), 2010 nawm 1, s 73, sch 2; Crime and Cts, 2013 c 22, sch 10 para 99
    Table; Children and Families, 2014 c 6, sch 3 paras 16(4)(c), 20(4)

c 22   **Electoral Administration**
    see (cert functions exerciseable concurrently)—SI 2010/1837, art 3
    trans of functions—SI 2015/1376, art 3(1) sch 1

2006

c 22 *continued*

   Pt 1 (ss 1-8) rep—Electoral Registration and Admin, 2013 c 6, s 23(1)

   s 13 rep in pt—SI 2008/1319, art 4

   s 32 am—SI 2007/1024, reg 3, sch 2

   ss 42-44—SI 2008/1848 (W 177), reg 8, sch 4

   s 42 appl (mods)—(E) SIs 2007/2089, regs 8, 11, 13, sch 4; 2012/323, sch 4 para 1 Table 5;
      444, sch 4 para 1 Table 5; 2031, regs 8, 12, 13, sch 4 pt 1 Table 5; ibid, reg 17
      sch 8 Table 4 (added by 2013/798, reg 7 sch 3)

   s 43 appl (mods)—(E) SI 2007/2089, regs 8, 11, 13, sch 4; SIs 2012/323, sch 4 para 1
      Table 5; 2031, regs 8, 12, 13, sch 4 pt 1 Table 5; ibid, reg 17 sch 8 Table 4
      (added by 2013/798, reg 7 sch 3)

   s 44 appl (mods)—(E) SI 2007/2089, regs 8, 11, 13, sch 4; SIs 2012/323, sch 4 para 1
      Table 5; 444, sch 4 para 1 Table 5; 2031, regs 8, 12, 13, sch 4 pt 1 Table 5;
      ibid, reg 17 sch 8 Table 4 (added by 2013/798, reg 7 sch 3)

     am—SIs 2007/1024, reg 3, sch 2; 2007/1388, art 3, sch 1

   s 46 appl (mods)—(E) SI 2007/2089, regs 8, 11, 13, sch 4; SIs 2008/1848 (W 177), reg 8,
      sch 4; 2012/323, sch 4 para 1 Table 5; 444, sch 4 para 1 Table 5; 2031, regs 8,
      12, 13, sch 4 pt 1 Table 5; ibid, reg 17 sch 8 Table 4 (added by 2013/798, reg 7
      sch 3)

   s 60 rep—NI (Misc Provns), 2006 c 33, s 30, sch 5

   s 62 am—Political Parties and Elections, 2009 c 12, s 19(4); SI 2012/1917, art 25(2),
      (3)(a)(c)(4); Recall of MPs, 2015 c 25, s 17(2)-(6)

     rep in pt—SI 2012/1917, art 25(3)(b)

   s 68 rep (prosp)—Electoral Admin, 2006 c 22, s 74, sch 2

   s 69 am—SI 2007/1024, reg 3, sch 2

     appl (mods)—(E) SIs 2007/2089, regs 8, 11, 13, sch 4; 2008/1848 (W 177), reg 8, sch
      4; 2010/2837, art 28, sch 5; 2012/323, sch 4 para 1 Table 5; 444, sch 4 para 1
      Table 5; 2031, regs 8, 12, 13, sch 4 pt 1 Table 5

   s 71 appl (mods)—Parly Voting System and Constituencies, 2011 c 1, sch 4 para 7

   s 74A added—SI 2010/1837, art 5, sch

     subst—SI 2015/1376, sch 2 para 12

   s 77 rep in pt—Electoral Registration and Admin, 2013 c 6, s 23(2)

   sch 1 rep in pt—NI (Misc Provns), 2006 c 33, s 30, sch 5; SI 2007/931, art 3; Electoral
      Registration and Admin, 2013 c 6, sch 4 para 23

     am—Electoral Registration and Admin, 2013 c 6, s 18(3)

c 23 **National Lottery**

   s 6 am—SI 2013/2329, sch para 28

c 24 *Appropriation (No 2)*—rep Appropriation (No 2), 2008 c 8, s 4, sch 3

c 25 **Finance**

   appl (mods)—SI 2007/1050, regs 3-12

   s 17 rep in pt—Income Tax, 2007 c 3, s 1031, sch 3

   s 20 rep—Finance, 2008 c 9, s 113, sch 36 para 92(i)

   s 25 rep—Corporation Tax, 2010 c 4, s 1181, sch 3 pt 1

   s 26 rep in pt—Corporation Tax, 2010 c 4, s 1181, sch 3 pt 1

   s 28 rep—Corporation Tax, 2009 c 4, s 1326, sch 3 pt 1

   s 30 rep—Finance, 2008 c 9, s 75(4)(b)

   ss 31-41 rep—Corporation Tax, 2009 c 4, ss 1322, 1326, sch 1 para 676, sch 3 pt 1

   s 42 rep in pt—Corporation Tax, 2009 c 4, ss 1322, 1326, sch 1 para 677, sch 3 pt 1

   ss 43-45 rep—Corporation Tax, 2009 c 4, ss 1322, 1326, sch 1 para 678, sch 3 pt 1

   s 46 am—SI 2006/3265, art 2; Corporation Tax, 2009 c 4, s 1322, sch 1 para 679

     appl (mods)—SI 2007/1050, reg 6

   s 47 am—SI 2006/3265, art 2; Corporation Tax, 2009 c 4, s 1322, sch 1 para 679

     appl (mods)—SI 2007/1050, reg 7

   ss 48-50 rep—Corporation Tax, 2009 c 4, ss 1322, 1326, sch 1 para 680, sch 3 pt 1

   s 51 am—SI 2006/3265, art 2

     appl (mods)—SI 2007/1050, reg 8

   s 52 rep—Corporation Tax, 2009 c 4, ss 1322, 1326, sch 1 para 681, sch 3 pt 1

   s 53 rep in pt—Corporation Tax, 2009 c 4, ss 1322, 1326, sch 1 para 682, sch 3 pt 1

   ss 54-58 rep—Corporation Tax, 2010 c 4, s 1181, sch 3 pt 1

   s 59 rep in pt—Finance, 2008 c 9, s 47(2)(b); Finance, 2010 c 13, s 58(16)

     rep—Finance, 2010 c 13, s 59(4)(a)

   s 65 am—Income Tax, 2007 c 3, s 1027, sch 1 paras 610, 612

   s 67 am—Income Tax, 2007 c 3, s 1027, sch 1 paras 610, 613

   s 68 am—Income Tax, 2007 c 3, s 1027, sch 1 paras 610, 614

2006
c 25 *continued*

s 69 rep—Finance, 2007 c 11, s 114, sch 27 pt 2
s 70 rep in pt—Finance, 2007 c 11, s 114, sch 27 pt 2
    am—(saving) Finance, 2007 c 11, s 32(4)-(6)(9)
s 71 rep in pt—Taxation (International and Other Provns), 2010 c 8, s 378, sch 10 pt 12
s 75 rep—Income Tax, 2007 c 3, s 1027, sch 1 paras 610, 615, sch 3
s 77 rep—Corporation Tax, 2009 c 4, s 1326, sch 3 pt 1
s 82 rep—Corporation Tax, 2010 c 4, ss 1177, 1181, sch 1 paras 480, 481, sch 3
s 83 am—Corporation Tax, 2010 c 4, s 1177, sch 1 paras 480, 482
    rep in pt—Corporation Tax, 2010 c 4, s 1181, sch 3 pt 1
s 84 rep in pt—Finance, 2009 c 10, s 126(6)(c)
s 86 rep—Finance, 2012 c 14, ss 146, 148, sch 16 paras 247(o)(i)
s 90 rep—Income Tax, 2007 c 3, s 1031, sch 3
s 91 rep in pt—Income Tax, 2007 c 3, s 1031, sch 3
s 93 rep—Corporation Tax, 2009 c 4, s 1326, sch 3 pt 1
s 95 rep in pt—Corporation Tax, 2010 c 4, s 1181, sch 3 pt 1; Taxation (International and
        Other Provns), 2010 c 8, s 378, sch 10 pts 7, 10
s 96 rep—Taxation (International and Other Provns), 2010 c 8, s 378, sch 10 pt 7
s 97 rep—Taxation (International and Other Provns), 2010 c 8, ss 374, 378, sch 8 paras 216,
        217, sch 10 pt 7
s 98 rep—Taxation (International and Other Provns), 2010 c 8, ss 374, 378, sch 8 paras 216,
        218, sch 10 pt 7
s 101 rep in pt—Corporation Tax, 2010 c 4, s 1181, sch 3 pt 1
ss 103-134 rep—Corporation Tax, 2010 c 4, ss 1177, 1181, sch 1 paras 480, 483(a), sch 3
s 136 rep—Corporation Tax, 2010 c 4, ss 1177, 1181, sch 1 paras 480, 483(b), sch 3
s 136A added—Finance, 2009 c 10, s 66, sch 34 para 8
    rep—Corporation Tax, 2010 c 4, ss 1177, 1181, sch 1 paras 480, 483(c), sch 3
s 138 rep—Corporation Tax, 2010 c 4, ss 1177, 1181, sch 1 paras 480, 483(d), sch 3
s 139 rep—Corporation Tax, 2010 c 4, ss 1177, 1181, sch 1 paras 480, 483(e), sch 3
ss 141, 142 rep—Corporation Tax, 2010 c 4, ss 1177, 1181, sch 1 paras 480, 483(f), sch 3
s 144 rep—Corporation Tax, 2010 c 4, ss 1177, 1181, sch 1 paras 480, 483(g), sch 3
s 145 rep in pt—Corporation Tax, 2010 c 4, ss 1177, 1181, sch 1 paras 480, 483(h), sch 3
s 151 rep in pt—Corporation Tax, 2010 c 4, s 1181, sch 3 pt 2; Taxation (International and Other
        Provns), 2010 c 8, s 378, sch 10 pt 6
s 154 rep in pt—Corporation Tax, 2010 c 4, s 1181, sch 3 pt 1
s 162 rep in pt—Stamp Duty Land Tax, 2015 c 1, sch para 21(a)
s 174 rep —Finance, 2008 c 9, s 113, sch 36 para 91
s 176 rep—Taxation (International and Other Provns), 2010 c 8, s 378, sch 10 pt 1
s 179 am—Income Tax, 2007 c 3, s 1027, sch 1 para 622; Corporation Tax, 2009 c 4, s
        1322, sch 1 para 692
sch 1 rep in pt—Corporation Tax, 2009 c 4, s 1326, sch 3 pt 1; Corporation Tax, 2010 c 4, s
        1181, sch 3 pt 1
sch 2 rep—Corporation Tax, 2009 c 4, s 1326, sch 3 pt 1
sch 3 rep in pt—Corporation Tax, 2009 c 4, s 1326, sch 3 pt 1
sch 4 rep—Corporation Tax, 2009 c 4, ss 1322, 1326, sch 1 para 693, sch 3 pt 1
sch 5 am—SI 2006/3265, art 2; Income Tax, 2007 c 3, s 1027, sch 1 paras 610, 623
    rep in pt—Corporation Tax, 2009 c 4, ss 1322, 1326, sch 1 para 694, sch 3 pt 1
    appl (mods)—SI 2007/1050, reg 10
sch 6 rep in pt—Finance, 2007 c 11, s 114, sch 27 pt 2; Corporation Tax, 2009 c 4, s 1326,
        sch 3 pt 1; Finance, 2009 c 10, s 48, sch 24 para 9(d); ibid, s 49, sch 25 para
        9(3)(g); Corporation Tax, 2010 c 4, s 1181, sch 3 pt 2; Taxation (International
        and Other Provns), 2010 c 8, s 378, sch 10 pt 10
sch 7 rep in pt—Income Tax, 2007 c 3, s 1031, sch 3
sch 8 am—Income Tax, 2007 c 3, s 1027, sch 1 paras 610, 624
    rep in pt—Corporation Tax, 2010 c 4, s 1181, sch 3 pt 1
sch 9 rep in pt—Corporation Tax, 2010 c 4, s 1181, sch 3 pts 1, 2; Taxation (International
        and Other Provns), 2010 c 8, s 378, sch 10 pts 8, 9
sch 10 rep—Corporation Tax, 2010 c 4, ss 1177, 1181, sch 1 paras 480, 484, sch 3
sch 11 rep—Finance, 2012 c 14, ss 146, 148, sch 16 para 247(o)(ii)
sch 12 rep in pt—Finance, 2008 c 9, s 8, sch 2 para 21(j), 55(h), 114(c); SIs 2009/2035, art
        2, sch; 2009/3001, reg 13, sch 2;
sch 13 rep in pt—Income Tax, 2007 c 3, ss 1027, 1031, sch 1 paras 610, 625, sch 3;
        Corporation Tax, 2010 c 4, s 1181, sch 3 pt 1; Taxation (International and
        Other Provns), 2010 c 8, s 378, sch 10 pts 1, 2, 12

2006

c 25 *continued*

    sch 14 rep in pt—Income Tax, 2007 c 3, s 1031, sch 3

    sch 15 am—Finance, 2007 c 11, s 91(10); Corporation Tax, 2009 c 4, s 1322, sch 1 para 696

    sch 16 rep—Corporation Tax, 2010 c 4, ss 1177, 1181, sch 1 paras 480, 485, sch 3

    sch 17 rep—Corporation Tax, 2010 c 4, ss 1177, 1181, sch 1 paras 480, 486, sch 3

    sch 18 rep in pt—Corporation Tax, 2010 c 4, s 1181, sch 3 pts 1, 2; Taxation (International and Other Provns), 2010 c 8, s 378, sch 10 pt 6

    sch 19 rep—Corporation Tax, 2010 c 4, s 1181, sch 3 pt 1

    sch 22 rep in pt—Finance, 2007 c 11, s 114, sch 27 pt 3; Finance, 2011 c 11, sch 16 para 84(b)

    sch 23 rep in pt—Finance, 2009 c 10, s 75(3)(a); Finance, 2013 c 29, s 51(4)

    sch 25 rep in pt—Scotland, 2012 c 11, sch 3 para 30; Finance, 2013 c 29, sch 41 paras 6(4), 7(2)(a)

c 26   **Commons**

    excl—SI 2013/3244, art 61(3)

    Pt 1 (ss 1-25) excl—SI 2009/1300L, arts 5, 46

    s 15 excl—SI 2011/41, art 49

        disappl—SI 2013/2587, art 5

        am—Growth and Infrastructure, 2013 c 27, s 14(2)(3)

    ss 15A, 15B added—Growth and Infrastructure, 2013 c 27, s 15

    s 15A rep in pt—(prosp) Planning (W), 2015 anaw 4, s 52

    s 15C added—Growth and Infrastructure, 2013 c 27, s 16(1)

        rep in pt—(prosp) Planning (W), 2015 anaw 4, s 53(2)(a)(i)

        am—(prosp) Planning (W), 2015 anaw 4, s 53(2)(a)(ii),(b)-(e)

    s 24 am—GSM C of E (Misc Provns), 2010 No 1, s 11; Growth and Infrastructure, 2013 c 27, s 17(b)

        rep in pt—Growth and Infrastructure, 2013 c 27, s 17(a); (prosp) Planning (W), 2015 anaw 4, s 54

    s 34 am—Crime and Cts, 2013 c 22, sch 9 para 52

    s 38 excl—(W) Nat Trust, 1971 c vi, s 23(2C); (E) SI 2007/2587, art 2

    s 39 appl—Ministry of Housing and Loc Govt Provnl O Conf (Greater London Parks and Open Spaces), 1967 c xxix, art 12(2A) of O; Nat Trust, 1971 c vi, s 23(2A); New Parishes, 1943 gsm 1, s 15(1)

    s 40 appl—Ministry of Housing and Loc Govt Provnl O Conf (Greater London Parks and Open Spaces), 1967 c xxix, arts 12(2A), 17(2A) of O; Nat Trust, 1971 c vi, s 23(2A); New Parishes, 1943 gsm 1, s 15(1)

    s 41 appl (mods)—Ministry of Housing and Loc Govt Provnl O Conf (Greater London Parks and Open Spaces), 1967 c xxix, art 12(2B) of O

        appl—Nat Trust, 1971 c vi, s 23(2B)

        rep in pt—Crime and Cts, 2013 c 22, sch 9 para 70

    s 46 am—Crime and Cts, 2013 c 22, sch 9 para 52

    s 59 am—Growth and Infrastructure, 2013 c 27, s 16(3); (prosp) Planning (W), 2015 anaw 4, sch 7 para 8

    s 61 am—(prosp) Planning (W), 2015 anaw 4, sch 7 para 9

    sch 1 am—(W) SI 2013/755 (W 90), sch 2 para 434

    sch 1A added—Growth and Infrastructure, 2013 c 27, sch 4

        am—SI 2014/257, art 3(2)-(7); (prosp) Planning (W), 2015 anaw 4, s 53(3)

    sch 1B added—Planning (W), 2015 anaw 4, sch 6

    sch 2 excl—SIs 2009/1300L, arts 5, 46; 2011/41, art 49

        disappl—SI 2013/2587, art 5

        —SI 2014/3038, reg 42(2)

c 27   **Housing Corporations (Delegation etc)**

    s 1 rep in pt—SI 2009/484, art 6, sch 2

c 28   **Health**

    s 5 am—Children and Families, 2014 c 6, s 95(2)

    s 9 appl (mods)—Children and Families, 2014 c 6, s 91(5)

        am—Children and Families, 2014 c 6, s 95(3)

    s 10 am—Children and Families, 2014 c 6, s 95(4)

    s 11 appl (mods)—Children and Families, 2014 c 6, s 91(6)

    s 12 am—SI 2007/1388, art 3, sch 1; SI 2008/3239 (W 286), reg 21

    s 18 am—SI 2013/602, sch 2 para 51(2)

    s 20 excl—SIs 2006/3148, reg 21; (temp to 31.3.2020) 2013/373, reg 18(3)

        appl—SI 2008/3239 (W 286), reg 20

2006

c 28 *continued*

s 25 am—Nat Health Service (Conseq Provns), 2006 c 43, s 2, sch 1 para 282

ss 27, 28 am—SI 2007/3101, reg 103

ss 34, 35 rep—Nat Health Service (Conseq Provns), 2006 c 43, s 6, sch 4

s 36 rep in pt—Nat Health Service (Conseq Provns), 2006 c 43, s 6, sch 4

ss 37-42 rep—Nat Health Service (Conseq Provns), 2006 c 43, s 6, sch 4

s 43 am—Nat Health Service (Conseq Provns), 2006 c 43, s 2, sch 1 para 283

ss 44-56 rep—Nat Health Service (Conseq Provns), 2006 c 43, s 6, sch 4

s 58 am—Nat Health Service (Conseq Provns), 2006 c 43, s 2, sch 1 para 284; Health and
    Social Care, 2008 c 14, s 127, sch 10 para 20

s 60 am—Health and Social Care, 2008 c 14, s 127, sch 10 para 21

    rep in pt—SI 2010/231, art 68, sch 4; Health and Social Care, 2012 c 7, sch 15 para
        74(1)

s 61 rep in pt—Health and Social Care, 2008 c 14, s 95, sch 15, sch 5 para 79

s 63 am—Health and Social Care, 2008 c 14, s 127, sch 10 para 22

    rep in pt—Health and Social Care, 2012 c 7, sch 15 para 74(2)

s 70-72 am—Nat Health Service (Conseq Provns), 2006 c 43, s 2, sch 1 paras 285-287

s 74 rep—Nat Health Service (Conseq Provns), 2006 c 43, s 6, sch 4

ss 75, 78 am—Nat Health Service (Conseq Provns), 2006 c 43, s 2, sch 1 para 288, 289

s 78 rep in pt—Nat Health Service (Conseq Provns), 2006 c 43, s 6, sch 4

s 79 am—Children and Families, 2014 c 6, s 95(5)

s 82 am—Nat Health Service (Conseq Provns), 2006 c 43, s 2, sch 1 para 290

    rep in pt—Nat Health Service (Conseq Provns), 2006 c 43, s 2, sch 1 para 290

sch 1 appl (mods)—Children and Families, 2014 c 6, s 91(5)

    am—Children and Families, 2014 c 6, s 95(6)

sch 2 appl (mods)—Children and Families, 2014 c 6, s 91(6)

sch 3 rep—Nat Health Service (Conseq Provns), 2006 c 43, s 6, sch 4

sch 4 am—SI 2006/2380, regs 2, 3; Health, 2009 c 21, s 19, sch 3 paras 8, 19

sch 5 rep in pt —Loc Govt and Public Involvement in Health, 2007 c 28, s 241, sch 18;
        Health and Social Care, 2008 c 14, ss 95, 127, 166, sch 5 para 80(a), sch 10
        para 23, sch 15; SI 2010/234, art 7, sch 3

    am—Health and Social Care, 2008 c 14, s 95, sch 5 para 80(b)

sch 6 am—SI 2010/231, art 68, sch 4

sch 8 am—Nat Health Service (Conseq Provns), 2006 c 43, s 2, sch 1 paras 291, 292,
    294-301

    rep in pt—Nat Health Service (Conseq Provns), 2006 c 43, ss 2, 6, sch 1 paras 293,
        299, sch 4; SI 2006/1407, art 3, sch 2; (S prosp) Loc Audit and Accountability,
        2014 c 2, sch 1 pt 2

c 29 **Compensation**

s 3 am—Financial Services, 2012 c 21, sch 18 para 109(2)(b)

    rep in pt—Financial Services, 2012 c 21, sch 18 para 109(2)(a)(3)

s 4 am—(prosp) Legal Services, 2007 c 29, s 187, sch 19 paras 1, 2

    mod—SI 2007/209, arts 4-12

s 5 am—(prosp) Legal Services, 2007 c 29, s 187, sch 19 paras 1, 3

    rep in pt—Legal Services, 2007 c 29, s 210, sch 23

s 6 am—(prosp) Legal Services, 2007 c 29, s 187, sch 19 paras 1, 4

s 7 am—Legal Services, 2007 c 29, s 187, sch 19 paras 1, 5

s 8 am—(pt prosp) Legal Services, 2007 c 29, s 187, sch 19 paras 1, 6; Crime and Cts, 2013
    c 22, sch 9 para 52

s 9 am—(prosp) Legal Services, 2007 c 29, s 187, sch 19 paras 1, 7

    mod—Legal Services, 2007 c 29, s 161(3)

s 11 am—Legal Services, 2007 c 29, s 187, sch 19 paras 1, 8

s 12 rep—SI 2010/22, art 5, sch 2

s 13 am—Legal Services, 2007 c 29, s 187, sch 19 paras 1, 9; SI 2010/22, art 5, sch 2;
    Financial Services (Banking Reform), 2013 c 33, s 139(8)

    rep in pt—SI 2010/22, art 5, sch 2

s 14 am—(prosp) Legal Services, 2007 c 29, s 187, sch 19 paras 1, 10

s 15 rep in pt—Legal Services, 2007 c 29, s 210, sch 23

    am—SI 2014/892, sch 1 para 170

sch am—(pt prosp) Legal Services, 2007 c 29, s 187, sch 19 paras 1, 11; Financial Services
    (Banking Reform), 2013 c 33, ss 139(2)-(7), 140(2)(3)

    mod—Legal Services, 2007 c 29, s 161(3)

2006

c 30 **Commissioner for Older People (Wales)**
ss 2-4 am—SI 2007/1388, art 3, sch 1
ss 6-8 am—SI 2007/1388, art 3, sch 1
s 10 am—SI 2007/1388, art 3, sch 1
s 12 am—SI 2007/1388, art 3, sch 1
s 14 am—SI 2007/1388, art 3, sch 1
s 15 am—SI 2007/1388, art 3, sch 1; Welsh Language (W), 2011 nawm 1, sch 3 para 8
s 16 am—SI 2007/1388, art 3, sch 1
s 17 am—SI 2007/1388, art 3, sch 1; Welsh Language (W), 2011 nawm 1, sch 3 para 9
s 18 am—SI 2007/1388, art 3, sch 1; Social Services and Well-being (W), 2014 anaw 4, sch
          3 para 33
s 27 am—Nat Health Service (Conseq Provns), 2006 c 43, s 2, sch 1 para 306; SI
          2007/1388, art 3, sch 1
     rep in pt—Nat Health Service (Conseq Provns), 2006 c 43, s 2, sch 1 para 306
s 28 am—SI 2007/1388, art 3, sch 1
sch 1 am—SI 2007/1388, art 3, sch 1
sch 2 am—SIs 2012/990 (W 130), art 10; 2013/755 (W 90), sch 2 para 435; Qualifications
          Wales, 2015 anaw 5, sch 1 para 39(b)
     rep in pt—Qualifications Wales, 2015 anaw 5, sch 1 para 39(a)
sch 4 rep in pt—Social Services and Well-being (W), 2014 anaw 4, sch 3 para 34

c 31 **International Development (Reporting and Transparency)**
s 3 rep—International Development (Official Development Assistance Target), 2015 c 12, s
         4
s 4 am—International Development (Gender Equality), 2014 c 9, s 2

c 32 **Government of Wales**
mod—Govt of Wales, 2006 c 32, s 162, sch 11
rep in pt—Wales, 2014 c 29, s 4(2)(a)
power to apply or incorporate (mods)—Police Reform and Social Responsibility, 2011 c 13,
          ss 54(5), 58(1)-(3)(7)
Pt 1 (ss 1-44) mod—Parly Voting System and Constituencies, 2011 c 1, s 13(5)
s 2 am—Parly Voting System and Constituencies, 2011 c 1, s 13(1)
    rep in pt—Parly Voting System and Constituencies, 2011 c 1, s 13(2)(a), sch 12
s 3 mod—Fixed-term Parliament(s), 2011 c 14, s 5(2)
    am—Wales, 2014 c 29, s 1(1)
s 7 am—Wales, 2014 c 29, s 2(2)
s 9 am—Wales, 2014 c 29, s 2(3)
s 11 rep in pt—Wales, 2014 c 29, s 2(4)(b)
     am—Wales, 2014 c 29, s 2(4)(a)
s 16 am—Wales, 2014 c 29, s 3(1)
ss 17A, 17B added —Wales, 2014 c 29, s 3(2)
s 18 am—Mental Health (Discrimination), 2013 c 8, sch para 5(1)(b)
     rep in pt—Mental Health (Discrimination), 2013 c 8, sch para 5(1)(a)
s 20 am—NAW (Remuneration), 2010 nawm 4, ss 16, 19, sch 3 paras 1-5
s 21 am—Constitutional Reform and Governance, 2010 c 25, s 38, sch 5 para 12
s 22 am—NAW (Remuneration), 2010 nawm 4, s 16, sch 3 paras 6, 7
     rep in pt—NAW (Remuneration), 2010 nawm 4, s 16, sch 3 para 6
s 24 am—NAW (Remuneration), 2010 nawm 4, ss 16, 19, sch 3 paras 8, 10, 11
     rep in pt—NAW (Remuneration), 2010 nawm 4, ss 16, 19, sch 3 paras 8, 9
s 37 am—Marine and Coastal Access, 2009 c 23, s 43(4), sch 4 para 6(2); Public Audit (W),
          2013 anaw 3, sch 4 para 71
s 44 rep—Bribery, 2010 c 23, s 17, sch 2
s 45 rep in pt—Wales, 2014 c 29, s 4(2)(b)
s 46 am—Wales, 2014 c 29, s 5
s 52 am—Constitutional Reform and Governance, 2010 c 25, s 19, sch 2 para 15(1)-(5)
s 53 am—NAW (Remuneration), 2010 nawm 4, ss 16, 19, sch 3 paras 12-16
s 54 am—NAW (Remuneration), 2010 nawm 4, s 16, sch 3 paras 17, 18
     rep in pt—NAW (Remuneration), 2010 nawm 4, s 16, sch 3 para 17
ss 58, 59 am—Marine and Coastal Access, 2009 c 23, s 43(4), sch 4 para 6(3)(4)
s 72 am—Police Reform and Social Responsibility, 2011 c 13, sch 16 para 352
s 78 am—Welsh Language (W), 2011 nawm 1, s 148(2)
s 79 subst (1.4.2016)—Well-being of Future Generations (W), 2015 anaw 2, s 16
ss 80, 82 am—Marine and Coastal Access, 2009 c 23, s 43(4), sch 4 para 6(5)(6)
s 83 mod—Commrs for Revenue and Customs, 2005 c 11, s 15(3)
s 94 am—SI 2009/3006, art 2

2006

c 32 s 94 *continued*

        mod—SI 2010/245, art 2

s 101 am—SI 2009/3006, art 2

s 106 am—SI 2011/1011(W 150), art 4(1)

s 106A added—SI 2011/1011(W 150), art 4(2)

s 108 am—Wales, 2014 c 29, s 6(3)

s 111 am—Wales, 2014 c 29, s 6(4)

s 113 am—SI 2012/1809, art 3(1), sch pt 1

s 115 am—SI 2011/1011(W 150), art 5

Pt 4A (ss 116A-116C) added —Wales, 2014 c 29, s 6(2)

s 116A am— (prosp)(conditionally) Wales, 2014 c 29, s 8(2) (with s 29(2)(b)(4) and s 14)

Pt 4A Ch 2 (ss 116D-116K) added (prosp) (conditionally)—Wales, 2014 c 29, s 8(3) (with s
        29(2)(b)(4) and s 14)

Pt 4A Ch 3 (s 116L) added—(17.2.2015 with qualifying provn) Wales, 2014 c 29, s
        15(1)(2) (with s 29(3)(a))

Pt 4A Ch 4 (s 116N) added—(17.2.2015 with qualifying provn) Wales, 2014 c 29, s
        18(1)(2) (with s 29(3)(b))

s 120 excl—Dormant Bank and Building Society Accounts, 2008 c 31, s 26(7)
        am—Public Audit (W), 2013 anaw 3, sch 4 para 72

s 121 am—(prosp) Wales, 2014 c 29, s 20(3)-(5)(7)(9)

s 122 rep in pt—(prosp) Wales, 2014 c 29, s 20(8)

s 122A added (prosp)—Wales, 2014 c 29, s 20(10)

s 124 am—Public Audit (W), 2013 anaw 3, sch 4 para 73

s 126A added—Constitutional Reform and Governance, 2010 c 25, s 44(2)

s 129 am—Public Audit (W), 2013 anaw 3, sch 4 para 74

s 134 am—SI 2008/948, art 3, sch 1

s 139 am—SI 2008/948, art 3, sch 1

s 141 am—SIs 2008/948, art 3, sch 1; 2009/1941, art 2, sch 1

s 143 rep in pt—Public Audit (W), 2013 anaw 3, sch 4 para 75

s 144 am—Public Audit (W), 2013 anaw 3, sch 4 para 76(2)(4)
        rep in pt—Public Audit (W), 2013 anaw 3, sch 4 para 76(3)

s 145 am—Public Audit (W), 2013 anaw 3, sch 4 para 77(3)
        rep in pt—Public Audit (W), 2013 anaw 3, sch 4 para 77(2)

s 147 trans of functions—SI 2015/1897, art 6(1)(d)
        am—SI 2015/1897, sch para 4(a)

s 148 am—Nat Health Service (Conseq Provns), 2006 c 43, s 2, sch 1 para 303; SI
        2013/755 (W 90), sch 2 para 437(3); Qualifications Wales, 2015 anaw 5, sch 4
        para 7; SI 2015/1897, sch para 4(b)
        rep in pt—SI 2013/755 (W 90), sch 2 para 437(2)
        trans of functions—SI 2015/1897, art 6(1)(d)

s 152 am—SI 2013/755 (W 90), sch 2 para 438

s 155 am—Marine and Coastal Access, 2009 c 23, s 43(4), sch 4 para 6(7)

s 155A added (prosp) (cond)—Wales, c 29, ss 10, 14(1),(6)(10)

s 158 rep in pt—Marine and Coastal Access, 2009 c 23, s 321, sch 22 pt 1
        am—Marine and Coastal Access, 2009 c 23, s 43(2)(3); Wales, 2014 c 29, s 6(5)

s 159 am—Marine and Coastal Access, 2009 c 23, sch 4 para 6(1)(8); Parly Voting System
        and Constituencies, 2011 c 1, sch 12 pt 2; Wales, 2014 c 29, s 6(6)

sch 1 rep—Parly Voting System and Constituencies, 2011 c 1, s 13(2)(b), sch 12

sch 3 am—Marine and Coastal Access, 2009 c 23, s 112(1), sch 8 para 3(2)(b), (3)
        rep in pt—Marine and Coastal Access, 2009 c 23, ss 112(1), 321, sch 8 para
        3(1)(2)(a), sch 22 pt 2

sch 4 excl—SIs 2008/1786, art 3; 2009/703, art 3, 3019, art 7; 2010/760, art 8

sch 5 am—Loc Govt and Public Involvement in Health, 2007 c 28, s 235, sch 17; Further
        Educ and Training, 2007 c 25, s 27; SI 2007/910, arts 1, 3, 4; Educ and Skills,
        2008 c 25, s 149; Loc Transport, 2008 c 26, s 122; Planning, 2008 c 29, s 202;
        SIs 2008/1036, art 2,1785, art 2, 3132, arts 2-5; Loc Democracy, Economic
        Development and Construction, 2009 c 20, s 33; Marine and Coastal Access,
        2009 c 23, s 310; SIs 2009/1757, art 2, 3006, art 2, 3010, arts 2, 3; 2010/236,
        arts 2, 3, 245, arts 3-5; 248, arts 2, 3; 1158, art 5, sch 2; 1208, arts 2-4; 1209,
        arts 2, 3; 1210, art 22; 1211, art 2, 1212, art 2; Budget Responsibility and Nat
        Audit, 2011 c 4, sch 5 para 27; ibid, sch 6 paras 3, 4; SI 2011/988, sch 4 para
        7(2)
        rep in pt—SIs 2008/3132, arts 3, 6; 2009/3006, art 2; 2010/1208, art 3

2006
c 32 *continued*

sch 7 am—SIs 2007/2143, arts 2-11; 2010/2968, arts 2-11; Budget Responsibility and Nat
Audit, 2011 c 4, sch 5 para 28; ibid, sch 6 paras 6, 7; Police Reform and Social
Responsibility, 2011 c 13, sch 16 para 353; Public Audit (W), 2013 anaw 3, sch
4 para 78(2)(3); Energy, 2013 c 32, sch 12 para 90; Anti-social Behaviour,
Crime and Policing, 2014 c 12, sch 11 para 43; (1.4.2016) Water, 2014 c 21, sch
7 para 135; Wales, 2014 c 29, ss 6(8)(9), 7(14), 22(2)(3); SI 2015/204, art 2
rep in pt—SIs 2008/960, art 22, sch 3; 2010/2968, arts 2, 3; Public Audit (W), 2013
anaw 3, sch 4 para 78(4)(a)(b)
sch 8 am—Serious Crime, 2007 c 27, s 73, sch 7 para 5; SIs 2008/948, art 3, sch 1;
2010/212, art 2; Constitutional Reform and Governance, 2010 c 25, s 44(3)-(6);
Public Audit (W), 2013 anaw 3, sch 4 para 79(3)-(5)
rep in pt—SI 2010/212, art 2; Public Audit (W), 2013 anaw 3, sch 4 para 79(2)(6)
sch 10 rep in pt—Mental Health (Discrimination), 2013 c 8, sch para 5(2); Social Services
and Well-being (W), 2014 anaw 4, sch 3 para 35; (prosp) Planning (W), 2015
anaw 4, sch 2 para 29
sch 11 rep in pt—Nat Health Service (Conseq Provns), 2006 c 43, s 2, sch 1 para 304; Parly
Voting System and Constituencies, 2011 c 1, s 13(2)(c), sch 12; Higher Educ
(W), 2015 anaw 1, sch para 23(a)(b); (1.4.2016) Well-being of Future
Generations (W), 2015 anaw 2, sch 4 para 18; (prosp) Planning (W), 2015
anaw 4, sch 7 para 2
mod—Nat Health Service (Conseq Provns), 2006 c 43, s 4, sch 2 para 17
am—SIs 2007/726, regs 2-7; 2007/1169, art 2; 2007/1270, art 2; Learning and
Skills (W), 2009 nawm 1, s 47, sch 1 paras 21, 22; SI 2010/1158, art 5, sch 2
sch 12 am—Police Reform and Social Responsibility, 2011 c 13, sch 16 para 353
sch 18 am—Localism, 2011 c 20, sch 13 para 79
c 33 **Northern Ireland (Miscellaneous Provisions)**
s 14 am—SI 2010/2061, art 2
s 17 am—Justice and Security (NI), 2007 c 6, s 44
s 28 rep—Northern Ireland, 2009 c 3, s 2, sch 5 para 9
sch 2 am—NI (St Andrews Agreement), 2006 c 53, ss 8, 9, sch 5 paras 8-14, sch 6 paras 1-4;
Justice and Security (NI), 2007 c 6, s 44, sch 5 paras 1, 2, 3
sch 4 rep in pt—(prosp) Political Parties and Elections, 2009 c 12, s 39, sch 7; SI 2010/976,
art 27
c 34 **Civil Aviation**
sch 2 rep in pt—Civil Aviation, 2012 c 19, sch 9 para 17
c 35 **Fraud**
s 9 am—SIs 2007/2194, art 10, sch 4; 2009/1941, art 2, sch 1
rep in pt—SI 2007/2194, art 10, sch 5
s 10 rep—SI 2009/1941, art 2, sch 2
c 36 **Wireless Telegraphy**
mod—SI 2006/3324, art 2, sch 1; 2006/3325, art 2, sch 1; 2007/278, art 2, sch 1
s 2 am—SI 2011/1210, sch 2 para 2
s 6 am—SI 2011/1210, sch 2 para 3
s 8 am—SI 2011/1210, sch 2 para 4
excl—Prisons (Interference with Wireless Telegraphy), 2012 c 20, s 1(7); SIs 2015/591,
regs 4,5,8,9,12,13,16,17,24,25,29,30; 2015/2066, reg 3
restr—SI 2010/2512, regs 9, 10 (added by SI 2014/953, regs 4, 5); 2014/1484, reg 2(3))
ss 8A-8C added—SI 2011/1210, sch 2 para 5
s 9 am—SIs 2009/2979, reg 13(2); 2011/1210, sch 2 para 6
ss 9ZA, 9ZB added—SI 2011/1210, sch 2 para 7
s 9A added—SI 2009/2979, reg 13(3)
am—SI 2010/419, reg 15
s 12 am—Digital Economy, 2010 c 24, s 38(1)-(3)
s 14 am—Digital Economy, 2010 c 24, s 38(4)-(7); SI 2011/1210, sch 2 para 8
s 30 am—SI 2011/1210, sch 2 para 9
ss 32A-32E added—SI 2011/1210, sch 2 para 10
s 33 am—SI 2011/1210, sch 2 para 11
s 34 am—SI 2011/1210, sch 2 para 12
s 39 am—SIs 2009/2979, reg 13(4); 2011/1210, sch 2 para 13(a)
rep in pt—SI 2011/1210, sch 2 para 13(b)
s 40 rep—SI 2011/1210, sch 2 para 14
s 41 am—SI 2011/1210, sch 2 para 15
s 43A added—Digital Economy, 2010 c 24, s 39(1)

2006
c 36 *continued*

s 44 am—Digital Economy, 2010 c 24, s 39(2)
ss 97, 98 appl—Wireless Telegraphy, 1967 c 72, s 5(6)
s 107 am—SI 2013/602, sch 2 para 52
s 111 am—SIs 2008/1277, reg 30, sch 2; 2014/892, sch 1 para 171(2)(i)(3)
    rep in pt—Enterprise and Regulatory Reform, 2013 c 24, sch 21 para 2; SI 2014/892,
        sch 1 para 171(2)(ii)
s 115 am—SIs 2009/2979, reg 13(5)-(7); 2010/1883, reg 7
s 118 rep in pt—Enterprise and Regulatory Reform, 2013 c 24, sch 21 para 2
sch 1 am—SI 2011/1210, sch 2 para 16(a)-(f)(h)-(j)
    rep in pt—SI 2011/1210, sch 2 para 16(g)
sch 4 am—Deregulation, 2015 c 20, s 80(5)(a),(b)(ii),(c),(d)(ii); SI 2015/664, sch 5 para 11
    rep in pt—Deregulation, 2015 c 20, s 80(5)(b)(i),(d)(i)
sch 7 rep in pt—(prosp) Serious Crime, 2007 c 27, s 92, sch 14; Enterprise and Regulatory
       Reform, 2013 c 24, sch 21 para 2
sch 8 rep in pt—Legislative and Regulatory Reform, 2006 c 51, s 30, sch 1

c 37   **Parliamentary Costs**
s 18 appl (mods)—SI 2011/2866, sch 3

c 38   **Violent Crime Reduction**
ss 1-7 rep —Anti-social Behaviour, Crime and Policing, 2014 c 12, sch 11 para 44(a)
s 8 rep —Anti-social Behaviour, Crime and Policing, 2014 c 12, sch 11 para 44(b); ibid, sch
      11 para 50
ss 9-14 rep —Anti-social Behaviour, Crime and Policing, 2014 c 12, sch 11 para 44(c)
ss 15-20 rep—Police Reform and Social Responsibility, 2011 c 13, s 140
s 26 rep—Anti-social Behaviour, Crime and Policing, 2014 c 12, sch 11 para 50
s 27 rep—Anti-social Behaviour, Crime and Policing, 2014 c 12, sch 11 para 45
s 32 rep (prosp)—Air Weapons and Licensing (S), 2015 asp 10, sch 2 para 3
s 47 am—Crim Justice and Immigration, 2008 c 4, s 6, sch 4 para 98
s 56 rep in pt—Anti-social Behaviour, Crime and Policing, 2014 c 12, sch 11 para 80
s 59 rep in pt—Anti-social Behaviour, Crime and Policing, 2014 c 12, sch 11 para 50
s 61 rep—Legal Aid, Sentencing and Punishment of Offenders, 2012 c 10, sch 12 para 54
sch 1 rep in pt—Legal Aid, Sentencing and Punishment of Offenders, 2012 c 10, s 64(5)(a)
sch 2 am—SI 2010/976, art 9, sch 11

c 39   **Emergency Workers (Obstruction)**
s 1 am—Health and Social Care, 2012 c 7, sch 5 para 138(a)(i)(b)
    rep in pt—Health and Social Care, 2012 c 7, sch 5 para 138(a)(ii)

c 40   **Education and Inspections**
am—SI 2010/1158, art 5, sch 2
Pts 1-7 (ss 1-111) am—SI 2010/1158, art 5, sch 2
s 5 rep—Educ, 2011 c 21, s 33(1)
s 6A added (pt prosp)—Educ, 2011 c 21, sch 11 para 2
Pt 2 (ss 7-32) rep in pt—Educ, 2011 c 21, sch 11 para 10(5)
s 7 appl (mods)—(E) SI 2007/2979, reg 3, sch 1; ibid, sch 1 para 23EA (added by SI
      2012/3158, reg 3(7))
    am—Educ, 2011 c 21, sch 11 para 3(a); ibid, sch 13 para 16(2)
    rep in pt—Educ, 2011 c 21, sch 11 para 3(b)-(d)
    mod—SI 2013/3109, sch 4 pt 1
s 7A added—Educ, 2011 c 21, sch 11 para 4
s 8 rep—Educ, 2011 c 21, sch 11 para 5
s 10 am—Educ, 2011 c 21, sch 11 para 6
    appl (mods)—(E) SI 2007/2979, reg 3, sch 1
    mod—SI 2013/3109, sch 4 Pt 2
s 11 appl (mods)—(E) SI 2007/1288, reg 29, sch 7
    am—Educ and Skills, 2008 c 25, s 169, sch 1 paras 37, 38; Educ, 2011 c 21, sch 11
      para 7
    rep in pt—Apprenticeships, Skills, Children and Learning, 2009 c 22, s 123, sch 16
    mod—SI 2013/3109, sch 4 Pt 2
s 11A added (prosp)—Children, Schools and Families, 2010 c 26, s 7
      am—Educ, 2011 c 21, sch 11 para 8
s 12 rep in pt—SI 2010/1080, art 2, schs 1, 2
    am—Educ, 2011 c 21, s 42(9), sch 11 para 9
ss 13 appl (mods)—SI 2009/276, reg 3
s 15 excl—Academies, 2010 c 32, s 6(9)
s 16 excl—Academies, 2010 c 32, s 6(9)

2006

c 40 s 16 *continued*

am—Children and Families, 2014 c 6, sch 3 para 81

s 17 excl—Academies, 2010 c 32, s 6(9)

appl (mods)—SI 2009/276, reg 3

s 21 am—Equality, 2010 c 15, s 211, sch 26 para 93 (added by SI 2010/2279, sch 1)

s 23 rep in pt—SI 2010/1080, art 2, schs 1, 2

s 24 am—SI 2010/1158, art 5, sch 2

s 28 am—Academies, 2010 c 32, s 14, sch 2 paras 19, 20

rep in pt—SI 2010/1080, art 2, schs 1, 2

s 41 rep in pt—Educ, 2011 c 21, sch 10 para 3

s 46 rep —Educ and Skills, 2008 c 25, s 169, sch 2

s 47 rep in pt—Educ and Skills, 2008 c 25, s 169, sch 2

s 48 am—Crime and Cts, 2013 c 22, sch 9 para 52

s 50 rep in pt—Educ and Skills, 2008 c 25, s 169, sch 2

s 52 rep in pt—Educ and Skills, 2008 c 25, s 169, sch 2

am—Crime and Cts, 2013 c 22, sch 9 para 52

s 54 rep in pt—(W) School Standards and Organisation (W), 2013 anaw 1, sch 5 para 23(2)

s 58 rep (W)—School Standards and Organisation (W), 2013 anaw 1, sch 5 para 34(2)

ss 59, 60 am—Apprenticeships, Skills, Children and Learning, 2009 c 22,

s 203, sch 13 paras 2, 3

s 60A added—Apprenticeships, Skills, Children and Learning, 2009 c 22,

s 203, sch 13 para 4

s 62 am—Crime and Cts, 2013 c 22, sch 9 para 52

ss 63, 64 am—Apprenticeships, Skills, Children and Learning, 2009 c 22,

s 203, sch 13 paras 5, 6

s 66 am—Apprenticeships, Skills, Children and Learning, 2009 c 22,

s 203, sch 13 para 7; Crime and Cts, 2013 c 22, sch 9 para 52

s 67 rep in pt—Apprenticeships, Skills, Children and Learning, 2009 c 22, ss 203, 266, sch

13 para 8, sch 16 pt 6

s 68 appl (mods)—(E) SI 2007/2979, reg 3, sch 1

rep in pt—SI 2010/1080, art 2, schs 1, 2

am—Educ, 2011 c 21, s 44(2)

s 69 rep in pt—Apprenticeships, Skills, Children and Learning, 2009 c 22, ss 203, 266, sch

13 para 9, sch 16 pt 6

am—Academies, 2010 c 32, s 14, sch 2 paras 19, 21

appl (mods)—SI 2007/2978, reg 24(1); ibid, reg 24(1) (added by SI 2012/1825, reg

2(10))

s 69A added—Apprenticeships, Skills, Children and Learning, 2009 c 22,

s 203, sch 13 para 10

am—Educ, 2011 c 21, s 44(3)(b)-(e)

rep in pt—Educ, 2011 c 21, s 44(3)(a)

s 69B added—Apprenticeships, Skills, Children and Learning, 2009 c 22,

s 203, sch 13 para 10

s 73 am—Apprenticeships, Skills, Children and Learning, 2009 c 22,

s 203, sch 13 para 11

s 74 am—Educ and Skills, 2008 c 25, s 169, sch 1 paras 86, 87; Educ, 2011 c 21, s 31(2),

sch 8 para 20(a)

rep in pt—Educ, 2011 c 21, s 31(3), sch 8 para 20(b)

s 75 rep—Apprenticeships, Skills, Children and Learning, 2009 c 22, ss 123, 266, sch 6

paras 58, 59, sch 16 pt 2

s 80 rep in pt—SI 2010/1158, art 5, schs 2, 3

s 81 rep—Apprenticeships, Skills, Children and Learning, 2009 c 22, ss 57(1)(5), 266, sch

16 pt 1

s 83 am—(W) Learner Travel (W), 2008 nawm 2, s 26, sch 2

s 87 rep in pt—(W) School Standards and Organisation (W), 2013 anaw 1, sch 5 para 34(3)

s 88 appl (mods)—SI 2007/958, reg 30

am—(prosp) Educ and Skills, 2008 c 25, s 169, sch 1 paras 37, 39; Deregulation, 2015

c 20, sch 16 para 1(2)-(4)

rep in pt—Deregulation, 2015 c 20, sch 16 para 1(5)

s 89 am—(W) Learner Travel (W), 2008 nawm 2, s 13; Educ, 2011 c 21, s 2(7)

rep in pt—Deregulation, 2015 c 20, sch 16 para 1(6)

s 91 am—Equality, 2010 c 15, s 211, sch 26 para 94 (added by SI 2010/2279, sch 1)

s 92 am—Educ, 2011 c 21, s 5

mod—(W) SI 2013/1793 (W 180), reg 12

2006
c 40 *continued*

s 93A added (prosp)—Apprenticeships, Skills, Children and Learning, 2009 c 22, s 246
s 94 am—Apprenticeships, Skills, Children and Learning, 2009 c 22,
    s 242(3)
s 97 am—Crime and Cts, 2013 c 22, sch 9 para 52
s 100 am—Educ, 2011 c 21, sch 13 para 16(3)
s 104 am—Educ, 2011 c 21, sch 13 para 16(4)
    mod—SI 2012/1107, art 7
s 111 am—Educ, 2011 c 21, sch 13 para 16(5)
s 116 mod—SI 2006/2991, reg 2
s 117 am—Children and Families, 2014 c 6, s 116(2)(a)
s 119 am—Children and Families, 2014 c 6, s 116(2)(b)
s 120 rep—Children and Families, 2014 c 6, s 116(1)
s 123 am—SIs 2010/1080, art 2, sch 1; 2010/1158, art 5, sch 2; Educ, 2011 c 21, sch 13
    para 16(6), sch 16 para 30(2)
    rep in pt—Educ, 2011 c 21, sch 16 para 30(3); Deregulation, 2015 c 20, sch 14 para
    51
s 124 am—SIs 2010/1080, art 2, sch 1; 2010/1158, art 5, sch 2;
    rep in pt—Educ, 2011 c 21, sch 16 para 31; Deregulation, 2015 c 20, sch 14 para 52
s 125 am—SI 2010/1080, art 2, sch 1; Educ, 2011 c 21, s 42(2), sch 13 para 16(7)
    rep in pt—Educ, 2011 c 21, sch 16 para 32; Deregulation, 2015 c 20, sch 14 para 53
s 126 am—SI 2010/1080, art 2, sch 1; Educ, 2011 c 21, s 42(4)-(8)
    rep in pt—Educ, 2011 c 21, sch 16 para 33; Deregulation, 2015 c 20, sch 14 para 54
s 127 am—Educ, 2011 c 21, s 42(10)
s 128 am—SI 2010/1080, art 2, sch 1; Educ, 2011 c 21, sch 16 para 34
    rep in pt—Deregulation, 2015 c 20, sch 14 para 55
    appl—SI 2015/1792, sch para 2
s 129 am—SI 2010/1080, art 2, sch 1
    rep in pt—Educ, 2011 c 21, sch 16 para 35; Deregulation, 2015 c 20, sch 14 para 56
s 130 am—SI 2010/1080, art 2, sch 1; Educ, 2011 c 21, sch 16 para 36(2)(3)
    rep in pt—Educ, 2011 c 21, sch 16 para 36(4); Deregulation, 2015 c 20, sch 14 para
    57
s 131 appl—SI 2015/1792, sch para 2
s 132 appl—SI 2015/1792, sch para 2
Pt 8 Ch 4 (ss 135-142) heading rep in pt—SI 2012/1879, art 4
s 135 am—SIs 2010/1158, art 5, sch 2; 2012/961, sch 1 para 8
s 136 rep in pt—SI 2012/1879, art 4(3)
s 138 rep—SI 2012/1879, art 3
s 139 rep in pt—SI 2012/1879, art 4(4)
    appl—SI 2015/1792, sch para 1
s 140 rep in pt—SI 2012/1879, art 4(5)
    appl—SI 2015/1792, sch para 1
s 141 appl—SI 2015/1792, sch para 1
ss 144, 145 appl—SI 2015/1792, sch para 4
s 146 am—Crim Justice and Cts, 2015 c 2, sch 9 para 22(2); Crim Justice and Cts, 2015 c 2,
    sch 9 para 22(3)
    rep in pt—Crim Justice and Cts, 2015 c 2, sch 9 para 22(4)
s 148 rep in pt—(W prosp) Children and Young Persons, 2008 c 23, ss 4(4), 42, sch 4
s 154 rep—Educ, 2011 c 21, s 41(2)
s 156 rep—SI 2012/2401, sch 1 para 21
s 159 am—SI 2010/1080, art 2, sch 1
    rep in pt—SI 2010/1080, art 2, schs 1, 2; Educ, 2011 c 21, sch 16 para 37;
        Deregulation, 2015 c 20, sch 14 para 58
s 162 am—Learner Travel (W), 2008 nawm 2, s 23(1), (2); Educ (W), 2009 nawm 5, sch
    sch paras 10-12; (W) Children and Families (W), 2010 nawm 1, s 72, sch 1
    paras 19, 20
s 166 am—SI 2010/1080, art 2, sch 1; Education (W), 2011 nawm 7, s 9(4)
s 167 rep (prosp)—(W) Children and Families (W), 2010 nawm 1, s 73, sch 2
s 171 am—Educ and Skills, 2008 c 25, s 169, sch 1 paras 37, 40; Policing and Crime, 2009
    c 26, s 81(2)(3)(l); SI 2012/3006, art 13(1)(2)(f)
s 176 rep—SI 2010/1080, art 2, schs 1, 2
ss 178, 179 rep—SI 2007/910, art 5
s 180 am—(spec retrosp effect) Educ and Skills, 2008 c 25, s 169, sch 1 paras 86, 88
s 181 am—(W) Learner Travel (W), 2008 nawm 2, s 23(1), (3)

2006

c 40 *continued*

s 182 am—Educ, 2011 c 21, s 42(11)

s 182A added—(W) Learner Travel (W), 2008 nawm 2, s 23(1), (3)

s 187 rep in pt—Educ, 2011 c 21, s 33(2)

sch 1 rep in pt—Equality, 2010 c 15, s 211, sch 27 pt 1 (subst by SI 2010/2279, sch 2)

sch 2 appl—Learning and Skills, 2000 c 21, sch 7A paras 5(1),7(2)

    appl (mods)—(E) SIs 2007/1288, regs 26, 29, schs 6, 7; 2013/3109, sch 3 paras 1-5

    am—Academies, 2010 c 32, s 14, sch 2, paras 19, 22(1)-(3); Educ, 2011 c 21, sch 11

        para 10, sch 13 para 16(8); Charities, 2011 c 25, sch 7 para 110

    rep in pt—SI 2010/1080, art 2, schs 1, 2; Educ, 2011 c 21, sch 11 para 10

    mod—SI 2013/3109, sch 4 pts 1, 2

sch 3 rep in pt—SI 2010/1080, art 2, schs 1, 2; Equality, 2010 c 15, s 211, sch 27 pt 1

        (subst by SI 2010/2279, sch 2); (W) School Standards and Organisation (W),

        2013 anaw 1, sch 5 para 23(3)

sch 4 rep in pt—Finance, 2007 c 11, s 114, sch 27 pt 4

sch 6 appl (mods)—SI 2007/2978, reg 24(2), sch 4

sch 7 am—Crime and Cts, 2013 c 22, sch 9 para 52

    rep in pt—(W) School Standards and Organisation (W), 2013 anaw 1, sch 5 para 9(2)

sch 10 rep in pt—(W) Learner Travel (W), 2008 nawm 2, s 26, sch 2

sch 11 mod—SI 2006/2991, reg 2

sch 12 am—Apprenticeships, Skills, Children and Learning, 2009 c 22, s 226(1)-(5)

    rep in pt—Apprenticeships, Skills, Children and Learning, 2009 c 22, ss 226(2)(4),

        266, sch 16 pt 8

sch 13 rep in pt—Loc Govt and Public Involvement in Health, 2007 c 28, s 146, sch 9 para

        1(1)(2)(y), sch 18; Health and Social Care, 2008 c 14, s 95, sch 5 para

        81(1)(2)(a), sch 15; SI 2012/2401, sch 1 para 22; Loc Audit and

        Accountability, 2014 c 2, sch 12 para 69(2)(a)(ii)

    am—Health and Social Care, 2008 c 14, s 95, sch 5 para 81(1)(2)(b)(3); Loc Audit

        and Accountability, 2014 c 2, sch 12 para 69(2)(a)(i)(b)(3)(4)

sch 14 rep in pt—Further Education and Training, 2007 c 25, s 30, sch 2; Loc Govt and

        Public Involvement in Health, 2007 c 28, s 241, sch 18; (prosp) Educ and Skills,

        2008 c 25, s 169, sch 2; Apprenticeships, Skills, Children and Learning, 2009 c

        22, s 266, sch 16 pt 4; SI 2012/2401, sch 1 para 23; (W) School Standards and

        Organisation (W), 2013 anaw 1, sch 5 para 23(4); Loc Audit and

        Accountability, 2014 c 2, sch 1 pt 2

sch 15 rep in pt—SI 2012/2401, sch 1 para 24

sch 17 rep in pt—School Standards and Organisation (W), 2013 anaw 1, sch 5 para 9(3)

c 41   **National Health Service**

appl (mods)—Health and Social Care, 2012 c 7, sch 6 para 8

s 1 subst —Health and Social Care, 2012 c 7, s 1

ss 1A-11 added —Health and Social Care, 2012 c 7, ss 2-10

s 1F am—Care, 2014 c 23, s 97(4)(a)

    power to appl—Care, 2014 c 23, s 97(2)

s 2 subst—Health and Social Care, 2012 c 7, sch 4 para 1(1)

    am—Health and Social Care, 2012 c 7, sch 4 para 1(2); Energy, 2013 c 32, sch 12 para

        91

s 2A added —Health and Social Care, 2012 c 7, s 11

s 2B added —Health and Social Care, 2012 c 7, s 12

s 3 am—Health and Social Care, 2012 c 7, s 13

    rep in pt—Health and Social Care, 2012 c 7, s 13(5)

    excl—SI 2013/350, reg 2(1)(a)

s 3A added —Health and Social Care, 2012 c 7, s 14

s 3B added —Health and Social Care, 2012 c 7, s 15

s 4 am—Health and Social Care, 2012 c 7, s 16

    rep in pt—Health and Social Care, 2012 c 7, sch 14 para 2

s 5 am—Health and Social Care, 2012 c 7, s 17(1)

s 6 am—Health and Social Care, 2012 c 7, sch 4 para 2

s 6A added—SI 2010/915, reg 2

    am—Health and Social Care, 2012 c 7, sch 4 paras 3(2)-(5)(6)(c)(d); SI 2013/2269,

        reg 7(1)

    rep in pt—Health and Social Care, 2012 c 7, sch 4 para 3(6)(a)(b)

s 6B added—SI 2010/915, reg 2

    am—Health and Social Care, 2012 c 7, sch 4 para 4(2)(3)

ss 6BA, 6BB added—SI 2013/2269, reg 7(2)

2006

c 41 *continued*

s 6C added —Health and Social Care, 2012 c 7, s 18(1)

s 6D added —Health and Social Care, 2012 c 7, s 19

s 6E added —Health and Social Care, 2012 c 7, s 20(1)

s 7 am—Health and Social Care, 2012 c 7, s 21(2)(4)

    rep in pt—Health and Social Care, 2012 c 7, s 21(3)

    mod—(temp) Health and Social Care, 2012 c 7, sch 6 paras 3-6

s 7A added —Health and Social Care, 2012 c 7, s 22

s 8 am—Health and Social Care, 2012 c 7, sch 4 para 5(2)(3)

    rep in pt—Health and Social Care, 2012 c 7, sch 4 para 5(1)(a)(b), sch 14 para 3

s 9 am—Health and Social Care, 2008 c 14, s 95, sch 5 para 82; Health and Social Care,

        2012 c 7, sch 21 para 6(a)(b); ibid, sch 17 para 10(2), sch 19 para 9(2); ibid, sch 4

        para 6(2)(a); Care, 2014 c 23, sch 5 para 16

    mod —(transtl provn) SIs 2008/2250, art 3(14); 2013/349, reg 103(1); 2015/1862, regs

        10-12; 1879, reg 9

    rep in pt—Health and Social Care, 2012 c 7, sch 4 para 6(2)(b)(c); ibid, sch 7 para 18,

        sch 14 para 4

    appl—SIs 2015/1862, reg 84(2); 1879, reg 77(3)

s 10A added —Health and Social Care, 2012 c 7, sch 21 para 7

s 11 am—Health and Social Care, 2012 c 7, sch 4 para 7(a)

    rep in pt—Health and Social Care, 2012 c 7, sch 4 para 7(b)(c)

s 12 am—Health and Social Care, 2012 c 7, sch 4 para 8(2)-(5)(a)(6)(7)

    rep in pt—Health and Social Care, 2012 c 7, sch 4 para 8(5)(b)(c)

s 12ZA added —Health and Social Care, 2012 c 7, sch 4 para 9

s 12A added—Health, 2009 c 21, s 11

    am—Health and Social Care, 2012 c 7, sch 4 para 10(2)(3)(a)(b)(4)(6)

    rep in pt—Health and Social Care, 2012 c 7, sch 4 para 10(3)(c)(5); SI 2013/1563,

        art 2

s 12B added—Health, 2009 c 21, s 11

    am—Health and Social Care, 2012 c 7, sch 4 para 11

s 12C added—Health, 2009 c 21, s 11

    rep in pt—SI 2013/1563, art 2

s 12D added—Health, 2009 c 21, s 11

    am—Health and Social Care, 2012 c 7, sch 4 para 12

s 12E added —Health and Social Care, 2012 c 7, s 147

Pt 2 Ch A1 (ss 13A-13Z4) added —Health and Social Care, 2012 c 7, s 23

s 13M am—Care, 2014 c 23, s 97(4)(b)

s 13N am—(prosp) Care, 2014 c 23, s 3(6)

s 13Q am—Care, 2014 c 23, s 120(15)

    rep in pt—Health and Social Care, 2012 c. 7, sch 14 para 4A

Pt 2 Ch A2 (ss 14A-14O and ss 14P-14Z24) added —Health and Social Care, 2012 c 7, ss

        25(1), 26

ss 14P-14Y mod—Health and Social Care, 2012 c 7, sch 6 para 11(2)(a)-(i)

s 14Z am—Care, 2014 c 23, s 97(4)(c)

s 14Z1 mod—Health and Social Care, 2012 c 7, sch 6 para 11(2)(j)

    am—(prosp) Care, 2014 c 23, s 3(7)

s 14Z2 rep in pt—Health and Social Care, 2012 c. 7, sch 14 para 4B

    am—Care, 2014 c 23, s 120(16)

s 14Z3 mod—Health and Social Care, 2012 c 7, sch 6 para 11(2)(k)

    am—SI 2014/2436, art 2

s 14Z4 mod—Health and Social Care, 2012 c 7, sch 6 para 11(2)(l)

s 14Z5 mod—Health and Social Care, 2012 c 7, sch 6 para 11(2)(m)

s 14Z7 mod—Health and Social Care, 2012 c 7, sch 6 para 11(2)(n)

s 14Z9 am—SI 2014/2436, art 3

s 14Z17 mod—Health and Social Care, 2012 c 7, sch 6 para 11(2)(o)

s 14Z19 mod—Health and Social Care, 2012 c 7, sch 6 para 11(2)(o)

s 14Z21 mod—Health and Social Care, 2012 c 7, sch 6 para 11(2)(o)

Pt 2 Ch 1 (ss 13-17) rep —Health and Social Care, 2012 c 7, s 33

s 15 am —Health, 2009 c 21, s 29(2)

s 16 am—Health, 2009 c 21, s 29(3)

s 17A added —Loc Govt and Public Involvement in Health, 2007 c 28, s 234(1)

Pt 2 Ch 2 (ss 18-24A) rep —Health and Social Care, 2012 c 7, s 34

s 23A added—Health and Social Care, 2008 c 14, s 139

s 24 am—Health and Social Care, 2012 c 7, s 206(2)

2006
c 41 *continued*

s 24A added —Loc Govt and Public Involvement in Health, 2007 c 28, s 234(2)
 am—Health and Social Care, 2012 c 7, s 206(3)
Pt 2 Ch 3 (ss 25-27) rep (pt prosp)—Health and Social Care, 2012 c 7, s 179
s 28 rep in pt—Health and Social Care, 2012 c 7, sch 4 para 13
s 28A added —Health and Social Care, 2012 c 7, s 48(1)
s 29 rep in pt—Health and Social Care, 2012 c 7, sch 4 para 14
s 30 am—Health and Social Care, 2012 c 7, s 159(1)
s 31 rep—Health and Social Care, 2012 c 7, sch 13 para 9(1)
s 32 rep (savings)—Health and Social Care, 2012 c 7, sch 13 para 10(1)
 mod (temp)—SI 2013/671, art 3
s 33 rep (prosp)—Health and Social Care, 2012 c 7, s 180(1)
 am—Health and Social Care, 2012 c 7, s 151(9)(a); (prosp) ibid, s 180(5)
 rep in pt—Health and Social Care, 2012 c 7, s 159(2)
s 34 rep—Health and Social Care, 2012 c 7, s 160(1)
s 35 rep (prosp)—Health and Social Care, 2012 c 7, s 180(2)
 rep in pt—Loc Govt and Public Involvement in Health, 2007 c 28, s 241, sch 18;
  Health and Social Care, 2012 c 7, s 160(2); ibid, s 159(5)
 am—Health and Social Care, 2008 c 14, ss 95, 151(9)(a), sch 5 para 83; (pt prosp) ibid,
  s 159(3)(4)
s 36 rep in pt—Health and Social Care, 2012 c 7, s 160(3); (prosp) ibid, s 180(3)
 am—(prosp) Health and Social Care, 2012 c 7, s 180(4)
s 37 am—Health and Social Care, 2012 c 7, s 161(1)(2)
s 38 rep —Health and Social Care, 2012 c 7, s 159(6)
s 39 rep in pt—Health and Social Care, 2012 c 7, ss 111(11)(a), 156(5), 159(7)
 am—Health and Social Care, 2012 c 7, ss 151(9)(a), 178(5)
s 39A added —Health and Social Care, 2012 c 7, s 162
s 40 am—(pt prosp) Health and Social Care, 2012 c 7, s 163(1), sch 14 para 5
s 41 rep —Health and Social Care, 2012 c 7, s 163(2)
s 42 am—Health and Social Care, 2012 c 7, s 163(5), sch 14 para 6
 rep in pt—Health and Social Care, 2012 c 7, s 163(3)(4)
s 42A added —Health and Social Care, 2012 c 7, s 163(6)
s 43 am—Health and Social Care, 2012 c 7, s 164(1)(2)(a)(b)(3); ibid, s 164(5)
 rep in pt—Health and Social Care, 2012 c 7, s 164(2)(c); ibid, s 164(4)
s 44 am—Health, 2009 c 21, s 33; Health and Social Care, 2012 c 7, s 165(2)
 rep in pt—Health and Social Care, 2012 c 7, s 165(1)
s 45 rep—Health and Social Care, 2012 c 7, s 163(7)
s 46 rep in pt—Health and Social Care, 2012 c 7, s 163(8)
s 48 subst—Health and Social Care, 2012 c 7, s 166
s 49 rep —Health and Social Care, 2012 c 7, s 159(8)
s 50 subst —Health and Social Care, 2012 c 7, s 163(9)
s 51 rep in pt—(prosp) Health and Social Care, 2012 c 7, sch 14 para 7
s 51A added —Health and Social Care, 2012 c 7, s 167
s 52 rep —Health and Social Care, 2012 c 7, s 111(11)
ss 52A-52E added—Health, 2009 c 21, s 15(1)
s 52C rep—Health and Social Care, 2012 c 7, s 173(1)
ss 53-55 rep —Health and Social Care, 2012 c 7, s 173(2)
s 56 rep in pt—Loc Govt and Public Involvement in Health, 2007 c 28, s 241, sch 18;
  Health and Social Care, 2012 c 7, s 168(3)(4)(6), sch 14 para 8(a)(b)
 am—Health and Social Care, 2008 c 14, s 95, sch 5 para 84; Health and Social Care,
  2012 c 7, ss 168(1)(2)(5)(7), 172(9)
s 56A added—Health and Social Care, 2012 c 7, s 169
 rep in pt—(prosp) Health and Social Care, 2012 c 7, sch 14 para 9
 am—Deregulation, 2015 c 20, s 96(2)
s 56AA added—Deregulation, 2015 c 20, s 96(3)
s 56B added —Health and Social Care, 2012 c 7, s 170
s 57 am—Health and Social Care, 2012 c 7, ss 172(1)-(6)(8), 173(2)(a)(i)(iii); Deregulation,
  2015 c 20, s 96(4)
 rep in pt—(prosp) Health and Social Care, 2012 c 7, ss 127(7), sch 14 para 10(a)(b)(c);
  ibid, s 173(2)(a)(ii)
s 57A added—Health and Social Care, 2012 c 7, s 171
s 58 rep—Finance, 2012 c 14, s 216(2)(b)
s 59 am—Health and Social Care, 2012 c 7, s 151(9)(a)
s 60 am—Health and Social Care, 2012 c 7, s 151(9)(a)(b)

2006
c 41 *continued*

s 61 am—Health and Social Care, 2012 c 7, s 153(1)(2)

s 64 am—Health and Social Care, 2012 c 7, s 158(2); ibid, s 172(10)(11); Deregulation, 2015 c 20, s 96(5)

    rep in pt—Health and Social Care, 2012 c 7, s 173(2)(b)

s 65 rep in pt—(prosp) Health and Social Care, 2012 c 7, sch 14 para 11

    am—Care, 2014 c 23, s 85(4)(5)

ss 65A-65O added—Health, 2009 c 21, s 16

s 65A rep in pt—Health and Social Care, 2012 c 7, s 174(1)(b); (prosp) ibid, sch 14 para 12

    am—Health and Social Care, 2012 c 7, s 174(1)(a)

s 65B rep (prosp)—Health and Social Care, 2012 c 7, sch 14 para 13(1)

    am—Health and Social Care, 2012 c 7, s 174(2)

s 65C rep (prosp)—Health and Social Care, 2012 c 7, sch 14 para 14

s 65D rep in pt—Health and Social Care, 2012 c 7, s 174(4)(c)(d)(7)

    am—Health and Social Care, 2012 c 7, s 174(3)(4)(a)(b)(e)(5)(6); Care, 2014 c 23, ss 84, 85(1)(2)

s 65DA added—Health and Social Care, 2012 c 7, s 175(1)

s 65E rep—Health and Social Care, 2012 c 7, s 173(3)

s 65F rep in pt—Health and Social Care, 2012 c 7, s 176(1)(b); (prosp) ibid, sch 14 para 15(3)(a)(6); ibid, sch 14 para 15(8); Care, 2014 c 23, s 85(3)(a)

    am—Health and Social Care, 2012 c 7, s 176(1)(a)(2); (prosp) ibid, sch 14 para 15(2)(3)(b)(4)(5); Care, 2014 c 23, ss 85(3)(b)(c)(6)(15), 120(2)-(4)

s 65G rep in pt—(prosp) Health and Social Care, 2012 c 7, sch 14 para 16; ibid, sch 14, para 16(2)-(4)

    am—Health and Social Care, 2012 c 7, s 176(3); Care, 2014 c 23, ss 85(7)-(9), 120(5)-(7)18)(e)

s 65H rep in pt—Health and Social Care, 2012 c 7, s 176(4)(b)(c)(5); (prosp) ibid, sch 14 para 17(2)(a); ibid, sch 14, para 17(4A)(a)

    am—Health and Social Care, 2012 c 7, ss 176(4)(a)(d)(6)(a)(b)(7), 189(5); (prosp) ibid, sch 14 para 17(2)(b)(3)-(5); Care, 2014 c 23, ss 85(10), 120(8)(9)(11)-(13)

s 65I rep in pt—(prosp) Health and Social Care, 2012 c 7, sch 14 para 18(4)

    am—Health and Social Care, 2012 c 7, s 176(8); (prosp) ibid, sch 14 para 18(2)(3)

s 65J rep in pt—(prosp) Health and Social Care, 2012 c 7, sch 14 para 19(3)

    am—Health and Social Care, 2012 c 7, s 176(9); (prosp) ibid, sch 14 para 19(2)

s 65K rep (prosp)—Health and Social Care, 2012 c 7, sch 14 para 20(1)

    am—Health and Social Care, 2012 c 7, s 177(1)(7)

ss 65KA-65KD added—Health and Social Care, 2012 c 7, s 177(2)

s 65KA rep in pt—(prosp) Health and Social Care, 2012 c 7, sch 14 para 21(2)

    am—(prosp) Health and Social Care, 2012 c 7, sch 14 para 21(3)-(5)

s 65KB am—Care, 2014 c 23, s 85(11)-(14)

s 65KD am—Care, 2014 c 23, s 85(13)(14)

s 65L rep in pt—Health and Social Care, 2012 c 7, s 177(4); (prosp) ibid, sch 14 para 22(4)

    am—Health and Social Care, 2012 c 7, s 177(3)(5); (prosp) ibid, sch 14 paras 22(2)(3)(a)(b)

s 65LA added—Health and Social Care, 2012 c 7, s 177(6)

    am—Deregulation, 2015 c 20, s 96(6)(7)

s 65M rep in pt—(prosp) Health and Social Care, 2012 c 7, sch 14 para 23(4)

    am—Health and Social Care, 2012 c 7, s 178(1); (prosp) ibid, sch 14 para 23(2)(3)

s 65N rep in pt—(prosp) Health and Social Care, 2012 c 7, sch 14 para 24(3); ibid, sch 14 para 24(2A)

    am—Health and Social Care, 2012 c 7, s 178(2)(3); (prosp) ibid, sch 14 para 24(2); Care, 2014 c 23, ss 84(6)(7), 120(14)

s 65O am—Health and Social Care, 2012 c 7, s 178(4); Care, 2014 c 23, s 120(1)

    rep in pt—Health and Social Care, 2012 c 7, sch 14 para 24A

Pt 2 Ch 5B (ss 65P-65Z3) added—Health, 2009 c 21, s 17

    rep —Health and Social Care, 2012 c 7, sch 4 para 15

s 66 am—(prosp) Health and Social Care, 2012 c 7, sch 21 para 8(1)

    rep in pt—(prosp) Health and Social Care, 2012 c 7, sch 14 para 25

    mod—(pt prosp) Health and Social Care, 2012 c 7, sch 21 para 8(2)(3)

s 67 rep in pt—Health and Social Care, 2012 c 7, sch 4 para 16; (pt prosp) ibid, sch 21 para 9(2)(3)

s 68 am—(prosp) Health and Social Care, 2012 c 7, sch 21 para 10(1)

    rep in pt—(prosp) Health and Social Care, 2012 c 7, sch 14 para 26

2006

c 41 s 68 *continued*

    mod—(temp) (prosp) Health and Social Care, 2012 c 7, sch 21 para 10(2)(3)

s 70 rep in pt—Health and Social Care, 2012 c 7, sch 4 para 17(a)(i)(ii); (prosp) ibid, sch 14
    para 27(1)

    am—Health and Social Care, 2012 c 7, sch 4 para 17(b); (prosp) ibid, sch 14 para
    27(2)

s 71 am—Health and Social Care, 2008 c 14, s 95, sch 5 para 85; ibid, s 142; Health and
    Social Care, 2012 c 7, sch 4 para 18(2)(a)(d)(e)(i)(ii),(3)(a)(b),(4)(a),(6)(a); ibid,
    sch 4 para 18(5), sch 7 para 19(b), sch 17 para 10(3), sch 19 para 9(3); Care,
    2014 c 23, sch 5 para 24(3); ibid, sch 7 para 18(9)

    rep in pt—(prosp) Health and Social Care, 2008 c 14, s 166, sch 15 pt 4; Health and
    Social Care, 2012 c 7, sch 4 para 18(2)(b)(c),(4)(b)(c),(6)(b)(c), sch 7 para
    19(a); (prosp) ibid, sch 14 para 28

    mod—(transtl provn) SI 2008/2250, art 3(15)

s 72 am—Health and Social Care, 2012 c 7, sch 17 para 10(4), sch 19 para 9(4); Care, 2014
    c 23, sch 5 para 15(2)

s 73 rep in pt—Health and Social Care, 2012 c 7, sch 4 para 19

s 73A added —Health and Social Care, 2012 c 7, s 30

s 73B added —Health and Social Care, 2012 c 7, s 31

s 73C added —Health and Social Care, 2012 c 7, s 32

s 74 am—Health and Social Care, 2012 c 7, sch 4 para 24(a)(b)

    rep in pt—Health and Social Care, 2012 c 7, sch 4 para 24(c)(d)

s 75 mod—Health Protection Agency, 2004 c 17, s 4(5)(c)

s 76 mod—Health Protection Agency, 2004 c 17, s 4(5)(b)

    am—Health and Social Care, 2012 c 7, sch 4 para 25(a)

    rep in pt—Health and Social Care, 2012 c 7, sch 4 para 25(b)(c)

s 77 am—Health and Social Care, 2012 c 7, s 200(1)(2)(4)-(7)(10)(d)(11)(12)

    rep in pt—Health and Social Care, 2012 c 7, s 200(3)(8)(9)(10)(a)-(c); ibid, sch 4 para
    26; (prosp) ibid, sch 14 para 29(a)(b)

s 78 rep (prosp)—Health and Social Care, 2012 c 7, sch 14 para 30

    rep in pt—Health and Social Care, 2012 c 7, sch 4 para 27, sch 21 para 11(b)

    am—Health and Social Care, 2012 c 7, sch 21 para 11(a)

s 79 rep (prosp)—Health and Social Care, 2012 c 7, sch 14 para 30

s 80 am—Health, 2009 c 21, s 13, sch 1; Health and Social Care, 2012 c 7, s 280(4), sch 4
    para 28(2)(4)-(6)(7)(a)(8)(9)(a)(b)(10)(11)

    rep in pt—Health and Social Care, 2012 c 7, sch 4 para 28(3)(a)(b)(7)(b)(c)(9)(c)

s 81 am—Health and Social Care, 2012 c 7, sch 4 para 29(2)(3)(5)(6)

    rep in pt—Health and Social Care, 2012 c 7, sch 4 para 29(4)

s 83 am—Health and Social Care, 2012 c 7, sch 4 para 30(2)(3)(5)

    rep in pt—Health and Social Care, 2012 c 7, sch 4 para 30(4)

s 84 am—Health and Social Care, 2012 c 7, sch 4 para 31

s 86 am—Health and Social Care, 2012 c 7, s 202(1), sch 4 para 32

s 87 am—Health and Social Care, 2012 c 7, sch 4 para 33

s 89 am—Health and Social Care, 2012 c 7, ss 28(1), 202(2), sch 4 para 34(1)

    mod—Health and Social Care, 2012 c 7, sch 4 para 34(2)

s 90 am—Crime and Cts, 2013 c 22, sch 9 para 52

s 91 am—Health and Social Care, 2012 c 7, sch 4 para 35(2)(3)

    rep in pt—Health and Social Care, 2012 c 7, sch 4 para 35(4)

s 92 am—Health and Social Care, 2012 c 7, sch 4 para 36(2)(5)

    rep in pt—Health and Social Care, 2012 c 7, sch 4 para 36(3)(4)

s 93 am—Health and Social Care, 2012 c 7, s 202(3), sch 4 para 37(2)(a)(4)

    rep in pt—Health and Social Care, 2012 c 7, sch 4 para 37(2)(b)(3)

s 94 am—Health and Social Care, 2012 c 7, s 28(2), sch 4 para 38(2)-(4); Crime and Cts,
    2013 c 22, sch 9 para 52

    mod—Health and Social Care, 2012 c 7, sch 4 para 38(5)

s 95 rep —Health and Social Care, 2012 c 7, sch 4 para 39

s 96 am—Health and Social Care, 2012 c 7, sch 4 para 40(2)(3)

s 97 am—Health and Social Care, 2012 c 7, sch 4 para 41(2)(3)(b)(4)(6)

    rep in pt—Health and Social Care, 2012 c 7, sch 4 para 41(3)(a)(5)

s 98A added —Health and Social Care, 2012 c 7, s 49(1)

Pt 5 (ss 99-114) rep—Health and Social Care, 2012 c 7, s 279

s 105 am—Crime and Cts, 2013 c 22, sch 9 para 52

s 109 am—Crime and Cts, 2013 c 22, sch 9 para 52

s 114A added —Health and Social Care, 2012 c 7, s 49(2)

2006
c 41 *continued*

s 115 am—Health and Social Care, 2012 c 7, sch 4 para 54(2)-(5)(7) (8)
rep in pt—Health and Social Care, 2012 c 7, sch 4 para 54(6)
s 117 am—Health and Social Care, 2012 c 7, sch 4 para 55
s 118 am—Health and Social Care, 2012 c 7, sch 4 para 56
s 119 am—SI 2010/22, art 5, sch 2; Health and Social Care, 2012 c 7, sch 4 para 57
s 120 am—Health and Social Care, 2012 c 7, sch 4 para 58
s 121 am—Health and Social Care, 2012 c 7, sch 4 para 59
s 122 am—Crime and Cts, 2013 c 22, sch 9 para 52
s 123 am—Health and Social Care, 2012 c 7, sch 4 para 60(2)(3)
rep in pt—Health and Social Care, 2012 c 7, sch 4 para 60(4)
s 124 am—Health and Social Care, 2012 c 7, sch 4 para 61(2)(3)
s 125 am—Health and Social Care, 2012 c 7, sch 4 para 62(2)(3)(b)(4)(5)
rep in pt—Health and Social Care, 2012 c 7, sch 4 para 62(3)(a)
s 125A added —Health and Social Care, 2012 c 7, s 49(3)
s 126 am—Health and Social Care, 2012 c 7, ss 213(7)(k), 220(7); ibid, sch 4 para
63(2)-(4)
rep in pt—Health and Social Care, 2012 c 7, sch 4 para 63(5)
s 127 am—Health and Social Care, 2012 c 7, sch 4 para 64(2)(3)
rep in pt—Health and Social Care, 2012 c 7, sch 4 para 64(4)
s 128 am—Health and Social Care, 2012 c 7, sch 4 para 65
s 128A added—Health, 2009 c 21, s 25
am—Health and Social Care, 2012 c 7, s 206(1)
s 129 am—Health, 2009 c 21, ss 26(1)-(4)(5)(a)(c)(d)(6)-(8), 27; SI 2010/231, art 68, sch 4;
Health and Social Care, 2012 c 7, s 207(8); ibid, s 207(3)(5)(6)(9), sch 4 para
66(2)-(7)(8)(a)(c)(9); Protection of Freedoms, 2012 c 9, sch 9 para 121
rep in pt—Health, 2009 c 21, ss 26(1)(5)(b), 38, sch 6; Health and Social Care, 2012
c 7, s 207(2)(b)(7), sch 4 para 66(8)(b)
excl—SIs 2012/1909, regs 23, 24(1)(2), 25(1), 26(1)(2), 27(1), 28(1), 29(1);
2013/349, regs 23, 24(1)92), 25(1), 26(1)(2), 27(1), 28(1), 29(1)
s 130 am—SI 2010/22, art 5, sch 2; Health and Social Care, 2012 c 7, s 207(10)(a); ibid,
sch 4 para 67
rep in pt—Health and Social Care, 2012 c 7, s 207(10)(b)
s 131 am—Health and Social Care, 2012 c 7, sch 4 para 68(2)(3)
rep in pt—Health and Social Care, 2012 c 7, sch 4 para 68(4)
s 132 am—SIs 2010/22, art 5, sch 2; 2010/231, art 68, sch 4; Health and Social Care, 2012
c 7, sch 4 para 69(2)-(5); Protection of Freedoms, 2012 c 9, sch 9 para 122
s 133 am—Health and Social Care, 2012 c 7, sch 4 para 70(2)(a)(3)(4)
rep in pt—Health and Social Care, 2012 c 7, sch 4 para 70(2)(b)
s 134 am—Health, 2009 c 21, s 13, sch 1 paras 6, 8; Health and Social Care, 2012 c 7, sch
4 para 71(2)(3)(a)(b)(4)
rep in pt—Health and Social Care, 2012 c 7, sch 4 para 71(3)(c)(d)
s 136 am—Health and Social Care, 2012 c 7, s 207(11), sch 4 para 72
s 137 am—Health and Social Care, 2012 c 7, sch 4 para 73
s 138 am—Health and Social Care, 2012 c 7, sch 4 para 74(2)(3)
s 139 am—Crime and Cts, 2013 c 22, sch 9 para 52
s 140 am—Health and Social Care, 2012 c 7, sch 4 para 75(2)(3)
s 144 am—Health, 2009 c 21, s 29(1)(4); Health and Social Care, 2012 c 7, sch 4 para
76(1)
s 146 rep (prosp)—Health and Social Care, 2012 c 7, s 208(1)(a)
Pt 7 Ch 4A (ss 147A, 147B) added (pt prosp)—Health and Social Care, 2012 c 7, s 208(2)
s 147A am—Protection of Freedoms, 2012 c 9, sch 9 para 123
Pt 7 Ch 5 (ss 148-150) am—(pt prosp) Health and Social Care, 2012 c 7, s 208(3)
s 148 am—SI 2010/22, art 5, sch 2; Health and Social Care, 2012 c 7, sch 4 para 77
s 149 am—SI 2010/22, art 5, sch 2
rep (prosp)—Health and Social Care, 2012 c 7, s 208(1)(b)
s 150 rep (prosp)—Health and Social Care, 2012 c 7, s 208(1)(c)
s 150A added—Health, 2009 c 21, s 28
am—Health and Social Care, 2012 c 7, sch 4 para 78(2)(3)
s 151 am—Health and Social Care, 2012 c 7, sch 4 para 79(2)-(4)
s 152 am—Health and Social Care, 2012 c 7, sch 4 para 80(2)(3)
s 154 am—SI 2010/22, art 5, sch 2; Health and Social Care, 2012 c 7, sch 4 para 81
s 155 am—SI 2010/22, art 5, sch 2; Health and Social Care, 2012 c 7, sch 4 para 82(2)(3)
s 157 am—SI 2010/22, art 5, sch 2; Health and Social Care, 2012 c 7, sch 4 para 83(2)(3)

2006
c 41 *continued*

s 158 am—SI 2010/22, art 5, sch 2; Health and Social Care, 2012 c 7, sch 4 para 84
  rep in pt—SI 2010/22, art 5, sch 2
s 159 am—SI 2010/22, art 5, sch 2; Health and Social Care, 2012 c 7, s 208(4)(b), sch 4
  para 85(2)-(6)
  rep in pt—(pt prosp) Health and Social Care, 2012 c 7, s 208(4)(a)
  mod—SIs 2012/1909, reg 87; 2013/349, reg 87
s 160 am—Health and Social Care, 2012 c 7, sch 4 para 86
s 161 am—Health and Social Care, 2012 c 7, sch 4 para 87
s 162 am—Health and Social Care, 2012 c 7, sch 4 para 88(2)(3)
s 164 am—Health and Social Care, 2008 c 14, s 141(1)(a); Health and Social Care, 2012 c
  7, sch 4 para 89(2)(3)
  rep in pt—Health and Social Care, 2008 c 14, ss 141(1)(b), 166, sch 15
s 165A added —Health and Social Care, 2012 c 7, s 51(1)
s 166 am—Health and Social Care, 2012 c 7, sch 4 para 90(2)(3)
s 167 am—Health and Social Care, 2012 c 7, sch 4 para 91(2)(4)-(6)
  rep in pt—Health and Social Care, 2012 c 7, sch 4 para 91(3)
s 168A added —Health and Social Care, 2012 c 7, s 49(4)
Pt 8 (ss 169-171) am—SI 2010/22, art 5, sch 2
s 169 am—SI 2010/22, art 5, sch 2
  rep in pt—SI 2010/22, art 5, sch 2
ss 171, 172 rep—SI 2010/22, art 5, sch 2
s 173 am —Health, 2009 c 21, s 13, sch 1 paras 6, 7(c)
s 176 am—Health and Social Care, 2012 c 7, sch 4 para 94(a)
  rep in pt—Health and Social Care, 2012 c 7, sch 4 para 94(b)
s 177 rep in pt—Health and Social Care, 2012 c 7, sch 4 para 95
s 180 am —Health, 2009 c 21, s 34; Health and Social Care, 2012 c 7, s 205(2)(3), sch 4
  para 96(2)-(5)(7)(9)
  rep in pt—Health, 2009 c 21, s 38, sch 6; Health and Social Care, 2012 c 7, sch 4 para
  96(6)(8)
s 181 am—SI 2010/22, art 5, sch 2
  rep in pt—Health and Social Care, 2012 c 7, sch 4 para 97(2)(3)
s 183 am—SI 2010/915, reg 3; Health and Social Care, 2012 c 7, sch 4 para
  98(2)(a)(3)(a)(c)(4)(a)(c); SI 2013/2269, reg 8
  rep in pt—Health and Social Care, 2012 c 7, sch 4 para 98(2)(b)(3)(b)(d)(4)(b)
s 185 am—Loc Govt and Public Involvement in Health, 2007 c 28, s 127; Health and Social
  Care, 2012 c 7, sch 4 para 99(a)
  rep in pt—Health and Social Care, 2012 c 7, sch 4 para 99(b); (prosp) ibid, sch 14
  para 31
s 186 am—Health and Social Care, 2012 c 7, sch 4 para 100(a)
  rep in pt—Health and Social Care, 2012 c 7, sch 4 para 100(b); (prosp) ibid, sch 14
  para 32
s 186A added —Health and Social Care, 2012 c 7, s 50(1)
s 187 am—Health and Social Care, 2012 c 7, sch 4 para 101
s 188 am—Health and Social Care, 2012 c 7, sch 4 para 102(a)
  rep in pt—Health and Social Care, 2012 c 7, sch 4 para 102(b)
s 194 rep in pt—Legal Services, 2007 c 29, s 208, sch 21 para 154, sch 23
s 195 am—Health and Social Care, 2012 c 7, sch 4 para 103(2)(3)
s 196 am—Health and Social Care, 2012 c 7, sch 4 para 104(2)(3)(a); ibid, sch 4 para
  104(4)
  rep in pt—Health and Social Care, 2012 c 7, sch 4 para 104(3)(b)(c); (prosp) sch 14
  para 33
s 197 am—Health and Social Care, 2012 c 7, sch 4 para 105(2)(3)
s 201 am—Health and Social Care, 2008 c 14, s 127, sch 10 para 24; Health and Social
  Care, 2012 c 7, sch 15 para 68(b); ibid, sch 4 para 106
s 206 am—SI 2007/289, art 67, sch 1
  rep in pt—Health and Social Care, 2012 c 7, s 178(11)
s 210 am—Health and Social Care, 2012 c 7, sch 4 para 107(2)(3)
s 211 am—Health and Social Care, 2012 c 7, sch 4 para 108(2)(3)
s 213 am—Health and Social Care, 2012 c 7, sch 4 para 109(a)
  rep in pt—Health and Social Care, 2012 c 7, sch 4 para 109(b)
s 214 am—Health and Social Care, 2012 c 7, sch 4 para 110(2)(a)(3)(a)
  rep in pt—Health and Social Care, 2012 c 7, sch 4 para 110(2)(b)(3)(b)
s 215 am—Health and Social Care, 2012 c 7, sch 4 para 111(3)(a)(4)(a)(c)

2006

c 41 s 215 *continued*

rep in pt—Health and Social Care, 2012 c 7, sch 4 para 111(2)(3)(b)(4)(b)

s 216 am—Health and Social Care, 2012 c 7, sch 4 para 112

s 217 am—Charities, 2011 c 25, sch 7 para 111; Health and Social Care, 2012 c 7, sch 4 para 113(a)

rep in pt—Health and Social Care, 2012 c 7, sch 4 para 113(b)(c); (prosp) ibid, sch 14 para 34

s 218 am—Health and Social Care, 2012 c 7, sch 4 para 114(c)

rep in pt—Health and Social Care, 2012 c 7, sch 4 para 114(a)(b)

s 220 am—Health and Social Care, 2012 c 7, sch 4 para 115

s 222 am—Health and Social Care, 2012 c 7, sch 4 para 116

s 223 am—SI 2009/1941, art 2, sch 1; Health and Social Care, 2012 c 7, sch 4 para 117(1)

s 223A added —Health and Social Care, 2012 c 7, sch 4 para 117(2)

ss 223B-223F added—Health and Social Care, 2012 c 7, s 24

s 223B am—Care, 2014 c 23, s 121(1)

ss 223G-223K added —Health and Social Care, 2012 c 7, s 27

s 223GA added—Care, 2014 c 23, s 121(2)

s 224 rep —Health and Social Care, 2012 c 7, sch 4 para 118

s 226 am—Health and Social Care, 2012 c 7, sch 4 para 119(3)(b)

rep in pt—Health and Social Care, 2012 c 7, sch 4 para 119(2)(3)(a)(4)-(8)

s 227 am—Health and Social Care, 2012 c 7, sch 4 para 120(5)

rep in pt—Health and Social Care, 2012 c 7, sch 4 para 120(2)-(4)(6)

ss 228-231 rep —Health and Social Care, 2012 c 7, sch 4 para 121

s 234 am—Health, 2009 c 21, s 13, sch 1 paras 6, 7(d)

rep in pt—Health and Social Care, 2012 c 7, sch 4 para 122

s 236 am—Health and Social Care, 2012 c 7, sch 4 para 123(2)(3)(a)(c)(d)

rep in pt—Health and Social Care, 2012 c 7, sch 4 para 123(3)(b)

s 238 rep —Loc Govt and Public Involvement in Health, 2007 c 28, s 241, sch 18 pt 18

s 239 rep —Loc Govt and Public Involvement in Health, 2007 c 28, ss 230(1), 241, sch 18 pt 18

s 240 rep —Loc Govt and Public Involvement in Health, 2007 c 28, ss 231(1), 241, sch 18 pt 18

s 241 rep —Loc Govt and Public Involvement in Health, 2007 c 28, ss 230(1), 231(1), 241, sch 18 pt 18

s 242 am—Loc Govt and Public Involvement in Health, 2007 c 28, s 233(1)-(4); Health, 2009 c 21, s 18(1)(7); Health and Social Care, 2012 c 7, s 206(4); (prosp) ibid, sch 14 para 35(a)(d); Care, 2014 c 23, s 120(17)

rep in pt—Health and Social Care, 2012 c 7, sch 4 para 126(2)(3); (prosp) ibid, sch 14 para 35(b)(c); ibid, sch 14 para 35(e)

s 242A added—Loc Govt and Public Involvement in Health, 2007 c 28, s 233(5)

rep —Health and Social Care, 2012 c 7, sch 4 para 127

s 242B added—Loc Govt and Public Involvement in Health, 2007 c 28, s 233(5)

rep—Health and Social Care, 2012 c 7, sch 4 para 127

s 243 rep —Loc Govt and Public Involvement in Health, 2007 c 28, s 232(1), sch 18

Pt 12 Ch 3 (ss 244-247A) am—Health and Social Care, 2012 c 7, s 190(8)

s 244 am—Loc Govt and Public Involvement in Health, 2007 c 28, s 121(4); Localism, 2011 c 20, sch 3 para 74; Health and Social Care, 2012 c 7, s 190(2)(b)-(d)(f)(3)-(7)

rep in pt—Health and Social Care, 2012 c 7, s 190(2)(a)(e)

s 245 am—Localism, 2011 c 20, sch 3 para 75(1)(2)(3)(a)(4)(5); Health and Social Care, 2012 c 7, s 191(2)-(4)

rep in pt—Localism, 2011 c 20, sch 3 para 75(1)(3)(b), sch 25 pt 4; Health and Social Care, 2012 c 7, s 191(5)

s 246 am—Health, 2009 c 21, s 13, sch 1 paras 6, 9; Localism, 2011 c 20, sch 3 para 76; Health and Social Care, 2012 c 7, s 191(7)-(9)

appl—SI 2013/218, reg 30(3)

s 247 am—Localism, 2011 c 20, sch 3 para 77(1)(2)(3)(a)(b)(4)(5); Health and Social Care, 2012 c 7, s 191(11)(12)(a)(13)

rep in pt—Localism, 2011 c 20, sch 3 para 77(1)(3)(c), sch 25 pt 4; Health and Social Care, 2012 c 7, s 191(12)(b)

s 247A added —Localism, 2011 c 20, sch 3 para 78

rep —Health and Social Care, 2012 c 7, s 191(14)

s 247B added —Health and Social Care, 2012 c 7, s 60(1)

s 247C added —Health and Social Care, 2012 c 7, s 52

2006

c 41 s 247C *continued*

  am—Care, 2014 c 23, sch 5 para 13(8)

s 247D added —Health and Social Care, 2012 c 7, s 53

s 248 rep —Health and Social Care, 2012 c 7, s 185(2)

s 249 am—Health and Social Care, 2012 c 7, s 29(3)

s 250 rep—Health and Social Care, 2012 c 7, s 283(1)

ss 250A-250D added—Health and Social Care, 2008 c 14, s 157(1)

  rep —Health and Social Care, 2012 c 7, s 280(2)

s 252 subst—Health and Social Care, 2008 c 14, s 158

  am—Health and Social Care, 2012 c 7, s 280(5)

s 252A added —Health and Social Care, 2012 c 7, s 46

s 253 am—Health and Social Care, 2012 c 7, ss 46, 47(2)-(5)

  rep in pt—Health and Social Care, 2012 c 7, s 47(6)

s 254 am—SI 2010/1158, art 5, sch 2

  rep in pt—SI 2015/914, sch para 82

s 254A added —Health and Social Care, 2012 c 7, sch 4 para 128

s 256 mod—Health Protection Agency, 2004 c 17, s 4(5)(a)(i); SI 2008/2839, arts 3, 6, sch

  am—SIs 2008/3002, arts 4, 5, schs 1, 2; 2010/866, art 5, sch 2; 2010/1158, art 5, sch 2; Localism, 2011 c 20, sch 19 para 44; ibid, 2011 c 20, sch 22 para 57; Health and Social Care, 2012 c 7, sch 4 para 129; SI 2013/2341, art 4

s 257 mod—Health Protection Agency, 2004 c 17, s 4(5)(a)(i)

  am—Health and Social Care, 2012 c 7, sch 4 para 130

s 258 am—Health and Social Care, 2012 c 7, sch 4 para 131(2)(3)(a)(b)

  rep in pt—Health and Social Care, 2012 c 7, sch 4 para 131(3)(c)(d)

s 259 trans of functions—SI 2008/1786, art 2

  am—Health and Social Care, 2012 c 7, sch 4 para 132

s 268 rep —Health and Social Care, 2012 c 7, sch 4 para 133

s 269 am—Health and Social Care, 2012 c 7, s 284(2)(3)(4)(6)-(8)

s 270 am—Health and Social Care, 2012 c 7, s 285(2)-(4)

s 271 am—Health and Social Care, 2008 c 14, s 160, sch 14 para 5; SI 2010/22, art 5, sch 2; Health and Social Care, 2012 c 7, ss 60(2), 172(12), 280(5)(b)(i), sch 4 para 134

  rep in pt—Health and Social Care, 2012 c 7, s 280(5)(b)(ii); ibid, sch 20 para 10(1)

s 271A added —Health and Social Care, 2012 c 7, sch 4 para 135

s 272 appl—Nat Health Service (W), 2006 c 42, ss 120(5), 209(4); Statistics and Registration Service, 2007 c 18, s 42(5B)

  am—Health, 2009 c 21, s 13, sch 1 paras 6, 10; (pt prosp) ibid, s 18(1)(8); Health and Social Care, 2012 c 7, ss 21(5), 178(6)(7)(8); ibid, ss 13(8), 18(2), 20(2), 23(2), 48(2), 50(2), sch 4 para 136(3)(b)

  rep in pt—Health and Social Care, 2012 c 7, s 173(6)(a)(b); ibid, sch 4 para 136(2)(a)(b)(3)(a)(b), sch 14 para 36(a)

s 273 appl—Nat Health Service (W), 2006 c 42, s 209(4)

  am—SI 2010/22, art 5, sch 2; Health and Social Care, 2012 c 7, s 21(6)(a)(b), sch 4 para 137(2)(3); ibid, s 47(7)

s 275 am—Mental Health, 2007 c 12, s 1, sch 1 para 24; SI 2007/3101, regs 104, 203; SI 2008/3002, arts 4, 5, schs 1, 2; Health, 2009 c 21, s 18(1)(9); SIs 2010/231, art 68, sch 4; 2010/915, reg 4; Health and Social Care, 2012 c 7, sch 4 para 138(2)(a)(c), sch 13 para 11; (prosp) ibid, s 40(5), sch 14 para 37; ibid, sch 17 para 10(5)

  rep in pt—SIs 2010/22, art 5, sch 2; 2010/1158, art 5, schs 2, 3; Health and Social Care, 2012 c 7, ss 173(7)(a)(b), 178(9); ibid, sch 4 para 138(2)(b)(3)

  mod—Health and Social Care, 2012 c 7, sch 4 para 138(4)(5); (temp) ibid, sch 4 para 138(4)(5)

s 276 rep in pt—Health, 2009 c 21, ss 13, 38, sch 1 paras 6, 11, sch 6; Health and Social Care, 2012 c 7, sch 4 para 139(2); ibid, s 208(5), sch 4 para 139(4); (prosp) ibid, sch 14 para 38

  am—Health and Social Care, 2012 c 7, sch 13 para 12; ibid, sch 4 para 139(3)(5)

sch A1 added —Health and Social Care, 2012 c 7, s 9(2), sch 1

sch 1 am—Health and Social Care, 2008 c 14, ss 143, 160, sch 14 para 6; SI 2010/1158, art 5, sch 2; Health and Social Care, 2012 c 7, s 17(3)(a)(b)(4)(a)(i)(b)(5)(6)(b)(ii)(iii)(7)(a)(c)(8)-(11)(12)(a)(iii)(13)

  rep in pt—Health and Social Care, 2012 c 7, s 17(4)(a)(ii)(c)(6)(a)(b)(i)(7)(b)(12)(a)(i)(b)

sch 1A added —Health and Social Care, 2012 c 7, s 25(2), sch 2

2006

c 41 sch 1A *continued*

        mod—Health and Social Care, 2012 c 7, sch 6 para 11(2)(p)

        am—Loc Audit and Accountability, 2014 c 2, sch 12 para 71

        appl in pt (mods)—SI 2015/192, sch para 18

sch 2 rep —Health and Social Care, 2012 c 7, sch 4 para 20

sch 3 rep —Health and Social Care, 2012 c 7, sch 4 para 21

sch 4 am—SI 2008/817, arts 5, 10; Health, 2009 c 21, s 18(1)(10); Deregulation, 2015 c 20, s 96(8)

        rep in pt—Health and Social Care, 2012 c 7, sch 4 para 22

        mod (temp)—Loc Audit and Accountability, 2014 c 2, sch 12 para 76

sch 6 am—Health, 2009 c 21, s 19, sch 3 paras 9, 11, 19; Health and Social Care, 2012 c 7, sch 4 para 23(2)(3)(a)(4)

        rep in pt—Health and Social Care, 2012 c 7, sch 4 para 23(3)(b)

sch 7 rep in pt—Loc Govt and Public Involvement in Health, 2007 c 28, s 146, sch 9 para 1(1)(2)(z), sch 18; Health and Social Care, 2012 c 7, ss 111(11)(b), 151(2), 154(7)(a), 156(6), 159(9); (pt prosp) ibid, s 180(6); Loc Audit and Accountability, 2014 c 2, sch 12 para 73(2)(b)(3)(b)(4)(5)(a); (prosp) ibid, sch 12 para 74(3)

        am—SI 2009/1941, art 2, sch 1; Health and Social Care, 2012 c 7, ss 151(1)(3)-(9), 152, 154(1)-(6)(7)(b)(8), 156(1)(2), 157, 158(1), 164(6), 178(10); (pt prosp) ibid, s 155, 156(4); SI 2012/2404, sch 2 para 57; Loc Audit and Accountability, 2014 c 2, sch 12 para 73(2)(a)(3)(a)(c)(5)(b); (prosp) ibid, sch 12 para 74(2)

        power to am conferred—(pt prosp) Health and Social Care, 2012 c 7, s 156(3)(a)

        power to rep conferred—(pt prosp) Health and Social Care, 2012 c 7, s 156(3)(b)

sch 8 rep—Health and Social Care, 2012 c 7, sch 13 para 9(1)

sch 8A added —Health, 2009 c 21, s 15, sch 2

        rep—Health and Social Care, 2012 c 7, s 173(4)

sch 9 rep—Health and Social Care, 2012 c 7, s 173(2)

sch 10 am—Health and Social Care, 2008 c 14, s 95, sch 5 para 86; Health and Social Care, 2012 c 7, s 151(9)(e)

sch 11 am—Health and Social Care, 2012 c 7, sch 4 para 92(2)-(6)(a)-(c)(7)

        rep in pt—Health and Social Care, 2012 c 7, sch 4 para 92(6)(d)

sch 12 am—Health, 2009 c 21, s 29(1)(5)-(7)(8)(a)(b)(9)-(15); Health and Social Care, 2012 c 7, s 207(12)(a), sch 4 para 93(2)(a)(i)(b)(i)(iii)(d)(e), (3)(a),(4)(a)(b)(i); Crime and Cts, 2013 c 22, sch 9 para 52

        rep in pt—Health, 2009 c 21, ss 29(1)(5)(8)(c), 38, sch 6; Health and Social Care, 2012 c 7, sch 4 para 93(2)(a)(ii)(b)(ii)(c)(f)(3)(b)(4)(b)(ii)

        mod—SI 2013/349, reg 99(1)

sch 12A added—Health and Social Care, 2012 c 7, s 51(2), sch 3

sch 13 rep—SI 2010/22, art 5, sch 2

sch 14 rep —Health and Social Care, 2012 c 7, sch 4 para 124

sch 15 rep in pt—Loc Govt and Public Involvement in Health, 2007 c 28, s 146, sch 9 para 1(1)(2)(z1), sch 18; Health and Social Care, 2012 c 7, sch 4 para 125; (prosp) ibid, sch 14 para 39(2)(3); Loc Audit and Accountability, 2014 c 2, sch 12 para 75(b)

        am—SI 2008/817, arts 6, 10; (pt prosp) Health and Social Care, 2012 c 7, sch 14 para 39(4)(5); Loc Audit and Accountability, 2014 c 2, sch 12 para 75(a)

        excl—SI 2012/2789, art 2

        appl in pt (mods)—SI 2015/192, sch para 19

sch 16 rep —Loc Govt and Public Involvement in Health, 2007 c 28, s 232(1), sch 18

sch 17 am—(pt prosp) Health and Social Care, 2012 c 7, s 208(6)

        appl—SI 2013/218, reg 30(3)

sch 19 rep—Health and Social Care, 2012 c 7, s 283(1)

sch 20 rep—SI 2015/914, sch para 83

sch 21 see—(trans of functions) SI 2008/1786, art 2

c 42   **National Health Service (Wales)**

ss 6A, 6B added—SI 2010/915, reg 5

s 6A am—SI 2013/2269, reg 10(1)

ss 6BA, 6BB added—SI 2013/2269, reg 10(2)

s 7 am—Health and Social Care, 2008 c 14, s 95, sch 5 para 87; Health and Social Care, 2012 c 7, sch 21 para 13(c)(d)(f); ibid, sch 17 para 11, sch 19 para 10(2)

        rep in pt—Health and Social Care, 2012 c 7, sch 21 para 13(e); ibid, sch 7 para 21, sch 21 para 13(a)(b)

s 8A added —Health and Social Care, 2012 c 7, sch 21 para 14

2006
c 42 *continued*

s 10 rep in pt—Health and Social Care, 2012 c 7, sch 21 para 15
s 13 am—Health and Social Care, 2012 c 7, sch 21 para 16(b)
    rep in pt—Health and Social Care, 2012 c 7, sch 21 para 16(a)
s 17 am—Health and Social Care, 2012 c 7, sch 21 para 17(a)(i)(iv)(b)(i)(iv)
    rep in pt—Health and Social Care, 2012 c 7, sch 21 para 17(a)(ii)(iii)(b)(ii)(iii)
s 22 rep in pt—Health and Social Care, 2012 c 7, sch 21 para 18
s 26 am—Health and Social Care, 2012 c 7, sch 21 para 19
s 27 rep in pt—Health and Social Care, 2012 c 7, sch 21 para 20
s 28 am—Health and Social Care, 2012 c 7, sch 21 para 21
s 30 am—Health and Social Care, 2008 c 14, s 95, sch 5 para 88(a); Health and Social Care,
      2012 c 7, sch 7 para 22(a)
    rep in pt—Health and Social Care, 2008 c 14, s 95, sch 15, sch 5 para 88(b); Health
        and Social Care, 2012 c 7, sch 7 para 22(b)
s 33 mod—Health Protection Agency, 2004 c 17, s 4(5)(c)
s 34 mod—Health Protection Agency, 2004 c 17, s 4(5)(b)
    am—Health and Social Care, 2012 c 7, sch 21 para 22(a)
    rep in pt—Health and Social Care, 2012 c 7, sch 21 para 22(b)(c)
s 36 rep in pt—Health and Social Care, 2012 c 7, sch 21 para 23
s 38 rep in pt—Health and Social Care, 2012 c 7, sch 21 para 24
s 39 rep in pt—Health and Social Care, 2012 c 7, sch 21 para 25
s 40 rep (1.4.2016)—Well-being of Future Generations (W), 2015 anaw 2, sch 4 para 19
    am—(prosp) Social Services and Well-being (W), 2014 anaw 4, s 14(3)
s 41 rep in pt—Health and Social Care, 2012 c 7, sch 21 para 26
s 50 mod—Nat Health Service (Conseq Provns), 2006 c 43, s 4, sch 2 para 15
s 51 rep in pt—Health and Social Care, 2012 c 7, sch 21 para 27
s 56 rep in pt—Health and Social Care, 2012 c 7, sch 21 para 28
s 64 mod—Nat Health Service (Conseq Provns), 2006 c 43, s 4, sch 2 para 15
s 65 rep in pt—Health and Social Care, 2012 c 7, sch 21 para 29
s 72 am—SI 2010/22, art 5, sch 2; Protection of Freedoms, 2012 c 9, sch 9 para 125
s 80 am—Health and Social Care, 2012 c 7, ss 213(7)(l), 220(8)
s 83 am—SI 2007/289, art 67, sch 1; (prosp) Health 2009 c 21, s 30; SI 2010/231, art 68,
      sch 4; Protection of Freedoms, 2012 c 9, sch 9 para 126
    rep in pt—(prosp) Health 2009 c 21, s 38, sch 6
s 84 am—SI 2010/22, art 5, sch 2
s 85 mod—Nat Health Service (Conseq Provns), 2006 c 43, s 4, sch 2 para 15
s 86 am—SI 2007/289, art 67, sch 1; 2010/22, art 5, sch 2; 2010/231, art 68, sch 4;
      Protection of Freedoms, 2012 c 9, sch 9 para 127
    rep in pt—SI 2007/289, art 67, sch 1
s 88 am—(pt prosp) Health and Social Care, 2008 c 14, s 141(2)(a)
    rep in pt—(pt prosp) Health and Social Care, 2008 c 14, ss 141(2)(b), 166, sch 15
s 99 mod—Nat Health Service (Conseq Provns), 2006 c 43, s 4, sch 2 para 15
s 104 am—SI 2010/22, art 5, sch 2
s 105 am—SI 2010/22, art 5, sch 2; Protection of Freedoms, 2012 c 9, sch 9 para 128
s 106 am—Health and Social Care, 2012 c 7, sch 21 para 30(b)
    rep in pt—Health and Social Care, 2012 c 7, sch 21 para 30(a)
s 106A added (prosp)—Health, 2009 c 21, s 31(1)
s 107 am—(prosp) Health, 2009 c 21, s 31(2)
ss 110, 111 am—SI 2010/22, art 5, sch 2
s 113 am—SI 2010/22, art 5, sch 2
s 114 am—SI 2010/22, art 5, sch 2
    rep in pt—SI 2010/22, art 5, sch 2
s 115 am—SI 2010/22, art 5, sch 2; Health and Social Care, 2012 c 7, sch 21 para
      31(2)(b)(c)(3)(a)(ii)(b)(ii)
    rep in pt—Health and Social Care, 2012 c 7, sch 21 para 31(2)(a)(d)(3)(a)(i)(b)(i)
s 131 am—SIs 2010/915, reg 6; 2013/2269, reg 11
    rep in pt—Health and Social Care, 2012 c 7, sch 21 para 32
s 142 rep in pt—Legal Services, 2007 c 29, s 208, sch 21 para 155, sch 23
s 144 am—Health and Social Care, 2012 c 7, sch 21 para 33
s 149 am—Health and Social Care, 2008 c 14, s 127, sch 10 para 25; Health and Social
      Care, 2012 c 7, sch 15 para 68(c)
s 161 am—Health and Social Care, 2012 c 7, sch 21 para 34(a)
    rep in pt—Health and Social Care, 2012 c 7, sch 21 para 34(b)
s 162 am—Health and Social Care, 2012 c 7, sch 21 para 35(2)(a)(3)(a)

2006

c 42 s 162 *continued*

rep in pt—Health and Social Care, 2012 c 7, sch 21 para 35(2)(b)(3)(b)

s 165 am—Charities, 2011 c 25, sch 7 para 112

s 170 am—SI 2009/1941, art 2, sch 1

s 174 rep in pt—Health and Social Care, 2008 c 14, s 140, sch 15, sch 12 para 7

s 175 rep in pt—Health and Social Care, 2008 c 14, s 140, sch 15, sch 12 para 8

am—Nat Health Service Finance (W), 2014 anaw 2, s 2

s 176 rep —Nat Health Service Finance (W), 2014 anaw 2, s 2(7)

s 181 rep in pt—Health and Social Care, 2012 c 7, sch 21 para 36(a)

am—Health and Social Care, 2012 c 7, sch 21 para 36(b)

s 184 am—Health and Social Care, 2012 c 7, sch 13 para 13

s 185 am—Loc Govt and Public Involvement in Health, 2007 c 28, s 127(4)

s 187 am—Social Services and Well-being (W), 2014 anaw 4, s 180(2)(a)(c)(3)

rep in pt—Social Services and Well-being (W), 2014 anaw 4, s 180(2)(b)

s 192 am—SI 2010/1158, art 5, sch 2

s 194 mod—Health Protection Agency, 2004 c 17, s 4(5)(a)(ii); SI 2008/2839, arts 3, 6, sch

am—SIs 2008/3002, arts 4, 5, schs 1, 2; 2010/866, art 5, sch 2; 2010/1158, art 5, sch 2

s 195 mod—Health Protection Agency, 2004 c 17, s 4(5)(a)(ii)

s 196 am —SI 2008/3002, arts 4, 5, schs 1, 2

s 197 am—Health and Social Care, 2012 c 7, sch 21 para 37(a)(b)

rep in pt—Health and Social Care, 2012 c 7, sch 21 para 37(c)(d)

s 199 am—SI 2008/3002, arts 4, 5, schs 1, 2

s 201 am—Health and Social Care, 2012 c 7, s 286(2)(3)

s 203 appl—Statistics and Registration Service, 2007 c 18, s 42(5C)

s 204 appl—Statistics and Registration Service, 2007 c 18, s 42(5C)

s 206 am—Mental Health, 2007 c 12, s 1, sch 1 para 25; SI 2007/3101, regs 105, 204; Health, 2009 c 21, s 18(1)(12); 2010/231, art 68, sch 4; 2010/915, reg 7; Health and Social Care, 2012 c 7, sch 21 para 38(1)(a)(b)

rep in pt—SIs 2010/22, art 5, sch 2; 2010/1158, art 5, schs 2, 3; Health and Social Care, 2012 c 7, s 173(8), sch 21 para 38(1)(c)(d); (prosp) ibid, sch 14 para 101

mod—(temp) Health and Social Care, 2012 c 7, sch 21 para 38(2)

s 244 appl (mods)—National Health Service, 2006 c 41, s 247A(3)(a)

ss 245, 246 appl (mods)—National Health Service, 2006 c 41, s 247A(3)(a)

sch 1 am—Health and Social Care, 2008 c 14, s 144; ibid, s 160, sch 14 para 7; (W) Children and Families (W), 2010 nawm 1, s 72, sch 1 paras 25, 26; SI 2010/1158, art 5, sch 2; School Standards and Organisation (W), 2013 anaw 1, sch 5 para 24(2)

sch 2 am—Health and Social Care, 2012 c 7, sch 21 para 39(c)

rep in pt—Health and Social Care, 2012 c 7, sch 21 para 39(a)(b)

sch 3 rep in pt—Health and Social Care, 2012 c 7, sch 21 para 40; Loc Audit and Accountability, 2014 c 2, sch 12 para 77

sch 5 am—Health, 2009 c 21, s 19, sch 3 paras 14, 15, 19; Health and Social Care, 2012 c 7, sch 21 para 41(3)

rep in pt—Health and Social Care, 2012 c 7, sch 21 para 41(2)

sch 7 am—(prosp) Health, 2009 c 21, s 32(1)(2)(a)(b)(3)-(5)

rep in pt—(prosp) Health, 2009 c 21, ss 32(1)(2)(c), 38, sch 6

sch 8 rep in pt—Health and Social Care, 2008 c 14, s 140, sch 15, sch 12 para 10(1), (2)(a), (3)(b), (4), (7)(b),(c)

am—Health and Social Care, 2008 c 14, s 140, sch 12 para 10(1), (2)(b), (3)(a), (7)(a), (8); Nat Health Service Finance (W), 2014 anaw 2, s 2(8)(9)

sch 10 rep in pt—Health, 2009 c 21, s 19, s 38, sch 3 paras 14, 16(1)(2), 19, sch 6; Health and Social Care, 2012 c 7, sch 21 para 42(2)(3)

am—Health, 2009 c 21, s 19, sch 3 paras 14, 16(1)(3), 19

sch 11 appl (mods)—National Health Service, 2006 c 41, s 247A(3)(a)

appl—SI 2013/218, reg 30(3)

sch 13 am—Health, 2009 c 21, s 19, sch 3 paras 14, 17, 19

sch 15 am—SI 2015/914, sch para 84

c 43 **National Health Service (Consequential Provisions)**

sch 1 rep in pt—Mental Health, 2007 c 12, s 55, sch 11 pt 3; Loc Govt and Public Involvement in Health, 2007 c 28, s 241, sch 18; Educ and Skills, 2008 c 25, s 169, sch 2; Corporation Tax, 2010 c 4, s 1181, sch 3 pt 1; SI 2010/22, art 5, sch 4; Equality, 2010 c 15, sch 27 pt 1A (added by SI 2011/1060, sch 3); Charities, 2011 c 25, sch 10; Finance, 2012 c 14, s 216(2)(c); Health and

2006

c 43 *continued*

> Social Care, 2012 c 7, sch 5 paras 31(2)(b), 139(a)(b), sch 7 para 23, sch 20
> para 7(a); (prosp) Welfare Reform, 2012 c 5, sch 14 pt 9; SI 2013/594, art 8;
> Loc Audit and Accountability, 2014 c 2, sch 1 pt 2

sch 2 am—SI 2009/1511, reg 7

> rep in pt—SI 2009/1511, reg 7

c 44　**NHS Redress**

s 1 am—Nat Health Service (Conseq Provns), 2006 c 43, s 2, sch 1 paras 308, 309, 310;
> Health and Social Care, 2012 c 7, sch 5 para 141(a)(d)

rep in pt—Health and Social Care, 2012 c 7, sch 5 para 141(b)(c)

s 5 am—Health and Social Care, 2008 c 14, s 95, sch 5 para 89

s 11 am—Nat Health Service (Conseq Provns), 2006 c 43, s 2, sch 1 para 311

s 13 am—Health and Social Care, 2008 c 14, s 95, sch 5 para 90

> rep in pt—Health and Social Care, 2012 c 7, s 281(3)

s 17 rep—SI 2007/910, art 5

s 18 am—Nat Health Service (Conseq Provns), 2006 c 43, s 2, sch 1 para 312

> rep in pt—Health and Social Care, 2012 c 7, sch 5 para 142

c 45　**Animal Welfare**

s 5 excl—(E) SI 2007/1100, regs 3, 4

s 8 rep in pt—Coroners and Justice, 2009 c 25, ss 177, 178, sch 21 para 96, sch 23 pt 5

s 32 am—SI 2015/664, sch 4 para 38

s 34 appl—SI 2014/3266 (W 333), reg 24

s 42 appl—SI 2014/3266 (W 333), reg 24

s 49 am—SSI 2015/338, sch 2 para 11

s 58 am—SI 2012/3039, reg 29(2)(3)

> rep in pt—SI 2012/3039, reg 29(4)

c 46　**Companies**

appl (mods)—SIs 2007/318, 3294; 2008/373, 374, reg 8, 432, 565, 567, 569, 1911, 1950,
> reg 4; 2009/1941, art 12, sch 3; 1804, regs 3(2)(a), 4-82 (and reg 83, sch 1);
> 2014/3348, art 220(4) sch 4

excl —Housing (S), 2010 asp 17, s 106(7)(c); SI 2014/3348, arts 217, 220(3)

mod—Land Registration, 2002 c 9, s 91; SIs 2008/373 reg 11(1) (substituted by 2013/2224,
> reg 10(a)); 432, art 17, sch; 2546, art 13, sch 1; 2009/317, art 3, sch; 814, art 7, sch

appl—Housing, 1996 c 52, sch 1 para 16D; SIs 2005/1788, reg 29; 2007/2974; 2007/3141;
> 2008/948, art 3, sch 1; 2009/2477, rule 58(2); 2013/1973, reg 9(1)

appl (mods)—SIs 2008/373 reg 3(4) (substituted by 2013/2224, reg 5); 2011/245, sch 6 pt
> 1

Pts 1-39 (ss 1-1181) appl (mods)—SIs 2009/2436, regs 3-5, sch 1 (and reg 9, sch 2);
> 2009/2437, regs 18, 19-23, 24

> ext—SI 2011/1265, sch 1 para 2

s 9 am—(30.6.2016) Small Business, Enterprise and Employment, 2015 c 26, sch 3 para 4;
> ibid, s 93(2)(3)

s 10 am—(prosp) Small Business, Enterprise and Employment, 2015 c 26, sch 6 para 2(a)

> rep in pt—(prosp) Small Business, Enterprise and Employment, 2015 c 26, sch 6 para
> 2(b)

s 12 am—Small Business, Enterprise and Employment, 2015 c 26, s 100(2); (prosp) ibid,
> sch 5 paras 12, 13

s 12A added (30.6.2016)—Small Business, Enterprise and Employment, 2015 c 26, sch 3
> para 5

s 14 appl (mods)—SI 2004/2326, reg 87(1) (substituted by SI 2014/2382, reg 32)

s 20 excl—Medicinal Products: Presecription by Nurses etc, 1992 c 28, s 4C(6) (subst by SI
> 2009/1941, art 2, sch para 140(3)); Commonhold and Leasehold Reform, 2002 c
> 15, s 74(c) (subst by SI 2009/1941, art 2, sch para 195(16)); ibid, sch 3 para
> 2(6) (added by SI 2009/1941, art 2, sch 1 para 195(4)(d))

s 21 am—Charities, 2011 c 25, sch 7 para 113

> excl—Small Business, Enterprise and Employment, 2015 c 26, s 85(2)(a)

s 22 excl—Small Business, Enterprise and Employment, 2015 c 26, s 85(2)(b)

s 30 appl—SI 1987/2048, art 9 (amended by SI 2009/1941, art 2, sch 1); Charities, 1993 c
> 10, s 64 (amended by SI 2009/1941, art 2, sch 1); Charities, 2011 c 25, s 198(5)

> appl (mods)—Companies (Audit, Investigations and Community Enterprise), 2004 c 27,
> ss 37, 54 (amended by SI 2009/1941, art 2, sch 1)

s 31 am—Charities, 2011 c 25, sch 7 para 114

s 32 am—(prosp) Small Business, Enterprise and Employment, 2015 c 26, sch 6 para 3(a)

2006

c 46 s 32 *continued*

rep in pt—(prosp) Small Business, Enterprise and Employment, 2015 c 26, sch 6 para 3(b)

s 33 saved—SI 2009/1941, art 11

s 43 appl (mods)—SI 2009/1917, reg 4

s 44 appl (mods)—SIs 2009/1917, reg 4; 2011/1347, art 24

s 45 appl (mods)—SIs 2011/1347, art 24; 2012/3012, reg 23(3)(4)(6)

s 46 appl (mods)—SI 2009/1917, reg 4

s 48 appl (mods)—SI 2009/1917, reg 5

am—Land Registration etc (S), 2012 asp 5, sch 5 para 50(2)

s 49 am—Land Registration etc (S), 2012 asp 5, sch 5 para 50(3)

s 51 appl (mods)—SI 2009/1917, reg 6

Pt 5 (ss 53-85) power to appl (mods)—Co-operative and Community Benefit Societies and Credit Unions, 2010 c 7, s 4(1); Co-operative and Community Benefit Societies, 2014 c 14, s 135

s 54 am—SI 2009/2958, arts 8, 9

s 63 am—SI 2015/664, sch 3 para 9(2)

s 64 am—SI 2015/664, sch 3 para 9(3)

s 90 appl—SI 2011/1265, sch 1 para 3(1)

ss 91-93 appl—SIs 2009/2437, regs 9, 24; 2011/1265, sch 1 para 3(1)

s 94 appl—SI 2011/1265, sch 1 para 3(1)

s 94 am—(prosp) Small Business, Enterprise and Employment, 2015 c 26, s 98(2)

s 95 appl—SI 2011/1265, sch 1 para 3(1)

am—Small Business, Enterprise and Employment, 2015 c

s 96 appl—SI 2011/1265, sch 1 para 3(1)

s 98 appl—SI 2011/1265, sch 1 para 4(2)

am —SI 1991/724, sch Pt 1

s 99 appl—SI 2011/1265, sch 1 para 4(2)

s 108 am—(prosp) Small Business, Enterprise and Employment, 2015 c 26, sch 6 para 4(a)

rep in pt—(prosp) Small Business, Enterprise and Employment, 2015 c 26, sch 6 para 4(b)

s 112 appl (mods)—Commonhold and Leasehold Reform, 2002 c 15, sch 3 (amended by SI 2009/1941, art 2, sch 1)

s 112A added (prosp)—Small Business, Enterprise and Employment, 2015 c 26, sch 5 para 2

s 120 am—(6.4.2016) Small Business, Enterprise and Employment, 2015 c 26, sch 3 para 6

s 122 am—Small Business, Enterprise and Employment, 2015 c 26, sch 4 para 23(a)

rep in pt—Small Business, Enterprise and Employment, 2015 c 26, sch 4 para 23(b)

s 127 am—(prosp) Small Business, Enterprise and Employment, 2015 c 26, sch 5 para 14

Pt 8 Ch 2A (ss 128A-128K) added (prosp)—Small Business, Enterprise and Employment, 2015 c 26, sch 5 para 3

s 129 am—(prosp) Small Business, Enterprise and Employment, 2015 c 26, sch 5 para 4

s 136 excl—Commonhold and Leasehold Reform, 2002 c 15, sch 3 (amended by SI 2009/1941, art 2, sch 1)

s 140 rep in pt—Pensions, 2014 c 19, sch 13 para 75

s 141 am—Corporation Tax, 2010 c 4, s 1177, sch 1 paras 487, 488

s 146 am—SI 2013/1970, sch para 2

s 145 am—SI 2009/1632, regs 12, 17

s 153 am—SI 2009/1632, reg 17

Pt 10 (ss 154-259) excl —Enterprise and Regulatory Reform, 2013 c 24, s 82(3) (4)

s 155 rep (prosp)—Small Business, Enterprise and Employment, 2015 c 26, s 87(2)

s 156 am—(prosp) Small Business, Enterprise and Employment, 2015 c 26, s 87(3)(a)(b); SI 2015/664, sch 3 para 9(4)

ss 156A-156C added (prosp)—Small Business, Enterprise and Employment, 2015 c 26, s 87(4)

s 161A added (prosp)—Small Business, Enterprise and Employment, 2015 c 26, sch 5 para 6

s 162 am—SI 2015/664, sch 3 para 9(5)

s 163 appl—SI 2004/2326, reg 10B (added by SI 2014/2382, reg 18); ibid, reg 85(4) (subst by SI 2014/2382, reg 29)

s 165 am—SI 2015/664, sch 3 para 9(6)

s 167 am—Small Business, Enterprise and Employment, 2015 c 26, s 100(4); SI 2015/664, sch 3 para 9(7)

2006
c 46 *continued*

ss 167A-167F added (prosp)—Small Business, Enterprise and Employment, 2015 c 26, sch 5 para 7

s 170 am—Small Business, Enterprise and Employment, 2015 c 26, s 89(1)

s 180 am—Enterprise and Regulatory Reform, 2013 c 24, s 81(2)

s 181 rep in pt—Charities, 2011 c 25, sch 10

s 190 am—Enterprise and Regulatory Reform, 2013 c 24, s 81(3)

s 215 am—Enterprise and Regulatory Reform, 2013 c 24, s 81(4)

s 226 rep—Charities, 2011 c 25, sch 10

Pt 10, Ch 4A (ss 226A-226F) added—Enterprise and Regulatory Reform, 2013 c 24, s 80

s 226D appl (mods)—Enterprise and Regulatory Reform, 2013 c 24, s 82(2)

s 232 excl—SIs 2008/432, art 11; 2546, art 9; 2644, art 30; 2674, art 32

s 246 am—(prosp) Small Business, Enterprise and Employment, 2015 c 26, sch 5 para 15; SI 2015/664, sch 3 para 9(8)

s 251 am—Small Business, Enterprise and Employment, 2015 c 26, s 90(3)

ss 252-255 appl (mods)—Co-operative and Community Benefit Societies, 2014 c 14, s 49(5)

s 252 appl—Pensions, 2008 c 30, s 75, sch 1 para 13(6)

Pt 11 (ss 260-269) excl—SI 2009/814, art 6

s 272 am—SI 2015/664, sch 3 para 9(9)

s 274A added (prosp)—Small Business, Enterprise and Employment, 2015 c 26, sch 5 para 9

s 275 am—SI 2015/664, sch 3 para 9(10)

s 276 am—Small Business, Enterprise and Employment, 2015 c 26, s 100(5); SI 2015/664, sch 3 para 9(11)

ss 277, 278 appl—SI 2004/2326, reg 85(7) (substituted by SI 2014/2382, reg 29)

ss 279A-279F added (prosp)—Small Business, Enterprise and Employment, 2015 c 26, sch 5 para 10

s 282 am—SI 2009/1632, regs 2, 5

s 283 am—SI 2009/1632, reg 5

s 284 am—SI 2009/1632, reg 2

s 285 subst—SI 2009/1632, reg 3

s 285A added—SI 2009/1632, reg 3

s 286 am—(prosp) Small Business, Enterprise and Employment, 2015 c 26, sch 5 para 16

s 303 am—SI 2009/1632, reg 4

s 303 rep in pt—SI 2009/1632, reg 4

s 307 am—SI 2009/1632, reg 9

s 307A added—SI 2009/1632, reg 9

s 311 am—SI 2009/1632, reg 10; (prosp) Small Business, Enterprise and Employment, 2015 c 26, sch 5 para 17

s 311A added—SI 2009/1632, reg 11

s 319A added—SI 2009/1632, reg 12

s 322A added—SI 2009/1632, reg 5

s 323 mod—SI 2013/1047, rule 20(3)

s 327 rep in pt—Deregulation, 2015 c 20, sch 6 para 29

s 330 rep in pt—Deregulation, 2015 c 20, sch 6 para 30

s 360B am—(prosp) Small Business, Enterprise and Employment, 2015 c 26, sch 5 para 18

ss 362-379 excl—SI 2007/2081, art 2

ss 380-414 appl (mods)—SI 2009/2436, sch 1 para 10 (amended by 2013/1972, reg 2(2)(a))

s 380 rep in pt—SI 2015/980, reg 4(2)

s 381 rep in pt—SI 2008/393, reg 6

s 382 am—SIs 2008/393, regs 2, 3; 2013/3008, reg 4(2); 2015/980, reg 4(3)

s 383 am—SIs 2008/393, regs 2, 3; 2013/3008, reg 4(3); 2015/980, reg 4(4)

s 384 am—SI 2007/2932, reg 3; Financial Services, 2012 c 21, sch 18 para 111; SI 2013/2005, reg 2(2)(a); 2015/980, reg 4(5)(b)

rep in pt—SIs 2013/2005, reg 2(2)(b); 2015/980, reg 4(5)(a)

ss 384A, 384B added—SI 2013/3008, reg 4(4)

Pt 15 Ch 2 (ss 386-389) appl—SI 2015/1493, reg 7(1)(a)

s 390 appl—SI 2015/1493, reg 7(1)(b)

s 391 appl (mods)—SI 2015/1493, reg 7(1)(c)

Pt 15 Ch 4 (ss 393-414) appl—SI 2015/1493, reg 7(1)(d)

s 393 am—SI 2013/3008, reg 5(2)

s 394 am—SI 2012/2301, reg 8

2006

c 46 *continued*

ss 394A-394C added—SI 2012/2301, reg 9
    appl (mods)—SI 2008/1911, reg 9
s 394A am—SI 2015/980, reg 5(2)
s 394B am—SI 2015/980, reg 5(3)
s 395 am—SIs 2008/393, reg 9; 2012/2301, regs 12, 13
    rep in pt—SI 2012/2301, reg 14
s 396 appl (mods)—SI 2008/308, reg 3
    am—SIs 2013/3008, reg 5(3); 2015/980, reg 5(4)
s 397 subst—SI 2015/980, reg 5(5)
s 399 am—SI 2015/980, reg 5(6)
s 400 am—SI 2015/980, reg 5(7)(a)-(d)
    rep in pt—SI 2015/980, reg 5(7)(e)
s 401 am—SI 2015/980, reg 5(8)(a)-(e)
    rep in pt—SI 2015/980, reg 5(8)(f)
s 403 am—SI 2012/2301, regs 15, 16
    rep in pt—SI 2012/2301, reg 17
s 404 am—SIs 2008/393, reg 10; 2015/980, reg 5(9)
s 405 am—SI 2015/980, reg 5(10)
s 406 subst—SI 2015/980, reg 5(11)
s 408 am—SIs 2008/393, reg 10; 2015/980, reg 5(12)(a)
    rep in pt—SI 2015/980, reg 5(12)(b)
s 410 rep—SI 2015/980, reg 5(13)
s 410A added—SI 2008/393, reg 8
    am—SI 2015/980, reg 5(14)
s 411 am—SIs 2008/393, reg 11; 2015/980, reg 5(15)
s 413 am—SI 2015/980, reg 5(16)
s 414 am—SI 2013/3008, reg 5(4)
Pt 15, Ch 5A (ss 414A-414D) added—SI 2013/1970, reg 3
s 414A appl (mods)—SI 2008/373 reg 4A(2) (added by 2013/2224, reg 6)
s 414B am—SI 2015/980, reg 6
s 414D appl (mods)—SI 2008/373 reg 4A (added by 2013/2224, reg 6)
Pt 15 Chs 5-12 (ss 415-475) specified ss appl (mods)—SI 2009/2436, sch 1 para 10 (added
    by 2013/1972, reg 2(2)(a))
Pt 15 Ch 5 (ss 415-419A) appl—SI 2015/1493, reg 7(1)(d)
s 415 am—SI 2015/980, reg 7
s 415A added—SI 2008/393, reg 6
    am—SI 2013/1970, reg 4(a)
    rep in pt—SI 2013/1970, reg 4(b)
s 416 am—SI 2008/393, reg 6
    rep in pt—SI 2013/1970, reg 6(2)(3)
s 417 rep—SI 2013/1970, reg 5
s 419 am—SI 2008/393, reg 6
    appl—SI 2005/1788, reg 29 (as subst by 2008/948, sch 1 para 242)
s 419A added—SI 2009/1581, reg 2
s 421 am—Enterprise and Regulatory Reform, 2013 c 24, s 79(1)
s 422A added—Enterprise and Regulatory Reform, 2013 c 24, s 79(2)
    appl (mods)—SI 2008/373 reg 6A (added by 2013/1971, reg 6)
Pt 15 Ch 7 (ss 423-436) appl—SI 2015/1493, reg 7(1)(d)
    appl (mods)—Housing and Regeneration, 2008 c 17, s 132(1)(2)
s 423 appl—SI 2005/1788, reg 29 (as subst by 2008/948, sch 1 para 242)
    am—SI 2013/1970, sch para 3
ss 424, 425 appl—SI 2005/1788, reg 29 (as subst by 2008/948, sch 1 para 242)
s 426 am—SI 2013/1970, reg 10(2)(3)
    rep in pt—SI 2013/1970, reg 10(4)
s 426A added—SI 2013/1970, reg 12(1)
ss 427, 428 rep —SI 2013/1970, reg 11
s 429 rep—SI 2013/1970, reg 11
s 430 appl—SI 2005/1788, reg 29 (as subst by 2008/948, sch 1 para 242)
    am—Enterprise and Regulatory Reform, 2013 c 24, s 81(6)-(9)
s 431 am—SI 2013/1970, sch para 4
s 432 am—SI 2013/1970, sch para 5
s 433 am—SI 2013/1970, sch para 6
s 434 rep in pt—SI 2013/1970, sch para 7

2006
c 46 *continued*

s 435 rep in pt—SI 2013/1970, sch para 8
s 436 appl—SI 2005/1788, reg 29 (as subst by 2008/948, sch 1 para 242)
s 438 am—SI 2015/664, sch 3 para 9(12)
s 439 am—Enterprise and Regulatory Reform, 2013 c 24, s 79(3)
s 439A added—Enterprise and Regulatory Reform, 2013 c 24, s 79(4)
    appl (mods)—Enterprise and Regulatory Reform, 2013 c 24, s 82(1)
s 440 am—Enterprise and Regulatory Reform, 2013 c 24, s 81(10)(a)(b)
    rep in pt—Enterprise and Regulatory Reform, 2013 c 24, s 81(10)(c)
s 441 appl—SI 2005/1788, reg 29A(2) (added by 2012/2335, reg 2(3))
    appl (mods)—Housing and Regeneration, 2008 c 17, s 132(1)(2)
    am—SI 2012/2301, reg 10
s 442 appl—SI 2005/1788, reg 29A(2) (added by 2012/2335, reg 2(3))
    appl (mods)—Housing and Regeneration, 2008 c 17, s 132(1)(2)
    am—SI 2015/980, reg 8(2)
s 443 appl—SI 2005/1788, reg 29A(2) (added by 2012/2335, reg 2(3))
    appl (mods)—Housing and Regeneration, 2008 c 17, s 132(1)(2)
s 444 appl (mods)—Housing and Regeneration, 2008 c 17, s 132(1)(2); SIs 2005/1788, reg
    29A(3) (added by 2012/2335, reg 2(3)); 2008/1911, reg 17
    am—SIs 2008/393, reg 12; 2013/3008, reg 6; 2015/980, reg 8(3)(a)-(c),(g)
    rep in pt—SI 2015/980, reg 8(3)(d)-(f)
s 444A added—SI 2008/393, reg 6
    appl (mods)—SI 2005/1788, reg 29A(3) (added by 2012/2335, reg 2(3))
    am—SI 2009/1581, reg 10
s 445 am—SIs 2008/393, reg 6; 2013/1970, sch para 9
    rep in pt—SI 2015/980, reg 8(4)(5)
s 446 rep in pt—SI 2008/393, reg 6
    am—SIs 2008/393, reg 13; 2009/1581, reg 3; 2013/1970, sch para 10
    appl—SI 2005/1788, reg 29A(2) (added by 2012/2335, reg 2(3))
s 447 appl—SI 2005/1788, reg 29A(2) (added by 2012/2335, reg 2(3))
    am—SIs 2009/1581, reg 4; 2013/1970, sch para 11
s 448 am—SI 2013/2005, reg 2(4)-(6)
ss 448A-448C added—SI 2012/2301, reg 11
    appl (mods)—SI 2008/1911, reg 19A (added by SI 2012/2301, reg 20(7))
s 448A am—SI 2015/980, reg 8(6)
s 448B am—SI 2015/980, reg 8(7)
ss 449, 450 rep—SI 2015/980, reg 8(8)(9)
s 451 appl—SI 2005/1788, reg 29A(2) (added by 2012/2335, reg 2(3))
    am—SI 2015/664, sch 3 para 9(13)
ss 452-453 appl—SI 2005/1788, reg 29A(2) (added by 2012/2335, reg 2(3))
Pt 15 Ch 11 (ss 454-462) appl (except s 456(2)(7))—SI 2015/1493, reg 7(1)(e)
s 454 appl—SI 2005/1788, reg 29 (as subst by 2008/948, sch 1 para 242)
    appl (mods)—Housing and Regeneration, 2008 c 17, s 132(1)(2)
    am—SI 2013/1970, sch para 12
s 455 am—SI 2013/1970, sch para 13
s 456 mod—SI 2012/1439, art 8(2)
    am—SI 2013/1970, sch para 14(a)(b)(c)(i)(d)
    rep in pt—SI 2013/1970, sch para 14(b)(c)(ii)
s 457 am—SI 2013/1970, sch para 15
s 458 am—SI 2008/948, art 3, sch 1
    mod—SI 2012/1439, art 8(3)
s 459 mod—SI 2012/1439, art 8(3)
    am—SI 2013/1970, sch para 16
s 460 am—SI 2008/948, art 3, sch 1
    mod—SI 2012/1439, art 8(3)
s 461 mod—SI 2012/1439, art 8(3)
    am—Financial Services, 2012 c 21, sch 18 para 112; SIs 2012/1439, art 6(2); 1741,
        sch para 2; Co-operative and Community Benefit Societies, 2014 c 14, sch 4
        para 100(3)(4)
    rep in pt—Co-operative and Community Benefit Societies, 2014 c 14, sch 4 para
        100(2)
s 463 am—SI 2013/1970, sch para 17(a)
    rep in pt—SI 2013/1970, sch para 17(b)
s 464 appl—SI 2015/1493, reg 7(1)(f)

2006

c 46 *continued*

    s 465 am—SI 2015/980, reg 9(2)

    s 466 am—SI 2015/980, reg 9(3)

    s 467 am—Financial Services, 2012 c 21, sch 18 para 113; SIs 2013/2005, reg 2(7)(a)(b); 2015/980, reg 9(4)

        rep in pt—SI 2013/2005, reg 2(7)(c)

    s 469 am—SI 2013/3008, reg 7(2)

        appl—SI 2015/1493, reg 7(1)(g)

    s 470 am—Financial Services, 2012 c 21, sch 18 para 114

    s 471 am—SIs 2012/2301, reg 18; 2013/3008, reg 7(3); 2013/1970, sch para 18

        appl—SI 2015/1493, reg 7(1)(h)

    s 472 am—SI 2013/3008, reg 7(4)

        appl—SI 2015/1493, reg 7(1)(i)

        rep in pt—SI 2015/980, reg 9(5)

    s 472A added—SI 2009/1581, reg 5

        am—SI 2013/636, sch para 9(2)

    s 474 am—SI 2007/2932, reg 3; Financial Services, 2012 c 21, sch 18 para 115; SIs 2013/636, sch para 9(3); 2013/2005, reg 2(8); 2013/3008, reg 7(5); 2015/980, reg 9(6)(a)

        mod—SI 2012/1439, art 8(4)

        rep in pt—SI 2015/980, reg 9(6)(b)

    s 475 am—SI 2012/2301, reg 6

        appl—SI 2015/1493, reg 7(1)(j)

    s 476 appl—SI 2015/1493, reg 7(1)(k)

    s 477 am—SIs 2007/2932, reg 3; 2008/393, reg 5; 2012/2301, reg 4(a)

        rep in pt—SI 2012/2301, reg 4(b)(c)

    s 478 am—SIs 2007/2932, reg 3; 2008/393, reg 5

    s 479 am—SIs 2007/2932, reg 3; 2008/393, reg 5; 2012/2301, reg 5(a)

        rep in pt—SI 2012/2301, reg 5(b)(c)

    s 479A added—SI 2012/2301, reg 7

        am—SI 2015/980, reg 10(2)

        appl (mods)—SI 2008/1911, reg 34A (added by 2012/2301, reg 20(4))

    s 479B added—SI 2012/2301, reg 7

        am—SI 2015/980, reg 10(3)

        appl (mods)—SI 2008/1911, reg 34A (added by 2012/2301, reg 20(4))

    s 479C added—SI 2012/2301, reg 7

        appl (mods)—SI 2008/1911, reg 34A (added by 2012/2301, reg 20(4))

    s 480 appl—SI 2015/1493, reg 7(1)(l)

    s 481 am—SIs 2007/2932, reg 3; 2015/980, reg 10(4)

        appl—SI 2015/1493, reg 7(1)(l)

    s 482 am—SI 2012/1809, art 3(1), sch pt 1

    s 493 am—SI 2013/1970, sch para 19

    s 494 am—SI 2013/1970, sch para 20

    s 495 am—SI 2013/3008, reg 8(2)(3)

        appl—SI 2015/1493, reg 7(1)(m)

    s 496 subst—SI 2015/980, reg 11(2)

        appl—SI 2015/1493, reg 7(1)(m)

    s 497A added—SI 2009/1581, reg 6

        subst—SI 2015/980, reg 11(3)

    s 498 am—SIs 2008/393, reg 6; 2013/1970, sch para 22

        appl—SI 2015/1493, reg 7(1)(n)

    s 498A added—SI 2009/1581, reg 7

    s 499 appl—SI 2015/1493, reg 7(1)(n)

        appl (mods)—Housing and Regeneration, 2008 c 17, s 132(1)(2)

    s 500 appl—SI 2015/1493, reg 7(1)(n)

        appl (mods)—Housing and Regeneration, 2008 c 17, s 132(1)(2)

    s 501 appl—SI 2015/1493, reg 7(1)(n)

        appl (mods)—Housing and Regeneration, 2008 c 17, s 132(1)(2)

    s 502 appl (mods)—Housing and Regeneration, 2008 c 17, s 132(1)(2)

    s 503 appl (mods)—Housing and Regeneration, 2008 c 17, s 132(1)(2); SI 2015/1493, reg 7(1)(o)

    s 504 appl (mods)—Housing and Regeneration, 2008 c 17, s 132(1)(2)

    s 505 appl (mods)—Housing and Regeneration, 2008 c 17, s 132(1)(2); SI 2015/1493, reg 7(1)(p)

2006

c 46 *continued*

s 506 appl (mods)—Housing and Regeneration, 2008 c 17, s 132(1)(2)

s 512 rep—Deregulation, 2015 c 20, sch 5 para 2

s 514 am—Deregulation, 2015 c 20, sch 5 para 14

s 515 am—Deregulation, 2015 c 20, sch 5 para 15(2),(3)(b)

    rep in pt—Deregulation, 2015 c 20, sch 5 para 15(3)(a)

s 516 am—Deregulation, 2015 c 20, sch 5 paras 3, 16

s 517 rep—Deregulation, 2015 c 20, sch 5 para 4

s 518 am—Deregulation, 2015 c 20, sch 5 paras 5, 17

s 519 am—SI 2008/948, art 3, sch 1; Deregulation, 2015 c 20, s 18(2); ibid, sch 5 paras 6,
    18

s 519A added—Deregulation, 2015 c 20, s 18(3)

s 520 am—Deregulation, 2015 c 20, sch 5 paras 7, 19

s 521 am—SI 2008/948, art 3, sch 1; Deregulation, 2015 c 20, sch 5 paras 8, 20

s 522 am—Deregulation, 2015 c 20, sch 5 para 9

s 523 am—Deregulation, 2015 c 20, s 18(4)

s 524 mod—SI 2012/1439, art 8(5)

    am—Deregulation, 2015 c 20, sch 5 para 11(2)

    rep in pt—Deregulation, 2015 c 20, sch 5 para 11(3)(4)

s 525 am—SIs 2007/3494, reg 41; 2012/1741, sch para 3

s 538A added—SI 2009/1581, reg 8

    am—SI 2013/636, sch para 9(5)(a)

    rep in pt—SI 2013/636, sch para 9(5)(b)

s 539 am—SI 2007/3494, reg 41; Financial Services, 2012 c 21, sch 18 para 116; SIs
    2013/636, sch para 9(6); 2013/2005, reg 2(9)

s 554 am—(prosp) Small Business, Enterprise and Employment, 2015 c 26, sch 5 para 19

s 555 am—(prosp) Small Business, Enterprise and Employment, 2015 c 26, sch 6 para 5(a)

    rep in pt—(prosp) Small Business, Enterprise and Employment, 2015 c 26, sch 6 para
    5(b)

s 557 am—SI 2015/664, sch 3 para 9(15)

s 558 am—(prosp) Small Business, Enterprise and Employment, 2015 c 26, sch 5 para 20

ss 584-587 appl—SI 2011/1265, sch 1 para 9

s 588 am—(prosp) Small Business, Enterprise and Employment, 2015 c 26, sch 5 para 21

s 593 am—SI 2011/1606, reg 2(4)(b)

s 595 am—SI 2011/1606, reg 2(2)(4)(a)

    rep in pt—SI 2011/1606, reg 2(3)

s 597 am—SI 2015/664, sch 3 para 9(16)

s 605 am—(prosp) Small Business, Enterprise and Employment, 2015 c 26, sch 5 para 22

s 616 am—(prosp) Small Business, Enterprise and Employment, 2015 c 26, sch 5 para 23

s 617 am—Small Business, Enterprise and Employment, 2015 c 26, sch 4 para 24

s 619 am—(prosp) Small Business, Enterprise and Employment, 2015 c 26, sch 6 para 6(a)

    rep in pt—(prosp) Small Business, Enterprise and Employment, 2015 c 26, sch 6 para
    6(b)

s 621 am—(prosp) Small Business, Enterprise and Employment, 2015 c 26, sch 6 para 7(a)

    rep in pt—(prosp) Small Business, Enterprise and Employment, 2015 c 26, sch 6 para
    7(b)

s 625 am—(prosp) Small Business, Enterprise and Employment, 2015 c 26, sch 6 para 8(a)

    rep in pt—(prosp) Small Business, Enterprise and Employment, 2015 c 26, sch 6 para
    8(b)

s 627 am—(prosp) Small Business, Enterprise and Employment, 2015 c 26, sch 6 para 9(a)

    rep in pt—(prosp) Small Business, Enterprise and Employment, 2015 c 26, sch 6 para
    9(b)

s 641 am—SIs 1991/724, sch Pt 1 (added by SI 2014/821, art 2(10)(a)(ii)); 2015/472, reg 3

s 644 am—(prosp) Small Business, Enterprise and Employment, 2015 c 26, sch 6 para 10(a)

    rep in pt—(prosp) Small Business, Enterprise and Employment, 2015 c 26, sch 6 para
    10(b)

s 649 am—(prosp) Small Business, Enterprise and Employment, 2015 c 26, sch 6 para 11(a)

    rep in pt—(prosp) Small Business, Enterprise and Employment, 2015 c 26, sch 6 para
    11(b)

s 651 appl—Small Business, Enterprise and Employment, 2015 c 26, sch 4 para 8(3)(4)

s 652 am—Small Business, Enterprise and Employment, 2015 c 26, sch 4 para 25

s 654 excl—(with savings) SI 2008/1915, art 3

s 655 am—(prosp) Small Business, Enterprise and Employment, 2015 c 26, sch 5 para 24

s 662 mod—SI 2011/1265, sch 1 para 7(1)

2006
c 46 *continued*

s 663 am—(prosp) Small Business, Enterprise and Employment, 2015 c 26, sch 6 para 12(a)
 rep in pt—(prosp) Small Business, Enterprise and Employment, 2015 c 26, sch 6 para
  12(b)
 mod—SI 2011/1265, sch 1 para 7(1)
s 664-667 mod—SI 2011/1265, sch 1 para 7(1)
s 668 mod—SI 2011/1265, sch 1 para 7(1)
 appl—SI 2011/1265, sch 1 para 7(2)
s 669 mod—SI 2011/1265, sch 1 para 7(1)
s 673 rep in pt—Pensions, 2014 c 19, sch 13 para 76
s 689 am—(prosp) Small Business, Enterprise and Employment, 2015 c 26, sch 6 para 13(a)
 rep in pt—(prosp) Small Business, Enterprise and Employment, 2015 c 26, sch 6 para
  13(b)
s 691 am—SI 2013/999, reg 3
s 692 am—SIs 2013/999, reg 4(2)(3); 2015/532, reg 3
s 693 am—SI 2013/999, reg 6
s 693A added—SI 2013/999, reg 7
s 694 am—SI 2013/999, reg 8
 rep in pt—SI 2013/999, reg 5(a)(b)
s 700 rep in pt—SI 2013/999, reg 5(c)
s 704 am—SI 2013/999, reg 9
s 707 am—SI 2015/664, sch 3 para 9(17)
s 708 am—(prosp) Small Business, Enterprise and Employment, 2015 c 26, sch 6 para 14(a);
  SI 2015/532, reg 4
 rep in pt—(prosp) Small Business, Enterprise and Employment, 2015 c 26, sch 6 para
  14(b)
s 709 am—SI 2015/532, reg 5
s 712 am—SI 2013/999, reg 10
s 713 am—SI 2013/999, reg 11
s 720A added—SI 2013/999, reg 12
s 720B added—SI 2013/999, reg 12
 am—(prosp) Small Business, Enterprise and Employment, 2015 c 26, sch 6 para
  15(a)
 rep in pt—(prosp) Small Business, Enterprise and Employment, 2015 c 26, sch 6
  para 15(b)
s 723 am—SIs 2013/999, reg 13; 2015/532, reg 6
s 724 am—SI 2013/999, reg 14(2); (prosp) Small Business, Enterprise and Employment,
  2015 c 26, sch 5 para 25; SI 2015/532, reg 7
 rep in pt—SI 2013/999, reg 14(3)
s 728 am—SI 2015/664, sch 3 para 9(18)
s 729 rep in pt—SI 2013/999, reg 15
s 730 am—(prosp) Small Business, Enterprise and Employment, 2015 c 26, sch 6 para 16(a)
s 730 rep in pt—(prosp) Small Business, Enterprise and Employment, 2015 c 26, sch 6 para
  16(b)
s 733 am—SI 2015/532, reg 8
s 734 am—SI 2015/532, reg 9
s 754 appl (mods)—SI 1999/2979, reg 14 (amended by SI 2009/1972, reg 4)
s 762 am—(prosp) Small Business, Enterprise and Employment, 2015 c 26, s 98(3)
s 766 am—SI 2011/1265, art 28(2)
Pt 21 (ss 768-790) appl (mods)—SI 2008/2546, art 4
s 770 am—(prosp) Small Business, Enterprise and Employment, 2015 c 26, sch 5 para 26
s 771 am—(prosp) Small Business, Enterprise and Employment, 2015 c 26, sch 5 para 27
s 772 am—(prosp) Small Business, Enterprise and Employment, 2015 c 26, sch 5 para 28
s 776 appl (mods)—SIs 2009/814, art 3; 2009/3226, art 3, sch 1
 excl—SI 2009/3226, art 3, sch 1
ss 777, 778 excl—SIs 2009/3226, art 3, sch 1; 2009/814, art 3
s 779 am—Small Business, Enterprise and Employment, 2015 c 26, s 84
s 780 rep—Small Business, Enterprise and Employment, 2015 c 26, sch 4 para 26(1)
s 785 am—Financial Services, 2012 c 21, s 112
s 786 am—(prosp) Small Business, Enterprise and Employment, 2015 c 26, sch 5 para 29
Pt 21A (ss 790A-790ZG) added (pt 6.4.2016) (pt 30.6.2016)—(pt 6.4.2016) (pt 30.6.2016)
  Small Business, Enterprise and Employment, 2015 c 26, sch 3 para 1
 see—Small Business, Enterprise and Employment, 2015 c 26, s 82
s 813 am—Small Business, Enterprise and Employment, 2015 c 26, s 83

2006

c 46 *continued*

Pt 23 (ss 829-853) excl—Postal Services, 2011 c 5, sch 1 para 18(a)

s 832 am—SI 2012/952, reg 2(2)(a)

rep in pt—SI 2012/952, reg 2(2)(b)(c)(3)

s 833 am—SI 2012/952, reg 2(4)(5)(a)(b)

rep in pt—SI 2012/952, reg 2(5)(c)(6)

ss 834, 835 rep—SI 2012/952, reg 2(7)

s 837 rep in pt—SI 2013/1970, sch para 23

s 839 am—SI 2009/1941, art 2, sch 1

s 843 am—SI 2007/3253, reg 2, sch 3; Financial Services, 2012 c 21, sch 18 para 117; SI 2015/575, sch 1 para 25

Pt 24 (ss 854-859) subst (by Pt 24 ss 853A-853L) (prosp—Small Business, Enterprise and Employment, 2015 c 26, s 92

s 854 mod—SIs 2008/432, art 17, sch; 2008/2546, art 13, sch 1

s 855 mod—SIs 2008/432, art 17, sch; 2008/2546, art 13, sch 1

am—SIs 2008/3000, regs 2-4; 2011/1487, reg 2(b); 2013/636, sch para 9(7)

rep in pt—SI 2011/1487, reg 2(a)

s 855A added—SI 2008/3000, reg 2

s 856 mod—SIs 2008/432, art 17, sch; 2008/2546, art 13, sch 1

rep in pt—SI 2008/3000, reg 7

am—SIs 2008/3000, reg 7; 2011/1487, reg 3

ss 856A, 856B added—SI 2008/3000, reg 7

s 856A am—SI 2011/1487, reg 4(1)

s 856B subst—SI 2011/1487, reg 4(2)

s 857 mod—SIs 2008/432, art 17, sch; 2008/2546, art 13, sch 1

s 858 am—SIs 2008/3000, reg 8; 2015/664, sch 3 para 9(19)

mod—SIs 2008/432, art 17, sch; 2008/2546, art 13, sch 1

s 859 rep—SI 2008/3000, reg 8

Pt 25 (Ch A1 and Ch 3) mod —SI 2014/3344, art 3(3)

Pt 25, Ch A1 (ss 859A-859Q) added—SI 2013/600, reg 2 sch 1

appl—SI 2009/1804 reg 32 (as amended by 2013/618, sch)

s 859A excl—SI 2015/912, sch 5 para 9

s 859C appl—SI 2014/3344, art 3(1)(2)

s 859F appl (mods)—Companies, 1985 c 6, s 466(4E)(4F)

s 859G appl (mods)—Companies, 1985 c 6, s 466(4E)(4F)

s 859I appl (mods)—Companies, 1985 c 6, s 466(4E)(4F)

s 859M appl (mods)—Companies, 1985 c 6, s 466(4E)(4F)

s 859N appl (mods)—Companies, 1985 c 6, s 466(4E)(4F)

Pt 25, Chs 1, 2 (ss 860-892) rep—SI 2013/600, reg 3

s 893 excl—Banking, 2009 c 1, s 252(1)

am—SI 2013/600, sch 2 para 3(2)

s 894 excl—Banking, 2009 c 1, s 252(1)

Pt 26 (ss 895-901) appl—SI 2008/948, art 3, sch 1

power to appl—Co-operative and Community Benefit Societies, 2014 c 14, s 118(1)(2)

appl (mods)—SI 2014/229, art 2(3) sch 2

s 896 am—SI 2008/948, art 3, sch 1

s 899 am—SIs 2008/948, art 3, sch 1; 2011/1265, art 28(3)

appl (mods)—SI 2009/3056, reg 29, sch 1

Pt 27 (ss 902-941) appl—SI 2008/948, art 3, sch 1

s 903 am—SI 2011/1606, reg 4

s 906 am—SI 2011/1606, reg 5

s 906A added—SI 2011/1606, reg 6

s 908 am—SI 2011/1606, reg 7

s 909 am—SIs 2008/690, reg 2; 2011/1606, reg 8

s 910 am—SI 2011/1606, reg 9

s 911 am—SI 2011/1606, reg 10

s 911A added—SI 2011/1606, reg 11

s 911B added—SI 2011/1606, reg 12

s 912 am—SI 2011/1606, reg 13

s 914 subst—SI 2008/690, reg 3

s 915 am—SI 2011/1265, art 28(4)

s 915A added—SI 2011/1606, reg 14

s 916 am—SI 2011/1606, reg 15

2006

c 46 *continued*

s 917 am—SI 2011/1606, reg 16
s 918 am—SI 2011/1606, reg 17
s 918A added—SI 2008/690, reg 2
    am—SI 2011/1606, reg 18
s 921 am—SI 2011/1606, reg 19
s 921A added—SI 2011/1606, reg 20
s 923 am—SI 2011/1606, reg 21
s 924 am—SI 2011/1606, reg 22
s 925 am—SI 2011/1606, reg 23
s 926 am—SI 2011/1606, reg 24
s 926A added—SI 2011/1606, reg 25
s 927 am—SI 2011/1606, reg 26
s 930 subst—SI 2008/690, reg 4
s 931 am—SI 2011/1606, reg 27(2)(3)
    rep in pt—SI 2011/1606, reg 27(4)
s 932 am—SI 2011/1606, reg 28
s 933A added—SI 2011/1606, reg 29
s 934 am—SI 2011/1606, reg 30
s 938 am—SIs 2008/948, art 3, sch 1; 2009/1941, art 2, sch 1
s 940A added—SI 2011/1606, reg 31
Pt 28 (ss 942-992) mod—SI 2014/3348, art 219(2)
ss 942-947 ext (mods)—SI 2008/3122, art 2, sch
s 948 am—Financial Services, 2012 c 21, sch 18 para 118
    ext (mods)—SI 2008/3122, art 2, sch
s 949 ext (mods)—SI 2008/3122, art 2, sch
s 950 am—Financial Services, 2012 c 21, sch 18 para 119
    ext (mods)—SI 2008/3122, art 2, sch
ss 951-965 ext (mods)—SI 2008/3122, art 2, sch
s 964 rep in pt—Financial Services, 2012 c 21, sch 19
s 966 am—SI 2007/1388, art 3, sch 1
s 980 am—SI 2015/664, sch 3 para 9(20)
s 984 am—SI 2015/664, sch 3 para 9(21)
s 993 appl (mods)—SI 2012/3012, reg 60(1)(3)
s 994 am—SI 2007/3494, reg 42
    rep in pt—Deregulation, 2015 c 20, sch 23 para 28(7)
s 995 am—Financial Services, 2012 c 21, sch 18 para 120
Pt 31 (ss 1000-1034) power to appl (mods)—Co-operative and Community Benefit Societies
    and Credit Unions, 2010 c 7, s 4(2)(c); Co-operative and Community Benefit
    Societies, 2014 c 14, s 135
s 1000 mod—SI 2014/1602, art 3(2)
    am—SI 2014/1602, art 2(2)(a)-(d); Small Business, Enterprise and Employment,
    2015 c 26, s 103(2)
    rep in pt—SI 2014/1602, art 2(2)(e)
s 1001 am—Small Business, Enterprise and Employment, 2015 c 26, s 103(3)
s 1002 am—SI 2014/1602, art 2(3)
    mod—SI 2014/1602, art 3(3)
s 1003 am—Small Business, Enterprise and Employment, 2015 c 26, s 103(4)
s 1004 appl (mods)—SI 2012/3013, reg 8(2)(3)
s 1005 appl—SI 2012/3013, reg 9(3)
s 1006 appl (mods)—SI 2012/3013, reg 12(5)(6)
s 1009 appl (mods)—SI 2012/3013, reg 14(3)(4)
s 1012 appl (mods)—Building Societies, 1986 c 53, s 90, sch 15 (amended by SI 2009/1941,
    art 2, sch 1); Friendly Societies, 1992 c 40, s 1217, sch 10 (amended by SI
    2009/1941, art 2, sch 1)
    appl—SI 2009/805, art 3, sch 1
s 1013 appl (mods)—Building Societies, 1986 c 53, s 90, sch 15 (amended by SI 2009/1941,
    art 2, sch 1); Friendly Societies, 1992 c 40, s 1217, sch 10 (amended by SI
    2009/1941, art 2, sch 1)
    appl—SI 2009/805, art 3, sch 1
s 1014 appl (mods)—Friendly Societies, 1992 c 40, s 1217, sch 10 (amended by SI
    2009/1941, art 2, sch 1)
    appl—SI 2009/805, art 3, sch 1
s 1015 appl (mods)—SI 2009/1941, art 2, sch 1

2006
c 46 s 1015 *continued*

  appl—SI 2009/805, art 3, sch 1

ss 1016-1021 appl (mods)—Friendly Societies, 1992 c 40, s 1217, sch 10 (amended by SI
  2009/1941, art 2, sch 1)

  appl—SI 2009/805, art 3, sch 1

s 1022 appl (mods)—Friendly Societies, 1992 c 40, s 1217, sch 10 (amended by SI
  2009/1941, art 2, sch 1)

  am—Land Registration etc (S), 2012 asp 5, sch 5 para 50(4)

  appl—SI 2009/805, art 3, sch 1

s 1023 appl (mods)—Friendly Societies, 1992 c 40, s 1217, sch 10 (amended by SI
  2009/1941, art 2, sch 1)

  appl—SI 2009/805, art 3, sch 1

s 1028A added—Small Business, Enterprise and Employment, 2015 c 26, sch 4 para 27(1)

s 1030 am—Damages (S), 2011 asp 7, sch 1 para 9

s 1032A added—Small Business, Enterprise and Employment, 2015 c 26, sch 4 para 28(1)

s 1033 am—SI 2015/664, sch 3 para 9(22)

s 1034 appl—SI 2009/805, art 3, sch 1

s 1034 appl (mods)—Building Societies, 1986 c 53, s 90, sch 15 (amended by SI 2009/1941,
  art 2, sch 1); Friendly Societies, 1992 c 40, s 1217, sch 10 (amended by SI
  2009/1941, art 2, sch 1)

s 1039 rep—SI 2015/664, sch 3 para 9(22)

s 1049 am—SI 2013/1970, sch para 24

s 1050 am—SI 2013/1970, sch para 25

s 1054 am—SI 2015/664, sch 3 para 17

Pt 35 (ss 1059A-1120) appl (mods)—SIs 2011/245, sch 6 pt 2 para 5(3); (specified ss in Pt
  35) SI 2014/3209, reg 20A Table A (added by 2015/1928, reg 3)

  mod—SI 2009/317, art 6

  saved—SI 2009/1804, reg 60

s 1059A added—SI 2009/1802, arts 2, 3

  am—SI 2014/1557, art 3; Small Business, Enterprise and Employment, 2015 c 26,
  s 95(2)

s 1061 am—SI 2009/1802, arts 2, 4

s 1061 rep in pt—SI 2009/1802, arts 2, 4

s 1064 appl—SI 2009/2437, regs 12, 24

s 1066 appl (mods)—SI 2004/2326, reg 14, sch 2 (amended by 2009/2400, regs 2, 3, 15, 16,
  38)

s 1067 am—SI 2009/1802, arts 2, 5

s 1068 am—SI 2009/1802, arts 2, 6; (30.6.2016) Small Business, Enterprise and
  Employment, 2015 c 26, sch 3 para 7; (prosp) ibid, sch 5 para 30

s 1070 am—SI 2009/1802, arts 2, 7

s 1075 am—SI 2009/1802, arts 2, 8

s 1076 am—SIs 2009/1802, arts 2, 9; 2013/600, sch 2 para 3(3)

s 1077 appl (mods)—SI 2009/2436, sch 1 para 19 (amended by SI 2012/2301, reg 23)

s 1078 appl (mods)—SI 2009/2436, sch 1 para 19 (amended by SI 2012/2301, reg 23)

  am—SIs 2012/2301, reg 19; 2014/1557, art 4; 2014/3209, reg 20(1); (prosp) Small
  Business, Enterprise and Employment, 2015 c 26, ss 93(5), 98(4

s 1079A added—SI 2014/1557, art 5

s 1079B added—Small Business, Enterprise and Employment, 2015 c 26, s 101(1)

s 1080 am—SI 2009/1802, arts 2, 10

s 1081 appl (mods)—SI 2004/2326, reg 13, sch 1A (amended by 2009/2400, regs 2, 3, 14,
  15, 37)

  am—SI 2013/600, sch 2 para 3(4); (prosp) Small Business, Enterprise and
  Employment, 2015 c 26, sch 5 para 31

s 1082 appl (mods)—SI 2004/2326, reg 14, sch 2 (amended by 2009/2400, regs 2, 3, 15, 16,
  38)

s 1083 am—SI 2009/1802, arts 2, 11

s 1084 appl (mods)—SI 2004/2326, reg 14, sch 2 (amended by 2009/2400, regs 2, 3, 15, 16,
  38)

s 1084A added—Small Business, Enterprise and Employment, 2015 c 26, s 95(1)

s 1085 appl (mods)—SI 2004/2326, reg 13, sch 1A (amended by 2009/2400, regs 2, 3, 14,
  15, 37)

s 1087 am—SIs 2009/1941, art 2, sch 1, 2009/1802, arts 2, 12; Small Business, Enterprise
  and Employment, 2015 c 26, ss 96(2), 99(2); (6.4.2016) ibid, sch 3 para 8

  rep in pt—SI 2013/600, sch 2 para 3(5)

2006

c 46 *continued*

ss 1087A, 1087B added (pt prosp)—Small Business, Enterprise and Employment, 2015 c 26, s 96(3)

s 1093 am—SI 2015/664, sch 3 para 9(23)

s 1094 am—(prosp) Small Business, Enterprise and Employment, 2015 c 26, sch 5 para 32(3)

s 1095 am—(prosp) Small Business, Enterprise and Employment, 2015 c 26, s 102

s 1096 am—SI 2013/600, sch 2 para 3(6)

s 1097A added—Small Business, Enterprise and Employment, 2015 c 26, s 99(1)

s 1099 am—Co-operative and Community Benefit Societies, 2014 c 14, sch 4 para 101

s 1103 appl (mods)—SI 2004/2326, reg 13, sch 1A (amended by 2009/2400, regs 2, 3, 15)
    appl—Small Business, Enterprise and Employment, 2015 c 26, sch 4 para 15

s 1104 appl—Small Business, Enterprise and Employment, 2015 c 26, sch 4 para 15

s 1105 appl (mods)—SI 2004/2326, reg 13, sch 1A (amended by 2009/2400, regs 2, 3, 15)
    appl—SI 2014/3209, reg 20B, Table B (added by 2015/1928, reg 4)
    am—SI 2013/600, sch 2 para 3(7)

s 1106 appl (mods)—SI 2004/2326, reg 13, sch 1A (amended by 2009/2400, regs 2, 3, 15)
    appl (mods)—SI 2014/3209, reg 20B, Table B (added by 2015/1928, reg 4)

s 1107 appl—Small Business, Enterprise and Employment, 2015 c 26, sch 4 para 15
    appl (mods)—SI 2014/3209, reg 20B Table B (added by 2015/1928, reg 4)

s 1109 am—SI 2009/1802, arts 2, 13

s 1112 appl—Small Business, Enterprise and Employment, 2015 c 26, sch 4 para 16

s 1113 appl—Small Business, Enterprise and Employment, 2015 c 26, sch 4 para 16
    appl (mods)—SI 2004/2326, reg 14, sch 2 (amended by 2009/2400, regs 2, 3, 15, 16, 38)

s 1115 am—SI 2009/1802, arts 2, 14

s 1116 am—SI 2009/1802, arts 2, 15

s 1117 appl (mods)—SI 2004/2326, reg 14, sch 2 (amended by 2009/2400, regs 2, 3, 15, 16, 38)

s 1120 rep—SI 2009/1802, arts 2, 16

s 1121 appl (mods)—SI 2012/3012, reg 23(5)-(7)
    appl—Small Business, Enterprise and Employment, 2015 c 26, sch 4 para 19(a)

s 1122 appl (mods)—SI 2012/3012, reg 23(5)(6)(8)
    appl—Small Business, Enterprise and Employment, 2015 c 26, sch 4 para 19(a)

s 1125 appl—Small Business, Enterprise and Employment, 2015 c 26, sch 4 para 19(b)

s 1126 am—(6.4.2016) Small Business, Enterprise and Employment, 2015 c 26, sch 3 para 9

s 1127 appl (mods)—SIs 2012/3012, regs 23(5)(6), 60(2)(3); 3013, reg 15(1)(a)(2)
    appl—Small Business, Enterprise and Employment, 2015 c 26, sch 4 para 19(c)

s 1128 appl (mods)—SIs 2012/3012, regs 23(5)(6), 60(2)(3); 3013, reg 15(1)(b)(2)
    appl—Small Business, Enterprise and Employment, 2015 c 26, sch 4 para 19(c)

s 1129 appl (mods)—SIs 2012/3012, regs 23(5)(6), 60(2)(3); 3013, reg 15(1)(c)(2)
    appl—Small Business, Enterprise and Employment, 2015 c 26, sch 4 para 19(d)

s 1131 appl (mods)—SIs 2012/3012, reg 60(2)(3); 3013, reg 15(1)(d)(2)

s 1132 appl (mods)—SIs 2012/3012, regs 23(5)(6)(9), 60(2)-(4); 3013, reg 15(1)(e)(2)(3)
    appl—Small Business, Enterprise and Employment, 2015 c 26, sch 4 para 19(e)

s 1136 am—SI 2013/600, sch 2 para 3(8); (6.4.2016) Small Business, Enterprise and Employment, 2015 c 26, sch 3 para 10; (prosp) ibid, ch 5 para 33

s 1139 appl—SI 2009/317, art 6
    appl (mods)—SI 2011/245, sch 6 pt 2 para 5(4)

s 1140 appl—SI 2009/317, art 6
    appl (mods)—SI 2011/245, sch 6 pt 2 para 5(4)
    am—SI 2009/1941, art 2, sch 1; Charities, 2011 c 25, sch 7 para 115(a)

ss 1143-1148 appl—Small Business, Enterprise and Employment, 2015 c 26, sch 4 para 14(4)

s 1154 am—SI 2009/1941, art 2, sch 1; Charities, 2011 c 25, sch 7 para 115(b)

s 1156 am—Crime and Cts, 2013 c 22, sch 9 para 43(a)
    rep in pt—Crime and Cts, 2013 c 22, sch 9 para 43(b)

s 1157 appl (mods)—Friendly Societies,1992 c.40, s 106 (amended by SI 2009/1941, art 2, sch 1)
    appl —Charities, 2011 c 25, s 192(1)

s 1162 mod—Charities, 2011 c 25, ss 55(3), 58

s 1164 am—Financial Services, 2012 c 21, sch 18 para 121

s 1165 am—Financial Services, 2012 c 21, sch 18 para 122

2006
c 46 *continued*

s 1169 am—(prosp) Small Business, Enterprise and Employment, 2015 c 26, s 93(6)

s 1170 am—SI 2007/732, reg 3

ss 1170A,1170B added—SI 2009/1941, art 2, sch 1

s 1173 am—SIs 2011/99, sch 4 para 5(a)(ii); 2013/3115, sch 2 para 42(2); 2015/980, reg 12(2)

s 1175 rep—Deregulation, 2015 c 20, sch 23 para 1

s 1183 am—Crime and Cts, 2013 c 22, sch 9 para 52

s 1193 am—SI 2009/2982, reg 5

s 1193 saved—SI 2009/2958, arts 8, 11

s 1201 subst—SI 2009/3182, reg 2

Pt 42 (ss 1209-1264) trans of functions—SI 2012/1741, arts 7-9
    appl (mods)—Loc Audit and Accountability, 2014 c 2, sch 5 para 1-27

s 1210 rep in pt—SI 2008/565, reg 15
    ext—SI 2008/1911, reg 48
    am—SIs 2011/99, sch 4 para 5(b)(ii); 2012/1809, art 3(1), sch pt 1; 2013/3115, sch 2 para 42(3)

s 1213 am—SI 2015/664, sch 3 para 9(24)

s 1214 appl—Budget Responsibility and Nat Audit, 2011 c 4, sch 2 para 25(4)

s 1215 am—SI 2015/664, sch 3 para 9(25)

s 1216 appl—Budget Responsibility and Nat Audit, 2011 c 4, sch 2 para 25(4)

s 1217 am—SI 2007/3494, reg 4

s 1219 am—SI 2007/3494, reg 5

s 1221 am—SI 2007/3494, reg 6

s 1223A added —SI 2007/3494, reg 7

ss 1224A, 1224B added —SI 2007/3494, reg 8

s 1224A am—SI 2011/1856, reg 3

s 1225 subst—SI 2012/1741, art 4

ss 1225A-1225G added—SI 2012/1741, art 4

s 1229 am—SI 2007/3494, reg 9; Public Audit (W), 2013 anaw 3, sch 4 para 81

s 1230 am—SI 2007/3494, reg 10; Public Audit (W), 2013 anaw 3, sch 4 para 82
    rep in pt—Budget Responsibility and Nat Audit, 2011 c 4, sch 5 para 30

s 1231 am—SI 2009/2958, arts 8, 12

ss 1239, 1240 see—(trans of functions) SI 2008/496, art 3

s 1239 am—SI 2007/3494, reg 30

s 1241 am—SI 2007/3494, reg 31

s 1242 am—SIs 2007/3494, reg 32; 2011/1856, reg 4
    rep in pt—SI 2013/1672, reg 14

s 1248 am—SI 2015/664, sch 3 para 9(26)

s 1251A added —SI 2007/3494, reg 11

s 1252 am—SI 2007/3494, reg 12

s 1253 am—SIs 2007/3494, reg 13; 2013/1672, reg 15

ss 1253A-1253C added —SI 2007/3494, reg 14

ss 1253D-1253F added —SI 2007/3494, reg 15

s 1253D subst—SI 2010/2537, reg 2
    rep in pt—SI 2010/2537, reg 4(1)

ss 1253DA-1253DE added—SI 2010/2537, reg 2

s 1253DE am—SI 2010/2537, reg 4(2)

s 1253E subst—SI 2010/2537, reg 3
    am—SI 2010/2537, reg 4(3)

s 1254 am—SI 2007/3494, reg 16

s 1256 appl (mods)—SI 2008/496, art 10
    mod—SIs 2012/1741, art 14; 2014/2009, art 9

s 1261 am—SIs 2007/3494, reg 2; 2010/2537, reg 6

s 1262 am—SIs 2007/3494, reg 3; 2010/2537, reg 6

s 1278 am—Corporation Tax, 2010 c 4, s 1177, sch 1 paras 487, 490
    rep in pt—SI 2013/1773, sch 1 para 42

Pts 45-47 (ss 1284-1300L) ext (mod)—SI 2009/1941, art 12, sch 3
    appl (mods)—SI 2009/2436, regs 3-5, sch 1 (and reg 9, sch 2)
    appl—SI 2009/2437, regs 18, 19-23, 24
    ext—SI 2011/1265, sch 1 para 2

s 1286 transtl provns and savings—SI 2009/1804, reg 84, sch 2

s 1293 am—Small Business, Enterprise and Employment, 2015 c 26, s 90(4)

s 1297 saved—SIs 2008/954, art 4; 2008/948, art 12

2006
c 46 *continued*

sch 1 am—SI 2009/1941, art 13; Charities, 2011 c 25, sch 7 para 116
appl—Charities, 2011 c 25, s 352(2)
schs 1A, 1B added (6.4.2016)—Small Business, Enterprise and Employment, 2015 c 26, sch
3 pt 1 para 2
sch 2 subst—SI 2009/1208, art 2, sch
am—SI 2010/22, art 5, sch 2; Budget Responsibility and Nat Audit, 2011 c 4, sch 5
para 31; Financial Services, 2012 c 21, sch 18 para 123; Co-operative and
Community Benefit Societies, 2014 c 14, sch 4 para 102(3)(4); SIs 2014/631,
sch 2 para 5(2)(b); 2014/892, sch 1 para 168(a); Consumer Rights, 2015 c 15,
sch 4 para 37(2)(b),(3)
appl (mods) —SI 2011/245, sch 6 pt 2 para 5(5); SIs 2013/2329, sch para 29(a);
2013/1882, art 10(4)(a); 2013/3134, sch 4 para 6(a)
rep in pt—Financial Services, 2012 c 21, sch 19; SI 2013/1881, sch para 11(a);
Co-operative and Community Benefit Societies, 2014 c 14, sch 4 para 102(2);
SIs 2014/631, sch 2 para 5(2)(a); 2014/892, sch 1 para 168(b); Consumer
Rights, 2015 c 15, sch 4 para 37(2)(a); Deregulation, 2015 c 20, sch 6 para
22(15)(a)
sch 3 excl—SI 2014/3038, reg 42(2)
sch 5 am—(prosp) Small Business, Enterprise and Employment, 2015 c 26, sch 5 para
34(a)(b)
sch 7 appl—Transport for London, 2008, c.i, s 49, sch 3; SIs 2008/409, regs 8, 10, sch 6;
2008/410, reg 9, sch 6; 2008/1913, sch 3
appl (mods)—SI 2008/1911, reg 52
mod—Charities, 2011 c 25, ss 55(3), 58
sch 8 am—SIs 2007/2932, reg 3; 2008/393, reg 6; 2008/3000, reg 9; 2009/1632, reg 21;
2009/1581, reg 9; 2009/1802, arts 2, 17; 2009/1941, art 2, sch 1; 2009/2561,
reg 2; 2011/1487, reg 5; Enterprise and Regulatory Reform, 2013 c 24, s 81(11)
(12); SI 2013/600, sch 2 para 3(9)(a)(b); Deregulation, 2015 c 20, sch 5 para
12(3); (6.4.2016) Small Business, Enterprise and Employment, 2015 c 26, sch 3
para 11; (prosp) ibid, s 93(7)(b); (prosp) ibid, sch 5 para 35; SI 2015/980, reg
13(3)-(5)
rep in pt—SIs 2009/1802, arts 2, 17; 2013/600, sch 2 para 3(9)(b)(c); 2013/1970, sch
para 26; Deregulation, 2015 c 20, sch 5 para 12(2); (prosp) Small Business,
Enterprise and Employment, 2015 c 26, s 93(7)(a); SI 2015/980, reg 13(2)
sch 9 rep—Deregulation, 2015 c 20, sch 23 para 1
sch 10 am—SIs 2007/3494, regs 17-28; 2010/2537, reg 5; 2011/1856, reg 5; 2012/1741,
art 5(2)-(6); 2013/1672, reg 16
appl—SI 2010/2537, reg 8
appl (mods)—Loc Audit and Accountability, 2014 c 2, sch 5 para 28
sch 11 am—SI 2007/3494, reg 44
trans of functions—SI 2008/496, art 3
sch 11A added —SI 2007/3494, reg 8, sch
mod—SI 2009/317, art 6
appl (mods)—SI 2011/245, sch 6 pt 2 para 5(6)
am—SI 2010/22, art 5, sch 2; Budget Responsibility and Nat Audit, 2011 c 4, sch
5 para 31; SIs 2011/1856, reg 6; 2013/2329, sch para 29(b); 2013/1882, art
10(4)(b); 2013/3134, sch 4 para 6(b); Loc Audit and Accountability, 2014 c 2,
sch 12 para 78; Co-operative and Community Benefit Societies, 2014 c 14, sch
4 para 103(3)(4); SIs 2014/631, sch 2 para 5(3)(b); 2014/892, sch 1 para
169(a)(i)(ii); Consumer Rights, 2015 c 15, sch 4 para 38
rep in pt—SI 2013/1881, sch para 11(b); Co-operative and Community Benefit
Societies, 2014 c 14, sch 4 para 103(2); SIs 2014/631, sch 2 para 5(3)(a);
2014/892, sch 1 para 169(b); Deregulation, 2015 c 20, sch 6 para 22(15)(b)
sch 12 am—SIs 2007/3494, reg 33; 2013/1672, reg 17
sch 13 rep in pt—Loc Audit and Accountability, 2014 c 2, sch 5 para 29(a)
am—Loc Audit and Accountability, 2014 c 2, sch 5 para 29(b)
c 47 **Safeguarding Vulnerable Groups**
trans of functions—SI 2012/3006, arts 98, 99
s 1 rep—SI 2012/3006, art 112
s 2 am—Policing and Crime, 2009 c 26, s 81(2)(3)(m); SI 2012/3006, art 3(a)
rep in pt—SI 2012/3006, art 4
s 4 am—SI 2008/2833, art 6, sch 3; Policing and Crime, 2009 c 26, s 81(2)(3)(m);
Protection of Freedoms, 2012 c 9, sch 9 para 44(b)(c); SI 2012/3006, art 3(a)

2006
c 47 s 4 *continued*

        rep in pt—SI 2008/2833, art 6, sch 3; Protection of Freedoms, 2012 c 9, sch 9 para 44(a), sch 10 pt 5

s 5 rep in pt—Protection of Freedoms, 2012 c 9, sch 9 para 45(a)(b), sch 10 pt 5

s 6 am—(prosp) Health and Social Care, 2008 c 14, s 160, sch 14 para 8; Health, 2009 c 21, s 13, sch 1 paras 12, 13; Policing and Crime, 2009 c 26, s 81(2)(3)(m); SI 2010/813, art 19; Health and Social Care, 2012 c 7, sch 5 para 144(b); Protection of Freedoms, 2012 c 9, sch 9 para 46(a)(c)

        rep in pt—Health and Social Care, 2012 c 7, sch 5 para 144(a); Protection of Freedoms, 2012 c 9, sch 9 para 46(b), sch 10 pt 5

s 7 rep in pt—Protection of Freedoms, 2012 c 9, sch 9 para 47, sch 10 pt 5

s 8 rep—Protection of Freedoms, 2012 c 9, sch 9 para 48, sch 10 pt 5

s 9 rep in pt—Protection of Freedoms, 2012 c 9, sch 9 para 49, sch 10 pt 5

ss 10-17 rep—Protection of Freedoms, 2012 c 9, sch 9 paras 50-57, sch 10 pt 5

s 18 rep in pt—Protection of Freedoms, 2012 c 9, sch 9 para 58(2)(a)(b)(3)(b), sch 10 pt 5

s 19 rep in pt—Protection of Freedoms, 2012 c 9, sch 9 para 59(3)(4)(5)(b)(6), sch 10 pt 5

        am—Protection of Freedoms, 2012 c 9, sch 9 para 59(5)(a)

s 20 rep in pt—Protection of Freedoms, 2012 c 9, sch 9 para 60, sch 10 pt 5

ss 21-24 rep—Protection of Freedoms, 2012 c 9, ss 68, 69, sch 10 pt 5

s 24A added —Policing and Crime, 2009 c 26, s 84(1)

        rep—Protection of Freedoms, 2012 c 9, s 69, sch 10 pt 5

ss 25-27 rep—Protection of Freedoms, 2012 c 9, s 69, sch 10 pt 5

s 28 ext (mod)—SIs 2009/3215, art 4, schs 3, 4; 2010/764, arts 4, 6-8, schs 2, 3; 2010/765, arts 4, 6-8, schs 2, 3

s 30 am—SI 2015/914, sch para 86

ss 30A, 30B subst for ss 30-32 (prosp)—Protection of Freedoms, 2012 c 9, s 72(1)

s 30A am—SI 2012/3006, art 48(a)

s 30B am—SI 2012/3006, art 48(b)

s 33 am—(prosp) Protection of Freedoms, 2012 c 9, s 72(2); SI 2012/3006, art 48(c)

s 34 am—(prosp) Protection of Freedoms, 2012 c 9, s 72(3)(a)(b)

s 34ZA added (prosp)—Protection of Freedoms, 2012 c 9, s 73

s 35 am—Policing and Crime, 2009 c 26, s 81(2)(3)(m); SI 2012/3006, art 3(b)

        rep in pt—Protection of Freedoms, 2012 c 9, sch 9 para 61(a)(b), sch 10 pt 5

s 36 am—Policing and Crime, 2009 c 26, s 81(2)(3)(m); SI 2012/3006, art 3(b)

        rep in pt—Protection of Freedoms, 2012 c 9, sch 9 para 62(2)(3), sch 10 pt 5

s 37 am—Policing and Crime, 2009 c 26, s 81(2)(3)(m); SI 2012/3006, art 3(b)

        rep in pt—Protection of Freedoms, 2012 c 9, sch 9 para 63(2)-(4), sch 10 pt 5

s 38 am—Policing and Crime, 2009 c 26, s 81(2)(3)(m); SI 2012/3006, art 3(b)

s 39 am—Policing and Crime, 2009 c 26, s 81(2)(3)(m); Protection of Freedoms, 2012 c 9, s 77(2)(a)(b)(i)(iii)(d); SI 2012/3006, art 3(b)

        rep in pt—Protection of Freedoms, 2012 c 9, s 77(2)(b)(ii)(c), sch 10 pt 5

s 40 am—Policing and Crime, 2009 c 26, s 81(2)(3)(m); SI 2012/3006, art 3(b)

s 41 am—SI 2009/1182, arts 4, 5-7, sch 5; Policing and Crime, 2009 c 26, s 81(2)(3)(m); SI 2010/231, art 68, sch 4; Educ, 2011 c 21, sch 2 para 27(2); Health and Social Care, 2012 c 7, s 213(7)(m), sch 15 para 52; Protection of Freedoms, 2012 c 9, s 75(1)(a)(i)(b)(i)(iii)(d), sch 9 para 64; SI 2012/3006, art 3(b)

        rep in pt—Protection of Freedoms, 2012 c 9, s 75(1)(a)(ii)(b)(ii)(c), sch 10 pt 5

s 42 am—Policing and Crime, 2009 c 26, s 81(2)(3)(m); SI 2012/3006, art 3(b)

s 43 rep in pt—SI 2009/1182, arts 4, 5-7, sch 5; Protection of Freedoms, 2012 c 9, s 75(4), sch 10 pt 5; SI 2012/3006, art 54

        am—Policing and Crime, 2009 c 26, s 81(2)(3)(m); Protection of Freedoms, 2012 c 9, s 75(5); (pt prosp) Protection of Freedoms, 2012 c 9, s 75(3), sch 10 pt 5; SI 2012/3006, arts 3(c), 48(d)

s 44 rep—Protection of Freedoms, 2012 c 9, s 75(6), sch 10 pt 5

s 45 am—Health and Social Care, 2008 c 14, s 95, sch 5 para 91(a), (c); Policing and Crime, 2009 c 26, s 81(2)(3)(m); SI 2010/1073, art 2; Educ, 2011 c 21, sch 2 para 27(3); Protection of Freedoms, 2012 c 9, s 76(1)(a)(i)(b)(i)(iii)(e); SI 2012/3006, art 3(d)

        rep in pt—Protection of Freedoms, 2012 c 9, s 76(1)(a)(ii)(b)(ii)(c)(d), sch 10 pt 5

s 46 am—Policing and Crime, 2009 c 26, s 81(2)(3)(m); SI 2012/3006, art 3(d)

s 47 am—Policing and Crime, 2009 c 26, s 81(2)(3)(m); Protection of Freedoms, 2012 c 9, s 76(2)(a)(b)(f); SI 2012/3006, arts 3(d), 48(e)

        rep in pt—Protection of Freedoms, 2012 c 9, s 76(2)(c)(d)(e), sch 10 pt 5

2006

c 47 *continued*

s 48 am—Protection of Freedoms, 2012 c 9, s 76(3)(f); (prosp) ibid, s
76(3)(a)(i)(iii)(iv)(b)-(e); SI 2012/3006, art 48(f)

rep in pt—(prosp) Protection of Freedoms, 2012 c 9, s 76(3)(a)(ii)(v), sch 10 pt 5

s 49 am—Protection of Freedoms, 2012 c 9, s 76(4)(f); (prosp) ibid, s
76(4)(a)(i)(iii)(iv)(b)-(e); SI 2012/3006, art 48(g)

rep in pt—(prosp) Protection of Freedoms, 2012 c 9, s 76(4)(a)(ii)(v), sch 10 pt 5

s 50 am—Policing and Crime, 2009 c 26, s 81(2)(3)(m); Protection of Freedoms, 2012 c 9, s
76(5); SI 2012/3006, arts 3(e), 48(h)

s 50A added—Policing and Crime, 2009 c 26, s 88

am—SI 2010/1154, art 12; Protection of Freedoms, 2012 c 9, s 77(3)-(5), sch 9 para
65; SIs 2012/3006, art 3(e); 2013/602, sch 2 para 53

s 51 rep in pt—Protection of Freedoms, 2012 c 9, sch 9 para 66, sch 10 pt 5

s 53 rep in pt—(W prosp) Children and Young Persons, 2008 c 23, ss 8, 42, sch 1 para 20,
sch 4

s 54 rep in pt—Protection of Freedoms, 2012 c 9, sch 9 para 67, sch 10 pt 5

s 56 am—Protection of Freedoms, 2012 c 9, sch 9 para 68(3)(a)(4)(b)(d)(f)

rep in pt—Protection of Freedoms, 2012 c 9, sch 9 para 68(2)(3)(b)(c)(4)(a)(c)(e)(g),
sch 10 pt 5

s 57 rep in pt—Protection of Freedoms, 2012 c 9, sch 9 para 69, sch 10 pt 5

s 59 rep—Protection of Freedoms, 2012 c 9, s 65(1), sch 10 pt 5

s 60 am—Protection of Freedoms, 2012 c 9, s 65(2); SI 2012/3006, art 5

rep in pt—Protection of Freedoms, 2012 c 9, sch 9 para 70, sch 10 pt 5

s 61 am—Protection of Freedoms, 2012 c 9, sch 9 para 71(b)

rep in pt—Protection of Freedoms, 2012 c 9, sch 9 para 71(a)(c), sch 10 pt 5

s 63 ext (mods)—SIs 2009/3215, art 4, schs 3, 4; 2010/764, arts 4, 6-8, schs 2, 3; 2010/765,
arts 4, 6-8, schs 2, 3

schs 1, 2 rep—SI 2012/3006, art 112

sch 3 appl (mods)—SIs 2008/473, regs 2, 4; 2009/12, art 5

am—SI 2008/3050, arts 2, 3; Policing and Crime, 2009 c 26, s 81(2)(3)(m); Police
Reform and Social Responsibility, 2011 c 13, sch 16 para 361; Educ, 2011 c 21,
sch 2 para 27(4)(a); SI 2011/565, art 2; Health and Social Care, 2012 c 7, sch 15
para 56(e); Protection of Freedoms, 2012 c 9, ss 67, 70(1)(a)(i)(ii)(b)(2), 71, 74,
sch 9 paras 72(3), 129; SI 2012/3006, arts 3(f), 48(i), 55, 56, 57, 58, 59

rep in pt—Educ, 2011 c 21, sch 2 para 27(4)(b); Protection of Freedoms, 2012 c 9, s
70(1)(a)(iii)(c), sch 9 para 72(2), sch 10 pt 5; SI 2012/3006, arts 60, 61

trans of functions—SI 2012/3006, arts 104, 106

sch 4 am—Educ and Skills, 2008 c 25, s 169, sch 1 para 41; Health and Social Care, 2008 c
14, s 95, sch 5 paras 92(2)(a), (4)(5), 93(3); Policing and Crime, 2009 c 26, s
81(2)(3)(m); Apprenticeships, Skills, Children and Learning, 2009 c 22, s 200;
SI 2009/2610, arts 25-27, 30; (W) Children and Families (W), 2010 nawm 1, s
72, sch 1 paras 27, 28; SIs 2010/1154, arts 2-7, 9, 10; 2010/1158, art 5, sch 2;
Charities, 2011 c 25, sch 7 para 117; Protection of Freedoms, 2012 c 9, ss 64,
66(2)(7), 77(6); SIs 2012/976, sch para 21; 1879, art 4(6); 2015/914, sch para
87

rep in pt—Health and Social Care, 2008 c 14, s 95, sch 15, sch 5 paras 92(2)(b), (3),
93(2); SI 2010/1154, arts 5, 8; Protection of Freedoms, 2012 c 9, ss
64(2)(6)(b)(d)(i)(vi)(viii)(x)(e)-(g)(7)(a)(b)(ii)(8)(9), 66(3)-(6)(8)(9), sch 10 pt 5

mod—SI 2009/2610, art 29

sch 5 rep—Protection of Freedoms, 2012 c 9, sch 9 para 51, sch 10 pt 5

sch 6 rep—Protection of Freedoms, 2012 c 9, sch 9 para 52, sch 10 pt 5

sch 7 am—SIs 2010/813, art 19; 2010/1080, art 2, sch 1; Educ, 2011 c 21, sch 16 para
38(b); Protection of Freedoms, 2012 c 9, s 72(5), sch 9 para 73(2)(a)(4)

rep in pt—Educ, 2011 c 21, sch 16 para 38(a); SIs 2012/2113, arts 8, 9; 2012/3006,
art 3(g); Protection of Freedoms, 2012 c 9, s 72(4)(6), sch 9 para 73(2)(b)(3),
sch 10 pt 5

sch 8 am—Policing and Crime, 2009 c 26, s 81(2)(3)(m); Educ, 2011 c 21, sch 2 para
27(5)(b)(c); SI 2012/3006, art 3(h)

rep in pt—Educ, 2011 c 21, sch 2 para 27(5)(a); Protection of Freedoms, 2012 c 9, sch
9 para 74, sch 10 pt 5

sch 9 ext (mods)—SIs 2009/3215, art 4, sch 3; 2010/764, arts 4, 6-8, schs 2, 3; 2010/765,
arts 4, 6-8, schs 2, 3

rep in pt—Protection of Freedoms, 2012 c 9, sch 10 pt 6

sch 10 ext (mods)—SIs 2009/3215, art 4, sch 3; 2010/764, art 4; 2010/765, art 4

2006

c 48   **Police and Justice**

savings—SI 2008/311, art 3

s 1 rep—Crime and Cts, 2013 c 22, sch 8 para 168

s 4 rep —Loc Govt and Public Involvement in Health, 2007 c 28, s 241, sch 18

s 6 rep in pt—Police Reform and Social Responsibility, 2011 c 13, sch 16 para 359

s 13 see—(trans of functions) SI 2008/678, sch 1

    am—SIs 2008/678, art 5, sch 2; 2010/976, art 12, sch 14; Crime and Cts, 2013 c 22, sch 8 para 169

    rep in pt—SI 2013/602, sch 2 para 54(2)

s 19 am—Loc Govt and Public Involvement in Health, 2007 c 28, s 126; Localism, 2011 c 20, sch 3 para 80(1)(2)(4)-(6)

    rep in pt—Localism, 2011 c 20, sch 3 para 80(1)(3), sch 25 pt 4

s 20 am—Loc Govt and Public Involvement in Health, 2007 c 28, ss 121(2)(3), 126

    rep in pt—Loc Govt and Public Involvement in Health, 2007 c 28, s 241, sch 18

s 26 rep —Anti-social Behaviour, Crime and Policing, 2014 c 12, sch 11 para 50

s 27 am—Mental Health, 2007 c 12, s 1, sch 1 para 26; Crime and Cts, 2013 c 22, sch 9 para 44(a)

    rep in pt—Crime and Cts, 2013 c 22, sch 9 para 44(b)

s 32 rep in pt—SI 2012/2401, sch 1 para 26

s 34 rep—Legal Aid, Sentencing and Punishment of Offenders, 2012 c 10, s 118(3)

s 35 rep in pt—Serious Crime, 2007 c 27, s 61(1)(2), sch 14

s 36 rep in pt—Serious Crime, 2007 c 27, s 92, sch 14

    am—Serious Crime, 2007 c 27, s 61(1)(3)

s 38 rep in pt—Serious Crime, 2007 c 27, s 61(1)(4), sch 14

s 41 am—Borders, Citizenship and Immigration, 2009 c 11, s 30

s 44 rep in pt—Crim Justice and Immigration, 2008 c 4, s 149, sch 28 pt 6

s 49 rep in pt—Crim Justice and Immigration, 2008 c 4, s 148, sch 26 para 81(1), (2)(a); ibid, s 149, sch 28 pt 8

    am—SIs 2010/976, art 12, sch 14; 2012/2595, art 13

sch 1 rep—Crime and Cts, 2013 c 22, sch 8 para 170

sch 2 rep in pt—(prosp) Crim Justice and Immigration, 2008 c 4, s 149, sch 28 pt 8

sch 3 am—(S prosp) Anti-social Behaviour, Crime and Policing, 2014 c 12, s 133(5)

sch 4 rep in pt—(prosp) Anti-social Behaviour, Crime and Policing, 2014 c 12, sch 11 para 102

sch 5 rep in pt—Policing and Crime, 2009 c 26, s 112, sch 8 pt 13

sch 8 am—Localism, 2011 c 20, sch 3 para 81

sch 13 rep in pt—Legal Aid, Sentencing and Punishment of Offenders, 2012 c 10, sch 16 para 19; Crime and Cts, 2013 c 22, sch 20 para 9

sch 14 rep in pt—Serious Crime, 2007 c 27, ss 61(1)(5), 92, sch 14; Loc Govt and Public Involvement in Health, 2007 c 28, s 241, sch 18; Crim Justice and Immigration, 2008 c 4, s 149, sch 28 pt 7; Anti-social Behaviour, Crime and Policing, 2014 c 12, sch 11 para 50

c 49   **Road Safety**

s 9 rep in pt—Road Safety, 2006 c 49, s 59, sch 7(4)

s 14 rep —Road Safety, 2006 c 49, s 59, sch 7(4)

ss 20, 21 rep in pt—(prosp) Coroners and Justice, 2009 c 25, s 178, sch 23 pt 1

s 39 am—SI 2012/977, sch 2 para 2(2)(a)

s 49A added—Loc Transport, 2008 c 26, s 129

    am—SI 2013/602, sch 2 para 55

s 49B added—Loc Transport, 2008 c 26, s 130

s 57 rep—Energy, 2013 c 32, sch 12 para 92

s 58 rep in pt—Road Safety, 2006 c 49, s 59, sch 7(4)

sch 1 rep in pt—Road Safety, 2006 c 49, s 59, sch 7(4)

sch 2 rep in pt—Road Safety, 2006 c 49, s 59, sch 7(4)

sch 3 rep in pt—Policing and Crime, 2009 c 26, s 112, sch 8 pt 13

    am—SIs 2012/977, sch 2 para 3(2); 2013/1644, sch 1; Immigration, 2014 c 22, sch 9 para 64

sch 6 rep in pt—Deregulation, 2015 c 20, sch 2 para 33

c 50   **Charities**

savings—SI 2008/3267, arts 3-17

ss 1-9 rep —Charities, 2011 c 25, sch 10

ss 11-44 rep —Charities, 2011 c 25, sch 10

Pt 3, Ch 1 (ss 45-66) see—(power to am or modify) (pt prosp) Charities, 1993 c 10, sch 1C, paras 6, 7 (added by 2006 c 50, s 8, sch 4)

2006
c 50 *continued*

s 54 am—Charities, 2011 c 25, sch 7 para 118
s 57 am—SI 2009/1834, art 4, sch 1
s 70 trans of functions—SI 2007/2914, art 3
    am—SIs 2007/2914, art 8, sch; 2010/1839, art 7, sch
s 72 rep in pt—Corporation Tax, 2010 c 4, ss 1177, 1181, sch 1 paras 491, 493, sch 3
    am—Charities, 2011 c 25, sch 7 para 119
s 73 am—Charities, 2011 c 25, sch 7 para 120
s 74 rep in pt—Charities, 2011 c 25, sch 7 para 121, sch 10
s 76 rep —Charities, 2011 c 25, sch 7 para 122, sch 10
s 78 rep in pt—Charities, 2011 c 25, sch 7 para 123(1)(a)(d)(2)(3), sch 10
    am—Charities, 2011 c 25, sch 7 para 123(1)(b)(c), sch 10
s 79 rep in pt—Charities, 2011 c 25, sch 7 para 124, sch 10
s 80 rep in pt—Charities, 2011 c 25, sch 7 para 125, sch 10
schs 1, 2 rep —Charities, 2011 c 25, sch 10
sch 3 rep—SI 2009/1834, art 4, sch 3
schs 4-7 rep —Charities, 2011 c 25, sch 10
sch 8 rep in pt—Housing and Regeneration, 2008 c 17, s 321, sch 16; SIs 2009/1834, art 4,
    sch 3, 1941, art 2, sch 2; Charities, 2011 c 25, sch 10; SI 2011/1725, sch para
    4; Co-operative and Community Benefit Societies, 2014 c 14, sch 7
sch 10 rep in pt—Charities, 2011 c 25, sch 10

c 51   **Legislative and Regulatory Reform**
ss 1, 4 am—SI 2007/1388, art 3, sch 1
s 11 subst—SI 2007/1388, art 3, sch 1
s 13 am—SI 2007/1388, art 3, sch 1
ss 15-19 appl (mods)—Fire and Rescue Services, 2004 c 21, s 5E(3); Localism, 2011 c 20, s
    7(3)
s 24 am—SIs 2007/1388, art 3, sch 1; 2015/1682, sch pt 1 para 4(r)
    excl—Marine and Coastal Access, 2009 c 23, s 3(2)
    rep in pt—Postal Services, 2011 c 5, sch 12 para 174
s 27 am—SI 2007/1388, art 3, sch 1
s 31 rep in pt—Loc Audit and Accountability, 2014 c 2, sch 12 para 123(d)

c 52   **Armed Forces**
see (provn for expiry (3.11.2011) unless continued—Armed Forces, 2006, s 382 (as subst by
    2011 c 18, s 1)
cont —(until 2.11.2015) Armed Forces, 2006, s 382(2) with SI 2014/1882, art 2; SI
    2015/1766, art 2
mod—SI 2009/826, reg 3
s 2 mod—SI 2009/826, reg 4
s 3A am—Armed Forces, 2011 c 18, s 6
s 9 am—Armed Forces, 2011 c 18, sch 2 para 7
s 11 mod—SI 2009/826, reg 4
s 12 mod—SI 2009/826, reg 5
s 20 mod—SI 2009/826, reg 4
s 20 am—Armed Forces, 2011 c 18, s 9
s 20A added—Armed Forces, 2011 c 18, s 10
s 22 mod—SI 2009/826, reg 4
s 39 am—Serious Crime, 2007 c 27, s 60, sch 5 paras 7, 8
s 40 subst —Serious Crime, 2007 c 27, s 60, sch 5 paras 7, 9, 10
s 46 subst —Serious Crime, 2007 c 27, s 60, sch 5 paras 7, 11
s 48 appl (mods)—Crim Justice, 1982 c 48, s 32(2A); Sexual Offences (Amdt), 1992 c 34, s
    6(1A); Powers of Crim Cts (Sentencing), 2000 c 6, s 114(3); Crim Justice and
    Ct Services, 2000 c 43, s 27(3); Sexual Offences, 2003 c 42, sch 3 para 93A(3),
    sch 5 para 172A(2); Crim Justice, 2003 c 44, s 233(2); Agriculture and
    Forestry (Financial Provisions),1991 c 53, s 33; Crim Justice, 2003 c 44, s
    255A; Crim Justice and Immigration, 2008 c 4, s 98(5)
    appl—Counter-Terrorism, 2008 c 28, s 95(5)
    am—Serious Crime, 2007 c 27, s 60, sch 5 paras 7, 12
s 50 am—Armed Forces, 2011 c 18, sch 4 para 3(2); Crim Justice and Cts, 2015 c 2, sch 14
    para 5
s 51 am—Domestic Violence, Crime and Victims (Amendment), 2012 c 4, sch para 11;
    Crim Justice and Cts, 2015 c 2, sch 14 para 6
s 52 mod—SI 2009/826, reg 6
s 53 am—Armed Forces, 2011 c 18, sch 4 para 4

2006
c 52 *continued*

s 58 am—Armed Forces, 2011 c 18, sch 4 para 5
s 67 mod—SI 2009/826, reg 3
　　　am—Armed Forces, 2011 c 18, sch 3 para 2
s 70 appl—SI 2013/1852, art 6(7)(a)
s 83 subst—Armed Forces, 2011 c 18, s 7
s 84 am—Anti-social Behaviour, Crime and Policing, 2014 c 12, s 176(7)
s 86 am—Armed Forces, 2011 c 18, s 8
s 87 am—Armed Forces, 2011 c 18, sch 4 para 6
s 88 am—Armed Forces, 2011 c 18, sch 4 para 7
s 90 am—Armed Forces, 2011 c 18, sch 3 para 3
　　　appl—SI 2013/1852, art 6(7)(b)
Ch 3A (ss 93A-93I) added—Armed Forces, 2011 c 18, s 11(1)
s 95 am—Armed Forces, 2011 c 18, s 15(2)(b)
s 96 am—Armed Forces, 2011 c 18, sch 3 para 4
s 97 am—Armed Forces, 2011 c 18, sch 4 para 8
Pt 4 (ss 98-112) mod—SI 2013/1852, art 25(3)(4)
ss 98-102 appl—SI 2013/1852, art 6(7)(c)
s 104 appl—SI 2013/1852, art 6(7)(c)
s 105 appl—SI 2013/1852, art 22(1)(a)
s 107 appl—SI 2009/2041, rule 136
　　　mod—SI 2013/1852, art 22(2)
s 108 appl—SI 2013/1852, art 22(1)
s 111 appl (mods)—SI 2009/1209, rules 28, 29
s 115A added—Armed Forces, 2011 c 18, s 3
s 116 am—Armed Forces, 2011 c 18, sch 3 para 5(1)
　　　mod—SI 2013/602, sch 3 para 9(2)
　　　excl—SI 2013/1852, art 7(5)
s 117 am—Armed Forces, 2011 c 18, sch 3 para 5(2)
s 119 mod—SI 2013/602, sch 3 para 9(2)
s 125 am—Armed Forces, 2011 c 18, sch 3 para 6(2)(a)
　　　rep in pt—Armed Forces, 2011 c 18, sch 3 para 6(2)(b)(3), sch 5
s 129 am—Armed Forces, 2011 c 18, sch 3 para 7
s 130 am—Armed Forces, 2011 c 18, sch 3 para 8
s 130A added—Armed Forces, 2011 c 18, sch 3 para 9
s 132 am—Armed Forces, 2011 c 18, s 12(1)
s 133 am—Armed Forces, 2011 c 18, sch 3 para 10
s 134 am—Armed Forces, 2011 c 18, sch 3 para 10
s 135 am—Armed Forces, 2011 c 18, s 12(2), sch 3 para 10
s 135A added—Armed Forces, 2011 c 18, sch 3 para 11
s 136 am—Armed Forces, 2011 c 18, sch 3 para 12
s 138 am—Armed Forces, 2011 c 18, s 13(1)
s 145 excl—SI 2009/1211, rule 90
s 153 am—Armed Forces, 2011 c 18, sch 3 para 13
s 155 excl—SI 2009/2041, rules 31(2), 33(1)
s 163A added—Crim Justice and Cts, 2015 c 2, sch 14 para 2
s 164 appl—Armed Forces, 1991 c 62, s 23(1A); Reserve Forces, 1996 c 14, s 127(4)
　　　rep in pt—Armed Forces, 2011 c 18, sch 4 para 9(a)(b), sch 5
　　　am—Armed Forces, 2011 c 18, sch 4 para 9(c)
s 165 excl—SI 2009/2041, rules 158, 159, sch
　　　subst—Armed Forces, 2011 c 18, s 14(1)
s 171 am—Mental Health, 2007 c 12, s 15(5)
s 172 appl (mods)—Courts-Martial (Appeals), 1968 c 20, s 22(3B)
　　　am—Health and Social Care, 2012 c 7, s 38(5)(e)
s 175 am—Legal Aid, Sentencing and Punishment of Offenders, 2012 c 10, s 63(2)
s 178 am—Crime and Cts, 2013 c 22, sch 16 para 32
s 180 am—(pt prosp) Legal Aid, Sentencing and Punishment of Offenders, 2012 c 10, s
　　　76(11)(a)
s 182 am—Legal Aid, Sentencing and Punishment of Offenders, 2012 c 10, s 78(2)(4); (pt
　　　prosp) ibid, s 78(3); Crime and Cts, 2013 c 22, sch 16 paras 33, 37(2)
s 183 am—SI 2008/912, art 3, sch 1; (prosp) Crime and Cts, 2013 c 22, sch 16 para 37(3);
　　　(Offender Rehabilitation, 2014 c 11, sch 6 para 8; ibid, sch 6 para 4(3)
　　　rep in pt—Offender Rehabilitation, 2014 c 11, sch 6 para 4(2)(4)
s 187 excl—Coroners and Justice, 2009 c 25, s 158(3)(d)

2006
c 52 *continued*

s 188 am—Crim Justice and Immigration, 2008 c 4, s 145, sch 25 paras 10, 11; Legal Aid, Sentencing and Punishment of Offenders, 2012 c 10, sch 22 para 23(2)(3)

s 190 am—Armed Forces, 2011 c 18, sch 3 para 14

s 191 am—Armed Forces, 2011 c 18, sch 3 para 14

s 193 am—Armed Forces, 2011 c 18, sch 3 para 14

s 194 am—Armed Forces, 2011 c 18, sch 3 para 15(2)

    rep in pt—Armed Forces, 2011 c 18, sch 3 para 15(3), sch 5

s 194A added—Armed Forces, 2011 c 18, sch 3 para 16

s 196 rep in pt—Legal Aid, Sentencing and Punishment of Offenders, 2012 c 10, sch 10 para 41(2)

ss 197-199 rep—Legal Aid, Sentencing and Punishment of Offenders, 2012 c 10, sch 10 para 41(3)

s 200 am—Armed Forces, 2011 c 18, sch 3 para 17; Legal Aid, Sentencing and Punishment of Offenders, 2012 c 10, sch 9 para 15(4)(5)

    rep in pt—Legal Aid, Sentencing and Punishment of Offenders, 2012 c 10, sch 9 para 15(2)(3)

s 201 rep—Legal Aid, Sentencing and Punishment of Offenders, 2012 c 10, sch 9 para 16

s 204 am—(pt prosp) Legal Aid, Sentencing and Punishment of Offenders, 2012 c 10, s 76(11)(b)

s 205 am—Offender Rehabilitation, 2014 c 11, sch 6 para 9

s 207 am—Legal Aid, Sentencing and Punishment of Offenders, 2012 c 10, sch 9 para 17(a)

    rep in pt—Legal Aid, Sentencing and Punishment of Offenders, 2012 c 10, sch 9 para 17(b), sch 10 para 41(4)

s 209 am—Crim Justice and Immigration, 2008 c 4, s 145, sch 25 paras 10, 12; Legal Aid, Sentencing and Punishment of Offenders, 2012 c 10, sch 22 para 24

s 211 am—Legal Aid, Sentencing and Punishment of Offenders, 2012 c 10, sch 22 para 25

s 213 am—Armed Forces, 2011 c 18, sch 3 para 18; Legal Aid, Sentencing and Punishment of Offenders, 2012 c 10, s 80(9); Offender Rehabilitation, 2014 c 11, sch 6 para 2

s 214 am—Offender Management, 2007 c 21, s 39, sch 3 para 17(1)(2); Armed Forces, 2011 c 18, sch 3 para 19

s 215 am—Offender Management, 2007 c 21, s 39, sch 3 para 17(1)(3)

s 218A added—Legal Aid, Sentencing and Punishment of Offenders, 2012 c 10, sch 22 para 2

    am—Crim Justice and Cts, 2015 c 2, s 5(3)

s 219 am—Crim Justice and Immigration, 2008 c 4, s 145, sch 25 paras 10, 13(1)-(3); Legal Aid, Sentencing and Punishment of Offenders, 2012 c 10, sch 22 paras 3(2), 4

    subst in pt—Crim Justice and Immigration, 2008 c 4, s 145, sch 25 paras 10, 13(4)

    rep in pt—Legal Aid, Sentencing and Punishment of Offenders, 2012 c 10, sch 22 para 3(3)

s 219A added—Legal Aid, Sentencing and Punishment of Offenders, 2012 c 10, sch 22 para 5

s 220 rep—Legal Aid, Sentencing and Punishment of Offenders, 2012 c 10, sch 22 para 6

s 221 am—Crim Justice and Immigration, 2008 c 4, s 145, sch 25 paras 10, 15(1)-(4); Legal Aid, Sentencing and Punishment of Offenders, 2012 c 10, sch 22 paras 7, 8, 26

    rep in pt—Crim Justice and Immigration, 2008 c 4, ss 145, 149, sch 25 paras 10, 15(1), (5), sch 28 pt 2

s 221A added—Legal Aid, Sentencing and Punishment of Offenders, 2012 c 10, sch 22 para 9

s 222 rep—Legal Aid, Sentencing and Punishment of Offenders, 2012 c 10, sch 22 para 10

s 223 am—Crim Justice and Immigration, 2008 c 4, s 145, sch 25 paras 10, 17(1)-(3); Legal Aid, Sentencing and Punishment of Offenders, 2012 c 10, sch 22 paras 27, 28

    rep in pt—Crim Justice and Immigration, 2008 c 4, ss 145, 149, sch 25 paras 10, 17(1), (4), sch 28 pt 2

s 224 subst—Legal Aid, Sentencing and Punishment of Offenders, 2012 c 10, sch 22 para 29

s 224A added—Crim Justice and Cts, 2015 c 2, sch 1 para 8

s 227A added—Legal Aid, Sentencing and Punishment of Offenders, 2012 c 10, sch 26 para 24

s 228 am—Crim Justice and Immigration, 2008 c 4, s 145, sch 25 paras 10, 18; Legal Aid, Sentencing and Punishment of Offenders, 2012 c 10, sch 22 para 30

2006

c 52 *continued*

ss 232A-232G added (pt prosp)—Armed Forces, 2011 c 18, s 17(1)

s 238 am—Coroners and Justice, 2009 c 25, s 144, sch 17 para 7(2)(b)(3)

    rep in pt—Coroners and Justice, 2009 c 25, ss 144, 178, sch 17 para 7(2)(a), sch 23 pt 5

s 237 am—Crim Justice and Immigration, 2008 c 4, s 145, sch 25 paras 10, 19; Legal Aid, Sentencing and Punishment of Offenders, 2012 c 10, sch 22 para 31, sch 26 para 25

s 239 am—Legal Aid, Sentencing and Punishment of Offenders, 2012 c 10, sch 26 para 26

s 241 am—Legal Aid, Sentencing and Punishment of Offenders, 2012 c 10, s 65(11)-(14)

ss 242, 243 appl (mods)—SI 2009/2041, rule 161

s 246 mod—Courts-Martial (Appeals), 1968 c 20, sch 1 para 4

    am—Legal Aid, Sentencing and Punishment of Offenders, 2012 c 10, sch 13 para 2(2)(3)(b), sch 22 para 32; Offender Rehabilitation, 2014 c 11, sch 6 para 3

s 247 mod—Courts-Martial (Appeals), 1968 c 20, sch 1 para 4

    am—Legal Aid, Sentencing and Punishment of Offenders, 2012 c 10, sch 13 para 3(2)(a)(3)(4)

    rep in pt—Legal Aid, Sentencing and Punishment of Offenders, 2012 c 10, sch 13 para 3(2)(b)

s 248 appl (mods)—SI 2009/2041, rule 161

s 252 appl —SI 2009/2041, rule 161

    rep in pt—Legal Aid, Sentencing and Punishment of Offenders, 2012 c 10, s 64(4)(a)

s 253 appl —SI 2009/2041, rule 161

    rep in pt—Legal Aid, Sentencing and Punishment of Offenders, 2012 c 10, s 64(4)(b)

s 254 am—(prosp) Crim Justice and Immigration, 2008 c 4, s 145, sch 25 paras 10, 25

s 256 am—Crim Justice and Immigration, 2008 c 4, s 145, sch 25 paras 10, 20; Legal Aid, Sentencing and Punishment of Offenders, 2012 c 10, sch 22 para 33(2)(3)

s 257 am—Health and Social Care, 2012 c 7, sch 15 para 57

s 258 am—Health and Social Care, 2012 c 7, s 38(5)(f)

s 259 am—Coroners and Justice, 2009 c 25, s 177, sch 21 para 89

s 260 am—Crim Justice and Immigration, 2008 c 4, s 145, sch 25 paras 10, 21; Legal Aid, Sentencing and Punishment of Offenders, 2012 c 10, sch 22 para 34(2)(3), sch 26 para 27

s 261 am—Crim Justice and Immigration, 2008 c 4, s 145, sch 25 paras 10, 22; Legal Aid, Sentencing and Punishment of Offenders, 2012 c 10, sch 22 para 35, sch 26 para 28

s 263 am—Coroners and Justice, 2009 c 25, s 144, sch 17 para 11

s 266 am—Crime and Cts, 2013 c 22, sch 16 para 38

s 267 am—SI 2013/3234, art 2

ss 269A-269C added—Armed Forces, 2011 c 18, s 16(1)

s 270 am—Crim Justice and Immigration, 2008 c 4, s 145, sch 25 paras 10, 26(1), (2); Armed Forces, 2011 c 18, sch 3 para 20(1); Crime and Cts, 2013 c 22, sch 16 para 34

s 270A added—Armed Forces, 2011 c 18, sch 3 para 20(2)

    am—Prevention of Social Housing Fraud, 2013 c 3, sch para 31

s 273 am—Crim Justice and Immigration, 2008 c 4, s 145, sch 25 paras 10, 23, 28; Legal Aid, Sentencing and Punishment of Offenders, 2012 c 10, sch 22 para 36, sch 26 para 29

s 276 am—Crim Justice and Immigration, 2008 c 4, s 145, sch 25 paras 10, 29, 34

ss 276A, 276B added—Crim Justice and Immigration, 2008 c 4, s 145, sch 25 paras 10, 30, 34

s 277 am—Armed Forces, 2011 c 18, s 18

s 280 saving—SI 2009/1209, rule 42

s 284 am—Crime and Cts, 2013 c 22, sch 16 para 36

s 285 ext—Crim Appeal, 1995 c 35, s 12B(2)(3)

s 286 mod—Crim Justice and Cts, 2015 c 2, sch 14 para 9

s 293 rep—Armed Forces, 2011 c 18, s 13(2), sch 5

s 295 mod—SI 2009/826, reg 3

s 299 ext —SI 1999/1736, sch 8

s 301 am—Armed Forces, 2011 c 18, sch 3 para 21

Pt 13 Ch 1 (ss 305-308) am—Armed Forces, 2011 c 18, sch 4 para 10

s 305 am—Armed Forces, 2011 c 18, sch 4 para 11(a)

    rep in pt —Armed Forces, 2011 c 18, sch 4 para 11(b), sch 5

s 306 rep —Armed Forces, 2011 c 18, s 11(2), sch 5

2006

c 52 *continued*

s 307 rep —Armed Forces, 2011 c 18, s 11(2), sch 5

s 308 am—Armed Forces, 2011 c 18, sch 4 para 12(2)(3)(a)(6)

    rep in pt—Armed Forces, 2011 c 18, sch 4 para 12(3)(b)-(d)(4)(5), sch 5

s 314 appl (mods)—Visiting Forces, 1952 c 67, s 13

    ext —SI 1999/1736, sch 8 (amended by SI 2009/2054, art 2, sch 1)

s 315 appl (mods)—Visiting Forces, 1952 c 67, s 13

s 316 appl (mods)—Visiting Forces, 1952 c 67, s 13

    ext —SI 1999/1736, sch 8 (amended by SI 2009/2054, art 2, sch 1)

Pt 13 Ch 4A (ss 321A-321B) added —Armed Forces, 2011 c 18, s 4

s 322 am—Armed Forces, 2011 c 18, s 16(2); Legal Aid, Sentencing and Punishment of

    Offenders, 2012 c 10, s 78(5)

s 323 appl—Crim Justice, 2003 c 44, s 94(1)

s 325 am—Armed Forces, 2011 c 18, sch 4 para 13

s 332 am—Armed Forces, 2011 c 18, s 19

ss 334-339 rep—Armed Forces (Service Complaints and Financial Assistance), 2015 c 19, s

    2(2)

s 340 excl—SI 2009/835, reg 2

Pt 14A (ss 340A-340O) added—Armed Forces (Service Complaints and Financial

    Assistance), 2015 c 19, s 2(1)

ss 343A, 343B added—Armed Forces, 2011 c 18, s 2

s 344 mod—SI 1999/1736, art 18 (amended by SI 2009/2054, art 2, sch 1)

s 365 am—(prosp) Armed Forces, 2011 c 18, s 21

    excl—SI 2013/1852, art 27(1)

s 365A added—Armed Forces, 2011 c 18, s 5

s 365B added—Armed Forces (Service Complaints and Financial Assistance), 2015 c 19, s

    1(1)

s 366 rep—Armed Forces (Service Complaints and Financial Assistance), 2015 c 19, s 1(3)

s 371A added—Armed Forces, 2011 c 18, s 23(1)

s 373 appl—Police and Crim Evidence, 1984 c 60, s 113(14)

    am—Crim Justice and Immigration, 2008 c 4, s 145, sch 25 paras 10, 31; Armed

        Forces, 2011 c 18, sch 4 para 14; Crim Justice and Cts, 2015 c 2, sch 14 para 7;

        Armed Forces (Service Complaints and Financial Assistance), 2015 c 19, sch

        para 10

    rep in pt—Legal Aid, Sentencing and Punishment of Offenders, 2012 c 10, sch 13 para

        4

s 374 transtl provns—SI 2008/1651, reg 20, sch 3

    am—Legal Aid, Sentencing and Punishment of Offenders, 2012 c 10, sch 22 para 37;

        Armed Forces (Service Complaints and Financial Assistance), 2015 c 19, sch

        para 11(b)

    rep in pt—Armed Forces (Service Complaints and Financial Assistance), 2015 c 19,

        sch para 11(a)

s 375 rep in pt—Armed Forces, 2011 c 18, sch 3 para 22, sch 5

    am—SI 2013/602, sch 2 para 56

s 376 appl—Police and Crim Evidence, 1984 c 60, s 113(12A); SI 1978/1908 (NI 27), art

    4(1A)

s 378 ext—SI 2009/3215, art 5; 2010/764, art 5; 2010/765, art 5

s 380 am—Armed Forces, 2011 c 18, sch 3 para 23, sch 5

    rep in pt—Armed Forces, 2011 c 18, sch 4 para 15, sch 5

s 382 subst —Armed Forces, 2011 c 18, s 1

s 384 appl—Crim Appeal, 1995 c 35, s 33(6); Armed Forces, 1991 c 62, s 24(4); Crim

    Justice, 2003 c 44, s 337(12A)

    mod—Legal Aid, Sentencing and Punishment of Offenders, 2012 c 10, s 153(4)

    am—SI 2012/2404, sch 2 para 59(2)

s 385 excl—Crim Justice and Cts, 2015 c 2, s 96(3)

sch 1 am—Crime and Cts, 2013 c 22, sch 22 para 17

sch 2 am—Serious Crime, 2007 c 27, s 60, sch 5 paras 7, 13; Crim Justice and Immigration,

    2008 c 4, s 148, sch 26 para 82; Coroners and Justice, 2009 c 25, s 177, sch 21

    para 64; Bribery, 2010 c 23, s 17, sch 1 para 11; Legal Aid, Sentencing and

    Punishment of Offenders, 2012 c 10, sch 26 para 30(2)(3), sch 27 para 11; Crim

    Justice and Cts, 2015 c 2, sch 14 para 8; Serious Crime, 2015 c 9, sch 4 para 75

    rep in pt—Bribery, 2010 c 23, s 17, sch 2

sch 2A added—Crim Justice and Cts, 2015 c 2, sch 14 para 3

sch 3A added—Armed Forces, 2011 c 18, s 14, sch 1

2006

c 52 sch 3A *continued*

rep in pt—Anti-social Behaviour, Crime and Policing, 2014 c 12, sch 11 para 81

sch 5 am—Crim Justice and Immigration, 2008 c 4, s 145, sch 25 paras 10, 32; Legal Aid, Sentencing and Punishment of Offenders, 2012 c 10, s 78(6)(8)(9); Offender Rehabilitation, 2014 c 11, sch 6 paras 5(2)(4)(6)(2)(a), 6(2)(3), 10, 11

rep in pt—Offender Rehabilitation, 2014 c 11, sch 6 para 5(3)

sch 6 rep in pt—Legal Aid, Sentencing and Punishment of Offenders, 2012 c 10, s 78(10)

sch 7 am—Crim Justice and Immigration, 2008 c 4, s 145, sch 25 paras 10, 33; Armed Forces, 2011 c 18, sch 3 para 24; Legal Aid, Sentencing and Punishment of Offenders, 2012 c 10, sch 9 para 18(2)(5); Offender Rehabilitation, 2014 c 11, sch 6 para 7(2)(4)

rep in pt—Legal Aid, Sentencing and Punishment of Offenders, 2012 c 10, sch 9 para 18(3)(4), sch 10 para 41(5); Offender Rehabilitation, 2014 c 11, sch 6 para 7(3)

sch 8 rep in pt—(prosp) Armed Forces, 2011 c 18, sch 5

sch 9 am—SI 2012/2404, sch 2 para 59(3)

sch 15 am—Armed Forces, 2011 c 18, s 22

sch 16 rep in pt—Armed Forces, 2006 c 52, s 378, sch 17; Housing and Regeneration, 2008 c 17, s 321, sch 16; Crim Justice and Immigration, 2008 c 4, s 149, sch 28 pt 2; Coroners and Justice, 2009 c 25, s 178, sch 23 pt 1; Legal Aid, Sentencing and Punishment of Offenders, 2012 c 10, sch 10 para 41(6), sch 13 para 5; ibid, sch 25 pt 2

ext—SI 2009/3215, art 5; 2010/764, art 5; 2010/765, art 5

2nd session of 54th Parliament

c 53 **Northern Ireland (St Andrews Agreement)**

mod—(retrosp) NI (St Andrews Agreement), 2007 c 4, s 1

s 1 rep in pt—NI (St Andrews Agreement), 2006 c 53, s 2, sch 2 para 7(a), sch 3 para 3(a)

sch 1 rep—NI (St Andrews Agreement), 2006 c 53, s 2, sch 2 para 7(b)

mod—(retrosp) NI (St Andrews Agreement), 2007 c 4, s 1(1)(b)

sch 2 mod—(retrosp) NI (St Andrews Agreement), 2007 c 4, s 1(1)(b)

sch 3 rep—NI (St Andrews Agreement), 2006 c 53, s 2, sch 4 para 3

sch 4 am—Northern Ireland Assembly Members, 2010 c 16, s 1(13)

c 54 *Consolidated Fund*—rep Appropriation (No 2), 2008 c 8, s 4, sch 3

c 55 **Investment Exchanges and Clearing Houses**

s 3 rep—Investment, Exchange and Clearing Houses, 2006 c 55, s 3(8)

2007

c 1 *Appropriation*—rep Appropriation (No 2) 2009 c 9, s 4, sch 3

c 2 **Planning-gain Supplement (Preparations)**

c 3 **Income Tax**

appl—SI 2009/470, reg 57; Corporation Tax, 2010 c 4, ss 332(2), 817(b); Taxation (International and Other Provns), 2010 c 8, s 220(2)

appl (mods)—Corporation Tax, 2010 c 4, s 996(2)

excl—Corporation Tax, 2009 c 4, s 3; Taxation (International and Other Provns), 2010 c 8, ss 79(2)(a), 174(2)(b)

ext—Corporation Tax, 2009 c 4, s 969(4)(b)

mod—Corporation Tax, 2009 c 4, s 294(2)

saved—Income Tax Act 2007 c 3, s 564V(4)

s 1 am—Taxation (International and Other Provns), 2010 c 8, s 374, sch 8 paras 71, 72; Finance, 2012 c 14, sch 1 para 6(2)

s 2 am—Finance, 2008 c 9, s 25, sch 7 paras 74, 75; Finance, 2009 c 10, s 49, sch 25 para 9(5); (retrosp to 6.4.2008) ibid, s 52(2); Taxation (International and Other Provns), 2010 c 8, s 371, sch 7 paras 50-51, 68-69, 75-76; ibid, s 374, sch 8 paras 219-220, 237-238, 256-257, 271-272, 280, 281(b); Finance, 2012 c 14, sch 6 para 7; Finance, 2013 c 29, sch 29 para 17(b); Finance, 2014 c 26, sch 11 para 4; Finance, 2015 c 11, s 21(2)

rep in pt—Finance, 2009 c 10, s 49, sch 25 para 9(5); Taxation (International and Other Provns), 2010 c 8, ss 374, 378, sch 8 paras 271, 272, 280, 281(a), sch 10 pts 10, 11; Finance, 2013 c 29, s 15(4)(a); ibid, sch 29 para 17(a); SI 2013/2819, reg 37(2)

s 3 am—Taxation (International and Other Provns), 2010 c 8, s 371, sch 7 paras 68, 70

s 5 subst—Corporation Tax, 2009 c 4, s 1322, sch 1 para 700

s 6 rep in pt—Finance, 2008 c 9, s 5(1)-(3)(5); Finance, 2014 c 26, sch 38 para 2(a)

2007

c 3 s 6 *continued*

          am—Finance, 2009 c 10, s 6(1)-(3)(5), sch 2 paras 1, 2; Scotland, 2012 c 11, s 26(2);
               Finance, 2014 c 26, sch 38 para 2(b); (prosp) (cond) Wales, 2014 c 29, ss 9(2),
               14(1)(2)-(4)

s 6A added—Finance, 2014 c 26, sch 38 para 3

s 6B added (prosp) (cond)—Wales, 2014 c 29, ss 9(3), 14(1)(2)-(4)

s 7 subst—Finance, 2008 c 9, s 5, sch 1 paras 1, 2
          am—Finance, 2014 c 26, s 3(1)

s 8 am—Finance, 2009 c 10, s 6(5), sch 2 para 3; Finance, 2012 c 14, s 1(3)(a)

s 9 am—Finance, 2009 c 10, s 6(4); Finance, 2012 c 14, s 1(3)(b), (c)

s 10 rep in pt—Finance, 2008 c 9, s 5, sch 1 paras 1, 3(1)(2)(4)(6); SI 2011/2926, art 2;
               Finance, 2011 c 11, s 2(1); Finance, 2014 c 26, sch 38 para 4(a)
          am—Finance, 2008 c 9, s 5, sch 1 paras 1, 3; SI 2008/3023, arts 1,2; Finance, 2009 c
               10, ss 2(1), 6(5), sch 2 para 4; SI 2010/2879, art 2; Scotland, 2012 c 11, s 26(3);
               Finance, 2012 c 14, s 2(1); SI 2012/3047, art 2(a); Finance, 2013 c 29, s 3(1); SI
               2013/3088, art 2(a); Finance, 2014 c 26, s 2(1)(a), sch 38 para 4(b); (cond) ibid, s
               1(3)(a); (prosp) (cond) Wales, 2014 c 29, ss 9(4), 14(1)(2)-(4); Finance, 2015 c
               11, s 4(1)

s 11 rep in pt—Finance, 2008 c 9, s 5, sch 1 paras 1, 4
          appl—Corporation Tax, 2010 c 4, s 538(4)

s 11A added—Finance, 2014 c 26, sch 38 para 5

s 11B added (prosp) (cond)—Wales, 2014 c 29, ss 9(5), 14(1)(2)-(4

s 12 subst—Finance, 2008 c 9, s 5, sch 1 paras 1, 5
          am—SIs 2008/3023, arts 1, 3; 2010/2879, art 3; 2012/3047, art 2(b); 2013/3088, art
               2(b); (temp) Finance, 2014 c 26, s 3(2)

s 13 rep in pt—Finance, 2008 c 9, s 5, sch 1 paras 1, 6; ibid, s 68(1)(a)
          am—Finance, 2008 c 9, s 68(2); Finance, 2009 c 10, s 6(5), sch 2 para 5; Finance,
               2014 c 26, sch 38 para 6; (prosp) (cond) Wales, 2014 c 29, ss 9(6), 14(1)(2)-(4)

s 14 rep in pt—SI 2013/2819, reg 37(3)

s 16 am—Scotland, 2012 c 11, s 26(4); Finance, 2014 c 26, sch 38 para 7; (prosp) (cond)
               Wales, 2014 c 29, ss 9(7), 14(1)(2)-(4)

s 17 am—Finance, 2008 c 9, s 5, sch 1 paras 1, 8

s 18 excl—Taxes Management, 1970 c 9, s 18E(2)(c)

s 20 rep—Finance, 2008 c 9, s 5, sch 1 paras 1, 10

s 21 rep in pt—Finance, 2008 c 9, s 5, sch 1 paras 1, 11(1)(2)
          am—Finance, 2008 c 9, s 5, sch 1 paras 1, 11(1)(3)-(6); Finance, 2014 c 26, s 4(2)
          excl—Finance, 2009 c 10, s 2(2); Finance, 2011 c 11, s 2(2); Finance, 2012 c 14, s
               2(2); Finance, 2013 c 29, s 3(2); Finance, 2014 c 26, ss 1(4)(a), 2(2)(a); (temp)
               ibid, s 3(3); Finance, 2015 c 11, s 4(2)

s 23 rep in pt—Finance, 2009 c 10, s 5, sch 1 para 6(o)(i)
          appl (mods)—Finance, 2009 c 10, s 23, s 72, sch 6 para 1(5)(a)(ii)(b)(ii), sch 35 para
               1(10)
          appl—Finance 2004 c 12, s 213A
          am—Finance, 2013 c 29, sch 3 para 2(2); Finance, 2014 c 26, sch 17 para 19

s 24 rep in pt—Finance, 2008 c 9, s 84, sch 27 para 27(1)(2); Finance, 2013 c 29, s 15(4)(b)
          am—SI 2013/2819, reg 37(4)

s 24A added—Finance, 2013 c 29, sch 3 para 1
          am—Finance, 2014 c 26, sch 11 para 5

s 25 rep in pt—Finance, 2008 c 9, s 84, sch 27 para 27(1)(3)
          appl (mods)—Finance, 2009 c 10, s 23, sch 6 para 6

s 26 rep in pt—Finance, 2009 c 10, s 5, sch 1 para 6(o)(ii); Taxation (International and
               Other Provns), 2010 c 8, ss 374, 378, sch 8 paras 71, 73(2)(3), sch 10 pt 1;
               Finance, 2012 c 14, sch 39 para 32(2)(a)
          am—Taxation (International and Other Provns), 2010 c 8, s 374, sch 8 paras 71, 73(4);
               Finance, 2012 c 14, sch 6 para 8; Finance, 2014 c 26, s 11(3), sch 11 para 6;
               Finance (No. 2), 2015 c 33, s 24(8)(9); SI 2015/1810, art 5(2)

s 27 rep in pt—Finance, 2009 c 10, s 5, sch 1 para 6(o)(ii); Finance, 2012 c 14, sch 39 para
               32(2)(a)
          am—Taxation (International and Other Provns), 2010 c 8, s 374, sch 8 paras 71, 74;
               Finance, 2012 c 14, sch 6 para 9; Finance, 2014 c 26, sch 11 para 7

s 28 am—Taxation (International and Other Provns), 2010 c 8, s 374, sch 8 paras 71, 75

s 29 am—(retrosp to 5.4.2007) SI 2009/2859, art 4; Taxation (International and Other
               Provns), 2010 c 8, s 374, sch 8 paras 71, 76; Finance, 2013 c 29, s 56(2); Finance,
               2014 c 26, sch 11 para 8

2007
c 3 *continued*

s 30 am—Finance, 2011 c 11, sch 3 para 8; ibid, sch 16 para 83; Finance, 2012 c 14, sch 1 para 6(3); SI 2015/1810, art 5(3)

s 31 rep in pt—Finance, 2008 c 9, s 5, sch 1 paras 1, 12
 am—Finance, 2014 c 26, s 11(4); SI 2015/1810, art 14(2)

s 32 am—Finance, 2007 c 11, s 26, sch 4 paras 4, 5, 21; Taxation (International and Other Provns), 2010 c 8, s 374, sch 8 paras 71, 77(4); Finance, 2013 c 29, s 56(3); Finance, 2014 c 26, sch 11 para 9
 rep in pt—Taxation (International and Other Provns), 2010 c 8, ss 374, 378, sch 8 paras 71, 77(1)-(3), sch 10 pt 1

s 33 am—Finance, 2014 c 26, s 11(5)

s 34 am—Finance, 2008 c 9, s 25, sch 7 paras 74, 76; ibid, sch 21 paras 1, 3; Finance, 2015 c 11, s 5(3)
 rep in pt—Finance, 2014 c 26, s 2(3)

s 35 am—SI 2007/3481, art 2; Finance, 2008 c 9, s 2(1)(a); SI 2008/3023, art 4; Finance, 2009 c 10, ss 3(1), 4(1); SI 2010/2879, art 4; Finance, 2011 c 11, s 3(1); SI 2011/2926, art 3(a); Finance, 2012 c 14, ss 3(1), 4(2); SI 2012/3047, art 3(a); Finance, 2013 c 29, s 2(1); SI 2013/3088, art 3(a); Finance, 2014 c 26, ss 1(3)(b)2(1)(b)(4)(a)(b); Finance, 2015 c 11, s 5(1)(4)

s 36 rep—Finance, 2014 c 26, s 2(5)

s 37 rep—Finance, 2015 c 11, s 5(5)

s 38 am—SIs 2007/3481, art 2; 2008/3023, art 4; 2010/2879, art 4; 2011/2926, art 3(d); 2012/3047, art 3(b); 2013/3088, art 3(b); 2014/3273, art 2(a); Finance, 2015 c 11, s 2(1)(b); SI 2015/914, sch para 88(2)(4)
 rep in pt—SI 2015/914, sch para 88(3)

s 40 am—Finance, 2008 c 9, s 118, sch 39 paras 54, 55

s 41 rep in pt—Finance, 2012 c 14, s 4(5)

Pt 3 Ch. 3 (ss 42-55) heading am—Finance, 2014 c 26, s 11(6)

s 42 am—Finance, 2008 c 9, s 25, sch 7 paras 74, 77

s 43 am—SIs 2007/3481, art 2; 2008/3023, art 4; 2010/2879, art 4; 2011/2926, art 3(e); 2012/3047, art 3(c); 2013/3088, art 3(c); 2014/3273, art 2(b)(c)(e); Finance, 2015 c 11, s 2(1)(c)

s 45 am—SIs 2007/3481, art 2; 2008/3023, art 4; 2010/2879, art 4; 2011/2926, art 3(f)(h); 2012/3047, art 3(d)(f); 2013/3088, art 3(d)(f); Finance, 2015 c 11, ss 2(1)(d)(e), 5(6)
 rep in pt—SL(R), 2013 c 2, s 1, sch 1 pt 10(1); Finance, 2014 c 26, s 2(6)

s 46 am—SIs 2007/3481, art 2; 2008/3023, art 4; Finance, 2008 c 9, s 118, sch 39 paras 54, 56; SI 2010/2879, art 4; 2011/2926, art 3(g)(h); 2012/3047, art 3(e)(f); 2013/3088, art 3(e)(f); 2014/3273, art 2(d)(e); Finance, 2015 c 11, ss 2(1)(f)(g), 5(7)
 rep in pt—SL(R), 2013 c 2, s 1, sch 1 pt 10(1); Finance, 2014 c 26, s 2(7)

s 47 rep in pt—SL(R), 2013 c 2, s 1, sch 1 pt 10(1)

s 48 rep in pt—SL(R), 2013 c 2, s 1, sch 1 pt 10(1)

s 53 am—Finance, 2008 c 9, s 118, sch 39 paras 54, 57; Taxation (International and Other Provns), 2010 c 8, s 374, sch 8 paras 71, 78

s 55 am—Finance, 2015 c 11, s 3(4)

Pt 3 Ch. 3A (ss 55A-55E) added—Finance, 2014 c 26, s 11(2)

s 55B am—SI 2015/1810, art 14(3)
 rep in pt—Finance, 2015 c 11, s 5(8)

s 55C rep in pt—Finance, 2015 c 11, s 5(9)
 am—SI 2015/1810, art 14(4)

s 56 am—Finance, 2008 c 9, s 70(2); Finance, 2009 c 10, s 4(3); Finance, 2014 c 26, s 11(7)

s 57 excl—Finance, 2008 c 9, s 2(2)(a); Finance, 2009 c 10, s 3(2); Finance, 2011 c 11, s 3(2); Finance, 2012 c 14, s 3(2); Finance, 2013 c 29, s 2(2); Finance, 2014 c 26, ss 1(4)(b), 2(2)(b); Finance, 2015 c 11, s 5(2)
 am—Finance, 2009 c 10, s 4(3); Finance, 2012 c 14, s 4(6)(a)(i), (b); Finance, 2014 c 26, ss 2(8)(a), 4(3); Finance, 2015 c 11, ss 2(2), 5(10)(a); Finance (No. 2), 2015 c 33, s 3(2)
 rep in pt—Finance, 2012 c 14, s 4(6)(a)(ii); SL(R), 2013 c 2, s 1, sch 1 pt 10(1); Finance, 2014 c 26, s 2(8)(b); Finance, 2015 c 11, s 5(10)(b)(c)

s 57A added—Finance (No. 2), 2015 c 33, s 3(1)

s 58 am—Finance, 2011 c 11, sch 3 para 9; SI 2015/1810, art 14(5)

s 60 am—Finance, 2010 c 13, s 24, sch 3 para 2

2007
c 3 continued

ss 61-63 appl (mods)—Finance, 2009 c 10, s 23, sch 6 para 2(4)
s 64 am—Finance, 2008 c 9, s 60, sch 21 para 4; Finance, 2010 c 13, s 24, sch 3 para
    3(a)(b); Finance, 2013 c 29, sch 4 para 54(2)
   rep in pt—Finance, 2008 c 9, s 66(4)(l)(i); Finance, 2010 c 13, s 24, sch 3 para 3(c)
s 65 am—Finance, 2013 c 29, sch 3 para 2(3)(a)
ss 66-68 appl—Finance, 2009 c 10, s 23, sch 6 para 11(a)
s 69 appl—Finance, 2009 c 10, s 23, sch 6 para 11(a)
   am—Corporation Tax, 2010 c 4, s 1177, sch 1 paras 494, 495
s 70 appl—Finance, 2009 c 10, s 23, sch 6 para 11(a); Corporation Tax, 2010 c 4, s 51(4)
s 72 am—Finance, 2008 c 9, s 60, sch 21 para 5; Finance, 2010 c 13, s 24, sch 3 para
    4(a)(b); Finance, 2013 c 29, sch 4 para 54(3)
   rep in pt—Finance, 2008 c 9, s 66(4)(l)(ii); Finance, 2010 c 13, s 24, sch 3 para 4(c)
s 73 am—Finance, 2013 c 29, sch 3 para 2(3)(b)
s 74ZA added—Finance, 2010 c 13, s 24, sch 3 para 5
s 74A added—Finance, 2008 c 9, s 60, sch 21 paras 2, 6
s 74B rep—Finance, 2010 c 13, s 24, sch 3 para 6
s 74C added—Finance, 2008 c 9, s 60, sch 21 para 2
   appl—Finance, 2009 c 10, s 23, sch 6 para 11(b)
   am—Finance, 2010 c 13, s 24, sch 3 para 7
s 74D added—Finance, 2008 c 9, s 60, sch 21 para 2
   appl—Finance, 2009 c 10, s 23, sch 6 para 11(b)
   am—Finance, 2010 c 13, s 24, sch 3 para 8
s 74E added—Finance, 2013 c 29, sch 4 para 54(4)
s 75 appl—Finance, 2009 c 10, s 23, sch 6 para 11(c)
s 76 am—Finance, 2008 c 9, s 74, sch 24 paras 20, 21
   appl—Finance, 2009 c 10, s 23, sch 6 para 11(c)
s 77 appl—Finance, 2009 c 10, s 23, sch 6 para 11(c)
s 78 am—Finance, 2008 c 9, s 74, sch 24 paras 22, 24
   appl—Finance, 2009 c 10, s 23, sch 6 para 11(c)
s 79 appl—Finance, 2009 c 10, s 23, sch 6 para 11(c)
s 80 appl—Finance, 2009 c 10, s 23, sch 6 para 11(d)
   am—Taxation (International and Other Provns), 2010 c 8, s 374, sch 8 paras 192, 193
s 81 rep—Finance, 2010 c 13, s 24, sch 3 para 9
s 82 am—Finance, 2007 c 11, s 26, sch 4 paras 4, 6, 21
s 96 am—Finance, 2012 c 14, s 9(2)
s 98 appl—Finance, 2012 c 14, s 9(8)
s 98A added—Finance, 2012 c 14, s 9(3)
s 102 am—Finance, 2007 c 11, s 26, sch 4 paras 4, 7, 21; Finance, 2014 c 26, sch 17 para
    8(2)
s 103A added—Finance, 2007 c 11, s 26, sch 4 paras 4, 8, 21
s 103B added—Finance, 2007 c 11, s 26, sch 4 paras 4, 8, 21
    am—Finance, 2008 c 9, s 61(1)
s 103C added—Finance, 2007 c 11, s 26, sch 4 paras 1, 2
   appl (mods)—Finance, 2007 c 11, s 26, sch 4 para 3
s 103D added—Finance, 2007 c 11, s 26, sch 4 paras 4, 9, 21
s 104 rep in pt—Finance, 2007 c 11, s 26, sch 4 paras 4, 10(a), 21, sch 27
s 105 am—Finance, 2007 c 11, s 26, sch 4 paras 4, 11(a), 21
s 106 rep—Finance, 2007 c 11, s 26, sch 4 paras 4, 12, 21, sch 27
s 107 rep in pt—Finance, 2007 c 11, s 26, sch 4 paras 4, 10(b), 21, sch 27
s 108 am—Finance, 2007 c 11, s 26, sch 4 paras 4, 11(b), 21
s 110 rep in pt—Finance, 2007 c 11, s 26, sch 4 paras 4, 10(c), 21, sch 27
s 111 am—Finance, 2007 c 11, s 26, sch 4 paras 4, 11(c), 21
s 112 am—Finance, 2007 c 11, s 26, sch 4 paras 4, 13, 21
   rep in pt—Finance, 2007 c 11, s 114, sch 27 pt 2
s 113A added—Finance, 2007 c 11, s 26, sch 4 paras 2(1)-(4)
   appl (mods)—Finance, 2007 c 11, s 26, sch 4 para 3
s 114 am—Finance, 2007 c 11, s 26, sch 4 paras 4, 14, 21
s 115 rep in pt—Finance, 2007 c 11, s 26, sch 4 paras 4, 10(d), 21, sch 27
   am—Finance, 2007 c 11, s 26, sch 4 paras 4, 15, 21
s 116 rep—Finance, 2007 c 11, s 26, sch 4 paras 4, 16, 21, sch 27
s 116A added—Finance, 2014 c 26, sch 17 para 8(2)
s 117 am—Finance, 2010 c 13, s 25(2); Finance, 2011 c 11, sch 14 para 3(2); Finance,
    2012 c 14, s 10(2); Finance, 2014 c 26, sch 17 para 9(2)

2007
c 3 *continued*

s 120 am—Finance, 2010 c 13, s 25(3); Finance, 2012 c 14, s 10(3)
s 121 am—Finance, 2013 c 29, sch 3 para 2(3)(c)
s 125 am—Finance, 2012 c 14, s 9(4)
s 127 appl (mods)—Finance, 2009 c 10, s 23, sch 6 para 2(5)
    am—Finance, 2011 c 11, sch 14 para 3(3)
s 127ZA added—Finance, 2011 c 11, sch 14 para 3(4)
s 127A added—Finance, 2010 c 13, s 25(4)
s 127B added—Finance, 2012 c 14, s 10(4)
s 127C added—Finance, 2014 c 26, sch 17 para 9(3)
s 128 am—Finance, 2009 c 10, s 68(1)-(3)
s 129 am—Finance, 2013 c 29, sch 3 para 2(3)(d)
s 133 am—Finance, 2013 c 29, sch 3 para 2(3)(e)
s 136 am—Corporation Tax, 2010 c 4, s 1177, sch 1 paras 494, 496
s 139 am—Corporation Tax, 2010 c 4, s 1177, sch 1 paras 494, 497
s 142 am—Finance, 2009 c 10, s 53, sch 28 para 8(a)
s 143 am—Finance, 2007 c 11, s 109, sch 26 para 12(1)(2)
s 146 am—Finance, 2007 c 11, s 51, sch 16 paras 11(6), 13
s 147 rep in pt—Finance, 2008 c 9, s 8, sch 2 paras 97, 98(1)(2)(a)
    am—Finance, 2008 c 9, s 8, sch 2 paras 97, 98(1)(2)(b)(3)
s 148 rep in pt—Finance, 2008 c 9, s 8, sch 2 paras 97, 99(1)-(3)
    am—Finance, 2008 c 9, s 8, sch 2 paras 97, 99(1)(4); Finance, 2013 c 29, sch 3 para
      2(4)
s 151 am—Finance, 2007 c 11, s 109, sch 26 para 12(1)(3); Corporation Tax, 2010 c 4, ss
      1177, 1180, sch 1 paras 494, 498, sch 2; Co-operative and Community Benefit
      Societies, 2014 c 14, sch 4 para 105
s 152 am—Finance, 2007 c 11, s 57(5)(9); Finance, 2009 c 10, s 69; SI 2009/3001, reg
      129(2); Finance, 2015 c 11, s 22(2)(a)-(g),(i)
    rep in pt—Finance, 2015 c 11, s 22(2)(h)
s 153 am—Finance, 2015 c 11, s 22(3)
s 154 am—Finance, 2015 c 11, s 22(4)
s 154A added—Finance, 2015 c 11, s 22(5)
s 155 am—Finance, 2008 c 9, s 118, sch 39 paras 54, 58; Finance, 2015 c 11, s 22(6)
s 157 rep in pt—Finance, 2012 c 14, sch 7 para 2
    am—Finance (No. 2), 2015 c 33, sch 5 para 2
s 158 am—Finance, 2008 c 9, s 5, sch 1 paras 1, 13; ibid, s 31(1); Finance, 2011 c 11, s
      42(2); Finance, 2012 c 14, sch 7 para 3(1)
    rep in pt—Finance, 2009 c 10, s 27, sch 8 para 6
s 161 rep in pt—Finance, 2008 c 9, s 8, sch 2 para 54
s 164A added—Finance (No. 2), 2015 c 33, sch 5 para 4
s 166 am—Finance (No. 2), 2015 c 33, sch 5 para 5
s 162 am—Finance (No. 2), 2015 c 33, sch 5 para 3
s 169 am—Finance, 2012 c 14, sch 6 para 10
s 170 am—Corporation Tax, 2010 c 4, s 1177, sch 1 paras 494, 499
    rep in pt—Finance, 2012 c 14, sch 7 para 4
s 172 am—(saving) Finance, 2007 c 11, s 51, sch 16 paras 5(1)(2)(5); Finance, 2012 c 14,
      sch 6 para 11; ibid, sch 7 para 5; Finance (No. 2), 2015 c 33, sch 5 para 6(a)(b),
      (d)
    rep in pt—Finance (No. 2), 2015 c 33, sch 5 para 6(c)
s 173 am—Finance, 2012 c 14, sch 7 para 6; Finance (No. 2), 2015 c 33, sch 5 para 7
s 173A added —(saving) Finance, 2007 c 11, s 51, sch 16 paras 5(1)(3)(5)
    am—Finance, 2012 c 14, sch 7 para 7(2), (3)(b); ibid, sch 6 para 12
    rep in pt—Finance, 2012 c 14, sch 7 para 7(3)(a)
s 173AA, 173AB added—Finance (No. 2), 2015 c 33, sch 5 para 8
s 173B added—Finance, 2012 c 14, sch 6 para 13
s 173B rep—Finance (No. 2), 2015 c 33, sch 5 para 9
s 174 am—Finance (No. 2), 2015 c 33, sch 5 para 10
s 175 am—Finance, 2009 c 10, s 27, sch 8 para 7; Finance, 2012 c 14, sch 7 para 8; Finance
      (No. 2), 2015 c 33, sch 5 para 11(2)
s 175A added—Finance (No. 2), 2015 c 33, sch 5 para 12
s 178A added—Finance, 2012 c 14, sch 7 para 9
s 179 rep in pt—Finance (No 3), 2010 c 33, s 5, sch 2 para 1(2); Finance, 2012 c 14, sch 7
      para 10

2007
c 3 *continued*

s 180 am—(saving) Income Tax, 2007 c 3, s 51, sch 16 paras 2(1)(2)(4); Finance (No 3), 2010 c 33, s 5, sch 2 para 1(3)
ss 180A, 180B added—Finance (No 3), 2010 c 33, s 5, sch 2 para 1(4)
s 184 am—Finance, 2007 c 11, s 109, sch 26 para 12(1)(4)
s 186 am—Finance, 2012 c 14, sch 7 para 11
s 186A added—(saving) Income Tax, 2007 c 3, s 51, sch 16 paras 2(1)(3)(4)
    am—Finance, 2012 c 14, sch 7 para 12; Children and Families, 2014 c 6, sch 7 para 70; Finance (No. 2), 2015 c 33, sch 5 para 13
s 190 am—Finance, 2007 c 11, s 51, sch 16 paras 16(2), 18; Corporation Tax, 2010 c 4, s 1177, sch 1 paras 494, 500
s 191A added—Finance (No 3), 2010 c 33, s 5, sch 2 para 1(5)
s 192 am—Finance, 2008 c 9, s 32, sch 11 paras 4, 5, 11; Finance, 2012 c 14, sch 7 para 13; Finance, 2014 c 26, s 56(2); Finance (No. 2), 2015 c 33, s 27(1)
s 195 am—Finance, 2007 c 11, s 51, sch 16 paras 11(7), 13
    rep in pt—Finance, 2007 c 11, s 114, sch 27 pt 2
    appl (mods)—Corporation Tax, 2010 c 4, s 79(7)(9)
s 196A added —Finance, 2008 c 9, s 32, sch 11 paras 4, 6, 11
s 196B added—Finance, 2008 c 9, s 32, sch 11 para 6
s 196C added —Finance, 2008 c 9, s 32, sch 11 para 11
s 198A added—Finance, 2012 c 14, sch 7 para 14
    am—Finance, 2014 c 26, s 56(3); Co-operative and Community Benefit Societies, 2014 c 14, sch 4 para 106; Finance, 2015 c 11, sch 6 para 3
    rep in pt—Finance, 2015 c 11, sch 6 para 4(1), 10(2)
s 198B added—Finance, 2014 c 26, s 56(4)
    rep in pt—Finance, 2015 c 11, sch 6 para 4(2), 10(3)
s 199 am—Corporation Tax, 2010 c 4, s 1177, sch 1 paras 494, 501; Finance, 2012 c 14, sch 7 para 15
s 200 rep—Finance (No. 2), 2015 c 33, sch 5 para 14
s 209 am—Finance, 2008 c 9, s 5, sch 1 paras 1, 14; Finance, 2011 c 11, s 42(3)(a); Finance, 2012 c 14, sch 7 para 17
s 210 am—Finance, 2008 c 9, s 5, sch 1 paras 1, 15; Finance, 2011 c 11, s 42(3)(b)
s 213 am—Finance, 2008 c 9, s 5, sch 1 paras 1, 16; Finance, 2011 c 11, s 42(3)(c)
s 220 am—Finance, 2008 c 9, s 5, sch 1 paras 1, 17; Finance, 2011 c 11, s 42(3)(d)
s 224 am—Finance, 2008 c 9, s 5, sch 1 paras 1, 18; Finance, 2011 c 11, s 42(3)(e); Finance (No. 2), 2015 c 33, sch 5 para 15
s 229 am—Finance, 2008 c 9, s 5, sch 1 paras 1, 19; Finance, 2011 c 11, s 42(3)(f)
s 230 am—SI 2008/954, arts 38, 39
    rep in pt—SI 2008/954, arts 38, 39
s 232 am—Corporation Tax, 2010 c 4, s 1177, sch 1 paras 494, 502
s 237 rep in pt—Finance, 2008 c 9, s 118, sch 39 paras 54, 59(1)(2)
    am—Finance, 2008 c 9, s 118, sch 39 paras 54, 59(1)(2)(b)(3)
s 239 am—(saving) Finance, 2007 c 11, s 51, sch 16 paras 5(1)(4)(5); Finance, 2009 c 10, s 105(1)(2)(a)(b)(3); Finance, 2012 c 14, sch 7 para 18
    rep in pt—Finance, 2009 c 10, s 105(1)(2)(c)
s 241 am—Finance (No. 2), 2015 c 33, sch 5 para 16
s 243 am—Finance, 2012 c 14, sch 7 para 19
s 246 am—Finance, 2012 c 14, sch 6 para 14
s 247 am—Finance (No. 2), 2015 c 33, sch 5 para 17
s 249 am—Finance, 2007 c 11, s 51, sch 16 paras 11(8), 13
s 251 am—Finance, 2007 c 11, s 51, sch 16 para 19
    rep in pt—Finance, 2012 c 14, sch 7 para 20
s 251A added—Finance (No. 2), 2015 c 33, sch 5 para 18
s 252A added—Finance (No. 2), 2015 c 33, sch 5 para 19
s 256A added—Finance, 2011 c 11, s 42(4)
s 257 am—Finance, 2007 c 11, s 109, sch 26 para 12(1)(5); Corporation Tax, 2010 c 4, s 1177, sch 1 paras 494, 503; Finance, 2012 c 14, sch 7 para 21
Pt 5A (ss 257A-257HJ) added—Finance, 2012 c 14, sch 6 para 1
    appl—Taxation of Chargeable Gains, 1992 c 12, sch 5BB para 8(4)
s 257A am—Finance, 2014 c 26, s 54(2)
    rep in pt—Finance, 2014 c 26, s 54(3)
s 257DG am—Finance, 2013 c 29, s 56(4)
s 257DJ am—Children and Families, 2014 c 6, sch 7 para 71
s 257EA appl—Taxation of Chargeable Gains, 1992 c 12, sch 5BB para 3(1)

2007

c 3 *continued*

Pt 5B (ss 257J-257TE) added—Finance, 2014 c 26, sch 11 para 1
s 257MQ rep in pt—Finance, 2015 c 11, sch 6 para 13(2)
s 257MS rep—Finance, 2015 c 11, sch 6 para 13(3)
s 257MW added—Finance, 2015 c 11, sch 6 para 1
ss 257P-257PD appl (mods)—Taxation of Chargeable Gains, 1992 c 12, sch 8B para 8(1))
s 257PE mod—Taxation of Chargeable Gains, 1992 c. 12, sch 8B para 8(2))
s 261 am—Finance (No. 2), 2015 c 33, sch 6 para 2
s 264A added—Finance, 2014 c 26, sch 10 para 2(1)
s 270 am—Finance, 2014 c 26, sch 10 para 1(1)
s 271 rep in pt—SI 2009/2035, art 2, sch
s 274 am—Finance, 2007 c 11, ss 51, 109, sch 16 para 20(1)(2)(4)(5), sch 26 para 12(1)(6);
　　　　Finance (No 3), 2010 c 33, s 5, sch 2 para 2(2); Finance, 2012 c 14, sch 8 para 2;
　　　　Finance (No. 2), 2015 c 33, sch 6 para 3
　　rep in pt—Finance, 2007 c 11, s 114, sch 27 pt 2
s 275 am—Finance (No 3), 2010 c 33, s 5, sch 2 para 2(3)
s 276 am—Corporation Tax, 2009 c 4, s 1322, sch 1 para 701; SI 2009/2860, art 5
s 278 am—Finance (No 3), 2010 c 33, s 5, sch 2 para 2(4)
s 280 am—Finance (No 3), 2010 c 33, s 5, sch 2 para 2(5)
s 280A added—Finance, 2007 c 11, s 51, sch 16 para 20(1)(3)(4)(5)
s 280B added—Finance, 2012 c 14, sch 8 para 3
　　　　am—Finance (No. 2), 2015 c 33, sch 6 para 4(5); Finance (No. 2), 2015 c 33, sch 6
　　　　　para 4
ss 280C, 280D added—Finance (No. 2), 2015 c 33, sch 6 para 5
s 281 am—Finance, 2014 c 26, sch 10 para 3(2)(3)
　　　　mod—Finance, 2014 c 26, sch 10 para 3(5)
　　　　appl (mods)—SI 2004/2199 reg 13(10) (added by 2015/361, reg 2(2))
s 284 am—Finance, 2007 c 11, s 51, sch 16 para 21, sch 27; Finance, 2014 c 26, sch 10
　　　　para 5
s 285 am—Finance (No 3), 2010 c 33, s 5, sch 2 para 2(6)
s 286 am—(saving) Finance, 2007 c 11, s 51, sch 16 paras 3(1)(2)(5)(6), 6(1)(2)(4)(5);
　　　　Finance (No 3), 2010 c 33, s 5, sch 2 para 2(7); Finance, 2012 c 14, sch 6 para
　　　　15; ibid, sch 8 para 4; Finance (No. 2), 2015 c 33, sch 6 para 6(2),(3)(a)(b)(d)(e)
　　rep in pt—Finance (No. 2), 2015 c 33, sch 6 para 6(3)(c)
ss 286A, 286B added—Finance (No 3), 2010 c 33, s 5, sch 2 para 2(8)
s 287 am—Finance, 2012 c 14, sch 8 para 5(2)-(5)
　　rep in pt—Finance, 2012 c 14, sch 8 para 5(6)
s 289 am—Finance (No 3), 2010 c 33, s 5, sch 2 para 2(9)
s 291 am—Finance (No 3), 2010 c 33, s 5, sch 2 para 2(10)(a)
　　rep in pt—Finance (No 3), 2010 c 33, s 5, sch 2 para 2(10)(b)
s 292A added—(saving) Finance, 2007 c 11, s 51, sch 16 para 6(1)(3)-(5)
　　　　am—Finance, 2012 c 14, sch 8 para 6(2), (3)(b); ibid, sch 6 para 16; Finance (No.
　　　　　2), 2015 c 33, sch 6 para 7
　　rep in pt—Finance, 2012 c 14, sch 8 para 6(3)(a), (4)
ss 292AA, 292AB added—Finance (No. 2), 2015 c 33, sch 6 para 8
s 292B added—Finance, 2012 c 14, sch 6 para 17
　　rep—Finance (No. 2), 2015 c 33, sch 6 para 9
s 293 am—Finance, 2009 c 10, s 27, sch 8 para 9(1)(2); Finance, 2012 c 14, sch 8 para 7;
　　　　Finance (No. 2), 2015 c 33, sch 6 para 10
　　rep in pt—Finance, 2009 c 10, s 27, sch 8 para 9(1)(3)
s 294A added—Finance (No. 2), 2015 c 33, sch 6 para 11
s 295 am—Finance, 2007 c 11, s 109, sch 26 para 12(1)(7)
s 297 am—Finance, 2012 c 14, sch 8 para 8
s 297A added—(saving) Income Tax, 2007 c 3, s 51, sch 16 para 3(1)(3)(5)(6)
　　　　am—Finance, 2012 c 14, sch 8 para 9; Children and Families, 2014 c 6, sch 7 para
　　　　　72; Finance (No. 2), 2015 c 33, sch 6 para 12
s 297B added—Finance (No. 2), 2015 c 33, sch 6 para 13
s 299A added—Finance, 2012 c 14, sch 8 para 10
s 300 am—Finance (No 3), 2010 c 33, s 5, sch 2 para 2(11)
s 301 am—Finance, 2007 c 11, s 51, sch 16 paras 17, 18; Corporation Tax, 2010 c 4, s
　　　　1177, sch 1 paras 494, 504
s 302A added—Finance (No 3), 2010 c 33, s 5, sch 2 para 2(12)
s 303 am—Finance, 2008 c 9, s 32, sch 11 paras 7, 8, 12; Finance, 2014 c 26, s 56(5);
　　　　Finance (No. 2), 2015 c 33, s 27(2)

2007
c 3 s 303 *continued*
   rep in pt—Finance, 2012 c 14, sch 8 para 11
  s 306 am—Finance, 2007 c 11, s 51, sch 16 paras 12, 13, sch 27
  s 307A added—Finance, 2008 c 9, s 32, sch 11 para 7
  s 307B added—Finance, 2008 c 9, s 32, sch 11 para 9,
  s 307C added—Finance, 2008 c 9, s 32, sch 11 para 12
  s 309A added—Finance, 2012 c 14, sch 8 para 12
   am—Finance, 2014 c 26, s 56(6); Co-operative and Community Benefit Societies,
    2014 c 14, sch 4 para 107; Finance, 2015 c 11, sch 6 para 7
   rep in pt—Finance, 2015 c 11, sch 6 paras 8(1), 11(2)
  s 309B added—Finance, 2014 c 26, s 56(7)
   rep in pt—Finance, 2015 c 11, sch 6 paras 8(2), 11(3)
  s 310 am—Corporation Tax, 2010 c 4, s 1177, sch 1 paras 494, 505; Finance, 2012 c 14,
    sch 8 para 13
  s 311 rep—Finance (No. 2), 2015 c 33, sch 6 para 14
  s 312A added—Finance, 2012 c 14, sch 8 para 15
  s 313 am—Corporation Tax, 2010 c 4, s 1177, sch 1 paras 494, 506; Finance (No 3), 2010
    c 33, s 5, sch 2 para 2(13)(a)(b); Finance, 2012 c 14, sch 8 para 16; Finance
    (No. 2), 2015 c 33, sch 6 para 15
   rep in pt—Finance (No 3), 2010 c 33, s 5, sch 2 para 2(13)(a)
  s 322 am—Finance, 2014 c 26, sch 10 para 4
  s 326 am—Finance (No. 2), 2015 c 33, sch 6 para 16
  s 326A added—Finance (No. 2), 2015 c 33, sch 6 para 17
  s 327 am—(saving) Finance, 2007 c 11, s 51, sch 16 paras 3(1)(4)(5)(6), sch 27; Finance
    (No. 2), 2015 c 33, sch 6 para 18
  s 330 rep in pt—SI 2009/2035, art 2, sch
  s 330A added—Finance, 2014 c 26, sch 10 para 5
  s 330B added—Finance (No. 2), 2015 c 33, sch 6 para 19
  s 331A added—Finance (No. 2), 2015 c 33, sch 6 para 20
  s 332 am—Finance, 2009 c 10, s 44, sch 22 para 11(5); Corporation Tax, 2010 c 4, s 1177,
    sch 1 paras 494, 507
  Pt VII (ss 333-382) appl (mods)—Finance, 2005 c 7, s 54A
  s 335 am—Finance, 2013 c 29, sch 27 para 2
  s 335A added—Finance, 2013 c 29, sch 27 para 3
  s 340 am—Corporation Tax, 2010 c 4, s 1177, sch 1 paras 494, 508
  s 341 am—SI 2009/56, art 3, sch 1 para 451; Corporation Tax, 2010 c 4, s 1177, sch 1
    paras 494, 509
  s 346 am—Corporation Tax, 2010 c 4, s 1177, sch 1 paras 494, 510
  s 348 rep in pt—Corporation Tax, 2010 c 4, ss 1177, 1181, sch 1 paras 494, 511(2)(a), sch
    3
   am—Corporation Tax, 2010 c 4, s 1177, sch 1 paras 494, 511(2)(b)-(3)(b)
  s 355 am—Corporation Tax, 2010 c 4, s 1177, sch 1 paras 494, 512
  s 356 rep in pt—Corporation Tax, 2010 c 4, ss 1177, 1181, sch 1 paras 494, 513(2), sch 3
   am—Corporation Tax, 2010 c 4, s 1177, sch 1 paras 494, 513(3)
  s 357 am—Finance, 2013 c 29, sch 27 para 4
  s 361 am—Corporation Tax, 2010 c 4, s 1177, sch 1 paras 494, 514; Finance, 2013 c 29,
    sch 27 para 5(2)
   rep in pt—Finance, 2013 c 29, sch 27 para 5(3)
  s 363 am—Corporation Tax, 2010 c 4, s 1177, sch 1 paras 494, 515
  s 364 rep in pt—Corporation Tax, 2010 c 4, ss 1177, 1181, sch 1 paras 494, 516, sch 3
  s 365 am—Corporation Tax, 2010 c 4, s 1177, sch 1 paras 494, 517
  s 368 am—Corporation Tax, 2010 c 4, s 1177, sch 1 paras 494, 518
  s 369 am—Corporation Tax, 2010 c 4, s 1177, sch 1 paras 494, 519
  s 372 am—Finance, 2008 c 9, s 118, sch 39 paras 54, 60
  s 372A added—Taxation (International and Other Provns), 2010 c 8, s 365, sch 2 paras 50,
    51
  s 372B added—Taxation (International and Other Provns), 2010 c 8, s 365, sch 2 paras 50,
    52
  s 372C added—Taxation (International and Other Provns), 2010 c 8, s 365, sch 2 paras 50,
    53
  s 372D added—Taxation (International and Other Provns), 2010 c 8, s 365, sch 2 paras 50,
    54
  s 373 am—Corporation Tax, 2010 c 4, s 1177, sch 1 paras 494, 520
  s 382 am—Finance, 2007 c 11, s 109, sch 26 para 12(1)(8)

2007

c 3 *continued*

s 383 am—Taxation (International and Other Provns), 2010 c 8, s 374, sch 8 paras 219, 221; Finance, 2013 c 29, sch 4 para 55(2); Finance, 2014 c 26, s 13(4)(a)

s 384 am—Finance, 2008 c 9, s 62, sch 22 para 21

s 384A added—Finance, 2009 c 10, s 61, sch 30 para 1(1)

s 384B added—Finance, 2013 c 29, sch 4 para 55(3)

s 392 am—Corporation Tax, 2010 c 4, s 1177, sch 1 paras 494, 521; Finance, 2014 c 26, s 13(2)(4)(b)(c), sch 11 para 10

s 393 rep in pt—Finance, 2007 c 11, s 114, sch 27 pt 6

s 393A added—Finance, 2014 c 26, s 13(3)

s 394 am—Corporation Tax, 2010 c 4, s 1177, sch 1 paras 494, 522

s 395 am—Corporation Tax, 2010 c 4, s 1177, sch 1 paras 494, 523

s 396 am—SI 2007/3506, art 3

s 397 am—Finance, 2007 c 11, s 109, sch 26 para 12(1)(9); Finance, 2014 c 26, s 14(1)

ss 399A, 399B added—Finance (No. 2), 2015 c 33, s 24(7)

s 413 am—Corporation Tax, 2010 c 4, s 1177, sch 1 paras 494, 524; Finance, 2011 c 11, sch 3 para 10; Finance, 2012 c 14, sch 15 para 8

s 414 am—Finance, 2008 c 9, s 5, sch 1 paras 1, 20; Finance, 2009 c 10, s 6(5), sch 2 para 6; SI 2015/1810, art 14(6)

s 415 am—SI 2015/1810, art 14(7)

s 416 am—Finance, 2010 c 13, s 32, sch 8 para 3(2)(a); Finance, 2014 c 26, sch 11 para 11; Finance, 2015 c 11, s 20(2)

    rep in pt—Finance, 2010 c 13, s 32, sch 8 para 3(2)(b)

s 418 am—Finance, 2007 c 11, s 60(1)(3); Finance, 2011 c 11, s 41(1)

s 422 rep—Finance, 2010 c 13, s 32, sch 8 para 3(3)

s 423 rep in pt—Finance, 2009 c 10, s 5, sch 1 para 6(o)(iii); Finance, 2012 c 14, sch 39 para 32(2)(b)(ii)

    am—Finance, 2012 c 14, sch 39 para 32(2)(b)(i)

s 424 am—SI 2009/2859, art 4(3); Taxation (International and Other Provns), 2010 c 8, s 374, sch 8 paras 71, 79

s 425 rep in pt—Finance, 2008 c 9, s 34, sch 12 paras 23, 24(a)

    am—Finance, 2008 c 9, s 34, sch 12 paras 23, 24(b); Taxation (International and Other Provns), 2010 c 8, s 374, sch 8 paras 71, 80

s 426 am—Corporation Tax, 2010 c 4, s 1177, sch 1 paras 494, 525

    rep in pt—Finance, 2012 c 14, s 50(2)(a)

s 428 am—Finance, 2015 c 11, s 20(3)

s 429 rep—Finance, 2012 c 14, s 50(1)

s 430 am—Corporation Tax, 2010 c 4, s 1177, sch 1 paras 494, 526; SI 2012/964, art 3(1) sch

    rep in pt—SI 2012/964, art 3(1) sch

s 431 am—Finance, 2011 c 11, sch 3 para 11

s 432 am—Finance, 2007 c 11, s 109, sch 26 para 12(1)(10); Corporation Tax, 2010 c 4, s 1177, sch 1 paras 494, 527

s 437 am—Finance, 2010 c 13, s 31, sch 7 para 2

s 438A added—Finance, 2010 c 13, s 31, sch 7 para 3

s 442 rep in pt—Finance, 2007 c 11, s 114, sch 27 pt 2

    am—Corporation Tax, 2010 c 4, s 1177, sch 1 paras 494, 528

s 443 rep in pt—Finance, 2007 c 11, s 114, sch 27 pt 2

    am—Corporation Tax, 2010 c 4, s 1177, sch 1 paras 494, 529

s 446 am—SI 2012/964, art 3(1) sch

    rep in pt—SI 2012/964, art 3(1) sch

Pt 8, Ch 4 (ss 447-452) rep in pt—Finance, 2013 c 29, s 15(4)(c)

s 448 rep in pt—Finance, 2008 c 9, s 66(4)(l)(iii); Finance, 2013 c 29, s 15(2)

s 449 rep in pt—Finance, 2008 c 9, s 66(4)(l)(iv); Finance, 2013 c 29, s 15(3)

s 450 appl—SI 2013/2819, reg 19(2)

s 451 rep—Finance, 2008 c 9, s 66(4)(l)(v)

s 459 rep—Finance, 2012 c 14, sch 39 para 32(1)

s 460 rep in pt—Finance, 2012 c 14, sch 39 para 32(2)(c)(i)

    am—Finance, 2012 c 14, sch 39 para 32(2)(c)(ii)

s 462 am—Finance (No 3), 2010 c 33, s 31, sch 14 para 3(2); Finance, 2014 c 26, sch 8 para 69

    rep in pt—SI 2013/2819, reg 37(5)

Pt 9, Ch 2 (ss 465-478) appl—Corporation Tax, 2010 c 4, s 1169(1)

s 465 rep in pt—Finance, 2013 c 29, sch 46 para 55

2007
c 3 *continued*

s 475 am—Finance, 2013 c 29, sch 45 para 103; ibid, sch 46 para 56
s 476 rep in pt—Finance, 2013 c 29, sch 46 para 57
s 479 am—Finance, 2010 c 13, s 30, sch 6 para 23(2); Finance, 2014 c 26, sch 8 para 70
    excl—SI 2013/2819, reg 12(3)(d)
s 480 am—Finance, 2007 c 11, s 65
s 481 am—Finance, 2010 c 13, s 30, sch 6 para 23(3); Finance, 2015 c 11, s 19(7)
s 482 am—Finance, 2007 c 11, s 55(2)(3); SI 2009/3001, reg 129(3); Finance, 2015 c 11, s
    19(8)
s 486 am—Finance, 2008 c 9, s 5, sch 1 paras 1, 21
s 488 am—Finance, 2014 c 26, sch 8 para 71(2)(3)(a)
    rep in pt—Finance, 2014 c 26, sch 8 para 71(3)(b)
s 489 am—Corporation Tax, 2009 c 4, s 1322, sch 1 para 702; Finance, 2014 c 26, sch 8
    para 72
s 490 rep in pt—Finance, 2014 c 26, sch 8 para 73
s 493 am —SI 2010/157, art 3
ss 494, 495 excl—SI 2013/2819, reg 12(4)
ss 496A, 496B added—SI 2010/157, art 3
s 496B excl—SI 2013/2819, reg 12(4)
s 497 am —SI 2010/157, art 3
s 498 am—Finance, 2007 c 11, s 56; Finance, 2008 c 9, s 5, sch 1 paras 1, 221)(2)(4)
    rep in pt—Finance, 2008 c 9, s 5, sch 1 paras 1, 22(1)(3)
s 500 appl—Corporation Tax, 2010 c 4, s 611(2)
s 503 appl—Corporation Tax, 2010 c 4, s 611(2)
s 504 rep—SI 2013/2819, reg 37(6)
s 504A added—SI 2009/23, art 5
s 505 rep —SI 2013/2819, reg 37(6)
s 505 rep in pt—Finance, 2008 c 9, s 66(4)(l)(vi)
    mod—Income and Corporation Taxes, 1988 c 1, s 339(3B)
s 506 rep—Finance, 2008 c 9, s 66(4)(l)(vii)
s 515 am—Finance, 2009 c 10, s 6(5), sch 2 para 7
s 518 am—Finance, 2010 c 13, s 32, sch 8 para 5(2)
s 519 rep—Finance, 2010 c 13, s 30, sch 6 para 23(4)
s 521 am—Finance, 2008 c 9, s 53, sch 19 para 9
s 521A added—Finance, 2010 c 13, s 32, sch 8 para 1(1)
s 527 am—Corporation Tax, 2010 c 4, s 1177, sch 1 paras 494, 530
    rep in pt—Taxation (International and Other Provns), 2010 c 8, ss 374, 378, sch 8
        paras 71, 81, sch 10 pt 1
s 529 am—SI 2011/1037, art 14(1)
s 530 am—Finance, 2007 c 11, s 105, sch 25 para 2
s 531 am—Finance, 2007 c 11, s 52, sch 17 para 18; Corporation Tax, 2010 c 4, s 1177,
    sch 1 paras 494, 531
s 532 am—SI 2013/2819, reg 37(7)
s 535 am—SI 2009/3001, reg 129(4)
s 538 rep in pt—SI 2009/56, art 3, sch 1 para 452; Finance, 2012 c 14, s 50(2)(b)
s 538A added—Finance, 2010 c 13, s 32, sch 8 para 5(3)
    am—Finance, 2012 c 14, sch 15 para 1
s 540 am—SI 2007/3506, art 3
s 543 rep in pt—Finance, 2011 c 11, sch 3 paras 12, 27(2)(3)
s 547 am—Finance, 2010 c 13, s 32, sch 8 para 2(1)
s 555 am—(as continuing to have effect) SI 2012/700, sch para 8
s 558 am—Charities, 2011 c 25, sch 7 para 126
s 559 am—Corporation Tax, 2010 c 4, s 1177, sch 1 paras 494, 536
Pt 10A (ss 564A-564Y) added—Taxation (International and Other Provns), 2010 c 8, s 365,
    sch 2 paras 1-26
s 564B am—Finance, 2012 c 14, sch 16 para 133; SI 2013/1881, sch para 12
s 564S appl—(S) Land and Buildings Transaction Tax (S), 2013 asp 11, sch 8 para 6
ss 565-595 rep —Finance, 2013 c 29, sch 29 para 18(a)
s 596 am—Finance, 2013 c 29, s 76(2)(3)
    rep in pt—Finance, 2013 c 29, sch 12 para 15(2)(a); ibid, sch 29 para 18(b)
ss 597-605 rep—Finance, 2013 c 29, sch 12 para 15(2)(b)
    am—Corporation Tax, 2010 c 4, s 1177, sch 1 paras 494, 544(a)(c)(d)
    rep in pt—Corporation Tax, 2010 c 4, ss 1177, 1181, sch 1 paras 494, 544(b), sch 3;
        Finance, 2013 c 29, sch 12 para 15(2)(c); ibid, sch 29 para 18(c)

2007
c 3 *continued*

ss 607-614 rep—Finance, 2013 c 29, sch 12 para 15(2)(d)
Pt 11ZA (ss 614ZA-614ZE) added —Finance, 2013 c 29, sch 29 para 1
Pt 11A added—Taxation (International and Other Provns), 2010 c 8, s 367, sch 3 paras 1-5
Pt 11A, Ch 1 (ss 614A, 614AA-614AC) added—Taxation (International and Other Provns),
     2010 c 8, s 367, sch 3 para 2
Pt 11A, Ch 2 (ss 614B, 614BA-614BY) added—Taxation (International and Other Provns),
     2010 c 8, s 367, sch 3 para 3
Pt 11A, Ch 3 (ss 614C, 614CA-614CD) added—Taxation (International and Other Provns),
     2010 c 8, s 367, sch 3 para 4
Pt 11A, Ch 4 (ss 614D, 614DA-614DG) added—Taxation (International and Other Provns),
     2010 c 8, s 367, sch 3 para 5
s 614DC appl —Taxation of Chargeable Gains 1992 c 12, s 37A
s 617 am—Finance, 2008 c 9, s 25, sch 7 para 157
s 620 am—SI 2007/1820, art 4
s 643 rep in pt—Finance, 2013 c 29, sch 46 para 58
s 644 rep—Finance, 2008 c 9, s 25, sch 7 para 158
s 647 am —Finance, 2013 c 29, sch 29 para 19
s 658 am —Finance, 2013 c 29, sch 29 para 20
s 668 am—Finance, 2008 c 9, s 118, sch 39 paras 54, 61
s 669 am—Finance, 2008 c 9, s 118, sch 39 paras 54, 62
s 670A added—Finance, 2008 c 9, s 25, sch 7 para 159
s 674 am—SI 2009/56, art 3, sch 1 para 454
s 680A rep in pt—Finance, 2008 c 9, s 5, sch 1 paras 50, 62(1)(2)(b)(3),(5)(b),(6),(8)
Pt 12A added—Taxation (International and Other Provns), 2010 c 8, s 368, sch 4 paras 1-5
Pt 12A, Ch 1 (ss 681A, 681AA-681AN) added—Taxation (International and Other Provns),
     2010 c 8, s 368, sch 4 para 2
Pt 12A, Ch 2 (ss 681B, 681BA-681BM) added—Taxation (International and Other Provns),
     2010 c 8, s 368, sch 4 para 3
Pt 12A, Ch 3 (ss 681C, 681CA-681CG) added—Taxation (International and Other Provns),
     2010 c 8, s 368, sch 4 para 4
Pt 12A, Ch 4 (ss 681D, 681DA-681DP) added—Taxation (International and Other Provns),
     2010 c 8, s 368, sch 4 para 5
s 681DP am—Finance, 2012 c 14, sch 16 para 134
ss 682-694 replaced (by ss 682-687) —Finance, 2010 c 13, s 38, sch 12 para 2
s 697 rep in pt—SI 2009/56, art 3, sch 1 para 456
s 698 am—SI 2009/56, art 3, sch 1 para 457
     rep in pt—Finance, 2010 c 13, s 38, sch 12 para 3
s 699 rep—Finance, 2010 c 13, s 38, sch 12 para 4
s 700 am—Finance, 2010 c 13, s 38, sch 12 para 5
s 701 am (heading am)—Finance, 2010 c 13, s 38, sch 12 para 6
s 703 rep—SI 2009/2035, art 2, sch
s 704 rep—SI 2009/56, art 3, sch 1 para 458
s 705 am—SI 2009/56, art 3, sch 1 para 459
ss 706-711 rep—SI 2009/56, art 3, sch 1 para 460
s 713 am—Finance, 2010 c 13, s 38, sch 12 para 7(2)
     rep in pt—Finance, 2010 c 13, s 38, sch 12 para 7(3)
Pt 13 Ch 2 (ss 714-751) appl—Income and Corporation Taxes, 1988 c 1, s 762ZA
     am—SI 2009/3001, reg 21
s 718 am—Finance, 2013 c 29, sch 10 para 2(2); ibid, sch 46 para 59
     rep in pt—Finance, 2013 c 29, sch 10 para 2(3)
s 720 am—Finance, 2008 c 9, s 25, sch 7 paras 163, 164; Finance, 2013 c 29, sch 10 para 3
     rep in pt—Finance, 2013 c 29, sch 46 para 60
s 721 am—Finance, 2013 c 29, sch 10 para 10(2)-(4); ibid, sch 46 para 61
     rep in pt—Finance, 2013 c 29, sch 10 para 10(5)
s 724 am—Finance, 2013 c 29, sch 10 para 11
s 725 am—Finance, 2012 c 14, sch 20 para 22; Finance, 2013 c 29, sch 10 para 12
s 726 subst—Finance, 2008 c 9, s 25, sch 7 paras 163, 165
     am—Finance, 2013 c 29, sch 10 para 13; ibid, sch 45 para 91(2); ibid, sch 46 para 19
s 727 am—Finance, 2008 c 9, s 25, sch 7 paras 163, 166; Finance, 2013 c 29, sch 10 para 4
     rep in pt—Finance, 2013 c 29, sch 46 para 62
s 728 am—Finance, 2013 c 29, sch 10 para 14(2)-(4); ibid, sch 46 para 63(2)(b)(3)(b)
     rep in pt—Finance, 2013 c 29, sch 10 para 14(5)
s 730 subst—Finance, 2008 c 9, s 25, sch 7 paras 163, 167

2007
c 3 s 730 *continued*

    am—Finance, 2013 c 29, sch 10 para 15; ibid, sch 45 para 91(3); ibid, sch 46 para 20

s 731 am—Finance, 2008 c 9, s 25, sch 7 paras 163, 168; Finance, 2013 c 29, sch 10 para 5

s 732 am—Finance, 2013 c 29, sch 46 para 64

s 734 am—Finance, 2008 c 9, s 25, sch 7 para 97; SI 2009/3001, reg 129(5)

s 735 subst—Finance, 2008 c 9, s 25, sch 7 paras 163, 169

    am—Finance, 2013 c 29, sch 45 para 91(4); ibid, sch 46 para 21

s 735A added—Finance, 2008 c 9, s 25, sch 7 paras 163, 169

s 736 am—Finance, 2013 c 29, sch 10 para 6

s 742A added—Finance, 2013 c 29, sch 10 para 7

s 743 am—Finance, 2013 c 29, sch 10 para 16(2)(3)

    rep in pt—Finance, 2013 c 29, sch 10 para 16(4)

s 744 am—Finance, 2013 c 29, sch 10 para 17(2)(3)(b)(4)

    rep in pt—Finance, 2013 c 29, sch 10 para 17(3)(a)

s 745 rep in pt—Finance, 2008 c 9, s 5, sch 1 paras 1, 24

    am—Finance, 2013 c 29, sch 10 para 18

s 746 am—Finance, 2013 c 29, sch 10 para 19

s 748 am—Legal Services, 2007 c 29, s 208, sch 21 paras 157, 158

s 749 am—Legal Services, 2007 c 29, s 208, sch 21 paras 157, 159

    rep in pt—Finance, 2013 c 29, sch 46 para 65(1)

s 751 am—SI 2009/56, art 3, sch 1 para 461; Finance, 2013 c 29, sch 10 para 8

s 771 am—Legal Services, 2007 c 29, s 208, sch 21 paras 157, 160

s 772 am—(retrosp to 5.4.2007) SI 2009/2859, art 4; Corporation Tax, 2010 c 4, s 1177,

    sch 1 paras 494, 547

s 777 am—(retrosp to 5.4.2007) SI 2009/2859, art 4

s 788 rep—SI 2009/2035, art 2, sch

s 792 am—Finance, 2007 c 11, s 26, sch 4 paras 4, 17, 21

s 809 am—Finance, 2007 c 11, s 26, sch 4 paras 4, 18, 21

Pt 13 Ch 5A (ss 809AZA-809AZG) added—Finance, 2009 c 10, s 49, sch 25 para 7

s 809AZE subst—Taxation (International and Other Provns), 2010 c 8, s 374, sch 8 para

    273

s 809AZF rep in pt—Finance, 2014 c 26, sch 17 para 23(2)(3)

Pt 13 Ch 5AA (ss 809AAZA-809AAZB) added—Finance, 2014 c 26, sch 17 para 24(1)

Pt 13, Ch 5B (ss 809BZA-809BZS) added—Taxation (International and Other Provns),

    2010 c 8, ss 369, 377, sch 5 para 2-6, sch 9

    restr—Finance, 2004 c 12, ss 196G(2)(3), 196I(5)(6)

s 809BZA am—Finance, 2012 c 14, sch 13 para 33(2)

s 809BZF am—Finance, 2012 c 14, sch 13 para 34

s 809BZH am—Finance, 2012 c 14, sch 13 para 35

s 809BZJ am—Finance, 2012 c 14, sch 13 para 36

Pt 13, Ch 5C (ss 809CZA-809CZC) added —Taxation (International and Other Provns),

    2010 c 8, ss 369, 377, sch 5 para 7, sch 9

s 809CZB am—SI 2013/2819, reg 37(8)

Pt 13 Ch. 5D (ss 809DZA-809DZB) added—Finance, 2014 c 26, sch 17 para 25(1)

s 809ZA added—Finance, 2008 c 9, s 55, sch 20 para 2(1)(3)

    am—Corporation Tax, 2010 c 4, s 1177, sch 1 paras 494, 548

s 809ZB rep—Corporation Tax, 2010 c 4, ss 1177, 1181, sch 1 paras 494, 549, sch 3

s 809ZC added—Finance, 2008 c 9, s 55, sch 20 para 2(1)(3)

    am—Corporation Tax, 2010 c 4, s 1177, sch 1 paras 494, 550

s 809ZD added—Finance, 2008 c 9, s 55, sch 20 para 2(1)(3)

ss 809ZE, 809ZF added—Corporation Tax, 2010 c 4, ss 1177, 1180, sch 1 paras 494, 551

Pt 13 Ch 5E (ss 809EZA-809EZH) added—Finance, 2015 c 11, s 21(1)

s 809EZA rep in pt—Finance (No. 2), 2015 c 33, s 45(2)

s 809EZB am—Finance (No. 2), 2015 c 33, s 44(1)

s 809EZDA added—Finance (No. 2), 2015 c 33, s 45(1)

s 809EZDB added—Finance (No. 2), 2015 c 33, s 45(1)

s 809EZDB excl—Taxation of Chargeable Gains, 1992 c 12, s 103KG(2)(4) (added by

    2015 c 33, s 43(1))

s 809EZG am—Finance (No. 2), 2015 c 33, s 44(2)

Pt 13, Ch 7 (s 809ZG) added—Taxation (International and Other Provns), 2010 c 8, s 371,

    sch 7 paras 50, 52

Pt. 13 Ch. 8 (ss 809ZH-809ZR) added—Finance, 2011 c 11, sch 3 para 1

s 809ZJ mod—Finance, 2011 c 11, sch 3 para 31(a)

Pt 14 Ch A1 (ss 809A-809Z7) added—Finance, 2008 c 9, s 25, sch 7 paras 1, 85-89

2007

c 3 Pt 14 Ch A1 *continued*

     mod—Income Tax (Earnings and Pensions), 2003 c 1 s 41F(8)

s 809A rep in pt—Finance, 2013 c 29, sch 46 para 2

s 809B appl—Income tax (Earnings and Pensions), 2003 c 1, s 41C

  am—Finance, 2013 c 29, sch 45 para 152(2)

  rep in pt—Finance, 2013 c 29, sch 46 para 3

s 809C am—(spec retrosp effect) Finance, 2009 c 10, s 51, sch 27 paras 2, 15(1); Finance, 2012 c 14, sch 12 para 2; Finance, 2015 c 11, s 24(2)

s 809D am—(spec retrosp effect) Finance, 2009 c 10, s 51, sch 27 paras 2, 3,15(1); Finance, 2013 c 29, sch 45 para 152(3)

  rep in pt—Finance, 2013 c 29, sch 46 para 4

s 809E am—(spec retrosp effect) Finance, 2009 c 10, s 51, sch 27 paras 2, 4,15(1); Finance, 2013 c 29, sch 45 para 152(4)

  rep in pt—Finance, 2013 c 29, sch 46 para 5

s 809F am—Finance, 2011 c 11, sch 2 para 41; Finance, 2013 c 29, sch 46 para 22

s 809G am—Finance, 2012 c 14, sch 39 para 32(2)(d); Finance, 2014 c 26, s 11(8)

s 809H am—(spec retrosp effect) Finance, 2009 c 10, s 51, sch 27 paras 2, 5,15(1); Finance, 2012 c 14, sch 12 para 3; Scotland, 2012 c 11, s 26(5); Finance, 2014 c 26, sch 38 para 8; (prosp) (cond) Wales, 2014 c 29, ss 9(8), 14(1)(2)-(4); Finance, 2015 c 11, s 24(3)

s 809I am—Finance, 2012 c 14, sch 12 para 20(2)

s 809K am—Finance, 2011 c 11, sch 2 para 42; Finance, 2013 c 29, s 21(2); Finance, 2014 c 26, sch 9 para 29

s 809L rep in pt—Finance, 2009 c 10, s 51, sch 27 para 6(1)(2)

  am—Finance, 2009 c 10, s 51, sch 27 para 6(1)(3)

s 809M am—Finance, 2009 c 10, s 51, sch 27 para 7; Corporation Tax, 2010 c 4, s 1177, sch 1 paras 494, 552; Finance, 2010 c 13, s 33; Finance, 2012 c 14, sch 12 para 13

s 809P am—Finance, 2009 c 10, s 51, sch 27 para 8

s 809Q am—Finance, 2013 c 29, sch 6 para 5

ss 809RA-809RD added—Finance, 2013 c 29, sch 6 para 6

s 809S am—Finance, 2010 c 13, s 38, sch 12 para 11

s 809T am—Finance, 2009 c 10, s 51, sch 27 para 9

s 809UA added—Finance, 2013 c 29, s 21(3)

s 809V subst—Finance, 2012 c 14, sch 12 para 4

  am—Finance, 2012 c 14, sch 12 para 6

ss 809VA-809VO added—Finance, 2012 c 14, sch 12 para 7

s 809W am—Finance, 2012 c 14, sch 12 para 8

s 809X rep in pt—(spec retrosp effect) Finance, 2009 c 10, s 51, sch 27 paras 10, 15(1)

  am—Finance, 2012 c 14, sch 12 para 9; Finance, 2013 c 29, sch 7 para 2

s 809Y am—Finance, 2012 c 14, sch 12 para 10; Finance, 2013 c 29, sch 7 para 3

ss 809YA-809YD added—Finance, 2012 c 14, sch 12 para 18

s 809YD rep in pt—Finance, 2013 c 29, sch 46 para 23

s 809YE added—Finance, 2012 c 14, sch 14 para 35

s 809YF added—Finance, 2013 c 29, sch 7 para 4

s 809Z am—Finance, 2013 c 29, sch 7 para 5(2)(4)

  rep in pt—Finance, 2013 c 29, sch 7 para 5(3)(5)

s 809Z1 rep—Finance, 2013 c 29, sch 7 para 6

s 809Z2 rep in pt—Finance, 2012 c 14, sch 12 para 11

s 809Z4 rep in pt—Finance, 2012 c 14, sch 12 para 12; Finance, 2013 c 29, sch 7 para 7(5)

  am—Finance, 2013 c 29, sch 7 para 7(2)-(4)

s 809Z5 rep in pt—(spec retrosp effect) Finance, 2009 c 10, s 51, sch 27 paras 11, 15(1)

s 809Z6 rep in pt—Finance, 2013 c 29, sch 7 para 8

s 809Z7 am—Finance, 2011 c 11, sch 2 para 43; Finance, 2012 c 14, sch 12 para 15; Finance, 2013 c 29, sch 46 para 24(b)

  rep in pt—Finance, 2012 c 14, sch 12 para 14; Finance, 2013 c 29, sch 46 para 24(a)

ss 809Z8-809Z10 added—Finance, 2012 c 14, sch 12 para 16

s 809Z9 am—Finance, 2013 c 29, s 21(4)

s 810 am—Finance, 2013 c 29, sch 45 para 152(5)

s 811 rep in pt—Finance, 2009 c 10, s 5, sch 1 para 6(o)(iv); Finance, 2012 c 14, sch 39 paras 28(1), 32(2)(e)

s 812 rep in pt—Finance, 2013 c 29, sch 46 para 66

s 812A added—Finance, 2013 c 29, sch 45 para 138

2007
c 3 *continued*

s 813 am—Taxation (International and Other Provns), 2010 c 8, s 374, sch 8 paras 280, 282
s 816 am—SI 2007/3506, art 3
s 817 rep in pt—Taxation (International and Other Provns), 2010 c 8, ss 374, 378, sch 8 paras 280, 283(2), sch 10 pt 11
    am—Taxation (International and Other Provns), 2010 c 8, s 374, sch 8 paras 280, 283(3)
s 818 am—Finance, 2008 c 9, s 38, sch 16 para 10(1)(2)
    rep in pt—Finance, 2008 c 9, s 38, sch 16 para 10(1)(3)
s 821 am—SI 2009/23, art 5
s 824 am—Taxation (International and Other Provns), 2010 c 8, s 374, sch 8 paras 280, 284
s 825 rep in pt—SI 2013/2819, reg 37(9)(a)
    am—SI 2013/2819, reg 37(9)(b)
s 827 am (with savings)—Finance, 2008 c 9, s 38, sch 16 paras 4, 5, 11(5)
Pt 14 Ch 1A (ss 828A-828D) added—(spec retrosp effect) Finance, 2009 c 10, s 52(1)
s 828B am—Finance, 2014 c 26, sch 38 para 9; (prosp) (cond) Wales, 2014 c 29, ss 9(9), 14(1)(2)-(4)
s 828C am—Taxation (International and Other Provns), 2010 c 8, s 374, sch 8 paras 71, 83
ss 829-832 rep—Finance, 2013 c 29, sch 45 para 152(6)
s 833 am—Finance, 2012 c 14, sch 37 para 5(2)-(6)
    rep in pt—Finance, 2009 c 10, s 5, sch 1 para 6(o)(v)
s 834 rep in pt—Finance, 2013 c 29, sch 46 para 67(1)
s 835 rep in pt—Corporation Tax, 2009 c 4, ss 1322, 1326, sch 1 para 705, sch 3 pt 1
s 835A added—Corporation Tax, 2009 c 4, s 1322, sch 1 para 706
Pt 14, Ch 2A (s 835B) added—Taxation (International and Other Provns), 2010 c 8, s 371, sch 7 paras 75, 77
Pt 14, Ch 2B (ss 835C-835S) added—Taxation (International and Other Provns), 2010 c 8, s 370, sch 6 paras 1-17
Pt 14, Ch 2C (ss 835T-835Y) added—Taxation (International and Other Provns), 2010 c 8, s 370, sch 6 paras 18-23
s 836 am—Corporation Tax, 2010 c 4, s 1177, sch 1 paras 494, 553; Finance, 2011 c 11, sch 14 para 3(5)
Pt 14, Ch 3A (ss 837A-837H) added—Taxation (International and Other Provns), 2010 c 8, s 371, sch 7 paras 68, 71
s 838 mod—Greater London Authy, 1999 c 29, s 34A(3))
s 838A added—Finance (No 3), 2010 c 33, s 31, sch 14 para 3(3)(6)
Pt 15 (ss 847-987) excl—Taxation (International and Other Provns), 2010 c 8, s 187(6)(b)
s 847 rep in pt—SI 2013/2819, reg 37(10)
s 848 am—Finance, 2010 c 13, s 40, sch 13 para 2(2)
    rep in pt—SI 2013/2819, reg 37(11)
s 849 am—Taxation (International and Other Provns), 2010 c 8, s 374, sch 8 paras 71, 84, 219, 222
s 851 am—Finance, 2008 c 9, s 5, sch 1 paras 1, 25
    excl—SI 2008/2682, reg 4; ibid, reg 4A(1)(4) (added by SI 2011/22, reg 7)
s 852 am—Finance, 2014 c 26, s 3(4)
s 853 am—SI 2009/1890, art 3; Co-operative and Community Benefit Societies, 2014 c 14, sch 4 para 108
s 858 am—Finance, 2013 c 29, sch 46 para 68(1)(a)
    rep in pt—Finance, 2013 c 29, sch 46 para 68(1)(b)
s 859 am—Finance, 2013 c 29, sch 46 para 69(1)(a)
    rep in pt—Finance, 2013 c 29, sch 46 para 69(1)(b)
s 860 am—Finance, 2013 c 29, sch 46 para 70(1)
s 861 rep in pt—Finance, 2013 c 29, sch 46 para 71(2)(3)
s 862 rep—SI 2009/2035, art 2, sch
s 866 am—Finance, 2012 c 14, s 18(1)
s 873 am—Finance, 2010 c 13, s 30, sch 6 para 23(5); SI 2013/2819, reg 37(12)
s 874 am—Finance, 2008 c 9, s 5, sch 1 paras 1, 26; Finance, 2013 c 29, sch 11 paras 2, 5; Co-operative and Community Benefit Societies, 2014 c 14, sch 4 para 109
    appl (mods)—SI 2009/2034, reg 16
    restr—SIs 2008/2692, reg 4A(1)(4) (added by 2011/22, reg 7); 2013/3209, reg 6
s 875 am—Finance, 2013 c 29, sch 11 para 3
s 878 mod—SI 2009/3227, reg 7(1)
    excl—SI 2013/3209, reg 9(a)
    am—Finance, 2013 c 29, sch 11 para 4

2007

c 3 *continued*

s 879 am—Finance, 2011 c 11, sch 13 para 19

s 885 excl—SI 2013/3209, reg 9(b)

s 886 am—Finance, 2007 c 11, s 47, sch 14 paras 21, 24; SI 2013/504, reg
    24(2)(a)(b)(c)(i)(iii)
  rep in pt—SI 2013/504, reg 24(2)(c)(ii)

s 887 am—Taxation (International and Other Provns), 2010 c 8, s 374, sch 8 paras 306, 307;
    Co-operative and Community Benefit Societies, 2014 c 14, sch 4 para 110

s 888A added—Finance, 2015 c 11, s 23(1)

s 889 am—Finance, 2008 c 9, s 5, sch 1 paras 1, 27
  excl—SI 2013/460, reg 3(1)(c)
  restr—SI 2013/3209, reg 6

s 892 am—Finance, 2008 c 9, s 5, sch 1 paras 1, 28

s 895 am—SI 2008/954, arts 38, 40

s 899 am—Corporation Tax, 2009 c 4, s 1322, sch 1 para 707; Corporation Tax, 2010 c 4, s
    1177, sch 1 paras 494, 554; SI 2013/2819, reg 37(13)

s 900 excl—SI 2010/2913, reg 3
  appl—SIs 2006/964 reg 46B(2) (added by 2013/1772, reg 2(2)); 2009/3001 reg
    124B(2) (added by 2013/1770, reg 2(3))

s 901 am—Finance, 2008 c 9, s 5, sch 1 paras 1, 29
  excl—SI 2010/2913, reg 3
  appl—SI 2009/3001 reg 124B(2) (added by SI 2013/1770, reg 2(3))

s 902 rep—Finance, 2008 c 9, s 5, sch 1 paras 1, 30

s 904 am—Corporation Tax, 2009 c 4, s 1322, sch 1 para 708; SIs 2009/23, art 5;
    2013/2819, reg 37(14)

s 910 am—Corporation Tax, 2009 c 4, s 1322, sch 1 para 709

s 918 appl—Finance, 2007 c 11, s 47, sch 13 para 13
  am—Corporation Tax, 2010 c 4, s 1177, sch 1 paras 494, 555; Finance, 2011 c 11,
    sch 13 para 20; Finance, 2013 c 29, sch 29 para 21

s 919 am—Finance, 2008 c 9, s 5, sch 1 paras 1, 31; Finance, 2011 c 11, sch 13 para 21;
    Finance, 2013 c 29, sch 29 para 22(a)(c)
  appl—Finance, 2007 c 11, s 47, sch 13 para 13
  rep in pt—Finance, 2013 c 29, sch 29 para 22(b)

s 920 rep —Finance, 2013 c 29, sch 29 para 23

s 921 appl—Finance, 2007 c 11, s 47, sch 13 para 13
  am—Finance, 2013 c 29, sch 29 para 24

s 922 rep —Finance, 2013 c 29, sch 29 para 25

s 923 rep —Finance, 2013 c 29, sch 29 para 25

ss 924, 925 rep —Finance, 2013 c 29, sch 29 para 25

ss 925A-925F added —Taxation (International and Other Provns), 2010 c 8, s 371, s 377,
    sch 7 paras 111, 112, sch 9

s 925A am—Finance, 2013 c 29, sch 29 para 26

s 925B rep —Finance, 2013 c 29, sch 29 para 27

s 925C am—Finance, 2013 c 29, sch 29 para 28(c)
    rep in pt—Finance, 2013 c 29, sch 29 para 28(a)(b)

s 926 appl—Finance, 2007 c 11, s 47, sch 13 para 13
  am—Taxation (International and Other Provns), 2010 c 8, s 371, s 377, sch 7 paras
    111, 113, sch 9

s 926 rep in pt—Finance, 2013 c 29, sch 29 para 29

s 927 appl—Finance, 2007 c 11, s 47, sch 13 para 13

s 928 am—Corporation Tax, 2010 c 4, s 1177, sch 1 paras 494, 556

s 933 appl—Small Charitable Donations, 2012 c 23, sch para 10
  appl (mods)—Small Charitable Donations, 2012 c 23, s 5(3)

s 934 am—Corporation Tax, 2009 c 4, s 1322, sch 1 para 710

s 935 appl (mods)—SI 2004/1450, reg 24(c) (amended by SI 2010/582, reg 12(d))

s 936 am—Corporation Tax, 2010 c 4, s 1177, sch 1 paras 494, 557

s 937 am—Corporation Tax, 2009 c 4, s 1322, sch 1 para 711

s 939 am—Finance, 2008 c 9, s 5, sch 1 paras 1, 32; ibid, s 134(1)(2); Corporation Tax,
    2009 c 4, s 1322, sch 1 para 712(1)-(3)(5); Finance, 2013 c 29, sch 11 para 8
  rep in pt—Finance, 2008 c 9, s 134(1)(3); Corporation Tax, 2009 c 4, s 1322, sch 1
    para 712(1)(4)

s 940A added—Finance, 2008 c 9, s 134(4)

Pt 15, Ch 13 (ss 941-943) rep —SI 2013/2819, reg 37(15)

ss 943A, 943B added—Finance, 2010 c 13, s 40, sch 13 para 1(4)

2007
c 3 *continued*

s 943C added —Finance, 2010 c 13, s 40, sch 13 paras 1(4), 4

s 943D added—Finance, 2010 c 13, s 40, sch 13 para 1(4)

Pt 15, Ch 15 (ss 945-962) appl (mods)—SI 2009/2034, reg 16

s 948 am—Corporation Tax, 2009 c 4, s 1322, sch 1 para 714

s 952 excl—Corporation Tax, 2010 c 4, s 610(3)(a)(iii)

s 953 am—Corporation Tax, 2010 c 4, s 1177, sch 1 paras 494, 558

s 955 am—Tribunals, Cts and Enforcement, 2007 c 15, s 62, sch 13 para 157

s 963A added—Finance (No 3), 2010 c 33, s 8

s 964 rep in pt—Finance, 2008 c 9, s 69(1); SI 2013/2819, reg 37(16)

s 965 am—Corporation Tax, 2009 c 4, s 1322, sch 1 para 715

s 966 excl—Finance, 2010 c 13, s 63, sch 20 para 4; SI 2010/2913, reg 3; Finance, 2012 c
            14, s 13(5); Finance, 2013 c 29, s 9(4); Finance, 2014 c 26, s 47(4); Finance
            (No. 2), 2015 c 33, s 30(4)

s 967 excl—Corporation Tax, 2010 c 4, s 610(3)(a)(i)

s 968 excl—Corporation Tax, 2010 c 4, s 610(3)(a)(ii)

s 971 am—Corporation Tax, 2009 c 4, s 1322, sch 1 para 716

s 972 am—Corporation Tax, 2010 c 4, s 1177, sch 1 paras 494, 559

s 973 am—Corporation Tax, 2010 c 4, s 1177, sch 1 paras 494, 560; Finance (No 3), 2010
            c 33, s 10, sch 4 para 2; Finance, 2013 c 29, sch 19 para 12

s 974 am—Corporation Tax, 2010 c 4, s 1177, sch 1 paras 494, 561; Finance, 2013 c 29,
            sch 19 para 12

s 975 am—Finance, 2013 c 29, sch 11 para 9

       rep in pt—SI 2013/2819, reg 37(17)

s 975A added—Finance, 2013 c 29, sch 11 para 10

s 976 am—Corporation Tax, 2009 c 4, s 1322, sch 1 para 717

s 979A added—(spec retrosp effect) Finance, 2009 c 10, s 33(4)

s 980 am—Corporation Tax, 2009 c 4, s 1322, sch 1 para 718

s 989 am—Statistics and Registration Service, 2007 c 18, s 60, sch 3 para 16; Finance, 2007
            c 11, s 109, sch 26 para 12(1)(12); Finance, 2008 c 9, s 5, sch 1 paras 1,
            33(1)(2)(4); ibid, s 34, sch 12 paras 23, 31; Finance, 2009 c 10, ss 6(5), 40, sch
            2 para 8, sch 19 para 13(c); SI 2009/56, art 3, sch 1 para 462; Corporation Tax,
            2010 c 4, s 1177, sch 1 paras 494, 562; Finance (No 3), 2010 c 33, s 9, sch 3
            para 2; Taxation (International and Other Provns), 2010 c 8, s 371, sch 7 paras
            91, 92; ibid, s 374, sch 8 paras 256, 258; Scotland, 2012 c 11, s 26(6); Finance,
            2012 c 14, sch 39 para 28(2); Finance, 2013 c 29, sch 45 para 107; Finance,
            2014 c 26, sch 38 para 10(b); (prosp) (cond) Wales, 2014 c 29, ss 9(10),
            14(1)(2)-(4)

       rep in pt—Finance, 2008 c 9, s 5, sch 1 paras 1, 33(1)(3); Corporation Tax, 2009 c 4,
            ss 1322, 1326, sch 1 paras 699, 719, sch 3 pt 1; Finance, 2010 c 13, s 30, sch 6
            para 23(6); Finance (No 3), 2010 c 33, s 5, sch 2 para 3(2); Finance, 2014 c 26,
            sch 38 para 10(a)

       appl—Finance (No 2), 2010 c 31, s 2, sch 1 para 2; Taxes Management, 1970 c 9, s
            12ZF(10)

s 989A added—Taxation (International and Other Provns), 2010 c 8, s 374, sch 8 paras 256,
            259

s 991 am—Corporation Tax, 2010 c 4, s 1177, sch 1 paras 494, 563; Financial Services
            (Banking Reform), 2013 c 33, sch 10 para 6; Co-operative and Community
            Benefit Societies, 2014 c 14, sch 4 para 111

s 992 am—Corporation Tax, 2010 c 4, s 1177, sch 1 paras 494, 564

s 993 appl—Finance 2004, ss 213D(4), 213O(8); ibid, s 228ZA; Finance, 2009 c 10, s 72,
            sch 35 para 2(5)(6); SI 2009/3001, regs 76, 82; Finance, 2010 c 13, s 22, sch 1
            para 49(3); SIs 2011/2999, reg 34(3)(a); 2014/685, reg 3(5)(a)

       appl (mods)—Taxation of Chargeable Gains, 1992 c 12, s 103KG(15)

       mod—Nat Insurance Contributions, 2014 c 7, sch 1 para 8(2)

s 994 appl—SIs 2009/3001, regs 76, 82; 2011/2999, reg 34(3)(a); 2014/685, reg 3(5)(a)

       am—Corporation Tax, 2010 c 4, s 1177, sch 1 paras 494, 565

s 995 appl—Income Tax (Earnings and Pensions), 2003 c. 1, s 312G(6)(b))

s 996 excl—Finance, 2013 c 29, s 8(4)

       rep in pt—Finance (No. 2), 2015 c 33, s 28(1)

s 997 am—Corporation Tax, 2010 c 4, s 1177, sch 1 paras 494, 566

       appl (mods)—Finance, 2011 c 11, s 53(6)

s 998 appl (mods)—Finance, 2008 c 9, s 53, sch 19 para 3(4)

s 999 am—Corporation Tax, 2010 c 4, s 1177, sch 1 paras 494, 567

2007
c 3 *continued*

s 1000 am—Corporation Tax, 2010 c 4, s 1177, sch 1 paras 494, 568

s 1005 subst—Finance, 2007 c 11, s 109, sch 26 para 1

    am—Taxation (International and Other Provns), 2010 c 8, s 365, sch 2 paras 50, 55

    appl—Finance, 1986 c 41, s 99A(2)

s 1007 am—SI 2009/23, art 5

s 1007A added—Finance (No 3), 2010 c 33, s 5, sch 2 para 3(3)

s 1010 rep—Finance, 2007 c 11, s 109, sch 26 para 12(1)(13), sch 27

s 1012 am —(spec retrosp effect) Finance, 2008 c 9, s 67(2)

s 1014 am—Finance, 2007 c 11, s 109, sch 26 para 12(1)(14); Finance, 2008 c 9, s 5, sch 1
    paras 1, 34; (with savings) ibid, s 38, sch 16 paras 2(2), 11(5); ibid, s 38, sch
    16 paras 4, 6(1)(3); Taxation (International and Other Provns), 2010 c 8, s 374,
    sch 8 paras 280, 285(3)(b), 326, 327; Finance, 2014 c 26, sch 11 para 12;
    Finance, 2015 c 11, s 125(2); Finance (No. 2), 2015 c 33, s 3(3)

    rep in pt—Finance, 2008 c 9, s 38, sch 16 paras 4, 6(1)(2); Taxation (International
    and Other Provns), 2010 c 8, ss 374, 378, sch 8 paras 280, 285(2)(3)(a), sch 10
    pt 11

    excl—Finance, 2008 c 9, s 31(4); Finance, 2009 c 10, s 44, sch 22 para 14(2);
    Finance (No 2), 2010 c 31, s 5(3); Finance, 2014 c 26, s 12(5), sch 37 para
    22(3); Finance, 2015 c 11, ss 16(6), 20(5), 23(4), sch 6 para 14(3)

s 1016 am—SI 2009/3001, reg 129(6)(b); Corporation Tax, 2010 c 4, s 1177, sch 1 paras
    494, 569(b); Taxation (International and Other Provns), 2010 c 8, s 374, sch 8
    paras 256, 260(1)-(3), 271, 274(2)

    rep in pt—Finance, 2009 c 10, s 49, sch 25 para 9(3)(h)(i); SI 2009/3001, regs 13,
    129(6)(a), sch 2; Corporation Tax, 2010 c 4, s 1177, sch 1 paras 494, 569(a);
    Taxation (International and Other Provns), 2010 c 8, ss 374, 378, sch 8 paras
    256, 260(4)(5), 271, 274(3), sch 10 pt 9, 10

s 1017 am—Corporation Tax, 2009 c 4, s 1322, sch 1 para 720; Corporation Tax, 2010 c 4,
    s 1177, sch 1 paras 494, 570; Taxation (International and Other Provns), 2010
    c 8, s 374, sch 8 paras 326, 328

s 1020 am—Taxation (International and Other Provns), 2010 c 8, s 371, sch 7 paras 91, 93

s 1022 am—SI 2008/954, arts 38, 41; Finance, 2014 c 26, sch 11 para 13

s 1023 am—Taxation (International and Other Provns), 2010 c 8, s 374, sch 8 paras 71, 85

s 1025 rep in pt—SI 2013/2819, reg 37(18)

s 1026 am—Taxation (International and Other Provns), 2010 c 8, s 374, sch 8 paras 71,
    86(a)

    rep in pt—Taxation (International and Other Provns), 2010 c 8, ss 374, 378, sch 8
    paras 71, 86(b), sch 10 pt 1

sch 1 am—SI 2007/3506, art 3; (retrosp to 5.4.2007) SI 2009/2859, art 4

    rep in pt—Finance, 2007 c 11, s 114, sch 27 pts 2, 6; Finance, 2008 c 9, s 5, sch 1
    paras 1, 35; ibid, s 8, sch 2 paras 21(k), 55(i), 102(b); ibid, s 36, sch 14 para
    17(o); ibid, s 41(7)(k); ibid, s 43, sch 17 para 35(2)(c); ibid, s
    66(3)(b)(4)(l)(viii); ibid, s 63, sch 23 para 12; ibid, s 84, sch 27 para 27(1)(4);
    ibid, s 113, sch 36 para 92(j); Finance, 2009 c 10, s 5, sch 1 para 6(o)(vi); ibid,
    s 27, sch 8 para 10(c); ibid, s 48, sch 24 para 9(e); ibid, s 49, sch 25 para
    9(3)(h)(ii); SIs 2009/56, art 3, sch 1 para 463; 2035, art 2, sch; 3001, reg 13,
    sch 2; Corporation Tax, 2010 c 4, s 1181, sch 3 pts 1, 2; Taxation
    (International and Other Provns), 2010 c 8, s 378, sch 10 pts 1, 2, 7, 9, 11, 12;
    Finance, 2011 c 11, sch 26 paras 1(2)(b)(i), 3(2)(c); Charities, 2011 c 25, sch
    10; Finance, 2012 c 14, sch 39 para 28(1); Finance, 2013 c 29, sch 12 para
    15(3); ibid, sch 29 para 30; SL(R), 2013 c 2, s 1, sch 1 pt 10(1); SI 2013/2819,
    reg 41(a)

sch 2 am—Finance, 2007 c 11, s 26, sch 4 paras 4, 19, 21; SIs 2007/940, art 2; 1820, art 4;
    Corporation Tax, 2010 c 4, s 1177, sch 1 paras 494, 571

    rep in pt—Finance, 2009 c 10, s 5, sch 1 para 6(o)(vii); SI 2009/2035, art 2, sch;
    Corporation Tax, 2010 c 4, s 1181, sch 3 pt 1; Finance, 2011 c 11, sch 26 para
    2(2)(c); ibid, sch 3 paras 14,27(2)(3); Finance, 2013 c 29, sch 12 para 15(4);
    ibid, sch 29 para 31; SI 2013/2819, reg 37(19)

sch 3 am—SI 2007/3506, art 3

    rep in pt—(retrosp to 5.4.2007) SI 2009/2859, art 4

    mod—Finance, 2007 c 11, s 41, sch 10 paras 7, 17(2)

sch 4 am—Finance, 2007 c 11, ss 26, 109, sch 4 paras 4, 20, 21, sch 26 para 12(1)(15);
    Finance, 2008 c 9, s 5, sch 1 paras 1, 36(1)-(3), 50, 63(1)(2); Finance, 2009 c 10,
    s 6(5), sch 2 para 9; ibid, s 49, sch 25 para 9(6)-(8); Corporation Tax, 2010 c 4, s

2007
c 3 *continued*

1177, sch 1 paras 494, 572(b); Finance (No 3), 2010 c 33, s 5, sch 2 para
4(1)-(4); Finance, 2010 c 13, ss 30, 31, 38, 40, sch 6 para 23(7)(a)(ii)(b), sch 7
para 4, sch 12 para 12, sch 13 para 2(3); Taxation (International and Other
Provns), 2010 c 8, ss 371, 374 sch 7 paras 68, 72, sch 8 paras 219, 223, 237,
239, 256, 261, 271, 275, 280, 286; Finance, 2011 c 11, s 42(5); ibid, sch 3 para
15; Finance, 2012 c 14, sch 6 para 18; Finance, 2013 c 29, sch 45 para 108;
Co-operative and Community Benefit Societies, 2014 c 14, sch 4 para 112(3);
Finance, 2014 c 26, sch 38 para 11; (prosp) (cond) Wales, 2014 c 29, ss 9(11),
14(1)(2)-(4); Finance, 2015 c 11, s 21(3)

rep in pt—Finance, 2008 c 9, s 5, sch 1 paras 1, 36(1)(4), 50, 63(1)(3); Corporation
Tax, 2009 c 4, ss 1322, 1326, sch 1 paras 699, 721, sch 3 pt 1; Corporation
Tax, 2010 c 4, ss 1177, 1181, sch 1 paras 494, 572(a), sch 3; Finance, 2010 c
13, s 30, sch 6 para 23(7)(a)(i); Finance, 2013 c 29, sch 12 para 15(5); ibid,
sch 29 para 32; SI 2013/2819, reg 37(20); Co-operative and Community
Benefit Societies, 2014 c 14, sch 4 para 112(2)

sch 7 rep in pt—Finance, 2008 c 9, s 36, sch 14 para 17(p)
sch 10 rep in pt—Finance, 2008 c 9, s 36, sch 14 para 17(p)

c 4   **Northern Ireland (St Andrews Agreement)**
c 5   **Welfare Reform**

Pt 1 (ss 1-29) mod —Jobseekers, 1995 c 18 Sch. 1 para. 2(2)
  appl (mods)—SI 2010/1907, regs 6, 16, schs 1, 2 (as amended by SI 2012/913, reg
    10(4))
  mod—SI 2012/360, art 2 sch 1 2
s 1 am—(prosp) Welfare Reform, 2009 c 24, s 124, sch 1 para 26; Welfare Reform, 2012 c
    5, ss 50(1), 52(2), 53, 62(2), (3); (prosp) ibid, s 54(2),(pt prosp) ibid, sch 3 para
    23
  rep in pt—(prosp) Welfare Reform, 2009 c 24, s 58, sch 7 pt 1; (pt prosp) Welfare
    Reform, 2012 c 5, sch 14 pt 1
s 1A added—Welfare Reform, 2012 c 5, s 51(1)
  am—(pt prosp) Welfare Reform, 2012 c 5, sch 3 para 26(a)
  rep in pt—(pt prosp) Welfare Reform, 2012 c 5, sch 14 pt 1
s 1B added—Welfare Reform, 2012 c 5, s 52(1)
  am—(pt prosp) Welfare Reform, 2012 c 5, sch 3 para 26(b)
  rep in pt—(pt prosp) Welfare Reform, 2012 c 5, sch 14 pt 1
s 1C added (prosp)—Welfare Reform, 2012 c 5, s 54(3)
  rep (pt prosp)—Welfare Reform, 2012 c 5, sch 14 pt 5
s 2 am—(pt prosp) Welfare Reform, 2012 c 5, sch 3 para 24; (prosp) ibid, sch 5 para 6(2),
    (3)
  rep in pt—(pt prosp) Welfare Reform, 2012 c 5, sch 14 pt 1
  excl in pt—SI 2013/379, reg 7(1)
s 3 am—(pt prosp) Welfare Reform, 2012 c 5, sch 3 para 26(c)
  rep in pt—(pt prosp) Welfare Reform, 2012 c 5, sch 14 pt 1
ss 4-6 rep (pt prosp)—Welfare Reform, 2012 c 5, sch 14 pt 1
ss 11-16 subst (by ss 11-11K) (pt prosp)—Welfare Reform, 2012 c 5, s 57(2)
s 12 am—Welfare Reform, 2009 c 24, s 3(3)
s 13 am—(prosp) Welfare Reform, 2009 c 24, s 3(4); Welfare Reform, 2012 c 5, s 55
s 14 am—(prosp) Welfare Reform, 2009 c 24, s 31(2) (as amended by Welfare Reform,
    2012 c 5, s 54(7))
s 15 am—Welfare Reform, 2009 c 24, s 10; (prosp) Welfare Reform, 2012 c 5, s 54(4)
s 15A added—Welfare Reform, 2009 c 24, s 11, sch 3 pt 2 para 6
  rep—Welfare Reform, 2012 c 5, s 60(2)
s 16 am—Welfare Reform, 2009 c 24, s 11, sch 3 pt 2 para 8(1)(2); (prosp) Welfare Reform,
    2012 c 5, s 54(5)
  rep in pt—Welfare Reform, 2012 c 5, sch 14 pt 6
s 16A added—Welfare Reform, 2012 c 5, s 56
  rep —Welfare Reform, 2012 c 5, sch 14 pt 5
s 18 am—(pt prosp) Welfare Reform, 2012 c 5, sch 3 para 26(d)
  excl in pt—SI 2013/379, reg 96(1)(3)
s 19 am—Welfare Reform, 2009 c 24, s 28(2); (prosp) Welfare Reform, 2012 c 5, s 57(3)
s 20 am—(prosp) Welfare Reform, 2009 c 24, s 6; (pt prosp) Welfare Reform, 2012 c 5, sch
    3 para 26(e); Children and Families, 2014 c 6, sch 7 para 73(2)(3)
  rep in pt—Children and Families, 2014 c 6, sch 7 para 73(4)
s 23 rep (pt prosp)—Welfare Reform, 2012 c 5, sch 14 pt 1

2007

c 5 *continued*

s 24 am—Welfare Reform, 2009 c 24, s 3(5); (pt prosp) Welfare Reform, 2012 c 5, s 57(4)
rep in pt—(prosp) Welfare Reform, 2009 c 24, s 58, sch 7 pt 1; (pt prosp) Welfare
Reform, 2012 c 5, sch 14 pts 1, 5
mod—SI 2013/983 art 11 9 (as modified by 2013/1511, art 9(2))

s 25 am—Welfare Reform, 2009 c 24, s 11, sch 3 para 8(1)(3); Welfare Reform, 2012 c 5, s
51(2); (pt prosp) ibid, s 57(5)
rep in pt—Welfare Reform, 2012 c 5, sch 14 pt 6

s 26 am—Welfare Reform, 2009 c 24, s 11, sch 3 para 8(1)(4); Welfare Reform, 2012 c 5, s
51(3); ibid, s 57(6)
rep in pt—(pt prosp) Welfare Reform, 2012 c 5, sch 14 pts 1, 5; ibid, sch 14 pt 6

s 27 am—(pt prosp) Welfare Reform, 2012 c 5, sch 3 para 25
rep in pt—(pt prosp) Welfare Reform, 2012 c 5, sch 14 pt 1

ss 29-34 rep (pt prosp)—Welfare Reform, 2012 c 5, sch 14 pt 1

ss 37-39 rep (pt prosp)—Welfare Reform, 2012 c 5, sch 14 pt 1

s 41 rep in pt—(pt prosp) Welfare Reform, 2012 c 5, sch 14 pt 1

ss 42, 43 rep—Welfare Reform, 2012 c 5, s 133(6)(a)

ss 46, 47 rep (pt prosp)—Welfare Reform, 2012 c 5, sch 14 pt 1

s 48 rep in pt—(pt prosp) Welfare Reform, 2012 c 5, sch 14 pts 1, 10

s 52 rep (prosp)—Welfare Reform, 2012 c 5, sch 14 pt 9

s 53 rep (prosp)—Welfare Reform, 2012 c 5, sch 14 pt 9
am —Identity Documents, 2010 c 40, s 12, sch 1 para 21(1)-(4)(a)(5)
rep in pt—Identity Documents, 2010 c 40, s 12, sch 1 para 21(4)(b)

s 54 rep in pt—(prosp) Welfare Reform, 2012 c 5, sch 14 pt 8

s 60 rep in pt—(prosp) Welfare Reform, 2012 c 5, sch 14 pt 9

s 69 rep in pt—Welfare Reform, 2012 c 5, s 133(6)(b)

sch 1 am—Pensions, 2007 c 22, s 3, sch 1 para 11; Welfare Reform, 2009 c 24, ss 5(2), 13;
Welfare Reform, 2012 c 5, sch 2 para 65; (pt prosp) ibid, sch 3 para 26(f); SIs
2014/560, sch 1 para 32(2); 3229, sch 5 para 17(2)
rep in pt—(prosp) Welfare Reform, 2009 c 24, s 58, sch 7 pt 1; (prosp) Welfare
Reform, 2012 c 5, sch 14 pt 1; SIs 2014/560, sch 1 para 32(3); 3229, sch 5
para 17(3)
excl in pt—SI 2013/379, reg 11
mod—SI 2013/379, reg 14

sch 1A added—Welfare Reform, 2009 c 24, s 11, sch 3 para 7
rep—Welfare Reform, 2012 c 5, s 60(2)

sch 2 am—Welfare Reform, 2009 c 24, s 11, sch 3 para 8(1)(5); (prosp) ibid, s 30(2);
Welfare Reform, 2012 c 5, s 54(6); (prosp) ibid, ss 57(7)-(9), 62(4); (pt prosp)
ibid, sch 3 para 26(g)
rep in pt—(pt prosp) Welfare Reform, 2012 c 5, sch 14 pt 1; ibid, sch 14 pt 6
excl in pt—SIs 2013/379, reg 85(2); 2013/381, reg 48(6)

sch 3 rep in pt—(prosp) Child Maintenance and Other Payments, 2008 c 6, s 58, sch 8; (pt
prosp) Welfare Reform, 2009 c 24, s 58, sch 7 pts 1-3; Welfare Reform, 2012 c
5, s 109(2); (prosp) ibid, sch 14 pt 1; ibid, sch 14 pt 13
mod—Welfare Reform, 2009 c 24, s 37(4)

sch 4 rep (prosp)—Welfare Reform, 2012 c 5, sch 14 pt 1
am—(prosp) Welfare Reform, 2009 c 24, s 9, sch 2 para 17; Welfare Reform, 2012 c
5, s 51(4)

sch 5 rep in pt—(prosp) Welfare Reform, 2012 c 5, sch 14 pt 1

sch 7 rep in pt—SI 2008/2833, art 6, sch 3; (prosp) Welfare Reform, 2012 c 5, sch 14 pts 1,
8, 9

c 6 **Justice and Security (Northern Ireland)**
s 1 am—Counter-Terrorism, 2008 c 28, s 28(6)
s 9 am—SI 2009/2090, art 2
sch 6 rep—SI 2009/3048, art 4

c 7 **International Tribunals (Sierra Leone)**

c 8 **Digital Switchover (Disclosure of Information)**
ss 1-5 ext (mods)—SI 2007/3472, art 2, sch
s 3 rep in pt—(W) SI 2013/3005 (W 297), art 2(2)
s 39 mod—SI 2011/2927, reg 4

c 9 **Rating (Empty Properties)**

c 10 *Appropriation (No 2)*—rep Appropriation (No 2) 2009 c 9, s 4, sch 3

2007
c 11 **Finance**

s 3 rep—Corporation Tax, 2010 c 4, ss 1177, 1181, sch 1 paras 573, 574, sch 3

s 4 rep—Finance, 2010 c 13, s 8(2)(b)

s 9 rep in pt—Finance, 2009 c 10, s 22(11)(b)

s 12 rep—Finance, 2009 c 10, s 17, sch 5 para 6(d)

s 16 am—Finance, 2008 c 9, s 164

s 17 rep—Corporation Tax, 2009 c 4, s 1326, sch 3 pt 1

s 27 rep in pt—Corporation Tax, 2010 c 4, s 1181, sch 3 pt 1

s 28 rep—Corporation Tax, 2009 c 4, s 1326, sch 3 pt 1

s 29 rep in pt—Finance, 2008 c 9, s 36, sch 14 para 17(p)

s 35 rep—Taxation (International and Other Provns), 2010 c 8, s 378, sch 10 pt 1

s 36 rep—Finance, 2008 c 9, s 84, sch 27 para 28

s 37 rep—Finance, 2008 c 9, s 75(4)(c)

s 44 rep—Finance, 2012 c 14, sch 18 para 23(e)(i)

ss 49, 50 rep—Corporation Tax, 2009 c 4, s 1326, sch 3 pt 1

s 53 rep in pt—Corporation Tax, 2010 c 4, s 1181, sch 3 pt 1, Taxation (International and
    Other Provns), 2010 c 8, s 378, sch 10 pt 7, 11

s 54 rep—Taxation (International and Other Provns), 2010 c 8, s 378, sch 10 pt 7

s 57 rep in pt—Corporation Tax, 2010 c 4, s 1181, sch 3 pt 1

s 58 rep in pt—Corporation Tax, 2009 c 4, s 1326, sch 3 pt 1

s 59 rep in pt—Corporation Tax, 2010 c 4, s 1181, sch 3 pt 1

s 60 rep in pt—Corporation Tax, 2010 c 4, s 1181, sch 3 pt 1; Finance, 2011 c 11, s 41(3)

s 72 rep in pt—Finance, 2008 c 9, s 97, sch 31 para 10
    appl—Finance, 2008 c 9, s 97(3)

s 73 rep—Finance, 2007 c 11, s 114, sch 27 pts 3, 4

s 81 rep—Finance, 2008 c 9, s 94, sch 30 para 15

s 84 am—Employment, 2008 c 24, s 12(1)

s 87 am—SI 2011/1739, art 7(1)

s 91 rep in pt—Finance, 2008 c 9, s 118, sch 39 para 65(e)

s 107 am—Finance, 2014 c 26, s 299(1)

s 108 rep in pt—SI 2009/56, art 3, sch 1 para 465

s 110 am—SI 2011/1431, reg 3

s 113 am—Corporation Tax, 2009 c 4, s 1322, sch 1 paras 722, 723

sch 3 rep in pt—Corporation Tax, 2009 c 4, ss 1322, 1326, sch 1 paras 722, 724, sch 3 pt 1

sch 5 rep in pt—Corporation Tax, 2009 c 4, s 1326, sch 3 pt 1; Corporation Tax, 2010 c 4, s
    1181, sch 3 pts 1, 2; Taxation (International and Other Provns), 2010 c 8, s 378,
    sch 10 pt 10

sch 6 rep in pt—(spec retrosp effect) Finance, 2009 c 10, s 63, sch 31 paras 11, 12;
    Corporation Tax, 2010 c 4, s 1181, sch 3 pt 1

sch 7 rep in pt—Finance, 2008 c 9, s 43, sch 17 paras 10(5)(7), 17(10)(11)(g), 18(5)(f);
    (spec retrosp effect) ibid, sch 17 para 27(2)(3); Finance, 2009 c 10, ss 36, 46,
    sch 16 para 5(i), sch 23 para 6(a); Corporation Tax, 2010 c 4, s 1181, sch 3 pt
    1; Taxation (International and Other Provns), 2010 c 8, s 378, sch 10 pt 1;
    Finance, 2012 c 14, sch 16 para 247(p)(i); ibid, sch 18 para 23(e)(ii)
    am—SI 2008/381, art 30; Corporation Tax, 2009 c 4, s 1322, sch 1 paras 722,
    725(2)(b)(3)-(5)

sch 8 rep in pt—Finance, 2008 c 9, s 43, sch 17 paras 17(10)(11)(g), 18(5)(f); Corporation
    Tax, 2009 c 4, s 1326, sch 3 pt 1; Finance, 2012 c 14, sch 16 para 247(p)(ii)

sch 9 rep in pt—Finance, 2008 c 9, s 8, sch 2 para 70(i); SI 2008/381, art 31, sch;
    Corporation Tax, 2009 c 4, s 1326, sch 3 pt 1; Finance, 2012 c 14, sch 16 para
    247(p)(iii)
    am—Finance, 2008 c 9, s 43, sch 17 para 38

sch 10 rep in pt—Finance, 2008 c 9, s 43, sch 17 para 3(d); Corporation Tax, 2009 c 4, s
    1326, sch 3 pt 1; Finance, 2012 c 14, sch 16 para 247(p)(iv)

sch 11 am—SIs 2008/954, art 42; 2009/2035, art 2, sch; Finance, 2012 c 14, sch 20 para 23

sch 12 rep—Finance, 2012 c 14, sch 18 para 23(e)(iii)

sch 13 am—Corporation Tax, 2009 c 4, s 1322, sch 1 paras 722, 726(2)(4)(5); Finance,
    2010 c 13, s 45(1)
    rep in pt—Corporation Tax, 2009 c 4, ss 1322, 1326, sch 1 paras 722, 726(3), sch 3
    pt 1; Taxation (International and Other Provns), 2010 c 8, ss 371, 378, sch 7
    paras 114, 115, sch 10 pt 12
    excl—SI 2007/2488, reg 1

sch 14 rep in pt—Finance, 2008 c 9, s 66(4)(m); Corporation Tax, 2009 c 4, s 1326, sch 3
    pt 1; Corporation Tax, 2010 c 4, s 1181, sch 3 pts 1, 2; Taxation (International

2007

c 11 *continued*

and Other Provns), 2010 c 8, s 378, sch 10 pts 1, 10; Finance, 2013 c 29, sch 12 para 14

sch 16 rep in pt—Corporation Tax, 2010 c 4, s 1181, sch 3 pt 1

sch 17 rep in pt—Corporation Tax, 2010 c 4, s 1181, sch 3 pt 1

sch 18 am—Equality, 2010 c 15, s 211, sch 26 para 95 (added by SI 2010/2279, sch 1)

sch 19 rep in pt—Finance, 2011 c 11, sch 16 para 84(c)(i); Taxation of Pensions, 2014 c 30, sch 2 para 19(4)(b)

sch 20 rep in pt—Finance, 2011 c 11, sch 16 para 84(c)(ii)

sch 21 rep—Finance, 2007 c 11, s 114, sch 27 pt 4

sch 24 am—Finance, 2008 c 9, s 122, sch 40 paras 1,2(1),(2)(a),(c),3-20; Corporation Tax, 2009 c 4, s 1322, sch 1 paras 722, 727(a)(b)(d); Finance, 2009 c 10, s 109, sch 57 paras 1-6, 7(1)(2)(a)(c)(3)(4), 9; SI 2009/56, art 3, sch 1 paras 466,467; Corporation Tax, 2010 c 4, s 1177, sch 1 paras 573, 575; Finance, 2010 c 13, s 35, sch 10 paras 1-6; Finance (No 3), 2010 c 33, s 28, sch 12 para 12; Finance, 2012 c 14, s 219; ibid, sch 24 para 29; Finance, 2013 c 29, sch 15 para 8; ibid, sch 18 para 7; ibid, sch 34 para 6; ibid, sch 50 para 1; Finance, 2014 c 26, sch 4 para 8, sch 22 para 19, sch 33 para 3; Finance, 2015 c 11, sch 7 para 56(2)(3); (prosp) ibid, sch 20 paras 2-8

rep in pt—Finance, 2008 c 9, s 122, sch 40 paras 1, 2(1),(3), 20(1),(2); Corporation Tax, 2009 c 4, s 1322, sch 1 paras 722, 727(c); Finance, 2009 c 10, s 109, sch 57 paras 1, 7(2)(b), 8

mod—VAT, 1994 c 23, sch 3BA para 34; Finance, 2008 c 9, s 113, sch 36 para 50(b)

appl—Finance, 1993 c 34, sch 20A para 9A(6) (added by SI 2014/3133, reg 5(4)); SIs 2009/470, regs 13,40; 2001/1004, sch 4 para 21A(8), 21D(9), 21F(12) (added SI 2012/821, reg 11)

appl (mods)—Social Security, Contributions and Benefits, 1992 c 4, s 11A(1)(3); Finance, 2010 c 13, s 22, sch 1 para 37; SI 2001/1004, reg 81 (as am by 2010/721, regs, 2, 4); 2013/938, reg 15

excl—Finance, 2014 c 26, sch 35 para 13(a)

sch 25 rep in pt—Finance, 2009 c 10, s 114(16)(b); Corporation Tax, 2010 c 4, s 1181, sch 3 pt 1

sch 26 rep in pt—Corporation Tax, 2010 c 4, s 1181, sch 3 pt 1; Finance, 2010 c 13, s 38, sch 12 para 13

sch 34 rep in pt—Corporation Tax, 2009 c 4, s 1326, sch 3 pt 1

c 12   **Mental Health**

s 15 rep in pt—Mental Health, 2007 c 12, s 15(6)

s 38 rep in pt—SI 2008/2833, art 6, sch 3

sch 1 rep in pt—Mental Health (Discrimination), 2013 c 8, sch para 6; Anti-social Behaviour, Crime and Policing, 2014 c 12, sch 11 para 50

sch 3 rep in pt—Health and Social Care, 2012 c 7, s 39(4)(f)

sch 6 am—SI 2008/912, art 3, sch 1

sch 10 am—SI 2008/2833, art 6, sch 3

c 13   **Concessionary Bus Travel**

s 9 am —Loc Transport, 2008 c 26, s 77, sch 4 para 67; Loc Democracy, Economic Development and Construction, 2009 c 20, s 119, sch 6 para 120

c 14   **Vehicle Registration Marks**

c 15   **Tribunals, Courts and Enforcement**

power to appl (mods)—Saving Gateway Accounts, 2009 c 8, s 24(4)(5)

s 2 am —SI 2010/21, art 5, sch 1

rep in pt—SI 2010/21, art 5, sch 1

s 4 rep in pt—SI 2010/21, art 5, sch 1

am—Crime and Cts, 2013 c 22, sch 14 para 13(1)

s 5 am & rep in pt—SI 2010/21, art 5, sch 1

rep in pt—SI 2010/21, art 5, sch 1

s 6 am—Crime and Cts, 2013 c 22, sch 14 para 8

s 6A added—Crime and Cts, 2013 c 22, sch 14 para 9

s 7 am—Crime and Cts, 2013 c 22, sch 13 para 43

s 8 am—Crime and Cts, 2013 c 22, sch 13 para 44

excl—Constitutional Reform, 2005 c 4 s 94B(6)

s 11 appl—Stamp, 1891 c 39, s 13A(7A); Taxes Management, 1970 c 9, ss 100B(3A), 100C(4A); Inheritance Tax, 1984 c 51, s 249(3A); Finance, 1999 c 16, sch 17 para 12 (2A); Tax Credits, 2002 c 21, sch 2 paras 2(2A), 4(1A); Employment,

2007
c 15 *continued*

2002 c 22, sch 1 paras 3(4A), 4(4A); Finance, 2003 c 14, sch 14 para 6(1A); Child Trust Funds, 2004 c 6, s 21(10A); SI 2009/1855, sch 4 para 3

power to appl (mods)—Social Security Contributions (Trans of Functions, etc), 1999 c 2, s 13(2A); SI 1999/761 art 12(2A)

mod—SIs 1999/1027, reg 12 (2); 2009/275, art 2 (amended by SI 2010/41, art 3); Charities, 2011 c 25, s 317(1)

excl—Taxes Management, 1970 c 9, ss 19A(11), 55(6A); Finance, 1988 c 39, s 130(4); Finance, 1994 c 9, s 60(4B); Value Added Tax, 1994 c 23, s 84(3C); Finance, 1996 c 8, s 55(3B); Finance, 2000 c 17, sch 6 para 122(2B); Finance, 2001 c 9, s 41(2B); Finance, 2003 c 14, schs 10 para 15(6), 11A para 9(6); SI 2003/96, reg 16(5); Finance, 2004 c.12, s 253(10); SI 2004/2622, reg 9(5); Income Tax (Trading and Other Income), 2005 c 5 s 646(7); SI 2007/1509, reg 7(2); Finance, 2008 c 9, sch 36 paras 6(4), 32(5); Finance (No 3), 2010 c 33, s 29, sch 13 paras 9, 12; Finance, 2011 c 11, sch 23 para 29(5); Finance, 2012 c 14, sch 38 paras 13(3), 20(6); Finance, 2014 c 26, ss 172(7), 256(7), 267(10)

am—Crime and Security, 2010 c 17, s 48, sch 2 para 5

appl (mods)—SI 2010/22, art 5, sch 5

s 12 appl—Land Registration, 2002 c 9, s 111(4) (added by SI 2013/1036, sch 1 para 231(c)); Commonhold and Leasehold Reform, 2002 c 15, s 176B(5) (added by SI 2013/1036, sch 1 para 144); Housing, 2004 c 34, s 231C(5) (added by SI 2013/1036, sch 1 para 176)

s 13 appl—SIs 2009/1307, sch 5 para 3; 2009/1885, sch 4 para 4

power to appl (mods)—Social Security Contributions (Trans of Functions, etc), 1999 c 2, s 13(2A); SI 1999/761 art 12(2A)

mod—SI 1999/1027, reg 12 (2); Charities, 2011 c 25, s 317(1)

excl—Taxes Management, 1970 c 9, ss 19A(11), 55(6A); Finance, 1988 c 39, s 130(4); Finance, 1994 c 9, s 60(4B); Value Added Tax, 1994 c 23, s 84(3C); Finance, 1996 c 8, s 55(3B); Finance, 2000 c 17, sch 6 para 122(2B); Finance, 2001 c 9, s 41(2B); Finance, 2003 c 14, schs 10 para 15(6), 11A para 9(6); SI 2003/96, reg 16(5); Finance, 2004 c 12, s 253(10); SI 2004/2622, reg 9(5); Income Tax (Trading and Other Income), 2005 c 5 s 646(7); SI 2007/1509, reg 7(2); Finance, 2008 c 9, sch 36 paras 6(4), 32(5); Finance (No 3), 2010 c 33, s 29, sch 13 paras 9, 12; Finance, 2011 c 11, sch 23 para 29(5); Finance, 2012 c 14, sch 38 paras 13(3), 20(6); Finance, 2014 c 26, ss 172(7), 256(7), 267(10)

appl (mods)—SIs 2010/22, art 5, sch 5; 2015/65, sch 2 para 8

am—Crime and Cts, 2013 c 22, s 23; Crim Justice and Cts, 2015 c 2, s 83(2)

ss 14A-14C added (prosp)—Crim Justice and Cts, 2015 c 2, s 64

s 15 see —(trans of functions) SI 2008/2684, art 7

am—(prosp) Crim Justice and Cts, 2015 c 2, s 84(4)

s 16 am—(prosp) Crim Justice and Cts, 2015 c 2, s 84(5)(6); (prosp) ibid, s 85(3)(4)

s 20 am—Borders, Citizenship and Immigration, 2009 c 11, s 53(3)

s 20A added—SI 2015/700, art 7

s 21 see —(trans of functions) SI 2008/2684, art 7

s 22 appl (mods)—SI 2012/605, reg 24(9)

s 27 am—Crime and Cts, 2013 c 22, sch 9 para 52

s 29 appl (mods)—SI 2012/605, reg 24(9)

s 36 rep in pt—Tribunals, Cts and Enforcement, 2007 c 15, s 146, sch 23 pt 1

s 39 am —SI 2010/21, art 5, sch 1

rep in pt—SI 2010/21, art 5, sch 1

s 42 rep in pt—SIs 2010/21, art 5, sch 1; 2013/2042, sch para 32

s 43 rep in pt—UK Borders, 2007 c 30, s 58, sch; SI 2010/21, art 5, sch 1

am—UK Borders, 2007 c 30, s 56(1); SI 2010/21, art 5, sch 1

ss 44, 45 rep—SI 2013/2042, sch paras 33, 34

s 46 am—Crime and Cts, 2013 c 22, sch 13 para 44(3)

s 47 am —SI 2010/21, art 5, sch 1; Crime and Cts, 2013 c 22, sch 14 para 13(1)

rep in pt—SI 2010/21, art 5, sch 1

Pt 2 (ss 50-61) appl—Welsh Language (W), 2011 nawm 1, sch 11 paras 3(3), 4(3)

s 51 am—Legal Services, 2007 c 29, s 208, sch 21 para 162

appl (mods)—London Building Acts Amdt 1939 c xcvii, s 109(5); Social Security, 1998 c 14, s 7(6B)

s 57 rep in pt—Crime and Cts, 2013 c 22, sch 13 para 35(7)

s 64 am—Crime and Cts, 2013 c 22, sch 9 para 46

s 72 appl (mods)—Law of Property, 1925 c 20, s 190(5)

2007
c 15 *continued*

s 78 am—Crime and Cts, 2013 c 22, sch 9 para 52
s 90 rep in pt—Crime and Cts, 2013 c 22, s 25(8)
s 92 am—Crime and Cts, 2013 c 22, sch 9 para 52
s 93 am—Crime and Cts, 2013 c 22, sch 9 para 52
s 95 am—Crime and Cts, 2013 c 22, sch 9 para 52; SI 2014/605, art 23
s 104 am—Crime and Cts, 2013 c 22, sch 9 para 52; SI 2014/605, art 24
s 106 am—Crime and Cts, 2013 c 22, sch 9 para 47(3)(5)(7)
    rep in pt—Crime and Cts, 2013 c 22, sch 9 para 47(2)(4)(6)(8)
s 107 am—Crime and Cts, 2013 c 22, sch 9 para 48(2)(5)(6)
    rep in pt—Crime and Cts, 2013 c 22, sch 9 para 48(3)(4)(7)-(9)
ss 115-118 am—Crime and Cts, 2013 c 22, sch 9 para 52
s 119 am—Crime and Cts, 2013 c 22, sch 9 para 52
s 121 am—Crime and Cts, 2013 c 22, sch 9 para 136(a)
s 122 am—Crime and Cts, 2013 c 22, sch 9 para 52
s 123 am—Crime and Cts, 2013 c 22, sch 9 para 52
    rep in pt—Crime and Cts, 2013 c 22, sch 9 para 136(b)
s 131 rep in pt—Crime and Cts, 2013 c 22, sch 9 para 136(b)
s 143 rep—Intellectual Property, 2014 c 18, s 10(11)
s 144 rep in pt—Crime and Cts, 2013 c 22, sch 13 para 35(7)
sch 1 rep in pt—SI 2010/21, art 5, sch 1
    am—Crime and Cts, 2013 c 22, sch 14 para 13(1)
sch 2 am—SI 2010/21, art 5, sch 1; Crime and Cts, 2013 c 22, sch 13 para 45; ibid, sch 14
    paras 10, 13(1)
    rep in pt—SI 2010/21, art 5, sch 1
sch 3 rep in pt—SI 2010/21, art 5, sch 1
    am—Crime and Cts, 2013 c 22, sch 13 paras 30, 46; ibid, sch 14 para 10(1)
sch 4 am—SI 2010/21, art 5, sch 1; Crime and Cts, 2013 c 22, sch 13 para 47
    rep in pt—SI 2010/21, art 5, sch 1
sch 5 am—SSI 2010/220, art 2, sch; Crime and Cts, 2013 c 22, sch 9 para 52
    rep in pt—SI 2013/2042, sch para 35
sch 6 am—SIs 2008/2833, art 2; 2009/1836, art 4; 2010/20, art 2; 2013/1034, arts 2, 4
    rep in pt—Financial Services, 2012 c 21, sch 19; SIs 2013/686, sch 1 para 9;
        2013/1034, art 3; 2014/3248, sch 3 pt 2; Deregulation, 2015 c 20, sch 6 para
        22(16)(a)
sch 7 rep—SI 2013/2042, sch para 36
sch 8 rep in pt—Tribunals, Cts and Enforcement, 2007 c 15, s 146, sch 23 pt 1; SI 2010/21,
    art 5, sch 3; Equality, 2010 c 15, sch 27 Pt 1A, (added by SI 2011/1060, sch 3);
    Crime and Cts, 2013 c 22, sch 13 para 28; Enterprise and Regulatory Reform,
    2013 c 24, s 12(5); SI 2013/2042, sch para 37
sch 10 rep in pt—SIs 2008/2833, art 6, sch 3; 2009/1307, art 5, sch 4, 1834, art 4, schs 3, 4,
    1835, art 4, schs 3, 4; 2010/22, art 5, schs 3, 4; Crime and Cts, 2013 c 22, sch
    13 para 89(2)(l); Deregulation, 2015 c 20, sch 6 para 22(16)(b)
sch 11 rep in pt—Crime and Cts, 2013 c 22, sch 9 para 141
sch 12 rep in pt—Finance, 2008 c 9, s 129, sch 43 para 10(1)(2); Crime and Cts, 2013 c 22,
    s 25(5)-(7)
    am—Finance, 2008 c 9, s 129, sch 43 para 10(1)(3); Crime and Cts, 2013 c 22, s
    25(2)-(4); ibid, sch 9 para 52
sch 13 rep in pt—Serious Crime, 2007 c 27, s 92, sch 14; Employment, 2008 c 24, s 20, sch
    1 pt 2; (prosp) Child Maintenance and Other Payments, 2008 c 6, s 58, sch 8;
    Finance, 2008 c 9, s 129, sch 43 para 11(d); (pt prosp) Welfare Reform, 2012 c
    5, sch 14 pt 1; Crime and Cts, 2013 c 22, s 25(9)(a); ibid, sch 9 para 136(b);
    Deregulation, 2015 c 20, sch 6 para 2(20); ibid, sch 23 para 32(5)
    am—Legal Aid, Sentencing and Punishment of Offenders, 2012 c 10, s 110(11);
    Crime and Cts, 2013 c 22, s 25(9)(b)-(e); ibid, sch 9 para 52
sch 15 am—Crime and Cts, 2013 c 22, sch 9 para 52
sch 16 rep in pt—Charities, 2011 c 25, sch 10
    am—Crime and Cts, 2013 c 22, sch 9 para 52
sch 20 rep in pt—(pt prosp) Enterprise and Regulatory Reform, 2013 c 24, sch 19 para 9(2)
sch 22 rep in pt—Housing and Regeneration, 2008 c 17, s 321, sch 16; Public Bodies, 2011
    c 24, sch 6
sch 36 am—Finance, 2009 c 10, sch 47 paras 5,6

2007

c 16   **Parliament (Joint Departments)**
            s 3 am—Constitutional Reform and Governance, 2010 c 25, s 19, sch 2 para 17; Public
                Service Pensions, 2013 c 25, sch 8 para 30

c 17   **Consumers, Estate Agents and Redress**
            trans of functions—Public Services Reform (S), 2010 asp 8, s 3(4)
            Pt 1 (ss 1-41) heading subst—SI 2014/631, sch 1 para 12(2)
            s 1 subst—SI 2014/631, sch 1 para 12(3)(4)
            s 2 rep —SI 2014/631, sch 1 para 12(5)
            s 3 am—Postal Services, 2011 c 5, sch 12 para 176
            s 4 am—Postal Services, 2011 c 5, sch 12 para 176; (prosp) Water, 2014 c 21, sch 7 para
                137; SI 2014/631, sch 1 para 12(6)
            s 5 am—Postal Services, 2011 c 5, sch 12 para 176; SI 2014/631, sch 1 para
                12(7)(a)-(c)(e)(f)(g)(h)(i)(iii)(i)
                rep in pt—SI 2014/631, sch 1 para 12(7)(d)(h)(ii)
            s 6 am—Pensions, 2011 c 19, sch 1 para 7; SI 2014/631, sch 1 para 12(8)(a)-(c)
                rep in pt—SI 2014/631, sch 1 para 12(8)(d)
            s 6A added—SI 2014/631, sch 1 para 12(9)
            s 7 rep—SI 2014/631, sch 1 para 12(10)
            s 7A added (S)—Public Services Reform (S), 2010 asp 8, s 3, sch 2 paras 15, 17
                rep—SI 2014/631, sch 1 para 12(11)
            s 8 am—SI 2014/631, sch 1 para 12(12)
            s 9 am—SI 2014/631, sch 1 para 12(13)
            s 10 am—SI 2014/631, sch 1 para 12(14)
            s 11 am—SI 2014/631, sch 1 para 12(15)
            s 12 am—SI 2014/631, sch 1 para 12(16)
            s 13 am—SI 2014/631, sch 1 para 12(17)
            s 14 am—SI 2014/631, sch 1 para 12(18)
            s 15 am—Postal Services, 2011 c 5, sch 12 para 177; SI 2014/631, sch 1 para 12(19)
            s 16 am—Postal Services, 2011 c 5, sch 12 para 178; SI 2014/631, sch 1 para 12(20)
            s 17 am—SI 2014/631, sch 1 para 12(21)(22)
            s 18 am—SI 2014/631, sch 1 para 12(23)
            s 19 am—SI 2014/631, sch 1 para 12(24)
            s 19A added—SI 2011/2704, reg 3(2)
                am—SI 2014/631, sch 1 para 12(25)
            s 20 rep—SI 2014/631, sch 1 para 12(26)
            s 20A added (S)—Public Services Reform (S), 2010 asp 8, s 3, sch 2 paras 15, 18
                rep—SI 2014/631, sch 1 para 12(26)
            ss 21-23 rep—SI 2014/631, sch 1 para 12(26)
            s 24 am —(S) Public Services Reform (S), 2010 asp 8, s 3, sch 2 paras 15, 19; Postal
                Services, 2011 c 5, sch 12 para 179; SIs 2014/631, sch 1 para 12(27); 2014/892,
                sch 1 para 173
            s 25 am—(S) Public Services Reform (S), 2010 asp 8, s 3, sch 2 paras 15, 20; Postal
                Services, 2011 c 5, sch 12 para 180; SIs 2012/2400, art 32; 2014/631, sch 1 para
                12(28); (prosp) Water, 2014 c 21, sch 7 para 138
            s 26 am—SI 2014/631, sch 1 para 12(29)
            s 27 am—SIs 2014/631, sch 1 para 12(30); 2014/892, sch 1 para 174
            s 28 am—SI 2014/631, sch 1 para 12(31)
            s 29 am—Postal Services, 2011 c 5, sch 12 para 181; SIs 2011/2704, reg 3(3)(b); 2014/631,
                sch 1 para 12(32)
                rep in pt—SI 2011/2704, reg 3(3)(a)
            s 31 am—SI 2014/631, sch 1 para 12(33)
            s 32 am—SI 2014/631, sch 1 para 12(34)
            s 33 am—SI 2014/631, sch 1 para 12(35)(a)-(c); (prosp) Water, 2014 c 21, sch 7 para 139
                rep in pt—SI 2014/631, sch 1 para 12(35)(d)
            s 35 am—SI 2014/631, sch 1 para 12(36)(b)-(e)
                rep in pt—SI 2014/631, sch 1 para 12(36)(a)
            s 36 am—SI 2014/631, sch 1 para 12(37)
            s 37 am—SI 2014/631, sch 1 para 12(38)(39)
            s 38 rep—SI 2014/631, sch 1 para 12(40)
            s 39 rep —Financial Services, 2012 c. 21, sch 19
            ss 40A, 40B added—SI 2014/631, sch 1 para 12(41)
            s 41 mod—SI 2008/1262, art 4
                am—Postal Services, 2011 c 5, sch 12 para 182; (prosp) Water, 2014 c 21, sch 7 para
                140(b)

2007
c 17 s 41 *continued*

rep in pt—SI 2014/631, sch 1 para 12(42); (prosp) Water, 2014 c 21, sch 7 para 140(a)

s 42 am—Postal Services, 2011 c 5, sch 12 para 183; (prosp) Water, 2014 c 21, sch 7 para 141(2)(3)(b)

rep in pt—(prosp) Water, 2014 c 21, sch 7 para 141(3)(a)

s 43 am—SI 2014/631, sch 1 para 12(43)

s 45 am—Postal Services, 2011 c 5, sch 12 para 184; SI 2014/631, sch 1 para 12(44)

s 49 am—SI 2014/631, sch 1 para 12(45)

s 52 rep in pt—Postal Services, 2011 c 5, sch 12 para 185
am—(prosp) Water, 2014 c 21, sch 7 para 142

s 57 rep—Deregulation, 2015 c 20, sch 6 para 2(20); ibid, sch 23 para 32(5)

s 58 rep in pt—Consumer Rights, 2015 c 15, sch 6 para 85(i)

s 60 am—Postal Services, 2011 c 5, sch 12 para 186

s 62 am—SI 2014/631, sch 1 para 12(46)(a)(b)
rep in pt—SI 2014/631, sch 1 para 12(46)(c)

s 65 am—SIs 2011/2704, reg 3(4); 2014/631, sch 1 para 12(47)(a)
rep in pt—Postal Services, 2011 c 5, sch 12 para 187; SI 2014/631, sch 1 para 12(47)(b)

sch 1 rep —SI 2014/631, sch 1 para 12(48)

sch 2 rep in pt—Postal Services, 2011 c 5, sch 12 para 188(b)

sch 4 am—SI 2014/631, sch 1 para 12(49)

sch 5 rep in pt—Postal Services, 2011 c 5, sch 12 para 188(c)

sch 7 rep in pt—Finance, 2008 c 9, s 8, sch 2 para 70(j); Postal Services, 2011 c 5, sch 12 para 188(d); Localism, 2011 c 20, sch 25 pt 29

c 18   **Statistics and Registration Service**
transtl provns—SI 2008/839, art 3
mod—SI 2011/2878, art 5
s 4 am—SI 2012/2404, sch 2 para 60
s 6 ext—SI 2008/928, art 2, sch
s 39 rep in pt—Counter-Terrorism, 2008 c 28, s 20, sch 9, sch 1 para 5(a)
appl—SI 2012/1711, reg 7 8
appl (mods)—(E) SIs 2009/244, reg 6; 3201, reg 6
s 42 am—Health and Social Care, 2012 c 7, s 287; SI 2014/3168, sch paras 13, 33
s 67 rep in pt—Counter-Terrorism, 2008 c 28, s 20, sch 9, sch 1 para 5(b)
sch 3 rep in pt—Loc Democracy, Economic Development and Construction, 2009 c 20, s 146, sch 7 pt 4

c 19   **Corporate Manslaughter and Corporate Homicide**
s 2 am—SI 2011/1868, art 2; Immigration, 2014 c 22, sch 9 para 15; Crim Justice and Cts, 2015 c 2, sch 9 para 23
s 6 am—Police and Fire Reform (S), 2012 asp 8, sch 7 para 71; Health and Social Care, 2012 c 7, sch 5 para 147(a), (b)(i); SI 2013/602, sch 1 para 9
rep in pt—Health and Social Care, 2012 c 7, sch 5 para 147(b)(ii), (iii); (prosp) ibid, sch 14 para 102
s 7 am—SIs 2008/912, art 3, sch 1; 2013/1465, sch 1 para 11
s 13 am—Police Reform and Social Responsibility, 2011 c 13, sch 16 para 365; Crime and Cts, 2013 c 22, sch 8 para 174; SI 2013/602, sch 2 para 57(2)(c)-(e)
rep in pt—SI 2013/602, sch 2 para 57(2)(b)
s 15 am—SI 2010/976, art 7, sch 9
s 18 am—Serious Crime, 2007 c 27, s 62
s 23A added—SI 2010/976, art 7, sch 9
s 24 am—SI 2010/976, art 7, sch 9
s 25 am—Energy, 2013 c 32, sch 12 para 93
s 27 am—SI 2010/976, art 7, sch 9
sch 1 am—SIs 2008/396, art 2; 2009/229, art 9, sch 2; 2748, art 8, sch; 2010/1836, art 6, sch; Budget Responsibility and Nat Audit, 2011 c 4, sch 5 para 32; Crime and Cts, 2013 c 22, sch 8 para 175
rep in pt—Serious Crime, 2007 c 27, ss 74, 92, sch 8 para 178, sch 14; SIs 2008/396, art 2; 2009/2748, art 8, sch; 2010/1836, art 6, sch; 2014/834, sch 2 para 44
sch 2 am—(prosp) Coroners and Justice, 2009 c 25, s 178, sch 23 pt 1

c 20   **Forced Marriage (Civil Protection)**
s 1 rep in pt—Crime and Cts, 2013 c 22, sch 11 para 210 Table
sch 1 trans of funtions—SI 2010/976, art 15, sch 17
am—SI 2010/976, art 15, sch 18
sch 2 rep in pt—Crime and Cts, 2013 c 22, sch 11 para 210 Table

2007

c 21   **Offender Management**

s 1 am—Crim Justice and Immigration, 2008 c 4, ss 6, 148, sch 4 para 99, sch 26 para 83;
Crim Justice and Cts, 2015 c 2, sch 9 para 25

s 3 am—Offender Rehabilitation, 2014 c 11, s 10; (prosp) Crim Justice and Cts, 2015 c 2,
sch 3 para 14

s 4 am—Offender Rehabilitation, 2014 c 11, sch 4 para 8

s 14 am—Crim Justice and Cts, 2015 c 2, sch 9 para 26; ibid, sch 10 para 37; (prosp) ibid,
sch 3 para 15

s 28 am—Legal Aid, Sentencing and Punishment of Offenders, 2012 c 10, sch 21 para 32

sch 1 am—Loc Govt and Public Involvement in Health, 2007 c 28, s 118(3)(4); SI
2012/854, art 4(2)

rep in pt—SI 2012/854, art 4(3)

sch 3 rep in pt—Equality, 2010 c 15, sch 27 Pt 1A (adde by SI 2011/1060, sch 3)

sch 5 am—Loc Govt and Public Involvement in Health, 2007 c 28, s 118(3)(5)

c 22   **Pensions**

s 13 rep in pt—Pensions, 2011 c 19, sch 1 para 9(a)

am—Pensions, 2011 c 19, sch 1 para 9(b)

s 15 am—Pensions, 2014 c 19, sch 13 para 78(2)(4)

rep in pt—Pensions, 2014 c 19, sch 13 para 78(3)

s 18 am—SI 2008/1432, regs 3, 8; Pensions, 2011 c 19, s 23

s 20 rep—SI 2010/911, art 8(1)(a)

s 21 rep—Pensions, 2008 c 30, ss 79(1), 148, sch 11, pt 1

s 22 rep—SI 2010/911, art 8(1)(a)

s 23 am—Pensions, 2008 c 30, s 86(1)(2)(4)(5)

rep in pt—Pensions, 2008 c 30, s 148, sch 11, s 86(1)(3)

s 27 am—Pensions, 2014 c 19, sch 13 para 79

sch 1 rep in pt—(pt prosp) Welfare Reform, 2009 c 24, s 58, sch 7 pts 1, 2; Pensions, 2011 c
19, sch 2 para 4(d); (pt prosp) Welfare Reform, 2012 c 5, sch 14 pts 1, 9;
Pensions, 2014 c 19, sch 12 para 91

sch 3 rep in pt—Pensions, 2011 c 19, sch 1 para 10

sch 4 rep in pt—Pensions, 2008 c 30, s 148, sch 11, pt 2, sch 11, pt 3; SI 2011/1730, art
8(1)(2)(a); Pensions, 2014 c 19, sch 13 para 80(3)

am—Pensions, 2011 c 19, s 27; SI 2011/1730, art 8(2)(b)(c); Pensions, 2014 c 19, sch
13 para 80(2)

sch 6 rep (with savings)—SI 2010/911, art 8

c 23   **Sustainable Communities**

s 3 am—Sustainable Communities Act 2007 (Amendment), 2010 c 21, s 1

s 5A-5D added—Sustainable Communities Act 2007 (Amendment), 2010 c 21, s 2(2)

s 7 rep—Deregulation, 2015 c 20, s 100(2)(c)

s 8 rep in pt—Public Bodies, 2011 c 24, sch 6

sch 1 am—Sustainable Communities Act 2007 (Amendment), 2010 c 21, s 2(3)

c 24   **Greater London Authority**

s 11 rep in pt—Equality, 2010 c 15, s 211, sch 27 pt 1 (as subst by SI 2010/2279, sch 2)

s 20 rep—Localism, 2011 c 20, sch 25 pt 32

s 30 rep in pt—Localism, 2011 c 20, sch 25 pt 16; ibid, sch 25 pt 17

s 36 rep (prosp)—Planning, 2008 c 29, s 238, sch 13

c 25   **Further Education and Training**

ss 1, 2 rep—Apprenticeships, Skills, Children and Learning, 2009 c 22, s 266, sch 16 pt 2

ss 4-10 rep—Apprenticeships, Skills, Children and Learning, 2009 c 22, s 266, sch 16 pt 2

ss 11-13 rep—Apprenticeships, Skills, Children and Learning, 2009 c 22, ss 123, 266, sch 6
paras 60, 61, sch 16 pt 2

ss 14-16 rep—Apprenticeships, Skills, Children and Learning, 2009 c 22, ss 123, 266, sch 6
paras 60, 62, sch 16 pt 2

s 18 rep in pt—Further and Higher Educ (Governance and Information) (W), 2014 anaw 1,
sch 2 para 4(a)

s 21 rep in pt—Further and Higher Educ (Governance and Information) (W), 2014 anaw 1,
sch 2 para 4(b)

s 22 rep (W)—Further and Higher Educ (Governance and Information) (W), 2014 anaw 1,
sch 2 para 4(c)

am—Educ, 2011 c 21, sch 12 para 45(a)

rep in pt—Educ, 2011 c 21, sch 12 para 45(b)

sch 1 rep in pt—SI 2010/1080, art 2, schs 1, 2; Charities, 2011 c 25, sch 10

2007

c 26   **Building Societies (Funding) and Mutual Societies (Transfers)**
    s 3 am—SI 2009/1941, art 2, sch 1; Co-operative and Community Benefit Societies, 2014 c
        14, sch 4 para 114
      rep in pt—SI 2009/1941, art 2, sch 1
    s 4 appl (mods)—SI 2009/509, art 7
      am—Co-operative and Community Benefit Societies, 2014 c 14, sch 4 para 115

c 27   **Serious Crime**
    s 1 am—(1.3.2016) Serious Crime, 2015 c 9, sch 1 para 2
    s 2 am—(1.3.2016) Serious Crime, 2015 c 9, sch 1 para 3
    s 2A added—(1.3.2016) Serious Crime, 2015 c 9, sch 1 para 4
    s 3 am—(1.3.2016) Serious Crime, 2015 c 9, sch 1 para 5
    s 4 am—SI 2010/976, art 8, sch 10; (1.3.2016) Serious Crime, 2015 c 9, sch 1 para 6
    s 5 am—Crime and Cts, 2013 c 22, sch 8 para 177; (1.3.2016) Serious Crime, 2015 c 9, sch
        1 para 7
    s 5A added—Serious Crime, 2015 c 9, s 50(2)
    s 7 subst—SI 2010/976, art 8, sch 10
      am—(1.3.2016) Serious Crime, 2015 c 9, sch 1 para 8
    s 8 rep in pt—SI 2014/834, sch 2 para 46
      am—(1.3.2016) Serious Crime, 2015 c 9, sch 1 para 9
    s 9 am—(1.3.2016) Serious Crime, 2015 c 9, sch 1 para 10; ibid, sch 4 para 76
    s 10 rep in pt—SI 2014/834, sch 2 para 47
       am—(1.3.2016) Serious Crime, 2015 c 9, sch 1 para 11
    s 12 am—(1.3.2016) Serious Crime, 2015 c 9, sch 1 para 12
    s 13 am—(1.3.2016) Serious Crime, 2015 c 9, sch 1 para 13
    s 16 am—Serious Crime, 2015 c 9, sch 4 para 77
    s 17 am—(1.3.2016) Serious Crime, 2015 c 9, sch 1 para 14
    s 18 am—(1.3.2016) Serious Crime, 2015 c 9, sch 1 para 15
    s 19 am—Serious Crime, 2015 c 9, sch 4 para 78
    s 21 am—Serious Crime, 2015 c 9, s 48; ibid, sch 4 para 79
    s 22 am—(1.3.2016) Serious Crime, 2015 c 9, sch 1 para 16
    s 22A-22D added—(1.3.2016) Serious Crime, 2015 c 9, sch 1 para 17
    s 22E added—Serious Crime, 2015 c 9, s 49
    s 24 am—SI 2010/976, art 8, sch 10
    ss 24A, 24B added—(1.3.2016) Serious Crime, 2015 c 9, sch 1 para 18
    s 27 am—SI 2009/1941, art 2, sch 1 para 265
       rep in pt—SI 2014/834, sch 2 para 48; Co-operative and Community Benefit Societies,
          2014 c 14, sch 4 para 116(2)(3); (1.3.2016) Serious Crime, 2015 c 9, sch 1
          para 19
    s 27A added—(1.3.2016) Serious Crime, 2015 c 9, sch 1 para 20
    s 28 am—SIs 2009/1941, art 2, sch 1 para 265; 2010/976, art 8, sch 10
    s 29 am —SI 2010/976, art 8, sch 10; (1.3.2016) Serious Crime, 2015 c 9, sch 1 para 21
      rep in pt—SI 2010/976, art 8, sch 10
    s 31 am—(1.3.2016) Serious Crime, 2015 c 9, sch 1 para 22(2)
      rep in pt—(1.3.2016) Serious Crime, 2015 c 9, sch 1 para 22(3)
    s 32 rep in pt—(1.3.2016) Serious Crime, 2015 c 9, sch 1 para 23
    s 34 am—SI 2012/1809, art 3(1) sch pt 1; (1.3.2016) Serious Crime, 2015 c 9, sch 1 para
        24
    s 36 am—Serious Crime, 2015 c 9, sch 4 para 80
    s 36A added—(1.3.2016) Serious Crime, 2015 c 9, sch 1 para 25
    s 39 rep in pt—Police Reform and Social Responsibility, 2011 c 13, sch 16 para 370(b)
      am—Police Reform and Social Responsibility, 2011 c 13, sch 16 para 370(a); Crime
        and Cts, 2013 c 22, sch 8 para 178; (1.3.2016) Serious Crime, 2015 c 9, sch 1
        para 26
    s 40 am—SI 2010/976, art 8, sch 10; (1.3.2016) Serious Crime, 2015 c 9, sch 1 para 27
    s 43 rep in pt—SI 2014/834, sch 2 para 49
      am—(1.3.2016) Serious Crime, 2015 c 9, sch 1 para 28
    Pt 2 (ss 44-67) restr—Corporate Manslaughter and Corporate Homicide, 2007 c 19, s
        18(1A)
    s 49 am—SI 2010/976, art 8, sch 10
    s 51A added —Coroners and Justice, 2009 c 25, s 177, sch 21 para 61(1)(2)
    s 53 am—Bribery, 2010 c 23, s 17, sch 1 paras 12, 13
    s 63 am—SI 2010/976, art 8, sch 10
    s 68 rep in pt—(prosp) (S) Crim Justice and Licensing (S), 2010 asp 13, s 98(a)
    s 69 rep in pt—(prosp) (S) Crim Justice and Licensing (S), 2010 asp 13, s 98(b)

2007

c 27 *continued*

s 70 am—SI 2014/834, sch 2 para 50

s 71 rep in pt—(prosp) (S) Crim Justice and Licensing (S), 2010 asp 13, s 98(c)

s 78 rep (pt prosp 1.3.2016)—Policing and Crime, 2009 c 26, s 112, sch 8 pt 4

s 80 rep in pt—Policing and Crime, 2009 c 26, s 112, sch 8 pt 5; Finance, 2013 c 29, sch 48 para 23

s 84 rep in pt—SI 2014/834, sch 2 para 51

s 89 am—SI 2010/976, art 8, sch 10; (1.3.2016) Serious Crime, 2015 c 9, sch 1 para 29
rep in pt—SI 2010/976, art 8, sch 10

s 93 rep in pt—(1.3.2016) Serious Crime, 2015 c 9, sch 1 para 30

sch 1 rep in pt—Marine and Coastal Access, 2009 c 23, s 321, sch 22 pt 5
am—Bribery, 2010 c 23, s 17, sch 1 paras 12, 14; Taxation (International and Other Provns), 2010 c 8, s 371, sch 7 paras 100,101; Protection of Freedoms, 2012 c 9, sch 9 para 142; Serious Crime, 2015 c 9, s 47(2)-(8); (1.3.2016) ibid, sch 1 para 31; ibid, sch 4 para 81(2)-(4); Modern Slavery, 2015 c 30, sch 5 para 7

sch 2 am—SI 2014/834, sch 2 para 52(2)
rep in pt—SI 2014/834, sch 2 para 52(3)(4)

sch 3 am—Coroners and Justice, 2009 c 25, s 177, sch 21 para 61(1)(3); Cluster Munitions (Prohibitions), 2010 c 11, s 31, sch 3 para 2; Serious Crime, 2015 c 9, sch 4 para 82

sch 6 rep in pt—Finance (No 3), 2010 c 33, s 29, sch 13 para 4; Civil Aviation, 2012 c 19, sch 9 para 17

sch 7 rep in pt—Loc Audit and Accountability, 2014 c 2, sch 1 pt 2

sch 8 rep in pt—(pt prosp) Policing and Crime, 2009 c 26, s 112, sch 8 pts 4, 5; Legal Aid, Sentencing and Punishment of Offenders, 2012 c 10, sch 5 pt 2; SI 2014/834, sch 2 para 53

sch 10 rep in pt—Policing and Crime, 2009 c 26, s 112, sch 8 pt 5

sch 13 rep in pt—Loc Audit and Accountability, 2014 c 2, sch 12 para 79

c 28　**Local Government and Public Involvement in Health**

ss 4-7 am—Loc Democracy, Economic Development and Construction, 2009 c 20, s 67, sch 4 paras 12-15

s 8 am—Loc Democracy, Economic Development and Construction, 2009 c 20, ss 65(1)-(3), 67, sch 4 para 16

s 9 am—Loc Democracy, Economic Development and Construction, 2009 c 20, s 67, sch 4 para 17

s 10 am—Loc Democracy, Economic Development and Construction, 2009 c 20, ss 65(4), 67, sch 4 para 18

s 11am—Loc Democracy, Economic Development and Construction, 2009 c 20, s 65(5)(a)
rep in pt—Loc Democracy, Economic Development and Construction, 2009 c 20, ss 65(5)(b), 146, sch 7 pt 3

s 12 am—Loc Democracy, Economic Development and Construction, 2009 c 20, ss 65(6), 67, sch 4 para 19
rep in pt—Loc Democracy, Economic Development and Construction, 2009 c 20, s 146, sch 7 pt 3

s 15 am—Police Reform and Social Responsibility, 2011 c 13, sch 10 para 14

s 16 appl (mods)—Loc Govt, 1970 c 70, s12(2)

s 23 am—Loc Democracy, Economic Development and Construction, 2009 c 20, ss 67, 119, sch 4 para 20(1)(3), sch 6 para 121(1)(2)
rep in pt—Loc Democracy, Economic Development and Construction, 2009 c 20, ss 67, 146, sch 4 paras 11, 20(1)(2), sch 7 pt 3

s 24 am—Localism, 2011 c 20, sch 7 para 49

s 25 am—Localism, 2011 c 20, sch 7 para 50

s 28 am—Localism, 2011 c 20, sch 7 para 51

s 31A added—Localism, 2011 c 20, s 24(6)

s 33 am—Localism, 2011 c 20, s 24(3)
rep in pt—Localism, 2011 c 20, s 24(2)(a), sch 25 pt 4

s 34 am—Localism, 2011 c 20, s 24(4)(5)
rep in pt—Localism, 2011 c 20, sch 25 pt 4

s 36 am—Loc Democracy, Economic Development and Construction, 2009 c 20, s 67, sch 4 para 21

s 38 rep in pt—Localism, 2011 c 20, s 24(2)(b), sch 25 pt 4

s 40 rep in pt—Localism, 2011 c 20, s 24(2)(c), sch 25 pt 4

ss 41-45 am—Loc Democracy, Economic Development and Construction, 2009 c 20, s 67, sch 4 paras 22-26

2007
c 28 *continued*

s 50-52 am—Loc Democracy, Economic Development and Construction, 2009 c 20, s 67,
    sch 4 para 27-29

ss 55-57 rep—Loc Democracy, Economic Development and Construction, 2009 c 20, s 146,
    sch 7 pt 3

s 59 am—Loc Democracy, Economic Development and Construction, 2009 c 20, s 67, sch 4
    para 30

s 62 rep in pt—Localism, 2011 c 20, sch 25 pt 4

s 63 rep in pt—Localism, 2011 c 20, sch 25 pt 4

s 64 rep—Localism, 2011 c 20, sch 25 pt 4

s 65 rep in pt—Localism, 2011 c 20, sch 25 pt 4

s 67 rep—Localism, 2011 c 20, sch 25 pt 4

s 69 rep in pt—Localism, 2011 c 20, sch 25 pt 4

s 70 rep in pt—Localism, 2011 c 20, sch 25 pt 4

s 78 rep —Deregulation, 2015 c 20, s 100(2)(d)

s 80 am—SI 2015/998, art 3

s 80A added—SI 2015/998, art 4

s 83 am—SI 2015/998, arts 5, 8

s 84 am—SI 2015/998, arts 6, 8

s 85 am—SI 2015/998, arts 7, 8

s 79 appl (mods)—SI 2008/2113, reg 7

s 86 appl (mods)—SI 2008/2113, reg 7
    am—Loc Democracy, Economic Development and Construction, 2009 c 20, s 67, sch 4
      para 31

s 92 appl (mods)—SI 2008/2113, reg 7
    am—Loc Democracy, Economic Development and Construction, 2009 c 20, s 67, sch 4
      para 32

s 93 am—SI 2015/998, art 10

s 96 appl (mods)—SI 2008/2113, reg 7
    am—Loc Democracy, Economic Development and Construction, 2009 c 20, s 67, sch 4
      para 32

s 97 appl (mods)—SI 2008/2113, reg 7

s 98 appl (mods)—SI 2008/2113, regs 7-8
    am—Loc Democracy, Economic Development and Construction, 2009 c 20, s 67, sch 4
      para 32

s 99 appl (mods)—SI 2008/2113, reg 7

s 100 appl (mods)—SI 2008/2113, reg 7
    am—Loc Democracy, Economic Development and Construction, 2009 c 20, s 67, sch
      4 para 32

s 102 am—Loc Democracy, Economic Development and Construction, 2009 c 20, s 67, sch
    4 para 33; SI 2015/998, art 9

Pt 5 (ss 103-128) appl (mods)—SI 2008/2113, regs 11-12
    rep in pt—Deregulation, 2015 c 20, s 101(2)

s 104 am—Loc Transport, 2008 c 26, s 77, sch 4 para 68; Housing and Regeneration, 2008
    c 17, s 56, sch 8 para 83; Loc Democracy, Economic Development and
    Construction, 2009 c 20, s 119, sch 6 para 121(1)(3); SI 2010/1080, art 2, sch 1;
    Police Reform and Social Responsibility, 2011 c 13, sch 16 para 367; SIs
    2013/594, art 6(a); 2014/469, sch 2 para 24
    rep in pt—Public Bodies, 2011 c 24, sch 6; Educ, 2011 c 21, sch 16 para 39; SI
      2013/594, art 6(b); Deregulation, 2015 c 20, sch 13 para 6(34)(a); ibid, sch 14
      para 59

ss 105-113 rep—Deregulation, 2015 c 20, s 101(1)(a)

s 114 rep—Deregulation, 2015 c 20, s 100(2)(d)

s 115 rep in pt—Localism, 2011 c 20, sch 25 pt 1

s 116 am—Health and Social Care, 2012 c 7, s 192
    mod—Nat Health Service, 2006 c 41, ss 13Z4(3), 14Z24(3)

s 116A added —Health and Social Care, 2012 c 7, s 193
    mod—Nat Health Service, 2006 c 41, ss 13Z4(3), 14Z24(3)

s 116B added —Health and Social Care, 2012 c 7, s 193
    mod—Nat Health Service, 2006 c 41, ss 13Z4(3), 14Z24(3)
    appl—Children and Families, 2014 c 6, ss 26(7), 27(4)

s 117 rep in pt—Deregulation, 2015 c 20, s 101(1)(b)

s 118 rep in pt—Deregulation, 2015 c 20, s 101(1)(c)

s 121 rep in pt—Localism, 2011 c 20, sch 25 pt 4

2007
c 28 *continued*

s 123 subst—Loc Democracy, Economic Development and Construction, 2009 c 20, s 32(1)
    mod —Local Government, 2000 c 22 s 9FH(6)
    am—Police Reform and Social Responsibility, 2011 c 13, sch 16 para 368
s 124 rep—Localism, 2011 c 20, sch 25 pt 4
s 127 rep in pt—Localism, 2011 c 20, sch 25 pt 4
s 136 rep in pt—Loc Govt and Public Involvement in Health, 2007 c 28, s 241, sch 18
s 138 rep—Deregulation, 2015 c 20, s 103(2)(b)
ss 145, 146 rep —Loc Audit and Accountability, 2014 c 2, sch 1 pt 2
s 147 rep in pt—(pt prosp) Welfare Reform, 2012 c 5, sch 14 pt 1
s 148 rep —Loc Audit and Accountability, 2014 c 2, sch 12 para 81
s 149 rep —Loc Audit and Accountability, 2014 c 2, sch 1 pt 2
s 150 rep in pt—(pt prosp) Welfare Reform, 2012 c 5, sch 14 pt 1
s 151 rep in pt—Loc Audit and Accountability, 2014 c 2, sch 1 pt 2
s 153 rep —Loc Audit and Accountability, 2014 c 2, sch 1 pt 2
s 155 rep in pt—Housing and Regeneration, 2008 c 17, s 321, sch 16; Loc Audit and
    Accountability, 2014 c 2, sch 1 pt 2
s 157 rep —Loc Audit and Accountability, 2014 c 2, sch 1 pt 2
s 158 rep —Loc Audit and Accountability, 2014 c 2, sch 12 para 123(e)
ss 159-165 rep —Loc Audit and Accountability, 2014 c 2, sch 1 pt 2
s 183 rep in pt—Localism, 2011 c 20, sch 4 para 55(1)-(4), sch 25 pt 5
ss 185-187 rep—Localism, 2011 c 20, sch 25 pt 5
s 188 rep in pt—Localism, 2011 c 20, sch 25 pt 5
ss 189-193 rep—Localism, 2011 c 20, sch 25 pt 5
s 194 rep in pt—Localism, 2011 c 20, sch 25 pt 5
ss 195, 196 rep —Localism, 2011 c 20, sch 25 pt 5
s 198 rep —Localism, 2011 c 20, sch 25 pt 5
s 201 rep in pt—Localism, 2011 c 20, sch 25 pt 5; Loc Audit and Accountability, 2014 c 2,
    sch 1 pt 2
ss 205-208 rep—Deregulation, 2015 c 20, sch 13 para 4
s 209 rep—Deregulation, 2015 c 20, sch 13 para 6(34)(b)
s 211 rep—Deregulation, 2015 c 20, sch 13 para 6(34)(b)
s 212 am—Localism, 2011 c 20, sch 25 pt 5; Loc Audit and Accountability, 2014 c 2, sch
    12 para 82
s 214 am—Loc Audit and Accountability, 2014 c 2, sch 12 para 83(2)(4)
    rep in pt—Loc Audit and Accountability, 2014 c 2, sch 12 para 83(3)(5)
s 217 rep in pt—Bribery, 2010 c 23, s 17, sch 2
s 221 am—Health and Social Care, 2012 c 7, s 182(2)-(8), (10)
    rep in pt—Health and Social Care, 2012 c 7, s 182(9)
s 222 am—Health and Social Care, 2012 c 7, s 183(2)-(8); ibid, sch 5 para 149(2)(a), (3)
    rep in pt—Health and Social Care, 2012 c 7, sch 14 para 104; ibid, sch 5 para
    149(2)(b), (c)
s 222A added —Health and Social Care, 2012 c 7, s 183(9)
s 223 am—Health and Social Care, 2012 c 7, s 184(2)-(5), (6)(a), (c)-(e)
    rep in pt—Health and Social Care, 2012 c 7, s 184(6)(b)
s 223A added —Health and Social Care, 2012 c 7, s 185(1)
s 224 am—Health and Social Care, 2012 c 7, sch 5 para 150(a), (b), (d); ibid, s 186(2)-(5)
    rep in pt—Health and Social Care, 2012 c 7, sch 14 para 105; ibid, sch 5 para 150(c)
s 225 am—Health and Social Care, 2012 c 7, s 186(7)-(9), (11)
    rep in pt—Health and Social Care, 2012 c 7, s 186(10); (prosp) ibid, sch 14 para 106;
    ibid, sch 5 para 151
s 226 am—Health and Social Care, 2012 c 7, s 186(13)-(16)
s 227 am—Health and Social Care, 2008 c 14, s 95, sch 5 para 94; Health and Social Care,
    2012 c 7, s 187(3)(a)(ii)-(iv), (4)(a), (b)(ii), (5)(a), (b), (6)(a)(ii), (iii), (8), (9)
    rep in pt—Health and Social Care, 2012 c 7, s 187(2), (3)(a)(i), (b), (c), (4)(b)(i), (c),
    (5)(c), (6)(a)(i), (b), (7); ibid, sch 5 para 152
s 228 rep—Health and Social Care, 2012 c 7, s 188(10)
s 236 rep in pt—Localism, 2011 c 20, sch 25 pt 4
s 240 am—Loc Democracy, Economic Development and Construction, 2009 c 20, s 67, sch
    4 para 34
    rep in pt—Deregulation, 2015 c 20, sch 13 para 6(34)(c)
s 244 rep in pt—Bribery, 2010 c 23, s 17, sch 2
sch 1 rep in pt—Loc Democracy, Economic Development and Construction, 2009 c 20, s
    146, sch 7 pt 3; (prosp) Coroners and Justice, 2009 c 25, s 178, sch 23 pt 1

2007

c 28 *continued*

    sch 3 rep in pt—Localism, 2011 c 20, sch 25 pt 4

    sch 8 rep in pt—SI 2010/866, art 7, sch 4

    sch 9 rep —Loc Audit and Accountability, 2014 c 2, sch 1 pt 2

    sch 10 rep —Loc Audit and Accountability, 2014 c 2, sch 12 para 84

    sch 11 rep —Loc Audit and Accountability, 2014 c 2, sch 1 pt 2

    sch 12 rep in pt—Localism, 2011 c 20, sch 25 pt 5

    sch 13 rep—Deregulation, 2015 c 20, sch 13 para 6(34)(b)

    sch 14 rep in pt—Bribery, 2010 c 23, s 17, sch 2; Loc Audit and Accountability, 2014 c 2,
        sch 12 para 123(e)

c 29   **Legal Services**

    s 57 am—Enterprise and Regulatory Reform, 2013 c 24, sch 6 para 109; SI 2014/892, sch 1
        para 176

    s 58 am—Enterprise and Regulatory Reform, 2013 c 24, sch 6 para 110

    s 59 am—Enterprise and Regulatory Reform, 2013 c 24, sch 6 para 111

    s 60 am—Enterprise and Regulatory Reform, 2013 c 24, sch 6 para 112; SI 2014/892, sch 1
        para 177

    s 61 am—Enterprise and Regulatory Reform, 2013 c 24, sch 6 para 113

    s 64 am—Financial Services, 2012 c. 21, sch 18 para 125(2)

    s 66 am—Enterprise and Regulatory Reform, 2013 c 24, sch 6 para 114

    s 67 am—Enterprise and Regulatory Reform, 2013 c 24, sch 6 para 115

    s 96 mod—SIs 2011/1712, art 1; 2014/1897, sch para 1; 1898, sch para 1

    s 104 am—Deregulation, 2015 c 20, sch 19 para 15

    s 125 mod—SI 2014/3307, art 3

    s 157 restr—Admin of Justice, 1985 c 61, s 43(3A)

    s 169 am—Financial Services, 2012 c. 21, sch 18 para 125(3); Crime and Cts, 2013 c 22,
        sch 8 para 187; SI 2013/602, sch 2 para 58

    s 174A added —Financial Services (Banking Reform), 2013 c 33, s 140(5)

    s 184 am—SI 2009/3339, art 2

    s 194 am—Charities, 2011 c 25, sch 7 para 127; Legal Aid, Sentencing and Punishment of
        Offenders, 2012 c 10, sch 5 para 68; ibid, s 61(1); Crime and Cts, 2013 c 22, sch
        9 para 101; SI 2014/605, art 25

    s 195 am—Financial Services, 2012 c. 21, sch 18 para 125(4)
        rep in pt—SI 2013/1881, sch para 13

    s 206 am—Financial Services (Banking Reform), 2013 c 33, s 140(6)

    s 207 am—Enterprise and Regulatory Reform, 2013 c 24, sch 6 para 116(a); SI 2013/2042,
        sch para 39

        rep in pt—Enterprise and Regulatory Reform, 2013 c 24, sch 6 para 116(b)

    sch 1 rep in pt—SI 2009/2035, art 2, sch
        am—SI 2012/2404, sch 2 para 61(2)

    sch 3 am—Crime and Cts, 2013 c 22, sch 10 para 98

    sch 4 am—SI 2009/3233, arts 2, 3; Enterprise and Regulatory Reform, 2013 c 24, sch 6
        para 117

    sch 5 am—SI 2009/3233, arts 2, 4; Deregulation, 2015 c 20, sch 19 para 16(2)-(8)

    sch 6 am—Enterprise and Regulatory Reform, 2013 c 24, sch 6 para 118

    sch 7 am—Enterprise and Regulatory Reform, 2013 c 24, sch 6 para 119

    sch 8 am—Enterprise and Regulatory Reform, 2013 c 24, sch 6 para 120

    sch 9 am—Enterprise and Regulatory Reform, 2013 c 24, sch 6 para 121

    sch 10 am—Enterprise and Regulatory Reform, 2013 c 24, sch 6 para 122

    sch 13 mod—SIs 2011/1712, art 2; 2014/1897, sch para 2

    sch 14 am—Postal Services, 2011 c 5, sch 12 para 189
        appl (mods)—SIs 2011/2038, sch para 1(5); 2014/3234, art 5; /3236, art 3; 3238,
          sch 2 para 12
        appl—SI 2011/2866, art 5(5)

    sch 15 am—SI 2012/2404, sch 2 para 61(3)

    sch 16 rep in pt—Legal Aid, Sentencing and Punishment of Offenders, 2012 c 10, sch 5 pt 2;
        Crime and Cts, 2013 c 22, sch 9 para 141; SI 2015/401, art 3(3)

    sch 19 rep in pt—SI 2010/22, art 5, sch 4

    sch 21 rep in pt—Crim Justice and Immigration, 2008 c 4, s 149, sch 28 pt 8; SI 2009/3054,
        art 3, sch; Equality, 2010 c 15, s 211, sch 27 pt 1 (subst by SI 2010/2279, sch
        2); ibid, sch 27, Pt 1A (added by SI 2011/1060, sch 3); Legal Aid, Sentencing
        and Punishment of Offenders, 2012 c 10, sch 5 pt 2; Finance, 2012 c 14, sch 39
        para 5(2)(f); SI 2012/2398, sch 1 para 10, sch 2 para 10; SL(R), 2013 c 2, s 1,

2007

c 29 *continued*

    sch 1 pt 5; Crime and Cts, 2013 c 22, sch 10 para 99 Table; Consumer Rights, 2015 c 15, sch 6 para 85(h)

   sch 23 rep in pt—Coroners and Justice, 2009 c 25, ss 177, 178, sch 21 para 97, sch 23 pt 9

   sch 24 am—Enterprise and Regulatory Reform, 2013 c 24, sch 6 para 123(a); Deregulation, 2015 c 20, sch 19 para 17

   rep in pt—Enterprise and Regulatory Reform, 2013 c 24, sch 6 para 123(b)

c 30 **UK Borders**

   mod—SI 1994/1405, art.7 (as am by SIs 2007/3579, art 3; 2015/856, arts 5,6)

   appl (mods)—SI 1994/1405, art 7 sch 4 (added by 2015/856, art 6)

   s 2 am—SI 1993/1813, sch 4 para 6(1)(a)(iii),(c)(d) (added by 2015/856, art 4); Borders, Citizenship and Immigration, 2009 c 11, s 52(1); Counter-Terrorism and Security, 2015 c 6, s 10(8)

    rep in pt—SI 1993/1813, sch 4 para 6(1)(a)(i)(ii),(b),(e) (added by 2015/856, art 4)

   s 3 am—Borders, Citizenship and Immigration, 2009 c 11, s 52(2)

   s 4 am—SI 1993/1813, sch 4 para 6(2) (added by 2015/856, art 4)

   s 5 rep in pt—Identity Documents, 2010 c 40, s 12, sch 1 para 19

   s 7 am—Immigration, 2014 c 22, s 11

   s 8 subst—Immigration, 2014 c 22, s 14(1)

    appl—British Nationality, 1981 c 61, s 41; Immigration and Asylum, 1999 c 33, s 144A; Nationality, Immigration and Asylum, 2002 c 41, s 126(8A)

   s 11 am—Crime and Cts, 2013 c 22, sch 9 para 138

   s 15 am—Immigration, 2014 c 22, s 12(3), sch 9 para 75

    rep in pt—Immigration, 2014 c 22, s 12(2)

   s 17 rep in pt—Immigration, 2014 c 22, sch 9 para 58

   s 19 rep—Immigration, 2014 c 22, sch 9 para 60 table

   s 20 rep—Immigration, 2014 c 22, sch 9 para 76(b)

   s 21 rep—Borders, Citizenship and Immigration, 2009 c 11, ss 55(8), 56, sch pt 4

   s 24 am—Policing and Crime, 2009 c 26, s 112, sch 7 para 113; SI 2012/2595, art 16(3); Crime and Cts, 2013 c 22, sch 21 para 39

    rep in pt—SI 2012/2595, art 16(2)

   s 31 rep —Protection of Freedoms, 2012 c 9, sch 10 pt 9

   s 33 am—Crim Justice and Immigration, 2008 c 4, s 146

   s 35 rep in pt—Immigration, 2014 c 22, sch 9 para 60 table

   s 40 am—SI 2014/834, sch 2 para 55

   s 41 am—SI 2014/834, sch 2 para 56

   s 41A added—Borders, Citizenship and Immigration, 2009 c 11, s 20(1)

    am—SI 2014/834, sch 2 para 57

   s 41B added—Borders, Citizenship and Immigration, 2009 c 11, s 20(1)

    am—SI 2014/834, sch 2 para 58

   s 42 am—Borders, Citizenship and Immigration, 2009 c 11, s 20(2); SI 2014/834, sch 2 para 59

   s 48 am—Borders, Citizenship and Immigration, 2009 c 11, s 28(1)(2)(3)(b)-(d), (4)(6); Equality, 2010 c 15, s 211, sch 26 para 94 (added by SI 2010/2279, sch 1); Immigration, 2014 c 22, sch 9 para 16

    rep in pt—Borders, Citizenship and Immigration, 2009 c 11, s 28(3)(a),(5)

   s 53 am—Borders, Citizenship and Immigration, 2009 c 11, s 28(7)(8)

   s 56 am—Borders, Citizenship and Immigration, 2009 c 11, s 28(9)

    rep in pt—SI 2010/21, art 5, sch 3

   s 56A added—Legal Aid, Sentencing and Punishment of Offenders, 2012 c 10, s 140

   s 60 rep in pt—Borders, Citizenship and Immigration, 2009 c 11, ss 52(3), 56, sch pt 3

   s 61 am—Immigration, 2014 c 22, s 73(5)

3rd session of 54th Parliament

c 31 *Consolidated Fund* —rep Appropriation (No 2) 2009 c 9, s 4, sch 3

2008

c 1 *European Communities (Finance)*—rep European Union (Finance), 2015 c 32, s 2(1)

c 2 **Banking (Special Provisions)**

   s 9 mod—Banking, 2009 c 1, s 237

    am—SI 2010/22, art 5, sch 2

   s 11 am—Financial Services (Banking Reform), 2013 c 33, sch 9 para 4(3)(c)

   s 12 saved—Banking, 2009 c 1, s 237

   s 15 am—SIs 2010/2628, regs 3, 13, sch 1; 2012/917, sch 1 para 3; 2013/3115, sch 2 para 43(2)

2008

c 2 s 15 *continued*

    rep in pt—SI 2013/3115, sch 2 para 43(3)

    s 16 excl—Banking, 2009 c 1, s 229(5)

    s 148 appl (mods)—SI 2008/2666, art 18

c 3   *Appropriation*—rep Appropriation (No 3), 2010 c 30, s 4, sch 3

c 4   **Criminal Justice and Immigration**

    Pt 1 (ss 1-8) appl—Crim Justice, 1991 c 53, s 234

    s 11 am—Coroners and Justice, 2009 c 25, s 177, sch 21 para 98(1)(2)

    ss 13-16 rep—Legal Aid, Sentencing and Punishment of Offenders, 2012 c 10, sch 21 para 35(b)(i)

    s 18 rep in pt—Legal Aid, Sentencing and Punishment of Offenders, 2012 c 10, sch 21 para 35(b)(i)

    s 20 rep in pt—Legal Aid, Sentencing and Punishment of Offenders, 2012 c 10, sch 10 para 42; ibid, sch 16 para 20(a)

    s 21 rep in pt—Legal Aid, Sentencing and Punishment of Offenders, 2012 c 10, s 110(14)(a)

    s 22 rep in pt—Legal Aid, Sentencing and Punishment of Offenders, 2012 c 10, s 110(14)(b)

    s 23 rep—Legal Aid, Sentencing and Punishment of Offenders, 2012 c 10, s 110(14)(c)

    s 26 rep—Legal Aid, Sentencing and Punishment of Offenders, 2012 c 10, sch 16 para 20(a)

    s 27 rep—Coroners and Justice, 2009 c 25, s 178, sch 23 pt 5

    s 28 rep—Legal Aid, Sentencing and Punishment of Offenders, 2012 c 10, sch 16 para 20(a)

    s 29 rep in pt—Legal Aid, Sentencing and Punishment of Offenders, 2012 c 10, s 114(5)

    s 32 rep—Legal Aid, Sentencing and Punishment of Offenders, 2012 c 10, sch 16 para 20(a)

    s 33 rep in pt—Legal Aid, Sentencing and Punishment of Offenders, 2012 c 10, sch 16 para 20(a); ibid, s 118(4)(a)

    s 34 rep in pt—Legal Aid, Sentencing and Punishment of Offenders, 2012 c 10, s 118(4)(b)

    s 48 rep in pt—Legal Aid, Sentencing and Punishment of Offenders, 2012 c 10, sch 24 para 29

    ss 56-58 rep—Legal Aid, Sentencing and Punishment of Offenders, 2012 c 10, sch 5 pt 2

    s 63 am—Crim Justice and Cts, 2015 c 2, s 37(2)

    s 66 am—Crim Justice and Cts, 2015 c 2, s 37(3)

    s 67 am—Crim Justice and Cts, 2015 c 2, s 37(4)

    s 76 am—Legal Aid, Sentencing and Punishment of Offenders, 2012 c 10, s 148; Crime and Cts, 2013 c 22, s 43

    appl (mods)—Dangerous Dogs, 1991 c. 65, s 3(1B) (added by 2014 c 12, s 106(2)(b))

    s 81 am—SI 2014/3141, sch 3 para 2

    s 82 am—SI 2010/976, art 15, sch 18

    s 83 rep in pt—SI 2010/976, art 15, sch 18

    am—SI 2014/3141, sch 3 para 3(2)

    s 84 am—SIs 2010/976, art 15, sch 18; 2014/3141, sch 3 para 4

    s 85 am—SI 2014/3141, sch 3 para 5(2)-(6)

    appl (mods)—SI 2014/3141, sch 3 para 5(8)(9)

    s 86 am—SI 2014/3141, sch 3 para 6

    s 87 am—SIs 2010/976, art 15, sch 18; 2014/3141, sch 3 para 7

    s 88 am—SIs 2010/976, art 15, sch 18; 2014/3141, sch 3 para 8

    s 89 am—SIs 2010/976, art 15, sch 18; 2014/3141, sch 3 para 9

    s 90 am—SIs 2010/976, art 15, sch 18; 2014/3141, sch 3 para 10

    s 90A added—SI 2010/976, art 15, sch 18

    am—SI 2014/3141, sch 3 para 11

    s 91 am—SIs 2010/976, art 15, sch 18; 2014/3141, sch 3 para 12(2)

    rep in pt—SI 2014/3141, sch 3 para 12(3)

    s 92 am—SIs 2010/976, art 15, sch 18; 2014/3141, sch 3 para 13

    s 98 am—Anti-social Behaviour, Crime and Policing, 2014 c 12, s 119(1)

    s 99 am—Anti-social Behaviour, Crime and Policing, 2014 c 12, s 119(3)

    s 118 rep—Anti-social Behaviour, Crime and Policing, 2014 c 12, sch 11 para 50

    s 119 rep in pt—Health and Social Care, 2012 c 7, sch 5 para 153; (pt prosp) ibid, sch 14 para 107(a)

    am—(pt prosp) Health and Social Care, 2012 c 7, sch 14 para 107(b)

    s 123 rep —Anti-social Behaviour, Crime and Policing, 2014 c 12, sch 11 para 50

    s 124 rep —Anti-social Behaviour, Crime and Policing, 2014 c 12, sch 11 para 50

    s 134 rep in pt—Housing and Regeneration, 2008 c 17, s 314, sch 16, sch 15 paras 23, 24

    s 135 rep in pt—Housing and Regeneration, 2008 c 17, s 314, sch 15 paras 23, 25; SI 2009/1307, art 5, sch 1

    s 141 rep in pt —(S) Crim Justice and Licensing (S), 2010 asp 13, s 100(1)

2008
c 4 *continued*

s 147 am—SI 2010/976, art 15, sch 18; Anti-social Behaviour, Crime and Policing, 2014 c 12, s 119(2)

rep in pt—SI 2014/3141, sch 3 para 14

s 152 am—SI 2014/3141, sch 3 para 15

sch 1 am—(W 6.4.2016) Children and Young Persons, 2008 c 23, s 8, sch 1 para 21; Coroners and Justice, 2009 c 25, s 177, sch 21 para 98(4)(a)(i)(b)(c); SIs 2009/1182, arts 4, 5-7, sch 5; 2010/813, art 20; 1158, art 5, sch 2; Legal Aid, Sentencing and Punishment of Offenders, 2012 c 10, ss 81(2), (3), 82(2)(b), 83(1); ibid, sch 5 para 69

rep in pt—Coroners and Justice, 2009 c 25, ss 177, 178, sch 21 para 98(1)(4)(a)(ii), sch 23 pt 1; Legal Aid, Sentencing and Punishment of Offenders, 2012 c 10, s 82(2)(a), (3)

appl —Crim Justice and Immigration, 2008 c 4, s 6, sch 4 paras 71, 73(1), (3)

sch 2 appl (mods)—Crim Procedure (S), 1995 c 46, s 234

appl—Powers of Crim Cts (Sentencing), 2000 c 6, s 73(4B)

am—Legal Aid, Sentencing and Punishment of Offenders, 2012 c 10, ss 83(2), (3), 84(2), (3), (4)(b)(ii)

rep in pt—Legal Aid, Sentencing and Punishment of Offenders, 2012 c 10, s 84(4)(a), (b)(i)

sch 3 am—SI 2010/1158, art 5, sch 2

sch 4 am—Coroners and Justice, 2009 c 25, s 177, sch 21 para 98(1)(3)

rep in pt—Coroners and Justice, 2009 c 25, s 178, sch 23 pt 4; Welfare Reform, 2009 c 24, s 58, sch 7 pt 3; (S) Crim Justice and Licensing (S), 2010 asp 13, s 14, sch 2 para 53; Legal Aid, Sentencing and Punishment of Offenders, 2012 c 10, ss 64(5)(b), 70(8), sch 25 pt 2

sch 5 rep—Legal Aid, Sentencing and Punishment of Offenders, 2012 c 10, sch 21 para 35(b)(ii)

sch 6 rep—Legal Aid, Sentencing and Punishment of Offenders, 2012 c 10, s 110(14)(c)

sch 9 rep in pt—Legal Aid, Sentencing and Punishment of Offenders, 2012 c 10, sch 24 para 30

sch 10 rep in pt—Legal Aid, Sentencing and Punishment of Offenders, 2012 c 10, sch 25 pt 2

sch 14 am—SI 2012/1809, art 3(1) sch pt 1; Crim Justice and Cts, 2015 c 2, s 37(5)(a)

rep in pt—Crim Justice and Cts, 2015 c 2, s 37(5)(b)

sch 18 am—SI 2010/976, art 15, sch 18

sch 19 am—SIs 2010/976, art 15, sch 18; 2012/1809, art 3(1) sch pt 1; 2014/3141, sch 3 para 16(2)(3)(5)(7)-(9)

rep in pt—SI 2014/3141, sch 3 para 16(4)(6)

sch 20 rep—Anti-social Behaviour, Crime and Policing, 2014 c 12, sch 11 para 50

sch 25 rep in pt—Armed Forces, 2011 c 18, sch 3 para 20(3), sch 5; Legal Aid, Sentencing and Punishment of Offenders, 2012 c 10, s 64(5)(c)

sch 26 rep in pt—Legal Aid, Sentencing and Punishment of Offenders, 2012 c 10, sch 12 para 55; ibid, sch 16 para 20(b); ibid, sch 21 para 35(b)(iii)

sch 27 rep in pt—Legal Aid, Sentencing and Punishment of Offenders, 2012 c 10, sch 16 para 20(c)

sch 28 rep in pt—Coroners and Justice, 2009 c 25, s 178, sch 23 pt 4

c 5 **Channel Tunnel Rail Link (Supplementary Provisions)**

s 50 am—SI 2008/2833, art 6, sch 3

rep in pt—SI 2008/2833, art 6, sch 3

s 51 rep—SI 2008/2833, art 6, sch 3

sch 3 rep in pt—SI 2008/2833, art 6, sch 3

c 6 **Child Maintenance and Other Payments**

ss 1-5 rep—SI 2012/2007, sch para 71

s 6 am—SI 2012/2007, sch para 72(2), (3); Welfare Reform, 2012 c 5, ss 140, 141

s 7 rep—SI 2012/2007, sch para 73

s 8 am—SI 2012/2007, sch para 74

ss 9-12 rep—SI 2012/2007, sch para 75

ss 13, 14 rep—SI 2012/2007, sch para 76

s 17 am—SI 2012/2007, sch para 77

s 18 am—SI 2012/2007, sch para 78

s 25 am—SI 2012/2007, sch para 79

s 27 am—SI 2012/2007, sch para 80

s 28 am—SI 2012/2007, sch para 81

2008

c 6 *continued*

    s 29 am—SI 2012/2007, sch para 82
    s 30 rep (prosp)—Welfare Reform, 2009 c 24, s 58, sch 7 pt 4
        am—SI 2012/2007, sch para 83
    s 32 am—SI 2012/2007, sch para 84
    s 33 am—SI 2012/2007, sch para 85
    s 34 am—SI 2012/2007, sch para 86
    s 39 am—SI 2012/2007, sch para 87
    s 40 am—SI 2012/2007, sch para 88
    s 44 rep—SI 2012/2007, sch para 89
    s 45 rep in pt—(prosp) Welfare Reform, 2012 c 5, sch 14 pt 1
    s 47 am—Mesothelioma, 2014 c 1, sch 2 para 2
    s 49 am—Welfare Reform, 2012 c 5, sch 11 para 16
    s 50 am—Welfare Reform, 2012 c 5, sch 11 paras 17, 18
    s 55 am—SI 2012/2007, sch para 90(a)
        rep in pt—SI 2012/2007, sch para 90(b)
    s 56 rep in pt—SI 2012/2007, sch para 91
    s 59 am—(prosp) Welfare Reform, 2009 c 24, s 51, sch 5 para 10
        rep in pt—(prosp) Welfare Reform, 2009 c 24, s 58, sch 7 pt 4; SI 2012/2007, sch para
            92
    s 61 rep in pt—SI 2012/2007, sch para 93
    sch 1 rep—SI 2012/2007, sch para 71
    sch 2 rep—SI 2012/2007, sch para 76
    sch 3 rep in pt—(prosp) Welfare Reform, 2009 c 24, s 58, sch 7 pt 4; SI 2012/2007, sch
           para 94
    sch 4 am—SI 2012/2007, sch para 95
    sch 5 am—Welfare Reform, 2012 c 5, s 136(2); SI 2012/2007, sch para 96(2), (3)(a), (4)
        rep in pt—SI 2012/2007, sch para 96(3)(b)
    sch 6 rep—SI 2012/2007, sch para 89
    sch 7 rep in pt—(prosp) Welfare Reform, 2009 c 24, s 58, sch 7 pts 1, 4; (prosp) Welfare
           Reform, 2012 c 5, sch 14 pt 1; ibid, sch 14 pt 13, 14
        am—SI 2012/2007, sch para 97

c 7   **European Union (Amendment)**
    s 5 am—European Union, 2011 c 12, s 14(1)
    s 6 rep—European Union, 2011 c 12, s 14(3)(d)

c 8   *Appropriation (No 2)*—rep Appropriation (No 3), 2010 c 30, s 4, sch 3

c 9   **Finance**
    saved—SI 2009/404, arts 3-12
    mod—SI 2009/317, art 3, sch
    appl (mods)—SI 2011/245, sch 6 pt 1
    s 2 rep in pt—Finance, 2009 c 10, s 5, sch 1 para 6(p)(i)
    s 3 rep in pt—Finance, 2009 c 10, s 5, sch 1 para 6(p)(ii)
    s 6 am—Corporation Tax, 2010 c 4, s 1177, sch 1 paras 576, 577
    s 7 rep—Corporation Tax, 2010 c 4, ss 1177, 1181, sch 1 paras 576, 578, sch 3
    s 20 rep in pt—Finance, 2009 c 10, s 64, sch 32 para 4
    ss 26-28 rep—Corporation Tax, 2009 c 4, s 1326, sch 3 pt 1
    s 29 rep—Corporation Tax, 2009 c 4, ss 1322, 1326, sch 1 paras 728, 729, sch 3 pt 1
    s 30 rep—Corporation Tax, 2009 c 4, s 1326, sch 3 pt 1
    s 31 rep—Finance, 2012 c 14, sch 7 para 3(2)
    s 35 rep—Corporation Tax, 2010 c 4, s 1181, sch 3 pt 1
    s 36 rep in pt—Corporation Tax, 2009 c 4, ss 1322, 1326, sch 1 paras 728, 730, sch 3 pt 1
    s 39 rep in pt—Finance, 2011 c 11, sch 23 para 61
    ss 40A-40G rep—Taxation (International and Other Provns), 2010 c 8, ss 374, 378, sch 8
           paras 169, 170, sch 10 pt 5
    ss 41, 42 rep—Taxation (International and Other Provns), 2010 c 8, ss 374, 378, sch 8 paras
           169, 170, sch 10 pt 5
    s 42A rep—Taxation (International and Other Provns), 2010 c 8, ss 374, 378, sch 8 paras
           169, 170, sch 10 pt 5
    s 44 rep—Finance, 2012 c 14, sch 18 para 23(f)(i)
    s 47 rep in pt—Finance, 2009 c 10, s 53, sch 28 para 9
    s 49 rep in pt—Corporation Tax, 2009 c 4, s 1326, sch 3 pt 1
    ss 54, 56 rep—Corporation Tax, 2010 c 4, s 1181, sch 3 pt 1
    s 57 rep—Taxation (International and Other Provns), 2010 c 8, s 378, sch 10 pt 1
    s 58 rep in pt—Corporation Tax, 2009 c 4, s 1326, sch 3 pt 1

2008

c 9 *continued*

s 59 rep—Taxation (International and Other Provns), 2010 c 8, s 378, sch 10 pt 1

s 64 rep in pt—Finance, 2009 c 10, s 36, sch 16 para 5(j)

s 65 rep—Corporation Tax, 2009 c 4, s 1326, sch 3 pt 1

s 73 rep in pt—Corporation Tax, 2009 c 4, s 1326, sch 3 pt 1

s 77 am—Corporation Tax, 2009 c 4, s 1322, sch 1 paras 728, 731

rep in pt—Finance, 2009 c 10, s 30, sch 11 para 64(a); Corporation Tax, 2009 c 4, s 1326, sch 3 pt 1; Finance, 2013 c 29, s 68(4)

s 80 rep in pt—Finance, 2011 c 11, s 57(7)

ss 85-87 rep —Finance, 2008 c 9, s 84, sch 27 para 29(a)

s 88 am—Finance, 2008 c 9, s 43, sch 17 para 18(4)

s 89 rep—Corporation Tax, 2010 c 4, s 1181, sch 3 pt 1

s 95 rep in pt—Finance, 2012 c 14, sch 39 para 8(2)(e)(i)

s 104 rep—Corporation Tax, 2010 c 4, s 1181, sch 3 pt 2; Taxation (International and Other Provns), 2010 c 8, s 378, sch 10 pt 6

s 105 rep—Finance, 2013 c 29, sch 31 para 12

s 111 rep in pt—Corporation Tax, 2010 c 4, s 1181, sch 3 pt 1

s 112 rep—Corporation Tax, 2010 c 4, s 1181, sch 3 pt 1

s 119 rep in pt—SI 2009/56, art 3, sch 1

s 130 rep in pt—Finance, 2012 c 14, s 50(3)(a)

mod—Finance, 2014 c 26, sch 22 para 8 (subst VAT, 1994 c 23, sch 3B para 16N)

s 131 rep in pt—Deregulation, 2015 c 20, sch 6 para 2(21)

s 133 rep in pt—Finance, 2012 c 14, s 50(2)(c)

s 147 rep—Finance, 2013 c 29, s 188(3)(a)

s 154 am—Corporation Tax, 2009 c 4, s 1322, sch 1 paras 728, 732

s 156 rep—Taxation (International and Other Provns), 2010 c 8, s 378, sch 10 pt 7

s 165 am—Corporation Tax, 2009 c 4, s 1322, sch 1 paras 728, 733; Corporation Tax, 2010 c 4, s 1177, sch 1 paras 576, 579

sch 1 rep in pt—Corporation Tax, 2009 c 4, s 1326, sch 3 pt 1; Corporation Tax, 2010 c 4, s 1181, sch 3 pt 1; Finance, 2012 c 14, sch 7 para 28; SI 2013/2819, reg 41(b)

sch 2 rep in pt—Corporation Tax, 2009 c 4, s 1326, sch 3 pt; Corporation Tax, 2010 c 4, s 1181, sch 3 pt 2; Taxation (International and Other Provns), 2010 c 8, s 378, sch 10 pt 8

sch 3 am—Finance (No 2), 2010 c 31, s 2, sch 1 paras 10, 11

sch 4 rep in pt—Finance, 2011 c 11, sch 16 para 84(d)(i)

sch 7 rep in pt—(prosp) Finance, 2008 c 9, s 41(7)(l); SIs 2009/3001, regs 13, schs 1, 2; 56, art 3, sch 1

am—SI 2009/3001, regs 13, 130, sch 1; (retrosp to 6.4.2009) Finance, 2009 c 10, s 51, sch 27 para 14, 15(1)

schs 8-10 rep —Corporation Tax, 2009 c 4, s 1326, sch 3 pt 1

sch 12 rep in pt—Finance, 2013 c 29, sch 29 para 33(2); SI 2013/2819, reg 41(b)

sch 13 rep—Corporation Tax, 2009 c 4, ss 1322, 1326, sch 1 paras 728, 735, sch 3 pt 1

sch 14 rep in pt—Finance, 2012 c 14, sch 16 para 247(q)(i)

sch 15 rep in pt—Corporation Tax, 2009 c 4, ss 1322, 1326, sch 1 paras 728, 736, sch 3 pt 1

sch 16 rep in pt—Corporation Tax, 2010 c 4, s 1181, sch 3 pt 1; Taxation (International and Other Provns), 2010 c 8, s 378, sch 10 pt 11

sch 17 rep in pt—(prosp) Finance, 2008 c 9, s 41(7)(l); SI 2009/3001, regs 13, schs 1, 2; Finance, 2009 c 10, ss 36, 46, sch 16 para 5(j), sch 23 para 6(b); Corporation Tax, 2009 c 4, s 1326, sch 3 pt 1; Taxation (International and Other Provns), 2010 c 8, s 378, sch 10 pt 1; Finance, 2012 c 14, sch 16 para 247(q)(ii)

am—Finance, 2009 c 10, s 46, sch 23 para 4(1); Taxation (International and Other Provns), 2010 c 8, s 374, sch 8 paras 87, 88

sch 18 rep—Finance, 2012 c 14, sch 18 para 23(f)(ii)

am—Finance, 2008 c 9, s 74, sch 25 para 8

sch 19 rep in pt—Corporation Tax, 2010 c 4, ss 1177, 1181, sch 1 paras 576, 580(2)(a), sch 3 pt 1

am—Corporation Tax, 2010 c 4, s 1177, sch 1 paras 576, 580(2)(b)-(3)

sch 20 rep in pt—(retrosp to 13.11.2008) Finance, 2009 c 10, s 64, sch 32 paras 2, 5(1); Corporation Tax, 2010 c 4, ss 1177, 1181, sch 1 paras 576, 581(3), sch 3 pt 1

am—Corporation Tax, 2010 c 4, s 1177, sch 1 paras 576, 581(2)

sch 22 rep in pt—Corporation Tax, 2009 c 4, s 1326, sch 3 pt 1

sch 23 rep in pt—Finance, 2013 c 29, sch 29 para 33(3)

sch 25 am—Corporation Tax, 2009 c 4, s 1322, sch 1 paras 728, 737

2008

c 9 sch 25 *continued*

      rep in pt—Finance, 2009 c 10, s 126(6)(d)

    sch 27 rep in pt—Corporation Tax, 2010 c 4, s 1181, sch 3 pt 2; Taxation (International and Other Provns), 2010 c 8, s 378, sch 10 pt 6

    sch 28 rep in pt—Finance, 2011 c 11, sch 16 para 84(d)(ii)

    sch 29 rep in pt—Finance, 2009 c 10, s 75(3)(b); Finance, 2011 c 11, sch 16 para 84(d)(iii)

    sch 32 rep in pt—(prosp) Finance, 2008 c 9, s 99, sch 32 para 23

    sch 30 rep in pt—Finance, 2012 c 14, sch 39 para 8(2)(e)(ii)

    sch 31 rep in pt—Finance, 2012 c 14, sch 39 para 8(2)(e)(iii)

    sch 35 rep in pt—Corporation Tax, 2009 c 4, s 1326, sch 3 pt 1; Corporation Tax, 2010 c 4, s 1181, sch 3 pt 1

    sch 36 appl (mods)—Customs and Excise Management, 1979 c 2, s 118G(2)(3); Social Security Administration, 1992 c 5, s 110ZA; SI 2009/470, regs 33, 60-61; Finance, 2010 c 13, s 22, sch 1 para 36; SIs 2006/208 reg 5 (added by 2013/2259, reg 21) (reg 5 am by 2015/673, reg 6(a)); 2013/938, reg 5

      mod—Corporation Tax, 2010 c 4, s 269DM(5) (added by 2015 c 33, sch 3 para 1); Nat Insurance Contributions, 2011 c 3, s 9(5); Finance, 2013 c 29, s 54(4)

      appl—Finance, 2004 c. 12, ss 153A(3)(6),153B(4)(7), 153C(3),153D(8),153E(2); ibid, ss 159A(2)(5), 159B(3)(6), 159C(3), 159D(2)); Finance, 2007 c 11, sch 11; Finance, 2009 c 10, s 97, sch 49 paras 4(2), 5(3); Finance (No 3), 2010 c 33, s 29, sch 13 paras 9, 12; SI 2013/938, reg 5(1)

      rep in pt—SIs 2009/2035, art 2, sch; 2009/56, art 3, sch 1; Finance, 2009 c 10, ss 95, 96, 109, sch 47 paras 1, 10(5), 11(3)(a)(7), 13(3)(a), 16(5), 17(2)(b), 18(3), 19, 20(4), 21(2)(a), sch 48 paras 1, 10, sch 57 para 14(a); Corporation Tax, 2010 c 4, ss 1177, 1181, sch 1 paras 576, 582(3)(a), sch 3, pt 1; Finance, 2010 c 13, s 30, sch 6 para 24; Finance, 2011 c 11, sch 23 paras 62(2)(3)(a)(c), 65; ibid, sch 24 paras 2(2)(3)(b)(4), 5(2)

      am—SIs 2009/3054, art 3, sch; 2009/56, art 3, sch 1; Finance, 2009 c 10, ss 95, 96, sch 47 paras 1-9, 10(1)-(4), 11(1)(2)(3)(b)(c)(4)-(6), 12, 13(1)(2)(3)(b), 14, 15, 16(1)-(4), 17(1)(2)(a)(c)(d)(3)-(5), 18(1)(2), 20(1)-(3), 21(1)(2)(b)(3), 22, sch 48 paras 1-9, 11-15; Corporation Tax, 2010 c 4, s 1177, sch 1 paras 576, 582(2)(3)(b); Finance, 2011 c 11, sch 23 para 62(3)(b); ibid, sch 24 paras 2(3)(a), 3, 4(1), 5(3), 6; Finance, 2012 c 14, s 224; SI 2012/3062, reg 6(1); Finance, 2013 c 29, s 54(2)(3); ibid, sch 34 paras 2-5; Finance, 2015 c 11, s 105(2); ibid, sch 7 para 57

    sch 39 rep in pt—Finance, 2009 c 10, ss 5, 34, 99, sch 1 para 6(p)(iii), sch 14 para 30(d), sch 51 para 42; Corporation Tax, 2009 c 4, s 1326, sch 3 pt 1; Corporation Tax, 2010 c 4, s 1181, sch 3 pts 1, 2; Taxation (International and Other Provns), 2010 c 8, s 378, sch 10 pts 1, 6; (as to events after 6.4.2015) Finance, 2012 c 14, sch 39 para 31(2)(d)(3)

    sch 40 rep in pt—SI 2009/56, art 3, sch 1; Finance, 2009 c 10, s 109, sch 57 para 14(b)

    sch 41 am—SI 2009/56, art 3, sch 1; Finance, 2009 c 10, s 109, sch 57 paras 10, 11, 12(1)(2)(a)(c)(3)(4); Corporation Tax, 2010 c 4, s 1177, sch 1 paras 576, 583; Finance, 2010 c 13, s 35, sch 10 paras 7-9; SI 2010/593, reg 90, sch 2; Finance, 2012 c 14, sch 23 para 15; ibid, sch 24 para 30; ibid, sch 25 para 11; Finance, 2013 c 29, sch 51 para 6; Finance, 2014 c 26, sch 28 para 27, sch 33 para 4; Finance, 2015 c 11, s 104(5)(6); (1.4.2016) ibid, sch 20 para 11(3)-(7),(9), 12; (prosp) ibid, sch 20 paras 10(2)-(4), 11(2), 13

      rep in pt—Finance, 2009 c 10, s 109, sch 57 paras 10, 12(1)(2)(b); Finance, 2012 c 14, sch 24 para 57; (1.4.2016) Finance, 2015 c 11, sch 20 para 11(8)

      appl (mods)—SI 2010/594, art 3, sch

    sch 42 rep in pt—Finance, 2012 c 14, s 187(2)(e)

c 10   **Sale of Student Loans**

    s 2 rep in pt—Educ, 2011 c 21, s 76(2)(b)

    s 8 am—SI 2013/1881, sch para 14

c 11   **Special Educational Needs (Information)**

    s 1 rep—Children and Families, 2014 c 6, sch 3 para 29(2)

c 12   **Statute Law (Repeals)**

c 13   **Regulatory Enforcement and Sanctions**

    Pt 1 (ss 1-21) trans of functions—SI 2012/246, art 2 4(1)(a) sch 1

    s 1 rep in pt—SI 2012/246, art 2 4(2) sch 1 para 1(a)

    s 2 rep—SI 2012/246, art 2 4(2) sch 1 para 1(b)

    s 5 am—SI 2012/246, art 2 4(2) sch 1 para 3

    s 6 am—SI 2012/246, art 2 4(2) sch 1 para 4

2008

c 13 s 6 *continued*

rep in pt—SI 2012/246, art 2 4(2) sch 1 para 1(c), (d)

s 7 rep—SI 2012/246, art 2 4(2) sch 1 para 1(e)

s 8 rep—SI 2012/246, art 2 4(2) sch 1 para 1(f)

s 9 rep—SI 2012/246, art 2 4(2) sch 1 para 1(g)

s 10 am—SI 2012/246, art 2 4(2) sch 1 para 5

rep in pt—SI 2012/246, art 2 4(2) sch 1 para 1(h)

s 11 am—SI 2012/246, art 2 4(2) sch 1 para 6

rep in pt—SI 2012/246, art 2 4(2) sch 1 para 1(i), (j)

s 12 am—SIs 2012/246, art 2 4(2) sch 1 para 7; 2014/892, sch 1 para 179

s 13 rep—SI 2012/246, art 2 4(2) sch 1 para 1(k)

s 14 rep—SI 2012/246, art 2 4(2) sch 1 para 1(l)

s 15 rep—SI 2012/246, art 2 4(2) sch 1 para 1(m)

s 16 am—SI 2012/246, art 2 4(2) sch 1 para 8(a), (b), (c)

rep in pt—SI 2012/246, art 2 4(2) sch 1 para 1(n)-(r)

s 17 rep—SI 2012/246, art 2 4(2) sch 1 para 1(s)

s 20 rep in pt—SI 2012/246, art 2 4(2) sch 1 para 1(t), (u)

s 21 rep in pt—SI 2012/246, art 2 4(2) sch 1 para 1(v)

Pt 2 (ss 22-35) trans of functions—SI 2012/246, art 2 4 sch 1

s 22 am—Enterprise and Regulatory Reform, 2013 c 24, s 67

s 24 am—Enterprise and Regulatory Reform, 2013 c 24, s 67(6)

s 25 am—SI 2012/246, art 2 4(2) sch 1 para 10

s 26 am—SI 2012/246, art 2 4(2) sch 1 para 11; Enterprise and Regulatory Reform, 2013 c 24, s 67(7)

s 28 am—SI 2012/246, art 2 4(2) sch 1 para 12

s 30 am—SI 2012/246, art 2 4(2) sch 1 para 13; Enterprise and Regulatory Reform, 2013 c 24, s 68(2)-(4)(6)-(9)

rep in pt—Enterprise and Regulatory Reform, 2013 c 24, s 68(5)

s 32 rep—SI 2012/246, art 2 4(2) sch 1 para 1(w)

s 33 am—SI 2012/246, art 2 4(2) sch 1 para 14

rep in pt—SI 2012/246, art 2 4(2) sch 1 para 1(x), (y)

s 35 rep in pt—SI 2012/246, art 2 4(2) sch 1 para 1(z)

Pt 3 (ss 36-71) mod—Video Recordings, 2010 c 1, s 1, sch para 5

s 37 am—SI 2013/602, sch 2 para 59

s 38 am—Equality, 2010 c 15, s 211, sch 26 para 98 (added by SI 2010/2279, sch 1)

s 39 excl —Waste (W), 2010 nawm 8, s 10(3)

am—SI 2015/664, sch 5 para 12(2)

s 42 excl—Waste (W), 2010 nawm 8, s 10(3)

am—SI 2015/664, sch 5 para 12(3)

s 49 mod —Waste (W), 2010 nawm 8, s 10(3)

am—SI 2015/664, sch 4 para 39

ss 63-66 appl (mods)—Waste (W), 2010 nawm 8, ss 10(4)(5), 14(4)(5)

s 67 appl (mods)—Waste (W), 2010 nawm 8, ss 10(4)(5), 14(4)(5); (W) SI 2013/755 (W 90), sch 7 para 12

ss 68, 69 appl (mods)—Waste (W), 2010 nawm 8, ss 10(4)(5), 14(4)(5)

s 73 am—Postal Services, 2011 c 5, sch 12 para 191; Civil Aviation, 2012 c 19, s 104; SIs 2014/892, sch 1 para 180; 2015/1682, sch pt 1 para 4(s)(i)

sch 1 am—SI 2012/246, art 2 4(2) sch 1 para 15

rep in pt—SI 2012/246, art 2 4(2) sch 1 para 1(aa)

sch 2 rep—SI 2012/246, art 2 4(2) sch 1 para 1(bb)

sch 3 rep in pt—Marine and Coastal Access, 2009 c 23, s 321, sch 22 pt 4; Equality, 2010 c 15, s 211, sch 26 para 99 (added by SI 2010/2279, sch 1); ibid, sch 27 pt 1 (subst by SI 2010/2279, sch 2); Charities, 2011 c 25, sch 7 para 130, sch 10; SIs 2013/1575, sch para 13; 2014/1637, sch 4 pt 1; Deregulation, 2015 c 20, sch 23 paras 25(3), 34(7)

am—Charities, 2011 c 25, sch 7 para 130; Scrap Metal Dealers, 2013 c 10, s 19(2); (W) (savings) Mobile Homes (W), 2013 anaw 6, sch 4 para 10; SI 2013/2215, art 2; Consumer Rights, 2015 c 15, sch 1 para 54; SIs 2015/776, art 17; 895, reg 6; 1726, sch para 5

sch 4 am—SI 2012/246, art 2 4(2) sch 1 para 16

sch 5 rep in pt—Marine and Coastal Access, 2009 c 23, s 321, sch 22 pt 4; Sports Grounds Safety Authy, 2011 c 6, sch 2 para 9, sch 3; (W) SIs 2013/755 (W 90), sch 2 para 439(2); 2014/892, sch 1 para 181(b)

2008

c 13 sch 5 *continued*

am—Sports Grounds Safety Authy, 2011 c 6, sch 2 para 9; Civil Aviation, 2012 c 19, s 103(2); Financial Services, 2012 c. 21, sch 18 para 126; (W) SIs 2013/755 (W 90), sch 2 para 439(3); 2014/892, sch 1 para 181(a); 2015/1682, sch pt 1 para 4(s)(ii)

sch 6 rep in pt—Marine and Coastal Access, 2009 c 23, s 321, sch 22 pt 4; Equality, 2010 c 15, s 211, sch 27 pt 1 (subst by SI 2010/2279, sch 2); SI 2010/2960, reg 36, schs 6, 8; Energy, 2013 c 32, sch 12 para 94; SIs 2013/1575, sch para 14; 2014/1637, sch 4 pt 1; 1639, sch 3 pt 1

sch 7 am—Civil Aviation, 2012 c 19, s 103(3)

c 14 **Health and Social Care**

Pt 1 (ss 1-97) mod—(prosp) Care, 2014 c 23, s 57(1)(2)

s 4 am—Health and Social Care, 2012 c 7, s 189(6)(a)(i), (b)
    rep in pt—Health and Social Care, 2012 c 7, s 189(6)(a)(ii)

s 10 excl —SI 2010/2484, art 3
    am—SI 2015/664, sch 4 para 40(2)

ss 12, 15 appl (mods) —SI 2010/2484, arts 4,16

s 17 mod—Care, 2014 c 23, s 57(3)

s 18 mod—Care, 2014 c 23, s 57(3)

s 19 appl (mods)—SI 2010/2484, arts 9,18
    am—Care, 2014 c 23, s 86

s 20 am—Care, 2014 c 23, ss 81, 95; Health and Social Care (Safety and Quality), 2015 c 28, s 1(2)(3)

s 20A added —Health and Social Care, 2012 c 7, s 280(3)

s 26 am—Care, 2014 c 23, s 87(1)

s 28 am—Care, 2014 c 23, s 87(2)(3)

s 29 am—Care, 2014 c 23, s 82(1)(2)

s 29A added —Care, 2014 c 23, s 82(3)

s 30 am—Health and Social Care, 2012 c 7, sch 5 para 155(a), (b)(i), (ii); ibid, sch 13 para 15
    rep in pt—Health and Social Care, 2012 c 7, sch 5 para 155(b)(iii), (c)

s 32 am—SI 2009/56, art 3, sch 1; Care, 2014 c 23, s 82(4)(a)
    rep in pt—SI 2009/56, art 3, sch 1

s 33 excl—SI 2010/2484, art 3
    am—SI 2015/664, sch 4 para 40(3)

s 34 am—SI 2015/664, sch 4 para 40(4)

s 35 am—SI 2015/664, sch 4 para 91

s 39 excl—SIs 2009/660; 2009/3112, reg 8
    am—Health and Social Care, 2012 c 7, sch 5 para 156(a), (b)(i), (ii); ibid, sch 13 para 16; Care, 2014 c 23, s 82(4)(b)
    rep in pt—Health and Social Care, 2012 c 7, sch 5 para 156(b)(iii), (c)

s 45 rep—Health and Social Care, 2012 c 7, sch 17 para 12(2)

ss 45A-45C added —Health and Social Care, 2012 c 7, s 181(4)

s 45D added —Health and Social Care, 2012 c 7, s 182(11)

s 46 subst—Care, 2014 c 23, s 91(2)

s 47 rep—Care, 2014 c 23, s 91(3)

s 48 am—Health and Social Care, 2012 c 7, s 293(2); ibid, s 40(6); ibid, sch 5 para 158(a); Care, 2014 c 23, s 91(4)(b)(6)-(8)
    rep in pt—Health and Social Care, 2012 c 7, sch 5 para 158(b); Care, 2014 c 23, ss 90(2), 91(4)(a)(5)

s 49 rep —Care, 2014 c 23, s 91(3)

s 50 rep in pt—Care, 2014 c 23, s 91(9)(a)

s 51 rep in pt—Care, 2014 c 23, s 91(9)(b)

s 53 am—Health and Social Care, 2012 c 7, sch 17 para 12(3)(a)
    rep in pt—Health and Social Care, 2012 c 7, sch 17 para 12(3)(b)

s 54 excl —Heath Protection Agency, 2004 c 17, s 10
    am—Health and Social Care, 2012 c 7, s 293(3); ibid, sch 5 para 160(b); Care, 2014 c 23, s 90(4)
    rep in pt—Health and Social Care, 2012 c 7, sch 5 para 160(a); Care, 2014 c 23, s 90(3)

s 55 rep in pt—Care, 2014 c 23, s 90(5)

s 56 rep —Loc Audit and Accountability, 2014 c 2, sch 12 para 87

s 57 am—Health and Social Care, 2012 c 7, s 293(4)
    rep in pt—Care, 2014 c 23, s 90(6)

2008

c 14 *continued*

s 59 am—Health and Social Care, 2012 c 7, sch 13 para 17; ibid, sch 5 para 161
s 61 rep in pt—Care, 2014 c 23, s 90(7)
ss 62, 63 appl—SI 2015/1792, sch para 5
s 64 restr—Care, 2014 c 23, s 92(9)
    am—Health and Social Care, 2012 c 7, sch 5 para 162(a); ibid, sch 19 para 11
    rep in pt—Health and Social Care, 2012 c 7, sch 5 para 162(b)
    appl—SI 2015/1792, sch para 5
s 70 am—Health and Social Care, 2012 c 7, s 289(2), (3), (4)(a), (b), (5), (6)
    rep in pt—(pt prosp) Health and Social Care, 2012 c 7, sch 5 para 163; Care, 2014 c 23,
      s 91(9)(c)
s 72 am—(pt prosp) Health and Social Care, 2012 c 7, sch 5 para 164(b)
    rep in pt—(pt prosp) Health and Social Care, 2012 c 7, sch 5 para 164(a); Care, 2014 c
      23, s 91(9)(d)
s 81 am—Health and Social Care, 2012 c 7, sch 5 para 165
s 82 am—Health and Social Care, 2012 c 7, s 181(6)-(10); ibid, s 294(1)-(3); ibid, s 181(5)
s 83 am—Health and Social Care, 2012 c 7, s 181(11), (12)
    rep in pt—Care, 2014 c 23, s 90(8)
s 87 am—SI 2015/664, sch 5 para 13
s 88 am—Care, 2014 c 23, s 82(5)
s 89 am—Care, 2014 c 23, s 82(4)(c)
s 93 am—SI 2009/3023, art 19
    appl—SIs 2009/3023, art 18; 2010/781, reg 28; 2014/2936, reg 24(7)
s 97 am—Health and Social Care, 2012 c 7, sch 5 para 166(2)(c), (4)(a), (5); ibid, s 40(7);
    SI 2012/961, sch 1 para 9
    rep in pt—Health and Social Care, 2012 c 7, sch 5 para 166(2)(a), (b), (3), (4)(b), (6);
      ibid, sch 14 para 109(a), (b)
ss 98-110 rep—Health and Social Care, 2012 c 7, s 231(2)
s 118 rep in pt—Health and Social Care, 2012 c 7, sch 15 para 73(2)
s 124 am—Health and Social Care, 2012 c 7, sch 15 para 45(1)(a), (b), (2)
    rep in pt—Health and Social Care, 2012 c 7, sch 15 para 45(1)(c)
s 125 am—Health and Social Care, 2012 c 7, sch 15 para 46(a)
    rep in pt—Health and Social Care, 2012 c 7, sch 15 para 46(b)
s 126 am—Health and Social Care, 2012 c 7, sch 15 para 47(2)(a), (4)
    rep in pt—Health and Social Care, 2012 c 7, sch 15 para 47(2)(b), (3)
s 128 rep in pt—Health and Social Care, 2012 c 7, sch 15 para 75(2)
s 144 am—SI 2010/1158, art 5, sch 2
s 145 rep—SI 2015/914, sch para 90
s 153 rep in pt—Health and Social Care, 2012 c 7, sch 5 para 167; (prosp) ibid, sch 14 para
    110
s 156 rep in pt—SI 2015/914, sch para 91(a)(c)
    am—SI 2015/914, sch para 91(b)
s 157 rep in pt—Health and Social Care, 2012 c 7, sch 20 para 11
s 158 rep —Health and Social Care, 2012 c 7, sch 20 para 11
s 159 rep in pt—Health and Social Care, 2012 c 7, sch 7 para 24
s 161 am—Health and Social Care, 2012 c 7, s 294(4)
s 162 rep in pt—Health and Social Care, 2012 c 7, sch 15 para 75(3)
s 165 am—Health and Social Care, 2012 c 7, s 294(5), (6)
s 171 am—Health and Social Care, 2012 c 7, sch 15 para 48
sch 1 am—Health and Social Care, 2012 c 7, s 181(2), (3); ibid, s 292; Care, 2014 c 23, ss
    88(1)-(6)(8), 89
    rep in pt—Care, 2014 c 23, s 88(7)
sch 4 rep in pt—SI 2012/2401, sch 1 para 31; Loc Audit and Accountability, 2014 c 2, sch
    12 para 88(2)(a)(ii)(b)(ii); Care, 2014 c 23, s 90(9)
    am—Loc Audit and Accountability, 2014 c 2, sch 12 para 88(2)(a)(i)(b)(i); ibid, sch
      12 para 88(3)
sch 5 rep in pt—Equality, 2010 c 15, sch 27 Pt 1A (added by SI 2011/1060, sch 3); (prosp)
    Health and Social Care, 2012 c 7, sch 14 para 40; ibid, sch 20 para 7(b);
    Protection of Freedoms, 2012 c 9, sch 10 pt 5; SI 2012/2401, sch 1 para 32;
    Loc Audit and Accountability, 2014 c 2, sch 1 pt 2
schs 6, 7 rep—Health and Social Care, 2012 c 7, s 231(2)
sch 8 rep in pt—Health and Social Care, 2012 c 7, sch 15 para 72(3)
sch 9 am—Health and Social Care, 2012 c 7, sch 15 para 49(2)-(4), (6)(b), (c), (8)
    rep in pt—Health and Social Care, 2012 c 7, sch 15 para 49(5), (6)(a), (7)

2008

c 14 *continued*

> sch 10 rep in pt—Equality, 2010 c 15, sch 27 Pt 1A (added by SI 2011/1060, sch 3); Health and Social Care, 2012 c 7, sch 15 paras 69(3), 71(2)-(4), 74(3), 75(4); ibid, sch 20 para 7(c)
>
> sch 11 rep in pt—Protection of Freedoms, 2012 c 9, sch 10 pt 2
>
> sch 14 rep in pt—Health and Social Care, 2012 c 7, sch 20 para 9(1)(c), 10(2); SI 2015/914, sch para 92
>
> > am—SI 2015/914, sch para 93

c 15 **Criminal Evidence (Witness Anonymity)**

> ss 1-9 rep—Coroners and Justice, 2009 c 25, ss 96, 178, sch 23 pt 3
>
> s 10 rep in pt—Coroners and Justice, 2009 c 25, s 178, sch 23 pt 3
>
> s 14 rep—Coroners and Justice, 2009 c 25, ss 96, 178, sch 23 pt 3

c 16 **National Insurance Contributions**

c 17 **Housing and Regeneration**

> am—Co-operative and Community Benefit Societies, 2014 c 14, sch 4 paras 122, 123
>
> s 2 am—Localism, 2011 c 20, s 189(2); ibid, sch 16 para 2
>
> s 4 am—Localism, 2011 c 20, sch 16 para 3; ibid, sch 19 para 47
>
> s 11 appl (mods)—SI 2009/1262, arts 2-7
>
> > am—Infrastructure, 2015 c 7, s 32(2)
>
> s 13 am—Planning, 2008 c 29, s 36, sch 2 para 65; Localism, 2011 c 20, s 189(3)(4)(5)(a); ibid, sch 12 para 31
>
> > rep in pt—Localism, 2011 c 20, s 189(3)(5)(b), sch 25 pt 31
>
> s 14 rep in pt—Localism, 2011 c 20, s 189(3)(6), sch 25 pt 31
>
> s 16 rep—Loc Democracy, Economic Development and Construction, 2009 c 20, s 146, sch 7 pt 4
>
> ss 17, 18 appl (mods)—GLA, 1999 c 29, s 333ZD(1); Localism, 2011 c 20, s 210
>
> s 26 am—Localism, 2011 c 20, s 189(3)(7)
>
> s 31 am—SI 2010/844, art 6, sch 2
>
> > rep in pt—SI 2010/844, art 6, sch 2; Localism, 2011 c 20, sch 16 para 4, sch 25 pt 26
> >
> > appl (mods)—GLA, 1999 c 29, s 333ZE(1)(2)
>
> s 32 rep in pt—Localism, 2011 c 20, sch 16 para 5, sch 25 pt 26
>
> > appl (mods)—GLA, 1999 c 29, s 333ZE(1)(2)
>
> s 33 appl (mods)—GLA, 1999 c 29, s 333ZE(1)(2)
>
> s 34 rep in pt—Localism, 2011 c 20, sch 16 para 6, sch 25 pt 26
>
> > appl (mods)—GLA, 1999 c 29, s 333ZE(1)(2)
>
> s 35 am—SI 2010/844, art 6, sch 2; Localism, 2011 c 20, s 189(3)(8)
>
> > appl (mods)—GLA, 1999 c 29, s 333ZE(1)(2)
>
> s 36 appl (mods)—GLA, 1999 c 29, s 333ZE(1)(2)
>
> s 37 rep—Localism, 2011 c 20, sch 16 para 7, sch 25 pt 26
>
> s 42 am—Localism, 2011 c 20, sch 16 para 7, sch 25 pt 26
>
> s 46 am—Localism, 2011 c 20, sch 16 para 7, sch 25 pt 26
>
> s 47 am—Localism, 2011 c 20, sch 16 para 7, sch 25 pt 26
>
> s 51 rep in pt—Public Bodies, 2011 c 24, sch 6
>
> > am—Infrastructure, 2015 c 7, s 31(3)
>
> s 53 am—Housing and Regeneration, 2008 c 17, s 56, sch 8 paras 44, 48
>
> > rep in pt—Housing and Regeneration, 2008 c 17, s 321, sch 16
>
> ss 53A, 53B added—Infrastructure, 2015 c 7, s 31(2)
>
> s 58 am—Localism, 2011 c 20, sch 16 para 11
>
> Pt 2 (ss 59-278) mod—Localism, 2011 c 20, sch 16 para 69(2)
>
> s 60 am—SI 2010/844, art 5, sch 1; Localism, 2011 c 20, sch 16 para 12
>
> ss 75-76 am—SI 2010/844, art 5, sch 1
>
> s 78 rep—Localism, 2011 c 20, sch 16 para 13, sch 25 pt 26
>
> s 79 am—SI 2010/844, art 5, sch 1; Co-operative and Community Benefit Societies, 2014 c 14, sch 4 para 124
>
> s 80 am—SI 2010/844, art 5, sch 1
>
> ss 81-92 rep—Localism, 2011 c 20, sch 16 paras 14-25, sch 25 pt 26
>
> ss 92A-92K added—Localism, 2011 c 20, sch 16 para 26
>
> s 93 am—Localism, 2011 c 20, sch 16 para 27
>
> ss 94-96 am—SI 2010/844, art 5, sch 1
>
> s 99 rep—Localism, 2011 c 20, sch 16 para 28, sch 25 pt 26
>
> s 100 am—Localism, 2011 c 20, sch 16 para 29
>
> ss 101-106 rep—Localism, 2011 c 20, sch 16 paras 30-35, sch 25 pt 26
>
> s 106A added—SI 2010/844, art 5, sch 1
>
> > rep (prosp)—(prosp) Loc Audit and Accountability, 2014 c 2, sch 12 para 90

2008

c 17 *continued*

s 107 am—SI 2010/844, art 5, sch 1
s 112 am—Loc Democracy, Economic Development and Construction, 2009 c 20, s 26(3);
    SI 2010/844, art 5, sch 1; Localism, 2011 c 20, sch 19 para 48
    rep in pt—Localism, 2011 c 20, sch 16 para 36, sch 25 pt 26
s 113 rep in pt—SI 2010/844, art 4
    am—SI 2010/844, art 5, sch 1
s 114A added—SI 2010/844, art 5, sch 1
ss 115, 116 am—SI 2010/844, art 5, sch 1
s 117 am—SI 2010/844, art 5, sch 1; Localism, 2011 c 20, sch 16 para 37
ss 118, 119 am—SI 2010/844, art 5, sch 1
s 120 am—SIs 2010/844, art 5, sch 1; 2013/496, sch 11 para 8(2)(3)(a)
    rep in pt—SI 2010/844, art 5, sch 1
s 122 am—Localism, 2011 c 20, s 177; ibid, sch 17 para 2
s 123 am—SI 2010/844, art 5, sch 1
s 126 rep—Deregulation, 2015 c 20, s 100(2)(e)
s 127 am—SI 2010/844, art 5, sch 1
s 128 am—SI 2010/844, art 5, sch 1; Loc Audit and Accountability, 2014 c 2, sch 12 para
    91
s 134 am—Co-operative and Community Benefit Societies, 2014 c 14, sch 4 para 125
s 135 am—Charities, 2011 c 25, sch 7 para 131
s 136 am—Charities, 2011 c 25, sch 7 para 132
s 138 am—Charities, 2011 c 25, sch 7 para 133
ss 141-143—SI 2010/844, art 5, sch 1
s 143A added—SI 2010/844, art 5, sch 1
s 144 am—SI 2010/844, art 5, sch 1
s 145 am—SI 2010/844, art 5, sch 1; Localism, 2011 c 20, sch 19 para 49
    rep in pt—Localism, 2011 c 20, sch 16 para 39, sch 25 pt 26
s 146 rep in pt—Localism, 2011 c 20, sch 16 para 39, sch 25 pt 26
    am—Localism, 2011 c 20, sch 19 para 50
s 147 am—SI 2010/844, art 5, sch 1; Localism, 2011 c 20, sch 19 para 51
    rep in pt—Localism, 2011 c 20, sch 16 para 40, sch 25 pt 26
s 148 am—Localism, 2011 c 20, sch 19 para 52(a)(b)(d)
    rep in pt—Localism, 2011 c 20, sch 19 para 52(c), sch 25 pt 31
s 152 am—SI 2014/3486, art 30(2)
s 153 am—SI 2013/496, sch 11 para 8(2)(3)(b)
s 157 am—SI 2013/496, sch 11 para 8(2)(3)(c); Co-operative and Community Benefit
    Societies, 2014 c 14, sch 4 para 126
ss 158, 159 am—SI 2010/844, art 5, sch 1
s 159A added—SI 2010/844, art 5, sch 1
s 161 am—Co-operative and Community Benefit Societies, 2014 c 14, sch 4 para 127
s 163 am—SI 2013/496, sch 11 para 8(2)(3)(d); Co-operative and Community Benefit
    Societies, 2014 c 14, sch 4 para 128
s 164 am—SI 2013/496, sch 11 para 8(4); Co-operative and Community Benefit Societies,
    2014 c 14, sch 4 para 129
s 165 am—SI 2013/496, sch 11 para 8(2)(3)(e); Co-operative and Community Benefit
    Societies, 2014 c 14, sch 4 para 130
s 167 am—Co-operative and Community Benefit Societies, 2014 c 14, sch 4 para
    131(2)(3)(b)
    rep in pt—Co-operative and Community Benefit Societies, 2014 c 14, sch 4 para
    131(3)(a)
Pt 2, Ch 5 (ss 170-191) am (heading am)—SI 2010/844, art 5, sch 1
ss 171-172 am—SI 2010/844, art 5, sch 1
s 174 am—Loc Democracy, Economic Development and Construction, 2009 c 20, s 26(3);
    SI 2010/844, art 5, sch 1; Localism, 2011 c 20, sch 19 para 53
    rep in pt—Localism, 2011 c 20, sch 16 para 41, sch 25 pt 26
s 175 am—SI 2010/844, art 5, sch 1
s 177—SI 2010/844, art 5, sch 1
s 178 am—SI 2010/844, art 5, sch 1; Localism, 2011 c 20, sch 19 para 54
ss 179-182 am—SI 2010/844, art 5, sch 1
s 180 rep in pt—Localism, 2011 c 20, s 165(1)(2), sch 25 pt 23
    am—SI 2010/844, art 5, sch 1; Localism, 2011 c 20, s 165(1)(3)
    restr—SI 2012/696, reg 4
ss 181, 182 am—SI 2010/844, art 5, sch 1

2008
c 17 *continued*

s 184—SI 2010/844, art 5, sch 1
ss 186-188—SI 2010/844, art 5, sch 1
s 190—SI 2010/844, art 5, sch 1
s 192 am—Localism, 2011 c 20, sch 17 para 3
s 193 am—Localism, 2011 c 20, s 176(1); ibid, sch 17 para 4(1)(2)
    rep in pt—Localism, 2011 c 20, sch 17 para 4(1)(3), sch 25 pt 27
s 194 am—SI 2010/844, art 5, sch 1; Localism, 2011 c 20, sch 17 para 5(1)(2)(4)(5)
    rep in pt—Localism, 2011 c 20, sch 17 para 5(1)(3), sch 25 pt 27
s 195 am—Localism, 2011 c 20, sch 17 para 6
s 196 am—Loc Democracy, Economic Development and Construction, 2009 c 20, s 26(4);
    Localism, 2011 c 20, sch 19 para 55
    rep in pt—Localism, 2011 c 20, sch 16 para 42, sch 25 pt 26; Loc Audit and
        Accountability, 2014 c 2, sch 12 para 92
s 197 am—Loc Democracy, Economic Development and Construction, 2009 c 20, s 26(5);
    Localism, 2011 c 20, s 152; ibid, s 176(2); ibid, sch 17 para 7; ibid, sch 19 para
    56
    rep in pt—Localism, 2011 c 20, sch 16 para 43, sch 25 pts 25, 26; Loc Audit and
        Accountability, 2014 c 2, sch 12 para 93
s 198 rep in pt—Localism, 2011 c 20, sch 17 para 8, sch 25 pt 27
ss 198A, 198B added—Localism, 2011 c 20, sch 17 para 9
s 201 am —SI 2010/844, art 5, sch 1; Localism, 2011 c 20, sch 17 para 10(1)(2)(5)(6)
    rep in pt—Localism, 2011 c 20, sch 17 para 10(1)(3)(4)(7), sch 25 pt 27; Loc Audit
        and Accountability, 2014 c 2, sch 12 para 94
s 202 rep in pt—Localism, 2011 c 20, sch 17 para 11(1)(2)(3)(b), sch 25 pt 27
    am—Localism, 2011 c 20, sch 16 para 44; ibid, sch 17 para 11(1)(3)(a)
s 203 am—Localism, 2011 c 20, sch 17 para 12
s 204 rep—Localism, 2011 c 20, sch 17 para 13, sch 25 pt 27
s 205 rep—Localism, 2011 c 20, sch 17 para 14, sch 25 pt 27
s 207 am—SI 2010/844, art 5, sch 1
s 210 am—SI 2010/844, art 5, sch 1
s 210A added—SI 2010/844, art 5, sch 1
    am—Loc Audit and Accountability, 2014 c 2, sch 12 para 95(2)(3)(5)-(7)
    rep in pt—Loc Audit and Accountability, 2014 c 2, sch 12 para 95(4)
s 212 am—SI 2013/496, sch 11 para 8(4); Co-operative and Community Benefit Societies,
    2014 c 14, sch 4 para 132
s 215 am—Localism, 2011 c 20, sch 17 para 15
s 216 am—Loc Democracy, Economic Development and Construction, 2009 c 20, s 26(6);
    Localism, 2011 c 20, sch 17 para 16(a); ibid, sch 19 para 57
    rep in pt—Localism, 2011 c 20, sch 16 para 45, sch 25 pt 26; ibid, sch 17 para 16(b),
        sch 25 pt 27
s 218 am—Localism, 2011 c 20, sch 17 para 17(1)(2)(4)
    rep in pt—Localism, 2011 c 20, sch 17 para 17(1)(3), sch 25 pt 27
s 220 am—SI 2010/844, art 5, sch 1
s 222 subst—SI 2010/844, art 5, sch 1
    rep in pt—Localism, 2011 c 20, sch 16 para 46, sch 25 pt 26
    am—Localism, 2011 c 20, sch 19 para 58
ss 226, 227 am—SI 2010/844, art 5, sch 1
s 229 am—SI 2015/664, sch 5 para 14
s 230 rep in pt—Localism, 2011 c 20, sch 16 para 47, sch 25 pt 26
    am—Localism, 2011 c 20, sch 19 para 59
s 232 rep—Localism, 2011 c 20, sch 16 para 48, sch 25 pt 26
s 232A added—Localism, 2011 c 20, sch 19 para 60
ss 236, 237 am—SI 2010/844, art 5, sch 1
s 239 am—Localism, 2011 c 20, s 180(2), sch 25 pt 28
    rep in pt—Localism, 2011 c 20, s 180(2), sch 25 pt 28
s 242 am—SI 2010/844, art 5, sch 1; Localism, 2011 c 20, sch 19 para 61
    rep in pt—Localism, 2011 c 20, sch 16 para 49, sch 25 pt 26
s 245 am—SI 2010/844, art 5, sch 1
s 247 am—SI 2010/844, art 5, sch 1
ss 248 am —SI 2010/844, art 5, sch 1; Localism, 2011 c 20, sch 19 para 62
    rep in pt—SI 2010/844, art 5, sch 1; Localism, 2011 c 20, sch 16 para 50, sch 25 pt
    26
s 249 am—Loc Audit and Accountability, 2014 c 2, sch 12 para 96

2008

c 17 *continued*

s 250 am —SI 2010/844, art 5, sch 1; Localism, 2011 c 20, sch 19 para 63
   rep in pt—SI 2010/844, art 5, sch 1; Localism, 2011 c 20, sch 16 para 51, sch 25 pt
     26
s 250A added—SI 2010/844, art 5, sch 1
s 251am—SI 2010/844, art 5, sch 1
s 252 am—SI 2010/844, art 5, sch 1; Localism, 2011 c 20, sch 19 para 64
   rep in pt—Localism, 2011 c 20, sch 16 para 52, sch 25 pt 26
s 252A added—SI 2010/844, art 5, sch 1
s 253 am—SI 2010/844, art 5, sch 1
s 255 am—SI 2013/496, sch 11 para 8(2)(3)(f); Co-operative and Community Benefit
    Societies, 2014 c 14, sch 4 para 133
s 256 am—SI 2010/844, art 5, sch 1
s 259 am—SI 2010/844, art 5, sch 1
s 266 am—Charities, 2011 c 25, sch 7 para 134
ss 269A, 269B added—SI 2010/844, art 5, sch 1
s 270 am —SI 2010/844, art 5, sch 1; Co-operative and Community Benefit Societies, 2014
    c 14, sch 4 para 134
s 271 am—Co-operative and Community Benefit Societies, 2014 c 14, sch 4 para 135
s 275 am—Charities, 2011 c 25, sch 7 para 135; Co-operative and Community Benefit
    Societies, 2014 c 14, sch 4 para 136(b); SI 2014/3486, art 30(3)
   rep in pt—Co-operative and Community Benefit Societies, 2014 c 14, sch 4 para
    136(a)
s 276 am—SI 2010/844, art 5, sch 1; Localism, 2011 c 20, sch 16 para 53(1)(3)-(6);
    Co-operative and Community Benefit Societies, 2014 c 14, sch 4 para 137(b); SI
    2014/3486, art 30(4)
   rep in pt—Localism, 2011 c 20, sch 16 para 53(1)(2), sch 25 pt 26; Co-operative and
    Community Benefit Societies, 2014 c 14, sch 4 para 137(a)
s 287A added—Loc Democracy, Economic Development and Construction, 2009 c 20, s
    26(1)(2)
s 290 rep in pt—Localism, 2011 c 20, sch 18 para 3, sch 25 pt 29
s 320 am—Localism, 2011 c 20, sch 17 para 18; Infrastructure, 2015 c 7, s 31(4)
sch 1 rep in pt—Bribery, 2010 c 23, s 17, sch 2
   am—Localism, 2011 c 20, sch 16 para 54
sch 2 am—SI 2009/1307, art 5, sch 1
   appl (mods)—GLA, 1999 c 29, s 333ZB(1); Localism, 2011 c 20, s 207(7)(8)
sch 3 appl (mods)—GLA, 1999 c 29, s 333ZA(6)(7); Localism, 2011 c 20, s 208(1)-(3)
   appl—GLA, 1999 c 29, s 333ZB(1) (subst by 2015 c 7, s 32(7)); Localism, 2011 c 20,
    s 208(1) (subst by 2015 c 7, s 32(10))
   am—Infrastructure, 2015 c 7, s 32(3)(4)
sch 4 am—SIs 2009/2748, art 8, sch; 2011/741, sch 2 para 2; 2012/2590, sch para 3
   appl (mods)—GLA, 1999 c 29, s 333ZB(3)(4); Localism, 2011 c 20, s 208(4)(5)
   trans of functions—SI 2011/741, art 3, sch 1
sch 7 am—SI 2008/3002, arts 4, 5, schs 1, 2
   rep in pt—SI 2008/3002, arts 5, 6, schs 2, 3
sch 8 rep in pt—Equality, 2010 c 15, sch 27 Pt 1A (added by SI 2011/1060, sch 3); Public
    Bodies, 2011 c 24, sch 6; Localism, 2011 c 20, sch 25 pt 31
sch 9 rep in pt—Equality, 2010 c 15, sch 27 Pt 1A (added by SI 2011/1060, sch 3); Finance,
    2011 c 11, sch 3 para 16; Localism, 2011 c 20, sch 25 pt 26; Loc Audit and
    Accountability, 2014 c 2, sch 1 pt 2
sch 11 appl (mods)—SI 2009/1260 (W 112), arts 2-7

c 18   **Crossrail**
see—SI 2014/310, art 18
s 4 am—SI 2009/229, art 9, sch 2
   trans of functions—SI 2009/229, art 4, sch 1
ss 6,7 am—SI 2010/988, art 3
s 8 am—SI 2010/988, art 3
   appl (mods)—SI 2014/310, art 18 sch 6 paras 1-3
   appl—SI 2015/781, sch 4 paras 1(a), 2, 3
s 9 am—SI 2010/988, art 4
   appl (mods)—SI 2014/310, art 18 sch 6 paras 1-3
   appl—SI 2015/781, sch 4 paras 1(a), 2, 3
s 10 appl (mods)—SIs 2014/310, art 18 sch 6 paras 1-3; 2015/781, sch 4 paras 1(a), 2, 3
ss 11-13 appl (mods)—SI 2014/310, art 18 sch 6 paras 1-3

2008

c 18 ss 11-13 *continued*

        appl—SI 2015/781, sch 4 paras 1(a), 2, 3

   s 15 appl (mods)—SI 2014/310, art 18 sch 6 paras 1-3

      appl—SI 2015/781, sch 4 paras 1(a), 2, 3

   s 20 appl (mods)—SI 2014/310, art 18 sch 6 paras 1-3

      appl—SI 2015/781, sch 4 paras 1(a), 2, 3

   s 22 am—SI 2015/1682, sch pt 1 para 4(t)(i)

   s 23 am—SI 2015/1682, sch pt 1 para 4(t)(ii)

   s 30 appl—SI 2015/781, sch 4 paras 1(a), 2, 3

      am—SI 2015/1682, sch pt 1 para 4(t)(iii)

   s 31 appl—SI 2015/781, sch 4 paras 1(a), 2, 3

   s 33 mod—SI 2010/988, art 5

   s 36 rep in pt—Localism, 2011 c 20, sch 25 pt 32

   s 42 mod—SI 2010/988, art 6

   s 44 mod—SI 2010/988, art 7

   s 46 appl—SI 2015/781, sch 4 paras 1(a), 2, 3

   s 47 am—SI 2010/988, art 3

   s 48 am—Planning, 2008 c 29, s 36, sch 2 para 66

   s 52 am—SI 2010/988, art 3

   s 54 am—SI 2015/1682, sch pt 1 para 4(t)(iv)

   sch 2 am—Localism, 2011 c 20, sch 22 para 58

      appl (mods)—SI 2014/310, art 18 sch 6 paras 1-3

      appl in pt—SI 2015/781, sch 4 para 1(b)

   sch 3 mod—SI 2010/988, art 8

      appl (mods)—SI 2014/310, art 18 sch 6 paras 1-3

   sch 4 am—SI 2009/229, art 9, sch 2

      trans of functions—SI 2009/229, art 4, sch 1

   sch 6 am—SIs 2009/1307, art 5, sch 1; 2010/988, art 3

   sch 7 appl (mods)—SI 2014/310, art 18 sch 6 paras 1-3

      appl in pt (mods)—SI 2015/781, sch 4 paras 1(c), 2, 3

   sch 9 am—SIs 2010/1551, art 11, sch; 2012/2590, sch para 4(a)

   sch 11 rep in pt—SL(R), 2013 c 2, s 1, sch 1 pt 9 Group 3(2)

      appl in pt—SI 2015/781, sch 4 paras 1(d), 2, 3

   sch 12 am—Constitutional Reform and Governance, 2010 c 25, s 19, sch 2 para 18

      rep in pt—Localism, 2011 c 20, sch 25 pt 32

   sch 13 am—Corporation Tax, 2009 c 4, s 1322, sch 1 paras 738, 739; Corporation Tax,

        2010 c 4, s 1177, sch 1 para 584

   sch 14 mod—SI 2010/988, art 9

      appl (mods)—SI 2014/310, art 18 sch 6 paras 1-3

      appl in pt—SI 2015/781, sch 4 paras 1(e), 2, 3

   sch 17 am—SIs 2009/2748, art 8, sch; 2009/229, art 9, sch 2; 2010/988, art 3; 2011/741,

        sch 2 para 3; 2012/1659, sch 3 para 19(2),(3)(b); 2012/2590, sch para 4(b)

      rep in pt—SI 2012/1659, sch 3 para 19(3)(a)

      trans of functions—SIs 2009/229, art 4, sch 1; 2011/741, art 3, sch 1

      mod—SI 2010/988, arts 10, 11

      appl (mods)—SI 2014/310, art 18 sch 6 paras 1-3

      appl in pt (mods)—SI 2015/781, sch 4 paras 1(f), 3(5)-(7)

c 19   *Appropriation (No 3)*—rep Appropriation (No 3), 2010 c 30, s 4, sch 3

c 20   **Health and Safety (Offences)**

      sch 3 rep in pt—SI 2014/1639, sch 3 pt 1

c 21   **Planning and Energy**

      s 1 am—Deregulation, 2015 c 20, s 43; (prosp) Planning (W), 2015 anaw 4, sch 2 para

        31(2)-(5)

      s 2 am—(prosp) Planning (W), 2015 anaw 4, sch 2 para 32

c 22   **Human Fertilisation and Embryology**

      s 33 appl (mods)—SI 2010/985, reg 5, sch 4

      s 35 am—Marriage (Same Sex Couples), 2013 c 30, sch 7 para 38; SI 2014/3229, sch 5

        para 18(2)

      s 38 appl (mods)—SI 2010/985, reg 5, sch 4

      s 40 am—Marriage (Same Sex Couples), 2013 c 30, sch 7 para 39; SI 2014/3229, sch 5

        para 18(3)

      s 42 am—Marriage (Same Sex Couples), 2013 c 30, sch 7 para 40; SI 2014/3229, sch 5

        para 18(4)

2008
c 22 *continued*
  s 46 am—Marriage (Same Sex Couples), 2013 c 30, sch 7 para 41; SI 2014/3229, sch 5
    para 18(5)
  s 54 am—Crime and Cts, 2013 c 22, sch 11 para 206
    appl (mods)—SI 2015/572, reg 18
  sch 6 rep in pt—Legal Aid, Sentencing and Punishment of Offenders, 2012 c 10, sch 5 pt 2;
    Crime and Cts, 2013 c 22, sch 10 para 99 Table
c 23 **Children and Young Persons**
  Pt 1 (ss 1-6) rep (prosp)—Children and Young Persons, 2008 c 23, s 42, sch 4
  ss 11-13 rep (prosp)—Children and Young Persons, 2008 c 23, s 42, sch 4
  s 31 am—SI 2010/1158, art 5, sch 2
  sch 1 rep in pt—Legal Aid, Sentencing and Punishment of Offenders, 2012 c 10, sch 12 para
    56
c 24 **Employment**
  s 4 rep—Deregulation, 2015 c 20, s 93(2)(b)
  s 5 rep—Enterprise and Regulatory Reform, 2013 c 24, sch 1 para 12
  ss 8, 9 rep in pt—(NI,S,W pt prosp) Enterprise and Regulatory Reform, 2013 c 24, sch 20
    para 2
c 25 **Education and Skills**
  am—SI 2010/1158, art 5, sch 2
  Pt 1 Ch 1 (ss 1-9) mod—SI 2013/1205, reg 8
  s 2 am—Apprenticeships, Skills, Children and Learning, 2009 c 22, s 37(1)(2)
  s 3 am—SI 2013/1242, art 2(2)(a)(b)
    rep in pt—SI 2013/1242, art 2(2)(c)
  s 4 am—SI 2010/1080, art 2, sch 1; Children and Families, 2014 c 6, sch 3 para 83(a)
    rep in pt—Children and Families, 2014 c 6, sch 3 para 83(b)
  s 6 am—SI 2013/1242, art 2(3)
  s 8 am—SI 2013/1242, art 2(4)(a)(b)(ii)(iii)
    rep in pt—SI 2013/1242, art 2(4)(b)(i)
  s 9 rep —Apprenticeships, Skills, Children and Learning, 2009 c 22, s 266, sch 16
  s 13 am—SI 2010/1080, art 2, sch 1; Educ, 2011 c 21, sch 16 para 41; Deregulation, 2015
    c 20, sch 14 para 61
  s 15 rep—Apprenticeships, Skills, Children and Learning, 2009 c 22, ss 254(1)(2), 266, sch
    16 pt 10
  s 16 am—SI 2010/1158, art 5, sch 2; Health and Social Care, 2012 c 7, sch 5 para 169(c)
    rep in pt—SI 2010/1080, art 2, schs 1, 2; Health and Social Care, 2012 c 7, sch 5 para
    169(a), (b)
  s 17 am —Apprenticeships, Skills, Children and Learning, 2009 c 22, s 254(1)(3)-(6); SI
    2010/1080, art 2, sch 1; Children and Families, 2014 c 6, sch 3 para 84(a)
    rep in pt—Children and Families, 2014 c 6, sch 3 para 84(b)
  s 47 am—SI 2010/1080, art 2, sch 1; Children and Families, 2014 c 6, sch 3 para 85(a)
    rep in pt—Children and Families, 2014 c 6, sch 3 para 85(b)
  s 48 am—Local Government (W), 2011 nawm 4, sch 3 para 7
  s 56 am—Crime and Cts, 2013 c 22, s 26(8); ibid, sch 9 para 52
  ss 57-59, 65 am—Crime and Cts, 2013 c 22, sch 9 para 52
  s 66 am—Apprenticeships, Skills, Children and Learning, 2009 c 22, s 37(1)(3); SI
    2015/1852, art 3(a)(b)
  s 68 rep in pt—Educ, 2011 c 21, s 28(3)(a)
  s 69 rep—Educ, 2011 c 21, s 28(2)
  s 70 rep in pt—Educ, 2011 c 21, s 28(3)(b)
  s 71 am—Educ, 2011 c 21, s 28(3)(c)
  s 72 am—SI 2010/1080, art 2, sch 1; Educ, 2011 c 21, sch 16 para 42; Deregulation, 2015
    c 20, sch 14 para 62
  s 73 rep—Educ, 2011 c 21, s 28(4)
  s 75 appl in pt—SI 2015/1792, sch para 3
  s 76 rep in pt—Apprenticeships, Skills, Children and Learning, 2009 c 22, ss 254(1)(7)(8),
    266, sch 16 pt 10
    am—Apprenticeships, Skills, Children and Learning, 2009 c 22, s 254(1)(7)(9)
  s 76A added—Apprenticeships, Skills, Children and Learning, 2009 c 22, s 255(1)(3)
    rep in pt—Educ, 2011 c 21, s 28(5)
  s 77 am—SIs 2010/1080, art 2, sch 1; 1158, art 5, schs 2, 3; Educ, 2011 c 21, sch 16 para
    43; Health and Social Care, 2012 c 7, sch 5 para 170(c)
    rep in pt—SI 2010/1158, art 5, sch 2; (Health and Social Care, 2012 c 7, sch 5 para
    170(a), (b); Deregulation, 2015 c 20, sch 14 para 63

2008

c 25 *continued*

s 78 am—SI 2010/1080, art 2, sch 1; 1158, art 5, sch 2; Children and Families, 2014 c 6, sch 3 para 86(a)

rep in pt—Children and Families, 2014 c 6, sch 3 para 86(b)

s 80 rep—Children and Families, 2014 c 6, sch 3 para 75(b)

s 81 rep in pt—Educ, 2011 c 21, s 29(9)(c)

s 82 rep—SI 2010/1080, art 2, schs 1, 2

ss 83, 84 saved—SI 2009/387, art 3

s 85 am—SI 2010/1158, art 5, sch 2

Pt 3 (ss 86-91) am—Small Business, Enterprise and Employment, 2015 c 26, s 78(4)(a)

s 86 rep—SI 2010/1080, art 2, schs 1, 2

s 87 rep in pt—Small Business, Enterprise and Employment, 2015 c 26, s 78(2),(4)(b)

s 91 rep in pt—Small Business, Enterprise and Employment, 2015 c 26, s 78(3)

Pt 4, Ch 1 (ss 92-148) mod—SI 2014/3364, art 3(2) and see Explanatory Note

s 93A added (with transtl mod)—SI 2012/976, arts 2, 3, sch para 22

s 94 am—Small Business, Enterprise and Employment, 2015 c 26, s 75(5)

s 111 mod—SI 2009/1513, art 2A

am—Children, Schools and Families, 2010 c 26, s 23

s 130 am—Policing and Crime, 2009 c 26, s 81(2)(3)(p)(4)(b); SI 2012/3006, art 13(1), (2)(f)

rep in pt—Educ, 2011 c 21, sch 2 para 20(a)

s 132 am—SI 2010/1080, art 2, sch 1; Educ, 2011 c 21, sch 16 para 44; Children and Families, 2014 c 6, sch 3 para 87

rep in pt—Deregulation, 2015 c 20, sch 14 para 64

s 141 am—Policing and Crime, 2009 c 26, s 81(2)(3)(p); SI 2012/3006, art 13(1), (2)(f)

s 147 rep in pt—Protection of Freedoms, 2012 c 9, sch 10 pt 5

s 158 rep (W) (prosp)—Children and Families (W), 2010 nawm 1, s 73, sch 2

s 159 rep in pt—Apprenticeships, Skills, Children and Learning, 2009 c 22, s 123, sch 16

s 160 rep in pt—Apprenticeships, Skills, Children and Learning, 2009 c 22, s 123, sch 16; Qualifications Wales, 2015 anaw 5, sch 4 para 8

s 161 rep—Apprenticeships, Skills, Children and Learning, 2009 c 22, s 266, sch 16

s 162 rep—Qualifications Wales, 2015 anaw 5, sch 4 para 8

s 163 rep—Apprenticeships, Skills, Children and Learning, 2009 c 22, s 266, sch 163

s 173 am—Educ, 2011 c 21, s 74

sch 1 rep in pt—Equality, 2010 c 15, s 211, sch 27 pt 1 (subst by SI 2010/2279, sch 2); Educ, 2011 c 21, sch 2 para 20(b); Welfare Reform, 2012 c 5, s 134(4); Protection of Freedoms, 2012 c 9, sch 10 pt 5; Children and Families, 2014 c 6, sch 3 para 75(a)

c 26   **Local Transport**

s 51 rep in pt—SI 2009/1885, art 4, schs 3, 4

ss 55, 56 rep (prosp)—Equality, 2010 c 15, s 211, sch 27 pt 1 (subst by SI 2010/2279, sch 2)

s 75 am—SI 2009/1885, art 4, sch 1

rep in pt—SI 2009/1885, art 4, sch 1

s 76 rep —SI 2009/1885, art 4, schs 3, 4

s 79 am—Loc Democracy, Economic Development and Construction, 2009 c 20, s 119, sch 6 paras 122, 123

s 85 appl—Loc Democracy, Economic Development and Construction, 2009 c 20, s 104(2)

s 86 am—Loc Democracy, Economic Development and Construction, 2009 c 20, s 119, sch 6 paras 122, 124

s 87 am—Loc Democracy, Economic Development and Construction, 2009 c 20, s 119, sch 6 paras 122, 125

s 88 appl—Loc Democracy, Economic Development and Construction, 2009 c 20, s 104(3)(a)

am—Loc Democracy, Economic Development and Construction, 2009 c 20, s 119, sch 6 paras 122, 126

s 89 appl—Loc Democracy, Economic Development and Construction, 2009 c 20, s 104(3)(b)

s 89A added—Loc Democracy, Economic Development and Construction, 2009 c 20, s 119, sch 6 paras 122, 127

s 90 am—Loc Democracy, Economic Development and Construction, 2009 c 20, s 119, sch 6 paras 122, 128

s 91 am—Loc Democracy, Economic Development and Construction, 2009 c 20, s 119, sch 6 paras 122, 129

2008

c 26 *continued*

s 97 appl—Loc Democracy, Economic Development and Construction, 2009 c 20, s 104(4)

s 102A am—Loc Democracy, Economic Development and Construction, 2009 c 20, s 119, sch 6 paras 122, 130

Pt 5, Ch 4 (ss 102B-102D) added —Localism, 2011 c 20, s 11

s 102C am—Co-operative and Community Benefit Societies, 2014 c 14, sch 4 para 138

s 123 am—SI 2011/1011(W 150), art 7

sch 4 rep in pt—Equality, 2010 c 15, sch 27 Pt 1A (added by SI 2011/1060, sch 3); Civil Aviation, 2012 c 19, sch 8 para 4; Loc Audit and Accountability, 2014 c 2, sch 1 pt 2

c 27   **Climate Change**

s 5 am—SI 2009/1258, art 2

rep in pt—SI 2009/1258, art 2

s 23 power to am conferred—Energy, 2013 c 32, s 1(8)(a)

s 71 rep in pt—Localism, 2011 c 20, s 47(a)(b), sch 25 pt 8

ss 72-75 rep—Localism, 2011 c 20, s 47(b), sch 25 pt 8

s 77 am —Waste (W), 2010 nawm 8, s 2

s 81 rep in pt—Deregulation, 2015 c 20, s 57(4)(b)

s 86 trans of functions—SI 2011/740, art 2

am—SI 2011/740, art 3

s 88 rep in pt—SI 2010/675, reg 109, sch 28

s 98 am —Waste (W), 2010 nawm 8, s 18, sch 1 para 2

rep in pt—Localism, 2011 c 20, sch 25 pt 8

sch 1 rep in pt—Equality 2010 c 15, sch 27 Pt 1A (added by SI 2011/1060, sch 3)

sch 5 rep—Localism, 2011 c 20, s 47(a), sch 25 pt 8

sch 6 am —Waste (W), 2010 nawm 8, s 1

c 28   **Counter-Terrorism**

s 1 am —(prosp) Crime and Security, 2010 c 17, s 56(3); Terrorism Prevention and Investigation Measures, 2011 c 23, sch 7 para 5(2)(b); Protection of Freedoms, 2012 c 9, sch 9 para 33

rep in pt—Terrorism Prevention and Investigation Measures, 2011 c 23, sch 7 para 5(2)(a)

s 7 am—SI 2013/602, sch 2 para 60(2)

ss 10-13 rep —Terrorism Prevention and Investigation Measures, 2011 c 23, sch 7 para 5(3)

s 14 rep in pt—Protection of Freedoms, 2012 c 9, sch 10 pt 1

ss 16, 17 rep—Protection of Freedoms, 2012 c 9, sch 10 pt 1

s 18 replaced (by ss 18, 18A-18E) —Protection of Freedoms, 2012 c 9, sch 1 para 4

s 18 am—Crime and Cts, 2013 c 22, sch 8 para 188; SI 2013/602, sch 2 para 60(3)

s 18D am—Anti-social Behaviour, Crime and Policing, 2014 c 12, sch 11 para 126(1)

s 18E am—Crime and Cts, 2013 c 22, sch 8 para 186; Anti-social Behaviour, Crime and Policing, 2014 c 12, sch 11 para 126(2)

s 28 am—Terrorist Asset-Freezing etc, 2010 c 38, s 35(4)

s 45 am—(S) Crim Justice and Licensing (S), 2010 asp 13, s 203, sch 7 para 85(a)(b); SI 2010/976, art 12, sch 14; Legal Aid, Sentencing and Punishment of Offenders, 2012 c 10, sch 21 para 33(3)

s 51 am—SI 2013/602, sch 2 para 60(4)

s 53 am—SI 2010/976, art 12, sch 14

s 63 am—SIs 2010/1197, reg 14, sch 2; 2937, reg 26; 2011/605, reg 19; 2011/1893, reg 19; 2011/2742, sch 2 para 1; 2012/925, reg 27

rep in pt—SIs 2011/2742, reg 19(2); 2012/925, reg 28(2)

s 64 rep in pt—SI 2009/1911, art 2; Terrorist Asset-Freezing etc, 2010 c 38, ss 45, 52, sch 2 pt 1

am—SI 2009/1911, art 2

ss 66-68 appl—Terrorist Asset-Freezing etc, 2010 c 38, s 28(4)

s 75 rep in pt—Terrorist Asset-Freezing etc, 2010 c 38, ss 45, 52, sch 2 pt 1

ss 78-81 rep—Terrorism Prevention and Investigation Measures, 2011 c 23, sch 7 para 5(4)

s 86 am—SI 2013/602, sch 2 para 60(5)

s 88 am—SI 2013/602, sch 2 para 60(6)

sch 4 am—SI 2013/602, sch 2 para 60(7)

sch 5 am—SI 2013/602, sch 2 para 60(8)(a)-(c)(e)(ii)

rep in pt—SI 2013/602, sch 2 para 60(8)(d)(e)(iii)(f)

sch 6 mod—SI 2009/1059, art 205, sch 2 para 17

am—Legal Aid, Sentencing and Punishment of Offenders, 2012 c 10, sch 22 para 38

2008

c 28 *continued*

      sch 7 am—SIs 2009/777, sch paras 2-4; 2009/1835, art 4, sch 1; Terrorist Asset-Freezing
            etc, 2010 c 38, ss 45, 48(1)(a)(b)(d)(2), 49, 50, 52, sch 1 paras 9, 10,
            11(2)(3)(5); ibid, s 51(1)(a); SI 2011/99, sch 4 para 6; Financial Services, 2012
            c 21, sch 18 para 127; SIs 2013/1881, sch para 15(2)(b); 2013/3115, sch 2 para
            44(2)(3)(b)(4)(b); Co-operative and Community Benefit Societies, 2014 c 14,
            sch 4 para 139
          rep in pt—SIs 2009/1835, art 4, sch 1; 2010/22, art 5, sch 2; Terrorist Asset-Freezing
            etc, 2010 c 38, ss 45, 48(1)(c), 52, sch 1 para 11(4), sch 2 pt 2; ibid, ss 45, 52,
            sch 2 pt 2; ibid, ss 45, s 51(1)(b)(2), 52, sch 2 pt 2; Financial Services, 2012 c.
            21, sch 18 para 127(4)(b); SIs 2013/1881, sch para 15(2)(a)(3)-(5); 2013/3115,
            sch 2 para 44(3)(a)(4)(a); 2014/834, sch 2 para 60
      sch 9 rep in pt—Terrorist Asset-Freezing etc, 2010 c 38, ss 45, 52, sch 2 pt 1

c 29   **Planning**

      saved—SIs 2009/400, art 6; 2010/101, art 6
      Pt 1 (ss 1-4) am—Localism, 2011 c 20, sch 13 para 3(1)(5)
      ss 1-3 rep—Localism, 2011 c 20, sch 13 para 2, sch 25 pt 20
      s 4 am—Localism, 2011 c 20, sch 13 para 3
      s 5 am—Localism, 2011 c 20, s 130(2)(3)
         rep in pt—Localism, 2011 c 20, s 130(4), sch 25 pt 20
      s 6 am—Localism, 2011 c 20, s 130(5)-(7)
      ss 6A, 6B added—Localism, 2011 c 20, s 130(8)
      s 8 am—Localism, 2011 c 20, s 130(9)-(12)
         excl in pt—SI 2015/1570, art 25(1)
      s 9 am—Localism, 2011 c 20, s 130(13)
      s 12 rep—Localism, 2011 c 20, s 130(14), sch 25 pt 20
      s 13 am—Crim Justice and Cts, 2015 c 2, s 92(3)
      s 14 am—SIs 2012/1645, art 2(2); 2015/949, art 2(2)
      s 16 am—SIs 2010/277, art 2; 2013/1479, art 2
         rep in pt—SI 2010/277, art 2
      s 22 subst—SI 2013/1883, art 3
         am—Infrastructure, 2015 c 7, sch 1 para 153
      s 25 am—SI 2013/1883, art 4
      s 29 am—SI 2012/1645, art 2(3)
      s 30A added—SI 2015/949, art 2(3)
      s 33 am—Localism, 2011 c 20, s 131(2)
         rep in pt—Growth and Infrastructure, 2013 c 27, s 18(3)(a)
      ss 35, 35ZA subst for s 35—Growth and Infrastructure, 2013 c 27, s 26(2)
      s 35A added—Localism, 2011 c 20, s 132(1)(10)
         am—Growth and Infrastructure, 2013 c 27, s 26(3)
      s 37 am—Localism, 2011 c 20, sch 13 para 5
      s 38 rep—Localism, 2011 c 20, sch 13 para 6, sch 25 pt 20
      s 39 am—Localism, 2011 c 20, sch 13 para 7
      s 42 am—Marine and Coastal Access, 2009 c 23, s 23(2)
      s 43 am—Marine and Coastal Access, 2009 c 23, s 23(1)(3)(a); Localism, 2011 c 20, s 133
      s 44 am—Marine and Coastal Access, 2009 c 23, s 23(1)(3)(b); Localism, 2011 c 20, s
            135(8)
      s 46 am—Localism, 2011 c 20, sch 13 para 8
      s 47 am—Localism, 2011 c 20, s 134
      s 50 rep in pt—Localism, 2011 c 20, sch 13 para 9, sch 25 pt 20
      s 51 am—Localism, 2011 c 20, sch 13 para 10
      s 52 am—Localism, 2011 c 20, s 135
      s 53 am—SI 2009/1307, art 5, sch 1; Localism, 2011 c 20, s 136(2)(3)(5); ibid, sch 13 para
            12
         rep in pt—Localism, 2011 c 20, s 136(4), sch 25 pt 20
      s 54 am—Localism, 2011 c 20, s 136(6)
      s 55 am—Marine and Coastal Access, 2009 c 23, s 23(1)(4); Localism, 2011 c 20, s
            137(3)(4); ibid, sch 13 para 13
         rep in pt—Localism, 2011 c 20, s 137(2), sch 25 pt 21
      s 56 am—Marine and Coastal Access, 2009 c 23, s 23(1)(5); Localism, 2011 c 20, s 138(2);
            ibid, sch 13 para 14
      s 56A added —Localism, 2011 c 20, s 138(3)
      s 57 am—Localism, 2011 c 20, s 135(9)
      s 58 am—Localism, 2011 c 20, sch 13 para 15

2008
c 29 *continued*

s 59 am—Localism, 2011 c 20, sch 13 para 16
s 60 am—Localism, 2011 c 20, s 138(4); ibid, sch 13 para 17
s 61 am—Localism, 2011 c 20, sch 13 para 18; Infrastructure, 2015 c 7, s 26
s 62 am—Localism, 2011 c 20, sch 13 para 19
s 63 rep—Localism, 2011 c 20, sch 13 para 20, sch 25 pt 20
s 64 am—Localism, 2011 c 20, sch 13 para 21
s 65 am—Localism, 2011 c 20, sch 13 para 22(1)(2); (prosp) Infrastructure, 2015 c 7, s
  27(1)
 rep in pt—Localism, 2011 c 20, sch 13 para 22(1)(3), sch 25 pt 20
s 66 rep in pt—Localism, 2011 c 20, sch 13 para 23(1)(2), sch 25 pt 20
 am—Localism, 2011 c 20, sch 13 para 23(1)(3)(4)
s 67 rep —Localism, 2011 c 20, sch 13 para 24, sch 25 pt 20
s 68 am—Localism, 2011 c 20, sch 13 para 25(1)-(3); (prosp) Infrastructure, 2015 c 7, s
  27(2)(b)
 rep in pt—Localism, 2011 c 20, sch 13 para 25(1)(4), sch 25 pt 20; (prosp)
  Infrastructure, 2015 c 7, s 27(2)(a)
s 69 am—Localism, 2011 c 20, sch 13 para 26(1)(2)
 rep in pt—Localism, 2011 c 20, sch 13 para 26(1)(3), sch 25 pt 20
s 70 rep—Localism, 2011 c 20, sch 13 para 27, sch 25 pt 20
s 71 am—Localism, 2011 c 20, sch 13 para 28
s 73 rep in pt—(prosp) Infrastructure, 2015 c 7, s 27(3)
s 74 rep in pt—Localism, 2011 c 20, sch 13 para 29(1)(2)(4), sch 25 pt 20
 am—Localism, 2011 c 20, sch 13 para 29(1)(3)
s 75 am—(prosp) Infrastructure, 2015 c 7, s 27(4)
Pt 6 Ch 3 (ss 78-85) am—Localism, 2011 c 20, sch 13 para 30(1)(6)
s 78 am—Localism, 2011 c 20, sch 13 para 30(1)-(5)
s 79 subst—Localism, 2011 c 20, sch 13 para 31
s 80 am—Localism, 2011 c 20, sch 13 para 32(1)(3)-(5)
 rep in pt—Localism, 2011 c 20, sch 13 para 32(1)(2), sch 25 pt 20
s 81 rep—Localism, 2011 c 20, sch 13 para 33, sch 25 pt 20
s 82 am—Localism, 2011 c 20, sch 13 para 34
s 83 am—Localism, 2011 c 20, sch 13 para 35(1)-(3)
 rep in pt—Localism, 2011 c 20, sch 13 para 35(1)(4)(5), sch 25 pt 20
s 84 rep (and cross-heading rep) —Localism, 2011 c 20, sch 13 para 36, sch 25 pt 20
s 85 rep —Localism, 2011 c 20, sch 13 para 36, sch 25 pt 20
s 86 am—Localism, 2011 c 20, sch 13 para 37
s 87 rep in pt—Localism, 2011 c 20, sch 13 para 38, sch 25 pt 20
s 88 am—Localism, 2011 c 20, s 138(5)
s 88A added —Localism, 2011 c 20, s 138(6)
s 89 am—Localism, 2011 c 20, s 138(7)
s 92 am—Localism, 2011 c 20, sch 13 para 39
s 93 am—Localism, 2011 c 20, sch 13 para 40
s 94 am—Localism, 2011 c 20, sch 13 para 41
s 95 rep in pt—SI 2013/2042, sch para 40(a)
s 95A added —Localism, 2011 c 20, sch 13 para 42
s 96 am—Localism, 2011 c 20, sch 13 para 43
s 97 rep in pt—SI 2013/2042, sch para 40(b)
s 98 am—Localism, 2011 c 20, s 139(2); ibid, sch 13 para 44
s 100 am—Localism, 2011 c 20, sch 13 para 45
s 101 am—Localism, 2011 c 20, sch 13 para 46
s 102 am—Marine and Coastal Access, 2009 c 23, s 23(1)(6); Localism, 2011 c 20, s
  138(8)(a)-(c); ibid, sch 13 para 47
 rep in pt—Localism, 2011 c 20, s 138(8)(d)-(f), sch 25 pt 21
ss 102A, 102B added —Localism, 2011 c 20, s 138(9)
s 103 am—Localism, 2011 c 20, sch 13 para 48(1)(4)
s 103 rep in pt—Localism, 2011 c 20, sch 13 para 48(1)-(3), sch 25 pt 20
s 104 am—Marine and Coastal Access, 2009 c 23, s 58(5); Localism, 2011 c 20, sch 13
  para 49
s 105 am—Localism, 2011 c 20, sch 13 para 50
s 106 am—Localism, 2011 c 20, sch 13 para 51
s 107 am—Localism, 2011 c 20, s 139(3); ibid, sch 13 para 52(1)(2)(4)(6)
 rep in pt—Localism, 2011 c 20, sch 13 para 52(1)(3)(5), sch 25 pt 20
s 108 am—Localism, 2011 c 20, sch 13 para 53

2008

c 29 *continued*

Pt 6 Ch 7 (ss 109-113) rep —Localism, 2011 c 20, sch 13 para 54, sch 25 pt 20

s 114 am—Localism, 2011 c 20, sch 13 para 55

s 115 rep in pt—Localism, 2011 c 20, sch 13 para 56, sch 25 pt 20

s 116 am—Localism, 2011 c 20, sch 13 para 57(1)(2)-(4)

 rep in pt—Localism, 2011 c 20, sch 13 para 57(1)(5), sch 25 pt 20

s 117 rep in pt—Localism, 2011 c 20, sch 13 para 58(1)(2)(6), sch 25 pt 20

 am—Localism, 2011 c 20, sch 13 para 58(1)(3)-(5)

s 118 am—Localism, 2011 c 20, sch 13 para 59(1)(2); Crim Justice and Cts, 2015 c 2, s 92(4)(a)-(c)

 rep in pt—Localism, 2011 c 20, sch 13 para 59(1)(3), sch 25 pt 20

s 120 am—Localism, 2011 c 20, s 140; ibid, sch 13 para 60

s 121 rep —Localism, 2011 c 20, sch 13 para 61, sch 25 pt 20

ss 122, 123 am—Localism, 2011 c 20, sch 13 para 62

s 124 rep —Localism, 2011 c 20, sch 13 para 63, sch 25 pt 20

s 127 am—Localism, 2011 c 20, sch 13 para 64(1)(2); Growth and Infrastructure, 2013 c 27, s 23(2)(a)(b)

 rep in pt—Localism, 2011 c 20, sch 13 para 64(1)(3), sch 25 pt 20; Growth and Infrastructure, 2013 c 27, s 23(2)(c)

ss 128, 129 rep—Growth and Infrastructure, 2013 c 27, s 24(1)

s 130 am—Localism, 2011 c 20, s 141(3); Growth and Infrastructure, 2013 c 27, s 24(5)

s 131 rep in pt—Localism, 2011 c 20, sch 13 para 65, sch 25 pt 20; Growth and Infrastructure, 2013 c 27, s 24(2)(c)

 am—Growth and Infrastructure, 2013 c 27, s 24(2)(a)(b)

s 132 rep in pt—Localism, 2011 c 20, sch 13 para 65, sch 25 pt 20; Growth and Infrastructure, 2013 c 27, s 24(3)(c)

 am—Growth and Infrastructure, 2013 c 27, s 24(3)(a)(b)

s 134 rep in pt—Localism, 2011 c 20, s 142(1)(2)(b), (4), sch 25 pt 21

 am—Localism, 2011 c 20, s 142(1)(2)(a), (3)

s 135 saved—SI 2012/2635, art 25(6)

s 136 am—Localism, 2011 c 20, sch 13 para 66(1)-(3)

 rep in pt—Localism, 2011 c 20, sch 13 para 66(1)(4), sch 25 pt 20

s 137 rep—Growth and Infrastructure, 2013 c 27, s 23(3)

s 138 am—Localism, 2011 c 20, sch 13 para 67; Growth and Infrastructure, 2013 c 27, s 23(4)(a)(b)

 rep in pt—Growth and Infrastructure, 2013 c 27, s 23(4)(c)

s 144 am—Growth and Infrastructure, 2013 c 27, s 27(2)

 rep in pt—Growth and Infrastructure, 2013 c 27, s 27(3)

s 147 am—Localism, 2011 c 20, sch 13 para 68(1)(2)

 rep in pt—Localism, 2011 c 20, sch 13 para 68(1)(3), sch 25 pt 20

ss 148, 149 rep —Marine and Coastal Access, 2009 c 23, ss 112, 321, sch 8 para 4(1)(7)(a)(b), sch 22 pt 2

s 149A added —Marine and Coastal Access, 2009 c 23, s 112(1), sch 8 para 4(1)(2)

s 152 am—SI 2009/1307, art 5, sch 1

 appl—SIs 2012/2284, art 19(5); 2012/2635, art 26(5); 2014/909, art 23(5); 2269, art 21(5); 3328, art 19(3)(a); 2015/1347, art 24(5); 1386, art 25(5)

s 155 excl—SI 2010/105, reg 4

s 156 appl in pt—SIs 2013/343, art 7(1); 2013/680, art 7(1)

s 158 mod—SI 2014/2441, art 9(4)

 excl in pt—SI 2014/1796, art 9

s 160 am—SI 2015/664, sch 4 para 41(2)(b)

 rep in pt—SI 2015/664, sch 4 para 41(3)(a)

s 161 am—Marine and Coastal Access, 2009 c 23, s 112(1), sch 8 para 4(1)(3)

 rep in pt—SI 2015/664, sch 4 para 41(3)(b)

s 165 am—SI 2009/1307, art 5, sch 1

s 171 am—Crime and Cts, 2013 c 22, sch 9 para 52

s 179 rep—Loc Democracy, Economic Development and Construction, 2009 c 20, s 146, sch 7 pt 4

s 181 rep—Loc Democracy, Economic Development and Construction, 2009 c 20, s 146, sch 7 pt 4

s 192 rep in pt—SI 2009/1307, art 5, sch 1

s 205 am—Localism, 2011 c 20, s 115

s 206 am—Localism, 2011 c 20, sch 22 para 61

s 210 am—Charities, 2011 c 25, sch 7 para 136

2008
c 29 *continued*

s 211 am—Localism, 2011 c 20, s 114(2); ibid, s 115(4)
    mod—SI 2010/948, reg 14(5) (added by 2014/385, reg 5(3)(b))
s 212 am—Localism, 2011 c 20, s 114(3)
s 212A added—Localism, 2011 c 20, s 114(4)
s 213 am—Localism, 2011 c 20, s 114(5)-(7)
s 216 am —SI 2010/948, reg 63; Localism, 2011 c 20, s 115(5)
    rep in pt—SI 2010/948, reg 63
ss 216A, 216B added —Localism, 2011 c 20, s 115(6)
s 218 rep in pt—SI 2015/664, sch 4 para 92
s 219 am—SI 2009/1307, art 5, sch 1
s 232 am—Localism, 2011 c 20, s 131(3); Growth and Infrastructure, 2013 c 27, s 26(4)
s 235 rep in pt—Localism, 2011 c 20, sch 13 para 69, sch 25 pt 20
s 237A added—Growth and Infrastructure, 2013 c 27, s 22(1)
s 240 am—SI 2015/949, art 2(4)
sch 1 rep —Localism, 2011 c 20, sch 13 para 2, sch 25 pt 20
sch 2 excl —Flood and Water Management, 2010 c 29, s 40(1)
    rep in pt—Growth and Infrastructure, 2013 c 27, s 18(3)(b)
sch 3 rep —Localism, 2011 c 20, sch 13 para 54, sch 25 pt 20
sch 4 am—Marine and Coastal Access, 2009 c 23, s 112(1), sch 8 para 4(1)(4); Localism,
    2011 c 20, sch 13 para 70(1)-(3)(5)-(7)
sch 4 rep in pt—Localism, 2011 c 20, sch 13 para 70(1)(4)(8), sch 25 pt 20
sch 5 am—Marine and Coastal Access, 2009 c 23, s 112(1), sch 8 para 4(1)(5); Localism,
    2011 c 20, sch 13 para 71
    rep in pt—Marine and Coastal Access, 2009 c 23, ss 112, 321, sch 8 para 4(1)(7)(c),
        sch 22 pt 2
sch 6 rep in pt—SI 2009/1307, art 5, sch 1; Localism, 2011 c 20, sch 13 para 72(1),
    (2)(6)(8)(10), sch 25 pt 20
    am—Marine and Coastal Access, 2009 c 23, s 112(1), sch 8 para 4(1)(6); Localism,
    2011 c 20, sch 13 para 72(1), (3)-(5)(7)(9)(11)(12); Infrastructure, 2015 c 7, s
    28
sch 8 am—(W) SI 2013/755 (W 90), sch 2 para 440
sch 9 rep in pt—Public Bodies, 2011 c 24, sch 6
sch 12 am—SI 2009/1307, art 5, sch 1; Localism, 2011 c 20, s 131(4)(a)(c)(d); ibid, s
    135(10); ibid, s 136(7); ibid, s 138(10); ibid, sch 13 para 73; Growth and
    Infrastructure, 2013 c 27, s 23(5); Crime and Cts, 2013 c 22, sch 9 para 52; SI
    2015/949, art 2(5)
    rep in pt—Localism, 2011 c 20, s 131(4)(b), sch 25 pt 20; ibid, sch 25 pt 21; Growth
    and Infrastructure, 2013 c 27, s 24(4)(a)

c 30   **Pensions**

Pt 1 (ss 1-33) appl (mods)—SI 2012/1388, art 2
s 2 am—Pensions, 2011 c 19, s 4(1)
    excl—SI 2010/772, reg 5A (added by SI 2012/1477, reg 2)
s 3 am—Pensions, 2011 c 19, s 5(1); ibid, s 6(1); SIs 2012/1506, art 2(1); 2013/667, art
    2(1); SI 2014/623, art 2(1)
    excl—SI 2010/772, reg 5A (added by SI 2012/1477, reg 2)
    mod—SIs 2010/772, regs 5B-5E (added by 2015/501, reg 5); 2012/1506, art 3;
    2014/623, art 3
s 4 subst—Pensions, 2011 c 19, s 6(2)
s 5 am—Pensions, 2011 c 19, s 4(2)(3); ibid, s 5(3); SIs 2012/1506, art 2(1); 2014/623, art
    2(1); Pensions, 2014 c 19, s 37(2)
    rep in pt—Pensions, 2011 c 19, s 4(4); ibid, s 6(3); Pensions, 2014 c 19, s 38(3)(b)
    excl in pt—SI 2010/772, reg 14 (substituted by SI 2012/215, reg 22); SI 2010/772, reg
    5A (added by SI 2012/1477, reg 2)
    mod—SIs 2010/772, regs 5B-5E (added by 2015/501, reg 5); 2012/1506, art 3;
    2014/623, art 3
s 6 am—Pensions, 2011 c 19, ss 4(5)(d), 6(4)(b)(c), 7
s 6 rep in pt—Pensions, 2011 c 19, ss 4(5)(a)-(c),6(4)(a)
s 7 rep in pt—Pensions, 2011 c 19, s 6(5)
    excl—SI 2010/772, reg 5A (added by SI 2012/1477, reg 2); ibid, reg 5E(2)(a)(ii) (added
    by 2015/501, reg 5)
    mod—SI 2010/772, reg 5B(2)(b) (added by 2015/501, reg 5)
s 9 am—Pensions, 2011 c 19, s 5(4)

2008
c 30 s 9 *continued*

    excl—SI 2010/772, reg 5A (added by SI 2012/1477, reg 2); ibid, reg 5E(2)(a)(ii) (added
     by 2015/501, reg 5)
    mod—SI 2010/772, reg 5B(2)(c) (added by 2015/501, reg 5)
  s 10 am—Pensions, 2014 c 19, s 38(1)(a)(i)(b)
   rep in pt—Pensions, 2014 c 19, s 38(1)(a)(ii)
  s 13 am —Pensions, 2011 c 19, s 8(2); SIs 2012/1506, art 2(2); 2013/667, art 2(2);
     2014/623, art 2(2); Children and Families, 2014 c 6, sch 7 para 74(a); ibid, sch 7
     para 74(b); SI 2015/468, art 2
   mod—SIs 2012/1506, art 3; 2014/623, art 3
  s 14 subst—Pensions, 2011 c 19, s 8(1)
  s 15A added—Pensions, 2011 c 19, s 9
  s 16 am—Pensions, 2011 c 19, s 10; Pensions, 2014 c 19, sch 18 para 11(3)
   excl—SI 2010/772, reg 47
   rep in pt—Pensions, 2014 c 19, sch 18 para 11(2)(4)
  s 20 mod—SI 2010/772, reg 45
   rep in pt—SI 2011/1724, reg 3
   am—(prosp) Pension Schemes, 2015 c 8, sch 2 para 40
  s 21 subst—Pensions, 2014 c 19, sch 13 para 82
   mod—SI 2010/772, reg 45
   am—(prosp) Pension Schemes, 2015 c 8, sch 2 para 41
  s 22 am—Pensions, 2011 c 19, s 11(1); Pensions, 2014 c 19, sch 13 para 83
  s 23 subst—Pensions, 2011 c 19, s 11(2)
  s 23A added—Pensions, 2014 c 19, s 39(2)
   am—(prosp) Pension Schemes, 2015 c 8, sch 2 para 42
  s 24 appl (mods)—SI 2010/772, reg 45
   am—Pensions, 2014 c 19, s 39(3); (prosp) Pension Schemes, 2015 c 8, sch 2 para 43
  s 26 rep in pt—SI 2011/1724, reg 3; (prosp) Pension Schemes, 2015 c 8, sch 2 para 44(3)
   am—(prosp) Pension Schemes, 2015 c 8, sch 2 para 44(2)(4)-(6)
  s 28 am—Pensions, 2011 c 19, s 12(1)(2)-(7); ibid, s 13; Pensions, 2014 c 19, s 39(4);
    (prosp) Pension Schemes, 2015 c 8, sch 2 para 45
  s 29 rep in pt—Pensions, 2014 c 19, s 39(5)
   am—(prosp) Pension Schemes, 2015 c 8, sch 2 para 46
  s 30 am—Pensions, 2011 c 19, ss 6(6), 14, 15(2); Pensions, 2014 c 19, ss 39(3)(7)-(9),
    40(2)-(5); (prosp) Pension Schemes, 2015 c 8, sch 2 para 47
   rep in pt—Pensions, 2011 c 19, s 15(3)
   appl (mods) (cond)—Pensions, 2014 c 19, s 40(7)
  s 32 am—Pensions, 2011 c 19, ss 12(8), 16
  s 35 am—(prosp) Pension Schemes, 2015 c 8, sch 2 para 48
  s 38 am—(prosp) Pension Schemes, 2015 c 8, sch 2 para 49
  s 40 am—SI 2010/22, art 5, sch 2; Pensions, 2014 c 19, s 41(1)
  s 41 am—SI 2010/22, art 5, sch 2; Pensions, 2014 c 19, s 41(1)
  s 42 am—Crime and Cts, 2013 c 22, sch 9 para 52
  s 44 am—SI 2010/22, art 5, sch 2
   rep in pt—SI 2010/22, art 5, sch 4
  s 53 am—SI 2010/22, art 5, sch 2
  s 54 am—Pensions, 2011 c 19, s 4(6)
   excl—SI 2010/772, reg 5A (added by SI 2012/1477, reg 2)
  s 56 am—Enterprise and Regulatory Reform, 2013 c 24, sch 2 para 41
  s 58 am—Enterprise and Regulatory Reform, 2013 c 24, s 23(1)(c); ibid, sch 1 para 13
  s 60 am—Pensions, 2011 c 19, s 36(2)
  s 67 am & rep in pt—Finance (No 3), 2010 c 33, s 30(2)(a)
  s 70 rep—SI 2015/178, art 3
  ss 79-85 rep—SI 2010/911, art 8
  s 87A added—Pensions, 2014 c 19, s 38(2)
  s 89 appl—Pension Schemes, 1993 c. 48, s 123(3A)
  s 95 am—Police Reform and Social Responsibility, 2011 c 13, sch 16 para 371
  s 99 am—Pensions, 2011 c 19, s 29(3); (prosp) Pension Schemes, 2015 c 8, sch 2 para
    50(2)(3)
   rep in pt—(prosp) Pension Schemes, 2015 c 8, sch 2 para 50(4)
  s 99A added—Pensions, 2011 c 19, s 29(4)
  ss 102, 103 rep—Pensions, 2014 c 19, sch 12 para 96(a)
  s 105 rep in pt—Pensions, 2014 c 19, s 29(2)(a)
  Pt 3, Ch 1 (ss 107-120) appl—SI 2014/1711, reg 42(1) 53 57

2008

c 30 *continued*

s 110 appl—Family Law (S), 1985 c 37, s 8(11)(b)
s 143 am—Pensions, 2011 c 19, s 8(3)
s 144A added —Pensions, 2011 c 19, s 36(1)
s 150 am—Pensions, 2011 c 19, s 36(3)
sch 1 appl (mods)—SI 2010/911, art 9
    rep in pt—Equality, 2010 c 15, sch 27 Pt 1A (added by SI 2011/1060, sch 3)
sch 3 rep—Pensions, 2014 c 19, sch 12 para 96(b)
sch 4 rep in pt—Pensions, 2014 c 19, sch 12 para 96(c)
sch 5 am—Pensions, 2011 c 19, s 20(5)-(7); ibid, sch 4 paras 30(2), 31(1)-(3)(4)(c), 32, 33,
    34(1)(b)(2), 35, 36; (prosp) Pensions, 2014 c 19, sch 20 para 7
    rep in pt—Pensions, 2011 c 19, sch 4 paras 30(1), 31(4)(a)(b), 34(1)(a)
    mod—(prosp) Pensions, 2014 c 19, sch 20 para 22(2)
    appl—SI 2014/1711, reg 42(1) 53 57
sch 8 rep in pt—Pensions, 2011 c 19, sch 4 para 20

c 31 **Dormant Bank and Building Society Accounts**

mod—SI 2009/317, art 3, sch
appl (mods)—SI 2011/245, sch 6 pt 1
s 1 appl—Finance, 2008 c 9, s 39(2)(a)
    mod—SI 2009/317, art 7
s 2 mod—SI 2009/317, art 7
s 7 am—Financial Services, 2012 c. 21, sch 18 para 128
ss 17 am—SI 2010/2967, art 3
ss 22-24 am—SI 2010/2967, art 3
s 26 am—SI 2010/2967, art 3
s 28 am—SI 2010/2967, art 3
sch 3 am—SI 2010/2967, art 3

c 32 **Energy**

s 1 am—Marine and Coastal Access, 2009 c 23, s 43; ibid, s 41, sch 4 para 5(2)(2)
s 2 am—Deregulation, 2015 c 20, s 14(2)
s 3A added—Deregulation, 2015 c 20, s 14(1)
s 17 restr—SI 2011/2305, reg 16(1)(b)
    am—SSI 2011/224, reg 2(2); SI 2011/2453, reg 2
s 18 am—SSI 2011/224, reg 2(3); SI 2011/2453, reg 3(1)(2)
s 19 am—SI 2011/2453, reg 4
s 21 am—SI 2011/2453, reg 5
s 22 am—SSI 2011/224, reg 2(4); SIs 2011/2453, reg 6; 2015/664, sch 4 para 42(2)(a)
    rep in pt—SI 2015/664, sch 4 para 42(2)(b)(c)
s 23 am—SIs 2011/2453, reg 7; 2015/664, sch 4 para 42(3)(a)
    rep in pt—SI 2015/664, sch 4 para 42(3)(b)
s 25 am—SI 2015/664, sch 4 para 42(4)
s 26 am—SSI 2011/224, reg 2(5); SI 2011/2453, reg 8
s 27 am—SI 2011/2453, reg 9
s 28 am—SI 2011/2453, reg 10
s 30 am—Energy, 2011 c 16, s 107(3)-(5); SI 2011/2453, reg 11
ss 30A, 30B added—Energy, 2011 c 16, s 107(2)
s 31 am—SI 2011/2453, reg 12
s 35 am—Marine and Coastal Access, 2009 c 23, s 43; ibid, s 41, sch 4 para 5(1)(3); SSI
    2011/224, reg 2(6); SI 2011/2453, reg 13
s 41am—Energy, 2013 c 32, s 146
s 45A added —Energy, 2013 c 32, s 149(2)
s 59 am—SI 2010/675, reg 107, sch 26
s 46 am—Energy, 2011 c 16, s 106(3); Energy, 2013 c 32, s 149(3); ibid, sch 12 para 96
s 49 excl—SI 2013/126, reg 11
    am—Energy, 2013 c 32, s 149(4)
s 50 am—Energy, 2013 c 32, sch 12 para 97
s 54 am—Energy, 2013 c 32, sch 12 para 98
s 59 am—Energy, 2013 c 32, sch 12 para 99(a)(b)
s 63 am—Energy, 2013 c 32, sch 12 para 100
s 65 rep —Energy, 2013 c 32, sch 12 para 30
s 66 am—Energy, 2013 c 32, s 149(5)
s 77 am—Land Registration etc (S), 2012 asp 5, sch 5 para 55
ss 80-82 rep—Energy, 2011 c 16, sch 2 para 17
s 82I am—SI 2015/664, sch 4 para 42(5)

2008

c 32 *continued*

        s 82K am—SI 2015/664, sch 4 para 42(6)

        s 82L am—SI 2015/664, sch 4 para 42(7)

        s 87 rep in pt—Deregulation, 2015 c 20, s 57(4)(c)

        Pt 4A (ss 82A-82Q) added —Marine and Coastal Access, 2009 c 23, s 314(1); SI 2011/556
            art 3(1),(2)(c)

        s 88 am—Energy, 2011 c 16, s 73(1)(2)-(6); SI 2012/2400, art 33(2), (3)

        s 100 am—SI 2011/2195, reg 2(2); Infrastructure, 2015 c 7, s 51(2),(3)(a)-(e),(4)
            rep in pt—Infrastructure, 2015 c 7, s 51(3)(f)-(i)

        s 105 am—Marine and Coastal Access, 2009 c 23, s 314(2); SI 2011/556 art 3(1),(2)(c);
            Infrastructure, 2015 c 7, s 51(5),(6)(b),(7)(8)
            rep in pt—Infrastructure, 2015 c 7, s 51(5),(6)(a)

        s 112 rep in pt—Energy, 2011 c 16, sch 2 para 18; Energy, 2013 c 32, sch 12 para 30

4th session of 54th Parliament

c 33   *Consolidated Fund*—rep Appropriation (No 3), 2010 c 30, s 4, sch 3

2009

c 1   **Banking**

        am—SI 2013/504, reg 25(2)

        Pt 1 (ss 1-89) appl (mods)—Banking, 2009 c 1, s 84

            excl—SI 2010/35, art 2

            mod—Banking, 2009 c 1, s 83A(1) with Table

            ext (mods)—Banking, 2009 c 1, s 89A, 89B(1)(2)-(6)

            power to am—Financial Services (Banking Reform), 2013 c 33, s 17(3)(f)

        Pt 1, Ch 1 (ss 1-3) (sections renumbered as Ch 1)—SI 2014/3329, art 3

        s 1 am—Financial Services, 2010 c 28, s 24, sch 2 paras 39, 40; Financial Services, 2012 c
            21, ss 99(3),100(2), 101(2),102(2); ibid, sch 17 para 2(2)(3); Financial Services
            (Banking Reform), 2013 c 33, sch 2 para 12; SI 2014/3329, art 4

        s 2 am—Financial Services, 2012 c 21, ss 101(3), 102(3); ibid, sch 17 para 3

        s 3 am—Financial Services, 2012 c 21, s 96(2); ibid, sch 17 para 4; SI 2014/3329, art 5

        Pt 1, Ch 2 (ss 3A, 3B) added—SI 2014/3329, art 6

        Pt 1, Ch 3 (ss 4-83) (sections renumbered as Ch 3)—SI 2014/3329, art 7

        s 4 am—(prosp) Financial Services, 2012 c 21, s 96(3); ibid, sch 17 para 5; SI 2014/3329,
            art 8(2)

        s 5 am—Financial Services, 2012 c 21, sch 17 para 6; SI 2014/3329, art 9

        s 6 am—Financial Services, 2012 c 21, sch 17 para 7(3)
            rep in pt—Financial Services, 2012 c 21, sch 17 para 7(2)

        ss 6A-6D and cross-heading added—SI 2014/3329, art 10

        s 6E and cross-heading added—SI 2014/3329, art 11

        s 7 appl (mods)—SI 2010/1188, art 5
            am—Financial Services, 2012 c 21, sch 17 para 8(2),(4)-(6); SI 2014/3329, art 12
            rep in pt—Financial Services, 2012 c 21, sch 17 para 8(3)

        s 7A added—SI 2014/3329, art 13

        s 8 subst—SI 2014/3329, art 14

        s 8ZA added—SI 2014/3329, art 15

        s 8A added—Financial Services (Banking Reform), 2013 c 33, sch 2 para 3
            rep—SI 2014/3329, art arts 2, 16

        s 9 am—Financial Services, 2012 c 21, sch 17 para 10; SI 2014/3329, art 17

        s 10 am—Financial Services, 2012 c 21, sch 17 para 11

        s 12 am—SI 2014/3329, art 18

        s 12ZA added—SI 2014/3329, art 19

        s 12A added —Financial Services (Banking Reform), 2013 c 33, sch 2 para 2
            am—SI 2014/3329, art 20

        s 12AA added—SI 2014/3329, art 21

        s 12B added—Financial Services (Banking Reform), 2013 c 33, sch 2 para 2
            rep—SI 2014/3329, arts 2, 22

        s 13 am—Financial Services (Banking Reform), 2013 c 33, sch 2 para 13; SI 2014/3329,
            art 23

        s 14 am—SIs 2010/2628, regs 3, 13, sch 1; 2012/917, sch 1 para 4; 2013/3115, sch 2 para
            45(2)

        s 17 am—Financial Services (Banking Reform), 2013 c 33, sch 2 para 14; SI 2014/3329,
            art 24

        s 18 am—Financial Services (Banking Reform), 2013 c 33, sch 2 para 15; SI 2014/3329,
            art 25

2009

c 1 *continued*

s 19 am—SI 2014/3329, art 26

s 20 am—Financial Services, 2012 c 21, s 100(3); SI 2014/3329, art 27

s 22 rep—SI 2014/3329, art 28

s 24 am—Financial Services, 2012 c 21, sch 17 para 12; SI 2014/3329, art 29

s 25 am—Financial Services, 2012 c 21, sch 17 para 13; SI 2014/3329, art 30

s 26 am—Financial Services, 2012 c 21, sch 17 para 14; SI 2014/3329, art 31

s 26A added —Financial Services, 2012 c 21, s 97(2)

s 27 am—Financial Services, 2012 c 21, sch 17 para 15

s 28 am—Financial Services, 2012 c 21, sch 17 para 16

s 29 am—Financial Services, 2012 c 21, s 97(3); ibid, sch 17 para 17

s 29A added—SI 2014/3329, art 32

s 30 am—Financial Services, 2012 c 21, sch 17 para 18; SI 2014/3329, art 33

s 31 am—Financial Services, 2012 c 21, s 97(4)(b)(c); SI 2014/3329, art 34
    rep in pt—Financial Services, 2012 c 21, s 97(4)(a); ibid, sch 17 para 19

s 33 am—SI 2014/3329, art 35

s 34 am—Financial Services, 2012 c 21, s 98(3)
    rep in pt—Financial Services, 2012 c 21, s 98(2)

s 36A added —Financial Services, 2012 c 21, s 100(4)
    am—SI 2014/3329, art 36

s 38 rep—SI 2014/3329, art 37

s 39 am—SI 2014/3329, art 38

s 39A added —Financial Services, 2012 c 21, s 102(4)
    am—SI 2013/504, reg 25(3)

s 39B added—SI 2014/3329, art 39

s 41 am—Financial Services, 2012 c 21, sch 17 para 20; SI 2014/3329, art 40(2)

s 41A added —Financial Services (Banking Reform), 2013 c 33, sch 2 para 5(1)
    am—SI 2014/3329, art 41

s 42 am—Financial Services, 2012 c 21, sch 17 para 21; Financial Services (Banking
    Reform), 2013 c 33, sch 2 para 5(2); SI 2014/3329, art 42

s 42A added —Financial Services, 2012 c 21, s 97(5)

s 43 am—Financial Services, 2012 c 21, sch 17 para 22; SI 2014/3329, art 43

s 44 am—Financial Services, 2012 c 21, s 97(6); ibid, sch 17 para 23; Financial Services
    (Banking Reform), 2013 c 33, sch 2 para 16; SI 2014/3329, art 44

ss 44A-44C added —Financial Services (Banking Reform), 2013 c 33, sch 2 para 5(3)

s 44A am—SI 2014/3329, art 45

s 44B am—SI 2014/3329, art 46

s 45 am—Financial Services, 2012 c 21, s 98(4); ibid, sch 17 para 24

s 46 am—Financial Services, 2012 c 21, s 97(7)(b)
    rep in pt—Financial Services, 2012 c 21, ss 97(7)(a), 98(5); ibid, sch 17 para 25

s 47 am—Financial Services, 2012 c 21, s 96(5); SI 2014/3329, art 47

s 48A added—Financial Services, 2010 c 28, s 21(2)
    am—Financial Services, 2012 c 21, s 97(8); Financial Services (Banking Reform),
    2013 c 33, sch 2 para 5(4)

ss 48B-48W added —Financial Services (Banking Reform), 2013 c 33, sch 2 para 4

s 48B am—SI 2014/3329, art 48(1)-(3)(4)(a)(b)(d)-(f)(5)(6)
    rep in pt—SI 2014/3329, art 48(4)(c)

s 48C am—SI 2014/3329, art 49

s 48D rep in pt—SI 2014/3329, art 50

s 48H am—SI 2014/3329, art 51

ss 48I-48K am—SI 2014/3329, art 52

s 48L am—SI 2014/3329, art 53

s 48M rep—SI 2014/3329, art 54

s 48N am—SI 2014/3329, art 55

s 48O am—SI 2014/3329, art 56

s 48T am—SI 2014/3329, art 57

s 48U am—SI 2014/3329, art 58

s 48V am—SI 2014/3329, art 59

s 48W am—SI 2014/3329, art 60

ss 48X, 48Y and cross-heading added—SI 2014/3329, art 61

s 48Z and cross-heading added—SI 2014/3329, art 62

s 49 am—Financial Services (Banking Reform), 2013 c 33, sch 2 para 6(1)

s 52 am—Financial Services (Banking Reform), 2013 c 33, sch 2 para 6(2); SI 2014/3329,
    art 63

2009
c 1 *continued*

s 52A added —Financial Services (Banking Reform), 2013 c 33, sch 2 para 6(3)

s 53 am—Financial Services, 2012 c 21, s 97(9); Financial Services (Banking Reform), 2013 c 33, sch 2 para 6(4); SI 2014/3329, art 64

s 54 am—Financial Services (Banking Reform), 2013 c 33, sch 2 para 6(5); SI 2014/3329, art 65

s 55 am—Financial Services, 2010 c 28, s 21(3)

s 56 am—Financial Services, 2010 c 28, s 21(4)(a)(b); Financial Services (Banking Reform), 2013 c 33, sch 2 para 6(6)

s 57 am—Financial Services, 2012 c 21, sch 17 para 26; Financial Services (Banking Reform), 2013 c 33, sch 2 para 6(7)

s 58 am—SI 2014/3329, art 66

s 60 am—SI 2014/3329, art 67

s 60A added —Financial Services (Banking Reform), 2013 c 33, sch 2 para 6(8)

s 60B added —Financial Services (Banking Reform), 2013 c 33, sch 2 para 6(8)
    am—SI 2014/3329, art 68(a)

s 61 am—Financial Services, 2010 c 28, s 24, sch 2 paras 39, 41; Financial Services (Banking Reform), 2013 c 33, sch 2 para 6(9)

s 62 am—Financial Services (Banking Reform), 2013 c 33, sch 2 para 6(10)

s 62A and cross-heading added—SI 2014/3329, art 69

ss 62B-62E and cross-heading added—SI 2014/3329, art 70

s 63 am—Financial Services (Banking Reform), 2013 c 33, sch 2 para 17; SI 2014/3329, art 71

s 64 am—SI 2014/3329, art 72

s 65 am—SI 2014/3329, art 73

s 66 am—Financial Services (Banking Reform), 2013 c 33, sch 2 para 18; SI 2014/3329, art 74

s 67 am—Financial Services (Banking Reform), 2013 c 33, sch 2 para 19; SI 2014/3329, art 75

s 68 am—Financial Services (Banking Reform), 2013 c 33, sch 2 para 20; SI 2014/3329, art 76

ss 70A-70D added—SI 2014/3329, art 77

s 71 am—Financial Services (Banking Reform), 2013 c 33, sch 2 para 21; SI 2014/3329, art 78

s 72 rep—SI 2014/3329, art 79

s 73 am—Financial Services (Banking Reform), 2013 c 33, sch 2 para 23; SI 2014/3329, art 80

s 74 am—Financial Services (Banking Reform), 2013 c 33, sch 2 para 24; SI 2014/3329, art 81

s 75 am—Financial Services, 2012 c 21, s 101(4); ibid, s 102(5)

s 76 am—SI 2014/3329, art 82

s 77 am—SI 2014/3329, art 83

s 78 am—SI 2014/3329, art 84

s 78A added—SI 2014/3329, art 85

s 79 am—SI 2014/3329, art 86

s 79A added—Financial Services, 2012 c 21, s 99(1)

s 80 am—SI 2014/3329, art 87

s 80A added —Financial Services (Banking Reform), 2013 c 33, sch 2 para 25

s 81A added—Financial Services, 2012 c 21, s 99(2)
    am—Financial Services (Banking Reform), 2013 c 33, sch 2 para 26; SI 2014/3329, art 88

s 81AA added—SI 2014/3329, art 89

s 81B added —Financial Services, 2012 c 21, s 100(5)
    am—SI 2014/3329, art 90

s 81ZBA added—SI 2014/3329, art 91

s 81BA added —Financial Services (Banking Reform), 2013 c 33, sch 2 para 7(1)
    am—SI 2014/3329, art 92

s 81C added —Financial Services, 2012 c 21, s 100(5)
    am—SI 2014/3329, art 93

s 81CA added —Financial Services (Banking Reform), 2013 c 33, sch 2 para 7(2)
    am—SI 2014/3329, art 94

s 81D added—Financial Services, 2012 c 21, s 100(5)
    am—Financial Services (Banking Reform), 2013 c 33, sch 2 para 7(3); SI 2014/3329, art 95

2009
c 1 *continued*

s 82 am—Financial Services, 2012 c 21, sch 17 para 27(2), (3)
s 83 am—Financial Services, 2012 c 21, s 97(10); SI 2014/3329, art 96(1)
    rep in pt—Financial Services, 2010 c 28, s 24, sch 2 paras 39, 42
Pt 1, Ch 4 (ss 83ZA-83Z2) added—SI 2014/3329, art 97
Pt 1, Ch 5 (ss 83A-89G) sections renumbered as Pt 1, Ch 5—SI 2014/3329, art 98
s 83A added —Financial Services, 2012 c 21, sch 17 para 28
    am—Financial Services (Banking Reform), 2013 c 33, sch 2 para 8; SI 2014/3329,
        art 99(2)(3)(a)(c)(4)(6)-(11)
    rep in pt—SI 2014/3329, art 99(3)(b)(5)
s 84 am—Financial Services, 2010 c 28, s 21(5); SI 2014/3344, art 2(2)
    rep in pt—SI 2014/3329, art 100(1)
ss 84A-84D added—SI 2014/3344, art 2(3)
s 85 am—Financial Services (Banking Reform), 2013 c 33, sch 2 para 27; SI 2014/3329,
    art 100
s 89A added —Financial Services, 2012 c 21, s 101(5)
    am—SI 2014/3329, art 101
s 89B added —Financial Services, 2012 c 21, s 102(6)
    am—Financial Services (Banking Reform), 2013 c 33, sch 2 para 9; ibid, sch 10 para
        7; SI 2014/3329, art 102
s 89C added —Financial Services, 2012 c 21, s 102(6)
    am—SI 2013/504, reg 25(3)
s 89D added —Financial Services, 2012 c 21, s 102(6)
    am—SI 2013/504, reg 25(3)
s 89E added —Financial Services, 2012 c 21, s 102(6)
    am—SI 2013/504, reg 25(3)
s 89F added —Financial Services, 2012 c 21, s 102(6)
    am—SI 2013/504, reg 25(3)
s 89G added —Financial Services, 2012 c 21, s 102(6)
    am—SI 2013/504, reg 25(5)(a)-(c)
    rep in pt—SI 2013/504, reg 25(5)(d)
Pt 1, Ch 6 (ss 89H-89J) added—SI 2014/3329, art 103
Pt 1, Ch 7 (ss 89K-89M) added—SI 2014/3329, art 103
Pt 2 (ss 90-135) appl (mods)—Building Societies, 1986 c.53, s 90C; SIs 2009/805, art 3,
    sch 1; 2011/245, sch 1 paras 6, 7
    excl—SI 2010/35, art 2
s 91 am—Financial Services, 2012 c 21, sch 17 para 30
s 93 am—Financial Services, 2012 c 21, sch 17 para 31
s 95 am—Financial Services, 2012 c 21, sch 17 para 32
s 96 am—Financial Services, 2012 c 21, sch 17 para 33; SI 2014/3329, art 104
s 97 am—Financial Services, 2012 c 21, sch 17 para 34
s 98 am—Financial Services, 2012 c 21, sch 17 para 35
s 100 am—Financial Services, 2012 c 21, sch 17 para 36
s 101 am—Financial Services, 2012 c 21, sch 17 para 37
s 103 appl (mods)—SI 2009/3056, reg 29, sch 1
    am—Financial Services, 2012 c 21, sch 17 para 38
s 104 appl (mods)—SI 2009/3056, reg 29, sch 1
s 108 am—Financial Services, 2012 c 21, sch 17 para 39
s 109 am—Financial Services, 2012 c 21, sch 17 para 40
s 113 am—Financial Services, 2012 c 21, sch 17 para 41
s 115 am—Financial Services, 2012 c 21, sch 17 para 42
s 117 am—Financial Services, 2012 c 21, sch 17 para 43
s 120 am—Financial Services, 2012 c 21, sch 17 para 44; Financial Services (Banking
    Reform), 2013 c 33, sch 2 para 10; SI 2014/3329, art 105(2)(3)(4)(a)
    rep in pt—SI 2014/3329, art 105(4)(b)
s 120A added—SI 2014/3329, art 106
s 129A added —Financial Services, 2012 c 21, sch 17 para 45
s 134 appl (mods)—SI 2009/3056, reg 29, sch 1
Pt 3 (ss 136-168) appl (mods)—Building Societies, 1986 c.53, s 90C; SIs 2009/805, art 3,
    sch 1; 2011/245, sch 2 para 6
    mod—SIs 2009/312, regs 2-4, sch; 2009/313, regs 2,3, sch 1
s 136 am—Financial Services (Banking Reform), 2013 c 33, sch 2 para 28
s 145 appl (mods)—SI 2009/3056, reg 29, sch 1
    am—Financial Services, 2010 c 28, s 21(6); SI 2015/989, sch para 4

2009
c 1 *continued*

s 145A added —Financial Services, 2012 c 21, s 103
 am—SI 2014/3329, art 107

s 147 am—Financial Services, 2012 c 21, sch 17 para 47

s 152A added —Financial Services (Banking Reform), 2013 c 33, sch 2 para 29

s 153 am—Financial Services, 2010 c 28, s 21(7); Financial Services, 2012 c 21, sch 17
 para 48

s 157 am—Financial Services, 2012 c 21, sch 17 para 49

s 157A added —Financial Services, 2012 c 21, sch 17 para 50

s 159A added —Financial Services, 2012 c 21, s 101(6)

s 166 am—Financial Services, 2012 c 21, sch 17 para 51

s 167 appl (mods)—SI 2009/3056, reg 29, sch 1

s 171 rep—Financial Services, 2010 c 28, s 24, sch 2 paras 39, 43

s 183 rep in pt—Financial Services, 2010 c 28, s 24, sch 2 paras 39, 44; Financial Services,
 2012 c 21, sch 17 para 53(2)(b)
 am—Financial Services, 2012 c 21, sch 17 para 53(2)(a),(3)

s 186 am—Financial Services, 2012 c 21, s 104(4)

s 186A added —Financial Services, 2012 c 21, s 104(2)

s 187 am—Financial Services, 2012 c 21, s 104(5)

s 191 subst —Financial Services, 2012 c 21, s 104(3)
 am—Financial Services (Banking Reform), 2013 c 33, sch 10 para 8

s 192 am—Financial Services, 2012 c 21, s 104(6)

s 202 am—SI 2010/22, art 5, sch 2

s 202A added —Financial Services, 2012 c 21, s 104(7)

ss 203A, 203B added—Financial Services, 2012 c 21, s 104(8)

s 204 am—Financial Services, 2010 c 28, s 24, sch 2 paras 39, 45; Financial Services, 2012
 c 21, s 104(9)

s 206A added—Financial Services, 2010 c 28, s 20
 am—Financial Services, 2012 c 21, s 104(10)

s 206B added —Financial Services, 2012 c 21, s 105

s 219 am—Financial Services, 2010 c 28, s 21(8)

s 220 am—Financial Services (Banking Reform), 2013 c 33, sch 2 para 30

s 223 am—Financial Services, 2012 c 21, sch 17 para 54

s 232 am—SI 2011/239, art 3; Financial Services, 2012 c 21, sch 17 para 55; SI 2013/636,
 sch para 10

s 234 am—Financial Services, 2012 c 21, sch 17 para 56

s 235 am—Financial Services, 2012 c 21, sch 17 para 57

s 244 am—Financial Services, 2012 c 21, sch 2 para 3; SI 2014/3329, art 108

s 246 am—Financial Services, 2012 c 21, sch 17 para 58; Financial Services (Banking
 Reform), 2013 c 33, s 95

s 248 rep—Financial Services, 2010 c 28, s 24, sch 2 paras 39, 46

s 249 am—Financial Services, 2012 c 21, sch 17 para 59(2)(3)
 rep in pt—Financial Services, 2012 c 21, sch 17 para 59(4); ibid, sch 19

s 250 am—Financial Services, 2010 c 28, s 24, sch 2 paras 39, 47(a)(b); Financial Services,
 2012 c 21, sch 17 para 60

s 251 rep in pt—Financial Services (Banking Reform), 2013 c 33, sch 9 para 4(3)(d)

s 256A added —Financial Services (Banking Reform), 2013 c 33, sch 2 para 11
 am—SI 2014/3329, art 109

s 258A added —Financial Services, 2012 c 21, s 101(7)
 am—SI 2013/3115, sch 2 para 45(3)

s 259 rep in pt—Financial Services, 2010 c 28, s 24, sch 2 paras 39, 48(2)(4); SI 2014/3329,
 art 110(2)
 am—Financial Services, 2010 c 28, s 24, sch 2 paras 39, 48(3); Financial Services,
 2012 c 21, s 100(6); ibid, s 101(8); ibid, s 102(7); ibid, sch 17 para 61(2)-(4);
 Financial Services (Banking Reform), 2013 c 33, sch 2 para 31; SIs 2013/504,
 reg 25(3); 2014/3329, art 110(3)

s 261 am—Financial Services, 2012 c 21, s 96(6); ibid, s 97(11); ibid, s 100(7); ibid, s
 101(9); ibid, s 102(8); ibid, sch 17 para 62(a)(c); Financial Services (Banking
 Reform), 2013 c 33, sch 2 para 32; SIs 2013/504, reg 25(6)(b); 2014/3329, art
 111
 rep in pt—Financial Services, 2012 c 21, sch 17 para 62(b); SI 2013/504, reg
 25(6)(a)(c)

c 2   **Appropriation**

2009

c 3   **Northern Ireland**
        sch 4 rep in pt—SI 2010/976, art 15, sch 18

c 4   **Corporation Tax**
        saved —Income Tax, 2007 c 3, s 564V(4)
        appl (mods)—SI 2011/245, sch 6 pt 1
        excl—Taxation (International and Other Provns), 2010 c 8, ss 79(2)(a), 174(2)(b), 639(4)
        am—Co-operative and Community Benefit Societies, 2014 c 14, sch 4 paras 141-143
        s A1 added—Taxation (International and Other Provns), 2010 c 8, s 374, sch 8 paras 308,
                309
            am—Finance, 2012 c 14, sch 20 para 25(b); ibid, sch 18 para 20
            rep in pt—Finance, 2012 c 14, sch 20 para 25(a); ibid, sch 16 para 136
        s 1 am—Finance, 2009 c 10, s 34, sch 14 paras 20, 21; Finance, 2011 c 11, sch 13 para 2
            rep in pt—Finance, 2009 c 10, s 123, sch 61 para 28; SI 2009/2035, art 2, sch
        s 2 am—Finance, 2013 c 29, sch 25 para 18; Finance, 2015 c 11, sch 7 para 58
        s 5 am—Finance, 2011 c 11, sch 13 para 3
        s 10 appl (mods)—Corporation Tax, 2010 c 4, s 631(3)(6)
            mod—Finance, 2012 c 14, s 149(2); ibid, s 179(2)
            appl—Finance, 2004 c 12, ss 196H(5), 196J(3); Taxation (International and Other
                Provns), 2010 c 8, s 371VB(4); Finance, 2012 c 14, sch 13 paras 8(3), 22(3)
        s 12 appl (mods)—Corporation Tax, 2010 c 4, s 619(3)(6)
            appl —Income Tax (Earnings and Pensions) 2003 c 1, s 554I(7)(d); Finance, 2004 c 12,
                s 196H(5), 196J(3); Taxation (International and Other Provns), 2010 c 8, s
                371VB(4); Finance, 2012 c 14, sch 13 paras 8(3), 22(3)
        Pt 2, Ch 3 (ss 13-18) appl—Taxes Management, 1970 c 9, s 109A; Taxation of Chargeable
                Gains, 1992 c 12, s 286A; Income Tax, 2007 c 3, s 835A
        Pt 2, Ch 3A (ss 18A-18S) added—Finance, 2011 c 11, sch 13 para 4
        s 18A rep in pt—Finance, 2012 c 14, sch 20 para 3
        ss 18CA, 18CB added—Finance, 2012 c 14, sch 20 para 4
        s 18F am—Finance, 2012 c 14, sch 20 para 5
        ss 18G-18I replaced (by ss 18G,18H,18HA-18HE,18I,18IA-18ID)—Finance, 2012 c 14,
                sch 20 para 6
        s 18P am—Finance, 2012 c 14, sch 20 para 7
        s 18Q rep in pt—Finance, 2012 c 14, sch 16 para 137
        Pt 2, Ch 4 (ss 19-32) appl (mods)—Taxation (International and Other Provns), 2010 c 8, s
                43
        s 20 am—Corporation Tax, 2010 c 4, s 1177, sch 1 paras 589, 590
        ss 21-28 appl—Finance, 2011 c 11, sch 19 para 26(3)
        s 24 subst—Finance, 2012 c 14, sch 16 para 138
        s 25 am—Corporation Tax, 2010 c 4, s 1177, sch 1 paras 589, 591
        Pt 3 (ss 34-201) mod—SI 3227/2009, reg 5
        s 35 excl—Finance, 2012 c 14, s 69(a)
            appl—Finance, 2012 c 14, s 71(1)
        s 36 am—Finance, 2012 c 14, sch 16 para 139
        s 38 am—Finance, 2012 c 14, sch 16 para 140
        s 39 am—Corporation Tax, 2010 c 4, s 1177, sch 1 paras 589, 592; Taxation (International
                and Other Provns), 2010 c 8, s 374, sch 8 paras 308, 310; Finance, 2012 c 14, sch
                16 para 141
        s 42 excl—Finance, 2006 c 25, s 104(3); Corporation Tax, 2010 c 4, s 519(2)
        s 46 rep in pt—Finance, 2012 c 14, sch 16 para 142
        s 51 rep in pt—Finance, 2009 c 10, s 30, sch 11 paras 45, 46
            am—Finance, 2013 c 29, s 78(3)
        s 54 am—Finance, 2014 c 26, sch 17 para 4(4)(b)
        s 56 am—Finance, 2009 c 10, s 30, sch 11 paras 45, 47(1)-(4); Finance, 2012 c 14, sch 16
                para 143(a); Finance, 2015 c 11, s 104; Finance (No. 2), 2015 c 33, s 38(7)(8)
            rep in pt—Finance, 2009 c 10, s 30, sch 11 paras 45, 47(1)(5)(6); Finance, 2012 c 14,
                sch 16 para 143(b)
        s 57 rep in pt—Finance, 2009 c 10, s 30, sch 11 paras 45, 48(1)(2)(4)(6); Corporation Tax,
                2010 c 4, ss 1177, 1181, sch 1 paras 589, 593(a), sch 3
            am—Finance, 2009 c 10, s 30, sch 11 paras 45, 48(1)(2)(4); Corporation Tax, 2010 c
                4, s 1177, sch 1 paras 589, 593(b)
        s 58 rep—Finance, 2009 c 10, s 30, sch 11 paras 45, 49
        ss 58A, 58B added—Finance, 2009 c 10, s 30, sch 11 paras 45, 50
        s 60 am—Finance, 2009 c 10, s 43, sch 21 paras 4, 5
        s 60A added—Finance, 2010 c 13, s 27, sch 5 para 2(2)

2009

c 4 *continued*

s 63 am—Finance, 2013 c 29, sch 28 para 6

s 71 am—SI 2010/1158, art 5, sch 2; (prosp) Educ, 2011 c 21, sch 13 para 18; SI 2012/976, sch para 23

s 75 rep in pt—SI 2009/2035, art 2, sch
    appl—Finance, 2012 c 14, s 81(4)

ss 86A, 86B added—Finance, 2015 c 11, sch 5 para 3

s 87 am—Corporation Tax, 2010 c 4, s 1177, sch 1 paras 589, 594

s 88 am—Corporation Tax, 2010 c 4, s 1177, sch 1 paras 589, 595

s 92A and cross-heading added—Finance, 2014 c 26, sch 17 para 4(2)

s 97 am—Corporation Tax, 2010 c 4, s 1177, sch 1 paras 589, 596; Taxation (International and Other Provns), 2010 c 8, s 374, sch 8 paras 262, 263

Pt 3 Ch 6A (ss 104A-104Y) added—Finance, 2013 c 29, sch 15 para 1

s 104BA added—Finance, 2013 c 29, sch 18 para 8
    am—Finance, 2014 c 26, sch 4 para 9

s 104WA added—Finance (No. 2), 2015 c 33, s 31(3)

s 104A am—Finance (No. 2), 2015 c 33, s 31(2)

s 104D am—Finance, 2015 c 11, s 28(4)(a)

s 104E am—Finance, 2015 c 11, s 28(4)(b)

s 104G am—Finance, 2015 c 11, s 28(4)(c)

s 104H am—Finance, 2015 c 11, s 28(4)(d)

s 104J am—Finance, 2015 c 11, s 28(4)(e)

s 104K am—Finance, 2015 c 11, s 28(4)(f)

s 104M am—Finance, 2015 c 11, s 27(2)

s 104N am—Finance, 2014 c 26, sch 1 para 10

s 104Y am—Finance, 2015 c 11, s 28(5)

s 105 am—Corporation Tax, 2010 c 4, s 1177, sch 1 paras 589, 597; Finance, 2011 c 11, sch 3 para 17; SI 2012/964, art 3(1) sch
    excl—Corporation Tax, 2010 c 4, s 203(3)
    rep in pt—SI 2012/964, art 3(1) sch

s 107 rep in pt—Finance, 2014 c 26, sch 9 para 31

s 126 rep—SI 2009/2035, art 2, sch

Part 2 Ch 8A (ss 127A-127G) added—SI 2012/266, art 10

s 130 subst—Finance, 2009 c 10, s 34, sch 14 paras 20, 22
    am—Finance, 2012 c 14, sch 16 para 144

s 132 am—Corporation Tax, 2010 c 4, s 1177, sch 1 paras 589, 598

ss 133A- 133N added—Finance (No. 2), 2015 c 33, s 18(1)

s 135 rep—Finance, 2012 c 14, sch 39 para 44(1)(a)

s 138 rep—Finance, 2012 c 14, sch 39 para 22(1)(a)

s 144 rep in pt—SI 2010/675, regs 107, 109, schs 26, 28
    am—SI 2015/374, art 8(2)

s 145 am—Finance, 2012 c 14, s 53(4)-(6)

s 146 am—SI 2012/266, art 5(2)

s 147 am—SI 2012/266, art 5(3)

ss 149A-149E added—SI 2012/266, art 5(4)

s 161 am—Taxation (International and Other Provns), 2010 c 8, s 374, sch 8 paras 123, 124; Finance (No. 2), 2015 c 33, s 40(1)

s 162 am—Taxation (International and Other Provns), 2010 c 8, s 374, sch 8 paras 123, 125; Finance (No. 2), 2015 c 33, s 41(1)

s 168 am—Corporation Tax, 2010 c 4, s 1177, sch 1 paras 589, 599

s 179 appl (mods)—SI 2009/2971, reg 18

s 180 am—Finance, 2012 c 14, s 54(2)

s 191 rep in pt—Finance, 2009 c 10, s 30, sch 11 paras 45, 51

s 201 am—Finance, 2012 c 14, sch 16 para 145

s 203 am—Finance, 2012 c 14, sch 16 para 146

s 208 mod—Finance, 2012 c 14, s 86(1)

s 209 mod—Finance, 2012 c 14, s 86(1)

s 210 rep in pt—Finance, 2009 c 10, s 30, sch 11 paras 45, 52(b)
    am—Finance, 2009 c 10, s 30, sch 11 paras 45, 52(a); Finance, 2014 c 26, sch 17 para 4(3); Finance, 2015 c 11, sch 5 para 4

s 214 rep in pt—Finance, 2009 c 10, s 30, sch 11 paras 45, 53
    am—Finance, 2013 c 29, s 78(4)

s 221A added—Corporation Tax, 2010 c 4, s 1177, sch 1 paras 589, 600

s 232 am—Finance, 2013 c 29, sch 28 para 7

2009

c 4 *continued*

s 241 rep in pt—Finance, 2011 c 11, sch 23 para 63

s 242 am—Taxation (International and Other Provns), 2010 c 8, s 371, sch 7 paras 23, 24

s 245 rep—SI 2009/2035, art 2, sch

ss 248A-248C added—SI 2011/1037, art 12(2)

s 258 rep—Finance, 2012 c 14, sch 39 para 44(1)(b)

s 260 am—Corporation Tax, 2010 c 4, s 1177, sch 1 paras 589, 601

s 264 am—Corporation Tax, 2010 c 4, s 1177, sch 1 paras 589, 602; Finance, 2011 c 11,
 sch 14 para 7(2)

s 267 am—Finance, 2011 c 11, sch 14 para 7(3)

s 268 am—Finance, 2011 c 11, sch 14 para 7(4)

s 268A added—Finance, 2011 c 11, sch 14 para 7(5)

s 269 am—Corporation Tax, 2010 c 4, s 1177, sch 1 paras 589, 603; Finance, 2011 c 11,
 sch 14 para 7(6); SI 2011/1037, art 12(3)

s 269A added—Finance, 2011 c 11, sch 14 para 7(7)

s 272 rep in pt—Finance, 2012 c 14, sch 39 para 44(2)

ss 273-276 rep—Finance, 2012 c 14, sch 39 para 44(1)(c)

s 283 rep in pt—Finance, 2009 c 10, s 30, sch 11 paras 45, 54

Pt 5 (ss 292-476) appl (mods)—Finance, 2009 c 10, s 48, sch 24 para 15(2)
 appl—Corporation Tax, 2010 c 4, s 990(5)
 mod—Budget Responsibility and Nat Audit, 2011 c 4, sch 4 para 2; Corporation Tax,
  2010 c 4, ss 356NB, 356NC; Localism, 2011 c 20, sch 24 para 5; Finance, 2012
  c 14, s 88; SIs 2013/2242, art 7; 2013/3209, reg 11(3)-(6)

s 297 am—Corporation Tax, 2010 c 4, s 1177, sch 1 paras 589, 604

s 298 am—Finance, 2012 c 14, sch 16 para 147(2)(a), (3)
 rep in pt—Finance, 2012 c 14, sch 16 para 147(2)(b)

s 302 appl—Finance, 2011 c 11, sch 19 para 26(7)

s 306 rep in pt—(prosp) Corporation Tax, 2009 c 4, s 1326, sch 3 pt 2
 am—Finance (No. 2), 2015 c 33, sch 7 para 2

s 306A added—Finance (No. 2), 2015 c 33, sch 7 para 3

s 307 am —Finance (No. 2), 2015 c 33, sch 7 para 4(2)(3),(5)
 rep in pt—Finance (No. 2), 2015 c 33, sch 7 para 4(4)

s 308 rep in pt —Finance (No. 2), 2015 c 33, sch 7 para 5(4)
 am—Finance (No. 2), 2015 c 33, sch 7 para 5(2)(3)

s 310 rep in pt—(prosp) Corporation Tax, 2009 c 4, s 1326, sch 3 pt 2; Finance (No. 2),
 2015 c 33, sch 7 para 6

s 311 am—Finance, 2009 c 10, s 61, sch 30 para 2(1)-(6); Finance (No 2), 2010 c 31, s 8,
 sch 5 para 1(1)-(6)(8); Finance, 2011 c 11, sch 4 para 2(2)(4)(a)(i), (5)
 rep in pt—Finance (No 2), 2010 c 31, s 8, sch 5 para 1(7); Finance, 2011 c 11, sch 4
 para 2(3) (4)(a)(ii)

s 312 rep in pt—Finance (No 2), 2010 c 31, s 8, sch 5 para 2(2); Finance, 2011 c 11, sch 4
 para 3(3)
 am—Finance (No 2), 2010 c 31, s 8, sch 5 para 2(3)(4); Finance, 2011 c 11, sch 4
 para 3(2)(4)

s 313 rep in pt —Finance (No. 2), 2015 c 33, sch 7 para 7(2),(3)(a)(b)(d),(4)
 am—Finance (No. 2), 2015 c 33, sch 7 para 7(3)(c),(5)-(8)

s 315 am—Finance (No. 2), 2015 c 33, sch 7 paras 8, 9(2)(3),(5)
 rep in pt —Finance (No. 2), 2015 c 33, sch 7 para 9(4)

s 316 subst—Finance (No. 2), 2015 c 33, sch 7 para 10

s 317 rep—Finance (No. 2), 2015 c 33, sch 7 para 11

s 318 am—Finance (No. 2), 2015 c 33, sch 7 para 12

s 320 am—Finance (No. 2), 2015 c 33, sch 7 para 3(2)(4)
 rep in pt —Finance (No. 2), 2015 c 33, sch 7 para 13(3)

s 320A added—Finance (No. 2), 2015 c 33, sch 7 para 14

s 321 rep—Finance (No. 2), 2015 c 33, sch 7 para 15

s 321A added—Finance, 2010 c 13, s 43(1)

s 322 am —Finance, 2010 c 13, s 44, sch 15 para 4; Finance, 2014 c 26, s 26(2)(3); SI
 2014/3329, art 123; Finance (No. 2), 2015 c 33, sch 7 para 16(2),(4)-(6)
 rep in pt—Finance (No. 2), 2015 c 33, sch 7 para 16(3)

s 323 am—Finance (No. 2), 2015 c 33, sch 7 para 17

s 323A added—Finance (No. 2), 2015 c 33, sch 7 para 18

s 324 am—Finance (No. 2), 2015 c 33, sch 7 para 19

s 326 am—Corporation Tax, 2010 c 4, s 1177, sch 1 paras 589, 605

s 328 rep (prosp)—Corporation Tax, 2009 c 4, s 1326, sch 3 pt 2 am—Finance, 2009 c 10, s 43, sch 21 paras 1, 2; Finance, 2011 c 11, sch 7 para 6; Finance (No. 2), 2015 c 33, sch 7 para 20(2),(4)(5),(7)

rep in pt —Finance (No. 2), 2015 c 33, sch 7 para 20(3),(6)

ss 328A-328H added—Finance, 2009 c 10, s 43, sch 21 paras 1, 3

rep—Finance (No. 2), 2015 c 33, sch 7 para 21

s 329 am—Finance (No. 2), 2015 c 33, sch 7 para 22

ss 330A-330C added—Finance (No. 2), 2015 c 33, sch 7 para 23

ss 331, 332 rep—Finance (No. 2), 2015 c 33, sch 7 para 24

Pt 5, Ch 4 (ss 335-347) appl (mods)—Corporation Tax, 2010 c 4, s 601

s 336 am—Finance, 2012 c 14, sch 16 para 148

s 337 am—Finance, 2012 c 14, sch 16 para 149; SI 2015/575, sch 1 para 26(2)

mod—Postal Services, 2011 c 5, sch 2 para 5

s 340 am—Taxation (International and Other Provns), 2010 c 8, s 374, sch 8 paras 123, 126; Finance (No. 2), 2015 c 33, sch 7 para 25(b)

rep in pt —Finance (No. 2), 2015 c 33, sch 7 para 25(a)

s 342 am—Finance (No. 2), 2015 c 33, sch 7 para 26(2)

rep in pt —Finance (No. 2), 2015 c 33, sch 7 para 26(3)

s 345 appl (mods)—SI 2009/2971, reg 25

am—Corporation Tax, 2010 c 4, s 1177, sch 1 paras 589, 606

rep in pt—Finance, 2014 c 26, s 28(2)(a)(b)

s 346 am—Corporation Tax, 2010 c 4, s 1177, sch 1 paras 589, 607

rep in pt—Finance, 2014 c 26, s 28(2)(a)(b)

s 347 rep—Finance (No. 2), 2015 c 33, sch 7 para 27

s 349 am—Finance (No. 2), 2015 c 33, sch 7 para 28(2)

rep in pt —Finance (No. 2), 2015 c 33, sch 7 para 28(3)

s 350, 351 rep —Finance (No. 2), 2015 c 33, sch 7 para 29

s 352 am—Finance (No. 2), 2015 c 33, sch 7 para 30

s 352A added—Finance (No. 2), 2015 c 33, sch 7 para 31

Pt 5, Chs 6-8 (ss 353-379) appl (mods)—Corporation Tax, 2010 c 4, s 601

s 353 rep in pt—Finance, 2009 c 10, s 41, sch 42(2)(a)

am—Finance, 2009 c 10, s 42(1)(2)(b); Finance, 2010 c 13, s 44, sch 15 paras 2(2), 4

s 354 am—Finance (No. 2), 2015 c 33, sch 7 para 32

s 358 am —Finance, 2010 c 13, s 44, sch 15 paras 2(3), 4; Finance (No. 2), 2015 c 33, sch 7 para 33

excl—Corporation Tax, 2010 c 4 s 814D(10)

s 359 am—Finance (No. 2), 2015 c 33, sch 7 para 34

s 361 am —Finance, 2010 c 13, s 44, sch 15 paras 2(4), 4; Finance (No. 2), 2015 c 33, sch 7 para 35(2),(4)

mod—Finance, 2012 c 14, s 23(8)-(12)

rep in pt —Finance (No. 2), 2015 c 33, sch 7 para 35(3)

ss 361A, 361B added—Finance, 2010 c 13, sch 15 para 2(1)(5)

rep —Finance (No. 2), 2015 c 33, sch 7 para 36

s 361C added —Finance, 2010 c 13, s 44, sch 15 paras 2(5), 4

s 361D added—Finance (No. 2), 2015 c 33, sch 7 para 37

s 362 am—Finance, 2012 c 14, s 23(2)(b), (c)(i), (ii) (d); Finance (No. 2), 2015 c 33, sch 7 para 38

rep in pt—Finance, 2012 c 14, s 23(2)(a), (c)(iii)

s 362A added—Finance (No. 2), 2015 c 33, sch 7 para 39

s 363 am —Finance, 2010 c 13, s 44, sch 15 paras 2(6), 4; Finance (No. 2), 2015 c 33, sch 7 para 40

appl—Finance, 2012 c 14, s 23(4)(b)

s 363A added—Finance, 2012 c 14, s 23(3)

s 364 am—Corporation Tax, 2010 c 4, s 1177, sch 1 paras 589, 608

s 371 am—Corporation Tax, 2010 c 4, s 1177, sch 1 paras 589, 609

s 372 rep in pt —Finance, 2015 c 11, s 25(3)(a)(c)

am—Finance, 2015 c 11, s 25(3)(b)

s 373 am—Finance, 2015 c 11, s 25(4)

s 374 rep —Finance, 2015 c 11, s 25(2)(a)

s 375 am—Finance, 2009 c 10, s 41, sch 20 paras 1, 3

s 376 am—Finance, 2009 c 10, s 41, sch 20 paras 1, 4; Corporation Tax, 2010 c 4, s 1177, sch 1 paras 589, 610; Taxation (International and Other Provns), 2010 c 8, s 374, sch 8 paras 123, 128

s 377 rep—Finance, 2015 c 11, s 25(2)(b)

2009
c 4 *continued*

s 383 am—(retrosp to 1.4.2009) SI 2009/2860, art 6(2); Corporation Tax, 2010 c 4, s 1177,
sch 1 paras 589, 611
s 384 rep (prosp)—Corporation Tax, 2009 c 4, s 1326, sch 3 pt 2
s 386 am—Finance, 2012 c 14, sch 16 para 150(2)(a), (3)(b), (c)
rep in pt—Finance, 2012 c 14, sch 16 para 150(2)(b), (3)(a)
s 387 am—Finance, 2012 c 14, sch 16 para 151
s 388 am—Finance, 2012 c 14, sch 16 para 152
s 389 am—Finance, 2012 c 14, sch 16 para 153
s 390 am—Corporation Tax, 2010 c 4, s 1177, sch 1 paras 589, 612; Finance, 2012 c 14,
sch 16 para 154(2)-(4)
s 391 am—Finance, 2012 c 14, sch 16 para 155
s 393 rep—Finance, 2012 c 14, sch 16 para 156
s 394 rep—Finance, 2012 c 14, sch 16 para 156
s 398 am—Finance, 2010 c 13, s 41, sch 14 para 2
s 399 am—Finance, 2010 c 13, s 41, sch 14 para 3, 4; Finance, 2011 c 11, s 60(1); Finance,
2012 c 14, sch 16 para 157
s 400 am—Finance, 2010 c 13, s 41, sch 14 para 5; SI 2010/614, art 2; Finance, 2011 c 11,
s 60(2)(a)
excl—Finance, 2012 c 14, s 112(1)
ss 400A-400C added—Finance, 2010 c 13, s 41, sch 14 para 6
s 400A am—Finance, 2011 c 11, s 60(2)(b)
excl—Finance, 2012 c 14, s 112(1)
ss 400B, 400C excl—Finance, 2012 c 14, s 112(1)
s 406 rep in pt—Finance, 2015 c 11, s 25(5)(a)
am—Finance, 2015 c 11, s 25(5)(b)
s 407 rep—Finance, 2015 c 11, s 25(2)(c)
s 408 rep—Finance, 2015 c 11, s 25(2)(d)
s 409 am—Finance, 2009 c 10, s 41, sch 20 paras 1, 7
s 410 am—Finance, 2009 c 10, s 41, sch 20 paras 1, 8; Corporation Tax, 2010 c 4, s 1177,
sch 1 paras 589, 613; Taxation (International and Other Provns), 2010 c 8, s 374,
sch 8 paras 123, 131
s 411 am—Corporation Tax, 2010 c 4, s 1177, sch 1 paras 589, 614
s 413 am—Finance, 2013 c 29, sch 11 para 11
s 415 excl—SI 2013/3209, reg 3(2)(a)
s 416 rep in pt—Finance, 2011 c 11, sch 5 para 7(2)(c)(3)(4)
excl—SI 2013/3209, reg 3(2)(a)
s 418 rep (saving)—Finance, 2011 c 11, sch 5 para 7(1)(3)(4)
am—Finance, 2009 c 10, s 61, sch 30 para 4(1)-(5)(6); (saving) (retrosp to
6.12.2012) Finance, 2011 c 11, s 29(1)(3)(4)
s 418A added—Finance, 2009 c 10, s 61, sch 30 para 4(7)
s 419 rep—(saving) Finance, 2011 c 11, sch 5 para 7(1)(3)(4)
am—Corporation Tax, 2010 c 4, s 1177, sch 1 paras 589, 615; (saving) (retrosp to
6.12.2012) Finance, 2011 c 11, s 29(2)(3)(4)
s 422 rep in pt—Finance (No. 2), 2015 c 33, sch 7 para 41(a)
am—Finance (No. 2), 2015 c 33, sch 7 para 41(b)
s 424 rep in pt—Finance (No. 2), 2015 c 33, sch 7 para 42(3)
am—Finance (No. 2), 2015 c 33, sch 7 para 42(2)
ss 427, 428 appl (mods)—Taxation (International and Other Provns), 2010 c 8, ss 117(6),
119(5)
s 430 am—SI 2011/1431, reg 4(2)
s 433 rep in pt—Finance (No. 2), 2015 c 33, sch 7 para 43(a)
am—Finance (No. 2), 2015 c 33, sch 7 para 43(b)
s 435 rep in pt—Finance (No. 2), 2015 c 33, sch 7 para 44(3)
am—Finance (No. 2), 2015 c 33, sch 7 para 44(2)
s 439 am—SI 2011/1431, reg 4(3)
s 440 rep in pt—Finance (No. 2), 2015 c 33, sch 7 para 45(a)(i),(b)
am—Finance, 2011 c 11, sch 4 para 4; Finance (No. 2), 2015 c 33, sch 7 para
45(a)(ii),(c)
s 441 excl—Corporation Tax, 2010 c 4, ss 938N, 938V(a)
am—Finance (No. 2), 2015 c 33, sch 7 para 46
s 442 am—Finance (No. 2), 2015 c 33, sch 7 para 47
s 443 rep —Finance (No. 2), 2015 c 33, sch 7 para 48
s 444 am—Taxation (International and Other Provns), 2010 c 8, s 374, sch 8 paras 123, 132

2009
c 4 *continued*

s 445 am—Taxation (International and Other Provns), 2010 c 8, s 374, sch 8 paras 123, 133
s 446 am—Taxation (International and Other Provns), 2010 c 8, s 374, sch 8 paras 123, 134
s 447 am—Taxation (International and Other Provns), 2010 c 8, s 374, sch 8 paras 123, 135
    appl—Taxation (International and Other Provns), 2010 c 8, ss 147(3)-(5)(6)(e);
        164(2); 174(4)
s 448 am—Corporation Tax, 2010 c 4, s 1177, sch 1 paras 589, 617
s 450 rep in pt—(prosp) Corporation Tax, 2009 c 4, s 1326, sch 3 pt 2
    am—Finance (No. 2), 2015 c 33, sch 7 para 49
s 452 am—Taxation (International and Other Provns), 2010 c 8, s 374, sch 8 paras 123, 136
s 453 rep—Finance, 2011 c 11, sch 5 para 8(1)
ss 454, 455 rep—Finance (No. 2), 2015 c 33, sch 7 para 50
s 455A added—Finance, 2011 c 11, sch 4 para 5
s 455B-455D added—Finance (No. 2), 2015 c 33, sch 7 para 51
s 457 am—Corporation Tax, 2010 c 4, s 1177, sch 1 paras 589, 618
s 459 am—Corporation Tax, 2010 c 4, s 1177, sch 1 paras 589, 619; SI 2010/614, art 3
s 461 am—Corporation Tax, 2010 c 4, s 1177, sch 1 paras 589, 620
s 463 am—Corporation Tax, 2010 c 4, s 1177, sch 1 paras 589, 621
s 464 am—Corporation Tax, 2010 c 4, s 1177, sch 1 paras 589, 622; Taxation
      (International and Other Provns), 2010 c 8, s 374, sch 8 paras 89, 90, 123, 138;
      Finance, 2011 c 11, sch 4 para 6; Finance, 2013 c 29, s 87(2)
    excl—Taxation (International and Other Provns), 2010 c 8, ss 31(5)(a), 112(5)(a);
      Corporation Tax, 2010 c 4, s 640(2); ibid, s 357YV(2) (added by 2015 c 33, s
      38(3))
    rep in pt—Finance, 2012 c 14, sch 16 para 158
s 465 am—Corporation Tax, 2010 c 4, s 1177, sch 1 paras 589, 623; Co-operative and
      Community Benefit Societies, 2014 c 14, sch 4 para 144; Finance, 2014 c 26, s
      27(2)
s 465A added—Finance, 2010 c 13, s 62, sch 19 para 1
s 465B added—Finance (No. 2), 2015 c 33, sch 7 para 52
s 466 appl—SI 2004/3256, reg 7A (as amended by SI 2009/1886, regs 3, 5); Corporation
      Tax, 2010 c 4, ss 357GD(11), 937K(8), 938K
ss 467-471 appl—Corporation Tax, 2010 c 4, s 938E(11); ibid, s 357GD(11)
s 471 am—Finance, 2012 c 14, sch 16 para 159
s 472 appl—Finance, 2010 c 13, s 44, sch 15 para 4(8); Corporation Tax, 2010 c 4, s
      357BC(10)
    am—Finance, 2012 c 14, sch 16 para 160
ss 473, 474 appl—Corporation Tax, 2010 c 4, ss 357GD(11), 357BC(10), 937K(8),
      938E(11)
s 473 am—Finance, 2012 c 14, sch 16 para 161
s 475 rep in pt—Finance (No. 2), 2015 c 33, sch 7 para 53
s 475A added—Finance (No. 2), 2015 c 33, sch 7 para 54
s 476 am—Finance, 2009 c 10, s 42(1)(3); Corporation Tax, 2010 c 4, s 1177, sch 1 paras
      589, 624; Finance (No. 2), 2015 c 33, sch 7 para 55
    excl—SI 2013/460, reg 3(1)(d)
s 477 am—Finance, 2009 c 10, s 48, sch 24 paras 1, 2; ibid, s 49, sch 25 para 8(1)(2)
s 479 rep in pt—Finance, 2009 c 10, s 42(1)(4)(5)(a)
    am—Finance, 2009 c 10, sch 42(1)(4)(5)(b)(c)(6)(7)
s 480 appl—SI 2009/2971, regs 19, 22, 24
s 481 am—Finance, 2009 c 10, s 42(1)(8)-(11)
s 484 am—Taxation (International and Other Provns), 2010 c 8, s 374, sch 8 paras 123, 139
s 486 am—Taxation (International and Other Provns), 2010 c 8, s 374, sch 8 paras 89, 91;
      Finance, 2012 c 14, sch 16 para 162
Pt 6, Ch 2A (ss 486A-486E) added—Finance, 2009 c 10, s 48, sch 24 para 3
        appl—Taxation (International and Other Provns), 2010 c 8, s 371SP(2)
ss 486B-486E excl—Income and Corporation Taxes 1988 c 1, sch 25 para 12F(6)
s 486D rep in pt—Finance, 2012 c 14, sch 20 para 26
s 486E am—Finance, 2012 c 14, sch 20 para 27(2), (3)
    rep in pt—Finance, 2012 c 14, sch 20 para 27(4)
Pt 6 Ch 2B (ss 486F-486G) added—Finance, 2009 c 10, s 49, sch 25 para 8(3)
s 486F am—Corporation Tax, 2010 c 4, s 1177, sch 1 paras 589, 625
s 486G am—Corporation Tax, 2010 c 4, s 1177, sch 1 paras 589, 626
s 488 am—Corporation Tax, 2010 c 4, s 1177, sch 1 paras 589, 627
s 489 rep—Taxation (International and Other Provns), 2010 c 8, s 374, sch 8 paras 171, 172

2009
c 4 *continued*

s 490 am—SIs 2009/3001, reg 131(3); 2011/1211, reg 45; Finance, 2014 c 26, s 27(3)
    excl—SI 2013/2819, reg 29A
    rep in pt—Finance, 2014 c 26, s 27(4)
s 492 subst—Finance, 2014 c 26, s 27(5)
s 493 am—Corporation Tax, 2010 c 4, s 1177, sch 1 paras 589, 628
s 495 am—Corporation Tax, 2010 c 4, s 1177, sch 1 paras 589, 629; Finance, 2014 c 26, s
    27(6)(a)(i)
    rep in pt—Finance, 2014 c 26, s 27(6)(a)(ii)(b)
s 498 excl—SI 2013/460, reg 3(1)(e)
s 499 am—Co-operative and Community Benefit Societies, 2014 c 14, sch 4 para 145
s 502 am—SI 2009/2568, art 3; Corporation Tax, 2010 c 4, s 1177, sch 1 paras 589, 630;
    Finance, 2012 c 14, sch 16 para 163; SI 2013/1881, sch para 16
    rep in pt—SI 2009/2568, art 3
s 506 am—SI 2009/2568, art 3
s 508 am—Taxation (International and Other Provns), 2010 c 8, s 374, sch 8 paras 123, 140
s 514 am—(retrosp to 1.4.2009) SI 2009/2860, art 6(3)
s 518 am—(retrosp to 1.4.2009) SI 2009/2860, art 6(4); Corporation Tax, 2010 c 4, s 1177,
    sch 1 paras 589, 631
s 519 am—Corporation Tax, 2010 c 4, s 1177, sch 1 paras 589, 632
s 520 am—Corporation Tax, 2010 c 4, s 1177, sch 1 paras 589, 633
s 521 rep—Taxation (International and Other Provns), 2010 c 8, ss 374, 378, sch 8 paras
    224, 225, sch 10
Pt 6 Ch 6A (ss 521A-521F) added—Finance, 2009 c 10, s 48, sch 24 para 4
s 521C appl—Taxation (International and Other Provns), 2010 c 8, s 371SQ(2)
s 521D am—Corporation Tax, 2010 c 4, s 1177, sch 1 paras 589, 634
s 521E rep in pt—Finance, 2012 c 14, sch 20 para 28
s 521F am—Finance (No. 2), 2015 c 33, sch 7 para 57(a)
    excl—Finance, 2009 c 10, s 48, sch 24 para 15(4)
    rep in pt—Finance (No. 2), 2015 c 33, sch 7 para 57(b)
Pt 6, Ch 7 (ss 522-535) rep—Finance, 2009 c 10, sch para 8(c)(i)
Pt 6, Ch 8 (ss 536-538) rep—Finance, 2009 c 10, s 48, sch 24 para 8(c)(ii)
s 539 am—Corporation Tax, 2010 c 4, s 1177, sch 1 paras 589, 635
    rep in pt—Finance, 2013 c 29, sch 29 para 35
s 540 am—(retrosp effect) Finance, 2009 c 10, s 61, sch 30 para 5(1); Corporation Tax,
    2010 c 4, s 1177, sch 1 paras 589, 636
    rep in pt—Finance, 2013 c 29, sch 29 para 36; Finance (No. 2), 2015 c 33, sch 7 para
    58
s 541 am—Corporation Tax, 2010 c 4, s 1177, sch 1 paras 589, 637
s 542 am—Finance, 2009 c 10, s 48, sch 24 para 10
s 547 rep—Finance, 2009 c 10, s 48, sch 24 para 8(c)(iii)
s 548 appl—Corporation Tax, 2010 c 4, s 938I(3)
s 549 am—SI 2009/2860, art 6(5)
    appl—Corporation Tax, 2010 c 4, s 938I(3)
s 550 am—Taxation (International and Other Provns), 2010 c 8, s 374, sch 8 paras 89, 92;
    Finance, 2010 c 13, s 45(2); Finance, 2013 c 29, sch 29 para 37(a)(b)
    rep in pt—Finance, 2013 c 29, sch 29 para 37(c)
s 556 appl—Finance, 2011 c 11, sch 19 paras 18(11), 22(3), 25(4), 31(3)
s 560 am—Finance, 2012 c 14, sch 16 para 164
s 561 am—Finance, 2012 c 14, sch 16 para 165
s 563 am—Finance, 2012 c 14, sch 16 para 166
s 564 am—Finance, 2012 c 14, sch 18 para 21
s 566 am —SI 2010/614, art 3
    rep in pt—SI 2010/614, art 3
Pt 7 (ss 570-710) appl (mods)—Corporation Tax, 2010 c 4, s 601
    mod—Finance, 2012 c 14, s 88
s 582 am—SI 2013/3218, art 2(2)
s 585 excl—SI 2013/3209, reg 3(2)(a)
s 587 am—SI 2013/1411, reg 13(a)
s 591 am—Finance, 2012 c 14, sch 16 para 167; SI 2013/636, sch para 11
s 594 am—Finance (No. 2), 2015 c 33, sch 7 para 60
s 594A added—Finance (No. 2), 2015 c 33, sch 7 para 61
s 595 rep in pt—Finance (No. 2), 2015 c 33, sch 7 para 62(2)(b),(4)
    am—Finance (No. 2), 2015 c 33, sch 7 para 62(2)(a),(3)

2009
c 4 *continued*

s 597 am—Finance (No. 2), 2015 c 33, sch 7 para 63(2)(3)
    rep in pt—Finance (No. 2), 2015 c 33, sch 7 para 63(4)
s 599A added—Finance, 2009 c 10, s 61, sch 30 para 3(1)
    am—Finance (No 2), 2010 c 31, s 8, sch 5 para 3(1)-(4)(6)(7); Finance, 2011 c 11,
        sch 4 para 8(2)(5)
    rep in pt—Finance (No 2), 2010 c 31, s 8, sch 5 para 3(5); Finance, 2011 c 11, sch 4
        para 8(3)(4)
s 599B added—Finance, 2009 c 10, s 61, sch 30 para 3(1)
    am—Finance, 2011 c 11, sch 4 para 9; Finance (No. 2), 2015 c 33, sch 7 para 64
s 604 rep in pt —Finance (No. 2), 2015 c 33, sch 7 para 65(3)
    am—Finance (No. 2), 2015 c 33, sch 7 para 65(2),(4)
s 604A added—Finance (No. 2), 2015 c 33, sch 7 para 66
s 605 rep—Finance (No. 2), 2015 c 33, sch 7 para 67
s 606 rep (prosp)—Corporation Tax, 2009 c 4, s 1326, sch 3 pt 2
    am—Finance, 2009 c 10, s 43, sch 21 paras 4, 6; Finance, 2011 c 11, sch 7 para 7;
        Finance (No. 2), 2015 c 33, sch 7 para 68(2),(4)(5),(7)
    excl—SI 2004/3256, reg 7A (am by SI 2009/1886, regs 3, 5)
    rep in pt —Finance (No. 2), 2015 c 33, sch 7 para 68(3),(6)
ss 606A-606H rep—Finance (No. 2), 2015 c 33, sch 7 para 69
s 607 am—Finance, 2009 c 10, s 43, sch 21 paras 4, 8; Finance (No. 2), 2015 c 33, sch 7
        para 70
ss 607A-607C added—Finance (No. 2), 2015 c 33, sch 7 para 71
s 608 rep—Finance (No. 2), 2015 c 33, sch 7 para 72
s 612 am—Finance (No. 2), 2015 c 33, sch 7 para 73
s 613 am—Finance (No. 2), 2015 c 33, sch 7 paras 74, 75(2)(3)
    rep in pt —Finance (No. 2), 2015 c 33, sch 7 para 75(4)
s 614 subst—Finance (No. 2), 2015 c 33, sch 7 para 76
s 615 am—Finance (No. 2), 2015 c 33, sch 7 para 77
s 622 am—Finance (No. 2), 2015 c 33, sch 7 para 78
s 625 am—Taxation (International and Other Provns), 2010 c 8, s 374, sch 8 paras 123, 141;
        Finance (No. 2), 2015 c 33, sch 7 para 79
    excl—SI 2004/3256, reg 6B(2)(a) (subst by 2015/1961, reg 6)
    appl—SI 2004/3256, reg 6C(2)(a) (subst by 2015/1961, reg 6)
s 628 excl—SIs 2004/3256, reg 6B(a) (added by 2014/3188, reg 6); 2004/3256, reg
        6B(2)(a) (subst by 2015/1961, reg 6); 2004/3256, reg 6C(2)(a) (subst by
        2015/1961, reg 6)
s 629 rep—Finance (No. 2), 2015 c 33, sch 7 para 80
s 631 appl (mods)—SI 2009/2971, reg 25
    am—Corporation Tax, 2010 c 4, s 1177, sch 1 paras 589, 640
    rep in pt—Finance, 2014 c 26, s 28(3)(a)(b)
s 632 am—Corporation Tax, 2010 c 4, s 1177, sch 1 paras 589, 641
    rep in pt—Finance, 2014 c 26, s 28(3)(a)(b)
s 634 am—Finance, 2012 c 14, sch 16 para 168(2)(4)
    rep in pt—Finance, 2012 c 14, sch 16 para 168(3)
s 635 am—Finance, 2012 c 14, sch 16 para 169
s 636 am—Finance, 2012 c 14, sch 16 para 170; SI 2015/575, sch 1 para 26(3)
s 643 am—Finance, 2013 c 29, s 41(2)
s 650 am—Finance, 2013 c 29, s 41(3)
s 653 am—Finance (No. 2), 2015 c 33, sch 7 para 81
s 654 am—Finance (No. 2), 2015 c 33, sch 7 para 82
s 658 am—Finance (No. 2), 2015 c 33, sch 7 para 83
s 659 am—Finance, 2013 c 29, s 41(4)
s 666 am—Finance (No. 2), 2015 c 33, sch 7 para 84
s 671 am—Finance (No. 2), 2015 c 33, sch 7 para 85
s 673 am—Finance (No. 2), 2015 c 33, sch 7 para 86
s 675 am—Finance (No. 2), 2015 c 33, sch 7 para 87
s 681 am—SI 2011/1431, reg 4(4)
s 684 am—Finance (No. 2), 2015 c 33, sch 7 para 88
s 688 am—SI 2011/1431, reg 4(5)
s 689 am—Finance, 2011 c 11, sch 4 para 10; Finance (No. 2), 2015 c 33, sch 7 para 89(b)
    rep in pt—Finance (No. 2), 2015 c 33, sch 7 para 89(a)
s 690 rep in pt—(prosp) Corporation Tax, 2009 c 4, s 1326, sch 3 pt 2; Finance (No. 2),
        2015 c 33, sch 7 para 90(3)

2009

c 4 s 690 *continued*

   am—Finance (No. 2), 2015 c 33, sch 7 para 90(2)
   excl—Corporation Tax, 2010 c 4, ss 938N, 938V(b))
s 691 am—Corporation Tax, 2010 c 4, s 1177, sch 1 paras 589, 642; Finance (No. 2), 2015
      c 33, sch 7 para 91
s 692 am—Finance (No. 2), 2015 c 33, sch 7 para 92(a)(b)
s 693 am—Taxation (International and Other Provns), 2010 c 8, s 374, sch 8 paras 123, 142
s 694 am—Taxation (International and Other Provns), 2010 c 8, s 374, sch 8 paras 123, 143
   appl—Taxation (International and Other Provns), 2010 c 8, ss 147(3)-(5)(6)(f),
      164(2), 174(4)
s 695 am—SI 2009/2860, art 6(6)
s 695A added—Finance, 2014 c 26, s 29(1)
s 697 am—Taxation (International and Other Provns), 2010 c 8, s 374, sch 8 paras 89, 93;
      SI 2013/504, reg 26(2)
s 698 rep—Finance (No. 2), 2015 c 33, sch 7 para 93
s 698A added—Finance, 2011 c 11, sch 4 para 11
ss 698B-698D added—Finance (No. 2), 2015 c 33, sch 7 para 94
s 699 am—Finance, 2012 c 14, sch 16 para 171(a)
   rep in pt—Finance, 2012 c 14, sch 16 para 171(b)
s 701A added—Finance, 2010 c 13, s 62, sch 19 para 2
s 702 subst—Finance (No. 2), 2015 c 33, sch 7 para 95
s 705 rep in pt—Finance (No. 2), 2015 c 33, sch 7 para 96
s 710 rep in pt —Finance (No. 2), 2015 c 33, sch 7 para 97(c)
   am—Corporation Tax, 2010 c 4, s 1177, sch 1 paras 589, 643; Finance, 2012 c 14,
      sch 16 para 172; Finance (No. 2), 2015 c 33, sch 7 para 97(a)(b)
   construed as one with reg 4 of SI 2014/685—SI 2014/685, reg 3(4)
Pt 8 (ss 711-906) mod—SI 3227/2009, reg 6(1); Budget Responsibility and Nat Audit,
      2011 c 4, sch 4 para 3(1); Postal Services, 2011 c 5, sch 2 para 6(1); Localism,
      2011 c 20, sch 24 para 1(3); Finance, 2012 c 14, s 88
   appl (mods)—Corporation Tax, 2010 c 4, s 601
s 712 am—Finance, 2009 c 10, s 70(1)(2)
s 715 am—Finance, 2009 c 10, s 70(1)(3); Finance (No. 2), 2015 c 33, s 33(2)
s 721 am—Taxation (International and Other Provns), 2010 c 8, s 374, sch 8 paras 123, 145
ss 728, 729 am—Taxation (International and Other Provns), 2010 c 8, s 374, sch 8 paras
      123, 145
ss 731 am —Taxation (International and Other Provns), 2010 c 8, s 374, sch 8 paras 123,
      145
s 736 am—Taxation (International and Other Provns), 2010 c 8, s 374, sch 8 paras 123, 145
s 738A added—Corporation Tax (NI), 2015 c 21, sch 2 para 1
ss 739, 740 am—Taxation (International and Other Provns), 2010 c 8, s 374, sch 8 paras
      123, 145
ss 742, 743 am—Taxation (International and Other Provns), 2010 c 8, s 374, sch 8 paras
      123, 145
s 746 am—Finance, 2012 c 14, sch 16 para 173; Finance, 2015 c 11, s 26(2); Finance (No.
      2), 2015 c 33, s 33(3)
s 748 am—Finance, 2011 c 11, sch 14 para 7(8)
s 753 am—Corporation Tax, 2010 c 4, s 1177, sch 1 paras 589, 644
s 768 am—Corporation Tax, 2010 c 4, s 1177, sch 1 paras 589, 645
s 772 am—Corporation Tax, 2010 c 4, s 1177, sch 1 paras 589, 646; SI 2010/2902, art 3
   rep in pt—SI 2010/2902, art 3
s 773 am—Corporation Tax, 2010 c 4, s 1177, sch 1 paras 589, 647
s 775 am—Corporation Tax, 2010 c 4, s 1177, sch 1 paras 589, 648; Taxation
      (International and Other Provns), 2010 c 8, s 374, sch 8 paras 123, 146; Finance,
      2011 c 11, sch 13 para 5
s 777 am—Corporation Tax, 2010 c 4, s 1177, sch 1 paras 589, 649
s 780 appl—SI 2009/2971, reg 13
   am—Finance, 2011 c 11, sch 10 para 7(2)
   excl—Finance, 2012 c 14, sch 17 para 24(3)
s 782 am—Taxation (International and Other Provns), 2010 c 8, s 374, sch 8 paras 89, 94
s 783 am—Finance, 2011 c 11, sch 10 para 7(3)
s 784 am—Corporation Tax, 2010 c 4, s 1177, sch 1 paras 589, 650
s 787 am—Corporation Tax, 2010 c 4, s 1177, sch 1 paras 589, 651
s 788 am—Finance, 2011 c 11, sch 10 para 7(4)

2009
c 4 *continued*

s 793 am—Corporation Tax, 2010 c 4, s 1177, sch 1 paras 589, 652; Taxation
(International and Other Provns), 2010 c 8, s 374, sch 8 paras 89, 95
s 796 am—Corporation Tax, 2010 c 4, s 1177, sch 1 paras 589, 653
s 800 rep in pt—Finance, 2012 c 14, sch 16 para 174
am—Finance (No. 2), 2015 c 33, s 33(4)
s 803 am—Finance, 2011 c 11, sch 13 para 6
s 806 am—Finance, 2012 c 14, sch 16 para 175
ss 808A, 808B added—Finance, 2013 c 29, sch 18 para 9
s 808C added—Finance, 2014 c 26, sch 4 para 10
s 809 am—Finance, 2011 c 11, s 62
s 810 rep in pt—Finance, 2012 c 14, sch 16 para 176
s 814 am—Corporation Tax, 2010 c 4, s 1177, sch 1 paras 589, 654
s 815 am—Finance, 2012 c 14, sch 16 para 177
s 816A added —Finance (No. 2), 2015 c 33, s 33(5)
s 818 am—Corporation Tax, 2010 c 4, s 1177, sch 1 paras 589, 655
s 819 am—SI 2011/1431, reg 4(6)
s 823 am—SI 2011/1431, reg 4(7)
s 826 am—Corporation Tax, 2010 c 4, s 1177, sch 1 paras 589, 656
s 827 am—Taxation (International and Other Provns), 2010 c 8, s 374, sch 8 paras 89, 96
s 841 am—Corporation Tax, 2010 c 4, s 1177, sch 1 paras 589, 657
s 844 rep in pt —Finance (No. 2), 2015 c 33, s 33(6)
am—Finance, 2013 c 29, s 61(3); Finance, 2015 c 11, s 26(3)
s 845 am—Finance, 2011 c 11, sch 13 para 7; Finance, 2013 c 29, s 61(4)
s 846 am—Taxation (International and Other Provns), 2010 c 8, s 374, sch 8 paras 123, 147;
Finance (No. 2), 2015 c 33, s 42(1)
s 847 am—Corporation Tax, 2010 c 4, s 1177, sch 1 paras 589, 658
s 848A added—Finance, 2011 c 11, sch 13 para 8
s 849A added—Finance, 2013 c 29, s 61(5)
ss 849B-849D added—Finance, 2015 c 11, s 26(4)
rep—Finance (No. 2), 2015 c 33, s 33(7)
s 855 rep in pt—Finance, 2012 c 14, sch 16 para 178
s 865 rep in pt—Finance, 2009 c 10, s 30, sch 11 paras 45, 55
s 870 rep—Finance, 2012 c 14, sch 20 para 29
s 870A added—Finance, 2014 c 26, s 62(2)
s 882 mod—Budget Responsibility and Nat Audit, 2011 c 4, sch 4 para 3(3); Postal Services,
2011 c 5, sch 2 para 6(3)
s 883 am—Finance, 2009 c 10, s 70(1)(4)(a)(c)
rep in pt—Finance, 2009 c 10, s 70(1)(4)(b)(d)
s 884 rep in pt—Finance, 2009 c 10, s 70(1)(5)(a)(c)
am—Finance, 2009 c 10, s 70(1)(5)(b)
s 885 rep in pt—Finance, 2009 c 10, s 70(1)(6)(a)
am—Finance, 2009 c 10, s 70(1)(6)
s 900 rep in pt—Finance, 2013 c 29, sch 46 para 138(1)
s 901 subst—Finance, 2012 c 14, sch 16 para 179
s 902 rep—Finance, 2012 c 14, sch 16 para 180
s 903 rep—Finance, 2012 c 14, sch 16 para 180
s 904 rep—Finance, 2012 c 14, sch 16 para 181
s 906 rep in pt—Taxation (International and Other Provns), 2010 c 8, ss 374, 378, sch 8
paras 89, 97(a), sch 10; Finance, 2012 c 14, sch 16 para 182
am—Taxation (International and Other Provns), 2010 c 8, s 374, sch 8 paras 89,
97(b)
excl —Taxation (International and Other Provns), 2010 c 8, ss 31(5)(b), 112(5)(b)
Pt 9A (ss 931A-931W) added—Finance, 2009 c 10, s 34, sch 14 para 1
appl (mods)—Corporation Tax, 2010 c 4, ss 787, 795
mod—Corporation Tax, 2010 c 4 s 814D(6))
s 931A am—Finance (No 3), 2010 c 33, s 9, sch 3 para 3(2)
rep in pt—Finance (No 3), 2010 c 33, s 9, sch 3 para 3(2)
s 931B am—Corporation Tax, 2010 c 4, s 1177, sch 1 paras 589, 659
s 931C am—Taxation (International and Other Provns), 2010 c 8, s 374, sch 8 paras 89, 98
s 931CA added—Finance, 2012 c 14, sch 20 para 30
s 931D am—Corporation Tax, 2010 c 4, s 1177, sch 1 paras 589, 660
s 931E am—Finance, 2012 c 14, sch 20 para 31

2009
c 4 *continued*

s 931H am—Finance (No 3), 2010 c 33, s 9, sch 3 para 3(3); Taxation (International and
          Other Provns), 2010 c 8, s 374, sch 8 paras 89, 99
s 931J am—Taxation (International and Other Provns), 2010 c 8, s 374, sch 8 paras 89, 100
s 931P am—Taxation (International and Other Provns), 2010 c 8, s 374, sch 8 paras 123,
          148
s 931RA added—Finance (No 3), 2010 c 33, s 9, sch 3 para 3(4)
s 931S am—Finance, 2012 c 14, sch 16 para 183; ibid, sch 18 para 22
s 931V am—Corporation Tax, 2010 c 4, s 1177, sch 1 paras 589, 661
s 931W rep in pt—Finance, 2012 c 14, sch 16 para 184
s 932 rep in pt—Finance, 2009 c 10, s 34, sch 14 paras 20, 23; SI 2013/2819, reg 38(2)
s 933 rep—Finance, 2009 c 10, s 34, sch 14 paras 20, 24
s 936 rep in pt—Finance, 2013 c 29, sch 46 para 139(1)
s 947 rep in pt—Finance, 2013 c 29, sch 46 para 140(1)
s 966 rep—SI 2009/2035, art 2, sch
s 968 rep—Corporation Tax, 2010 c 4, ss 1177, 1181, sch 1 paras 589, 662, sch 3
Pt 10 Ch 5 (ss 971-973) rep —SI 2013/2819, reg 38(3)
s 974 am—Finance, 2009 c 10, s 34, sch 14 paras 20, 25; Corporation Tax, 2010 c 4, s
          1177, sch 1 paras 589, 664
s 976 rep in pt—Finance, 2012 c 14, sch 39 para 22(2)
s 978 rep—Finance, 2012 c 14, sch 39 para 22(1)(b)
s 982 rep in pt—Finance, 2009 c 10, s 34, sch 14 paras 20, 26; SI 2013/2819, reg 38(4)
s 983 am—Finance, 2014 c 26, sch 8 para 75
s 985 am—Finance, 2012 c 14, sch 16 para 185; Finance, 2013 c 29, sch 18 para 21(2)
s 987 am—Finance, 2014 c 26, sch 8 para 76(2)(3)(5)(6)
          rep in pt—Finance, 2014 c 26, sch 8 para 76(4)
s 988 am—Finance, 2014 c 26, sch 8 para 77
s 989 am—Finance, 2010 c 13, s 42(4)-(6); Finance, 2014 c 26, sch 8 para 78
s 994 am—Finance, 2014 c 26, sch 8 para 79
s 995 am—Finance, 2014 c 26, sch 8 para 80
s 997 am—Finance, 2014 c 26, sch 8 para 81
s 998 am—Finance, 2014 c 26, sch 8 paras 82, 83
s 999 am—Finance, 2012 c 14, sch 16 para 186; Finance, 2013 c 29, sch 18 para 21(2);
          Finance, 2014 c 26, sch 8 para 142(3)(a)(b)(4)(5)
          rep in pt—Finance, 2014 c 26, sch 8 para 142(2)(3)(c)
s 1000 appl—Finance, 2012 c 14, s 81(2)s 81(3)(a)(7)
          am—Finance, 2012 c 14, sch 16 para 187(2); Finance, 2013 c 29, sch 18 para 21(2)
          rep in pt—Finance, 2012 c 14, sch 16 para 187(3)
s 1002 am—Finance, 2014 c 26, sch 9 para 40
s 1004 am—Corporation Tax, 2010 c 4, s 1177, sch 1 paras 589, 665
s 1005 am—Finance, 2013 c 29, sch 23 para 22; Finance, 2014 c 26, sch 9 para 41
s 1007 am—Finance, 2011 c 11, sch 13 para 9
s 1007A added—Finance, 2014 c 26, sch 9 para 42
s 1009 am—Finance, 2013 c 29, sch 23 para 23
          rep in pt—Finance, 2013 c 29, sch 46 para 141(1)
s 1010 am—Finance, 2013 c 29, sch 23 para 24
s 1011 am—Finance, 2013 c 29, sch 23 para 25
s 1013 am—Finance, 2012 c 14, sch 16 para 188; Finance, 2013 c 29, sch 18 para 21(2)
s 1015 am—Finance, 2011 c 11, sch 13 para 10
ss 1015A, 1015B added—Finance, 2014 c 26, sch 9 para 43
s 1016 am—Finance, 2014 c 26, sch 9 para 44
s 1017 rep in pt—Finance, 2013 c 29, sch 46 para 142(1)
s 1018 am—Finance, 2013 c 29, sch 23 para 26
s 1019 am—Finance, 2013 c 29, sch 23 para 27
s 1021 am—Finance, 2012 c 14, sch 16 para 189; Finance, 2013 c 29, sch 18 para 21(2)
s 1022 am—Finance, 2013 c 29, sch 23 para 28
s 1025 rep in pt—Finance, 2013 c 29, sch 46 para 143(1); Finance, 2014 c 26, sch 9 para
          32
ss 1025A, 1025B added—Finance, 2014 c 26, sch 9 para 45
s 1026 am—Finance, 2013 c 29, sch 23 para 29
s 1027 am—Finance, 2013 c 29, sch 23 para 30
ss 1030A, 1030B added—Finance, 2014 c 26, sch 9 para 45
s 1032 rep in pt—Finance, 2013 c 29, sch 46 para 144(1); Finance, 2014 c 26, sch 9 para
          33

s 1033 am—Finance, 2013 c 29, sch 23 para 31

s 1034 am—Finance, 2013 c 29, sch 23 para 32

Pt 12 Ch 6 (ss 1037, 1038) am (heading am)—Finance, 2013 c 29, sch 23 para 33(2)

s 1038 subst—Finance, 2013 c 29, s 40(2)

s 1038A added—Finance, 2013 c 29, s 40(3)

s 1038B added—Finance, 2013 c 29, sch 23 para 33(1)

s 1039 am—Finance, 2012 c 14, sch 3 para 16(2)(3)(a); (with spec commencing effect)
Finance, 2013 c 29, sch 15 paras 13(2)(a)(4)(a), 28,29

rep in pt—Finance, 2012 c 14, sch 3 para 16(3)(b); (with spec commencing effect)
Finance, 2013 c 29, sch 15 paras 13(2)(b)(3)(4)(b), 28,29

s 1040ZA added—Finance, 2013 c 29, sch 18 para 10
am—Finance, 2014 c 26, sch 4 para 11

s 1040A added—Finance, 2013 c 29, sch 15 para 2(2)

s 1041 am—Corporation Tax, 2010 c 4, s 1177, sch 1 paras 589, 666

s 1042 rep in pt—Finance, 2012 c 14, sch 3 para 17

s 1043 rep in pt—Finance, 2012 c 14, sch 3 para 3(2)

s 1044 am—Finance, 2011 c 11, s 43(3); Finance, 2012 c 14, sch 3 para 2(2); Finance,
2015 c 11, s 27(3)(a)

rep in pt—Finance, 2012 c 14, sch 3 para 3(3)

s 1045 am—Finance, 2011 c 11, s 43(4); Finance, 2012 c 14, sch 3 para 2(3); Finance,
2015 c 11, s 27(3)(b)

rep in pt—Finance, 2012 c 14, sch 3 para 3(4)

s 1046 am—Finance, 2012 c 14, sch 3 para 10
rep in pt—Finance, 2012 c 14, sch 3 para 18

s 1048 am—Corporation Tax, 2010 c 4, s 1177, sch 1 paras 589, 667

s 1049 am—Corporation Tax, 2010 c 4, s 1177, sch 1 paras 589, 668

s 1050 rep—Finance, 2012 c 14, sch 3 para 3(5)

s 1052 am—Finance (No 3), 2010 c 33, s 13(2)(a); Finance, 2015 c 11, s 28(4)(g)
rep in pt—Finance (No 3), 2010 c 33, s 13(2)(b)

s 1053 am—Finance (No 3), 2010 c 33, s 13(3)(a); Finance, 2015 c 11, s 28(4)(h)
rep in pt—Finance (No 3), 2010 c 33, s 13(3)(b)

s 1055 am—Finance, 2011 c 11, s 43(5); Finance, 2012 c 14, sch 3 para 2(4); Finance,
2015 c 11, s 27(3)(c)

s 1056 am—Corporation Tax, 2010 c 4, s 1177, sch 1 paras 589, 669

s 1057 am—Finance, 2012 c 14, sch 3 para 11
rep in pt—Finance, 2012 c 14, sch 3 para 19

s 1058 am—Finance, 2011 c 11, s 43(6); Finance, 2012 c 14, sch 3 para 2(5); Finance,
2014 c 26, s 31(1)

rep in pt—Finance, 2012 c 14, sch 3 para 15(2)

s 1059 rep—Finance, 2012 c 14, sch 3 para 15(3)

s 1062 am—Corporation Tax, 2010 c 4, s 1177, sch 1 paras 589, 670

Pt 13 Ch 3 (ss 1063-1067) rep (with spec commencing effect)—Finance, 2013 c 29, sch 15
paras 14, 28,29

s 1063 rep in pt—Finance, 2012 c 14, sch 3 para 4(2)

s 1064 rep—Finance, 2012 c 14, sch 3 para 4(3)

s 1066 am—Finance, 2015 c 11, s 28(4)(i)

s 1067 am—Finance, 2015 c 11, s 28(4)(j)

Pt 13 Ch 4 (ss 1068-1073) rep (with spec commencing effect)—Finance, 2013 c 29, sch 15
paras 15, 28,29

s 1068 rep in pt—Finance, 2012 c 14, sch 3 para 5(2)

s 1069 rep—Finance, 2012 c 14, sch 3 para 5(3)

s 1071 am—Finance (No 3), 2010 c 33, s 13(4)(a); Finance, 2015 c 11, s 28(4)(k)
rep in pt—Finance (No 3), 2010 c 33, s 13(4)(b)

s 1072 am—Finance (No 3), 2010 c 33, s 13(5)(a); Finance, 2015 c 11, s 28(4)(l)
rep in pt—Finance (No 3), 2010 c 33, s 13(5)(b)

Pt 13 Ch 5 (ss 1074-1080) rep (with spec commencing effect)—Finance, 2013 c 29, sch 15
paras 16, 28,29

s 1074 rep in pt—Finance, 2012 c 14, sch 3 para 6(2)

s 1075 rep—Finance, 2012 c 14, sch 3 para 6(3)

s 1077 am—Finance, 2015 c 11, s 28(4)(m)

s 1078 am —Finance, 2015 c 11, s 28(4)(n)

s 1080 am—Finance, 2012 c 14, sch 16 para 190(2)(3)
rep in pt—Finance, 2012 c 14, sch 16 para 190(4)

2009
c 4 *continued*

s 1081 am—Finance, 2013 c 29, sch 15 para 17(2)
s 1082 rep (with spec commencing effect)—Finance, 2013 c 29, sch 15 paras 18, 28,29
    am—Corporation Tax, 2010 c 4, s 1177, sch 1 paras 589, 671
s 1083 rep (with spec commencing effect)—Finance, 2013 c 29, sch 15 paras 19, 28,29
    rep in pt—Finance, 2012 c 14, sch 16 para 191
s 1084 am—(with spec commencing effect) Finance, 2013 c 29, sch 15 paras 20, 28,29
Pt 13, Ch 7 (ss 1085-1142) am—Finance, 2012 c 14, sch 3 para 30
s 1085 am—Finance, 2012 c 14, sch 3 para 21(2), (3), (5)
    rep in pt—Finance, 2012 c 14, sch 3 paras 7(2), 21(4), (6), (7)
s 1087 am—Finance, 2012 c 14, sch 3 para 22(2)-(4), (5)(c)
    rep in pt—Finance, 2012 c 14, sch 3 paras 7(3), 22(5)(a), (b)
s 1088 am—Finance, 2012 c 14, sch 3 para 23(2)
    rep in pt—Finance, 2012 c 14, sch 3 para 23(1)
s 1089 rep—Finance, 2012 c 14, sch 3 para 24
s 1090 rep—Finance, 2012 c 14, sch 3 para 24
s 1091 am—Finance, 2012 c 14, sch 3 para 25(2)
    rep in pt—Finance, 2012 c 14, sch 3 para 25(1)
ss 1092-1096 rep—Finance, 2012 c 14, sch 3 para 26
s 1097 rep—Finance, 2012 c 14, sch 3 para 7(5)
s 1099 rep—Finance, 2012 c 14, sch 3 para 26
s 1100 am—Finance, 2012 c 14, sch 3 para 27
s 1101 am—Finance, 2015 c 11, s 28(4)(o)
s 1102 am —Finance, 2015 c 11, s 28(4)(p)
s 1103-1111 rep—Finance, 2012 c 14, sch 3 para 28
s 1112 am—Finance, 2012 c 14, sch 3 para 29(2), (4)(a), (5)
    rep in pt—Finance, 2012 c 14, sch 3 para 29(3), (4)(b)
s 1113 rep in pt—Finance, 2012 c 14, sch 3 para 31(2)
s 1114 am—Finance, 2014 c 26, sch 1 para 11
s 1115 rep in pt—Finance, 2012 c 14, sch 3 para 31(3)
s 1116 am—Corporation Tax, 2010 c 4, s 1177, sch 1 paras 589, 675
s 1119 am—(with spec commencing effect) Finance, 2013 c 29, sch 15 paras 21, 28,29
s 1122 appl—Finance (No 2), 2010 c 31, s 3, sch 2 para 8
s 1126 am—Finance, 2015 c 11, s 28(2)
ss 1126A, 1126B added—Finance, 2015 c 11, s 28(3)
s 1128 am—Finance, 2012 c 14, sch 3 para 34
s 1129 am—Finance, 2012 c 14, sch 3 para 35
s 1130 am—Finance, 2012 c 14, sch 3 para 36
s 1131 am—Finance, 2012 c 14, sch 3 para 37
s 1133 rep in pt—(with spec commencing effect) Finance, 2013 c 29, sch 15 paras 22, 28,29
s 1138 am—Finance, 2013 c 29, sch 15 para 2
s 1139 rep—Finance (No 3), 2010 c 33, s 13(6)
s 1142 am—Corporation Tax, 2010 c 4, s 1177, sch 1 paras 589, 676
Pt 14 (ss 1143-1179) am—Finance, 2009 c 10, s 26, sch 7 para 2
s 1143 am—Finance, 2009 c 10, s 26, sch 7 para 3; Finance, 2012 c 14, sch 16 para 192
s 1144 am—Finance, 2009 c 10, s 26, sch 7 para 4
s 1145 subst—Finance, 2009 c 10, s 26, sch 7 para 5
    excl—(retrosp effect) SI 2009/2037, arts 1, 3
ss 1145A, 1145B added—Finance, 2009 c 10, s 26, sch 7 para 5
s 1146 am—Finance, 2009 c 10, s 26, sch 7 para 6
    rep in pt—Finance, 2009 c 10, s 26, sch 7 para 6(3)(b)
s 1146A added—Finance, 2009 c 10, s 23, sch 7 para 7
Pt 14, Ch 2 (ss 1147-1150) am—Finance, 2009 c 10, s 26, sch 7 para 8
s 1147 am—Finance, 2009 c 10, s 26, sch 7 para 9
s 1149 am—Finance, 2009 c 10, s 26, sch 7 para 10
s 1150 am—Finance, 2009 c 10, s 26, sch 7 para 11
s 1153 am—Corporation Tax, 2010 c 4, s 1177, sch 1 paras 589, 677; Finance, 2012 c 14,
    sch 16 para 193
s 1158 am—Corporation Tax, 2010 c 4, s 1177, sch 1 paras 589, 678; Finance, 2012 c 14,
    sch 16 para 194(2), (3)
Pt 14, Ch 4 (ss 1159-1168) am—Finance, 2012 c 14, sch 16 para 195
s 1159 rep—Finance, 2012 c 14, sch 16 para 196
s 1160 am—Finance, 2012 c 14, sch 16 para 197

2009
c 4 *continued*

s 1161 am—Finance, 2009 c 10, s 26, sch 7 para 12(2)(3)(4)(a); Finance, 2012 c 14, sch 16
 para 198
 rep in pt—Finance, 2009 c 10, s 26, sch 7 para 12(4)(b)(5)-(8)
s 1162 subst—Finance, 2009 c 10, s 26, sch 7 para 13
 am—Finance, 2012 c 14, sch 16 para 199
s 1163 am—Finance, 2009 c 10, s 26, sch 7 para 14
s 1164 am—Finance, 2012 c 14, sch 16 paras 200, 201
s 1165 am—Finance, 2009 c 10, s 26, sch 7 para 15; Finance, 2012 c 14, sch 16 para 202
s 1166 am—Finance, 2012 c 14, sch 16 para 203
s 1167 am—Finance, 2012 c 14, sch 16 para 204
s 1168 am—Finance, 2012 c 14, sch 16 para 205
s 1169 am—Finance, 2009 c 10, s 26, sch 7 para 15; Finance, 2012 c 14, sch 16 para 206
s 1173 am—Finance, 2009 c 10, s 26, sch 7 para 17
s 1174 rep—Finance, 2009 c 10, s 26, sch 7 para 18
s 1175 am—Finance, 2009 c 10, s 26, sch 7 para 19
s 1176 rep—Finance, 2009 c 10, s 26, sch 7 para 20
s 1178 am—Finance, 2009 c 10, s 26, sch 7 para 21
s 1178A added—Finance, 2009 c 10, s 26, sch 7 para 22
s 1179 rep in pt—Finance, 2009 c 10, s 26, sch 7 para 23
 am—Corporation Tax, 2010 c 4, s 1177, sch 1 paras 589, 679
s 1184 rep in pt —Finance, 2015 c 11, s 29(2); SI 2015/1741, art 2
s 1195 am—Finance, 2013 c 29, sch 18 para 12
s 1198 am—Finance, 2014 c 26, s 32(2)
 power to am—Finance, 2014 c 26, s 32(7)
s 1200 am—Finance, 2015 c 11, s 29(3); SI 2015/1741, art 2
s 1201 am—Finance (No 3), 2010 c 33, s 14(1)-(5)
s 1202 am—Finance (No 3), 2010 c 33, s 14(6); Finance, 2014 c 26, s 32(3); Finance, 2015
 c 11, s 29(4)(a); SI 2015/1741, art 2
 power to am—Finance, 2014 c 26, s 32(7)
 rep in pt—Finance, 2015 c 11, s 29(4)(b); SI 2015/1741, art 2
s 1206 am—Finance, 2013 c 29, sch 18 para 13
s 1207 am—SI 2014/834, sch 2 para 62
s 1209 am—Corporation Tax, 2010 c 4, s 1177, sch 1 paras 589, 680
s 1210 am—Corporation Tax, 2010 c 4, s 1177, sch 1 paras 589, 681
s 1211 am—Corporation Tax, 2010 c 4, s 1177, sch 1 paras 589, 682
s 1215 rep—Finance, 2015 c 11, s 29(5); SI 2015/1741, art 2
Pt 15A (ss 1216A-1216EC) added—Finance, 2013 c 29, sch 16 para 1
s 1216A am—Finance, 2014 c 26, s 33(2)
s 1216B am—Finance, 2014 c 26, s 33(3)
s 1216AB am—Finance, 2015 c 11, s 30(2)(3)
s 1216AC am—Finance, 2015 c 11, s 30(4)
s 1216AD am—Finance, 2015 c 11, s 30(5)
s 1216ADA added—Finance, 2015 c 11, s 30(6)
s 1216CE am—Finance, 2015 c 11, s 31(1)
s 1216CN am—SI 2014/834, sch 2 para 63
Pt 15B (ss 1217A-1217EC) added—Finance, 2013 c 29, sch 16 para 1
s 1217A am—Finance, 2014 c 26, s 34(2)
s 1217AE am—Finance, 2014 c 26, s 34(3)
s 1217B am—Finance, 2014 c 26, s 34(4)
s 1217C am—Finance, 2014 c 26, s 34(6)(a)
s 1217CE am—Finance, 2014 c 26, s 34(6)(b)-(d)
s 1217CF am—Finance, 2014 c 26, s 34(5)
s 1217CG am—Finance, 2014 c 26, s 34(6)(e)
s 1217CN am—SI 2014/834, sch 2 para 64
s 1217EB am—Finance, 2014 c 26, s 34(6)(f)(g)
Pt 15C (ss 1217F-1217OB) added—Finance, 2014 c 26, sch 4 para 1
s 1218A renumbered from s 1217—Finance, 2013 c 29, sch 18 para 21(1)(a)
s 1218B renumbered from s 1218—Finance, 2013 c 29, sch 18 para 21(1)(b)
s 1219 am—Corporation Tax, 2010 c 4, s 1177, sch 1 paras 589, 683
s 1220 am—Corporation Tax, 2010 c 4, s 1177, sch 1 paras 589, 684
s 1221 rep in pt—Corporation Tax, 2010 c 4, ss 1177, 1181, sch 1 paras 589, 685(a), sch 3
 am —Corporation Tax, 2010 c 4, ss 1177, 1180, sch 1 paras 589, 685(b), sch 2;
 Finance, 2013 c 29, sch 29 para 38; Finance, 2015 c 11, sch 5 para 5

2009
c 4 *continued*

s 1223 am—Corporation Tax, 2010 c 4, s 1177, sch 1 paras 589, 686(2)(4); Finance, 2015
     c 11, sch 2 para 3
    rep in pt—Corporation Tax, 2010 c 4, ss 1177, 1181, sch 1 paras 589, 686(3), sch 3
s 1223A added—Finance, 2012 c 14, sch 16 para 207
s 1224 am—Finance, 2014 c 26, sch 17 para 4(4)(a)
s 1225 am—Corporation Tax, 2010 c 4, s 1177, sch 1 paras 589, 687
s 1227A added—Finance, 2014 c 26, sch 17 para 4(4)(b)
s 1229 am—Corporation Tax, 2010 c 4, s 1177, sch 1 paras 589, 688
s 1231 rep in pt—Finance, 2009 c 10, s 30, sch 11 paras 45, 56
s 1234 appl—Finance, 2012 c 14, s 81(2)s 81(3)(b)(7)
s 1235 appl—Finance, 2012 c 14, s 81(2)s 81(3)(c)(7)
s 1237 appl—Finance, 2012 c 14, s 81(2)s 81(3)(d)(7)
ss 1238-1242 appl—Finance, 2012 c 14, s 81(2)s 81(3)(f)(7)
s 1238 appl—Finance, 2012 c 14, s 81(2)s 81(3)(e)(7)
s 1243 appl—Finance, 2012 c 14, s 81(2)s 81(3)(g)(7)
s 1244 appl—Finance, 2012 c 14, s 81(2)s 81(3)(h)(7)
s 1244A added—Finance, 2015 c 11, sch 5 para 6
s 1248 am—Corporation Tax, 2010 c 4, s 1177, sch 1 paras 589, 689
    rep in pt—Finance, 2013 c 29, sch 29 para 39
s 1249 appl—Finance, 2012 c 14, s 82(2), (3), (5)
s 1251 am—Finance, 2009 c 10, s 30, sch 11 paras 45, 57(1)-(4)(7)(b)(8); Finance, 2012 c
     14, sch 16 para 208(2), (3)(a)
    rep in pt—Finance, 2009 c 10, s 30, sch 11 paras 45, 57(1)(6)(7)(a)(9); Finance,
     2012 c 14, sch 16 para 208(3)(b)
    appl—Finance, 2012 c 14, s 82(4), (5)
s 1253 appl—Finance, 2012 c 14, s 81(6)
s 1253A added—Finance, 2015 c 11, sch 5 para 7
s 1256 am—Corporation Tax, 2010 c 4, s 1177, sch 1 paras 589, 690
ss 1259-1261 appl (mods)—Corporation Tax, 2010 c 4, ss 765(2), 768(4)
s 1261 appl—Corporation Tax, 2010 c 4, s 357GB(5)
s 1262 appl (mods)—Corporation Tax, 2010 c 4, ss 765(2), 768(4)
    am—Corporation Tax, 2010 c 4, s 1177, sch 1 paras 589, 691(2); Finance, 2014 c
     26, sch 17 para 10(2)
    rep in pt—Corporation Tax, 2010 c 4, ss 1177, 1181, sch 1 paras 589, 691(3), sch 3
s 1263 appl (mods)—Corporation Tax, 2010 c 4, ss 765(2), 768(4)
s 1264 appl (mods)—Corporation Tax, 2010 c 4, ss 765(2), 768(4)
s 1264A added—Finance, 2014 c 26, sch 17 para 10(3)
s 1265 appl (mods)—Corporation Tax, 2010 c 4, ss 765(2), 768(4)
s 1266 am—Taxation (International and Other Provns), 2010 c 8, s 374, sch 8 paras 89,101
s 1269 am—Taxation (International and Other Provns), 2010 c 8, s 374, sch 8 paras 308,
     311
s 1273A added—Finance, 2014 c 26, sch 17 para 2
s 1274 mod—Taxation (International and Other Provns), 2010 c 8, s 371SN(1)(2))
s 1283 rep—Finance, 2012 c 14, sch 39 para 53(1)(b)
s 1285 rep—Finance, 2009 c 10, s 34, sch 14 paras 20, 27
Pt 20, Ch 1 (ss 1288-1305) appl (mods)—Finance, 1989 c 26, s 85(2BA)
    appl—Finance, 2012 c 14, s 92
s 1288 am—Finance, 2012 c 14, sch 16 para 209(a)
    rep in pt—Finance, 2012 c 14, sch 16 para 209(b)
s 1291 am—Finance, 2011 c 11, sch 2 para 45
s 1292 am—Finance, 2011 c 11, sch 2 para 46; Finance, 2013 c 29, sch 23 para 34; Finance,
     2014 c 26, sch 37 para 23(1)
s 1293 am—Finance, 2011 c 11, sch 2 para 47(2)-(5); Finance, 2013 c 29, sch 23 para 35
s 1296 am—Finance, 2011 c 11, sch 2 para 48
s 1297 am—Finance, 2012 c 14, sch 16 para 210
s 1298 am—Finance, 2012 c 14, sch 16 para 211
s 1301A added—Taxation (International and Other Provns), 2010 c 8, s 371, sch 7 paras 38,
     39
s 1301B added—Corporation Tax, 2010 c 4, s 1177, sch 1 paras 589, 692
s 1303 am—SIs 2010/530, art 2, sch; 2014/1283, sch para 6
s 1304 am—Finance, 2012 c 14, sch 16 para 212
s 1305A added—Finance, 2014 c 26, s 30(1)
s 1306 am—Corporation Tax, 2010 c 4, s 1177, sch 1 paras 589, 693

2009

c 4 *continued*

s 1307 am—Corporation Tax, 2010 c 4, s 1177, sch 1 paras 589, 694

s 1308 am—Corporation Tax, 2010 c 4, s 1177, sch 1 paras 589, 695

s 1310 am—Finance, 2009 c 10, s 34, sch 14 paras 20, 28; Finance, 2010 c 13, s 62, sch 19 para 3; Finance, 2013 c 29, sch 18 para 14(2); Finance, 2014 c 26, sch 4 para 12; Finance, 2015 c 11, s 28(6); Finance (No. 2), 2015 c 33, s 31(4)

rep in pt—Taxation (International and Other Provns), 2010 c 8, ss 374, 378, sch 8 paras 224, 226, sch 10

s 1311 rep—Corporation Tax, 2010 c 4, ss 1177, 1181, sch 1 paras 589, 696, sch 3

s 1312 am—Corporation Tax, 2010 c 4, s 1177, sch 1 paras 589, 697; Taxation (International and Other Provns), 2010 c 8, s 374, sch 8 paras 329, 330

s 1316 am—Corporation Tax, 2010 c 4, s 1177, sch 1 paras 589, 698

s 1317 rep—Corporation Tax, 2010 c 4, ss 1177, 1181, sch 1 paras 589, 699, sch 3

s 1318 rep—Corporation Tax, 2010 c 4, ss 1177, 1181, sch 1 paras 589, 700, sch 3

s 1319 rep in pt—Corporation Tax, 2010 c 4, ss 1177, 1181, sch 1 paras 589, 701(2), sch 3; Finance, 2010 c 13, s 30, sch 6 para 25(2)

am—Corporation Tax, 2010 c 4, s 1177, sch 1 paras 589, 701(3); SI 2011/1431, reg 4(8)

s 1320 rep in pt—Corporation Tax, 2010 c 4, ss 1177, 1181, sch 1 paras 589, 702, sch 3

s 1325 rep in pt —Finance (No. 2), 2015 c 33, sch 7 para 101(3)

s 1329 rep in pt—Finance (No. 2), 2015 c 33, sch 7 para 101(4)

sch 1 rep in pt—Finance, 2009 c 10, s 30, sch 11 para 64(b);ibid, s 30, sch 11 paras 45, 58; ibid, s 34, sch 14 para 30(e); ibid, s 48, sch 24 para 9(f); Corporation Tax, 2010 c 4, s 1181, sch 3 pts 1, 2; Taxation (International and Other Provns), 2010 c 8, s 378, sch 10 pts 1-3, 6-12; Finance, 2011 c 11, sch 3 para 18; ibid, sch 9 para 5(f); Finance, 2012 c 14, s 26(2)(d); ibid, sch 16 para 247(r); ibid, sch 39 para 39(c); SL(R), 2013 c 2, s 1, sch 1 pt 10(1); SI 2013/2819, reg 41(c)

sch 2 rep in pt—SIs 2009/2035, art 2, sch; (retrosp to 1.4.2009) 2009/2860, art 6(7)(d)(f); Finance (No. 2), 2015 c 33, sch 7 para 101(2)

am—(pt retrosp to 1.4.2009) SI 2009/2860, art 6(7); Corporation Tax, 2010 c 4, s 1177, sch 1 paras 589, 703; Taxation (International and Other Provns), 2010 c 8, s 374, sch 8 paras 308, 312; SI 2010/614, art 3; Finance, 2012 c 14, sch 16 para 213(2), (3)

sch 3 am—(retrosp to 1.4.2009) SI 2009/2860, art 6(8)

sch 3 rep in pt—Finance (No. 2), 2015 c 33, sch 7 para 101(5)

sch 4 am—Finance, 2009 c 10, s 26, sch 7 para 26(1)(2)(4)- (6); ibid, s 34, sch 14 paras 20, 29; ibid, s 43, sch 21 para 9; ibid, s 48, sch 24 para 7(1)(2)(4)-(6)(8)(9); Corporation Tax, 2010 c 4, s 1177, sch 1 paras 589, 704; Finance, 2010 c 13, s 30, sch 6 para 25(3); Finance, 2011 c 11, sch 13 para 11; Finance, 2012 c 14, sch 16 para 214(a),(d)-(f),(h),(j),(l); SIs 2012/266, art 11; 2012/735, art 7; Finance, 2013 c 29, sch 15 para 3; ibid, sch 18 paras 15(1)(2), 21(3); ibid, sch 23 para 36; SI 2013/1411, reg 13(b)(i); Co-operative and Community Benefit Societies, 2014 c 14, sch 4 para 146(b); Finance, 2014 c 26, s 34(7)(b), sch 1 para 12, sch 4 para 13, sch 16 para 5; Finance (No. 2), 2015 c 33, sch 7 para 99(2)(3)

rep in pt—Finance, 2009 c 10, s 26, sch 7 para 26(1)(3)(7); ibid, s 48, sch 24 para 7(1)(3)(7); (retrosp to 1.4.2009) SI 2009/2860, art 6; Corporation Tax, 2010 c 4, ss 1177, 1181, sch 1 paras 589, 704(28), sch 3; Finance (No 3), 2010 c 33, s 13(7); Finance, 2012 c 14, sch 3 paras 8, 32(a); Finance, 2012 c 14, sch 16 para 214(b)(c),(g)(i),(k),(m); (with spec commencing effect) Finance, 2013 c 29, sch 15 paras 23, 28,29; SI 2013/1411, reg 13(b)(ii); Co-operative and Community Benefit Societies, 2014 c 14, sch 4 para 146(a); Finance, 2014 c 26, s 34(7)(a); Finance, 2015 c 11, s 29(6); SI 2015/1741, art 2; Finance (No. 2), 2015 c 33, sch 7 para 99(4)

c 5   **Industry and Export (Financial Support)**

c 6   **Geneva Conventions and United Nations Personnel (Protocol)**

s 1 ext (mods)—SIs 2010/2965, art 3, sch 1; (to Jersey) 2012/2589, art 2 sch

s 2 ext (mods)—(to the Isle of Man) SI 2012/2594, arts 2, 3

sch ext (mods)—SIs 2010/2965, art 3; (to Jersey) 2012/2589, art 2 sch

c 7   **Business Rate Supplements**

s 4 am—(W prosp) Localism, 2011 c 20, s 68(2)

s 7 rep in pt—Localism, 2011 c 20, s 68(3), sch 25 pt 9

s 8 am—(W prosp) Localism, 2011 c 20, s 68(4)

2009
c 7 *continued*

s 10 rep in pt—Localism, 2011 c 20, s 68(5)(a), sch 25 pt 9
sch 1 am—(W prosp) Localism, 2011 c 20, s 68(6)
sch 2 mod—SI 2014/3204, regs 18(5)(b), 19(3)(b)
appl (mods)—SI 2014/3204, sch 5 para 2

c 8   *Saving Gateway Accounts*—rep Savings Accounts and Health in Pregnancy Grant, 2010 c 36, s 2(1)

c 9   **Appropriation (No 2)**

c 10   **Finance**

s 3 rep in pt—Finance, 2009 c 10, s 5, sch 1 para 6(q)
s 7 am—Corporation Tax, 2010 c 4, s 1177, sch 1 paras 706, 707
s 8 am—Corporation Tax, 2010 c 4, s 1177, sch 1 paras 706, 708
ss 28, 29 rep—Corporation Tax, 2010 c 4, s 1181, sch 3 pt 1
s 29 rep—Finance, 2015 c 11, s 22(7)
s 35 rep—Taxation (International and Other Provns), 2010 c 8, ss 374, 378, sch 8 paras 158, 159, sch 10 pt 4
s 38 rep—Corporation Tax, 2010 c 4, ss 1177, 1181, sch 1 paras 706, 709, sch 3
s 44 rep in pt—Taxation (International and Other Provns), 2010 c 8, s 378, sch 10 pt 5
s 45 am—Corporation Tax, 2010 c 4, s 1177, sch 1 paras 706, 710
s 46 rep—Finance, 2012 c 14, sch 16 para 247(s)(i)
s 47 rep—(accounting periods ending on or after 1.1.2016) Finance, 2012 c 14, s 30(2)(3); SI 2015/1999, art 2
s 49 rep in pt—Finance, 2010 c 13, s 30, sch 6 para 26
s 56 am—Taxation (International and Other Provns), 2010 c 8, s 374, sch 8 paras 102, 103
s 57 rep—Taxation (International and Other Provns), 2010 c 8, s 378, sch 10 pt 1
s 58 rep—Corporation Tax, 2010 c 4, s 1181, sch 3 pt 1
ss 59, 60 rep—Taxation (International and Other Provns), c 8, s 378, sch 10 pt 1
ss 62, 63 rep—Corporation Tax, 2010 c 4, s 1181, sch 3 pt 1
s 66 rep—Corporation Tax, 2010 c 4, s 1181, sch 3 pt 1
s 68 rep in pt—SI 2011/702, art 15(a)
s 77 rep in pt—Finance, 2012 c 14, sch 29 para 13(b)
s 83 rep (prosp)—Finance, 2009 c 10, s 83(3)
s 90 rep—Corporation Tax, 2010 c 4, ss 1177, 1181, sch 1 paras 706, 711, sch 3 pt 1
s 94 appl—Finance, 2012 c 14, sch 38 para 28(4)
appl (mods)—SI 2013/938, reg 16
s 101 rep in pt—Finance (No 3), 2010 c 33, s 25, sch 9 paras 2, 13, 14
appl—SIs 2009/470, reg 39(2)(b) (subst by 2011/784, reg 8); 2013/938, reg 14
am—Finance, 2014 c 26, sch 22 para 20(2)
ss 101, 102 appl (mods)—Social Security, Contributions and Benefits, 1992 c 4, s 11A(1)(3)
s 102 rep in pt—Finance (No 3), 2010 c 33, s 25, sch 9 para 3(2)
am—Finance (No 3), 2010 c 33, s 25, sch 9 paras 3(3), 13, 15
appl—SI 2009/470, reg 39(5)(b) (subst by SI 2011/784, reg 8)
mod—Nat Insurance Contributions, 2014 c 7, s 4(9)
s 103 appl—SIs 2009/470, reg 39(2)(b), (5)(b) (subst by SI 2011/784, reg 8); 2013/938, reg 14
s 103A added—Finance (No 3), 2010 c 33, s 25, sch 9 para 4
s 104 am—Finance (No 3), 2010 c 33, s 25, sch 9 para 5
s 108 appl (mods)—SIs 2001/1004, reg 90K (am by 2009/2028, reg 3); 2003/2682, reg 203 (am by 2009/2029, reg 4); 2005/2045, reg 48 (am by 2009/2028, reg 3)
s 108 am—SI 2011/702, art 15(b); Finance, 2014 c 26, sch 22 para 20(3)
s 111 rep—Taxation (International and Other Provns), 2010 c 8, ss 371, 378, sch 7 paras 83, 84, sch 10
s 123 am—Taxation (International and Other Provns), 2010 c 8, s 374, sch 8 paras 227, 228
s 124 am—Co-operative and Community Benefit Societies, 2014 c 14, sch 4 para 147
s 125 mod—SI 2015/623, reg 65(1)
s 126 am—Corporation Tax, 2010 c 4, s 1177, sch 1 paras 706, 712; Taxation (International and Other Provns), 2010 c 8, s 374, sch 8 paras 331, 332
s 444BA appl (mods)—(retrosp to 31.12.2008) SI 2009/2039, regs 1, 3, 4
s 767 rep—Finance, 2009 c 10, s 37, sch 17 para 1(d)
sch 2 rep in pt—Finance, 2011 c 11, sch 17 para 26(1)(a); Finance, 2012 c 14, sch 39 para 28(1)
sch 3 am—Corporation Tax, 2010 c 4, s 1177, sch 1 paras 706, 713
sch 5 rep in pt—Finance, 2009 c 10, s 99, sch 51 paras 17, 24(2)(a)(3)(5)

2009
c 10 *continued*

sch 6 am—Corporation Tax, 2010 c 4, s 1177, sch 1 paras 706, 714; Finance, 2010 c 13, s 24, sch 3 para 10(a)(b)
rep in pt—Finance, 2010 c 13, s 24, sch 3 para 10(c)
sch 7 rep in pt—Finance, 2012 c 14, sch 16 para 247(s)(ii)
schs 9, 10 rep—Corporation Tax, 2010 c 4, s 1181, sch 3 pt 1
sch 11 rep in pt—Finance, 2012 c 14, sch 16 para 247(s)(iii)
sch 12 rep in pt—Corporation Tax, 2010 c 4, s 1181, sch 3 pt 1; Finance, 2011 c 11, sch 10 para 8(d)
sch 14 rep in pt—Corporation Tax, 2010 c 4, s 1181, sch 3 pt 1; Taxation (International and Other Provns), 2010 c 8, s 378, sch 10 pts 1, 2
sch 15 rep in pt—Taxation (International and Other Provns), 2010 c 8, ss 374, 378, sch 8 paras 158, 160, sch 10 pts 2, 4
sch 16 am—Taxation (International and Other Provns), 2010 c 8, s 374, sch 8 paras 102, 104; Finance, 2011 c 11, sch 12 para 9(2)-(5); Finance, 2012 c 14, sch 20 paras 33(b), 35(a), 36
rep in pt—Finance, 2011 c 11, sch 12 para 13(b); Finance, 2012 c 14, sch 20 paras 33(a), 34, 35(b)
sch 17 am—Taxation (International and Other Provns), 2010 c 8, s 374, sch 8 paras 149, 150
sch 18 rep (with savings)—Corporation Tax, 2010 c 4, ss 1177, 1180, 1181, sch 1 paras 706, 715 schs 2, 3
sch 19 rep in pt—Corporation Tax, 2010 c 4, s 1181, sch 3 pt 1; Finance, 2013 c 29, sch 29 para 40; SI 2013/2819, reg 41(d)
sch 21 rep in pt —Finance (No. 2), 2015 c 33, sch 7 para 100
sch 22 am—Corporation Tax, 2010 c 4, s 1177, sch 1 paras 706, 716
rep in pt—Taxation (International and Other Provns), 2010 c 8, ss 374, 378 sch 8 paras 173, 174, sch 10 pt 5; SI 2012/952, reg 4(a)
sch 23 rep in pt—Finance, 2011 c 11, sch 9 para 5(g); Finance, 2012 c 14, sch 16 para 247(s)(iv)
sch 24 rep in pt—Taxation (International and Other Provns), 2010 c 8, s 378, sch 10 pt 3
sch 25 rep in pt—Corporation Tax, 2010 c 4, ss 1177, 1181, sch 1 paras 706, 717, sch 3 pt 1
sch 28 rep in pt—Finance, 2010 c 13, ss 58(17), 59(4)(b)
sch 29 rep—Corporation Tax, 2010 c 4, s 1181, sch 3 pt 1
sch 30 rep in pt—Finance, 2011 c 11, sch 4 para 12(a); ibid, sch 5 para 7(2)(b)
sch 31 rep—Corporation Tax, 2010 c 4, s 1181, sch 3 pt 1
sch 32 rep in pt—Corporation Tax, 2010 c 4, s 1181, sch 3 pt 1
sch 33 am—Corporation Tax, 2010 c 4, s 1177, sch 1 paras 706, 718(2)
rep in pt—Corporation Tax, 2010 c 4, ss 1177, 1181, sch 1 paras 706, 718(3)-(7), sch 3
sch 34 rep—Corporation Tax, 2010 c 4, s 1181, sch 3 pt 1
sch 35 rep (saving) (2011-12 and subsequent tax years)—SI 2010/2939, art 2(1)(2)
appl (mods)—SI 2009/2031, arts 2, 3, 6
am—SIs 2009/2031, arts 2, 4, 6-11; 2010/572, art 2; 2010/429, arts 2-10; Corporation Tax, 2010 c 4, s 1177, sch 1 paras 706, 719; Taxation (International and Other Provns), 2010 c 8, s 374, sch 8 paras 102, 105
rep in pt—SI 2010/429, arts 2-5; (as continuing to have effect) Finance, 2011 c 11, sch 17 para 26(1)(b)
sch 37 rep (prosp)—Finance, 2009 c 10, s 83(3)
sch 44 rep (2010-11 and subsequent tax years) —Corporation Tax, 2010 c 4, ss 1177, 1181, 1184, sch 1 paras 706, 720, sch 3 pt 1
am—(as continuing to have effect) Finance, 2011 c 11, s 63(5)
sch 45 rep in pt—Corporation Tax, 2010 c 4, s 1181, sch 3 pt 1
sch 46 am—Corporation Tax, 2010 c 4, s 1177, sch 1 paras 706, 721
sch 51 rep in pt—Finance (No 3), 2010 c 33, s 28, sch 12 para 13(a)
sch 52 rep in pt—Finance (No 3), 2010 c 33, s 28, sch 12 para 13(b)
sch 53 am—Corporation Tax, 2010 c 4, s 1177, sch 1 paras 706, 722; Finance (No 3), 2010 c 33, s 25, sch 9 paras 6-8, 13, 16-19; Finance, 2013 c 29, sch 51 para 7; (prosp) Finance (No. 2), 2015 c 33, s 15(2)
appl (mods)—Finance, 2010 c 13, s 22, sch 1 para 30(2)
appl—SI 2013/938, reg 14
sch 54 am—Finance (No 3), 2010 c 33, s 25, sch 9 paras 9-11; SIs 2010/157, art 4; 2011/1037, art 8

2009

c 10 sch 54 *continued*

  rep in pt—Finance, 2012 c 14, sch 39 para 28(1)

 sch 54A added—Finance (No 3), 2010 c 33, s 25, sch 9 para 12

  am—Finance, 2013 c 29, sch 18 para 16; Finance, 2014 c 26, sch 4 para 14

 sch 55 appl (mods)—Social Security, Contributions and Benefits, 1992 c 4, s 11A(1)(3); SI
   2001/1004, sch 4 para 21G (added by SI 2014/2397, reg 3(5)); Finance, 2010
   c 13, s 22, sch 1 para 38

  appl—SI 2009/470, reg 40 (am by SI 2011/784, reg 9)

  am—Finance, 2010 c 13, s 35, sch 10 paras 10-12, 13(2), 14; Finance (No 3), 2010
   c 33, s 26, sch 10; Finance, 2012 c 14, sch 24 paras 31-34; Finance, 2013 c 29,
   sch 34 para 7(1); ibid, sch 50 paras 3-9; ibid, sch 51 para 8; Finance, 2014 c 26,
   sch 21 para 7, sch 28 para 29, sch 33 para 5; Finance, 2015 c 11, sch 7 para
   59(1); (1.4.2016) ibid, sch 20 paras 16(3)-(7),(9), 17; (prosp) ibid, sch 20 paras
   15, 16(2), 18, 19

  rep in pt—Finance, 2010 c 13, s 35, sch 10 paras 10, 13(3); (1.4.2016) Finance,
   2015 c 11, sch 20 para 16(8)

 sch 56 rep in pt—Finance (No 3), 2010 c 33, s 27, sch 11 para 2(5)(12), 5(4)(b); Finance,
   2013 c 29, sch 50 para 14(3)

  am—Finance (No 3), 2010 c 33, s 27, sch 11 paras 1-2(4)(6)-(11)(13)-5(4)(a),
   5(5)-10; Finance, 2013 c 29, sch 34 paras 9, 10(2)(a); ibid, sch 49 para 7; ibid,
   sch 50 paras 11, 12, 13, 14(2); Finance, 2014 c 26, sch 21 para 8, sch 28 para
   30; Finance, 2015 c 11, s 104; Finance (No. 2), 2015 c 33, s 38(7)(8)

  appl (mods)—Social Security, Contributions and Benefits, 1992 c 4, s 11A(1)(3); SI
   2001/1004, regs 67A, 67B (added by SI 2010/721, regs 2, 3); Finance, 2010 c
   13, s 22, sch 1 para 39; Finance, 2014 c 26, s 226(7)

  appl—SI 2009/470, reg 36 (subst by SI 2011/784, reg 7)

  mod—(temp) Finance, 2013 c 29, sch 34 paras 10(1), 11

 sch 61 am—Corporation Tax, 2010 c 4, s 1177, sch 1 paras 706, 724; Taxation
   (International and Other Provns), 2010 c 8, s 374, sch 8 paras 227, 229;
   Scotland, 2012 c 11, sch 3 para 31(3)(a),(4),(6)(a),(8)(9),(11)(12),(13)(a);
   (with qualifying provn) Wales, 2014 c 29, s 16(3)(4)-(7), sch 2 para 14

  rep in pt—Taxation (International and Other Provns), 2010 c 8, s 378, sch 10 pt 7;
   Scotland, 2012 c 11, sch 3 para 31(3)(b),(6)(b),(7),(10),(13)(b),(14); (with
   qualifying provn) Wales, 2014 c 29, s 16(3)(4)-(7), sch 2 para 15

c 11 **Borders, Citizenship and Immigration**

 s 1 am—Energy, 2013 c 32, sch 12 para 101(2)

 s 7 am—Finance, 2012 c 14, sch 24 para 49; Energy, 2013 c 32, sch 12 para 101(3)

  rep in pt—Finance, 2012 c 14, sch 24 para 58

 s 15 am—SI 2014/834, sch 2 para 66

 s 18 rep in pt—SI 2014/834, sch 2 para 67

 s 22 am—SI 2013/1542, art 32(4)

  rep in pt—SI 2013/1542, art 32(2)(3)(5)

 s 29 am—SI 2013/602, sch 2 para 61

 s 31 rep—SI 2014/834, sch 2 para 68

 s 37 rep in pt—SI 2014/834, sch 2 para 69

 s 39 am—Citizenship (Armed Forces), 2014 c 8, s 1(4)

 s 51 rep in pt—Immigration, 2014 c 22, sch 9 para 60 table

 s 53 rep—Crime and Cts, 2013 c 22, s 22(4)

 s 54A added—Immigration, 2014 c 22, s 3

c 12 **Political Parties and Elections**

 see (cert functions made exerciseable concurrently)—SI 2010/1837, art 3

 trans of functions —SI 2015/1376, art 3(1) sch 1

 s 1 rep in pt—Transparency of Lobbying, Non-Party Campaigning and Trade Union Admin,
   2014 c 4, s 38(5)

 s 23 rep in pt—Electoral Registration and Admin, 2013 c 6, sch 4 para 24(a)

 s 38A subst—SI 2015/1376, sch 2 para 13

c 13 **Parliamentary Standards**

 s 2 rep in pt—Constitutional Reform and Governance, 2010 c 25, s 38, sch 5 para 2(a)

  am—Constitutional Reform and Governance, 2010 c 25, s 38, sch 5 para 2(b)

 s 3 am—Constitutional Reform and Governance, 2010 c 25, s 26(1)

 s 3A added—Constitutional Reform and Governance, 2010 c 25, s 28(2)

 s 4 subst —Constitutional Reform and Governance, 2010 c 25, s 29(1)-(3)

 s 4A added —Constitutional Reform and Governance, 2010 c 25, s 29(1)-(3)

2009

c 13 *continued*

s 5 am—Constitutional Reform and Governance, 2010 c 25, ss 25, 28(3), 30, 38, sch 5 para
3; ibid, s 40, sch 6 para 47(1)

s 6 am—Constitutional Reform and Governance, 2010 c 25, ss 28(4), 31(3)(4)
rep in pt—Constitutional Reform and Governance, 2010 c 25, s 31(2)

s 6A added—Constitutional Reform and Governance, 2010 c 25, s 31(5)

s 7 am—Constitutional Reform and Governance, 2010 c 25, s 31(6)(a)
rep in pt (heading)—Constitutional Reform and Governance, 2010 c 25, s 31(6)(b)

s 8 rep—Constitutional Reform and Governance, 2010 c 25, s 32

s 9 subst—Constitutional Reform and Governance, 2010 c 25, s 33

s 9A added—Constitutional Reform and Governance, 2010 c 25, s 33

s 9B added—Constitutional Reform and Governance, 2010 c 25, s 34(1)

s 10A added—Constitutional Reform and Governance, 2010 c 25, s 35

s 11 rep—Constitutional Reform and Governance, 2010 c 25, s 36

s 12 am—Constitutional Reform and Governance, 2010 c 25, s 38, sch 5 para 4(2)(a)(3)
rep in pt—Constitutional Reform and Governance, 2010 c 25, s 38, sch 5 para 4(2)(b)

s 13 rep in pt—Constitutional Reform and Governance, 2010 c 25, s 38, sch 5 para 5(2)
am—Constitutional Reform and Governance, 2010 c 25, s 38, sch 5 para 5(3)
appl —Constitutional Reform and Governance, 2010 c 25, s 40, sch 6 para 48(3)

s 14 rep in pt—Constitutional Reform and Governance, 2010 c 25, s 38, sch 5 para 6

s 15 rep—Constitutional Reform and Governance, 2010 c 25, s 37

ss 28, 29 rep—Electoral Registration and Admin, 2013 c 6, s 23(2)

ss 30-37 rep —Electoral Registration and Admin, 2013 c 6, sch 4 para 24

sch 1 rep in pt—Constitutional Reform and Governance, 2010 c 25, s 38, sch 5 para
7(2)(3)(c)(4)(c)
am—Constitutional Reform and Governance, 2010 c 25, s 38, sch 5 para
7(3)(a)(b)(4)(a)(b)(d)(5); ibid, s 40, sch 6 para 47(2)(3); Budget Responsibility
and Nat Audit, 2011 c 4, sch 5 para 33

sch 2 subst—Constitutional Reform and Governance, 2010 c 25, s 26, sch 3

sch 3 rep in pt—Constitutional Reform and Governance, 2010 c 25, s 27(2)(a)
am—Constitutional Reform and Governance, 2010 c 25, s 27(2)(b)(3)(4)

sch 4 added—Constitutional Reform and Governance, 2010 c 25, s 34, sch 4
am—Crime and Cts, 2013 c 22, sch 9 para 117

c 14 **Law Commission**

c 15 **Autism**

s 4 am—Health and Social Care, 2012 c 7, sch 5 para 171(c)
rep in pt—Health and Social Care, 2012 c 7, sch 5 para 171(a), (b); (pt prosp) ibid, sch
14 para 111

s 20 am—Crime and Cts, 2013 c 22, s 22(2)(a)(i)(iii)
rep in pt—Crime and Cts, 2013 c 22, s 22(2)(a)(ii)(b)

c 16 **Holocaust (Return of Cultural Objects)**

s 1 am—Nat Library of S, 2012 asp 3, sch 2 para 8(a)

s 2 am—Nat Library of S, 2012 asp 3, sch 2 para 8(b)

c 17 **Driving Instruction (Suspension and Exemption Powers)**

s 4 rep in pt—(prosp) Driving Instruction (Suspension and Exemption Powers), 2009 c 17, s
4, sch 2

sch 1 rep (prosp)—Driving Instruction (Suspension and Exemption Powers), 2009 c 17, s 4,
sch 2

c 18 **Perpetuities and Accumulations**

c 19 **Green Energy (Definition and Promotion)**

c 20 **Local Democracy, Economic Development and Construction**

am—Co-operative and Community Benefit Societies, 2014 c 14, sch 4 para 149

Pt 1 Ch 1 (ss 1-9) rep —Localism, 2011 c 20, s 45, sch 25 pt 6

Pt 1 Ch 2 (ss 10-22) rep—Localism, 2011 c 20, s 46, sch 25 pt 7

s 23 rep in pt—Public Bodies, 2011 c 24, sch 6
am—Police Reform and Social Responsibility, 2011 c 13, sch 16 para 375; SI
2014/469, sch 2 para 25

s 31 rep—Localism, 2011 c 20, sch 25 pt 4

s 35 am—Police Reform and Social Responsibility, 2011 c 13, sch 16 para 376
rep in pt—Localism, 2011 c 20, sch 25 pt 32; Deregulation, 2015 c 20, sch 13 para
6(35)(a)

s 36 am—Loc Audit and Accountability, 2014 c 2, sch 12 para 98(2)(a)
rep in pt—Loc Audit and Accountability, 2014 c 2, sch 12 para 98(2)(b)(3)(4)

s 37 rep in pt—Loc Audit and Accountability, 2014 c 2, sch 12 para 99

2009

c 20 *continued*

s 38 am—Loc Audit and Accountability, 2014 c 2, sch 12 para 100(2)(3)(5)(7)

    rep in pt—Loc Audit and Accountability, 2014 c 2, sch 12 para 100(4)(6)

s 39 am—Loc Audit and Accountability, 2014 c 2, sch 12 para 101

s 40 am—Co-operative and Community Benefit Societies, 2014 c 14, sch 4 para 150; Loc Audit and Accountability, 2014 c 2, sch 12 para 102

s 41 am—Loc Audit and Accountability, 2014 c 2, sch 12 para 103

s 42 am—Loc Audit and Accountability, 2014 c 2, sch 12 para 104(2)

    rep in pt—Loc Audit and Accountability, 2014 c 2, sch 12 para 104(3)

s 43 am—Co-operative and Community Benefit Societies, 2014 c 14, sch 4 para 151; Loc Audit and Accountability, 2014 c 2, sch 12 para 105

s 44 am—Co-operative and Community Benefit Societies, 2014 c 14, sch 4 para 152; Loc Audit and Accountability, 2014 c 2, sch 12 para 106

s 45 am—Loc Audit and Accountability, 2014 c 2, sch 12 para 107

s 46 am—Public Audit (W), 2013 anaw 3, sch 4 para 90

    rep in pt—Loc Audit and Accountability, 2014 c 2, sch 12 para 108

s 50 am—Public Audit (W), 2013 anaw 3, sch 4 para 91(2)-(8)(10); Loc Audit and Accountability, 2014 c 2, sch 12 para 109(3)(5)(b)(6)(8)

    rep in pt—Public Audit (W), 2013 anaw 3, sch 4 para 91(9); Loc Audit and Accountability, 2014 c 2, sch 12 para 109(2)(4)(5)(a)(7)

s 51 am—Loc Audit and Accountability, 2014 c 2, sch 12 para 110

s 52 rep—Loc Audit and Accountability, 2014 c 2, sch 12 para 111

s 53 am—Loc Audit and Accountability, 2014 c 2, sch 12 para 112(2)

    rep in pt—Loc Audit and Accountability, 2014 c 2, sch 12 para 112(3)(4)

s 54 am—Co-operative and Community Benefit Societies, 2014 c 14, sch 4 para 153(2)(4)

    rep in pt—Co-operative and Community Benefit Societies, 2014 c 14, sch 4 para 153(3); Loc Audit and Accountability, 2014 c 2, sch 12 para 113

s 57 am—Localism, 2011 c 20, s 24(7)

s 69 functions made exercisable concurrently—SIs 2014/865, sch 2 para 4; 1012, art 12(1), sch 2 para 4

s 70 mod—SI 2010/490, reg 39

    rep in pt—Localism, 2011 c 20, s 109(1), sch 25 pt 15

    am—Localism, 2011 c 20, sch 8 para 18

ss 71-81 rep—Localism, 2011 c 20, s 109(1)(b), sch 12 pt 15

s 82 rep in pt—Localism, 2011 c 20, s 109(1), sch 25 pt 16

    am—Localism, 2011 c 20, sch 8 para 19

s 83 rep —(prosp) Localism, 2011 c 20, s 109(1)(a), sch 25 pt 16; (prosp) Public Bodies, 2011 c 24, sch 6

s 84 rep—Localism, 2011 c 20, s 109(1)(b), sch 25 pt 15

s 85 rep in pt—Localism, 2011 c 20, s 109(1)(b), sch 25 pt 15

ss 86, 87 rep—Localism, 2011 c 20, sch 25 pt 15

ss 113A-113C added —Localism, 2011 c 20, s 13(1)

s 113B am—Co-operative and Community Benefit Societies, 2014 c 14, sch 4 para 154

s 117 am—Localism, 2011 c 20, s 13(2)

Pt 7 (ss 121-137) rep—Deregulation, 2015 c 20, s 102(1)

s 147 rep in pt—Localism, 2011 c 20, sch 25 pt 15

s 148 rep in pt—Localism, 2011 c 20, sch 25 pt 6; ibid, sch 25 pt 7

sch 1 am—Deregulation, 2015 c 20, s 95(2)-(7)

sch 2 appl—Loc Gov and Public Involvement in Health, 2007 c 28, s 8

sch 5 rep in pt—Localism, 2011 c 20, sch 25 pt 16; ibid, sch 25 pt 32

sch 6 rep in pt—Equality, 2010 c 15 sch 27 Pt 1A (added by SI 2011/1060, sch 3); Localism, 2011 c 20, sch 25 pt 5; Loc Audit and Accountability, 2014 c 2, sch 1 pt 2

c 21   **Health**

Pt 1 (ss 1-14) am—Health and Social Care, 2012 c 7, sch 5 para 174(a)

s 2 am—Health and Social Care, 2012 c 7, sch 5 para 174(b); ibid, 175(2), (3)(c), (4)-(6); ibid, sch 17 para 13; ibid, sch 19 para 12; ibid, sch 13 para 18; Care, 2014 c 23, s 99(3)

    rep in pt—Health and Social Care, 2012 c 7, sch 5 para 175(3)(a), (b); (pt prosp) ibid, sch 14 para 113

s 3 am—Health and Social Care, 2012 c 7, sch 5 para 174(c)

    rep in pt—Health and Social Care, 2012 c 7, sch 5 para 176(2), (3)

s 8 excl —SI 2010/279, regs 2, 3

    am—Health and Social Care, 2012 c 7, sch 5 para 177(2), (4), (5)

2009

c 21 s 8   *continued*

        rep in pt—Health and Social Care, 2012 c 7, sch 5 para 177(3); (pt prosp) ibid, sch 14
            para 114

        s 9 am—Health and Social Care, 2012 c 7, sch 5 para 178

        s 15 rep—Health and Social Care, 2012 c 7, s 173(5)

        s 18 rep in pt—Health and Social Care, 2012 c 7, s 173(2)(c)

        s 29 rep in pt—Health and Social Care, 2012 c 7, sch 4 para 76(2); ibid, sch 4 para 93(5)

        s 33 rep—Health and Social Care, 2012 c 7, s 165(3)

        s 36 am—Health and Social Care, 2012 c 7, sch 5 para 179

        sch 1 rep in pt—Protection of Freedoms, 2012 c 9, sch 10 pt 5

        sch 3 rep in pt—Health and Social Care, 2012 c 7, s 283(2); ibid, sch 13 para 9(2); ibid, sch
            20 para 3(b); ibid, sch 20 para 7(d)

c 22   **Apprenticeships, Skills, Children and Learning**

        savings—SI 2010/303, arts 8-12

        am—SI 2010/1158, art 5, sch 2

        mod—SIs 2011/908, art 14; 1012, art 16

        Pt 1 Ch. A1 (ss A1-A7) added—Deregulation, 2015 c 20, sch 1 para 1

        Pt 1 Ch. 1 (ss 1-39) am—Deregulation, 2015 c 20, sch 1 para 6

        s 1 rep—Deregulation, 2015 c 20, sch 1 para 7

        ss 3-6 rep—Deregulation, 2015 c 20, sch 1 para 8

        s 5 am—Educ, 2011 c 21, s 71(2)

        s 6 subst—Educ, 2011 c 21, s 71(3)

        s 11 am—Deregulation, 2015 c 20, sch 1 para 9(a)

          rep in pt—Deregulation, 2015 c 20, sch 1 para 9(b)(c)

        s 12 rep in pt—Deregulation, 2015 c 20, sch 1 para 10

        ss 13-17 rep—Deregulation, 2015 c 20, sch 1 para 11

        s 18 am —Deregulation, 2015 c 20, sch 1 para 25

        s 19 am —Deregulation, 2015 c 20, sch 1 para 26(a)

          rep in pt—Deregulation, 2015 c 20, sch 1 para 26(b)

        s 20 am—Deregulation, 2015 c 20, sch 1 para 27

        ss 23-27 rep—Deregulation, 2015 c 20, sch 1 para 12

        s 32 rep in pt —Deregulation, 2015 c 20, sch 1 paras 13, 14

        s 36 rep in pt—Educ, 2011 c 21, sch 18 para 3

        s 38 am —Deregulation, 2015 c 20, sch 1 para 15

        s 39 rep in pt—Deregulation, 2015 c 20, sch 1 para 16

        s 39 am—Educ, 2011 c 21, s 71(4)

        s 45 am—Educ, 2011 c 21, s 30(1)

        s 48 rep in pt—Educ, 2011 c 21, s 30(7)(a)

          am—Educ, 2011 c 21, s 30(7)(b)

        s 50 am—SI 2010/1158, art 5, sch 2

          rep in pt—SI 2010/1158, art 5, sch 3

        s 51 am—SI 2010/1158, art 5, sch 2

        ss 60-80 rep —Educ, 2011 c 21, s 66

        Pt 4 (ss 81-121) am—Deregulation, 2015 c 20, sch 14 para 31(a)

        Pt 4 Ch. 1 (ss 81-99) am—Deregulation, 2015 c 20, sch 14 para 31(b)

        s 81 rep—Deregulation, 2015 c 20, sch 14 para 2

        s 82 rep —Deregulation, 2015 c 20, sch 14 para 3

        s 83 am—Educ, 2011 c 21, sch 18 para 5; Children and Families, 2014 c 6, sch 3 para
            89(a)(b); Deregulation, 2015 c 20, sch 1 para 17; ibid, sch 14 para 4

          rep in pt—Children and Families, 2014 c 6, sch 3 para 89(c)

        ss 83A, 83B added —Educ, 2011 c 21, s 69(2)

        s 83A am—Deregulation, 2015 c 20, sch 1 para 18(a); ibid, sch 14 para 5(2)

          rep in pt —Deregulation, 2015 c 20, sch 1 para 18(b); ibid, sch 14 para 5(3)

        s 83B am—Deregulation, 2015 c 20, sch 1 para 19(2)(3); ibid, sch 14 para 6

          rep in pt—Deregulation, 2015 c 20, sch 1 para 19(4)

        s 84 rep—Deregulation, 2015 c 20, sch 14 para 7

        s 85 rep—Deregulation, 2015 c 20, sch 14 para 8

        s 86 am—Educ, 2011 c 21, s 30(8)(b); ibid, sch 18 para 7; Children and Families, 2014 c 6,
            sch 3 para 90; Deregulation, 2015 c 20, sch 14 para 9(2)

          rep in pt—Educ, 2011 c 21, s 30(8)(a); Deregulation, 2015 c 20, sch 14 para 9(3)

        s 87 am—Children and Families, 2014 c 6, sch 3 para 91; Deregulation, 2015 c 20, sch 14
            para 10(2)(3)

          rep in pt—Deregulation, 2015 c 20, sch 14 para 10(4)

        s 88 am—Educ, 2011 c 21, s 73(2); Deregulation, 2015 c 20, sch 14 para 11

2009

c 22 *continued*

s 90 am—Deregulation, 2015 c 20, sch 1 para 20; ibid, sch 14 para 12

ss 91-99 rep —Educ, 2011 c 21, sch 18 para 8

Pt 4 Ch. 2 (ss 100-111) am—Deregulation, 2015 c 20, sch 14 para 31(c)

s 100 rep in pt—Educ, 2011 c 21, sch 18 para 9; Deregulation, 2015 c 20, sch 14 para 13(2)(c),(3)

    am—Deregulation, 2015 c 20, sch 1 para 2; ibid, sch 14 para 13(2)(a)(b),(4)(5)

s 101 am—Children and Families, 2014 c 6, sch 3 para 92(a); Deregulation, 2015 c 20, sch 1 para 3(2)(a); ibid, sch 14 para 14

    rep in pt—Children and Families, 2014 c 6, sch 3 para 92(b); Deregulation, 2015 c 20, sch 1 para 3(2)(b)(3)

s 102 am—Deregulation, 2015 c 20, sch 14 para 15

s 103 am—Deregulation, 2015 c 20, sch 1 para 4; ibid, sch 14 para 16(2)

    rep in pt—Deregulation, 2015 c 20, sch 14 para 16(3)

s 104 rep —Educ, 2011 c 21, sch 18 para 10

s 105 rep—Deregulation, 2015 c 20, sch 1 para 21

s 106 rep—Deregulation, 2015 c 20, sch 14 para 18

s 107 rep in pt—Educ, 2011 c 21, sch 16 para 47; Deregulation, 2015 c 20, sch 14 para 19(3)(4)

    am—Deregulation, 2015 c 20, sch 14 para 19(2),(5)

ss 108, 109 rep —Deregulation, 2015 c 20, sch 14 para 20

s 110 rep—Deregulation, 2015 c 20, sch 14 para 21

s 111 rep—Deregulation, 2015 c 20, sch 14 para 22

ss 112-114 rep —Educ, 2011 c 21, s 73(3)

s 115 am—Children and Families, 2014 c 6, sch 3 para 93(a)(b)(d); Deregulation, 2015 c 20, sch 14 para 23

    rep in pt—Children and Families, 2014 c 6, sch 3 para 93(c)

s 116 am—Deregulation, 2015 c 20, sch 14 para 24

s 117-120 rep—Deregulation, 2015 c 20, sch 14 para 25

s 120A added—Deregulation, 2015 c 20, sch 14 para 26

s 121 am—Educ, 2011 c 21, sch 18 para 12; Deregulation, 2015 c 20, sch 1 para 22(b); ibid, sch 14 para 27(3)

    rep in pt —Deregulation, 2015 c 20, sch 1 para 22(a); ibid, sch 14 para 27(2)

s 122 am—SI 2010/1158, art 5, sch 2; Educ, 2011 c 21, sch 16 para 48; Deregulation, 2015 c 20, sch 14 para 28(b)

    rep in pt—Deregulation, 2015 c 20, sch 14 para 28(a),(c)(d)

s 128 am—Educ, 2011 c 21, s 22

s 129 rep in pt—Educ, 2011 c 21, sch 8 para 23; Children and Families, 2014 c 6, sch 3 para 94(b)

    am—Children and Families, 2014 c 6, sch 3 para 94(a)

s 132 am—Qualifications Wales, 2015 anaw 5, s 35(2)

s 151 am—Educ, 2011 c 21, s 23(2)

ss 151A-151D added —Educ, 2011 c 21, s 23(3)

s 152 am—Educ, 2011 c 21, s 23(4)

ss 152A-152C added —Educ, 2011 c 21, s 23(5)

s 153 am—Educ, 2011 c 21, s 23(6)

s 173 rep —Educ, 2011 c 21, sch 8 para 24

ss 175-191 rep —Educ, 2011 c 21, s 25

s 194 am —SI 2010/1158, art 5, schs 2, 4

    rep in pt —SI 2010/1158, art 5, schs 2-4

ss 196, 197 am—SI 2010/1158, art 5, sch 2

s 205 rep (W) —School Standards and Organisation (W), 2013 anaw 1, sch 5 para 12

ss 206-224 rep —Educ, 2011 c 21, s 45(1)

ss 227-241 rep —Educ, 2011 c 21, s 18(1)

s 246 am—SI 2010/1158, art 5, sch 2

    rep in pt—SI 2010/1158, art 5, sch 3

s 247 rep in pt—SI 2010/1158, art 5, schs 2, 3

s 248 rep—Educ, 2011 c 21, s 6

s 249 am—Educ, 2011 c 21, s 51(2)(b)(3)

    rep in pt—Educ, 2011 c 21, s 51(2)(a)

s 250 rep —Educ, 2011 c 21, s 29(9)(d)

s 252 rep in pt—SI 2010/1158, art 5, schs 2, 3

    am—SI 2010/1158, art 5, sch 2

s 253A added—Small Business, Enterprise and Employment, 2015 c 26, s 79(1)

2009

c 22 s 253A *continued*

　　　　am—Qualifications Wales, 2015 anaw 5, sch 4 para 9(2)

　　s 255 rep in pt—Educ, 2011 c 21, s 28(6)

　　s 256 rep in pt—Educ, 2011 c 21, sch 12 para 46(2)

　　s 262 am—Educ, 2011 c 21, s 23(7); ibid, sch 18 para 13(2)(4)(a); Small Business,
　　　　　　Enterprise and Employment, 2015 c 26, s 79(2)

　　　　rep in pt—Educ, 2011 c 21, s 45(2)(f); ibid, sch 18 para 13(3)(4)(b)

　　s 267 am—Deregulation, 2015 c 20, sch 1 para 23

　　s 269 rep in pt—Educ, 2011 c 21, sch 18 para 14

　　sch 3 rep —Educ, 2011 c 21, s 66

　　sch 4 rep—Deregulation, 2015 c 20, sch 14 para 29

　　sch 5 rep in pt—Educ, 2011 c 21, sch 8 para 25; Deregulation, 2015 c 20, sch 14 para 30(b)

　　　　am—Deregulation, 2015 c 20, sch 14 para 30(a)

　　sch 6 rep in pt—Equality, 2010 c 15, sch 27 Pt 1A (added by SI 2011/1060, sch 3); Educ,
　　　　　　2011 c 21, sch 12 para 46(3); Further and Higher Educ (Governance and
　　　　　　Information) (W), 2014 anaw 1, sch 2 para 5; Qualifications Wales, 2015 anaw
　　　　　　5, sch 4 para 9(3)

　　sch 8 rep in pt—Educ, 2011 c 21, sch 12 para 46(4)

　　sch 9 am—Educ, 2011 c 21, sch 7 paras 2(2)(a)(b)(3)(4), 3-8

　　　　rep in pt—Educ, 2011 c 21, sch 7 paras 2(2)(c), 9

　　sch 10 rep—Educ, 2011 c 21, sch 8 para 24

　　sch 11 rep —Educ, 2011 c 21, s 25

　　sch 12 rep in pt—Equality, 2010 c 15, sch 27 Pt 1A (added by SI 2011/1060, sch 3); Educ,
　　　　　　2011 c 21, sch 8 para 26; ibid, sch 16 para 50; Charities, 2011 c 25, sch 10;
　　　　　　Protection of Freedoms, 2012 c 9, sch 10 pt 5; Qualifications Wales, 2015
　　　　　　anaw 5, sch 4 para 9(4)

　　sch 14 rep (W) —School Standards and Organisation (W), 2013 anaw 1, sch 5 para 12

　　sch 15 rep—Educ, 2011 c 21, s 18(1)

　　sch 16 rep in pt—Educ, 2011 c 21, s 45(2)(g)

c 23　　**Marine and Coastal Access**

　　appl in pt—SI 2014/3102, art 4(12)

　　s 12 rep in pt—SI 2010/490, reg 132, sch 6

　　s 16 am—(W) SI 2013/755 (W 90), sch 2 para 442

　　Pt 4 (ss 65-100) excl—SIs 2015/318, art 8(6)(10); 1592, art 8(7)

　　Pt 4, Ch 1 (ss 65-73) mod—SIs 2013/1873, art 27; 2014/1873, art 11, sch 13 pt 2, sch 14 pt
　　　　　　2

　　s 68 excl—Planning, 2008 c 29, s 149A(5)

　　s 69 excl—Planning, 2008 c 29, s 149A(5)

　　　　am—SI 2011/1210, sch 1 para 101

　　s 72 appl—SI 2013/343, sch 2 para 2(5); 2014/2950, sch 10 para 3(6)

　　　　appl (mods)—SIs 2014/1599, sch 10 pt 1 para 5, sch 11 pt 1 para 5; 1873, sch 13 pt 1
　　　　　　para 5, sch 14 pt 1 para 5; 2594, sch 2 pt 1 para 5, sch 3 pt 1 para 5; 3331, sch
　　　　　　8 pt 1 para 2(5), sch 9 pt 1 para 2(5), sch 10 pt 1 para 2(6), sch 11 pt 1 para
　　　　　　2(8); 2015/1561, sch 7 para 5

　　s 73 am—SI 2015/374, art 9(2)

　　ss 73A, 73B added —SI 2015/374, art 9(3)

　　s 75 am—SI 2011/405, reg 2

　　s 85 am—SI 2015/664, sch 4 para 43(2)

　　s 92 am—SI 2015/664, sch 4 para 43(3)

　　s 93 am—SI 2015/664, sch 5 para 15

　　s 103 am—SI 2015/664, sch 4 para 43(4)

　　s 105 am—SI 2015/664, sch 4 para 43(5)

　　Pt 5, Ch 1 (ss 116-147) appl—SI 1994/2716 reg 36(3)(4) (subst by 2009 c 23, sch 11 para
　　　　　　4(1))

　　　　appl (mods)—SI 2010/490, reg 38

　　s 123 am—SI 2010/490, reg 132, sch 6

　　　　mod—SI 2007/1842, reg 6(6) (added by SI 2012/1928, reg 3(b)); SI 2010/490, reg
　　　　　　9A(6) (substituted by SI 2012/1927, reg 8)

　　s 124 mod—SI 2007/1842, reg 6(6) (added by SI 2012/1928, reg 3(b)); SI 2010/490, reg
　　　　　　9A(6) (substituted by SI 2012/1927, reg 8)

　　s 140 am—SI 2015/664, sch 4 para 43(6)

　　s 147 am—(W) SI 2013/755 (W 90), sch 2 para 443

　　s 149 am—(W) SI 2013/755 (W 90), sch 2 para 444

　　s 152 am—(W) SI 2013/755 (W 90), sch 2 para 445

2009

c 23 *continued*

s 158 am—SI 2010/490, reg 132, sch 6
s 163 am—SI 2015/664, sch 4 para 43(7)
s 168 am—(W) SI 2013/755 (W 90), sch 2 para 446
s 190 am—SI 2015/664, sch 4 para 43(8)
ss 194-195 ext to S —Marine (S), 2010 asp 5, s 158(1)
ss 197-199 ext to S—Marine (S), 2010 asp 5, s 158(1)
s 199 rep in pt—SI 2015/664, sch 4 para 102(2)
ss 200, 201 ext to S—Marine (S), 2010 asp 5, s 158(1)
s 203 ext to S —Marine (S), 2010 asp 5, s 160(2)
s 204 ext to S —Marine (S), 2010 asp 5, s 161(1)(a)
s 205 rep—SI 2015/664, sch 4 para 102(3)
s 206 ext to S —Marine (S), 2010 asp 5, s 161(1)(b)
s 207 ext to S —Marine (S), 2010 asp 5, s 161(1)(c)
s 209 ext to S —Marine (S), 2010 asp 5, s 161(1)(d)
s 210 ext to S —Marine (S), 2010 asp 5, s 161(1)(e)
s 211 ext to S —Marine (S), 2010 asp 5, s 161(1)(f)
s 214 ext to S —Marine (S), 2010 asp 5, s 161(1)(g)(4)
s 220 rep in pt—SI 2015/664, sch 4 para 102(4)
s 232 am—(W) SI 2013/755 (W 90), sch 2 para 447; SI 2015/664, sch 4 para 93
s 235 appl—SI 2015/1711, reg 14(1)
s 237 am—SI 2010/490, reg 132, sch 6
    rep in pt—SI 2010/490, reg 132, sch 6
s 238 am—(W) SI 2013/755 (W 90), sch 2 para 448
    appl—SI 2015/1711, reg 14(1)
s 292 appl in pt—SI 2015/1711, reg 14(2)
    rep in pt—SI 2015/664, sch 4 para 43(9)(c)
    am—SI 2015/664, sch 4 para 43(9)(a)(b)
s 313 rep—(W) SI 2013/755 (W 90), sch 2 para 449
sch 1 am—Marine and Coastal Access, 2009 c 23, s 253(7)
sch 2 rep in pt—Equality, 2010 c 15, sch 27 Pt 1A (added by SI 2011/1060, sch 3)
sch 6 rep in pt—(prosp) Localism, 2011 c 20, sch 8 para 20(a), sch 25 pt 16; (prosp)
            Planning (W), 2015 anaw 4, sch 2 para 35(3)(4)
    am—(prosp) Planning (W), 2015 anaw 4, sch 2 paras 34, 35(2), 36
sch 7 am—SI 2013/602, sch 2 para 62(2)
sch 9 excl—SI 2011/556, art 4
    mod—SI 2012/698, art 2
sch 10 am—SI 2013/602, sch 2 para 62(3)
sch 11 rep in pt—SI 2010/490, reg 132, sch 6
sch 14 rep in pt—Energy, 2013 c 32, sch 12 para 30
sch 15 ext to S —Marine (S), 2010 asp 5, s 158
sch 17 appl—SI 2010/2870, art 10
sch 22 ext to S —Marine (S), 2010 asp 5, ss 158(1), 161(1)(h)

c 24   **Welfare Reform**

s 1 rep in pt—Welfare Reform, 2012 c 5, sch 14 pt 3; (pt prosp) ibid, sch 14 pt 4
s 2 rep (prosp)—Welfare Reform, 2012 c 5, sch 14 pt 1
s 3 am—Welfare Reform, 2012 c 5, s 58(2)
    rep in pt—(prosp) Welfare Reform, 2009 c 24, s 58, sch 7 pt 1; (pt prosp) Welfare
            Reform, 2012 c 5, sch 14 pts 1, 5
s 4 rep (prosp)—Welfare Reform, 2012 c 5, sch 14 pt 1
    rep in pt—Welfare Reform, 2012 c 5, sch 14 pt 2
s 5 rep (prosp)—Welfare Reform, 2012 c 5, sch 14 pt 1
    rep in pt—(prosp) Welfare Reform, 2009 c 24, s 58, sch 7 pt 1
s 8 rep (pt prosp)—Welfare Reform, 2012 c 5, sch 14 pt 5
    rep in pt —(prosp) Welfare Reform, 2012 c 5, sch 14 pt 1; ibid, sch 14 pt 2
    am—(prosp) Welfare Reform, 2012 c 5, s 58(3)
s 9 rep (prosp)—Welfare Reform, 2012 c 5, sch 14 pt 1
s 10 rep (pt prosp)—Welfare Reform, 2012 c 5, sch 14 pt 5
s 11 rep—Welfare Reform, 2012 c 5, s 60(3)
s 14 rep (prosp)—Welfare Reform, 2012 c 5, sch 14 pt 9
ss 16-21 rep —Welfare Reform, 2012 c 5, s 73
s 22 rep —Welfare Reform, 2012 c 5, s 101(2)
s 25 rep—Welfare Reform, 2012 c 5, sch 14 pt 3
s 29 rep (pt prosp)—Welfare Reform, 2012 c 5, sch 14 pt 4

2009

c 24 s 29 *continued*

         am—(prosp) Welfare Reform, 2012 c 5, sch 7 para 14

    s 31 am—(prosp) Welfare Reform, 2012 c 5, s 54(7); (prosp) ibid, sch 7 para 15(2)

    s 32 am—(prosp) Welfare Reform, 2012 c 5, sch 7 para 16(2)(a), (b), (3)

         rep in pt—(pt prosp) Welfare Reform, 2012 c 5, sch 14 pt 4; ibid, sch 7 para 16(2)(c);

           ibid, sch 14 pts 2, 3, 6

    s 33 rep—Welfare Reform, 2012 c 5, sch 14 pt 3

    s 34 rep in pt—(prosp) Welfare Reform, 2012 c 5, sch 14 pt 1

    s 35 rep (pt prosp)—Welfare Reform, 2012 c 5, sch 14 pt 1

    s 36 rep (pt prosp)—Welfare Reform, 2012 c 5, sch 14 pt 1

    s 37 rep in pt—(prosp) Welfare Reform, 2012 c 5, sch 14 pt 1

    s 50 am—SI 2015/914, sch para 94; SSI 2015/157, sch para 9

    s 51 am—SI 2012/2007, sch para 99

    sch 1 rep—Welfare Reform, 2012 c 5, sch 14 pt 2

    sch 2 rep (prosp)—Welfare Reform, 2012 c 5, sch 14 pt 1

    sch 3 rep—Welfare Reform, 2012 c 5, s 60(3)

    sch 4 rep in pt—(prosp) Welfare Reform, 2009 c 24, s 58, sch 7 pt 1; (prosp) Welfare

           Reform, 2012 c 5, sch 14 pt 1

    sch 5 am—SI 2012/2007, sch para 100

    sch 6 am—SI 2014/560, sch 1 para 34

    sch 7 rep in pt—(prosp) Welfare Reform, 2012 c 5, sch 14 pt 1; ibid, sch 14 pts 2, 3, 6

c 25   **Coroners and Justice**

    s 8 am—Crime and Cts, 2013 c 22, sch 9 para 73

    ss 9A, 9B added—Crim Justice and Cts, 2015 c 2, sch 13 para 1

    s 19 am—Health and Social Care, 2012 c 7, s 54(2)

    s 20 am—Health and Social Care, 2012 c 7, s 54(3)

    s 24 am—Police Reform and Social Responsibility, 2011 c 13, sch 16 para 372

    s 36 rep in pt—Public Bodies, 2011 c 24, s 33(2)

    s 39 rep—SI 2012/2401, sch 1 para 34

    s 40 rep —Public Bodies, 2011 c 24, s 33(1)

    s 42 rep in pt—Public Bodies, 2011 c 24, s 33(2)

    s 45 rep in pt—Public Bodies, 2011 c 24, s 33(2)

    s 51 rep —Legal Aid, Sentencing and Punishment of Offenders, 2012 c 10, sch 5 pt 2

    s 54A am—Crim Justice and Cts, 2015 c 2, sch 13 para 2(2)

    s 55 am—Crim Justice and Cts, 2015 c 2, sch 13 para 2(3)

    s 71 rep (EW)—Modern Slavery, 2015 c 30, sch 5 para 8

    s 74 am—SI 2010/976, art 12, sch 14

    s 75 am—SI 2010/976, art 12, sch 14; Crime and Cts, 2013 c 22, sch 8 para 186

    s 77 am—SI 2010/976, art 12, sch 14; Crime and Cts, 2013 c 22, sch 8 para 188

         rep in pt—SI 2014/834, sch 2 para 71

    s 78 am—SI 2010/976, art 12, sch 14

    s 80 rep in pt—SI 2014/834, sch 2 para 72

    s 81 am—Crime and Cts, 2013 c 22, sch 8 para 187

         rep in pt—SI 2014/834, sch 2 para 73

    s 116 am—SI 2010/976, art 12, sch 14

    s 125 am—Legal Aid, Sentencing and Punishment of Offenders, 2012 c 10, sch 19 para 23;

         ibid, sch 26 para 31(2), (3); Crim Justice and Cts, 2015 c 2, sch 5 para 17(2)(3)

    s 126 am—Legal Aid, Sentencing and Punishment of Offenders, 2012 c 10, sch 21 para

         34(2)(b), (c), (3)(b), (c), (4)

         rep in pt—Legal Aid, Sentencing and Punishment of Offenders, 2012 c 10, sch 21 para

           34(2)(a), (3)(a)

    s 131 am—(prosp) Crim Justice and Cts, 2015 c 2, sch 3 para 16

    s 142 rep in pt—SI 2013/2853, art 2(2)(d)

    s 145 rep—Legal Aid, Sentencing and Punishment of Offenders, 2012 c 10, sch 16 para

         21(a)

    ss 149-153 rep —Legal Aid, Sentencing and Punishment of Offenders, 2012 c 10, sch 5 pt 2

    s 156 rep in pt —(S) Crim Justice and Licensing (S), 2010 asp 13, s 203, sch 7 para

         87(a)(i)(b)(i)

         am—(S) Crim Justice and Licensing (S), 2010 asp 13, s 203, sch 7 para

         87(a)(ii)(b)(ii)

    s 161 am—SI 2010/976, art 12, sch 14

    s 162 am—Crime and Cts, 2013 c 22, sch 8 para 186

    s 166 am—SI 2010/976, art 12, sch 14; Crime and Cts, 2013 c 22, sch 8 para 186

    s 170 rep in pt—Crime and Cts, 2013 c 22, sch 8 para 189

2009

c 25 *continued*

ss 176, 177 am—SI 2010/976, art 12, sch 14

s 182 am—SI 2010/976, art 12, sch 14

sch 1 rep in pt—Crim Justice and Cts, 2015 c 2, sch 6 para 12(2)

am—Domestic Violence, Crime and Victims (Amendment), 2012 c 4, sch para 12; Crim Justice and Cts, 2015 c 2, sch 6 para 12(3)

sch 2 am—SI 2010/976, art 12, sch 14

sch 6 am—Crim Justice and Cts, 2015 c 2, sch 13 paras 4-7

sch 10 rep in pt—Public Bodies, 2011 c 24, s 33(2)

sch 12 am—SI 2012/1809, art 3(1) sch pt 1

sch 13 am—SI 2012/1809, art 3(1) sch pt 1

sch 16 am—SI 2010/976, art 12, sch 14

sch 17 rep in pt—Armed Forces, 2011 c 18, sch 5; Legal Aid, Sentencing and Punishment of Offenders, 2012 c 10, s 79(3)

sch 18 rep —Legal Aid, Sentencing and Punishment of Offenders, 2012 c 10, sch 5 pt 2

sch 21 rep in pt—Legal Aid, Sentencing and Punishment of Offenders, 2012 c 10, s 64(5)(d); SI 2012/2401, sch 1 para 35; Anti-social Behaviour, Crime and Policing, 2014 c 12, sch 11 para 50; Crim Justice and Cts, 2015 c 2, sch 7 para 22

am—(pt prosp) Crime and Cts, 2013 c 22, sch 13 para 49(6)(a)(b)

sch 22 rep in pt—Legal Aid, Sentencing and Punishment of Offenders, 2012 c 10, sch 16 para 21(b)

sch 23 rep in pt—(prosp) Armed Forces, 2011 c 18, sch 5

c 26 **Policing and Crime**

s 2 rep in pt—Equality, 2010 c 15, sch 27 Pt 1A (added SI 2011/1060, sch 3); Police Reform and Social Responsibility, 2011 c 13, sch 16 para 378

s 12 rep in pt—(prosp) Anti-social Behaviour, Crime and Policing, 2014 c 12, sch 11 para 102

s 18 rep in pt—Legal Aid, Sentencing and Punishment of Offenders, 2012 c 10, sch 25 pt 2

s 31 rep—Anti-social Behaviour, Crime and Policing, 2014 c 12, sch 11 para 50

s 33 rep in pt—Police Reform and Social Responsibility, 2011 c 13, ss 105(10), 107(8)

Pt 4 (ss 34-50) am—Serious Crime, 2015 c 9, sch 4 para 83

s 34 subst—Serious Crime, 2015 c 9, s 51

s 35 am—Serious Crime, 2015 c 9, sch 4 para 84

s 36 am —Crime and Security, 2010 c 17, s 35(2)

s 38 am —Crime and Security, 2010 c 17, s 36

s 42 am —Crime and Security, 2010 c 17, s 37; ibid, s 35(3)

s 43 am—Crime and Cts, 2013 c 22, s 18(3)

s 46A added—Crime and Security, 2010 c 17, by s 39(2)

s 46B added —Crime and Cts, 2013 c 22, sch 12 para 2

s 48 am—Crime and Cts, 2013 c 22, s 18(4); ibid, sch 12 para 3(b)

rep in pt—Crime and Cts, 2013 c 22, sch 9 para 51(2); ibid, sch 12 para 3(a)

s 49 am—Crime and Cts, 2013 c 22, s 18(2); ibid, sch 12 para 4; Serious Crime, 2015 c 9, sch 4 para 85

s 57 am—SI 2012/2595, art 18

s 71 rep in pt—Legal Aid, Sentencing and Punishment of Offenders, 2012 c 10, sch 10 para 43

s 81 rep in pt—Protection of Freedoms, 2012 c 9, sch 10 pt 5

ss 82-87 rep—Protection of Freedoms, 2012 c 9, sch 10 pt 5

ss 89, 90 rep—Protection of Freedoms, 2012 c 9, sch 10 pt 5

ss 92 rep—Protection of Freedoms, 2012 c 9, sch 10 pt 5

s 93 rep—Protection of Freedoms, 2012 c 9, s 79(1) sch 10 pt 6

s 101 am—Identity Documents, 2010 c 40, s 12, sch 1 para 20

s 113A added—SI 2010/976, art 12, sch 14

sch 2 am—SI 2010/976, art 12, sch 14

sch 5 am —Crime and Security, 2010 c 17, s 38; Crime and Cts, 2013 c 22, sch 9 para 51(3)(a); ibid, sch 12 para 5

rep in pt—Crime and Cts, 2013 c 22, sch 9 para 51(3)(b)

sch 5A added—Crime and Security, 2010 c 17, s 39(3)

am—Legal Aid, Sentencing and Punishment of Offenders, 2012 c 10, sch 12 para 58; Crime and Cts, 2013 c 22, sch 12 paras 7(2), 8-13, 14(a), 15; Crim Justice and Cts, 2015 c 2, sch 9 para 27

rep in pt—Crime and Cts, 2013 c 22, sch 12 para 7(3)(4)(14)(b)(c)

sch 7 rep in pt—Legal Aid, Sentencing and Punishment of Offenders, 2012 c 10, sch 5 pt 2; Finance, 2013 c 29, sch 48 para 24

2009

c 26 *continued*

sch 8 rep in pt—Protection of Freedoms, 2012 c 9, sch 10 pt 5

sch 9 am—SI 2012/1534, art 3

5th session of the 54th Parliament

c 27　　**Consolidated Fund**

2010

c 1　　**Video Recordings**

c 2　　*Terrorist Asset-Freezing (Temporary Provisions)*—rep Terrorist Asset-Freezing etc, 2010 c 38, ss 45, 46(2), 52, sch 2

c 3　　*Fiscal Responsibility*—rep Budget Responsibility and Nat Audit, 2011 c 4, s 10(c)

c 4　　**Corporation Tax**

appl—Taxation (International and Other Provns), 2010 c 8, s 220(2); Land and Buildings Transaction Tax (S), 2013 asp 11, sch 7 para 20

appl (mods)—SI 2011/245, sch 6 pt 1

excl—Corporation Tax, 2010 c 4, s 639(4); Taxation (International and Other Provns), 2010 c 8, ss 79(2)(a), 174(2)(b)

saved —Income Tax, 2007 c 3, s 564V(4)

am—Co-operative and Community Benefit Societies, 2014 c 14, sch 4 para 156

s 1 am—Finance, 2010 c 13, s 46, sch 16 para 2; Finance, 2011 c 11, sch 3 para 20; ibid, sch 5 para 1; Finance, 2013 c 29, sch 14 para 2(1), sch 20 para 2; ibid, sch 29 para 42(b); Finance, 2014 c 26, sch 1 para 2(a), sch 16 para 2; Finance, 2015 c 11, sch 2 para 4(a)(b); ibid, sch 3 para 2; Finance (No. 2), 2015 c 33, s 38(2); (prosp) Corporation Tax (NI), 2015 c 21, sch 2 para 5

rep in pt—Finance, 2010 c 13, s 46, sch 16 para 2; Finance, 2013 c 29, sch 29 para 42(a); SI 2013/2819, reg 39(2); Finance, 2014 c 26, sch 1 para 2(b)

s 3 subst—Finance, 2014 c 26, sch 1 para 3

s 5 am—Finance, 2013 c 29, s 66(2)

s 6 am—Finance, 2011 c 11, sch 7 para 1

appl (mods)—Taxation (International and Other Provns), 2010 c 8, s 371SI(2)

s 7 am—Finance, 2011 c 11, sch 7 para 2

appl (mods)—Taxation (International and Other Provns), 2010 c 8, s 371SI(3))

ss 9A, 9B added—Finance, 2011 c 11, sch 7 para 3

s 9A am—Finance (No. 2), 2015 c 33, s 34(3)(5)

rep in pt—Finance (No. 2), 2015 c 33, s 34(4)

s 9B am—Finance (No. 2), 2015 c 33, s 34(7),(9)-(12)

s 9C added—Finance, 2013 c 29, s 66(3)

s 17 appl —Corporation Tax, 2010 c 4, s 937M

am—Finance, 2011 c 11, sch 7 para 4; Finance, 2012 c 14, sch 16 para 216(a); Finance (No. 2), 2015 c 33, s 34(13)

rep in pt—Finance, 2012 c 14, sch 16 para 216(b)

Pt 3 (ss 18-34) rep—Finance, 2014 c 26, sch 1 para 4

s 37 appl (mods)—Finance, 2009 c 10, sch 6 para 3(1)

appl—Finance, 2012 c 14, s 123

s 38 appl (mods)—Finance, 2009 c 10, sch 6 para 3(1)

s 40 am—Finance, 2012 c 14, sch 21 para 5; Finance, 2013 c 29, s 92(8)

s 43 am—Finance, 2013 c 29, s 92(9)

s 45 appl—Finance, 2014 c 26, sch 16 para 9(1)

s 47 am—Corporation Tax, 2010 c 4, s 1177, sch 1 paras 206, 208

heading subst—Co-operative and Community Benefit Societies, 2014 c 14, sch 4 para 157

s 54 am—Finance, 2012 c 14, sch 16 para 217

Pt 4 Ch 4 (ss 62-67) excl—Finance, 2012 c 14, s 87

s 63 rep in pt—Finance, 2012 c 14, sch 22 para 20

s 65 am—Finance, 2011 c 11, sch 14 para 8(2)

s 67A added—Finance, 2011 c 11, sch 14 para 8(3)

appl—Capital Allowances, 2001 c 2, s 250A(2)

s 67B added—Finance, 2012 c 14, sch 16 para 218

s 90 am—Co-operative and Community Benefit Societies, 2014 c 14, sch 4 para 158

Pt 5 (ss 97-188) appl—Finance, 2012 c 14, s 125

appl (mods)—Land and Buildings Transaction Tax (S), 2013 asp 11, sch 10 paras 47, 48; ibid, sch 11 paras 40, 41

s 105 am—Finance, 2013 c 29, s 29

s 107 am—Finance, 2013 c 29, s 30

2010
c 4 *continued*

s 129 am—Finance (No 3), 2010 c 33, s 12, sch 6 para 2; Finance (No. 2), 2015 c 33, s
      35(2)(a)
s 130 am—Finance (No 3), 2010 c 33, s 12, sch 6 para 3; Finance (No. 2), 2015 c 33, s
      35(2)(b)
s 133 rep in pt—Finance (No 3), 2010 c 33, s 12, sch 6 para 4(2)(a)(3)(a); Finance (No. 2),
      2015 c 33, s 35(1)(a)(ii)(b)(ii)(c)
      am—Finance (No 3), 2010 c 33, s 12, sch 6 para 4(2)(b)(3)(b)(4); Finance (No. 2),
      2015 c 33, s 35(1)(a)(i)(b)(i)
s 134A added—Finance (No 3), 2010 c 33, s 12, sch 6 para 5
      rep—Finance (No. 2), 2015 c 33, s 35(2)(c)
s 143 rep in pt—Finance (No 3), 2010 c 33, s 12, sch 6 para 7(2)(a)
      am—Finance (No 3), 2010 c 33, s 12, sch 6 para 7(2)(b)(3)
s 144 rep in pt—Finance (No 3), 2010 c 33, s 12, sch 6 para 8(2)(a)
      am—Finance (No 3), 2010 c 33, s 12, sch 6 para 8(2)(b)(3); SI 2013/463, art 10
s 146 rep in pt—Finance (No 3), 2010 c 33, s 12, sch 6 para 6(2)(a)(4)(a)
      am—Finance (No 3), 2010 c 33, s 12, sch 6 para 6(2)(b)(3)(4)(b)
ss 146A, 146B added—Finance (No 3), 2010 c 33, s 12, sch 6 para 9
s 148 am—SI 2013/463, art 11
s 149 am—SI 2013/463, art 12
s 151 am—Co-operative and Community Benefit Societies, 2014 c 14, sch 4 para 159
s 154 am—SI 2012/266, art 13(2); Finance, 2013 c 29, s 31(2)
s 155 am—SI 2012/266, art 13(3); Finance, 2013 c 29, s 31(2)
ss 155A, 155B added—SI 2012/266, art 13(1)
s 156 am—SI 2012/266, art 13(4); Finance, 2013 c 29, s 31(1)
Pt 5, Ch 6 (ss 157-182) appl—Taxation of Chargeable Gains, 1992 c. 12, s 236T(2);
      Capital Allowances, 2001 c 2, ss 212G(5), 212H(2); Income Tax, 2007 c. 3, s
      257MV(8); Taxation (International and Other Provns), 2010 c 8, s 345(7)-(10);
      Finance, 2015 c 11, sch 16 para 7(5)
      appl (mods)—Income Tax, 2007 c 3, s 257BF(3)(4)
ss 158, 159 mod—SI 2013/3209, reg 4
s 160 excl—SI 2013/460, reg 3(2)(c)
s 161 am—Financial Services, 2012 c 21, sch 18 para 129(2)
s 162 am—Finance, 2012 c 14, s 32(2); Finance, 2013 c 29, s 43(2)
      rep in pt—SI 2013/3209, reg 12(a)(i)
s 164 am—Finance, 2012 c 14, s 32(3)-(5)
s 164A added—Finance, 2013 c 29, s 43(3)
      rep—SI 2013/3209, reg 12(a)(ii)
s 166 mod—Income Tax, 2007 c 3, s 257MV(9)
s 169 am—Finance, 2014 c 26, s 40(2)
s 173 am—SI 2012/266, art 14(2)
ss 174A, 174B added—SI 2012/266, art 14(1)
s 188 am—Finance, 2013 c 29, s 31(3); Finance, 2014 c 26, s 40(3)
s 189 am—Finance, 2011 c 11, sch 3 para 21; Finance, 2014 c 26, s 35(2)
s 192 am—Finance, 2014 c 26, s 35(3)
s 194 rep in pt—Finance, 2012 c 14, s 33(5)(a)
s 197 am—Finance, 2011 c 11, s 41(2)
s 200 appl (mods)—Income Tax, 2007 c 3, s 809ZJ(9)
      am—Finance, 2014 c 26, s 35(4)
s 202 am—Finance, 2010 c 13, s 30, sch 6 para 27(2)(a); SI 2012/964, art 3(1) sch; Finance,
      2014 c 26, s 35(5)
      rep in pt—Finance, 2010 c 13, s 30, sch 6 para 27(2)(b); SI 2012/964, art 3(1) sch
s 202A added—Finance, 2014 c 26, s 35(6)
Pt 6, Ch 2A (ss 202B-202C) added—Finance, 2014 c 26, s 35(7)
s 209 am—Finance, 2010 c 13, s 31, sch 7 paras 5, 6
s 210A added—Finance, 2010 c 13, s 31, sch 7 paras 5, 7
s 217 am—Finance, 2010 c 13, s 30, sch 6 para 27(3)(a); SI 2012/964, art 3(1) sch
      rep in pt—Finance, 2010 c 13, s 30, sch 6 para 27(3)(b); SI 2012/964, art 3(1) sch
s 220 am—Finance, 2013 c 29, sch 27 para 8
s 220A added—Finance, 2013 c 29, sch 27 para 9
s 220B added—Finance, 2013 c 29, sch 27 para 13(1)
s 240 am—Finance, 2013 c 29, sch 27 para 10
s 244 am—Finance, 2013 c 29, sch 27 para 11(2)
      rep in pt—Finance, 2013 c 29, sch 27 para 11(3)

2010
c 4 *continued*

s 257 am—Finance, 2012 c 14, sch 4 para 19
Pt 7A Ch 1 (s 269A) added—Finance, 2015 c 11, sch 2 para 1
s 269A am—Finance (No. 2), 2015 c 33, sch 3 para 5
Pt 7A Ch 2 (ss 269B, 269BA-269BE) added—Finance, 2015 c 11, sch 2 para 1
s 269B am—Finance (No. 2), 2015 c 33, s 20(10)
s 269BA rep in pt—Finance (No. 2), 2015 c 33, s 20(11)
s 269C rep in pt—Finance (No. 2), 2015 c 33, s 20(12)
Pt 7A Ch 3 (ss 269C, 269CA-269CN) added—Finance, 2015 c 11, sch 2 para 1
Pt 7A Ch 4 (ss 269D, 269DA-269DN) added—Finance (No. 2), 2015 c 33, sch 3 para 1
s 270 am—Finance, 2012 c 14, sch 22 para 18(2); Finance, 2014 c 26, sch 1 para 5(2), sch
      14 para 2; Finance, 2015 c 11, sch 14 para 2(2),(4)(5)(a)
   rep in pt—Finance, 2015 c 11, sch 11 para 11; ibid, sch 14 para 2(3),(5)(b)
s 279 appl—Taxation (International and Other Provns), 2010 c 8, s 206(3)(b)(4)(b)
Pt 8, Ch 3A (ss 279A-279H) added—Finance, 2014 c 26, sch 1 para 5(3)
ss 279F, 279G mod—Finance (No. 2), 2015 c 33, s 39(1)(2)(a)
s 285A and cross-heading added—Finance, 2014 c 26, sch 16 para 3
s 287A added—Finance, 2013 c 29, s 87(1)
s 292 am—Finance, 2013 c 29, sch 31 paras 2(2), 18(3)(4)
   rep in pt—Finance, 2013 c 29, sch 31 paras 7(2), 18(2)
s 293 rep—Finance, 2013 c 29, sch 31 para 7(3)
ss 294, 295 rep—Finance, 2013 c 29, sch 31 para 19
s 296 am—Finance, 2013 c 29, sch 31 paras 2(3)(b)-(d), 20
   rep in pt—Finance, 2013 c 29, sch 31 para 2(3)(a)
s 298 rep—Finance, 2013 c 29, sch 31 para 10
s 298A added—Finance, 2013 c 29, sch 31 para 21
s 307 am—Finance, 2015 c 11, sch 11 para 2
s 309 am—Finance, 2015 c 11, sch 11 para 3
s 310 am—SI 2011/2885, art 2
s 311 am—Finance, 2015 c 11, sch 11 para 4
s 312 rep in pt—Finance, 2013 c 29, sch 15 paras 24(2), 28, 29
s 316 am—Finance, 2015 c 11, sch 11 para 5
s 317 am—Finance, 2015 c 11, sch 11 para 6
s 318A added—Finance, 2015 c 11, sch 11 para 7
s 326 am—Finance, 2015 c 11, sch 11 para 8
s 327 am—Finance, 2015 c 11, sch 11 para 9
s 328A added—Finance, 2015 c 11, sch 11 para 10
Pt 8, Ch 5A (ss 329A-329T) added—Finance, 2014 c 26, sch 14 para 1
   rep—Finance, 2015 c 11, sch 11 para 13(1)
s 330 am—Finance, 2011 c 11, s 7(1); Finance, 2012 c 14, s 182(1); ibid, sch 21 para 2;
      ibid, sch 22 para 18(3); Finance, 2015 c 11, s 48(1); ibid, sch 14 para 3
s 330ZA added—Finance, 2015 c 11, sch 14 para 4
ss 330A-330C added—Finance, 2012 c 14, sch 21 para 3
s 330A excl—Finance, 2015 c 11, s 48(5)(6)
s 330B am—Finance, 2013 c 29, s 88(2)-(5)(6)(b)
   rep in pt—Finance, 2013 c 29, s 88(6)(a)
   excl—Finance, 2015 c 11, s 48(5)(6)
Pt 8 Ch 6A (ss 332A-332KA) added—Finance, 2015 c 11, sch 12 para 2
   restr (condtionally)—Finance, 2015 c 11, sch 13 para 6(2)(3)
Pt 8 Ch 7 (ss 333-356AA) am—Finance, 2012 c 14, sch 22 paras 17, 21(2)
   rep—(savings) Finance, 2015 c 11, sch 12 paras 3, 6-8
   (as saved) restr (conditionally)—Finance, 2015 c 11, sch 13 para 6(2)(3)
s 333 am—Finance, 2014 c 26, sch 15 para 5(3)(a)
   rep in pt—Finance, 2014 c 26, sch 15 para 5(3)(b)
s 334 am—Finance, 2012 c 14, sch 22 paras 2, 21(2)
s 337 am—Finance, 2011 c 11, s 63(1); Finance, 2012 c 14, sch 22 paras 3(2), (4), 21(2);
      SI 2013/2910, art 4
   rep in pt—Finance, 2012 c 14, sch 22 paras 3(3), 21(2)
s 338 am—Finance, 2012 c 14, sch 22 paras 4, 21(2)
s 339 am—Finance, 2012 c 14, sch 22 paras 5, 21(2)
s 340 am—Finance, 2012 c 14, sch 22 paras 6, 21(2); SI 2013/2910, art 5
s 341 am—Finance, 2012 c 14, sch 22 paras 7, 21(2); SI 2013/2910, art 6
s 342 am—Finance, 2012 c 14, sch 22 paras 8, 21(2); SI 2013/2910, art 7
s 343 am—Finance, 2012 c 14, sch 22 paras 9, 21(2)

2010
c 4 *continued*

s 344 am—Finance, 2012 c 14, sch 22 paras 10, 21(2); SI 2013/2910, art 8
s 345 am—Finance, 2012 c 14, sch 22 paras 11, 21(2)
s 346 am—Finance, 2012 c 14, sch 22 paras 12, 21(2)
s 347 am—Finance, 2012 c 14, sch 22 paras 13, 21(2)
s 349 am—Finance, 2012 c 14, sch 22 paras 14, 21(1)
s 349A added—Finance, 2012 c 14, sch 22 paras 15, 21(1)
    am—SI 2013/2910, art 9
    mod (as saved)—Finance, 2015 c 11, sch 13 para 3
s 350 subst—Finance, 2011 c 11, s 63(2)
    mod (as saved)—Finance, 2015 c 11, sch 13 para 4
s 352 am—Finance, 2014 c 26, sch 15 para 4
s 355 am—SI 2010/1899, arts 2, 3
s 356 am—SI 2010/1899, arts 2, 4
s 356A added—SI 2013/2910, art 10
s 356AA added—(s 357 renumbered as s 356AA) Finance, 2014 c 26, sch 15 para 2
    am—Finance, 2011 c 11, s 63(3); Finance, 2012 c 14, sch 22 paras 16(3), 21(1);
      ibid, sch 22 paras 16(2)(5), 21(2); SI 2013/2910, art 11; Finance, 2014 c 26,
      sch 15 para 5(4)
    rep in pt—Finance, 2012 c 14, sch 22 paras 16(4), 21(2)
Pt 8, Ch 8 (ss 356B-356JB) added—Finance, 2014 c 26, sch 15 para 3
s 356C am—Finance, 2015 c 11, sch 14 para 5
s 356DB rep—Finance, 2015 c 11, sch 14 para 6
s 356IB added—Finance, 2015 c 11, sch 14 para 7
s 356JB am—Finance, 2015 c 11, sch 14 para 8
Pt 8 Ch 9 (ss 356JC-356JNB) added—Finance, 2015 c 11, sch 13 para 2
    restr (conditionally)—Finance, 2015 c 11, sch 13 para 6(2)(3)
Pt 8ZA (ss 356K-356NG) added—Finance, 2014 c 26, sch 16 para 4
Pt 8A (ss 357A-357GE) added—Finance, 2012 c 14, sch 2 para 1
s 357CG am—Finance, 2013 c 29, sch 15 para 10(a); ibid, sch 18 para 18; Finance, 2014 c
    26, sch 4 para 15(2)(3)(b)
    rep in pt—Finance, 2014 c 26, sch 4 para 15(3)(a)
s 357CHA added—Finance, 2013 c 29, sch 18 para 19
s 357CK am—Finance, 2013 c 29, sch 15 para 11; ibid, sch 18 para 20(2)(3)
s 357CL am—Finance, 2014 c 26, sch 1 para 13(2)(a)(b)
    rep in pt—Finance, 2014 c 26, sch 1 para 13(2)(c)
s 357CM am—Finance, 2014 c 26, sch 1 para 13(3)(a)(b)
    rep in pt—Finance, 2014 c 26, sch 1 para 13(3)(c)
Pt 8B (ss 357H-357XI) added—Corporation Tax (NI), 2015 c 21, s 1
Pt 8C (ss 357YA-357YB) added—Finance (No. 2), 2015 c 33, s 38(3)
s 382 am—Finance, 2010 c 13, s 61, sch 18 para 2
s 383 am—Finance, 2010 c 13, s 61, sch 18 para 3
s 385 am—Finance, 2012 c 14, s 24(2)
s 387 am—Finance, 2011 c 11, sch 6 para 2
s 389 am—Finance, 2011 c 11, sch 6 para 3
s 390 am—Finance, 2011 c 11, sch 6 para 4
s 391 am—Finance, 2011 c 11, sch 6 para 5
s 392 subst—Finance, 2010 c 13, s 61, sch 18 para 4
    am—Finance, 2012 c 14, s 24(3)
s 393 rep in pt—Finance, 2010 c 13, s 29(2)
s 394 am—Finance, 2010 c 13, s 29(3)(a)
    rep in pt—Finance, 2010 c 13, s 29(3)(b)
s 394ZA added—Finance, 2012 c 14, s 24(4)
s 394A added—Finance, 2010 c 13, s 61, sch 18 para 5
    am—Finance, 2012 c 14, s 24(5)
s 398 rep in pt—Finance, 2010 c 13, s 29(4)
ss 398A-398G added —Finance, 2010 c 13, s 61, sch 18 para 6
s 398A am—Finance, 2011 c 11, sch 6 para 6(2)
s 398D am—Finance, 2012 c 14, sch 20 para 38
    rep in pt—Finance (No. 2), 2015 c 33, s 36(2)(a)
s 398G rep in pt—Finance, 2011 c 11, sch 6 para 6(3)
    am—Finance, 2011 c 11, sch 6 para 6(3)
s 401 am—Finance, 2011 c 11, sch 6 para 7
s 402 am—Finance, 2011 c 11, sch 6 para 8

2010
c 4 *continued*

s 403 am—Finance, 2011 c 11, sch 6 para 9
s 405 am—Finance, 2010 c 13, s 29(5)
s 408 am—Finance, 2010 c 13, s 29(6)
s 410 am—Finance, 2011 c 11, sch 6 para 11
s 412 am—Finance, 2011 c 11, sch 6 para 12
s 413 am—Finance, 2011 c 11, sch 6 para 13
s 414 am—Finance, 2011 c 11, sch 6 para 14
s 421 am—Finance, 2011 c 11, sch 6 para 15
s 427 am—Finance, 2012 c 14, s 24(6)
s 432 am—Finance, 2013 c 29, sch 14 para 2(2)
s 434 am—Finance, 2011 c 11, sch 6 para 17
s 435 am—Finance, 2011 c 11, sch 6 para 18
s 436 am—Finance, 2011 c 11, sch 6 para 19
s 437 am—Finance, 2010 c 13, s 61, sch 18 para 7
     rep in pt—Finance, 2011 c 11, sch 6 para 21
ss 437A-437C added—Finance, 2011 c 11, sch 6 para 22
Pt 10 (ss 438-465) appl (mods)—Nat Insurance Contributions, 2014 c 7, sch 1 pt 1
s 438 am—Finance, 2013 c 29, sch 30 para 2(1)
Pt 10, Ch 2 (ss 439-454) appl (mods)—Income Tax (Trading and Other Income), 2005 c 5,
     s 456(7); Corporation Tax, 2009 c 4, s 376(1)
s 449 appl—Income Tax (Earnings and Penions), 2003 c 1, s 312G(6)(a))
s 450 appl—Water Industry, 1991 c 56, sch 2B para 9 (added by Water, 2014 c 21, sch 3);
     SI 2014/1686, sch 2 paras 40(4), 41(4)(5) (applying 1988 c 1, s 216 now
     re-stated)
s 451 appl—Water Industry, 1991 c 56, sch 2B para 9 (added by Water, 2014 c 21, sch 3);
     SI 2014/1686, sch 2 paras 40(4), 41(4)(5) (applying 1988 c 1, s 216 now
     re-stated)
s 454 appl—Taxation (International and Other Provns), 2010 c 8, s 341(5)
s 455 am—Finance, 2013 c 29, sch 30 para 3(1)
s 459 am—Finance, 2013 c 29, sch 30 para 4(1)
Pt 10, Ch 3A (ss 464A, 464B) added—Finance, 2013 c 29, sch 30 para 5(1)
Pt 10, Ch 3B (ss 464C, 464D) added—Finance, 2013 c 29, sch 30 para 6(1)
s 465 rep in pt—Finance, 2011 c 11, sch 23 para 64(2)
     am—Finance, 2013 c 29, sch 30 para 7
s 467 rep—Finance, 2010 c 13, s 30, sch 6 para 27(4)
s 468 am—SI 2012/964, art 3(1) sch
     rep in pt—SI 2012/964, art 3(1) sch
s 472 rep in pt—Finance, 2012 c 14, s 50(2)(d)
s 472A added—Finance, 2010 c 13, s 32, sch 8 para 1(2)
s 475 rep in pt—Finance, 2012 c 14, s 50(2)(e)
s 477A added—Finance, 2010 c 13, s 32, sch 8 para 7
     am—Finance, 2012 c 14, sch 15 para 3
s 486 am—SI 2013/2819, reg 39(3)
s 491A added—Finance, 2012 c 14, sch 15 para 4
s 496 rep in pt—Finance, 2011 c 11, sch 3 paras 22, 27(2)(3)
s 500 am—Finance, 2010 c 13, s 32, sch 8 para 2(2)
ss 502-510 rep —(subject to transtl provns) Finance, 2011 c 11, sch 3 paras 23,27(2)(3), 30
s 508 am (as continuing to have effect)—SI 2012/700, sch para 9
s 511 am—Charities, 2011 c 25, sch 7 para 142
     rep in pt—Charities, 2011 c 25, sch 7 para 142, sch 10
s 525 am—Finance, 2012 c 14, sch 4 para 2(2), (3)
     rep in pt—Finance, 2012 c 14, sch 4 para 2(4)
s 527 am—Finance, 2012 c 14, sch 4 paras 3, 14
s 528 am—Finance, 2012 c 14, sch 4 paras 4, 15; SI 2014/518, reg 2(2)
ss 528A, 528B added—Finance, 2012 c 14, sch 4 para 16
s 530 rep in pt—Finance (No 3), 2010 c 33, s 10, sch 4 paras 3, 4(1)-(3)
     am—Finance (No 3), 2010 c 33, s 10, sch 4 paras 3, 4(4); Finance, 2012 c 14, sch 4
     para 22; Finance, 2013 c 29, sch 19 para 2
s 530A added—Finance, 2012 c 14, sch 4 para 23
     am—Finance, 2013 c 29, sch 19 para 3
s 531 am—Finance, 2012 c 14, sch 4 para 27; Finance, 2013 c 29, sch 19 para 4
s 534 rep in pt—Finance, 2014 c 26, sch 1 para 14(2)
s 535 rep in pt—Finance, 2014 c 26, sch 1 para 14(3)

2010

c 4 *continued*

ss 538-540 rep—Finance, 2012 c 14, sch 4 para 33

s 543 am—Finance, 2012 c 14, sch 4 para 40

 rep in pt—Finance, 2014 c 26, sch 1 para 14(4)

s 544 am—Finance, 2012 c 14, sch 4 para 41; SI 2014/518, reg 2(3)

s 545 rep in pt—Finance, 2012 c 14, sch 4 para 34(1)

s 547 rep in pt—Finance, 2012 c 14, sch 4 para 28

s 548 am—Finance, 2013 c 29, sch 19 para 5

s 549 am—Finance (No 3), 2010 c 33, s 10, sch 4 paras 3, 5; Finance, 2013 c 29, sch 19
 para 6

s 549A added—Finance, 2013 c 29, sch 19 para 7

s 550 am—Finance (No 3), 2010 c 33, s 10, sch 4 paras 3, 6; Finance, 2013 c 29, sch 19
 para 8

s 551 rep in pt—Finance, 2014 c 26, sch 1 para 14(5)

s 552 am—Finance, 2014 c 26, sch 1 para 14(6)

s 553 am—Finance (No 3), 2010 c 33, s 10, sch 4 paras 3, 7

s 554A added—Finance (No 3), 2010 c 33, s 10, sch 4 paras 3, 8
 appl —Income Tax, 2007 c 3, s 973(3A)

s 556 am—Finance, 2012 c 14, sch 4 para 43

 rep in pt—Finance, 2012 c 14, sch 4 para 35(1)

s 558 am—Finance, 2012 c 14, sch 4 para 5

 rep in pt—Finance, 2012 c 14, sch 4 para 36(1)

s 559 am—Finance, 2012 c 14, sch 4 para 6

 rep in pt—Finance, 2012 c 14, sch 4 para 37(1)

s 561 am—Finance, 2012 c 14, sch 4 paras 7, 17

s 562 am —Finance, 2012 c 14, sch 4 para 8(2)-(4), (6)(a)

 rep in pt—Finance, 2012 c 14, sch 4 para 8(5), (6)(b)

s 562A added—Finance, 2012 c 14, sch 4 para 9

ss 562B, 562C added—Finance, 2012 c 14, sch 4 para 18

s 564 rep in pt—Finance (No 3), 2010 c 33, s 10, sch 4 paras 3, 9(2); Finance, 2012 c 14,
 sch 4 para 24; Finance, 2014 c 26, sch 1 para 14(7)

 am—Finance (No 3), 2010 c 33, s 10, sch 4 paras 3, 9(3)

s 565 am—Finance, 2012 c 14, sch 4 para 25

s 566 rep in pt—Finance, 2012 c 14, sch 4 para 29

s 567 rep—Finance, 2012 c 14, sch 4 para 30

s 568 am—Finance, 2012 c 14, sch 4 para 31

s 572 am—Finance, 2012 c 14, sch 4 para 10

s 573A added—Finance, 2012 c 14, sch 4 para 11

s 573B added—Finance, 2012 c 14, sch 4 para 20

s 577 am—Finance, 2012 c 14, sch 4 para 12(2), (3)(b), (4)

 rep in pt—Finance, 2012 c 14, sch 4 para 12(3)(a)

s 583 rep in pt—Finance, 2012 c 14, sch 4 para 38

s 588 am—Finance, 2013 c 29, sch 19 para 9

s 589 am—Finance, 2013 c 29, sch 19 para 10

ss 595-597 rep—Finance, 2012 c 14, sch 4 para 39

s 599A added—Finance (No 3), 2010 c 33, s 10, sch 4 paras 3, 10
 appl—Income Tax, 2007 c 3, s 973(3B)

s 605 am—Finance (No 3), 2010 c 33, s 10, sch 4 paras 3, 11; Finance, 2013 c 29, sch 19
 para 11

s 606 am—Finance, 2012 c 14, sch 16 para 219

s 610 rep in pt—Finance, 2010 c 13, s 30, sch 6 para 27(5)

Pt 13, Ch 3 (ss 611, 612) rep —SI 2013/2819, reg 39(4)

s 614 rep in pt—Finance, 2014 c 26, sch 1 para 15(2)

s 618 rep in pt—Finance, 2014 c 26, sch 1 para 15(3)

s 620 am—SI 2012/2595, art 21
 appl (mods)—Land and Buildings Transaction Tax (S), 2013 asp 11, s 45(7)

Pt 13 Ch 3A (s 622A) added—Finance, 2011 c 11, s 50

s 627 am—Finance, 2014 c 26, sch 1 para 15(4)

s 628 am—Finance, 2014 c 26, sch 1 para 15(5)

s 630 am—Finance, 2014 c 26, sch 1 para 15(6)

s 635 am—Financial Services, 2012 c. 21, sch 18 para 129(3)

s 645 am—Co-operative and Community Benefit Societies, 2014 c 14, sch 4 para 160

s 653 am—Co-operative and Community Benefit Societies, 2014 c 14, sch 4 para 161

s 654 am—Co-operative and Community Benefit Societies, 2014 c 14, sch 4 para 162

2010
c 4 *continued*

s 658 am—Finance, 2010 c 13, s 30, sch 6 paras 30, 31; Finance, 2012 c 14, s 52(1);
    Finance, 2013 c 29, sch 21 para 4; SI 2015/725, reg 3(a)(b)
  rep in pt—Finance, 2010 c 13, s 30, sch 6 paras 30, 31
s 659 am—Finance, 2013 c 29, sch 21 para 2
s 660 am—Finance, 2013 c 29, sch 21 para 3; SI 2015/725, reg 10
s 660A added—Finance, 2013 c 29, sch 21 para 5
s 661A-661C added—Finance, 2010 c 13, s 30, sch 6 paras 30, 32
s 661CA added—SI 2015/725, reg 4
s 661D added—Finance, 2012 c 14, sch 15 para 6
    rep in pt—Finance, 2014 c 26, s 35(12)(a)
s 661E added—Finance, 2014 c 26, s 35(9)
s 662 am—Finance, 2013 c 29, sch 21 para 6; SI 2014/3327, art 2
s 663 am—Finance, 2013 c 29, sch 21 para 7; SI 2014/3327, art 3
s 664 am—Finance, 2014 c 26, s 35(10)(12)(b)
s 665 am—Finance, 2014 c 26, s 35(12)(c)
s 665A added—Finance, 2012 c 14, sch 15 para 7
    am—Finance, 2014 c 26, s 35(11)
s 672 am—Finance, 2013 c 29, sch 13 para 1
s 676 subst—Finance, 2013 c 29, s 32(1)
s 688 am—Finance, 2014 c 26, s 37(2)
Pt 14, Ch 5A (ss 705A-705G) added—Finance, 2013 c 29, sch 13 para 1(3)
s 721 am—Finance, 2013 c 29, sch 13 para 1(4)
s 723 am—Finance, 2014 c 26, s 37(3)
s 724A added—Finance, 2014 c 26, s 37(4)
s 725 am—Finance, 2013 c 29, sch 13 para 1(5)
s 726 am—Finance, 2014 c 26, s 37(5)
s 728 rep —Finance, 2011 c 11, sch 23 para 64(2)
s 730 am—Finance, 2013 c 29, sch 13 para 1(6)
Pt 14A (ss 730A-730D) added—Finance, 2013 c 29, sch 14 para 1
s 730B am—Finance, 2014 c 26, s 38(1)
Pt 14B (ss 730E-730H) added—Finance, 2015 c 11, sch 3 para 1
s 730G am—Finance (No. 2), 2015 c 33, s 37(2)-(5)
s 730H am—Finance (No. 2), 2015 c 33, s 37(6)
s 733 rep in pt—Finance, 2010 c 13, s 38, sch 12 paras 8, 9
s 735 rep—Finance, 2010 c 13, s 38, sch 12 paras 8, 10
s 756 rep in pt—Finance, 2014 c 26, sch 17 para 27
Pt 16, Ch 1A (ss 757A-757B) added—Finance, 2014 c 26, sch 17 para 28(1)
Pt 16, Ch 2 (ss 758-779) restr—Finance, 2004 c 12, ss 196G(2)(3), 196I(5)(6)
s 758 am—Finance, 2012 c 14, sch 13 para 38
s 763 am—Finance, 2012 c 14, sch 13 para 39
s 765 am—Finance, 2012 c 14, sch 13 paras 40, 41, s 196L(4), (6)
ss 774-776 appl—Finance, 2004 c 12, ss 196J(5)
s 778 am—SI 2013/2819, reg 39(5)
Pt 16, Ch 4 (ss 779A-779B) added—Finance, 2014 c 26, sch 17 para 29(1)
Pt 17 (ss 780-814) rep —Finance, 2013 c 29, sch 29 para 43
Pt 17A (ss 814A-814D) added —Finance, 2013 c 29, sch 29 para 2
s 835 am—Finance, 2012 c 14, sch 16 para 224
s 836 am—Finance, 2012 c 14, sch 16 para 225
s 839 am—Finance, 2012 c 14, sch 16 para 226(2), (3)
    rep in pt—Finance, 2012 c 14, sch 16 para 226(4)
s 840 am—Finance, 2012 c 14, sch 16 para 227
Pt 19, Ch 2 (ss 849-862) appl (mods)—Income Tax, 2007 c 3, s 681BD(4)
s 860 am—Finance, 2012 c 14, sch 16 para 228
s 886 am—Finance, 2012 c 14, sch 16 para 229
Pt 21A (ss 937A-937O) added—Finance, 2010 c 13, s 46, sch 16 para 3
Pt 21B (ss 938A-938N) added—Finance, 2011 c 11, sch 5 para 2
s 938M am—Finance, 2012 c 14, sch 20 para 39
Pt 21BA (ss 938O-938V) added—Finance, 2013 c 29, sch 20 para 3
Pt 21C (ss 939A-939I) added—Finance, 2011 c 11, sch 3 para 2
s 939C mod—Finance, 2011 c 11, sch 3 para 31(b)
s 940A added—(s 938 renumbered as s 940A) Finance, 2011 c 11, sch 5 para 3(1)(a)
    am—Finance, 2011 c 11, sch 5 para 3(2)
s 940B added—(s 939 renumbered as s 940A) Finance, 2011 c 11, sch 5 para 3(1)(b)

2010
c 4 *continued*

s 940C added—(s 940 renumbered as s 940C) Finance, 2011 c 11, sch 5 para 3(1)(c)
s 948 am—Finance, 2011 c 11, sch 6 para 24
s 950 am—Finance, 2011 c 11, sch 6 para 25(2)(3)(a); Finance, 2012 c 14, s 24(7)
    rep in pt—Finance, 2011 c 11, sch 6 para 25(3)(b)
Pt 22, Ch 4 (ss 963-966) appl—Finance, 2010 c 13, s 22, sch 1 para 41
        appl (mods)—SI 1998/3175, reg 9 (subst by 2011/1785, reg 12)
        mod—Finance, 2014 c 26, sch 16 para 8(3)
s 967 am—Finance, 2012 c 14, sch 15 paras 10, 17(2)
Pt 22 Ch 6 (ss 969-972) mod—Finance, 2015 c 11, sch 16 para 1
s 984 mod—GLA, 1999 c 29, s 34A(3)
s 986 rep in pt—(prosp) Health and Social Care, 2012 c 7, sch 14 para 115
    am—Finance, 2013 c 29, s 37
s 987A added—Finance, 2013 c 29, s 38(1)
ss 991-995 rep—Finance, 2012 c 14, sch 39 para 16
s 998 am—Finance, 2012 c 14, s 33(5)(b)
s 1000 excl —Taxation (International and Other Provns), 2010 c 8, s 155(6)(b)
s 1001 rep in pt—Finance, 2012 c 14, s 33(5)(c)
    am—Co-operative and Community Benefit Societies, 2014 c 14, sch 4 para 163
s 1002 rep—Finance, 2012 c 14, s 33(2)
s 1020 am—Finance, 2012 c 14, s 33(3)(b)
s 1021 rep—Finance, 2012 c 14, s 33(4)
s 1027A added—Finance (No 3), 2010 c 33, s 9, sch 3 para 1(3)
s 1029 am—SI 2012/266, art 16(2); Finance, 2013 c 29, s 43(4); Co-operative and
        Community Benefit Societies, 2014 c 14, sch 4 para 164
    rep in pt—SI 2013/3209, reg 12(a)(iii)
ss 1030A, 1030B added—SI 2012/266, art 16(3)
s 1032 appl (mods)—SI 2010/665, art 2
s 1032A added—Finance, 2013 c 29, s 43(5)
    rep —SI 2013/3209, reg 12(a)(iv)
s 1034 rep in pt—Finance, 2013 c 29, sch 46 para 145
s 1038 subst—Finance, 2013 c 29, s 40(2)
s 1038A added—Finance, 2013 c 29, s 40(3)
s 1046 rep in pt—Finance, 2011 c 11, sch 23 para 64(2)
s 1054 excl—SI 2013/460, reg 3(1)(f)
s 1055 am—Co-operative and Community Benefit Societies, 2014 c 14, sch 4 paras 165,
        166
s 1056 am—Co-operative and Community Benefit Societies, 2014 c 14, sch 4 para 167
s 1065 am—Finance, 2015 c 11, sch 1 para 26
s 1097 rep—Finance, 2011 c 11, sch 23 para 64(2)
s 1100 am—Finance, 2015 c 11, s 19(9)
s 1102 rep in pt—Finance, 2011 c 11, sch 23 para 64(2)
s 1104 appl (mods)—SI 2013/2819, reg 28(2)
s 1107 appl (mods)—SI 2013/2819, reg 28(2)
s 1109 am—Finance, 2011 c 11, sch 23 para 64(3); Finance, 2013 c 29, sch 29 para 44(3)
    rep in pt—Finance, 2013 c 29, sch 29 para 44(2)
s 1112 appl—Finance, 2004 c 12, s 196L(3)
s 1119 rep in pt—Finance, 2010 c 13, s 30, sch 6 para 27(6); Co-operative and Community
        Benefit Societies, 2014 c 14, sch 4 para 168(2)
    am—Co-operative and Community Benefit Societies, 2014 c 14, sch 4 para 168(3);
        Finance, 2014 c 26, sch 1 para 16
s 1120 appl—Corporation Tax, 2009 c 4, s 18D(4); Taxation (International and Other
        Provns), 2010 c 8, s 49(4)
    am—Financial Services, 2012 c. 21, sch 18 para 129(4); SI 2013/636, sch para 12;
        Co-operative and Community Benefit Societies, 2014 c 14, sch 4 para 169
s 1121 am—SI 2013/1388, reg 5
s 1122 appl—Taxes Management, 1970 c 9, s 77E(3); betting and Gaming Duties, 1981 c
        63, sch 1A para 8(6); Value Added Tax, 1994 c 23, sch 9 Pt 2 Note (19);
        Finance, 2000 c 17, sch 6 paras 42B(7), 42C(7), 152B(5); Finance, 2003 c 14,
        sch 2A para 20; ibid, sch 6B para 6(8); Taxation (International and Other
        Provns), 2010 c 8, s 34(3), 44(5), 45(6), 49(4), 68(6), 70(3)(b), 112(7), 259(2);
        SI 2011/2999, reg 34(3)(b); Land and Buildings Transaction Tax (S), 2013 asp
        11, s 58; SI 2014/685, reg 3(5)(b)
s 1122 mod—Land and Buildings Transaction Tax (S), 2013 asp 11, sch 17 para 49

2010

c 4 *continued*

s 1122 appl (mods)—Finance, 2003 c 14, sch 4A para 5A(10); Finance, 2013 c 29, ss
136(6), 172; Corporation Tax, 2009 c 4, s 133D(5)(6) (added by 2015 c 33, s
18(1))

s 1123 appl—SIs 2011/2999, reg 34(3)(b); 2014/685, reg 3(5)(b)

s 1124 appl —Taxation of Chargeable Gains, 1992 c 12, s 151K(6); Taxation (International
and Other Provns), 2010 c 8, s 365, sch 2 paras 31; Finance, 2011 c 11, sch 13
para 33(4)

s 1127 appl (mods)—Finance, 2011 c 11, s 53(6)
appl—Finance, 2015 c 11, s 87(8)

s 1139 am—Finance, 2011 c 11, sch 19 para 48; Finance, 2012 c 14, sch 20 para 40;
Finance, 2015 c 11, s 115(3)

Pt 24, Ch 2 (ss 1141-1153) appl—Income Tax, 2007 c 3, s 1007A; Taxation (International
and Other Provns), 2010 c 8, s 78(2)(b)

s 1141 mod—Finance, 2015 c 11, s 114(1)

Pt 24, Ch 3 (ss 1154-1157) appl in pt (mods)—Taxation (International and Other Provns),
2010 c 8, s 345(7)-(10) (subst by 2014 c 26, s 39(2))

s 1154 saved —Corporation Tax, 2010 c 4, s 351(1A)

s 1158 subst—Finance, 2011 c 11, s 49(2)
am—Finance, 2013 c 29, s 45(1)

s 1159 subst—Finance, 2011 c 11, s 49(3)

ss 1160-1165 rep—Finance, 2011 c 11, s 49(4)

s 1171 am—Finance, 2012 c 14, sch 16 para 230(b); Finance, 2015 c 11, s 125(3)
rep in pt—Finance, 2012 c 14, sch 16 para 230(a)
excl—Finance, 2015 c 11, s 29(10); ibid, sch 13 para 6(6); Corporation Tax (NI)
2015, c 21, s 5(7)

s 1172 appl—Finance (No. 2), 2015 c 33, s 33(12)

s 1173 rep in pt—Finance, 2012 c 14, sch 16 para 231; (with spec commencing effect)
Finance, 2013 c 29, sch 15 paras 24(3), 28, 29

sch 1 rep in pt —Savings Accounts and Health in Pregnancy Grant, 2010 c 36, s 2(5);
Finance, 2010 c 13, s 38, sch 12 para 14; Finance (No 3), 2010 c 33, s 5, sch 2
para 5; Finance, 2011 c 11, sch 5 para 7(2)(d); ibid, sch 25 pt 10; ibid, sch 3
paras 24, 27(2)(3); (prosp) Public Bodies, 2011 c 24, sch 6; Charities, 2011 c
25, sch 10; Finance, 2012 c 14, sch 3 para 32(b); ibid, sch 16 para 247(t); ibid,
sch 39 paras 7(2)(c), 17(b); SI 2012/952, reg 4(b); Finance, 2013 c 29, sch 12
para 16, sch 15 para 24(4); ibid, sch 29 para 45; SL(R), 2013 c 2, sch 1 pt
10(1); SI 2013/2819, reg 41(e)

sch 2 am—SI 2010/2902, art 4
rep in pt—Finance, 2011 c 11, sch 3 paras 25,27(2)(3); Finance, 2013 c 29, sch 29
para 46

sch 4 rep in pt—Finance, 2010 c 13, ss 29(7), 30, sch 6 para 27(7)(a)(i); Finance, 2011 c 11,
s 49(5), sch 6 para 26(1); Finance, 2013 c 29, sch 29 para 47; Co-operative and
Community Benefit Societies, 2014 c 14, sch 4 para 170(a); Finance, 2014 c
26, sch 1 para 17(3); Finance, 2015 c 11, sch 11 paras 9(2), 12(3)
am—Finance, 2010 c 13, ss 30, 31, 46, 61, sch 6 para 27(7)(a)(ii)(b)-(d), sch 7 paras
5, 8, sch 16 para 4, sch 18 para 8; Finance, 2011 c 11, sch 5 para 4; ibid, sch 6
para 26(2); ibid, sch 3 paras 26,27(2)(3); Finance, 2012 c 14, sch 2 para 1(2);
ibid, sch 22 para 19; Finance, 2013 c 29, sch 13 para 2; ibid, sch 14 para 2(2);
ibid, sch 20 para 4; SI 2013/2910, art 12; Co-operative and Community Benefit
Societies, 2014 c 14, sch 4 para 170(b); Finance, 2014 c 26, sch 1 para
17(2)(4)-(6), sch 14 para 3, sch 15 para 5(5); Finance, 2015 c 11, sch 2 para 5;
ibid, sch 3 para 3; ibid, sch 11 para 12(2); ibid, sch 14 para 9(3); Finance (No. 2),
2015 c 33, sch 3 para 6; (prosp) Corporation Tax (NI), 2015 c 21, sch 2 para 6

c 5   **Appropriation**

c 6   **Marriage (Wales)**

c 7   **Co-operative and Community Benefit Societies and Credit Unions**
ss 1, 2 rep—Co-operative and Community Benefit Societies, 2014 c 14, sch 7
s 4 rep—Co-operative and Community Benefit Societies, 2014 c 14, sch 7

c 8   **Taxation (International and Other Provisions)**
appl—Corporation Tax, 2010 c 4, ss 332(2), 817(b)
appl (mods)—Corporation Tax, 2010 c 4, s 996(2); SI 2011/245, sch 6 pt 1
s 1 am—Finance, 2014 c 26, s 289(5)(a)
Pt 2 (ss 2-134) appl—Corporation Tax, 2010 c 4, s 269DL(6) (added by 2015 c 33, sch 3
para 1)

2010

c 8 *continued*

s 18 am—Finance, 2011 c 11, sch 13 para 26

s 34 am—Finance, 2014 c 26, s 292(2)(3)

s 42 am—Finance, 2013 c 29, sch 47 para 12; Finance, 2014 c 26, s 292(6)
excl—Corporation Tax, 2010 c 4, s 269DL(8)(a) (added by 2015 c 33, sch 3 para 1)

s 43 subst—Finance, 2011 c 11, sch 13 paras 27, 37
rep in pt—Finance, 2012 c 14, sch 16 para 233

s 49A added—Finance, 2013 c 29, sch 47 para 13

s 49B added—Finance, 2014 c 26, s 292(7)

ss 59, 62 am—SI 2010/2901, art 4

s 72 rep in pt—Finance, 2012 c 14, sch 16 para 234

s 78 am—Finance, 2011 c 11, sch 13 para 28

s 85 am—Finance, 2010 c 13, s 36, sch 11 paras 2, 5(1)(a)(b)(c)(i)
rep in pt—Finance, 2010 c 13, s 36, sch 11 para 5(1)(c)(ii)

s 85A added—Finance, 2010 c 13, s 36, sch 11 para 4(1)
rep in pt—Finance, 2010 c 13, s 36, sch 11 para 5(2); Finance, 2013 c 29, sch 29 para 48(2)

s 86 rep in pt—Finance, 2010 c 13, s 36, sch 11 para 6(1)(a)
am—Finance, 2010 c 13, s 36, sch 11 para 6(1)(b)

s 96 am—Finance, 2012 c 14, sch 16 para 235(c)
rep in pt—Finance, 2012 c 14, sch 16 para 235(a), (b)

ss 97, 97A subst for s 97—Finance, 2012 c 14, sch 16 para 236

s 98 rep—Finance, 2012 c 14, sch 16 para 237

s 99 am—Finance, 2012 c 14, sch 16 para 238

s 102 rep—Finance, 2012 c 14, sch 16 para 239

s 103 rep in pt—Finance, 2012 c 14, sch 16 para 240

s 104 am—Finance, 2012 c 14, sch 16 para 241

s 112 am—Finance, 2010 c 13, s 36, sch 11 para 7(1); Finance, 2013 c 29, sch 47 para 14;
Finance, 2014 c 26, s 292(4)(5)

s 118 am—Co-operative and Community Benefit Societies, 2014 c 14, sch 4 para 171(2)(3)

s 123 am—SI 2011/1431, reg 5

s 130A added—Finance, 2011 c 11, s 72(1)

s 143 appl (mods)—Finance, 2012 c 14, sch 36 para 16(6)

Pt 4 (ss 146-217) excl—Corporation Tax, 2010 c 4, s 938N; Budget Responsibility and Nat
Audit, 2011 c 4, sch 4 para 3(2); Postal Services, 2011 c 5, sch 2 para 6(2);
Finance, 2012 c 14, s 129

s 147 am—Finance, 2011 c 11, sch 5 para 5(1); Finance, 2013 c 29, sch 32 para 13

s 157 appl in pt—Finance, 2015 c 11, s 106(7)(a)

s 158-163 appl (mods)—Finance, 2015 c 11, s 106(7)(b)

s 164 am—Finance, 2011 c 11, s 58(1)

ss 166-171 excl—Corporation Tax, 2010 c 4, s 542(2)

s 166 am—Finance, 2012 c 14, sch 2 para 3

s 167A added—Finance, 2012 c 14, sch 2 para 4

s 170 am—Finance, 2012 c 14, sch 2 para 5

s 171 am—Finance, 2012 c 14, sch 2 para 6

s 174 am—Finance, 2014 c 26, s 75(2)

s 174A added—Finance, 2014 c 26, s 75(3)

s 179 am—Finance, 2012 c 14, sch 20 para 42

s 187A added—Finance, 2014 c 26, s 75(4)

s 206A added—Finance, 2013 c 29, sch 32 para 14

s 210 am—SI 2010/2901, art 4

s 213 am—Finance, 2013 c 29, sch 32 para 15

Pt 6 (ss 231-259) excl—Corporation Tax, 2010 c 4, ss 938N, 938V(c)

s 231 am—Finance, 2011 c 11, sch 5 para 5(2); Finance, 2013 c 29, sch 20 para 5

s 236 am—Finance, 2013 c 29, sch 47 para 15

s 254 appl—Corporation Tax, 2010 c 4, ss 4(4), 37(9), 45(6), 62(6), 66(4)

Pt 7 (ss 260-353B) see (retrosp effect for amdmts) —Finance (No 3), 2010 c 33, s 11, sch 5
paras 1
excl—Corporation Tax, 2010 c 4, s 938N, 938V(d)

s 260 am—Finance (No 3), 2010 c 33, s 11, sch 5 para 2

s 262 am—Finance (No 3), 2010 c 33, s 11, sch 5 para 3; Finance, 2012 c 14, sch 5 para 2

s 263 am—Finance (No 3), 2010 c 33, s 11, sch 5 para 4; Finance, 2011 c 11, sch 13 para 29

s 264 am—Finance (No 3), 2010 c 33, s 11, sch 5 para 5

2010

c 8 *continued*

s 265 am—Finance (No 3), 2010 c 33, s 11, sch 5 para 6(2)

rep in pt—Finance (No 3), 2010 c 33, s 11, sch 5 para 6(3)

s 265A added—Finance (No 3), 2010 c 33, s 11, sch 5 para 7

s 266 am—Finance (No 3), 2010 c 33, s 11, sch 5 para 8

s 269 am—Finance, 2012 c 14, sch 16 para 242

s 270 am—Finance (No 3), 2010 c 33, s 11, sch 5 para 9; SI 2013/636, sch para 13(2)

s 271 rep in pt—Finance (No 3), 2010 c 33, s 11, sch 5 para 10(2)

am—Finance (No 3), 2010 c 33, s 11, sch 5 para 10(3)

s 273 rep in pt—Finance (No 3), 2010 c 33, s 11, sch 5 para 11

s 273A added—Finance (No 3), 2010 c 33, s 11, sch 5 para 12

s 275A added—Finance (No 3), 2010 c 33, s 11, sch 5 para 13

s 276 am—Finance, 2012 c 14, sch 5 para 3

s 280 am—Finance, 2012 c 14, sch 5 para 4

s 280A added—Finance (No 3), 2010 c 33, s 11, sch 5 para 14

s 284 am—Finance (No 3), 2010 c 33, s 11, sch 5 para 15

s 284A added—Finance (No 3), 2010 c 33, s 11, sch 5 para 16

s 288 am—Finance, 2012 c 14, sch 5 para 5

s 292 am—Finance (No 3), 2010 c 33, s 11, sch 5 para 17; SI 2012/3045, reg 3; Finance, 2012 c 14, sch 5 para 6

s 293 subst—SI 2012/3045, reg 4

s 296 am—Finance, 2012 c 14, sch 5 para 7; SI 2012/3045, reg 5

s 298 am—SI 2012/3045, reg 6

s 298A added—Finance, 2012 c 14, sch 20 para 43

s 305 am—Finance (No 3), 2010 c 33, s 11, sch 5 para 18

s 305A added—Finance, 2012 c 14, sch 5 para 8

s 310 am—Finance, 2012 c 14, sch 16 para 243(a)

s 310 rep in pt—Finance, 2012 c 14, sch 16 para 243(b)

s 313 am—Finance, 2012 c 14, sch 5 para 9

s 314 am—Finance (No 3), 2010 c 33, s 11, sch 5 para 19; Finance, 2012 c 14, sch 5 para 10; ibid, sch 20 para 44

s 314A added—Finance, 2012 c 14, sch 20 para 45

am—SI 2012/3045, reg 7

s 315 rep in pt—Finance (No 3), 2010 c 33, s 11, sch 5 para 20

s 316 am—Finance (No 3), 2010 c 33, s 11, sch 5 para 21; Finance, 2013 c 29, s 44(1); SI 2013/636, sch para 13(3)

rep in pt—Finance, 2012 c 14, sch 5 para 11

s 317A added—Finance, 2011 c 11, sch 13 para 30

s 318A added—Finance (No 3), 2010 c 33, s 11, sch 5 para 22

s 321 rep in pt—Finance (No 3), 2010 c 33, s 11, sch 5 para 23

s 326 rep in pt—Finance, 2010 c 13, s 30, sch 6 para 28

s 327 rep in pt—Finance (No 3), 2010 c 33, s 11, sch 5 para 24(1)-(3)

am—Finance (No 3), 2010 c 33, s 11, sch 5 para 24

s 329 am—Finance, 2012 c 14, sch 5 para 12

s 330 am—Finance, 2012 c 14, sch 5 para 13

s 331ZA added—Finance, 2012 c 14, sch 5 para 14

s 331A added—Finance (No 3), 2010 c 33, s 11, sch 5 para 25

s 332 am—Finance (No 3), 2010 c 33, s 11, sch 5 para 26

ss 332A-332C added—Finance (No 3), 2010 c 33, s 11, sch 5 para 27

s 332AA added—SI 2015/662, reg 2(2)

s 336A added—Finance (No 3), 2010 c 33, s 11, sch 5 para 28

Pt 7, Ch 10 (ss 337-353) am —(heading am) Finance (No 3), 2010 c 33, s 11, sch 5 para 29

s 337 am—Finance, 2012 c 14, sch 5 para 15

s 339 am—Finance (No 3), 2010 c 33, s 11, sch 5 para 30; Finance, 2012 c 14, sch 5 para 16(2)

rep in pt—Finance, 2012 c 14, sch 5 para 16(3)

s 345 am—Finance (No 3), 2010 c 33, s 11, sch 5 para 31; Finance, 2014 c 26, s 39(2)

s 346 am—SI 2015/662, reg 2(3)

s 348 am—Finance, 2012 c 14, sch 5 para 17; SI 2015/662, reg 2(4)

s 348A added—Finance, 2012 c 14, sch 5 para 18

s 351 am—Finance (No 3), 2010 c 33, s 11, sch 5 para 32; Finance, 2012 c 14, sch 5 para 19

s 353 am—Finance, 2012 c 14, sch 5 para 20; SI 2013/636, sch para 13(4)(a)(c)

rep in pt—SI 2013/636, sch para 13(4)(b)

2010
c 8 *continued*

s 353A added—Finance (No 3), 2010 c 33, s 11, sch 5 para 33
　　am—Finance, 2014 c 26, s 39(3)
s 353AA added—Finance, 2012 c 14, sch 5 para 21
s 353B added—Finance (No 3), 2010 c 33, s 11, sch 5 para 33
Pt 8 (ss 354-363) am—Finance, 2014 c 26, s 289(5)(b)
s 363A added—Finance, 2011 c 11, s 59
　　am—Finance, 2013 c 29, sch 46 para 146; Finance, 2014 c 26, s 289(2)-(4)(5)(c)
Pt 9A (ss 371AA-371VJ) added—Finance, 2012 c 14, sch 20 para 1
s 371BB appl (mods)—Corporation Tax, 2009 c 4, ss 18H-18HE
s 371BC am—Finance (No. 2), 2015 c 33, sch 3 para 8; Corporation Tax (NI), 2015 c 21,
　　sch 2 para 2
s 371BH mod—SI 2012/3044, reg 5
s 371BI added—Finance (No. 2), 2015 c 33, sch 3 para 9
Pt 9A, Ch 3 (ss 371CA-371CG) appl (mods)—Corporation Tax, 2009 c 4, s 18HA
s 371CE am—Finance, 2013 c 29, sch 47 para 17
s 371CG am—SI 2013/636, sch para 13(5)
Pt 9A, Ch 4 (ss 371DA-371DL) appl (mods)—Corporation Tax, 2009 c 4, s 18HB
Pt 9A, Ch 5 (ss 371EA-371EE) appl (mods)—Corporation Tax, 2009 c 4, s 18HC
s 371ED rep in pt—Finance, 2013 c 29, sch 47 para 3
s 371EE am—Finance, 2013 c 29, sch 47 para 4
Pt 9A, Ch 7 (s 371GA) appl (mods)—Corporation Tax, 2009 c 4, s 18HD
Pt 9A, Ch 9 (ss 371IA-371IJ) appl (mods)—Corporation Tax, 2009 c 4, s 18HE
s 371IB am—Finance, 2013 c 29, sch 47 para 19
s 371IE am—Finance, 2013 c 29, sch 47 para 20
s 371IH am—Finance, 2014 c 26, ss 293(1), 294(1)
Pt 9A, Ch 11-14 (ss 371KA-371NE) appl (mods)—Corporation Tax, 2009 c 4, s 18HF
s 371KB mod—SI 2012/3024, reg 4
s 371RB appl (mods)—Corporation Tax, 2009 c 4, s 931E(4)(6)
s 371RD appl—Corporation Tax, 2009 c 4 s 931E(5)(6)
s 371RE rep in pt—SI 2014/3237, reg 2(a)
　　am—SI 2014/3237, reg 2(b)-(d)
s 371UBA added—Finance (No. 2), 2015 c 33, sch 3 para 10
s 371UD rep—Finance (No. 2), 2015 c 33, s 36(1)
s 371VA am—Finance, 2013 c 29, sch 47 para 6
s 371VG am—Finance, 2013 c 29, sch 47 para 7(2)
　　rep in pt—Finance, 2013 c 29, sch 47 para 7(3)
s 371VH rep in pt—Finance, 2013 c 29, sch 47 para 8(2)
　　am—Finance, 2013 c 29, sch 47 para 8(3)
s 371VIA added—Finance, 2013 c 29, sch 47 para 9
sch 7 rep in pt—Finance, 2013 c 29, sch 29 para 48(3)
sch 8 rep in pt—Finance, 2012 c 14, s 26(2)(e); ibid, sch 16 para 247(x); SL(R), 2013 c 2, s
　　1, sch 1 pt 10(1); Finance, 2013 c 29, sch 29 para 48(4)
sch 9 am —Finance (No 3), 2010 c 33, s 11, sch 5 para 34
sch 11 am—Finance (No 3), 2010 c 33, s 11, sch 5 para 35; Finance, 2012 c 14, sch 16 para
　　244; SI 2013/636, sch para 13(6)(b)
　　rep in pt—SI 2013/636, sch para 13(6)(a)
c 9　**Child Poverty**
s 6 rep in pt—Welfare Reform, 2012 c 5, sch 13 para 5
ss 8-8C subst for s 8—Welfare Reform, 2012 c 5, sch 13 para 2
s 9 am—Welfare Reform, 2012 c 5, s 146(2), (3), (4)(a)-(c), (5)
　　rep in pt—Welfare Reform, 2012 c 5, s 146(4)(d)
s 10 am—Welfare Reform, 2012 c 5, sch 13 para 6(a)
　　rep in pt—Welfare Reform, 2012 c 5, sch 13 para 6(b)
s 13 am—Welfare Reform, 2012 c 5, sch 13 para 7(a)
　　rep in pt—Welfare Reform, 2012 c 5, sch 13 para 7(b)
s 14 rep—Welfare Reform, 2012 c 5, sch 13 para 8(2)
s 15 am—Welfare Reform, 2012 c 5, sch 13 para 9
s 16 am—Welfare Reform, 2012 c 5, sch 13 para 10
s 18 am—Welfare Reform, 2012 c 5, sch 13 para 11
s 20 am—Police Reform and Social Responsibility, 2011 c 13, sch 16 para 379; Health and
　　Social Care, 2012 c 7, sch 5 para 183(a)
　　rep in pt—Health and Social Care, 2012 c 7, sch 5 para 183(b), (c)
s 24 rep—Deregulation, 2015 c 20, s 100(2)(f)

2010

c 9 *continued*

> s 28 am—Welfare Reform, 2012 c 5, sch 13 para 12
> sch 1 subst—Welfare Reform, 2012 c 5, sch 13 para 3
> sch 2 am—Welfare Reform, 2012 c 5, sch 13 para 13(2), (3)
>> rep in pt—Welfare Reform, 2012 c 5, sch 13 para 13(4)

c 10 **Third Parties (Rights against Insurers)**
> excl —Merchant Shipping, 1995 c 21, s 225P(7)(c) (added by 2011 c 8, s 1(2))
> s 1 am—(prosp) Insurance, 2015 c 4, sch 2 para 4
> s 4 rep in pt—Deregulation, 2015 c 20, sch 6 para 2(22)
>> am—(prosp) Insurance, 2015 c 4, sch 2 para 2
> s 6 am—(prosp) Insurance, 2015 c 4, sch 2 para 3
> s 19 subst—Insurance, 2015 c 4, s 19
> s 19A added—(prosp) Insurance, 2015 c 4, sch 2 para 6
> sch 3 am—(prosp) Insurance, 2015 c 4, sch 2 para 5(2)-(6)

c 11 **Cluster Munitions (Prohibitions)**
> ext (mods)—(Isle of Man) SI 2011/2443, art 2, sch

c 12 **Appropriation (No 2)**

c 13 **Finance**
> s 2 am—Finance (No 2), 2010 c 31, s 1; Finance, 2011 c 11, s 4(1)
> s 16 rep—Finance, 2011 c 11, s 24(1)
> s 23 rep—SI 2010/2938, art 2
> s 40 rep —SI 2013/2819, reg 41(f)
> s 47 rep in pt—Finance, 2012 c 14, sch 16 para 247(u)
> s 58 rep in pt—Finance, 2010 c 13, s 59(4)(c)
> s 64 am—SI 2013/636, sch para 14(2)
> sch 1 am—Financial Services, 2012 c. 21, sch 18 para 130; SI 2013/636, sch para 14(3);
>> Co-operative and Community Benefit Societies, 2014 c 14, sch 4 para 173
>> rep in pt—Finance, 2012 c 14, sch 39 para 5(2)(g)
> sch 2 rep—SI 2010/2938, art 2
> sch 6 rep in pt—Finance, 2011 c 11, sch 26 para 1(2)(b)(ii); Finance, 2012 c 14, s 52(2);
>> Finance, 2013 c 29, sch 12 para 17; ibid, sch 35 para 3(a); Finance, 2014 c 26,
>> s 114(3)(e)
>> am—Charities, 2011 c 25, sch 7 para 143; Finance, 2013 c 29, sch 35 para 3(b)
> sch 8 rep in pt—Finance, 2012 c 14, s 50(3)(b); ibid, sch 15 paras 12, 16
> sch 13 rep —SI 2013/2819, reg 41(f)
> sch 14 rep in pt—Finance, 2011 c 11, s 60(3)

c 14 **Anti-Slavery Day**

c 15 **Equality**
> s 1 rep in pt—Public Bodies, 2011 c 24, sch 6; Health and Social Care, 2012 c 7, sch 5 para
>> 181; Deregulation, 2015 c 20, s 100(2)(g)
>> am—Police Reform and Social Responsibility, 2011 c 13, sch 16 para 381
> s 7 rep in pt—Stamp Duty Land Tax, 2015 c 1, sch para 21(b)
> s 9 rep in pt—Enterprise and Regulatory Reform, 2013 c 24, s 97(2)
>> power to rep or am conferred—Enterprise and Regulatory Reform, 2013 c 24, s
>> 97(7)-(10)
>> am—Enterprise and Regulatory Reform, 2013 c 24, s 97(3)(4)
> s 23 am—Marriage (Same Sex Couples), 2013 c 30, sch 7 para 43
> Pt 5 (ss 39-83) appl (mods)—SI 2010/1835, art 2
>> appl—SI 2011/1771, regs 3(1)-(3), 4, 5
>> excl—Constitutional Reform, 2005 c 4, ss 27(5A)(b), 63(4)
> s 40 rep in pt—Enterprise and Regulatory Reform, 2013 c 24, s 65
> s 42 am—Crime and Cts, 2013 c 22, sch 8 para 181; SI 2013/602, sch 2 para 63(2)(a)(b)
>> rep in pt—SI 2013/602, sch 2 para 63(2)(c)
> s 43 am—Police Reform and Social Responsibility, 2011 c 13, sch 16 para 382; Crime and
>> Cts, 2013 c 22, sch 8 para 182; SI 2013/602, sch 2 para 63(3)(a)(c)(d)
>> rep in pt—SI 2013/602, sch 2 para 63(3)(b)
> s 50 am—Crime and Cts, 2013 c 22, sch 13 para 50
> s 51 am—Crime and Cts, 2013 c 22, sch 13 para 51
> s 67 am—SIs 2014/560, sch 1 para 35(2); 3229, sch 5 para 19(2)
> s 76 am—SI 2010/2622, art 2
> s 80 rep in pt—SIs 2014/560, sch 1 para 35(3); 3229, sch 5 para 19(3)
> s 85 am—SI 2012/976, sch para 25
> s 87 am—SI 2010/2279, arts 2, 3; SI 2012/976, sch para 26; School Standards and
>> Organisation (W), 2013 anaw 1, sch 5 para 11

2010

c 15 *continued*

s 91 am—Educ, 2011 c 21, sch 13 para 20(2)

s 94 am—SI 2010/2279, arts 2, 4

s 108 am—SI 2010/2279, arts 2, 5

s 110 am—Marriage (Same Sex Couples), 2013 c 30, s 2(5); SI 2014/3229, sch 5 para 19(4)

s 114 am—Crime and Cts, 2013 c 22, sch 9 para 52

s 115 am—Justice and Security, 2013 c 18, sch 2 para 12; Immigration, 2014 c 22, sch 9 para 59

s 118 am—SIs 2011/1133, reg 55; 2015/1392, reg 7(2)
    rep in pt—Enterprise and Regulatory Reform, 2013 c 24, s 64(13)

s 119 am—Crime and Cts, 2013 c 22, sch 9 para 52

s 121 am—(1.1 2016) Armed Forces (Service Complaints and Financial Assistance), 2015 c 19, sch para 13(2)(4)(5)
    rep in pt—(1.1 2016) Armed Forces (Service Complaints and Financial Assistance), 2015 c 19, sch para 13(3)

s 120 am—Crime and Cts, 2013 c 22, sch 9 para 52

s 123 am—SI 2011/1133, reg 56; Enterprise and Regulatory Reform, 2013 c 24, sch 2 para 43

s 124 am—Crime and Cts, 2013 c 22, sch 9 para 52; Deregulation, 2015 c 20, s 2(1)(a)
    rep in pt—Deregulation, 2015 c 20, s 2(1)(b),(2)(a)

s 125 rep—Deregulation, 2015 c 20, s 2(2)(b)

s 127 am—Crime and Cts, 2013 c 22, sch 9 para 52; (1.1 2016) Armed Forces (Service Complaints and Financial Assistance), 2015 c 19, sch para 14

s 129 am—SI 2011/1133, reg 57; Enterprise and Regulatory Reform, 2013 c 24, sch 2 para 44

s 132 am—SI 2010/2279, arts 2, 6

s 134 am—SI 2010/2279, arts 2, 6

s 135 am—SI 2010/2279, arts 2, 7

s 138 rep—Enterprise and Regulatory Reform, 2013 c 24, s 66(1)

s 139A added—Enterprise and Regulatory Reform, 2013 c 24, s 98(2)

s 140 am—Crime and Cts, 2013 c 22, sch 9 para 52

s 140A added—SI 2011/1133, reg 58

s 140AA added—SI 2015/1392, reg 7(3)
    rep in pt—SI 2015/1972, reg 5(2)

s 140B added —Enterprise and Regulatory Reform, 2013 c 24, sch 2 para 45

s 141 am—(1.1 2016) Armed Forces (Service Complaints and Financial Assistance), 2015 c 19, sch para 15

s 143 am—Crime and Cts, 2013 c 22, sch 9 para 52

s 144 am—Enterprise and Regulatory Reform, 2013 c 24, s 23(5)

s 147 am—SI 2012/334, art 2; Enterprise and Regulatory Reform, 2013 c 24, s 23(6)

Pt 11 (ss 149-159) appl (mods)—SI 2012/2734, regs 3-6, sch pt 1, 2, 3

s 159 excl—Constitutional Reform, 2005 c 4, s 27(5A)(a)

s 182 am—SI 2011/3066, sch para 1(a), (b)(ii)
    rep in pt—SI 2011/3066, sch para 1(b)(i)

s 183 rep in pt—Deregulation, 2015 c 20, sch 10 para 29(2)
    am—Deregulation, 2015 c 20, sch 10 para 29(3)

s 184 rep—Deregulation, 2015 c 20, sch 10 para 30(a)

s 185 rep in pt—Deregulation, 2015 c 20, sch 10 para 30(b)(i)
    am—Deregulation, 2015 c 20, sch 10 para 30(b)(ii)

s 194 am—Charities, 2011 c 25, sch 7 para 144

s 207 am—Enterprise and Regulatory Reform, 2013 c 24, s 98(3)

s 208 am—Enterprise and Regulatory Reform, 2013 c 24, s 98(4)
    rep in pt—Deregulation, 2015 c 20, sch 10 para 30(c)

sch 3 am—SI 2010/2279, arts 2, 8, 9; (savings) Mobile Homes (W), 2013 anaw 6, sch 4 para 11; Marriage (Same Sex Couples), 2013 c 30, s 2(6); ibid, sch 7 para 44; SI 2013/1865, reg 13(4); SI 2014/3229, sch 5 para 19(5)

sch 6 am—GSM Bishops and Priests (Consecration and Ordination of Women), 2014 No 2, s 2
    mod—Finance, 2015 c 11, s 123

sch 8 am—SI 2011/1060, art 6(2)

sch 9 rep in pt—SI 2011/1069, reg 2(2)(3)
    am—SI 2011/1069, reg 2(4); (pt prosp) Marriage (Same Sex Couples), 2013 c 30, sch 4 para 17

2010

c 15 *continued*

sch 10 am—Educ, 2011 c 21, sch 13 para 20(3); SI 2012/976, sch para 27

sch 11 am—SI 2012/976, sch para 28; School Standards and Organisation (W), 2013 anaw 1, sch 5 para 28(2)(a)

rep in pt—SI 2010/2279, arts 2, 10; School Standards and Organisation (W), 2013 anaw 1, sch 5 para 28(2)(b)

sch 17 am—Education (Wales), 2009 nawm 5, ss 9(2)(3), 10, 11(2)(a)(b), 12-16; Educ, 2011 c 21, sch 1 para 12; ibid, sch 1 para 13(a)(b); ibid, sch 13 para 20(4); ibid, sch 15 para 2; SI 2011/1060, art 6(3); Children and Families, 2014 c 6, s 60

rep in pt—Educ, 2011 c 21, sch 1 para 13(c); Enterprise and Regulatory Reform, 2013 c 24, s 64(14)

sch 18 am—SI 2010/2279, arts 2, 11

sch 19 am—Budget Responsibility and Nat Audit, 2011 c 4, sch 1 para 28; ibid, sch 5 para 34; Police Reform and Social Responsibility, 2011 c 13, sch 16 para 383; (Localism, 2011 c 20, sch 22 para 62; SSI 2011/233, art 2; SIs 2011/1060, sch 1 para 2-9, sch 2; 2011/1063(W 154), art 2; Health and Social Care, 2012 c 7, sch 5 para 182(a); ibid, sch 5 para 182(b); ibid, sch 13 para 19; ibid, sch 17 para 14; ibid, sch 19 para 13; Financial Services, 2012 c. 21, sch 18 para 131; SSI 2012/55, art 2; SI 2012/990 (W 130), art 11; Public Audit (W), 2013 anaw 3, sch 4 para 92; Enterprise and Regulatory Reform, 2013 c 24, sch 4 para 26; Energy, 2013 c 32, sch 12 para 102; Financial Services (Banking Reform), 2013 c 33, sch 4 para 16; SSI 2013/170, art 2; SIs 2013/602, sch 2 para 63(4)(b)-(d); 2013/755 (W 90), sch 2 para 450(3); Anti-social Behaviour, Crime and Policing, 2014 c 12, sch 11 para 96; Care, 2014 c 23, sch 7 para 27; ibid, sch 5 para 35; (prosp) Crim Justice and Cts, 2015 c 2, sch 3 para 17; Planning (W), 2015 anaw 4, sch 1 para 7; Qualifications Wales, 2015 anaw 5, sch 1 para 40; SSI 2015/83, art 2

rep in pt—Localism, 2011 c 20, sch 16 para 62, sch 25 pts 26, 32; Public Bodies, 2011 c 24, sch 6; Health and Social Care, 2012 c 7, sch 5 para 182(c), (d); (prosp) ibid, sch 14 para 116; Legal Aid, Sentencing and Punishment of Offenders, 2012 c 10, sch 5 para 70; SI 2012/2007, sch para 109(e); Crime and Cts, 2013 c 22, sch 8 para 183; SIs 2013/602, sch 2 para 63(4)(a)(e); 2013/755 (W 90), sch 2 para 450(2); Loc Audit and Accountability, 2014 c 2, sch 12 para 114; SIs 2014/892, sch 1 para 182; 3184, sch para 15

sch 20 rep—Equality 2010 c 15, s 186(2)

sch 21 appl (mods)—SI 2010/2128, reg 14

am—Crime and Cts, 2013 c 22, sch 9 para 52

sch 22 am—Educ, 2011 c 21, s 62(4)(c)

sch 23 am—SI 2014/3229, sch 5 para 19(6)

sch 25 am—SI 2012/1809, art 3(1) sch pt 1

sch 26 am —SIs 2010/2279, art 12, sch 1; 2011/1060, art 3(2)

sch 27 am —SI 2010/2279, art 13, sch 2; 2011/1060, schs 3, 4

c 16 **Northern Ireland Assembly Members**

c 17 **Crime and Security**

s 6 rep in pt—Terrorism Prevention and Investigation Measures, 2011 c 23, sch 7 para 6(2)

s 12 rep in pt—Terrorism Prevention and Investigation Measures, 2011 c 23, sch 7 para 6(3)

s 13 am—SI 2012/2595, art 22(2)

s 14 rep —Protection of Freedoms, 2012 c 9, sch 9 para 4(2) sch 10 pt 1

ss 16-19 rep —Protection of Freedoms, 2012 c 9, sch 9 para 4(2) sch 10 pt 1

s 20 rep—Terrorism Prevention and Investigation Measures, 2011 c 23, sch 7 para 6(4)

ss 21-23 rep —Protection of Freedoms, 2012 c 9, sch 9 para 4(2) sch 10 pt 1

s 31 am—Crime and Cts, 2013 c 22, sch 8 para 179(a)

rep in pt—Crime and Cts, 2013 c 22, sch 8 para 179(b)

s 34 rep—Serious Crime, 2015 c 9, sch 4 para 86

ss 40, 41 rep —Anti-social Behaviour, Crime and Policing, 2014 c 12, sch 11 para 46

s 42 am—SI 2012/2595, art 22(3)

rep in pt—Protection of Freedoms, 2012 c 9, sch 10 pt 3

s 44 am—SI 2012/2595, art 22(5)

s 55 rep—Police Reform and Social Responsibility, 2011 c 13, s 119(4)

s 56 rep—Terrorism Prevention and Investigation Measures, 2011 c 23, sch 7 para 6(5)(a)

s 58 rep in pt—Terrorism Prevention and Investigation Measures, 2011 c 23, sch 7 para 6(5)(b); Protection of Freedoms, 2012 c 9, sch 9 para 4(3) sch 10 pt 1

s 59 am—SI 2012/2595, art 22(5)

sch 1 rep in pt—Protection of Freedoms, 2012 c 9, sch 10 pt 3

2010
c 18   **Personal Care at Home**
          s 1 am—SI 2015/914, sch para 95
c 19   **Mortgage Repossessions (Protection of Tenants etc)**
c 20   **Sunbeds (Regulation)**
          s 2 am—SI 2015/664, sch 4 para 44
          s 10 am—SI 2015/664, sch 4 para 94
          sch appl (mods)—SI 2011/1130(W 156), reg 9(3)(4)
c 21   **Sustainable Communities Act 2007 (Amendment)**
c 22   **Debt Relief (Developing Countries)**
          cont—SI 2011/1336, art 2
c 23   **Bribery**
          s 10 am—SI 2014/834, sch 2 para 74(2)(a)(3)-(5)
                  rep in pt—SI 2014/834, sch 2 para 74(2)(b)
          s 17 am—SI 2012/2595, art 19
c 24   **Digital Economy**
          s 17, 18 rep—Deregulation, 2015 c 20, s 56
          s 42 rep—SI 2015/664, sch 4 para 103
          s 43 am—SI 2013/2352, sch 1 para 14
c 25   **Constitutional Reform and Governance**
          s 1 am—SI 2012/2595, art 20
          ss 10-14 excl—Crime and Cts, 2013 c 22, sch 1 para 7(7)
          s 23 rep in pt—European Union, 2011 c 12, s 14(2)(a)
                  am—European Union, 2011 c 12, s 14(2)(b)(c); Finance, 2011 c 11, sch 19 para 69;
                      Finance, 2012 c 14, s 218(3)
          s 41 rep in pt—Finance, 2013 c 29, sch 46 para 147(1)
          s 43 rep in pt—SI 2014/1372, sch para 12
          s 46 power mod—Protection of Freedoms, 2012 c 9, s 104(2)
          sch 6 am—Public Service Pensions, 2013 c 25, s 34; Public Service Pensions, 2013 c 25, sch
                      11 para 1(3)(a)
                  rep in pt—Public Service Pensions, 2013 c 25, sch 11 paras 1(2)(3)(b), 7
          sch 7 rep in pt—Protection of Freedoms, 2012 c 9, s 104(1)(b)
c 26   **Children, Schools and Families**
          s 2 rep—Children and Families, 2014 c 6, sch 3 para 19(2)
          s 5 am—Academies, 2010 c 32, s 14, sch 2 para 26(2)(a)(b)(3)
          Pt 2 (ss 11-22) rep—Crime and Cts, 2013 c 22, s 17(4)
          s 22 rep—Educ, 2011 c 21, s 45(2)(h)
          s 29 rep in pt—Crime and Cts, 2013 c 22, s 17(4)
          schs 1, 2 rep—Crime and Cts, 2013 c 22, s 17(4)
          sch 3 rep in pt—Crime and Cts, 2013 c 22, s 17(4)
          sch 4 rep in pt—Crime and Cts, 2013 c 22, s 17(4)
c 27   **Energy**
          s 5 power to rep conferred—Energy, 2013 c 32, s 1(8)(b)
c 28   **Financial Services**
          s 1 rep—Financial Services, 2012 c. 21, sch 19
          s 2 rep in pt—Financial Services, 2012 c. 21, sch 19
          s 3 rep in pt—Financial Services, 2012 c. 21, sch 19
          ss 6, 7 rep—Financial Services, 2012 c. 21, sch 19
          sch 2 rep in pt—Financial Services, 2012 c. 21, sch 19
c 29   **Flood and Water Management**
          ss 1-3 appl—Income Tax (Trading and Other Income), 2005 c 5, s 86B(4) (added by 2015 c
                      11, sch 5 para 1)
          s 6 am—SI 2013/755 (W 90), sch 2 para 452; (prosp) Water, 2014 c 21, sch 7 para
                      144(b)(c)
                  rep in pt—(prosp) Water, 2014 c 21, sch 7 para 144(a)
          s 11 am—SI 2013/755 (W 90), sch 2 para 453
          s 12 am—SI 2013/755 (W 90), sch 2 para 454
          s 13 am—SI 2013/755 (W 90), sch 2 para 455
          s 14 am—SI 2013/755 (W 90), sch 2 para 456
          s 15 am—SI 2013/755 (W 90), sch 2 para 457
          s 17 am—SI 2013/755 (W 90), sch 2 para 458
          s 18 am—SI 2013/755 (W 90), sch 2 para 459
          s 22 am—SI 2013/755 (W 90), sch 2 para 460
          s 23 am—SI 2013/755 (W 90), sch 2 para 461
          s 25 am—SI 2013/755 (W 90), sch 2 para 462

2010
c 29 *continued*
    s 26A added—SI 2013/755 (W 90), sch 2 para 463
    s 35 rep in pt—(prosp) Water, 2014 c 21, sch 7 para 145
    s 38 am —SI 2013/755 (W 90), sch 2 para 464
    s 39 am—SI 2013/755 (W 90), sch 2 para 465
    s 42 rep in pt—(prosp) Water, 2014 c 21, sch 7 para 146
    s 44 am—Water, 2014 c 21, sch 7 para 147
    sch 1 am—SI 2013/755 (W 90), sch 2 para 466
    sch 2 rep in pt—Localism, 2011 c 20, sch 25 pt 4
    sch 3 am—SIs 2012/1659, sch 3 para 20; 2013/755 (W 90), sch 2 para 467; Water, 2014 c
        21, ss 21(3), 88(a)(b)
    sch 4 am—SIs 2013/755 (W 90), sch 2 para 468; 2015/48, art 15
1st session of 55th Parliament
c 30   **Appropriation (No 3)**
c 31   **Finance (No 2)**
    s 6 rep—Finance, 2011 c 11, sch 16 para 84(e)(i)
    s 9 rep—Finance, 2012 c 14, sch 16 para 247(v)
    sch 3 rep—Finance, 2011 c 11, sch 16 para 84(e)(ii)
    sch 5 rep in pt—Finance, 2011 c 11, sch 4 para 12(b)
c 32   **Academies**
    s 1 am—Educ, 2011 c 21, s 53(2)(4)-(7)
        rep in pt—Educ, 2011 c 21, ss 52, 53(3); Children and Families, 2014 c 6, sch 3 para 95
    s 2 rep in pt—Educ, 2011 c 21, sch 15 para 3
    s 3 am—Educ, 2011 c 21, s 57(2)
        appl (mods)—SI 2007/2979, sch 1 para 23B (added by 2012/1201, reg 4)
    s 4 am—Educ, 2011 c 21, ss 55, 57(3); ibid, sch 13 para 2
        appl (mods)—SI 2007/2979, sch 1 para 23C (added by 2012/1201, reg 4)
    s 5 subst —Educ, 2011 c 21, s 56
        appl (mods)—SI 2007/2979, sch 1 para 23D (added by 2012/1201, reg 4)
    s 6 am—Educ, 2011 c 21, s 58; ibid, sch 13 para 3
        appl (mods)—SI 2007/2979, sch 1 paras 23E, 23F (added by 2012/1201, reg 4)
    s 7 am—Educ, 2011 c 21, s 57(4)
    s 8 am—Educ, 2011 c 21, s 59
    s 9 subst—Educ, 2011 c 21, s 60(1)
        mod—SI 2012/1107, art 8
    s 10 subst —Educ, 2011 c 21, s 60(2)
    s 10A added—Educ, 2011 c 21, s 61
        am—Educ, 2011 c 21, sch 13 para 4
    s 12 am—Educ, 2011 c 21, sch 14 para 20
        rep in pt—Charities, 2011 c 25, sch 10
    s 17 am—Educ, 2011 c 21, s 57(5)
    sch 1 am—Educ, 2011 c 21, sch 13 para 5
        subst—Educ, 2011 c 21, sch 14 para 1
    sch 2 rep in pt—Educ, 2011 c 21, sch 11 para 11
c 33   **Finance (No 3)**
    s 13 rep in pt—(with spec commencing effect) Finance, 2013 c 29, sch 15 paras 25, 28, 29
    s 15 rep—Finance, 2012 c 14, sch 16 para 247(w)
    sch 3 rep in pt—Finance, 2012 c 14, s 33(5)(d)
    sch 6 am—Finance, 2015 c 11, s 115(2)
        rep in pt—Finance (No. 2), 2015 c 33, s 35(2)(d)
    sch 10 rep in pt—Finance, 2013 c 29, sch 50 para 15
        am—Finance, 2014 c 26, sch 22 para 21
    sch 11 am—Finance, 2014 c 26, sch 22 para 22
c 34   **Equitable Life (Payments)**
c 35   **Local Government**
c 36   **Savings Accounts and Health in Pregnancy Grant**
c 37   **Superannuation**
    s 3 rep (with savings)—SI 2010/2996, art 2
c 38   **Terrorist Asset-Freezing etc**
    power to rep —Terrorist Asset-Freezing etc, 2010 c 38, s 47
    Pt 1 (ss 1-47) ext (mods)—(Isle of Man) SIs 2011/749, art 2, sch; 2011/750, art 2 3, sch 1-3;
        (Guernsey) 2011/1082, art 3 4, sch
    s 20 am—Counter-Terrorism and Security, 2015 c 6, s 45(3)(a)
        rep in pt—Counter-Terrorism and Security, 2015 c 6, s 45(3)(b)

2010

c 38 *continued*

> s 23 am—Financial Services, 2012 c. 21, sch 18 para 132(2)
>> rep in pt—Legal Aid, Sentencing and Punishment of Offenders, 2012 c 10, sch 5 para 71
> s 31 am—Counter-Terrorism and Security, 2015 c 6, s 45(2)
> s 41 am—Financial Services, 2012 c. 21, sch 18 para 132(3)
> sch 2 ext (mods)—(Isle of Man) SI 2011/749, art 2, sch

c 39   **Consolidated Fund**
c 40   **Identity Documents**
c 41   **Loans to Ireland**

2011

c 1   **Parliamentary Voting System and Constituencies**
> trans of functions—SI 2015/1376, art 3(1) sch 1
> s 9 rep—SI 2011/1702, art 2(a)
> sch 10 rep—SI 2011/1702, art 2(b)
> sch 12 rep in pt—SI 2011/1702, art 2(c)
> s 13 am—SI 2015/1376, sch 2 para 14(2)(a)
> s 14 am—SI 2015/1376, sch 2 para 14(2)(b)

c 2   **Appropriation**
c 3   **National Insurance Contributions**
c 4   **Budget Responsibility and National Audit**
c 5   **Postal Services**
> s 16 funct made exercisable concurrently—SI 2014/500, art 2(2)(a)(i)
> s 17 am—SI 2014/500, art 5(2)
>> funct made exercisable concurrently—SI 2014/500, art 2(2)(a)(ii)
> s 20 funct made exercisable concurrently—SI 2014/500, art 2(2)(a)(iii)
>> rep in pt—SI 2014/500, art 5(3)(a)(i)
>> am—SI 2014/500, art 5(3)(a)(ii)(iii)(b)(c)
> s 21 am—SI 2014/500, art 5(4)
> s 24 funct made exercisable concurrently—SI 2014/500, art 2(2)(a)(iv)
>> am—SI 2014/500, art 5(5)(a)(b)
> s 25 funct made exercisable concurrently—SI 2014/500, art 2(2)(a)(v)
>> am—SI 2014/500, art 5(6)
> s 26 am—SI 2014/500, art 5(7)
> s 29 excl—Communications, 2003 c 21, ss 370(11)(12), 371(11)(12)
> s 51 am—SIs 2013/783, art 6; 2014/631, sch 1 para 13(2)(a)(iii)(iv)(b)-(e); 892, sch 1 para 185
>> rep in pt—SI 2014/631, sch 1 para 13(2)(a)(i)(ii)
> s 56 am—SIs 2014/631, sch 1 para 13(3); 892, sch 1 para 186
> s 57 am—SI 2014/631, sch 1 para 13(4)
> s 59 am—Enterprise and Regulatory Reform, 2013 c 24, sch 6 para 125
> s 60 am—Enterprise and Regulatory Reform, 2013 c 24, sch 6 para 126
> s 61 subst in pt—SI 2014/631, sch 1 para 13(5)(a)
>> am—SI 2014/631, sch 1 para 13(5)(b)
> s 65 am—SI 2014/631, sch 1 para 13(6)
> s 89 am—SI 2014/500, art 5(8)
> s 91 funct made exercisable concurrently—SI 2014/500, art 2(2)(b)
>> am—SI 2014/500, art 5(9)
> sch 5 rep in pt—SI 2014/631, sch 1 para 13(7)(a)(b)
>> subst in pt—SI 2014/631, sch 1 para 13(7)(c)
> sch 7 am—Enterprise and Regulatory Reform, 2013 c 24, sch 14 para 19; SI 2014/631, sch 1 para 13(8)
> sch 10 am—Financial Services, 2012 c. 21, sch 18 para 133
> sch 12 rep in pt—Localism, 2011 c 20, sch 25 pt 19; Public Bodies, 2011 c 24, sch 6

c 6   **Sports Ground Safety Authority**
c 7   **Estates of Deceased Persons (Forfeiture Rule and Law of Succession)**
c 8   **Wreck Removal Convention**
c 9   **Police (Detention and Bail)**
> s 10 rep—Pensions, 2014 c 19, sch 18 para 12
c 10   **Supply and Appropriation (Main Estimates)**
> mod—Supply and Appropriation (Anticipation and Adjustments), 2013 c 12, s 5, sch 2; Supply and Appropriation (Anticipation and Adjustments), 2014 c 5, s 7, sch 3

2011

c 11 **Finance**

s 5 am—Finance, 2012 c 14, s 5(1)

s 7 am—Finance, 2012 c 14, sch 21 para 4

s 11 rep in pt—Finance, 2013 c 29, sch 1 para 5(4)

s 29 rep—(saving for its retrospective effect to 6.12.2010) Finance, 2011 c 11, sch 5 para 7(2)(e)(3) (and see s 29(3))

s 43 rep in pt—Finance, 2012 c 14, sch 3 para 32(c)

s 56 rep—Finance, 2012 c 14, sch 16 para 247(y)

s 63 rep in pt—Finance, 2012 c 14, sch 22 para 20

s 78 rep in pt—Finance, 2013 c 29, sch 42 para 1(2)(a)

s 79 am—Finance, 2012 c 14, sch 30 paras 18(2)(b), 22

rep in pt—Finance, 2012 c 14, sch 30 para 18(2)(a)

s 80 rep—Finance, 2012 c 14, sch 30 para 18(3)

sch 3 mod—SI 2012/700, sch paras 8, 9

sch 13 rep in pt—Finance, 2013 c 29, sch 29 para 49

sch 16 am—Finance, 2013 c 29, s 50(3)(a)(c); Taxation of Pensions, 2014 c 30, sch 1 para 52

rep in pt—Finance, 2013 c 29, s 50(3)(b)(d); Taxation of Pensions, 2014 c 30, sch 1 para 32(2), 66(2)(b); ibid, sch 2 paras 17(5), 19(4)(a); (1.4.2016) Finance (No. 2), 2015 c 33, ss 21(9), 22(11)(a)

sch 18 mod—SI 2012/764, reg 21

rep in pt—Finance, 2013 c 29, s 47(2)(a)(b); Finance, 2014 c 26, s 42(3); Taxation of Pensions, 2014 c 30, sch 1 paras 74(5), 75(2)

am—Finance, 2013 c 29, s 47(2)(c)(3); SI 2013/1740, reg 2

sch 19 am—SI 2011/3015, arts 3(2)(b)(3)(a)(d), 4(2)(b)(3)(a)(b)(e)(4), 5(2)(b)(3)(a)(b)(e), 6(2)(b)(3)(a)(c), 7(2)(b)(3)(a)(c); Finance, 2012 c 14, sch 16 para 246; ibid, sch 34 paras 2, 3, 5, 6, 8(2), (3), 9, 11(1), (2); ibid, sch 18 para 134; Finance, 2013 c 29, ss 202, 203, 204, 205(1); SI 2013/636, sch para 15(2)-(5)(6)(a)(ii)(iii)(b)(c)(7); Finance, 2014 c 26, s 119(2)(a)(b), 3(a)-(c); ibid, sch 26 paras 2(a)(b), 3(a)-(c), 4(a)-(c), 5(a)(b), 6(a)(b), 10(1), 11(1)-(3), 12; Finance, 2015 c 11, s 76(2)(3); (retrosp to 1.1.2014) Finance (No. 2), 2015 c 33, s 20(2)(3)(a),(4)-(7),(8); (1.1.2016) ibid, sch 2 para 1; (1.1.2017) ibid, sch 2 para 2; (1.1.2018) ibid, sch 2 para 3; (1.1.2019) ibid, sch 2 para 4; (1.1.2020) ibid, sch 2 para 5; (1.1.2021) ibid, sch 2 para 6

rep in pt—SI 2011/3015, arts 3(2)(a)(3)(b)(c)(4), 4(2)(a)(3)(c)(d), 5(2)(a)(3)(c)(d)(4), 6(2)(a)(3)(b)(4), 7(2)(a)(3)(b)(4); Finance, 2012 c 14, sch 34 para 11(3); SI 2013/636, sch para 15(6)(a)(i); Finance, 2014 c 26, sch 26 para 8(2)-(4); (retrosp to 1.1.2014) Finance (No. 2), 2015 c 33, s 20(3)(b),(8)

subst in pt—Finance, 2014 c 26, sch 26 para 9(2)

sch 20 rep—Finance, 2013 c 29, sch 42 para 1(2)(a)

sch 22 rep in pt—Finance, 2012 c 14, sch 39 para 8(2)(f)

sch 23 am—SI 2012/3062, reg 6(2); Finance, 2013 c 29, s 228(1); Finance, 2015 c 11, s 105(1)

appl—SIs 2009/470, reg 33 (amended by 2012/836, reg 4); 2009/470, reg 33(1) (subst by 2013/607, reg 9)

sch 25 am—SI 2014/834, sch 2 para 75

c 12 **European Union**

c 13 **Police Reform and Social Responsibility**

see (specified sections) functions of S of S made exercisable concurrently with the Chancellor of the Duchy of Lancaster—SIs 2015/1376, art 3(1), sch 1 para (o); ibid, art 7; 1526, art 3(1),(2)(a)-(h)

s 7 subst in pt—Anti-social Behaviour, Crime and Policing, 2014 c 12, sch 11 para 97

s 9 rep—Anti-social Behaviour, Crime and Policing, 2014 c 12, sch 11 para 98

s 18 am—Localism, 2011 c 20, sch 7 para 53; Loc Audit and Accountability, 2014 c 2, sch 12 para 116

s 19 am—Loc Audit and Accountability, 2014 c 2, sch 12 para 117

s 22 am—Localism, 2011 c 20, sch 7 para 54

s 24 rep in pt—Anti-social Behaviour, Crime and Policing, 2014 c 12, sch 11 para 102

s 42 am—Anti-social Behaviour, Crime and Policing, 2014 c 12, s 140(5)(6)

s 50 am—SI 2015/1526, sch para 1(2)(a)

s 51 restr—SI 2014/1963, art 6

s 54 am—SI 2015/1376, sch 2 para 15(2)

s 55 am—SI 2015/1526, sch para 1(3)

s 58 rep in pt—SI 2015/1526, sch para 1(4)

2011

c 13 s 58 *continued*

　　　　funct exercisable concurrently—SI 2014/268, art 2

　　　　am—SIs 2014/268, art 4(2)(a)(b); 2015/1376, sch 2 para 15(4)(a); 1526, sch para
　　　　　　1(2)(b)

　　　　s 61 rep in pt—Crime and Cts, 2013 c 22, sch 8 para 184

　　　　s 65 am—SI 2015/1526, sch para 1(2)(c)

　　　　s 66 am—SI 2015/1526, sch para 1(2)(d)

　　　　s 70 am—SI 2015/1526, sch para 1(2)(e)

　　　　s 71 am—SI 2015/1526, sch para 1(2)(f)

　　　　s 72 am—Loc Govt (Democracy) (W), 2013 anaw 4, sch 1 para 5

　　　　s 75 am—SI 2015/1526, sch para 1(2)(g)

　　　　s 111 rep in pt—Deregulation, 2015 c 20, sch 18 para 15

　　　　s 118 rep in pt—SI 2015/664, sch 4 para 104

　　　　s 119 am—SI 2012/1659, sch 3 para 22

　　　　Pt 3 (ss 141-149) am—Anti-social Behaviour, Crime and Policing, 2014 c 12, s 153(11)

　　　　s 142 am—Anti-social Behaviour, Crime and Policing, 2014 c 12, s 153(10)

　　　　s 142A added—Anti-social Behaviour, Crime and Policing, 2014 c 12, s 153(2)

　　　　s 143 am—Anti-social Behaviour, Crime and Policing, 2014 c 12, s 153(3)(a)(b)

　　　　s 144 am—Anti-social Behaviour, Crime and Policing, 2014 c 12, s 153(4)

　　　　s 145 am—Anti-social Behaviour, Crime and Policing, 2014 c 12, s 153(5)(a)-(e)

　　　　s 146 am—Anti-social Behaviour, Crime and Policing, 2014 c 12, s 153(6)(a)-(c)

　　　　s 147 am—Anti-social Behaviour, Crime and Policing, 2014 c 12, s 153(7)(a)(b)

　　　　s 148 am—Anti-social Behaviour, Crime and Policing, 2014 c 12, s 153(8)(a)(b)

　　　　s 149 am—Anti-social Behaviour, Crime and Policing, 2014 c 12, s 153(9)

　　　　s 154 am—SIs 2014/268, art 4(3); 2015/1376, sch 2 para 15(4)(b)

　　　　sch 2 mod (temp)—SI 2013/2319, art 2(1)

　　　　　　am—Anti-social Behaviour, Crime and Policing, 2014 c 12, s 141(1)

　　　　　　rep in pt—Anti-social Behaviour, Crime and Policing, 2014 c 12, sch 11 para 99

　　　　sch 4 mod (temp)—SI 2013/2319, art 2(2)

　　　　　　am—Anti-social Behaviour, Crime and Policing, 2014 c 12, s 141(2)

　　　　　　rep in pt—Anti-social Behaviour, Crime and Policing, 2014 c 12, sch 11 para 100

　　　　sch 8 am—Anti-social Behaviour, Crime and Policing, 2014 c 12, s 140(2)(3)

　　　　sch 16 rep in pt—Anti-social Behaviour, Crime and Policing, 2014 c 12, sch 11 para 50;
　　　　　　　　ibid, sch 11 para 102; Loc Audit and Accountability, 2014 c 2, sch 1 pt 2;
　　　　　　　　Deregulation, 2015 c 20, ss 102(2)(a), 103(2)(c)

c 14　　**Fixed-term Parliaments**

　　　　s 1 excl in pt —Recall of MPs, 2015 c 25, s 5(3)

　　　　s 2 excl in pt—Recall of MPs, 2015 c 25, s 5(3)

　　　　s 3 am—Electoral Registration and Admin, 2013 c 6, s 14(1)

　　　　s 5 rep —Wales, 2014 c 29, s 1(2)

c 15　　**Sovereign Grant**

c 16　　**Energy**

　　　　s 11 am—SI 2012/3170, reg 2(2), (3)

　　　　s 20 am—SI 2013/1881, sch para 17(2)

　　　　ss 25, 26 rep—SI 2013/1881, sch para 17(3)

　　　　s 30 am—SI 2013/1881, sch para 17(4)

　　　　ss 76-78 rep —Energy, 2013 c 32, s 142(4)

　　　　ss 82, 83 mod—Pipe-Lines, 1962 c 58, s 9(9)(a)

　　　　s 84 excl—Pipe-Lines, 1962 c 58, s 9(9)(b)

　　　　s 91 appl—Gas, 1995 c 45, s 12(7)

　　　　ss 93-102 mod—SI 2013/1046, rule 205(2)

c 17　　**Coinage (Measurement)**

c 18　　**Armed Forces**

　　　　s 17 rep —Anti-social Behaviour, Crime and Policing, 2014 c 12, sch 11 para 82(1)

　　　　s 20 rep (1.1.2016)—Armed Forces (Service Complaints and Financial Assistance), 2015 c
　　　　　　19, sch para 16

　　　　s 28 rep—Defence Reform, 2014 c 20, s 45(10)

　　　　sch 4 rep in pt—Anti-social Behaviour, Crime and Policing, 2014 c 12, sch 11 para 82(2)

c 19　　**Pensions**

　　　　s 2 rep in pt—(6.4.2016) Pensions, 2014 c 19, sch 12 para 97(a)

　　　　s 3 rep—Pensions, 2014 c 19, sch 12 para 97(b)

　　　　s 18 rep—Pensions, 2014 c 19, s 38(3)(c)

　　　　s 19 rep in pt—(prosp) Pension Schemes, 2015 c 8, sch 1 para 11(b)

　　　　s 21 rep in pt—(prosp) Pension Schemes, 2015 c 8, s 41(2)

2011

c 19 *continued*

Pt 4 (ss 29-33) excl—SI 2014/1711, regs 6, 41, 44(1), 47(1), 72(1), 76(1)

s 29 restr—SI 2014/1711, reg 69(2)

sch 2 rep (6.4.2016)—Pensions, 2014 c 19, sch 12 para 97(a)

sch 3 rep—Pensions, 2014 c 19, sch 12 para 97(b)

c 20 **Localism**

s 1 funct exercisable concurrently—SI 2014/863, sch 2 para 1; 864, sch 3 para 1; 865, sch 2 para 1

s 4 am—Co-operative and Community Benefit Societies, 2014 c 14, sch 4 para 175

s 25 appl (mods)—SI 2012/2734, regs 3-6 sch pts 1, 2

Pt 1, Ch 7 (ss 26-37) appl (mods)—SI 2012/2734, regs 3-6 sch pts 1, 2

s 27 rep in pt—Localism, 2011 c 20, s 36(a), sch 25 pt 5

ss 30-34 appl—Humber Bridge, 1959 c xlvi, s 11(3)(a)-(e) (subst by 2013 c vi, sch 1 para 1)

ss 38, 39 appl in pt (mods)—(26.1.2016) Loc Govt (W), 2015 anaw 6, s 28(5)

ss 41,42 appl in pt (mods)—(26.1.2016) Loc Govt (W), 2015 anaw 6, s 28(5)

s 95 excl—SI 2012/2421, reg 13(2), sch 3

s 141 rep in pt—Growth and Infrastructure, 2013 c 27, s 24(4)(b)

s 155 rep in pt—Anti-social Behaviour, Crime and Policing, 2014 c 12, sch 11 para 50

s 158 excl—SI 2012/696, reg 3

s 159 am—Crime and Cts, 2013 c 22, sch 9 para 52

s 185 rep in pt—Co-operative and Community Benefit Societies, 2014 c 14, sch 7

s 190 am—Co-operative and Community Benefit Societies, 2014 c 14, sch 4 para 176

s 191 am—Co-operative and Community Benefit Societies, 2014 c 14, sch 4 para 177

s 200 rep in pt—SI 2014/3184, sch para 16(a)(i)(ii)

am—Co-operative and Community Benefit Societies, 2014 c 14, sch 4 para 178

s 208 am—Infrastructure, 2015 c 7, s 32(10)

s 216 am—Co-operative and Community Benefit Societies, 2014 c 14, sch 4 para 179

sch 3 rep in pt—Health and Social Care, 2012 c 7, s 191(15)

sch 8 rep in pt—Localism, 2011 c 20, sch 25 pt 16

sch 14 am—Anti-social Behaviour, Crime and Policing, 2014 c 12, s 100(3)(a)(b); ibid, sch 11 para 47(2)(3)(5)(6); (W prosp) ibid, sch 11 paras 47(4)(b)(c), 48

rep in pt—(W prosp) Anti-social Behaviour, Crime and Policing, 2014 c 12, sch 11 para 47(4)(a); ibid, sch 11 para 47(7)

sch 17 rep in pt—Loc Audit and Accountability, 2014 c 2, sch 12 para 123(g)

sch 20 rep in pt—Loc Audit and Accountability, 2014 c 2, sch 1 pt 2

sch 22 rep in pt—Growth and Infrastructure, 2013 c 27, s 24(4)(c); SI 2014/3184, sch para 16(b)

c 21 **Education**

s 24 rep—Qualifications Wales, 2015 anaw 5, sch 4 para 10

s 30 rep in pt—Deregulation, 2015 c 20, sch 14 para 65(a)

s 35 rep in pt—School Standards and Organisation (W), 2013 anaw 1, sch 5 para 36

s 70 rep—Deregulation, 2015 c 20, sch 14 para 65(b)

s 72 rep—Deregulation, 2015 c 20, sch 14 para 65(c)

s 76 restr—SI 2012/1309, reg 15

s 77 rep in pt—Higher Educ (W), 2015 anaw 1, sch para 25(3)

am—Higher Educ (W), 2015 anaw 1, sch para 25(2)

sch 5 rep in pt—Loc Audit and Accountability, 2014 c 2, sch 1 pt 2; Higher Educ (W), 2015 anaw 1, sch para 26

sch 12 rep in pt—Further and Higher Educ (Governance and Information) (W), 2014 anaw 1, sch 2 para 7

sch 13 rep in pt—Deregulation, 2015 c 20, sch 16 para 2(2)(d)

sch 16 rep in pt—Deregulation, 2015 c 20, s 102(2)(b)

sch 18 rep in pt—Deregulation, 2015 c 20, sch 14 para 65(d)

c 22 **London Olympic Games and Paralympic Games (Amendment)**

s 1 rep in pt—SI 2014/3184, sch para 17

ss 4-9 rep—London Olympic Games and Paralympic Games (Amdt), 2011 c 22, s 10(2)

c 23 **Terrorism Prevention and Investigation Measures**

s 2 am—Counter-Terrorism and Security, 2015 c 6, s 17(2)

s 3 am—Counter-Terrorism and Security, 2015 c 6, s 20(1)

s 4 am—Counter-Terrorism and Security, 2015 c 6, s 20(2)

s 10 am—Crime and Cts, 2013 c 22, sch 8 paras 186, 188; SI 2013/602, sch 2 para 64(2)(a)(i)(b)(i)

rep in pt—SI 2013/602, sch 2 para 64(2)(a)(ii)(b)(ii)

2011

c 23 *continued*

s 23 am —Counter-Terrorism and Security, 2015 c 6, s 17(3)(4)

s 31 mod —Counter-Terrorism and Security, 2015 c 6, s 51(5)

sch 1 am—Financial Services, 2012 c. 21, sch 18 para 135; Counter-Terrorism and Security, 2015 c 6, ss 16(2)(3)(5), 17(5), 18, 19

rep in pt—Counter-Terrorism and Security, 2015 c 6, s 16(4)

sch 3 rep in pt —SSI 2015/338, sch 2 para 14(2)(a)

am—SSI 2015/338, sch 2 para 14(2)(b)(c),(3)

sch 6 am—Protection of Freedoms, 2012 c 9, sch 1 para 5; Legal Aid, Sentencing and Punishment of Offenders, 2012 c 10, sch 24 para 32(a); SI 2013/602, sch 2 para 64(3)(a)(i)(b)

rep in pt—Legal Aid, Sentencing and Punishment of Offenders, 2012 c 10, sch 24 para 32(b); SI 2013/602, sch 2 para 64(3)(a)(ii)

c 24 **Public Bodies**

s 14 rep in pt—(prosp) Water, 2014 c 21, s 40(2)(a)

s 26 rep in pt—SI 2013/1821, art 3(2)

s 36 rep in pt—(conditionally on coming into force of 2010 c 7, s 1) Public Bodies, 2011 c 24, s 36(3); Co-operative and Community Benefit Societies, 2014 c 14, sch 7

am—SI 2013/1821, art 3(3); Co-operative and Community Benefit Societies, 2014 c 14, sch 4 para 180(2)(a)(b)(3)(a)(b)

schs 1-5 see—(entries cease to have effect on 14.2.2017) Public Bodies, 2011 c 24, s 12

sch 1 rep in pt—SIs 2012/964, art 3(2); 1206, art 3; 1923, sch; 2007, sch para 109(f); 2398, arts 2(4), 3(3); 2401, sch 1 para 37; ibid, sch 2 para 4; 2407, art 3; 2654, sch; 2013/64, art 5; 252, art 6; 686, sch 1 para 10; 687, sch 1 para 15(2); 2042, sch para 41(a); 2314, art 9; 2352, sch 1 para 15; 2853, art 2(3); 2014/631, sch 1 para 14; 1068, art 3(3); 1924, sch; 2015/850, art 3(4); 978, sch pt 1

am—Infrastructure, 2015 c 7, s 54

sch 2 rep in pt—SIs 2013/2329, art 9; 2014/892, sch 1 para 183

sch 3 rep in pt—SI 2013/2042, sch para 41(b)

sch 4 rep in pt—SI 2013/2042, sch para 41(c); (prosp) Water, 2014 c 21, s 40(2)(b)

sch 5 rep in pt—SIs 2013/2042, sch para 41(d); 2014/631, sch 2 para 6

c 25 **Charities**

s 1 restr—SI 2012/735, arts 5(1), 6(1)

s 29 mod—SI 2012/3012, reg 6(2)(a)

ss 30-34 excl—SI 2012/3012, reg 6(3)

s 31 appl—Places of Worship Registration, 1855 c 81, s 9(1) (subst by 2011 c 25, sch 7 para 5(1)(a)); School Standards and Framework, 1998 c 31, sch 1 para 10 (subst by 2011 c 25, sch 7 para 78)

s 35 mod—SI 2012/3012, reg 6(4)

s 36 mod—SI 2012/3012, reg 6(5)(a)

s 38 mod—SI 2012/3012, reg 6(6)

s 43 appl—SI 2012/3013, reg 37(6)

s 44 appl—SI 2012/3013, reg 37(6)

s 57 mod—SI 2013/1764, reg 5

s 70 appl—Coal Industry, 1987 c 3 s 5(8) (subst by 2011 c 25, sch 7 para 47(2))

s 70 excl—Reserve Forces, 1996 c 14, sch 5 para 6 (subst by 2011 c 25, sch 7 para 69(3))

s 71 appl—Coal Industry, 1987 c 3, s 5(8) (subst by 2011 c 25, sch 7 para 47(2))

s 73 appl—Coal Industry, 1987 c 3, s 5(8) (subst by 2011 c 25, sch 7 para 47(2))

s 74 appl—Coal Industry, 1987 c 3, s 5(8) (subst by 2011 c 25, sch 7 para 47(2))

excl—SI 2013/1775, art 3, sch 2 para 2

s 80 am—SI 2012/2404, sch 2 para 62(2)

s 88 appl—Coal Industry, 1987 c 3, s 5(8) (subst by 2011 c 25, sch 7 para 47(2))

appl (mods)—SI 2012/3013, reg 25(4)(5)

s 89 appl—Coal Industry, 1987 c 3, s 5(8) (subst by 2011 c 25, sch 7 para 47(2))

s 97 am—SI 2013/1773, sch 1 para 44(b)

s 101 am—SI 2013/1773, sch 1 para 44(b)

ss 104A, 104B added—Trusts (Capital and Income), 2013 c 1, s 4

s 109 am—Financial Services, 2012 c. 21, sch 18 para 136

Pt 8 (ss 130-176) appl (mods)—SI 2012/3013, reg 41

s 144 am—SI 2015/321, art 3

s 145 am—SI 2015/321, art 4

s 149 am—Health and Social Care, 2012 c 7, sch 5 para 184(c); (1.4.2017) Loc Audit and Accountability, 2014 c 2, sch 12 para 119(2)(3)(a)-(c)(4)(6)

2011

c 25 s 149 *continued*

  rep in pt—Health and Social Care, 2012 c 7, sch 5 para 184(a), (b), (d); (pt prosp) ibid, sch 14 para 118; (1.4.2017) Loc Audit and Accountability, 2014 c 2, sch 12 para 119(5)(7)

 s 150 rep in pt—(pt prosp) Health and Social Care, 2012 c 7, sch 14 para 119

 s 151 am—(1.4.2017) Loc Audit and Accountability, 2014 c 2, sch 12 para 120(2)(3)(a)(b)

 s 152 am—(1.4.2017) Loc Audit and Accountability, 2014 c 2, sch 12 para 121(2)(a)-(c)

 s 154 am—(1.4.2017) Loc Audit and Accountability, 2014 c 2, sch 12 para 122

 s 178 am—SI 2012/2404, sch 2 para 62(3)

 s 180 am—SIs 2012/2404, sch 2 para 62(4); 2012/3014, art 5

 s 181 am—SI 2012/3014, art 6

 s 183 am—SIs 2012/2404, sch 2 para 62(5); 2012/3014, art 7

 s 229 am—Co-operative and Community Benefit Societies, 2014 c 14, sch 4 para 182(2)(3)

 s 230 am—SI 2013/496, sch 11 para 11

 s 310 appl (mods)—SI 2012/3012, reg 61

 s 312 appl (mods)—SI 2012/3012, reg 61

 Pt 17, Ch 2 (ss 319-324) appl—Redundant Churches and Other Religious Buildings, 1969 c 22, s 4(8A) (subst by 2011 c 25, sch 7 para 17(1)); Coal Industry, 1987 c 3, s 5(8B) (subst by 2011 c 25, sch 7 para 47(2)); Reverter of Sites, 1987 c 15, s 4(2) (subst by 2011 c 25, sch 7 para 48)

 s 336 appl—SI 2012/3012, regs 26(5), 27(2)

 s 337 appl—Places of Worship Registration, 1855 c 81, s 9(2) (subst by 2011 c 25, sch 7 para 5(2)); Open Spaces, 1906 c 25, s 4(4) (subst by 2011 c 25, sch 7 para 8(2)); GSM New Parishes, 1943 No 1, s 14(4) (subst by 2011 c 25, sch 7 para 9(2)); Reverter of Sites, 1987 c 15, s 4(4) (subst by 2011 c 25, sch 7 para 48); SI 2012/3012, regs 26(5), 27(2)

 s 339 appl—Reverter of Sites, 1987 c 15, s 4(4) (subst by 2011 c 25, sch 7 para 48)

 sch 3 am—Co-operative and Community Benefit Societies, 2014 c 14, sch 4 para 183(2)(3)

 sch 6 appl—Redundant Churches and Other Religious Buildings, 1969 c 22, s 4(8A) (subst by 2011 c 25, sch 7 para 17(1)); Coal Industry, 1987 c 3, s 5(8B) (subst by 2011 c 25, sch 7 para 47(2)); Reverter of Sites, 1987 c 15, s 4(2) (subst by 2011 c 25, sch 7 para 48)

  am—SI 2012/3014, art 8

 sch 7 rep in pt—Co-operative and Community Benefit Societies, 2014 c 14, sch 7

 sch 9 rep in pt—Co-operative and Community Benefit Societies, 2014 c 14, sch 7

2012

c 1 **Supply and Appropriation (Anticipation and Adjustments)**

c 2 **Live Music**

c 3 **Public Services (Social value)**

 s 1 am—SI 2015/102, sch 6 para 8(2),(4)(a)(c)(d),(5)

 rep in pt—SI 2015/102, sch 6 para 8(3),(4)(b)

c 4 **Domestic Violence Crime and Victims (Amendment)**

c 5 **Welfare Reform**

 Pt 1 (ss 1-43) mod—Jobseekers, 1995 c 18 sch 1 2(3) (added by 2013/630, reg 10(b))

 s 1 appl—SI 2003/2382 reg 2 (amended by 2013/475, reg 17(7))

 rep in pt—Finance, 2014 c 26, s 79(11)(a)(i)(b)

 am—Finance, 2014 c 26, s 79(11)(a)(ii)

 s 4 mod—SI 2013/376, regs 8, 12, 15

 excl —SI 2013/376, reg 14

 s 11 excl—SI 2013/376, sch 4 para 4; ibid, sch 5 para 4

 s 39 am—SIs 2014/560, sch 1 para 36(2)(4)(a)(b); 3229, sch 5 para 20(2)(4)(a)(b)

 rep in pt—SIs 2014/560, sch 1 para 36(3); 3229, sch 5 para 20(3)

 s 44 rep in pt—(pt prosp) Welfare Reform, 2012 c 5, sch 14 pt 4

 s 45 rep (pt prosp)—Welfare Reform, 2012 c 5, sch 14 pt 4

 s 46 rep in pt—(pt prosp) Welfare Reform, 2012 c 5, sch 14 pt 4

 s 50 rep in pt—(prosp) Welfare Reform, 2012 c 5, sch 14 pt 1

 s 52 rep in pt—(prosp) Welfare Reform, 2012 c 5, sch 14 pt 1

 s 54 rep in pt—(pt prosp) Welfare Reform, 2012 c 5, sch 14 pt 5

 ss 55, 56 rep (pt prosp)—Welfare Reform, 2012 c 5, sch 14 pt 5

 s 58 rep in pt—(prosp) Welfare Reform, 2012 c 5, sch 14 pt 1; (pt prosp) ibid, sch 14 pt 5

 s 59 rep (prosp)—Welfare Reform, 2012 c 5, sch 14 pt 1

 s 63 rep in pt—Children and Families, 2014 c 6, sch 7 para 75

 s 69 rep (prosp)—Welfare Reform, 2012 c 5, sch 14 pt 1

2012

c 5 *continued*

ss 71, 72 rep (prosp)—Welfare Reform, 2012 c 5, sch 14 pt 8

s 83 excl—SIs 2013/377, regs 25, 27; 2013/387, reg 27(1)

s 87 excl—SI 2013/377, reg 31(1)(3)(6)

s 96 am—(6.4.2016) Pensions, 2014 c 19, sch 12 para 52

s 105 rep in pt—(prosp) Welfare Reform, 2012 c 5, sch 14 pt 1
am—Crime and Cts, 2013 c 22, sch 9 para 52

s 106 rep in pt—(prosp) Welfare Reform, 2012 c 5, sch 14 pts 1, 8

s 111 rep (prosp)—Welfare Reform, 2012 c 5, sch 14 pt 1

s 120 rep in pt—(prosp) Welfare Reform, 2012 c 5, sch 14 pt 12

s 127 am—SI 2012/2007, sch para 102; (pt prosp) Childcare Payments, 2014 c 28, s
27(6)(b); SI 2014/606, reg 4
rep in pt—(pt prosp) Childcare Payments, 2014 c 28, s 27(6)(a)

s 128 am—SI 2012/2007, sch para 103

s 129 am—SI 2012/2007, sch para 104

s 130 rep in pt—(prosp) Welfare Reform, 2012 c 5, sch 14 pt 1

s 131 rep in pt—(prosp) Welfare Reform, 2012 c 5, sch 14 pt 1

s 132 appl—SIs 2012/1483, reg 10(2) (subst by 2013/454, reg 3(10)); 2015/124, reg 8

s 136 am—SI 2012/2007, sch para 105

s 137 am—SI 2012/2007, sch para 106

s 138 am—SI 2012/2007, sch para 107

sch 7 rep in pt—(prosp) Welfare Reform, 2012 c 5, sch 14 pt 1; (pt prosp) ibid, sch 14 pt 4

sch 9 rep in pt—(prosp) Welfare Reform, 2012 c 5, sch 14 pt 1

sch 11 am—SI 2012/2007, sch para 108
rep in pt—(prosp) Welfare Reform, 2012 c 5, sch 14 pt 1

sch 12 rep in pt—(prosp) Welfare Reform, 2012 c 5, sch 14 pt 1

c 6 **Consumer Insurance (Disclosure and Representation)**

s 2 rep in pt—(12.8.2016) Insurance, 2015 c 4, s 14(4)

s 11 rep in pt—(12.8.2016) Insurance, 2015 c 4, s 21(6)

c 7 **Health and Social Care**

s 58 am—Energy, 2013 c 32, sch 12 para 103

s 67 rep in pt—Health and Social Care, 2012 c 7, s 114(1)

s 72 am—Enterprise and Regulatory Reform, 2013 c 24, sch 15 para 48; SI 2014/892, sch 1
para 188

s 73 am—SI 2014/892, sch 1 para 189(2)(3)(a)-(c)(4)(a)-(c)(5)(6)

s 74 am—SI 2014/892, sch 1 para 190

s 76 excl—SIs 2013/257, reg 17; 2013/500, reg 17
am—SI 2015/102, sch 6 para 9

s 79 am—SI 2014/892, sch 1 para 191

s 80 am—SI 2014/892, sch 1 para 192(2)-(4)

s 87 am—Health and Social Care, 2012 c 7, s 114(1)(c)
rep in pt—Health and Social Care, 2012 c 7, s 114(1)(d)

s 88 rep (prosp)—Health and Social Care, 2012 c 7, s 180(3)

s 97 am—SI 2014/892, sch 1 para 193

s 101 am—Enterprise and Regulatory Reform, 2013 c 24, sch 6 para 128

s 102 am—Enterprise and Regulatory Reform, 2013 c 24, sch 6 para 129; SI 2014/892, sch
1 para 194

s 103 am—Enterprise and Regulatory Reform, 2013 c 24, sch 6 para 130

s 105 am—Enterprise and Regulatory Reform, 2013 c 24, sch 14 para 21

s 106 am—Enterprise and Regulatory Reform, 2013 c 24, sch 14 para 22

s 111 rep (prosp)—Health and Social Care, 2012 c 7, s 112
am—Care, 2014 c 23, s 83(2)(3)

ss 112-114 rep —Health and Social Care, 2012 c 7, s 114

s 120 am—Enterprise and Regulatory Reform, 2013 c 24, sch 6 para 131(2)(4)
rep in pt—Enterprise and Regulatory Reform, 2013 c 24, sch 6 para 131(3)

s 121 am—Enterprise and Regulatory Reform, 2013 c 24, sch 6 para 132

s 122 am—Enterprise and Regulatory Reform, 2013 c 24, sch 6 para 133

s 123 am—Enterprise and Regulatory Reform, 2013 c 24, sch 6 para 134

s 142 am—Enterprise and Regulatory Reform, 2013 c 24, sch 6 para 135

s 145 am—Financial Services, 2012 c. 21, sch 18 para 137

s 149 am—Enterprise and Regulatory Reform, 2013 c 24, sch 6 para 136

s 150 am—Enterprise and Regulatory Reform, 2013 c 24, sch 6 para 137

s 155 rep in pt—(prosp) Loc Audit and Accountability, 2014 c 2, sch 12 para 123(h)

s 174 rep in pt—(prosp) Health and Social Care, 2012 c 7, sch 14 para 13(2)

2012
c 7 *continued*

s 176 rep in pt—(pt prosp) Health and Social Care, 2012 c 7, sch 14 paras 15(7), 17(6), 18(5), 19(4)

s 177 rep in pt—(prosp) Health and Social Care, 2012 c 7, sch 14 para 20(2), 22(5)

s 178 rep in pt—(prosp) Health and Social Care, 2012 c 7, sch 14 para 23(5), 24(4)

s 197 mod—National Health Service, 2006 c 41,s 13Z4(3)

s 199 mod—National Health Service, 2006 c 41, ss 13Z4(3), 14Z24(3)

Pt 9 Ch. 1A (ss 251A-251C) added—Health and Social Care (Safety and Quality), 2015 c 28, ss 2-4

s 253 am—Care, 2014 c 23, s 122(2)

s 261 am—Care, 2014 c 23, s 122(3)

s 262A added —Care, 2014 c 23, s 122(4)

s 290 mod—National Health Service, 2006 c 41,s 13Z4(3)
    excl—Care, 2014 c 23, s 111(9)
    am—Care, 2014 c 23, sch 5 para 15(3)

s 291 mod—National Health Service, 2006 c 41,ss 13Z4(3),14Z24(3)

s 293 rep in pt—Care, 2014 c 23, ss 90(10), 91(9)(e)

sch 5 rep in pt—Care, 2014 c 23, s 91(9)(f); Deregulation, 2015 c 20, s 102(2)(c)

sch 6 mod—National Health Service, 2006 c 41,s 14Z24(3)

sch 8 am—Enterprise and Regulatory Reform, 2013 c 24, sch 15 para 49

sch 10 am—Enterprise and Regulatory Reform, 2013 c 24, sch 6 para 138; SI 2014/892, sch 1 para 195(2)-(5)(6)(a)(7)
    subst in pt—SI 2014/892, sch 1 para 195(6)(a)

sch 12 am—Enterprise and Regulatory Reform, 2013 c 24, sch 6 para 139(2)(3)(4)(b)(d)(5)-(13)
    rep in pt—Enterprise and Regulatory Reform, 2013 c 24, sch 6 para 139(4)(a)(c)(8)(d)(ii)

sch 14 am—Care, 2014 c 23, s 84(8); ibid, s 85(15)(a)(b)(c)(i)-(iii); ibid, s 120(18)(a)-(j)

c 8   **Water Industry (Financial Assistance)**

c 9   **Protection of Freedoms**

ss 1-12 appl—SI 2013/1813, art 2(a)

s 1 mod—SI 2013/1813, art 6

s 3 mod—SI 2013/1813, art 4

s 13 appl (mods)—SI 2013/1813, arts 2(b), 3

ss 14-18 appl—SI 2013/1813, art 2(c)

s 14 mod—SI 2013/1813, art 5

s 18 mod—SI 2013/1813 art 5A (added by 2013/2580, art 4)

s 22 appl—SI 2013/1813, art 2(d)

s 95 am—Crime and Cts, 2013 c 22, sch 8 para 185

ss 109, 110 rep—Modern Slavery, 2015 c 30, sch 5 para 9(2)

sch 1 appl—SI 2013/1813, arts 7(a)(c)(d), 8
    appl (mods)—SI 2013/1813, art 7(b)

sch 9 rep in pt—Modern Slavery, 2015 c 30, sch 5 para 9(3)

c 10   **Legal Aid, Sentencing and Punishment of Offenders**

s 24 am—Crime and Cts, 2013 c 22, sch 9 para 52

s 36 am—Crime and Cts, 2013 c 22, sch 9 para 52

s 57 am—Financial Services, 2012 c. 21, sch 18 para 138(2)

s 58 am—Financial Services, 2012 c. 21, sch 18 para 138(3)

s 59 am—Financial Services, 2012 c. 21, sch 18 para 138(4)

s 67 rep in pt—Crime and Cts, 2013 c 22, sch 16 para 22(1)

s 72 rep in pt—(prosp) Crime and Cts, 2013 c 22, sch 16 paras 12(6), 13(6)

s 85 appl (mods) (cond)—Children and Families, 2014 c 6, s 137(2)-(4); (prosp) Defence Reform, 2014 c 20, sch 5 paras 2(5), 6(4); ibid, sch 7 para 12; Loc Audit and Accountability, 2014 c 2, sch 9 para 4(9); Transparency of Lobbying, Non-Party Campaigning and Trade Union Admin, 2014 c 4, ss 30(10), 33(9), 35(10)(a), 36(3)
    appl mods—Consumer Rights, 2015 c 15, sch 5 para 37(3)(a)
    excl in pt—Finance, 2014 c 26, s 174(5); SI 2015/664, reg 2(1) sch 1

Pt 3 Ch 3 (ss 91-107) appl—SI 2014/3141, reg 91(10)

s 91 mod—SI 1991/1505, reg 6 (amended by 2012/2824, reg 2(2))
    appl—SI 2014/3141, reg 91(10)

s 102 am—Crime and Cts, 2013 c 22, s 19(5); Crim Justice and Cts, 2015 c 2, sch 9 para 29

s 103 am—Crim Justice and Cts, 2015 c 2, sch 9 para 30

s 128 am—Crim Justice and Cts, 2015 c 2, sch 1 para 25; (prosp) ibid, s 11(3)

2012

c 10 *continued*

> s 139 mod—Police, 1997 c 50 s 113(6F)
> ss 145-147 rep—Scrap Metal Dealers, 2013 c 10, s 19(1)(f)
> sch 1 am—Crime and Cts, 2013 c 22, sch 9 para 52; SI 2013/748, arts 3-7; (pt prosp)
>> Anti-social Behaviour, Crime and Policing, 2014 c 12, sch 11 para 49(2)(3);
>> Children and Families, 2014 c 6, s 9(12)(a)(b); ibid, sch 2 para 70; ibid, sch 3
>> para 96(a)(b); Housing (W), 2014 anaw 7, sch 3 para 20(2)(a)(b); SIs 2014/605,
>> art 26(a)(b); 3305, art 2(2)-(4); Counter-Terrorism and Security, 2015 c 6, s 1(2);
>> Serious Crime, 2015 c 9, sch 4 paras 87, 88; Modern Slavery, 2015 c 30, s
>> 47(2)(3); ibid, sch 5 para 10; SI 2015/914, sch para 96(b)
> restr —SI 2013/451, reg 4
> rep in pt—Immigration, 2014 c 22, sch 9 para 6; SI 2015/914, sch para 96(a)
> sch 2 am—Crime and Cts, 2013 c 22, sch 9 para 52
> sch 4 am—Public Service Pensions, 2013 c 25, sch 8 para 31
> sch 5 rep in pt—Children and Families, 2014 c 6, s 18(3)(e)(i)(ii)
> sch 13 rep in pt—Crim Justice and Cts, 2015 c 2, s 30(3); ibid, s 30(3)
> sch 26 rep in pt—Crime and Cts, 2013 c 22, sch 16 para 23(2)
> sch 27 rep in pt—SI 2015/583, sch 1 Table 1

c 11 **Scotland**

> s 20 rep in pt—Deregulation, 2015 c 20, sch 11 para 1(5)
> s 24 rep in pt—SI 2014/3294, art 4(2)
> ss 26A-26M rep—Finance, 2014 c 26, sch 38 para 17(a)
> sch 2 rep in pt—Finance, 2014 c 26, sch 38 para 17(b)(c)
> sch 3 rep in pt—Finance, 2013 c 29, sch 41 para 7(2)(b); (17.2.2015 with qualifying provn)
>> Wales, 2014 c 29, s 16(3)(4)-(7), sch 2 para 16

c 12 **Sunday Trading (London Olympic and Paralympic Games)**

> ss 1, 2 rep—Sunday Trading (London Olympic Games and Paralympic Games), 2012 c 12,
>> s 3(1)

c 13 **Supply and Appropriation (Main Estimates)**

> mod—Supply and Appropriation (Anticipation and Adjustments), 2013 c 12, s 3 sch 1

c 14 **Finance**

> s 13 mod—Finance, 2013 c 29, sch 45 para 159
> s 22 rep —Finance, 2013 c 29, sch 29 para 50(2)
> s 26 appl in pt (mods)—SI 2015/1983, regs 3, 4
> s 27 appl (mods)—SI 2015/1983, regs 3, 4
> s 74 rep in pt—SI 2013/2819, reg 40(a)
> am—SI 2013/2819, reg 40(c)
> s 78 rep in pt—(with spec commencing effect) Finance, 2013 c 29, sch 15 paras 26(2), 28,29
> am—Finance, 2013 c 29, sch 29 para 50(3)
> s 102 rep in pt—Finance, 2014 c 26, sch 1 para 18
> s 129 am—SI 2015/1959, reg 2
> s 139 am—SI 2013/636, sch para 16(2)(3)(a)
> rep in pt—SI 2013/636, sch para 16(3)(b)
> s 213 rep in pt —Stamp Duty Land Tax, 2015 c 1, sch para 21(c)(i)
> s 221 am—Finance, 2014 c 26, s 295(2)(3)
> sch 3 rep in pt—Finance, 2015 c 11, s 27(4)
> sch 6 rep in pt —Finance (No. 2), 2015 c 33, sch 5 paras 20(1),22(1)
> sch 7 rep in pt—Co-operative and Community Benefit Societies, 2014 c 14, sch 7; Finance
>> (No. 2), 2015 c 33, sch 5 paras 20(2)(3)
> sch 8 rep in pt—Co-operative and Community Benefit Societies, 2014 c 14, sch 7; Finance
>> (No. 2), 2015 c 33, sch 6 paras 21, 22(2)(3)
> sch 14 am—Finance, 2014 c 26, s 118(1)
> sch 16 rep in pt—(with spec commencing effect) Finance, 2013 c 29, sch 15 paras 26(3), 28,
>> 29; ibid, sch 29 para 50(4)
> sch 17 am—SIs 2012/3009, reg 16; 2013/2244, reg 2(2); 2015/1959, regs 3, 4
> Sch 20 rep in pt —Finance (No. 2), 2015 c 33, s 36(2)(b)
> sch 24 subst in pt—Finance, 2014 c 26, s 124(2)(4); SI 2014/47, art 3(1)(2)
> am—Finance, 2014 c 26, s 124(3); ibid, sch 28 para 31(2)-(4); SI 2015/664, sch 2
>> para 13
> sch 32 rep in pt—Finance, 2013 c 29, sch 42 para 1(2)(b)
> sch 34 rep in pt—Finance, 2013 c 29, ss 202(4)(a), 203(7)
> am—Finance, 2013 c 29, s 202(4)(b)
> sch 35 rep in pt—Stamp Duty Land Tax, 2015 c 1, sch para 21(c)(ii)
> sch 36 am—Finance, 2013 c 29, s 221(1)

2012

c 14 sch 36 *continued*

appl (mods)—SI 2013/938, reg 6

sch 38 appl—Social Security Admin, 1992 c 5,s 110ZA(2A); SIs 2009/470, reg 33(1)
(subst by 2013/607, reg 9); 2013/622, reg 41

c 15   **European Union (Approval of Treaty Amendment Decision)**

c 16   **Infrastructure (Financial Assistance)**

c 17   **Local Government Finance**

sch 3 rep in pt—Loc Audit and Accountability, 2014 c 2, sch 1 pt 2

c 18   **Mental Health (Approval Functions)**

c 19   **Civil Aviation**

s 24 am—Enterprise and Regulatory Reform, 2013 c 24, sch 6 para 141

s 25 am—Enterprise and Regulatory Reform, 2013 c 24, sch 6 para 142

s 26 am—Enterprise and Regulatory Reform, 2013 c 24, sch 6 para 143

s 27 am—Enterprise and Regulatory Reform, 2013 c 24, sch 6 para 144

s 28 am—Enterprise and Regulatory Reform, 2013 c 24, sch 6 para 145

s 29 am—Enterprise and Regulatory Reform, 2013 c 24, sch 6 para 146

s 30 am—Enterprise and Regulatory Reform, 2013 c 24, sch 6 para 147

s 60 am—SI 2014/892, sch 1 para 197(2)(a)(b)(3)(a)-(c)(4)(a)(b)(5)(6)(b)(c)(7)
rep in pt—SI 2014/892, sch 1 para 197(3)(d)(6)(a)

s 61 am—SI 2014/892, sch 1 para 198(2)-(4)(5)(a)(b)(6)(a)(b)(7)(8)

s 62 am—Enterprise and Regulatory Reform, 2013 c 24, sch 15 para 51; SI 2014/892, sch 1
para 199(2)(a)(b)(3)(4)

s 63 am—Enterprise and Regulatory Reform, 2013 c 24, sch 15 para 52; SI 2014/892, sch 1
para 200

s 64 am—SI 2014/892, sch 1 para 201(a)(b)

s 65 am—SI 2014/892, sch 1 para 202

sch 2 am—Enterprise and Regulatory Reform, 2013 c 24, sch 6 para
148(2)-(16)(17)(b)(19)-(32)(33)(a)(d)
rep in pt—Enterprise and Regulatory Reform, 2013 c 24, sch 6 para
148(17)(a)(c)(18)(33)(b)(c)

sch 6 am—SIs 2014/469, sch 2 para 26; 892, sch 1 para 203(2)(a)(3); 2015/1682, sch pt 1
para 4(u)
rep in pt—SI 2014/892, sch 1 para 203(2)(b); Deregulation, 2015 c 20, sch 6 para
22(17)

c 20   **Prisons (Interference with Wireless Telegraphy)**

s 4 am—Crim Justice and Cts, 2015 c 2, sch 9 para 31

c 21   **Financial Services**

power to appl (temp until 15.5.2039)—(prosp) Water, 2014 c 21, s 79(4); (prosp) ibid, s
81(10)

s 14 rep in pt—(prosp) Financial Services (Banking Reform), 2013 c 33, sch 3 para 18

s 61 am—SI 2014/3329, art 124

s 68 mod—SI 2013/1881, art 65(3)(d)
am—Financial Services (Banking Reform), 2013 c 33, s 105

s 73 am—Financial Services (Banking Reform), 2013 c 33, sch 10 para 9

s 76A added—Financial Services (Banking Reform), 2013 c 33, s 106(2)

s 77 am—Financial Services (Banking Reform), 2013 c 33, s 106(5)

s 78 am—Financial Services (Banking Reform), 2013 c 33, s 106(6)

s 79 am—Financial Services (Banking Reform), 2013 c 33, s 106(7)

s 80 am—Financial Services (Banking Reform), 2013 c 33, s 106(8)

s 81 am—Financial Services (Banking Reform), 2013 c 33, s 106(9)

s 83 am—Financial Services (Banking Reform), 2013 c 33, ss 105(4), 106(10)

s 84 appl (mods)—SI 2013/442, arts 61(3)(a), 63(2)
appl—SI 2001/2326 art 18(2) (amended by 2013/472, sch 2 para 49(b)(ii)(bb)-(ff))

s 85 mod—SI 2013/442, art 61(3)(b)
appl (mods)—SI 2013/442, art 63(2)
am—Financial Services (Banking Reform), 2013 c 33, sch 3, para 19(2)(b)(i)(3)(b)(i);
(7.3.2016) sch 3 para 19(2)(b)(ii)(3)(b)(ii); ibid, sch 10 para 10; SI 2013/1388,
reg 6; Pension Schemes, 2015 c 8, sch 3 para 17
rep in pt—(7.3.2016) Financial Services (Banking Reform), 2013 c 33, sch 3 para
19(2)(a)(3)(a)
appl—SI 2001/2326 art 18(2) (amended by 2013/472, sch 2 para 49(b)(ii)(bb)-(ff))

s 86 appl—SI 2001/2326 art 18(2) (amended by 2013/472, sch 2 para 49(b)(ii)(bb)-(ff))

s 87 am—Small Business, Enterprise and Employment, 2015 c 26, s 20

2012

c 21 *continued*
s 107 rep in pt—Consumer Rights, 2015 c 15, sch 6 para 84(2)
am—Consumer Rights, 2015 c 15, sch 6 para 84(3)

c 22   **Police (Complaints and Conduct)**
c 23   **Small Charitable Donations**
s 1 am—SI 2015/2027, art 3
s 4 am—SI 2015/2027, art 4
s 6 am—SI 2015/2027, art 5(a)(b)
s 9 am—SI 2015/2027, art 6

2013

c 1   **Trusts (Capital and Income)**
c 2   **Statute Law (Repeals)**
c 3   **Prevention of Social Housing Fraud**
s 4 rep in pt—Modern Slavery, 2015 c 30, sch 5 para 27(2)(b)
am—Modern Slavery, 2015 c 30, sch 5 para 27(2)(a)
s 7 am—Housing (W), 2014 anaw 7, sch 3 para 21
sch rep in pt—Serious Crime, 2015 c 9, sch 4 para 89; (17.3.2016) Modern Slavery, 2015 c 30, sch 5 para 27(3)

c 4   **Disabled Persons' Parking Badges**
c 5   **European Union (Croatian Accession and Irish Protocol)**
c 6   **Electoral Registration and Administration**
trans of functions—SI 2015/1376, art 3(1) sch 1
s 1 rep in pt—Electoral Registration and Admin, 2013 c 6, s 1(5)
s 25 am—SI 2015/1376, sch 2 para 16
sch 1 rep in pt—Electoral Registration and Admin, 2013 c 6, sch 1 para 2(3)
sch 5 mod—SI 2015/1520, art 2

c 7   **HGV Road User Levy**
excl—SI 2014/800, art 2
s 14A added—Finance, 2014 c 26, s 93(1)
sch 1 am—Finance, 2014 c 26, ss 82(2), 92(2)(3)

c 8   **Mental Health Discrimination**
c 9   **European Union (Approvals)**
c 10   **Scrap Metal Dealers**
c 11   **Prisons (Property)**
c 12   **Supply and Appropriation (Anticipation and Adjustments)**
mod —Supply and Appropriation (Anticipation and Adjustments), 2014 c 5, ss 3, 5 schs 1, 2

c 13   **Presumption of Death**
c 14   **Mobile Homes**
s 8 am—SI 2014/1900, sch 1 para 17

c 15   **Antarctic**
c 16   **Welfare Benefits Up-rating**
s 1 am—SI 2014/2888, reg 7(2)(a)

c 17   **Job Seekers (Back to Work Schemes)**
c 18   **Justice and Security**
c 19   **Groceries Code Adjudicator**
s 13 am—SI 2014/892, sch 1 para 205
s 14 am—SI 2014/892, sch 1 para 206
s 15 am—SI 2014/892, sch 1 para 207(a)
rep in pt—SI 2014/892, sch 1 para 207(b)
sch 1 am—SI 2014/892, sch 1 para 208

c 20   **Succession to the Crown**
c 21   **Partnerships (Prosecution) (Scotland)**
c 22   **Crime and Courts**
s 51 rep in pt—Immigration, 2014 c 22, sch 9 paras 7 table, 60 table
ss 52, 53 rep—Immigration, 2014 c 22, sch 9 para 60 table
sch 1 excl—Regulation of Investigatory Powers, 2000 c 23 s 55(3A)
sch 4 excl—Health and Safety at Work,1974 c 37 s 51A(2D)(2E)(f)
sch 8 rep in pt—SI 2014/834, sch 2 para 76
sch 9 rep in pt—(S prosp) Loc Audit and Accountability, 2014 c 2, sch 1 pt 2; Co-operative and Community Benefit Societies, 2014 c 14, sch 7; Consumer Rights, 2015 c 15, sch 6 para 85(n)
sch 13 rep in pt—Crime and Cts, 2013 c 22, sch 13 para 81
sch 22 rep in pt—Deregulation, 2015 c 20, sch 11 para 15

2013
c 23   **Marine Navigation**
c 24   **Enterprise and Regulatory Reform**
    s 52 am—Financial Services (Banking Reform), 2013 c 33, s 67(4); ibid, sch 8 para 11; SI
            2015/1682, sch pt 1 para 4(v)(i)
    s 53 am—SI 2015/1682, sch pt 1 para 4(v)(ii)
    s 72 excl—Agric Sector (W), 2014 anaw 6, s 12(2)(a)
    sch 4 rep in pt—SI 2015/16, reg 2(2)(a),(4)
        am—Financial Services (Banking Reform), 2013 c 33, s 67(5); ibid, sch 5 para
            2(2)-(4); ibid, sch 8 para 12; SIs 2015/16, reg 2(2)(b)(c),(3); 1682, sch pt 1 para
            4(v)(iii)
        mod—SI 2003/1592, sch 4 para 18 (added by SI 2014/891, art 19(5))
    sch 19 rep in pt—(prosp) Small Business, Enterprise and Employment, 2015 c 26, sch 10
        para 12
        mod—Finance (No. 2), 2015 c 33, sch 8 para 33(2)
    sch 20 excl—Agric Sector (W), 2014 anaw 6, s 12(2)(a)
c 25   **Public Services Pensions**
    s 18 excl—SI 2014/1964, sch 2 para 10(2)(b); SSI 2014/217, sch 3 paras 7(2), 10(2); SIs
            2015/95, reg 6; 182, sch 2 paras 6(2)(b), 10(2)(b); SSI 2015/142, sch 4 paras
            13(2)(b), 16(2)(b), 19(2)(b)
    sch 5 am—Pension Schemes, 2015 c 8, s 80
    sch 7 appl—SSI 2014/217, sch 3 para 21; SIs 1992/129, sch 2 rule G1(10) (added by
            2015/589, sch 3 para 7(a)(ii)); 2006/3432, sch 1 pt 11 rule 1(7) (added by
            2015/589, sch 2 para 5(a)(ii)); 2015/432, reg 5(2)(a)
        appl (mods)—SI 2014/2848, sch 2 paras 32, 33, 42, 43 (added by 2015/589, sch 1
            para 7(d)); SSI 2015/19, regs 32, 33 (added by 2015/141, reg 22(d))
        restr—SI 2015/95, reg 16
c 26   **Defamation**
    s 9 am—SI 2014/2947, sch 4 para 7
c 27   **Growth and Infrastructure**
    s 7 rep in pt—Growth and Infrastructure, 2013 c 27, s 7(4)
c 28   **Supply and Appropriation (Main Estimates)**
c 29   **Finance**
    s 6 am—Finance, 2014 c 26, sch 1 para 19(a)
        rep in pt—Finance, 2014 c 26, sch 1 para 19(b)(c)
    s 7 am—Finance, 2014 c 26, sch 2 para 6(2)(3)
        rep in pt—Finance, 2014 c 26, sch 2 para 6(4)
    s 23 rep in pt—Finance, 2014 c 26, s 24(16)
    s 43 rep —SI 2013/3209, reg 12(b)
    s 50 rep in pt—Finance, 2014 c 26, s 41(5)
    Pt 3 (ss 91-174) appl—Finance, 2014 c 26, ss 223(8), 223(9)(e)
    s 94 am—Finance, 2014 c 26, ss 109(2), 110(2)
    s 99 am—Finance, 2014 c 26, ss 109(3), 110(3); Finance, 2015 c 11, s 70(1)
    s 101 excl in pt—Finance, 2015 c 11, s 70(3)
        mod—Finance, 2015 c 11, s 70(4)
    s 102 am—Finance, 2015 c 11, s 71
    s 110 rep in pt—Finance, 2015 c 11, s 72(3)(a)
        am—Finance, 2015 c 11, s 72(2),(3)(b)(c),(4)
    s 147 appl—Finance, 2003 c 14 sch 4A para 5E(9)
    s 159 mod—Finance, 2014 c 26, s 109(5)(6); Finance, 2015 c 11, s 73(7)(8)
    s 159 am—Finance, 2015 c 11, s 73(2)
    s 159A added—Finance, 2015 c 11, s 73(3)
    s 161 am—Finance, 2015 c 11, s 73(4)
    s 163 mod—Finance, 2014 c 26, s 109(5)(7)
    s 172 appl—Finance, 2003 c 14 sch 4A para 5A(10)(b)
    s 203 rep—Finance, 2014 c 26, s 119(4)
    Pt 5 (ss 206-215) ext—Nat Insurance Contributions, 2014 c 7, s 10(1)
    s 206 mod—Nat Insurance Contributions, 2014 c 7, s 10(2)
        am—Finance, 2015 c 11, s 115(1)
    s 207 mod—Nat Insurance Contributions, 2014 c 7, s 10(3)
    s 209 mod—Nat Insurance Contributions, 2014 c 7, s 10(4)
    s 210 am—Nat Insurance Contributions, 2014 c 7, s 10(5)
    s 222 am—Finance (No. 2), 2015 c 33, s 50
    sch 1 am—Finance, 2014 c 26, sch 2 para 7(2)(4)(a)(i)(c)
        rep in pt—Finance, 2014 c 26, sch 2 para 7(3)(4)(a)(ii)(b)

2013

c 29 *continued*

> sch 22 rep in pt—Finance, 2014 c 26, s 42(4)
> sch 25 rep in pt—Finance, 2014 c 26, sch 1 para 20
> sch 33 am—Finance, 2014 c 26, ss 224(5)(6), 225(3), 277(6); Finance, 2015 c 11, s 73(5); Finance (No. 2), 2015 c 33, sch 8 para 42
> excl—Finance, 2014 c 26, s 208(10)s 208(11)(e)
> mod—Finance, 2014 c 26, s 227(9)(d)

c 30 **Marriage (Same Sex Couples)**

> mod—SIs 1995/300, reg A4(4) (added by SI 2014/78, reg 4); 1995/866, reg 2B(4) (added by SI 2014/78, reg 26); 2000/619, reg 2A(4) (added by SI 2014/78, reg 19); 2002/1311, reg 2A(4) (added by SI 2014/78, reg 23); 2008/653, reg 2.A.1A(4) (added by SI 2014/78, reg 12); ibid, reg 3A.1A(4) (added by SI 2014/78, reg 15);
> s 9 am—Deregulation, 2015 c 20, s 99(3)
> s 11 excl—SI 2014/560, sch 2 paras 1-5
> mod—SIs 1992/129, sch 2 Scheme sch 1 Pt 3 rules 1(5), 2(5) (added by SI 2014/560, sch 3 para 17); 1992/1612, regs 42B(5), 42C(5) (added by SI 2014/560, sch 3 para 17); 2006/3432, rules 4(4), 5(5) (added by SI 2014/560, sch 3 para 17); 2010/990, regs 2A(5), 2B(5) (added by SI 2014/560, sch 3 para 17); 2012/687, rules 2A(5), 2B(5) (added by SI 2014/560, sch 3 para 17)
> sch 3 excl—SIs 1987/257, reg J1(7) (added by SI 2014/79, reg 5(c)); 1992/129, sch 2 Scheme sch 1 Pt 3 rules 1(4), 2(4) (added by SI 2014/560, sch 3 para 17); 1997/1612, regs 42B(4), 42C(4) (added by SI 2014/560, sch 3 para 17); 2006/3432, rules 4(4), 5(4) (added by SI 2014/560, sch 3 para 17); 2010/990, regs 2A(4), 2B(4) (added by SI 2014/560, sch 3 para 17); 2012/687, rules 2A(4), 2B(4) (added by SI 2014/560, sch 3 para 17); 2014/560, sch 2 para 5
> mod —SIs 1992/129, sch 2 Scheme sch 1 Pt 3 rules 1(5), 2(5) (added by SI 2014/560, sch 3 para 17); 1997/1612, regs 42B(5), 42C(5) (added by SI 2014/560, sch 3 para 17); 2006/3432, rules 4(5), 5(5) (added by SI 2014/560, sch 3 para 17); 2010/990, regs 2A(5), 2B(5) (added by SI 2014/560, sch 3 para 17); 2012/687, rules 2A(5), 2B(5) (added by SI 2014/560, sch 3 para 17); SI 2014/560, sch 2 para 4
> sch 4 rep in pt—Pensions, 2014 c 19, sch 12 para 77
> sch 7 rep in pt—SI 2014/3229, sch 5 para 21

c 31 **High Speed Rail (Preparation)**

c 32 **Energy**

> mod (temp)—SI 2014/469, art 7(2)art 7(3)(c)(4)-(9)
> s 33 appl—SI 2014/2043, reg 66
> s 84 am—SI 2015/1682, sch pt 1 para 4(w)(i)
> s 89 am—SI 2015/1682, sch pt 1 para 4(w)(ii)
> s 90 am—SI 2015/1682, sch pt 1 para 4(w)(iii)
> s 97 mod—SI 2014/469, sch 1 para 5(2)(3)(a)(4)
> s 105 mod—SI 2014/469, sch 1 para 5(4)(5)(b)
> ss 109, 110 appl—SI 1975/335, reg 11(2) (substituted by SI 2014/469, sch 3 para 175)
> s 111 mod—Atomic Weapons Establishment, 1991 c. 46, sch para 10D
> s 132 restr—Electricity, 1989 c 29 s 32Z(6)(b)
> sch 8 mod—SI 2014/469, sch 1 para 5(2)(3)(b)(c)(4),(5)(c)
> sch 9 rep in pt—Deregulation, 2015 c 20, sch 13 para 6(36)
> am—SI 2015/1682, sch pt 1 para 4(w)(iv)
> mod—SI 2014/469, sch 1 para 5(4)(5)(d)
> excl—SI 2005/2042, reg 54A (added by SI 2014/469, sch 3 para 192)
> sch 10 excl—SI 2014/469, sch 1 paras 4, 5(6)
> mod—SI 2014/469, sch 1 para 5(4),(5)(e)
> sch 12 rep in pt—SI 2014/1638, sch 13 para 8(2) sch 14 pt 1

c 33 **Financial Services (Banking Reform)**

> s 17 am—SI 2014/3348, sch 3 para 6(a)(b)(ii)
> rep in pt—SI 2014/3348, sch 3 para 6(b)(i)
> s 40 appl (mods)—SI 2015/1911, reg 15(1)
> s 58 am—Small Business, Enterprise and Employment, 2015 c 26, s 14(3)(4)
> ss 81-93 appl (mods)—SI 2015/1911, reg 14(1)
> s 98 am—SI 2015/1911, reg 19(a)-(c)
> s 104 appl (mods)—SI 2015/1911, reg 15(2)
> s 108 am—Small Business, Enterprise and Employment, 2015 c 26, s 14(5)
> sch 4 appl in pt (mods)—SI 2015/1911, reg 15(3)

2014

c 1   **Mesothelioma**

c 2   **Local Audit and Accountability**
appl —SI 2015/192, sch pt 1 2
s 12 appl (mods)—SI 2014/1710, reg 9(5)
s 20 appl—Housing and Regeneration, 2008 c 17, s 210A(1B)
ss 22, 23 appl—Housing and Regeneration, 2008 c 17, s 210A(1B)
s 25 appl—GLA, 1999 c 29, s 134(4)
ss 26-31 excl—GLA, 1999 c 29, s 134(5)
s 32 appl—(pt prosp) GLA, 1999 c 29, s 134(6) (amended by 2014 c 2, sch 12 para
43(4)(a))
mod (temp)—SI 2015/179, art 3
sch 2 rep in pt—Deregulation, 2015 c 20, sch 13 para 6(37)
am—SI 2015/975, reg 2(2)
sch 4 am—SI 2014/2845, reg 2
sch 7 appl (mods)—SI 2014/1629, reg 23
sch 8 excl—GLA, 1999 c. 29, s 134(5)
sch 11 see (disclosure powers ext)—Anti-terrorism, Crime and Security, 2001 c 24, s 17 127
Sch 4 para 53F
sch 13 am—SI 2015/972, art 2(2)(3)

c 3   **European Union (Approvals),**

c 4   **Transparency of Lobbying, Non-Party Campaigning and Trade Union Administration**
trans of functions—SI 2015/1376, art 3(1), sch 1
s 25 am—SI 2015/1376, sch 2 para 17(2)(a)
s 33 am—SI 2014/1530, reg 64(1)(b)(2) sch 3 pt 2

c 5   **Supply and Appropriation (Anticipation and Adjustments)**

c 6   **Children and Families**
appl—SI 2014/2270, art 20(1)
Pt 3 (ss 19-83) mod—SI 2015/62, regs 31(1), 32(1)
s 37 rep in pt —SI 2015/914, sch para 97
s 58 rep (13.3.2019)—Children and Families, 2014 c 6, s 58(5)
s 91 am —SI 2015/895, reg 2

c 7   **National Insurance Contributions**
s 2 am—SI 2015/578, reg 2

c 8   **Citizenship (Armed Forces)**

c 9   **International Development (Gender Equality)**

c 10   **Leasehold Reform (Amendment)**
rep (W)—Housing (W), 2014 anaw 7, s 140(2)

c 11   **Offender Rehabilitation**

c 12   **Anti-social Behaviour, Crime and Policing**
s 48 am—SI 2015/664, sch 4 para 45
s 63 ext—Police Reform, 2002 c 30 Sch 4 para 5
s 116 am—Serious Crime, 2015 c 9, sch 4 para 90

c 13   **Northern Ireland (Miscellaneous Provisions)**

c 14   **Co-operative and Community Benefit Societies**
restr—Credit Unions, 1979 c 34, s 2(3)
mod—Credit Unions, 1979 c 34, s 31(3)
appl—Housing, 1996 c. 52, Sch 1 para 9(5)
excl—Housing and Regeneration, 2008 c 17 s 167(5)(ca)
s 2 excl—Credit Unions, 1979 c 34, s 2(1)
s 3 mod —Credit Unions, 1979 c 34, s 6(1A)
appl (mods)—Credit Unions, 1979 c 34, s 2(2)
s 4 excl—Credit Unions, 1979 c 34, s 2(1)
s 5 appl (mods)—Credit Unions, 1979 c 34, s 20(1)-(1ZD)
mod—Credit Unions, 1979 c 34, s 6(1A)
s 7 appl (mods)—Credit Unions, 1979 c 34, s 6(1A)
s 9 appl (mods)—Credit Unions, 1979 c 34 s 20(1D)
s 10 mod—Credit Unions, 1979 c 34, s 3(4)
s 14 excl—Credit Unions, 1979 c 34, s 2(1)
s 16 mod—Credit Unions, 1979 c 34, s 4(3)
s 21 excl—Credit Unions, 1979 c 34, s 4(5)
s 53 mod—Land Registration, 2002 c 9, s 91(9A)
s 62 subst—Bankruptcy and Diligence, etc, 2007 asp 3, s 49(1)
s 63 rep—Bankruptcy and Diligence, etc, 2007 asp 3, s 49(2)
s 64 am—Bankruptcy and Diligence, etc, 2007 asp 3, s 49(3)(a)

2014
c 14 *continued*

s 67 excl—Credit Unions, 1979 c 34, s 31(4)
ss 77, 78 excl—Credit Unions, 1979 c 34, s 31(4)
s 81 excl—Credit Unions, 1979 c 34, s 31(4)
s 85 mod —Housing, 1996 c 52, Sch 1 para 17(2)
appl (mod)—Housing and Regeneration, 2008 c 17, s 134(2)
s 87 appl—Loc Democracy, Economic Development and Construction, 2009 c 20, s 44(4)(b)
ss 89, 90 excl—Credit Unions, 1979 c 34, s 31(4)
s 97 mod—Friendly Socieities, 1974 c 46, s 40(3)
s 107 appl—Credit Unions, 1979 c 34, s 18(3)
ss 109, 110 mod—Credit Unions, 1979 c 34, s 21(1)-(3A)
s 111 mod —SI 2014/229, art 13 (subst by SI 2014/1822, art 4)
ss 112-114 excl—Credit Unions, 1979 c 34, s 22
s 113 mod—SI 2014/229, art 14 (subst by SI 2014/1822, art 4)
s 115 mod—Credit Unions, 1979 c 34, s 6(1A); ibid, s 23(3)
s 116 excl—Credit Unions, 1979 c 34, s 23(5)
s 126 mod—SI 2014/229, art 15 (subst by SI 2014/1822, art 4)
Pt 10 (ss 127-133) mod—Credit Unions, 1979 c. 34, s 28(1)
s 127 appl—Loc Democracy, Economic Development and Construction, 2009 c. 20, s 44(4)(c)
ss 141, 143-146, 148, 149 appl—Credit Unions, 1979 c. 34, s 31(2)
sch 3 excl—Credit Unions, 1979 c. 34 s 32(1)
sch 4 rep in pt—Finance, 2015 c 11, sch 6 para 12(b)
am—Finance, 2014 c 26, sch 39 paras 3-14
c 15 **Deep Sea Mining**
c 16 **Inheritance and Trustees' Powers**
c 17 **Gambling (Licensing and Advertising)**
c 18 **Intellectual Property**
s 13 am—SI 2014/2329, reg 3(1)(2)
c 19 **Pensions**
Pt 1 (ss 1-24) excl—SI 2007/1398, reg 8(3) (as am by 2015/1985, art 30(4)(a))
s 24 rep in pt—(6.4.2021) Pensions, 2014 c 19, s 24(8)
appl (mods)—SI 2015/118, regs 13-15
s 34 am—Pension Schemes, 2015 c 8, sch 4 para 45
s 35 rep (conditionally)—Pensions, 2014 c 19, s 35
s 36 rep in pt—(prosp) Pension Schemes, 2015 c 8, s 39(6)
sch 14 rep (6.4.2021)—Pensions, 2014 c 19, s 24(8)
appl (mods)—SI 2015/118, regs 13-15
sch 17 am—(prosp) Pension Schemes, 2015 c 8, sch 2 para 51(2); ibid, sch 4 para 46
rep in pt—(prosp) Pension Schemes, 2015 c 8, sch 2 para 51(3)
c 20 **Defence Reform**
c 21 **Water**
ss 64-81 rep (14.5.2039)—(with power to bring forward date of repeal) Water, 2014 c 21, s 83(1),(2)-(8)
s 69 am—SI 2015/1902, reg 29
c 22 **Immigration**
s 24 mod—SI 2014/2873, art 6 sch paras 1, 3
s 26 mod—SI 2014/2873, art 6 sch para 2; ibid, art 7, sch para 4
s 40 am—SI 2014/3074, art 2
s 48 am—SI 2015/396, sch 4 para 2
s 49 appl—Finance, 1977 c 36, s 3A(10) (added by SI 2015/396, sch 1 para 2); Civil Partnership, 2004 c 33, s 88A(9) (added by SI 2015/396, sch 3 para 2)
s 50 am—SI 2015/396, sch 4 para 3
s 62 am—SI 2015/396, sch 4 para 4
s 67 ext (mods) —(Jersey) SIs 2015/1532, art 2(2)(a) sch 2; (Guernsey) 1533, art 5 sch 2
ss 68-70 ext (mods) —(Isle of Man) SI 2008/680, art 22, sch 9A (added by 2015/1765, arts 5, 7)
s 73 ext in pt (mods) —(Jersey) SIs 2015/1532, art 2(2)(a) sch 2; (Guernsey) 1533, art 5 sch 2
sch 1 rep in pt—Immigration, 2014 c 22, sch 9 para 7 table
sch 8 ext (mods) —(Jersey) SIs 2015/1532, art 2(2)(b), sch 2; (Guernsey) 1533, art 5, sch 2
sch 9 ext in pt —(Jersey) SI 2015/1532, art 2(2)(c), sch 2
ext (mods) —(Guernsey) SI 2015/1533, art 5, sch 2

2014

c 23 **Care**
Pt 1 (ss 1-80) appl in pt (mods)—SI 2015/305, regs 2(1)(a)(2), 4-12
s 39 appl in pt—Mental Capacity, 2005 c 9, sch A1 para 183(2A) (added by SI 2015/914, sch para 80)
s 55 appl—SI 2015/314, reg 2 3
s 67 excl—SI 2014/2824, reg 4
    restr—SI 2014/2889, reg 4
s 78 appl—Loc Authy Social Services, 1970 c 42, s 7(1A) (added by SI 2015/914, sch para 17)
Pt 3 Ch. 2 (ss 109-117) mod—SI 2015/642, art 2(2)(b)
sch 1 appl in pt—Social Work (S), 1968 c. 49, s 86(2) (as amended by 2014 c 23, sch 1 para 7(2)); Mental Capacity, 2005 c 9, sch A1 para 183(2A) (added by SI 2015/914, sch para 80)

c 24 **House of Lords Reform**
s 6 am—H of L (Expulsion and Suspension), 2015 c 14, s 2

c 25 **Supply and Appropriation (Main Estimates)**

c 26 **Finance**
s 2 am—Finance, 2015 c 11, s 3(2)(3)
s 32 rep in pt—Finance, 2015 c 11, s 29(7)(a)(c); SI 2015/1741, reg 2
    am—Finance, 2015 c 11, s 29(7)(b)(d); SI 2015/1741, reg 2
s 56 rep in pt—Finance, 2015 c 11, sch 6 para 12(a)
s 69 rep—Finance, 2015 c 11, sch 11 para 13(2)
s 94 rep (retrosp to 1.8.2015)—Finance (No. 2), 2015 c 33, s 48(2)(6)
s 95 rep—Finance (No. 2), 2015 c 33, s 48(2)
Pt 4 (ss 199-233) appl (mods)—Social Security, Contributions and Benefits, 1992 c 4, s 11A(1)(3) (added by 2015 c 5, sch 1 para 3); ibid, s 16(1)(d) (added by 2015 c 5, sch 2 para 32)
s 199 am—Finance, 2015 c 11, sch 18 para 2
s 220 am—Finance, 2015 c 11, sch 18 para 3
s 221 am—Finance, 2015 c 11, sch 18 para 4
s 222 am—Finance, 2015 c 11, sch 18 para 5
s 223 am—Finance, 2015 c 11, sch 18 para 6
s 225A added—Finance, 2015 c 11, sch 18 para 7
s 227 am—Finance, 2015 c 11, sch 18 para 8
s 227A added—Finance, 2015 c 11, sch 18 para 9
Pt 5 (ss 234-283) appl (mods)—Social Security, Contributions and Benefits, 1992 c 4, s 11A(1)(3) (added by 2015 c 5, sch 1 para 3); ibid, s 16(1)(d) (added by 2015 c 5, sch 2 para 2)
    mod—Nat Insurance Contributions, 2015 c 5, sch 2 pt 2
s 237 rep in pt—Finance, 2015 c 11, sch 19 para 2(7)
    am—Finance, 2015 c 11, sch 19 para 2(2)-(6),(8)
s 283 am—Finance, 2015 c 11, sch 19 para 3
sch 1 excl in pt—Finance (No. 2), 2015 c 33, s 39(1)(2)(b)
sch 14 rep—Finance, 2015 c 11, sch 11 para 13
sch 32 am—Finance, 2015 c 11, sch 18 para 10(2)(3)
sch 34 am—Finance, 2015 c 11, sch 19 paras 4, 6-8
sch 36 rep in pt—Finance, 2015 c 11, sch 19 para 5

c 27 **Data Retention and Investigatory Powers**
ss 1-7 rep (31.12.2016)—Data Retention and Investigatory Powers, 2014 c 27, s 8(3)
s 2 am—Counter-Terrorism and Security, 2015 c 6, s 21

c 28 **Childcare Payments**
s 11 appl (mods)—SI 2015/448, reg 16
ss 12, 13 appl (mods)—SI 2015/448, reg 17
s 19 am—SI 2015/537, reg 2

c 29 **Wales**
s 13 trans of functions—SI 2015/1376, art 3(1), sch 1
    am—SI 2015/1376, sch 2 para 18(2)(a)
sch 1 trans of function—SI 2015/1376, art 3(1), sch
sch 1 am—SI 2015/1376, sch 2 para 18(2)(b)

c 30 **Taxation of Pensions**
sch 1 rep in pt—Finance (No. 2), 2015 c 33, s 22(11)(b)(i)
sch 2 rep in pt—Finance (No. 2), 2015 c 33, s 22(11)(b)(ii)

Chronological Table of the

Acts of the Parliaments of Scotland

1424 – 1707 (a)

(a) Following the practice of the 1908 Revised Edition, the Acts recorded in the Parliamentary Proceedings prior to the reign of James 1 (contained in Volume 1 of the Record Edition), are not included. See also Preface at page x.

Record Edition	Title or Subject Matter	How Affected	12mo Edition
James I			**James I**
1424 (May 26)			**Parl. 1–1424**
c. 1	Church	rep. SLR(S) 1906	c. 1
c. 2	Public peace	"	c. 2
c. 3	Treason	"	c. 3
c. 4	Treason	"	c. 4
c. 5	Riders and gangers	"	c. 5
c. 6	Officers of law	"	c. 6
c. 7	Sorners	"	c. 7
c. 8	Customs and burgh mails	"	c. 8
c. 9	Crown revenues	"	c. 9
c.10	Supply	"	—
c.11	Salmon	"	c.10
c.12	Salmon	rep. SLR(S) 1964	c.11
c.13	**Royal Mines**		c.12
c.14	Clergy	rep. SLR(S) 1906	c.13
c.15	Clergy	"	c.14
c.16	Export duty	"	c.15
c.17	Export duty	"	c.16
c.18	Football	"	c.17
c.19	Archers	"	c.18
c.20	Rooks	"	c.19
c.21	Muirburn	"	c.20
c.22	Customs	"	c.21
c.23	Customs	"	c.22
c.24	Coinage	"	c.23
c.25	Innkeepers	rep. SL (Reps.) 1989 (c.43)	c.24
—	Beggers	rep. SLR(S) 1906	c.25
c.26	Not public and general		
c.27	Supply	"	—
1424 (Mar. 12)			**Parl. 2–1424**
			c.26
c. 1	Church	rep. SLR(S) 1906	c.27
c. 2	Hospitals	"	c.28
c. 3	Heretics and Lollards	"	c.29
c. 4	Observance of Statutes	"	c.30
c. 5	Leagues	"	—
c. 6	Trade in Flanders	"	c.31
c. 7	Horses	"	c.32
c. 8	Tallow	"	—
c. 9	Price of food	"	
c. 10	Theft of Green Wood, etc.	"	c. 33
c. 11	Stolen Wood	"	c. 34
c.12	Salmon	rep. Salmon Fisheries(S) 1828 c. 39 s.1	c.35
c.13	Deer	rep. SLR(S) 1906	c.36
c.14	Reset	"	—
c.15	Treason	"	c.37
c.16	Foreign Trade	"	c.38

Record Edition	Title or Subject Matter	How Affected	12mo Edition
James I			**James I**
c.17	Deacons of crafts	rep. SLR(S) 1906	c.39
c.18	Prayers for Royal Family	"	—
c.19	Customs	"	c.40
c.20	Labourers	"	c.41
c.21	Beggars	"	c.42
c.22	Leasing making	"	c.43
c.23	Wapinschaws	"	c.44
c.24	[Poor's Counsel]	rep. Legal Aid and Solicitors (S) 1949 c.63 s.17(3)(5), sch. 8 Pt. I rep. SL (Reps.) 1973 c.39	c.45
c.25	Remissions	rep. SLR(S) 1906	c.46
1425			**Parl. 3–1425**
c. 1	Church	rep. SLR(S) 1906	—
c. 2	Armour to be imported		c.47
c. 3	The law of the land	rep. SLR(S) 1964	c.48
c. 4	Registration of King's letters	rep. SLR(S) 1906	—
c. 5	Export of coin	"	c.49
c. 6	Jurymen	"	c.50
c. 7	Forethought felony	"	c.51
c. 8	Attendance in Parliament	"	c.52
c. 9	Attorneys	"	c.53
c.10	Statute Law Revision	"	cc.54-55
c.11	Travellers	"	c.56
c.12	Prayers for Royal Family	"	—
c.13	Measures	"	—
c.14	Weights	"	c.57
c.15	Water measures	"	c.58
c.16	Ferries	"	c.59
c.17	Wapinschaws	"	c.60
c.18	Trade with Ireland	"	cc.61–64
c.19	Lords of Session	"	c.65
c.20	Poor	"	c.66
c.21	Proclamation of Acts of Parliament	"	c.67
			Parl. 4–1426
c.22	Weights and measures	"	cc.68–70
c.23	Fire in Towns	"	cc.71–75
1426			**Parl. 5–1426**
c. 1	Customs	rep. SLR(S) 1906	c.76
c. 2	Deacons of crafts	rep. 1427 (July 1) c.46	c.77
c. 3	Craftsmen's work	rep. SLR(S) 1906	c.75
c. 4	Wages	"	c.79
c. 5	Workmen	"	c.80
c. 6	Agriculture	"	c.81
c. 7	Castles	"	c.82
1427 (July 1)			**Parl. 6–1426**
c. 1	Oaths	rep. SLR(S) 1906	c.83
c. 2	Travellers abroad	"	c.84
c. 3	Travellers	"	c.85
c. 4	Deacons of crafts	"	c.86
c. 5	Spiritual Court of Procedure	"	c.87
c. 6	Arbitrations	"	c.87
c. 7	Exceptions	"	—
c. 8	Jurisdiction over Scotsmen dying abroad	rep. SLR(S) 1964	c.88
1427 (Mar. 1)			**Parl. 7–1427**
c. 1	Customs	rep. SLR(S) 1906	c.100
c. 2	Members of Parliament	"	c.101
c. 3	Craftsmen	"	c.102
c. 4	Beggars	"	c.103

Record Edition	*Title or Subject Matter*	*How Affected*	*12mo Edition*
James I			**James I**
c. 5	*Wolves*	rep. SLR(S) 1906	c.104
c. 6	*Salmon*	"	—
c. 7	*Shipping*	"	—
c. 8	*Lepers*	"	c.105
c. 9	*Barratry*	"	c.106
c.10	*Attendance at Court*	"	—
c.11	*Interpretation of Acts*	"	c.107
c.12	*Wild birds*	"	c.108
1428			**Parl. 8–1428**
Vol. II, p. 17	*Oath by Queen*	rep. SLR(S) 1906	c.109
1429 (Apr. 26)			
c. 1	*Treason*	rep. SLR(S) 1906	c.110
c. 2	*Husbandmen*	"	—
1429 (Mar. 6)			**Parl. 9–1429**
c. 1	*Mayors of Fee*	rep. SLR(S) 1906	c.111
c. 2	*Summons*	"	c.112
c. 3	*Brieves*	rep. SLR(S) 1964	c.113
c. 4	*Essonvies*	rep. SLR(S) 1906	c.114
c. 5	*Caution to abide judgment*	"	c.115
c. 6	*Appeals*	"	c.116
c. 7	*Procedure in appeals*	"	c.117
c. 8	*Sumptuary law*	"	c.118
c. 9	*Sumptuary law*	"	—
c.10	*Sumptuary law*	"	—
c.11	*Defence of the realm*	"	c.120
c.12	*Defence of the realm*	"	c.121
c.13	*Defence of the realm*	"	c.122
c.14	*Defence of the realm*	"	c.123
c.15	*Shipwrecks*	"	c.124
c.16	*Advocates' oath*	"	c.125
c.17	*Galleys*	"	c.126
c.18	*Brief of sasine*	"	c.127
c.19	*Fugitives of England*	"	c.128
c.20	**Lawburrows**	rep. in pt.SLR(S) 1906; 1964	c.129
c.21	*Service of inquests and retours*	rep. SLR(S) 1906	c.130
c.22	*Salmon*	"	c.131
1431			**Parl. 10–1431**
c. 1	*Supply*	rep. SLR(S) 1906	—
c. 2	*Salmon*	"	c.132
c. 3	*Treason*	"	—
c. 4	*Alienation of Crown lands*	"	c.133
1432			**Parl. 6–1426**
c. 1	*Murder*	rep. SLR(S) 1906	c.89
c. 2	*Murder*	"	c.90
c. 3	*Murder*	"	c.91
c. 4	*Murder*	"	c.92
c. 5	*Murder*	"	c.93
c. 6	*Murder*	"	c.94
c. 7	*Murder*	"	c.95
c. 8	*Murder*	"	c.96
c. 9	*Murder*	"	c.97
c.10	*Murder*	"	c.98
c.11	*Officer's wands*	"	c.99
1433			**Parl. 11–1433**
c. 1	*King's protection*	rep. SLR(S) 1906	c.134
c. 2	*Mill lades*	"	—
c. 3	*Defaulting Sheriffs*	"	—
1434			**Parl. 12–1434**
c. 1	Not public and general		c.135
c. 2	*Fealty to Queen*	rep. SLR(S) 1906	c.136

Record Edition	Title or Subject Matter	How Affected	12mo Edition
James I			**James I**
1436			**Parl. 13–1436**
c. 1	*Thieves*	rep. SLR(S) 1906	c.137
c. 2	*Jury oath*	"	c.138
c. 3	*Arrestments*	"	c.139
c. 4	*Pursuit by Sheriffs*	"	c.140
c. 5	*Englishmen*	"	c.141
c. 6	*Thieves*	"	c.142
c. 7	*Import of bullion*	"	c.143
c. 8	*Taverns*	"	c.144
c. 9	*English cloth*	"	c.145
c.10	*Selling salmon to English men*	"	c.146
c.11	*Flemish wine trade*	"	c.147
c.12	*Place of trial*	"	c.148
c.13	*Gold, silver and jewels*	"	c.149
James II.			**James II.**
Undated			**Parl. 1–1437**
Vol. II, p. 31	*Crown lands*	rep. SLR(S) 1906	c. 2
1437			
Vol. II, p. 31	*Coronation*	rep.SLR(S) 1906	c. 1
1438 (Nov. 27)			
c. 1	*Inquisitions in last reign*	rep. SLR(S) 1906	—
c. 2	*Robbery*	"	—
1438 (Mar. 13)			**Parl. 2–1438**
c. 1	*Sittings of Parliament*	rep. SLR(S) 1906	—
c. 2	*Rebels*	"	c. 3
1440			**Parl. 3–1440**
c. 1	*Church*	rep. SLR(S) 1906	c. 4
c. 2	*Circuit courts*	"	c. 5
c. 3	*Crimes*	"	c. 6
1443			**Parl. 4–1443**
c. 1	*Church*	rep. SLR(S) 1906	c.7
c. 3	*Jurisdiction of Pope*	rep. 1592 c.8	—
1445			
Vol. II, p. 33	*Crown lands*	rep. SLR(S) 1906	—
1449			**Parl. 6–1449**
c. 1	*Church censure*	rep. SLR(S) 1906	c.12
c. 2	*Public peace*	"	c.13
c. 3	*Treason*	"	cc.14–15
c. 4	*Borders*	"	c.16
c. 5	*Officers of law*	"	c.17
c. 6	**Leases**	rep.in pt. SLR(S) 1906 ext. Freshwater and Salmon Fisheries (S), 1976 c.22, s.4. appl.(except as relating to rivers Tweed or Upper Esk) Salmon and Freshwater Fisheries (Consolidation) (S), 2003 asp 15, ss 66(1), 71(3)(4) appl.(River Tweed District) SI 2006/2913, art 73	cc.18–19
	excl	Registration of Leases (S), 1857 c 26, s 20C (added by Land Registration (S), 2012 asp 5, sch 2 para 16)	
c. 7	*Spuilyies*	rep. SLR(S) 1906	c.20
c. 8	*Officers of law*	"	c.21
c. 9	*Sorners and beggars*	"	c.22

Record Edition James II.	Title or Subject Matter	How Affected	12mo Edition James II.
c.10	Statute Law Revision	rep. SLR(S) 1906	—
c.11	Price of food	"	cc.23–24
c.12	Treason	"	c.25
c.13	Regalities	"	c.26
c.14	Theft and robbery	"	c.27
c.15	Justice clerks	"	c.28
c.16	Castles	"	—
c.17	Coinage	"	c.29
c.18	Parties summoned to King's Council	"	c.30
1450			**Parl. 7–1450**
c. 1	Poison	rep. SLR(S) 1906	c.31
c. 2	Poison	"	c.32
1451			**Parl. 8–1451**
c.1–18	Coinage	rep. SLR(S) 1906	cc.33–37
1452			**Parl. 9–1452**
c. 1	English money	rep. SLR(S) 1906	—
c. 2	Meeting of Parliament	"	—
c. 3	Corn	"	c.38
c. 4	Food	"	c.39
c. 5	Food	"	c.40
1454			**Parl. 10–1454**
c. 1	Criminal Law	rep. SLR(S) 1906	—
c. 2	Food	"	c.40
1455 (Aug. 4)			**Parl. 11–1455**
c. 1	Crown lands	Not public and general	c.41
c. 2	Not public and general		—
c. 3	Warden in the Borders	rep. SLR(S) 1906	c.42
c. 4	Regalities	"	c.43
c. 5	Tenure of offices	"	c.44
c. 6	Compensation for offices revoked	"	c.44
c. 7	Coiners	"	—
c. 8	Sorners	"	c.45
c. 9	Burghs	"	c.46
c.10	Embassy to Pope	"	—
c.11	Sumptuary laws	"	c.47
c.12	Sumptuary laws	"	c.47
c.13	Continuation of Parliament	"	—
c.14	Not public and general		—
1455 (Oct. 13)			**Parl. 12–1455**
c. 1	War in England	rep. SLR(S) 1906	c.48
c. 2	Traitors in England	"	c.48
c. 3	Treason	"	c.49
c. 4	War with England	"	c.50
c. 5	War with England	"	c.51
c. 6	War with England	"	c.51
c. 7	War with England	"	c.51
c. 8	War with England	"	c.52
c. 9	War with England	"	c.52
c.10	War with England	"	c.53
c.11	War with England	"	c.54
c.12	War with England	"	c.54
c.13	Sorners	"	—
c.14	Border garrisons	"	c.55
James III			**James III**
1456			**Parl. 13–1456**
c. 1	Taking prisoners	rep. SLR(S) 1906	—
c. 2	Borders	"	—

Record Edition	Title or Subject Matter	How Affected	12mo Edition
James III			**James III**
c. 3	Defence of realm	rep. SLR(S) 1906	c.56
c. 4	Artillery	"	—
c. 5	France	"	—
c. 6	Pestilence	"	c.57
c. 7	Coinage	"	c.58
c. 8	Sittings of Justices	"	—
c. 9	Sheriffs	"	c.59
c.10	Constables' fees	"	c.60
c.11	War with England	"	—
1457			**Parl. 14–1457**
c. 1	Lords of the Session	rep. SLR(S) 1906	—
c. 2	Jurisdiction of Lords of the Session	"	c.61
c. 3	Procedure before Lords of the Session	"	c.62
c. 4	Expenses of the Lords of the Session	"	c.63
c. 5	Successors of Lords of the Session	"	—
c. 6	Wapinschaws	"	c.64
c. 7	Coinage	"	—
c. 8	Gold and Silver work	"	c.65
c. 9	Dyers	"	c.66
c. 10	Shipping	"	c.67
c. 11	Sumptuary	"	c.68
c. 12	Hospitals	"	c.69
c. 13	Sumptuary	"	c.70
c. 14	Circuit courts	"	c.70
c. 15	Feuing	"	c.71
c. 16	Regalities	"	c.72
c. 17	Beggars	"	—
c. 18	Measures	"	c.73
c. 19	Remissions	"	c.74
c. 20	Chamberlain aires	"	—
c. 21	Members of Parliament	"	c.75
c.22	Constables' fees	"	—
c.23	Officers of law	"	c.76
c.24	Leagues in burghs	"	c.77
c.25	Squatters	"	c.78
c.26	Sorners and beggars	"	c.79
c.27	Woods, hedges and broom	"	c.80
c.28	Agriculture	"	c.81
c.29	Attendance at Court	"	c.82
c.30	Fencing	"	c.83
c.31	Wild Birds	"	c.84
c.32	Rooks, crows, etc.	"	c.84
c.33	Salmon	"	c.85
c.34	Salmon	"	c.86
c.35	Wolves	"	c.87
c.36	Hares and rabbits	"	c.88
c.37	Leasing makers	"	—
c.38	Muirburn	"	—
c.39	Proclamation of Acts of Parliament	"	c.89
c.40	Execution of Acts of Parliament	"	c.89
1466 (Oct. 9)			**Parl. 1–1466**
c. 1	Church	rep. SLR(S) 1906	c. 1
c. 2	Commission of Parliament	"	—
c. 3	Queen's dowry	"	c. 2
c. 4	Benefices	"	c. 3
c. 5	Pensions out of benefices	"	c. 4
c. 6	Lawburrows	"	c. 5

Record Edition **James III**	Title or Subject Matter	How Affected	12mo Edition **James III**
c. 7	*Induciae of Summons*	rep. SLR(S) 1906	c. 6
c. 8	*Pupils and minors*	,,	—
c. 9	*Benefices*	,,	c. 7
c.10	*Money*	,,	c. 8
c.11	*Money*	,,	—
c.12	*Coinage*	,,	c. 9
c.13	*Hospitals*	,,	c.10
1466 (Jan. 31)			**Parl. 2–1466**
c. 1	*Foreign trade*	rep. SLR(S) 1906	c.11
c. 2	*Craftsmen and merchants*	,,	c.12
c. 3	*Merchants*	,,	c.13
c. 4	*Charter party*	,,	c.14
c. 5	*Restraint on shipping*	,,	c.15
c. 6	*Restraint on trade*	,,	c.16
c. 7	*Trade with Middleburg*	,,	
c. 8	*Trade with France and Norway*	,,	c.17
1467 (Oct. 12)			**Parl. 3–1467**
c. 1	*Foreign money*	rep. SLR(S) 1906	c.18
c. 2	*Currency*	,,	c.19
c. 3	*Ferries*	,,	c.20
c. 4	*Currency*	,,	c.21
1467 (Jan. 12)			**Parl. 4–1467**
c. 1	*King's marriage*	rep. SLR(S) 1906	—
c. 2	*Norway*	,,	—
c. 3	*Currency*	,,	c.22
c. 4	*Currency*	,,	c.22
c. 5	*Currency*	,,	c.22
c. 6	*Currency*	,,	c.22
c. 7	*Currency*	,,	c.22
c. 8	*Import of bullion*	,,	—
c. 9	*Weights and measures*	,,	c.22
c.10	*Assessment on barons*	,,	—
c.11	*Receivers of taxes*	,,	—
1468			**Parl. 4–1467**
c. 1	*Currency*	rep. SLR(S) 1906	c.23
c. 2	*The Session*	,,	—
c. 3	*Export of cattle*	,,	c.24
c. 4	*Sessions of Parliament*	,,	—
c. 5	*Circuit courts*	,,	—
c. 6	*Fines imposed by Sessions*	,,	—
c. 7	*Vacancies in Lords of Session*	,,	—
1469			**Parl. 5–1469**
c. 1	*Church*	rep. SLR(S) 1906	c.25
c. 2	*Sheriffs*	,,	c.26
c. 3	*Reversion*	rep. SLR(S) 1906; Title Conditions (S), 2003 asp 9, s 89	c.27
c. 4	*Prescription*	rep. Prescription and Limitation (S.), 1973 c.52, s.16(2), sch. 5 pt. I	c.28
c. 5	*Officers of burghs*	rep. SLR(S) 1906	c.29
c. 6	*Notaries*	,,	c.30
c. 7	*Measures of cloth*	,,	c.31
c. 8	*Brieves*	,,	c.32
c. 9	*Constables' fees*	,,	c.33
c.10	*Tenants*	,,	c.34
c.11	*Murder*	,,	c.35
c.12	**Diligence**	rep. in pt.—SLR(S) 1906 rep. in pt.—SLR(S)1964	c.36
c.13	*Salmon and trout*	rep. SLR(S) 1906	c.37

Record Edition	Title or Subject Matter	How Affected	12mo Edition
James III			**James III**
c.14	Continuation of Parliament	rep. SLR(S) 1906	c.38
c.15	Holy days	rep. 1592 c.8	—
c.16	Hospitals	rep. SLR(S) 1906	—
c.17	Ferries	"	—
c.18	Registers	"	c.39
c.19	Currency and coining	"	c.40
			Parl. 14–1480
c.20	Remit to Committee	rep. SLR(S) 1906	c.115
c.21	Not public and general		—
1471 (May 6)			**Parl. 6–1471**
c. 1	Church	rep. SLR(S) 1906	—
c. 2	Embassy to France	"	—
c. 3	Murder	"	c.42
c. 4	Barratry	"	c.43
c. 5	Artillery	"	—
c. 6	Armour	"	c.44
c. 7	Sumptuary	"	c.45
c. 8	Currency	"	c.46
c. 9	Manswearing	"	c.47
c.10	Sea fishing	"	c.48
c.11	Fines imposed by Lords of Council	"	c.49
c.12	Committee of Parliament	"	—
1471 (Aug. 2)			
Vol. II, p. 101	Brieves	rep. SLR(S) 1906	c.41
1474			**Parl. 7–1474**
c. 1	Church	rep. SLR(S) 1906	—
c. 2	Embassy to England	"	—
c. 3	Commission to Denmark	"	—
c. 4	Money and Bullion	"	c.50
c. 5	Artillery	"	—
c. 6	Tutors	rep. Age of Legal Capacity (S.) 1991 c.50 s.10(2) sch.2	c.51
c. 7	Arrestments	rep. SLR(S) 1906	c.52
c. 8	Moveable succession	"	c.53
c. 9	Prescription	rep. Prescription and Limitation (S) 1973 c.52, s.16(2), sch. 5 pt. I	c.54
c.10	Brieves of inquest	rep. SLR(S) 1906	c.55
c.11	Civil causes	"	—
c.12	Burgh councils	"	c.56
c.13	Entry to lands	"	c.57
c.14	Apprehension of criminals	"	c.58
c.15	Stealing hawks and hounds	"	c.59
c.16	Deers and rabbits	"	c.60
c.17	Ferries	"	c.61
c.18	Continuation of Parliament	"	—
1475			**Parl. 8–1475**
c. 1	Church	rep. SLR(S) 1906	—
c. 2	Circuit courts	"	—
c. 3	Civil causes	"	c.62
c. 4	Criminal juries	"	c.63
c. 5	Royal marriage	"	—
c. 6	Currency	"	c.64
c. 7	Coin	"	c.65
c. 8	Brieves of idiotry	"	c.66
c. 9	Currency	"	c.67
c.10	Currency	"	c.68

Record Edition	Title or Subject Matter	How Affected	12mo Edition
James III			**James III**
c.11	Courts of Guerra	rep. SLR(S) 1906	c.69
Vol.II, p.113	Crown lands	"	c.70
Vol.II, p.113	Crown lands (Not public and general)	"	c.71
Vol.II, p.114	Continuation of Parliament	"	—
1478			**Parl. 10–1477**
c. 1	Church	rep. SLR(S) 1906	—
c. 2	Remissions	"	—
c. 3	Coin	"	—
c. 4	Embassy to Burgundy	"	—
c. 5	Imports	"	c.72
c. 6	Salmon	"	c.73
c. 7	Ferries	"	c.74
c. 8	Muirburn	"	c.75
c. 9	Salmon	"	c.76
c.10	Beggars and sorners	"	c.77
c.11	Horse shoeing	"	c.78
c.12	Committee of Parliament	"	—
1481 (Apr. 2)			**Parl. 11–1481**
c. 1	Defence of the realm	rep. SLR(S) 1906	—
c. 2	Defence of the realm	"	c.80
c. 3	Defence of the realm	"	—
c. 4	Defence of the realm	"	c.81
c. 5	Defence of the realm	"	—
c. 6	Defence of the realm	"	c.82
c. 7	Benefices	"	—
1481 (Mar. 18)			
c. 1	England	rep. SLR(S) 1906	—
c. 2	Defence of the realm	"	—
c. 3	Administration of justice	"	—
c. 4	Defence of the realm	"	—
c. 5	Defence of the realm	"	—
c. 6	Defence of the realm	"	—
c. 7	Defence of the realm	"	—
c. 8	Defence of the realm	"	—
c. 9	Defence of the realm	"	—
c.10	Defence of the realm	"	—
c.11	Defence of the realm	"	—
c.12	Defence of the realm	"	—
c.13	Embassy to France	"	—
c.14	Wife's ratification	"	c.83
c.15	Not public and general		—
c.16	Benefices	"	c.84
c.17	Barratry	"	c.85
c.18	Imports	"	—
			Parl. 10–1481
Vol. II, p. 141	Courts of Purprision	rep. SLR(S) 1906	c.79
1482			**Parl. 12–1482**
c. 1	Peace with England	rep. SLR(S) 1906	—
c. 2	Lieutenant-General	"	—
c. 3	Defence of the realm	"	—
c. 4	Administration of justice	"	—
c. 5	Warden's courts	"	c.86
c. 6	Safe conducts	"	c.87
c. 7	Wine	"	c.88
c. 8	Money	"	—
c. 9	Benefices	"	—

Record Edition James III	Title or Subject Matter	How Affected	12mo Edition James III
			Parl. 14–1487
c.10	Foreign trade	"	c.114
c.11	Scots traders in France	"	—
1483			**Parl. 13–1483**
c. 1	Defence of the realm	rep. SLR(S) 1906	c. 89
c. 2	Dunbar Castle	"	—
c. 3	Duke of Albany	"	—
c. 4	Circuit courts	"	—
c. 5	Remissions	"	—
c. 6	King's rents	"	c.90
c. 7	Attendance at Parliament	"	—
c. 8	Internal discords	"	c.91
c. 9	Barratry	"	—
c.10	Money and bullion	"	c.93
c.11	Barratry	"	—
1485			
c. 1	Church	rep. SLR(S) 1906	—
c. 2	England	"	—
c. 3	Esk water	"	—
c. 4	Circuit courts: remissions	"	c.94
c. 5	Embassy to Pope.	"	—
cc.6–12	Embassy to Pope	"	—
c.13	Ferries	"	c.95
c.14	Letters to Pope as to benefices	"	—
c.15	Fineness of silver work	"	c.96
c.16	Money	"	—
c.17	Barratry	"	—
1486			
c. 1	Currency	rep. SLR(S) 1906	c.97
c. 2	Tallow	"	—
c. 3	Hides	"	—
1487 (Oct. 1)			**Parl. 14–1487**
c. 1	Remissions	rep. SLR(S) 1906	—
c. 2	Circuit courts	"	—
c. 3	Treason	"	c.98
c. 4	Coroners	"	c.99
c. 5	Murder	"	c.100
c. 6	Detention of prisoners	"	c.101
c. 7	Goods of convicts	"	c.102
c. 8	Sheriffs and coroners at circuit courts	"	c.103
c. 9	Attendance at courts	"	c.104
c.10	Jurisdiction and process in civil factions	"	c.105
c.11	Embassy to Rome	"	—
c.12	Foreign traders	"	c.106
c.13	Craftsmen	"	c.107
c.14	Burgh Officers	"	c.108
c.15	Shipping	"	c.109
c.16	Salmon barrels	"	c.110
c.17	**Royal Burghs**	rep. in pt.—SLR(S) 1906	c.111
c.18	Sea fishing	rep. SLR(S) 1906	—
c.19	(Not public and general)		—
Vol. II, p.179	(Not public and general)		c.112
1487 (Jan. 11)			**Parl. 14–1487**
c. 1	Church	rep. SLR(S) 1906	—
c. 2	Royal marriages	"	—
c. 3	Berwick	"	—
c. 4	Truce with England	"	—

Record Edition	Title or Subject Matter	How Affected	12mo Edition
James III			**James III**
c. 5	*Appointment of Justices*	rep. SLR(S) 1906	—
c. 6	*Appointment of Justices*	,,	—
c. 7	*Circuit courts*	,,	—
c. 8	(Not public and general)		
c. 9	*Money*	,,	—
c.10	*Coining*	,,	—
c.11	*Import of bullion*	,,	—
c.12	*Barratry*	,,	—
c.13	*Export of money*	,,	—
c.14	*Crime*	,,	—
c.15	*Sea fishing*	,,	—
c.16	*Legates from Rome*	,,	—
c.17	*Civil jurisdictions*	,,	—
c.18	*Goods of convicts*	,,	c.113
c.19	*See of Aberdeen*	,,	—
James IV.			**James IV.**
1488 (Oct. 6)			**Parl. 1–1488**
c. 1	*Church*	rep. SLR(S) 1906	—
c. 2	*Royal marriage*	,,	—
c. 3	*France*	,,	—
c. 4	*Goods of rebels*	,,	—
c. 5	*Goods of burgesses and merchants*	,,	—
c. 6	*Rebel officers of law*	,,	—
c. 7	*Heirs of rebels*	,,	—
c. 8	*Administration of Justice*	,,	—
c. 9	*Crime*	,,	—
c.10	*Burgh jurisdiction*	,,	c. 1
c.11	*Coin and bullion*	,,	c. 2
c.12	*Shipping*	,,	c. 3
c.13	*Barratry*	,,	
c.14	*Barratry*	,,	c. 4
c.15	*King's death*	,,	—
c.16	*Salmon*	,,	—
c.17	*Edinburgh Castle*	,,	—
c.18	*Dunbar Castle*	,,	—
c.19	*King's revocation*	,,	c. 5
c.20	*Heirs of those slain in battle*	,,	c. 6
1488 (Jan. 14)			
c. 1	*Coin and bullion*	rep. SLR(S) 1906	—
c. 2	Not public and general		—
c. 3	*Salmon barrels*	,,	—
cc.4–5	Not public and general		—
1489 (Jan. 26)			
c. 1	*Church*	rep. SLR(S) 1906	—
c. 2	*England*	,,	—
c. 3	*France*	,,	—
c. 4	*Denmark*	,,	—
c. 5	*Galloway cawps*	,,	—
c. 6	*Warden of the Marches*	,,	—
c. 7	*Siege of castles held by rebels*	,,	—
c. 8	*King's Council*	,,	—
c. 9	*Money*	,,	—
c.10	*Gold and Silver coin*	,,	—
c.11	*Rebels*	,,	—
1489 (Feb. 3)			**Parl. 2–1489**
c. 1	*Church*	rep. SLR(S) 1906	c. 7

Record Edition James IV.	Title or Subject Matter	How Affected	12mo Edition James IV.
c. 2	*Circuit Courts*	rep. SLR(S) 1906	—
c. 3	*Public peace*	”	c. 8
c. 4	*Supply*	”	c. 9
c. 5	*Foreign treaties*	”	—
c. 6	*Embassy to Denmark*	”	—
c. 7	*King's revocation*	”	c.10
c. 8	*Duke of Ross*	”	—
c. 9	*Truce with England*	”	c.11
c.10	*Auditors of King's Accounts*	”	—
c.11	*Appointment of King's Privy Council*	”	—
c.12	*King's Privy Council*	”	c.12
c.13	*Goldsmith's*	”	c.13
c.14	*Trade*	”	c.14
c.15	*Ferries*	”	—
c.16	*Salmon*	”	c.15
c.17	*Free tenants*	”	c.16
c.18	*Money*	”	c.17
c.19	*Galloway cawps*	”	c.18
c.20	*Carrick cawps*	”	c.19
c.21	*Annual rents in burghs*	”	c.20
c.22	*King's tenants*	”	c.21
cc.23–24	(Not public and general)		—
c.25	*King's revocation*	”	c.22
c.26	*Dumbarton Castle*	”	—
c.27	*Administration of Justice*	”	—
1491 (Apr. 28)			**Parl. 3–1491**
c. 1	*Church*	rep. SLR(S) 1906	—
c. 2	*France*	”	c.23
c. 3	*Royal marriage*	”	—
c. 4	*Embassy to Denmark*	”	—
c. 5	*Brieves*	”	c.24
c. 6	**Liferent Caution**	rep. in pt.—SLR(S) 1964	c.25
c. 7	**Leases**	”	c.26
c. 8	*Lawburrows*	rep. SLR(S) 1906	c.27
c. 9	*Murder*	”	c.28
c.10	*Circuit court*	”	c.29
c.11	*Decrees for expenses*	”	c.30
c.12	*Currency*	”	c.37
c.13	*Wapinschaws*	”	cc.31–32
c.14	*Truce on the borders*	”	—
c.15	*Measures*	”	c.33
c.16	*Sessions*	”	—
c.17	*Leagues in burghs*	”	c.34
c.18	*Brieves of error*	”	c.35
c.19	**Common Good**	rep. in pt.—SLR(S) 1906	c.36
c.20	*Proclamation of Acts*	rep. SLR(S) 1906	—
1491 (Feb. 6)			
c. 1	*Royal marriage*	rep. SLR(S) 1906	—
c. 2	*Late King's treasure*	”	—
c. 3	*Late King's murderers*	”	—
c. 4	*Administration of Justice*	”	—
1493			**Parl. 4–1493**
c. 1	*Church*	rep. SLR(S) 1906	—
c. 2	*Privileges granted by Pope*	”	—
c. 3	*Benefices*	”	c.38
c. 4	*Benefices*	”	—
c. 5	*Papal legates*	”	—
c. 6	*St. Andrews and Glasgow*	”	—

Record Edition James IV.	Title or Subject Matter	How Affected	12mo Edition James IV.
c. 7	St. Andrews and Glasgow	rep. SLR(S) 1906	—
c. 8	Pleas in Court of Rome	"	—
c. 9	Benefices	"	c.39
c.10	Currency	"	c.40
c.11	Royal marriage	"	—
c.12	Customs	"	c.41
c.13	Craftsmen	"	c.42
c.14	Deacons of craft	"	c.43
c.15	Multures	"	c.44
c.16	Execution of statutes	"	c.45
c.17	Taxation	"	cc.46–47
c.18	Muirburn	"	c.48
c.19	Herons	"	—
c.20	Seafishing	"	c.49
c.21	Donations by late King	"	c.50
c.22	King's revocation	"	c.51
c.23	Salmon barrels	"	c.52
c.24	Sea-fishing	"	c.52
1496			**Parl. 5–1494**
c. 1	Church	rep. SLR(S) 1906	—
c. 2	Barratry	"	c.53
c. 3	Education	"	c.54
c. 4	Money	"	c.55
c. 5	Workmen's prices	"	c.56
c. 6	Summons of error	"	c.57
1503			**Parl. 6–1503**
Vol. II, p. 240	Renovation	rep. SLR(S) 1906	c.100
c. 1	Church	"	—
c. 2	King's Council	"	c.58
c. 3	Administration of Justice	"	c.59
c. 4	Administration of Justice	"	c.60
c. 5	Administration of Justice	"	c.61
c. 6	Remissions	"	c.62
c. 7	Remissions for murder	"	c.62
c. 8	Notaries	"	c.64
c. 9	Spuilzie	rep. in pt.—SLR(S) 1906 rep. SL (Reps.), 1973 (c.39)	c.65
c.10	Sheriff's expenses	rep. SLR(S) 1906	c.66
c.11	Sheriff Court expenses	"	c.67
c.12	Money	"	c.68
c.13	Fish ponds	"	c.69
c.14	Beggars	"	c.70
c.15	Sea fishing	"	—
c.16	Green wood	"	c.71
c.17	Salmon	"	c.72
c.18	Sheriffdoms	"	c.73
c.19	Dovecots	"	c.74
c.20	Wapinschaws	"	c.75
c.21	Heirs and executors	rep. SLR(S) 1964	c.76
c.22	Terce	rep. Succession (S) 1964 (c.41) s.34(2), sch. 3	c.77
c.23	Attendance in Parliament	rep. SLR(S) 1906	c.78
c.24	The law of the land	"	c.79
c.25	Jurisdiction of burghs officers	"	c.80
c.26	Jurisdiction in foreign countries	"	c.81
c.27	The conservator	"	c.82
c.28	Fairs	"	c.83
c.29	Privileges of burghs	"	c.84
c.30	Burgh taxes	"	c.85

Record Edition James IV.	Title or Subject Matter	How Affected	12mo Edition James IV.
c.31	Guild brethren	rep. SLR(S) 1906	c.86
c.32	Shipping	"	—
c.33	Leagues in burghs	"	c.87
c.34	Wool, hides, skins	"	c.88
c.35	Precepts of sasine	"	c.89
c.36	Feuing Crown Lands	"	c.90
c.37	Fueing lands	"	c.91
c.38	Malt makers	"	c.92
c.39	Sheriff's jurisdiction	"	c.93
c.40	Brieves of inquest	"	c.94
c.41	Brieves of right	"	c.95
c.42	Measures and Weights	"	c.96
c.43	Bullion	"	—
c.44	Currency	"	c.97
c.45	Diligence	rep. Debtors (S.) 1987 c.18, s.108 (3), sch.8	c.98
c.46	Appeals	rep. SLR(S.), 1906	c.99
1504			
cc.1–4	Not public and general		
c. 5	Sheriffdoms	rep. SLR(S) 1906	—
c.6–7	(Not public and general.)		
c. 8	Holyrood House	"	—
1509			**Parl. 7–1509**
c. 1	Church	rep. SLR(S) 1906	—
c. 2	Sheriffdoms	"	c.101
James V.			**James V.**
1515			**Parl. 1–1515**
c. 1	Church	rep. SLR(S) 1906	c. 1
c. 2	Theft	"	c. 2
1522			**Parl. 2–1522**
c. 1	Estates of those slain in battle	rep. SLR(S) 1906	c. 3
c. 2	Leases of tenants slain in battle	"	c. 4
1524 (Nov. 14)			
c. 1	Church	rep. SLR(S) 1906	—
c. 2	Regent	"	—
c. 3	Guardianship of King	"	—
c. 4	Casualties falling to King	"	—
c. 5	Privy Council	"	—
c. 6	Embassy to England	"	—
c. 7	Administration of Justice	"	—
c. 8	Administration of Justice	"	—
c. 9	Theft	"	—
c.10	Coin	"	—
c.11	Crown rents	"	—
c.12	Crown lands	"	—
c.13	Remissions	"	—
1524 (Feb. 15)			
c. 1	Privy Council	rep. SLR(S) 1906	—
c. 2	King's person	"	—
c. 3	Benefices	"	—
c. 4	King's person	"	—
c. 5	Government of the realm	"	—
c. 6	Borders	"	—
c. 7	Trade with England	"	—
c. 8	Salt	"	—
c. 9	Seals	"	—
c.10	Crown property	"	—
c.11	Edinburgh Castle	"	—
c.12	Earl of Morton	"	—

Record Edition	Title or Subject Matter	How Affected	12mo Edition
James V.			**James V.**
1525			
c. 1	*Church*	rep. SLR(S) 1906	—
c. 2	*Barratry*	"	—
c. 3	*Subscription of writs*	"	—
c. 4	*Heresy*	"	—
c. 5	*Quorum of Lords*	"	—
c. 6	*Sentence of cursing*	"	—
c. 7	*Treaty with England*	"	—
c. 8	*Criminal procedure*	"	—
c. 9	*Public peace*	"	—
c.10	*Fire raising and rape*	"	—
c.11	*Privy Council*	"	—
1526 (Jan. 12)			
c. 1	*Church*	rep. SLR(S) 1906	—
c. 2	*King's majority*	"	—
cc.3–5	Not public and general		
c. 6	*Privy Council*	"	—
c. 7	*King's Acts in minority*	"	—
c. 8	Not public and general		
c. 9	*King's person*	"	—
c.10	*Crown property*	"	—
c.11	*Money and bullion*	"	—
c.12	*King's privileges from Pope*	"	—
c.13	*King's marriage*	"	—
c.14	*Observance of penal statutes*	"	—
c.15	*Estates of minors deceased*	"	—
c.16	*Legates*	"	—
c.17	*Criminal law*	"	—
1526 (Nov. 12)			**Parl. 3–1528**
c. 1	*Church*	rep. SLR(S) 1906	—
c. 2	*Bread*	"	—
c. 3	*Flesh*	"	—
c. 4	*Tallow*	"	—
c. 5	*Coining*	"	—
c. 6	Not public and general		
c. 7	*Circuit courts*	"	—
c. 8	*Maltmakers*	"	—
c. 9	*King's privileges*	"	—
c.10	*Fire raising*	"	c. 8
1528			**Parl. 3–1528**
c. 1	*Coroner's arrestments*	rep. SLR(S) 1906	c. 5
c. 2	*Responsibility for tenants*	"	c. 6
c. 3	*Assythment*	"	c. 7
1532			**Parl. 5–1537**
c. 1	*Church*	rep. SLR(S) 1906	—
c. 2	**College of Justice**	rep. in pt.—SLR(S) 1906	cc.36–41
c. 3	*Money*	rep. SLR(S) 1906	—
c. 4	Not public and general		—
1535			**Parl. 4–1535**
c. 1	*Church*	rep. SLR(S) 1906	—
c. 2	*Hersey*	"	—
c. 3	*Sentence of cursing*	"	c. 9
c. 4	*General Provincial Council*	"	—
c. 5	*Supply*	"	—
c. 6	*Coin*	"	—
c. 7	*Afforestation*	"	c.10
c. 8	*Woods and muirburn*	"	c.11
c. 9	*Forests*	"	c.12

Record Edition	Title or Subject Matter	How Affected	12mo Edition
James V.			**James V.**
c.10	Deer	rep. SLR(S) 1906	—
c.11	Dovecots, etc.	”	c.13
c.12	Orchards	”	—
c.13	Hares	”	c.14
c.14	**Liferent Caution**	rep. in pt.—SLR(S) 1964	c.15
c.15	Supply	rep. SLR(S) 1906	—
c.16	Salmon	”	c.16
c.17	Salmon	”	c.17
c.18	Sea fishing	”	—
c.19	Wapinschaws	”	—
c.20	Artillery	”	—
c.21	Artillery	”	—
c.22	Border strongholds	”	—
c.23	Travellers	”	c.18
c.24	Horses	”	c.19
c.25	Trade with England	”	c.20
c.26	Forestallers	”	c.21
c.27	King's rents	”	—
c.28	Murder	”	—
c.29	Beggars	”	c.22
c.30	Sanctuary	”	c.23
c.31	Burghs	”	—
c.32	Foreign shipping trade	”	c.24
c.33	Foreign shipping trade	”	c.25
c.34	Foreign shipping trade	”	c.31
c.35	Burgh officers	”	c.26
c.36	Burghs	”	c.27
c.37	Lord Chancellor's sittings	”	—
c.38	Hornings	rep. SLR(S) 1964	c.32
c.39	Criminal procedure	rep. SLR(S) 1906	cc.33–35
c.40	Theft	”	—
c.41	Peace of the country	”	c.28
c.42	Maltmakers	”	c.29
c.43	Craftsmen within burgh	”	c.30
1540 (Dec. 3)			**Parl. 6–1540**
c. 1	Summons of treason against a deceased person	rep. SLR(S) 1906	c.69
c. 2	Ratification of last Parliament's Acts	”	—
c. 3	Excommunication	”	c.36
c. 4	King's revocation	”	c.70
c. 5	Church	”	—
c. 6	Sheriff's courts	”	c.71
c. 7	Civil procedure	”	c.72
c. 8	Sheriff's deputes	”	c.73
c. 9	Indorsing of letters	”	c.74
c.10	**Citation**		c.75
c.11	Notaries	”	c.76
c.12	Sasines	”	c.77
c.13	Notaries	”	c.78
c.14	Protocols of Sasines	”	c.79
c.15	Perjury	”	c.80
c.16	Notaries	”	c.81
c.17	Sheriff's deputes	”	c.82
c.18	Leasing making	”	c.83
c.19	Crown Lands Not public and general	”	c.84
c.20	Procedure in forfeitures	”	—
c.21	Wapinschaws	”	c.85
c.22	Defence of the realm	”	c.86
c.23	Defence of the realm	”	c.87
c.24	Defence of the realm	”	c.88
c.25	Defence of the realm	”	c.89

Record Edition	Title or Subject Matter	How Affected	12mo Edition
James V.			**James V.**
c.26	Defence of the realm	rep. SLR(S) 1906	c.90
c.27	Defence of the realm	"	c.91
c.28	Remission	"	c.92
1540 (Mar. 14)			**Parl. 7–1540**
c. 1	Church	rep. SLR(S) 1906	—
c. 2	Virgin Mary	"	—
c. 3	Pope	"	—
c. 4	Church	"	—
c. 5	Church	"	—
c. 6	Heresy	"	—
c. 7	Heresy	"	—
c. 8	Heresy	"	—
c. 9	Saint's images	"	—
c.10	**College of Justice**	rep. in pt.SLR(S) 1906; SLR(S) 1964	c.93
c.11	Defence of the realm	rep. SLR(S) 1906	c.94
c.12	Defence of the realm	"	c.95
c.13	Crown rents	"	c.96
c.14	Murder	"	c.97
c.15	Theft	"	—
c.16	Food supply	"	c.98
c.17	Coinage	"	c.99
c.18	Wine, salt and timber	"	c.100
c.19	Hospitals	"	c.101
cc.20–21	Not public and general		cc.102–3
c.22	Judges	rep.SL (Reps.), 1973 (c.39)	c.104
c.23	Fraud	rep. SLR(S) 1964	c.105
c.24	Entry to lands	rep. SLR(S) 1906	c.106
c.25	Burghs	"	—
c.26	Burghs	"	c.107
c.27	Coin	"	c.108
c.28	Measures	"	c.109
c.29	Expenses of process	"	c.110
c.30	Craftsmen	"	c.111
c.31	Clothmakers	"	c.112
c.32	Forestallers	"	c.113
c.33	Weights	"	c.114
c.34	Not public and general		c.115
c.35	Dissolution of Crown lands	"	c.116
c.36	Not public and general		—
c.37	Subscription of Deeds	rep. Requirements of Writing (S) 1995 (c.7), s.14(2), sch.5	c.117
c.38	Crime	rep. SLR(S) 1906	c.118
c.39	King's privileges from Rome	"	c.119
c.40	Intestate succession	"	c.120
c.41	Legates	rep. SLR(S) 1964	—
cc.42–3	Not public and general		cc.121–2
c.44	Tallow	rep. SLR(S) 1906	c.123
c.45	Coining	"	c.124
c.46	Bishoprics and abbacies	"	c.125
c.47	Printing Acts of Parliament	"	c.127
Mary			**Mary**
1542			**Parl. 1–1542**
c. 1	Lord Governor	rep. SLR(S) 1906	—
c. 2	Lord Governor	"	—
c. 3	Embassy to England	"	—
c. 4	Lord Governor	"	—
cc.5–6	Not public and general		—
c. 7	Privy Council	"	—
c. 8	Queen's person	"	—

Record Edition	Title or Subject Matter	How Affected	12mo Edition
James V.			**James V.**
c. 9	Queen's person	rep. SLR(S) 1906	—
c.10	Heresy	”	—
c.11	Heresy	”	—
c.12	Bible in vulgar tongue	”	—
c.13	Treason of persons deceased	”	—
Vol. II, p. 424	Passing of signatures	”	c. 1
1543			**Parl. 2–1543**
c. 1	Services to Queen	rep. SLR(S) 1906	—
c. 2	Expiry of Treaty with England	”	—
c. 3	Treaty with France	”	—
c. 4	Great Council	”	—
c. 5	Not public and general		—
c. 6	Heresy	”	—
c. 7	College of Justice	”	c. 1
c. 8	Publication of Acts	”	—
c. 9	Not public and general		—
1545			**Parl. 3–1546**
c. 1	Defence of the realm	rep. SLR(S) 1906	—
c. 2	Defence of the realm	”	—
c. 3	Defence of the realm	”	—
cc.4–5	Defence of the realm	”	—
c. 6	Defence of the realm	”	—
c. 7	Queen's person	”	—
c. 8	Defence of the realm	”	—
c. 9	Defence of the realm	”	—
c.10	Defence of the realm	”	—
c.11	Treaties with England and France	”	—
c.12	St. Andrews Castle	”	—
c.13	Removal of tenants	”	c. 3
c.14	Royal marriage	”	—
c.15	Supply	”	—
1551 (May 29)			**Parl. 4–1551**
c. 1	Excommunication	rep. SLR(S) 1906	c. 7
c. 2	Traitors	”	c. 8
c. 3	Game	”	c. 9
1551 (Feb. 1)			**Parl. 5–1551**
c. 1	Wine	rep. SLR(S) 1906	c.11
c. 2	Prices of fowls	”	c.12
c. 3	Defence of the realm	”	c.13
c. 4	Defence of the realm	”	c.14
c. 5	Defence of the realm	”	c.15
c. 6	Not public and general		—
c. 7	Blasphemy	”	c.16
c. 8	Disturbance in church	”	c.17
c. 9	Excommunication	”	c.18
c.10	Excommunication	”	—
c.11	Bigamy	rep. SLR(S) 1964	c.19
c.12	Adultery	rep. SLR(S) 1906	c.20
c.13	Maltmakers	”	—
c.14	Ferries	”	c.21
c.15	Meat	”	—
c.16	Beggars	”	—
c.17	Notaries	”	c.22
c.18	Craftsmen	”	c.23
c.19	Notaries	”	—
c.21	Deer	”	—
c.22	Sumptuary	”	c.25
c.23	Packing and peeling	”	—

Record Edition	Title or Subject Matter	How Affected	12mo Edition
James V.			**James V.**
c.24	Forestallers	rep. SLR(S) 1906	—
c.25	Sea fish	,,	—
c.26	Printers	,,	c.27
c.27	French Ambassador	,,	—
c.28	Lord Governors' actings	,,	—
c.29	Royal contract	,,	—
			Parl. 4–1551
c.30	Rents of burnt tenements	,,	c.10
1555			**Parl. 6–1555**
c. 1	Church	rep. SLR(S) 1906	—
c. 2	Reversions	,,	c.29
c. 3	**Lands Redemption**		c.30
c. 4	Murder	,,	c.31
c. 5	Citation	,,	c.32
c. 6	Citation	rep. SL Reps, 1986	c.33
c. 7	Saines	rep. SLR(S.) 1906	c.34
c. 8	Minors	rep. Administration of Justice (S) 1933 (c.41) s.12(2)	c.35
c. 9	Lent	rep. SLR(S) 1906	c.36
c.10	Reversions	,,	c.37
c.11	Resignations	,,	c.38
c.12	Removings	rep. SLR(S) 1964	c.39
c.13	Murders	rep. SLR(S) 1906	—
c.14	Export of food	,,	c.40
c.15	Criminal Procedure	,,	c.41
c.16	Civil procedure	rep. SLR(S) 1964	c.42
c.17	Bonds of manrent	rep. SLR(S) 1906	c.43
c.18	Notaries	,,	c.43
c.19	Export to England	,,	c.45
c.20	Weights and measures	,,	—
c.21	Sasines	,,	c.46
c.22	Perjury	,,	c.47
c.23	Not public and general		c.48
c.24	Burghs	,,	c.49
c.25	Game	rep. SLR(S) 1964	c.51
c.26	Craftsmen	rep. SLR(S) 1906	c.52
c.27	Highways	,,	c.53
c.28	Sea fishing	,,	c.54
c.29	Hornings	,,	c.55
c.30	Lambs	,,	—
c.31	Ferries	,,	—
c.32	Chickens	,,	—
c.33	Woods	,,	—
c.34	Goldsmiths	,,	c.56
c.35	Wine, salt, etc.	,,	c.57
c.36	Game	,,	c.58
c.37	Shipping trade	,,	c.59
c.38	Beggars	,,	—
c.39	Treason	,,	c.60
c.40	Robert Hood, etc.	,,	c.61
c.41	Queen's revocation	,,	c.28
1557			**Parl. 7–1557**
c. 1	Commissioners to France	rep. SLR(S) 1906	—
c. 2	Commissioners to France	,,	—
c. 3	Commissioners to France	,,	—
c. 4	Caution in improbations	,,	c.62
c. 5	Exceptions	,,	c.63
c. 6	Expenses of process	,,	c.64
1558			**Parl. 8–1558**
c. 1	Commissioners to France	rep. SLR(S) 1906	—
c. 2	Commissioners to France	,,	—
c. 3	Queen's Marriage	,,	—
c. 4	Queen's Marriage	,,	—

Record Edition	Title or Subject Matter	How Affected	12mo Edition
James V.			**James V.**
c. 5	Queen's Marriage	rep. SLR(S) 1906	—
c. 6	French subjects	"	c.65
c. 7	Grants by Queen Regent	"	—
1560			
c. 1	**Confession of Faith Ratification**		—
c. 2	**Papal Jurisdiction**		—
c. 3	Abolition of idolatry	rep. SLR(S) 1906	—
c. 4	Abolition of Mass	"	—
1563			**Parl. 9–1563**
c. 1	Act of oblivion	rep. SLR(S) 1906	c.67
c. 2	Exceptions thereto	"	c.67
c. 3	Salmon	rep. SLR(S) 1964	c.68
c. 4	Gold and silver	rep. SLR(S) 1906	c.69
c. 5	Coining	"	c.70
c. 6	Food	"	—
c. 7	Salt	"	c.71
c. 8	Manses and glebes	rep. SLR(S) 1964	c.72
c. 9	Witchcraft	rep. Witchcraft 1735 (c.5)	c.73
c.10	Adultery	rep. SLR(S) 1906	c.74
c.11	Armed Forces	"	c.75
c.12	Parish churches	"	c.76
c.13	Tenants of Church lands	"	c.77
c.14	Measures and weights	"	—
c.15	Game	"	—
c.16	Notaries	"	c.78
c.17	Notaries	rep. SL (Reps.), 1973 (c.39)	c.79
c.18	Sasines	rep. SLR(S) 1906	c.80
c.19	Resignations	"	c.81
c.20	Burghs	"	c.82
c.21	Burghs	"	c.83
c.22	Coals	"	c.84
c.23	Flesh	"	c.85
c.24	Burghs	"	c.86
c.25	Letters of marque	"	—
c.26	St. Andrews	"	—
c.27	Embassy to Denmark	"	—
1564			**Parl. 10–1564**
c. 1	Queen's majority	rep. SLR(S) 1906	c.87
c. 2	Church Lands	"	c.88
1567			**Parl. 1–1567**
c. 1	Edinburgh Castle	rep. SLR(S) 1906	—
c. 2	Religion	"	c.31
cc.3–6	Not public and general		
c. 7	Act of oblivion	"	—
c. 8	Bill posting	"	—
cc. 9–30	Not public and general		—
James VI.			**James VI.**
1567			**Parl. 1–1567**
c. 1	Accession and coronation	rep. SLR(S) 1906	—
c. 2	Regent	"	c. 1
c. 3	Abolition of Papal authority	"	c. 2
c. 4	Repeal of Acts in support of Papacy	"	c. 3
Vol. III, p. 14.	Confession of Faith	"	Vol.I,p 337
c. 5	Mass	"	c. 5
c. 6	Church	"	c. 6
c. 7	Thirds of benefices	"	c. 7
c. 8	**Coronation Oath**		c. 8

Record Edition James VI.	Title or Subject Matter	How Affected	12mo Edition James VI.
c. 9	*Holders of public offices*	rep. SLR(S) 1906	c. 9
c.10	*Ministers*	"	c.10
c.11	*School teachers*	"	c.11
c.12	**Church Jurisdiction**	rep. in pt.SLR(S) 1906	—
c.13	*College bursaries*	rep. SLR(S) 1906	c.12
c.14	*Fornication*	"	c.13
c.15	*Incest*	rep. Incest and Related Offences (S.), 1986, c.36, s.2(2), sch.2.	c.14
c.16	*Marriage*	rep.—Marriage (S.), 1977 c.15, s.28 (2), sch. 3.	c.15
c.17	*Game*	rep. SLR(S) 1906	c.16
c.18	*Queen*	"	—
c.19	*Queen*	"	—
c.20	*Queen at Lochleven*	"	—
c.21	*Coinage*	"	c.17
c.22	*Court of Session*	rep. SLR(S) 1964	c.18
c.23	*Firearms*	rep. SLR(S) 1906	c.18
c.24	*Coining*	"	c.19
c.25	*Commission to report on Articles*	"	—
c.26	*Benefices*	"	c.20
c.27	*Theft*	"	c.21
c.28	*Horses*	"	c.22
c.29	*Court of Session*	"	—
c.30	*Escheat*	"	c.23
c.31	*Churchmen*	"	c.24
c.32	*Barons*	"	c.25
c.33	*Burghs*	"	c.26
c.34	*Sasines with burgh*	"	c.27
c.35	*Dunbar Castle*	"	—
c.36	*Commissariot procedure*	"	c.28
c.37	*Maltman*	"	c.29
c.38	*Salmon, etc.*	"	c.30
c.39	*Printing of Acts*	"	c.32
c.40	*Fire Raising*	"	c.33
1571			**Parl. 2–1571**
c. 1	*Regent*	rep. SLR(S) 1906	c.34
c. 2	*Church*	"	c.35
c. 3	*Ratification of previous Parliament*	"	—
c. 4	*Darnley's murderers*	"	c.36
c. 5	*Forfeited persons*	"	c.37
c. 6	Not public and general		c.38
c. 7	*Burghs*	"	—
c. 8	*Alienations by rebel burgesses*	"	c.39
c. 9	*Shipping*	"	c.40
c.10	*Officers at arms*	"	—
cc.11–14	Not public and general		
c.15	*Chapel Royal of Stirling*	"	—
cc.16–17	Not public and general		
c.18	*Churchmen slain in service*	"	c.41
c.19	*Men slain in service*	"	c.42
c.20	*Men in slain service*	"	c.43
c.21	*Treaty with England*	"	—
1572			**Parl. 3–1572**
c. 1	*Regent*	rep. SLR(S) 1906	c.44
c. 2	*Church*	"	c.45
c. 3	*Church property*	"	c.46
c. 4	*Pardon to rebels*	"	c.47
c. 5	*Manses and glebes*	rep. SLR(S) 1964	c.48

Record Edition James VI.	Title or Subject Matter	How Affected	12mo Edition James VI.
c. 6	Regent	rep. SLR(S) 1906	—
c. 7	Crown jewels, etc.	,,	—
c. 8	Hornings	,,	c.49
c. 9	Regent's Acts	,,	c.50
c.10	Not public and general		—
c.11	Edinburgh	,,	—
c.12	Bulls fraudulently obtained	,,	c.51
c.13	Benefices	,,	c.52
c.14	Excommunication	,,	c.53
c.15	Parish Churches	rep. SLR(S) 1964	c.54
1573			**Parl. 4–1573**
c. 1	Divorce for desertion	rep. Divorce (S) 1938 c.50 s.7	c.55
c. 2	Wine	rep. SLR(S) 1906	—
c. 3	Salt	,,	c.56
c. 4	Measures	,,	c.57
c. 5	Edinburgh	,,	c.58
c. 6	Export prohibitions	,,	c.59
c. 7	Sea fishing	,,	c.60
1578			**Parl. 5–1578**
c. 1	Freedom of Parliament	rep. SLR(S) 1906	—
c. 2	Regent	,,	—
c. 3	Church	,,	—
c. 4	Election of King's Council	,,	—
c. 5	Universities and Colleges	,,	—
c. 6	Glebes	rep. SLR(S) 1964	c.61
c. 7	Hospitals	rep. SLR(S) 1906	c.63
cc.8–10	Not public and general		—
c.11	**Burghs**		c.64
c.12	Darnley's murderers	,,	c.65
c.13	Crown lands	rep. SLR(S) 1964	c.66
c.14	Not public and general		—
c.15	Flesh	rep. SLR(S) 1906	c.67
c.16	Vacation	,,	—
c.17	Commissary Courts	,,	—
c.18	Commission on law	,,	—
c.19	Church	,,	—
cc.20–22	Not public and general		—
c.23	Coin	,,	—
c.24	Tay Bridge	,,	—
cc.25–32	Not public and general		—
c.33	Recognition of burgh lands	,,	—
c.34	Not public and general		—
1579			**Parl. 6–1579**
cc.1–5	Not public and general		—
c. 6	**Church**		c.68
c. 7	**Church Jurisdiction**	rep. in pt.SLR(S) 1906	c.69
c. 8	Sunday	rep. SL(Reps.) 1989 (c.43)	c.70
c. 9	Converts to Papacy	rep. SLR(S) 1906	c.71
c.10	Bibles	,,	c.72
c.11	Drawing teind	,,	c.73
c.12	Beggars and poor	,,	c.74
c.13	Registration	rep. Debtors (S.), 1987 (c.18), s.108(3), sch. 8	c.75
c.14	Officers at arms	rep. SLR(S) 1906	c.76
c.15	Lawburrows	,,	c.77
c.16	**Criminal letters**	rep. in pt.SLR(S) 1964	c.78
c.17	Perambulations	rep. SLR(S) 1906	c.79
c.18	Subscription of Deeds	rep. Requirements of Writing (S) 1995 (c.7), s.14(2), sch.5	c.80

Record Edition James VI.	Title or Subject Matter	How Affected	12mo Edition James VI.
c.19	Prescription (Ejections)	rep. Prescription and Limitation (S.), 1973 (c.52), s.16(2), sch. 5 pt.I	c.81
c.20	Prescription	rep. SLR(S) 1964	c.82
c.21	Prescription	rep. Prescription and Limitation (S.), 1973 (c.52), s.16(2), sch. 5 pt.I	c.83
c.22	Woods	rep. SLR(S) 1906	c.84
c.23	Burghs	,,	c.85
c.24	Sea fishing	,,	c.86
c.25	Firearms	,,	c.87
c.26	Forestallers	,,	c.88
c.27	Salmon	,,	c.89
c.28	Coals	,,	c.90
c.29	Expenses of process	,,	c.91
c.30	King's Revocation	,,	—
c.31	Coinage	,,	—
c.32	King's Council	,,	—
c.33	Forfeitures	,,	—
c.34	Low Countries	,,	c.96
c.35	Low Countries	,,	c.97
c.36	Privy Council	,,	—
c.37	Court of Session	rep. SLR(S) 1964	c.92
c.38	Court of Session	,,	c.93
cc.39–40	Not public and general		—
c.41	Regent	rep. SLR(S) 1906	—
cc.42–44	Not public and general		—
c.45	Hornings	rep. Debtors (S.), 1987 (c.18), s.108(3), sch.8	c.94
c.46–53	Not public and general		—
c.54	Regent	rep. SLR(S) 1906	—
c.55	Loyal subjects	,,	—
c.56	Spirits	,,	—
c.57	Burghs	,,	—
c.58	Education	,,	c.98
cc.59–76	Not public and general		—
1581			**Parl. 7–1581**
c. 1	Church	rep. SLR(S) 1906	c.99
c. 2	Stipends	rep. SL(Reps.) 1974 (c.22)	c.100
c. 3	Benfices	rep. SLR(S) 1906	c.101
c. 4	Presentation of ministers	,,	c.102
c. 5	Blasphemy	,,	c.103
c. 6	Pilgrimages	,,	c.104
c. 7	Adultery	,,	c.105
c. 8	Papists	,,	c.106
c. 9	Committee on Articles	,,	—
c.10	Coin	,,	c.106
c.11	Bullion	,,	c.107
c.12	Customs	,,	c.108
c.13	King's Protection	,,	c.109
c.14	Killing and maiming cattle	,,	c.110
c.15	Salmon	,,	c.111
c.16	Thieves	,,	c.112
c.17	Hospitals	,,	—
c.18	Sumptuary	,,	c.113
c.19	Sumptuary	,,	c.114
c.20	Jurisdiction of Rome	,,	c.115
c.21	Residence of land owners	,,	c.116
c.22	**Lawburrows**	rep. in pt.SLR(S) 1906	c.117
c.23	**Breach of Arrestment**	rep. in pt.SLR(S) 1906; SLR(S.) 1964	c.118
c.24	Inhibitions	rep. SLR(S) 1906	c.119
c.25	Prescription	,,	p.466
c.26	Convention of Burghs	rep. Debtors (S),1987 (c.18) s.108(3), sch.8	c.119
c.27	Shipping	rep. SLR(S) 1906	c.120
c.28	Regulation of prices	,,	c.121

Record Edition James VI.	Title or Subject Matter	How Affected	12mo Edition James VI.
c.29	*Horses*	rep. SLR(S) 1906	c.122
c.30	*Firearms*	"	c.123
c.31	*Export of Cattle*	"	c.124
c.32	*Captains of castles*	"	c.125
c.33	*Wine*	"	c.126
c.34	*Heirs of forfeited persons*	"	—
cc.35–36	Not public and general		—
c.37	*Proclamation of Acts*	"	c.128
c.38	*King's Council*	"	—
c.39	*Suitors to King*	"	—
c.40	*Factories*	"	—
c.41	Not public and general		—
c.42	*Ward holdings*	"	—
cc.43–64	Not public and general		—
c.65	*Lords of Session*	"	—
cc.66–67	Not public and general		—
c.68	*Revocation*	"	—
c.69	*Revocation*	"	—
c.70	*Revocation*	"	—
cc.71–113	Not public and general		—
1584 (May 19)			**Parl. 8–1584**
c. 1	*Church*	rep. SLR(S) 1906	—
c. 2	**Sovereignty**		c.129
c. 3	*Authority of Parliament*	"	c.130
c. 4	**Unlawful Jurisdictions**		c.131
c. 5	*Deprivation of ministers*		c.132
c. 6	**Disqualification of Ministers**		c.133
c. 7	*Treason*	"	—
c. 8	*Treason*	"	c.134
c. 9	*Treason*	"	—
c.10	*Revocation*	"	—
c.11	*Reduction of forfeitures*	"	c.135
c.12	*Remissions*	"	c.136
c.13	*Kings' Guard*	"	c.137
c.14	*Murders*	"	c.138
c.15	*Execution of decrees*	rep. Debtors (S) 1987 (c.18) s.108(3), sch.8	c.139
c.16	*Officers of State*	rep. SLR(S) 1906	—
c.17	*Attendance at courts of law*	"	c.140
c.18	Not public and general		—
c.19	*Measures*	"	c.141
c.20	*Commissioners in ecclesiastical causes*	rep. 1592 c. 8	—
c.21	*Rebels*	rep. SLR(S) 1906	c.142
c.22	*Ministers' stipends*	"	—
c.23	Not public and general		—
c.24	*Rebels*	"	—
c.25	Not public and general		—
c.26	*Revocation*	"	—
c.27	*College of Justice*	"	—
c.28	*Coinage*	"	—
c.29	*Coinage*	"	—
cc.30–49	Not public and general		—
1584 (Aug. 20)			**Parl. 9–1584**
c. 1	Not public and general		—
c. 2	*Ministers and schoolmasters*	rep. SLR(S) 1906	—
c. 3	*Prelacies*	"	c. 1
c. 4	Not public and general		—
c. 5	*Feuing of Crown Lands*	"	c. 6

Record Edition James VI.	Title or Subject Matter	How Affected	12mo Edition James VI.
c. 6	Forfeited lands	rep. SLR(S) 1906	c. 2
c. 7	Lands of those accused of treason	"	—
c. 8	Church lands	"	c. 7
c. 9	Not public and general		c. 8
c.10	**Decrees in absence**	rep (prosp) Bankruptcy and Diligence etc. (S), 2007 asp 3, s 226, sch 6	c. 3
c.11	Subscription of deeds	rep. SLR(S) 1964	c. 4
c.12	Sumptuary	rep. SLR(S) 1906	c. 5
c.13	Export prohibitions	"	c. 9
c.14	Burghs	"	—
c.15	Sumptuary	"	—
c.16	Treason	"	—
cc.17–19	Not public and general		—
c.20	King's revocation	"	—
cc.21–38	Not public and general		—
1585			**Parl. 10–1585**
c. 1	Leasing making	rep. SLR(S) 1964	c.10
c. 2	Execution of Acts of Parliament	rep. SLR(S) 1906	—
c. 3	Fees	"	—
c. 4	College of Justice	"	—
c. 5	Benefices	"	c.11
c. 6	Leagues	rep. SLR(S) 1964	c.12
c. 7	Style of signatures	rep. SLR(S) 1906	c.13
c. 8	Extortions by keepers of castles	"	—
c. 9	Double poinding	"	c.19
c.10	Privy Council	"	—
c.11	Burghs	"	c.14
c.12	Prohibited exports	"	c.15
c.13	Thieves	"	c.16
c.14	Factors and tenants	"	—
c.15	Church lands	"	—
c.16	Signatures	"	c.20
c.17	Chancellor	"	—
c.18	Treaty with England	"	—
c.19	Forfeited persons	"	c.17
c.20	King's revocation	"	c.17
c.21–23	Not public and general		—
c.24	Ministers and schoolmasters	"	—
c.25	Curators	rep. SLR(S) 1906; Adults with Incapacity (S), 2000, asp 4, s. 88(3), sch. 6	
cc.26–73	Not public and general		—
c.74	Commissioners of the shires	rep. SLR(S) 1906	—
1587			**Parl. 11–1587**
c. 1	King's majority	rep. SLR(S) 1906	c.22
c. 2	Church	"	c.23
c. 3	Religion	"	c.24
c. 4	Papal books	"	c.25
c. 5	Benefices	"	c.26
c. 6	Disorders in church	rep. SLR(S) 1964	c.27
c. 7	Dilapidations	rep. SLR(S) 1906	c.28
c. 8	Not public and general		c.29
c. 9	Coin	"	—
c.10	King's marriage	"	—
c.11	Measures and weights	"	—
c.12	Clergy liferents	"	—
c.13	Not public and general		c.30
c.14	King's revocation	"	c.31

Record Edition James VI.	Title or Subject Matter	How Affected	12mo Edition James VI.
c.15	Non resident ministers	rep. SLR(S) 1906	c.32
c.16	Parliament	"	cc.33–40
c.17	Parliament	"	c.41
c.18	Parliament	"	—
c.19	Privy Council	"	—
c.20	College of Justice	"	—
c.21	Lords of Session	"	—
c.22	Not public and general		—
c.23	Court of Session	"	c.42
c.24	Vexatious litigants	"	c.43
c.25	Court of Session	"	—
c.26	Court of Session	"	—
c.27	Court of Session	"	c.44
c.28	Privy Council	"	—
c.29	Notaries	"	c.45
c.30	Officers of Arms	rep. Debtors (S.) 1987 (c.18) s.108(3), sch.8	c.46
c.31	Supersederes	rep. SLR(S) 1906	c.47
c.32	Teinds	"	c.48
c.33	Treason	"	c.49
c.34	Treason	"	cc.50–51
c.35	Usury	"	c.52
c.36	Wine and timber	"	c.53
c.37	**Tolls**	rep. in pt.SLR(S) 1964	c.54
c.38	Forestallers	rep. SLR(S) 1906	—
c.39	Export of victuals	"	c.55
c.40	Horses	"	c.56
c.41	Sea fishing	"	c.57
c.42	Lent	"	c.58
c.43	Game	rep. SLR(S) 1964	c.59
c.44	Brieves	rep. SLR(S) 1906	c.64
c.45	Payments to factors	"	—
c.46	Commendator of Kelso	"	—
c.47	Patronage	"	c.61
c.48	Gifts of pensions	"	c.62
c.49	Exchequer	"	c.63
c.50	Sasines	"	c.64
c.51	Exchequer	"	—
c.52	Crown lands	"	cc.65–69
c.53	Crown-wadsets	"	—
c.54	Jurors	rep. SLR(S) 1906; SLR(S) 1964; Crim. Procedure (S.), 1975 (c.21), s.461 (2), sch. 10 pt.I.	cc.70–81
c.55	Ratifications	rep. SLR(S) 1906	—
c.56	King's peace	"	—
c.57	**Criminal Justice**	rep. in pt.—SLR(S.) 1906; Legal Aid and Solicitors 1949 c.63 s.17(3)(5) sch. 8; SL(Reps.)1973 c.39; Crim. Procedure((S), 1975 c.21, s.461(2) sch.10 pt.I.	cc.82–92
c.59	King's peace	rep. SLR(S) 1906	cc.93–110
c.60	Pacification	"	—
cc.71–76	Not public and general		
c.77	Churchmen's warrandice	"	c.111
cc.78–108	Not public and general		—
c.109	Burghs	"	c.112
cc.110–113	Not public and general		
c.114	**Burghs**		c.113
cc.115–119	Not public and general		—
c.120	Barons in Parliament	"	c.114
cc.121–122	Not public and general		
c.123	Defence of the realm	"	—
c.124	Supply	"	—
c.125	Bullion	"	—

Record Edition James VI.	Title or Subject Matter	How Affected	12mo Edition James VI.
cc.126–131	Not public and general		—
c.132	*Administration of justice*	"	—
c.133	*Commission on law*	"	—
c.134	Not public and general		—
c.135	*Commission on prices of food*	"	—
c.136	*Measures and weights*	"	c.115
1592			**Parl. 12–1592**
cc.1–3	Not public and general		—
c. 4	*Obligations of forfeited persons*	rep. SLR(S) 1906	—
cc.5–7	Not public and general		—
c. 8	**General Assembly**	rep.in pt. SLR(S) 1906	c.116
c. 9	*Deposition of ministers*	rep. SL(Reps.) 1974 (c.22).	c.117
c.10	*Manses and glebes*	rep. SLR(S) 1964	c.118
c.11	*Adultery*	rep. Succession (S) 1964 (c.41) s.34(2), sch. 3	c.119
c.12	**Murder in churches**	rep. SLR(S) 1906	c.120
c.13	*Erection of church lands and teinds*	"	c.121
c.14	*Jesuits*	"	c.122
c.15	*Ministers' stipends*	"	c.123
c.16	Not public and general		—
c.17	*Market-days*	"	c.124
c.18	*Pacification*	"	c.125
c.19	*Hospitals*	"	—
cc.20–26	Not public and general		—
c.27	*Ministers' Stipends*	"	—
c.28	*Sheriff's deputes*	"	c.126
c.29	**Lyon King of Arms**	rep.in pt. SLR(S.) 1906 ss.3, 5 rep. in pt Debtors (S) 1987 c.18 s.108(3), sch.8.	c.127
c.30	*Crown-rents*	rep. SLR(S) 1906	c.128
c.31	*Mines and metals*	rep. SLR(S) 1906; Abolition of Feudal Tenure etc.(S), 2000 asp 5, s. 76(2), sch. 13 pt. I	—
c.32	*King's revocation*	rep. SLR(S) 1906	—
c.33	Not public and general		—
c.34	*Crown lands*	"	c.129
c.35	*King's parks*	"	c.130
c.36	*Burgh mails*	"	—
c.37	*Customs*	"	c.131
c.38	*Salvo jure cujuslibet*	"	c.132
cc.39–40	Not public and general		—
c.41	*Privy Council*	"	—
c.42	*Treasurer*	"	—
c.43	Not public and general		—
c.44	*Rentals and feus*	"	c.133
c.45	*Printing Acts of Parliament.*	"	—
c.46	*King's marriage*	"	—
c.47	*King's marriage*	"	—
c.48	*King's marriage*	"	—
c.49	*King's marriage*	"	—
c.50	*Lords of Session*	rep. SLR(S) 1964	c.134
c.51	*Signatures*	rep. SLR(S) 1906	c.135
c.52	*Reduction of redemptions*	"	c.136
c.53	*Redemptions*	"	c.137
c.54	*Bounding charters*	"	c.138
c.55	*Pensions*	"	c.139
c.56	*Unlawful conditions in contracts*	"	c.140
c.57	*Repossessions*	"	—

Record Edition James VI.	Title or Subject Matter	How Affected	12mo Edition James VI.
c.58	*Bonds by prisoners*	rep. SLR(S) 1906	—
c.59	**Citation**		c.141
c.60	*General charges*	"	c.142
c.61	**Compensation**		c.143
c.62	**Expenses**		c.144
c.63	*Escheats*	"	c.145
c.64	*Commissariot*	"	—
c.65	*Treason*	"	c.146
c.66	*Escheats*	"	c.147
c.67	*Remissions*	"	c.157
c.68	*Fire raising in coal mines*	"	c.148
c.69	*Beggars and poor*	"	c.149
c.70	*Forestallers*	"	c.150
c.71	*Export of bestial*	"	c.151
c.72	**Deforcement**	rep. in pt. SLR(S) 1964	c.152
c.73	*Criminal libel*	rep. SLR(S) 1906	c.153
c.74	*Burghs*	"	c.154
c.75	*Burghs*	rep. SLR(S) 1964	c.155
c.76	*Craftsmen in suburbs*	rep. SLR(S) 1906	c.156
c.77	*Export of hides*	"	c.158
c.78	*Streets in burgh*	"	c.159
c.79	*Admiral*	"	c.160
cc.80–81	Not public and general		—
c.82	Not public and general		c.162
cc.83–87	Not public and general		—
c.88	*Remit to Privy Council*	"	—
c.89	*Provostries*	"	c.161
cc.90–181	Not public and general		—
1593			
cc.1–5	Not public and general		—
c. 6	*Markets on Sundays*	rep. SLR(S) 1906	c.163
c. 7	*Jurisdiction of Church*	"	c.164
c. 8	*Glebes*	rep. SLR(S) 1964	c.165
c. 9	*Ministers*	"	c.166
c.10	*Benefices*	rep. SLR(S) 1906	c.167
c.11	*Mass*	"	c.168
c.12	*Ministers' livings*	rep. SLR(S) 1964	c.169
c.13	*Lawburrows*	rep. SLR(S) 1906	c.170
c.14	Not public and general		c.171
c.15	*Customs officers*	"	c.172
c.16	*Remissions*	"	c.173
c.17	*Vassals of forfeited persons*	"	—
c.18	*Crown lands*	"	c.175
c.19	*Patronage*	"	c.176
c.20	*Church lands*	"	c.190
c.21	Not public and general		—
c.22	*Assault in courts*	rep. SLR(S) 1964	c.177
c.23	*Remissions*	rep. SLR(S) 1906	c.178
c.24	*College of Justice*	"	c.174
c.25	*Execution of deeds*	rep. SLR(S) 1964	c.179
c.26	*Benefices*	rep. SLR(S) 1906	c.186
c.27	Not public and general		c.192
cc.28–29	Not public and general		c.192–194
c.30	*Suspensions*	"	—
c.31	*Coinage*	"	—
c.32	Not public and general		c.180
c.33	*Burghs*	"	—
c.34	*Hornings*	rep. Debtors (S) 1987 (c.18) s.108(3), sch.8.	c.181
c.35	Not public and general		c.187
c.36	*Export of hides*	rep. SLR(S) 1906	c.182
c.37	*Customs*	"	c.183

Record Edition **James VI.**	*Title or Subject Matter*	*How Affected*	*12mo Edition* **James VI.**
c.38	*Dean of Guild*	rep. SLR(S) 1906	c.184
c.39	*Common good of burghs*	rep. SLR(S) 1964	c.185
c.40	Not public and general		—
c.41	Not public and general		c.188
cc.42–44	Not public and general		—
c.45	*Ministers' stipends*	rep. SLR(S) 1906	—
c.46	*Privy Council*	”	—
cc.47–56			
c.57	Not public and general		c.189
c.58	Not public and general		c.191
c.59	Not public and general		c.195
1594			**Parl. 14–1594**
cc.1–2	Not public and general		—
c. 3	*Mass*	rep. SLR(S) 1906	c.196
c. 4	*Papists*	”	c.197
c. 5	*Erections after annexation*	”	c.198
c. 6	*Provision of churches*	”	c.199
c. 7	*Excommunication*	”	c.200
c. 8	*Sunday*	rep. SLR(S) 1964	c.201
c. 9	*Manses and glebes*	”	c.202
c.10	*Patron's consent to tacks*	rep. SLR(S) 1906	c.203
c.11	*Repeal of Acts*	”	c.204
c.12	*Forfeited persons*	”	c.205
c.13	*Annexation*	”	c.207
c.14	*Dissolution*	”	c.208
c.15	*Leasing makers*	”	c.209
c.16	*Wines*	”	c.210
c.17	*Pensions*	”	c.211
c.18	*Officers of arms*	”	c.212
c.19	*Suspensions*	”	c.213
c.20	*King's Parks*	”	c.210
c.21	*College of Justice*	”	c.211
c.22	*Declinature*	rep. Ct of Session 1988 c. 36 s.52(2), sch.2.	c.212
c.23	*Vacation*	rep. SLR(S) 1906	c.227
c.24	*Prescription*	rep. Prescription and Limitation (S), 1973 (c.52), s.16(2), sch. 5 pt.I	c.218
c.25	Not public and general		c.219
c.26	**Land Purchase**	rep. in pt.SLR(S) 1964	c.220
c.27	*Ejection caution*	rep. Bankruptcy and Diligence etc. (S), 2007 asp 3, s 226, sch 6	c.217
c.28	*Consideration of Articles*	rep. SLR(S) 1906	c.218
c.29	*Murder*	”	c.219
c.30	**Parricide**		c.224
c.31	*Lent*	”	c.225
c.32	*Usury*	”	c.222
c.33	*Student and bursars*		c.223
c.34	*Salmon*	”	c.224
c.35	*Burghs*	rep. SLR(S) 1964	c.225
c.36	*Burghs*	”	c.226
c.37	*Theft*	rep. SLR(S) 1906	c.231
cc.38–44	Not public and general		—
c.45	*Prelates*	”	c.232
c.46	Not public and general		c.223
c.47	*Skinners*	”	—
cc.48–73	Not public and general		—
c.74	*Currency*	”	—
c.75	*Bullion*	”	c.206
c.76	*Forestallers*	”	—
c.77	*Caution for Exchequer accounts*	”	c.230
cc.78–97	Not public and general		—
c.98	*Hospitals*	”	—

Record Edition James VI.	Title or Subject Matter	How Affected	12mo Edition James VI.
cc.99–100	Not public and general		—
1597			**Parl. 15–1597**
c. 1	Not public and general		—
c. 2	*Prelates in Parliament*	rep. SLR(S) 1906	c.235
c. 3	**Kirk Dykes**		c.232
c. 4	*Crown lands*	”	c.233
c. 5	Not public and general		c.234
c. 6	Not public and general		c.235
c. 7	Not public and general		c.236
c. 8	*Assyis hering*	”	c.241
c. 9	*Heritable chamerlains*	”	c.242
c.10	*Feu-duties*	”	c.243
c.11	*Tacks and pensions of thirds.*	”	c.244
c.12	*Thirds of Benefices*	”	c.245
c.13	*Benefices*	”	c.246
c.14	*Ratifications*	”	c.247
c.15	*Possessors of benefices*	”	c.248
c.16	*Feuars of temporalities*	”	c.249
c.17	*Feu-Duty*	rep. Abolition of Feudal Tenure etc.(S), 2000 asp 5, s. 76(2), sch. 13 pt. I	c.250
c.18	*Usury*	rep. SLR(S) 1906	c.251
c.19	*Firearms*	”	c.252
c.20	*Gold and silver*	”	c.253
c.21	*Wool*	”	c.254
c.22	*Customs*	”	c.255
c.23	*Woollen goods*	”	c.256
c.24	*Coal*	”	c.257
c.25	*Customs*	”	c.258
c.26	*Cocquets*	”	c.259
c.27	*Shipping*	”	c.260
c.28	*Foreign Trade*	”	c.261
c.29	*Imports*	”	c.262
c.30	*Usury*	”	c.263
c.31	*Foreign trade*	”	c.264
c.32	*Salmon*	”	c.265
c.33	*Titles to land*	”	c.266
c.34	*Burghs*	”	c.267
c.35	*Registration of hornings*	”	c.268
c.36	*Registration of hornings*	”	c.269
c.37	*Game*	”	c.270
c.38	*Fines*	”	c.271
c.39	*Beggars and gipsies.*	”	c.272
c.40	**Lawburrows**	rep.in pt. SLR(S) 1964	c.273
c.41	*General Band*	rep. SLR(S) 1964	c.274
c.42	*Sheriff clerks*	rep. SLR(S) 1906	c.275
c.43	*Baron's commissioners*	”	c.276
c.44	*Prisons*	”	c.277
c.45	*Benefices*	”	c.278
c.46	*Burgh*	”	c.279
c.47	*Burgh taxation*	”	c.280
c.48	*Supply*	”	c.281
cc.49–65	Not public and general		—
c.66	*Coin*	”	—
cc.67–95	Not public and general		—
1600			**Parl. 16–1600**
cc.1–2	Not public and general		—
c. 3	*Thanksgiving day*	rep. SLR(S) 1906	c. 1
c. 4	Not public and general		c. 2
cc.5–9	Not public and general		—
c.10	Not public and general		c. 3
c.11	Not public and general		—

Record Edition	*Title or Subject Matter*	*How Affected*	*12mo Edition*
James VI.			**James VI.**
c.12	*Privy Councillors*	rep. SLR(S) 1906	c. 4
c.13	*Purprision*	"	c. 5
c.14	*Firearms*	"	c. 6
c.15	*Ursury*	"	c. 7
c.16	*Coal mines*	"	c. 8
c.17	Not public and general		—
c.18	*Currency*	"	c. 9
c.19	*Herring*	"	c.10
c.20	*Salmon*	"	c.11
c.21	*Duels*	rep. Duelling (S) 1819 (c. 70)	c.12
c.22	*Hornings*	rep. Debtors (S) 1987 (c.18) s.108(3), sch.8.	c.13
c.23	**Crown Proceedings**		c.14
c.24	*Customs*	rep. SLR(S) 1906	c.15
c.25	*Church*	"	c.16
c.26	*Non-communicants*	"	c.17
c.27	*Jesuits*	"	c.18
c.28	*Beggars*	"	c.19
c.29	*Marriage of adulterers*	rep. SLR(S) 1964	c.20
c.30	*Registers*		c.21
c.31	*Public peace*	rep. SLR(S) 1906	c.22
c.32	*Defence of the realm*	"	c.23
c.33	*Border hostages*	"	c.28
c.34	*Game*	"	—
c.35	*Theft and redress*	"	—
c.36	*Sasines*	"	—
c.37	*Customs*	"	c.24
c.38	*Hornings*	"	c.25
c.39	*Royal Palaces*	"	c.26
cc.40–50	Not public and general		—
c.51	Not public and general		c.27
c.52	*Precedence*	"	—
c.53	*Wool*	"	—
cc.54–57	Not public and general		—
1604			**Parl. 17–1604**
c. 1	*Union with England*	rep. SLR(S) 1906	c. 1
c. 2	*Church*	"	—
cc.3–8	Not public and general		—
1606			**Parl. 18–1606**
c. 1	**Sovereignty**		c. 1
c. 2	*Bishops*	rep. 1690 c.7	c. 2
c. 3	Not public and general		c. 4
c. 4	*Tweed and Annan*	rep. SLR(S) 1906	c. 5
c. 5	*Customs*	"	c. 6
c. 6	*Glebes*	rep. SLR(S) 1964	c. 7
c. 7	*Teinds*	rep. SLR(S) 1906	c. 8
c. 8	*Ejections and spuilyies*	"	c. 9
c. 9	*Hornings*	rep. SLR(S) 1964	c.10
c.10	*Colliers and salters*	rep. SLR(S) 1906	c.11
c.11	*Feuing of wardlands*	"	c.12
c.12	*Lint in lochs*	rep. SLR(S) 1964	c.13
c.13	*Crown vassals' duties*	rep. SLR(S) 1906	c.14
c.14	*Sasines*	"	c.15
c.15	*Royal Burghs*	"	c.16
c.16	*Royal Burghs*	rep. SLR(S) 1964	c.17
c.17	*Royal residences*	rep. SLR(S) 1906	—
c.18	*Supply*	"	—
c.19	*Supply*	"	—
cc.20–22	Not public and general		—
c.23	*Commission on erections*	"	—
c.24	Not public and general		—
c.25	Not public and general		c.18
cc.26–37	Not public and general		—

Record Edition James VI.	Title or Subject Matter	How Affected	12mo Edition James VI.
c.38	College of Justice	rep. SLR(S) 1906	—
cc.39–60	Not public and general		—
c.61	Not public and general		c.19
cc.62–67	Not public and general		—
c.68	Not public and general		c.20
cc.69–70	Not public and general		—
c.71	Dilapidation of bishoprics	"	c. 3
cc.72–102	Not public and general		—
1607			**Parl. 19–1607**
c. 1	Union with England	rep. SLR(S) 1906	—
c. 2	Mass	"	c. 1
c. 3	Not public and general		c. 8
c. 4	Not public and general		—
c. 5	Erection of kirks	"	—
c. 6	**Theft**	rep.in pt. SLR(S) 1964; Salmon and Freshwater Fisheries (Consolidation) (S), 2003 asp 15, s 70(2), sch 4 pt 2; SI 2006/2913, sch 4 pt 2	c. 3
c. 7	Weights and measures	rep. SLR(S) 1906	c. 2
c. 8	Craftsmen	"	c. 4
c. 9	Education	"	—
c.10	Not public and general		c. 7
c.11	Not public and general		—
c.12	Royal Burghs	"	c. 5
c.13	Convention of burghs	rep. Debtors (S.),1987 c.18, s.108(3), sch.8.	c. 6
cc.14–15	Not public and general		—
c.16	Regiam Majestatem	rep. SLR(S) 1906	—
cc.17–27	Not public and general		—
c.28	Not public and general		c. 9
cc.29–35	Not public and general		—
1609			**Parl. 20–1609**
cc.1–2	Not public and general		—
c. 3	Education	rep. SLR(S) 1906	c. 1
c. 4	Perverts to Papacy	"	c. 2
c. 5	Excommunication	"	c. 3
c. 6	Excommunication	"	c. 4
c. 7	Jesuits	"	c. 5
c. 8	Commissiariots	"	c. 6
c. 9	Commission on erections	"	—
cc.10–13	Not public and general		—
c.14	Justices of Peace	"	c. 7
c.15	Sumptuary	"	c. 8
c.16	Slander	"	c. 9
c.17	Borders	"	c.10
c.18	Lords of Session	"	c.11
c.19	Patronage	"	c.12
c.20	Gipsies	"	c.13
c.21	Resignations	"	c.14
c.22	Hornings	rep. SLR(S) 1964	c.14
cc.23–29	Not public and general		—
c.40	Registers	rep. SLR(S) 1906	—
cc.41–46	Not public and general		—
c.47	Submission of disputes	"	—
c.48	Rape	"	—
cc.49–64	Not public and general		—
1612			
c. 1	Acts of Assembly	rep. 1690 c.7	c. 1
c. 2	Extradition with England	rep. SLR(S) 1906	c. 2
c. 3	Hornings in case of murder	"	c. 3
c. 4	Rape	"	c. 4
c. 5	Teinds	"	c. 5

Record Edition James VI.	Title or Subject Matter	How Affected	12mo Edition James VI.
c. 6	*Borders*	rep. SLR(S) 1906	c. 6
c. 7	*Hornings*	rep. SLR(S) 1964	c. 7
c. 8	*Bishops' manses*	rep. SLR(S) 1906	c. 8
c. 9	*Pardons*	"	c. 9
c.10	Not public and general		c.10
c.11	Not public and general		c.11
c.12	*Supply*	"	—
c.13	*Supply*	"	—
cc.14–15	Not public and general		—
c.16	*Bishop's land in Orkney*	"	—
cc.17–23	Not public and general		—
c.24	*Mint*	"	—
cc.35–46	Not public and general		—
c.47	*Burghs*	"	—
cc.48–75	Not public and general		—
1617			**Parl. 22–1617**
c. 1	*Bishops*	rep. 1690 c.7	c. 1
c. 2	*Chapters*	rep. SLR(S) 1906	c. 3
c. 3	*Plantation of kirks*	rep. SLR(S) 1964	c. 3
c. 4	*Leases by prelates*	rep. SLR(S) 1906	c. 4
c. 5	*Dilapidation of benefice*	"	c. 5
c. 6	*Communion elements*	rep. SLR(S) 1964	c. 6
c. 7	*Attendance in Parliament*	rep. SLR(S) 1906	c. 7
c. 8	*Justice of Peace*	"	c. 8
c. 9	*Teinds*	"	c. 9
c.10	*Poor*	"	c.10
c.11	*Queen's Council*	"	c.11
c.12	*Prescription*	rep. Prescription and Limitation (S.), 1973 c.52, s.16(2) sch. 5 pt.I.	c.12
c.13	*Reduction*	rep. Prescription and Limitation (S.), 1973 (c.52), s.16(2), sch. 5 pt.I	c.13
c.14	**Executors**		c.14
c.15	*Escheats*	rep. SLR(S) 1964	c.15
c.16	**Registration**	rep. in pt. SLR(S) 1906; Title Conditions (S), 2003 asp 9, s 128(2), sch 15	c.16
c.17	*Arrestments*	rep. Bankruptcy and Diligence etc. (S), 2007 asp 3, s 226, sch 6	c.17
c.18	*Forests*	rep. SLR(S) 1906	c.18
c.19	*Dovecotes*	rep. SL(Reps.) 1974	c.19
c.20	*Drunkards*	rep. SLR(S) 1906	c.20
c.21	*Cawps*	"	c.21
c.22	*Protocols .*	"	c.22
c.23	Not public and general		c.23
c.24	*Commission on heritable offices*	"	—
c.25	*Commission on Justice Courts.*	"	—
cc.26–36	Not public and general		
c.37	*Commission on tanning*	"	—
cc.38–62	Not public and general		—
1621			**Parl. 23–1621**
c. 1	*Articles of Perth*	rep. 1690 c. 7	c. 1
c. 2	*Supply*	rep. SLR(S) 1906	c. 2
c. 3	*Supply*	"	c. 3
c. 4	*Ratification*	"	c. 4
c. 5	*Plantation of kirks*	rep. SLR(S) 1964	c. 5
c. 6	**Diligence**	rep (prosp) Bankruptcy and Diligence etc. (S), 2007 asp 3, s 226, sch 6 rep. in pt. SLR(S) 1906; Age of Majority (S) 1969 c.39), s.1 (3), sch. 1 pt.I	c. 6
c. 7	**Adjudication**	rep (prosp) Bankruptcy and Diligence etc. (S), 2007 asp 3, s 226, sch 6	c. 7

Record Edition James VI.	Title or Subject Matter	How Affected	12mo Edition James VI.
		rep. in pt.SLR(S) 1906	
c. 8	Registration	rep. SLR(S) 1906	c. 8
c. 9	Feuing by bishops	"	c. 9
c.10	Glebes to be teind free	rep. SLR(S) 1964	c.10
c.11	Restitution of chapters	rep. SLR(S) 1906	c.11
c.12	Packing and peeling	"	c.12
c.13	Protections	"	c.13
c.14	Gaming	rep. Betting and Gaming 1906 (c.60), s.15, sch. 6	c.14
c.15	Church lands	rep. SLR(S) 1906	c.15
c.16	Measures	"	c.16
c.17	Sale by measure	"	c.17
c.18	Bankruptcy	rep. Bankruptcy (S.) 1985 (c.66), s.75(2) sch.8	c.18
c.19	Table of fees	rep. SLR(S) 1906	c.19
c.20	Hornings	rep. Debtors (S.) 1987 (c.18), s.108(3), sch.8.	c.20
c.21	Servants	rep. SLR(S) 1906	c.21
c.22	Forgery	rep. SLR(S) 1964	c.22
c.23	Pardon	rep. SLR(S) 1906	c.23
c.24	Registration	"	c.24
c.25	Sumptuary	"	c.25
c.26	Houses in Edinburgh	"	c.26
c.27	Comprisings	"	c.27
c.28	Usury	"	c.28
c.29	Tradesmen	"	c.29
c.30	Game	"	c.30
c.31	Hunting and hawking	rep. SLR(S) 1964	c.31
c.32	Hunting and hawking	rep. SLR(S) 1906	c.32
c.33	Not public and general		c.33
c.34	Money	"	—
c.35	Supply	"	—
c.36	Mines and minerals	"	—
c.37	Commission as to erected prelacies	"	—
c.38	Measures	"	—
c.39	Edinburgh water supply	"	—
cc.40–80	Not public and general		—
c.81	King's castles	"	—
c.82	Burghs	"	—
cc.83–110	Not public and general		—
c.111	Supply	"	—
c.112	Supply	"	—
c.113	Not public and general		—
c.114	Clerks of Session	"	—
Charles I.			**Charles I.**
1633			**Parl. 1–1633**
c. 1	Supply	rep. SLR(S) 1906	c. 1
c. 2	Supply	"	c. 2
c. 3	**Sovereignty**	rep. in pt.SLR(S) 1906	c. 3
c. 4	Religion	rep. SLR(S) 1906	c. 4
c. 5	Education	"	c. 5
c. 6	Charitable bequests	"	c. 6
c. 7	Invading of ministers	rep. SLR(S) 1964	c. 7
c. 8	Minister's stipends	"	c. 8
c. 9	Revocation	rep. SLR(S) 1906	c. 9
c.10	Not public and general		c. 9
c.11	Not public and general		c. 9
c.12	Interruptions	"	c.12
c.13	Not public and general		c.13
c.14	Not public and general		c.14
c.15	Teinds	rep. SLR(S) 1964	c.15
c.16	Ward holding	rep. SLR(S) 1906	c.16

Record Edition	Title or Subject Matter	How Affected	12mo Edition
Charles I.			**Charles I.**
c.17	*Teinds*	rep. SLR(S) 1964	c.17
c.18	*Exchequer*	rep. SLR(S) 1906	c.18
c.19	*Valuation of teinds*	rep. SLR(S) 1964	c.19
c.21	*Usury*	"	c.21
c.22	*Supply*	"	c.22
c.23	*College of Justice*	"	c.23
c.24	*Royal Burghs*	"	c.24
c.25	*Justices of Peace*	"	c.25
c.26	*Lords of Session*	"	c.26
c.27	*Pardon*	"	c.27
cc.28–31	Not public and general	cc.28–31	
c.32	*Commission for surveying laws*	rep. SLR(S) 1906	—
c.33	*Commission anent Admiralty*	"	—
c.34	*Commission to Privy Council*	"	—
c.35	*Commission to Privy Council*	"	—
c.35	*Commission to Privy Council*	"	—
cc.36–37	Not public and general		—
c.38	*Commission as to exchange*	"	—
c.39	*Commission as to criminal procedure*	"	—
c.40	Not public and general		—
c.41	*Commission to Exchequer*	"	—
c.42	*Commission to Privy Council*	"	—
cc.43–168	Not public and general		
Charles II			**Charles II**
1661			**Parl. 1–1661**
c. 1	*Oaths*	rep. Promissory Oaths 1871 s. 1, sch. 2, Pt. 2	c. 1
cc.2–3	Not public and general		—
c. 4	*Commission to Lords of Articles*	rep. SLR(S) 1906	—
c. 5	*Commission on trade*	"	—
c. 6	**Crown appointments**	rep.in pt. SLR(S) 1906	c. 2
c. 7	**Parliament**	"	c. 3
cc.8–10			
c.11	*Remonstrators*	rep. SLR(S) 1906	—
c.12	*King's prerogative*	rep. SLR(S) 1964	c. 4
c.13	**Prerogative**	rep.in pt. SLR(S) 1906	c. 5
c.14	Not public and general		
c.15	*Guard for Parliament*	rep. SLR(S) 1906	—
cc.16–17	Not public and general		—
c.18	*Repeal*	"	c. 6
c.19	*Anabaptists*	"	—
c.20	Not public and general		—
c.21	*Repeal*	"	—
c.22	*League and Covenant*	"	c. 7
c.23	*Vacant stipends*	"	—
cc.24–36	Not public and general		—
c.37	*Mass*	"	c. 8
cc.38–45	Not public and general		—
c.46	*Annulling 1649 Parliament*	"	c. 9
c.47	*Messengers of Arms*	rep. SL(Reps.) 1986	—
c.48	*Signet*	rep. SLR(S) 1906	—
cc.49–51	Not public and general		—
c.52	*King's person*	"	c.10

Record Edition Charles II	Title or Subject Matter	How Affected	12mo Edition Charles II
cc.53–56	Not public and general		—
c.57	*Persons coming from Ireland*	"	—
cc.58–61	Not public and general		—
c.62	*Oath of allegiance*	rep. Promissory Oaths 1871, s.1, sch. 2, Pt. 2	c.11
cc.63–66	Not public and general		—
c.67	*Teind Commission*		c.61
cc.68–86	Not public and general		—
c.87	*Judicial proceedings ratified*	rep. SLR(S) 1906	c.12
c.88	*Apparent heirs*	rep. Succession (S)1964 (c.41), s.34 (2), sch. 3	c.24
cc.89–91	Not public and general		—
c.92	*Tobacco pipes*	rep. SLR(S) 1906	—
cc.93–111			—
c.112	*Supply*	"	c.13
cc.113–125	Not public and general		—
c.126	*Rescissory Act*	"	c.15
c.127	*Religion and Church*	"	c.16
c.128	*Supply*	"	c.14
cc.129–135	Not public and general		—
c.136	*Duns*	"	—
cc.137–156	Not public and general		—
c.157	*Royal burghs*	"	—
cc.158–166	Not public and general		—
c.167	*Education*	"	—
cc.168–193	Not public and general		—
c.194	*Sittings of Session*	"	—
c.195	*Clan Gregor*	rep. 1693 c. 62	—
cc.196–198	Not public and general		—
c.199	*Sittings of Session*	rep. SLR(S) 1906	—
cc.200–209	Not public and general		—
c.210	*Thanksgiving*	rep. 1690 c. 58	c.17
c.211	**Precedence**	rep. in pt.SLR(S) 1964	—
cc.212–214	Not public and general		—
c.215	*Cursing and beating parents.*		c.20
c.216	*Blasphemy*	rep. 53 Geo. III, c.160 s.III	c.21
c.217	*Homicide*	rep. SLR(S) 1906	c.22
c.218	*Poinding*	rep. Debtors (S) 1987 (c.18), s.108(3), sch 8	c.29
c.219	*Soapworks*	rep. SLR(S) 1906	c.48
cc.220–237	Not public and general		—
c.238	*Excommunication*	rep. 1663 c. 77, and 1690 c. 58	c.25
c.239	*Restoration of stolen goods*	rep. SLR(S) 1964	c.26
c.240	*Pardon*	rep. SLR(S) 1906	c.27
c.241	*Quots*	"	c.28
c.242	*Feuars of church lands*	"	c.30
c.243	*Registration*	rep. Abolition of Feudal Tenure etc. (S), 2000 asp 5, s. 76(2), sch. 13 pt. I	c.31
c.244	**Bonds**	rep. in pt.SLR(S) 1964	c.32
c.245	*Salmon*	rep. SLR(S) 1906	c.33
c.246	*Clandestine marriages*	rep. SLR(S) 1964	c.34
c.247	*Redemptions*	rep. Title Conditions (S), 2003 asp 9, s 128(2), sch 15	—
cc.248–252	Not public and general		—
c.253	*Parliamentary elections*	rep. SLR(S) 1906	c.35
c.254	*Payment of members*	"	—
c.255	*Oath of allegiance*	"	—
cc.256–259	Not public and general		—
c.260	*College of Justice*	"	c.23
c.261	*Redemption in reversions*	"	—

Record Edition **Charles II**	Title or Subject Matter	How Affected	12mo Edition **Charles** **II**
cc.262–264	Not public and general		—
c.265	*Minister's stipends in Edinburgh*	″	—
cc.266–269	Not public and general		—
c.270	*Lords of Session*	″	c.50
c.271	*Lords of Session*	″	—
c.272	*Bullion*	″	c.37
c.273	*Coinage*	″	—
c.274	*Mint*	″	—
c.275	*Linen companies*	″	c.42
c.276	*Linen*	″	c.43
c.277	*Shipping*	″	c.44
c.278	*Hides*	″	c.45
c.279	*Fishings*	″	c.39
c.280	*Manufacturies*	″	c.40
c.281	*Sunday*	rep. SL(Reps.) 1989 (c.43)	c.18
c.282	*Swearing and drinking*	rep. SLR(S) 1906	c.19
c.283	**Arrestments**	rep.in pt. SLR(S) 1964	c.51
c.284	**March Dykes**	rep.in pt. SLR(S) 1906	c.41
cc.285–290	Not public and general		—
c.291	*Presentation of ministers*	rep. SLR(S) 1906	c.36
c.292	*Council for trade*	″	—
cc.293–295	Not public and general		—
c.296	*Signet*	″	—
cc.297–307	Not public and general		—
c.308	*Prohibited exports*	″	c.46
c.309	*Registration*	″	—
c.310	*Tradesmen.*	″	c.47
cc.311–319	Not public and general		—
c.320	*Salmon*	″	—
c.321	*Supply*	″	—
cc.322–323	Not public and general		—
c.329	Not public and general		c.53
c.330	*Vacant stipends*	″	c.52
c.331	*Patrons*	rep. SLR(S) 1964	c.54
c.332	*Shipping*	rep. SLR(S) 1906	c.55
c.333	*Colliers*	″	c.56
c.334	*Customs*	″	c.57
c.335	*Ward holdings*	″	c.58
c.336	*Exchequer*	″	c.59
c.337	*Signatures*	″	c.60
c.338	*Justices of the Peace*	rep. District Cts. (S) 1975 (c.20), s.24(2), sch. 2.	c.38
c.339	*Public debt*	rep. SLR(S) 1906	—
c.340	*Amendment of Acts*	″	—
c.341	*Commissaries of Edinburgh.*	″	—
c.342	*Trial of certain prisoners*	″	—
c.343	Not public and general		—
c.344	**Diligence**	rep (prosp) Bankruptcy and Diligence etc. (S), 2007 asp 3, s 226, sch 6 rep.in pt. SLR(S) 1906	c.62
c.345	*Usury*	rep. SLR(S) 1906	c.49
cc.346–351	Not public and general		—
c.352	*Supply*	″	—
c.353	*Supply*	″	—
cc.354–356	Not public and general		—
c.357	*Aberdeen Commissary Courts*	″	—
cc.358–391	Not public and general		—
c.392	**Saving third party rights**		c.63
c.393	*Adjournment*	″	—

Record Edition	Title or Subject Matter	How Affected	12mo Edition
Charles II			**Charles II**
1662			**Parl. 1–Sess.2 1662**
c. 1	*Bishops in Parliament*	rep. SLR(S) 1906	c. 1
c. 2	*Attendance in Parliament*	"	—
c. 3	*Re-establishment of Prelacy.*	rep. 1689 (June 5) c.4 and 1690 c.7	c. 1
cc.4–6	Not public and general		—
c. 7	*Benefices*	rep. SLR(S) 1906	c. 3
c. 8	*Thanksgiving.*	"	—
cc.9–10	Not public and general		—
c.11	*Creditors of forfeited persons.*	"	—
c.12	*King's persons and authority.*	"	c. 2
c.13	*Universities*	rep. 1690 c.57	c. 4
cc.14–15	Not public and general		—
c.16	*Lords of Sessions*	rep. SLR(S) 1906	c. 7
c.17	*Theft and robbery*	"	c. 6
cc.18–24	Not public and general		—
c.25	*Bishops' teinds*	"	c. 9
cc.26–27	Not public and general		—
c.28	*Relief*	"	—
cc.29–37	Not public and general		—
c.38	*Registers*	rep. SLR(S)1906	—
cc.39–49	Not public and general		—
c.50	*Revocation*	rep. SLR(S) 1906	c. 8
cc.51–52	Not public and general		—
c.53	*Lyon King of Arms*	rep. 1693 c.15	—
c.54	*Declaration de fideli*	rep. 1690 c.57	c. 5
cc.55–70	Not public and general		—
c.71	*Pardon*	rep. SLR(S) 1906	c.10
c.72	Not public and general		—
c.73	*Forfeited persons*	"	—
c.74	*Abatement of exercise*	"	—
cc.75–82	Not public and general		—
c.83	*Public debt*	"	—
c.84	*Debtor and creditor*	"	—
cc.85–110	Not public and general		—
c.111	Not public and general		c.11
c.112	*Adjournment*	"	c.12
1663			**Parl. 1–Sess.3**
Vol. VII, p. 449	*Lords of the Articles*	rep. 1690 c.3	c. 1
c. 1	*Billeting*	rep. SLR(S) 1906	Vol. 2 after p. 37
c. 2	*Protections*	"	c. 4
c. 3	*Advocations*	"	c. 9
c. 4	**Minority**	rep (prosp) Bankruptcy and Diligence etc. (S), 2007 asp 3, s 226, sch 6 am.- Age of Majority (S), 1969 (c.39), s.1(3), sch.1 pt.I	c.10
c. 5	*Beer in Shetland*	rep. SLR(S) 1906	—
cc.6–8	Not public and general		—
c. 9	*Ecclesiastical authority*	rep. 1689 (June 5) c.4 and 1690 c.57	c. 2
c.10	*Stipend for 1662*	rep. SLR(S) 1906	—
c.11	Not public and general		—
c.12	*Ruinous houses in burghs*	rep. SLR(S) 1964	c. 6
c.13	*Import of spirits*	rep. SLR(S) 1906	c. 7
c.14	*Tin*	"	c. 8
c.15	*Lyon King*	"	—
c.16	Not public and general		—

Record Edition Charles II	Title or Subject Matter	How Affected	12mo Edition Charles II
c.17	Declaration de fideli	rep. 1690 c.57	c. 3
c.18	Irish corn	rep. SLR(S) 1906	c.14
c.19	Forfeited persons	"	—
cc.20–21	Not public and general		—
c.22	National synod	rep. 1690 c.7	c. 5
c.23	Customs	rep. SLR(S) 1906	c.13
c.24	Customs	"	—
c.25	Silkweavers	"	—
c.26	Not public and general		—
c.27	Forfeited persons	"	—
c.28	Supply	"	c.25
c.29	Money	"	c.11
c.30	Repeals of Acts	"	Vol. 2, p. 373
c.31	Manses	rep. SL(Reps.) 1974 (c.22).	c.21
c.32	Not public and general		c.32
c.33	Attendance in Parliament	rep. SLR(S) 1906	—
c.34	Teind commission	rep. SLR(S) 1964	c.28
c.35	Agriculture	"	c.12
c.36	Comprisings	rep. SLR(S) 1906	c.22
cc.37–41	Not public and general		—
c.42	Tender of loyalty	"	c.26
c.42	Markets	"	c.19
cc.44–51	Not public and general		—
c.52	Beggars	"	c.16
cc.53–55	Not public and general		—
c.56	Coal	"	c.17
c.57	Measures	"	c.18
c.58	Not public and general		—
c.59	Cards	"	—
cc.60–61	Not public and general		—
c.62	Universities	rep. 1672 c.46	c.24
c.63	Linsteed	rep. SLR(S) 1906	c.20
cc.64–65	Not public and general		—
c.66	Crown rents	"	c.15
cc.67–71	Not public and general		—
c.72	Table of fees	"	—
c.73	Not public and general		—
c.74	Public debts	"	—
cc.75–76	Not public and general		—
c.77	Excommunication	rep. 1690 c.58	c.23
cc.78–80	Not public and general		—
c.81	King's prerogative	rep. 1701 c.7	—
c.82	Penal statutes	rep. SLR(S) 1906	c.27
c.83	Justices of the Peace	"	c.29
cc.84–112	Not public and general		—
c.113	Not public and general		c.30
1669			**Parl. 2–1669**
c. 1	Election of Commissioners.	rep. SLR(S) 1906	—
c. 2	King's supremacy	rep. 1690 c.1	c. 1
c. 3	Militia	rep. SLR(S) 1906	c. 2
c. 4	Registration	"	c. 3
c. 5	Poinding	rep. Debtors (S.) 1987 (c.18) s.108(3), sch.8	c. 4
c. 6	Ministers	rep. SLR(S) 1906	c. 5
c. 7	Benefices and stipends	rep. SLR(S) 1964	c. 6
cc.8–11	Not public and general		—
c.12	Naturalization	rep. SLR(S) 1906	c. 7
c.13	Bullion	rep. 1686 c.38	c. 8
c.14	Prescription	rep. Prescription and Limitation (S.), 1973 (c.52), s.16(2), sch. 5 pt.I	c. 9

Record Edition **Charles II**	Title or Subject Matter	How Affected	12mo Edition **Charles II**
c.15	*Interruptions*	rep. Prescription and Limitation (S.), 1973 (c.52), s.16 (2), sch. 5 pt.I	c.10
c.16	Not public and general		—
c.17	*Rebels*	rep. 1690 c.60 and SLR(S) 1906	c.11
c.18	*Excise and customs*	rep. SLR(S) 1906	c.11
c.19	Not public and general		c.13
c.20	*Export of corn*	"	c.14
cc.21–35	Not public and general		—
c.36	*Ale*	"	c.15
c.37	*Highways and bridges*	rep. SLR(S) 1964	c.16
c.38	**March dykes**		c.17
c.39	*Ajudications*	"	c.18
c.40	*Confirmation and quots*	rep. SLR(S) 1906	c.19
c.41	*Moratorium*	"	—
cc.43–94	Not public and general		—
c.95	**Lyon King of Arms**	rep. in pt. Debtors (S.), 1987 c.18, s.108 (3) sch.8.	—
cc.96–114	Not public and general		—
c.115	*Printers and stationers*	rep. SLR(S) 1906	—
cc.116–126	Not public and general		—
c.127	*Commission as to inferior courts*	"	—
cc.128–131	Not public and general		—
c.132	*Commission for trade*	"	—
cc.133–135	Not public and general		—
c.136	Not public and general		c.21
c.137	*Adjournment*	"	c.22
1670			**Parl. 2–Sess.2 1670**
c. 1	*Treaty with England*	rep. SLR(S) 1906	c. 1
c. 2	*Delinquents*	rep. 1690 c.7	c. 2
c. 3	*Supply*	rep. SLR(S) 1906	c. 3
c. 4	*Invading of ministers*	"	c. 4
c. 5	*Conventicles*	rep. 1690 c.57	c. 5
c. 6	*Irregular baptisms*	"	c. 6
c. 7	*Lauder and Duns*	rep. SLR(S) 1906	—
c. 8	*Divine Worship*	rep. 1690 c.57	c. 7
cc.9–11	Not public and general		—
c.12	*Lords of Session*	rep. SLR(S) 1906	c. 8
c.13	*Highways*	"	c. 9
cc.14–61	Not public and general		—
c.62	Not public and general		c.10
c.63	*Adjournment*	"	c.11
1672			**Parl. 2–Sess.3 1672**
c. 1	*Militia*	rep. SLR(S) 1906	c. 1
c. 2	*Tutors and Curators*	rep. Age of Legal Capacity, 1991 (c.50), s.10(2), sch.2	c. 2
c. 3	*Irish victual*	rep. SLR(S) 1906	c. 3
c. 4	*Supply*	"	c. 4
c. 5	*Royal burghs*	"	c. 5
c. 6	*Summons execution*	rep. Court of Session, 1988 (c.36), s.52(2) sch.2.	c. 6
cc.7–15	Not public and general		—
c.16	**Writs**	rep.in pt. SLR(S) 1906	c. 7
c.17	*Arrestments*	rep. SLR(S) 1906	c. 8
cc.18–19	Not public and general		—
c.20	*Unlawful ordinations*	rep. 1690 c.57	c. 9
c.21	*Sumptuary*	rep. SLR(S) 1906	c.10
c.22	*Baptism*	"	c.11
c.23	*Thanksgiving*	rep. 1690 c.58	c.12

Record Edition Charles II	Title or Subject Matter	How Affected	12mo Edition Charles II
c.24	*Ann*	rep. SLR(S) 1906; Abolition of Feudal Tenure etc. (S), 2000 asp 5, s. 76(2), sch.13 pt. I	c.13
c.25	*Taxed marriages*	rep. SLR(S) 1906	c.14
cc.26–38	Not public and general		—
c.39	*Teind commission*	rep. SLR(S) 1964	c.15
c.40	**Courts**	rep.in pt. 1681 c.109; SLR(S) 1906; SLR(S) 1964; Crim. Procedure (S) 1975 (c.21), s.461 (2) sch.10 pt.I.	c.16
c.41	*Conventicles*	rep. 1690 c.57	c.17
c.42	*Correction houses*	rep. SLR(S) 1906	c.18
cc.43–44	Not public and general		—
c.45	**Adjudications**	rep (prosp) Bankruptcy and Diligence etc. (S), 2007 asp 3, s 226, sch 6 rep.in pt. SLR(S) 1906	c.19
c.46	*Vacant stipends*	rep. SLR(S) 1906	c.20
c.47	**Lyon King of Arms**	rep.in pt. SLR(S) 1906; Debtors (S) 1987 (c.18), s.108(3), sch.8; Requirements of Writing (S) 1995 (c.7), sch.5	c.21
cc.48–54	Not public and general		—
c.55	*Moratorium*	rep. SLR(S) 1906	—
cc.56–57	Not public and general		—
c.58	*Profaneness*	"	c.22
cc.59–147	Not public and general		—
c.148	Not public and general		c.23
c.149	*Adjournment*	"	c.24
1673			**Parl. 2–Sess.4 1673**
c. 1	*Salt*	rep. SLR(S) 1906	Vol. 2, p. 157
c. 2	*Brandy*	"	Vol. 2, p. 519
c. 3	*Sumptuary*	"	Vol. 2, p. 520
c. 4	*Tobacco*	"	Vol. 2, p. 521
1681			**Parl. 3–1681**
c. 1	*Protestant religion*	rep. SLR(S) 1906	c. 1
c. 2	*Sussession to Crown*	rep. 1690 c.7	c. 2
c. 3	*Supply*	rep. SLR(S) 1906	c. 3
c. 4	*Public peace*	rep. 1689 (June 5) c.4 and 1690 c.57	c. 4
c. 5	*Subscription of Deeds*	rep. Requirements of Writing (S) 1995, c.7, sch.5	c. 5
c. 6	*Religion and the test*	rep. 1690 cc.7 and 58	c. 6
c. 7	*Summer session*	rep. 1686 c.6	c. 7
cc.8–9	Not public and general		—
c.10	*Excise*	rep. SLR(S) 1906	c. 8
c.11	*Personal protections*	"	c. 9
c.12	*Terce*	rep. Succession (S) 1964 (c.41), s.34(2) sch.3	c.10
c.13	*Registration in Burgh*	rep. Burgh Registers (S) 1926 (c.50), s.4, sch. 2	c.11
cc.14–76	Not public and general		—
c.78	*Trade*	rep. SLR(S) 1906	c.12
c.79	**Declinature**	rep.(as to Ct of Session) Ct of Session, 1988 (c.36), s.52(2) sch.2 ext. Civil Partnership, 2004 c 33, ss 246, 247, sch 21 para 1	c.13
c.80	*Sumptuary*	rep. SLR(S) 1906	c.15
c.81	*Assassinations*	"	c.15
c.82	*Admiralty Court*	rep. SLR(S) 1964	c.16
c.83	*Judicial sale*	rep. SL(Reps.) 1973 (c.39)	c.17
c.84	*Royal prerogative*	rep. 1690 c. 58	c.18

Record Edition	Title or Subject Matter	How Affected	12mo Edition
Charles II			**Charles II**
c.85	Oaths of Minors	rep. Age of Legal Capacity, 1991 c.50 s.10(2), sch.2	c.19
c.86	**Bills of Exchange**	rep. in pt. Debtors (S.),1987 (c.18), s.108(3), sch.8.	c.20
c.87	Election of Commissioners.	rep. SLR(S) 1906	c.21
c.88	Quorum of Justice Court	"	c.22
c.89	St. Andrews University	"	c.23
c.90	Bread and meat	"	c.24
c.91	Test	"	c.25
c.92	Public debt	"	c.26
c.93	Salt	"	c.27
c.94	Revision of laws	"	—
c.95	Lyon King at Arms	"	—
c.96	Not public and general		—
c.97	Thatching houses	"	—
cc.98–107	Not public and general		—
c.108	Coal and salt	rep. SLR(S) 1964	—
c.109	Advocates, etc.	rep. SLR(S) 1906	—
cc.110–191	Not public and general		—
c.192	Not public and general		c.28
c.193	Adjournment	"	Vol. 2, p. 568
James VII.			**James VII**
1685			**Parl. 1–1685**
c. 1	Protestant religion	rep. SLR(S) 1906	c. 1
c. 2	Supply	rep. 1690 c.58, and SLR(S) 1906	c. 2
c. 3	Treason	rep. SLR(S) 1906	c. 3
c. 4	Treason	"	c. 4
c. 5	The Covenants	rep. 1690 c.58	c. 5
c. 6	Attendance at Ordinances	rep. 1690 cc.57 and 58	c. 6
c. 7	Treason	rep. 1690 c.58	c. 7
c. 8	Conventicles	rep. 1690 cc.57 and 58	c. 8
c. 9	Crown rents	rep. SLR(S) 1906	c. 9
c.10	Judicial confessions	"	c.10
c.11	Refusal of office	rep. 1690 c.58	c.11
c.12	Supply	rep. SLR(S) 1906	c.12
c.13	Test	rep. 1690 c.58	c.13
c.14	Prescription	rep. Prescription and Limitation (S.), 1973 (c.52), s.16 (2), sch. 5 pt.1	c.14
c.15	Interruptions	rep. SLR(S) 1964	c.15
c.16	Justices of Peace	rep. 1690 c.58	c.16
cc.17–20	Not public and general		—
c.21	Oath of allegiance	"	c.17
c.22	Vacant stipends	rep. SLR(S) 1906	c.18
c.23	College of Justice	"	c.19
c.24	Game	"	c.20
c.25	Theft of dogs and hawks	"	c.21
c.26	Entail	rep. 1690 c.104, and SLR(S) 1906; Abolition of Feudal Tenure etc. (S), 2000 asp 5, s. 76(2), sch. 13 pt. 1	c.22
c.27	Trade	rep. SLR(S) 1906	—
c.28	Manufactories	"	—
c.29	Refusals to depone	rep. 1690 c.58	c.23
c.30	Adjudications	"	c.26
c.31	Rebels	"	c.25
c.32	Citations	rep. SLR(S) 1906	c.29
c.33	Sea passengers	rep. 1690 c.58	c.27
c.34	Tenants	rep. 1690 c.57	c.24
c.35	Teind Commission	rep. SLR(S) 1964	c.28
c.36	The Plot	rep. 1690 c.58	c.30

Record Edition	Title or Subject Matter	How Affected	12mo Edition
James VII.			**James VII**
c.37	*Militia*	rep. SLR(S) 1906	c.32
c.38	*Poll money*	″	c.34
c.39	*Records*	rep. 1686 c.42	c.33
c.40	*Messengers' fees*	rep. SLR(S) 1964	c.35
c.41	*Officers of state*	rep. SLR(S) 1906	c.31
c.42	*Ross-shire*	rep. 1686 c.36	—
cc.43–44	Not public and general		—
c.45	*Earl of Argyle*	rep. 1686 c.40 and 1690 c.58	c.36
c.46	*Clergy*	rep. 1690 c.58	c.37
c.47	*Registration*	rep. SLR(S) 1906	c.38
c.48	*Earl of Argyle*	rep. 1686 c.39	—
c.49	*Enclosing ground*	rep. SLR(S) 1906	c.39
c.50	Not public and general		c.45
c.51	*Greenland fishing*	″	c.41
c.52	Not public and general		—
c.53	*Annexation*	rep. 1690 c.58	c.42
c.54	Not public and general		—
c.55	*Annexation*	″	c.40
c.56	*Orkney and Shetland*	rep. SLR(S) 1964	c.43
c.57	*Regulation of Judicatories*	rep. SLR(S) 1906	—
c.58	Not public and general		—
c.59	*Measures*	″	c.44
cc.60–119	Not public and general		—
c.120	Not public and general		c.46
c.121	*Adjournment*	″	c.47
1686			**Parl. 1–Sess.2 1686**
c. 1	*Dissolution*	rep. 1690 c.58	c. 1
c. 2	Not public and general		—
c. 3	*Supply*	rep. SLR(S) 1906	c. 2
c. 4	*Interlocutors*	rep. S.I. 1986/1937	c. 3
c. 5	**Citation**		c. 4
c. 6	*Court of Session*	rep. SLR(S) 1906	c. 5
c. 7	*Christmas vacation*	rep. 1690 c.58	c. 6
c. 8	*Dissolution*	″	c.26
c. 9	Not public and general		—
c.10	*Supply*	rep. SLR(S) 1906	—
c.11	*Dissolution*	rep. 1690 c.58	c. 7
c.12	*Dissolution*	″	c.27
c.13	*Highways and bridges*	rep. SLR(S) 1906	c. 8
c.14	*Supply*	″	—
c.15	Not public and general		—
c.16	*Dissolution*	″	—
c.17	*Annexation*	rep. 1690 c.58	c. 9
c.18	Not public and general		—
c.19	*Dissolution*	″	c.13
c.20	*Process*	rep. SLR(S) 1906	c.10
c.21	*Winter herding*	rep. and superseded, Animals (S.), 1987 (c.9), ss.1, 8(2), sch.	c.11
c.22	Not public and general		c.12
c.23	*Supply*	rep. SLR(S) 1906	—
c.24	*Dissolution*	rep. 1690 c.58	c.28
c.25	Not public and general		c.29
c.26	*Irish victual and cattle*	rep. SLR(S) 1906	c.14
c.27	*Inhibitions*	″	c.15
c.28	*Linen*	″	c.16
c.29	*Sasines*	rep. SLR(S) 1964	c.17
c.30	*Evidence*	rep. S.I. 1986/1937	c.18
c.31	*Regulation of Judicatories.*	rep. SLR(S) 1906	c.23
c.32	*Prohibited imports*	″	—
c.33	*Registration of Sasines*	rep. SLR(S) 1964	c.19

Record Edition James VII.	Title or Subject Matter	How Affected	12mo Edition James VII
c.34	*Teind Commission*	rep. SLR(S) 1964	c.22
c.35	*Clerk to Justices of Peace*	rep. SLR(S) 1906	c.20
c.36	*Repeal of Act*	rep. 1690 cc.47 and 58	—
c.37	Not public and general		c.21
c.38	*Supply*	rep. SLR(S) 1906	c.24
c.39	*Argyle*	”	—
c.40	*Earl of Argyle*	”	c.25
c.41	*Bark*	”	c.30
c.42	*Records*	”	—
c.43	Not public and general		c.31
cc.44–46	Not public and general		—
c.47	*Supply*	”	—
c.48	*Macers of Parliament*	”	—
cc.49–101	Not public and general		—
c.102	Not public and general		c.32
c.103	*Adjournment*	”	c.33
William and Mary			**Estates of Scotland**
1689 (Mar. 14)			**1689**
c. 1	*Declaration as to this meeting*	rep. SLR(S) 1906	c. 2
c. 2	*Public revenue*	”	c. 3
c. 3	*Defence of the realm*	”	c. 4
c. 4	*Militia*	”	—
c. 5	*Military oath*	rep. Promissory Oaths 1871 (c.48), s.1, sch. 2, pt.2	c. 5
c. 6	*Address to Prince of Orange.*	rep. SLR(S) 1906	c. 6
c. 7	*Papists*	”	c. 7
cc.8–9	Not public and general		—
c.10	*Suspect persons*	”	c. 8
c.11	*Defence of the realm*	”	—
Vol. IX, p. 22	*Committee for settling government*	”	c.10
c.12	*Services in western shires*	”	—
c.13	*Glasgow*	”	—
c.14	Not public and general		—
c.15	*Militia*	”	c.11
c.16	*Militia*	”	—
cc.17–19	Not public and general		—
c.20	*Edinburgh*	”	—
c.21	*Glasgow*	”	—
c.22	*Edinburgh*	”	—
c.23	*Suspect persons*	”	c.12
c.24	*Fiars prices*	”	—
cc.25–26	Not public and general		—
c.27	*Glasgow*	”	—
c.28	**The Claim of Right**		c.13
c.29	*Proclamation of King and Queen*	”	c.14
c.30	*Government until acceptance of Crown*	”	c.15
c.31	Not public and general		—
c.32	*Dundee*	”	—
c.33	*Attendance at meeting*	”	—
c.34	*Allegiance to William and Mary*	”	c.16
c.35	*Proclamation of King and Queen*	”	c.17
c.36	*Militia*	”	—
c.37	Not public and general		—
c.38	*Shipping on west coast*	”	c.19

Record Edition	Title or Subject Matter	How Affected	12mo Edition
William and Mary			**Estates of Scotland**
cc.39–42	Not public and general		—
c.43	*Edinburgh*	"	—
c.44	*Rothesy*	"	—
c.45	*Levy of horsemen*	"	c.20
c.46	*Oath by King and Queen*	"	c.21
c.47	*Protestants from Ireland*	"	—
c.48	*Elections of magistrates*	"	c.22
c.49	*Infantry*	"	c.23
c.50	*Irvine*	"	—
c.51	*Shipping*	"	—
c.52	*Two ships for public service*	"	—
c.53	Not public and general		—
c.54	*Cavalry*	"	c.24
c.55	*Garrison in Arran*	"	—
c.56	*Dunnottar Castle*	"	—
c.57	*Shipping*	"	c.25
c.58	*Forage for army*	"	—
c.59	Not public and general		—
c.60	*Union with England*	"	c.26
c.61	*Offer of Crown*	"	c.28
cc.62–67	Not public and general		—
c.68	*Thanksgiving*	"	c.31
c.69	*Collection of Customs*	"	—
cc.70–73	Not public and general		—
c.74	*Supply*	"	c.32
c.75	*Forfeited persons*	"	c.33
cc.76–78	Not public and general		—
c.79	*Irish and French Protestants.*	"	c.34
c.80	*Committee of Estates*	"	c.35
c.81	*Ayr*	"	—
cc.82–83	Not public and general		—
c.84	*Adjournment*	"	c.36
c.85	*Attendance of absent members*	"	—
c.86	*Supply*	"	—
c.87	*Supply*	"	—
cc.88–89	Not public and general		—
c.90	*Montrose*	"	—
c.91	*Supply*	"	—
c.92	*Fencibles in Fife*	"	—
c.93	*Supply*	"	—
c.94	Not public and general		—
c.95	*Glasgow*	"	—
Vol. IX, p. 92	*Payment of forces*	"	c.37
c.96	Not public and general		—
c.97	*Adjournment*	"	c.40
1689 (June 5)			**Parl. 1–1689**
c. 1	*Declaration as to meeting of Estates*	rep. SLR(S) 1906	c. 1
c. 2	*Oath of allegiance*	"	c. 2
c. 3	*Attendance of absent members*	"	—
c. 4	**Prelacy**	rep.in pt. SLR(S) 1906	c. 3
c. 5	*Army*	rep. SLR(S) 1906	—
c. 6	Not public and general		—
c. 7	*Defence of the realm*	"	—
c. 8	Not public and general		c. 4

Record Edition William and Mary	Title or Subject Matter	How Affected	12mo Edition Estates of Scotland
c. 9	Not public and general		c. 5
Vol. IX, p. 100	Adjournment	,,	c. 6

1690 (Apr. 15)

Parl. 1–Sess.2 1690

c. 1	Repeal	rep. SLR(S) 1906	c. 1
c. 2	Presbyterian ministers	,,	c. 2
c. 3	Committees of Parliament	,,	c. 3
c. 4	Oath of allegiance	rep. Promissory Oaths 1871 (c.48), s.1, sch. 2 pt.2	c. 4
c. 5	Not public and general		
c. 6	Courts of Judicature	rep. SLR(S) 1906	—
c. 7	**Confession of Faith Ratification**	rep.in pt. SLR(S) 1906	c. 5
c. 8	Supply	rep. SLR(S) 1906	c. 6
c. 9	Oath of allegiance	,,	c. 7
c.10	Public fast	,,	—
c.11	Oath of allegiance	,,	c. 8
c.12	Poll money	,,	c. 9
c.13	Supply	,,	c.10
c.14	Representation of shires	,,	c.11
c.15	Royal burghs	,,	c.12
c.16	Hornings	rep. SLR(S) 1964	c.13
c.17	Suspect persons	rep. SLR(S) 1906	c.14
c.18	Not public and general		c.15
c.19	Not public and general		—
c.20	Not public and general		c.16
cc.21–22	Not public and general		—
c.23	Sittings of Courts	,,	—
c.24	Not public and general		—
c.25	Universities	,,	c.17
c.26	Recission of forfeitures	,,	c.18
cc.27–36	Not public and general		—
c.37	Supply	,,	—
cc.38–44	Not public and general		—
c.45	Glasgow	,,	—
cc.46, 47	Not public and general		—
c.48	Dissolution	,,	c.19
c.49	Judicial sale	rep. S.L.(R.),1973 (c.39)	c.20
c.50	Child murder	rep. Concealment of Birth (S) 1809 (c.14)	c.21
c.51	Coin	rep. SLR(S) 1906	—
c.52	Christmas vacation	rep. Yule vacance 1711 (c.22)	c.22
c.53	Patronage	rep. SLR(S) 1964	c.23
c.54	Vacant stipends	rep. SLR(S) 1906	c.24
c.55	Profaneness	,,	c.25
c.56	**Confirmation**		c.26
c.57	Repeal	,,	c.27
c.58	Repeal	,,	c.28
c.59	Not public and general		c.29
c.60	Rescission of forfeitures	,,	c.31
c.61	Udal Tenure	rep. SLR(S) 1906; Abolition of Feudal Tenure etc. (S), 2000 asp 5, s. 76(2), sch. 13 pt. I	c.32
c.62	Poindings	rep. SLR(S) 1906	—
c.63	Teinds	rep.SLR(S) 1964; Abolition of Feudal Tenure etc. (S), 2000 asp 5, s. 76(2), sch. 13 pt. I	c.30
cc.64–82	Not public and general		—
c.83	Not public and general		Vol. 3, p. 462

Record Edition	Title or Subject Matter	How Affected	12mo Edition
William and Mary			**Estates of Scotland**
c.84	Not public and general		Vol. 3, p. 464
cc.85–94	Not public and general		—
c.95	Not public and general		c.41
c.96	*Annual rents*	rep. SLR(S) 1906	c.42
c.97	*Prescription*	"	c.40
c.98	*Removings*	"	c.39
c.99	*Security of government*	"	c.38
c.100	*Army*	"	c.37
c.101	*Mint*	"	c.36
c.102	*Ministers*	"	c.35
c.103	*Fishery*	"	c.34
c.104	*Persons forfeited*	"	c.33
c.105	*Process of treason*	"	c.43
cc.106–109	Not public and general		—
c.110	Not public and general		c.44
Vol. IX, p. 230	*Adjournment*	"	c.45
1690 (Sept. 3)			**Parl. 1–Sess.3**
c. 1	Not public and general		—
c. 2	*Highland depredations*	rep. SLR(S) 1906	c. 4
c. 3	*Robbing the packet*	"	c. 3
c. 4	Not public and general		—
c. 5	*Supply*	"	c. 2
c. 6	*Absent members*	"	c. 1
c. 7	*Supply*	"	—
c. 8	*Supply*	"	—
c. 9	Not public and general		—
Vol. IX, p. 238	*Adjournment*	"	c. 6
1693			**Parl. 1–Sess.4 1693**
c. 1	*Members of Parliament*	rep. SLR(S) 1906	—
c. 2	*Members of Parliament*	"	—
c. 3	*Absent members*	"	—
c. 4	*Absent noblemen*	"	—
c. 5	Not public and general		—
c. 6	*Monthly fast*	"	c. 1
c. 7	Not public and general		—
c. 8	*Supply*	"	c. 2
c. 9	*Seamen*	"	—
c.10	*Excise*	"	c. 3
c.11	*Defence of the realm*	"	c. 4
c.12	*Herring and salmon*	"	c. 5
c.13	Not public and general		—
c.14	*Oath of allegiance*	rep. Promissory Oaths 1871 (c.48), s.1, sch. 2, pt.2	c. 6
c.15	*Defence of the realm*	rep. SLR(S) 1906	c. 7
c.16	*France*	"	c. 8
c.17	*Poll money*	"	c. 9
c.18	*Bishop's rents*	"	c.10
c.19	Not public and general		—
c.20	*Adjournment of Session*	"	c.11
c.21	**Citation**	rep.in pt. SLR(S) 1906	c.12
c.22	**Real rights**	rep.in pt. SLR(S) 1906; Land Registration (S.)1979 c.33, s.29(4), sch. 4. am. Abolition of Feudal Tenure etc. (S), 2000 asp 5, s. 76(1), sch. 12 pt. I para. 3	c.13
c.23	**Register of sasines**	mod. Public Registers and Records (S) 1948 (c.57), s.7, sch.	c.14

Record Edition **William and Mary**	Title or Subject Matter	How Affected	12mo Edition **Estates of Scotland**
		rep.in pt. SLR(S.) 1964; Land Registration (S)1979 c.33, s.29(4), sch. 4.	
c.24	**Registration**	c.15	
cc.25–28	Not public and general		—
c.29	*Excise*	rep. SLR(S) 1906	c.16
c.30	*Court of Session*	"	c.17
c.31	*Interlocutors*	rep. S.I. 1986/1937	c.18
c.32	*Court of Session*	rep. SLR(S) 1906	c.19
c.33	*Court of Session*	"	c.20
c.34	*Court of Session*	"	c.21
cc.35–36	Not public and general		—
c.37	*Fast*	"	—
c.38	**Ministers**	rep.in pt. Churches(S) 1905 c.12, s.6(2), sch.2; SLR(S)1906; SLR(S) 1964	c.22
c.39	*Teind Commission*	rep. SLR(S) 1964	c.24
c.40	*Removings*	rep.Term and Quarter Days (S.), 1990 (c.22), s.2(3).	c.23
c.41	*Parsonages*	rep. SLR(S) 1964	c.25
c.42	**Court of Session**	rep.in pt. SLR(S) 1906	c.26
c.43	*Criminal Procedure*	rep.Crim. Procedure(S) 1975 (c.21), s. 461 (2), sch. 10 pt. I.	c.27
c.44	Not public and general		Vol. 3, p. 382
c.45	*Common good*	rep. SLR(S) 1964	c.28
c.46	*Forfeited persons*	rep. SLR(S) 1906	c.31
c.47	Not public and general		—
c.48	*Linen*	"	c.29
c.49	*Baize*	"	—
c.50	*Foreign trade*	"	c.32
c.51	*Burghs*	rep. SLR(S) 1964	c.30
cc.52–59	Not public and general		—
c.60	*Oath of allegiance*	rep. SLR(S) 1906	c.37
c.61	*Court of Session*	"	c.38
c.62	*Justiciary*	"	c.39
c.63	Not public and general		**Parl. 1–Sess.5**
c.64	*Profaneness*	rep. SLR(S) 1906	c.40
cc.64–66	Not public and general		—
c.67	*Universities*	"	c.41
cc.68–70	Not public and general		—
c.71	*Treason*	"	c.33
c.72	*Judicatories*	"	c.34
c.73	*Resignations and sasines*	"	c.35
c.74	Not public and general		c.36
cc.75–88	Not public and general		—
c.89	Not public and general		c.42
Vol. IX, p. 346	*Adjournment*	"	c.43
William 1695			**William Parl. 1–Sess.5 1695**
c. 1	*Fast*	rep. SLR(S) 1906	c. 1
cc.2–3	Not public and general		—
c. 4	*Citations before Parliament.*	"	c. 2
c. 5	*Adjournment of Session*	rep. SLR(S) 1964	c. 3
c. 6	*Justice Court*	"	c. 4
c. 7	*Cautioners*	rep. Prescription and Limitation (S.), 1973 (c.52), s.16 (2), sch. 5 pt.I	c. 5
c. 8	*Judicial sale*	rep. SL(Reps.),1973 (c.39)	c. 6
c. 9	*Supply*	rep. SLR(S) 1906	c. 7

Record Edition	Title or Subject Matter	How Affected	12mo Edition
William			**William**
c.10	Africa Company	rep. SLR(S) 1906	c. 8
c.11	Adjournment of Session	"	c. 9
c.12	Supply	"	c.10
c.13	Not public and general		—
c.14	Blasphemy	rep. 53 Geo. III c.160s.III	c.11
c.15	Baptisms and marriages	rep. Scottish Episcopalians 1711 (c.10)	c.12
c.16	Profaneness	rep. SLR(S) 1906	c.13
c.17	Markets on Sundays	"	c.14
cc.18–25	Not public and general		—
c.26	Vacant churches	rep. Church Patronage (S) 1711 (c.21)	c.15
c.27	Persons restored from forfeiture	rep. SLR(S) 1906	c.16
c.28	Mint	"	c.17
c.29	Teind Commission	"	c.18
c.30	Muslin	rep. 1705 c. 52	c.19
c.31	Post Office	rep. Post Office (Revenues) 1710 (c.11)	c.20
c.32	Brandy	rep. SLR(S) 1906	c.21
cc.33–34	Not public and general		—
c.35	Intrusion into churches	rep. SLR(S) 1964	c.22
c.36	**Runrig Lands**	rep. in pt.SLR(S) 1906	c.23
cc.37–38	Not public and general		—
c.39	Apparent heirs	rep. SLR(S) 1906	c.24
c.40	Fines	"	c.25
c.41	Not public and general		—
c.42	Succession to Papists	"	c.26
cc.43–50	Not public and general		—
c.51	Church	rep. SLR(S) 1964	c.27
c.52	Excise	rep. SLR(S) 1906	c.28
c.53	Excise	"	c.29
c.54	Soil Preservation	rep. SL(Reps.) 1974 (c.22)	c.30
c.55	Supply	rep. SLR(S) 1906	c.31
c.56	Not public and general		—
c.57	Statute law revision	"	—
cc.58–62	Not public and general		—
c.63	Exportation of victual	"	c.32
c.64	Defence of the realm	"	c.33
c.65	Import duties	"	c.34
c.66	Linen	"	c.35
c.67	Skinners	"	c.36
c.68	Justiciary	"	c.37
c.69	**Division of Commonties**	ext. Sheriff Cts (S) 1907 (c.51) s.5(3) mod. (1.4.2015) Courts Reform (S), 2014 asp 18, s 38(3)	c.38
c.70	Rum	rep. 1696 c. 7	c.39
c.71	Signet letters	rep. SLR(S) 1964	c.40
c.72	**Confirmation**		c.41
c.73	Common good	rep. SLR(S) 1906	c.42
c.74	Poor	"	c.43
cc.74–145	Not public and general		—
c.146	Not public and general		c.44
Vol. IX, p. 523	Adjournment	rep.— SLR(S) 1906	c.45
1696			**Parl. 1–Sess.6**
			1696
c. 1	Supply	rep. SLR(S) 1906	c. 1
c. 2	Excise	"	c. 2
c. 3	Public Officers	"	c. 3
c. 4	Death bed	"	c. 4
c. 5	Bankruptcy	rep. Bankruptcy (S), 1985 (c.66), s.75(2), sch.8.	c. 5
c. 6	Meal	rep. SLR(S) 1906	c. 6
c. 7	Rum	"	c. 7

Record Edition	Title or Subject Matter	How Affected	12mo Edition
William			**William**
c. 8	*Tutors and Curators*	rep. Age of Legal Capacity, 1991 (c.50), s.10(2), sch.2	c. 8
c. 9	*Prescription*	rep. Prescription and Limitation (S.), 1973 (c.52), s.16(2), sch. 5 pt.I	c. 9
c.10	*Procedure in Parliament*	rep. SLR(S) 1906	c.10
c.11	*Apparent heirs*	"	c.11
c.12	*Packing and peeling*	"	c.12
c.13	*Vacant churches*	rep. Church Patronage(S) 1711 (c.21)	c.13
c.14	*Universities*	rep. SLR(S) 1964	c.14
c.15	*Deeds*	rep. Requirements of Writing (S) 1995 (c.7), s.14(2), sch.5	c.15
c.16	*Greenlaw*	rep. Berwickshire County Town 1903 (c.5)	c.16
c.17	*Security of kingdom*	rep. 1704 c. 3	c.17
c.18	*Registration of Sasines*	rep. SLR(S) 1964	c.18
c.19	*Interruptions*	rep. Prescription and Limitation (S), 1973 (c.52), s.16(2), sch. 5 pt.I	c.19
c.20	**Vitious Intromitters**		c.20
c.21	*Aliments*	rep. SLR(S) 1906	c.21
c.22	*Suspensions*	"	c.22
c.23	*Defence of the realm*	"	c.23
c.24	*Forfeited estates*	"	c.24
c.25	*Blank Bonds and Trusts*	rep. Requirements of Writing (S) 1995 (c.7), s.14(2), sch.5 excl. Companies, 2006 (c.46), s 742	c.25
c.26	*Education*	rep. Education(S) 1872 (c.62)	c.26
c.27	*Import of victual*	rep. SLR(S) 1906	c.27
c.28	*Servants to Papists*	"	c.28
c.29	*Poor*	"	c.29
c.30	*Supply*	"	c.30
c.31	*Profaneness*	"	c.31
c.32	*Prisons*	"	c.32
cc.33–34	Not public and general		
c.35	*Salmon*	rep. Salmon, 1986 (c.62), s.41, sch.5	c.33
c.36	*Doune*	rep. SLR(S) 1906	c.34
c.37	*Duels*	rep. Duelling(S) 1819 (c.70)	c.35
c.38	**Inland Bills**		c.36
c.39	*Malt measures*	rep. SLR(S) 1906	c.37
c.40	*Coinage*	"	c.38
c.41	**Registration**		c.39
c.42	Not public and general		—
c.43	*Justiciary*	"	c.40
c.44	*Pupils*	"	c.41
c.45	*Coining*	"	c.42
c.46	*Salt in ale*	"	c.43
c.47	*Salt*	"	c.44
cc.48–81	Not public and general		—
c.83	Not public and general		c.45
Vol. X, p. 112	*Adjournment*	"	c.46
1698			**Parl. 1–Sess.7 1698**
c. 1	*Supply*	rep. SLR(S) 1906	c. 1
c. 2	*Vacant churches*	rep. SLR(S) 1964	c. 2
c. 3	*Salmon*	"	c. 3
c. 4	*Registration*	rep. Requirements of Writing (S) (c.7), s.14(2), sch.5	c. 4
c. 5	*Minors*	rep. SLR(S) 1906	c. 5
c. 6	*Clandestine marriages*	rep. SLR(S) 1964	c. 6
c. 7	*Sumptuary*	rep. SLR(S) 1906	c. 7
c. 8	Not public and general		c. 8
c. 9	*Quartering of soldiers*	"	c. 9
c.10	*Quartering for deficiency*	"	c.10
c.11	*Vassals of bishops' lands*	rep. SLR(S) 1964	c.11

Record Edition	Title or Subject Matter	How Affected	12mo Edition
William			**William**
c.12	*Supply*	rep. SLR(S) 1906	c.12
c.13	Not public and general		c.13
c.14	*Macers of Court of Session.*	,,	—
cc.15–32	Not public and general		—
c.33	*College of Justice*	,,	c.14
c.34	*Game*	,,	c.15
c.35	*Planting*	rep. SLR(S) 1964	c.16
c.36	*Travellers to France*	rep. SLR(S) 1906	c.17
c.37	*Tonnage*	,,	c.18
c.38	*Burghs*	,,	c.19
c.39	*Trade*	rep. SLR(S) 1964	c.20
c.40	*Poor*	rep. SLR(S) 1906	c.21
c.41	*Personal protections*	,,	c.22
c.42	*Brandy*	,,	c.23
c.43	*Sea fishing*	,,	c.24
c.44	*Supply*	,,	c.26
cc.45–46	Not public and general		—
c.47	*Supply*	,,	c.26
c.48	Not public and general		—
c.49	Not public and general		c.27
Vol. X, p. 182	*Adjournment*	,,	c.28
1700			**Parl. 1 – Sess.8 & 9 1700**
c. 1	*Adjournment of Session*	rep. SLR(S) 1906	c. 1
c. 2	*Act of Security*	,,	c. 2
c. 3	*Popery*	,,	c. 3
c. 4	*Adjournment of Session*	,,	c. 4
c. 5	*Adjournment of Session*	,,	c. 5
c. 6	**Criminal Procedure**	rep. in pt.Criminal Procedure(S) 1887 c.35 s.43; SLR(S)1906; SLR(S) 1964; Crim. Procedure(S) 1975 c.21, s.461 (2), sch. 10 pt.I.	c. 6
c. 7	*King's prerogative*	rep. SLR(S) 1906	c. 7
c. 8	*Foreign wool*	,,	c. 8
c. 9	*Export of wool*	,,	c. 9
c.10	Not public and general		—
c.11	*French wines*	,,	c.10
c.12	*Profaneness*	,,	c.11
c.13	*Import of silks*	,,	c.12
c.14	*African Company*	,,	c.13
c.15	*Quots of testaments*	,,	c.14
c.16	*Supply*	,,	c.15
cc.17–52	Not public and general		—
c.53	*Supply*	,,	c.16
c.54	Not public and general		c.17
Vol. X, p. 341	*Adjournment*	,,	c.18
Anne			**Anne**
1702			**1702**
c. 1	*Queen's authority*	rep. SLR(S) 1906	c. 1
c. 2	*Adjournment of Session*	,,	c. 2
c. 3	*Act of Security*	,,	c. 3
c. 4	*Declaration as to present meeting*	,,	c. 4
c. 5	*Fast*	,,	c. 5
c. 6	*Supply*	,,	c. 6
c. 7	*Union*	,,	c. 7
c. 8	*Justiciary*	,,	c. 8
Vol. XI, p. 28	*Adjournment*	,,	c. 9

Record Edition	Title or Subject Matter	How Affected	12mo Edition
Anne			**Anne**
1703			**Parl. 1–Sess.1**
			1703
c. 1	*Queen's authority*	"	c. 1
c. 2	*Act of Security*	"	c. 2
c. 3	*Parliament of 1689*	"	c. 3
c. 4	*Leasing makers*	"	c. 4
c. 5	Not public and general		—
c. 6	*Peace and war*	rep. 1707 (6 Ann) (c.36)	c. 5
c. 7	*Public accounts*	rep. SLR(S) 1906	c. 6
c. 8	*Butchers*	"	c. 7
c. 9	*African Company*	"	c. 8
c.10	*Importation of Irish victual.*	"	c. 9
c.11	*Export of wool*	"	c.10
c.12	Not public and general		—
c.13	*Importation of wines*	"	c.11
1704			**Parl. 1–Sess.2**
			1704
c. 1	*Adjournment of Session*	rep. SLR(S) 1906	c. 1
c. 2	Not public and general		c. 2
c. 3	*Security of kingdom*	rep. 1707 (6 Ann) (c.36)	c. 3
c. 4	*Supply*	rep. SLR(S) 1906	c. 4
c. 5	*Commissioners of Justiciary.*	"	c. 5
c. 6	*Export of wood*	"	c. 6
c. 7	*Public accounts*	"	c. 7
c. 8	Not public and general		—
c. 9	*Duty on foreign shipping*	"	c. 8
1705			**Parl. 1–Sess.3**
			1705
cc.1–46	Not public and general		—
c.47	*Butter and cheese*	rep. SLR(S) 1906	c. 1
c.48	**Fisheries**	rep. in pt.SLR(S) 1906	c. 2
c.49	*Council of trade*	rep. SLR(S) 1906	c. 3
c.50	*Treaty with England*	"	c. 4
c.51	*Beef and pork*	"	c. 5
c.52	*Linen and wool*	"	c. 6
c.53	*Supply*	"	c. 7
c.54	Not public and general		—
c.55	Not public and general		c. 8
c.56	Not public and general		c. 9
Vol. XI, p. 299	*Adjournment*	"	c.10
1706-7			**Parl. 1–Sess.4**
			1706
c. 1	*Adjournment of Session*	rep. SLR(S) 1906	c. 1
c. 2	*Supply*	"	c. 2
c. 3	*Musters of fencibles*	"	c. 3
c. 4	*Adjournment of Session*	"	c. 4
			1707
c. 5	*Adjournment of Session*	rep. SLR(S) 1906	c. 5
c. 6	**Protestant Religion and Presbyterian Church**	rep. in pt.Churches(S) 1905 (c.12) s.6(2) S. 6(2) sch.2; SLR(S)1964: mod. Universities(S) 1932 c.26 s.5	c. 6
c. 7	**Union with England**	rep. in pt.SLR(S) 1906; Criminal Justice 1948 (c.58) s.83 (3) sch. 10, Pt. III; Peerage 1963 (c.48), s.7(2), sch.2; SLR(S) 1964	c. 7
c. 8	*Election*	rep. in pt.SLR(S) 1906; Peerage 1963 (c.48), s.7(2), sch. 2; SLR(S) 1964; Representation of the People, 1969 (c.15), s.24 (4), sch. 3, pt.II	

Record Edition **Anne**	*Title or Subject Matter*	*How Affected*	*12mo Edition* **Anne**
		residue rep. Electoral Admin, 2006 c 22, s 17(7)(b), sch 2	
c. 9	Not public and general		—
c.10	*Kirks and teinds*	rep. SLR(S) 1964	c. 9
c.11	*Musters of fencibles*	rep. SLR(S) 1906	c.10
cc.12–83	Not public and general		—
c.84	Not public and general		c.11
c.85	Not public and general		—
c.86	Not public and general		c.12
cc.87–90	Not public and general		—
c.91	*Game*	rep. SLR(S) 1964	c.13
cc.93–93	Not public and general		—
c.94	*Wool*	rep. SLR(S) 1906	c.14
c.95	Not public and general		—
c.96	*African Company*	,,	c.15
c.97	*Public debts*	,,	c.16
c.98	Not public and general		c.17
Vol. XI, p. 491	*Adjournment*	,,	c.18

Chronological Table of the

Acts of the Scottish Parliament

1999

asp 1   *Mental Health (Public Safety and Appeals) (Scotland)*—rep Mental Health (Care and
            Treatment) (S), 2003 asp 13, s 331(2), sch 5 pt 1

2000

asp 1   **Public Finance and Accountability (Scotland)**
            s 4 mod—Budget (S), 2014 asp 6, s 6(4); Budget (S), 2015 asp 2, s 6(4)
            s 9 am—Finance (No 2), 2005 c 22, s 47(1); Land Registration etc (S), 2012 asp 5, sch 5
                    para 37; Revenue Scotland and Tax Powers, 2014 asp 16, sch 4 para 3
                rep in pt—Scotland, 2012 c 11, sch 3 para 32
            s 10 mod—Local Govt (S), 1973 c 65, s 103H
                am—Public Services Reform (S), 2010 asp 8, s 118(2)
                restr —SSI 2010/322, art 4
            s 11 am—Crim Justice and Licensing (S), 2010 asp 13, s 97(2)(a), (b)
            s 12 am—Public Services Reform (S), 2010 asp 8, s 118(3)
            s 13 rep in pt—SI 2007/825, reg 4
                am—Public Services Reform (S), 2010 asp 8, s 118(4)
                restr—SSI 2010/322, art 6
            s 21 am—SI 2008/948, art 3, sch 1; SSI 2013/177, sch para 4(b)
                rep in pt—SSI 2013/177, sch para 4(a)
            s 22 am—Public Services Reform (S), 2010 asp 8, s 118(5)
            s 23 am—Water Industry (S), 2002 asp 3, s 71(2), sch 7 para 27(1)(2); Water Services etc
                    (S), 2005 asp 3, s 32, sch 5 para 5; Public Services Reform (S), 2010 asp 8, s
                    118(6)
                mod—Police and Fire Reform (S), 2012 asp 8, s 43
            s 23A added—Public Services Reform (S), 2010 asp 8, s 118(7)
                appl—Police and Fire Reform (S), 2012 asp 8, s 42(7)
            s 24 appl—Police and Fire Reform (S), 2012 asp 8, s 42(7)
            Pt 2A (ss 26A-26G) added—Crim Justice and Licensing (S), 2010 asp 13, s 97(3)
            s 26D am—Budget Responsibility and Nat Audit, 2011 c 4, sch 5 para 24; (prosp) Loc
                    Audit and Accountability, 2014 c 2, sch 12 para 47(2)(3)
            sch 1 rep in pt—Housing (S), 2001 asp 10, s 112, sch 10, para 28(1); Water Industry (S),
                    2002 asp 3, s 71(2), sch 7 para 27(1)(3)(a); (prosp) Nat Health Service Reform
                    (S), 2004 asp 7, s 11(2), sch 2
            sch 2 am—Public Services Reform (S), 2010 asp 8, s 118(8)
                rep in pt—Public Services Reform (S), 2010 asp 8, s 118(8)(a)(ii), (e)(i)
                restr—SSI 2010/322, art 4
                excl—SSI 2010/322, art 5
            sch 3 am—Public Services Reform (S), 2010 asp 8, s 118(9)
            sch 4 rep in pt—Housing (S), 2001 asp 10, s 112, sch 10, para 28(2); Water Industry (S),
                    2002 asp 3, s 71(2), sch 7, para 27(1)(3)(b); Smoking, Health and Social Care
                    (S), 2005 asp 13, s 42(2), sch 3; Further and Higher Educ (S), 2005 asp 6, s 32,
                    sch 3 para 8; Nat Library of S, 2012 asp 3, sch 3

asp 2   **Budget (Scotland)**
            s 4 am—SSIs 2001/7, art 2(1)(2); 68, art 2(1)(2)
            Pt 2 (s 5) am—Budget (S), 2001 asp 4, s 8
            sch 1 am—SSIs 2000/307, art 2(2); 2001/7, art 2(1)(3), sch 1; 68, art 2(1)(3)(b), sch 1
                rep in pt—SSI 2001/68, art 2(1)(3)(a)
            sch 2 am—SSIs 2000/307, art 2(3)(4); 2001/7, art 2(1)(4); 268, art 2(1)(4)
            sch 3 am—SSIs 2000/307 art 2(5); 2001/7, art 2(1)(5); 68, art 2(1)(5), sch 2

asp 3   **Census (Amendment) (Scotland)**
asp 4   **Adults with Incapacity (Scotland)**
            appl—Equal Pay, 1970 c 41, s 11(2A)(b); Human Tissue, 2004 c 30, s 45, sch 4 pt 2,
                    para 12(1)(a)(ii); SI 2005/3448, reg 7(3)(b)
            appl (mods)—SI 2010/1907, reg 16(2)(c), (3)

2000
asp 4 *continued*

s 1 appl—Regulation of Care (S), 2001 asp 8, s 25(7)(a)(14)(a); Licensing (S), 2005 asp 16, ss 28(5)(c)(ii), 34(3)(a)(ii)
 am—SSI 2005/465, art 2, sch 1 para 28(1)(2)
s 3 am—Adult Support and Protection (S), 2007 asp 10, s 55
s 4 am—Adult Support and Protection (S), 2007 asp 10, s 56
s 6 am—Adult Support and Protection (S), 2007 asp 10, ss 67, 77, sch 1 para 5(a); SSI 2015/157, sch para 4(2)
s 9 rep in pt—Mental Health (Care and Treatment) (S), 2003 asp 13, s 331(2), sch 5 pt 1
 am—SSI 2015/157, sch para 4(3)
s 10 power to am—Joint Inspection of Children's Services and Inspection of Social Work Services (S), 2006 asp 3, s 7(2)(3)
s 12 rep in pt—Mental Health (Care and Treatment) (S), 2003 asp 13, s 331(2), sch 5 pt 1
s 15 am—Adult Support and Protection (S), 2007 asp 10, s 57(1)(2)
s 16 am—Human Tissue (S), 2006 asp 4, s 57(2); Adult Support and Protection (S), 2007 asp 10, s 57(1)(2)
s 16A added—Adult Support and Protection (S), 2007 asp 10, s 57(3)
s 19 am—Adult Support and Protection (S), 2007 asp 10, s 57(4)
s 19A added—SSI 2008/380, art 2
s 20 rep in pt—Adult Support and Protection (S), 2007 asp 10, s 57(5)
s 22 rep in pt—Adult Support and Protection (S), 2007 asp 10, s 57(6)
s 22A added—Adult Support and Protection (S), 2007 asp 10, s 57(7)
s 23 rep in pt—Adult Support and Protection (S), 2007 asp 10, s 57(8)
s 24 am—Family Law (S), 2006 asp 2, s 36
Pt 3 (ss 25-34) replaced by Pt 3 (ss 24A-24D, 25, 26, 26A-26G, 27, 27A-27H, 28A, 29, 30, 30A, 30B, 31, 31A-31E, 32, 33)—Adult Support and Protection (S), 2007 asp 10, s 58
Pt 4 (ss 35-46) appl —Regulation of Care (S), 2001 asp 8, s 8
s 35 am —Regulation of Care (S), 2001 asp 8, s 79, sch 3, para 23(1)(2); Mental Health (Care and Treatment) (S), 2003 asp 13, s 331(1), sch 4, para 9(1)(2); SSIs 2005/610, reg 2; 2011/211, sch 1 para 8(2), sch 2 para 5(2)
 rep in pt—Mental Health (Care and Treatment) (S), 2003 asp 13, s 331(2), sch 5 pt 1
s 36 rep—Regulation of Care (S), 2001 asp 8, s 80(1), sch 4
s 37 appl—SSIs 2003/155, reg 3(4); 266, reg 3(4)
 am—SSI 2005/465, art 2, sch 1 para 28(1)(4)
s 38 rep —Regulation of Care (S), 2001 asp 8, s 80(1), sch 4
s 39 am—Adult Support and Protection (S), 2007 asp 10, s 77, sch 1 para 5(b); Welfare Reform, 2007 c 5, s 28, sch 3 para 22(1)(2); SSI 2013/137, reg 6(2)
s 40 am—Regulation of Care (S), 2001 asp 8, s 79, sch 3, para 23(1)(3); SSI 2011/211, sch 1 para 8(3), sch 2 para 5(3)
s 41 am—SSI 2005/465, art 2, sch 1 para 28(1)(5); Adult Support and Protection (S), 2007 asp 10, s 77, sch 1 para 5(c); Welfare Reform, 2007 c 5, s 28, sch 3 para 22(1)(3); SSI 2013/137, reg 6(3)
s 45 am—Regulation of Care (S), 2001 asp 8, s 79, sch 3, para 23(1) (4)(a)(b)(e)
 rep in pt—Regulation of Care (S), 2001 asp 8, s 79, sch 3, para 23(1)(4)(c)(d)
s 47 am—Mental Health (Care and Treatment) (S), 2003 asp 13, s 331(1), sch 4, para 9(1)(3); Smoking, Health and Social Care (S), 2005 asp 13, s 35(1)(2); Adult Support and Protection (S), 2007 asp 10, s 77, sch 1 para 5(d)
 rep in pt—Mental Health (Care and Treatment) (S), 2003 asp 13, s 331(2), sch 5 pt 1; Adult Support and Protection (S), 2007 asp 10, s 77, sch 2
s 48 rep in pt—Mental Health (Care and Treatment) (S), 2003 asp 13, s 331(2), sch 5 pt 1
ss 49, 50 am—Smoking, Health and Social Care (S), 2005 asp 13, s 35(1)(3)(4)
s 51 appl—SI 2004/1031, reg 2(1), sch 1 pt 1 para 2
 am—SIs 2004/1031, reg 54, sch 10 pt 1 para 21; 2006/2984, reg 3
s 53 am—Adult Support and Protection (S), 2007 asp 10, s 59(1)
s 55 am—Adult Support and Protection (S), 2007 asp 10, s 59(2)
s 56 am—Land Registration etc (S), 2012 asp 5, sch 5 para 38(2)
s 56A added—Adult Support and Protection (S), 2007 asp 10, s 59(3)
s 57 am—Mental Health (Care and Treatment) (S), 2003 asp 13, s 331(1), sch 4, para 9(1)(4); Adult Support and Protection (S), 2007 asp 10, s 60(1)(2)
 rep in pt—Mental Health (Care and Treatment) (S), 2003 asp 13, s 331(2), sch 5 pt 1
 appl—SI 2003/762, reg 2(2)(k)
s 58 am—Adult Support and Protection (S), 2007 asp 10, s 60(1)(2)
s 60 am—Adult Support and Protection (S), 2007 asp 10, s 60(3)

2000

asp 4 *continued*

s 61 am—Adult Support and Protection (S), 2007 asp 10, s 60(4); Land Registration etc (S), 2012 asp 5, sch 5 para 38(3)

s 62 am—Adult Support and Protection (S), 2007 asp 10, s 60(5)

s 63 am—Adult Support and Protection (S), 2007 asp 10, s 60(6)

s 64 am—Human Tissue (S), 2006 asp 4, s 57(3); Adult Support and Protection (S), 2007 asp 10, s 60(7)

s 66 am—SSI 2005/465, art 2, sch 1 para 28(1)(6)(7)(8)

s 70 am—Adult Support and Protection (S), 2007 asp 10, s 60(8)

s 71 am—Adult Support and Protection (S), 2007 asp 10, s 60(9)

s 72 am—SSI 2005/465, art 2, sch 1 para 28(1)(6)(7)(8); Adult Support and Protection (S), 2007 asp 10, s 60(10)

s 73 am—SSI 2005/465, art 2, sch 1 para 28(1)(6)(7)(8); Adult Support and Protection (S), 2007 asp 10, s 60(11)

s 73A added—Adult Support and Protection (S), 2007 asp 10, s 60(12)

s 74 am—Adult Support and Protection (S), 2007 asp 10, s 60(13)

s 75 am—Adult Support and Protection (S), 2007 asp 10, s 60(13)

s 75A added—Adult Support and Protection (S), 2007 asp 10, s 60(15)

s 79A added—Adult Support and Protection (S), 2007 asp 10, s 60(16)

s 81A added—Adult Support and Protection (S), 2007 asp 10, s 61
  mod —(temp) SSI 2007/334, art 3

s 84 am—Regulation of Care (S), 2001 asp 8, s 79, sch 3, para 23(1)(5)

s 84A added—Human Fertilisation and Embryology, 2008 c 22, s 65, sch 7 para 18

s 84B added—Human Fertilisation and Embryology, 2008 c 22, s 65, sch 7 para 18

s 87 am—Mental Health (Care and Treatment) (S), 2003 asp 13, s 331(1), sch 4, para 9(1)(5); SSI 2005/465, art 2, sch 1 para 28(1)(9); Adult Support and Protection (S), 2007 asp 10, ss 57(9), 77, sch 1 para 5(e)

  rep in pt—Mental Health (Care and Treatment) (S), 2003 asp 13, s 331(2), sch 5 pt 1; Civil Partnership, 2004 c 33, s 261(4), sch 30

  appl—SI 2004/1031, reg 2(1), sch 1 pt 1 para 2

sch 1 am—Regulation of Care (S), 2001 asp 8, s 79, sch 3, para 23(1)(6); SSI 2011/211, sch 1 para 8(4), sch 2 para 5(4)

  rep in pt—Mental Health (Care and Treatment) (S), 2003 asp 13, s 331(2), sch 5 pt 1

sch 2 am—SI 2001/3649, Pt. 7, Ch I, art 235; Adult Support and Protection (S), 2007 asp 10, s 77, sch 1 para 5(f)-(h)

sch 3 am—Adult Support and Protection (S), 2007 asp 10, s 77, sch 1 para 5(f)-(h)

sch 4 am—Adult Support and Protection (S), 2007 asp 10, ss 60(17), 77, sch 1 para 5(f)-(h)

sch 5 am—Regulation of Care (S), 2001 asp 8, s 79, sch 3, para 23(1)(7)

  rep in pt—Regulation of Care (S), 2001 asp 8, s 80(1), sch 4; Mental Health (Care and Treatment) (S), 2003 asp 13, s 331(2), sch 5 pt 1; Adult Support and Protection (S), 2007 asp 10, s 77, sch 2

asp 5   **Abolition of Feudal Tenure etc (Scotland)**

s 4 rep —Land Registration etc (S), 2012 asp 5, sch 5 para 39(2)

Pt IV (ss 17-49) appl—Conveyancing and Feudal Reform (S), 1970 c 35, s 9(2B)

s 17 rep in pt—Title Conditions (S), 2003 asp 9, s 128(2), sch 15

  am—Title Conditions (S), 2003 asp 9, ss 81(2)(a), 114(6), sch 13 paras 1, 2

  excl—Title Conditions (S), 2003 asp 9, s 63(9)

s 18 am—Title Conditions (S), 2003 asp 9, s 114(6), sch 13 paras 1, 3

s 18A added—Title Conditions (S), 2003 asp 9, s 114(1)(2)

  am—Land Registration etc (S), 2012 asp 5, sch 5 para 39(3)

s 18B added—Title Conditions (S), 2003 asp 9, s 114(1)(2)

s 18C added—Title Conditions (S), 2003 asp 9, s 114(1)(2)

  rep in pt—(prosp) Nat Health Service Reform (S), 2004 asp 7, s 11(2), sch 2

s 20 rep in pt—Title Conditions (S), 2003 asp 9, ss 114(6), 128(2), sch 13 paras 1, 4(a)(b)(ii), sch 15; SSI 2003/503, art 2, sch 1 pt I, paras 3, 4(a)

  am—Title Conditions (S), 2003 asp 9, s 114(6), sch 13, paras 1, 4(b)(i); SSI 2003/503, art 2, sch 1 pt I, paras 3, 4(b)

s 23 rep—Title Conditions (S), 2003 asp 9, s 128(2), sch 15

s 24 rep in pt—Title Conditions (S), 2003 asp 9, s 128(2), sch 15

s 25 am—Title Conditions (S), 2003 asp 9, s 114(6), sch 13, paras 1, 5

s 26 rep—Title Conditions (S), 2003 asp 9, s 128(2), sch 15

s 27 am—Title Conditions (S), 2003 asp 9, s 114(6), sch 13, paras 1, 6

s 27A added—Title Conditions (S), 2003 asp 9, s 114(1)(3)

s 28 rep in pt—Title Conditions (S), 2003 asp 9, s 128(2), sch 15

2000
asp 5 *continued*

    s 28A added—Title Conditions (S), 2003 asp 9, s 114(1)(4)

    ss 29-32 rep—Title Conditions (S), 2003 asp 9, s 128(2), sch 15

    s 42 am—Title Conditions (S), 2003 asp 9, s 114(6), sch 13, paras 1, 7

    s 43 am—Title Conditions (S), 2003 asp 9, s 114(6), sch 13, paras 1, 8

    s 46 rep—Land Registration etc (S), 2012 asp 5, sch 5 para 39(4)

    s 49 am—Title Conditions (S), 2003 asp 9, s 114(6), sch 13, paras 1, 10

        rep in pt—Title Conditions (S), 2003 asp 9, s 128(2), sch 15

    s 54 am—Title Conditions (S), 2003 asp 9, s 114(6), sch 13, paras 1, 11

    s 56 am—Title Conditions (S), 2003 asp 9, s 114(6), sch 13, paras 1, 12

    s 60 rep in pt—Title Conditions (S), 2003 asp 9, s 128(2), sch 15

    s 63 am—Land Registration etc (S), 2012 asp 5, sch 5 para 39(5)

    s 65 rep—Land Registration etc (S), 2012 asp 5, sch 5 para 39(6)

    s 65A added—Title Conditions (S), 2003 asp 9, s 114(1)(5)

        appl—Land Registration (S) 1979 c 33, s 28(1)

        rep in pt—Land Registration etc (S), 2012 asp 5, sch 5 para 39(7)

    s 67 excl—Glasgow Airport Rail Link, 2007 asp 1, s 30(4); Edinburgh Airport Rail Link,
        2007 asp 16, s 36(5)

    s 73 am—Title Conditions (S), 2003 asp 9, s 114(6), sch 13, paras 1, 13(a)(i)(iii), (b)(c)

        rep in pt—Title Conditions (S), 2003 asp 9, s 114(6), sch 13, paras 1, 13(a)(ii)

    s 75 am—Title Conditions (S), 2003 asp 9, s 114(6), sch 13, paras 1, 14

    s 77 am—Title Conditions (S), 2003 asp 9, s 114(6), sch 13, paras 1, 15

        rep in pt—Title Conditions (S), 2003 asp 9, s 128(2), sch 15; SSI 2003/503, art 2,
        sch 1 pt I, paras 3, 5

    schs 1-11A power to am—Title Conditions (S), 2003 asp 9, s 128(3)(b)

    schs 5A-5C added—Title Conditions (S), 2003 asp 9, s 114(6), sch 13, paras 1, 16

    sch 8 rep in pt—Title Conditions (S), 2003 asp 9, s 128(2), sch 15

        am—Title Conditions (S), 2003 asp 9, s 114(6), sch 13, paras 1, 17

    sch 8A added—Title Conditions (S), 2003 asp 9, s 114(6), sch 13, paras 1, 18

    sch 11A added—Title Conditions (S), 2003 asp 9, s 114(6), sch 13, paras 1, 19

    sch 12 rep in pt—Title Conditions (S), 2003 asp 9, s 128(2), sch 15; (prosp) Housing (S),
        2006 asp 1, s 192(2), sch 7; SI 2008/1277, art 30(3), sch 4; Flood Risk
        Management (S), 2009 asp 6, s 96, sch 3, para 11; Corporation Tax, 2010 c 4, s
        1181, sch 3, pt 1; (1.8.2016) Housing (S), 2014 asp 14, sch 2 para 9

        am—Title Conditions (S), 2003 asp 9, s 114(6), sch 13, paras 1, 20

    sch 13 rep in pt—Title Conditions (S), 2003 asp 9, s 128(2), sch 15

asp 6   **Standards in Scotland's Schools etc (Scotland)**

    s 2A added—Schools (Health Promotion and Nutrition) (S), 2007 asp 15, s 1

    s 5 am—Gaelic Language (S), 2005 asp 7, s 9(3); Scottish Schools (Parental Involvement),
        2006 asp 8, s 2(6); Schools (Health Promotion and Nutrition) (S), 2007 asp 15, s 2

    s 6 am—Scottish Schools (Parental Involvement), 2006 asp 8, ss 3, 18(5)

    s 7 am—Scottish Schools (Parental Involvement), 2006 asp 8, s 4

    ss 10A-10C added—School Educ (Ministerial Powers and Independent Schools (S), 2004
        asp 12, s 2

    s 24 rep in pt —School Educ (Ministerial Powers and Independent Schools (S), 2004 asp 12,
        s 8(2), sch 2

    ss 26-31 rep—Scottish Schools (Parental Involvement), 2006 asp 8, s 23, sch

    s 34 am—Children and Young People (S), 2014 asp 8, sch 5 para 7(1)(b)

    ss 43,44 rep in pt—Educ (Additional Support for Learning) (S), 2004 asp 4, s 33, sch 3 para
        11

    ss 45-54 rep—SSI 2011/215, sch 7

    s 58 am—Title Conditions (S), 2003 asp 9, s 128(1), sch 14, para 12; School Educ
        (Ministerial Powers and Independent Schools (S), 2004 asp 12, s 8(1), sch 1 para
        2; Land Registration etc (S), 2012 asp 5, sch 5 para 40

        rep in pt—Scottish Schools (Parental Involvement), 2006 asp 8, s 23, sch; SSI
        2011/215, sch 7

    sch 1 rep—Scottish Schools (Parental Involvement), 2006 asp 8, s 23, sch

    sch 2 rep in pt—Scottish Schools (Parental Involvement), 2006 asp 8, s 23, sch; Equality,
        2010 c 15, s 211(2), sch 27 pt 1 (as subst by SI 2010/2279, sch 2); SSI
        2011/215, sch 7

    sch 3 rep in pt—SSI 2011/215, sch 7

2000

asp 7 **Ethical Standards in Public Life etc (Scotland)**
trans of functions—S Parl Commn and Commrs, 2010 asp 11, s 2(1)(a)
s 8 am—S Public Services Ombudsman, 2002 asp 11, s 25(1), sch 6 para 21; S Parl Commn and Commrs, 2010 asp 11, s 29, sch 2, para 1
s 9 subst—S Parl Commn and Commrs, 2010 asp 11, s 2, sch 1 pt 1, para 1
am—SSI 2013/197, sch 2 para 2
s 10 am—S Parl Commn and Commrs, 2010 asp 11, s 2, sch 1 pt 1, paras 2-4, 9; SSI 2013/197, sch 2 para 3
s 11 am —S Parl Commn and Commrs, 2010 asp 11, s 2, sch 1 pt 1, paras 2, 5, 6, 9; SSI 2013/197, sch 2 para 3
s 12 am—S Parl Commn and Commrs, 2010 asp 11, s 2, sch 1 pt 1, paras 2, 4, 9
rep in pt—SSI 2013/197, sch 2 para 4
s 13 am —S Parl Commn and Commrs, 2010 asp 11, s 2, sch 1 pt 1, paras 2, 4, 6, 9
rep in pt—SSI 2013/197, sch 2 para 5
s 14 am —S Parl Commn and Commrs, 2010 asp 11, s 2, sch 1 pt 1, paras 2, 4, 9
rep in pt—SSI 2013/197, sch 2 para 5
s 16 am—S Parl Commn and Commrs, 2010 asp 11, s 2, sch 1 pt 1, paras 2, 4
s 17 am—S Parl Commn and Commrs, 2010 asp 11, s 29, sch 2, para 2
s 19 rep in pt—Water Services etc (S), 2005 asp 3, s 32, sch 5 para 6(a)
s 21 am —S Parl Commn and Commrs, 2010 asp 11, s 2, sch 1 pt 1, paras 2, 4
s 22 am—SSI 2015/402, sch para 4
s 23 am—S Parl Commn and Commrs, 2010 asp 11, s 2, sch 1 pt 1, para 2
ss 25, 26 rep—Water Services etc (S), 2005 asp 3, s 32, sch 5 para 6(b)
s 27 rep—SSI 2013/197, sch 2 para 6
s 28 am—S Parl Commn and Commrs, 2010 asp 11, s 2, sch 1 pt 1, para 7; SSI 2013/197, sch 2 para 7
s 30 rep in pt—Water Services etc (S), 2005 asp 3, s 32, sch 5 para 6(c)
sch 1 rep in pt—Water Services etc (S), 2005 asp 3, s 32, sch 5 para 6(d); S Parl Commn and Commrs, 2010 asp 11, s 29, sch 2, paras 4, 11, 15
am—S Parl Commn and Commrs, 2010 asp 11, ss 2, 29, sch 1 pt 1, paras 2, 8, sch 2, paras 4, 5-10, 12-14, 16; SSI 2013/197, sch 2 para 8(a)(b)
sch 2 rep —S Parl Commn and Commrs, 2010 asp 11, s 29, sch 2, para 17
sch 3 rep in pt—Water Industry (S), 2002 asp 3, s 71(2), sch 7 para 28(a); Public Appointments and Public Bodies etc.(S), 2003 asp 4, s 17, sch 4, para 15; SSI 2003/119, art 2(1)(2)(a); Further and Higher Educ (S), 2005 asp 6, s 32, sch 3 para 9(b); Public Services Reform (S), 2010 asp 8, s 1, sch 1, para 28; ibid, s 43, sch 10 para 1(b); ibid, s 106, sch 14, para 1(a); ibid, s 110, sch 17, para 24(a); Police and Fire Reform (S), 2012 asp 8, sch 8 pt 1; Historic Environment Scotland, 2014 asp 19, sch 6 para 1(a)
am—Water Industry (S), 2002 asp 3, s 71(2), sch 7 para 28(b); SSI 2002/201, art 15(1); 2003/1, art 15(1); 119, art 2(1)(2)(b); 279, art 2; 2004/543, art 2; Water Services etc (S), 2005 asp 3, s 32, sch 5 para 6(e); Further and Higher Educ (S), 2005 asp 6, s 32, sch 3 para 9(a); Transport (S), 2005 asp 12, s 4, sch 1 para 17; Gaelic Language (S), 2005 asp 7, s 12, sch 2 para 1; Charities and Trustee Investment (S), 2005 asp 10, s 104, sch 4 pt 1 para 12; Management of Offenders etc (S), 2005 asp 14, s 21(9); Smoking, Health and Social Care (S), 2005 asp 13, s 42(2), sch 3; Police, Public Order and Crim Justice (S), 2006 asp 10, sch 6 para 7; Tourist Boards (S), 2006 asp 15, sch 2 para 6; Legal Profession and Legal Aid (S), 2007 asp 5, s 81, sch 5 para 4; Judiciary and Cts (S), 2008 asp 6, s 9, sch 1 para 19; Climate Change (S), 2009 asp 12, s 99, sch 2 para 3; SSI 2009/286, art 2; Public Services Reform (S), 2010 asp 8, s 43, sch 10 para 1(a); ibid, s 106, sch 14, para 1(b); ibid, s 110, sch 17, para 24(b); Crofting Reform (S), 2010 asp 14, s 55, sch 4, para 4; Housing (S), 2010 asp 17, s 162, sch 2, para 6; SSI 2011/113, art 2; Nat Library of S, 2012 asp 3, sch 2 para 4; Police and Fire Reform (S), 2012 asp 8, sch 1 para 14; ibid, sch 7 para 61; SI 2012/1659, sch 3 para 23; Post-16 Educ (S), 2013 asp 12, sch para 4; Revenue Scotland and Tax Powers, 2014 asp 16, sch 4 para 4; Historic Environment Scotland, 2014 asp 19, sch 6 para 1(b); Food (S), 2015 asp 1, s 17(1); SSI 2015/157, sch para 5

asp 8 **Education and Training (Scotland)**
s 1 am—SSI 2000/292, reg 10

asp 9 **Bail, Judicial Appointments etc (Scotland)**
ss 8-10 rep —Crim Proceedings etc. (Reform) (S), 2007 asp 6, s 80, sch para 27(a)
s 11 rep —Crim Proceedings etc. (Reform) (S), 2007 asp 6, s 80, sch para 27(b)
sch rep in pt—Crim Proceedings etc. (Reform) (S), 2007 asp 6, s 80, sch para 27(c)

2000

asp 10　　**National Parks (Scotland)**

　　　　　s 9 mod—Town and Country Planning (S), 1997 c 8, s 26(6J)

　　　　　ss 11, 12 mod—SSI 2007/268, art 4

　　　　　s 15 am—Land Registration etc (S), 2012 asp 5, sch 5 para 41(a)(b)

　　　　　　　rep in pt—Land Registration etc (S), 2012 asp 5, sch 5 para 41(c)

　　　　　ss 23-26 appl (mods)—SSIs 2002/201, art 14; 2003/1, art 14

　　　　　s 27 rep in pt—Public Records (S), 2011 asp 12, s 14(d)

　　　　　sch 1 excl —SSIs 2002/201, art 7(5); 2003/1, art 7(18)

　　　　　　　restr —(para 18 restr) SSI 2004/473, art 2

　　　　　sch 2 am—SI 2009/1941, art 2, sch 1 para 186

　　　　　sch 5 rep in pt—S Public Services Ombudsman, 2002 asp 11, s 25(1), sch 6 para 22

asp 11　　**Regulation of Investigatory Powers (Scotland)**

　　　　　appl—Regulation of Investigatory Powers, 2000 c 23, s 76A

　　　　　s 2 am—Constitutional Reform, 2005 c 4, s 40(4), sch 9 pt 1 para 73; SI 2009/1941, art 2,
　　　　　　　sch 1 para 187 aw check

　　　　　s 5 am—Police and Fire Reform (S), 2012 asp 8, sch 7 para 15(2)

　　　　　s 8 am—SSI 2010/420, art 2; Police and Fire Reform (S), 2012 asp 8, sch 7 para 15(3)

　　　　　　　rep in pt—SSI 2010/350, art 4

　　　　　s 9 rep —Police and Fire Reform (S), 2012 asp 8, sch 8 pt 1

　　　　　s 10 am—Police, Public Order and Crim Justice (S), 2006 asp 10, sch 6 para 9(3); Crim
　　　　　　　Justice and Licensing (S), 2010 asp 13, s 106(2)(a), (b); Police and Fire Reform
　　　　　　　(S), 2012 asp 8, sch 7 para 15(4)

　　　　　　　rep in pt—Police and Fire Reform (S), 2012 asp 8, sch 8 pt 1

　　　　　s 10A added —Crim Justice and Licensing (S), 2010 asp 13, s 106(3)

　　　　　　　rep —Police and Fire Reform (S), 2012 asp 8, sch 8 pt 1

　　　　　s 11 am—Police, Public Order and Crim Justice (S), 2006 asp 10, sch 6 para 9(4); Crim
　　　　　　　Justice and Licensing (S), 2010 asp 13, s 106(4); Police and Fire Reform (S),
　　　　　　　2012 asp 8, sch 7 para 15(5)

　　　　　s 11 rep in pt—Police and Fire Reform (S), 2012 asp 8, sch 8 pt 1

　　　　　s 12 rep —Police and Fire Reform (S), 2012 asp 8, sch 8 pt 1

　　　　　s 12A added—Police, Public Order and Crim Justice (S), 2006 asp 10, sch 6 para 9(6)

　　　　　　　rep —Police and Fire Reform (S), 2012 asp 8, sch 8 pt 1

　　　　　s 12ZA added —Police and Fire Reform (S), 2012 asp 8, sch 7 para 15(6)

　　　　　s 13 see—SSI 2000/340, arts 3-5

　　　　　s 14 am—Police, Public Order and Crim Justice (S), 2006 asp 10, sch 6 para 9(7); Crim
　　　　　　　Justice and Licensing (S), 2010 asp 13, s 106(6)(a); Police and Fire Reform (S),
　　　　　　　2012 asp 8, sch 7 para 15(7)

　　　　　　　rep in pt —Crim Justice and Licensing (S), 2010 asp 13, s 106(6)(b); Police and Fire
　　　　　　　　Reform (S), 2012 asp 8, sch 8 pt 1

　　　　　s 15 am—Police, Public Order and Crim Justice (S), 2006 asp 10, sch 6 para 9(8)

　　　　　　　rep in pt—Police and Fire Reform (S), 2012 asp 8, sch 8 pt 1

　　　　　s 16 am—Police, Public Order and Crim Justice (S), 2006 asp 10, sch 6 para 9(9); Crim
　　　　　　　Justice and Licensing (S), 2010 asp 13, s 106(7); Police and Fire Reform (S),
　　　　　　　2012 asp 8, sch 7 para 15(8)

　　　　　　　rep in pt—Police and Fire Reform (S), 2012 asp 8, sch 8 pt 1

　　　　　s 18 am—Police, Public Order and Crim Justice (S), 2006 asp 10, sch 6 para 9(10); Police
　　　　　　　and Fire Reform (S), 2012 asp 8, sch 7 para 15(9)

　　　　　　　rep in pt—Police and Fire Reform (S), 2012 asp 8, sch 8 pt 1

　　　　　s 19 mod—SSI 2014/339 arts 6, 8

　　　　　s 20 am—Police, Public Order and Crim Justice (S), 2006 asp 10, sch 6 para 9(11); Police
　　　　　　　and Fire Reform (S), 2012 asp 8, sch 7 para 15(10)

　　　　　　　rep in pt—Police and Fire Reform (S), 2012 asp 8, sch 8 pt 1

　　　　　s 23 am—Police, Public Order and Crim Justice (S), 2006 asp 10, sch 6 para 9(12)' Police
　　　　　　　and Fire Reform (S), 2012 asp 8, sch 7 para 15(11)(a)(b)

　　　　　　　rep in pt—Police and Fire Reform (S), 2012 asp 8, sch 7 para 15(11)(c)

　　　　　s 24 see—SSIs 2003/181, art 2, 183, art 2

　　　　　　　am—Police, Public Order and Crim Justice (S), 2006 asp 10, sch 6 para 9(13); Police
　　　　　　　　and Fire Reform (S), 2012 asp 8, sch 7 para 15(12)(a)(b)

　　　　　　　rep in pt—Police and Fire Reform (S), 2012 asp 8, sch 7 para 15(12)(c)

　　　　　s 26 am—Police and Fire Reform (S), 2012 asp 8, sch 7 para 15(13)

　　　　　s 31 am—Police, Public Order and Crim Justice (S), 2006 asp 10, sch 6 para 9(14); Crim
　　　　　　　Justice and Licensing (S), 2010 asp 13, s 106(8); Police and Fire Reform (S),
　　　　　　　2012 asp 8, sch 7 para 15(14)

　　　　　　　rep in pt—Police and Fire Reform (S), 2012 asp 8, sch 8 pt 1

2000

asp 12   **Sea Fisheries (Shellfish) Amendment (Scotland)**

2001

asp 1   *Abolition of Poindings and Warrant Sales*—rep Debt Arrangement and Attachment (S), 2002
        asp 17, s 61, sch 3 pt 1 para 27

asp 2   **Transport (Scotland)**
        cert functions trans—SSIs 2006/527, art 3, sch 1; 538, art 3, sch 1
        s 5 am—SSI 2001/218, reg 5; Police and Fire Reform (S), 2012 asp 8, sch 7 para 16
        ss 28, 29 mod—Edinburgh Tram (Line Two), 2006 asp 6, s 54(2); Edinburgh Tram (Line
              One), 2006 asp 7, s 54(2)
        s 41 am—Transport (S), 2005 asp 12, s 50
        s 48 am—Transport (S), 2005 asp 12, s 51(1)(2); Police and Fire Reform (S), 2012 asp 8,
              sch 8 pt 1
        s 49 am—Abolition of Bridge Tolls (S), 2008 asp 1, s 3, sch 1 para 2
        s 53 am—Statistics and Registration Service, 2007 c 18, s 60, sch 3 para 12
        s 54 am—Transport (S), 2005 asp 12, s 51(1)(3)
        s 64 am—Transport (S), 2005 asp 12, s 51(1)(4)
        s 66 am—Transport (S), 2005 asp 12, s 51(1)(5)
        s 68 am—Loc Govt in S, 2003 asp 1, s 44(2)
            power to am—Loc Govt in S, 2003 asp 1, s 44(3)
        s 69 rep in pt—Abolition of Bridge Tolls (S), 2008 asp 1, s 3, sch 2 pt 1
        s 70 am—Transport (S), 2005 asp 12, s 45(3)-(6); Transport and Works (S), 2007 asp 8, s
              27
        s 79 am—Transport (S), 2005 asp 12, s 51(1)(6)
        s 81 am—Transport (S), 2005 asp 12, s 51(1)(7)
        s 82 am—Transport (S), 2005 asp 12, s 51(1)(8)
        sch 1 am—Transport (S), 2005 asp 12, s 51(1)(9)(b)
            rep in pt—Transport (S), 2005 asp 12, s 51(1)(9)(a)

asp 3   **Salmon Conservation (Scotland)**
        rep (except in relation to rivers Tweed and Upper Esk)—Salmon and Freshwater Fisheries
              (Consolidation) (S), 2003 asp 15, s 70(2), sch 4 pt 2
        rep (river Tweed)—SI 2006/2913, art 76(3), sch 4 pt 2

asp 4   **Budget (Scotland)**
        s 3 am—SSIs 2001/480, art 2(1)(2), sch 1; 2002/134, art 2(1)(2), sch 1; Budget (S), 2003
              asp 6, s 8(a)
        s 5 am—SSIs 2001/480, art 2(1)(3); 2002/134, art 2(1)(3)
        Pt 2 (s 6) rep—Budget (S), 2002 asp 7, s 8
        sch 1 subst—SSI 2001/480, art 2(1)(4), sch 2
            am—SSI 2002/134, art 2(1)(4)(a)(c), sch 2; Budget (S), 2003 asp 6, s 8(b)
            rep in pt—SSI 2002/134, art 2(1)(4)(b)
        sch 2 am—SSIs 2001/480, art 2(1)(5); 2002/134, art 2(1)(5), sch 3
        sch 3 am—SSIs 2001/480, art 2(1)(6), sch 3; 2002/134, art 2(1)(6)
        sch 4 am—SSI 2002/134, art 2(1)(7)

asp 5   **Leasehold Casualties (Scotland)**
asp 6   **Education (Graduate Endowment and Student Support) (Scotland)**
        ss 1, 2 rep—Graduate Endowment Abolition (S), 2008 asp 3, s 1(1)
asp 7   **Convention Rights (Compliance) (Scotland)**
        s 10 rep in pt—Sexual Offences (S), 2009 asp 9, s 61, sch 6
        sch am—Crim Justice (S), 2003 asp 7, ss 39(a)(b), 85, sch 4 para 5
asp 8   **Regulation of Care (Scotland)**
        appl —SI 1987/1971, reg 27(h); Adoption and Children, 2002 c 38, s 131(1)(d); SSI
              2002/217, reg 2(5); Protection of Children (S), 2003 asp 5, s 18(1), sch 2 para 12
        Pt 1 (ss 1-32) rep —Public Services Reform (S), 2010 asp 8, s 106, sch 14, para 37
            transtl saving—SSI 2011/169, arts 2,3
        Pt 2 (ss 33-42) rep —Public Services Reform (S), 2010 asp 8, s 106, sch 14, para 37
        s 44 am—SI 2007/3101, reg 257
        s 45 am—SI 2007/3101, reg 258
        s 46 am—SI 2007/3101, reg 259; Public Services Reform (S), 2010 asp 8, s 107, sch 15,
              para 2(b)
            rep in pt—Public Services Reform (S), 2010 asp 8, s 107, sch 15, para 2(a), (c)
        ss 46A, 46B added—SI 2007/3101, reg 260
        s 47 am—SI 2007/3101, reg 261; Public Services Reform (S), 2010 asp 8, s 107, sch 15,
              para 3

2001

asp 8 *continued*

s 48 am—Smoking, Health and Social Care (S), 2005 asp 13, s 30(1)(4); Public Services Reform (S), 2010 asp 8, s 107, sch 15, paras 4(b), 5

rep in pt—Public Services Reform (S), 2010 asp 8, s 107, sch 15, para 4(a)

s 49 am—Public Services Reform (S), 2010 asp 8, s 107, sch 15, para 6

s 50 am—SI 2007/3101, reg 262; Public Services Reform (S), 2010 asp 8, s 107, sch 15, para 7(d)(i)(iii), (e), 8

rep in pt—Public Services Reform (S), 2010 asp 8, s 107, sch 15, para 7(a)-(c), (d)(ii)

s 51 am—Smoking, Health and Social Care (S), 2005 asp 13, s 30(1)(5); SI 2007/3101, reg 263; Public Services Reform (S), 2010 asp 8, s 107, sch 15, para 9(a)(b), (c)(i)(iii)

rep in pt—Public Services Reform (S), 2010 asp 8, s 107, sch 15, para 9(c)(ii)

s 53 am —Public Services Reform (S), 2010 asp 8, s 106, sch 14, para 3; ibid, s 107, sch 15, para 10

s 57 am—SI 2007/3101, reg 264

ss 57A, 57B added—Smoking, Health and Social Care (S), 2005 asp 13, s 32

s 59 rep in pt —Public Services Reform (S), 2010 asp 8, s 106, sch 14, para 4(a)

am —Public Services Reform (S), 2010 asp 8, s 106, sch 14, para 4(b)

s 60 rep in pt —Public Services Reform (S), 2010 asp 8, s 106, sch 14, paras 2, 5(a)

am —Public Services Reform (S), 2010 asp 8, s 106, sch 14, para 5(b)(c)

s 61 rep in pt —Public Services Reform (S), 2010 asp 8, s 106, sch 14, para 6

s 62 rep in pt —Public Services Reform (S), 2010 asp 8, s 106, sch 14, paras 7(a)(b)

am —Public Services Reform (S), 2010 asp 8, s 106, sch 14, para 7(c)(d)

s 63 rep in pt —Public Services Reform (S), 2010 asp 8, s 106, sch 14, para 8(a)

am —Public Services Reform (S), 2010 asp 8, s 106, sch 14, para 8(b)

s 64 am —Public Services Reform (S), 2010 asp 8, s 106, sch 14, para 9; ibid, s 107, sch 15, para 11(a)(i), (b)

rep in pt—Public Services Reform (S), 2010 asp 8, s 107, sch 15, para 11(a)(ii)

s 65 rep in pt —Public Services Reform (S), 2010 asp 8, s 106, sch 14, para 10(a)-(d), (e)(i), (f)

am —Public Services Reform (S), 2010 asp 8, s 106, sch 14, para 10(e)(ii)-(v)

s 66 rep—S Public Services Ombudsman, 2002 asp 11, s 25(1), sch 6 para 24

s 68 am—SSI 2013/211, sch 1 para 11

s 70 rep—SSI 2014/90, sch pt 1

s 73 am—Children and Young People (S), 2014 asp 8, sch 5 para 8

s 74 rep—SSI 2013/211, sch 2

s 76 rep—SSI 2013/211, sch 2

s 77 subst—SSI 2011/211, art, sch 1, para 9

am—SSI 2013/177, sch para 5

s 78 am—Smoking, Health and Social Care (S), 2005 asp 13, s 31(1)(3); Protection of Vulnerable Groups (S), 2007 asp 14, s 83

sch 1 rep —Public Services Reform (S), 2010 asp 8, s 106, sch 14, para 37

sch 3 rep in pt—SI 2001/2478, art. 2; Mental Health (Care and Treatment) (S), 2003 asp 13, s 331(2), sch 5 pt 1; Serious Organised Crime and Police, 2005 c 15, s 174(2), sch 17 pt 2; Adoption and Children (S), 2007 asp 4, s 120, sch 3; Sexual Offences (S), 2009 asp 9, s 61, sch 6; Taxation (International and Other Provns), 2010 c 8, s 378, sch 10, pt 13

asp 9   **Scottish Local Authorities (Tendering) (Scotland)**

asp 10   **Housing (Scotland)**

appl—Civil Partnership, 2004 c 33, s 112(12)

restr—Immigration, Asylum and Nationality, 2006 c 13, s 43(5)

s 5 am—(prosp) Housing (S), 2014 asp 14, sch 2 para 10(2)

s 11 am—SSI 2003/331, art 2, sch pt 1, para 8(1)(2)(a)(i)(b); (prosp) Housing (S), 2014 asp 14, s 12(1)(b)

rep in pt—SSI 2003/331, art 2, sch pt 1, para 8(1)(2)(a)(ii); (prosp) Housing (S), 2014 asp 14, s 12(1)(a)

s 14 am—Homelessness etc. (S), 2003 asp 10, s 11(2), sch para 4(1)(2); Housing (S), 2010 asp 17, s 155(a); Housing (S), 2014 asp 14, s 14(1)

s 14A added—Housing (S), 2010 asp 17, s 155(b)

s 16 am —Housing (S), 2010 asp 17, s 153(a); (1.8.2016) Housing (S), 2014 asp 14. sch 2 para 10(3)

s 23 am—(1.8.2016) Land Registration etc (S), 2012 asp 5, sch 5 para 42(a)

rep in pt—(1.8.2016) Housing (S), 2014 asp 14, sch 2 para 10(3)

s 24 am—Land Registration etc (S), 2012 asp 5, sch 5 para 42(b)

2001

asp 10 *continued*

s 31 am—Civil Partnership, 2004 c 33, s 261(2), sch 28 pt 4 para 63

s 32 rep in pt—(prosp) Housing (S), 2014 asp 14, s 12(2)(a)(i)(c)(i)
   am—(prosp) Housing (S), 2014 asp 14, s 12(2)(a)(ii)-(iv)(b)(c)(ii)

s 34 am—Housing (S), 2014 asp 14, s 7(1)(b); (prosp) ibid, s 9(1)(a)(b)
   rep in pt—(prosp) Housing (S), 2014 asp 14, s 7(1)(a)

s 35 am—Antisocial Behaviour etc (S), 2004 asp 8, s 144(1), sch 4 para 6(1)(2); (prosp)
      Housing (S), 2014 asp 14, ss 7(2)(a)(b)(ii)(iii)(c), 9(2)(a)(b)
   rep in pt—(prosp) Housing (S), 2014 asp 14, s 7(2)(b)(i)

s 35A added (prosp)—Housing (S), 2014 asp 14, s 10(1)

s 36 am—Homelessness etc. (S), 2003 asp 10, s 11(2), sch para 4(1)(3); (prosp) Housing (S),
      2014 asp 14, s 11(a)-(f)

s 37 rep in pt—(prosp) Housing (S), 2014 asp 14, s 10(2)(a)(i)
   am—(prosp) Housing (S), 2014 asp 14, ss 9(3), 10(2)(a)(ii)(iii)(b)(c)

ss 42-51 rep (prosp)—Housing (S), 2014 asp 14, sch 2 para 10(4)

s 52 rep—Housing (S), 2014 asp 14, s 1(2)

s 56 am—SSI 2003/331, art 2, sch pt 1, para 8(1)(3)

s 57 rep —Housing (S), 2010 asp 17, s 162, sch 2, para 7(2)

s 58 rep —Housing (S), 2010 asp 17, s 162, sch 2, para 7(2)

ss 59-68 rep —Housing (S), 2010 asp 17, s 162, sch 2, para 7(2)

s 68A added—Housing (S), 2006 asp 1, s 177

ss 69-75 rep —Housing (S), 2010 asp 17, s 162, sch 2, para 7(3)

s 76 rep in pt —Housing (S), 2010 asp 17, s 162, sch 2, para 7(4)

s 79 rep —Housing (S), 2010 asp 17, s 162, sch 2, para 7(5)

ss 80-82 rep —Housing (S), 2010 asp 17, s 162, sch 2, para 7(5)

s 83 am—SI 2009/1941, art 2, sch 1 para 191(4); Co-operative and Community Benefit
      Societies, 2014 c 14, sch 4 para 79(2)(a)(b)(3)

s 89 am—Housing (S), 2006 asp 1, s 10

s 92 saved—Loc Govt in S, 2003 asp 1, s 22(14)
   rep in pt—Housing (S), 2006 asp 1, s 192(2), sch 7

s 93 rep in pt—Housing (S), 2006 asp 1, s 192(2), sch 7

s 94 rep in pt—Loc Govt Finance (Unoccupied Properties etc.) (S), 2012 asp 11, s 4(c)

Pt 6 (ss 96-105) rep —Housing (S), 2006 asp 1, s 192(2), sch 7

s 108 ext—Civil Partnership, 2004 c 33, ss 246, 247, sch 21 para 50
   am—Civil Partnership, 2004 c 33, s 261(2), sch 28 pt 4 para 64

s 109 am —Housing (S), 2010 asp 17, ss 153(b), 155(c); SSI 2011/445, art 2

s 111 rep in pt —Housing (S), 2010 asp 17, s 162, sch 2, para 7(6)

sch 1 am—Fire (S), 2005 asp 5, s 89(1), sch 3 para 20; SI 2005/1379, sch para 15; SSI
      2009/248, art 2, sch 1 para 9; Housing (S), 2010 asp 17, s 154(b), (c); SSI
      2013/119, sch 1 para 18
   rep in pt —Housing (S), 2010 asp 17, s 154(a); Police and Fire Reform (S), 2012 asp
      8, sch 8 pt 2

sch 2 am—Civil Partnership, 2004 c 33, s 261(2), sch 28 pt 4 para 65; (prosp) Housing (S),
      2014 asp 14, s 15(a)(b)

sch 3 am—Civil Partnership, 2004 c 33, s 261(2), sch 28 pt 4 para 66; (prosp) Housing (S),
      2014 asp 14, s 13(a)-(d)

sch 5 am—Housing (S), 2006 asp 1, s 54(a)(b); Equality, 2006 c 3, s 40, sch 3 para 62

sch 6 am—Antisocial Behaviour etc (S), 2004 asp 8, s 144(1), sch 4 para 6(1)(3); (prosp)
      Housing (S), 2014 asp 14, ss 7(4)(a)(b), 8

sch 7 rep —Housing (S), 2010 asp 17, s 162, sch 2, para 7(2)

sch 8 rep —Housing (S), 2010 asp 17, s 162, sch 2, para 7(2)

sch 9 rep in pt —Housing (S), 2010 asp 17, s 162, sch 2, para 7(7)

sch 10 rep in pt—(prosp) Housing (S), 2006 asp 1, s 192(2), sch 7; Co-operative and
      Community Benefit Societies, 2014 c 14, sch 7; Hosuing (S), 2014 asp 14, sch
      2 para 10(5)(a); (1.8.2016) ibid, sch 2 para 10(5)(b); (prosp) ibid, sch 2 para
      10(5)(c)

asp 11 **Mortgage Rights (Scotland)**

ss 1-3 rep—Home Owner and Debtor Protection (S), 2010 asp 6, s 8(4)(a)

s 4 am—Title Conditions (S), 2003 asp 9, s 128(1), sch 14, para 13; Homelessness etc. (S),
      2003 asp 10, s 11(2), sch, para 5(a)(ii)(b)(c)
   rep in pt—Homelessness etc. (S), 2003 asp 10, s 11(2), sch, para 5(a)(i); Home Owner
      and Debtor Protection (S), 2010 asp 6, s 8(4)(b)

sch am —SSI 2010/318, art 2, sch, pt 2

asp 12 *Erskine Bridge Tolls*—rep Abolition of Bridge Tolls (S), 2008 asp 1, s 3, sch 2 pt 1

2001

asp 13   **International Criminal Court (Scotland)**
      mod—SI 2009/317, art 3, sch
      appl (mods)—SI 2011/245, sch 6 pt 1
      s 4 am —Bribery, 2010 c 23, s 17, sch 1, para 6
      s 7 appl—Extradition, 2003 c 41, ss 64(7)(f), 65(7)(f), 137(6)(f), 138(6)(f) (see SI
            2003/3103, arts 2-5)
      s 8A added —Crim Justice and Licensing (S), 2010 asp 13, s 32(2)
      ss 9A, 9B added —Crim Justice and Licensing (S), 2010 asp 13, s 33
      s 10 rep—Sexual Offences (Procedure and Evidence) (S), 2002 asp 9, s 9
      s 15 am—Police and Fire Reform (S), 2012 asp 8, sch 7 para 17
      s 24 am—Management of Offenders etc (S), 2005 asp 14, s 21(10)
      s 25 rep—Mental Health (Care and Treatment) (S), 2003 asp 13, s 331(2), sch 5 pt 1
      s 28 rep in pt —Crim Justice and Licensing (S), 2010 asp 13, s 32(3)
      sch 6 rep in pt—(prosp) Bankruptcy and Diligence etc. (S), 2007 asp 3, s 226, sch 6 pt 1
            am—SSI 2014/293, sch para 2

asp 14   **Protection from Abuse (Scotland)**
      s 1 am—Family Law (S), 2006 asp 2, s 32(2)(3)
        rep in pt—Family Law (S), 2006 asp 2, s 45(2), sch 3
      s 3 am—Police and Fire Reform (S), 2012 asp 8, sch 7 para 18
      s 6 rep—Family Law (S), 2006 asp 2, s 45(2), sch 3

asp 15   *Police and Fire Services (Finance) (Scotland)*—rep Police and Fire Reform (S), 2012 asp 8,
      sch 8 pt 1
      s 2 rep—Fire (S), 2005 asp 5, s 89(2), sch 4

2002

asp 1   **Scottish Local Government (Elections)**
      s 1 rep —S Loc Govt Elections, 2009 asp 10, s 1, sch 1 para 3
      s 5 am—Loc Electoral Admin and Registration Services (S), 2006 asp 14, ss 25, 35, sch 2
      para 14

asp 2   **School Education (Amendment) (Scotland)**
      s 2 rep in pt—S Schools (Parental Involvement), 2006 asp 8, s 23, sch

asp 3   **Water Industry (Scotland)**
      Pt 1 (ss 1-6C) am —Public Services Reform (S), 2010 asp 8, s 3, sch 2, para 7
      s 1 subst—Water Services etc (S), 2005 asp 3, s 1(1)
      s 2 rep —Public Services Reform (S), 2010 asp 8, s 3, sch 2, para 21
      s 2A added —Public Services Reform (S), 2010 asp 8, s 3, sch 2, para 2
            am—SI 2014/631, sch 1 para 15(2)(a)-(c)
      s 3 am—Water Services etc (S), 2005 asp 3, s 32, sch 5 para 7(1)(2)
        rep in pt—Water Services etc (S), 2005 asp 3, s 3(2)
      s 4 am—Water Services etc (S), 2005 asp 3, s 32, sch 5 para 7(1); Public Services Reform
            (S), 2010 asp 8, s 3, sch 2, para 3; SI 2014/631, sch 1 para 15(3)
      s 5 am—Water Services etc (S), 2005 asp 3, ss 1(3), 32, sch 5 para 7(1)(3)(a); Public
            Services Reform (S), 2010 asp 8, s 3, sch 2, para 4(a), (b), (c)(i); SI 2014/631, sch
            1 para 15(4)
        rep in pt—Water Services etc (S), 2005 asp 3, s 32, sch 5 para 7(3)(b); Public Services
            Reform (S), 2010 asp 8, s 3, sch 2, para 4(c)(ii)
      s 6 am—Water Services etc (S), 2005 asp 3, s 32, sch 5 para 7(1); Public Services Reform
            (S), 2010 asp 8, s 3, sch 2, paras 1, 5, 6; SI 2014/631, sch 1 para 15(5)(a)-(c)
      ss 6A-6C added—Water Services etc (S), 2005 asp 3, s 3(3)
          rep —Public Services Reform (S), 2010 asp 8, s 3, sch 2, para 21
      s 11 am—Water Services etc (S), 2005 asp 3, s 32, sch 5 para 7(1); SSI 2010/95, reg 6
      s 25 am—SI 2009/1941, art 2, sch 1 para 200; Water Resources (S), 2013 asp 5, s 23
      s 26 am—Water Services etc (S), 2005 asp 3, s 32, sch 5 para 7(1)(4)(a)
        rep in pt—Water Services etc (S), 2005 asp 3, s 32, sch 5 para 7(1)(4)(b)
      s 27 am—Water Services etc (S), 2005 asp 3, s 32, sch 5 para 7(1); Public Services Reform
            (S), 2010 asp 8, ss 3, 130(2), sch 2, para 8; SI 2014/631, sch 1 para 15(6)(a)(b)
      s 28 am —Public Services Reform (S), 2010 asp 8, ss 3, 130(3), sch 2, para 9; SI 2014/631,
            sch 1 para 15(7)(a)(b)
      s 29 replaced (by ss 29-29G)—Water Services etc (S), 2005 asp 3, s 21(1)
      s 29B am—Public Services Reform (S), 2010 asp 8, ss 3, 130(4)(b), sch 2, para 10; SI
            2014/631, sch 1 para 15(8)
        rep in pt—Public Services Reform (S), 2010 asp 8, s 130(4)(a)
      s 29D am —Public Services Reform (S), 2010 asp 8, ss 3, 130(5), sch 2, para 11; SI
            2014/631, sch 1 para 15(9)

2002

asp 3 *continued*

s 30 am—Water Services etc (S), 2005 asp 3, s 21(2)

ss 31-34 rep—Water Services etc (S), 2005 asp 3, s 21(3)

s 35 am—Water Services etc (S), 2005 asp 3, s 21(4)

s 35A added—Water Services etc (S), 2005 asp 3, s 21(5)

s 40 rep —Water Services etc (S), 2005 asp 3, s 32, sch 5 para 7(5)

s 42 rep in pt—Water Resources (S), 2013 asp 5, s 27(2)

    am—Water Resources (S), 2013 asp 5, s 27(3)

ss 42A, 42B added—Water Resources (S), 2013 asp 5, s 27(1)

s 43 am—SI 2009/1941, art 2, sch 1 para 200

s 46 am—Water Environment and Water Services (S), 2003 asp 3, s 33(2), sch 3, para 24

s 49 am—Water Services etc (S), 2005 asp 3, s 32, sch 5 para 7(6)

s 50A added—Water Resources (S), 2013 asp 5, s 24

s 51A added—Water Resources (S), 2013 asp 5, s 25

s 54 am—Nature Conservation (S), 2004 asp 6, s 57, sch 7 para 13(a)(d)(i)(ii)

s 56 am—Climate Change (S), 2009 asp 12, s 74

s 56A added —Water Services etc (S), 2005 asp 3, s 22

    am—Public Services Reform (S), 2010 asp 8, ss 3, 130(6), sch 2, para 12; SI 2014/631, sch 1 para 15(10)

s 56B added—Water Services etc (S), 2005 asp 3, s 22

s 57 am—Water Services etc (S), 2005 asp 3, s 32, sch 5 para 7(1)(7); Public Services Reform (S), 2010 asp 8, ss 3, 130(7), sch 2, para 13; SI 2014/631, sch 1 para 15(11)

s 58 rep in pt—Public Records (S), 2011 asp 12, s 14(e)

s 68 am—Water Services etc (S), 2005 asp 3, s 32, sch 5 para 7(8)

s 70 appl—Control of Pollution, 1974 c 40, s 62(2)(a); Loc Govt in S, 2003 asp 1, s 47(2)

    am—Water Services etc (S), 2005 asp 3, s 32, sch 5 para 7(9)(a)(b); Public Services Reform (S), 2010 asp 8, s 130(8); Water Resources (S), 2013 asp 5, s 26; SI 2014/631, sch 1 para 15(12)

sch A1 added—Water Services etc (S), 2005 asp 3, s 1(4), sch 1

sch 1 rep in pt—Water Services etc (S), 2005 asp 3, s 32, sch 5 para 7(10); Public Services Reform (S), 2010 asp 8, s 3, sch 2, para 21

    am—Water Services etc (S), 2005 asp 3, s 32, sch 5 para 7(1)

sch 4 am—Debt Arrangement and Attachment (S), 2002 asp 17, s 61, sch 3 pt 1 para 28; Bankruptcy and Diligence etc. (S), 2007 asp 3, s 226, sch 5 para 26

sch 7 rep in pt—Fire (S), 2005 asp 5, s 89(2), sch 4; Transport and Works (S), 2007 asp 8, s 29, sch 3; Flood Risk Management (S), 2009 asp 6, s 96, sch 3 para 13; Marine (S), 2010 asp 5, s 167, sch 4, para 9; (prosp) Reservoirs (S), 2011 asp 9, s 112(3); Regulatory Reform (S), 2014 asp 3, sch 3 para 15; (prosp) Housing (S), 2014 asp 14, sch 2 para 11

asp 4   **Criminal Procedure (Amendment) (Scotland)**

s 1 am—SSI 2002/233, art 2

s 13 saved—Nat Health Service (S), 1978 c 29, s 16A(5)

asp 5   **Community Care and Health (Scotland)**

power to am—Joint Inspection of Children's Services and Inspection of Social Work Services (S), 2006 asp 3, s 7(2)(3)

s 1 am—SSI 2011/211, sch 1 para 10(a)

s 2 am—Mental Health (Care and Treatment) (S), 2003 asp 13, s 28(2)(a); Adult Support and Protection (S), 2007 asp 10, s 65(2)

s 4 am—Mental Health (Care and Treatment) (S), 2003 asp 13, s 331(1), sch 4, para 12(1)(2)

rep in pt—Adult Support and Protection (S), 2007 asp 10, s 62(3)

s 5 am—Care, 2014 c 23, sch 1 para 3(4)(a)-(c); (prosp) ibid, para 10(2)

    mod—SSI 2015/202, reg 2(1)

s 6 am—Mental Health (Care and Treatment) (S), 2003 asp 13, s 331(1), sch 4, para 12(1)(3)

s 7 rep—SSI 2014/90, sch pt 1

s 12 am—SSI 2011/211, sch 1 para 10(b)

ss 13-15 ext—Health Protection Agency, 2004 c 17, s 4(5)(d)(e)

ss 15-17 rep—Public Bodies (Joint Working) (S), 2014 asp 9, s 71(3)

    cont for specified purpose—SSI 2015/157, art 3(1)-(3)

s 18 rep—Primary Medical Services (S), 2004 asp 1, s 8, sch para 3(1)(2)

s 19 rep—SSI 2004/167, art 2, sch para 6(a)

2002
asp 5 *continued*

  s 20 rep in pt—Health and Social Care (Community Health and Standards), 2003 c 43,
        s 196, sch 14 pt 3
  s 22 am—Mental Health (Care and Treatment) (S), 2003 asp 13, s 28(2)(b)(ii)-(iv); SSI
        2011/211, sch 2 para 6
      rep in pt—Mental Health (Care and Treatment) (S), 2003 asp 13, s 28(2)(b)(i); (prosp)
        Nat Health Service Reform (S), 2004 asp 7, s 11(2), sch 2
  sch 1 am—SSI 2009/137, art 2
  sch 2 rep in pt—Primary Medical Services (S), 2004 asp 1, s 8, sch para 3(1)(3); SSI
        2004/167, art 2, sch para 6(b); Smoking, Health and Social Care (S), 2005 asp
        13, s 42(2), sch 3; SI 2014/90, sch pt 1

asp 6   **Protection of Wild Mammals (Scotland)**
  s 9 am—SSI 2015/338, sch 2 para 6
  sch rep in pt—SSI 2006/536, art 2(3), sch 3; Wildlife and Natural Environment (S), 2011
        asp 6, sch pt 2

asp 7   **Budget (Scotland)**
  s 3 am—SSI 2003/157, art 2(1)(2)
  s 5 am—SSIs 2002/542, art 2(1)(2); 2003/157, art 2(1)(3)
  s 6 (Pt 2) rep—Budget (S), 2003 asp 6, s 9
  sch 1 am—SSIs 2002/542, art 2(1)(3); 2003/157, art 2(1)(4)
  sch 2 am—SSIs 2002/542, art 2(1)(4); 2003/157, art 2(1)(5)
  sch 3 am—SSIs 2002/542, art 2(1)(5); 2003/157, art 2(1)(6)
  sch 4 am—SSIs 2002/542, art 2(1)(6); 2003/157, art 2(1)(7)
  sch 5 am—SSI 2003/157, art 2(1)(8)

asp 8   **Marriage (Scotland)**
asp 9   **Sexual Offences (Procedure and Evidence) (Scotland)**
  s 6 rep in pt—Crim Proceedings etc. (Reform) (S), 2007 asp 6, s 80, sch 1 para 28
asp 10   **Fur Farming (Prohibition) (Scotland)**
  s 2 am—SSI 2015/338, sch 2 para 7
asp 11   **Scottish Public Services Ombudsman**
  appl (mod) —Water Services etc. (S) 2005 asp 3, s 11A(1)-(4)
  s 3 am—Further and Higher Educ (S), 2005 asp 6, s 27(1); Post-16 Educ (S), 2013 asp 12,
        sch para 5(2)
  s 5 am—S Parl Commn and Commrs, 2010 asp 11, s 29, sch 3, para 1
  s 7 am—Statistics and Registration Service, 2007 c 18, s 63(4)(5); Climate Change, 2008 c
        27, s 32, sch 1 para 34(2); Loc Electoral Admin (S), 2011 asp 10, s 18(a)
      rep in pt—Health and Social Care, 2012 c 7, sch 7 para 14
      restr (subsection 6D added by 2011 asp 10, s 18(a) restr)—S Independence Referendum,
        2013 asp 14, s 30
  s 11 am—S Parl Commn and Commrs, 2010 asp 11, s 29, sch 3, para 2(a)-(d)
  s 12 am—S Parl Commn and Commrs, 2010 asp 11, s 29, sch 3, para 3
  s 13 am—S Parl Commn and Commrs, 2010 asp 11, s 29, sch 3, para 4
  s 14 am—(1.4.2016) Welfare Funds (S), 2015 asp 5, s 13(2)
  s 15 am—S Parl Commn and Commrs, 2010 asp 11, s 29, sch 3, para 5(a)-(d)
  ss 16A-16G added—Public Services Reform (S), 2010 asp 8, s 119
  s 16H added—(1.4.2016) Welfare Funds (S), 2015 asp 5, s 13(3)
  s 17 am—S Parl Commn and Commrs, 2010 asp 11, s 29, sch 3, para 6(a)-(f)
  s 17A added —S Parl Commn and Commrs, 2010 asp 11, s 29, sch 3, para 7
  s 18 am—(1.4.2016) Welfare Funds (S), 2015 asp 5, s 13(4)
  s 19 am—Freedom of Information (S), 2002 asp 13, ss 71(2), 75, sch 4 para 1; S Parl
        Commn and Commrs, 2010 asp 11, s 29, sch 3, para 8(a), (b) (1.4.2016) Welfare
        Funds (S), 2015 asp 5, s 13(5)
      excl—Loc Govt, 1974 c 7, s 34M
  s 20 am—(1.4.2016) Welfare Funds (S), 2015 asp 5, s 13(6)
  s 21 am—Public Services Ombudsman (W), 2005 c 10, s 39(1), sch 6 para 73; Health, 2009
        c 21, s 35, sch 5 para 15
  s 23 am—(1.4.2016) Welfare Funds (S), 2015 asp 5, s 13(7)
  s 23 rep in pt—S Parl Commn and Commrs, 2010 asp 11, s 29, sch 3, para 9
  s 24 am—Further and Higher Educ (S), 2005 asp 6, s 27(2)
  sch 1 rep in pt—SI 2006/1031, reg 49(2), sch 9
      am—S Parl Commn and Commrs, 2010 asp 11, s 29, sch 3, para 10-19
  sch 2 am—Freedom of Information (S), 2002 asp 13, ss 71(1), 75; Public Appointments and
        Public Bodies etc.(S), 2003 asp 4, s 17, sch 4, para 16(a); Primary Medical
        Services (S), 2004 asp 1, s 8, sch para 4(1)(2); Transport (S), 2005 asp 12, s 4,

2002
asp 11 *continued*

sch 1 para 19; Further and Higher Educ (S), 2005 asp 6, ss 27(3), 32, sch 3 para 11(a); Fire (S), 2005 asp 5, s 89(1), sch 3 para 21; Licensing (S), 2005 asp 16, s 144, sch 6 para 9; Gaelic Language (S), 2005 asp 7, s 12, sch 2 para 2; Management of Offenders etc (S), 2005 asp 14, s 21(11); Water Services etc (S), 2005 asp 3, s 32, sch 5 para 8(a)(b); Serious Organised Crime and Police, 2005 c 15, s 171(2); Police, Public Order and Crim Justice (S), 2006 asp 10, s 101, sch 6 para 10(2); Tourist Boards (S), 2006 asp 15, s 4, sch 2 para 7; S Commn for Human Rights, 2006 asp 16, s 10, sch 2 para 16; Statistics and Registration Service, 2007 c 18, s 63(4)(6); Climate Change, 2008 c 27, s 32, sch 1 para 34(3); Judiciary and Cts (S), 2008 asp 6, s 9, sch 1 para 20(1); (prosp) Climate Change (S), 2009 asp 12, s 99, sch 2 para 4; SI 2009/1941, art 2, sch 1 para 201; Public Services Reform (S), 2010 asp 8, s 29, sch 7, para 2(a); ibid, ss 106, 110, sch 14, para 11(b), sch 17, para 25; S Parl Commn and Commrs, 2010 asp 11, s 29, sch 3, para 20; ibid, s 26(2); (prosp) Crim Justice and Licensing (S), 2010 asp 13, s 1, sch 1, para 13; Housing (S), 2010 asp 17, s 162, sch 2, para 8; Loc Electoral Admin (S), 2011 asp 10, s 18(b); SSI 2011/208, art 2(2); Nat Library of S, 2012 asp 3, sch 2 para 5; Police and Fire Reform (S), 2012 asp 8, sch 7 paras 19(2), 62; SSI 2012/43, art 2(a); SI 2012/1659, sch 3 para 24; Post-16 Educ (S), 2013 asp 12, sch para 5(3); SSI 2013/197, sch 2 para 9(a); Children and Young people (S), 2014 asp 8, s 81(10); Historic Environment Scotland, 2014 asp 19, sch 6 para 2(a); Food (S), 2015 asp 1, s 17(2); SSI 2015/286, art 2

rep in pt—SSI 2002/468, art 2; Public Appointments and Public Bodies etc.(S), 2003 asp 4, s 17, sch 4, para 16(b); (prosp) Nat Health Service Reform (S), 2004 asp 7, s 11(2), sch 2; Health Protection Agency, 2004 c 17, s 11(2), sch 4; Further and Higher Educ (S), 2005 asp 6, s 32, sch 3 para 11(b); Railways, 2005 c 14, s 59, sch 13 pt 1; Natural Environment and Rural Communities, 2006 c 16, s 105, sch 11 para 171, sch 12; Police and Justice, 2006 c 48, s 52, sch 15 pt 1A; SSI 2009/236, art 2; Public Services Reform (S), 2010 asp 8, s 1, sch 1, para 29; ibid, s 3(2), sch 2, para 21, sch 7, para 2(b); ibid, s 106, sch 14, para 11(a); S Parl Commn and Commrs, 2010 asp 11, s 2, sch 1, para 10; Police and Fire Reform (S), 2012 asp 8, sch 8 pt 1; Health and Social Care, 2012 c 7, sch 7 para 15; SSI 2012/85, art 2; SSI 2013/197, sch 2 para 9(b); Housing (S), 2014 asp 14, sch 2 para 12; Historic Environment Scotland, 2014 asp 19, sch 6 para 2(b); SI 2014/631, sch 1 para 16

sch 3 am—Mental Health (Care and Treatment) (S), 2003 asp 13, s 331(1), sch 4, para 13; Housing (S), 2006 asp 1, s 192(1), sch 6 para 19

rep in pt—School Educ (Ministerial Powers and Independent Schools (S), 2004 asp 12, s 8(2), sch 2; SI 2007/477, reg 5, sch

sch 4 am—Primary Medical Services (S), 2004 asp 1, s 8, sch para 4(1)(3); Further and Higher Educ (S), 2005 asp 6, s 27(4); (prosp) Smoking, Health and Social Care (S), 2005 asp 13, s 42(1), sch 2 para 6; SSI 2005/465, art 2, sch 1 para 31; Police, Public Order and Crim Justice (S), 2006 asp 10, s 101, sch 6 para 10(3); S Parl Commn and Commrs, 2010 asp 11, s 29, sch 3, para 21; Police and Fire Reform (S), 2012 asp 8, sch 7 para 19(3)

rep in pt—Police and Fire Reform (S), 2012 asp 8, sch 8 pt 1

sch 5 am—Freedom of Information (S), 2002 asp 13, ss 71(2),75, sch 4 para 2

sch 6 rep in pt—Mental Health (Care and Treatment) (S), 2003 asp 13, s 331(2), sch 5 pt 1

asp 12 **Education (Disability Strategies and Pupils' Education Records) (Scotland)**

s 6 am—Equality, 2010 c 15, s 211(1), sch 26 para 101 (added by SI 2010/2279, sch 1 para 6)

asp 13 **Freedom of Information (Scotland)**

s 5 am—Freedom of Information (Amdt) (S), 2013 asp 2, s 1(1)

s 7A added—Freedom of Information (Amdt) (S), 2013 asp 2, s 1(2)

s 11 am—Equality, 2010 c 15, s 211(1), sch 26 para 103 (added by SI 2010/2279, sch 1 para 6)

s 12 am—Equality, 2010 c 15, s 211(1), sch 26 para 104 (added by SI 2010/2279, sch 1 para 6)

s 18 am—Freedom of Information (Amdt) (S), 2013 asp 2, s 2

s 20 excl—Statistics and Registration Service, 2007 c 18, s 40(3)

s 25 am—Freedom of Information (Amdt) (S), 2013 asp 2, s 3

s 37 excl—Inquiries, 2005 c 12, s 18(4)

s 39 appl (mods)—SSI 2004/520, reg 20

2002

asp 13 *continued*

s 42 rep in pt—SI 2006/1031, reg 49(2), sch 9; S Parl Commn and Commrs, 2010 asp 11, s 29, sch 4, para 1(e)

am—S Parl Commn and Commrs, 2010 asp 11, s 29, sch 4, para 1(a)-(d),(f)-(h), 2-4

s 43 appl (mods) —SSI 2004/520, reg 18(5)(6)

am—S Parl Commn and Commrs, 2010 asp 11, s 29, sch 4, para 5

ss 44, 45 appl (mods)—SSI 2004/520, reg 18(5)(6)

s 46 appl (mods) —SSI 2004/520, reg 18(5)(6)

am—S Parl Commn and Commrs, 2010 asp 11, s 29, sch 4, para 6(a)-(d)

s 46A added —S Parl Commn and Commrs, 2010 asp 11, s 29, sch 4, para 7

Pt 4 (ss 47-56) appl (mods)—SSI 2004/520, reg 17

ss 47-51 appl (mods)—SSI 2009/440, reg 12(1)(2), sch

ss 53-56 appl (mods)—SSI 2009/440, reg 12(1)(2), sch

s 57 am—SSI 2013/365, art 2

s 59 rep in pt—Freedom of Information (Amdt) (S), 2013 asp 2, s 4(1)(a)

am—Freedom of Information (Amdt) (S), 2013 asp 2, s 4(1)(b)(c)

s 63 appl (mods)—SSI 2004/520, reg 18(5)(6)

appl—SSI 2009/440, reg 12(3)

s 65A added—Freedom of Information (Amdt) (S), 2013 asp 2, s 5

s 70 rep in pt—Public Services Reform (S), 2010 asp 8, s 4(5)(a)

s 72 am—Freedom of Information (Amdt) (S), 2013 asp 2, s 4(2)

sch 1 am—Public Appointments and Public Bodies etc.(S), 2003 asp 4, s 17, sch 4, para 17(c)(ii); (prosp) ibid, s 17, sch 4, para 17(c)(i); Primary Medical Services (S), 2004 asp 1, s 8, sch para 5(a)(b); Fire (S), 2005 asp 5, s 89(1), sch 3 para 22; Transport (S), 2005 asp 12, ss 4, 17(5), 41(4), sch 1 para 20, sch 2 para 4; Further and Higher Educ (S), 2005 asp 6, s 32, sch 3 para 12(a)(b); Licensing (S), 2005 asp 16, s 144, sch 6 para 10; Gaelic Language (S), 2005 asp 7, s 12, sch 2 para 3; Management of Offenders etc (S), 2005 asp 14, s 21(12); Water Services etc (S), 2005 asp 3, s 32, sch 5 para 9(a)(b); Police, Public Order and Crim Justice (S), 2006 asp 10, s 101, sch 6 para 11; Tourist Boards (S), 2006 asp 15, s 4, sch 2 para 8; Joint Inspection of Children's Services and Inspection of Social Work Services (S), 2006 asp 3, s 8(2); S Commn for Human Rights, 2006 asp 16, s 10, sch 2 para 17; Legal Profession and Legal Aid (S), 2007 asp 5, s 81, sch 5 para 5; Judiciary and Cts (S), 2008 asp 6, ss 9, 60, sch 1 para 21, sch 3 para 18; SSI 2008/297, art 2, sch 1; (prosp) Climate Change (S), 2009 asp 12, s 99, sch 2 para 5; Public Services Reform (S), 2010 asp 8, s 29, sch 7, para 3(a); S Parl Commn and Commrs, 2010 asp 11, s 27(1), (2); (prosp) Crim Justice and Licensing (S), 2010 asp 13, s 1, sch 1, para 14; Housing (S), 2010 asp 17, s 162, sch 2, para 9; SSIs 2011/211, sch 1 para 11(b), sch 2 para 7(a); 2011/113, art 4; Post-16 Educ (S), 2013 asp 12, sch para 6; SSI 2013/126, art 2(a)(c) sch; 2013/197, sch 2 para 10(a); SI 2013/783, art 8; Historic Environment Scotland, 2014 asp 19, sch 6 para 3(a); Children and Young People (S), 2014 asp 8, s 81(11)(a)(b); Housing (S), 2014 asp 14, sch 2 para 13(2); Revenue Scotland and Tax Powers, 2014 asp 16, sch 4 para 5; SSI 2014/354, art 2(a)-(d), sch; SI 2014/631, sch 1 para 17(2)(a)(b); Food (S), 2015 asp 1, s 17(3)

rep in pt—Public Appointments and Public Bodies etc.(S), 2003 asp 4, s 17, sch 4, para 17(a)(b); (prosp) Nat Health Service Reform (S), 2004 asp 7, s 11(2), sch 2; Smoking, Health and Social Care (S), 2005 asp 13, s 42(2), sch 3; Further and Higher Educ (S), 2005 asp 6, s 32, sch 3 para 12(c); SSI 2008/297, art 3, sch 2; Public Services Reform (S), 2010 asp 8, ss 1, 2(4), 4(5)(b), 5(4), 7(4), 29, sch 1, para 30, sch 7, para 3(b); ibid, s 3, sch 2, para 21; Flood and Water Management, 2010 c 29, s 46(5); SSI 2011/211, sch 1 para 11(a), sch 2 para 7(b); SSI 2013/126, art 2(b); 2013/197, sch 2 para 10(b); Historic Environment Scotland, 2014 asp 19, sch 6 para 3(b); Housing (S), 2014 asp 14, sch 2 para 13(3)

sch 2 am —S Parl Commn and Commrs, 2010 asp 11, s 29, s 4, paras 8-14

sch 3 appl (mods)—SSI 2004/520, reg 17

asp 14 **Scottish Qualifications Authority**

asp 15 **University of St Andrews (Postgraduate Medical Degrees)**

asp 16 **Scottish Parliamentary Standards Commissioner**

trans of functions—S Parl Commn and Commrs, 2010 asp 11, s 2(1)(b)

ss 1, 2 rep —S Parl Commn and Commrs, 2010 asp 11, s 2, sch 1, para 11

s 3 am —S Parl Commn and Commrs, 2010 asp 11, s 2, sch 1, para 12; SSI 2013/197, sch 2 para 12

2002

asp 16 *continued*

s 13 ext—SI 2003/2278, art 2(a)

rep in pt —S Parl Commn and Commrs, 2010 asp 11, s 29(5), (6)

s 14 ext—SI 2003/2278, art 2(b)

s 16 am—S Parl Commn and Commrs, 2010 asp 11, s 2, sch 1, para 13(a), (b)(i), (ii); SSI 2013/197, sch 2 para 13(a)

rep in pt—SSI 2013/197, sch 2 para 13(b)

s 17 rep—SSI 2013/197, sch 2 para 14

s 18 rep —S Parl Commn and Commrs, 2010 asp 11, s 29(5), (6)

appl—S Parl Commn and Commrs, 2010 asp 11, s 29, sch 7, para 6(2)

s 20 ext—SI 2003/2278, art 2(c)

rep in pt—Arbitration (S), 2010 asp 1, s 2, sch 1, para 14(a)

am—S Parl Commn and Commrs, 2010 asp 11, s 2, sch 1, para 14(b); SSI 2013/197, sch 2 para 15

sch 1 rep —S Parl Commn and Commrs, 2010 asp 11, s 2, sch 1, para 11

asp 17   **Debt Arrangement and Attachment (Scotland)**

mod—SI 2009/317, art 3, sch

appl (mods)—SI 2011/245, sch 6 pt 1

s 1 am—Bankruptcy and Debt Advice (S), 2014 asp 11, s 53(2)

s 2 am—Bankruptcy and Diligence etc. (S), 2007 asp 3, s 211(1)(2)

rep in pt—Bankruptcy and Diligence etc. (S), 2007 asp 3, s 212(1)(2)

s 3 am—Bankruptcy and Diligence etc. (S), 2007 asp 3, s 212(1)(3)

rep in pt—SSI 2011/141, reg 20(5)

s 4 am—SSIs 2004/468, reg 35(5); 404, regs 2, 11(d); 2011/141, reg 33(5)(a)(b)

rep in pt—Bankruptcy and Diligence etc. (S), 2007 asp 3, s 226, sch 6

s 5 rep in pt—Bankruptcy and Diligence etc. (S), 2007 asp 3, s 212(1)(4)

s 7 am—Bankruptcy and Diligence etc. (S), 2007 asp 3, s 212(1)(5); Bankruptcy and Debt Advice (S), 2014 asp 11, ss 3(2), 53(3)

s 7A added—Bankruptcy and Diligence etc. (S), 2007 asp 3, s 211(1)(3)

s 9 am—Bankruptcy and Diligence etc. (S), 2007 asp 3, s 212(1)(6)

rep in pt—Bankruptcy and Debt Advice (S), 2014 asp 11, s 53(4)

Pt 1A (ss 9A-9S) added—Bankruptcy and Diligence etc. (S), 2007 asp 3, s 173

s 10 am—Bankruptcy and Diligence etc. (S), 2007 asp 3, s 212(1)(7); ibid, s 226, sch 5 para 30(1)(2); (prosp) Child Maintenance and Other Payments, 2008 c 6, s 57, sch 7 para 5

rep in pt—Bankruptcy and Diligence etc. (S), 2007 asp 3, s 209(1)

s 11 am—Bankruptcy and Diligence etc. (S), 2007 asp 3, ss 213, 226, sch 4 para 10, sch 5 para 30(1)(3)

s 13A added—Bankruptcy and Diligence etc. (S), 2007 asp 3, s 226, sch 5 para 30(1)(4)

s 14 am—Bankruptcy and Diligence etc. (S), 2007 asp 3, s 226, sch 5 para 30(1)(5)

s 15 am—Bankruptcy and Diligence etc. (S), 2007 asp 3, s 226, sch 5 para 30(1)(6)

rep in pt—(prosp) Bankruptcy and Diligence etc. (S), 2007 asp 3, s 226, sch 6 pt 1

s 19 am—Bankruptcy and Diligence etc. (S), 2007 asp 3, s 212(1)(8)

s 19A added—Bankruptcy and Diligence etc. (S), 2007 asp 3, s 212(1)(9)

s 20 am—Bankruptcy and Diligence etc. (S), 2007 asp 3, s 212(1)(10)(12)

s 21 am—Bankruptcy and Diligence etc. (S), 2007 asp 3, s 212(1)(10)(12)

s 26 am—Bankruptcy and Diligence etc. (S), 2007 asp 3, s 212(1)(12)

s 27 rep in pt—Bankruptcy and Diligence etc. (S), 2007 asp 3, s 212(1)(13)

s 28 am—Bankruptcy and Diligence etc. (S), 2007 asp 3, s 226, sch 5 para 30(1)(7)

s 31 am—Bankruptcy and Diligence etc. (S), 2007 asp 3, s 212(1)(14)

s 32 am—Bankruptcy and Diligence etc. (S), 2007 asp 3, s 226, sch 5 para 30(1)(8)(a)

s 33 am—Bankruptcy and Diligence etc. (S), 2007 asp 3, s 226, sch 5 para 30(1)(9)

s 34 am—Bankruptcy and Diligence etc. (S), 2007 asp 3, s 226, sch 5 para 30(1)(10)

s 40 am—Bankruptcy and Diligence etc. (S), 2007 asp 3, s 226, sch 5 para 30(1)(11)

s 41 am—Bankruptcy and Diligence etc. (S), 2007 asp 3, s 226, sch 5 para 30(1)(12)

s 45 rep in pt—Public Services Reform (S), 2010 asp 8, s 13, sch 4, para 33

s 47 rep in pt —SSI 2004/468, reg 5, sch 3 para 4

am—SSIs 2004/468, reg 5, sch 3 para 4; 2011/141, sch 2 para 3

s 60 am—Bankruptcy and Diligence etc. (S), 2007 asp 3, s 226, sch 5 para 30(1)(14)

rep in pt—Bankruptcy and Diligence etc. (S), 2007 asp 3, s 226, sch 6

s 60A added—Bankruptcy and Diligence etc. (S), 2007 asp 3, s 212(1)(15)

s 62 am—Bankruptcy and Diligence etc. (S), 2007 asp 3, s 211(1)(4); Bankruptcy and Debt Advice (S), 2014 asp 11, sch 3 para 38(a)(b)

2002

asp 17 *continued*

   sch 1 am—Bankruptcy and Diligence etc. (S), 2007 asp 3, s 226, sch 5 para 30(1)(15); ibid,
     s 212(1)(16)
    rep in pt—(prosp) Bankruptcy and Diligence etc. (S), 2007 asp 3, s 226, sch 6
   sch 3 rep in pt—Income Tax, 2007 c 3, s 1031, sch 3; Public Health etc. (S), 2008 asp 5, s
     126, sch 3 pt 1

2003

asp 1 **Local Government in Scotland**
   saved—SSI 2010/119, art 4
   ss 1,2 ext (mods)—Loc Govt, 2003 c 26, s 101(1)(3)(5) (see SI 2003/2938)
   ss 3-5 mod—SSI 2013/121, art 7, sch
   s 7 am—Building (S), 2003 asp 8, s 58, sch 6, para 25
   s 11 rep in pt—Fire (S), 2005 asp 5, s 89(2), sch 4
   ss 12, 13 mod—SSI 2013/121, art 7, sch
   Pt 2 (ss 15-19) rep (prosp)—Community Empowerment (S), 2015 asp 6, sch 5
   s 15 appl—Antisocial Behaviour etc (S), 2004 asp 8, s 1(11)
   s 16 am—Fire (S), 2005 asp 5, s 89(1), sch 3 para 23(1)(2); Transport (S), 2005 asp 12, s 4,
     sch 1 para 11; Police and Fire Reform (S), 2012 asp 8, s 46(1)(b); ibid, sch 7 para
     64; SSI 2015/157, sch para 6
    rep in pt—Police and Fire Reform (S), 2012 asp 8, s 46(1)(a)
   s 17 am—Transport (S), 2005 asp 12, s 4, sch 1 para 11
   Pt 3 (ss 20-22) mod—Waverley Railway (S), 2006 asp 13, s 39
   s 22 am—Fire (S), 2005 asp 5, s 89(1), sch 3 para 23(1)(3); pt 2
   s 25 rep—Police and Fire Reform (S), 2012 asp 8, sch 8 pt 3
   s 33 rep in pt—Loc Govt Finance (Unoccupied Properties etc.) (S), 2012 asp 11, s 2(2)(a),
     (b)(i), (4)(a)
    am—Loc Govt Finance (Unoccupied Properties etc.) (S), 2012 asp 11, s 2(2)(b)(ii), (3),
     (4)(b),(5)-(7)
   s 46 appl—Road Traffic, 1988 c 53, s 95
    rep in pt—Police and Fire Reform (S), 2012 asp 8, sch 8 pt 1
   s 50 rep—Scottish Schools (Parental Involvement), 2006 asp 8, s 23, sch
   s 57 am—(prosp) Community Empowerment (S), 2015 asp 6, sch 4 para 7
    rep in pt—(prosp) Community Empowerment (S), 2015 asp 6, sch 5
   s 61 am—Fire (S), 2005 asp 5, s 89(1), sch 3 para 23(1)(5); Transport (S), 2005 asp 12, s 4,
     sch 1 paras 15(5), 16(5)(b)
    rep in pt—Transport (S), 2005 asp 12, s 4, sch 1 paras 15(5), 16(5)(a); Police and Fire
     Reform (S), 2012 asp 8, sch 8 pts 1,2

asp 2 **Land Reform (Scotland)**
   s 1 excl—Serious Organised Crime and Police, 2005 c 15, s 131(1)(c)
   s 7 am—SSIs 2005/65, art 2(a); 2013/356, art 2
    rep in pt—SSI 2005/65, art 2(b)
   s 29 am—SSI 2015/271, art 4
   s 32 am—SSIs 2003/2155, art 3(1), sch 1 pt 2, para 15(1)(2); 2011/2085, sch 1 para 52
    rep in pt—SI 2003/2155, art 3(2), sch 2, Table 1
    appl—SSI 2010/348, art 3
   Pt 2 (ss 33-67) appl—Title Conditions (S), 2003 asp 9, s 43(9)
   s 33 am—(15.4.2016) Community Empowerment (S), 2015 asp 6, s 36(1)(a)(ii),(b)(c),(2)
    rep in pt—(15.4.2016) Community Empowerment (S), 2015 asp 6, s 36(1)(a)(i),(d)
   s 34 am—Charities and Trustee Investment (S), 2005 asp 10, s 104, sch 4 pt 1 para 13(a);
     SI 2009/1941, art 2, sch 1 para 218(2); (15.4.2016) Community Empowerment
     (S), 2015 asp 6, s 37(2)-(8)
    rep in pt—(15.4.2016) Community Empowerment (S), 2015 asp 6, s 37(3)(d),(7)(a)
   s 35 am—(15.4.2016) Community Empowerment (S), 2015 asp 6, s 338(2)-(4)
   s 36 am—(15.4.2016) Community Empowerment (S), 2015 asp 6, s 39(2)(3)
    rep in pt—(15.4.2016) Community Empowerment (S), 2015 asp 6, s 39(2)(a)(ii)
   s 37 am—(15.4.2016) Community Empowerment (S), 2015 asp 6, s 40; (15.4.2016) ibid,
     sch 4 para 8(2)
   s 38 am—(15.4.2016) Community Empowerment (S), 2015 asp 6, s 41(a)(i)(iv)-(vi),(b)-(d)
    rep in pt—(15.4.2016) Community Empowerment (S), 2015 asp 6, s 41(a)(ii)(iii);
     (15.4.2016) ibid, sch 5
   s 39 am—(15.4.2016) Community Empowerment (S), 2015 asp 6, s 42(2)-(7)(9)
   s 39 rep in pt—(15.4.2016) Community Empowerment (S), 2015 asp 6, s 42(8)
   s 39A added—(15.4.2016) Community Empowerment (S), 2015 asp 6, s 43

2003

asp 2 *continued*

s 40 am—SSIs 2005/623, art 23; 2012/38, sch para 3
 rep in pt—(1.8.2016) Housing (S), 2014 asp 14, sch 2 para 14(2); (15.4.2016)
  Community Empowerment (S), 2015 asp 6, sch 5
s 41 am—(15.4.2016) Community Empowerment (S), 2015 asp 6, s 44
s 44 am—(15.4.2016) Community Empowerment (S), 2015 asp 6, s 45
s 44A added—(15.4.2016) Community Empowerment (S), 2015 asp 6, s 46
s 50 am—(15.4.2016) Community Empowerment (S), 2015 asp 6, s 47
 rep in pt—(15.4.2016) Community Empowerment (S), 2015 asp 6, sch 5
s 51 am—(15.4.2016) Community Empowerment (S), asp 6, ss 48(a), 51(2); (15.4.2016)
  ibid, sch 4 para 8(3)(b)(i)
 rep in pt—(15.4.2016) Community Empowerment (S), 2015 asp 6, s 48(b)(c);
  (15.4.2016) ibid, sch 4 para 8(3)(a),(b)(ii)(iii), sch 5
s 51A added—(15.4.2016) Community Empowerment (S), 2015 asp 6, s 49
s 51B added—(15.4.2016) Community Empowerment (S), 2015 asp 6, s 50
s 51C added—(15.4.2016) Community Empowerment (S), 2015 asp 6, s 51(1)
s 52 am—(15.4.2016) Community Empowerment (S), 2015 asp 6, ss 52, 53(1); (15.4.2016)
  ibid, sch 4 para 8(4)(a)(i)-(iv),(b)
 rep in pt—(15.4.2016) Community Empowerment (S), 2015 asp 6, sch 4 para
  8(4)(a)(v), sch 5
s 56 am—(15.4.2016) Community Empowerment (S), 2015 asp 6, s 54
s 57 am—(15.4.2016) Community Empowerment (S), 2015 asp 6, s 55
s 60 am—(15.4.2016) Community Empowerment (S), 2015 asp 6, ss 53(2), 56
s 60A added—(15.4.2016) Community Empowerment (S), 2015 asp 6, s 57
s 61 am—(15.4.2016) Community Empowerment (S), 2015 asp 6, s 58
 rep in pt—(15.4.2016) Community Empowerment (S), 2015 asp 6, sch 5
s 62 am—(15.4.2016) Community Empowerment (S), 2015 asp 6, s 59
 rep in pt—(15.4.2016) Community Empowerment (S), 2015 asp 6, sch 5
s 65 rep in pt—(1.8.2016) Housing (S), 2014 asp 14, sch 2 para 14(3)
s 67A added—(15.4.2016) Community Empowerment (S), 2015 asp 6, s 60
s 67B added—(15.4.2016) Community Empowerment (S), 2015 asp 6, s 61
s 68 am—Crofting Reform etc., 2007 asp 7, s 39, sch 1 para 5(1)(2); (15.4.2016)
  Community Empowerment (S), 2015 asp 6, sch 4 para 8(5)
s 69A added—Crofting Reform etc., 2007 asp 7, s 31(1)(2)
s 71 am —Charities and Trustee Investment (S), 2005 asp 10, s 104, sch 4 pt 1 para 13(b);
  SI 2009/1941, art 2, sch 1 para 218(3); (prosp) Community Empowerment (S),
  2015 asp 6, s 62(2)-(9)
 rep in pt—(prosp) Community Empowerment (S), 2015 asp 6, s 62(3)(e)
s 72 am—(prosp) Community Empowerment (S), 2015 asp 6, s 63
s 73 am—(prosp) Community Empowerment (S), 2015 asp 6, s 64(2)(a),(b)(i),(d),(3)-(5)
 rep in pt—(prosp) Community Empowerment (S), 2015 asp 6, s 64(2)(b)(ii),(c)
s 74 am—(prosp) Community Empowerment (S), 2015 asp 6, s 65
s 75 am—(prosp) Community Empowerment (S), 2015 asp 6, s 66
s 76 am—(prosp) Community Empowerment (S), 2015 asp 6, s 67
s 81 am—(prosp) Community Empowerment (S), 2015 asp 6, s 68
s 88 am—(prosp) Community Empowerment (S), 2015 asp 6, s 69
s 89 am—(prosp) Community Empowerment (S), 2015 asp 6, s 70
s 92 am—(prosp) Community Empowerment (S), 2015 asp 6, s 71
s 94 am—(prosp) Community Empowerment (S), 2015 asp 6, s 72(2)(a)(i),(b),(3)(4)
 rep in pt—(prosp) Community Empowerment (S), 2015 asp 6, s 72(2)(a)(ii)
ss 73-76 am—Crofting Reform etc., 2007 asp 7, s 39, sch 1 para 5(1)(3)-(6)
ss 81, 82 am—Crofting Reform etc., 2007 asp 7, s 39, sch 1 para 5(1)(7)(8)
s 84 rep in pt—(1.8.2016) Housing (S), 2014 asp 14, sch 2 para 14(4)
ss 85-88 am—Crofting Reform etc., 2007 asp 7, s 39, sch 1 para 5(1)(9)-(12)
s 88A added—Crofting Reform etc., 2007 asp 7, s 31(1)(3)
ss 89-92 am—Crofting Reform etc., 2007 asp 7, s 39, sch 1 para 5(1)(13)-(16)
ss 95, 96 am—Crofting Reform etc., 2007 asp 7, s 39, sch 1 para 5(1)(17)(18)
s 97ZA added (prosp)—Community Empowerment (S), 2015 asp 6, s 73
s 97A added—Crofting Reform etc., 2007 asp 7, s 31(1)(4)
Pt 3A (ss 97B-97Z) added (prosp)—Community Empowerment (S), 2015 asp 6, s 74
s 97Z1 added (pt. 15.4.2016) (pt prosp)—Community Empowerment (S), 2015 asp 6, s 75
s 98 am—(prosp) Community Empowerment (S), 2015 asp 6, sch 4 para 8(6)
 rep in pt—(prosp) Community Empowerment (S), 2015 asp 6, sch 5

2003

asp 2 *continued*

     sch 1 am—SI 2003/2155, art 3(1), sch 1 pt 2, para 15(1)(3)

     sch 2 rep in pt—SSI 2012/228, sch

asp 3   **Water Environment and Water Services (Scotland)**

     Pt 1 (ss 1-28) ext (mods)—SIs 2003/3245, reg 6; 2004/99, reg 5(1), sch 4

     s 1 am—SSI 2015/270, reg 2(a)

     s 2 rep in pt—Flood Risk Management (S), 2009 asp 6, s 96, sch 3 para 14

        am—Regulatory Reform (S), 2014 asp 3, sch 3 para 8(2); SSI 2015/270, reg 2(b)

        mod—SSI 2009/420, reg 3(a)

     s 5A added—Aquaculture and Fisheries (S), 2013 asp 7, s 54(2)

     s 7 am—Aquaculture and Fisheries (S), 2013 asp 7, s 54(3)

     s 9 am—Aquaculture and Fisheries (S), 2013 asp 7, s 54(4)

     s 11 am—Aquaculture and Fisheries (S), 2013 asp 7, s 54(5); Food (S), 2015 asp 1, sch

        para 8

     s 20 am—SSI 2005/348, reg 3; (prosp) Regulatory Reform (S), 2014 asp 3, sch 3 para 8(3)

     s 21 rep in pt—(prosp) Regulatory Reform (S), 2014 asp 3, sch 3 para 8(4)

     s 22 am—Reservoirs (S), 2011 asp 9, s 109(1); (prosp) Regulatory Reform (S), 2014 asp 3,

        sch 3 para 8(5)(b)

        rep in pt—(prosp) Regulatory Reform (S), 2014 asp 3, sch 3 para 8(5)(a)

     s 23 am—(prosp) Regulatory Reform (S), 2014 asp 3, sch 3 para 8(6)(b)

        rep in pt—(prosp) Regulatory Reform (S), 2014 asp 3, sch 3 para 8(6)(a)

     s 24 rep in pt—Planning etc. (S), s 53, 2006 asp 17, sch

     s 26 rep—Water Resources (S), 2013 asp 5, sch 4 para 2

     s 28 mod—SSI 2009/420, reg 3(b)

        am—Aquaculture and Fisheries (S), 2013 asp 7, s 54(6)

        rep in pt—(prosp) Regulatory Reform (S), 2014 asp 3, sch 3 para 8(7)

     s 36 rep in pt—Planning etc. (S), s 53, 2006 asp 17, sch; (prosp) Regulatory Reform (S),

        2014 asp 3, sch 3 para 8(8)(a)(b)

     sch 1 am—(prosp) Regulatory Reform (S), 2014 asp 3, sch 3 para 8(9)

     sch 2 rep (prosp)—Regulatory Reform (S), 2014 asp 3, sch 3 para 8(10)

        am—Antisocial Behaviour etc (S), 2004 asp 8, s 66, sch 2 pt 1 para 6; Water Services

           etc (S), 2005 asp 3, s 32, sch 5 para 10(b); Further and Higher Educ (S), 2005

           asp 6, s 32, sch 3 para 13(a); Gaelic Language (S), 2005 asp 7, s 12, sch 2 para 4;

           Charities and Trustee Investment (S), 2005 asp 10, s 104, sch 4 pt 1 para 14; SSI

           2005/540, art 2(1)(3)(a)(4)(a)(6)

        rep in pt—Water Services etc (S), 2005 asp 3, s 32, sch 5 para 10(a); Further and

           Higher Educ (S), 2005 asp 6, s 32, sch 3 para 13(b); SSI 2005/540,

           art 2(1)(2)(3)(b)(4)(b)(5)

     sch 2A added—Reservoirs (S), 2011 asp 9, s 109(2)

asp 4   **Public Appointments and Public Bodies etc (Scotland)**

     trans of functions—S Parl Commn and Commrs, 2010 asp 11, s 2(2)

     s 1 rep —S Parl Commn and Commrs, 2010 asp 11, s 2, sch 1, para 15

     s 2 ext—SSI 2006/303, art 2

        am —S Parl Commn and Commrs, 2010 asp 11, s 2, sch 1, para 16; SSI 2013/197, sch 2

           para 16(a)

     s 3 am —S Parl Commn and Commrs, 2010 asp 11, s 29(8), (9)

     s 5 rep in pt—(prosp) Nat Health Service Reform (S), 2004 asp 7, s 11(2), sch 2

     s 6 rep (prosp)—Nat Health Service Reform (S), 2004 asp 7, s 11(2), sch 2

     s 7 am—(prosp) Nat Health Service Reform (S), 2004 asp 7, s 11(1), sch 1 para 4(1)(2)

        rep in pt—(prosp) Nat Health Service Reform (S), 2004 asp 7, s 11(2), sch 2

     s 8 rep in pt—(prosp) Nat Health Service Reform (S), 2004 asp 7, s 11(2), sch 2

     s 9 am—(prosp) Nat Health Service Reform (S), 2004 asp 7, s 11(1), sch 1 para 4(1)(3)

        rep in pt—(prosp) Nat Health Service Reform (S), 2004 asp 7, s 11(2), sch 2

     s 10 rep in pt—(prosp) Nat Health Service Reform (S), 2004 asp 7, s 11(2), sch 2

     s 15 rep—Public Services Reform (S), 2010 asp 8, s 7(3)(a)

     s 16 rep—Public Services Reform (S), 2010 asp 8, s 7(3)(b)

     s 20 am —S Parl Commn and Commrs, 2010 asp 11, s 2, sch 1, para 17; SSI 2013/197, sch

        2 para 16(b)

        rep in pt—Public Services Reform (S), 2010 asp 8, s 7(3)(c)

     sch 1 rep —S Parl Commn and Commrs, 2010 asp 11, s 2, s 1, para 15

     sch 2 rep in pt—(prosp) Nat Health Service Reform (S), 2004 asp 7, s 11(2), sch 2; Natural

        Environment and Rural Communities, 2006 c 16, s 105(2), sch 11 para 173,

        sch 12; Tourist Boards (S), 2006 asp 15, s 4, sch 2 para 9(a); Crim Proceedings

        etc. (Reform) (S), 2007 asp 6, s 80, sch 1 para 29; SSI 2008/348, art 2; Public

2003
asp 4 *continued*

Services Reform (S), 2010 asp 8, ss 1, 2(5), 4(6), 5(5), 6(3), 7(3)(d), 29, sch 1, para 31, sch 7, para 4(b); ibid, s 106, sch 14, para 12(a); Flood and Water Management, 2010 c 29, s 46(4); SSI 2011/215, sch 7; Police and Fire Reform (S), 2012 asp 8, sch 8 pt 1

am—Police, Public Order and Crim Justice (S), 2006 asp 10, s 101, sch 6 para 12; Tourist Boards (S), 2006 asp 15, s 4, sch 2 para 9(b); SSI 2007/110, art 2; Legal Profession and Legal Aid (S), 2007 asp 5, s 81, sch 5 para 6; Judiciary and Cts (S), 2008 asp 6, s 9, sch 1 para 18(1); SSI 2008/348, art 2; Health Boards (Membership and Elections) (S), 2009 asp 5, s 8, sch 1 para 2; (prosp) Climate Change (S), 2009 asp 12, s 99, sch 2 para 6; SSIs 2009/390, art 2; 2010/50, art 2; Housing (S), 2010 asp 17, s 162, sch 2, para 10; Public Services Reform (S), 2010 asp 8, s 29, sch 7, para 4(a); ibid, ss 106, 110, sch 14, para 12(b), sch 17, para 26; SSIs 2011/22, art 2, 186, art 3, 236, art 2; Police and Fire Reform (S), 2012 asp 8, sch 1 para 16; ibid, sch 7 para 65; Post-16 Educ (S), 2013 asp 12, sch para 7; Victimes and Witnesses (S), 2014 asp 1, s 31(3); Children and Young People (S), 2014 asp 8, s 81(12); Revenue Scotland and Tax Powers, 2014 asp 16, sch 4 para 6; Historic Environment Scotland, 2014 asp 19, sch 6 para 4(a)(b); Food (S), 2015 asp 1, s 17(4)

sch 3 rep—Public Services Reform (S), 2010 asp 8, s 7(3)(e)

sch 4 rep in pt—SSI 2004/167, art 2, sch para 7; S Parl Commn and Commrs, 2010 asp 11, s 2, sch 1, paras 18, 19

asp 5 **Protection of Children (Scotland)**
rep (except ss 13, 16) —Protection of Vulnerable Groups (S), 2007 asp 14, s 88, sch 4 para 42

savings (for spec provns)—SSI 2010/180, arts 3-12

s 13 rep—SSI 2011/215, sch 7

asp 6 **Budget (Scotland)**
s 3 am—SSIs 2003/330, art 2(1)(2); 603, art 2(1)(2); 2004/147, art 2(1)(2)

s 5 am—SSIs 2003/603, art 2(1)(3); 2004/147, art 2(1)(3)

Pt 2 (s 6) rep—Budget (S), 2004 asp 2, s 8

sch 1 am—SSIs 2003/330, art 2(1)(3); 603, art 2(1)(4); 2004/147, art 2(1)(4)

rep in pt—SSI 2003/603, art 2(1)(4)

sch 2 am and rep in pt—SSIs 2003/603, art 2(1)(5); 2004/147, art 2(1)(5)

sch 3 am—SSIs 2003/330, art 2(1)(4); 603, art 2(1)(6); 2004/147, art 2(1)(6)

sch 5 am—SSI 2004/147, art 2(1)(7)

asp 7 **Criminal Justice (Scotland)**
s 1 am—SSI 2005/465, art 2, sch 1 para 34(1)(2)

s 3 am—Crim Justice and Licensing (S), 2010 asp 13, s 203, sch 7, para 71

s 7 am—SSI 2005/465, art 2, sch 1 para 34(1)(3)

s 11 am—Management of Offenders etc (S), 2005 asp 14, s 13(1)(2)

s 14 am—Civil Partnership, 2004 c 33, s 261(2), sch 28 pt 4 para 67; SSI 2011/211, sch 1 para 12(a); (pt prosp) Victims and Witnesses (S), 2014 asp 1, s 23(2)(a)(b),(3)(a), (4)(a),(5),(6)(a)(b); (prosp) ibid, s 23(7)

rep in pt—(pt prosp) Victims and Witnesses (S), 2014 asp 1, s 23(3)(b)-(d),(4)(b)

s 15A rep —Crim Justice and Licensing (S), 2010 asp 13, s 89

s 16 am—Crim Proceedings etc. (Reform) (S), 2007 asp 6, s 36; SSI 2008/185, art 2; SSI 2011/211, sch 1 para 12(b); Victims and Witnesses (S), 2014 asp 1, ss 23(9)(a)-(c), (10)(a)(b),(12),(13), 27(a)(b); (prosp) Mental Health (S), 2015 asp 9, s 54

rep in pt—SSI 2008/185, art 2; Victims and Witnesses (S), 2014 asp 1, ss 23(9)(b)(ii), (d),(11)

ss 16A-16C added (prosp)—Mental Health (S), 2015 asp 9, s 55

s 17 am—Victims and Witnesses (S), 2014 asp 1, s 28

s 17A added—Victims and Witnesses (S), 2014 asp 1, s 29

ss 17B-17D added (prosp)—Mental Health (S), 2015 asp 9, s 56

s 17E added (prosp)—Mental Health (S), 2015 asp 9, s 57

s 18A added (prosp)—Mental Health (S), 2015 asp 9, s 58

s 18B added (prosp)—Mental Health (S), 2015 asp 9, s 59(2)

s 19 rep in pt—Sexual Offences (S), 2009 asp 9, s 61, sch 6

s 21 am—Sexual Offences, 2003 c 42, c 42, s 139, sch 6, para 49; SI 2009/1182, arts 4, 5-7, sch 5; Health and Social Care, 2012 c 7, s 213(8)(c)

s 22 rep (prosp)—Human Trafficking and Exploitation (S), 2015 asp 12, sch para 2
am —Crim Justice and Licensing (S), 2010 asp 13, s 46(1)(a)-(e),(f)(ii)

2003

asp 7 s 22 *continued*

    rep in pt —Crim Justice and Licensing (S), 2010 asp 13, s 46(1)(f)(i)

    s 23 rep in pt—Crim Justice and Licensing (S), 2010 asp 13, s 64(4)

    s 40 rep in pt—Management of Offenders etc (S), 2005 asp 14, s 21(13)

        am—(prosp) Custodial Sentences and Weapons (S), 2007 asp 17, s 66, sch 4 para 4

    s 42 rep in pt—Crim Proceedings etc. (Reform) (S), 2007 asp 6, s 80, sch 1 para 30(a); Crim Justice and Licensing (S), 2010 asp 13, s 14, sch 2, para 47(2)(c)(i),(e)(ii),(f)

        am —Crim Justice and Licensing (S), 2010 asp 13, s 14, sch 2, para 47(2)(a)(b),(c)(ii), (d),(e)(i)

    ss 44,45 rep—Antisocial Behaviour etc (S), 2004 asp 8, s 144(2), sch 5

    s 46 rep —Crim Justice and Licensing (S), 2010 asp 13, s 14, sch 2, para 47(3)

    s 50 rep in pt—Crim Justice and Licensing (S), 2010 asp 13, s 14, sch 2, para 47(4)

    s 53 am—SSI 2013/211, sch 1 para 12

        rep in pt—SSI 2013/211, sch 2

    s 56 am —Crim Justice and Licensing (S), 2010 asp 13, s 82(2)(a)-(c), (e), (g); SI 2011/2298, sch para 2(a)(b); Police and Fire Reform (S), 2012 asp 8, sch 7 para 21(2)(a)

        rep in pt —Crim Justice and Licensing (S), 2010 asp 13, s 82(2)(d), (f)

    s 59 rep (prosp)—Crim Proceedings etc. (Reform) (S), 2007 asp 6, s 80, sch 1 para 30(b)

    s 60 rep in pt —Crim Justice and Licensing (S), 2010 asp 13, s 14, sch 2, para 47(5)(a), (b)

    ss 68, 69 rep —Bribery, 2010 c 23, s 17, sch 2

    s 70 rep in pt—Serious Organised Crime and Police, 2005 c 15, s 174(2), sch 17 pt 2

    s 73 rep in pt—Crim Justice and Licensing (S), 2010 asp 13, s 112(2)

    s 74 am—Crim Justice and Licensing (S), 2010 asp 13, s 25(2)(a), (c)

        rep in pt—Crim Justice and Licensing (S), 2010 asp 13, s 25(2)(b)

    s 75 rep —Police and Fire Reform (S), 2012 asp 8, sch 8 pt 1

    s 76 rep in pt—Police and Fire Reform (S), 2012 asp 8, sch 8 pt 1

    s 83 rep—Antisocial Behaviour etc (S), 2004 asp 8, s 144(2), sch 5

    s 88 am—(prosp) Victims and Witnesses (S), 2014 asp 1, s 23(14); (prosp) Mental Health (S), 2015 asp 9, s 59(3)

    sch 2 am—Management of Offenders etc (S), 2005 asp 14, s 13(1)(3)

asp 8   **Building (Scotland)**

    appl—Licensing (S), 2005 asp 16, ss 45(11), 47(7), 50(8)

    excl—SI 2009/822, art 3

    s 1 rep in pt—Public Services Reform (S), 2010 asp 8, s 6(2)(a)

    s 3 rep in pt—Public Services Reform (S), 2010 asp 8, s 6(2)(b)

    s 24 am—Housing (S), 2006 asp 1, s 192(1), sch 6 paras 21,22; Housing (S), 2014 asp 14, s 89(1)(a)(ii)(b)

        rep in pt—Housing (S), 2014 asp 14, s 89(1)(a)(i)

    s 31 rep—Public Services Reform (S), 2010 asp 8, s 6(2)(c)

    s 35 am—SSI 2015/271, art 3(1)

    s 44 am—Buildings (Recovery of Expenses) (S), 2014 asp 13, s 1(a)(i)(ii)

    ss 46A-46H added —Buildings (Recovery of Expenses) (S), 2014 asp 13, s 1(b)

    s 47 am—Buildings (Recovery of Expenses) (S), 2014 asp 13, ss 1(c)(i)-(iv)

    s 55 am—Reservoirs (S), 2011 asp 9, s 112(4)

    s 56 rep in pt—Public Services Reform (S), 2010 asp 8, s 6(2)(d)

    sch 1 am—SSI 2014/364, reg 49

    sch 6 rep in pt—SSIs 2006/475, art 2, sch 2; 2009/248, art 2, sch 2

asp 9   **Title Conditions (Scotland)**

    appl in pt (mod)—SI 2009/729, art 5(1)(3)(4)

    excl in pt—SI 2009/729 art 5(2)

    appl—SSI 2010/188, art 17

    mod—SSI 2010/188, art 38

    s 3 am—Tenements (S), 2004 asp 11, s 25, sch 4, paras 1,2

    s 4 am—SSI 2003/503, art 2, sch 1 pt I, paras 6,7; Tenements (S), 2004 asp 11, s 25, sch 4, paras 1,3

        excl—SSI 2010/188, art 31

        rep in pt—Land Registration etc (S), 2012 asp 5, sch 5 para 43(2)

    s 8 am—SSI 2006/379, art 3

    s 10 am—Tenements (S), 2004 asp 11, s 25, sch 4, paras 1,4

    s 10A added—Tenements (S), 2004 asp 11, s 25, sch 4, paras 1,5

        am—Housing (S), 2014 asp 14, s 86(1)

    s 11 am—Tenements (S), 2004 asp 11, s 25, sch 4, paras 1,6

    s 12 am—Long Leases (S), 2012 asp 9, sch para 3(2)

2003

asp 9 *continued*

s 20 am—Long Leases (S), 2012 asp 9, sch para 3(3)

s 25 am—Tenements (S), 2004 asp 11, s 25, sch 4, paras 1,7

s 29 am—Tenements (S), 2004 asp 11, s 25, sch 4, paras 1, 8(a)(i),(b)–(h)

    rep in pt—Tenements (S), 2004 asp 11, s 25, sch 4, paras 1, 8(a)(ii)

s 31A added—Tenements (S), 2004 asp 11, s 25, sch 4, paras 1,9

s 33 am—Tenements (S), 2004 asp 11, s 25, sch 4, paras 1, 10(b)

    rep in pt—Tenements (S), 2004 asp 11, s 25, sch 4, paras 1, 10(a)

s 35 rep in pt—Tenements (S), 2004 asp 11, s 25, sch 4, paras 1, 11

s 37 am—SSI 2003/503, art 2, sch 1 pt I, paras 6,8

s 41 am—Land Registration etc (S), 2012 asp 5, sch 5 para 43(3)

s 43 am—Tenements (S), 2004 asp 11, s 25, sch 4, paras 1, 12

s 45 rep in pt—Tenements (S), 2004 asp 11, s 25, sch 4, paras 1, 13

s 46 rep in pt—Nat Health Service Reform (S), 2004 asp 7, s 11(2), sch 2

s 46A added —Climate Change (S), 2009 asp 12, s 68

s 51 rep —Land Registration etc (S), 2012 asp 5, sch 5 para 43(4)

s 53 am—Tenements (S), 2004 asp 11, s 25, sch 4, paras 1, 14

s 58 rep —Land Registration etc (S), 2012 asp 5, sch 5 para 43(4)

s 60 am—Land Registration etc (S), 2012 asp 5, sch 5 para 43(5)(a)

    rep in pt—Land Registration etc (S), 2012 asp 5, sch 5 para 43(5)(b)

s 63 am—Long Leases (S), 2012 asp 9, sch para 3(4)

s 71 rep in pt—Land Registration etc (S), 2012 asp 5, sch 5 para 43(6)

s 73 rep in pt—Land Registration etc (S), 2012 asp 5, sch 5 para 43(7)

s 75 excl—Waverley Railway (S), 2006 asp 13, s 44(2); Glasgow Airport Rail Link, 2007

    asp 1, s 42(3); Edinburgh Airport Rail Link, 2007 asp 16, s 55(2);

    Airdrie-Bathgate Railway and Linked Improvements, 2007 asp 19, ss 37(2),

    54(2); SSI 2010/188, art 31

    excl in pt—Forth Crossing, 2011 asp 2, s 27(2)

    rep in pt—Land Registration etc (S), 2012 asp 5, sch 5 para 43(8)

s 84 am—Land Registration etc (S), 2012 asp 5, sch 5 para 43(9)

s 90 am—SSI 2003/503, art 2, sch 1 pt I, paras 6,9(b)(c); Tenements (S), 2004 asp 11, s 25,

    sch 4, paras 1, 15

    rep in pt—SSI 2003/503, art 2, sch 1 pt I, paras 6,9(a)

    excl—SSI 2010/188, art 17

s 98 am—Tenements (S), 2004 asp 11, s 25, sch 4, paras 1, 16

s 99 am—SSI 2003/503, art 2, sch 1 pt I, paras 6,10; Tenements (S), 2004 asp 11, s 25,

    sch 4, paras 1, 17

s 104 am—SSI 2003/503, art 2, sch 1 pt I, paras 6,11; Tribunals, Courts and Enforcement,

    2007 c 15, s 48, sch 8, paras 56, 57

    rep in pt—SI 2013/2042, sch para 25

s 105 am—Long Leases (S), 2012 asp 9, sch para 3(5)

s 106 am—SSI 2003/503, art 2, sch 1 pt I, paras 6,12

    appl—SSI 2010/188, art 32

s 109 am—SSI 2003/503, art 2, sch 1 pt I, paras 6,13(b)-(d)

    rep in pt—SSI 2003/503, art 2, sch 1 pt I, paras 6,13(a)

s 110 rep in pt—SSI 2003/503, art 2, sch 1 pt I, paras 6,14

s 119 rep in pt—Tenements (S), 2004 asp 11, s 25, sch 4, paras 1, 18; Land Registration etc

    (S), 2012 asp 5, sch 5 para 43(10)

s 122 am—SSI 2003/503, art 2, sch 1 pt I, paras 6,15; Tenements (S), 2004 asp 11, s 25,

    sch 4, paras 1, 19(b)(c); Land Registration etc (S), 2012 asp 5, sch 5 para 43(11);

    Long Leases (S), 2012 asp 9, sch para 3(6)

    rep in pt—Tenements (S), 2004 asp 11, s 25, sch 4, paras 1, 19(a)

s 126 am—Tribunals, Courts and Enforcement, 2007 c 15, s 48, sch 8, paras 56, 58

    rep in pt—SI 2013/2042, sch para 26

s 128 am—SSI 2004/551, art 2

sch 1A added—Tenements (S), 2004 asp 11, s 25, sch 4, paras 1, 20

    am—SSI 2004/552, art 2

asp 10   **Homelessness etc. (Scotland)**

ss 1–3 rep—SSI 2012/330, art 13

s 4 rep in pt—SSI 2012/330, art 14

ss 5, 6 rep—SSI 2012/330, art 13

s 11 am—Home Owner and Debtor Protection (S), 2010 asp 6, s 8(5)(a)(i), (ii)

    rep in pt—Home Owner and Debtor Protection (S), 2010 asp 6, s 8(5)(a)(iii)

sch rep in pt—Home Owner and Debtor Protection (S), 2010 asp 6, s 8(5)(b)

2003

asp 11   **Agricultural Holdings (Scotland)**
    s 5 am—SSI 2011/232, arts 7, 8
    s 9 am—Agricultural Holdings (Amdt) (S), 2012 asp 6, s 2
    s 16 am—SSI 2011/232, art 9
    Pt 2 (ss 24-38) mod—SSI 2004/557, regs 3–5
    s 27 am—(1.8.2016) SSI 2012/38, sch para 4
        rep in pt—(1.8.2016) Housing (S), 2014 asp 4, sch 2 para 15
    s 71 am—Civil Partnership, 2004 c 33, s 261(2), sch 28 pt 4 para 68
    s 72 rep in pt—SSI 2014/98, arts 2(2)(a)-(c), 3
    s 72A added—SSI 2014/98, art 2(3)
    s 73 appl—SSI 2014/98, art 5

asp 12   **Dog Fouling (Scotland)**
    s 3 am—Police and Fire Reform (S), 2012 asp 8, sch 7 para 22
    s 9 rep in pt—Crim Proceedings etc. (Reform) (S), 2007 asp 6, s 80, sch 1 para 31
    s 16 am—Equality, 2010 c 15, s 211(1), sch 26 para 105 (added by SI 2010/2279, sch 1
        para 6)

asp 13   **Mental Health (Care and Treatment) (Scotland)**
    power to am—Joint Inspection of Children's Services and Inspection of Social Work
        Services (S), 2006 asp 3, s 7(2)(3)
    appl—Crim Justice, 2003 c 44, s 180, sch 9 pt 1, paras 2(4),4(4)
    appl (mod)—SSI 2008/356, reg 33
    s 1 am—(prosp) Mental Health (S), 2015 asp 9, s 53(4)
    s 3 rep in pt—(prosp) Nat Health Service Reform (S), 2004 asp 7, s 11(2), sch 2
        am—SSI 2011/211, sch 2 para 8(2)
    Pt 2 (ss 4-20) excl—(prosp) Care, 2014 c 23, sch 1 para 2(4)(5)
    s 4 am —Public Services Reform (S), 2010 asp 8, s 111(2)
    ss 4ZA-4ZD added—Victims and Witnesses (S), 2014 asp 1, s 30
    s 4A added —Public Services Reform (S), 2010 asp 8, s 111(3)
    s 5 am —Public Services Reform (S), 2010 asp 8, s 111(4)
    s 7 am—Public Services Reform (S), 2010 asp 8, ss 106, 110, sch 14, paras 13, 14, sch 17,
        paras 27, 28
    s 8 am—Public Services Reform (S), 2010 asp 8, ss 106, 110, sch 14, paras 13, 15, sch 17,
        paras 27, 29; SSI 2011/211, sch 1 para 13(2); Police and Fire Reform (S), 2012
        asp 8, sch 7 para 23(2)
    s 8A added —Public Services Reform (S), 2010 asp 8, s 111(5)
    s 9 am —Public Services Reform (S), 2010 asp 8, ss 106, 110, sch 14, paras 13, 16, sch 17,
        paras 27, 30
    s 9A added —Public Services Reform (S), 2010 asp 8, s 111(6)
    s 10 am —Public Services Reform (S), 2010 asp 8, s 111(7)
    s 11 am —Public Services Reform (S), 2010 asp 8, s 111(8)
    s 12 am —Public Services Reform (S), 2010 asp 8, s 111(9)
    s 13 rep in pt —Public Services Reform (S), 2010 asp 8, s 111(10)(b)(ii),(d)
        am —Public Services Reform (S), 2010 asp 8, s 111(10)(a),(b)(i)(iii),(c),(e)
    s 14 rep in pt —Public Services Reform (S), 2010 asp 8, s 111(11)(e)
        am —Public Services Reform (S), 2010 asp 8, s 111(11)(a)-(d)
    s 15 am —Public Services Reform (S), 2010 asp 8, s 111(12)(a)(b)
        rep in pt —Public Services Reform (S), 2010 asp 8, s 111(12)(c)
    s 16 am —Public Services Reform (S), 2010 asp 8, s 111(13)(a)
        rep in pt —Public Services Reform (S), 2010 asp 8, s 111(13)(b)(c)
    s 17 am —Public Services Reform (S), 2010 asp 8, ss 106, 110, 111(14), sch 14, paras 13,
        17, sch 17, paras 27, 31; Police and Fire Reform (S), 2012 asp 8, sch 7 para
        23(3)
    s 19 rep in pt—(prosp) Mental Health (S), 2015 asp 9, s 36(2)(a)
        am—(prosp) Mental Health (S), 2015 asp 9, s 36(2)(b)-(d)
    s 24 am—(prosp) Mental Health (S), 2015 asp 9, s 31
    ss 25-27 excl—Care, 2014 c 23, sch 1 paras 1(3), 2(3), 4(3)(b)
    s 25 am—SSI 2011/211, sch 1 para 13(3)
        mod—SSI 2015/202, reg 2(2)
    s 30 am—SSI 2015/157, sch para 7(2)
    s 31 am—SSI 2013/211, sch 1 para 13
    s 32 appl—Emergency Workers (S), 2005 asp 2, s 2(3)(h)(i)
    s 34 am—Public Services Reform (S), 2010 asp 8, s 106, 110, sch 14, paras 13, 18, sch 17,
        paras 27, 32
    s 35 am—Police and Fire Reform (S), 2012 asp 8, sch 7 para 23(4)

2003

asp 13 *continued*

s 36 am—SSI 2005/465, art 2, sch 1 para 32(1)(2); (prosp) Mental Health (S), 2015 asp 9, ss 4(2), 11(2)

    rep in pt—(prosp) Mental Health (S), 2015 asp 9, s 29(3)(a)

s 38 am—(prosp) Mental Health (S), 2015 asp 9, s 4(3)

    rep in pt—(prosp) Mental Health (S), 2015 asp 9, s 4(3)(c)(iii)

s 39 am—SSI 2005/465, art 2, sch 1 para 32(1)(3)

s 40 am—(prosp) Mental Health (S), 2015 asp 9, s 4(4)

s 42 am—(prosp) Mental Health (S), 2015 asp 9, s 4(5)

s 43 am (and title am)—(prosp) Mental Health (S), 2015 asp 9, s 7(2)(3)

s 44 am—SSI 2005/465, art 2, sch 1 para 32(1)(4); (prosp) Mental Health (S), 2015 asp 9, ss 5(2), 11(3)

    rep in pt—(prosp) Mental Health (S), 2015 asp 9, s 29(3)(b)

s 46 am—SSI 2005/465, art 2, sch 1 para 32(1)(5); (prosp) Mental Health (S), 2015 asp 9, s 5(3)(b)

    rep in pt—(prosp) Mental Health (S), 2015 asp 9, s 5(3)(a)

s 47 am—SSI 2005/465, art 2, sch 1 para 32(1)(6)

    rep in pt—(prosp) Mental Health (S), 2015 asp 9, s 29(3)(c)

s 49 am—SSI 2005/465, art 2, sch 1 para 32(1)(7)

s 50 am—SSI 2005/465, art 2, sch 1 para 32(1)(8)

s 51 am—SSI 2005/465, art 2, sch 1 para 32(1)(9)

s 55 am—SSI 2005/465, art 2, sch 1 para 32(1)(10)

s 56 am—(prosp) Mental Health (S), 2015 asp 9, s 8(2)(3)

s 58 rep in pt—(prosp) Mental Health (S), 2015 asp 9, s 29(3)(d)

s 64 am—(prosp) Mental Health (S), 2015 asp 9, s 1(2)

s 65 am—(prosp) Mental Health (S), 2015 asp 9, s 1(3)

s 71A added (prosp)—Mental Health (S), 2015 asp 9, s 11(4)

s 76 am—SSI 2005/465, art 2, sch 1 para 32(1)(11)

    appl (mods)—SSIs 2005/467, reg 42(1)(2); 2008/356, reg 29

s 77 mod—SSI 2008/356, reg 33

s 78 mod—SSI 2008/356, reg 33

s 87A added (prosp)—Mental Health (S), 2015 asp 9, s 2(2)

s 93 am—SSI 2004/533, art 2(1)(2)

s 95 am—SSI 2004/533, art 2(1)(3)

s 101 am—Adult Support and Protection (S), 2007 asp 10, s 68; (prosp) Mental Health (S), 2015 asp 9, s 21(2)

s 124 am—(prosp) Mental Health (S), 2015 asp 9, s 3(2)

s 124A added (prosp)—Mental Health (S), 2015 asp 9, s 13(2)

s 127 rep in pt—(prosp) Mental Health (S), 2015 asp 9, ss 9(2)(a)(d), 10(2)(a)

    am—SSI 2005/465, art 2, sch 1 para 32(1)(12); (prosp) Mental Health (S), 2015 asp 9, ss 9(2)(b)(c)(e), 10(2)(b),(3)

s 130 am—SSI 2005/465, art 2, sch 1 para 32(1)(13)

    rep in pt—SSI 2005/465, art 3, sch 2

s 133 am—SSI 2005/465, art 2, sch 1 para 32(1)(14)

s 135 rep —Crim Justice and Licensing (S), 2010 asp 13, s 14, sch 2, para 48(a)

s 136 am—(prosp) Mental Health (S), 2015 asp 9, ss 12(2), 34(2)

s 137 appl (mods)—SSIs 2005/467, reg 42(1)(3); 2008/356, reg 29

s 139 mod—SSI 2008/356, reg 33

s 140 mod—SSI 2008/356, reg 33

s 153A added (prosp)—Mental Health (S), 2015 asp 9, s 50

s 157 rep in pt—(prosp) Mental Health (S), 2015 asp 9, s 51(2)

s 158 am—SSI 2004/533, art 2(1)(4)(b)

    rep in pt—SSI 2004/533, art 2(1)(4)(a)

s 159 am—SSI 2004/533, art 2(1)(5)

s 160 am—(prosp) Mental Health (S), 2015 asp 9, s 51(3)

s 161 am—SSI 2004/533, art 2(1)(6)

s 167 am—SSI 2005/465, art 2, sch 1 para 32(1)(15)

s 168 am—SSI 2005/465, art 2, sch 1 para 32(1)(16)

s 171 am—SSI 2005/465, art 2, sch 1 para 32(1)(17)

s 172 rep in pt—SSI 2005/465, art 3, sch 2

s 179 am—SSI 2005/465, art 2, sch 1 para 32(1)(18)

s 183 appl (mods)—SSI 2005/467, reg 39

    am—Adult Support and Protection (S), 2007 asp 10, s 69(1)

s 184 am—Adult Support and Protection (S), 2007 asp 10, s 69(2)

2003
asp 13 *continued*

s 188 am—Adult Support and Protection (S), 2007 asp 10, s 69(3)

s 189 am—(prosp) Mental Health (S), 2015 asp 9, s 21(3)

s 193 am—Adult Support and Protection (S), 2007 asp 10, s 69(4); (prosp) Mental Health
    (S), 2015 asp 9, s 60(2)

s 198 am—(prosp) Mental Health (S), 2015 asp 9, s 52

s 200 am—(prosp) Mental Health (S), 2015 asp 9, s 60(3)

s 207 appl (mods)—SSI 2005/467, reg 40
    am—Adult Support and Protection (S), 2007 asp 10, s 70(1)

s 208 am—Adult Support and Protection (S), 2007 asp 10, s 70(2)

s 210 am—Adult Support and Protection (S), 2007 asp 10, s 70(3)

s 212 am—Adult Support and Protection (S), 2007 asp 10, s 70(4)

s 213 am—(prosp) Mental Health (S), 2015 asp 9, s 21(4)

s 215 am—Adult Support and Protection (S), 2007 asp 10, s 70(5)

s 218A added (prosp)—Mental Health (S), 2015 asp 9, s 48(2)

s 221 am—(prosp) Mental Health (S), 2015 asp 9, s 9(3)(a)(b)(d)
    rep in pt—(prosp) Mental Health (S), 2015 asp 9, s 9(3)(c)

s 224 am—(prosp) Mental Health (S), 2015 asp 9, ss 9(4)(a)(c)(d)(f), 10(4)(a); (prosp) ibid,
    s 60(4)
    rep in pt—(prosp) Mental Health (S), 2015 asp 9, s 9(4)(b)(e), 10(4)(b)

s 229 appl (mods)—SSIs 2005/467, regs 4, 28; 2008/356, reg 17

s 230 appl (mods)—SSIs 2005/467, regs 4, 29; 2008/356, reg 18
    rep in pt—(prosp) Mental Health (S), 2015 asp 9, s 6(2)

s 245 am—(prosp) Mental Health (S), 2015 asp 9, s 30(2)

s 246 am—SSI 2004/533, art 2(1)(7)

s 248 am—SSI 2005/465, art 2, sch 1 para 32(1)(19)

s 250 am—(prosp) Mental Health (S), 2015 asp 9, s 23(2)

s 251 rep (prosp)—Mental Health (S), 2015 asp 9, s 22(2)

s 252 rep (prosp)—Mental Health (S), 2015 asp 9, s 22(2)
    am—SSI 2005/465, art 2, sch 1 para 32(1)(20)
    rep in pt—SSI 2005/465, art 2, sch 1 para 32(1)(20)(d)(i)

s 254 am—Civil Partnership, 2004 c 33, s 261(2), sch 28 pt 4 para 69; SSI 2005/465, art 2,
    sch 1 para 32(1)(21)

s 255 rep in pt—(prosp) Mental Health (S), 2015 asp 9, s 24(2)

s 256 rep in pt—(prosp) Mental Health (S), 2015 asp 9, s 24(3)(a)
    am—(prosp) Mental Health (S), 2015 asp 9, s 24(3)(b)

s 257 rep in pt—(prosp) Mental Health (S), 2015 asp 9, s 24(4)(a)
    am—(prosp) Mental Health (S), 2015 asp 9, ss 23(3), 24(4)(b)(c)

s 257A added (prosp)—Mental Health (S), 2015 asp 9, s 25(2)

s 259A added (prosp)—Mental Health (S), 2015 asp 9, s 27(2)

s 260 appl (mods)—SSI 2008/356, reg 30

s 261 appl (mods)—SSIs 2005/467, reg 43; 2008/356, reg 31

s 261A added (prosp)—Mental Health (S), 2015 asp 9, s 28(2)

s 262 appl (mods)—SSI 2005/467, reg 44

s 264 am—Mental Health (S), 2015 asp 9, s 14(2); SSI 2015/364, reg 3(a)

s 266 rep—Mental Health (S), 2015 asp 9, s 15(2)

s 267 am—Mental Health (S), 2015 asp 9, s 15(3)(4)

s 268 rep in pt—Mental Health (S), 2015 asp 9, s 16(2)(a),(d),(e)(i),(f)
    am—Mental Health (S), 2015 asp 9, ss 14(3), 16(2)(b)(c),(e)(ii); SSI 2015/364, reg
    3(b)

s 269 rep in pt—Mental Health (S), 2015 asp 9, s 16(3)(a)
    am—Mental Health (S), 2015 asp 9, s 16(3)(b)(c)

s 270 rep—Mental Health (S), 2015 asp 9, s 15(5)

s 271 am (and title am)—Mental Health (S), 2015 asp 9, ss 15(6)(7), 16(4)(b)
    rep in pt—Mental Health (S), 2015 asp 9, s 16(4)(a)

s 271A added—Mental Health (S), 2015 asp 9, s 16(5)

s 272 am—Mental Health (S), 2015 asp 9, s 15(8)

s 273 am—Mental Health (S), 2015 asp 9, ss 16(6), 18(2)

s 274 am—SSI 2004/533, art 2(1)(8)

ss 276A-276C added (prosp)—Mental Health (S), 2015 asp 9, s 26(2)

s 281 am—SSI 2011/211, sch 2 para 8(3)

s 289 am—SSI 2004/533, art 2(1)(9); Adult Support and Protection (S), 2007 asp 10, s
    71(1); (prosp) Mental Health (S), 2015 asp 9, s 32(2)

s 290 am—SSI 2004/533, art 2(1)(10); (prosp) Mental Health (S), 2015 asp 9, s 32(3)

2003

asp 13 *continued*

s 291A added (prosp)—Mental Health (S), 2015 asp 9, s 29(2)

s 292 am—Police and Fire Reform (S), 2012 asp 8, sch 7 para 23(5)

s 295A added (prosp)—Mental Health (S), 2015 asp 9, s 19

s 298 am—SSI 2011/211, sch 1 para 13(4), sch 2 para 8(4)

s 299 am—(prosp) Mental Health (S), 2015 asp 9, s 20(2)(a)(ii),(b)
   rep in pt—(prosp) Mental Health (S), 2015 asp 9, s 20(2)(a)(i),(c)

s 300 am—SSI 2011/211, sch 1 para 13(5)

s 301 appl (mods)—SSIs 2005/467, reg 22(4); 2008/333, regs 2-3; 2008/356, reg 12

s 302 appl (mods)—SSIs 2005/467, reg 22(5); 2008/181, reg 2; 2008/333, regs 4-5

s 303 am—(prosp) Mental Health (S), 2015 asp 9, s 33(2)
   appl (mods)—SSIs 2008/181, reg 2; 2008/333, regs 6-7
   appl—SSI 2008/356, reg 12

s 309 am—Adult Support and Protection (S), 2007 asp 10, s 71(2); (prosp) Mental Health
   (S), 2015 asp 9, s 33(3)

s 309A added—Adult Support and Protection (S), 2007 asp 10, s 72(1)
   am—(prosp) Mental Health (S), 2015 asp 9, s 32(4)

s 310 am—SSI 2004/533, art 2(1)(11); (prosp) Mental Health (S), 2015 asp 9, s 33(4)
   appl (mods)—SSI 2005/467, reg 22(6)

ss 311-313 rep—Sexual Offences (S), 2009 asp 9, s 61, sch 6

s 314 rep —SSI 2005/465, art 3, sch 2

s 316 am—SSI 2005/465, art 2, sch 1 para 32(1)(22); Adult Support and Protection (S),
   2007 asp 10, s 71(3)

s 318 rep in pt—(prosp) Mental Health (S), 2015 asp 9, s 22(3)

s 319 rep —Sexual Offences (S), 2009 asp 9, s 61, sch 6

s 320 appl (mods)—SSIs 2005/467, reg 14; 2008/356, reg 9
   rep in pt—(prosp) Mental Health (S), 2015 asp 9, s 24(5)

s 321 appl (mods)—SSIs 2005/467, reg 15; 2008/356, reg 9

s 323 am —Constitutional Reform, 2005 c 4, s 40(4), sch 9 pt 1 para 83

s 326 am—SSI 2005/465, art 2, sch 1 para 32(1)(23)(a); Adult Support and Protection (S),
   2007 asp 10, ss 71(4), 72(2); Sexual Offences (S), 2009 asp 9, s 61, sch 5 para 6;
   Public Services Reform (S), 2010 asp 8, s 111, sch 18, para 1; Mental Health (S),
   2015 asp 9, s 16(7); (prosp) ibid, s 36(3)
   rep in pt—SSI 2005/465, art 2, sch 1 para 32(1)(23)(b)

s 328 appl—Crim Procedure (S),1995 c 46, s 271

s 329 am—SSIs 2005/465, art 2, sch 1 para 32(1)(24)(a); 2011/211, sch 1 para 13(6), sch 2
   para 8(5); Children and Young People (S), 2014 asp 8, sch 5 para 9; (prosp)
   Mental Health (S), 2015 asp 9, ss 6(3), 22(4), 53(5), 60(5); SSI 2015/157, sch
   para 7(3)
   rep in pt—SSI 2005/465, art 2, sch 1 para 32(1)(24)(b)

s 331 am—SSI 2005/465, art 2, sch 1 para 32(1)(25)

sch 1 am—Adult Support and Protection (S), 2007 asp 10, s 77, sch 1 para 6; Public
   Services Reform (S), 2010 asp 8, s 111, sch 18, paras 2, 4-7, 9; Victims and
   Witnesses (S), 2014 asp 1, s 31(1)(a)-(c)
   rep in pt —Public Services Reform (S), 2010 asp 8, s 111, sch 18, paras 2, 3, 8

sch 1A added—Victims and Witnesses (S), 2014 asp 1, s 31(2)

sch 2 am—SSI 2005/465, art 2, sch 1 para 32(1)(26); Adult Support and Protection (S),
   2007 asp 10, s 73
   rep in pt—Smoking, Health and Social Care (S), 2005 asp 13, s 42(2), sch 3; Court
   Reform (S), 2014 asp 18, sch 4 para 5; (prosp) Mental Health (S), 2015 asp 9, s
   21(5)

sch 3 am—(prosp) Mental Health (S), 2015 asp 9, s 35(3)

sch 4 am—SSI 2005/465, art 2, sch 1 para 32(1)(27)
   rep in pt—SSI 2005/465, art 3, sch 2; Joint Inspection of Children's Services and
   Inspection of Social Work Services (S), 2006 asp 3, s 8(4)(h); Crim Justice and
   Licensing (S), 2010 asp 13, s 14, sch 2, para 48(b)

sch 5 am—SSI 2005/465, art 2, sch 1 para 32(1)(28)
   rep in pt—SSI 2005/465, art 3, sch 2

sch 7 am—(prosp) Mental Health (S), 2015 asp 9, s 35(2)

asp 14 **Council of the Law Society of Scotland**

asp 15 **Salmon and Freshwater Fisheries (Consolidation) (Scotland)**

s 3 am—Aquaculture and Fisheries (S), 2007 asp 12, s 19

s 3A added—Aquaculture and Fisheries (S), 2007 asp 12, s 20(1)

s 4 am—Aquaculture and Fisheries (S), 2007 asp 12, ss 20(2), 24(2)

2003

asp 15 *continued*

      s 5A added—Aquaculture and Fisheries (S), 2007 asp 12, s 21
      s 8 rep in pt—SSI 2009/85, reg 48, sch 2
      s 14 am—Aquaculture and Fisheries (S), 2013 asp 7, s 31
      s 17 am—Aquaculture and Fisheries (S), 2007 asp 12, s 41, sch 1 para 6(1)(2)
      ss 17A, 17B added—Aquaculture and Fisheries (S), 2007 asp 12, s 22
      s 21A added—Aquaculture and Fisheries (S), 2013 asp 7, s 26(2)
      s 24 rep—Aquaculture and Fisheries (S), 2007 asp 12, s 35(1)
      s 27 am—Aquaculture and Fisheries (S), 2013 asp 7, s 33(2)
      s 28 rep in pt—SSI 2006/181, art 2, sch pt 1
           am—Aquaculture and Fisheries (S), 2007 asp 12, s 23(1); Aquaculture and Fisheries
               (S), 2013 asp 7, s 33(3)
      s 30 am—Aquaculture and Fisheries (S), 2007 asp 12, s 23(2); Aquaculture and Fisheries
               (S), 2013 asp 7, ss 26(3), 33(4)
      s 31 am—Aquaculture and Fisheries (S), 2007 asp 12, s 41, sch 1 para 6(1)(3)
      s 33 am—Aquaculture and Fisheries (S), 2013 asp 7, ss 25(2)(a), 29(2), 30(2)
      s 33A added—Aquaculture and Fisheries (S), 2007 asp 12, s 35(2)
           am—Aquaculture and Fisheries (S), 2013 asp 7, s 32(2)
      s 33B added—Aquaculture and Fisheries (S), 2013 asp 7, s 32(3)
      s 35 am—Aquaculture and Fisheries (S), 2013 asp 7, s 25(2)(b)
           rep in pt—Aquaculture and Fisheries (S), 2013 asp 7, s 30(3)
      s 36 am—Aquaculture and Fisheries (S), 2013 asp 7, s 25(2)(c)
      s 37 am—Aquaculture and Fisheries (S), 2013 asp 7, ss 25(2)(d), 29(3)
      s 38 am—Aquaculture and Fisheries (S), 2013 asp 7, s 29(4)
      s 39 am—Aquaculture and Fisheries (S), 2013 asp 7, s 30(4)
      s 44 am—Aquaculture and Fisheries (S), 2013 asp 7, s 24(2)
      ss 46A–46G added—Aquaculture and Fisheries (S), 2013 asp 7, s 24(3)
      s 48 am—Aquaculture and Fisheries (S), 2007 asp 12, s 41, sch 1 para 6(1)(4)
      s 51A added—Aquaculture and Fisheries (S), 2007 asp 12, s 24(1)
      s 64 am—Water, 1989 c 15, sch 17, para 4; Aquaculture and Fisheries (S), 2013 asp 7, s
            28(2)(a)(3)(4)
           rep in pt—Aquaculture and Fisheries (S), 2013 asp 7, s 28(2)(b)
      s 64A added—Aquaculture and Fisheries (S), 2013 asp 7, s 27(2)
      s 67 subst—Aquaculture and Fisheries (S), 2013 asp 7, s 34
      s 68 am—Aquaculture and Fisheries (S), 2013 asp 7, ss 24(4), 26(4)
      s 69 am—SSI 2009/85, reg 48, sch 2
      sch 1 am—Aquaculture and Fisheries (S), 2007 asp 12, s 41, sch 1 para 6(1)(5);
               Aquaculture and Fisheries (S), 2013 asp 7, s 25(3)
      sch 3 am—Aquaculture and Fisheries (S), 2007 asp 12, s 41, sch 1 para 6(1)(6)(7)

asp 16 **National Galleries of Scotland**
asp 17 **Commissioner for Children and Young People (Scotland)**
      s 2 am —S Parl Commn and Commrs, 2010 asp 11, s 29, sch 5, para 1
      s 3 am —S Parl Commn and Commrs, 2010 asp 11, s 29, sch 5, para 2
      s 7 am—(prosp) Children and Young People (S), 2014 asp 8, s 5(2)(a)-(c)
      s 8 am—(prosp) Children and Young People (S), 2014 asp 8, s 5(3)(a)-(c)
      s 10 am —S Parl Commn and Commrs, 2010 asp 11, s 29, sch 5, para 3
      s 11 am—(prosp) Children and Young People (S), 2014 asp 8, ss 5(4)(a)-(c), 6(2)(a)(b)
      s 14A added —S Parl Commn and Commrs, 2010 asp 11, s 29, sch 5, para 4
      s 14AA added (prosp)—Children and Young People (S), 2014 asp 8, s 6(3)
      sch 1 am—S Parl Commn and Commrs, 2010 asp 11, s 29, sch 5, para 5-15

asp 18 **Education (School Meals) (Scotland)**
asp 19 **Robin Rigg Offshore Wind Farm (Navigation and Fishing) (Scotland)**

2004

asp 1 **Primary Medical Services (Scotland)**
      s 2 rep in pt—Tobacco and Primary Medical Services (S), 2010 asp 3, s 41, sch 2, para 7
      s 5 rep in pt—Smoking, Health and Social Care (S), 2005 asp 13, s 42(2), sch 3
      sch rep in pt—(prosp) Smoking, Health and Social Care (S), 2005 asp 13, s 42(2), sch 3
asp 2 **Budget (Scotland)**
      s 3 am—SSIs 2004/290, art 2(1)(2); 365, art 2(1)(2); 2005/164, art 2(1)(2)
      Pt 2 (s 6) rep—Budget (S), 2005 asp 4, s 8
      sch 1 am—SSIs 2004/565, art 2(1)(3); 2005/164, art 2(1)(3)
           rep in pt—SSI 2005/164, art 2(1)(3)(a)(ii)(aa)(bb)(dd)
      sch 2 am—SSIs 2004/565, art 2(1)(4); 2005/164, art 2(1)(4)

2004

asp 2 sch 2 *continued*

    rep in pt—SSI 2005/164, art 2(1)(4)(e)(ii)(iii),(k)(i)(ii)

  sch 3 am—SSIs 2004/290, art 2(1)(3); 365, art 2(1)(5); 2005/164, art 2(1)(5)

  sch 4 am—SSIs 2004/565, art 2(1)(6); 2005/164, art 2(1)(6)

  sch 5 am—SSIs 2004/565, art 2(1)(7); 2005/164, art 2(1)(7)

asp 3   **Vulnerable Witnesses (Scotland)**

  s 11 am—Children's Hearings (S), 2011 asp 1, s 176(2); Victims and Witnesses (S),2014
    asp 1, s 22(a)(c)

    rep in pt—Victims and Witnesses (S), 2014 asp 1, s 22(b)

  s 12 am—Children's Hearings (S), 2011 asp 1, s 176(3)

  s 16A added—Children's Hearings (S), 2011 asp 1, s 176(4)

  s 22A added—Children's Hearings (S), 2011 asp 1, s 176(5)

  sch 2 appl (mods)—SSI 2006/464, art 4

asp 4   **Education (Additional Support for Learning) (Scotland)**

  s 1 am—Educ (Additional Support for Learning) (S), 2009 asp 7, ss 1(2), 6, 8(1); Children
    and Young People (S), 2014 asp 8, sch 5 para 10(2)(a)(b)

  s 5 am—Educ (Additional Support for Learning) (S), 2009 asp 7, s 9; Children and Young
    People (S), 2014 asp 8, sch 5 para 10(3)

  s 6 am—Educ (Additional Support for Learning) (S), 2009 asp 7, s 8(2)

  s 7 am—Educ (Additional Support for Learning) (S), 2009 asp 7, s 1(3)

  s 8A added—Educ (Additional Support for Learning) (S), 2009 asp 7, s 7

  s 10 am—Educ (Additional Support for Learning) (S), 2009 asp 7, s 1(4)

  s 11 rep in pt—Educ (Additional Support for Learning) (S), 2009 asp 7, s 1(5)

  s 12 am—Educ (Additional Support for Learning) (S), 2009 asp 7, s 1(6)

  s 13 am—Educ (Additional Support for Learning) (S), 2009 asp 7, s 17

  s 14A added —Educ (Additional Support for Learning) (S), 2009 asp 7, s 10

  s 15 am—Educ (Additional Support for Learning) (S), 2009 asp 7, ss 2(a)(b)(d)(e), 11

    rep in pt—Educ (Additional Support for Learning) (S), 2009 asp 7, s 2(c)

  s 16 am—Educ (Additional Support for Learning) (S), 2009 asp 7, s 12

    rep in pt—Educ (Additional Support for Learning) (S), 2009 asp 7, s 3

  s 17 rep in pt—Equality, 2010 c 15, s 211, sch 17, para 12(a); ibid, s 211(2), sch 27 pt 1 (as
    subst by SI 2010/2279, sch 2)

    am —Equality, 2010 c 15, s 116, sch 17, para 12(b)

  s 18 am—Educ (Additional Support for Learning) (S), 2009 asp 7, ss 1(7)(a)-(c)(d)(ii)(e),
    18(1), 19(1)(b)

    rep in pt—Educ (Additional Support for Learning) (S), 2009 asp 7, ss 1(7)(d)(i),
    19(1)(a)

  s 19 am—Educ (Additional Support for Learning) (S), 2009 asp 7, ss 1(8), 18(2), 19(2)

  s 26 am—SSI 2005/267, reg 2; Educ (Additional Support for Learning) (S), 2009 asp 7, ss
    13(a)(ii)(b), 14-16

    rep in pt—Educ (Additional Support for Learning) (S), 2009 asp 7, s 13(a)(i)

  s 26A added —Educ (Additional Support for Learning) (S), 2009 asp 7, s 22

  s 27A added —Educ (Additional Support for Learning) (S), 2009 asp 7, s 23

  s 29 am—Educ (Additional Support for Learning) (S), 2009 asp 7, s 5; Children and Young
    People (S), 2014 asp 8, sch 5 para 10(4)(a)(b)

  sch 1 am—Educ (Additional Support for Learning) (S), 2009 asp 7, ss 20, 21; Equality,
    2010 c 15, s 116, sch 17, para 12(c)

    rep in pt—Court Reform (S), 2014 asp 18, sch 4 para 6

  sch 2 am—Educ (Additional Support for Learning) (S), 2009 asp 7, s 1(9); Equality, 2010 c
    15, s 211(1), sch 26 para 106 (added by SI 2010/2279, sch 1 para 6)

  sch 3 rep in pt—SSI 2011/215, sch 7

asp 5   **Criminal Procedure (Amendment) (Scotland)**

  s 4 rep in pt —Crim Justice and Licensing (S), 2010 asp 13, s 203, sch 7, para 74(a)

  s 9 am—SSI 2005/40, art 3(1)(2)

  s 10 am—SSI 2005/40, art 3(1)(3)

  s 17 rep —Crim Justice and Licensing (S), 2010 asp 13, s 203, sch 7, para 74(b)

  s 18 am—SSI 2005/40, art 3(1)(4)

  s 24 rep in pt—Protection of Vulnerable Groups (S), 2007 asp 14, s 88, sch 4 para 43

  sch am—SSI 2005/40, art 3(1)(5)

    rep in pt —Crim Justice and Licensing (S), 2010 asp 13, s 203, sch 7, para 74(c)

asp 6   **Nature Conservation (Scotland)**

  s 1 see—(defn of public bodies ext) Flood Risk Management (S), 2009 asp 6, s 59(4)

  s 2A added—Wildlife and Natural Environment (S), 2011 asp 6, s 36

  Pt 2 (ss 3-39) appl (mods)—SI 1994/2716, regs 19-22 (as subst by SSI 2004/475, regs 3, 9)

2004

asp 6 *continued*

     s 5A added—Wildlife and Natural Environment (S), 2011 asp 6, s 37(2)

     s 9 am—Wildlife and Natural Environment (S), 2011 asp 6, s 38

     s 13 am—Wildlife and Natural Environment (S), 2011 asp 6, s 39(2)

     s 14 am—Wildlife and Natural Environment (S), 2011 asp 6, ss 39(3), 40(1)(b)

     s 17 am—Wildlife and Natural Environment (S), 2011 asp 6, ss 39(4), 40(1)(c)

     s 20A added—Wildlife and Natural Environment (S), 2011 asp 6, s 40(1)(a)

     s 21 trans of functions—Public Services Reform (S), 2010 asp 8, s 2(2)

        rep in pt—Public Services Reform (S), 2010 asp 8, s 2(3)(a)

        am—Public Services Reform (S), 2010 asp 8, s 2(3)(b), (c)

     s 44 am—Wildlife and Natural Environment (S), 2011 asp 6, s 40(1)(d)(e)

     s 48 am—Wildlife and Natural Environment (S), 2011 asp 6, s 37(3)

     s 58 rep in pt—Public Services Reform (S), 2010 asp 8, s 2(3)(d)

        am—Wildlife and Natural Environment (S), 2011 asp 6, s 37(4); SI 2011/2085, sch 1 para 58

     sch 1 am—Public Services Reform (S), 2010 asp 8, s 2(3)(e)(i)-(iii), (v)

        rep in pt—Public Services Reform (S), 2010 asp 8, s 2(3)(e)(iv)

asp 7   **National Health Service Reform (Scotland)**

     s 2 rep —Public Bodies (Joint Working) (S), 2014 asp 9, s 71(4)

asp 8   **Antisocial Behaviour etc (Scotland)**

     s 1 am—Police and Fire Reform (S), 2012 asp 8, sch 7 para 24(2)

        rep in pt—Police and Fire Reform (S), 2012 asp 8, sch 8 pt 1

     s 2 rep n pt—Police and Fire Reform (S), 2012 asp 8, sch 8 pt 1

        am—Police and Fire Reform (S), 2012 asp 8, sch 7 para 24(3)

     s 8 am—SI 2011/2085, sch 1 para 59

     s 12 am—Children's Hearings (S), 2011 asp 1, sch 5 para 3

     s 15 am—Police and Fire Reform (S), 2012 asp 8, sch 7 para 24(4)

     s 18 am—Police and Fire Reform (S), 2012 asp 8, sch 7 para 24(5)

     s 20 rep in pt—Police and Fire Reform (S), 2012 asp 8, sch 8 pt 1

     s 26 am—Crim Justice and Licensing (S), 2010 asp 13, s 99(1)

     s 27 am—Crim Justice and Licensing (S), 2010 asp 13, s 99(2)

     s 30 am—Crim Justice and Licensing (S), 2010 asp 13, s 99(3)

     s 31 am—Police and Fire Reform (S), 2012 asp 8, sch 7 para 24(6)

     s 32 am—Crim Justice and Licensing (S), 2010 asp 13, s 99(4)

     s 33 am—Crim Justice and Licensing (S), 2010 asp 13, s 99(5)

     s 35 am—Police and Fire Reform (S), 2012 asp 8, sch 7 para 24(7)

     s 36 am—Crim Justice and Licensing (S), 2010 asp 13, s 99(6)

     s 37 am—Crim Proceedings etc (Reform) (S), 2007 asp 6, s 44(3)

     s 40 am—SSI 2015/150, sch para 7

     s 40A added—Crim Justice and Licensing (S), 2010 asp 13, s 99(7)

        rep in pt—(31.5.2016) Human Trafficking and Exploitation (S), 2015 asp 12, sch para 3(a)

        am—(31.5.2016) Human Trafficking and Exploitation (S), 2015 asp 12, sch para 3(b)(c)

     s 51 am—Crim Proceedings etc (Reform) (S), 2007 asp 6, s 80, sch 1 para 32(a)

     s 68 am—SSI 2011/201, art 3)

     s 69 am—SSI 2011/201, art 4

     s 71 am—SSI 2011/201, art 5

     s 74 am—SSI 2011/201, art 6

     s 78 am—SSI 2011/201, art 7

     s 79 am—SSI 2011/201, art 8

     s 81 rep in pt—Housing (S), 2006 asp 1, s 192(2), sch 7; SSI 2011/211, sch 2 para 9(a)(i)

        am—SSI 2011/211, sch 1 para 14(2); ibid, sch 2 para 9(a)(ii)(iii)

     s 82 rep in pt—Housing (S), 2006 asp 1, s 176(2)

     s 83 rep in pt—SSI 2005/650, art 2(a); (prosp) Housing (S), 2006 asp 1, s 192(2), sch 7; SSI 2011/211, sch 2 para 9(b)(i)(ii)(iii)

        am—SSI 2005/650, art 2(b); Housing (S), 2006 asp 1, s 176(3)(a)(b); SSI 2009/33, art 2; SSI 2011/211, sch 1 para 14(3)

     s 84 am—Housing (S), 2006 asp 1, s 176(4); Private Rented Housing (S), 2011 asp 14, s 3(1); ibid, sch para 2

     s 85 appl—Housing (S), 2006 asp 1, s 130(3)

        am—Housing (S), 2006 asp 1, ss 175(2), 176(5); Private Rented Housing (S), 2011 asp 14, s 1(1)

     s 85A added—Private Rented Housing (S), 2011 asp 14, s 2

2004

asp 8 *continued*

s 86 am—Private Rented Housing (S), 2011 asp 14, s 3(2); ibid, sch para 3
s 87A added—Housing (S), 2006 asp 1, s 176(6)
s 88 am—Private Rented Housing (S), 2011 asp 14, s 4
s 88A added—Housing (S), 2006 asp 1, s 176(7)
    am—Private Rented Housing (S), 2011 asp 14, s 5(1)
s 89 am—Private Rented Housing (S), 2011 asp 14, sch para 4
s 90 am—Private Rented Housing (S), 2011 asp 14, sch para 5
s 91 am—Private Rented Housing (S), 2011 asp 14, sch para 6
s 92 am—Private Rented Housing (S), 2011 asp 14, sch para 7; (prosp) Housing, 2014 asp
    14, sch 1 para 57(b)(i)(c)
    rep in pt—(prosp) Housing, 2014 asp 14, sch 1 para 57(a)(b)(ii)
s 92ZA added —Private Rented Housing (S), 2011 asp 14, s 5(2)
    am—(prosp) Housing, 2014 asp 14, sch 1 para 58(a)(i)-(iv)(b)(i)-(iv)
s 92A added—Housing (S), 2006 asp 1, s 175(3)
s 92B added —Private Rented Housing (S), 2011 asp 14, s 6
s 93 am—Housing (S), 2006 asp 1, s 176(8); Private Rented Housing (S), 2011 asp 14, s 7;
    ibid, sch para 8
s 93A added —Private Rented Housing (S), 2011 asp 14, s 8
s 97 am—Housing (S), 2006 asp 1, s 176(9)(10); (prosp) Housing, 2014 asp 14, sch 1 para
    59(a)(b)
ss 97A, 97B added —Private Rented Housing (S), 2011 asp 14, s 9
s 99A added—Private Rented Housing (S), 2011 asp 14, s 10
s 101 am—Housing (S), 2006 asp 1, s 176(11); Private Rented Housing (S), 2011 asp 14, s
    3(3); (prosp) Housing, 2014 asp 14, sch 1 para 60(1)(b)
s 112 am—SSI 2013/211, sch 1 para 14(2); SSI 2015/402, sch para 5
s 116 rep—SSI 2013/211, sch 2
s 117 am—SSI 2013/211, sch 1 para 14(3)
s 119 am—Police and Fire Reform (S), 2012 asp 8, sch 7 para 24(8)
s 120 rep —Crim Justice and Licensing (S), 2010 asp 13, s 14, sch 2, para 50(a)
s 128 am—SSI 2009/248, art 2, sch 1 para 10; Offensive Behaviour at Football and
    Threatening Communications (S), 2012 asp 1, s 3
ss 130, 131 am—Crim Proceedings etc (Reform) (S), 2007 asp 6, s 80, sch 1 para 32(b)
s 132 am—Crim Proceedings etc (Reform) (S), 2007 asp 6, s 80, sch 1 para 32(b)
    rep in pt—Crim Proceedings etc (Reform) (S), 2007 asp 6, s 80, sch 1 para 32(c)
ss 135-137 rep—SSI 2013/211, sch 2
s 139 am—Police and Fire Reform (S), 2012 asp 8, sch 7 para 24(9)
s 141 am—Private Rented Housing (S), 2011 asp 14, s 1(2)
s 143 appl—Licensing (S), 2005 asp 16, ss 21(6), 65(6)
    am —Housing (S), 2010 asp 17, s 162, sch 2, para 11
sch 2 rep in pt—Regulatory Reform (S), 2014 asp 3, sch 3 para 37
sch 4 rep in pt —Crim Justice and Licensing (S), 2010 asp 13, s 14, sch 2, para 50(b); SSI
    2012/330, art 15; SSI 2013/211, sch 2

asp 9   **Local Governance (Scotland)**
s 3 am—Loc Electoral Admin and Registration Services (S), 2006 asp 14, s 34(6)
s 3A added —Scottish Loc Govt Elections, 2009 asp 10, s 2(1)
s 16 am—Scottish Loc Govt Elections, 2009 asp 10, s 2(2)

asp 10   **Stirling-Alloa-Kincardine Railway and Linked Improvements**
s 12 rep in pt—SSI 2006/181, art 2, sch pt 1
s 16 am—Land Registration etc (S), 2012 asp 5, sch 5 para 45

asp 11   **Tenements (Scotland)**
s 1 rep in pt—Land Registration etc (S), 2012 asp 5, sch 5 para 46(2)(a)
    am—Land Registration etc (S), 2012 asp 5, sch 5 para 46(2)(b)
s 4 am—Housing (S), 2014 asp 14, s 85(1)(a)
s 4A am—Housing (S), 2014 asp 14, s 85(1)(b)
s 13 am—Housing (S), 2014 asp 14, s 85(1)(c); ibid, s 86(2)(a)
s 29 am—Housing (S), 2014 asp 14, s 86(2)(b)
s 84 am—(prosp) Housing (S), 2014 asp 14, s 60(1)
s 85B added—(prosp) Housing (S), 2014 asp 14, s 21(1)
s 86 am—(prosp) Housing (S), 2014 asp 14, s 21(2)
s 88 rep in pt—(prosp) Housing (S), 2014 asp 14, s 60(2)(a)(i)
    am—(prosp) Housing (S), 2014 asp 14, s 60(2)(a)(ii)(b)(c)
s 89 am—(prosp) Housing (S), 2014 asp 14, s 60(3)(a)(b)
s 90 am—(prosp) Housing (S), 2014 asp 14, s 60(4)

2004

asp 11 *continued*

        s 91 am—(prosp) Housing (S), 2014 asp 14, s 60(5)

        s 92 am—(prosp) Housing (S), 2014 asp 14, ss 19(2), 60(6)

        s 92A am—(prosp) Housing (S), 2014 asp 14, s 60(8)

        s 92ZA am—(prosp) Housing (S), 2014 asp 14, s 60(7)

        s 97 am—(prosp) Housing (S), 2014 asp 14, s 19(3)(a)(b)

        s 101 am—(prosp) Housing (S), 2014 asp 14, s 60(9)

        sch 1 am—Climate Change (S), 2009 asp 12, s 69; (1.4.15) Housing (S), 2014 asp 14, s
            85(1)(d)(e)

        sch 2 am—SSI 2004/490, art 2

           rep in pt—SI 2014/1924, sch

        sch 3 am—Land Registration etc (S), 2012 asp 5, sch 5 para 46(3)

asp 12   **School Education (Ministerial Powers and Independent Schools) (Scotland)**

2005

asp 1   **Breastfeeding etc (Scotland)**

        s 1 am—SSI 2009/248, art 2, sch 1 para 11

asp 2   **Emergency Workers (Scotland)**

        s 1 am—Fire (S), 2005 asp 5, s 38; SSI 2008/37, art 2; Police and Fire Reform (S), 2012
            asp 8, sch 7 para 67

          appl (mods)—SI 2013/602, art 24

        s 2 rep in pt—SSI 2008/37, art 3

          am—SSI 2013/211, sch 1 para 15

        ss 3, 4 appl (mods)—SI 2013/602, art 24

        s 6 am—Crim Proceedings etc (Reform) (S), 2007 asp 6, s 44(4)

        s 7 rep in pt—Fire (S), 2005 asp 5, s 89(1), sch 3 para 25

          subst (by s 7A)—Police and Fire Reform (S), 2012 asp 8, sch 7 para 25

asp 3   **Water Services etc (Scotland)**

        s 3 rep —Public Services Reform (S), 2010 asp 8, s 3, sch 2, para 21

        s 6 am—Water, 2014 c 21, s 7(3)(a)(b)

        s 11A added —Public Services Reform (S), 2010 asp 8, s 131

        s 13 am—SI 2009/1941, art 2, sch 1 para 248

        s 14 am—Water Resources (S), 2013 asp 5, s 28

        s 18 see—SSI 2006/464, arts 5, 6, schs 2, 3

        s 19 am—Public Services Reform (S), 2010 asp 8, s 3, sch 2, para 14; SI 2014/631, sch 1
            para 18(2)

        s 20 see—SSI 2006/464, arts 5, 6, schs 2, 3

        ss 20A, 20B added (1.4.2016)—Water Resources (S), 2013 asp 5, s 32

        s 20B am—SI 2014/631, sch 1 para 18(3)

        ss 20C, 20D added (pt prosp)—Water Resources (S), 2013 asp 5, s 33(2)

        s 25 see—SSI 2006/155, art 2

          am—Regulatory Reform (S), 2014 asp 3, sch 3 para 9

        s 26 see—SSI 2006/155, art 2

          am—Public Health etc (S), 2008 asp 5, s 115

        s 34 am—Water Resources (S), 2013 asp 5, s 33(1); (prosp) Water, 2014 c 21, s 7(4)

        sch 2 mod—SSI 2006/464, art 4

          am—(1.4.2016) Water, 2014 c 21, s 7(2)

          see—SSI 2006/464, art 7

        sch 5 rep in pt —Public Services Reform (S), 2010 asp 8, s 3, sch 2, para 21

asp 4   **Budget (Scotland)**

        s 3 am—SSIs 2006/56, art 2(2); 162, art 2(2)

        Pt 2 (s 6) rep—Budget (S), 2006 asp 5, s 8

        sch 1 am—SSIs 2005/383, art 2(1), sch 1 para 12(1)(2); 2006/56, art 2(3); 162, art 2(3)

        sch 2 am—SSIs 2005/383, art 2(1), sch 1 para 12(1)(3); 2006/56, art 2(4); 162, art 2(4)

        sch 3 am—SSIs 2006/56, art 2(5); 162, art 2(5)

        sch 4 am—SSIs 2006/56, art 2(6); 162, art 2(6)

        sch 5 am—SSI 2006/162, art 2(7)

asp 5   **Fire (Scotland)**

        Pt 1 (ss 1-6) am (title subst) —(Police and Fire Reform (S), 2012 asp 8, sch 7 para 68(2)

        s 1 rep —Police and Fire Reform (S), 2012 asp 8, sch 8 pt 2

        s 1A added —Police and Fire Reform (S), 2012 asp 8, s 101(1)

        ss 2-7 rep —Police and Fire Reform (S), 2012 asp 8, sch 8 pt 2

        s 8 am—Police and Fire Reform (S), 2012 asp 8, s 102

        s 9 am—Police and Fire Reform (S), 2012 asp 8, s 104

2005
asp 5 *continued*

s 10 am—Police and Fire Reform (S), 2012 asp 8, s 105
s 11 am—Police and Fire Reform (S), 2012 asp 8, s 106
s 12 rep—Police and Fire Reform (S), 2012 asp 8, sch 8 pt 2
s 13 am—Police and Fire Reform (S), 2012 asp 8, s 107
s 14 am—Police and Fire Reform (S), 2012 asp 8, s 108
s 15 am—Police and Fire Reform (S), 2012 asp 8, s 109
s 16 am—SI 2005/2060, art 2(1)(2); Police and Fire Reform (S), 2012 asp 8, s 110
s 16 rep in pt—Police and Fire Reform (S), 2012 asp 8, sch 8 pt 2
s 16A added—SI 2005/2060, art 2(1)(3)
        am—SI 2013/602, sch 2 para 47
s 17 am—Police and Fire Reform (S), 2012 asp 8, sch 7 para 68(3)
s 18 am—Police and Fire Reform (S), 2012 asp 8, sch 7 para 68(4)
s 19 am—Police and Fire Reform (S), 2012 asp 8, sch 7 para 68(5)
s 20 am—Police and Fire Reform (S), 2012 asp 8, sch 7 para 68(6)
s 21 am—Police and Fire Reform (S), 2012 asp 8, sch 7 para 68(7)
s 23 am—Police and Fire Reform (S), 2012 asp 8, sch 7 para 68(8)
s 24 am—Police and Fire Reform (S), 2012 asp 8, sch 7 para 68(9)
s 24A added—SSI 2006/367, art 8
s 25 am—Police and Fire Reform (S), 2012 asp 8, sch 7 para 68(10)
        appl (mods)—SI 2013/602, arts 21(2), 22(2)
s 27 am—Police and Fire Reform (S), 2012 asp 8, sch 7 para 68(11)
        appl (mods)—SI 2013/602, arts 21(3), 22(3)
s 29 am—Police and Fire Reform (S), 2012 asp 8, sch 7 para 68(12)
        appl (mods)—SI 2013/602, arts 21(4), 22(4)
s 30 am—Police and Fire Reform (S), 2012 asp 8, sch 7 para 68(13)
ss 33, 34 rep —Police and Fire Reform (S), 2012 asp 8, sch 8 pt 2
s 35 am —(Police and Fire Reform (S), 2012 asp 8, s 111
s 36 am—Police and Fire Reform (S), 2012 asp 8, s 112
s 37 rep —Police and Fire Reform (S), 2012 asp 8, sch 8 pt 2
s 39 am—Crim Proceedings etc (Reform) (S), 2007 asp 6, s 44(5); Police and Fire Reform
        (S), 2012 asp 8, sch 7 para 68(14)
ss 39A-39C added—Police and Fire Reform (S), 2012 asp 8, s 113
s 40 am—Police and Fire Reform (S), 2012 asp 8, sch 7 para 68(15)
s 41 am—Police and Fire Reform (S), 2012 asp 8, sch 7 para 68(16)
s 41 rep in pt—Police and Fire Reform (S), 2012 asp 8, sch 8 pt 2
Pt 2 Ch 8A (ss 41A-41C) added —Police and Fire Reform (S), 2012 asp 8, s 114
ss 41D-41K added —Police and Fire Reform (S), 2012 asp 8, s 115
s 41E am—(prosp) Community Empowerment (S), 2015 asp 6, sch 4 para 9(a)
s 41J am—(prosp) Community Empowerment (S), 2015 asp 6, sch 4 para 9(b)
s 41L added —Police and Fire Reform (S), 2012 asp 8, s 116
s 41M added—Police and Fire Reform (S), 2012 asp 8, s 117
s 42 rep—Police and Fire Reform (S), 2012 asp 8, sch 8 pt 2
s 42A added —Police and Fire Reform (S), 2012 asp 8, s 118
s 43 rep —Police and Fire Reform (S), 2012 asp 8, sch 8 pt 2
Pt 2 Ch 8B (ss 43A-43G) added—Police and Fire Reform (S), 2012 asp 8, s 119
ss 44, 45 rep Pt 2 Ch 8A (ss 41A-41C) added—Police and Fire Reform (S), 2012 asp 8, sch
        8 pt 2
Pt 2 Ch 8C added —Police and Fire Reform (S), 2012 asp 8, sch 7 para 68(17)
s 46 rep—Police and Fire Reform (S), 2012 asp 8, sch 8 pt 2
s 47 am—Police and Fire Reform (S), 2012 asp 8, sch 7 para 68(18)
ss 48-50 rep —Police and Fire Reform (S), 2012 asp 8, sch 8 pt 2
s 51 am—Police and Fire Reform (S), 2012 asp 8, s 120; ibid, sch 7 para 68(19)
s 52 am—Police and Fire Reform (S), 2012 asp 8, sch 7 para 68(20)
s 59 am—Police and Fire Reform (S), 2012 asp 8, sch 7 para 68(21)
s 60 mod—SSI 2006/456, reg 24(3)(b)(i)
s 61 appl —Licensing (S), 2005 asp 16, s 21(1)(e)
        am—SIs 2005/2060, art 2(1)(4); 2007/320, reg 48, sch 5; 2008/960, art 22, sch 3;
                Police and Fire Reform (S), 2012 asp 8, s 103(1); Energy, 2013 c. 32, sch 12 para
                86
        mod—SSI 2006/456, reg 24(3)(a)(i)(b)(ii)
        rep in pt—Police and Fire Reform (S), 2012 asp 8, sch 8 pt 2; Energy, 2013 c. 32, sch
                12 para 86(5)(a)
s 62 mod—SSI 2006/456, reg 24(3)(a)(ii)(b)(iii)

2005
asp 5 *continued*

s 64 mod—SSI 2006/456, reg 24(3)(a)(iii)(b)(iv)
s 67 mod—SSI 2006/456, reg 24(3)(b)(v)
    am—Police and Fire Reform (S), 2012 asp 8, s 103(2)
    rep in pt—Police and Fire Reform (S), 2012 asp 8, sch 8 pt 2
s 72 am—SI 2005/2060, art 2(1)(5)
    mod—SSI 2006/456, reg 24(3)(c)
s 77 am—SI 2005/2060, art 2(1)(6)
    mod—SSI 2006/456, reg 24(3)(a)(iv)
s 77A added—SI 2005/2060, art 2(1)(7)
    mod—SSI 2006/456, reg 24(3)(a)(v)
s 78 am—SI 2005/2060, art 2(1)(8)(a)(ii)(b)(c); Housing (S), 2006 asp 1, s 192(1), sch 6
    para 23; Protection of Vulnerable Groups (S), 2007 asp 14, s 83; SSIs 2011/211,
    sch 1 para 15, 369, art 2
    rep in pt—SI 2005/2060, art 2(1)(8)(a)(i)(iii); SSI 2005/352, reg 2; Housing (S), 2006
    asp 1, s 192(2), sch 7
s 79 am—SI 2005/2060, art 2(1)(9); Police and Fire Reform (S), 2012 asp 8, sch 7 para
    68(22)
    rep in pt—Police and Fire Reform (S), 2012 asp 8, sch 8 pt 2
s 80 am—Police and Fire Reform (S), 2012 asp 8, sch 7 para 68(23)
s 81 am—Police and Fire Reform (S), 2012 asp 8, sch 7 para 68(24)
s 85 am—Police and Fire Reform (S), 2012 asp 8, sch 7 para 68(25)
s 86 am—Police and Fire Reform (S), 2012 asp 8, sch 7 para 68(26)
s 86A added —Police and Fire Reform (S), 2012 asp 8, sch 7 para 68(27)
s 88 rep in pt—Police and Fire Reform (S), 2012 asp 8, sch 8 pt 2
sch 1 rep —Police and Fire Reform (S), 2012 asp 8, sch 8 pt 2
sch 1A added—Police and Fire Reform (S), 2012 asp 8, s 101(2)
    am—Bankruptcy and Debt Advice (S), 2014 asp 11, sch 3 para 39
sch 3 rep in pt—(prosp) Road Safety, 2006 c 49, sch 7(7); (1.8.2016) Housing (S), 2014 asp
    14, sch 2 para 16

asp 6   **Further and Higher Education (Scotland)**

s 3 am—Post-16 Educ (S), 2013 asp 12, sch para 8(2)
s 4 am—Post-16 Educ (S), 2013 asp 12, sch para 8(3)
s 6 am—Post-16 Educ (S), 2013 asp 12, sch para 8(4)
s 7 am—Post-16 Educ (S), 2013 asp 12, sch para 8(5)
s 7A added —Post-16 Educ (S), 2013 asp 12, s 5(1)
s 7B added—Post-16 Educ (S), 2013 asp 12, s 8(1)
s 7C added —Post-16 Educ (S), 2013 asp 12, s 8(3)
s 7D added—Post-16 Educ (S), 2013 asp 12, sch para 8(6)
s 9 am—Post-16 Educ (S), 2013 asp 12, sch para 8(7)
    rep in pt—Post-16 Educ (S), 2013 asp 12, sch para 8(7)(h)(iii), (i)(ii)(iii)
s 9A added —Post-16 Educ (S), 2013 asp 12, s 2
s 9B added —Post-16 Educ (S), 2013 asp 12, s 14
s 9C added—Post-16 Educ (S), 2013 asp 12, s 3
s 9D added —Post-16 Educ (S), 2013 asp 12, s 4
s 10 am—Post-16 Educ (S), 2013 asp 12, sch para 8(8)
s 11 am—Post-16 Educ (S), 2013 asp 12, sch para 8(9)
s 12 am—Post-16 Educ (S), 2013 asp 12, s 9(1)(a)(c)
    rep in pt—Post-16 Educ (S), 2013 asp 12, s 9(1)(b)
ss 12A, 12B added —Post-16 Educ (S), 2013 asp 12, s 9(2)
s 13 am—Post-16 Educ (S), 2013 asp 12, sch para 8(10)
s 13A added —Post-16 Educ (S), 2013 asp 12, sch para 8(11)
s 14 am—Post-16 Educ (S), 2013 asp 12, sch para 8(12)
s 14A added —Post-16 Educ (S), 2013 asp 12, s 17
s 18 am—Post-16 Educ (S), 2013 asp 12, sch para 8(13)
s 19A added —Post-16 Educ (S), 2013 asp 12, s 16
s 20 am—Post-16 Educ (S), 2013 asp 12, sch para 8(14)
s 22 am—Housing (S), 2010 asp 17, s 162, sch 2, para 12; Post-16 Educ (S), 2013 asp 12,
    sch para 8(15)(a), (b)(i),(d),(e)
    rep in pt—Post-16 Educ (S), 2013 asp 12, sch para 8(15)(b)(ii), (c)
ss 23A-23D added —Post-16 Educ (S), 2013 asp 12, s 5(2)
ss 23E-23O added —Post-16 Educ (S), 2013 asp 12, s 10
s 23N am—SSI 2015/153, sch para 3(2)
s 23P added —Post-16 Educ (S), 2013 asp 12, s 11

2005

asp 6 *continued*

s 23Q added —Post-16 Educ (S), 2013 asp 12, s 12

s 23R added —Post-16 Educ (S), 2013 asp 12, s 13

s 24 am—Post-16 Educ (S), 2013 asp 12, sch para 8(16)

s 25 am—Post-16 Educ (S), 2013 asp 12, sch para 8(17)

    rep in pt—Post-16 Educ (S), 2013 asp 12, sch para 8(17)(a)(ii)

s 25A added —Post-16 Educ (S), 2013 asp 12, sch para 8(18)

s 26 am—Post-16 Educ (S), 2013 asp 12, sch para 8(19)

s 26A added —Post-16 Educ (S), 2013 asp 12, s 19

s 28 am—Post-16 Educ (S), 2013 asp 12, sch para 8(20)

s 31 am—Post-16 Educ (S), 2013 asp 12, sch para 8(21)

s 34 am—Post-16 Educ (S), 2013 asp 12, sch para 8(22)

s 35 am—Post-16 Educ (S), 2013 asp 12, sch para 8(23)(a)(c); SSI 2015/153, sch para 3(3)

    rep in pt—Post-16 Educ (S), 2013 asp 12, sch para 8(23)(b)

sch 1 am—Post-16 Educ (S), 2013 asp 12, sch para 8(24)(a)

sch 2 appl—SSI 2005/565, sch 1 pt II

    am—SSIs 2005/660, art 2; 2006/480, art 2; 2007/255, art 2; 2008/241, art 2; 412, art

      2; 2011/227, art 2, 229, art 2; Police and Fire Reform (S), 2012 asp 8, sch 7 para

      26(2)(a); SSIs 2013/319, art 2(b)(d)(e)(g)(h)(j)(k)(m)(n); 2014/250, art 3(a)(b)

    rep in pt—SSIs 2007/524, art 2; 2008/412, art 2; 2012/216, art 2(d); 2013/319, art

      2(a)(c)(f)(i)(l)

sch 2A added —Post-16 Educ (S), 2013 asp 12, s 8(2)

sch 2B added —Post-16 Educ (S), 2013 asp 12, s 11(2)

    am—SSI 2015/153, sch para 3(4)

sch 3 rep in pt—Graduate Endowment Abolition (S), 2008 asp 3, s 1(2)

asp 7   **Gaelic Language (Scotland)**

s 1 am—SI 2009/1941, art 2, sch 1 para 249

s 10 am—SSI 2006/367, art 7

    rep in pt—Food (S), 2015 asp 1, sch para 9

asp 8   **Prohibition of Female Genital Mutilation (Scotland)**

s 3 rep in pt—Serious Crime, 2015 c. 9, s 70(2)(a)

s 4 rep in pt—Serious Crime, 2015 c. 9, s 70(2)(b)

s 6 am—Serious Crime, 2015 c. 9, s 70(2)(c)

asp 9   **Protection of Children and Prevention of Sexual Offences (Scotland)**

s 1 am—Sexual Offences (S), 2009 asp 9, s 61, sch 5 para 7

s 2 am —Crim Justice and Licensing (S), 2010 asp 13, s 103(2)(a), (b); SSI 2012/216, art

    2(a)-(c)

    rep in pt—Police and Fire Reform (S), 2012 asp 8, sch 7 para 26(2)(b)

s 4 am —Crim Justice and Licensing (S), 2010 asp 13, s 103(3); Police and Fire Reform (S),

    2012 asp 8, sch 7 para 26(3)(a)(b)(ii)(c)

    rep in pt—Police and Fire Reform (S), 2012 asp 8, sch 7 para 26(3)(b)(i); ibid, sch 8 pt 1

s 5 am —Crim Justice and Licensing (S), 2010 asp 13, s 103(4)

s 7 am —Crim Justice and Licensing (S), 2010 asp 13, s 103(5); Anti-social Behaviour,

    Crime and Policing, 2014 c 12, sch 11 para 78(2)(3)

s 8 rep in pt —Crim Justice and Licensing (S), 2010 asp 13, s 203, sch 7, para 75(a)(i)

    am —Crim Justice and Licensing (S), 2010 asp 13, s 203, sch 7, para 75(a)(ii), (b)(i),

      (ii); Anti-social Behaviour, Crime and Policing, 2014 c 12, sch 11 para 79(2)-(5)

s 9 am—Crim Justice and Licensing (S), 2010 asp 13, s 40(2)(a)

s 10 am—Crim Justice and Licensing (S), 2010 asp 13, s 40(2)(b)

s 11 am—Crim Justice and Licensing (S), 2010 asp 13, s 40(2)(c)

s 12 am—Crim Justice and Licensing (S), 2010 asp 13, s 40(2)(d)

s 14A added—Crim Justice and Licensing (S), 2010 asp 13, s 40(3)

s 17 ext —(to EWNI) Violent Crime Reduction, 2006 c 38, s 56(1)(a)

s 18 ext —(to EWNI) Violent Crime Reduction, 2006 c 38, s 56(1)(b)

sch rep in pt—Sexual Offences (S), 2009 asp 9, s 61, sch 6

asp 10   **Charities and Trustee Investment (Scotland)**

s 7 excl—SSI 2006/219, art 2

    see—SSI 2008/268, art 2

s 12 excl in pt—SI 2011/237, reg 2(2) (amended by SSI 2013/362, reg 2(2))

s 15 am—Public Services Reform (S), 2010 asp 8, s 120(1)

s 16 excl in pt—SSI 2011/237, reg 2(1)

s 18 excl—SSI 2011/237, reg 2(2); SI 2011/237, reg 2(2) (as amended by SSI 2013/362,

    reg 2(2))

s 19 excl—SSI 2006/220, art 2

2005
asp 10 s 19 *continued*

    am —Housing (S), 2010 asp 17, s 162, sch 2, para 13(2)

    s 30 am—Public Services Reform (S), 2010 asp 8, s 121(1)

    s 34 am—Public Services Reform (S), 2010 asp 8, s 122

    s 36 am—Charities, 2006 c 50, sch 8 para 210

    s 38 rep in pt —Housing (S), 2010 asp 17, s 162, sch 2, para 13(3)(a), (c)-(e)

    am—Housing (S), 2010 asp 17, s 162, sch 2, para 13(3)(b); Public Services Reform (S), 2010 asp 8, s 123

    s 39 am—Public Services Reform (S), 2010 asp 8, s 124(1); Charities, 2011 c 25, sch 7 para 106

    s 40 am—Public Services Reform (S), 2010 asp 8, s 124(2)

    s 42 rep in pt—Public Services Reform (S), 2010 asp 8, s 124(3)(a)

    am—Public Services Reform (S), 2010 asp 8, s 124(3)(b)

    Pt 1 Chapter 5A (ss 43A-43D) added —Public Services Reform (S), 2010 asp 8, s 125(1)

    s 46 am—SI 2008/948, art 3, sch 1

    rep in pt—SI 2008/948, art 3, sch 1

    s 52 am—Public Services Reform (S), 2010 asp 8, s 120(2)

    s 56 am—SIs 2007/2194, art 10, sch 4; 2009/1941, art 2, sch 1 para 250(2); Co-operative and Community Benefit Societies, 2014 c 14, sch 4 para 97(2)(3)

    s 58 am —SIs 2009/1941, art 2, sch 1 para 250(3); 2013/496, sch 11 para 7;); Co-operative and Community Benefit Societies, 2014 c 14, sch 4 para 98

    rep in pt—SI 2009/1941, art 2, sch 1 para 250(3)

    s 67 am—Public Services Reform (S), 2010 asp 8, s 127(1)

    s 68A added—Public Services Reform (S), 2010 asp 8, s 127(2)

    s 69 am—Charities, 2006 c 50, sch 8 para 211; Charities, 2011 c 25, sch 7 para 107

    s 70A added—Public Services Reform (S), 2010 asp 8, s 126

    Pt 1 Chapter 10 (ss 71-78) appl—SSI 2011/237, reg 3(10)

    s 71 am—Public Services Reform (S), 2010 asp 8, s 121(2)

    am —Public Services Reform (S), 2010 asp 8, s 125(2)

    s 73 am—Public Services Reform (S), 2010 asp 8, s 121(3)

    s 86 am—Police and Fire Reform (S), 2012 asp 8, sch 7 para 27

    s 96 am—Charities, 2011 c 25, sch 7 para 108

    s 105 am—SI 2008/948, art 3, sch 1

    s 106 am—SI 2009/1941, art 2, sch 1 para 250(4); Public Services Reform (S), 2010 asp 8, s 125(3)

    sch 2 rep in pt—Courts Reform (S), 2014 asp 18, sch 4 para 7

    sch 4 rep in pt—Protection of Vulnerable Groups (S), 2007 asp 14, s 88, sch 4 para 44; SI 2009/1941, art 2, sch 2; Equality, 2010 c 15, s 211(2), sch 27 pt 1 (as subst by SI 2010/2279, sch 2)

asp 11   **Baird Trust Reorganisation**

asp 12   **Transport (Scotland)**

    s 1 am—SI 2009/1941, art 2, sch 1 para 251

asp 13   **Smoking, Health and Social Care (Scotland)**

    s 3 mod—SSI 2006/90, reg 2

    s 9 rep —Tobacco and Primary Medical Services (S), 2010 asp 3, s 41, sch 2, para 5 (with SSI 2010/77, art 2)

    s 28 am—Patient Rights (S), 2011 asp 5, s 22(2)(a)(i)(ii)(b)(i)(ii)(c), (3)-(5)

    rep in pt—Patient Rights (S), 2011 asp 5, ss 22(2)(a)(iii), (b)(iii)

    s 30 rep in pt —Public Services Reform (S), 2010 asp 8, s 110, sch 17, para 33

    s 36 rep—Public Health etc (S), 2008 asp 5, s 126, sch 3 pt 1

    sch 2 rep in pt—Public Health etc (S), 2008 asp 5, s 126, sch 3 pt 1

asp 14   **Management of Offenders etc (Scotland)**

    s 2 am—Joint Inspection of Children's Services and Inspection of Social Work Services (S), 2006 asp 3, s 8(3)(a); SSI 2011/211, sch 1 para 16(a)

    s 3 see—SSI 2006/63, art 2

    s 6 am—Joint Inspection of Childrens Services and Inspection of Social Work Services (S), 2006 asp 3, s 8(3)(b); SSI 2011/211, sch 1 para 16(b)

    s 10 am —Crim Justice and Licensing (S), 2010 asp 13, s 14, sch 2, para 51(2); ibid, s 203, sch 7, para 76(a)(b); Police and Fire Reform (S), 2012 asp 8, sch 7 para 28

    s 12 rep —Crim Justice and Licensing (S), 2010 asp 13, s 14, sch 2, para 51(3)

    s 21 ext —(to EWNI) SI 2006/art 3

    rep in pt—SSI 2015/39, sch para 7

asp 15   **Environmental Assessment (Scotland)**

    s 3 am—SSI 2015/271, art 5(1)

2005

asp 16   **Licensing (Scotland)**
appl (mods)—SSI 2009/277, art 7
power to modify—Alcohol etc (S), 2010 asp 18, s 15(1)(c)(i)
s 1 appl—SI 2006/1115, art 3
   mod—SSI 2007/545, reg 2
   rep in pt —Crim Justice and Licensing (S), 2010 asp 13, s 195(2)(a)
s 2 rep in pt—(prosp) Air Weapons and Licensing (S), 2015 asp 10, s 54
ss 2, 3appl—SI 2006/1115, art 3
s 4 am—(prosp) Air Weapons and Licensing (S), 2015 asp 10, s 41
   appl—SI 2006/1115, art 3
   rep in pt —Crim Justice and Licensing (S), 2010 asp 13, s 198, sch 6, paras 1, 2
s 5 appl—SI 2006/1115, art 3
s 6 am —Alcohol etc (S), 2010 asp 18, ss 9, 11(2)(a)(ii), (b)(ii); Police and Fire Reform (S),
      2012 asp 8, sch 7 para 29(2)(3); (30.9.2016) Air Weapons and Licensing (S),
      2015 asp 10, s 42(a)-(d)
   appl—SI 2006/1115, art 3
   rep in pt —Alcohol etc (S), 2010 asp 18, s 11(2)(a)(i), (b)(i)
s 7 appl—SI 2006/1115, art 3
   am —Alcohol etc (S), 2010 asp 18, s 11(3); Police and Fire Reform (S), 2012 asp 8, sch
      7 para 29(2)(3); (30.9.2016) Air Weapons and Licensing (S), 2015 asp 10, s 55(2)
   rep in pt—(30.9.2016) Air Weapons and Licensing (S), 2015 asp 10, s 55(2)(b)(i)(iii)
s 8 appl—SI 2006/1115, art 3
ss 9A, 9B added (prosp)—Air Weapons and Licensing (S), 2015 asp 10, s 56(2)
s 10 appl—SI 2006/1115, art 3
s 12A added —Alcohol etc (S), 2010 asp 18, s 12
   am—Police and Fire Reform (S), 2012 asp 8, sch 7 para 29(4)(a)(5);
   rep in pt—Police and Fire Reform (S), 2012 asp 8, sch 7 para 29(4)(b)
s 14 am—(prosp) Air Weapons and Licensing (S), 2015 asp 10, s 57
s 15 am —(prosp) Crim Justice and Licensing (S), 2010 asp 13, s 197(2), (3)(b), (4)-(6)
   rep in pt —(prosp) Crim Justice and Licensing (S), 2010 asp 13, s 197(3)(a)
s 19 mod—SSI 2007/545, regs 4, 5
s 20 mod—SSI 2007/545, regs 4, 5
   rep in pt —(prosp) Crim Justice and Licensing (S), 2010 asp 13, s 179(2)(a)
   am—(prosp) Crim Justice and Licensing (S), 2010 asp 13, s 179(2)(b), (3)
s 21 appl—SSI 2007/454, art 10
   rep in pt—Crim Justice and Licensing (S), 2010 asp 13, ss 180(3)(4), 198, sch 6, para 3
   am—Crim Justice and Licensing (S), 2010 asp 13, s 180(2); Alcohol etc (S), 2010 asp
      18, s 11(4); Police and Fire Reform (S), 2012 asp 8, sch 7 para 29(2)(3)
s 22 rep in pt—Crim Justice and Licensing (S), 2010 asp 13, s 198, sch 6, para 4
   am—Crim Justice and Licensing (S), 2010 asp 13, s 183(2); Police and Fire Reform (S),
      2012 asp 8, sch 7 para 29(2)(3); (prosp) Air Weapons and Licensing (S), 2015
      asp 10, s 43(2)
s 23 am—Crim Justice and Licensing (S), 2010 asp 13, ss 181, 198, sch 6, para 5; Police
      and Fire Reform (S), 2012 asp 8, sch 7 para 29(2)(3); (30.9.2016) Air Weapons
      and Licensing (S), 2015 asp 10, ss 43(3), 55(3)
s 24 appl (mod)—SSI 2007/513, reg 3
   am—Crim Justice and Licensing (S), 2010 asp 13, s 198, sch 6, para 6(1)-(3); Police
      and Fire Reform (S), 2012 asp 8, sch 7 para 29(2)(3)
s 24A added—Crim Justice and Licensing (S), 2010 asp 13, s 183(3)
   am—Police and Fire Reform (S), 2012 asp 8, sch 7 para 29(2)(3)
s 26 am—Crim Justice and Licensing (S), 2010 asp 13, s 187(2); Police and Fire Reform (S),
      2012 asp 8, sch 7 para 29(2)(3)
s 27 am —Alcohol etc (S), 2010 asp 18, s 7
s 27A added —Alcohol etc (S), 2010 asp 18, s 10(1)
   am—Police and Fire Reform (S), 2012 asp 8, sch 7 para 29(2)(3)
s 28 am—(prosp) Air Weapons and Licensing (S), 2015 asp 10, sch 2 para 4(2)
s 29 am—(prosp) Air Weapons and Licensing (S), 2015 asp 10, sch 2 para 4(3)
s 33 am—Crim Justice and Licensing (S), 2010 asp 13, s 198, sch 6, para 7(1)-(3); Police
      and Fire Reform (S), 2012 asp 8, sch 7 para 29(2)(3); (prosp) Air Weapons and
      Licensing (S), 2015 asp 10, ss 44(2), 49(2)(3)
s 33A added (prosp)—Air Weapons and Licensing (S), 2015 asp 10, s 49(4)
s 34 rep (prosp)—Air Weapons and Licensing (S), 2015 asp 10, s 49(5)
s 35 rep in pt—(prosp) Air Weapons and Licensing (S), 2015 asp 10, sch 2 para 4(4)
s 36 am—(prosp) Air Weapons and Licensing (S), 2015 asp 10, s 45(2)

2005
asp 16 *continued*

s 37 am—(prosp) Air Weapons and Licensing (S), 2015 asp 10, s 45(3); (prosp) ibid, sch 2
    para 4(5)
s 38 appl—SSI 2007/454, art 17
s 39 am—(prosp) Air Weapons and Licensing (S), 2015 asp 10,s 45(4)
s 39A added—Crim Justice and Licensing (S), 2010 asp 13, s 182(2)
    am—(prosp) Air Weapons and Licensing (S), 2015 asp 10, s 45(5)
s 39B added (prosp)—Air Weapons and Licensing (S), 2015 asp 10, s 45(6)
s 40A added —(pt prosp) Crim Justice and Licensing (S), 2010 asp 13, s 184(2)
    rep in pt—(prosp) Air Weapons and Licensing (S), 2015 asp 10, s 59(2)(a)(b)
    am—Police and Fire Reform (S), 2012 asp 8, sch 7 para 29(2)(3); (prosp) Air
        Weapons and Licensing (S), 2015 asp 10, s 59(2)(c)(3)
s 43 appl (mod)—SSI 2007/513, reg 3
s 44 am—Crim Justice and Licensing (S), 2010 asp 13, s 198, sch 6, para 8; Police and Fire
        Reform (S), 2012 asp 8, sch 7 para 29(2)(3); (prosp) Air Weapons and Licensing
        (S), 2015 asp 10, s 50
s 45 am—Crim Justice and Licensing (S), 2010 asp 13, s 185
s 47 am—Crim Justice and Licensing (S), 2010 asp 13, s 187(3); Police and Fire Reform (S),
        2012 asp 8, sch 7 para 29(2)(3)
s 48 am —Crim Justice and Licensing (S), 2010 asp 13, s 184(3)(b); (pt prosp) ibid, s
        184(3)(a)(ii); Police and Fire Reform (S), 2012 asp 8, sch 7 para 29(2)(3)
    rep in pt—Crim Justice and Licensing (S), 2010 asp 13, s 184(3)(a)(i); (prosp) Air
        Weapons and Licensing (S), 2015 asp 10, s 59(4)
s 49 am—Crim Justice and Licensing (S), 2010 asp 13, s 187(4); Police and Fire Reform (S),
        2012 asp 8, sch 7 para 29(2)(3)
    rep in pt—(prosp) Air Weapons and Licensing (S), 2015 asp 10, sch 2 para 4(6)
s 50 am—SSI 2009/256, art 4; Crim Justice and Licensing (S), 2010 asp 13, s 186(1)-(4)
s 51 am—Police and Fire Reform (S), 2012 asp 8, sch 7 para 29(2)(3)
s 56 am —Alcohol etc (S), 2010 asp 18, s 13(2); Crim Justice and Licensing (S), 2010 asp
        13, s 187(5); Police and Fire Reform (S), 2012 asp 8, sch 7 para 29(2)(3)
s 57 rep in pt —Crim Justice and Licensing (S), 2010 asp 13, s 198, sch 6, para 9
    am—Crim Justice and Licensing (S), 2010 asp 13, s 189(2); Police and Fire Reform (S),
        2012 asp 8, sch 7 para 29(2)(3); (prosp) Air Weapons and Licensing (S), 2015
        asp 10, sch 2 para 4(7)
s 59 rep in pt —Crim Justice and Licensing (S), 2010 asp 13, s 198, sch 6, para 10(1)-(3)
    am —Alcohol etc (S), 2010 asp 18, s 13(3)
s 60 am —Alcohol etc (S), 2010 asp 18, s 8(2)
s 61 am—Police and Fire Reform (S), 2012 asp 8, sch 7 para 29(2)(3)
s 63 am —Crim Justice and Licensing (S), 2010 asp 13, s 188(2)
s 67 am—Police and Fire Reform (S), 2012 asp 8, sch 7 para 29(2)(3)
s 69 am—Crim Justice and Licensing (S), 2010 asp 13, s 190(1)-(3); ibid, s 198, sch 6, para
        11; Police and Fire Reform (S), 2012 asp 8, sch 7 para 29(2)(3)
s 70 am—Police and Fire Reform (S), 2012 asp 8, sch 7 para 29(2)(3)
s 70A added —Crim Justice and Licensing (S), 2010 asp 13, s 191
s 73 am—Crim Justice and Licensing (S), 2010 asp 13, s 198, sch 6, para 12; Police and
        Fire Reform (S), 2012 asp 8, sch 7 para 29(2)(3); (prosp) Air Weapons and
        Licensing (S), 2015 asp 10, s 46(2)
s 73A added—Air Weapons and Licensing (S), 2015 asp 10, s 46(3)
s 74 am—Crim Justice and Licensing (S), 2010 asp 13, ss 192(2)(a)(ii), (b)(ii), (c), 198, sch
        6, para 13(1)-(4); Police and Fire Reform (S), 2012 asp 8, sch 7 para 29(2)(3);
        Air Weapons and Licensing (S), 2015 asp 10, s 60(2); (prosp) ibid, s 46(4)
    rep in pt—Crim Justice and Licensing (S), 2010 asp 13, s 192(2)(a)(i),(b)(i)
s 75 appl (mod)—SSI 2007/513, reg 3
    am—Crim Justice and Licensing (S), 2010 asp 13, s 198, sch 6, para 14(2), (3)(b);
        Police and Fire Reform (S), 2012 asp 8, sch 7 para 29(2)(3)
    rep in pt—Crim Justice and Licensing (S), 2010 asp 13, s 198, sch 6, para 14(3)
s 76 am—Crim Justice and Licensing (S), 2010 asp 13, s 192(3)
s 77 am—(prosp) Air Weapons and Licensing (S), 2015 asp 10, s 60(3)
    appl (mod)—SSI 2007/454, art 23
s 78 am—(prosp) Air Weapons and Licensing (S), 2015 asp 10, ss 46(5), 60(4)
s 79 am—Police and Fire Reform (S), 2012 asp 8, sch 7 para 29(2)(3)
s 82 appl (mod)—SSI 2007/513, reg 3

2005

asp 16 *continued*

s 83 am—Crim Justice and Licensing (S), 2010 asp 13, s 198, sch 6, para 15(1)-(3); Police and Fire Reform (S), 2012 asp 8, sch 7 para 29(2)(3); (prosp) Air Weapons and Licensing (S), 2015 asp 10, ss 47(2), 51

s 84 am—(prosp) Air Weapons and Licensing (S), 2015 asp 10, s 48(2)

s 84A added—Crim Justice and Licensing (S), 2010 asp 13, s 198, sch 6, para 16

    am—Police and Fire Reform (S), 2012 asp 8, sch 7 para 29(6); (prosp) Air Weapons and Licensing (S), 2015 asp 10, ss 48(3), 60(5)

s 84B added (prosp)—Air Weapons and Licensing (S), 2015 asp 10, s 58

s 92 am—Crim Justice and Licensing (S), 2010 asp 13, s 192(4)

ss 94-95 appl (mod)—SSI 2007/454, art 26

s 96 appl (mod)—SSI 2007/454, art 26

    am—Crim Justice and Licensing (S), 2010 asp 13, s 24(4)

s 97 am—Crim Justice and Licensing (S), 2010 asp 13, s 193(2)

s 98 am—Crim Justice and Licensing (S), 2010 asp 13, s 193(3)

s 99 am—Crim Justice and Licensing (S), 2010 asp 13, s 193(4)

s 103 rep in pt —Crim Justice and Licensing (S), 2010 asp 13, s 195(2)(b)

ss 104A, 104B added (prosp)—Air Weapons and Licensing (S), 2015 asp 10, s 53(1)

s 105 appl—SI 2006/1115, art 3

    rep in pt—(prosp) Air Weapons and Licensing (S), 2015 asp 10, s 53(2)(a)

    am—Police and Fire Reform (S), 2012 asp 8, sch 7 para 29(7); (prosp) Air Weapons and Licensing (S), 2015 asp 10, s 53(2)(b)

s 106 rep in pt —Crim Justice and Licensing (S), 2010 asp 13, s 195(2)(c);

s 107 rep in pt —Crim Justice and Licensing (S), 2010 asp 13, s 195(2)(d)

s 117 am—Crim Justice and Licensing (S), 2010 asp 13, s 188(3)

s 118 rep in pt —Crim Justice and Licensing (S), 2010 asp 13, s 195(2)(e)

s 120 rep in pt —Crim Justice and Licensing (S), 2010 asp 13, s 195(2)(f)

s 121 rep in pt —Crim Justice and Licensing (S), 2010 asp 13, s 195(2)(g)

s 122 mod—SSI 2007/545, reg 3

s 127 rep in pt —Crim Justice and Licensing (S), 2010 asp 13, s 195(2)(h)

s 128 rep in pt —Crim Justice and Licensing (S), 2010 asp 13, s 195(2)(i)

s 129 am —Crim Justice and Licensing (S), 2010 asp 13, s 24(5)

    rep in pt—(prosp) Air Weapons and Licensing (S), 2015 asp 10, s 52

s 131 rep in pt—Crim Justice and Licensing (S), 2010 asp 13, s 194

s 134 am—(prosp) Air Weapons and Licensing (S), 2015 asp 10, s 62(2)(3)

s 134A added—Crim Justice and Licensing (S), 2010 asp 13, s 196

ss 134ZA-134ZC added (prosp) —Air Weapons and Licensing (S), 2015 asp 10, s 61(2)

ss 141A, 141B added —Crim Justice and Licensing (S), 2010 asp 13, s 195(3)

s 146 am —Alcohol etc (S), 2010 asp 18, ss 8(3), 10(2); (prosp) Alcohol (Minimum Pricing) (S), 2012 asp 4, s 1(4); (prosp) Air Weapons and Licensing (S), 2015 asp 10, s 56(3)

s 147 appl (mod)—SSI 2007/76, reg 4

    am —Alcohol etc (S), 2010 asp 18, s 11(5); (prosp) Crim Justice and Licensing (S), 2010 asp 13, s 184(4); Police and Fire Reform (S), 2012 asp 8, sch 7 para 29(8)

    rep in pt—(prosp) Air Weapons and Licensing (S), 2015 asp 10, s 59(5)

s 148 rep in pt —Crim Justice and Licensing (S), 2010 asp 13, s 198, sch 6, para 17

    am—Alcohol etc (S), 2010 asp 18, s 11(6); (prosp) Crim Justice and Licensing (S), 2010 asp 13, s 184(5); Police and Fire Reform (S), 2012 asp 8, sch 7 para 29(9)

sch 1 appl—SI 2006/1115, art 3

    restr in pt—SSI 2007/128, art 4

    rep in pt—Crim Justice and Licensing (S), 2010 asp 13, s 198, sch 6, para 18

    am —Crim Justice and Licensing (S), 2010 asp 13, s 189(3)

sch 2 excl in pt—(temp) SSI 2007/128, art 5

    am —Alcohol etc (S), 2010 asp 18, s 11(7); SSI 2011/130, art 2; Police and Fire Reform (S), 2012 asp 8, sch 7 para 29(10)

sch 3 am—SSIs 2007/457, reg 2; 2007/546, regs 2, 3; 2009/270, reg 2; Alcohol etc (S), 2010 asp 18, ss 2(2), 3(1)-(3), 4(2), 5(2)(3),(4)(b)-(5); (prosp) (with provn for cesser) Alcohol (Minimum Pricing) (S), 2012 asp 4, ss 1(2),2

    rep in pt —Alcohol etc (S), 2010 asp 18, s 5(4)(a)

sch 4 am —Alcohol etc (S), 2010 asp 18, ss 2(3), 3(4)(5), 4(3), 6(3); (prosp) (with provn for cesser) Alcohol (Minimum Pricing) (S), 2012 asp 4, ss 1(3),2

sch 5 am—(prosp) Air Weapons and Licensing (S), 2015 asp 10, ss 45(7), 47(3), 48(4), 49(6)(b)(c)

    rep in pt—(prosp) Air Weapons and Licensing (S), 2015 asp 10, s 49(6)(a)

2006

asp 1   **Housing (Scotland)**
        power to am—Housing (S), 2014, s 20(2)(b)
        s 2 am —Housing (S), 2010 asp 17, s 149(1)
        s 5 rep in pt —Housing (S), 2010 asp 17, s 149(2)
        s 13 rep in pt—Housing, 2014 asp 14, s 22(a)
           am—Housing, 2014 asp 14, s 22(b)(c); ibid, s 23(1)
        s 18 am—(prosp) Housing, 2014 asp 14, s 17(2)(a)(b)(3)
        ss 19A, 19B added —Housing, 2014 asp 14, s 23(2)
        s 20A added —Housing, 2014 asp 14, s 24(1)
        s 21 am—Private Rented Housing (S), 2011 asp 14, s 35(2); Housing, 2014 asp 14, s 96(1)
        s 22 am —Housing (S), 2010 asp 17, s 162, sch 2, para 14; Housing (S), 2014 asp 14, s 25(1)(b)-(e)
           rep in pt—Housing (S), 2014 asp 14, sch 2 para 17(a)(b)
        s 22A added —Private Rented Housing (S), 2011 asp 14, s 11
           am—Housing (S), 2014 asp 14, s 25(3)
        s 23 am—Housing (S), 2014 asp 14, s 25(4)(a)-(e)
        s 24 am—Housing (S), 2014 asp 14, s 25(5); (prosp) ibid, sch 1 para 50(a)(b)
        ss 28A-28C added —Private Rented Housing (S), 2011 asp 14, s 35(4)
        s 29 am—Private Rented Housing (S), 2011 asp 14, s 35(5)
        s 30 rep in pt—Housing (S), 2014 asp 14, s 87(a)
           am—Housing (S), 2014 asp 14, s 87(b)
        s 42 rep in pt—Housing (S), 2014 asp 14, s 88(a)
           am—Housing (S), 2014 asp 14, s 88(b)(c)
        s 47 am—Housing (S), 2014 asp 14, 89(2)(a)(b)
        s 50 am —Housing (S), 2010 asp 17, s 150(1)
        s 53 am—Housing (S), 2014 asp 14, s 87(b)
        s 57 am—(prosp) Housing (S), 2014 asp 14, s 17(4)(a)(b)
        s 59 am —Housing (S), 2014 asp 14, s 87(b)
        s 61 am —Housing (S), 2010 asp 17, s 150(3)
           rep in pt—Housing (S), 2014 asp 14, s 89(3)
        s 64 am—Housing (S), 2014 asp 14, s 27(1)(a)-(c); (prosp) ibid, sch 1 para 53(b)
           rep in pt—(prosp) Housing (S), 2014 asp 14, sch 1 para 53(a)
        s 65 am—Housing (S), 2014 asp 14, s 27(2)
           rep in pt—(prosp) Housing (S), 2014 asp 14, sch 1 para 54
        s 66 am—Housing (S), 2014 asp 14, s 27(3)
        s 66A added (prosp)—Housing (S), 2014 asp 14, s 18(1)
        s 67 rep (prosp)—Housing (S), 2014 asp 14, sch 1 para 55
           am—Equality, 2006 c 3, sch 3 para 63(c)
        s 71 am —Housing (S), 2010 asp 17, s 151
        s 75 am—Financial Services, 2013 c 21, sch 18 para 240; SI 2013/1881, sch para 46(a)(b)
           rep in pt—SI 2013/1881, sch para 46(c)
        s 117 am—SI 2014/631, sch 2 para 7(1)(a)(b)
        s 125 am—Private Rented Housing (S), 2011 asp 14, s 13(1)(a)(b)
           rep in pt—Private Rented Housing (S), 2011 asp 14, s 13(1)(c)
        s 126 am—SSI 2011/211, sch 1 para 17, sch 2 para 10
        s 129A added —Private Rented Housing (S), 2011 asp 14, s 13(2)
        s 131 am—Private Rented Housing (S), 2011 asp 14, s 13(3)
        s 131A added —Private Rented Housing (S), 2011 asp 14, s 13(4)
        s 135 am—Private Rented Housing (S), 2011 asp 14, s 13(5)
        s 138 am—SSI 2006/475, sch 1 para 17(2)(3)(a)
        s 139 am—SSI 2006/475, sch 1 para 17(2)(3)(b)
        s 156 am—Private Rented Housing (S), 2011 asp 14, s 14
        s 158 am—SSI 2006/475, sch 1 para 17(2)(3)(c)(4); Private Rented Housing (S), 2011 asp 14, s 15(1)
        s 159 am—Private Rented Housing (S), 2011 asp 14, s 15(2)
        s 163 am—Private Rented Housing (S), 2011 asp 14, s 16
        s 164 am—SSI 2006/475, sch 1 para 17(2)(3)(d)
        s 166 am—SSI 2006/475, sch 1 para 17(5); Police and Fire Reform (S), 2012 asp 8, sch 7 para 30
        s 172 am—Housing (S), 2010 asp 17, s 150(4); Housing (S), 2014 asp 14, ss 85(2)(a)-(c), 90(1)(a)-(f), 91(1)(a)(ii)(b)(c)
           rep in pt—Housing (S), 2014 asp 14, s 91(1)(a)(i)
        s 172A added—Housing (S), 2014 asp 14, s 91(2)
        s 173 rep in pt—Public Health etc. (S), 2008 asp 5, s 126, sch 3 pt 1

2006

asp 1 s 173   *continued*

    am—Housing (S), 2014 asp 14, s 90(a)-(d)

    s 174A added—Housing (S), 2014 asp 14, s 85(3)

    s 179 rep—Climate Change (S), 2009 asp 12, s 99, sch 2 para 7

    s 181 am—Private Rented Housing (S), 2011 asp 14, s 35(6); Housing (S), 2014 asp 14, s 25(6)(a)(b)

    s 182 am—Private Rented Housing (S), 2011 asp 14, s 35(7); Housing (S), 2014 asp 14, s 25(7)

    s 184 am—Housing (S), 2014 asp 14, s 25(8)

    s 187 appl—Housing (S), 2014 asp 14, s 92(1)(b)

    am—Housing (S), 2014 asp 14, s 25(9)

    s 191 am—Private Rented Housing (S), 2011 asp 14, ss 13(6), 35(8); Housing (S), 2014 asp 14, ss 24(2), 85(4); Housing (S), 2014 asp 14, s 25(10); (prosp) ibid, sch 1 para 51

    rep in pt—Police and Fire Reform (S), 2012 asp 8, sch 8 pt 2

    sch 1 am —Housing (S), 2010 asp 17, s 149(3)(a)(i)(ii),(b),(e)(f)

    rep in pt —Housing (S), 2010 asp 17, s 149(3)(a)(iii),(c)(d)

    sch 2 am—Police and Fire Reform (S), 2012 asp 8, sch 7 para 70; SSI 2013/137, reg 7; Housing (S), 2014 asp 14, s 26(1)-(4),(5)(a),(6)(7)

    rep in pt—Housing (S), 2014 asp 14, s 26(5)(b)

    sch 4 am—SSI 2006/475, sch 1 para 17(2)(3)(e)

    sch 5 am—SSI 2015/271, art 6(1)

asp 2   **Family Law (Scotland)**

    s 28 am—SSI 2011/234, reg 9(2)

    s 29 am—SSI 2011/234, reg 9(3)

    s 29A added—SSI 2011/234, reg 9(4)

    s 35 rep—Damages (S), 2011 asp 7, sch 2

    s 38 am—SIs 2014/560, sch 1 para 31; 2014/1110 art 18

asp 3   *Joint Inspection of Children's Services and Inspection of Social Work Services (Scotland)*—rep Public Services Reform (S), 2010 asp 8, s 106, sch 14, para 37

asp 4   **Human Tissue (Scotland)**

    s 13 am —Public Services Reform (S), 2010 asp 8, s 110, sch 17, para 34

    s 17 excl—SSI 2006/390, regs 2-5

    s 18 see—SSI 2006/368, reg 3

asp 5   **Budget (Scotland)**

    s 3 am—SSIs 2006/589, art 2(2); 2007/244, art 2

    Pt 2 (s 6) rep—Budget (S), 2007 asp 9, s 8

    sch 1 am—SSIs 2006/589, art 2(3); 2007/244, art 2

    sch 2 am—SSIs 2006/589, art 2(4); 2007/244, art 2

    sch 3 am—SSIs 2006/589, art 2(5); 2007/244, art 2

    sch 4 am—SSIs 2006/589, art 2(6); 2007/244, art 2

    sch 5 am—SSI 2006/589, art 2(7)

asp 6   **Edinburgh Tram (Line Two)**

    s 13 am—SI 2013/2314, art 6(1)(2)

    ss 23, 24 see (time limit for exercise of powers)—(with power to ext) Edinburgh Tram (Line Two), 2006 asp 6, ss 40,41

    s 25 am—Land Registration etc (S), 2012 asp 5, sch 5 para 47

    s 40 ext—SSI 2011/127, art 2

    s 62 am—Police and Fire Reform (S), 2012 asp 8, sch 7 para 31

    rep in pt—Police and Fire Reform (S), 2012 asp 8, sch 8 pt 1

asp 7   **Edinburgh Tram (Line One)**

    ss 23, 24 see (time limit for exercise of powers)—(with power to ext) Edinburgh Tram (Line One), 2006 asp 7, ss 40,41

    s 25 am—Land Registration etc (S), 2012 asp 5, sch 5 para 48

    s 40 ext—SSI 2011/126, art 2

    s 62 am—Police and Fire Reform (S), 2012 asp 8, sch 7 para 32

asp 8   **Scottish Schools (Parental Involvement)**

asp 9   *Senior Judiciary (Vacancies and Incapacity) (Scotland)*—rep Judiciary and Cts (S), 2008 asp 6, s 73, sch 5 para 4

asp 10   **Police, Public Order and Criminal Justice (Scotland)**

    ss 1-32 rep —Police and Fire Reform (S), 2012 asp 8, sch 8 pt 1 (with transtl savings in SSI 2013/121, art 11)

    Pt 1 Ch. 2 (ss 33-50) mod—SSI 2013/121, art 16

    s 33 am—Police and Fire Reform (S), 2012 asp 8, s 61

2006

asp 10 *continued*

s 33A added —Police and Fire Reform (S), 2012 asp 8, s 62

s 34 am—Police and Fire Reform (S), 2012 asp 8, sch 7 para 33(2)

s 34 rep in pt—Police and Fire Reform (S), 2012 asp 8, sch 8 pt 1

s 35 am—Police and Fire Reform (S), 2012 asp 8, sch 7 para 33(3)

s 36 am—Police and Fire Reform (S), 2012 asp 8, sch 7 para 33(4)

s 40A added —Police and Fire Reform (S), 2012 asp 8, sch 7 para 33(5)

s 41 am—Police and Fire Reform (S), 2012 asp 8, sch 7 para 33(6)

 rep in pt—Police and Fire Reform (S), 2012 asp 8, sch 8 pt 1

s 41A added —Police and Fire Reform (S), 2012 asp 8, s 63

s 41B added—Police and Fire Reform (S), 2012 asp 8, s 64

s 41C added —Police and Fire Reform (S), 2012 asp 8, s 65

s 41D added—Police and Fire Reform (S), 2012 asp 8, s 66

s 41E added —Police and Fire Reform (S), 2012 asp 8, s 67

s 41F added —Police and Fire Reform (S), 2012 asp 8, s 68

s 42 rep —Police and Fire Reform (S), 2012 asp 8, sch 8 pt 1

s 42A added —Police and Fire Reform (S), 2012 asp 8, s 69

s 43 am—Police and Fire Reform (S), 2012 asp 8, sch 7 para 33(7)

s 44 am—Police and Fire Reform (S), 2012 asp 8, sch 7 para 33(8)

s 45 am—Police and Fire Reform (S), 2012 asp 8, sch 7 para 33(9)

s 46 am—Police and Fire Reform (S), 2012 asp 8, sch 7 para 33(10)

s 46A added —Police and Fire Reform (S), 2012 asp 8, s 70

s 47 subst —Police and Fire Reform (S), 2012 asp 8, sch 7 para 33(11)

 am—SSI 2013/119, sch 1 para 21

ss 48-50 rep —Police and Fire Reform (S), 2012 asp 8, sch 8 pt 1

s 52 am—Police and Fire Reform (S), 2012 asp 8, sch 7 para 33(12)(a)

 rep in pt—Police and Fire Reform (S), 2012 asp 8, sch 7 para 33(12)(b)

s 53 rep in pt—Policing and Crime, 2009 c 26, s 112, sch 8 pt 11

s 55 am—SSIs 2007/125, art 2; 2013/228, art 2

s 57 am—Police and Fire Reform (S), 2012 asp 8, sch 7 para 33(13)(a)

 rep in pt—Police and Fire Reform (S), 2012 asp 8, sch 7 para 33(13)(b)

s 60 am—SSI 2015/338, sch 2 para 9(2)

s 67 am—SI 2011/2085, sch 1 para 65

s 68 ext—(to EW, NI) Policing and Crime, 2009 c 26, s 106(1)

s 69 am—Police and Fire Reform (S), 2012 asp 8, sch 7 para 33(14)

s 87 am—SI 2011/2085, sch 1 para 65

s 91 am—(prosp) Custodial Sentences and Weapons (S), 2007 asp 17, s 66, sch 4 para 5(1)(2)

s 92 am—(prosp) Custodial Sentences and Weapons (S), 2007 asp 17, s 66, sch 4 para 5(1)(3)

s 94 am—(prosp) Custodial Sentences and Weapons (S), 2007 asp 17, s 66, sch 4 para 5(1)(4)

s 95 am—SSI 2015/338, sch 2 para 9(3)

s 96 am—SSI 2015/338, sch 2 para 9(4)(a)(d)(5)

 rep in pt—SSI 2015/338, sch 2 para 9(4)(b)(c)

s 96A added—SSI 2015/338, sch 2 para 9(6)

s 99 rep in pt—Police and Fire Reform (S), 2012 asp 8, sch 8 pt 1

s 103 am—Police and Fire Reform (S), 2012 asp 8, sch 7 para 33(15)

sch 1 rep—(with transtl saving for para 16 in SSI 2013/121, art 11) Police and Fire Reform (S), 2012 asp 8, sch 8 pt 1

schs 2, 3 rep—Police and Fire Reform (S), 2012 asp 8, sch 8 pt 1

sch 4 am—SI 2009/1941, art 2, sch 1 para 261(3); Police and Fire Reform (S), 2012 asp 8, sch 7 para 33(16), (17); Crime and Cts, 2013 c. 22, sch 8 para 172(b)(ii),(c)

 rep in pt—Police and Fire Reform (S), 2012 asp 8, sch 8 pt 1; Crime Cts, 2013 c. 22, sch 8 para 172(a),(b)(i)

sch 6 am—SSI 2007/260, art 2; (prosp) Anti-social Behaviour, Crime and Policing, 2014 c 12, sch 11 para 102

 rep in pt—Police and Fire Reform (S), 2012 asp 8, sch 8 pt 1

asp 11   **Animal Health and Welfare (Scotland)**

s 20 excl—SSI 2007/256, reg 3

s 43 am—SSI 2015/338, sch 2 para 10

s 49 am—Police and Fire Reform (S), 2012 asp 8, sch 7 para 34

2006

asp 12   **Interests of Members of the Scottish Parliament**
       s 19 rep in pt and am—SI 2009/1941, art 2, sch 1 para 262
       sch am—SSIs 2011/40, Annex; 2011/196, art 2

asp 13   **Waverley Railway (Scotland)**
       s 16 am—Land Registration etc (S), 2012 asp 5, sch 5 para 49
       s 27 am—SSI 2011/14, art 2

asp 14   **Local Electoral Administration and Registration Services (Scotland)**
       ss 1-3 rep—Loc Electoral Admin (S), 2011 asp 10, s 13(2)
       ss 8-11 rep—Loc Electoral Admin (S), 2011 asp 10, s 11(7)
       s 57 am—Statistics and Registration Service, 2007 c 18, s 60
       s 58 am—SSI 2010/21, art 2, sch
           appl (mod)—SI 2010/985, reg 5, sch 4
       sch 2 rep in pt—SSI 2012/31, art 4

asp 15   **Tourist Boards (Scotland)**
       sch 2 rep in pt—Equality, 2010 c. 15, sch 27 pt 1A (added by SI 2011/1060, sch 3)

asp 16   **Scottish Commission for Human Rights**
       s 7 am —S Parl Commn and Commrs, 2010 asp 11, s 29, sch 6, para 1(a)(ii), (b)
           rep in pt —S Parl Commn and Commrs, 2010 asp 11, s 29, sch 6, para 1(a)(i)
       s 14 am—SSIs 2013/211, sch 1 para 16; 2015/402, sch para 6
       s 15 am —S Parl Commn and Commrs, 2010 asp 11, s 29, sch 6, para 2(a)-(c)
       sch 1 am —S Parl Commn and Commrs, 2010 asp 11, s 29, sch 6, paras 3-12

asp 17   **Planning etc. (Scotland)**
       see—(transtl provns) SSI 2009/222
       s 20 am—SSI 2009/256, art 5(2)
       s 21 am—SSI 2009/256, art 5(3)

2007

asp 1   **Glasgow Airport Rail Link**
       s 15 am—Land Registration etc (S), 2012 asp 5, sch 5 para 51

asp 2   **St Andrew's Day Bank Holiday (Scotland)**

asp 3   **Bankruptcy and Diligence etc. (Scotland)**
       saving—SSI 2008/45, art 3
       mod—SIs 2009/317, art 3, sch; 2010/2993, reg 5
       appl (mods)—SI 2011/245, sch 6 pt 1
       s 15 rep in pt—Bankruptcy and Debt Advice (S), 2014 asp 11, sch 4
       s 21 rep —Bankruptcy and Debt Advice (S), 2014 asp 11, sch 4
       Pt 2 (ss 37-49) appl (mods)—Industrial and Provident Societies, 1967 c 48, s 3(1); SI
               2015/428, art 5(2) sch 2
       s 38 am—Banking, 2009 c 1, s 253(2)
       s 39 am—Banking, 2009 c 1, s 253(3)
       s 40 mod—Industrial and Provident Societies, 1967 c 48, s 3(2)
       s 42 am—Banking, 2009 c 1, s 253(4)
       s 43 am—Banking, 2009 c 1, s 253(5)
       s 44 am—Banking, 2009 c 1, s 253(6)
       s 45 mod—Industrial and Provident Societies, 1967 c 48, s 3(3)
       s 47 am—Banking, 2009 c 1, s 253(7); SI 2009/1941, art 2, sch 1 para 267
       s 49 am—Co-operative and Community Benefit Societies, 2014 c 14, sch 4 para 120(2)(3)
       Pt 3 (ss 50-78) am —Public Services Reform (S), 2010 asp 8, s 13, sch 4, paras 9, 10
       s 50 rep —Public Services Reform (S), 2010 asp 8, s 13, sch 4, para 33, table
       s 51 am —Public Services Reform (S), 2010 asp 8, s 13, sch 4, paras 9, 11(1)(b), (c)(ii), (iii),
               (d), (e), (2)(3)
          rep in pt —Public Services Reform (S), 2010 asp 8, s 13, sch 4, paras 9, 11(1)(a), (c)(i),
             (f)
       s 52 rep —Public Services Reform (S), 2010 asp 8, s 13, sch 4, para 33, table
       s 53 rep in pt —Public Services Reform (S), 2010 asp 8, s 13, sch 4, paras 9, 12(a)
          am —Public Services Reform (S), 2010 asp 8, s 13, sch 4, paras 9, 12(b)
       ss 54-60 rep —Public Services Reform (S), 2010 asp 8, s 13, sch 4, para 33, table
       s 61 am —Public Services Reform (S), 2010 asp 8, s 13, sch 4, paras 9, 13(1)(a), (c), (2)
          rep in pt —Public Services Reform (S), 2010 asp 8, s 13, sch 4, paras 9, 13(1)(b), 33,
             table
       s 62 am—Public Services Reform (S), 2010 asp 8, s 13, sch 4, paras 9, 14
       s 63 am—Public Services Reform (S), 2010 asp 8, s 13, sch 4, paras 9, 15
       s 63A added —Public Services Reform (S), 2010 asp 8, s 13, sch 4, paras 9, 16
       s 64 am —Public Services Reform (S), 2010 asp 8, s 13, sch 4, paras 9, 17(1)

2007

asp 3 s 64   *continued*

    rep in pt —Public Services Reform (S), 2010 asp 8, s 13, sch 4, paras 9, 17(2)

 s 65 am —Public Services Reform (S), 2010 asp 8, s 13, sch 4, paras 9, 18

 s 65A added —Public Services Reform (S), 2010 asp 8, s 13, sch 4, paras 9, 19

 s 66 am —Public Services Reform (S), 2010 asp 8, s 13, sch 4, paras 9, 20

 ss 67-74 rep —Public Services Reform (S), 2010 asp 8, s 13, sch 4, para 33, table

 s 75 am —Public Services Reform (S), 2010 asp 8, s 13, sch 4, paras 9, 21

 s 76 rep —Public Services Reform (S), 2010 asp 8, s 13, sch 4, para 33, table

 s 77 am —Public Services Reform (S), 2010 asp 8, s 13, sch 4, paras 9, 22

 s 78 rep in pt —Public Services Reform (S), 2010 asp 8, s 13, sch 4, paras 9, 23

 s 83 am —Public Services Reform (S), 2010 asp 8, s 13, sch 4, paras 9, 24

 s 85 am—Land Registration etc (S), 2012 asp 5, sch 5 para 52(2)

 s 114 am—SSI 2015/150, sch para 9

 s 117 am —Public Services Reform (S), 2010 asp 8, s 13, sch 4, paras 9, 25(a)

 s 121 am —Public Services Reform (S), 2010 asp 8, s 13, sch 4, paras 9, 25(a)

 s 128 am —Public Services Reform (S), 2010 asp 8, s 13, sch 4, paras 9, 26; Land
    Registration etc (S), 2012 asp 5, sch 5 para 52(3)

    rep in pt —Public Services Reform (S), 2010 asp 8, s 13, sch 4, para 33, table

 s 139 am —Public Services Reform (S), 2010 asp 8, s 13, sch 4, paras 9, 25(a)

 s 145 am —Public Services Reform (S), 2010 asp 8, s 13, sch 4, paras 9, 27

    rep in pt —Public Services Reform (S), 2010 asp 8, s 13, sch 4, para 33, table

 s 152 am—SSI 2009/129, arts 2, 4

 s 157 am —Public Services Reform (S), 2010 asp 8, s 13, sch 4, paras 9, 25(a)

 ss 176, 177 am—Public Services Reform (S), 2010 asp 8, s 13, sch 4, paras 9, 24

 s 178 am —Public Services Reform (S), 2010 asp 8, s 13, sch 4, paras 9, 24,28

 ss 179-182 am —Public Services Reform (S), 2010 asp 8, s 13, sch 4, paras 9, 24

 s 183 am —Public Services Reform (S), 2010 asp 8, s 13, sch 4, paras 9, 24, 25(a)

 ss 184-189 am —Public Services Reform (S), 2010 asp 8, s 13, sch 4, paras 9, 24

 s 189 am —Public Services Reform (S), 2010 asp 8, s 13, sch 4, paras 9, 24

    rep in pt —Public Services Reform (S), 2010 asp 8, s 13, sch 4, para 33, table

 s 191 am —Public Services Reform (S), 2010 asp 8, s 13, sch 4, paras 9, 24

 s 198 am—Public Services Reform (S), 2010 asp 8, s 13, sch 4, paras 9, 29

    rep in pt —Public Services Reform (S), 2010 asp 8, s 13, sch 4, para 33, table

 s 212 rep in pt —Public Services Reform (S), 2010 asp 8, s 13, sch 4, para 33, table

 s 216 am—Public Services Reform (S), 2010 asp 8, s 13, sch 4, paras 9, 24; Housing (S),
    2010 asp 17, s 152(3)

 s 217 am —Public Services Reform (S), 2010 asp 8, s 13, sch 4, paras 9, 24

 s 221 am—(prosp) Child Maintenance and Other Payments, 2008 c 6, s 57, sch 7 para 6;
    Public Services Reform (S), 2010 asp 8, s 13, sch 4, paras 9, 30; SSI 2012/301,
    sch para 3

    rep in pt —Public Services Reform (S), 2010 asp 8, s 13, sch 4, para 33, table

 sch 1 rep in pt —Public Services Reform (S), 2010 asp 8, s 13, sch 4, para 33, table

 sch 2 rep —Public Services Reform (S), 2010 asp 8, s 13, sch 4, para 33, table

 sch 3 am —Public Services Reform (S), 2010 asp 8, s 13, sch 4, paras 9, 25(b)

 sch 5 am —Public Services Reform (S), 2010 asp 8, s 13, sch 4, paras 9, 31

    rep in pt —Public Services Reform (S), 2010 asp 8, s 13, sch 4, para 33, table

 sch 6 am—Public Services Reform (S), 2010 asp 8, s 13, sch 4, paras 9, 32; Bankruptcy and
    Debt Advice (S), 2014 asp 11, sch 3 para 40

    rep in pt —Public Services Reform (S), 2010 asp 8, s 13, sch 4, para 33, table

asp 4   **Adoption and Children (Scotland)**

 power to mod—Human Fertilisation and Embryology, 2008 c 22, s 55

 appl (mods)—SSI 2009/182, regs 53, 54-61

 s 2 am—SSI 2011/211, sch 1 para 18

 s 4 rep (prosp)—Children and Young People (S), 2014 asp 8, sch 5 para 11(2)

 s 6 am—(prosp) Children and Young People (S), 2014 asp 8, sch 5 para 11(3)(4)

 s 7 rep —Public Services Reform (S), 2010 asp 8, s 106, sch 14, para 37

 s 9 appl (mods)—SSI 2009/152, reg 4

 s 10 rep in pt—SSI 2010/21, art 2, sch

 Pt 1, Ch 1A added (prosp)—Children and Young People (S), 2014 asp 8, s 75

 Pt 1, Ch 2 (ss 14-38) appl (mods)—SSI 2009/182, reg 9(1)(2)-(4)

 s 14 appl (mods)—SI 2010/985, reg 4, sch 3

 s 21 excl—SSI 2009/182, reg 6

 s 22 appl (mods) —SI 2010/985, reg 4, sch 3

 s 23 rep in pt—SSI 2013/211, sch 1 para 17(2)(a)(b)

2007

asp 4 s 23 *continued*

    am—SSI 2013/211, sch 1 para 17(2)(c)

s 24 appl (mods)—SI 2010/985, reg 4, sch 3

s 25 appl (mods)—SSI 2009/182, reg 6

s 26 rep in pt—SSI 2010/21, art 2, sch

ss 27, 28 appl (mods)—SI 2010/985, reg 4, sch 3

s 30 am—Human Fertilisation and Embryology, 2008 c 22, s 56, sch 6 para 56

s 33 appl (mods) —SI 2010/985, reg 4, sch 3

s 35 appl (mods) —SI 2010/985, reg 4, sch 3

s 36 am—SSI 2013/211, sch 1 para 17(3)

ss 40-43 appl (mods) —SI 2010/985, reg 4, sch 3

ss 53-55 appl (mods)—SSI 2009/182, reg 9(5); SI 2010/985, reg 4, sch 3

ss 56-58 appl (mods)—SI 2010/985, reg 4, sch 3

s 72 am—SSI 2013/211, sch 1 para 17(4)

s 76 am—SSI 2010/21, art 2, sch

s 77 appl (mods)—SI 2010/985, reg 4, sch 3

s 79 am—SSI 2013/211, sch 1 para 17(5)

s 89 am—SSI 2013/211, sch 1 para 17(6)

s 90 am—SSI 2013/211, sch 1 para 17(7)

s 95 am—SSI 2013/211, sch 1 para 17(8)

s 96 am—SSI 2013/211, sch 1 para 17(9)

    rep in pt—SSI 2013/211, sch 2

s 97 am—SSI 2013/211, sch 1 para 17(10)

s 106 am—SSI 2013/211, sch 1 para 17(11)

    rep in pt—SSI 2013/211, sch 2

s 108 appl (mods)—SI 2010/985, reg 4, sch 3

s 109 appl (mods)—SI 2010/985, reg 4, sch 3

    am—SSI 2010/21, art 2, sch

    rep in pt—SSI 2010/21, art 2, sch

s 110 am—SSI 2013/211, sch 1 para 17(12)

s 111 appl (mods)—SI 2010/985, reg 4, sch 3

ss 113, 114 appl (mods)—SI 2010/985, reg 4, sch 3

s 117 appl (mods)—SI 2010/985, reg 4, sch 3

    am—(prosp) Children and Young People (S), 2014 asp 8, sch 5 para 11(5)

s 118 appl (mods)—SI 2010/985, reg 4, sch 3

s 119 appl (mods)—SI 2010/985, reg 4, sch 3

    am—SSI 2013/211, sch 1 para 17(13); (prosp) Children and Young People (S), 2014

    asp 8, sch 5 para 11(6)

    rep in pt—SSI 2013/211, sch 2

sch 1 appl (mods)—SSI 2009/182, reg 9(5); SI 2010/985, reg 4, sch 3

sch 2 rep in pt—SSI 2013/211, sch 2

asp 5 **Legal Profession and Legal Aid (Scotland)**

appl—Legal Services, 2007 c 29, s 195(1)

Pt 1 (ss 1-46) appl mods—SSI 2012/153, reg 2

s 2 am—SSI 2014/232, reg 2(2)(a)(i)(ii)(b)(c)

s 4 am—SSI 2014/232, reg 2(3)(a)(i)-(iv)(b)(c)

s 5 rep —SSI 2014/232, reg 2(4)

s 6 transtl provns—SSI 2009/17, art 2

    am—SSI 2014/311, reg 2(5)(a)-(c)(i)(ii)

s 7 am—SSI 2014/311, reg 2(6)(a)-(c)(i)(ii)

s 8 am—SSI 2014/311, reg 2(7)

s 9 am—SSI 2014/311, reg 2(8)(9)(a)(b)

s 9A added—SSI 2014/311, reg 2(10)

s 15 am—SSI 2014/311, reg 2(8)(11)

s 17 rep in pt—SSI 2014/311, reg 2(12)(a)(b)

s 23 am—SSI 2014/311, reg 2(11)(13)(a)-(c)(i)-iii)(d)(i)(ii)(e)(i)-(iii)(f)

    rep in pt—SSI 2014/311, reg 2(13)(c)(iv)(e)(iii)

s 24 am—SSI 2014/311, reg 2(14)(a)(b)(d)(i)-(iii)(e)(i)-(iii)(f)(ii)(g)

    rep in pt—SSI 2014/311, reg 2(14)(c)(e)(iv)(f)(i)

s 29 am —Legal Services (S), 2010 asp 16, s 144(a)

s 33 am—SSI 2014/311, reg 2(11)

s 36 am—SSI 2014/311, reg 2(11)

s 37 am—SSI 2014/311, reg 2(11)

s 46 am —Legal Services (S), 2010 asp 16, ss 143, 144(b); SSI 2014/311, reg 2(15)

2007

asp 5 *continued*

   s 47 am—SSI 2014/311, reg 2(11)

   Pt 2A (ss 57A-57G) added—Legal Services (S), 2010 asp 16, s 81

   Pt 2B (ss 57H-57L) added (prosp)—Legal Services (S), 2010 asp 16, s 114

   s 75 am—SSI 2011/235, art 7

   s 77 rep—Legal Services, 2007 c 29, s 195(4), sch 23

   s 78 am —Legal Services (S), 2010 asp 16, s 145(1); SSI 2012/212, reg 4(2)

   s 79 am —Legal Services (S), 2010 asp 16, s 145(2)

   sch 1 mod—SSI 2008/332, art 5

    ext—SI 2008/2341, art 5

    am —Legal Services (S), 2010 asp 16, s 144(c); SSI 2010/415, art 2; SSIs 2014/311,

     reg 2(16); 2014/272, art 2(a)-(c)

   sch 3 am —Legal Services (S), 2010 asp 16, s 144(d); SSI 2014/311, reg 2(17)(a)(b)

asp 6 **Criminal Proceedings etc. (Reform) (Scotland)**

   saving—SSI 2008/42, arts 4-6

   s 3 am—SSI 2007/540, art 3

   s 7 am—SSI 2008/109, art 3

    rep in pt —Crim Justice and Licensing (S), 2010 asp 13, s 203, sch 7, paras 78, 79

   s 20 am—SSI 2007/540, art 4

   s 45 excl—SIs 2008/295, reg 6; 296, regs 6, 7

   s 49 rep in pt —Crim Justice and Licensing (S), 2010 asp 13, s 14, sch 2, para 52(a)

   s 56 am—SI 2007/1655, reg 5, sch 1; SI 2014/2947, sch 4 para 6

   s 57 rep —Crim Justice and Licensing (S), 2010 asp 13, s 14, sch 2, para 52(b)

   s 59 rep in pt —Judiciary and Cts (S), 2008 asp 6, ss (2)(a), 57(1), 73, sch 5 para (3)(a),

     5(1)

    am—Judiciary and Cts (S), 2008 asp 6, ss (2)(b), (c), (d), 57(1); Courts Reform (S),

     2014 asp 18, s 127(2)(3)

   s 60 rep —Judiciary and Cts (S), 2008 asp 6, s 73, sch 5 para (3)(b), 5(1),

   s 61 subst—Judiciary and Cts (S), 2008 asp 6, s 58(1), (2)

    am—(prosp) Courts Reform (S), 2014 asp 18, sch 5 para 40(2)

   s 62 rep in pt—(prosp) Courts Reform (S), 2014 asp 18, sch 5 para 40(3)(a)-(c)

   s 63 rep in pt—Judiciary and Cts (S), 2008 asp 6, s 73, sch 5 para (3)(c), 5(1)

    am—Judiciary and Cts (S), 2008 asp 6, s 57(1), (3); (prosp) Courts Reform (S), 2014

     asp 18, sch 5 para 40(4)

   s 66 saving—SSIs 2008/328, art 6; 363, art 6; 2009/331, art 6(6); 332, art 6(6)

   s 67 am—SSIs 2007/540, art 5; 2014/155, art 4(2)

   s 69 am—Judiciary and Cts (S), 2008 asp 6, s 42(1), (2)

    rep in pt—Judiciary and Cts (S), 2008 asp 6, s 42(1), (3)

   s 70 am—SSIs 2007/540, art 6; 2014/155, art 4(3)

   s 71 am—Judiciary and Cts (S), 2008 asp 6, s 41

   ss 71A, 71B added—SSI 2014/155, art 4(4)

   s 74 rep (prosp)—Courts Reform (S), 2014 asp 18, sch 5 para 40(5)(a)

    am—Judiciary and Cts (S), 2008 asp 6, s 58(1), (3); SSI 2014/155, art 4(5)

    rep in pt —Crim Justice and Licensing (S), 2010 asp 13, s 203, sch 7, paras 78, 80

   s 74A added —Crim Justice and Licensing (S), 2010 asp 13, s 203, sch 7, paras 78, 81

    rep (prosp)—Courts Reform (S), 2014 asp 18, sch 5 para 40(5)(b)

   s 75 rep (prosp)—Courts Reform (S), 2014 asp 18, sch 5 para 40(5)(c)

    am—SSI 2014/155, art 4(6)(a)(b)

   s 76 am —Crim Justice and Licensing (S), 2010 asp 13, s 203, sch 7, paras 78, 82(a)

    rep in pt —Crim Justice and Licensing (S), 2010 asp 13, s 203, sch 7, paras 78, 82(b);

     (prosp) Courts Reform (S), 2014 asp 18, sch 5 para 40(6)(a)(b)

   s 77 rep in pt—(prosp) Courts Reform (S), 2014 asp 18, sch 5 para 40(7)(a)-(c)

   s 81 am—Judiciary and Cts (S), 2008 asp 6, s 73, sch 5 para 5(1), (2); Courts Reform (S),

     2014 asp 18, s 127(4)

   sch am—SI 2007/3480, art 2(2)(a)(b)

    rep in pt —Crim Justice and Licensing (S), 2010 asp 13, s 14, sch 2, para 52(c); ibid, s

     203, sch 7, paras 78, 83(a), (b)

asp 7 **Crofting Reform etc.**

asp 8 **Transport and Works (Scotland)**

   s 11 am—SSI 2011/396, art 19(a)(b)

   s 12 am—SSI 2011/396, art 20; SI 2015/1682, sch Pt 3 para 11(b)

   s 13 am—SSI 2011/396, art 21

    rep in pt—SSI 2011/396, art 21(c)(ii)

   s 21 am—SSI 2011/396, art 22

2007

asp 9 **Budget (Scotland)**
s 3 am—SSIs 2007/551, art 2; 2008/107, art 2; 2009/120, art 2
Pt 2 (s 6) rep—Budget (S), 2008 asp 2, s 8
sch 1 am—SSIs 2007/551, art 3; 2008/107, art 3; 2009/120, art 3
sch 2 am—SSIs 2007/551, art 4; 2008/107, art 4; 2009/120, art 4
    rep in pt—SSI 2009/120, art 4
sch 3 am—SSIs 2007/551, art 5; 2008/107, art 5
sch 4 am—SSI 2008/107, art 6
sch 5 am—SSI 2008/107, art 7

asp 10 **Adult Support and Protection (Scotland)**
Pt 1 (ss 1-53) mod—SSI 2012/66, art 2
s 5 am —Public Services Reform (S), 2010 asp 8, ss 106, 110, sch 14, paras 19, 20, sch 17,
    para 35(a); Police and Fire Reform (S), 2012 asp 8, sch 7 para 35(2)
s 27 am—Police and Fire Reform (S), 2012 asp 8, sch 7 para 35(3)
s 42 am —Public Services Reform (S), 2010 asp 8, ss 106, 110, sch 14, paras 19, 21, sch 17,
    para 35(b); Police and Fire Reform (S), 2012 asp 8, sch 7 para 35(4)
s 43 am —Public Services Reform (S), 2010 asp 8, s 106, sch 14, paras 19, 22
s 44 am —Public Services Reform (S), 2010 asp 8, s 106, sch 14, paras 19, 23
s 45 am —Public Services Reform (S), 2010 asp 8, s 106, sch 14, paras 19, 24
s 46 am —Public Services Reform (S), 2010 asp 8, s 106, sch 14, paras 19, 25
s 53 am —Public Services Reform (S), 2010 asp 8, s 106, sch 14, paras 19, 26(b)
    rep in pt —Public Services Reform (S), 2010 asp 8, s 106, sch 14, paras 19, 26(a)
s 63 rep—SSI 2014/90, sch, pt 1

asp 11 **Prostitution (Public Places) (Scotland), sch pt 1**
asp 12 **Aquaculture and Fisheries (Scotland)**
ss 4A, 4B added—Aquaculture and Fisheries (S), 2013 asp 7, s 1(2)
s 5 am—Aquaculture and Fisheries (S), 2013 asp 7, s 2(2)
s 5A added—Aquaculture and Fisheries (S), 2013 asp 7, s 2(3)
s 6 am—Aquaculture and Fisheries (S), 2013 asp 7, s 1(3)
s 12 am—SSI 2011/427, reg 3(2)
Pt 4 (ss 25-33) am and renumbered as Pt 4 (ss 25-31) and Pt 4A (ss 32,33)—Aquaculture
    and Fisheries (S), 2013 asp 7, s 60(5)-(7)
s 25 am—Aquaculture and Fisheries (S), 2013 asp 7, s 60(2)(a),(b)(ii),(c)(d)
    rep in pt—Aquaculture and Fisheries (S), 2013 asp 7, s 60(2)(b)(i)
s 27 am—Aquaculture and Fisheries (S), 2013 asp 7, s 60(3)
s 31 am—Aquaculture and Fisheries (S), 2013 asp 7, s 60(4)
s 32 am—Aquaculture and Fisheries (S), 2013 asp 7, s 60(7)
s 37 am—SSI 2011/427, reg 3(3)
s 43 am—Aquaculture and Fisheries (S), 2013 asp 7, s 1(4)
s 44 am—SSI 2011/427, reg 3(4)

asp 13 **Christmas Day and New Year's Day Trading (Scotland)**
s 7 rep in pt—SI 2012/1916, sch 34 para 45(a)
    am—SI 2012/1916, sch 34 para 45(b)

asp 14 **Protection of Vulnerable Groups (Scotland)**
s 8 rep in pt —Public Services Reform (S), 2010 asp 8, s 106, sch 14, paras 27, 28(a)(i),
    (b)(i), (iii)
    am—Public Services Reform (S), 2010 asp 8, ss 106, 110, sch 14, paras 27, 28(a)(ii),
    (b)(ii), (iv), sch 17, para 36(a); SI 2010/231, art 68, sch 4; SSI 2011/215, sch 6
    para 2(2)
s 13 ext—SSI 2010/180, art 5
s 17 rep in pt —Public Services Reform (S), 2010 asp 8, s 106, sch 14, paras 27, 29(a), (b)
    am —Public Services Reform (S), 2010 asp 8, s 106, sch 14, paras 27, 29(c); Health
    and Social Care, 2012 c 7, sch 15 para 56(f)
s 18 am—SSI 2010/446, arts 3, 5; Police and Fire Reform (S), 2012 asp 8, sch 7 para
    36(2)(a)(i)(b)(c)(ii)
s 19 rep in pt —Public Services Reform (S), 2010 asp 8, s 106, sch 14, paras 27, 30(a); SSI
    2011/211, sch 1 para 19(a)
    am—Public Services Reform (S), 2010 asp 8, ss 106, 110, sch 14, paras 27, 30(b), sch
    17, para 36(b); SI 2010/231, art 68, sch 4
s 30 rep in pt —Public Services Reform (S), 2010 asp 8, s 106, sch 14, paras 27, 31(a)
    am —Public Services Reform (S), 2010 asp 8, ss 106, 110, sch 14, paras 27, 31(b), sch
    17, para 36(c)
s 30A added —SI 2009/1182, arts 4, 5-7, sch 5
    am—Health and Social Care, 2012 c 7, sch 15 paras 56(f), 58

2007
asp 14 *continued*

s 32 am —Crim Justice and Licensing (S), 2010 asp 13, s 203, sch 7, para 84

s 38 am—SSI 2010/446, arts 3, 6; (Police and Fire Reform (S), 2012 asp 8, sch 7 para 36(3)

s 39 am—SSI 2010/446, arts 3, 7
    rep in pt—SSI 2010/446, arts 3, 7
    am—Policing and Crime, 2009 c 26, s 81(2)(3)(n)

s 40 am—Policing and Crime, 2009 c 26, s 81(2)(3)(n); SSI 2010/446, arts 3, 8

s 41 am—SSI 2010/446, arts 3, 9

Pt 2 (ss 44-77) mod—SI 2010/2660, art 21

s 46 rep in pt—(8.2.2016) SSI 2015/423, art 4(3)

s 49 am—(8.2.2016) SSI 2015/423, art 4(3)

s 51 am—(8.2.2016) SSI 2015/423, art 4(4)

s 52ZA added (8.2.2016)—SSI 2015/423, art 4(5)

s 52 replaced (by ss 52, 52A) (8.2.2016)—SSI 2015/423, art 4(6)

s 53 am—(8.2.2016) SSI 2015/423, art 4(7)(a)-(c)
    rep in pt—(8.2.2016) SSI 2015/423, art 4(7)(d)

s 57A added (8.2.2016)—SSI 2015/423, art 4(8)

s 73 am—Public Services Reform (S), 2010 asp 8, s 106, sch 14, paras 27, 32; SSI
    2011/215, sch 6 para 2(3)

s 75 am—SSI 2010/446, arts 3, 10; Police and Fire Reform (S), 2012 asp 8, sch 7 para
    36(4)

s 76 am—SSI 2010/446, arts 3, 11; Police and Fire Reform (S), 2012 asp 8, sch 7 para
    36(5)

s 94 am—Public Services Reform (S), 2010 asp 8, ss 106, 110, sch 14, paras 27, 33, 34,
    sch 17, para 36(d); SI 2014/90, sch pt 3

s 96 am—SSI 2013/211, sch 1 para 18(2)
    rep in pt—SSI 2013/211, sch 2

s 97 am—Policing and Crime, 2009 c 26, s 81(2)(3)(n); SI 2010/231, art 68, sch 4; Police
    and Fire Reform (S), 2012 asp 8, sch 7 para 36(6)(a); SSI 2015/153, sch para 4
    rep in pt—SSI 2011/211, sch 1 para 19(b); Police and Fire Reform (S), 2012 asp 8, sch
    7 para 36(6)(b)

sch 1 rep in pt—SSI 2010/246, arts 2, 3
    am—SSI 2010/246, arts 2, 4-11

sch 2 am —Public Services Reform (S), 2010 asp 8, ss 106, 110, sch 14, paras 27, 35, sch
    17, para 36(e); SSIs 2010/240, arts 3-8; 446, arts 3, 12; SSI 2011/211, sch 1
    para 19(c); Post-16 Educ (S), 2013 asp 12, sch para 9; SSI 2013/203, arts 3, 4

sch 3 am —Public Services Reform (S), 2010 asp 8, ss 106, 110, sch 14, paras 27, 36, sch
    17, para 36(f)(i)(iii), (g); SSIs 2010/245, arts 3, 5; 446, arts 3, 12; SSI
    2011/211, sch 1 para 19(d)
    rep in pt —Public Services Reform (S), 2010 asp 8, s 110, sch 17, para 36(f)(ii); SSI
    2010/245, art 4

sch 4 rep in pt—SSIs 2010/446, art 21; 2011/215, sch 7

sch 5 am—Policing and Crime, 2009 c 26, s 81(2)(3)(n); SI 2010/231, art 68, sch 4
    rep in pt—SSI 2011/211, sch 1 para 19(e)

asp 15   **Schools (Health Promotion and Nutrition) (Scotland)**

asp 16   **Edinburgh Airport Rail Link**

s 9 am—Land Registration etc (S), 2012 asp 5, sch 5 para 53(2)

s 20 am—Land Registration etc (S), 2012 asp 5, sch 5 para 53(3)

s 38 am—Police and Fire Reform (S), 2012 asp 8, sch 7 para 37

asp 17   **Custodial Sentences and Weapons (Scotland)**

s 4 am—(prosp) Crim Justice and Licensing (S), 2010 asp 13, ss 18(2)(a)(ii)-(iv), 71, sch 4,
    para 12
    rep in pt —(prosp) Crim Justice and Licensing (S), 2010 asp 13, s 18(2)(a)(i),(b)

s 5 subst —(prosp) Crim Justice and Licensing (S), 2010 asp 13, s 18(3)

Pt 2, Chapter 3 (ss 28-57) —(prosp) Crim Justice and Licensing (S), 2010 asp 13, s 18(4)

s 29 rep in pt —(prosp) Crim Justice and Licensing (S), 2010 asp 13, s 18(5)(a)(b)
    am—(prosp) Crim Justice and Licensing (S), 2010 asp 13, s 18(5)(c)-(e)

s 29A added (prosp)—Crim Justice and Licensing (S), 2010 asp 13, s 18(6)

s 34 am —(prosp) Crim Justice and Licensing (S), 2010 asp 13, s 18, sch 3, para 2

s 35 am —(prosp) Crim Justice and Licensing (S), 2010 asp 13, s 18, sch 3, para 3(a)

s 36 am —(prosp) Crim Justice and Licensing (S), 2010 asp 13, s 18, sch 3, para 3(b)

s 37 am —(prosp) Crim Justice and Licensing (S), 2010 asp 13, s 18, sch 3, para 3(c)

s 40 am —(prosp) Crim Justice and Licensing (S), 2010 asp 13, s 18, sch 3, para 4

s 42 am —(prosp) Crim Justice and Licensing (S), 2010 asp 13, s 18, sch 3, para 5

2007

asp 17 *continued*

s 42A added (prosp)—Crim Justice and Licensing (S), 2010 asp 13, s 18, sch 3, para 6
s 45 am —(prosp) Crim Justice and Licensing (S), 2010 asp 13, s 18, sch 3, para 7
s 46 am —(prosp) Crim Justice and Licensing (S), 2010 asp 13, s 18, sch 3, para 8
s 46A added (prosp)—Crim Justice and Licensing (S), 2010 asp 13, s 18(7)
s 47 am —(prosp) Crim Justice and Licensing (S), 2010 asp 13, s 18(8)
s 51 am —(prosp) Crim Justice and Licensing (S), 2010 asp 13, s 18, sch 3, para 9
s 55 am —(prosp) Crim Justice and Licensing (S), 2010 asp 13, s 18, sch 3, para 10
s 56 am —(prosp) Crim Justice and Licensing (S), 2010 asp 13, s 18, sch 3, para 11
s 65 am —(prosp) Crim Justice and Licensing (S), 2010 asp 13, s 18, sch 3, para 12
sch 2 am —(prosp) Crim Justice and Licensing (S), 2010 asp 13, s 18, sch 3, para 13
sch 3 am —(prosp) Crim Justice and Licensing (S), 2010 asp 13, s 18, sch 3, para 14
    rep in pt —(prosp) Crim Justice and Licensing (S), 2010 asp 13, s 18, sch 3, para
      14(6)(a)
sch 6 subst—Crim Justice and Licensing (S), 2010 asp 13, s 19

asp 18   *Rights of Relatives to Damages (Mesothelioma) (Scotland)*—rep Damages (S), 2011 asp 7,
      sch 2

asp 19   **Airdrie-Bathgate Railway and Linked Improvements**
s 30 am—Land Registration etc (S), 2012 asp 5, sch 5 para 54(2)
s 37 am—Land Registration etc (S), 2012 asp 5, sch 5 para 54(3)

2008

asp 1   **Abolition of Bridge Tolls (Scotland)**
asp 2   **Budget (Scotland)**
s 3 am—SSIs 2008/424, art 2; 2009/120, art 5
Pt 2 (s 6) rep—Budget (S), 2009 asp 2, s 8
sch 1 am—SSIs 2008/424, art 3; 2009/120, art 6
    rep in pt—SSIs 2008/424, art 3; 2009/120, art 6
sch 2 am—SSIs 2008/424, art 4; 2009/120, art 7
    rep in pt—SSIs 2008/424, art 4; 2009/120, art 7
sch 3 am—SSIs 2008/424, art 5; 2009/120, art 8
sch 4 am—SSI 2009/120, art 9
sch 5 am—SSIs 2008/424, art 6; 2009/120, art 10

asp 3   **Graduate Endowment Abolition (Scotland)**
asp 4   *Glasgow Commonwealth Games*—rep Glasgow Commonwealth Games, 2008 asp 4, s 50
asp 5   **Public Health etc (Scotland)**
saved—SSI 2009/319, art 3, schs 2, 3
s 6 am —Public Services Reform (S), 2010 asp 8, s 110, sch 17, para 37(a); SSI 2015/157,
      sch para 8(2)
s 8 am—SSI 2015/157, sch para 8(3)
s 117 am—Public Services Reform (S), 2010 asp 8, s 110, sch 17, para 37(b)

asp 6   **Judiciary and Courts (Scotland)**
am—Courts Reform (S), 2014 asp 18, sch 4 para 1(2)
Pt 2, Ch 2 (ss 4-8) ext—(to EW, NI) SI 2009/2231, art 4
s 2 am—Courts Reform (S), 2014 asp 18, sch 5 para 16(2)(a)(b)
s 10 rep in pt—(prosp) Tribunals (S), 2014 asp 10, sch 9 para 12(2)(a)
    am—(prosp) Tribunals (S), 2014 asp 10, sch 9 para 12(2)(b)(c); (prosp) Courts Reform
      (S), 2014 asp, sch 5 para 9(3)
ss 20A-20G added (subst ss 21-23) —Courts Reform (S), 2014 asp 18, s 123
ss 24-26 rep —Courts Reform (S), 2014 asp 18, sch 5 para 9(2)(a)
s 30 am—(prosp) Tribunals (S), 2014 asp 10, sch 9 para 12(3)
s 40 rep —Courts Reform (S), 2014 asp 18, sch 5 para 9(2)(b)
s 43 rep in pt—Courts Reform (S), 2014 asp 18, sch 5 para 9(2)(c)
    am—Courts Reform (S), 2014 asp 18, sch 5 paras 9(4)(a)(b), 16(3), 38(2)
ss 47-56 rep —Courts Reform (S), 2014 asp 18, sch 5 para 9(2)(c)
Pt 4 (ss 60-70) am—Courts Reform (S), 2014 asp 18, sch 4 para 1(12)(a)
s 60 am—Courts Reform (S), 2014 asp 18, sch 4 para 1(3)(12)(b)
s 61A added (prosp)—(part prosp) Courts Reform (S), 2014 asp 18, s 130(2)
    appl (temp)—Courts Reform (S), 2014 asp 18, sch 4 para 3(1)
s 62 am—S Civil Justice Council and Crim Legal Assistance, 2013 asp 3, s 15(3)(a);
      Courts Reform (S), 2014 asp 18, sch 4 para 1(4)(a)(b); ibid., sch 5 paras 9(5),
      16(4)
    rep in pt—S Civil Justice Council and Crim Legal Assistance, 2013 asp 3, s 15(3)(b)
s 64 rep in pt—Courts Reform (S), 2014 asp 18, sch 5 paras 9(2)(d), 38(3)

2008
asp 6 *continued*

> s 70 appl (temp)—Courts Reform (S), 2014 asp 18, sch 4 para 3(1)
> s 70 am—Courts Reform (S), 2014 asp 18, sch 4 para 1(5)
> s 72 rep in pt—Courts Reform (S), 2014 asp 18, sch 5 para 9(2)(e)
>> am—Courts Reform (S), 2014 asp 18, sch 5 paras 9(6)(a)-(c), 38(4)
> sch 1 rep in pt—(prosp) Tribunals (S), 2014 asp 10, sch 9 para 12(4)(a)
>> am—Courts Reform (S), 2014 asp 18, s 131(1)(a)(b); (prosp) Tribunals (S), 2014 sch 9 para 12(4)(b)(c)(5)
> sch 3 rep in pt—Courts Reform (S), 2014 asp 18, sch 4 para 1(7) (8)(b)
>> am—Courts Reform (S), 2014 asp 18, sch 4 para 1(8)(a)(c)(d)(8)-(11)(12)(c)
>> appl (mods)(temp)—Courts Reform (S), 2014 asp 18, sch 4 para 3(3)
>> mod (temp)—Courts Reform (S), 2014 asp 18, sch 4 para 3(3)
> sch 5 rep in pt—Courts Reform (S), 2014 asp 18, sch 5 para 9(2)(f)

asp 7 **Scottish Register of Tartans**
> s 15 rep—Public Services Reform (S), 2010 asp 8, s 4(7)

2009

asp 1 **Scottish Parliamentary Pensions**
> s 3 am—SSI 2011/196, art 3
> sch 1 am—Pension Schemes, 2015 c. 8, sch 4 para 43(2)(3)
> sch 1 rep in pt (rule 13 rep)—SSI 2011/244, Annex para 1
> sch 1 am (rules 49, 85 am)—SSI 2011/244, Annex paras 2, 3
> sch 1 am (rule 85A added)—SSI 2011/244, Annex para 4
> sch 3 am—SSI 2011/244, Annex para 5

asp 2 **Budget (Scotland)**
> s 3 am—SSIs 2009/434, art 2; 2010/118, art 2
> Pt 2 (s 6) rep—Budget (S), 2010 asp 4, s 8
> sch 1 am—SSIs 2009/434, art 3; 2010/118, art 3
>> rep in pt—SSIs 2010/118, art 3
> sch 2 am—SSIs 2009/434, art 4; 2010/118, art 4
>> rep in pt—SSI 2010/118, art 4
> sch 3 am—SSIs 2009/434, art 5; 2010/118, art 5

asp 3 **Disabled Persons Parking Places (Scotland)**
asp 4 **Damages (Asbestos-related Conditions) (Scotland)**
asp 5 **Health Boards (Membership and Elections (Scotland)**
> s 1 rep in pt—(conditionally) Health Boards (Membership and Elections) (S), 2009 asp 5, s 6(2)(3)
> ss 2-5 rep—(conditionally) Health Boards (Membership and Elections) (S), 2009 asp 5, s 6(2)(3)
> s 6 rep in pt—(conditionally) Health Boards (Membership and Elections) (S), 2009 asp 5, s 6(2)(3)
>> restr—SSI 2013/364, art 3(2)
> s 7 rep—(conditionally) Health Boards (Membership and Elections) (S), 2009 asp 5, s 6(2)(3)
> sch rep in pt—SSI 2010/50, art 3

asp 6 **Flood Risk Management (Scotland)**
> s 12 am—SI 2010/1102, regs 26, 27
> s 13 am—SI 2010/1102, regs 26, 28
> s 14 am—SI 2010/1102, regs 26, 29
> s 25 am—SI 2010/1102, regs 26, 30
> s 30 am—SI 2010/1102, regs 26, 31
> s 32 am—SI 2010/1102, regs 26, 32
> s 50A added—SI 2010/1102, regs 26, 33
> s 55 rep in pt—SI 2010/1102, regs 26, 34
>> am—SI 2010/1102, regs 26, 34
> s 78 rep—Regulatory Reform (S), 2014 asp 3, sch 3 para 44
> Pt 7 (ss 84-90) rep—Reservoirs (S), 2011 asp 9, s 112(5)
> sch 2 appl (mods)—SSI 2010/426, reg 9

asp 7 **Education (Additional Support for Learning) (Scotland)**
> s 9 am—Equality, 2010 c 15, s 211(1), sch 26 para 107 (added by SI 2010/2279, sch 1 para 6)

asp 8 **Offences (Aggravation by Prejudice) (Scotland)**

2009

asp 9 **Sexual Offences (Scotland)**
s 9 am—Crim Justice and Licensing (S), 2010 asp 13, s 43(2)(a)-(c)
s 10 am—Crim Justice and Licensing (S), 2010 asp 13, s 43(3)
s 26 am—Crim Justice and Licensing (S), 2010 asp 13, s 43(4)(a)-(d)
s 36 am—Crim Justice and Licensing (S), 2010 asp 13, s 43(5)(a)-(d)
s 39 am—Crim Justice and Licensing (S), 2010 asp 13, ss 44, 71; sch 4, para 13(1)-(4)
s 44 am—SSI 2011/211, sch 1 para 20(2), sch 2 para 11; SSI 2015/153, sch para 5
s 46 am—SSI 2011/211, sch 1 para 20(3)
s 55 am—Crim Justice and Licensing (S), 2010 asp 13, s 203, sch 7, para 86
sch 3 am—SSI 2010/421, art 2, sch para 4

asp 10 **Scottish Local Government Elections**
asp 11 *Convention Rights Proceedings (Amendment) (Scotland)*—Scotland, 2012 c 11, s 14(2)
asp 12 **Climate Change (Scotland)**
s 10 am—SSI 2015/197, art 2
s 11 am—SSI 2015/197, art 3
s 82A added (18.4.2016)—Procurement Reform (S), 2014 asp 12, s 36
s 88A added—Regulatory Reform (S), 2014 asp 3, s 43(2)
sch 1A added—Regulatory Reform (S), 2014 asp 3, s 43(3)

2010

asp 1 **Arbitration (Scotland)**
Act appl (temp until coming into force generally for "statutory arbitration")—Food Safety,
1990 c 16, s 15B(18) (added by Food (S), 2015 asp 1, s 33); (prosp)
Mesothelioma, 2014 c 1, s 16(4)
power to am—(prosp) Mesothelioma, 2014 c 1, s 16(5)
ss 1-15 excl—SSI 2010/220, sch
sch 1 excl—SSI 2010/220, sch

asp 2 **Schools (Consultation) (Scotland)**
s 1 am—Children and Young People (S), 2014 asp 8, s 80(5)
s 2A added—Children and Young People (S), 2014 asp 8, s 77
s 4 am—Children and Young People (S), 2014 asp 8, s 81(6); ibid, s 78
s 5 rep in pt—Children and Young People (S), 2014 asp 8, s 79(2)(a)
am—Children and Young People (S), 2014 asp 8, 79(2)(b)-(d)(3)(4)
s 10 am—Children and Young People (S), 2014 asp 8, s 79(5)(a)-(d)
s 11A added—Children and Young People (S), 2014 asp 8, s 80(1)
s 12 rep in pt—Children and Young People (S), 2014 asp 8, s 80(2)(a)
am—Children and Young People (S), 2014 asp 8, s 80(2)(b)(c)
s 12A added—Children and Young People (S), 2014 asp 8, s 80(3)
s 13 subst—Children and Young People (S), 2014 asp 8, s 80(4)
s 15 rep in pt—Children and Young People (S), 2014 asp 8, s 81(1)(d)
am—Children and Young People (S), 2014 asp 8, s 81(1)(a)-(c)
s 16 rep—Children and Young People (S), 2014 asp 8, s 81(2)
s 17 rep in pt—Children and Young People (S), 2014 asp 8, s 81(3)(a)(i)(ii)
am—Children and Young People (S), 2014 asp 8, s 81(3)(b)
ss 17A, 17B added—Children and Young People (S), 2014 asp 8, s 81(4)
ss 17C, 17D added —Children and Young People (S), 2014 asp 8, s 81(4)
s 19 am—Children and Young People (S), 2014 asp 8, s 81(7)(a)(b)
s 20 am—Children and Young People (S), 2014 asp 8, s 81(8)(a); ibid, s 81(8)(b)
s 21 am—Children and Young People (S), 2014 asp 8, s 81(9)(a)(b)
sch 2 am—(prosp) Community Empowerment (S), 2015 asp 6, sch 4 para 10(a)(b)
sch 2A added —Children and Young People (S), 2014 asp 8, s 81(5)

asp 3 **Tobacco and Primary Medical Services (Scotland)**
mod—SSI 2013/85, reg 17
s 2 rep in pt—Courts Reform (S), 2014 asp 18, sch 5 para 18(b)(i)
am—Courts Reform (S), 2014 asp 18, sch 5 para 18(a)(b)(ii)
Pt 1 Ch 2 (ss 10-24) appl (mods)—SSI 2011/23, reg 2-4

asp 4 **Budget (Scotland)**
s 3 am—SSIs 2010/282, art 2; 445, art 2; 2011/212, art 2
Pt 2 (s 6) rep—Budget (S), 2011 asp 4, s 8
sch 1 am—SSIs 2010/282, art 3; 445, art 3; 2011/212, art 3(2)-(4)
rep in pt—SSI 2011/212, art 3(2)(c)(iv)
sch 2 am—SSIs 2010/282, art 4; 445, art 4; 2011/212, art 4
sch 3 am—SSI 2011/212, art 5

2010

asp 5   **Marine (Scotland)**
 s 15 appl—SI 2010/2870, art 3
 Pt 4 (ss 20-64) mod—Forth Crossing, 2011 asp 2, s 8
 s 20 excl—SSI 2011/202, art 8(1)
 s 27 am—SI 2011/1210, sch 1 para 102
 s 38 am—Regulatory Reform (S), 2014 asp 3, s 54(2)
 ss 63A, 63B added —Regulatory Reform (S), 2014 asp 3, s 54(3)
 s 79 mod—SSI 2012/228, reg 4
 s 80A added —Historic Environment Scotland, 2014 asp 19, sch 4 para 3(a)
 ss 82-84 appl—SI 2010/2870, art 4
 s 82 am—Historic Environment Scotland, 2014 asp 19, sch 4 para 3(a)-(g)
 s 83 am—Historic Environment Scotland, 2014 asp 19, sch 4 para 4(a)-(c)
 s 84 am—Historic Environment Scotland, 2014 asp 19, sch 4 para 5
 s 104 rep—Wildlife and Natural Environment (S), 2011 asp 6, sch pt 2
 s 97 excl in pt—(temp until 18.8.2016) SSIs 2015/302, art 5; (8.2.2016) 437, art 6(1)
 Pt 7 (ss 131-157) mod—Aquaculture and Fisheries (S), 2013 asp 7, s 35(6)
 s 131 mod—SI 2010/2870, art 6
 s 132 mod—SI 2010/2870, art 7
  am—SSI 2012/215, sch para 2
 s 151 appl (mod) (savings)—SI 2010/2870, art 9
  mod—Aquaculture and Fisheries (S), 2013 asp 7, ss 7(3), 35(7)
 s 152 appl (mod) (savings)—SI 2010/2870, art 9
  mod—Aquaculture and Fisheries (S), 2013 asp 7, ss 7(3), 35(7)
 s 153 appl (mod) (savings)—SI 2010/2870, art 9
  mod—Aquaculture and Fisheries (S), 2013 asp 7, ss 7(3), 35(7)
 s 154 appl (mod) (savings)—SI 2010/2870, art 9
  mod—Aquaculture and Fisheries (S), 2013 asp 7, ss 7(3), 35(7)
 s 155 appl—SI 2010/2870, art 9
  mod—Aquaculture and Fisheries (S), 2013 asp 7, ss 7(3), 35(7)
 ss 156, 157 mod—Aquaculture and Fisheries (S), 2013 asp 7, ss 7(3), 35(7)
 sch 2 am—Police and Fire Reform (S), 2012 asp 8, sch 7 para 39; Aquaculture and Fisheries
  (S), 2013 asp 7, s 61

asp 6   **Home Owner and Debtor Protection (Scotland)**
 s 13 rep in pt—Bankruptcy and Debt Advice (S), 2014 asp 11, sch 4

asp 7   **Ure Elder Fund Transfer and Dissolution**

asp 8   **Public Services Reform (Scotland)**
 s 3 am—SI 2014/631, sch 1 para 19(2)(a)-(c)
 ss 14-30 see —(provn for expiry on 3.6.2020) Public Services Reform (S), 2010 asp 8, s
  134(3), (4)-(6) (with SSI 2015/234, art 2)
 s 31 excl—SSI 2010/322, art 3
 s 51 am—SSI 2015/157, sch para 10(2)
 s 53 am—Public Bodies (Joint Working) (S), 2014 asp 9, s 54(a)-(d)
 s 105 am—SSIs 2013/211, sch 1 para 19(2); 2015/157, sch para 10(3)
 s 114 am—Police and Fire Reform (S), 2012 asp 8, sch 7 para 40(2)
 s 115 am —Housing (S), 2010 asp 17, s 162, sch 2, para 15(2); Police and Fire Reform (S),
  2012 asp 8, sch 7 para 40(3); Public Bodies (Joint Working) (S), 2014 asp 9, s
  56(2); (prosp) Community Empowerment (S), 2015 asp 6, sch 4 para 11
 s 116A added—Public Bodies (Joint Working) (S), 2014 asp 9, s 56(3)
 s 117 am—Public Bodies (Joint Working) (S), 2014 asp 9, s 56(4)
 sch 2 rep in pt—SI 3024/631, sch 1 para 19(3)
 sch 5 see—(provn for expiry on 3.6.2020) Public Services Reform (S), 2010 asp 8, s 134(3),
  (4)-(6) (with SSI 2015/234, art 2)
  rep in pt —S Parl Commns and Commrs, 2010 asp 11, s 2, sch 1, para 20(a); Police
   and Fire Reform (S), 2012 asp 8, sch 8 pt 1; SSIs 2013/192, art 2(a); 2013/197,
   sch 2 para 17(b)(c); Historic Environment Scotland, 2014 asp 19, sch 6 para
   5(a)(ii); SSI 2015/39, art 3(2)(a)
  am —S Parl Commns and Commrs, 2010 asp 11, s 2, sch 1, para 20(b), (c); Nat
   Library of S, 2012 asp 3, sch 2 para 9(a); Police and Fire Reform (S), 2012 asp
   8, sch 1 para 17(2); ibid, sch 7 paras 40(4), 72(2); SI 2012/1659, sch 3 para
   26(2); SSIs 2013/192, art 2(b); 197, sch 2 para 17(a); Historic Environment
   Scotland, 2014 asp 19, sch 6 para 5(a)(i); SSIs 2015/39, art 3(2)(b)(c); 157, sch
   para 10(4)
  sch 6 see—(provn for expiry on 3.6.2020) Public Services Reform (S), 2010 asp 8, s 134(3),
   (4)-(6) (with SSI 2015/234, art 2)

2010

asp 8 sch 6 *continued*

   am —S Parl Commns and Commrs, 2010 asp 11, s 2, sch 1, para 21(a), (b), (d); SSI
    2013/197, sch 2 para 17(a)

   rep in pt —S Parl Commns and Commrs, 2010 asp 11, s 2, s 1, para 21(c); SSI
    2013/197, sch 2 para 17(b)(c)

  sch 7 see—(provn for expiry on 3.6.2020) Public Services Reform (S), 2010 asp 8, s 134(3),
   (4)-(6) (with SSI 2015/234, art 2)

  sch 8 rep in pt —S Parl Commns and Commrs, 2010 asp 11, s 2, sch 1, para 22(a); Police
   and Fire Reform (S), 2012 asp 8, sch 8 pt 1; SSIs 2013/197, sch 2 para 17(b)(c);
   2013/211, sch 2; Historic Environment Scotland, 2014 asp 19, sch 6 para
   5(b)(ii); SSI 2015/39, art 3(3)

   am —S Parl Commns and Commrs, 2010 asp 11, s 2, sch 1, para 22(b), (c); Nat
    Library of S, 2012 asp 3, sch 2 para 9(b); Police and Fire Reform (S), 2012 asp
    8, sch 1 para 17(3); ibid, sch 7 paras 40(5), 72(3); SI 2012/1659, sch 3 para
    26(3); SSIs 2013/197, sch 2 para 17(a); 2013/211, sch 1 para 19(3); Historic
    Environment Scotland, 2014 asp 19, sch 6 para 5(b)(i); Revenue Scotland and
    Tax Powers, 2014 asp 16, sch 4 para 7; Food (S), 2015 asp 1, s 17(5)(a)

  sch 12 am—SSI 2013/211, sch 1 para 19(4)

  sch 14 rep in pt—SSI 2011/211, sch 1 para 21

  sch 19 am —Housing (S), 2010 asp 17, s 162, sch 2, para 15(3); Police and Fire Reform (S),
   2012 asp 8, sch 7 paras 40(6), 72(4); Food (S), 2015 asp 1, s 17(5)(b)

  sch 20 am —Housing (S), 2010 asp 17, s 162, sch 2, para 15(4); Police and Fire Reform (S),
   2012 asp 8, sch 7 para 40(7); Food (S), 2015 asp 1, s 17(5)(c)

   rep in pt—Police and Fire Reform (S), 2012 asp 8, sch 8 pt 2

asp 9 **Control of Dogs (Scotland)**

  s 5 am—SSI 2015/338, sch 2 para 12(2)

  s 11 am—SSI 2015/338, sch 2 para 12(3)

  s 13 am—Police and Fire Reform (S), 2012 asp 8, sch 7 para 41

asp 10 **Interpretation and Legislative Reform (Scotland)**

  s 28 appl (mods)—(pt prosp) Health and Social Care, 2012 c 7, ss 224(3), 304(7)

  s 30 excl—SSI 2011/88, art 5

  s 31 appl (mods)—Nat Health Service Reform and Health Care Professions, 2002 c 17, s
   38(3C); Health and Social Care, 2012 c 7, s 304(7)

  s 32 appl—Nat Health Service Reform and Health Care Professions, 2002 c 17, s 38(3D);
   Health and Social Care, 2012 c 7, s 304(8)

  s 41 appl (mods)—Interests of Members of the Scottish Parliament, 2006 asp 12, sch para
   10(3)-(5) (as subst by SSI 2011/196, art 2)

   appl (mods)—S Parl Pensions, 2009 asp 1, s 3(5)-(7) (as subst by SSI 2011/196, art 3)

  Pt 4 (ss 48-53) excl—SSI 2011/88, art 3(1)(a)

  sch 1 rep in pt—Police and Fire Reform (S), 2012 asp 8, sch 8 pt 1

   am—Marriage and Civil Partnership (S), 2014 asp 5, s 4(15); Courts Reform (S),
    2014 asp 18, sch 5 para 45

  sch 3 excl—SSI 2011/88, art 5

  sch 4 excl—SSI 2011/88, art 4(2)

asp 11 **Scottish Parliamentary Commissions and Commissioners**

  Pt 1 (ss 1-28) am—SSI 2013/197, sch 1 para 31

  s 1 subst—SSI 2013/197, art 3(1)

   am—SSI 2013/197, sch 1 para 8

  s 2 rep—SSI 2013/197, sch 1 para 2

  s 3 subst—SSI 2013/197, sch 1 para 3

  s 4 am—SSI 2013/197, sch 1 para 4

  s 5 subst—SSI 2013/197, sch 1 para 5

  s 6 rep—SSI 2013/197, sch 1 para 6

  s 7 am—SSI 2013/197, sch 1 para 7(a)(c)(d)

   rep in pt—SSI 2013/197, sch 1 para 7(b)(e)(f)

  s 8 am—SSI 2013/197, sch 1 para 9

  s 9 am—SSI 2013/197, sch 1 para 10

  s 10 am—SSI 2013/197, sch 1 para 11

  s 11 am—SSI 2013/197, sch 1 para 12

  s 12 am—SSI 2013/197, sch 1 paras 13(a)-(c), (d)(i), 18

   rep in pt—SSI 2013/197, sch 1 para 13(d)(ii)

  s 13 am—SSI 2013/197, sch 1 para 14

  s 14 am—SSI 2013/197, sch 1 para 15(a),(b)(ii),(c)(d)

   rep in pt—SSI 2013/197, sch 1 para 15(b)(i)

2010

asp 11 *continued*

s 15 rep in pt—SSI 2013/197, sch 1 para 16(a)
am—SSI 2013/197, sch 1 para 16(b)(c)
s 16 rep in pt—SSI 2013/197, sch 1 para 17(a),(b)(ii)
am—SSI 2013/197, sch 1 para 17(b)(i)(iii),(c)
s 17 am—SSI 2013/197, sch 1 para 19(a)(i)(iii),(b)
rep in pt—SSI 2013/197, sch 1 para 19(a)(ii)
s 18 am—SSI 2013/197, sch 1 para 20
s 19 am—SSI 2013/197, sch 1 para 21
s 20 am—SSI 2013/197, sch 1 para 22
s 20 appl (mods)—SSI 2013/197, sch 4 para 4
s 21 am—SSI 2013/197, sch 1 para 23(a)(b), (c)(ii)(iii),(d)
rep in pt—SSI 2013/197, sch 1 para 23(c)(i)
s 22 am—SSI 2013/197, sch 1 para 24
s 23 am—SSI 2013/197, sch 1 para 25
s 24 am—SSI 2013/197, sch 1 para 26
s 25 am—SSI 2013/197, sch 1 para 27(a)-(c),(e)
rep in pt—SSI 2013/197, sch 1 para 27(d)
s 26 rep—SSI 2013/197, sch 1 para 28
s 27 rep—SSI 2013/197, sch 1 para 29
s 28 rep in pt—SSI 2013/197, sch 1 para 30(a)
am—SSI 2013/197, sch 1 para 30(b)(c)
s 29 rep in pt—SSI 2013/197, sch 1 para 32(a)
am—SSI 2013/197, sch 1 para 32(b)
s 30 rep—SSI 2013/197, sch 1 para 33
sch 1 rep—SSI 2013/197, sch 1 para 2

asp 12 **William Simpson's Home (Transfer of Property etc.)**

asp 13 **Criminal Justice and Licensing (Scotland)**

s 6 am—Courts Reform (S), 2014 asp 18, sch 5 para 17(2)(a)(b)
s 8A added—Courts Reform (S), 2014 asp 18, sch 5 para 17(3)
s 9 am—Courts Reform (S), 2014 asp 18, sch 5 para 17(4)(a)-(c)
s 13 rep in pt—Courts Reform (S), 2014 asp 18, sch 5 para 17(5)(a)
am—Courts Reform (S), 2014 asp 18, sch 5 para 17(5)(b)
s 31 rep in pt—Police and Fire Reform (S), 2012 asp 8, sch 8 pt 1
s 47 rep (prosp)—Human Trafficking and Exploitation (S), 2015 asp 12, sch para 5
s 56 rep —Police and Fire Reform (S), 2012 asp 8, sch 8 pt 1
s 116 am—Double Jeopardy (S), 2011 asp 16, sch para 18
s 117 am—Police and Fire Reform (S), 2012 asp 8, sch 7 para 42(2)
s 132 am—SI 2013/728, art 3
ss 140A-140F added—Double Jeopardy (S), 2011 asp 16, s 13
s 141 am—Double Jeopardy (S), 2011 asp 16, sch para 19
s 142 am—Double Jeopardy (S), 2011 asp 16, sch para 20
s 143 am—Double Jeopardy (S), 2011 asp 16, sch para 21
s 145 am—Double Jeopardy (S), 2011 asp 16, sch para 22
s 146 am—Double Jeopardy (S), 2011 asp 16, sch para 23
s 147 am—Double Jeopardy (S), 2011 asp 16, sch para 24
s 150 am—Double Jeopardy (S), 2011 asp 16, sch para 25
s 152 am—Double Jeopardy (S), 2011 asp 16, sch para 26
s 153 am—Double Jeopardy (S), 2011 asp 16, sch para 27; SSI 2015/338, sch 2 para
13(2)(3)
s 155 am—Double Jeopardy (S), 2011 asp 16, sch para 28
s 156 am—Double Jeopardy (S), 2011 asp 16, sch para 29
s 158 am—Double Jeopardy (S), 2011 asp 16, sch para 30
s 160 am—Double Jeopardy (S), 2011 asp 16, sch para 31
s 162 am—Double Jeopardy (S), 2011 asp 16, sch para 32
s 164 am—Police and Fire Reform (S), 2012 asp 8, sch 7 para 42(3)
s 166 am—Double Jeopardy (S), 2011 asp 16, sch para 33
s 167 am—Double Jeopardy (S), 2011 asp 16, sch para 34
sch 1 am—SSI 2015/388, art 2
sch 2 rep in pt—Welfare Reform, 2012 c 5, sch 14 pt 3
sch 7 rep in pt—(prosp) Mental Health (S), 2015 asp 9, s 49(b)

asp 14 **Crofting Reform (Scotland)**

s 4 am—Crofting (Amdt) (S), 2013 asp 10, sch para 2(2)
s 5 am—Crofting (Amdt) (S), 2013 asp 10, sch para 2(3)

2010

asp 14 *continued*

    s 10 am—Crofting (Amdt) (S), 2013 asp 10, sch para 2(4)
    s 15 am—Crofting (Amdt) (S), 2013 asp 10, sch para 2(5)
    sch 2 am—Crofting (Amdt) (S), 2013 asp 10, sch para 2(6)

asp 15   **Criminal Procedure (Legal Assistance, Detention and Appeals) (Scotland)**

asp 16   **Legal Services**

    s 8 am—Enterprise and Regulatory Reform, 2013 c. 24, sch 6 para 193
    s 15 am—Enterprise and Regulatory Reform, 2013 c. 24, sch 6 para 194
    s 28 am—Enterprise and Regulatory Reform, 2013 c. 24, sch 6 para 195
    s 49 am—Enterprise and Regulatory Reform, 2013 c. 24, sch 6 para 196
    s 76 am—Enterprise and Regulatory Reform, 2013 c. 24, sch 6 para 197
    s 92 am—Enterprise and Regulatory Reform, 2013 c. 24, sch 6 para 198
    s 103 am—Enterprise and Regulatory Reform, 2013 c. 24, sch 6 para 199
    s 113 am—Enterprise and Regulatory Reform, 2013 c. 24, sch 6 para 200
    s 122 am—Enterprise and Regulatory Reform, 2013 c. 24, sch 6 para 201
    s 125 am—Enterprise and Regulatory Reform, 2013 c. 24, sch 6 para 202
    s 147 am—Enterprise and Regulatory Reform, 2013 c. 24, sch 6 para 203
    s 149 am—Enterprise and Regulatory Reform, 2013 c. 24, sch 6 para 204(a)
        rep in pt—Enterprise and Regulatory Reform, 2013 c. 24, sch 6 para 204(b)
    sch 2 am—Enterprise and Regulatory Reform, 2013 c. 24, sch 6 para 205
    sch 5 am—Enterprise and Regulatory Reform, 2013 c. 24, sch 6 para 206
    sch 6 am—Enterprise and Regulatory Reform, 2013 c. 24, sch 6 para 207
    sch 7 am—Enterprise and Regulatory Reform, 2013 c. 24, sch 6 para 208
    sch 9 am—Enterprise and Regulatory Reform, 2013 c. 24, sch 6 para 209(a)
        rep in pt—Enterprise and Regulatory Reform, 2013 c. 24, sch 6 para 209(b)

asp 17   **Housing (Scotland)**

    s 18 am—Localism, 2011 c. 20, sch 16 para 60; SI 2013/496, sch 11 para 10(2)
    s 30 am—SI 2013/496, sch 11 para 10(3)(4)(a)
    s 58 am—Housing (S), 2014 asp 14, sch 2 para 18(2)
    s 67 am—(pt prosp) Housing (S), 2014 asp 14, s 97(a)
        rep in pt—Housing (S), 2014 asp 14, s 97(b)
    s 68 am—Localism, 2011 c. 20, sch 16 para 61
    s 80 am—SIs 2013/496, sch 11 para 10(3)para 10(4)(b); 2014/3486, art 31(2)(a)-(d)
    s 82 am—SI 2013/496, sch 11 para 10(3)para 10(4)(c)
    s 87 am—SI 2013/496, sch 11 para 10(3)para 10(4)(d)
    s 94 am—SI 2013/496, sch 11 para 10(3)para 10(4)(e)
    s 96 am—SI 2013/496, sch 11 para 10(3)para 10(4)(f)
    s 97 am—SI 2013/496, sch 11 para 10(3)para 10(4)(g)
    s 98 am—SI 2013/496, sch 11 para 10(3)para 10(4)(h)
    s 99 am—SI 2013/496, sch 11 para 10(3)para 10(4)(i)
    s 104A added—Housing (S), 2014 asp 14, s 98(1)
    s 108 rep in pt—(1.8.2016) Housing (S), 2014 asp 14, sch 2 para 18(3)
    s 110 am—Housing (S), 2014 asp 14, sch 2 para 18(4)
    s 124 am—Housing (S), 2014 asp 14, sch 2 para 18(5)
    Pt. 10 Ch 3 (ss 124A, 124B) added—Housing (S), 2014 asp 14, s 98(2)
    ss 140-144 rep (1.7.2017)—Housing (S), 2014 asp 14, sch 2 para 18(6)
    ss 145-147 rep (1.7.2017)—Housing (S), 2014 asp 14, s 1(3)
    s 164 rep in pt—Housing (S), 2014 asp 14, s 98(3)
    s 165 mod—SSI 2011/96, art 4(2)
    s 165 am—Housing (S), 2014 asp 14, s 98(4) Bankruptcy and Debt Advice (S), 2014 asp
        11, sch 3 para 41
    sch 2 rep in pt—(1.8.2016) Housing (S), 2014 asp 14, sch 2 para 18(7)(a); ibid, sch 2 para
        18(7)(b)

asp 18   **Alcohol etc (Scotland)**

    s 1 rep (prosp)—Alcohol (Minimum Pricing) (S), 2012 asp 4, s 4
    s 14 am—Police and Fire Reform (S), 2012 asp 8, sch 7 para 43(2)
    s 15 am—Police and Fire Reform (S), 2012 asp 8, sch 7 para 43(3)
        rep in pt—Police and Fire Reform (S), 2012 asp 8, sch 8 pt 1

2011

asp 1   **Children's Hearings (Scotland)**

    s 5 appl—Child Abduction and Custody, 1985 c 60, s.20(6) (added by SI 2013/1465, sch 1
        para 1(2))
    s 6 am—SSI 2013/211, sch 1 para 20(2)

2011

asp 1 *continued*

Pt 2 (ss 14-24) appl—SSI 2003/179, reg 3A (added by SSI 2013/200, reg 3(3))

s 19 am—SSI 2015/402, sch para 7(2)

s 26 am—SSI 2013/211, sch 1 para 20(3)

s 27 am—SSI 2013/211, sch 1 para 20(4)

s 29A added—SSI 2013/211, sch 1 para 20(5)

s 31 am—SSI 2013/211, sch 1 para 20(6)

s 33 am—Children and Young People (S), 2014 asp 8, s 82(a)(b)

s 54 am—Children and Young People (S), 2014 asp 8, s 83

s 61 am—Police and Fire Reform (S), 2012 asp 8, sch 7 para 44

s 62 am—Forced Marriage etc. (Protection and Jurisdiction) (S), 2011 asp 15, s 13(2)

s 66 am—SSI 2013/211, sch 1 para 20(7)

s 67 rep in pt—Forced Marriage etc. (Protection and Jurisdiction) (S), 2011 asp 15, s
13(3)(a)

am—Forced Marriage etc. (Protection and Jurisdiction) (S), 2011 asp 15, s 13(3)(b);
SSI 2013/211, sch 1 para 20(8)

s 78 am—SSI 2013/211, sch 1 para 20(9)

rep in pt—SI 2013/2042, sch para 42

s 79 am—Children and Young People (S), 2014 asp 8, s 84(2)(a)-(c)

s 80 am—Children and Young People (S), 2014 asp 8, sch 5 para 12(2)

s 81 am—Children and Young People (S), 2014 asp 8, sch 5 ppara 12(3)(a)(b)

s 81A added—Children and Young People (S), 2014 asp 8, s 84(3)

s 83 rep in pt—SSI 2013/211, sch 2

s 90 am—Children and Young People (S), 2014 asp 8, s 85(a)(b)

s 91 appl (mods)—SSI 2013/194, rule 68(2)

s 93 appl (mods)—SSI 2013/194, rule 68(3)(a)

s 94 am—Children and Young People (S), 2014 asp 8, sch 5 para 12(4)

s 95 am—Children and Young People (S), 2014 asp 8, s 86

s 96 appl (mods)—SSI 2013/194, rule 68(3)(b)

am—Children and Young People (S), 2014 asp 8, s 87

s 98 am—SSI 2013/211, sch 1 para 20(10)

s 105 am—Children and Young People (S), 2014 asp 8, sch 5 para 12(5)

s 106 am—Children and Young People (S), 2014 asp 8, sch 5 para 12(6)

s 115 am—SSI 2013/211, sch 1 para 20(11)

s 117 am—SSI 2013/211, sch 1 para 20(12)

s 138 rep in pt—SSI 2013/211, sch 2

s 140 am—SSI 2013/211, sch 1 para 20(13)

s 142 am—Children and Young People (S), 2014 asp 8, sch 5 para 12(7)

s 155 am—SSI 2013/211, sch 1 para 20(14)

s 156 am—SSI 2013/211, sch 1 para 20(15)

s 159 am—SSI 2013/211, sch 1 para 20(16)

s 160 am—Children and Young People (S), 2014 asp 8, sch 5 para 12(8)

s 162 am—SSI 2015/402, sch para 7(3)

s 168 rep in pt—SSI 2013/211, sch 1 para 20(17)

s 175 am—SSI 2013/211, sch 1 para 20(18)

s 182 am—SSI 2013/211, sch 1 para 20(20)

s 193 appl—SSIs 2013/212, reg 3; 2013/149, reg 2(2); 2013/194, rule 99

s 202 am—SSI 2013/211, sch 1 para 21; Children and Young People (S), 2014 asp 8, sch 5
para 12(9)

sch 1 rep in pt—Children and Young People (S), 2014 asp 8, s 88(2)(a)(i)

am—Children and Young People (S), 2014 asp 8, ss 88(2)(a)(ii)(b)(i)-(iv), 89(2)

sch 6 rep in pt—Children and Young People (S), 2014 asp 8, sch 5 para 12(10)(b)

am—Children and Young People (S), 2014 asp 8, sch 5 para 12(10)(a)

asp 2   **Forth Crossing**

s 70 rep in pt—Regulatory Reform (S), 2014 asp 3, sch 3 para 38

asp 3   **Historic Environment (Amendment) (Scotland)**

asp 4   **Budget (Scotland)**

s 3 am—SSI 2011/434, art 2; SSI 2012/105, art 2

Pt 2 (s 6) rep—Budget (S), 2012 asp 2, s 8

sch 1 am—SSIs 2011/434, art 3(2)(a)(b)(d), (3)(4); 2012/105, art 3

rep in pt—SSIs 2011/434, art 3(2)(a)-(c)(e)(f); 2012/105, art 3(2)(a)(ii)(iv)

sch 2 am—SSIs 2011/434, art 4; 2012/105, art 4

sch 3 am—SSI 2012/105, art 5

2011

asp 5 **Patient Rights (Scotland)**
    s 17 rep in pt—Public Bodies (Joint Working) (S), 2014 asp 9, s 71(5)
        am—Public Bodies (Joint Working) (S), 2014 asp 9, s 63(4)

asp 6 **Wildlife and Natural Environment (Scotland)**

asp 7 **Damages (Scotland)**
    mod—SSI 2011/268, art 4(1)
    s 2 am—Domestic Abuse (S), 2011 asp 13, s 1(5)
    s 14 mod—SSI 2011/268, art 4(2)

asp 8 **Property Factors (Scotland)**
    s 16 am—Housing (S), 2014 asp 14, s 96(2)

asp 9 **Reservoirs (Scotland)**
    s 9 excl—SSI 2015/48, art 14
    ss 78-81 rep—Regulatory Reform (S), 2014 asp 3, sch 3 para 13(2)
    s 82 rep in pt—Regulatory Reform (S), 2014 asp 3, sch 3 para 13(a)(ii)(b)
        am—Regulatory Reform (S), 2014 asp 3, sch 3 para 13(b)
    s 83 rep in pt—Regulatory Reform (S), 2014 asp 3, sch 3 para 13(4)
    s 84 rep in pt—Regulatory Reform (S), 2014 asp 3, sch 3 para 13(5)
    s 86 rep in pt—Regulatory Reform (S), 2014 asp 3, sch 3 para 13(6)(7)
    s 87 rep in pt—Regulatory Reform (S), 2014 asp 3, sch 3 para 13(8)
    s 89 rep in pt—Regulatory Reform (S), 2014 asp 3, sch 3 para 13(10)
    s 90 rep in pt—Regulatory Reform (S), 2014 asp 3, sch 3 para 13(11)(a)(b)
    s 114 rep in pt—Regulatory Reform (S), 2014 asp 3, sch 3 para 13(12)
    sch rep in pt—Regulatory Reform (S), 2014 asp 3, sch 3 para 13(13)

asp 10 **Local Electoral Administration (Scotland)**

asp 11 **Certification of Death (Scotland)**

asp 12 **Public Records (Scotland)**
    s 1 mod—Victims and Witnesses (S), 2014 asp 1, s 30
    sch am—Nat Library of S, 2012 asp 3, sch 2 para 10; Police and Fire Reform (S), 2012 asp
        8, sch 1 para 18; ibid, sch 7 paras 45, 73; SI 2012/1659, sch 3 para 27; SSI
        2013/197, sch 2 para 18(a); Revenue Scotland and Tax Powers, 2014 asp 16, sch
        4 para 8; Historic Environment Scotland, 2014 asp 19, sch 6 para 6(a); Food (S),
        2015 asp 1, s 17(6); SSIs 2015/39, sch para 8(a)(b); 157, sch para 11; 335,
        art.2(a)(c)
        rep in pt—Police and Fire Reform (S), 2012 asp 8, sch 8 pt 1; SSI 2013/197, sch 2 para
            18(b)(c); Historic Environment Scotland, 2014 asp 19, sch 6 para 6(b); SSIs
            2015/39, sch para 8(c); 335, art.2(b)

asp 13 **Domestic Abuse (Scotland)**

asp 14 **Private Rented Housing (Scotland)**
    s 35 rep in pt—Housing (S), 2014 asp 14, s 25(11)

asp 15 **Forced Marriage etc. (Protection and Jurisdiction) (Scotland)**

asp 16 **Double Jeopardy (Scotland)**

2012

asp 1 **Offensive Behaviour at Football and Threatening Communications (Scotland)**

asp 2 **Budget (Scotland)**
    s 4 am—SSIs 2012/346, art 2; 2013/117, art 2
    s 6 rep—Budget (S), 2013 asp 4, s 8
    sch 1 am—SSIs 2012/346, art 3(3)-(6); 2013/117, art 3
        rep in pt—SSI 2012/346, art 3(2)
    sch 2 am—SSIs 2012/346, art 4; 2013/117, art 4

asp 3 **National Library of Scotland**

asp 4 **Alchohol (Minimum Pricing) (Scotland)**

asp 5 **Land Registration etc. (Scotland)**
    s 27 rep in pt—SSI 2015/265, art 2
    Pt 4 (ss 56-64) appl (mods)—SSI 2014/190, art 4
    sch 1 am—SSI 2014/190, art 5(a)(b)
    sch 4 am—SSIs 2014/190, art 6; 2014/346, arts 4(1)(2)
    sch 5 rep in pt—SI 2013/1575, sch para 16; Co-operative and Community Benefits Societies,
            2014 c 14, sch 7; SSI 2014/190, art 2(2)(b)
        am—SSI 2014/190, art 2(2); 2014/346, art 3

asp 6 **Agricultural Holdings (Amendment) (Scotland)**

asp 7 **Criminal Cases (Punishment and Review (Scotland)**

2012

asp 8　　**Police and Fire Reform (Scotland)**
　　　　savings—SSI 2013/121, art 3
　　　　s 10 appl—Railways and Transport Safety, 2003 c 20, 24(4) (subst by SI 2013/602, sch 2
　　　　　　　para 41(2)); ibid, s 25(4) (subst by SI 2013/602, sch 2 para 41(3))
　　　　s 24 appl—SI 2013/602, arts 5(5), 7
　　　　s 46 am—(prosp) Community Empowerment (S), 2015 asp 6, sch 4 para 12(a)
　　　　s 47 am—(prosp) Community Empowerment (S), 2015 asp 6, sch 4 para 12(b)
　　　　Pt 1 Ch 10 (ss 60-70) mod—SSI 2013/121, art 16(1)-(4)
　　　　s 84 appl—SSI 2013/121, art 4(4)(5)
　　　　ss 90, 91 appl—SI 2013/602, art 10(1)
　　　　s 92 appl (mods)—SI 2013/602, art 10(2)
　　　　sch 7 rep in pt—SI 2013/602, sch 2 para 65; Anti-social Behaviour, Crime and Policing,
　　　　　　　2014 c 12, sch 11 para 102; Housing (S) 2014, asp 14, sch 2 para 19

asp 9　　**Long Leases (Scotland)**
　　　　s 78 mod—SSI 2014/8, art 2
asp 10　**Welfare Reform (Further Provision) (Scotland)**
asp 11　**Local Government Finance (Unoccupied Properties, etc.) (Scotland)**

2013

asp 1　　**Social Care (Self-directed Support) (Scotland)**
　　　　s 5 mod—SSI 2014/25, reg 11
　　　　s 7 mod—SSI 2014/25, reg 11
　　　　s 8 mod—SSI 2014/25, reg 11
　　　　s 20 rep —Public Bodies (Joint Working) (S), 2014 asp 9, s 71(6)
　　　　s 24 am—SSI 2015/157, sch para 12
asp 2　　**Freedom of Information (Amendment) (Scotland)**
asp 3　　**Scottish Civil Justice Council and Criminal Legal Assistance**
　　　　Pt 1 (ss 1-16) power to appl—Tribunals (S), 2014 asp 10, ss 65(2), 66(2)
　　　　s 2 am—Tribunals (S), 2014 asp 10, sch 9 para 13(2)(a)(b)(3)(4); Courts Reform (S), 2014
　　　　　　　asp 18, sch 5 para 31(2)(a)(b)
　　　　s 4 am—Tribunals (S), 2014 asp 10, sch 9 para 13(5)(a)(b); Courts Reform (S), 2014 asp
　　　　　　　18, sch 5 para 31(3)(a)(b)(c)(i)(ii)
　　　　s 6 am—Tribunals (S), 2014 asp 10, sch 9 para 13(6)(a)-(c)
　　　　s 8 am—Tribunals (S), 2014 asp 10, sch 9 para 13(7)(a)(b)
　　　　s 13 am—Tribunals (S), 2014 asp 10, sch 9 para 13(8)
　　　　s 13A added —Tribunals (S), 2014 asp 10, sch 9 para 13(9)
　　　　s 16 am—Tribunals (S), 2014 asp 10, sch 9 para 13(10)
asp 4　　**Budget (Scotland)**
　　　　s 4 am—SSIs 2013/328, art 2; 2014/81, art 2(a)-(c)
　　　　Pt 2 (s 6) rep—Budget (S), 2014 asp 6, s 8
　　　　sch 1 am—SSIs 2013/328, art 3(2)-(4); 2014/81, art 3(2)(a)-(n)(3)(a)-(c)
　　　　sch 2 am—SSIs 2013/328, art 4; 2014/81, art 4(2)(a)(b((i)(ii)(3)(a)-(c)
asp 5　　**Water Resources (Scotland)**
　　　　s 5 am—(prosp) Regulatory Reform (S), 2014 asp 3, sch 3 para 10(2)
　　　　s 21 am—(prosp) Regulatory Reform (S), 2014 asp 3, sch 3 para 10(3)
　　　　s 50 am—(prosp) Regulatory Reform (S), 2014 asp 3, sch 3 para 10(4)
asp 6　　**High Hedges (Scotland)**
asp 7　　**Aquaculture and Fisheries (Scotland)**
asp 8　　**Forth Road Bridge**
asp 9　　**National Trust for Scotland (Governance etc.)**
asp 10　**Crofting (Amendment) (Scotland)**
asp 11　**Land and Buildings Transaction Tax (Scotland)**
　　　　excl—SSI 2014/377, arts 6(2), 9
　　　　s 9 appl—SSI 2014/377, art 4(2)
　　　　s 10 appl—SSI 2014/377, art 4(2)
　　　　　　appl (mods)—SSI 2014/377, arts 3(4), 4(4)
　　　　　　am—Revenue Scotland and Tax Powers, 2014 asp 16, sch 4 para 9(2)
　　　　s 11 am—Revenue Scotland and Tax Powers, 2014 asp 16, sch 4 para 9(3)
　　　　s 25 am—SSI 2015/123, art 2
　　　　s 27 am—Revenue Scotland and Tax Powers, 2014 asp 16, sch 4 para 9(4); SSIs 2015/93,
　　　　　　　art 2(2); 123, art 3
　　　　s 31 appl—SSI 2014/375, reg 12
　　　　s 32 appl—SSI 2014/375, reg 12
　　　　s 32 am—Revenue Scotland and Tax Powers, 2014 asp 16, sch 4 para 9(5)(a)(b)

2013

asp 11 *continued*

  s 33 am—SSI 2015/123, art 4

  s 35 rep in pt—Revenue Scotland and Tax Powers, 2014 asp 16, sch 4 para 9(6)(a)
    am—Revenue Scotland and Tax Powers, 2014 asp 16, sch 4 para 9(6)(b)

  s 37 rep —Revenue Scotland and Tax Powers, 2014 asp 16, sch 4 para 9(7)

  s 37A added—Revenue Scotland and Tax Powers, 2014 asp 16, sch 4 para 9(8)

  s 41 rep in pt—Revenue Scotland and Tax Powers, 2014 asp 16, sch 4 para 9(9)

  s 48 am—Revenue Scotland and Tax Powers, 2014 asp 16, sch 4 para 9(10)

  s 50 am—Revenue Scotland and Tax Powers, 2014 asp 16, sch 4 para 9(11)

  s 54 rep in pt—Revenue Scotland and Tax Powers, 2014 asp 16, sch 4 para 9(12)(b)
    am—Revenue Scotland and Tax Powers, 2014 asp 16, sch 4 para 9(12)(a)

  s 55 rep —Revenue Scotland and Tax Powers, 2014 asp 16, sch 4 para 9(13)

  s 56 rep —Revenue Scotland and Tax Powers, 2014 asp 16, sch 4 para 9(14)

  s 58 am—SSI 2015/123, art 5

  s 63 am—Revenue Scotland and Tax Powers, 2014 asp 16, sch 4 para 9(15)

  s 65 am—SSI 2015/123, art 6(1)

  s 68 rep in pt—Revenue Scotland and Tax Powers, 2014 asp 16, sch 4 para 9(16)(a)(b)
    am—Revenue Scotland and Tax Powers, 2014 asp 16, sch 4 para 9(16)(c)

  s 70 rep in pt—Revenue Scotland and Tax Powers, 2014 asp 16, sch 4 para 9(17)

  sch 2 am—Revenue Scotland and Tax Powers, 2014 asp 16, sch 4 para 9(18); SSI 2014/351,
    art 2

  sch 5 am—Revenue Scotland and Tax Powers, 2014 asp 16, sch 4 para 9(19); SSI 2015/123,
    art 8

  sch 6 am—SSI 2015/93, art 2(3)

  sch 9 am—SSI 2015/93, art 2(4)

  sch 10 am—Revenue Scotland and Tax Powers, 2014 asp 16, sch 4 para 9(20)(a)(b)

  sch 10A added—SSI 2015/123, art 7 sch

  sch 11 am—Revenue Scotland and Tax Powers, 2014 asp 16, sch 4 para 9(20)(a)-(d)

  schs 13A, 13B added—SSI 2015/93, art 2(5)

  schs 16A-16C added—SSI 2015/93, art 2(6)

  sch 17 appl—SSI 2014/377, arts 7(2), 8(2)(a)(b)
    am—Revenue Scotland and Tax Powers, 2014 asp 16, sch 4 para 9(20)(a)(b)
    mod—SSI 2014/377, art 9

  sch 19 appl—SSI 2014/377, arts 10(1), 11(2)(a)(b)
    am—Revenue Scotland and Tax Powers, 2014 asp 16, sch 4 para 9(23)
    mod—SSI 2014/377, arts 10(2), 11(2)(c)

  sch 20 am—SSI 2015/123, art 6(2)

asp 12 **Post-16 Education (Scotland)**

asp 13 *Scottish Independence Referendum Franchise)*—rep S Independence Referendum (Franchise),
    2013 asp 13, s 14

asp 14 **Scottish Independence Referendum**

2014

asp 1 **Victims and Witnesses (Scotland)**

  s 1A added—SSI 2015/444, reg 2

  s 3A added—SSI 2015/444, reg 3

  ss 3B-3D added—SSI 2015/444, reg 4

  ss 3E, 3F added—SSI 2015/444, reg 5

  s 3G added—SSI 2015/444, reg 6

  s 3H added—SSI 2015/444, reg 7

  s 3I added—SSI 2015/444, reg 8

  s 3J added—SSI 2015/444, reg 9

  s 4 am—SSI 2015/444, reg 10

  s 5 am—SSI 2015/444, reg 11

  s 8 am—(31.5.2016) Human Trafficking and Exploitation (S), 2015 asp 12, sch para 6);
    SSI 2015/444, reg 12

  ss 9A-9C added—SSI 2015/444, reg 13

  ss 9D, 9E added—SSI 2015/444, reg 14

  s 27A added—SSI 2015/444, reg 15

  ss 29A, 29B added—SSI 2015/444, reg 16

  s 32 am—SSI 2015/444, reg 17

asp 2 **Landfill Tax (Scotland)**

  s 15 am—Revenue Scotland and Tax Powers, 2014 asp 16, sch 4 para 10(2)(a)-(c)

  s 18 am—Revenue Scotland and Tax Powers, 2014 asp 16, sch 4 para 10(3)

2014

asp 2 *continued*

      s 22 rep in pt—Revenue Scotland and Tax Powers, 2014 asp 16, sch 4 para 10(4)

      s 23 rep in pt—Revenue Scotland and Tax Powers, 2014 asp 16, sch 4 para 10(5)

      s 25 am—Revenue Scotland and Tax Powers, 2014 asp 16, sch 4 para 10(6)

      ss 25A, 25B added—Revenue Scotland and Tax Powers, 2014 asp 16, sch 4 para 10(7)

      s 26 rep—Revenue Scotland and Tax Powers, 2014 asp 16, sch 4 para 10(8)

      s 28 rep —Revenue Scotland and Tax Powers, 2014 asp 16, sch 4 para 10(9)

      s 29 rep —Revenue Scotland and Tax Powers, 2014 asp 16, sch 4 para 10(10)

      s 30 am—Revenue Scotland and Tax Powers, 2014 asp 16, sch 4 para 10(11)

      s 31 rep in pt—Revenue Scotland and Tax Powers, 2014 asp 16, sch 4 para 10(12)(a)(b)

      ss 32, 33 rep —Revenue Scotland and Tax Powers, 2014 asp 16, sch 4 para 10(13)

      s 34 rep in pt—Revenue Scotland and Tax Powers, 2014 asp 16, sch 4 para 10(14)(b)

        am—Revenue Scotland and Tax Powers, 2014 asp 16, sch 4 para 10(14)(a)

      s 35 rep —Revenue Scotland and Tax Powers, 2014 asp 16, sch 4 para 10(15)

      s 36 rep —Revenue Scotland and Tax Powers, 2014 asp 16, sch 4 para 10(16)

      s 39 am—Revenue Scotland and Tax Powers, 2014 asp 16, sch 4 para 10(17)

      s 41 rep in pt—Revenue Scotland and Tax Powers, 2014 asp 16, sch 4 para 10(18)(a)(ii)(b)

        am—Revenue Scotland and Tax Powers, 2014 asp 16, sch 4 para 10(18)(a)(i)

      s 43 rep in pt—Revenue Scotland and Tax Powers, 2014 asp 16, sch 4 para 10(19)

asp 3   **Regulatory Reform (Scotland)**

      excl—Landfill Tax (S), 2014 asp 2, s 12(4)

      sch 1 am—Food (S), 2015 asp 1, s 17(7); SSI 2015/271, art 8

        rep in pt—Food (S), 2015 asp 1, sch para 10

asp 4   **Burrell Collection (Lending and Borrowing) (Scotland)**

asp 5   **Marriage and Civil Partnership (Scotland)**

      s 10 am—SSI 2015/371, art 5

      s 11 appl—SI 2014/3229, art 14

        mod—SSI 2015/371, art 6

asp 6   **Budget (Scotland)**

      s 4 am—SSIs 2014/363, art 2; 2015/138, art 2

      Pt 2 (s 6) rep—Budget (S), 2015 asp 2, s 8

      sch 1 rep in pt—SSIs 2014/363, art 3(2)(a)(b)(e); 2015/138, art 3(2)(d),(e)(ii)(iii),(g)

        am—SSIs 2014/363, art 3(2)(c)(d)(f)(3)(4); 2015/138, art 3(2)(3)(4)

      sch 2 am—SSIs 2014/363, art 4(2); 2015/138, art 4

asp 7   **City of Edinburgh Council (Leith Links and Surplus Fire Fund)**

asp 8   **Children and Young People (Scotland)**

      s 7 am—Public Bodies (Joint Working) (S), 2014 asp 9, s 58

      sch 1 am—SSI 2015/157, sch para 13(2)

      sch 2 am—SSI 2015/157, sch para 13(3)

      sch 3 am—SSI 2015/157, sch para 13(4)

      sch 4 am—SSI 2015/157, sch para 13(5)

asp 9   **Public Bodies (Joint Working) (Scotland)**

      s 23 rep in pt—SSI 2014/342, art 2(2)

      s 24 rep in pt—SSI 2014/342, art 2(3)

      s 26 am—SSI 2014/342, art 2(4)

      s 36 am—SSI 2014/342, art 2(5)

      s 59 am—SSI 2014/342, art 2(6)

      s 62 am—SSI 2014/342, art 2(7)

asp 10   **Tribunals (Scotland)**

      appl —Tribunals (S), 2014 asp 10, sch 9 paras 11(3), 12(4)(c)(5)

      s 13 appl—Tribunals (S), 2014 asp 10, sch 9 para 12(5)

      s 57A added —Courts Reform (S), 2014 asp 18, sch 5 para 24

      sch 1 am—Revenue Scotland and Tax Powers, 2014 asp 16, sch 4 para 11(2)(3); SSI

        2015/404, reg 2

asp 11   **Bankcuptcy and Debt Advice (Scotland)**

asp 12   **Procurement Reform (Scotland)**

      s 4 am—SSI 2015/446, sch 6 para 2(2)

      s 11 am—SSI 2015/446, sch 6 para 2(3)

      s 41 am—SSI 2015/446, sch 6 para 2(4)(a)(b)

        rep in pt—SSI 2015/446, sch 6 para 2(4)(c)

      sch am—Revenue Scotland and Tax Powers, 2014 asp 16, sch 4 para 12; Food (S), 2015

        asp 1, s 17(8); SSI 2015/271, art 7(b)

        rep in pt—SSI 2015/271, art 7(a)

asp 13   **Buildings (Recovery of Expenses (Scotland)**

2014

asp 14   **Housing (Scotland)**

asp 15   **City of Edinburgh Council (Portobello Park)**

asp 16   **Revenue Scotland and Tax Powers**
        s 74 appl—SSI 2015/130, reg 4(2)
           am—SSI 2015/130, reg 4(3)
        ss 76-79 appl—SSI 2015/130, reg 4(2)
        s 182 mod—SSI 2015/3 reg 39(2) (added by 2015/152, reg 11)
        s 183 appl—SSI 2015/3 reg 39(2) (added by 2015/152, reg 11)

asp 17   **Disabled Persons' Parking Badges (Scotland)**

asp 18   **Courts Reform (Scotland)**
        s 39 excl—SSI 2000/301 rule 4(2) (amended by 2015/338, sch 1 para 2); SI 2015/700, art
           4
        s 58 rep —Courts Reform (S), 2014 asp 18, sch 4 para 9(2)
        s 59 am—Courts Reform (S), 2014 asp 18, sch 4 para 9(3)(a)
           rep in pt—Courts Reform (S), 2014 asp 18, sch 4 para 9(3)(b)
        s 79 rep —Courts Reform (S), 2014 asp 18, sch 4 para 8
        sch 4 am—SSI 2015/405, art 2
        sch 9 am—Courts Reform (S), 2014 asp 18, s 131(2)

asp 19   **Historic Environment Scotland**

2015

asp 1   **Food (Scotland)**

asp 2   **Budget (Scotland)**
        s 4 am—SSI 2015/434, reg 2(a)-(c)
        sch 1 rep in pt—SSI 2015/434, reg 3(2)
           am—SSI 2015/434, reg 3(3)(a)-(o)
        sch 2 am—SSI 2015/434, reg 4(2)(3)

asp 3   **Community Charge Debt (Scotland)**

asp 4   **Legal Writings (Counterparts and Deliveries) (Scotland)**

asp 5   **Welfare Funds (Scotland)**

asp 6   **Community Empowerment (Scotland)**

asp 7   **Scottish Elections (Reduction of Voting Age)**

asp 8   **Prisoners (Control of Release) (Scotland)**

asp 9   **Mental Health (Scotland)**

asp 10   **Air Weapons and Licensing (Scotland)**

asp 11   **British Sign Language (Scotland)**

asp 12   **Human Trafficking and Exploitation (Scotland)**

asp 13   **Harbours (Scotland)**

Chronological Table of the Acts of

The National Assembly for Wales

2012

anaw 1   **National Assembly for Wales (Official Languages)**

anaw 2   **Local Government Byelaws (Wales)**
        sch 1 am (Table 1 am)—SI 2014/3111 (W 311), art 2
        sch 1 am (Table 2 am)—SI 2014/3111 (W 311), art 3
        sch 2 am—Loc Govt (Democracy) (W), 2013 anaw 4, sch 1 para 6

2013

anaw 1   **School Standards and Organisation (Wales)**
        Pt 2 Ch 1 (ss 2-20) power to mod—Education (W), 2011 nawm 7 s 18(1)(a)) (as subst by
            2013 anaw 1, sch 5 para 13(3)(a))
            mod—Educ Reform, 1988 c. 40 s 219(3A) (added by 2013 anaw 1, sch 5 para 1(3));
                Teaching and Higher Educ, 1998 c 30 s 19(12)(13) (as subst by 2013 anaw 1,
                sch 5 para 3); Education, 2002 c 32, s 34(7) (as amended by 2013 anaw 1, sch
                5 para 6(2)); Children, 2004 c 31, s 50A(3) (added by 2013 anaw 1, sch 5 para
                7(3)); Education, 2005 c 18, s 114(8)(c) (added by 2013 anaw 1, sch 5 para
                8(3)(c))
            appl (mods)—School Standards and Framework, 1998 c. 31 s 89C(2)(a)(b) (as
                subst by 2013 anaw 1, sch 5 para 4(5)); Loc Govt, 2000 c 22, sch 1 para 10 (as
                subst by 2013 anaw 1, sch 5 para 5(2)); Children, 2004 c 31, s 50A(1)(2)
                (added by 2013 anaw 1, sch 5 para 7(3)); Childcare, 2006 c 21, s 29 (as subst
                by 2013 anaw 1, sch 5 para 10); Equality, 2010 c 15, s 87(3) (added by 2013
                anaw 1, sch 5 para 11(3))
            excl—Education, 1996 c 56 ss 484(7),560(6) (as amended by 2013 anaw 1, sch 5
                para 2(6)(7)); ibid., sch 1 para 6(4) (as amended by 2013 anaw 1, sch 5 para
                2(8)); Equality, 2010 c 15, s 87(4) (added by 2013 anaw 1, sch 5 para 11(3)))
        Pt 2 Ch 2 (ss 21-31) mod—Education (W), 2014 anaw 5, s 20
        s 25 am—Education (W), 2014 anaw 5, s 44(2)
        s 26 am—Education (W), 2014 anaw 5, s 44(3)
        s 80 mod—SI 2014/1132, reg 58(5)

anaw 2   **Food Hygiene Rating (Wales)**

anaw 3   **Public Audit (Wales)**
        s 23 am—(1.4.2016) Well-being of Future Generations (W), 2015 anaw 2, sch 4 para 32
        sch 4 rep in pt—Loc Audit and Accountability, 2014, sch 12 para 123(i)

anaw 4   **Local Government (Democracy) (Wales)**
        s 29 excl—Loc Govt (W), 2015 anaw 6, s 21(5)
            power to am—Loc Govt (W), 2015 anaw 6, s 24
        s 74 am—Loc Govt (W), 2015 anaw 6, s 43

anaw 5   **Human Transplantation (Wales)**

anaw 6   **Mobile Homes (Wales)**
        power to am—Housing (W), 2014 anaw 7, s 109(2)
        s 33 rep in pt—Housing (W), 2014 anaw 7, sch 3 pt 5, para 30(3)(a)
            am—Housing (W), 2014 anaw 7, sch 3 pt 5, para 30(3)(b)(c)
        s 39 rep in pt—Housing (W), 2014 anaw 7, sch 3 pt 5, para 30(4)
        s 49 am—Housing (W), 2014 anaw 7, sch 3 pt 5, para 30(5)
        s 53 am—Housing (W), 2014 anaw 7, sch 3 pt 5, para 30(6)
        s 56 mod—Environment, 1995 c 25 sch 9 para 4A(a)(b) (added by 2013 anaw 6, sch 4 para
                8(3)); (16.3.2016) Housing (W), 2014 anaw 7, s 103
        s 61 rep in pt—Housing (W), 2014 anaw 7, sch 3 pt 5, para 30(7)
        s 62 am—Housing (W), 2014 anaw 7, sch 3 pt 2 para 26(2), ibid, sch 3 pt 5 para 30(4)
        sch 1 am—Housing (W), 2014 anaw 7, sch 3 pt 2 para 26(3)

anaw 7   **Active Travel (Wales)**

2014

anaw 1	**Further and Higher Education (Governance and Information) (Wales)**
anaw 2	**National Health Service Finance (Wales)**
anaw 3	**Control of Horses (Wales)**
anaw 4	**Social Services and Well-being (Wales)**

excl—Care, 2014 c 23, sch 1 paras 1(1), 3(2), 4(2)(b)

s 14 rep in pt—(1.4.2016) Well-being of Future Generations (W), 2015 anaw 2, sch 4 para 33

s 14A added (6.4.2016)—Well-being of Future Generations (W), 2015 anaw 2, sch 4 para 34

s 34 appl—Care, 2014 c 23, s 52(3)

ss 46, 47 appl—Care, 2014 c 23, s 52(8)

s 48 appl—Care, 2014 c 23, s 52(8)

    am—Housing (W) 2014 anaw 7 sch 3 pt 1, para 22(2)

s 49 appl—Care, 2014 c 23, s 52(8)

s 50 power to mod—(prosp) Care, 2014 c 23, sch 1 para 9(2)(a)

s 52 power to mod—(prosp) Care, 2014 c 23, sch 1 para 9(2)(a)

s 53 am—(6.4.2016) Care, 2014 c 23, s 75(8)

s 119 excl—SI 2015/1988 (W 298), reg 14

    mod—SI 2015/1988 (W 298), reg 15

    appl (mods)—SI 2015/1988 (W 298), reg 16

s 134 am—Crim Justice and Cts, 2015 c 2, sch 9 para 32(2)(3)

s 188 am—Crim Justice and Cts, 2015 c 2, sch 9 para 32(4)(5)

s 190 am—SI 2015/914, sch para 98

s 194 am—(6.4.2016) Care, 2014 c 23, sch 1 para 13

sch A1 added—(6.4.2016) Care, 2014 c 23, sch 4 pt 2

sch 2 rep in pt—Housing (W) 2014 anaw 7 sch 3 pt 1, para 22(3)(a)

    am—Housing (W) 2014 anaw 7 sch 3 pt 1, para 22(3)(b)

anaw 5	**Education (Wales)**
anaw 6	**Agricultural Sector (Wales)**
anaw 7	**Housing (Wales)**

2015

anaw 1	**Higher Education (Wales)**

Pt 2 (ss 2-16) mod—SI 2015/1353, art 3

s 5 mod—SI 2015/1484 (W 163), reg 5(1)

Pt 3 (ss 17-26) mod—SI 2015/1353, art 4(1)

s 17 mod—SI 2015/1484 (W 163), reg 5(2)

sch mod—SI 2015/1484 (W 163), reg 6

anaw 2	**Well-being of Future Generations (Wales)**

s 15 excl in pt—SI 2015/1924 (W 287), reg 3

sch 2 mod—SI 2015/1924 (W 287), reg 4

anaw 3	**Violence against Women, Domestic Abuse and Sexual Violence (Wales)**
anaw 4	**Planning (Wales)**
anaw 5	**Qualifications Wales**
anaw 6	**Local Government (Wales)**

Chronological Table of Measures of

The National Assembly for Wales 2008-2011

2008

nawm 1   **NHS Redress (Wales)**

nawm 2   **Learner Travel (Wales)**
>ss 14A-14N added—Safety on Learner Transport, 2011 nawm 6, ss 1-14
>s 24 am—SI 2010/1148 (W 103), art 2
>>rep in pt—School Standards and Organisation (W), 2013 anaw 1, sch 5 para 25(2)
>s 27 am —Safety on Learner Transport, 2011 nawm 6, s 15
>sch A1 added—Safety on Learner Transport, 2011 nawm 6, s 7(2), sch

2009

nawm 1   **Learning and Skills (Wales)**
>am—SI 2010/1148 (W 103), art 3(2)
>s 44 am—SI 2010/1148 (W 103), art 3(3)
>>rep in pt—School Standards and Organisation (W), 2013 anaw 1, sch 5 para 26(2)
>sch rep in pt **—Further and Higher Educ (Governance and Information) (W), 2014 anaw 1, sch 2 para 6**

nawm 2   **Local Government (Wales)**
>s 12A added—Loc Govt (W) 2011, nawm 4, s 161
>s 16 am—SI 2012/990 (W 130), art 12
>>rep in pt—Public Audit (W), 2013 anaw 3, s 11(2)
>s 21 appl (mods)—Fire and Rescue Services, 2004 c 21, s 24(4)(5) (added by 2009 nawm 2, s 51(1), sch 1 para 33
>>am—Public Audit (W), 2013 anaw 3, sch 4 para 84
>s 22 appl (mods)—Fire and Rescue Services, 2004 c 21, s 24(4)(5) (added by 2009 nawm 2, s 51(1), sch 1 para 33
>>rep in pt—Public Audit (W), 2013 anaw 3, sch 4 para 85
>s 26 appl (mods)—Fire and Rescue Services, 2004 c 21, s 24(4)(5) (added by 2009 nawm 2, s 51(1), sch 1 para 33
>>am—Public Audit (W), 2013 anaw 3, sch 4 para 86
>s 27 appl (mods)—Fire and Rescue Services, 2004 c 21, s 24(4)(5) (added by 2009 nawm 2, s 51(1), sch 1 para 33
>>am—Public Audit (W), 2013 anaw 3, sch 4 para 87(2)-(6)
>>rep in pt—Public Audit (W), 2013 anaw 3, sch 4 para 87(7)
>s 27A added—Public Audit (W), 2013 anaw 3, sch 4 para 88
>Pt 2 (ss 37-47) rep (1.4.2016)—Well-being of Future Generations (W), 2015 anaw 2, sch 4 para 21
>s 38 am—SI 2014/1713 (W 173), art 2(2)
>s 48 rep in pt—(1.4.2016) Well-being of Future Generations (W), 2015 anaw 2, sch 4 para 22
>s 50 rep in pt—(1.4.2016) Well-being of Future Generations (W), 2015 anaw 2, sch 4 para 22
>s 51 rep in pt—(1.4.2016) Well-being of Future Generations (W), 2015 anaw 2, sch 4 para 22
>sch 2 rep in pt —Localism, 2011 c 20, sch 5 pt 1; Deregulation, 2015 c. 20, s 100(2)(h)
>sch 3 rep (1.4.2016)—Well-being of Future Generations (W), 2015 anaw 2, sch 4 para 23

nawm 3   **Healthy Eating in Schools (Wales)**
>s 7 am—SI 2010/1148 (W 103), art 4(2)
>s 8 am—SI 2010/1148 (W 103), art 4(2); School Standards and Organisation (W), 2013 anaw 1, sch 5 para 35
>s 11 am—SI 2010/1148 (W 103), art 4(3)
>>rep in pt—School Standards and Organisation (W), 2013 anaw 1, sch 5 para 27(2)

nawm 4   **National Assembly for Wales Commissioner for Standards**

nawm 5   **Education (Wales)**
>am—SI 2010/1148 (W 103), art 5(2)
>s 9 subst—SI 2011/ 1651 (W187), art 3
>s 10 subst—SI 2011/ 1651 (W187), art 4

2009

nawm 5 *continued*

    s 11 subst—SI 2011/ 1651 (W187), art 5
    s 12 subst—SI 2011/ 1651 (W187), art 6
    s 13 subst—SI 2011/ 1651 (W187), art 7
    s 14 subst—SI 2011/ 1651 (W187), art 8
    s 15 subst—SI 2011/ 1651 (W187), art 9
    s 16 subst—SI 2011/ 1651 (W187), art 10
    s 17 am—SI 2011/ 1651 (W187), art 11
    s 18 am—SIs 2011/ 1651 (W187), art 12; 2011/1651 (W187), art 13(1)
    s 19 am—SI 2010/1148 (W 103), art 5(4)
    s 26 am—SI 2011/1651 (W187), art 13(2)
    sch rep in pt—SI 2011/1651 (W187), art 13(3)

2010

nawm 1   **Children and Families (Wales)**
    s 2 rep in pt—(1.4.2016) Well-being of Future Generations (W), 2015 anaw 2, sch 4 para 25
    s 4 rep in pt —(heading rep in pt) SI 2010/1148 (W 103), art 6(2); (1.4.2016) Well-being of Future Generations (W), 2015 anaw 2, sch 4 para 26(b)
      am—SI 2010/1148 (W 103), art 6(3); (1.4.2016) Well-being of Future Generations (W), 2015 anaw 2, sch 4 para 26(a)
    s 5 rep in pt —(1.4.2016) Well-being of Future Generations (W), 2015 anaw 2, sch 4 para 27(a)
      am—(1.4.2016) Well-being of Future Generations (W), 2015 anaw 2, sch 4 para 27(b)
    s 6 am—SI 2013/755 (W 90), Sch 3 para 1
    s 34 am—Crime and Cts, 2013 c. 22, Sch 11 para 208
    s 43 rep in pt—Crime and Cts, 2013 c. 22, Sch 11 para 209(a)
      am—Crime and Cts, 2013 c. 22, Sch 11 para 209(b)
    s 48 am—SI 2015/664, sch 5 para 16

nawm 2   **Social Care Charges (Wales)**

nawm 3   **Red Meat Industry (Wales)**
    sch 2 am—SI 2011/2946 (W 319), art 2(1)(2)

nawm 4   **National Assembly for Wales (Remuneration)**
    sch 1 rep in pt—SI 2014/1004 (W 93), art 2(a)(b)

nawm 5   **Carers Strategies (Wales)**

nawm 6   **Playing Fields (Community Involvement in Disposal Decisions) (Wales)**

nawm 7   **Mental Health (Wales)**
    s 2 am—(1.4.2016) Well-being of Future Generations (W), 2015 anaw 2, sch 4 para 29
    s 11 rep (1.4.2016)—Well-being of Future Generations (W), 2015 anaw 2, sch 4 para 30
    s 50 am—(prosp) Housing (W), 2014 anaw 7, sch 3 para 19

nawm 8   **Waste (Wales)**
    s 8 am—SI 2013/755 (W 90), Sch 3 para 2
    s 11 am—SI 2013/755 (W 90), Sch 3 para 2
    s 16 am—SI 2013/755 (W 90), Sch 3 para 2

2011

nawm 1   **Welsh Language (Wales)**
    sch 3 rep in pt—Social Services and Well-being (W), 2014 anaw 4, sch 3 para 36
    sch 6 rep in pt —Financial Services, 2012 c 21, sch 18 para 144; School Standards and Organisation (W), 2013 anaw 1, sch 5 para 30(2); SIs 2013/755 (W 90), sch 3 para 3(2); 2014/892, sch 1 para 259
      am—Loc Govt (Democracy) (W), 2013 anaw 4, sch 1 para 4; SI 2013/755 (W 90), sch 3 para 3(3); (prosp) Planning (W), 2015 anaw 4, sch 1 pt 2, para 8; SI 2015/1682, sch pt 3 para 12(a)(b)

nawm 2   **Rights of Children and Young Persons (Wales)**

nawm 3   **Domestic Fire Safety (Wales)**
    s 6 am—SI 2013/2723 (W 261), art 2

nawm 4   **Local Government (Wales)**
    s 1 am—Loc Govt (W), 2015 anaw 6, s 42(2)-(4)
      rep in pt—Loc Govt (W), 2015 anaw 6, s 42(5)
    s 4 am—Loc Govt (Democracy) (W), 2013 anaw 4, s 59
      rep in pt—Loc Govt (Democracy) (W), 2013 anaw 4, sch 2 Table 1
    s 11A added—Loc Govt (Democracy) (W), 2013 anaw 4, s 60(1)
    s 19 am—Loc Govt (Democracy) (W), 2013 anaw 4, s 60(2)

2011

nawm 4 *continued*

      s 36 rep in pt —Localism, 2011 c 20, sch 25 pt 4

      s 82 am—Loc Govt (Democracy) (W), 2013 anaw 4, s 61

      s 87 rep in pt—Loc Govt (W), 2011 nawm 4, s 36(2), sch 4 pt 4B

      s 128 rep (1.4.2016)—Well-being of Future Generations (W), 2015 anaw 2, sch 4 para 31

      Pt 8 (ss 141-160) rep in pt—Loc Govt (Democracy) (W), 2013 anaw 4, s 63(2)

               appl (mods)—(25.1.2015) Loc Govt (W), 2015 anaw 6, ss 25(3)(4), 26

      s 142 am—Loc Govt (Democracy) (W), 2013 anaw 4, s 62

      s 143A added—Loc Govt (Democracy) (W), 2013 anaw 4, s 63(1)

         excl—Loc Govt (W), 2015 anaw 6, s 29(7)(8)

         ext (temp until 31.3.2020)—Loc Govt (W), 2015 anaw 6, s 39

         am—Loc Govt (W), 2015 anaw 6, s 40(2)-(4)

      s 144 am—Loc Govt (Democracy) (W), 2013 anaw 4, s 64; (prosp) Planning (W), 2015

         anaw 4, sch 1 pt 2 para 9

      s 147 am—Loc Govt (Democracy) (W), 2013 anaw 4, s 65

      s 148 rep in pt—Loc Govt (Democracy) (W), 2013 anaw 4, s 66(a)

         am—Loc Govt (Democracy) (W), 2013 anaw 4, s 66(b)

      s 151 am—Loc Govt (Democracy) (W), 2013 anaw 4, s 67(a)(b)

      s 167 rep—Loc Govt (Democracy) (W), 2013 anaw 4, sch 2 Table 1

      sch 2 am—Loc Govt (W), 2015 anaw 6, s 41(2)

         rep in pt—Loc Govt (W), 2015 anaw 6, s 41(3)

nawm 5   **Housing (Wales)**

nawm 6   **Safety on Learner Transport (Wales)**

nawm 7   **Education (Wales)**

      s 8 rep in pt—School Standards and Organisation (W), 2013 anaw 1, sch 5 para 29(2)

      s 13 am—School Standards and Organisation (W), 2013 anaw 1, sch 5 para 29(3)

      s 16 rep—School Standards and Organisation (W), 2013 anaw 1, sch 5 para 13(2)

      s 18 am—School Standards and Organisation (W), 2013 anaw 1, sch 5 para 13(3)

      s 20 rep—School Standards and Organisation (W), 2013 anaw 1, sch 5 para 29(4)

      s 21 rep in pt—School Standards and Organisation (W), 2013 anaw 1, sch 5 para 29(5)

      ss 26-30 rep—School Standards and Organisation (W), 2013 anaw 1, sch 5 para 29(6)

Chronological Table of Church Assembly and General Synod Measures

1920 (10 & 11 Geo 5)

No 1   **Convocations of the Clergy**
        am—CAM Synodical Govt, 1969 No 2, s 1(5)

1921 (11 & 12 Geo 5)

No 1   *Parochial Church Councils (Powers)*—rep CAM Parochial Church Councils (Powers), 1956
        No 3, s 10(4)
No 2   *Ecclesiastical Commissioners*—rep CAM Clergy Pensions, 1926 No 6, s 39 sch 4
No 3   *Union of Benefices*—rep SLR, 1950

1922 (12 & 13 Geo 5)

No 1   *Representation of the Laity (Amendment)*—rep CAM Representation of the Laity, 1929 No 2,
        ss 1, 2
No 2   *Pluralities Act, 1838 Amendment*—rep SLR, 1950
No 3   **Revised Table of Lessons**

1923-1924 (14 & 15 Geo 5) (a)

No 1   *Benefices Act, 1898 (Amendment)*—rep GSM Patronage (Benefices), 1986 No 3, s 41, sch 5
No 2   *Union of Benefices*—rep (saving), CAM Pastoral, 1968 No 1, ss 94, 95, sch 8 paras 3,5, sch 9
No 3   **Ecclesiastical Dilapidations**—rep (exc s 52) (saving), GSM Repair of Benefice Buildings,
        1972 No 2, s 35, sch 2
        s 52 am—CAM Ecclesiastical Dilapidations (Amdt), 1929 No 3, s 18; Trustee, 2000 c 29,
        s 40(1), sch 2 pt III para 50
        rep in pt—GSM Endowments and Glebe, 1976 No 4, s 47(4), sch 8
No 4   **Bishopric of Blackburn**—rep (exc ss 1, 13) (saving) SL(R), 1973 c 39
        s 13 rep—GSM C of E (Misc Provns), 1976 No 3, s 7
No 5   *Diocese of Southwell (Division)*—rep (saving), SL(R), 1973 c 39
No 6   *Diocese of Winchester (Division)*—rep (saving), SL(R), 1973 c 39

(a) These Measures though passed in 1924 describe themselves as 1923

1925 (15 & 16 Geo 5)

No 1   **Interpretation**
        am—CAM Synodical Govt, 1969 No 2, s 2(2)
        s 1 rep—Interpretation, 1978 c 30, s 25(1), sch 3
        s 4 rep—SL(R), 2004 c 14, s 1(1), sch 1 pt 6/5
No 2   *Bishopric of Leicester*—rep (saving) SL(R), 1973 c 39
No 3   **Diocesan Boards of Finance**
        s 3 am—GSM Team and Group Ministries, 1995 No 1, s 7

1926 (16 & 17 Geo 5)

No 1   **Brislington Parishes (Transfer)**
        s 3 rep—SLR, 1950
No 2   **Rural Deaneries of Pontefract and Hemsworth (Transfer)**
        s 3 rep—SLR, 1950
No 3   *Parish of Manchester Division Act, 1850 (Amendment)*—rep (saving) CAM Cathedrals, 1963
        No 2, s 54(1) (4), sch 2
No 4   **Ecclesiastical Commissioners**
        s 1 rep—CAM Archdeaconries (Augmentation), 1953 No 4, s 2, sch
        s 2 rep—CAM Cathedrals, 1963 No 2, s 54(1), sch 2
        s 3 rep—SLR, 1964
        s 4 rep—CAM Ecclesiastical Commissioners (Powers), 1936 No 5, s 9
        s 5 rep—CAM Ecclesiastical Jurisdiction, 1963 No 1, s 87, sch 5
        s 7-9, sch rep—SLR, 1964
No 5   *First Fruits and Tenths*—rep SL(R), 1993 c 50, s 1(1), sch 1 pt VI
No 6   *Clergy Pensions*—rep CAM Clergy Pensions, 1948 No 1, s 63, sch 8
No 7   *Episcopal Pensions*—rep Clergy Pensions, 1961 No 3, s 48(1), sch 3
No 8   *Benefices (Ecclesiastical Duties)*—rep CAM Incumbents (Discipline), 1947 No 1, s 27; GSM
        Endowments and Glebe, 1976 No 4, s 47(4), sch 8

1927 (17 & 18 Geo 5)

No 1   *Indian Church*— rep SL(R), 1976 c 16, sch 1 pt VII
No 2   *Clergy Pensions (Amendment)*—rep CAM Clergy Pensions, 1948 No 1, s 63 sch 8
No 3   *New Dioceses (Transitional Provisions)*—rep GSM Dioceses, 1978 No 1, s 9(8)

1928 (18 & 19 Geo 5)

No 1   *Ecclesiastical Commissioners (Provision for Unbeneficed Clergy)*—rep GSM Endowments
               and Glebe, 1976 No 4, s 47(4), sch 8
               [1928 Measure ext to Sodor and Man—CAM Ecclesiastical Commissioners (Sodor and
                    Man), 1930 No 5, s 1]
No 2   **Tithe (Administration of Trusts)**
               s 1-5 rep—SLR, 1964
               ss 7-16 rep—SLR, 1964
               sch rep—SLR, 1964
No 3   *Clergy Pensions (Amendment)*—rep CAM Clergy Pensions, 1948 No 1, s 63 sch 8

1929 (19 & 20 Geo 5)

No 1   *Parochial Registers and Records*—rep GSM Parochial Registers and Records, 1978 No 2,
               s 26(2), sch 4
No 2   *Representation of the Laity*—rep CAM Representation of the Laity, 1956 No 2, s 2(1)
No 3   **Ecclesiastical Dilapidations (Amendment)**
               rep (exc s 18)—GSM Repair of Benefice Buildings, 1972 No 2, s 35, sch 2
No 4   **Westminster Abbey**
               s 2 rep—Westminster Abbey and St Margaret Westminster, 1972 c xxvi, s 25, sch 2

1930 (20 & 21 Geo 5)

No 1   *Parsonages*—rep CAM Parsonages, 1938 No 3, s 23
No 2   *Archdeaconry of Surrey*—rep CAM Cathedrals, 1963 No 2, s 54(1), sch 2
No 3   *Marriage*—rep Marriage, 1949 c 76, s 79, sch 5 pt II
No 4   *Ecclesiastical Commissioners (Pensions of Church Estates Commnrs)*—rep CAM Church
               Property (Misc Provns), 1960 No 1, s 20(4)
No 5   **Ecclesiastical Commissioners (Sodor and Man)**
               s 1 rep in pt—GSM Endowments and Glebe 1976 No 4, s 47(4), sch 8
No 6   *Clergy Pensions (Older Incumbents)*—rep CAM Clergy Pension 1961 No 3 s 48(1) sch 3
No 7   *Pluralities*—rep CAM Pastoral, 1968 No 1, s 95, sch 9
No 8   **Benefices (Transfer of Rights of Patronage)**
               rep (except as applied by s 6(3) of City of London (Guild Churches)—GSM Patronage
                    (Benefices), 1986 No 3, s 41, sch 5
               expld—CAM Pastoral, 1968 No 1, ss 32(10, 41, sch 3 para 5(1)
               power to excl—GSM Dioceses, 1978 No 1, sch para 10
               excl—GSM Pastoral, 1983 No 1, ss 20–22, 24, 27, 29, 31, 32, 40, sch 3 para 6(1)

1931 (21 & 22 Geo 5)

No 1   *Episcopal Pensions (Sodor and Man)*—rep CAM Clergy Pensions, 1961 No 3, s 48(1), sch 3
No 2   **Ecclesiastical Commissioners (Loans for Church Training Colleges)**
               s 3 am—SI 2007/1556, sch, para 1
No 3   *Benefices (Exercise of Rights of Presentation)*—rep GSM Patronage (Benefices), 1986 No 3,
               s 41, sch 5
No 4   **Channel Islands (Church Legislation)**
               appl—GSM C of E (Misc Provns), 1992 No 1, s 19(4); GSM Priests (Ordination of Women),
                    1993 No 2, s 12(4); GSM Ordination of Women (Financial Provns), 1993 No 3,
                    s 13(2); GSM Pastoral (Amdt), 1994 No 1, s 15(3) GSM Pensions 1997 No 1,
                    s 11(3)
               s 1 appl—C of E (Misc Provns), 1976 No 3, s 8(6); GSM Endowments and Glebe, 1976
                    No 4, s 48(1)
               ss 2,3 rep in pt—CAM Channel Is (Church Legislation), 1931 (Amdt), 1957 No 1, s 1
               sch am—CAM Channel Is (Church Legislation), 1931 (Amdt), 1957 No 1, s 2;
                    SI 2001/3500, art 8, sch 2 pt II, para 10
               trans of functions—SI 2001/3500, arts 3, 4(1)(c)(3)–(8), sch 1, para 3(a)
No 5   **Channel Islands (Representation)**
No 6   *Ecclesiastical Commissioners (Provision for Unbeneficed Clergy), 1928 (Amdt)*—rep GSM
               Endowments and Glebe, 1976 No 4, s 47(4), sch 8
No 7   *Cathedrals*—rep GSM C of E (Misc Provns), 1992 No 1, s 17(2), sch 4, pt I

1932 (22 & 23 Geo 5)

No 1   *Benefices (Diocesan Boards of Patronage)*—rep GSM Patronage (Benefices), 1986 No 3,
        s 41, sch 5

1933 (23 & 24 Geo 5)

No 1   *Benefices (Purchase of Rights of Patronage)*—rep GSM Patronage (Benefices), 1986 No 3,
        s 41, sch 5
No 2   **Wythenshawe Parishes (Transfer)**
        s 3 rep—SLR, 1950
No 3   **Parish of Manchester Revenues**
No 4   **Benefices (Sequestrations)**
        expld—CAM Vacancies in Sees, 1959 No 2, s 5
        ext—CAM Pastoral, 1968 No 1, s 68(4), sch 7 paras 1, 3(1) (d)
        s 1 am—GSM C of E (Misc Provns), 1976 No 3, s 5
            rep in pt—GSM Endowments and Glebe, 1976 No 4, s 47(4), sch 8
        s 3 rep—GSM Endowments and Glebe 1976 No 4, ss 38(1), 47(4) sch 8
        s 4 rep —GSM Endowments and Glebe, 1976 No 4, s 47(4), sch 8
        s 6 rep—GSM C of E (Misc Provns), 1992 No 1, s 17(2), sch 4, pt II

1934 (24 & 25 Geo 5)

No 1   **Clerical Disabilities Act, 1870 (Amendment)**
No 2   *Banns of Marriage*—rep Marriage, 1949 c 76, sch 5 pt II
No 3   *Cathedrals (Amendment)*—rep CAM Cathedrals, 1963 No 2, s 54(1), sch 2

1935 (25 & 26 Geo 5)

No 1   *Diocese of Southwell (Transfer)*—rep (saving) SL(R), 1973 c 39
No 2   *Farnham Castle*—rep CAM Farnham Castle, 1961 No 1, s 4

1936 (26 Geo 5 & Edw 8)

No 1   *Clergy Pensions (Amendment)*—rep CAM Clergy Pensions, 1948 No 1, s 63, sch 8
No 2   *Union of Benefices (Amendment)*—rep CAM Pastoral, 1968 No 1, s 95, sch 9
No 3   *Clergy Pensions (Widows and Dependants)*—rep CAM Clergy Pensions, 1948 No 1, s 63,
        sch 8
No 4   *Cathedrals (Houses of Residence)*—rep CAM Cathedrals, 1963 No 2 s 54(1), sch 2
No 5   **Ecclesiastical Commissioners (Powers)**
        s 1 rep—CAM New Housing Areas (Church Buildings), 1954 No 1, s 2
        s 2 rep in pt—GSM Cathedrals, 1999 No 1, ss 38(3), 39(1), sch 2 para 1; SL(R), 2004
            c 14, s 1(1), sch 1 pt 6/2(5)
        s 3 rep—GSM Church Commissioners (Misc Provns), 1975 No 1, s 1(2)
        s 4 rep—CAM Pastoral, 1968 No 1, s 95, sch 9
        s 5 rep—GSM Endowments and Glebe, 1976 No 4, s 47(4), sch 8
        s 6 excl—CAM Cathedrals, 1963 No 2, s 53, sch 1
            rep (as to incumbents)—GSM Endowments and Glebe, 1976 No 4, s 47(3), sch 7
        ss 7, 8 rep—GSM Endowments and Glebe, 1976 No 4, s 47(4), sch 8
        s 9 rep—CAM Ecclesiastical Jurisdiction, 1963 No 1, s 87, sch 5
        s 12 rep in pt—GSM Church Commissioners (Misc Provns), 1975 No 1, s 1(2)

1937 (1 Edw 8 & 1 Geo 6)

No 1   *Queen Anne's Bounty (Powers)*—rep GSM Endowments and Glebe, 1976 No 4, s 47(4), sch 8
No 2   *House of Laity (Co-opted Members)*—rep CAM Representation of the Laity, 1956 No 2,
        s 2(2)
No 3   **Southwark Cathedral**
        ss 2, 5 ,8 rep—CAM Cathedrals, 1963 No 2, s 54(1), sch 2
        schs 1, 2 rep—CAM Cathedrals, 1963 No 2, s 54(1), sch 2

1938 (1 & 2 Geo 6)

No 1   *Marriage (Licensing of Chapels)*—rep Marriage, 1949 c 76, s 79, sch 5 pt II
No 2   *Guildford Cathedral*—rep CAM Guildford Cathedral, 1959 No 3, s 10
No 3   **Parsonages**
        see—CAM Loans (Postponement of Repayment), 1942 No 2, s 2, sch; CAM Parsonages
            (Amdt), 1947 No 2, s 1
        saved—CAM New Parishes, 1943 No 1, s 16(6)
        ext (mods)—GSM Pastoral, 1983 No 1, s 33(4)

1938 (1 & 2 Geo 6)
No 3 *continued*

   am—GSM C of E (Misc Provns), 2000 No 1, s 2, sch 1 para 2
   appl—GSM Mission and Pastoral, 2011 No 3, s 47(4)
  s 1 am—CAM Church Property (Misc Provns), 1960 No 1, ss 1, 4(1), sch; GSM C of E
    (Misc Provns), 1983 No 2, s 4; GSM Team and Group Ministries, 1995 No 1,
    s 8(2); GSM C of E (Misc Provns), 2000 No 1, s 2, sch 1 para 3(a)(ii)(b)-(d); GSM
    C of E (Misc Provns), 2005 No 3, s 1, sch 1 paras 1, 2(a)(b); SI 2005/3129,
    art 4(3), sch 3 para 2; (prosp) GSM C of E (Misc Provns), 2006 No 1, s 1, sch 1
    para 2; GSM C of E (Misc Provns), 2010 No 1, s 12(1)
   rep in pt—CAM Church Property (Misc Provns)1960 No 1, s 4(1), sch; GSM
    Endowments and Glebe, 1976 No 4, s 47(4), sch 8; GSM Team and Group
    Ministries, 1995 No 1, s 8(2); GSM C of E (Misc Provns), 2000 No 1, ss 2,20,
    sch 1 para 3(a)(i), sch 8 pt II; (prosp) GSM C of E (Misc Provns), 2006 No 1, s
    1, sch 1 para 3
   expld—GSM Endowments and Glebe, 1976 No 4, s 34
   saved—GSM Endowments and Glebe, 1976 No 4, s 10(4)
  s 2 rep in pt—CAM Church Property (Misc Provns), 1960 No 1, ss 2(1), 14(2); GSM
    Endowments and Glebe 1976 No 4, s 47(4), sch 8; GSM C of E (Misc Provns),
    2000 No 1, s 2, sch 1 para 4(a)
   am—CAM Church Property (Misc Provns), 1960 No 1, s 4(1), sch; GSM C of E (Misc
    Provns), 2000 No 1, s 2, sch 1 para 4(b)(c); GSM C of E (Misc Provns), 2005 No 3,
    s 1, sch 1 paras 1, 3
  s 2A added—CAM Church Property (Misc Provns), 1960 No 1, s 3(1); GSM Team and
    Group Ministries, 1995 No 1, s 8(3)
   am—GSM Patronage (Benefices), 1986 No 3, ss 34(a), 41, sch 4 para 2
   rep in pt—GSM C of E (Misc Provns), 2000 No 1, s 2, sch 1, para 5
  s 3 am—CAM Church Property (Misc Provns), 1960 No 1, s 3(2); GSM Patronage
    (Benefices), 1986 No 3, s 41, sch 4 para 3; GSM Team and Group Ministries, 1995
    No 1 s 8(4); (prosp) GSM C of E (Misc Provns), 2006 No 1, s 1, sch 1 para 4
   rep in pt—GSM Patronage (Benefices), 1986 No 3, s 41, sch 4 para 3, sch 5; GSM C of
    E (Misc Provns) 2000 No 1, ss 2,20, sch 1, para 6(b), sch 8 pt II
  s 4 rep—GSM Patronage (Benefices), 1986 No 3, s 41, sch 5
  s 5 subst (prosp)—GSM C of E (Misc Provns), 2006 No 1, s 1, sch 1 para 5
   am & rep in pt—GSM C of E (Misc Provns), 2000 No 1, ss 2,20, sch 1, para 7(a), sch 8
    pt II
   am—CAM Parsonages (Amdt), 1947 No 3, s 3; CAM Church Property (Misc Provns),
    1960 No 1, s 4(1), sch; GSM Endowments and Glebe, 1976 No 4, s 35(3); GSM
    Pastoral (Amdt), 1982 No 1, s 70; GSM Pastoral, 1983 No 1, s 91; GSM C of E
    (Misc Provns), 2000 No 1, s 2, sch 1, para 7(b)(c)
  s 5 rep in pt—GSM Repair and Benefice Buildings, 1972 No 2, s 35, sch 2; GSM
    Endowments and Glebe, 1976 No 4, s 47(4), sch 8
   saved—GSM Endowments and Glebe, 1976 No 4, s 36(2)
   excl—GSM Pastoral, 1983 No 1, s 33(5); GSM Mission and Pastoral, 2011 No 3, s
    47(5)
  s 6 am—CAM Church Property (Misc Provns), 1960 No 1, s 4(1), sch
   rep in pt—(prosp) GSM C of E (Misc Provns), 2006 No 1, s 1, sch 1 para 6
  s 7 subst—GSM C of E (Misc Provns), 2000 No 1, s 2, sch 1, para 8
   am—GSM C of E (Misc Provns), 2005 No 3, s 1, sch 1 paras 1, 4; (prosp) GSM C of E
    (Misc Provns), 2006 No 1, s 1, sch 1 para 7
  s 9 am—CAM Church Property (Misc Provns), 1960 No 1, s 4(1), sch; GSM C of E (Misc
    Provns), 2000 No 1, s 2, sch 1, para 9; GSM C of E (Misc Provns), 2005 No 3, s 1,
    sch 1 paras 1, 5; (prosp) GSM C of E (Misc Provns), 2006 No 1, s 1, sch 1 para 8
   rep in pt—Charities, 1960 c 58, s 48(2), sch 7 pt II
  s 10 rep—GSM Endowments and Glebe, 1976 No 4, s 47(4), sch 8
  s 11 am—CAM Church Property (Misc Provns), 1960 No 1, s 4(1) sch; GSM C of E (Misc
    Provns), 2005 No 3, s 1, sch 1 paras 1, 6, 7
  s 12 am—GSM C of E (Misc Provns), 2005 No 3, s 1, sch 1 paras 1, 6, 7
  s 13 am—GSM Patronage (Benefices), 1986 No 3, s 41, sch 4 para 5
  s 14 rep—GSM C of E (Misc Provns), 1976 No 3, s 3(9), sch pt II
  s 15 expld—CAM Church Property (Misc Provns), 1960 No 1, s 4(2)
   rep in pt—GSM Patronage (Benefices), 1986 No 3, s 41, sch 4 para 6
   am—GSM C of E (Misc Provns), 2000 No 1, s 2, sch 1, para 10; (prosp) GSM C of E
    (Misc Provns), 2006 No 1, s 1, sch 1 para 9
  s 16 am—GSM Patronage (Benefices), 1986 No 3, s 41, sch 4 para 7

1938 (1 & 2 Geo 6)
No 3 *continued*

  s 19 rep—GSM Patronage (Benefices), 1986 No 3, s 41, sch 5
  s 20 am—CAM Church Property (Misc Provns), 1960 No 1, s 2(2); GSM Patronage
    (Benefices), 1986 No 3, s 41, sch 4 para 8; GSM C of E (Misc Provns), 2000
    No 1, s 2, sch 1, para 11
  s 21 rep—SL(R), 2004 c 14, s 1(1), sch 1 pt 6/2(2)
  s 23 rep—SLR, 1950

No 4 **Ecclesiastical Commissioners (Powers)**
    rep (exc ss 2(1) (2) (4), 9, 13)—GSM Endowments and Glebe, 1976 No 4, s 47(4), sch 8
No 5 **Liverpool City Churches Act, 1897 (Amendment)**
No 6 *Faculty Jurisdiction*—rep (saving) CAM Faculty Jurisdiction, 1964, No 5, s 16

1939 (2 & 3 Geo 6)

No 1 *Queen Anne's Bounty (Powers)*—rep GSM Endowments and Glebe, 1976 No 4, s 47(4), sch 8
No 2 *Ecclesiastical Officers' Remuneration*—rep CAM Ecclesiastical Fees 1962 No 1, s 8(2), sch
    pt II
No 3 *Clergy (National Emergency Precautions)*—rep SLR, 1950

1939 (3 & 4 Geo 6)

No 1 *House of Laity (Postponement of Election)*—rep SL(R), 1977 c 18, s 1(1), sch 1 pt V

1940 (3 & 4 Geo 6)

No 2 *Benefice Buildings (Postponement of Inspections and Repayment of Loans)*—rep SLR, 1953;
    GSM Repair of Benefice Buildings, 1972 No 2, s 35, sch 2
No 3 *Ecclesiatical Dilapidations (Chancel Repairs)*—rep GSM C of E (Misc Provns), 2000 No 1,
    s 20, sch 8 pt I

1941 (4 & 5 Geo 6)

No 1 *Diocesan Reorganisation Committees*—rep CAM Pastoral 1968 No 1, s 95, sch 9

1942 (5 & 6 Geo 6)

No 1 *Ecclesiastical Commissioners (Powers)*—rep CAM Church Property (Misc Provns), 1960
    No 1, s 12(2); SL(R), 2004 c 14, s 1(1), sch 1 pt 6/2(1)
No 2 *Loans (Postponement of Repayment)*—rep SLR, 1964

1943 (6 & 7 Geo 6)

No 1 **New Parishes**
    s 1 rep—(saving) CAM Pastoral 1968 No 1, ss 94,95, schs 8 paras 4, 9
    ss 2-12 rep—CAM Pastoral, 1968 No 1, s 95, sch 9
    s 13 am—CAM Church Property (Misc Provns), 1960 No 1, s 5; GSM C of E (Misc Provns),
        1983 No 2, s 1(1); GSM C of E (Misc Provns), 1992 No 1, s 8(a)(i)-(iii); GSM C
        of E (Misc Provns), 2010 No 1, s 1, sch 1 para 2(a)-(c)
      rep in pt—Charities, 1960 c 58, s 48(2), sch 7 pt II; GSM Ecclesiastical Offices (Terms
        of Service), 2009 No 1, s 12, sch 3; GSM C of E (Misc Provns), 2010 No 1, ss
        1, 12, sch 1 para 2(d), sch 2
      excl—Sharing of Church Buildings, 1969 c 38, s 3(3)
      appl—GSM Sharing of Church Buildings 1970 No 2, s 2(2)
      saved—GSM Endowments and Glebe, 1976 No 4, s 23(2)
    s 14 rep in pt—Charities 1960 c 58, s 48(2), sch 7 pt II; GSM Endowments and Glebe, 1976
        No 4, s 47(4), sch 8
      mod—CAM Pastoral, 1968 No 1, s 76(1)
      expld—CAM Pastoral, 1968 No 1, s 76(2); GSM Pastoral, 1983 No 1, s 76(2)
      am—Charities, 1960 c 58, s 48(1), sch 6; GSM C of E (Misc Provns), 1983 No 2, s 2;
        Charities, 1993 c 10, s 98(1), sch 6 para 3(2)(4); Charities, 2006 c 50, s 75, sch 8
        para 30; GSM C of E (Misc Provns), 2010 No 1, s 1, sch 1 para 3; Charities,
        2011 c 25, sch 7 para 9
      saved—Crown Estate, 1961 c 55, s 4(3)
      excl—Sharing of Church Buildings, 1969 c 38, s 3(3)
      appl—GSM Sharing of Church Buildings 1970 No 2, s 2(2); GSM Endowments and
        Glebe, 1976 No 4, s 23(1)
      ext—GSM Pastoral, 1983 No 1, s 76(1)
    s 15 expld—Admin of Justice, 1965 c 2, s 17(2)
      certain functions trans—SI 1965/143, arts 2, 3(1), sch

1943 (6 & 7 Geo 6)
No 1 s 15 *continued*

appl—GSM Sharing of Church Buildings 1970 No 2, s 2(2)

am—Commons, 2006 c 26, s 44, sch 4 para 5; GSM C of E (Misc Provns), 2010 No 1, s 1, sch 1 para 4

s 16 subst—CAM Church Property (Misc Provns), 1960 No 1, s 6(2)

appl—GSM Sharing of Church Buildings 1970 No 2, s 2(2)

am—GSM Endowments and Glebe, 1976 No 4, s 41(2); GSM C of E (Misc Provns), 1983 No 2, ss 1(2), 3; GSM C of E (Misc Provns), 1992 No 1, s 8(b)(i)(ii); GSM C of E (Misc Provns), 2010 No 1, s 1, sch 1 para 5

rep in pt—GSM Endowments and Glebe, 1976 No 4, ss 41(1), 47(4), sch 8; GSM Ecclesiastical Offices (Terms of Service), 2009 No 1, s 12, sch 3; GSM C of E (Misc Provns), 2010 No 1, s 12, sch 2

s 17 subst—CAM Church Property (Misc Provns), 1960 No 1, ss 6(2), 7

am—GSM Endowments and Glebe, 1976 No 4, s 18(4) (5); GSM C of E (Misc Provns), 1978 No 3, s 7; GSM C of E (Misc Provns), 1992 No 1, s 8(c); GSM C of E (Misc Provns), 2010 No 1, s 1, sch 1 para 6(a)(b)(d)(e); GSM C of E (Misc Provns), 2014 No 1, sch 2 para 2

rep in pt—GSM Endowments and Glebe, 1976 No 4, ss 18(4), 47(4), sch 8; SL(R), 2004 c 14, s 1(1), sch 1 pt 6/2(2); GSM C of E (Misc Provns), 2010 No 1, ss 1, 12, sch 1 para 6(a)(c), sch 2

s 18 appl—GSM Sharing of Church Buildings, 1970 No 2, s 2(2)

s 19 rep—GSM C of E (Misc Provns), 2010 No 1, s 12, sch 2

s 20 am—GSM C of E (Misc Provns), 2010 No 1, s 1, sch 1 para 7

s 21 am—GSM C of E (Misc Provns), 2010 No 1, s 1, sch 1 para 8

s 22 rep—(saving) CAM Pastoral, 1968 No 1, ss 94, 95, schs 8 para 2, 9

ss 23,24 rep—CAM Pastoral, 1968 No 1, s 95, sch 9

s 25 rep—Marriage, 1949 c 76, s 79, sch 5 pt II

ss 26,27 rep—CAM Pastoral, 1968 No 1, s 95, sch 9

s 28 am—GSM Patronage (Benefices), 1986 No 3, s 41, sch 4 para 9

s 29 rep in pt—GSM Patronage (Benefices), 1986 No 3, s 41, sch 5

am—GSM C of E (Misc Provns), 2010 No 1, s 1, sch 1 para 9

s 30 rep—CAM Pastoral, 1968 No 1, s 95, sch 9

s 31 am—Charities, 1960 c 58, s 48(1), sch 6; Charities, 1993 c 10, s 98(1), sch 6 para 3(4); Charities, 2006 c 50, s 75, sch 8 para 31; GSM C of E (Misc Provns), 2010 No 1, s 1, sch 1 para 10; Charities, 2011 c 25, sch 7 para 10

rep in pt—Education, 1973 c 16, s 1(4) (5), sch 2 pt III

s 32 rep in pt—SLR, 1950

sch rep—SLR, 1950

No 2 **Episcopal Endowments and Stipends**

appl—GSM Care of Places of Worship, 1999 No 2, s 6(1)

s 1 rep in pt—SL(R), 2004 c 14, s 1(1), sch 1 pt 6/2(1)

s 3 excl—GSM Ecclesiastical Offices (Terms of Service), 2009 No 1, s 11(5)

s 4 ext—GSM Ecclesiastical Offices (Terms of Service), 2009 No 1, s 11(5)

s 5 subst—GSM C of E (Misc Provns), 2014 No 1, s 3

s 6 rep—CAM Episcopal Pensions, 1945 No 2, s 9(2)

s 8 rep in pt—SL(R), 2004 c 14, s 1(1), sch 1 pt 6/2(1)

No 3 *Diocesan Education Committees*—rep SL(R), 1986 c 12, s 1(1), sch 1 pt XIII

1944 (7 & 8 Geo 6)

No 1 *Reorganisation Areas*—rep (saving), CAM Pastoral, 1968 No 1, ss 94, 95, sch 8 paras 1, 7, sch 9

s 15 cont—GSM Pastoral, 1983 No 1, s 92, sch 8 para 4

1944 (8 & 9 Geo 6)

No 1 *Emergency Legislation*—rep SLR, 1964

1945 (8 & 9 Geo 6)

No 2 *Episcopal Pensions*—rep CAM Clergy Pensions, 1961 No 3, s 48(1), sch 3

No 3 *Incumbents (Disability)*—rep GSM Incumbents (Vacation of Benefices), 1977 No 1, s 20(2)

1946 (9 & 10 Geo 6)

No 1 **Ecclesiastical Commissioners (Curate Grants)**

s 1 rep in pt—GSM Endowments and Glebe, 1976 No 4, s 47(4), sch 8

1946 (9 & 10 Geo 6)

No 2   *Clergy Pensions (Supplementary Pensions)*—rep CAM Clergy Pensions 1948 No 1, s 63, sch 8

No 3   *Benefices (Suspension of Presentation)*—rep CAM Benefices (Suspension of Presentation), 1953 No 5, s 8

1947 (10 & 11 Geo 6)

No 1   *Incumbents' Discipline*—rep CAM Ecclesiastical Jurisdiction, 1963 No 1, s 87, sch 5

No 2   **Church Commissioners**

appl—CAM Pastoral, 1968 No 1, s 44(2); GSM Mission and Pastoral, 2011 No 3, s 56(3)

ext—GSM Pastoral, 1983 No 1, s 43(2)

s 1 rep in pt—Charities, 1960 c 58, s 48(2), sch 7 pt II

s 3 am—CAM Church Commnrs, 1964 No 8, s 2(1) (a)

s 4 rep in pt—CAM Church Commnrs, 1964 No 8, s 2(3); GSM Nat Institutions, 1998 No 1, s 7(1), sch 4 para 2

    am—GSM C of E (Misc Provns), 2014 No 1, sch 2 para 3(2)

s 5 am—CAM Church Commnrs, 1964 No 8, s 2(1) (b); GSM C of E (Misc Provns), 1992 No 1, s 17(1), sch 3, para 4; GSM Nat Institutions, 1998 No 1, s 7(1), sch 4 para 3; GSM C of E (Misc Provns), 2014 No 1, sch 2 para 3(3)

    rep in pt—GSM Nat Institutions, 1998 No 1, s 7(1), sch 4 para 3

s 6 am—CAM Church Commnrs, 1964 No 8, s 1; CAM Church Commnrs, 1970 No 3, s 1; GSM C of E (Misc Provns), 1995 No 2, s 6; GSM Pensions, 1997 No 1, s 10(1), sch 1 pt I para 2; GSM Nat Institutions, 1998 No 1, s 7(1), sch 4 para 4; GSM C of E (Misc Provns), 2005 No 3, s 2(a)(b); GSM C of E (Misc Provns), 2010 No 1, s 2; GSM C of E (Misc Provns), 2014 No 1, sch 2 para 3(4)(b)-(e)

    rep in pt—GSM Nat Institutions, 1998 No 1, s 7(1), sch 4 para 4

    mod—GSM C of E (Misc Provns), 2014 No 1, para 3(4)(a)

s 6A added—GSM C of E (Misc Provns), 2014 No 1, s 4(1)

s 7 am—CAM Church Commnrs, 1964 No 8, s 2(1) (c); GSM Nat Institutions, 1998 No 1, s 7(1), sch 4 para 5

s 8 rep in pt—Charities, 1960 c 58, s 48(2), sch 7 pt I; CAM Church Commnrs, 1964 No 8, s 2(3)

s 9 subst—GSM C of E (Misc Provns), 2006 No 1, s 2, sch 2 para 2

    am—GSM C of E (Misc Provns), 2014 No 1, sch 2 para 3(5)

s 10 am—GSM C of E (Misc Provns), 1978 No 3, s 3(1); GSM Pensions 1997 No 1, s 10(1), sch 1 pt I para 3; GSM Nat Institutions, 1998 No 1, s 7(1), sch 4 para 6

    rep in pt—GSM Nat Institutions, 1998 No 1, s 13(2)

s 11 rep in pt—GSM C of E (Misc Provns), 2005 No 3, s 2(c)

s 12 trans of functions—SI 2001/3500, arts 3, 4(1)(c)(3)–(8), sch 1, para 9

    am—SI 2001/3500, art 8, sch 2 pt II, para 11

s 15 rep in pt—SLR, 1966; SL(R), 2004 c 14, s 1(1), sch 1 pt 6/2(1)

s 16 rep—SLR, 1966

s 17 expld—CAM Church Property (Misc Provns), 1960 No 1, s 18

    am—CAM Church Commnrs, 1964 No 8, s 2(1) (d); Superannuation, 1972 c 11, s 29(1), sch 6 paras 21, 22;GSM Nat Institutions, 1998 No 1, s 7(1), sch 4 para 7

    rep in pt—SL(R), 2004 c 14, s 1(1), sch 1 pt 6/2(1)

s 18 rep in pt—GSM C of E (Misc Provns), 2006 No 1, s 2, sch 2 para 3

sch 1 power to am—GSM Nat Institutions, 1998 No 1, s 5(2)

    am—GSM C of E (Misc Provns), 1978 No 3, s 4; GSM C of E (Misc Provns), 1992 No 1, s 17(1), sch 3, para 5; GSM Nat Institutions, 1998 No 1, sch 4 para 8; SI 2003/2922, art 3; GSM C of E (Misc Provns), 2006 No 1, s 2, sch 2 para 4; SI 2006/164, art 3, sch 1; SI 2007/2128 sch para 1; GSM C of E (Misc Provns), 2014 No 1, sch 2 para 3(6)(a)(7)(8)

    rep in pt—GSM C of E (Misc Provns), 2006 No 1, s 2, sch 2 para 4; GSM C of E (Misc Provns), 2014 No 1, sch 2 para 3(6)(b)

sch 2 rep—GSM Nat Institutions, 1998 No 1, s 13(2)

sch 3 rep—CAM Church Commnrs, 1964 No 8, s 2(3)

sch 4 am—CAM Church Commnrs, 1964 No 8, s 2(1) (e)(f); GSM Nat Institutions, 1998 No 1, s 7(1), sch 4 para 9; GSM C of E (Misc Provns), 2014 No 1, sch 2 para 3(9)

    rep in pt—CAM Church Commnrs, 1964 No 8, s 2(1)(f); GSM Nat Institutions, 1998 No 1, s 7(1), sch 4 para 9

No 3   **Parsonages (Amendment)**

s 1 am—GSM Patronage (Benefices), 1986 No 3, s 41, sch 4 para 10

1948 (11 & 12 Geo 6)

No 1   *Clergy Pensions*—rep CAM Clergy Pensions, 1961 No 3, s 48(1), sch 3

1949 (12, 13 & 14 Geo 6)

No 1   **Church Dignitaries (Retirement)**
        appl—GSM Ecclesiastical Offices (Terms of Service), 2009 No 1, s 3(7)
        s 3 rep in pt—CAM Clergy Pensions, 1961 No 3, s 47, sch 2
           am—CAM Clergy Pensions, 1961 No 3, s 47, sch 2
        Pt II (ss 4-11) rep—CAM Ecclesiastical Jurisdiction, 1963 No 1, s 87, sch 5
        s 13 rep in pt—CAM Ecclesiastical Jurisdiction, 1963 No 1, s 87, sch 5
        s 14 subst—GSM Incumbents (Vacation of Benefices), 1977 No 1, s 20(1)
        s 18 rep in pt—CAM Ecclesiastical Jurisdiction, 1963 No 1, s 87, sch 5
No 2   *Parochial Church Councils (Powers) (Amendment)*—rep CAM Parochial Church Councils
        (Powers), 1956 No 3, s 10(4)
No 3   *Pastoral Reorganisation*—rep (saving) CAM Pastoral, 1968 No 1, ss 94, 95, sch 8 paras 1, 9,
        14, sch 9
No 4   *Benefices (Suspension of Presentation), 1945(Amendment)*—rep CAM Benefices
        (Suspension of Presentation), 1953 No 5, s 8
No 5   *Reorganisation Areas, 1944 (Amendment)*—rep CAM Reorganisation Areas, 1944 (Amdt),
        1954 No 2, s 4

1950 (14 Geo 6)

No 1   *Incumbents (Discipline), 1947 (Amendment)*—rep CAM Ecclesiastical Jurisdiction, 1965
        No 1, s 87, sch 5

1951 (14 & 15 Geo 6)

No 1   *Diocesan Education Committee 1943 (Amendment)*—rep CAM Diocesan Education
        Committees, 1955 (4-5 Eliz 2 No 1, s 4(1)
No 2   *Bishops (Retirement)*—rep GSM Bishops (Retirement), 1986 No 1, s 12(2) sch
No 3   *Ecclesiastical Dilapidations Measures 1923 to 1929 (Amendment)*—rep GSM Repair of
        Benefice Buildings, 1972 No 2, s 35, sch 2
No 4   *Cathedrals (Appointed Commissioners)*—rep CAM Cathedrals, 1963 No 2, s 54(1), sch 2
No 5   *Benefices (Stabilization of Incomes)*—rep GSM Endowments and Glebe 1976 No 4, s 47(4),
        sch 8

1952 (1 & 2 Eliz 2)

No 1   *Union of Benefices (Disused Churches)*—rep CAM Pastoral 1968 No 1, s 95, sch 9

1952 (15 & 16 Geo 6 & 1 Eliz 2)

No 1   *Church of England Pensions Board (Powers)*—rep CAM Clergy Pensions 1961 No 3,
        s 48(1), sch 3

1953 (1 & 2 Eliz 2)

No 2   **Diocesan Stipends Funds**
        s 1 trans of functions—GSM C of E (Misc Provns), 2000 No 1, s 1(1)(a)
           subst—GSM C of E (Misc Provns), 2000 No 1, s 4, sch 1, para 2
        s 2 am & rep in pt—GSM C of E (Misc Provns), 2000 No 1, ss 4, 20, sch 2, para 3, sch 8
           pt I
           am—GSM Endowments and Glebe, 1976 No 4, s 35(1)
           rep in pt—GSM Endowments and Glebe, 1976 No 4, s 47(4), sch 8; GSM C of E (Misc
           Provns) 2000 No 1, s 20, sch 8 pt I
        s 3 rep in pt—GSM C of E (Misc Provns) 2000 No 1, s 20, sch 8 pt I
        s 4 subst—GSM Endowments and Glebe, 1976 No 4, s 35(2)
           restr—GSM Endowments and Glebe, 1976 No 4, s 37(2)
           am—GSM C of E (Misc Provns), 1992 No 1, s 17(1), sch 3, para 6; GSM C of E (Misc
           Provns), 2000 No 1, s 4, sch 2, para 4; Trustee Act, 2000 c 29, s 40(1), sch 2 pt III,
           para 51; GSM C of E (Misc Provns), 2006 No 1, s 3(2)(a)
           rep in pt—GSM C of E (Misc Provns), 2006 No 1, s 3(2)(b)
        s 5 subst—GSM Endowments and Glebe, 1976 No 4, s 9
           restr—GSM Endowments and Glebe, 1976 No 4, s 37(2)
           am—GSM C of E (Misc Provns), 1992 No 1, s 17(1), sch 3, para 7; GSM C of E (Misc
           Provns), 2000 No 1, s 4, sch 2, para 5; GSM C of E (Misc Provns), 2006 No 1, s
           3(3)

1953 (1 & 2 Eliz 2)
No 2 *continued*
    s 6 rep—CAM Pastoral, 1968 No 1, s 95, sch 9
    s 7 rep—GSM C of E (Misc Provns), 2005 No 3, s 3
    s 8 rep in pt—GSM C of E (Misc Provns), 1976 No 3, s 3(9), sch pt II
        am—GSM C of E (Misc Provns), 1992 No 1, s 17(1), sch 3, para 8
    s 10 rep—SL(R), 2004 c 14, s 1(1), sch 1 pt 6/2(2)
    s 11 rep in pt—SL(R), 2004 c 14, s 1(1), sch 1 pt 6/2(2)
No 3   *Incumbents (Discipline) and Church Dignitaries (Retirement) Amendment*—rep CAM
        Ecclesiastical Jurisdiction, 1963 No 1, s 87, sch 5
No 4   *Archdeaconries (Augmentation)*—rep GSM Endowments and Glebe, 1976 No 4, s 47(4),
        sch 8
No 5   *Benefices (Suspension of Presentation)*—rep (saving), CAM Pastoral, 1968 No 1, ss 94, 95,
        sch 8 para 9(c), sch 9

1954 (2 & 3 Eliz 2)
No 1   **New Housing Areas (Church Buildings)**
    s 1 excl—Sharing of Church Buildings, 1969 c 38, s 3(3)
        am—GSM Sharing of Church Buildings 1970 No 2, s 2(1); GSM Church
            Commissioners (Assistance for Priority Areas), 1988 No 2, s 1(1)(2)
        rep in pt—GSM Church Commissioners (Assistance for Priority Areas), 1988 No 2,
            s 1(1)(b) (2)
        appl—GSM Church Commissioners (Assistance for Priority Areas), 1988 No 2, s 2(2)
    s 2 rep—SL(R), 2004 c 14, s 1(1), sch 1 pt 6/2(1)
No 2   *Reorganisation Areas Measure, 1944 (Amendment)*—rep CAM Pastoral, 1968 No 1, s 95,
        sch 9
No 3   *Cathedrals (Grants)*—rep CAM Cathedrals, 1963 No 2, s 54(1), sch 2
No 4   *Clergy Pensions*—rep CAM Clergy Pensions, 1961 No 3, s 48(1), sch 3

1955 (3 & 4 Eliz 2)
No 1   **Inspection of Churches**
        am—GSM Care of Churches and Ecclesiastical Jurisdiction, 1991 No 1, s 3, sch 3, para 5(b)
        appl—GSM Faculty Jurisdiction, 1964 No 5, s 3
        excl—GSM Mission and Pastoral, 2011 No 3, s 61(3)
    s 1 am—GSM Care of Churches and Ecclesiastical Jurisdiction, 1991 No 1, s 3, sch 3,
        para 2
    ss 1A,1B added—GSM Care of Churches and Ecclesiastical Jurisdiction, 1991 No 1, s 3,
        sch 3 para 3
    s 2 am—GSM Care of Churches and Ecclesiastical Jurisdiction, 1991 No 1, s 3, sch 3 para 4
    s 6 am—GSM Care of Churches and Ecclesiastical Jurisdiction, 1991 No 1, s 3, sch 3,
        para 5; Architects, 1997 c 22, s 26(a)

1956 (4 & 5 Eliz 2)
No 1   *Diocesan Education Committees*—rep GSM Diocesan Bds of Education 1991 No 2, s 11(2)
No 2   *Representation of the Laity*—rep (saving) CAM Synodical Govt 1969 No 2, s 7(3)
No 3   **Parochial Church Councils (Powers)**
        mod—CAM Cathedrals, 1963 No 2, s 12(4); (savings) Cathedrals, 1999 No 1, ss 12(5),
            38(2)(3)
    s 1 appl—GSM Dioceses, 1978 No 1, s 3, sch para 15 (3)
    s 2 subst—CAM Synodical Govt, 1969 No 2, s 6
        am—GSM C of E (Misc Provns), 1983 No 2, s 5
    s 3A added—GSM C of E (Misc Provns), 2014 No 1, s 5(2)
    s 4 appl—CAM Pastoral, 1968 No 1, s 41, sch 3 para 12(4)
        ext—GSM Pastoral 1983 No 1, ss 20-22, 24, 27, 29, 31, 32, 40, sch 3 para 12(4)
        see (powers cont)—GSM Mission and Pastoral, 2011 No 3, sch 3 para 10(4)
    s 6 ext—GSM Endowments and Glebe, 1976 No 4, s 23(3)
        appl—GSM C of E (Misc Provns), 1992 No 1, s 10(3)
        excl—GSM C of E (Misc Provns), 1992 No 1, s 10(2); (retrosp) ibid s 10(1)
        excl in pt—SI 2015/1545, art 2(1)
        am—GSM Team and Group Ministries, 1995 No 1, s 9; GSM Ecclesiastical Property,
            2015 No 2, s 1(2)(3),(5)(6)
        rep in pt—Charities, 2006 c 50, s 75, sch 8 para 38; GSM Ecclesiastical Property, 2015
            No 2, s 1(4)
    s 6A added—GSM Ecclesiastical Property, 2015 No 2, s 1(7)

1956 (4 & 5 Eliz 2)
No 3 *continued*
    s 7 rep in pt—GSM C of E (Legal Aid and Misc Provns), 1988 No 1, ss 13, 14, sch 3
       am—GSM C of E (Misc Provns), 2014 No 1, s 5(3)
    s 8 subst—GSM C of E (Misc Provns), 2005 No 3, s 4

1957 (5 & 6 Eliz 2)
No 1   **Channel Islands (Church Legislation) Measure, 1931 Amendment**
    appl—GSMC of E (Misc Provns) 1992 No 1, s 19(4); GSM Priests (Ordination of Women)
       1993 No 2, s 12(4); (Ordination of Women (Financial Provns) 1993 No 3, s 13(2)

1958 (6 & 7 Eliz 2)
No 1   **Church Funds Investment**
    s 2 am—Charities, 2006 c 50, s 75, sch 8 para 40, sch 9
       rep in pt—GSM C of E (Misc Provns), 2010 No 1, s 3
    s 5 rep—GSM C of E (Misc Provns), 2006 No 1, s 4
    s 7 rep—Govt Trading, 1990 c 30, s 4(2), sch 2 pt I
    sch appl—CAM Pastoral, 1968 No 1, s 45(6); SI 1979/1204
       am—GSM C of E (Misc Provns) 1995 No 2, s 7, sch paras 2-13; GSM C of E (Misc
          Provns), 2000 No 1, s 14(2)(3)(5); Trustee, 2000 c 29, s 40(1), sch 2 pt III,
          para 52
       rep in pt—GSM C of E (Misc Provns), 2000 No 1, s 14(4)
No 2   *Church Schools (Assistance by Church Commissioners)*—rep GSM C of E (Misc Provns),
       2000 No 1, s 20, sch 8 pt I

1959 (7 & 8 Eliz 2)
No 1   **Truro Cathedral**
    s 2 rep in pt —(savings) Cathedrals, 1999 No 1, ss 38(3), 39(2), sch 3
    s 7 rep—(savings) CAM Cathedrals, 1963 No 2, s 54(1),'sch 2; (saving) Cathedrals 1999
       No 1 ss 38(3), 39(2), sch 3
    ss 8,9 rep—(savings) CAM Cathedrals, 1963 No 2, s 54(1), sch 2
No 2   **Vacancies in Sees**
    s 1 rep—GSM Patronage (Benefices), 1986 No 3, s 41, sch 5
    s 2 rep—GSM C of E (Misc Provns) 1992 (No 1, s 17(2), sch 4, pt I
    s 3 rep—GSM C of E (Misc Provns), 1976 No 3, s 3(9), sch pt II
    s 4 rep—GSM Endowments and Glebe, 1976 No 4, s 47(4), sch 8
    s 6 rep—CAM Cathedrals, 1963 No 2, s 54(1), sch 2
    s 7 rep—GSM Endowments and Glebe, 1976 No 4, s 47(4), sch 8
    s 8 rep—CAM Ecclesiastical Fees, 1962 No 1, s 8(2), sch pt II
    sch rep—GSM Patronage (Benefices), 1986 No 3, s 41, sch 5
No 3   **Guildford Cathedral**
    ss 1, 2-8 rep—CAM Cathedrals, 1963 No 2, s 54(1), sch 2
    s 9 rep in pt—CAM Cathedrals, 1963 No 2, s 54(1), sch 2
    s 10 rep—CAM Cathedrals, 1963 No 2, s 54(1), sch 2

1960 (8 & 9 Eliz 2)
No 1   **Church Property (Miscellaneous Provisions)**
    s 3 rep in pt—GSM Patronage (Benefices), 1986 No 3, s 41, sch 5
    s 7 am—GSM C of E (Legal Aid and Misc Provns), 1988 No 1, s 9; GSM C of E (Misc
       Provns), 2000 No 1, s 5, sch 3, para 2; GSM C of E (Misc Provns), 2006 No 1, s 5
    s 8 am—GSM C of E (Misc Provns), 2000 No 1, s 5, sch 3, para 3; GSM C of E (Misc
       Provns), 2010 No 1, s 12(2)
    s 9 am—GSM Patronage (Benefices), 1986 No 3, s 34(2) (b); GSM C of E (Misc Provns),
       2000 No 1, s 5, sch 3, para 4(b)
       rep in pt—GSM Patronage (Benefices), 1986 No 3, s 41, sch 5; GSM C of E (Misc
          Provns), 2000 No 1, s 5, sch 3, para 4(a)
    s 10 am—GSM C of E (Misc Provns), 2000 No 1, s 5, sch 3, para 5
    s 11 rep in pt—GSM Patronage (Benefices), 1986 No 3, s 41, sch 5; GSM C of E (Misc
       Provns), 2000 No 1, s 5, sch 3, para 6(a)
       am—GSM C of E (Misc Provns), 2000 No 1, s 5, sch 3, para 6(a)(b)
    s 12 rep—GSM C of E (Misc Provns), 2000 No 1, s 20, sch 8 pt I
    ss 13,14 rep—GSM Endowments and Glebe 1976 No 4, s 47(4), sch 8
    s 15 rep—SL(R), 2004 c 14, s 1(1), sch 1 pt 6/2(2)
    s 16 rep—GSM C of E (Misc Provns), 2000 No 1, s 20, sch 8 pt I

1960 (8 & 9 Eliz 2)

No 1 *continued*

s 17 am—GSM C of E (Misc Provns), 2000 No 1, s 5, sch 3, para 7

s 18 rep in pt—SL(R), 2004 c 14, s 1(1), sch 1 pt 6/2(2)

s 19 rep in pt—SLR, 1964

s 20 am—GSM Church Commissioners (Misc Provns), 1975 No 1, s 2; GSM C of E (Misc Provns), 2005 No 3, s 5(1)(2)(4)–(7); SIs 2005/3325, arts 78, 79; 2014/3061, Sch 3 para 1

    rep in pt—GSM C of E (Misc Provns), 2005 No 3, ss 5(1)(3)(7), 10, sch 5

s 21 rep—GSM C of E (Misc Provns), 2000 No 1, s 20, sch 8 pt I

s 22 rep—SL(R), 2004 c 14, s 1(1), sch 1 pt 6/2(2)

s 23 rep—Charities, 1960 c 58, s 48(2), sch 7 pt II

s 24 rep in pt—SL(R), 2004 c 14, s 1(1), sch 1 pt 6/2(2)

s 25 am—GSM C of E (Misc Provns), 2000 No 1, s 5, sch 3, para 8

s 26 rep—GSM C of E (Misc Provns), 1976 No 3, s 3(9), sch pt II

s 27 am—GSM C of E (Misc Provns), 2000 No 1, s 5, sch 3, para 9

1961 (9 & 10 Eliz 2)

No 1   **Farnham Castle**

    ss 1-3 rep in pt—GSM C of E (Misc Provns), 2006 No 1, s 6

No 2   **Baptismal Registers**

    ss 1, 3 am—GSM Parochial Registers and Records 1978, No 2, s 26(1), sch 3 paras 5, 6

No 3   **Clergy Pensions**

    power to am—GSM Clergy Pensions (Amdt), 1972 No 5, s 6

    power to cont certain provns—Social Security (Consequential provns), 1992 c 6, s 5, sch 3, pt II, para 15

    ext—GSM Diocese in Europe, 1980 No 2, s 5(1)

    appl—GSM Pastoral, 1983 No 1, s 26, sch 4 para 13

    mod—GSM Pastoral, 1983 No 1, s 26, sch 4 para 13

    constr with—GSM Pensions, 1997 No 1, s 9(3)

    saved—GSM Nat Institutions, 1998 No 1, s 5(1)

    Pt I (ss 1-9) rep—SI 1988/2265

    Pt II (ss 10-16) rep—SI 1988/2265

    Pt III (ss 17-34) ext—GSM Deacons (Ordination of Women) 1986 No 4, s 3(1)

    s 17 am—GSM Clergy Pensions (Amdt) 1982 No 2, s 1; GSM C of E (Pensions), 1988 No 4, s 11; GSM Pensions, 1997 No 1, s 10(1), sch 1 pt I para 5; SI 2005/3325, arts 80, 81(1)

    s 18 am—GSM C of E (Pensions), 1988 No 4, s 18(1), sch 2 pt I para 7(a)(b)

        rep in pt—GSM C of E (Legal Aid and Misc Provns) 1988 No 1, s 12(a)

    ss 19, 20 rep—GSM C of E (Pensions), 2003 No 2, s 6, sch

    s 21 am—GSM C of E (Pensions), 1988 No 4, s 18(1), sch 2 pt I para 9; GSM C of E (Misc Provns), 1995 No 2, s 8(b);GSM Pensions, 1997 No 1, ss 8(1),10(1), sch 1 pt I para 6; GSM C of E (Misc Provns), 2010 No 1, s 4; GSM C of E (Misc Provns), 2014 No 1, sch 2 para 4(2)

        rep in pt—GSM C of E (Pensions), 1988 No 4, s 18(1), sch 2; GSM C of E (Misc Provns), 1995 No 2, s 8, GSM Pensions,1997 No 1 s 10(2), sch 2 pt I

    s 21 trans of functions—SI 1998/1751, art 2, sch 1

    s 22 am—GSM Pensions, 1997 No 1, s 10(1), sch 1 pt I para 7

    s 23 rep—GSM Pensions, 1997 No 1, s 10(2), sch 2 pt I

    s 24 am—GSM C of E (Pensions), 1988 No 4, s 18(1) sch 2 pt I para 10; GSM Pensions, 1997 No 1, s 10(1), sch 1 pt I para 8

    s 25 am—GSM Pensions, 1997 No 1, s 10(1), sch 1 pt I para 9

    s 26 am—CAM Clergy Pensions (Amdt), 1967 No 1, s 4(1); GSM Clergy Pensions (Amdt), 1982 No 2, s 2(1); GSM Deacons (Ordination of Women), 1986 No 4, s 3(3) para 3; GSM C of E (Pensions), 1988 No 4, s 12(1) (a) (2) (3); GSM C of E (Pensions), 2003 No 2, s 3; SI 2005/3325, arts 80, 81(2)(3)

        ext—CAM Clergy Pensions (Amdt), 1967 No 1, s 4(4)

        rep in pt—GSM C of E (Pensions) 1988 No 4, ss 12(1)(b),18(2), sch 3; GSM C of E (Pensions), 2003 No 2, s 6, sch

        mod—GSM Ordination of Women (Financial Provns) 1993 No 3, s 2

    s 27 am—GSM Clergy Pensions (Amdt), 1982 No 2, s 3; GSM C of E (Pensions), 1988 No 4, s 13; SI 2005/3325, arts 80, 81(2)(3)

    s 28 am—CAM Clergy Pensions (Amdt), 1967 No 1, s 4(2) (3); GSM Clergy Pensions (Amdt), 1982 No 2, s 2(2); GSM C of E (Pensions), 1988 No 4, s 18(1), sch 2 pt I para 11

1961 (9 & 10 Eliz 2)
No 3 s 28 *continued*

      ext—CAM Clergy Pensions (Amdt), 1967 No 1, s 4(4)
  s 29 am—GSM C of E (Pensions) 1988 No 4 s 18(1) sch 2 pt I para 12
  s 30 am—GSM C of E (Pensions), 1988 No 4, s 18(1), sch 2 pt I para 13; SI 2005/3325,
          arts 80, 81(4)
  s 32 am—GSM Clergy Pensions (Amdt), 1982 No 2, s 4; Financial Services, 1986 c 60, s
          212(2), sch 16 para 3; GSM C of E (Pensions), 1988 No 4, s 14; Trustee, 2000 c
          29, s 40(1), sch 2 pt III, para 53(1); GSM C of E (Misc Provns), 2014 No 1, s
          4(2)
      rep in pt—GSM C of E (Pensions), 1988 No 4, s 18(2), sch 3; Trustee, 2000 c 29,
            s 40(1)(3), sch 2 pt III, para 53(2), sch 4 pt II
  s 32A added—GSM Clergy Pensions (Amdt), 1982 No 2, s 5
  s 33 rep—GSM Pensions 1997 No1, s 10(2), sch 2 pt I
  s 34 am—GSM Clergy Pensions (Amdt), 1972 No 5, s 5(3); GSM C of E (Pensions), 1988
          No 4, s 18(1), sch 2 pt I para 14; GSM Pensions, 1997 No 1, s 10(1), sch 1 pt I
          para 10
      rep in pt—GSM C of E (Legal Aid and Misc Provns) 1988 No 1, s 12(b); GSM
            Pensions 1997 No1, s 10(1), sch 1 pt I para 10
  Pt IV (ss 35-50) ext—GSM Deacons (Ordination of Women) 1986 No 4, s 3(1)
  ss 35-37 rep—SI 1988/2256
  s 38 am—GSM C of E (Pensions), 1988 No 4, s 18(1), sch 2 para 16; Arbitration, 1996
          c 23, s 107(1), sch 3 para 15; SI 2005/3325, arts 80, 81(5)(6)
  s 38A added—SI 1988/2239
      am—GSM Pensions, 1997 No 1, s 10(1), sch 1 pt I para 11; SI 2005/3325, arts 80,
          81(5)(6)
  s 39 rep—GSM C of E (Pensions), 1988 No 4, s 18(2), sch 3
  s 40 am—GSM C of E (Pensions), 1988 No 4, s 18(1), sch 2 pt I para 17(2); SI 2005/3325,
          arts 80, 81(7)
  s 40A rep—GSM Pensions 1997 No 1, s 10(2), sch 2 pt I
  ss 41, 42 rep—SI 1988/2256
  ss 42A-42C added—GSM C of E (Pensions), 1988 No 4, s 15
  s 44 am—GSM Clergy Pensions (Amdt) 1972 No 5, s 5(4); SI 1988/2256; GSM Pensions,
          1997 No 1, s 10(1), sch 1 pt I para 12
  s 45 rep—SI 1988/2256
  s 46 am—(retrosp) SI 1977/1146; GSM Deacons (Ordination of Women), 1986 No 4, s
          3(2) (3); GSM C of E (Pensions), 1988 No 4, s 18(1), sch 2 pt I para 20; SI
          1988/2256; GSM Pensions, 1997 No 1, s 10(1), sch 1 pt I para 13; GSM C of E
          (Misc Provns), 2014 No 1, sch 2 para 4(3); SI 2014/3061, sch 3 para 2
      rep in pt— GSM Pensions, 1997 No 1, s 10(2) pt I
  s 48 rep in pt—SL(R), 1977 c 18, s 1(1), sch 1 pt V; SI 1988/2256
  sch 1 rep—SI 1988/2256
  sch 2 rep in pt—SL (Reps) 1977 c 18, s 1(1), sch 1 pt V; GSM Bishops (Retirement), 1986
          No 1, s 12(2), sch
  sch 3 rep—SI 1988/2256

1962 (10 & 11 Eliz 2)

No 1   *Ecclesiastical Fees*—rep GSM Ecclesiastical Fees 1986 No 2, s 11(1)
          excl—GSM Bishops (Retirement), 1986 No 2, s 9
          appl—GSM Bishops (Retirement), 1986 No 2, s 9

1963

No 1   **Ecclesiastical Jurisdiction**
          appl—CAM Pastoral, 1968 No 1, s 19(8); GSM Mission and Pastoral, 2011 No 3, s 34(9)
          expld—CAM Synodical Govt, 1969 No 2, s 3(6)
          ext—GSM Priests (Ordination of Women), 1993 No 2, s 5
          s 1 rep in pt —GSM Clergy Discipline, 2003 No 3, s 46, sch 2
           am —GSM Clergy Discipline, 2003 No 3, s 44(2), sch 1 paras 1, 2
          s 2 rep in pt—GSM C of E (Worship,etc), 1974 No 3, s 6(3), sch 2; GSM C of E (Misc
               Provns), 1992 No 1, s 17(2) sch 4, pt II; GSM C of E (Misc Provns), 1995
               No 2, s 9
           am—GSM Ecclesiastical Judges and Legal Officers 1976 No 2, s 1(1); Cts and Legal
               Services, 1990 c 41, s 71(2), sch 10 para 17; GSM Care of Churches and
               Ecclesiastical Jurisdiction, 1991 No 1, s 8, sch 4 para 2; GSM C of E (Misc
               Provns), 2006 No 1, s 7(2); (spec retrosp effect) GSM C of E (Misc Provns), 2010

1963

No 1 s 2 *continued*

No 1, s 5(1); GSM C of E (Misc Provns), 2014 No 1, s 6(2); GSM Care of Churches and Ecclesiastical Jurisdiction (Amdt), 2015 No 1, s 9(1)(2)

s 2A added—GSM Ecclesiastical Judges and Legal Officers1976 No 2, s 2

s 3 rep in pt—GSM C of E (Worship, etc), 1974 No 3, s 6(3), sch 2; GSM C of E (Misc Provns), 1995 No 2, s 9; GSM Clergy Discipline (Amdt), 2013 No. 2, s 9(2)(4)

am—GSM Ecclesiastical Judges and Legal Officers, 1976 No 2, s 1(2); Cts and Legal Services, 1990 c 41, s 71(2), sch 10 para 18(1); GSM Care of Churches and Ecclesiastical Jurisdiction, 1991 No 1, s 8, sch 4 para 3; GSM Clergy Discipline, 2003 No 3, s 44(2), sch 1 paras 1, 4; GSM Clergy Discipline (Amdt), 2013 No. 2, s 9(2)(3)(5)(6); GSM C of E (Misc Provns), 2014 No 1, s 6(3)

s 4 rep in pt—GSM C of E (Worship, etc), 1974 No 3, s 6(3), sch 2; GSM C of E (Misc Provns), 2006 No 1, s 7(4)

am—GSM Care of Churches and Ecclesiastical Jurisdiction, 1991 No 1, s 8, sch 4 para 4(c); GSM C of E (Misc Provns), 2006 No 1, s 7(4)(5)

s 6 rep in pt—GSM Repair of Benefice Buildings 1972 No 2, s 35, sch 2; GSM Clergy Discipline, 2003 No 3, s 46, sch 2; SL(R), 2004 c 14, s 1(1), sch 1 pt 6/1

am—GSM Care of Churches and Ecclesiastical Jurisdiction, 1991 No 1, s 8, sch 4 para 5

excl—SIs 2009/1300, art 5(10); 2015/2044, art 5

s 7 am—GSM Care of Churches and Ecclesiastical Jurisdiction, 1991 No 1, s 8, sch 4 para 6; GSM Care of Cathedrals (Supplementary Provns), 1994 No 2, s 8 Sch, para 2(a)(b); GSM Clergy Discipline (Amdt), 2013 No. 2, s 9(2)(7); GSM Care of Churches and Ecclesiastical Jurisdiction (Amdt), 2015 No 1, ss 7(1), 8

rep in pt—GSM Clergy Discipline, 2003 No 3, s 46, sch 2; GSM Care of Churches and Ecclesiastical Jurisdiction (Amdt), 2015 No 1, s 7(2)

s 8 am—GSM C of E (Misc Provns), 2000 No 1, s 15; GSM Care of Churches and Ecclesiastical Jurisdiction (Amdt), 2015 No 1, s 7(3)

s 9 rep —GSM Clergy Discipline, 2003 No 3, s 46, sch 2

s 10 am—GSM Care of Churches and Ecclesiastical Jurisdiction, 1991 No 1, s 8, sch 4 para 7; GSM Care of Churches and Ecclesiastical Jurisdiction (Amdt), 2015 No 1, s 7(4),(6)(c),(8)(b)

rep in pt—GSM Care of Churches and Ecclesiastical Jurisdiction (Amdt), 2015 No 1, s 7(5)(6)(a)(b),(7),(8)(a)

s 11 rep in pt —GSM Clergy Discipline, 2003 No 3, s 46, sch 2

am—Constitutional Reform, 2005 c 4, s 145, sch 17 pt 2 para 16(1)(2)

s 12 am—GSM Clergy Discipline, 2003 No 3, s 44(2), sch 1 paras 1, 5

ss 14-16 rep in pt —GSM Clergy Discipline, 2003 No 3, s 46, sch 2

Pts IV,V (ss 22-37) rep—GSM Clergy Discipline, 2003 No 3, s 46, sch 2

s 27 rep in pt—GSM C of E (Worship, etc), 1974 No 3, s 6(3), sch 2; GSM C of E (Misc Provns), 1995 No 2, s 9

s 33 am—Cts and Legal Services, 1990 c 41, s 71(2), sch 10 para 19

s 43 am—Cts and Legal Services, 1990 c 41, s 71(2), sch 10 para 18(2)

s 46 rep in pt —GSM Clergy Discipline, 2003 No 3, s 46, sch 2

mod—GSM Care of Places of Worship, 1999 No 2, s 3(3)

s 47 am—GSM Care of Churches and Ecclesiastical Jurisdiction, 1991 No 1, s 8, sch 4, para 8; GSM Clergy Discipline, 2003 No 3, s 44(2), sch 1 paras 1, 6; GSM Care of Churches and Ecclesiastical Jurisdiction (Amdt), 2015 No 1, s 10

s 49 am—GSM Clergy Discipline, 2003 No 3, s 44(2), sch 1 paras 1, 7

s 50 am—GSM Clergy Discipline, 2003 No 3, s 44(2), sch 1 paras 1, 8

s 52 am—GSM Clergy Discipline, 2003 No 3, s 44(2), sch 1 paras 1, 9

s 54 rep—GSM Clergy Discipline, 2003 No 3, s 46, sch 2

Pt IX (ss 55-57) rep—GSM Clergy Discipline, 2003 No 3, s 46, sch 2

s 55 subst—GSM Ecclesiastical Jurisdiction (Amdt), 1974 No 2, s 1

mod—GSM Ecclesiastical Jurisdiction (Amdt), 1974 No 2, s 2(4)

am—Supplementary Benefits, 1976 c 71, s 35(2), sch 7 para 4; GSM C of E (Misc Provns), 1992 No 1, ss 7(a) (ii) (iii), 17(1), sch 3, para 9

rep in pt—Supplementary Benefits, 1976 c 71, s 35(2), sch 7 para 4; Social Security, 1986 c 50, s 86, sch 10 pt II para 40; GSM C of E (Misc Provns), 1992 No 1, s 7(a)(i)(ii)

s 56 subst—GSM Ecclesiastical Jurisdiction (Amdt), 1974 No 2, s 1

am—GSM C of E (Misc Provns), 1992 No 1, s 7(b) (ii)

rep in pt—GSM C of E (Misc Provns), 1992 No 1, s 7(b(i)

s 57 am—GSM Ecclesiastical Jurisdiction (Amdt), 1974 No 2, s 2(1)

s 58 am—GSM Care of Cathedrals (Supplementary Provns), 1994 No 2, s 8, sch para 3

1963

No 1 s 58 *continued*

   saved—GSM Nat Institutions, 1998 No 1, s 5(1), sch 2 pt I

   appl (mods)—GSM Clergy Discipline, 2003 No 3, s 35

  s 59 rep—GSM C of E (Legal Aid and Misc Provns), 1988 No 1, s 14, sch 3

  s 60 am—GSM C of E (Legal Aid and Misc Provns), 1988 No 1, s 14, sch 2 para 1(a) (c);
    GSM Care of Churches and Ecclesiastical Jurisdiction, 1991 No 1, s 8, sch 4
    para 9; GSM Care of Cathedrals (Supplementary Provns), 1994 No 2, s 8, sch
    para 4; GSM C of E (Legal Aid), 1994 No 3, s 7(2), sch 2

   appl—SI 1990/2335

   appl (mods)—GSM Clergy Discipline, 2003 No 3, s 35

  s 61 appl—SI 1990/2335

   appl (mods)—GSM Clergy Discipline, 2003 No 3, s 35

  s 62 am—GSM Care of Cathedrals (Supplementary Provns), 1994 No 2, s 8, sch para 5; SI
    2007/1556, sch, para 2(a)

   appl (mods)—GSM Clergy Discipline, 2003 No 3, s 35

  s 63 am—GSM Ecclesiastical Fees 1986 No 2, s 11 (2); GSM Care of Cathedrals
    (Supplementary Provns), 1994 No 2, s 8, sch para 6

   appl (mods)—GSM Clergy Discipline, 2003 No 3, s 35

  s 64 rep—GSM Care of Churches and Ecclesiastical Jurisdiction, 1991 No 1, s 32(2), sch 8

  s 65 rep—GSM Care of Churches and Ecclesiastical Jurisdiction, 1991 No 1, s 32(2), sch 8

  s 66 am—GSM Care of Churches and Ecclesiastical Jurisdiction, 1991 No 1, s 8, sch 4
    para 10; GSM Clergy Discipline, 2003 No 3, s 44(2), sch 1 paras 1, 10;
    Constitutional Reform, 2005 c 4, s 145, sch 17 pt 2 para 16(1)(3); SI 2007/1556,
    sch, para 2(b)

  s 67 rep in pt —GSM Clergy Discipline, 2003 No 3, s 44(2), sch 1 paras 1,11

  s 69 rep in pt—GSM Clergy Discipline, 2003 No 3, s 46, sch 2

   am—GSM Clergy Discipline, 2003 No 3, s 44(2), sch 1 paras 1,12

  s 70 rep in pt—GSM Clergy Discipline, 2003 No 3, s 46, sch 2

  s 71 am—GSM Endowments and Glebe 1976 No 4, s 47(1), sch 5 para 2

   appl (mods)—GSM Clergy Discipline, 2003 No 3, s 35

  s 72 rep in pt—GSM Repair of Benefice Buildings, 1972 No 2, s 35, sch 2

   appl (mods)—GSM Clergy Discipline, 2003 No 3, s 35

  s 73 appl (mods)—GSM Clergy Discipline, 2003 No 3, s 35

  s 74 am—GSM Clergy Discipline, 2003 No 3, s 44(2), sch 1 paras 1, 13

   appl (mods)—GSM Clergy Discipline, 2003 No 3, s 35

  ss 75,76 appl (mods)—GSM Clergy Discipline, 2003 No 3, s 35

  s 77 rep—GSM Clergy Discipline, 2003 No 3, s 46, sch 2

  s 78 appl (mods)—GSM Clergy Discipline, 2003 No 3, s 35

  s 79 am—GSM Ecclesiastical Jurisdiction (Amdt), 1974 No 2, s 2(2)

  s 80 am—GSM Care of Cathedrals (Supplementary Provns), 1994 No 2, s 8, sch para 7

   appl (mods)—GSM Clergy Discipline, 2003 No 3, s 35

  s 81 am—GSM Care of Churches and Ecclesiastical Jurisdiction, 1991 No 1, s 8, sch 4,
    para 11; GSM Care of Cathedrals (Supplementary Provns), 1994 No 2, s 8, sch
    para 8

   appl (mods)—GSM Clergy Discipline, 2003 No 3, s 35

  s 82 rep—SL(R), 2004 c 14, s 1(1), sch 1 pt 6/1

  s 83 appl (mods)—GSM Clergy Discipline, 2003 No 3, s 35

  s 88 rep—SL(R), 2004 c 14, s 1(1), sch 1 pt 6/1

  sch 1 rep in pt—GSM C of E (Worship, etc), 1974 No 3, s 6(3), sch 2; GSM C of E (Misc
    Provns), 1995 No 2, s 9

  sch 2 rep—GSM Clergy Discipline, 2003 No 3, s 46, sch 2

   am—Cts and Legal Services, 1990 c 41, s 71(2), sch 10 para 20

  sch 3 rep—GSM Ecclesiastical Jurisdiction (Amdt), 1974 No 2, s 2(3)

  sch 4 rep in pt—SL(R), 1977 c 18, s 1(1), sch 1 pt V; SL(R), 2004 c 14, s 1(1), sch 1 pt 6/1

No 2 **Cathedrals**

  cont—(temp) GSM Cathedrals, 1999 No 1, s 38(3)

  am—GSM Cathedrals, 1976 No 1, s 8(1)

  appl (mods)—GSM Dioceses, 1978 No 1, s 22(1)

  appl—Admin of Justice, 1982 c 53, s 41(3); GSM Priests (Ordination of Women), 1993
    No 2, s 8; Leasehold Reform, Housing and Urban Development, 1993 c 28, ss 9, 40,
    61, sch 2 para 8(1) (a), sch 14, para 11(a)

  saved—GSM Nat Institutions, 1998 No 2, s 5(1), sch 2 pt II

  ss 1-38 rep—(savings) GSM Cathedrals, 1999 No 1, ss 38(3), 39(2), sch 3

  s 21 mod—Trustee, 2000 c 29, s 40(2), sch 3, para 8

1963

No 2 *continued*

s 39 am—GSM C of E (Misc Provns), 2000 No 1, s 6

s 40 am—(savings) GSM Cathedrals, 1999 No 1, ss 38(3), 39(1), sch 2 para 3

s 41 am—(savings) GSM Cathedrals, 1999 No 1, ss 38(3), 39(1), sch 2 para 4

s 42 am—GSM Cathedrals, 1976 No 1, s 7; GSM Cathedrals, 1999 No 1, s 38(3), 39(1), sch 2 para 5

s 43 subst—GSM C of E (Misc Provns), 2010 No 1, s 10(2)

s 44 am—GSM Cathedrals, 1999 No 1, ss 38(3), 39(1), sch 2 para 6

ss 45-51 rep—(savings) GSM Cathedrals, 1999 No 1, ss 38(3), 39(2), sch 3

s 52 rep in pt—GSM Cathedrals, 1976 No 1, s 8(2); GSM Cathedrals, 1999 No 1, ss 38(3), 39(2), sch 3

    appl—GSM Dioceses, 1978 No 1, s 22(1)

    am—Housing Grants, Construction and Regeneration, 1996 c 53, ss 118, 125, sch 2 pt II, para 19; Architects, 1997 c 22, s 26(b)

's 54 rep in pt—SL(R), 1977 c 18, s 1(1), sch 1 pt V

sch 1 rep in pt—SL(R), 1971; SL(R), 1977 c 18, s 1(1), sch 1 pt V

sch 2 rep—SL(R), 1977 c 18, s 1(1), sch 1 pt V

1964

No 1   **Church Commissioners (Loans for Theological Colleges and Training Houses)**

No 2   **Incumbents and Churchwardens (Trusts)**

s 1 am—Charities, 1993 c 10, s 98(1), sch 6 para 7; Charities, 2011 c 25, sch 7 para 13

    rep in pt—Trusts of Land and Appointment of Trustees, 1996 c 47, s 25(2), sch 4; GSM Ecclesiastical Property, 2015 No 2, s 2(2)

s 2 rep in pt—GSM Endowments and Glebe, 1976 No 4, s 47(4), sch 8

    am—Charities, 2006 c 50, s 75, sch 8 para 42; GSM Ecclesiastical Property, 2015 No 2, s 2(3)

s 3 am—Charities, 2006 c 50, s 75, sch 8 para 43; GSM Ecclesiastical Property, 2015 No 2, s 2(5)

    rep in pt—GSM Ecclesiastical Property, 2015 No 2, s 2(4)

s 4 excl—SI 2015/1545, art 2(2)

s 5 excl—SI 2015/1545, art 2(2)

    am—Charities, 2006 c 50, s 75, sch 8 para 44; GSM Ecclesiastical Property, 2015 No 2, s 2(6)(a)(b)

    rep in pt—GSM Ecclesiastical Property, 2015 No 2, s 2(6)(c)(d)

s 5A added—GSM Ecclesiastical Property, 2015 No 2, s 2(7)

sch 1 am—Charities, 2006 c 50, s 75, sch 8 para 45

    rep in pt—GSM Ecclesiastical Property, 2015 No 2, s 2(8)

No 3   *Churchwardens (Appointment and Resignation)*—rep (saving) (transtl provns) GSM Churchwardens, 2001 No 1, ss 9, 11, 15(2), sch 1, para 1, sch 3

No 4   *Holy Table*—rep GSM C of E (Worship, etc), 1974 No 3, s 6(3), sch 2

No 5   **Faculty Jurisdiction**

    am—GSM Care of Churches and Ecclesiastical Jurisdiction, 1991 No 1, s 32, sch 7

s 1 appl in pt (mods)—SI 2011/2866, sch 2

s 2 rep—GSM Care of Churches and Ecclesiastical Jurisdiction, 1991 No 1, s 32(2), sch 8

s 3 am—GSM C of E (Misc Provns), 2014 No 1, s 7

s 4 rep in pt—GSM Care of Churches and Ecclesiastical Jurisdiction, 1991 No 1, s 32(1) (2), sch 7 para 1, sch 8

    am—Charities, 2006 c 50, s 75, sch 8 para 46

s 5 rep—GSM Care of Churches and Ecclesiastical Jurisdiction, 1991 No 1, s 32(2), sch 8

s 6 saved—CAM Pastoral, 1968 No 1, s 29(2); GSM Pastoral, 1983 No 1, s 29(4)

    am—GSM Ecclesiastical Fees 1986 No 2, s 11(2); GSM Care of Churches and Ecclesiastical Jurisdiction, 1991 No 1, s 32(1), sch 7 para 2

s 7 excl—SIs 2009/1300, art 5(10); 2015/2044, art 5

s 9 rep—GSM Care of Churches and Ecclesiastical Jurisdiction, 1991 No 1, s 32(2) sch 8

s 10 rep—GSM Care of Churches and Ecclesiastical Jurisdiction, 1991 No 1, s 32(2), sch 8

s 11 appl—GSM Mission and Pastoral, 2011 No 3, s 68(12)

s 12 rep—GSM Care of Churches and Ecclesiastical Jurisdiction, 1991 No 1, s 32(2), sch 8

s 13 rep—GSM Care of Churches and Ecclesiastical Jurisdiction, 1991 No 1, ss 2(8), 32(2), sch 8

s 14 rep—GSM Care of Churches and Ecclesiastical Jurisdiction, 1991 No 1, s 32(2) sch 8

s 15 am—GSM Care of Churches and Ecclesiastical Jurisdiction, 1991 No 1, s 32, sch 7 para 3(a); GSM Dioceses, Pastoral and Mission, 2007 No 1, sch 7

1964

No 5 *continued*

s 24 am—(EW) Building, 1984 c 55, s 133(1), sch 6 para 12

sch rep—GSM Care of Churches and Ecclesiastical Jurisdiction, 1991 No 1, s 32(2), sch 8

No 6 **Clergy (Ordination and Miscellaneous Provisions)**

s 1 am—GSM Deacons (Ordination of Women), 1986 No 4, s 1(3)(4)

r in pt—SL(R), 2004 c 14, s 1(1), sch 1 pt 6/1

ss 3-6 rep—GSM C of E (Worship, etc), 1974 No 3, s 6(3), sch 2

s 7 rep—CAM Overseas and Other Clergy (Ministry and Ordination), 1967, s 7(1)

s 9 subst—GSM Clergy (Ordination), 1990 No 1, s 1

s 10 rep—GSM C of E (Legal Aid and Misc Provns), 1988 No 1, s 14 sch 3

s 11,12 rep—SL(R), 2004 c 14, s 1(1), sch 1 pt 6/1

No 7 *Vestures of Ministers*—rep GSM C of E (Worship, etc), 1974 No 3, s 6(3), sch 2

No 8 **Church Commissioners**

s 2 rep in pt—SL(R), 2004 c 14, s 1(1), sch 1 pt 6/2(1)

s 3 rep—SL(R), 2004 c 14, s 1(1), sch 1 pt 6/2(1)

1965

No 1 *Prayer Book (Alternative and other Services)*—rep (saving), GSM C of E (Worship, etc)1974 No 3, s 6(3) (4), schs 2, 3

No 2 *Benefices (Suspension of Presentation) (Continuance)*—rep with saving, CAM Pastoral, 1968 No 1, ss 94, 95, sch 8 para 9(c), sch 9

No 3 *Prayer Book (Miscellaneous Provisions)*—rep (saving), GSM C of E (Worship, etc), 1974 No 3, s 6(3)(4), schs 2, 3

No 4 **Prayer Book (Versions of the Bible)**

am—CAM Synodical Govt, 1969 No 2, s 3(4)

1966

No CAM were passed during 1966

1967

No 1 **Clergy Pensions (Amendment)**

s 1 rep—GSM C of E (Pensions), 1988 No 4, ss 7(3), 18(2), sch 3

s 2 rep—SI 1977/1146

s 3 am—GSM C of E (Pensions), 1988 No 4, s 5(a) (b) SIs 1988/2239, 2256; 1992/1748; GSM Pensions, 1997 No 1, s 10(1), sch 1 pt I para 1

rep in pt—GSM Pensions, 1997 No 1, s 10(2), sch 2 pt I

s 4 rep in pt—GSM Clergy Pensions (Amdt), 1982 No 2, s 2(3)

am—GSM C of E (Pensions), 2003 No 2, s 2(5); Charities, 2006 c 50, s 75, sch 8 para 48

s 5 rep—(saving) SI 1985/2081

No 2 **Extra-Parochial Ministry**

s 2 rep in pt—Education, 1973 c 16, s 1(4), sch 2 pt II; GSM C of E (Legal Aid and Misc Provns), 1988 No 1, s 5

am—GSM C of E (Legal Aid and Misc Provns)

saved—GSM C of E (Misc Provns), 1992 No 1, s 2(3)

No 3 **Overseas and Other Clergy (Ministry and Ordination)**

am—GSM Dioceses in Europe, 1980 No 2, s 6

s 1 excl—GSM C of E (Ecumenical Relations) 1988 No 3, s 4

am—GSM C of E (Misc Provns), 2014 No 1, s 8(2)

s 1A added—GSM C of E (Misc Provns), 2014 No 1, s 8(3)

1968

No 1 *Pastoral*—rep GSM Pastoral, 1983 No 1, s 93, sch 9

No 2 **Prayer Book (Further Provisions)**

ss 1-4 rep—(saving) GSM C of E (Worship, etc), 1974 No 3, s 6(3)(4), schs 2, 3

s 5 am—GSM C of E (Worship, etc), 1974 No 3), s 6(2), sch 1

rep in pt —(saving) GSM C of E (Worship, etc), 1974 No 3, s 6(3) (4), schs 2, 3

1969

No 1 *Clergy Pensions (Amendment)*—rep SI 1975/136

No 2 **Synodical Government**

s 3 rep in pt—GSM C of E (Worship, etc), 1974 No 3, s 6(3), sch 2; SL(R), 2004 c 14, s 1(1), sch 1 pt 6/5

1969

No 2 *continued*

s 4 excl—GSM Dioceses, 1978 No 1, s 4(4)

    am—GSM Synodical Govt (Amdt), 2003 No 1, ss 1(1)

s 7 rep in pt—(except in IOM) SL(R), 2004 c 14, s 1(1), sch 1 pt 6/5

s 9 rep in pt—SL(R), 2004 c 14, s 1(1), sch 1 pt 6/5

sch 2 (Constitution of the General Synod) am—Synodical Govt (Special Majorities), 1971
        No 1, s 1; GSM Synodical Govt (Amdt), 1974 No 1, ss 2, 3; GSM C of E
        (Worship, etc), 1974 No 3, s 6(2), sch 1; GSM C of E (Misc Provns), 1978
        No 3, s 1; GSM Diocese in Europe, 1980 No 2, s 3(1); SI 1998/1715, art 4(4),
        sch 2 para 1; GSM C of E (Misc Provns), 2006 No 1, s 8(a)

    trans of functions—SI 1998/1715, art 2, sch 1

    saved—GSM Nat Institutions, 1998 No 1, s 10

    ext—GSM Diocese in Europe, 2013 No. 1, s 2(1)(2)(a)

sch 3 (Church Representation Rules) am—SI 1973/1865; GSM Diocese in Europe, 1980
        No 2, s 2, sch 2; SI 1984/1039; GSM Patronage (Benefices), 1986 No 3, s 41,
        sch 4 para 13; SI 1989/2094; GSM Care of Churches and Ecclesiastical
        Jurisdiction, 1991 No 1, s 32, sch 7 para 4; GSM Priests (Ordination of
        Women), 1993 No 2, s 10, sch 3 para 3; SIs 1994/3118; 1995/3243 paras 1-11;
        GSM Nat Institutions 1998 No 1, s 13(1), sch 5 para 2; SI 1998/319 paras 1-4;
        GSM Cathedrals, 1999 No 1, ss 38(3), 39(1), sch 2 para 8; SI 1999/2112
        paras 1,4,9,16,18,20-23; GSM Synodical Govt (Amdt), 2003 No 1, ss 1(2),
        3(1), sch paras 1, 2-5,7,9; SI 2004/1889, rules 1-10,12,14-16,19(4); Charities,
        2006 c 50, s 75, sch 8 para 54; GSM Dioceses, Pastoral and Mission, 2007 No
        1, ss 49, 63(6), sch 7; Charities, 2011 c 25, sch 7 para 21(2)-(6); GSM C of E
        (Misc Provns), 2014 No 1, s 9(a); SI 2014/2113, paras 2, 4-10, 12-18, 20

    rep in pt—SIs 1984/1039; 1989/2094; 1994/3118; 1995/3243 paras 1-11;
        SI 1999/2112, paras 3, 5-7,8,11,12-15,17,19; ibid., paras 2,7,23; (saving)
        (transtl provns) GSM Churchwardens, 2001 No 1, ss 9, 11, 15(1)(2), sch 1,
        para 1, sch 2, para 1, sch 3; GSM Synodical Govt (Amdt), 2003 No 1, ss 1(2),
        3(1), sch paras 6,8; SI 2004/1889, rules 12(a)(c)(d),19(4)(c); GSM C of E
        (Misc Provns), 2014 No 1, s 9(b); GSM Bishops and Priests (Consecration and
        Ordination of Women), 2014 No 2, sch; SI 2014/2113, paras 3, 11,19, 20

    mod—CAM Cathedrals, 1963 No 2, s 12(3); GSM Cathedrals, 1999 No 1, ss 12(4),
        38(2)(3)

    appl —GSM Clergy Discipline, 2003 No 3, s 21(4)

sch 4 rep in pt—SL(R), 2004 c 14, s 1(1), sch 1 pt 6/5

sch 5 am—GSM C of E (Misc Provns), 2006 No 1, s 8(b)

1970

No 1   **Collegiate Churches (Capital Endowments)**

No 2   **Sharing of Church Buildings**

    s 1 rep—GSM Pastoral, 1983 No 1, s 93, sch 9

    s 2 am—GSM Church Commissioners (Assistance for Priority Areas), 1988 No 2, s 2(3)

No 3   **Church Commissioners**

1971

No 1   **Synodical Government (Special Majorities)**

1972

No 1   **Admission to Holy Communion**

No 2   **Repair of Benefice Buildings**

    appl—GSM Patronage (Benefices), 1986 No 3, s 34(5)

    ext—GSM Endowments and Glebe, 1976 No 4, s 33(1)

    s 1 am—GSM C of E (Misc Provns), 2005 No 3, s 6, sch 2 paras 1, 2

    s 2 rep in pt—GSM Endowments and Glebe, 1976 No 4, s 47(2) (4), sch 6 para 3, sch 8
        am—GSM C of E (Misc Provns), 2000 No 1, s 7, sch 4, para 2

    s 4 rep in pt—GSM Endowments and Glebe, 1976 No 4, s 47(2) (4), sch 6 para 3, sch 8

    ss 6,7 rep—GSM Endowments and Glebe, 1976 No 4, s 47(2) (4), sch 6 para 3, sch 8

    s 8 rep in pt—GSM Endowments and Glebe, 1976 No 4, s 47(2) (4), sch 6 para 3, sch 8

    s 12 am—GSM Patronage (Benefices Measure), 1986 No 3, s 41, sch 4 para 14

        rep in pt—GSM Endowments and Glebe, 1976 No 4, s 47(2) (4), sch 6 para 3, sch 8;
            GSM C of E (Misc Provns), 2000 No 1, s 7, sch 4, para 3

1972

No 2 *continued*

s 14 am—GSM C of E (Misc Provns), 2000 No 1, s 7, sch 4, para 4; GSM C of E (Misc
 Provns), 2005 No 3, s 6, sch 2 paras 1, 3, 5
 rep in pt—GSM C of E (Misc Provns), 2005 No 3, s 6, sch 2 paras 1, 4
s 15 rep in pt—GSM C of E (Misc Provns), 2000 No 1, s 7, sch 4, para 5
 am—GSM C of E (Misc Provns), 2005 No 3, s 6, sch 2 paras 1, 6, 7
s 16 am—GSM Endowments and Glebe,1976 No 4,s 47(1),sch 5 para 4(2); GSM C of E
 (Misc Provns), 2005 No 3, s 6, sch 2 paras 1, 6, 7
 rep in pt—GSM C of E (Misc Provns), 2000 No 1, s 7, sch 4, para 6
s 17 subst—GSM C of E (Misc Provns), 2005 No 3, s 6, sch 2 paras 1, 8
s 18 rep—GSM C of E (Misc Provns), 2005 No 3, ss 6, 10, sch 2 paras 1, 9, sch 5
s 19 rep in pt—GSM Endowments and Glebe, 1976 No 4, s 47(2)(4), sch 6 para 3, sch 8
 am—GSM C of E (Misc Provns), 2000 No 1, s 7, sch 4, para 8; GSM C of E (Misc
 Provns), 2005 No 3, s 6, sch 2 paras 1, 10
s 20 am—GSM Endowments and Glebe, 1976 No 4, s 47(1), sch 5 para 4(3); GSM C of E
 (Misc Provns), 2006 No 1, s 9
 rep in pt—GSM Endowments and Glebe, 1976 No 4, s 47(2) (4), sch 6 para 3, sch 8;
 GSM Care of Churches and Ecclesiastical Jurisdiction, 1991 No 1, ss 6(4),
 32(2), sch 8; GSM C of E (Misc Provns), 2000 No 1, s 7, sch 4, para 9
s 21 rep in pt—GSM Endowments and Glebe, 1976 No 4, s 47(2) (4), sch 6 para 3, sch 8;
 GSM C of E (Misc Provns), 2000 No 1, s 7, sch 4, para 10; GSM C of E (Misc
 Provns), 2005 No 3, s 6, sch 2 paras 1, 11(a)
 am—GSM Patronage (Benefices), 1986 No 3, ss 34(6), 41, sch 4 para 15; GSM C of E
 (Misc Provns), 2000 No 1, s 7, sch 4, para 10; GSM C of E (Misc Provns), 2005
 No 3, s 6, sch 2 paras 1, 11(b)
s 22 rep—GSM Endowments and Glebe, 1976 No 4, s 47(2) (4), sch 6 para 3, sch 8
s 26 am—GSM Endowments and Glebe, 1976 No 4, s 47(1), sch 5 para 4(4)
 rep in pt —(saving) GSM Endowments and Glebe, 1976 No 4, s 47(2) (4), sch 6 para 3,
 sch 8
s 27 rep in pt—GSM Patronage (Benefices), 1986 No 3, s 41 sch 5
 am—GSM C of E (Misc Provns), 2000 No 1, s 7, sch 4, para 11
s 28 rep—GSM C of E (Misc Provns), 1976 No 3, s 3(9), sch pt II
s 30 am—GSM C of E (Misc Provns), 2000 No 1, s 7, sch 4, para 12
s 31 am—GSM Endowments and Glebe, 1976 No 4, s 47(1), sch 5 para 4(5)(a) (c) (6);
 GSM Patronage (Benefices), 1986 No 3, s 41, sch 4 para 16; GSM C of E (Misc
 Provns), 2006 No 1, s 9
 rep in pt—GSM Endowments and Glebe, 1976 No 4, s 47(1) (2) (4), sch 5 para 4(5)
 (b), sch 6 para 3, sch 8; GSM Nat Institutions, 1998 No 1, s 13(1), sch 5 para 3
s 32 rep—SL(R), 2004 c 14, s 1(1), sch 1 pt 6/2(2)
 sch 1 rep in pt—GSM Endowments and Glebe, 1976 No 4, s 47(2) (4), sch 6 para 3, sch 8;
 SL(R), 2004 c 14, s 1(1), sch 1 pt 6/2(2); GSM C of E (Misc Provns), 2005 No
 3, s 10, sch 5

No 3 **Benefices**
 saved—GSM Patronage (Benefices Measure), 1986 No 3, s 17(1)
 s 1 am—GSM C of E (Misc Provns), 1992 No 1, s 17(1), sch 3, para 11

No 4 **Deaconesses and Lay Ministry**
 s 1A added—GSM Team and Group Ministries, 1995 No 1, s 13
 am—GSM Ecclesiastical Offices (Terms of Service), 2009 No 1, s 11, sch 2 para 1

No 5 **Clergy Pensions (Amendment)**
 s 1 rep—(saving) SI 1977/1146
 s 2 rep—SI 1988/2256
 s 3 am—GSM C of E (Pensions), 1988 No 4, s 18(1), sch 2 pt II para 21
 s 4 rep in pt—SI 1975/136; (saving) SI 1985/2081
 s 5 rep in pt—SI 1988/2256
 am—GSM Pensions, 1997 No 1, s 10(1), sch 1 pt I paras 15,16
 s 6 am—GSM C of E (Pensions), 1988 No 4, s 16(a)-(d); GSM Pensions, 1997 No 1, s
 10(1), sch 1 pt I, paras 15,17; SIs 2005/3325, arts 82, 83; 2014/3061, Sch 3 para 3
 rep in pt—GSM C of E (Misc Provns), 1995 No 2, s 14
 ext—GSM Ordination of Women (Financial Provns), 1993 No 3, s 4(4)
 trans of functions—SI 1998/1715, art 2, sch 1

1973

No GSM were passed during 1973

1974

No 1   **Synodical Government (Amendment)**
No 2   **Ecclesiastical Jurisdiction (Amendment)**
    appl—GSM Mission and Pastoral, 2011 No 3, s 34(9)
No 3   **Church of England (Worship and Doctrine)**
    s 2 saved—GSM C of E (Misc Provns), 1976 No 3, s 1(2)

1975

No 1   **Church Commissioners (Miscellaneous Provisions)**
    saved—GSM Nat Institutions, 1998 No 1, s 5(1), sch 2 pt I
    s 1 rep in pt—SL(R), 2004 c 14, s 1(1), sch 1 pt 6/2(1)
    s 2 rep—GSM C of E (Misc Provns), 2005 No 3, s 10, sch 5
No 2   **Ecclesiastial Offices (Age Limit)**
    appl (mods)—GSM Pastoral, 1983 No 1, s 20(9A); (Channel Is) SI 2000/2767, art 3, sch
      para 1 of Scheme
    appl—GSM Mission and Pastoral, 2011 No 3, s 34(10)
    excl—GSM C of E (Misc Provns), 1978 No 3, s 2(3)
    s 1 expld—GSM C of E (Misc Provns), 1978 No 3, s 2(1)
      mod—GSM C of E (Misc Provns), 1978 No 3, s 2(2)
    s 3 am—GSM Bishops (Retirement), 1986 No 1, s 11(1)
    s 4 rep—GSM Bishops (Retirement), 1986 No 1, s 12(2), sch
    s 5 rep in pt—GSM C of E (Misc Provns), 1983 No 2, s 8(11)
    sch am—GSM Ecclesiastical Offices (Terms of Service), 2009 No 1, s 3(10)

1976

No 1   **Cathedrals**
    saved—GSM Nat Institutions, 1998 No 1, s 5(1), sch 2 pt II
    appl (mods)—GSM Dioceses, 1978 No 1, s 22(1)
    s 3 am—GSM C of E (Misc Provns), 1992 No 1, s 9(2) (a)-(d)(5)
    s 4 rep in pt—GSM C of E (Misc Provns), 1992 No 1, ss 9(3) (a), 17(2), sch 4, pt II
      am—GSM C of E (Misc Provns), 1992 No 1, s 9(3)(b)
    s 5 am—GSM C of E (Misc Provns), 1992 No 1, s 9(4)
No 2   **Ecclesiastical Judges and Legal Officers**
    s 3 rep in pt—GSM C of E (Misc Provns), 1983 No 2, s 6(1)
      am—GSM C of E (Misc Provns), 1983 No 2, s 6(2); GSM Care of Churches and
      Ecclesiastical Jurisdiction, 1991 No 1, s 9, sch 5 para 2
    s 5 am—GSM Clergy Discipline, 2003 No 3, s 44(3)
    s 7 expld—GSM C of E (Misc Provns), 1992 No 1, s 13
No 3   **Church of England (Miscellaneous Provisions)**
    s 1 rep in pt—SL(R), 2004 c 14, s 1(1), sch 1 pt 6/1
    s 2 rep —GSM Ecclesiastical Offices (Terms of Service), 2009 No 1, s 12, sch 3
      rep in pt—SL(R), 2004 c 14, s 1(1), sch 1 pt 6/1
    s 3 rep—GSM C of E (Misc Provns), 1983 No 2, s 8(11)
    s 4 am—GSM Care of Churches and Ecclesiastical Jurisdiction, 1991 No 1, s 9, sch 5 para 3
    s 6 am—GSM C of E (Misc Provns), 1992 No 1, s 17(1), sch 3,para 12
    s 7 rep—SL(R), 2004 c 14, s 1(1), sch 1 pt 6/1
    s 8 rep in pt—SL(R), 2004 c 14, s 1(1), sch 1 pt 6/1
No 4   **Endowments and Glebe**
    appl—GSM Pastoral, 1983 No 1, s 31(4); GSM Care of Churches and Ecclesiastical
      Jurisdiction, 1991 No 1, s 31(1); Compulsory Purchase, 1965 c 56) s 31; London
      Underground, 1992 c iii s 35(4); London Docklands Railway (Lewisham), 1993 c vii;
      s 24(4); London Underground (Jubilee), 1993 c ix, s 27(4); Charities, 1993 c 10,
      s 96(2) (b); Leasehold Reform, Housing and Urban Development, 1993 c 28, ss 9, 40,
      61, sch 2 para 8(5), sch 14, para 12(2)
    s 3 am—GSM C of E (Misc Provns), 1978 No 3, s 11(1)
    s 6 rep in pt—SL(R), 2004 c 14, s 1(1), sch 1 pt 6/2(1)
      am—GSM C of E (Misc Provns), 2014 No 1, s 10(1)
    s 8 rep—GSM Stipends (Cessation of Special Payments), 2005 No 1, s 2(2)(3)
    s 10 rep in pt—SL(R), 2004 c 14, s 1(1), sch 1 pt 6/2(2)
    s 11 rep in pt—GSM C of E (Misc Provns), 2000 No 1, s 8, sch 5, para 2(a)
      am—GSM C of E (Misc Provns), 2000 No 1, s 8, sch 5, para 2(b)(c); Charities, 2006 c
      50, s 75, sch 8 para 59; GSM C of E (Misc Provns), 2006 No 1, s 10, sch 3 para 2;
      Charities, 2011 c 25, sch 7 para 34
    s 13 rep—SL(R), 2004 c 14, s 1(1), sch 1 pt 6/2(2)

1976

No 4 *continued*

s 14 am—GSM C of E (Misc Provns), 2006 No 1, s 10, sch 3 para 3

s 17 rep—GSM C of E (Misc Provns), 2000 No 1, s 20, sch 8 pt I

s 18 rep in pt—GSM Pastoral (Amdt), 1982 No 1, s 24(2); GSM C of E (Misc Provns), 2000 No 1, s 8, sch 5, para 3

    am—Charities, 2006 c 50, s 75, sch 8 para 60

s 19A added—GSM C of E (Misc Provns), 2000 No 1, s 8, sch 5, para 4

    am—GSM C of E (Misc Provns), 2006 No 1, s 10, sch 3 para 4

s 20 am—GSM C of E (Misc Provns), 1992 No 1, s 17(1), sch 3, para 13; GSM Team and Group Ministries, 1995 No 1, s 14(2); GSM C of E (Misc Provns), 2000 No 1, s 8, sch 5, para 5(a)-(k); GSM C of E (Misc Provns), 2005 No 3, s 7, sch 3 paras 1, 2(a)–(d),(f), (h); GSM C of E (Misc Provns), 2006 No 1, s 10, sch 3 para 5(a)(c); GSM C of E (Misc Provns), 2010 No 1, s 6(a)

    rep in pt—GSM C of E (Misc Provns), 2000 No 1, s 20, sch 8 pt I; GSM C of E (Misc Provns), 2005 No 3, s 7, sch 3 paras 1, 2(e)–(g); GSM C of E (Misc Provns), 2006 No 1, s 10, sch 3 para 5(b); GSM C of E (Misc Provns), 2010 No 1, s 6(a)

s 21 rep—GSM C of E(Misc Provns), 2000 No 1, s 20, sch 8 pt I

s 23 am—GSM C of E (Misc Provns), 1983 No 2, s 1(3); GSM C of E (Misc Provns), 1992 No 1, s 17(1), sch 3, para 14; GSM C of E (Misc Provns), 2010 No 1, s 6(b); GSM C of E (Misc Provns), 2014 No 1, sch 2 para 6(2)

    rep in pt—GSM C of E (Misc Provns), 2014 No 1, sch 2 para 6(3)

s 24 am—GSM C of E (Misc Provns), 1992 No 1, s 17(1), sch 3, para 15; GSM C of E (Misc Provns), 2005 No 3, s 7, sch 3 paras 1, 3

s 25 subst—GSM C of E (Misc Provns), 2000 No 1, s 8, sch 5, para 6

s 26 rep in pt—GSM C of E (Misc Provns), 2000 No 1, ss 8, 20, sch 5, para 7(a), sch 8, pt II; GSM C of E (Misc Provns), 2005 No 3, ss 7, 10, sch 3 paras 1, 4, sch 5

s 27 am—GSM C of E (Misc Provns), 2000 No 1, s 8, sch 5, para 8

s 28 rep—GSM C of E (Misc Provns), 2000 No 1, s 8, sch 5, para 8

s 32 am—GSM Team and Group Ministries, 1995 No 1, s 14(2); GSM C of E (Misc Provns), 2000 No 1, s 8, sch 5, para 9; GSM C of E (Misc Provns), 2005 No 3, s 7, sch 3 paras 1, 5

s 35A added—GSM Nat Institutions, 1998 No 1, s 13(1), sch 5 para 4

    rep in pt—GSM C of E (Misc Provns), 2000 No 1, ss 8, 20, sch 5, para 10(c) sch 8 pt I

s 36 rep in pt—GSM C of E (Misc Provns), 2006 No 1, s 10, sch 6

s 37 rep—GSM C of E (Misc Provns), 2000 No 1, s 20, sch 8 pt I

s 38 rep in pt—GSM Pastoral, 1983 No 1, s 93, sch 9; GSM C of E (Misc Provns), 1992 No 1, s 17(1), sch 3, para 16; SL(R), 2004 c 14, s 1(1), sch 1 pt 6/2(2)

    am—GSM C of E (Misc Provns), 2000 No 1, s 8, sch 5, para 11; GSM Dioceses, Pastoral and Mission, 2007 No 1, s 63(2)

s 42 rep—GSM C of E (Misc Provns), 2000 No 1, ss 8, 20, sch 5, para 12, sch 8, pt II

    restored—GSM C of E (Misc Provns), 2005 No 3, s 7, sch 3 paras 1, 6

s 43 rep—GSM C of E (Misc Provns), 1983 No 2, s 8(11)

s 44 rep—Charities, 1993 c 10, s 98(2), sch 7

s 45 am—GSM C of E (Misc Provns), 1992 No 1, s 17(1), sch 3, para 17; GSM C of E (Misc Provns), 2000 No 1, s 8, sch 5, para 13(a)(b)(c); GSM C of E (Misc Provns), 2005 No 3, s 7, sch 3 paras 1, 7; GSM C of E (Misc Provns), 2006 No 1, s 10, sch 3 para 6

s 49 rep in pt—SL(R), 2004 c 14, s 1(1), sch 1 pt 6/2(2)

sch 3 rep—GSM C of E (Misc Provns), 2000 No 1,s 20, sch 8 pt II

    revived—GSM C of E (Misc Provns), 2005 No 3, s 7, sch 3 paras 1, 8

sch 5 rep in pt—Land Registration, 2002 c 9, s 135, sch 13

sch 6 rep in pt—SL(R), 2004 c 14, s 1(1), sch 1 pt 6/2(2)

1977

No 1   **Incumbents (Vacation of Benefices)**

    restr—GSM Ecclesiastical Offices (Terms of Service), 2009 No 1, s 11(6)

    rep in pt—GSM Incumbents (Vacation of Benefices) (Amdt), 1993 No 1, ss 4,15

    s 1 added—GSM Incumbents (Vacation of Beneifces) (Amdt), 1993 No 1, ss 1, 15

    s 1 renumbered as s 1A—GSM Incumbents (Vacation of Benefices) (Amdt), 1993 No 1, ss 1, 14(1), 15, sch 3 para 1

    s 1A am—GSM Incumbents (Vacation of Benefices) (Amdt), 1993 No 1, ss 2(2), 14(1) (3), 15, sch 3 para 1

1977

No 1 *continued*

s 2 saved—GSM C of E (Misc Provns), 1983 No 2, s 9(4)
 am—GSM Incumbents (Vacation of Benefices) (Amdt), 1993 No 1, s 14(1), sch 3 para 2
 rep in pt—GSM Incumbents (Vacation of Benefices) (Amdt), 1993 No 1, s 14(1) (2), sch 3 paras 2, sch 4
s 3 am—GSM Incumbents (Vacation of Benefices) (Amdt), 1993 No 1, ss 3(2) (3), 15
 rep in pt—GSM Incumbents (Vacation of Benefices) (Amdt), 1993 No 1, ss 3(4), 14(2), 15, sch 3 paras 3, sch 4
s 5 subst—GSM Incumbents (Vacation of Benefices) (Amdt), 1993 No 1, s 14(1), sch 3 para 3
s 6 am—GSM Incumbents (Vacation of Benefices) (Amdt), 1993 No 1, s 14(1), sch 3 para 4
s 7 am—GSM Incumbents (Vacation of Benefices) (Amdt), 1993 No 1, s 14(1), sch 3 para 5
s 7A added—GSM Incumbents (Vacation of Benefices) (Amdt), 1993 No 1, ss 5, 15
 rep in pt—GSM Incumbents (Vacation of Benefices) (Amdt), 1993 No 1, s 14(2), 15, sch 4
s 8 rep in pt—GSM Incumbents (Vacation of Benefices) (Amdt), 1993 No 1, s 14(2), 15, sch 4
s 9 rep in pt—GSM Incumbents (Vacation in Benefices) (Amdt), 1993 No 1, s 14(2), 15, sch 4
 am—GSM Incumbents (Vacation of Benefices) (Amdt), 1993 No 1, s 14(1), sch 3 para 6
s 9A added—GSM Incumbents (Vacation of Benefices) (Amdt), 1993 No 1, ss 6, 15
s 10 rep in pt—GSM Incumbents (Vacation of Benefices) (Amdt), 1993 No 1, ss 7, 14(1), 15 sch 3 para 7, sch 4
s 11 rep in pt—GSM Incumbents (Vacation of Benefices) (Amdt), 1993 No 1, s 14(2), sch 4
s 12A added—GSM C of E (Misc Provns), 2014 No 1, s 11(1)
s 13 subst—(saving) GSM Incumbents (Vacation of Benefices) (Amdt), 1993 No 1, ss 8, 15
s 14 am—GSM C of E (Pensions), 1988 No 4, s 18(1), sch 2 pt II para 22; GSM C of E (Pensions) (Amdt), 2015 No 3, s 2(2)(a)
 rep in pt—GSM Incumbents (Vacation of Benefices) (Amdt), 1993 No 1, s 14(2) sch 4
s 15 rep—GSM C of E (Legal Aid and Misc Provns), 1988 No 1 s 14, sch 3
s 16 rep in pt—GSM Incumbents (Vacation of Benefices) (Amdt), 1993 No 1, s 14(2), sch 4
 am—GSM Incumbents (Vacation of Benefices) (Amdt), 1993 No 1, s 14(1), para 8
s 18 subst—GSM Incumbents (Vacation of Benefices) (Amdts), 1993 No 1, ss 9, 15
 trans of functions—SI 1998/1715, art 2 sch 1
s 19 am—GSM Incumbents (Vacation of Benefices) (Amdt), 1993 No 1, s 14(1), sch 3 para 9
s 19A added—GSM Incumbents (Vacation of Benefices) (Amdt), 1993 No 1, ss 10, 15
 appl—GSM C of E (Legal Aid and Misc Provns), 1988 No 1, s 7(1A)
s 21 am—GSM Incumbents (Vacation of Benefices) (Amdts), 1993 No 1, ss 11, 15
sch replaced (by sch 1)—GSM Incumbents (Vacation of Benefices) (Amdt), 1993 No 1, ss 12, 15, sch 1
sch 2 added—(saving) GSM Incumbents (Vacation of Benefices) (Amdt), 1993 No 1, ss 13, 15, sch 2
 am—GSM C of E (Misc Provns), 2000 No 1, s 9(a)(b); GSM C of E (Misc Provns), 2014 No 1, sch 2 para 7(a)-(e)(f)(i)
 rep in pt—GSM C of E (Misc Provns), 2000 No 1, s 9(c); GSM C of E (Misc Provns), 2014 No 1, sch 2 para 7(f)(ii)

1978

No 1 *Dioceses*—rep GSM Dioceses, Pastoral and Mission, 2007 No 1, sch 7
No 2 **Parochial Registers and Records**
 ss 2-5 am—GSM C of E (Misc Provns), 1992 No 1, s 4(1), sch 1, paras 2-4
 s 9 subst—GSM C of E (Misc Provns), 1992 No 1, s 4(1), sch 1, para 5
 s 9A added—GSM C of E (Misc Provns), 1992 No 1, s 4(1), sch 1, para 6
 s 10 am—GSM C of E (Misc Provns), 1992 No 1, s 4(1), sch 1, para 7(a) (b)
 s 11 am—Priests (Ordination of Women), 1993 No 2, s 10, sch 3 para 5
 s 12A added—GSM C of E (Misc Provns), 1992 No 1, s 4(1), sch 1, para 8
 s 19 rep in pt—GSM Pastoral, 1983 No 1, s 93, sch 9
 am—Charities, 1993 c 10, s 98(1), sch 6 para 30
 s 20 am—GSM C of E (Misc Provns), 1978 No 3, s 6; GSM C of E (Misc Provns), 1992 No 1, s 4(1), sch 1, para 9; GSM C of E (Misc Provns), 1995 No 2, s 10; GSM Ecclesiastical Fees (Amdt), 2011 No 2, sch 2 para 4
 s 23 rep—SL(R), 2004 c 14, s 1(1), sch 1 pt 6/5
 s 25 am—GSM C of E (Misc Provns), 1992 No 1, s 4(1), sch 1, para 10

1978

No 2 *continued*

 s 27 rep in pt—SL(R), 2004 c 14, s 1(1), sch 1 pt 6/5

 sch 1 am—GSM C of E (Misc Provns), 1992 No 1, s 4(1)(3) sch 1, para 11

 sch 2 subst—GSM C of E (Misc Provns), 1992 No 1, s 4(1), sch 1, para 12

No 3 **Church of England (Miscellaneous Provisions)**

 s 3 rep in pt—SL(R), 2004 c 14, s 1(1), sch 1 pt 6/2(2)

 s 5 rep—GSM C of E (Misc Provns), 2000 No 1,s 20, sch 8 pt I

 s 8 am—GSM C of E (Misc Provns), 2006 No 1, s 11

 s 9 rep—GSM Care of Churches and Ecclesiastical Jurisdiction, 1991 No 1, s 32(2), sch 8

 s 11 rep in pt—GSM C of E (Misc Provns), 1983 No 2, s 8(11)

 s 12 rep—SL(R), 2004 c 14, s 1(1), sch 1 pt 6/2(2)

 s 13 rep in pt—SL(R), 2004 c 14, s 1(1), sch 1 pt 6/2(2)

1979

 No GSM were passed during 1979

1980

No 1 **Deaconesses and Lay Workers (Pensions)**

 ext—GSM Diocese in Europe, 1980 No 2, s 5(2)

 s 1 am—GSM C of E (Pensions), 1988 No 4, s 18(1), sch 2 pt II para 23; GSM Pensions, 1997 No 1, s 10(1), sch 1 pt I para 18; SIs 2005/3325, arts 84, 85; 2014/3061, sch 3 para 4

No 2 **Dioceses in Europe**

 saved—GSM Nat Institutions, 1998 No 1, s 5(1), sch 2 pt I

 s 3 rep—GSM Diocese in Europe, 2013 No. 1, s 2(2)(b)

 s 5 am—GSM C of E (Pensions), 1988 No 4, s 18(1), sch 2 pt II para 24; GSM C of E Pensions (Amdt), 2009 No 2, s 2(3); GSM C of E (Pensions) (Amdt), 2015 No 3, s 2(2)(b)

 rep in pt—GSM C of E (Pensions), 1988 No 4, s 18(1), sch 2 pt I para 24

1981

 No GSM were passed during 1981

1982

No 1 *Pastoral (Amendment)*—rep GSM Pastoral, 1983 No 1, s 93, sch 9

No 2 **Clergy Pensions (Amendment)**

 ss 2,12 rep in pt—GSM C of E (Pensions), 2003 No 2, s 6, sch

 s 28 rep—GSM C of E (Pensions), 2003 No 2, s 6, sch

1983

No 1 *Pastoral*—rep GSM Mission and Pastoral, 2011 No 3, sch 9

No 2 **Church of England (Miscellaneous Provisions)**

 s 7 rep—GSM Bishops (Retirement), 1986 No 1, s 12(2), sch

 s 8 rep—GSM Dioceses, Pastoral and Mission, 2007 No 1, s 65, sch 7

 s 10 rep—GSM Dioceses, Pastoral and Mission, 2007 No 1, s 65, sch 7

 s 11 rep—GSM Pastoral, 1983 No 1, s 93, sch 9

 s 12 rep—SL(R), 2004 c 14, s 1(1), sch 1 pt 6/1

 s 13 rep in pt—SL(R), 2004 c 14, s 1(1), sch 1 pt 6/1

1984

 No GSM were passed during 1984

1985

 No GSM were passed during 1985

1986

No 1 **Bishops (Retirement)**

 saved—GSM Nat Institutions, 1998 No 1, s 5(1), sch 2 pt I

 s 3 excl—GSM Ecclesiastical Offices (Terms of Service), 2009 No 1, s 3(8)

 s 6 rep —GSM Ecclesiastical Offices (Terms of Service), 2009 No 1, ss 3(7), 12, sch 3

 s 7 excl—GSM Ecclesiastical Offices (Terms of Service), 2009 No 1, s 3(7)(8)

 rep in pt—GSM Ecclesiastical Offices (Terms of Service), 2009 No 1, s 12, sch 3

1986
No 1 *continued*

    s 8 ext—GSM Ecclesiastical Offices (Terms of Service), 2009 No 1, s 3(9)

    s 11 am—GSM Dioceses, Pastoral and Mission, 2007 No 1, sch 7

No 2   **Ecclesiastical Fees**

    s 1 trans of functions—SI 1998/1715, art 3

      subst—GSM Ecclesiastical Fees (Amdt), 2011 No 2, s 1(1)

    s 2 rep in pt—GSM C of E (Misc Provns), 1995 No 2, s 14

      trans of functions—SI 1998/1715, arts 2,3, 4, sch 1

      am—SI 1998/1715, art 4(4), sch 2 para 2(1); GSM Ecclesiastical Fees (Amdt), 2011 No 2, s 2

    s 3 rep—GSM Ecclesiastical Fees (Amdt), 2011 No 2, s 4(1)(a)

    s 4 subst—GSM Ecclesiastical Fees (Amdt), 2011 No 2, s 3(a)

    s 5 am—GSM Care of Churches and Ecclesiastical Jurisdiction, 1991 No 1, s 10, sch 6 para 2; GSM Ecclesiastical Fees (Amdt), 2011 No 2, s 3(b)

      rep in pt—GSM Care of Churches and Ecclesiastical Jurisdiction, 1991 No 1, s 10, sch 6 para 2(a)(ii)

      trans of functions—SI 1998/1715, art 2, sch 1

    s 6 am—GSM Care of Churches and Ecclesiastical Jurisdiction, 1991 No 1, s 10, sch 6, para 3; GSM C of E (Misc Provns), 1995 No 2, s 14; GSM Care of Places of Worship, 1999 No 2, s 4, sch 2 paras 1-3

      trans of functions—SI 1998/1715, art 2, sch 1

    s 7 appl—SI 2005/2018, art 4, sch 2 para 1(14)(b)

    s 8 saved—GSM Nat Institutions, 1998 No 1, s 5(1), sch 1 pt I

    s 10 am—GSM Care of Churches and Ecclesiastical Jurisdiction, 1991 No 1, s 10, sch 6 para 4; GSM Clergy Discipline, 2003 No 3, s 44(4); GSM Ecclesiastical Fees (Amdt), 2011 No 2, s 4(1)(b)(i)(iii); GSM Clergy Discipline (Amdt), 2013 No. 2, s 9(8); GSM C of E (Misc Provns), 2014 No 1, sch 2 para 8

      rep in pt—GSM Ecclesiastical Fees (Amdt), 2011 No 2, s 4(1)(b)(ii)

    sch A1 added—GSM Ecclesiastical Fees (Amdt), 2011 No 2, s 1(2), sch 1

      rep in pt—SI 2012/993, art 2

      am—SI 2014/813, arts 2, 3

No 3   **Patronage (Benefices)**

    appl—GSM Priests (Ordination of Women), 1993 No 2, s 7(3); Mental Capacity, 2005 c 9, s 18(4), sch 2 para 10(3)(4)

    s 3 am—GSM C of E (Misc Provns), 2000 No 1, s 17

    s 5 am—Mental Capacity, 2005 c 9, s 67(1), sch 6 para 34(1)(2)

    s 6 rep—Land Registration, 2002 c 9, s 135, sch 13

    s 7 appl—GSM Priests (Ordination of Women), 1993 No 2, ss 2(4)(h), 3(5)(e)

      restr—GSM Mission and Pastoral, 2011 No 3, s 88(a)

    s 9 am—GSM C of E (Misc Provns), 1992 No 1, s 17(1), sch 3, para 26; Mental Capacity, 2005 c 9, s 67(1), sch 6 para 34(1)(3)

    s 10 am—GSM C of E (Misc Provns), 2014 No 1, sch 2 para 9

    s 11 am—GSM Priests (Ordination of Women), 1993 No 2, ss 3(7), 10, sch 3 para 10; SI 2005/3129, art 4(3), sch 3 para 3

      rep in pt—GSM Priests (Ordination of Women), 1993 No 2, ss 3(7), 10, sch 3 para 10; GSM Bishops and Priests (Consecration and Ordination of Women), 2014 No 2, sch

    s 12 am—GSM Priests (Ordination of Women), 1993 No 2, ss 3(7),10, sch 3 para 11; SI 2005/3129, art 4(3), sch 3 para 3

    s 13 am—GSM Priests (Ordination of Women), 1993 No 2, ss 3(7),10, sch 3 para 12

      rep in pt—GSM Bishops and Priests (Consecration and Ordination of Women), 2014 No 2, sch

    s 16 am—GSM Dioceses, Pastoral and Mission, 2007 No 1, s 63(3)

    s 16A added—GSM C of E (Misc Provns), 2014 No 1, s 12(2)

    s 24 am—GSM C of E (Misc Provns), 2014 No 1, s 12(3)

    s 33 am—Trusts of Land and Appointment of Trustees 1996 c 47, s 25(1) sch 3, para 24

    s 34 rep in pt—GSM C of E (Misc Provns), 2000 No 1, s 20, sch 8 pt III

    s 35 am—GSM Priests (Ordination of Women), 1993 No 2, ss 3(7),10, sch 3 para 13; GSM Crown Benefices (Parish Representatives), 2010 No 3, s 1; GSM C of E (Misc Provns), 2014 No 1, s 12(4); ibid., sch 2 para 9(3)(5)

      rep in pt—GSM C of E (Misc Provns), 2014 No 1, sch 2 para 9(4); GSM Bishops and Priests (Consecration and Ordination of Women), 2014 No 2, sch

    s 36 rep—(prosp) Constitutional Reform, 2005 c 4, ss 145, 146, sch 17 pt 1 para 7, sch 18 pt 4

1986

No 3 *continued*

   s 37 am—GSM C of E (Misc Provns), 2014 No 1, sch 2 para 9(6)

   s 38 rep in pt—GSM C of E (Misc Provns), 1995 No 2, s 14

    trans of functions—SI 1998/1715, art 2 sch 1

   s 39 appl—GSM Priests (Ordination of Women), 1993 No 2, s 3(5)

    am—GSM C of E (Misc Provns), 2014 No 1, sch 2 para 9(7)

   sch 2 am—GSM C of E (Misc Provns), 1992 No 1, s 17(1), sch 3, para 27

   sch 4 rep in pt—GSM Mission and Pastoral, 2011 No 3, sch 9

No 4 **Deacons (Ordination of Women)**

1987

   No GSM were passed during 1987

1988

No 1 **Church of England (Legal Aid and Miscellaneous Provisions)**

   Pt I (ss 1-4) rep—(saving) GSM C of E (Legal Aid), 1994 No 3, ss 5, 7(1)

   s 6 rep—GSM Dioceses, Pastoral and Mission, 2007 No 1, sch 7

   s 7 am—GSM Team and Group Ministries, 1995 No 1, s 15; GSM Ecclesiastical Offices

    (Terms of Service), 2009 No 1, s 11, sch 2 para 19

    rep in pt—GSM Ecclesiastical Offices (Terms of Service), 2009 No 1, s 12, sch 3

   sch 1 rep—(saving) GSM C of E (Legal Aid), 1994 No 3, ss 5, 7(1)

   sch 2 rep in pt—GSM Mission and Pastoral, 2011 No 3, sch 9

No 2 **Church Commissioners (Assistance for Priority Areas)**

No 3 **Church of England (Ecumenical Relations)**

   s 2 am—GSM Dioceses, Pastoral and Mission, 2007 No 1, s 63(4)

   s 5 am—GSM C of E (Misc Provns), 1992 No 1, s 6; GSM C of E (Misc Provns), 2014 No

    1, sch 2 para 10

No 4 **Church of England (Pensions)**

   ss 1-4, 6, 15 rep—SI 1988/2256

   s 14 rep in pt—Trustee, 2000 c 29, s 40(1)(3), sch 2 pt III, para 56, sch 4 pt II

   s 17 rep—GSM Pensions, 1997 No 4, s 10(2), sch 2 pt I

   sch 1 rep—SI 1988/2256

   sch 2 rep in pt—SIs 1988/2256; 2239; GSM C of E (Pensions), 2003 No 2, s 6, sch

1989

   No GSM were passed during 1989

1990

No 1 **Clergy (Ordination)**

   s 2 rep —GSM Dioceses, Pastoral and Mission, 2007 No 1, sch 7

No 2 *Care of Cathedrals* —rep GSM Care of Cathedrals, 2011 No 1, sch 3

1991

No 1 **Care of Churches and Ecclesiastical Jurisdiction**

   appl—GSM Care of Places of Worship, 1999 No 2, s 2(4), sch 1 para 5(1)

   s 6 am—GSM C of E (Misc Provns), 1995 No 2, s 13; GSM Care of Churches and

    Ecclesiastical Jurisdiction (Amdt), 2015 No 1, s 1(a)

    rep in pt—GSM Care of Churches and Ecclesiastical Jurisdiction (Amdt), 2015 No 1, s

     1(b)

   Pt 3 (ss 8-19) excl—SIs 2009/1300, art 5(10); 2015/2044, art 5

   s 11 rep in pt—GSM Care of Churches and Ecclesiastical Jurisdiction (Amdt), 2015 No 1, s

    5(2)

   s 13 saved—GSM Care of Places of Worship, 1999 No 2, s 2(3)

   s 14 excl—GSM Pastoral, 1983 No 1, s 56(2L); GSM Mission and Pastoral, 2011 No 3, s

    68(14)

    am—GSM Care of Churches and Ecclesiastical Jurisdiction (Amdt), 2015 No 1, s

     2(1)-(3)

   s 15 am—GSM Care of Churches and Ecclesiastical Jurisdiction (Amdt), 2015 No 1, s

    3(1)(2)

   s 16 appl—GSM Pastoral, 1983 No 1, s 56(2K); GSM Mission and Pastoral, 2011 No 3, s

    68(13)

   s 17 subst—GSM C of E (Misc Provns), 2014 No 1, s 13(2)

   s 18 rep in pt—GSM C of E (Misc Provns), 2014 No 1, s 13(3)(b)(c)

1991

No 1 s 18 *continued*

am—GSM C of E (Misc Provns), 2014 No 1, s 13(3)(a)

s 18A added—GSM Care of Churches and Ecclesiastical Jurisdiction (Amdt), 2015 No 1, s 4

ss 18B,C added—GSM Care of Churches and Ecclesiastical Jurisdiction (Amdt), 2015 No 1, s 5(1)

s 22 am—SI 2009/1307, sch 3 para 2

s 25 trans of functions—SI 1998/1715, art 2, sch 1

am—GSM Clergy Discipline, 2003 No 3, s 45(3); GSM Care of Cathedrals (Amdt), 2005 No 2, s 19, sch 3 para 6; GSM Ecclesiastical Offices (Terms of Service), 2009 No 1, s 11, sch 2 para 21; GSM Care of Churches and Ecclesiastical Jurisdiction (Amdt), 2015 No 1, s 6(1)(b),(2)(3)

rep in pt—GSM Care of Churches and Ecclesiastical Jurisdiction (Amdt), 2015 No 1, s 6(1)(a)

s 26 ext—GSM Care of Places of Worship, 1999 No 2, s 5

am—GSM Care of Places of Worship, 1999 No 2, s 5; GSM Clergy Discipline, 2003 No 3, s 45(1)(2)(b)(c); ibid, s 45(2)(a) (as am by 2013 No 2, sch para 13); GSM Ecclesiastical Offices (Terms of Service), 2009 No 1, s 11, sch 2 para 22

s 27 rep in pt—GSM C of E (Misc Provns), 1995 No 2, s 5

trans of functions—SI 1998/1715, art 2, sch 1

s 31 am—GSM Team and Group Ministries, 1995 No 1, s 16; Constitutional Reform, 2005 c 4, s 145, sch 17 pt 2 para 25; GSM Dioceses, Pastoral and Mission, 2007 No 1, sch 7

s 52 am and rep in pt—GSM Pastoral (Amdt), 1994 No 1, s 5

sch 7 rep in pt—GSM Mission and Pastoral, 2011 No 3, sch 9

No 2 **Diocesan Boards of Education**

s 3 rep in pt—Education, 1993 c 35, s 307(1)(3), sch 19, para 163, sch 21 pt II; School Standards and Frameworks, 1998 c 31, s 140(1), sch 30 para 30, sch 31; (W) School Standards and Organisation (W), 2013 anaw 1, sch 5 para 15(2)

am—Education, 1996 c 56, s 582(1), sch 37 pt I paras 102(2)(3); School Standards and Frameworks, 1998 c 31, s 140(1), sch 30 para 30; Educ, 2002 c 32, s 51, sch 4, para 13; Educ and Inspections, 2006 c 40, s 30, sch 3 para 4; (W) School Standards and Organisation (W), 2013 anaw 1, sch 5 para 15(2)

s 5 rep—School Standards and Frameworks, 1998 c 31, s 140(3), sch 31

s 6 am—Education, 1993 c 35, s 307(1), sch 19 para 165; Education, 1996 c 56, s 582(1), sch 37 pt I para 104(2)(3)

rep in pt—School Standards and Frameworks, 1998 c 31, s 140(3), sch 31

s 7 am—Education, 1993 c 35, s 307(1), sch 19 para 166; Education, 1996 c 56, s 582(1), sch 37 pt I para 105; School Standards and Frameworks, 1998 c 31, s 140(1), sch 30 para 31; Educ and Inspections, 2006 c 40, s 30, sch 3 para 5; (W) School Standards and Organisation (W), 2013 anaw 1, sch 5 para 15(3)

rep in pt—School Standards and Frameworks, 1998 c 31, s 140(3), sch 31; (W) School Standards and Organisation (W), 2013 anaw 1, sch 5 para 15(3)

s 9 rep—School Standards and Frameworks, 1998 c 31, s 140(3), sch 31

s 10 am—Education, 1996 c 56, s 582(1), sch 37 pt I para 107; School Standards and Frameworks, 1998 c 31, s 140(1), sch 30 para 32(2)(4); Educ, 2002 c 32, s 65(3), sch 7 pt 2, para 3(1)-(3)

rep in pt—Education 1996 c 56, s 582(1)(2), sch 37 pt I para 107(a) sch 38 pt I; School Standards and Frameworks, 1998 c 31, s 140(1)(3), sch 30 para 32(2)(3), sch 31

s 26 am—GSM Care of Cathedrals (Supplementary Provns), 1994 No 2, s 9, GSM C of E (Legal Aid), 1994 No 3, s 7(2), sch 2

1992

No 1 **Church of England (Miscellaneous Provisions)**

s 1 am—GSM Team and Group Ministries, 1995 No 1, s 17(2)(3)

sch 3 am—GSM Dioceses, Pastoral and Mission, 2007 No 1, sch 7

rep in pt—GSM Mission and Pastoral, 2011 No 3, sch 9

1993

No 1 **Incumbents (Vacation of Benefices) (Amendment)**

s 9 rep in pt—GSM C of E (Misc Provns), 1995 No 2, s 14

No 2 *Priests (Ordination of Women)*—rep GSM Bishops and Priests (Consecration and Ordination of Women), 2014 No 2, s 1(3)

1993

No 3 **Ordination of Women (Financial Provisions)**
ext (Channel Is)—SI 1999/1317, art 2, sch
s 10 trans of functions—SI 1999/1715 art 2 sch 1

1994

No 1 *Pastoral (Amendment)*—rep GSM Mission and Pastoral, 2011 No 3, sch 9
No 2 *Care of Cathedrals (Supplementary Provisions)*—rep GSM Care of Cathedrals, 2011 No 1,
sch 3
saved—GSM Nat Institutions, 1998 No 1, s 5(1), sch 2 pt I; GSM Cathedrals, 1999 No 1,
ss 6(8), 38(2)(3)
am—GSM Cathedrals, 1999 No 1, s 36
No 3 **Church of England (Legal Aid)**
s 1 trans of functions—SIs 1998/1715, art 2, sch 1; 2007/1556, art 2
s 4 trans of functions—SI 1998/1715, art 2, sch 1
s 2 am—SI 2005/3129, art 4(3), sch 3 para 4
sch 1 am—GSM Clergy Discipline, 2003 No 3, s 44(5)
sch 2 rep in pt—GSM Mission and Pastoral, 2011 No 3, sch 9

1995

No 1 **Team and Group Ministries**
Pt 1 (ss 1–6) rep —GSM Mission and Pastoral, 2011 No 3, sch 9
sch 1 rep —GSM Mission and Pastoral, 2011 No 3, sch 9
sch 2 rep —GSM Mission and Pastoral, 2011 No 3, sch 9
No 2 **Church of England (Miscellaneous Provisions)**
s 2 am—GSM C of E (Misc Provns), 2014 No 1, s 19
s 4 rep —GSM Ecclesiastical Offices (Terms of Service), 2009 No 1, s 12, sch 3
saving—SI 2010/2847, art 2, sch 1
s 6 rep—GSM Nat Institutions, 1998 No 1, s 13(3)
s 11 rep—GSM Mission and Pastoral, 2011 No 3, sch 9
rep in pt—GSM Dioceses, Pastoral and Mission, 2007 No 1, sch 7
s 12 rep —GSM Dioceses, Pastoral and Mission, 2007 No 1, sch 7

1996

No GSM were passed during 1996

1997

No 1 **Pensions**
s 1 am—SIs 2005/3325, arts 88, 89; 2014/3061, sch 3 para 6
s 2 am—GSM C of E (Misc Provns), 2014 No 1, sch 2 para 12(2)
s 4 am—GSM C of E (Pensions), 2003 No 2, s 4
s 7 subst—GSM C of E (Pensions), 2003 No 2, s 5
am—GSM C of E Pensions (Amdt), 2009 No 2, s 1; GSM C of E (Pensions) (Amdt),
2015 No 3, s 1
s 9 am—GSM C of E (Misc Provns), 2014 No 1, sch 2 para 12(3)

1998

No 1 **National Institutions**
s 2 mod—GSM Diocese in Europe, 2013 No. 1, s 1(2); (retrosp) GSM C of E (Misc Provns),
2014 No 1, sch 2 para 13(2)
s 3 am—Charities, 2011 c 25, sch 7 para 80
s 8 mod—GSM Diocese in Europe, 2013 No. 1, s 1(2)
s 10 rep in pt—GSM C of E (Misc Provns), 2014 No 1, sch 2 para 13(3)
sch 1 am—SIs 2001/3701, s 2; 2003/2922, art 3; GSM C of E (Misc Provns), 2006 No 1, s
13; GSM C of E (Misc Provns), 2014 No 1, sch 2 para 13(4)
sch 5 rep in pt—GSM Mission and Pastoral, 2011 No 3, sch 9

1999

No 1 **Cathedrals**
s 4 am—Charities, 2011 c 25, sch 7 para 82
s 9 am—GSM Care of Cathedrals (Amdt), 2005 No 2, s 19, sch 3 para 7
s 15 excl—GSM Ecclesiastical Offices (Terms of Service), 2009 No 1, s 11(8)
am—Charities, 2011 c 25, sch 7 para 83
s 16 rep in pt—Trustee, 2000 c 29, s 40(1)(3), sch 2 pt III, para 57(b), sch 4 pt III

1999

No 1 s 16 *continued*

        am—Trustee, 2000 c 29, s 40(1), sch 2, pt III, para 57(a)

        s 17A added—GSM C of E (Misc Provns), 2014 No 1, s 14(2)

        s 20 am—GSM Care of Cathedrals (Amdt), 2005 No 2, s 19, sch 3 paras 8, 9

        s 27 am—Charities, 2011 c 25, sch 7 para 84; GSM C of E (Misc Provns), 2014 No 1, s 14(3)

        s 34 am—Charities, 2006 c 50, s 75, sch 8 para 196; Charities, 2011 c 25, sch 7 para 85

        s 36 am—GSM Care of Cathedrals (Amdt), 2005 No 2, s 19, sch 3 para 10; GSM C of E (Misc Provns), 2014 No 1, sch 2 para 14

        sch A1 added—GSM C of E (Misc Provns), 2014 No 1, s 14(5), sch 1

No 2   **Care of Places of Worship**

2000

No 1   **Church of England (Miscellaneous Provisions)**

        s 10 rep—GSM Mission and Pastoral, 2011 No 3, sch 9

        s 11 rep—Charities, 2011 c 25, sch 10

        s 18 rep—GSM Dioceses, Pastoral and Mission, 2007 No 1, sch 7

        sch 1 rep in pt—GSM C of E (Misc Provns), 2006 No 1, s 15, sch 6

        sch 2 rep in pt—GSM C of E (Misc Provns), 2005 No 3, s 10, sch 5; GSM C of E (Misc Provns), 2006 No 1, s 15, sch 6

        sch 4 rep in pt—GSM C of E (Misc Provns), 2005 No 3, s 10, sch 5

        sch 5 rep in pt—GSM C of E (Misc Provns), 2005 No 3, s 10, sch 5

        sch 6 rep—GSM Mission and Pastoral, 2011 No 3, sch 9

        rep in pt—GSM C of E (Misc Provns), 2005 No 3, s 10, sch 5

2001

No 1   **Churchwardens**

        s 2 am—Charities, 2006 c 50, s 75, sch 8 para 198; Charities, 2011 c 25, sch 7 para 93

        s 5 am—GSM C of E (Misc Provns), 2014 No 1, sch 2 para 15

2002

      No GSM were passed during 2002

2003

No 1   **Synodical Government (Amendment)**

        s 2 am—GSM Dioceses, Pastoral and Mission, 2007 No 1, sch 7

No 2   **Church of England (Pensions)**

        ss 1, 2 am—SI 2005/3325, arts 90, 91

        s 7 am—SI 2014/3061, Sch 3 para 7

        sch 4 am—SI 2014/3061, Sch 3 para 8

        No 3—**Clergy Discipline**

s 4 am   GSM Clergy Discipline (Amdt), 2013 No. 2, s 9(1), sch paras 2, 3

        s 8 am—GSM Clergy Discipline (Amdt), 2013 No. 2, s 1(2)(3)

        s 16 am—GSM Clergy Discipline (Amdt), 2013 No. 2, s 2

        s 20 am—GSM Clergy Discipline (Amdt), 2013 No. 2, s 3

        s 21 am—GSM Clergy Discipline (Amdt), 2013 No. 2, s 9(1), sch para 4

        s 23 am—GSM Clergy Discipline (Amdt), 2013 No. 2, s 9(1), sch para 5

        s 30 am—GSM Clergy Discipline (Amdt), 2013 No. 2, s 4

        s 31 am—GSM Clergy Discipline (Amdt), 2013 No. 2, s 5

        s 34 subst—GSM Clergy Discipline (Amdt), 2013 No. 2, s 9(1), sch para 6

        s 34A added—GSM Clergy Discipline (Amdt), 2013 No. 2, s 9(1), sch para 7

        s 36 am—GSM Clergy Discipline (Amdt), 2013 No. 2, s 6(2)-(4); ibid., s 9(1), sch para 8

        rep in pt—GSM Clergy Discipline (Amdt), 2013 No. 2, s 6(5)

        s 37 am—GSM Clergy Discipline (Amdt), 2013 No. 2, s 7(2)(3); ibid., s 9(1), sch para 9

        rep in pt—GSM Clergy Discipline (Amdt), 2013 No. 2, s 7(4)

        s 38 am—GSM Clergy Discipline (Amdt), 2013 No. 2, s 8

        s 39 am—GSM Clergy Discipline (Amdt), 2013 No. 2, s 9(1), sch para 10

        s 43 am—Constitutional Reform, 2005 c 4, s 145, sch 17 pt 2 para 35; GSM Clergy Discipline (Amdt), 2013 No. 2, s 9(1), sch para 11

        s 44 rep in pt—GSM Clergy Discipline (Amdt), 2013 No. 2, s 9(1), sch para 12(a)

        am—GSM Clergy Discipline (Amdt), 2013 No. 2, s 9(1), sch para 12(b)

        s 45 am—GSM Clergy Discipline (Amdt), 2013 No. 2, s 9(1), sch para 13

2004

No GSM were passed during 2004

2005

No 1 **Stipends (Cessation of Special Payments)**
No 2 *Care of Cathedrals (Amendment)* —rep GSM Care of Cathedrals, 2011 No 1, sch 3
No 3 **Church of England (Miscellaneous Provisions)**
    s 8 rep—GSM Mission and Pastoral, 2011 No 3, sch 9
    sch 4 rep—GSM Mission and Pastoral, 2011 No 3, sch 9

2006

No 1 **Church of England (Miscellaneous Provisions)**
    s 12 rep —GSM Mission and Pastoral, 2011 No 3, sch 9
    sch 4 rep —GSM Mission and Pastoral, 2011 No 3, sch 9
    sch 5 rep in pt—GSM C of E (Misc Provns), 2010 No 1, s 12, sch 2
No 2 *Pastoral (Amendment)*—GSM Mission and Pastoral, 2011 No 3, sch 9

2007

No 1 **Dioceses, Pastoral and Mission**
    s 1 rep in pt—GSM Mission and Pastoral, 2011 No 3, sch 9
    s 4 am—GSM C of E (Misc Provns), 2014 No 1, s 16(2)(3)
    s 13 rep in pt—GSM Bishops and Priests (Consecration and Ordination of Women), 2014
        No 2, sch
    s 14 excl—GSM Vacancies in Suffragan Sees and other Ecclesiastical Office, 2010 No 2, s 2
        rep in pt—GSM Bishops and Priests (Consecration and Ordination of Women), 2014
        No 2, sch
    s 15 excl—GSM Vacancies in Suffragan Sees and other Ecclesiastical Office, 2010 No 2, s 2
    s 17 rep in pt—GSM Bishops and Priests (Consecration and Ordination of Women), 2014
        No 2, sch
    Pt 3 (ss 33–39) rep —GSM Mission and Pastoral, 2011 No 3, sch 9
    Pt 4 (ss 40–46) rep —GSM Mission and Pastoral, 2011 No 3, sch 9
    Pt 5 (ss 47–51) rep —GSM Mission and Pastoral, 2011 No 3, sch 9
    Pt 6 (ss 52, 53) rep —GSM Mission and Pastoral, 2011 No 3, sch 9
    ss 58–61 rep —GSM Mission and Pastoral, 2011 No 3, sch 9
    s 62 am—Charities, 2011 c 25, sch 7 para 128
        rep in pt—GSM Mission and Pastoral, 2011 No 3, sch 9
    s 63 rep in pt—GSM Care of Cathedrals, 2011 No 1, sch 3
    sch 1 sm—GSM C of E (Misc Provns), 2014 No 1, s 16(4)
    sch 2 am—Charities, 2011 c 25, sch 7 para 129
    sch 3 rep —GSM Mission and Pastoral, 2011 No 3, sch 9
    sch 5 rep —GSM Mission and Pastoral, 2011 No 3, sch 9
    sch 6 rep in pt—GSM Mission and Pastoral, 2011 No 3, sch 9
        am—GSM C of E (Misc Provns), 2014 No 1, sch 2 para 16

2008

No 1 **Church of England Marriage**
    s 1 am—GSM C of E Marriage (Amdt), 2012 No 1, s 1(2)-(4)
    s 1A added—GSM C of E Marriage (Amdt), 2012 No 1, s 1(1)

2009

No 1 **Ecclesiastical Offices (Terms of Service)**
    s 3 am—GSM C of E (Misc Provns), 2014 No 1, sch 2 para 17(a)(c)
        rep in pt—GSM C of E (Misc Provns), 2014 No 1, sch 2 para 17(b)
    sch 2 rep in pt—GSM Mission and Pastoral, 2011 No 3, sch 9
No 2 **Church of England Pensions (Amendment)**

2010

No 1 **Church of England (Miscellaneous Provisions)**
    s 6 rep in pt—GSM C of E (Misc Provns), 2014 No 1, sch 2 para 6(3)
    s 7 rep—GSM Mission and Pastoral, 2011 No 3, sch 9
    s 8 rep—GSM C of E (Misc Provns), 2014 No 1, sch 2 para 18(1)
    s 10 am—Charities, 2011 c 25, sch 7 para 145
        rep in pt—GSM Care of Cathedrals, 2011 No 1, sch 3

2010
No 1 *continued*

s 12 rep in pt—GSM Mission and Pastoral, 2011 No 3, sch 9
savings—GSM C of E (Misc Provns), 2014 No 1, sch 2 para 18(2)
sch 2 savings—GSM C of E (Misc Provns), 2014 No 1, sch 2 para 18(2)

No 2 **Vacancies in Suffragan Sees and other Ecclesiastical Office**
No 3 **Crown Benefices (Parish Representatives)**

2011

No 1 **Care of Cathedrals**
No 2 **Ecclesiastical Fees (Amendment)**
No 3 **Mission and Pastoral**

mod—GSM C of E (Misc Provns), 2014 No 1, sch 2 para 19(10)
s 6 rep in pt—GSM C of E (Misc Provns), 2014 No 1, sch 2 para 19(2)
s 7 am—GSM C of E (Misc Provns), 2014 No 1, sch 2 para 19(3)
s 21 rep in pt—GSM C of E (Misc Provns), 2014 No 1, sch 2 para 19(4)
s 34 am—SI 2012/992, art 2, sch para 1
rep in pt—GSM Bishops and Priests (Consecration and Ordination of Women), 2014
No 2, sch
s 35 rep in pt—GSM Bishops and Priests (Consecration and Ordination of Women), 2014
No 2, sch
s 39 am—SI 2012/992, art 2, sch para 2; GSM C of E (Misc Provns), 2014 No 1, sch 2 para
19(5)
s 40 am—SI 2012/992, art 2, sch para 3
appl—SI 2014/2083, reg 2(4)
s 45 am—SI 2012/992, art 2, sch para 4; GSM C of E (Misc Provns), 2014 No 1, sch 2 para
19(6)
s 57 am—GSM C of E (Misc Provns), 2014 No 1, sch 2 para 19(7)
s 67 am—Charities, 2011 c 25, sch 7 para 146
s 77 am—Charities, 2011 c 25, sch 7 para 147
s 80 rep in pt—GSM Bishops and Priests (Consecration and Ordination of Women), 2014
No 2, sch
s 88 excl in pt—GSM C of E (Misc Provns), 2014 No 1, s 12(2)
s 90 am—GSM C of E (Misc Provns), 2014 No 1, sch 2 para 19(8)
s 95 am—GSM C of E (Misc Provns), 2014 No 1, sch 2 para 19(9)
s 101 am—GSM C of E (Misc Provns), 2014 No 1, sch 2 para 19(11)
s 106 am—Charities, 2011 c 25, sch 7 para 148; SI 2012/992, art 2, sch para 5
sch 3 am—Charities, 2011 c 25, sch 7 para 149(2)(3)
sch 4 am—SI 2012/992, art 2, sch para 6; GSM C of E (Misc Provns), 2014 No 1, sch 2
para 19(12)
rep in pt—GSM C of E (Misc Provns), 2014 No 1, sch 2 para 19(12)(b)(c)
appl (mods)—SI 2014/2083, reg 2(3)
appl—SI 2014/2083, reg 2(4)

2012

No 1 **Church of England Marriage (Amendment)**

2013

No 1 **Diocese in Europe**
No 2 **Clergy Discipline (Amendment)**

2014

No 1 **Church of England (Miscellaneous Provisions)**
No 2 **Bishops and Priests (Consecration and Ordination of Women)**

2015

No 1 **Care of Churches and Ecclesiastical Jurisdiction (Amendment)**
No 2 **Ecclesiastical Property**
No 3 **Church of England (Pensions) (Amendment)**